VIEW OF JERUSALEM FROM OLIVET AS IT WAS IN THE TIME OF CHRIST.

REVISED EDITION

With maps and five hundred illustrations

COMPILED FROM
DR. WILLIAM SMITH'S
DICTIONARY OF THE BIBLE

SMITH'S BIBLE DICTIONARY

INCLUDING

Four Thousand Questions and Answers
On The Old and New Testaments

A History of the Books of the Bible

Analytical and Comparative Concordance

HOLMAN BIBLE PUBLISHERS
NASHVILLE

Published by
Holman Bible Publishers
Nashville, TN 37234
3 4 5 6 7 8 9   89 88 87 86
Printed in the United States of America

ISBN-0-87981-033-5
ISBN-0-87981-035-1 (Thumb-Indexed Edition)

LIST OF ILLUSTRATIONS.

LIST OF ILLUSTRATIONS.

INDEX.

INDEX.

CHRONOLOGICAL TABLES.

A NEW ANALYTICAL AND COMPARATIVE CONCORDANCE,

Embracing the salient and ready-working features of the larger Concordances. In its analytical arrangement it shows the different shades of meaning attached to the originals. In its comparative presentation it notes the word-changes made in the Revised Version.

It is the only Concordance of a convenient size now published that embraces the aforenamed special features.

KEY TO PRONUNCIATION

Every reader has found that Biblical proper names are very difficult to pronounce. In this Bible Dictionary the proper names are divided with the accent (') placed upon the syllable to which it belongs.

In addition to this, the vowels are marked to show what sound they should receive. These and marks for consonant sounds are shown in the tables below. By attention to this Key the reader can easily pronounce correctly all the proper names.

ā as in āge	ī as in vīne	y as in lyre
ă as in ădd	ï as in pïque	y as in typical
â as in câre	o as in do	ç (soft) as s as in cite
ä as in ärms	o as in done	çh as sh
ạ as in ạll	o as in wolf	c, ch as k
ȧ as in pȧst	ô as in fôr	g (soft) as in gem
a as in what	ōō as in fōōd	g as in get
ē as in mēte	ŏŏ as in fŏŏt	s as z as in wise
e as in veil	û as in ûrn	x as gz as in exist
ĕ as in mĕt	u as in rude	n as in linger
ê as in thêre	u as in push	th as in thine
ẽ as in makẽr		

SMITH'S
BIBLE
DICTIONARY

SMITH'S
DICTIONARY OF THE BIBLE.

AÂ'RON. The son of Amram and Jochebed, and the elder brother of Moses and Miriam (Num. xxvi. 59; xxxiii. 39). He was a Levite, and is first mentioned in Ex. iv. 14, as one who could "speak well." He was appointed by Jehovah to be the Interpreter and "Mouth" (Ex. iv. 16) of his brother Moses, who was "slow of speech;" and accordingly he was not only the organ of communication with the Israelites and with Pharaoh (Ex. iv. 30; vii. 2), but also the actual instrument of working most of the miracles of the Exodus. (See Ex. vii. 19, etc.) Thus on the way to Mount Sinai, during the battle with Amalek, Aaron is mentioned with Hur, as staying up the weary hands of Moses, when they were lifted up for the victory of Israel (not in prayer, as is sometimes explained, but) to bear the rod of God. (See Ex. xvii. 9.) Through all this period he is mentioned as dependent upon his brother, and deriving all his authority from him. The contrast between them is even more strongly marked on the arrival at Sinai. Moses at once acts as the mediator (Gal. iii. 19) for the people, to come near to God for them, and to speak his words to them. Aaron only approaches with Nadab, and Abihu, and the seventy elders of Israel, by special command, near enough to see God's glory, but not so as to enter his immediate presence. Left, then, on Moses' departure, to guide the people, Aaron is tried for a moment on his own responsibility, and he fails from a weak inability to withstand the demand of the people for visible "gods to go before them." Possibly it seemed to him prudent to make an image of Jehovah, in the well-known form of Egyptian idolatry (Apis or Mnevis), rather than to risk the total alienation of the people to false gods; and his weakness was rewarded by seeing a "feast to the Lord" (Ex. xxxii. 5) degraded to the lowest form of heathenish sensuality, and knowing, from Moses' words and deeds, that the covenant with the Lord was utterly broken. He repented of his sin, and Moses gained forgiveness for him (Deut. ix. 20).—Aaron was now consecrated by Moses to the new office of the high priesthood. The order of God for the consecration is found in Ex. xxix., and the record of its execution in Lev. viii. The only occasion on which his individual character is seen is one of presumption. The murmuring of Aaron and Miriam against Moses clearly proceeded from their trust, the one in his priesthood, the other in her prophetic inspiration, as equal commissions from God (Num. xii. 2). On all other occasions he is spoken of as acting with Moses in the guidance of the people. Leaning as he seems to have done wholly on him, it is not strange that he should have shared his sin at Meribah, and its punishment [MOSES] (Num. xx. 10–12). Aaron's death seems to have followed very speedily. It took place on Mount Hor, after the transference of his robes and office to Eleazer (Num. xx. 28). This mount is still called the "Mountain of Aaron." [HOR.]—The wife of Aaron was Elisheba (Ex. vi. 23); and the two sons who survived him, Eleazar and Ithamar. The high priesthood descended to the former, and to his descendants until the time of Eli, who, although of the house of Ithamar, received the high priesthood, and transmitted it to his children; with them it continued till the accession of Solomon, who took it from Abiathar, and restored it to Zadok (of the house of Eleazar). [ABIATHAR.]

AÂR'ONITES. Priests, descendants of Aaron (1 Chr. xii. 27). An important family in David's time.

ÂB (*father*). Absalom, *makes peace;* Abner, *causes light.* ABBA, father, as used by Jesus (Mark xiv. 36) and Paul (Rom. viii. 15; Gal. iv. 6).—2. The name of the fifth (sacred) month, as used after the captivity.

ABAD'DON (*destruction, or the place of the dead*). ASMODEUS in the Apocrypha; APOLLYON, Rev. ix. 11; Job xxvi. 6 (destruction).

ABADÎ'AS. Obadiah, son of Jehiel (1 Esd. viii. 35).

ABÂG'THA (*father or cause of fortune*). An officer of the presence before King Ahasuerus (Esd. i. 10).

AB'ÀNA (*perennial*). Amana. The main river of Damascus, now called Barada. It has several channels, and irrigates the whole city and suburbs. Rises in Anti-Lebanon, near Zebedany (and a tributary at Ain-Fijy), 23 miles N. W. of Damascus, and 2300 feet higher. It empties into the lake and marsh of Ateibeh, 15 miles E. of the city. See 2 Kings v. 12.

AB'ARIM (*beyond*). A mountain range east of the Dead Sea and the Jordan. Nebo is its highest peak, and Pisgah is the top of Nebo. Average height 2000 to 4000 feet.

AB'BA. Father. The ancient Aramaic word. The peculiar term for the father-God used by Jesus.

AB'DĂ. Father of Adoniram (1 K. iv. 6)—2. Son of Shammua (Neh. xi. 17), called Obadiah in 1 Chr. ix. 16.

AB'DEEL. Father of Shelemiah (Jer. xxxvi. 26).

AB'DI. Ancestor of Ethan the singer (1 Chr. vi. 44).—2. Father of Kish (2 Chr. xxix. 12).—3. One of the sons of Elam (Ezr. x. 26).

AB'DIAS. Obadiah the prophet, in 2 Esd. i. 39.

AB'DIEL (*servant of God*), Abdallah in Arabic. Son of Guni (1 Chr. v. 15). The name is noted for its use by Milton in his Paradise Lost, for an angel—"Among the faithless, faithful only he."

AB'DON (*servile*). BEDAN in 1 Sam. ii. 11. A judge of Israel.—2. Son of Shishak.—3. Eldest son of Jehiel, son of Gibeon.—4. Son of Micah, also called Achbor.—Had forty sons and thirty nephews.

ABED'NEGO (*servant of Nego—that is, Mercury the God*). The name given by the Chaldeans to Daniel's companion Azariah (Dan. i. 3).

A'BEL (*weakness, breath*). In Hebrew HEBEL.

Second son of Adam; killed by his brother Cain (Gen. iv).

A′BEL (*meadow*). Several places so named.—1. A′BEL-BETH-MAA′CHAH, or ABEL-MAIM; a strong city on the slope of Mt. Hermon, near the Jordan, where Joab besieged Sheba (2 Sam. xx. 14).—2. A′BEL-KERA-MIM (*of the vineyards*). Near Rabbath, and even now famous for its wines (Judg. xi. 33).—3. A′BEL-MEHO-LAH (*of dancing*). South of Bethshan near Jordan. The birth-place of Elisha

THE SO-CALLED TOMB OF ABSALOM.

(1 K. xix. 16), and noted for Gibeon's victory over Midian (Judg. vii. 22).—4. ABEL-MIZ-RAIM (*of the Egypts*). Near Hebron, where Joseph, his brethren, and the Egyptians mourned for Jacob (Gen. l. 11). Lost.—5. ABEL-SHITTIM (*of the acacias*). In Moab, near the head of the Dead Sea. The last camping ground of the Exodus (Num. xxxiii. 49). Acacia trees are now found wherever there is water in that region.

A′BEZ. Town in Issachar (Josh. xix. 20). Now Tubas, near Shunem.

A′BI (*father*). Abijah. Mother of King Hezekiah (2 K. xviii. 2).

ABI′AH (*Jehovah his father*). Son of Becher (1 Chr. vii. 8).—2. Wife of Hezron (1 Chr. ii. 24).—3. Son of Samuel, and a judge in Beersheba (1 Sam. viii. 2).—4. Mother of Hezekiah. Abi.—5. Son of Rehoboam (1 Chr. iii. 10).—6. Descendant of Eleazar. See ABIJAH.

ABI′ASAPH (*the gatherer*). Head of a family of Kohathites (Ex. vi. 24). Noted persons of this family were Samuel the prophet, and Elkanah his father, and Heman the singer. The family lived in Mount Ephraim (1 Sam. i).

ABI′ATHAR (*abundance*). The only son of Ahimelech the priest, who escaped Saul's massacre at Nod (1 Sam. xxii.), and who joined David in his flight, and was afterwards priest with Zadok in David's reign. "Solomon thrust out Abiathar from being priest unto the Lord," fulfilling the doom of Eli's house.

ABI′DAH (*wise*). Grandson of Abraham by Keturah (Gen xxv. 4; 1 Chr. i. 33).

AB′IDAN (*father of the judge*). Chief in Benjamin at the Exodus (Num. i. 2).

A′BIEL Abi′el (*strong*). Father of Kish, grandfather of Saul and Abner.—2. One of David's 30 "mighty men."

ABIE′ZER (*helper*). Eldest son of Gilead (Josh. xvii. 2), formerly of the east of Jordan, later of Ophrah, a lost place, which was near the south border of Esdraelon. Gideon was of this family

(Judg. vi. 34).—2. One of David's "mighty men." ABIEZRITES, the family title.

AB′IGAIL (*maker of joy*). Nabal's beautiful wife, who saved her husband from David's anger—Nabal having died ten days after, David made her his wife (1 Sam. xxvi. 14).—2. A sister of David, mother of Amasa.

ABIHA′IL (*mighty*). Father of Zuriel, chief of the Merari (Num. iii. 35).—2. Abishur's wife (1 Chr. ii. 29).—3. Son of Huri of Gad (1 Chr. v. 14). —4. Rehoboam's wife (2 Chr. xi. 18), a descendant of Eliab, David's elder brother.—5. Father of Esther, and uncle of Mordecai (Esth. ii. 15).

ABI′HU (*God is father*). Second son of Aaron by Elizabeth. He was consecrated, with his father and brothers, for the ministry. Abihu and his brother Nadab lost their lives for an error in the altar service, while intoxicated (?).

ABI′JAH (*father God.*) A son of Samuel, whose misconduct gave the Israelites the occasion to demand a change of government to a monarchy. (1 Sam. viii. 1).—2. Son and successor of Rohoboam (B. C. 958). He followed the idolatries of his father (1 K. xiv. 23).

ABI′LA, ABILE′NE (*grassy meadow*). On the E. slope of Mt. Hermon. Mentioned by Josephus (Ant. 14, 13, 3). The name is derived from Abel, the first martyr (by tradition). ABILA was the capital city of the district, under the Romans, and its ruins are now seen on the banks of the Barada ravine, 12 miles N. W. of Damascus. The district is well watered by the Abana, and by many other streams from Anti-Lebanon ; is fertile and affords good pasture. When Luke wrote (iii. 1) the tetrarchy was divided between Lysanias and Philip. There is a coin bearing the name and title of Lysanias of Abilene.

ABIM′AEL (*father of Mael*). Of Joktan (Gen. x. 28). A supposed trace of the name is in Mali, a town in Arabia (the Minæans).

ABIM′ELECH (*father of the king*), the name of several Philistine kings, was probably a common title of these kings, like that of Pharaoh among the Egyptians, and that of Cæsar and Augustus among the Romans. Hence in the title of Ps. xxxiv. the name of Abimelech is given to the king, who is called Achish in 1 Sam. xxi. 11.—1. A Philistine, king of Gerar (Gen. xx., xxi.), who, exercising the right claimed by Eastern princes, of collecting all the beautiful women of their dominions into the harem (Gen. xii. 15 ; Esth. ii. 3), sent for and took Sarah. A similar account is given of Abraham's conduct on this occasion, to that of his behavior toward Pharaoh. [ABRAHAM.] 2. Another king of Gerar in the time of Isaac, of whom a similar narrative is recorded in relation to Rebekah (Gen. xxvi. 1, etc.). 3. Son of the judge Gideon by his Shechemite concubine (Judg. viii. 31). After his father's death he murdered all his brethren, 70 in number, with the exception of Jotham, the youngest, who concealed himself ; and he then persuaded the Shechemites to elect him king. Shechem now became an independent state, and threw off the yoke of the conquering Israelites. When Jotham heard that Abimelech was made king, he addressed to the Shechemites his fable of the trees choosing a king (Judg. ix. 1). After Abimelech had reigned three years, the citizens of Shechem rebelled. He was absent at the time, but he returned and quelled the insurrection. Shortly after he stormed and took Thebez, but was struck on the head by a woman with the fragment of a millstone (comp. 2 Sam. xi. 21); and lest he should be said to have died by a woman, he bade his armor-bearer slay him. Thus God avenged the murder of his brethren and fulfilled the curse of Jotham.

ABIN'ADAB (*princely*). A Levite of Kirjathaim, in whose house the ark "rested" for 20 years (1 Sam. vii. 1).—2. Second son of Jesse (1 Sam. xvi. 8).—3. Son of Saul, killed on Mt. Gilboa (1 Sam. xxxi. 2).—4. Father of one of Solomon's cabinet officers (1 K. iv. 11).

AB'INER. Hebrew form of ABNER.

ABIN'OAM (*gracious*). Barak's father (Judg. iv. 6).

ABI'RAM (*high*). Reubenite and conspirator. See KORAH—2. Eldest son of Hiel, who died because his father undertook to rebuild Jericho (1 K. xvi.; Josh. vi.).

ABISE'I. Son of Phinehas (2 Esd. i. 2).

AB'ISHAG (*cause of error*). The beautiful Shunemite wife of David in his old age.

ABISH'AI (*gift-maker*). Son of David's sister

Asahel, *in blood revenge* (Num. xxv. 19). David mourned his untimely loss, following his bier.

ABOMINA'TION. Any thing or custom detested or disliked for religious reasons. The Egyptians would not eat with any foreign people, or eat anything touched by them; and the Hebrews adopted a similar rule. The ABOMINATION OF DESOLATION (Matt. xxiv. 15; Dan. ix. 27), is a reference to an idol worship (of images) on or near the sacred altar on Moriah. See ANTIOCHUS EPIPHANES.

A'BRAHAM (*father of a multitude*). First named ABRAM (*of elevation*). His name was changed, and he received from God the PROMISE of the blessing to all nations in his posterity, when he was 99 years old. Son of TERAH, born in UR, "of the Chaldees," B. C. 1996; had two elder brothers, HARAN and NAHOR, and a half sister, SARAH, (Iscah), who was his wife and the mother of Isaac. The *spiritual* element in the life of Abraham is the chief topic in the Bible narrative, very few incidents of his natural life being recorded. He was

ABRAHAM'S OAK, NEAR HEBRON.

Zeruiah, brother of Joab, and one of David's chief and best officers.

ABISH'ALOM (*peaceful*). Father of Maachah, wife of Rehoboam and mother of Abijah (1 K. xv. 2). Same as Absalom.

ABISHU'A (*of happiness*). Son of Bela (1 Chr. viii. 4).—2. Son of Phinehas, father of Bukki (1 Chr. vi. 4). High-priest after Phinehas and before Eli. Iosepos, in Josephus (Ant. 8, 1, 3).

AB'ISHUR (*upright*). Son of Shammai (1 Chr. ii. 28).

AB'ISUM. Son of Phinehas (1 Esd. viii. 2).

AB'ITAL (*protection*). Wife of David (2 Sam. iii. 4).

ABI'TUB (*goodness*). Son of Shaharaim by Hushim (1 Chr. viii. 2).

ABI'UD. Grandson of Zerubbabel by Shelomith (Matt. i. 13).

AB'NER (*light-maker*). Cousin of Saul and commander-in-chief of his army. After Saul's death he made Ishbosheth, Saul's son, king, but betrayed him to David, and was killed by the friends of

60 when his father's family left Ur and went to Haran (where Terah died, aged 215), and 75 when the promise was first made, when, as directed, he entered Canaan, and fixed his camp under a sacred oak near Shechem, where he built an altar and worshiped God, receiving a promise of the inheritance of the land by his descendants.

Abraham is the first recorded worshiper of the one true God. The promise made to him was two-fold—temporal and spiritual: that his descendants should be many and prosperous, and that by him all the families of the earth should be blessed. The promise has been fulfilled in both ways: his descendants, both Jews and Arabs, have been and are now countless, and the spiritual blessings, by the rapid distribution of the Bible through the world, are reaching all the "families."

Besides Sarah he had a wife named KETURAH, who bore him several sons; and also a *handmaid*, Hagar, whose son, Ishmael, was the head of a great family (see ISHMAEL).

Before Isaac was born, Lot, his nephew, was regarded as his heir, and lived with him. He built an altar between Bethel and Hai. From here he went south "going and pulling up" his tent-pins, towards Beersheba, whence a famine drove him into Egypt.

Pharaoh hearing of the beauty of Sarai, according to the kingly privilege, took her into his family, but soon returned her to Abraham with presents—"a blessing" of cattle and servants, so that when Abram returned into Canaan he was much richer in cattle, silver and gold. Lot had been with him, and again they camped near Bethel.

Their cattle having increased to a great number, and contentions among their servants arising, Abram and Lot separated, one choosing the plains of Jericho and the other the hills of Judea. After this time the promise was again repeated; and Abram pitched his tent in the oak grove near Mamre, where he built another altar.

He is first called THE HEBREW on the rescue of his nephew Lot from Chedorlaomer; but his language is supposed to have been Chaldaic, rather than the Hebrew of the Old Testament.

and the destruction of the cities of the plain announced, Abraham discovered that he "had entertained angels unawares." He begged to save his nephew Lot and his family, and the next morning, when offering the daily sacrifice, as he saw the ascending smoke from the plain, he probably felt sure of Lot's safety.

During the next few months he practiced the same deception on the Abimelech of Gerar that he had 23 years before on the Pharoah of Egypt. The king was warned of his danger in a dream, and dismissed Sarah with presents.

Isaac was born B. C. 1896, and Ishmael (with his mother) was dismissed at the time Isaac was weaned (at 3 years), because Ishmael mocked at the child (probably offered pretended worship to the child of the promise).

Isaac was 25 when he was laid on the altar, and saved from burning by the angel's voice, Abraham's faith having proved true. His mother died at Hebron 12 years after, at the age of 127, and was

HEBRON.

At this time he could arm 318 of his *trained servants*, showing that his family must have been very large. The Bedawins of Syria are now exact representatives of the ancient patriarch, in their manner of living in tents, by keeping flocks, in habits and religion, and in being ready on the shortest notice to make a raid for defence or reprisal. At Mamre his faith was made stronger by having the promise once more repeated, and by the prophesy of the bondage in Egypt, with the deliverance.

Ishmael was born of Hagar when Abram was 85 years old, and Sarah 75, and was to have been considered a son of Sarai, but the childless woman could not restrain her envy and jealously of the favored mother Hagar. When Abram was 99 the promise was renewed, a distinction being made—of *temporal* blessings for Ishmael and *spiritual* for Isaac who was promised to Sarai. Abram's name was changed to Abraham and his wife's to Sarah, and the covenant of circumcision was renewed to all the family and servants.

A few days after he entertained "three men," who appeared at his tent door in the dress and manner of the natives. This is one of the most beautiful instances on record of ancient customs. The patriarch and his wife, with their own hands, prepared refreshments, and stood by while their guests ate. Travelers in Syria meet with such attentions now among Abraham's descendants. When the promise of a son to Sarah was renewed,

buried in Machpelah, which Abraham bought of the sons of Heth. This legal conveyance of land is the oldest on record.

Abraham sent Eliezer to renew family ties with his family in Haran, and get a wife for Isaac, when that beautiful and touching incident of "Rebekah at the Well" occurred. This brilliant picture includes all the requisites of a perfect marriage—the sanction of parents, favor of God, domestic habits of the wife, her beauty, modest consent, kindness, and her successful hold on her husband's love even while living in the same tent with her mother-in-law.

Abraham's descendants occupy the land from Egypt to the Euphrates, besides those that are "scattered and peeled" all over the world.

He died aged 175, and was buried in the cave of Machpelah by his sons Isaac and Ishmael. To this day he is called the "friend of God," and is reverenced alike, as the Father of the Faithful by Jew, Mohammedan and Christian.

ABRAHAM'S BOSOM. Meaning a place of peace, repose and happiness. See LORD'S SUPPER.

ABRŌ'NAH (*passage*). Station in the desert near Eziongeber.

ABRŌ'NAS. Torrent near Cilicia, perhaps NAHR-ABRAIM, the ancient Adonis. Arbonai in Judg. ii. 24.

ĂB'SALOM (*peacemaker*). Third son of David, only son of his mother, Maachah, daughter of Talmai, king of Geshur, born at Hebron. He is described as a very handsome man, having a very heavy head of hair. Absalom killed his half-brother, Amnon, for an outrage on his sister Tamar, and fled for security to his grandfather, king Talmai, where he stayed 3 years. Joab, by the help of a talented woman of Tekoah, induced David to pardon Absalom and recall him, but kept him two years longer out of his presence. By the death of Amnon, and it may be of Chilead also, Absalom was the oldest son of the king living, and he was ambitious for the throne, plotted for the

John D'Acre. Seaport 8 miles north of Carmel, by the bay of Acre. The ancient port is filling with sand, and large ships must land at Hepha, near Carmel. The plain of Acre is 6 miles wide, to the hills of Galilee, and is one of the most fertile in Palestine. It was given to Asher by Joshua, but never conquered (Judg. i.). Paul stayed here one day. Very few antiquities are to be found in the modern town, except such as have been used in rebuilding the walls and houses. Napoleon failed to capture Acre in 1799. During the crusades it was an important city, next to Jerusalem. It has

ACRE—ANCIENT ACCHO OR PTOLEMAIS.

place of power, "stole the hearts of the people" by flatteries and promises, and proclaimed himself king at Hebron. His father, David, was obliged to fly to Mahanaim, and Absalom took possession of Jerusalem. The crafty Hushai, whom David sent to advise and assist Ahithophel in counseling Absalom, gained time for the true king, and the forces of Absalom were defeated in the wood of Ephraim, and Absalom himself, having entangled his hair in a tree, was killed by Joab, David's general, and buried under a heap of loose stones as a mark of contempt. David waited in the gate of Mahanaim for the news of the battle, and mourned bitterly when he knew his son was dead.

Absalom raised a pillar "in his lifetime," in the king's dale, but the pillar and its place have disappeared, leaving no trace. The monument called Absalom's tomb, in the Kidron valley, is a modern structure, nearly all cut from the solid rock, and on a side hill, not in a dale.

AB'SALON. Ambassador to Lysias (2 Macc. xi. 17)

ABŪ BUS. Father of Ptolemeus, son-in-law to Simon Maccabeus (1 Macc. xvi. 11).

ĂC'CĂD. In Shinar, built by Nimrod. *Akkerkoof* (Arabic name) is 9 miles E. of the Tigris. A ruined brick mound 400 feet around, 125 high, cemented by bitumen, and divided into layers of 12 to 20 feet by reeds, and remains of canals, reservoirs, and other works, show the size and importance of the ancient city.

ĂC'CHŌ. ĀCRE. (*hot sand?*). PTOLEMAIS. St.

been taken by many people ; Egyptian who named it Ptolemais; Antiochus the Great; the Maccabees (?); Alexander Balas; Alexander Janneus failed, but Cleopatra succeeded; Tigranes; the Romans; Crusaders; Mohammedans; Ibrahim Pasha; and is now ruled by the Turks. Pop. 5000 to 10,000.

ĂCEL'DĂMA (*field of blood*). Bought for the 30 pieces of silver that Judas received for betraying Jesus and returned. Potter's Field. On the steep south slope of Hinnom, opposite the Siloam pool. A few old olive trees grow near an old ruin called the house of Ananus. The hill side is full of rock-hewn tombs. Ship-loads of earth have been carried away from this spot as holy earth, and the Campo Santo (holy field) at Pisa is filled with it.

ĂCHĀ'IĂ. Province of Rome in Greece. Gallio was proconsul when Paul was there (Acts xviii. 12).

Ā'CHĂN (*troubler*). Stoned at Jericho for stealing public property (Josh. vii.).

Ā'CHĂR (*trouble*). Variation of Achan.

ĂCH'BOR (*mouse*). Father of Baal-hanan, king of Edom (Gen. xxxvi. 38).—2. Son of Michaiah, in Josiah's time (2 K. xxii. 12).

ĂCHIĂCH'ARUS. Keeper of the seal of Esarhaddon, king of Nineveh (Tobit i. 21). Nephew to Tobit, son of his brother Anael. Supposed to be the Hebrew for Mordecai.

ĂCHĪ'AS. Son of Phinees, high-priest (2 Esd. i. 2). AHIJAH?

Ā'CHIM. Son of Sadoc, father of Eliud. In Hebrew JACHIN (Gen. xlvi. 10; Mat. i. 14).

A-CHIOR (*fighter*). A general in the army of Holofernes (Judg. v.), after, a convert to Judaism (Judg. xiv.).

A'CHISH. King at Gath (Ps. xxxiv. Abimelech). David fled twice to him from Saul. (1 Sam. xxvii. 3-12, etc.)

ACHI'TOB. AHITUB, high-priest (1 Esd. viii. 2).

A'CHOR (*valley of trouble*). Near Jericho, in *Wady Kelt*. Where Achan was stoned.

ACH'SA. Daughter of Caleb (1 Chr. ii. 49).

ACH'SAH (*anklet*). Daughter of Caleb, given to his nephew, Othniel, in reward for leading the attack on Debir The "upper and lower springs"

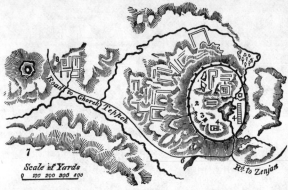

Scale of Yards
100 200 300 400

ACHMETHA.

that were given her as a dower, with the south land (Negeb), are located 6 miles S. W. of Hebron.

ACH'SHAPH (*incantation*). Royal city of Canaan (Josh. xi.). HEPHA on the bay of Acre.

ACH'ZIB. Judah in the Shefela.—2. In Asher, from which the Canaanites were not driven out. Ecdippa. Now *Es Zib*, 7 miles N. of Acre. After the return from captivity this was the most northern limit of Israel.

ACTS OF THE APOSTLES. The similarity of words and forms of sentences between the ACTS and LUKE leads to the belief that Luke wrote both. The book repeats a part of Christ's history, especially the ascension and what attended that event, and the advent of the Holy Spirit at the Pentecost, with the wonderful success of their preaching. The Church in Jerusalem is then noticed; its persecutions, and the conversion of one of its most violent enemies (Paul); and then the narrative includes the efforts made to spread the Gospel by

EARTHEN LAMP. 1.

Peter and by Paul. The chief interest in the book, after the introduction, is the activity, success, sufferings and teachings of the great apostle. The book seems unfinished. The author was a companion of Paul, and a witness of most of the acts he records. His design was to show the co-operation of God in spreading Christianity, and to prove the perfect equality of right and privilege in the new Church of Gentile and Jew, and to give illustrations of the power and working of the religion of Jesus. Written after A. D. 63. The place is not

known. Perhaps in fragments as they traveled or lived in different cities, finishing the work at Rome. See HISTORY OF THE BIBLE.

There are several spurious books called Acts; of Christ, of Paul, and others. See APOCRYPHA.

AD'AH (*beauty*). First wife of Lamech, mother of Jabal and Jubal.—2. Daughter of Elon the Hittite, one of the three wives of Esau, mother of Eliphaz, and so of the Edomites (Gen. xxxvi.). BASHEMATH in Gen. xxvi.

ADA'IAH (*adorned by Jehovah*). Maternal grandfather of Josiah (2 K. xxii. 1).—2. Gershonite, ancestor of Asaph (1 Ch. vi. 41). Iddo in v. 21.—3. Son of Shimhi, a Benjamite (1 Chr. viii. 21).—4. Son of Jeroham.—5. Of the descendants of Bani (Jedeus in Esd. ix. 30; Ezr. x. 29).—6. Son of another Bani—both 5 and 6 took foreign wives.—7. Of the line of Pharez.—8. Ancestor of Maaseiah (2 Chr. xxiii. 1).

ADA'LIA. Son of Haman (Esth. ix. 8).

AD'AM (*the man; or reddish tint*). The peculiar work of the 6th day of the creation, the crown of the whole fabric, was man, made in the divine image, he alone of all animals having a spiritual life. Adam was made male and female, and the two were placed in the garden Eden (EDEN), where proper food abounded. Some believe that a pair of each race were made, black, brown, red, yellow, white, and many others, because there are such great differences in complexion and figure among mankind.

The original state of man was one of activity and enjoyment. God assumed form and speech, and instructed His children how to dress and keep the garden, and exercised their faculties in naming the animals that He had made; and taught them something of the qualities and relations of vegetables, earths, the heavens, and external objects to which they were related.

The forming of the woman from a rib of Adam has been declared a poetic myth; but the lesson is just as surely taught, whether it is a fact or a fable, that woman stands in a peculiarly close relation to man. The "tree of the knowledge of good and evil," and the "tree of life," were tests of obedience, and as such might have been of any kind. The serpent is described as if it had been a special agent—perhaps one of those spirits that are believed to be superior to man, invisible to his eyes, good and bad, powerful, and always contending for his soul (2 Cor. ii. 11).

Woman was sentenced to endure the pains of child-bearing, and the humiliating dependance on a husband; and man to labor, with or without reward, and both to be subject to death (spiritual?). The sentence of the serpent is hard to interpret. The serpent is not CURSED literally, but rather blessed in having an extra means of protection in the dread of all other animals; he does not suffer by crawling on his belly because he is especially made to go in that way; and he does not eat dust. The denunciation of the serpent was symbolical, and is by some said to be the *first gospel promise*. "I will put enmity between thee and the woman, and between thy seed and her seed; he will attack thee on the head, and thou wilt attack him at the heel." The serpent was the spirit of lying and cruelty, as opposed to God, holy, good and wise.

It is probable that the first garments were made of the skins of animals, offered in sacrifice.

Cain was born the year after the expulsion; Abel a few years later, and Seth at least 130 years after Cain. Other sons and daughters were born to them of whose history nothing is recorded.

Adam's death at the age of 930 is stated, but that of Eve is not given.

AD'AM (*red earth*). City on the Jordan near Zarthan (Josh. iii. 16).

AD'AMAH. N. W. of the Sea of Galilee (Josh. xix. 36). Lost.

Probably the horned viper, the asp of Cleopatra, found in great numbers in the deserts. Arabia *Siffon*. It is extremely venomous, only 15 inches long, but fatal even in slight scratches.

AD'DI. Son of Cosam, father of Melchi (Luke iii. 28).—2. See ADNA (1 Esd. ix. 31).

ANCIENT EGYPTIAN FUNERAL PROCESSION.

AD'AMI. DAMIN.

Ā'DÄR. Name after the captivity of the 6th month. The holy days in it were: 7th, a fast for the death of Moses; 9th, a fast for the memory of the School of Hillel; 13th, Fast of Esther, and for the death of Nicanor; 14th and 15th, the fast of Purim (Esther ix. 21).

AD'ASA. Ephraim near Beth-horon (Jos. Ant. xii. 10, 5; 1 Macc. vii. 40, 45).

AD'BEEL (*Sign of God*). Son of Ishmael (Gen. xxv. 13).

AD'DAN (*strong*). ADDON (Ezra ii. 59).

AD'DAR. Son of Bela (1 Ch. viil. 3). ARD in Num. xxvi. 40.

ADDER.

ADDER. There are four Hebrew names translated adder.—1. *Acshub*, in Ps. cxl. 3, quoted by Paul in Rom. iii. 13. The original (coiled and hiding) would apply to any kind of serpent.—2.

AD'DO. Grandfather of Zechariah (1 Esd. vi. 1). IDDO.

ADDUS. His sons returned with Zerubbabel (1 Esd. v. 34).—2. A priest removed for losing his family record (1 Esd. v. 38). Called Barzillai, in Ezra and Nehemiah, whose daughter Augia he married.

A'DER. Son of Beriah, of Aijalon (1 Chr. vii. 15). EDER.

ĀDIAB'ENE. The chief of the six provinces of Assyria, watered by the great and little Zab, which flow into the Tigris.

AD'ĪDÄ. In the Shefela, fortified by Simon Maccabeus against Tryphon.—2. Mentioned by Josephus near Jordan. HADID. ADITHAIM.

A'DIEL (*ornamented*). Prince in Simeon (1 Chr. iv. 36).—2. Priest (1 Chr. ix. 12).—3. Ancestor of Azmaveth (1 Chr. xxvii. 25).

A'DIN. 454 of his family returned with Zerubbabel (Ezr. ii. 15), and 51 with Ezra (viii. 16).

AD'INA (*pliant*). Son of Shiza, David's captain east of Jordan (1 Chr. xi. 42); next in rank to the "30 mighty men."

AD'INO, THE EZNITE. JASHOBEAM.

AD'INUS. JAMIN (1 Esd. ix. 48).

ADITHA'IM (*two shares of booty*). In the Shefela. HADID. (Josh xv. 36.)

AD'LAI. Ancestor of Shaphat, David's shepherd (1 Chr. xxvii. 29).

AD'MÄH (*fort*). In the vale of Siddim, always with Zeboim (Gen. x.). It had a king (xiv.), and was destroyed with Sodom and Gomorrah.

ADMA'THA. One of the 7 princes of Persia.

AD'NA (*pleasure*). Returned with Ezra (x. 30).

MODERN EGYPTIAN FUNERAL PROCESSION.

Pethen, the cobra.—3. *Tsepha*, in Prov. xxiii. 32, adder; in Is. xi. 8; Je. viii. 17, cockatrice. The original means *to hiss*. In the Septuagint, basilisk—which is a fabulous serpent.—4. *Shephiphon*, only in Gen. xlix. 17, of Dan, "a serpent by the way."

and married a gentile wife.—2. Priest in Joiakim's reign (Neh. xii. 12).

AD'NAH (*pleasure*). A Manassite; deserted Saul for David (1 Chr. xii. 20).—2. General of 300,000 in Jehoshaphat's army (2 Chr. xvii. 14).

ADŌ'NĀI (*Lord, Master*). Hebrew word for Lord, God, and Lord of Hosts.

The Hebrews did not pronounce the sacred name J. A. H. which we now call Jehovah, and its true pronounciation is supposed to be lost; instead of doing so, they said ADONAI when J. A. H. occurred in the text.

ADŌ'NI-BĒ'-ZEK (*lord of Bezek*). Canaanite king of Bezek, 17 miles E. of Shechem. He was head of the Canaanite and Perizzite bands, and was beaten and taken prisoner, maimed and died in Jerusalem, B. C. 1449 (Judg. i.).

ADŌNĪ'JÄH (*my lord is Jehovah*). Fourth son of David, born of Haggith at Hebron (2 Sam. iii.). After the death of Amnon and Absalom he made pretensions to the throne of David, supported by Joab and Abiathar, the high priest; but David caused Solomon to be proclaimed and crowned, and invested with authority. Adonijah was pardoned; but after David's death he renewed his attempt on the throne and was executed by Solomon's order (1 K.).

ADŌNĪ'RÄM (*lord, high*). ADORAM. Chief of the tribute receivers in the reigns of David, Solomon and Rehoboam. He became hateful to the people and was stoned to death (1 K.).

ÄDŌNĪZĒ'DEK (*lord of justice*). King of Jerusalem when Joshua entered Canaan. He joined with four Amorite kings to punish the Gibeonites for their league with Joshua. Being beaten by Joshua, they fled to a cave in Makkedah, where they were taken; had their necks trod upon as a sign of subjection, and were killed and buried in the cave (Josh. x.).

ADŎP'TION. Placing as a son one who is not so by birth. Never done by the Hebrews. Paul alluded to the Roman custom (Gal. iv.), where the law gave the adopted son equal rights with a real son. Abraham did not adopt Hagar's son, nor Jacob the sons of the maids of Leah and Rachel, nor the sons of Joseph; Moses was not adopted by Pharaoh's daughter according to law, but as an exception.

ADŌRÄ'-IM. SHEFELA. Built by Rehoboam (2 Chr. xi.). *Dura,* a large village 5 ms. S. W. of Hebron, marks the site.

ADŌRÄ'TION. The acts and postures in worship are similar in all Oriental nations, and have come down to the present from remote antiquity unchanged. It is believed that the Hebrews in *all* their prayers used all the forms of posture and prostration that the modern Arabs have grouped into *one* prayer, which are nine positions. All of these are found on the monuments of Egypt and Assyria. Prayer is made standing, with the hands lifted or crossed or folded; this is the posture before kings or great men. The hands are also stretched forth as in supplication; one hand only is lifted in taking an oath (Gen. xiv.). Kneeling is a common mode (1 K. vii.; Ezra ix.; Dan. vi.; Luke xxii.);

PRIEST.

prostration of the body, resting on the knees and arms, the forehead touching the ground, and the whole body lying along, the face being down. The monuments show figures kneeling on one knee and smiting the breast; sitting on the heels, the hands being folded, is a very respectful attitude (1 Chr. xvii. 16; 1 K. xviii. 42). Among the Romans

ADORATION—MODERN EGYPTIAN.

prostration was the peculiar act of adoration and worship (Acts x. 26), but Orientals do so in respect or reverence only. Kissing the head (1 Sam. x.), the hand, the hem of the garment, or the earth near the object of respect, and kissing one's own hand (Job xxxi. 27; Hosea xiii. 2), to persons or idols. Holding the hand on the mouth as in kissing it is the highest act of respect and adoration.

A-DRÄM'-MĒ-LECH (*fire king*). An idol worshiped by the colonists from Assyria in Samaria (2 Kings xvii. 31), by sacrificing children by fire. The idol represented the male power of the sun-god, ANAMMELECH, the female.

AD-RÄ-MYT'-TĬUM (*named after Adramys, brother of Croesus, king of Lydia*). Seaport in Asia Minor, where the ship belonged in which Paul was wrecked. The gulf of the same name was opposite the island of Lesbos. Pop. 1500, with some commerce.

Ā'-DRĬÄ. A'DRIAS. Sea named from Adria on the Po, Italy. At first the name was given to the upper end of the Gulf of Venice; afterwards to the whole gulf; and in Paul's time to the Mediterranean as bounded by Sicily, Italy, Greece and Africa (Acts xxvii. 27).

ÄD'-RĬ-ĒL (*God's flock*). Son of Barzillai, to whom Saul gave his daughter Merab, who had been promised to David (1 Sam. xvii. 19).

Ā-DUL'-LAM (*people's justice*). Judah, in the Shefela (Josh. xvi. 35). A place of great antiquity. Fortified by Rehoboam.

The CAVE OF ADULLAM is located 6 miles N. of Beit Jibrin, and now called Deir Dubban. There are many caves in this region. Some think the cave must have been nearer the Dead Sea, among the mountains, 6 miles S. W. of Bethlehem, in *Wady Khureitun.*

A-DÜL'-TERY. Crime of a married woman with a man not her husband. Or of either man or woman who is bound, with any other person not their mate. Orientals do not include the man in the condemnation. ADULTERY in the O. T. means symbolically idolatry and apostasy from the Hebrew church. In the N. T. "an adulterous generation" (Matt. xii. 39), means a faithless and impious generation — who did not worship the true God, but did worship false gods.

ĀDUM'MIM (*red pass*). BENJ.— (Josh. xv. 7). On the road from Jericho to Jerusalem, in *Wady Kelt.* It was always noted for robbers, and was therefore selected for the locality of the parable of the Good Samaritan. (Luke x.) Eight miles E. of Jerusalem there are ruins of a convent and a khan, on opposite sides of the road.

ADORATION—ANCIENT EGYPTIAN.

AD'-VENT, THE SECOND. The second coming of Jesus Christ, often foretold by Jesus, and frequently mentioned by the apostles. This event has been looked for and expected in every age and every year since the ascension. Some hold that Christ reigns now, at the right hand of the Father, and must reign until all enemies are put under his feet. They hold that the judgment is now going on; the wicked are passing away; and that men become *consciously* the subjects of this judgment as they pass into the invisible world.

AD'VŌCATE (*Greek* Paraclete). The name given to the Holy Spirit by Jesus (John xiv. 16); and to Jesus by John (1 John ii.).

Æ'NEAS. A paralytic healed by Peter (Acts ix. 33), at Lydda.

Æ'NŎN. Enon. (*Springs*). Near Salim, where John baptized (John iii. 22). Six miles S. of Bethshan, at Tell Redgah. A tomb near is called Shekh Salim. The brook in *Wady Chusneh* runs near, and many rivulets wind about in all directions. Here is "much water."

AG'ĀBUS (*locust*). One of the 70 disciples. Two prophesies of his are recorded, and their fulfilment (Acts xi. 27-30; xxi. 10). The famine through "all the world" was only through the world in Palestine—the Jews' world. It is mentioned by Josephus (xx. 2, 5), about A. D. 42, 14 years after Agabus met Paul at Cæsarea, and warned him of his sufferings at Jerusalem if he went up there.

MODERN EGYPTIAN HEAD DRESSES.

Ā'GAG (*burn*). A title of the king of the Amalekites, like Pharaoh of the Egyptians, Cæsar of the Romans, and Abimelech of the Philistines (Num. xxiv. 7; 1 Sam. xv. 8). AGAGITE for Amalekite in Esther iii. 1, 10; viii. 3, 5.

AG'A-PE (*Gr. agapœ, to love*). The Church perpetuated the commemoration of the death of Jesus by certain symbols at meals; a custom most beautiful and most beneficial; for it was a supporter of love, a solace of poverty, a moderator of wealth, and a discipline of humility. Tertullian, speaking of the Agape does not mention the Eucharist as distinct from the meal. "The nature of our supper may be gathered from its name, the Greek term for love. However much it may cost us, it is real gain to incur such expense in the cause of piety; for we aid the poor by this refreshment; we do not sit down to it till we have first tasted of prayer to God; we eat to satisfy our hunger; we drink no more than benefits the temperate; we feast as those who recollect they are to spend the night in devotion; we converse as those who know that the Lord is an ear-witness. After water for washing hands, and lights have been brought in,

every one is required to sing something in the praise of God, either from the Scriptures or from his own thoughts. By this means, if any one has indulged in excess, he is detected. The feast is closed with prayer." Pliny mentions this custom of the Christians, and says they eat common food (not such as was used for idol worship). Paul speaks of the abuse of this custom in 1 Cor. xi. 21; and, perhaps to avoid such abuse, the Eucharist was celebrated apart from any meal from about the year A. D. 150.

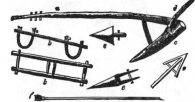

a, Plow. *b*, yoke. *f*, goad &c. *e*, points.

AG'ATE. Second precious stone in the high-priest's breastplate (SHEVO in Ex. xxviii. 19). In Is. liv. 12, and Ez. xxvii. 16, CADCOD, meaning a ruby. The same word is also translated chrysoprase and emerald. See PRECIOUS STONES.

ĀGE. Old age. Peculiar respect to old age is a general custom in the Orient, and has been from most remote times. The Scriptures record many instances of such respect and honor. The young rose and stood up in their presence (Lev. xix. 32); and even old men before one especially honored (Job xxix. 8). They were privileged to give the first words of counsel (Job xxxii.; Eccl. xxxii.); and old men, ELDERS, became a class, such as the FATHERS, and SENATORS in Rome, and were regarded as the depositaries of knowledge and experience (Job xv.). The attainment of old age was set forth as a blessing (Gen. xv.; Job v.), in prolonging the enjoyment of life, and a sign of peaceful times (Zech. viii.; Is. lxv.); a reward for piety, and a token of God's favor. Of all marks of respect, that to age is most willingly paid; because we may ourselves become aged, and receive such homage.

AGŌ'RA. A public place, broad street, market-place, forum; where goods are sold, meetings held for debate, and trial, and to idle away the time. See AREOPAGUS.

PLOW. HOE.

AG'RICULTURE. The earliest records are of the best men engaged in this pursuit. Laws regulating its affairs formed the chief code of the Hebrews, and tended to produce an equality in interest, binding the son and elevating the slave to a common servitude. The earth was the Lord's, and all were tenants to him, payable in the rent of the Sabbatical year. The family possession was inherited, and if sold must be returned on the year of Jubilee to the original owner, and wealthy owners of many fields were denounced (Is. v. 8). IRRIGATION was always needed for the best re-

hillsides, are a constant feature, and a necessity, in the hill country. On these narrow levels the vines, fruits and crops were raised, and frequent reference to fertilizers show a high state of culture, probably when the population was the greatest. Fences were not used, but watchmen guarded the ripening products, and the view was variegated by

PLOWING AND SOWING.

sults in Palestine—being neglected now, the soil is dry and sterile—although the rains of Canaan distinguished the country from the rainless Nile valley. There is in Palestine almost every variety of climate. Perpetual snow on Mt. Hermon and Mt. Lebanon; at Jericho, 60 or 80 miles distant, there is tropical heat, and snow is never seen. The hills of Bashan, Gilead, Galilee, Samaria, and Judea are the homes of forests, vines, fig-trees, and all kinds of fruit trees and vegetables; the plains produce bananas, oranges, lemons, besides all these, and frost is almost unknown. Palms formerly grew all over the country, as far north as Beirut and Baalbek. The greatest heat at Jerusalem is 90° (Fah.), and the cold 30°. Damascus is in a cooler latitude, and the record is 88° and 29°. The sky is almost cloudless for a large part of the year; the variations of sunshine and rain affecting only the autumn and winter months. The autumnal rains begin in the latter part of October, and gently continuing through November and December; and rain is rare after March, seldom or never so late as May. The ground is not often frozen in winter, snow lying during the night only; and in the plain of Jericho no snow or frost is ever seen, but there is on the hills around a spring-like temperature and air. The summer heat is oppressive, and fatal on exposure, but not on the higher hills, where heavy dews fall, and the nights are cool. The winter is the season of green fields and foliage, the summer heat destroying the grass. The HARVEST begins in the plain early in April; in Esdraelon in May, and on the hills in June.

The seasons were usually counted as two in the Scriptures, but we find six terms altogether (used by the Rabbins):—1. SEED-TIME, Oct. to Dec.; 2. WINTER, Dec. to Feb.; 3. COLD, Feb. to April; 4. HARVEST, April to June; 5. HEAT, June to Aug.: 6. SUMMER, Aug. to October.

The terraces, formed by stone walls along the

their different colors. The boundaries were marked by trees or piles of stones (Job xxiv.; Deut. xix. 14), and about gardens, orchards and vineyards there were walls (or hedges), having towers for watching and defense.

The monuments bear the sculptured figures of many implements, and pictures of the modes of using them in field and garden work. The PLOW is a kind of heavy hoe, used in the hand or drawn by animals or men (Job i. 14). It was made of a crooked root, shod with iron and fitted with one or two handles. The yoke was a straight or bent stick with rope or bent bows. The ox-goad was a pole six or eight feet, sharp at one end, and fitted with a spade at the other for clearing the plow, or for breaking clods (Is. xxviii. 24; Hosea x. 11; Job. xxxix. 10, where "harrow the valleys" should be "break the clods," as in the Hebrew). *Seed was sown* and hoed (harrowed) or plowed in, in drills or broadcast. Moses alluded in Deut. xi. 10 to the mode of sowing during the inundation, or by irrigation, in Egypt by using the foot (to open or stop the little rills of water). *Reaping* was of several modes: pulling up by the roots (as barley and doora are now in Egypt); and as wheat and barley do not grow very high (20 to 30 inches), it is pulled for convenience; by the sickle, at the ground, or just under the heads, as the straw may be wanted or not. Ears were carried in baskets; the whole stalk in sheaves (Gen. xxxvii. 7), and a cart is mentioned in Micah ii. 13. Camels or other animals are used to carry the produce. The poor were allowed to glean (Ruth ii. 7; Lev. xix. 9). *Threshing* was done on level places made in the

THRESHING AND WINNOWING.

field, called floors, about fifty feet across, circular. The grain was trodden out with cattle, arranged three or four abreast, and driven around, and the cattle were not to be muzzled (Deut. xxv. 4). Sticks and flails were used to thresh out small quantities (Ruth ii. 17; Is. xxviii. 27). Threshing machines were made of frames filled with sharp stones or pieces of iron set in holes, or fitted with circular saws (Land and Book ii. 315), which were drawn over the grain (Is. xxviii. 27; xli. 15; Amos i. 3). *Winnowing* was done, and is now, by tossing the grain against the wind with a fork or fan (Matt. iii. 12; Jer. iv. 11), and then passing it through a sieve (Amos ix. 9). It was stored in granaries cut in the rock, built underground, or above (Jer. xli. 8).

Ā'GUR (*one of the assembly*). Author of the

sessor of Ahab, and 8th king of Israel. B. C. 897 to 896.—2. Son of Jehoram, 6th king of Judah. B. C. 885.

AH'BAN (*brotherly*). Son of Abishur by Abihail (1 Chr. ii. 29).

A'HER (*another*). Ancestor of the Hushim (1 Chr. vii. 12).

A'HI (*brother*). Chief of a family in Gad, Gi-

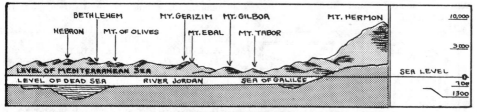

PROFILE OF PALESTINE, N. TO S.

sayings in Prov. xxx. Native of Massa, East Arabia, and lived about B. C. 600. Some have supposed that this was an assumed name of Solomon, such as was "Koheleth," translated "preacher."

A'HAB (*father's brother*). Son of Omri, king of Israel, and reigned 22 years, B. C. 918 to B. C. 897. His wife was JEZEBEL, daughter of Ethbaal, king of Tyre, a woman of strong character, and an idolatress. She succeeded in introducing the worship of Baal into Israel, a temple being built at Samaria for the worship. Elijah, the prophet, pronounced the judgment of God on Ahab's house, and he died of wounds received in battle (see 1 Kings).—2. A false prophet, son of Kolaiah, who deceived the Jewish exiles in Babylon (Jer. xxix. 21).

AHAR'AH. Third son of Benjamin (1 Chr. viii. 1).

AHAR'HEL. The family (in Judah) traced its descent from Ashur, a posthumous son of Hezron, through Coz (1 Chr. iv. 8).

AHA'SAI. Priest; ancestor of Amashia (Neh. xi. 13).

AHAS'BAI (*refuge in God*). Father of Eliphelet (2 Sam. xxiii. 34).

AHASUĒ'RUS (*Achashverosh*). The title of the Persian king, and means *lion-king*. Four persons are mentioned by this title, who were, 1. ASTYAGES (Dan. ix.); 2. CAMBYSES (Ezra iv.); 3. The husband of Vashti and Esther, the same who was

lead (1 Chr. v. 15).—2. A descendant of Shamer, of Asher (1 Chr. vii. 34). AHIJAH?

AHĪ'AH (*friend of God*). AHIJAH.

AHĪ'AM (*father's brother*). One of David's 30 heroes (2 Sam. xxiii. 33).

AHĪ'AN. Of Shemida, Manasseh (1 Chr. vii. 19).

AHĪ'EZER (*helper*). Chief in Dan, in the Exode (Num. i. 12).—2. Chief of a band of bowmen with David (1 Chr. xii. 3).

AHĪ'HUD (*brother of Jews*). Chief in Asher; one of Joshua's assistants in the allotment (Num. xxxiv. 27).—2. Chief in Benjamin (1 Chr. viii. 7).

AHĪ'JAH, or AHIAH (*friend of Jehovah*). Son of Ahitub; grandson of Phinehas (1 Sam. xiv. 3, 18). He was a priest at Shiloh, in care over the ark; giving oracles by the aid of the ark and the ephod. It is not known what caused the neglect of the ark in the latter day of Saul's reign. Saul's rash curse, Jonathan's danger, the failure to get an answer from the oracle, the peoples' rescue of Jonathan, led to coolness between the king and the high priest, which ended in a terrible revenge, after Ahimelech's favor to David. Ahimelech may have been Ahijah's brother.—2. Son of Bela. ACHIA (1 Chr. viii. 7).—3. Son of Jerahmeel.—4. One of David's 30 (1 Chr. xi. 36).—5. Levite in David's reign; treasurer in the temple (1 Chr. xxvi. 20).—6. AHIAT. Son of Shisha, an officer of Solomon (1 K. iv. 3).—7. AHIAS. Prophet in Shiloh (Shilonite), in the time of Solomon and Jeroboam (1 K. xiv. 2), who prophesied the breaking loose

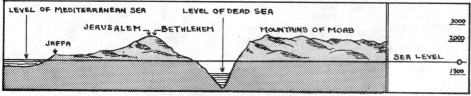

PROFILE ACROSS—JAFFA TO MOAB.

called XERXES by the Greeks; the marriage with Esther is assigned to his 7th year, in which he returned to Shushan from his disastrous expedition to Greece; 4. Mentioned in Tobit xiv. 15, who was Cyaxares I.

ĀHĀ'VA (*river*). River in Babylonia, on whose banks Ezra collected the Jewish exiles for the return to Jerusalem (Ezra viii. 15, 31). Hit.

Ā'HAZ (*possessor*). Son and successor of Jotham, and 11th king of Judah. Reigned 16 years, B. C. 714 to 729. He respected neither God, the law nor the prophets.

AHĀZĪ'AH (*holden of Jehovah*). Son and suc-

of the ten tribes from Solomon's kingdom in punishment for his idolatry (1 K. xi. 31-39) ; and the death of Ahijah, the king's son, and at the same time the captivity of Israel (1 K. xiv. 6-16). See 2 Chr. ix. 29, for a reference to work by Ahijah, now lost.—8. Father of Baasha, king of Israel (of Issachar), (1 K. xv. 27).—9. A chief who signed the covenant with Nehemiah (Neh. x. 26).

AHĪ'KAM (*enemy's brother*). Son of Shaphan the scribe (2 K. xxii. 12). He was one of the delegates sent to Huldah, the prophetess, by the king. He protected Jeremiah, the prophet, after he was taken out of the pit (Jer. xxxix. 14).

AHI′LUD (*maker*). Father of Jehoshaphat the recorder (2 Sam. viii. 16).—2. Father of Baanä (1 K. iv. 12).

Ā-HĪ-MA′-AZ (*choleric*). 1. Father of Saul's wife, Ahinoam.—2. Son and successor of Zadok, high priest, in David's reign.—3. Son-in-law of Solomon, and one of his 12 chief purveyors, or tax collectors; whose district was Naphtali.

AHI′MAN (*giver*). One of three famous giants. Anakim of Hebron (Num. xiii. 22).

ĀHIM′ELECH (*king's brother*). Great grandson

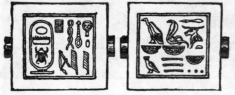

THOTHME'S RING.

of Eli, priest at Nob, who gave David some of the sacred bread from the presence-table, and the sword of Goliath, which had been in safe keeping there.

AHI′MOTH (*deathly*). Kohathite in David's reign (1 Chr. vi. 25).

AHIN′ADAB. One of 12 officers who gathered monthly supplies for Solomon's household at Mahanaim, in Manasseh (1 K. iv. 14).

AHI′O (*brotherly*). Son of Abinadab. Ahio went before and his brother behind the ark, when it was carried from their father's house (2 Sam. vi. 3).—2. Benjamite, a son of Beriah (1 Chr. viii 14).—3. Benjamite, son of Jehiel, founder of Gibeon (1 Chr. viii. 31).

AHI′RAM (*exalted brother*). Son of Benjamin; Ehi in Gen. xlvi. 21. AHI′RAMITES. Descendants of Ahiram.

AHIS′AMACH (*supporter*). Danite, father of Aholiob, architect on the tabernacle (Ex. xxxi. 6).

AHISH′AHAR (*morning dawn*). Son of Bilhan, grandson of Benjamin (1 Chr. vii. 10).

AHI′SHAR (*upright*). Controller of king Solomon's household. Always an office of great trust and influence in the east (1 K. iv. 6).

ĀHITH′OPHEL (*foolish*). A statesman of brilliant talents in David's time. His counsels were regarded as oracles (2 Sam. xvi.). When his counsels to Absalom were neglected for those of Hushai (whom David had sent), he went home and hanged himself at Giloh. The only suicide mentioned in the O. T., except those engaged in war.

AHITUB (*goodness*). Father of Ahimelech.—2. Son of Amariah, grandfather of Zadok, the high priest (1 Chr. vi. 7).

AH′LAB (*fertility*). City in Asher (Judg. i. 31). Gush Caleb in after times, and now El Jish, near Safed.

AH′LAI (*a wish*). Daughter to Sheshan, wife of Jarha an Egyptian slave (1 Chr. ii. 31, 35). Zabad, one of David's heroes descended from her (1 Chr. xi. 41), and Azariah, one of Joash's captains (2 Chr. xxiii. 1).

AHŌ′AH (*friend of God*). Son of Bela, of Benjamin (1 Chr. viii. 4). Ahoite in 2 Sam. xxiii. 9.

AHŌ′LAH (*her own tent*). AHOLI′BAH (*my tent in her*). Two fictitious names used by the prophet Ezekiel for Israel (Samaria) and Judah. Describing their neglect of the true worship of Jehovah, and their consequent disgrace and ruin.

ĀHŌ′LĬ-AB (*father's tent*). Skilful artizan of the tribe of Dan, who, with Bezaleel, constructed the Tabernacle.

AHŪ′MAI. Son of Jahath, Judah (1 Chr. iv. 2).

AHŪ ZAM. Ahuzzam. Son of Ashur, founder of Tekoa (1 Chr. iv. 6).

AHUZ′ZATH (*possession*). The "friend" or "favorite" who was with Abimelech II on his visit to Isaac (Gen. xxvi. 26). Some interpret the word ahuzzath to mean a company, or a retinue.

Ā-Ī (*heap of ruins*). Benj. (Gen. xii. 8). HAI E. of Bethel. The second city taken by Joshua in Canaan. Eight miles N. of Jerusalem.—2. Burial place of Elon, in Zebulon (Judg. xii.).

A′IAH (*clamor*). Son of Zibeon. Ajah in Gen; xxxvi. 24 (1 Chr. i. 40).

A′IATH (Is. x. 28). AI. AI′JA.

AI′JALON (*gazelle place*). A city of the Kohathites (Josh. xxi. 24), in Dan. (xix. 42); fortified by Rehoboam (2 Chr. xi. 10). Celebrated in the poem on the battle of Joshua in the "Book of Jasher" (Josh. x. 12). Now Ain Yalo, 12 miles N. W. of Jerusalem.—2. City of Zebulun; birth-place of Elon, and his burial-place. JALUN, east of Acre.

AI′JELETH. AYELETH HAS-SHACHAR (*hind of the dawn*). Only in Ps. xxii. in the introduction. as the name of the tune in which that psalm might be chanted.

Ā′IN (*fountain*). En. Prefix to many names, as Engedi, Enrogel.—1. Num. xxxiv. 11, a source of the Jordan, or a town near.—2. City in Judah (Josh. xv. 32).

Ā′JĀLON (*stag*). Valley and town in Benj. noted in Joshua's exploits (Josh. x. 12). Several other towns of the same name, in Dan, Ephraim and Zebulun.

A′KAN (*keen-sighted*). Descendant of Esau (Gen. xxxvi. 27). Jakan in 1 Chr. i. 42.

AK′KUB (*insidious*). Descendant of Zerubbabel; one of the 7 sons of Elioenai (1 Chr. iii. 24). 2. Doorkeeper at the east-gate of the temple. His descendants are reported among the returned from Babylon (1 Chr. ix. 17). Dacobi in 1 Esd. v. 28.— 3. A Nethinim (Ezr. ii. 45). Acub in 1 Esd. v. 30.— 4. A Levite (Neh. viii. 7). Jacubus in 1 Esd. ix. 48.

AK-RĀB′-BIM (*scorpions*). Maa′leh Akrab′bim, *scorpion pass*, in the mountains south of the Dead Sea.

AL′EMA. City in Gilead, large and strong (1 Macc. v. 26). BEER-ELIM?

ALABASTER VASES.

ALABĀS′TER. So named from the town of Alabastron, in Middle Egypt, where there are quarries of this fine-grained, pink-colored gypsum. It is not clear, but is colored in stripes, much varied in width and tint—very near the tint of their fingernails, including the crescent light place at the upper end of the nails. It was made into cups, boxes, etc. for holding perfumes, ointments, and other precious articles. Boxes for the same uses of any substance—wood, glass, stone, metal—were also called alabasters (Matt. xxvi. 7; Mark xiv. 3; Luke vii. 37).

ALEXAN′DER (*men helper*). King of Macedon. Called the Great. Born at Pella B. C. 356, son of Philip and Olympias. Educated by the famous philosopher Aristotle. Alluded to in Daniel's prophesy. He destroyed the Persian empire and placed Greeks in power there; conquered Asia,

332, by the help of the same architect who rebuilt the Temple of Diana, at Ephesus. For centuries this was the largest city in the world. Pop. 600,000 (Diodorus). The lighthouse of its spacious port was famous in the world of commerce as the PHAROS, one of the 7 wonders. The great library is said to have had 700,000 volumes (Strabo), even after losing 400,000 by fire (B. C. 47), and was finally destroyed by the Saracens, A. D. 642.

ALEXANDRIA.

Egypt, Syria, and founded the city of ALEXANDRIA (B. C. 332), which may be said to have been built on the ruins of Sidon and Tyre, for it grew rich and powerful on the Oriental trade which formerly fed those cities, and was then diverted from the Euphrates to the Red Sea route. Alexander's toleration of Oriental customs and religions, guaranteeing to all people (and especially the Jews, who were exempted from tax on the 7th year,) the free observance of their hereditary laws, showing the same respect to their gods as to the gods of Greece, thus combining and equalizing the West and the East, weakened all the nationalities of his empire, and tended to dissolve the old religions. The Greek and Hebrew learning of Alexandria greatly influenced the planting of Christianity there, as well as in Asia. He married Roxana and Parysatis, Eastern princesses, an example followed by 80 generals and 10,000 soldiers of his army, who married Oriental wives. Josephus gives an ac-

TETRADRACHM OF ALEXANDER THE GREAT. B. C. 350.

count of a visit of Alexander to Jerusalem, and his reception by the high priest, which has been called fabulous (Ant. xi. 8). He died at Babylon B. C. 323, only 32 years old, of intemperance.

ALEXAN′DER BĀLĀS. A pretended son of Antiochus Epiphanes. He reigned four years over Syria (1 Macc. x. 11; Jos. Ant. xiii. 2).

ALEXAN′DER JÁNNÆUS. The first prince of the Maccabees, who called himself king.

ALEXAN′DER. Four persons so named in the Gospels.—1. Son of Simon the Cyrenean, who bore the cross part of the way (Mark xv.).—2. A powerful opponent of the apostles, related to the high priest (Acts iv. 6).—3. Son of Herod the Great and Marianne.—4. A Jew of Ephesus, who took part in the uproar in the temple of Diana, against Paul.—5. A coppersmith, excommunicated by Paul for errors.

ALEXAN′DRIA. Greek, Roman, and Christian capital of Egypt, founded by Alexander, B. C.

Among the learned men were Philo, a Jew (author of works which contain the best array of Hebrew Platonism—almost an imitation of Christian ethics), and Origen and Clement, Christians, whose writings have influenced and directed religious men in all Christian nations to the present. Ptolemy Philadelphus favored the translation from Hebrew into Greek of the Holy Scriptures (Old Testament), and the work was called the SEPTUAGINT, finished about B. C. 280. It is now the oldest known version, and is called the Codex Alexandrinus (Jos. c.; Apion ii. 4). See WRITING.

The Museum was the means of spreading a knowledge of Aristotle through the civilized world, and at one time it gathered 14,000 students from all the world. Modern astronomy arose there, under the direction of Eratosthenes, who taught the globe shape of the earth, its poles, axis, equator, arctic circles, equinoctial points, solstices, horizon, eclipses, and the distance of the sun. Callimachus (poet) wrote a treatise on birds; Apollonius one on mathematics and geometry, and invented a clock. Hipparchus was the great astronomer of the age, and discovered the precession of the equinoxes, gave methods of solving all triangles, and constructed tables of chords, tables of latitude and longitude, and a map of more than 1000 stars. The Almagest of Ptolemy (A. D. 138), was for 1500 years the highest authority on the phenomena and mechanism of the universe. The same author described the world from the Canaries to China.

These systems were supplanted by the discoveries of Newton of the law of gravitation, and of Columbus of the New World. There was a very extensive botanical and zoological garden, and a school for the study of Anatomy and dissection. The temples of Isis and Sarepis were among the finest ever built, and were partly

ALEXANDER BALAS.

used for scientific purposes, having the most perfect instruments for astronomical observations then known. They were destroyed by Bishop Theophilus A. D. 390. Present pop. about 60,000 from all nations.

AL'LÓN (*oak?*). ELON. Naphtali (Josh. xix. 33). Zaananim, *loading tents*, near Kedesh (Judg. iv. 11).—2. ALLON-BAC'HUTH (*oak of weeping*), under which Rebekah's nurse, Deborah, was buried (Gen. xxxv. 8). Palm tree of Deborah in Judg. iv. 5, between Ramah and Bethel.

AL'MOND. Nut tree, larger than a peach tree; thrives from China to Spain, and on both sides of the Mediterranean, and nowhere better than in Syria. It is the earliest to blossom in spring (February), the pink-white blossoms appearing some weeks before the leaves.

ALMOND TREE AND BLOSSOMS.

ALMS. The Hebrews had no word for a free gift to the poor, such as alms, but used *righteousness* for such acts, as in Job xxix. 10–16; Prov. x. 2; Deut. xiv. 29; xxiii. 24, 25; xxiv. 19; xxvi. 12; Lev. xix. 9, 10; xxiii. 22; xxv. 5. The laws of Moses made ample provision against poverty, and if they had been strictly kept, in letter and spirit, there could not have been any destitution. The gospel recognizes the duty of alms-giving and enforces it, and this virtue was a peculiar mark of a Christian in the early age. This was not made a definite rule, but was left to the constraint of inward principle and feeling, "to prove the sincerity of their love." Encouragement of idle vagrancy was denounced as wrong, and such idlers were scorned (2 Thess. iii. 10–12). The Jews, since the destruction of Jerusalem, have regarded their poor as the people of God, and those who give to them are credited with as much virtue as if they kept all the commandments, and they teach that alms-giving atones for their sins. As Jesus sought the needy and the sick, and kindly ministered help and consolation, so it is his will that his Church shall show the same spirit towards the poor and afflicted.

AL'MUG. ALGUM. Fragrant sandal-wood, white and yellow, found in the mountains of Malabar. The trees are 9 to 12 inches through, 25 to 30 feet high. Its uses were for perfume, incense, beads, rosaries, fans, elegant boxes, and cabinets, and for musical instruments. Solomon used it for pillars in the houses he built, and for musical instruments (1 K. x. 12; 2 Chr. ix. 10).

AL'NATHAN. ELNATHAN (1 Esd. viii. 44; Ezr. viii. 16).

AL'OE. An ordoriferous, precious tree of Siam, where it is worth its weight in gold, and is used for perfuming garments and rooms, and as a medicine. It is not our gum aloes.

AL'PHÆUS (Alpheus, *exchange*). Father of the lesser James (Matt. x. 3). Called Cleopas in John xix. 25. Alphæus and Cleopas are synonymous in Hebrew and Greek.

ALPHABET. WRITING.

AL'TAR. The central point of religious worship, as a mount, table or structure of turf, wood, stone or metal, on which sacrifice was made to some deity. The first one mentioned in the Bible is that built by Noah. Moses restricted the building of altars to those for the temple service only; but the law was often broken (Lev. xvii.; Deut. xii.; Judg. vi.; 1 Sam. vii.; 2 Sam. xxiv.; 1 K. iii.). Moses directed two kinds to be made: 1. ALTAR OF BURNT-OFFERING, the table of the Lord (Ex. xxvii. 8), having horns to which the animal to be sacrificed might be bound (Ps. cviii. 27); and a ledge half way up, on which the priests could stand, which was fenced below with a net work of metal; —2. ALTAR OF INCENSE, the golden altar, Ex. xxxix. 38, (the other being the brazen) (Ex. xxxviii. 30). This was not strictly an altar, as no sacrifice was offered on it. Both had rings for carrying by poles.

ALTÁS'CHITH (*destroy not*). In the introduction to Psalms lvii., lviii., lix., lxxv., indicating the melody to which the psalms were to be sung.

Ā'LUSH (*wild place*). Station in the Exodus, not identified (Num. xxxiii. 13).

AL'VAN (*thick*). Horite, son of Shobal (Gen. xxxvi. 23). ALIAN (1 Chr. i. 40).

A'MAD (*station*). In Asher, lost (Josh. xix. 26).

AMAD'ATHA. AMADATHUS. (Est. xii. 6; xvi. 10.) HAMMEDATHA.

A'MAL. Descendant of Ashur, son of Jacob (1 Chr. vii. 35).

AM'ALEK (*to lick up*). Son of Eliphaz, grandson of Esau, and a Shekh of Edom (Gen. xxxvi.).

AMAL'EKITES. An ancient nomadic race, found from Petræa to the Persian Gulf, and may have been descendants of the grandson of Esau. The mention of this country in Gen. xv. 7, does not imply that they were a people at that early time, but that they were a people in that country when the history was written. They were doomed to extinction because they opposed the Hebrews; and they were fewer and weaker from age to age up to the last mention in David's time (1 Sam. xxvii.; xxx. 17), who destoyed their remnant.

A'MAN. HAMAN. (Tobit xiv. 10; Esth. x. 7., etc.).

AM'ANA. Mt. near the S. end of Anti-Lebanon, where the Abana rises (Cant. iv. 8).

AMARI'AH (*whom Jehovah promised*). 1. Father of Ahitub.—2. High priest in the reign of Jehoshaphat.—3. A Kohathite Levite.—4. Priest in Hezekiah's time. —5. Son of Bani (Ezr. x.).—6. Priest with Zerubbabel.—7. A descendent of Pharez.—8. Ancestor of Zephaniah the prophet.

AM'ASA (*burden*). Son of Ithra, by David's sister Abigail. Was general to Absalom, and was defeated by Joab, but pardoned by David, and appointed Joab's successor as general. Joab killed him treacherously (2 Sam.).

EARTHEN LAMP. 2.

AMA'SHAI. Son of Azareel, priest in the time of Nehemiah (xi. 13). Amash'sai, correctly.

AMASI'AH (*whom God bears*). Son of Zichri, Jehoshaphat's general of 200,000 in Judah (2 Chr. xvii. 16).

A'MATH. HAMATH.

AMATHE'IS (1 Esd. ix. 29). ATHLAI.

AM'ATHIS (*the land of*). HAMATH. (1. Macc. xii. 25).

AMAZI'AH (*whom Jehovah strengthens*). Son of Joash and 8th king of Judah. Began to reign at 25, B. C. 838, and reigned 29 years. He was the first to hire men to fill his army. He conquered Edom and carried home the idols for worship, and so brought on his own ruin, and was killed by conspirators at Lachish.—2. Priest of the golden calf at Bethel, under Jeroboam II, in the time of the prophet Amos (vii. 10).

GLASS LAMP.

AMEDA'THA. (Esth. iii. 1) HAMMEDATHA.

A'MEN' (*truth*). Hebrew word, usually translated *verily;* or at the end of sentences not translated, but meaning *so be it.* In Rev. iii. 14 it is used as a name of the Lord, "the Amen, the faithful and true witness." It is used as a word of confirmation, binding a saying, or an oath (Num. v. 22; Deut. xxvii. 15; Neh v. 13; Ps. cvi. 48), and as a response or closing of a prayer (Matt. vi. 13; Rom. xi. 36).

AM'MI (*my people*). The name of Israel when they shall have been restored to God's favor (Hos. ii. 1).

AM'MIDOI. Returned with Zerubbabel (1 Esd. v. 20). Humtah in Josh. xv. 54. AMMIDIOI.

AM'MIEL (*people of my God*). Spy from Dan, in the Exodus (Num. xiii. 12).—2. Father of Machir of Lodebar (2 Sam. ix. 4).—3. Father of Bathshua, wife of David (1 Chr. iii. 5); ELIAM in 2 Sam. xi. 3. Son of Ahithophel.—4. Sixth son of Obed-edom (1 Chr. xxvi. 5), a doorkeeper of the temple.

AMMI'HUD (*people of Judah*). Father of Elishama; chief in the Exodus; an Ephraimite (Num. i. 10); ancestor of Joshua (1 Chr. vii. 26).—2. Simeonite chief in the allotment; father of Shemuel (Num. xxxiv. 20).—3. Father of Pedahel, chief in the allotment (ib. 28).—4. Father of Talmai, king of Geshur (2 Sam. xiii 37).—5. Descendant of Pharez (1 Chr. ix. 4).

AMMIN'ADAB (*bounteous people*). Son of Aram, father of Elizabeth, wife of Aaron; an ancestor of Jesus (Matt. i. 4).—2. Kohathite Levite in David's time.—3. One of the most noted charioteers of his day (Cant. vi. 12). If this last is read *ammi-nadib*, it will mean *my loyal people.*

AMMIN'ADIB. (Cant. vi. 12).

AMMISHAD'DAI (*people of the Almighty*). Father of Ahiezer, chief in Dan in the Exodus (Num. i. 12).

AMMIZ'ABAD (*people of the giver*). Son of Be-naiah, and his father's lieutenant over the 3d division of David's army, in the 3d monthly course (1 Chr. xxvii. 6).

AM'MON (*son of my relative*). AMMONITES. Ben Ammi in Gen. xix. 38. Descended from Lot. The people occupied the territory afterwards given to Reuben and Gad, after driving out the Zamzummim (Deut. ii. 20). Jabbok was their border on the N. They were nomadic, restless and predatory, as the Moabites were settled, civilized and industrious. They opposed the march of Israel to Canaan, and although favored by Moses (Deut. ii. 9), yet they were hated and warred with always. They worshipped *Moloch*, also called *Milcom*, and *Malcham.* Saul was made king (the second time) on account of his relief of Jabesh from the Amalekites (1 Sam. xi.). Women of this people were in Solomon's house. The last mention of them is in 1 Macc. v. 6, 30–43.

AM'NON (*faithful*). Eldest son of David by Ahinoam, born at Hebron B. C. 1056. Killed by Absalom 1032.

A'MOK (*deep*). Priest; returned with Zerubbabel (Neh. xii. 7).

AM'OMUM. An aromatic plant growing in India, Armenia, Media, and Pontus, described by Pliny, but not identified in our day. In Rev. xviii. 13 of the Hebrew—not in the A. V. The oily extract was used for the hair; and the name given to any fine perfume.

A'MON (*builder*). Son of Manasseh, and king of Judah. An idolater, and reigned only two years, B. C. 644–2 (2 K. xxi.).

A'MON (*multitude*). Egyptian deity. The name is translated generally in the O. T., which confuses the meaning. In Jer. xlvi. 25 "multitude of No" should be "Amon of No." And in Nahum iii. 8 "populous No" means No-Amon. The Greeks called this god Jupiter Ammon. On the monuments the name is Amun-re—Amon the son. He was supposed to be in the form of man, and was the supreme god of Egypt—king of gods.

AMON.

AM'ORITE (*mountaineers*). On both sides of Jordan (Num. xxi.; Gen. xv. 16; Deut. i. 20). From Emor, 4th son of Canaan. Og and Sihon, their kings E. of Jordan, opposed Moses, but were beaten, and their land was given to Reuben, Manasseh, and Gad. This district was good pasture, and is now. Five Amorite kings on the W. of Jordan opposed Joshua, and were defeated. The Jebusites were a branch, who held Zion 400 years after Joshua, until David took it (2 Sam. v. 6). Solomon imposed a tribute on the remnant of the people (1 K ix. 20).

A'MOS (*burden*). Prophet in the days of Isaiah and Hosea. Native of Tekoa, and was a dresser of sycamore (fig) trees. He prophesied at Bethel. His book is one of the finest in style, being full of pure language, vivid pictures, and often sublime thoughts; most of his imagery is taken from rural life. B. C. 780. See HISTORY.

A'MOZ (*strong*). Father of Isaiah.

AMPHIP'OLIS. Capital of a district in Macedonia (Acts xvii). On a height on the east bank of the river Strymon, 3 miles from the sea. The gold mines of Mt. Pangæus made the city famous

Now *Newtown.* Xerxes sacrificed nine young men and maids, and several white horses, on the bank of the Strymon (Herod. vii. 113).

AMPLI'AS. Disciple at Rome, beloved of Paul in the Lord (Rom. xvi. 8).

AM'RAM (*high ones*). Son of Kohath, father of Moses and Aaron.

AM'RAPHEL (*keeper of the gods*). Hamite king of Shinar (Gen. xiv. 1, 9).

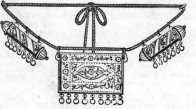

MODERN EGYPTIAN AMULET.

AM'ULET (*pendant*). Any object carried as a magical protection against evil or danger. Tickets with writing; stones and metal with pictures and writing. Moses tried to turn the practice to good use by directing his laws to be written on them (Ex. xiii. 9, 16; Deut. vi. 8; xi. 18). They are now very common in oriental countries, and not unknown in our own land. Jacob found some worn as earrings (Gen. xxxv.).

AM'ZI. Merarite; ancestor of Ethan the singer (1 Chr. vi. 46).—2. Ancestor of Adaiah, priest in Nehemiah's time (xi. 12).

A'NAB (*grapery*). Judah (Josh. xi. 21), from which Joshua expelled the Anakim. A tower marks the site near Maon (Rob. ii. 195).

A'NAH (*answer*). Son of Zibeon, father of Esau's wife, Aholibamah (Gen. xxxvi. 24). He discovered the hot springs of Callirohoe. He was a Horite, that is, a mountaineer. He is also called BEERI (fountains) the Hittite, in honor of his finding the springs.

ANAHA'RATH (*pass*). Place in Issachar (Josh. xix. 19). ARANEH, 2 miles E. of Jenin (Rob. ii. 316, 319. Hackett).

ANA'IAH (*whom God answers*). Who stood at Ezra's right hand during the reading of the law (Neh. viii. 4). ANANIAS in 1 Esd. ix. 43.

A'NAK. AN'AKIM (*neck-chain*). Name of a race of tall people, who lived at Hebron, and vicinity (Num. xiii. 33; Josh. xv. 14), descended from ARBA. They appear on the monuments of Egypt as tall and light colored, and are called Tammahu, from the Hebrew Talmai.

ANAM'MELECH (*kingly image*). The Assyrian Moloch, in whose worship the people passed their children through the fire. This was the *female* power as ADRAMMELECH was the *male* power of the sun-god.

A'NAN (*cloud*). A chief who signed the covenant with Nehemiah (x. 26).

ANA'NI (*protected*). Seventh son of Elioenai, of the royal line of Judah (1 Chr. iii. 24).

ANANI'AH (*protected by Jah*). Priest; ancestor of Azariah; assisted in rebuilding the wall (Neh. iii. 23).

ANANIAH. Place between Nob and Hazor (Neh. xi. 32).

ANANI'AS. A disciple at Jerusalem who, with his wife, Sapphira, tried to impose on Peter and the brethren, and defile the house of God, died suddenly, and was buried at once (Acts v).—2. Made high priest (Acts xxiii.) about A. D. 477 by Herod, king of Chalcis (Ant. xx. 5, 2). He made himself great wealth out of his office. Paul when before the Sanhedrin called him a white wall, and prophesied his ruin, which came in a time of trouble, and he fell by an assassin (Wars ii. 17; vi. 69).—3. Disciple at Damascus, who was directed (by the Lord) to go to Saul and lay hands on him, to ordain him to the ministry (Acts ix. 10–17). Tradition makes him bishop of Damascus, and a martyr.

ANAN'IEL. Forefather of Tobit (i. 1). HANANEEL.

A'NATH (*answer*). Father of Shamgar (Judg. ii. 31).

ANATH'EMA (*suspended*). When said of things given to God, it is pronounced anathema (Luke xxi. 5). It was also the religious curse of the Hebrews. It means also *devoted*—any person or thing devoted to God. Paul means *devoted* where he says *accursed*, in Rom. ix. 3. Those Jews *devoted* themselves to the work of killing Paul (Acts xxiii. 12). *Anathema maranatha* (*the Lord comes*), means that the curse (as well as a blessing) has its operation in Christ's kingdom, and rises to its highest power at his coming, and he will surely come to bless as well as to curse (1 Cor. xvi. 22). It was used as the church censure, or final excommunication, and it is so used now, of those who are excluded from the company of the believers.

AN'ATHOTH (*echoes*). Ben., near Nob and Hazor (Neh. xi. 32). *Anata*, 3½ ms. N. E. of Jerusalem, where there are remains of walls and buildings in the midst of orchards of figs and olives. The quarries still supply Jerusalem.

JEWISH HIGH PRIEST.

ANDREW (*strong man*). Brother of Peter, and native of Bethsaida in Galilee (John i. 44). He was first a disciple of John the Baptist, but followed Jesus on John's testimony, and informed his brother Peter of what he had found—that Jesus was the Christ (verses 35, 36, 41). He did not leave his business of fishing until some time after (Mark i. 14). He was present at the feeding of the 5000 at Jerusalem, when the Greek Jews wished to see Jesus (John vi. 8); and, with others, on Olivet, asked privately of Jesus what he meant by his strange words about destroying and rebuilding the temple. Of his after-life and death nothing is recorded. Tradition says he preached in Scythia, or Achaia, and was crucified on a cross, now called St. Andrew's, which is of a peculiar shape, and still bears his name. The early writers mention the "Acts of Andrew," and the "Gospel of St. Andrew," but they were rejected, and are lost.

ANDRŌ′NICUS (*man conquerer*). Fellow-prisoner of Paul, and his kinsman, and a disciple before Paul's conversion. The allusion in Romans xvi. 7 probably has reference to some part of Paul's history, now lost.

Ā′NEM (*two springs*). In Issachar (1 Chr. vi. 37). ENGANNIN.

by Quirinus), and then deposed by **Valerius Gratus.** Father-in-law to Caiaphas, who was high priest when Jesus was crucified (John xviii.; Acts iv. 6). The office of high priest was judicial, in addition to the temple service, and Annas for a long period held this honored place, his term having been 20 years. Five of his sons succeeded each other to

CITY OF ASKELON.

Ā′NER (*boy*). A Canaanite sheikh who joined Abram, Eshcol and Mamre in pursuit of Chedorlaomer (Gen. xiv).—2. Town of the Levites in Manasseh (1 Chr. vi. 70).

AN′ETHOTHITE, THE. Resident of ANATHOTH. ANTOTHITE (2 Sam. xxiii. 27).

ANGAREU′O (*compel*). From the Tartar language, meaning forced service (as a mounted courier) without pay (Matt. v. 41; Mark xv. 21).

AN′GEL (*messenger*). Whatever God employs to do his will. In Ps. civ. 4 (quoted in Heb. i. 7), the wind (spirit) is His angel. Haggai was called the Lord's angel (i. 13), as was John the Baptist by Malachi (iii. 1). Israel was God's angel, sent to enlighten the world (Is. xlii. 19), as well as the priests (Mal. ii. 7), meaning the priests as a body. Jesus spoke of *angels of God*, who were neither married nor given in marriage, but were *spirits*, not in the flesh, but above, more free, more powerful, more wise (Matt. xxii. 30; xxvi. 53; Gen. xvi. 7; Heb. xii. 22). There are angels of light (of heaven), and angels of darkness, "that kept not their first estate." Isaiah speaks of the *angel of the presence* (lxiii. 9), and Moses of the angel that went before Israel (Ex. xxiii. 21), who has the whole world as his heritage (Rev. viii. 3), and who is believed to be the Lord Jesus, whom the Father sent to reveal Him to men.

ANK′LET. Ornament of gold, silver, brass iron or glass, for the ankles, worn in ancient and modern days in the East by women. Isaiah (iii. 16) says they made a tinkling with the feet; that is, the women tinkled them together when they walked in a mincing way. A string of little bells is worn by some Arab girls.

AN′NA. Prophetess of the tribe of Asher, daughter of Phanuel. She was 84 when in the temple, as mentioned by Luke (ii. 36), she recognized the Messiah.

AN′NAS. High priest for 15 years (appointed

the same office, and then his son-in-law; and in all these changes he had exercised the highest judicial authority. He might have been a member of the Sanhedrin, and possibly was its president or vice-president.

ANNUN′CIĀTION. This word means the announcement of the selection of the Virgin Mary as the favored mother of Jesus. About the year 800 the church decreed (council of Trullo) a day for celebrating the event.

ANNŪ′US. Error in 1 Esd. viii. 48; "with him" in A. V. Ezra viii. 19.

ANOINT. Anointing. Use of oil on the head or any object to be honored. Jacob poured oil on his stone pillow at Bethel, consecrating it to God.

ANOINTING

Guests were honored by having their hair oiled. The monuments have pictures of the act. It was a common custom among the Hebrews, and is often referred to in the O. T. (Ps. xxiii. 5; xlv. 7; Prov. xxi. 7; xxvii. 9). To omit the use of this perfumed oil was a sign of grief and mourning (Dan. x. 3; Is. lxi. 3). It was also used as a medicine (Is. i. 6; Mark vi. 13; James v. 14). Kings were called "the anointed of the gods," and both kings and priests were confirmed in their office by the anointing of oil, both in Egypt and Palestine. Anointing the eyes denoted a spiritual recovery of sight—knowledge of divine truth. The Holy Spirit descended on the head of Jesus, like a spiritual

![Altar of burnt offering illustration]

ALTAR OF BURNT OFFERING.

anointing, a divine confirmation of his office of Messiah.

The bodies of the dead were also anointed, or embalmed, with spiced oil. See PERFUMES.

A'NOS. Son of Bani (1 Esd. ix. 34). VANIAH.

ÂNT. The Hebrew word for this insect was *namal, cut off* (Gen. xvii. 11). The males and females have four wings, which soon fall off. The workers are wingless. They feed on vegetables, animals and insects. They will rob a granary in a few days, or even hours. Solomon alluded to the ant as an instance of the use of *proper seasons* for collecting provisions (Prov. vi. 6).

ANTI'AM (*sighing of the people*). Son of Shemidah, Manasseh (1 Chr. vii. 19).

AN'TI-CHRIST (*against Christ*). Unbelievers, heretics, and persecutors (1 John ii. 18, 22). Some understand this term to mean all men (or an organized body), who oppose Christ, and whom he will overcome or destroy (Rev. xi. 13, 17).

AN'TIOCH in Syria. On the Orontes, 30 miles from the sea, 300 from Jerusalem. Founded by Seleucus Nicator (*conqueror*), B. C. 300, and named in honor of his father, Antioch. It was the capital of the Greek and Roman governors of Syria for nearly 1000 years. Its suburb Daphne was famous for its sanctuary to Apollo and Diana (2 Macc. iv. 33); the sacred grove extending its cool shades and brooks of water for ten miles around. It was a sensual paradise, where pleasure, under the disguise of religion, dissolved the firmness of manly virtue. The first GENTILE CHURCH was founded here by Paul, and the disciples were here first called CHRISTIANS in derision by the pagans (Acts xi. 21-26). Ignatius who suffered martyrdom under Trajan, at Rome, was bishop of Antioch 40 years. In the time of Chrysostom (born here A. D. 344), the pop. was 200,000, one half being Christians. The city had a street colonnade from end to end, built by Antiochus Epiphanes, and paved with granite by Antoninus Pius; most sumptuous marble baths, built by Caligula, Trajan and Hadrian; a marble palace of Diocletian, and was the finest and largest city in Western Asia. It lost greatly in wealth and population in several earthquakes: one in A. D. 526, destroying 250,000 people, at the time of the festival of the Ascension,

when many strangers were gathered; and in 1822 one-fourth of the city and people, about 5000. It was of great importance during the Crusades, and is often mentioned for its sieges, battles, and the brilliant exploits of both Christian and Moslem in and about its walls. Am. Prot. missionaries began to preach there in 1856. Pop. now about 20,000. Ar. name *Antakia*. Ruins of aqueducts, marble pavements, columns, and other evidences of its ancient splendor are often found buried under rubbish.

AN'TIOCH in Pisidia. Founded by the same king (who built 10 or 15 others of the same name), and peopled them by hired immigrants from Magnesia on the Mæander. On the S. side of Mt. Paroreia, on the boundary between Pisidia and Phrygia, overlooking a broad plain. Recent discoveries of ancient inscriptions prove the site correct. There are ruins of several churches, temples, a theatre, and an aqueduct of which 21 arches are now entire. The ancient city was often visited by Paul (Acts), with Barnabas, Silas, and Timothy who was a native of this district.

ANTIOCHIA (2 Macc. iv. 33), for Antioch.

ANTIO'CHIANS. Partizans of A. Epiphanes, or Jason (2 Macc. iv. 9). "Sinful men" in Doway.

ANTI'OCHIS. In the family of A. Epiphanes (2 Macc. iv. 30).

ANTI'OCHUS (*who lasts out*). There are several of this family name. 1. ANTIOCHUS II. THEOS (*the god*). Son of A. Soter (*savior*.) He succeeded his father B. C. 261. He was the "king of the north" of Daniel (xi.), who joined "the king of the south" (Ptolemy) by marrying his daughter Berenice.—2. ANTIOCHUS III, THE GREAT, succeeded his brother Seleucus Keraunus (*thunderer*), who was poisoned after ruling 3 years), and was the first really strong man since Seleucus, who founded the family and empire in Syria. He was only 15 when he began to rule, and his great rival, Ptolemy IV, Philopator (*father loving*), of Egypt, was crowned only two years later. Ptolemy began his reign by murdering nearly all of his relations, including his mother and father. Antiochus did no violence to his friends, but planned how to in-

TETRADRACHM OF ANTIOCHUS IV EPIPHANES.

crease the wealth and power of his people, and passed his whole life in war. One part of his policy was to put a great trust in the Jews as a people, and especially as soldiers (Ant. xii. 3, 4). At one time he moved 2000 families of Jews from Mesopotamia to Lydia and Phrygia for garrison service. He increased the honors and privileges of the Jews in Palestine, when he became master there, and they were very near to the actual enjoyment of social and religious liberty. He is also mentioned by Daniel (xi. 41), as one who should stand "in the glorious land which by his hand was to be consumed." His own daughter, Cleopatra, whom he gave to Ptolemy Epiphanes as a wife, opposed him in favor of her husband. Hannibal influenced him to war against Rome, and he was beaten finally at Magnesia in Lydia, B. C. 190. He lost his life B. C. 187, in an attempt to plunder the temple of Belus in Elymais.—3. ANTIOCHUS IV EPIPHANES (*illustrious*), youngest son of A. the Great, succeeded to his brother Seleucus Philopator, who reigned 10 years, chiefly as "a raiser of taxes" (Dan. xi. 20). Epiphanes gained the kingdom *by flatteries* (s. 21), that is, by a system of lavish bribery. These and other acts caused the Greeks to call him Epimanes (*crazy*), a very sharp and sarcastic pun on his title. He wished to plun-

ANTIOCHUS TRYPHON.

der the Jewish temple, because he needed money, and to do this it was his policy to make the Jews hateful, and destroy their nationality. But he raised up the Maccabees who, after many years of war and suffering, delivered their people (B. C. 143), as is recorded on the coins of that period (MONEY). He was a type of Antichrist, so made by his want of respect to God and religion, and the disregard of every higher feeling among men. He worshiped the Roman war-god, whose forts were his temples.—4. ANTIOCHUS V EUPATOR (*of noble descent*), succeeded his father A. IV, B. C. 164, while a child, and was under the guardian Lysias, and they were killed by Demetrius Soter, when the rule fell to Antiochus VI, son of Alexander Balas and Cleopatra, who while a child was under the care of Tryphon, B. C. 145, who contended for the throne against Demetrius Nicator. Tryphon, by treachery and success in war, gained supreme power, killed Antiochus, and assumed the throne. The coins bear his head as Antiochus and Trypho, and on some the title of Theos is added. The books of Daniel and the Maccabees give a large space to the life and deeds and bad character of this king.—5. ANTIOCHUS VII SIDETES (*from Side in Pamphylia*). Called also EUSEBES (*pious*). This was the last king of the Seleucid family, who ruled B. C. 141–128. There were some who assumed the name Antioch as a title until the Romans made Syria a province, B. C. 63.

ANTOTHI'JAH (*Jah's answers*). Son of Shashak (1 Chr. viii. 24).

ANTIPAT'RIS (*against father*). Built by Herod the Great, on the edge of Sharon, now *Kefer Saba*, 12 ms. N. E. of Joppa. Capharsaba in Josephus. Dr. Eli Smith found and identified the place while on a journey expressly to follow Paul's night march from Jerusalem to Cæsarea (Acts xxiii. 31). There are remains of the Roman road, which led by Gophna.

ANTO'NIA. Fort built by Herod on the N. W. corner of the temple site, and named after his friend. JERUSALEM.

A'NUB (*bound*). Son of Coz, of Judah (1 Chr. iv. 8).

A'NUS. A Levite (1 Esd. ix. 48). BANI?

APA'ME. Of Darius' family; daughter of Bartacus (1 Esd. iv. 29).

APE. Brought by Solomon's ships (1 K. x. 22) from India or Malabar, where they are now found, called KAPI (Heb. KOPH). They were prized as curiosities then as now.

APEL'LES (*Apollo's gift*). A disciple saluted by Paul (Rom. xvi. 10). Tradition says he was bishop of Smyrna.

APHAR'SACH'ITES. Persians transplanted into Samaria (Ezr. iv. 9). Fars—Persia.

APHEK (*firmness* or *strength*). 1. Issachar (Josh. xii. 18; xv. 53). APHAKAH.—2. Asher (Josh. xix. 30; Judg. i. 31). APHIK. (Josh. xiii. 4). W. of Baalbek 15 ms., on the E. slope of Lebanon. AFKA. A temple to Venus made this city famous.—3. Where the Philistines encamped before the battle in which the sons of Eli were killed and the Ark was taken (1 Sam. ix. 1). In the mountains N. W. of Jerusalem.—4. The site of another battle, where Saul was killed (1 Sam. xxix. 1), near Shunem, or Jezreel.—5. Aphik, now called Fik, E. of the sea of Galilee 6 ms.; the site of several battles with the Syrians (1 K. xx. 26; 2 K. xiii. 17). Ben Hadad was defeated here; and Joash at the word of Elisha drew a bow at a venture, and afterwards gained several battles over the Syrians. The houses occupy a crescent-shaped cliff, at the base of which are three fine fountains, which send a stream into the lake below the hill on which Gamala stood.

APOCH'RYPHA (*hidden*). The name of a certain class of books, offered as genuine, but not received as of divine origin, and of equal authority with the other books of the Bible. These are, as they stand in the A. V.:

1. Esdras, 1 and 2.
2. Tobit.
3. Judith.
4. Addition to Esther.
5. Wisdom of Solomon.
6. Wisdom of Jesus, Son of Sirach.
7. Baruch, and Jeremiah's Epistle.
8. The Song of the Three Holy Children.
9. The History of Susanna.
10. Bel and the Dragon.
11. Prayer of Manasseh.
12. Maccabees, 1 and 2, and the Book of Enoch, accepted in Abyssinia.

APE

Besides these there are a number that never were admitted to a position among the Sacred writings, such as, The Assumption of Moses, Testament of the Twelve Patriarchs, and many others attributed to Abraham, Eldad, Modad, etc.

The original meaning of apochrypha was *hidden*, but it is now used to mean *spurious*.

The real value of these books is in their being specimens of Jewish literature, and books of their history, throwing light on their religion and theological opinions, although more or less colored by fancy or fable. They are assigned to a period dating since 300 B. C., the latest, Esdras, dating about 30 B. C., or even later. The books themselves do not assert the use of the prophetic gift, but do say that this gift had departed from Israel (1 Macc. ix. 27), but it was hoped that prophets would again appear (iv. 46; xiv. 41). The style and power of the writing is inferior, and especially so is the poetry, excepting only the Song of the Three Children, which may be the reproduction of some ancient sacred service. There are many blunders and anachronisms in their historical allusions. The books of the New Testament era that have been regarded as doubtful are, 2d Ep. of St. Peter; Ep. of St. James; Ep. of St. Jude; 2d and 3d Eps. of St. John; the Apocalypse, and the Ep. to the Hebrews. Those condemned as spurious: Acts of Paul; Shepherd of Hermas; Revelation of Peter; Ep. of Barnabas, and Instructions of the Apostles. Those denounced as impious are, Gospels of Peter, Thomas, Matthias, and the Acts of Andrew, John, and the other apostles.

Some of these books were read in the churches for instruction, but not for a rule and guide. The Westminster Confession says, "The books called Apochrypha, not being of divine inspiration, are no part of the canon of Scripture, and therefore are of no authority in the Church of God, nor to be any otherwise approved, or made use of, than other human writings." See HISTORY OF THE BOOKS.

APOLLŌ′NIA, a city of Macedonia, through which Paul and Silas passed in their way from Philippi and Amphipolis to Thessalonica (Acts xvii. 1). According to the *Antonine Itinerary*, it was distant 30 Roman miles from Amphipolis, and 37 Roman miles from Thessalonica.

APOLLOPH′ANES, a Syrian, killed by Judas Maccabæus at Gazara (2 Macc. x. 37).

APOL′LOS, a Jew from Alexandria, eloquent (which may also mean *learned*) and mighty in the Scriptures; one instructed in the way of the Lord, according to the imperfect view of the disciples of John the Baptist (Acts xviii. 25), but on his coming to Ephesus during a temporary absence of St. Paul, A.D. 54, more perfectly taught by Aquila and Priscilla. After this he became a preacher of the gospel, first in Achaia and then in Corinth (Acts xviii. 27; xix. 1), where he watered that which Paul had planted (1 Cor. iii. 6). When the apostle wrote his First Epistle to the Corinthians, Apollos was with or near him (1 Cor. xvi. 12), probably at Ephesus in A.D. 57: we hear of him then that he was unwilling at that time to journey to Corinth, but would do so when he should have convenient time. He is mentioned but once more in the N. T., in Tit. iii. 13. After this nothing is known of him. Tradition makes him bishop of Cæsarea. It has been supposed by some that Apollos was the author of the Epistle to the Hebrews.

APOL′LYON, or, as it is literally in the margin of the A. V. of Rev. ix. 11, "a destroyer," is the rendering of the Hebrew word ABADDON, "the angel of the bottomless pit." The angel Apollyon is further described as the king of the locusts which rose from the smoke of the bottomless pit at the sounding of the fifth trumpet. From the occurence of the word in Ps. lxxxviii. 11, the Rabbins have made Abaddon the nethermost of the two regions into which they divide the lower world. But that in Rev. ix. 11 Abbadon is the angel, and not the abyss, is perfectly evident in the Greek. There is no authority for connecting it with "the destroyer" alluded to in 1 Cor. x. 10.

APŌS′TLE (*sent forth*). The Jews so called those who carried about letters from their rulers. There were but few who had this honor, and to whom Jesus entrusted the organization of his Church. There were twelve originally whom he ordained, that they should be with him; and he gave them power over unclean spirits, and to heal all manner of diseases; commissioning them to preach the kingdom of God (Mark iii.; Matt. x.; Luke vi.), saying, "As the Father hath sent me, so send I you." It seems to have been essential to this high office, 1. That they should have seen the Lord, and have been eye and ear witnesses of what they testified to the world (John. xv. 27; Acts i. 21). Paul claims equal authority from having seen Jesus in a vision (1 Cor. ix. 1; xv. 8).—2. Called and chosen by the Lord himself (Acts i. 24).—3. Infallible inspiration (John xvi. 13; 1 Cor. ii. 10), because it was their office to explain the O. T., and to set forth the New (Luke xxiv. 27).—4. The power of working miracles (Mark xvi. 20; Acts ii. 43).—5. To these were added the power to settle points of faith, and determine all controversies. Jesus is once called "the apostle of our profession" (Heb. iii. 1). THE APOSTLE'S CREED is not of their own making, but contains their doctrine as set forth by Christian men in later times. THE APOSTOLIC AGE dates from the day of Pentecost, and is usually divided into two periods, before and after the destruction of Jerusalem A. D. 70, the latter period ending at the death of John A. D. 99. There was not a revelation of the Lord's commands and the duties they involved complete as final at one time, but rather a progressive illumination—a peculiar succession and combination of events—from the first call to be apostles, the day of pentecost, the visions at Cæsarea and Joppa, the conversion and call of Paul—by which the five heralds of the Gospel were instructed, and enabled to teach its free and comprehensive spirit. The first Christian church was composed of Jews only, and they observed the Mosaic ritual strictly, and were continually in the temple (Luke xxiv. 53; Acts ii. 46; iii. 1); and the Jews spoke of them as the SECT of the Nazarenes, as the Pharisees and Sadducees and Essenes were sects within the Jewish church (Acts xxiv. 5; xxviii. 22; xv. 5; xxvi. 5; v. 17). A community of goods was required at first, but was soon abandoned. The Greeks (and other Gentiles) were admitted and elevated the tone of the society, and increased its power for diffusion, for the Gentiles so outnumbered the Jews at Antioch as to require a new name—which was given by their scorners—Christian. Shortly before the destruction of Jerusalem the members of the church found a refuge in Pella, east of Jordan, away from the power of the Sanhedrin, which held its sessions at Jamnia on the Great Sea, and this ended the connection of the new church with the old—Moses was to be thereafter second to Jesus in authority, and from that time an enmity grew up between

ASSYRIAN ARMLET.

them which has not yet been healed—and can never be (2 Cor. iii). The second period is almost a blank, since there is no account of any of the apostles except John, and with his death the age closes. Since then the church has been left to the guidance of man only, assisted by the invisible spirit, towards its spiritual maturity.

APOTHECARIES. Hananiah, one of the rebuild-ers of the wall, was a perfumer, or maker of ointment (Neh. iii. 8).

APPĀ'IM (*nostrils*). Son of Nadab, of Judah (1 Chr. ii. 30).

APPHĬ'A. Disciple (Philemon 2): member of Philemon's household. Appii in Acts xxviii. 15.

AP'PHUS. Surname of Jonathan Maccabeus (1 Macc. ii. 5).

AP'PĬĪ-FŌ'RUM (*market place of Appius*). On the Appian bay, between Naples and Rome, 43 ms. from Rome. Appius Claudius, who built the famous road from Rome to Brundusium, had a statue in his honor here (Acts xxviii. 15).

AQ'UĬLÄ (*eagle*). Jew at Corinth, tent maker and friend of Paul (Acts xviii. 2). He and his wife Priscilla had been banished from Rome with all Jews, by Claudius. They became zealous promoters of the cause, as Paul says "helpers in Christ Jesus," "who have for my life laid down their own necks" (Rom. xvi. 3, 4). The Greek church honor Aquila as a bishop, on July 12. The Romans call him bishop of Heraclea, and the festival of Aquila and Priscilla is on July 8.

ÄR. Capital of Moab, on the Arnon (Num. xxi. 15–28). The place is still called Rabba, and is 17 miles E. of the Dead Sea, 10 S. of the Arnon, and its ruins occupy a low hill over looking a plain, where are found the remains of two Roman temples and some water-tanks. It was burnt by King Sihon (Is. xv. 1). Rabbath Moab.

A'RA (*lion*). Son of Jether, of Asher (1 Chr. vii. 38).

AR'AB. Judah. (Josh. xv. 52). Near Hebron. Lost.

AR'ABAH (*waste—sterile*). The valley of depression from Mt. Hermon to the Red Sea at Ezion Geber (Akabah). (Deu. i. 1; Job xxiv. 5; Is. xxxiii. 9). Now restricted to the valley from the Sea of Galilee to the S. end of the Dead Sea, and called El Ghor. It is 150 miles long by 1 to 10 or 12 miles wide. ARBOTH, the plural of Arabah was the name given to the plain of Jericho (Josh. v. 10; Num. xxii. 1; 2 Sam. xv. 28). The region is called KIKKAR in Gen. xiii. 10. From the Dead Sea to Akabah the Arabs name the valley *Wady el Arabah*. The desert of TIH bounds the A. on the west, by long walls of limestone, 1500 to 1800 feet above its floor. The mts. of Edom form the E. wall, and are of granite, basalt, and porphyry, 2,000 to 2,300 ft. in elevation, and covered with vegetation. Mt. Hor, the highest peak, is 5,000 ft. above the sea. A line of chalk cliffs, 150 ft. high, 6 ms. S. of the Dead Sea, running E. and W., divides the A. from El Ghor. W. EL JEIB is the principal water-course—flowing only in winter. The A. is a desert of sand, gravel, low hills, and cut by numberless water-courses. The sirocco blows almost constantly. There are a very few shrubs and plants, as rushes, tamarinds, oleanders, anemones, lilies, and palms. The water-shed is 40 ms. N. of Akabah, from which the water flows both N. and S. The pass up out of the A. near Akabah, upon the plateau of Tih, is now used by pilgrims on the route from Suez to Mecca, and is called NUKB, the pass. From this plateau to 1000 ft. above it is another pass, on the route from Mt. Hor to Hebron, called *es Sufah*, where Israel was repulsed by Canaan (Deut. i. 44; Num. xiv. 43–45). On the E. side *Wady Ithm* leads through the mts.

near Akabah, where there are remains of a Roman road, leading to the country E. of the Dead Sea, over the same route traversed by the Exodus, when Edom was compassed (Num. xxi. 4).

ARĀ'BIA (*east country*). E. of Palestine, including all the descendants from Ishmael and Keturah (Gen. x. 30; xxix. 1; Judg. vi. 3.) Sons of the East (Num. xxiii. 7; 2 Chr. ix. 14). Sons of Kedem (s. xxi. 13). "Forest in A." (Ex. xii. 38; Neh. xiii. 3; 1 K. x. 15), "Mixed multitude" are Arabians. Now called by the Arabs BILAD EL ARAB—country of the Arba. Bedawin are people of the open country, not living in towns. Extends from the Euphrates and the Persian Gulf to Egypt and the Red Sea; and from the Indian Ocean to the Mediterranean, or Great Sea. The ancients divided it into ARABIA FELIX, A. DESERTA, and A. PETRÆA. The modern divisions are the Peninsula of Sinai, Arabia, and North A. (See Sinai, Edom, Petra, Mt. Hor, Arabah, Syria, Aram.) The original settlers were the sons of Shem and Ham

ARIMATHEA.

(Gen. x. 21, 15). There are many ruins in Arabia of a more ancient people than any known to history—(Marib, Sana, Reydan, Riam, Inen, Rien). There are many allusions in the Bible to the Arabs; and the manners and customs of the modern people are a help to the interpretation of those texts that refer to the ancients, and especially in Job. The Bedawin constantly remind us of the accounts of the patriarchs, or later Israelites. Respect to age (Lev. xix. 32); deference to superiors (2 K. v. 13); engravings on signets of sentences having the name of God (Ex. xxxix. 30; John iii. 33). As a pledge, the ring is given (Gen. xli. 42); they wear an inkhorn in the girdle (Ezek. ix. 2, 3, 11). Many of the most obscure passages are explained by a knowledge of the present customs.

The people have in all ages been active, enterprising, restless; ambitious in commerce, conquest, and religion.

The country of A. was never conquered.

ARĀ'BIANS (2 Chr. xvii. 11). Nomades, east and south of Palestine, a part being descended from Keturah. The Sheikh (*king*) was called Aretas (2 Macc. v. 8).

A'RAD (*wild ass*). Son of Beriah, a Benjamite (1 Chr. viii. 15).

Ā'RĂD. S. of Judah (Num. xxi. 1; King of A., Josh. xii. 14; Judg. i. 16). Tell Arad, 20 ms. S. of Hebron. (R.)

AR'ĀDUS. ARVAD (*wandering*). Phœnicia (Ezek. xxvii. 8; Gen. x. 18). An island 3 ms. from the coast, near the river Eleutherus, Nahr el Kebir; and opposite to it is the site of Antaradus, now called Ruad (1 Macc. xv. 23). The island was settled by fugitives from Sidon. High and rocky, about a mile in extent, near Tripoli.

A'RAH (*traveler*). Son of Ulla, of Asher (1 Chr. vii. 39).—2. 775 of the "sons of Arah" returned with Zerubbabel (Ezr. ii. 5). Ares (1 Esd. v. 10).

A'RAM (*hight*). N. E. of Palestine. Called also Syria—which see (Gen. xxxi. 18; xxxiii. 18). 1. A. *Dammesek*, Syria of Damascus (2 Sam. viii. 5, 6).—2. A. Naharaim (*two rivers*), the country of Abraham (Gen. xxv. 20).—3. Padan A., Aram at the foot of the mountains.—4. A. Zobah (2 Sam. x. 6, 8).—5. A. Beth Rehob.—6. A. Maachah (1 Chr. xxi. 6). Geshur (2 Sam. xv. 8; 1 K. xi. 25). Aram was a son of Shem, and his brethren were Elam, Asshur, Arphaxad. Aram is also Assyria (2 K. xviii. 26; Is. xxxvi. 11; Jer. xxxv. 11; 2 K. xvi. 6).— 2. Aram, of whose family was Elihu who visited Job (xxxii. 2).

A'RAMITESS. Woman of Aram (1 Chr. vii. 14).

ARAM-NAHARAIM. Mesopotamia. (Plain of Damascus?)

A'RAM ZOBAH. Aram and Zobah (Ps. lx.).

A'RAN (*wild goat*). A Horite (Gen. xxxvi. 28).

AR'ARAT (*holy land*). A mountainous district, or lofty plateau, nearly 5000 ft. above the sea, between the Black and Caspian seas, where rise the Euphrates and Tigris, which flow into the Persian Gulf; the Araxes and Cyrus, into the Caspian; and the Acampsis, into the Black Sea. The range of Mt. Taurus begins at the N. E. end of the Great Sea, near Antioch in Syria, runs N. E., meeting the range of Abus, from the head of Persian Gulf running N. W., at the Mt. Ararat, which is 17,750 feet high. It is alluded to in Scripture as—1. *Ararat* (Gen. viii. 4), the land on which the Ark rested; and where the sons of Sennacherib fled after killing their father (2 K. xix. 37).—2. *Minni* (Jer. li. 27). Josephus says there is a great mountain in Armenia called Baris (Ant. i. 3, 6).—3. *Togarmah.* In Gen. x. 3, this is the name of the youngest son of Gomer. Ezek. (xxxviii. 6) says, "the house of Togarmah of the north." Tyre traded in horses with Togarmah (Ezek. xxvii. 14).

ÄR'ARATH. ARARAT (Tobit i. 21).

ÄRAU'NAH (*Jah is strong*). The Jebusite who sold his threshing-floor to David for a place for an altar to God (2 Sam. xxiv.). He was one of the royal family of the Jebusites (2 Sam. xxiv. 23). David bought the whole hill Moriah for 600 shekels of gold, and the treshing-floor and oxen for 50 shekels (1 Chr. xxi. 25).

AR'BA. See HEBRON.

AR'BA (*hero-baal*). Ancestor of the Anakim—named Hebron Kirjath-arba (city of Arba. Josh. xiv. 15; xv. 13). Arbah in Gen. xxxv. 27.

AR'BATHITE. Resident in the Arabah, the Jordan valley (2 Sam. xxiii. 31).

ARBAT'TIS. Error for Acrabattine; or meaning *Ard el Butihah* in Galilee (1 Macc. v. 23).

ARBE'LA (1 Macc. ix. 2), Arabella, near Maisaloth. Beth Arbel, or what is now called *Irbil*, a few miles W. of Magdala. (Hos. x. 14.)

AR'BITE THE. Resident of Arab (2 Sam. xxiii.

35). Paarai, the Arbite, one of David's guard; Naarai, the son of Ezbai in 1 Chr. xi. 37.

ARBŌNAI (Judg. ii. 14, Mambre). See ABRONAS.

ARCHELÄ'US (*leading the people*). Son of Herod by Malthace, a Samaritan, brought up at Rome. Appointed by Augustus Ethnarch after his father's death. Banished to and died in Gaul at Vienne. He had a bad reputation (Matt. ii. 22) for cruelty and oppression.

THRESHING WITH THE SLED.

AR'CHEVITES. People from Erech(?) living in Samaria (Ezr. iv. 9).

ARCHIP'PUS (*driver of horses*). Disciple in Colossæ, "our fellow soldier" (Philemon 2). He is supposed to have been a teacher, one of the 70 sent out, as well as deacon, in Colossæ and Laodicea, and to have suffered as a martyr at Chonæ.

ARCHĪTE. Hushai, the Archite in 2 Sam. xv. 32. No town of Arca is known in Palestine; the one north of Tripoli is in Phœnicia. Josh. (xvi. 2) has "the borders of Archi" near Bethel and Luz.

ARCTŪ'RUS. Heb. ASH, AYISH, in Job ix. 9; xxxviii. 32. The Arabians name the cluster of four stars in the body of the "Great Bear" *en nash*, and those in the tail *el Benat*, the daughters.

ÄRD (*descent*). Son of Benjamin, the youngest (Gen. xlvi. 21).—2. Son of Bela (Num. xxvi. 40). Addar in 1 Chr. viii. 3. Ardites, from him.

AR'DATH. The field in 2 Esd. ix. 26, meaning that all Palestine was but a field or waste (Arboth?) to the Jews.

AR'DON (*fugitive*). Son of Caleb by Azubah (1 Chr. ii. 18).

ARE'LI (*hero's son*). ARIEL. Son of Gad (Gen. xlvi. 16). Arelites (Num. xxvi. 17).

ÄREŌP'AGUS (*hill of Ares*). Mars Hill. Athens. A rocky height opposite the west end of the Acropolis, used from the earliest times as a place of assembly for the honorable men who had held the office of Archon. On this hill Paul stood, in the midst of these august men, when he said, "Whom ye ignorantly worship, Him declare I unto you." Dionysius, the Areopagite (Acts xvii. 23–34). "In the market daily." The AGORA, or market, was a public place, surrounded on three sides by the architectural glories of Athens. It may be described thus: To the northeast was the Acropolis, a rocky height 150 feet above the street below, crowned with the *Parthenon* and other temples; north the *Areopagus;* west the Pnyx (pulpit); and south the *Museum*, with other buildings. (See plan of Athens.)

At the time of Paul's visit, Athens was a magnificent city, ornamented in every quarter with memorials sacred to religion and patriotism, showing the highest achievements in art. The famed Academy had its groves of plane and olive trees, retired walks and cooling fountains, altars and statues and temples, near which was the house of Plato, the great teacher.

The Acropolis had clustered on its summit memorials and monuments of religion and art, such as were never seen on an equal space. Pericles had adorned it with a flight of steps and a Propylæa, with five entrances and two flanking temples of Pentelican marble, where were placed the equestrian statues of the Roman emperors Augustus and Agrippa, the temple of the Wingless Victory; a picture-gallery; and there still stands the ruin of the unequaled Parthenon, which was then adorned with the masterpieces of the sculptor Phidias.

The Erechtheium, containing the holy olive-tree, sacred to Minerva, the holy salt-spring, and other sacred things. A colossal bronze statue of Pallas Promachus, by Phidias, stood near, the plume of whose lofty helmet was visible from the sea between Sunium and Athens.

Pausanias gives an account of a great number of statues on the Acropolis, so that we wonder how there could be any space left for the people.

It is no wonder, however, that Paul, with his natural genius and vast experience, should have been inspired by the surroundings. (See Life of Paul.)

AREOP'AGITE. A member of the council at Athens (Acts xvii. 34). DIONYSIUS.

AR'ETAS (*graver*). Title of the kings of Arabia, as Ptolemy of Egypt, and Augustus of Rome.—1. In the time of Antiochus Epiphanes, B. C. 170 (2 Macc. v. 8).—2. Father-in-law of Herod Antipas, whose Ethnarch ruled in Damascus when Paul escaped in a basket (2 Cor. xi. 32).

ARE'US. King of the Lacedemonians, whose letter to the high-priest Onias is given in 1 Macc. xii. 20–23; about 300 B. C.

AR'GOB (*stony*). Manasseh, east of Jordan, in Bashan. Had sixty fortified cities (Deut. iii. 4, 13, 14; 1 K. iv. 13), called *Trachonitis*, a translation of the Hebrew name. The Samaritans called it *Rigobaah=stony*. The Arabs named it *Mujeb=stony*, and it is now *El Lejah*. It lies fifteen miles south of Damascus, is triangular, twenty-two miles from north to south, and fourteen from east to west. The region is elevated above the surrounding country, and is very rocky, like an ocean of basaltic rocks and boulders; thickly studded with deserted cities and villages, in all of which the houses are solidly built and of remote antiquity. A Roman road runs through the district, probably leading from Damascus to Bosra. *Kenath* and *Edrei* are on the border, to the southwest. The *Hauran* presents the utmost contrast to the Lejah, in being a country of the richest agricultural soil, in rolling downs, from the Sea of Galilee to the desert, far beyond the Lejah.

AR'GOB. The two princes, Argob and Ariel, were killed with Pekahiah, in the palace at Samaria, by Pekah.

ARIARA'THES. Mithridates, king of Cappadocia, B. C. 163–130.

ARI'DAI. Son of Haman (Esth. ix. 8).

ARIDA'THA. Son of Haman (Esth. ix. 8).

ARI'EH. ARJEH (*the lion*). See ARGOB. ARIEL.

A'RIEL (*lion of God*). Poetical name of Jerusalem (Is. xxix. 1, 2, 7).

A'RIEL (*lion of God*). Chief under Ezra (viii. 16), in his caravan. One of the Gileadite chiefs killed by Pekah. See ARGOB. The same word occurs in 2 Sam. xxiii. 20, where it is rendered "two lion-like men"—and might be "two sons of Ariel." 2. Isaiah (xxix. 1) so names Jerusalem.—Lion of God, or hearth of God; the same word in Ezekiel xliii. 15) translated altar. means *hearth of God*.

ARIMATHE'A. A city of Judea (Luke xxiii. 51). King Demetrius writes (1 Macc. xi. 34): "We have ratified unto them the borders of Judea, with the three governments of Aphereum, Lydda, and Ramathaim, that are added unto Judea from the country of Samaria." Joseph of Arimathea (Matt. xxvii. 57; Mark xv. 43; John xix. 38). The place has been identified as the village of Renthieh, ten miles east of Joppa, on the road from Lydda to Antipatris, but this is doubted on the authority of Josephus.

A'RIOCH (*lion-like*). 1. King of Ellasar (Gen. xiv.1).—2. Captain of the guard (Dan. ii. 14).—3. King of the Elymæans. In Judith i. 6, Erioch king of the Eliceans; in DOWAY, Deioces, king in Media.

ARI'SAI. Son of Haman (Esth. ix. 9).

ARISTAR'CHUS (*excellent ruler*). A Thessalonian, companion of Paul; with him at Ephesus (Acts xix.), and on the voyage, and at Rome, a fellow-prisoner and laborer (Col. iv. 10; Philem. 24). Tradition makes him bishop of Apamea.

ARISTOBU'LUS (*best advised*). 1. Jewish priest in Egypt in the reign of Ptolemy VI, B. C. 165. Judas Maccabeus addressed him as a counsellor of the king (2 Macc. i. 10). He wrote and dedicated to Ptolemy an allegorical exposition of the Pentateuch. Eusebius and Clement of Alexandria preserve fragments of his works.—2. A resident at Rome, whose household is the subject of a salutation in Rom. xvi. 10.—3. Son and successor of John Hyrcanus.—4. Second son of Alexander Jannæus.—5. Grandson of No. 3, and the last of the Maccabæans; murdered by the designs of Herod, B. C. 34.—6. Son of Herod the Great by Mariamne.

ARITH'METIC (*numbering*). The Hebrews were not a scientific, but a religious and practical people; but it must be in ferred from what they did, in certain trades and arts, that they had the needed skill, and reckoning by numbers was not an exception. For figures, after the captivity, they used their letters, as is seen on the Samaritan coins; and this may have been their earliest custom also.

EGYPTIAN ARK.

ARK. A word adopted from the Egyptian. A chest. The word for Noah's ark is TEBAH, the same as used for that of Moses (Gen. vi.; viii.; Ex. ii). ARK OF THE COVENANT. An oblong chest of acacia wood, gilded, 45 inches long, 27 wide, and 27 deep (Ex. xv. 10; Num. vii. 9.) It was to contain (or by its side), the book of the law, the covenant, and perhaps also the pot of manna, and Aaron's rod (Heb. ix. 4). When Solomon's temple was dedicated the ark contained only the "two tables" of stone (1 K. viii. 9). It was to be kept in the most holy place, excluding all idols, and itself be the centre of regard, as denoting the presence of God, on the Mercy Seat, which was on the lid, overshadowed by two images with wings. Jeremiah predicted (iii. 16), that it should be finally abandoned as a sacred object. It "rested" at Shiloh until the superstitious warriors took it into battle and lost it to the Philistines. Not long after its recovery it was placed in the temple. It is believed to have been burnt when the Babylonians destroyed Solomon's temple.

ARK, NOAH'S. The form and size cannot be learned from the text. The figures are given as 300 cubits long, 50 wide, and 30 high. The cubit was of several kinds, 18, 19, and 21 inches in length. The present opinion (among some), is that the Deluge was a local inundation, extending only far enough to destroy the human race, which is supposed to have dwelt in the valley of the Euphrates and Tigris. The form of the ark may be seen in that of the great rafts on those rivers, which have a flat-roofed cabin on them, like a rude house. The Apameans had a tradition that the ark rested near their city, in Phrygia, of which the coin here shown, dating from A. D. 150, is a memorial, now in Paris.

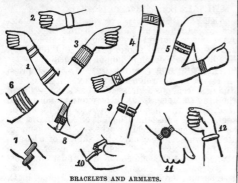

BRACELETS AND ARMLETS.

AR'KITE. Canaanite people living at Arka, under Mt. Lebanon on the sea (Gen. x. 17). Alexander Severus was born there, and it was then named Cæsarea Lebani. The ruins are on a hill looking over a fine plain, the sea, and mts.

ARMAGED'DON. A name for the plain of Jezreel. ESDRAELON. Mount Megiddo (Rev. xvi. 16). There is a symbolical meaning attached to this name and place which it is impossible to explain in this limited space. It may be interesting to recount the several great battles fought on the plain, which have given it a solemn importance in history. The great victory of Barak over the Canaanites (Judg. iv., v.), and of Gideon over the Midianites (Judg. vii); and two great disasters—the death of Saul (1 Sam. xxi. 8) in the invasion of the Philistines, and the death of Josiah in the invasion of the Egyptians (2 K. xxiii. 29). See JEZREEL.

ARME'NIA. ARARAT. Christianity was established here in the 4th century. The whole number of the Armenians is about two millions. They have a rich convent on Zion (See Jerusalem). The ARMENIAN VERSION of the Bible was made in A. D. 410 by (the patriarch Isaac and) Miesrob, aided by his pupils Joannes Ecelensis and Josephus Palnensis, from the Syriac. It was afterwards corrected from the Greek, and was finished in the year 431.

ARM'LETS. Ornaments worn by men, as *bracelets* are by women.

ARMS. ARMOR. Offensive. 1. Club, mace, bar, hammer, or maul (*shevet-barzel*, Ps. ii. 9). At first of wood, then of metal.—2. Throw-stick (*maphietz*) figured on the monuments, and called by Arabs *lissan*. The Australian *boomerang* is an instance. —3. Dirk or sword, of flint, a deer's horn (*chereb*, now used in the East), of wood as now in Nubia, or of metal. The sword is carried in a belt or slung (girded, 1 Sam. xvii. 39).—4. Spear (*romach*), a short blade of a deer's horn straightened, or of metal, on a pole of wood. The horn of the oryx is about 40 inches long. Some were very heavy (*chanith*, 1 Sam. xvii. 7).—5. Javelin (*cidon*), a light spear for throwing; a dart (*shelach*, 1 Sam. xiii. 22). SHEBET, baton, or sceptre, with which

Joab killed Absalom, (2 Sam. xviii. 14).—6. Bow (*kesheth*), and arrow (*hitz*), of a reed, branch, rib of palm, wood and horn, ivory, iron or brass. There were cases for the bow and for the arrows. —7. Sling (*kela*), for throwing stones; of plaited thongs. Stones were cast 400 feet and lead bullets 600. Balista were strong bows or springs rigged to throw stones (1 Chr. xii. 2).—8. Ram (*car*), a loaded car with a heavy pole shod with iron, sometimes shaped like a ram's head. Some were large towers on wheels, holding soldiers. Defensive. 1. Shield (*tsinnah*), buckler, (*magen*) roundel, (*parma*) target, (*shelet*), made of wood, or wickerwork, covered with hide, bordered with metal; kings and chiefs had them made of gold, silver or brass.—2. HELMET (*koba*); of rushes, osiers, skins, wood, cloth (*turban*), and metal.—3. ARMOR for the body; of leather, iron, brass. Shown on the monuments, covering the breast, or breast and back, or the whole body, with separate pieces for the arms and legs (Goliath wore them). Armor was also placed on the horse.

AR'MY. The Hebrews began, continued, and ended their national life in war. The law of Moses enrolled in the army every male from 20 to 50 years (Num. i. 3; 2 Chr. xxv. 5; Ant. iii. 12, 14), except the Levites. The divisions were 10, 50, 100, 1000, with proper officers (1 Macc. iii. 56; Num. xxxi. 14; 1 Sam. viii. 12). Messengers with trumpets summoned to the camp (Judg. iii. 27). The head of the nation was leader, as Moses, until the time of David, when the office of "captain of the host" was made distinct from that of king. Foot soldiers were the only kind at first used (Num. xi. 21), even while the Canaanites had chariots of iron (Judg. i. 19). David introduced horses and chariots contrary to the divine direction (Deut. xvii. 16), and was followed by his successors. The soldiers had to provide their own arms and food (1 Sam. xvii. 17), until a STANDING ARMY was made by the kings (1 Sam. viii. 11, 12; xiii. 2; 1 Macc. xiv. 32). David had 600 chosen men (2 Sam. xv. 18), "mighty men," perhaps his body guard (1 K. xiv. 28). A division served in each month, changing through the year. Foreigners were admitted to the service, and even advanced to high places (1 Sam. xv. 19; Ant. xiii. 13, 5).

HEAVY ARMED WARRIOR.

AR'NA. Forefather of Ezra (2 Esd. i. 2).

AR'NAN (*active*). Son of Rephaiah (1 Chr. iii. 21, "sons of").

ÄR′NON (*swift—noisy*). River forming the boundary between Moab and Ammon, east of the Dead Sea (Num. xxi.; Judg. xi.). Fords of Arnon (Is. xvi. 2). Near the Dead Sea the stream is eighty-two feet wide, four feet deep, and flows between almost perpendicular walls of red, brown, and yellow sandstone. Now the Wady Mojeb. (Josh. xiii. 9), "Aroer that is upon the bank of the river Arnon, and the city that is in the midst of the river." There is a ruin at the junction of the Lejum with the Arnon, name not known.

A′ROD (*wild ass*). Son of Gad (Num. xxvi. 17). **ARODI** (Gen. xlvi. 17). **ARODITES.**

ÄR′OER (*ruins*). Name of several places east of Jordan. 1. On the Arnon, north bank, ten miles from the Dead Sea, now in ruins. A Roman road connected it with cities north and south (Deut. ii. 36; iii. 12; iv. 48; Josh. xii. 2; xiii. 9; Judg. xi. 26; 2 K. x. 33; 1 Chr. v. 8).—2. Gad, facing Rabbah (Num. xxxii. 34; Josh. xiii. 25). Ayra, six miles east from the Jordan, two miles north of W. Sheriah.—3. The cities of Aroer (Is. xvii. 2). Supposed to be in Bashan.—4. Judah (1 Sam. xxx. 28). Ararah, on the road from Gaza to Petra, eleven miles southwest of Beer-sheba (Rob).

AR′OERITE. Hothan, father of two of David's captains (1 Chr. xi. 44).

A′ROM. 32 sons of Arom returned with Zorobabel (1 Esd. v. 16). Asom? Hasom in Ezr. ii. 19.

COIN OF APAMEA.

ÄRPHAX′AD (*region of the Chasdim*). Third son of Shem, born B. C. 1658, and lived 438 years (Gen. x. 22; xi. 12—). Arrapachitis, in N. Assyria, was the original home of the Chaldeans.—2. King of the Medes (Deioces) who founded Ecbatana. Another account says he was Astyages, their last king.

ÄRSĀ′CES (*prince of the noble*). Title of the kings of Parthia and Media. Mithridates I took Demetrius II, of Syria, prisoner B. C. 139 (1 Macc. xiv. 2), and treated him with respect, giving him his daughter in marriage. Persians now call their king SHAH.

ÄR′SARETH. Region beyond the Euphrates (2 Esd. xiii. 45).

ÄRTAXERX′ES (*great king*). *Artachshast.* 1. One who hindered the rebuilding of the temple (Ezr. iv. 7), from his time to that of Darius. He is believed to be the Magian imposter Smerdis, B. C. 521). —2. Artaxerxes Longimanus in whose 7th year Ezra led the second colony of exiles back to Judea (c. 7). He was son of Xerxes who was defeated in Greece.—3. Who allowed Nehemiah, in the 20th year of his reign to go to Jerusalem on civil business, and to remain in office there 12 years, B. C. 425. Some think that 2 and 3 were the same person.

AR′TEMAS. Companion to Paul (Tit. iii. 12). Bishop of Lystra?

AR′TEMIS. DIANA (Acts xix. 24).

ARTIL′LERY. Bows and arrows, slings, etc., in 1 Sam. xx. 40.

ÄR′UBOTH. Commissariat district of Solomon (1 K. iv. 10). Probably Shefelah.

ÄRU′MAH. Near Shechem. Residence of Abimelech (Judg. ix. 41).

ÄR′VAD (*wandering*). Phœnicia. On the island of Ruad, and on the mainland. Lately examined by Renan (Phœnicia, Paris, 1869). The island is a steep rock on every side, and has ruins of walls, some still very high (Strabo).

ÄRVĀDI′TES. Descendents of Arvad, son of Canaan (Gen. x. 18). They lived on the island, and mainland (above) and were described as a colony of Sidon, and as noted mariners (Ez. xxvii. 8; Strabo 16, p. 754), and had a king of their own (1 Macc. xv. 23).

AR′ZA (*earth*). King Elah's prefect at Tirzah (1 K. xvi. 9). In the Targum, Jonathan, "idol of Beth-Arza."

Ā′SĂ (*physician*). Son of Abijah, grandson of Rehoboam, and 3d king of Judah, from B. C. 955 to 914, 41 years. "He walked in the steps of his ancestor David" (1 K. xv. 11).

ASADI′AS. HASADIAH (Baruch i. 1; 1 Chr. iii. 20).

AS′AEL. Ancestor of Tobit (i. 1). JAHZEEL?

AS′ĀHEL (*made by God.*) Son of David's sister Zeruiah, brother to Joab and Abishai. Noted as a swift runner, and so lost his life (2 Sam. ii. 18).

ASAHI′AH (*God-made*). One of Josiah's messengers to Huldah the prophetess, to inquire about the newly found book of the law of Moses (2 K. xxii. 12). ASAIAH.

ASĀ′IAH (*God-made*). Chief in Hezekiah's reign (1 Chr. iv. 36).—2. Levite in David's reign (ib. vi. 30).—3. First-born of the Shilonite (ib. ix. 5).

AS′ANA (1 Esd. v. 31). ASNAH in Ezr. ii. 50.

Ā′SAPH (*choir leader*). Levite, son of Barachias (1 Chr. vi. 39), and David's choir leader. The "sons of Asaph" succeeded him as leaders (1 Chr. xxv.; 2 Chr. xx. 14). Eleven of the Ps. have his name in their titles (Ps. lxxiii.-lxxxiii.).—2. Recorder to king Hezekiah.—3. Keeper of the royal forest under Artaxerxes (Neh. ii. 8).

BATTERING RAM.

ASĀ′REEL (*God-bound*). Son of Jehaleleel (1 Chr. iv. 16).

ASARE′LAH. Son of Asaph, instrumental musician (1 Chr. xxv. 2).

ASBAZ′ARETH (1 Esd. x. 69). ESARHADDON. See AZBAZZARETH.

ASE'AS (1 Esd. ix. 32). ISHIJAH?

ASEBEBI'A. Levite in 1 Esd. viii. 47. SHEREBIAH?

ASEBI'A. HASHABIAH.

ASE'NATH (*worshiper of Neith*). Daughter of Potipherah, priest of On, Joseph's wife.

A'SER (Tobit i. 2). City in Galilee. HAZOR? (Luke ii. 36; Rev. vii. 6). ASHER.

ASE'RER (1 Esd. v. 32). SISERA?

A'SHAN. Al Ghuweir, in Simeon (Josh. xv. 42; xix. 7).

goddess (2 K. xxi. 7; xxiii. 6). Grove in A. V. Perhaps a head or bust on a straight pillar.

ASH'IMA (*goat with short hair*). A god of the Hamathites, in Samaria, brought from Assyria (2 K. xvii. 30). The Mendesian god of Egypt was a goat (as the Greek Pan), and the Phœnician Esmun.

ASH'KELON. One of the five cities of the Lords of the Philistines (Josh. xiii. 3; 1 Sam. vi. 17). Samson retired to A. as to a remote place (Judg. xiv. 19). Since the crucifixion it has been more noted than before. There was a temple and sacred

ASHDOD

ASHBE'A (*I adjure*). Eshba in the Targum of Joseph. It is not known whether this means a house or a place.

ASH'BEL (*God's charge*). Son of Benjamin (Gen. xlvi. 21).

ASHDOD. AZO'TUS. Eighteen miles south of Joppa, in Philistia. On an elevation above the plain, was strongly fortified, and was one of the seats of the worship of the god Dagon (1 Sam. v. 5; Josh. xv. 47). The birthplace of Herod the Great, who adorned it with baths. It was on the high road to Egypt, and besieged by the Assyrian Tartan, B. C. 716 (Is. xx. 1). Psammetichus besieged it for 29 years, B. C. 630 (Jer. xxv. 20). Philip was found at Azotus (Acts viii. 40; Neh. xiii. 23, 24). It was noted during the Crusades. Now called Usdud. The modern village is built among the ruins of the ancient city, and is embowered in groves, tall sycamores, and hedged with cactus, while the sand drifting with the wind is creeping up to the very doors, two miles from the sea, and burying every green thing.

ASH'DOTH-PIS'GAH (*to pour forth*). Springs E. of the Dead Sea (Deut. iii. 17; Josh. xii. 3; xiii. 20; Num. xxi. 15). Ravine on the E. slope of Pisgah.

ASHER (*happy*). The eighth son of Jacob, by Zilpah, Leah's handmaid (Gen. xxx. 13). The names of one of the 12 tribes. The boundaries are extremely difficult to trace, but were N. of Carmel, on the Great Sea (Josh. xix. 24–31). It contained some of the richest soil in Palestine, and minerals. Anna, who lived in the temple, watching for the coming of Christ, was of this tribe.

ASHE'RAH (*straight*). Idol of the Phœnician

lake to Derceto, the Syrian Venus. It was celebrated for its groves of cypress, figs, olives, pomegranates, vines, and for henna, which grew best here of any place, except only Canopus, and also for the peculiar onions called shallot. Richard I of England, during the Crusades, fortified and held his court at A. The Muslim called it the Bride of Syria. The ancient city was enclosed in a natural wall of hills forming an amphitheatre on the shore of the sea, and on the top of this ridge was the wall, which was very high, thick, and built of small stones and old columns of granite and marble. The modern village Askulan, is very beautiful in its groves, orchards, and shade-trees (Gen. xx. 2). Gerar is supposed to be A. by the Samaritans.

ASH'KENAZ.. One of the sons of Gomer, son of Japhet. The tribe or nation was located in or near Armenia, Ararat, Minni (Jer. li. 27). The name is a compound, As-kenz = As-race. Probably the origin of ASIA.

ASH'NAH. Judah. Two cities. 1. 9 ms. W. of Jerusalem, near Zanoah (Josh. xv. 33). 2. S. W. of Jer. 16 ms., near Nezib (Josh. xv. 43).

ASH'PENAZ (*horse-nose*). Chief of the eunuchs in Assyria (Dan. i. 3).

AS'PHAR, THE POOL OF. Jonathan and Simon encamped in the vicinity of this pool before the battle with Bacchides (1 Macc. ix. 33; Jos. Ant. xiii. 1, § 2). Is it lake Asphaltitis?

ASH'RIEL. Son of Manasseh (1 Chr. vii. 14). ASRIEL?

ASH'TERATHI'TE. Resident in Ashtaroth (1 Chr. xi. 44). Uzzia was one.

ASH'TORETH. ASHTAROTH (*star*). BASHAN.

The seat of the idolatry of the goddess Asntaroth, or Astarte. *Tell Ashareh*, a mound 70 feet high, at one time occupied by a village or buildings. A fine spring issues near some ruins at the base. Following the Samaritan Pentateuch, which reads Afinit Karnaim, instead of Ashtaroth Karnaim, the site of the temple and city of Astarte, is looked for on the S. W. slope of Jebel Hauran, 8 miles N. E. from Bozrah at a place called *El Afineh.*—2. *A. Karnaim (of the two horns).* Now supposed to be Es Sunamein, 25 miles S. of Damascus on the pilgrim route to Mecca. *Sunamein=two idols.*

ASH'UR (*hero*). Son of Hezron; "father" (chief) of Tekoa (1 Chr. ii. 24).

ASH'URITES. In the list of Ishbosheth (2 Sam. ii. 9). House of Asher, meaning the whole of Galilee (Judg. i. 32).

COIN OF LAODICEA—STRUCK BY THE ASIARCH.

ASH'VATH. Son of Japhlet, of Asher (1 Chr. vii. 33).

Ā'SIA (*orient*). Found only in 1 Macc. viii. 6, and the N. T. Now Asia Minor.—2. The country of the king of Pergamos, Mysia, Lydia, Phrygia. 3. Name claimed by the kings of Antioch, now Cilicia (1 Macc. xii. 39). Chief town, Ephesus (Acts ii. 9).

ASIAR'CHÆ. Chief of Asia in Acts xix. 31. A religious office in Asia (Minor), under the Romans, annual, and subject to the proconsul. There are coins of several cities which show by their inscriptions that this office was a great honor. Their duties were the control of the public GAMES and SPECTACLES in the theatres (which were at their own expense?). Philip was the Asiarch when Polycarp was killed at Smyrna. Only wealthy men could have it. Each city sent one person annually to the council, ten were chosen from the whole number, one was made president, or Asiarch. Others think the ten were all Asiarchs.

ASIHĪ'AS. Son of Phorosh, or Parosh (1 Esd. ix. 26).

A'SIEL (*God-made.*) Ancestor of Jehu of Hezekiah's reign (1 Chr. iv. 35).—2. One of the five writers employed by Esd. on the law and history (2 Esd. xiv. 24).

ASĪ'PHA (1 Esd. v. 29). HASUPHA.

ASMODĒ'US (*to destroy*). "King of the demons." (Tobit, iii, 8, etc.)

ASNAP'PER (*general*). "The great and noble" officer who settled the Assyrians in Samaria (Ex. iv. 10).

A'SOM (1 Esd. ix. 33). HASHUM.

ASP. Cobra of Egypt. See ADDER.

ASPAL'ATHUS. A sweet perfume (Ecclus. xxiv. 15).

ASPĀ'THA. Son of Haman (Esth. ix. 7).

AS'PHAR, THE POOL. In the wilderness of Thecoe (1 Macc. ix. 33). ASPHALTITIS?

ASPHAR'ASUS. MISPERETH (1 Esd. v. 8).

AS'RIEL (*vow of God*). Son of Gilead (Num. xxvi. 31). ASRIELITES.

ASSAHĪ'AS (1 Esd. i. 9). HASHABIAH. ASEHIA.

ASSAL'IMOTH (1 Esd. viii. 36). SHELOMITH?

ASSANĪ'AS (1 Esd. viii. 54). HASHABIAH?

ASSARĒ'MŌTH (1 Macc. iv. 15). Margin. GAZERA?

AS'SHUR. Son of Shem. Named Assyria.

ASSHŪ'RIM. From Dedan, grandson of Abraham (Gen. xxv. 3). Ashur in Ezr. xxvii. 23.

ASSIDÆ'ANS (*pious*). A sect who upheld the doctrine of the unity of God, and opposed Grecian manners and idolatries (1 Macc. vii. 13). The name afterwards denoted a life of austerity and religious exercises, in the hope of hastening the coming of the Messiah, and of making an atonement for their own and others' sins. (There is a sect of the name of Assidians now in Poland).

AS'SIR (*captive*). Son of Korah (Ex. vi. 24).—2. Son of Ebiasaph (1 Chr. vi. 23). 3. Son of Jeconiah (1 Chr. iii. 17). Jeconiah the captive?

AS'SOS. Seaport in Mysia, on a peninsula in the Ægean Sea (Acts xx. 13). The ruins are very extensive, and give a more perfect idea of an entire ancient Greek city than any other known site. Paul met Luke and others here after walking from Troas.

ASSYR'IA. Country on the Tigris (Gen. ii. 14), the capital of which was Nineveh (x. 11): named from *Asshur*, the Son of Shem, who was deified and worshiped as their chief god by the Assyrians: 500 ms. N. E. to S. W. and 350 to 100 ms. wide. Divided from Armenia by a high range of mountains. Its northern part is mountainous, the middle hilly, with fertile plains, and the southern is the great plain of *Mesopotamia (midst of rivers)*—the district now called *El Jezira.* This plain is 250 miles long, divided by the rocky ridge, *Sinjar*—a limestone range, sparsely wooded, and of a golden color, with purple lines of shade at a distance. 80 ms. N. of the Sinjar the plain extends to the hilly region, and was once densely populated, but is now a wilderness. The mounds are the only relics of antiquity, and these contain (in those of Nineveh, and others recently partly explored by Layard), proofs of their greatness, in sculptures, inscriptions, and remnants of architecture. The first king of A. who oppressed Israel was Chushan-Rishathaim, B. C. 1400 (Judg. iii. 8). Art and architecture, civil and religious institutions, were in a very advanced state. They used the arch, tunnels, drains, the level, and roller; engraved on gems; enamelled, inlaid, and plated with metals; made glass, optical instruments, ivory, bronze, and precious metal ornaments. The prophesies against A. are those of Nahum, B. C. 645; Zephaniah ii., B. C. 608; and Ezekiel xxxi. B. C. 584.

ASSYRIAN KING.

ASSYR'IANS. In Heb. ASSHUR (Is. x. 5., etc.).

ASTAR'TE. ASHTORETH.

ASTATH (1 Esd. viii. 38). AZGAD?

ASTRON'OMY (*star-naming*). The knowledge of this science by the Hebrews was very limited, as may be judged from their writings; but they in no case oppose scientific fact or truth. Some special knowledge was needed for the temple service. Worship of the stars was denounced with other idolatries (Job xxxviii. 32; K. xxiii. 5. MAZZAROTH. 2. Signs of the Zodiac. MAZZALOTH—planets). The Chaldeans and Egyptians were more cultivated in this and other sciences, and used them in their religious systems.

ASSYRIAN KING PUTTING OUT THE EYES OF HIS CAPTIVES.

ASY'LUM (*inviolable refuge*). The earliest recorded was the temple of pity at Athens, or perhaps one made by Cadmus at Thebes, Greece. Christians adopted the pagan custom and made their churches asylums, and this is still the case in Italy. Moses set apart 6 cities of refuge in the Holy Land. (CITIES OF REFUGE). He also made the "horns of the altar" an asylum; which privilege afterwards attached to the temple and its courts (1 Macc. x. 43).

ASYN'CRITUS. Disciple at Rome (Rom. xvi. 14).

A'TAD (*thorn*). Threshing-floor on the W. of Jordan, near Hebron, (Gen. l. 10–11). ABEL-MIZRAIM.

AT'ARAH (*crown*). Wife of Jerahmeel, mother of Onam (1 Chr. ii. 26).

AT'AROTH (*crowns*). 1. A. Beth Joab, Judah (1 Chr. ii. 54).—2. A. Addar, Eph. (Josh. xvi. 2), 6 ms. N. W. of Bethel.—3. A. Shophan-Gad (Num. xxxii. 34), S. of Heshban, near Jebel Atarus.—4. A. Reuben (Num. xxx. 3).

A'TER (*dumb*). Gate-keepers in the temple (Ezr. ii. 42). Sons of Jatal (1 Esd. v. 28).—2. 98 sons of Ater returned with Zerubbabel (Num. viii. 21).

ATERE'ZIAS (1 Esd. v. 15). See ATER 2.

ATHARI'AS (1 Esd. v. 40). Correctly "the Tirshatha."

ATHENO'BIUS. Envoy by Antiochus Sidetes to Simon (1 Macc. xv. 28).

ATH'ENS. Capital of Greece, founded by Cecrops, B. C. 1556. Visited by Paul (Acts xvii.; 1 Thess. iii.). He founded a church. The people were lovers of music, painting, sculpture, architecture, and oratory, and took part in politics. The fine arts, history, and philosophy were a part of the education of all freemen. The plan shows the position of the Agora (*market-place*), between the four hills. Pausanias says the Athenians surpassed all others in attention to the gods; and their city was crowded with temples, altars, statues, and other sacred works. Paul said they were "too religious." See AREOPAGUS.

ATH'LAI. ATHALIAH. Error in Ezr. x. 28.

ATIPHA (1 Esd. v. 32). HATIPHA?

ATONE'MENT (*at-one-ment*). Satisfaction for sin by which forgiveness is had. When Jacob sent a present to his brother Esau, he said, "I will cover his face, so that he shall forgive my offence, I will make atonement before him, I will placate him" (Gen. xxxii. 21). In Ps. xvi. 14, "a wise man will pacify it" (the wrath of the king). Only once in the N. T., in Rom. v. 11, where it means reconciling. THE DAY OF ATONEMENT was a great feast of the Jews, on the 10th of Tisri, and was held as a day of rest, a kind of Sabbath of Sabbaths, the only day in the year when the whole people fasted. The service was peculiar. The high-priest, clothed in white linen, without ornaments, took a young bull and a ram for himself and his house, and two goats as a sin-offering, and a ram as a burnt offering for the people. The goats were selected by lot, one for Jehovah and one for Azazel in the wilderness (*that is to be sent away surely*). The blood of the victims was taken into the most holy place and sprinkled upon and before the mercy-seat. The scape-goat, to be sent away, was brought forth and the high-priest confessed over his head his sins and those of the people, and he was sent into the wilderness by a trusty man. The bullock and the goat were not eaten, but entirely burnt. This was a symbol of the great truths of the redemptory system by means of propitiation, and it is understood as a type of the vicarious intercession of Jesus Christ.

AT'TAI (*timely*). Grandson of Sheshan, son of Ahlai and Jarha, the Egyptian slave (1 Chr. ii. 35). 2. One of David's "lion-faced" warriors (1 Chr. xii. 11).—3. Second son of Rehoboam by Maachah, daughter of Absalom (2 Chr. xi. 20).

ATTAL'IA. Maritime city in Pamphylia, named from Attalus Philadelphus, king of Pergamos. (Acts xiv. 25). Now Adalia, whose ruins witness its former greatness. Pop. 8000.

ATTHARA'TES (1 Esd. ix. 49). Error for "the Tirshatha" in Neh. viii. 9.

AU'GIA. Daughter of Barzillai (1 Esd. v. 38).

AUGUS'TUS (*venerable*). Title of the Roman Emperors. First assumed by Caius Julius Cæsar Octavianus (nephew of the great Julius Cæsar), when at the battle of Actium he became sole ruler of the empire, B. C. 29. Born B. C. 63, died A. D. 14, aged 76. He gained his great power by gradually uniting in himself all the principal state offices. Tiberius was associated with him in the empire long before his death. He was truly venerable and worthy of regard, for he used his absolute power with great moderation and prudence.

PLAN OF ATHENS.

AUGUSTUS' BAND (Acts xxvii. 1). Independent guard of the governor.

AURA'NUS. Leader of a riot in Jerusalem (2 Macc. iv. 40).

AUTEAS. Levite (1 Esd. ix. 48). HODIJAH?

A'VA (*overturning*). In Assyria; AHAVA—IVAH (2 K. xvii).

ĀV′ARAN (*killer of the royal elephant*). (1 Macc. vi. 43–46). Title of honor given to Eleazar, brother of Judas Maccabeus.

Ā′VEN (*nothing*). 1. Plain of AVEN, perhaps the Bukaa, of Baalbek (Amos i. 5).—2. High places of AVEN (Hos. x. 8), BETHEL.—3. In Ezr. xxx. 17, AVEN—ON, HELIOPOLIS in Egypt.

Ā′VIM, (*ruins*). AVITES. 1. Inhabitants of AVA. (2 K. xvii).—2. Town in Benj., ruins-town (Josh. xviii, 23). It is supposed, from Joshua, xiii. 3, that the country of the Avim was taken from them by the Philistines; called Hazerim in Deut. ii. 23.

Ā′VITH. Chief city of Hadad, king of Edom, (Gen. xxxvi. 35). Jebel Ghoweythe, N. E. of Kerak.

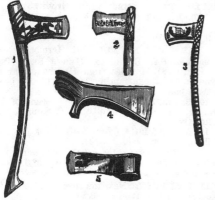

AXES.

AX. The Hebrew words are KARDOM, or GARZEN, the softer form, for a heavy ax with a long handle. MAATZAD, a carving knife (Is. xliv. 12), and also a file for wood or iron (Jer. x. 3); CHEREB, a longer knife, or sword; CASH SHIL (Ps. lxxiv. 6), a carpenter's hatchet; MAGZERAH, ax or clever; MAPPETS, a maul or battle-ax. In some the ax is fastened to the handle with a thong or strip of leather, wound around a great many times; in others there is a hole or eye through the head. See KNIFE, HOE.

AZ′AEL (1 Esd. ix. 14). ASAHEL. AZAE′LUS

A′ZAL ATZAL (Zech. xiv. 5). The limit of the Mt. of Olives in a poetical passage of Zechariah.

AZALĪAH (*God-spared*). Father of Shothan, the scribe (2 K. xxii. 3).

AZANĪAH (*God hears*). Father of Jeshua, the Levite (Neh. x. 9).

AZA′PHION. SOPHERETH ? (1 Esd. v. 33).

AZAR′AEL. AZA′REEL (*God helps*). Korhite, with David at Ziklag (1 Chr. xii. 6).—2. Levite musician in David's time (1 Chr. xxv. 18) ; Uzziel in xxv. 4.—3. Son of Johoram, of Dan (1 Chr. xxvii. 22).—4. Son of Bani (Ezr. x. 41). Esril in 1 Esd. ix. 34. —5. Father of Amashai, priest in Jerusalem (Neh. xi. 13).

AZARĪAS (1 Esd. ix. 21). Uzziah in Ezr. x. 21. Several errors in the Apocrypha of this name, the correct form being found in Ezra and Nehemiah, Azariah. AZARIAS, the angel Raphael (Tobit v. 12).

A′ZAZ (*strong*). Father of Bela (1 Chr. v. 8). REUBENITE.

AZĀ′ZEL. Scape-goat in Lev. xvi. 8. See ATONEMENT.

AZAZĪAH (*God strengthens*). Musician in David's choir (1 Chr. xv. 21). Harpist.—2. Father of Hosea, prince in Ephraim (1 Chr. xxvii. 20).—3. Treasurer of tithes in Hezekiah's time (2 Chr. xxxi. 13).

AZBAZ′ARETH. ESAR-HADDON (1 Esd. v. 69).

AZ′BUK. Father of Nehemiah, prince of Beth-zur (Neh. iii. 16).

Ā′ZEKĀH. In the plain of Judah, having "daughters," suburbs (Josh. 10). *Tell Zakariya?*

A′ZEL. Descendant of Saul (1 Chr. viii. 37). ASEL.

A′ZEM (*bone*). EZEM.

AZEPHŪRITH. ARSIPHURITH (1 Esd. v. 16);—Jorah, in Ezr. ii. 18, and Hariph in Neh. vii. 24; combined by an error of the scribe.

AZĒ′TAS. Family that returned (1 Esd. v. 15); not in Ezra and Nehemiah.

AZ′GAD. Family of 1222 returned with Ezra (ii. 12); and 110 in his second caravan (viii. 12). Sadas in 1 Esd. v. 13, and 3222. Astath in 1 Esd. viii. 38.

AZĪA. Porter in the temple (1 Esd. v. 31). UZZA.

AZĪEI (2 Esd. i. 2). Ancestor of Esdras. AZARIAH. EZARIAH. EZIAH.

A′ZIEL. JAAZIEL.

AZĪZA (*strong*). Of the family of Zattu (Ezr. x. 27). SARDEUS (1 Esd. ix. 28).

AZMĀ′VETH (*strong as death*). One of David's "valiant men" of Bahurim (2 Sam. xxiii. 31).—2. Descendant of Mephibosheth (1 Chr. viii. 36).—3. Father of Jeziel and Pelet, Benjamite slingers and archers who joined David at Ziklag (1 Chr. xii. 3). 4. Overseer of the royal treasures in David's reign.

AZMĀ′VETH. City in Benj. now Hizmeh, S. E. of Er-Ram (Ramah). The sons of the singers settled there (Neh. xii. 29).

AZ′MON. S. border of Palestine, near Hazaraddar (Num. xxxiv. 5). Now ASEI′MEH, west of Kedesh.

AZ′NOTH TĀBOR (*ears of Tabor*). W. in Naphtali, near Dio Cæsarea (*Eusebius*).

A′ZOR. Son of Eliakim in the genealogy of Jesus (Matt. i. 13).

AZŌ′TUS. ASHDOD.

AZŌTUS, MOUNT. Battle-field in which Judas Maccabeus was killed (1 Macc. ix. 15). Hill on which Ashdod was built?

AZ′RIEL (*God's help*). Patriarch in Manasseh (1 Chr. v. 24).—2. Ancestor of Jerimoth, chief in Naphtali (1 Chr. xxvii. 19). Uzziel in the lxx.— 3. Father of Serriah (Jer. xxxvi. 26).

AZ′RIKAM (*help against an enemy*). Son of Neariah, of Judah (1 Chr. iii. 23).—2. Son of Azel (1 Chr. viii. 38).—3. Ancestor of Shemaiah (1 Chr. ix. 14).—4. Prefect in the palace of Ahaz, in Pekah's invasion (2 Chr. xxviii. 7).

AZŪ′BAH. Wife of Caleb (1 Chr. ii. 18).—2. Mother of Jehoshaphat (1 K. xxii. 42).

COIN OF HADRIAN AUGUSTUS.

A′ZUR. AZ′ZUR. Father of Hananiah, the false prophet (Jer. xxviii. 1).—2. Father of Jaazaniah (Ezr. xi. 1).

AZŪ′RAN (1 Esd. v. 15). Azzur in Neh. x. 17.

AZ′ZAH (*strong*) (Deut. ii. 23, etc.). Correct name of Gaza.

AZ'ZAN (*sharp*). Father of Paltiel, of Issachar, a prince (Num. xxxiv. 26).

AZ'ZUR (*helper*). Signer of the marriage covenant (Neh. x. 17). AZUR.

B

BA'AL. 1. A Reubenite, whose son or descendant Beerah was carried of by the invading army of Assyria under Tiglath-Pileser (1 Chr. v. 5). 2. The son of Jehiel, father or founder of Gibeon, by his wife Maachah; brother of Kish, and grandfather of Saul (1 Chr. viii. 30; ix. 36).

BA'AL (*sun or lord*), the supreme male divinity of the Phœnician and Canaanitish nations, as ASHTORETH was their supreme female divinity. There can be no doubt of the very high antiquity of the worship of Baal. We find it established amongst the Moabites and their allies the Midianites in the time of Moses (Num. xxii. 41), and through these nations the Israelites were seduced to the worship of this god under the particular form of Baal-peor (Num. xxv. 3–18; Deut. iv. 3). In the times of the kings the worship of Baal spread greatly, and together with that of Asherah became the religion of the court and people of the ten tribes (1 K. xvi. 31–33; xviii. 18, 22). And though this idolatry was occasionally put down (2 K. iii. 2; x. 28), it appears never to have been permanently abolished among them (2 K. xvii. 16). In the kingdom of Judah also Baal-worship extensively prevailed. The worship of Baal amongst the Jews seems to have been appointed with much pomp and ceremonial. Temples were erected to him (1 K. xvi. 32; 2 K. xi. 18); his images were set up (2 K. x. 26); his altars were very numerous (Jer. xi. 13), were erected particularly on lofty eminences (1 K. xviii. 20), and on the roofs of houses (Jer. xxxii. 29); there were priests in great numbers (1 K. xviii. 19), and of various classes (2 K. x. 19); the worshippers appear to have been arrayed in appropriate robes (2 K. x. 22); the worship was performed by burning incense (Jer. vii. 9) and offering burnt sacrifices, which occasionally consisted of human victims (Jer. xix. 5). The officiating priests danced with frantic shouts around the altar, and cut themselves with knives to excite the attention and compassion of the god (1 K. xviii. 26–28). Throughout all the Phœnician colonies we continually find traces of the worship of this god; nor need we hesitate to regard the Babylonian Bel (Is. xlvi. 1) or Belus as essentially identical with Baal, though perhaps under some modified form. Among the compounds of Baal which appear in the O. T. are: 1. BA'AL-BE'RITH (Judg. viii. 33; ix. 4). The name signifies the *Covenant-Baal*, the god who comes into covenant with the worshippers. 2. BA'AL-ZE'BUB, worshipped at Ekron (2 K. i. 2, 3, 16). The meaning of the name is *Baal* or *Lord of the fly*. The name occurs in the N. T. in the well-known form BEELZEBUB. 3. BA'AL-HA'NAN. 1. The name of one of the early kings of Edom (Gen. xxxvi. 38, 39; 1 Chr. i. 49, 50). 2. The name of one of David's officers, who had the superintendence of his olive and sycamore plantations (1 Chr. xxvii. 28). 4. BA'AL-PE'OR. We have already referred to the worship of this god.

BA'AL, *geographical.* The word occurs as the prefix or suffix to the names of several places in Palestine, as follows:

1. Simeon (1 Chr. iv. 33). Baalath Beer.

2. **BA'ALAH.** Kirjath Jearim, Judah, 7 miles W. of Jerusalem (Josh. xv. 9).—3. Town of the same name in Dan (Josh. xix. 44).

4. **B. BEER** (*B. of the well*, or *holy well*), south Judah, and given to Simeon. Other sacred wells in this region were called Beer-lahai-roi (*of the vision of God*), and Beersheba (*of the oath*).

5. **B. GAD** (*fortune*). The most northern point of Joshua's victories (xi. 17; xii. 7). Supposed to have been a Phœnician sanctuary. Robinson thought it the same as Banias, which has been a sanctuary of the god Pan from a remote age.

6. **B. HA'MON** (*of multitude*). Where Solomon had a vineyard (Cant. viii. 11). May have been not far north of Samaria (Judith viii. 3).

7. **B. HA'ZOR** (*village*). Where Absalom had a sheep-farm, and where Amnon was murdered (2 Sam. xiii. 23).

8. **MT. BA'AL HERMON.** Mt. Hermon.

9. **B. ME'ON.** BETH-BAAL-MEON. BETH-MEON (1 Chr. v. 8). 9 miles from Heshbon, near the mountain of the hot springs, and reputed to be the native place of Elisha.

10. **B. PER'AZIM** (*destructions*). Scene of David's victory over the Philistines (2 Sam. v. 20; 1 Chr. xiv. 11).

11. **B. SHAL'ISHA** (*third idol*). Not far from Gilgal, Sharon (2 K. iv. 42).

12. **B. TA'MAR** (*of the palm*). Benjamin, near Gibeah (Judg. xx. 33). The palm-tree of Deborah is supposed to be meant by some. Lost.

13. **B. ZE'PHON.** Near the crossing-place of the Red Sea in the Exodus. Lost.

BA'ALAH. BAAL.

BA'ALATH. BAAL.

BA'ALE, of Judah. BAAL.

BA'ALIM. BAAL.

BA'ALIS. King of the Bene-Ammon (Jer. xl. 14).

BA'ANA. Son of Ahilud (1 K. iv. 12).

BA'ANAH. 1. Son of Rimmon (2 Sam. iv).—2. Fathers of Heleb (2 Sam. xxiii. 29).—3. Correctly Baana, Son of the Cushai (1 K. iv. 16).—4. Returned with Zerubbabel (Ezr. ii. 2).

BA'ARA. Wife of Shaharaim.

BAASEI'AH. A Gershonite, ancestor of Asaph (1 Chr. vi. 40).

BAASHA (*bad*). The first king of the second line which reigned over the ten tribes. He was an idolater—worshiped the calves, and compelled the people to break off intercourse with Jerusalem.

BA'ALBEK (*city of the sun*). BAAL GAD (Josh. xi. 17; xii. 7), in Cœle-Syria, the valley of Lebanon, under Mt. Hermon. The ruins are the most important and remarkable in the whole country; the site pleasantly located on the lowest slopes of Anti-Lebanon, at the opening of a small valley into the plain El Bukaa. A small stream, divided into many rills for irrigation, waters the fertile soil.

The city was not regular in plan, and heaps of ruins scattered over a space of two miles indicate its size. The chief attractions are the three temples. 1. The Great Temple, whose ruins are very grand and picturesque, but seems to have been left unfinished. The Great Gate is ornamented with every device that could be used in the most florid Corinthian style. Ears of grain, vine-leaves and grapes, with little figures of genii, or elves half-hid among them, and many choice touches of scroll-work, attract the eye and gratify the taste. Only 6 columns of the peristyle of this temple are now standing (75 ft. high, 7 ft. thick, the pediment 120 ft. above the ground), besides two courts and a portico. These are on an artificial platform, which is elevated 30 feet, and has vaults underneath. The three great stones forming a part of the wall of this platform measure (1) 64 ft., (2) 63 ft. 8 in., (3) 63 ft. Thickness, 13 feet. The large stone left in the quarry is 69 ft. long, 17 ft. wide, and 14 ft. thick. 2. The Octagon Temple is Ionic and Corinthian in style, circular inside and outside, having niches which are seen each between two columns. Carved wreaths ornament the space above each. This has been used as a Christian church, but is now ruinous. 3. The Temple of the Sun, also Corinthian, is the most beautiful work there. The great work of Wood and Dawkins contains drawings and plans of every object of interest at Baalbek, and also at Palmyra.

BA'ASHA (*lays waste*). Son of Ahijah, 3d king of Israel, for 24 years. B. C. 953 to 930.

BA'BEL, BAB'YLON (*gate of God*). Capital of the Plain of Shinar (Gen. x. 10). Built B. C. 2600 (ver. 25), on both sides of the river Euphrates: a vast square, 56 miles in circuit. About 5 miles above *Hillah*, on the E. bank of the river, are a great many artificial mounds of enormous size, in three groups: 1. Babil, or Mujellibe (*overturned*), a high pile of unbaked bricks; 2. The palace or *Kasr*; and 3. The mound on which the modern tomb of *Amram ibn Ali* stands. In a line with the Amram mound, on both sides of the river, are the ruins of a great palace, the bricks of which bear the name of Nergal-Sharezer (Neriglissar), who was the chief magician (Rab-mag) and officer of Nebuchadnezzar (Jer. xxxix. 3). Similar mounds, but smaller, are scattered over the country on both sides of the river, one of which, 6 miles S. W. of Hillah is called *Birs Nimrud*, which some say is the tower of Babel. Inscriptions found here, of the date of Nebuchadnezzar, mark the site of Borsippa, outside of Babylon. A broad and deep moat, kept full of water, surrounded one wall of the ancient city, outside of which was another wall 200 royal cubits high and 50 thick. (*Pliny* says 200, *Strabo* 75, and *Rawlinson* 60 to 70 feet). Scarcely a trace of these walls can be found now, except it may be a few mounds which are supposed to mark the sites of some of the gates. Ctesias says there were 250 towers on the walls. The houses were generally built of bricks made of the river mud, sundried, or burnt in kilns, cemented with bitumen, and were three and four stories high.

The streets were straight, and crossed each other at right angles, the cross streets having gates of bronze at the river. Ctesias mentions a bridge of stone 3,000 feet long and 30 feet wide, connecting two palaces on opposite sides of the river. There were 3 walls around the royal palace on the Eastern side, the second or middle wall being 300 ft. high and the towers 420 ft., and 4½ miles in circuit, made of colored brick, representing hunting scenes, with figures of Ninus and Semiramis. A tunnel under the river also connected the two palaces (Jer. li. 58, 53; l. 15). There were a hundred gates of bronze with posts and lintels of the same. The banks of the river had quays, whose ruins still exist, and on the bricks was written in arrow-head characters the name of the last king. The most imposing ruin examined by Layard is called *Birs Nimrud*, and was found to be in seven stories, with a chamber on the top, each story smaller, forming an

oblique pyramid with a square base. It was called the *Temple of the Seven Spheres*, and is not the Tower of Babel of the Scriptures, which is not yet identified. The stories were colored, and were, beginning at the lower—1st, 272 ft. square, 26 ft. high, colored black; 2d, 230 sq. 26 h., orange; 3d, 188 sq. 26 h., red; 4th, 146 sq. 15 h., golden color; 5th, 104 sq 15 h., yellow; 6th, 62 sq. 15 h., blue; 7th, 20 sq. 15 h., silver color; and the ark nearly covering the entire upper platform and 15 feet high, color not given: making, in all, 153 feet above the platform, which was three feet above the plain. The empire lasted 1300 yrs. (Jer. xxv. 12, 14). It is now a desolation, the great city has become heaps (li. 37), the land a wilderness for wild beasts, and even the Arabs refuse to pitch the tent, and the shepherd to fold sheep there (Is. xiii. 19–22).

BA'BI (1 Esd. viii. 37). BEBAI.

BA'CA (*weeping*). The valley (Ps. lxxxiv. 6). Located in Hinnom (2 Sam. v. 23). A valley of the same name is now found in Sinai. (*Burck.*).

BACCHI'DES (*son of Bacchus*). Friend of Antiochus Epiphanes, and governor of Mesopotamia; after Judas Maccabeus fell he reëstablished the power of the Syrian faction in Judæa. B. C. 161-158.

BACCHU'RUS. A holy singer who married a foreign wife (1 Esd. ix. 24).

BAC'CHUS. Greek *Dionysus.* (2 Macc. vi. 7; xiv. 33). A god of special abhorence to the Jews. He

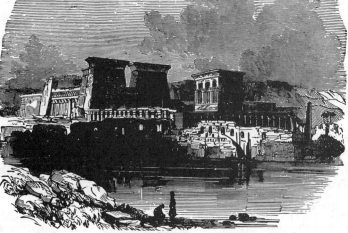

BABYLON.

was the god of wine, and of general festivity and jollity, and his rites sanctioned the most frantic excesses of revelry and excitement. Nicanor threatened to build a temple to Bacchus on the site of the temple of Solomon.

BACE'NOR. Captain under Judas Maccabæus (2 Macc. xii. 35).

BACH'RITES. Family of Becher, son of Ephraim.

BADG'ER (Heb. *Tachash*). The antelope. Tachaitze of Eastern Africa, bluish slaty-gray in color. Sculptured in Egypt.

BA'GO. BIGVAI.

BAGO'AS. EUNUCH (Judith xii. 11).

BA'GOI (1 Esd. v. 14). BIGVAI.

BAHARU'MITE, THE. BAHURIM.

BAHŪ'RIM (*young men's village*). Near the Jerusalem-Jericho road; where in the *Wady Ruwaby*, there are some ruins.

BALA'AM (*stranger*). Son of Beor, and a prophet (Num. xxii. 5). This strange man worshiped Jehovah, and at the same time knew and practiced the forbidden arts of divination. His prophesies are distinguished for dignity, compression, vividness, and fulness of imagery: there is scarcely any work equal to them in the later prophets (Rev. ii. 14).

BA'LAC (Rev. ii. 14). BALAK.

BAL'ADAN. MERODACH—BALADAN.

BA'LAH (Josh. xix. 3). BAAL.

BĀ'LĀK (*empty*). Son of Zippor, king of Moab, who hired Balaam to curse the Israelites (Num. xxii. 24).

BAL'ĀMO. BAAL. (Judith. viii. 3).

BALAS'AMUS (1 Esd. ix. 43).

BALDNESS, is natural and artificial. The artificial is caused by shaving the head, in token of mourning for the dead (Jer. xvi. 6), which Moses forbade to the Jews because it was a heathen custom. Baldness was ridiculed (2 K. ii. 23), perhaps on suspicion of leprosy. A bald man was declared unfit for the priestly office (Lev. xxi. 20).

BALM. TSORI.

BALNU'US (Esd. ix. 31). BINNUI.

BALTHA'SAR. (Bar. i. 11–12). BELSHAZZAR.

BA'MAH (*High-place*) (Ezr. xx. 29). Jehovah gave this name to every place of idolatrous worship.

BA'MOTH. Station in the Exodus (Num. xxi. 19.)

BA'MOTH-BA'AL. BAAL. High-place in Moab (Josh. xiii. 17).

BAN (1 Esd. v. 37). TOBIAH.

BANAI'AS (1 Esd. ix. 35). BENAIAH.

BA'NI. 1. Gadite; one of David's 30 (2 Sam. xxiii. 36).—2. A Levite (1 Chr. vi. 46).—3. Father of Imri (1 Chr. ix. 4). 4. Children of Bani, returned with Zerubbabel (Ezr. ii. 10—5. An Israelite—son of Bani (Ezr. x. 38).—6. A Levite (Neh. iii. 17). 7. A Levite [ANUS] (Neh. viii. 7).—8. Another Levite (Neh. ix. 4).—9. Levite—son of Asaph (Neh. xi. 22).

BA'NID (1 Esd. viii. 36). Lost out of Ezr. viii. 10.

BANNAI'A (1 Esd. ix. 33). SABAD in Ezra

BAN'NUS (1 Esd. ix. 34). BANI or BINNUI.

BAN'QUET. Entertainment furnished at the expense of one man; usually towards the close of the day, between 5 and 6, and called supper. On grand occasions the invitations were given out some days before, and on the day appointed a servant was sent to announce that the time had arrived, and the guest was expected (Matt. xxii. 8; Luke xiv. 17). After accepting the invitation, to neglect to attend was no less than an insult. When all who had been invited had arrived the master of the house shut the door (Luke xiii. 24). The first act of welcome was washing the feet and anointing the hair with perfumed oil; and among the wealthy, on great days, a handsome cloak was furnished to each guest, to be worn during the festivity (Ecc. ix. 8; Rev. iii. 4).

BAN'UAS. Returned from captivity (1 Esd. v. 26).

BĀP'TISM. Washing before prayer or sacrifice was a custom among all ancient nations, as a sign of spiritual purity in the physical cleanness, and baptism was instituted as an initiatory rite of his religion by the Lord Jesus Christ. To be baptized for Moses (1 Cor. x. 2) means to become subject to the law of Moses; to be baptized for Christ, shows an intention to become a true follower of Christ. John baptized with water unto repentance—not causing repentance but as a sign of it. Perhaps only a sign of their willingness to enrol themselves among John's followers. Jesus himself did not baptize with water, but with the Spirit, and Christian baptism was only instituted after the resurrection, when the Lord gave the commission to his apostles "to go into all the world and preach the gospel to every creature." There are different views of Baptism. 1. That it is a direct instrument of grace, when applied by a properly qualified person; infusing into the soul positive moral goodness; or, as some believe, giving only the *capacity*

PHENECIAN VASE.

to receive goodness, which if rightly used will lead to salvation; while others again see that the good will only be enjoyed by those who are predestined to salvation.—2. It is a seal of grace, divine blessings being thereby confirmed to the soul.—3. Some hold that it is only a sign of initiation into Church membership.—4. Or a token of regeneration, to be received only by those who give evidence of being really regenerated.—5. A symbol of purification. The *mode* of baptism differs; and there is practiced immersion and affusion or sprinkling. The Marcionites, and the Gnostics baptized the dead (1 Cor. xv. 29), by proxy, some one answering for the dead, while the water was applied to the dead body; and parents were baptized for their children, from a mistaken reading of the words of Paul. He meant "If the dead rise not at all, what benefit do they expect who baptize vicariously for the dead?"

BARAB'BAS (*son of Abba*). One who had forfeited his life for sedition and murder (Mark xv. 7). The Armenian Version reads "Whom will ye that I shall deliver unto you, Jesus Barabbas, or Jesus that is called Christ?"

BAR'ACHEL. Father of Elihu, a Buzite (Job xxxii. 2–6).

BARACHI'AS (Matt. xxiii. 25). ZACHARIAS.

BA'RAK (*lightning*). Son of Abinoam of Kedesh, Naphtali (Judg. iv. 6). Summoned by Deborah to fight against Jabin and Sisera.

BARBA'RIAN. Any nation but the Greek, was the Greek definition. The term meant to the Greeks what Gentile did to the Jews—any people but Jews. The Egyptians had a similar term; and the oriental nations all had, and have now some term for distinction between their own and other people.

BARHU'MITE. BAHURIM. AZMARETH.

BARI'AH. Son of Shemaiah, of Judah (1 Chr. iii. 22).

BAR-JE'SUS. ELYMAS.

BAR-JO'NA. PETER.

BARKOS. A Nethinim returned with Zerubbabel (Ezr. ii. 53).

BAR'LEY. Used, by the poor only, for bread, mixing it with wheat, beans, lentils, millet, etc., and as fodder for horses (Judg. vii. 13 ; 2 K. iv. 42 ; Ezr. iv. 9 ; 1 K. iv. 28). The barley harvest is in March and April, earlier than the wheat harvest by three weeks.

Barley bread is a sign of poverty, and is little esteemed (Ezr. xiii. 19). Its value was one-third that of wheat (Rev. vi. 6).

BARN. Ten different Hebrew and Greek words are translated barn. Barns, as we know them, for storing hay, grain, etc., are unknown in the East. Rooms, or pits (granaries) are often made underground or cut into the solid rock. It is the custom to keep animals, produce, grain, and all kinds of goods, in the lower story of the dwelling. Poor people often sleep in the same room with their cattle.

BAR'NABAS (*exhorter*). Joses, a Levite of Cyprus, an early disciple and companion of Paul, was called Barnabas—son of eloquence—because of his ready oratory (Acts. iv. 36). He was the first to recognize Paul's sincerity, and introduce him to the church in Jerusalem (ix. 27). Being honored with the mission to Antioch, he sought for Saul (Paul) in Tarsus as a helper, and they worked together a year. Barnabas' sister's son, Mark, was the Evangelist. He is not counted as an apostle (see APOSTLE), although Luke so speaks of him in Acts xiv. 14 ; and they were equally honored by the church until after the quarrel and separation of Barnabas from Saul. After that Barnabas is lost sight of The Epistle called by his name is believed to be spurious, because it has in it errors in the Jewish history and worship, and very feeble grasp of divine truth, unworthy of a Levite and a disciple. It is assigned to the 2d century A. D. by Alford.

BARO'DIS. Servant of Solomon, returned with Zerubbabel (1 Esd. v. 34).

BARSABAS. See JOSEPH and JUDAS.

BAR'TACUS. Father of Apame. "The admirable" was probably an official title belonging to his rank (1 Esd. iv. 29).

BARTHOL'OMEW (*son of Talmai*). One of the 12. The same as Nathanael. Born at Cana. Philip had some difficulty in bringing him to regard Jesus as the Christ. He was one of the 7 to whom Jesus appeared after the resurrection at the lake of Tiberias, and a witness of the ascension. Tradition only gives any account of him after that time, when he is supposed to have gone as a preacher

into "the East" (India). A spurious gospel bears his name.

BARTIME'US (*son of Timai*), a blind beggar of Jericho (Mark x. 46).

BA'RUCH (*blessed*). 1. Friend and amanuensis of Jeremiah (Jer. xxxii. 12). See HISTORY OF THE BOOKS.—2. Son of Zabbai (Neh. iii. 20).—3. Son of Col-hozeh (Neh. xi. 5).

BARZILLA'I. A wealthy Gileadite who was hospitable to David when he fled from Absalom (2 Sam. xvii. 27) ; but declined David's invitation to reside at court, because of his great age.—2. Whose son married Saul's daughter Michal.

BAS'ALOTH. BAZLITH. (1 Esd. v. 31).

BAS'CAMA. Gilead, where Tryphon killed Jonathan Maccabeus, whose bones were afterwards

ORIENTAL BANQUET.

removed to Modin by Simon (1 Macc. xiii. 23-25). Lost.

BA'SHAN, (*soft, rich soil, or basalt soil*). Land of Bashan. E. of Jordan, N. of Jabbok ; from the border of Gilead to Hermon, and from the Jordan to Salcah (Josh. xii. 4, 5 ; Deut. iii. 10–14). At Edrei, Og, king of B., was defeated, and the land given to the half-tribe of Manasseh, with half of Gilead. It was famous for its oaks (Is. ii. 13 ; Zech. xi. 12), and cattle ; and now the granary of Damascus. Modern travelers speak of its delightful forests, of its flocks and herds, and grain fields. ARGOB, with its 60 cities, was in Bashan.

BA'SHAN-HA'VOTH-JA'IR. Name given to Argob after its conquest by Jair (Deut. iii. 14.)

BASH'EMATH (*fragrant*). Daughter of Ishmael, Esau's 3d wife (Gen. xxxvi. 3). MAHALATH (xxviii. 9).—2. Daughter of Elon the Hittite, and wife of Esau (Gen. xxvi. 34).

BA'SIN. The translation of four Hebrew words, and one Greek word. The forms of some kinds have been preserved on the monuments, and are given in the article WASHING THE HANDS AND FEET.

EGYPTIAN BASKETS.

BAS'KET. Five Hebrew words are translated basket. The form of the bread-basket is shown in the cut. They were made of grass, or willow twigs.

BAS'MATH. Daughter of Solomon (1 K. iv. 4), wife of Ahimaaz, one of the king's officers.

BAS'SA. Bezai. (1 Esd. v. 16).

BA'STAI. Besai. (1. Esd. v. 31).

BAS'TARD (Heb. *mamzer*). A child born to those who marry within the limited degrees of relationship, as two of the same family; or a Jew and a gentile.

BAT. Among the animals forbidden to be eaten (Lev. xi. 20). The peculiar habitation of bats, in the dark recesses of rocky caves, and their nocturnal habits, give great force to the prophesy that the idols shall be cast to the bats and the moles. Baruch shows (among other images) that the idols are no gods because bats sit on their heads, with birds and cats.

BĀTHING. Baptism. In Palestine, Syria and Egypt, bathing is a luxury as well as a necessity, and is now a religious ceremony, as in ancient times.

BATH-RABBIM. Gate of the ancient city of Heshbon. The two pools were near this gate; were likened to the eyes of Shelomith's beloved (Cant. vii. 4).

BÁTHSHĒ'BA (*promised—sworn*). A daughter of Eliam, wife of Uriah, and grand-daughter of Ahitophel, the statesman. Mother of Solomon. There are recorded instances of her vigorous understanding and kindness of heart.

BATH'SHUA. Daughter of the oath.

BÁTH ZACHĀRĪ'AS (*house of Z.*). Now *Beit Sakarieh.* 8 ms. N. of Beit Sur.

BAVAI. Ruler of Keilah (Neh. iii. 18).

BAY-TREE. A native—not an exotic (Ps. xxxvii. 35). Grows near Antioch.

BAZ'LITH (*stripping*). "Children of B." returned with Zerubbabel (Neh. vii. 54).

BDELLIUM. The gum of a tree that grew in the land of India and Arabia—used in sacrifice and as a perfume and flavor for wine. The word may mean pearls (Gen. ii. 12; Num. xi. 7).

BEALI'AH. A Benjamite who went over to David at Ziklag (1 Chr. xii. 5).

BE'ALOTH. A town in the extreme South of Judah (Josh. xv. 24).

BE'AN, CHILDREN OF. Beon. (1 Macc. v. 4), probably Bedouins.

BEANS. A native of Palestine, Syria and Asia Minor. (2 Sam. xvii. 28). Blossoms from January to March. Planted in November; gathered in February. Both the green pod and ripe beans, boiled with oil and garlic, are commonly used by persons of all classes. There are several kinds, some of which are fed to horses.

BEARDS.

BEAR. The Hebrew name (*dob*) is still in use for the bear in the East, which is found on Mts. Hermon, Lebanon, and other parts of the country;

and naturalists have shown that it is a species peculiar to Syria.

BEARD. The beard in the East is a badge of manhood and a mark of freedom. The Egyptians shaved it off and wore a false beard of plaited hair, in style and length to suit their rank. The Hebrews were distinct from both their Egyptian and Assyrian neighbors, as may be shown on the monuments, where captives are drawn in their proper costume and feature. It was a shame to lose the hair or beard (Is. l. 6), and also a sign of mourning. It was carefully dressed and oiled (Ps. cxxx. iii), and a full, long beard was, and is, a highly coveted ornament.

BE'BAI. 1,623 sons of Bebai returned with Zerubbabel (Ezr. ii. 11); 28 more with Ezra; 4 took foreign wives (Ezr. x. 28).—2. Father of Zechariah.—3. Bebai—Chobai (Judg. xv. 4).

BE'CHER (*first-born—young camel*). 1. Second son of Benjamin (Gen. xlvi. 21).—2. Son of Ephraim (Num. xxvi. 35).

ELEPHANT.

BECHO'RATH. Son of Aphiah—grandson of Be'cher (Sam. ix. 1.)

BEC'TILETH, THE PLAIN OF (*house of slaughter*) between Nineveh and Cilicia (Judg. ii. 2). Bactiali was a plain 21 miles from Antioch. (Peutinger tables).

BED. 1. A mat of grass, reeds, straw, hemp, or one or more cloths.—2. A quilt or mattress, filled with cotton, wool, grass, or straw. The pillow for the head is a frame of wood, a stone, or a stuffed bag, or sheep-skin. The bed was laid on the *divan* (platform 6 to 8 feet wide, and 8 to 15 inches high, on one or more sides of a room). *Bedsteads*, or movable frames (1 Sam. xix. 15; bier, 2 Sam. iii. 31), were used, perhaps, only, by the wealthy. Some were made of palm-sticks, and others of iron (Deut. iii. 11). Sculptures in Asia Minor show many elegant shapes of bedsteads, and couches. The *canopy* (Judith xvi. 23) was, and is still used in the East, for display, and for protection against light, dust and insects (Esth. i. 6; Ps. vii. 16). The people seldom or never change their dress on going to bed; only taking off the outer garment (see Dress), excepting in hot weather.

BE'DAD (*separation, part*). Father of Hadad, king of Edom (1 Chr. i. 46).

BE'DAN (*son of Dan—servile*), judge of Israel (1 Sam. xii. 11).

BE-DEI'AH. Son of Beni (Ezr. x. 35).

BEE (*děbôrâh*). Palestine abounded in bees, for it was a land "flowing with milk and honey"

(Deut. xxxii. 13). The banded bee of Palestine is not found in this country. So plentiful was wild honey that it was exported. It was eaten mixed with butter. There is a vegetable substance called honey which is a thick juice of grapes.

BEELI'ADA (*known by Baal*). Son of David; born in Jerusalem (1 Chr. xiv. 7).

BEEL'SARUS. BIL-SHAN (1 Esd. v. 8).

BEELTETH'MUS (*chancelor*). Officer of Artaxerxes in Palestine (1 Esd. ii. 16–25.)

BEEL'ZEBUB (*fly-god*). BEEL'ZEBUL (*lord of dirt*). *House-god*, and *dung-god*, by some. A belief that demons possessed persons, led to a belief in a *prince* of demons, who was supposed to rule over them.

BE'ER. 1. One of the latest halting-places of the Israelites, lying beyond the Arnon, and so called because of the well which was there dug by the "princes" and "nobles" of the people, and is perpetuated in a fragment of poetry (Num. xxi. 16–18). This is possibly the BEER-ELIM referred to in Is. xv. 8. 2. A place to which Jotham the son of Gideon fled for fear of his brother Abimelech (Judg. ix. 21).

BE'ER (*well*). 1. A well dug by the "princes" beyond Arnon, near one of the last stations of the Exode, and celebrated in poetry (Num. xxi. 16, 18). —2. Jotham, son of Gideon, fled to this place (Judg. ix. 21). Site lost.

BE'E-RA (*well*). Son of Zophah (1 Chr. vii. 37).

BE'ER-AH (*well*). Prince of the Reubenites (1 Chr. v. 6.)

BEER-ELIM (*well of heroes*). BEER 1 (Is. xv. 8).

BE'ER-I. 1. The father of Judith, one of the wives of Esau (Gen. xxvi. 34). [ANAH.] 2. Father of the prophet Hosea (Hos. i. 1).

BE'ER-LAHA'I-ROI, a well, or rather a living spring (A. V. *fountain,* comp. Jer. vi. 7), between Kadesh and Bered, in the wilderness, "in the way to Shur," and therefore in the "south country" (Gen. xxiv. 62), which, according to the explanation of the text, was so named by Hagar, because God saw her there (Gen. xvi. 14). By this well Isaac dwelt both before and after the death of his father (Gen. xxiv. 62; xxv. 11). In both these passages the name is given in the A. V. as "the well Lahai-roi." Mr. Rowland announces the discovery of the well Lahai-roi at *Moyle* or *Moilahi,* a station on the road to Beersheba, 10 hours south of *Ruheibeh;* near which is a hole or cavern bearing the name of *Beit Hagar* (Ritter, *Sinai,* 1086, 7); but this requires confirmation.

BEE'ROTH (*wells*). One of the 4 cities of the Hivites; the other 3 being Gibeon, Chephirah, and Kirjath Jearim (Josh. ix. 17; xviii. 25, 26, 28). 10 ms. N. of Jerusalem, on the Shechem road, the customary resting-place of travelers (*Rob*).—Bene Jaakan. Edom, a station (Deut. x. 6).

BEER'SHEBA (*well of swearing or well of seven*). S. border of Judah. Dug by Abraham (Gen. xxi. 31). The compact of Abraham and Abimelech was ratified by setting apart 7 ewe-lambs (sheba, seven). Isaac's servants also "digged" a well (xxvi. 32). Two principal wells and five smaller ones are on the N. bank of Wady Seba on the edge of the desert. One is 12½ ft. diameter, 44½ ft. to the water (*Rob.,* Apr. 12). The other is 5 ft. diam. and 42 ft. to the water. Watering-troughs of stone lie around the wells, and among the grass are crocuses and lilies. The 5 lesser wells are at some distance from the 2 larger. The ruins of a town are on the hills N. of the wells. It is very frequently mentioned as one of the boundaries of all Israel: From Dan

to Beer-sheba. The Arab name is Bir es Seba', Well of the Lion.

BEESHTE'RAH. MAN. (Josh. xxi. 27). ASHTAROTH.

BEE'TLE. LOCUST.

BEEVES. BULL; OX.

BEGGAR. ALMS; POOR.

BEGOTTEN. Jesus Christ, the Son of God (John i. 14, 18; Rev. i. 5).

BEHEADING. PUNISHMENTS.

BEHE'MOTH. There can be little or no doubt that by this word (Job xl. 15–24) the hippopotamus is intended, since all the details descriptive of the *behemoth* accord entirely with the ascertained habits of that animal. Since in the first part of Jehovah's discourse (Job xxxviii., xxxix.) *land animals and birds* are mentioned, it suits the general purpose of that discourse better to suppose that *aquatic or amphibious* creatures are spoken of in the last half of it; and since the leviathan, by almost universal consent, denotes the crocodile, the behemoth seems clearly to point to the hippopotamus, his associate in the Nile. The description of the animal's lying under "the shady trees" amongst the "reeds" and willows is peculiarly appropriate.

BE'KAH (*part-half*). WEIGHTS AND MEASURES.

BE'LEMUS (1 Esd. ii. 16). BISHLAM.

BEL. The national god of the Babylonians (Is. xlvi. 1; Jer. l. 2). Zeus Bel is the male, and Hera the female, of the same deity. Writers are divided as to whether Bel (Baal) was the sun or the planet Jupiter: if the sun, then Ashtoreth was the moon-goddess.

BEL AND DRA'GON. DANIEL, ADDITIONS TO.

BELA. 1. One of the five cities of the plain which was spared at the intercession of Lot, and received the name of Zoar (Gen. xiv. 2; xix. 22). It lay on the southern extremity of the Dead Sea, on the frontier of Moab and Palestine (Jerome on Is. xv.), and on the route to Egypt, the connection in which it is found, Is. xv. 5; Jer. xlviii. 34; Gen. xiii. 10. We first read of Bela in Gen. xiv. 2, 8. 2. Son of Beor, who reigned over Edom in the city of Dinhabah eight generations before Saul, king of Israel, or about the time of the Exodus. He is supposed by some to be the same as Balaam. It is not improbable that he was a Chaldean by birth, and reigned in Edom by conquest. He may have been contemporary with Moses (Gen. xxxvi. 31–33; 1 Chr. i. 43, 44). 3. Eldest son of Benjamin, according to Gen. xlvi. 21 (A. V. "Belah"); Num. xxvi. 38, 40; 1 Chr. vii. 6; viii. 1, and head of the family of the BELAITES. 4. Son of Ahaz, a Reubenite (1 Chr. v. 8).

BE'LAITES. Descendants of Bela 3.

BELI'AL. The translators of our A. V., following the Vulgate, have frequently treated this word as a proper name, and given it in the form *Belial,* in accordance with 2 Cor. vi. 15. There can be no question, however, that the word is not to be regarded as a proper name in the O. T.; its meaning is *worthlessness,* and hence *recklessness, lawlessness.* The expression *son* or *man of Belial* must be understood as meaning simply a worthless, lawless fellow. The term as used in 2 Cor. vi. 15 is generally understood as an appellative of Satan, as the personification of all that was bad.

BEL-TE-SHAZ'ZAR. Name given to Daniel (Dan. i. 7). Correctly BEL-SHAT-ZAR (*favored by Bel*)

BELLS. Large bells were not used in ancient times, nor are they in use now. Small hand bells were used by the Greeks, Romans and Jews. The high priest wore round the hem of his dress seventy-two gold bells, which were placed alternately with pomegranates. The little girls of Cairo wear strings of them round their feet. They were sometimes attached to the harness of horses and camels.

BEL'LOWS. The ancients used two kinds, according to the monuments, ingeniously contrived to be worked by the feet (Jer. vi. 29).

ELIJAH AT PRAYER.

BEL'MA-IM. BELMEN. Place S. of Dothaim (Judg. vii. 3).

BEL'MEN. ABEL-MAIM. Place in Samaria (Judg. iv. 4). ABEL-MEHOLAH.

BE'LIEVE. Faith in the Lord Jesus Christ (Acts xiii. 35).

BE'LIEV'ERS. Christians (Acts v. 14).

BÉLSHÁZZAR (*Bel's prince*). The last king of Babylon. A mysterious writing appearing on the wall during a great feast, and his magicians not being able to read it, Daniel was called, and explained its meaning. He died the same night (Dan. v.).

BEN (*son*). A Levite—a porter of the ark (1 Chr. xv. 18).

BEN-A-BIN'A-DAB. Son of Abinadab (1 K. iv. 11).

BENA'IAH (*god-built*). 1. Son of Jehoiada, of Kabzeel, a Levite (2 Sam. xxiii. 20–23).—2. One of David's 30 valiant men; an Ephraimite. Seven others of this name, but none very noted.

BEN-AM'MI (*son of my kindred*). Son of the younger daughter of Lot (Gen. xix. 38).

BENCH'ES. Hatches, or "thy deck" (Ez. xvi. 15 ff).

BEN-DE'KAR (*Lance-bearer*). Son of Dekar (1 K. iv. 9).

BE'NE-BE'RAK (*sons of lightning*). City of the tribe of Dan (Josh. xix. 45).

BEN-E-FAC'TOR (*a doer of good*). Title of honor (Luke xxii. 25).

BENEJÁAKAN. Tribe descended from Jaakan (AKAN), a Horite chief (Gen. xxxvi.), and who owned wells where Israel encamped in the Exode (Num. xxxiii. 31).

BENEKÉDEM (*people of the East*). Kedem was the name for the whole country E. of Palestine, far or near. They lived (as now) in tents, kept flocks and herds, and were always ready for robbing expeditions.

BEN-GE'BER. Son of Geber (1 K. iv. 13).

BENHĀ'DAD (*son of Adad, a god of Syria*). **1.** King of Syria, who was hired by Asa, king of Judah, to invade Israel (1 K. xv. 18). Supposed to be the same as Hadad, the Edomite, who rebelled against Solomon (1 K. xi.).—2. King of Syria, son of the former, and always at war with Ahab (1 K. xxi. 30). He consulted the prophet Elisha, by means of Hazael, and was smothered by him soon after, B. C. 884 (2 K. viii.).—3. A king of Syria, son of Hazael (2 K. xiii.).

BEN-HA'IL (*warrior*). A prince Jehoshaphat sent to teach in Judah (2 Chr. xvii. 7).

BEN-HA'NAN (*son of one gracious*). Son of Shimon (1 Chr. iv. 20).

BEN-HE'SED (*son of Hesed*), (1 K. iv. 10).

BEN'-HUR (*son of Hur*), (1 K. iv. 8).

BE-NĪ'NU (*our son*). A Levite, who sealed the covenant with Nehemiah (Neh. x. 13).

BEN'JAMIN (*fortune*). Named Benoni by his dying mother. Youngest son of Jacob, second of Rachel, born near Bethlehem ; his father's favorite, next to Joseph, and the mark of special honors from him. He had the affection of his brothers, and received their favors as a matter of course, and was not very positive, but a quiet, gentle spirit. He had ten sons and grand-sons at the migration into Egypt (Gen. xlvi.). He made no special history for himself. The *tribe* was always of least consequence. At the Exodus there were 35,400 of full age, and at the passage over Jordan 45,600. There were 26 cities in their portion (see map). The tribe was almost destroyed for violating the rights of hospitality (Judg. xix. 20), 600 only escaping to the rock Rimmon (see RIMMON and SHILOH). The first deliverer of Israel (from Moab) in the time of the judges, was Ehud, a Benjamite. The first king of Israel was Saul, a Benjamin ; and Saul (Paul), the apostle, was also of this tribe.

BEN'JAMIN, GATE OF. In Jerusalem.

BEN'JA-MITE. Decandant of Benjamin (Judg. iii. 15).

BE'NO (*his son*). A Levite, son of Merari (1 Chr. xxiv. 26, 27).

BENO'NI (*son of my sorrow*). Name given by Rachel to her son (Gen. xxxv. 18).

BEN-ZO'HETH (*son of Zoheth*). Decandant of Judah (1 Chr. iv. 20).

BE'ON. Place E. of Jordan (Num. xxxii. 3). (Compare verse 38).

BE'OR (*torch or lamp*). 1. Father of Bela. Edomite king (Gen. xxxvi. 32).—2. Father of Balaam.

BE'RA (*son of evil*). King of Sodom (Gen. xiv. 2).

BERĀ'CHAH (*blessing*). 6 miles S. of Bethlehem, 1 mile E. of the Hebron road, now called *Bereikut* (2 Chr. xx. 26).

BER-A-CHI'AH. A Levite (1 Chr. vi. 39). BERE-CHIAH.

BE-RAI'AH or **BER-A-I'AH** (*Jehovah created*). Son of Shimhi. A Benjamin chief (1 Chr. viii. 21).

BERE'A. Macedonia (Acts xvii. 10). Visited by Paul and Silas, Paul's companion. Sopater of Berea (xx. 4 ; Rom. xvi. 21). Sosipater. Now called Verria, on the E. slope of Olympus, well watered, and commanding a fine view of the plains of Axius and Haliacmon; 15,000 population. The ruins are Greek, Roman, and Byzantine.—2. A name of Aleppo.—3. Judea, near Jerusalem (1Macc. iv. 4; Jos. Ant. xi. § 1). Jerome says certain persons lived in this city who had, and used St. Matthew's Hebrew Gospel.

BER-E-CHI'AH (*God blessed*).—1. son of Zerubbabel (1 Chr. iii. 20).—2. Father of Meshullam 13 (Neh. iii. 4, 30).—3. A Levite (1 Chr. ix. 16).—4. A doorkeeper for the Ark (1 Chr. xv. 23).—5. A chief in Ephraim (2 Chr. xxxviii. 12).—6. Father of Asaph (1 Chr. xv. 17).—7. Father of Zechariah. (Zech. i. 1, 7).

BE'RED. In the wilderness, near Kadesh (Gen. xvi. 14). Located at Elusa, Khulasa (Ar.), 12 ms. S. of Beersheba, where there is a well. Supposed to be Shur, and also Gerar.

BERE'ITES. Descendants of Beriah 1.

BERE-NI'CE (*gift*). Eldest daughter of Herod Agrippa. 1. Married to her uncle Herod, king of Chalcis, and was after his death wife of Polemon, king of Cilicia. She was also with Vespasian and Titus (Ant. xix. 5, 1; xx. 7, 2, 3).

BE'RI. BEERI. Son of Zophah (1 Chr. vii. 36).

BE-RI'AH (*in evil, or a gift*).—1. Son of Asher (Gen. xlvi. 17), descended from the Bereites.—2. Son of Ephraim (1 Chr. vii. 20, 23).—3. A Benjamite (1 Chr. viii. 13, 16).—4. A Gershonite Levite, son of Shimre (1 Chr. xxiii. 10, 11).

BE'RITES (*well*). People visited by Joab in his search after Sheba (2 Sam. xx. 14).

BE'RITH (*The God*) (Judg. ix. 46).

BE-RO'DACH—BAL'A-DAN. MERODACH (2 K. xx. 12).

BE'ROTH (1 Esd. v. 19). BEEROTH.

BERŌTHĀH. BERO'THAI; BERY'TUS; BEI'RUT (*ba-root*). Chief seaport in North Palestine (Syria). (2. Sam. viii. 8; Ezr. xlvii. 16). A city of the Phœnicians, named after Baal Berith (*god of wells*). Van de Velde proposes for the Scripture place *Tell el Byruth*, between Tadmor and Hamoth. See PHŒNICIA.

BEROTH'ITE, THE (1 Chr. xi. 39), from Beroth or Beeroth.

BERRIES. Fruit of the olive-tree (Is. xvii. 6; Jas. iii. 12).

BER'YL. See PRECIOUS STONE.

BER-ZE'LUS (1 Esd. v. 38). BARZILLAI 1.

BE'SAI (*victory?*) Returned with Zerubbabel (Ezr. ii. 49).

BES-O-DE'IAH. Father of Meshullam—(*Intimate of Jehovah*) (Neh. iii. 16).

BE'SOM. A broom or brush of twigs (Is. xiv. 23).

BE'SOR (*cool*), THE BROOK. Judah (1 Sam. xxx. 9). A winter torrent, rising south of Hebron, and reaching the sea a few miles S. of Gaza.

BESTEAD' (Is. viii. 21). Distressed.

BE-STOW'. To give or confer (Ex. xxxii. 29).

BE'-TAH (*trust, confidence*). City of Hadadezer king of Zobah (2 Sam. viii. 8). TIBHATH (Gen. xxii. 24).

BETA'NE. BETHANIN of Eusebius, two miles from Terebinth, or Oak of Abraham, and four from Hebron. This has been variously identified with Betharath, Bethainun (Beth-anoth) and Betaneh, or Ectabana, in Syria.

BE'TEN (*belly*). A city on the border of Asher (Josh. xix. 25), 8 miles E. of Ptolemais.

BĒTH. House of any kind. TENT. HANGINGS. FAMILY. TEMPLE.—AB'ARA (*house of the ford*), where John was baptizing (John i. 28). The oldest MSS. read BETHANY. It was beyond Jordan, and nearly opposite Jericho.—A'NATH. Naph. Fenced city (Josh. xix. 38; Judg. i. 33). Site lost. —A'NOTH. Judah (Josh. v. 59).' Beit ainun, near Halhul, and Beit Sur. (*Rob.*) 3 ms. N. of Hebron.

BETH'ANY (*house of dates*). One of the most interesting places in Palestine. The residence of Lazarus, who was raised from the dead; the frequent resting-place of Jesus; the home of Mary and Martha, and of Simon, the leper; and from whence the triumphal entry began; and near this place was the scene of the Ascension. On the Mt. of Olives (Mark xi. 1; Luke xix. 29); 15 furlongs off (John xi. 18); on the road to Jericho (Luke xix. 1, 29), and near it was Bethphage. It is now called El Azariyeh, the city of Lazarus. Is in a hollow, surrounded with olives, almonds, pomegranates, oaks, and carobs. The buildings are ruinous and wretched. The house of Lazarus is pointed out as a square tower, very ancient; and his tomb, a cave in the rock, descended by 26 steps.

BETH-AR'ABAH (*house of the desert*). One of the six cities of Judah in the Arabah—sunk valley of the Jordan (Josh. xv. 6, 61; xviii. 22).

BETH-ĀRAM. Gad, E. of Jordan (Josh. xiii. 27, xxxii. 36). Site located two miles E. of Jordan in W. Seir. *Livias. Tell Haran.*

OLIVES.

BETH-ÄRBEL (Hos. x. 14). Site lost. Supposed to refer to Judg. viii.

BETH-ĀVEN (*house of naught*). Benj. E. of Bethel (Josh. vii. 2).

BETH-ĀZ'MAVETH. Benj. (Neh. vii. 28). On the hills S. E. of Jeba.

BETH-BĀAL-MEON. Reuben, on the downs E. of Jordan (Josh. xiii. 17). Baal Meon (Num. xxxiii. 38). The name is still given to a ruin of large size, two miles S. W. of Hesban (*Burck.*) in W. Zurka Main, where there are remains of a Roman road.

BETH-BĀ'RAH (*house of the ford*) (Judg. vii. 24). Gideon's victory was near Bethshean, and the fords were probably the outlets of the brooks coming down from the mountains of Ephraim. The place where Jacob crossed on his return from Mesopotamia, and at which Jephtha slew the Ephraimites. Located by Van de Velde on the Jordan, at the ford on the Nablus-Es—Salt road.

BETH-BĀ'SI. In the Jordan valley, not far from Jericho (1 Macc. ix. 62, 64; Jos. Ant. xiii. 1, § 5).

BETH-BIR'ĒI. Simeon (1 Chr. iv. 31), near Beersheba.

BETH'-CAR (*house of lambs*). West of Mizpeh (1 Sam. vii. 11; Jos. Ant. vi. 2, § 2).

BETH-DĀ'GON (*house of Dagon*).—1. In the Shefelah, Judah (Josh. xv. 41). Site supposed to be found at Beit dejan, between Lydda and Jaffa (*Rob*).—2. Asher, near the coast (xix. 27).—3. Beit dejan, about 5 ms. S. E. of Nablus, Shechem.

BETH-DIBLĀ-THĀ'IM (*house of the double cake*). Moab (Jer. xlviii. 22).

BETH-ĒDEN (*house of pleasantness*) (Amos i. 5.)

BETH-E'-KED (*shearing house*).

BETH-EL (*house of God*). Ten miles north of Jerusalem, to the right of the Shechem road, where Jacob saw the ladder in his dream (Gen. xxviii. 19). The name of the city was originally Luz. Another account is, that Jacob set up a stone to mark the spot where God spake with him (Gen. xxxv. 14, 15; Hosea xii. 4, 5). In Abram's time it was called Bethel (xii. 8). Jeroboam, the king, set up a golden calf at Bethel (1 K. xiii). Jehu continued the worship of the calf. It was near Bethel that the event of the bears and Elisha and the forty-two children took place. It was a royal residence (Amos vii. 13). There were winterhouses and summer-houses and houses of ivory at B. (iii. 14, 15; 2 K. xxvii. 28). Josiah destroyed it. The worship of God and of idols went on side by side for many years (Amos v. 14, 22). Was a strong place in later times (1 Macc. ix. 50). It is not mentioned in the N. T. Josephus relates its capture by Vespasian (Wars iv. 9, § 9). The ruins cover four or five acres: on a low hill between two valleys, which run into es Suweinit (*Rob*).—2. Judah (Josh. xii. 16; 1 Sam. xxx. 27). Chesil, Bethul. HIEL, the BETHELITE, the rebuilder of Jericho (1 K. xvi. 34.)

BETH'-EL-ITE. Hiel, the Bethelite, re-built Jericho (1 K xvi. 34).

BETHĒ'MEK (*house of the valley*). Asher, on the border of Jipthah-el. 'Amkah, 8 miles N. E. of Akka (*Rob*).

BĒ'THER. Mountains of (Cant. ii. 17). Lost.

BETHES'DA (*house of mercy* or *place of flowing water*). A pool at Jerusalem, near the sheep-gate, or "market," with five porches, extensive enough to accommodate a large number of sick and infirm people, who resorted there for relief (John v. 2). Supposed to be the great excavation near St. Stephen's gate, now called Bethesda. The porches and water are gone, and all around it are ruins, but it is very large, cemented as if for holding water, and there might have been buildings on its east and north sides anciently. See JERUSALEM.

SECTION OF POOL.

BETHĒ'ZEL (*fixed*). Philistia (Micah i. 11).

BETH'GĀDER (*wall*). Geder (Josh. xii. 13).

BETH'GA-MUL (*house of the weaned*, or *camel*). Moab, in the plains. Um-el Jemail, a few miles south of Busrah, in the Hauran (*Rob*.).

BETH-HĀC'CĒREM (*house of the vine*). New Tekoa (Jer. vi. 1; Neh. iii. 14).

BETH-HAG'GAN (*garden--house*).

BETH-HĒ'RAN. East of Jordan, at the mouth of Wady Seil Now Tell Haran-Livias. Built by the Gadites (Num. xxxii. 36; Josh. xiii. 27).

BETH-HŌG'LAH (*house of partridge*). On the border of Judah (Josh. xv. 6) and Benjamin, near Jericho. A great spring and ruin in the Jericho plain is now called Ain Hajla (*Rob*.).

BETH-HŌ'RON (*house of caverns*). Two cities, on the Jerusalem-Jaffa upper road, built by Sherah, a woman of Ephraim, on the boundary between Ephraim and Benjamin (Josh. xvi. 3, 5; xviii. 13, 14; xxi. 22). Two of the most memorable victories

INN. CARAVANSERAI.

of the Jews occurred here—Joshua over the five Amorite kings, when the sun and moon stood still at his command (Josh. x.), and that of Judas Maccabæus over the forces of Syria, under Seron (1 Macc. iii. 13-24). The Roman army, under Cestius Gallus, was defeated here in the reign of Nero, with a loss of 5,680 men (Jos. Wars, ii. § 8).

BETH-JESH'IMOTH (*house of the wastes*). East of Jordan, in the deserts of Moab (Num. xxxiii. 49). Was one of the cities which were "the glory of the country" (Ez. xxv. 9). Beth Jisimuth is now half a mile east of the Jordan, and a mile north of the Dead Sea.

BETH-LEB'ĀOTH (*house of lionesses*). Simeon (Josh. xix. 6; 1 Chr. iv. 31). BETHBIREI.

BETH'LĒHĒM (*house of bread*). Four and a half miles south of Jerusalem. One of the most ancient cities in Palestine. Called EPHRATH (*fruitful*) (Gen. xxxv. 16; xlviii 7). The residence of Boaz and Ruth, the birthplace of David, and the residence of Saul. Rehoboam fortified it (2 Chr. xi. 16). The INN OF CHIMHAM was a halting place for those who would "go to enter into Egypt" (Jer. xli. 17); which was probably the same inn in which Jesus was born (Matt. ii. 1, 5; Luke ii. 4, 5). Called also B. JUDAH and CITY OF DAVID. Justin Martyr (A. D. 150) speaks of our Lord's birth as having taken place "in a certain cave very close to the village" The village is not again mentioned after the birth of Jesus, in the Scripture. The Emperor Hadrian planted a grove of Adonis over the cave, which stood 180 years (A. D. 135-315). The Empress Helena, after clearing away this grove, built a church on the spot, which has been continued, with additions, making it "a half church and half fort," until the present day. The modern town is built on the low hill behind the convent (or church), facing the east. The hill is an offshoot of the main ridge, and ends in a little valley or narrow plain. The village is walled in, and is triangular. The plain east of the ridge is that on which tradition says the angels appeared to the shepherds, and it is called the Shepherds' Field (Arabic, *Beit Sahur*—house of Sahur). As the plains were always, anciently, cultivated, it is probable that the shepherds would have been found on the hill, where they now may be found, with their flocks.

A church containing the monuments of the three shepherds is mentioned by an early writer (Arculfus), as standing in the midst of the fields and terraced gardens. Jerome lived here, in a cell which is now pointed out, next to the great church, where he wrote most of his commentaries, and compiled the Latin Vulgate, the best ancient version of the Scriptures, A. D. 385–420. The present town has about 3,000 people, nearly all Christians, who are makers of crucifixes, beads, models of the holy places, and other articles for sale to pilgrims.—2. Zebulon, 7 ms. W. of Nazareth (Josh. xix. 15). Birthplace of Ibzan, the judge (Judg. xii. 8).

BETH'LEHEMITE. One from Bethlehem (1 Sam. xvi. 1, 18; 2 Sam. xxi. 19).

BETH-MĀ'ĀCHAH. See ABEL.

BETH-MÄR'CĀBOTH (*house of chariots*). HAZAR-SUZIM, MADMANNAH (Josh. xix. 5). Of Simeon in Judah, extreme S. A station on the way to Egypt, where Solomon's chariots were kept (1 K. ix. 19; 2 Chr. viii. 6). Post-station.

BETH-ME'ON. House of habitation (Jer. xlviii. 23).

BETH-MILLO (*wall-house*). Near Shechem (Judg. ix. 20, 46–49). Perhaps a part of the fortification of Shechem.—2. A fort or tower on Zion (2 K. xii. 20). MILLO (2 Sam. v. 9).

BETH-NIM'RAH (*house of pure water*). E. of Jordan, N. of Beth-aram, in the Jordan valley,

xi. 1; Luke xix. 29). Probably W. of Bethany (Matt. xxi. 19). The locality of the miracle of the withered fig-tree.

BETH-PHĒLET (Neh. xi. 26).

BETH-RĀ'PHA (*house of the giant*). Judah (1 Chr. iv. 12). Lost.

BETH-RĒ'HOB (*house of room*). Naph. Near Dan Laish (Judg. xviii. 28). A little kingdom of Aram (2 Sam. x. 6). Now called Hunin, and was one of the strongest forts in the North P., and commanded the plain of Huleh. Its beveled masonry marks its Phœnician origin (Rob. iii. 371).

BETHSĀ'IDA (*house of fish*). Two places on the Sea of Galilee. 1. B. of Galilee (John xii. 21). The city of Andrew, Peter and Philip (John i. 44). In the land of Gennesaret.—2. B. on the E. of Jordan, raised to importance by Philip the Tetrarch, and named Julias, after the daughter of the emperor (Jos. A. xviii. 2, § 1). The 5,000 were fed near this place (Luke ix. 10; John vi. 3–10; Mark vi. 39; Matt. xiv. 19). A blind man was healed here (Mark viii. 22–26). About two miles N. of the lake, and half a mile E. of the Jordan, is a long hill called Tell Julias, now covered with extensive ruins (Rob. ii. 413).

JULIAS.

BETHLEHEM.

opposite Jericho · a fenced city (Num. xxxii. 36; Josh. xiii. 27; Is. xv. 6; Jer. xlviii. 34). Eusebius mentions it as a large place. A group of ruins 2 m. E. of the Jordan are now called Nimrim or Wady Shoaib. Supposed to be the Bethabara of John i. 28; Matt. iii. 5; Mark i. 5.

BETH-O'RON. BETH-HORON (Judg. iv. 4).

BETH-PĀ'LET (*house of flight*). Judah (Josh. xv. 27; Neh. xi. 26). Near Moladah and Beersheba. Lost. PALTITE (2 Sam. xxiii. 26).

BETH-PĀZ'ZEZ. ISSA. (Josh. xix. 21). Lost.

BETH-PE'OR. E. of Jordan, opposite Jericho, 6 m. N. of Libias; a place dedicated to Baal (Josh. xiii. 20). It is supposed that Moses was buried in this ravine (Deut. iii. 29, iv. 46, xxxiv. 6). Beth is used for Baal.

BETH-PHĀ'GE (*house of figs*). On the Mt. of Olives near the Jericho road (Matt. xxi. 1; Mark

BETHSĀ'MOS. BETH-AZMAVETH.

BETH-SAN. BETH-SHEAN. (1 Macc. v. 52; xii. 40, 41).

BETH-SHAN. BETH-SHEAN (1 Sam. xxxi. 10, 12).

BETH-SHĒ'AN. BETHSHAN (*house of rest*). Town of Manasseh in Issachar (1 Chr. vii. 29; Josh. xvii. 11). In the Ghor, 18 ms. S. of the lake of Galilee, 4 ms. W. of the Jordan. Called Scythopolis, from the Scythians, B. C. 631 (2 Macc. xii. 29; Judith iii. 10; Col. iii. 11). The corpses of Saul and his sons were fastened on its walls by the Philistines (1 Sam. xxi. 10, 12). Three or four large brooks run near, and Ain Jalud, one of these, was the fountain which was near Jezreel, referred to in 1 Sam. xxix. 1. The ruins of Beisan now cover about 3 ms. in circuit, among which is a tower of Phœnician origin. The ruins are on several hills, high, steep, between whose black, rocky bases the four brooks run. The highest hill is nearly 200 feet high, and overlooks the Jordan for many miles N. and S. It must have been a city of temples (Rob. iii. 328; 1 Chr. i. 10). Josephus names it as the chief city of the Decapolis (Jos. Wars, iii. 9, 7).

BETH-SHĒ′MESH (*house of the sun*). Several places of this name. 1. Judah, near Kirjath Jearim (Josh. xv. 10; 1 Sam. v. 13). The ark was sent here by the Philistines from Ekron (1 Sam. vi. 9–12, 18). Now *Ain Shems.*—2. Issachar (Josh. xix. 22).—3. A fenced city of Naphtali (Josh. xix. 38).—4. An idolatrous temple in Egypt (Jer. xliii. 13). AVEN. ON.

BETH-SHITTAH (*house of the acacia*). In the N. of Palestine, to which the Midianites fled before Gideon (Judg. vii. 22). In the valley of the Jordan (Rob. ii. 356).

BETH-TĂP′PŪAH (*house of the citron*). Judah, near Hebron (Josh. xv. 53; 1 Chr. ii. 43). Now called Teffuh, and surrounded by olive groves, vines and fig-trees.

BETH′SUA. BETH-ZUR (1 Macc. iv. 29, 61; vi. 7, 26, 31, 49–59; ix. 52).

BETHŪ′EL (1 Chr. iv. 30). BETHUL. Simeon (Josh. xix. 4).

BETHŪLIA. S. of the Plain of Esdrælon, near Dothan, in which the chief events of the book of Judith occurred (Rob. ii. 313). The Frank Mountain was called Bethulia in the middle ages. Safed was also called by the name of the lost city.

BETH-ZACH-ARĪ′AS. BATHZACHARIAS.

BETH′ZUR (*house of rock*). Judah (Josh. xv. 58). Josephus says it was the strongest fortress in Judea. Built by Rehoboam, or fortified by him, and built by the people of Maon (1 Chr. ii. 42, 45). In the days of Jerome this was considered as the place of the baptism of the eunuch by Philip. Robinson finds it in Beit Sur, 4 ms. N. of Hebron, near the Jerusalem road.

BE′TOLI-US (Esd. v. 21). BETHEL 1.

BET-O-MES′-THAM and **BETOMASTHEM.** Lost.

BETROTHING. See MARRIAGE.

BETŌ′NIM (*pistachio nuts*). Gad (Josh. xiii. 26; Gen. xliii. 11).

BEŪ′LAH (*married*) (Is. lxii. 4). The name which the land of Israel is to bear when it is married.

JESUS CHRIST, KING OF KINGS.

BĒZEK (*lightning*). Two places.—1. ADONI-BEZEK (*lord of B*). Judah (Judg. i. 5).—2. Where Saul mustered his army (1 Sam. xi. 8). Supposed to have been in the Jordan valley, between Shechem and Bethshean (Jos. Ant. vi. 5, § 3). Lost.

BĒZER (*gold or silver ore*). A city of refuge in Reuben. In the wilderness (Deut. iv. 43; Josh. xx. 8). E. of Jericho (xxi. 36; 1 Chr. vi. 78). Bosor in Maccabees. East of the Dead Sea. Site lost. Supposed to have been near Um er Russas.

BĒZETH. Part of the Mt. of Olives (1 Macc. vii. 19; Jos. Ant. 10, § 2). Lost. (Judg. iv. 6, xv. 4). BEZETHA?

BE-ZAI. BESAI. Returned with Zerubbabel (Neh. vii. 23; x. 18).

BEZ′ALUL (*in the shadow of God*). Of Judah, son of Uri (1 Chr. ii. 20).

BI′ATAS (1 Esd. ix. 48). PELAIAH 2.

BIBLE. See History of the Books.

BICH′RI, (*first-born—youthful*). Ancestor of Sheba (2 Sam. xx. 1, etc.).

BID′KAR (*stabber*). Jehu's captain (2 K. ix. 25).

BIER. BURIAL 2.

BIG′THA (*garden—gardener*, or *given by fortune*). ABAGTHA, one of the seven princes of Ahasuerus' court (Esth. i. 10).

BIG′THAN and **BIG′THA-NA.** BIGTHA, fellow-conspirator with Teresh (Esth. ii. 21).

BIG′VAI or **BIG′VA-I**, (*husbandman*). 2056 children came home from captivity with Zerubbabel (Ezr. ii. 14).

EARTHEN LAMP. 3.

BIK′ATH. A′VEN (Amos. i. 5). AVEN I.

BIL′DAD (*son of contention*). The second of Job's three friends (Job. ii. 11, etc.).

BIL′EAM. BALAAM. Manasseh, near Megiddo (1 Chr. vi. 70).

BIL′GAH (*cheerfulness*). 1. A priest in David's time (1 Chr. xxiv. 14).—2. A priest who returned from Babylon with Zerubbabel (Neh. xii. 5, 18).—3. BILGAI.

BĬL′HAH. Simeon. BAALAH. BALAH. (1 Chr. iv. 29).

BIL′GAI or **BIL′GA-I.** BILGAH, a priest who sealed the covenant with Nehemiah (Neh. x. 8). BILGAH 2.

BIL′HAN (*modest*). 1. A Benjamite (1 Chr. iv. 29).—2. Son of Ezer (Gen. xxxvi. 27; 1 Chr. i. 42).

BIL′SHAN (*eloquent*). Companion of Zerubbabel (Ezr. ii. 2).

BIM′HAL (*circumcised*). Son of Japhet (1 Chr. vii. 33).

BIN′EA (*fountain—gushing forth*). Son of Moza. Descendant of Saul (1 Chr. viii. 37, ix. 43).

BIN′NU-I (*a building*). 1. Levite—father of Noadiah (Ezr. viii. 33).—2. Son of Pahath-Moab (Ezr. x. 30).—3. Son of Bani (Ezr. x. 38).—4. Bani (Neh. vii. 15).—5. Levite—son of Henadad (Neh. iii. 24, x. 9).

BIRTHDAY. Birthday feasts were common (Job i. 4), and martyrs and heroes were honored on that day. It was the king's day (Matt. xiv. 6). and kept holy, without work.

BIRTHRIGHT. The privilege of the firstborn son to a double share of the inheritance (Elisha asked for a double share of Elijah's spirit). Great respect was (and is) paid to him as the expected successor of his father as head of the family. He is supposed to have been a kind of priest of the family, but there is no allusion to this in Scripture. Reuben lost his birthright, which was given to Joseph, whose two sons enjoyed it, one share each. There was a sacredness in the title, as is seen in the "first-begotten," as applied to the Messiah, and to the Jewish people as the chosen of God.

BIR'ZAVITH (*olive source*). In the line of Asher (1 Chr. vii. 31); probably a place. Lost. MALCHIEL?

BISH'LAM (*son of peace*). Officer in Persia at the time of the return from captivity (Ezra iv. 7). Belemus in 1 Esd. ii. 16.

BISH'OP (*overseer*). An old title of the Romans adopted in the early church for its officers who were charged with its superintendance. Originally the same as *elder*. Both deacons and elders were preachers as well as overseers. In Paul's time the two titles had already become descriptive of different duties required of the different officers. The church elected them, and the apostles confirmed them by laying on their hands (sometimes also the hands of the presbytery—ELDERS), (2 Tim. i. 6; 1 Tim. iv. 14). They were to lead blameless lives, be the husband of one wife; have a spiritual care over the flocks (1 Peter v. 2); teach in private and public; visit the sick (James v. 14), receive and entertain strangers (1 Tim. i. 2). Bishops succeeded to the authority of the apostles.

BI-THI'AH (*worshiper—daughter of Jehovah*). Wife of Mered of Judah, and daughter of a Pharaoh (1 Chr. iv. 18).

BITH'RON (*the broken-up place*). A district in the Jordan valley, E. of the river (2 Sam. ii. 29). Not determined.

BITHYN'IA. Province in Asia Minor, on the Black Sea (Acts xvi. 7). Paul was not suffered to visit B., but the gospel was preached there (1 Peter i. 1). The country is mountainous and well watered.

BIT'TER. BITTER HERBS. A *bitter* day (Amos viii. 10). A *bitter* and hasty nation (Acts viii. 23). Simon at Samaria being in the gall of *bitterness*. The passover was eaten with *bitter herbs* (Ex. xii. 8).

BIT'TERN (Heb. *kippod*). The Hebrew word is translated both hedgehog and bittern. The Arabic name of hedgehog is *kunfod*. Is. xxxiv. 7, &c., corrected would read, "The pelican and hedgehog" instead of "cormorant and bittern." (See Wood's Bible Animals). Others refer to porcupine as offering all the required points (Imp. Bible Dict., p. 227).

BITU'MEN. SLIME.

BIZJÖTH'JAH (*contempt of Jehovah*). Judah, near Beersheba (Josh. xv. 28). *Deir el Belah*, on the coast 10 ms. from Gaza? *Bewaty*, 15 ms. S. of Gaza?

BIZ'THA. The second of the seven eunuchs of king Ahasuerus (Esth. i. 10).

BLACK. COLORS.

BLAINS (*to boil up*). Violent ulcerous inflammations, the sixth plague of Egypt (Ex. ix. 9, 10). In Deut. xxviii. 27, 35, called the botch of Egypt.

BLAS'PHEMY (*speaking evil of God*). This crime was punished with death (by stoning) by the Jews, and both Jesus and Stephen were condemned on a charge of breaking the law. The *Blasphemy against the Holy Ghost* (Matt. xii. 31) has never been determined, unless it was the saying that the miracles of Jesus were the work of Satan.

BLAST'ING A scorching of grain by the E. wind (Deut. xxviii. 22; Gen. xii. 6, ff.).

BLAS'TUS (*a bud, sprout*). The chamberlain of Herod Agrippa I. An officer of great influence with the people of Tyre and Sidon when they aimed at a reconciliation with the king (Acts xii. 20).

BLEM'ISH. All priests and animals for sacrifice were required to be without blemish or bodily defect (Lev. xxi. 17, 86). Jesus Christ is compared to "a lamb without blemish" (1 Pet. ii. 13).

BLESSING. Favors or benefits specially given by

God. Men bless God by thankfully acknowledging his goodness and excellence. The same acts and returns among men have the same name.

BLINDING. PUNISHMENTS.

BLIND'NESS. Is very common in the East from many causes (Matt. ix. 27, ff, xi. 5, xii. 22, xx. 30 ff). "Opening the eyes of the blind" is mentioned as a peculiar attribute of the Messiah (Is. xxix. 18). Blindness was wilfully inflicted as a punishment (Judg. xvi. 21). See cut on p. 28.

BLOOD. Among the Hebrews called the life (Lev. xvii. 11–14). In sacrifices the blood was caught and disposed of in a prescribed manner (Lev. iv.). Murder was held to curse the place where it was done (a superstition still strong in nearly every country (Gen iv. 10).

The Jewish people from the time of Noah were forbidden to eat blood (Gen. ix. 4), when at the same time animal food was permitted, because the blood was specially offered to God in sacrifice (Lev. xvii. 11). Since animal sacrifices have been

BITTERN.

abolished by the one great sacrifice of Jesus, blood is eaten by Christians. THE AVENGER OF BLOOD is the nearest relative (to the fifth degree) to any person who has been murdered, whose duty it is to avenge the death (Gen. ix. 5). A money payment is often accepted for a life in the East. The 6 Cities of Refuge were appointed as a refuge for any who accidentally killed another [not for murderers, for whom there was no refuge or pardon]. The "blood-revenge" has, more than any other custom or power, prevented the tribes of Arabia from exterminating each other.

BLOT. Blame, or blameworthiness (Job xxxi. 7; Prov. ix. 7).

BLUE. COLORS.

BOANER'GES (*sons of thunder—loud voiced?*). Names given to the two zealous sons of James and John (Mark. iii. 17).

BOAR. SWINE.
BOAT. SHIP.

BO'AZ (*agile*). Married Ruth as directed by the law (Deut. xxv. 5). He was a pure and high-minded man, fearing the Lord and keeping his obligations among men.

BOC'CAS (1 Esd. viii. 2). BUKKI.

BOCH'ERU (*youth or first-born*). Son of Azel (1 Chr. viii. 38).

BŌ'CHIM (*the weepers*). W. of Jordan, N. of Gilgal (Judg. ii. 1, 5).

BŌ'HAN. A stone set up on the border of Benjamin and Judah, between Betharabah and Bethhoglah on the E., and Adummim and Enshemesh on the W. (Josh. xv. 6; xviii. 17).

and Love are expressed by this word when we speak of *bosom* friends; it was well known to the ancients (Luke xvi. 20).

BŌ'SOR. E. of Jordan, in Gilead (1 Macc. v. 26, 36).

BŌSŌ'RA. Gilead. A strong city taken by Judas Maccabæus; probably the same as Bozrah (1 Macc. v. 26, 28).

BOSS. ARMS.

BOTCH. BLAINS. MEDICINE.

BOT'TLE. One Greek and four Hebrew words are

BOZRAH.

BOIL. MEDICINE.

BOLLED (*formed into seed-vessels*). The flax was *bolled* (Ex. ix. 31).

BOLSTER. BED.

BOND. Bondage. See SLAVE.

BON'NET. HEAD-DRESS.

BOOK. WRITING.

BOOTHS. Huts made of branches of trees or other very perishable materials.

BOTTLES.

BO'OZ. BOAZ (1 Matt. i. 5; Luke iii. 32).

BO'RITH (2 Esd. 1, 2). BUKKI.

BOR'ROW. LOAN.

BOS'CATH (*stony*). BOZKATH (2 K. xxii. 1).

BO'SOM. Abraham's bosom. DRESS. Intimacy

translated bottle (*chemeth, nebel, bakbuk, nod* and *askos.*) Bottles are of skins, or of earth or glass. Skins of goats and kids are used for the smaller, and of the ox for the larger. These skin bottles are mentioned by Homer, Herodotus and Virgil, and are now used in Spain and all over the Orient. Earthen and glass bottles were also used, and are often mentioned.

BOWELS. In the Bible meaning the seat of the feelings as we now use heart; also mercy and compassion (Gen. xliii. 30).

BOWING. ADORATION.

BOWL. CUPS.

BOX. ALABASTER; VIAL.

BOX-TREE. This elegant shrub, or small tree, is twice named by Isaiah for its beauty (Is. xli. 19, lx. 13; 2 Esd. xiv. 24). It is thought that the word ivory ought to be translated box-wood in Ezr. xxvii. 6. Box is still used for combs, and by the carver and the turner. It is the best material for blocks for the wood-engraver.

BŌZEZ (*shining.—Teeth of the cliff*). The rock on the N. of the pass by which Jonathan entered the Philistine camp (1 Sam xiv. 4, 5). In the Wady Suweinit, near Michmash.

BŌZKATH. Judah, in the Shefelah (Josh. xv. 39; 2 K. xxii. 1). The native place of King Josiah.

BŌZ'RAH (*enclosure; sheepfold*). Chief city in Edom (Gen. xxxvi. 33). The modern name is Buseireh—*little Busreh* (Rob., ii. 167). It is still a strong fort on a hill-top among the mts., about 25 ms. S. E. of the Dead Sea, half way to Petra (Is. xxxiv. 6, lxiii. 1; Jer. xlix. 13, 22; Amos i. 12; Micah ii. 12). It is the centre of a pastoral region.—

2. In the plain country—the land of Mishor—(Jer. xlviii. 24). E. of the Dead Sea and Lower Jordan are high table-lands, called Belka, where there are three ruins, named Um-el-Jemal (Beth-gamul), Kureiyeh (Kerioth), and Busrah (Bozrah), in the N. E. section, which is a rich district near the Hauran. The walls of Bozrah were 4 ms. in extent, and they did not include the suburbs. Temples, churches, mosques, and a beautiful theatre, are all in ruins; only a strong castle is left entire.

BRĂCELET. Armlet, wristlet. Ornament worn around the arm, above or below the elbow.

BRAMBLES. Thorns.

BRĂNCH. Limb of a tree—figuratively a person related to another, or to a family—as Jesus to the line of David (Is. iv. 2; xi. 1; Jer. xxiii. 5; xxxiii. 15; Zech. iii. 8, vi. 12)—Christians to Christ.

BRIDLE. Bridles were in the lips of captives, as seen in the Assyrian sculptures. The prisoners are all fettered and have in the under lip a ring to which is attached a cord held by the king (Is. xxxvii. 29; 2 K. xix. 28). See page 28.

BRI'ER. THORNS.

BRIG'AN-DINE. ARMS.

BROID'ERED. "Broidered Hair" (1 Tim. ii. 9).

BROTH or **SOUP** (Judg. vi. 19, 20; Is. lxv. 4). FOOD.

BRIM'STONE. Sulphur. Found on the shore of the Dead Sea.

BROOK. See RIVER.

BROTH'ER. 1. Kinsman, brother, nephew, cousin.—2. Of the same tribe.—3. Of the same people. —4. An ally in war.—5. Any friend (Job. vi. 15).

BRICK-MAKING IN EGYPT.

BRASS. The Hebrews did not mix copper and zinc, as we do, to make brass, but used the copper pure, or mixed tin with it, forming *bronze;* of which metal is nearly all of the antique coins not gold and silver.

BRA'VERY. In Is. iii. 18, beauty, splendor.

BRAY. To make a noise like an ass (Job vi. 5, etc.) or to break in pieces (Prov. xxviii. 22).

BRA'ZEN SEA. SEA, molten.

BRA'ZEN SERPENT. SERPENT. Brazen.

BREACHES (Judg. v. 17), a rent, notch. HOUSE, WAR.

BREAD (Hebrew *lehem,* or *lechem*). First mentioned in Gen. xviii. 6. Bread was a term for the whole meal; as meal (ground grain) is for all that is eaten at any time. The best was made of wheat, ground and sifted, leavened and baked. Poorer kinds were made of barley, rye, beans, and lentiles. The bread was kneaded with the hands or with the feet (as shown on the monuments), in a trough, and if unleavened baked thin and quickly, as now by the Bedawins. There were private and public ovens (Jer. xxxvii. 21; Neh. iii. 11). Hot, smooth stones are used for baking now. The objectionable passage in Ez. iv. 12 is explained when we know that dried dung of all kinds, in the East where there is no wood, is used for burning. Ephraim is a cake not turned (Hosea vii. 8). The baking-pan was used (Lev. ii. 5; 2 Sam. xiii. 9), and the frying-pan.

BREAST-PLATE. See ARMS.

BREECHES. Under-drawers (Ex. xxviii. 42).

BRETHREN. Brothers.

BRIBE. Bribery of magistrates was forbidden (Ex. xxiii. 8; Deut. xvi. 19), and when Samuel's sons took bribes, and perverted justice, the people asked for a king (1 Sam. viii.).

BRICK. Made of clay, clay and sand, mud with straw, burnt in kilns, or dried in the sun. They were sometimes colored or painted in patterns. Houses of sundried bricks had layers of reeds or straw at intervals. David made the prisoners work in brick-kilns (2 Sam. xii. 31). Bitumen, mud, and and a very hard cement, were used to join the bricks.

BRIDE and BRIDEGROOM. MARRIAGE.

BRIDGE. The only mention of a bridge is in 2 Macc. xii. 13. The Romans made the first bridges in Syria and Palestine.

—6. One in the same office (1 K. ix. 13).—7. Fellow man (Luke xix. 17).—8. One of a similar character (Job xxx. 29).—9. Disciples (Matt. xxv. 40).—10. Of the same faith (Amos i. 9; Acts ix. 30). A term meaning similarity, as "brother of dragons," in Job xxx. 29. See JAMES for brethren of the Lord.

BROWN. COLORS.

BRUIT. NEWS or RUMOR (Jer. x. 22).

BUBAS'TIS. PI-BESETH.

BUCK'LER. See ARMS and ARMOUR.

BUFFET. To smite, to maltreat (Matt. xxvi. 67).

BUILDING. ARCHITECTURE.

BŬK'KI (*mouth of God*). Fifth in the line of high priests after Aaron. Son of Abishua (1 Chr. vi. 5). Boccas in Esdras viii. 2.—2. One of Joshua's assistants in the allotment. Of the tribe of Dan (Num. xxxiv. 22).

BUK-KI'AH (*hasting from Jehovah*). A Levite. Son of Heman. Musician in the temple (1 Chr xxv. 4, 13).

BUL (*rain*). Eighth month. CLIMATE.

BULL. BULL'OCK. CATTLE.

BUL-RUSH. REED.

BUL'WORKS. FENCED CITY.

BOTTLES.

BU'NAH. Son of Jerahmeel, of Pharez and Judah (1 Chr. ii. 25).

BUN'NI (*built*). A Levite (Neh. ix. 4).—2. A chief (x. 15).—3. Ancestor of Shemaiah (xi. 15).

BUR'IAL. The custom was to bury in tombs or graves, and there were no exceptions, not even criminals (Deut. xxi. 23). The tombs cut in the rocks of Palestine and Egypt have been found to be depositories of much valuable information on the manners and customs of antiquity. Sepulchres for families were cut near the residence, in a garden, or by the road, long before they were expected to be needed. Only kings and prophets were buried in towns (1 K. ii. 10; 2 K. x. 35; 1 Sam. xxv. 1). Rachel's tomb was a monument erected on the spot where she died. It was a misfortune and a dishonor to fail of burial in the family tomb (1 K. xiii. 22); and an honor to a person or family to wish to be buried with them (Ruth i. 17); or to give one a place in a sepulchre (Gen. xxiii. 6; Luke xxiii. 50). It was the custom to wash them with lime ("white"), each year (Matt xxiii. 27). Spices were used to prepare the body for the grave (2 Chr. xvi. 14; John xix. 40), which were omitted as a mark of popular dishonor (2 Chr. xxi. 19). Burning was very rare, and only recorded of Saul and his sons. The next of kin presided over the whole offices, but there were public buriers (Ez. xxxix. 12; Acts v. vi. 10). The body was wrapped in its usual dress, and with bandages. Coffins were rarely used. A stone sarcophagus was used for a great person—king, etc. The dead were carried on a bier, by the relatives or hired persons, or by any who wished to honor the dead or the relatives. The desire was to be buried in the native place, as Jacob and Joseph wished to be carried to Canaan, because of a superstition that only those buried in the Promised Land would rise in the resurrection.

BU'ZI. Buzite, father of Ezekiel (Ez. i.).

BUZ'ITE. Descendant of Buzi (Job xxxii. 2, 6).

BY. Sometimes meaning *against* (1 Cor. iv. 4).

BYB'LUS. GEBAL. The Greeks changed the name of Gebal to Byblus, and the Septuagint uses that name in 1 K. v. 18, etc. In mythology this was the birth-place of Adonis, and contained the principal temple and sanctuary of that god. Byblus had a fleet of war vessels in the time of Alexander. For many centuries it was a place of importance, and in Christian times had a bishop.

C

CAB. WEIGHTS AND MEASURES.

CAB'BON. Judah, in the Shefelah (Josh. xv. 40).

CĀ'BUL (*little*). 1. Asher (Josh. xix. 27; Jos. vi. § 43, 45). Modern site, 8 ms. E. of Acre.—2. Region in Galilee given by king Solomon to Hiram, king of Tyre, which "pleased him not" (1 K. ix. 12, 13; Jos. Ant. viii. 5, § 3).

CAD'DIS. Eldest brother of Judas Maccabæus (Macc. ii. 2).

CÆSARĒ'A. On the shore of the Great Sea, N.

SITE OF CANA.

BURN'ING. BURIAL.

BURN'ING-AGUE (Lev. xxvi. 16). FEVER.

BURNT'-OFFERING. TEMPLE.

BUSH. MOSES.

BUSH'EL. MEASURES.

BUT'LER. Cup-bearer.

BUT'TER. The term usually means *curdled milk*, curds, milk, and cheese. Butter (churned cream) is made by shaking a skin of cream, or milk, and when formed, melting, and pouring into skin bottles, or earthern jars. It is more like oil than our butter.

BUY'ING. AGRICULTURE.

BUZ.—1. 2d son of Nahor and Milcah (Gen. xxii. 21). Elihu, the Buzite (Job xxxii. 2, 6), was of this family (of Aram) which settled in Arabia (Jer. xxv. 23).

W. of Jerusalem 70 ms., and 35 N. of Joppa, on the ancient road from Tyre to Egypt (Jos. Wars, i. 21, § 5). The political capital of Palestine, and a very important city in the time of the apostles (Acts viii. 40; ix. 30; x. 1. 24; xi. 11; xii. 19; xviii. 22; xxi. 8, 16; xxiii. 23, 33; xxv. 1, 4, 6, 13). In Strabo's time there was at this place Strato's Tower, and a landing-place; and Herod the Great, at immense cost, built an artificial breakwater and founded a city, B. C. 22. The sea-wall was built of very large blocks of stone, 50 feet long, and extended into water of 120 feet depth, enclosing several acres, on which a large fleet could safely ride (Jos. Ant. xv. 9). Named, in honor of Augustus, C. Sebaste (Jos. Ant. xvi. 5, § 1). Sometimes called C. Palestina, and C. Stratonis. Called Sebastos on coins. The residence of Philip, one of the 7 deacons of the early church, and the home of the historian Eusebius; the scene of some of Origen's labors and the birthplace of Procopius. Was noted in the time of the Crusades. Is now utterly desolate.

It was at Cæsarea that Origen (A. D. 185-201), a man of great natural ability, collated the text of the Septuagint, Hebrew and other Greek versions, making a page of six columns, each version in its proper column, thus forming what was called the *Hexapla—Six-ply* version of the Scriptures, which is the most important contribution to biblical literature in ancient times. Of some books he gave eight versions.

CÆSARÉ'A PHILIP'PI. PANEAS (*Pan*). At the S. W. foot of Mt. Hermon, on a broad terrace overlooking the Huleh plain; behind the mountain range rises in rugged bold peaks, wooded and capped with snow. Groves of evergreens, oaks and olives, hawthorns, myrtles, oleanders, and beautifully carpeted with grass. One of the chief sources of the Jordan is in a cave near the castle, and pours out an abundance of water, spreading fertility in its course. Named by Philip in honor of Tiberius Cæsar and himself. Agrippa II named it Neronias, after Nero. Titus exhibited gladiators there (Jos. Wars vii. 2, § 1). On the coins it is C. Paneas. Its most ancient name is now only known at the spot. The castle (Subeibeh) is of Phœnician work, and one of the largest in the land. Supposed to be Baal Gad (Josh. xi. 17). The charge to Peter was given here by Jesus (Matt. xvi. 18), and near it was probably the scene of the Transfiguration (xvii. 1, 2).

CAIA'PHAS (*rock, or dépression*). Joseph Caiaphas, high-priest of the Jews, under Tiberius at the crucifixion—appointed by Valerius Gratus, A. D. 25, holding it till removed by Marcellus, A. D. 37. His long term indicates unusual power and fitness. Son-in-law of Annas. He pronounced judgment that Jesus was guilty of blasphemy (Matt. xxvi. 57-66), and uttered a prophesy of Jesus without being conscious of it.

CAIN (*acquisition*). The first-born of the Adamic race. Son of Adam and Eve (Gen. iv. 1). Eve said, "I have got a man, by the help of Jehovah." It is supposed that he worked in the field, and that his brother Abel kept the flocks. After the murder of Abel (through envy and jealousy) he went into the land of Nod (*wandering land*); saw a sign from heaven, and was assured that no attempt would be permitted against his life; he married *Save*, and built the city of Enoch. Society was thoroughly organized in his time, and we find such names as Zillah (*shadow*), Naamah (*pleasant*), and Adah (*ornamental*); and Jabal living in tents; Jubal making musical instruments; Tubal Cain in the shop of the smith; Lamech composing poetry; while history and genealogy were carefully preserved.—2. CAIN. A place in Judah, in the mts., near Zanoah and Gibeah (Josh. xv. 57).

CAI'NAN (*possessor*). Son of Enos. Greatgrandson of Adam. Father of Mahalaleel. Died aged 910 (Gen. v. 9; Luke iii. 37).—2. Son of *Arphax'ad* and father of Sala. The name is supposed to have been *added* to the genealogy for some reason by the scribes or some compiler.

CA'LAH (*old age*). One of the most ancient cities of Assyria, built by Asshur (Gen. x. 11). HALAH (2 K. xvii. 6). Shalmaneser carried Israel captive to this city. The Nimrud ruin, which has yielded vast quantities of Assyrian remains, is believed to be the ancient Calah, once capital of the empire.

CAL'COL (*sustenance*). Son or descendant of Zerah (1 Chr. ii. 6).

CALD'RON. A pot or kettle (2 Chr. xxxv. 13).

CA'LEB (*dog*). The only one besides Joshua, of all those who left Egypt, who was permitted to enter Canaan. Son of Jephunneh, the Kenezite (Josh. xiv. 14), not a Hebrew, but so adopted, and the city of Hebron was given to him as his portion.—

2. Son of Hezron—Pharez—Judah—and father of Hur; his wives were Azubah, Jerioth and Ephrath, Ephah and Maachah.—3. Son of Hur.—4. CALEB EPHRATA. BETHLEHEM.

CALF. Image for worship made at Sinai in imitation of the Apis (Mnevis?) of Egypt, from the jewelry borrowed of the Egyptians (Ex. xxxii. 2). Not solid gold, but of wood, gilded or plated with gold (as the emblem of Osiris—Apis—was made). Moses burnt the image as an allegorical act (Job xv. 16; Hos. viii. 56; x. 6). Another was set up at Bethel, and one at Dan.

CAL'NE (*fort of Ann*), Calno, Calnah, Canneh, Assyria, on the E. bank of the Tigris, opposite Seleucia (Gen. x. 10), Ctesiphon, 200 ms. below Nineveh, 20 below Bagdad, 6 N. of Babel. *Tauk Kesra* is its present name, and the ruins are very interesting.

CALIS'THENES. Burnt by the Jews (2 Macc. viii. 33).

CAL'PHI Father of Judas (1 Macc. xi. 70).

CALVARY (*a bare skull*). GOLGOTHA. Place of the crucifixion of Jesus. Wm. C. Prime this year found a wall in Jerusalem which he thinks is the long-lost second wall of Josephus, running south of the so-called Church of the Holy Sepulchre, and so far proves the claim that the true site of calvary, and the sepulchre are known and in that church (Matt. xxvii. 33; Mark xv. 22; Luke xxiii. 33; John xix. 17).

FLESH HOOKS.

CAM'EL (Heb. *gamal*). Mentioned in Gen. xii. 16; Ex. ix. 3, as abundant (2 Chr. xiv. 15). Used as a means of traveling, especially across the desert (1 K. x. 2), both for riding and for burdens; and also used in war. The coarse hair (shed in the spring) was made into tent-cloth, and heavy cloaks for rough weather, and used in the desert or open country (Matt. iii. 4); and the fine hair into the delicate "camel's hair shawls." Its meat was forbidden as food or sacrifice, because it does not divide the hoof. Many trinkets and ornaments are hung on the neck and sides of favorite camels (Judg. viii. 21, 26). Its foot is provided with pads under the two toes which do not easily sink in the sand; its nostrils can be closed against the dust or fine sand, or hot wind; its sharp, long teeth are exactly adapted to cut off the prickly shrubs of the desert; its hump is almost pure fat, which can be absorbed on a long journey, where food is scanty; and its stomach has several extra water-bags, holding many days supply. The desert would be uninhabitable without the camel (and the palm-tree). Camel's milk is a luxury much esteemed in the East. The swiftness of the dromedary (*swift-camel*) is proverbial, 900 miles in 8 days having been done.

CA'MON (*full of grain*). GILEAD? (Ant. 5, 7, 6). Where Jair was buried (Judg. x. 5). Lost. CYAMON.

CAM'PHIRE. Camphor (Cant. i. 14; iv. 13). Hebrew *kopher*, Greek *kupros*, Arabic *alcana*.

Lawsonia inermis, a privet, with clusters of delicate little lilac blossoms, and exquisite in perfume. The ladies wear them in their bosoms as a boquet. The dried leaves are mixed with citron juice and used to stain the nails and palms with a yellowish brown (rust-color), very much liked (and is compelled by fashion), in the East. In Persia men also dye the nails. The hair is colored also, by adding indigo, black. Deut. xxi. 12, should read "adorn her nails" instead of "pare her nails."

CĀ′NA (*the nest*). Galilee (John ii. 1). 7 ms. N. of Nazareth. Scene of the first miracle of Christ, turning water into wine; and another, healing the son of a nobleman (iv. 46–54). The native place of Nathanael, Bartholomew. Now called Kana el Jelil, and in ruins, occupying a beautiful side-hill overlooking the plain of Buttauf. (Robinson ii. 346–9, iii. 108). Howard Crosby, D.D. (*Life of Jesus*), decides in favor of Kefr Kenna, 4 ms. N. E. of Nazareth. The text is equally explained by either place.

CĀ′NĀAN (*bowed down*). 4th son of Ham (Gen. x. 6), progenitor of the Phœnicians. The word is also translated "traffickers" (Is. xxiii. 8), "merchant" (11), "the land of traffic" (Ezr. xvii. 4), "merchant people" (Zeph. i. 11), and in scorn by Hosea (xii. 7), "he is a merchant; the balances of deceit are in his hand," speaking of degenerate Israel. Ham, the younger son of Noah, behaved with indecent levity towards his father, becoming a shame and reproach to him in his old age, and so Ham was punished in his youngest son, for indecent levity, shameless profligacy, and insufferable abominations, have poisoned the whole line, taking the shape and plea of religion, the most hateful being worshiped as the most holy. Mt. Lebanon is now the harbor of the most revolting types of idolatry, the relics of. antiquity.

CĀ′NĀAN (*lower country*). That is, lower than Gilead. The ancient name of the country between the Jordan and the Great Sea, extending from Hamath on the N. to the desert below Beersheba on the S. (Gen. xii. 5; xiii. 12; Zeph. ii. 5; Is. xix. 18; Judg. iii. 1; Ex. xv. 15). In Matt. xv. 22, the name is applied to Philistia and Phœnicia, the low lands.

CANDLESTICK.

CĀ′NĀANITE. Simeon the Zealot (Canaanite—from the Syriac *kannean*, of which the Greek is *zelotes*).

CĀ′NĀANITE. Dwellers in the land—lowland—as lower than Gilead. And again, dwellers in the lower lands of the plains by the sea; and in the Jordan valley (Num. xiii. 29; Gen. x. 18–20).—2. Any people in the land not Hebrew (Gen. xii. 6; Num. xxi. 3).

CAN′DĀCE (Greek, *kandake*). Title of the queens

of *Meroe*, whose capital was Napata. A prime minister from this court was converted by Philip, on his way back from Jerusalem to Ethiopia (Acts viii. 27). Queens of this country were sculptured on the ancient monuments, mentioned by Herodotus (Nitocris, ii. 100), Pliny (vi. 35), Strabo (xvii. 820), Dio Cassius (liv. 5), and Eusebius.

CAN′DLE. LAMP.

CANDLESTICK. LAMPSTAND. The only light of the tabernacle, and afterwards of the temple, was that of the 7 lamps on the golden stand; or *ten*, according to 1 K. vii. 49, and *one* in 1 Macc. i. 23; iv. 49; Wars vii. 5. The only ancient figure we have of this is the sculpture on the Arch of Titus at Rome.

CĀNE (*reed, grass*). A sweet-scented vernal grass, much valued for its perfume (Is. xliii. 24; calamus (*reed*) in Cant. iv. 14. There is no notice of the sugar-cane.

CĀNKERWORM. LOCUST.

QUEEN CANDACE.

CĀ′NON (*rule*). The authoritative standard of religion and morals, composed only of divinely inspired writings, which have been added from the time of Moses to that of John. In making the selection of the books, the four conditions were kept in view: 1. Divine authority; 2. Entire and incorrupt work as made by the writer; 3. The whole complete as a rule, and guide; and 4. Therefore needing no further addition. The Holy Bible is then the only and supreme standard of religious truth and duty. The evidences are: The decision of the Church in council; the concurrent testimony of ancient Jewish and Christian writers; and the internal evidence of the books themselves. Inquiring, we wish to know—1. Were the books written by their reputed authors? 2. Were the writers believed to be divinely inspired by their cotemporaries? and 3. Have the books been kept as they were written, unchanged? In Exodus and the earlier books of the Old Testament, the term used for the Sacred Writings is *The Law*, or the Book of the Covenant (Ex. xxiv. 7). After the return from the captivity (about 400 B. C.) they are called recitations, or the words read or recited (Neh. viii. 8). They were also called *The Books* in Ecclesiasticus. Josephus, Philo, and the writers of the New Testament call them *Sacred Writings, Sacred Letters*, and *Scriptures* (Matt. xxi. 42, xxii. 29; John v. 39; Acts viii. 32, 35; Rom. xvi. 26; 2 Pet. i. 20), and Paul, twice, Holy Scriptures (Rom. i. 2; 2 Tim. iii. 15). After the New Testament was written, Jerome (A. D. 400) called them the Sacred Books (following 2 Macc. ii. 13), the name *Bible* being first applied by Chrysostom A. D. 400, adding the title *Divine*, or, as we now write it, *Holy Bible*. The word *Bible* is Greek, and means *book*. The sacred book of Mohammed is called *Korawn—the book* (i. e., the thing to be read). The word *Scriptures* is Latin, and means writings. The Bible is divided into the Old and New Testaments (2 Cor. iii. 14), and according to the *Canon* (*Kanon*, Gr., *rule*, meaning *The Catalogue of the Sacred Books*), consisting of 39 books in the Old and 27 in the New Testament. The Roman church adds 10 other books (or parts). The Old Testament collection was completed by Ezra, having been begun by the ancient patriarchs, continued by Moses (Deut. xxxi. 9), by Joshua (xxiv. 26), by Samuel (1 Sam. x. 25), by David, Solomon, and others; and his arrangement has been preserved up to the present time. It was divided into three classes of writings: the *Law* (*Thorah*), the *Prophets* (*Nebiim*), and the *Psalms* (*Chethubim*), (Luke xxiv. 4). Josephus names the same divisions (c. Apion i. 8). The first canon on record is that of Laodicea in Phrygia,

A. D. 365, which•fixed the names and order and number of the books very much as we find them now. The Council of Hippo in 393, of Carthage in 419, in which Augustine (Bishop of Hippo), had great influence, held (A. D. 397) that the entire canon of Scripture is comprised in these books— Genesis, Exodus, Leviticus, Numbers, Deuteronomy, Joshua, Judges, 1 small book of Ruth, * * the 4 books of the Kingdoms, and 2 of the Remains. These are the historical books: Job, Tobit, Esther, Judith, 2 books of Maccabees, and 2 books of Ezra. Next are the prophets; 1 book of the Psalms of David, 3 of Solomon—viz., Proverbs, Canticles, and Ecclesiastes. The 2 books Wisdom and Ecclesiasticus are called Solomon's only because they resemble his writings, and they were written by Jesus, the son of Sirach, which are to be reckoned among the prophetical books. The rest are the prophets, 12 of them being reckoned together as one book; and after these the four prophets of large volumes— Isaiah, Jeremiah, Daniel and Ezekiel. The New Testament was the same as now received.

BOOKS OF THE OLD TESTAMENT, WRITTEN IN HEBREW.

NAME.	CHAP.	WRITTEN BY	B. C.	YEARS.	REMARKS.
1. Genesis, - - - -	50	Unknown, - - - - -		2278	⎫
2. Exodus, - - - - -	40	Moses, - - - - - -	1491	145	⎪ These five are called
3. Leviticus, - - - -	27	Moses, - - - - - -	to		⎬ Pentateuch, Greek for
4. Numbers, - - - -	36	Moses, - - - - - -		38	⎪ *five* books.
5. Deuteronomy, - - -	34	Moses, - - - - - -	1450		⎭
6. Joshua, - - - - -	24	Joshua, - - - - -	1433	17	
7. Judges, - - - - -	21	Several, - - - - -	721–562	299 (430)	
8. Ruth, - - - - - -	4	Unknown, - - - - -			Written long after the
9. 1 Samuel, - - - -	31	⎫		72	events narrated.
10. 2 Samuel, - - - -	24	⎪		40	
11. 1 Kings, - - - -	22	⎬ Compiled by Jeremiah,	550	(427	
12. 2 Kings, - - - -	25	⎭		⸆26)	
13. 1 Chronicles, - - -	29	⎱ Compiled by Daniel	580	2969	
14. 2 Chronicles, - - -	36	⎰ and Ezra.	450	500	
15. Ezra, - - - - - -	10	⎱ Daniel, Nehemiah, ⎰ Haggai, Ezra.	450	79	
16. Nehemiah, - - - -	13	Nehemiah, - - - - -	440	36	
17. Esther, - - - - -	10	Unknown, - - - - -	425?		
18. Job, - - - - - -	42	Unknown, - - - - -			
19. Psalms, - - - - -	150	⎱ Compiled by Ezra or ⎰ by Simon.	450 300		Written by David 73; Asaph 12; Korah 11;
20. Proverbs, - - - -	31	Compiled by Solomon, -	1000		Heman 1 (78th); Ethan
21. Ecclesiastes, - - -	12	Unknown, - - - - -	400?		(89th); Solomon (72d,
22. Song of Songs, - - -	8	Unknown, - - - - -	900?		127th); Moses (90th);
23. Isaiah, - - - - -	66	Isaiah, - - - - -	700		and others.
24. Jeremiah, - - - -	52	Jeremiah, - - - - -	550		Dr. Stanley urges that
25. Lamentations, - - -	5	Jeremiah, - - - - -	550		there were two prophets
26. Ezekiel, - - - - -	48	Ezekiel, - - - - -	525		named Isaiah and two
27. Daniel, - - - - -	12	Daniel, - - - - -	525		Zechariah.
28. Hosea, - - - - -	14	Hosea, - - - - -	750		The age of prophesy
29. Joel, - - - - - -	3	Joel, - - - - -	700		is chiefly included be-
30. Amos, - - - - -	9	Amos, - - - - -	780		tween 800 and 400, B. C.
31. Obadiah, - - - -	1	Obadiah, - - - - -	?		Several prophets, as
32. Jonah, - - - - -	4	Jonah, - - - - -	800		Shemaiah, Ahijah, Eli-
33. Micah, - - - - -	7	Micah, - - - - -	725		jah and Elisha, left no
34. Nahum, - - - - -	3	Nahum, - - - - -	725		writings.
35. Habakkuk, - - - -	3	Habakkuk, - - - - -	550		
36. Zephaniah, - - - -	3	Zephaniah, - - - - -	600		
37. Haggai, - - - - -	2	Haggai, - - - - -	500		
38. Zechariah, - - - -	14	Zechariah, - - - - -	500		
39. Malachi, - - - -	4	Malachi, - - - - -	420		

BOOKS OF THE APOCRYPHA, OF THE OLD TESTAMENT AGE, IN THE ORDER GIVEN IN THE AUTHORIZED VERSION.

1. 1 and 2 Esdras; 2. Tobit; 3. Judith; 4. Esther; 5. Wisdom of Solomon; 6. Wisdom of Jesus, son of Sirach—Ecclesiasticus; 7. Baruch; 8. Song of the Three Holy Children; 9. History of Susanna; 10. Bel and the Dragon; 11. Prayer of Manasseh; 12. 1 and 2 Maccabees. The Book of Enoch is accepted by the Abyssinians. There have been also included in the Apocrypha—3 and 4 Esdras, the Book of Elias the Prophet; 3, 4 and 5 Maccabees (now received by the Greek Church); the Ascension of Isaiah; the Assumption of Moses, and others.

BOOKS OF THE NEW TESTAMENT, WRITTEN IN GREEK.

NAME.	CHAP.	WRITTEN BY	A. D.	REMARKS.
1. Matthew, - - - -	28	Matthew, - - - -	50–60	Palestine, Aramaic and Greek.
2. Mark, - - - - -	16	Mark, - - - - -	63–70	At Rome, directed by Peter.
3. Luke, - - - - -	24	Luke, - - - - -	58–60	Cæsarea, when Paul was there.
4. John, - - - - -	21	John, - - - - -	78	Ephesus.
5. Acts, - - - - -	28	Luke, - - - - -	63	
6. Romans, - - - -	16	Paul, - - - - -	58	Corinth.
7. 1 Corinthians, - - -	16	" - - - - -	57	Ephesus.
8. 2 Corinthians, - -	13	" - - - - -	58	Philippi.
9. Galatians, - - -	6	" - - - - -	54	Ephesus.
10. Ephesians, - - -	6	" - - - - -	62	Rome.
11. Philippians, - - -	4	" - - - - -	62	Rome.
12. Colossians, - - -	4	" - - - - -	62	Rome.
13. 1 Thessalonians, - -	5	" - - - - -	53	Corinth.
14. 2 Thessalonians, - -	3	" - - - - -	53	Corinth.
15. 1 Timothy, - - -	6	" - - - - -	67	Macedonia.
16. 2 Timothy, - - -	4	" - - - - -	68	Rome.
17. Titus, - - - - -	3	" - - - - -	67	Ephesus.
18. Philemon, - - -	1	" - - - - -	62	Rome.
19. Hebrews, - - - -	13	" - - - - -	58	Corinth, in Hebrew and Greek.
20. James, - - - - -	5	James, - - - - -	45–62	Brother of the Lord.
21. 1 Peter, - - - -	5	Peter, - - - - -	60–67	Babylon.
22. 2 Peter, - - - -	3	" - - - - -		
23. 1 John, - - - -	5	John, - - - - -	78	Ephesus.
24. 2 John, - - - -	1	" - - - - -	78	} Addressed to individuals.
25. 3 John, - - - -	1	" - - - - -	78	
26. Jude, - - - - -	1	Judas, - - - - -	60–67	Brother of James (Luke vi. 16.)
27. Revelation, - - -	22	John, - - - - -	80–99	In Patmos.

APOCRYPAL BOOKS OF THE NEW TESTA-MENT AGE.

EUSEBIUS, in his list of the sacred books, makes a distinction against certain ones which were doubtful or heretical, and which were: 1. The doubtful—Acts of St. Paul, Shepherd of Hermas, Apocalypse of Peter, Epistle of Barnabas, Doctrine of the Apostles, Gospel to the Hebrews. 2. The heretical—Gospels of Peter, Thomas, Matthias, and others; the acts of Andrew, John, Epistle of Clement, and others. The oldest version in any language of which there is a record, is the *Septuagint*, written in Greek, at Alexandria, Egypt, B. C. 286–280. The oldest known copy of this version is written on thin vellum, contains the whole Bible, and is dated in the 5th century: now in the British Museum, and is called the *Codex Alexandrinus*.

$\frac{Γ}{5}$ ΚΕΤΙΕΠΤΛΗΘΥΝΘΗϹΛΝΟΙΘΛΙΒΟΝ
ΤΕϹΜΕ
ΠΟΛΛΟΙΕΠΛΝΕϹΤΗϹΛΝΕΠΕΜΕ.

Codex Alexandrinus. 5th century. (Ps. iii. 2).

The *Codex Vaticanus* is a manuscript in the Vatican Library, Rome; contains the whole Bible, except a few lost leaves, and belongs to the 4th century.

'ΜΙϹΘΟϹΟΥΛΟΓΙΖΕΤΑΙ' *Codex Vaticanus. 4th C.*
'ΚΑΤΑΧΑΡΙΝΑΛΛΑΚΑΤΑ' *(Rom. iv. 4).*

The *Codex Sinaiticus* was found in the Convent on Mount Sinai. It belongs to the 6th century, but

ΚΛΙΟΜΟΛΟΓΟΥΜΕ *C. Sinaiticus. 6th C.*
ΝΩϹΜΕΓΛΕϹΤΙΝ *(1 Tim. iii. 16).*

is a copy of one of an earlier date. Besides the O. and N. T., it has the Gospel and Epistles of Barnabas and the Epistle of Hermas.

Fragments of the Gospel are contained in a palimpsest MS. in a library at Wolfenbuttel, **Ger**

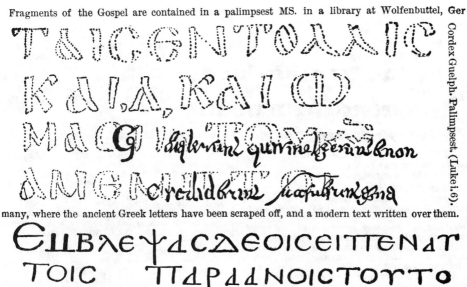

Codex Guelph. Palimpsest. (Luke i. 6).

many, where the ancient Greek letters have been scraped off, and a modern text written over them.

This specimen is from a copy in the library of Trinity College, Dublin, a palimpsest, and belongs to the 6th century. It is dated A. D. 200 (about), and shows a very neat and clear text, as well as all the others. The oldest Hebrew MS. known is dated A. D. 489; is a roll, and was found in the Karaite Synagogue in the Crimea. The specimen given here is from a Pentateuch written on a roll of leather, preserved in Odessa, originally brought from Derbend, in Daghestan. It was "corrected" in 580, and therefore probably written some time before.

From a copy of the Book of Genesis, in Greek, written for Origen, A.D. 185–255.

Ancient Hebrew MS. A.D. 580. (Mal. iv. 6).

As a specimen of the ancient Hebrew letter used about the time that Paul was a pupil of Gamaliel, here is a copy from a gravestone in the Crimea, of the year A. D. 6. This style of letter is like that on the coins of the Maccabees, B. C. 139, and other coins down to A. D. 130, given in the chapter on *Coins*. We have records of Origen's work, in which he placed side-by-side six different versions of each book of the Bible, thus forming the most valuable contribution to the critical study of the Scriptures known to scholars; but no specimen of his MS. is extant. The oldest known MSS. in our own, or the Anglo-Saxon language, is the Durham Bible, dated A. D. 688. The oldest *printed* Hebrew Bible (Old Testament) was issued at Soncino, Italy, A. D. 1487, in folio. The Complutensian Polyglott was published at the expense of Cardinal Ximenes in 1514–1522, in 6 vols. folio, and sold at 6½ ducats. The Hebrew Vulgate, and Greek texts of the O. T. (with a Latin translation of the Greek), were printed in three parallel columns; the Targum of Onkelos, with a Latin translation in two columns below. The oldest known version in the Latin language is the *Vulgate* (current text), which was the work of Jerome, A. D. 385–420, while he lived at Bethlehem. Tertullian (160–245) mentionsa Latin version, but there is nothing known of any belonging to his age. The first book

(*On a gravestone at Simpheropol, Crimea.*) "This is the grave Buki, son of Isaac, the priest; may his rest be in Paradise! [Died] at the time of the deliverance of Israel, in the year 702 of our captivity," (*i. e. A. D. 6*).

printed was the Bible, in Latin; and the splendid pages of the Mazarin Vulgate, printed by Gutenburg and Fust in 1455, at Mainz, are not surpassed at this day as specimens of typography.

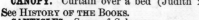

A.D. 688

Anglo Saxon. "Durham Bible.

CANOPY. Curtain over a bed (Judith x. 21). See HISTORY OF THE BOOKS.

CANTICLES. Song of Solomon.

CÃ-PER'NA-UM (*village of Nahum*). On the N. W. shore of the Lake of Galilee. The scene of many of the works of Christ. Not mentioned in the O. T. or the Apocrypha. Site now located at Tell Hum, where there are ruins of a magnificent synagogue, with beautiful specimens of columns, some of which are double; cornices and massive walls; and a great extent of ruins, half a mile long by a quarter wide. The home of Jesus after leaving Nazareth on being rejected (Mark ii. 1). Here Matthew was chosen (ix. 10). Simon, Peter and Andrew belonged here (i. 29). (For the miracles wrought here, see LIFE OF CHRIST). The son of the nobleman was healed here by words spoken at Cana. The woes denounced against this city and others near it have been so literally fulfilled that even their sites cannot be determined (*Stanly*, S. & P., ch. x.; *Rob.* ii. 403–4, iii. 344–358). Mentioned by Josephus (Wars, iii. 10 § 8). *Wilson*, Lands of the Bible (ii. 139, 149). The Palestine Exploration has this last year added new facts to the evidence in favor of Tell Hum being the true site. (The Recovery of Jerusalem, p. 265, &c.)

ASSYRIAN KITCHEN.

CÃ'PHAR. A village (1 Chr. xxvii. 25).

CÃ'PHAR-SAL-AMA. A place where a battle was fought between Judas and Nicanor (1 Macc. vii. 31).

CÃPHEN'ATHA. A place on the E. of Jerusalem (1 Macc. xii. 37).

CÃPH'TOR. CRETE. CAPHTORIM. Mentioned three times as the origin of the Philistines (Deut. ii. 23; Jer. xlvii. 4; Amos ix. 7). By some supposed to be an ancient name of a part of Egypt. KEBT-HOR in hieroglyphics.

CAPPADO'CIA. Asia Minor (Acts ii. 9; 1 Peter i. 1; Jos. Ant. xii. 3, § 4). The road from Palestine passed through the famous Cilician Gates, which led through Mt. Taurus. It is an elevated table-land divided by chains of mountains, well watered but scantily wooded. Mazaca, afterward called Cæsarea, was the Roman capital, and at the base of Mt. Argæus, the highest in Asia Minor. The people were mixed, Scythian and Persian.

CAP'TAIN. Some times a civil and at others a military chief is meant. The Lord is called the captain of his people's salvation (Heb. ii. 10).

CAPTIVITY. The Hebrews reckon four captivities: Babylonian, Median, Grecian and Roman. The expatriation of the people belongs to two periods only—the first and second captivity. In the first—the Babylonish—the best of the nation were carried to Assyria. They were not slaves, but were free under their own civil laws (they would not obey the divine law of ceremonies away from the temple, and it is thought that the custom of building synagogues in every city arose during the captivity), and were ruled by their own elders (Ez. xiv. 1; xx. 1), and held slaves themselves (Tobit viii. 18); while some filled high offices at the court, as Mordecai and Daniel. This event occupied, from beginning to end, 150 years, ending B. C. 588. Judah was carried away captive by Nebuchadnezzar about a hundred years after the first deportation of Israel (Jer. lii). The decree of Cyrus granting the return of the Jews, was dated B. C. 536. A part of the people, under Zerubbabel, returned B. C. 535; and more under Ezra B. C. 458; and of others, under Nehemiah, B. C. 445. The return thus extending over a period of 145 years. (See Nehemiah, Ezra, Haggai and Zechariah). The number of those who remained in Assyria was about six times those who returned to Jerusalem, and they were known in the time of Christ as the DISPERSED (John vii. 35; James i. 1). Besides those who remained in Assyria, there were many Jews who fled into Egypt (Zech. x. 6–10), and into Arabia, settling in Yemen (Sheba). After this time the TEN TRIBES were lost to history. It is supposed that they intermarried with each other and with the people among whom they lived, and so became lost as distinct tribes, or even as a people. During and after the captivity the Jews laid aside their prejudices, forgot their peculiar tribal pride, and became one nation (Is. xi. 13; Ez. xxxvii. 22); and since that time no one of them is able to trace his lineage to any particular tribe, but may reasonably claim to have the blood of the whole twelve mingled in his veins. So Paul seems to have felt (Acts xxvi. 7) when pleading before Agrippa.

CARBUNCLE (Is. liv. 12). PRECIOUS STONES.

CARCAS. One of the seven princes of Ahasuerus (Esth. i. 10).

CARCHE'MISH (*fort of Chemosh*). Assyria (Is. x. 9). By Euphrates (Jer. xlvi. 2; 2 Chr. xxv. 20). Assyrian inscriptions discovered in modern times show it to have been a chief city of the Hittites, from B. C. 1100 to B. C. 850, who were masters of Syria. Taken by Pharaoh Necho, B. C. 608, and 3 yrs. after by Nebuchadnezzar.

CÃ'RIA. S. W. in Asia Minor.

CARMA'NIANS. People of Carmania, north of the Persian Gulf (2 Esd. xv. 30).

CARE'AH. Father of Johanan (2 K. xxv. 23).

CÃR'MEL (*park—fruitful field*). A mountain range branching off to the north-west from the mountains of Samaria, 15 miles long, 2 to 4 wide, and 600 to 1800 feet high, ending in a steep cape far out into the Great Sea, dividing the plain of

Acre from Sharon (Josh. xii. 22, xix. 26; Jer. xlvi. 18). The plain of Esdraelon lies east, and the river Kishon washes its north side. No part of Palestine equals it in picturesque beauty and variety of scenery, the luxuriance of its herbage, and the brilliance and variety and abundance of its flowers (Is. xxxv. 2; Cant. vii. 5). There are many deep ravines, which abound in partridges, quails, woodcock, hares, jackals, wolves, hyenas, and wild-boars; and it is said, anciently also lions and bears. There are many caves in the vicinity of the convent, which were once occupied by hermits; and one of these is said to be the one referred to in 1 K. xviii. 4; and also see Amos ix. 3. The chief incident in its history is Elijah's sacrifice, the site of which is now located at el Mukrakah (*the burning—the sacrifice*), on a rock terrace, Tell el Kusis (*hill of the priests*), at the east end; from which was seen the whole of the plain of Esdraelon, the river Kishon, Gilboah with Jezreel at its base, Jezebel's temple and Ahab's palace in full view, the sea being hid by the hill to the west, up which the servant could climb in a few minutes and see the sea in its entire expanse (1 K. xviii. 30; 2 K. iv. 23). Pythagoras visited it, and Vespasian, the emperor, came to consult the oracle of Carmel. Elijah was sitting on the mountain when the "fifties" were sent by Ahaziah to take him prisoner for stopping his messengers to Baal at Ekron, and two bands were consumed by fire from heaven (2 K. i. 9–15). After the ascent of Elijah, Elisha went to reside on Carmel for a time (2 K. ii. 25), and was here when the woman from Shunem found him, and told him of her son's death (iv. 25). Called now Jebel Mar Elias. The convent was built A. D. 1830, over ancient ruins, and is famous for having been founded by St. Louis of France, and its name given to the Barefoot Carmelite Friars.—2. Judah, 6 miles southeast of Hebron. City of Nabal (1 Sam. xxv. 2), and of Abigail, David's favorite wife (xxv. 3), where Saul set up a "place" after his victory over Amalek (xxv. 12), and Uzziah had vineyards (2 Chr. xxvi. 10). It is mentioned by Jerome and Eusebius as having a Roman garrison; and in the history of the Crusades, A. D. 1172. The heaps of ruins now called Kurmul, lie around the sloping sides of an oval valley, the head of which is shut in by rocky ridges. The castle (*Kasr el Birkeh*) had walls 10 feet thick of beveled stones, 60 feet long, 40 wide, and 30 high. Near it was a round tower, and there are the remains of several churches, one of which was 150 by 50 feet. There is a fine reservoir of sweet water supplied from springs near (*Van de Velde*).

CAR'MELITE. Of Carmel in the mountains of Judah (1 Chr. xi. 37).

CARMELITESS. Woman of Carmel in Judah (1 Sam. xxvii. 3).

CARMI. (*a vine-dresser*).—1. Father of Achan (Josh. xii. 1, 18).—2. 4th son of Reuben (Gen. xlvi. 9).

LOCUST.

CAR'MITES. Of Reuben (Num. xxvi. 6).

CARNAIM. In the land of Galaad, Gilead. Ashteroth Karnaim.

CARPENTER. Since wood was always too scarce and precious in Palestine for any use besides for doors, windows, etc., and for decorations, the carpenter was probably a carver of such finishing as is now seen in the best rooms of the East.

CAR'PUS. A disciple at Troas with whom Paul left his cloak (2 Tim. iv. 13), books and parchments. He is mentioned as bishop of Berytus in Thrace by Hippolytus.

CARRIAGE. This word means baggage in the A. V.

CAR'SHENA. One of the seven princes (Esth. i. 14).

CART.

CART. Wagon. Were open or covered (Num. vii. 3), and used to carry persons and burdens (Gen. xlv. 19; 1 Sam. vi. 7), or produce (Amos ii. 13). There were no roads, and the only ones now in use have been lately made, from Joppa to Jerusalem, and from Beirut to Damascus.

CAR'VING. Carving and engraving have always been much used for the decoration of houses, furniture, arms, jewelry, etc. The occupation of Joseph was that of a carver and not a carpenter, as wood has always been too scarce and expensive to use in the framework of houses.

CASIPH'IA. Place between Babylon and Jerusalem (Ezr. viii. 17).

CAS'LEU (1 Macc. i. 54).

CAS'LU'HIM. Mizraite people (Gen. x. 14). In Upper Egypt. Bochart thinks they were the Colchians of the Greeks.

CAS'PHON (1 Macc. v. 36).

CAS'PHOR. Fortified city in the land of Galaad (1 Macc. v. 26). The Jews took refuge there from the Ammonites.

CAS'PIS. A strong, fortified city. Was taken by Judas Maccabaeus (2 Macc. xii. 13, 16).

CAS'SIA. One of the principal spices in the composition of the "oil of holy ointment" (Ezr. xxx. 24); a choice perfume. Also, an article among the precious merchandise of Tyre (Ezr. xxxvii. 19).

CAS'TOR and **POL'LUX** (*sons of Jupiter*), (Acts xxviii. 11). Name of the vessel in which Paul sailed from Malta to Rome; derived from the name of the two stars called "the twins," the fabled sons of Jupiter and Leda.

CATS (Bar. vi. 22). The cat was a favorite of the Egyptians, and is found embalmed among their mummies.

CAT'-ER-PIL-LAR. See LOCUST.

CATHUA. GIDDEL (1 Esd. v. 30).

CAUL. A head-dress, made in checker-work; long, like a scarf; worn by women for ornament.

CAUSE'-WAY. Raised path (1 Chr. xxvi. 16, 18).

CAVE. Mentioned in the early history as often useful to men. There are a great number in the limestone region of Palestine and Syria, many of which have been cut out larger for shelter or defence. Several Hebrew words are used to denote caves, holes and fissures, and many places were named from noted caves, and some people, as the Horites (caveites), were so named from their dwellings. The great cave near Aleppo will hold 3000 horse-soldiers. Maundrell described a large system of caves, containing 200 rooms, near Sidon. Lot is the first who is recorded as living in a cave. The cave of Machpelah is the first mentioned as a burial-place. Other noted caves were Makkedah (five kings taken in by Joshua); Adullam (where David cut Saul's skirt off); and in Josephus, the famous robber-caves of Arbela, near Gennesaret.

CEDAR (Heb. EREZ; Ar. ARZ, *the larch*). There are eleven groves of cedars on the Lebanon mountains, which have been visited by travelers recently. One, near the highest peak, 6000 feet above the sea, N. E. of Beirut, and long famous for its 400 ancient trees of immense size, standing near the summits, which are covered with perpetual snow; the second, near Deir El Kamr. The six largest of this northern group measured, in 1868, 48, 40, 38, 33½, 30, 29¾ feet; and a third, near Ain Zehalteh, on the Beirut-Damascus stage road, lately found. Dr. Robert Morris recently brought several camel loads of cones from these trees for distribution among Sunday-School scholars. The references to cedar-wood in the Scripture do not always mean the cedar of Lebanon—as, for instance, when at Sinai (Lev. xii. 6). The word EREZ means also pine, cyprus, fir and juniper. Rev. Henry H. Jessup, an American missionary in Syria, thinks the whole range of Lebanon, from 3000 to 7000 feet altitude, was at one time covered with cedar groves.

CE'DRON. Near Jamnia and Azotus; fortified by Antiochus Sidetes.—2. Kidron, the torrent E. of Jerusalem, which see.

CEI'LAN (1 Esd. v. 15). AZETAS.

CEILING. The ceilings of the principal apartments in Eastern houses are the parts on which the chief care is expended in adorning. The Jews bestowed much care on these parts in their houses (Jer. xxii. 14; Hag. i. 4).

CEN'CHREÆ. Harbor of Corinth, on the Saronic Gulf, east, whence Paul sailed for Ephesus (Acts xviii. 18). There was a church here, of which PHŒBE was a member (Rom. xvi. 1), and Lucius its first bishop, appointed by Paul. There was a temple at the end of each mole, and a statue of Neptune on a rock between, as may be seen on an ancient coin of Corinth.

CENDEBE'US, correctly CENDEBÆ'US. One of Antiochus' generals in Palestine (1 Macc. xv. 38, ff).

HIPPOPOTAMUS.

CENSER. A small portable vessel of metal, fitted to contain burning coals (2 Chr. xxvi. 18; Luke i. 9).

CENTU'RION. Captain of 100. CENTURY. A Roman military officer. Cornelius, a centurion, was one of the first disciples. Several others are mentioned.

CE'RAS (1 Esd. v. 29). KEROS.

CE'TAB (1 Esd. v. 30).

CHA'BRIS. Son of Gothoniel (Judith vi. 15; viii. 10; x. 6).

CHA'DIAS (1 Esd. v. 20). AMMIDOI.

CHAFF (Is. v. 24; xxxiii. 11). The carrying away of chaff by the wind in Scripture is used as a symbol of the destruction of the wicked (Is. xvii. 13).

CHAIN. Chains were in use by the ancients; they were made of precious metal for ornaments, and were worn alike by men and women—of iron for other purposes. The gold chain given to Joseph (Gen. xii. 42), and the one promised to Daniel (Dan. v. 7), were the first mentioned.

CHAL'CE-DO-NY. PRECIOUS STONES.

CHAL'COL (1 K. iv. 31).

CHALK (Is. xxvii. 9). Limestone.

CHAL'DÆA, CHALDEA, CASDIM (*Khaldi in Armenian, the moon*). Babylonia—the whole, or sometimes the southern part (Dan. v. 30, ix. 1; Gen. xi. 28). Haran died in Ur of Casdim (Ezek. i. 3). The whole of Mesopotamia occupied by Chaldeans. The Chaldeans were one out of many Cushite tribes peopling Babylonia. Hence came Sabæans to afflict Job (i. 15-17). Recently discovered inscriptions on ancient works show that there were two languages in use: one a Semitic, for civil purposes, and another a Cushite, for learned and religious purposes (Dan. i. 4; v. 11). The Chaldeans were priests, magicians or astronomers—the depositaries of learning and science. The plains were formerly irrigated by canals led from the river, spread over the country like a network. Groves of palm-trees, pleasant gardens, fields of grain and vineyards, proved the richness of the soil, and supported a dense population. It is now a waste of drifting dust and sand, with heaps of bricks and rubbish (Is. xiv. 23; Jer. l. 38). The chief cities were Accad, Babel, Borsippa, Calneh, Cutha, Erech, Sippara and Teredon. Herodotus mentions a vast number of cities, and the mounds over all the country prove his statements true.

CHAMBERS OF IMAGERY. Used by Ezekiel (viii. 12) in denouncing the idolatrous corruptions of the kingdom of Judah, or that part which imitated the Egyptians in painting on the walls of a chamber pictures of idols, &c., for worship. (See *Wilkinson's Manners and Customs of the Ancient Egyptians*). Every man has a chamber in his own mind filled with his idols—his dearest objects of regard.

CHAM BER-ING (Rom. xiii. 13).

CHAM BER-LAIN. Erastus, "the chamberlain." An officer who had charge of a king's lodgings and wardrobe (2 K. xxiii. 11).

CHAME'LEON (Heb. KO-ACH, *strength*). There are two lizards, each of which has been proposed as the animal meant. Lizards are very plentiful in Palestine and Egypt. 1. The chameleon is noted for its strong grasp, by which it sustains its position for a long time on twigs and branches. The normal color is black or slaty, but can be changed in an instant to many other tones, as green, yellow, spotted, which changes seem to be independent of the will of the animal.—2. The Nile Monitor is sometimes called the land crocodile, being about 6 feet in length. It eats the eggs and young of the crocodile.

CHAM'OIS. A specie of wild goat found in Arabia (Deut. xiv. 5).

CHAM-PAIGN (*a plain*) (Deut. xi. 30).

CHA'NAAN (Judg. v. 39, 10).

CHA'NAANITE (Judg. v. 16).

CHAN'CEL-LOR (Ezr. iv. 8, 9, 17).

CHAN'EL-BONE (Job xxvi. 22). The bone of the arm above the elbow.

CHAN'GERS (Judg. ii. 15). MONEY CHANGERS.

CHANGERS OF MONEY. A class who made a business, in accommodating the temple worshipers at the annual feasts of the Jews, by exchanging the money of those who came from foreign countries for the half-shekel which was the lawful tribute to the treasury. They probably crept gradually nearer the temple until they occupied the corners and passages of the sacred courts. From these Jesus drove them, because no trading was lawful there, and certainly not dishonest, sharp practices, which had made God's house a "den of thieves."

CHAN-NU-NE'US. MERARI (1 Esd. viii. 48).

CHA'NOCH. ENOCH (Gen. iv. 17).

CHAP'EL (*a holy place, sanctuary*). Idol's temple (1 Macc. i. 47). Bethel was crowded with altars (Amos iii. 14).

CHAP'ITER. The upper part of a pillar (Ex. xxxviii. 17).

CHAP'MEN. Traders (2 Chr. ix. 14). Foot-peddlers,

CHARAATH'ALAR (1 Esd. v. 36).

CHAR'A-CA. A place E. of Jordan (2 Macc. xii. 17). Lost.

CHAR'A-SHIM, THE VALLEY OF. A place settled by Joab 2 (1 Chr. iv. 14), and reinhabited by Benjamites after the captivity (Neh. xi. 35).

CHAR'CHĀMIS (1 Esd. i. 25). CARCHEMISH.

CHAR'CHĒMIS (2 Chr. xxxv. 20).

CHAR'CUS (1 Esd. v. 32). BARKOS.

CHA'RE-A. HARSHA (1 Esd. v. 32).

CHAR'GER. (Heb. AGARTAL). Basin in Ezra i. 9, that is, a tank for catching the blood from the victims on the altar.—2. KEARAH, deep dishes (Num. vii. 13).—3. PINAX, a tray, or server, of wood inlaid, or of metal (such as is now used for the common table), (Matt. xiv. 8).

CHARIOT. Heb. *merkabah*, and *rekeb*, and *agaloth* for war-chariots, or wagons or carts. The Egyptian monuments present paintings of several kinds of chariots, all of two wheels only, differing chiefly in the ornaments. The king's was different only in being more richly ornamented, and as having the king alone—as a sign that to him belonged the entire glory of the victory. In the Assyrian sculptures are some 4-wheeled carriages. Three persons usually ride in them—the king, his umbrella-bearer, and the charioteer. The Persian chariots were heavier than those of Egypt or Assyria.

CHARITY. Greek *agape*, which is properly love (1 Cor. viii. 1, 13; Luke xi. 42; Rom. v. 5, 8.) AGAPE.

CHAR'MIS. Son of Melchiel; one of the three rulers of Bethulia (Judg. vi. 15).

CHAR'RAN. HARAN (Acts vii. 2, 4).

CHASTE-BA (1 Esd. v. 31).

CHĀ'VAH (Gen. iii. 20). Eve.

CHE'BAR (*great river*). Chaldea (Ez. i. 3). Some of the Jews were located here during the captivity (Ez. i. 1, 3, iii. 15; 2 K. xxiv. 15). HABOR. This was the largest artificial canal of Babylonia, and was cut by the Jewish captives.

CHE'DORLĀ'OMER (Gen. 14). King of Elam, perhaps a part of Persia and Media. His marauding excursion, aided by four other kings, was brought to an abrupt and disastrous end by Abraham.

CHEESE. There is no Hebrew word for cheese. The three words translated cheese are: 1. *gebinah*, curdled milk (Job x. 10); 2. *charitse hechalab*, slices of curds (1 Sam. xvii. 18); 3. *shephoth bakar*, curd rubbed fine—of kine (2 Sam. xvii. 29). Cheese now in use in the East is in small round cakes (4

inches), white, very salt, and hard. The Bedawins coagulate buttermilk, dry it, and grind to powder.

CHEL'LAL. Son of Pahath-moab (Ezr. x. 30).

CHELCI'AS. 1. Of Baruch (Bar. i. 1).—2. Highpriest (Bar. i. 7)—3. Father of Susanna (Sus. ii. 29, 63).

CHEL'LIANS (Judg. ii. 23). CHELLUS.

CHEL'LUH (*strong*). Son of Bani (Ezr. x. 35).

CHEL'LUS. Place west of Jordan (Jud. i. 9).

CHE'LOD (corrupted text in Jud. i. 6).

CHE'LUB (*basket*). 1. Father of Mehir, of Judah

CHARIOT.

(1 Chr. iv. 11).—2. Father of Ezri, David's officer (xxvii. 26).

CHE-LU'BAI. Caleb, son of Hezron (1 Chr. ii. 9)

CHEM'ARIM (*idol-priests*). An ascetic; one who goes about dressed in black (Zeph. i. 4). Idolatrous priests in 2 K. xxiii. 5. Priests of false worship (Hos. x. 5).

CHĒ'MOSH (*subduer*). The national god of the Moabites (1 K. xi. 7; Jer. xlviii. 7), who were called the people of Chemosh (Num. xxi. 29). Also of the Ammonites, though Moloch was afterwards their god (Jer. xlix). Moloch and Chemosh may mean the same god, who might have been also called Baal Peor. Traces of the same worship are found at Babylon, Tyre, and it was introduced among the Hebrews by Solomon, who built a high place on the Mt. of Offense, so named for that act. The Arabs worshiped a black stone as his emblem—as a black stone in the Kaaba at Mecca is an emblem now worshiped by all Mohammedans. This idol represented some of the planets: perhaps Saturn.

CHE'NA-AN (Gen. ix. 18). CANAAN.

CHE-NĀ'ANAH. Son of Bilhan, a Benjamite (1 Chr. vii. 10).—2. Father of Zedekiah (1 K. xxii. 11, 24).

CHENA'NI. A Levite (Neh. ix. 4).

CHENANI'AH. Chief of the Levites (1 Chr. xv. 22, 27).

CHE'PHAR-HAAMMO'NAI (*village of the Ammonites*); a city of Benjamin (Josh. xviii. 24).

CHEPH'IRAH (*the village*). Benjamin (Josh. ix. 17). East of Yalo, two miles. Kefir (Rob., iii. 146). The Gibeonites of this place (and also Kirjath Jearim and Beeroth) played the trick on Joshua mentioned in Josh. ix. 3, which led them to make a treaty with them.

CHE'RAN. Son of Dishon (Gen. xxxvi. 26).

CHE'REAS. Brothers of Timotheus; governor of Gazara where he was slain by the Jews (2 Macc. x. 32, 37).

CHER'ETHIM. Cher'ethims; pl. of Cherethites (Ez. xxv. 16).

CHERĒTHĪ'TES and **PELETHITES.** Body-guard

of David. No other king had one, that is recorded, but they had runners. Their captain was Benaiah the son of Jehoiadah (2 Sam. viii. 18). Under Solomon, Benaiah was made general instead of were *round about* the throne. They are especially called *living creatures* (Ezekiel and John), and so full of eyes, the peculiar sign of life. The cherubim were designed as symbols of faith and hope to

ENTRANCE OF PALACE AT KONYUNJIK.

Joab. The names are of Philistine origin, and the men may have been partly of Philistine and partly of Hebrew (refugee) origin, attached to David in his adversity, and rewarded by him in his prosperity.

CHE′RITH. The brook Cherith, in a valley now called Kelt, running by Jericho to the Jordan (1 K. xvii. 3, 5; Jos. Ant. viii. 13, § 2). Some have supposed that it must be looked for on the east of Jordan.

CHER′UB (*mystic figure on the ark*). Cherubim, plural. A keeper, warder or guard of the Deity. Josephus said no one in his day could even conjecture the shape of the cherubim that Solomon made for the Holy of Holies (Ant. viii. 3, 3). They were of wood, gilded, and 15 feet high (1 K. vi. 23). Ezekiel describes them as having each four faces and four wings; but he gives only two faces (or it may be but one) to those in the temple on the walls. The cherubim of Rev. iv. 7, 8, are living creatures, with one body, four faces full of eyes, and six wings. The fourfold combination was of man, lion, ox, and eagle. Monstrous combinations of this kind are figured and sculptured both in Assyria and Egypt. These combined forms are symbolical of united powers; the lion of strength, royal majesty; the ox of patient industry; wings of swiftness, quickness, and the human head the intelligence to guide all these for one purpose; and

SPHINX.

thus showing that the divine government is sustained by intelligence, power, patience, and speed. They were servants of God, and they were ministers of vengeance (Ez. x. 7; Rev. xv. 7), and attendants of the heavenly king, praising and extolling the wonders of his grace (Rev. v. 11), and thus always nearest to God, "*in the midst of the throne*" (Rev. iv. 4–6), while others as angels and elders,

man, pointing to the possibility of man attaining to the highest and holiest places. (See EGYPT for picture of the Sphinx, and NINEVEH for winged figures).

CHE′SALON (*flank*). Judah (Josh. xv. 10). Now Kesla, 7 ms. W. of Jerusalem.

CHE′SED (*increase*). Son of Nahor (Gen. xx. 22).

CHE′SIL. Simeon (Josh. xv. 30). Near the desert, S.

CHEST (Heb. ARON and GENAZIM). Meaning Ark of the Covenant, Joseph's coffin, and the contribution box in the temple. Treasuries in Esther iii. 9.

CHESTNUT TREE. In the A. V. (Gen. xxx. 37; Ez. xxxi. 8) the translation of the Heb. ARON, the plane tree. In Ecclus xxiv. 14, wisdom is a plane tree by the water.

CHESUL′LOTH (*loins*). Issa. Between Jezreel and Shunem (Josh. xix. 18). Iksal? Chisloth Tabor?

CHET′TIM. CHITTIM (1 Macc. i. 1).

CHE̅′ZIB (*false*). Birthplace of Shelah (Gen. xxxviii. 5). AIN KUSSABEH. A fountain and ruins 10 ms. S. W. of Beit Jibrin.

CHI̅′DON (*javelin*). Near Kirjath Jearim (1 Chr. xiii. 9; 2 Sam. vi.). An accident happened here to the ark while on its way to Jerusalem.

CHICKENS (2 Esd. i. 30; Matt. xxiii. 37). HEN.

CHILD. CHILDREN. Were regarded as God's gifts. Parents were bound to teach them their own faith and fit them to occupy the place of true members of the covenant (Gen. xviii. 19; Deut. vi. 7; xi. 19), and required of children a kind of sacred reverence, sanctioned in the Decalogue; the parent standing to his children as God does to the parent. At five the child was placed under the father's special care, and at twelve the son was called *the son of the law.* Very severe laws regulated the conduct of the child and punished misconduct (Lev. xix. 3; Ex. xxi. 15, 17; Deut. xxvii. 16), in the father as well as the son (Deut. xxi. 21). Property descended to the sons in equal shares, the oldest having a double portion, no wills being necessary. The child might be sold for a debt of the parent (2 K. iv. 1; Is. i. 1; Neh. v. 5), until the year of jubilee. The word child also means a person noted for certain qualities, as "children of the world"—selfish; "children of light" having religion; "child of song," a good singer.

CHIL′ION (*sickly*). Son of Elimelech. An Ephrathite (Ruth i. 2–5, iv. 9).

CHIL′MAD. On the Euphrates; mentioned by Xenophon (Anab. i. 5, 10). Had traffic with Tyre (Ez. xxvii. 23).

CHIM′HAM (*longing*). Son of Barzillai—returned with David (2 Sam. xix. 37, 38, 40; Jer. xli. 17). See BETHLEHEM.

CHIN′NERETH. Naph. Fortified city (Josh. xix. 35). Lost. It is a question which was named first, the lake or the city. Gennesar is a proper change of the same name. (See GENNESARETH).

CHI′OS. Island in the Ægean Sea, 5 ms. from the shore of Asia Minor, 32 ms. long, 8 to 18 ms. wide (Acts xx. xxi.).

CHIS′LON (*confidence—hope*). Father of Elidad, the prince of Benjamin (Num. xxxiv. 21).

CHIS′LOTH-TA′BOR (*loins—flanks*). West end of Mt. Tabor (Josh. xix. 12). Iksal?

CHIT′TIM, KITTIM (*maritime*). Josephus says it was Cyprus. Mentioned many times (Gen. x. 4; 1 Chr. i. 7; Num. xxiv. 24). Fleets from Tyre sailed there (Is. xxiii. 1, 12; Jer. ii. 10). Cedar or box-wood was got there (Ez. xxvii. 6). Some suppose the name means all the islands settled by the Phœnicians, as Crete, the Cyclades, &c.

CHLO′E (*verdant—short*). A disciple mentioned by Paul (1 Cor. i. 11).

CHO′BA. Ephraim (Judg. iv. 4). CHO′BAI (xv. 4, 5). Hobah?

CHORA′SHAN (*smoking furnace*). Visited or haunted by David (1 Sam. xxx. 30). May be the ASHAN of Simeon, S. of Hebron (Josh. xv. 42).

CHORA′ZIN. One of the cities in which the mighty works of our Lord were done (Matt. xi. 21; Luke x. 13), 2 ms. from Capernaum. Supposed to be Kerazeh, a small Arab village 3 ms. inland from Tell Hum. The woes pronounced upon this city have come to pass. Its site even is doubtful.

CHOZE′BA. CHEZIB. ACHZIB (1 Chr. iv. 22).

CHRIST. Title of Jesus as the Messiah. See JESUS.

CHRISTIAN. Followers of the highest and best known divine laws as taught by Jesus Christ. The name Christian was given to the disciples of Jesus at Antioch by the Greeks in derision, in the reign of Claudius. They were before that called Nazarenes and Galileans.

COIN OF CYPRUS.

CHRŌNOL′OGY. The chronology of the Bible is that of the Jews and their ancestors, from the earliest records to the end of the writing of the New Testament. Since the Bible is not a complete history of the whole time it represents, nor of the whole world, it must not be expected to have a continuous chronology. Designed alterations by bad men and careless copying have changed many points, and have made it necessary to exercise the greatest care in determining and correcting the errors. The Jews were not a mathematical people, or scientific in any respect, and computed the year by observation only. The Egyptians and Chaldees were far in advance of the Hebrews in science, and attained to a high standard of mathematical knowledge and chronological computation. The observation of the moon was the basis of the year's reckoning. Messengers were stationed on the heights around Jerusalem, on the 30th day of the month, to announce the appearance of the new moon, who reported to the Sanhedrin. This custom, among the Jews, was older than Moses, as appears in the regulation of it in Num. xxviii. 11. The year was made of twelve moons; and every fourth or fifth year a month was added at the end of the year, after the month Adar, called Veadar, *Second Adar*. The sacred year began with the month Nisan, in which Moses brought Israel out of Egypt (Ex. xii. 2; Esth. iii. 7). The civil year began as now, with the month Tishri, which was supposed to be the month of the creation.

CHART OF MONTHS, FEASTS, ETC.

Modern.	Sacred No.	Months.	Civil No.	Festivals.
April,	1,	Nisan or Abib,	7,	Passover, 15.
May,	2,	Iyar-Zif,	8,	2d Passover, 14.
June,	3,	Sivan,	9,	Pentecost, 6.
July,	4,	Tammuz,	10,	4th mo., 17.
August,	5,	Ab,	11,	Temple taken by Chaldees, 9.
September,	6,	Elul,	12,	{ Nehemiah dedicated the walls, 7. Wood-offerings, 21.
October,	7,	Tishri,	1,	{ Trumpets, 1. Atonement, 10. Tabernacles, 15.
November,	8,	Marchesvan,	2,	Fast, 19.
December,	9,	Chislev,	3,	Dedication, 25.
January,	10,	Tebeth,	4,	{ Feast of 10th mo., 8. Siege of Jerusalem, 10.
February,	11,	Shebet,	5,	Beginning of year of trees, 15.
March,	12,	Adar,	6,	2d Temple, 3; Purim, 14, 15.

The year was also dated from the king's reign, as in Esther, Chronicles, Kings, etc.; from the building of King Solomon's temple; and from the beginning of the Babylonish captivity. The week was of seven days, ending with the Sabbath. The Egyptians and Greeks divided the month into periods of ten days, called decades. The day was divided into night and day: thus, in Gen. i. 5, "the evening and the morning were the first day." The evening began at sunset, the morning at sunrise. There were four divisions of the day in common use—evening, morning, double light (noon), and half night (midnight). The night was divided into watches, the first and the second. A middle watch is mentioned once in Judg. vii. 19; and the morning watch in Ex. xiv. 24, and 1 Sam. xi. 11. Four night-watches were adopted from the Romans in later times (Mark viii. 35). The day and the night were divided into 12 hours each (Dan. iv. 19, 33). The Egyptians divided the day and night into hours from about 1200 B. C. The division into 24 hours was unknown before the fourth century B. C. The most common usage was to divide the day by the position of the sun, as the Arabs do now. The length of the day was longer in summer than in winter, and the hour longer in proportion. There were many contrivances for measuring time, such as dials, gnomons and clepsydræ, which had long been known by other nations. The day was divided into four parts only for the Temple service (Acts ii. 15; iii. 1; x. 9). The Sabbath (a day of *rest*), at the end of the week, was kept up by the patriarchs, and continued by the law of Moses, as a memorial of the deliverance from Egypt (Deut. v.), and was a day of joy and rejoicing. The morning and evening sacrfice in the Temple were doubled, the shew-bread changed for fresh, the law was publicly read and expounded; and this custom, simple at first, finally developed into the grand ceremonials of the Synagogue, especially under Ezra, after the return from Babylon. The resurrection of our Lord Jesus, the Christ, occurred on the FIRST day of the week (John xx.), and several of his appearances to his friends and disciples happening on that day also, the day of Pentecost in that year fell on that day, when the miraculous gift of tongues prepared the apostles for their peculiar work among all nations; therefore it was adopted as the day for stated meetings of the believers, and called the Lord's day. The seventh day, the seventh month, the seventh year, and the YEAR OF JUBILEE (the 49th or 50th), were sacred, and had their festivals and privileges. The seventh month contained the FEAST OF TRUMPETS, the DAY OF ATONEMENT and the FEAST OF TABERNACLES (which was the most joyful of all the Hebrew festivals), and the opening of the New Year. On the seventh year the land was to rest (Ex. xxiii. 10), in which no field was to be tilled nor vineyard dressed, nor even grain gathered that had sowed itself, nor grapes plucked. All debts were released. The Sabbatical year completed the Sabbatical scale. It began on the seventh month, and was marked by high and holy occupation, connected with sacred reflection, and was completed in the YEAR OF JUBILEE. It is quite certain that the year of jubilee was the 49th. It was to begin on the tenth day of the seventh month, at the sound of a horn (trumpet) all through the land (Lev. xxv.). The laws respecting this year were: 1. Rest for the soil; 2. Restoration of land to its original owner; 3. Freedom to all slaves, whether by poverty or other causes. A notable instance of the release from debt is recorded in Nehemiah v., after the captivity, when the people were rebuilding the walls. There were several eras used in reckoning, by writers, and as national customs. 1. The Exodus (1 K. vi. 1; Num. xxxiii. 38), counting from the first starting out of Egypt.—2. The foundation of King Solomon's Temple.—3. The captivity of Jehoiachin (Ezek. i. 2; xxix. 1; 2 K. xxv. 27; Jer. lii. 31).—4. The return from the captivity of Babylon (Ez. iii. 1, 8).—5. The era of the Seleucidæ.—6. The year of liberation under Simon Maccabæus, marked by coins (1 Macc. xiii. 41). And the years of the reign of each king in his own time, reckoned from the beginning of the new year next after his accession. The original records are so few, and so indefinite, that it is difficult to fix on the precise date of any event, either in the Old or the New Testament. The Bible does not give a connected chronology from Adam down, nor from Noah, nor even from Abraham; nor is there any apparent purpose or system of dates that we can find. At one time it was expected that a better acquaintance with the originals would disclose a perfect system of chronology, giving periods, years, months, and even days; but such close study has unexpectedly shown us that the Bible treats of men and character, and God's dealing with man, and of certain distinct and separate periods of time only as were occupied in the passing events recorded. The people of the East, and the Arabs of the desert in particular, have never been mathematical, founding their chronology on astronomy; but have from

the first regulated their calendar by observation only. Since they did not have the exact machinery of our modern clocks for determining the precise times of the sun's, moon's or stars' rising and setting, eclipses, &c. (which are the foundation of our most exact calculations), they never could have had more than a moderate degree of accuracy in their observations. The new moon would be expected on a certain day, and the precise moment of its appearance would depend on the place of observation, on a hill or in a valley, and the careful watch and good eyesight of the sentinel. The true figures of the original Hebrew chronology are very obscure in many instances, because there are three different versions—the Hebrew, the Samaritan and the Septuagint—each of which gives a different series of figures for the ages of the patriarchs, as shown in the following

TABLE OF THE AGES OF THE PATRIARCHS.

Date B. C.	Name.	Age of each when the next was born			Whole life of each.		
		Heb.	Sam.	Sept.	He.	Sa.	Sep
4004	Adam . . .	130	130	230	930	930	930
3874	Seth	105	105	205	912	912	912
3769	Enos . . .	90	90	190	905	905	905
3679	Cainan . .	70	70	170	910	910	910
3609	Mahalaleel	65	65	165	895	895	895
3544	Jared . . .	162	62	162	962	962	847
3382	Enoch . . .	65	65	165	365	365	365
3317	Methuselah	187	67	187	969	720	969
3130	Lamech . .	182	53	188	777	653	753
2948	Noah . . .	502	502	502	950	950	950
2446	Shem . . .	100	100	100	600	600	600
2348	FLOOD . .	1656	1307	2262			
2346	Arphaxad	35	135	135	438	438	535
	Cainan . .			130			460
2311	Salah . . .	30	130	130	433	433	460
2281	Eber	34	134	134	464	404	404
2247	Peleg . . .	30	130	130	239	239	339
2217	Reu	32	132	132	239	239	339
2185	Serug . . .	30	130	130	230	230	330
2155	Nahor . . .	29	79	79	148	148	208
2126	Terah . . .	130	70	70	205	145	205
1996	Abraham .	100					
1896	Isaac . . .	60					
1836	Jacob . . .	91					
1726	Joseph . .						

1. Here is a continuous chronology from Adam to Joseph, subject to only three questions : 1. Are the numbers given in either version of the text genuine? If so, which is correct? 2. What was Terah's age at the birth of Abraham? 3. When did the 430 years (of the period from the Promise to the Exodus) begin? A synopsis of the debates on these points may be found in Smith and Kitto. The accuracy of the *original Hebrew* is not doubted; but the alterations cannot be pointed out, so as to harmonize the three records in the Hebrew, the Septuagint, and the Samaritan. The Hebrew text, as interpreted by Ussher, is adopted here for convenience.

2. From the call of Abraham to the Exodus, 430 years; estimated as follows;

Abraham to Jacob .	85	Abraham to Isaac . .	25
Levi's age	137	Isaac to Jacob	60
Kohath's age	133	Joseph entered Egypt	130
Amram's age	137	Joseph lived after . .	71
Moses at Exodus . .	80	Oppression after Joseph.	
	572	Moses at Exodus . .	80
			366

B.C. 1921—430=1491.

From the number 572 we may take the average years of each before the birth of the next, making a sum of 142, and this will leave 430. To the 366 we may add the years of oppression (Ex. i. 8–22) after Joseph died, say 64, and this gives the number required. Joshua's ancestry, from Ephraim, is given in 1 Chr. vii. 23–27; and if their ages were equal to their brethren of the other tribes mentioned, 430 years is not too long a period.

The specimen of ancient Egyptian papyrus preserved in the Bibliotheque at Paris, and published in *fac-simile* (pl. V. in the Astor Library), gives independent and disinterested evidence on the question of the long life of Jacob and others of this age. At the close of the essay (on morals) the writer says: "I have become an elder on the earth; I have traversed 110 years of life by the gift of the king and the approval of the elders, fulfilling my duty toward the king in the place of favor." The inscriptions at Memphis corroborate this account, and show that the writer *Ptah-hotp*, was eldest son of *Assa*, 5th king of the 15th dynasty (B. C. 1960–1860), whose father's age must have been at least 130. Manetho also verifies the same point. The increase of the Jews in Egypt was from *seventy families* to about *three millions.*

From Exodus to the Foundation of King Solomon's Temple, 480 years (1 K. vi. 1).

	Ussher.	B. C.	Poole.	Josephus.	Crosby.	Miner.	Hales.	B. C.
Exodus to Joblhua, - - - - - - -	40	1491	40	40	40	40	40	1648
Joshua and Elders, } - - - - -	6.4m	1451	13	25	37	17	26	1608
		1438	32				27	1553
First Servitude, } Mesopotamian,	40	1398	430	18	390	Book of Judges.	8	1526
Othniel, 1st Judge, }				40			40	1518
Second Servitude, } Moabite, - -	80	1323		81	}	317	18	1478
Ehud and Shamgar, }							80	1460
Third Servitude, } Canaanite, -	40	1265		20			20	1426
Deborah and Barak, }				40			40	1406
Fourth Servitude, } Midianite, - -	40	1245		7			7	1368
Gideon, }				40			40	1359
Abimelech, - - - - - - - -	9.2m			3			3	1319
Tola, }	48	1232		22			23	1316
Jair, } - - - - - - - -		1210		22			22	1293
Fifth Servitude, } Ammon, - - -	6	1188		18			18	1271
Jephthah, }				6			6	1253
Ibzan, }		1182		7			7	1247
Elon, } - - - - - - - -	25	1175		10			10	1240
Abdon, }		1165					8	1230
Sixth Servitude, }				40	1 Sa. vii.		40	1222
Samson, } Philistia, - - -	40			20	Samson,	Eli xxx.		
Interim, }					Samuel,	Sam. x.		1182
Eli, - - - - - - - -		1157		40	and Eli, cotemporaries.	Book of 1 Sam.	20	1152
Seventh Servitude, }				12		72	Samuel.	1142
Samuel and Saul, 18, } Anarchy, - -	40	1095	40	18	40	2 Sam.	12	1122
Saul, 22, }			40	2	32	40	40	1110
David, - - - - - - - -	40	1014	40	40	40		40	1070
Solomon, - - - - - - - - -	3		3	3	3		3	1030
	478½		638	592	580	749	621	
Solomon's Temple (foundation B. C.),		1012			1008	1012		1027
Destruction, - - - - - - - -	424	588						
Return from captivity, - - - - -	145	536						
Under Zerubbabel, - - - - -		535						
" Ezra, - - - - - - - -		458						
" Nehemiah, - - - - - - -		445						

B. C.
445. Walls of Jerusalem rebuilt by Nehemiah. Herodotus reads his history at Athens. The age of Phidias (sculptor), Euripides (poet) Pericles in Greece. Military tribunes in Rome.
425. Xerxes II, king of Persia (Darius II, 424). Thucydides (historian. His book ends B. C. 410, and Xenophon's begins).
414. Amyrtæus, king of Egypt, revolts from Persia. The Athenians being alarmed by an eclipse, are defeated before Syracuse, Sicily. —413. Archelaus, king of Macedon. The 400 rule in Athens.
404. Artaxerxes II, king of Persia.—401. Xenophon and the 10,000 retreat. Socrates dies.
383. Mithridates, king of Pontus. Bithynia made a kingdom. Plato (philosopher). Aristæus (mathematician).
368. A *celestial globe* brought from Egypt to Greece.
366. Jeshua slain by Johanan in the temple of Jerusalem.—361. Darius Ochus king of Persia.
360. Cappadocia made a kingdom. Tachos, king

of Egypt. Philip II, king of Macedon. Demosthenes.
356. Temple of Diana burnt at Ephesus. Alexander born.
349. Darius Ochus takes Egypt and robs the temples. Aristotle (tutor to Alexander, 343). —345. 12 cities in Italy buried by an earthquake.—336. Eclipses first calculated by Calippus of Athens.
330. Alexander conquers Persia. He enters Jerusalem. Seeing the high priest, Jaddua, in his sacred robes, he respects him, and offers sacrifice to Jehovah.—323. Alexander died at Babylon.
100,000 Jews carried into Egypt by Ptolemy. Onias I, high priest.—312. Seleucus Nicator, king of Syria.
311. Judæa subject to Antigonus. Appian Way made.
301. Judæa under the Ptolemies. Euclid, mathematician in Alexandria. Chinese wall built.
284. Colossus of Rhodes. Sect of Saducees. The Pharos (first light-house) at Alexandria.

267. Ptolemy makes a canal from the Nile to the Red Sea. Silver money coined. Parthia.

248. Onias II, high priest.—246. Ptolemy Euergetes conquers Syria.—237. Simon II, high priest.

241. Attalus 1, king of Pergamus. Archimedes, mathematician.

203. Judæa conquered by Antiochus. Onias III, high priest.—200. Jesus, son of Sirach (Ecclesiasticus). First mention of the Sanhedrin (70 rulers).

187. Syria a Roman province.—175. Jason, high priest. The temple plundered by Antiochus Epiphanes, and dedicated to Jupiter Olympus (168). See head on page 11.

165. Judas Maccabæus expels the Syrians and purifies the temple. Rise of the Pharisees.

161. First treaty with the Romans.—146. Carthage destroyed.

135. End of the Apocrypha. Antiochus IV, (Sidetes) besieged Jerusalem.

130. John Hyrcanus delivers Judæa from the Syrians, and reduces Samaria and Idumæa.

107. Aristobulus, king of Judæa.—116. Ptolemy Lathyrus, king of Egypt.—107. Alexander I, king of Egypt.

105. Alexander Jannæus at war with Egypt. Libraries of Athens sent to Rome by Sylla (86).

92. Tigranes, king of Armenia. See portrait in COINS.

79. Alexandra, widow of Jannæus, governs Judæa. Pompey in Africa. Julius Cæsar.

70. Hyrcanus II, high priest, deposed by his brother Aristobulus. They appeal to Pompey, who conquers Judæa and Syria, and makes them Roman provinces.—63. Antiochus XII, the last of the race of the Seleucidæ.

53. The temple plundered by Crassus (proconsul of Syria). Augustus born.—31. Cæsar passes the Rubicon.

48. Antipater of Idumæa. Calphurnius Bibulus, governor of Syria. Battle of Pharsalia.

45. Cæsar reformed the calendar, using solar years instead of lunar. Gives the Jews privileges.

44. Cæsar assassinated.—42. Battle of Philippi.

40. Herod the Great marries Mariamne, granddaughter of Hyrcanus, and is made king by the Romans (at Rome, with Pagan sacrifices).—30. Mariamne, and all the Sanhedrin but Pollio and Sameas, killed by Herod.

37. Romans assist Herod by taking Jerusalem. Antigonus, last Asmonean, killed at Antioch.

30. The Roman Republic becomes a monarchy. Antony and Cleopatra in Egypt.

27. Battle of Actium. The title of Augustus (Venerable) created and given to Cæsar Octavius.

20. Augustus (nephew of Julius Cæsar) visited Judæa and enlarged Herod's kingdom, by Paneas, where Herod built a temple in honor of Augustus (Cæsarea Philippi), ordering heathen games to be celebrated every fifth year. Herod built a temple at Samaria and called the city Sebaste (Venerable). He began to rebuild the temple, which was finished in the reign of Herod Agrippa II, A. D. 65.

15. Augustus (Germanicus) assumes the title of Pontifex Maximus (Pope).—11. Germany conquered by the Romans.

5. Varrus, gov. of Syria; Cyrenius (Quirinius) of Judæa. Cymbeline, king of Britain. Dionysius of Halicarnassus, historian. Herod robs the tomb of David.

4. Jesus the Christ born in Bethlehem. Flight into Egypt. Herod dies: his son Archelaus succeeds as Ethnarch. Herod Antipas tetrarch of Galilee. (For events in the life of Jesus and of Paul, see BIOGRAPHY).

A. D.

14. Tiberius, emperor.—19. Jews banished from Rome. Herod builds the city of Tiberias.

25. Pontius Pilate, gov. of Judæa.—26. John the Baptist's ministry begins. Thrace becomes a Roman province.—27. Jesus baptized.

30. Crucifixion Friday, April 7th (Nisan 15th) Philo, a Jew of Alexandria. Seneca.

37. Apion of Alexandria (grammarian). See Josephus. Caligula emperor.—40. First Christians at Antioch, Syria.

41. Herod's persecution.—52. Council of Apostles at Jerusalem.

48. Population of Rome, 1,200,000.

CHRYS'OLITE, CHRYS'OPRASE, CHRYSO'PRASUS. See PRECIOUS STONES.

CHUB. A country or people associated with Egypt. Lud, Phut and others in Ez. xxx. 5.

CHUN (to stand up). A city of Hadadezer (1 Chr. xviii. 8). BEROTHAI in 2 Sam. viii. 8.

CHURCH (called). The Lord's faithful people. The Lord's house, where his people gather. A church is any number of souls, called and united in one vow, in one place, for divine worship, where the pure word is preached, and the sacraments duly administered, and godly living, after his law, as given by the head of the church, the Lord Jesus Christ. The church in Galatia means all the societies or churches in that country.

CHU'SHAN or **CUSHAN-RISHATHAIM** (Ethiopian of wickedness). King of Mesopotamia, who oppressed the Israelites 8 years. Probably a sheikh, not a king.

CHU'SI (Judg. vii. 18). A place near Ekrebel.

CHUZA (seer). Steward of Herod Antipas (Luke viii. 3).

CILIC'IA (Cilix, son of Agenor). (Herodotus vii. 91). Asia Minor, southeast on the sea. Separated from Pamphylia, W., Lycaonia and Cappadocia, N., and Syria E., by lofty mountains. Chief rivers are Calycadnus, Cydnus, and Sarus. Fertile and populous. Tarsus was its capital. Josephus supposed it was the Tarshish of Gen. x. 4 (Ant. i. 6, § 1.) Native land of Paul the Apostle. The high road between Syria and the West. The Roman general Pompey destroyed the pirates and robbers of Cilicia.

CASTOR AND POLLUX.

CI'MAH (cluster), (Job. ix. 9).

CIN'NAMON. A native of Ceylon and other islands of the Indian Ocean. It was one of the principal spices in the precious ointment used in the Tabernacle, and highly valued for its perfume (Ex. xxx. 23; Prov. vii. 17).

CIN'NEROTH. NAPHTALI (1 K. xv. 20). CHINNEROTH.

CIRA'MA (1 Esd. v. 20). Ramah in Ezr. ii. 26.

CIRCUMCIS'ION (cutting around). The cutting off of the foreskin of man, first practised by Abraham by divine command, as a token of a covenant between God and man. It was a very ancient custom founded on (supposed) sanitary laws, by the Egyptians and Ethiopians, and the practise is widespread in modern days; the Abyssinian Christians holding to the rite strictly. The Egyptian priests were required to observe this rite, and it was only strictly binding on those who entered the priesthood. So it became the badge of a religion that made undue account of outward distinctions, and merely natural virtues. The Hebrews were to practice it because they were to be *a nation of priests* (Ex. xix. 6), and it was to signify spiritual purity, being so considered by the leading men, implying a call to a holy life and purity of heart. The time was the 8th day after birth; among other people at full age—20 years. Foreigners on adoption into the Hebrew nation were required to submit to it.

CIS. KISH (Acts xiii. 21).

CI'SAI (Esth. xi. 2). KISH.

CIS'TERN. A dug place, for the water of a spring, or from rain. Some were built up of stone and cement, and the best were cut in the solid rock. The largest are called pools, such as Solomon's, the Royal Cistern, Bethesda, etc. (See JERUSALEM.) A wheel is used to pan the rope over for drawing up the water, alluded to in Eccl. xii. 6. Keeping to one's own sources of pleasure, and not meddling with the property of others, is taught in the Proverbs (v. 15), by the figure of the cistern. Idolatry is compared to broken cisterns (Jer. ii. 3).

CIT'TIMS. CHITTIM (1 Macc. viii. 5).

CITIZEN. Among Romans, etc.. a member of the state, or of a city. Among the Hebrews a member of the nation at large. Paul was an instance of one born to the rights of a Roman citizen, which protected and benefited him on three occasions (Acts vi. 37; xxii. 25; xxv. 11). The Roman law made two classes of citizens—the first entitled to hold office and vote, and carry on public and private business—the second to enjoy only the protection of the laws as a free man. The sacred law was the basis of the civil among the Jews, and citizenship was acquired by complying with the terms of the covenant, and lost by certain transgressions. Christians are counted as citizens of the celestial state.

CIT'Y. Any inhabited place, large or small.

CLAU'DA. An island S. W. of Crete (Acts xxvii. 16). Now Gozzo.

CLAU'DIA. A British maiden; wife of Pudens, daughter of King Cogidubnus, an ally of Rome and a disciple (2 Tim. iv. 21).

CLAU'DIUS. 5th emperor of Rome, A. D. 41 to 54. Tiberius Claudius Nero Germanicus. He succeeded Caligula. The famine mentioned in Acts xi. 28, happened in his reign; and he banished all Jews from Rome (xvii. 2). His head is on the coin of Cyprus. Agrippina, his fourth wife, poisoned him.

JEWISH SCRIBES.

CLAY. A beautiful symbol of the divine power over the destinies of man was derived from the potter's use of clay, as he produced such elegant and useful forms from such a crude material (Is. lxiv. 8; Rom. ix. 21). "It is turned as clay to the seal" (Job xxxviii. 14), refers to the use of clay in

stopping up doors in tombs or granaries, and the use of a seal engraved with a private design on the soft surface, leaving its impression as a protection against intrusion. Bricks were stamped also as may be seen on the numberless specimens from the ruins. Locks on the storehouses in the East are now further secured by the clay, stamped with a seal.

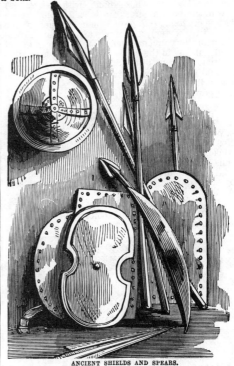

ANCIENT SHIELDS AND SPEARS.

CLEAN and **UNCLEAN.** Terms of frequent occurrence in the Bible, concerning the rites and usages of the Abrahamic covenant, having both a natural and a symbolical meaning. It is mentioned as in use at the sacrifice made by Noah and it is probable that it was then an ancient distinction. Animals, birds, beasts and reptiles were pronounced good for food without distinction (Gen. ix. 3). It then has no foundation in the laws of diet or health. The line was fixed by man between the wild, obnoxious, poison-fanged animals, filthy in habit and suggestive of evil, and the tame, docile creatures, more cleanly in their habits and more akin to the better instincts of mankind. The Egyptians sacrificed dogs, cats, crocodiles, etc., and held them as sacred. Moses, to separate his people from those pagans, confined sacrifices to animals from the flock and herd, sheep, goats and cattle, and to the dove species among birds; while, for food, a larger limit was allowed, but in the same time, the animals allowed being those that chew the cud and divide the hoof, among wild animals only the deer species, and of birds, a few were prohibited by name, and the rest allowed; of fishes those that had both fins and scales; and of insects, locusts and grasshoppers. The unclean were called *abominations*, and were to work a *spiritual defilement* if eaten. The clean and unclean animals had a counterpart in the soul, and the restrictions laid on the appetite became a bit and bridle to the soul. This law was abolished by the Lord in a vision to Peter at Joppa. There were other laws relating to ceremonial impurity, touching certain animals, dead bodies, diseased persons, the intercourse between man and wife, and the office of the mother. Particulars in Leviticus.

CLEAVE. To adhere to; "clave to" (Ruth i. 14); to divide; separated (Acts iii. 2).

CLEFT. (Deut. xiv. 6; Cant. ii. 14, etc.).

CLEMENT. Mentioned by Paul in Phil. iv. 3, with much esteem and honor, as his fellow laborer at Philippi, whose name (with the others) was in the book of life. He is said to have been bishop of Rome (Pope Clemens Romanus, the third from Peter), and wrote a letter to the Corinthians very much esteemed by the ancients and read publicly in the churches. It is in the Alexandrian MS. copy of the Scriptures as Codex A.

CLEO'PAS. One of the two disciples that saw Jesus on the way to Emmaus.

CLEOPAT'RA. Daughter of Antiochus III (the Great), and the name of several queens of Egypt. **1.** Wife of Ptolemy V, called Epiphanes, B. C. 193; **2.** Wife of Ptolemy VI, Philometer (Esth. xi. 1); **3.** Wife of Alexander Balas, B. C. 150, daughter of No. 2; afterwards given by her father to Demetrius Nicator (1 Macc. xi. 12); also wife of Antiochus VII, Sidetes, B. C. 125, who killed Demetrius. She murdered her son Seleucus, and died by a poison she had prepared for her second son, A. VIII.

CLEO'PHAS ALPHEUS (John. xxix. 25).

CLIFF, anciently called CLIFT (Is. xxxii. 14). A steep rock split off by violence.

THE GRAVE OF DAVID.

CLIMATE. There is no country in the world which has such a variety of climate and temperature, within the same limits, as Palestine. On Mts. Hermon and Lebanon there is perpetual snow; and at Jericho, only 60 or 80 miles, there is tropical heat. The hills of Bashan, Gilead, Galilee, Samaria, and Judæa, are the home of forests, vines, fig-trees, and all kinds of fruits and vegetables; and the plains produce bananas, oranges, etc. From Jerusalem to Jericho, in a direct line, is about 15 miles. At one place snow and ice sometimes are seen in the winter, but at the other frost is never known. Frost is also unknown in the plains of Sharon and Philistia. The temperature at Engedi is as high as that of Thebes, in Egypt. Palms grow as far north as Beirut, and bear fruit also at Damascus in sheltered positions.. The greatest heat on the hills of Judæa, Hebron, and Jerusalem, is seldom above 90° Fahrenheit, and the cold only once so low as 28° in five years (*Barclay*.).

Damascus is cooler, the highest being 88°, and the lowest 29°.

TABLE OF MEAN MONTHLY TEMPERATURE RAINFALL, PRODUCTS, ETC.

Months.	Jerusalem. Degrees.	Rain-fall inches.	Damascus.	Beirut.
Jan.	49.4	13	47	58
Feb.	54.4	16	53	61
Mar.	55.7	8	55	62
Apr.	61.4	2	57	63
May	73.8	1	73	72
June	75.2		78	75
July	79.1		86	82
Aug.	79.3		81	82
Sept	77.		79	80
Oct.	74.2	2	72	80
Nov.	63.8	2	62	66
Dec.	54.5	12	45	54
Annual	66.5	56	67	69

Highest in Judea 90°, shade at noon; lowest 28°, night.

Damascus 88°, noon: 29°, night; winter.

On Lebanon, Shumlan, highest 82°, in August.

In Gennesaret, 450 ft. above the sea, from March 17 to April 5, average, 63°, and 73° from 8 A. M. to 8 P. M. In May 78°, and day only 83°.

Dead Sea shore, 42°; average, night 47°, day 67°, in Jan. In April 105°, in the shade.

The Arabs leave for the high lands in the hot months, June to Sept.

Beersheba, Feb., night 31°, noon 72°; in summer 65° night, and 90° day, highest range.

Nablus is sheltered and warmer than Jerusalem; and Nazareth also.

January.—Last sowing of wheat and barley. Last roasting ears of corn (the 3d crop of the year!). Trees in leaf. Almond blossoms, apricot, peach, plum, beans. Winter figs still on the trees. Cauliflowers, cabbages, oranges, lemons, limes, citrons. Mandrake in bloom; wormwood also. New leaves on the olive-trees. Fire is needed in the house. Many flowers.

February.—Barley may be sown. Beans, onions, carrots, beets, radishes, etc. Oranges, etc. Apple trees in bloom. Flowers in the fields abundant.

March.—Beans and peas in the market. Trees in full leaf. Barley ripe at Jericho. Fig tree blossoms while the winter fig is still on. First clusters of grapes. Pear trees, apple, palm, and buckthorn in bloom. Sage, thyme, mint, etc. Carob pods ripe. Celery. Rue, parsley, hyssop, leeks, onions, garlic, etc. Flowers carpet the fields.

April.—Barley and wheat harvest. Sugar-cane set. Beans, etc., lettuce, cucumbers; lavender, rosemary, mulberries. Oleander blossoms; also rose of Sharon. Great variety of flowers. Early ears of corn. Apricots.

May.—Harvest in the plains and on the hills. Almonds, apples, mandrakes, and many vegetables. Grass begins to wither for want of rain. Melons of all kinds, onions, cucumbers, tomatoes, potatoes, corn. Walnuts, blackberries, sycamore and mulberry figs.

June.—Threshing grain. Figs, cherries, plums cedar-berries, olives, almonds, quinces, plaintain fruit, bananas, grapes, liquorice plant, dandelion, egg-plant, doum palm dates. Henna (for dyeing the nails) and roses gathered.

July.—Pears, nectarines, peaches, grapes, melons, potatoes, tomatoes, egg-plant, Indian figs, prickly pear (cactus fruit), gourds. Millet, doura, linseed, tobacco, grapes.

August.—All fruits and vegetables before named, and also citrons, pomegranates. Olives now perfect. Grapes. The fruit month.

September.—Every fruit and vegetable still in market. Cotton and hemp mature. Millet, doura, maize, lentils, chick-peas, lupines, beans, fenngreek, fennel, castor-oil plant. Grapes.

October.—Sesame (for lamp oil) ripe. Wheat and barley may be sown. Vegetables planted. Olives yield the last berries. Pomegranates, pistachio nuts. Lettuce, radishes, and other garden sauce. Cotton mature. Fig leaves fall. Plowing.

November.—Principal sowing of wheat and barley. Trees lose their leaves. Early dates. Very few olives. Grapes. Plowing.

December.—Grass abundant. Wheat and barley may still be sown, and pulse also. Sugar cane, cauliflowers, cabbage, radishes, lettuce, lentils. Plowing.

This calendar is mainly true of Jerusalem and the hill country. Some weeks allowance must be made for the higher temperature of the Jordan valley, and the plains by the Mediterranean sea.

RAIN. The average rain-fall at Jerusalem for the year is 56; in very wet seasons it has gone higher, 85, 44—66 average. The average in London is only 25, in the highlands of England 60, in New York, 62, and the highest in the lake country 65. There is a wet and a dry season. In the wet, the winter, the rains fall in two series of showers, called the early (*yoreh*) and the latter rain (*malkosh*), with occasional lighter showers between, and many clear sunny days. The loss of rain is sure to affect the harvest, and a total want of rain would destroy all crops (Amos iv. 7). From April to November there is scarcely ever a cloud. The dews are heavy often like a small shower. Chilly nights, succeeding hot days have always been a constant feature in the East (Gen. xxxi. 40). The different climate of Jericho has been often noticed. Josephus says, and it is true now, that linen clothing can be worn at Jericho when there is snow in the hills around Jerusalem. The plains along the sea shore are but little hotter than the hills. Beirut is much hotter the year round than Jerusalem. In the desert are found the greatest extremes of heat and cold. In winter the heat will be greater than our summer in the day, and the night colder than our average winter. The winds are very regular in their season and effects. West or S. W. wind invariably brings rain in winter (Luke xii. 54). The North wind is cool, but rare. The South wind is always hot (55; Job xxxvii. 17). The East wind is very rare in the winter, and, blowing on the desert in summer, is dry and hot (Ez. xvii. 10; Hos. xiii. 15). In the Jordan valley there is an under and an upper current. The under current blows down the valley in winter and up in summer. There are no East and West winds in the Arabah.

CLOUD. See CLIMATE. Pillar of a cloud. The peculiar sign and symbol of the Lord's presence with his ancient people, during the exodus (Ex. xiii. 21), as of a cloud by day and of fire by night. It disappeared (or is not mentioned) from the passage of the river Jordan until the dedication of Solomon's temple (2 Chr. v. 13), and then only as a momentary sign for that occasion. The figurative use of the cloud has reference to the peculiar climate. "A cloud of the latter rain" (Prov. xvi. 15) means the gladdening influence of the king's countenance when well favored toward his subjects. The commanding the clouds to rain not was a sign of desolation (Is. v. 6; Deut. xi. 17). Dark clouds were emblems of gloom and sadness (Joel ii. 2). Swift wind-driven clouds, with lightning, were an emblem of Jehovah (Ps. civ. 3). Their height expressed loftiness (Ps. lvii. 10).

CLOUTED (Josh. ix. 5). Mended. Spotted.

CLOUTS (Jer. xxxviii. 11, 12). Cast-off rags or torn clothes.

ÇNI'DUS. Caria, S. W., in Asia Minor (Acts xxvii. 7). Passed by Paul. Celebrated for the worship of the goddess Venus (Strabo xiv. 965).

COACHES (Is. lxvi. 20).

COAL (PEHHAN—*black*, and GAHHELETH—*burning*). There are veins of coal in Mt. Lebanon, a few miles from Beirut, and it is probable that the Hebrews and Phœnicians knew and used it. But charcoal must have been specially meant in Psalm cxx. 4, in coals of juniper; and only charcoal was used in the censer at the temple service.

COAST. border, bound (Ex. x. 4; xiv. 19).

COCK. Domestic poultry are not mentioned in the O. T., unless in Is. xxii. 17, 18. The compassion of the Lord towards Jerusalem is compared to the tender care of a hen over her chickens (Matt. xxii. 37; Luke xiii. 34). The cock-crowing of Matt. xiii. 35, refers to a certain hour of the night, just before dawn, and the special signal given at that hour to Peter (Matt. xxvi. 34, 74). They are on the monuments in Assyria but not in Egypt; also on the Etruscan pottery of great antiquity (Mrs. Gray's *Etruria*), and on the coins of Greeks and Romans. The ancient Britons kept them, but did not think it right to eat them (Cæsar's Wars, 5).

COFFER. A box hanging from the side of a cart (1 Sam. vi. 8, 11, 15; Ezr. vi. 2). "In a coffer."

COLHŌZEH (*all-seeing*). A man of Judah (Neh. iii. 11, 5).

CO'LIUS (1 Esd. ix. 23) KELAIAH.

COLLARS (Judg. viii. 26). EAR-RINGS.

COL'LEGE (2 K. xxii. 14; and *second* in Zeph. i. 10). Where Huldah the prophetess lived "in the lower (or *second*) part of the city" (Neh. xi. 9).

COL'LOPS OF FAT (Job xv. 27). Slices of fat.

COL'ONY. Philippi, in Macedonia, is so called (Acts xvi. 12). A body of citizens sent out to found a new state for themselves, under the same laws and rights.

COL'ORS. There are about twenty different words, meaning color, in the O. T.; but only white, black, red, yellow or green are distinctly named. In the N. T. there are seven words meaning color. 1. *Leben*, white (Lebanon, white mts). Milk is leben, and so is manna, snow, horses, clothing, the moon, the pale face, and white hair. It was the symbol of joy, of innocence, purity; the clothing of angels, saints, and of Jesus.—2. *Shahor*, black: as hair, complexion of the sick, horses, mourners' robes, clouded sky, night, turbid brook; and as opposed to white, the symbol of evil.—3. *Adom*, red

ASSYRIAN GALLEY.

(Adam). Blood, pottage of lentiles, a horse, wine, complexion, leprous spot, a grape-vine; and the symbol of bloodshed.—4. *Argaman*, purple. Made at Tyre, from a shell-fish. The color was only a drop in the throat of each animal. It was purple, violet, or blue, according to the fixing. Some say the violet (or blue) was had from a different shell-fish, and called—5. *Tekeleth*, blue. The deep blue of the sky, violet, and sometimes as black; the ribands and fringes of the Hebrew dress (Num. xv. 38), tapestries of Persia (robes of perfection in Ez. xxiii. 12).—6. *Shani,* shine (as scarlet); *tolaath,* worm scarlet (our word vermillon means *worm* color). Lips, in Cant. iv. 3, fire; scarlet robes were luxuries, and appropriate for a warrior's cloak (Na. ii. 3). The vermillion of the ancients was like our Venitian-red—dull red—such as is seen on the monuments, where it has preserved its tint for many ages.

chief word), with many definitions, in alphabetical order, with a reference to the place where each may be found. They are useful for comparing passages bearing on the same subject, which may explain each other, and for finding the place where any particular text or subject is located. So, in a few minutes, all the texts on the subject of the Lord's Supper may be found and read. The first work of the kind was made by Antony of Padua (born A. D. 1195, died 1231). Cruden's is the best now in use.

TABLE OF THE SHEW BREAD. (From the Arch of Titus, Rome.)

COLOS'SE, COLOSSÆ. On the Lycus, a branch of the Mæander, in Phrygia, near Laodicea (Col. ii. 1; iv. 13). Pliny (Nat. Hist. v. 41) describes it as a celebrated city in Paul's time. Paul founded a church here, on his third tour. The ruins of the ancient city are near the modern village of Chonas.

COM'FORTER. A name given to the Holy Spirit (2 Sam. x. 3).

COM'MERCE (trade, Heb. REKEL, traffic). The first record of bargain and sale is of Abraham's purchase of the burial-place for Sarah of Ephron, at Hebron, for 400 shekels weight (as sovereigns are weighed at the Bank of England) of silver. Job throws much light on the commerce, manufactures and science of his age. He mentions gold, iron, brass (copper or bronze), lead, crystal, jewels, weaving, merchants, gold from Ophir, topazes from Ethiopia, building of swift ships, writing in books, engraving on plates of metal and stone, and fine seal or gem engraving; fishing with hooks, nets, spears; harp, organ, and names of stars. The history of Sidon and Tyre is a record of commercial affairs; and that of the building of King Solomon's Temple is also. Foreigners were the principal traders before the Captivity, but after that, and especially after the destruction of Jerusalem by Titus, the Jews have been an entire people of traffic.

COM'PEL (Mark xv. 21). To press into service.

CONANI'AH (*whom Jehovah hath sent*). Chief of the Levites in time of Josiah (2 Chr. xxxv. 9).

CON'CIS'ION (*cutting off*). A term of contempt for outward circumcision (Phil. iii. 2).

CON-CŎR'DANCE. A book which gives the names of persons, places and things (and ideas by their

CON'-CU-BINE. A wife of second rank, where more than one wife was allowed. Her condition was assured and provided for by Moses. She was either 1. A Hebrew girl bought; 2. A captive taken in war from the Gentiles; 3. A foreign slave bought; 4. Or a Canaanite woman, bond or free. She could not be sold, but might be sent away free.

CON'DUIT (French, aqueduct), (2 K. xviii. 17). The largest mentioned is from Solomon's Pool to the Temple site.

CŌ'NEY (Heb. SHAPHAN, *rabbit*). The Syrian Hyrax. Its habits are very much like the rabbit, only it is a little larger. Its teeth and hoofs (instead of claws on each toe), are like those of the rhinoceros (Lev. xi. 5; Deut. xiv. 7; Ps. civ. 18; Prov. xxx. 26).

CONFEC'TION (*a compound*), (Ex. xxx. 35).

CON-GRE-GĀ'-TION (*edah*). The Hebrew people collected as a holy community, held by religious bonds (for political ends). Circumcision and full age (20), were the requisites for membership, which might be forfeited for certain faults (Deut. xxiii. 1–8). During the Exodus the whole nation could gather from their tents, but when they occupied the country on both sides of Jordan, it became a necessity to appoint representatives, who are called, in Num. i. 16, persons "wont to be called to the Congregation"; and, in xvi. 2, they are styled "chiefs of the Congregation, who are called to the Convention"; and, in Ex. xxxviii. 25, their name is, "those deputed to the assembly" (numbered in A. V.). Besides these, the heads of families (patriarchs—sheikhs now), and a fourth class, the judges of cities, magistrates (cadi, now). They met at the door of the tabernacle, or in some other noted places, as Shechem by Joshua; Mizpeh by the Levite (Judg. xx. i.); Gilgal by Samuel. In the Exodus the sound of the trumpet called the assembly together (Num. x. 2-4), but in Canaan messengers were used of necessity. It did not have legislative powers, for the law of Moses was supreme, but *by-laws* could be made. They could not lay taxes. The divine law was submitted to the assembly for acceptance or rejection (Ex. xix. 3-9, xxiv. 3). Chiefs were confirmed in their office (or rejected) by this body (Num. xxvii. 19; 1 Sam. xi. 15, 2 Sam. v. etc.). The assembly could arrest the execution of the king's sentence, as Jonathan was "rescued" (2 Sam. xiv. 44, 45), by the action of the *Edah.* Peace and war with foreign powers were considered in it (Josh. ix. 15, 18). It was the high court of appeal, and had control of death-penalties. After Jeroboam's usurpation, it was called the C. of Jerusalem (2 Chr. xxx. 2), or of Judah (v. 25). It finally was reduced to the 72 members of the Sanhedrin.

money, in quantities, is often found buried, dated many centuries back. See MONEY.

CORAL (*lofty*). Coral is mentioned only twice in Scripture (Job xxviii. 18; Ez. xxvii. 16). It often occurs in ancient Egyptian jewelry. The coral which is described as being brought from Syria was probably that of the Red Sea where coral abounds.

CORBAN (*a sacred gift*). A present devoted to God or to his temple (Matt. xxiii. 18). The Jews were reproved by Christ for cruelty to their parents in making a *corban* of what should have been theirs (Mark ii. 7).

CORIANDER. An aromatic plant found in Egypt, Persia and India, mentioned twice in Scripture (Ex. xvi. 31; Num. xi. 7).

CORD. The word cord means line, band, rope thread, string, etc. It is made of various mate. rials according to its uses. Strips of camel hide are still used by the Bedawins. The finer sorts were made of flax (Is. xix. 9); others of the fibre of the date palm, and of reeds and rushes. The tent

RIVER EUPHRATES.

CONI'AH. JEHOIACHIN (Jer. xxii. 24).

CONONI'AH. A Levite; ruler of the offerings in Hezekiah's time (2 Chr. xxxi. 12, 13).

CONSCIENCE. Internal knowledge; moral faculty which judges between right and wrong (John viii. 9.)

CONVER-SA'-TION. The whole tenor of one's life, acts, and thoughts.

COOKING. MEALS.

CON-VO-CA'TION. The religious gathering on the Sabbath and the great feast-days.

COOS. COS. Island at the E. entrance to the Archipelago, and between Miletus and Rhodes, and the peninsulas on which are Halicarnassus and Cnidus (Acts xxi. 1) 21 ms. long, N. E. to S. W., and 6 ms. wide. Was an important island in Jewish history from early times (1 Macc. xv. 23; Jos. Ant. xiv. 7 § 2). Stanchio.

COPPER. (Heb. NEHOSHETH). Copper was and is now used more extensively in the East than any other metal. There is no certain mention of iron in the Scriptures, and all kinds of instruments, weapons and tools must have been made of copper or bronze, which is a mixture of copper and tin. Wherever brass, iron and steel are mentioned copper was the metal meant in the original. Copper

being an image of the human body, the cords which held it represented the principle of life (Job iv. 21). For leading or binding animals (Ps. xviii. 27). For bow-strings made of catgut (Ps. xi. 2). A line of inheritance (Josh. xvii. 14; xix. 9).

CORINTH'. On the isthmus that joins Peloponnesus to Greece. The rock, Acrocorinthos, south of the city, stood 2,000 feet above the sea, on the broad top of which there was once a town. The Acropolis of Athens can be seen from it, 45 miles (Liv. xlv. 28). It has two harbors: CENCHRÆA (now Kenkries), on the Saronic gulf, 7½ ms. distant, east; and LECHÆUM, on the Gulph of Lepanto, 1½ ms. west (Strabo viii. 6). Corinth was the natural capital of Greece, and was the commercial centre. Eminent for painting, sculpture, and works in metal and pottery. Famous for a temple to Venus of great wealth and splendor, the most ancient in Greece. Was the military centre during the Achaian league. Destroyed by the Romans, B. C. 146, and after 100 years of desolation the new city visited by Paul was built by Julius Cæsar, and peopled with freedmen from Rome (Pausanias—Strabo). Paul lived here eighteen months, and became acquainted with Aquila and Priscilla. The Posidonium, the sanctuary of Neptune was the scene of the Isthmian games, which were celebrated, every other year, and gave Paul some of his most striking imagery. It was N. E. of the city, near the harbor of Schœnas, now Kalamaki, on the Saronic gulf (1 Cor. ix. 24, 26). The foot-races were run in the stadium; the boxing held in the theatre; and the victor's wreaths were made from the pines that grew near.

CRANE.

CORINTH'IANS. The people of Corinth. For Paul's epistles to, see PAUL.

COR'-MO-RANT. The cormorant (Heb. SHALAK, Lev. xi. 17; Deut. xiv. 17); and Pelican (Heb. KAATH, Ps. cii. 6). Common in Syria, among the rocks on the coasts.

CORN. A term for all kinds of grain. The grains and loaves of Indian corn (maize), were found under the head of an Egyptian mummy, and it is supposed to be mentioned by Homer and Theophrastus. The offering in Lev. ii. 14, was of green corn, roasted, which was eaten with oil, etc. (ver. 15). The "seven ears of corn" on one stalk is possible, and has been noticed (N. Y. *Evening Post*, Aug. 26, 1863) lately in this country and is in accord with the proper character of maize, but not of wheat, and we may so understand the dream interpreted by Joseph.

COR-NE'LIUS. A Roman centurion, commander of 100 (Acts x. 1). He seems to have worshiped the true God before his conversion (x. 2), and not the pagan deities. He was the first Gentile convert, and was received by Peter.

CORNER. The Levitical law gave a portion of the field called a "corner" to the poor, and the right to carry off what was left, also the gleanings of the trees and the vines (Lev. xix. 9). See also RUTH, GLEANING.

COR'NER STONE. A stone of size and importance in the corner of a building, uniting two walls. This is laid with ceremonies in large buildings. Christ is the corner stone of our salvation (Eph. ii. 20; 1 Pet. ii. 6; Matt. xxi. 42).

CORNET. MUSICAL INSTRUMENTS.

CORRUP'TION, MOUNT OF (2 K. iii. 13.) MT. OF OLIVES.

CO'SAM (*a diviner*). Son of Elmodam, in the line of Joseph (Luke iii. 28).

COTES. Enclosures for sheep (2 Chr. xxxii. 28).

COTTAGE (*house*), (Is xxiv. 20). A tent or shelter made of boughs.

COTTON (Heb. KAR-PAS; Sans., *karpasam;* Arabic, *karfas*); mentioned in Esther i. 6, as *green* hangings. "Hanging curtains of calico, in stripes, and padded, are used, in India, as a substitute for doors." In the king of Delhi's palace there is a roof supported by beautiful pillars, between which hangs striped and padded curtains, easily rolled up or removed. Some of the passages where *fine linen* is said, in our version, *cotton* was probably the article meant in the original.

COUL'TER (1 Sam. xiii. 20, 21). "Plowshare."

COUN'CIL. An assembly of people, rulers, priests or apostles. See SANHEDRIN.

COURT (Heb. CHATSER). An inclosed space, or yard, belonging to a house.

COU'THA. A servant of the temple (1 Esd. v. 32).

COV'ENANT (Heb. BERITH). Contracts between men, and between God and men. Various rites were used: joining hands (Ez. xvii. 18); by an oath (Gen. xxi. 31); by a heap of stones; (ib. xxxi. 46); by a feast (ib. xxvi. 30); by sacrificing victims, dividing the parts, and both parties to the covenant walking between the parts of the sacrifice (xv. 8–17); and, more common and above all others, eating salt (Num. xviii. 19; Lev. ii. 13).

The covenants between God and men were also ratified by signs. By the sacrifice, when a symbol of deity, a smoking furnace and a burning lamp, passed between the parts (Gen. xv. 17); by the 12 loaves on the table of shew-bread (Lev. xxiv. 6–8); and the crucifixion of the Christ (Heb. ix. 15, xiii. 20; Is. lv. 3).

COZ (*thorn*). A man of Judah, also a Levite. (1 Chr. iv. 8, xxiv. 10).

COZBI, (*false*). A Midianite woman, daughter of Zur (Num. xxv. 15, 18).

CRACK'NELS. Hard, brittle cakes (1 K. xiv. 3).

CRAFTS'MAN. A mechanic (Deut. xxvii. 15). CHARASHIM.

CRANE (Heb. AGUR). Is a wader, migratory, utters a twittering cry, and goes in vast flocks (Is. xxxviii. 14; Jer. viii. 7).

CRE-A-TION. The origin of all things, material and living, in the world, and this heavens around it (Gen. i; Ps. cxlviii. 5). When rightly understood God's works and His Word are in harmony. The Mosaic account in Genesis opens with a notice of the work of God in the original creation of the world and the heavens, in the vastly remote past, and passes at once to the final preparation of the earth for man's occupation, which has extended through six (geological) periods of unknown extent, which are called days. It is supposed by the geologist that the first formations were rocks, either in water by deposit, or both water and fire. There are traces of living things in the rocks, called *fossils*, and they are without eyes; perhaps because there was no light—for light was made after the heavier materials. Both vegetables and animals appear at the same time. These oldest rocks are called the CAMBRIAN, and are 5 miles thick.

The next in the series is the SILURIAN, of sediment, whose thickness is 6 miles. Fossils are very numerous, and of low types, having no animal with vertebræ (back-bone), except a few fishes on the very top. Vegetation first appears in this place. There was light, and there were *eyes* in the living things. The firmament (expanse) divided the waters above (clouds) from the waters below (the ocean).

The third in the series is the OLD RED SAND-STONE, which marks the time when the great mountain ranges of the world were lifted into their present position. Sedimentary, and two miles thick, and having fossils of animals found in the other two, and of vertebrates. Dry land appeared, grass, herbs and trees. No land animals.

The fourth was the CARBONIFEROUS (coal bearing), in which we find coal, minerals, limestone. Coal is made of wood, and the fossil wood found in the coal series does not show the *rings* which we now find in all wood as marks of the yearly growth, which is evidence of dense fogs and very pale light. The lifting of the fogs towards the end of this period, letting the sunshine on the earth, is described by Moses as the events of the fourth day. The fossil remains in these rocks are the same at the equator and everywhere, indicating a uniform heat all over the earth. Animal life on land is first seen: insects, such as beetles, scorpions, and reptiles—such as frogs.

The fifth series was the PERMIAN, which has remains of a higher order of vegetation and of animals, such as the *saurians* (lizards), and birds, whose fossils are in the NEW RED SANDSTONE of this series.

The TRIAS and OOLITE show fossils of more advanced orders, both vegetable and animal. Palm, pine, cypress, insects, and three kinds of lizards, called by Moses "the moving creature that hath life"—a better translation of the original being "the reptile that hath the breath of life"—and also great sea monsters (called *whales* in Genesis). The fossils of these animals exist in such amazing numbers as to give the name *age of reptiles* to this day, which was the fifth in the account of Moses.

ARK.

The next was the CHALK, which has but few remains, while the Tertiary, which followed, is full of mammals, such as cattle, beasts and creeping things, which mark the progress of the sixth day, which ended on the creation of man.

There are no fossil remains of man among all the vast number of living things in all the series. And there are no animals now living on the earth whose origin cannot be traced in the fossil remains

of similar races living on the earth before man was placed here.

The discovery of flint implements (hatchets, spears, arrow-heads and wedges) in the gravel quarries of Abbeville and Amiens, France, does not carry back the history of man into the age of the extinct species of elephant, whose bones were found in the same deposit, because no human bones were found there.

The truth of the Mosaic account is thus peculiarly shown in the records of the rocks.

The account is true as it would appear if shown to a man in a vision, every item agreeing with the optical appearances.

CART.

It may be that there was a race of men living on the earth before the birth of Adam ; and if so, the passages which seem to imply other races besides Adam's would have an explanation. The several species of men, with their distinct languages, indicate more than one origin.

The most skeptical scientist of the present day admits that the breath of life was breathed into at least one original form—if not three or four—and that is the whole question. God did create a living being, or several; and since the most careful examination shows that species and groups of animals were from the first—in the oldest rocks, and in all of them—distinct, as distinct as they are now, and so may have been created each by itself, "after its own kind." The history of the past is proved true by the discoveries of the present. However short the account, the *order* of the events is correct, according to science.

CRES'CENS (*growing*), (2 Tim. iv. 10). One of the seventy disciples. An assistant of Paul.

CRÊTE. CANDIA. S. of the Archipelago; 160 ms. long from E. to W., and 6 to 35 ms. wide. Homer says it had 100 cities (Iliad ii. 649; Virgil, Æ. iii. 106). Minos, the great legislator, was a native. Very mountainous, but full of fruitful valleys. There was a very early connection with the Jews (1 Sam. xxx. 14; 2 Sam. viii. 18; Ez. xxv. 16; Zeph. ii. 5; 1 Macc. x. 67, xv. 23; Jos. Ant. xvii. 12, § 1). Cretans were at the feast of Pentecost at Jerusalem (Acts ii. 11). Visited by Paul (see Life).

CRETES (Acts iii. 11). CRE'TANS (Tit. i. 12). People of Crete.

CRIB (Job xxxix. 9), (*to fodder*). Feeding-box for animals, made of small stones and mortar, or cut from a single stone.

CRISP'ING-PINS (Is. iii. 22).

CRIS'PUS (*curled?*). Ruler of the Jewish synagogue (Acts xviii. 8).

CROC'ODILE (Heb. LEVIATHAN). The Jewish translations of Job xli. gives crocodile for leviathan, and the description is very poetical as well as true. Herodotus says the Egyptians paid divine honors to this reptile, keeping a tame one, whose ears were hung with rings and fore-paws circled with bracelets; and when he died they embalmed his body. The worship began in the fear of man for the most terrible animal in the river Nile.

CROSS. An upright stake, with one or more cross-pieces, on which persons were suspended for punishment. It was an emblem of pain, guilt and ignominy, but has been adopted by Christians as the most glorious badge of a servant and follower of the Christ, who was crucified on it. Constantine was the first emperor who adopted it as an ensign, whose coins bear its form, with monograms of Christ or of Constantine. The image was added to the cross, forming the crucifix, in the 6th century. The term *cross* was used for self-denial by Jesus and others (Matt. xvi. 24). See cut, p. 40.

CROWNS.

CROWN. Originally the band or ribbon about the head or hair of a king or a priest. The ornamented cap differed in style in every country, as is shown on the sculptures and coins. A wreath of leaves crowned the winners in the Grecian games. The final inheritance of the saints is figured as *a crown of righteousness* (2 Tim. iv. 8). The figures are of crowns from Egypt: 1. Upper E.; 2. Lower E.; 3. Upper and Lower united; 4. Assyria; 5. Assyria (Sardanapalus 3d); 6. Assyrian (Sennacherib); 7. Tigranes (Syria); 8. At Persepolis; 9. Crown of leaves, Roman coin of Galba. The Roman soldiers crowned Jesus with a wreath of thorn twigs, made from what is now called Christ's thorn (*zizyphus*), and by the Arabs *nubk*, the jujube tree. It is very abundant, and forms dense thorny hedges (growing or laid in rows two or three feet high), through which no large animal can pass.

CRUCIFIX'ION. Putting a person to death on a cross was a very common practice in ancient days, as hanging is now. Jesus was condemned to the cross by the Sanhedrin for blasphemy, and by Pilate for sedition against Cæsar. The scarlet robe, crown of thorns, and other insults were the inventions of those engaged in the execution, and were peculiar to his case. Whipping was a part of the punishment, but in the case of Jesus was not the legal act, being applied before sentence. The sufferer was to carry his cross, or a part of it. The clothes were perquisites to the guards. A cup of stupefying liquor was often given in mercy, just before the hands and feet were nailed. The body was often left to waste away naturally on the cross, or be eaten by birds and beasts, by the Ro-

mans, but they allowed the Jews to bury then dead on account of the law of Moses (Deut. xxi. 22, 23). Constantine abolished crucifixion.

CRUSE (Heb. TSAPPAHATH, *a flask*). A small vessel for holding water and other liquids (1 Sam. xxvi. 11, 12, 16), still used in the East.

GATE AT SIDON.

CRYS'TAL. Three Hebrew words, 1. ZEKUKITH, 2. GABISH, and 3. KERACH, are translated crystal. 1. is, no doubt, the word for glass; 2. means (like) clear ice; and 3. means ice or frost. "Clear as crystal," is a figure in Ez. i. 22; Rev. iv. 6; xxi. 11, etc.

CUCK'OO (Heb. SHACHAPH), (Lev. xi.; Deut. xiv.). The Arabs think its note sounds like *yakoob*, and so call it Jacob's bird. It migrates, and winters in Palestine. Tristram suggests the shore petrel as the bird of the Hebrew text.

CU'-CUM-BER (Heb. KISHUIM, heavy, hard to digest). Grown only in the fertile land which is overflowed by the Nile, and is esteemed the coolest and most pleasant fruit in the East (Is. i. 8).

CUM'BER. Overload, harass (Luke x. 40)

CUM'BRANCE. Burden (Deut. i. 12).

CUM'MIN (Heb. KAMMON). An umbelliferous plant (fennel), bearing aromatic seeds, like anise, coriander, dill and caraway. Used as a styptic after circumcision. Cultivated for export (Is. xxviii. 25; Matt. xxiii. 23).

CUN'NING. Skilful, expert as a workman (Gen. xxv. 27).

CUP OF THE PTOLEMIES.

CUP (Heb. 1. COS, 2. KESAOTH, 3. GEBIA; Greek, *poterion*). The designs were imitated from those of Egypt and Assyria, Phœnicia, etc., as shown by the Scriptures and specimens from antiquity. They were of metal, earthenware, wood, etc. The "sea" or "laver" of Solomon's temple was called a cup, and was of brass (bronze?), and highly ornamented with sculptured lilies.

EGYPTIAN CUPS.

Nos. 1, 2, 3. From paintings at Thebes, Egypt. 4. Porcelain. 5. Green earthenware. 6. Coarse pottery. 7. Wood. 8. Arragonite. 9. Earthen. Bronze cups (and other vessels) are often found in the ancient tombs. A kind of stone was wrought into jugs and bottles, vases and cups at Alabastron, in Upper Egypt, now called *alabaster*. Matt. xxvi. 7, should read alabaster *vase*, not *box*. The "Cup of the Ptolemies" is a work of the time of Nero, 5 inches high, of a single sardonyx, set in a base. See SIDON and ALABASTER.

ASSYRIAN CUPS.

1. Lion head, Khorsabad. 2. Lion-head with handle. 3. From Khorsabad, all of bronze. 4. Red pottery, Nimroud. 5. Painted cup, Karamles. 6, 7. Bronze, Nimroud. The workmanship is excellent, and they are often ornamented with jewels, and embossed with sculptures of animals, or groups of men and animals. Cups of brass and silver are now in use all over the East; generally decorated with some sentence in Arabic of a mystical sense. See BOTTLES and BOWLS.

The office of CUP-BEARER is of great antiquity, being mentioned at the courts of the Pharaoh, the Assyrian, Persian, and Jewish kings. RAB-SHAKEH of 2 K. xviii. 17, should read *chief cup-bearer*, as in Luther's bible, (*der Erzschenke*). The cup is used as a figure: of a man's lot (Ps. xi. 6, etc.); of a nation's great riches (Jer. li. 7); as a contrast in "cup of God," true worship, and "cup of devils" idolatry (Ps. lxxv. 8; Is. li. 17, 22); signifying afflictions (Matt. xx. 22, xxvi. 39); of salvation (Ps. cxvi. 13), and of blessing (Luke xxii. 17; 1 Cor. x. 16).

CUR'TAIN (Heb. TERIAH). Made of linen goats' hair, silk, and cotton; used for beds, partitions in tents, and for doors in houses. Heaven compared to a curtain (Ps. civ. 2; Is. xl. 22). The curtains of the tabernacle were embroidered with many colors, in figures on fine linen. Curtains of Solomon (Cant. i. 5).

CUSH. Son of Ham (Gen. x. 6). Country in Africa. Ethiopia (Ez. xxxix. 10; 2 Chr. xii. 3). Tirhakah, king of C. (Is. xxxvii. 9). Modern name Kesh. Geez. People were black (Jer. xiii. 23).

CUSH'ITE. "Ethiopian" (Num. xii. 1).

CUTH'AH. CUTH. In Asia. Shalmaneser transplanted people from here to Samaria during the Jews' captivity (2 K. xvii. 24, 30). Mixing with the Jews of the 10 tribes they became the Samaritans, and were called Cuthæans (Jos. Ant. ix. 14, § 3, xl. 8, § 6, xii. 5, § 5). Between Tigris and Euphrates rivers.

CUT'TINGS IN THE FLESH. Mutilations of the body, practised by the Heathens in mourning for the dead (Jer. xvi. 6, 7. xli. 5); prohibited to the Jews (Lev. xix. 28).

CY'A-MON (*beans*). *Tell Kaimon* on the E. slope of Mt. Carmel (Judith, vii. 3; Chelmon in *Doway* V). Burial place of Jair.

CYM'BAL and CYM'BALS. MUSICAL INSTRUMENTS.

CY'PRUS. Island off the coast of Phœnicia and Cilicia, 148 miles long, 40 wide, and irregular; (see map). The highest mountain is Olympus, 7000 feet. Gold, silver, and copper are mined. Its cities were, Salamis, Citium (now Larneka), and Paphos (now Baffa), and many others. Alexander got 120 ships there for his siege of Tyre. It was the birth-place of Barnabas (Acts iv. 36), and was visited by Barnabas and Paul (Acts xiii). The Pagans worshiped Astarte (Venus), in a licentious manner. Barnabas and Mark (Acts xv) Cyprians, the people, in 2 Macc. iv. 29.

CY'RENE. Lybia, Africa. Founded B.C. 632, by Greeks. Built on a table-land 1800 ft. above the sea, in a region of great beauty and fertility, 500 ms. W. of Alexandria. The Pentapolis of Cyrenaica were Cyrene, Apollonia, Ptolemais, Arsinoe, and Berenice (Strabo, xvii.). After Alexander the Great's death Jews were settled there with many privileges. In the time of Christ the Cyreneans had a synagogue in Jerusalem (Acts vi. 9; Philo). Simon, who bore the cross, was from C. (Matt. xxviii., etc.). Lucius of C. was with Paul and Barnabas (xiii. 1). Lucius and Mark are named as bishops of the church at C. Arabic name *Ghrenna*.

CYRE'NIUS (Latin). Publius Sulpicus Quirinus was governor of Syria twice: before A. D. 1 (B. C. 4); and again, the second time, A. D. 6. Died A. D. 21 (Luke ii. 2).

CY'RUS. The Persian name for the sun (Heb. KORESH), and the same as the Egyptian name *Phrah*. Thus, Cyrus is a title for the king, as Pharaoh, Augustus, etc. The Bible mentions only the one who conquered Babylon, unless the Cyrus, the Persian, of Daniel, was the uncle of Cyrus, who issued the decree permitting the return of the captive Jews to Judæa. It is impossible to separate the history of Cyrus from the fables connected with it, and now more than when Herodotus found the same difficulty, only a century after the events. The work of a resident historian. Ctesias, in the court of Persia, about fifty years later than Herodotus, has been lost, except a few extracts by Photius, and that of Xenophon, are both historical romances.

That he became supreme king of Persia, and conquered Babylon, is undoubted. The turning of the course of the river Euphrates and capture of Babylon during a great feast, are also facts.

Daniel's Darius, the Mede, is the Astyages of history, and was a viceroy of the Cyrus who first ruled over Babylon.

It is supposed that the Persian religion, which is almost purely a monotheism, prepared Cyrus to sympathize with the Jews, and that Daniel's explanation of the prophesies, that he had been helping to fulfil, unknown to himself, concluded him to issue the decree for the Jews' return to their native land and temple.

A tomb of Cyrus is shown at Parsargadæ near Persepolis.

D

DAB'AREH (Josh. xxi. 28). DABERATH.

DAB'BA-SHETH (*hump* of a camel). Town on a hill. ZEBULON.

DAB'ERATH. Is. Lev. (Josh. xxi. 28). Now Deburieh, W. of Mt. Tabor. Beautifully situated on a rocky platform, with Tabor behind and the broad plain of Esdrælon in front. Boundary of Zebulon (Josh. xix. 12).

DAB'RIA. One of 5 scribes employed by Esdras (2 Esd. xiv. 24).

DACO'BI (1 Esd. v. 28). AKKUB.

DAD DEUS. SADDEUS (1 Esd. viii. 45). IDDO.

DAGON.—FROM A GEM.

DA'GON (Heb. DAG, *little fish, dear*). The type of the god of the Philistines. His temples were at Gaza and Ashdod (Judg. xvi. 21: 1 Sam. v. 5). Traces of the worship are left in the names Cephar-dagon and Beth-dagon. Sanconiatho says the name is derived from dagon, grain, and it was the god of agriculture: but this origin does not agree so well with the *idea*, which was *to multiply, increase*, as fish do by millions. This god was known in Assyria, and is sculptured there, as shown in the large cut. Miss Fanny Corbeaux ("*The Re-*

a woman's face, and fishbody. Atergatis, Argatis, Arathis, and Argata, are different forms of Derceto.

DAGON, THE FISH GOD.

DAI'SAN (1 Esd. v. 31). Error for REZIN.

DALA'IAH (*Jehovah delivers*). Son of Elioenai, of Judah (1 Chr. iii. 24).

DALE (Gen. xiv. 17): valley.

DALMANU'-THA. On the shore of the Sea of Galilee; visited by Jesus (Mark, viii. 10). Near Magdala. Possibly it is the same as Zalmon, near Tiberias, now called Ain el Barideh (*the cold fountain*), where are fine fountains and the ruins of a city (Rob. ii. 396).

DALMA'TIA. Illyricum. On the E. shore of the Adriatic Sea, N. W. of Greece. Visited by Paul (Rom. xv. 19), and Titus (2 Tim. iv. 10) during Paul's imprisonment in Rome.

DAL'PHON. Son of HAMAN (Esth. ix. 7).

DA'MA. Capital of the Ledja. See TRACHONITIS.

DAMASCUS.

phaim") shows that the Chaldean Oannes, the Philistine Dagon, and Egyptian On, are identical. DERCETO was the female (as Dagon was the male), and was worshiped at Ashkelon. She had

DAM'ARIS (*heifer*). A disciple in Athens (Acts xvii. 34), and (perhaps) the wife of Dionysius the Areopagite. Correctly, DAMALIS.

DAMAS'CUS. On the E. of Anti-Lebanon, 2,200

feet above the sea, in a fertile plain near the desert. The oldest city known to history. It is cut through by the Barada river, which divides into many branches, and together with the Helbon on the N. and the Awaj on the S., fertilizes a region 30 ms. in extent, which being favored by the finest climate, produces almost every valuable product of forest, field and garden. First mentioned in Gen. xiv. 15 and in Gen. xv. 2, as the city of Abraham's steward. For 800 yrs., from Abraham to David, the Scriptures are silent on Damascus. David put a garrison in D. (1 K. xi. 23; 2 Sam. viii. 6; Jos. Ant. vii. 5, § 2). During Asa's reign Benhadad pillaged cities in Naphtali (1 K. xv. 19, 20). After this it is mentioned many times. Naaman, the leper, who was cured by Elisha the prophet, was of D. (2 K. v. 1). The Assyrian king, Tiglath Pilē'ser, took the city and carried captive the people to Kir (2 K. xvi. 7–9). Isaiah's prophesy (xvii. 3; Amos i. 4, 5). Jeremiah described it, B. C. 600: "D. is waxed feeble, and turneth herself to flee, and fear hath seized on her" (xlix. 24). At the time of the Apostle Paul the city was under Roman rule, and Aretas, the Arabian, king (2 Cor. xi. 22; Jos. Ant. xvi. 11, § 9). Has now 150,000 people: Christians 15,000; Jews, 6,000

The fine fabrics of D. were celebrated as early as 800 B. C. (Amos iii. 12). The damask silk and sword-blades are still famous. Certain localities are pointed out as having a historical connection with Paul's time. The "street called straight" is now the street of Bazaars; there is a "house of Judas;" the house of Ananias; the scene of the conversion, which is an open green spot surrounded with trees, now used as a Christian burial-ground; the place where Paul was let down by the wall in a basket; and also several spots connected with the history of the prophet Elisha. The old city stands on the S. bank of the principal river, surrounded by a ruinous wall of ancient Roman foundations, and a patchwork of all the succeeding ages. The city is splendid, when viewed at a distance, but the houses are rudely built; the narrow streets, paved with big rough stones, or not at all, partly roofed across with mats, or withered branches: the bazaars are covered ways with a few stalls on both sides, each trade having its own quarter. Although rough and rude on the street, yet the interior of the private houses is neat, paved, with fountain and fruit-trees, with grateful shade, and the rooms opening from the court decorated with carving, gilding, and all that wealth and taste can provide. Modern name Esh Shaum.

DAMASCENES. Inhabitants of Damascus (2 Cor. xi. 32).

DAMNATION (*condemnation*), (Mark xvi. 16).

DA'MON. Near Shefa Amer. E. of Acre.

DAN (*judge*). Fifth son of Jacob. First son of Bilhah, Rachel's maid (Gen. xxx. 6.) One of the twelve tribes. The last to receive its portion, and the least portion, but among the most fertile in the land.—2. The city originally called Laish. Leshem (Josh. xix. 47). They were idolaters from the beginning (Gen. xiv. 14; Deut. xxxiv. 1; Judg. xviii). The worship was continued by Jeroboam (1 K. xii. 29, 30; Amos viii. 14). "From Dan to Beersheba," was the common form of speaking of the extent of Palestine (Judg. xx. 1; 1 Sam. iii. 20, etc.). Tell el Kadi (*judge's mound*) is the modern name, and is a long, steep hill, covered with ruins, from the base of which flows one of the largest fountains in the world (Rob. 396).

DANCE (Heb. machol), to move or leap in a circle, twist or turn around, as the dancing Dervishes now do in the East. The sacred song and dance always go together (Ex. xv. 20); words, and music and motion, aiding each other in expressing the joy or sorrow of the soul (Judg. xi. 34; Eccl. iii. 4). The Romans also danced in their worship; so, also, the Egyptians.

In the modern Oriental dance a woman leads off, and goes through a number of graceful and artistic attitudes, and then all the others of the party follow her in every motion. The two companies of dancers are called by an error *armies* in Cant. vi. 13.

DAN'IEL (*God's Judge*). 1. David's son (1 Chr. iii. 1).—2. A Levite (Ezra viii. 2).—3. A celebrated prophet in the Chaldean and Persian period, and a (princely) descendant of Judah. He was taken with other captives (Ananiah, Mishael, and Azariah) to Babylon, B. C. 607, at the age of 12 to 16, educated thoroughly and made a cupbearer at the court, when he was given a new name Belshatzar (*favorite of Bel*). He kept the Jewish law of clean and unclean meat (Dan. i. 8, 16), and was constant and faithful in his devotions to God. After three years service he interpreted a dream (v. 17) on the occasion of the king's decree against the magi, and for this service was made "ruler" and "chief governor" over the province and magistrates of Babylon. He interpreted Nebuchadnezzar's second dream, and the handwriting on the wall, thus introducing the knowledge of the true God, and alluding to the profane use (and consequent insult to God) of the holy vessels of the temple, as one of the crowning sins of the king and his people, which were the means of ending the nation's life, by the conquest of the Medes and Persians (v. 10, 28), while he lived at Susa, and after he had been removed from office, when he was again placed in one of the highest offices of trust and honor. During an interval in which no event in Daniel's life is recorded, his three companions were delivered from a fiery furnace.

Darius made him first of the three presidents of the empire. Having exercised the rites of his religious faith, contrary to law, he was thrown to the lions, but was delivered alive (vi. 10, 23). He was in favor with the king in the third year of Cyrus, and saw his last vision on the banks of the Tigris (B. C. 534), when the prophesy of the 70 weeks was delivered to him (ch. ix.). He died at the age of over 90, at Susa, where there was a monument to his memory in the 12th century, described by Benjamin of Tudela.

DANJĀ'AN (Ps. ii. 26). Laish.

DAN'NAH. Town in Judah (Josh. xv. 49), S. W. of Hebron. Lost.

DANCE OF PRIESTS—EGYPTIAN.

DAPH'NE. A grove and sanctuary sacred to Apollo, 5 miles S. W. of Antioch, Syria, founded by Seleucus Nicator. See Antioch. The right of asylum—where criminals could shelter themselves from justice, because it was thought to be sacrilege to take any one away by force—was an honor attached to this place (2 Macc. iv. 33). The sacred right was often violated, especially when a good man sought safety from the wicked, as in the case of Onias. Now called *Beit el Maa—house of water* (Jos. Wars, i. 12, § 5).

DĀ'RA. Darda. Son of Mahol; a wise man, in

Solomon's age (1 K. iv. 31). Son of Zerach (1 Chr. ii. 6). Sirach or Esrachite?

DÄR′IC. Gold coin of Persia, current in Palestine after the captivity (Ezr. ii. 69; viii. 27; Neh. vii. 70, etc.). The darics that have been found among the ruins are thick pieces of pure gold, stamped, as in the engraving. The gold pieces found at Sardis are of older date, and were made by Crœsus.

DARIC.

The name daric may be derived from "DARA," the Persian name for king, or from "Darius, the king." Plutarch mentions silver darics. See MONEY.

DA-RĪUS (in Heb. DARJAVESH). The Assyrian title lord-king—Dara, *lord;* shah, *king.* 1. The first mentioned is DARIUS, THE MEDE (Dan. v. 31, etc.), called also Cyáx′ares (B. C. 538). The gold coin was named Daric—that is, king's money.—2. DARIUS, SON OF HYS-TAS-PES (*Vashtaspa*), made king B. C. 521. He conquered Babylon, Scythia, Libya, Thrace, Macedonia and some of the islands in the Ægean sea, but the Greeks defeated him at Marathon (B. C. 490). Died B. C. 485 (Ezr. iv. 7.).—3. DARIUS, THE PERSIAN. Darius II, Nothus, king of Persia, B. C. 424–404. Perhaps DARIUS CODOMANUS (Neh. xii. 22).

DARK′NESS. Opposite of light, absence of light (Gen. i. 2). Three times mentioned in the Bible. In Genesis, at the creation; at the Exodus, as one of the plagues of Egypt, and at the crucifixion. Used as a figure of adversity and misery (Job xviii. 6; Ps. cvii. 10). "Works of darkness," heathen rites and ceremonies (Eph. v. 11), "outer darkness," shut out of heaven (which is glorious with light).

FRUIT OF DATE PALM.

DÄR′KON. Children of Darkon were among the servants of Solomon, who returned from the captivity (Ezr. ii. 56).

DARLING. My only one (Ps. xxii. 20).

DÄ′ROM (*south*), (Deut. xxxiii. 23). Naphtali was to possess the sea and Darom. Jerome and others so name Philistia and the plain toward Egypt.

DÄ′RON (*south*). Fort built by the Crusaders at Deir el Belah (*convent of dates*), near Gaza, on ancient ruins.

DÄTES. Fruit of the palm tree, called *clusters* in Cant. vii. 7, and *honey* in 2 Chr. xxxi. 5, dates in the margin. In many parts of Arabia the staple product and the main source of landed wealth, is the date-palm, of which there are many species. The ripening season is August and September. The fruit is a substitute for the bread of other countries. To cut down the date trees is a great achievement in war—and the absence of those trees from Palestine indicates a long period of wars and an unsettled condition. To plant the palm on new ground is a sign of prosperity—as now in Egypt. The Arabs believe the tree is a blessing granted only to them, and denied to all other people. Mohammed taught, "Honor the date tree, she is your mother." There are 139 varieties, 70 of which are well known, each of which has its peculiar name. Some six kinds are superior. El Shelebi, the best, are two inches long, with small stones. The value in Arabia is about three cents a pound.

DÄTH′AN (*fountain*). Chief in Reuben, who joined Korah in rebellion against Moses and Aaron.

DÄTH′EMA. Fort in Gilead (1 Macc. v. 9), near Mizpeh.

DAUGH′TER. 1. Female offspring; of the wife; or adopted; or of a sister; or of a cousin (Ruth iii. 18; Gen. xxxiv. 17); or a grand-daughter.—2. The female inhabitants of a place, or those who hold the faith of a certain place, as "daughters of Zion" (Is. iii. 16), "daughters of the Philistines," "daughters of Jerusalem," "daughters of Aaron" (Num. xxv. 1; 2 Sam. i. 20; Luke i. 5). Cities were named or spoken of under female names, and were said to have daughters, suburbs or villages near. A vine had daughters (branches, in Gen. xlix. 22). Sarah was the daughter of 90 years—that is, she was 90 years old.

DAVID (*beloved*). SYNOPSIS OF HIS LIFE. Born at Bethlehem in Judah, B. C. 1084. His father, Jesse; his mother's name not recorded (1 Sam. xvi. 10, 17, 58). Had 7 elder brothers—Eliab, Abinadab, Shammah, Nethaneel, Raddai, Ozem, and Elihu; and two sisters—Zeruiah, and Abigail.

He watched the flocks in the field, and in their defense killed a lion and a bear. He was short, light, "comely," had red hair and blue eyes; was strong, and swift of foot; valiant and prudent.

At a yearly family feast he was anointed king by Samuel "from the sheep-cote" (2 Sam. vii. 8). He went to carry food to his three brothers in Saul's army, and was introduced to the king as valiant and brave. He killed Goliath with a stone from a sling. The sword and armor of the giant were first taken to his tent in Bethlehem, afterwards to Nob, and laid up in the Tabernacle (Ps. viii. 19, 29). Saul takes David into his service as a minstrel. Jonathan, his friend. Women sing his praise as superior to Saul. Saul jealous; seeks twice to kill David. Being afraid of David he made him captain of 1,000. David behaved wisely, and all Israel and Judah loved him. Merab is offered to David as a wife as a reward for his service against Goliath, the Philistine. But Saul gave Merab to Adriel. Michal, Saul's daughter, loved David, and Saul offered her to David for a price, and David paid double the price, for he killed 200 Philistines. He paid twice for his wife, killed Goliath and the 200. He is made armor-bearer and captain of the body guard, with a place at the king's table. Saul seeks to kill him; sets men to watch for him; Michal assists his escape. Goes to Ramah to Samuel (Ps. lix). Michal is given to Phaltiel. Secret meeting with Jonathan. The sign of the arrow. David flies. Saul tries to take him at Ramah. David eats consecrated bread, and gets Goliath's sword at Nob (Ps. lii); against

Doeg, who informed against David and killed the priests. David goes to Abimelech (Achish), and feigning madness, escapes (Ps. xxxiv. 56). In the cave of Adullam. Joined by his family beside outlaws, debtors, etc. The incident of the water at Bethlehem (1 Chr. xi. 17). Moves to Herodium or to Masada. Takes his parents to the king of Moab; (they are never mentioned again). Nahash, of Ammon, treats him kindly. Gadites swim the Jordan at its flood and join him. God influences a move to the forest of Hareth. Amasai, a Benjamite, joins him. Relieves Keilah, where

sins. Reigned in Hebron 7½ years. David crowned (3d time) king of all Israel (Ps. lxxviii., lxx.). Constitutional law. Festival 3 days; the tribes send produce, fruits, etc., to the feast, and contingents to the army, which was "like the host of God" (1 Chr. xii. 22). Joab (his nephew) commander: Issacharites his counselors. Jehoiada and Zadok join him. (Ps. xxvii.). Jebus taken. Joab made commander-in-chief. Royal residence in the City of David—Zion. His wives were increased by hostages from surrounding princes. Two attacks by Philistines repulsed: their idols burned.

POOL AT HEBRON.

Abiathar the priest joins him with an ephod. His troop is now 600. Saul appears; David flies to Ziph.

Twice the Ziphim betray him to Saul, who hunts him "like a partridge" with 3,000 men (Ps. liv.), in the wilderness of Maon. Sees Saul two or three times, once at the cliff of divisions, again in a cave near Engedi, when he cuts off his skirt, and then in a fortified camp, when David carried off by night the water-jar and spear from Saul's bedside.

Twice Saul repented, and said he was reconciled to David. Psalms of this date liv., lvii., lxiii., cxli. Nabal and Abigail; marries Ahinoam, and Abigail. David again goes to Achish, with his troop. Achish gives him Ziklag. Benjamite archers join him. Studies the Philistines' art of war. Attacks the Bedawins to deceive Achish. Philistine nobles suspicious, and cause him to be sent back from the army. Saul and Jonathan killed on Gilboa. Manassites join David. Amalekites plunder Ziklag. Abiathar prophesies victory, and David recovers the spoil from the Amalekites. Makes a present to many friends, whose places "he was wont to haunt." Makes a law of division of the spoils (1 Sam. xxx.). News of the battle on Gilboa: kills the messenger. Laments for Saul and Jonathan. David anointed king at Hebron (30 years old). Thanked the men of Jabesh-Gilead for burying Saul. ISHBOSHETH, king in Mahanaim. David the only king west of Jordan. War between the two sections. Abner kills Asahel, David's nephew. Abner quarrels with Ishbosheth, and comes to David. Michal restored to David. Abner and Ishbosheth murdered. David executes the two assas-

Hiram of Tyre an ally: sends cedar-wood for David's palace.

The ark removed from Kirjath Jearim—Obed Edom. The new Tabernacle on Zion; the old left standing at Gibeon. The great assembly on Zion. Musical art developed. Zadok and Abiathar. Nathan the prophet. David, as a priest and minstrel, in the procession. He blesses the people from the new Tabernacle on Zion (Ps. xv. xxiv., xxix., xxx., lxviii., ci., cxxxii.): "The Lord of Hosts, he is the King of Glory" (Ps. xxiv., x.). Michal reproaches him, and is rebuked. God's house designed. Prophesy by Nathan of a Messiah (2 Sam. vii. 12–17). David organizes a court and camp. Mephibosheth cared for, in memory of Jonathan. Hanun, son of Nahash, abuses David's messengers. Ammon and Syria beaten. Joab commander-in-chief (1 Chr. xi. 6): 12 divisions of 24,000 men, one for each month, all infantry, without cavalry. Chain armor in use. Benaiah captain of David's body-guard, the Cherethites and Pelethites—Ittai. The band of 600 continued as Gibborim, heroes; Abishai, David's nephew, captain. Social and moral institutions formed. Ahithophel and Jonathan, Hushai, Shera the scribe, Jehoshaphat, and Adoram, councillors. Gad the seer and Nathan the prophet advisers. Abiathar and Zadok high priests; the musicians, under Asaph, Heman, and the Levites, guardians of the gates and treasures. The Philistines, Moabites, Syrians, Edomites (Ps. lx.), and Ammonites, subdued. Rabbah taken. David wears the gold crown of Milcom (Ps. xxi. 3, lxxxix. 39). Uriah murdered. Nathan's rebuke (Ps. xxii. 51), "Thou art the man." Bathsheba taken. David fasts for his sick child. The child dies: "I shall go to him, but he shall not return to me." Solomon, "the peaceful," born, (Ps. xx. 21). Educated by Nathan the prophet. His daughter Tamar outraged; his eldest son Amnon murdered. Absalom fled to Geshur. The artifice of Joab and the widow of Tekoa, to restore Absalom. Absalom waits two years to see his father; burning Joab's field, is brought to the king. Absalom plots—rebels: David a wanderer again. Leaves the city; a vast multitude go with him. Ittai the faithful, Zadok and Abiathar with the ark, which David sent back. Hushai, "the friend", sent to watch Ahithophel (grandfather of Bathsheba), who was untrue.

Absalom arrives from Hebron. At Bahurim, Ziba's deceit—Shimei's curses. David rested in the Jordan valley, near the ford (Ps. iii. 143). They cross the Jordan to Mahanaim (Ps. xlii.) against Ahithophel (lv., lxix., cix.). Barzillai, Shobi, and Machir his friends. Ahithophel kills himself. Joab, Abishai, and Ittai, were there. Amasa, David's nephew, was with Absalom. Battle in the forest of Ephraim. Absalom killed by Joab. David waiting in the gate. The two messengers, Ahimaaz, and Cushi. David vows to supersede Joab by Amasa. The return to Jerusalem. Shimei forgiven. Mephibosheth partly reinstated; Barzillai rewarded in his son Chimham. Judah and Israel are reconciled.

Sheba's rebellion. David's ten women shut up. Amasa sent to assemble the militia. The forces sent after Sheba. Joab killed Amasa. Sheba's head cast out of Abel. Adoram over the tribute; Jehoshaphat, recorder; Sheva, scribe; Zadok and Abiathar, priests; and Ira, a chief ruler.

A famine of three years on account of the Gibeonites' murder by Saul. David delivered 7 sons of Saul to be hanged, as an atonement. The bones of Saul and Jonathan buried in Zelah. David grows faint in the fight with the Philistines. Ishbibenob, the giant, thought to kill David. Abishai kills the giant. Psalm of thanksgiving (2 Sam. xxii.).

EGYPTIAN DOOR.

David numbered the people unlawfully, in pride. Joab and the captains opposed it. Gad, the prophet, warns of 3 calamities; David would not choose, and the 3 days' pestilence killed 70,000, and was stayed at the threshing-floor of Ornan. David bought the site for a sanctuary, and it is now marked by an ancient church—the Dome of the Rock (see Jerusalem). David renews his resolve to build a house for the Lord, and gathers materials. Charges Solomon with the solemn duty (1 Chr. xxii.).

The young Abishag. Adonijah's rebellion. Joab and Abiathar helped (Ps. xcii.). By David's order Solomon is anointed king at Gihon. Adonijah pardoned by Solomon. David's last song (2 Sam. xxiii. 1–7). David's last words (1 K. ii. 1–9), describe the perfect ruler fearing God. Died at the age of 70. Buried "between Siloah and the guard-house." Reigned in Jerusalem 33 years (Neh. iii. 16). The site of his tomb is lost.

DAVID'S FAMILY.—1. Michal (no children, 2 Sam. vi.). 2. Ahinoam—son Amnon (1 Chr. iii. 1). 3. Abigail—son Daniel (ib.) Maachah—son Absalom, 3 sons died. Tamar (2 Sam. xiii.). 5. Haggith—son Adonijah (2 Sam. iii.). 6. Abital—son Shephatiah (1 Chr. iii.). 7. Eglah—son Ithream. Sons whose mothers are not named: Ibhar, Elishua, Eliphelet, Nogah, Nepheg, Japhia, Elishama, Eliada, Eliphalet and Jerimoth (1 Chr. xiv. 7; 2 Chr. xi. 18). 8. Bathsheba—sons: one died—Shammua, Shobab, Nathan and Jedidjah or Shelomoh = Solomon (2 Sam. xii. 25). The children of the 10 concubines, and their mothers, are not named. There is no reason to suppose he had more than eight wives. The text of 2 Sam. v. 13, probably refers to Michal, Bathsheba and the 10 women whom he took at Jerusalem.

David was a soldier, shepherd, poet, prophet, priest, statesman and king, a romantic friend, chivalrous leader, devoted father. He represents the Jewish people at the point of the change from the lofty writers of their older system to the higher civilization of the newer, and was a type of the Messiah, who is called the Son of David.

David as king is almost above reproach; his private life only proved him a man. Next to Abraham's, David's is the most dearly cherished name of all the ancient patriarchs. The Psalms, whether his own or others' writings, have been the source of consolation and instruction far beyond any other of the holy scriptures, and are the only expressions of devotion that have been equally used by all branches of the Christian church and by the Jews.

It is now thought that the saying that David was a man after God's own heart meant only that he was chosen, while Saul was rejected—and his excellence as a king justified the choice.

The noble qualities of his soul, his sublime piety, which was the habit of his life, his intense struggle against fiery passions, and his mournful remorse over occasional sins, far outweighed his faults.

Because he passed through temptation, passion and humiliation, we are instructed and comforted; and through the divine psalms which he wrote we are provided with language for our times of distress and trouble.

DAY. See Chronology.

DAY'S JOURNEY. Sabbath. See Weights.

DAYS'MAN. Arbitrator; one to appeal to (Job. ix. 33).

DAVID, CITY OF. Zion in Jerusalem, and also Bethlehem.

DEACON. Assistant, helper. Christ is called a deacon (A. V. minister, Rom. xv. 8). The Apostles appointed officers and made rules as circumstances required. The 7 deacons appointed to care for the widows (serving tables), had special duties which passed away with the occasion. But there was then a difference made between the ministers of spiritual and of material things. They also assisted at the communion by carrying the food and drink to the members. They received the contributions; cared for the sacred vessels; read the gospel sometimes, and baptized. They were to be grave, venerable, of good report in life, sincere, truthful, temperate, not using their office for profit, keeping the faith in a pure conscience, husband of one wife, ruling their children and house well (1 Tim. iii.; Acts vi.).

DĒA'CONESS (Rom. vi.). The records show that they were useful in the early centuries—a service which was afterwards absorbed into the nunneries.

DEAD SEA. This name is first met in history, about 200 years after Christ. In the O. T. it is called the Salt Sea, sea of the Plain. See SALT SEA.

DĒATH. 1. Natural death; end of the life of the body. 2. Spiritual death; insensible to holiness; alienation from God (Matt. viii. 22; Eph. ii.; Rom. vi. 21). The poetic expressions are "return to dust" (Gen. iii. 19); "removal from the body" (Job x. 21); "asleep" (Jer. li. 39; John xi. 11); "losing the breath" (Ps. civ. 29); the soul laying off its clothing" (2 Cor. v. 3); "to depart" (Phil. i. 23); "for a great trial" (2 Cor. i. 10). GATES OF DEATH (Job xxxviii. 17); doors of the shadow. Some believe that we should be able to live forever if we did not break God's law. But the Bible is a spiritual book and not a treatise on Natural History.

DEB'IR (*oracle*). 1. Ancient royal city of Canaan (Josh. x. 33). Kirjath-Sepher (*book city*). Now Dibeh, 6 ms. S. W. of Hebron, where there is a fine spring and aqueduct.—2. Judah near the valley of Achor. Wady Daborat the N. W. corner of the Dead Sea (Josh. xv. 7).—3. Boundary of Gad, near Mahanaim. Lo-debar (Josh. xiii. 26.—4. A king of Eglon, hanged by Joshua (x. 3).

DEB'ORA. Mother of Tobeil, the father of Tobit, (Tobit i. 8).

DEB'ORAH (*bee*). 1. Rebekah's nurse (Gen. xxxv. 8). Buried under an oak called Allon-bachuth.—2. A prophetess, wife of Lapidoth who lived near a palm tree between Ramah and Bethel (Judg. iv. 4). She composed a song (ch. v.) in memory of the victory over Sisera (by Barak and Deborah) which, for poetic beauty, is much valued, and gives her the title of prophetess (singer).

DEBT'OR. The strict law of inheritance, of Moses, provided against commercial speculation and debts, by requiring all landed property and slaves to be freed on the year of jubilee (7th) (Lev. xxv. 39). No debtor could be sent to prison, or whipped, or oppressed unfairly, except by breaking the law. In Egypt the creditor could send the debtor to prison, and seize his family tomb and prevent burials there. The Roman laws were very severe against the debtor, and hard on slaves (made by debt). Bankers and sureties in the commercial sense were unknown (Prov. xxii. 26). No interest could be lawfully taken from a poor person, but relief was to be given without price, laws being made to prevent evading this rule (Ex. xxii. 25; Lev. xxv. 35, etc.). Nehemiah corrected such abuses (Neh. v.), and Jesus approved of the law of Moses, although in the later times the custom of usury had become popular, and usurers had their tables in the courts of the Temple. Loans could be secured by pledges, under certain rules: 1. The cloak, which was used day and night by the poor, must be returned at sundown. A bedstead (a luxury) might be taken (Ex. xxii.); no widow's garments, or a millstone, could be taken (Deut. xxiv. 6, 17). The creditor could not enter a house for his pledge but must wait outside (Deut. xxiv. 10). Debtors held as slaves must be released at the jubilee, and might be redeemed for a price. Foreign slaves were not released (Lev. xxv. 44). A year was allowed to redeem houses sold for debt. The Romans superseded the law of the jubilee year, and the debtor could be held *in prison* until the last farthing was paid (Matt. v. 26).

DEC'ALŌGUE (*ten words*). TEN COMMANDMENTS (Ex. xx). The basis of all laws. The *number ten* was regarded as perfect or complete, therefore the TEN GREAT WORDS were the perfect law of God (Ps. xix. 7) given on Sinai. They were cut on two tables of stone, and kept for several centuries in the ark, in the very centre of the holy place, as a symbol of the centre of the whole system. The *two* tables indicate a division of the law, into duties towards God, and duties toward our neighbor (Matt. xx. 37–39). Some critics point out more than 20 decalogues in the laws of Moses. See LEVITICUS in the HISTORY.

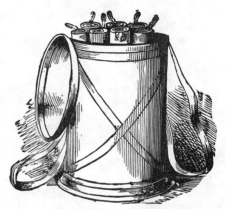

ANCIENT WRITING MATERIALS.

DECAP'OLIS (*ten cities*). Mentioned three times in the N. T. (Matt. iv. 25; Mark v. 20, vii. 31), and many times in Josephus and other ancient writers. Soon after the Romans conquered Palestine they rebuilt and colonized ten cities, and gave them especial privileges. The list of the names of these ten cities is given differently by various writers. Pliny names Scythopolis, Hippos, Gadara, Pella, Philadelphia, Gerasa, Don Canatha, Damascus, and Raphana. Ptolemy includes Capitolias; and an inscription in Palmyra makes Abila one. The name was probably given to a large district in Christ's time. Damascus is the only one of the ten cities left, all the others being in ruins.

DĒ'DAN (*low country*). 1. Son of Raamah, grandson of Cush (Gen. x. 7). An island on the shore of the Persian Gulf is called *Dadan*, and another *Sheba*.—2. A son of Jokshan, grandson of Abraham by Keturah (Gen. xxv. 3). In each case the brother is named Sheba, and both tribes may have intermarried and occupied the same country. "The travelling companies of Dedanim" of Is. xxi. 13, are caravans, They traded with Tyre (Ez. xxvii. 15, 20) in ivory, ebony and fine dry goods (precious cloths).

DEDICĀ'TION, FEAST OF THE. Instituted in memory of the purification of the temple by Judas Maccabæus after driving out the Syrians (B. C. 164), (1 Macc. iv. 52; Jer. x. 22). It lasted 8 days—Dec. 25 (CHISLEV) to Jer. 3. Carrying branches of trees and singing, especially the Hallelujah song, every day.

DEEP, THE. Abyss. Bottomless pit in A. V. (Luke viii. 31; Rev. ix. 1, 2, 11; xx. 1, 3; 2 Cor. xi. 25). In Rev. x. 6, 7, "ascend into heaven," "descend into the deep," the place of the dead. This does not include Hades, which is supposed to include the deep, which is, then, only a part of the great unknown place of the dead,

DEGRĒE. 1 Tim. iii. 13, should read: "For they who well served as deacons obtain for themselves a good degree, and much confidence in faith in Christ Jesus." That is, in spiritual matters.

DEGREES, THE SONG OF (*stairs* or *steps*), is a title of 15 Psalms by different authors. Pilgrim songs, sung by the people as they went up to Jerusalem (Ex. xxxiv. 24; 1 K. xii. 27; Ezr. vii. 9; Ps. cxxii. 4). 5 were written by David (4) and Solomon (1), and the other 10 after the return from Captivity. See Ps. cxx. to cxxxiv. See PSALMS in the HISTORY.

DEHA'VITES (*villagers*), (Ezr. iv. 9). Planted in Samaria by Assyria. Dahi (Herodotus i. 125), in Persia; and Daci, in Europe (Dacia).

DĒ'KAR. An officer of Solomon's in Judah (1 K. iv. 9).

VIEW OF BETHLEHEM.

DELĀI'AH (*Jehovah's freedman*). 1. Priest in David's time, leader of the 23d course (1 Chr. xxiv. 18).—2. Children of D. returned from Captivity (Ezr. ii. 60).—3. Son of Mehetable (Neh. vi. 10).—4. Son of Shemaiah, in Jehoikim's time (Jer. xxxvi. 12).

DELĪ'LAH (*drooping, languishing*). Samson's love; lived in the valley of Sorek, Philistia. She was a wily seducer, who loved the bribes, and not her honor or her lover's safety, and captivated only to destroy. Her bribe was large—5,500 pieces of silver—shekels ($2,750), equal to 33,000 as to our standard of wages. See MONEY.

DĒL'UGE. Flood (Heb. HAMMABAL the fulness of waters), from *yubal*, a river (fulness). Deluge is used instead of flood.

The belief in a deluge of greater or less extent is of very ancient date, in all nations who have kept records, or have traditions. It is very often noticed in the Bible, as a fact from which a great lesson is to be learned (Matt. xxiv. 38), and its history is given in Gen. vi. viii. The account next in value to this is that of the Greeks (Ovid)—the flood of Deucā'lion and Pyr'rhā. The Hindus (Sir Wm. Jones, *Asiatic Res.* iii. 116) also have an account, which, with the Greek, agrees with that in Genesis in many points. The Chinese legend is not very parallel, but agrees in a few items. The Parsee account says the flood washed away all the wickedness which Ah'rī-män (the Evil One) had brought about. The Chaldee (Jos. Ap. i. 19), that Noa saved Sem, Japet, and Chem. The Assyrian is (Eusebius, *Ev. Præp.* c. ix.) similar. The Scandinavian, Mexican, Peruvian, and others, have each a story to tell, of a great flood, and a few persons saved.

The Scripture account is, the God sent the deluge as a punishment for sin, destroying all flesh but such as he directed Noah to place in the ark.

The time occupied was 358 days, 7 days less than our year, or 1 year and 10 days by the Jews' calendar. The present majority opinion is, that the subject has a *moral* rather than a *physical* character. That mankind had not spread beyond the valley of the Euphrates and Tigris, and Syria; and that the deluge only extended far enough to be universal as to *mankind*. There has been no evidence yet brought to light, such as human bones, or teeth, proving any great destruction of life in this, or any other region, which can be dated to the time of the deluge. The *size of the ark* is a great argument against the deluge being so universal as to cover the whole globe. There are now known 1700 species of animals, about 1000 of which are *clean*, of whom 7 of each species were to be kept; 6000 species of birds, 1000 of reptiles, and 550,000 of insects; and the entire space in the ark—547 by 91 feet (21 ins. to the cubit) 3 stories high—is 150,000 sq. ft. too small, by many times, for standing-room, besides food and storage And how could 8 persons attend to so many animals daily? Many animals, some in the polar regions, others in the tropics, cannot bear a change of climate, even if they could be carried so far from their homes. Peculiar species belong to each quarter of the globe, whose ancestors have left their record in the ancient rocks, fossilized, showing an unbroken succession. It was also impossible to lay up provision for the wild beasts. Seeds and plants must have perished by so long a soaking in water, and fresh-water fish also, if covered by the salt ocean several months. The notion of a universal deluge is at variance with the light of reason. Geological records (in the rocks, etc.) show the results of many floods in the past history of the earth. Vast extents of the earth's surface have been raised or depressed in modern times (in Chili 100,000 sq. ms., 2 ft. high), and the work of sinking is now going on in Holland. The temple of Jupiter, near Naples, shows that it has been sunk, with the island on which it stands, under the waters of the Bay of Baiæ, half its hight, by the holes halfway up the marble columns, all round the temple on a water-line that were bored by a shell-fish that lives under water only. Those who suppose the deluge related only to the ancestors of the Hebrews, and had no reference to any other races, are answered by a denial of the remote antiquity of Egypt and Assyria. The evidences of the antiquity of Egypt and Assyria are far more convincing than any yet offered for the deluge. Only by limiting the deluge to a small part of the earth's surface can the account of Moses be made to harmonize with science.

DĒLUS (G. *delos, visible*). The smallest of the Cyclades, islands in the Grecian Archipelago, the chief seat of the worship of Apollo and his sister Diana (1 Macc. xv. 23). The island was said to have suddenly appeared anciently, as several others have in our time. It was the center of an extensive commerce B. C. 146.

DĒ'MAS, DEMETRIUS or DEMARCHUS. Companion to Paul (Philemon 24; Col. iv. 14; 2 Tim. iv. 10). One of Keble's grandest hymns is founded on the association of Demas and Luke with Paul in his earlier trials, and of the desertion of Demas after.

DE-MÈ'TRI-US (*votary of Demeter, Ceres*). Maker of silver shrines of Artemis at Ephesus (Acts xix. 24). They were small models of the great statue of Diana. He made an adroit speech against Paul, exciting their religious and selfish feelings against the new sect, which aimed to spoil the business of shrine-making. — 2. Another Demetrius is commended by John as having a character so purely Christian as to carry its own testimony with it (3 John 12). — 3. DEMETRIUS SOTER, king of Syria, son of Seleucus IV. (See SYRIA and ANTIOCHUS). — 4. D. NICATOR, son of No. 3, who was excluded by Alexander Balas from the throne until B. C. 146. He first treated the Jews well, but afterwards so badly that they took sides with Antiochus Theos. Killed at Tyre, B. C. 126.

DÈ'MON (Gr. *daimon, god*). At first the Supreme, then a god, and later, to spirits believed to be between gods and men; a kind of messenger, who became tutelary deities of men and cities; and finally the notion of *evil* demons the latest form. Some believed they were the spirits of evil men after death. It was used to denote fortune, chance, fate. In the Hebrew it is used for a pestilence (Ps. xci. 6), idols (xcvi. 5; Lev. xix. 4), devils (Deut. xxxii. 17), God (*troop* in A. V.), the goddess of fortune (Is. lxv. 11), satyrs (Is. xiii. 21; xxxiv. 14). The Hebrews meant evil spirits. In the N. T. they are spiritual, evil, at enmity with God, having power to work evil to man with disease and sin, positively and actively wicked. Called devils in 1 Cor. x. 20; 1 Tim. iv. 1; Rev. ix. 20. The modern notion is that there is but one devil (Lardner), although demons are innumerable (Dr. Campbell). The devil, the old serpent, the adversary, satan, prince of the power of the air, etc., are one. God and his angels are opposed to the devil and his angels, the demons. The angels are sent forth from God's presence to minister on earth to the heirs of salvation; it is the spirit of God which gives his people that character of life-giving and blessed fruits by which they are known; on the contrary, the devil and his demon agency are discovered in the strong delusions and grievous oppressions which men have suffered and do suffer from their power.

DE-MÒ'NI-ACS. Men subject to the power of demons, and who are deaf, dumb, blind, epileptic, frenzied, hypochrondriac, imbecile, and suffer ills both of body and mind. Demons cannot be known to our senses, nor their powers distinguished from natural causes; and the few words about them in the scripture do not help to a clear idea of them. Some suppose that the demoniacs were madmen— under the influence of melancholia or mania—in neither case using reason. There are accounts of some who were maniacs and others lunatics. Some also ascribe every form of disease, bodily or mental, to demons. Jesus said the casting out of demons was a part of his work, and by this work he brought the kingdom of God to us (Lev. xiii. 32; Matt. xii. 28).

DEM'OPHÒN. Syrian general, under Antiochus V, (2 Macc. xii. 2).

DENÀ'RIUS. Penny. 12 to 15 cents. See MONEY.

DEP'UTY. Proconsul (Acts xiii. 7, etc.).

DER'BE. Lycaonia, on the road from Tarsus to Iconium (Acts xiv. 6), which passes through the famous CILICIAN GATES, and where the pass opens upon the plains of Lycaonia, the city of Derbe stood. Gaius belonged here (Acts xx. 14).

DESCRY To reconnoitre (Judg. i. 23).

DES'ERT. Four words of the Hebrew text are translated desert, and they are: 1. ARABAH. The Ghor—the Jordan valley; Jericho at the S., and Bethshean at the N. (Ezek. xlvii. 8; Is. xxxv. 1, 6, xl. 3, xli. 19, etc.; Jer. ii. 6, v. 6, etc.). —2. MIDBAR. Pasture grounds, or the wilderness of the

wanderings, where the Israelites had flocks and herds with them during the whole of the passage from Egypt to Canaan (Ex. iii. 1, v. 3, x. 26, xii. 38, xix. 2; Num. xi. 22, xxxii. 21, xxx. 15). —3. CHARBAH. Waste places, dryness, desolation (Ps. cii. 6; Is. xlviii. 21); W. of Sinai (Ez. xiii. 4; Job iii. 14). —4. JESHIMON. Waste places on each side of the Dead Sea. Usually translated Beth Jeshimon (Num. xxi. 20; 1 Sam. xxiii. 19). Is more expressive of utter desolation than any of the others (Deut. xxxii. 10).

DEMETRIUS I.

DES'SAU. Judah (2 Macc. xiv. 16.) Nicanor's army encamped there. Supposed to be Adasa.

DEÜ'EL (*El knows*). Father of Eliasaph (Num. i. 14). REUEL.

DEU-TER-Ò'NO-MY (Gr. *second law*). Fifth book of the Pentateuch. Named in Hebrew ELLEH HADDEVARIM, *these are the words*. See HISTORY.

DEV'IL (Gr. *Diabolos, slanderer, false accuser*). Called SATAN (*to lie in wait, oppose*) by the Hebrews, and *Shatan* by the Arabs. This character expresses the antagonistic, malicious, and perverse nature of the enemy of God and man. See DEMON. It is not believed (by all) that he is an independent, self-existent spirit of evil, though some do so believe, with the Manicheans. He is also called Dragon, Evil One, Angel of the Bottomless Pit, Prince of this World, the God of this World, Prince of the Power of the Air, Apollyon, Abaddon, Belial, Beelzebub. The word Satan is used also to mean an adversary. Hadad the Edomite was an adversary (Heb. SATAN) to Solomon (1 K. xi. 14); David is suspected of being an adversary (satan in 1 Sam. xxix. 4) to the Philistines; the angel of the Lord was a satan (adversary) to Balaam (Num. xxii. 22); a wicked man is a satan in Ps. cix. 6. The wicked wives are adversaries (satans, diabolous; the Hebrew Satan is the Greek Diabolos) in 1 Tim. iii. 1; false accusers, 2 Tim. iii. 3, and Titus ii. 3; and Jesus said one of the 12 was a devil (diabolos, Satan), an adversary. The Hebrew marks, by the article, a difference between a satan, an adversary, and the Satan, a person, the chief. In Zech. iii. 1, 2, it is the Satan, and also in Job 1st and 2d chapters, and 1 Chr. xxi. 1: Matt. iv. 1–11; Luke viii. 12; John viii. 44; Acts xiii. 10; Eph. vi. 11; 1 Pet. v. 8; 1 John iii. 8; Rev. xii. 9.

DEMETRIUS II.

It is said that the Devil is spiritual, but not spirit— not eternal. He works by deceiving, producing or keeping in ignorance, misunderstanding, evil thoughts, unholy desires, pride, anger, revenge, discontent and repining; and besides these moral, he works in physical ways, producing disease (Job ii. 7; Luke xiii. 6; Acts x. 38), which is sometimes used as a divine chastisement (1 Tim. i. 20). As

God is the only supreme self-existence, and Satan is not eternal nor in accord with God, but an adversary, he will be overcome, when he has served the will of God, and will go down into the abyss, with death and hell, into utter and final annihilation (Rev. xx. 2, 10, 14).

HEAD-DRESSES.

DEVŌ'TIONS. Objects of worship—temples, images, altars, etc. Paul meant *objects* of devotion in Acts xvii. 23.

DEW.—The dew falls copiously in Palestine, at night, in spring and autumn, but very little in the summer—May to August. It falls some weeks before, and also after the rains, and so shortens the dry season. It is used as a figure of God's goodness in Hos. xiv. 5, "I will be as the dew unto Israel;" and in Job, of his prosperity (xxix. 19), "the dew lay all night on my branch;" in Ps. cx. 3, of freshness and energy, ' dew of his youth" (Christ); of eloquent speech, "distilling like the dew" (Deut. xxxii. 2); of brotherly love, as the "dew of Hermon" (Ps. cxxxiii. 3); and as a sign of calamity, if wanting, in 2 Sam. i. 21, indicating barrenness.

DI'-A-DEM (*bound around*). CROWN. Only four passages have this, and they might be read, "fillet," "mitre," "tiara," or "turban," the original meaning *rolled together*, or around, like the modern Eastern head-dress (Is. iii. 23). The diadem as worn by kings, as a badge of absolute power, was a band about two inches wide, made of silk, ornamented with gold, tied behind, as in No. 7. The ends of the ribbon are frequently shown on the coins. Gibbon describes one as "a broad white fillet, set with pearls" like No. 5. Nos. 1, 2 and 3 are Egyptian; 4, 5, 6, Assyrian; 7, from a coin of Tigranes, king of Syria; 8, sculpture at Persepolis; 9, Roman, civic, of leaves, from a coin. See page 66.

DIVAN.

DI'-AL. (Heb. MAALOTH, *degrees*). The earliest mention of the sun-dial is among the Babylonians, 540 B. C. Herodotus says the Greeks adopted it from them, as also the division of the day into 12 parts, being introduced to Greece by the astronomer Berosus, the Chaldean. The first notice of "the hour" is by Daniel (iii. 6). The degrees of Ahaz (2 K. xx. 11), cannot be explained. It may have reference to a dial with degrees (lines numbered). This might have been a present from Tiglath Pileser, the ally of Ahaz, and made in Babylon.

DI'-A-MOND (Heb. YAHALOM, *precious stone*, and SHAMER, *sharp point*). The hardest and most precious of all the gems. One was in the sacred breast-plate of the high priest, though some say that (*yahalom*) was an onyx. Ezekiel speaks of making his forehead hard as a diamond (SHAMIR, adamant in A. V. Ez. iii. 9), and Jeremiah of an iron pen pointed with a diamond (Jer. xvii. 1), and Zechariah, of hearts as hard as an adamant stone (vii. 12). The same word *shamir* is Hebrew for brier.

DĬ-AN'-A, Latin. (Greek, ARTEMIS). The twin sister of Apollo, the sun-god. She is the moon goddess. The Assyrians named them Adrammelech and Anamelech. Diana was called the goddess of hunting, chastity, marriage, and nocturnal incantations. In Palestine the name was ASHTORETH. The services were performed by women (*melissai*), and eunuchs (*megabissoi*),with a high priest (*essene*). The great temple at Ephesus, and grove at Daphne were the most noted shrines of this worship. The image at Ephesus was said to have fallen out of heaven complete! The great temple was 425 by 220 feet, and had 127 columns of marble, each 60 feet high. See EPHESUS.

DIANA.

DIB'LAIM. Mother of Hosea's symbolical wife Gomer (Hos. i. 3).

DIB'LATH. By some supposed to be the same as **RIBLAH.** By others it is located in Moab, where it is applied to a district in which was Almon-Diblathaim (Num. xxxiii. 46), and Beth D. (Jer. xlviii. 22). S. E. of Heshbon.

DI'BON. E. border of Moab, 3 ms. N. of Arnon river (Num. xxxiv. 45). Rebuilt by the Gadites. Dibon-Gad (xxxii. 34). In Reuben (Josh. xiii. 9, 17). The ruins are still called *Diban*, and are extensive. Dimon (Is. xv. 9).—2. Judah. DIMONAH (Neh. xi. 25).

DIB'RI. Father of Shelomith, who had married an Egyptian, and her son having "blasphemed the name" was stoned (Lev. xxiv. 11).

DID'YMUS (*twin*). The apostle Thomas (John xi. 16).

DIKLÄH (*palm-tree*). There is a district in Arabia, extending along the Red Sea, from Edom to Medina, called *Dakalah*, from its fruitful palmgroves. Another district is Yemen, now called *Minæi*, also fruitful in palms, is thought to be the the real location; where there is a tribe of Arabs *Duklai*. (Burckhardt). (Gen. x. 27, 31; 1 Chr. i. 21).

DIL'EAN (*place of cucumbers*). Judah (Josh. xv. 38). Lost. Possibly Tima, near Ekron.

DIL'LY. Hauran, 6 ms. W. of Edraa, on the edge of a large marsh: the aqueduct for conveying water to Gadara begins here.

DIMAS. Village on E. slope of Hermon; on Damascus—Beirut road.

DIM'NAH. Zeb. (Josh. xxi. 35; Lev.) Damon, near Accho.

DI'MON, WATERS OF. Streams E. of the Dead Sea. Moab (Is. xv. 9). DIBON.

DIMO'NAH. Judah. S., near the desert (Josh. xv. 22).

DIM'REH. V. 8 ms. S. of Askulan, on the W. Esneid.

DINAH (*acquitted*) Dau. of Jacob by Leah. Her history is a short tragedy (Gen. xxxiv.). Her two full brothers took her part against Shechem, and for their deceit and cruelty were condemned by Jacob on his death-bed. Among all the tribes of the East, to this day, any wrong to a sister must be avenged by her brothers or father, or the whole family is disgraced. She may have gone with Jacob into Egypt (xlvi. 15), but she is not mentioned again, nor is her death recorded.

DI′NAITES Cuthæan colonists who were placed in Samaria (Ezr. iv. 9).

DINHĀ′BAH (*present*) (Gen. xxxvi. 32). Capital city and birthplace of Bela, son of Beor, king of Edom. 8 ms. from Ar. toward the river Arnon. —7 ms. from Heshbon, on Mt. Peor (Eusebius). DANABA was a bishop's see in Palmyrene, Syria (Zosimus iii. 27).

DIONYSIA. Feast of Bacchus (2 Macc. vi. 7).

DIONYS′IUS, THE AREOPAGITE. (Acts xvii. 34). Dionysus or Bacchus. He was a member of the supreme court of the Areopagus, and one of the few converts of Paul at Athens. A. D. 420, a writer called Pseudo-Dionysius wrote a book in the name of the disciple, which was believed to be genuine for a long time, but is now condemned.

DIONY′SUS. BACCHUS (3 Macc. ii. 29).

DIOCÆSAREA. SEPPHORIS.

DIOT′REPHES (*Jove-nurtured*). A disciple who resisted the apostle John, in Asia-Minor.

DIR′WEH. Ruin and fountain E. of Beth-Zur, 4 ms. N. of Hebron.

DISCIPLE. Believer. Member of the Church of Christ.

DISCOV′ER. To uncover. "The voice of the Lord—discovereth the forests," that is, the lightning strips off the bark and branches (Ps. xxix. 9).

DIS′CUS. A quoit of iron, copper, or stone, for throwing in play, in the gymnasium. Jason introduced Greek games into Jerusalem in the time of Antiochus Epiphanes, which the priests indulged in to the neglect of their duties (2 Macc. iv. 14).

DISH (Heb. SEPHEL, TSALLACHATH, and KERAH, and Greek *trublion*). Bowl, charger. See MEALS, CUPS.

DI′SHAN. Youngest son of Seir the mountaineer (Horite). (1 Chr. i. 38). DISHON (Gen. xxxvi. 21).—2. Son of Anah, and grandson of Seir (1 Chr. i. 41).

DISSOLVE. To explain (Dan. v. 16).

DISPER′SION, THE JEWS OF THE. Those who remained in Babylonia after the return from captivity were called the "dispersed, or "of the dispersion," or in Heb. "stripped naked." "Removed" in Deut. xxviii. 25; Jer. xxxiv. 17. This included the 12 tribes. The Jewish *faith* succeeded to the *kingdom* of David at the return of the remnant, and faithful Jews everywhere contributed the half-shekel to the temple services (Jos. Ant, xviii. 9, 1). Three sections of the dispersion are noticed in history, of Babylon, of Syria, and of Egypt. The Greek conquests extended the limits of the dispersed, by securing greater liberties to the Jews. See ANTIOCHUS, THE GREAT. The African dispersion centred at Alexandria, the best fruit of which is the Septuagint. After the rise of the Jews, in Trajan's time, they were nearly exterminated and the remnant driven into Europe. Those in Rome followed Pompey after his victories in the East. They were banished from the city under Claudius, because they "were continually raising disturbances, Chrestus being their leader" (Suetonius, c. 25). Probably on account of their opposition to the preaching of Christ by Paul and others. The dispersion influenced the spread of the gospel, because the apostles and preachers followed the Jews into "all the world" (Acts ii.).

DIS′TAFF. SPINNING. (Prov. xxxi. 19).

DI′VES. A Greek word meaning *rich*, which Jesus used in the parable of Lazurus and the "rich" man (Luke xvi. 19). It has since Chaucer's time (see Sompnoure's Tale, "Lazar and Dives") been used in theological literature as a proper name.

DIVINĀ′TION (Heb. KESEM, *to divide*) Imitation of prophesy; the art of pretending to foretell future events, from the appearance of cards, dice, liquids in a vial, or sediment in a cup (Gen. xliv. 4) which had magical writing on it, or engraving on it; of the earth, sea, and sky; the entrails of animals; the flight of birds; of graves; in dreams; (Num. xii. 6), ("good dreams are one of the great parts of prophesy."—*Koran*) by talismans, images,

THE KING, CHIEF OFFICERS, AND GODS OF ASSYRIA DIVINING WITH A CUP.

oracles; by arrows (see Assyrian sculptures, where the king holds divining arrows, or a rod); and also by magic arts. Plato calls it science without reason. It was taught that the gods gave signs of future events, all through the universe, and that men of observation and study could read those signs. Moses condemned the whole system (Deut. xviii. 10–12), and those who practiced it as impious impostors. The desire to know the future was proper, and would be gratified by God's own *prophet*, who should speak as he was inspired. This superstition is found among all people, at this day, and is even now practiced under the name of clairvoyants, second-sight, trance-mediums, seventh daughter or son, by cards, water, rods, palm, etc. The result of such practices is the same in all ages, a certain loss of judgment, of purity, and piety, and is as hateful now as ever (1 Sam. xv. 23). The divination by lot seems to be an exception, and is said to be divine (Prov. xvi. 33), and with the Hebrews was conducted solemnly and with religious preparations (Josh. vii. 13), as in the case of Achan and of the division of the Promised Land (Num. xxvi. 55), the election of Saul as king (1 Sam. x. 20), and the chosing of Matthias to the vacant apostleship (Acts i. 26). Many appearances are recorded as of the direct work of God, as the serpent rod of Moses; leprous hand; burning bush; plagues; cloud; Aaron's budding rod; the dew of Gideon, etc., and also visions (Num. xii. 6). See CUP on p. 37.

SHEKEL.

DIVŌRCE. The law of Moses is found in Deut. xxiv. 1-4, and xxii. 19, 29. The original words are *some uncleanness* (Heb. ERVATH DABAR), and are very loosely explained by the Jewish doctors, so that many causes for divorce were admitted. One school (Shammai) limited it to a moral cause, and another (Hillel) included many others: as a bad breath, snoring, a running sore, and burning the food when cooking. When Jesus was appealed to (Matt. v. 31, with a view to entangle him in their disputes), he said, The practice allowed by the Mosaic law of divorcing a wife without crime on her part, and on the ground of dislike or disgust, is opposed to the original, divine idea of marriage: according to which a man and his wife are joined together by God, to be one flesh, and are not to be put asunder by man. He who puts away his wife by a bill of divorce without her crime, causes her to commit adultery by placing it within her power to marry another man. The party who permits the divorce is criminal in marrying again. The mere exchange of a piece of writing will not dissolve the spiritual bond. Unless the union is dissolved by crime, any who unite with either party are criminal.

The apostle Paul allowed (1 Cor. viii.) *separation* of a believer from an *unbeliever*, but not to marry another, but to seek reconciliation and reunion. In the Roman church a marriage with an unbeliever may be annulled by the believer, who may marry another. Some Protestants follow the same custom, and also in case of desertion. See MARRIAGE.

DĬZ'AHAB (*place of gold*). On the Red Sea, now Dohab (Deut. i. 1).

DOCTOR. Teacher (Luke iii. 46). SCRIBE.

DŌ'CUS (*small fort*). Near Jericho (1 Macc. xvi. 15). Built by Ptolemeus, son of Abubus, in which he entertained and murdered his father-in-law, Simon Maccabæus and his two sons (Ant. xiii. 8). Dagon, ruins near Ain Duk, are supposed to mark the site (*Rob.* ii. 309).

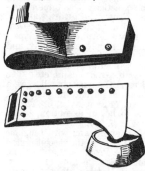

ANCIENT HINGES.

DŌ'DĀI (*loving*). An Ahohite, captain of the course of the army (24,000), who served in the 2d month (1 Chr. xxxii. 4). Dodo? Brother of JESSE?

DODĀ'NIM. Descendants of the 4th son of Javan (Gen. x. 4). Rodanim. The island of Rhodes and the river Rhone are relics of the name.

DODĀ'VAH (*love of Jah*). Father of Eliezer, who denounced Jehoshaphat's alliance with Ahaziah (2 Chr. xx. 37).

DŌ'DŌ (*God his friend*). 1. Of Bethlehem, father of Elhanan, one of David's noted 30 captains (1 Chr. xi. 26).—2. Dodai, the 2d in chief command of David's army (2 Sam. xxiii. 9, 24; 1 Chr. xi. 12). 3. Of Issachar, forefather of Tola, the judge (Judg. x. 1).

DŌ'EG (*fearful*). Chief of Saul's herdsmen (1 Sam. xxii. 9). He obeyed king Saul, and killed the priests of Nob (85, and their families also). He was a proselyte to the Jewish faith, attending there to fulfil a vow.

DOG (Heb. KELEB, *seizer;* Ar. *kelb*). From most ancient times the humble friend and servant of man. Sculptured on the monuments of Assyria and Egypt. Mentioned as shepherd dogs by Job (xxx. 1); Moses as property (Deut. xxiii. 18), and Solomon (Eccles. ix. 4). The vile rulers of Israel were compared to dogs by Isaiah (lvi. 10, 11). The dog is almost universal in the East, and runs, half-wild, in the streets; never caressed, or made pets of, and seldom admitted to a house or tent. They eat anything that comes in their way, and also each other, if a dog strays from his proper district. Jezebel's fate (2 K. ix.) might be repeated any day or night in any city of the East. Byron writes in his Siege of Corinth:

> " He saw the lean dogs, beneath the wall,
> Hold o'er the dead their carnival;
> Gorging and growling o'er carcass and limb,
> They were too busy to bark at him."

David wrote of Saul's hired assassins lying in wait to kill him: "They return at evening: they make a noise like a dog, and go round about the city. Let them wander up and down for meat, and grudge if they be not satisfied" (Ps. lix. 6). He also speaks of them in Ps. xxii. 16, 20. The caravans to Mecca have many dogs, going from Egypt, Syria and Persia. The dog was held to be unclean, and was despised, and is now, the name being a term of reproach, commonly applied to Christians by the Mohammedans.

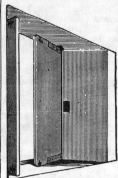

STONE DOOR.

DŌOR. (Heb. SHAAR, *to divide, gate;* PETHAH, *entering;* SAPH, *threshold;* DALETH, *to hang down as a curtain, a door;* TERA, PULE, PULON, *gate*). The door had a threshold, side posts and lintel in houses, and was an opening in the side of a tent. The door is generally of wood, and sometimes of cedar, handsomely carved, and also a cloth for inside use. In the Hauran are now to be seen doors of stone, turning on hinges of stone, dating from antiquity. Doors and doorways in the East are generally small and mean in appearance compared with ours, or with the interior to which they open.

MODERN EGYPTIAN DOOR.

The gates of cities are built strong for defense, with towers and chambers (2 Sam. xviii. 24), and rooms inside for public assembly, for hearing the news, buying or selling, or judicial affairs. In Assyrian cities they were similar; and in the temples were highly ornamented with sculpture and colors. The doorway in the engraving from the ruins of the palace (or temple) at Koyunjik (a part of Nineveh), shows the magnificent style of sculpture, in the use of ideal figures combining men, and animals, and birds. (See cut on page 54.)

The principal doorways in the palaces were guarded by symbolic bulls, or winged gods. Images of the gods were hidden in the walls and floor as a kind of protection.

The Egyptian temple was a kind of fort, with massive walls, and a gate with strong, high towers. The doors had double leaves, often plated with metal. They were provided with locks and bars of metal.

The gates of Babylon are said to have been of bronze (brass). On the doors of Egypt in our day, there are sentences from the holy book, following the ancient custom (Deut. vi. 9; Is. liv. 12; Rev. xxi. 21; Lane, Mod. Egyptians, Wilkinson). Petitions were presented to the king at the gate; and the gate was sometimes made a place of sanctuary—a refuge for criminals.

The doors of Solomon's Temple are described as being very valuable, richly carved, and overlaid with gold (1 K. vi. 34, etc). Those of the holy place were double. The Beautiful Gate of Herod's Temple is said to have been of Corinthian brass (bronze), (Jos. Wars, v. 5, § 3), and required twenty men to move it.

The gates of precious stones of Revelations and Isaiah were suggested to the writers by the stone doors of the Hauran, which are often several inches thick, of fine hard bazalt, beautifully carved.

To open, or lift up as a curtain, a door to a coming guest, was and is an especial honor, as alluded to in Ps. xxiv. 7.

"I would rather be a door-keeper in the house of my God than dwell in the tents of wickedness (Ps. lxxxiv. 10), may be better understood as meaning "I would rather lay at the door of the house of my God (like Lazarus), than have a home in their tents."

DOPH'KAH (*cattle driving*). Station of the Exodus (Num. xxxiii. 12). See WILDERNESS.

DOR (*habitation*). Royal city of the Canaanites (Josh. xvii. 11; 1 K. iv. 11). On the Great Sea, 14 miles S. of Carmel, 7 ms. N. of Cæsarea. Its king was defeated with others near the waters of Merom (Judg. i. 27), in Manasseh, but the ancient people were never expelled. Solomon made them pay tribute. This was the most southern city built by the Phœnicians. The ruins are on a hill and extend half a mile, the most conspicuous being an old tower, which is a landmark, called Tantura (*the horn*).

DO'RA (1 Macc. xv. 11). DOR.

DOR'CAS. See TABITHA.

DORYM'ENES. Father of Ptolemy (1 Macc. iii. 38). He fought against Antiochus the Great (Polybius, v. 61).

DŌSĬTH'EUS. 1. Captain under Judas Maccabæus against Timotheus (2 Macc. xii. 19).—2. A horseman of Bacenor's band (2 Macc. xii. 35).—3. Son of Drimlus, an apostate Jew at Raphia (3 Macc. i. 3).—4. "Said he was a priest and Levite," messenger to carry the translation of Esther to Egypt (Esther xi. 1, Doway). Another mentioned by Josephus (c. Apion ii. 5).

DO'THAN. Dothaim (*two wells*). 14 ms. N. of Shechem (Gen. xxxvii. 17). Joseph was sold by his brethren here to the Egyptians (ib. 25). Elisha, the prophet, lived at D. when Benhadad thought to capture him (2 K. vi. 8-23). Tell Dothan is now at the S. end of a rich plain, separated by slight hills from Esdraëlon, and the ruins are on a very large hill; with a fine spring at

its foot. The massive ancient Jewish or Roman pavement is to be seen in the road that runs near, from Beisan to Egypt.

DO TO WIT. To make known. Not used. (2 Cor viii. 1).

DOVE (Heb. YONAH). Two species are mentioned in the law—turtle-dove and pigeon. Both were to be offered in burnt offering (Deut. i. 14). It is a symbol of peace, and the most exalted of animals, as symbolizing the Holy Spirit, and the meekness, purity and splendor of righteousness. Two ancient relics show its use as a national ensign—one on a Phœnician coin, where the dove, with rays about its head and wings closed, stands on a globe; and the other, a sculpture in the Hauran, where the dove's wings are spread, also stands on a globe, the rays behind terminating in stars. Carrier pigeons are figured in Egypt. A dove has carried a letter from Babylon to Aleppo in two days. The DOVE'S DUNG of 2 K. vi. 2, has been explained as chick-peas or the roots of the *ornithogalum umbellatum*, or the Star of Bethlehem, used now by the poor. Pigeon cotes are common all over the East, usually made of coarse stone jars piled into a kind of house, by itself or on a roof.

DRACH'MA. See MONEY.

DRAG'ON (Heb. TANNIM, dragons). A mammal, living in the desert (Is. xiii. 22), crying like a child (Job xxx. 29); probably the jackal, which has a mournful howl. Another (Heb. TANNIN) was a great sea monster. Used as a metaphor of the Pharaoh (Is. li. 9; Ez. xxix. 3), where it means the crocodile (see Jer. li. 34). The word is also used as a metaphor for the devil in Rev. xii.

DREAM. We know that God needs no rest, and

DOVE.

is as active when we sleep as when we wake, and therefore we may suppose that divine influences fashion our dreams, as well as direct our waking thoughts. It is supposed that God appeared to Moses, Abraham, Jacob and Joseph, in dreams. So the Greeks believed (Homer, Il. i. 63). Moses promised such visitations (Num. xii. 6); Peter (Acts 10), and Paul (2 Cor. xii. 1), had such dreams. Jeremiah condemns those who pretended to have revelations in dreams (xxiii. 25), and in visions, etc. xxvii. 9), and Ezekiel also (xiii. 2-9). The modern imitators of Spiritism pretend to a divine converse—perhaps deluding themselves—believing that the wild fancies of their trances are the work of the divine mind.

DRESS. Oriental dress has preserved a peculiar uniformity in all ages, from Abraham to the modern Bedawin. The monument at Behistun exhibits the antiquity of the costume, which can be compared with that of figures of modern Syrians and Egyptians. The dress for men and women differed but very little; many articles being worn by both in common, varied only by the manner of putting them on. Men wore the shawl over the head and shoulders, or over the shoulders, while the women used it around the waist.

The *drawers* are scant or full, gathered around the waist. They are fastened just below the knee by garters.

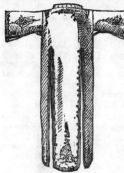

The *shirt* reaches to or falls a little below the knees, and is worn outside of the drawers generally. When dressed in the drawers and shirt only, a person was said to be n a k e d (Mark xiv. 51). They also wear a vest, like ours, buttoned up to the chin. The buttons are sewed on the edge of the garment, and passed through

YELEK. GOWN.

a loop, never using a buttonhole.

The *coat* has sleeves to the wrist, or longer, and skirts to the knees or ankles.

Over the coat is worn the *girdle* (Acts xxi. 11), which is two or three yards long and about half a yard wide, and is made of any material, from a strip of leather or a rope, to the finest silk, with embroidery. The coat, when cut off at the hips, is sometimes embroidered very highly. The same garment is worn by women, and is called Yelek. This is the robe of ceremony for both sexes, referred to in 1 K. v. 5, and 2 Chr. ix. 4, and (the long skirt) the present that Jehu gave the prophets of Baal (2 K. x. 22).

CLOAK.

The *cloak* (ABBA, LEBUSH) is a large square bag, open on one side, with holes at the upper corners for the hands, and a band around the neck. Goat's or camel's hair is used in the desert (Matt. iii. 4) as worn by John the Baptist. Joseph's coat of (many) colors was of this pattern; and such rich garments are common among the wealthy, being made of silk or wool, and richly embroided. The same garment is called a *burnoos* when it has a hood, as worn in Algeria. The *hyke* is a square shawl, folded cornerwise, and worn as in the cut of Egyptians. Bedawins use a cloth woven with threads of silver or gold, called *Akal*. The head is covered first with a white cotton cap (*libdeh*), over which is worn the *tarbush* (see HEAD-DRESS), a red woolen cap, generally with a blue tassel. Around the tarbush a narrow shawl (three or more yards

long) is wound, forming the turban. Women cover themselves with a thin cloak and a veil, leaving only the eyes (or only one eye) visible, as in the figure (Oriental street costume). The ancient

TUNIC. CAFTAN. COAT.

Jewesses did not vail their faces, but covered the hair only. Women wear the hair long, braided, curled, etc., and decorated with jewels and coins. Men generally shave the head (2 Sam. xiv. 26). The ancient Jews probably wore the hair as low as the ears or neck, and, as Josephus says of the body-guard of Solomon, used powder (Ant. viii. 7, 3). In mourning the head was shaved (Is. xxii. 12, etc.).

EGYPTIANS.

There are many ornaments in use for the hair, head, ears, nose, and neck, not very much different from those in use here; except the nose-ring. The eyebrows and lashes are frequently colored.

The feet are loosely covered, and are seldom deformed as ours are by tight shoes. The inner slippers are very soft, and only worn in the house; the over-shoes and boot being worn out doors, and always left at the door. Stockings and leggings for cold weather are in common use.

SANDALS.

Sandals are still used in the house, but could never have been in common use out doors, because of the many thorns and briers. The *Kubcobs* are high wooden stilts, used in the bath, or on wet floors. SANDALS.

Jos. Ant. iii. 7, § 7: "The vestments of the high priest, being made of linen, signified the earth; the blue denoted the sky, being like lightning in its pomegranates; and in the noise of the bells, resembling thunder. And for the Ephod, it showed that God had made the universe of four elements; and as for the gold interwoven, I suppose it related to the splendor by which all things are enlightened. He also appointed the breast-plate to be placed in the middle of the ephod, to resemble the earth, for that has the very middle place. And the girdle which encompassed the high priest round, signified the ocean, for that goes round about and includes the universe. * * * * And for the turban, which was of a blue color, it seems to me to mean heaven, for how otherwise could the name of God be inscribed upon it?"

Exodus xxviii.: "And these are the garments which they shall make—the breast-plate, and the ephod, and the robe, and the coat of checker-work, the turban, and the girdle;" all of which were peculiar to and worn only by the high priest.

In this description the under-garments are not mentioned. In verse 42, linen drawers are directed to be worn, and it may be presumed that the other undergarments worn by the upper classes were used by the priests.

Breastplate (v. 4, 15). This was embroidered, in two halves sewed together, the front to receive the 12 stones, and the back to shield the studs; and besides, so as to fit the chest better, because the stuff was thick and stiff from embroidery, and the fine wires of gold worked into the design. The making of the wires is described in xxxix. 3. In it were set four rows of engraved stones, bearing the names of the twelve tribes of Israel. Each stone was set in a rim of gold, like a cameo (or breast-pin), with a button or stud at the back, which was put through a button-hole in the breast-plate. Putting the twelve stones into their places was a solemn service, showing the presence of the twelve tribes before the altar of Jehovah, and they were called LIGHTS and PERFECTIONS—(Urim and Thummim). It was two spans high, and one wide.

Two cord-like chains of gold wire were fastened to the upper corners of the breast-plate by two rings of gold (v. 14), which were attached to the engraved stones on the shoulders, one to each stone. Two gold rings on the lower corners of the breastplate were opposite two rings in the girdle; and a blue cord tied the rings together and kept the breast-plate in its place (v. 26, 27, 28).

The other garments were peculiar only in color and ornament, their pattern being similar to those already described.

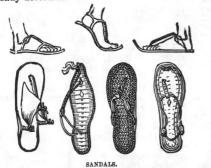

SANDALS.

DRINK (Heb. SHECAR, *any intoxicating beverage*). Strong drink was made from several fruits besides grapes: as pomegranates (Cant. viii. 2), figs, apples, dates, carob fruit, and from grain: as wheat, barley, millet, and from honey. A fine wine is made by putting raisins in water and burying the jars in the ground until after fermentation.

DROM'EDARY (Heb. BECHER, BICRAH, RECESH, RAMMAC). See CAMEL. The A. V. translates in error RECESH in 1 K. iv. 28, and Esth. viii. 10, 14, dromedaries, when the original means swift horses; also RAMMAC in Esther viii. 10, 14, mules instead of mares.

ORIENTAL STREET COSTUME.

DROPPING, A CONTINUAL (Prov. xxvii. 15). Drops of rain in a wintry day drive a man out of his house; in the same manner also does an abusive woman (Lam. xx.). See HOUSE.

DRUSIL'LA (feminine of Lat. *Drusus*). Daughter of Herod Agrippa I, and Cypros (Acts xii. 1). She was betrothed to Antiochus Epiphanes, but on his refusing to become a Jew she was married to Azizus, king of Emesa. She afterwards left her husband for Felix (ib. xxiv. 24). She, with her son perished in an eruption of Mt. Vesuvius.

DUKE. Translation of the Heb. ALLUPH, which means patriarch, head of a family, or, in Arabic, *sheikh*, chief, leader.

DUL'CIMER (Heb. or Chal. SUMPHONYAH). Musical instrument mentioned by Daniel (iii. 5, 15). The modern dulcimer is a box, strung with about 50 wires—the longest 36 inches, the shortest 18—played with two small hammers, held in the hands. MUSICAL INSTRUMENTS.

DU'MAH (*silence*). Son of Ishmael, founder of a tribe of Ishmaelites. The DISTRICT was in the N. of Arabia, near Edom (Gen. xxv. 15; Is. xxi. 11), where there is now a city called *Doomah el*

Jendel, 240 miles E. of Petra, in a circular valley, surrounded by very fine gardens and orchards. An ancient castle, of massive masonry, is in ruins. Another DUMAH is in Judah, 17 miles from Eleutheropolis, 6 miles S. W. of Hebron.

DUMB. Unable to speak (Ex. iv. 11). See MIRACLES.

ROMAN STANDARD BEARER.

DUNG (Heb. GILALA). Used both for manure and for fuel. Its use as manure is very much the same as with us. For fuel it is carefully dried. Many poor people spread cow dung on the outside of their houses to dry for fuel (Ezr. iv. 12.) See Deut. xxiii. 12. The word was omitted in writing, as in 2 K. x. 27, where *draught-house* is substituted. One of the gates of Jerusalem was named Dunggate (Neh. iii. 13, Dung Port). Public execration or insult was shown by using his house as a "draught-house."

DUNG-GATE. JERUSALEM.

DUN'GEON. PRISON.

DU'RA (Heb. CIRCLE). Where Nebuchadnezzar set up an image (Dan. iii. 1). Oppert found the pedestal of a colossal image in a plain called Dowair, S. E. of Babylon, where he thinks the plain of Dura was.

DUST. An image of what is low, mean and impure. Abraham calls himself but dust and ashes (Gen. xviii. 27). In times of grief and mourning the custom in the East is to sit in the dust, and to sprinkle it over the head. To throw dust on one is to show contempt (as Shimei to David, 2 Sam. xvi. 13), and the Jews to Paul (Acts xxii. 23). Shaking the dust off the feet was to leave it as a testimony to the great wickedness of the persons who had offended. To lick the dust is to be prostrated or subdued; to put the mouth in the dust is to show great humility. To return to the dust is a term for death. The dust of the desert sometimes is carried by whirlwinds to great distances, land falling, covers a caravan or the fertile land, leaving desolation in its track.

E

EAGLE (Heb. NESHER; Ar. *niss'r, to tear with the beak*). Eagles are found in all parts of the world, and there are several species in Palestine. 1. Imperial. 2. Short-toed. 3. Golden. 4. Spotted. 5. White-tailed. 6. Bonelli's eagle. 7. Gier eagle, or Egyptian vulture, and others. The NESHER is not an eagle, but a Griffon-vulture, which is found in all hot countries of the old world. It measures nearly five feet; eight feet extent of wing. The allusion in Matthew (xxiv. 28), "whereseover the carcase is, there will the eagles be gathered together," refers to vultures, because eagles do not gather more than two or three, while vultures assemble in large flocks. Its bare head is alluded to in Micah i. 16. Job mentions its strong eye-sight and wing (xxxix. 27-30). "The cliffs are perforated with caves at all hights, wholly inaccessible to man, the secure resting place of hundreds of noble griffons." (*Tristram, Land of Israel*.) This gorge was the one Josephus describes near Arbela as inhabited by robbers, who were dislodged with great labor and hard fighting. The god NISROCH, specially worshiped by Sennacherib, the Assyrian, was a vulture-headed figure, with wings. Ezekiel and John use this vulture as one of the heads in their symbolic figure (Ez. x. 14; Rev. iv. 6). Its longevity is alluded to in Ps. ciii. 5. "Thy youth is renewed like the eagle's," (NESHER). One was kept in Vienna 104 years. They are always in sight in the East, every day in the year. Its care for its young is twice used as an example of God's fatherly care (Deut. xxxii. 11; Ex. xix. 4).

The gier eagle (Lev. xi. 18), called in Hebrew and Arabic RACHMAH, and is the modern Pharaoh's Hen, or Egyptian Vulture. It is migratory in Palestine, and ranges from Asia Minor to the Cape of Good Hope. The DAYAH is probably a kite (Lev. xi. 14), of which four kinds are known in Palestine. (See KITE.)

The golden eagle lives in pairs only, and requires a wide range of country, five pairs occupying as much as twenty miles. It is smaller than the Griffon, and not so strong.

The short-toed eagle is strong, heavy, and handsome, about two feet long, dark brown, and marked with black spots. There are twice as many of these as of all the other eagles put together in Palestine.

E'ANES (1 Esd. ix. 21). HARIM, MASSEIAH and ELIJAH.

EAR (*to plow*) (Deut. xxi. 4; Is. xxx. 24.)

EAR'NEST. (Heb. ARABON), a pledge, security (Gen. xxxviii. 17, 18, 20. Prov. xvii. 18).

EAR'RINGS (Heb. NEZEM). Ear-rings were made of gold, silver, brass or bronze, and glass, and in a great variety of forms, and varying in size from half an inch to three inches across. The nose ring is peculiar to the East, and is mentioned in Genesis (xxiv. 47), where Abraham's servant gave one to Rebekah. Except the nose ring men wear nearly all of these ornaments among oriental nations, and have from remote antiquity, as appears on the monuments in Egypt and Assyria. Rings were especially used for purposes of superstition and idolatry. The ring of ABRAXAS is an instance of superstitious use, as adopted by Christian Gnostics, and the museums of Europe and America furnish a great many other curious

NOSE-RING.

specimens of similar designs. Rings, coins and medals are hung in strings around the neck, by the sides of the face, and across the forehead sewed to the edge of the tarbush (see HEAD DRESS). Some ear-rings in the East are very large; two or even three inches across, and are loaded with pearls, precious stones, or glass.

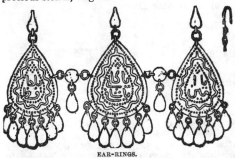

EAR-RINGS.

EARTH (Heb. ERETZ, Gr. *Ge*). Land and water, the whole visible surface of the globe. The Hebrew writers often used the term as we now use it, if meaning a local and limited space (James v. 17; Lev. iv. 25), and especially in the account of the crucifixion, where the darkness may have been over all the land of Israel, but probably not over all the globe (Matt. xxvii. 45; Luke xxiii. 44).

EARTH'QUAKES. Earthquakes have been frequent in all ages in Palestine, and their ravages may be traced at Aleppo (1616, 1812), Antioch (1737), Laodicea, Beirut, Sidon, Tyre, Safed, and Tiberias (1837). One is mentioned in the time of King Uzziah (Zech. xiv. 5): another in 31 B. C., when a great part of Jerusalem was destroyed and 10,000 persons killed. Josephus speaks of one about the time of the crucifixion (Ant. ix. 10, 4), when a large rock fell from Olivet.

EAST (Heb. KEDEM) (*before or in front*). By the east was often meant sun-rise. The Jews used to designate the lands lying east and north-east of Palestine (Gen. xxv. 6).

EAS'TER (Acts xii. 4). PASSOVER.

EAST'GATE (Neh. iii. 29). A gate of Jerusalem.

EATING. MEALS.

E'BAL. Mt. N. of Shechem (Deut. xi. 29). Moses charged the Israelites to put the blessing upon Mt. Gerizim, and the curse upon Mt. Ebal. Both mts. are now terraced and cultivated, from bottom to top, by fine gardens. Ebal is 2700 feet high; Gerizim 2600 above the sea, and about 1000 above Shechem. The valley is about 600 ft. wide.

E'BED (Heb. *servant*).—1. Father of Gaal (Judg. ix. 26, xxviii. 30, xxxi. 35).—2. Son of Jonathan (Ezr. viii. 6); Obeth in 1 Esd.

LOCUST.

E'BEDME'LECH. Ethiopian eunuch of Zedekiah, who released the prophet Jeremiah from prison, and was therefore saved when Jerusalem was taken (Jer. xxxviii. 7, ff).

E'BEH (Heb. EBEH)—*reed, bulrushes, papyrus* (Job. ix. 26). Boats or skiffs made of papyrus—light and swift.

EBEN-EZER (*stone of departure*). (1 Sam. xx. 19).

EBEN-E'ZER (*stone of help*). Set up by Samuel between Mizpeh and Shem (1 Sam. vii. 12). Site lost.

EBER (*beyond*), HEBER.—1. Son of Salah, great-grandson of Shem; from whom the Hebrews were named.—2. Son of Elpaal, a Benjamite (1 Chr. viii. 12).—3. A priest of Amok under Joiakim (Neh. xii. 20).

EBI'ASAPH (Heb. ABIASAPH). A Levite (1 Chr. vi. 23). The prophet Samuel and Heman the singer descended from him. ASAPH.

EBONY. True Ebony is a native of the coast of Malabar and of Ceylon. The tree is large, the stem nine feet in circumference, and shoots up, before it branches, to 29 ft. in hight; the branches are stiff, irregular and numerous. This elegant plant furnishes valuable materials for inlaying; its fine-grained wood being sometimes black, gray, or green.

EBRO'NAH. Near Ezion-geber.

E-CA'NUS. One of the five swift scribes who assisted Esdras (2 Esd. xiv. 24) ASIEL 2.

ECBATA'NA. ACHMETHA (Ezr. vi. 2). Two cities of this name.—1. Capital of N. Media. Atropatene of Strabo. The 7-walled town of Herodotus, and said to have been the capital of Cyrus. Where the roll was found which proved to Darius that Cyrus had really made a decree allowing the Jews to rebuild their temple. Ruins the most massive and antique, now called Takht-i-Suleiman, are on a conical hill 150 ft. above the plain, enclosing 2400 by 1200 ft. An artificial lake, 300 ft. across, is filled with clear, sweet water. The walls of the Temple were colored 7 tints—black, white, orange, blue, scarlet, silver and gold, in the order of the days dedicated to the planets. Was an important city as late as the 13th century, called Gaza, Gazaca, Cauzaca, by Greeks and Romans, and Shiz by Orientals.—2. The southern city, capital of Greater Media, is now called Hamadan, and is one of the great cities of Persia, with 20,000 inhabitants. Was the summer residence of the Persian kings from Darius downward. Was occupied by Alexander. The Jews say it was the residence of Ahasuerus, and show the tombs of Esther and Mordecai near it. See cut on page 6.

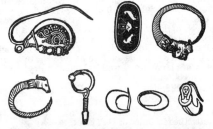

EAR-RINGS.

ECCLESIAS'TICUS. See HISTORY OF THE BOOKS.

ECLIPSE OF THE SUN. Supposed to be alluded to in Amos viii. 8, 9; Mic. iii. 6; Zech. xiv. 6· Jer. xv. 9.

ED (Heb. *witness*), (Josh. xxii. 34).

E'DAR (*flock-tower*). Where Jacob first pitched his tent after the death of Rachel (Gen. xxxv. 21). Near Bethlehem. Eder? There is a Jewish tradition that the Messiah is to be born there.

EDDIAS (1 Esd. ix. 26). JEZIAH.

EDEN (*garden of God*). The idea of a paradise of purity and happiness is found in all nations and in every religion. The location of the garden is lost.

Dr. Robinson proposed as the site of Eden the ruin called Jusieh el Kadimeh, in the valley of the Orontes, 30 ms. N. of Baalbek, 3 ms. S. E. of Riblah. A fortress in it was 396 ft. sq., having towers at the corners. Houses and streets are traced among the ruins over a space of 2½ ms. Much material has been carried away to build a new town of Jusieh, 1 m. N. W., toward Riblah. Ptolemy, Strabo and Pliny mention Paradisus in this same district. It is now dreary and barren, and water is found only in cisterns.—2. Beit-Jenn (*the house of Paradise*), S. W. of Damascus, on the E. slope of Hermon, near Mejdel, on a branch of the Pharpar.—3. Ez. xxiv. 23. In Assyria, with Haran, Canneh and Sheba, trading with Tyre. Supposed to be Aden.—4. Beth E. A country residence of the kings of Damascus (Amos i. 5). Near the cedars of Lebanon is a village of Ehden, but it is not identified with any historical event.

SIGNET RING OF SUPHIS.

ED'NA (Heb. *pleasure*). Wife of Raguel (Tob. vii. 2; viii. 14, 16).

E'DOM. IDUMEA (Mark iii. 8). The name of Esau (Gen. xxv. 29–34). The country settled by Esau's descendants. The ruddy hue of the mountains may have given the name Edom, which is *red* in the original. The ancient name was Mt. Seir. Seir means rugged. On the E. side of W. Arabah, from Elath on the S. to Moab on the N., at the brook Zered (Deut. ii. 13, 14, 18), about 100 ms. long by 20 ms. wide. The whole country is wild, rugged, and full of deep glens, but is also very fertile on the terraces; while the desert on each side is barren. The people dwelt amid the rocky hights, in caves and houses perched on dizzy crags, like eagles in their nests, living by their swords (Gen. xxvii. 40; Jer. xlix. 16); yet, as Isaac promised, this land possessed "the fatness of the earth, and of the dew of heaven" (Gen. xxvii. 39). The ancient capital was Bozrah. Sela (*Petra*) was the stronghold, and Ezion-geber its seaport, where Solomon built a fleet (2 Sam. viii. 14; 1 K. ix. 26). The crusaders built a fortress 12 ms. N. of Petra, on Mons. Regalis, now a ruin, called Shobek. The people were always idolaters (2 Chr. xxv. 14; Jos. Ant. xv. 17, § 9). The rock temples and dwellings of Edom were cut in a soft rock; were large, airy, well lighted and dry, and a safe protection against robbers.

E'DOMITES. Descendants of Edom (Gen. xxxvi. 1, ff.). See EDOM.

E'DREI. Bashan, one of its two capitals, the residence of Og (Deut. i. 4). In Manasseh (Josh. xiii. 12, 31). Two modern places claim this ancient name—(1) Edhra, at the S. W. angle of the Lejah, and (2) Dera, in the open plain of the Hauran, 14 ms. S. of the former. The ruins of Edhra are extensive and important above any other of the region; on a rocky projection from the Lejah, 3 ms. in circuit, raised 30 feet above the plain, which is wide and of unequalled fertility. The walls, roofs and doors are of a dark stone. There were many public buildings.—2. Naphtali, 3 ms. S. of Kedesh (Josh. xix. 37).

EGYPTIAN KING. RHAMSES IV.

EDUCATION. The Jews were strictly charged in the law to educate their children (Deut. iv. 9), but probably only in moral and religious discipline. The exceptions were those who were intended for priestly or civil office, as in the cases of Moses, Paul, Ezra, Daniel. There were schools of prophets (singers?) one of which, kept by Samuel, David attended. The sect of Essenes instructed children.

EG'LAH (Heb. *a heifer*). Wife of David at Hebron (2 Sam. iii. 5; 1 Chr. iii. 3). See DAVID.

ECLA'IM (2 *pounds*). (Is. xv. 8). Moab. Lost.

EGLON. Judah, in the Shefelah (Josh. xv. 39; x. 3–5). Now Ajlan, a shapeless mass of ruins, 10 ms. S. W. of Beit Jibrin, on the road to Gaza, from which it is 13 ms. Name of a very fat king of Philistia (Judg. iii. 14).

SIGNET OF THOTHMES III.

EGYPT. It would be interesting and valuable if we could give here a full account of all the monuments which confirm scripture, found in Egypt; but as that would fill a large volume, we must admit only a few illustrations, referring the student to the larger works.

Concerning Abraham, we find that the account of his visit to Egypt is confirmed by many facts which may be compared with the history, laws and customs of the country as found in Wilkinson, Lane, and other writers. The principal points illustrated by evidence derived from Egypt are: 1. That Egypt was then a rich, powerful, and civilized nation. 2. The lower part, or Delta, was dry. 3. Its kings were called Pharaoh. 4. Slavery was an institution. 5. There was a famine in Canaan and an abundance in Egypt. 6. Abraham's wife, Sarah, was fair and did not wear a veil. 7. Pharaoh wished to place Sarah in his harem. 8. Abraham was well received as a shepherd. 9. He had sheep, oxen, asses, men and maid servants, and camels. 10. Abraham accepted Pharaoh's gifts because he dared not refuse them, for the custom of the time then, as well as now, makes the refusal of a present an insult.

Joseph was sold to the Ishmaelites for a household servant; was bought by Potiphar, an officer of Pharaoh; made an overseer in the king's house; was

KING OF JUDAH.

tempted by Potiphar's wife; thrown in prison; interpreted the king's dream; was elevated to office; was invested with a ring and robes of office, a gold chain; had his name changed to an Egyptian one; and was married to Asenath, daughter to a priest of On.

The ring of Suphis, here engraved, was found on a mummy in the necropolis of Sakkara, near Memphis, is of pure gold, massive, and is now in the Abbott Egyptian Museum of the Historical Society, New York. The mummy was entirely cased in pure gold, every limb, even to the fingers' ends, being wrapped separately, and the whole was inscribed with hieroglyphics. Joseph was embalmed and put in a coffin (Gen. l. 26). The mummy cased in gold is of the age of Thothmes III, the Pharaoh who reigned in the time of Joseph, whose signet was found attached to a chain of gold, around his neck. The seal turns on a swivel, and so has two tablets, which are engraved. The whole is of very pure gold. Pharaoh made Joseph a ruler over all the land of Egypt, and called him ZAPHNATH-PAANE-AH (*preserver of the world*) (Gen. xli. 37-45.) The seal bears the name of Pharaoh, and also the title "Paaneah." (These, with the chain, are now in the Leyden Museum.) "He made him to ride in the second chariot" (v. 43).

MERCHANT OF CAIRO CARRYING HIS KEYS.

"Now there arose up a new king over Egypt, which knew not Joseph," and there was a period of bondage in which the Jews were held until the time of Moses and the Exodus.

The monuments show us the taskmaster and his men, the several kinds of work, punishment by the bastinado, etc.

The picture on p. 43, is in the tomb of Roschere, at Thebes. Rosellini (See his great work on Egypt, in the Astor Library) says: "Of the laborers, some are bringing clay in vessels; some mingling the straw with it; others taking the bricks out of the moulds and arranging them in order for burning; others carrying away the burnt bricks: all are different from the three overseers at the right-hand end of the picture (a fourth is sitting), in com-

the skill requisite to make a golden image of a calf, such as they made in Sinai?" As proof that they had, we offer the pictures on the monuments, showing men actually at work at the furnaces, "the refiner's fire," weighing, etc. The "calf" they made was an image of the Egyptian god Apis, which was a live bull, kept at Memphis; and they had probably, while slaves, made many images of him for use in all parts of the country.

Selections might be made showing workers in nearly every industry known in the East, but the student will be better satisfied with the larger works; and we have given enough here to point the argument, that the scriptures are true.

Long after the Exodus, "Shishak, king of Egypt, came up against Jerusalem" (2 Chr. xii. 2), and on one of the walls in a temple at Karnac there is a picture of 63 prisoners, each one representing a city, tribe, or nation, and among them is a "king of the country of Judah." The names of Beth-horon, Megiddo, Mahanaim, and other cities in Palestine, are there, on shields. There are 84 names of persons or places of Canaan on the monuments at Abu Simbel, Thebes, and other ruins in Egypt, written in hieroglyphics. (See SHISHAK.) The word mizraim (*the two Egypts*) in the Hebrew Scriptures is translated Egypt in many passages (Ez. xxix. 10, etc.). Misr is *red mud* in Arabic. The name on the monuments is KEM (black). Upper E. extended from the cataracts to Memphis, and was called THEBAIS; and Lower E. from Memphis to the sea called the DELTA. Upper E. was also called PATHROS (Is. xi. 11). Land of Ham (Ps. cv. 23). The sign for Upper E. was a bent reed, and for Lower E. a bee (Is. vii. 18).

E'HI (Heb. *connection*), a Benjamite chief (Gen. xlvi. 21). AHIRAM.

E'HUD (Heb. *union, powerful*). 1. Son of Bilhan (Zech. vii. 10, viii. 6).—2. Son of Gera, tribe of Benjamin (Judg. iii. 15, ff), the second Judge of the Israelites (B. C. 1336), called a deliverer.

E'KER (Heb. *transplanted*). Descendant of Judah (1 Chr. ii. 27).

SPHINX AND PYRAMIDS.

plexion, physiognomy and beard. The original is in colors and the figures are very large.

The inscription at the top is translated, "Captives brought by his majesty to build the temple of the great God."

The question has been asked. "Had the Jews

EK'REBEL (Judg. vii. 18), AKRABEH A village 7 miles S. E. of Nablûs.

EK'RON (Heb. *eradication*). A royal city in the north of Philistia (Josh. xiii. 3), now AKIR, built on the accumulated rubbish of past ages. The deity worshiped was Baal-zebub. Ekron was the last place to which the Ark was carried before its return to Israel.

EK'RONITES. People of Ekron (Josh. xiii. 3).

E'LAH (valley of Terebinth). Where David slew Goliath (1 Sam. xvii. 2, 19; xxi. 9).

E'LAH (*strength*), (Heb. TEREBINTH or *oak*).—1. Son of Baasha, king of Israel (1 K. xvi. 8–14).—2. Father of Hoshea (2 K. xv. 30).

EL'AH. Duke of Edom (Gen. xxxvi. 41).—2. Father of Shimei (1 K. iv. 18).—3. Son of Caleb (1 Chr. iv. 15).—4. Son of Uzzi, a Benjamite chief (1 Chr. ix. 8).

EL'AHDAH (Heb. ELADA), (*whom God adorns*). A descendant of Ephraim (1 Chr. vii. 20).

E'LAM. Oldest son of Shem (Gen. x. 22). The country peopled by his descendants was along the Ulai, and its capital was Shushan, one of the most powerful and magnificent cities of antiquity. The name is found in the ancient inscriptions. Called also Nuvaki. Extended from the Persian Gulf to Assyria on the N., to the Zagron mts. on the E., and the Tigris on the W. In the time of Abram, the king of Elam was one of the most powerful in Asia (Jer. xlix. 34–39). The people were idolaters, and their images are found in the ruins. Elamites were at the Pentecostal feast (Acts ii. 9).

E'LAMITES. They were the original inhabitants of ELAM (Gen. x. 22; Ezr. iv. 9).

E'LASAH (*God-created*). ELASA. 1. A priest of Pashur (Ezr. x. 22).—2. Son of Shaphan. Sent on a mission by king Zedekiah to Babylon. (Jer. xxxi. 3).

E'LATH. Idumæa, on the E. gulf of the Red Sea. First named in Deut. ii. 8; and the reference in 1 K. ix. 26, shows that E. was more ancient than Ezion-gaber. King Solomon built a navy here. A fort is kept garrisoned here now, called Akaba, for the benefit of the pilgrims to Mecca.

EL'BETH'EL (*God of Bethel*). The place where God appeared to Jacob when he was fleeing from Esau (Gen. xxxv. 7).

EL'CIA. HILKIAH (Judg. viii. 1).

EL'DA-AH (Heb. *whom God called*) (Gen. xxv. 4). Son of Midian.

EL'DAD (*whom God loves*) and **MEDAD.** Two of the seventy Elders who had the gift of prophesy (Num. xi. 16, 26).

EL'DER (Heb. ZAKEN, Gr. *presbyter*). An old man. A title of honor and respect given to persons in authority (Gen. xxiv. 2; l. 7), as stewards or as master workmen. The elder was a political officer among the Hebrews, Moabites, Midianites and Egyptians (Num. xxii. 7). The office is the keystone of the political system among the modern Syrians, who use the name SHEIKH, which means *old man*, for the chief or head of the tribe. Moses adopted the idea and regulated its use by laws (Ex. iii. 16; iv. 29). Their authority was almost unlimited, within the law and customs (Josh. ix. 18). They became judges or magistrates in Canaan, in the local towns, sitting in the gates (Deut. xix. 12). They are called the Senate in 1 Macc. xii. 6. See SYNAGOGUE. The office of elder in the Christian church was adopted from the Jewish custom.

E'LEAD (*whom God applauds*). A decendant of Ephraim (1 Chr. vii. 21). SHUTHELAH.

ELE'ALEH (*God's hight*). E. of Jordan, on the plateau of Moab, 1 m. N. E. of Heshbon, on the summit of a conical hill. Was once strongly fortified; and there are ruins of walls, cisterns, etc. Rebuilt by Reuben (Num. xxxii. 37).

ELEA'SA. Near Azotus (1 Macc. ix. 15).

ELE'ASAH (Heb. ELASAH.) 1. Son of Helez of Judah (1 Chr. ii. 39).—2. Son of Rapha (1 Chr. viii. 37, ix. 43).

ELEA'ZAR (Heb. *whom God helps*). 1. Son of Aaron (Lev. x. 1, ff). Eleazar was chief over the Levites (Num. iii. 32).—2. Son of Abinadab (1 Sam. vii. 1).—3. Son of Dodo the Ahohite; one of the three chiefs of David's army (2 Sam. xxiii. 9, ff).—4. A Levite, son of Mohli (1 Chr. xxiii. 21, 22).—5. A priest (Neh. xii. 42).—6. A decendant of Parosh; an Israelite (Ezr. x. 25).—7. Son of Phinehas (Ezr. viii. 33).—8. Elizzer (1 Esd. viii. 43).—9. Avaran (1 Macc. ii. 5).—10. A distinguished scribe of great age, who was a martyr in the time of Antiochus Epiphanes (2 Macc. vi. 18, 31).—11. Father of Jason (1 Macc. viii. 18).—12. Son of Eliud (Matt. i. 15).

ELECT' (*chosen, selected*). Election. The designation of persons to office (Acts ix. 15); of people or nations to the enjoyment of peculiar privileges (Deut. vii. 6–8) and of a definite number of persons to eternal life (2 Thess. ii. 13). This subject belongs to the mysteries of God and cannot be so clearly stated as to leave no uncertainty in the mind. The position is: that God does and will save a number of persons, and He does this according to a plan which he formed before the world was made; and he has never, and never will change that plan (Eph. i. 4; 2 Tim. i. 9); their election is of free grace and love, and not for any good in the person (Eph. i. 5); the redemption of Christ is included in the great plan. This plan enters into our destiny as a controlling element; as, it may be said by analogy, the patriotic determination of Washington resulted in the independence of our country; and the plans of a father determines where his family shall reside, the college his son shall attend, and the studies he shall pursue.

EL-ELOHE-ISRAEL (*Almighty, God of Israel*). Name of the altar that Jacob built facing Shechem (Gen. xxxiii. 19, 20).

ELEPH (*ox*). Benj. (Josh. xviii. 18).

ELEPHANTS (Heb. SHEN-HABBIM). Elephants were used in warfare (1 Macc. i. 17, iii. 34). See IVORY.

ELEUTHEROP'OLIS. On the E. border of the plain of Philistia, at the foot of the hills of Judæa, in S. Palestine, 25 ms. S. W. from Jerusalem. Not mentioned in Scripture, but was an important city

WORKING IN METALS.

in the early Christian ages, when its name was Betogabra, *House of Bread.* Eusebius mentions it as the seat of a bishop, and reckons distances to other cities from it as a centre. The ruins are still shown of a fine chapel, and of a fort built by the Crusaders, 200 ft. square, in the 12th cent. Now Beit Jibrin, having 50 or more houses. The great attractions here are the caverns, or houses cut in the solid rocks. Rooms 100 feet or more in length, with smooth and ornamented walls, and lofty, arched roofs; some 40 to 70 ft. by 60 ft. high; most

WORKING IN METALS.

of them lighted by openings in the roof, and connected by doorways. Jerome says they were built by Idumæans.

ELEU'THERUS. River in Syria (1 Macc. xi. 7, xii. 30). Strabo says it divided Syria from Phœnicia. Now the Nahr el Kebir, *Great River;* rising in Lebanon, passing through the entrance to Hamath (Num. xxxiv. 8), emptying into the Great Sea 18 miles N. of Tripolis.

ELHA'NAN (*God-endowed*). 1. A great warrior in David's time (2 Sam. xxiii. 24). Son of Dodo, one of David's thirty men.—2. Son of Jair (or Jaor).

ELI (*hight*). A high-priest descended from Aaron (1 K. ii. 27; 2 Sam. viii. 17).

E'LI LA'MA (*my God*) **SABACH'THA-NI**—*wherefore hast thou forsaken me?*—words uttered by Christ on the cross (Matt. xxvii. 46; Ps. xxii.).

ELI'AB (*God is father*). 1. Son of Helon (Num. i. 9).—2. Son of Phallu (Num. xxvi. 8, 9).—3. One of David's brothers, son of Jesse (1 Chr. ii. 13).—4. A Levite, porter and musician (1 Chr. xv. 18, 20).—5. A Gadite leader in David's time (1 Chr. xii. 9).—6. Son of Nohath (1 Chr. vi. 27).—7. Son of Nathanael (Judg. viii. 1).

ELI'ADA (*whom God knows or cares for*). 1. Son of David (2 Sam. v. 16).—2. A Benjamite who led 200,000 men to the army of Jehoshaphat (2 Chr. xvii. 17).

ELI'ADAH (Heb. ELIADA). Father of Rezon (1 K. xi. 23). ELI'ADAS (1 Esd. ix. 28)—ELIOENAI.

ELI'AH (Heb. ELIJAH). 1. Son of Jeroham (1 Chr. viii. 29).—2. Son of Elam (Ezr. x. 26).

ELI'ABA (*whom God hides*). One of David's thirty men (2 Sam. xxii. 32).

ELI'ĀKIM (*whom God has set up*). 1. Son of Hilkiah I (2 K. xviii. 26, 37); he was a prefect in the king's house (Is. xxii. 20).—2. The original name of Jehoiakim, king of Judah (2 K. xxii. 34). —3. A priest who assisted at the dedication of the new wall of Jerusalem (Neh. xii. 41).—4. Son of Abiud, and father of Azor (Matt. i. 13).—5. Son of Melea (Luke iii. 30, 31).

ELIAM. ELIAB (*God's people*): 1. Father of Bathsheba (2 Sam. i. 3).—2. Son of Ahithophel (2 Sam. xxiii. 34).

ELIAS. See ELIJAH.

ELI'ASAPH (*whom God has added*). 1. Son of Deuel (Num. i. 14).—2. Son of Lael (Num. iii. 24).

ELI'ASHIB (*God restores*). 1. A priest in David's time (1 Chr. xxiv. 12).—2. Son of Elioenai (iii. 24).—3. High-priest at Jerusalem (Neh. iii. 1, 20, 21).—4. A singer (Ezr. x. 24).—5. Son of Zattu (x. 27).—6. Son of Bani (x. 36).

ELI'ATHAH (*God comes*). Son of Hernan (1 Chr. xxv. 4, 27).

ELI'DAD. Son of Chislon; a prince who assisted in the division of the land of Canaan (Num. xxxiv. 21).

E'LIEL (*God is strength*). A common name among the Hebrews, but nothing of any note is known of any one bearing it (1 Chr. viii. 20; ii. 46).

ELIE'NAI. Son of Shimhi (1 Chr. viii. 20). Elioenai, a chief.

ELIE'ZER (*God helps*). 1. Steward of Abraham's

house (Gen. xv. 5).—2. Son of Moses and Zipporah (Ex. xviii. 4).—3. Son of Becher (1 Chr. vii. 8).—4. Priest in David's reign (xxv. 24).—5. Son of Zichri (xxvii. 16).—6. Son of Dodavah (2 Chr. xx. 37).—7. A chief Israelite—a learned assistant to Ezra (Ezr. viii. 16).—8, 9, 10. Priests (Ezr. x 18, 23, 31).—11. Son of Jorim (Luke iii. 29).

ELIHOE'NAI. Son of Zerahiah, who, with 200 men, returned from the captivity with Ezra (Ezr. viii. 4).

CARMEL.

ELIHO'REPH (*God rewards*). Son of Shisha, scribe of Solomon.

ELI'HU (*Jehovah*). 1. Son of Barachel (Gen. xxii. 21).—2. Son of Tohu (1 Sam. i. 1).—3 (1 Chr. xxvii. 18). "Of the brethren of David."—4. Captain of the thousands of Manasseh (1 Chr. xii. 20). A Levite (1 Chr. xxvi. 7).

ELI'JAH (Heb. ELI'AHU, *God-Jah, El-Jehovah*). On his first appearance he is simply denominated "Elijah the Tishbite, of the inhabitants of Gilead" (1 K. xvii. 1). It is supposed that Thisbe, in Galilee, was the birth-place of Elijah, but there is no proof. Such points were left in doubt that he might be known and thought of simply as *the great prophet reformer*. In this light alone he appears in the sacred history. His one grand object was to awaken Israel to the conviction that Jehovah, *Jehovah alone is God*. The period of Israelitish history at which Elijah appeared was one that emphatically called for the living exhibition of this great truth. It was that period of Ahab's apostasy, when, through the influence and example of his wife Jezebel he formally introduced the worship of other gods into Israel. In the language of the sacred historian, "It seemed a light thing for him to walk in the sins of Jeroboam, the son of Nebat; he took the daughter of Ethbaal to wife, and served Baal, and worshiped him. He reared up an altar for Baal in the house of Baal, in Samaria" (1 K. xvi. 31). He did not rest, like his predecessors, with the corrupt worship of Jehovah under the form of a calf, but brought in the worship of the Tyrian Baal, with its usual accompaniment of the Asherah pollutions—the rites of the Syrian Venus. Hence he enters on the work assigned him as the special servant of Jehovah, and in his name announces what shall absolutely come to pass, confident that there is no power in heaven or earth capable of reversing the word. "And Elijah said unto Ahab, As Jehovah, God of Israel liveth, before whom I stand,

WILLOW BOAT.

there shall not be dew nor rain these years, but according to my word" (1 K. xvii. 1). After the utterance of a word by which the genial influences of heaven were to be laid under arrest for a series of years, it became necessary that a hiding place should be provided for Elijah, that he might escape from the violence of those in high places, and from the importunities of others, who might try to prevail upon his pity. Such a hiding-place was found for him to the east —beyond the limits of the kingdom of Israel— beside the brook Cherith, that flowed into the Jordan. There he found not only water from the brook, but also supplies of bread and flesh, morning and evening, ministered at God's command by ravens. The brook Cherith, however, in course of time dried up, and another place of refuge had to be provided for the prophet. This was found in the house of a poor widow, with an only son—and she not in the land of Israel, but at Zarephath (Sarepta), in the territory of Zidon, the native region of the infamous Jezebel (1 K. xvii. 9). Brought by divine direction to the place and to the woman, he found her near the gate of the city, gathering a few sticks to prepare her last meal, that she and her son might thereafter die. In the confidence of faith he bids her go and bake the bread as she intended, but in the first instance to bring a portion of it, with a little water, to him, demanding such faith from her as he himself exercised toward God. And he added, as the ground for her belief and his own demand, "For thus saith Jehovah, God of Israel, the barrel of meal shall not waste, neither shall the cruse of oil fail till the day that Jehovah sendeth rain on the earth." On the occasion of a severe illness befalling her son, she said to Elijah in a petulant tone, "What have I to do with thee, O thou man of God? Art thou come unto me to call my sin to remembrance, and to slay my son?"

Josephus does not understand that the child died. Jewish tradition says that this boy afterwards became a servant to the prophet, and also the prophet Jonah.

This seems to imply that she looked upon him as the occasion of her calamity, and that it would have been better for her had she not known him. However she graciously overlooked what might be wrong in it; as it was, the calamity proved a heavy trial to Elijah, and with holy freedom he laid it before God, and said, "O Jehovah, my God, hast thou also brought evil upon the widow with whom I sojourn, by slaying her son? I pray thee, let this child's soul come into him again." The child began to breathe, and presently was delivered alive to his mother. She said, "Now, by this I know that thou art a man of God, and the word of Jehovah in thy mouth is truth."

It was in the third year of Elijah's sojourn with the widow, that the Lord came to him, announcing the near prospect of rain, and bid him go and show himself to Ahab (1 K. xviii. 1). Returning to King Ahab, he procured the great assembly at Mount Carmel, where God "answered by fire," and the prophets of Baal were destroyed. (See CARMEL.) Now the long terrible drought was broken, and a plentiful rain descended at the prophet's prayer. He fled from the fury of Jezebel, first to Beersheba where he left his servant (Jonah), and went on alone into the wilderness (of Sinai.—Dr. Crosby), where he wished for death. "It is enough, Lord, let me die, for I am not better than my fathers." (The oratorio of Elijah, by Mendelssohn, is a beautiful and effective commentary on this part of the prophet's life.) Here the prophet saw the Lord pass by, in answer to his complaint. The wind rent the mountains, and brake in pieces the rocks of Sinai; then an earthquake; and after that a fire, burning in the constant blaze of lightning. These were symbols of the angry frame of mind that the prophet had. Then, after a profound stillness, there came a small voice, soft and gentle. This was Jehovah's method of winning men—not by exhibitions of terrible power. The persecutions of Ahab and Jezebel, the slaughter of Baal's priests, had nothing of God in them; but he was to be found as truly worshiped by the few who had not bowed the knee to Baal. These commands were given him:—To return to the wilderness of Damascus, and at a proper time annoint Hazael, king of Syria, Jehu, king of Israel, and Elisha as his successor. Elisha was appointed by having Elijah's cloak (of coarse camel hair, or wool) cast on him, when, from that time "He poured water on the hands of Elijah," that is, served him daily. Six years after he denounces Ahab and Jezebel for their crime against Naboth, in taking his vineyard. He foretells the death of Ahaziah, the king. The warning letter to Jehoram is by a later hand, of the same school. Two bands of guards having been sent by Ahab to arrest him, he calls down fire from heaven on their heads. Soon after that he crossed the Jordan with Elisha "on dry ground," and was separated from him by fire and carried away by a wind "into heaven." Elisha asked for the first born's double portion, as the eldest follower of Elijah. His whole life as a prophet was one of trial and conflict. The Jews, in the time of Jesus, expected Elijah to reappear, and Jesus alludes to the belief (Matt. xi. 14), explaining the fulfilment as in John the Baptist. Elijah (Elias in Greek) became a name for any or all true prophets, as David for the king, Abraham or Israel for the Hebrews.

ĒLIM (*trees*). Had twelve fountains (not wells), and a palm grove, being a kind of desert paradise (Ex. xv. 27). *Wady Ghurundel* has now several fine fountains, supplying a perennial stream, and has more trees, shrubs, and bushes than any other spot in the desert. Here the plain ends and the mountain begins.

ELIM'ELECH (*God is King*). The Bethlehemite husband of Noomi; the father of Mahlon and Chilion. See RUTH in the HISTORY OF THE BOOKS.

MULBERRY.

ELIOĒ'NĀI (*eyes turned to El-God*).—1. Benjamite, and head of a family (1 Chr. vii. 8).—2 Simeonite, and head of a family (1 Chr. iv. 36).—3. Korhite Levite, and doorkeeper in the Temple of Solomon (1 Chr. xxvi. 3). Two before, and two others after the captivity, were not noted.

EL'IPHAL (*judged by El*). Son of Ur (1 Chr. xi. 35).

ELIPH'ALET. Son of David, the last of 13, born in Jerusalem (2 Sam. v. 16).—2. One of David's 30 heroes.—3. A Benjamite. ELIPHELET.

EL'IPHAZ, or **ELĪPHAZ** (*God for strength*). 1. Son of Esau, and father of Teman (Gen. xxxvi. 10).—2. Chief of the three friends of Job, called the Temanite (Job. ii. 11). See JOB in the HISTORY OF THE BOOKS.

ELIPH'ELET (*God distinguishes*).—1. Son of David (1 Chr. iii. 6). ELPALET.—2 ELIPHALET 1.—3. Son of ABASBAI (2 Sam. xxiii. 34). ELIPHAL in 1 Chr. xi.—4. Son of Eshek, and of Saul through Jonathan (1 Chr. viii. 39).—5. One of the Bene-Adonikam who returned with Ezra (Ezr. viii. 13).—6. One of the Bene-Hashum in Ezra's time (Ezr. x. 33).

TORTOISE.

ELIS'ABETH (*fulness of God*).—1. Wife of Zacharias, and mother of John the Baptist (Luke i. 5, 42), and cousin to Mary, the mother of Jesus.—2. The wife of Aaron (Ex. vi. 23).

ELISĒUS. The name of Elisha in the Apocrypha and the N. T. (Luke iv. 27).

ELĪ'SHA (*God for Salvation*). Son of Shaphat, and a native of Abel-Meholah, where Elijah found him, whose pupil and successor he was from B. C. 903 to 838 (1 K. xix. 16), He was with Elijah when he divided the Jordan, and was carried away by a whirlwind and chariot of fire. Elijah's mission was to show that El was the God of Israel—Elisha to show that God should also be the salvation of his people. Beneficent working and kindly blessing were Elisha's chief work. His first act was to heal the bitter waters of Jericho. Following this were: the anathema on the young lads who mocked at God's prophet; refusing to prophesy for Jehoram the son of Ahab, "the son of a murderer," he did so to Jehoshaphat, giving them counsel which secured victory; he multiplied the widow's pot of oil; restored the Shunemite's son; cured the poisoned pottage; he multiplies a scant supply (twenty barley loaves and some roasted corn) to enough for 100 men; cured Naaman's leprosy; Gehazi lies, and is cursed with leprosy; restored the ax lost in the Jordan; showed a host of spiritual warriors to his servant, and struck blind the whole Syrian army, but he saved them from destruction by the Jews, caused the king to feed and send them away; he predicts plenty and the death of the king; the king restores her land to the Shunemite; predicts the death of king Ben-hadad, and the succession of Hazael; anoints Jehu king over Israel; the incident of the smiting with the bundles of arrows. Even after death he restored the dead to life. Elisha is seen to resemble Christ in his miracles, and in his loving, gentle character. He had no successor. The Greek church honors Elisha as a saint, on June 14.

ELĪSHA (*firm bond*). Son of Javan (Gen. x. 4), who named the "Isles of Elisha," which traded with Tyre (Ez. xxvii. 7). ELIS is from the same source. HELLAS, ancient Greece.

ELISHĀ'MA (*God hears*). Prince in Ephraim (Num. i. 10).—2. Son of David (2 Sam. v. 16).—3. Son of David, also called ELISHUA (1 Chr. iii. 6).—4. Of Judah, son of Jekamiah (1 Chr. ii. 41), and father of Nethaniah, grandfather of Ishmael of the Captivity (2 K. xxv. 25); ELISHAMAH in some editions.—5. Scribe to Jehoiakim (Jer. xxxvi. 12).—7. Priest to Jehoshaphat, and sent to teach (2 Chr. xvii. 8).

ELĪSH'APHAT (*God judges*). Captain of "hundreds," in the service of Jehoiada (2 Chr. xxiii. 1).

ELĪSH'EBA (*God of the oath*). Daughter of Amminadab, of Judah, wife of Aaron; same as Elisabeth (Ex. vi. 23; Num. i. 7). Her marriage to Aaron united the royal and priestly tribes, Judah and Levi.

ELISHU'A (*El is salvation*). David's son, born at Jerusalem (2 Sam. v. 15). ELISHAMA in 1 Chr. iii. 6).

ELĪU. Ancestor of Judith (viii. 1), of Simeon.

ELĪ'UD (*Jews' God*). Son of Achim (Matt. i. 15). From Abina.

ELIZ'APHAN (*God protects*).—1. Son of Uzziel, a Levite (Ex. vi. 22). The family are mentioned in the times of David and Hezekiah. ELZAPHAN. 2. Son of Parnach, appointed by Moses, from Zebulon, to assist in dividing the land (Num. xxxiv. 25).

ELĪ'ZUR (*God the rock*). Son of Shedeur, of Reuben (Num. i. 5).

ELKĀ'NAH (*El creates*). Son of Korah (Ex. vi. 24). Several generations of Korah's sons are given in 1 Chr. vi. 22, etc.—2. Son of Joel, in the same line as 1 (vi. 25, 36).—3. Another, in the line of Ahimoth, or Mahath (vi. 26, 35).—4. A Kohathite Levite, in the line of Heman. Son of Jeroham, and father of Samuel the prophet (1 Sam. i. 1, etc). He lived in Mt. Ephraim, or Ramah, and attended yearly meeting for worship and sacrifice at Shiloh. He was rich enough to give three bullocks when Samuel was presented at the house of the Lord.—5. A Levite living in Netopha (ix. 16).—6. Doorkeeper in David's time, for the Ark (xv. 23).—7. Joined David at Ziklag (xii. 6).—8. The second in command in the house of Ahaz, killed by Zichri (2 Chr. xxviii. 7).

BULBUL.

ELKŌSH' (*El's power*). Birthplace of Nahum (i. 1). There is a place so named in Assyria (34 ms. N. of Mosul), and modern Jews and the resident Chaldee Christians show a tomb of Nahum there. Jerome says the place was in Galilee, where there is now a traditional tomb of the prophet at *kefr tanchum*, near Tiberias.

ELKOSH'ITE. From Elkosh.

EL'LASAR (Gen. xiv. 1). THELASAR TELASSAR. The country and kingdom of Arioch in the days of Abraham.

ELM. Error for *oak* (Heb. ALAH), in Hos. iv. 13.

ELMO'DAM. Son of Er, in Joseph's line (Luke iii. 28). Almodad in Gen. x. 26.

ELNA'AM (*El his delight*). Father of Jeribai and Joshaviah, two of David's guard (1 Chr. xi. 46).

ELNA'THAN (*whom El gave*). Maternal grandfather of Jehoiachin (2 K. xxiv. 8).—2. Three Levites of this name in Ezra's time (Ezr. viii. 16). In 1 Esd. viii. 44, etc., the names are ALNATHAN and EUNATAN. Elnathan was sent by the king into Egypt to bring back the fugitive Urijah (Jer. xxvi. 20); and he was present at the burning of Jeremiah's roll, protesting against the act. See JEHOIAKIM.

ELO HIM. A plural word in Hebrew, meaning the true God. JAH.

ELO I. When applied to heathen idols, it means gods. My God (Mark xv. 34).

E'LON (Heb. ALLON, *an oak*). 1. Father of Esau's wife Adah, a Hittite (Gen. xxvi. 34).—2. Founder of the Elonites (Gen. xlvi. 14).—3. Judge for ten years (Judg. xii. 11); from the tribe of Zebulon. E'LON (*oak*). Dan (Josh. xix. 43). Same place as E LON-BETH-HANAN (*oak of the house of grace*). Dan (1 K. iv. 9). Lost.

EL'PAAL (*El, his reward*). Son of Hushim, a Benjamite, and founder of a family (1 Chr. viii. 12).

ELPA'RAN. Terebinth of Paran (Gen. xiv. 6).

EL'TEKEH (*El fearing*). Place in Dan (Josh. xix. 44). Levitical.

ELTEKON (*God its foundation*). In Judah, 4 miles from Hebron (Josh. xv. 59). Lost.

ELTO LAD (*El's kindred*). In Judah, near Beersheba (Josh xv. 30). Wilton thinks it was in *Wady Lussan*, 60 miles S. of Gaza. Rowland places it in *Wady Salud*, 40 miles S. E. of Gaza.

ELUL. Name of the sixth Hebrew month.

ELU'ZAI (*God my praise*). Soldier who joined David at Ziklag (1 Chr. xii. 5).

ELYMA'IS. ELAM. City in Persia, containing a very rich temple, in which were many trophies deposited by Alexander the Great (1 Macc. vi. 1). Antiochus Epiphanes failed to capture it (Ant. xii. 9, § 1). In Tobit, ii. 10, Elymais is the name of a province.

ELYÆ'MANS. Elamites (Judith i. 6). See ELAM.

EL'YMAS (Ar. *wise*). Arabic name of Barjesus (Acts xiii. 6), the sorcerer. The Orientals called fortune-tellers by their true names, sorcerers, imposters.

EL'ZABAD (*given by El*). Warrior from Gad, who joined David in the wilderness (1 Chr. xii. 12).—2. A Korhite Levite, son of Shemaiah (1 Chr. xxvi. 7), a doorkeeper in the Temple.

MUMMY.

EL'ZAPHAN (*protected by El*). Cousin to Moses, and son of Uzziel (Ex. vi. 22). He was one of the two bearers of Nadab and Abihu (Lev. x. 4). ELIZAPHAN.

EMBALMING (*em-bă-ming*). Preserving by spices, gums, etc., dead bodies from decay. Two instances are mentioned in the O. T.: Jacob's and Joseph's bodies (Gen. l. 2, 26). The soft parts of the interior were removed, and spices, gums, etc., filled in their stead, and the whole was then steeped for 70 days in natron (petroleum or asphaltum), after which the body was carefully wrapped in strips of linen, dipped in gum, and delivered to the friends, who put it in the coffin, which was of wood carved and painted, or of stone, sculptured. The whole art was carefully guarded by strict laws. The body could only be cut by an authorized person, with a stone knife (see KNIFE). Embalming was not practiced by the Hebrews. Asa was laid in a bed of spices (2 Chr. xvi. 14), and Jesus had a hundred pound weight of spices placed in the tomb (John xix. 39, 40).

The Egyptians practiced the art because of their belief in the doctrine of transmigration of souls. (See Pettigrew's *Hist. of Eg. Mummies*).

EMBROIDERED ROBE.

EMBROIDERY (Heb. ROKEN), (Ex. xxxv. 35). Needlework. Two kinds of extra fine cloth was made, one by the *roken* of various colors and figures, called *rikmah*, and the other by the *chosheb* (*cunning workmen*), into which gold or other metallic threads are woven, besides the usual colors, both of which were made in the loom. The needle was used where the figure was wanted on one side only of the cloth. Wilkinson says that "Many of the Egyptian stuffs presented various patterns, worked in colors by the loom, independent of those produced by the dyeing or the printing process, and so richly composed that they vied with the cloths embroidered by the needle." The art was known in Assyria also, as the sculptures show. Ezekiel mentions embroidered work as the production of Egypt and Assyria, imported by way of Tyre (Ez. xxvii. 7, 23, 24). See DRESS.

EM'ERALD (Heb. NOPEK). A precious stone in the 2d row in the breastplate of the high-priest (Ex. xxviii. 18).

EM'ERODS. Some kind of tumors which afflicted the Philistines, because of their want of respect for the ark of the covenant (1 Sam. v. 6).

E'MIM (Heb. *terrors*). Moabite name for a race of giants or strong men, on the east of the Dead Sea (Gen. xiv. 5; Deut. ii. 10).

EMMAN'UEL. IMMANUEL (Matt. i. 23).

EMMA'US. Now called Kuriet El Enab, 7½ ms. west of Jerusalem. Josephus mentions it (Wars vii. 6, 9). Jerome mistook Nicopolis, the present *Amwas*, for this place, a proof of how early some scripture localities of the N. T. times were lost.— 2. In the plain of Philistia; fortified by Bacchides (Ant. xiii. 1, 3; Macc. ix. 50). Destroyed A. D. 4, by the Romans. Rebuilt A. D. 220, and called Nicopolis.—3. A village on the shore of the Sea of Galilee, S. of Tiberias, the same as Hammath (*hot baths*).

EM'MOR. See HAMOR (Acts vii. 16).

EN. AIN Hebrew for *fountain*. The word means *an eye*. See AIN.

ENA'JIM. ENAM. An open place (Gen. xxxviii. 11, 21), in the gate of Enam.

E'NAM (*double spring*). Judah, in the Shefelah (Josh. xv. 34). The residence of Tamar. (Gen. xxxviii. 14).

E'NAN (*having eyes or fountains*). Ahiram Ben Enan was a chief of the tribe of Naphtali, at Sinai (Num. i. 15).

ENCAMPMENT (Heb. MAHANEH). The camp of the Lord's host, with the Lord himself symbolically resident among them. The whole camp was a sacred place, and all impurities both actual and ceremonial must go outside of its limits (Deut. xxiii. 14). Criminals were also executed outside, as also of the cities. It was managed and guarded in a military style, with sentinels, etc. See WILDERNESS OF THE WANDERING. The modern Bedawins now camp in any fit place, near water, if possible. The Sheikh marks his place by his spear standing in front of his tent. The walled cities were fortified camps.

above the level plain; the water is sweet and warm (81° Fahr.). Ruins of the ancient city are scattered tered over the hills and plain. The soil is rich and fertile, and the variety of trees even now produced gives evidence of its ancient fruitfulness. The vineyards mentioned in Cant. i. 14, are still represented by fine vines. Its history is 4000 years, but may be told in a few words. The Amorites dwelt here (Gen. xiv. 7; 2 Chr. xx. 2). David cut off the skirt of Saul's robe in a cave at E. (1 Sam. xxiv. 1-4). The early hermits of Palestine, the Essenes, had their chief seat at Engedi, and not far from there is the convent of Mar Saba (Saint Saba), in the gorge of Kidron.

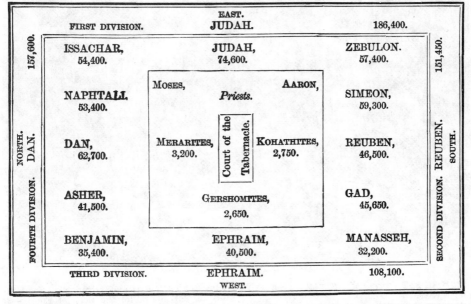

EAST.

		JUDAH.			186,400.
FIRST DIVISION.					

157,600.	ISSACHAR, 54,400.	JUDAH, 74,600.	ZEBULON. 57,400.	151,450.
	NAPHTALI. 53,400.	MOSES, *Priests.* AARON,	SIMEON, 59,300.	
NORTH. DAN.	DAN, 62,700.	MERARITES, 3,200. Court of the Tabernacle. KOHATHITES, 2,750.	REUBEN, 46,500.	SOUTH. REUBEN.
FOURTH DIVISION.	ASHER, 41,500.	GERSHOMITES, 2,650.	GAD, 45,650.	SECOND DIVISION.
	BENJAMIN, 35,400.	EPHRAIM, 40,500.	MANASSEH, 32,200.	

THIRD DIVISION.	EPHRAIM.	108,100.

WEST.

ENCHANTMENTS. Several Hebrew words are so translated.—1. LATIM (Ex. vii. 11); secret arts. —2. CESHAPHIM (2 K. ix. 22); witchcrafts, sorceries. in Isaiah xlvii. 9, meaning muttered spells. —3. LAHASH (Eccl. x. 11); ear-rings, amulets in Is. iii. 20. Used in the charming of serpents.—4. NAHASH (Num. xxiii. 23), augury, omen.—5. HEBER, spell. See MAGIC, DIVINATION.

EN'DOR (*spring of Dor*). In Issacher, but belonging to Manasseh (Josh. xvii. 11). The great victory over Sisera and Jabin (Ps. lxxxiii. 9, 10). Saul visited the witch (1 Sam. xxviii. 7). Now a little village at the N. of Jebel Duhy, Little Hermon. The rocks around are full of caves.

ENE AS. A paralytic healed by Peter at Lydda (Acts ix. 33, 34).

ENEGLA IM (*spring of two heifers*). On the shore of the Dead Sea. Lost. (Ez. xlvii. 10).

ENGANNIM (*spring of gardens*). Judah, in the Shefelah near Zanoah (Josh. xv. 34). —2. Issachar (Josh. xix. 21; Lev. xxi. 29). Now Jenin, at the head of the plain of Esdraelon (Jos. Ant. xx. 6, § 1). The spring and orchards are stil famous.

ENGE'DI (*spring of the kid*). In the wilderness of Judah, on the W. shore of the Dead Sea (Josh. xv. 62). HAZEZON TAMAR (*the pruning of the palms*) was its original name, from its palm-groves (2 Chr. xx. 2; Eccl. xxiv. 14; Jos. Ant. ix. 1, § 2). A rich plain half a mile square, gently sloping up from the water to the base of the mts., watered by a fountain a mile from the sea, up a ravine 400 ft.

EN'GINE. In military affairs, machines for throwing things, first mentioned of Uzziah's time (2 Chr. xxvi. 15). They were: 1. *balista*, cross-bows, for arrows or stones, and *catapulta*, the same, much larger,—2. the *battering ram* (see cut on page 25), for breaking walls (Ez. iv. 2).

ENGRA'VER (*harash*, in Ex. xxviii. 11, etc.).

SPHINX.

Any worker in wood, stone, or metal. The work was cutting names or devices on rings or seals; as on the high-priest's dress, breast-plate, etc. The art was known among all ancient nations, as evidences from the ruins prove. Many beautiful specimens of engravings on rings, etc., are preserved in the museums of Europe and in the Abbott Egyptian Museum, New York.

ENHAD'DAH (*swift spring*). In Issachar, near ENGANNIM (Josh. xix. 21).

ENHAKKŌ'RE (*spring of the crier*). The spring which came forth in answer to the call of Samson (Judg. xv. 19). See LEHI.

ENHĀ'ZOR (*spring of the village*). Naph., a fenced city. near Kedesh (Josh. xix. 37). Lost.

means a spiritual, upright life. The Greek and Latin fathers used the instances of Enoch and Elijah as evidences of the possibility of a resurrection and a future life. He is supposed to be one of the two witnesses alluded to in Rev. xi. 3. He is called Edris (*the learned*) in the Koran, and is credited with inventing the art of writing and the

VALLEY OF SALT, BETWEEN CANAAN AND EDOM.

ENMISH'PAT (*spring of judgment*), (Gen. xiv. 7). KADESH.

E'NOCH. HENOC (*teacher*). Eldest son of Cain, who named his city after himself (Gen. iv. 17).—2. The son of Jared, and father of Methuselah, the seventh from Adam (Jude, 14). Enoch was a type of perfected humanity, "a man raised to heaven by pleasing God, while angels fell to earth by transgression." Some have thought Enoch was the

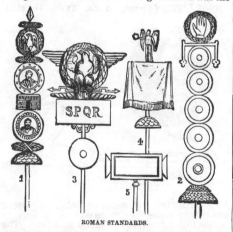

ROMAN STANDARDS.

god of the new year, because he lived 365 years, and did not die. The phrase "walked with God," is also used of Noah (Gen. vi. 9), and of Abraham (xvii. 1), and of others, as well as of people, and

sciences of arithmetic and astronomy. See HISTORY OF THE BOOKS for the Book of Enoch.—3. Third son of Midian (1 Chr. i. 33, Henoch).—4. Son of Reuben (Gen. xlvi. 9, Hanoch), from whom came the Hanochites (Num. xxvi. 5).—5. In 2 Esd. vi. 49, 51, Enoch is found in the Latin and English versions, and Behemoth in the Æthiopic.

E'NON (John iii. 23). AENON.

ENOS (Heb. ENOSH, *man*). Son of Seth (Gen. iv. 26). Enosh (1 Chr. i. 1).

ENRIM'MON. Reinhabited after the return from the Bab. Cap. (Neh. xi. 29). Probably Ain and Rimmon (Josh. xv. 32).

EN-RŌGEL (*fuller's fountain*). Spring near Jerusalem, at the junction of the valleys of Jehoshaphat and Hinnom (Josh. xv. 7; xviii. 16). Jonathan and Ahimaaz hid here (2 Sam. xvii. 17). Adonijah held a feast here, by the stone Zoheleth; his first and last attempt on the crown (1 K. i. 9). Josephus (Ant. vii. 14, § 4; ix. 10, § 4) mentions the royal gardens. The well is 125 feet deep, walled up square with large stones, and arched over. It overflows underground most of the time, over the top only a little while in the rainy season. "It is a singular work of ancient enterprise" (Thomson, *Land and Book*, ii. 528).

ENSHE'MESH (*spring of the sun*). Landmark on the N. of Judah (Josh. xv. 7). The only spring now known east of the Mt. of Olives is the Well of the Apostles, so called because it is supposed that Christ and his apostles rested there often, about a mile east of Bethany. The sun shines on the spring all day long.

EN'SIGN. STANDARD. Several Hebrew words are so rendered: NES, an elevated signal, not a military standard, having on it a device, emblem or inscription, as "Jehovah nissi" (Ex. xii. 15); the pole on which the brazen serpent was lifted is so called (Num. xxi. 8), which was an ensign of deliverance. DEGEL was the standard given to each of the four divisions (see ENCAMPMENT) of the Israelite host in the Wilderness (Num. i. 52). The Egyptia banners had on them sacred emblems—

EGYPTIAN STANDARDS.

as a boat, an animal, a bird, or the king's name. The Hebrew banners are described by the Rabbis as follows: Judah, a lion; Reuben, a man; Ephraim, an ox; Dan, an eagle. It is more probable that each tribe and each company in a tribe had a particular ensign for its own use—as a figure or inscription. The Romans made images on their standards of certain gods and of deified men, which they worshiped. The Assyrian standards were very similar to those represented here as Egyptian and Roman.

ENSUE'. In 1 Pet. iii. 11, ensue means to follow after and overtake—a meaning now obsolete.

ENTAP'PUAH (*citron-spring*). Boundary of Manasseh, near Shechem (Josh. xvii. 7). TAPPUAH.

ENTRE'AT. INTREAT. TREAT. To be entreated means in Scripture to be persuaded, as in 1 Chr. v. 20; Is. xix. 22, etc.

EPŒN'ETUS. EPENETUS (*praised*). Disciple at Rome, mentioned in Rom. xvi. 5, as the first fruit of Asia unto Christ. Tradition says he was first bishop of Carthage.

EP'APHRAS (*lovely*). Paul's assistant at Colossæ (Col. i. 7), of which he was a native, and very kind to Paul, who was in prison in Rome.

EPAPHRODI'TUS (*favored by Venus*). A disciple at Philippi, who was sent to Paul at Rome with contributions (Phil. ii. 25). He preached in North Greece and Macedonia.

E'PHAH (*darkness*). Son of Midian (Gen. xxv. 4; Is. xl. 6, 7). There is a town in Arabia, near Bilbeys, called Gheyfer (jä-fĕr), which is sup-

posed to be Ephah.—2. Woman in Caleb's family, in the line of Judah (1 Chr. ii. 46).—3. Son of Johdai, in the same line (ib. 47).—4. See WEIGHTS AND MEASURES.

E'PHAI (*weary*). OPHAI (*languid*). Of Netopha, whose sons were officers left in Judah during the Captivity (Jer. xl. 8). Killed with Gedaliah by Ishmael (xli. 3—compare xl. 13). Ishmael 6.

E'PHER (*calf*). Son of Midian (Gen. xxv. 4). The Arabs have a town named Ghifr (*jiffer*, a calf), but trace to Amalek and Ishmael, and not to Midian.—2. Son of Ezra, of Judah, in Caleb's line (1 Chr. iv. 17).—3. Chief in Manasseh, E. of Jordan (1 Chr. v. 24).

E'PHES-DAM'MIM (*end of blood*). Between Socoh and Azekah, where the Philistines encamped the evening before David slew Goliath (1 Sam. xvii. 1). PAS-DAMMIM (1 Chr. xi. 13).

EPHE'SIAN. Trophimus, the Ephesian (Acts xxi. 29).

EPHE'SIANS. Citizens of Ephesus, who worshiped Diana (Acts xix. 28, etc.). The Epistle to the Ephesians is described in the HISTORY OF THE BOOKS.

EPH'ESUS. About the middle of the W. of Asia Minor, opposite the island of Samos. The capital of Asia, which province under the Romans included only the W. part of the peninsula. Built partly on hills and partly on the plain. The climate was excellent. The country around the city was very fertile, and its position most convenient for traffic with other regions of the Levant. In the time of Augustus it was the great metropolis of this section of Asia Minor. Paul's journeys indicate the facilities for travel by sea and land.

The harbor was elaborately constructed, and at its head stood the famous temple of Diana. The first temple was burnt on the night Alexander the Great was born; the second, which stood in Paul's time, was built by the contributions of all Asia: 425 feet long by 220 wide, with 127 marble columns, each 60 feet high. Built in the Ionic order, perfected here first. The magnificence of this great temple was a proverb throughout the world. Here the people held an "uproar" against Paul for two hours (Acts xix. 23. See PAUL). Public games were held in the month of May, which was

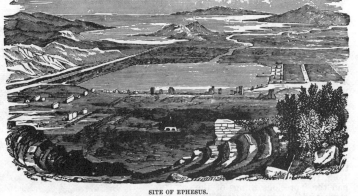

SITE OF EPHESUS.

sacred to Diana, and Paul was probably there at that time (1 Cor. xvi. 8). Plutarch mentions the charms and amulets which were made and sold here, and accounts of faith in their value reach as far down as the 6th century. The coins of E. have many allusions to the Diana worship. Josephus says the Jews were numerous there. Disciples of

John the Baptist were found here after the ascension of Christ (Acts xviii. 25; xix. 3). Paul established a church here, of which Timothy was at one time the head. It is supposed that St. John the Divine wrote his Gospel and Epistles here; the Apocalypse being written on Patmos. E. was one of the *seven churches*, and is named first; and its

attempts to conquer E. were ever made, and Shalmaneser only succeeded through the internal divisions of the kingdom of Samaria (721 B. C. See SHECHEM; SAMARIA).—2. A city on a hill N. E. of Jerusalem, 10 ms. See OPHRAH.—3. A forest E. of Jordan, near Mahanaim, where Absalom was caught by his hair in a tree and killed, when fighting against his father David, the king (2 Sam. xviii. 6).

THEATRE AT EPHESUS.

E'PHRAIN. EPHRON (2 Chr. xiii. 19). Supposed to be Ophrah.

E'PHRAIM, THE GATE OF. See JERUSALEM.

E'PHRAIM, MOUNT, means the whole hill country of the district between Jordan and the plain of Sharon.

E'PHRAIM, THE WOOD OF. EPHRAIM 3.

E'PHRAIMITE. Ephrathite (Judg. xii. 5), of E.

EPH'RATAH, EPH'RATH. The ancient name of Bethlehem. Ephratites, cities of Bethlehem-Judah (Ruth i. 2). The second wife of Caleb, the son of Hezrom, mother of Hur, and grandmother of Caleb the spy, was named

"candlestick" has been removed surely, for all is desolation now where the city once stood. The fine columns have been carried to other cities, chiefly Constantinople and Italy. Ruins cover the hills and a swamp the plain. There is a tradition that the mother of Jesus was buried here, and also Timothy and St. John.

There is now a railroad from Smyrna to Aidin, with a station near the ruins of Ephesus, called Aysaluk (ā-sa-look, *city of the moon*). The whole district covered by the ancient city and suburbs are now desolate. The map was copied from one constructed on the spot by Prof. Eddy, 1870. See LIFE OF PAUL, of JOHN, DIANA.

EPH'LAL (*judgment*). Son of Zabad (1 Chr. ii. 37), in the tribe of Judah.

EPH'OD (*girded on*). Part of the high-priest's dress—the peculiar badge of his office.

E'PHOD (*oracle-giving*). Father of Hanniel, chief in Manasseh (Num. xxxiv. 23).

E'PHRAIM (*double fruitfulness*). Second son of Joseph by his wife Asenath. Blessed by Jacob above his elder brother, Manasseh (Gen. xlviii.). Joshua, the son of Nun, was of E. The portion of E. in Canaan was 55 ms. from E. to W. and 70 ms. from N. to S. in extent; elevated, hilly, and having the plain of Sharon, a narrow strip, on the W., Esdraëlon on the N., and the Jordan valley on the E., in the centre of the country, the whole called Mt. E. (1 Sam. i. 1, vii. 17; 2 Chr. xiii., xv. 8). It had the "precious things of the earth, and the fulness thereof," as blessed by Moses. The finest and most fruitful of all the land. Afterward called Samaria. Its wealth and importance were increased by the presence of the Ark of the Covenant and the Tabernacle at Shiloh within its borders. The people were jealous, and at enmity with the tribe of Judah from the time of David. Very few

Ephrath (1 Chr. ii. 19), Ephratah in verse 50. Caleb-ephratah in verse 24.

E'PHRON (*fawn*). Son of Zohar (Heb. ZOCHAR), a Hittite, who sold the field to Abraham (Gen. xxiii. 8, etc.).

E'PHRON. E. of Jordan, a strong city between Carnaim and Bethshan (1 Macc. v. 46-52; 2 Macc. xvi. 27). Lost.

E'PHRON, MOUNT, Cities of, were landmarks (Josh. xv. 9). Said to be Ain Lifta (Nephtoah), and Kuriet el Enab (Kirjath-Jearim).

EPICU'REANS. Disciples and followers of the philosopher Epicurus (lived B. C. 342-271), who taught at Athens. He tried to find in philosophy a practical guide to happiness. True pleasure, and not absolute truth, was his aim. He endeavored to remove superstitious fears, and made the study

EPHRAIM.

of physics (nature) useful for the good of mankind. Epicurus was a follower of Diogenes Laërtius. His system had degenerated into mere materialism at the time when Paul was at Athens (Acts xvii. 18). The Stoics were their opponents; who were named from a portico (Greek *stoa*) in which the philosopher Zeno taught, at Athens, a system of ethics based on *pride*, as Christianity is on humility. This school taught the Fatherhood of God, the common bonds of mankind, and the sovereignity of the soul. Christianity was a practical union of the two schools of Epicureans and Stoics. The same ideas among the Jews produced the sect of Sadducees. The teaching of the Hebrew patriarchs and prophets was independent of any system of philosophy, and it is curious that Greek philosophy arose just after the Hebrew prophets closed their oracles, Malachi being cotemporary with Socrates.

EPIPH'ANES. ANTIOCHUS EPIPHANES (1 Macc. i x.)

EP'IPHI. The 11th month of the Egyptian year, the third of the "season of waters," inundation. Named from the goddess Apapt. The Hebrews derived from this their name Abib, the 1st sacred, and the 7th civil month in their calendar.

EPIS'TLES. See HISTORY OF THE Books.

E'QUAL. Means to make equal in Lam. ii. 13.

ER (*watchful*). First-born of Judah, son of Bath-Shuah, a Canaanite. He married Tamar, who became mother of Pharez and Zarah by Judah. He probably sinned by idolatry (prompted by his wife ?) (Gen. xxxviii. 3-7).—2. In the line of Judah, son of Shelah (1 Chr. iv. 21).—3. Son of Jose, a cotemporary with king Uzziah (Luke iii. 28).

E'RA. CHRONOLOGY. The Era of Jesus Christ is dated four years too late, and was fixed by the Abbot Dionysius Exiguus, in the 6th century, so that the true date would be now not 1878 but 1882.

E'RAN. Son of Shuthelah, and ancestor of the Eranites.

E'RANITES. Descendants of Eran (Num. xxvi. 36).

ERAS'TUS (*beloved*). Chamberlain of Corinth, and a disciple (Rom. xvi. 23). He was with Paul on some of his journeys (Acts xix. 23), and probably settled at Corinth (2 Tim. iv. 20).—2. A deacon in the church at Ephesus. Supposed to be different from No. 1.

E'RECH. Land of Shinar. Built by Nimrod (Gen. x. 10). Now Irak, 43 ms. E. of Babylon. The place seems to have been the metropolis of the Assyrian kings, mounds and the remains of bricks and coffins being found through a wide district. People from this city were transplanted to Samaria by Asnapper (Ezr. iv. 9). See *Rawlinson's Five Great Monarchies.*

E'RES. Hebrew word for a species of pine. See CEDAR.

E'RI (*watching.*) HERL. HER. Son of Gad (Gen. xlvi. 16).

E'RITES. Branch of the tribe of Gad, from Eri (Num. xxvi. 16).

ESA'IAS. The Greek form of the Hebrew Isaiah (ISAIAHU), (Matt. iii. 3, etc).

E'SAR-HAD'DON (*fire-given*). King of Assyria, son of Sennacherib (2 K. xix. 37). He first appears in history B. C. 680, as king, after his father's murder (Is. xxxvii. 38). The monuments exhibit him as one of the most powerful of the Assyrian kings, conquering all Asia, from the Persian

Gulf to the mountains in Armenia, and the Mediterranean Sea. He is the only Assyrian king who dwelt (a part of the time) at Babylon, where bricks are found bearing his name. It is while living there (B. C. 680-667), that Manasseh, king of Judah, was brought before him at Babylon (2 Chr. xxxiii. 11). He proved his great clemency by restoring Manasseh to his throne in Jerusalem, and by giving territory on the Persian Gulf to a son of Merodach-Baladan, whom he had conquered, and who submitted to him and became a refugee at his court. He was a builder of great works, such as his palace at Babylon, and three others, in different cities, for himself and his son ; and one inscription mentions thirty temples in Assyria and Mesopotamia. These works were ornamented highly with silver and gold. The palace at Nimroud is the best preserved of any. Mr. Layard found its plan to agree quite closely with that of Solomon's palace (1 K. vii. 1-12), but much larger, the great

THE VALLEY OF TOPHET.

hall being 220 by 100 feet, and the porch 160 by 60. The sculptures were winged bulls, sphinxes and slabs, most of which were almost destroyed by fire. It is believed that Phœnician and Greek artists were employed as assistants on these works. His son, Asshur-banipal, succeeded him (SARDANAPALUS).

ESAU (Heb. ESAV, *hairy*). Oldest son of Isaac, twin of Jacob. The bitter enmity of the two brothers, and the strife between the two nations derived from them, were foreshadowed even in the womb (Gen. xxv. 22 to 27). Esau was a robust, active, real Bedawy, "son of the desert," and was loved for his wild, roaming disposition, but his brother Jacob was more crafty, and, succeeding in buying his birthright for a dinner ("mess of pottage," verse 34), Esau attempted to get from his blind father the blessing belonging to the first-born, and which he had sold to Jacob, but Jacob again was too crafty for his brother, and succeeded in deceiving Isaac, and received the blessing. From this time he was called Edom (*red*), which was given to the country that he afterwards lived in. At the age of 40 he married, against the will of his parents, two Canaanite women. Jacob was sent to Padan-aram, out of the way of Esau, who took another wife, Mahalath, his cousin, daughter of Ishmael (xxviii. 8, 9). He then went to Mt. Seir, where he was living when Jacob returned from Padan-aram, and had become rich and powerful. The brothers met on the east of Jordan, when Jacob again acted in a double-faced way, and parted to meet again only at the side of their dead father, twenty years after, at Machpelah. From this time he lived in Mt. Seir, but nothing is recorded of his later history. See EDOM, EDOMITES.

ESCHEW. To flee from, as used in Job i. 1, 8, ii. 3; 1 Pet. iii. 11. Obsolete.

GOLDEN EAGLE.

ESDRAE'LON. The Greek name of Jezreel (Judith iii. 9), the Great Plain of Josephus, the valley of Megiddo. It is very rich in soil, lying on a volcanic basalt, but there is not an inhabited village in its whole extent, which is triangular, 18, 15, by 12 miles, on the three sides. See Map. It is noted for the number and importance of the battles fought on its surface. "Warriors from every nation have pitched their tent in the plain of Esdraelon." The names Deborah, Barak, Gideon, Josiah, Holofernes, Vespasian, the Crusaders, Saracens, Turks, and French, give a hint of the events which have made the valley memorable.

ES'DRAS. The form of Ezra in the Apocrypha. —2. The books of Esdras. See the HISTORY OF THE BOOKS.

E'SEK (*strife*). Well dug in the valley in Gerar (Gen. xxvi. 20) by the herdsmen of Isaac.

ESHBA'AL (*baal's man*). ISHBOSHETH? Fourth son of Saul (1 Chr. viii. 33).

ESH'BAN (*wise hero*). HESHBON. A Horite, son of Dishon (Gen. xxxvi. 26).

ESH'COL (*cluster*). Valley N. W. of Hebron, visited by the spies who were sent by Moses from Kadesh Barnea, from which place they brought away a huge cluster of grapes, so remarkable as to name it the valley of the cluster (Num. xiii. 24). The valley was named from Eshcol, the brother of Mamre, the Amorite, in Abraham's time (Gen. xiv. 13, 24).

ESH'EAN. Judah, near Hebron (Josh. xv. 52). Lost.

E'SHEK. A Benjamite, descendant of Saul, founder of a noted family of archers (1 Chr. viii. 39).

ESH'KALONITES. Citizens of Ashkelon (Josh. iii. 3).

ESH'TAOL. Judah, in the Shefelah, allotted to Dan. The residence, during his youth, of Samson; and here he was buried (Judg. xiii. 25; xvi. 31). Some of the Danites who were sent to look for a new home in the N. were from E. (xviii. 2, 8, 11). Lost. In the time of Jerome it was said to lie between Azotus and Ascalon, and named Astho; and another, named Esthaül, 10 miles N. of Eleutheropolis, probably near the present Yeshua.

ESH'TAULITES. Among the citizens of Kirjath-Jearim (1 Chr. ii. 53).

ESHTEMO'A (*women of note*). Judah, in the mountains (Josh. xv. 50; 1 Chr. vi. 57). Frequented by David (1 Sam. xxx. 28). Now Semna, 7 ms. S. of Hebron. Founded by the descendants of the Egyptian wife of Mered (1 Chr. iv. 17).—2. Name of a person in 1 Chr. iv. 19, as a Maachathite.

ESH'TON (*uxorious*). In the line of Judah (1 Chr. iv. 11).

ES'LI. Son of Naggai, father of Naum (Luke iii. 25).

ESO'RA. Perhaps Hazor or Zorah. Fortified by the Jews on the approach of Holofernes (Jud. iv. 4). Possibly Bethhoron.

ESPOU'SAL. MARRIAGE.

ES'ROM. In the geneology of Jesus (Matt. i. 8; Luke iii. 33). HEZRON.

ESSE'NES. Josephus says they combined the ascetic virtues of the Pythagoreans and Stoics with a spiritual knowledge of the Divine Law, and arose about 200 B. C. Their chief city was Engedi (Pliny). The name is supposed to mean *silent, mysterious* or *pious* (Dr. Ginsburg). The origin of the party was rather in a certain tendency of religious thought among all classes towards an ideal purity. Special doctrines had for their object a life of absolute purity and divine communion. Next to God, Moses was honored; the Sabbath was carefully kept; food was eaten only when prepared by their own members, and never cooked on the Sabbath; and they practiced self-denial, temperance, and agriculture. Slavery, war, and commerce were forbidden. They were very regular in their devotions; before sunrise they began their prayer and praise; said grace before and after meals; ate from only one kind of food at a meal; disallowed oaths, holding truth to be sacred; held all things in common. Their system was a compound of mystical and ceremonial elements. The applicant for membership was obliged to live a year outside of the order, but keeping its rules (?), having received as badges an ax, a white apron, and a white dress. One year more he would share in the ablutions but not in the meals. After two more years he was admitted to full membership, solemnly binding himself to piety to God, justice to men, to hate the wicked, assist the righteous, injure no one, speak the truth, avoid robbery and theft, and keep the rules and secrets of the society. Some of their rules were: 1. To bathe, if touched by a stranger, or a lower grade of their own order, and before and after meals, and other natural acts; not to spit in an assembly, and if so not on the *right side;* the social meal was a sacrament. 1. Baptisms produced bodily purity, which led to 2. celibacy, and 3, spiritual purity, and 4, to a meek and lowly spirit, banishing all anger and malice, thus reaching 5, holiness, arriving at 6, a state wherein he is a Holy Temple for the Holy Spirit, and could prophesy, and advancing to 7, could perform miraculous cures, raising the dead, attaining finally to the lofty state of Elias, the forerunner of the Messiah, and no longer subject to death.

Jesus alludes to the Essenes in Matt. v. 34, "swear not at all," and in xix. 12, "who abstain from marriage for the kingdom of heaven's sake," and Paul in 1 Cor. vii., which is hardly intelligible without a knowledge of the tenets of the Essenes, and by James in v. 12, and the first church held all things in common as they did (Acts iv. 32–34). Their number was never larger than 4000. See Josephus and Eusebius. They disappeared after the destruction of Jerusalem, and are not heard of again, although various orders of monks follow more or less strictly their rules and practices.

ES'THER (*the planet* VENUS, ASTER, ASTARTE, ASHTORETH, meaning *good fortune*). The Persian form of the Hebrew name HADASSAH (*a myrtle*). She was daughter of Abihail, son of Shimei, a Benjamite, cousin of Mordecai. Her parents did not return from captivity, but died, leaving her in care of her relative (cousin?) Mordecai. The Persian king having divorced his queen, Vashti (*a beauty*), for contempt, the royal choice fell on Esther, after passing many others by. In this position she delivered her people, who were still very numerous, from a threatened calamity, which was the origin of the yearly feast of Purim. See HISTORY OF THE BOOKS, Esther and Apocrypha.

E'TAM (*place of wild beasts*). Simeon (1 Chr. iv. 32).—2. Judah; fortified and garrisoned by Rehoboam (2 Chr. xi. 6)   Near Bethlehem and Tekoah.

E'TAM (*the rock*). To which Samson retired after his slaughter of the Philistines (Judg. xv. 8, 11). Probably in the valley of Urtas.

ETER'NAL (Heb. OLAM, *hidden, time long past*, and of future *to the end*).

ETER'NITY (Heb. AD), only once, in Is. lvii. 15, meaning duration in time.

E'THAN (*limit of the sea*). Station in the Exodus, near the Red Sea, east.

ETHAN (*firmness*) 1. The Ezrahite, son of Mahal, a wise man, only excelled by Solomon (1 K.iv. 31; Ps. lxxxix).—2. Son of Kish, a Levite in David's time (1 Chr. vi. 44). Played cymbals with Heman and Asaph (xv. 17, 19).—3. Levite ancestor of Asaph, the singer (1 Chr. vi. 42).

ETH'ANIM. MONTH.

ETH'BAAL (*with Baal*). A king of Sidon, father of Jezebel (1 K. xvi. 31). Josephus said he was king of Tyre and Sidon. Menander says that

INK BOTTLE.

Ithobalus, a priest of Astarte, killed Pheles and usurped the throne, reigning 32 years, B. C. 940–908.

E'THER (*abundance*). Judah, in the Shefelah (Josh xv. 42), in Simeon.   Now Attarah near Gaza.

ETHIO'PIA (*burnt*). The country called in Hebrew CUSH. S. of Egypt, from Syene (Ez. xxix. 10). Libyan desert W., Abyssinian highland E. and S. The Hebrews traded with E. (Is. xlv. 14) in ebony, ivory, frankincense, gold and precious stones (Job xxviii. 19; Jos. Ant. viii. 6, § 5). Settled by a Hamitic race (Gen. x. 6), dark (Jer. xiii. 23), men of stature (Is. xviii. 2), and fine-looking (xxxviii. 7). The Sabæans were the most noted tribe. There are ruins of many temples in E. built during the reigns of the Hyksos kings of Egypt. Queen Candace is mentioned in Acts viii. 27.

The official title of the queen was CANDACE, and there was a line of queens who governed the country about the time of Christ, who successfully resisted even the Romans.

ETHIOPIANS.

ETHIŌ'PIAN (Heb. CUSHITE).   Black man (Jer. xiii. 23).   Zereh (2 Chr. xiv. 9) and Ebed-melech (Jer. xxxviii. 7, etc.,) were Ethiopians.

ETHIO'PIAN WOMAN. Wife of Moses. A CUSH-ITE (Num. xii. 1). She is also said to be a Midianite, and so supposed to be a second wife.

ETHIŌ'PIANS. In several passages meaning CUSHITES.

ETHIŌ'PIC VERSION.   See HISTORY OF THE BOOKS, page 4.

ETH'NAN (*gift*). Son of Hela, the wife of Ashur (1 Chr. iv. 7).

ETH'NI (*giving*). Ancestor of Asaph (1 Chr. vi. 41).

EUBU'LUS (*prudent*). Disciple at Rome (2 Tim. iv. 21).

EUER'GETES (*benefactor*). Title of honor among the Greeks. Two of the Ptolemies were so honored—Ptolemy III and VII.

EUME'NES (*friendly*). Eumenes II, king of Pergamus, succeeded his father, Attalus I, B. C. 197. He served the Romans against the Greeks in the battle of Magnesia (B. C. 190), for which he was rewarded with the provinces of Mysia, Lydia, Ionia, Phrygia, Lycaonia and Thracian Chersonese. Died probably B. C. 159 (1 Macc. viii. 8).

EU'NICE (*victorious*). Mother of Timothy (2 Tim. i. 5); a disciple of pure faith (Acts xvi. 1).

EU'NUCH (Heb. SARUS). Officer, chamberlain. The word indicates the incapacity which certain mutilation produces—a practice contrary to the law in Deut. xxiii. 1. The origin of the custom is ascribed to queen Semiramis, but is probably as old as Eastern despotism itself, which delights in servants who excite no jealousy. It is supposed that the prophet Daniel and his companions were so treated, because it was so prophesied (2 K. xx. 17). The ETHIOPIAN EUNUCH was probably an officer of the queen, perhaps a Jew.

EUŌ'DIA. EUŌ'DIAS (*good journey*). Disciple, a woman of Philippi (Phil. iv. 2).

EUPHRĀ'TES (*the good river*). Now called Frat. Called in Scripture *the river*. The largest, longest, and most important river in W. Asia. Rises in the mts. of Armenia, near Erzeroum and Mt. Ararat. Of two branches: one is called Frat, and Black River (*Kara su*), and is 400 ms. long; the other, Murad Chai (*chief*), 270 ms. long; and both unite at Kebban Meden, in a stream 360 ft. wide, and from this point to the Persian Gulf it is 1,000 ms. making in all nearly 1,800 ms., 1,200 of which is navigable for steamers. Nebuchadnezzar dug canals to carry the water of the annual inundation across the wide plains of Chaldea. Herodotus describes the river and its traffic (i. 185). First mentioned in Gen. xv. 18, in the description of the promised land (Deut. i. 7, xi. 24; Josh i. 4). Fulfilled partially by Reuben (1 Chr. v. 9), and completely by David (Ps. cxxxvii. 1).

EUPŎL'EMUS (*good warrior*). Son of John the son of Accos, KOZ (Neh. iii. 4, etc.). Envoy sent to Rome by Judas, about B. C. 161 (1 Macc. viii. 17). He was a well known historian, mentioned by Eusebius and Josephus.

EURŎC'LYDON. Name of a wind from a certain quarter (Acts xxvii. 14). See PAUL.

EUTY'CHUS (*fortunate*). The youth who was resuscitated by Paul after having fallen out of a window at Troas (Acts xx. 9).

EVAN'GELIST (*publisher of glad tidings*). An order of men in the Christian Church. They were not attached to any particular locality, but worked wherever there was a field, by preaching or writing. Philip (Acts xxi. 8), and Timothy (2 Tim. iv. 5), and the four, Matthew, Mark, Luke, John are examples.

ĒVE (Heb. CHAVVAH, *living*). Name of the first woman. It is the feminine form of the noun which means life. There are two accounts of her creation

21 to 25, give the account of Eve's formation out of the rib of Adam. The story—or two stories—may mean simply that God holds both man and woman equal in duty and accountability, and one in nature and origin. Eve is not mentioned after the birth of Seth, and her death is not recorded.

E'VENING. CHRONOLOGY.

EV'ER, AND FOREV'ER. Eternal. Eternity. The whole period.

Ē'VI (*desire*.) Prince of Midian (Num. xxxi. 8).

EV'IDENCE. In Jer. ˙xxxii. 10, etc., means bill of sale, in the prophet' petition; purchase of a field. This symbolic act meant that though desolation must come, God's promise was sure, and houses, fields and vineyards should again be possessed in Palestine by the Hebrews.

ĒVIL MERO'DACH (*Merodak's fool*). Son and successor of Nebuchadnezzar, B. C. 561; murdered and succeeded by Neriglissar, B. C. 559. Joachin was kindly treated by him (2 K. xxv. 27). The historian Berosus says that his change of policy from severe to mild caused his death by the violent men of his party.

ĒVIL-SPIRIT. Devil. DEMON.

EXCELLENCY OF CARMEL (Is. xxxv. 2). See CARMEL.

EX'CELLENT. Surpassing (Dan. ii. 31). Excellent glory (2 Peter i. 17). "Most excellent" was a title of rank and honor given to Theophilus (Luke i. 3), and to Felix (Acts xxiii. 23; xxiv. 3); and to Festus (Acts xxvi. 25).

EXCHAN'GERS. Money changers (Matt. xxv. 27).

EXCOMMUNICĀ'TION. Putting one out of church society. The Jews had three modes: 1. For twenty-four minor offenses an offender was under NIDDUI. Keeping a fierce dog, swearing, etc., were instances. The penalty was to abstain

THE PYRAMIDS OF TIZEH FROM THE NILE, LOOKING EAST. SHOWING THE SITE OF THE SPHINX.

In Genesis. 1. Gen. i 27: "So God created man in his own image, in the image of God created he him; male and female created he them;" 2. ii. 18: "And the Lord God said 'It is not good that the man should be alone,'" (his creation is noticed in verse 7), "'I will make him a help meet for him.'" Then, in verses 19 and 20, is the account of the creation of the beasts, and that among them there was not found a help meet for Adam. Verses

from the use of the bath, the razor, wine, etc., and to keep at 6 feet (4 cubits) distance from every one. He could not worship in the temple in the usual manner, and this lasted 30 days.—2. The second was CHEREM. He could not teach or be taught to work for or buy any object not intended for food. —3. The SHAMMATHA, an entire cutting off from the congregation. Moses did not make this law, but the natural right of societies for self-preservation gave rise to it. The cases in Num. xvi. (of Korah, etc.), Judg. v. 23 (Meroz), Ezr. vii. 26; x. 8; Ex. xxx. 33, and Lev. xiii. 46; xvii. 4, are precedents. One instance is recorded in the N. T., John ix., of the young man who confessed that Jesus was the Christ. The fear of the result prevented some from such a confession (xii. 42). The blessing in Luke vi. 22, refers to the three forms of this law. The excommunication founded by Jesus was to be executed only after due trial, and a settled contempt for the church in refusing to atone for a trespass which the person has committed (Matt. xviii. 15–18). The final act of exclusion was to be done only after two warnings. Paul commanded the same (1 Tim. i. 20; 1 Cor. v. 11 Tit. iii. 10), and frequently used the power. Restoration was possible, and is urged in 2 Cor. ii. 6. The censure of the church was not to include enmity, curses, and persecution, as among some sects, but rather to look upon the excluded "as a heathen and a publican," that may be brought in again. It is a spiritual penalty, not physical, separating from the communion of the church, aiming to benefit the person and the church, by excluding heresy, immorality, and only put in force by the authority of the church at large (by a vote?) and the sanction of the highest officer, whose sentence was declared in the congregation to which the offender belonged; and that penitence is a condition of restoration, which is to be as public as the exclusion.

EXECU′TIONER (Heb. TABBACH, *slaughter*). The duties were both those of an executioner and of the leader of the body-guard of the king, as in Egypt (Gen. xxxvii. 36), whose official residence was the prison. It was a post of high dignity. The Septuagint says Potiphar was *chief-cook.*

EX′ILE. CAPTIVITY.

EX′ODUS (*going out*). For the book, see HISTORY OF THE BOOKS. The date of the Exodus of the Hebrews from Egypt, led by Moses, is fixed by different writers: as Poole, B. C. 1652, Hales, 1648, Usher, 1491, Bunsen, 1320. The patriarchal institution ended and the era of the Law began at the Exodus—the family had become a nation. The departure was begun at Raamses (Rameses) in the early morning of the 15th of Nisan, which was from that time called the first month. Three stages brought them to the Red Sea, where they were overtaken by Pharaoh and delivered by Moses, as celebrated in the songs of Moses and Miriam (Ex. xv.).

The great difficulty in tracing the route of the Israelites from Egypt to Canaan has called out a large number of travelers in our day, who have minutely examined the district (or a part of it, omitting the region of the 38 years wandering, because there are no records from which to form a base of exploration), and from their researches it is "possible by the internal evidence of the country itself to lay down not indeed the actual route of the Israelites in every stage, but in almost all cases, and in some cases the very spots themselves."

The question of the passage of the Red Sea is referred to MIRACLES.

ETHAM was a district on both sides of the N. end of the Red Sea. The place of crossing might have been anywhere between Suez and Jebel Ata-

kah, which is a steep, high promontory standing out into very deep water.

SHUR (*wall*) is a name for the whole desert from Suez to Beersheba, N. of the plain Er Ramleh, also called PARAN. The first water found was at MARAH (*bitter*), and the rest at ELIM (*stags,*) where there were twelve fountains, and a kind of desert paradise, among a grove of palm trees. *Wady Ghurundel* has several fine fountains, a perennial stream, and more trees, shrubs and bushes than any other place in the desert. Here the mountain district begins. The next camp was by the Red Sea, where, in a wild and lonely plain, there is a sublime view of Sinai's granite peaks on one side, and the blue sea on the other.

The WILDERNESS OF SIN is a continuation of

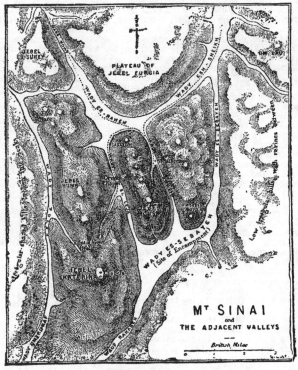

MAP OF SINAI.

this valley on the south, widening into the broadest plain in the whole region. Here they first murmured, and the quails were sent in answer to their cry, and the first fall of manna. DOPHKA and ALUSH were probably in the same plain. REPHIDIM (*supports*) is located in Wady esh Sheikh, the most spacious valley in this region, and the most fertile. Here the people found no water to drink, and Moses brought water out of a rock (Ex. xvii. 5, 6). The Amalekites attacked the people, and were routed. Jethro, Moses' father-in-law, visited him here and counseled him. They next pitched in the plain of Rahah (*rest*, Ex. xix.) in front of SINAI. *Jebel Musa* (Mount Moses), the Sinai of recent tradition, is in the midst of a group of mountains, and is 7,000 feet high. Katerin is 8,700, and Om Shomer is 9,300 feet high. On the summit of Jebel Musa is a platform nearly 100 feet across, partly covered with ruins, a chapel at the east end, and a small mosque. *Ras es Sufsafeh* (peak of the willow) is the Sinai of many scholars, because from it the plain can be seen, and every other requirement of the text answered, and every incident illustrated by the features of the surrounding district. They stayed almost a year at Sinai. While Moses was on the mount, receiving the two tables, Aaron (his brother) made a calf of gold, probably in imitation of the Egyptians. Aaron's sons offered strange fire (Lev. x.), and were destroyed, and the second passover was held.

On leaving Sinai a certain order of march and of camping was adopted (Num. x.), and Hobab was engaged as a guide, to be unto them "instead of eyes" (ver. 31), as is the custom now in crossing the desert. From Sinai to Kadesh the route cannot be clearly laid down. After three days they pitched in Paran, at a place afterwards called TA-BERAH (*burning*, Num. xi. 3). Quails were sent here (ver. 31), the people suffered from a plague after eating them, and the place was named a second time KIBROTH-HATTAAVAH (*graves of lust*, ver. 33). The next station, HAZEROTH, has been identified with *Ain Hudherah*, a little fountain in a wild, dreary waste, among naked hills, 40 miles from Sinai. The place was noted for the foolish rebellion of Miriam and Aaron (xii.). The fountain of *El Ain*, north of *Hudherah*, is the most important watering-place in the district. The next station that can be located is EZION-GEBER, at the head of the Gulf of Akabah. Between this station and Kadesh, in the *Arabah*, there were many stations, and, as appears from the two accounts in Num. xxxiii. and in Deut. ii. 8, x. 6, they wandered up and down the valley several times.

KADESH (*holy*), next to Sinai, was the most important of all the resting-places in the wilderness. From here the twelve spies were sent into the promised land, and from Kadesh the rebellious people were turned back into the wilderness by the way of the Red Sea (Deut. i. 40) to wander for 38 years. And when they attempted to go up (by the pass Es Sufah) against the command of the Lord, they were defeated at Hormah with disgrace and slaughter (Num. xiv. 40).

Of the "great and terrible wilderness" of the wandering not one station is recorded, nor even a hint of its locality, and the only events noticed are (besides the ceremonial law) the execution of the man who gathered sticks on the Sabbath day (Num. xv.), the rebellion of Korah (xvi.), and (either during that time or soon after) the writing of the ninetieth Psalm by Moses. The great desert from Akabah to Gaza, is now called Et Tyh (the wandering), and it may be the very region; but having no names to locate or compare, there is nothing left us but conjecture.

HOUSE IN DAMASCUS.

They visited Kadesh a second time, where Miriam, the sister of Moses, died and was buried (Num. xx. 1). Moses brought water out of the rock, and the people and their beasts drank. Their flocks had survived through 38 years. Then they sent messengers to the king of Edom, asking permission to pass through his country, and making the fairest proposals, but they were denied their request (xx. 14).

They then left Kadesh and moved to Mt. Hor, where their first high-priest, Aaron, died and was buried, and Eleazar his son was invested with the "holy garments" and the office of his father. See AARON.

The next place that is identified is the pass through the east wall of the Arabah, up into the Arabian desert— *Wady Ithm*—by the way of the Red Sea (to compass the land of Edom, xxi. 4). Here the fiery serpents were sent, killing many; and the brazen serpent was set up, which became a type of the greater salvation. IJE ABARIM was reached, and then the willow brook (ZERED), and and soon also the ARNON, and they were out of the desert. Sihon, king of the Amorites, opposed their advance, and Israel smote him, and possessed his land from the Arnon to the Jabbok. They next conquered Og, the king of BASHAN. His "giant cities" are still standing, deserted but not ruined, all over the vast plain of the *Hauran*. The king of *Moab* sent the prophet Baalam to curse Israel as they were encamped in the plains of Moab, and he blessed them, but laid a snare which caught them, and caused the loss of thousands of lives (xxxi. 16).

INTERIOR OF HOUSE.

Moses numbered the pleople in the plain of Moab, and found 601,730 men above the age of 20 (being only 1820 less than the number at Sinai, 39 years before), and of all these only three were among those who came out of Egypt, all the rest having fallen in the desert (Num. xiv. 29), leaving only Moses, Caleb and Joshua. After looking at the land from the hights of Nebo, Moses died, and was buried (by the Lord), "but no man knoweth of his sepulchre" (Deut. xxxiv. 6). With his death the wanderings ended.

EX'ORCISM. The formal ejection of evil spirits from persons or places. Those who do this are called EXORCISTS. This pretense is usually accompanied with incantations and magical arts of various kinds, and was common to all nations of antiquity (Jos. Ant. viii. 2, 5, Wars, vii. 6, 3). Jesus implied that such a power did exist, and might be used after peculiar preparation (Matt. xii. 27; Luke ix. 49). There was an order of Exorcists in the Christian church in the 3d century, which led to a great increase of superstition, fraud, and imposture. Some introduced forms of exorcism into baptism, saying, "as the soul before baptism is in bondage to the devil, so at baptism it should be formally released from the evil spirit." The priest was instructed to breathe three times on the face of the subject, and say, Depart from him, foul spirit— give place to the Holy Spirit, the Paraclete. Then another breathing on the face, with the words, Receive the Holy Spirit. The order still is in the Roman ritual. It was originally practiced by the Lutherans, but it is now disused. John wrote his Gospel in Asia, where medical science was advanced, and he seems to have known that the diseases attributed to demons were merely natural diseases, for he nowhere mentions possessions of evil spirits, except as being spoken of by Jews, whom he is reporting.

EXPIĀ'TION. Sacrifice. DAY OF ATONEMENT.

EYE (Heb. AYIN). Used as a symbol of many objects and ideas. Among the Hebrews a few uses were: 1. A *fountain*, or *spring* (AIN). 2. Color (Num. xi. 7; Prov. xxiii. 31). 3. Face; as in eye to eye (face to face), (Num. xiv. 14). 4. Look, as in Cant. iv. 9. 5. "In the eyes," means in his presence, or in his judgment (Gen. xix. 8, xxix. 20; 2 Sam. x. 3). 6. "To set eyes on one," is to look with favor (Job xxiv. 23), and also to express anger (Amos ix. 8). 7. Evil eye (Matt. xx. 15); wanton eyes, etc. In Zech. iv. 10, God's angels are "his eyes," and in Persia the ministers of state are "the king's eyes." In the East servants watch the hands of their master, receiving orders and directions by motion of the hand. PAINTING THE EYES is an ancient practice among Orientals, and referred to in 2 K. ix. 30, where Jezebel is spoken

PAINTED EYE.

of as "painting her eyes," not "face," in Jer. iv. 30, where "rending the face," means "painting the eyes," and by Ezekiel in xxiii. 40. Lane says, of painting eyes: "Their charming effect is much hightened by the concealment of the other features (however pleasing they may be) and is rendered still more striking by a practice, universal among the females of the higher and middle classes, and very common among those of the lower orders, which is, blackening the edge of the eyelids, both above and below the eyes, with a black powder called *kohl*. The paint is made by burning a resin and catching the smoke on glass or any hard substance. Almond shells also make good black smoke. The black is moistened with rose-water. The ancient sculptures show the antiquity of the practice.

ĒZ. Hebrew word for she-goat, and in some passages also he-goat.

ESBĀ'I (*shining*). Father of Naarai, one of David's chiefs (1 Chr. xi. 37).

EZ'BON (*working*). 1. Son of Gad (Gen. xlvi. 16); OZNI.—2. Son of Bela (1 Chr. vii. 7).

EZĒ'KIEL (Heb. YEHEZEKEL, *God will strengthen*). One of the four greater prophets. Son of Buzi, a priest, and carefully educated. We know that he was in captivity because his prophesy is dated on the banks of the river Chebar, in the 5th year of Jehoiachin's captivity. Josephus gives other particulars. His age is not known. It is supposed, from several concurring allusions in his writings, that he was twenty-five when carried to Assyria a captive, and thirty at the time he wrote his first prophesy. He was energetic, earnest, spiritually minded. He prophesied twenty years, B. C. 595-575, ending with the 14th year after the last deportation from Judæa. The first 8 years were cotemporary with Jeremiah. See HISTORY OF THE Books, for the BOOK OF EZEKIEL.

E'ZEL. (1 Sam. xx. 19). Where David parted from Jonathan.

E'ZEM. Simeon (1 Chr. iv. 29; Josh. xix. 3).

Ē'ZER (*treasure*). 1. Horite duke, in the line of Seir (Gen. xxxvi. 21; 1 Chr. i. 42; Ezar in 38).—2. Father of Hushah, in the line of Judah (1 Chr. iv. 4).—3. Son of Ephraim (ib. vii. 2).—4. Gadite, who joined David (ib. xii. 9).—5. Levite, who repaired the wall under Nehemiah (Neh. iii. 19).—6. Priest, assisting Nehemiah (xii. 42).

E'ZION-GE'BER (*giant's backbone*). At the head of the eastern arm of the Red Sea. Now Akabah (Num. xxxiii. 35; Deut. ii. 8; 1 K. ix. 26, xxii. 48; 2 Chr. viii. 17). Station of the Exodus. Port for Solomon's fleet. Jehoshaphat's fleet was broken here (2 Chr. xx. 37).

EZ'NITE (Heb. EZNI). Adine, the Eznite; also called Josheb-bassebet, the Tachmonite (2 Sam. xxiii. 8).

EZRA (*help*). 1. In the line of Judah (1 Chr. iv. 17).—2. The famous Scribe and Priest (Esdras in the Apocrypha), son of Seraiah 7 and descendant of Hilkiah 2, high priest in Josiah's reign (Ezra vii. 1). His history is given partly in Ezra vii. to x. and in Nehemiah viii., xii. 26, 36. His narrative includes 80 years, during which period, in Persia there were Cyrus, Cambyses, Smerdis, Darius Hystaspis, Xerxes and Artaxerxes Longimanus. The last named gave Ezra men, money and letters of power, and permission to return and rebuild the house at Jerusalem.

He collected and revised the books of the O. T. Tradition says he died at Babylon (or Zamzumu on the Tigris), aged 120. A tomb is shown as his, 20 ms. above the junction of the Euphrates and Tigris.

The works credited to him are: 1. Founding the

PEREGRINE FALCON.

Great Synagogue; 2. Forming the Canon of the O. T.; 3. Introduction and use of the Chaldee instead of the Old Hebrew letters; 4. Authorship of Chronicles, Ezra, Nehemiah, and Esther. Some also add Ezekiel and Daniel; 5. Institution of Synagogues.—3. Another Ezra was head of one of the 22 courses of priests which returned with Zerubbabel and Joshua.—4. One who assisted at the dedication of the wall (Neh. xii. 33) For Book of Ezra, see HISTORY OF THE BOOKS.

EPHESIAN TEMPLE OF DIANA.

EZ'RAHITE (*of Ezra*, or *of Zerah*). A title of Ethan (1 K. iv. 31). There is no reason to believe that the Ethan and Heman, authors or singers, mentioned in the titles of the Psalms, are the same as those in 1 Kings. The two passages, in Chronicles and Kings have become mixed. There was no Heman an Ezrahite.

EZ'RI (*Jehovah's help*). Son of Chelub, over David's farmers (1 Chr. xxvii. 26).

F

FA'BLE. The deliberate choice of statements known to be inventions, which are intended to teach general truth. The Mythus is an unconscious evolution of traditional thought or fancy. The parable assumes that what is related might have been true, and deals with matters of human life, using the acts of men to figure those of a higher order of being. The fable draws its materials from the brute creation and inanimate nature, attributing the qualities of humanity to brutes, trees, &c.

The fable of Jotham about the trees of Shechem is the oldest extant (B. C. 1209), and as beautiful as any made since (Judg. ix. 8–15). The fable in Ezekiel xvii. 1–10, brings before us the lower forms of creation as representatives of human characters and destinies. The great Lokman, the Arabian writer of fables, lived about the time of David (B. C. 1025), Hesiod and Æsop of the Greeks are still later (B. C. 550). The fable exhibits relations between man and man, the parable those between man and God. The fables and inventions

alluded to in 1 Tim. iv. 7; Titus, i. 14; 2 Pet. i. 16, were false and weak, probably, and unfit for instruction.

FACE. The most peculiarly indicative part of the human figure. The face is the presence; to stand before the face is to stand in the presence. The face is also the favor—as the prince's face, or favor. To turn away the face is to deny a favor. And the *face of the Lord* means His presence. "No one can see the face of God and live," but Jacob did see it, as he says so, and lived (Gen. xxxii. 30.) Jacob first mentions God's face, at Peniel. God's grace or favor is indicated in such passages as "seeking face," "lift on us the light of thy face," "pour out thine heart like water before the face of the Lord" (Lam ii. 19).

FAIR HA'VENS. Harbor on the south side of Crete, east of Cape Matala, and near Lasea (Acts xxvii. 8). Visited by Paul on his voyage to Rome, A. D. 60. (Gr. *Kaloi Limenes*).

FAIRS (Heb. IZEBONIM). Only in Ezekiel xxvii., where it is found seven times, once translated wares in verse 33. The word means *exchange*, and the sense of the chapter is much improved by this rendering.

FAITH (Heb. EMUN, *faith;* EMUNAH, *faithful;* Greek *elpis; faith* or *hope; pistis, one belief*). Faith is the assent of the mind to the truth of God's revealed will. There are two kinds: 1. *Historical*, which assents to the statements about the life and works of Jesus and the apostles, as historical truths. 2. *Evangelical*, or *saving faith*, is an assent to the truth of revelation, and an entire trust and confidence in God's character, and Christ's teachings, with an unreserved surrender of the will. Jesus Christ is then received into the heart as the Saviour, Prophet, Priest, and King, to be loved and obeyed. This is instrumentally a means of salvation, an essential grace, and a mainspring of Christian life.

FALLOW-DEER (Heb. YACHMUR). Permitted as food by the law, and supplied to Solomon's table (Deut. xiv. 5; 1 K. iv. 23). Two kinds of deer were known to the Hebrews in Palestine. Jacob refers to one in his blessing on Naphtali Its beauty, speed and agility are frequently used by the poets and prophets. The opening of the xlii. psalm is as beautiful as familiar:

"As the hart pants after the water-brooks,
　So does my soul pant for thee, O God."

This was written by David when Saul was hunting him from one place to another like a deer or "a partridge." Figures of deer are sculptured on the ancient monuments in Egypt. The bubale is classed among cattle in the East, and is found from Gibraltar to the Persian Gulf, living in small herds. The fallow-deer is quite rare, a few living around Mt. Tabor, and Lebanon, and is not found in Arabia, but Persia and Armenia are its peculiar home.

FAL'LOW-GROUND. Land that has been left to rest untilled a year or more. Figuratively, backsliding, unfruitful in spiritual things (Hosea x. 12).

FAMIL'IAR-SPIRIT. DIVINATION. MAGIC.

FAM'INE. A scarcity of food. Several are noticed: Gen. xii. 10; xxvi. 1, xli; Ruth i. 1; 2 K. vi. 25; Acts xi. 27. The most noted is that of seven years in Egypt, by which the whole people were reduced to dependence on the king, when Joseph was prime minister. Famine results from want of rain, visits of locusts and other insects. Amos predicted a spiritual famine (viii. 11).

FAN. 1. A hand machine, like a flat basket, for winnowing grain (Is. xxx. 24).—2. A large fork with a long handle, with which the grain is thrown up against the wind (Jer. xv. 7; Matt. iii. 12).

FAR'THING (Gr. *quadrans, one fourth of the as, or assarion*). Equal to two lepta (mites), about ⅜ of a cent. The specimens now extant are very neatly and artistically made, of copper or bronze, except that, like all ancient coin, the edge is unfinished.

ASSARION.

FAST. There is no word in the Pentateuch which means *to fast.* It was a voluntary, not a legal, act. This was probably a silent protest against the tendency to asceticism, so prevalent in the East. The vow of the Nazarite was voluntary, and only included wine and things related to it in origin, and the cases where it was necessary were few. Once a year, at the yearly atonement, the people were called to do what became, after a while, a fast in common terms (Lev. xvi. 29; Acts xxvii. 9), but there is no rule against eating or drinking, while there is against work—it was to be "a Sabbath of rest." Isaiah notices that when the spiritual element declined the ceremonial increased, and fasts became popular as an easy means of atonement (Is. lviii. 5). The true fast is to have a serious and heartfelt sorrow for sin, with earnest strivings to be delivered from it, as Isaiah says. Holiness and mourning are always, in the Hebrew mind, contrasts—opposite states of feeling. The public fast anciently among the Hebrews as well as among the modern Arabs, was a total abstinence from food for twenty-four hours, beginning at sunset. The forty days fast of Moses, Elijah and Jesus were miraculous. Jesus did not institute a fast, except the life-long fast of his disciples, after his death, intimated in Luke v. 34, 35, and directed those who did fast to conceal the fact by washing and dressing as usual, so as not to appear to fast before men and not really fast before God (Matt. vi. 17). The mere fast is no essential part of the gospel plan, although it was practiced by the apostles (1 Cor. vii. 5; Acts xiii. 2, etc.). The real fast is *the sacrifice of the personal will,* which is meant by the term *afflicting the soul* (Is. lviii. 5).

FAT. The fat, as being the choice part of animals, and especially sacred to the Lord, was always to be burned in sacrifice, even when other parts were to be eaten. The fat and the blood were not to be eaten (Lev. iii. 16, 17; vii. 23–27). The term *fat* was applied to the best and most excellent of all things, as the fat of the earth, of the wheat, of the oil, the vine, and even the fat of the mighty. The burning of it in the sacrifice is typical of the offering of what was best and loftiest in Christ's pure humanity. In him alone was there anything strictly good to offer. The offering of his followers is only acceptable through the working of his grace in their hearts (Ps. xii. 1).—2. Fat, for vat, in wine fat.

FATHER. 1. Male parent.—2. Any male ancestor, as Father Abraham.—3. Any man in the position of a father, as Joseph to Pharaoh.—4. The inventor or teacher of an art was called its father, and the father of those who practiced it. "Jubal was the father of all such as handle the harp or organ," that is, he was a teacher of music, if not its inventor; and "Jabal, the father of such as dwell in tents" (Gen. iv. 20, 21).—5. The builder or founder of a city, as Salma, the father of Bethlehem (1 Chr. ii. 51).—6. Any one who makes a thing or produces it, or tells a story, or recites a poem, is called the father of such a thing or poem. The authority of the father was sanctioned by the law of Moses, as standing between God and man. His blessing conferred special benefits, and his curse special injury. His sins affected his children, but they were not liable to punishment for them. The command to honor the parents was the only one to which a promise was attached, in the decalogue, while disrespect and filial insubordination were the worst of crimes.

The principle of respect to age and authority, so universal in the East, is derived from the patriarchal spirit, which still prevails outside of the walled cities, especially among the Arabs.

FATHOM. See WEIGHTS AND MEASURES.

FAT'LING. Fat beast. In good condition.

FANCHION. Falchion, a short crooked sword (Judith xiii. 6; xvi. 9). Cimeter.

FEASTS. See FESTIVALS.

FEET. See WASHING FEET, SANDALS.

FE'LIX. Claudius Antonius Felix was the Roman governor (procurator) of Judæa, from A. D. 53 to 60. He was originally a slave and was freed by the Emperor Claudius. His brother Pallas was also freed by the Emperor's mother Antonia, and deservedly had great influence with Claudius. Felix is said to have ruled Judæa in a mean, cruel, and profligate manner. Under the pretense of destroying robbers he crucified hundreds of good and patriotic Jews. He had trouble with false Mes-

GATE OF NICEA. BITHYNIA.

siahs also, followers of a "certain Egyptian magician." He married Drusilla, a Jewess, sister of the younger Agrippa; whom he enticed from her second husband Azizus. He kept Paul in prison two years, hoping that his friends would buy his liberty with a heavy bribe (see PAUL). Felix being recalled to Rome, was succeeded by Festus, and being charged with crimes by citizens of Cæsarea, would have been condemned to death but for the influence in his favor of his brother Pallas.

FELLER. Who cuts trees down, for timber or wood (Is. xiv. 8).

FENCED CITIES (Heb. MIBZAR, *cut off, separate*). The difference between a city and a village in the Bible is the wall around the city. The village had a watch-tower only. Sometimes the houses are built close together around a space, forming a wall, the entrance having a gate. Jerusalem, as described by Josephus, had three walls on some sides, with towers and battlements. Some of the cities in Assyria were surrounded with very wide and high walls, with a ditch outside for water, and a palisade in the middle of the ditch. These are found drawn in the sculptures.

FER'RET (Heb. ANAKAH, *sighs* or *groans*). Formerly translated shrew-mouse, but now the Gecko, of which there are several in Palestine. It is also called the Fan-foot. It is a lizard, with padded feet, and can move up and down walls like a fly, without noise, except what it makes with its voice, which sounds like its name—geck-o. They are red,

SIEGE OF JERUSALEM.

brown, green, or bright blue, and all studded with clear white spots over the back and flanks.

FER'RY-BOAT (Heb. ABARAH). Perhaps a raft (2 Sam. xix. 18).

FESTIVALS. The law plainly intended stated and regular meetings for worship, at shorter or longer intervals. No rule was made for any particular form of gathering, but each community was left to direct its own affairs. When synagogues were built, after the Captivity, the service was made more uniform. These gatherings were intended to be holy (Is. i. 13; Ps. lxxxi. 3, etc.). They were sacred seasons—feasts of the soul.

1. THE WEEKLY SABBATH (Heb. SHABBATH, *a day of rest*). The 7th day of the week (Gen. ii. 3), was established by law (Ex. xvi. 23, 29), to be kept by the whole people (Ex. xxv. 25). Isaiah utters solemn warning against profaning, and promises blessings for the due observance of it (Is. lviii. 13). The Scribes and Pharisees invented many strict rules, which hedged about the day and bound the people hand and foot, so that Jesus found it necessary to repeat the saying that "the Sabbath was made for man, and not man for the Sabbath." It was the key-note to a system consisting of 7th day, 7th week, 7th month, 7th year, and year of jubilee, which was at the end of 7 times 7 years. Each of these periods had its sacred day. It was lawful and customary for the priests to light fires, bake the shew-bread, and do other needed work about the Temple. "There was no Sabbath in holy things."

2. PASSOVER OR FEAST OF UNLEAVENED BREAD. It was kept in the 14th day of the first month, "between the two evenings"—that is, late in the evening is the Lord's Passover. On the next day, the 15th, is the feast of the unleavened bread, continuing 7 days (Lev. xxiii. 5). The lamb sacrificed for the passover must be of the first year, and without blemish (1 Cor. v. 7). The flesh of the paschal lamb was eaten to show the actual fellowship which the partakers of the feast held with God as the result of the atoning sacrifice.

THE PASSOVER was the annual national birthday festival, and was held in the first month when the ears of grain were forming. The lamb was roasted (not boiled), not a bone broken, and was entirely eaten, the persons standing, with loins girt, a staff in hand, shoes on, ready for a journey, in memory of the Exodus. The Pharisees excused the custom of reclining at the table in their day, by saying that it was a sign of the rest that the Lord had granted his people. The bitter herbs eaten with the lamb were reminders of the bondage in Egypt, and of the anxiety and trouble mingled with blessings in life, an emblem of the crucifixion of nature. Leavened bread was not to be eaten for a week—unleavened bread was "the bread of affliction," "for they came out of Egypt in haste." Leaven is a species of corruption—against which Jesus warned his disciples as in the peculiar errors of the Pharisees (Matt. xvi. 6). The feast also pointed to the future—to the sacrifice of the Paschal Lamb (Luke xxii. 15, 16).

THE FEAST OF WEEKS (Greek name PENTECOST.) The presentation of the first ripe ears of barley. It was also the feast of *first-fruits* and of *harvest*. The offering was made by the priest waving two loaves, made of the best of the crop, of fine wheat flour, leavened and baked, but not put on the altar (where no leaven could be placed), (Deut. xxvi. 2). This feast was in memory of the giving of the Law. It was the end of the harvest, as the second day of the Passover was the first, and it was the end of the Week of Weeks—seven times seven days. Canaan was in a peculiar sense God's land, and as He manifests his care in providing, He should be honored by those who are partakers of his bounty. In spiritual matters it was also the harvest season—the end of Christ's personal ministry on earth.

THE FEAST OF TRUMPETS, OR NEW MOON. The year was reckoned by the moon, twelve or more moons making a year (see CHRONOLOGY). Besides the usual offerings (Num. xxii. 11-15), there was a blowing of trumpets, as sung in Ps. lxxxi. 3. It occurred on the first of the 7th month, near our October. The voice of God and the voice of the trumpet on Mt. Sinai were heard together (Ex. xix. 16-19). It was a symbol of the mighty voice of God. The first was the *sacred month*, and was therefore placed *seventh* in the calendar. Four days were sabbaths, the 10th was the Day of Atonement, the 15th was the Feast of Tabernacles.

THE FEAST OF THE DAY OF ATONEMENT (see ATONEMENT). It was the occasion above all others, on which the ideas of sin and atonement rose to their highest potency in the ritual of the old covenant, exhibiting those ideas in their clearest light, how one ordained from among men, for the purpose of drawing near to God, mediates in behalf of his fellow men in things pertaining to sin and salvation.

THE FEAST OF TABERNACLES, the last of the appointed festivals under the old covenant, beginning on the 15th of the 7th month, and lasting seven days. The real name is *booths*, and was celebrated "in the end of the year, when they had gathered in their labors out of the field" (Ex. xxiii. 16). The crops and the vintage are supposed to be ended, and this was practically the end of the year. The booths were temporary and slight structures of sticks and leaves (Neh. viii. 16). Its object was to keep in memory the sojourn in the wilderness, a sort of perpetual renewing of their religious youth, when the covenant of the Law was first given. There was the same sin-offering for each day, and double the other offerings, two rams and fourteen lambs each day, and thirteen bullocks on the first day, one less each day, ending with seven on the seventh day.

After the Captivity, and in later times, there was

the Feast of the DEDICATION, in memory of the fresh consecration of the temple after it had been profaned by Antiochus Epiphanes (1 Macc. iv. 52 -59), B. C. 164 (John x. 22). It was held beginning on the 15th day of the 9th month (December) and lasted eight days. The modern Jews light one light on the first day, two on the next, etc. (8 on the last), making it a "Feast of Lights" (Ant. xii. 7, 7). Business and jollity going on as usual.

The FEAST OF PURIM is kept on the 14th and 15th of the 12th month, Adar (March). See BOOK OF ESTHER in the HISTORY.

FEASTS OF CHARITY or LOVE FEAST. See AGAPE.

FES'TUS PORCIUS. The successor of Felix as governor of Judæa, A. D. 60. His term was short, for he died in a little while (A. D. 62). He was superior to Felix, and would have set Paul at liberty, if he had understood the case, which Paul seeing, he appealed to Cæsar (Acts xxiv. 27). He gave the apostle a hearing in the presence of Agrippa and Berênice, and was astonished at his preaching, but supposed it came from a heated imagination aided by the peculiar dreamy speculations of the East. He got into a quarrel with the priests at Jerusalem by building a dining room in the governor's house, which overlooked the temple courts, when the priests built a high wall, cutting off the view. The emperor afterward sustained the priests (Ant. xx. 8). He was a good man and governor, but indifferent to religion.

FET'TERS. Chains to confine the feet, made of bronze or iron (Judg. xvi. 21; brass, iron in Ps. cv. 15).

FÉ'VER (Heb. KADDACHATH). Burning ague in Lev. xxvi. 21. DALLEKETH is translated inflammation in Deut. xxviii. 22, and CHARCHUR, extreme burnings. Greek *puretos*, fever in Matt. viii. 15, etc. Malignant fevers are still met with in Palestine, near water, in the spring and autumn, especially about the Sea of Galilee (*Land and Book*, i. 547).

FIELD (Heb. SADEH). A field which is not fenced; an open field (Num. xxii. 23, 24). Separate plots were marked by stones (Deut. xix. 14), which might be removed (Job. xiv. 2); and it was necessary to watch the flocks and herds day and night to prevent trespass. FULLER'S FIELD, POTTER'S FIELD.

FIG (Heb. TEENAH; Arab. *tin, the ficus carica tree;* Gr. *sukē*, fig-tree; *suka* (sycamore) figs. Three kinds are cultivated: 1. The early fig (Heb. BOKKORE, *early fig;* BICCURAH, *first ripe*), ripe in June, green in color.—2. The summer fig (KERMOUS), ripe in August, is sweet and the best, purple in color; and the green fig (*pag*) which remains on the tree all winter. (*Beth-phâge*, place of figs). DEBELAH, cake of figs in 1 Sam. xxx. 12. It is still used in the East as the most convenient and the best poultice (2 K. xx. 7; Is. xxxviii. 21). It is one of the few plants which grow wild all over the country. The fig tree puts forth its earliest fruit buds before its leaves, and the foliage forms a very dense shade. "To sit every man under his vine and under his fig tree," indicates in the East the fullest idea of peace, security and prosperity. Jeremiah (as well as several other prophets) uses the fig through all of his books as an emblem of good or evil, and particularly in chap. xxiv. Jesus made frequent use of the tree or its fruit as an emblem or a means of instruction, especially in the case of the barren fig tree, as a lesson against deceit. It grows best near a fountain or stream. The sycamore fig grows to a large size in Palestine and Egypt—sometimes 50 feet in circumference— and is evergreen. The fruit is purple, smaller than the other kinds, sweetish, and not so valuable. They ripen from November to June. The wood is used for many purposes, as it is almost the only large tree in Egypt.

FILE (Heb. PETSIRSAH). In 1 Sam. xiii. 21, translated file. The word means notched.

FIN'GER (Heb. ETSABA). The priest sprinkled with his forefinger (Lev. iv. 6). A certain gesture of the finger indicated contempt (Is. lviii. 9). The FINGER OF GOD, is his power (Ex. viii. 19).

FIR (Heb. BEROSH, BEROTH, *to cut up into boards*). Pine, cypress, juniper, or various evergreen trees. Found in the mountains. The timber was supplied to King Solomon by Hiram for the temple, for the floors and doors. It was used for musical instruments (2 Sam. vi. 5). The tree is next in size to the cedar. It is used by the poets and prophets among their figures.

SYCAMORE FIG.

FIRE (Heb. ESH). The symbol of Jehovah's presence, and first kindled by the Lord (Lev. vi. 9; 2 Chr. vii. 1). Sacred fire could only be had from the altar, and the crime of Nadab and Abihu was in using "strange fire" from some other source. No fire could be kindled on the Sabbath, except by the priests for holy purposes. Fire for cooking is made with sticks, grass and dried dung. To set fire to a grain field is a capital offense. Any damage by a careless fire must be made good (Ex. xxii. 6).

Fire was used to burn certain criminals and prisoners, and in some cases to destroy an enemy's city, and in the art of metallurgy. Fire was a symbol of fierce passion, calamities etc., and an emblem of healing spiritually (Mal. iii. 2). A baptism by fire.

FIRE-PAN (Heb. MACHTAH). Snuff-dish, or some utensil used about the altar.

FIRKIN (John ii. 6; Greek *metretes*). The firkin is a larger vessel than the one meant in the text.

FIR'MAMENT (Heb. RAKIA). The expanse; the sky over our heads. On the second day the expanse was made; on the fourth, *in the expanse* was made the sun, moon and stars.

FIRST-BORN (Heb. BECHOR). See BIRTHRIGHT. The religious bearing was the most important. Christ is the first born of all creation (Col. i. 16, 18), and the first born from the dead.

FIRST-FRUITS (BICCURIM). Among fruits what the first-born is among men and beasts. The first or best of the oil, of the wine, of the wheat, of all the harvest, was sacred to the Lord, to be given in a quantity, according to the will and inclination of each person. The faithful priest reaped a rich reward from the holy zeal that he instilled into the hearts of his people. The doctors limited the gifts to the 60th part as the least that would be accepted. In the later times the Jews turned the gifts into money. This custom was not peculiar to Israel. The first-fruits were often sent to Jerusalem from foreign countries.

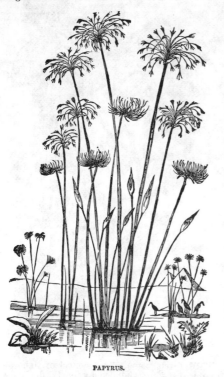

PAPYRUS.

FISH (Heb. DAG, DAGAH; Gr. *icthus*). No particular kind of fish is mentioned by name in the Bible; but there are frequent references to fish generally. It is a little remarkable that the apostles, who were professed fishermen, did not designate by name any kinds of fish, saleable or unsaleable, and especially the one bearing the tribute-money. It would have been interesting to know the name of the fish, as well as that of the coin. Even the law of Moses does not mention names (as among animals), but character only, as fins and scales for pure or clean, that might be eaten. Solomon's treatise on fishes (1 K. iv. 33), is lost. The Greek furnishes 400 names for varieties of fishes, but the Hebrew has not one. Jacob knew how rapidly they increase, for he alludes to this fact in his blessings (Gen. xlviii. 16), "multitude," etc., meaning in the original "as fishes do increase." Fish were eaten from the earliest times (Num. xi. 22), and one of the gates of Jerusalem was called Fish Gate. In Egypt, the monuments show many pictures of fish and fishing. The historians speak of the vast quantities of fish taken, from which the royal revenue was derived for the queen's special

use, for jewelry, perfumery, etc., of $350,000 a year. The Assyrian sculptures also show men fishing. The Egyptians also dried and salted fish, as shown in the sculptures.

FITCHES (Heb. KETZACH). "The fitches are beaten out with a staff," (Is. xxviii. 27). The fennel-flower, a coarse kind of pea, hard, but nutritious. In the great famine in England in 1555 wild fitches saved many people from starving. It grows all over Europe and Asia. The "fitches" in Ezekiel's symbolized bread (iv. 9), was spelt (Heb. KUSSEMETH), a grain something like wheat.

FLAG (Heb. SUPH, and ACHU). The ark of Moses was floated among the flags (Ex. ii. 3), SUPH. Isaiah predicts that the reeds and flags shall wither (xix. 6) in Egypt: "Can the flag grow without water?" (ACHU, Job. viii. 11). It is rendered meadow or marsh in Gen. xli. 2, 18. Any waterplant would answer the case. The Edible Rush, and Flowering Rush grow both in Egypt and Palestine. The name of the Red Sea is Yam Suph.

FLÄG'ON (Heb. ASHISHAH). In 2 Sam. vi. 19; Cant. ii. 15, and Hosea iii. 1, it is a cake of raisins. —2. (Heb. NEBEL). In Is. xxii. 24 is a bottle of skin or pottery.

FLÄX (Heb. PISHTAH, *peeled*). Very few plants are so beautiful and so useful as the slender flax, with its tall, taper leaves, large purple flowers, and its strong fibre from which the most delicate lawn or coarsest canvas is made. The holy garments of Aaron, and the curtains of the tabernacle were partly of linen. Its whiteness, in linen, was a symbol of purity. The ancient sculptures represent the manufacture of linen (Prov. xxxi. 13).

FLEA (Heb. PAROSH). "The king of the fleas holds his court in Tiberias," now as ever in old times. Frequent change of linen is the only means of keeping clear of them in the East. They almost disappear in the heat of summer. They swarm on travelers, when scarcely touching natives. They are said to produce a healthy irritation in the skin. David says: "After whom is the king of Israel come out? * * * after one flea?" (1 Sam. xxiv. 14, xxvi. 20).

FLESH (BASAR). All that is of flesh and blood (Gen. vi. 13); and the human race (Luke iii. 6, etc.). The weakness, and frailty of man is also flesh (Rom. iv. 1). Flesh is also the antipathy to spirit (viii. 1).

FLIES FLY (Heb. ZEBUB, AROB). Common house-flies swarm in great numbers in the East. The peculiar gray fly (Ar. *thebab*) which comes with the rise of the Nile is productive of disease in both man and animals. The *arob* was the fly, or swarm of insects of one of the plagues in Egypt. Flies in the East are very persistent in settling on persons, never quitting until dark, and are the means of carrying diseases from one to another. The Philistines had a god, Baal-zebub, whose special duty it was to take care of flies. Judging from their number they are well cared for. The "ointment (perfume) of the apothecary" (Eccles. x. 1) was attractive to flies, and their dead bodies spoiled its odor, and so would little follies spoil the reputation of a wise man. The man is the perfume, his little folly the dead fly, his disgrace the bad odor.

FLINT (CHALLAMISH). Used in Deut. viii. 15; and Psalms cxiv. 8, in reference to God's bringing water and oil out of the naturally barren rocks for the sake of his people. In Is. i. 7, it is a metaphor of the firmness of the prophet in resisting his enemies, as also in Ez. iii. 9.

FLOOD. DELUGE.

FLOOR. PAVEMENT.

FLOUR. BREAD.

FLOWERS. Flowering plants and shrubs are found in great numbers and variety all over Palestine, except in the highest regions of the mountains, and in the shifting sands of the desert. 2500 have been named and classified, 500 of which are well known in Europe. The most abundant families of plants are Leguminous, pod-bearing, such as peas, beans, pulse; the Astragalus and the Acacia. A vast number of thistles, centauries, and other like plants, cover the richest plains and the stony hills. Many sweet flowering shrubs, such as marjoram, thyme, lavender, calaminth, sage, and others similar. A vast number and variety of weeds, mustard being the king of all. Fennel, Bupleurum, and Eryngium form dense rows of foliage and flowers along the border of woods, and in damp hollows. Soap plant is conspicuous, and the Boragineæ, annual weeds, besides which are the Echiums, Anchusas, and other fine species. Scrophularia, Veronica, Linaria and Verbascum (mulleins) are very abundant. Grasses are very numerous, many species bearing silky plumes of flowers of great beauty and grace. The variety and beauty of the family of lilies is no where exceeded. The lily springs up everywhere, and the Amaryllids are of great size, beauty, and variety. Fritillarias and squills are in abundance, and bear pretty flowers. Violets and geraniums are very numerous and finely colored. Roses are a subject of profitable cultivation for attar, and a valley near Jerusalem is called the Valley of Roses (Wady el Werd). The Narcissus is very beautiful, abundant and in several varieties, and is believed to be the flower alluded to by the poet in Cant. ii. 1, and the prophet in Is. xxxv. 1. Several other Amaryllids are found in great numbers, and almost the most showy plants in the field. Iris, crocus, and gladiolus grow very large and showy. Broom, ivy, dog-rose, elder, honeysuckle, berberry, hawthorn, and jasmine are found in Lebanon and Anti-Lebanon, at and above 4000 feet elevation. Rhododendrons, primrose, and a great variety of plants, from 5000 to 7000, and some kinds are found even up to the limits of the snow line; at 8000 Vicia forms tufts of pale blue, at 9000 there are Arenaria, Arabis, Drabas, Festuca, and Potentilla, while the little Nocea and the Oxyria grows on the very summit of Khodib, 10,200 feet high. From the sands of the desert to the snows of the mountain summits there are flowers of many varieties, blooming in every month of the year.

FLUTE (Chaldee, *mashrokitha*). Made of one or more pipes. Pipe in 1 K. i. 40. One of the simplest and oldest of musical instruments. Used at banquets (Is. v. 12), at public worship (Dan. iii. 5, etc.), marriages, funerals, and by pilgrims on the way to the yearly meeting.

FLUX. Dysentery of a very severe kind in the East, attended with fever (Acts xxviii. 8). The Oriental custom of wearing a bandage around the bowels is a preventive of bowel disorder by protecting against the sudden changes from hot to cold which always follows sundown. When bound the dysentery is less dangerous. King Jehorum had a chronic dysentery, with *prolapsus ani* (2 Chr. xxi. 15).

FOOD. Some kind of prohibition in what may be eaten or may not has been known from the earliest times. The human race can eat "every herb bearing seed," and "every tree in which is the fruit of a tree" (Gen. i. 29), and also "every moving thing that liveth," but flesh with the life thereof, which is the blood, was prohibited (Gen. ix. 3, 4). And other rules made distinctions of clean and unclean among animals, fowls and fishes, for food. (See CLEAN.) The climate influences the diet all over the world. Animal food is not needed, and cannot be used, during the greater part of the year, nor can it be kept in a healthy state for any length of time in the hot season. The sacrificial feasts occurring at long intervals when animal food was eaten, were very acceptable, on account of the abstinence preceding them. Bread is the chief food

besides fruit and vegetables. Rice is much used. (BREAD.) Neither eggs nor fowls are mentioned among gifts of first-fruits, although they are largely used now in the East. Almost every known fruit and vegetable can be had, in plenty and of good quality. Milk, cheese, butter (melted as oil), oil of olives, and honey, or molasses from grapes (dibs) can be found everywhere. Condiments of many kinds are in common use; and much use is made of aromatic herbs in cookery. Nuts cooked with meat adds delicacy to the flavor. Highly seasoned food, with spices, salt, onions, garlic, lemons, pomegranates, and verjuice, makes a savory dish. Cracked wheat is boiled with meat. "Killing, cooking, and eating in rapid succession is a very old custom" (*Land and Book*, ii. 162). The Arabs have many caustic terms of contempt for the man who neglects to honor a guest with a "sacrifice" of a lamb, kid, or calf, as required by the laws of hospitality. (See MEALS, WINE, WATER). Milk and honey, and oil with honey, or butter with honey, are choice dishes, eaten with bread, usually for breakfast.

FOOL. Used of moral more than of intellectual deficiencies, of one who does not fear God, and acts without regard to His law (Ps. xiv. 1).

FOOT. (See WASHING FEET). The foot was used as a symbol of many ideas. Such phrases as "slipping of the foot," "stumbling," and "from head to foot," need no explanation. "To be under the feet," means subject to a king, or as a servant to the master (Ps. viii. 6; Heb. ii. 8); derived from the symbolical act of a conquerer who placed his foot on the neck of his subdued enemies in token of triumph (Josh. x. 24), as may be seen in the sculptures on the ancient monuments. To be at any one's feet meant service or pupilage (Judg. iv. 10), and Paul actually sat at the feet of Gamaliel (who sat on a raised seat), as was the custom then (Acts xxii. 3). "Lameness of feet" is affliction or calamity (Ps. xxxv. 15). To set one's foot in a place is to take possession (Deut. i. 36). To water with the foot is to turn the little rills easily (this was a mark of the superiority of Palestine to Egypt, because rain and brooks were there instead of the Nile and the artificial canals); (xi. 10.) To walk with a straight foot "uprightly" in Gal. ii. 14. Naked feet (out of doors) was poverty or mourning

FITCHES.

(Ez. xxiv. 17). Uncovering the feet, or taking off the overshoe in the East, is equivalent to taking off the hat with us. Uncovering the feet was a part of the act of adoration (Ex. iii. 4), as Moses before the burning bush. "How beautiful on the mountains are the feet of him who brings glad tidings" (Is. lii. 7).

The Hebrews were modest in their writings, and used the word foot for certain parts and actions which could not be named. "Hair of the foot," "water of the foot," "between the feet" (Deut. xxviii. 57), "he covereth his feet" (Judg. iii. 24 for "dismisses the refuse of nature.")

FOOT'MEN (Heb. RAGLI). 1. Soldiers; not horsemen.—2. (Heb. ROOTZ.) Swift runners (1 Sam. viii. 11; xxii. 17). Paul refers to them (1 Cor. ix. 24). Elijah ran before Ahab as a footman.

FORDS. Places for crossing a river by wading. See JORDAN.

FOUN'DER (Judg. xvii. 4; Jer. vi. 29). METALS.

FOUN'TAIN (Heb. AYIN, *to flow;* MAYAN, *a gushing;* BOR, *a cistern;* MABBUA, *to bubble out;* MAKOR, *to dig*). These several words are translated fountain, but only one, AYIN, really means a spring of water. The springs of Palestine are remarkable for their great number, and some of them for their immense volume. Water there is fertility and life, and the whole land is full of great fountains, such as those of the Dog River; of the River of Beirut;

RUINS OF CAPERNAUM.

FORE'HEAD (Ez. ix. 4). It was (and is now in India) the custom in the East to mark or color the forehead, to distinguish the holy from the profane (Rev. xiii. 16), the devotees of certain idols, and also slaves. "Jewels for the forehead" (Ez. xvi. 12), means nose-rings, or, it may be, strings of coins.

FOREST (Heb. YAAR, abundance, forest; CHORESH, thick wood; PARDES, orchard). Since the historical era, Palestine has had few forests, the trees being mostly fruit or ornamental. The highlands were probably once well wooded. Several forests are mentioned: of Lebanon, which must have been one of great extent (see CEDAR, FIR); of Hareth; of Carmel; of Ephraim, etc. There are now extensive forests in Persia, of oak, terebinth (Is. ii. 13; Ez. xxvii. 6). "The house of the forest of Lebanon" was built of cedar and fir from Lebanon, with many pillars like a forest, in Jerusalem (1 K. vii. 2). The forest supplies the poets and prophets with many fine figures.

FORKS (1 Sam. xiii. 21). Hay-forks with three or more prongs; used, also, in winnowing grain.

FORNICA'TION. ADULTERY.

FORTIFICA'TION. FENCED CITIES (Micah vii. 12).

FOR'TRESS (2 Sam. xxii. 2; Ps. xviii. 2; Is. xxv. 12). FENCED CITIES.

FORTUNA'TUS. Disciple at Ephesus, native of Corinth (1 Cor. xvi. 17). He is also mentioned in Clement's Epistle.

FOUNDA'TION, GATE OF THE (2 Chr. xxiii. 5). JERUSALEM.

Damur; Owely; Zahrany; Litany at Baalbek; Zahleh; Ainjar, and Mushgarah; Ras el Ain at Tyre; Kabery and Naamany near Acre; of the Kishon at Janin, Lejjun, and Wady Kusaby; Zerka near Cæsarea; Aujeh at Antipatris, and the Ras in Sharon. And so we might go all through Palestine, on both sides of the Jordan. Some are hot, as at Tiberias, Gadara, and Callirrhoë; others are intermittent as the Fuarr, the source of the Sabbatic River, and the Menbej, east of Beit Jenn, Mt. Hermon (*Land and Book*, i. 405). The fountain at Nazareth has a traditional antiquity and importance. Wealthy men in the East build handsome structures over fountains for their preservation, and the benefit of residents and travelers.

FOUNTAIN-GATE. JERUSALEM (Neh. xii. 37).

FOWL (Heb. BARBURIM (1 K. iv. 23) *fatted fowl*). Barn-door fowl, or geese. The Egyptian paintings represent catching, keeping, feeding, killing, salting, cooking, and eating of fowl.

FOX (Heb. SHUAL, *to dig through*). The Arab name for jackal is *shikal*, but a little different from the Hebrew SHUAL, and is it evident from the habits of the animal referred to that the jackal is meant. They are plenty now in Palestine, and are night-prowlers, lying concealed in the day-time, in caves, holes, or among the ruins. They go in packs of hundreds. They eat any carcase of either animal or man (Ps. lxiii. 9, 10). The Orientals never spare pain in men or animals, and Samson, who was revengeful and unscrupulous, tied a firebrand between two jackals and sent them into the dry wheat-fields of the Philistines, destroying vast fields probably. (See FIRE.) Jackals are very fond of grapes (Matt. viii. 20; Luke ix. 58).

FRANK'INCENSE (Heb. LEBONAH). Resin of the *Boswellia tree*, which grows 40 feet high in India and Arabia Felix. It has a balsamic smell, and burns with a white flame and fragrant odor. Its burning was symbolical of the holiness of Jehovah (1 Chr. ix. 29) and of prayer (Ps. cxli. 2; Luke i. 10; Rev. viii. 3).

FRAY (Deut. xxviii. 26, etc.). To terrify. Not used now.

FREEDOM. CITIZEN. SLAVE.

FREE-WILL OFFERING (Lev. xxii. 18). Free gifts. SACRIFICE.

FRET (Lev. xiii. 55). A plague spot in a leprous garment.

FRINGES (Heb. ZITHZITH, *flourish*). Bobs, tassels or fringes (Num. xv. 38). They are shown on many ancient figures. ASSYRIA; DRESS; EMBROIDERY.

FROG (Heb. ZEPHARDEA, *marsh-leaper*). Mentioned but three or four times in the Bible (always of the plague), but very common in Palestine and Egypt (Ex. viii. 2–14; Ps. lxxviii. 45; cv. 30; Wisdom xix. 10). It is believed that the frogs of the plague were the edible variety. Their noise is heard from one end of the land to the other (L. & B. i. 368). In Egypt they were regarded as a type of the Creator (Pthah).

FRONT'LET (Heb. TOTAPHOTH). Something bound on the forehead, "between the eyes," and as a sign or token in the hand (a ring?). Originally the meaning of the law or direction was to keep in memory, as in Prov. vi. 21: "Bind them on the heart, and tie them on the neck." But after the return from captivity the Jews made the law literal, and wrote it out (Ex. xiii. 2–10, 11–16; Deut. vi. 5–9; xi. 13–21) on bits of parchment, called Phylacteries, which were put in little cases of leather (metal in our day), and tied on the forehead and left arm. The ribbon for tying them was colored purple by the Pharisees, and made showy and broad (Mark vii. 3, 4), and were worn by all Jews except Karaites, women and slaves. The Rabbis made many rules about their uses. They were not worn on the Sabbath, because the Sabbath was itself a sign; the person reading them in the morning must stand; in the evening he may sit; the color of the thread might be changed to red in times of persecution; both hands must be used in writing them; the parchment must not have a hole in it; only one blot or error was permitted; a person wearing them must keep six feet off from a cemetery—and many others. They were a means of religious vanity, hypocrisy and display, and were so denounced by Jesus. The Rabbis said (by a kind of pious fraud) that God wore them, arguing from Is. xlix. 16; lxii. 8; Deut. xxxiii. 2. They were a kind of amulet, such as the modern Arabs use. AMULET.

FROST (Heb. HANAMAL, *hail-stones*, Ps. lxxviii. 47); KERACH, *ice* (Gen. xxxi. 40); KEPHOR, *hoar-frost* (Ex. xvi. 40). There is a great difference between the temperature of the day and night in the East. CLIMATE.

FRUIT (Heb. PERI, *fruit in general;* KAYITS, *summer fruits*). Their great variety and excellence would fill a volume.

FRYING-PAN. BREAD.

FUEL. DUNG.

FULLER. Business of cleaning and whitening cloth. It was carried on outside the city of Jerusalem, where was the *Fuller's Field*, mentioned three times in the Bible (2 K. viii. 17; Is. vii. 3; xxxvi. 2), so close, that one speaking in the field could be heard by one standing on the city wall. Perhaps near the pool of Gihon, or it might have

been at En Rogel. Rabshakeh and his great host must have come on the north side.

FUNERAL. BURIAL. See cuts on pages 7 and 110.

FURLONG. The stadium; Roman, 201 $\frac{45}{100}$ yards; English, 220 yards (Luke xxiv. 13).

FURNACE. Several kinds are mentioned: **1.** TANNER, *oven* (Gen. xv. 17); KIBSHAN, *lime-kiln* (Gen. xix. 28); KUR, *furnace for smelting metals;* ATTUN, *furnace* (Dan. iii. 6); Gr. *kaminos, baker's oven* (Matt. xiii. 42).

FRINGE.

FUR'NITURE (Heb. KELI, *apparatus*, Ex. xxxi. 7). The furniture of Eastern dwellings is very simple. Many articles deemed necessary with us would find no place there.—2. Heb. KAR, *a camel's saddle and its canopy* (Gen. xxxi. 34).

G

GA'AL (*loathing*). Son of Ebed (Judg. ix). A brigand who was ready to sell his services to the highest bidder.

GA'ASH (*earthquake*). Mount Gaash on the north side of which was Timnathcheres, the city given to Joshua at his request (Josh. xix. 49, 50), and where he resided and was buried (Josh. xxiv. 30; Judg. ii. 9). Lost.

GA'BA. GEBA.

GAB'AEL (*God's highest*). **1.** Descendant of Tobit (Tob. i. 1).—2. A poor Jew (Tob. i. 17), to whom Tobit lent money.

GABBAI (*tax-gatherer*). An important person in the family of Benjamin (Neh. xi. 8).

GAB'BATHA. Pavement (John xix. 13). Outside the Prætorium (judgment hall), where Pilate delivered Jesus to death. The *bema* was an elevated pavement, the usual place of justice.

GABDES. GABA (1 Esd. v. 20).

GA'BRIAS (*man of Jehovah*, Tob. i. 14). Brother of Gabael.

GABRIEL (*man of God*). Angel (Dan. viii. 16; Luke i. 19). In Jewish and Christian traditions the archangel of God.

GAD (*troop*). Jacob's seventh son, first-born of Zilpah, Leah's maid; brother to Asher (Gen. xxx. 11–13; xlvi. 16, 18). The country given to the

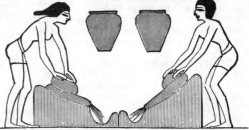

EGYPTIAN FULLER.

tribe was the centre of the east of Jordan (Deut. iii. 12), from Heshbon to Mahanaim. On the east was Aroer, that faces Rabbah (Josh. xiii. 25); west was Jordan (v. 27), and including the Arabah, from the Jabbok to the Sea of Chinnereth. The most beautiful district in Syria. It is a high range of purple-tinted mountains, cut down by deep ravines, partially clothed with forests of oak, terebinths, sycamores, ilex, beech, fig, and evergreen shrubs. The climate is fine and soil fertile, affording the best pasturage. At one time the tribe possessed the land as far east as Salcah (1 Chr. v. 11, 16). Jephthah was a Gadite of Mizpah (Judg. xi. 34). Carried into captivity, and its cities inhabited by Ammonites (1 Chr. v. 26; Jer. xlix. 1).

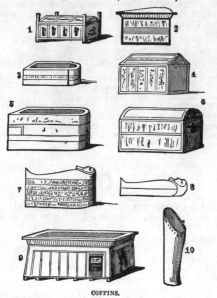

COFFINS.

GAD'ARA. Five miles southeast of the Sea of Galilee, three miles from the river Hieromax. There were warm springs near the river, called Amatha. Josephus says it was a Greek city, and the capital of Peræa (Jos. B. J. iv. 7, § 3; Mark v. 1; Luke viii. 26-37). Here the Lord healed the demoniacs (Matt. viii. 28-34; Mark v. 1-21; Luke viii. 26-40). The most interesting ruins at Gadara are the tombs, which are very numerous in the cliffs around the city, cut in the solid rock, being rooms ten to twenty feet square, and some larger, with small recesses out of them for bodies, the doors being stone, turning on stone hinges. The space over which the ruins are scattered is about two miles, on a narrow, high ridge, sloping east, anciently walled all around. There was a straight street from end to end, with a colonade on each side, and two very large theatres, now in ruins. Not a house or a column is standing.

GADARENES'. People of Gadara.

GAD'DI (*fortunate*). Son of Susi (Num. xiii. 11).

GAD'DIAL (*fortune of God*). A Zebulonite spy.

GA'DI. A Gadite. Father of King Menahem (2 K. xv. 14, 17).

GADITES. Of the tribe of Gad.

GA'HAM (*swarthy*). Son of Nahor, brother of Abraham (Gen. xvii. 24), son of Reumah.

GA'HAR (*hiding-place*). Ancestor of Nethinim (Ezr. ii. 47).

GA'IUS. A common Roman name.

GAL'AAD (1 Macc. v. 9, 56; Jud. i. 8).

GA'LAL (*worthy*). 1. A Levite (1. Chr. ix. 15). —2. Son of Jeduthun (ix. 16; Neh. xi. 17).

GAL'ATIA (*country of the Galli, Asia*). Used in two senses.—1. Some suppose France (Gaul) is meant in 2 Tim. iv. 10, and 1 Macc. viii. 2. France (Gaul) may have been the origin of the people who invaded Greece and Asia Minor in the 4th century, B. C., and were first checked by Antiochus, who

was called Soter (*saviour*) for the success, and were finally subdued by the Roman Manlius, B. C. 189, when they gathered into a district in the central region of Asia Minor. Visited twice by Paul (Acts xviii. 23). The Epistle to the Galatians was written after the second visit.

GALA'TIANS (1 Macc. viii. 2; 2 Macc. viii. 20; Gal iii. 1). People of any race, or Jews, or Gauls from France, living in Galatia. For Epistle to the Galatians, see HISTORY OF THE BOOKS.

GAL'BANUM (HELBENAH). A perfume used in the preparation of the sacred incense (Ex. xxx. 34). Resinous, yellow-brown, but it is not known from what plant or tree it is derived.

GAL'EED (*heap of witness*). The name which Jacob gave to the heap which he and Laban made on Mount Gilead (Gen. xxxi. 47, 48, xxiii. 25). JEGAR-SAHADUTHA.

GALGALA (1 Macc. ix. 2). MAGDALA?

GALILE'AN. Native of Galilee (Mark xiv. 70).

GALILEE (GALIL, *a circle*). At first applied to a small district about Kedesh, on the N. W. shore of the Sea of Galilee (Is. ix. 1). Afterward, during the Roman rule, the name of the whole country north of the Kishon river and Mount Gilboa, to the Leontes and Hermon, from the Jordan to the sea (Josephus Life, 12, Wars, iii.). Divided into Upper, as far as the N. W. angle of the Sea of Galilee, and Lower, as far south as Ginea (Jenin), including the great plain of Esdraëlon. The hills are now wooded, with gentle slopes, and are fruitful of all that man uses, and luxuriant in flowers of every variety (Deut. xxxiii. 18; Gen. xlix. 20). The chief towns were Capernaum, Kedesh, Bethsaida, Tiberias, Nazareth, Cana, besides many other smaller, the ruins of which are scattered over nearly every hill-top or hill-side. Here was the scene of the greater part of the works and life of Jesus, which are the subject of the first three Gospels almost wholly. THE SEA OF GALILEE, GENNESARET.

GALL (Heb. MERERAH, *bitter*; ROSH, *poison-hemlock*, or *poppies*). Gall means the bitter nature of the drink offered Jesus (Matt. xxvii. 34).

GAL'LERY (Heb. RAHIT, *ceiling*; rafters in Cant. i. 17; RAHAT, *braided*, in Gen. xxx. 28, gutters; ATTIK, *pillar* for the support of a house, Ez. xli. 15).

GAL'LEY. SHIP.

GAL'LIM (*heaps*). Twice mentioned (1 Sam. xxv. 44; Is. x. 30). It was probably near Dan, Laish, but is lost.

GAL'LIO, JUNIUS ANNÆUS. Elder brother of the philosopher Seneca, who dedicated to him his treatise *De Vita Beta*, and in another work describes him as a man universally loved, and who especially abhorred flattery. He was the proconsul of Achaia, and by his prudent course much assisted Paul (Acts xviii. 12-17). He was a victim to Nero's cruelty.

GAMA'LA (*camel*). Built on a hill, near the middle of the E. shore of the Sea of Galilee. Described by Josephus as an important town.

GAMA'LIEL (*benefit of God*). 1. Son of Padahzur (Num. i. 10, ii. 20), head of the tribe of Manasseh, in the Exodus.—2. A Pharisee, and a celebrated doctor (Acts v. 34; xxii. 3); a Rabbi, teacher of Paul. He was grandson of the famous Hillel, and son of Rabbi Simeon, and president of the Sanhedrin during the time of Tiberius, Caligula, and Claudius. He lived 18 years after the destruction of Jerusalem.

GAMES. The ancient (and modern) Orientals are represented as very fond of games of many kinds, private and public, frequently mentioned in Scripture. The sculptures and paintings of antiquity exhibit these in every variety. Job alludes to one in xli. 5, and Jeremiah in xxx. 19, and Jesus, in Matt. xi. 16. Music, dancing, and song were always enjoyed on festive occasions (Ps. xxx. 11; Luke xv. 25). Armed men jousted (2 Sam. ii. 14); they played with single-stick; with the cestus; wrestled; quoits; at leaping; running; and all Grecian games. The rewards in the Grecian games were of several kinds: A chaplet of wild olive; palm branches; and the honors freely given him by his friends and fellow-citizens, of sacrifices to the gods, and poems in his praise, exemption from public service, and a pension. There were four more celebrated: Olympic, Pythian, Nemean, and Isthmian, among the Greeks, in which the most eminent men contended for the prizes, which fact made them a fitting illustration of the Christian life. Temperance in eating and drinking was the rule, and severe exercise at stated times. The Romans added brutality and cruelty, and men were required to fight each other, and wild beasts also. Paul witnessed the games, in various cities where he preached, and is the only one in the N. T. who makes use of them as illustrations of the strife for good against evil in the theatre of life.

GAM'MADINE (Ez. xxvii. 11). Hired soldiers. Mercenaries.

GA'MUL (*weaned*). A priest (1 Chr. xxiv. 17), leader of the 22d course.

GAR. "Sons of Gar," servants of Solomon (1 Esd. v. 34).

GAR'DEN (Heb. GAN, GINNAH; Gr. *keros*). The garden was essential in Egypt. They made constant and general use of fruits and flowers at the table, which required careful cultivation. Their residences were surrounded with gardens, laid out with skilful care, with ornamental beds of curious devices, arbors of trellis-work, basins and rills of water with fish, and paved walks. The Israelites remembered the gardens when they were in the desert, and did not neglect them when in Palestine. Everywhere we find traces of such cultivation: in terraces, cisterns for water, springs cared for, and names of places compounded with Gan or Gen (Engannim, Gennesaret). The garden was often away from the village or house a half a mile perhaps, in some favored spot for water and good soil. The summer-house was decorated with handsome designs and showy colors. It was a place of retirement (John xxviii. 1), and also of merry-making (Is. li. 3). They were inclosed with walls, hedges, and had watch-towers; and even the poorest a booth to shelter the watchman (Is. i. 8; Mark xii. 1; Job. xxvii. 18). A family tomb was sometimes built in the garden (2 K. xxi. 18, 26; John xix. 41, 42).

GARDEN-HOUSE. Place where king Ahaziah II fled from Jehu (2 K. xix. 27); the modern Jenin (Engannim).

GA'REB, THE ITHRITE. A hero of David's army, from Jattir (2 Sam. xxiii. 38).

GA'REB, THE HILL. Near Jerusalem (Jer. xxxi. 39). Now occupied by the new and fine buildings of the Russian mission.

GAR'LIC (SHUM). A vegetable, something like the onion, found in Egypt (Num. xi. 5). The Egyptians have always made use of it as a stimulant, for it quickens the circulation.

GAR'MITE (*bony*), (1 Chr. iv. 9). Keilah, from Gerem.

GARNER. BARN.

GAR'RISON (Heb. MAZZAH, *garrison;* NEZIB, *a garrison*, or also *a column* (1 Sam. xiii. 3); MAZZEBAH, *a pillar* (Ez. xxvi. 11); Gr. *phoureo, to keep watch* (2 Cor. xi. 32). The garrison at Jerusalem was a citadel, or the tower of Antonia (Acts xxi. 34, 37). Another, in Damascus, was used to prevent Paul's escape.

GA'TAM (*burnt valley*). Fourth son of Eliphaz (Gen. xxxvi. 11); head of an Edomite tribe. Jethema is a modern town in Arabia.

GATE (Heb. SHAAR, *gate;* PETHAH, *entry;* SAPH, *threshhold, door-post;* DELETH, *door, two leaved gate;* Chal. *tera, gate, door;* Gr. *thura, pule, pulon*). An entrance into a camp, a house, a tent, a temple, a city, etc. "To possess the gate," was a term meaning power and wealth (Gen. xxii. 17). It was the place of assembly (Prov. i. 21) for social (Ps. lxix. 12) and legal purposes (Ruth iv. 1). Daniel sat in the gate of the king of Babylon (iv. 49); for attracting the notice of the king (Esth. ii. 19), and for marketing (2 K. vii. 1). The gate was spoken of as meaning the city (Gen. xiv. 60; Ps. lxxxvii. 2) or

GATE.

the people of the city (2 Sam. xv. 2). There was (and is) generally an open place both outside and inside the gate. In such a one the king of Ai was buried (Josh. viii. 29), and Jeremiah the prophet was set in the stocks (Jer. xx. 2).

The Assyrian palaces furnish many illustrations of Scripture, and especially in the architecture, paintings and sculptures of the gates. They were lofty, magnificent, built for the ages, guarded by symbolic figures, never used inside of buildings, who present to the visitor the fir-cone, a symbol of life. In the floor of the door-way are usually found concealed curious, small images of baked clay, with animal heads on human (or lion) bodies and bull's legs and tail, which were the guardian divinities of the gate (TERAPHIM, Arabic *tarf*, boundary).

GATH, one of the five royal cities of the Philistines (Josh. xiii. 3; 1 Sam. vi. 17), and the native place of the giant Goliath (1 Sam. xvii. 4, 23). It probably stood upon the conspicuous hill now called *Tell-es-Safieh*, upon the side of the plain of Philistia, at the foot of the mountains of Judah; 10 miles E. of Ashdod, and about the same distance S. by E. of Ekron. It is irregular in form, and about 200 ft. high. Gath occupied a strong position (2 Chr. xi. 8) on the border of Judah and Philistia (1 Sam. xxi. 10; 1 Chr. xviii. 1); and from its strength and resources, forming the key of both countries, it was the scene of frequent struggles, and was often captured and recaptured (2 Chr. xi. 8; xxvi. 6; 2 K. xii. 17; Am. vi. 2). The ravages of war to which Gath was exposed appear to have destroyed it at an early period, as it is not mentioned among the other royal cities by the later prophets (Zeph. ii. 4; Zech. ix. 5, 6).

GATH-HE'PHER (*wine-press of the well*). Zebulon, near Japhia (Josh. xix. 13). Gittah-hepher. Benjamin of Tudela says that in his time (A. D. 1140) the tomb of Jonah was shown on a hill near Sepphoris.

GATH-RIM'MON. Dan, in the plain (Josh. xxi. 24). Lost.—2. Manasseh, west of Jordan (ib. 25). Probably Bethshan.

GA'ZA (*strong*). AZ'ZAH (*desert*). The last town in the southwest of Palestine, on the coast toward Egypt. On the high road between Egypt and Syria. Mentioned in Genesis (x. 19), one of the oldest cities in the world (Gen. x. 17), and is a town now. Joshua could not subdue it (x. 41). Held by Judah a short time (Judg. i. 18; iii; xii. 1). Samson carried off its gates (xvi. 1–31). Gaza is mentioned in the inscriptions at Nineveh (*Layard*, p. 144). The Ethiopian was baptized by Philip on the way to Gaza. There are deep wells of good water, orchards of varieties of fruit, and palm trees and olive groves. Settled by Avim or Hivites, who were driven out by the Caphtorim from Egypt. Became one of the five royal Philistine cities, the last home of the giant Anakim (Josh. xi. 22). Taken by Alexander the Great, who was wounded there (Arrian ii. 26). A church was established there early, but idolatry was only abandoned publicly when the last eight temples were destoyed, A. D. 406. Taken by the Saracens A. D. 634. The Crusaders built a fort in 1152. The ancient harbor is covered by the sands. Now called Guzzeh.

7). A district S. of Moab, from W. el Ahsy S. to Shobek, near W. Shuweir. The cities were Arindela, Bozrah, Shobek, Tophel, and others smaller — 2. A very ancient city on a spur of Lebanon, close to the shore, anciently having a fine harbor, which is now choked up with sand and ruins of buildings, quays, etc. The castle is one of the best specimens of ancient masonry, having stones 20 feet long and beveled. The columns and walls, and their great extent especially, prove the splendor and importance of the city (Ez. xxvii. 9 ; Joshua xiii. 5). Workers in stone from G. were employed on Solomon's temple (1 K. v. 18—*stone-squarers* being a translation of Giblites—people of Gebal). Jebail.

GE'BER (*a man*). 1. Son of Geber (1 K. iv. 13). —2. Son of Uri (iv. 19).

GE'BIM (*ditches*). Village N. of Jerusalem, near Anathoth (2 K. iii. 16; Is. x. 31). Now *El Isawiyeh*.

GEDALI'AH (*Jehovah made him great*). 1. Son

GAZA.

GAZ'ARA. Near Azotus, Philistia (1 Macc. xiv. 34; Strabo xvi. 2). A very strong hold (2 Macc. x. 32). Supposed the same as Gazer—Gezer of 2 Sam. v. 25. Taken by Pharaoh, father-in-law to Solomon. 1 K. ix. 16; Josh. x. 33, xxi. 12, xvi. 3 point to a site between Bethhoron the nether and the sea, probably at the foot of the hills in the border of the Shefelah. There may have been two cities of the same name. Neither is located.

GA'ZATHITES. People of Gaza (Josh. xiii. 3).

GA'ZER (2 Sam. v. 25). GEZER.

GA'ZEZ (*shearer*). 1. Son of Caleb.—2. Son of Haran (1 Chr. ii. 46).

GA'ZITES (Judg. xvi. 2). GAZA.

GAZ'ZAM (*devouring*). Ancestor of Nethinim (Exr. ii. 48).

GE'BA (*the hill*). Benjamin (Josh. xxi. 17; 1 Chr. vi. 60). Was held by the Philistines (1 Sam. xiii. 3), who were expelled by Jonathan (1 Sam. xiv. 5). Isaiah (x. 28) describes the march of the Assyrians, and their halt at Geba.—2. (Judith iii. 10), where Holofernes is said to have encamped.

GE'BAL (*a line*, or *mountain ridge*). (Ps. lxxxiii.

of Ahikam (Jer. xl. 5), the secretary of King Josiah. He was appointed the executive officer of Nebuchadnezzar, after the Captivity, and was popular for his piety and gentleness, but was murdered soon after his appointment by Baalis and Ishmael. 2. A Levite, one of the musicians of Jehovah (1 Chr. xxv. 3, 9).—3. A priest (Ezr. x. 18).—4. Son of Pashur (Jer. xxxviii. 1).—5. Grandfather of Zephaniah (Zeph. i. 1).

GED'DUR (1 Esd. v. 30). GAHAR.

GED'EON. GIDEON. 1. Ancestor of Judith (Jud. xiii. 1).—2. Gideon (Heb. xi. 32). Greek form of the Hebrew Gideon.

GE'DER. Judah, extreme S. (Josh. xii. 13). Lost.

GED'ERAH (*sheep-cote*). Judah, in the Shefelah (Josh. xv. 36). Lost.

GEDERASHITE. The natives of Gederah (1 Chr. xii. 4).

GEDERITE. Inhabitants of Geder (1 Chr. xxvii. 28).

GED'EROTH (*sheep-cotes*). GEDEROTHAIM (*two sheep-cotes*), Lost.

GE'DOR. Judah, in the Mts. (Josh. xv. 58),

near Hebron, or half-way to Bethlehem. The modern name is Jedur.—2. Benj. (1 Chr. xii. 7).— 3. (1 Chr. iv. 39). A place from whence Simeon expelled the Hamites, dwellers in tents, and the Maonites. Probably on the way to Petra. Lost.

GEHA'ZI (*valley of vision*). Servant of Elisha. An unfaithful messenger of the good Shunammite (2 K. iv., v.).

GEHEN'NA. The Greek name of Hinnom.

GELIL'OTH (*to roll or wind as a river*). Benj., near Adummim, the same as Gilgal (Josh. xviii. 17).

GEMAL'LE (*camel-driver*). Father of Ammiel. A spy (Num. xiii. 12).

GEMARI'AH (*Jehovah has made perfect*). 1. Son of Shophan, a noble of Judah, who had a chamber in the house of the Lord (Jer. xxxvi.).—2. Son of Hilkiah (xxix.).

GEMS. PRECIOUS STONES.

GENEAL'OGY. The Orientals are peculiar in keeping genealogies of their families, and also of horses and camels. They made them the means of proving titles to property and offices. No list is so long or complete as that of Jesus.

GEN'ERAL (1 Chr. xxvii. 34). ARMY.

GENERATION (Heb. DOR, *a period of time*). Now about thirty years. The Hebrews had no fixed limit. One term is mentioned as 86 years (Gen. xv. 16), another 130 (v. 3), and one 500 years (v. 32). Its average was 30 to 40, probably, as now.

GEN'ESIS. HISTORY OF THE BOOKS.

GENNES'ARET, SEA OF (*the garden*). The Sea of Tiberias; the Sea of Chinnereth; the Sea of Galilee (Num. xxxiv. 11; Josh. xii. 3). Named from a town of the same name (Josh. xix. 35), which is lost, if it is not the site between Tiberias and the hot baths (Josh. xi. 2; Deut. iii. 17). Most of the life of Jesus was passed near this lake. Capernaum was on its shore, "His own city" (Matt. iv. 13). He called his first disciples from among its fishermen (Luke v.). Near it were spoken many of his parables, the Sermon on the Mount, and a number of the miracles were performed. There were 9 cities on its shores, and many others near. It is about 13 ms. long and 6 ms. wide, and the surface is 700 feet below the level of the ocean. The water is, in some places, 250 feet deep. The E. shore is 2,000 feet high, bare of trees, and cut down by deep ravines, quite flat and uniform on the summits. The W. banks are similar, but not so regular in hight, and being opened for the plain of G. The whole basin has a scathed, volcanic look. The climate is quite tropical. Palms and all kinds of trees and vegetables grow luxuriantly, and indigo is cultivated. The beach is pebbly everywhere, and is covered by small, twisted shells, purplish grey. Only one of the 9 cities now remains, Tiberias, almost in ruins, and even the sites of the others are disputed and in doubt.

GENNI'US (*high-born*). Father of Apollonius IV (2 Macc. xii. 2).

GENTILES (Heb. GOYIM, *foreigners, not Jews;* Gr. *ethnos, people; hellene, Greeks*). Any people not Hebrews, and who do not worship Jehovah.

GENUBATH (*theft*). Son of Hadad 4, a member of Pharaoh's court (1 K. xi. 20).

GE'ON. GIHON. One of the four rivers of Paradise (Gen. ii. 13). Perhaps only used as a poetic figure (Eccl. xxiv. 27).

GERA (*a grain*). Descendant of Benjamin (Gen. xlvi. 21). Son of Bela (1 Chr. viii. 3).

GE'RAH (*berry*). WEIGHTS AND MEASURES.

GE'RAR. A very ancient city S. of Gaza (Gen. x. 19; xx. 1; xxvi. 1). Near Kedesh in Shur; peopled by pastoral Philistines. Isaac was born there (xxi. 2, 3), and found it a very fertile land (xxvi. 12), and grew so rich that the Philistines envied him (14).

GER'ASA. In Matt. viii. 28, mistaken for Gadarenes. On the E. border of Peræa (Jos. Wars iii. 3, § 3), in the Mts. of Gilead, 20 ms. E. of the Jordan, 25 N. of Rabbath Ammon, Philadelphia. It was once one of the proudest cities of Syria, as its abundant ruins testify. The Saracens have never occupied it. Built in a narrow valley, on both the sloping sides, 5 miles from the Jabbok. Through it a small creek winds, fringed with many trees and shrubs. There was a colonnade from end to end of the city, with a circular forum at one end. Hundreds of columns are still standing.

It was one of the cities of the Decapolis, but is not mentioned by name in the Bible. The present people are active and prosperous.

GERGESENES. People of Gergesa on the E. of the Sea of Galilee (Matt. viii. 28). GADARENES.

GERIZ'IM (*desert* or *shorn*). S. of Shechem. The law was given on Mt. Sinai, and the blessing and cursing on the two mountains Ebal and Gerizim. (See EBAL). Jotham stood on G. when he denounced Abimelech (Judg. ix.). When Alexander took Palestine he gave Sanballat (the Persian governor under Darius) permission to build a temple on Mt. G.; and Manasseh, brother of Jaddua the high priest at Jerusalem, was made high priest at Shechem, about 420 B. C. This temple was destroyed by the Jews, 129 B. C. The ruins are still shown. The Samaritans worship here yet, without temple or altar. The view from the summit is one of the finest in Palestine, commanding the deep blue of the Great Sea, snowy Mt. Hermon, purple Gilead and Moab, and the lovely green valley of Mokhna at its foot.

GER'IZITES (*dwelling in a desert land*). GERZITES.

GERRHE'NIANS, THE (2 Macc. xiii. 24). Inhabitants of Gerar.

FIG.

GER'SHOM. 1. Son of Moses (Ex. ii. 22, xviii. 3).—2. Son of Levi (1 Chr. vi. 16, 17, 20).—3. A member of the family of Phinehas (Ezr. viii. 2. GERSON.

GER'SHON (*expulsion*). Son of Levi (Gen. xlvi. 11).

GERSHO'NITES, THE. Descendants of Gershom (1 Chr. xxvi. 21). They had charge of the coverings, curtains, hangings, cords, etc., of the Tabernacle, and of transporting them.

GER'SON (1 Esd. viii. 29). Error for Gershon.

GER'ZITES (*dwelling in a desert*), people who occupied the land S. of Palestine and Egypt (1 Sam. xxvii. 8).

GE'SEM. GOSHEN. (Jud. i. 9).

GE'SHAM (*filthy*). Son of Jahdai (1 Chr. ii. 47).

GĒS'HEM (*carcase*). An Arabian (Neh. ii. 19, vi. 2). An inveterate enemy of the Jews in the time of Nehemiah.

MT. GERIZIM.

GĒSH'UR (*bridge*). N.E. in Bashan (Deut. iii. 14). David married Maachah, the daughter of Talmai, king of G. (2 Sam. iii. 3), mother of Absalom. Joab found Absalom in this place (2 Sam. xiii. 37, xv. 8). It is supposed to be the district now called El Lejah.

GĒSHURI and **GESHURITES.** People of Geshur (Deut. iii. 14).—2. Ancient tribe, in the desert between Arabia and Philistia (Josh. xiii. 2).

GETH'ER (*fear*). Son of Aram (Gen. x. 23).

GETHSEM'ANE (*oil-press garden—wine-press*, GATH, *wine*). "A small farm." In the Kidron valley, on the lower slope of Olivet, 850 feet from St. Stephen's Gate, and 800 feet from the closed Gate, at the angle between the direct road up Olivet and that leading to the right around the hill (both leading to Bethany). Tradition only locates the "garden" (John xviii. 1) here; the "place" (Matt. xxvi. 36; Mark xiv. 32) was "over the brook Kidron, on Olivet somewhere, perhaps nearer Bethany on the road to the right; or rather away from any road. From the days of Eusebius, Jerome, and Adamnanus, some such place has been spoken of as "a place of prayer for the faithful" (Jerome), and having a church built on it. The place might have been selected by the Empress Helena (as many others were), to represent that mentioned in the Gospels. It is now walled in, enclosing eight very old olive-trees, and ornamented with beds of flowers. One of the trees is 25 feet in girth. The city walls and the top of the dome on the Great Mosque are in plain view. The Turks have pleasure-grounds, or gardens, further up the valley, where they resort to enjoy the cool shade of the olive-trees, some of which are quite

as large as those in "Gethsemane." The antiquity of these trees is argued from the tax of one medina for each tree, which rate was fixed for trees that stood at the time of the conquest; all those planted since being taxed one-half their produce (Chateaubriand). This would carry the date back to A. D. 634, when Omar took Jerusalem; or, if the tax was decreed after the Turks took the city, to A. D. 1087. Pilgrims pay the guide for showing this place, with others at the Holy City.

GEU'EL (*God's majesty*). Son of Machi; a spy (Num. xiii. 15).

GEZ'ER. City of Canaan, not far from Beth-horon, the west limit of the tribe of Ephraim, (1 Chr. vii. 28). Horam, king of Gezer, came up to help Lachish, and was killed by Joshua (x. 33). David smote the Philistines from Geba to Gezer (2 Sam. v. 25). Site lost.

GEZ'RITES. Inhabitants of Gezer (1 Sam. xxvii. 8).

GHOST (*Spirit*). SPIRIT, HOLY.

GI'AH (*breaking forth*) (2 Sam. ii. 24). To distinguish the position of the hill Ammah.

GIANTS. (Heb. NEPHILIM, REPHAIM). Persons of great strength. The Nephilim were living in Canaan at the time of the Exodus (Num. xiii. 33). The sons of Anak were afterwards identified with the same race, living at Hebron. The Rephaim were a tribe living in Canaan, Og being a king of the branch on the east of Jordan (Deut. iii. 11). The same name was in later times given to any large and strong people. The Emim and Zamzummim were also of the giants (ii. 10, 20). These merely strong men gave way before the skilful, and disappear from the history of the cultivated people. Goliath and his brother are the last mentioned.

GIB'BAR (*hero*). 95 of this family returned with Zerubbabel (Ezr. ii. 20). Gibeon in Neh. vii.

GIB'BETHON (*hill*). Town in Dan (Josh. xix. 44). Levitical.

GIBEAH (*rounded—a hill*). 1. G. OF SAUL (1 Sam. xv. 34). The native place of Saul (1 Sam. x. 26; 2 Sam. xxi. 6), where he was a farmer. He made it his capital (xxii. 6). Seven of his descendants were hanged by the Amorites (Is. x. 29). The site is pointed out, four miles north of Jerusalem, at Tuleil el Ful (*little hill of beans*, where there is an ancient ruin on the top of a conical hill.—2. G. OF JUDAH (Josh. xv. 57). Jeba, in Wady Masurr, near Hebron.—3. G. IN BENJAMIN (Josh. xviii. 28), near to Kirjath Jearim, where the Ark of God was kept for a while (2 Sam. vi. 3), in the time of Saul.—4. G. OF PHINEAS (Josh. xxiv. 33). Where Eleazar, son of Aaron, was buried, in Mt. Ephraim, 12 miles north of Jerusalem, near a glen of the same name.—5. G. OF BENJAMIN (Judg. xix., xx.). A city, having a square, and 700 "chosen men," near Bethel; mentioned during the Philistine wars of Saul and Jonathan (1 Sam. xiii., xiv.). *Jeba* in the *Wady Suweinit*.—6. G. IN THE FIELD (Judg. xx. 31). On one of the highways leading from Gibeah of Benjamin. Lost.—7. Several other places are also called Gibeah. 1. (Josh. v. 3), called afterward Gilgal.—2. The hill of Moreh (Judg. vii. 1).—3. *Gibeath-ha-Elohim*, the hill of God (1 Sam. x. 5). Lost.—4. G. *of Hachilah* (1 Sam.

xxiii. 19, xxvi. 1).—5. *G. of Ammah* (2 Sam. ii. 24).—6. *G. of Gareb* (Jer. xxxi. 39).

GIB'EATH (Josh. xviii. 28). GIB'EATHITE (1 Chr. xii. 3).

GIBEON (*belonging to a hill*). (Josh. ix. 3–15). One of the 4 cities of the HIVITES, the people who made a league with Joshua by an artifice, and so escaped the fate of Jericho and Ai. It was in Benjamin (xviii. 25). TULEIL EL FUL (*hill of beans*). The contest of the two parties of 12, of David and of Ishbosheth, was by the pool of Gibeon. Joab killed Amasa (2 Sam. xx. 10) at the great stone in Gibeon; and Joab himself fled to Gibeon for sanctuary, when condemned by Solomon, and was killed by Benaiah (1 K. ii. 34).

GIB'EONITES (Josh. ix. 17). Hivites who played a trick on Joshua, saving their lives, but accepting a life of servitude (v. 23, 27). Saul attempted their destruction (2 Sam. xxi.), and his sons were "crucified" to appease them.

GIB'LITES. Natives of Gebal (Josh. xiii. 5). The "land of the Giblites" was, among the Promised Land, to be governed by Joshua. They were noted as ship-carpenters in Solomon's time, and as stone-masons. Their chief city, Byblus, was the seat of the worship of Adonis (Ez. viii. 14).

GIDDAL'TI (*I have made great*). Son of Heman (1 Chr. xxv. 4).

GID'DEH (*giant*). 1. Children of G., returned with Zerubbabel (Ezr. ii. 47).—2. Children of G. were "servants of Solomon" (Ezr. ii. 56).

GIDEON (*destroyer*), also, JERUBBAAL (*striver against Baal*). The 5th Judge. He destroyed the Midianite host, with the "300 men that lapped" (Judg. viii. 10).

GIDEŌ'NI (*cutting down*). Father of Abidan (Num. i. 11).

GI'DOM. Near Rimmon (Josh. xx. 45).

GIFT. This is a formal business in the East. You are compelled by custom to accept and to return a gift from any person, or take the consequences of an insult by refusing. There are 15 names for gift: MINHAH, is a gift from one to a superior (Judg. iii. 15); MASOTH, from a king or any superior (Esth. ii. 18); NISSETH, is similar (2 Sam. xiv. 42); BERACHAH (*blessing*), complimentary; SHOCHAD, bribe; MATTAN, MATTANAH, present (Gen. xxv. 6); METTATH, false gift (Prov. xxv. 14); Greek *doma*, gift (Matt. vii. 11); *dorea, dorema, doron*, gift or offering; *anathema*, devoted; *charisma*, gift; *charis*, grace; and several others. It was no less an insult to neglect to give a present when custom led one to expect such a mark of respect (1 Sam. x. 27).

GI'HON. The second river of Paradise (Gen. ii. 13).—2. Near Jerusalem, where Solomon was anointed and proclaimed king (1 K. i. 33, 38, 45). The waters of Gihon were "stopped" by Hezekiah; that is, were conducted "straight down to the west side of the city of David" (2 Chr. xxxii. 30). See JERUSALEM.

GIL'ALAI (*heavy*). The son of a priest at the consecration of the wall of Jerusalem (Neh. xii. 36).

GIL'BOA (*bubbling fountain*). A mountain range between the plain of Esdraelon and the Jordan, near which is the city of Jezreel (1 Sam. xxviii. 4; xxix. 1). Mentioned only in connection with the death of Saul and Jonathan (xxxi. 1; 2 Sam. i. 6, xxi. 12; 1 Chr. x. 1, 8). The fountain from which it was named is at its northern base, and was called the well of Harod (Judg. vii. 1), and the spring of Jezreel (1 Sam. xxix. 1). The modern name is *Jebel Fukuah*, and it is 600 feet high above the plain, and there is on its highest summit a village and ruin called *Gelbus* by Eusebius, and *Wezar* by the Arabs.

GIL'EAD (*rugged*), MOUNT, THE LAND OF (Gen.

xxxi. 21). First known in Jacob's time. It next appears when the Israelites were on the march from Egypt, as divided in two sections and governed by Og and Sihon. It is rich in pastures and forests, well watered, and the great number of ruins bear witness of a former numerous population. It was occupied by Reuben and Gad. The whole extent, from Rabbath Ammon to the Hieromax, is one broad, elevated region or mountain (Deut. iii. 12). The same elevation is called Bashan, north of that river. The Lord showed Moses, from the top of Pisgah, all the land of Gilead unto Dan. Probably a popular phrase, as was "from Dan to Beersheba" (Josh. xx. 8). The Gadites are supposed to have imitated the habits of the people they displaced, which are now preserved by the Bedawins in the same district. Thus Jephthah appears like an Arab sheikh of our day (Judg. xi.); and some of David's captains were trained there (1 Chr. xii. 8, 15). RAMOTH GILEAD was its chief city (1 K. xxii. 4). Gilead first fell before the Assyrians (2 K. xv. 29). It was an asylum for refugees (2 Sam. ii. 8), David fleeing there from Absalom. It is now known south of the Jabbok as *Jebel Jilad*, and north of that river as *Jebel Ajlun*, and the capital is *Es Salt*, on the site of the ancient Ramoth Gilead. The whole country is like a fine park. Graceful hills, rich vales, luxuriant herbage, bright wild-flowers, noble forests, wooded heights, and winding glens clothed with tangled shrubbery, open glades and flat meadows of richest green, all so strongly in contrast with the general barren aspect of Western Palestine.

GIL'EADITE, THE (Judg. x. 3). A branch of the tribe of Manasseh.

BALM OF GILEAD.

GIL'GAL (*circle*), (Josh. iv. 19). Near Jericho; the first encampment of the Israelites in Palestine, where they set up twelve stones as a memorial of the passage of the Jordan. An ancient city (Deut. xi. 30). It was for centuries the great place of the nation's assembly (ix. 6, x. 6, 43). The Tabernacle was pitched here until it was removed to Shiloh (xviii. 1). It was visited by Samuel and Saul and David (1 Sam. x. 8, xi. 14, xiii. 4, xv. 12, xix. 15). There was a high place there for idolaters (Hos. iv. 15; Amos iv. 4, v. 5). As prophesied, the place is utterly desolate. It is impossible now to find where the city was. It was probably not far from Jericho.—2. A royal city of the Canaanites, near Dor (Josh. xii. 23). *Jiljuleh* (?) 4 miles south of Antipatris.—3. G. IN THE MOUNTAINS (2 K. ii. 1), *Jiljilia*, 6 miles north of Bethel.

GI'LOH (Josh. xv. 51). Judah. Native place of Ahithophel (2 Sam. xv. 12). Lost.

GI'LONITE (2 Sam. xv. 12).

GIM'ZO (2 Chr. xxviii. 18). Judah, near Dan. Jimzu, a large village on a hill, well shaded with trees, 3 miles S. W. of Lydda, where the two roads from Jerusalem (by the Beth-horons and by the Wady Suleiman, which parted at Gibeon) join and go on to Jaffa. There are some large underground granaries here.

GIN. A trap for birds and beasts (Is. viii. 14; Amos iii. 5).

GI'NATH (*protection*). Father of Tibni (1 K. xvi. 21, 22). He disputed the throne with OMRI.

GIN'NETHO. A priest who returned with Zerubbabel (Neh. xii. 4).

GIN'NETHON (*gardener*). A priest (Neh. x. 6).

GIR'DLE (Heb. HAGOR, EZOR, MEZAH, ABNET; Gr. *zone*). DRESS.

GIR'GASHITES, THE (Gen. x. 16, xv. 21). The descendants of the fifth son of Canaan, who settled on the east of the Sea of Galilee. Called Gergesenes in Matt. viii. 28.

GIS'PA (*caress*). An overseer of Nethinim (Neh. xi. 21).

GIT'TAHHEPHER—GATH-HEPHER. (Josh. xix. 13).

GIT'TAIM (*two wine-presses*). (2 Sam. iv. 3). A place built by the Gibeonites after they had been expelled from Beeroth (Josh. ix. 17). Inhabited by Benjamites after the return from captivity.

GIT'TITES. People of Gath. 600 men who went with David from Gath (2 Sam. xv. 18, 19).

GIT'TITH. A musical instrument. (Ps. viii., lxxvi., iv.).

GI'ZONITE (*pass, ford*) (1 Chr. xi. 34). Gouni. GUNI.

GLASS BLOWERS.

GLASS. So many specimens of ancient glass vessels have been found lately, there is no longer any doubt as to the remote antiquity of the manufacture of glass. It was practiced in Egypt, where the ancient paintings represent men at work over the furnaces, and in the laboratory blowing vessels of glass, at least 1400 B. C. Images, beads, cups, vases, bottles, even coffins, and a great variety of useful and ornamental articles, were made of this material, which are now shown in the Museums at New York and in Europe. The emperor Hadrian was presented by an Egyptian priest with some glass vases, so rare and excellent as to be reserved for unusual occasions of display. Clear glass was not valued, but colored, every variety of tone and tint were sought after. The allusions to glass in the Bible are never to a transparent substance, but to a shining, brilliant, colored mass (Rev. iv. 4). But two colorless, transparent drinking cups were bought by Nero, at a great price. Glass was not used in windows; a thin stone, mica, or talc being used until long after

our era. Mirrors (looking-glasses in Ex. xxxviii. 8) were made of metal, not of glass. (MIRROR). The Egyptians (and other ancients) practiced the art of grinding, engraving, and inlaying it with gold enamel, and of working elaborate designs in colors (as an image of a duck with the feathers imitated in form and color) in the midst of masses of clear glass. Precious stones were very successfully imitated by colored glass.

GLEAN'ING. CORNER. The poor had rights of gleaning fruit and grain-fields.

GLĒDE (RAAH). *Kite.* Probably the buzzard. (Deut. xiv. 13).

GLŌRY. The heart, soul, intelligence, feeling, will, and so the glory of a man as a living, rational being. Of God, it is the manifestation of the divine attributes and perfections, or such a visible effulgence of light as indicates these (Ex. xxxii. 18; John i. 14). The chief end of the Christian is, to live "to the glory of God." "Give God the glory," is to confess the truth (Josh. viii. 19; John ix. 24). "My glory" is my soul, in Ps. xvi. 9, . 12, etc.

GLŌSS. Explanation. A glossary is a collection of notes intended to illustrate or explain the text. Many words in the Scriptures and the Gospels were obscure to the common people, and needed to be explained, in a theological, historical, geographical, biographical, allegorical and mystical manner. Some glosses were written in the margin (marginal notes), or between the lines in a smaller letter. These were sometimes transferred into the body of the text by ignorant or careless copyists, a few instances being pointed out. Only the most competent scholars can detect these errors. The great exegetical thesaurus of the middle ages was collected by Walafrid Strabo from Augustine, Ambrose, Jerome, Gregory, Isidore, Beda, Alcuin, Rhabanus, Maurus and his own writings.

GNAT (NAT, Greek *konops*). *Mosquito.* One of the smallest of insects (Matt. xxiii. 24). The bite in the East often produces sores, with fever. Sleeping on high ground, away from water or trees, is one way of avoiding them.

GOAD (Heb. MALMAD, *a pole* (Judg. iii. 31); DORBAN, *the spike point* (1 Sam. xiii. 12). AGRICULTURE.

GOAT (AKKO, YEELIM, AZELAH, *wild goat*, ATTUD, ZAFIR, SAIR, *hairy*, *he-goat* (Greek *satyr*), EZ, *she-goat*, or *goat*, TAISH, GEDI, *kid*, Gr. *eriphion* (Matt. xxv. 33). Goats are an important part of pastoral wealth in the East. Neither Abraham or Job had them, unless they were included in the "flocks." Jacob tended them (ATTUDIM, he-goats, is rendered *rams* in Gen. xxxi. 10, 12). The goat was used in sacrifice as the type of the Christ, and the paschal-lamb could be from the sheep or the goats (Ex. xii. 5), as also the burnt-offering (Lev. i. 10), the peace-offering (iii. 12), the sin-offering (iv. 23), and the trespass-offering (ver. 6); the scapegoat (see ATONEMENT) was a peculiar type of Christ as the sin-bearer (xvi). The flesh of the kid is excellent; of the old goat not very palatable. An old Karaite gloss says: "The idolaters seethed a kid in its mother's milk, and sprinkled the broth on their trees, gardens, etc., and Moses therefore condemned the practice." Goat's milk is

GEM. FLORENCE.

very valuable (Prov. xxvii. 26, 27), and is milked at the door of customers every morning. The skin is used for bottles. The hair for cloth, for cloaks, or tents (Cant. i. 5; Ex. xxxvi. 14), or pillows (1 Sam. xix. 13). The Angora goat has the longest and best hair for cloth. The long-eared Syrian goat is peculiar to Syria. (The ears are sometimes 2 ft. long). A delicate grey wool under the long hair is the valued stuff for cloth, only three ounces being had from each goat, but of extreme fineness. The goat was a symbol of Macedonia. It is used often by the prophets, poets, and evangelists, as a symbol or type.

GOAT, SCAPE. ATONEMENT.

GO'ATH (*to low*, as a cow). Goath, (*heifer's pool*). (Jer. xxxi. 39). Near the hill Gareb.

GOB (*pit*). (2 Sam. xxi. 18, 19). The scene of two battles between David's soldiers and the Philistines. GE'ZER, in 1 Chr. xx. 4.

GOB'LET (Heb. AGGAN). A vessel for wine or other liquid (Cant. vii. 2). BASIN, CUP.

GODLINESS, MYSTERY OF (1 Tim. iii. 16). Jesus, the Christ.

GOD-SPEED (2 John 10, 11). Good speed.

GŎG (*mountain*). 1. Son of Shemaiah, of Reuben (1 Chr. v. 4).—2. MAGOG.—3. In the Septuagint of Num. xiv. 9, Gog is instead of Agag. Gog, as used by Ezekiel (xxxviii. xxxix), means the head or chief of Magog; and also John (Rev. xx. 8–10), making Gog and Magog persons.

GO'LAN (Deut. iv. 43). A Levitical city of Bashan in Manasseh (Josh. xxi. 27). One of the cities of refuge (xx. 8). The site is lost. The city is not mentioned after the time of Joshua in the Scriptures, but the city and the district of the same name is often mentioned by Josephus. Gamala (*El Husn*), on the east shore of the Sea of Galilee, was in the district (B. J. iv. i. 1). Its principal cities were Golan, Hippos, Gamala, Julias or Bethsaida, Seleucia, and Sogane (Josephus), and about 121 others, nearly all of which are unknown. The country is high (2500 feet), flat, and fertile, well watered, with good pasture. This is the MISHOR of 1 K. xx. 23, 25, where the Syrians were defeated near Aphek (now called *Fik*). The low, rounded hills, called *Tells*, extending south from Hermon for about 20 miles, are partly covered with forests or groves of oak and terebinth. The wandering Bedawins (*Anazeh*) visit the *Jaulan* every year in May, with their flocks and herds.

GOLD (Heb. ZAHAB; Gr. *chrusion, chrusos*). Gold has been known from the earliest times, and seems to have been very abundant among the ancients. It was a representative of wealth, and much used for ornaments and for the decoration and utensils of public buildings. Coined money of gold is not mentioned very early. See MONEY.

GOLDSMITH. Alluded to in Prov. xvii. 3; Is. xlvi. 6; Judg. xvii. 4; Neh. iii. 8, etc.

GOL'GOTHA (*a skull*), (Matt. xxvii. 33, etc.). Where Jesus was crucified, outside of the city gate (Heb. xiii. 12), but near the city (John xix. 20), and a road leading from the country, where there were passers-by (Matt. xxvii. 39); and there was a garden or orchard at the place (Mark xv. 46). The place is not mentioned again until A. D. 355, when a church was built to honor the spot.

The city at that time had a wall about Zion, and another about Acra. Beyond these, to the north, the *suburbs* were enclosed by another wall by Agrippa. This seems to leave no place for the site on that side, and therefore denies the claim of the present Church of the Holy Sepulchre, in the centre of the modern city. Another theory places the site on Mt. Moriah, where now stands the great mosque called the Dome of the Rock, which is claimed to be the real church built by Constantine. There is a cave in a rock under this building, which is claimed to be the tomb; and also that it was Araunah's threshing-floor. Another theory is, that the site was not far from St. Stephen's gate.

Wm. C. Prime has discovered (1871) a wall which he thinks is a part of the ancient 2d wall so long in question, and found it in the right position and direction to exclude the Holy Sepulchre Church, and so arguing for that as the site which was accepted by Constantine (or Helena) as the true one. JERUSALEM.

GOLI'ATH (*exile*) A giant of Gath, who defied the armies of Israel, "morning and evening for forty days," and whose defeat (1 Sam. xvii.) threw such glory around the youthful career of David.

GO'MER (Gen. x. 2, 3; Ezek. xxxviii. 6). Eldest son of Japheth. Progenitor of the Cimmerians, whose traces are found in the Cimmerian Bosporus, C. Isthmus, Mt. Cimmeriun, Cimmeria, and the C. walls (Herodotus, iv. 12, 45, 100), and also in the modern name Crimea. The Cymri of Wales, Cambria, and Cumberland in England are assigned to the same origin.

GOAT.

GOMOR'RAH (*submersion*). One of the 5 cities of the plain or vale of Siddim, whose kings joined battle against four kings (Chedorlaomer and his allies, Gen. xiv. 2–8), when Abram came to the rescue. Four of them were destroyed, leaving only Zoar or Bela, which was spared at Lot's request (xix. 23–29). Their fate is alluded to by the prophets as a warning to Israel (Deut. xxix. 23; Is. xiii. 19); to Edom (Jer. xlix. 18; l. 40), to Moab (Zeph. ii. 9); and again to Israel by Amos (iv. 11); and by Peter (2 Pet. ii. 6); and by Jude (verses 4–7), as a warning to those who should "deny Christ."

The site of these cities is a question that it has been impossible to solve. They were said to be in the vale of Siddim, which *became* (is) the Salt Sea (Gen. xiv. 3), or sea of the plain (Josh. xii. 3). Josephus says the region was not submerged (B. J. iv. 8, 4), but remained visible, and parched. It is now known that the Dead Sea was a lake from the creation, being a natural formation which has been undisturbed, not even by a volcano, and the water being very deep (500 to 2,300 feet), leaves no place for sites of cities; and although the south bog (below Lisan) is shallow (3 to 12 feet), its bed has been elevated by the rivers which flow north from the Arabah. Not one of the cities has ever been found, except it may be Zoar. GOMORRHA in the Apocrypha.

GO'PHER (*pitch*). A hard, strong tree, from the wood of which Noah's ark was made (Gen. vi. 14). Cypress or pine.

GOR/GIAS. General of Antiochus Epiphanes (1 Macc. iii. 38).

GORTY/NA. In Crete (1 Macc. xv. 23). It was the capital of the Island under the Romans. The famous Cretan labyrinth was here, the ruins of which are found at the foot of Mt. Ida. Paul may have preached here, while his vessel was at Fair Havens, where "much time" was spent (Acts xxvii. 9).

GO/SHEN. That part of Egypt, east of the Delta, near the way of the land of the Philistines (Ex. xiii. 17), where there was pasture-land, suited to the habits of Joseph's brethren. The only limits that can be indicated from the ancient accounts are the present *Wady El Tumeylat*, and the desert lakes, *Temsah* and *Bitter Lakes*. This region is still very productive wherever it is watered, either from the Nile or from wells (Gen. xlv. 10, xlvi. 28, xlvii. 27, l. 8; Ex. viii. 22, ix. 26). The plagues of Egypt did not effect this land. The soil is capable of tillage to an indefinite extent.

GOS/PELS. Good news. See HISTORY. BOOKS.

SHORT-TOED EAGLE.

GOTHO/NIEL. Othniel, father of Chabris (Judith vi. 15).

GOURD (Heb. KIKAYON; Jonah iv. 6–10). Perhaps the castor-oil plant, which grows like a tree in the East. Some think it was a pumpkin, which grows very large and rapid. The PAKKUOTH (2 K. iv. 39) was a poisonous fruit, gathered by the pupils of Elisha. Thought to be the colocynth. Knops in 1 K. vii. 24.

GOV/ERNOR (Heb. ALLSEPH). A sheikh (Zech. ix. 7); duke in some places.—2. HOKEK, cadi, a justice (Judg. v. 9).—3. MEHOKEK (v. 14).—4. MO-SHEL, pasha, judge (Gen. xlv. 26; ruler in Josh. xii. 2).—5. NAGID.—6. NASI.—7. PECHAH.—8. PA-KIA.—9. SHALLIT.—10. SAR.—11. SEGAN.—12. Gr. *ethnarches*, ruler.—13. *hegemon*, leader.—14. *oiko-nomos*, steward.—15. *architriklinos*, ruler of the feast (Eccl. xxxii).

GOZAN (*quarry*), (1 Chr. v. 26). The Gauza-nites of Ptolemy, watered by the Habor, in Assyria, where the Israelites were carried captive. Mygdonia.

GRACE (*favor*). (Heb. CHEN; Gr. *charis*.) Kindness towards mankind shown by the Lord Jesus (John i. 14, 16, etc.).

GRASS. (Heb. HATZIO; *herbage*). (1 K. xviii. 5) ; DASHA, first-shoots, in Jer. i. 11; YEREK, green (Num. xxii.4); ESEB, *herbs* (Gen. i. 30). Gr. *chor-tos* (Matt. vi. 30); blade in Mark iv. 28.

GRASSHOPPER. LOCUST.

GRAY/HOUND. GREY-HOUND. Alluded to in Prov. xxx. 31, as one of "four things which are comely in going." Some prefer "horse," and others "cock."

GRE/CIAN. Believing Greeks from Greece (Acts vi. 1, etc.). Also such Jews as had been born in other lands, as well as in Palestine, but who had been educated abroad.

GREECE (Greek *Hellas;* Heb. JAVAN). Greece included the four provinces of Macedonia, Epirus, Achaia (Hellas) and Peloponnesus (Morea). Generally only Hellas and Peloponnesus are meant. The grand features are mountain and sea, which exerted a strong influence on the character of the people, as appears in their poetry, religion, and history. The climate is very temperate, the air salubrious, and the soil fertile. Its history extends back to B. C. 776, in authentic records, and beyond that in traditions and myths, such as that of Ægialus, who founded Sicyon B. C. 2089, and of Uranus, who settled there B. C. 2042. The Greeks said they received from Asia Minor, Phœnicia, and Egypt letters and laws, and certain tenets in religion. The Egyptian Inachus found-ed Argos B. C. 1856, and Cecrops led a colony 300 years earlier to Attica, carry-ing with him the worship of the goddess Neith (Athenæ). The Phœnician Cad-mus founded Thebes in Bœotia, and taught the Greeks letters. (See Page 173.)

The Phrygian Pelops took possession of the south, B. C. 1283, naming it after him-self. The famous expedition of Jason and the Argonauts in search of the golden fleece, is dated B. C. 1263, and the siege of Troy, 1193. From the First Olympiad, B. C. 776, to B. C. 300, Greece was a leader power in politics and religion. It is chiefly from Alexander's time down, that the Bible has to do with Greece. First known to the Jews in the slave-market of Tyre, where the prophet Joel charges the Tyrians with selling Hebrew children to the Grecians (Joel iii. 6), B. C. 800; and Ezekiel says, "traded the persons of men and vessels of brass in thy market" (Ez. xxvii. 13). Greek slaves were highly valued in all the East (Bochart i., c. iii. 175). Daniel mentions Greece (viii. 21, etc.) in his sketch of Alexander and his successors. Alexander visited Jerusalem, and respected its religion (Ant. xi. 8, 3). The Lacedæmonians sent an embassy and a letter to the Jews, B. C. 300 (Ant. xii. 4, 10), when king Areus claims kinship for his people with the Jews. Paul visited Greece (Acts xx. 2), staying there three months. The Greeks, and their lan-guage, were so influential in Paul's time that the name Greek stands in the N. T. as Gentile does in the O. T. Their influence on the spread of the Gospel by a peculiar preparation of the mind for the Gospel teachings was very great, in quickening thought and destroying indifference to religion. (See GOSPELS in the HISTORY.) The arts of war, and the fine-arts of peace were carried to a great perfection. Their Asiatic empire spread their in-stitutions, and filled half of Asia Minor with tem-ples, theatres, aqueducts, and well-built cities. The Church did not flourish in Athens, but was more eminent in Corinth.

GREEK. Educated in the religion and language of Greece. Barbarian was any one who was not a Greek.

GREEK VERSIONS OF THE O. T. See HISTORY, BOOKS.

GRINDING. MILL.

GROVE (Heb. ASHERAH, *an image worshiped in the grove*), (2 K. viii. 6). A wood dedicated to idolatry. The sacred symbolic tree of Assyria refers to the same idea. The Hebrew word ELON also means grove (translated oak of Mamre, in Gen. xiii. 18, and of Moreh, in xii. 6, etc.). The grove took the place of the church building in the ancient heathen religions, where altars were erected to the gods. Pliny says trees were the first temples. Afterwards the temples were built in the groves. The Temple of Solomon had figures of trees on its interior walls for ornaments. The mosque which stands on its site now has olive, palm and cedar trees growing around it. Tree-worship was widespread, and is not yet passed away. The Buddhists of India venerate the banian (fig tree). The Etrurians worshiped a palm, the Druids and Celts an oak.

GUARD (Heb. 1. TABBACH, *a cook*, afterwards *an executioner*), (Gen. xxxvii. 36).— 2. RAZ, *a runner* (2 Sam. xv. 1). They also carried dispatches. "Guard-chamber" (1 K. xiv. 28).—3. MISHMERETH, *watching* (Neh. iv. 9). "Which goeth at thy bidding," in 1 Sam. xxii. 14, should be " captain of the body-guard."

GUD'GODAH (*thunder*), (Deut. x. 7). HAGIDGAD.

GUEST. HOSPITALITY. Guest-chamber. HOUSE.

GUILTY. Bound by his oath (Matt. xxiii. 1). Deserving death (Num. xxxv. 31).

GUL'LOTH (Josh. xv. 19). Springs, upper and lower, added by Caleb to his daughter Achsah's dower. They were near Debir, but cannot now be identified. Possibly *Ain Nunkar*, and *Devir Ban*, east of Hebron.

GU'NI (*colored*). 1. Son of Naphtali (Gen. xlvi. 24).—2. Descendants of Gael (1 Chr. v. 15), father of Abdiel.

GU'NITES, THE. Sons of Naphtali (Num. xxvi. 48).

GUR (*ascent*). Where Ahaziah was wounded (2 K. ix. 27) at Ibleam, between Jezreel and Bethhaggan (*garden-house*), which is now said to be Jenin. The pass may be the very steep place on the road from Jezreel to the plain of Esdraelon, near Megiddo.

GUR'BA'AL (*ascent of Baal*), (2 Chr. xxvi. 7). "And God helped him (Uzziah) against the Arabians that dwelt in Gur-baal." Supposed to mean Gerar.

GUTTER (correctly, *a water-course*). 2 Sam. v. 6, should read "but the blind and the lame will turn thee away;" and verse 8, "Any one that smites a Jebusite, and gets to the water-course."

H

HAAHASH'TARI (Heb. *the Ahashtarite messenger*). Father (builder) of Tekoa (1 Chr. iv. 6).

HABA'IAH (*Jehovah protects*), (Ezr. ii. 61; Neh. vii. 63). Sons of Chebaijah were among the returned from captivity.

HABAK'KUK. See HISTORY OF THE BOOKS.

HABAZINI'AH (*light of Jah.*) Ancestor of Jaazaniah (Jer. xxxv. 3).

HABERGEON. A coat of mail covering the neck and breast. See ARMS.

HABOR (1 Chr. v. 26). A river and district in Assyria, where Tiglath Pileser placed some of the Jews of the tribes of Reuben and Gad, during the First Captivity; and where, 17 years after, Shalmaneser, his successor, settled captives from Samaria and Israel (2 K. xvii. 6, xxviii. 11). The Khabur (name of a river) is found in an Assyrian inscription of the date of 900 B. C.

HACHILI'AH (*Jehovah enlivens*). Father of Nehemiah (Neh. i. 1, x. 1).

HACHI'LAH, THE HILL (1 Sam. xxiii. 13, 19). On the S. of Jeshimon (the barren district), near Ziph, in a forest, where David and his 600 men hid from Saul, and David in the night took away Saul's spear and bottle of water from his couch, and showed them to Abner, the captain of Saul's guard, next morning from the opposite bank of the ravine (xxvi. 5-20). See DAVID.

HACHMO'NI (*wise*). *Son of* and *The Hachmonite* (1 Chr. xxvii. 32, xi. 11). Head of a large family. TACHMONITE.

HADAD, CHADAD (*mighty*). 1. Son of Ishmael (Gen. xxv. 15).—2. A king of Edom (Gen. xxxvi. 35).—3. The last king of Edom at Pai (1 Chr. i.

COIN OF VESPASIAN.

50).—4. Member of the royal house of Edom (1 K. xi. 14). He married the sister-in-law of the Pharaoh of Egypt. After David died, he attempted to recover his lost dominion from Solomon.

HADAD'EZER (*Hadad is his help*) (2 Sam. viii. 3, 12). HADAREZER.

HA'DAD RIM'MON (both words are names of Syrian idols). The city was a stronghold before Abraham's time. Here king Josiah "went against" Pharaoh Necho, was wounded, and died at Jerusalem (2 K. xxiii. 29; 2 Chr. xxxv. 20-23). Mentioned by the prophet Zechariah (xii. 11). Four or five miles south of *Lejjun* is a ruin on a hill, which (*Rumana*) is supposed to be the ancient site.

HA'DAR (*chamber*). Hadad, in 1 Chr. i. 30. Eighth son of Ishmael. The Mt. Hadad on the borders of the Syrian desert north of El Medineh, is supposed to mark the locality of this branch of Ishmael's family.

HA'DAREZER. Son of Rehob (2 Sam. viii. 3). King of ZOBAH (1 Chr. xviii. 3, ff). David captured from him 1000 "shields of gold" besides other great spoil.

HAD'ASHAH (*new*), (Josh. xv. 37). Judah, in the Shefelah. Adasa (1 Macc. vii. 40), where Nicanor was killed by Judas Maccabæus. Lost.

HADAS'SAH (*myrtle*), (Esth. ii. 7).

HADAT'TAH (*new*), (Josh. xv. 25). Judah, between Beersheba and Kedesh. Hazor-Hadattah; New Hazor.

HELL. This is the word generally and unfortunately used by our translators to render the Hebrew *Sheol*. It would perhaps have been better to retain the Hebrew word *Sheol*, or else render it always by "the grave" or "the pit." It is deep (Job xi. 8) and dark (Job xi. 21, 22), in the centre of the earth (Num. xvi. 30; Deut. xxxii. 22), having within it depths on depths (Prov. ix. 18), and fastened with gates (Is. xxxviii. 13) and bars (Job xvii. 16). In this cavernous realm are the souls of dead men, the Rephaim and ill spirits (Ps. lxxxvi. 13 ; lxxxix. 48; Prov. xxiii. 14; Ez. xxxi. 17; xxxii. 21). it is clear that in many passages of the O. T. *Sheol* can only mean "the grave," and is so rendered in the A. V. (see, for example, Gen. xxxvii. 35 ; xlii. 38 ; 1 Sam. ii. 6 ; Job xiv. 13). In other passages, however, it seems to involve a notion of punishment, and is therefore rendered in the A. V. by the word "Hell." But in many cases this translation misleads the reader. It is obvious, for instance, that Job xi. 8 ; Ps. cxxxix. 8 ; Am. ix. 2 (where "hell" is used as the antithesis of "heaven"), merely illustrate the Jewish notions of the locality of *Sheol* in the bowels of the earth. In the N. T. the word Hades, like *Sheol*, sometimes means merely "the grave" (Rev. xx. 13; Acts ii. 31; 1 Cor. xv. 55), or in general "the unseen world." It is in this sense that the creeds say of our Lord, "He went down into hell," meaning the state of the dead in general, without any restriction of happiness or misery—a doctrine certainly, though only virtually, expressed in Scripture (Eph. iv. 9 ; Acts ii. 25–31). Elsewhere in the N. T. Hades is used of a place of torment (Luke xvi. 23 ; 2 Pet. ii. 4; Matt. xi. 23, etc.). Consequently, it has been the prevalent, almost the universal, notion that Hades is an *intermediate state* between death and resurrection, divided into two parts, one the abode of the blessed, and the other of the lost. In holding this view main reliance is placed on the parable of Dives and Lazarus ; but it is impossible to ground the proof of an important theological doctrine on a passage which confessedly abounds in Jewish metaphors. The word most frequently used in the N. T. for the place of future punishment is *Gehenna* or *Gehenna of fire*.

HA′DID (*sharp*), (Ez. ii. 33; Neh. vii. 37, xi. 34). Three ms. from Lydda, 10 ms. from Joppa (1 Macc. xii. 38). Alexander was defeated here by Aretas (Ant. xiii. 15, 2), and Vespasian made it an outpost during his siege of Jerusalem. ADIDA. ADITHAIM.

HAD′LAI (*resting*). Father of Amasa 2 (2 Chr. xxviii. 12).

HAD′ŌRAM. Fifth son of Joktan (Gen. x. 27; 1 Chr. i. 21). Probably located, with Joktan's other descendants, in South Arabia, but not yet identified. The Adramitæ, and Hadramaut have been suggested, but rejected on philological grounds.

HA′DRACH (Zech. ix. 1). A district somewhere in the vicinity of Damascus. Lost.

HA′GAB (*locust*). Ancester of Nethinim who returned with Zerubbabel (Ezr. ii. 41.)

HAG′ABA. Ancestor of Nethinim who came with Zerubbabel (Neh. vii. 48). HAGABAH (Ezr. ii. 45).

HA′GAR (*stranger*). An Egyptian slave (Gen. xii. 16, xvi. 1), presented to Abraham by Pharaoh. Mother of Ishmael. The Hagarites settled in Paran (Gen. xxi. 21; Gal. iv. 22). They are mentioned in 1 Chr. xi. 38, where Mibhar, a Hagarite, is one of David's captains. Jaziz, a Hagarite, had charge of David's flocks, and an Ishmaelite of his camels, because they had experience in the care of such animals (1 Chr. xxvii. 31). The HAGARITES occupied the country south of Palestine, from the sea to the Euphrates, as the Bedawins do now.

Hejer is the capital of a district in the province of El Bahreyn, in N. Arabia, near the Persian Gulf.

HAG′GAI (*festive*). The 9th in order of the minor prophets, who returned with Zerubbabel from captivity. See HISTORY OF THE BOOKS.

HAG′GERI. Descendant of Hagar. Mibhar, son of Haggeri, was an officer of David's guard (1 Chr. xi. 38).

HAG′GI. Son of Gad (Gen. xlvi. 16). Haggites (Num. xxvi. 15).

HAGGI′AH (*festival of Jah*). A Levite (1 Chr. 30).

HAG′GITH (*festive*). Mother of Adonijah (2 Sam. iii. 4).

HAIL. Was one of the plagues of Egypt. Hail is more common than snow in the hill country of Palestine (Ps. cxlviii. 8). God smote the Amorites with "hail-stones" (Josh. x. 11). RAIN.

HAIR. The Egyptians were very uniform in their habits of dressing the hair. Herodotus says that they let their hair and beard grow only in mourning. The priests, who were to be clean to the highest possible degree, had to shave their whole bodies every third day. Other men shaved the head only—or the beard also. The women wore their hair natural, but braided, and dressed with strings of silk with ornaments. The Assyrian men wore the hair combed and curled, falling quite low about the neck; wearing the whiskers curled also. Among the Greeks and Romans, the fashion of wearing the hair passed through many changes. One style is shown on p. 76. The Hebrews cut the men's hair quite short, almost to the ears (Ez. xliv. 20), and to keep the beard a proper length by trimming it, but not to shave either head or beard. The NAZARITE was an exception, who let both hair and beard grow uncut or uncombed.

HAK′KATAN (*little*). Father of Johanan, who was a chief, and returned with Ezra from Babylon (Ezr. viii. 12).

HAK′KOZ (*thorn*). A priest in the service of David (1 Chr. xxiv. 10).

HAKU′PHA (*bent*). Ancestor of Nethinim; came from Babylon with Zerubbabel (Ezr. ii. 51).

HA′LAH (2 K. xvii. 6). In Assyria, where Tiglath Pileser planted some of the captive Jews. Now called Kalah, an ancient ruin on the side of the upper Khabur.

HEAD DRESS.

HA′LAK, THE MOUNT (*the smooth, bald mountain*). (Josh. xi. 17, xii. 7). The south limit of Joshua's conquests near Mt. Seir. The name of the east end of Akrabbim.

HAL′HUL (Josh. xv. 58). Judah. Four miles north of Hebron, on the top of a hill, is a ruin, and at its foot is a village bearing the ancient name.

HA′LI (Josh. xix. 25). On the border of Asher. May be Alia, 5 ms. N. E. of Acre.

HALICARNAS′SUS (1 Macc. xv. 25). In Caria, on the Ceramian gulf. The birth-place of Herodotus, and of Dionysius. The Jews residing here were, by a decree of the Romans, allowed the exercise of all their sacred rites. Alexander destroyed the city by fire.

HALL. Court of the high-priest's house (Luke xxii. 55; in Matt. xxvii. 27, and Mark xv. 16). Hall, in John xviii. 28, "judgment-hall." A covered space, surrounded by rooms opening into it; or, perhaps, a large audience chamber. The court of a dwelling-house is not covered.

HALLELŪʹJAH (*praise ye Jah*). Praise ye the Lord. Alleluia in Rev. xix. 1–6; Ps. cxiii.–cxviii., were called *hallel* (praise), and were used on special occasions.

HALLŌʹHESH (*enchanter*). A chief, who signed the covenant with Nehemiah (Neh. x. 24).

HALŌʹHESH. Son of Halohesh, ruler of half of Jerusalem (Neh. iii. 12).

HAM (*warm*), (Egyptian *chem, dark*). One of the sons of Noah (Gen. vi. 10), perhaps the third, if Japheth was the elder brother (x. 21). Settled in Africa (Ps. lxxviii. 51, cv. 23, cvi. 22), and also sent many branches into Asia (Canaanites). There is no ancient name so well preserved and located. Ham is identified with JUPITER AMMON, and also ZEUS, because both words are derived from a root meaning hot, fervent, or sunburnt. For the last 3000 years the world has been mainly indebted for its advancement to the Semitic races; but before this period the descendants of Ham—Egypt and Babylon—led the way as the pioneers in art, literature and science. Mankind at the present day lies under infinite obligations to the genius and industry of those early ages, more especially for alphabetic writing, weaving cloth, architecture, astronomy, plastic art, sculpture, navigation and agriculture. The art of painting is also represented, and music indirectly, by drawings of instruments.

THE SONS AND GRANDSONS OF HAM, AND THEIR LOCATION.

HAM.	**CUSH.**	Seba, - - - -	Meroe, in Egypt.
		Havilah, - - - -	Abyssinia.
		Sabtah, - - - -	S. W. coast Red Sea.
		Raamah, { Sheba, Dedan. }	Arabia, Persia.
		Sabtechah, - - -	Ethiopia.
		Nimrod (Belus), -	Shinar. Chaldæa.
	MIZRAIM.	Ludim, - - - -	West, in Africa.
		Anamim, - - - -	Mareotis.
		Lehabim, - - - -	Libyans.
		Naphtuhim, - - -	Memphis.
		Pathrusim, - - -	Thebes. Pathros.
		Casluhim, - - -	Arabia Petræa.
		Caphtorim, - - -	Damietta.
	PHUT, - - - - -		Lybians.
	CANAAN.	Sidon, - - - -	Sidon and Tyre.
		Heth, - - - -	Hittites.
		Jebusites, - - - -	Jerusalem.
		Amorites, - - - -	Judæa.
		Girgasite, - - - -	Gergesenes.
		Hivite, - - - -	Shechem.
		Arkite, - - - -	Arke.
		Sinite, - - - -	Sinnas.
		Arvadite, - - -	Island of Arvad.
		Zemarite, - - -	Sumrah (ruin).
		Hamathite, - - -	Hamath.

HĀʹMAN (*magnificent*). Prime minister of King Ahasuerus (Esth. iii. 1). After he failed in his conspiracy he was hanged on the same gallows he had made for Mordecai. He is called a Macedonian in Esther xvi. 10 (Apoc.).

HAMATH (*to defend*). The principal city of North Syria and capital of a district of the same name (Gen. x. 18). In the centre of the Orontes valley. Toi, king of Hamath, paid tribute to David (2. Sam. viii). Hamath was conquered by Solomon (2 Chr. viii. 3). Alexander took it

and changed its name to Epiphania, in honor of Antiochus Epiphanes. It has now 30,000 people, is a well-built city, in a narrow and rich valley. Four bridges span the rapid river. The chief trade is in silk, woollen, and cotton. "The entrance to Hamath," so often used as a landmark in the O. T. (*Land and Book* i. 354), and Tristram (*Land of Israel*, 621), the entrance into the valley as you look north from Baalbek.

HAMATHZOBAH (*fortress of Zobah*), (2 Chr. viii. 3).

HAMATHITE (*from Hamath*). A family descended from Canaan (Gen. x. 18).

SHEKEL.

HAMʹMATH (*warm baths*). One of the fenced cities of Naphtali (Josh. xix. 35). Josephus mentions a city called Ammaus (*warm water*), one mile from Tiberias, on the shore of the Sea of Galilee. Ibrahim Pacha built spacious baths over these four warm springs. The water is 144° Fahr., very salt and bitter, with a strong, sulphurous odor. There are ancient ruins for a mile or more around.

HAMMEDĀʹTHA (*double*). Father of Haman (Esth. iii. 1, 10).

HAMʹMELECH (Jer. xxxvi. 26; xxxviii. 6). Hebrew term for "the king."

HAMʹMER. 1. A tool used by the gold-beaters (Is. xli. 7). Carpenter (Jer. xxiii. 29).—2. A tool for hollowing (1 K. vi. 7); a weapon of war (Prov. xxv. 18). See ARMS. The Maccabees were so named from Hammer (MACBEH).

HAMMOLʹEKETH (*the queen*). Daughter of Machir (1 Chr. vii. 17, 18).

HAMʹMON (*hot*). In Asher (Josh. xix. 28). *Hamul*, near Zidon.—2. Levitical, in Naphtali (1 Chr. vi. 76); the same as HAMMOTH DOR, (Josh. xxi. 32). Levitical city in Naph. HAMMATH.

HAMŌʹNAH (*mul-titude*). A city in which the people of Gog will be buried (Ez. xxxix. 16).

HAʹMONGOG, THE VALLEY OF (*Gog's multitude*). Name to be given to a glen on the east of the sea (Ez. xxxix. 11, 15).

HAʹMOR (*a he-ass*). Father of Shechem (Gen. xxxiii. 19).

HAMʹUEL (*God's wrath*). Son of Mishma (1 Chr. iv. 26).

HAʹMUL (*pillared*). Son of Pharez, son of Judah by Tamar (Gen. xlvi. 12).

HAʹMULITES. The descendants of Hamul of Judah (Num. xxvi. 21).

HAMŪʹTAL (*dew's brother*). Daughter of Jeremiah (2 K. xxiii. 31).

HANʹAMEEL (*safety*). Son of Shallum (Jer. xxxii. 7–9, 12, 44).

HAʹNAN (*merciful*). A chief of Benjamin (1 Chr. viii. 23). There are eight others of this name, but none famous.

HANʹANEEL, THE TOWER OF. In the wall of Jerusalem (Neh. iii. 1). Between the sheep-gate and the fish-gate, on the N. E. corner of the city.

HANĀʹNI. 1. Son of Heman (1 Chr. xxv. 4, 25).—2. A seer (B. C. 941), king of Judah (2 Chr. xvi. 7).—3. A priest (Ezr. x. 20).—4. Brother of

Nehemiah (Neh. i. 2). Governor of Jerusalem B. C. 445 (vii. 2).—5. A priest (xii. 36).

HANANI'AH (*Jah is kind*). 1. Son of Heman (1 Chr. xxv. 4, v. 23).—2. Captain in King Uzziah's army (2 Chr. xxvi. 11).—3. Father of Zedekiah (Jer. xxxvi. 12).—4. Son of Azur, a false prophet (Jer. xxvii. xxviii.). He opposed Jeremiah in predicting a return from Babylon in 2 years, when the time had been fixed at 70.—5. Grandfather of Irijah (Jer. xxxvii. 13).—6. Head of a Benjamite house (1 Chr. viii. 24).—7. Shadrach, of the house of David (Dan. i. 3, 6, 7, 11).—8. Son of Zerubbabel (1 Chr. iii. 19).—9. Son of Bebai (Ezr. x. 28).—10. A priest (Neh. iii. 8)—11. Head of Jeremiah's priestly course (xii. 12).—12. Steward of the palace at Jerusalem vii. 2, 3).—13. A chief who signed the covenant with Nehemiah (x. 23).

HAND (YAD, *power, agency*). Laying on of hands, sign of authority, or of a blessing conferred (Num. xxvii. 18). Sitting at the right hand of power, man of my right hand.

HAN'DICRAFT. Special workmen were among the great benefactors of ancient times, and were honored as the chief favorites. God is honored for his "handiwork" (Ps. viii. 3; xix. 1; Gen. ii. 2; Job xxxiv. 19). Several men are honored in the O. T. for their work, as Tubal-Cain, Jabal, Jubal, and Bezaleel. The Hebrews were more agricultural than scientific or artistic, and invented little, yet their skill is recorded in the cases of the tabernacle and the temple. Among the metal workers were goldsmiths, silversmiths, coppersmiths, and ironworkers, whose work is often mentioned. The tools noticed are forceps (tongs, in Is. vi. 6), hammer, anvil, bellows. The carpenters (woodcarvers) were skilful (Is. xli. 7). Their implements were the rule (chalk-pencil), measuring-inel, compasses, plane or smoothing instrument, saw, hatchet, knife, awl, nail, hone, drill, mallet, chisel, etc. There were boat-builders also. Spinners, weavers, fullers, dyers, tent-makers, embroiderers. Tanning and dressing leather. Masons, bakers, butchers, cheese-makers, shoemakers, barbers, are mentioned in the Bible, and drawn on the monuments engaged in their proper avocations.

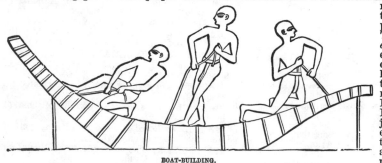

BOAT-BUILDING.

HANDKERCHIEF (*napkin, apron*), (Luke xix. 20). Larger and longer than ours, and of stronger cloth, fit for various uses, as a girdle or turban.

HA'NES. In Egypt (Is. xxx. 4). ANASIEH on the W. branch of the Nile. Perhaps Tahpanhes.

HANGINGS. (Heb. MASACH, *curtain*, Ex. xxvi. 10). KELAIM, *tapestry* (xxvii. 9).

HAN'IEL. Son of Ulla (1 Chr. vii. 39).

HAN'NAH (*grace*). Wife of Elkanah, and mother of Samuel (1 Sam. i. 2.).

HAN'NATHON (*graceful*). Zebulon (Josh. xix. 14). Lost.

HAN'NIEL (*grace of God*). Son of Ephod. A prince (Num. xxxiv. 23).

HA'NOCH (*initiated*). ENOCH and HENOCH. 1. Children of Midian (Gen. xxv. 4).—2. Son of Reuben (Gen. xlvi. 9).

SILVERSMITHS.

HA'NOCHITES, THE. Descendants of Hanoch (Num. xxvi. 5).

HA'NUN (*favored*). 1. Son of Nahash (2 Sam. x. 1, 2).—2. A man who repaired the wall of Jerusalem (Neh. iii. 13).—3. Son of Zalaph, who also assisted in the repairs (iii. 30).

HAPH'RAIM (*two pits*), (Josh. xix. 19). Issa. Six miles E. of Lejjun, two W. of Shunem; now called El Fuleh.

HA'RA (*mountain land*), (1 Chr. v. 26). Province in Assyria, where some of the Jews of the tribe of Reuben and Gad were carried captive.

HAR'ADAH. Station in the wandering (Num. xxxiii. 24). Lost.

HĀ'RAN (Gen. ix. 31). Terah and his family (including Abraham) came to Haran and dwelt there; where Terah died. Called Padan Aram (plain of Aram). Aram Naharaim (A. of the two rivers). In 2 K. xix. 12, it is connected with Gozan, Mesopotamia, taken by the Assyrians. Ezekiel groups it with Canneh, Eden, and other cities in Assyria (xxvii. 23). Harran (of the Arabs) stands on the banks of the small river *Belilk*, a branch of the Euphrates. From it a number of roads radiate to the great fords of the Tigris and Euphrates. Being in the route of the trade between Central and Western Asia it attracted Terah, and explains the allusion of the prophet Ezekiel. There is a *Harran el Awamid* 10 ms. east of Damascus, on the shore of the lake Ateibeh, between "the two rivers" Abana and Pharpar. In 1861 Dr. Beke made a journey to Palestine especially to follow the route of Laban and Jacob from Haran, and walked over the ground in about 5 days, which agrees with the Bible narrative. The flocks, herds, and little children could not have been driven across the desert, 300 miles, 25 days without water. The route in the Hauran is well watered, and has good pasture all the way.

HAR'ARITE (*mountain*). One of David's men. 1. Father of Shammah (2 Sam. xxiii. 11).—2. Shammah, the Hararite (xxiii. 33.)—3. Sharar (xxiii. 33); father of Ahiam.

HARBONA (*ass-driver*). A eunuch in the service of King Ahasuerus (Esth. i. 10). Harbonah in Esth. vii. 9.

HARE (ARNEBETH). Unclean under the law, "because he cheweth the cud but divideth not the hoof." It is of the squirrel kind, and does not chew the cud, but moves the jaw as though it did. There are two kinds in Palestine, the Syrian and Egyptian, and are very plentiful in some parts, and afford good returns to the hunter. There are no rabbits.

HAR'EL (*the mountain of*), (Ez. xliii. 15).

HA'REPH (*early-born*). Son of Caleb, and father of Beth-gader (1 Chr. ii. 51).

HA'RETH, THE FOREST OF (1 Sam. xxii. 5). Forest in Judah, to which David fled after leaving the cave of Adullam. See DAVID.

HARHAĪ'AH (*dry*). Father of Uzziel 6 (Neh. iii. 8).

HAR'HAS (*poverty*). Ancestor of Shallum (2 K. xxii. 14).

HAR'HUR (*inflammation*). The sons of Harhur returned with Zerubbabel (Ezr. ii. 51).

HA'RIEL. HADID (Ezr. ii. 33).

HA'RIM (*flat-nosed*). 1. A priest in the house of God (1 Chr. xxiv. 8).—2. 1,017 "children of Harim," returned from captivity (Ezr. ii. 39).—3.—4. Families of the children of Harim, 320 in number. who came from the Captivity (Ezr. ii. 32). REHUM.

HA'RIPH (*autumnal rain*.) 112 "children of Hariph," who returned with Zerubbabel (Neh. vii. 24). People who sealed the covenant (x. 19).

HAR'LOT (ZONAH, NOCHRI-YAH, KEDHISHA, *set apart for a sacred use*). They had a certain way of wearing their dress, and sometimes sat in a public place (Prov. vii. 10; Gen. xxxviii. 14), and might have been foreign women, not Hebrews. They sang in the streets (Is. xxiii. 16; Eccles. ix. 4). Some had houses (1 K. iii. 16). Jephthah's mother was a harlot, or "strange woman" (Judg. xi. 2). Gods were anciently, and are now actually worshiped in brothels (see Herodotus). This licentious worship was found at Baal-Peor, and among the Samaritans who came from Assyria (2 K. xvii. 30). The law of Moses was very strong against the practice, not even allowing the money earned by such a trade to come into the treasury (Lev. xix. 29), and made very severe laws in some cases (xxi. 9), which were sometimes carried out (Gen. xxxviii. 24), and neglected at others (Micah i. 7), as in the case of Samaria.

HAR'NEPHER (*panting*). Son of Zophah (1 Chr. vii. 36).

HAR'NESS (*armor*), (1 K. xx. 11). See HORSE. **HAR'NESSED** (Josh. i. 14, iv. 12). Armed men.

HA'ROD, THE WELL OF. Correctly, the fountain (Judg. vi. 33). The fountain by which Gideon pitched, having the Hill of Moreh on the north, in the valley of Jezreel (vii. 1). Now called *Ain Jalud*, at the foot of Mount Gilboa. It is a very large spring, and is visited constantly by a great number of flocks and herds (Judg. vi. 5).

HA'RODITE (*from Harod*). Descendants of David's strong men (2 Sam. xxiii. 25).

HA'ROEH (*the seer*). Son of Shobel (1 Chr. ii. 52).

HA'RORITE, THE. One of David's guard (1 Chr. xi. 27).

HARO'SHETH OF THE GENTILES (Judg. iv. 2). In the north of Palestine, the home of Sisera. *Tell Harothieh* is an immense double hill, covered with the ruins of old walls and buildings, commanding a narrow pass where the Kishon flows close to the foot of Carmel. Barak and Deborah chased Sisera and his scattered host as far as this pass, after their terrible defeat and slaughter along the plain of Esdraelon. (*Thomson, Land and Book*).

HARP (Heb. KINNOR; Gr. *kithara*). A stringed instrument of music. Josephus says it had 10 strings, and was played with a plectrum; others say it had 24 or 47 (1 Sam. xvi. 23, xviii. 10).

HARROW (1 Chr. xx. 3). See AGRICULTURE.

HAR'SHA (*worker*). Ancestor of Nethinim, who returned with Zerubbabel (Ezr. ii. 52).

HART. A clean animal (Deut. xii. 15). Permitted by the law for food. See FALLOW-DEER.

HĀ'RUM (*exalted*). Father of Aharhel (1 Chr. iv. 8).

HARU'MAPH (*snub-nosed*). Father of Jedaiah 2 (Neh. iii. 10).

HARU'PHITE (*strong*). A Korhite, who joined David at Ziklag (1 Chr. xii. 5).

HĀ'RUZ (*active*). Father of Meshullemeth (2 K. xxi. 19).

HAR'VEST. AGRICULTURE.

HASHADI'AH (*whom Jah loves*). A descendant of Judah (1 Chr. iii. 20).

HASENŪ'AH (*bristling*). A Benjaminite (1 Chr. ix. 7).

HASHABI'AH (*Jah regards*). Son of Amaziah

SARCOPHAGUS.

(1 Chr. v. 45). There are 13 of this name, but none of them were noted.

HASHAB'NAH. Chief of the people who signed the covenant with Nehemiah (Neh. x. 25).

HASHABNĪ'AH. 1. Father of Hattush 2 (Neh. iii. 10).—2. A Levite (ix. 5).

HASHBĀD'ANA (*thoughtful judge*). One who stood with Ezra when he read the law to the people of Jerusalem (Neh. viii. 4).

HĀ'SHEM (*fat*). The sons of Hashim were among David's strong men (1 Chr. xi. 34). Joshen.

HASHMAN'NIM (*opulent nobles*). (Ps. lxviii. 31).

HASHMŌ'NAH (*fatness*). (Num. xxxiii. 29). Near Mt. Hor. HESHMON(?)

HĀ'SHUB. HASSHUB. 1. Son of Pahath-moab (Neh. iii. 11).—2. Another, who assisted in the repairs of the Jerusalem wall (iii. 23).—3. One of the heads of the people who signed the covenant (x. 23).—4. A Levite (xi. 15).

HĀSHŪ'BAH (*esteemed*). Part of the family of Zerubbabel (1 Chr. iii. 20). HASADIAH.

HĀ'SHUM (*rich*). 1. 1,023 "children of Hashum," returned with Zerubbabel (Ezr. ii. 19; x

33).—2. One who stood on Ezra's left, when he read the law to the people (viii. 4).

HASHŪ'PHA. Ancestor of Nethinim (Neh. vii. 46).

HAS'RAH. Harhas (2 Chr. xxxiv. 22).

HASSENĀ'AH (*thorny*). "Sons of Hassenaah" rebuilt the fish-gate in the wall of Jerusalem (Neh. iii. 3).

HASŪ'PHA (*stripped*). Ancestor of Nethinim (Ezr. ii. 43).

HĀ'TACH (*verity*). Eunuch in Ahasuerus' court (Esth. iv. 5, 6 9, 10).

HĀ'THATH (*terror*). Son of Othniel (1 Chr. iv. 13).

HĀT'IPHA (*captive*). Ancestor of Nethinim (Ezr. ii. 54).

HĀT'ITA (*exploring*). Ancestor of the gate-keepers who returned with Zerubbabel (Ezr. ii. 42).

ARABIAN HAWK

HĀT'TEL (*wavering*). Ancestor of the "children of Solomon's servants," who returned with Zerubbabel (Ezr. ii. 57).

HĀT'SIHAMMENŪ'CHOTH (*midst of resting-places*).

HĀT'TUSH (*assembled*). 1. Son of Shechaniah (1 Chr. iii. 22; Ezr. viii. 2).—2. A priest (Neh. x. 4, xii. 2).—3. Son of Hashabnia (Neh. iii. 10).

HAU'RAN. Part of the district of Bashan. Ezekiel (xlvii. 16, 18) probably meant a region inclu-

ding the Lejah, Batanæa in the mountains (where the oaks of Bashan still grow around the ruins of ancient cities), and what is now Hauran. The Hauran is a vast fertile plain, the "granary of Damascus." Not a rock or stone encumbers its soil. More than a hundred ruined cities are found—though only deserted, not ruined; for the houses are quite perfect and habitable still, being built of stone, even to the doors and window-shutters, hinges and all, and roofs—of fine solid stone. Some of the dates are before our era, and it is quite probable that these cities are the very same that Moses described (Deut. iii. 5).—*Porter's Five Years in Damascus*.

HĀVĪ'LAH (*sand*). 1. Son of Cush (Gen. x. 7); and, 2. A son of Joktan (x. 29).—1. On the Red Sea, in Arabia, between Mecca and Sanaa. It is a fertile region, abounding in fruit, gum and myrrh; mountainous, well watered, and has a numerous population. The people were called by Eratosthenes (in Strabo), Chaulanitæ.—2. A district southeast of Sanaa. A third district of the same name is sought for in answer to Gen. ii. 11, which was compassed by one of the rivers of Eden. In Gen. xxv. 18, it is stated that the tribes of Ishmael dwelt from "Havilah unto Shur;" and this seems to call for a locality on the Persian Gulf or the Euphrates.

HĀ'VOTH JĀÏR (Num. xxxii. 41). Jair took a number of small towns in Gilead, in the mountain district south of the Hieromax, and named them "Jair's villages." A descendant of his, of the same name, was a judge of Israel, and lived here in 30 cities (Judg. x. 3, 4.) Bashan-havoth-jair were among the 60 cities of Argob (Deut. iii. 14, etc.).

HAWK (NEZ; Arabic *nez*). In Job xxxix. 26 "does the nez fly by thy wisdom?" It was migratory, as are 10 or 12 kinds now. The *sak'r* is used to catch partridges, grouse, quail, herons, hares and gazelles.

HĀY (CHATZIR, Gr. *herba;* Prov. xxvii. 25; Is. xv. 6). The modern Orientals do not make hay for such uses as we do, but the ancients mowed grass, and used the dried hay (Ps. lxxii. 6) for burning, or perhaps for feeding (Ps. xxvii. 2).

HĀ'ZAEL (*El is seeing*). A king of Damascus, B. C. 886–840 (see ELISHA). The Assyrian inscriptions furnish some accounts of wars in Syria in his day, which are also mentioned in Scripture. Hazael fulfiled a prophesy of Elisha in ravaging Gilead, etc. (2 K. x. 32, 33).

HĀ'ZAEL, THE HOUSE OF (Amos i. 4). Damascus, or Hazael's palace, or perhaps his family.

HAZAI'AH (*Jah beholds*). Son of Judah (Neh. xi. 5).

HĀZ'AR AD'DAR (*called space for a camp, named Addar*), (Num. xxxiv. 4). A south boundary of the promised land, near Kadesh-Barnea. There are walled-in places all over this district, but without names known to history.

HĀZARMĀVETH. Third son of Joktan (Gen. x. 26). Located in the south of Arabia, on the Indian Ocean. Now called *Hadramaut*. Capital city Shibam. Chief ports Mirbat, Zafari (SEPHAR), Kisheem. The native name of a person is *Hadramee*—very similar to their name in ancient history, Adramitæ. The country is well cultivated, and exports frankincense, myrrh, aloes (from Socotra), gum arabic, and dragon's blood. North of Hadramaut, the Great Red Desert of Arabia, called

DAHNA (*red sand*), extends to Nejed and the Persian Gulf, occupying a third of the whole peninsula.

HA′ZEL (Gen. xxx. 37). (Heb. LUZ.) The hazel or the wild almond tree, the cultivated being named SHAKED. The Heb. for hazel is EGOZ.

HAZELELPŌ′NI (*shade upon me*). Sister of the sons of Etam (1 Chr. iv. 3). The Zelelpo′nite.

HA′ZER (*enclosed, as a court-yard or camp*). These walls are found in many parts of Palestine and Arabia. Sometimes they are roofed in with a tent and become a dwelling for a short time (Is. xxxviii. 12) by shepherds. The name is used with others for several places : 1. *H. addar* (which see). 2. *H. enan* (*village of springs*). The north boundary of the promised land (Num. xxxiv. 9), the N. E. corner (ver. 10). *Kuryetein* (village of fountains), 40 ms. east of Riblah, and 60 north of Damascus. It is a large place, and has the only fountains in the region. There are ruined columns, probably of the city called by the Greeks Coradæa. 3. *H. gaddah* (Josh. xv. 27). In the south of Judah, between Moladah and Beersheba, now *Jerrah*. 4. *H. shual* (1 Chr. iv. 28). A city near the last named, now called *Saweh*. Both of these places are in ruins, on low hills. 5. *H. hatticon* (Ez. xlvii. 16). On the boundary in Hauran. Lost. 6. *H. Susah* (*horse village*). (Josh. xix. 5). Allotted to Simeon, near Ziklag. 7. *H. susim* (*village of horses*). Probably the same as the last. 8. *Hazeroth*. Station in the wilderness on the route from Sinai to Ezion-geber. See WILDERNESS.

HAZERE. 4 ms. W. of Bint Jebeil, has extensive ruins, and the right location (*Land and Book*, i. 439).—2. (Josh. xix. 37). 10 ms. S. W. of Safed, Hazur, near El Mughar.

HAZE′ROTH (Num. xi. 35). A place 25 ms. N. of Sinai.

HAZEZON TAMAR (*palm forest*). ENGEDI.

HĀ′ZIEL (*vision of God*). A Levite (1 Chr. xxiii. 9).

HA′ZIRIM. Hazer (Deut. ii. 3). Villages.

HA′ZO (Gen. xxii. 22). Azon of Nahor, settled on the Euphrates, in Chazene (Strabo).

COIN OF SARDIS.

HA′ZOR (Josh. xi. 1-12). An ancient, royal city, fortified, near Lake Merom. "The head of all those kingdoms," i. e., the chief city in North Canaan. Taken by Joshua, and given to Naphtali. In after-times, a king Jabin, of Hazor, held the Israelites in subjection 20 years. Jabin's army, including 600 chariots of iron, led by Sisera (perhaps intending to conquer all Palestine), were routed by Barak and Deborah (Judg. iv.). Fortified by Solomon (1 K. ix. 15.) Referred to by Josephus, and in Macc. xi. 67.—2. (Josh. xv. 23). Judah, south. Lost.—3. (Neh. xi. 33. Benjamin, after the Captivity. Tell Azur. 5 ms. N. E. of Bethel.—4. (Jer. xlix. 28). Some noted camping-ground of the Arabs. Lost. There are two or three Hazors named in Josh. xv. 23–25; one of them a *new* village (Hadattah); and one changed to Hezron. There were also BAAL HAZOR and EN HAZOR.

HEAD (Heb. ROSH, Gr. *kephale*). Used for the top of anything, as the summit of a mountain, top of a tree.

HEAD-DRESS. The head-dress is a very important matter in the hot climate of the East, besides its use "for glory and for beauty" (Ex. xxviii. 40). There are several names of different articles used by different persons, or at various times. 1. ZANIPH, (*to roll or wind*) worn by nobles (Job xxix. 14), and ladies (Is. iii. 23), and kings (lxii. 3; *mitre* in Zech. iii. 5), was a turban, intended for display. 2. PEER, modern name tarbush (or kaook) the red cap. The Bedawin head-dress (*keffieh*) is formed by folding a square cloth across from the corners, and tying it on the head, so as to have one (double) corner behind and one on each side of the neck. The Assyrian was probably made of bright and mingled colors (Ez. xxiii. 15). See cuts on pps. 9, 76 and 120.

EGYPTIAN HEAD-DRESS.

HEART (Heb. LEB, Gr. *kardia*). The supposed seat of the intellect, soul, etc. (Judg. xvi. 17).

HEARTH (Heb. AH, ACH, MOKED, KIYOR). A floor of stones on which a fire is made. Used for the whole house. Jehoiakim's was probably a brazier of charcoal (Jer. xxxvi. 23).

HEATH (AROER, ARAR). A shrub used in thatch, for brooms, beds, etc., probably juniper or savin (Jer. xvii. 6, xlviii. 6).

HEATHEN (GOI, GOYIM). All nations have a term for distinguishing other people from their own. The Hebrews were very particular in this matter, because they were forbidden to marry out of their own nation, or even to mingle in society with them. The heathen were worshipers of false gods. After the Greeks came into power their name meant the same as heathen (Greek *hēthen*), and is the same or similar to "uncircumcised." Goyim also meant wicked as opposed to the righteous Jews.

HEAVEN. 1. RAKIA, *firmament, expanse*.—2. SHAMAYIM, *the high*, the heavens (air, and earth). Always plural in the Hebrew of the O. T.—3. MAROM (*mountain*), hight, *high region;* SHAHAKIM, *expanse, skies*.—4. ARABAH (*the desert*), *the heaven;* ARIPHIM (*distilling*), *clouds;* Greek, *ouranos* (*air*), *heaven;* hupsos (hight), *on high; another* (*from above*) *heaven*. The "third heaven" of Paul, in 2 Cor. xii. 2, is explained from the Jewish way of naming three parts in heaven, as: 1. The place of clouds in the air; 2. The place of the sun, moon and stars; 3. The place of God and his angels. Heavens and earth meant the entire universe. Once heaven, earth, and under the earth (Phil. ii. 10).

HĒ′BER (*society*). 1. Grandson of Asher (Gen. xlvi. 17).—2. Father of Socho, of Judah (1 Chr. iv. 18).—3. Gadite (v. 13).—4. Son of Elpaal, a Benjamite (viii. 17).—5. Son of Shashak (xxii.). —6. Husband of Jael, a Kenite (Judg. iv. 11-17). —7. The patriarch Eber (Luke iii. 35). Heberites (Num. xxvi. 45).

HEBREW. This name was first used of Abraham in Gen. xiv. 13. Four sources have been offered: 1. From Abram; 2. From ABAR; 3. From EBER (*country beyond*); and 4. From EBER, the patriarch (this would have been IBRI). Hebrew of the Hebrews; a pure-minded Jew.

HEBREWS, EPISTLE TO THE. See HISTORY OF THE BOOKS.

HE′BRON (*the friend*). Third son of Kohath, who was second son of Levi (Ex. vi. 18). The clan is mentioned in the time of David (1 Chr. xv. 9, xxiii. 19), as of the sons of Levi, who only ought to carry the ark of God; and also mighty men of valor of Jazer, in Gilead (xxvi. 31), who were officers in David's government; and another branch held the same rank on the west side of Jordan. There was a Hebron among the sons of Caleb. The CITY OF HEBRON is one of the most ancient, built 7 years before Zoan (Num. xiii. 22), and even older than Damascus (Gen. xii. 18). See cut of Hebron on page 4. Its original name was Arba, or Kirjath Arba (city of Arba), from Arba, the father of Anak (xxxiii. 2; Josh. xiv. 15, xv. 13). It was also called MAMRE (Gen. xxiii. 19, xxxv. 27). The ancient city was in a valley, and its pools help fix its site and identity (2 Sam. iv. 12). Many years of the lifetime of Abraham, Isaac and Jacob were spent here, where they were all buried; and from Hebron Jacob and his family set out for Egypt, by way of Beersheba. The city was given to Caleb by Joshua, who drove out the Anakim. One of the CITIES OF REFUGE. It was David's royal residence for 7 years and a half; where most of his sons were born; and here he was crowned king over all Israel (2 Sam. ii.), when David changed the royal residence to Jerusalem. Fortified by Rehoboam. It was occupied after the Captivity; but fell into the hands of the Edomites, from whom it was recovered by Judas Maccabæus (1 Macc. v. 65). It was called Hebron or Castle of Abraham during the Crusades. The modern town is called Khulil (*the friend* "of God"), by the Arabs, and lies on the eastern and southern side of a beautiful valley. The houses are all of stone, well built, having flat roofs with many domes. The streets are only a few feet wide, and the bazaars are covered either by awnings or arches. Glass is the only manufacture; lamps, and the bracelets and rings worn by women. The court in which the mosque over the tombs of the patriarchs is built is surrounded by an extensive and lofty wall, formed of large stones, strengthened by square buttresses, the greatest antiquity in Hebron, and probably the same as that seen and described by Josephus (Ant. i. 14; B. J. iv. 9, 7).

MELON.

The only other antiquities are the two cisterns for rain-water (pools). The one close to the south gate of the city is 133 feet square, 22 feet deep, and built of hewn limestone, with steps at each corner, down to the water. The other pool at the north end of the town is 85 by 55 feet, and 19 feet deep. The surrounding country is productive, and the many ruins show a once dense population and high state of cultivation. Population 5000.—2. In Asher (Josh. xix. 28). ABDON?

HE'BRONITES, THE. Descendants of Hebron, son of Kehath (Num. iii. 27).

HEDGE (GADER, GEDER, *a stone wall*, or other fence; MESUKAH, *hedge of thorns or cactus*). Besides stones, walls are made of sun-dried mud, (es-

pecially in Egypt); and the *nukb* thorn tree makes an impassable hedge, as well as the cactus.

HE'GAI or **HEG'AI.** *Eunuch* (prime-minister) of the court of Ahasuerus (Esth. ii. 8–15).

HE'GE. HEGAI (Esth. ii. 3). Aja or Aga in Sanscrit. Name of a modern Turkish officer.

HEIFER (AGLAH, *the young of kine*). They worked with other cattle, in treading out grain (Hosea x. 11), and in plowing (Judg. xiv. 18). Egypt was "a fair heifer" (Jer. xlv. 20), in allusion to the bull Apis worshiped there. Several names are made from it, as Eglah, En-eglaim, and Parah (*young mother cow*). Heifers are used at the plow now as anciently.

THE ORDINANCE OF THE RED HEIFER (Num. xix.), is a very peculiar item in the ancient religion, concerning cleansing rather than atonement. It was intended to cleanse from the ceremonial defilement which followed from touching a dead body, or a bone of a dead man, or entering a house where there was a person dead. Purification in the usual way required 7 days of time. A son of the high priest sprinkled the blood of a red heifer before the tabernacle (temple, not on the altar), and the carcase was to be burned entire, outside of the camp, in a clean place (with a bit of cedar wood, and of scarlet cloth), reserving nothing; the ashes were to be kept for use. Mixed with fresh water they were sprinkled on the unclean, on the third, and on the seventh day, with a bunch of hyssop. After changing his clothes and bathing he was clean. His house or tent was also to be sprinkled, with all its furniture, etc.

HE'LAH (*rust*). Wife of Ashur (1 Chr. iv. 5).

HE'LAM. On the west bank of the Euphrates, where David met and defeated the army of Hadarezer (2 Sam. x. 16). Alamatha of Ptolemy.

HEL'BAH (Judg. i. 31). Asher, not far from Sidon.

HEL'BON (Ezek. xxvii. 18). "In the wine of Helbon." A village 10 miles north of Damascus, in a wild and beautiful glen, which is clothed in vineyards. There are many ruins of temples, some with Greek inscriptions, and many other marks of ancient wealth.

HEL'DAI (*long-lived*). 1. Captain for the temple-service (1 Chr. xxvii. 15).—2. An Israelite (Zech. vi. 10).

HE'LEB (*fat*). Son of Baanah (2 Sam. xxiii. 29). Heled.

HE'LED (*strength*), (1 Chr. xi. 30). HELDAI 1.

HE'LEK (*possession*). Son of Gilead (Num. xxvi. 30).

HE'LEKITES, THE. Family from Helek (Num. xxvi. 30).

HE'LEM (*stroke*). 1. A descendant of Asher (1 Chr. vii. 35). Hotham?—2. (*strength*), (Neh. vi. 14). HELDAI 2.

HE'LEPH (Josh. xix. 33.) Where the north boundary of Naphtali began. *Beit Lif*, east of Ras Abyad and west of Kades.

HE'LEZ (*loin*). 1. One of David's guard (2 Sam. xxxii. 26; xxvii. 10).—2. Son of Azariah (ii. 39).

HE'LI, ELI. 1. Father of Joseph, the husband of the Virgin Mary (Luke iii. 23).—2. (2 Esd. i. 2; Ezr. vii. 2, 3).

HELIODO'RUS (*given by the sun*). The treasurer of Seleucus Philopator (2 Macc. iii. ff). He was appointed to carry away the private treasures in the Temple at Jerusalem, but fell down speechless and was restored by the high priest Onias.

HEL'KAI (*Jah, his portion*). A priest (Neh. xii. 15).

HEL'KATH (Josh. xix. 25). Boundary of Asher. Lost. Ikkrith? Hukkok in 1 Chronicles vi. 75.

HEL'KATH HAZZURIM (2 Sam. ii. 16). Near

the pool of Gibeon, where 12 of Joab's men and 12 of Abner's killed each other and brought on a general battle.

HELL. See page 119.

HELLENIST. GRECIAN.

HEL'MET. ARMS.

HELPS (Gr. *antilepseis*). Care of the poor and sick, by the deacons and deaconesses, by a gift of the spirit. "From time to time God raises up heroes of Christian charity, angels of mercy, for the benefit of humanity."

HE'LON (*strong*). Father of Eliab, prince of Zebulon (Num. i. 9., ii. 7).

HEM OF THE GAR'MENT. The Jews attached a symbolical importance to the hem or fringe, because of the regulation in Num. xv. 38. See FRINGE.

HE'MAM. HOMAM. Son of Lotan (Gen. xxxvi. 22).

HEMAN (*faithful*). 1. Son of Zerah (1 Chr. ii. 6).—2. Son of Joel, a Levite and musician (1 Chr. vi. 33), to whom the vocal and instrumental music of the temple service, in the reign of David, was committed (xv. 16–22). He was also connected with the family of Zerah, the Ezrahite, and his name is in the title to Ps. lxxxviii.

HE'MATH. HAMATH (Amos vi. 14).

HE'MATH. HAMMATH. A person or place named as the origin of the Kenites (1 Chr. ii. 55), and the house of Rechab.

HEM'DAN (Gen. xxxvi. 26). East of Akaba there is an Arab tribe of the name of Hamran.

HEMLOCK (LAANAH and ROSH, *gall*).

HEN (*grace*). Son of Zephaniah (Neh. vi. 14). TOBIJAH 2.

HEN (Gr. *ornis, fowl*), (Matt. xxiii. 37; Luke xiii. 34), also (2 Esd. i. 30). Nowhere noticed besides in these passages, but were always kept as now, in every village or farm house.

HE'NA (2 K. xix. 13). Some ancient ruins, called Ana, are found on the Euphrates, near Mosaib. (Sippara).

HEN'ADAD (*favor of Hadad*). A chief Levite who helped rebuild the temple (Ezr. iii. 9; Neh. iii. 18, 24).

HE'NOCH. 1. Enoch 2 (1 Chr. i. 3).—2. Hanoch 1 (i. 33).

HE'PHER (Josh. vii. 17). West of Jordan, as was also the land of Hepher. Lost.

HE'PHER (*a well*). 1. Son of Gilead (Num. xxvi. 32).—2. Son of Ashur (1 Chr. iv. 6).—3. One of David's men (xii. 36).

HEPHERITES. The family of Hepher (Num. xxvi. 32).

HEPH'ZIBAH (*my delight in her*). 1. Name given to the new Jerusalem (Is. lxiii. 4).—2. Queen to Hezekiah and mother of Manasseh (2 K. xxi. 1).

ORANGEE.

HE'RA. HERCULES.

HER'ALD (Chal. *karoza*). An officer (Dan. iii. 4).

HERBS. Bitter herbs. FOOD.

HER'CULES (*Hera's glory*). The national god of Tyre, called MELKART (*king of the city*). The worship extended to all colonies of Tyre, especially to Carthage. This was the Baal also. The Greeks make him the most famous hero of their fabulous history, remarkable for his great strength (SAMSON), and especially for 12 "labors" which were connected with the health and safety of men. Hera was the Greek name of Juno, who was the guar-

dian deity of married women. In Assyria she was *Astarte*, "Queen of Heaven;" and as such is sculptured at Hierapolis, in Asia Minor.

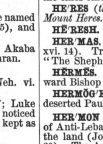

HERA.

HERD. Herdman. The herd was one of the chief sources of wealth, and the ox the most precious, next to the horse and mule. The herd yielded the most esteemed sacrifice. Its supply for sustenance was most important, in flesh, milk, butter and cheese. The cattle were broken to service in the third year, after which they were rarely killed. The ox eats grass and browses on foliage also. The harvest is gathered and threshed by the help of cattle. Pharaoh made some of Joseph's brothers overseers of herds, and David's herdsmen were among the chief officers of his court.

HE'RES (*the sun*), (Is. xix. 18)—Irhaheres, for *Mount Heres*. See Judg. i. 35. IRSHEMESH.

HE'RESH. A Levite (1 Chr. ix. 15).

HER'MAS. HERMES. A disciple of Rome (Rom. xvi. 14). Tradition says he was the author of "The Shepherd of Hermas."

HERMES. One of the seventy disciples, afterward Bishop of Dalmatia (Rom. xvi. 14).

HERMOG'ENES (2 Tim. i. 15). A disciple who deserted Paul without cause.

HER'MON (*nose of mountain*). The highest peak of Anti-Lebanon, on or beyond the north border of the land (Josh. xi. 17; Deut. xxxiv. 1; 1 Sam. iii. 20). The Amorites called it *Shenir* (*to shine, as a coat of mail*); the Sidonians, *Sirion* (*to glitter*); also called *Sion* (*elevated*); and now by the Arabs *Jebel esh Sheikh* (*chief mountain*), and *Jebel eth Thelj* (*snowy mountain*). Its head is crowned with perpetual snow; and when the whole lowland country is burnt by the summer sun, long lines of snow streak down the sides of Hermon, like the white locks of an old man about his shoulders. There are three summits, about a quarter of a mile from each other in a triangular position, and 10,000 feet high. They are visible (at a distance as one peak) from every part of Palestine north of Shiloh, from the Jordan valley near the Dead Sea, and from the Moab mountains as far south as Nebo. Its rivers are Jordan, Abana, Pharpar, Orontes, and Leontes. It was the religious centre of pagan Syria, and the temples of Baal gave it a name. The ruins of these temples are now found on many of its lower shoulders, as at Rakleh, Sed Dan, Bustra, Mutaleih, Kefr Kuk, Burkush, Aiba, Hibariyeh, Tilthatha, Ain Hersha, Asheir, Bekkeh, Munseh, and Paneas. At Rakleh there is a god's face, 40 inches in diameter, surrounded by a wreath, all well cut in bold relief, and set in the wall of the temple, which is a ruin, and one of a circle of temples all around, facing the summit of Hermon. The temple at Asheir is on an elevated platform (which is ornamented with a frieze and cornice), 126 by 69 feet, and itself 89 by 40 feet, and 54 feet high. In the Ionic style, with cup and ball ornaments. On the very highest peak are the foundations of a circular wall of large stones, enclosing hewn stones (some beveled), in heaps, disclosing the plan of a small temple (Deut. xii. 2; 2 K. xvii. 10). The central peak is a bald cone of gray limestone, 2,000 feet higher than the surrounding ridges. These lower ridges are thinly clothed with evergreen oaks. The whole of Palestine can be seen from the summit.

HERMONITES, THE. "The Hermons" (Ps. xlii. 6).

HERMONS (Ps. xlii. 6). The three summits of Hermon.

HEROD FAMILY, TABLE OF THE.

Father.	Son.		
	1. Antipater, governor of Idumea.		
	2. Antipater. See Josephus.		
2. Antipater,	3. Phasael.		
2. Antipater,	4. HEROD (the king in Matt. iii).		
		Mother.	
"	5. Joseph,	⎱ Cypros, an Ara-	
"	6. Pheroras,	⎰ bian.	
"	7. Salome,	"	"
3. Phasael.	8. Phasael.		
4. Herod,	9. Antipater,	Doris.	
"	10. Aristobulus,	Mariamne, g. d. of Hyrcanus.	
"	11. Alexander,	"	"
"	12. Salampio,	"	"
"	13. Cypros,	"	"
"	14 Herod,	Mariamne, daugh. of Simon.	
"	15. Antipas,	⎱ Malthac, a Sama-	
"	16. Archelaus,	⎰ ritan.	
"	17. Olympias,		
"	18. Herod,	Cleopatra.	
"	19. Philip,	"	
"	20. Phasael,	Pallas.	
"	21. Roxana,	Phædra.	
"	22. Salome,	Elpis.	
"	Two wives, no name or children.		
5. Joseph,	23. Joseph.		
7. Costabarus,	24. Berenice.		
	25. Herod.		
10. Aristobulus,	26. Aristobulus,	24. Berenice	
"	27. Agrippa,	"	
"	28. Herodias,	"	
11. Alexander,	29. Alexander,	16. D. Archelaus.	
"	30. Tigranes,	"	
14. Herod,	31. Salome,	28. Herodias.	
23. Joseph,	32. Mariamne,	17. Olympias.	
8. Phasael.	33. Cypros,	12. Salampio.	
25. Herod,	34. Aristobulus,	32. Mariamne.	
26. Aristobulus,	35. Jotape,	Jotape.	
27. Agrippa,	36. Agrippa, K.,	33. Cypros.	
"	37. Drusus,	"	
"	38. Berenice,	"	
"	39. Mariamne,	"	
"	40. Drusilla,	"	
29. Alexander,	41. Tigranes.		
34. Aristobulus,	42. Herod,	31. Salome.	
"	43. Agrippa,	"	
"	44. Aristobulus,	"	
Felix,	45. Agrippa,	40. Drusilla.	
Tigranes,	46. Alexander.		

Josephus says the Herods were Edomites (xiv. 15 § 2), but Nicolaus of Damascus, a historian of the times, says they returned from exile with other Jews (a story invented to please Herod). Antipater (1.) gained power, first in Idumea, and then

HEROD COIN.

by fomenting the divisions between Hyrcanus, the high priest and his brother Aristobulus. He also came into power in Judæa, although Hyrcanus was nominal ruler. Herod (4.) the Great was only 15 years (20?) when he began to rule, and soon won a popular enthusiasm by good measures of public safety and quiet. Being summoned before the Sanhedrin, he appeared robed in purple, with a strong guard of soldiers, and was not sentenced. Not long after receiving favor from Sextus, president of Syria, and Cassius, he punished Ma-

lichus his father's murderer. He was made governor of Judæa jointly with his brother Phasael, B. C. 41. Antigonus being driven out of Judæa, joined the Parthians and got possession of Judæa, 40 B. C., Herod flying to Rome, while Phasael killed himself. Octavius Cæsar confirmed Herod in his office and Herod returned to Judæa, where he tried to gain the favor of the Jews by rebuilding and ornamenting the temple (commenced B. C. 24), and restoring such cities as Cæsarea, Antipatris, Sebaste (Samaria), and others, besides public buildings in Damascus, Tripoli, Ptolemais, Tyre, Sidon, Askelon and Antioch (a large open space, paved with marble, having a cloister), and also frequent public games and feasts, all at his own expense. He also made costly presents to Cæsar and Agrippa. He is said to have destroyed the genealogies of the Jewish priestly families. These deeds were prompted by the ambition to connect his name with the prosperity of his country, like Solomon's. The close of his career was stained with many cruel and barbarous crimes. His wives and children plotted against each other. (He had ten wives, two of whom were his own nieces.)

HEROD COIN.

Three of his sons (9, 10, 11) he had killed, with the mother of two (10, 11). In the midst of these family troubles, and of seditions in the city, he was seized with a terrible disorder in the bowels, and tried to kill himself, after giving orders for a magnificent funeral. He attempted to destroy the infant Jesus by killing all the children in Bethlehem (about 12), to get rid of an object of jealousy, for Jesus was spoken of as born king of the Jews. He died B. C. 4. He maintained peace at home and abroad by his vigor and timely generosity, and conciliated the good-will of the Romans. Many coins of his reign are still extant. (See MONEY.)

HEROD ANTIPAS (15) had been destined as his father's successor, but was appointed "tetrarch of Galilee and Peræa." He first married a daughter of Aretas (king of Arabia Petræa), and afterwards Herodias, his half-brother "Herod-Philip's" wife. This Herodias caused the death of John the Baptist. Aretas, in revenge for the slight put on his daughter, invaded Herod's territory and defeated him. He went to Rome, at the suggestion of Herodias, to ask for the title of a king, but being there opposed by the friends of Agrippa, he was banished to Lugdununi, A. D. 39, where he died, his wife being with him. It was to this Herod that Jesus was sent for examination by Pilate. He built Tiberias, and restored Sepphoris, and Bethharem in Peræa, naming it Julias after the emperor's wife.

ARCHELAUS (16). The kingdom which had been once intended for his brother Antipas, was left to Archelaus, who was educated in Rome, and Augustus confirmed the choice, giving him Idumea, Judæa, Samaria, Cæserea, Joppa, and Jerusalem, with the title of Ethnarch. He broke the Mosaic law by marrying his brother's widow, Glaphyra; was denounced by his subjects, appealed to Cæsar, and was banished to Vienne, in Gaul, where he died (A. D. 39).

HEROD PHILIP I (14). His mother was daughter of the high-priest Simon. He married Herodias, sister of Agrippa I, and their daughter was Salome (31). Herodias left him for his half-brother Antipas (Matt. xiv. 3). He was excluded from all share in his father's possessions because of his mother's treachery, and lived a private life.

HEROD PHILIP II (19). He was brought up at Rome, and after his father's death was appointed governor (tetrarch) of Batanæa, Trachonitis, Auranitis, and Jamnia, which he ruled with justice and moderation, without taking part in the intrigues of the rest of his family. He rebuilt Paneas, and named it Cæsarea Philippi, and raised Bethsaida beyond Jordan to a city, naming it Julias after the daughter of the emperor, and died there (A. D. 31). He married Salome (31), but left no children.

HEROD AGRIPPA I (26)—Was educated in Rome with Claudius and Drusus, where Tiberius imprisoned him for an unguarded speech. Caius Caligula, the succeeding emperor, liberated him, and made him tetrarch of Galilee and Perea (Lysanias). Herod Antipas and Herodias tried in vain to have him deposed, but he defeated their plans by a countercharge of treason with the Parthians. Agrippa rendered important service to Claudius, and had his dominions enlarged by Samaria and Judæa, so that they equaled in extent those of Herod the Great. He was a strict keeper of the law, and was respected by the Jews. It is supposed that it was to increase their favor that he put to death James the Less, and put Peter in prison (Acts xii). In the fourth year of his reign over Judæa (A. D. 44), he attended some games in honor of the emperor. Appearing in a robe ornamented with silver embroidery, his flatterers saluted him as a god, when he was seized with a sudden illness, and died in five days (eaten of worms).

HEAD OF TITUS. COIN OF HEROD AGRIPPA II.

HEROD AGRIPPA II (36). He was educated at Rome, and was only 17 at his father's death. His first appointment was the kingdom of Chalcis, and afterwards the tetrarchies of Philip and Lysanias, with the title of king (Acts xxv). Nero added several cities. He built many splendid public buildings in Jerusalem and Berytus. Juvenal in his satires notices his relation to his sister Berenice. He died at Rome in the 3d year of Trajan, A. D. 100, the last of the Herods.

HERODIANS. Formed a party very keenly opposed to the claims of Jesus, who favored the Herod family and watched its interests. They "watched him, and sent forth spies, which should feign themselves just men, that they might take hold of his words, so that they might deliver him unto the power and authority of the governor" (Luke xx. 20). Herodias, daughter of Aristobulus, son of Herod the Great (4), and wife first of Herod Philip, and then, contrary to the law of Moses, of Herod Antipas, who had a wife, the daughter of the king of Arabia (Aretas). John the Baptist reproved her, and she in revenge caused his death (Matt. xiv. 8) at Machærus. She went with her husband Antipas into exile (see HEROD ANTIPAS), at a place now called St. Bertrand de Comminges, in France, near Spain, on the Garonne river, anciently Lugdunum Converarum, at the foot of the Pyrenees.

HERODION. A relative of Paul at Rome (Rom. xvi. 11). Tradition says he was bishop of Tarsus, or of Patræa.

HERON (ANAPHAH). An unclean bird (Lev. xi. 19; Deut. xiv. 18). There are several species "after its kind" in Palestine, one of which is called the White Ibis, which are found in immense flocks about the Huleh lake and marsh. The flesh is excellent.

HE'SED (favor). Commissary for Solomon in the Aruboth (1 K. iv. 10).

HESH'BON (Num. xxi. 26). Capital city of Si-

hon, king of the Amorites, on the western border of the Mishor (Josh. xiii. 17), and on the boundary between Reuben and Gad. The ruins are 20 miles east of Jordan, opposite the north end of the Dead Sea, on an insulated hill, scattering over a space more than a mile in circuit, with not a single edifice entire. Many cisterns are whole, and a large reservoir near the base of a hill recalls the text in Cant. vii. 4, "Thine eyes are like the fishpools of Heshbon." The view from the summit is very extensive over the great undulating plateau, embracing the ruins of a great number of cities, whose names resemble those of the Scriptures. (See Tristram's Land of Israel).

HESH'MON (Josh xv. 27). On the south border of Palestine. Lost. Azmon? (Num. xxxiv. 4).

HES'RON (enclosed). Son of Reuben (Num. xxvi. 6). HEZRON. HESRONITES.

HETH (terror). CHETH. Ancestor of the Hittites, son of Canaan (Gen. x.) In Abraham's time they were called Bene Cheth, sons of Cheth. The name CHAT is found on the Egyptian monuments for Palestine.

HETH'LON (stronghold). On the N. border of Palestine (Ez. xlvii. 15), at the north end of Lebanon.

HEZ'EKI. A Benjamite, son of Elpaal (1 Chr. viii. 17). HEZEKIAH.

HEZEKI'AH (HIZEKIYAH, strength of Jah). 12th king of Judah, son of the idolator Ahaz. Made king at 25 (or 20), B. C. 726. He destroyed the images and the instruments of idol worship, even the image of the brazen serpent, which had been preserved to his time as a precious relic of the wilderness, and repaired the temple and its furniture. He then held a solemn assembly, and after that a feast of the Passover, to which a great many came, and others sent gifts, and the seven days were fully honored, so much so that another seven days were added "with gladness" (2 Chr. xxx. 23). He refused submission and tribute to the king of Assyria, which brought the Assyrian army to Samaria in the fourth year of his reign, and in the

ANCIENT WELL.

14th year the assault on Judæa was made (2 K. xviii. 13), when Hezekiah made peace, being compelled to rob the temple to pay the tax. A strong confirmation of the leading facts in the Bible narrative has lately been discovered at Nineveh, sculptured in stone, with the names of Hezekiah and others familiar, which leave no doubt in the matter. Sennacherib insisted on an unconditional surrender, in the most offensive manner. Hezekiah humbled himself before God, and being assured by Isaiah of the favor of Jehovah, he called his army together and prayed for help, which came as a plague upon the hosts of the Assyrians (2 K. xix. 35). Sennacherib was killed soon after his return home, in the house of his idol, by two of his sons. Hezekiah only lived a year longer, dying in his 54th year. He was one of the best kings of both Israel and Judah.—2. Son of Neariah, in the royal line of Judah (1 Chr. iii. 23).—3. Hizkiah in Zeph. i. 1.

HĒ'ZION (*vision*). King of Aram, father of Tabrimon (1 K. xv. 18).

HE'ZOR (*swine*). 1. A priest (1 Chr. xxiv. 15). —2. Head of the layman who signed the covenant (Neh. x. 20).

HEZ'RĀĪ (*enclosed*). One of David's strong men (2 Sam. xxiii. 35.) Hezro (1 Chr. xi. 37).

HEZ'RON. HEZRAI. 1. Son of Reuben (Gen. xlvi. 9).—2. Son of Pharez (2 Gen. xlvi. 12).—3. Hazor (Josh. xv. 25).

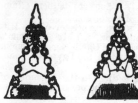

EAR-RINGS.

HEZRONITES, THE. 1. Descendants of Hezron (Num. xxvi. 6).—2. Part of the tribe of Judah. Son of Pharez (xxvi. 31).

HID'DAI (*mighty*). One of David's guard (2 Sam. xxiii. 30). HURAI.

HID'DEKEL (Gen. ii. 14). One of the rivers of Eden—the 3d, "flowing *toward* the E. of Assyria." Daniel saw one of his poetic visions near its banks (Dan. x. 4). The Aramæan name of the river Tigris is *Digla*—Arabic, *Diklah;* and the Hebrew name seems to be compounded of the ancient name with the prefix for active, HIDDIKLAH or HIDDE-KEL. Pliny writes it Diglito, "an arrow;" Josephus, Diglath, "swift" (Ant. i. 1, 3), all of which refer to the great swiftness of its current. (See TIGRIS).

HI'EL. JEHIEL (*El is animation*). Native of Bethel (1 K. xvi. 34; Josh. vi. 26).

HIERAP'OLIS (Col. iv. 13). Five miles north of Laodicea. There are mineral springs, whose waters form stalactites, which gave it an ancient celebrity (Strabo xiii. 629). A great number of sepulchres are found in its vicinity. The ruins show its ancient greatness, and traces are still distinct of a temple of Apollo, a theatre (346 feet), a gymnasium (400 feet sq.), and three Christian churches (one 300 feet).

HIERON'YMUS (*hallowed*). A general of Syria (2 Macc. xii. 2).

HIGGAI'ON (Ps. ix. 17). Meditation. Soft music. A direction for singing.

HIGH PLACES (*bāmoth*). From the top of Hermon to the crest of the low hills, all over the land, there are evidences that they were used for religious rites, both in idolatrous and in pure worship. The temple on Moriah was intended to supersede all other high places, and no other worship was allowed, except on special occasions.

HIGH PRIEST. The office of the (COHEN, *priest*) high priest was legal, theological and historical. The legal included all the law of Moses alluding to it, as the substitute for the first-born. He alone was consecrated by the anointing oil, the underpriests being sprinkled only (Ps. cxxxiii.). His dress was symbolical. (See DRESS). He alone could enter the Holy of Holies, which he did but once a year (DAY OF ATONEMENT) clothed in pure white. The accidental man-slayer was safe in the City of Refuge during his life-time, and at his death could return to his friends. He could not follow a funeral, nor disfigure himself by mourning. There was an assistant, called

SAGAN (second priest), who could act in his stead (Luke iii. 2). The elders or Sanhedrin appointed him before the monarchy. No one could hold the office who was blemished, or was under 20 years (2 Chr. xxxi. 17), and it ended only at death, although one could be, or was deposed for ill-conduct. Theologically he was a type of Jesus the Christ. Historically his office concerns the history of the Jews for 1370 years, including nearly 80 different persons, from Aaron to Phannias. See pages 8, 16.

HIGHWAY. Roads or paths were used in ancient times, but the Romans made the first paved ways, traces of which still remain.

HI'LEN (1 Chr. vi. 58). Judah. Levitical.

HILKI'AH (*Jah's portion*). Son of Shallum, ancestor of Ezra the scribe (Ezr. vii. 1). Josiah effected the great reformation in his time, when the book of the law of Moses (see DEUTERONOMY in History of the Books) was found in the temple, where it had been hidden for centuries. Six others of this name were of little note.

HILL (GIBEAH, *knoll;* HAR *mountain;* MAALEH, *hight, ascent;* Gr. *bounos, mount; heoreine, mountain*).

HIL'LEL (*praise*), Judge of Israel, father of Abdon (Judg. xii. 13-15).

HIN. WEIGHTS AND MEASURES.

HIND (Heb. AYYALAH, AYYELETH). Female stag. (HART). (Gen. xlix. 21). See FALLOW DEER.

HINGE (POTH, TSIR). Stone hinges are peculiar to Palestine and Assyria. See DOOR.

HIN'NOM, THE VALLEY OF (Josh. xviii. 16). On the S. and W. of Mt. Zion. The origin of the name is unknown (Jer. vii. 31). An idol of bronze of great size was set up in the valley, facing Olivet, where children were sacrificed in the fire, which seems to have been kindled inside the idol. Josiah abolished the worship, and strewed human bones over the place, making it unclean, and thus prevented the renewal of worship there (2 K. xxiii. 10). These inhuman practices gave the place a horrible character, and caused its name to be detested and used as a figure for a place of torment.

EAR-RINGS.

HIPPOPOT'AMUS (*river horse*). BEHEMOTH. See p. 35.

HI'RAH (*noble birth*). The friend of Judah (Gen. xxxviii. 1, 12).

HIRAM or **HURAM** (*high-minded*). 1. King of Tyre (2 Sam. v. 11; 1 Chr. xiv. 1). He built a palace for David (1 K. v. 1), also a temple for Solomon (1 K. vi. 1)—2. An artificer (vii. 13, 40, 45).

HIRCĀ'NUS. Son of Tobias (2 Macc. iii. 11).

HITTITES. Children of Heth. See HAM. The name is found in the Egyptian hieroglyphics, where are also found the names of their gods, Ashtoreth and others.

HI'VITES. Of the sons of Canaan. See HAM. They lived under Hermon, in the land of Mizpeh (Josh. xi. 3), and in Lebanon as far as Hamath (Judg. iii. 3). Jacob bought a small field of Hamor, the Hivite, at Shalem near Shechem (Gen xxxiii. 18, xxxiv. 2). Esau married Aholibamah, a Hivite. The Hivites of Gibeon made a treaty with Joshua by a deceit (Josh. ix. 3); and for this act they were condemned to the temple service. AVIM.

HIZKI'AH. HEZEKIAH. Ancestor of Zephaniah (Zeph. i. 1).

HIZKI'JAH (Neh. x. 17). "Ater of Hizkijah."

HO'BAB (*beloved*). The father-in-law of Moses,

or, more probably, his brother-in-law (Num. x. 29 –32). He was an experienced sheikh, and valuable as a guide. See EXODUS.

HO'BAH (*hidden*; Gen. xiv. 15). Where Abraham's pursuit of the kings he defeated at Dan ended, north of Damascus. Three miles north-east of Damascus is a village called Jobar, where there is a synagogue dedicated to Elijah; and another village, Buzeh, near, in which there is a very ancient sanctuary of Abraham. Both places are offered as the site of Hobah.

HOD (*splendor*). Son of Zophah (1 Chr. vii. 37), of Asher.

HODAI'AH (*praise ye Jah*). Son of Elioenai (1 Chr. iii. 24).

HODAVI'AH. HODAIAH. 1. A man of Manasseh (1 Chr. v. 24).—2. Son of Hassenuah (1 Chr. ix. 7).—3. A Levite (Ezr. ii. 40). HODEVAH.

HO'DESH (*new moon*). Wife of Shaharaim (1 Chr. viii. 9).

HODE'VAH (Neh. vii. 4, 3). HODIJAH.

HODI'AH. Wife of Ezra (1 Chr. iv. 19).

HODI'JAH (*splendor of Jehovah*). 1. A Levite (Neh. viii. 7).—2. A Levite (x. 13).—3. Layman (x. 18).

HOG'LAH (*partridge*). Daughter of Zelophehad (Num. xxvi. 33). Heir.

HO'HAM (*Jah impels*). Canaanite. King of Hebron (Josh. x. 3).

HOLD. Place held by a garrison (Judg. ix., 46, 49).

HOLM-TREE. A species of oak. (History of Susanna, 58 v).

HŎLŌFER'NĒS (*symbolical*), (Jud. ii. 4). King over the Assyrians.

HO'LON (*abode*), (Josh. xv. 51). Judah, between Goshen and Giloh. Lost.—2. In Moab, in the Mishnor. HILEN. Lost.

HO'LY CHIL'DREN, THE SONG OF THE THREE. See HISTORY OF THE BOOKS.

HOMAM (*extermination*), (1 Chr. i. 39). Homaima, a ruin south of Petra, half-way to Ailath, on the ancient Roman road. The native city of the Abassides (Rob., B. R., ii. 572).

HO'MER (*a heap*). WEIGHTS AND MEASURES.

HON'EY (DEBASH, YAAR, NOPHET). The product of bees, of sweet gum bearing trees, of dates, of grapes, and other vegetables or fruit. Butter and honey mingled are eaten with bread in the morning.

HOOD. DRESS. HEAD DRESS.

HOOK, Hooks. Fishing hooks (HACCAH, Am. iv. 2); ring for the nose (CHOACH, Job xli. 2). (See page 28, for ring in the lips of prisoners). Hooks in the pillars of the tabernacle (VAVIM, Ex. xxvi. 32); pruning-hook (MAZMERAH, Is. ii. 4); pot-hook for a cook (MAZLEG, 1 Sam. ii. 13); butcher's hooks (SHEPHATTAYIM, Ez. xl. 43).

HOPH'NI (*fighter*), and PHIN'EAS. Two sons of Eli, priests at Shiloh.

HOR, MOUNT (HAR, *mountain*), (Num. xx. 25). On the edge of Edom, not far from Kadesh and Zalmonah. Aaron was buried here (22–29). The ascent is very steep and difficult—rocky; and on its summit is a rude building called Aaron's tomb. (See page 1.) Juniper grows almost to the top. The view from the summit is very extensive in every direction; on the north the passes of Akrabbim, where the Jews were defeated, and the mountains around the Dead Sea; on the east, the rugged range of Edom (with the Deir, or convent of Petra, in sight), red, bare, and desolate; southward,

the wide downs of Mt. Seir; and westward the Arabah, with its hundred water-courses; and above it the great white wilderness, fading into the hot and trembling distance. 5,000 feet high.

HŌ'RAM (*hight*). King of Gezer (Josh. x. 33).

HŌ'REB (*dried up*). SINAI. EXODUS.

HŌ'REM (Josh. xix. 38). Naphtali. Hurah, a ruin on a low tell in Wady Ain, west of and near Merom.

HORHAGID'GAD. GUDGODAH. (Num.xxxiii.32).

HŌRI (*lives in caverns*). 1. Son of Lotan (Gen. xxxvi. 22).—2. (Gen.xxxvi.30) "Hori."—3. Father of Shaphet (Num. xiii. 5).

HORITE. **HORITES**. Inhabitants of Mount Seir. (Gen. xiv. 6).

HORMAH (*destruction, cursed*), (Judg. i. 17). Zephath. City of a king, in the south of Palestine (Josh. xii. 14). El Sufa, S. E. of the Dead Sea. See EXODUS.

HORN (KEREN). Horns on cattle; often used as weapons—for which see ARMS—and for trumpets for calling workmen to dinner, the soldiers to the field, and for announcing religious ceremonies. Used also for bottles. The elephant's tusks were called horns (from their shape), as also trumpets of metal. The summit of a hill was a horn, as also the corners of the altar for burnt-offerings. The modern

EGYPTIAN PRIESTS.

Druses wear a horn on the head for ornament, but it was not an ancient custom of the Hebrews. In poetry the horn is strength, and also a nation, or a king, or a god.

HORNET (ZIRAH). A winged insect, used as a figure by the poets and prophets (Ex. xxiii. 27, 28; Deut. vii. 20; Josh. xxiv. 11, 12) of a persistent warrior. There are four kinds in Palestine, all different from the European varieties. ZOREAH, hornet-town.

HORONA IM (*two caverns*), (Is. xv. 5; Jer. xlviii. 3, 5). Near Zoar, Luhith, Nimrim, on a declivity, beside a noted road. Lost.

HŌR'ONITE, or **HŌ'RONITE**. One from Horonaim. Sanballat (Neh. ii. 10).

HORSE (SUS). Not mentioned among Abraham's cattle, but first as coming from Egypt (Gen. xlvii. 17). The horse is almost exclusively used in war in Scripture, and is so sculptured on the monuments both of Egypt and Assyria. Job gives a most elegant description of a war-horse in ch. xxxix.19–25. "An horse is a vain thing for safety" (Ps. xxxiii. 17), said the poet and the prophet also (Deut. xvii. 16). Solomon disobeyed the letter and spirit of the prohibition not to multiply horses, and his successors also. Horses are used as symbols by the prophets, as in Zech. i. 8, "a man riding on a red horse;" and he also mentions speckled (or bay) and white horses. John, in Rev. vi., saw four horses go forth: white, red, black and livid (green), indicating the spiritual condition of the nations. White horses are an emblem of triumph and power. Successful generals rode in triumph on white horses (Rev. xix. 11–15).

HORSE-LEECH (ALUKAH). Very common in all

the stagnant waters and in the running brooks, clinging to stones. Used as a figure in Prov. xxx. 15.

HO′SAH (*refuge*), (Josh. xix. 29). Asher, not far from Tyre.—2. A Levite (1 Chr. xxvi. 10, 38).

HO′SAI (*seer*), (2 Chr. xxxiii. 19). CHOZAI.

HŌSAN′NA (*save now*). Ps. cxviii. was sung on joyful occasions, such as the feast of Tabernacles. Verses 25 and 26 were sung with loud acclamation. "Hosanna to the Son of David" in Matt. xxi. 9.

HOSĒ′A (*salvation*). A prophet, called of God, with Amos, to declare his word to Israel. See HISTORY OF THE BOOKS.

HOSHA′IAH (*Jah helps*). A leader of the princes of Judah to the wall of Jerusalem (Neh. xii. 32). —2. Father of Azariah (Jer. xlii. 1).

LIONS.

HOSH′AMA (*Jah hears*). A son of king Jeconiah (1 Chr. iii. 18).

HOSHE′A (*safety*). Hosea I, son of Nur (Deut. xxxii. 44). OSHEA, the prophet.—2. The last king of Israel (Is. vii. 16). Shalmanezer, king of Assyria, besieged and ended the kingdom of Israel B. C. 721 (2 K. xvii).—3. Son of Azaziah (1 Chr. xxvii. 30), and ruler of Ephraim.—4. One of the people who signed the covenant (Neh. x. 23).

HOSPITAL′ITY. One of the chief virtues among the Orientals, and it is most highly esteemed on the desert, being less needed and less valued in the towns. The ancient Egyptians limited their practice to their own people, having a superstitious dread of all foreigners. The O. T. is full of allusions to the rites and the divine commands for their practice, and instances of the national belief of the Hebrews in their value. The laws of Moses give many directions for special cases, as with the stranger, "for ye were strangers in the land of Egypt" (Lev. xix. 34), the poor, and the traveler. To break the law was a very great offense, as in the case of Benjamin at Gibeah (Judg. xiii 15, xix. 17–21). The good Samaritan stands for all ages as an example of Christian hospitality. The account of Abraham entertaining the three angels is a perfect picture of how a modern Bedawin sheikh would treat a traveler in our day. (See ABRAHAM). Oriental respect for the covenant of salt (and bread) is a part of the law of hospitality. To taste another's salt is to make yourself his friend for the time. In every village there is a *mewsil*, inn, for the use of travelers, where they are supplied with food by certain families near it. No money is paid, but presents may be made equivalent to the value of the articles used.

HOS′TAGES (2 K. xiv. 14; 2 Chr. xxv. 24).

HOTHAM (*a seal*). Son of Heber (1 Chr. vii. 32). HELEM 1.

HO′THAN. HOTHAM. Father of Shama (1 Chr. xi. 44).

HO′THIR (*superior*). Son of Heman (1 Chr. xxv. 4, 28).

HOUR. See CHRONOLOGY, p. 55.

HOUSE (BETH, *to pass the night*). A dwelling for man or cattle. House, tent, palace, tomb, tabernacle, temple; heaven; family. The houses of the rich are made of stone with two or more stories arched over the rooms and passage-ways, with fine stair-ways, supplied with wide galleries or verandahs, and open places for light and air, generally built around two or three sides of a court, in which is a fountain or pool of water. The wall next to the street is usually blank, with a small door, and a window or two, high up, and latticed. (See WINDOW). The door often has an inscription, seldom the name of the resident. The poor live in houses of mud, sun-dried, usually of one story, roofed with mud laid on poles which are covered with grass or palm-leaves. In the rainy season the rain leaks through (see DROPPING), if not prevented by rolling the mud with a stone roller. When of two storys the lower is for the use of animals and for storage. In hot countries people sleep on the roofs under tents of cloth, or booths of branches. The cool of the evening is also passed on the roof, when proclamation is made by the public crier of any command of the ruler, or news of any public kind. It is also a place for prayer. Some roofs have vines so trained as to form a shelter from the sun or neighbors. The space is found useful for drying grain, fruit, and clothing from the wash. Stairways lead from the roof to the ground in the court without passing into the house. It is quite usual to build pigeon-houses of bottles on the battlements, and sparrows build their own nests in any corner or hole, even plugging up the chimneys (Ps. lxxxiv., cii. 7), and are caught in great numbers, being almost worthless (Matt. x. 29.) Very large houses, convents, and inns, have several courts, connected by passages. South of Nablus (Shechem) the roof is supplied with domes for lighting and enlarging the rooms below. The upper room or chamber is the choice place, given only to strangers or friends of distinction. The sculptures in Egypt and Assyria present houses of more than one story. The guest room, or divan, is provided with seats all around the room, except by the doors, like wide, low sofas; no chairs are used. The Romans and Greeks used chairs and reclining seats or sofas around the table at banquets. (See p. 33). The walls are often ornamented with carvings of wood, and sometimes painted in beautiful patterns. (See CARPENTER). The furniture is much more simple than ours, and less expensive, except in the houses of the rich. (See CORNERSTONE, BRICK, ROOF).

HUK′KOK (*incision*), (Josh. xix. 34). On the south border of Asher and Naphtali. *Yakuk*, in the Wady el Amud. An ancient Jewish tradition locates the tomb of Habakkuk here (Benj. of Tudela, ii. 421).

HUL (*region*), (Gen. x. 23). Second son of Aram, grandson of Shem. The plain or valley of the Jordan north of Lake Merom is called Ard el Huleh, and the lake's most ancient name is Huleh, and it is still so called by the Arabs.

HUL′DAH (*weasel*), a prophetess (2 K. xxii. 14; 2 Chr. xxxiv. 22), whose husband, Shallum, was master of the wardrobe to king Josiah (2 K. xxii.

14). Huldah was famous as an oracle when Jeremiah was a boy in the school at Anathoth.

HUM'TAH (*lizards*), (Josh. xv. 54). Judah, in the hill country.

HUNTING. The Hebrews were not given to hunting, except for the protection of their fields or families from wild beasts. The names of many places indicate that wild game was plentiful, even to a degree of danger. Thomson (*Land and Book*) says it is still plenty in some places, especially in Galilee.

HU'PHAM (*coast-man*). Son of Benjamin (Num. xxvi. 39). HUPPIM.

HU'PHAMITES. Descendants of Hupham (Num. xxvi. 39).

HUP'PAH (*covering*) A priest (1 Chr. xxiv. 13), of the 13th course.

HUP'PIM (*screen*). A Benjamite (1 Chr. vii. 12).

HUR. A man with Moses and Aaron in the battle with Amalek (Ex. xvii. 10); husband of Miriam.—2. Son of Hur (Ex. xxxi. 2).—3. One of the 5 kings of Midian (Num. xxxi. 8).—4. Father of Rephaiah (Neh. iii. 9).—5. Son of Hur; an officer for Solomon (1 K. iv. 8).

HU'RAI (*noble*). One of David's guard (1 Chr. xi. 32). HIDDAI.

HURAM (*high-born*). 1. Son of Bela (1 Chr. xiii. 5).—2. King of Tyre (1 Chr. xiv. 1).—3. Hiram, the artificer (ii. 13). He was called Ab (father), a title of respect, used now in the East, and the origin of the title of the Bishop of Rome (*pope, father*).

HU'RI. Father of Abihail (1 Chr. v. 14).

HU'SHAH (*haste*), (1 Chr. iv. 4) A town built by Ezer.

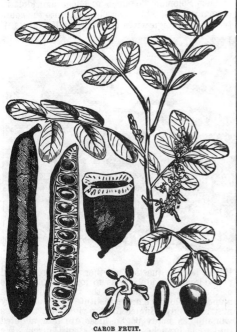

CAROB FRUIT.

HU'SHAI (*hasting*). An Archite (2 Sam. xv. 32 ff.). A friend of David (xv. 37). Probably the father of Baanah 3. (1 K. iv. 16).

HU'SHAM (*haste*). King of Edom (Gen. xxxvi. 34, 35).

HU'SHATHITES. One from Husha. Two of David's guard. 1. Sibbechai (Hittite?), (2 Sam. xxi. 18).—2. Mebunnai (2 Sam. xxiii. 27).

HU'SHIM. 1. Children of Dan (Gen. xlvi. 23). —2. A Benjamite (1 Chr. vii. 12).—3. One of the wives of Shaharaim (viii. 8).

HUSKS (Gr. *keratia*). The fruit of the carob tree, which is very common in the East, and the Greek islands, where it is in great request for fattening hogs. It has a sweetish pulp when tender. The ripe pods (10 inches long) are dry and have seeds like beans. See HONEY. The leaves are like our ash, but dark and glossy. It blossoms in February and the pods are ripe in May.

HUZ. Nahor's elder son (Gen. xxii. 21) "And Buz his brother." There is a district of Kaseem, in Arabia, which some suppose to be the land of Uz (Job i. 1). See Palgrave's *Journey in Arabia*.

HUZ'ZAB (*fixed*). Queen of Nineveh? (Nah. ii. 7). Country of Zab, that is, the river.

HYDAS'PES. A river (Judith i. 6), in connection with the Euphrates and Tigris. Choaspes of Susiana.

HY'ENA. Not mentioned by name in the O. T. as translated, but meant in the original by the word ZEBUA (Ar. *dabba*), which is rendered *streaked bird* in Jer. xii. 9 (Hyena in the Sept.). Valley of Zeboim (hyenas in 1 Sam. xiii. 18). It is still found in numbers, ready to attack wounded, dying, or dead animals, eating all, even the very bones, its jaws being most powerful. Their flesh is not eaten, having a bad odor.

HYMENE'US One of the earliest Gnostics, who argued that the resurrection was passed already (1 Tim. i. 20; 2 Tim. ii. 17, 18).

HYMN. "In psalms, and hymns, and spiritual songs." The Greek word *Umnos*, or *humnos*, means a song (in praise of Deity), as a part of worship, and there are several collections of such as were used in ancient times, written by Callimachus, Orpheus, Homer, Linus, Sappho, and others. Jesus and his disciples sang a hymn before going out, on the eve of the last supper (Matt. xxvi. 30). The words used are supposed to have been Ps. cxv; cxviii, called the Hallel. Paul and Silas sang hymns in prison at Philippi (Acts xvi. 25; Gr. *humnoun*, praises); and Paul commends their use in his epistles (Eph. v. 19; Col. iii. 16). The hymn differs from the psalm in thought and composition. The different meters were adopted from the Greek models.

HYSSOP (EZOR; Gr. *hussopos*). The Arabic *zufä* is a plant growing on a slender square stem, free from thorns, or spreading branches, ending in a cluster of heads, having

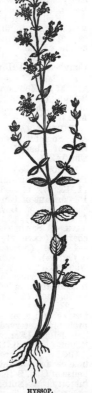

HYSSOP.

a pleasant aromatic odor, growing on the walls in Palestine. No plant in the East is better fitted for purposes of sprinkling. Its leaves are often eaten (like summer savory) with bread.

I

I AM, and **I AM THAT I AM.** JAH.

IB'HAR (*chosen*). Son of David (2 Sam. v. 15).

IB'LEAM. Bil'eam (1 Chr. vi. 70; Josh. xvii. 11). Given to Manasseh, but in Asher. Jelama, north of Jenin, is perhaps the site. Ahaziah was wounded here by Jehu's soldiers (2 K. ix. 27).

IBNEI'AH (*Jah will build*). Son of Jehoram (1 Chr. ix. 8).

IBNI'JAH. IBNEIAH. A Benjamite (1 Chr. ix. 8).

IB'RI. HEBREW. A Levite (1 Chr. xxiv. 27).

IB'ZAN (*of tin*). A native of Bethlehem. Judge of Israel for seven years (Judg. xii. 8, 10). He had thirty sons and thirty daughters. BOAZ.

ICE. FROST. Ice is very rare in the plains and hills, and only familiar on the highest mountains.

ICHABOD (*wo, or departed glory*). Son of Phinehas (1 Sam. iv. 21). So named by his mother, who died at hearing of the loss of the Ark of God, her husband, and father-in-law, at the battle of Aphek.

ICO'NIUM (Acts xiii. 51). Konieh, a large city; is on a table-land, a fertile plain, near a semicircle of snow-capped mountains in Asia Minor. This level district was Lycaonia, of which Cicero says it was the capital. It was on the route leading from Ephesus to Tarsus, Antioch, and the Euphrates. Here Paul was stoned, and left for dead (xiv. 19). The city is built out of the ruins of the ancient structures, and pieces of marble columns, capitals, and carved cornices appear everywhere in the masonry. It is now quite large, the residence of a pasha, surrounded with beautiful groves and gardens, well watered, and the resort of pilgrims who visit a saint's tomb. In the middle ages it was the capital of the Seljukian Sultans, and is called the cradle of the Ottoman empire. The traditional story of Paul and Thecla is located here. (See Conybeare and Howson's Life of Paul).

ID'ALAH (Josh. xix. 15). Zebulon. Semuniyeh, 3 ms. S. of Beit-lahur, was near it.

ID'BASH (*honey-ed*). Son of "the father of Elam," (1 Chr. iv. 3).

ID'DO (*timely*). 1. Father of Ahinadab (1 K. iv. 14).—2. Descendant of Gershom, son of Levi (1 Chr. vi. 21). ADAIAH.—3. Son of Zechariah (xxvii. 21). —4. YEDOI, (*born on a festival*). A seer who had a "vision" which concerned Jeroboam and alluded to Solomon (2 Chr. ix. 29). He wrote a history and a genealogy, which are lost, but are probably preserved in part in "Chronicles."—5. Son of Id'do (Ezr. v. 1).—6. A chief; one of the Nethinim (Ezr. viii. 17, 20).

IDOL. There are 21 Hebrew words for idols or images for worship. 1. AVEN, *nought* (Beth*el*, house of God, Beth*aven*, house of vanity), nothing, iniquity; 2. ELIL, *no god*, as contrasted with ELOHIM, *God;* 3. EMAH, *terror;* 4. MIPHLETSETH, *horror* (Phallus, the productive power of nature and the nature-goddess Ashera; Priapus); 5. BOSHETH, *shameful;* 6. GILLULIM, *filthy gods;* 7. SHIKKUZ, *impurity;* 8. SEMEL, *likeness;* 9. ZELEM,

shadow; 10. TEMUNAH, *model;* 11. ATSAB, *shape;* 12. EZAB, *fashion;* 13. OTSEB, *figure;* 14. ZIR, *a shape;* 15. MAZZEBAH, *statue;* 16. CHAMMANIM, *sun-images;* 17. MASCHITH, *device;* 18. TERAPHIM, *idols* (see TERAPHIM); 19. PESEL, *carved image;* 20. PESILIM, *graven images* (quarries, in Judg. iii. 19, 26); 21. NESEC, *molten image;* MASSEKAH, *shaped in a mould.* These various terms are obscure, because very little material has come down to us from antiquity which fixes the form of these images. Jeremiah described in a sarcastic way how these so-called gods were made, but he did not give an idea of the particular shape. All of these terms expressed worthlessness and vanity, contempt and abhorrence.

IDOLATRY (TERAPHIM; Gr. *idolatreia*). The worship of deity made visible, whether of true or false ideas, in images, pictures, stars, fire, or ideal statements, as shown in business pursuits or in pleasure, or for honor, where self is preferred above the honor and glory of God. Nearly three in four of all the human race are open idolaters; and if judged by the strict moral sense of the term, very many of the other fourth worship self rather than God (Col. iii. 5). By the Jewish law the idolater was to be stoned to death, and a city given up to it was to be wholly destroyed, with all it contained (Deut. xiii. 12, xvii. 2). The laws of Moses imply that idolatry was known to him, and the paintings and sculptures of Egypt prove its existence there before the time of Moses, but the earliest mention in the Bible is in the incident of Rachel stealing her father's teraphim (images in Gen. xxxi. 19), by which he was guided, as some who consult the clairvoyant or other "fortune-tellers" of our day (a species of idolatry very prevalent among the ignorant and superstitious). The story of Micah and his images shows how widespread the custom was in the age succeeding Joshua and the elders. Solomon did much to encourage idolatry of many kinds, which were brought into the country by his foreign wives (1 K. xi. 7; 2 K. xxiii. 13).

ICONIUM.

It has been a question whether the Hebrews did not so lapse into idolatry as to lose all knowledge of the true God. They lost the true sound of his name, for which we now substitute Jehovah. They may have only mingled foreign rites with the true worship, as many pagan ideas are now adopted into some branches of the Christian Church. We know that the Hebrews worshiped the sun (Baal), moon (Astarte, Diana), the stars (Ashtoreth, Mazzaloth in Job), planets Chiun or Remphan (Saturn, Acts vii. 40–43), and made representations of celestial bodies or ideas, in human form, for worship, as of the sun, moon and stars (Hera, Diana, see

HERA, Cybele, Apollo, Adonis [Tammuz, in 2 K. xxi. 3], Venus, etc.); of KEN, in Egypt, and MY-LITTA, in Nineveh; and also images of beasts, as the ox (Ps. cvi. 20); Aaron's and Jeroboam's bull-calf; and of a goat (Ashima); fly (Beelzebub); a cock (Nergal); and fish (Dagon); the dog (Nibhaz); the mule and peacock (Adrammelech); the horse and pheasant (Anammelech). The Assyrians (Samaritans also) had a system of ancestor-worship (Asshur and others), and also a lower nature-worship, including the elements, trees, etc. The scape-goat of the Day of Atonement is a re-cognition of the existence of Satan (Typhon in Egyptian system), but was not a worship of that being, for only sins were sent to Azazel, nothing choice or precious.

The Christian Church now holds that God has sanctioned but one image, which was made by himself, for man's worship, which is the intelli-gent, rational, holy nature of man, which appears in all completeness and perfection in Jesus the Christ, and is reflected in his followers as they have more or less received the spirit of the gospel. "God is a spirit, and they that worship him must worship in spirit and in truth" (John iv. 24).

IDUME'A. Greek form of EDOM.

IDUME'ANS. EDOMITES. People of Idumea (2 Macc. x. 15, 16).

I'GAL (*El will avenge*). 1. A spy, son of Jo-seph (Num. xiii. 7).—2. One of David's men, son of Nathan (2 Sam. xxiii. 36; Joel 8).

IGDALI'AH (*Jah will make great*). Father of Hanan (Jer. xxxv. 4).

I'GEAL—IGAL. Son of Shemaiah (1 Chr. iii. 22).

I'IM (*ruins*). Ije Abarim (Num. xxxiii. 45). Lost.—2. Judah, south; near Beersheba (Josh. xv. 28). Lost. AZEM?

I'IM. JIM (Is. xiii. 22). BEAST.

IJE-AB'ARIM (*heaps, or ruins of Abarim*), (Num. xxi. 11). This region, east of the Dead Sea, is still unexplored by any Christian traveler in our day, and therefore it is impossible to say whether the stations of the Israelites can be located or not.

I'JON (*ruin*), (1 K. xv. 20; 2 K. xv. 29). In the N. Jordan valley, now called Tell Dibbin. The hill is a favorable site for a city, overlooking the whole plain of Merj Aiyun, and on the road leading from the coast into the interior.

IK'KESH (*perverse*). Father of Ira (2 Sam. xxiii. 26).

I'LAI (*supreme*). An Ahohite (1 Chr. xi. 29). ZALMON.

ILLYR'ICUM (Rom. xv. 19). Paul preached the gospel of Christ "from Jerusalem round about unto Illyricum." A country on the east shore of the Adriatic Sea, north of Epirus. Illyricum was at one time one of the four great divisions of the Roman empire, and included the whole country between the Adriatic, the Danube, the Black Sea, and Macedonia (Gibbon, c. i).

IM'LA (*full*). Father of Micaiah (2 Chr. xviii. 7, 8). Im'lah in 1 K. xxii. 8, 9.

IMMAN'UEL (*with us El, or God with us*). The name of the child (prophetic) which was to be given to the house of David (Is. vii. 14). Isaiah bids Ahaz ask a sign of Jehovah, which he, with pretended humility, refused to do, when this sign of a child by a virgin (virgin is a young woman), was given, and, as some think, the prophesy was fulfilled within a few years, and others look on the child as a type of Jesus the Christ, as seems to be the meaning in Matt. i. 23.

IM'MER (*talkative*). 1. Head of a family of priests (1 Chr. ix. 12; Ezr. ii. 37, x. 20).—2. A place in Babylonia (Ezr. ii. 59; Neh. vii. 61).

IMMORTAL'ITY (Gr. *athanasia*, deathless, not mortal). The Christian believes that the human

soul will never die. Some hold the doctrine that only those who believe on Christ will be blessed with immortality, while those who deny him will die (Rom. ii. 7; 2 Tim. i. 10). The same Greek word is also rendered incorruption in 1 Cor. xv. 42, etc., and sincerity in Eph. vi. 24, etc.

IM'NA (*whom God keeps back*). Son of Helem (1 Chr. vii. 55).

IM'NAH (*good fortune*) (JIMNA, JIMNAH). 1. First born of Asher (1 Chr. vii. 30).—2. Father of Kore (2 Chr. xxxi. 14).

BROAD-TAIL SHEEP.

IMPUTE' (*to reckon to one what does not belong to him*). (Heb. HASHAB Lev. vii. 18; Ps. xxxii. 2); and rendered "to think" in Gen. l. 20; and "to count" in Lev. xxv. 27, etc., "to reckon," "to es-teem," "to devise," and "to imagine," in other places.—SUM, in 1 Sam. xxii. 15; "to put" in Gen. ii. 8; "to make" in xxi. 13.—3. Greek *ellegeo* in Rom. v. 13; "to put on account" in Philemon 18. —4. *logizomai*, in Rom. iv. 6, etc.; "to reason" in Mark xi. 31; and by several other terms.

IM'RAH (*refractory*). A chief of Asher (1 Chr. vii. 36).

IM'RI (*eloquent*). 1. A man of the family of Pharez (1 Chr. ix. 4).—2. Father of Zaccur 4 (Neh. iii. 2).

IN'CENSE (Heb. KETORAH, LEBONAH; Gr. *thu-miama*). A compound of sweet-smelling gums used in acts of worship, and forbidden in private life (Ex. xxx. 27). The mixture is said to have been equal parts of stacte, onycha, frankincense, galbanum. The altar of incense was placed in front of the veil, from which on the great Day of Atonement the high-priest could raise a cloud of perfume which covered the mercy-seat (entered within and filled the holy of holies). It was a type of Christian prayer.

IN'DIA (Esth. i. 1, viii. 9). The extent of the kingdom of Ahasuerus was from India to Ethiopia, 127 provinces. Acts ii. 9, instead of Judæa read India. The country around the river Indus, now the Punjaub, which Herodotus describes as part of Darius' empire (iii. 98). At a later period it was conquered by Alexander. The name is found in the inscriptions at Persepolis (1 Macc. viii. 8). Modern India, or Hindostan, is more extensive than the ancient. The articles obtained by Solo-mon from the East were Indian, such as horns of ivory, ebony, broidered work and rich apparel, sandal-wood, apes, peacocks, and tin.

IN'GATHERING, FEAST OF (Ex. xxiii. 16). TABERNACLES, FEAST OF.

INN (Heb. MALON). A lodging-place for the night. Only a room is to be had, the traveler must supply himself with furniture, bed, etc. They were built generally two stories high, and near wa-ter. One is mentioned in the history of Joseph (Gen. xlii. 27), and by Moses in his day (Ex. iv. 24), by Jeremiah; the habitation (inn) of Chimham (xli. 17), and the same by Luke, where Jesus was born (ii. 7). The Good Samaritan is said to have left money (in our standard about $2.50) to pay charges at the inn (Luke xxii). The inn is usually built around a yard, having a well or fountain, and entered by a gate which can be closed against intruders at night. The baggage and animals occupy the lower rooms and the people the upper and better chambers. When the upper rooms were full of crowds at feast times, the late comers would be obliged to take a lower room, among the animals ("in the manger").

INSPIRA'TION (from the Latin, *in-breathing*). The supernatural influence of God's spirit on the human mind, by which prophets, apostles, and other sacred writers were qualified to record divine truth without error. Others hold that is only a divine impression on the mind, by which the understanding is informed. "All Scripture is given by inspiration of God" (2 Tim. iii. 16).

I'RAD. ARAD? JARED. Son of Enoch (Gen. iv. 18).

I'RAM (*duke, sheikh*), (Gen. xxxvi. 43). Where Iram was is not known. Probably either in or near Edom, if not an original component of Idumea.

IRHA'HERES (*the city of the sun*). The sacred city Heliopolis (its Greek name), or On, in Egypt (Is. xix. 18). Beth Shemesh, in Jer. xliii. 13. (See ON).

I'RI. IRAM. 1. Son of Bela (1 Chr. vii. 7). IR.—2. URIAH.—3. (1 Esd. viii. 62).

IRI'JAH (*founded*). Son of Shelemiah (Jer. xxxvii. 13, 14).

IR'NAHASH (*serpent city*). BETHLEHEM? (1 Chr. iv. 12). NAHASH.

I'RON (Josh. xix. 38). Naphtali. Sarun.

I'RON (Heb. BARZEL; Chal *parzlah*. The references are many to iron, and as early as the time of Tubal-Cain (Gen. iv. 22). A furnace of iron is taken as the image of the bondage in Egypt (Deut. iv. 20). Iron knives (or steel) are drawn on the monuments in Egypt. The remains of ancient Nineveh furnish articles of iron coated with bronze, which has preserved them. Tin melts at 470°, copper, silver and gold at 1800°, and cast iron at 3000°, while malleable iron requires a higher degree, but furnaces of clay, fed with charcoal and supplied with a blast of air from two skin-bellows, are used successfully in the East.

IR'PEEL (*restored by God*), (Josh. xviii. 27). Benjamin. Lost.

IR'SHEMESH (*mount of the sun*), (Josh. xix. 41). Danite city. MOUNT HERES. BETHSHEMESH?

I'RU (IRAM?). Son of CALEB (1 Chr. iv. 15).

I'SAAC (Heb. YIZHAK, *laughing*). Born at Gerar, B. C. 1896, of Sarah (who was 90) and Abraham (who was 100), in fulfilment of a divine promise (Gen. xxi. 17; Gal. iv. 29). When three years old,

BUTTERFLIES OF PALESTINE.

INSTANT. IN'STANTLY (Luke xii. 4; xxiii. 23). Pressing, at once.

INTERCES'SION. Prayer for (or against) others (Jer. vii. 16; Rom. xi. 2).

INTERPRETATION (*explanation*). Making known clearly.

IO'NIA. That part of the coast of Asia Minor which is between Doris and Æolis. Ionia was celebrated for its 13 cities and its islands. The chief cities were Ephesus, Smyrna, Samos, Chios and Miletus (Jos. Ant. xvi. 2, 3). India in 1 Macc. viii. 8.

IPHEDEI'AH (*Jah sets free*). Son of Shashak (1 Chr. viii. 25).

IR (*city*). IRI (1 Chr. vii. 12).

I'RA (*wakeful*). 1. "The JAIRITE," one of David's officers (2 Sam. xx. 26).—2. "The ITHRITE," one of David's guard (xxiii. 38; 1 Chr. xi. 40).—3. Son of Ikkesh, captain of the 6th monthly course (2 Sam. xxiii. 26).

at the feast made on the day he was weaned, he was mocked by Ishmael with pretended homage (as the child of the promise and type of the Messiah) which so offended his mother that his half-brother and his mother Hagar were sent away (Heb. xi. 17; James ii. 20). At maturity he almost fell a victim to his father's faith on the altar as a burnt-offering. He was married at the age of 40 to his beautiful cousin Rebekah, but was tormented with jealous fear (as his father was) that some powerful chief would carry her off for her beauty. In his old age he was deceived by his wife and her favorite son Jacob, who got from him the patriarchal blessing which belonged to Esau by birth-right. At the age of 60 his two sons, Esau and Jacob were born. In his 75th year he and his brother Ishmael buried their father Abraham, who died at Mamre, in the cave of Machpelah, beside Isaac's mother, Sarah. He lived in tents, and mostly in the south-country (Negeb), where several places are mentioned as his residence for a time. When his father died he was at Beer-lahai-roi, from which the famine drove him to Gerar, where Abimelech put him in fear of losing his wife, when he practiced the same deception that his father did in the same place a few years before. The Philistines envied his prosperity, and jealous of his increasing power (and disliking his religion?), tried to drive him out by filling up his wells; but he dug new ones. One of those which he was permitted to use in peace, quite a distance fronf Gerar, he named Rehoboth (*room*, i. e., *room enough at last*). The promise to Abraham was repeated to Isaac at Beersheba, where he sunk a well as a memorial, and built an altar. The well remains, but the altar has disappeared. He made peace with Abimelech there also, and dug another well as a memorial (well of the oath). His first great grief was the undutiful conduct of his son Esau in marrying two young Canaanite women. His eyesight failed many years before his death; but he lived to enjoy the return to him at Hebron of Jacob, with his large family and great wealth in flocks and herds. He died at the age of 180, and was buried beside his father, in the cave of Machpelah, by his sons Esau and Jacob. His character is very severely criticised, especially for the denial of his wife at Gerar, and so exposing her to danger; and in allowing Jacob to enjoy the fruit of his deception. He was a gentle and dutiful son, and a faithful and constant husband of one wife.

ISA'IAH (*Jah is helper*). See HISTORY OF THE BOOKS.

ISCAH (*she looks forth*). Niece of Abraham, daughter of Haran, and sister of Milcah and Lot. A Jewish tradition identifies her with Sarah. Abraham said she was the daughter of his father, but not of his mother (Gen. xx. 12). She might have been a grandchild, or any degree of descent (see DAUGHTER).

ISH'BAH (*praising*). In the line of Judah, father of Eshtemoa (1 Chr. iv. 17).

ISH'BAK (*leaving*). Son of Abraham and Keturah (Gen. xxv. 2), progenitor of a tribe in N. Arabia, called *Sabak* or *Sibak*, an extensive and fertile tract in Nejed, inhabited by the Beni Temeem. Shobek is the name of a ruined castle on a hill 12 ms. N. of Petra, which was a stronghold of the Crusaders, and called by them Mons Regalis.

ISH'BIBENOB (*his seat at Nob*). Son of Rapha, a Philistine giant, killed by Abishai (2 Sam. xxi. 16).

ISHBO'SHETH (*of shame*). Youngest of Saul's 4 sons, and his legal successor. His name was originally Esh'baal. He was 40 years old when he began to reign, and reigned two years at Mahanaim, while Abner was contending with David's generals (2 Sam. iii. 10). He fell a victim to revenge for some crime of his father, but David punished the murderers.

ISH'I (*saving*). 1. A descendant of Judah, son of Appaim (1 Chr. ii. 31).—2. Son of Zoheth (iv. 20).—3. Head of a family of Simeon (iv. 42).—4. A chief of Manasseh E. of Jordan (v. 24).

ISH'I (*my husband*), (Hos. ii. 16). Symbolical name.

ISHI'AH (*whom Jah lends*). The last one of Izrahiah's five sons, a chief in David's time (1 Chr. vii. 3).

ISHI'JAH. ISHIAH. One of the sons of Harim (Ezr. x. 31).

ISH'MA (*waste*). A descendant of Etam (1 Chr. iv. 3), in the line of Judah.

ISH'MAEL (*whom God hears*). Son of Abraham and Hagar (Gen. xvi. 15, 16). First-born of the patriarch. Born at Mamre, but was sent into the wilderness south of Beersheba, Paran, when he was 16 years old. He had a wife from Egypt (xxi. 21), who was mother of his 12 sons, besides a daughter. Esau married his daughter. His sons were Nebajoth, Kedar, Abdeel, Mibsam, Mishma, Dumah, Massa, Hadar, Tema, Jetur, Naphish, and Kedema. The Arabic historians divide the Arabs into two races: 1. Pure Arabs, descendants of Joktan; and 2. Mixed Arabs, descendants of Ishmael. Like the sons of Isaac his brother, or rather Jacob, Ishmael's sons were founders of tribes, some of which are known in history by their names; and "they dwelt from Havilah unto Shur that is before Egypt" (Gen. xxv. 18). Their language is spoken all over Arabia, with very few exceptions, and is the same in all rules and idioms now as in most ancient times; and the poetical, or rhyming, and the current language, are one and the same, with a different arrangement of words only. The prophesy, "He shall be a wild ass of a man, his hand against every man, and every man's hand against him," is now and ever has been true;

PHARAOH'S PALACE.

and also the other saying, Ishmael "shall dwell in the presence of all his brethren," for they have always been free. The desert is called in Arabic, Bedu, and the genuine Arab calls himself Bedawee (*desert-man*), Bedawin (*desert-men*). 4000 years have not changed their disposition, manners, habits, occupation, government, or dress.

ISHMAI'AH (*Jah hears*). Son of Obadiah (1 Chr. xxvii. 19).

ISH'MEELITE (1 Chr. ii. 17), and Ishmelites (Gen. xxxvii. 25, 27, 28). Descendants of Ishmael.

ISH'MERAI (*Jehovah keeps*). A Benjamite (1 Chr. viii. 18).

I'SHOD (*man of glory*). Son of Hammoleketh (1 Chr. vii. 18).

ISH'PAN (*bald*). A Benjamite (1 Chr. viii. 22).

ISH'TOB (2 Sam. x. 6, 8). A small kingdom on the east of Jordan, in Aram.

ISH'ŪAH (*even*). Son of Asher (Gen. xlvi. 17).

ISH'UĀI. (ISHUAH.) Son of Asher (1 Chr. vii. 30).

ISH'UI. (ISHUAI.) Son of Saul (1 Sam. xiv. 49), by Ahinoam.

ISLE (Heb. IYIM; Greek *nesion, nesos, a habitable place*). Dry land (Is. xlii. 15); islands, coasts of the sea, or land in the sea, which were far away, and to be reached by crossing the sea (Ps. lxxii. 10).

ISHMACHI'AH (*Jah upholds*). An overseer of offerings under King Hezekiah (2 Chr xxxi. 13).

ISHMAI'AH or ISMAIAH. A chief (1 Chr. xii. 4).

IS'PAH. ISHPAN. A Benjamite chief (1 Chr. viii. 16).

IS'RAEL (*soldier of God*). The name given to Jacob at the time he wrestled with the angel at Peniel.—2. It was also used as the name of the Hebrew nation.—3. The north kingdom, not including Judah.

KINGS OF IS-RAEL.	REIGN	B. C.	KINGS OF JU-DAH.	REIGN	QUEENS IN JUDAH.
1 Jeroboam -	22	975	Rehoboam	7	Naamah.
		957	Abijah - -	3	Michaiah.
			Asa - - - -	41	Maachah.
2 Nadab - - -	2	954			
3 Baasha - - -	24	953			
4 Elah - - - -	2	930			
5 Timri - - - -	0	929			
6 Omri - - - -	12	929			
7 Ahab - - - -	22	918			
		914	Jehoshaphat	25	Azubah.
8 Ahaziah - -	2	898			
9 Jehoram - -	12	896			
		892	Jehoram -	8	
		885	Ahaziah - -	1	Athaliah.
10 Jehu - - - -	28	884	Athaliah -	6	
		878	Jehoash -	40	Zibiah.
11 Jehoahaz -	17	856			
12 Jehoash - -	16	841			
		839	Amaziah -	29	Jehoaddan.
13 Jeroboam II	41	825			
		810	Uzziah - -	52	Jecholiah.
Interregnum.	11				
14 Zachariah -	0	773			
15 Shallum - -	0	772			
16 Menahem -	10	772			
17 Pekahiah -	2	761			
18 Pekah - - -	20	759			
		758	Jotham - -	16	Jerusha.
		742	Ahaz - - -	16	
2d Interregnum.	9				
19 Hoshea - - -	9	730			
			Hezekiah -	29	Abi.
Samaria taken -		721			
		698	Manasseh -	55	Hephzibah.
		643	Amon - - -	2	Meshullemeth.
		641	Josiah - - -	31	Jedidah.
		610	Jehoahaz -	0	Hamutal.
		610	Jehoiachim	11	Zebudah.
		599	Jehoiachin	0	Nehushta
		599	Zedekiah -	11	Hamutal.
		588	Jerusalem destroyed.		

ISRAEL, KINGDOM OF. The ten tribes which were divided to Jeroboam by the prophet Ahijah of Shiloh (1 K. xi. 31, 35), leaving Judah alone to the house of David; Benjamin, Simeon, and Dan joining Judah afterward. SHECHEM was the first capital (1 K. xii. 25); TIRZAH the second (xiv. 17); and SAMARIA the third. Jezreel was occasionally a royal residence. The holy cities were Dan (Paneas) and Bethel. The population was at one time over 3 millions, if the number in the armies is correct as given in 2 Chr. xiii. 3. The area of the whole country, in the time of Solomon, occupied by the twelve tribes, was 12,810 sq. ms., of which 9,375 belonged to Israel and 3,435 to Judah. New Hampshire has about 9,000 sq. ms. Ephraim and Judah had always been rivals, and were nearly matched in numbers from the first, and the two largest of the twelve. For three, or, perhaps, nearly four centuries, the ark was in the territory of Ephraim, at Shiloh, until the time of Eli. But when the theocracy was superseded by the kingdom, Saul, the king, was a Benjamite, and Solomon, the son of David, of Judah; but Jeroboam, the leader of the revolt, was an Ephraimite, and, before Solomon's death was accused of treason, and fled to Egypt. The burdensome taxes of Solomon's reign probably hastened, if it did not cause the revolt of the ten tribes; and the death of Solomon was the notice for Jeroboam's return, and the establishment of the new kingdom of Israel, B. C. 975. This was the most important event, and the greatest misfortune, since Joshua crossed the Jordan. Some of the mistakes which were fatal were: The driving out of the Levites from their possessions, for they carried with them their sacred character and powerful support of the king; the alliance with the kings of Egypt and Damascus; the marriage of Ahab with Jezebel, of Phœnicia. The want of a system of union among the tribes composing the kingdom, and the presence of a large number of slaves, were other elements of weakness. The Philistines took some towns; Damascus took its chances for plunder and revenge; Edom and Moab rescued themselves; and Assyria, after many visits to the once rich and prosperous country, finally carried away the gleanings of so many years of religious decline, moral debasement, national degradation, anarchy, bloodshed, and deportation.

IS'RAELITE. Descendant of ISRAEL. HEBREW. JEW (2 Sam. xvii. 25).

IS'SACHAR (*hire*), (Gen. xxx. 17), (Heb. ISASCAR). Ninth son of Jacob and fifth son of Leah. He is not mentioned again as a person—his name only, as the name of a tribe. In the order of march in the desert, Issachar's place was on the east of the tabernacle, with Judah and Zebulon. Only the tribes of Judah and Dan outnumbered them at the passage of the Jordan, Issachar having 64,300 fighting men. (For location, see map of the Twelve Tribes). Its location and boundaries are recorded in Josh. xix. 17-23. Its land was and is now the richest in Palestine. Esdraëlon, the plain (called Jezreel, the seed-plot of God, on account of its rich soil), Mt. Tabor, and Gilboa were in its border, and the river Kishon ran through it. Jacob blessed Issachar in the image of "a strongboned he-ass, couching down between two hedgerows," which is a picture of contented ease and quiet. When David took the census, near the close of his reign, Issachar had 87,000, of whom 36,000 were mercenary "bands." Shalmaneser carried the tribe captive to Assyria. It was not known as a tribe after the return. We are left to suppose that the tribe fell into idolatry, because there is nothing recorded in favor of its religious history.—2. The seventh son of Obed Edom (1 Chr. xxvi. 5).

ISSHI'AH (*Jah lends*). ISHIAH. JESIAH. 1. Descendant of Moses (1 Chr. xxiv. 21).—2. A Levite (xxiv. 25). JESIAH 2.

IS'SUE, RUNNING. The law for males is in Lev. xv. 1-15; that for females in verses 19-31. It is supposed that the disease intended in men (gonorrhœa) arose from over-use or impure connection; and that in woman, the natural monthly purification of nature.

IS'UAH. ISHUAH. Son of Asher (1 Chr. vii. 30). ISUI (Gen. xlvi. 17).

ĪTAL'IAN (*from Italy*), (Acts x. 1).

IT'ALY. In the time of Paul the whole peninsula south of the Alps was included under this name (Acts x. 1). The ITALIAN BAND were soldiers recruited in Italy. Rome was the capital of the Roman Empire. The church was planted in Italy very early, since the Epistle to the Romans was written only about 25 years after the crucifixion, when a large number of Jews must have been there. From that day to this it has been the seat of civil and religious power, with many fortunes of revolution and persecution, the church always profiting, in all ages, so far as increasing in influence and power.

ITCH (HERES). A disease inflicted on the Israelites as a punishment (Deut. xxviii. 27). MEDICINE.

I'THAI or **ITH'AI.** (ITTAI.) Son of Ribai (1 Chr. xi. 31).

ITH'AMAR. Youngest son of Aaron (Ex. vi. 23). After the death of Nadab and Abihu, he and Eleazar were appointed to their places in the priestly office (Ex. xxviii. 1). The high priesthood passed into Ithamar's line by Eli.

ITH'IEL (*God with me*). 1. Son of Jesaiah (Neh. xi. 7).—2. Ithiel and Ucal, to whom Agur delivered his lecture (Prov. xxxi. 1).

ITH'MAH (*orphanage*). One of David's guard (1 Chr. xi. 46).

ITH'NAN (*given*). A town in the south of Judah (Josh. xv. 23).

ITHRA. JETHER. An Israelite (2 Sam. xvii. 25). Father of AMASA.

ITHRAN. JETHER. 1. Son of DISHON (Gen. xxxi. 26).—2. A descendant of Asher (1 Chr. vii. 37).

ITH'REAM (*residue of the people*). Son of David (2 Sam. iii. 5; 1 Chr. iii. 3), born in Bethlehem.

ITH'RITE, THE. Descendant of Jether. Two of David's guard (2 Sam. xxiii. 38) were Ithrites.

IT'TAH KAZIN (*people of a judge*), (Josh. xix. 13). Boundary of Zebulon. Lost.

ITTAI, the Gittite. Native of Gath; a Philistine in David's army, in the revolution of Absalom; commander of the 600 who were with David in his wanderings. He seems to have had equal command afterwards with Joab and Abishai, at Mahanaim (2 Sam. xviii. 2). Tradition says Ittai took the crown from the head of the idol Milcom. —2. Son of Ribai, one of David's guard. Ithai in 1 Chr. xi.

ITURÆ'A (*from Jetur, the son of Ishmael*). (Gen. xxv. 15). N. E. of Palestine, along the base of Hermon (Luke iii. 1). Philip was "tetrarch of Ituræa and the region of Trachonitis." Now Jedur. It is table-land, with conical hills at intervals, well watered, rich soil, and excellent pasture. The rock is basalt, and the houses are built of it. Its ancient cities are deserted, but standing. Bedawins still pitch their tents there.

I'VAH (2 K. xviii. 34). Hit, on the Euphrates. Ahava of Ezra (viii. 15). The ancient city was dedicated to Iva, the god of air. Shalmaneser brought people from it to Samaria, who carried their gods with them, according to custom among all ancient people.

IVORY (SHEN, *a tooth*). The tusks of the elephant are called teeth, and also horns (Ez. xxvii. 15). Solomon made use of it (Ps. xlv. 8), and had a throne of ivory (1 K. v. 18), overlaid (inlaid) with gold. The tusk of the African elephant sometimes weighs 120 pounds, and measures 10 feet long. There are many beautiful relics of carved ivory that were found in the ruins of Nineveh, and from Egypt, of figures on boxes, and various toilet ornaments—works of art of a high order.

I'VY (*Hederah helix*). A creeping plant, sacred to Bacchus (2 Macc. vi. 7). It grows wild in Palestine.

IZ'EHAR. IZHAR. (Num. iii. 19).

IZ'EHARITES, THE. The Izharites (Num. iii. 27).

IZ'HAR (*anointed with oil*). Son of Kohath (Ex. vi. 18, 21; Num. iii. 19).

IZ'HARITES. Descendants of Izhar (1 Chr. xxiv. 22).

IZRAHI'AH (*Jah brings forth*). Son of Uzzi (1 Chr. vii. 3).

IZ'RAHITE, THE. Descendant of Zerahi (1 Chr. xxvii. 8).

IZ'RI. Descendant of Jezer. A Levite (1 Chr. xxv. 11—in verse 3, ZERI).

J

There is no distinction in the Hebrew between J and i. The proper sound is that of y when placed before a vowel, as Jah, yäh; Jonah, yōnah.

JA'AKAN (*intelligent*). The Israelites encamped around the wells of the tribe "of the sons" (*Bene*) Jaakan (Deut. x. 6). Tayibeh (*Rob.*).

JA'AKOBAH (1 Chr. iv. 36). JACOB. Simeonite chief.

JA'ALA (*wild goat*). Sons of his were among the returned from captivity (Neh. vii. 58).

JA'ALAH (Ezra ii. 56). JAALA. Jeelin in Esdras.

JA'ALAM (*God hides*). Son of Aholibamah, wife of Esau (Gen. xxxvi. 5), and a sheikh in Edom. He was a phylarch (duke in Genesis).

JA'ANAI (*answers*). Chief in Gad (1 Chr. v. 12).

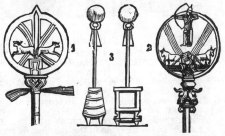

ASSYRIAN STANDARDS. SEE ENSIGN.

JA'ARE-ORE'GIM (*Jair, the weaver?*). The Targum says. "And David, the son of Jesse, weaver of the veils of the house of the sanctuary, who was of Bethlehem, slew Goliath the Gittite." In 1 Chr. xx. 5, the account is "Elhanan, the son of Jair, slew Lahmi, the brother of Goliath," etc. JAIR.

JA'ASAU (*made by Jah*). A son of Bani, who had to put away his Gentile wife (Ezr. x. 37).

JA'ASIEL (*made by El*). Judge in Benjamin in David's time (1 Chr. xxvii. 21).

JAAZANI'AH (*Jah hears*), (Heb. YA'AZANYA'HU) Captain under Johanan (2 K. xxv. 3). Son of Hoshaiah (xlii. 1), the Maachathite (Jer. xl. 8).— 2. Son of Shaphan (Ez. viii. 11), leader of seventy elders, seen by Ezekiel worshiping idols.—3. Son of Azur, a chief, subject of Ezekiel's prophesy (Ez. xi. 1).—4. A Rechabite (Jer. xxxv. 3).

JA'AZER (*Jah helps*) Amorite town, E. of Jordan in Gilead (Num. xxxii. 1). Rebuilt by Gad, and assigned to the Levites (Merarites, v. 35).

Famous for its vineyards (Is. xvi. 8, 9). The land of Jazer; *Seir*, west of Ammon, north of Heshbon.

JĀAZĪ'AH (*Jah consoles*). 3d son of Merari, the Levite (1 Chr. xxiv. 26).

JĀĀ'ZĪEL (*El consoles*). Musician in David's time (1 Chr. xv. 18). AZIEL.

JĀ'BAL (*stream*). Son of Lamech, "father" of dwellers in tents and graziers (Gen. iv. 20).

JAB'BOK (*flowing*). River in Gilead, falling into the Jordan about mid-way between the Sea of Tiberias and the Dead Sea (Josh. xii. 2). The border of the Ammon was strong (Num. xxi. 24), the river running in a defile, deep, narrow and wild, fringed with willows, cane, and oleanders, evergreen oak, pine and arbutus. *Wady Zurka.* Some think it was the Hieromax, *Wady Yarmuk.*

EGYPTIAN TEMPLE.

JĀ'BESH (*dry*). 1. Father of Shallum, 15th king of Israel (2 K. xv. 10).—2. Short form of

JĀ'BESH GIL'EAD. Jabeth, in Gilead, the largest city in the half-tribe of Manasseh, 6 miles from Pella, now called *Ed Deir,* on *Wady Yabis.* It did not send its contingent against Benjamin (Judg. xxi. 8), and was punished by the destruction of all its people but 400 young women, who were given to the Benjamites for wives. Nahash attacked it (1 Sam. xi.), but Saul came to the rescue. When the bodies of Saul and his sons hung on the walls of Bethshan, the valiant men of Jabesh Gilead made a raid at night and carried them off, and buried them honorably (1 Sam. xxxi. 11–13).

JĀ'BEZ (*causes sorrow*). 1. Town in Judah, where the Kenite scribes resided (1 Chr. ii. 55).—2. In the minute genealogy of Judah (iv. 9, 10) Jabez was more honorable than his brethren, who are not recorded.

JĀ'BIN (*intelligent*). King of N. Canaan, at Hazor, who headed a most powerful army against Joshua (xi. 1–4), and was surprised and defeated near the waters of Merom (7). Joshua afterwards burnt Jabin's city.—2. King of Hazor, in the time of the Judges, who lived in the same city of Hazor (rebuilt), raised an army against Israel, and was defeated, etc. Some have thought that the two accounts were of one event, or of two victories over one Jabin: one by Joshua and another by Barak, but it is more probable that there were two kings of that name, as recorded, and there were 150 years between the two kings.

JAB'NEEL (*El builds*). In Judah, near the sea,

north (Josh. xv. 11), held at one time by the Philistines (2 Chr. xxvi. 6), who were driven out by Uzziah. Jamnia, in 1 Macc. iv. 15, and a strong place. Now called *Yebna* or *Ibna,* on a little hill, near the *Rubin* river, 11 miles S. of Joppa, where the Crusaders built the castle of Ibelin, and a church, whose ruins are still visible.—2. In Naphtali. Lost. Josephus mentions Iamnith, in Upper Galilee.

JAB'NEH. JABNEEL.

JĀ'CHAN (*afflicted*). A chief in Gad (1 Chr. v. 13).

JĀ'CHAN (*he will establish*). Name of one of the pillars in the porch of Solomon's temple (1 K. vii. 21).

JĀ'CHIN. 1. 4th son of Simeon (Gen. lxvi. 10). Jachinites (Num. xxvi. 12).—2. Head of the 21st course of priests (1 Chr. ix. 10); some of this course returned from captivity (Neh. xi. 10).

JĀ'CHINITES. Family founded by Jachin.

JĀ'CINTH (Gr. *ya-cinth*). 1. A dark purple flower. — 2. PRECIOUS STONES.

JĀ'COB (*supplanter*). Esau and Jacob were twins, sons of Rebekah, wife of Isaac, born B. C. 1836, at the well Lahai-roi. Jacob was the favorite of his mother, and was a shepherd. He bought the birthright of his elder brother Esau (at an unfair price in his brother's distress) and got the patriarchal blessing from his father by a stratagem, in which he was aided by his mother. This blessing was material only, and did not include the spiritual promises. His quiet life ended when, at the age of 78 he was obliged to leave home, and was sent to Padan-Aram to find a wife among his mother's relatives. On the way there he had the dream of the ladder reaching from earth to heaven, at Bethel. Isaac had repeated his blessing when he left home, with the addition of the spiritual promises made to Abraham, and they were confirmed in the dream at Bethel. (Jacob seems to have thought only of *a local God who lived at Bethel,* with whom he was disposed to make a bargain for service on conditions). The beautiful incident of the meeting of Jacob with Rebekah at the well exhibits the pure and simple habits of the time, and the courtesy and kindness so native to those who follow the shepherd's life. Laban drove a very hard and shrewd bargain with Jacob, compelling him to serve 14 years for Rachel and marry Leah besides, but this was repaid by Jacob in his sharp practice in making himself rich in "much cattle," by skilful management. At the age of nearly 100 he returned to Canaan, and on the way his name was changed from Jacob to Israel (God's soldier) at Peniel, where he met his brother Esau, who was then a kind of Bedawin wanderer, such as now roam over the same district, although Esau appeared to be much the better man of the two.

The images (gods) that Rachel stole from her father's house, were small figures of certain designs, (TERAPHIM), such as are often found buried among the ruins in Palestine, and were used in Pagan worship. The value put on them by Laban shows how little real knowledge he had of the true God. Jacob stayed awhile at Shechem, where he buried under a sacred tree the stolen images; and also at Bethel where he built an altar. While on the way to Hebron, where his father was, his son Benjamin was born, and the mother, Rachel, died and was buried near Bethlehem, where a tomb preserves her memory to this day.

Esau and Jacob met again at Hebron, when they buried their father Isaac.

Soon after this Joseph was sold into Egypt.

Jacob was living at Hebron with his eleven sons, when a famine brought about the migration to Egypt (see JOSEPH), where he was assigned a home in the pasture land of Goshen, by the Pharaoh, and where he died, aged 130 (147). His body was borne to the cave of Machpelah, and laid in the tomb with those of Abraham, Sarah and Isaac. The blessing that Jacob gave his sons was a proof that his faith in God's promise was strong—had increased—and that his idea of the true God had become clearer and more elevated. It is full of fine thoughts, poetic language, and abounds in the most beautiful images.

JA'DAU. IDDO. A son of Nebo, who married a Gentile (Ezr. x. 43).

JAD'DUA (*known*). 1. A layman, who signed the covenant with Nehemiah (x. 21).—2. Son(?) and successor of Jonathan, high-priest, the last whose name is recorded in the O. T. Josephus relates of him a ceremonious reception of Alexander (Ant. xi. 8, § 7).

JA'DON (*judge*). The Meronothite who assisted in repairing the wall of Jerusalem (Neh. iii. 7).—2. A man of God, from Judah, who withstood Jeroboam at Bethel, as said by Josephus, in error for Iddo (2 Chr. ix. 29).

JA'EL (*climber, Ibex*). Wife of Heber (of the family of Hobab), the Kenite, a sheikh of a Bedawin tribe, who had pitched his tent under an oak, called on that account "oak of the wanderers" (plain of Zaanaim in Judg. iv. 11), near Kedesh-Naphtali (HEBER, ELON). When his army was routed, Sisera fled in another direction, away from the flying host, and sought safety in the woman's private tent, where he would have been safe, under Jael's cloak, if the woman herself had not betrayed him, which she did do, killing him with one of the tent-pins. God's judgment on Sisera was celebrated in the song of Deborah, but not

JACOB'S WELL.

JACOB'S WELL. Is in a low spur of Mt. Gerizim, at the mouth of the valley of Shechem. "Formerly there was a square hole opening into a carefully built vaulted chamber, 10 ft. sq., in the floor of which was the true mouth of the well. Now a part of the vault has fallen in, and completely covered up the mouth, so that it looks like a shallow pit." The well is 9 feet diameter, circular, cut through limestone rock nearly 100 feet deep. It sometimes has water in it, but is often quite dry. There was a small church over it in the 4th century, and to the south-west there are a few shapeless ruins still left.

JA'DA (*skilful*). Son of Onam by Atarah (1 Chr. ii. 28).

Jael's treacherous and violent method.—2. A judge of Israel (Judg. v. 6).

JA'GUR (*lodging-place*). Town in the south of Judah (Josh. xv. 21). KINAH.

JAH (*yäh*). The shorter form of Jehovah. Used in forming such names as Eli-jah, Isa-jah, Jerem-jah (Jeremiah). GOD (German *Gött*). The Hebrew names are: 1. EL, *might*, as EL-SHADDAI, *God almighty* (Gen. xiv.); EL-ELOHIM, *God mightier than all gods, God of gods;* EL-BETH-EL, *the place of the mighty God;* also in compounds, as AREZE-EL, *the cedars of God,* that is tall and strong; and peculiarly in poetry.—2. ELOAH, *strong;* ELOHIM, the plural. ELOAH is used only in poetry, and ELOHIM in both poetry and prose

The plural is used in Hebrew to enlarge and intensify the idea expressed by the singular. ELOHIM is not *the gods*, but is the strongest of all strong beings, the fullness of divine perfections, the sum of all the powers of all imaginable gods. There is nothing in this name either for against the idea of a trinity. That belongs to the New Testament age. The unity of God was guarded with the utmost jealousy against idolatrous polytheists (Deut. vi. 4, xxxii. 39; Is. xliv. 6). The word was often used for the heathen gods and other ideas of divinity (Ps. viii. 6, xcvii. 7), as angels; and also to the rulers and judges of Israel (Ex. xxii. 9, 28), and God (Elohim) is said to judge among the rulers (Elohim in Ps. lxxxii. 1). All true sons of Israel were called sons of God (Elohim, John x. 35). The Cainites claimed to be "sons of God" in distinction from the Sethites, who took the more humble name of "sons of Adam," or "sons of the Man" (Gen. vi. 4). The peculiar name of God in relation to the covenant, is—3. JEHOVAH; but in reading the Scriptures the Jews always pronounced

BOAT OF THE NILE.

the word ADONAI, which is *Lord*. The vowel points now in use were not invented for centuries after the Hebrew ceased to be a living language, so that the true pronounciation of the name Jehovah was lost, and the word was written YHVH, and pronounced Adonai or Elohim. The vowel points of Adonai (ADONAI) were placed in Jehovah (JAHOVAH), but this is not found in the old copies, and not older than about 1500 A. D. Diodorus Siculus gives the Greek IAO for the Hebrew JHVH. The meaning of Jehovah is *underived existence*, HE IS, or I AM BECAUSE I AM, the God of Abraham, of grace, and truth, and love; self-existence, eternity. Elohim is God *in nature*, Jehovah is God *in grace*. (The temple of Isis, at Sais, had this inscription: "I am all that has been, that is, and that will be," meaning Isis, the universal mother.) The word Jehovah is supposed to mean YAHU, *joy;* VAH, *pain*—the God of good and evil. See HISTORY, page xiv. In Greek, the word is—4. THEOS, any deity, idol, or the true God (Matt. i. 23), and Satan (God of this world).—5. KURIOS, Lord in Matt. i. 20; and in the Septuagint as the translation of Jehovah; also of a man, a lord.

JA'HATH (*union*). 1. Son of Libni (1 Chr. vi. 20). Ancestor of Asaph.—2. Head of a family in the line of Gershom (1 Chr. xxiii. 10).—3. In the line of Judah (1 Chr. iv. 2).—4. A Levite, son of Shelomoth (xxiv. 2).—5. Merarite Levite in Josiah's time (xxxiv. 12); an overseer of repairs in the temple.

JA'HAZ. JAHA'ZA (Josh. xiii. 18). JAHA'ZAH. JAH'ZAH (Num. xxi. 23). A place where the battle was fought between the Israelites and Sihon, king of the Amorites. Jeremiah mentions it (xlviii. 21) as in Moab. Not yet identified.

JAHAZI'AH (*seen by Jah*). Son of Tikvah, and assistant to Ezra (x. 15). Ezechias in Esdras.

JAHA'ZIEL (*seen by El, that is, made strong*). 1. Deserted Saul for David at Ziklag (1 Chr. xii. 4). —2. Priest in David's time, who blew the trumpet at ceremonials (1 Chr. xvi. 6).—3. 3d son of Hebron, a Levite. The family is mentioned in David's time (1 Chr. xxiii. 19).—4. Levite of the sons of Asaph who prophesied the destruction of the army that was coming to attack Jerusalem (2 Chr. xx. 14).—5. A son of Jehaziel returned from captivity as chief of the Bene-Shecariah (Ezr. viii. 5). Zattu (for Shecariah) in 1 Esdras viii. 32 (Bene Zathoe). JEZELUS.

JAH'DAI (*led by Jah*). In Caleb's line, father of 6 sons (1 Chr. ii. 47).

JAH'DIEL (*made joyful by El*). Chief in Manasseh, E. of Jordan (1 Chr. v. 24).

JAH'DO (*united*). Son of Buz, a Gadite (1 Chr. v. 14).

JAH'LEEL (*hope in El*). 3d son of Zebulon (Gen. xlvi. 14). JAHLEELITES (Num. xxvi. 26).

JAH'MAI (*Jah guards*). Chief in the house of Tola, Issachar (1 Chr. vii. 2).

JAH'ZAH (*threshing-floor*). JAHAZ (1 Chr. vi. 78).

JAH'ZEEL (*El divides*). 1st son of Naphtali (Gen. xlvi. 24). Jahzeelites (Num. xxvi. 48). Jahziel in 1 Chr. vii. 13. JAHZEEL.

JAH'ZERAH (*led back by Jah*). Priest of the family of Immer (1 Chr. ix. 12).

JA'IR (*splendid*). 1. Descended from both Judah and Manasseh. Leader in the conquest of Bashan, B. C. 1451. See HAVOTH-JAIR.—2. 8th judge of Israel, B. C. 1210, a Gileadite. Buried in Camon. —3. 2 Sam. xxi. 19.

JAIRITE, IRA, THE (2 Sam. xx. 26). (Pasha ?)

JAI'RUS (Gr. for the Heb. JAIR). Ruler in a synagogue in Galilee, whose daughter Jesus restored to life and health (Luke viii. 14).

JA'KAN. JAAKAN. Akan.

JA'KEH (*pious*). Father of Agur (Prov. xxx. 1). Supposed by some to be a name for David, father of Solomon, but without evidence.

JA'KIM (*lifted by Jah*). Chief of the 12th course of priests in David's reign (1 Chr. xxiv. 12). JACHIN ?—2. One of the Bene Shimhi (1 Chr. viii. 19).

JA'LON (*abiding*). A son of Ezra, in the line of Judah (1 Chr. iv. 17).

JAM'BRI, children of (i. e. some of the tribe) attacked the Maccabees, and suffered reprisals (1 Macc. ix. 36). Amorites?

JAMES. Three persons are mentioned by this name in the N. T. The original form of the name in Hebrew is Jacob, and is so called now by the church in the East; St. Jacob (*Mar Yacoob*). The name has passed through several changes, through many languages. It was in Greek, Iakobos; Latin, Jacobus; Italian, Iacomo, or Giacomo, and Jacopo; Spanish, Iago (Diego), and Xayme, or Jayme (*hayme*); French, Jacques, and Jame, which is in English James. (See Robertson's *Becket*, p. 139). The modern derivatives are framed on the original form, as Jacobin, and Jacobite.

1. JAMES, THE SON OF ZEBEDEE. He first appears as a fisherman, A. D. 27, when he, with his brother John, was called by Jesus to be his disciple (Mark i. 20). His father owned a boat (ship) and employed help. On another occasion he, his brother John, with Simon and Andrew, were directed by Jesus, and caught a very large number of fish at one haul, which was explained by the

Great Teacher to mean that they all should become successful fishers of men. James was numbered with the 12, among the first 4. He was always selected for any special duty. He was present at the raising of Jairus' daughter (Mark i. 29); one of the three on the Mt. of Transfiguration (Matt. xviii. 1); one of the 4 who heard the sermon on the last days (Mark xiii. 3); and one of 3 in Gethsemane (Matt. xxvi. 37). He joined his brother John in the request that fire should be called down on the Samaritans (Luke ix. 54); and in the ambitious request, with their mother, to sit nearest to Christ in his kingdom (Matt. xx. 20). These requests were refused with indignation by Jesus, and they were named Boanerges (Mark ii. 17). They were at the Feast of Pentecost. He was a man of very resolute purpose and determined action, and was given a high position among the apostles (Acts xii. 2); and he is the only one of the 12 whose death is recorded, which took place about 10 years after the crucifixion.

2. JAMES THE LORD'S BROTHER. The children of Joseph and Mary were Jesus, James, Joses, Jude (Judas), Simon, and three daughters whose names are not given (Matt. xiii. 55, 56; Gal. i. 19, ii. 9, 12). His brethren did not believe in Jesus as the Christ at the first (John vii. 5), and some of them not until a few days before the Day of Pentecost (1 Cor. xv. 7). James occupied a prominent position among the apostles, and was surnamed "the Just." James and Peter seem to have been in authority on equal terms when Paul was admitted to the fellowship of the apostles on the word of Barnabas (Acts ix. 27; Gal. i. 18), and after that time he acts as the president of the council in Jerusalem (Acts xii. 17, xv. 13), whose decrees he delivered formally, a position recognized and recorded by Paul (Gal. ii. 9), and honored by a formal visit of ceremony in the presence of all the presbyters (Acts xxi. 18). He is believed to have been appointed Bishop of Jerusalem by Jesus in a vision, as is reported by Epiphanius and others of the early historians of the Church, only that Eusebius says the appointment was by the apostles. Hegesippus, a Jewish disciple in the 2d century, gives the most minute and interesting account, in which he is described as the brother of Jesus, holy from the womb, drinking neither wine nor spirits, nor eating animal food, and wearing both his hair and whiskers without shaving (but with trimming), and he avoided the use of perfumes and ceremonious bathing, and wore only linen clothes. He was a very constant attendant on the services in the temple, and prayed "on his knees" for the salvation of the people, so that he was looked upon as the "bulwark of the church," and it is said that "all who became believers believed through James." This same authority relates that he was thrown from the gable of the temple to the ground, and then stoned to death, shortly before the siege of Jerusalem. See the HISTORY for the EPISTLE OF JAMES.

3. JAMES THE SON OF ALPHÆUS (Clopas), and Mary (John xix. 25), one of the apostles (Matt. x. 3; Mark iii. 18, etc.), (Matt. xxvii. 56; Mark xv. 40), and is also called James the Less. He had a brother named Joses, and a sister Salome. The occurrence of the same name in the mother and children of two families does not argue a relation, rather the contrary, and it is not likely that these were relatives of Jesus.

JĀ′MIN (*right hand*). Son of Simeon, founder of the Jaminites (Gen. xlvi. 10).—2. Son of Ram of Hezron in Judah (1 Chr. ii. 27).—3. Reader under Ezra (Neh. viii. 7).

JAM′LECH (*Jah makes the king*). Chief in Simeon in the time of Hezekiah (1 Chr. iv. 34, 41).

JAM′NIA for JABNEEL in the Apocrypha.

JANGLING (Gr. *mataiologia*). Babbling, idle talk. "Jangling is whan a man spekith to moche biforn folk, and clappith as a mille, and taketh no keep what he saith." (Chaucer. *Parson's Tale*).

JAN′NA. Father of Melechi in the line of Jesus. JOHN?

JAN′NES and JAM′BRES. The two Egyptian magicians who imitated Moses. Their names were given by Paul only (2 Tim. iii. 8, 9). The origin of the names is obscure. Jannes may be Greek for the Egyptian AAN (Ian), two kings having that name (meaning *valley*), one of which lived before Joseph. It is supposed that Paul found the names in some history (or tradition), now lost.

JANŌ′AH (*quiet*). In Naphtali, taken by Tiglath-Pileser (2 K. xv. 29). Janohah in Eusebius and Jerome.

JANŌ′HAH (*into rest*). On the N. boundary of Egypt (12 ms. E. of Neapolis—*Eusebius*). YANUN is in that locality (Van de Velde, ii. 303), in a valley which slopes toward the Jordan, a small village among extensive ancient ruins. *Khirbet Yanun*, N. E. of Yanun, may be the more ancient (Rob. 297).

JĀ′NUM (*slumber*). Judah in the mts., near Hebron (Josh. xv. 53). Jā′nus.

JĀ′PHETH (*extent*). Second son of Noah (Gen. x. 2, 6). YAPHAH (*fair*) may be the root-wood, in allusion to the light complexion of the people of the Japhetic races who occupied the Isles of Greece (shores and islands), coasts of the Great Sea, and Asia Minor, Asia and Europe.

JAPHI′A (*fair*). Zebulon's boundary ran from Daberath to Japhia, and Gath-hepher (Josh. xix. 12). YAFA is two miles S. of Nazareth. A tradition says Zebedee was born here, and therefore the Latins call it San Giacomo (St. James).

JAPHI′A (*shining*). 1. King of Lachish (Josh. x. 3).—2. Son of David, born in Jerusalem. Nephia in the Peshito. See DAVID.

JAPH′LET. In the line of Asher, through Beriah (1 Chr. vii. 32).

JAPH′LETI. Boundary of the Japhletite on the S. of Ephraim (Josh. xvi. 3). Probably an ancient Canaanite tribe.

JĀ′PHO (*beauty*). JOPPA. (Josh. xix. 46).

JĀ′RAH (*honey*). Son of Micah (1 Chr. ix. 42). Jehoadah in ch. viii. 36.

COIN OF CORINTH.

JĀ′REB (*hostile*). A king of Assyria (Hos. v. 13; x. 6). The title of "avenger" (YAREB), was assumed by him, as "defender of the faith" was by Henry VIII.

JĀ′RED (*low ground*). A patriarch, son of Māhāl′alēel, father of Enoch (Gen. v. 15).

JĀRESI′AH (*Jah nourishes*). Chief in Benjamin (1 Chr. viii. 27).

JAR′HA. Egyptian servant of Sheshan, husband of his daughter Ahlai (1 Chr. ii. 34).

JĀ′RIB (*adhering*). 1. Jachin in Gen. xlvi.; Ex. vi.; Num. xxvi.—2. Chief with Ezra (Ezr. viii. 16).—3. A priest, son of Jozadak (x. 18).—4. Joarib.

JĀR′MUTH (*hill*). In the Shefelah near Socoh (Josh. xv. 35). Its king, *Piram*, was routed (with the 5 kings) at Beth-horon by Joshua (Josh. x. 3, 25). *Yarmuth*, about 9 miles N. E. of Beit Jibrin. —2. City in Issa. (Josh. xix. 17). Remeth in verse 21, and in 1 Chr. vi. 73, Ramoth.

JARO'AH (*moon*). Chief in Gad (1 Chr. v. 14).

JA'SHEN (*sleeping*). Sons of J. were in David's guard (2 Sam. xxiii. 32). Sons of Hashem in 1 Chr. xi. 34.

JA'SHER, THE BOOK OF (*book of the upright*). A book of heroic poetry and history mentioned in two places in the O. T. (Josh. x. 13, and 2 Sam. i. 18), and probably a book of songs and eulogies of distinguished men in Israel. The Vulgate has "the book of the just one;" the Septuagint, "the book of the upright one;" the Syriac, "the book of praises," or "psalms." There is an English forgery of 1751 (Bristol, 1829). The original was probably published first in the time of Joshua, and again in David's reign with additions. A scheme was started for gathering the supposed fragments of this work from the various books of the O. T. The supposed plan of the work is that it was written to supply a popular demand in Solomon's time, and its object was to show that God made man upright, but carnal wisdom led him away from the law (spiritual wisdom), when the Hebrews were chosen to keep the law; David was made (perpetual) king for his religious integrity. The compiler named is the prophet Nathan, and it contained the pith, or marrow of the religious system of the Hebrews. This is only a conjecture.

LAMP STAND.

JASHO'BEAM (*return*). Son of Zabdiel (1 Chr. xxvii. 2), a Korhite (xii. 6), or a Hachmonite (xi. 11). He slew 800 at one time (2 Sam. xxiii. 8). Chief in David's guard, over the 1st monthly course of 24,000 men.

JA'SHUB (*who returns*). 1. 3d son of Issachar (1 Chr. vii. 1). Job in Gen. xlvi.—2. son of Bani (Ezr. x. 29).

JASH'UBI-LE'HEM (*returns to bread*). Son of Judah by Bathshua (1 Chr. iv. 22). It may also be the name of a place—Chozeba, Chezib, or Achzib. The Targum (or Chronicles) says Chozeba is Elimelech; Joash and Saraph are Mahlon and Chilion, who had the dominion in Moab from marrying the two girls; Jashubi-Lehem is Noomi and Ruth who returned (jashub, *return*) to Beth-lehem (lehem, *bread*), after the famine. A poem derived from the book of Ruth.

JA'SHUBITES. Family of Jashub (Num. xxvi. 24).

JA'SIEL (*made by El*). One of David's guard (1 Chr. xi. 47). A Mesobaite.

JA'SON. Greek form of the name Jesus; Hebrew, Joshua.—1. Son of Eleazar, sent by Judas Macc. to treat with the Romans, B. C. 161 (1 Macc. viii. 17). —2. Father of Antipater, an envoy to Rome (1 Macc. xii. 16), perhaps the same as No. 1.—3. Of Cyrene, a Jewish author of "Five Books of the War of Jewish Liberation," from which the 2d book of Maccabees was compiled. (See MACCABEES in the HISTORY).—4. Jason the high-priest, 2d son of Simon 2, and brother of Onias 3. He got his office by fraud, and attempted to Hellenize the Jews by building a gymnasium on the Greek model in Jerusalem, which even the priests attended to the neglect of their duties (2 Macc. iv. 9), and by sending a deputation to the games in honor of Hercules at Tyre. Menelaus supplanted him by fraud and a bribe.—5. The Thessalonian who entertained Paul and Silas, for which the Jewish mob attacked him (Acts xvii. 5). He was a companion of Paul (Rom. xvi. 21). SECUNDUS? (Acts xx. 4).

JAS'PER (YASHEFEH). PRECIOUS STONES.

JATH'NIEL (*whom El gives*). Door-keeper in the temple (1 Chr. xxvi. 2). Of the family of Meshelemiah.

JAT'TIR (*eminent*). Judah in the mts. (Josh. xv. 48). David sent a part of the spoils of Ziklag to this place (1 Sam. xxx. 27). 12 ms. S. of Hebron is Attir, in ruins, on a hill.

JA'VAN. 4th son of Japheth, father (settler) of Elisha, Tarshish, Kittim, and Dodanim. The Hebrew name of Greece. In the Cuneatic it is *Yanun.* Homer says that early settlers of Greece were *Iaonas* (Iliad xiii. 685).—2. The Javan of Ez. xxvii. 19 is an error for UZAL in Arabia (*Yemen*).

JA'ZER. JAAZER.

JA'ZIZ (*shining*). A Hagarite shepherd in David's employ (1 Chr. xxvii. 31). Perhaps stationed in the country of his ancestors, east of Jordan (verses 19-22).

JE'ARIM, MOUNT. Chesalon (*Keslu*), is on a steep ridge, between *Wady Ghurab* and *Wady Ismail*, 7. ms W. of Jerusalem.

JEAT'ERAI (*following one*). Son of Zerah, a Levite (1 Chr. vi. 21). Ethni?

JEBERECHI'AH (*Jah blesses*). Father of Zechariah, in Ahaz's time (Is. viii. 2). Berechia?

JE'BUS (*trodden down*). JERUSALEM. JEBUSI.

JEB'USITE. Third son of Canaan (Gen. x. 16). First mentioned in the account of the spies (Num. xiii. 29). Jabin's army contained men from the Amorites, Hittites, Perizzites and Jebusites (Josh. xi. 3). The king was killed at Bethhoron (x. 1, 5, xii. 10); a part of it was taken and burned by Judah (Judg. i. 21), but the citadel held out for 300 years, until David's time (2 Sam. v. 6). Araunah, the Jebusite, is made immortal by his dealing with David. The remnant of the tribe was made tributary to Solomon (1 K. ix. 20), and are heard of as late as the captivity (Ezr. ix. 1).

JECAMI'AH (*Jah assembles the people*). Son of Neri, of the line of Nathan and of Jesus (Luke iii. 27).

JECHOLI'AH (*Jah is mighty*). Wife of Amaziah, king of Judah (2 K. xv. 2). Jecoliah in Chr. She was a native of Jerusalem.

JECHONI'AS. Greek form of Jechoni'ah.

JECONI'AH (*Jah builds*). Jehoiachin, the last but one of the kings of Judah.

JEDA'IAH (*Jah knows*). Head of the 2d course of priests (1 Chr. xxiv. 7). Some of this course returned from captivity (Ezr. ii. 36), and there were two priestly families (Neh. xii. 6, etc.).—2. A priest in the time of Joshua, the high-priest (Zech. vi. 10).

JEDA'IAH (*Jah's praise*). The Hebrew differs in these two names, but it is not easy to show the difference in English letters. 1. Ancestor of Ziza, of Simeon (1 Chr. iv. 37).—2. Son of Harumaph, who assisted in rebuilding the wall (Neh. iii. 10).

JEDI'AEL (*El knows*). Chief in Benjamin (1 Chr. vii. 6), whose family, with its branches, numbered 17,200 fighting men in David's time.—2. Son of Meshelemiah, a Levite, a doorkeeper in the temple (1 Chr. xxvi.).—3. Son of Shimri, of David's guard (1 Chr. xii. 45).—4. A "head" of 1000, who joined David near Ziklag (1 Chr. xii. 20).

JEDI'DAH (*only one*). Queen of Amon, mother of Josiah (2 K. xxii. 1). She was a native of Bozkath.

JEHEZ'EKEL (*El makes strong*). Priest in charge of the 20th course (1 Chr. xxiv. 16).

JEHI'AH (*Jah lives*). Door-keeper with Obed-edom for the ark (1 Chr. xv. 24).

JEHI'EL (*El lives*). 1. A Levite assistant in the temple (1 Chr. xv. 18).—2. Son of Jehoshaphat (2 Chr. xxi. 2).—3. Ruler in the temple in Josiah's time (xxxv. 8).—4. Levite, head of Laadan's sons (1 Chr. xxiii. 8).—5. Son of Hachmoni, in David's guard (xxvii. 32). Jerome says Jehiel was David's son Chileab (Daniel), and Achamoni David himself.—6. Levite in the time of Hezekiah (2 Chr. xxix. 14).—7. A Levite and an overseer of the sacrifices (xxxi. 13).—8. Father of Obadiah, who returned from captivity at the head of 218 sons of

DOME OF THE ROCK, JERUSALEM.

JEDIDI'AH (*Jah's darling*). The name given to Solomon by the prophet Nathan. David named him Shelomoh, *peaceful*.

JEDU'THUN (*praising*). One of the conductors of the temple music in the time of David (1 Chr. xv. 17; xxiii. 6). The three were ETHAN, the son of Kushaiah, the Merarite; HEMAN, the Kohathite; and ASAPH, the Gershonite. He played on cymbals in the procession, when the ark was brought to Zion, but he was appointed to duty at Gibeon (Ps. cl. 5). His name is in the titles of several psalms (xxxix.; lxii.; lxxvii.), as choir leader.

JE'EZER (Num. xxvi. 20). ABIEZER. JEEZERITES.

JE'GAR-SAHADU'THA (*witness heap*). Name in Aramaic of the pillar, or heap of stones set up by Laban and Jacob. There are two accounts of the same heap (Gen. xxxi. 47), Jacob naming it Galeëd.

JEHALE'LEEL (*who praises El*). Four sons of his are named in Judah's line (1 Chr. iv. 16).

JEHALE'LEEL (*who praises El*). Father of Azariah who assisted in restoring the temple in Hezekiah's time (2 Chr. xxix. 12).

JEHDE'IAH (*Jah makes joyful*). Descendant of Gershom, in David's time (1 Chr. xxiv. 20). Shubael was head of the house in xxvi. 24.—2. A Meronothite who took care of David's she-asses (xxvii. 30).

Joab (Ezr. viii. 9).—9. Father of Shekaniah, who assisted Ezra (x. 2).—10. Another of the same family who had to part with his Gentile wife (Ezr. x. 26). —11. A priest of the sons of Harim, who also put away his wife (x. 21).

JEHI'EL (different from the last in the Hebrew). Father of Gibeon in the line of Saul the king (1 Chr. ix. 35).—2. Son of Hotham the Aroerite, in David's guard (1 Chr. xi. 44).

JEHIE'LI. The Bene-Jehieli were treasurers of the temple (1 Chr. xxvi. 21).

JEHIZKI'AH (*Jah strengthens*). Son of Shallum, Chief in Ephraim in the time of Ahaz. He saved a large number of captives, and had them clothed, fed, tended, and returned to Jericho (2 Chr. xxviii. 12).

JEHO'ADAH (*Jah adorns*). Great-grandson of Merib-baal, in the time of Saul (1 Chr. viii. 36).

JEHOAD'DAN of Jerusalem, Josiah's queen, and mother of Amaziah of Judah (2 K. xiv. 2).

JEHO'AHAZ (*Jah holds*). Son and successor of Jehu, who reigned 17 years, B. C. 856-840, in Samaria (2 K. xiii. 1-9).—2. Shallum, 4th son of Josiah, whom he succeeded as king of Judah, being chosen over his elder brother, B. C. 610, after a short reign he was deposed (2 K. xxiii. 32; Jer. xxii. 10), by Pharaoh Necho, taken to Riblah, put in chains, and taken to Egypt, where he died. The people lamented for him, and he was the first king of Judah who died in exile.—3. Youngest son of king Jehoram. His name as king of Judah was Ahaziah.

JEHŌ′ASH (*Jah's gift*). Joash, 8th king of Judah.—2. 12th king of Israel.

JEHOHĀ′NAN (*Jah's gift*). Johanan (John). 1. Levite and doorkeeper in the tabernacle (1 Chr. xxvi. 3).—2. Chief of Judah, general of 280,000 under Jehoshaphat (2 Chr. xvii. 15). Father of Ishmael, a captain of 100 (xxiii. 1).—3. A Bene-Bebai who was parted from his Gentile wife (Ezr. x. 28). —5. A priest under Joiakin, h.-p. (Neh. xii. 13), after the captivity.—6. Priest and musician at the dedication of the wall (Neh. xii. 42).

JEHOI′ACHIN (*appointed by Jah*). Jeconiah, Coniah, Jeconias, Joiakim and Joacim. Son of Jehiakim and Nehushta, and 19th king of Judah, reigning 3 mos. 10 days. He was 18 years old (2 K. xxiv. 8), or 8 (2 Chr. xxxvi. 9), and was carried captive by Nebuchadnezzar, in revenge for the alliance that his father had made with Egypt. The best of the people, the sacred vessels of the temple, and all the treasure of the people, were taken to Babylon, leaving a poor and feeble remnant. Jehoiachin was kept a close prisoner nearly all the rest of his life, 36 years, when Evil-Merodach liberated him. (See ÉVIL-MERODACH). He was the last of Solomon's line, as predicted by Jeremiah (xxii. 30), the succession passing over to Nathan's line.

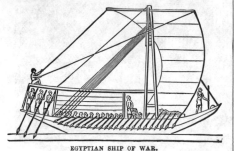

EGYPTIAN SHIP OF WAR.

JEHOI′ADA (*Jah favors*). 1. Father of Benaiah, David's general (2 Sam. viii. 18). He was also chief-priest, and leader of 3,700 Aaronites who joined David at Hebron (1 Chr. xii. 27).—2. Son of Benaiah, who succeeded Ahithophel as counselor to David—unless there is an error in position and Benaiah is meant.—3. High-priest at the time of Athaliah's usurpation, and in Joash's reign, B. C. 884–878. He succeeded Amariah. Married Jehosheba, daughter of king Jehoram, and sister of king Ahaziah (2 Chr. xxii. 11). He stole Joash when Athaliah killed all the other royal line of Judah, and hid him 6 years in the Temple, finally placing him on the throne.—4. 2d priest (sagan) to Seraiah the h.-p., and was deposed for friendship to the prophet Jeremiah (Jer. xxix. 25–29).—5. Son of Paseah, who repaired the Old Gate at Jerusalem (Neh. iii. 6).

JEHOI′AKIM (*Jah appoints*). 19th king of Judah (B. C. 609–598), 25 years old at his accession. He was first named Eliakim, and was the son of Joash and Zebudah, but Pharaoh Necho changed his name when he made him king in his brother Jehoahaz's stead (2 K. xxiii. 33), who died in Egypt, in captivity (v. 34), and he also collected a heavy fine ($200,000) from Judah for Josiah's part with Babylon against Egypt. The battle at Carchemish ended the rule of Egypt in Palestine for that time, and Nebuchadnezzar besieged and took Jerusalem, and carried some of the royal family to Babylon as hostages, among whom were Daniel and his three companions. The prophets Jeremiah and Ezekiel warned the king and people of the re-

sults of their idolatries, but instead of repenting, they burned Jeremiah's prophesy, put him in prison and drove Urijah the prophet into Egypt, where he was killed, and his corpse treated in a barbarous manner (Jer. xxvi. 21–23; xxxvi.). According to the warnings of Ezekiel (xvii.) and Jeremiah (ii. xxvii.), enemies attacked them on all sides (2 K. xxiv. 7); the king lost his life, and was buried without honor (Jer. xxii. 18, 19). The king of Babylon came in a few weeks after his death and carried his son and all the best men and their families and treasures to Babylon. This act of the king in burning Jeremiah's book was the first recorded attack on the liberty of the public press, and it did not succeed; the second edition was enlarged and improved (Jer. xxxvi. 32).

JEHOI′ARIB (*Jah a defender*). Head of the 1st course of priests in David's reign (1 Chr. xxiv. 7). His descendants were among the returned captives (Neh. xi. 10).

JEHŌ′NADAB (*Jah incites*). The son of Rechab (a Kenite), who assisted Jehu in his reforms, and in the destruction of the Baal worshipers (2 K. x. 15). Jeremiah holds up to the people the obedience of the Rechabites (pilgrims) who kept the law of abstinence from wine, and that to live only in tents, in contrast to the general disregard of the law of Moses (Jer. xxxv.), and prophesies an immortality of the house of Rechab. There is no historical trace of them after the Jewish nation went to pieces, and it is supposed that they became disciples of Jesus.

JEHON′ATHAN (*Jah's gift*). JONATHAN. 1. Son of Uzziah, steward to David (1 Chr. xxvii. 25).— 2. A Levite instructor of the people (2 Chr. xvii. 8).—3. A priest after the return from captivity (Neh. xii. 18).

JEHŌ′RAM (*Jah has. exalted*). JORAM. 1. Son of Ahab, king of Israel, and successor to his brother Ahaziah, B. C. 896. His reign was noted for the lives of the two great prophets Elijah and Elisha. He was killed by an arrow from Jehu's bow in Naboth's vineyard (1 K. xxi. 21). He was the last of the line of Omri.—2. Eldest son of Jehoshaphat, succeeding him as king of Judah at the age of 32, reigning 8 years, B. C. 893–885. He murdered his 6 brothers, and (by the help of his wife Athaliah, the daughter of Ahab) revived the Baal worship (see ELIJAH). The latter part of his reign was a series of calamities to the nation, and death to his family, himself dying of a painful malady, not regretted, and being buried without honor.—3. A priest sent to teach the law to the people (2 Chr. xvii. 8).

JEHOSHAB′EATH (*Jah's worshiper*). Jehosheba the wife of Jehoiada, the high priest.

JEHOSHA′PHAT (*Jah is judge*). 1. Son of Asa and Azubah; succeeded to the throne of Judah at the age of 35, and reigned 25 years, B. C. 914–889 (1 K. xv. 24; 2 K. viii. 16; 2 Chr. xvii., xxi.). "The Lord was with Jehoshaphat, because he walked in the first ways of his father David, and sought not unto Baalim; but sought to the Jehovah God of his father." * * "He took away the high-places and groves out of Judah" (2 Chr. xvii. 6; 1 K. xxii. 43). He sent out teachers among the people to instruct them in the law, set up just judges in the walled cities, forming a supreme court in Jerusalem, for references and appeals. He built castles and store-cities, and aimed to restore commerce in the Red Sea. The army was reformed in five sections; and the Arabians, Philistines, and Edomites were laid under tribute. He was saved from a very great danger by his trust in God (2 Chr. xx.; Ps. lxxxiii., xli., xlvii., xlviii.). He made a friendly alliance with the idolatrous kingdom of Israel, and to secure peace married his son Jehoram to Athaliah, the daughter of Ahab. He was saved by a miracle with his army in the desert (2 K. iii.), at the request of a prophet of Jehovah. The mutual relations between prophet and king in this reign is a sign of the high attainments which the king had made in the divine life. He was prudent enough to appoint his successor (Jehoram, 2 Chr. xxi. 3) in his life-time, as David had done to Solomon.—2. Son of Ahilud, a historian in David's reign (2 Sam. viii. 16). Such officers were attached to all eastern courts (Esther vi. 1).—3. A priest who blew a trumpet before the ark, on its way from the house of Obed-edom to Zion.—4. Son of Paruah, one of 12 commissaries (1 K. iv. 17). His district was Issachar.—5. Son of Nimshi, father of king Jehu (2 K. ix. 2).

JEHOSH'APHAT, VALLEY OF (*valley where Jah judges*), (Joel iii. 12). The valley between Scopus and Olivet and Jerusalem, so named after the greatest king after Solomon (2 Chr. xx.). The nations are to assemble for judgment, where Christ will appear the second time (Acts i. 11). Kidron. The Mohammedans point out a stone in the east wall of the temple area, near the S. end, from which a bridge will be stretched across the valley to Mt. Moriah, over which all souls must pass—the just in safety, the wicked falling off into Gehenna. This valley has been used as a burial-ground from the days of Josiah (2 K. xxiii. 6); and both Jews and Mohammedans look on the place as a most sacred resting-place; but the modern name cannot be traced beyond the 4th century A. D. Joel's prophesy was a poetical and symbolical figure, intended to teach that God is always present with and defending his faithful children. See JERUSALEM.

JEHOSH'EBA (*oath to Jah*). Daughter to Jehoram, king of Judah, but her mother is not mentioned. She married Jehoiada, the high-priest, being the only woman of Aaron's line who married into a royal family. She assisted her husband in preserving the young Joash (see JEHOIADA), (2 K. xi. 2).

JEHOSH'UA (*his help is Jah*). JOSHUA. (Num. xiii. 16).

JEHO'VAH. See JAH.

JEHO'VAH-JI'REH (*Jah will see*). The place where Abraham was about to sacrifice Isaac. Lost. (Gen. xxii. 14).

JEHO'VAH-NIS'SI (*Jah my banner*). Place of an altar built by Moses in memory of a victory over the Amalekites, on Horeb (Ex. xvii. 15).

JEHO'VAH-SHA'LOM (*Jah is peace*). Place of an altar built by Gideon in Ophrah, in memory of the salutation of the angel, "Peace be unto thee" (Judg. vi. 24).

JEHO'VAH-SHAM'MAH (*Jah is there*). The name of the city in Ezekiel's vision (Ez. xl., xlviii.).

JEHO'VAH-TSID'KENU (*Jah our righteousness*, in Jer. xxiii. 6). Supposed to be one of the titles of the Messiah. It was the prophetic name of a king to be raised up (a branch of David), who will reign and prosper, executing judgment and justice, Also, it is to be the name of the Jerusalem of the future, as the city of the great king (xxxiii. 16).

JEHOZ'ABAD (*gifted by Jah*). JOZABAD. There were several of this name: 1. The murderer of Joash (2 K. xii. 21), whose mother was a Moabitess.—2. A general of 180,000 in Jehoshaphat's army, a Benjamite (2 Chr. xvii. 18).—3. A porter or door-keeper of the south gate of the temple (1 Chr. xxvi. 4; Neh. xii. 25).

JEHOZ'ADAK (*Jah makes just*). JOZADAK. Son of Seraiah, the last high-priest before the captivity (2 K. xxv. 18), who was carried into captivity, and died there, but left a son Jeshua, who returned and revived the office (Ezr. iii. 2). JOZEDEC in the Greek, and in Haggai and in Zechariah.

JE'HU (*Jah is he*). 1. First in the 5th dynasty in Israel (see ISRAEL). He was the son of Jehoshaphat (2 K. ix. 2). His grandfather was Nimshi, who was better known than his father. Twenty years before he began to reign he was divinely singled out as the king of Israel by Elijah, and he was anointed by a servant of Elisha, when he was a general in the army, fighting against Hazael, king of Syria, at Ramoth-Gilead (vrs. 4–10). He carried out the directions of the prophesy to the very letter, and also destroyed the Baal (and Astarte) worshipers, their temple and images, but did not entirely purify the national worship, and therefore his line went to destruction in the 4th generation (2 K. xxix. 30; Hos. i. 4).—2. Son of Hanani, a prophet of Judah, whose prophesy was directed against Israel. He also wrote a life of Jehoshaphat (2 Chr. xvi. 7; xx. 34; 1 K. xvi. 1).—3. Man of the house of Hezron, in Judah (1 Chr. ii. 38).—4. Chief in Simeon (iv. 35).—5. "Jehu, the Anthothite," joined David at Ziklag (xii. 3).

SHIP.

JEHUB'BAH (*will be hidden*). Son of Shomer of Asher (1 Chr. vii. 34).

JEHU'CAL (*potent*). Son of Shelemiah (Jucal), "prince of the king" (Jer. xxxvii. 3, xxxviii. 1).

JE'HUD (*praise*). City in Dan (Josh. xix. 45). El Yehudiyeh, near Lydd, 7 miles east of Jaffa (Rob.).

JE'HUDI (*Jews*). Son of Nethaniah, sent to bring Baruch with Jeremiah's denunciation to be read to the king (Jer. xxxvi. 14, 21, 23).

JEHUDI'JAH (*Jewess*). Correctly Hajehudijah, a wife of Merod, sister of Naham (1 Chr. iv. 18). Hodijah in verse 19.

JE'HUSH (*collecting*). Son of Eshek in the line of Saul (1 Chr. viii. 39).

JEI'EL (*El's treasure*). There are eight of this name, but none are famous.

JEKAB'ZEEL (*El collects*). Kabzeel was so named after the return from captivity (Neh. ix. 25).

JEKAME'AM (*assembler*). Levite in David's time, in the line of Hebron (1 Chr. xxiii. 19).

JEKAMI'AH (*Jah collects*). Son of Shallum (in Ahab's time). Another person is called Jekamiah in 1 Chr. ii. 41.

JEHU'THIEL (*piety*). Son of Mered (see JEHUDIJAH), who built Zanoah.

JEMI'MA (*dove*). Job's eldest daughter after his recovery (Job xlii. 14). JEMAMA is a name of a province in the centre of Arabia, said to have been named after an ancient queen of the Arabians.

JEM'INI (*right hand*). A Benjamite (1 Sam. ix. 1).

JEM'NAAN. JABNEEL. JAMNIA. (Judith ii. 28).

JEM'UEL (*El's day*). Son of Simeon (Gen. xlvi. 10).

JEP'THÆ for **JEPHTHAH**, in Heb. xi. 32.

JEPH'THAH (Heb. YIFTAH, *he will open*, Judg.

xxii). Son of Gilead and a concubine. Driven out of the family by the other children, he went to Tob, where he became a leader of a band of marauders, ready for any service but not of robbery. Samuel names him among those who were raised up by God for his people (1 Sam. xii. 11), and Paul mentions his special faith (Heb. xi. 32). The Elders of Israel not finding any one offering to lead against the Ammonites, who had been masters for 18 years, appealed to Jephthah, who solemnly accepted the position. He tried to secure the aid of Ephraim, but in vain, and also to reason with the king of Ammon; and then after making a rash vow he completely overthrew the enemy, taking 20 cities; when having punished the Ephraimites, he held his office for 6 years. The story of his daughter's sacrifice by his vow has been variously understood. Josephus says she was made a burnt-offering, but modern scholars have inclined to the notion that she was devoted to perpetual virginity, and the sacred service of God in the temple. The story of Iphgenia (doomed as a sacrifice to Diana, and made a priestess in her temple) has been cited as a parallel example of the spirit of the Greeks in that age. The vow was that the first person that came out of his house to meet him should be the Lord's, that is, should be devoted to the Lord; if a man he should serve as a priest's servant: if a woman she should be devoted to the sacred duties of religion as a holy virgin (Judg. xi. 39), a companion to the women of the Gibeonites.

PISTACHIO.

Human sacrifice was contrary to the Hebrew idea of true worship of God, and is specially rebuked in the story of Abraham and Isaac. The idea of *sacrifice* is just as strongly brought out in the perpetual virginity of the young woman who, in common with all the daughters of Israel, might hope to become a mother, or the mother even of the Messiah. Besides, burnt-offerings must in all cases be males; and again, the vow to offer some animal would have been a small matter, unworthy of the important occasion. It is quite reasonable to suppose that Jephthah thought of his daughter when he made the vow, for he was a husband of one wife, and had but one child, who was his only hope of posterity, thus making it a real sacrifice. The Levites also were *devoted* in this same sense to the service of God, made dependent, sacred to the

Lord, and *offered as an offering.* Samuel was also devoted to the Lord.

JEPHUN'NEH (*for whom a way is made*). The father of Caleb, a Kenezite of Edom.—2. Eldest son of Jether, in Asher (1 Chr. vii. 38).

JĔ'RAH (*new moon*). 4th Son of Joktan (Gen. x. 26). *Yerakh* in Yemen, and (more probable) the Alilœi (*the moon people*) of Herodotus; not those who are named from Mohammed's relative, Bene-Hilāl, living near the Red Sea, south, near Zafari. There is also a locality called El-Latt (*lah*), meaning the rock where a peculiar worship was offered (to the serpent?); a species of fetishism.

JERAH'MEEL (*El's mercy*). 1. Eldest son of Hezron (1 Chr. ii. 9).—2. A Levite of the family of Kish (xxiv. 29).—3. Son of Hammelech, or the king, the keeper of Jeremiah and Baruch in prison (Jer. xxxvi. 26).

JERAH'MEELITES. From No. 1 (1 Sam. xxvii. 10), lived in the S. of Judah.

JĔ'RED (*descent*). JARED. Son of Mahalaleel, father of Enoch (1 Chr. i. 2).—2. Builder of Gedor, in Judah (iv. 18).

JEREMAI (*living in the hights*). Son of Hashum (Ezr. x. 33).

JEREMĪ'AH (*Jah throws*). 1. The great Hebrew prophet. (See HISTORY OF THE BOOKS). Seven others of the same name.—2. Jeremiah of Libnah, father of Hamutal, wife of Josiah (2 K. xxiii. 31). —3, 4, 5, in David's army (1 Chr. xii. 4, 10, 13).— 6. A hero in Manasseh, beyond Jordan (v. 24).— 7. Priest of high rank, and head of the 3d course (Neh. x. 2–8), which assisted in the dedication of the wall of Jerusalem (xii. 34).—8. Father of Jaazaniah, the Rechabite (Jer. xxxv. 3).

JEREMIAH, LAMENTATIONS OF. See HISTORY OF THE BOOKS.

JEREMĪ'AS. Greek form of Jeremiah. JEREMAI.

JER'EMOTH (*hights*). 1. Chief of the House of Beriah, of Benjamin (1 Chr. viii. 14), who lived in Jerusalem.—2. A Levite, son of Mushi (xxiii. 23).—3. Son of Heman, head of the 13th choir of musicians (1 Chr. xxv. 22). Jerimoth in v. 4.—4. Son of Elam.—5. Son of Zattu, who complied with Ezra's reform in putting away his Gentile wives, and sacrificed for each (Ezr. x. 26, 27).—6. Ramoth in the Hebrew in verse 29.

JEREMY. The short English form of Jeremiah.

JEREMY, THE EPISTLE OF. See Baruch in the HISTORY.

JERI'AH (*built by Jah*). A Levite chief of the House of Hebron (1 Chr. xxiii. 19). JERIJAH.

JER'IBAI (*Jah defends*). Son of Elnaan, in David's guard (1 Chr. xi. 46).

JER'ICHO (*city of the moon;* and another, *a fragant place*). (Num. xxii. 1). In the Jordan valley, 8 miles from the Dead Sea and 6 from the Jordan. When the Jews crossed the Jordan, Jericho was a large and strong city, whose origin is not recorded. Since it is not mentioned in Gen. xiii., when Abraham and Lot looked over the plain, it must have been built after that time. It was anciently surrounded by palm-trees, of which there were many kinds (Deut. xxxiv. 3; Jos. B. J., 8, § 3), thickly dotted about in pleasure gardens; besides balsam, figs, rose-plants, cypress, and many others. Josephus says, "It will not be easy to light on any climate in the habitable earth that can well be compared to it." It was the first city W. of the Jordan taken by the Israelites. Joshua cursed the city (Josh. vi. 26), and the curse was fulfilled in the person of Hiel the Bethelite (1 K. xvi. 34).

The Roman general Pompey camped there one night, and Gabinius made it one of the five cities of assembly. Under Herod the Great it rose to some importance; was full of treasure of all kinds and had valuable revenues. Antony gave it to Cleopatra. Herod built a fort there, which he named Cyprus, in honor of his mother; and a tower, Phasælis. He also built a new town higher up the plain, which he also called Phasælis. Norman McLeod thinks the modern village marks the site of Gilgal (*Eastward*, p. 198).

Near Jericho was a copious spring, which was healed by Elisha (2 K. ii. 19-21), and is now called *Ain es Sultan*. It is about a mile and a half from the modern village of Er Riha.

There are extensive ruins, rubbish and foundations, in several places, on both sides the Wady Kelt (Brook Cherith) and at the Ain es Sultan, marking ancient sites—the most ancient at the fountain. The city of the New Testament was on the banks of the Wady Kelt, on the direct route from Peræa to Jerusalem. It was visited several times by Jesus. Approaching it he cured one blind man (Luke xviii. 35), and leaving it he cured another (Mark x. 46). In the house of Zaccheus (probably in a garden in the suburbs) he related the parable of the Ten Pounds.

Vespasian made it the head of a toparchy. It was destroyed during the siege of Jerusalem. It revived under Saracen rule, and in the time of the Crusades was one of the most fertile regions in Palestine.

The Latins have a tradition that Jesus was baptized in the Jordan, opposite Jericho, and the Greeks point to another place, not far off. Both places are visited by great numbers of pilgrims, especially at Easter. Many bottles and cans of the water of the Jordan are carried away as mementoes of the place.

daughter Mahalath was a wife of Rehoboam, her cousin, Abihail, being another (2 Chr. xi. 18).—8. A Levite, custodian of offerings, under Azariah the high-priest (xxi. 13).

JERI'OTH (*curtains*). Wife of Caleb (the ancient), (1 Chr. ii. 18). The Vulgate says she was Caleb's daughter by his first wife.

JEROBO'AM (Heb. YARAB'AM, *many people*). The founder of the Kingdom of Israel, an Epraimite, the son of Nebat by Zeruah, a widow, (1 K. xi. 26). He was obliged to fly to Egypt for plotting against Solomon, when a young man, even after Solomon had given him an office of honor and profit (ver. 28). He found an asylum and a kind reception in Egypt, from the Pharaoh Shishak (Sesonchis), successor of the father-in-law of Solomon, who had also received kindly Hadad another enemy of Solomon. On the death of Solomon, and on the request of his friends, Rehoboam hastened to fulfil Ahijah's prophesy in forming a kingdom out of the 10 tribes, being chosen king B. C. 975. He made haste to change the religion of his people, in order to more certainly separate them from Jerusalem, and set up the calf-worship at Bethel (*Bethaven*), and Dan, and changed the time of holding the feasts. His hand was paralyzed because he attempted to arrest the prophet from Judah who predicted the overthrow of his idolatry, but was restored sound on the prayer of the same prophet. His political policy also was unsound, and did not perpetuate itself. He warred with Judah all his days, and died after a reign of 22 years.

JEROBO'AM II. Son of Joash, of the dynasty of Jehu, 13th king of Israel (B. C. 825). Corrup-

JERICHO.

JER'ICHO, PLAINS OF. The wide valley of the Jordan around Jericho, about 8 or 10 miles across (2 K. xxv. 5; Jer. xxxix. 5).

JERI'EL (*founded by El*). Chief in the house of Tola, of Issachar (1 Chr. vii. 2).

JER'IMOTH (*hights*). 1. Son of Bela (1 Chr. vii. 7).—2. A hero who joined David at Ziklag (1 Chr. xii. 5).—3. A son of Becher (1 Chr. vii. 8).— 4. Son of Musha, chief of a family of Meraites (xxiv. 30).—5. Son of Heman, head of the 15th choir of musicians (xxv. 4, 22).—6. Son of Azriel, of Naphtali (xxvii. 19). Princes in ver. 22.— 7. Son of David, and of a concubine, whose

tions of all kinds, political and religious, were notorious, and were condemned by the prophet Amos (vii.) He. reigned 41 years, and extended his father's conquests, taking Hamath, Damascus, the Hauran, Gilead, Ammon and Moab, and advanced his kingdom to its highest point of prosperity. These successes had been predicted by Jonah (2 K. xiv. 25-28). Amos was falsely reported by Jeroboam's high-priest at Bethel as having said that the king should die by the sword, but Amos meant (vii. 9-17) the *house* of Jeroboam, which was the recognized idea in the N. T. times (John viii. 52; Mark xiv. 57; Acts vi. 13). Ps. xlv. may refer to Jeroboam. He was buried in state with his ancestors.

JERŌ'HAM (*one beloved*). 1. Father of Elkanah, and about the same age as Eli (1 Chr. vi. 27).—2. A Benjamite, and founder of a family (viii. 27).—3. Father of Ibneiah (ix. 8).—4. Leader of the 16th course of priests (i. 12).—5. Sons of Jeroham of Gedor joined David at Ziklag (xii. 7).—6. Father of Azareel, chief, in David's time, of Dan (xxvii. 22.)—7. Father of Azariah, a captain of hundreds, who aided in the matter of the young king Joash (2 Chr. xxiii. 1).

kingdom (Ez. v. 5); leaving Hebron, where he had reigned 7½ years. The seat of the religion had been before this at Shechem, Shiloh, Gibeah, Nob, and Gibeon. Zion was now called the CITY OF DAVID, and was soon enlarged by walls, strengthened by towers, and beautified by a palace for the king, built by the mechanics of Hiram, king of Tyre. After the ark, which had rested at Kirjath-Jearim 20 years after Eli's death, was brought to Zion, David assumed the duties of priest as well as king, offering burnt-offerings and peace-offerings under a new tent in the citadel of

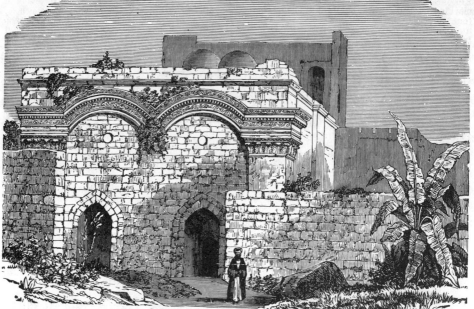

REMAINS OF THE GOLDEN GATES, JERUSALEM.

JERUBBA'AL (*Baal pleads*). Surname of Gideon, because he threw down an altar of Baal (Judg. vi. 32), and when the Abiezites complained to his father he replied, let Baal plead (his own cause).

JERUBBE'SHETH (*with whom the idol contends*). That is *shemeth* (the idol) a shameful thing. Same as Jerubbaal, and a name of Gideon.

JERU'EL (*founded by El*), **THE WILDERNESS OF** (2 Chr. xx. 16). Between Tekoa and Engedi, near Berachah, now Bereikut. There was a watch-tower (ver. 24), from which the enemy was seen, and re-ported to Jehoshaphat. The forces of Moab and Ammon were at the end of the brook (*wady*) facing the wilderness of Jeruel.

JERU'SALEM (*foundation of peace*). First mentioned in Gen. xiv. 18, by the name of Salem, whose king was Melchizedek (who is said by the Rabbis to be the patriarch Shem). The name Sha-laim (Ps. lxxvi. 2) means two cities, and is applied to the cities or quarters on (modern) Zion and in the Tyropœon valley. At the conquest of Canaan the name of its king was Adoni-zedek (*lord of jus-tice*), (Josh. x. l. 3), almost the same as Melchize-dek (*king of righteousness*). Joshua speaks of the city as "The Jebusite" (xv. 8), after the name of its occupiers. In the time of the Judges the name was JEBUS (xix. 10, 11). Judah could not, and Benjamin did not drive out the Jebusites (Josh. xv. 63; Judg. i. 21), and the city only became the capital of the nation after about 450 years from the time of Joshua, when David made it his royal residence, and the sanctuary, near the centre of his

Zion. The ark was only removed from here to the Temple of Solomon. David's royal gardens were in the valley at En Rogel. David and most of his successors were buried in the citadel, but there are no traces of their tombs. (See p. 71). The sepul-chres of David were in or near Ophel (Neh. iii. 16, xii. 37). The three great works of Solomon were the Temple, with its east wall and cloister, the Pal-ace, and wall of Jerusalem (Josephus). Also a a palace for his Egyptian wife; which was not on Zion (1 K. vii. 8, ix. 24; 2 Chr. viii. 11). "All of these were costly stones, * * *sawed with saws*," just such stone as is now found in the great quarry under the city, north of the Temple area, which may be sawed almost as easy as chalk; the build-ings probably required for residences by the thou-sand women of Solomon's house, who were of sev-eral nations and of different religions; the colleges for the several priests (very much such a state of things as is now found in the city, except that the various sects support themselves independently of each other); the 1400 chariots, and 12,000 riding-horses requiring stables; and besides all these, "all that he desired to build in Jerusalem and in Leba-non," shows the activity of his reign. And we are compelled to notice that he also built shrines for Ashtoreth, Chemosh, and Milcom, heathen divinities, on the site now occupied by the village of Siloam, on that part of Olivet called the Mt. of Corruption (1 K. xi.; 2 K. xxiii); which Josiah de-stroyed, together with an image of Molech in Hin-nom, 360 years after.

The first relic that we have in our day of the time of Solomon is a part of the foundation wall of the Temple platform, lately uncovered, an outline sketch of which is in the margin. These are the kind of stones that were "sawed," now very much harder, after long exposure.

The Son of Sirach (and also Tacitus) speaks of a "sea" of waters that was under the Temple, and this was recently brought to light by *Robinson* and *Barclay*, (City of the Great King, 526). It is 736 feet in circuit, 42 in depth, and capable of holding two million gallons.

The columns were once covered with metal, but are now bare, or plastered stone. The rain from the mosque of Aksa and other buildings is drained into it. No fountain has been discovered.

Under the S. E. corner of the Temple area are approach from Zion to the temple enclosure. Solomon's aqueduct from the Pools above Etham passes over this arch, and under the street above. This arch has at one time been used as a cistern. The rock was found on sinking a shaft 51 feet 6 inches below the floor. Below this room there were found vaults, tanks, etc., and a secret passage east and west, probably connecting the Temple with Zion.

The extent of the filling up above the original rock can be seen from the plan, where the debris is 85 feet deep at the S. W. corner of the Haram wall. The "chippings" of the stones and absence of any pieces of pottery, etc., show that this dirt, close to the wall, has never been disturbed since Hiram's builders put it there. The spring of "Robinson's Arch" is seen in its place; and the stones composing the arch were found by Lieut.

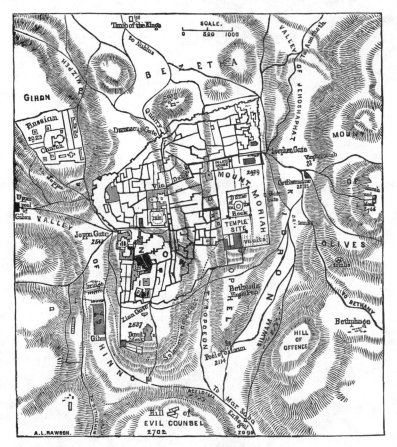

PLAN OF JERUSALEM.

many columns, arched over, supporting the platform above at its level, resting on the uneven surface of the original hill. The piers or columns are from 3 to 8 feet in diameter, from 5 to 23 feet apart, and there are 15 rows; and opening into this place, which is called Solomon's stables, is a triple gate, under the Aksa mosque. West of these, under the actual temple site, now under the Aksa mosque, is another series of piers and vaults, which seems to have been built up from more ancient materials. Besides the citadel, now called David's tower, there are scarcely any very ancient remains in the city that have not been thrown down and built up again several times.

"Wilson's" arch is one of a series forming an Warren buried under 40 feet of rubbish; one stone having broken through the roof of an aqueduct, lay on the rocky bottom at the depth of 63 feet.

This plan is of the city as it now is; with a few signs indicating ancient works, sites of ancient walls, churches, towers, and other structures in different ages; as many as could be laid down without confusing the work.

The city is small, but there is scarcely a place of any note, not even Nineveh or Babylon, that has been, to modern scholars, such a profound puzzle. The descriptions of Josephus are minute, his knowledge being exact and complete; and the hills on which the city stands are so marked and distinct from each other, that it seems almost marvelous that there could have been any difficulty, until we are reminded of the fact that during the middle ages, and especially during the Crusades, it

JAFFA GATE (JERUSALEM)

was regarded as a peculiarly sacred city, and as such must needs have every event that is mentioned in the Bible as having happened in or near it located and honored with some monument, costly and showy in proportion to the importance of the event so honored.

els inside the edifice. To describe these various "stations" would require a volume, and it has been already done completely by Bartlett (*Walks about Jerusalem: Jerusalem Revisited*); Barclay (*City of the Great King*); Thomson (*Land and Book*); in *Smith's Dictionary of the Bible; Kitto's Cyclopædia;* by Tristram, and others. The numbers on the plan of the church indicate:—1. The entrance. 2. Chapel of the Angel; a small model of a church, 10 ft. wide and 20 ft. high, standing under the great dome, built of marble, and containing The Holy Sepulchre (3). 4. Is the "centre of the world," according to the Greeks (based on Ez. v. 5). 5. Latin church. 6. 49 steps of solid rock lead down to the Chapel of the "Finding of the Cross." 7. Calvary; to which there is an ascent of marble steps from near 1. Although it is no proof of the truth of the traditions which locate the "stations" in this church, yet De Vogue and others (Sandys) give us a great mass of historical evidence that there has been a Church of the Holy Sepulchre for many ages in the city. The oldest engraved *seal of the city* is that here given, dated A. D. 1150; and there seems to have been a small church inside the larger one at that time, as there is now. The next one, dated 1162–'72, gives the Tower of David and the Temple, besides the Sepulchre; which would favor the opinion of Fergusson, in *Smith's Dict.* (article Jerusalem), that Moriah, Zion, the City of David, and the Holy Sepulchre were all on the same hill, now called the Haram. The history is continued in the seal of Baldwin IV, 1174, with the inscription "Tower of David;" and also by many others, which may be seen in De Vogue's work. The plan of the church of those ancient

CHURCH OF THE HOLY SEPULCHRE.

One of the most extensive of these monuments is the Church of the Holy Sepulchre, a collection of buildings in a vast mass, without order, 350 ft. long by 280 wide, including 70 sacred localities, presided over by 17 different sects in separate chap-

times is very much like that of the present day. That in Sandys, of 200 yrs. ago, is almost identical. The Knights of St. John, the ruins of whose hospital are in the next block south of the Sepulchre Church, have left a seal of their order, which gives a hint of their objects and duties also. Jerusalem is now a sort of collection of churches and hospitals, with a great many vacant places strewed with ruins. Pilate's house, where Jesus was judged, is located at the N. W. corner of the Haram area, and it probably stood on the site of the Citadel of David. The Crusaders respected the Dome of the Rock, and held sacred service in it, but used the Aksa mosque for a stable, despising it as a work of Jews, the Temple of Solomon. It was so only in location, for El Aksa was built by the Mohammedans in the seventh century, on the

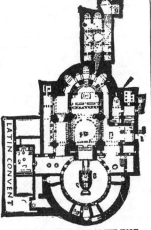

PLAN OF THE CHURCH OF THE HOLY SEPULCHRE.

site of the Temple of Solomon, whom they reverence among the prophets, as well as David, and also Jesus, the son of David.

The twelve columns around the centre (with four square piers at equal intervals) are of porphyry, and have gilded capitals; the canopy is of crimson silk. The outside of this church is eight-sided, of marble, covered in the upper part with the finest glazed tiles, in colors, to the top of the dome, which is finished with a spire and bronze crescent. The piece of native rock, the top of which shows white in the picture, is 60 feet long by 55 feet wide, and 12 feet high above the floor at the highest point, and is hollowed out underneath—forming a large room, which is believed by many to have been the real sepulchre of Jesus, now very much enlarged.

The Temple has so entirely disappeared, that "not one stone is left on another." And, besides, its very location is still a matter of guesses and speculation. Several churches, a pagan temple, and other buildings, have occupied the platform for ages, and have disappeared, leaving very few traces.

The first mention of a street in the city is in 2 Chr. xxix. 4, where Hezekiah gathered the priests and Levites into the East street and his soldiers in the street of the City of David (xxxii. 5, 6). The Bakers' street is mentioned as that from

HOLY SEPULCHRE, A. D. 1150.

which the prophet Jeremiah was to receive his daily allowance while he was in prison (Jer. xxxvii. 21). The Cheesemongers' street of Josephus is supposed to have been in the Tyropœon valley.

The circuit of the outer wall in the time of Christ was about four miles. Josephus says (Wars, v. 4) there were many towers 30 feet square (some larger), and solid for a hight of 30 feet. Above the base there were rooms for the soldiers; and over these again rooms and cisterns

for water. There were on the third wall 90 towers, 300 feet apart; 40 on the middle wall, and on the old wall 60. Psephinus, the most northern, was on high ground, N. W. of the city, was 105 feet high, and eight-sided. From its top could be seen the Jordan and the Dead Sea eastward, and the Great Sea westward. The tower Hippicus was named by Herod after his friend; and Phasælus after his (Herod's) brother, and it was 135 feet high; finished inside and outside "like a royal palace." Another was named after Mariamne, Herod's queen. It was 75 feet high, and equally splendid. The Castle of Antonia, at the N. W. corner of the Temple area, was built by John Hyrcanus. Pilate's judgment-hall was in this castle, which was probably on the site of David's citadel (John xviii. 28, xix. 9). The towers of Meah and Hananeel are also mentioned in Neh. iii. 1; Jer. xxi. 38.

The ancient plans located St. Stephen's Gate on the north side of the city, at what is now called Damascus Gate. The view shows a few of the tombs and gravestones, of which there are thousands in this valley of Jehoshaphat. The lions on each side of the gateway may date from the Crusades.

The water supply of the city has been remarkable in all ages for being sufficient in times of extreme drought, siege and famine. Hezekiah "stopped" some sources, which have remained hidden to the present; and it can only be supposed

CAVITAS. REGIS REGUM OMNIUM.
HOLY SEP. TOWER OF DAVID. TEMPLE.
Amorium I. 1162–1137.

that they were north of the city (2 Chr. xxxii. 4, etc.). Nearly every house has its cistern, or several, large or small. But the one pool of all others was Bethesda, which was near the Sheep-gate.

The masonry is of large blocks of stone, 18 to 20 inches square (A). (See cut on page 38, SECTION OF POOL). The joints are hollowed out, and blocks 16 inches deep inserted half their length (B); the spaces between these blocks being filled by others 8 inches deep. Over these is a coarse plaster with gravel (D); and the inside finish is a thick coat of cement.

The identity of this pool with that mentioned in the Gospel has been the source of many and long arguments, but the conclusion that it is the real Bethesda seems to be gaining in favor.

Siloam is supplied by an underground passage from the Virgin Fountain, 1700 ft. long. Recent explorations have discovered a water supply of the Virgin Fountain

TURIS DAVID.
Baldwin IV. 1174–1185. A. D.

from a vault in the side of Ophel above it, shown in the plan and section here given. From this and many other recent discoveries it appears that Jerusalem is undermined with a series of water-courses, which are frequently alluded to by Josephus and other ancient writers.

In all the accounts of the sieges of the city we read of the besiegers suffering from thirst, but of the besieged from hunger only, since there never was a scarcity of water inside of the walls.

HOSPITALIS JERUSALEM.
Knights of St. John.

The proof of the connection, by an underground passage, of the Fountain of the Virgin with the Pool of Siloam was obtained, with great labor and peril and imminent risk of life by Lieut. Warren, Sergeant Birtles and an Arab laborer. They were obliged to crawl along on their backs, carrying instruments, books and pencil, a lighted candle in the mouth, and in a stream of dirty water 12 inches deep, in a passage which was sometimes only 16 to 20 inches high. The passage is about 1700 feet between the two pools, crooked, and occupied the party about four hours in its exploration.

in this valley, seen by Sir John Maundeville as late as 1322: the *waters of Gihon* were called "the brook that flowed through the land," and was brought straight down to the west side of the City of David (2 Chr. xxxii. 30). Solomon was anointed king at the lower *fountain* of Gihon (1 K. i. 33–45), which was located somewhere between Acra, Bezetha, and Moriah, and not in Hinnom, as now stated (*Barclay*); the Gihon valley would then commence north of the Damascus Gate, and end in the Tyropœon: *Siloam; En Rogel; Motza* (*spring-head*), Ain el Durrage (?), S. E. of En Rogel; *Dragon's Well* (in Hinnom, not far from the Jaffa Gate, the ancient Valley Gate); *Aqueduct of Pilate*, "whereby he brought water from a distance of 400 furlongs" (Josephus, Wars, ii. ix. 4); the *Stone Aqueduct* described by Aristeus; *Solomon's Pools* at Etham, and the aqueduct from them to the city, giving off a branch to the *Great Pool*, now Lower Gihon. Barclay thinks Herod brought the water from Etham by a more direct route than Solomon, and supplied the Upper Gihon Pool, the *Serpent's Pool* of Josephus. *Pool of Hezekiah*, built by Herod; a very large Pool near the Fish Gate (near St. Ann Church, Brocardus, in 1283; *Lacus Quidam*, not located; *The Pool that was made* somewhere in the Tyropœon, of which there are no traces; *Ditch* between Zion and Ophel—bears all the marks of having been an ancient pool; a large Pool (100 feet around, near the Absalom Pillar; the Well of Flagellation and two large tanks near Damascus Gate; the "Sea" under the Temple site, into which there are eight well-holes, from

VIEW OF JERUSALEM.

Abundance of water was required in the Jewish public worship, a part of which was a ceremonial of ablution. The many sources of supply and the means of storing it for use during the dry season, sieges, and times of drought, may be seen in the following list of fountains, pools, etc.

The brook *Kidron*. There was "a little river"

the platform above; 43 well-mouths in the Haram area lead down to wells or reservoirs; Well of the Healing, in Valley street; the Pilgrim Pool, near the Herod Gate; Helena's Cistern, in the Coptic convent; Cotton Megara Pool; Lady Mary Pool, near the St. Stephen Gate; Bath of Tiberius, on Zion, near the English Cemetery; several very large pools, or tanks, within a mile radius of the city, more or less in ruins; and the great number of cisterns, before mentioned, under private houses, into which rain-water is conducted.

SOLOMON'S CISTERNS UNDER THE TEMPLE AREA.

A picture of a siege of the city was found sculptured on a slab in the ruins of Khorsabad (see cut on page 104), in the "Retiring Chamber" of the palace, and is a concise and interesting record. At that time, it seems that the brook Kidron was full of water, and there was a plenty of olive trees on the hills about the city. There are now but a very few trees near the walls, the most interesting being those in the Garden of Gethsemane. Titus cut down all the trees around Jerusalem, and his tenth legion was camped on Olivet, building their part of the wall surrounding the city, along the bottom of the valley of Kidron. The Turks have pleasure-grounds, or gardens, farther up the valley (half a mile or so), where they resort to enjoy the cool shade of the olive-trees, some of which are quite as large as those in Gethsemane, and, it may be, as old. The antiquity of those in Gethsemane is argued from the tax, which is fixed by the Turks at *one medina* for each tree, which rate dates from before or at the time of their conquest; all those planted since everywhere in the empire being taxed one-half their produce. This would carry the date back to A. D. 634, when Omar took Jerusalem; or to the time when the Turks took it, A. D. 1087.

There are no level streets, and the passenger is always ascending or descending, over rough and uncared-for ways. The houses are built on heaps of rubbish, which have been gathering for ages. The foundations for the Church of St. James (English) rest on piers, built up from the rock through 40 to 50 feet of debris. The streets are often very narrow, the widest being only eight to ten feet. The houses are often built across the street on arches; and the custom of shading them with awnings of mats or boards, suspended by ropes, makes them dark and cool, which is very grateful in that hot climate. Only two or three streets have a name, except such as are being adopted lately by the Franks, generally those used by the Crusaders. The materials used for building is the native limestone, generally broken into squares, not hewn, or sawn, except by the most wealthy. In many walls may be found fragments of ancient structures, such as cornices, columns, capitals, and mutilated sculptures, built in as raw material.

Timber is only brought from other countries, and therefore very costly, and is only used for window-frames and doors, but not for floors or roofs. The windows are always small, and, if large enough to admit a thief, are barred with iron, and give the houses a jail-like appearance. Window-glass is only found in the houses of the rich. Only one door opens on the street, and there are no windows in the lower story opening on the street, secluding the houses, but making dismal streets. The interior of the rooms is pleasing, because of the arches and domes required in forming the upper stories and roof. The floors are frequently laid with colored stones, arranged in most beautiful patterns.

The principal trade is in beads, crosses, incense, crucifixes, pilgrim-shells, staffs, pressed flowers, and other keepsakes (besides relics, which are made in great quantities), with the thousands of pilgrims and other travellers, who visit the country every year. Soap-making, and weaving of coarse cotton cloth, are almost the only active manufactures in the city.

A vast number live professedly on charity. There are separate bazaars, frequented by the different people: By the Jews, in the street near their great synagogue, on the east slope of Mount Zion; by the Turks, in David, Damascus, and Temple streets; by the Arabs, in Via Dolorosa (El Wad), near the St. Ann church; and by the Christians, in Patriarch street. The Cotton Bazaar was once a very grand structure, but it is now abandoned to rubbish, and only used as a passage-way to the Haram area.

This short account of the "Holy City" would be still more incomplete without some brief notice of Solomon's Temple, and its successors.

Whatever we know about them is to be found in the First Book of Kings, in Jeremiah, in Ezekiel (who saw the first temple in a vision, ch. xl.), in Josephus, in Aristeas; and after these, the modern books of Williams, Robinson, Barclay, and Paine, in our language; and of those in foreign, the best is the German of Dr. Neumann, of Gotha (*Die Stiftshutte*). Mr. Paine's plan is copied here, because of its simplicity, and seeming fidelity to the original, as critically and clearly interpreted by the

INTERIOR OF THE DOME OF THE ROCK.

author (*Solomon's Temple*—T. O. Paine). Of the temple of Zerubbabel there is a very short account in Ezra, and in Hecatæus, quoted by Josephus. The size was a third larger than Solomon's, but its ornamentation was less showy. The size of either was less than the average of our churches in the country villages. Josephus is almost the only authority for all we know about the Temple of Herod, which was the one seen by Jesus. There is not a word in the New Testament about its appearance, nor even its location. But it is supposed that while the figures of Josephus are correct as to the ground-plan, his figures of the elevation are twice the real height (*Ant.*, xv. 11, 3).

The bridge on which Titus stood at the siege and destruction of the city (described by Josephus) had fallen long ago, but its remains have been discovered by Robinson and Lt. Warren, and minute accounts published. The view engraved here shows the spring of the arch, which rested against the temple wall (Br. in the plan of Herod's Temple). The bridge was 51 ft. wide, and extended across the valley to Zion, 350 ft.; probably resting on 5 or 6 arches. One of the

JESHA'IAH (*Jah's salvation*). Son of Jeduthun, choir-leader in the temple, of the 8th division (1 Chr. xxv. 3).—2. A Levite, eldest son of Rehabiah, in the line of Amram (xxvi. 25).—3. Son of Athaliah and chief of the sons of Elam, who returned with Ezra (viii. 7).—4. A Merarite who returned with Ezra (viii. 19).

JESHA'NAH (*ancient*). A town which, with its dependent villages, was one of the three taken from Jeroboam by Abijah (2 Chr. xiii. 19). A place of importance in Benjamin, and now *Ain Sinia*, a well-watered village with vineyards, fruit-trees and gardens (Rob. iii. 80), three miles N. of Bethel.

JESHARE'LAH (*upright toward El*). Son of Asaph, chief of the 7th choir (1 Chr. xxv. 14). ASARELAH.

JESHEBE'AB (*father's abode*). Head of the 14th course of priests (1 Chr. xxiv. 13).

BROOK KIDRON

stones, shown in the cut, is 21 ft. long, and another 29, by nearly 6 wide.

The famous "Wailing-place" of the Jews (where they go to bewail the desolation of Zion) is a few rods north of this place.

"The past of Jerusalem is overflowing with thought. But the future is equally impressive. These ruins are not always to remain. The future Temple, and the restored Israel, when "Jerusalem shall be the throne of the Lord to all nations," claim the most earnest thought. The day when "the feet" of the Lord "shall stand on the Mount of Olives, which is over against Jerusalem toward the east," is full of importance; and whether we look back or forward, we have to speak of Zion as "the joy of the whole earth," for "salvation is of the Jews." The present missionary work in Jerusalem is deeply interesting. * * But surely there is no spot on earth like Jerusalem."—(Dr. Tyng).

JERU'SHA (*possessed*). Daughter of Zadok, queen of Uzziah (2 K. xv. 33). In Chronicles the name is JERUSHAH (2 Chr. xxvii. 1).

JESAI'AH (Heb. ISAIAH). 1. Son of Hananiah, grand-son of Zerubbabel (1 Chr. iii. 21).—2. A Benjamite whose descendants were chosen by lot to reside in Jerusalem after the return from captivity (Neh. xi. 7).

JE'SHER (*upright*). Son of Caleb by Azubah (1 Chr. ii. 18). JETHER.

JESH'IMON (*desert*). A more desolate region or place than a MIDBAR (*wilderness*), and applied to the plain and hillsides at the N. end and on the W. side of the Dead Sea. It consists of a level plain of nitrous earth, into which the feet sink several inches as into ashes, and hills of chalky limestone, without herbage, except a few alkaline plants and the usual fringe of the Jordan river. The Hill of Hachilah (*dark red cone*) may have been *Sebbeh*, (Masada), so well described by Josephus, as Metsadoth (strong-holds in 1 Sam. xxiii. 19), and the word CHORESH (Heb. for wood in verse 19) means a thicket, dense and thorny, such as is found along the shore there now.

JESHI'SHAI (*son of the old man*). Ancestor of the Gadites in Gilead (1 Chr. v. 14).

JESH'UA (*Jah saves*). JOSHUA or JEHOSHUA. 1. Joshua the son of Nun (Neh. viii. 17).—2. A priest in David's time, head of the 9th course (Ezr. ii. 36).—3. A Levite in the reign of Hezekiah (2 Chr. xxxi. 15).—4. Son of Jehozadak, the first high-priest after the return from captivity. His family succeeded for 14 times, down to Onias (Ezr. ii. 2; Neh. vii. 7). He took a leading part in the rebuilding of the Temple, and restoration of the nation. He was a man of earnest piety, patriotism, and courage. After a disuse for 50 years he restored the daily sacrifice on a new altar.— 5. Head of a Levitical house, who returned from captivity (Ezr. ii. 40).—6. A branch of the family of Pahath-Moab, of Judah (Neh. x. 14).

JESH'UA. *Yeshua,* S. near Moladah, occupied after the return from captivity (Neh. xi. 26).

JESH'URUN. Symbolical name for Israel in Deut. xxxii. 15, etc., meaning *most upright, or to be blessed,* in an endearing sense also, as little one, or dear one, therefore *good little people.*

JESI'AH (*Jah lends*). A Korhite, a hero with David at Ziklag (1 Chr. xii. 6).—2. Son of Uzziel (xxiii. 20). Jeshiah (error) in xxiv. 25.

JESIM'IEL (*whom El places*). A Simeonite, of Shinei's family (1 Chr. iv. 36).

JES'SE (YISHAI, *manly*). Son of Obed, father of David. His name is never mentioned again, not even when David took his parents to Nahash in Moab for security from Saul (1 Sam. xxii. 3). He was grandson of Boaz, one of the wealthy ones in that favored place. His wife's name is not mentioned. Tradition says that the king of Moab killed both Jesse and his wife, with their attendants.

JES'UI (Heb. ISHUAI). Son of Asher. The Jesuites were numbered in the plains of Moab (Num. xxvi. 44).

JE'SUS (Gr. and Latin form of the Heb. Joshua, or Jehoshua, *the help of Jah,* or *Saviour*). 1. The father of SIRACH, and grandfather of—2. The SON OF SIRACH (Eccles. i. 27), author of the Book of ECCLESIASTICUS, or the WISDOM OF JESUS, THE SON OF SIRACH. See HISTORY OF THE BOOKS. He was also known as Ben Sira, a writer of proverbs which closely resemble those in Wisdom.

2. **JE'SUS,** called JUS'TUS (*the just*). A disciple Paul at Rome (Col. iv. 11). Tradition makes him Bishop of Eleutheropolis.

3. **JESUS CHRIST.** The name Jesus means Saviour, and was a common name, derived from the ancient Hebrew Jehoshua.

The title CHRIST means anointed, consecrated, sacred, and is used only for the MESSIAH, who came in fulfilment of prophesy.

The prophets, from the time of Moses, hold up to view an illustrious person who was to appear, and should belong to the highest order of being, since the name of the Eternal One is His; and he should also be called Wonderful, Counselor, the Mighty God, the Everlasting Father; that he should assume human nature and be born of a virgin of the family of David (Is. xi. 1), in Bethlehem of Judæa, (Mic. v. 2), and his mission should be the salvation of his people and all mankind (Is. xlix. 6); that He should be despised and rejected of his people; be cut off, but not for himself; be wounded for men's transgressions, bruised for their iniquities; by His stripes men should be healed (Is. liii.); the Lord should lay on Him the iniquity of men; He should make his soul an offering for sin; and should be exalted and made very high; should see of the travail of his soul and be satisfied, and by his knowledge justify many; and Jehovah say to Him, "Sit thou at my right hand, until I make thine enemies thy footstool" (Ps. cx. 1); to Him should be given dominion, glory, and a kingdom, and all people should serve Him,—an everlasting dominion which shall not pass away (Dan. vii. 13, 14): all of which has been completely fulfilled in Jesus, the son of Mary of Nazareth, who was divinely appointed to be the Messiah, from everlasting, before the foundations of the world (Prov. viii. 23; 1 Pet. i. 20; Luke ii.).

Jesus was born in Bethlehem, and though the Christian Era is dated from his birth, modern chronologists insist upon a date for the momentous event at least four years earlier—that is to say, about B. C. 4. Some say B. C. 6. Joseph and

Mary were espoused and had gone up from Naza, reth to answer to the census-roll ordered by Augustus, for taxation; and they came to Bethlehem because they were of the house of David. The event was announced by an angel to some shepherds who were watching their flocks by night in the field near the village; and the heavenly host, who were with the angel, praised God, saying, "Glory to God in the highest, and on earth peace, good-will toward men" (Luke ii. 14).

The coming of Christ was an event of general expectation, and the Gentiles were next to the shepherd Jews in rendering homage to Him, in the visit of the Wise Men from the East, who brought offerings and rich presents (Matt. ii. 1).

Herod the king, who is described as a cruel tyrant, having been made jealous of the wonderful child, who was born King of the Jews, ordered that all the children (about 12) in Bethlehem from two years old and under should be killed; and Jesus was saved only by Joseph hurrying him and his mother away to Egypt, where it is supposed that they stayed about a year.

On the way from Egypt the family avoided Bethlehem and returned to Nazareth.

When he was twelve years old, his parents took him with them to attend the annual feast of the Passover, when he was one day found in the Temple, questioning and answering the Jewish priests, and displaying astonishing wisdom (Luke ii. 47).

The account of his childhood and youth, and even maturity, up to "about thirty years of age," besides the incident in the Temple, is given in two grand sentences by Luke, indicative of the increase and development of the human powers, the spiritual being perfect from the beginning: "And the child grew, and waxed strong in spirit, filled with wisdom, and the grace of God was upon him. And Jesus increased in wisdom and stature, and in favor with God and man" (ii. 40, 52).

The modesty and brevity of the Gospels on this part of the life of Jesus, is one great evidence of its truth, as compared with tales of fiction, wherein the hero is perfected in minute and wonderful details.

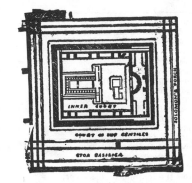

PLAN OF HEROD'S TEMPLE.

Joseph (the reputed father of Jesus, and so called by his mother Mary, ii. 48), is not again mentioned in the Scriptures after this event. Whether he lived to witness the wonderful events and profit by the teaching of the Saviour, does not appear.

The question of the family of Jesus, as to whether his mother Mary had any other children besides him, is unsettled, although Matthew distinctly mentions four brothers, besides sisters. Some have held that these were brothers and sisters-in-law, children of Joseph by a former wife, and others, that they were the children of the sister of Jesus' mother, who was also named Mary, and was the wife of Clopas; this would have them to be cousins of Jesus. See MARY.

The person, the life, and the work of Jesus are the subject of the whole New Testament, (and, in prophesy, of the Old), and, as a whole, are the *historical* and *doctrinal* foundation of Christianity.

His life may be studied in several sections by students, as here arranged :

1. Birth, including the appearances to Zechariah, Elizabeth, Mary, and Joseph, and the birth of John the Baptist.

2. The witnesses of the Messiah—the Shepherds, the Magi and Herod.

3. Preparation and baptism.

4. Fasting, temptation and public manifestation in Galilee, Judæa and Samaria.

5. His offered proof of his divinity in his miracles, may by classed in two groups :

(1). Of Love. { In raising the dead. Curing mental disease. Healing the body.

(2). Of Power. { In creating; destroying; overcoming men's wills.

6. The instruction in his discourses and parables.

7. Incidents showing the effect of his contact with various persons.

8. The scene of his ministry, of which details are given in the GEOGRAPHY.

Matthew, Mark and Luke's records are mainly of the events in Galilee, never mentioning his visits to Jerusalem until the time near the crucifixion, and only implying such visits and teaching by his lamentations, and the visits of the scribes, etc., besides the intimacy with the family at Bethany. John records a few acts in Galilee, and gives all the rest of his book to the events in Judæa—nearly one-half being about the last three months; and seven chapters (one-third), on the last few days. Neither writer attempted a com-*plete chronology*, but aimed at a general picture of *the life*. See GOSPELS, in the HISTORY OF THE BOOKS.

9. The duration of the ministry cannot be determined exactly. Those who interpret the prophesy of Isaiah literally, limit it to one year (Is. lxi. 2). But John mentions *six feasts*, at five of which Jesus was present. 1. (ii. 13), soon after his baptism; 2. (v. 1), a feast when he went up to Jerusalem; 3. (vi. 4), and another, from which he stayed away, in Galilee; 4. (vii. 2), the feast of Tabernacles, to which he went privately; 5. (x. 22), the feast of the dedication; 6. (xii. xiii), and the last, the Passover, at which he was crucified—extending through three years.

10. And, while on this subject of time, it may be valuable to consider, by the help of the map, tracing each movement as closely as possible, the amount of labor, traveling—mainly on foot (or on animals)—that must be compressed into a single year, if the short period is chosen.

The date of the birth of Jesus, and the month and the day, have each been the subject of much debate, without any definite settlement. The various opinions have ranged through four years of time, and have suggested nearly every month in the year. Tischendorf and Wieseler say that Jesus could hardly have been born before the first of January, A. U. C. 750; and suggest February as the latest date probable. Gresswell says that April 5 or 6 must be the day of his birth (A. U. C. 750). Dr. Robinson supposes it could not have been later than in the autumn of A. U. C. 749; while it *may* have occurred one or two years earlier; Lardner fixes the time about the middle of August or the middle of November, A. U. C. 748 or 749; Winer, Ideler and others say 747; Dr. Wordsworth says in the spring of 749 (B. C. 5); Clement of Alexandria says some placed the day on April 20, and others on May 20; the 25th of December as the day dates from the traditions of the 4th century.

HARMONY OF EVENTS FROM THE FOUR GOSPELS.

	Matthew.	Mark.	Luke.	John.
Genealogy, - - - - - - - - -	i. 1–17		iii. 23–38	
Angel appeared to Elizabeth, Yuttah, - -			i. 5	
Angel appeared to Mary, Nazareth, - - -			i. 25	
Mary visits Elizabeth, Yuttah, - - - -			i. 39	
Jesus born, Bethlehem, - - - - -	i. 18–25		ii. 1	
Shepherds watch, Bethlehem, - - - -			ii. 8	
Circumcision, Bethlehem, - - - - -			ii. 21	
Presentation, Jerusalem, - - - -			ii. 22	
Visit of Wise Men, Bethlehem, - - - -	ii. 1			
Flight into Egypt, - - - - - -	ii. 13			
Jesus with the Doctors, - - - -			ii. 40	
Baptism of Jesus the Christ, - - - -	iii. 13	i. 9	iii. 21	i. 32
Temptation, Quarantana, - - - - -	iv. 1	i. 12	iv. 1	
Andrew and Peter follow him, - - - -				i. 37
Nathanael's witness, - - - - -				i. 49
Water made wine, Cana, - - - - -				ii. 1
Cleanses the temple, 1st passover, - - -				ii. 12
Nicodemus, Jerusalem, - - - - -				ii. 23
Jesus and John baptizing, Enon, - - -				iii. 22
Woman of Samaria, Shechem, - - - -				iv. 1
Nazareth, Nobleman's son healed, - - -				iv. 46
Draught of fishes, Capernaum, - - -			v. 6	
Four apostles called, Capernaum, - - -	iv. 13	i. 16	v. 1	
Demoniac healed, Capernaum, - - - -		i. 21	iv. 31	
Simon's wife's mother healed, Capernaum, -	vii. 14	i. 29	iv. 38	
Circuit in Galilee, - - - - -	iv. 23	i. 35	iv. 42	
Leper healed, Galilee, - - - - -	viii. 1	i. 40	v. 12	
Stills the storm, Galilee, - - - -	viii. 18	iv. 35	viii. 22	
Land of the Gadarenes, - - - - -	viii. 28	v. 1	viii. 26	
Jairus' daughter raised, Capernaum, - - -	ix. 18	v. 21	viii. 41	
Woman healed, Capernaum, - - - -	ix. 18	v. 21	viii. 41	
Blind man, Demoniac, Capernaum, - - -	ix. 27			
Paralytic, Capernaum, - - - - -	ix. 1	ii. 1	v. 17	

	Matthew.	Mark.	Luke.	John.
Matthew called, Capernaum, - - - -	ix. 9	ii. 13	v. 27	
Second Passover, Jerusalem, - - - -				v. 1
Pool of Bethesda, Jerusalem, - - -				v. 2
Plucking grain on the Sabbath, - - -	xii. 1	ii. 23	vi. 1	
Withered hand healed, Samaria, - -	xii. 9	iii. 1	vi. 6	
Jesus by the sea, Capernaum. The twelve chosen,	x. 24	iii. 13	vi. 12	
Sermon on the mount, Hattin, - - -	v. 1		vi. 17	
Centurion's servant healed, Capernaum, - -	viii. 5		vii. 1	iv. 6
Widow's son raised, Nain, - - - - -			vii. 11	
Messengers from John, - - -	xi. 2		vii. 18	
Woe to the cities of Galilee, - - -	xi. 20			
Jesus' feet anointed, Capernaum, - -			vii. 06	
The two debtors, - - - - -			vii. 41	
Second circuit in Galilee, - - -			viii. 1	
Parable of the sower, Capernaum, - -	xii. 1	iv. 1	viii. 4	
" Candle under a bushel, -		iv. 21	viii. 16	
" Sower, - - - - -		iv. 26		
" Wheat and tares, - -	xiii. 24		xiii. 18	
" of grain of mustard-seed,	xiii. 31	iv. 30	xiii. 20	
" of the leaven, - -	xiii. 33			
Wheat and tares explained, - - -	xiii. 36			
The treasure, pearl and net, - - -	xiii. 44			
His mother and brethren, - - -	xii. 46	iii. 31	viii. 19	
Reception at Nazareth, - - -	xiii. 53	vi. 1		
Third circuit in Galilee, - - -	ix. 35	vi. 6		
Twelve sent out, Capernaum, - -	x.	vi. 7	ix. 1	
Herod's opinion Jesus (Tiberias), -	xiv. 1	iv. 14	ix. 7	
Death of John the Baptist, - - -	xiv. 3	vi. 17		
Third passover, - - - -			vi. 4	
5000 fed near Bethsaida, - - -	xiv. 13	vi. 30	ix. 10	vi. 1
Walks on the sea of Galilee, - - -	xiv. 22	vi. 45		vi. 16
Miracles in Gennesaret, - - -	xiv. 34	vi. 53		
Bread of life, - - - -				vi. 22
Washen hands, Capernaum, - - -	xv. 1	vii. 1		
Syrophœnician woman, coast, - -	xv. 21	vii. 24		
Miracles of healing in Galilee - -	xv. 29	vii. 31		
4000 fed in Decapolis, - - - -	xv. 32	viii. 1		
The sign from heaven, Magdala, - -	xvi. 1	viii. 10		
Leaven of the Pharisees, - - -	xvi. 12	viii. 14		
Blind man healed, Bethsaida, - -		viii. 22		
Peter's profession near Cæsarea, - -	xvi. 13	viii. 27	ix. 18	vi. 66
His passion foretold, - - - -	xvi. 20	viii. 30	ix. 21	
Transfiguration on Mt. Hermon, - -	xvii. 1	ix. 2	ix. 28	
Of Elijah, - - - - - -	xvii. 10	ix. 11		
Lunatic healed, - - - -	xvii. 14	ix. 14	ix. 37	
His passion foretold in Galilee, - -	xvii. 22	ix. 30	ix. 43	
Fish caught with the tribute, Capernaum, -	xvii. 24			
The little child, Capernaum, - - -	xviii. 1	ix. 33	ix. 46	
One casting out devils, - - - -		ix. 38	ix. 49	
Offenses, - - - - - -	xviii. 6	ix. 42	xvii. 2	
The lost sheep, - - - - -	xviii. 10		xv. 4	
Forgiveness of injuries, - - -	xviii. 15			
Binding and loosing. Forgiveness, - -	xviii. 18			
Parable unmerciful servant, - -	xviii. 21			
Salted with fire, - - - - -		ix. 49		
Journey to Jerusalem, - - - -			ix. 51	vii. 1
Fire from heaven, Samaria, - - -			ix. 52	
Foxes have holes, birds have nests, etc., -	viii. 19		ix. 57	
The seventy sent out, Capernaum, - -			x. i	
Feast of Tabernacles, Jerusalem, - -				vii.
Woman taken in adultery, Jerusalem, -				viii. 1
Dispute with the Pharisees, Jerusalem, -				viii. 12
The man born blind healed, Jerusalem, -				ix. 1
The good shepherd, Jerusalem, - -				x. 1
The seventy return, Jerusalem, - -			x. 17	
The good Samaritan, Jerusalem, - -			x. 25	
Mary and Martha, Bethany, - - -			x. 38	
The Lord's Prayer, - - - -	vi. 9		xi. 1	
Prayer effectual, - - - - -	vii. 7		xi. 5	
"By Beelzebub," Jerusalem, - -	xii. 22	iii. 20	xi. 14	
The unclean spirit, Jerusalem, - -	xii. 43		xi. 24	
The sign of Jonah, Jerusalem, - -	xii. 38		xi. 29	
The light of the body, - - - - {	v. 15 / vi. 22		xi. 33	
The Pharisees, - - - - -	ii. 3		xi. 37	
What to fear, - - - - -	x. 26		xii. 1	
Master, speak to my brother. - - -			xii. 13	

	Matthew.	Mark.	Luke.	John.
Covetousness. Watchfulness, - - - -	vi. 25		xii. 16	
Galileans that perished, - - -			xiii. 1	
Woman healed on the Sabbath, Perea, -			xiii. 10	
The grain of mustard-seed, Perea, - -	xiii. 31	iv.	xiii. 18	
The leaven, Perea, - - - -	xiii. 33		xiii. 20	
Toward Jerusalem, Perea, - - -			xiii. 22	
Are there few? Bethany, - - -			xiii. 23	
Warning against Herod, - - -			xiii. 31	
O Jerusalem! Jerusalem! - - -	xxiii. 37		xiii. 34	
Dropsy healed on the Sabbath, - -			xiv. 1	
Chief rooms. Great supper, - -	xxii. 1		xiv. 7	
Following Christ with the cross, -	x. 37		xiv. 25	
Parables—Lost sheep, Piece of money, Prodigal Son,			xv.	
Unjust steward, Rich man and Lazarus, -			xvi.	
Offenses, - - - - - -				
Faith and merit, - - - - -	xviii. 6		xvii. 1	
Ten lepers healed, Samaria, - -	xvii. 20		xvii. 5	
How the kingdom cometh, Perea, -			xvii. 11	
Parable of unjust judge, Perea, -			xvii. 20	
Parable of Pharisee and Publican, Perea, -			xviii. 1	
Of divorce, Perea, - - - -			xviii. 9	
Infants brought to Jesus, Perea, -	xix. 1	x. 1		
Rich young man inquiring, Perea, -	xix. 13	x. 13	xviii. 15	
Promises to the disciples, Perea, -	xix. 16	x. 17	xviii. 18	
Laborers in the vineyard, Perea, -	xix. 27	x. 28	xviii. 28	
His death foretold the third time, Perea, - -	xx. 16			
Request of James and John, Perea, - -	xx. 17	x. 32	xviii. 31	
Heals two blind men, Jericho - -	xx. 20	x. 35		
Zaccheus. Parable of ten talents, Jericho -	xx. 29	x. 46	xviii. 35	
Feast of Dedication, Jerusalem, -	xxv. 14		xix. 11	x. 22
Beyond Jordan, Bethabara, - - -				xi. 1
A. D. Raising Lazarus, Bethany, -				xi. 45
29　Meeting of the Sanhedrin, Caiaphas -				xi.
Apr.　Jesus in Ephraim, - - -				xi. 54
" 1. Mary anoints his feet, Bethany, -				xii. 3
" 2. Triumphal entry into Jerusalem, -	xxvi. 6	xiv. 3	vii. 36	xii. 12
2d cleansing of the temple, - -	xxi. 1	xi. 1	xix. 29	ii. 13
" 3. The barren fig-tree, Olivet, -	xxi. 12	xi. 15	xix. 45	
Fig-tree withered, between Bethany and the	xxi. 17	xi. 11		
city, - - - - - -		xi. 19		
" 4. Pray and forgive, - - -	vi. 14	xi. 24		
By what authority—parable of the two sons, - - - - -	xxi. 23	xi. 27	xx. 1	
Parable of the wicked husbandman,	xxi. 28			
Parable of the wedding garment, -	xxi. 33			
The tribute money, - - - -	xxii. 1	xii. 1	xx. 9	
The state of the risen, - - -	xxii. 15	xii. 13	xiv. 16	
The great commandment, - -	xxii. 18	xii. 18	xx. 20	
David's son and David's Lord, -	xxii. 34	xii. 28	xx. 27	
Against the Pharisees, - - -	xxii. 41	xii. 35	xx. 41	
The widow's mite, - - - -	xxiii. 1	xii. 38	xx. 45	
Christ's second coming, - - -		xii. 41	xxi. 1	
Parable of ten virgins, - - -	xxiv. 1	xiii. 1	xxi. 5	
Parable of five talents, - - -	xxv. 1			
The Last Judgment, - - -	xxv. 14		xix. 11	
Greeks ask to see Jesus. The voice,	xxv. 31			
John's reflections on the Jews' unbelief,				xii. 20
His crucifixion foretold, - -				xii. 36
The priests, scribes and elders conspire,	xxvi. 2			xii. 32
" 5. Judas Iscariot, - - -	xxvi. 3	xiv. 1	xxii. 1	
" 6. Pascal supper, last passover, -	xxvi. 14	xiv. 10	xxii. 3	
Disciples' feet washed, - -	xxvi. 17	xiv. 12	xxii. 7	xiii. 1
The disciples contend, - -				xiii. 5
The Lord's Supper, - - -			xxii. 24	
Peter's fall foretold, - -	xxvi. 26	xiv. 22	xxii. 19	
Last discourse. Departure—Comforter,	xxvi. 30	xiv. 26	xxii. 31	xiii. 36
Vine and branches. Abiding in love,				xiv. 1
Work of Comforter, - - -				xv. 1
Prayer of Jesus Christ, - -				xvi.
" 7. Gethsemane, on Olivet, - -				xvii. 1
The betrayal, Gethsemane, - -	xxvi. 36	xiv. 32	xxii. 40	xviii. 1
Malchus' wounded ear healed, -	xxvi. 47	xiv. 43	xxii. 47	xviii. 2
Before Annas. Hill of Evil Counsel, -	xxvi. 51	xiv. 47	xxii. 50	xviii. 10
Peter's denial, - - - -	xxvi. 57	xiv. 53	xxii. 54	xviii. 12
Jesus before the Sanhedrin, Jerusalem,	xxvi. 69	xiv. 66	xxii. 56	xviii. 17
Before Pilate, Jerusalem, - - -	xxvi. 59	xiv. 55	xxii. 63	xviii. 19
	xxvii. 1	xv. 1	xxiii. 1	xviii. 28

Note: Column bracket annotations in the table read "In the Temple." (for rows from "By what authority" through "The widow's mite"), "On Olivet." (for rows from "Christ's second coming" through "His crucifixion foretold"), and "Jerusalem." (for rows from "The priests, scribes and elders conspire" through "Prayer of Jesus Christ").

	Matthew.	Mark.	Luke.	John.
Judas dies, - - - - -	xxvii. 3			
Jesus before Herod silent, - - -			xxiii. 4	
Accused and condemned, - - -	xxvii. 15	xv. 6	xxiii. 13	xviii. 29
Mocked by soldiers, - - -	xxvii. 27	xv. 16	xxiii. 36	xix. 3
Crowned with thorns, - - -	xxvii. 29	xv. 17		xix. 2
The crucifixion, Calvary, - - -	xxvii. 35	xv. 24	xxiii. 33	xix. 18
The veil rent—Darkness, - - -	xxvii. 51	xv. 38	xxiii. 45	
The body buried by Joseph, - - -	xxvii. 57	xv. 43	xxiii. 50	xix. 38
" 8. The sepulchre guarded, - - -	xxvii. 62			
" 9. The Resurrection, - - -	xxviii. 1	xvi. 1	xxiv. 1	xx. 1
Appearance of Emmaus, - - -		xvi. 12	xxiv. 13	
Appearance of Jerusalem, - - - .		xvi. 14	xxiv. 36	xx. 19
Appearance Sea of Tiberias—Charge to Peter,				
Appearance on a mount in Galilee—(Paul),	xxviii. 16			xxi. 1
Appearance in Jerusalem—(Peter in Acts), .				
Ascension, Olivet, - - - - -		xvi. 19	xxiv. 50	
Unrecorded works, - - - - -				xxi. 25

(bracketed group at left labeled "40 days")

The life of Jesus combined in a three-fold character the offices of prophet, priest and king. His prophesies pointed both to the manner and the time of the mission and work of redemption; and, as John said, were really clear light shining; his priestly office was shown in his vicarious atonement for the sins of men; and his kingly office appears in his royal power of subduing all men to his will for the good of his people. To his church he was also prophet, priest, and king above all others who had held either of those offices. He first said, "No one hath seen God at any time, the only begotten Son, who is in the bosom of the Father, he hath declared him" (John iii. 16). Jesus founded a system of ethics, revised and overruled all the old systems of morals, and so purified the system that it will stand for all the coming ages without changing. This was done among those men who thought they were learned and wise, and that they needed only to extend Phariseeism or Essenism to perfect the moral system of mankind, when Jesus showed them that such ascetic notions were born in the desert and would die there. An obscure Galilean wood carver readily and surely did what so many eminent men had failed to accomplish—he laid the foundations of a universal religion—on a perfect morality, showing how the divine and human elements can be made to appear in harmonious action in every soul. He is therefore superior to all the prophets who preceded him.

The priestly element was almost peculiar in Judaism. The Pharisees enlarged upon the hint of Moses and declared the whole people to be a nation of priests; but that the sacrifices and oblations (while so many fell short of the ceremonial purity) had to be offered by a mediating priesthood, and by them alone, as having immediate access to God, and only acceptable from them, while it was held to be blasphemy to attempt to change the institutes of Moses (Acts vi. 11, 14,) even although the prophets had so distinctly said, something higher and purer was needed, and would be given from above, being brought by the Messiah, the great spiritual king, successor of David (Ps. civ). The sufferings and glory, struggle with temptation and sin, ransom paid, and atonement made, whereby the guilt of iniquity was to be forever atoned, and sacrifice and oblation cease, and a new temple consecrated (Zech. vi. 12), in every heart, was the burden Jesus bore in his character and office of the great high-priest (Heb. x.). The necessity for his work was not seen until after it had been done, and he was gone from among men. His priesthood was more perfect than any before him.

The Jews had expected a temporal king, a King of Zion, as announced in the letter of the prophets, the spiritual meaning being overlooked. The angel said to Mary that the throne of his father David should be given to him; the Eastern Magi inquired after him, and did obedience to him as King of the Jews (Luke i. 32). Herod struck at the infant as at a pretender to his throne; John announced him as coming to set up the Kingdom of Heaven; and even when he declared before Pilate the spiritual nature of his kingdom, the Jews failed to see what sort of a King he was. However feeble and powerless he may have seemed then as a king before Pilate, and when wearing the crown of thorns and the purple robe, succeeding history has proved his actual power among men, above and beyond all other kings, moving and controlling their hearts and minds, and this power is extending throughout the world, not by force or violence, but as gently and surely as the light of the sun. As a king he is more winning, powerful, more enduring, and more holy and good than any who have reigned before him.

GOAT OF AOUDAD.

Christians in all ages have wished for some picture or figure of Jesus, which should represent the Saviour or the Man of Sorrows, and a great number of attempts have been made to represent one or the other of those phases of the great character: some with an expression of calm serenity and dignity, without grief; and others with the crown of thorns, purple robe, and face of sorrowful aspect. Except a few crude outlines, painted on the walls of sepulchres, (as in the Catacombs under Rome), or on tablets, or rude engravings of the early ages, no work of this kind, claiming excellence, can be dated earlier than Leonardo da Vinci's or Raphael's time, who have made the most acceptable works, from which nearly all others have been imitated; and even theirs were reproductions of the traditionary likeness, fashioned after the Greek model of the young hero-god Apollo, or the Egyptian Serapis. The story that Pilate had a likeness engraved on an emerald is a fable, and the likeness in question is a copy from Raphael's cartoon of the Miraculous Draught of Fishes. The likeness, the actual birth-place, the several places of his residence, of his crucifixion, and of the sepulchre have one and all been lost beyond all hope of authentic recovery. We know that he was born in Bethlehem, raised in Nazareth, began his work in Cana and Capernaum, was crucified and buried near Jerusalem, but the exact places have, perhaps by divine intention, been purposely forgotten.

QUARRY CAVE UNDER JERUSALEM.

JĒ'THER (*excellence*). 1. Jethro, father-in-law to Moses (Ex. iv. 18), who is also called Hobab (Num. x. 31).—2. Gideon's eldest son (Judg. viii. 20).—3. Father of Amasa, general of Absalom's army. ITHRA (2 Sam. xvii. 25). He was an Ishmaelite, or a Hebrew living among Ishmaelites. He married Abigail, David's sister (probably in the land of Moab).—4. Son of Jada (1 Chr. ii. 32). 5. Son of Ezra, in the line of Judah (1 Chr. iv. 17).—Ezra and Amram being one, this Jether may be Aaron, as some suggest.—6. Chief in Asher, father of Jephunneh (1 Chr. vii. 38).

JĒ'THETH (*a tent-pin*). A duke in Edom (Gen. xxxvi. 40). There is a place called *El Wetidah* in Nejed (in the *Dahna*, sandy desert), and an *El Wetid* range of mountains, which may preserve the name of the ancient family, for Wetedeh is stable, firm, as a tent-pin.

JETH'LAH (*hanging*). In Dan, near Ajalon (Josh. xix. 42). Lost.

JĒ'THRO (*superiority*). JETHER. Father-in-law of Moses (Ex. iv. 18, xviii. 1), and also called Hobab (Num. x. 31; Judg. iv. 11). Reuel (Raguel) was the head of the family into which Moses married (Ex. ii. 18), but was probably his wife's grandfather, for Hobab was his son (Num. x. 29). He became a convert to the worship of Jehovah, and sacrificed (Ex. xviii. 12).

JĒ'TUR (*camp*). Son of Ishmael (Gen. xxv. 15). ITURÆA.

JEŪ'EL (*El's treasure*). Chief in Judah, of the sons of Zerah, at the first occupation of Jerusalem (1 Chr. ix. 6).—2. A son of Adonikam, returned from captivity (1 Esd. viii. 39).

JĒ'USH (*Jah hastens*). 1. Son of Esau by Aho-

libamah (Gen. xxxvi. 5).—2. Benjamite chief, son of Bilhan (1 Chr. vii. 10).—3. Levite of the house of Shimei (xxiii. 10).—4. Son of king Rehoboam and Abihail (2 Chr. xi. 18).

JĒ'UZ (*Jah counsels*). Benjamite chief (1 Chr. viii. 10). Born in Moab, son of Shaharaim and Hodesh.

JEW. Short form of JĔHŪDĪ (*people of Judah*). First mentioned in 2 K. xvi. 6, when the king of Syria drives the (Jehudim) Jews from Elath. Jeremiah frequently uses it, perhaps because the tribe of Judah was very numerously represented in the captivity. In the N. T. the Jews are spoken of as the determined opponents of the gospel.

The history of the Jews, as a people, may be divided into three eras: 1. From Abraham (or Heber) to the close of the collection of the Laws, originally oral, then written, B. C. 536;—2, ending A. D. 600,—and 3. From then to the present. The chief interest to the Bible student is found in the history before A. D. 70, since which time the affairs of this people have had but little value in the world, as compared to them during the ages before. The influence of foreign people and native powers may be distinctly traced from age to age: of Persia, in organization, order, and the ritual; of Greece, by liberty and speculation; of the Asmonean leaders, in independent thinking and faith; of the Herods, the separation of the church and state, with the falling to pieces of the Jewish Church in favor of its successor, the Church of Jesus Christ.

JEW'ESS. Born a Hebrew, of any tribe (Acts xvi. 1), as the mother of Timothy, and Drusilla the wife of Felix (xxiv. 24). See HEROD.

JEW'ISH. Paul warns Titus (i. 14) against Jewish fables. See FABLE.

JEW'RY. Judah, Judæa (Dan. v. 13; Luke xxiii. 5; John vii. 1).

JEWS' LANGUAGE. Jewishly (2 K. xviii. 26).

JEZANI'AH. JAAZANI'AH. AZARIAH.

JEZ'EBEL (*chaste*). Wife of king Ahab, mother of Athaliah, queen of Judah, and Ahaziah and Joram, kings of Israel. She was daughter of Ethbaal, king of the Zidonians, who had proved himself a powerful and wise king. Jezebel brought her religion with her, and transplanted it into the willing hearts of the Hebrews (1 K. xvi. 31), and the king of Israel and his people adopted formally the worship of the Phœnician gods. Elijah, Carmel, Naboth, Jehu, and Jezreël, are names that recal the main points in her history, which may be read in those articles.

Jezebel is charged with sorcery in the O. T. (2 K. ix. 22), and in the New (Rev. ii. 20), where her name is used as the symbol of a wife given over to unholy practices. As human nature is the same from age to age, so do persons enact the same deeds over and again.

JĒ'ZER (*image*). Son of Naphtali (Num. xxvi. 49). Jezerites.

JEZI'AH (*Jah sprinkles*). Of the family of Parosh; married a Gentile wife (Ezr. x. 25).

JEZI'EL (*El's assembly*). Benjamite with David at Ziklag (1 Chr. xii. 3).

JEZLI'AH (*Jah preserves*). Benjamite, son of Elpaal (1 Chr. viii. 18).

JEZŌ'AR (*whiteness*). Son of Helah, wife of Asher (1 Chr. iv. 7).

JEZRAHI'AH. A Levite, chief chorister at the dedication of the wall (Neh. xii. 42).

JEZRĒ'EL (*El has planted*). Founder of Etam

(1 Chr. iv. 3). "These are the families of the father of Etaus."

JEZ'REEL (*what God plants*). At the west foot of Mt. Gilboa, on a hill overlooking the great plain of Jezreel (Esdraelon, Judith iv. 5). The hill is rocky and steep on the N. E. side, and about 100 ft. high. Carmel can be seen to the west, and the Jordan valley to the east. There was a temple here to Astarte, with 400 priests, supported by Jezebel; Ahab's palace (ivory house, 1 K. xxiii. 39); a watch-tower (2 K. ix. 17), which may be also the tower in Jezreel near which Pharaoh encamped when Josiah "went against him" and was wounded (xxiii. 25). The spring of Harod is about 1 m. E. where the story of Gideon's night adventure with lamps and pitchers is located, and also the defeat and death of Saul and Jonathan. To this city Elijah ran before Ahab from Carmel, 12 ms.; here Naboth was murdered, that Ahab might have his vineyard; and the "house of Ahab" (the whole family) were killed; and Jezebel was thrown from a window and eaten by dogs in the same field that was taken from Naboth. There are about a dozen poor houses and a ruined tower in the modern village, which is called Zerin.—2. A town in Judah, near Carmel (Josh. xv. 56). Here David took Ahinoam the Jezreelitess for his first wife (1 Sam. xxvii. 3).—3. Eldest son of the prophet Hosea (i. 4).

JIB'SAM (*pleasant*). Son of Tola, of Issachar (1 Chr. vii. 2).

JID'LAPH (*tearful*). Son of Nahor (Gen. xxii. 22).

JIM'NA. Jimnah, eldest son of Asher (Num. xxvi. 44). IMNAH.

JIMNI'TES. Descendants of Jimna.

JIPH'TAH (*freed*). Judah, in the Shefelah (Josh. xv. 43). Lost.

JIPH'THAH-EL (*El opens*), **THE GORGE OF.** Jotapata (the same city) was besieged by Vespasian, held out, and stood a long time (B. J. iii. 7). Now Jefat, 12 ms. N. W. of Nazareth. The valley (*gorge*) of Abilin extends from near Jefat to the plain of Acre. It is inclosed with steep, wooded hills.

JO'AB (*Jah his father*). Son of Zeruiah, David's sister. He and his brothers Abishai and Asahel cast their lot with David (1 Sam. xxii. 3), and their history runs close to his. Joab's native power and and martial deeds made him the most famous of the three brothers, and he was ambitious and crafty, jealous and revengeful, as is shown in his history as "captain of the host." Joab earned at Jebus his title of commander-in-chief. The duel between 12 young heroes on each side, between the forces of Joab and Abner, took place at the pool of GIBEON, and brought on a general battle, which turned in favor of Joab and David's forces. Abner quarreled with Ishbosheth and went over to David, when Joab killed him, treacherously pretending it was "in blood-revenge" for his brother Asahel, whom Abner had killed. David dared not punish Joab, because he and his two brothers were so useful to him in the army. In the war against Hanun, Joab made a speech which is justly noticed as a perfect model of military address: "Be of good courage, and let us play the men for our people and for the cities of our God, and the Lord do as seemeth him good," (2 Sam. x. 12). It was in the second year of this war that Uriah was murdered by David, by the help of Joab. He also, at the close of the siege, sent for David, and gave him his share of the spoil, generously waiving his own right.

Joab was very kind and generous to Absalom in restoring him to his father's favor, after his flight from killing his brother Amnon, but was equally ready to kill Absalom when in rebellion against David, especially since Absalom preferred Amasa

as his commander. Joab met at the great stone in Gibeon, his cousin Amasa, who had been appointed commander-in-chief over him, and treacherously murdered him as he did Abner. David prayed often to be released from such a terrible man. He opposed David's desire to number the people with true religious fervor (2 Sam. xxiv. 3). In the last days of David, Joab joined Adonijah in rebellion to the king, but Solomon was proclaimed, and executed his father's injunction, even taking Joab from the sacred sanctuary of the altar (Ex. xxi. 14), and killing him by the hand of Benaiah.—2. Son of Seraiah, of Kenaz (1 Chr. iv. 14).—3. Sheikh of a family which outnumbered any other in the return from captivity (Ezr. ii. 6).

JO'ACHAZ. JEHOAHAZ. The son of Josiah (Matt. i. 11).

JO'ACHIM. 1. JEHOIAKIM, JOACIM.—2. A high-priest in the time of Baruch, at Jerusalem (Bar. i. 7).

JO'ACIM. 1. JEHOIAKIM.—2. JEHOIACHIM (1 Esd. i. 43).—3. Joiakim, the son of Jeshua (v. 5).—4. High-priest in Jerusalem (Judith iv. 6, 14).—5. Husband of Susanna. See HISTORY OF THE Books.

JOADA'MUS. GEDALIAH.

JO'AH (*Jah is helper*). 1. Son of Asaph, historian to Hezekiah. Commissioned to treat with the Assyrian general Rabshakeh (Is. xxxvi. 3).—2. Son of Zimmah (1 Chr. vi. 21), brother of Ethan (ver. 42).—3. Son of Obed-edom (xxvi. 4), door-keeper.—4. Father of Eden, assisted in Hezekiah's reformation (2 Chr. xxix. 12).—5. Son of Joahaz, a recorder or historian to Josiah (xxxiv. 8).

JO'AHA (*Jah sustains*). Father of Joah.—5. Jo'anan. Johanan, son of Eliashib.

JOAN'NA (*Jah's gift*). Son of Rhesa (Luke iii. 27). Hananiah in 1 Chr. iii. 19?

JOAN'NA (*Jah's gift*). Wife of Chuza, Herod's steward, contributed to the support of Jesus, and brought spices to put into the tomb where his body was laid (Luke viii. 3, xxiv. 10). Joan.

JOAN'NAN. Jehohanan, surnamed Caddis, eldest brother of Judas Maccabæus (1 Macc. ii. 2).

JO'ASH. JEHOASH (*Jah gave*). Father of Gideon, a wealthy man of the Abiezrites, who permitted the worship of idols, but also defended his son for destroying them (Judg. vi.).—2. Son of Ahaziah and 8th king of Judah. The only child of Ahaziah who escaped the massacre by Athaliah, being saved by a pious aunt and kept in the temple 6 years (2 Chr. xxii. 11). Athaliah counseled the murder of all Jehoram's relatives as a security against rebellion or conspiracy (2 Chr. xxi. 4, 6), and also advised her son Ahaziah (xxii. 10), until his death, when she reigned 6 years, until Joash was brought out. Pure religion was restored (ex-

LION WEIGHT.

cept that some high places were not destroyed), sacrifice and contributions restored the temple. After 23 years, Jehoiada, the high-priest, died; Joash had evil counselors and revived the worship of Baal and Ashtaroth, and being rebuked by a son of Jehoiada, Zechariah, he caused him to be stoned in the court of the temple (Matt. xxiii. 35). After an invasion by Hazaël, king of Syria, who carried off a great sum in treasure, Joash was murdered in his bed by servants. The prophets Elisha and Joel lived in this age. He reigned 40 years, from B. C. 878 to 838. His name is omitted in Matthew's genealogy.—3. Son and successor of Jehoahaz on the throne of Israel, B. C. 840-825 (2 K. xiv. 1; comp. xiii. 1 with xiii. 10). The kingdom was in a very reduced condition from the inroads of Hazael, and Joash, either from pity or policy, visited the prophet Elisha just before the prophet's death, receiving from him a promise of success against the king of Syria, when the incident of the arrows occurred (2 K. xiii. 14–19). He gained victories over Syria, and also over Judah, and carried off immense treasures from Jerusalem, and threw down 600 feet of the walls.—4. Several others of this name are only known in the lists.

JŌ'ATHAM. Jotham, son of Uzziah (Matt. i. 9).

JŌAZAB'DUS. Jozabad, the Levite.

JŌB (Heb. YOB, *convert*). 3d son of Issachar (Gen. xlvi. 13). Jashub in 1 Chr. vii. 1.

JŌB (Heb. IYOB, *afflicted*). The hero of the BOOK OF JOB; see HISTORY.

JŌ'BAB (YOBAB, *howling*). Son of Jokban (Gen. x. 29). The etymology points to a district or locality which is a *howling desert*, and may be anywhere in the desert region of Arabia, S.—2. King of Edom (Gen. xxxvi. 33), in the line of Esau, son of Zerah of Bozrah. The Septuagint identifies this king with Job, the suffering patriarch.—3. King of Madon, routed by Joshua at Merom (Josh. xi. 1).—4. Chief in Benjamin.

JOCH'EBED (Heb. YOKEBED, *Jah's glory*). The aunt and wife of Amram, and mother of Moses and Aaron (Ex. vi. 20). The Sept. says "cousin" instead of aunt.

instead of Joel, *Vashni* is given as a name; the word vashni (VESHENI) means "and the second." The word may also mean (VESHNI) *Jah is strong*, as Joel is sometimes rendered, and so be used as a substitute.—4. Chief in Simeon (1 Chr. iv. 35).—5. Son of Hanoch, in the line of Carmi, in Reuben (1 Chr. v. 4).—6. Chief in Gad (v. 12).—7. Son of Izrahiah, in Issachar, general of a division of 36,000 (1 Chr. vii. 3). Son of Uzzi, according to the Syriac. Seven others of this name were not very noted, except as leaders and officers about the temple.

JŌE'LAH (*Jah helps*). Son of Jeroham of Gedor, with David at Ziklag.

JŌE'ZER (*Jah's help*). With David among the Philistines (1 Chr. xii. 6).

JOG'BĒHAH (*elevated*). Built and fortified by the tribe of Gad (Num. xxxii. 35). Mentioned with Jaazer and Beth Himram, and now called *Jebeiha*, 4 ms. N. of *Amman* (Burck. Rob.).—2. In the account of Gideon's pursuit of the Midianites (Judg. viii. 11). Gideon's route can be traced to *Nowa* (KARKOR). The village of *Jabieh*, near *Tell Jabieh*, a few miles N. E. of *Fik*, is the ancient Jogbehah.

JOG'LI (*exiled*). Father of Bukki, chief in Dan (Num. xxxiv. 22).

JŌ'HA (*Jah revives*). Son of Beriah, a Benjamite (1 Chr. viii. 16).—2. One of David's guard, a Tizite, son of Shimri (xi. 45).

JOHA'NAN (*Jah's gift*). JEHOHANAN. 1. Son of Azariah in the line of Zadok (1 Chr. vi. 9), high-priest in Rehoboam's reign.—2. Son of Elioenai, in the line of Zerubbabel (1 Chr. iii. 24).—3. Son of Kareah, captain in the siege of Jerusalem, and one of the first to submit to the Chaldean governor. He arrested the murderers of this governor. (Jer. xl. 8, xli. 11). He, with others, passed a night at the Khan of Chimham (see BETHLEHEM), and settled in Egypt (2 K xxv. 23). 8 others of this name were but little known.

JOHAN'NES (1 Esd. ix. 29). Jehohanan in Ezr. x. 28.

JOHN. Short form of Jehohanan (*Jah's gift*). 1. Father of Mattathias, of the Maccabees (1 Macc. ii. 1).—2. Eldest son of Mattathias; Caddis (ii. 2; ix. 36).—3. Father of Eupolemus, Envoy to Rome (viii. 17).—4. Son of Simon (xiii. 53).—5. Envoy to Lysias (2 Macc. xi. 17).—6. One of the high-priest's family who sat in judgment, with Annas and Caiaphas, on the Apostles Peter and John (Acts iv. 6). Rabbi Johanan ben Zaccai, president of the Great Synagogue at Jamnia.—7. Surname of Mark (Acts xii. 12).

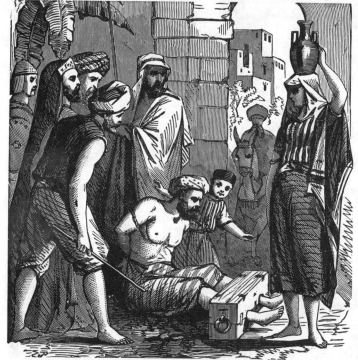

SYRIAN CULPRIT IN THE STOCKS.

JŌ'DA. Judah the Levite in 1 Esd. v. 38 (Ezr. iii. 19); Hodaviah (ii. 40); Hodevah (Neh. vii. 43); Hodijah (x. 10); Sudias (1 Esd. v. 26).

JŌ'ED (*Jah is witness*). Son of Pedaiah, a Benjamite (Neh. xi. 7).

JŌ'EL (*Jah is El*). The prophet. See HISTORY OF THE BOOKS.—2. In 1 Chr. vi. 36 an error for Shaul of ver. 24.—3. Eldest son of Samuel, the prophet (1 Sam. viii. 2), and father of Heman, the singer. He and his brother Abiah were judges in Beersheba, and disgraced their office by corruption, bribes, and perverted judgment. A singular error of some copyist has occurred in 1 Chr. vi. 28, where

8. **JOHN**, THE APOSTLE. Was a native of Bethsaida, on the Sea of Galilee, the son of Zebedee and Salome. He was acquainted with the character of Jesus as the Messiah before the call to be an apostle. In company with his brother James, and

Peter he was specially favored by Jesus on several occasions: at the Transfiguration; the restoring of Jairus' daughter; in the garden Gethsemane; and (including Andrew) at the discourse on the fall of Jerusalem. He was mistaken, with the others of the twelve, in his idea of the temporal mission of the Messiah; and with James joined his mother in the ambitious request for places of dignity and honor. He and James were called Boanerges, for their zeal. John was called also the DIVINE and the REVELATOR, from his writings. His family could not have been poor, because they kept servants, and contributed to the support of Jesus; and he received Mary into his home at Jerusalem, after the crucifixion. He also enjoyed social privileges, and the acquaintance of the high-priest.

Jesus loved John, who was the youngest of the twelve. Twice he showed himself to him as the Lord, by a miracle touching his own occupation, that he could understand without doubt. He was probably more intimate with him than any other, as the leaning on his bosom at the supper would indicate. After the ascension Paul found him living in Jerusalem, where he was a pillar in the church; and he was yet there when Paul was in Ephesus, A. D. 58. After Paul left Ephesus, John was sent there, about A. D. 65. From there he is believed to have been taken to Rome during one of the persecutions of the time, where he was thrown into boiling oil, from which he emerged unscathed. He was exiled to Patmos, where he wrote the Apocalypse, about A. D. 96. (*Patmos and 7 Churches*). Polycrates (A. D. 200) calls him a martyr, but does not record either the time, place, or manner of his death. His epistles give evidence of a large diocese, requiring many journeys of pastoral visitation. He is described as a mild man, affectionate almost to effeminacy; but as a true Oriental, sometimes firing up as in the case of the Samaritans, when they rejected Jesus.

9. **JOHN,** THE BAPTIST. Son of Zacharias, and Elisabeth (Luke i. 5). Birth foretold in their old age by an angel; preceded our Lord's by six months. Dwelt alone in barren region west of Dead Sea; his dress of woven camel's hair, his food, locusts and wild honey. When he emerged to preach the baptism of repentance for the remission of sins, crowds gathered because of his preternatural birth, his life and the expectation that some great one was about to appear (Matt. iii). Baptized Jesus. Reproved Herod for taking to himself Herodias, wife of his brother Philip; cast into prison by Herod (Luke iii. 20), and beheaded at behest of Salome, prompted by her mother Herodias, and Herod, charmed by her grace, promised her whatsoever she would ask (Matt. xiv. 1–12).

JOI′AKIM. From Jehoiakim. High-priest, son of Jeshua (Neh. xii. 10).

JOI′ARIB. From Jehoi′arib. 1. Three of this name, but little known.

JOK′DEAM (*by the people*). City in Judah, near Hebron (Josh. xv. 56).

JŌ′KIM. JOIAKIM. Son of Shelah son of Judah (1 Chr. iv. 22).

JOK′MEAM (Kitzaim in Josh. xxi. 22). In the Jordan Valley, near the east end of Esdraëlon (1 K. iv. 12).

JOK′NEAM (*had by the people*). City in Zebulon (Josh. xxi. 34). *Tell Kaimon* near the east end of Carmel.

JOK′SHAN (*fowler*). Son of Abraham and Keturah (Gen. xxv. 2), whose sons were Sheba and Dedan. The Arabs have a Yokshan in their literature, but there is no trace of connection with the son of Abraham.

JOK′TAN (*made small*). Son of Eber (Gen. x. 25), father of the Joktanite Arabs in the S. of Arabia. Their dwelling was from Mesha to Sephar, a mount of the East (v. 30). The ancestor of the southern Arabs was KAHTAN, who is said to be the same as Joktan. The Jewish tradition may have been adopted by the Mohammedans. There is undisputed evidence of the settlement of Joktan's sons in that region, who founded a great kingdom which existed for ages before our era, and was renowned in the world of classical antiquity.

JOK′THEEL (*subdued by El*). City in the Shefelah of Judah (Josh. xv. 38), near Lachish, now *Keitulaneh.*—2. The cliff *Selah*, the stronghold of the Edomites (2 K. xiv. 7; 2 Chr. xxv. 11–13).

JŌNA. JOHANAN or JONAH. BAR-JONA (PETER).

JON′ADAB. JEHONADAB. 1. Son of Shimeah, nephew of David (2 Sam. xiii. 3). He was "very subtle," and a friend of his cousin Amnon, heir to the throne, and gave him the fatal advice concerning his sister Tamar, and he knew of Absalom's purpose to kill Amnon (verse 32).

JO′NAH (YONAH, dove). Son of Amittai, of Gath-hepher, in Zebulon. See JONAH, in the HISTORY OF THE BOOKS.

JO′NAN. Son of Eliakim (Luke iii. 30). JOHN.

JO′NAS. Greek for Jonah.

JON′ATHAN (*Jah gave*). JEHONATHAN. 1. Eldest son of Saul the king. He is first mentioned at the age of 30, when his father was made king (1 Sam. xiii. 2). He was married, and had one son, Mephibosheth (if no more), born about 5 years before his death (2 Sam. ii. 8, iv. 4). He was the heir to the throne. His courage was shown in the night exploit at Michmash, and his strength and skill in the use of the bow and spear (i. 22). He was a friend to David, and stood between him and his father as a peacemaker. The story of the friendship of David and Jonathan is one of the most pathetic in history. The people knew his value and sustained the elders in saving his life when in danger from Saul's foolish vow. He nobly yielded his own expectations of the kingdom to David, whom he believed to have been divinely selected. He perished with his father on Gilboa (1 Sam. xxxi.). David sung a eulogy over their graves that is unmatched for pathos and elevation (2 Sam. i. 18). Jonathan's son Mephibosheth was cared for by David in his own family.—2. A Levite, son of Gershom, who after the death of Joshua, impiously served as a priest, first to Micah, and then to the Danites in Dan Laish (Judg. xvii. 18).—3. Son of Abiathar the priest, who took an active part in Absalom's revolt, aiding David as a spy (2 Sam. xv. 36, xvii. 17); and also in the revolt of Adonijah (1 K. i. 42).—4. A soldier, son of Shimeah, and nephew to David, who killed a gigantic Philistine of Gath (2 Sam. xxi. 20).—5. Uncle to David, "a counselor, a wise man, and a scribe," (1 Chr. xxvii. 32). The word DOD, *uncle*, means any near relation, or even a friend (Is. v. 1).—6. Son of Jashen, a hero (2 Sam. xxiii. 32), who may be the one called the son of Shage, the Hararite (1 Chr. xi. 34). Nine others of this name are mentioned, one of whom owned the house in which Jeremiah was in prison (Jer. xxxvii. 15).

JŌ′NATH-Ē′LEM-RĒCHŌ′KIM. The name of a musical instrument which produced soft, mellow sounds, and found only in the title of Ps. lvi., as a direction to the choir leader.

JOP′PA (YAFA, *beauty*). In Dan on the seashore, a seaport in Solomon's time (Josh. xix. 46; 2 Chr. ii. 16). The cedar for the two temples, Solomon's and Zerubbabel's, and the palaces of David and Solomon was landed here (Ezr. iii. 7). Jonah embarked here when trying to escape from the unpleasant mission to Nineveh. During the wars of the Maccabees it was a stronghold (1 Macc. x. 75). Peter's "vision of tolerance" was on a house-top in this city (Acts x. 9–18). A Christian bishop resided here until the Saracens took the place. Pilgrims from all lands have landed here for many ages to go up to Jerusalem.

It was taken and retaken many times during the crusades. Saladin destroyed and Richard (Lionheart) rebuilt the fortifications. In the 13th century there was not a house entire on the site. It has now 5,000 people, 3 convents, Greek, Latin, and Armenian, and several mosques. The bazaars are interesting and antique. The city is on a hill, close to the sea, and is surrounded by miles of orchards—orange, lemon and many other fruits, besides gardens, which are scarcely surpassed.

The poet Ovid located here the beautiful myth of Andromeda and the sea-monster, a poetical allusion to the rocky barriers of the port, which to this day make approach to Joppa impossible by sea in a storm.

JŌ'RAH (*watering*). Ancestor of a family of 112 who returned from captivity (Ezr. ii. 18). Hariph in Neh. vii. 24.

JŌ'RAI (*Jah teaches*). A Gadite (1 Chr. v. 13).

JŌ'RAM. JEHORAM.

RINGS.

JŌR'DAN (*the descender*). Heb. YARDEN; Ar. *El Urdon*, descender, and *Esh Sheriah*, the wateringplace. The largest river in Palestine. Rises in Mt. Hermon and empties into the Dead Sea. The sources are in the south, west and north-west slopes of Hermon, whose melting snows supply the fountains, some of which are so copious that each one of three forms a full stream at once. These three are: the Hasbany, the most northern, longest and muddiest; the Leddan (Ar. *El-ed-Dan*), the largest but shortest; and the Baniasy (of Paneas), the clearest.

There are, also, a fountain and stream from Ijon; one from Belat, 3 miles N. W. of the Huleh lake, another from *Ain Mellahah* one mile N. W.; all of which are perennial, and large enough, each one, to turn a mill. About a mile S. of Hasbaiya the fountain of Shiba, 5 miles up the slope of Hermon, sends a stream north of the hill on which stands the Pagan temple of Hibbariyeh in ruins; another stream from the same direction is the Lūsiäny, and flows into the Jordan at El Gujar, after coursing around the ruined castle of Bostra. These streams flow in deep, rocky channels, several feet below the general level of the country. The slopes of Hermon are "alive with streams" which supply the Jordan. The Hasbany, Leddan, and Baniasy unite in the Huleh marsh, pass S. into the lake Huleh, and flowing west from its S. angle, tumbles down a rocky ravine, with cliffs on each side, full of rapids, sinking 700 feet in 9 miles, to the Sea of Galilee.

From the S. of this sea the Jordan flows in a channel 100 feet wide, rocky, winding, *always descending;* falling over about forty cascades and rapids, sinking 600 feet in 60 miles, in a straight line, but making nearly 200 by its windings, to the Dead Sea, where it is a shallow stream, 500 feet wide, and deep in the rainy, or shallow in the dry season. The surface is there 1300 feet below the ocean. (SEA).

The tributaries below Genessaret on the east are the Yarmuk (Jabbok?), 5 ms. S. of the sea, 120 feet wide and 4 deep; and the Jabbok, which has two outlets into the Jordan, about midway between the two seas.

There are many winter torrents, dry in summer, and several fountains, as at Pella, Wä'dy Shē'riah, Nim'rin, on the east; and on the west, Bethshan (from the well of Harod), Sä'lim, Wä'dy Fer'räh (from Mokhua), Wä'dy Fasä'il, Wä'dy Nemäirah,

Wä'dy Kelt, and the Fountain of Elisha at Jericho, besides many small and nameless fountains and streams on both sides.

This section is the only part referred to in the Bible.

Nearly the whole course is below the ocean level. Fountain at Hasbaiya 1700 feet above.

"	" Paneas	1147	"	"
"	" Dan	350	"	"
Lake Huleh		100	"	"
Sea of Galilee		650	"	below.
Dead Sea		1312	"	"

JORDAN VALLEY (ARABAH) is a long, narrow plain, N. to S., bordered by steep and nearly parallel ridges; Gilead on the east, rising 3,000 to 5,000 ft., and Samaria, on the W., rising from 2,000 to 3,000; and is about 6 ms. wide in the northern part, widening to 10 or 12 at Jericho. The sides are not regular, but are broken by ridges, or spurs, from the mountains, which run out into the plain at several places, indicated on the map, as at Bethshan, and SURTABEH (Zarthan). See GEOLOGY in PALESTINE. The surface is not level, but lifted into low hills and ridges. The map shows the course of the river through the Ghor as very winding. The upper Jordan, above the lake and marsh Huleh, is fordable in many places, the brooks being shallow, with stony beds. In the rainy season they often overflow, and are then impassable for a few days at a time. S. of the lake Huleh there is more water, and the fords are fewer. Just north of the Sea of Galilee, near Bethsaida Julias, there is a ford over sand-bars in the dry season. The road from Damascus into Galilee passes over a bridge about 2 ms. S. of the Huleh, called Jacob's Daughters (after a mythical race, said to live in oak trees), ½ a m. S. of the Sea of Galilee there is a Roman bridge, in ruins, and a ford called SEMAKH. The bridge Mejamia is Saracenic, 5 ms. further S., but there is no ford.

There is no mention of a bridge over the Jordan in the Scriptures, and the Mejamia is the only one now in use, S. of the Sea of Galilee. Opposite Bethshan the river is fordable in the dry season. Near Succoth, just N. of Wady Yabesh (Jabesh), there is an island with sand-bars on each side, forming a ford in summer. This is probably the Bethabara of Judges vii. 24. S. from this place to the mouth of the Jabbok there are several fords at low water. 10 ms. S. of the Jabbok is the ford on the Shechem Es Salt road, and traces of a Roman bridge. There is a ford both above and below the pilgrim's bathing-place, opposite Jericho. The upper one, called El Mashrää, is the supposed one crossed by Joshua.

The banks of the river are fringed with trees, flowering shrubs, cane and reeds; oleanders, hollyhocks, purple thistles, marigolds, anemones, willows, tamarisk, cedar, arbutus, aspen, and ghurräh; where beasts and birds in great numbers find shelter.

JŌ'RIM. Son of Matthat (Luke iii. 29).

JOR'KOAM (*people spreading*). City near Hebron (1 Chr. ii. 44).

JOSA'BAD. Soldier with David at Ziklag (1 Chr. xii. 4).

JOS'APHAT for Jehoshaphat in Matt. i. 8.

JŌ'SE. Son of Eliezer (Luke iii. 29).

JOS'EDEC. JOHOZADAK.

JŌ'ŞEPH (*he will increase*). The son of Jacob by Rachel, was born in Haran, (near Damascus?) B. C. 1726. Of his youth, up to the age of 17, we know nothing; but at that age he had so excited the envy and hate of his brothers, by simply receiving his father's gifts and attentions, and by telling his ominous dreams, and also by his acts of filial fidelity, that his brothers, prompted by Judah, sold him for a slave at Shechem, for 20 shekels of silver, to a band of Ishmaelites, who took him to

Egypt (Gen. xxx. xxxvii.). Reuben had intended to rescue Joseph, and had him cast into a dry pit, from which he might be taken afterward; but he was too late. His coat (of many colors) was a long tunic with sleeves, striped or embroidered. (See DRESS). The brothers dipped this in a kid's blood, and sent it to Jacob, who was deceived by the trick, and believed Joseph had been killed by some wild beast.

The merchants sold him to Potiphar (chief of the executioners), a native of Egypt, and an officer of the Pharaoh (B. C. 1709), in the reign of Thothmes III, whose ring is engraved on page 7 (Gen. xxxix.).

In Potiphar's house he prospered, rising to the highest position of honor and confidence. Being tempted by his master's wife, and honorably denying her request, he was falsely accused by her, and thrown into prison. Here he again prospered, and was advanced to the charge of all the other prisoners (Ps. cv. 17–18).

While in the prison, two other prisoners, a butler and a baker, dreamed dreams which Joseph interpreted (Gen. xl.). These accounts are interesting, because they agree with the manners of the ancient Egyptians, as recorded on their monuments (Anc. Egypt ii. 152).

Joseph begged the butler, when he should be restored to favor, as he showed from his dream, to think of him, and speak of him to the Pharaoh; but he did not do so (Gen. xl. 13–16, 23), until the Pharaoh dreamed two prophetic dreams, which found in Joseph a successful interpreter, on the recommendation of the butler (xl.). He was then released, after two years' confinement. The dreams foreboded the approach of a seven years' famine; and on consultation with his advisers, Joseph was chosen by the Pharaoh to exercise full power over all Egypt, except the throne, as one whose wisdom was of divine origin, in token of which he put his ring on Joseph's hand, invested him with royal garments, and gave him a new name, Taphnath-paaneah (saviour of the world); and gave him for a wife Asenath, daughter of Potipherah, a priest of On.

He was now thirty years old. His two sons, Manasseh and Ephraim, were born during the seven years of plenty. His wisdom appeared when the famine was known to extend to "all lands" i. e. bordering on Egypt, and their people came to buy corn in Egypt (xli. 56–57). Among others, the ten brothers of Joseph came also, and he recognized them; but they did not know him, for he had probably adopted the dress and speech of Egypt, and besides, the boy of seventeen that they sold for a slave was now a man over thirty, and a governor.

Joseph severely tried and punshed his brothers by calling them spies, putting them in prison for three days, and detaining one (Simeon) while the others returned with corn to Canaan, with orders to bring Benjamin down to Egypt. But even while pretending this severity his good heart caused him to weep; it may be as much from joy at seeing them, as from anxiety about Benjamin and his father.

As soon as Benjamin came his manner changed—with difficulty only could he act longer in a false character, and he gave orders to prepare for them to dine with him at noon (hiding himself to weep in his room). The account of the dinner agrees exactly with the monuments as to the customs of the Egyptians, which were also adopted by the Jews. Joseph was served by himself—his brethren by themselves, and the Egyptians also apart by themselves; and when each one was seated in order, according to his birthright, Simeon being released and with them, they wondered that any one should know their ages.

Joseph wished to try how far his brothers would be faithful to his father, and laid a plan to trap

them and detain Benjamin by putting a cup in Benjamin's sack. On being arrested when a little way out of the city, and brought back before Joseph, with Benjamin as the detected criminal, Judah showed the deepest regard for his aged father's feelings, and offered himself a ransom, that Benjamin might return to him. This, in the Scripture, is one of the most touching passages in the whole course of literature (Gen. xliv. 18–34).

Joseph could bear it no longer, but made himself known to his brothers, and then his first question was, "Is my father alive?" and he hastens to relieve them of anxiety and fear, by showing them that it was God's providence that sent him to Egypt to prepare the way for their salvation from death by famine (xlv. xlvi.).

Pharaoh gave Joseph leave, and ordered him to bring his father and his household into Egypt; and accordingly they were brought and settled in Goshen, where Joseph met his father, honored him by presenting him before the king, and sustained him and his through the remaining years of famine (xlvii. 12).

Joseph's prudence and policy made Pharaoh absolute master and owner of all Egypt, except the priest's land, by the sale of the stores which had been laid up during the years of plenty. This is the greatest social revolution recorded in history—the reduction of an entire nation to slavery or dependence by famine (13–26).

Jacob died, and Joseph had his body embalmed and carried to the cave of Machpelah (l. 13).

BAAL.

Joseph's brothers feared him after his father's death, and coming near, begged his forgiveness, when he made the noble reply: "Fear not; I will nourish you and your little ones."

He lived to the age of 110 years, and saw Ephraim's children to the third generation; and Manasseh's also were brought up on his knees.

When he died, they embalmed his body, and put it in a coffin in Egypt. (B. C. 1616.)

He had reminded them of God's promise to bring them again into Canaan, and required them to carry his bones with them when they went. So they carried the body in the desert for forty years, and laid it in its final resting-place at Shechem (Josh. xxiv. 32).

Joseph is above all others the purest character known to history, (always excepting Jesus). Unlike David, Solomon, and any other, he left only good reports of his heart and hands. His trials, resistance to temptation, degradation, exaltation, saving his people, and confounding his enemies, mark him as a type of the Christ.

JŌ′ṢEPH. The son of Heli, the husband of Mary, and the legal father of Jesus (Matt. i.). The first fact we learn of him is his descent from David. He is then mentioned as the betrothed husband of Mary.

This custom of espousal was the beginning of marriage, and was made by the parents if the parties were under age. It was a public and formal proceeding, confirmed by oaths, and presents to the bride (Gen. xxiv. 22, 53). Twelve months were allowed to pass before the marriage ceremony; and the betrothal could only be broken off by a bill of divorce. Mary was the daughter and heir of Joseph's uncle, Jacob.

The age at which marriage was legal was 18; but probably, then as now, in Palestine, many married much younger—from 12 years upward; so if this was a first marriage, with Joseph as well as Mary, they were most probably under 20 years, and it may be that Mary was only 15 to 18. During the twelve months after the betrothal, Joseph was grieved at the discovery that Mary was with child, and intended to divorce her as privately as possible; but being reconciled by divine instruction in a dream, he accepted her as his wife. Mary bore several children to Joseph, two of whom became believers after the crucifixion, and James was the first Christian bishop of Jerusalem. We have also the names of Joseph, Simon, and Jude. Of the daughters no names are given (Matt. i. 18, 24, 25, xxvi. 56, xiii. 55, 56).

Joseph was an artisan of some kind (the original Greek word meaning *smith*, or maker of articles out of any material); and it is probable that he was a carver of wood for interior decoration (a carpenter), and that his son Jesus was taught the same trade. All handicraft were held in honor, and they were learned and followed by the sons of the best men.

The decree of Augustus Cæsar, taxing all the people, required them to appear for that purpose at their proper places, according to their tribes; so Joseph and Mary were at Bethlehem (if they did not reside there) when Jesus was born. At the proper age for presenting the child in the temple, Joseph went with the child and his mother, and heard Simeon's and Anna's prophetic words. He was also present when the magi visited the child; and being warned in a dream, "took the young child and his mother at night and departed into Egypt." On his return, after Herod's death, "he turned aside" and dwelt at Nazareth.

When Jesus was 12 years old, they went up to Jerusalem, to the annual feast of the Passover, and the incident of the child among the doctors occurred.

Joseph is not mentioned again in the gospels after this time.

It is supposed that he died before the crucifixion, from the words of Jesus when on the cross, recommending his mother to the care of the beloved disciple (John xix. 26). The question of his neighbors at Nazareth, as recorded by Mark, seems to indicate that he was then dead.

COIN OF ANTIOCHUS III.

JOSEPH 3, of Issachar, one of the spies (Num. xiii. 7).—4. One who had married a Gentile wife (Ezr. x. 42).—5. Four of the ancestors of Jesus had this name (Luke iii. 23, 24, 26, 30).—6. Of Arimathea. All we know of him is that he had some wealth, and was a member of the Sanhedrin, a secret disciple of Jesus, and that he appeared for a time, taught one great lesson, and was heard of no more. He was looking and waiting for the Messiah; did not consent to the judgment against Jesus, and begged for his body, that it might be properly buried. A tradition says he went to England, and settled there, near Glastonbury.

JOSEPH, called **BARSÁ'BAS** (*son of the old man, or wisdom*). Nominated but not chosen to fill a vacancy in the 12 (Acts i. 23). Also called Justus. The fact that he was nominated to be an apostle shows that he had seen Jesus, heard and believed, and had been with the others, perhaps constantly. Eusebius says he was one of the 70.

JŌ'SES (*Jesus, or Joseph*). 1. Son of Eliezer (Luke iii. 29).—2. Brother of Jesus (Matt. xiii. 55). —3. Joses Barnabas (Acts iv. 36).

JŌSĒ'PHUS (Greek-Latin form of Joseph). FLA-

vius Josephus is the ancient historian, whose works were composed from materials found in the Scripture, the Apocrypha, the Targums, and in Jewish traditions. It is believed that he intended to tell the truth so far as he knew, except when the Jewish people, or the Roman power were to be flattered, when his text was colored for that purpose. This may be the reason why he so carefully omitted any account of Jesus and his teachings, which must have caused a great commotion in the Jewish church, if considered only in the light of a new sect—the Nazarenes. Recent explorations confirm his statements in matters of history, except in minute figures, in which exaggeration seems to have been sometimes the design.

JŌ'SHAH (JOSHAVIAH, *Jah lets dwell*). Chief in Simeon. Son of Amaziah (1 Chr. iv. 34).

JOSHA'PHAT (JEHOSHAPHAT), the Mithnite, a hero in David's guard (1 Chr. xi. 43).

JOSHÁVĪ'AH (*Jah lets dwell*). Son of Elnaam, one of David's guard (1 Chr. xi. 46).

JOSHBEKĀ'SHAH (*Jah sits firm*). Son of Heman, leader of the 16th choir (1 Chr. xxv. 4).

JOSHEBBAS'SEBET (*the people turn to Jah*). The Ethnite (in the margin of 2 Sam. xxiii. 9).

JOSH'ŪA ((*Jah his help*). (The same in the Hebrew as the original of Jesus). The son of Nun, and successor of Moses as leader of the people. His name was first Oshea (Num. xiii. 8), and in the N. T. he is called Jesus (Acts vii. 45; Heb. iv. 8). He was of the tribe of Ephraim (1 Chr. vii. 27). He is first mentioned in Ex. xvii., at the time of the attack of the Amalekites, but in such a manner as to convey that he was well known before; and Moses at that time indicated him as his successor by giving him a new name (or title), Jehoshua (*salvation*). He was one of the 12 spies (Num. xiii. 16). He opposed Aaron's calf-worship, and he with Caleb were the only two souls excepted from the judgment of wandering and dying without seeing Canaan, and was specially selected even when Moses was rejected at the waters of Meribah-Kadesh. He did not originate, his office and work being completion—leading the people into the Land of Promise, dividing and occupying Canaan, and destroying their enemies. His personal and official life is without a blemish, except the hasty treaty with the Gibeonites. The people of Israel under Joshua were nearest to the original conception of a united, obedient, willing, company of children serving a father. But he was not perfect; since he did not occupy all the land, nor prevent the bitter quarrels which divided the people after his day. He received his commission (or had it confirmed), in the same manner as Paul did, in a vision (Josh. v. 13–15), from the Lord Jesus (when he was 84). He was a type of Jesus the Christ, as was also Jeshua, the high-priest, in the second redemption of the nation (Zech. iii.). See BOOK OF JOSHUA in the HISTORY OF THE BOOKS, and TIMNATH SERAH. He died at the age of 110.

JOSH'ŪA. JESHUA. The son of Josedech, who was carried away by Nebuchadnezzar (1 Chr. vi. 15), and high-priest after the return from Babylon. There are several other persons of this name, of whom very little is known.

JOSĪ'AH (YOSHIAHU, *Jah heals*). 1. Son of Amon, and 15th king of Judah, from B. C. 641 to 610, reigning 31 yrs., from 8 yrs. old. His history is given in 2 K. xxii., xxiv.; 2 Chr. xxxiv., xxxv., and Jeremiah i. to xii. In his day the Temple was repaired and the BOOK OF THE LAW was found (see HISTORY OF THE BOOKS). He was wounded in a battle against Pharaoh Necho, and died near Jerusalem, where he was buried with great display.—2. Son of Zephaniah (Zech. vi. 9).

JOSIBĪ'AH (*Jah makes to dwell*). Father of Jehu (1 Chr. iv. 35).

JOSIPHI'AH (*Jah increase him*). Ancestor of Shelomith, who returned with Ezra (viii. 10).

JOT (Heb. YOD, *the hand*). The smallest letter in the Hebrew alphabet. Used as a symbol of the least. Jot or tittle (Matt. v. 28); not even the finishing touch.

JOT'BAH (*goodness*). Native town of Haruz and his daughter Meshullemeth (2 K. xxi. 19). *Et Taiyibeh* (see OPHRAH). Arabic, *Et Tayib, good*. There are three sites so named. 1. S. of Hebron; 2. W. of Hebron; 3. N. of Jerusalem.

JOT'BATH. JOTBA'THAH (*goodly*). *Wady el Athbeh*, in the desert, N. W. of Akabah.

JŌ'THAM (*Jah is upright*). 1. Son of Gideon (Judg. ix. 5). His parable of the bramble is the oldest of its kind. He lived at Beer.—2. Son of king Uzziah, succeeding him to the throne of Judah B. C. 158, at the age of 25, and reigning 16 years (2 K. xv.; 2 Chr. xxvii.).—3. Son of Jahdai, in Judah's line (1 Chr. ii. 47).

JOZ'ABAB. JEHOZABAD. There were seven of this name, without special note.

JOZ'ĀCHAR (*Jah remembers*). Son of Shimeath (2 K. xii. 2). Zabad in 2 Chr. xxiv. 26.

JŪ'BAL (*music*). Son of Lamech, by Adah (Gen. iv. 21); a teacher, and perhaps inventor of musical instruments, both for string and wind.

JŪ'BILEE (YOBEL, *rushing sound*). See CHRONOLOGY, p. 56. The year of Jubilee was the 49th, so as to count full 7's, and no more. If on the 50th, the count by 7's would be interrupted.

JŪ'DA (*Judas*). Son of Joseph, father of Simeon (Luke iii. 30).—2. Son of Joanna (Hananiah), (iii. 26). Abiud in Matt. i. 13.—3. Brother of Jesus (Mark vi. 3).—4. JUDAH.—5. Juda, for the land of Judah in Matt. ii. 6, etc.

JUDÆ'A. Latin form of Judea.

JŪ'DAH (YEHUDAH, *praise Jah*). The Jew or Hebrew. JUDA. JUDAH. 1. Fourth son of Jacob, by Leah. His brothers were Reuben, Simeon, Levi (Judah), Issachar, Zebulon. He was a leader in family matters from his youth up, and more is known of him than of any other except Joseph. Reuben advised the brothers to throw Joseph into the pit, and Judah proposed the sale to the traders, both acting honorably to themselves, wishing to save the life of Joseph (Gen. xxvii. 26). See JOSEPH for Judah's conduct in Egypt (Gen. xliv. 14, 16–34). Judah went before Jacob into Egypt (xlvi.). Jacob honors Judah first in his blessings (xlix. 8–10). He had 5 sons, 3 by a Canaanite, the daughter of Shuah—ER, ONAN and SHELAH—and 2 by the widow of Er (TAMAR), Pharez and Zerah. (See 12 TRIBES). The boundaries of Judah are more carefully noted than any of the others (Josh. xv. 20–63). The district was about 45 miles N. to S., and nearly 50 wide E. to W. See PALESTINE, GEOLOGY, CLIMATE, KINGDOM OF JUDAH.—2. A Levite ancestor of Kadmiel (Ezr. iii. 9).—3. A Levite, who had a Gentile wife (x. 23).—4. A Benjamite, son of Senuah (xi. 9). —5. Assisted in dedicating the wall (xii. 34).

JŪ'DAH, KINGDOM OF. The kingdom actually began with the revolt of the 10 tribes, but was really a continuation of the kingdom of Saul and David. The kingdom was an original element in the system that Moses projected, and the first elections, of Saul, David and Solomon, were divinely directed. See list of kings in ISRAEL. Rehoboam, Solomon's son and successor, lost the ten tribes, and also suffered from the Pharaoh SHISHAK, who robbed the temple (2 Chr. xii.).

Jehoshaphat was the greatest king after David, and increased the power and wealth of his people. His ships being destroyed in a storm, his scheme for commerce was given up.

A grave error was committed in a marriage with the house of Ahab, Jehoram taking Athaliah for a wife, who introduced her mother Jezebel's image-worship.

The treasures of the temple or of the king were several times carried away from Judah. All the vast hoards of David and Solomon were lost by Rehoboam to Shishak (1 K. xiv. 26); Benhadad took from Asa the savings of 40 years. Jehoash sent to Hazael all that Jehoshaphat, Jehoram, Ahaziah, and himself had dedicated, besides his private wealth (2 K. xii. 18); Jehoash of Israel took from Amaziah all the treasures (xiv. 11–14); Ahaz surrendered to Tiglath Pileser (xvi. 8); Hezekiah to Sennacherib 300 talents of silver, and 30 of gold (xviii. 14–16); in the days of Josiah (or after he was killed) the Pharaoh could only collect 100 talents of silver, and 1 talent of gold, by taxation, there being no treasure in the temple, and (perhaps a mistake) Nebuchadnezzar carried off all the treasures of the temple, with the very vessels that Solomon had made (xxiv. 13), 5400 in number (Ezra i. 11). The royal line was twice almost destroyed, by Jehu, and by Athaliah. The real cause of decay in this power was the contest between the Church and the State; the priest grew stronger as the king was weaker. Faction grew bold and fierce, and bloodshed was common (Ez. xxii.). The nation grew wealthy, luxurious, superstitious, idolatrous, with only a formal show of true religion. The king appointed the high-priest, but did not dare to depose one. The high-priests gained more honor than the kings—especially it was a great honor to trace to Zadok the priest. But the nation could not be saved even by a pure high-priesthood. Society was corrupt, and full of contention, and unable to defend itself against Egypt and Babylon. The kingdom lasted 487 yrs.; 387 after Israel seceded, and 133 after Israel's captivity.

SPHINX.

JŪ'DAS (Greek-Latin form of Judah). 1. In 1 Esd. ix. 23.—2. 3d son of Mattathias, the Maccabæus (1 Macc. ii. 4, etc.).—Son of Calphi (xi. 70). —4. A Jew in Jerusalem (2 Macc. i. 10).—5. Son of Simon, and brother of John Hyrcanus (1 Macc. xvi. 2).—6. The patriarch Judah, in Matt. i. 2, 3. —7. A man in Damascus, who lodged Paul (Saul) after his conversion (Acts ix. 11).—8. BAR'SABAS a leading member of the Church at Jerusalem (Acts xv. 22), a prophet (v. 32), chosen with Silas to go with Barnabas and Saul to Antioch as delegates on the Gentile convert question (v. 27).—9. Of Galilee, the leader of a revolt in the time of Quirinus (A. D. 6), mentioned by Gamaliel in his speech before the Sanhedrin (Acts v. 37). He was a religious enthusiast, whose motto was, "We have no Lord or Master but God." See Jos. xviii. 1, § 1.

JŪ'DAS ISCĀR'IOT (from KERIOTH, his native place). Son of Simon (John vi. 71). His early life is not recorded. He was awarded the unhappy notoriety of betraying Jesus, his Lord and Master. He must have been a useful man among the 12, because he was appointed their steward (John xii. 6). Jesus knew his character from the first (vi. 64); but no one else even suspected him up to the very last day, when Peter and John were only made to know by a private sign from the Master who was the betrayer (xiii. 26). He got from the high-priest

30 shekels, the price of a slave, but returned the money when repentance overtook him, after the crucifixion. His tender heart and quick conscience appears in the fact that he killed himself rather than live with the feeling of remorse for his crime.

Some have thought that he believed that Jesus would be able to free himself from the priests, and stand higher than ever for the trial; others think that he as well as the rest believed Jesus was delaying the opening of his temporal kingdom, and that he would only force him to declare his power and majesty by bringing him face to face with his enemies. While these theories are only possibly true in a slight degree, the love of money was beyond question a motive. The other 11 were weak, perplexed, vascillating, faint-hearted, but Judas was active and speculative, in the trying moment, his religion is only a servant to his worldly interest, and he perhaps discovered that the spiritual kingdom would not pay. This is why he was dishonest in his stewardship (John xii. 4), and grudged the value of the perfume that Mary honored Jesus with at Bethany. His presence among the 12 is explained in "The presence of such a false friend in the company of his disciples was needed to complete the circle of Christ's trials and temptations." David in the Psalms describes such a character, whose words were smooth as butter; whose actions were drawn swords; who ate his meat, and lifted his heel against him.

It seems probable that Judas did not stay to the Lord's Supper.

JUDAS. JUDE. A disciple, writer of the Epistle (see HISTORY OF THE BOOKS). He was "brother of James" (Jude 1), "the Lord's brother" (Gal. i. 19; ii. 9, 12; Matt. xiii. 55; Mark vi. 3). He was not an apostle, for he did not believe on Jesus as the Christ until after the crucifixion (John vii. 5). Only one question of his to Jesus is all that is recorded of him (John xiv. 22). Eusebius (History iii. 20, 32), says the Lord's relatives were feared by the Emperor Domitian, and were known as late as the end of Trajan's reign.

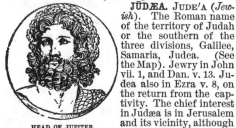

JUDÆA. JUDE'A (*Jewish*). The Roman name of the territory of Judah or the southern of the three divisions, Galilee, Samaria, Judea. (See the Map). Jewry in John vii. 1, and Dan. v. 13. Judea also in Ezra v. 8, on the return from the captivity. The chief interest in Judæa is in Jerusalem and its vicinity, although there are many names of

HEAD OF JUPITER.

cities all over its territory, connected with interesting persons and events.

JUDÆA, THE WILDERNESS OF. Was along the W. shore of the Dead Sea.

JUDG'ES (SHOFETIM). Patriarchal seniors who administered justice, usually the chief or head of a tribe (Sheikh). Moses introduced the system on the advice of his father-in-law, Jethro (Ex. xviii). There were two distinct orders of judges. 1. The leader, or chief of the whole nation, instead of or before the kings were elected.—2. The elder princes or chiefs of families. A list of judges over all Israel is given in CHRONOLOGY, page 57. For BOOK OF JUDGES see HISTORY OF THE BOOKS.

JUDG'MENT. Judicial decision. Sentence of a judge. The Day of Judgment (Matt. x. 5; xi. 22), the great day (Jude 6), last day (John xi. 24), in which Christ will judge the world (Acts xvii. 31; John v. 22), in righteousness (Matt. xxv. 31–46; 2 Cor. v. 10; Rev. xx.). See ADVENT. Some believe that resurrection follows immediately after death, and that judgment is already pronounced

on ourselves by our lives, the Christ only carrying out the sentence, so that the world may continue without end, and souls go to their final account, the judgment never ending.   Others hold that the resurrection is reserved to the end of the world, when there will be no more souls born, and all the dead from the beginning will be raised at one time. It seems more probable that the spirit world, heaven, is entered at once by the blessed soul, recognizing friends, relatives, the ancient worthies, Jesus and God the Father. See RESURRECTION.

JUDG'MENT HALL (Gr. *praitorion*), (John xviii. 28). This has been located in Pilate's house, and in Herod's palace, and in the Castle Antonia. There was another hall at Cæsarea (Jos. Ant. xv. 9, § 6).

JU'DITH (YEHUDITH, *Jewess*). 1. Wife of Esau, dau. of Beeri; also called Aholibama (Gen. xxvi. 34, xxxvi. 2).—2. Judith the heroine of the BOOK OF JUDITH; see HISTORY.

JU'LIA (feminine of Julius). A disciple at Rome, wife(?) of Philologus (Rom. xvi. 15).

JU'LIUS. Centurion of the "Augustus Band," who conducted Paul to Rome from Cæsarea, and used him courteously (Acts xxvii. 1, 3).

JU'NIA. A disciple at Rome (Rom. xvi. 7).

JU'NIPER (ROTHEM). A white-blossomed broom, found in Spain, Barbary, Syria, and the desert of Sinai, and called Spanish broom, in Arabic *Bethem*. The bush is the largest in the desert, and gives shade from the sun, wind, and rain, and the Bedawins make charcoal from the twigs (illustrating Ps. cxx. 4). Job speaks of eating rothem roots (xxx. 4), as a picture of abject poverty and want. Elijah slept under a broom bush (Rob. i. 203).

JU'PITER (Gr. *Zeus*, Latin *Jupiter, Divumpater, heaven-father*). The son of Saturn and Ops, brother and husband of Juno, father and king of gods and men, and supreme ruler of the universe, in the Greek and Roman mythology. Jupiter *Tonans*, the thunderer; *fulminator*, the lightning-wielder; *Pluvius*, the rain-giver. See PAUL. The worship of Jupiter was general in all Greek countries, and was once attempted on Mt. Moriah, in the temple, by order of ANTIOCHUS EPIPHANES. See MACCABEES.

JU'SHABHE'SED (*loving kindness is returned*). Son of Zerubbabel (1 Chr. iii. 20).

JUSTIFICĀ'TION (Gr. *dikaio*). Used in the Bible to mean passing sentence or giving a decision (Deut. xxv. 1; Prov. xvii. 15; Is. v. 22; Ps. cxliii. 2). It is opposed by condemn (Gr. *katakrino*), in Rom. viii. 33, 34. By the deeds of the law there shall no flesh be justified in God's sight (iii. 20). It is a judicial act of God, by which the sinner is declared innocent, as if he had never sinned, not because of works, but of Christ's righteousness; the means by which it is apprehended is faith. Justified by faith and through faith (iii. 28, iv. 5; Gal. ii. 16, iii. 8).

JUS'TIFY. The faith that justifies is a working living faith, and must so prove itself whenever occasion demands.

JUS'TUS (*just*). 1. Surname of Joseph Barsabas (Acts i. 23).—2. A disciple at Corinth (xviii. 7).—3. Surname of Jesus, a friend of Paul (Col. iv. 11).

JUT'TAH (YUTAH, *inclined*). An ancient city of Judah, allotted to the priests (Josh. xv. 55). The residence of Zacharias, a priest, the father of John the Baptist. It is now a large village, five miles south of Hebron. (See Luke i.). It is found on the Egyptian monuments as *tah-n-nu*, a fort of the Anakim, near Hebron. Called "a city of Juda" in Luke i. 39.

K

KAB'ZEËL (*gathered by El*). Judah in the S. E. (Josh. xv. 21). The native place of Benaiah, one of David's "mighty men" (2 Sam. xxiii. 20; 1 Chr. xi. 22). Jekabzeel in Neh. xi. 25, where it is one of the places occupied after the return from captivity. It was probably a shepherd settlement (so many of which are known), its name being derived from "the gathering of the flocks."

KAB'BALAH. Reception; doctrine received orally. The teachings are: 1. God is above everything; even above being and thinking. Therefore it cannot be said truly that he has either a will, desire, thought, action—language, because these belong to finite man. He cannot be comprehended by the intellect, nor described with words. He is in a peculiar sense without life, for He cannot die, and He in a certain sense does not exist, because that which is incomprehensible does not exist to us. He therefore made known some properties of His existence to us.

The will to create implies limit, therefore the imperfect world, limited and finite, is no work of the infinite; but since there cannot be any accident or chance where infinite wisdom resides, the world (and universe) must have been indirectly created by the 10 intelligences (SEFIROTH), which emanate from the One original emanation, the infinite intelligence (EN SEF). These 10 powers have bodies, the one original emanation (not created) has a form also. They are divided into 3 groups; which operate on the 3 worlds, of intellect, of souls, and of matter.

All human souls are pre-existent in the world of *sefiroth*, and must live the life of probation on the earth. If its life is pure it rises to the sphere of the *sefiroth;* but if it sins, it will have to live over and over again until it becomes pure. (Some say the limit is to 3 trials.) The souls that have lived have the first right to new-born bodies, and so there are many waiting even for the first chance, and Messiah cannot be born until all others have been born, at the end of days. This is a hermeneutical (explaining Scripture) system, invented to satisfy those Jews who did not agree with the descriptions of heaven by the prophets.

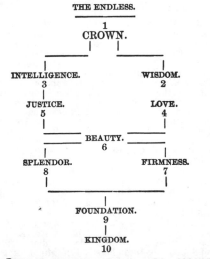

THE ENDLESS.

```
                    1
                  CROWN.
                  |    |
         |                        |
  INTELLIGENCE.               WISDOM.
       3                         2
       |                         |
   JUSTICE.                    LOVE.
       5                         4
       |                         |
       |_____   BEAUTY.   _____|
                    6
       |                         |
  SPLENDOR.                  FIRMNESS.
       8                         7
       |                         |
       |_____|
                    |
               FOUNDATION.
                    9
                    |
                KINGDOM.
                   10
```

KĀDES (Judith, i. 9). Summoned to aid him by Nebuchadnezzar. Kadesh Naphtali (Josh. xv. 23).

KĀDES. Greek form of *Kadesh* (Judg. i. 9.)

KĀ'DESH. K. BARNEA (*holy places*). El Mishpat (*spring of judgment*), which is Kadesh (Gen. xiv. 7). The most northern place reached by the Israelites in their direct road to Canaan. Located at Ain el Weibeh, on the western side of the Arabah, N. W. of Petra, where there is the most copious fountain and the most important wateringplace in that valley. There are no ruins of any "city" (v. 16), nor of the tomb of Miriam (Jerome, Onom.). See EXODUS.

KAD'MIEL (*one stands before El*). A Levite who returned with Zerubbabel (Ezr. ii. 40, iii. 9: Neh. vii. 43).

WASHING HANDS BEFORE MEALS.

KAD'MONITES THE. Children of the East (Gen. xv. 19).

KĀ'IN. CAIN (Num. xxiv. 22).

KAL'LAI (*swift messenger of Jehovah?*) A priest (Neh. xii. 20).

KĀ'NAH (*reed*) (Josh. xix. 28). Asher. Seven miles S. E. of Tyre, a village of 300 families. A mile north of it is the ancient site (Em el Awamid, *mother of columns*), with ruins, some of which are colossal—foundations, oil-presses, cisterns, and posts of houses, and great numbers of columns (L. and B. 298). AIN KANAH, five miles S. E. of Sidon, is also claimed as the true site.

KĀ'NAH, THE RIVER. Boundary between Ephraim and Manasseh, flowing into the Mediterranean two miles S. of Cæsarea (Josh. xvi. 8, xvii. 9), now called *Nar Ahkar*.

KA'REAH (*bald-head*). Father of Johanan and Jonathan (Jer. xl. 8), called CAREAH.

KAR'KAA (*flat*). On the boundary, next to Azmon, on the south side of Judah (Josh. xv. 3). Lost.

KAR'KOR (*level place*). Where Zeba and Zalmunna felt "secure" with their host, and Gideon smote them (Judg. viii. 10, 11). Somewhere on the level Mishor, but not identified.

KAR'TAH (*city*). (Josh. xxi. 34). In Zebulon. Lost.

KAR'TAN (*two towns*). Naphtali (Josh. xxi. 32). Kirjathaim?

KATT'ATH (*small*). Zebulon (Josh. xix. 13). Lost.

KĒ'DAR (*black*). Second son of Ishmael (Gen. xxv. 13). Settled his tribe in the N. W. of Medina, in Arabia, bordering Palestine. The glory of the sons of Kedar is mentioned by Isaiah (xxi. 13–17), their villages (xlii. 11), and their princes by Ezekiel (xxvii. 21), who supplied Tyre with sheep and goats; and in Canticles (i. 5) their tents are noticed as "black, but comely." Mohammed traces his lineage to Abraham through the celebrated Koreish tribe, which sprang from Kedar. The Arabs in the Hejaz are called Beni Harb (*men of war*), and are Ishmaelites as of old, from their beginning. Palgrave says their language is as pure now as when the Koran was written (A. D. 610), having remained unchanged more than 1200 years; a fine proof of the permanency of Eastern institutions.

KEDE'MAH (*eastward*). Son of Ishmael (Gen. xxv. 15).

KĔD'EMOTH (*beginnings*). Reuben, east of the Dead Sea, near the Arnon (Deut. ii. 26). Name of a city and a wilderness (*i. e.* the pasture-land) near it. Lost. This district has not been explored.

KĔ'DESH (*sanctuary*). 1. Kĕdesh in Galilee, one of the Cities of Refuge. A fortified city in Naphtali (Josh. xix. 37). The residence of Barak (Judg. iv. 6), where he and Deborah assembled their army. The tree of Zaanaim, under which was pitched the tent in which Sisera was killed, was in the vicinity. It was captured by Tiglath Pileser, with other towns, and its people removed to Assyria (2 K. xv.). The tomb of Barak was shown in the 12th century (*Benjamin of Tudela*). The site is beautiful. A little green plain among the mountains, with a border of wooded hills, and well watered. The ruins on a rounded *tell*, which was once fortified, and the broken columns and handsome capitals, sarcophagi, and heaps of hewn stones, show its former grandeur.—2. In Issachar (Josh. xxi. 28 has Kishon, and 1 Chr. vi. 72, Kedesh).—3. South, in Judah (Josh. xv. 23). Kadesh Barnea ?

KĔ'DRON. KIDRON.

KEHE'LATHAH (*assembly*). (Num. xxxiii. 22). Between Sinai and Kadesh. Lost.

Now called *Kenawat*, and beautifully situated on the west slope of the Hauran, in the midst of oak groves. The ruins extend a mile and a half long by half a mile wide, and consist of temples, palaces, theatres, towers, churches (of the early Christians), and many private houses with doors and roofs of stone. A colossal head of Ashtoreth, found by Porter, shows that this goddess was worshiped there.

KĔ'NAZ (*hunting*). One of the "dukes" (sheikhs) of Edom (Gen. xxxvi. 15; 1 Chr. i. 53). Caleb and Othniel were of this race. The modern tribes of the *Anezeh*, the most powerful of all the Bedawins in Arabia, cover the desert from the Euphrates to Syria, and from Aleppo to Nejed. Their army numbers 90,000 camel-riders and 10,000 horsemen.

KĔ'NEZITE (Gen. xv. 19.) An ancient tribe of unknown origin, inhabiting the land promised to Abraham, east of Palestine.

KĔ'NITE (*smith*). A tribe much mentioned, but whose origin is not recorded. They may have been a branch of Midian, for Jethro is a Kenite, and lived in Midian when first known by Moses. The RECHABITES are the most noted of this people. Jael, who killed Sisera, was a Kenite (Judg. iv. 11).

KEN'IZZITES (*hunter*). (Gen. xv. 19). Lost.

KĔ'RENHAP'PUCH (*paint-horn*). Daughter of Job (Job. xlii. 14). Horn of plenty. See EYES.

EGYPTIANS WEIGHING A SOUL IN THE BALANCE.

KEI'LAH (*fort*). Judah, in the Shefelah (Josh. xv. 44). David rescued it from the Philistines in harvest-time (1 Sam. xxiii. 1). It was then fortified (ver. 7). After the return from Babylon the people of Keilah assisted Nehemiah in rebuilding the walls of Jerusalem (Neh. iii. 17, 18). The tomb of the prophet Habakkuk was said to be here, by Josephus and Jerome. The site is located N. W. of Hebron about ten miles; on a projecting cliff on the right bank of Wady el Feranj, where there is a large ruined castle called *Kilah*.

KEI'LAH, THE GARMITE. Descendant of Caleb (1 Chr. iv. 19).

KELAI'AH (*assembly*). KELITA (Ezr. x. 23).

KEL'ITA (*dwarf*). A Levite who returned with Ezra (Ezr. x. 23). KELAIAH.

KEM'UEL (*assembly of El?*). 1. A son of Nahor (Gen. xxii. 21).—2. Son of Shiptan, appointed by Moses to assist in dividing the land of Canaan (Num. xxxiv. 24).—3. Father of Hashabiah (1 Chr. xxvii. 17).

KĔ'NAN. CAINAN. Son of Enos (1 Chr. i. 2; Gen. v. 9).

KĔ'NATH (*possession*). A strong city of Bashan, or rather Argob. Taken by Nobah, who changed its name to Nobah (Num. xxxiii. 42). One of 60 cities, all fenced, with high walls, gates, and bars, taken by Jair in Argob (Deut. iii. 3, etc.). Gideon went up by Nobah after Zeba and Zalmunna.

KER'CHIEFS (Ez. xiii. 18, 21). DRESS.

KĔ'RIOTH (*cities*). (Josh. xv. 25). Judah, south. Kuryetein (*two cities*), 15 miles S. of Hebron. The town from which Judas Iscariot was named.—2. A town in Moab, mentioned with Dibon, Bozrah and others (Jer. xlviii. 24). Now Kureiyeh, six miles east of Busrah, on the west slope of the Hauran. There are many ruined columns; and a cistern having a stone roof supported on a triple row of columns, under which are benches, rising like a theatre. A Greek inscription on one of the benches dates the cistern A. D. 296. The houses had walls four to eight feet thick, of solid basalt, with roofs of slabs of stone reaching across from wall to wall. In Amos ii. 2, Kirioth means the "cities of Moab."

KĔ'ROS (*weaver's comb*). A Nethinim, who returned with Zerubbabel (Ezr. ii. 44).

KET'TLE (*dud*). A vessel used for sacrifices or cooking (1 Sam. ii. 14).

KETU'RAH (*incense*). Wife of Abraham (Gen. xxv. 1). See ABRAHAM. The sons of Keturah were Zimran, Jokshan, Medan, Midian, Ishbak and Shuah. Keturah herself is lost to history.

KEY (*mafteah*). Keys are sometimes very large in the East, two feet or more long. It is a symbol of authority (Is. xxii. 22, etc.).

KEZI'A (*cassia*). Daughter of Job (Job xlii. 14).

KĒ'ZIZ, THE VALLEY OF (*destruction*). A city of Benjamin, named Emekkeziz, and mistranslated in Josh. xvii. 21. Near Jericho. Lost.

KIB'ROTH HATTĀ'AVAH (*graves of lust*). Station of the wandering.

KIBZA'IM (*two heaps*). In Ephraim (Josh. xxi. 22). JOKMEAM.

KID. Young goat. MILK.

KID'RON (*turbid*). In the original Hebrew it is always called a dry water-course or wady (*nachal*. See RIVER). East of the walls of Jerusalem, at the foot of Olivet (2 Sam. xv. 23; John xviii. 1). Now called the Valley of Jehoshaphat. It is in most places narrow, with steep, naked banks, and only a few strips of cultivable land. The Tyropœon joins it at the Pool of Siloam, and the Hinnom at En Rogel, all three forming what is now called the Wady en Nar (*fire*), leading to Mar Saba and the Dead Sea. The whole valley is filled with tombs and graves. The most ardent desire of every dying Jew (or Mohammedan) of Palestine is to be buried there. Dr. Barclay mentions a fountain in the north end of the valley, flowing in winter several hundred yards, and sinking out of sight, probably running under ground, being covered many feet deep by rubbish, as proved by recent digging through the accumulation, near the temple area (see JERUSALEM), and heard murmuring at En Rogel, and also two miles down the valley, where water was found in midsummer. William of Tyre and Brocardus heard the subterranean waters in their day. Where the path from St. Stephen's Gate crosses the valley there is a bridge, with one arch 17 feet high, near which are the church and tomb of the Virgin and the garden of Gethsemane. Another bridge, on a single arch, crosses near the Absalom tomb. The temple area wall is here 150 feet above the bottom of the valley.

KILN. KIL. Brick.

KĪ'NAH (*lamentation*). Judah, next to Edom (Josh. xv. 22). Lost.

KIN'DRED. Relatives.

KING (MELECH; Gr. *basileus*). A title applied to men. Sometimes it is used of men who were only leaders or rulers of one city, as the king of Sodom, etc. This form of government seems to be native to the East. The will of one man rather than the union of many. The true king of Israel, as designed by Moses, was God; and that form of government is called a theocracy (Gr. *theos*, god). Moses saw that a visible king would be wanted, and provided for such a state (Deut. xvii. 14–20). The king was to be anointed with oil (1 Sam. x. 1), and was called, therefore, "the Lord's anointed." This was an ancient Egyptian custom. ANOINTING.

KINGDOM OF GOD. The divine kingdom of Jesus the Christ. Matthew only says "kingdom of the heavens" for the state of things to be expected at the coming of the Messiah, as soon as converted sinners become citizens of the heavenly kingdom (Rev. i. 6). For BOOK OF KINGS, see HISTORY.

KING'S DALE (Gen. xiv. 17; 2 Sam. xviii. 18). (SHAVEH, *level place*). The Plain of Rephaim. Absalom's pillar, a name given to a modern structure (of the later Roman age in style), is a mistake, for his pillar was reared up in a plain or broad valley (*Emek*. See PLAIN). See cut of Absalom's Tomb, page 2.

KIR (*a wall*). Where the people of Damascus were carried by the king of Assyria (2 K. xvi. 9). Elam and Kir are mentioned together by Isaiah (xxii. 6). The river Cyrus, flowing from the Caucasus to the Caspian Sea, still bears its ancient name, *Kur*. But it is not yet known where the city or district was located. *Kerend* is offered, and also *Carna*, both cities in Media. Elam (which see) was near the Persian Gulf, and Kir may have been a variant name for Kish, the eastern Ethiopia.

KIR HĀ'RESH, KIR HAR'ASETH, KIR HAR'E-SETH, KIR HE'RES (*brick fort*) and **KIR MŌ'AB** (2 K. iii. 25; Is. xvi. 7; Jer. xlviii. 31, 36). One of the chief fortified cities of Moab (built of brick—heres). When Joram, king of Israel, invaded Moab, Kir was the only city not taken, and this was saved by the sacrifice by the king of Moab of his eldest son, on the wall (2 K. iii. 27). *Kerak* (the modern name) stands on the top of a rocky hill, about 10 miles from the Dead Sea, and 3,000 feet above its level. It was at one time strongly fortified, on the top of a high hill, surrounded on all sides by a deep valley, and again enclosed by mountains higher than the town, from which hights the slingers threw stones into the city, as mentioned in 2 K. iii. 25. The entrances to the ancient city were only two, and tunnelled through the solid rock for a hundred feet, on the north and south. On the western side stands the citadel, a strong building, built by the Crusaders, containing a chapel, on the walls of which are some rude paintings. On clear days Bethlehem and Jerusalem may be seen from here.

MOABITE STONE.

Rev. Mr. Klein (of the Palestine Exploration) in 1868 found a Semitic monument in Moab, on which there is an inscription (translated by Mr. Deutsch, of the British Museum), giving an account of many cities named in the Bible, which king Mesha built, among which is *Karkha* (Kerak). This is the oldest monument in the Phœnician language that is known. It adds to our knowledge of that day. In 2 K. i. 1, is a mention of a rebellion of Moab, which was put down by Israel and Judah. This stone gives particulars, not in the Bible, of the acts of the king of Moab; his conquest of cities; rebuilding others; his religious wars; and that he believed himself divinely guided by the god Chemosh.

Almost the whole of the Greek alphabet is found on this stone, such as is in use now, and identical with the Phœnician, even including those letters which were supposed to have been added during the Trojan war; and also the Greek letter ūpsilon, which was supposed to have been added later. The most ancient letters are here shown to be the most simple—mere outlines.

KIR'IAH (*town*). Kerioth. Kartah, Kartan,

Kiriathaim .(Ez. xxv. 9). In Moab. One of the "glories of the country," named among the denunciations of Jeremiah (xlviii. i. 23).

KIR'JATH (Josh. xviii. 28). In Benjamin. Lost. —2. KIRJATHAIM, KIRIATHAIM (*double city*). Reuben, a little south of Heshbon (Num. xxxii. 27). It was a large Christian village in the time of Eusebius and Jerome. *Kureiyat* is a ruin near *Jebel Attarus*, south of Wady Zurka Main, south of which is a level plateau called *el Koura* (*plain*), which may be the Plain of Moab. It is one of the oldest of Bible cities (Gen. xiv. 5). It was on the "Plain" (shaveh) Kiriathaim that the Emims were smitten by the eastern kings who plundered Sodom. —3. A town of Naphtali (1 Chr. vi. 76). Kartan.— 4. KIRJATH ARBA. Hebron. It is supposed that Hebron was the ancient name, the Canaanites calling it Kirjath Arba on their taking possession, when the Israelites restored the ancient name. A tradition says the city was called Arba, or *four*, because Adam, Abraham, Isaac, and Jacob were buried there. But Joshua says *Arba* was a great man (xiv. 15).—5. KIRJATH BAAL (*Baal's city*), (Josh. xv. 60, xviii. 14). Kirjath Jearim.—6. KIRJATH HUZOTH. Where Balaam was conducted by Balak to offer sacrifice (Num. xxii. 30). Kureiyat. —7. KIRJATH JEARIM (*city of forests*), (Josh. ix. 17). One of the 4 cities of the Gibeonites, who tricked Joshua. Also Kirjath Arim, peopled after after the Captivity (Ezr. ii. 25). A boundary (Josh. xv. 9). The ark remained here 20 years after it was brought from Bethshemesh, until it was removed by David to Jerusalem (1 Sam. vii.). Now *Kuryet el Enab* (*city of grapes*).

The Danites pitched "behind Kirjath Jearim" on the eve of their expedition to Laish, and the name Mahaneh Dan (camp of Dan) remained for a long time after they left (Judg. viii. 12). EMMAUS, where Jesus appeared after his resurrection (Mark xvi. 12; Luke xxiv. 13–35), is located here by recent scholars. The exploits of a noted robber sheikh who lived here has given it the name of Abu Gosh (father of lies) village. There are a few houses around an old convent (Minorite), and a Latin church, one of the most solidly built in Palestine.—8. KIRJATH SANNAH (*city of palms*), (Josh. xv. 49). KIRJATH SEPHER (*city of the book*). Judah. Called also Debir.

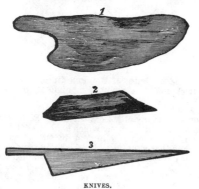

KNIVES.

KISH (*a bow?* see ARMS, i. 3). Father of Saul 2 (1 Sam. x. 21).—2. Son of Jehiel (1 Chr. viii. 30; ix. 36).—3. Great-grandfather of Mordecai (Esth. ii. 5).—4. Levite (1 Chr. xxiii. 21).

KISH'I (KUSHAIAH). A Merarite, ancestor of Ethan (1 Chr. vi. 44). KISH 4.

KISH'ION (*hard*). Issachar, in Esdraëlon (Josh. xix. 20). Kedesh (1 Chr. vi. 72).

KISH'ON, THE RIVER (Judg. iv. 7). Drains Esdraëlon and neighboring hills, being fed by the large spring of water at Daberath (*Deburieh*) at the N. W. foot of Mt. Tabor, and by another large fountain at En Gannim (*Jenin*), which is its most remote source; and also by the waters of Megiddo (a spring at *Lejjun*), running along the north base of Carmel. After receiving many small tributaries from the hills on each side, it enters the plain of Acre by the narrow pass between Harosheth (*Tell Harotieth*) and Carmel, just below which it receives Wady Malik, with the drainage from the plain of Zebulon (*Buttauf*), as far as Mt. Kurn Hattin, Araba, and Jabel Kaukab, near Cana. Below this point it is fed by the very copious fountains (*Saadiyeh*) three miles S. E. of Hepha (*Caiffa*), and others from under Carmel (Shaw), when it empties into the Bay of Acre near Caiffa, the last few miles only being a river with water the year round, flowing between banks of loamy soil fifteen feet high, with a stream 50 to 75 feet across. The whole system of tributaries above Harosheth are dry wadys through the summer or dry season. There are many historical associations belonging to this river, referred to in other places. See Armageddon. (*Land and Book*, c. xxix.).

KI'SON. KISH'ON (Ps. lxxxiii. 9).

KISS (NASHAK; Gr. *phileo*). The kiss is used to denote: 1. on the lips, affection; 2. on the cheek, respect, or salutation; 3. a symbol of charity in the early Church (Rom. xvi. 6; 1 Cor. xvi. 20; 2 Cor. xiii. 12, etc.); 4. on the beard, respect to age or authority; 5. on the forehead, condescension; 6. on the back, or palm, of the hand, submission; as also to kiss the feet; 7. on the ground near, a mark of respect; 8. to kiss the hand to an idol, worship (1 K. xix. 18; Hos. xiii. 2).

KITE (AYAH, vulture, in Job xxviii. 7). See page 124 for cut. A bird of prey (Lev. xi. 14; Deut. xiv. 13). The word AYAH was probably the name of the species, and is well translated kite.

KITH'LISH (Josh. xv. 40). Judah, in the Shefelah, near Eglon. Lost.

KIT'RON (Judg. i. 30). The Canaanites were not driven out, but remained as tributaries. Lost.

KIT'TIM (Gen. x. 4; 1 Chr. i. 7). CHITTIM.

KNIFE (CHEREB), (Josh. v. 2), sword; MAAK'E-LETH (Judg. xix. 29) table-knife; MACHALAPHIM (Ezr. i. 9) slaughter-knives; SAKKIN, knife (Prov. xxiii. 2). The most ancient historians mention knives of stone and of iron. The Easterns make little use of the knive at the table. Jeremiah speaks of a pen-knife (xxxvi. 23). The razor was used to shave the head of the Nazarite (Num. vi. 5, etc.), and the bodies of priests in Egypt (Herodotus ii. 86).

KNOP (CAPTOR, crown, Ex. xxv. 31). Imitation of the blossom of an almond tree; and a small gourd or cucumber (PEKAIM, cucumbers, in 1 K. vi. 18; vii. 24). See FRINGE, on page 109. Fringes, tassels and borders were symbolical in the dress of the high priest and of the Jews generally.

KŌ'A (Ez. xxiii. 23). Lost.

KŌ'HATH (*assembly*). Son of Levi (Gen. xlvi. 11). KEHATH. He died aged 133 (Ex. vi. 18). Moses and Aaron were of his line. The posterity of Kohath in the Exodus numbered 8600 males, 2750 being over 30. They (except Aaron and his sons) bore the ark and its furniture (Num. iii. 31).

KŌ'HATHITES. Descendants of KOHATH (Num. iii. 27, 30).

KOLI'AH (*voice of Jah*). 1. A Benj mite (Neh. xi. 7).—2. Father of Ahab (Jer. xxix. 21).

KOPH (*back of the head*), (Ps. cxix.). WRITING.

KŌ'RAH (*bald*). 1. Son of Esau (Gen. xxxvi. 5, 14, 18), one of the "dukes" of Edom.—2. Another duke, son of Esau (xxxvi. 16).—3. Son of Hebron (1 Chr. ii. 43).—4. Son of Izhar, a Levite, and ringleader of a rebellion against Moses and Aaron; the only person of note in it. His sons were not guilty, and escaped his doom. Samuel the prophet was of this family (1 Chr. vi. 22.). Ten psalms bear their names in the titles, as choristers in the temple.

KŌ'RAHITE (1 Chr. ix. 19, 31). Kōr'hite, or Kō'rathite, descendant of Korah.

KO'RAHITES, THE. Descendants of Korah 4 (Num. xxvi. 58). KORAHITE.

KŌ'RE (*partridge*). 1. A Korahite, ancestor of Shallum (1 Chr. ix. 19, xxvi. 1).—2. Son of Imnah, an overseer of offerings (2 Chr. xxxi. 14).—3. (1. Chr. xxvi. 19). "Sons of Kore."

KOR'HITES, THE. Descendants of Korah 4 (Ex. vi. 24). KORAHITE.

KOZ (*thorn*). ACCOZ, COZ, HAKKOZ (Ezr. ii. 61).

KUSHAI'AH (*rainbow*). KISH, father of Ethan (1 Chr. xv. 17).

L

LĀ'ADAH (*order*). Son of Shelah (1 Chr. iv. 21).

LĀ'ADAN (*put in order*). 1. Ancestor of Joshua (1 Chr. vii. 26).—2. Son of Gershon; Libni (xxiii. 7, 9; xxxi. 21).

LA'BAN (*white*). (Deut. i. 1). Libnah? (Num. xxxiii. 29). Ptolemy mentions an *Auara;* the Peutinger tables a *Hauarra;* and the Arabs have a place called *Ain Howara*—all of which mean *white*, and may refer to the same locality.

LĀ'BAN (*white*). Son of Bethuel, brother of Rebekah, father of Leah and Rachel.

LAB'ANA. LEBANA (1 Esd. v. 29).

LACE (*thread, cord*). (Ex. xxviii. 28, 37).

LACEDEMO'NIANS. Inhabitants of Sparta (1 Macc. xii. 2, 5, 6, 20, 21).

way to Egypt, and required all his power (2 Chr. xxxii. 9). This siege has been found pictured on one of the chambers of the palace at Koyunjik, under the name Lakhisha.

The inscription sculptured with the picture is translated: "Sennacherib, the mighty king, king of the country of Assyria, sitting on the throne of judgment before the city of Lakhisha. I give permission for its slaughter." There are several pictures, one of which gives a plan of a circular city with double walls and many towers. The expedition moved on to Egypt, and on its return Lachish was a second time besieged, at the same time that the great host of the Assyrians were slain by a miracle on the plain north of Jerusalem (Is. xxxvii. 36). It was rebuilt, and suffered a siege by Nebuchadnezzar (Jer. xxxiv. 1–7). The Jews occupied it after the return from Babylon.

LACU'NUS. Son of Addi (1 Esd. ix. 31). CHE-HAL.

LADDER OF TYRE. A high mountain, 10 ms. north of Acre, which stands out into the deep sea without a beach, and is only passed by a zigzag road cut in its face. The cape 6 ms. further north is passed by a similar way, which was built by Alexander. Simon was made governor of the country from the Ladder of Tyre to the borders of Egypt (1 Macc. xi. 59). Now called *Ras en Nakhura* (the excavated cape), and there is a small village of the same name on the hight.

LA'EL (*of God*). Father of Eliasaph (Num. iii. 24).

LA'HAD (*oppression*). Son of Jahath (1 Chr. iv. 2).

LAHA'IROI, THE WELL (*the well where God was seen by one who still lives*). Where Hagar took refuge from her imperious mistress, in the desert, between Kadesh and Bered, in the way to Shur (Gen. xvi. 14). It was afterward a favorite camping-ground of Isaac (xxiv. 62; xxv. 11).

"THE NORTH BAY OF THE SALT SEA, AT THE SOUTH END OF JORDAN."—Josh. xviii. 19.

LA'CHISH (*obstinate*). An ancient royal Amorite city (Josh. x. 3), whose king, Japhia, joined the alliance with Adonizedec, king of Jerusalem, to smite Gibeon for making a treaty with Joshua. The allied kings were defeated at Beth-horon, and were hanged at Makkedah (v. 26). The city was taken on the second day. Dr. Robinson found the site on a rocky hill, having but few ruins, 11 miles S. W. of *Beit Jibrin*, only two miles W. of Eglon. Lachish was fortified by Rehoboam, after the separation of the kingdom of Israel (2 Chr. xi. 9). Amaziah fled to it as a secure place (2 K. xiv. 19). It is supposed that the city was not taken, because it is said, in 2 Kings xix. 8, that "Sennacherib had departed from Lachish," and, in 2 Chr. xxxii. 1, that he had "thought to win" the fenced cities of Judah. It was taken by Sennacherib when on his

LAH'MAM (*place of contest*). In the Shefelah (Josh. xv. 40). Lahmas?

LAH'MI (*Bethlehemite*). Brother of Goliath (1 Chr. xx. 5).

LA'ISH (*strong, lion*). An ancient Phœnician city, occupied by a colony of Sidonians, in the valley between Hermon and Lebanon, at one of the great fountains of the Jordan. Its ancient name was Leshem (Josh. xix. 47), and it was an ancient sanctuary.

The LAISH of Isaiah x. 30 was near Jerusalem. Another (Laisa) is mentioned, where Judas encamped, in 1 Macc. ix. 5.

LA'ISH. Father of Phaltiel (1 Sam. xxv. 44).

LA'KUM (*to stop up a way*). In Naphtali (Josh. xix. 33). Perhaps near the bridge of the "Daughters of Jacob."

LAMB (Chal. *Immar*), Heb. 1. KEBES, (Ez. vi. 9), a male, and KIBSAH, female of the first year.—2. TALEH (1 Sam. vii. 9), the young of any animal, especially a sucking lamb.—3. KAR (2 K. iii. 4), a fat ram.—4. TSON (Ex. xii. 26), flock of lambs.—5. SEH (ib. 3), the individuals of the flock.—6. Greek *Amnos* (John i. 29, 36; Acts viii. 32; 1 Pet. i. 19), a lamb, and, figuratively, of Christ as the lamb for sacrifice.—7. Gr. *Aren* (Luke x. 3), *Arnion*, little lamb. See PASSOVER.

LÄ′MECH (*powerful*). 1. A descendant of Cain (Gen. iv. 18, 24). He is the only one except Enoch whose history is sketched with a few particulars, before the flood, and is the first recorded polygamist, having two wives, Adah and Zillah. His daughter was Naamah. His sons were Jabal, Jubal, and Tubal Cain. Josephus says he had 77 sons. The earliest recorded poem in the Bible is by him, supposed to have been an exultation over the invention of the sword.—2. Father of Noah (Gen. v. 29).

LÄ′MED (*ox-goad*). Twelfth letter of the Hebrew alphabet (Ps. cxix.). WRITING.

LAMENTA′TIONS OF JEREMIAH, THE. See HISTORY OF THE BOOKS.

EARTHEN LAMP. NO. 6.

LAMP. NER, *light*, (Ex. xxv. 37; 1 K. vii. 49, etc.). The lamp used in the tabernacle, and the ten in the temple. The ancient lamps were rude in design, small, and were supplied with olive oil, and trimmed with a wick of flax. Many specimens have been found lately in Palestine, among ancient ruins. See cuts on pages 6, 14, 15, 40, etc. There are several other names for lamp. 1. IYER; 2. LAPPID, *torch* (Judg. vii. 16, 20); 3. Gr. *lampas*, *a light* (Acts xx. 8). The lamp was carried in marriage processions (Matt. xxv.), and the Mohammedans use very ornamental and showy patterns in their ceremonies. The wick now used is generally of cotton twisted around a straw. Gideon's lamps might have been of similar make to the modern paper or cloth lanterns. The cloth is waxed, and stretched over a wire frame or rings, and is contrived so as to close up in a small space when not in use. The small size of the lamp made it necessary to carry a little jug of oil, or to have the lamp filled if a whole evening was passed away from home. The lantern is a protection against the wild dogs of the streets, who are sure to attack any one in the dark.

LAN′CET (1 K. xviii. 28). ARMS.

LAN′TERN (*light*), (John xviii. 3).

LAODICE′A (Rev. i. 11, iii. 14; Col. iv. 13, 15). There were four of the same name : 1. In Phrygia, near Hierapolis ;—2. In the east of Phrygia ; —3. On the coast of Syria, the port of Aleppo ; —4. East of Lebanon. The first is the only one mentioned in Scripture, as one of the SEVEN CHURCHES (which see).

LAODICE′A. An ancient city on the Lycus, in the valley of the Meander, forty miles east of Ephesus. Its site was on seven hills, which were drained by two brooks, the Asopus and Caprus. The ruins are of a stadium, in very complete pre-servation, three theatres (one of which was 450 feet in diameter), bridges, aqueducts, and a gymnasium, which testify to its ancient wealth and importance. Its original name was Diospolis, (the city of Jupiter), which was changed to Rhoas, under which title it became the largest city in Phyrgia (Pliny). Antiochus II gave it the name of his wife, Laodike.

It became the seat of an archbishop, and in its cathedral church were gathered several councils; in one of which, a system of supplying the villages or small societies in the interior with church services by itinerating presbyters, was adopted (somewhat similar to the Methodist plan now in use), under the direction of the bishop of Laodicea. Here was also adopted a rule "that Christians should not Judaize by resting on the seventh day, but to work on it as usual, and rest on the Lord's day as far as possible, like Christians."

The city was utterly destroyed A. D. 1230, since when it has lain in shapeless ruins, only visited for its marble and other materials.

The aqueduct (which supplied the city, and is now almost perfect), which conveyed water *down* one hill, across the plain, and *up* another, in *stone pipes*, proves the Romans to have been acquainted with the hydrostatic law of water finding its level. The stone pipes have a diameter of two feet, and are fitted into each other at the ends, and the calcareous deposit from the water has incrusted them, forming almost a continuous pipe without a visible joint.

The seats in the stadium have letters and numbers, their owner's or the keeper's marks.

A recent visitor found a number of workmen sawing up the richly sculptured entablature of the ancient theatre, having been busy there for six years, cutting up the marble. Near them was a colossal statue, sawn into several pieces. In this manner, have disappeared, during the past twenty years, two agate pillars, 18 inches in diameter ; a great number of composite richly sculptured columns, adorned with busts and heads in relief, vases with wreaths of leaves and fruits, and statues and busts and architectural ornaments without number.

Colossæ is about ten miles east from Laodicea, near the village of Chonas, but is without any interesting ruins, although it was an important city in the time of the expedition of Xerxes. Hierapolis (which see in the Geography) has lately afforded a fine proof of the truth of an account of Strabo (xiii. iv. 14), who speaks of a deadly vapor (carbonic acid gas ?) which killed any animal that approached the place. The experiment was tried by Svoboda recently on two fowls, and resulted fatally to both in a few seconds.

LAODICE′ANS. People of Laodicea (Col. iv. 16 ; Rev. iii. 14).

LAP′IDOTH (*torches*). Husband of Deborah (Judg. iv. 4).

LAP′WING (Lev. xi. 19). An unclean bird. Its feathers are long and very beautiful. The hoopoe (Solomon's bird with the golden crown) is supposed by some to be the one. The Sadducees supposed it was the common hen (DUKIFATH), and others that it was the cock of the woods. There are many legends about the hoopoe, one of which is that a vast flock flew over King Solomon's head, while on a desert journey, shadowing him from the sun, in reward for which he gave them a crown of golden feathers.

LASÆ′A (Acts xxvii. 8). City in Crete, identified in 1856 by Rev. G. Brown, 5 miles inland from Fair Havens. A Venitian MS. of the 16th century describes Lapsæa, with a temple in ruins, and other remains in the harbor. This city is one proof of the accuracy of Luke's account, even in minute details. 16 miles east of Gortyna.

LA'SHA (*fissure*). Southeast in Palestine, the limit of the country (Gen. x. 19). Callirhoë answers to the text in its position and character. Herod built a residence there; and recently there have been found on the site tiles, pottery and coins. En Englaim?

LAS'THENES (*strength*). An officer of nobility (1 Macc. xi. 31, 32; xiii. 4).

LATCH'ET. The fastening used to hold the sandal on the foot (Luke iii. 16).

LAT'IN (John xix. 20; Luke xxiii. 38). The language of the Romans.

LAT'TICE. A window (Judg. v. 28; Prov. vii. 6). 1. ESHNAB, casement in Prov. vii. 6; the word means *to be cool*, and we understand the use of the term for the latticed windows, in which water-jars are set to cool, and air is admitted also to the room. —2. HARAKKIM, *a net-work before a window* (Cant. ii. 9). Orientals are very jealous of observation by neighbors, and screen their windows by carved work, lattices of wood, coarse mats, or open work of bricks.—3. SEBAKAH, *net-work;* the same word is used for a net in Job xviii. 8, and also for the ornamental net-work on the columns before Solomon's Temple (1 K. vii. 18).

term law is used for the Old Testament as a whole in John x. 34, etc.

The Law of Moses depended on the Abrahamic covenant, which concerned the temporal promises, which were conditional on the keeping of the spiritual laws. Its principles were universal, but it had special rules for the Jews also. There were several kinds of laws: 1. Civil; 2. Criminal; 3. Judicial; 4. Constitutional; 5. Ecclesiastical; and 6. Ceremonial.

1. CIVIL.—Of the authority of a father over his family ; of husband and wife (the wife was *nothing* without the husband, not even recognized as a person (Num. xxx. 6–15). The degrees of relation in the matter of marriage; of divorce; of slave-wives; slander against a wife; the vicious before marriage to be put to death; the Levirate marriage; master and slave; master's power limited; no one could kill a slave or maim one; the slave free at the year of jubilee, except foreign slaves, who were perpetual; fugitive slaves from foreign nations were not given up; protection and kindness to foreigners (strangers) was a sacred duty, as they had very few rights under the law.

THE LAWS OF LAND AND PROPERTY.—All land was God's alone, and men were only tenants (Lev.

MOUNTAIN OF MOAB, PLAINS OF JORDAN.

LAUGH (Job ix. 23; 2 K. xix. 21; Ps. lxxx. 6), LAAG; TASHAK in Gen. xvii. 17, to mock; SACHAK (Ps. ii. 4), to play, to make sport; SEHOK, laughter in several passages, and derision in others; Gr. *Gelos*; in James iv. 9, laughter; *katagelao*, to laugh to scorn (Matt. ix. 24, etc.).

LAVER (KIYOR). A vessel containing water for washing hands and feet before offering sacrifice, and standing between the altar and the tabernacle (Ex. xxx. 19).

The form is not given, and can only be supposed to have been round, and to have had a movable stand, perhaps on wheels for convenience in moving. In the temple, besides the SEA, there were ten lavers, all of brass, on bases (1 K. vii. 27, 39), 5 on the north and 5 on the south side. They contained each 160 gallons of water used for washing the sacrifices for burnt-offerings (2 Chr. iv. 6). They are particularly described in Josephus viii. 3, § 6.

LAW (TORAH). The Mosaic Law. A guide in the way of moral conduct. Greek *nomos*. The

xxv. 23); all sold land returned to the original owner at the jubilee; houses were sold to be redeemed in a year, or not at all; the Levitical houses redeemable at all times; lands or houses sanctified were redeemable at prices according to the time before the jubilee; if devoted by the owner, to sacred purposes, and not redeemed at the jubilee, then they were a perpetual property of the priests. INHERITANCE descended to 1. sons, 2. daughters, 3. brothers, 4. uncles on father's side, 5. on mother's side, 6. other relatives.

LAW OF DEBT.—All debts between Israelites to be released on the year of jubilee; interest for loans of money not to be taken; pledges not to be insolently exacted (Deut. xxiv. 19, 20).

TAXATION.—The poll-tax for the support of the temple service was ½ shekel each year; spoil taken in war was halved, and 1-500 of one, and 1-50 of the other paid to the temple treasury; tithes of all farm produce 1-10; a second tithe for feasts and charity, 1-60 of first fruits of corn, wine, and oil;

firstlings of clean beasts; the redemption money for man 5 shekels, and for unclean beasts ½ shekel, to be given to the priests.

POOR.—They had a right to the gleaning of the fields; and to eat fruit, or grapes, etc., on the spot, but not to carry away; wages to be paid day by day; the priests reckoned as poor; the price of all devoted things was fixed for redemption; for a man 50 shekels, a woman 30, a boy 20, a girl 10.

2. CRIMINAL.—Offenses against God: Idolatry; witchcraft and false prophesy; divination; magic; blasphemy; Sabbath breaking (punishment in all these cases, death by stoning).

Offenses against man: Cursing, smiting, or disobedience to parents and to the judges (penalty, death by stoning); murder to be punished without reprieve, or satisfaction in money; death by negligence, or of a slave by whipping; accidental murder or killing must be avenged by the next of kin, but could be avoided by fleeing to one of the Cities of Refuge; where the murderer was not known the elders of the nearest city must disavow and sacrifice retaliation and damages for assault.

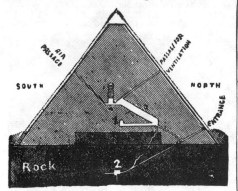

SECTION OF PYRAMID.

ADULTERY was to be punished by death to both offenders; rape of a married woman, of betrothed maid, by death to the offender; seduction of a young woman to be compensated by marriage, with a dowry of 50 shekels, without privilege of divorce; or, if she choose, a full dowry without marriage; unlawful marriages punished in various ways (Lev. xx.).

Theft, double or four-fold retribution; a night-robber could be killed; trespass or injury to things lent to be made good; perversion of justice strictly forbidden; kidnapping punished with death; false-witness, slander, by law of retaliation.

JUDICIAL LAWS. Judges were appointed, and were usually Levites; their sentence was final, and it was a capital offense to reject their judgment; two witnesses were required in capital matters; whipping must be limited so as not to leave marks. The KING set aside by his laws much of the law of Moses, and its scheme of officers, even deposing the high-priest (1 Sam. xxii. 17). 70 elders were appointed by the king with a religious sanction, forming the Sandhedrin (see SANHEDRIN), of priests, scribes, and elders (2 Chr. xix. 8–11). The king's power was limited by the law, and he was directly forbidden to be despotic (Deut. xvii. 14–20). He could tax 1-10; compel service; declare war.

The chiefs of each tribe or family acted for that tribe or family (Josh. xi. 15); and in some reigns controlled both the king and the priests (Jer. xxvi. 10).

The king's revenue was raised from the tenth, from confiscation of criminal's land (1 K. xxi. 15); the bound service of foreigners; his flocks and herds; tributes from foreign kings; commerce (in Solomon's time, 1 K. x. 22).

RELIGIOUS. There were laws for sacrifices, on many occasions; as the various offerings on the altar (where the fire must never be left to go out), for priests, women, lepers, the Day of Atonement and Festivals.

THE LAW OF HOLINESS (which resulted from the union with God through sacrifice), was shown in the dedication of the first-born, and the offering of all first-fruits (Ex. xiii. 2, etc.; Deut. xxvi.); the distinction of clean and unclean food; the rules for purification; against maiming; unnatural marriages; and the laws regulating the orders of priests, holy places and things, and also the times of holding services; as the Sabbath, the Sabbatical year (7th), the year of Jubilee; passover; feast of weeks (Pentecost); of tabernacles; of trumpets; and Day of Atonement.

The law is purely theocratic—derived from God, and not from man, and depended on the faith of the nation, the belief in God as the head of the Jewish people.

LAW'YER (Gr. nomikos). Scribe was the official title, and lawyer meant one learned in the law (Matt. xxii. 35; Luke x. 25; Tit. iii. 13).

LAZ'ARUS (ancient ELEAZAR, God is his helper). 1. Lazarus of Bethany, brother of Martha and Mary (John xi. 1).—2. Lazarus in the parable of the rich man and Lazarus (Luke xvi. 19–31). This is the only instance of a proper name in any of the parables.

It is supposed that "Simon the leper" was the father of Lazarus and the two sisters Martha and Mary, and that when the leprosy had made Simon an outcast, his children managed the house, and the daughters especially, since it is they who gave the feast when Jesus was there (Luke x. 38; John xii. 2), and was perfumed with the costly spikenard by Mary. The family were moderately wealthy, as appears in their having a house that could accommodate a large party, in their giving a feast, having so expensive a perfume (300 pence, that is the price of 300 days wages), and a family tomb cut in the rock. Simon may have been a Pharisee, as would seem from their friendly acquaintance with the Nicodemus branch of that sect in Jerusalem, and the ready use of their creed by Martha (John xi. 24). Simon may have been sent to Galilee with others to watch Jesus as a teacher of a new sect in the church, and partly through reverence, and also in the line of his duty he took him to his house. His disease might have been developed afterwards, and he have been removed, either by death or by the seclusion required by the law for a leper, when his daughters continued the hospitality their father began. This explains why Lazarus was a young man of some importance in his circle, had many acquaintances and friends, and perhaps held the position of an archōn (ruler in the village). His description agrees with this in its details, the salutation of Jesus as the "Good Master" (Mark x. 17), his respectful attitude, and his quick and earnest inquiry after the most important truth. The answer of Jesus to him was the same as that to his sister (to him "One thing thou lackest;" to her "One thing is needful"). Jesus is said by Mark to have loved him, which term is only applied to John and the sisters of Lazarus (John xi. 5). The craving for truth and holiness in Lazarus was that which Jesus loved. Martha was apparently occupied and contented with outward activity, and the teachings of the Pharisees, not suspecting the great truth that eternal life is even now present to the faithful. Lazarus hesitates between his old faith which he had "kept from his youth up" and the new light, and in this condition he is struck down by the fever, which does its work quickly in the East.

The words and conduct of Jesus show the deep concern of the friend and the restoration especially the affectionate work of the Great Teacher, who brought truth home to many hearts by one lesson.

The sisters believed that he would have healed him of his sickness if he had been there at the time (John xi. 21), and their want of faith even after the loss of their brother brings tears of sympathy mingled with indignation to his eyes. The raising of Lazarus cannot be told in more fitting words than are used by John (xi.), who writes as an eye witness, and one who saw also with a spiritual eye. A tradition states that the first question Lazarus asked after being raised was whether he should die again, and when told he must go the way of all men, it touched him with a deep sadness, and he never smiled again. What he saw during his four days' sleep was never made known, nor whether he was even conscious.

Lazarus was naturally made the subject of the spite of the Scribes and Pharisees for his part in the seeming assistance that he gave to Jesus, whose works were denounced by them as imposture and the work of the devil, or Beelzebub (Matt. ix. 34; x. 25; Mark iii. 22, etc.).

There is an explanation of the remark of Judas at the feast which is, that he, with others, had expected at this feast a distribution of large sums to the poor, and therefore the perfume used on one of themselves was "waste" because it lessened the amount expected to be distributed.

Nothing is recorded of Lazarus after the feast.

The whole story of Lazarus, so full of beauty and simplicity, sympathy and truthfulness, is above criticism, and the work of a man who, in his old age and ripe faith was a witness in this account that Jesus was "the resurrection and the life."

LEAD (OFERETH; Gr. *molibdos*). Was known very early to the ancient Hebrews, being found in Sinai and Egypt (Ez. xxvii. 13). It was used for weights (Ex. xv. 10 ; Eccles. xxii. 14). Oxide of lead was used to glaze pottery then as now.

LEAF (ALEH, *to grow up ;* TEREF, *to pluck off ;* ZELAIM, *two-leaved doors*), (DELETH). Leaves of a book or roll.

LE'AH (*wearied*). Daughter of Laban, 1st wife of Jacob, mother of Reuben, Simeon, Levi, Judah, Issachar, Zebulon, Dinah. She had but little share of her husband's love, and she suffered the pain of witnessing Dinah's dishonor at Shechem, with the terrible retribution that followed. She lived longer than Rachel, and died in the Negeb, and was buried in the cave of Machpelah.

LEAS'ING (*falsehood*), (Ps. iv. 2; v. 6). Lies, in Ps. xl. 4; lviii. 3.

LEATH'ER (2 K. i. 8; Matt. iii. 4). There are very few notices of leather, unless the word skin means leather in use, as in Lev. xi. 32; xiii. 48; Num. xxxi. 20, etc. TANNER.

LEAVEN (SEOR, *fermentation*). There was also besides fermented (KAMEZ), sharpened (MAZZOTH) bread, unleavened (Ex. xii. 7). Leaven was strictly forbidden in all sacrifices, as typical of corruption or decay. Jesus uses leaven as a figure in describing the peculiar corruption of ideas of the Scribes and Pharisees. The pagans also avoided it in their offerings to their gods. It is also used as a figure for the gospel for its secretly penetrating and diffusive power (1 Cor. v. 6).

LEB'ANA (*white*). A Nethinim, who returned with Zerubbabel (Neh. vii. 48).

LEB'ANAH (Ez. ii. 45).

LEBANON (*white*). The white mountain of Palestine, on the north of the country given to the Israelites (Deut. i. 7; xi. 24; Josh. i. 4). There

are two ranges, Lebanon on the west, and Anti-Lebanon on the east, almost parallel, extending from near Tyre to Hamath, about 110 miles. See GEOLOGY and HERMON.

The valley of Lebanon is alluded to in the description of the extent of the land taken by Joshua (xi. 17). It is 5 to 8 miles wide, the whole length of the Lebanon, and watered by the two rivers Leontes and Orontes. The original name was Bukaa (*the valley*), which was changed to Cœle-Syria (*hollow Syria*), by the Romans, and is now restored by the Arabs. Lebanon toward the sunrising, was the name for Anti-Lebanon in Joshua xiii. 5. (The best description is in *Porter's Damascus*).

Lebanon, from the Leontes to the Eleutherus, has an average elevation of 6,000 to 8,000 feet, with two higher groups of peaks—Sunnin, 8,500, and Makhmel (Khodib)—10,051 (10,200 by one authority). The view of Lebanon from the sea is exceedingly grand. The wavy top is covered with snow during winter and spring, and the two highest peaks capped with ice on the sultriest days of summer. Cultivation, chiefly by terraces, extends to a hight of 6,000 feet. Little fields and gardens are often seen on high places, difficult of approach, where it would seem that the eagles only could have planted the seed. Fig trees and vines cling to steep rocks and narrow ledges; long rows of mulberry trees fringe the winding terraces, and olive orchards fill the ravines. Hundreds of villages and convents cling like swallows' nests to the steep cliffs. The mountain seems to be built of thousands of terrace walls, rising like steps from the sea to the snow. Seen from below, the rocky

LOCUST.

walls alone appear, divided by many deep and wild ravines. Looking down upon the terraces from a hight, the vegetation is seen everywhere clothing the slopes with a great variety of tints from fields of grain, gardens of vegetables, vineyards, and different fruit and forest trees. One of the most striking and beautiful scenes in the world is from the upper slopes of Lebanon, where far away, over and beyond some deep, dark glen, clothed with dense foliage, the broad and bright Mediterranean reposes under a cloudless sky. The beauties of Lebanon were noticed by the poets and prophets of Israel (Cant. iv. 11; Hosea xiv. 5, 6, 7). The coolness of its snows and waters was appreciated by Jeremiah in contrast to the heats of summer in the lower lands (Jer. xviii. 14). The finest view of Lebanon from the east is at Baalbek, where the snowy crests extend north and south as far as the eye can see. The view from the range of Anti-Lebanon is more grand and extensive, but less picturesque, because more distant.

The glory of Lebanon was its cedar, pine and oak forests, which were used in Solomon's Temple and his other grand edifices, for temples and palaces, in Rome and Assyria, and in ship-building (1 K. vi.; 2 Sam. v. 11; Ezr. iii. 7; Is. xiv. 8; Ez.

xxvii. 4–6; Jos. Wars v. 5, 2; Pliny xiii. 11; Layard 356). There are two groups of cedars now standing as witnesses of past grandeur. One is in a basin formed by the highest summits of Lebanon, which rise in a semi-circle around the head waters of the Kadisha, 6,172 feet above the sea. The other is on the slope of Keniseh, near the new stage-coach road from Beirut to Damascus, from which our sketch was taken. The rivers are not very large nor long, but are among the most famous in the world's history. Beginning at the north, the Eleutherus (*Nahr el Kebir*) rises in the plain of Emesa, flows around the north end of Lebanon, and falls into the sea between Arvad and Tripolis. The *Kadisha* (*sacred river*), now *Nahr Abu Aly*, rises near the cedars under the highest summits of Lebanon, and flows through a gorge of surpassing grandeur, to the sea, at Tripolis. The perpendicular walls of rock at one place are 1000 feet high. The *Nahr Ibrahim*, the classic Adonis (the scene of the romantic story of Venus and Adonis. Adonis being killed by a boar, his blood now annually colors the water of the river, which runs red to the sea). Ezekiel mentions Adonis under the name Tammuz (viii. 14). It rises near the ancient Apheka, where there is a ruined temple of Venus, and falls into the sea near Gebel. The Lycus (*Nahr el Kelb*, Dog river) rises on Sunnin and empties into St. George's Bay, a few miles north of Beirut. At its mouth are the famous sculptured rocks on the side of the pass, where the armies of Assyria, Egypt, Greece, Rome and France have left records of their deeds. Pliny mentions the Magoras, which is probably the *Nahr Beirut*. The Tamyras or Damuras of Strabo rises near *Deir el Kamar*, the modern capital of Lebanon, and reaches the sea about ten miles south of Beirut.

The Bostrenus (*Nahr el Awaly*) is a small stream, 8 miles further south.

The Leontes (see SYRIA), in the lower part, rushes through a wild chasm, the banks of which are a thousand feet or more high, almost perpendicular, and are spanned at one place by a natural bridge 60 feet long and 100 feet above the stream. All of these are on the western slope; and there are none on the eastern, except those in the valley of Lebanon, the Orontes and the Leontes. The rivers of Anti-Lebanon are the Abana, *Barada* (the golden-flowing stream), which rises in the beautiful little plain of Zebedany, flows along the western side of the ridge, and then down through a wild gorge into the plain of Damascus, where it divides into several channels, and is lost in the

TEMPLE.

marsh and lake east of that city. The Pharpar (*Nahr Awaj*) rises high up on the eastern side of Hermon, flows across the Hauran, and is also lost in a marsh and lake south of the former. The Helbon waters the fertile glen of Helbon.

It is supposed that the Maronites in Lebanon are descendants of the ancient Syrians, but there is no direct evidence. The Druses are Arabs. No other country has such a mixture of many races, holding to their ancient religions, more or less idolatrous. There are very few remains of ancient temples on

Lebanon, while Hermon is crowded with them. The American Mission has a station at Abeih, a few miles S. E. of Beirut, not far from *Deir el Kamar*. Young men, and also young women, of every class and of every faith, are seeking education for its uses in commerce and benefits in social and private life; and the Syrian college, lately established in Beirut, will complete the work.

LEB'AOTH (*lioness*). Judah in the south (Josh. xv. 32). Given to Simeon out of Judah's lot. Beth Lebaoth (*place of lions*). The place may have been invested by wild beasts, and therefore so named.

LEBBÆ'US (*courageous*), (Matt. x. 3). THADDEUS.

LEBO'NAH (*frankincense*). Three miles west of Shiloh, now *El Lubban*. The village stands on the slope of a hill bordering the wady Lubban, and its houses have a gray and antique appearance. In the cliffs above are caves and sepulchres, witnesses of a former importance (Judg. xxi. 19).

LE'CAH (*journey*), (1 Chr. iv. 21). A town built by Er. Lost.

LEEKS (CHAZIR, *grass*). There are several plants offered in explanation of the 20 allusions in the O. T. to "leeks." The *trigonella* grows in gardens in Egypt, and is eaten in large quantities in the fall, as greens are with us. The seeds are also eaten boiled. Radishes, onions, garlic (and leeks) were supplied to the workmen who built the pyamids. The priests were not permitted to eat any of these, as Plutarch explains.

LEES (SHEMER, *preservation*). Wine was left standing on the lees to give it color and body (Is. xxv. 6). The wine undisturbed was thick, and before it was used it was necessary to strain off the lees.

LE'GION (Matt. xxvi. 53; Luke viii. 30). A portion of the Roman army, about 6,000 infantry.

LEHA'BIM (Gen. x. 13). Mizraim's third son, perhaps the ancestor of the Lubim, allies of the Egyptians, mentioned in the inscriptions on their monuments at Medinet Habu (dated 1250 B. C.); and also of the Libyans. Jeremiah noticed them in the 6th century B. C., and Daniel still later. They are located on the African coast, west of Egypt, as far as and beyond Cyrene. The great Arab tribe, the Beni Ali, now extends from Egypt to the Atlantic, and illustrates the probable extent of the ancient Lubim and their accessions. There has been from the earliest times a constant stream of colonization flowing along the coast of Africa, north of the Great Desert, from the Nile to the Straits of Gibraltar, from different nations and people. The Phœnicians and Greeks drove the Lubim into the desert and the mountains, where they still remain.

LE'HI. The place where Samson slew a thousand men with a jaw-bone (Judg. xv. 9-19). L'chi is the Hebrew word for *jaw-bone*, but the name of the place was Ramath lehi (v. 17). It was on the border of Judah and Philistia. The spring of Enhakkore was known in Jerome's time, near Morasthi, the prophet Micah's birth-place, east of Eleutheropolis. Now Lost.

LE'MECH. LAMECH 2 (Gen. v. 25).

LEM'UEL (*devoted*), (Prov. xxxi. 1-9).

LEN'TILES (ADASHIM). A bean-like plant much esteemed in the East as an article of food. There are several kinds (Gen xxv. 34; Ez. iv. 9). They were used in making bread in times of scarcity. The present Arabic name (ADAS) is the same as the Hebrew. Red pottage is made of the red lentile, and is a very palatable dish, called ADOM in Gen. xxv. 30. The poor in Egypt now use it because it is cheaper than wheat. There is a tradition that Esau sold his birthright at Hebron, and in memory of this the Arab monks (dervishes) distribute daily a supply of lentile soup to the poor, and strangers.

LEOPARD (NAMER; *spotted*). Mentioned in 7 passages. The word was compounded into several of towns as Beth-nimrah, Nimrah, Nimrim (Leopard-town, etc.), (Is. xi. 6; Jer. v. 6, etc.).

Habakkuk compares the Chaldæan horses to the swift leopard (i. 8), and Daniel alludes to the "winged leopard," as a type or figure of the rapid conquests of Alexander. The hills of Palestine were frequented by the leopard in ancient times, as may be inferred from Cant. iv. 8., and it is now found in the mountains of Hermon and Lebanon, and sometimes in the gorges near Jerusalem, especially the lower Kidron, where it retreats into caves from the heat of the sun.

The Chēĕtah may be included in this description, as it was used by the ancient Egyptians in hunting, and so sculptured on the monuments. Their skins were worn by the priests during their religious ceremonies, and are so worn by the modern dervishes.

LEPER (ZARUA; leprosy, ZARAATH; Gr. *lepra, levros*). Supposed to be the peculiar scourge of an offended deity. The white variety was more common (if there is more than one) covering the entire body, or the most of it, and was called the leprosy of Moses. This was the "clean" kind. The symptoms were first a swelling, a scab or baldness, and a shiny spot. The hair changed to a white or yellowish-white over the swelling. Sometimes raw flesh ("proud flesh") appeared in the sore. It often disappeared after going so far. If it went farther it became "unclean." While disease was active and spreading it was unclean, but when it had spread all over the body, and could go no farther, the person became clean again. The object of the disease seems to have been to create a nameless horror, and dread of contagion. It is not known whether it was propagated by contagion. Some passages mean any disease that spreads in the skin (Lev. xiii., xiv.). The modern Elephantiasis (*Barbadoes leg, swelled leg*) is not the leprosy of the Hebrews, although sometimes called "black leprosy." The leprosy of garments and of walls has caused many ingenious explanations. One of walls is that of a fungus growth on the wall producing spots; another of the nitrous efflorescence in red spots.

LE'SHEM (*glancing*—the stone *jacinth*). The city Laish (Josh. xix. 47; Rev. xxi. 20).

LE'THECH (*pouring*). A measure for grain (Hos. iii. 2). WEIGHTS AND MEASURES.

LET'TUS. HATTUSH (1 Esd. viii. 29).

LETU'SHIM. Second son of Dedan (Gen. xxv. 3), who founded a tribe in Arabia called by Ptolemy *Allumœoti* (Heb. LEUMMIM). There was a city called Luma in Arabia Deserta.

LEUM'MIM (*nations*). Sons of Dedan (Gen. xxv. 3).

LE'VI (*to adhere*). Third son of Leah, wife of Jacob. Born in Mesopotamia, B. C. 1750 (Gen. xxix. 34). When Dinah went out to see the young women of Shechem, as Josephus says, at an annual festival of nature-worship, such as that mentioned in Numbers xxv. 2, of the people in Moab, she was taken by Shechem as a wife; which was resented as an insult by her brothers, Jacob, Simeon, and Levi, who executed their revenge on the city in a fearful manner (Gen. xxxiv.), destroying the whole city for the error of one man. This is an early instance of a blood feud, which are so common in the East now. Levi plotted with others against Joseph. He went into Egypt with his three sons, Gershon, Kohath, and Merari, and as one of the eldest, was presented to Pharaoh. The descendants of Levi, among whom were Moses and Aaron, were made the ministers of religion and the repre-

sentatives of the national faith; Jacob prophesied that Levi should be scattered among his brothers, which was fulfilled in the distribution of the tribe among the 48 Levitical cities, which were scattered throughout the whole country. The tribe displaced the earlier priesthood of the first-born as representatives of the holiness of the people.

LENTILES.

Their first enumeration gave 22,000, which was nearly equal to the number of the first-born males of all the other tribes, which was 22,263—reckoning from one month old upward. The 273 were redeemed by 5 shekels each, being paid to Aaron. They guarded the ark, and were reckoned separately as the host (of the Lord), and were not counted in the army. Their special duties were the daily sacrifice, and the work about the tabernacle (and Temple), in a certain appointed order (Num. iii., iv., vii.).

A table of the family will show the division of the tribe into the three seperate brances according to their functions (Ex. vi. 16–25).

Father	1 Levi.	4 Merari	12 Mushi.
Levi	2 **GERSHON.**	7 Amram	13 Moses.
"	3 **KOHATH.**	"	14 Aaron.
"	4 **MERARI.**	8 Izhar	15 Korah.
2 Gershon	5 Libni.	"	16 Nepheg.
"	6 Shimei.	"	17 Zithri.
3 Kohath	7 Amram.	10 Uzziel	18 Mishael.
"	8 Izhar.	"	19 Elzaphar
"	9 Hebron.	"	20 Zithri.
"	10 Uzziel.	14 Aaron	21 Eleazar.
4 Merari	11 Mahali.	"	22 Ithamar.

The Levitical order proceeded from the people, and were not a privileged class (Ex. xxviii.); nor was the monarchy designed to be so (Deut. xvii. 14–20), and the people always took part in the coronation of the king and the installation of the high-priest (1 Chr. xxix. 22; 1 Macc. xiv. 35). They did not cultivate land or work at trades, but were to receive a tenth as tithes from the people; a part of which was again divided to the priests (Num. xviii. 21, etc.). Their duty was to instruct the people in the law, and to enable them to spread this knowledge through the land. 48 cities were assigned for residences to them, 6 of which were cities of refuge, and 13 were for the priests, distributed as follows: KOHATHITES—Priests: Judah and Simeon 9; Benjamin 4. Not priests: Ephraim 4; Dan 4; half Manasseh (west) 2. GERSHONITES—Half Manasseh (east) 2; Issachar 4; Asher 4; Naphtali 3. MERARITES—Zebulon 4; Reuben; Gad 4. Each of these cities was to have a suburb for pasture-ground, for the Levites' cattle (Num. xxxv. 4, 5). Saul massacred the priests at Nob, slew the Gibeonites in their service, and assumed the priestly office; but David reorganized and restored them to their proper service. The CHORAL SERVICE is first mentioned in David's time (1 Chr. xv. 16, and minutely in ch. xxv.). Ethan (1 Chr. 19), one of the singers, was a man of great talent (1 K. iv. 31), and author of the 89th Psalm. The tribe was divided into 12 orders or courses, to serve each one month in rotation. The porters served only a week, but the four chief porters lived in the temple court (1 Chr. ix. 27). Psalm cxxxiv. was a song of the night-watchmen around the temple. The Levites appear as SCRIBES first in 2 Chr. xxxiv. 13, under Josiah. The books of Chronicles were probably compiled by scribes, under the direction of Daniel and Ezra. The age at which service was to be required was originally 30 years, but was reduced to 20 in the tribe of Solomon (1 Chr. xxiii. 24–27). Ezekiel records the idolatry of the Levites in chs. xliv. and xlviii. Psalm cxxxvii. is a mournful and touching record of the Levites' experience in captivity. The priests, Levites, singers, and porters who returned from Babylon were (it seems from Ezr. ii. 36–42) a very small "remnant" (iii. 8). None of the Levites came to the first meeting of preparation for the return (viii. 15). Their service and residence were established as of old, and they joined in the last great song of praise which is recorded (Neh. ix. 6–38). From this time down we have scarcely any account in the Old, and but a very few notices of them in the N. T. (as in Luke x. 32; John i. 19, etc.). They were also dispersed among the Gentiles, with the other tribes (Acts iv. 36).

The religious system established by custom from Abraham's time was changed when Aaron was made the high-priest. The eldest son of each house inherited the priestly office, and performed the duties (Ex. xxiv. 15), and this idea led to that other that Israel was a nation of priests. The great change was made when the entire tribe of Levi was set aside as a priestly caste—an order—as witnesses and guardians of the national worship. The Levites took the place of the first-born in the nation which were numbered, being 22,273, the Levites being 22,000, counting all from a month old upward, and the difference was balanced by paying for each one of the odd number the price of a victim vowed in sacrifice. The tabernacle was a sign of the presence of God among the people, and the Levites were the royal guard of this invisible king. They were not included in the armies, although called the Lord's Host. The Kohathites held the highest offices, guarding and bearing the sacred vessels, including the ark, after these had been covered with the dark-blue cloth by the priests. The Gershonites bore the tent-cloths, curtains, etc., and the Merarites carried the boards, bars, and pillars, using oxen and carts. They purified them selves by a ceremonious washing and sprinkling, and were solemnly consecrated by the people (Num. viii. 10).

CROWN.

LEVI'ATHAN (LIVYATHAN, an animal wreathed). The crocodile.

Described as living in the sea (or river), and probably a term including several kinds of monsters of the deep (Ps. civ. 26), and also serpents. Job iii. 8 has mourning for leviathan. The practice of enchantment is referred to, which was similar to the modern snake-charming. The description in Job xli. is of the crocodile (so in the version of T. J. Conant), and also in Ps. lxxiv. 14. The

Arabic name is Timsah, which is given to the lake near Suez, through which the Suez canal runs. The word is translated dragon in Ezekiel (xxx. 3). The leviathan of Is. xxvii. 1 (NACHASH, serpent), is used as a type of Egypt, and the crocodile was an emblem of that country. The python (satan) was worshiped by the Egyptians as well as the crocodile.

LEV'IRATE (husband's brother). The law by which a younger brother married the widow of the elder brother, and raised children in his name.

LE'VIS. Corruption of "the Levite" in Ezr. x. 13.

LIB'ANUS. LEBANON (1 Esd. iv. 48, v. 55).

LIB'ERTINES (Acts vi. 9). Two explanations of this difficult text are offered: 1. People or disciples from Libertum near Cyrene, Africa.—2. That the Libertines were Jews who had been made prisoners in various wars, reduced to slavery, and afterward liberated, converted, and received into the synagogues with disciples from other cities (Jos. Ant. xviii. 3, § 5).

LIB'NAH (whiteness). Station in the desert (Num. xxxiii. 20), between Sinai and Kadesh, near Rissah, perhaps on the Red Sea. Laban Deut. i. 1).—2. A city in the S. W. of Palestine, taken by Joshua next after Makkedah, on the day that "the sun stood still." Sennacherib besieged it (2 K. xix. 8). The great destruction of his army, when 185,000 died in one night (Is. xxxvii. 8–36; 2 K. xix. 8), took place either here (where Rabshakeh, his general, joined him with the force that had camped at Jerusalem), or, according to Josephus and Herodotus, at Pelusium (Ant. x. 1, 4). King Zedekiah's mother was of this place (Jer. lii. 1). A little village called El Menshieh, 5 ms. W. of Eleutheropolis, on the direct road between Makkedah and Eglon, with a few ruins which are evidences of its former strength, marks the site of the ancient Libnah.

LIB'NI (white). 1. Son of Gershom (Ex. vi. 17). —2. Son of Mahli (vi. 29).

LIB'NITES, THE. Descendants of LIBNI.

LIB'YA (Acts ii. 10). Libya about Cyrene. LUBIM.

LIB'YANS. People of LIBYA (Jer. xlvi. 9).

LICE (KINNIM). Only in Ex. viii. 16–18, and Ps. cv. 31; both references applying to the plague in Egypt. It is urged by some that the original means gnats and not lice: 1. Because the Greek knips (knipes) may mean that insect.—2. Plant-lice may have been meant, and an Arabic word (kaml, a louse) is referred to in proof, when describing "a thistle black with plant-lice," which is often seen in Egypt. The Egyptians were very scrupulous on the subject of purity, and especially avoided lice and all vermin. The plague of lice was therefore especially obnoxious to them.

LIEUTENANTS. The official title of one who governed the Persian empire (Esth. iii. 12, viii. 9).

LIFE (HAY, or CHAY), living thing (Gen. i. 20); NEPHESH, soul (xii. 5; Ps. xi. 1); mind (xxiii. 8); person (xiv. 21); heart (Ex. xxiii. 9); Greek bios, present life (Luke viii. 14); zoe, (Matt. vii. 14); zao, to live; pneuma, spirit, ghost (Rev. xiii. 19); psuche, soul (Matt. ii. 20). Life and to live used of the existence of men and animals, and of the enjoyment of what makes life valuable, as happiness (Ps. xvi. 11), and the favor of God (Rom. vi. 4). The true life is immortality in blessedness and glory, and it is believed by some that Jesus taught that such a life was only to be won by a pure life of faith and deeds, believing on him who is the Lord of Life (Matt. xix. 16, 17, 29; Rom. ii. 7, v. 17, vi. 23.

LIGHT (OR; Gr. phos). The element light; that which enables us to see. Also, figuratively, the intellectual, moral, and spiritual element by which we may see (Matt. vi. 23; John i. 4, v. 35). God is the source of this light, as the sun is of the other. Children of light is a term for true disciples (Luke xvi. 8; Eph. v. 8). Jesus Christ is the Light of the world.

LI'GURE (LESHEM). PRECIOUS STONES.

LIK'HI (*learned*). Son of Shemida (1 Chr. vii. 19).

LIL'Y (SHU-SHAH, SHOSHAN-NAH; Gr.*Krinon*). There is a great difference of opinion on this question as to what flower was meant by the Hebrews, or by Jesus, which appears in our translation as the lily. Dr. Thomson, (*Land and Book*, i. 394),says, "The Huleh lily is very large, and the three inner petals meet above and form a gorgeous canopy, such as art never approached, and king never sat under, even in his utmost glory.

LILIES.

Nothing can be in higher contrast than the luxuriant, velvety softness of this lily, and the crabbed, tangled hedge of thorns about it."

The Phœnician architects ornamented the temple with lily work, probably imitating the use of the lotus in Egypt about the columns, and the rim of the brazen sea. These ideas are wrought into visible shape in T. O. Paine's *Temple of Solomon*.

LIME. Limestone is the common rock of Palestine (Deut. xxvii. 2, 4). Lime-kilns are frequent, and where limestone is not easily accessible, as in Asia Minor, the Turks are in the habit of breaking up the marble columns, capitals, handsomely carved entablatures, and even statues of the gods, to be burnt into lime.

LINEN. Heb. 1. SHESH, fine linen (Gen. xli. 42); 2. BAD, linen used for the under clothes of the priests (Ex. xxviii. 42; Lev. vi. 10); 3. BUTS, fine linen, perhaps from the Greek *Bussos* (2 Chr. v. 12), of which the vail of the temple was made (iii. 14), and Mordecai was arrayed (colored purple), and the rich man arrayed in the parable (Luke xvi. 19); 4. ETUN, made of fine flax (Prov. vii. 16); 5. MIKVE, linen yarn (1 K. x. 28); 6. SADIN, linen garments (Judg. xiv. 12); 7. Gr. *sindon*.

Egypt, from the most ancient time, was celebrated for its fine linen, which was used for the sacred garments of the priests, for mummy wrappers, and to write upon. Some specimens may be seen in the Abbot Egyptian Museum, in New York (Hist. So. Building, on 2d Ave., near 9th st.).

LIN'TEL. The upper framework of a door (1 K. vi. 31) correctly "upper door-post" (Ex. xii. 7). Heb. AYIL, post (Ez. xl., xli.). Some say that ayil meant a wall along an entrance way which could be divided into panels; 2. KAFTAR, knop (Amos ix. 1; Zeph. ii. 14); 3. MASHKOF (upper door-post in Ex. xii. 22). Aben Ezra translates

mashkof by window, because it means "to look, as from the window over the door upon any one below. See WINDOW.

LI'NUS (*flax*). A disciple at Rome (2 Tim. iv. 21).

The first bishop of Rome after the apostles was Linus (A. D. 68–80), and no lofty pre-eminence was attached to the office at that time, as appears from the simple mention of his name among others. He is said to have written an account of the dispute between Peter and Simon Magus.

LI'ON. There are no lions now in Palestine, but they abound in the deserts, and the swamps of the Euphrates. There are several names of places compounded of the name of lion which show that the animal was known there anciently, as Leboath, Laish (Josh. xv. 32; Judg. xvii. 7).

These seven names for lion, indicating different ages: 1. GUR, or GOR, a cub (Gen. xlix. 9); 2. KEFIR, a young lion (Judg. xiv. 5); 3. ARI, ARYEH, full grown lion (Gen. xlix. 9); 4. SHAKHAL, (*the roarer*) large, strong lion (Job iv. 10); 5. SHAKHAZ, in full vigor (xviii. 8); 6. LABI, or LEBBIYA, an old lion (Gen. xlix. 9), (Coptic, *labai*, lioness); 7. LAISH, old, decrepit, feeble (Job xi. 11).

The lion of Palestine was probably the African, which was shorter and rounder, and had less mane than the Asiatic variety. Sometimes a "multitude of shepherds" turned out to hunt the lion (Is. xxxi. 4), and a few instances are recorded of a single person attacking him (1 Sam. xvii. 34), or perhaps two or more (Amos iii. 12). The Arabs now dig a pit for the lion, covering it slightly, and decoying him with some small animal, as a kid.

The kings kept lions for amusement (Ez. xix. 9), and for hunting in Assyria (Anc. Egyptians iii. 17), as represented on the monuments (Layard, *Nin. and Bab.* 138). Poets and other writers made much use of the lion for his strength (Judg. xiv. 18), courage (Prov. xxviii. 1), and ferocity (Gen. xlix. 9); qualities which were attributed to brave, or other noted men. The lion's roar is given by four Hebrew words: 1. SHAAG, thunder (Judg. xiv. 5), his roar when hunting; 2. NAHAM, the cry when the prey is seized (Is. v. 29); 3. HAJAH, growl of defiance; 4. NAAR, the yelp of young lions (Jer. li. 38). Besides these there are terms for other qualities and acts; as RABATS, crouching (Ez. xix. 2); SHACHAT, lying in wait in a den; ARAB, secret watching for prey; RAMAS, creeping in a stealthy manner (Ps. civ. 20); ZINNEK, the spring upon the prey (Deut. xxxiii. 22). The lion was used in poetry and in sculpture as a symbol of majesty and power, as in the Assyrian compound figures. In Egypt it was worshiped at Leontopolis. It was the emblem of the tribe of Judah, and is mentioned as a symbol by John in Revelation v. 5. Solomon's throne was ornamented with lions, as also the brazen laver (1 K. vii. 29, 36).

LITTER. A couch or sedan chair, borne by men, between mules or on camels, now in use by

LITTER.

the Egyptians (Num. vii. 3; Is. lxvi. 20). They are shown in use on the ancient sculptures and paintings.

LIV'ER. Internal organ of the body (Prov. vii. 23).

LIZ'ARD (Heb. LETAAH). The fan-foot lizard is reddish brown, spotted with white, and lives on insects and worms. It is named from its note which sounds like "Gecko." They lay small, round eggs. Their feet cling to the wall like a fly's, and they run around the house without noise, always at night.

LOAM'MI (*not my people*). Second (symbolical) son of Hosea (Hos. i. 9).

LOAN. The law of Moses required the rich to lend to the poor without interest, only taking security against loss. Foreigners were not included in this rule. The practice of usury was always discreditable among the Hebrews (Prov. vi. 1, 4, xi. 15, xvii. 18, etc.), and Nehemiah restrained its exercise (v. 1, 13). The MONEY CHANGERS of the Temple were useful to the worshipers from a distance, and especially from foreign countries, in changing their money to the only lawful coin, the half-shekel, the annual temple dues from each person; but their presence in the temple itself was illegal and a desecration of the holy place. Their proper place was among business men, on the street with the merchants.

LOCK. The common wooden lock of the East is a clumsy wooden bolt kept in place by a few loose pins which may be lifted by a key with pegs fitted to match (see KEY). Bolts and locks were used (Judg. iii. 23; Cant. v. 5; Neh. iii. 3).

WELL OF THE VIRGIN (JERUSALEM).

LO'CUST. Heb. ARBEH (*multitude*) locust in Ex. x. 4, and many other passages; CHAGAB (*locust generally*) grasshopper in Num. xiii. 33, and others; CHARGOL (*locust*) grasshopper; beetle in Lev. xi. 22; SALAM (*bald locust*) locust in Lev. xi. 22; GAZAM (*palmer-worm*); GOB (*great grasshopper*) in Nahum iii. 17; Is. xxiii. 4; CHANAMAL (*hail or frost?*) locust in Ps. lxxviii. 47; YELEK (*rough*) cankerworm in Nahum iii. 15; caterpillar in Ps. cv. 34; CHASIL (*caterpillar*); ZELAZAL, locust in Deut. xxviii. 42. The clouds of locusts sometimes obscure the sun, and they are very destructive, eating every green thing in their way. See cuts on pages 51, 83.

Their great voracity is alluded to in Ex. x. 12; Joel i. 4; and several other passages, and they are compared to horses in Joel ii. 4, 5, and in Rev. ix. 7, 9, where the noise they make in flying (like a heavy shower of rain) is also noticed, and their irresistable progress. Sometimes they enter the houses and eat the wood work. They do not travel in the night. Some kinds of birds eat them (Starling, Ar. smurmur); and they are eaten by men also, after being roasted, fried or stewed, mixed with flour and ground or pounded fine, and by boiling in water. Vast quantities are drowned in the sea, being carried into it by the wind. They generally die in a day or two. The children catch some kinds, as they do handsome butterflies, for their beauty, being marked with many colors, streaked and spotted. The women often put the eggs of the locust (chargol) into their ears as a cure for, or a preventive of, ear-aches.

LOD. Built by Shamer (1 Chr. viii. 12). Always connected with Ono. It is called Lydda in the Acts (ix. 32), where Peter healed Æneas of palsy. One of the murderers of Julius Cæsar (Cassius Longinus) was stationed in Palestine, and sold the whole people of Lydda into slavery (Ant. xiv. 11, 2); and Antony restored them. Cestius Gallus burnt it, and Vespasian, some time after, colonized it. The Romans gave it a new name, Diospolis (on the coins of Septimus Severus), and it became a seat of Jewish learning, and a large and wealthy town. It was the seat of a bishopric at an early date. Tradition connects the birth of St. George with the ruins of a church in the town, once a splendid structure, built by Justinian (Rob. ii. 244). There are about 1000 people now in the place, which is called by its ancient name, as near as an Arab can speak it (Lud).

LODE'BAR (*without pasture*). The native place Machir ben Ammiel, in whose house Mephibosheth found a home, after his father's death, on the E. of Jordan (2 Sam. xvii. 27, ix. 4, 5). This same Machir was one of the first to supply the wants of David when he fled from Absalom. It was near Mahanaim. Lost.

LODGE. (Is. i. 8). COTTAGE. Shelter made of boughs.

LODGE, to. To "tarry all night" (Gen. xix. 2; Judg. xix. 10; Matt. xxi. 17). HOSPITALITY. INN.

LOINS. The lower region of the back, the seat of strength (Gen. xxxv. 11, xxxvii. 34). Figuratively the source of progeny.

LO'IS (*better*). Grandmother of TIMOTHY, (2 Tim. i. 5, iii. 15).

LORD. See JAH.

LORD'S DAY, THE. (Greek, *He kuriakē hēmera*, in Rev. i. 10). The first day of the week, the weekly festival in memory of the resurrection of the Lord on that day. Some of the "fathers of the early Church" understand it to mean Easter day.

The first day of the week was chosen for the weekly meetings and feasts by those who "preached Jesus and the Resurrection." The appearance to the disciples, apostles, and others, were all on the Lord's day, and the custom of assembling on that day was adopted without a recorded exception in all the Churches. Besides the evidence of the early fathers there is that of Pliny in his letter to Trajan, from Pontus, "The Christians were accustomed to meet together on a stated day, before it was light, and sing hymns to Christ or God, and to bind themselves by a sacrament, and after separating they met again to take a general meal. Justin Martyr calls it Sunday, saying the exercises were prayer, the celebration of the Holy Eucharist, and the collection of alms, because it was the first day on which God dispelled the darkness, and because Jesus Christ rose from the dead on it." This is not the SABBATH, for that was the 7th day, and was a day of rest and a "Holy day" to Jehovah (Is. lviii. 13), and the two are carefully separated in character and intention. The Lord's day was to be a day of joy, cheerfulness, and of relaxation, and of religious meetings, no work being formally forbidden or rest commanded, and the law of Moses in the 4th commandment is nowhere in the Gospels applied to the day.

Some deny any religious character or obligation to the day; others hold it to be an institution of the Church only, without divine sanction; and a third opinion is that it is a continuation under the new order of spiritual things, of the original Sabbath, and the 4th commandment applies equally to the Lord's day.

The first legal act affecting the day that is recorded is that of Constantine, A. D. 321, "Let all judges and city people, and the business of all arts, rest on the venerable Day of the Sun. Yet let those in the country freely and without restraint attend to the cultivation of the fields, since it frequently happens that not more fitly on any day may corn be planted in furrows, or vines in the trenches, lest through the moment's opportunity the benefit granted by heavenly foresight be lost."

Constantine had a nation of many kinds of people with many kinds of religion, and he so framed the laws in favor of his new faith as to do as little violence as possible to the old institutions. This law was acceptable to the Christians who could keep it with joy, and not burdensome to the Pagans, who could feel no interest in it. He certainly did not honor the day, but rather accepted the honor that it brought to him as a convert to the new faith.

The Council of Nice, A. D. 325, notices the day incidentally as already an old institution, and makes some rules concerning the posture of worshipers.

LORD'S PRAYER, THE. The name (not in the Scriptures) of the prayer spoken by Jesus as a model to his disciples, given in Matt. vi. 9–13; Luke xi. 2–4.

LORD'S SUPPER, (Gr. *kuriakon deipnon*, 1 Cor. xi. 20). The great central act of Christian worship, described by Paul (verses 23–26), as having been instituted on the night of the betrayal. It was a continuation or a substitute for the Passover (Matt. xxvi. 19, etc.). See AGAPE.

The Paschal Feast was kept, not precisely as Moses directed (Ex. xii.), but in this manner: The members of the company met in the evening, reclined on couches (John xiii. 23, etc.), the head of the company or house asking a blessing "for the day and for the wine," over a cup, of which he and all the others tasted. Then all present washed their hands. Then the table was set out with the Paschal lamb, unleavened bread, bitter herbs and sauce of dates, figs, raisins and vinegar (HAROSETH), the herbs being dipped into the sauce and eaten, by the leader first. After this the dishes were changed and the cup of wine was again blessed and passed around. Then the real supper began with the solemn introductory words and a thankgiving, with the psalms cxiii., cxiv., after which the hands were again washed. Then the leader broke a loaf of bread and gave thanks, dipping a piece with the bitter herbs into the sauce (sop in A. V.), and eating it, followed by all the company. The lamb was then eaten, with bread and herbs, after which the third cup of wine, called "the cup of blessing," was passed around. A fourth cup (of the Hallel) was passed around during the chanting of psalms cxv., cxviii. The fifth cup was passed during the chanting of the GREAT HALLEL (Ps. cxx.–cxxxviii.).

The Lord's Supper was to take the place of this feast, and the bread and wine instead of being memorials of the deliverance from Egypt, were to be memorials of the Lord and Master. The Paschal feast was annual, but no rule was given for the new supper, which was left to be settled by inclination and custom.

The unleavened bread broken was a memorial of his broken body; the wine of his blood (see Matt. xiii. 38, 39; Gen. xli. 26; Dan. vii. 17), which was the New Testament (Jer. xxxi. 31), symbolical of the new covenant. The custom was well observed from the beginning (Acts ii. 42). Some even suppose that the blessing of the bread and wine occurred at every meal, and at least one a day, each assembly around a table being known as the church of such a place, the materials being paid for out of the common fund.

The bread was such as was commonly used, for they did not propose to continue the obligation of the Passover in using unleavened bread; the wine, as is the general custom in the East, was mixed with water. A part of the ceremony was "a holy kiss" (1 Cor. xvi. 20).

The original supper of "fellowship" passed by degrees into the "communion" service, as taking the place of the feast of charity, which had been abused by selfish souls. The new rule given by Paul separated the idea of a full meal from the celebration of the Lord's Supper, or the Eucharist, and instead of daily it was to be only on the Lord's Day, and also the time was changed from evening to the morning (Acts xx. 11).

The practice of Paul himself seems to have joined the Feast of Charity and the Eucharist, especially shown on board the ship in the storm (xxvii. 35).

BRONZE LOCK, FULL-SIZE, FOUND AT JERUSALEM.

LORUHA'MAH (*the uncompassionated*). Daughter of HOSEA (Hos. i. 6). ROHAMAH.

LOT. Son of Haran, nephew of Abraham (Gen. xi. 27), born in Ur of the Chaldees, and settled in Canaan. He took refuge in Egypt with Abram during the famine (xii. 4, xiii. 1), and returned with him into the south of Palestine. He chose the Arabah for his pasture-land, leaving Abram on the hills of Benjamin and Judah. When the four kings captured him, he was rescued by his uncle (xiv.). Lot had probably entered into the cities, adopted some of their customs, and gathered other property besides cattle and tents (v. 12), including women (servants). The last scene in his life is recorded in connection with the destruction of the cities of the plain, when there appears in contrast with some of the darkest traits of human nature in the people of the cities, the pleasant habits and customs of Lot's wandering life; the chivalrous hospitality —washing feet, unleavened bread, the ready feast, such as we read of on the hills of Hebron among Abram's tents, and was referred to by Paul in the beautiful passage, "Be not forgetful to entertain strangers, for thereby some have entertained angels unawares" (Heb. xiii. 2). The traveler now meets with these traits among the Bedawin, which are almost identical with those of their ancestors of that early age. Where Zoar was, or in what mountain Lot dwelt, has not been determined (see ZOAR). The story of Lot's wife, and especially the strange conclusion, might have been passed by as a mystery, but for the use of it as an example in one of the discourses of Jesus (Luke xvii. 31, 32), where he says, "In that day he that is in the field let him not return back: remember Lot's wife" (who did). The author of the Book of Wisdom (x. 7), and Josephus (Ant. i. 11, 4), seem to have believed in an actual monument of salt; and many travelers from their day to this have seen and described pillars of salt which they accepted as Lot's wife.

Ammon and Moab were the children of Lot (Deut. ii. 9, 19), and as such were exempted from conquest by Moses. (See Ps. lxxxiii.) The Arabs have traditions of Lot (Koran, ch. vii., xi.), in which he is described as a preacher sent to the cities of the plain, which they call Lot's cities. The Dead Sea is also called the Sea of Lot (Bahr Loot).

LO′TAN (*covering*). Son of Seir (Gen. xxxvi. 20).

LOVE (Heb. AHABA, Gr. *agape*). Natural affection. Also spiritual affection for holy things (Rom. xiii. 10; 1 John. iv. 7, etc.), which is a fruit of the Spirit, opposed to all evil, and only satisfied with a likeness to Jesus Christ and God.

LOVE-FEAST. See AGAPE.

LOW COUN′TRY (2 Chr. xxvi. 10). PLAIN. Arabah?

LO′ZON. Ancestors of Solomon's servants, who returned with Zerubbabel (1 Esd. v. 33). DARKON.

LU′BIM (*people of a dry land*). LEHABIM. In Shishak's army (2 Chr. xii. 3). Mentioned by the prophets (Nahum iii. 9; Dan. xi. 43), and on the Egyptian monuments, where they are called LEBU, who contended with Egypt in war, and were subdued about 1250, B. C. They are painted as a Shemitic race, fair and strong. Perhaps the same as the LEHABIM. They occupied the shores of the Great Sea, and the Desert inland, west of Egypt. The Kabyles and Berbers of that district may be descendants, as they are the successors of the Lubim (Libyans).

LU′CAS. LUKE. Companion of Paul at Rome (Col. iv. 14).

LU′CIFER (*light bearing*). Son of the morning, morning star (Is. xiv. 12), a symbol of the king of Babylon. Since the time of Jerome it is a name for Satan. See DEMON, DEVIL.

LU′CIUS (*born in the day-time*). 1. A Roman consul (1 Macc. xv. 10), and uncertain whether 1. L. Furius, B. C. 136; 2. L. Cæcilius Metellus Calvus, B. C. 142; or 3. L. Calpurnius Piso, B. C. 139, who is probably the one referred to. —2. A kinsman of Paul (Rom. xvi. 21), afterwards bishop of Cenchræa.—3. Lucius of Cyrene, was probably at the Feast of Pentecost, if not one of the 70, and also one of the "men of Cyrene," who preached in Antioch (Acts xi. 20). Different traditions make him bishop of Cenchræa, Cyrene and Laodicea in Syria.

LU′CRE. That which is gained unworthily (1 Sam. viii. 3; 1 Tim. iii. 8).

LUKE (Gr. *Loukas*; Latin *Lucas, born at daylight*). A common name among Romans. A Gentile born at Antioch in Syria, educated a physician, and an artist (Nicephorus ii. 43). Some have supposed him one of the 70, and also one of the two who saw Jesus at Emmaus, but without good reason. He first appears historically at Troas with Paul, going with him into Macedonia (Acts xvi.·9, 10), and writing his history after that as an eye witness. See GOSPEL and ACTS in the HISTORY.

It is supposed that he died a martyr between A. D. 75 and 100, but no locality is given.

LU′NATIC (*moon-struck*), (Matt. iv. 24, xvii. 15). Disease of the body and mind. MADNESS.

LUST. Desire (Ps. lxxviii. 18, 30), inordinate and sensual (Rom. i. 27).

LUZ. LUZAH (*almond-tree*). An ancient city of Canaan, named Bethel by Jacob (Gen. xxviii. 19).

It is likely that the place of Jacob's pillar, of the El-Beth-el sanctuary (xxxv. 6, xlviii. 3), and of Jeroboam's idolatry (1 K. xii. 29), were not *in*, but *south* of the city of Luz (Josh. xvi. 1, 2, xviii. 13). —2. One of the men of Luz was allowed by the house of Joseph to escape, when the city was destroyed, and he went into the land of the Hittites, where he built another Luz. Probably on the Orontes river (Porter).

LYCAO′NIA (*Lucos*, a wolf, *wolf-country*). An undulating plain, 20 miles by 13, among the mountains in Asia Minor, north of Cilicia.

Iconium (its capital), Derbe, and Lystra were there, and visited by Paul. The speech of this district was a corrupt form of Greek (Acts xiv. 11). It was a Roman colony, and had a good road. The streams are brackish, and there are several small salt-lakes; but flocks find good pasture.

LY′CIA (LI′KEA). A province and peninsula southwest in Asia Minor, opposite the island of Rhodes; mountainous and well watered with small creeks.

Bellerophon, one of its ancient kings, is celebrated in Greek mythology. The Romans took it from Antiochus the Great, after the battle of Magnesia (B. C. 190). There are many ruined cities in this region, described in the excellent works of Fellows, Spratt, and Forbes, full of architecture, sculpture, and inscriptions of the ancients. It is mentioned in 1 Macc. xv. 23, during its golden period, just after its emancipation from the rule of the island Rhodes. Paul visited two of its cities, Patara and Myra.

LYDDA.

LUD. Fourth son of Shem (Gen. x. 22), from whom descended the Lydians; who first settled north of Palestine, and afterward in Asia Minor. The name is found on the Egyptian monuments of the 13th, 14th and 15th centuries B. C. as a powerful people called Luden. (See LYDIA).

LU′DIM (Gen. x. 13). Allies of the Egyptians (2 Chr. xii. 3, xvi. 8; Nahum iii. 9). Probably the same people as the Lehabim.

LU′HITH, THE ASCENT OF (Is. xv. 5; Jer. xlviii. 5). A famous pass somewhere in Moab, not yet identified.

LYD′DA. Greek form of Lod. The first historical notice of this city, since Christ, is the signature of Ætius Lyddensis to the acts of the Council of Nicæa (A. D. 325); after which it is frequently mentioned, especially during the Crusades. The Arabs have a tradition that the final contest between Christ and Antichrist will be at Lydda. (Sale's *Koran*, c. 43, note).

LY′DIA (*from king Lydus*). A province in Asia Minor, on the Sea, south of Mysia, and north of Caria. Taken by the Romans from Antiochus the Great, after the battle of Magnesia, B. C. 190, and given to the king of Pergamus, Eumenes II (1

Macc. viii. 8). The *India and Media* of this passage in Maccabees should be corrected to read *Ionia and Mysia*.

LYD'IA (*from Lydia?*). The first convert in Europe, by Paul, and his hostess at Phillippi (Acts xvi. 14, 15, 40). She was a Jewess and was found by Paul attending Jewish Sabbath worship by the side of a stream. She was by occupation a traveling dealer in dyed goods and dyes, and belonged in Thyatira, which was noted for such products. The mention of the conversion of her household indicates some wealth and importance, whether as head of a family or only of hired servants. Her character as a Christian woman is shown in her acceptance of the Gospel, her urgent hospitality, and continued friendship for Paul and Silas when they were persecuted. Her death is not recorded.

LYD'IANS. People of Lydia (Jer. xlvi. 9).

LYSA'NIAS (*ending sorrow*). Tetrarch of Abilene, in the 15th year of Tiberius, when Herod Antipas was tetrarch of Galilee, and Herod Philip was tetrarch of Ituræa and Trachonitis.

Josephus mentions a Lysanias who ruled in that district, near Lebanon, in the time of Antony and Cleopatra, 60 years before the one mentioned by Luke, and also another of the time Caligula and Claudius, 20 years after Luke's reference. The name may have been a common one to several rulers; and the last one mentioned by Josephus the one referred to by Luke.

LYS'IAS (*relaxing*). 1. A nobleman who was intrusted with the government of Syria, B. C. 166 (1 Macc. iii. 32.)—2. Clau'dius Lys'ias, a military tribune who commanded Roman troops at Jerusalem under Felix.

He rescued Paul from the mob of Jews, and afterwards sent him to Cæsarea, under a guard. Since he bought his freedom, and bore a Greek name, it is supposed that he was a Greek by birth (Acts xxi. 31–40, etc.).

LYSIM'ACHUS (*ending strife*). 1. Son of Ptolemæus (Esth. xi. 1).—2. Brother of Menelaus, the high-priest, and his deputy at the court of Antiochus (2 Macc. iv. 29–42). He was killed by a mob, B. C. 170, on account of his tyranny and sacrilege.

LYS'TRA. In Lycaonia. Where divine honors, after the Greek manner, were offered to Paul, and where he was at once stoned. It was the home of Paul's companion, Timothy. The extensive ruins of *Bin bir Kilissi* (*one thousand and one churches*) lie along the eastern declivity of the Karadagh (black mountain), where are to be seen the remains of about 40 churches, some 25 of which are quite entire (*Hamilton*, Asia Minor).

M

MA'ACAH. 1. Mother of Absalom (2 Sam. iii. 3).—2. Daughter of Nahor (Gen. xxii. 24).—3. Father of Achish, king of Gath (1 K. ii. 39).—4. Grand-daughter of Abishalom (1 K. xv. 2, 10, 13). —5. Second wife of Caleb, mother of five of his children (1 Chr. ii. 48).—6. Daughter of Talmai and mother of Absalom (iii. 2).—7. Wife of Jehiel (1 Chr. viii. 29, ix. 35).—8. Wife of Machir (1 Chr. vii. 15, 16).—9. Father of Hanan (xi. 43).—9. Father of Shephatiah (xxvii. 16).

MA'ACAH (*oppression*). MAACHAH. A small kingdom on the N. E. of Palestine, near Argob (Deut. iii. 14), and Bashan (Josh. xii. 5), founded by a son of Nahor, Abraham's brother (Gen. xxii. 24). The people were not expelled, but mingled with the Jews. Eliphelet, of this nation, was one of David's 30 captains (2 Sam. xxiii. 34), and Jaazaniah was a captain in the army of Israel at the time of the Captivity.

MAACH'ATHI, MAACHATHITES, THE. People of Maachah (Deut. iii. 14).

MA'ADAI. Son of Bani (Ezr. x. 34).

MAADI'AH (*ornament of Jehovah*). A priest who returned from captivity (Neh. xii. 5).

MA'AI or **MAA'I** (*compassion*). Son of a priest at the dedication of the wall of Jerusalem (Neh. xii. 36).

MA'ALEH-ACRAB'-BIM. See AKRABBIM.

MA'ANI. BANI 4 (1 Esd. ix. 34).

MA'ARATH (*a bare place*). In the hill country of Judah (Josh. xv. 59).

TRYPHON.

MAASEI'AH (*work of Jehovah*). 20 persons of this name, but none very famous. 1. A descendant of Jeshua (Ezr. x. 18).—2. A priest (21).—3. Another priest (22).—4. A descendant of Pahath-Moab (30).—5. Father of Azariah (Neh. iii. 23).—6. An assistant of Ezra (viii. 4).—7. A Levite (viii. 7).—8. A chief (x. 25).—9. Son of Baruch (xi. 5.)—10. Ancestor of Sallu (xi. 7).—11. Ten priests who assisted Ezra (xii. 41, 42).—12. Father of Zephaniah (Jer. xxi. 1, xxix, 25).—13. Father of Zedekiah (xix. 21).—14. A porter of the temple (1 Chr. xv. 18, 20).—15. Son of Adaiah (2 Chr. xxiii. 1).—16. An officer of high rank (xxvi. 11).—17. The "king's son" (2 Chr. xxviii. 7).—18. Governor of Jerusalem (xxxiv. 8).—19. Son of Shallum (Jer. xxxv. 4).—20. A priest (Jer. xxxii. 12).

MA'ASAI. A priest who returned from captivity and lived in Jerusalem (1 Chr. ix. 12). AMASHAI.

MAASI'AS. MAASEIAH 20 (Bar. i. 1).

MA'ATH. Son of Mattathias (Luke iii. 26).

MA'AZ (*anger*). Son of Ram (1 Chr. ii. 27).

MAAZI'AH (*consolation of Jah*). 1. A priest (1 Chr. xxiv. 18).—2. A priest who signed the coven-ant (Neh. x. 8).

MAB'DAI. BENAIAH 8 (1 Esd. ix. 34).

MABNAD'EBAI (Ezr. x. 40). MACHMADEBAI.

MAC'ALON (1 Esd. v. 21). MICHMASH.

MAC'CABEES. See HISTORY OF THE BOOKS.

THE FAMILY OF THE MACCABEES.

ASMONÆANS.	
	1 Chasmon.
	2 Johanan.
	3 Simeon.
	4 Mattathias.
4 Mattathias.	5 Johanan
"	6 Simon.
"	7 Judas.
"	8 Eleazar.
"	9 Jonathan.
6 Simon.	10 Judas.
"	11 Johannes Hyrcanus 1.
"	12 Mattathias.
"	13 Daughter, m. Ptolemæus.
11 J. Hyrcanus.	14 Aristobulus I, m. Salome.
"	15 Antigonus.
"	16 Jannæus Alexander.
"	17 Son, 18 Son.
16 J. Alexander.	18 Hyrcanus II.
"	19 Aristobulus II.
19 Aristobulus II.	20 Alexander.
"	21 Antigonus.
20 Alexander.	22 Mariamne, m. Herod (Gt.)
"	23 Aristobulus.

MACEDO'NIA. The country N. of Thessaly and the Ægean Sea, S. of the Balkan mts., extending to Trace on the E., and to Illyria on the W. There are two great plains, one watered by the Axius, which empties into the Thermaic gulf near Thessalonica, and the other by the Strymon, which flows by Philippi and Amphipolis into the Ægean Sea. Mt. Athos is a peninsula between these two plains. Philip and Alexander ruled here, and the Romans conquered it from Perseus (B. C. 168.) In the N. T. times a proconsul of one district resided at Thessalonica, ruling over Macedonia, Thessaly, and a tract along the Adriatic (Acts xvi. 9, 10, 12, xix. 21, etc.). In the Apocrypha there are some notices of this country. Haman is called a Macedonian (Esth. xvi. 10). The Maccabees mention Alexander, son of Philip (1 Macc. i. 1), who came out of the land of the Chettiim and smote Darius, king of the Persians and Medes. This was the first part of Europe that received the Gospel, by the labor of Paul and his companions (Acts xvi. 9), who first preached to a small congregation of women (v. 13), on the banks of the Strymon near Philippi; and the first convert was a woman, LYDIA.

MACEDO'NIAN. From MACEDONIA (Esth. xvi. 10, 14). See HISTORY OF THE BOOKS.

MACH'BANAI (*thick one*). Soldier of David at Ziklag (1 Chr. xii. 13).

MACHBE'NAH (*a mantle*). A town built by Shevah. Lost. (1 Chr. ii. 49).

MA'CHI (*diminution*). Father of Genel (Num. xiii. 15).

MACHIR (*sold*). 1. Son of Manasseh (1 Chr. vii. 14). His children were caressed by Joseph (Gen. l. 21).—2. Son of Ammiel, a chief on the E. side of Jordan (2 Sam. ix. 4, 5).

MA'CHIRITES, THE. People of Machir (Num. xxvi. 29).

MACHMAD'EBAI (*gift of the noble*). Son of Bani (Ezr. x. 40).

LYSIMACHUS.

MACH'PELAH. The district in which was the field of Ephron the Hittite, containing the cave which was bought by Abraham, and became the burial-place of Abraham himself, Sarah, Isaac, Rebekah, Leah and Jacob. This cave and the field around it was the only spot which belonged to Abraham in the country. The Haram at Hebron (see view of Hebron) is said to stand over this cave. It is a massive stone structure, in the ancient style, of dark gray stone, 200 ft. long, 115 wide, and 50 high. Some of the stones are 12 to 20 ft. long, by 4 to 5 thick, with beveled edges, like the temple wall at Jerusalem, and must be as old as Solomon's time.

There are shown inside of this building, which is now called a mosque, several small monuments, standing on the floor, each enclosed in a shrine, with iron railings. The first on the right as you enter is that of Abraham; on the left that of Sarah, each guarded by a silver gate. Isaac and Rebekah are also honored, each with a separate chapel; and also Jacob and Leah, opposite the entrance. The cave is under the floor, is in two rooms, and most strictly guarded from intrusion. The best description is given by Stanley (*Jewish*

Church, etc.). This is almost the only spot on earth which attracts all who profess the simple creed "I believe in God." And this is only the grave of an old shepherd, who lived under a tent there 4,000 years ago, whose only title was "The Friend," which is now the Arab name of Hebron, *Al Khulil*.

MA'CRON (*long head*). Son of Dorymenes (1 Macc. iii. 38), governor of Cyprus (2 Macc. x. 12).

MAD'AI (Gen. x. 2). Third son of Japheth, from whom descended the Medes. See 2 K. xvii. 6; Dan. xi. 1; Esth. i. 3, in all of which passages the same original word is found, although differently translated in each.

MADI'ABUN. The son of Madiabun assisted at the Temple dedication (1 Esd. v. 58).

MA'DIAN. MIDIAN (Judg. ii. 26).

MADMAN'NAH (*dunghill*). South in Judah, not far from Gaza (Josh. xv. 21, 31). Beth Marcaboth?

MAD'MEN (Jer. xlviii. 2). Included in the curse of Moab. Near Heshbon.

MADME'NAH (Is. x. 31). A small village between Anathoth and Nob. The prophet said Madmenah *flies* (before the Assyrian).

MAD'NESS (SHAGA, *to be stirred* or *excited*), (1 Sam. xxi. 13); HALEL, *to flash out*, as light or sound (Prov. xxvi. 18); MAINOMAI or *mania* (John x. 20). Among Oriental nations madmen were looked upon with reverence, as possessed of a sacred character. LUNATICS.

MA'DON. City of Canaan before the conquest, whose king, Jobab, was killed at the waters of Merom by Joshua (xi. 1-9). Somewhere in north.

MAE'LUS (1 Esd. ix. 26). MIAMIN.

MAG'BISH (*freezing*). One hundred and fifty-six of the children of Magbish returned from captivity (Ezr. ii. 30). In Benjamin. Lost.

MAG'DALA (*tower*). In most of the MSS. the name is MAGADAN. Christ came into the limits of Magdala after the miracle of feeding the 4,000 on the other side of the lake (Matt. xv. 89). Now called *El Mejdel*, on the west shore of the Sea of Galilee, close to the water, about three miles north of Tiberias, at the southeast corner of the plain of Gennesaret. There was a watch-tower here that guarded the entrance to the plain. Here was the home of Mary Magdalene. Dalmanutha in Mark viii. 10.

MAGDALE'NE, MARY OF. MAGDALA (Mark xvi. 9).

MAG'DIEL (*praise of El*). A Duke of Edom (Gen. xxxvi. 43).

MA'GED (1 Macc. v. 36).

MA'GI (Heb. CHARTUMIM; Gr. *Magoi*). Wise men, magicians, magians. They are credited all over the East with certain secret learning which in remote antiquity distinguished Egypt and Chaldæa. Among the Jews they were considered a sort of *sacred scribes*, skilled in divining, and interpreting the hidden meaning of certain passages of the Scriptures. In Egypt and Chaldæa they seem to have been the sole interpreters of secret things, the past and the future, but in Palestine they never ranked with the prophets, unless among the idolatrous people. The Books of Exodus and Daniel show their eminent position and influence, and pretense to occult knowledge. Some among them were probably free from superstition; men of sound minds, and finding in their books sounder views of the Divine government of the world than the great body of their associates were capable of understanding. The exiled Jews carried to such as these the welcome knowledge of the true Jehovah. Of this class were the three who, as "wise men from the East," came to see him who was born king of the Jews.

The Gospel narrative is simple and direct. They were guided by a star, in which they saw the sign of the expected Messiah, which was then the "hope of all nations." As magianism was then the chief religion of the kingdom of Parthia, it is supposed they came from that country, or it may be from Eastern Chaldæa. Their dress and appearance commanded respect at Jerusalem, and their presents also indicated persons of no ordinary rank. (The presents do not seem to have raised Joseph and Mary above their condition of poverty). In the apocryphal book of Seth it is said that this "star" was a circle of light with a figure of a child and a cross over its head inside. The general opinion now is that it was a meteoric substance, divinely guided. The office of the star ended at the "manger," for the magi were sent back by a dream (Matt. ii. 12).

The number of the magi was not stated, but has been since fixed by the Roman Church as three, with the names Gaspar, Melchoir, Balthasar, and the title of kings, whose relics are shown in Cologne, where they are honored as saints, and have a gorgeous monument. Ps. lxxii. 10 is the foundation for this invention; "The kings of Tarshish and of the isles shall bring presents, the kings of Sheba and Saba shall offer gifts." There is also a legend that they were converted by the apostle Thomas. The number three was supposed from the gifts being three, gold, frankincense, and myrrh. "The gold was a symbol of a king; the myrrh of the bitterness of the Passion, and the preparation of the tomb; the frankincense was offered in adoration of the divinity of the Son of God."

The Greek Church makes the occasion magnificent and important. The magi arrive with a grand escort of 1000, who were part of an army of 7000 who rested on the East bank of Euphrates. They came on the expedition in obedience to a prophesy of Zoroaster, who said that in the latter days there should be a Mighty One, a Redeemer, and that a star should announce his coming. Twelve of the holiest priests had kept watch for this star for many ages, on the Mount of Victory. When the star appeared it was in the form of an infant with a cross, and a voice bade them to follow it to Judea, which they did, traveling two years, during all of which time their provisions and water were supplied by a miracle. The gifts were the identical ones that Abraham gave to the sons of Keturah, the Queen of Sheba returned to Solomon, and which had found their way back East again. The other fanciful legends would fill a volume.

MAGIC. Wonder-working, in some way beyond the ordinary powers of man. This is only a pretense, and has nothing to do with Natural Philosophy. The belief in magic as a reality is very wide-spread in the East, and is simply an undue exercise of certain mental faculties, which take the place of religion in undeveloped persons. Some races in Africa have no higher conception of God and religion than the supposed magical powers of the air, minerals, etc., and worship by incantations. Even the Shemites were not exempt, as appears in the notices of Laban's images, but with them it took a kind of second rank to the true religion, being considered unlawful, but still very valuable as an aid to men in various selfish desires (Gen. xxxi. 19, 30, 32-35). This is the first notice of that superstition which in after time worked so much mischief in the Hebrew community. The name TERAPHIM has been derived from Egypt, TER, a shape, figure, or rather, in Coptic, *to change figure.*

The next instance in the history of the magician is in the account of Moses before Pharaoh. There is a little doubt as to the intention of the writer, whether he means to represent the Egyptians were natural philosophers or practicers of magic arts (supernatural magic). They had notice of what Moses was to do, and had time to prepare an imitation, but in no case did they undo what the Hebrew workers did ; for they did not restore the purity of the river Nile water, nor drive away the frogs, lice, and locusts, but they did increase the evil in each case, or appeared to do so. The Pharaoh did not expect anything more of them. When the last plague came, which they could not imitate, nor dare to increase, they acknowledged the "finger of God." The Egyptian magicians counted Moses and Aaron as members of their own profession, possessed of a little more of the secret knowledge, or of some strange device unknown to them, and the Pharaoh seems to have thought the same, until the miracle of the boils appeared, which seems to have convinced him. When the plague of boils attacked the magicians they disappeared. They could not imitate that, nor dare to increase it in themselves.

COIN OF MACEDONIA.

Some writers accept the theory that magic is an imitation of the Divine sign-work—miracle—but the work of the Satan, or his inferior demons. The original Hebrew account of the work before Pharaoh says "the revealers (magicians) did so with their fumigations."

The tricks of the magicians in the case of Pharaoh were paralleled by that of Artabanus, who caused the wine in the cup of Xerxes to change from white to red, which he interpreted to mean that the gods were displeased with the expedition (the displeased one was Artabanus.)

The NACHASHISM (enchantment, or serpent-divining) of Balaam is the next point in this history. But it appears that this prophet knew the true Jehovah, and consulted him instead of the "evil demons."

All through the history of the Jews, as recorded in the Scriptures, in both the Old and New Testaments, the belief in the actual power of evil spirits is recognized, and called into use in many cases. The same superstition is still very powerful among the poorly informed, and leads to consulting fortune-tellers, clairvoyants, and other professors of the "black art." Pliny's Natural History is full of curious fables on this topic, and these fables were the only storehouse of the so-called wisdom of the magicians. The Roman Church has perpetuated this belief and practice in its miracle fables, such as in the life of Gregory of Neo Cæsarea, the Thaumaturgist (wonder-worker), and the "Our Lady of Lourdes," besides many other books of "Lives of Saints." (See DEMON).

The notion of the "Elixir of Life" arose from the belief that Adam would have lived forever if he could have eaten from time to time of the fruit of the tree of life; but that being excluded from the garden, he died; and therefore if the true composition of the fruit can be discovered and used by men, it will restore youth from time to time, and so make man immortal. The "philosopher's stone" is the same notion applied to minerals, which are to be purified by contact with a pure substance, which changes all metals into gold—the purest known metal. The early Christian did not dispute the theory, but denied the possibility of discovering the true "Elixir" or the true "Stone."

The immediate mischief of this "black art" is in promising power, pleasure, riches, wisdom, without the necessary sacrifice of study and labor.

The Easterns now make Solomon a sort of king of magicians, ruling them with a certain "seal" (a six-pointed star—made of two triangles), and credit all manner of wonderful deeds. (See SOLOMON.

Paul met this "imposition and crime" as it deserved on several occasions, the most noted that was recorded being at Ephesus, when so many of the books of magic were burned (Acts xix. 19), estimated at the value of $85,000.

There is no evidence in the Scriptures that any real results were ever produced by these magicians; it was all trick, effect on the imagination and fancy, based on the known superstition and false instruction of the dupes.

The Greek and Roman magicians were of the same character, and it is probable that all nations and tribes have a set of impostors of a like kind, descending from the magician to the serpent-charmers, fetish-men, clairvoyants, and medicine men of the Indians.

MAGNIF ICAL (1 Chr. xxii. 5). Grand, splendid.

MA'GOG. Second son of Japheth (Gen. x. 2), and founder of a race (Rev. xx. 8), the great Scythian tribe, now called Russian. Ezekiel places the nation in the north (xxxix. 2), near Togarmah, and the maritime regions of Europe (v. 6). They had cavalry and used bows. In the 7th century B. C. they were a formidable power, felt through the whole of Western Asia. They took Sardis (B. C. 629), and overran the country as far as Egypt, where they were turned back by a bribe given by Psammetichus, and took Ascalon.

MA'GOR-MIS'SABIB (*terror on every side*). Name given to Pashur by Jeremiah (Jer. xx. 3). The same words are found in other passages, but not as a name (vi. 25, xx. 10, xlvi. 5; xlix. 29; Lam. ii. 22; Ps. xxxi. 13).

COLUMN AT PERSEPOLIS.

MAGPI-ASH (*moth-killer*). A chief who signed the covenant (Neh. x. 20). Magabish in Ezra ii. 30.

MA'HALAH (*sickness*). One of the children of Hammoleketh (1 Chr. vii. 18).

MAHALA'LEEL (*praise of God*). 1. Son of Cainan (Gen. v. 12, 13, 15, 17).— 2. Descendant of Perea, son of Judah (Neh. xi. 4).

MĀ'HĀLATH (*a lyre*). 1. Daughter of Ishmael (Gen. xxviii. 9).—2. First wife of King Rehoboam (2 Chr. xi. 18).—3. Mahalath, a stringed instrument like the kithara, (harp), and used in the sacred chant (Ps. liii. title; Gen. iv. 21). —4. Ma'halath Lean'noth, the beginning of a song (Ps. lxxxviii. 1).

MA'HALI (Ex. vi. 19). MAHLI (*sick, infirm*).

MAHANA'IM (*two camps*). 18 ms. E. of Jordan, and 10 N. of Jerash, now Birket Manneh (Tristram). Here Jacob divided his people and flocks into two bands, through fear of Esau. At the conquest it was a city on the border of the two tribes, Gad and Manasseh, but given to Gad (Josh. xiii. 26, 30, xxi. 38). Abner selected it as the capital of the kingdom of Ishbosheth, crowning him there king over all Israel (2 Sam. ii. 8, 9). David took refuge there when Absalom rebelled, and sat between the two gates of the walled city when the news of the death of his son was brought to him (2 Sam. xvii. 24, xviii. 24, 33), and retired to the chamber over the gate to weep for him. It was the seat of an officer of Solomon, and is alluded to in Cant. vi. 13—"Two armies"—Mahanaim. The name is found on the monuments in Egypt, at Karnak. See EGYPT.

MAHA'NEHDAN (*camp of Dan*). Behind Kirjath Jearim (Judg. xviii. 12, see 22–26). Where the Danites camped just before setting out for their northern home.

MA'HARAI (*impetuous*). General of the tenth division in David's army, numbering twenty-four thousand (1 Chr. xxvii. 13).

MA'HATH (*grasping*). 1. Son of Amasai (1 Chr. vi. 35). AHIMOTH.—2. A Kohathite who had charge of the tithes in the reign of Hezekiah (2 Chr. xxix. 12).

MA'HAVITE, THE. One of David's strong men (1 Chr. xi. 46).

MAHA'ZIOTH (*visions*). Son of Heman, chief of the twenty-third choir of musicians (1 Chr. xxv. 4, 30).

MA'HER-SHA'LAL-HASH'BAZ. The name was given by divine direction and means that Damascus and Samaria now soon to be plundered by the king of Assyria (Is. viii. 1–4).

MAH'LAH (*disease*). Daughter of Zelophehad (Num. xxvii. 1–11).

MAH'LI (*sickly*). 1. Son of Merari (Num. iii. 20).—2. Son of Mushi (1 Chr. vi. 47).

MAH'LITES, THE. Descendants of MAHLI (Num. iii. 33; xxvi. 58).

MAH'LON (*sickly*). First husband of RUTH. Son of Elimelech (Ruth i. 2, 5; iv. 9, 10).

MA'HOL (musical instrument, Ps. cl. 4). Teacher of ETHAN, HEMAN, CHALCOL and DARDA, musicians, and famous for wisdom next to Solomon (K. iv. 31).

MAIA'NEAS (1 Esd. ix. 48).

MA'KAZ (*end*. 1 K. iv. 9). In Dan.

MA'KED (1 Macc. v. 26). A strong and great city in Gilead. Where Judas Maccabæus delivered the Jews from the Ammonites. Lost.

MAK'HELOTH (*assemblies*). Desert camp (Num. xxxiii. 25).

MAK'KEDAH (*shepherd camp*). An ancient royal city of Canaan taken by Joshua after the defeat of the allied kings at Gibeon (Josh. x. 28, xii. 16). This stronghold was the first one taken in this region. *El Klediah*, in Wady es Sumt. There are many caves in this part of the country, but no one has been identified as *the cave*.

MAK'TESH (*mortar*). A quarter, or part of Jerusalem (Zeph. i. 11). The merchants and mechanics gathered their shops in and around the Tyropœon valley. The Bazaar is now in the same ancient place.

MAL'ACHI. HISTORY OF THE BOOKS.

MAL'CHAM. 1. Son of Shaharaim (1 Chr. viii. 9).—2. An idol invested with honors by its worshipers (Zeph. i. 5).

MAL'CHIA (*Jah's king*). 1. Son of Levi (1 Chr. vi. 40).—2. Son of Parosh (Ezr. x. 25).—3. Son of Harim (x. 31).—4. Son of Rechab, ruler of the circuit of Beth-haccerem (Neh. iii. 14).—5. Son of Zephaniah, who assisted in rebuilding the wall of Jerusalem (Neh. iii. 31).—6. A priest who stood with Ezra when he read the Law to the people (viii. 4).—7. Father of Pashur (xi. 12).—8. Son of Hammelech (2 Chr. xxviii. 7).

MAL'CHIEL (*God's king*). Son of Beriah (Gen. xlvi. 17). Founder of Birzavith (1 Chr. vii. 31).

MALCHIELITES. The descendants of Malchiel (Num. xxvi. 45).

MALCHI'JAH. 1. A priest, father of Pashur (1

Chr. ix. 12).—2. Chief of the fifth of the twenty-four courses by David (xxiv. 9).—3. A layman (Ezr. x. 25).—4. Descendant of Harim (Neh. iii. 11).—5. A priest who sealed the covenant (x. 3). —6. A priest who assisted in the dedication of the wall of Jerusalem (xii. 42).

MALCHI'RAM (*king of altitude*). Son of Jeconiah (1 Chr. iii. 18).

MAL'CHISHU'A (*king of help*). Son of Saul (1 Sam. xiv. 49).

MAL'CHUS. Servant of the high-priest maimed by Peter and restored by Jesus (John xviii. 10; Luke xxii. 51).

MALE'LEEL. Son of Cainan (Luke iii. 37).

MAL'LOS (*a lock of wool*), (2 Macc. iv. 30). A city of Cilicia, 20 ms. from Tarsus, at the mouth of the river Pyramus.

MALLO'THI (*fulness*). Pupil of Heman and leader of the nineteenth choir (1 Chr. xxv. 4, 26).

MAL'LOWS (MALLUAH). The leaves and pods used as a pot-herb, eaten in Arabia and Palestine (Job. xxx. 4).

MAL'LUCH (*reigning*). 1. Ancestor of Ethan (1 Chr. vi. 44).—2. Son of Bani (Ezr. x. 29).—3. Descendant of Harim (32).—4. A priest (Neh. x. 4). —5. A chief who signed the covenant (x. 27).—6. A priest who returned from captivity (xii. 2).

MAMA'IAS (1 Esd. viii. 44).

MAM'MON (*riches*), (Matt. vi. 24).

MAM'RE (*fruitfulness*). An ancient Amorite in alliance with Abram (Gen. xiv. 13–24); his name was given to the site on which HEBRON was built (xxiii. 17, 19).

MAM'RE. Faces Machpelah (Gen. xxiii. 17, etc). One of Abraham's favorite camping-grounds. In its grove he had a sanctuary, which he called his Bethel (house of God). Here Abraham entertained the 3 angels, and Isaac was promised. The name has not been preserved in any locality.

MAM'UCHUS (1 Esd. ix. 30).

MAN. Four Hebrew words are rendered man: 1. ADAM, ruddy, like Edom.—2. ISH, a man; ENESH, a woman.—3. GEBER, to be strong.—4. METHIM, (mortal) men (as in Methusael, Methuselah). The Adam (HA-ADAM, *the man*) was the person created in the image of God. The term red in the Eastern languages means many different tints or tones of red; as a red horse or camel, and, when used of a man, means "fair." Some explain the word as derived from *adamah*, earth, because he was made from the dust or earth. The word Enoch (*strong, or nobleman*) is a compound of the word ISH. The variant Enoch is only apparent in orthography, the meaning being the same.

MAN'AEN. Teacher in the church at Antioch (Acts xiii. 1). Josephus says he was in high repute among the Essenes for wisdom and piety. He foretold to Herod the Great that he was to attain royal honors.

MAN'AHATH (*offering*). MAN'AHETHITES. A place called Manocho in a list of eleven towns given in the Septuagint, but omitted in the A. V., as not far from Bethlehem.

MAN'AHATH. Son of Shobal (Gen. xxxvi. 23).

MANASSE'AS. Son of Pahath-Moab (1 Esd. ix. 31; Ezr. x. 30).

MANASSEH. There is no reason given for depriving Manasseh of his birthright, as there was in the case of his grand-uncle Esau. On leaving Egypt at the Exode this was the least of the twelve tribes, numbering at Sinai only 32,200, but at the census, just before the crossing of the Jordan, they had increased to 52,700 men over 20 years old, at which Manasseh is honored with a first mention before Ephraim. The division of the tribe is one of the singular facts in the history of the Israelites, and seems to be at variance with the national feeling and laws. Some of this tribe were warriors, and made entensive conquests: as Machir, who took Gilead and Bashan; Jair, who took 60 cities in Argob; and Nobah, who captured Kenath and its vicinity, a tract of country the most difficult in the whole land, being full of fortified cities, and in the possession of Og and Sihon. (See HAURAN, BASHAN, HESHBON, ARGOB, KENATH, NOBAH, etc.).

The lot of the half-tribe west of the Jordan was small, lying along the north border of Ephraim, but since the boundary is so slightly recorded it is very difficult to follow it. The line is drawn from the river Kanah (supposing that river to have been just south of Cæsarea), to a place on the Jordan "before Shechem" (Josh. xvii. 7, 9, 11; Jos. Ant. v. i. 22). See DOR, IBLEAM, ENDOR, TAANACH, and MEGIDDO). There is no account of this tribe separate from Ephraim, and it is likely that the two neighbors were spoken of as one people (2 Chr. xxxi. 1, xxxiv. 6, 9).

MANAS'SES. 1. (1 Esd. ix. 33).—2. King of Judah (Matt. i. 10). See HISTORY OF THE BOOKS.— 3. Son of Joseph (Rev. vii. 6).—4. Husband of Judith (Jud. viii. 2, 7). See BOOK OF JUDITH.

MANASS'ITES, THE. Members of the tribe of Manasseh (Deut. iv. 43).

MANDRAKE.

MAN'DRAKES (Cant. vii. 13). The mandrake is now called ATROPA MANDRAGORA. The odor or flavor of the plant is a matter of opinion. They have a delightful smell, and the taste is agreeable, though not to every body. The Orientals especially value strongly smelling things, that to more delicate senses are unpleasing. The fruit was ripe as the time of wheat harvest. From a rude resemblance of old roots of the mandrake to the human form, some strange superstitious notions have arisen concerning it (Jos. Wars, vii. 6, § 3). The leaves are dark-green, the flowers white, with veins of purple, and the fruit orange, and the size of nutmegs.

MAN'GER (Gr. *phatne*). The feeding-place for animals, or a trough made of mortar or cut out of single stones. See INN.

MA'NI (1 Esd. ix. 30).

MAN'LIUS, TITUS (*born early in the morning*). Ambassador of the Romans (2 Macc. xi. 34-38).

MAN'NA (Heb. MAN). A month after leaving Egypt the people were in want of food, and murmured against their leaders, when the quails were sent in the evening and the manna appeared in the morning, after the "dew was gone up." It was a small round thing, like hoar-frost or corrianderseed, and the people said "what is this?" (MAN-HU). Moses answered that it was the bread that

SARCOPHAGUS AT SIDON.

the Lord had given them to eat (Ex. xvi. 1-3, 11-15). Its flavor was like wafers of flour-bread and honey. The gummy drops which form on the leaves of the tamarisk are of a similar sweetish substance, as also the tarfa gum, and several other articles called manna in Arabia; but the true manna was none of these, and probably a distinct thing made for the occasion. Its similarity to other things offers no explanation of its character. It came without notice, and as abruptly discontinued. Botanists have tried to explain the thing by references to many articles, as esculent lichen, which is eaten in Northern Africa. It is a species of moss. Some have considered the miracle as multiplying the natural supples of the desert as that of the loaves and fishes was at Bethsaida, increasing five loaves and two fishes.

MANO'AH (*rest*). Father of SAMSON (Judg. xiii. 2).

MAN-SLAYER. Not an intentional murderer. Death by a blow in a quarrel (Num. xxxv. 22). Death by a stone thrown at random (xxii. 23). In these and like cases the man-slayer could escape to a CITY OF REFUGE. An animal, not known to be vicious, causing death to a person was put to death; but if it was known to be vicious, the owner was liable to be fined or put to death (Ex. xxi. 28, 31). A thief taken at night might lawfully be put to death; but if the sun had risen, killing him was regarded as MURDER (Ex. xxii. 23).

MAN'TLE (Heb. SEMICHAH). See cloak in DRESS.

MA'OCH (*breast-band*). Father of ACHISH. King of Gath (1 Sam. xxvii. 2).

MA'ON. In the mts. of Judah (Josh. xv. 55), near Juttah. It was in the wilderness near this place (bleak and hilly pasture-lands) that David hid himself from Saul. Main 7 ms. S. E. of Hebron (*Rob.*). On a conical hill, 200 ft. high, are ruins of foundations of hewn stone, a square enclosure, towers, and cisterns. The people use the caves near for dwellings, as of old.

MA'ONITES (Judg. x. 12). An ancient and powerful nomad tribe, allied to the Phœnicians, first settled with the Amalekites in the vale of Sodom, and afterward migrated eastward into Arabia. They named Maon in Judah, Beth-Maon in Moab, and Maan in Edom, 15 ms. E. of Petra. This last is now an important pilgrim station, on the caravan route to Mecca. A castle and other antiquities mark its ancient strength. Mehunim (2 Chr. xxvi. 7). Among the descendants of Caleb, the son of Shammai, the builder of Beth-zur (1 Chr. ii. 45).

MA'RA (*bitter*). The name given to NOOMI at Bethlehem (Ruth i. 20).

MA'RAH (*bitter*). Well, on the route of the Exodus. See EXODUS.

MAR'ALAH (*trembling*). On the border of Zebulon (Josh. xix. 11). 4 ms. S. W. of Nazareth, the little village of Malul stands on a hill, and contains the ruins of a temple and other antiquities.

MARANATH'A (*our lord cometh*), (1 Cor. xvi. 22). See ANATHEMA.

MAR'BLE. Called by Josephus white stone, quarried from under Jerusalem (Esth. i. 6).

The vast excavation under the N. E. section of Jerusalem, so long lost, was discovered a few years ago by Dr. J. T. Barclay, author of "The City of the Great King," and since that time has been visited by many travelers. It is entered from outside of the wall of the city, east of the Damascus Gate. A guide is necessary to avoid getting lost, there are so many chambers running into each other for nearly 800 feet from the entrance. There is water in the cave, but it is limy and bitter. On the walls are carved crosses, Hebrew letters, and other marks, showing that the place has been known since the crucifixion.

The chalky limestone of Palestine is full of caves, many of which are noted. (See ADULLAM).

The white stone of this quarry is nearly as soft as chalk, and is easily cut out with a saw. The cream-colored is also streaked with orange-tawney and other similar tints, in coarse and fine, wavy lines; is much harder than the white, and is called dolomite.

The marble columns of Tyre, Cæsarea, Joppa and other ruins, were probably imported, as there are no quarries of such hard, fine, white marble known in the country.

MAR'CUS (*a large hammer*). Both a first and a surname (Col. iv. 10).

MARDOCHI'US. MORDECAI. 1. Uncle of Esther (Esth. x. 1).—2. (1 Esd. v. 8).

MARE'SHAH (*head-town*). 1. A city of Judah (Josh. xv. 44). Hebron was founded by Mareshah (1 Chr. ii. 42). It was one of the cities fortified by Rehoboam (2 Chr. xi. 8). It was the native place of Eliezer, who prophesied the destruction of Jehoshaphat's fleet at Ezion Geber.—2. Father of Hebron (1 Chr. ii. 42).—3. Mareshah, grandson of SHELAH (1 Chr. iv. 21),

MAR'IMOTH. A priest (2 Esd. i. 2).

MAR'ISA (2 Macc. xii. 35).

MARK. HISTORY OF THE BOOK.

MAR'KET (MAARAB). An open place, where people came for business or to converse (Ez. xxvii. 13, 17).

The market-place was a resort for news and

social chat (Matt. xi. 16; Luke vii. 32). There justice was administered, especially if it was at a gate. They were generally open places just inside the gate, although there were other localities for certain occupations, as Bakers' street (Jer. xxxvii. 21), and many others mentioned by Josephus. They were probably covered by a roof, forming a piazza.

MAR'MOTH. A priest (1 Esd. viii. 62).

MA'ROTH (*bitterness*). Mentioned by the prophet Micah (i. 12), and probably near Jerusalem.

MARRIAGE. Instituted in the garden of Eden (Gen. i. 27, 28; ii. 18, 24). The Saviour advocated the divine character of marriage apart from civil laws. He opposed divorces except for one cause (Matt. v. 32, xix. 3, 6, 9), and all breaches of the marriage vow (Matt. v. 28). Betrothal preceded the marriage rite and was a binding engagement (Matt. i. 18–25). Groomsman referred to as "the friend of the bridegroom" in John iii. 29. A procession formed part of the ceremony, and took place at night accompanied by young unmarried women bearing lamps (Matt. xxv.).

The modern Jews make a solemn contract before witnesses, in writing, which is signed. The ceremony consists of the bride standing in her best garments, and jewelry (borrowed if necessary), under a canopy, beside the bridegroom, where the contract is read to them by a Rabbi, and their hands are joined in the presence of witnesses. A glass of wine is tasted by both, when the glass is broken by the bridegroom, and a ring is given to the bride, of plain gold. In nearly all cases in the East a dower is given for the wife, which belongs to her. Some few parents (as the Circassians) take the dower as a price paid for the daughter. The Mohammedan custom is to pay the bride two-thirds of the dower, reserving the other part until her death or divorce. The Hebrews called the husband lord (BAAL). The first wife was the only one recognized by the civil law, but all others were valid in the Church (2 Chr. xxiv. 3, 2 Sam. xii. 8), where (in the law of Moses) the second, or other wife, was called maid-servant (Ex. xxi. 7). The rich often married poor relatives to give them support and protection. The strongest motive for a plurality of wives was the great desire for many children, and the fact that many women are barren (1 Sam. i. 2). The Talmudists limited the number to four, except in the case of the king who could have eighteen. Polygamy was only prohibited by an imperial edict of Honorius, A. D. 400.

Just before the Christian era the idea arose that marriage affected the intellectual and spiritual nature. Up to that time the Hebrews taught it as a duty, but then it was urged that its effect was to lessen man's holiness, the teaching of the Essenes, an ascetic order of celibates (Jos. Wars, ii. 8; 2, 13). The Therapeutæ and Gnostics adopted the same idea, from whom the Christians copied it, forming monastic orders (a monk is a living insult to woman), in direct opposition to the instruction of Jesus and his apostles, who recognized the duty and holiness of the state, and enjoined respect to its laws. In the case of a widow it was regarded as a sign of holiness to remain a widow, in the latter time only, for it is expressly charged upon a brother to raise up children to a deceased brother (Gen. xxxviii. 8,) by his widow (by Moses, Matt. xxii. 23). The same custom (Levirate marriage, from Levir, a brother-in-law,) was and is held among other people, as in the case of the Ossetes in Georgia (Asia), and Arabia, with some changes, which include the privilege of the father of the deceased husband to claim the widow for a wife if the brother refuses. (Perhaps in consequence of Judah's example).

The laws regulating legal marriage were very strict, and were of two kinds, 1. when between two Hebrews, and 2. when a Hebrew married a Gen-

tile. (1). The first restriction was based on ideas of health and propriety among relatives (Lev. xviii. 6–18), both of blood kin, and by marriage, because the husband and wife were "one flesh" (Matt. xix. 5). Surprising exceptions were made in the cases of the daughter and the niece; a man might marry his daughter and his niece; but the mother could not marry a son or a nephew. An heiress could not marry out of her tribe (out of policy, in keeping the land in the original owner's tribe). The high-priest must only marry a young unmarried woman, a Hebrew, never a widow, or one divorced, or a Gentile. No person physically defective could marry. The apostle restricted church officers to one wife, and prohibited a second marriage during the life-time of the first, even after divorce. The wife could divorce her husband for some causes. There was no rule in regard to age, except that early marriage is commended (Prov. ii. 17; v. 18; Is. lxii. 5). The age at which marriage may be consummated is from 12 (or even 10), upwards, in a woman; and was limited to 13 in a man. The usual age varies from 16 to 18. The first marriage (of virgins) is usually on a Wednesday; a second, as of a widow, etc., on Thursday.

The wife is almost always chosen for a man by his parents, if living, or by his guardian, or a friend, or relations (Gen. xxiv.). The son could request such favors (xxiv. 4); but if the son broke this custom the parents had "a grief of mind" (xxvi. 35). The maid's consent was asked in some cases (but not as a rule), after her father's decision. A friend sometimes did the whole business of selecting the bride for the bridegroom; and in modern days the bridegroom seldom sees the face of his wife until the actual moment of marriage, or until after the ceremony. The espousal was legal and binding, confirmed by oaths, a feast, sometimes a ring to the "bride," and exchange of presents, or at least presents to the bride. A year passed between betrothal and marriage in the case of a first marriage of the woman, a few weeks or days if a second. The custom of a settlement of property on the wife came into use after the Captivity.

VINE.

The bridegroom wore a new dress, if able, and a crown of gold, silver, roses, myrtle or olive. The bride's dress, among the wealthy, was a magnificent display of fine clothes and curious traditions. Both parties perfumed themselves. The bride took a bath (Ruth iii. 3; Eph. v. 26) in a formal manner, accompanied by her relatives and friends (Ez. xxiii. 40). After putting on her finest garments, around her waist was wound a peculiar girdle (KISHURIM, the attire, Jer. iii. 32); and over her head was thrown the veil or long shawl (Gen. xxix. 25), covering the whole figure; while on her head was set a crown ornamented with jewels, or a chaplet of leaves and flowers (KALLAH, chaplet, also bride). A pair of ornamented slippers were a gift from the husband before marriage. The moderns carry the presents to the bride in procession through the street, with bands of music, instrumental and vocal, nearly every one carrying a lantern; arriving at the bride's house, she is escorted to the bridegroom's house, where the marriage-feast is held. The very wealthy prolong the feast several days, furnishing garments for each guest, to be worn only during the time. Amusements of many kinds are in order.

There were three kinds of legal marriage: 1. By written contract; 2. By payment of a sum of money (or an equivalent) before witnesses; and 3. By force—as a man compelling a woman to submit to him, or by seduction.

The wife's rights were food, raiment (including house), and conjugal privileges (Ex. xxi. 10). Her duties were as extensive as the entire household, as shown in Prov. xxxi.

Marriage is used as a type in both the Old and New Testaments of true religious union with God in many beautiful passages.

SWIFT.

MARS HILL. AREOPAGUS.

MAR′SENA (*worthy man*). A prince of Persia (Esth. i. 14).

MARTHA. Daughter of Simon the leper, and sister of LAZARUS and MARY of BETHANY. She was the elder sister, the head and manager of the household. She was present at the supper at Bethany (John xii. 2).

When Jesus first visited Martha's house (Luke x. 38–42), she hastened to provide the repast, while Mary was attracted by the teaching of the Master, when Martha complained of Mary's neglect of the work to be done, forgetting the *one* thing needful (the thirst for spiritual waters?).

Martha's character appears again in the same light at the time of the sickness, death and resurrection of Lazarus. She hastened out of the village to meet the coming Saviour, while Mary sat still in the house and awaited his coming (John xi. 20, 22). Her anxiety clouded her perception of the true meaning of the words of Jesus, "He shall rise again," supposing that he referred only to the general belief in the resurrection beyond the grave. When she learned the truth she made a confession of faith in him as "The resurrection and life," and acknowledged his power and goodness, although a moment before she had objected to rolling away the stone from the door of the tomb, supposing the body of Lazarus to be decayed. Her death is not recorded.

MARY (*rebellion*). Greek form of Miriam. There are six Marys in the New Testament:
1. The betrothed of Joseph and mother of Christ, Matt. i. 18–25; Matt. xii. 46; Mark vi. 3; Luke viii. 19; John ii. 1–5; John xix. 26; Acts i. 14.
2. Wife of Cleophas, Matt. xxvii. 56, 61; Matt. xxviii. 1–9; Mark xvi. 1–8; Luke xxiv. 1–10.
3. Mother of John Mark, Acts xii. 12; Col. iv. 10.
4. Sister of Martha and Lazarus, Luke x. 41, 42; John xi. 12.
5. Mary Magdalene, Matt. xxviii. 1–10; Mark xvi. 1–10; Luke xxiv. 10, John xx. 1–18.

6. A Roman Convert, Rom. xvi. 6.
Three Marys were at the cross, John xix. 25.

MAR′TYR (Gr. *martus*). "Witnesses" in Matt. xviii. 16. Simply witness. Witnesses of the gospel, suffering persecution, became *martyrs* in the modern sense.

MAS′ALOTH (*terraces*). Near Arbela: the great caverns in the Wady al Humam (*pigeon valley*), which were fortified by Josephus (Josephus, Life, 37). Kulaet Ibu Maan. Herod drove a band of robbers out of them by letting soldiers down the face of the cliff to the mouth of the caves in large boxes.

MAS′CHIL. A musical term denoting a melody requiring great skill in execution (Ps. xxxii., xlii.).

MASH (Gen. x. 23). 4th son of Aram; settled in Mesopotamia. Mt. Masius (between the Euphrates and the Tigris, in the N.), and the river Mafche flowing at its base, preserve the name. A prince of Masou was taken by Rameses II on the Orontes, at Kedesh.

MASH′EL. City of Asher (1 Chr. vi. 74). Misheal (Josh. xix. 26).

MASI′AS. Servant of Solomon (1 Esd. v. 34).

MAS′MAN (1 Esd. viii. 43).

MAS′PHA (1 Macc. iii. 46). Massepha, or Mizpeh?—2. A city taken by Judas Maccabæus, E. of Jordan (1 Macc. v. 35). It may be the same as Mizpeh of Gilead, or Mizpeh of Moab.

MASRE′KAH (*vineyard*). Native city of Samlah, king of Edom (Gen. xxxvi. 36). The region called Jebal, N. of Edom, is now famous for its vineyards (owned by the Refaya tribe), and this place may have been located there, as Eusebius and Jerome say.

MAS′SA (*burden*). Son of Ishmael (Gen. xxv. 14).

MAS′SAH (*temptation*). In the Sinai desert (Ex. xvii. 2, 7). REPHIDIM. WILDERNESS.

MAS′SIAS (1 Esd. ix. 22).

MAS′TICH-TREE. The gum is used to strengthen the teeth and gums. It was prized by the ancients on this account, and for its medical properties. It is used in the preparation of spirits, as a sweetmeat, and in varnishes. The trees are very wide, and circular, 10 or 12 ft. high, and are found on the shores of the Mediterranean.

MATHANI′AS. A descendant of Pahath-Moab (1 Esd. ix. 31).

MATHU′SALA. Son of Enoch (Luke iii. 37).

MA′TRED (*propelling*). Daughter of Mezahab (Gen. xxxvi. 39).

MA′TRI (*rain of Jah*). Family of Benjamin (1 Sam. x. 21).

MAT′TAN (*a gift*). 1. Priest of Baal (2 K. xi. 18).—2. Father of Shephatiah (Jer. xxxviii. 1).

MAT′TANAH (*gift.*) Station S. E. of the Dead Sea (Num. xxi. 18).

MATTANI′AH (*gift of Jah*). 1. Original name of ZEDEKIAH, king of Judah (1 K. xxiv. 17).—2. Son of Asaph (1 Chr. ix. 15). He was leader of a Temple-choir (xi. 17).—3. A descendant of Asaph (2 Chr. xx. 14).—4. Son of Elam (Ezr. x. 26).—5. Son of Zattu (27).—6. Descendant of Pahath-Moab (30).—7. Son of Bani (37).—8. Father of Zaccur (Neh. xiii. 13).—9. Pupil of Heman (1 Chr. xxv. 4, 16).—10. Descendant of Asaph, who assisted in the purification of the Temple (2 Chr. xxix. 13).

MAT′TATHA. Son of Zathan (Luke iii. 31).

MAT′TATHAH. A descendant of Hashum (Ezr. x. 33).

MATTATHI′AS. 1. An assistant to Ezra (1 Esd. ix. 43).—2. Father of MACCABEES (1 Macc. ii. 1). —3. Son of Absalom (xi. 70; xiii. 11).—4. Son of Simon Maccabæus (xvi. 14).—5. Nicanor's envoy

(2 Macc. xiv. 19).—6. Son of Amos (Luke iii. 25). —7. Son of Semei (26).

MAT'TENAI. 1. Of the family of Hashum (Ezr. xi. 33).—2. Descendant of Bani (37).—3. A priest (Neh. xii. 19).

MAT'THAN. Son of Eleazar (Matt. i. 15).

MAT'THANI'AS. Descendant of Elam (1 Esd. ix. 27).

MAT'THAT. 1. Son of Levi (Luke iii. 24).—2. Son of Levi (29).

MATTHE'LAS (1 Esd. ix. 19).

MATTHEW (Mattathias, *the gift of Jehovah*). Is only mentioned at the time of his call to be an apostle, when he was in "the receipt of custom," (Matt. ix. 9). Mark gives him another name— Levi, the son of Alphæus (Mark ii. 14; iii. 18) who has been supposed to have been the same as the Alphæus the father of James the Less, but without reason. On his call he gave a feast by way of a farewell to his friends, to which Jesus was invited (Luke v. 27). His humility is seen in his styling himself "the publican" (Matt. x. 3). He was with the other apostles after the resurrection (Acts i. 13). After this there is no record of him or his acts. It is not known how or where he died. There is a tradition that he lived in Jerusalem 15 years after the crucifixion, and that he became a martyr in Persia. See HISTORY OF THE BOOKS for the GOSPEL.

MATTHI'AS. 1. MATTATHAH (1 Esd. ix. 33).—2. An apostle chosen to succeed Judas (Acts i. 26). Tradition says he preached in Cappadocia.

MATTITHI'AH (*gift*). 1. First born of Shallum (1 Chr. ix. 31).—2. A musician of David's choir (1 Chr. xvi. 5).—3. Of the family of Zebo (Ezr. x. 43).—4. A priest who assisted Ezra (viii. 4).—5. Son, or pupil of Jeduthun, leader of the 14th Temple choir (1 Chr. xxv. 3, 21).

MAT'LOCK (CHEREB). A single-headed pickaxe. The Egyptian hoe was of wood, and answered for hoe, spade and pick (1 Sam. xiii. 20, 21).

MAUL (MEPHITS). A heavy, war-like instrument (Prov. xxv. 18). See ARMS.

MĀUZ'ZIM (*forts*). Layard (*Nin.* ii. 456) after describing Hera, the Assyrian Venus, as "standing erect on a lion, and crowned with a tower or mural coronet, which, we learn from Lucian, was peculiar to the Semetic figure of the goddess," adds, "May she be connected with the 'El Maozem,' the deity presiding over bulwarks and fortresses, the 'god of forces' of Dan. xi. 38."

MAZITI'AS (1 Esd. ix. 35).

MAZ'ZAROTH. See ASTRONOMY.

MEAD'OW (Heb. ACHU), (Gen. xli. 2, 18). Translated meadow. Rendered *cave* in the Peshito-Syriac.

ME'AH (*a hundred*). The tower of Meah was on the city wall north of the sheep-gate, when rebuilt by Nehemiah (iii. 1, xii. 39). Located by some at the N. W. corner of the Temple area, where the fortress of Antonia was afterwards built, and now called Pilate's house. Porter locates it at the N. E. corner of the Harem area, where there are massive foundations.

MEALS. The Jews generally eat their dinner before noon, and their supper after sundown. The chief meal of the Jews was in the evening; of the Egyptians it was at noon. The early Hebrews sat or squatted round a low table upon which the meal was served, but in later times couches were used to recline upon before the tables. The guests were ranged in order of rank side by side (Gen. xliii. 33), resting upon the left elbow, the right arm being free—this posture explains the text "leaning on Jesus's bosom (John xiii. 23, xxi. 20). The dishes, as they are to this day, were generally stews of rice, beans, and burgal (cracked wheat),

with soups or sauces. The meats were so cooked that when served they fell to pieces. Knives and forks were not used at the table, but spoons, and generally thin slices of bread, were doubled up and dipped into the dishes, all eating from the same dish. These pieces of bread also served the purpose of napkins. It was after this manner that Judas eat of the sauce or *sop* at the Last Supper (John xiii. 26). Washing of the hands, from being a necessity, was elevated to a form and ceremony.

MEA'NI (1 Esd. v. 31).

MEA'RAH (*cave*). Boundary of the unconquered land near Zidon (Josh. xiii. 4). Half way between Tyre and Sidon are ruins called *Adlan*, and in the cliffs near are many caves and grottos (*Rob.*). William of Tyre mentions a fortified cave near Sidon, occupied by the Crusaders.

MEAT. LEHEM, *bread* (1 Sam. xx. 24); TEREF, *spoil* (Ps. cxi. 5); Gr. *bromu* and *brosis* (Matt. iii. 4; Acts xxvii. 33; Heb. v. 12). Anything that may be eaten. This word was never used for flesh-meat, unless it was included in a general sense, as we now say food.

MEAT-OFFERING. See SACRIFICE.

MEBUN'NAI (*strong one*). One of David's guard (2 Sam. xxiii. 27). Called SIBBECHAI (xxi. 18; 1 Chr. xx. 4).

MECHE'RATHITE, THE. "The Maachathite (2 Sam. xxiii. 34).

MED'ABA. Greek form of Medeba (1 Macc. ix. 36).

ME'DAN (*strife*). Son of Abraham by Keturah (Gen. xxv. 2). Traces of this people are supposed to be found in the village of Madan, on the Euphrates, and the city Maadan in Hejaz, Arabia. Maadan, *mines*.

ME'DEBA (*quiet waters*). In Moab (Num. xxi. 30). Name of the Mishor south of Heshbon (Josh. xiii. 9, 16). The Ammonites were defeated here by Joab, David's general (1 Chr. xix.). Not recorded as possessed by Reuben, and was probably only tributary. It was a strong fortress in the

AT DINNER.

time of the Maccabees (1 Macc. ix. 35; Ant. xiii., i. 4, 9, 1). Ptolemy locates a Medeba between Bostra and Petra. Eusebius and Jerome mention a Christian village east of Medeba. It was a noted bishopric of the patriarchate of Bitira Arabiæ, and so named in the acts of the Council of Chalcedon (A. D. 451). A large tank, columns, and extensive foundations, on a rocky hill 4 miles S. E. of Heshbon, on the Roman road, mark the site.

MEDES. Media (Gen. x. 2, Madia; 2 K. xvii. 6, Medes; Esth. i. 3, Media; Dan. xi. 1, Mede). 3d son of Japhet, and founder of a great race. 1500 years of their history is a blank, from their first mention to the time when Isaiah threatened to stir them up against Babylon (xiii. 7, B. C. 72). Berosus (Chaldæan historian) says that the Medes conquered Babylonia B. C. 2458. This date may be very much too ancient, for the word Mede is first found on the Assyrian monuments at the date of B. C. 880 (Rawlinson); but there is no doubt that both Cushite and Semitic races occupied Mesopotamia together from a very early date. They were called Arians in the time of which Herodotus writes; and traces of them are found from Hindustan to Thrace. It is supposed that the race had its origin on the banks of the Indus, from whence its people found their way into Persia, Media, Greece, etc.

In Media, Sargon, Sennacherib, and Esar-haddon reigned from B. C. 720 to B. C. 660, over a country which before that time had been ruled by a great many sheikhs (chiefs of families or tribes). About the middle of the 7th century B. C., Cyaxares (the Mede) led a fresh immigration of Arians into Media, and is called the first king of Media by Diodorus. In his reign the three kingdoms, Media, Lydia, and Babylon, were united by treaty and marriages. The empire extended from the Halys river to the Caspian gates, 1500 miles long, and from the Euphrates and the Persian Gulf to the Black and Caspian Seas, 450 miles wide. It lasted only 75 years.

The Persians, led by Cyrus, conquered Media and terminated the kingdom, B. C. 558.

One of the tribes of Media, the Budii, are mentioned in the Scripture by the name of Phut (Ez. xxvii. 10), whose soldiers were in the army of Tyre, together with Persians and others.

VICTORY.

The ancient religion was a belief in two nearly equal divinities of opposite principles, Ormazd the good, and Ahriman the evil—both self-existent and irresistible, and both always contending with each other. Ormazd was worshiped; and also the sun, moon, and stars, and respect paid to genii. The fire-worship of Armenia was more or less blended with this system. Magism consisted of the worship of the elements, chiefly fire. Altars on mountaintops were kept continually burning, and sacrifices were frequent. The priesthood formed a distinct class, and professed ability to interpret dreams, explain visions, and to divine future events.

The captive Israelites were placed in certain cities of the Medes by the king of Assyria (2 K. xvii. 6, etc.). Both Isaiah and Jeremiah prophesied the part which the Medes were to take in destroying Babylon (Jer. li. 11, 28). Daniel interpreted the writing on the wall as the sign of the coming conquest by the Medes and Persians (xi. 25–28). Ezra

mentions the palace of Achmetha, where the decree of Cyrus was found (vi. 2, 5), which the monuments prove to have been the residence of Cyrus at that time. See ECBATANA.

In the Apocrypha, Media is the chief scene of the book of Tobit, and a large part of that of Judith.

ME'DIAN. Citizen of MEDIA (Dan. ix. 1).

MEDIATOR (*interpreter*). Moses was the Mediator between Jehovah and the Isralites (Gal. iii. 19, 20). JESUS CHRIST is the one Mediator between God and men (1 Tim. ii. 5).

MED'ICINE. The Egyptian physicians (barbers?) were skilled, and perhaps also educated, if we may believe the Greeks, before the Exodus. The first mention of a physician was of the "servants of Joseph" who embalmed his father (Gen. l. 2); they were probably regular attendants on the royal house. Specialists are mentioned by Herodotus (ii. 84), 'each physician is for one kind of sickness, such as for the eyes, teeth, head, stomach, etc. The practice of medicine was largely superstitious. The medicines mostly used were salves, balms, (Jer. viii. 22), plasters or poultices (2 K. xx. 7); bathing (2 K. v. 10), oils, and mineral baths. Charms and amulets were used by the Jews, also charming by the hand, as in 2 K. v. 11. Knowledge of anatomy is suggested in Job x. 11, and also shown in monumental figures. Physicians received public salaries, and their office was held in high esteem. The Jews at a later period, overcame much of their abhorrence of uncleanness, and of their reverence for human remains, in the pursuit of medical knowledge. Alexandria became the centre for medical study. (See ALEXANDRIA.) Luke is referred to as "the beloved physician," and his medical education was probably Greek.

MEE'DA (1 Esd. v. 32).

MEEK. Heb. ANAV, *oppressed, afflicted, humble.* Applied to those who rather suffer wrong than do wrong, and therefore enjoy God's favor (Num. xii. 3). The word translated meek in Num. xii. 3, in reference to Moses, means "disinterested."

MEGIDDO (*place of troops*). An ancient royal city of the Canaanites, on the south border of the plain of Esdraëlon, commanding a pass leading from the plain to the Samarian hills (Josh. xii. 21). In the territory of Issachar, but belonging to Manasseh. The people were not driven out, but paid tribute (Judg. i. 27, 28). It is made famous in the song of victory of Deborah, when Barak defeated Sisera (Judg. iv. 13, etc.). One of Solomon's officers was placed here, and some important works built (1 K. ix. 15). Ahaziah fled here from Jehu, and died (2 K. ix. 27). The "good king" Josiah "went against" Pharaoh Necho, as an ally of the king of Assyria, was wounded here, and died at Jerusalem (2 Chr. xxxv. 22–24). From this event the name of the place became a poetical synonym for terrible conflict and grief; as in the Revelation (xvi. 16. See also Zech. xii. 11; 2 Chr. xxxv. 25). El Lejjun. Waters of Megiddo. See KISHON.

MEGID'DON (Zech. xii. 11). PLAIN OF.

MEHETA'BEEL. Ancestor of Shemaiah (Neh. vi. 10).

MEHET'ABEL (*El benefits*). Daughter of Matred (Gen. xxxvi. 39).

MEHI'DA (*junction*). Ancestor of Nethinim, returned from captivity (Ex. ii. 52; Neh. vii. 54).

ME'HIR (*price*). Son of Chelub (1 Chr. iv. 11).

ME'HOLATHITE, THE. (1 Sam. xviii. 19). See ABEL MEHOLAH. This place was called Meadow of the Whirlpool, and was near some rapid or whirlpool in the river Jordan.

MEHU'JAEL (*smitten by El*). Son of Irad, and fourth in descent from Cain (Gen. iv. 18).

MEHU'MAN (*faithful*). A chamberlain of Ahasuerus (Esth. i. 10).

MEHU'NIMS. Maonites. (See MAON). Josephus speaks of a city built by king Uzziah on the Red Sea to overawe the Arabs, who adjoined Egypt (Ant. ix. 10, 3). Probably near or in the valley of Gerar. One of the three friends of Job was Sophar, king of the Minæans, who is also called Zophar the Naamathite. (See NAAMAH). This people were located by Strabo and Ptolemy in the S. W. corner of Arabia, in Hadramaut. There is a Minyay S. E. of Gaza, a station on the road to Sinai, mentioned in the Christian records of the 6th century with some distinction. *Main*, a ruin south of Heshbon (BAAL MEON), is another relic of the tribe. Some of them returned from captivity with Zerubbabel (Ezr. ii. 50).

MEJARKON (*yellow waters*). In Dan (Josh. xix. 46), near Joppa. Torrent?

MEKO'NAH (*a place*). A city of some size, having suburbs, in the south, near Ziklag; occupied after the return from captivity (Neh. xi. 28).

MELATIAH (*Jah delivers*). A Gibeonite who assisted in building the wall (Neh. iii. 7).

MEL'CHI (*my king*). 1. Son of Jamra (Luke iii. 24).—2. Son of Addi (iii. 21).

MELCHI'AH. Father of Pashur (Jer. xxi. 1).

MELCHI'AS. 1. MALCHIAH 2 (1 Esd. ix. 26).

MEL'CHIEL. Son of Melchiel, governor of Bethulia (Judg. vi. 15).

MELCHIS'EDEC (Heb. v., vi., vii.).

MEL'CHISHU'A. Son of Saul (1 Sam. xiv. 49; xxxi. 2).

MELCHIZ'EDEK (*king of righteousness*). He lived in the time of Abraham, worshiped God, and was "a priest of the most high God," perhaps a first-born, and a patriarch or elder in the city of Salem (Gen. xiv.). He received Abraham's homage and presents or tithes, and gave him a blessing, and gave bread and wine to his tired and hungry army.

Some have thought that the bread and wine were sacrificial, and that Melchizedek was a type of Christ. Others have strangely imagined that it was an appearance of Christ himself in the disguise of the priest.

He really was both a king and a priest—and so far typical of the spiritual king and priest, Jesus the Christ.

The "order of Melchizedek" (Ps. cx. 4) means "likeness in official dignity," being both king and priest. The object of the Hebrews was to show that Christ was the king and priest of the new dispensation, and it was objected that he was not of the tribe of Levi, and his father was not a high-priest (Ex. xxix. 29, 30), nor even any priest, and his mother fell short of the requirements of the law (Lev. xxi. 13, 14). His descent must have been preserved in the records, and have been pure from stains on both father and mother's side; and he was to become a priest by education and high-priest by consecration (Ex. xxix. 9) with the holy oil, while wearing the holy garments of Aaron; and he must hand over his holy office to a successor before his death. Jesus did not carry out this Leviti-

cal idea, and was not therefore a priest after that order. Paul, in his letter to the Hebrews, discusses the question very freely and clearly. See SALEM.

MEL'COM (Heb. MALCAM), (Jer. xlix. 1, 3).

ME'LEA (*full*). Son of Menan (Luke iii. 31).

ME'LECH (*king*). Son of Micah (1 Chr. viii. 35, ix. 41).

MEL'ICU (Neh. xii. 14). MALLUCH.

MEL'ITA. MALTA. A small island, 20 by 12 miles in extent, and 60 miles south of Sicily, where Paul was wrecked when on his way to Rome (Acts xxvii. xxviii.). The island is full of mementoes of Paul, who is its tutelary saint. The bay where the shipwreck occurred is called St. Paul's, and is a deep inlet on the north side of the island, 5 miles from the port of Malta, and is one mile wide and

SCULPTURED COLUMNS FROM TADMOR.

two miles long, inland, having the small island Salmonetta on the western side of the entrance. The whole island is a barren rock, but has been made fertile to some extent by great labor. The Phœnicians colonized it, from whom the Greeks took it about 736 B. C.; and in turn the Carthaginians became its masters in the Second Punic War, 528 B. C., and the Romans in 242 B. C., whose officer, Publius, governed it when Paul was there. Its history since then has been full of changes in its masters, in which we read of Vandals, Greeks (A. D. 553), Arabs, Normans (A. D. 1090), Germans (1530, by whom it was given to the Knights of St. John, of Jerusalem), the French (1798), and finally the English, who hold it now. The Anglican Bishop of Gibraltar resides there. The island is a station for several lines of steamers and submarine telegraph cables. The island of Meleda, in the Adriatic Sea, on the coast of Dalmatia, 125 miles southeast of Venice, was once supposed to be the one on which Paul was wrecked; but a more careful examination of all the facts, and of the course of the prevailing winds, and position of the islands and places mentioned, both before and after the shipwreck, have determined the question in favor of Malta. The "barbarous people" of Acts xxviii. 2, were simply not Greeks. The Greeks called every nation or tribe barbarians who did not speak the Greek language.

MEL'ONS (Heb. ABATICHIM). Melons are extensively cultivated in the East, and used as a common article of diet; here we make a luxury of them. Thomson says "Nothing could be regretted in the burning desert more than these delicious (water) melons, whose exuberant juice is so refreshing to the thirsty pilgrim," (Num. xi. 5).

MEL'IZAR (Heb. MELZAR, *steward*), (Dan. i., ii. 16).

MEM (Heb. MEYM). The thirteenth letter of the Hebrew alphabet (Ps. cxix.).

MEM'MIUS, QUIN'TUS. A common first name among the Romans (2 Macc. xi. 34).

MEMPHIS (*the abode of the good one*). In Hebrew MOPH or NOPH (Hosea ix. 6). The ancient

PETRA. EDOM.

Egyptian name was Men-nefru, the *pyramid city*. On the west bank of the Nile, just south of the junction of the three branches, Canopic, Sebennytic and Pelusiac. It was built on a district which was reclaimed by Menes from a marsh, by turning the Nile into a new channel, east of the ancient one which ran close to the Libyan mountains; and in a position which commanded both the Delta and Upper Egypt. Of all the temples, palaces, walls, and houses which the ancient historians describe, not one stone is left on another—the pyramids only remaining. The necropolis in the vicinity witnesses the ancient importance of the city. The principal pyramid field extends along the west bank of the Nile for about 15 miles; and the whole district, including many ruins and small pyramids, for nearly 60 miles. There are from 40 to 60 pyramids, according to the count of various travelers, who include more or less large and small pyramids and ruins of supposed pyramids. The Hebrew prophets distinctly predicted the fall of Memphis (Is. xix. 13; Jer. ii. 16, xlvi. 14, 19; Ez. xxx. 16), the latest about 525 B. C., 50 years before the invasion of Cambyses, and their words seem to have been fulfilled to the very letter. Only one of all its multitude of images and idols now remains, fallen, broken, half buried in sand and mud (the statue of Rameses II, the finest known work of Egyptian sculpture). There is a vast collection of antiquities from Egypt in the Abbott Museum, New York, where may be seen a countless number of relics of the past, of cloth, papyrus, wood, stone and metal, with works of art from Memphis and other localities throughout Egypt. The pyramids stand on a rocky shelf of the desert, 150 feet above the Nile basin.

The Great Pyramid was 480 feet high, and built of stone quarried near, and (the finest) across the river, at Toura. The surface was smooth, when complete, being finished with polished marble, or with a hard cement. This is now taken off, leaving the surface in rude steps, 3 to 6 feet high, varied by the thickness of the layers of stone. The interior walls were also polished, and are now. The king's chamber is of red granite, and contains the lower part of a porphyry sarcophagus, the lid having been removed. Cambyses nearly destroyed the city, B. C. 470, and the rise of Alexandria into importance completed its overthrow.

MEMU'CAN (*in authority*). A privy council of

the king (Esth. i. 14, 16, 21). They were "wise men who knew the times" (skilled in the planets, according to Aben Ezra) and appeared to have formed a council of state, interpreting the laws.

MEN'AHEM (*consoler*). Son of Gadi, king of Israel from B. C. 772 to 761. He continued the idolatrous calf-worship of Jeroboam. The cotemporary prophets Hosea and Amos devoted their lives and talents to attempts at reform of the Church in Israel, but without success. Their books are a picture of society in their time, poetically expressed, but certainly not flattering to either king or people.

ME'NAN. Son of Mattatha (Luke iii. 31).

ME'NE. MENA, (*numbered*). The first word in the mysterious writing on the wall in Belshazzar's palace, interpreted by Daniel (v. 25-28).

MENELA'US. A high-priest, appointed to the office from Antiochus Epiphanes by a bribe, B. C. 172 (2 Macc. iv. 23-25).

MENES'THEUS (*one who abides*). The father of APOLLONIUS (2 Macc. iv. 21).

MENI (*destiny*). An object of idolatrous worship, the moon goddess, LUNA (Is. xv. 11).

MEN-STEALERS were put to death (Ex. xxi. 16).

MENU'CHA (*place of rest*), (Jer. li. 59). SERAIAH II.

MENU'CHAH (*without noise or tumult*). With ease in Judg. xx. 43.

MENU'CHITES (1 Chr. ii. 52).

MEON'ENIM, THE PLAIN OF. Correctly, The OAK of Meonenim (*the enchanters*); (Judg. ix. 37). There were five noted trees near Shechem. 1. The oak of Moreh (not *plain*, as in Gen. xii. 6) where Abram built his first altar in the Promised Land.— 2. Jacob took from his family all the strange gods, and ear-rings, and hid them under an oak at Shechem (xxxv. 4).—3. The oak under which Joshua set up the stone-witness (Josh. xxiv. 26).—4. The oak of the pillar (not *plain*, as in Judg. ix. 6), under which Abimelech was made king.—5. The oak of the enchanters, where Gaal, son of Ebed, saw the soldiers of Abimelech coming, as he stood in the gate of Shechem (Judg. ix. 37). Jacob and Joshua may have chosen the same tree, and the words used by the two men are almost identical in form and spirit. Probably, also, the holy place and the crowning of the king were under the same tree : altogether making four references to the same sacred oak. These sacred trees were found all over the land, and this one may have been connected with the shrine of Baal Berith in its vicinity (Judg. viii. 33, ix. 46).

MEON'OTHAI (*my dwellings*). Son of OTHNIEL (1 Chr. iv. 14).

MEPHA'ATH (*sightly*). Moabite city in Reuben, near Heshbon (Josh. xiii. 18; Jer. xlviii. 21), given to the Merarite Levites. The Romans had a garrison here in the time of Eusebius. Lost.

MEPHIB'OSHETH (*shame-destroyer*, or *image-breaker*). The name is given in Chr. as Meribbaal—Baal and Bosheth being synonymous. (See IDOL.) 1. Son of Saul by Rizpah (2 Sam. xxi. 8). He was crucified, with six others by the Gibeonites (as an offering to the god of Famine?), and hung on the cross for five months. Their bones were buried by David in the cave of Kish, at Zelah, when the famine, which had continued for three years, ended.—2. Son of Jonathan, Saul's son. His life was full of trial and suffering. He was but an infant of 5 yrs. when his father and grandfather were killed on Mt. Gilboa, living at Gibeah, when he was dropped from the arms of his nurse, both of his feet being permanently injured (2 Sam. iv. 4). He was taken to Lodebar, where he was cared for by Machir, the sheikh.

ME'RAB (*increase*). Eldest daughter of king Saul (1 Sam. xiv. 49). She was betrothed to David (xviii. 17), but married Adriel, to whom she bore five sons (2 Sam. xxi. 8). See DAVID.

MERAI'AH (*rebellion*). A priest of the family of Seraiah (Neh. xii. 12).

MERAI'OTH (*rebellious*). 1. He was the immediate predecessor of Eli in the office of HIGH PRIEST (1 Chr. ix. 11).—2. Another priest in the time of Joiakim (Neh. xii. 15).

ME'RAN. A place mentioned with Theman as famous for its merchants and wise men (Baruch iii. 23). In Arabia, but not identified. MEDAN?

MERA'RI (*sorrowful*). Third son of Levi, head of the great division. For their position and duties in the service, see LEVI. The history of the family is traced from Exodus to after the Captivity. —2. Father of Judith (Jud. viii. 1).

MERA'RI (*unhappy*). Head of the 3d division of the tribe of Levi. The Merarites carried the boards, bars, pillars, sockets, pins, and cords of the Tabernacle, by the help of oxen and carts (Num. iii. 20, etc.). In the division of the land they had 12 cities, in Reuben, Gad, and Zebulon (Josh. xxi. 7). They furnished a third part of the musicians, and a third of the doorkeepers. They are frequently mentioned in the history until the return from captivity (Ezr. viii. 18). The family and its branches may be seen in the table:

GENEALOGY OF MERARI.

LEVI.

	1 Merari.
1 Merari.	2 Mushi.
2 Mushi.	3 Mahli.
"	4 Eder.
	5 Jerimoth.
3 Mahli.	6 Libni.
6 Libni.	7 Shimei.
"	8 Uzza.
"	9 Shimei.
"	10 Haggiah.
	11 Asariah.
3 Mahli	12 Abihael.
11 Abihail.	13 Zuriel.
3 Muhli.	14 Shamer.
13 Shamer.	15 Bani.
"	16 Amzi.
	17 Hilkiah.
16 Hilkiah.	18 Amaziah.
17 Amaziah.	19 Hashabiah.
16 Hilkiah.	20 Jeduthum?
18 Hashabiah.	21 Malluch.
20 Mallach.	22 Abdi.
21 Hashabiah.	23 Jaaziah or Jaaziel.
22 Jaaziah or Jaaziel.	24 Shoham.
" "	25 Zaccur, or Zechariah.
" "	26 Ibri or Abdi.
21 Abdi.	27 Eleazar.
"	28 Kishi, Kish, or Kashaiah.
19 Jeduthun?	29 Hosah.
"	30 Obed-Edom.
"	31 Galal, or Gedaliah.
"	32 Zeri or Izri.
"	33 Jeshaiah.
"	34 Hashabiah.
	35 Mattethiah.
27 Kishi.	36 Jerameel.
"	37 Ethan, or Jeduthan.
28 Hasah.	38 Simri.
"	39 Hilkiah.
"	40 Tabaliah.
	41 Zecariah.
34 Hashabiah.	42 Azriham.
42 Azrikan.	43 Hasshub.
43 Hushub.	44 Hashabiah.
"	45 Shemaiah.
	46 Hashabiah.
	47 Jeshaiah.
	48 Sherebiah.

MERATHA'IM (*bitter affliction*). A name given by Jeremiah to Babylon (l. 21).

MERCU'RIUS. In Greek and Roman mythology, the son of JUPITER and Maia (Acts xiv. 12).

MER'CY (Heb. CHESED). In the Scriptures it is a development of benevolence, a feeling of kindness or compassion toward the needy and helpless, and an attribute of God toward mankind (Ex. xx. 6).

MER'CY-SEAT (Heb. KAPPÔRETH). The lid of the Ark of the Covenant. See ARK.

ME'RED (*rebellion*). Son of Ezra (1 Chr. iv. 17). He took for a wife BITHIAH a daughter of Pharaoh. Perhaps a poetical or Kenite name of Moses. Others say of Caleb instead.

MER'EMOTH (*hights*). Son of Uriah, of the family of Hakkoz (Ezr. viii. 33), and appointed a register of gifts and treasure in the Temple. He worked on the repairs of the wall (Neh. iii. 4, 21).—2. Layman, son of Bani (Ezr. x. 36).—3. Family of priests who signed the covenant (Neh. x. 5). Mentioned a century before in ch. xii. 3.

ME'RES (*worthy*). Counselor to Ahasuerus (Esth. i. 14).

MER'IBAH (*strife*). A fountain in the desert of Sin, which flowed at the command of Moses (Ex. xii. 1–7). The place was called Massah (*temptation*), and Meribah (*chiding*).—2. Another fountain of the same character was near Kadesh (Num. xx. 13; Deut. xxxiii. 8). This is also called the Waters of Meribah (Ps. lxxxi. 7, cvi. 32). It was here that Moses sinned in impatience and assumption of power, for which offense he was not permitted to cross over Jordan (Num. xx. 12).

MERIBBA'AL (*against Baal*). MEPHIBOSHETH.

MERŌ'DACH (*bold*). The Babylonian Bel, a gilded image of which was worshiped at Babylon. The planet Jupiter.

MERO'DACH BAL'A-DAN. BALADAN. Berodach is an error. Reigned twice over Babylon, B. C. 721 to 709, and in 702 six months.

The Assyrian inscriptions give his name distinctly, and have records of both reigns. Sargon deposed him the first time, and Sennacherib the second, appointing Belib in his place. There is no certainty of the date of the embassy sent by him to Hezekiah, king of Judah (2 Chr. xxxii. 31), but it was probably between B. C. 721 and 709. If the real object of the league was to effect a political union for strength against Assyria, of Babylon, Judæa, and Egypt, then the business failed, for Sargon seized Babylon and Ashdod.

CHERUB.

ME'ROM, THE WATERS OF (Josh. xi. 5, 7). Where Jabin, king of Hazor, and his allies were defeated by Joshua. The lake El Huleh or Samochonitis (Jos. Ant. v. 5, 1). This lake lies in the south end of a marshy plain, between the foot of Hermon and the hills of Galilee, which is 15 miles long by 5 wide; the lake being triangular and 3 to 5 miles across, according to the dry or wet season. It is 120 feet above the ocean. Several streams (see JORDAN) unite in the marsh, form the Jordan, and flow through the lake. The plain on each side of the lake is of rich soil, and is cultivated by the Bedawin Arabs from Lebanon and merchants of Damascus,—a repetition of life 3,000 years ago, as recorded in Judges xviii. The modern is really the most ancient name, being derived from Hul, the second son of Aram (Gen. x. 23). A district near Hamah is named after him, and also the town Huleh, near the castle of Hunin. The large spring on the west bank of the plain, Ain Mellahah, which pours out a brook 50 feet wide, once gave its name to the lake, Meleha (*William of Tyre*).

MERO'NOTHITE, THE. Native of Meronoth (1 Chr. xxvii. 30).

ME'ROZ (*asylum*), (Judg. v. 23). Whose people refused to help Deborah and Barak against Sisera. *El Murussus*, north of Bethshan 4 miles (*Rob.* ii. 356).

ME'RUTH (1 Esd. v. 24). A corruption of IMMER.

COIN OF TARSUS.

MES'ECH. The sixth son of Japheth (Gen. x. 2), and founder of a nation (Ps. cxx. v.), which traded with Tyre (Ez. xxvii. 13), and was ruined with Egypt (xxxii. 26), and a neighbor of Gog and Magog (xxxviii. 2). Herodotus speaks of the Moschi and Tiburini in Persia (iii. 94), who formed a part of the army of Xerxes; and these are the Meshech and Tubal of the Scriptures. They were settled in the mountains of Caucasus, and in north Armenia; and their descendants to-day follow the customs mentioned by Ezekiel, and sell their daughters for wives and for slaves (to the Turks). The name is written *Muskai* on the Assyrian monuments and *Mashoash* on the Egyptian, of the time of the third Rameses (*Wilkinson*). They are the *Muskovs* of Russia (*Rawlinson*).

ME'SHA. The Joktanites dwelt from Mesha unto Mt. Sephar (Gen. x. 30). The mountain range of Zames (Mesha) runs from near the Persian Gulf S. W., nearly across Arabia. There is a mount Zafara on the Indian Ocean. Here is now, and has been from remote times, the country of the *Beni Kahtan* (Joktanite Arabs), inhabiting Yemen, Hadramaut and Oman, separated from the Ishmaelites by the Nejed mountain range.

ME'SHA (*safety*). 1. King of MOAB (2 K. iii. 4), who revolted from the 10 tribes after the death of Ahab, against whom Jehoshaphat and Jehoram led their armies. He was a great sheep-breeder. A monument erected by him is mentioned in the article KIR HARESH, with an engraving of "THE MOABITE STONE," on page 173.—2. Son of Caleb, who founded Ziph (1 Chr. ii. 42).—3. (*retreat*). Son of Shaharaim (1 Chr. viii. 9).

ME'SHACH (*ram*). The name given to MISHAEL 3, companion of Daniel (Dan. i. 4). It was a name of the sun-god of the Chaldæans.

ME'SHECH (*drawing out*). 1. Son of Japheth (Gen. x. 2), and of the race in connection with Tubal, Magog and other northern nations.—2. MASH (1 Chr. i. 17).

MESHELEMI'AH (*whom Jah repays as a friend*). Son of Kore, a porter in the house of Jehovah (1 Chr. ix. 21). Shelemiah in 1 Chr. xxvi. 1.

MESHEZ'ABEEL (*delivered*). 1. Ancestor of MESHULLAM 13 (Neh. iii. iv.).—2. A family who sealed the covenant (x. 21).—3. Father of Pethahiah (xi. 24).

MESHIL'LEMITH. Son of Immer, a priest (Neh. xi. 13).

MESHIL'LEMOTH (*requital*). 1. A chief under Pekah, ancestor of Berechiah (2 Chr. xxviii. 12).—2. MESHILLEMITH (Neh. xi. 13).

MESHO'BAB (*returned*). A prince in Hezekiah's reign (1 Chr. iv. 34).

MESHUL'LAM (*friend*). 1. Ancestor of Shaphan (2 K. xvii. 3).—2. Son of Zerubbabel (1 Chr. iii. 19).—3. A Gadite chief in the time of Jotham (v. 13).—4. A Benjamite chief (viii. 17).—5. Son of Hodaviah, and father of Sallu (ix. 7; Neh. xi. 7).—6. Son of Shephathiah (1 Chr. ix. 8).—7. Father of Hilkiah (ix. 11).—8. A priest and son of MESHIL'LEMITH (1 Chr. ix. 12).—9. Overseer of the workmen in rebuilding the Temple (2 Chr. xxxiv. 12).—10. A chief sent by Ezra to Iddo (Ezr. viii. 16, 17).—11. A chief who assisted Jonathan and Jahaziah in examining the marriages which the people had contracted with foreign wives (x. 15).—12. Descendant of Bani (x. 29).—13. Son of Berechiah (Neh. iii. 4, 30, vi. 18).—14. Son of Besodeiah; he assisted in restoring the gate of Jerusalem (iii. 6).—15. One who stood with Ezra when he read the law (viii. 4).—16. A priest who sealed the covenant (x. 7).—17. One who sealed the covenant (20).—18. A priest (xii. 13).—19. Another priest.—20. A porter (25).—21. A prince who assisted at the dedication of the wall (xii. 33).

MESHUL'LEMETH (*friend*). Daughter of Haruz, wife of Manasseh (2 K. xxi. 19).

MESO'BAITE (MEZOBAYAH, *gathering-place of Jah*). A title of JASIEL (1 Chr. xi. 47).

MESOPOTA'MIA (*between the rivers*). Between the Tigris and Euphrates, 700 miles long by 20 to 250 wide. The Aram Naharaim (in the Hebrew) of Gen. xxiv. 10, and Padan Aram of xxv. 20. It is a plain, but is crossed by the Sinjar hills east to west, near its centre, not far from Mosul. The nomade tribes are the only people, and they are driven to the hills in the hot season, when the pastures become dry, dusty and parched, except near the streams. (See Assyria.) It is becoming the belief among scholars that the Mesopotamia (the city of Nahor) of Terah and Haran of Abraham were near Damascus (*Dr. Beke*), where Bethuel and Laban lived, and Abraham sent a servant to fetch Rebekah to be Isaac's wife; and a hundred years after that Jacob earned his two wives in 21 years. It was also the residence of Balaam (Deut. xxiii. 4). All of these references may apply to the region around Damascus, between the rivers Pharpar and Abana.

MESSI'AH. CHRIST. The anointed (as a king). The word is found in the original Hebrew many times, in all of which it is translated anointed, except in Daniel ix. 25, 26. The ceremony of ANOINTING was intended to mark what God had set apart for his own purposes. It was His royal stamp, which was to be applied to the high priest (Ex. xxviii. 41), the offerings, the tabernacle, table, ark, candlestick, altar of incense, laver and vessels attached to them, "to sanctify them, and they shall be most holy; whatsoever toucheth them shall be holy."

Samuel anointed Saul and David (three times), while Absalom was anointed by the rebels. The ceremony was performed by the prophets or the priests.

The prophetic use of the title was historic among the Hebrews, and well known to Herod, who was affected by the idea, although he doubted the truth of the divine claim to a belief and hope for the Messiah. The Messiah was to be a son of David (the great king), by the covenant (Ps. lxxxix.) who is described as "the mighty God, the Father of Ages, the Prince of Peace" (Is. ix. 6). See JESUS, page 157. Some expected a temporal king, a literal king, like David. In their view "Son of

David'' meant one who inherited his wisdom and kingly power, who should make the Jews as great a people as ever, or even greater.

In view, also, of the spiritual darkness and ignorance of their oppressors, and all of their neighbors—as judged by their standard—there seemed to be a real need of a deliverer, not only for Israel, but for "all nations.'' The true Messiah was to be an instrument by whom God's great purpose to man was to be carried out by a sacrificial work. The idea of a Messiah is as old as the history of the Hebrew race, being found, or rather alluded to, in the oldest writings, before the time of Moses, and especially in the blessing of Jacob, and in the psalms of David, and the prophesies of Isaiah, Daniel, etc. The expectation of a "golden age" was common among the ancient nations, to which the Jews added the particular personage, the Messiah, who was to reign in that good time; and this is still kept up by the modern Jews, who pray, at every meal, "Merciful God, make us worthy of seeing the days of the Messiah.''

Historians give accounts of about 30 different pretended Messiahs, since the destruction of Jerusalem by Titus (Matt. xxiv. 24); Mark xiii. 22); which are so many proofs of the real Messiah, who foretold them.

METALS. The earliest record of the production and manufacture of metals is in the reference to Tubal Cain, a Cainite, the son of Lamech (Gen. iv. 22). The first mention of metal as money is in Gen. xxiii. 16. The gold and silver possessed by the Jews was of vast amount even allowing for over statements (1 Chr. xxii. 14, xxix. 4). The trade in metals was mostly held by the Phœnicians (Ez. xvii. 7). Metals were also supplied worked in thin plates (Jer. x. 9). The holy vessels used in the Temple were mostly gold (Ezr. v. 14). Tin is mentioned among the spoils of the Midianites (Num. xxxi. 22), and lead in Ez. xv. 10. In the earliest times copper (NECOSHETH) and bronze were used for many purposes in the place of iron introduced at a later period. The passage in Job xxviii. 2, "Molten out of stone," refers to the smelting of copper ore. In Jer. vi. 28, the word copper is used as a term of vileness (by its comparison with silver and gold). It is also used as a term of strength (Ps. cvii. 16; Jer. i. 18, xv. 20). The word brass is frequently used for copper. The art of coating with brass (?) and silver was known to the Hebrews (Ex. xxxviii. 2, and Prov. xxvi. 23). The working of copper into weapons and utensils (Num. xvii. 4); of castings in 1 K. vii. 45, and of gilding (Is. xl. 19). Iron (Barzel) found in the hills of Palestine as well as copper. Probably steel was known to the Hebrews, but this word appearing in 2 Sam. xxii. 35; Job xx. 24; Ps. xviii. 34; Jer. xv. 12, might be translated *brass*, or more correctly, *copper*. Arms were made of bronze (2 Sam. xxi. 16; Job xx. 24; Ps. xviii. 34), and armor in 1 Sam. xvii. 5, 6, 38. See MONEY.

METE'RUS. Sons of Meterus returned from captivity (1 Esd. v. 17).

ME'THEGAM'MAH (*bridle of the mother city*). A place David took from the Philistines (2 Sam. viii. 1).

METHU'SAEL (*man of God*). Son of Mehujael. and father of LAMECH 1 (Gen. iv. 18).

METHU'SELAH (*man of offspring*). Son of Enoch (Gen. v. 25–27). He lived 969 years, longer than any other PATRIARCH, and died the year of the flood.

MEU'NIM (Neh. vii. 52).

MEU'ZAL (Ez. xxvii. 19).

MEZA'HAB (*water*). Father of Matred (Gen. xxxvi. 39).

MIA'MIN (*from the right hand*). 1. A layman (Ezr. x. 25).—2. A priest who returned from captivity (Neh. xii. 5).

MIB'HAR (*choice*). Son of Haggeri, one of David's men (1 Chr. xi. 38).

MIB'SAM (*sweet odor*). 1. Son of Ishmael (Gen. xxv. 13).—2. Son of Simeon (1 Chr. iv. 25).

MIB'ZAR (*fort*). A duke of Edom (1 Chr. i. 53).

MI'CHA. 1. Son of Mephibosheth (2 Sam. ix. 12). —2. A Levite who signed the covenant (Neh. x. 11).—3. Father of Mattaniah (xi. 17, 22).—Father of Ozias, governor of Bethulia (Jud. vi. 15). See MICAH, in HISTORY OF THE BOOKS.

MI'CHAEL (*like God*). 1. Father of Sethur (Num. xiii. 13).—Son of Abihail (1 Chr. v. 13).—3. A Gadite ancestor of Abihail (ver. 14).—4. Ancestor of Asaph (vi. 40).—5. One of the chief men of Issachar (vii. 3).—6. Of the sons of Beriah (viii. 16). —7. A captain who joined David (xii. 20).—8. Ancestor of Omri (xxvii. 18).—9. Son of Jehoshaphat (2 Chr. xxi. 2, 4).—10. Ancestor of Zebadiah (Ezr. viii. 8).

MI'CHAH. Eldest son of Uzziel (1 Chr. xxiv. 24).

MI'CHAIAH (*like Jah*). 1. Father of Achbor, of high rank in the time of Josiah (2 K. xxii. 12).—2. Son of Zaccur (Neh. xii. 35).—3. A priest at the dedication of the wall of Jerusalem (xii. 41).—4. Daughter of Uriel (2 Chr. xiii. 2).—5. A prince sent to teach in Judah (xvii. 7).—6. Son of Gemariah (Jer. xxxvi. 11–14).

MI'CHAL (*who like El ?*). The youngest daughter of Saul, espoused to David. Saul had intended to make her a party to his designs, but was foiled by her devotion to David. This was especially illustrated in the incident in 1 Sam. xix. 11–17, by which she assisted the escape of David. Saul afterwards canceled the marriage, but a reunion followed through the mission of Abner (2 Sam. iii. 12–21). Through her conduct on meeting David, after his return from celebrating the entry of the ark into Jerusalem, she was punished with the curse of barrenness (2 Sam. vi. 16–23). Thus it was that the races of Saul and David were not united.

MICHE'AS. The prophet Micah 7 (2 Esd. i. 39).

MICH'MAS (Ezr. ii. 27). MICHMASH.

COIN OF TROAS.

MICH'MASH (*something hidden*). In Benjamin. A pass celebrated by the exploit of Jonathan, Saul's son (1 Sam. xiii., xiv. 4, 16). Jonathan Maccabæus also resided there (1 Macc. ix. 73), on account of the military strength of the pass (Ant. xiii. 1, 6). *Mukhmas*, in the *Wady Es Suweinit*, has ruins of many foundations of hewn stones, columns, cisterns, etc., indicating a once strong place, perhaps a city devoted to the heathen deity Chemosh (the two names being similar). The two rocks (see BOZEZ and SENEH), may still be seen; one on each side of the narrow and precipitous valley (*Rob.*). Isaiah, in speaking of the invasion of Judah by Sennacherib, says he laid up his carriages at Michmash (x. 28), which agrees with the character of the place, it being too steep for wheels.

MICH'METHAH (*hiding-place*). Boundary of Ephraim and Manasseh, west of Jordan, facing Shechem (Josh. xvii. 7).—2. Between Ephraim and Benjamin (xvi. 6), toward the Great Sea.

MICH'RI (*price of Jah*). Ancestor of Elah, a chief after the Captivity (1 Chr. ix. 8).

MICHTAM. A musical term applied to three Psalms (xvi., lvi., lx).

MID'DIN (*measures*). Judah, in the wilderness. Um el Bedun, S. W. of the Dead Sea? (Velde).

MID'IAN (*strife*). Fourth son of Abraham by Keturah, and founder of a nation (Gen. xxv. 2; Num. xxii.), the rulers of Northern Arabia for a long time; inhabiting the peninsula of Sinai, where Moses fled after killing the Egyptian (Ex. ii. 15), and the country east of Edom and Palestine (xxxvii. 28). They were a snare to the Israelites, and Moses denounced their mischief-making (Num. xxv. 15, 17). Gideon's night-attack with trumpets, and lamps in pitchers, was on a host of Midianites in the valley of Jezreel (Judg. vi. to viii.). They were nomadic, pastoral, wealthy, and delighted in plunder, exactly as their descendants the Bedawins do now. There is no mention of this great nation, which has had an existence for 30 centuries, in any other book but the Bible, unless the accounts of the Arabs of the city of Medyen (the ruins of which are shown on the Akabah Gulf) refer to a city of this people. There is a tradition (in the *Marasid*, and a history of the people in *El Makhreezee*), that this is the city visited by Moses, and they point out a well at which he watered his flocks. They are also mentioned in the Koran (vii., xi.). It is conjectured that Jethro, who is called a priest of Midian, was of the Kenites, who were a branch of this people, and who remained friendly to the Israelites when the main body of the Midianites made war, and incurred the Divine vengeance.

MID'IANITE. One from MIDIAN (Gen. xxxvii. 28, 36).

MID'IANITISH. Belonging to MIDIAN (Num. xxv. 6 ff).

MID'RIFF. CAUL (Ex. xxix. 13).

MID'WIFE. Childbirth in the East, on account of open-air living, is usually easy. The office of midwife, when necessary, is performed by relatives, and sometimes by a professional. Two or three days before the time of delivery, the midwife carried to the house a chair, of peculiar form, upon which the patient is seated during birth (Ex. i. 16). CHILD. The modern Egyptian practice explains that alluded to in Exodus. See MEDICINE.

MIG'DAL E'DAR. Translated "O tower of the flock," in Micah iv. 8. A poetic name of Zion, because of its strength and watchfulness over Israel (Jer. xiii. 17).

TIMBREL.

MIG'DAL EL (*tower of God*). A fenced city in Naphtali (Josh. xix. 38). A place is mentioned in the Wady Kerkerah, 8 ms. E. of Nakura, called Mujeidel. But it is supposed Magdala is referred to in the text.

MIG'DAL GAD (*tower of Gad*). Judah, in the Shefelah (Josh. xv. 37), near Lachish and Eglon. El Mejdel, 2 ms. E. of Askulan, is a large and fine village, in the midst of groves, orchards, and cultivated fields. Large hewn stones, columns, etc., indicate an antiquity of importance; probably of a city devoted to the worship of the heathen deity Gad, as Baal Gad was, under Mt. Hermon.

MIG'DOL (*tower*). 1. A place between which and the Red Sea the Israelites were directed to camp on leaving Egypt (Ex. xiv. 2).—2. A bound-ary town mentioned by Jeremiah and Ezekiel, on the N. as Syene was on the S. of Egypt. Hecatæus of Miletus places Magdolo 12 ms. S. of Pelusium.

MIG'RON (*precipice*). Near Saul's city (1 Sam. xiv. 2), where there was a pomegranate tree, under which Saul and the remnant of his host "tarried" while Jonathan went on his famous exploit against the Philistines. Isaiah (x. 28) names it in the list of places passed by Sennacherib, on the S. side of the Wady Suweinit. Whether it was a rock or a town is not known.

MIJ'AMIN. 1. Chief of the 6th course of priests (1 Chr. xxiv. 9).—2. A priest who signed the covenant with Nehemiah (Neh. x. 7).

MIK'LOTH (*staves*). 1. Son of Jehiel (1 Chr. viii. 32).—2. A leader of the 2d division of David's army (xxvii. 4).

MIKNEI'AH (*possession of Jah*). One of the gate-keepers of the Ark (1 Chr. xv. 18, 21).

MIL'ALAI (*eloquent*). A priest who assisted at the wall of Jerusalem (Neh. xii. 36).

MIL'CAH (*queen*). 1. Daughter of Haran (Gen. xi. 29).—2. Fourth daughter of Zelophehad (Num. xxvi. 33).

MIL'COM (*little Molech*). The abomination of the children of Ammon (1 K. xi. 7).

MIL'DEW (*pale*). Blasting and turning yellow from disease (Deut. xxviii. 22).

MILE. The Roman measure of a mile was equal to 1618 English yards. (The English is 1760 yds.). "To go a mile" (Matt. v. 41). The Jewish mile was of two kinds, long or short, according to the length of pace. The Roman measurement was ultimately introduced into Palestine.

MILE'TUS. Seaport and the ancient capital of Ionia, Asia Minor, 36 ms. S. of Ephesus. The presbyters of the Church of Ephesus met Paul at this place on his return from his third missionary journey (Acts xx. 6). Several men of renown were born here—Democritus (460 B. C.), Anaximenes (504), Hecatæus, Anaximander (611), Thales (639), and Timotheus. There were four harbors, one of which would hold a fleet. The oracle of its famous temple of Apollo was consulted as late as the 4th century. Christian bishops of Miletus were present at several councils from the 5th to the 8th centuries. It is now a ruin called Melas, near the mouth of the river Meander. The sea has receded from the site several miles.

MILK. There are two Hebrew terms for milk, one (CHELEB), meaning *fresh milk*, the other (CHEMAH) *curdled*. Both are frequently used in Scripture; fresh milk is figuratively used to mean abundance (Gen xlix. 12; Ez. xxv. 4; Joel iii. 18, etc.). It is often mentioned with honey, as a "land flowing with milk and honey," applied to describe Egypt as well as Palestine (Num. xvi. 13). As a term of simplicity it occurs in 1 Cor. iii. 2; Heb. v. 12, 13; 1. Pet. ii. 3; Is. lv. 1). The milk was from goats, cows, sheep and camels (Prov. xxvii. 27; Deut. xxxii. 14). "Thirty milch camels" were given by Jacob to Esau (Gen. xxxii. 15). The word butter used in the A. V. generally means curdled milk (Gen. xviii. 8; Judg. v. 25). The meaning in Deut. xxxii. 14 and Prov. xxx. 33 is butter. The plan of preparation of butter by the Hebrews was probably the same as that now in use in the East. The milk, mixed with a little sour milk, is heated over a slow fire, in a copper pan. The separated milk is put into a goatskin, which is tied to a stake or tent pole, and shaken until the butter comes. The water is pressed from this butter and it is put into another skin. After two days the butter is returned to the fire, wheat, boiled with leaven, being added—the whole is boiled and then skimmed, the butter remaining on the top, foreign matter being precipitated, *burgoul* or wheat and leaven. See CHEESE.

MILL (RECHAIM, *the two mill-stones*, Ex. xi. 5); also in the preparation of manna for food in Num. xi. 8. The ordinary mill was a household machine of two stones two feet in diameter and six inches thick, the lower one hollowed out a little, and the upper fitted to it, and turned from right to left around by a wooden handle. This is the work of women or slaves. Captives (as Samson) were often forced to grind (Judg. xvi. 21); but more generally women were thus employed, as in Ex xi. 5 and Matt. xxiv. 41. The use of the mill in each household was incessant, so that when the mill was not working it was a sign of desolation (Jer. xxv. 10; Rev. xviii. 22; Eccles. xii. 3, 4). So necessary to the daily subsistence was the use of the mill that there was a law against pledging either of the stones (Deut. xxiv. 6). In the East, to this day, these hand-mills are seen worked by two women. There are mills on nearly every running stream, with the most primitive machinery, where the wheels are fitted with wooden pins for cogs. Other mills are turned by animals. Millstone is used figuratively, as in Matt. xviii. 6; Job xli. 24; Mark ix. 24; Luke xvii. 2. See MORTAR.

MIL'LET (DOCHAN). Mentioned only in Ez. iv. 9. There was the "common millet" (*Panicum Miliacum*), and the "Turkish millet." It was probably the latter. Millet produced a bread of inferior quality.

MIL'LO (*fulness*). An ancient Jebusite name of a part of the citadel of Jerusalem (2 Sam. v. 9). Solomon raised a levy to build or enlarge this work (and others, 1 K. ix. 15). Hezekiah repaired Millo, *the City of David* (2 Chr. xxxii. 5). The HOUSE OF MILLO was a chief clan of Shechem (Judg. ix. 6, 20). King Joash was murdered by his slaves at "the house of Millo that goeth down to Silla" (2 K. xii. 20), which is supposed to have been the place mentioned first.

MI'NA (Luke xix. 13).

MIN'CING (Heb. TAFOF). Short, quick step; refers to an affectation of gait (Is. iii. 16).

MINES. MINING. (See METALS). The ancients were skilful miners, and their operations are alluded to by Job (xxviii. 1–11). Evidences remain of Egyptian copper mining in the Sinai desert. Palestine produced iron and copper. The Phœnicians brought tin from Spain, and possibly Cornwall, in England. There were lead mines bordering the coast of the Red Sea. Iron mining is referred to in Deut. iv. 20. See cut, p. 122. SILVERSMITH.

MIN'GLED PEOPLE (Heb. HAEREB). Mixed population (Jer. xxv. 20; Ez. xxx. 5). Rulers over mingled tribes (1 K. x. 15) and mercenaries.

MIN'IAMIN. 1. A Levite (2 Chr. xxxi. 15).—2. A priest (Neh. xii. 17).—3. A priest at the dedication of the wall (xii. 41).

MINNI (*division*). Armenia (Jer. li. 27). The Minnai of the Assyrian inscriptions were located near lake *Urumieh*. (See ARMENIA).

MIN'ISTER (Heb. MESHARETH). One who serves another; the term to distinguish from master; Solomon's servants and ministers (1 K. x. 5). "Moses rose up and his *minister* Joshua" (Ex. xxiv. 13). He who *administers* an office. "God's ministers" (Rom. xiii. 4, 6). "Ministers of Christ" (1 Cor. iv. 1). "Christ came not to be ministered unto, but to minister." Minister "of the circumcision" (Rom. xv. 8).

MIN'NITH (*given*). A town east of Jordan (Judg. xi. 33), celebrated for its wheat (Ez. xxvii. 17), which was exported at Tyre. *Menjah*, a ruin, 4 ms. N. E. of Heshbon (*Velde*).

MIN'STREL. In the A. V. the word minstrel only occurs twice in 2 K. iii. 15. "But now bring me a minstrel;" and in Matt. xix. 23, "When Jesus saw the minstrel." The Hebrew in the first text means a player upon a stringed instrument, as David was (1 Sam. xvi. 23; also 1 Sam. x. 5). In Matthew minstrel means pipe-player. Pipe-playing was used by professional mourners. See MUSIC and MUSICAL INSTRUMENTS.

MINT (Gr. *heduosmon*). One of those herbs, the tithe of which the Jews were most exact in paying. Mint was used by the Greeks and Romans in medicine and cookery. The horse-mint (*Mentha sylvestris*) is common in Syria. Mint is only mentioned in Matt. xxiii. 23, and Luke xi. 42, as a tithe. Probably the horse-mint (*Mentha sylvestris*).

COIN OF PERSEUS.

MIPH'KAD, THE GATE (*number*). A gate of Jerusalem in the time of Nehemiah (iii. 31); perhaps in the City of David.

MIRACLES. Two Hebrew words, OTH, sign, and MOFETH, wonder, (plural NIFLAOTH, wonders), and three Greek words, *terata*, wonders; *semeia*, signs; *dunameis*, powers, mighty works, are translated miracles. None of these words imply supernatural power, or religious purpose, because those points are always left to be inferred from the simple narrative of the event, for many wonderful events are recorded which were not supernatural, as in the case of Isaiah who walked naked and barefoot for three years, for a sign (Is. xx. 3). Natural and common events may be used for signs, and do indicate the miracle if they were predicted.

The meaning of miracle in our day is a work or sign that is above and beyond nature. A miracle may be defined as a violation of a law of nature by a particular volition of the Deity, or by the interposition of some visible agent. This is not quite correct, for the miracle is the result of a new power, or new law, which produces effects not included in our ordinary experience. It is simply one law operating on another so far as to neutralize it, and produce unexpected results.

In the case of healing sickness, the word, or touch, or gesture, is the prediction of the cure, and the supernatural is seen in the prediction, or seeing before time what will come to pass. The prediction and the fulfilment may occur near together, or at a great length of time apart, and two sets of independent witnesses depose to the prediction and the fulfilment, leaving no room for doubt or fraud.

Viewed as mere wonderful events for man's astonishment miracles are highly improbable occurrences, but considered as signs of a moral and religious revelation, and witnesses or evidences of the commission of the teachers of religion to instruct and inform mankind, they are no longer improbable, but are signs of the presence of God in action.

The prediction of an eclipse appears supernatural to the ignorant savage who is not aware that the laws of the motions of the heavenly bodies are known and can be calculated precisely; to the scholar it is no wonder, for he can either compute the exact time for himself, or can understand by what means another can do it. The means are natural, the foreknowledge is also within the province of nature. If we could be elevated to a spiritual plane where we should be able to see the powers which move and control the human frame, we should be able to see how Peter cured the lame man, or Jesus healed the blind, and should no longer wonder, for we should recognize the source of the power as God himself manifested in Jesus. We should only recognize the source, not see the means, except that we should see the result, and the agent, for God cannot be seen and followed by us.

The miracles of Jesus were a necessary part of his mission, and formed an integral part of his teaching, and were therefore more than mere signs or specimens of the presence of God, and more than mere proofs of a divine commission. The life and teaching of Jesus form one column or set of columns, and his miracles another, on which rest the roof and dome of the church.

The mission of the Christ was to teach and redeem mankind; to tell them what to believe, and how to be saved, and to be himself the author of their salvation, the worker of a new creation. The Christ was God in the flesh, and Christianity is God in action, made known, or communicated to man, so that we are partakers of the divine nature, through faith in Christ.

The miracles of the Old Testament are nearly all found in two groups, being almost wholly absent from other periods in the track of the Jewish history; and Moses and Elijah are the two central figures, who are the impersonations of the law and the prophets. One of the evidences of the truth of the Bible history is that there are no miracles ascribed to many of the prominent characters, not even such as David, Solomon, or Abraham. The period of over 400 years from Malachi to Christ are without any authentic record of a miracle.

The Old Testament miracles are nearly all of power, and were wrought for the destruction of the enemies of the Hebrew Church or the preservation of its members. A few were works of mercy also, as of Elijah's restoration of the widow's son. The miracles of Christ were both of power and love. (See JESUS.) The miracle attested by eye witnesses and the teaching of Christ were the foundation of the Christian religion, which still remains the belief of a large part of the enlightened sections of the world.

Miracles ceased when the Christian Church was established. The ecclesiastical miracles of the ages since the Apostles are totally different in purpose and kind from those recorded in the Scriptures, and very closely resemble the legendary inventions with which Pagans in all ages have amused or astonished and imposed on mankind. The accounts of the miracles are always simple and direct, without attempt to explain, or even a notice of the wonderful character of the event. The reports of modern "miracles" are so minute as to suggest the novel or fable.

MIR'IAM (*bitter*). Sister of Moses, who it is supposed watched her infant brother when he was exposed in the Nile (Ex. ii. 4). Upon the flight of the Israelites from Egypt, Miriam is called prophetess (Ex. xv. 20), where she celebrates the passage of the Red Sea with music. The arrival of Zipporah, Moses' Ethiopian wife, excited the enmity of Miriam, who incited Aaron to sedition (Num. xii.); for this conduct Miriam was stricken with leprosy, and was recovered by the intercession of Moses. She died in the 1st month of the 40th year after the Exodus, at Kadesh-Barnea (Num. xx. 1). See EXODUS, HISTORY OF THE BOOKS.

MIR'MA (*deceit*). Son of Shaharaim (1 Chr. viii. 10).

MIR'ROR (Heb. MARAH, REI). Mirrors were of polished metal. The Israelitish women probably brought Egyptian-made mirrors out of Egypt. These were given to make the "laver of brass and the foot of it" for the Temple (Ex. xxxviii. 8). Figuratively mentioned in Job xxxvii. 18.

MIS'AEL. 1. MISHAEL 2 (1 Esd. ix. 44).—2.

MISHAEL 3. (SONG OF THE THREE HOLY CHILDREN.)

MIS'GAB (*lofty fort*). City of Moab (Jer. xlviii. 1). Mizpeh (1 Sam. xxiii. 3).

MISH'AEL (*who is what God is*). 1. Son of Uzziel (Ex. vi. 22). He assisted in removing the bodies of Nadab and Abihu from the sanctuary (Lev. x. 4, 5).—2. One who stood with Ezra (Neh. viii. 4).—3. Companion of Daniel (Dan. i. 6, 7, 11, 19).

MI'SHAL (Josh. xxi. 30).

MI'SHAM (*swift-going*). Son of Elpaal (1 Chr. viii. 12).

MISHEAL (*entreaty*). A city of Asher (Josh. xix. 26).

MISH'MA (*hearing*). 1. Son of Ishmael (Gen. xxv. 14).—2. Son of Simeon (1 Chr. iv. 25).

MISHMAN'NAH (*fatness*). A Gadite, who joined David at Ziklag (1 Chr. xii. 10).

MISH'RAITES (*slippery place*). People from Mishra (1 Chr. ii. 53).

MIS'PERETH (*number*). One who returned from captivity (Neh. vii. 7).

MIS'REPHOTHMAIM (*burnings of waters*). Near Sidon (Josh. xi. 8); not conquered at Joshua's death (xiii. 6). Zarephath. Sarepta.

MIST (Heb. ED). Vapor rising from the earth, and forming clouds (Gen. ii. 6).

ROSE.

MITE (Gr. *lepton*). See MONEY.

MITH'CAH (*sweetness*). Desert station. Lost. (Num. xxxiii. 28).

MITH'NITE, THE (*extension*). The native place of JOSHAPHAT (1 Chr. xi. 43).

MITH'REDATH (*given by Mithra*). 1. Treasurer of Cyrus (Ez. i. 8).—2. An officer at Samaria (Ezr. iv. 7).

MITHRIDA'TES. 1. MITHRIDATH 1 (1 Esd. ii 11).—2. MITHREDATH 2 (ii. 16).

MITYLE'NE. Chief town in Lesbos (Acts xx. 14, 15). The Romans called it "the beautiful," from its fine buildings. It was a free city in Paul's time. It is a city now, and gives its name to the whole island.

MIXED MULTITUDE (*a medley of people*). Mentioned as amongst the Israelites in their journey from Rameses to Succoth (Ex. xii. 38). See Num. xi. 4. In the return from the Babylonish Captivity, *mixed multitude* refers to Arabians (Neh. xii. 4), which is probably the meaning in the other references.

MIZ'AR, THE HILL (*little*). From which the Psalmist uttered the pathetic appeal recorded in Ps. xlii. E. of Jordan. Lost. (Not Little Hermon.)

MIZPAH, MIZPEH, (*watch-tower*, or *look-out*). 6 places of this name: 1. Mispah (also Galeed), where Jacob and Laban set up a memorial stoneheap (Gen. xxxi. 45), saying, The Lord *watch* between us. Mizpah was the Hebrew form of the ancient name of the place. N. of Mahanaim, on some hill-top. Jebel Osha, near Es Salt? The top is broad and flat—a fine place for an assembly—and on the N. slope is a ruin, called Jilad (Gilead). (Grove, in *Smith's Dict.*).—2. THE LAND OF MISPAH. The Hivites of this land helped Jabin against the Israelites (Josh. xi. 3).—3. THE VALLEY OF MISPEH. Where Joshua chased Jabin and his multitude (ver. 8). Cœle-Syria, or Bukaa? Perhaps the reference is to the Hauran, "eastward" from the waters of Merom.—4 (Ib. xv. 38). In the Shefelah. Tell es Safieh (Velde).—5. A city of Benjamin (Ib. xviii. 26), on Neby Samwil, 4 ms. N. W. of Jerusalem. Here the whole nation assembled to avenge the Levite (Judg. xx.); and to sacrifice before attacking the Philistines by order of

Samuel (1 Sam. vii.); and again to elect Saul king (x.): the city of Gibeon was about 1 m. N. of the hill; and perhaps on this very hight Solomon offered sacrifice, and was endowed with wisdom (1 K. iii. 4). It was fortified by Asa, who took the materials from Ramah, 3 ms. N. E. Gedaliah, Nebuchadnezzar's governor, lived here when he was killed by the fanatic Ishmael (Jer. xl. 7, 8). After the destruction of the Temple it was held as a holy place, where sacrifice was made (xli. 5) in a house of the Lord. This character continued as late as the time of the Maccabees (1 Macc. iii. 46). There is a village and a mosque (formerly a church) on the summit of *Neby Samwil*. The hill rises steeply 600 ft. above the plain, and commands a very extensive view, especially E., as far as Kerak, in Moab, and W. to the Mediterranean.—6. MIZPEH OF MOAB (1 Sam. xxii. 3). Where David sought an asylum for his father and mother, with the king of Moab (among the relatives of Ruth?).

MIZ′RAIM (*the two Egypts*). EGYPT (Gen. x. 6). This name (not of a man but of a country) represents a centre from which colonies went out from the remotest antiquity. Egypt is now called *Misr* in Arabic. See EGYPT.

MIZ′ZAH (*fear*). Son of Reuel (Gen. xxxvi. 13, 17).

MNA′SON (*remembering*). An old disciple, a resident of Jerusalem, and a native of Cyprus (Acts iv. 36, xxi. 16).

MO′AB (*from father*). Son of Lot, and founder of a tribe, located E. of the Dead Sea (Gen. xix. 37), in the district once occupied by the Emims (Gen. xiv. 5; Deut. ii. 11). Zoar, the city of this tribe, was most probably N. E. of the Dead Sea, from which the Amorites drove them, and which was given to Reuben. The whole region is undulating, without any high ridges or sudden hills, except near the Dead Sea and Jordan, is covered with sites of ruined towns, on every hill or other convenient place, and its soil is rich. The country must, when prosperous, have presented a scene of plenty and happiness scarcely equalled. The Roman roads have not entirely disappeared, on which there are still milestones of the time of Trajan, Marcus Aurelius, and Severus, with the numbers yet readable. The argument in favor of the truth of prophesy receives great strength from the consideration of the past and present condition of Moab, especially when it is known that the prophets spoke at the time of its greatest prosperity (Is. xv., xvi., xxv., B. C. 720; Jer. xlviii., B. C. 600), 12 yrs. before the invasion of Nebuchadnezzar (xxvii. 3); and the country was promised to the Arabs of the east (Bedawins), who now occupy it (Ez. xxv. 8–11). Sanballat, the Moabite (Horonite), was a chief among those who laughed the Jews to scorn, after their return from captivity, and when they attempted to rebuild the walls of Jerusalem (Neh. ii. 19). Manasseh, a son of Joiada, the high-priest, married his daughter (xiii. 28), and became high-priest of the Samaritans in the temple built by his father-in-law on Mt. Gerizim (Josephus). The Moabites probably had a national record of events, from which the account of Balak and Balaam (Num. xxii.-xxiv.) was borrowed. Of Mesha, a king of Moab, an interesting relic has this [1870] year been found by the Palestine Exploration (see KIR HARESH).

MO′ABITE. Descendant of MOAB (Deut. ii. 9).

MO′ABITESS. A female of MOAB (Ruth i. 22).

MOADI′AH (*festival of Jah*). One who returned from captivity (Neh. xii. 17).

MOCH′MUR (*foaming*). Probably the Wady Ahmur.

MO′DIN. The native city of the Maccabees, who were of the race of the priests (1 Macc. ii. 1, xiii. 25), where their ancestral sepulchre was located (Jos. Ant. xiii. 6, 6; 1 Macc. xiii. 27–30, **11.** 70; ix. 19). Here the resistance to Antioch was begun by Mattathias; and here the Jewish armies encamped on the eve of two of their most noted victories—that of Simon over Cendebæus (1 Macc. xvi. 4), and that of Judas over Eupator (2 Macc. xiii. 14). The site of Modin is located at Latrun, on the road from Jerusalem to Ramleh, 12 miles from the former, where there are ancient remains of importance (*Rob.*).

MO′ETH. Son of Sabban (Ezr. viii. 33).

MO′LADAH. South, in Judah (Josh. xv. 26); given to Simeon. Reoccupied after the Captivity (Neh. xi. 26). Herod retired to a tower in Malatha of Idumæa (Josephus). *El Milh* is a ruin of great extent, with two large wells, and is on the regular road from Petra to Hebron.

MOLE (TINSHEMETH). Mentioned in Lev. xi. 18, as the name of a bird (*swan*) or in Lev. xi. 30, as *male*—amongst "creeping things" that are unclean. Probably a *chameleon* on a general allusion. In Is. ii. 20 it is more likely to mean a mole (CHEFOR PEROTH).

MOLECH (MELEK, *king*). The chief god of the Phœnicians—mentioned as the god of the Ammonites. Probably known to the Israelites before the time of Solomon. Human sacrifices (infants) were offered up to this idol, the victims being slowly burnt to death in the arms of the idol, which were of metel, hollow, and could be heated on the inside. Manasseh sacrificed his son to Molech. Solomon erected an altar to this god on one of the summits of Mount Olivet (see JERUSALEM, p. 150), described in 1 Kings xi. 7. This idol worship being continued, both there and in Tophet, until Josiah abolished it and defiled the altars (2 Kings xxiii. 10, 13). His son Jehoahaz revived this worship (2 Kings xxiii. 32). Molech was worshiped by the Phoenician colonies, as at Carthage, where there were at one time sacrificed 200 boys, believing this would relieve the city from a siege. See PHŒNICIA.

MO′LI. Son of Merari (1 Esd. viii. 47).

MO′LID (*begetter*). Son of Abishur (1 Chr. ii. 29).

MO′LOCH (Amos v. 26; Acts vii. 43). MOLECH.

MOM′DIS. Son of Bani (1 Esd. ix. 34).

WEIGHING MONEY.

MON′EY. The most ancient notices of money refer to certain weights of precious metals, but not to coins. The first mention of wealth in the Bible is of the wealth of Abraham when he left Egypt to return to Canaan; and of the 1000 pieces of silver that the Abimelech gave Abraham for Sarah's use (Gen. xiii. 2, xx. 16), unless Job lived before his time, when the "kesitah and ring of gold," which each of his friends gave him after his recovery, would belong to an earlier age.

Abraham bought the cave of Machpelah and weighed to Ephron 400 shekels of silver, current with the merchant (xxiii. 6). Jacob paid 100 kesitahs for a field at Shalem; Achan stole 200 shekels of silver, and a tongue of gold weighing 50 shekels (Josh. vii.).

Jewels in the East have in all ages been a convenient and recognized means of keeping property, the precious metals being always weighed, as in the case of the presents to Rebekah (Gen. xxiv. 22). Egyptian (and perhaps also other) money was made into rings, for convenience, as when the sons of Jacob carried bundles of money of certain weight to Egypt to buy corn (xlii. 35, xliii. 21). The Midianites were "spoiled" of jewels of gold, chains and bracelets, rings, ear-rings, and tablets, of 16,750 shekels' weight.

Jehoiada "took a chest, and bored a hole in the lid of it, and set it beside the altar, on the right side, and the priests put therein all the money" (2 K. xii. 9.) This is the first mention of a contribution box, 850 B. C. These small pieces *may* have been coins.

Saul's servants said that they had only the fourth part of a shekel to give the prophet, and it seems to have been customary to give more (1 Sam. ix. 8). A half-shekel was the yearly temple dues (Ex. xxx. 13, 15).

HALF-SHEKEL.

The credit for making the first coins, is given to the Lydians, Asia Minor, by Herodotus (i. 94), which were of gold; and to Phidra of Argos, in the island of Ægina, 860 B. C., of silver, by the Parian chronicle (a series of inscriptions, or records, on marble, dated 200 B. C.).

The earliest coins used in Palestine were Persian, and called Daric (*king's money*, from Darius), 450 B. C. (Ezr. ii. 69; Neh. vii. 70; 1 Chr. xxix. 7). (See cut on page 70). The stater (*standard*) was another Persian coin, of silver and of gold, and also the siglos (Greek for *shekel?*).

There are still to be found in the museums of Paris, Gotha, London, and in some private collections, coins of Sardis (see cut on page 125), Scythopolis (Bethshan), Joppa, Tarsus, Sycamina, Ascalon, Ephesus, Philadelphia, and several other cities of Palestine, of the date of Alexander, 350 B. C.

Antiochus VII, 139 B. C. granted the privilege of coining money among the Jews to Simon Maccabæus, and the various pieces are dated "In the first, or second, year of Simon (see cut on page 121), benefactor of the Jews, High-Priest" (1 Macc. xiii. 34, 42; Ant. xiii. 6). The date was always given in letters. (See NUMBER). Some coins have "ethnarch." There are some shekels with the inscription SHEKEL HAKODESH, shekel of the Sanctuary, that is the Temple.

Eleazar, son of Simon, struck coins both of silver and bronze (see cut on page 77). Jehonathan, high-priest, struck coins, B. C. 105–78, of which some are still extant.

The money of Herod is less interesting, because of its Greek character, and being of bronze only. The farthing of the New Testament was the smallest of Herod's coins, unless the mite was smaller. The text in Mark xii. 42, is explained, "she threw in two *leptra*, (mites) which is a quadrans" (farthing), (see page 103), as though we should say two mills, which are a quarter of a cent (nearly). Such very small coins are often found buried, with others, among the ancient ruins of Palestine. The

modern Arabs also use small pieces which look very much like fish scales, in size and thickness.

The coin which Peter found in the mouth of the fish, was probably the stater, or tetradrachm, the only Greek silver coin in use at that time, equal in value to the shekel, which was not then coined, or in use, unless for Temple dues (see pages 13 and 18 for cuts of tetradrachm). The tribute money (Matt. xxii. 15–21) bore the head of a Cæsar, Tiberius or some earlier one, and was a day's wages of a soldier, and such as was paid the laborers in the vineyard (Matt. xviii. 28, xx. 2, 9, 13, xxii. 19; Mark vi. 37, xii. 15, xiv. 5; Luke vii. 41, x. 35, xx. 24; John vi. 7, xii. 15; Rev. vi. 6).

The piece of money paid Judas is represented by the tetradrachm of Antiochus III (cut on page 168), which was equal to the shekel. As there were money-changers in the Temple, who changed Gentile coins for the Temple money (shekel of the sanctuary), the thirty pieces may have been Jewish shekels of Simon or Eleazar (pages 77, 121).

The last coins struck by the Jews are those of Barkokab, A. D. 130. (This is doubted by some numismatists).

The Romans struck several coins and medals in memory of the fall of Jerusalem, one of which is given on page 77. Herod Agrippa also gives a head of Titus, when Emperor, on one of his coins. The Aretas who ruled Damascus when Paul was there struck coins, one of which is now well known. The coin of Ephesus bears a model of the temple of Diana, and a head of Nero.

There is a curious medal with a head of Christ on a cross, which was found at Urfa, Syria (by Rev. G. B. Nutting, missionary, who loaned it to me), and is engraved on page 40. It is very ancient, but cannot be dated, except that it is probably later than the time of Constantine.

A coin if genuine is often the very best evidence concerning ancient persons and places, which cannot be denied or explained away. Even if they were forged, in some age near the true date, they have still a value according to their antiquity. It is often found that ancient records are confirmed by coins, as for instance in the case of the port of Cenchræa, where the coin of Corinth explains the text. See page 143.

The frequent allusions to burying money and treasure was confirmed as true records a few years ago by the discovery of some earthen jars in a garden at Sidon, containing nearly 8000 pieces of gold, the coinage of Philip of Macedon, and Alexander, his son. There were no banks or places of secure deposit, and the only safety was in burying money or treasure in some secret place, as alluded to in Prov. ii. 4; and also in Jer. xli. 8, where the treasures hid were produced.

MONTH (HODESH or CHODESH, YERAH or YERACH). The Hebrew months were divided into twenty-nine and thirty days alternately. The period of New Moon marked the first day called New Moon day or New Month. (See CHRONOLOGY). The months were numbered, as first, second; and also named in the calendar (Gen. vii. 11; 2 Kings xxv. 3; Esth. viii. 9). The Hebrew month does not run even with ours, being regulated by the moon, and having about 29 days, while ours has an arbitrary number given it, varying from 28 to 31 days.

MONUMENT (Is. lxv. 4). Various terms used, as *preserved* in Is. xlix. 6; *hidden* (xlviii. 6); *besieged* (i. 8, and Ez. vi. 12). It is a general reference to retired places.

MOON. Three names of the moon were used by the Hebrews: YAREAH, *paleness;* LEBONAH, *white;* and HODESH (*renewing*) *new moon.* The hodesh moon was the means of reckoning the months and fixing the feasts, etc. In the account of the festivals it appears that the authorities set a watch on the hills about Jerusalem, who looked for the new moon, and when it was seen they were to report to the Sanhedrin. (See NEW MOON). The new moon regulated the month, and if any cloud or other cause prevented the discovery, the month would vary by a day.

The names of the moon in the account of the creation were framed on its light-giving property and color.

It is (and was anciently) a common superstition in Palestine that the moon has a powerful effect on both animal and vegetable life. That sleeping in the open air, exposed to the light of the moon, produces serious ills, blindness (Ps. cxxi. 6), etc. That as dew fell most abundantly on clear cool nights, the moon was the cause of its falling; and also the cause of all fertility.

The moon was worshiped (as also the sun) as a power, and was personified, several moon-goddesses being recorded. Some nations directly addressed the moon itself in their ceremonies, as the Pelasgians, Carthaginians, Teutons, Celts and others made images of women in certain drapery and attitude, called by the Armenians, Anaitis; by the Phœnicians, Astarte (Job xxxi. 26; 2 K. xxiii. 13; Jer vii. 18; viii. 2; xix. 13; xliv. 17–19). Queen of heaven; Syrians, Ashtoreth; Babylonians, Sin; Egyptians, Isis or Neith; Greeks, Artemis; Romans, Diana. The Chaldæans called the moon (and the woman-image) Queen of Heaven. See cut on page 127.

The worship was very widely known and practiced, and was specially denounced by Moses (Deut. iv. 19; xvii. 3), but in spite of his laws it was introduced with other idolatries by Manasseh, B. C. 698. Josiah reformed the Church in his day, but not permanently (2 K. xxiii. 5). The moon was worshiped as the power to which women were peculiarly subject; and women offered incense, drink-offerings and cakes, and by the kissing of the hand towards the bright orb.

MOR'DECAI (*little man*), (Esth. ii. iii. iv. v.). He was the guardian of Esther, who was selected to succeed Vashti as queen of Ahasuerus, king of Persia, her Jewish descent remaining unknown to the king. Mordecai, who was an officer at the court, became informed of a plot against the king's life; this he communicated to Esther, who warned the king; this service, however, was, at the time, unrewarded. Haman at this time rose into favor and the highest office in court; he was an Agagite, and to him Mordecai showed no reverence. The anger of Haman was excited, and he obtained the king's order for the immediate massacre of all Jews throughout the kingdom. Esther becoming informed, through Mordecai, of this decree, hastened, uncalled for, to the king's presence, and with boldness pleaded the cause of the Jews. This, together with the memory of Mordecai's previous service, recalled by the reading of the records, determined the king to counteract the effect of the order (which by the Persian law could not be recalled), and by giving the Jews facilities for defense. Mordecai was promoted to the highest position, and Haman was ordered to be executed upon the gibbet he had prepared for Mordecai. Mordecai used his influence to the service of the Jews with wisdom and goodness. See ESTHER in the HISTORY OF THE BOOKS.

MO'REH (*a teacher*). THE OAK OF MOREH (not plain), was the first halting-place of Abram in Canaan (Gen. xii. 6), and was near Shechem. (Land of Moriah?) The field which Jacob bought probably included this sacred grove. The name Morthia is found on some ancient coins as a title of Neopolis—Shechem. Josephus has a Mamortha, or Mabortha, which he says was a local name (B. J. v. 8, 1). THE HILL OF MOREH. At the base of this hill the Midianites encamped on the night when Gideon attacked them with his 300 (Judg.

vii. 1). Now called Little Hermon or *Jabel ed Duhy*.

MORESH'ETH GATH (*possession of the wine-press*), (Micah i. 14). In the Shefelah, near Lachish. The prophet Micah was a native of *a* Moresheth, but whether this is the one is not certain.

PENNY.

MORI'AH. Found only in two passages—Gen. xxii. 2, and 2 Chr. iii. 1. 1. THE LAND OF MORIAH (Gen. xxii. 2) was more than two days' journey from Gerar, where Abram then lived (Beersheba being mentioned just before and just after the event of the journey), and probably in the same region with the oak of Moreh, Shechem.— 2. MOUNT MORIAH would in that case be Mt. Gerizim, according to the tradition of the Samaritans; but it is said, in 2 Chr. iii. 1, that Solomon began to build the house of the Lord at Jerusalem, in Mount Moriah. There must have been two mountains of that name, or the one at Jerusalem is the only one. This mount, then, has witnessed the offered sacrifice of Isaac, the vision of God's judgment and mercy, the presence of His Temple and worship, and the crucifixion.

MOR'TAR (MEDOKAH). Mill or mortar, in which grain was pounded for domestic use (Num. xi. 8). The Arabs use the same simple machine now. They were made of stone or hard wood. (See MILL). The mortar for olives (KUTTASH) was made expressly for that use, of a heavy stone roller or wheel, which rolled around in a circular trough or tub, of stone also, moved by a long handle of wood. This squeezed or bruised the pulp, but did not crush the pits.

MO'SERAH (*bond*). Station in the Arabah, near Mt. Hor (Deut. x. 6). Moseroth (*bonds*), in Num. xxxiii. 30. *Wady Mousa* is supposed to be a remnant of the name Moserah. Aaron died while the people were encamped here.

MO'SES (MOSHEH, *drawn out of the water*). The son of Amram and Jochebed, of the tribe of Levi. Aaron was his brother, and Miriam his sister. He was saved from the Pharaoh's decree, of death to all male infants born to the Hebrews, by being laid in an ark (boat) of papyrus (A. V. bulrushes), and left among the reeds near the Nile bank, where the daughter of the Pharaoh was in the habit of bathing, where she found and drew him out of the water. He was educated as an Egyptian in the priest's college at Heliopolis, and was probably initiated into the sacred order of the priests (Acts vii. 22), and named Osarsiph, or Tisithen (Strabo, Ant. ii. 9, 7). It is probable, also, that he became acquainted in that seat of learning with Greek, Chaldæan, and Assyrian literature.

The great importance of selecting proper nurses may be learned from the history of Moses, whose mother, a Hebrew woman, nursed him, although he was brought up by the Egyptians; and when he became of age he chose the religion and people of his own race, although he was offered a place in the Pharaoh's family as an adopted son.

He became the champion of his people from the first, and showed his compassion for their sufferings by killing one of the task-masters who was abusing a Hebrew. Pharaoh would have punished him with death for the murder, if he had not fled into Arabia, and "sat down by a well" in the land of Midian, where his first act was to defend the daughters of Reuel (Jethro), a priest of Midian, against their oppressors, the shepherds. (See MIDIAN). He became a shepherd in the service of Jethro, and married Zipporah, his daughter, by whom he had two sons, Gershom and Eliezer. During the seclusion of his shepherd life, in the valley of Shoayb (or Hobab), he received a divine commission to deliver his people Israel from the Egyptian bondage, and at the same time the divine name Jehovah (Heb. YEHEVEH = self-existence), which was explained to him, and a confirmation of his mission in the three miracles of the burning bush, the serpent rod, and the leprous hand. Supported by his brother Aaron, sustained in a wonderful way by the miracles of the ten plagues, the last of which was the most terrible, in the death of the first-born in all Egypt, Moses led out the Israelites to the E. side of the Red Sea, blessed with liberty, and a large tribute from their late oppressors.

On this occasion Moses wrote his first recorded poem (Ex. xv.). His sister Miriam also sang a song, the title, or subject only, of which is known.

Moses was at this time 80 years old. His life during the next 40 years is a part of the history of the Israelites, inseparable, and for 38 years entirely unknown. He died at the age of 120, and was not careful of his memory, leaving no monument of stone to mark his grave, which is unknown (Deut. xxiv.).

Moses is the only character to which Jesus compares himself, as a revealer of a new name of God, and the founder of a new religious faith, as a lawgiver, and as a prophet; and they both were misunderstood in their office as peacemakers; and the death of Moses suggests the ascension of Jesus (John v. 46; Heb. iii. xii.).

DOOR OF A TOMB.

The laws framed by Moses have influenced and even controlled the larger part of civilized mankind since his time; and the religion which he found scattered in traditions and shaped into a beautiful system still holds millions to its faith; while its successor, Christianity, claims present hold of a large part of mankind, and promises a universal sway in the future.

Besides the song on the passage of the Red Sea, Moses wrote others, of which only fragments have been preserved.

1. A war-song against Amalek (Ex. xvii. 16).

"As the hand is on the throne of Jehovah,
So will Jehovah war with Amalek
From generation to generation."

2. On the revelries at the calf-worship at Sinai (Ex. xxxii. 18):

"Not the voice of them that shout for mastery,
Nor the voice of them that cry for being overcome,
But the noise of them that sing, do I hear."

3. The songs recorded (and lost) in the Book of the Wars of the Lord, and the fragment of the Song at the Well, in Moab.

4. The Song of Moses in Deut. xxxii. was probably written in Moab.

5. The Blessing on the Twelve Tribes, which contains a concise statement of the characteristics of the different tribes.

6. The 90th Psalm (if not also some others following), is a sublime view of the eternity of God, which he describes as more enduring than the "everlasting" mountains.

Moses is called a prophet by one of the later prophets.

The word translated *meek*, in Num. xii. 3, means *disinterested*, which describes Moses better. He always forgot himself when the good of his people was to be served. Gave up his position in Pharaoh's house; avenged his people's wrongs; desired Aaron to take the lead; wished all were gifted as he was; preferred that his name be blotted out to save his people, when he was offered the promise of Abraham; not his sons, but Aaron's, were raised to the honor of priests, nor even to leaders, for after his death the leadership passed to Joshua, of another tribe; and although he earned the title of the father of his people, yet they were never called the children of Moses but of Abraham.

MOSOL'LAM (1 Esd. ix. 14). MESHULLAM.

MOSOL'LAMON (1 Esd. viii. 44).

MOTE (*a twig* or *mote*). The emblem of lesser faults (Matt. vii. 3–5).

MOTH (Heb. ASH; Gr. *sēs*). A destructive insect. Nearly every instance where this insect is mentioned it is in reference to its destroying garments (Job. xiii. 28).

MOTHER (Heb. EM; Gr. *mētēr*). The mother was honored and esteemed in the Hebrew system, and far above the station given her in any other system of the age (1 K. ii. 19; Ex. xx. 12; Lev. xix. 3; Deut. v. 16; Prov. x. 1, xv. 20, xvii. 25, xxix. 15, xxxi. 30). See WOMEN.

MOULD'Y (Heb. MIKKUDIM), (Josh. ix. 5, 12).

MOUNTAIN. The Hebrew words are, HAR, HARER, or HARAR, and the Chaldee, *tur;* which are translated mount, mountain, and hill. The various parts of a mountain were described by the names of parts of the human body: 1: Head (ROSH, Gen. viii. 5), meaning tops or summits.—2. Ears (AZNOTH, Josh. xix. 34); projections or spurs. Uzzen Sherah.—3. Shoulder (KATHEF, Deut. xxxiii. 12), meaning side or slope.—4. Side (ZAD, 1 Sam. xxiii. 26).—5. Loins (KISLOTH, Josh. xix. 12): Ha-Cesulloth (*loins-village*).—6. Rib (ZELA, 2 Sam. xvi. 13).—7. Back (SHEKEM), the origin of the name Shechem, which is on the back of Gerizim.—8. Thigh (JARKAH, Judg. xix. 1, 18).—9. In Chaldee *tur* is mountain, and this is borrowed in the modern name of Olivet, Jebel et Tur.

MOUNTAIN OF THE AMMONITES (Deut. i. 19, 20). On the plateau of Et Tyh, from Jebel Araif en-Nakah to Jebel el Mukrah, but also extended in lower ranges as far as Hebron.

MOURN'ING. There are a great many allusions to mourning in the Bible. Its customs include: Beating the breast and body; weeping and screaming in an excessive manner; wearing dark-colored garments; songs and shouts of lamentation; funeral feasts; hired mourners; the disuse of perfumes, oil, and fine food, and the use of ashes, and coarse food and clothes. The time of mourning lasted from 7 to 30 days. Outward expression of sorrow for the dead, and also signs of repentance. The earliest notice is in Job (i. 20), who, on hearing of the calamities to his children, "arose, rent his mantle, shaved his head, and fell down upon the ground, and worshiped," uttering words of submission, and sitting down in the ashes. 7 days and nights the mournful rites were prolonged, with the use of sack-cloth and dust. On his recovery the friends held a kind of congratulatory mourning over him for his past sufferings (xlii. 11). The next instance is of Abraham, who wept for Sarah (B. C. 1871), in words which indicate a formal mourning (Gen.

xxiii. 2). The time usually given was 7 days as for Saul, in 1 Sam. xxxi. 13. The oak under which Deborah, the nurse of Rebekah, was buried was called Allan-bakuth, oak of weeping. The instances of mourning and weeping are very many in the Scriptures, in all the ages. The Egyptians decreed a mourning for a king of 72 days (Herodotus), and the people tore their garments, closed the temples, forbid sacrifices, and held no festivities, but instead they wandered through the streets, throwing dust on their heads, singing a funeral dirge. Ornaments were left off (Ex. xxxiii. 4; Joel ii. 16): but the Jews were forbidden to cut their flesh, as the pagans did (1 K. xviii. 28; Lev. xix. 28), or to shave the eyebrows or hair. The priests were denied all outward signs of grief (Lev. x. 6, xxi. 1, 4, 11), and the Nazarite also (Num. vi. 7). The mourning ordered by David for Abner was in form, with all the required rites, ceremonies, and processions. David also wrote an elegy and lamentation for Abner (2 Sam. iii. 31, 35). Elegies were very often composed for the dead (Ez. xxvi. 1-18, xxvii. 1-36; Amos v. 1, etc.). The customs did not change until the days of Christ, when "many of the Jews came to comfort Martha and Mary" (John xi. 19): "much people" were with the widow of Nain (Luke vii. 12). Mourning apparel is mentioned in 2 Sam. xiv. 2; ashes were put on the head, and oil was denied. The head was shaved. Mourning women were hired, and the custom is still in use. The monuments in Egypt show all these customs in actual practice. It was the custom, also, to give food to the mourners at funerals. The cries and songs used are peculiarly mournful and affecting. Idolatrous mourning (for Tammuz) was prohibited (Ez. viii. 14). The most singular custom of wailing every week, at the wall of the Temple in Jerusalem, has been kept up for ages, by those Jews who still look for the Christ, and hope for the deliverance of Zion.

MOUSE (AKBAR, *field-ravager*). An unclean animal (Lev. xi. 29), forbidden as food. Five golden mice were made for a trespass offering (1 Sam. vi. 4, 5). It is not known what they were, and some think jerboas answer the meaning of the original.

MOUTH (PEH). Is used in the Scriptures both literally of men and beasts (Gen. viii. 11).

MOW'ING. The heat of the climate in Palestine is so great it soon dries up the herbage so that hay-making is not in use (Amos vii. 1). Grass and green grain were cut for immediate use (Ps. cxxix. 7; Amos vii. 1).

MO'ZAH (*spring-head*). Benjamin (Josh. xviii. 26), near Cephirah, the modern Kefir.—2. Son of Zimri, and in the line of Saul—Mephibosbeth—Micah (1 Chr. ix. 42).

MUF'FLERS (*veils*). A female ornament (Is. xii. 19).

MUL'BERRY TREES (BACA, BEKAIM). It is not certain that mulberry trees are meant in 2 Sam. v. 23, 24; 1 Chr. xiv. 14. Some think it was a species of poplar. See cut on p. 88.

MULE (PERED, *mule;* REKESH, *dromedary;* and YEMIM, *warm springs;* are all translated mule. First mentioned in David's time, when horses became common, and they appear to have become favorites all at once, being mentioned in hundreds (Neh. vii. 68). The king's sons rode on mules. The law forbid the Jews from raising mules, and they either imported them or broke the law (Lev. xix. 19). Yemim, warm springs, were found by Anah (and not mules as in Gen. xxxvi. 24), east of the Dead Sea, now called Machærus or Callirhoe.

MUP'PIN (*sorrow*). A descendant of Rachel (Gen. xlvi. 21).

MURDER. Was an outrage on the likeness of God in man, and also a damage to society in the loss of a member. There was to be no reprieve of the murderer, for money, as the pagans allowed. The accidental man-slayer might escape to the City of Refuge.

The custom of blood-revenge is very ancient, and Moses regulated it by certain restrictions, which protected the accidental homicide, but punished the wilful criminal. Bloodshed, even in war, was polluting (Num. xxxv. 33; Deut. xxi. 1; 1 Chr. xxviii. 3). Some of the ancients held that an attempt to murder was equally criminal as an actual murder. Child murder, parricide, poisoning, are not included among other particular things mentioned in the law (Ex. xxi.).

If an animal, known to be unruly and violent, caused the death of a person by the neglect of its owner or keeper, both the animal and its owner were destroyed.

The question of guilt was to be determined by the judges, but the execution of the sentence was the duty and privilege of the next of kin to the sufferer originally, but was directed by the king and his officers in later times. At least two witnesses were required on a capital offense.

Private revenge caused many assassinations in some ages, several instances of which are recorded in 1 K. xv. 27; xvi. 9, 10; 2 K. viii. 15; x. 7; xi. 1, 16; and there are many others.

Burglars, if taken in the act, before day light (or sunrise), could be killed, but not after sunrise.

MULBERRY.

MUR'RAIN (DEBER). A plague among cattle.

MU'SHI (*forsaken*). Son of MERARI (Ex. vi. 19).

MU'SHITES. Descendants of Mushi (Num. iii. 33).

MUSIC. The first record of music is in Gen. iv. 21, referring to Jubal (brother of Tubal-Cain) as the father (teacher?) of musicians upon the harp and organ; probably the lyre and the Pandean pipes. Music was used socially from an early date, as in Gen. xxxi. 27, both as an accompaniment to song and dance. Music was an especial employment of women, and, at a later period, "foreign girls" visited Palestine as musicians (Is. xxiii. 16). David was an accomplished musician, and gave much attention to its cultivation, and introduction into the Temple worship (1 Chr. xxv. 1). It is probable that in this service were female choirs (Ezr. ii. 65). The prophets were great cultivators of music, and it was an important branch of the instruction in the schools of the prophets.

From the time of Abraham, the Israelites were essentially a musical people, as the Arabs are to this day, living in the same country, exhibiting their musical nature in their constant habit of singing. The Egyptians were practical musicians, and introduced music upon all festive occasions. During the Israelitish bondage, the Hebrews, naturally musical, became acquainted with the musical instruments of the Egyptians, which they carried with them across the desert into Canaan, and their use has been recorded in every succeeding age. In the titles of the Psalms both tunes and musical terms appear. See MUSICAL INSTRUMENTS. We have no records of any tunes used by the ancient Hebrews, and can only suppose that they had a system of musical notation. The most eminent composers of music (especially sacred music) in our age are Hebrews.

Εναρχηηνολογοσκαιολογοςῆ
προστονθεν·καιθεηνολογος·
ουτοσηνεναρχηιπροστονθεν
πανταδιλγτουεγενετοικιχω
ρεισαυτουεγενετοουδεν·
ογεγονενεναυτωζωηην _
καιηζωηηντοφωστωνανῶν
καιτοφωσεντηςκοτιαφαι ·
νεικαιηςκοτιααυτοουκατθ
λαβεν·

MUSICAL INSTRUMENTS. There were three kinds in use. 1. Stringed, (harp, viol, sackbut). 2. Wind, (trumpet, horn, cornet, pipe, flute, organ, dulcimer). 3. Of percussion, (bells, cymbals, timbrel). See cut, p. 202.

The cornet (SHOFAR) was made of the horn of a ram or wild goat, or ox. Its use was for signals, as for the jubilee (Lev. xxv. 9), new year, and muster for war (Jer. iv. 5), and for giving alarm by the sentinels on the approach of an enemy (Ez. xxxiii. iv). KEREN was a horn of any kind. Two silver trumpets were ordered by Moses, for calling the assembly together; for the signal to march in the wilderness, for the muster for war, and for festivals (Num. x. 10). YOBEL was probably the name of a distinct style of horn or trumpet (Ex. xix. 13), called ram's horn in Job vi. 5, 6. The modern cornet is not a successor of the ancient in tone and effect, being of brass and much more harsh and noisy.

The horn (KEREN) was probably the primitive trumpet, being a horn of an ox, ram, or goat, with a mouthpiece, or simple open end. The same word is used for the horn which held the oil used in consecration or anointing the king, priests or sacrifices (1 Sam. xvi. 1, etc.). The word KEREN meant also to shine, and is so used in the account of Moses at Sinai, where, instead of horns, it was more likely to have been light reflected from his face.

The pipe (CHALIL) or flute (1 K. i. 40), was an instrument *bored out,* as of wood. The form of the flute was very much the same in all ancient countries. We know what the Greek flute was, both single and double, and may guess at the Hebrew very closely. The flute is very much improved in modern days by keys, especially in the Bœhm variety, which is really the ancient instrument improved by modern keys. The bore is the same size throughout, differing from the common flute, which is very large at the mouth end, tapering towards the other. The small sizes are called fife and picolo. The flute was used in mourning,

for its soft, sad tones (Matt. ix. 23), and in the Temple choirs (Ps. lxxxvii. 7, "pipers"). They were made of reeds also for the altar service because of their softer tones.

The flute (MASHROKUTHA, *the hisser*), was made of one, two, or several pipes, and was not the organ. The dervishes use the flute in their sacred dances.

The organ (UGGAB, *the blower*), a general term for all musical instruments that are blown (Gen. iv. 21; Job xxi. 12, xxxi. 31; Ps. cl. 4). Supposed to be the same as the Pandean pipe, which was the favorite with the shepherds in Homer's age.

The dulcimer (SUMFONIAH), an Assyrian instrument (Dan. iii. 5, 15); a triangular chest, with 50 wires (18 to 36 inches), played with two small hammers.

There are several words rendered musical instruments about which there are doubts; as DAHAVAN, 2d wife (Dan. vi. 8); MINNIM, *stringed instruments* (Ps. cl. 4; xlv. 8); NEBEL ASOR, *ten stringed psaltery* (Ps. xxxiii. 2, cxliv. 9); SHIDDAH *palanquin* (Eccl. ii. 8); SHALISHIM, *triangle,* or *cymbals* (1 Sam. xviii. 6).

MUSTARD, (*sinapis nigra*). Is found abundantly in Palestine both in a wild and cultivated state. The mustard plant grows to a very large size on the banks of the Jordan. In comparison with any other "garden herb" it would be a "tree."

MUTH-LAB'BEN. Occurs in the title of Ps. ix. Muthlab'ben either referred to the instrument or the tune to which the Psalm was to be sung.

MYN'DUS. Between Miletus and Halicarnassus, the residence of Jews for convenience in trade (1 Macc. xv. 23). Mentioned by Herodotus and Strabo for its ships and harbor. There is an ancient pier and other ruins at the site.

MY'RA. In Lycia, where Paul changed vessels on the way to Rome (Acts xxvii. 5). The city was on a hill, at the foot of which flowed a navigable stream, with a good harbor at its mouth (Pliny). There are ruins of various periods of its history; ornamented tombs, with inscriptions in the Lycian character; a very large theatre, of the Greek age; and a Byzantine church.

MYRRH (MOR). One of the ingredients in the "oil of holy ointment," and used as a perfume (Prov. vii. 17). It was one of the gifts brought to the infant Jesus (Matt. ii. 11). Myrrh was used for EMBALMING (John xix. 39).

The tree which produces the myrrh of commerce (*Balsamodendron myrrha*), has a hard wood and bark, with a strong odor. The gum is at first soft, like thick turpentine, hardening on exposure.

LOT (Gen. xxxvii. 25, xliii. 11), is also rendered myrrh, and is believed to refer to the odorous gum of the *cistus creticus,* ladanum. It is used as a stimulant in medicine, and also as a perfume.

MYR'TLE-TREE (Heb. HADAS). It is a shrub or tree common in Southern Europe, North Africa and Syria. Its berries are used as a substitute for spices. The Jews use it in their adornments at the Feast of Tabernacles (Neh. viii. 15).

MY'SIA. Province in the N. W. of Asia Minor, west of Bithynia, north of Eolis, or Lydia. It was celebrated for its corn and wine. Paul passed through it on his first journey (Acts xvi. 7, 8). Assos and Adramyttium were in Mysia, but Troas was independent.

MYS'TERY (Gr. *mustēriŏn*). One initiated. Truths hidden from the natural sense and from the merely natural reason (1 Cor. xiii. 2). The New Testament idea is a hidden truth to the natural sense, but seen by the spiritual sense, as

Paul says to the Colossians (ii. 2), and Jesus to his disciples (Matt. xiii. 11; Mark v. 11).

The word was used of those doctrines and facts which had been hidden, and were then unveiled both by outward facts and spiritual experience, as the kingdom of heaven, the doctrine of the cross, the resurrection, and the entire life of Jesus, which was the mystery of Godliness. It also refers to the meaning of parables and symbols.

N

NA'AM (*grace*). A Son of Caleb.

NA'AMAH (*pleasing*). 1. Daughter of Lamech, by Zillah.—2. Wife of Solomon and mother of king Rehoboam; she was an Ammonite.

NA'AMAH. Judah in the Shefelah (Josh. xv. 41), in the group with Lachish, etc. Lost.

NA'AMAN (*pleasantness*). 1. "Na'aman, the Syrian," Aramite warrior, cured of leprosy by Elisha (2 K. v.). See LEPROSY. This incident is referred to by Jesus (Luke iv. 27).—2. One of the family of Benjamin, who came down to Egypt with Jacob (Gen. xlvi. 21).

There is a Jewish tradition in Josephus (Ant. viii. 15, 5), which says that Naaman was the archer whose arrow struck Ahab with his mortal wound, and thus "gave deliverance to Syria." This feat gave the warrior a great place and favor at the court of king Benhahad and command of the army. He was also privy counselor to the king, and attended him to the Temple when he worshiped in state. In Judæa his leprosy would have compelled him to seclusion, and kept him away from the king and all others, but the Syrians were not so cautious. It was Naaman who went in and told his master (lord, the king, in verse 4). His carrying away earth has been imitated many times in ancient and modern times. The Campo Santo at Pisa is filled with earth carried from Aceldama. Pilgrims to Mecca always bring away something: dirt, sand or stones. Elisha was made known in Damascus by this cure, and well received by Naaman's successor, Hazael.

NA'AMATHITE (Job ii. 11, etc.). Zophar, one of Job's friends, was from NAAMAH; but it is supposed that it must be looked for in Arabia, where the Temanite and Shuhite, his other two friends, lived. Lost.

NA'AMITES. The descendants of Na'aman 2, mentioned in Num. xxvi. 40.

NA'ARAH (*a girl*). Second wife of Ashur, a descendant of Judah (1 Chr. iv. 5, 6).

NA'ARAI. Son of Ezbai, one of David's "valient men" (1 Chr. xi. 37).

NA'ARAN (*boyish*). An eastern limit of Ephraim (1 Chr. vii. 28. See GEZER). Naarath in Josh. xvi. 7. Perhaps Neara, from which Archelaus conducted water to irrigate the royal gardens at Jericho (Ant. xvii. 13, 1). It was between Ataroth and Jericho. There are large ruins at the foot of the hills and in the deep ravines a few miles north of Jericho, where there are also ruins; but no place has been pointed out as the site in question. *Wady Nawaimeh*, 3 miles N. of Jericho?

NAASH'ON or **NA'ASHON** (Heb. NAHSHON) (Ex. vi. 23).

NAAS'SON (Gr. *Naasson*), (Matt. i. 4; Luke iii. 32).

NA'ATHUS. Of the family of Addi (1 Esd. ix. 31).

NA'AZUZ. The name of a tree, translated thorn, in Isaiah vii. 18, 19, lv. 13, a thorn tree.

NA'BAL (*fool*). A large owner of sheep and goats, near Carmel of Judah, descended from Caleb. He refused to supply provisions requested by David, through his young men, whom he insulted

(1 Sam. xxv. 10, 11). His wife Abigail saved his life by appeasing the wrath of David. The excitement caused by the danger and rescue of Na'bal hastened his death, after which David married Abigail (1 Sam. xxv.). See ABIGAIL.

The history of Nabal is one of the few glimpses given of the private life of the Hebrews. Josephus says he was a Ziphite (Ant. vi. 13, 6), residing at Emmaus, south of Carmel in Judah. The vast flocks were pastured on the downs, and gathered yearly at shearing time, when there was feasting, and a joyous time (xxv. 2, 4, 36). David's ten messengers came to Nabal on one of these feast days, and were recognized by his shepherds as friends who had guarded them in the wilderness. They mentioned their services and David, and claimed a reward as for servants, but were denied by the churlish farmer. Josephus says he was not descended from Caleb, but was the son of a caleb, that is, a dog. The violence of his nature and manner on this occasion prevented his shepherds from telling him who David was, but his beautiful wife was ready to hear, and hastened to mend the mischief her hasty and obstinate husband had done. David had already vowed not to leave "a dog" even of the whole household of Nabal, when Abigail met him, and saluting him in the Eastern manner as a prince, explained to him in truly poetic phrases her husband's folly. David changed his mind, and Abigail returned, but finding her husband drunk, waited until next morning before telling him the news. When Nabal learned of the danger that had been only just averted by his wife's quick wit, his heart "became as a stone?" Probably a stroke of paralysis followed, terminating in death in ten days (v. 37, 38). David never forgot Nabal's death but when the great general Abner was murdered he said, mournfully, "Died Abner as Nabal (a fool) died." The death of Nabal was a divine judgment on unrestrained passion and vice.

NA'BOTH (*fruit produce*). A Jezreelite who was the owner of a vineyard coveted by king Ahab (see AHAB), near whose palace it was (1 K. xxi. 1, 2). Naboth declined to part with his land. Through the order of Jezebel, Ahab's wife, Naboth was publicly accused of blasphemy, conveyed beyond the walls and stoned to death with his children (2 K. ix. 26), the punishment for that crime (Lev. xxiv. 16; Num. xv. 30). Ahab then took possession. Elijah uttered the prophetic curse "In the place where the dogs licked the blood of Naboth, shall dogs lick thy blood even thine" (1 K. xxi.).

ROMAN MEDAL.

The trial of Naboth was a fearful mockery of justice. He, as an Elder, was set "on high," that is, in the seat of honor, at the head of the divan among the rulers, and then false witnesses, hired for the business, swore away his life. The prophet denounced the crime, and retribution followed the judicial murder. The same crime was planned against Jesus, and carried out. The retribution in this case being a total loss of judicial power, which had been so grossly abused.

Tristram thinks the site of the vineyard can be identified on the rocky slope near the ruins of ancient Jezreel, where "not a shrub now clothes the bare hillside. A watch tower there would have given a view of the country for many miles over the route of Jehu " (*Land of Israel*, page 130).

NA'CHON'S. Threshing floor (2 Sam. vi. 6). Called also Chiden's (1 Chr. xiii. 9), and after the sad event of Uzzah's death by the ark, it was named Perez Uzzah (perez, broken). (Ant. vii. 4, 2). Between Kirjath Jearim and Jerusalem.

NACHOR. NAHOR. 1. Mother of Abraham (Josh. xxiv. 2). Also spelled Nahor. The Hebrew H is a strong breathing, and is often written CH.—2. Grand father of Abraham (Luke iii. 34).

NA'DAB (*spontaneous*). 1. Eldest son of Aaron and Elisheba (Ex. vi. 23; Num. iii. 2).

Aaron, Nadab and Abihu, with seventy elders (Ex. xxiv. 1), were selected from the assembly of the people to worship "afar off," whilst Moses awaited God upon Mount Sinai. Nadab and his brother were afterwards destroyed by fire (Lev. x. 1) for burning in their censers fire not taken from that which perpetually burnt on the altar (Lev. vi. 13).—2. King Jeroboam's son (Jeroboam I), second king of Israel. He ascended the throne B. C. 954, reigned two years (1 K. xv. 25–31), and was slain at the siege of Gibbethon by his officer Baasha, who succeeded him, B. C. 953. (See ISRAEL).—3. Son of Shammai (1 Chr. ii. 28), of the tribe of Judah.—4. Son of Gibeon (viii. 30, ix. 36), of the tribe of Benjamin.

PAPYRUS, 1ST CENTURY.

NADAB'ATHA (1 Macc. ix. 3; Ant. xiii. 1, 4). GABATHA. From which the children of Jambi were escorting a bride with great pomp and music, when they were attacked by Jonathan and Simon. On the east of Jordan, near *Es Salt?* Josephus says the bride was the daughter of an illustrious Arabian.

NAG'GE (Heb. NOGAH, *splendor*). An ancestor of Jesus Christ (Luke iii. 25), who lived in the time of Onias I.

NA'HALAL (*pasture*). In Zebulon (Josh. xxi. 35). Na'hallal (error in xix. 15). Na'halol (Judg. i. 30). *Malul*, 4 miles southwest of Nazareth, in the plain of Esdraëlon.

NAHA'LIEL (*torrent of El*). One of the latest halting places; N. of the Arnon (Num. xxi. 19). Wady Encheyle, a branch of the Mojeb (Arnon). The word Encheyle is the Hebrew name Nahaliel reversed, or transposed. The identification of places by their names, even after the names have been changed by passing through several languages, is a work of patient research and thought, and was very successful in the case of Edward Robinson, who recovered several hundred localities in this way. There are many yet waiting for future research on the E. of Jordan.

NA'HAM (*consolation*). Brother of Hodiah, or Jehudijah, wife of Ezra (1 Chr. iv. 19).

NAHAMA'NI (*compassionate*). Returned with Zerubbabel and Jeshua from Babylon (Neh. vii. 7).

NA'HARAI (Heb. SNORER). Joab's armor-bearer (2 Sam. xxiii. 37).

NA'HASH (*serpent*). 1. King of the Ammonites (see AMMON). He treated the people of Jabesh-Gilead with the utmost cruelty, at which Saul attacked and destroyed the Ammonite force (1 Sam. xi. 1, 2–11). He retained the favor of David.—2. Mentioned only once (2 Sam. xvii. 16). The first husband of Jesse's wife; not Na'hash, the Ammonite.

NA'HATH (*rest*). 1. A duke, or sheikh, of Edom, eldest son of Reuel, the son of Esau (Gen. xxxvi. 13, 17; 1 Chr. i. 37).—2. A Kohathite Levite, son of Zophai (1 Chr. vi. 26).—3. A Levite in Hezekiah's reign: a collector of taxes, etc. (2 Chr. xxxi. 13).

NAH'BI (*hidden*). The son of Vophsi; a Naphtalite, one of the 12 spies (Num. xiii. 14).

NA'HOR (*snorting, snoring*). 1. Abraham's grand-father, the son of Serug (Gen. xi. 22–25). —2. Grand-son of Na'hor, called Na'hor, brother to Abraham. He married Milcah. Eight of his sons were by this wife (Gen. xxii. 20–24). Na'hor remained in the land of his birth.

GENEALOGY OF NAHOR'S DESCENDANTS TO JACOB.

		1. NAHOR.	
1.	Nahor.	2. Terah.	
2.	Terah.	3. Abraham.	
"		4. Nahor.	
"		5. Haran.	
3.	Abraham.	6. Isaac	(mother).
4.	Nahor.	7. Tebah.	Reumah.
"		8. Gaham.	"
"		9. Thahash.	"
"		10. Maacah.	"
"		11. Huz.	Milcah.
"		12. Buz.	"
"		13. Kemuel.	"
"		14. Chesed.	"
"		15. Hazo.	"
"		16. Pildash.	"
"		17. Jidlaph.	"
"		18. Bethuel.	"
11.	Huz, Uz.	19. Job.	
12.	Buz.	20. Elihu.	
13.	Kemuel.	21. Aram.	[dæans.
14.	Chesed.	22. Chasidim or Chal-	
18.	Bethuel.	23. Laban.	
"		24. Rebekah.	
23.	Laban.	25. Leah.	
"		26. Rachel.	
	Isaac.	27. Esau. 24. Rebekah	
"		28. Jacob.	"

NAHOR, THE CITY OF (Gen. xxiv. 10).

NAH'SHON (*enchanter*). Also written Naason and Naashon; son of Amminadab, and prince of the children of Judah (1 Chr. ii. 10), at the numbering in the wilderness (Ex. vi. 23; Num. i. 7, etc.). Elisheba, the wife of Aaron, was his sister. His son Talmon became the husband of Rahab after the fall of Jericho.

NA'HUM (*consolation*). See HISTORY OF THE BOOKS.

NAIL.—1. (T'FAR). A nail or claw of man or animal (Deut. xxi. 12; Dan. iv. 33, vii. 19). A point used in writing, as signets are engraved on gems or hard stones (Jer. xvii. 1). The captive wife was "to make herself neat," that is, to *stain* her nails (not *pare*), with the henna dye (Deut. xxi. 12). A nail (Is. xxii. 23–25, xxxiii. 20), a stake (xxxiii. 20). Tent peg (Judg. iv. 21, etc.). See JAEL—TENT. Tent pegs of wood and iron. Nails of the cross (John xx. 25, and Col. ii. 14).

NA'IN (*pleasant*). The scene of one of the greatest miracles of Jesus, the raising of the widow's son (Luke vii. 12). It is now a small village, of 20 huts, on a rocky slope, in the midst of extensive ruins of an ancient place, on the northwestern end of Little Hermon (*Jebel ed Duhy*). There are sepulchral caves along the steep eastern approach from the plain, and also on the other side of the town (*Rob.*) It is but a few miles from Nazareth, in the vicinity of Endor and Shunem, places noted in the history, and its name remains unchanged from its ancient form. The custom of carrying the dead out of the villages, or cities, is still practiced in the East, as it was when Jesus met the procession coming out of Nain. And there is now on a hill side, about ten minutes walk from the village, the grave yard, with a few whitewashed grave stones, unfenced. The extent of the ruins of Nain indicate an ancient city of some extent, with a wall and gates. But now there is a painful desolation around the few stone and mud hovels, with flat earth roofs, and doors only three feet high. Fountains never change, and the one here close to the village on the west side, is the best reason for the location of the dwelling place. It is a square cistern, arched over with masonry, being supplied with water through an acqueduct from the hills.

NAI'OTH (*college buildings*). Where Samuel and his disciples lived (1 Sam. xix. 18, etc.). Where David fled for refuge from Saul. Samuel had a school here. Verse 20 is rendered by the Targum—Jonathan, "They saw the company of scribes singing praises, and Samuel teaching, standing over them." As Naioth was *in* Ramah (ver. 19), it was probably a dwelling used for a school in the town of Ramah. See 2 K. xxii. 14. Huldah lived in a college in Jerusalem.

NAME (Heb. SHEM). The root GNA, to know, has given rise to the Sanscrit *naman*, Greek *ŏnŏma*, Latin *nomen*, Gothic *nama*, and our *name*.

No monuments are more enduring than names. Sometimes they are the most ancient records of persons, places and things. They are fossils of thought. Bible names have almost always a meaning, which is often given by the writer for a purpose. The meaning of a name being known, we are able to get a better knowledge of persons and their history, especially if the name was given for some special reason or act. This work is very difficult because men's names are so constantly changing with the growth or decay of language, and the substitution of one language for another.

The Hebrews gave but one name to a child, except in peculiar cases (as Solomon, Jedidjah), or where it was necessary to add the father's or mother's name, if the mother was the more noted. There is but one David, but there are several named Jesus, as the Son of Sirach, etc. The ancient custom was more simple than the modern, which (among the Arabs) exalts a man's external affairs by giving him names and titles carrying terms of flattery and display. The custom of naming—simple, compound, or ornamental—indicates very nearly the age of the person so named. There were 3 kinds: 1. Simple. 2. Compound. 3. Derived. 1. Simple names are numerous, and quite plain in their meaning, as—ARIEH, lion; DEBORAH, bee; DAN, judge; TAMAR, palm-tree; JONAH, dove; DISHAN, gazelle. Diminutives were often used, as, Zebulon, (*my little dweller with me*), and Jeduthun (*little praiser*), a director of musical affairs in David's cabinet. 2. Compound names express more complete ideas than the simple, and are therefore more important in history. Abiezer, Abital, Abigail, Abraham, compounded of Ab, father, or maker. Abijail (*joymaker*, or *cheerful*), at first, probably, an epithet only, but afterward a name by consent and use. The Arabs have a habit of giving names in sport, or derision, which the Hebrews did not indulge in, as—Abul-Hussain, the father of the little castle, that is, a fox who lives in a hole; Abu-Ayuba, the father of Job, that is, the camel, because it is as patient as Job. A man is often called father of a place, village, or city, who was the settler, or builder, or only the ruler, of that place. See FATHER. The prefix AB was often joined to a term or name, to show dignity or character, as—ABNER, father of light, that is, a wise counselor. Sometimes AB appears to mean brother, as, Achiram, brother of Ram (perhaps one who was accidentally fortunate). The word HUD, splendor, was compounded with Jehovah, as Jehudi, a Jewess (correctly Hajehudiah), that is, Jehovah's splendor (God's work). CHUR, free (Hur in Ex. xvii. 10), and ISH, a man, forms Asshur, a freeman. ISHOD, man of beauty.

The word, AM people, forms with many names of countries, cities, etc., names of the people, as distinguished from families; as AMMINADAB, that is he who belongs to the whole people; ITHREAM,

the residue of the people; YORKOAM (1 Chr. ii. **44,** Jorkoam), increaser of the people, at first a man's name, then the name of the place founded or enlarged by him.

Many compound names carry a religious sense with them, containing some divine name. These are found, in some cases, to contain a name and a verb, or a complete sentence; as NATHANAEL given by El (Theodore and Dorothea in Greek are on the same model). HOSHEA, help, with JAH becomes Jehoshua, God's help, or salvation. MELEH, king, with AB, father, becomes Abimelech, father king; with ZEDEK, righteousness, becomes Melchizedek, king of righteousness; ADONAI, lord, RAM, hight, Adoniram, lord of exaltation.

3. The names of men became names of women by a change of termination; as Meshullum, Meshullumeth; Haggai, Haggith; Dan, Dinah; Judah, Judith. (This does not account for the use of names of men which are used for women without change, and which were probably used as a kind of monument, being compound words, and incapable of regular feminine forms). Ai (imperfect form of Jah) with AMIT, truth, means truth of Jah; JEDID, darling, with Jah, Jedidiah, Jah's darling. Some names seem to have been used for both men and women, even the feminine forms, as Shelomith, feminine of Shelomo (Solomon), for a man (1 Chr. xxvi. 25). Many titles of men in office were feminine, as PEKAH, governer, KOHELETH, preacher. AB, father, becomes in the plural ABOTH (feminine) not ABIM (masculine). ZERUB-BABEL (*scattered in Babylon*), was a hint of the man's history. Many names indicate the condition of the National history at the time they were given; as a time of religious elevation in Hodaiah, praise ye Jah; Elioënai, mine eyes look to El; Zephaniah, watcher of the Lord.

The pure Hebrew names Eleazar became Grecized into Lazarus; Joshua became Jason, and Jesus; Alcimus from Eleakim.

In the Old Testament there are many names which are derived from the heathen idols, as Bethaven, house of idols; Gurbaal, place of baal; Hadarazer, whose help is Hadad; and in the New Testament, as Apollonius, Phœbe, Artemas.

The Hebrews gave their children the names of many natural objects, as Tamar, a palm tree; Hadassah, myrtle; Zipporah, sparrow; and Zillah, shadow; Shimrath, vigilant; Tabitha, gazelle; Rachel, ewe; Shual, fox; Cheran, lamb. The right of naming belonged to the father, but was allowed to the mother in many cases. The

PLAN OF ANCIENT TOMB.

time was usually at the day of circumcision, the 8th for boys, and for girls at any time during the first year. The boy often was called son of his father if he became noted, or to distinguish him from other relatives of the same name.

When a man had no sons he was the subject of his friends' sympathy who gave him an imaginary son, whose name was added to his. If a son became famous the father was honored by being called the father of such a one.

The name often indicated the character or office of the person, as Isaiah, Jah is helper. When God elects a man for a certain work he is said to call him by name, as Bezaleel, the shadow of God (Ex. xxxi. 1). Receiving a new name from God is an expression founded on the custom of giving children or others new names when some act of theirs, or event in their history, or other cause, made them noted, as the change of Abram to Abraham; and means a new personal relation to God (Is. lxv. 15, lxii. 2; Rev. ii. 17, iii. 12).

NANE'A, THE TEMPLE OF. At Elymais, rich with the trophies of Alexander, and plundered by Antiochus Epiphanes (1 Macc. vi. 1–4; 2 Macc. i. 13–16).

NA'OMI (*my pleasantness*). Wife of Elimelech, mother-in-law of Ruth (Ruth i. 2, iii. 1, iv. 3). She buried her husband and sons, Mahlon and Chilion, in the land of Moab. She returned to Bethlehem with Ruth. Correctly, NOOMI.

family of Christians in Rome, alluded to by Paul in Rom. xvi. 11.

NARD. (See SPIKENARD).

NAS'BAS. Tobit's nephew, who, with Achiacharus, attended the wedding of Tobias (Tob. xi. 18).

NASITH. NEZIAH (1 Esd. v. 32).

NASOR, THE PLAIN OF. Near Kedesh Naphtali, the scene of a battle between Jonathan and Demetrius (1 Macc. xi. 67). HAZOR.

NA'THAN (*gift*). 1. Hebrew prophet in the reign of David and Solomon. In the consultation with David upon the building of the Temple (2 Sam. vii.

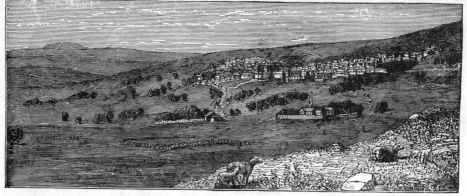

NAZARETH.

NA'PHISH (*refreshment*). (1 Chr. v. 19). A tribe descended from the last but one of the sons of Ishmael; settled in the Hauran and Gilead; allies of Jetur (who was in Ituræa). Traces of this tribe may be looked for in Arabia, for they were driven out by Reuben, Gad, and Manasseh. They were wealthy when dispossessed, having lost to the Israelites 50,000 camels, 250,000 sheep, and 2,000 asses. Ptolemy says the Agræi were a people of N. Arabia.

NAPH'ISI (1 Esd. v. 31). NEPHUSIM.

NAPH'TALI (NIPHTALI, *wrestled*). 6th son of Jacob, 2d-born of Bilhah (Gen. xxx. 8). He had 4 sons when Jacob went into Egypt (xlvi. 24). There is not a word said about him personally in the Scriptures. See EXODUS, TWELVE TRIBES.

NAPHTALI, MOUNT. The high land of the district occupied by the tribe (Josh. xx. 7).

NAPH'THAR (*a cleaning*). The name given to the substance said to have been found in the pit in which the sacred fire of the altar had been concealed at the destruction of the temple. This fable is related in 2 Macc. i. 19–36.

NAPH'TUHIM. Called on the Egyptian monuments Na-Petu, the people of (*Nine*) *bows.* The chief city of this nation (Naputa) is now in ruins, on the island of Meroë, on the Upper Nile, where there are found pyramids, temples (one of Osiris and Ammon), sphinxes, and many beautiful sculptures. In the British Museum are two lions, sculptured in red granite, fine works of art, brought from this ruined city.

NAPKIN. (See HANDKERCHIEF). As a wrapper to fold up money (Luke xix. 20). As a cloth bound round the head of a corpse (John xi. 44, xx. 7). As an article of dress; probably as a turban, or as the Bedawin *keffieh* (Acts xix. 12). Possibly the napkin was a cloth adapted to a variety of uses, such as described; also for a girdle; worn over the face, etc.

NARCIS'SUS (*the Narcissus plant*). One of a

2, 3, 17) Nathan reproves David for his sin with Bath-sheba, and prophesies in the form of a parable of "the rich man and the ewe-lamb" (2 Sam. xii. 1–12). Nathan was the educator of Solomon (2 Sam. xii. 25). In the last days of David Nathan assisted the cause of Solomon. He assisted in the inauguration of Solomon (1 K. i. 8). He had a son, Zabud, who was the "king's friend." He wrote a Life of David (1 Chr. xxix. 29) and a Life of Solomon (2 Chr. ix. 29). The loss of his biography of David is a heavy one to history.—2. Son of David by Bath-sheba (1 Chr. iii. 5, xiv. 4, and 2 Sam. v. 14). He appears as one of the forefathers of Joseph in Christ's genealogy (Luke iii. 31).— 3. Related to one of David's "valiant men" (2 Sam. xxiii. 36; 1 Chr. xi. 38).—4. One of the chief men who returned from Babylon with Ezra on his second expedition (Ezr. viii. 16; 1 Esd. viii. 44).

NATHAN'AEL (*given of God*). Born at Cana of Galilee. One of the Twelve, under the name of Bartholomew (son of Talmai). (See BARTHOLOMEW). He was one of the seven Apostles to whom Jesus appeared after the resurrection at the Sea of Tiberias. When introduced to Jesus by Philip, Jesus said, "Behold an Israelite indeed, in whom there is no deceit," thus making his name almost a synonym for sincerity. Tradition says he preached in Arabia Felix, having Matthew's gospel, and was crucified in Armenia or Cilicia.

NATHANI'AS. Nathan, of the sons of Bani (1 Esd. ix. 34; Ezr. x. 39).

NA'THAN-ME'LECH (*placed by the king*). Steward in the court of Josiah (2 K. xxiii. 11).

NATION. Genesis x. gives the descendants of Noah. A record of primitive geography and ethnology of the utmost importance. By this record the geographical distribution of Noah's descendants can be ascertained, as also the origin of the earliest nations. The dispersion of these nations and the circumstances related to that important event, are recorded in Gen. xi. The date of this event of the dispersion can be fixed from the genealogy of Shem, here recorded. (See BABEL).

Many nations and countries have been named after Shem, whose descendants wandered and divided into distinct tribes. This tendency is still a characteristic of the Arabs. See HAM. JAPHETH.

NA'UM. Son of Esli (Luke iii. 25).

NAVE (Heb. GAV). The central part of a wheel.

NA'VE (Gr. *Nauè*). Joshua's father NUN (Eccl. xlvi. 1): so called in the Septuagint.

NAZARENE. An inhabitant of NAZARETH. Especially associated with the name of Christ and his followers, who were called Nazarenes (Acts xxiv. 5). It was used as a name of contempt to Christ's followers. In Christ's family making their home in Nazareth, the prophesy of Isaiah was fulfilled (Is. xi. 1; Jer. xxiii. 5), Christ being the young branch from the royal family of David.

NAZ'ARETH (*the branch*). First mentioned in Matt. ii. 23, or rather, in the order of time, in Luke i. 26, as the scene of the Annunciation to Mary of the birth and character of Jesus (v. 31–33). Before this event the place was unknown to history, but since then its name has become a household word through all the Christian world, equally reverenced with Bethlehem and Jerusalem.

A low, undulating ridge of hills encloses the green plain that lies like a lake, with Nazareth built on one of its shores. The valley runs nearly east and west, is about a mile long, and a quarter of a mile wide; the hills vary in hight from 100 to 500 ft. above its level; the highest, Neby Ismail, being 1800 feet above the ocean. The soil is rich, and well cultivated, producing a great variety of fruit, grain, vegetables, and flowers, which ripen early and in rare perfection. Population about 4,000, nearly all Christians (Latin and Greeks), except a few Arabs, and not one Jew.

The parents of Jesus came here soon after their return from Egypt (Luke ii. 39); and after the visit to the Temple, when he was twelve years old, Jesus returned here with them (ii. 51); he grew up here to manhood (iv. 16); from here he went down to Jordan to be baptized by John (Mark i. 9; Matt. iii. 13); his first teaching in public was in its synagogue (xiii. 54); here he was first rejected (Luke iv. 29); and Jesus of Nazareth was a part of the inscription on the cross (John xix. 19).

The view from the top of Neby Ismail is very extensive, and includes many interesting Scripture localities, being one of the most noted in Palestine, combining the elements of the beautiful and the sublime. In the north are the white peaks of Lebanon, and Hermon towering high above them, because nearer. Eastward, the Hauran, Gilead, Tabor, Little Hermon, and Gilboa. South, the Plain of Esdraëlon, the hills of Samaria; and west, Carmel and the Mediterranean. The villages in the view are Cana, Nain, Endor, Jezreel, Taanach, and many ruins not yet identified.

The rock of this whole region is a soft, white marl, easily crumbled; and there is probably not a house, or structure of any kind, nor even a loose stone, remaining of the time of Christ's residence there. Since the general features of hill and valley, fountains and water-courses, could not have greatly changed, we may accept the location of the "steep place," near the Maronite Church, and the Fountain of the Virgin, as historical. A great many other localities are pointed out by the residents as traditional sites of every event mentioned in the Gospels as having occurred there, but they

MAP OF NAZARETH.

have no other interest than in so far as they recall the gospel narrative.

NAZ'ARITE (Heb. NAZIR). Either a man or woman who, under ancient Hebrew law, bound himself or herself to abstain from wine and all products of the grape; to wear the hair long and uncut, and to observe purification in abstaining from contact with the dead. If they witnessed death or otherwise approached death, their consecration had to be entirely recommenced. The period of observance of this vow varied from eight days to a month, or even a life time. When this period had concluded, offerings were made, the hair was cut off and burnt, and the Nazarite was discharged from his vow (Num vi.; Amos ii. 11, 12). Paul assisted four Christian Jews in this ceremony (Acts xxi. 20–26).

NEAH (*the shaking*). Landmark on Zebulon's west border (Josh. xix. 13). *El Ain*, 3 miles N. W. of Nazareth.

NEAP'OLIS (*new city*). The first place visited by Paul in Macedonia (Acts xvi. 11). On a rocky promontory, in a wide and beautiful bay, stands the Turkish village Kavala (5,000 inhab.), in the midst of the ruins of the ancient city. There was an aqueduct for bringing water from a distance of 12 miles; near the city, it passed a ravine over a double tier of arches, 80 feet above the brook below, in Roman style, hewn and cemented; fine sarcophagi, with inscriptions, of the age of Claudius, Ionic columns, and sculptured figures, besides foundations of ancient houses, etc., are witnesses of its ancient importance.

2. Shechem was also called Neapolis in Vespasian's time.

3. The bishops of Neapolis in Arabia were present at the councils of Chalcedon and Constantinople; a place now called Suleim, on Jebel Hauran (*Porter*, Damascus, ii. 85).

NEARI'AH (*servant of Jah*). 1. Son of Shemaiah (1 Chr. iii. 22, 23).—2. Son of Ishi, captain of 500 Simeonites (iv. 42).

NE'BAI (*fruit-bearer*). One who sealed the covenant (Neh. x. 19).

NEBAI'OTH. NEBA'JOTH. Ishmael's first-born (Gen. xxv. 13). Esau married Mahalath, the sister of Nebajoth (xxviii. 9). The country from the Euphrates to the Red Sea was called in Josephus' time Nabatene (Ant. i. 13, 4; Gen. xxv. 18). They were called by the Arabs *Nabat* (or *Nabeet*), and were celebrated for their agriculture, astronomy, magic and medicine, accounts of which have been recently discovered in some ancient books of theirs, written from 2500 to 600 B. C., consisting of a book of agriculture, one of poisons, the works of Tenkeloosha, the Babylonian, and the Book of the Secrets of the Sun and Moon; all of which were translated in A. D. 904 by Ibn Washiyeh (*Keysee*). The rock-temples of Petra, in Edom, were the works of this people, who are thus proved to have been a highly cultivated race many ages before the Greeks.

NEBO.

NEBAL'LAT (*secret folly*). Benjamite town, after the Captivity (Neh. xi. 34). *Beit Nebala*, 4 miles N. E. of Lydda (*Rob.*).

NE'BAT (*look*). Father of JEROBOAM (1 K. xi. 26).

NE'BO, MOUNT. From which Moses took his first and last view of the Promised Land (Deut. xxxii. 49), and where he died and was buried in one of its ravines (xxxiv. 6). Located by Tristram (*Land of Israel*, 535) 3 miles S. W. of Heshbon; overlooking the mouth of the Jordan, over against Jericho, meeting every condition of the text.

NE'BO (*project*). Town east of Jordan, on the Mishor, in Gad (Num. xxxii. 3, 38); a ruin, 3 miles west of Heshbon, on the side of *Wady Heshban*.—2. In Benjamin, now called *Beit Nubah*, 12 miles N. W. of Jerusalem, in *Wady Mansur*. The Crusaders built the Castle of Arnaldi here (*William of Tyre*, xiv. 3).

NE'BO (*interpreter of the gods*). A Babylonish god. Nebo was the god of learning and letters among the Chaldæans, Babylonians and Assyrians (Is. xlvi. 1; Jer. xlviii. 1). Nebo was the Babylonian name of the planet Mercury. This word is in the formation of several names, such as Nebuchadnezzar, Nebuzaradan, Nebushasban, etc. The cut represents the statue of the god set up by Pul, king of Assyria, in the Bristish Museum, London.

NEBUCHADNEZ'ZAR, or **NEBUCHADREZ'ZAR** (NEBO THE MIGHTY). The son of Nabopolassar, king of Chaldæa and founder of the Babylonian Empire. Nebuchadnez'zar, after having succeeded in recovering Carchemish, by defeating Necho, king of Egypt (Jer. xlvi. 2–12), and conquering Phœnicia, Palestine and Jerusalem, marched into Egypt, when he was informed of the death of his father. He hurried back, accompanied by his light troops, to secure his succession to the throne, which he ascended B. C. 604; the main army and captives (amongst whom were Daniel, Hananiah, Mishael and Azariah) following him by a longer route. These captives were of royal lineage, and the king had them educated in the language and learning of the Chaldæans, with a view to their employment in court (2 K. xxiv. 1; 2 Chr. xxxvi. 6; Dan. i. 1). Nebuchadnez'zar had left the conquered Jehoiakim, king of Judah, upon the throne as a tributary prince, but he soon after rebelled, probably anticipating support from Egypt (2 K. xxiv. 1). Phœnicia followed in the rebellion, and Nebuchadnez'zar, after having invested Tyre, advanced upon Jerusalem, which immediately submitted. He punished Jehoiakim with death, placing that king's son, Jehoiachin, upon the throne of Judah.. This king soon after revolting, caused Nebuchadnez'zar for a third time to march to Jerusalem; he took Jehoiachin captive, together with ten thousand, amongst whom were Ezekiel the prophet, and Mordecai, the uncle of Esther (Esth. ii. 6). He also stripped the Temple and the treasury of riches, and placed the king's uncle, Zedekiah, upon the throne. After nine years, Zedekiah rebelled, the neighboring princes assisting him. The king of Babylon again marched to Judah, and after an obstinate siege of nearly a year, during which time he repelled an incursion of the Egyptians, he entered Jerusalem, seized Zedekiah, whose children he put to death before his eyes, and sent him, fettered, to Babylon, after having put out his eyes (2 K. xxiv. 25; 2 Chr. xxxvi.). Nebuchadnezzar raised his kingdom and city to the greatest splendor; the marvellous hanging gardens are ascribed to him, erected to please Amytis, his queen, by imitating the groves of her native country, Media. The ruins of Birs Nimroud attest the magnificence of his works; these are situated a few miles from the site of the city of Babylon. He died about B. C. 562, after reigning forty years.

NEBUSHAS'BAN (*adherent of Nebo*); an officer at the capture of Jerusalem. He was chief of the eunuchs (Jer. xxxix. 13).

NEBUZAR'ADAN (*favors*). Captain of the GUARD, an officer of high rank in the court of Nebuchadnezzar, especially engaged in the sieges of Jerusalem (1 K. xxv. 8–20; Jer. xxxix. 9, xl. 1, lii. 12, 30).

NECHO. PHARAOH 9 (2 Chr. xxxv. 20, 22).

NECH'OSHETH. Sometimes translated *brass*, but properly means *copper*—sometimes bronze. See METALS, p. 201. (Job xxviii. 2).

NECK. Used both literally (Gen. xxvii. 16) and figuratively (Luke xiv. 20). Burdens were borne on the neck (Gen. xxvii. 40). The neck was used figuratively for several ideas: To denote subjection, by placing the foot on it (Josh. x. 24); seizing a person by the neck securely (Job xvi. 12). To be stiff-necked was to be stubborn, rebellious.

NECO'DAN (1 Esd. v. 37).

NĔC'ROMANCER (Deut. xviii. 11). DIVINATION.

NEDABI'AH (*whom Jah impels*). A son of Jeconiah (1 Chr. iii. 18).

NEEANI'AS. Son of Hachaliah (Ecclus. xlix. 13).

NEEDLE'S EYE. Supposed to mean a narrow door, or gateway, too low for a camel to pass through, standing. They are unloaded, and forced to creep through on their knees.

NE'GEB (*south*). The country S. of Beersheba. Its character is that of wide-rolling downs, green in winter, but bare in summer, affording pasturage, but not grain-crops.

NEG'INAH. (Heb.) A term by which all stringed-instruments are described (Ps. lxi.; Job xxx. 9): is the singular form of the next word.

NEG'INOTH. A general term for stringed-instruments: Ps. iv., vi., xlv., liv., lv. lxxvi., are addressed to leaders of stringed-instruments. See MUSIC, and MUSICAL INSTRUMENTS.

NEHEL'AMITE (*strong one*) **THE.** A false prophet (Jer. xxix. 24, 31, 32).

NEHEMIAH (*comforter of Jah*). His genealogy is not known, although he was perhaps of the tribe of Judah. He was the son of Hachaliah (Neh. i. 1). His brother was Hanani (Neh. vii. 2); most probably of royal descent and not of the priesthood as supposed from Neh. x. 1-8, but as a prince in Neh. ix. 38. His office was that of cup-bearer to King Artaxerxes Longimanus. At his own request he was appointed governor of Jerusalem about B. C. 444, when he relieved the people from the oppression of the Samaritans. In this good work he was assisted by Ezra (Neh. viii. 1, 9, 13, xii. 36). See HISTORY OF THE BOOKS.

NE'HILOTH (Heb. CHALAL). A term for perforated wind instruments of all kinds (1 Sam. x. 5).

NE'HUM (*comfort*). One who returned from captivity (Neh. vii. 7).

NEHUSH'TA (*brass*). Daughter of Elnathan (2 K. xxiv. 8).

NEHUSH'TAN (*brazen*), (Num. xxi. 8). The brazen serpent which Moses set up in the wilderness. It was destroyed by Hezekiah as it had become debased to the service of idolatry in the reign of Ahaz his father. Hezekiah gave the name Nehushtan to it as a term of derision, implying it to be mere brass (2 K. xviii. 4).

NE'IEL (*treasure of God*). Landmark of Asher, now *Miar*, on a lofty hight 10 ms. N. W. of Nazareth (Josh. xix. 27).

NEK'EB (*cavern*). On the N. border of Naphtali (Judg. iv. 11). Lost.

NE'KODA (*distinguished*). 1. The children of Nekoda who returned from captivity (Ezr. ii. 48). —2. The same who were unable to prove their descent from Israel (Ezr. ii. 60).

NEM'UEL (Heb. JEMUEL). 1. Son of Eliab (Num. xxvi. 9).—2. Son of Simeon (xxvi. 12).

NEM'UELITES, THE. Descendants of NEMUEL (Num. xxvi. 12).

NE'PHEG (*sprout*). 1. Son of Izhar (Ex. vi. 21).—2. Son of David (2 Sam. vi. 15).

NEPH'EW (Heb. NECHED), (*progeny*). Has

various meanings, as in Judg. xii. 14, Job xviii. 19. In Gen. xxi. 23, son's son.

NE'PHI (NAPHTHAR), (2 Macc. i. 36).

NE'PHIS. Children of Nebo (Ezr. ii. 29).

THE TOXICOA.

NE'PHISH (NAPHISH), (1 Chr. v. 19).

NEPHISH'ESIM. Those who returned from captivity (Neh. vii. 52).

NEPH'THALI (Tob. i. 1, 2, 4, 5).

NEPH'THALIM (Tob. vii. 3).

NEPHTO'AH, THE WATER OF. Landmark between Judah and Benjamin (Josh. xv. 9). *Ain Lifta*, 2½ miles N. W. of Jerusalem. Another fountain, *Ain Yalo*, in *Wady el Werd* (*roses*), is urged as the site by some, on account of the text in 1 Sam. x. 2.

NEPHU'SIM (*expansions*), (Ezr. ii. 50).

NER (*light*). Son of Jehiel (1 Chr. ix. 36).

NERD or **NARD.** See SPIKENARD.

NE'REUS. Name of an ancient sea-god. A Christian at Rome (Rom. xvi. 15).

NER'GAL (Heb.). An Assyrian deity (2 K. xvii. 30) represented in the Hellenic mythology by Mars. He presided over wars. In the monuments he is entitled "the storm ruler," "the king of battle," "the champion of the gods," "the god of the chase," etc. The allusion to Nergal in the Scriptures is in 2 K. xvii. 30, equivalent to the man-lion of Nineveh.

NER'GAL SHARE'ZER. 1. One of Nebuchadnezzar's military chiefs (Jer. xxix. 3).—2. The chief magi under the same king (Jer. xxxix. 3, 13) with the title Rab-Mag. Babylonian inscriptions suggest the identification of 2 with Neriglissar, who murdered Evil Merodach and became king of Babylon.

NE'RI. Son of Melchi (Luke iii. 27).

NERI'AH (*lamp of Jah*). Son of Maaseiah (Jer. xxxii. 12).

NERI'AS. NERIAH (Bar. i. 1).

NE'RO (*brave*). The Roman emperor (Lucius Domitius Ahenobardus) born A. D. 37. He was named Nero Claudius, etc., by his grand uncle Claudius, who had adopted him. Made emperor, A. D. 54. Accused of having burnt Rome, but Nero tortured and burnt Christians charging them with the crime. Both Paul and Peter suffered martyrdom during his reign. He committed suicide A. D. 68, to avoid retribution. The Cæsar mentioned in Acts xxv. 8, xxvi. 32, xxviii. 19; Phil. iv. 22, is Nero; also Augustus in Acts xxv. 21, 25.

NEST (KEN). As in Job xxxix. 27; Matt. viii. 20: also as a dwelling as in Num. xxiv. 21. In Gen. vi. 14, *rooms* mean *nests or cribs*.

NET. The terms for net in the Bible are numerous, and refer to its application or construction. In the N. T. there appears *sagênê*, denoting a large, hauling-net (Matt. xiii. 47); *amphiblestron*, a casting-net (Matt. iv. 20; Mark i. 16); and *diktuon*, a similar kind of net (Matt. iv. 20; Mark i. 18; Luke v. 2). Nets were used for hunting, as well as fishing. The Egyptians made their nets of flax, with wooden needles. In Egypt bird and animal nets were used, which last also appear on the Nineveh marbles. These nets were so constructed that the sides closed in upon the prey, or with movable frames. Net has frequently a figurative use, as in Ps. ix. 15, xxv. 15, xxxi. 4, as expressing God's vengeance, as in Ez. xii. 13; Hos. vii. 12.

NETHAN'EEL (*given of God*). 1. Son of Zuar (Num. 1, 8).—2. Son of Jesse (1 Chr. ii. 14).—3. A priest in David's reign (xv. 24).—4. Father of Shemaiah (xxiv. 6).—5. Son of Obed-edom (xxvi. 4).—6. A prince of Judah (2 Chr. xvii. 7).—7. A chief Levite (xxxv. 9).—8. A priest of Pashur (Ezr. x. 22).—9. Another priest (Neh. xii. 21).—10. A Levite (ver. 36).

NETHANI'AH (*given of Jah*). 1. Son of Elishama (2 K. xxv. 23), of the royal family of Judah.— 2. Son of Asaph, a chief in the course of the Temple-choir (1 Chr. xxv. 2, 12).—3. One of the Levites who taught the law in Judah (2 Chr. xvii. 8).—4. Father of Jehudi (Jer. xxxvi. 14).

NETH'INIM (*dedicated*). A body of men *given* to assist the Levites in the performance of the rites of the Temple (Ezr. vii. 24) as the Levites were given to Aaron (Num. ii. 9, viii. 19). The Nethinim performed the menial offices of the Temple, living near it. They assisted in rebuilding the Temple walls, etc., after the return from captivity.

CHERUB.

NET'OPHAH (*a dropping*). Peopled after the return from captivity (Ezr. ii. 22). Two of David's captains were natives of this place (2 Sam. xxiii. 28). At the dedication of the wall built by Nehemiah, the singers were found residing in the *villages* of this people; so there were more than one town, perhaps a district, near Bethlehem. Seraiah (*warrior of Jehovah*), a native of this place, was an accomplice of Ishmael in the murder of Gedaliah (2 K. xxv. 23). Um Tuba, 2 ms. N. E. of Bethlehem. Beit Nettif, in the Wady Sumt, is mentioned in the Jewish traditions as famous for "oil of Netopha" (Rob. ii. 17).

NETOPH'ATHI (Neh. xii. 28).

NETO'PHATHITE (Heb. NETOPHATHI) THE. One from NETOPHAH (2 Sam. xxiii. 28, 29).

NET'TLE (Heb. CHARUL), (Job xxx. 7). A plant of rapid growth, and well known for its power of stinging. They have minute tubular hairs, which emit a poisonous fluid when pressed.

NEW MOON. Marked the commencement of each month (see MONTH), and was celebrated as a holy-day. Offerings were made as ordained (Num. xxviii. 11, 15). All business was suspended (Amos viii. 5). The Day of the N. M. was recognized as a family festival with religious observances, although not especially ordained. It was proclaimed by the trumpet-sound (Ps. lxxxi. 3). After the establishment of Christianity the observance was discontinued.

NEW TESTAMENT. See HISTORY OF THE BOOKS.

NE'ZIAH (*illustrious*). Ancestor of Nethinim (Ezr. ii. 54).

NE'ZIB (Josh. xx. 43). Beit Nusib, in the low, hilly district between Beit Jibrin and Hebron. There are ruins of a building, 120 × 30 ft., and a tower 60 ft. sq., of ancient, massive masonry, besides broken columns.

NIB'HAZ (Heb. NABACH), (*to bark*). A deity of the Avites; the figure of a dog, or dog-headed man (2 K. xvii. 31). The Syrians worshiped the dog, and there was a colossal figure of one between Beirut and Tripolis, which has been lately destroyed.

NIB'SHAN (*light-soil*). A city on the W. shore of the Dead Sea (Josh. xv. 62). DESERT. 2. EN-GEDI.

NICA'NOR. 1. Son of Patroclus (2 Macc. viii. 9). A general under Antiochus Epiphanes and Demetrius I. He assisted in the first expedition of Lycias, B. C. 166 (1 Macc. iii. 38). He was defeated, but, after the death of Antiochus, Demetrius made him governor of Judæa (2 Macc. xiv. 12).

NICODE'MUS (NAKDIMON, *innocent of blood*). A Pharisee, ruler of the Jews, teacher of the law (John ii. 23, iii. 1, 10), a member of the Sanhedrin. He was probably wealthy, as his valuable tribute to the tomb of the Lord indicates. His timidity was shown in his night visit to the Great Teacher, where he received divine instruction, and a prediction of the crucifixion. When that prediction had been fulfilled and Joseph of Arimathea had begged for and was permitted by Pilate to take the body from the cross, Nicodemus assisted. Tradition says that he lived in intimacy with Gamaliel, and was buried near the grave of Stephen.

NICOLAI'TANS. A sect of heretics of the Apostolic period. They held it lawful to eat food sacrificed to idols; to join in idolatrous worship; and that God did not create the universe. They held their women in common. John's Gospel and also his Apocalypse opposes their teaching. (See HISTORY OF THE BOOKS). These doctrines have been supposed to have originated with the prophet Balaam. They are sometimes called Shuaibites, from the Midianite Shuaib, which is Balaam.

NIC'OLAS, NICH'OLAS, NICO'LAUS. One of the first seven deacons of the Church of Jerusalem (Acts vi. 5). He was a native of Antioch.

NICOP'OLIS (*city of victory*). Built by Augustus, in Epirus, on the site where his army encamped the night before the battle of Actium. The Temple of Neptune was placed on the spot occupied by his own tent. Paul requested Titus (iii. 12), to come to him from Crete, or from Dalmatia (2 Tim. iv. 10), to Nicopolis. He also urged Timothy in the same manner (v. 21). There are on the peninsula, N. W. of the Bay of Actium (*Gulf of Arta*), ruins of a temple, a theatre, walls, and other structures, on the hill and the low marshy plain; now deserted. It is possible that Paul was arrested here, and taken to Rome for his final trial (*Conybeare* and *Howson*).

NI'GER (*black*). A name given to SIMEON 6 (Acts xiii. 1).

NIGHT ((Heb. TO SINK; THE SINKING OF THE DAY). See CHRONOLOGY, p. 56.

NIGHT-HAWK (Heb. TACHMAS). In the enumeration of unclean animals in Lev. xi. 16, and in Deut. xiv. 15, this word appears. There is much controversy as to its meaning, whether the *night-hawk* or the *white owl*.

NILE. The Hebrew names of the river were SHICHOR (*black*); Yeor (*the river*); Sihor, in Jer. ii. 18. The Sanscrit *Nilah* means *dark blue;* and one of the upper branches of the river is now called the Blue Nile. The name Yeor is Egyptian, and is written AUR on the monuments. It is also called HAPEE MU (*the abyss*). Dr. Livingstone's late accounts show this to be the longest river in the world; rising

NILE EMBLEM.

in or beyond the lake Victoria Nyanza, south of the equator, and emptying into the Mediterranean at N. lat. 31°; its course running through 36 degrees, having been traced more than 2700 ms., while it is quite certain that it will be found to be 1000 ms. longer. (The Amazon extends through 30 degrees, and the Missouri and Mississippi together about 35 degrees). There are three chief branches: 1. The Blue (*Bahr el Azrak*) drains Abyssinia, and brings down the alluvial soil which fertilizes Egypt. 2. The White (*Bahr el Abyad*), joins the Blue at Khartoom, the capital of Soodan. 3. The Atbara (*black river*), rises also in Abyssinia, and joins the Nile at the north point of the Island of Meroë. There are no tributaries below the Atbara. The stream is interrupted by several cataracts formed by granite projected up through the sandstone of its bed. The first cataract is at the south boundary of Egypt (lat. 24°), the ancient Syene, now *Assouan;* the second, or Great Cataract, is in lat. 22°; the third in lat. 19° 45′; the fourth in lat. 18° 45′; and the fifth in 18° 20′, 100 miles above the fourth. The river parts into several branches below the pyramids of Memphis and Cairo, and encloses the Delta. The ancients mention seven branches: 1. Pelusiac; 2. Tanitic; 3. Mendesian; Bucolic (Damietta); 5. Sebennytic; 6. Bolbytene (Rosetta); 7. Canopic (Is. xi. 15). The width, in its lower course, is from half a mile to a mile wide, where there are islands. The water is sweet, especially during the inundation, and quickly becomes clear by settling its sediment. As Egypt has no rain (Zech. xiv. 17–19), the river supplies water to the soil by its overflow. The annual rise is noticed at Khartoom in April, but is not visible in Lower Egypt before June, and continues until September. The prophet Amos refers to the inundation as a symbol of great power and utter desolation (viii. 8, ix. 5). Job was acquainted with the Nile floods, for the word that he uses in ch. xxviii., ver. 10, for *rivers*, is the plural of the name of the Nile, in the original. Jeremiah also uses it as a figure when speaking of Pharaoh Necho's army (xlvi.). Its waters abound in fish of many kinds (Num. xi. 5); but crocodiles (described minutely by Job (xli.), and mentioned by Ezekiel (xxix. 3), are becoming very scarce, and are only found in Upper Egypt. The monuments and the ancient writers give accounts of the banks of the Nile as being bordered with flags, reeds, and flowers, especially the lotus, and full of wild-fowls. Now the banks are nearly bare, as prophesied by Isaiah (xix. 6, 7). The papyrus, which was used for making paper, and for boats (which were remarkable for their swiftness—Is. xviii. 2), has entirely disappeared, except in the marshes of the Delta. Ezekiel compares Pharaoh to a crocodile (great dragon) in the Nile, fearing no one (xxix. 1–5; whale, in xxxii. 2). Moses was exposed on its waters in a boat of papyrus (bulrushes, Ex. ii.

3). It is said traditionally that Jesus lived on its banks, near Heliopolis; and its name is associated with many other Bible characters, such as Absalom, Jacob, Joseph, Solomon (whose wife was a daughter of Pharaoh), besides the captive king of Judah, pictured on the walls of the temple at Karnac. See MEMPHIS.

NIM'RAH (*pure water*). In the "land of Jazer," afterward called Beth Nimrah (Num. xxxii. 3, 36); in the tribe of Gab. The name Nimrim (*panthers*) is found in several localities east of Jordan (*Porter*). Two miles east of the Jordan, on the road from Jericho to Es Salt, are ruins near copious fountains (Is. xv. 6; Jer. xlviii. 34). Eusebius says it was a village north of Zoar. If our location of Nimrah is correct, Zoar must have been north of the Dead Sea.

NIM'ROD (*the extremely impious rebel*). Son of Cush (Gen. x. 8, 9). He established an empire in Shinar (Babylonia), the chief cities of which were Babel, Erech, Accad, and Calneh; and extended it northward over Assyria, including the cities Nineveh, Rehoboth, Calah, and Resen. There is no authentic account of his life. The tales of Ctesias, and others, except that in the Bible, are guesses or inventions; and of the great cities which he built very little has been known until within the last twenty-five years, when Layard exhumed the palaces, sculptures and inscriptions of *Nimroud*. See NINEVEH.

NIM'SHI (*drawn out*). Grandfather of Jehu, generally called the SON of Nimshi (1 K. xix. 16).

NIN'EVEH (*Nin-navah=Nin-town*). The ancient capital of Assyria. First mentioned in Gen. x. 11). The country was also called the land of Nimrod by Micah (v. 6). Balaam prophesied the captivity of Israel by Assyria (Num. xxiv. 22), and Asaph sings of their alliance with Moab (Ps. lxxxiii. 8). Jonah was sent to the city about 800 B. C., and Nahum devotes the whole of his book to "the burden of Nineveh," about 725 B. C. Isaiah says that Sennacherib resided in the city; and it was probably the scene of his death (Is. xxxvii. 37), while worshiping in the temple of Nisroch, his god. The last notice of it is by Zephaniah, B. C. 630 (ii. 13). Assyria is alluded to as having been destroyed, according to prophesy by Ezekiel (xxxi.), and Jeremiah omits it from his catalogue of all nations (xxv.). The city is not mentioned in the inscriptions of the Persian dynasty. Herodotus passed very near, if not over, the site of the city, about 200 years after its destruction, but does not mention it, except as having once been there. Xenophon, with his 10,000 Greeks, encamped near the site (B. C. 401), but does not mention its name (*Anab.* iii. 4, 7), although he describes the mounds as they appear now. Alexander marched over the very place, and won a great victory at Arbela, in sight of it, but his historians make no note of it. The Emperor Claudius planted a colony there, and restored the name Nineve. Tacitus calls it Ninos, when taken by Meherdates. On the coins of Trajan it is Ninus, and on those of Maximinus it is Niniva; Claudeopolis being added on both coins. Many relics of the Romans have been found; vases, sculptures, figures in bronze and marble, terra-cottas, and coins. The site was again deserted when Heraclius gained a victory over the Persians, A. D. 627.

The Arabs named their fort, on the east bank of the Tigris, *Ninawi* (A. D. 637). The accounts of its immense extent are various, and not very reliable. Diodorus Siculus says the dimensions were (according as we estimate his figures, from 32 to 60, or even) 74 miles in circuit. The walls were 100 feet high, and wide enough for three chariots to drive abreast; flanked by 1500 towers, each 200 feet high (accounts which have not yet been verified). Layard says: "If we take the four great mounds of Nimrud, Koyunjik, Khorsabad, and

Karamles, as the corners of a square, it will be found to agree pretty accurately with the 60 miles of Herodotus, which make the three days' journey of Jonah.'' Within this space there are many mounds, and remains of pottery, bricks, etc.

The name of Nineveh is found on the Egyptian monuments of the date of Thothmes III, about 1400 B. C.

The first notice in modern times of the ruins were by Mr. Rich, in 1820, who brought to London a few bricks, with inscriptions, some cylinders, gems, and other remains. Layard next visited them, in 1840; but Botta, a French consul at Mosul, found the first Assyrian monument, which was of value as a confirmation of Scripture. It was soon followed by a great variety of works of art, in 1844, at Khorsabad, the results of which exploration are in the Assyrian room at the Louvre, Paris. The great work of disentombing the remains of ancient Nineveh was performed by Layard, from 1845 to 1850.

BLACK OBELISK OF NIMROUD.

The accounts of Layard's discoveries are published in minute detail, filling volumes, and will repay the time spent in reading them; for, besides giving undoubted and truthful glimpses of antiquity, in almost every phase of society, they are as startling and exciting as the wildest romance, both in text and illustration. But far beyond these in value to us are their uses in confirmation of the Scriptures.

Place and Fresnel discovered, at Khorsabad, colossal, human-headed, winged bulls, which were in groups on each side of great doorways; besides other mythic figures. The most important inscription that has been brought to light, is that on two of the human-headed bulls from Koyunjik (now in the British Museum), giving an account of Sennacherib; his wars with Hezekiah, and the capture of Lachish, with pictures illustrating it (See LACHISH). Nearly equal in value is the Black Obe-

lisk of Nimroud; a piece of black marble, 6 ft. 6 in. high, 1 ft. 6½ in. sq. at the top, and 2 ft. sq. at the bottom, the upper half covered with 5 panels of figures, with inscriptions between each panel, and also many lines below the lower one: altogether 210 lines. One side, only, is engraved here: the four may be seen in the work on '' Nineveh and its Palaces,'' by Bonomi. The story may be inferred from the text in 2 K. xvii., xviii. The first panel, at the top, exhibits the king, attended by his eunuch, and a bearded officer (perhaps the returned conqueror); a captive kisses his foot, and two officers wait the king's orders. The image of Baal, and a circle enclosing a star (the sun?) are similar to those on the rocks at Nahr el Kelb. The same images, reversed in position, are in the second panel. One may mean Morning, and the other Evening; and both, with the figures in the other panels bringing and presenting tribute, indicate that the captives were so many, and the tribute so vast, that they consumed the whole day in their presentation. Some of the figures on the obelisk resemble those on the wall of the small temple of Kalabshe, who are enemies of Râamses II, and are understood to represent Jews in both cases. The inscription, as interpreted by Rawlinson, mentions the receiving by the king of tribute from the cities of Tyre, Sidon, and Gebal, in his 21st year; defeating the king of Hamath, and 12 other kings of the upper and *lower* country (Canaan, lower). Dr. Hincks reads the names of Jehu, king of Israel, and dates the obelisk 875 B. C. Dr. Grotefend reads the names of Tiglath Pileser, Pul, and Shalmanassar, and refers to the accounts in Isaiah (xx.), and Nahum (iii.).

Sargon's name was found in another inscription, with his title, Shalmaneser, and the account of the capture of Samaria (which in Assyrian is SAMARINA). He carried off 27,280 families, and placed colonies, in their stead, of people from Assyria (2 K. xviii.). The king of Egypt is called PIRHU (Pharaoh), and Heliopolis is RABEK (Ra—*sun*, bek—*city*). Ashdod, Jamnia, Hamath, Beræa, Damascus, Bambyce, and Charchemish, are mentioned among his captures. He is also styled the conqueror of remote Judæa. He had a statue and inscription in his honor on the island of Cypress. The son of this king was Sennacherib, who built Koyunjik; and in the great palace there were found inscriptions in honor of his capture of Babylon from Merodach-Baladan (2 K. xx. 12; Is. xxxix. 1); and of Sidon, under King Luliya; and of his expedition into Judæa, in which occur the names KHAZAKIYAHU (Hezekiah), URSALIMA (Jerusalem), and YAHUDA (Jews). The king of Pelusium is mentioned. The tribute of Hezekiah, as recorded, consisted of 30 talents of gold, 300 talents of silver, the vessels and ornaments of the Temple, slaves, both boys and girls, maid-servants and men-servants—confirming the Scripture account (2 K. xviii. 13–16).

The tells or mounds (see Ezr. ii. 59; Ez. iii. 15; 2 K. xix. 12) which are scattered all over the region watered by the Euphrates and Tigris and their confluents, contain the remains of Assyrian, Babylonian, and Persian occupation. They vary in size from 50 to 150 feet high, and also much more in length, being from a few rods to several miles in extent. Those forming what is now called Nineveh are *Koyunjik*, which is 3,900 feet long by 1500 wide and 96 high; *Neby Yunas* (traditional tomb of Jonah), about 40 acres in extent; *Khorsabad*, 6,000 feet square; *Selamieh*, 410 acres; *Nimrud*, 1,000 acres: and in this group of mounds (called Nimroud) there are indications of more than 100 towers, at regular intervals. On the S. W. of this group there is a mound 2,100 feet by 1,200, with a cone at one corner (N. W.) 140 feet high.

A **treasure-house of records**, such as is alluded

to by Ezra (v. 17, vi. 2), was found at Koyunjik, filled with the archives of the empire, written on tablets of terra-cotta, and in perfect order and preservation, piled from the floor to the ceiling, most of which were sent to the British Museum.

NIN′EVITES. Inhabitants of Nineveh (Luke xi. 30).

NI′SON (Esth. xi, 2).

NIS′ROCH (Heb.). The name of an idol of Nineveh (2 K. xix. 37).

NI′TRE (Heb. NETHER). Used as a wash (Jer. ii. 22). This substance is not the same as our nitrate of potassa. Natron was and is now used by the Egyptians for washing clothes, for yeast and for soap; also as a cure for toothache mixed with vinegar. It is found in the soda lakes of Egypt, 50 miles W. of Cairo. The Natron lakes of Egypt were early occupied by hermits, who built large and fortlike monasteries, where, for ages, the study of the Christian religion was pursued, and its practice kept up, with the severest ritualistic forms. Their libraries were found, after several centuries of neglect, to contain valuable copies of the Gospels, homilies, and books of church services.

NOADI′AH (*with whom Jah convenes*). 1. Son of Binnui (Ezr. viii. 33).—2. Noadiah the prophetess (Neh. vi. 14).

NO′AH (NOACH, *to rest*, or *give comfort*.) The second head of the human race, as Adam was the first. From his birth to the age of 500 years there is a blank in his history. Society in his day had become sadly corrupted by the custom of intermarriage of different races, especially of two distinct religious communities, called "The sons of God" (Elohim) and "The Sons of the Man" (Ha-Adam). There were also Nephilim, men of violence, who turned peaceable society upside down. The "Sons of God" (BENE-ELOHIM) were the descendants of Seth, and worshipers of God; the "Sons of the Man" were descendants of Cain, and probably idolaters. The union of the two families or races produced a mixed condition of religion, which could not be pure.

Another interpreter understands Bene Elohim to have been a race distinct from Adam's, and dating long before his creation, and therefore an inferior race, idolatrous and wicked, and therefore the name means "worshipers of false gods," as the Israelites are called children of God the Father. The daughters of men would then be of Adam's race. This supposition is against the received text in the first three chapters of Genesis. Another theory was long popular in the Church: that the "Sons of God" were angels, an intermediate race of spirits who have the power of assuming the human form. But as we have no evidence of any such appearance in our day it is very difficult to have faith in the supposition. If we were to receive the Book of Enoch as inspired, which claims a date of 1000 years before the Flood, we should have the record of a belief in such occurrences in that age, and some excuse for such a belief in our day. But that book is rejected by all Christians, except the Abyssinians.

The offspring of this mixture of races were men noted for strength and courage, Nephilim (giants in the A. V.), violent men. If the Nephilim of Canaan were descendants of those mentioned in Genesis (vi. 4), the fact is a strong evidence against the universality of the Deluge (See GIANTS, DELUGE, GENESIS). Noah's Ark, and the Deluge are described in other places. The first act of Noah, after the Deluge, and the escape from the Ark, was to build an altar, and offer sacrifice to God, of every clean beast, and every clean fowl. New blessings and new laws are given to man, especially concerning human life. Noah's last act was the cursing of Ham, and the blessing of his other sons. This is believed to have been the origin of the *color* of the Negro (sons of Ham), and of the idolatrous tendencies of the Canaanites. When the sons of Israel (Shem) took possession of the country of Canaan, then Canaan became a servant to Shem; he became the slave of Japhet when Tyre and Carthage were taken by the Greeks and Romans (Japhet). For

DETAILS AT NOBAH.

Japhet to dwell in the tents of Shem, was when Japhet received the knowledge of the true God from Shem, that is, by the Hebrew Scriptures. Noah lived 350 years after the Deluge, and must have witnessed the confusion of tongues, and the dispersion from Babel. It is supposed that he had no other children than those named. See GENESIS, in the HISTORY OF THE BOOKS, for a notice of several traditions of Noah, and the Flood, in various countries.

NO′AH (*motion*). Daughter of ZELOPHEHAD (Num. xxvi. 33).

NO-A′MON (*populous No*). (Nahum iii. 8; Ez. xxx. 14, 15). Identical with Thebes. Multitude of No (Jer. xlvi. 25). See Thebes.

NOB (*high*). David fled from Saul and came to Nob (1 Sam. xxi. 1), which was near Anathoth (Neh. xi. 32). There are on a conical hill, 2¾ miles N. of Jerusalem, traces of a small, but very ancient city—cisterns hewn in the rock, large hewn stones, and ruins of a small tower, besides other indications. From the summit, Zion is in plain view (Is. x. 32).

NO′BAH (*a barking*). (See KENATH). Most of the chief towns of the Hauran have traces of the architectural magnificence that Rome lavished on her colonies. The tanks, bridges, and many houses are solidly built, and even at this late day nearly as good as new.

NO′BAH. An Israelite warrior (Num. xxxii. 42).

NO′BLEMAN. A man of high rank (John iv. 46, 49).

NOD (*flight*).

NO′DAB (*nobility*). The name of an Arab tribe (1 Chr. v. 19).

NO′E. The patriarch NOAH (Job iv. 12).

NO′EBA. NEKODA 1 (1 Esd. v. 31).

NO′GAH (*bright*). Son of David (1 Chr. iii. 7).

NO′HAH (*rest*). Son of Benjamin (1 Chr. viii. 2).

NON. NUN. Father of Joshua (1 Chr. vii. 27).

NOPH. Moph, Memphis. (Is. xix. 13). See MEMPHIS.

NO′PHAH (*blast*). Only mentioned in the fragment of an ode, composed by the Amorites after their capture of Heshbon from the Moabites (Num. xxi. 30), and quoted by Moses. A city between Heshbon and Medeba. Lost.

NORTH (Heb. ZAPHON; Gr. *borrhas*). As denoting the northern quarter (Gen. xiii. 14; Ex. xxvi. 20, 35; Luke xiii. 29); "Land of the North" (Jer.

iii. 18). Also expressed, relatively, to the direction of the hand.

NOSE (Heb. AF, *the organ of smell*), (Prov. xxx. 33). Figuratively, as "anger" in Gen. xxvii. 45, or "wrath," (Gen. xxxix. 19) suggested by hard breathing. Heb. APPAYIM (*two breathing holes*), is translated "nostrils" in Gen. ii. 70.

NOSE-JEWEL (Heb. NEZEM). A ring of metal—gold or silver—passed through the right nostril, worn for ornament by women in the East (Gen. xxiv. 22). It is usually from 1 to 3½ ins. in diameter. Beads, corals, and jewels, are strung upon it. ORNAMENTS. (See Cut, p. 82.)

NOV'ICE (Gr. *neophutos*). A new convert (1 Tim. iii. 6).

NUM'BER. Hebraic numerals were denoted by letters. At a later period this was the mode of notation, as seen in the Maccabæan coins. Certain numbers were used as figurative representations, and not actual quantities, such as, 7, 10, 40, 100, which represent completeness. 7 is thus used as "seven-fold" in Gen. iv. 24; seven times (meaning completely) in Lev. xxv. 24, and Ps. xii. 6; as also the general use of the number 7. 10 was a number of especial selection. The number 12 was specially mystical, and is found in many instances; as 12 months, 12 tribes, 12 loaves of shewbread, 12 disciples or apostles. 40 was also very mystical; as 40 days of Moses; 40 years in the wilderness; 40 days and nights of Elijah in the wilderness, and of Jesus on the mount; 40 years each the life of several kings and judges. Seventy-fold, as in Gen. iv. 24, Matt. xviii. 22, etc. The mystic number 666, in Rev. xiii. 18, still remains the subject of controversy. One theory suggests the numerals to mean Lx., in Gr. *lateinos* (Lat. *latinus*), *beast*, or *kingdom*.

NUMBERS. See HISTORY OF THE BOOKS.

NUME'NIUS (*new moon*). Son of Antiochus. He was sent on an embassy to Rome and Sparta to renew the friendly connections with the Jews, B. C. 144 (1 Macc. xii. 16, 17). He was again sent, B. C. 141 (xiv. 24).

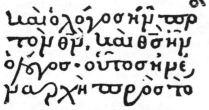

GREEK MS. A. D. 1000.—St. John i. 1, 2.

NUN (*a fish*). 1. Father of JOSHUA (Ex. xxxiii. 11).—2. The fourteenth letter of the Hebrew alphabet (Ps. cxix). WRITING.

NURSE. The position of the nurse when one was wanted, was one of much honor and importance (Gen. xxiv. 59). CHILD.

NUTS (*Botnim and Egoz*). Spoken of as among the good things of the land to be taken by Jacob's sons to propitiate the governor of Egypt. This nut was most likely the Pistachio. BOTNIM (Pistachio Town), a town of Gad (Josh. xiii. 26), probably derives its name therefrom. The word EGOZ occurs in Cant. vi. 11, and probably means walnut. One Arabic term (derived from the Persian) for walnut is *jaws;* another is *chusf*, which means *tall tree*. Walnuts were anciently very plenty around the Sea of Galilee. They are still cultivated near Sidon as an article of commerce.

NYM'PHAS (*bridegroom*). A rich and devoted Christian in Laodicea. His house was used as a chapel (Col. iv. 15). Some ancient manuscripts say Nymphas was a woman, a view which is adopted by the Greek Church.

O

OAK. There are several Hebrew words which are rendered oak in the A. V., as EL, to be strong (Gen. xiv. 6); ELAH, terebinth (Is. vi. 13); ELON, oak (Gen. xii. 6); ILAN, strong tree (Dan. iv.); ALLAH, *an oak* (Josh. xxiv. 26); ALLON, evergreen oak (Hos. iv. 13). The most noted trees were Abraham's oak at Mamre, the oak at Shechem, of Deborah, Rebekah's nurse, of the wanderers. 1. EL (AEL), *to be strong* (Gen. xiv. 6); the plural of EL is ELIM, also ELOTH and ELATH. Elim is the name of the place where there were 70 palm trees, the word EL, instead of meaning oak, is used in that instance for grove, ELIM, groves (Ex. xv. 27). There was also a palm grove at Akabah. In Is. i. 29, ELIM means oaks, the same word in Is. lxi. 3, and Ez. xxxi. 14, means any thrifty, large tree.—2. ALAH, *the terebinth*. The most noted one was Abraham's Oak at Mamre, where the three angels appeared to him. It is now represented by an oak (Thomson thinks it was an oak and not the terebinth) of the species *Quercus-pseudo-coccifera*. (See cut on page 3).—3. ELON, *some kind of oak*. Translated plain in the A. V. and in the Targum.—4. ILAN, *strong tree* (Dan. iv., only), and possibly an oak.—5. ALLAH, *an oak* (Josh. xxiv. 26, only).—6. ALLON, *evergreen oak* (Hos. iv. 13), and also the Holly-leaved oak; the Hairy-cupped oak; the prickly-cupped; the Kermes, which furnishes the insect used in dyes (Is. i. 18, scarlet).

The oak forests of Bashan were noted in the earliest times (Is. ii. 13; Ez. xxvii. 6; Zech. xi. 2), and they are still extensive and contain several varieties of very fine trees. Besides these, there are others scattered all over the country, both in the hilly districts and on the mountains. Mount Carmel, Anti-Lebanon (west slopes), Lebanon (east slopes, and many ravines), and the Hill Country of Galilee and Judæa, are supplied with scrubby oaks 10 to 15 feet high, bearing acorns in great quantities, useful for bread. Where the ground is now stripped of trees of all kinds, its roots are often found and dug for fuel. The largest tree of this species is that near Hebron, called "Abraham's Oak," which is 23 feet in girth, and shades a space 90 feet across. The nut-gall bearing oak is plentiful in Galilee and Asia Minor. The Valonia oak is valuable for its tannin, contained in the acorn cups. It is probable that this was the "Oak of Bashan" (Q. *ægilops*).

There are many storied oaks in Palestine. Rebekah's nurse, Deborah, was buried under one at Bethel (Gen. xxxv. 8); Saul and his sons, under another in Jabesh (1 Chr. x. 12). The national covenant was commemorated by a monument under an oak at Shechem, by Joshua (xxiv. 26); Jacob hid the stolen images under the same tree (Gen. xxxv. 4); Absalom was caught by his hair in one in Bashan; Gideon saw an angel under an oak in Ophrah (Judg. vi. 11), and many were the shelters of altars for both true and false worship. The Arabs now have a superstition that spirits, *jin* (called Jacob's daughters), live in oak trees, and they hang rags of all kinds on the branches as charms against them.

OATH. An appeal to Divine authority to ratify the truth of an assertion (Heb. vi. 16). Calling God to witness, as, "God do so to me, and more, also, if," etc. (Ruth i. 17; 1 Sam. ii. 17). Idolators swore by their false gods. Many frivolous forms were used, as, "By the blood of Abel;" "By my head;" "By the Temple," etc. Jesus was asked by the high-priest to swear, "By the living God," to the truth of what he was teaching of himself (Matt. xxvi. 63). Jesus is believed to have prohibited profane and careless, or false swearing—not telling the truth under oath. It appears that Jesus gave testimony on oath before the high-priest, and Paul did not teach against it (Gal. i. 20; 1 Cor. xv. 31;

2 Cor. i. 23). There would seem to be no use for oaths among genuine Christians, living in the presence of God, but they are useful in dealing with those who do not live a Christian life. When men everywhere, and at all times, prefer the truth to lies, then oaths may be dispensed with. The forms or actions in taking an oath, anciently, were :—1. Lifting up the hand (Gen. xiv. 22). 2. Putting the hand on the head of the accused (Lev. xxiv. 14). 3. Putting the hand under the thigh (Gen. xxiv. 2), by both parties (Jos.). 4. Standing before the altar, or looking towards Jerusalem (1 K. viii. 31). 5. Dividing a victim (as a lamb), and passing between the pieces (Gen. xv. 10). 6. Placing the hands on the Book of the Law (Ex. xxiii. 1). The crime of PERJURY was strongly condemned. It was taking the Lord's name in vain. If a man gave false witness, he received the punishment that he tried to inflict on another by his perjury (Ex. xx. 7; Lev. xix. 12). Women were not permitted to give evidence on oath (Deut. xix. 17). The Mohammedan swears on the open Koran : Mohammed swore "By the setting of the stars." Bedawin Arabs touch the middle tent-pole, and swear by the life of the owner. The Romans were strict with men under oath (authority in Matt. viii. 9; Acts xvi. 27, xxvii. 42).

OBADI'AH (*servant of Jah*), also written ABADIAS and ABDIAS. 1. Ancestor of some mentioned in the genealogies of Judah (1 Chr. iii. 21),—2. Son of Izrahiah (vii. 3).—3. Son of Azel (viii. 38, ix. 44).—4. Son of Shemaiah (ix. 16). ABDA 2 a musician in the Temple-choir (Neh. xii. 25).—5. A captain in David's army (1 Chr. xii. 9).—6. A prince who taught in Jehoshaphat's reign (2 Chr. xvii. 7).—7. Son of Jehiel (Ezr. viii. 9).—8. A priest who signed the covenant with Nehemiah (xi. 5).—9. One of the twelve prophets. See HISTORY OF THE BOOKS.—10. An officer of high rank in Ahab's palace (1 K. xviii. 3). During the fierce persecution of the prophets by Jezebel he concealed a hundred of them in caves and fed them with bread and water (vs. 4, 13).—11. Father of Ishmaiah (1 Chr. xxvii. 19).—12. A Levite, overseer of the workmen on the Temple (2 Chr. xxxiv. 12).

O'BAL (*bare district*). Son of Joktan (Gen. x. 28). EBAL.

OBDI'A (1 Esd. v. 38; Ezr. ii. 61).

O'BED (*serving*). 1. Son of Boaz and Ruth (Ruth iv. 17). The Book of Ruth gives an interesting account of his birth and the social and religious life of the Israelites at that time.—2. A descendant of Jarha (1 Chr. ii. 37, 38).—3. One of David's men (xi. 47).—4. Son of Shemaiah, firstborn of Obed-edom (xxvi. 7).—5. Father of Azariah. A captain (2 Chr. xxiii. 1).

O'BED-E'DOM (*serving Edom*). 1. A member of the family of Kohath (2 Sam. vi. 10, 11). After the death of Uzzah, the ark which was being taken to the city of David was carried into the house of Obed-edom, where it remained three months (1 Chr. xv. 25).—2. Son of Jeduthun (1 Chr. xvi. 38).—3. Treasurer of the Temple (2 Chr. xxv. 24).

O'BETH. EBED, the son of Jonathan (1 Esd. viii. 32).

O'BIL (*chief of the camels*). An Ishmaelite who had charge of a herd of camels (1 Chr. xxvii. 30).

O'BOTH (*bottles*). Encampment in Moab. Lost. (Num. xxi. 10).

OCHI'EL (1 Esd. i. 9).

O'CHIM. Heb. translated "doleful creatures" in Is. xiii. 21. Some creature uttering doleful screeches, perhaps an owl.

OCIDE'LUS. Error for Jozabad in 1 Esd. ix. 22 (Ezr. x. 22).

OCI'NA (Judith ii. 28). Name for Accho. (See William of Tyre).

OC'RAN (*afflicted*). Father of Pagiel (Num. i. 13).

O'DED (*erecting*). 1. Father of Azariah (2 Chr. xv. 1, 8).—2. A prophet who secured the release of the captives from Judah (xxviii. 9). This incident in the history of the Kingdom of Israel is in pleasant contrast to many others. A whole army were liberated, clothed and fed.

ODOL'LAM. ADULLAM. *Beit Ula.*

ODONAR'KES. Chief of a tribe slain by Jonathan (1 Macc. ix. 66).

OFFENCE. The Heb. HET or CHET (Eccl. x. 4), is translated sin (Lev. xix. 17; xx. 20, etc.), also fault in Gen. xli. 9. MICHSHOL (1 Sam. xv. 31; Is. viii. 14), "stumbling block," Gr. *skandalon* in Matt. xvi. 23; xviii. 7; Luke xvii. 1. To eat with offence is to eat so as to be an occasion of sin in another (Rom. xiv. 20). "A temptation to sin," "perplexity," "danger," "that which produces disgust," etc.

BAAL.

OFFEND, TO (from Lat. *offendo*). Offence, as a breach of the law, is alluded to in Rom. v. 15, 17; as an offered excuse for sin in Matt. xv. 12; John vi. 61.

OFFERING. (See SACRIFICE).

OF'FICER (Heb. NEZIB, SARIS, PEKAH, PEKUDDAH, PAKID, RAB, SHOTER), and others, are terms conveying various meanings, from a commander of an army to a simple messenger of a court of justice (John vii. 32, 45, etc.). In Luke xii. 58, there appears *prakter* (*a doer*)—Revenue officers, (1 Macc. x. 41, xiii. 37). *Huperites*, bailiff or some inferior officer (Matt. v. 25).

OG (*crooked*). King of BASHAN, ruler over sixty cities. He was one of the giant (violent, strong) race of Rephaim (Josh. xiii. 12). This race was probably Shemite in origin, dating earlier than the Canaanites. Og's couch (palanquin, Amos iii. 12), is described as of iron, 15 ft. 9 in. long, and 6 ft. wide (Deut. iii. 11). This would indicate Og's hight at 9 feet at least.

O'HAD (*union*). Son of Simeon (Gen. xlvi. 10).

O'HEL (*house*). Son of Zerubbabel (1 Chr. iii. 20). HASADIAH.

OIL. The Olive was the chief source of oil (See OLIVES). (Ez. xvi. 13). It was used in the preparation of meat offerings in the Temple (Lev. v. 11, vi. 21). The second pressing was used for lamps. Oil was an important article of merchandise (1 Chr. xxvii. 28; Ez. xxvii. 17). See OINTMENT. OLIVE.

OIL-TREE (Heb. 'EZ SHEMEN). A tree bearing fruit resembling that of the olive (Is. xli. 19). OLIVE.

OINT'MENT (Heb. SHAMAN, *to be fat;* ROKAH, *to anoint;* MIRKAHATH, the vessel for holding the perfume, or ointment; MISHAH, *oil*. Ointment was a general term for perfumes, cosmetics, for substances used for medicinal, sacred, and ceremonial purposes. Olive oil formed the body of these ointments. A particular ointment was appointed for use in consecration (Ex. xxx. 23, 33, xxix. 7, xxxvii. 29, xl. 9, 15), of myrrh, cassia, sweet cinnamon, sweet calamus and olive oil. With this, also, the furniture of the Tabernacle was anointed. Dead bodies were anointed with both ointment and oil. Christ refers to this in Matt. xxvi. 12; Mark xiv. 3, 8; Luke xxiii. 56. It was largely used in medical treatment, alluded to by Christ in curing the blnid man (Is. i. 6; John ix. 6; Jer. viii. 22; Rev. iii. 18). As a cosmetic for the face, so common with the Greeks and Romans, it was also used by the Egyptians and Jews, and is now by the inhabitants of Palestine to this day. Allusion is made to the use of ointments in Ruth iii. 3; Eccl. vii. 1, ix. 8; Prov. xxvii. 9, 16; Matt. xxvi. 7; Luke vii. 42; Rev. xviii. 13.

OL'AMUS. Son of Bani (1 Esd. ix. 30).

OLD-GATE. A gate of JERUSALEM (Neh. iii. 6).

OLD TES'TAMENT. See HISTORY OF THE BOOKS.

GREEK MS., A. D. 960.—John i. 1–3.

OL'IVE. (Heb. ZAYITH, or ZAIT). A tree from 15 to 30 ft. high, bearing berries, smooth, like an oval plum, violet color when ripe, having an oily pulp, and a hard, rough stone. The leaves are like the willow, and of a dull, *olive* green, on the smooth, upper surface, and silvery pale on the downy, under surface. The flowers are small and white. See cut, p. 37.

The body of the tree dies at the heart and stands up on several legs. The bark of old trees is very rough, like that on old willow trees. They live to a great age. (See GETHSEMANE.) A sacred olive tree was kept in the court of the Temple of Pandrosus, on the Acropolis, Athens; and the allusion in Ps. iii. 8 would imply that they were grown in the Temple Court on Zion.

The best olive-oil is now raised where, before the Christian era, the tree was almost unknown, in Italy and Spain, and where millions depend on it for half their living. The trees are planted by cuttings. If the slip is from a wild olive it must be grafted from a good one. The Church is a cultured olive tree, and Gentilism a wild olive tree (Rom. xi. 10–24). The wild tree bears but very few berries, and scarcely any oil can be got from them.

Olive orchards are as common in the East around every village as apple orchards are in the United States. Anciently it was exported from Palestine to Egypt (Ez. xxvii. 17; Hos. xii. 1). Moses sings of "oil out of the flinty rock," in one of his odes (Deut. xxxii. 13), which indicates that then, as now, the best soil for the olive was the chalky marl, with flint, and just mould enough to cover the roots. The text may have alluded to the oil mills and presses, where the oil comes out of the rock, for the press vat is often hollowed out of a large rock.

The tree bears in its seventh year, and a good crop in its fifteenth, and continues to bear for several hundred years. The crop is yielded every other year, and a large tree will produce from ten to fifteen gallons of oil. The yield by the acre is about one hundred dollars.

It is their substitute for our butter and lard. Many dishes are cooked in olive oil. The lamp is supplied with it; and the second pressing (not so pure), is used in making soap. The orchards or groves are carefully guarded near harvest time, and the rulers announce the day for gathering the berries, which begins in October. The general harvest is in November. The trees are shaken, and beaten with poles, but a few always remain for the gleaning of the poor. The shaking of the olive tree is a cold, wet, laborious operation, as it

occurs in the winter, when rain and cold winds, and frost are frequent.

OLIVES, MOUNT OF (HAR-HAZZATHIM, Zech. xiv. 4). "Before Jerusalem, on the east." Referred to as the "ascent of Olivet" in other places (2 Sam. xv. 30, etc.) in the Old Testament, and the various changes of the same in the New (Luke xix. 29; Acts i. 12). The first mention of the mount is at the time David fled over it, and the last is the triumphal progress of the Son of David over its slopes. The description, written, perhaps over 2,500 years ago, is now a good one. It is near Jerusalem—a ravine between them—olive-trees (Neh. viii. 15; Mark xi. 8), and gives a very distinct view of the Temple site and the city from its summit, where there is now a chapel (2 Sam. xv 23, 32). Solomon built chapels for the worship of Ashtoreth, Chemosh, and Milcom, heathen divinities, on a part of Olivet called the "Mount of Corruption" (2 K. xxiii. 13), which some believe to be the highest summit, where the chapel of the Ascension now stands—the same spot that was held sacred by David.

Olivet is a ridge, 300 feet higher than the Temple site, and a mile long, north and south, divided into three or four summits, which are named—commencing at the north—1. Viri Galilæi, also Vineyard of the Sportsman; 2. Ascension, by the Arabs *Jebel et Tur;* 3. Prophets; and 4, Offense, Arab *Baten el Hawa*, Belly of the Winds. During the middle ages the mount was dotted all over with chapels, or monuments of some kind, marking the localities selected as the sites of interesting events recorded in Scripture; among which are the tombs of the Virgin, Joachim, and Anna, near Gethsemane (in which are the Cave of Christ's Prayer and Agony, the rock on which the three disciples slept, and the place of the capture of Christ; spot on which the Virgin witnessed the stoning of Stephen; where her girdle dropped at the time of her Assumption; where Jesus wept over the city (Luke xix. 41); where Jesus first said the Lord's Prayer —(the Beatitudes were also pronounced here); where the woman taken in adultery was brought to him; Tombs of the Prophets (containing Haggai and Zechariah); cave in which the Apostles wrote the Creed; where Christ spoke of the judgment to come; Cave of St. Pelagia, and of Huldah, the prophetess; Place of the Ascension; where the Virgin was warned of her death by an angel; spot from which the Apostles witnessed the Ascension (viri Galilæi=men of Galilee); where the three Marys saw Jesus after his resurrection. All of these places on the side toward the city. On the slopes, south and east, the place of the barren fig-tree; Bethphage; Bethany (house of Lazarus, and the cave, or tomb); stone on which Christ sat when Mary and Martha saw him. Only three of these command our special attention—Gethsemane, the place of the Lamentation, and the place of Ascension. (See GETHSEMANE). Stanley says that the Lord's "triumphal entry" must have been on the road, not over the summit, but the longer and easier route round the south shoulder of the mount (between the summit called the Prophets and that called the Mt. of Corruption), which has the peculiarity of presenting two successive views of the city, just before and after passing a slight elevation in the path. Ezekiel mentions Olivet in his wonderful vision (xi. 23); and Zechariah says of the Messiah, "His feet shall stand in that day (of the destruction of Jerusalem) on the Mount of Olives" (xiv. 4).

Jesus stood somewhere on its brow when he predicted the overthrow of the city (Mark xiii. 1).

The whole mount is now called by the Jews Har-hammishkah, *mount of corruption* or *destruction.*

There are three paths leading from near Gethsemane to the top of Olivet, besides the road to

Jericho. The first leads north of the central summit (Ascension) to the little village near the top (see map, p. 151). The second passes the Cave of Pelagia, in a direct course up the mount to the church and village. The third runs near the Tomb of the Prophets and ends at the same village. The fourth is the road to Bethany and Jericho, and passes between the Mt. of Offense and the Tomb of the Prophets. This is now, as it must have been anciently, the usual route for caravans and all large parties. Coming from Bethany you may get two views of the city: the first, of the southeast corner of the Temple site and Zion. The road then descends a slight declivity, and the city is hid behind a ridge of Olivet. A few rods further the path rises steeply up to a ledge of smooth rock, where the whole city is seen in one view. It is almost the only really authentic spot on Olivet or near Jerusalem that is not marked by a church, chapel or tower, and is the only one that is located without controversy (see view, p. 154).

OLYM'PAS (Gr. *given by heaven*). A disciple at Rome (Rom. xvi. 15). Tradition says he was of the 70, and died A. D. 69.

OLYM'PIUS. A title given to the Greek deity, Zeus (JUPITER), (2 Macc. vi. 2), from his residence on Mt. Olympus, in Greece.

OMAE'RUS. AMRAM, son of Bani (1 Esd. ix. 34).

O'MAR (*eloquent*). Son of Eliphaz (Gen. xxxvi. 11, 15). The name now found in the *Amir* tribe of Arabs, in Gilead.

Ō'MEGA (Gr. **Ō**). The last letter of the Greek alphabet (Rev. i. 8, 11). Symbol of "the last," as **A** is of "the first."

O'MER (*handful*). See WEIGHTS and MEASURES.

OM'RI (*servant of Jah*). 1. "Captain of the host" to Elah, also the 6th king of Israel, a vigorous and unscrupulous ruler (1 K. xvi. 21), in Tirzah, his capital. He transferred his residence to the hill Shomron, (Samaria), which he bought of Shemer, where he reigned 6 years more.—2. Son of Becher (1 Chr. vii. 8).—3. Son of Judah, a descendant of Pharez (ix. 4).—4. Son of Michael (xxvi. 18).

ON (*power*). Son of Peleth. A chief who revolted against Moses (Num. xvi. 1).

ON. (*Heliopolis*). BETHSHEMESH (Jer. xliii. 13). Egyptian sacred name *ha-ra* (the *city of the sun*), and common name *an*. It was on the E. bank of the Nile, 20 miles N. E. of Memphis; once the capital of the district. Joseph's wife was a daughter of a priest of On (Gen. xli. 45). The site is now marked by low mounds, enclosing a space about ¾ of a m. each way, where once stood the temple of the sun and the city, only a solitary obelisk (70 ft. high, and covered with hieroglyphics) being left of the former splendors of the place. The emperor Augustus carried a great many works of art, and an obelisk from this city to Rome; and Constantine adorned Constantinople from the same source. Tradition says that Joseph brought Mary and the infant Jesus to On, and points out a large fig-tree as the one under which they camped.

O'NAM (*strong*). 1. Son of Shobal (Gen. xxxvi. 23).—2. Son of Jerahmeël (1 Chr. ii. 26, 28), by Atarah.

O'NAN. Son of Judah (Gen. xxxviii. 4). It was Onan's duty to marry his brother's widow, and perpetuate the race; but he took means to prevent the consequences of marriage. Jehovah was angry with him, and slew him as he had slain his brother (ver. 9).

ONĒ'SIMUS. A slave who had escaped from his master Philemon of Colossæ, and had fled to Rome, where Paul converted him and recommended his forgiveness by his master in an epistle (Philemon). (See HISTORY OF THE BOOKS). Onesimus left Rome in the company of Tychicus, carrying the epistles to Philemon, to the Colossians, and Ephesians (Col. iv. 9). There is a tradition that Onesimus became Bishop of Beræa, where he is said to have been martyred.

ONĒSIPH'ORUS (*profit-bringing*). An Ephesian mentioned in 2 Tim. i. 16–18, who rendered Paul generous service during his second captivity in Rome, in acknowledging which, the apostle alludes

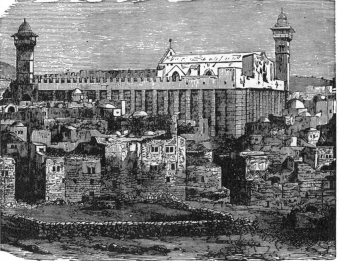

MOSQUE AT HEBRON.

to the "house of Onesiphorus," and in 2 Tim. iv. 19, to "the household of Onesiphorus," which suggests that the family might have shared in rendering services to Paul.

ONIA'RES. An error in 1 Macc, xii. 20, for AREUS to ONIAS.

ONI'AS (Heb. ONIYAH, *strength of Jah*). The name of five high priests; two only are mentioned in the A. V., I and III.

JADDUA
JADDUA 1. ONIAS I	- - - - B. C. 330.
1. ONIAS 2. SIMON the Just.	
2. SIMON 3. ONIAS II.	
3. ONIAS 4. SIMON II.	
4. SIMON 5. ONIAS III	- - - B. C. 198.
" " 6. ONIAS IV (Menelaus).	
5. ONIAS 7. ONIAS V.	

Onias IV assumed the Greek name Menelaus to gain the favor of the Greek party. He had been reproved by his eldest brother, Onias III, for appropriating the sacred treasures, at which he murdered his brother through an assassin (Andronicus) about 171 B. C. (2 Macc. iii. 4).

ONI'AS, THE CITY OF. Where stood a temple built by Onias V, and the Jewish settlements in Egypt. The site of the city of Onias was in the district north of Heliopolis.

ONIONS (Heb. BETSALIM). A bulbous plant; a

favorite article of food with the Egyptians. They are very mild in Egypt, and grow to a large size.

O'NO (*strong*). Built by the sons of Elpaal. In Benjamin (1 Chr. viii. 12). 725 of the people of Lod, Hadid, and Ono returned from Babylon (Ezr. ii. 33). There was a plain near the city (Neh. vi. 2), where Nehemiah was invited (but he declined) five times to come to a village in it to meet Sanballat. *Beit Anna*, 4½ ms. N. of Lud.

ONY'CHA (Heb. SHEHELETH, or SHECHELETH). The origin of our word *shell*. The Hebrew word is only mentioned in Ex. xxx. 34, as an ingredient of the sacred perfume. This word has been variously rendered—As the horny lid closing the open part of a shell, a kind of mollusk. Gosse thinks it was some gum resin, as all marine animals, except fish with fins and scales, were unclean.

EAR-RING, NATURAL SIZE.

O'NYX (Heb. SHOHAM). See PRECIOUS STONES.

O'PHEL. A part of ancient Jerusalem, first mentioned as having its wall built "much" upon by Jotham (2 Chr. xxvii. 3). Manasseh enclosed it with a wall (xxxiii. 14). It was near the water-gate (Neh. iii. 26), and a great corner-tower (v. 27). Josephus calls it Ophla (Ant. ix. 11, 2; B. J. ii. 17, 9). The prophet Micah (iv. 8) calls Ophel the daughter of Zion, which would indicate that Zion was the Temple-site, for Ophel is the hill S. of the S. wall of the Temple.—2. The Ophel of 2 K. v. 24, was the residence of the prophet Elisha, to which Gehazi returned after begging a present from Naaman, near Samaria.

O'PHIR (*dust—red dust?*). In the Himyarite language *ofir* is *red*, and the people of Mahra call their country red, and the Red Sea *Bahr Ofir*. Ophir was a region from which Solomon obtained gold in Tyrian ships, by the way of Eziongeber. It was in Arabia (Gen. x. 29), where several sons of Joktan settled, giving their names to regions or tribes. Sophir is the form of the name in the Septuagint and Josephus. The gold, silver, precious stones, ivory, apes, peacocks, and almug-wood are Indian articles, but may have been imported there. Jeremiah (x. 9) and Daniel (x. 5), say gold of *Uphaz*, probably meaning Ophir. On the shore of the Red Sea, in Arabia.

OPH'RAH (*a faun*). Two places of this name. 1. In Benjamin (Josh. xviii. 23), 5 ms. E. of Bethel, now called *Et Taiyibeh* a small village on a conical hill, containing ancient ruins. Jesus retired to this obscure place, after the miracle of raising Lazarus, with his disciples (John xi. 54). (See cut on page 94.) 2. In Manasseh, the native place of Gideon (Judg. vi. 11, viii. 27), and where he was buried. The prophet Micah calls it Aphrah (*dust*, i. 10).

OR. Used in the now obsolete sense of *ere* or *before* (Ps. xc. 2).

OR'ACLE (Heb. DEBIR). The inner sanctuary of the Temple (1 K. vi. 5, 16 ff.).

OR'ATOR (*a speaker*). The title given to TERTULLUS, the advocate of the Jews against Paul (Acts xxiv. 1). TRIAL.

OR'CHARD. See GARDEN. The East is naturally a country of orchards.—Of oranges, lemons, pomegranates, apples, olives, cherries, dates, apricots, figs, and other fruits. Nearly the whole support of a family can be had from the orchard. Trees are taxed very heavily, whether bearing or not, and from the time they are planted, which prevents enterprise.

ORDAIN. To order, constitute, appoint, found, or establish, as a priest or a deacon over a church. Heb. YASAD, founded in 1 Chr. ix. 22; 2. KUN, to establish (Ps. viii. 3); 3. MENAH, to set, or to number (Dan. v. 26; MENE in v. 25); 4. NATHAN to give (2 K. xxiii. 5); 5. AMAD, to raise up (Ex. ix. 16); 6. ARACA, to set in order (Ps. cxxxii. 17); 7. PAAL, work (Job xi. 8); 8. KUM, to confirm (Esth. ix. 27); 9. SUM, to appoint (1 Chr. xvii. 9); 10. SHAFATH, to set (Is. xxvi. 12); 11. ASAH, to make (1 K. xi. 31); 12. Greek, *diatasso*, to arrange (1 Cor. vii. 17); 13. *Kathistemi*, to place (Heb. v. 1); 14. *Kataskouazo*, to prepare fully (Heb. ix. 6); 15. *Krino*, to separate (Acts xvi. 4), and "to judge" over 80 times; 16. *Horizo*, to bound, limit (Acts x. 42); 17. *Poieo*, to make (Mark iii. 14); 18. *Proorizo*, predetermine (1 Cor. ii. 17); 19. *Tasso*, to set in order (Acts xiii. 48); 20. *Tithemi*, to lay (John xv. 16); 21. *Cheirotoneo*, to stretch (Acts xiv. 23); 22. *Ginomai*, to begin to be (Acts i. 22), this word is repeated 700 times in the N. T.; 23. *Prographo*, to write before (Rom. xv. 4); 24. *Proëtoimazo*, to appoint (Eph. iii. 3).

O'REB (*raven*). A chief of the Midianites who invaded Israel and was defeated by GIDEON. The disaster in which Oreb and Zeeb lost their lives (by the hands of Ephraimites), was one of the most awful on record. Two large rocks, near the scene, were named in memory of the event.

O'REB, THE ROCK (*the raven's crag*). (Judg. vii. 25; Is. x. 26). Not far from Bethshemesh, on the east (or west) side of Jordan. The Jews have a tradition that the prophet Elijah was fed by the people of Oreb (*ravens*). (See *Reland*).

O'REN (*pine*). Son of Jerahmeël (1 Chr. ii. 25).

OR'GAN. A musical instrument consisting of a combination of metal and reed pipes of different lengths and sizes. MUSICAL INSTRUMENTS.

ORI'ON. "God who made Arcturus, Orion and the Pleiades" (Job ix. 9; xxxviii. 31, 32; Amos v. 8). KESIL in Hebrew. Called the giant by the Arabs, which was Nimrod among the Chaldæans. Aben Ezra says Orion means the constellation now called Scorpion, or the bright star in it called Antares

ORNAMENTS. The ancient monuments show that ornaments were used in great variety in ancient as well as modern times. Every rank uses them, rich or poor, and as many as their means permit. If gold cannot be had, then silver, or brass, or tin, or glass, is used. Engraved gems were in use only by the most wealthy and educated. These bore besides the words or letters, figures of gods or mythical animals, or the portraits of relatives or friends (see PRECIOUS STONES). A few of the articles were: 1. NEZEM, ring; nose ring in Gen. xxiv. 22, 27.—2. ZAMID, bracelet.—3. KELI, jewels.—4. NEZEM-BEAZNOTH, rings in the ears.—5. CHOTHAM, seal, signet. — 6. PATHIL, string of beads (?).—7. TABBAATH, a signet ring (the badge of authority).—8. RABID, chain (of gold, Ez. xvi. 11).— 9. CHACH, buckle.—10. KUMAZ, tablets strung together, as hearts, diamonds, etc. (Ex. xxxv. 22).—11. MAROTH, looking-glasses.— 12. EZ'ADAH, chains (Num. xxxi. 20).—13. AGIL, circular ear-ring, solid. — 14. SAHARONIM, moonshaped little pieces, strung on a cord.—15. NETIFOTH, pendents (Judg. viii. 26).—16. TORIM, beads (rows), Cant. i. 10, 11, of gold or silver, or pearls.—17. CHARUZIM, any perforated small articles.—18. ANAK, perhaps a hanging lock of hair, in Cant. iv. 9. — 19. CHALAIM, necklace (Cant. vii. 1). — 20. GELILOM, garland (v. 12). — 21. LIVYAH, wreath. — 22. AKASIM, tinkling ornaments (Is. iii. 23).—23. SHEBISIM, lace caps.—24. SHEROTH, bracelets made of twisted wires.—25. REALOTH, spangles.—26. PEERIM, bonnets.—27. ZEADOTH, a chain to shorten the steps, worn on the legs.—28. KISSHURIM, girdle.—29. BOTTE-HANNEFESH, scent bottles.—30. LECASHIM, amulets used as earrings.—31. CHARITIM, purses (round, conical).—32. GILYONIM, a thin veil, gauze. Scarcely any new thing has been added in modern days. The *ckoôrs*, a saucer-shaped ornament of metal, sewed to the top of the cap and ornamented with stones, or engraved, now used by the Arabs, was probably very ancient; as may be inferred from the "golden tower" of the Mishna. (See cut on p. 9).

OR'NAN (*active*). ARAUNAH the Jebusite (1 Chr. xxi. 15, 18, 20, 25, 28).

OR'PAH (*forelock*). Wife of Chilion, son of Nöomi. She accompanied her sister-in-law on the road to Bethlehem, but went back to her people and her gods (Ruth i. 4, 14).

ORTHO'SIAS. Described by Pliny (v. 17) as near Tripolis, south of the river Eleutherus (which was the northern boundary of Phœnicia), in a strong pass; and a city of great importance, as commanding the route between Phœnicia and Syria. Tryphon fled there when besieged by Antiochus in Dora (1 Macc. xv. 37). The ruins are on the south bank of the *Nahr el Barid* (*cold river*).

OSE'A. Hoshea, king of Israel (2 Esd. xiii. 40).

OSE'AS. The prophet Hosea (2 Esd. i. 39).

OSE'E. The prophet Hosea (Rom. ix. 25).

OSHE'A. The original name of Joshua, son of Nun (Num. xiii. 8, 16).

OS'PRAY (Heb. OZNIYAH). An unclean bird. Very powerful; often weighing five pounds. It plunges under the water to catch fish. It belongs

ANTS OF PALESTINE.

to the *Falconidæ*, or falcon family, and is found in Europe, North America, and occasionally in Egypt (Deut. xiv. 12).

OS'SIFRAGE (Heb. PERES), (*bone-breaker*). The Lammergeier. An unclean bird (Lev. xi. 13). It attacks the wild goat, young deer, sheep, calves, etc. It is found in the highest mountains of Europe, Asia and Africa, and is frequently seen in the sky flying alone. See EAGLE, page 136.

OS'TRICH (Heb. BATH HAYYA'ANAH, daughters of the wilderness—*female ostriches*. YA'ENIM, *ostriches*, and RANAN, *to wail*—sometimes rendered *peacocks*). The words are generally accepted to mean the ostrich. In Lam. iv. 3, appears the word YA'ENIM (plural) which rightly translates ostrich. NOTSEH, *feathers*, in Job. xxxix. 13. Several lay their eggs in the same nest, which is usually a hollow scooped in the sand, where (covered only by the sand, about a foot deep), the sun warms them during the day. A few eggs are left out of the nest, intended for food for the young brood. The supposed cruel habit of the bird is used as a type of the cruelty and indifference of the Hebrews (Lam. iv. 3; Job xxxix. 16). This supposition is an error. for the ostrich cares for, and defends its young, even risking its own life. The brood numbers 20 to 30, are gray when young, and can run at once. The old birds are black and white. The valued plumes are pure white. They are easily tamed, and will live among the goats and camels. The Arabs hang great numbers of the eggs in their mosques, and also use them for cups, jars, etc. When chased they run in a circle, and can run a mile in about 2'. By running inside the circle, the horse gains on the ostrich, and comes up with him.

OTH'NI (*lion of Jah*). Son of Shemaiah (1 Chr. xxvi. 7). OTHEN (*lion*).

OTH'NIEL (*lion of El*). Descendant of Kenaz, and brother of CALEB 1 (Josh. xv. 17). He is first mentioned as the captor of Kirjath-Sepher (Debir), near Hebron, where he won his wife (his cousin Achsah), as a prize for leading the attack (Josh. xiv. 12–15; see ACHSAH). He is next called to be a judge (Judg. iii. 9), holding the office 40 years, or giving the nation rest in peace for that time.

OTHONI'AS. Error for Mattaniah (Ezr. x. 27), in 1 Esd. ix. 28.

OUCHES. Sockets in which the precious stones of the breast-place were set. (Nouches in Chaucer). (Ex. xxviii. 11, 13, xxxix. 6, etc.).

OV'EN (Heb. TANNUR). The ovens in the East are of two kinds. The stationary ones are found only in towns, where regular bakers are employed (Hos. vii. 4). The portable ones consist of a large jar made of clay, three feet high, larger at the bottom, with a hole for removing the ashes. Every house possesses such an article (Ex. viii. 3). It was heated with twigs, grass or wood (Matt. vi. 30), sometimes with dung, and the loaves were placed both inside and outside of it. FIRE.

OVERSEERS. A ministerial title, perhaps elder or bishop (Acts xx. 28).

OWL. Heb. 1. BATH HAYYA'ANAH (*daughters of the waste places*). (See OSTRICH). 2. YANSHUF or YANSHOF. The Ibis, an unclean bird, as in Lev. xi. 17 and Deut. xiv. 16. Probably not known in Palestine, but a native of Egypt. In Is. xxxiv. 11 it is mentioned in the desolation of Idumæa (Edom). 3. COS (*cup*), little owl (Lev. xi. 17, etc.). 4. KIPPOZ, the owl, which is common in the vicinity (and even in the city) of Jerusalem. LILITH, screech-owl, in Is. xxxiv. 14. The *lilith* was to the Hebrews what the *ghost* or *ghoul* is to the Arab, a "night-monster," and so they called the screech-owl by that name.

OWL.

OX. Heb. 1. BAKAR, horned cattle, of full age (Is. lv. 25).—2. FAR, BENBAKAR, calf.—3. SHOR, one of a drove of full grown cattle. THOR (the Chaldee form) in Ezr. vi. 9.—4. AGAL, calf of the first year; EGLAH, a heifer (Hos. x. 11), giving milk (Is. vii. 21), or plowing (Judg. xiv. 18).—5. AGIL, a bull two (?) years old (vi. 25).—6. ABARIM (*strong*) bulls.—7. TEO, wild bull (Is. li. 20); possibly the ORYX. Stall-fed cattle are alluded to in Prov. xv. 17, and 1 K. iv. 23. The cattle on the monuments are long-horned, short-horned, polled, or muley, besides the Abyssinian; and of every variety in color, as ours are. (See p. 10). The ox was the most important of all animals to the ancient Hebrews (as well as nearly all other nations). They were used for plowing (Deut. xxi. 10); threshing grain (Mic. iv. 13); for draught (1 Sam. vi. 7); to carry burdens (1 Chr. xii. 40), and riders; their flesh was eaten (1 K. i. 9); they were used for sacrifice, and the cow supplied milk, butter, tallow, hides, etc. The law contains many favorable clauses for its protection from misuse, abuse, starvation, and cruelty, and providing for its well-being, food and rest. The Hebrews did not castrate animals, but used them in their natural condition. Cattle grazing in distant pastures often became quite wild, as in Ps. xxii. 13. The present cattle in Palestine are small in size, and not good in quality. The buffalo is common now, and it was known anciently. The habits of this animal very nearly, if not entirely, answer the points in the text of Job xl. 15–24. They frequent the muddy pools, and the swift stream of Jordan, avoiding insects by keeping entirely under water, except their eyes and nose, under the covert of the reeds and willows. They are trained to the plow, and are much stronger than the ox.

O'ZEM (*strength*). 1. Son of Jesse (1 Chr. ii. 15).—2. Son of Jerahmeël (ii. 25).

OZI'AS. 1. Son of Micha, one of the governor's of Bethulia (Judg. vi. 15).—2. Uzzi, ancestor of Ezra (2 Esd. ii. 2).—3. Uzziah, king of Judah (Matt. i. 8, 9).

O'ZIEL. Ancestor of Judith (Jud. viii. 1). Uzziel.

OZ'NI (*attentive*). Son of Gad (Num. xxvi. 16). Ezbon.

OZ'NITES. Descendants of Ozni (Num. xxvi. 16).

OZO'RA. Nathan, Adaiah, Machnadebai, are corrupted into the sons of Ozora (1 Esd. ix. 34).

P

PA'ARAI (*open*). NAARAI, son of Ezbai (1 Chr. xi. 37).

PA'DAN (Heb. PODDAN, *a plain*). (Gen. xlviii. 7).

PA'DAN A'RAM. The family of the founder of the Jewish race settled here, with whom the descendants of Abraham married, as with an aristocratic people. (See HARAN.) *Padan* is Arabic for field, or ploughed land. The wife of the heir of the promise was sought here; and it was, probably, near Damascus, only a few days' journey from where Abraham was living, and not many weeks' (or months') travel, far away in Mesopotamia (Gen. xxxviii. xxxix).

PA'DON (*deliverance*). Ancestor of Nethinim, who returned from captivity (Ezr. ii. 44).

PAG'IEL (*event of El*). Son of Ocran (Num. i. 13).

PA'HATH-MOAB (*governor of Moab*). Head of one of the principal houses of the tribe of Judah. This title is obscure, but in 1 Chr. iv. 22 allusion is made to a family of Shilonites, of the tribe of Judah, who once had dominion in Moab. The family was of exalted rank, as is shown by its appearing fourth in the lists of both Ezr. ii. 6, and Neh. vii. 11. Among the lay princes PA'HATH-MOAB signs second (Neh. x. 14).

PA'I. A town in Edom (1 Chr. i. 50).

PAINTS. The only reference to paint is that of its universal use among women as a cosmetic to paint the eyes. (See EYE, p. 101).

PAL'ACE. The buildings, court-yards, etc., enclosed within the walls of a royal residence. The particular allusion to palace is that by the Herods, which was afterwards the residence of the Roman governor or prætor, hence it was called in Greek Pretorium. Christ was brought before the Roman procurator, Pontius Pilate, in this palace (Mark. xv. 16). The most celebrated palace mentioned in the Scriptures, is that of Solomon, a detailed description of which occurs in 1 K. vii. 1–12, and in Josephus (Ant. viii. 5, 1, 2). The Palace of Solomon was in the city on Mount Zion, opposite the Temple. It is estimated to have covered some 150,000 or 160,000 square feet. The first of the buildings upon entering, was "the House of the Forest of Lebanon." This was a hall so named from the cedars of Lebanon, worked into pillars and beams of which there were rows (1 K. vii. 2). The dimensions were 150 feet long by 75 feet in width and thirty high. This was the audience chamber. The next building of importance was the Hall of Judgment (1 K. vii. 7), 75 feet square. There was also a colonnade on "The Porch," 75 by 45 feet, used for reception and for the transaction of ordinary business.

There was further the inner court, with gardens and fountains, and accommodation for the harem officers of the court and guard.

PA'LAL (*judge*). Son of Uzai, who assisted at the Jerusalem walls (Neh. iii. 25).

PAL'ESTINE, PALÆSTI'NA. The translation of the Heb. PELESHETH, which is found only four times, and always in poetical passages in the O. T. (Ex. xv. 14; Is. xiv. 29, 31; Joel iii. 4). The same word is translated "Philistia" in Ps. lx. 8, lxxxiii. 7, lxxxvii. 4, cviii. 9. The two words were synonymous at the time our version was made, and Palestine in the Scriptures means only so much of the country as we now call Philistia.

On the Assyrian monuments there is a country described as PALAZTU on the West Sea, separate from Tyre, Damascus, Samaria and Edom. The Egyptians wrote it at Karnak PULUSATU. The Greeks called it Philistine Syria. Jerome (A. D. 400), also restricts the name to Philistia, and is followed by Procopius.

In our day the name is used of the whole country, including all that the Jews or Hebrews ever occupied.

It was originally called The Land of Canaan, low land (as compared with the high plateaus of Bashan and Gilead, Ps. cv. 11). The land of the Hebrews in Gen. xl. 15, only. The land of the Hittites in Josh. i. 4, and CHETU or CHITA on the Egyptian monuments.

The name HOLY LAND (TA-NETR) is as old as the Pharaoh Rameses II, and Thothmes III. The Phœnicians called their own country Holy Land, and the Egyptians may have borrowed the term, which argues that the idea of Holy Land belonged to the country before the Hebrews took possession, and is the most generally known now.

The Land of Israel (1 Sam. xiii. 19), land of Jah (Hos. ix. 3), the holy land (Zech. ii. 12), and the glorious land (Dan. xi. 41), were names in use during the monarchy.

There is no record of any division of the land, except the names of the several peoples inhabiting it, until the 12 tribes took possession, when the several divisions were known by the names of the tribes.

After the Captivity (if not before, 2 Chr. ix. 11), it was called Judæa, meaning the land of the Jews. The Romans divided it into Galilee, Samaria, Judæa, Perea, and gave names and limits to the surrounding country; as Phœnicia, Cœle-Syria, Lysania, Hauran, Edom, etc.

The land is about 140 ms. (Dan to Beersheba) long, and 40 ms. average width, between the Jordan valley and the West Sea; fenced in by this valley on the east, the Lebanon on the north, the desert on the south, and the Great Sea on the west. The whole of this district is high land, from 100 to 3000 feet above the sea level. The divisions are into Plain, Hill Country, Jordan Valley, and Mountains; each almost a strip from north to south, with a distinct history as well as structure.

1. The Plains lie along the shore of the Great Sea; are narrow at the north, and become wider southward, and are elevated from 100 to 500 feet; the surface sandy, rolling, with few forest trees, but many orchards, vines and shrubs, watered by brooks, fed by fountains. The great plain of Esdraëlon cuts the country into two sections, between Galilee and Samaria. There are no safe harbors on the coast, and only a few such as they are, at Tripolis, Jebail, Beirut, Acre, Joppa. Tyre and Sidon have almost entirely lost their harbors with sand which comes across from the great Sahara desert, and is destroying all the harbors, and creeping inland in many places, as at Beirut, Askulan, and Gaza.

2. The Hill Country, on both sides of the Jordan is elevated from 1000 to 4000 feet, has a few isolated peaks, and many deep ravines. The torrents flow mostly in winter, and there are many fountains and wells, and two rivers, Kishon and Leontes.

Galilee is about 20 miles wide, undulating, with plains, and several mountain peaks, as Safed, Jermuk (4000), Hattin, Kaukab, Tabor and Gilboa, rugged and sharp, with forests of oak, terebinth, thorns, and fruit orchards. The whole region is carpeted with flowers in the rainy season. The dews of Hermon increase the length of the green season and continues its freshness long after the southern section is dried up. There are many brooks flowing the year round, numerous fountains, and few wells.

HEAD-DRESS.

Carmel rises from the sea, south of Esdraëlon (see CARMEL), joins the hills of Samaria, which extend south through Judæa to the desert. (See EPHRAIM and SAMARIA). The hill-tops are rounder than those in Galilee, and well wooded. The noted peaks are Gerizim, Ebal, Samaria, Jedua, Haskin, Farsi and Kurn Surtabeh, none of which are very high. The noted valleys (or plains) are Mukhna, 6 miles long by one wide; Sanur, 2 miles; Kubatiyeh, 2½, and Dothan, 2½ miles. Orchards and groves of fruit are numerous, and the soil is excellent for raising grain.

The hills of Judæa are drier, with fewer fountains or permanent brooks, and the soil is poorer and less productive than Galilee or Samaria, which are nearer the mountains. There are few plains and no high peaks. The forests are few, shrubs many, and orchards and vineyards are cultivated extensively.

The country S. of Hebron and Beersheba is called the South (NEGEB). In the hot season it is dry and parched, hot and dusty, but the first rains bring up the grass, and start the fresh leaf on the trees, and all through the winter it is a delightfully fresh and green pasture. Very few orchards and vineyards; fountains are rare, and wells numerous, with no running brooks, all being winter-torrents. Very little grain is raised. See GILEAD, HAURAN. 3. The mountains are a continuation of Lebanon, on the W. of Jordan, and of Anti-Lebanon on the E., ending at Hebron and Kerak, nearly. The highest peaks in both ranges are N. of the Holy Land, on each side of the Leontes river. On Lebanon there are Dhor el Khodib (thŏr el kŏdib), 10,051 ft.; Sunnin,

8,500; Keniseh, 6,824; and Tomat Niha (*twin-peaks*) 6,500; on Anti-Lebanon, Mt. Hermon, 10,000: the range runs N. E., and varies in hight from 4,500 to 7000 ft. The peaks S. of Hermon are, Osha,

country are limestone, having few fossils. Over that there is a white cretaceous deposit, full of fossils, flints, ammonites, echinites (cidaris, petrified olives), fish, and others. This deposit is most noticeable on the western slopes of Lebanon, and the eastern slopes of Anti-Lebanon. Geodes of chalcedony, from an oz. weight to a 100 lbs., are numerous in Galilee, besides jasper and agate. Soft, friable sandstone, is found in extensive beds in both ranges. Coal is found near Beirut, in thin veins, and of poor quality. Iron and copper mines were worked anciently (Deut. viii. 9, xxxiii. 25; Eusebius viii. 15, 17). There are two kinds of limestone, the lower, white, and the upper, creamy, with streaks. The great quarry under Jerusalem (cut on p. 162), affords both kinds. The white (Arabic *melekeh*) is chalky, and may be easily cut, and sawed into blocks; the dark (Ar. *mezzeh*) is much harder, and takes a fine polish. Many of the caves are in limestone, some of which, as those in the north, at Paneas, and on the Dog river, are immense fountains. Many are used for storing grain, etc., and some for dwellings. The chalk deposits are found on summits only, N. of Hebron, as at Olivet, Bethlehem, Carmel, etc.; S. of Hebron it is more abundant, and near the surface, especially on the E. side of the Arabah, where the Romans named one place *Gypsaria* (Chalk-town). Flints are very abundant in the

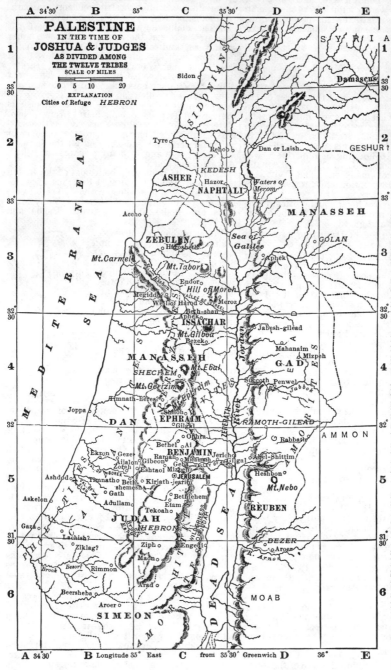

PALESTINE
IN THE TIME OF
JOSHUA & JUDGES
AS DIVIDED AMONG
THE TWELVE TRIBES
SCALE OF MILES
0 5 10 20
EXPLANATION
Cities of Refuge HEBRON

5000, near Es Salt (Ramoth Gilead); Nebo, 4,600, near Heshbon; and Zumla, E. of Gilead, about 4000 to 5000 ft. 4. The most remarkable feature of Palestine is the valley of the Jordan, the ancient Arabah (see ARABAH; DEAD SEA; JORDAN).

GEOLOGY. The great masses of rock under the

chalk on the W. shore of the Dead Sea. Sandstone is the under-stratum, in two layers, or series: one dusky-red, twisted, full of caverns, and colored with iron and other minerals, the other is dark grey, compact, bearing fossils—the chief underlying rock of the whole region E.

of Jordan. The chalk is of not so recent a deposit on the E. of Jordan, and is capped with a soft, friable sandstone, without fossils. The Abarim mountains are different, being sandstone, capped with chalk, bearing fossils. The red sandstone appears at Kerak. Both the sandstone and the limestone, on the E. are of an earlier age than those on the W. of Jordan. At Zurka Main, and at Wady Mojib, they form cliffs 400 ft. high. From Hermon to Kerak the whole region is limestone; 1000 ft. higher than Canaan, W. of Jordan.

EARTHQUAKES have been frequent, even in the historical period, the most noted, since that in the days of Uzziah, being those at Aleppo, in 1616–1812; Antioch, 1737; Laodicea, Beirut, Sidon, Tyre, Safed, and Tiberias, 1837. The principal sources of lava-streams on the E. of Jordan were at Phiala (so called), on Hermon, which is an extinct crater, now full of water; Tell Abu Tumeis; Kuleib; and El Hish, on Jebel Hauran, from which streams flowed over the whole district bounded by the Pharpar, the Jordan, and the Yarmuk. The Yarmuk was once dammed up by the stream from Phiala, and has made a new channel through the limestone beside the black basalt. There are many extinct craters in the Hauran (see TRACHONITIS, ARGOB). Lava and basalt have been traced eastward over the summits of Jebel Hauran (Alsadamum), but have not been followed beyond El Hish and Salcah. Basalt underlies Esdraëlon, extending through the district bounded by Delata on the N. Tiberias on the E., Tabor on the S., and Turan and Sefuriyeh on the W. One centre of eruption was at Hattin—the most ancient—which sent out a stream of dark, iron-grey, solid, and massive basalt, towards the Sea of Galilee, forming cliffs near Tiberias, 500 ft. high, overlaying limestone; and another, more recent, from three craters near Safed, El Jish, Taiteba, and Delata, which poured out a dark brown and a reddish-grey lava—porous. The Arabah is a deep ditch, from Hermon to the Red Sea, with a dividing ridge (see AKRABBIM) just S. of the Dead Sea. The width is an average of 10 ms., and the surface is everywhere below the ocean level; being deepest at the Dead Sea, where it is 1312 ft. below in the wet, and 5 or 6 ft. lower in the dry season. Tertiary and alluvial deposits are found in the valley, along the whole course of the Jordan, and on both shores of the Dead Sea, at the mouths of the rivers. There are two terraces of chalky marl: the upper extending across from side to side, between the mountains, and the lower, 50 to 150 ft. below; forming a ditch in which the river has worn a still lower channel of 10 or 20 ft. deep. The whole plain is worn into rounded knolls, by water from the high land on both sides; most distinctly seen on the edges of the terraces.

The strata exposed are limestone, rolled boulders, pebbles of flint, sandstone, tufas, marl, chalky deposits, pure chalk, conglomerates, sand, gravel, clay and detritus. South of Massada there are tall, conical knolls, shaped like hay-stacks, with pointed tops.

The shores of the Dead Sea are cut down on all sides, through crystalline rocks, into ravines, 600 to 1200 feet deep, with traces of extinct waterfalls and other evidences of remote antiquity. At Wady Derejeh there are eight terraces of gravel, marking different beaches, one above another—the highest 44 feet above the present level. There is no evidence that the Dead Sea was ever connected with either the Mediterranean or the Red Sea; but it was at one time 350 feet higher than at present, if not 540, as we may learn from the chalky deposits at Wady Hasasah. The ocean level is marked very distinctly all around the sea, indicating that there has been no general disturbance since the present arrangement of strata was completed. See MT. SEIR, MT. SINAI, RED SEA; also, CLIMATE, FLOWERS, TREES.

Mr. Tristam described 322 species of birds gathered by him and his party, and now safely deposited by him in a museum in London. Swimmers and waders were not well represented; 27 species are native to Palestine. He caught an ostrich in the Belka, east of the Dead Sea. (See the articles on the name of each bird). The whole country abounds in birds of every kind known in the temperate zone. Caged birds are found in almost every house.

Fish are caught in great plenty on the Great Sea and in Galilee; and one at least of its varieties is painted on the monuments in Egypt.

Reptiles are abundant, especially lizards, tortoises, geckos and chameleons. The common frog and tree-toad abound in wet places. Snakes are not very numerous, and none large. There are 3 species of scorpion. Mollusks are very numerous, in more than a hundred-varieties. Butterflies are as numerous, in proportion, as the flowers.

PALESTI′NA (*Palestine*). (Heb. PELESHETH); (Ex. xv. 14; Is. xiv. 29; Joel iii. 4; in Ps. lx. 8. Philistia, which was a synonymous term at one time). Palestine in the Scripture means Philistia, only (which see)

PAL′LU (*distinguished*). Son of Reuben (Ex. vi. 14).

PAL′LUITES, THE. Descendants of Pallu (Num. xxvi. 5).

TEMPLE OF DIANA.

PALM′ERIST (*palm of Christ*). Castor-oil plant (Jon. iv. 6).

PALMER-WORM. A voracious, hairy caterpillar, which does great damage to fruit-trees, and other vegetation (Joel i. 4).

PALMO′NI ("*that certain*"). An expression used to designate a person without calling him by name (Dan. viii. 13).

PALM-TREE (Heb. TAMAR; Gr. *phoinix*). The variety most common in the East is the date-palm (*phœnix dactylifera*). The palm-tree was always associated with Palestine; the name Phœnix being probably derived from Phœnicia. The coins of Vespasian, commemorating the conquest of Jerusalem by Titus, represent a woman of Judæa, weeping under a palm-tree. The date-palm is endogenous (growing from the end); its average hight is about 70 ft. About 8 yrs. after being planted, it yields fruit, averaging about 100 lbs., and continues productive for 100 yrs. Dates take the place of bread to a large extent in the East, and all the other parts of the tree are used for building, fencing, roofs, mats, baskets, couches, bags, etc. There is a saying with the Arabs that "The palm-tree has 360 uses." Jericho, "The City of Palm-Trees" (Deut. xxiv. 3; Judg. i. 16, iii. 13). The palm-groves of Jericho were always famous.

HAZE′ZON-TAMAR (*the pruning of the palm-tree*). Is alluded to in Gen. xlv. 7, and in 2 Chr. xx. 2. TAMAR (*the palm*), in the vision of Ezekiel (Ez. xlvii. 19, xlviii. 28). BETHANY (*the house of dates*) suggests that there were palms in the district of the Mt. of Olives, whence the people "took branches of palm-trees and went forth to meet Him" (John xii. 13): "Dwelt under the palm-tree of Deborah" (Judg. iv. 5). Women were named after the palm-tree, as the wife of ER, named TAMAR (Gen. xxxviii; also in 2 Sam. xiii. 1, and xiv. 27). Its form used in decoration in the Temple (2 Chr. iii. 5; 1 K. vi. 29, 32, 35, vii. 36), and in Ezekiel's vision (Ez. xl. 16, xli. 18). "The righteous shall flourish like the palm-tree" (Ps. xcii. 12). Its grace—the lofty and ever-green foliage, cresting the top of the tree, near to heaven—all suggest abundant illustration. The Jews commemorated victories by carrying palms (1 Macc. xiii. 51; Esd.

ii. 44-47), etc. Also, the glorified are mentioned in Rev. vii. 9, as "clothed with white robes, and palms in their hands. See DATES.

PAL'SY, (Gr. *paralusis, relaxation*). An abolition of function, whether of intellect, special sensation, or voluntary motion.

To destroy action or energy; *a disabling of the nerves* of a part of a body, afterward also of the whole body (Matt. iv. 24). The withered hand was an instance, cured by Jesus (Mark iii. 1).

PAL'TI (*deliverance of Jah*). Son of Raphu, a spy (Num. xiii. 9).

PAL'TIEL (*deliverance of God*). Son of Azzan and prince of Issachar (Num. xxiv. 26).

PAL'TITE (*descendants of Pelet, the*). One of David's men (2 Sam. xxiii. 26).

PAMPHY'LIA. A province of Asia (Minor), on the south coast, bordering the same sea as, and west of Cilicia (Acts xx. v. ii. 5). The sea is now called *Adalia*, from the ancient Attalia. The region was only 20 ms. wide, inland, between Taurus and the sea. Paul here first entered Asia, having just left Cyprus, landing at Perga (Acts xiii. 13), where John Mark left him and Barnabas. The language seems from Luke's account (Acts ii. 10), to have been corrupted to some local dialect. The region is now thinly peopled, with a few towns along the coast, in the midst of fine orchards, surrounded by fertile fields. Ruins here and there mark ancient sites.

PAN'NAG. Some kind of spice, or aromatic plant exported from Palestine at Tyre (Ezr. xxvii. 17). It may possibly have been a flavoring substance used in bread. The Syriac renders it millet.

PAPER-REEDS. PAPYRUS. "Paper reeds by the brooks" in Is. xix. 7, should read "meadows by the river" (Nile).

PANE'AS. (See CÆSAREA PHILIPPI.)

PA'PHOS. In Cyprus at the west end of the island (Salamis being at the east end and a road between); the seat of the Roman governor, Sergius Paulus, who "believed" after hearing Paul and Barnabas (Acts xiii. 12). Elymas (*magician, sorcerer*), was struck with blindness (for a season), as a punishment for deceiving people with his magic. They had a fine temple in honor of Aphrodite (Venus), who was worshiped, and was fabled to have risen from the sea at this place (Homer, Od. viii. 362). The temple was at a place now called *Kuklia*, some distance from the new town called *Baffa*.

COIN OF RHODES.

PAPY'RUS (*Reed*). (Heb. names: AGMON, GOME, AROTH, KANEH). A tall reed (3 to 6 ft., angular), with a broom-shape head, formerly lining the Nile banks, and growing elsewhere in marshes in Egypt and Palestine. Its lower part was used for food, after cooking. It is without leaves, and the pulp was used for making paper. Some ancient specimens of the papyrus (covered with writing and drawings), are to be found in the Abbott Museum, New York, (and in several museums in Europe). See page 106.

The several words translated reed in the A. A. are: 1. AGMON, *a rush*. In Job xl. 26, it is asked, "Canst thou put a rush through the nose of the crocodile?" as you do through the gills of a fish!— 2. GOME, *the papyrus, paper-reed;* translated rush and bulrush. The word occurs four times: when

Moses was hid in a boat made of papyrus, in Ex. ii. 3; in the notice of the skiffs or canoes of the Ethiopians (Is. xviii. 2); and as a reed in Is. xxxv. 7, and in Job viii. 11. The stem is three inches thick at the base, and ten to sixteen feet long.

The Abyssinians use it for light boats. There were other similar plants of which boats were also made. See cut, Egyptians making a papyrus boat, on page 122.

The papyrus (paper) was made from the soft pulp, which is cellular, and could be sliced very thin. These slices were cut as long as the paper was to be wide, and were laid side by side, and other slips laid over the seams and gummed into place, until the whole was of the required size and thickness. The papyrus-reed grows in Syria, in the marsh of the Huleh (from which place Antigonus got it to make cordage for his ships), on Gennesaret, in Sicily, in Abyssinia, along the White Nile, and in Nubia.

There is another species in Palestine, growing near Caiffa, under Carmel. This has a top like an umbrella. The true papyrus hangs the top on one side, like a broom. See cut on page 106. The Arabs use both kinds for mats, roofs and walls for their huts.—3. AROTH (once only as paper-reeds in Is. xix. 7), green herbage, such as grows in wet, marshy places.—4. ACHU (flag in Job viii. 11, and meadow in Gen. xli. 2, 18). Some water-plant, eaten by cattle; perhaps the beautiful Flowering Rush, or it may be the Edible Rush.—5. SUF (flags in Ex. ii. 3, 5, where the boat containing Moses was laid; flags in Is. xix. 6, and reeds in Jonah ii. 5). Weeds. The Red Sea is called *Yam Suf*, by the Arabs—Sea of Weeds. Suf is a term for all marine vegetation.—6. KANEH, *a cane* (*stalk* of wheat or corn in Gen. xli. 5, 22; *branches* of a candlestick in Ex. xxv. 31; a measure equal to six cubits in Ez. xl. 5; and in anatomy, the name of the bone between the shoulder and the elbow in Job xxxi. 22).—7. Greek *kalamos*. Used for a reed growing, a measuring-rod (Rev. xi. 1, etc.), and a reed-pen (3 John 13).

There was a fragrant reed also, KENEH BOSEM (Ez. xxx. 23), and KANEH HATTOB (Jer. vi. 20). The *Calamus aromaticus* is very fragrant, and is used for perfume in ointments. The lemon-grass is another aromatic reed or grass.

PAR'ABLE (Heb. MASHAL; Greek *parabole;* Latin *parabola*). A similitude, a comparison. See FABLE. The Hebrews used the term mashal (similitude) for the Proverbs (1 Sam. x. 12, xiv. 13), prophesy (Num. xxiii. 7), enigmas (Ps. lxxviii. 2), and narrative (Ez. xii. 22). The parable was used by the Hebrew teachers from the earliest times, and especially by Hillel, Shammai and other great Rabbis just before the Christian era. The parable is a low form of speech, adapted to the ignorance of the great mass of mankind. The Scribes had a kind of parable that was understood by the few only, and therefore it is said that the Sermon on the Mount was open and plain instruction, and "not as the Scribes." Jesus chose this form of teaching the people, who were spiritually blind and deaf (Matt. xiii. 13). The parable attracts, and if understood, is remembered, yet sometimes the meaning is lost. There were probably many spoken which were not recorded (ib. 34). The number is about 30 or 31.

The parables of Jesus are the most characteristic and beautiful portions of his teachings, full of interest to the youngest and instruction to the oldest, conveying, in delightful narratives, the profoundest truths relating to his kingdom, of which we become sensible in proportion as our views of religion rise into the spiritual and ideal. All outward things take on a fuller meaning and have a richer color and brighter light. The great object of Jesus was to manifest himself, and his parables do this by laying bare the hearts of men.

The interpretation of the parables belongs to the highest order of Biblical exegesis, requiring knowledge, spiritual discernment, taste and tact, and a well-balanced mind. There are no rules applicable to this work.

It may be noticed that there seems to be but one leading idea in each parable. The aim is ethical, and is not poetical, the story being told for the sake of the lesson.

It is extremely difficult to classify the parables. The chronological order is given as near as may be in the article JESUS. It does not appear that they were delivered in any order or sequence, but in answer to inquiries, or called forth by certain circumstances from time to time. In the following table only one reference is given; the others can be found in the article JESUS.

GROUP 1.—RELATING TO CHRIST'S KINGDOM.

1. Wicked Husbandmen (Matt. xxi. 33–44). The fate of those who abuse their privileges and refuse to enter the kingdom.
2. The Rich Fool (Luke xii. 16–21). The vanity of all worldly things without the kingdom.
3. The Marriage of the King's Son (Matt. xxii. 1–14). Danger of rejecting the invitations of the kingdom.
4. The Barren Fig-tree (Luke xiii. 6–9). Danger of delay.
5. The Great Supper (Luke xiv. 15–24). Outward privileges useless without a personal use of the means of salvation.
6. The Pearl of Great Price (Matt. xiii. 45, 46). The kingdom to be sought for alone.
7. The Hid Treasure (Matt. xiii. 44). Sacrifice for the kingdom when found.
8. The Rich Man and Lazarus (Luke xvi. 19–31). The kingdom in the estimate of God and of man.

GROUP 2.—CHRIST'S KINGDOM IN THE HEART.

9. The Sower (Matt. xiii. 3–8). Preparation of the heart.
10. The Seed Growing Secretly (Mark iv. 26–29). The kingdom grows in the heart silently and constantly.

GROUP 3.—MANIFESTATION OF THE KINGDOM.

14. The Two Debtors (Luke vii. 41–43). The kingdom appears in obedience springing from love.
15. The Good Samaritan (Luke x. 30–37). Aid in love, which knows no limits and spares no pains.
16. The Two Sons (Matt. xxi. 28). In the obedience of deeds not words.
17. The Unmerciful Servant (Matt. xviii. 23–35). In mercy and forgiveness without limit.
18. The Unjust Steward (Luke xvi. 1–9). In wise and energetic improvement of temporal advantages.
19. The Friend at Midnight (Luke xi. 5–8). In constant prayer.
20. The Unjust Judge (Luke xviii. 1–8). Persevering prayer.
21. The Pharisee and Publican (Luke xviii. 9–14). In humility and contrition.
22. The Laborers in the Vineyard (Matt. xx. 1–16). Unselfish rejoicing in the salvation of others.
23. The Lost Sheep (Matt. xvii.).
24. The Lost Piece of Money (Luke xv. 8–10).
25. The Prodigal Son (Luke xv. 11–32).
    In acknowledging the wisdom and beauty of receiving sinners, and in a missionary spirit.
26. The Unprofitable Servant (Luke xvii. 7–10). Confessing all that we can do is nothing.
27. The Ten Virgins (Matt. xxv. 1–13). Preparation for the coming of the Lord.
28. The Talents (Matt. xxv. 14–30). Active preparation for the coming of the Lord.

GROUP 4.—THE CONSUMMATION OF THE KINGDOM.

29. The Pounds (Luke xix. 11–27). The final reckoning.
30. The Draw-net (Matt. xiii. 47–50). The final separation.

PA′RAH (*cow*). Five miles N. E. of Jerusalem. The name is continued in *Wady Farah* (*mouse*), the Arabs keeping the *sound* only of the ancient name, as they have done in many other cases. Dr. Barclay claims this wady for the ancient locality of ÆNON, where John was baptizing; for there is a large intermitting fountain there (John iii. 23; City of the Great King, 558). Khurbet Farah (*ruin of*) lies on the fork between Wady Tuwar and Wady Farah (Josh. xviii. 23).

PA′RAN (*place of caves*). Name of a mountain and a wilderness. The mountain is only mentioned in two poetical passages (Deut. xxxiii. 2; Hab. iii. 3). This name is preserved in Wady FARAN

WADY FARAN.

11. The Tares and the Wheat (Matt. xiii. 24–30). Difficulties in the way of the kingdom.
12. The Mustard-seed (Matt. xiii. 31, 32). Outward growth of the kingdom.
13. The Leaven in the Meal (Matt. xiii. 33). Inward growth.

(*faran*), in Sinai; and the mountain is probably that now called Serbal, one of the grandest in the region (*Bartlett*, Forty Days; *Stanley*). The wilderness is described minutely in the Scriptures; and had Palestine on the north, Arabah on the east, and Sinai on the south; corresponding to the

desert *Et Tyh* (*the wandering*) of the present (see
SINAI). This region is not a desert, or a wilderness, but is called by the Hebrews *Midbar* (*pasture-land*).

PAR'BAR (1 Chr. xxvi. 18). An open porch,
or some structure on the west side of the Temple
court.

PARCHED GROUND. In Is. xxxv. 7. Heb.
SHARAB, should be read "mirage," a peculiar de-
ceptive appearance of the heated air, by which
you are led to think you see trees, houses, water,
etc., at a distance.

GREEK PARTRIDGE.

PAR'LOR. The king's audience chamber (Judg.
iii. 20–25).

PARMASH'TA (*superior*). Son of Haman (Esth.
ix. 9).

PAR'MENAS (*abiding*). A deacon (Acts vi. 5).

PAR'NACH (*delicate*). Ancestor of Elizaphan
(Num. xxxiv. 25).

PA'ROSH (*a flea*). 2,172 descendants of Parosh
who returned from captivity (Ezr. ii. 3). Another
150 males accompanied Ezra (Ezr. viii. 3). They
assisted in building the wall of Jerusalem (Neh.
iii. 25), and sealed the covenant (x. 14).

PARSHAN'DATHA (*interpreter*). Eldest of Haman's sons, slain by the Jews (Esth ix. 7).

PART. (Heb. PELECH, *circuit or district*). Used
in reference to Jerusalem, Beth-haccerem, Mizpah, Beth-zur and Keilah (Neh. iii. 9).

PAR'THIA (Acts ii. 9). The Parthians here
meant were Jews only, who were present at Jerusalem on the day of Pentecost. Originally it was
a small mountainous district N. E. of Media, between Aria and Hyrcania, but afterward included
a large district. The country is mountainous, climate pleasant, soil fertile, well watered by many
small streams (which do not reach the seas, but
are absorbed in the ground), and has many ruins
of ancient cities, such as Ctesiphon, Akker-kuf,
El Hammam and Takt-i-Bostan, some of the most
remarkable Oriental remains, which are evidence
of a former state of prosperity and wealth. It is
now a part of Persia. The first known of this
Scythian people is of the time of Darius Hystaspis; although it is supposed that Cyrus annexed
their territory to his empire (B. C. 550). They
were in Xerxes' great army in Greece. Alexander gave their country to Eumenes. The Parthian
Empire began under Arsaces, B. C. 256, and extended from the Tigris to India, and from the
Chorasmian desert to the Southern Ocean. It was
the only power that opposed Rome with final success. The Roman general, Crassus, was defeated
by them at Carrhæ (Harran). (*R. K. Porter*).

PAR'TRIDGE (KORE). The desert partridge,
used as a simile by David when pursued by Saul
(Sam. xxvi. 20), and as a simile of a man who
reaps what he does not sow (Jer. xvii. 11). They
are very prolific, laying 20 or more eggs. There

are several species in Palestine. The word KORE
may also include the black partridge of India and
the sand grouse, which latter is very common in
Syria.

PARU'AH (*blossoming*). Father of Jehoshaphat
(1 K. iv. 17).

PARVA'IM. From whence gold was brought for
the ornamentation of the Temple (2 Chr. iii. 6).
The Sephar of Gen. x. 30, which was a mountain,
and probably the same as Ophir. Others hold that
Parvaim means Eastern, as the modern *Levant*
does, and therefore say that the text means only
eastern gold. Pliny mentions a Barbatia on the
Tigris (vi. 32).

PA'SACH (*cut up*). Son of Japhlet (1 Chr. vii.
33).

PASDAM'MIM (*hand of confusion*). Ephes Dam-
mim (1 Chr. xi. 13). Where a fierce conflict with
the Philistines occurred. *Damun* is a ruin, 3 miles
east of Socho, but it is not identified beyond
dispute.

PASE'AH (*lame*). 1. Son of Eshton (1 Chr. iv.
12).—2. Ancestor of Nethinim, who returned from
captivity (Ezr. ii. 49). PHASEAH.—3. Ancestor of
the Jehoiada who assisted in repairs of the "old
gate" (Neh. iii. 6).

PASH'UR (*prosperity*). 1. Son of Malchiah,
one of the princes in the court (Jer. xxxviii. 1).
The name of a family of priests of the house of
Malchijah (Jer. xxi. 1).—2. Another priest, son of
IMMER, and governor of the house of the Lord. He
was opposed to Jeremiah in Jehoiakim's reign, and
for this indignity his name was changed to MAGOR-
MISSABIB (*terror on every side*), (xx. 1–6).—3. Father of GEDALIAH 4 (xxxviii. 1).

PAS'SAGE (Heb. EBER, MAABAR, MAEBARAH).
A river ford or mountain pass (1 Sam. xiii. 23).
See JORDAN.

PAS'SENGERS (Heb. OBERIM). Those who go
right on their ways. "The valley of the passengers" means the valley where Gog's multitude
were to be buried (Ez. xxxix. 11).

PASSION. Suffering of the Lord JESUS CHRIST
on the cross (Acts i. 3).

PASS'OVER (Heb. PESACH; Greek *Pascha*). The
first of the three great annual festivals of the Hebrews, held in Nisan, 14th to 21st. There are several distinct passages relating to the Passover in
Exodus and Deuteronomy, where its original intention, the unleavened bread, the first-born sanctified, are mentioned, and the paschal lamb. In
Ex. xxiii. 14–19, the paschal lamb is mentioned as
My Sacrifice, and the feast is called "of unleavened
bread." The redemption of the first-born is noticed
in xxiv. 18–26. In Deut. xvi. 1–8, the command is
given to keep the passover in Jerusalem. A lamb
was roasted whole—not a bone of it to be broken—
and eaten entirely, the same night, with bitter
herbs; if not all eaten, the remnant to be burnt.
The blood of the victim was to be sprinkled on the
door-post.

The meaning was to commemorate the Exodus
from Egypt, when the Lord passed over the first-
born of the Hebrews and smote those of the
Egyptians. The Rabbis affixed the penalty of
whipping to any one who should not kill the
paschal lamb in the Court of the Temple, and
separated the people into three companies at that
time to avoid confusion. During the killing trumpets were blown and the Hallel was sung by the
Levites. See LORD'S SUPPER, AGAPE.

The position of sitting down to the meal or reclining was adopted by the Hebrews as a sign of
their freedom, as though just out of Egypt.

The use of wine had no place in the original institution, but was sanctioned by Jesus both in the
Passover and the Lord's Supper.

It has been debated whether the Lord ate the

Passover the last time on the same day as the Jews did or the evening before; but the frequent references to the event by all the Evangelists, without hesitation as to the time, leaves no doubt that it was eaten at the usual time. The Sadducees and Pharisees differed as to the proper day.

Jesus, the Christ, was himself the Paschal Lamb, the spiritual Passover, of whom the Hebrew rite was a type.

PAS'TOR (Heb. ROEH, *a shepherd*), (Jer. ii. 8); also applied to CHRIST, the Great "Shepherd" (Jer. xxvi. 31), and to the spiritual ministers of a church (Eph. iv. 11). BISHOP. ELDERS.

PAS'TURE. To those who had large flocks and herds, an abundance of pasturage and water were of great importance. ABRAHAM, ISAAC, and JACOB, moved from place to place in order to obtain these essentials. Palestine is well adapted to grazing. Figuratively it is applied to the spiritual wants of the people of God (Ps. xxiii. 2). PASTOR.

PAT'ARA. The seaport of Xanthus, near the coast, in Lycia. It was devoted to the worship of Apollo (Hor. Odes, iii. 4, 64), and the coins of the district exhibit traces of the respect paid to the divinity. Some of the ruins—among which are a triple arch of a gate of the city, and a ruined theatre, baths, temples, etc.—indicate a once populous and important city; such as it probably was at the time of Paul's visit (Acts xxi. 1, 2), when it was an emporium of commerce between the east and west coasts of the Levant (see Livy, xxxvii. 16; Beaufort's *Karamania, Ionian Ant. of the Dilettanti Soc.*, and Fellows).

PATHE'US. PETHAHIAH, the Levite (1 Esd. ix. 23).

on a hill, to the S. is the monastery of "St. John the Divine" (built by Alexius Comnenus). In the library of this church are many ancient MSS., two of which contain an account of John after the Ascension. There are no forest-trees, but many flowering shrubs and plants. Walnut and fruit-trees are grown in orchards; and the wine is famous for its strength and flavor. Now called Patina, and Palmosa. Pop. 4,000. (See *Patmos and the Seven Churches*).

PAT'ROBAS. A Christian at Rome (Rom. xvi. 14).

PATRO'CLUS (*famous from his father*). Father of Nicanor (2 Macc. viii. 9).

PA'U (*bleating*). The capital of Hadar (Gen. xxxvi. 39).

PAUL (Heb. SAUL). He was a Benjamite, a native of Tarsus, Cilicia, and was born about A. D. 5, a free Roman citizen (by descent from his father). He had a sister (whose son is mentioned), and perhaps other sisters, as well as brothers, some of whose names may possibly be those given by Paul in his Epistle to the Romans, as Andronicus, Junia, and Herodion. Tarsus was then the rival of Athens and Alexandria as a seat of learning, where Paul began that acquaintance with the classical writers which was continued when he went to Jerusalem as a pupil of Gamaliel, who was a strict Pharisee, and well known by his title of "The Glory of the Lord," and "Rabban" (Our Master). It seems to have been the intention of his parents to fit him for the rabbinical profession. It was the custom to teach every son a trade, and he was brought up to the making of tent-cloth (from goats' hair, called cilicia). These black tents are now

PATMOS.

PATH'ROS. A district in Egypt, and a Mizraite tribe.

PA'TRIARCH (Greek *patriarches*). Head of a family or tribe (Heb. vii. 4; Acts vii. 8, ii. 29). It is a title of many of the ancestors of the Hebrews, as David, Abraham, Noah.

They were the head of the religious faith and practice, as well as leader and judge in civil affairs, and represented God who is the great father of all men. When the Temple worship took the place of family worship the patriarch became a sheikh, and was no longer a priest.

The Arabs still keep up this form of government in civil affairs, but not in religious.

PAT'MOS (Rev. i. 9). A rocky island, S. of Samos—one of the Sporades, in the Icarian Sea, a part of the Ægean Sea—15 ms. around; divided almost in two by a narrow isthmus, on the E. side of which are the town and harbor, and near them,

used in Syria, and are mentioned by the ancient poets. While yet a young man he showed a great zeal for the law of Moses (Judaism), in consenting and assisting at the stoning of Stephen, by holding the cloaks of those who threw the stones. The main events of his life, as given by Luke, and by himself, are:—His conversion; labors at Antioch; the first missionary journey, in which he assumed the character of the Apostle to the Gentiles; the visit to Jerusalem, to settle the relation of the Gentile and Jewish converts; the introduction of the Gospel into Europe; the third missionary journey, during which time he wrote the four great Epistles; the arrest, imprisonment, voyage to Rome, and death. The chronology and details are given in the table below. Personally, Paul is almost unknown to us, unless we accept tradition and the statements of the ancients. The portrait given (p. 237) represents the idea that the artist formed of him hundreds of years after his death, and it is only interesting to us as a relic of early Christian art. From the Gospels we learn that he was of a subtile, tenacious and versatile intellect; intolerant before, but, after his conversion, tolerant of the opinions of others; of a weak bodily presence, and a poor voice; but full of fresh ideas, and so thoroughly systematic and persistent as to deserve the name of the chief founder of the Christian Church.

Stephen is called the forerunner of Paul ("the blood of the first martyr, the seed of the greatest apostle"); and he was his anticipator in spirit and power, as may be seen in his defense before the Sanhedrin, wherein he gave a critically just and true summary of the Jewish Church—denouncing the local worship, and bringing out the spiritual element in its history. The substance of the whole speech, and its style, seems to have been thrown over Paul's spirit, like the mantle of the prophet.

His mission to Damascus was to arrest the disciples of Jesus there, and bring them to Jerusalem for trial and punishment, as apostates from the Jewish Church. On the way he was arrested by a miracle, converted by receiving knowledge of the truth; was consecrated by Ananias; and, after his recovery from the temporary blindness, began his work for the new cause, in the synagogue at Damascus, by preaching Jesus the Christ to the Jews, and Jesus the Son of God to the Gentiles.

His preaching naturally excited the rage of his late friends and employers, who regarded him as an apostate and a dangerous man, and aimed at his life; when he was obliged to escape from the city by night, his friends letting him down from a window in the wall in a basket. See DAMASCUS.

His return to Jerusalem (after three years' absence), as a disciple, only caused alarm to the brethren, who remembered his zeal against them, in the case of Stephen and as the high-priest's officer, until he was introduced as a believer by Barnabas. Being driven out of the city in a short time by the Jews, he returned by Cæsarea to Tarsus, from whence he was summoned by Barnabas to come to Antioch to help in the gospel work. On account of the famine, predicted by Agabus, Barnabas and Saul were sent to Jerusalem with a contribution for the poor there; and on their return, John Mark (nephew of Barnabas), accompanied them as an assistant.

It was on the first mission-ary journey, while they were in Cyprus, that his name was changed from Saul to Paul, which was the Greek form of the name,—as Jason is for Jesus, Pollio for Hillel, Al-phæus for Clopas, etc.

HEAD-DRESS.

Paul and Barnabas were again sent to Jerusalem, to have a decision made, by the apostles and elders, on the question of circumcision; when Peter declared the fact that God himself had set the seal of the gift of the Holy Ghost on the Gentile as well as on the Jew convert.

Before setting out on his second missionary journey Paul separated from Barnabas, because he could not trust Mark, who had left them at a critical time on their first journey; so Paul took Silas instead of Barnabas, and Barnabas took Mark with him. The business of the next year was founding churches in Phrygia and Galatia, which he did with great success.

In a vision, the spirit of Jesus turned him back from Bithynia; and while at Troas, in the form of a man of Macedonia (in another vision), directed him to carry the gospel into Europe, in the memo-rable words, "Come over into Macedonia and help us."

The style of the narrative in Acts intimates, in the change from "they" to "we," that Luke, the writer went with Paul from Troas.

They preached from city to city for nearly a year, and passed on into Greece (to Athens). Here he set forth the gospel in the synagogue, the market-place, and, by invitation, in the venerable assembly of the Areopagus, where were gathered the most polished men of the foremost seat of learning in the world, who were acute, witty, shrewd, and most intensely scornful. He exposed the folly of their superstitions with exquisite tact and ability, and unfolded the character and claims of the "un-known God" whom they were already worshiping unintelligently. But he made very little impression on the popular religion, probably because his simple faith, having no splendid show of material accession, could not be expected to take the place of their highly poetical mythology, which was celebrated by the most magnificent displays of temples, vestments, processions, and sacrifices.

A year and a half in Corinth was spent in preaching and working at his trade, with better results than at Athens.

Again at Ephesus, he made so many friends that the idol-makers became alarmed for the business, and stirred up a tumult against Paul. They made small copies of the temple and image of Diana, which were used in private houses, or carried on journeys; and Paul declared that they were "no gods," but that Jesus the Christ was the only proper object of worship as the Son of God. See EPHESUS and SEVEN CHURCHES.

After another visit to Macedonia, Greece, and Illyria, he turned toward Jerusalem for the fifth and last time. On the way there occurred, at Miletus, one of the most affecting incidents in the whole story of his life. The elders of the church at Ephesus had come to Miletus to meet him. He was over sixty years of age, naturally feeble of body, always a hard worker, and it seemed probable that this was their last interview. He recalled his labors among them, assuring them that his single object had always been the preaching of the gospel of Jesus; and referred to the dangers through which they all had passed, and those that the Holy Spirit had predicted were to come, and to his determination to press on, as though his life was in his hand, and entreated them to follow him for the sake of their Lord Jesus.

The visit to Jerusalem seemed to his friends at Cæsarea also to be dangerous; and Agabus, who had 17 years before proved himself a prophet, showed Paul that he would be put in bonds if he went up to the city.

The story cannot be told in better words than Luke uses, in the 21st and the following chapters of Acts. His enemies had determined on his destruction, and watched for an opportunity, and were finally compelled to invent an accusation on the pretext that Paul had taken some Greeks into the Temple, and thereby had broken the Law of Moses, and had polluted the Holy House. He was rescued from the furious mob of Jews by the Roman soldiers, and also protected on account of his Roman citizenship; but was for years kept in chains, without trial, with occasional examinations before the governor and the king (which, it is more than suspected, were for the purpose of extorting a bribe from Paul or his friends), and was finally sent to Rome, on his appeal to Cæsar. Luke's account of the voyage has been most severely criticised, and found to agree with the nature of the region, climate, winds, coasts, habits and superstitions of the people, and even the make of the ships at that age; and since its purpose was to follow the spiritual Paul chiefly, has been shown to be one of the finest and truest records extant (see MELITA).

Of Paul's death almost nothing is known. Tradition affirms that he was beheaded at Rome, where a grave is now shown, which is honored with a monument.

His personal appearance had little to command admiration, or even respect. A small figure, a bald head, with weak eyes and a hooked nose, like some of the Jews of our day—and, added to these, feeble health—makes a whole that would excite, besides ridicule, only sympathy, until we become acquainted with the great soul and ardent spirit that was the tenant of this poor frame.

PAUL.
Engraved on copper an ideal portrait, found in a cemetery, dated 480, A. D.

He is one of the most wonderful characters known to history. Called to a peculiar work, he was most peculiarly adapted to that work from nature, education and circumstances, and most nobly did he succeed. His labor in establishing the Church in many cities and countries occupied nearly thirty years of constant application—in traveling, preaching, writing and working with his own hands at his trade; some of the time, even while a prisoner, chained to a guard, or in a cell, ending, when he was "ready to be offered," in his death at the age of nearly 70 years. See ROME.

He was a poor mechanic, and in the eyes of the Greeks and Romans was of an origin as hateful as that of the Jews, who are called the enemies of mankind; and, as his enemies said, he was of a bodily presence that was weak, and had a contemptible speech; yet he did more than any other man to set in motion those new ideas that were to lift mankind up out of the darkness of superstition, purify their minds from the errors of ages, open their hearts to the great truths of the oneness of God, and the brotherhood of men, and the value of a good and true life; enforcing these great truths by a life equally great, full of bravery, self-sacrifice, and self-denial, and which have gained power to crush and scatter the Paganism of the Greek and Roman world.

This work was not done without pain, and danger, and toil. From the very beginning he suffered hardship, risk of life from his former associates; continued in long journeys by sea and land; shipwreck; stoning by an infuriated mob; exposure to the fury of wild beasts in the amphitheatre; and finally loss of life by violence.

If privation, suffering, patience, and perseverance—warmed by zeal and tempered with wisdom and love, elevated and polished by scholarship and brilliant talents, inspired with the knowledge of the Divine Spirit, and all these qualities softened with a charming urbanity that was never laid aside—if all these rare endowments can build an enduring memorial in the earth, surely among the immortals in the memory of men will be found, along with the names of Adam, Moses, David,

Solomon, and Jesus, the noble name of **Paul the Apostle.** Already his epistles are printed in **a** hundred and fifty languages; read by as many millions, and churches are dedicated to his name in every Christian city in the world.

TABLE OF EVENTS IN THE LIFE OF PAUL THE APOSTLE.

A. D.			
5 Born in Tarsus, in Cilicia	Acts	xxii.	3
A Roman citizen by birthright.			
A Pharisee	Phil.	iii.	5
By trade a tent-maker. (Goat's hair—Cilicia)	Acts	xviii.	3
20 At the school of Gamaliel, Jerusalem	"	xxii.	3
30 Assists in stoning Stephen	"	vii.	58
Makes havoc of the Church	"	viii.	4
36 Goes to Damascus to persecute the disciples	"	ix.	2
Baptized. Begins to preach Jesus the Crucified	"	ix.	18, 20
Journey into Arabia; return to Damascus	Gal.	i.	17, 18
38 Escape from Damascus in a basket (2 Cor. xi. 33)	Acts	ix.	25
Goes up to Jerusalem. Disciples afraid of him	"	"	26
Introduced by Barnabas: preach'd the Lord Jesus	"	"	27
39 Driven out of Jerusalem; goes to Tarsus	"	"	30
40 At Antioch. Preaches to the Gentiles	"	xi.	25
Disciples first called Christians in Antioch	"	"	26
Two Roman, three Jewish scourgings (2 Cor. xi. 24–26).			
42 Agabus prophesies a famine	"	"	28
44 Barnabas and Saul sent to Jerusalem with money	"	"	30
45 Joined by Mark, Barnabas' sister's son	"	xii.	25
46 Barnabas and Saul "separated" for the work	"	xiii.	2
FIRST MISSIONARY JOURNEY. Antioch to Seleucia	"	"	4
In Cyprus at Salamis. Paphos - Saul's name changed to Paul.	"	"	8
Elymas blinded	"	"	9
Sailed from Paphos to Perga, in Pamphylia	"	"	13
Antioch in Pisidia. Discourse to the Jews	"	"	14
The Gospel preached to the Gentiles	"	"	46
Paul and Barnabas expelled from Pisidia	"	"	50
They come to Iconium	"	"	51
To Lystra. A cripple healed	"	xiv.	6
The people propose to sacrifice to them	"	"	13
Paul stoned, and supposed to be dead	"	"	19
He recovers, and they go to Derbe	"	"	20
Lystra, Iconium, and Antioch	"	"	21
Passed through Pisidia to Pamphylia	"	"	24
Preached in Perga, Attalia, and Antioch	"	xiv.	25, 26
48 End of the first missionary jour'ey	"	"	27
50 Visit to Jerusalem with Barnabas and Titus (Gal. ii.).			
51 The Council at Jerusalem	"	xv.	
Barnabas and Silas sent with Paul to Antioch	"	"	22
Paul and Barnabas preach in Antioch	"	"	35
THE SECOND MISSION'Y JOURN'Y	"	"	36
Paul and Silas go through Syria and Cilicia	"	"	41

VESTIBULE WITHIN THE GOLDEN GATE

A. D.
Aug.—Storm in Adria. Clauda - - Acts xxvii. 14
  The ship lightened by casting
    overboard the tackle - - - - "   " 19
  Vision of the angel by Paul - - "   " 23
  Prophesies the events of the
    voyage - - - - - - - - - "   " 26
  All escaped safe to land. Ship
    wrecked - - - - - - - - "   " 44
  A viper fastens on Paul's hand.
    Malta - - - - - - - - - Acts xxviii. 3
  The father of Publius healed by
    Paul - - - - - - - - - "   " 8
  After three months they sail for
    Syracuse - - - - - - - "   11, 12
  Rhegium. Puteoli. Appii Forum "   " 13
  Three Taverns - - - - - - "   13–15
61 Rome. In his own house - - "   " 16
  He persuades the Jews - - - - "   " 23
62 Writes to Philemon, Colossians, Ephesians and
    Philippians at Rome.
63 Goes to Macedonia (Phil. ii. 24).
  Asia Minor (Phil. xx. ii.).
64 Spain. Supposed visit (Rom. xv. 24).
66 Asia Minor (1 Tim. i. 3).
67 Writes First Epistle to Timothy from Mace-
    donia.
  Epistle to Titus from Ephesus. Nicopolis.
68 In prison at Rome. Writes Second Epistle to
    Timothy.
  Beheaded in May or June.
  PAVEMENT (*Gabbatha*).

RACHEL'S TOMB, BETWEEN JERUSALEM AND BETHLEHEM.

PAVIL'ION. A general term for an awning or
tent. Three different words are thus translated in
the Scriptures: "He shall hide me in his pavilion," in Ps. xxvii. The Heb. soc means a hut. In
Jer. xliii. 10, Nebuchadnezzar is alluded to as
"spreading his royal pavilion"—the word SHAF-
RUR or SHAFRIR is the one used—meaning bright,
or rich tapestry, famed in Babylonian times.

PE (PE, *mouth*). The 17th letter of the Hebrew
alphabet (Ps. cxix). WRITING.

PEACE (Heb. SHALOM, *soundness, health, welfare,
prosperity*). "Peace be unto thee" (Judg. vi. 23;
1 K. ii. 33; Ps. xxxvii. 11, 37, etc.). Peace as the
opposite of war: "And I will give peace in the
land" (Lev. xxvi. 6; Judg. iv. 17, etc.). Peace, as
friendship, in Ps. xxviii. 3, xli. 9. "Peace be unto
you," was a common form of Eastern salutation
(John xx. 19, 21, 26, etc.); "Your peace!" (Matt.
x. 13).

PEACE-OFFERING (Heb. SHELEM); (Lev. iii.–
vii. 11). There were three kinds: 1. Praise or
thanksgiving. 2. Votive. 3. Voluntary or free-
will offerings. The sacrifice was accompanied by
an offering of "unleavened cakes mingled with
oil, and unleavened wafers anointed with oil, of
fine flour, fried" (Lev. vii. 12–13). From the
peace-offering the fat was burned on the altar; the
right shoulder of the animal sacrificed was given
to the priest; the breast was a *wave-offering*. The
rest was to be eaten by the offerer upon the day of
offering. This was the characteristic of the peace-
offering, suggesting, figuratively, peace with God.
See OFFERING ; SACRIFICE.

PEA'COCK (Heb. TUKIIM). Imported into Palestine through the Tarshish navies of King Solomon (1 K. x. 22; 2 Chr. ix. 21). The importation
of peacocks is named with that of ivory and apes.
The birds were probably brought from India or
Ceylon, where there is reason to believe the navies
visited. (See TARSHISH.) The Cingalese word
(*tokei*) for peacock, bears a close resemblance to
the Hebraic.

PEARL (Heb. GABISH). They are formed inside
the shells of several species of *mollusca*, and
consist of carbonate of lime and animal matter;
are hard and smooth, and have a silvery-white lustre. Pearls were held among the most precious
stones in the ancient world. Their beauty is due to
Nature, alone, as they are not improved by Art.
The "pearl of great price" is a fine specimen
yielded by the pearl oyster, which is found in the
Persian Gulf (Matt. xiii. 45, 46).

PED'AHEL (*God delivers*). Son of Ammihud
(Num. xxxiv. 28).

PEDAH'ZUR (*God delivers*). Father of Gamaliel
(Num. i. 10).

PEDAI'AH (*Jah delivers*). 1 Father of Zebudah
(2 K. xxiii. 36).—2. Father of ZER-
UBBABEL, brother of SALATHIEL (1
Chr. iii. 17–19).—3. Descendant of
Parosh (Neh. iii. 25).—4. A priest
who assisted Ezra (viii. 4).—5. Ancestors of Sallu (xi. 7).—6. A treasurer (xiii. 13).—7. Father of Joel (1
Chr. xxvii. 20).

PEDIGREE. GENEALOGY (Num. i.
18).

PEEL, TO (Heb MARAT). "Peeled" in Ez. xxix. 18, translates literally that the skin of the shoulder was
peeled by the carrying of earth to
form earth-works at the siege of
Tyre. In Is. xviii. 2, 7, "a nation
scattered and *peeled*" is variously
rendered. Gesenius suggests "a people drawn out and smoothed."

PE'KAH (*open-eyed*). Son of Remaliah, captain of Pekahiah whom he
assassinated, and succeeded to his throne B. C. 758,
and thus became eighteenth king of Israel. He
reigned twenty years, in the seventeenth of
which he combined with Rezin, king of Damascus, against Ahaz, king of Judah, (2 K.
xvi. and 2 Chr. xxviii.). (See prophesies of
Isaiah, Is. vii.–ix.) The result was the seizure of
Damascus and all the lands east of the Jordan and
north of Galilee, by Tiglath-Pileser king of Assyria. Pekah was killed by Hosea, son of Elah,
who headed a conspiracy, and afterwards mounted
the throne (2 K. xv. 25–38, xvi. 1–9). Assyrian
inscriptions record the taking of Damascus by
TIGLATH-PILESER.

PEKAHI'AH (*Jah has opened his eyes*). Son
and successor of MENAHEM; was the seventeenth
king of Israel. He reigned two years, and was
killed by Pekah, his general, who succeeded him.
His death took place B. C. 758 (2 K. xv. 22–25).

PE'KOD. A name given to the Chaldæans in
Jer. l. 21 and Ez. xxiii. 23. The meaning of this
word is uncertain; in one sense it would appear to
be *to visit, to punish*. In another it means a *prefect*
(officer).

PELAI'AH (*whom Jah distinguished*). 1. Son of
Elioenai (1 Chr. iii. 24).—2. A Levite who as-

sisted Ezra (Neh. viii. 7), and also sealed the covenant (x. 10).

PELALI'AH (*whom Jah judges*). Son of Amzi, a priest (Neh. xi. 12).

PELATI'AH (*whom Jah delivers*). 1. Son of Hananiah (1 Chr. iii. 21).—2. A captain of the Simeonites (iv. 42).—3. One who sealed the covenant (Neh. x. 22).—4. Son of Benaiah (Ez. xi. 5-12, 13).

PE'LEG (*division*). Son of EBER; brother of JOKTAN (Gen. x. 25). CHRONOLOGY.

PE'LET (*deliverance*). 1. Son of Jahdai (1 Chr. ii. 47).—2. Son of AZMAVETH 3 (xii. 3).

PE'LETH (*swiftness*). 1. Father of On who joined in the Rebellion (Num. xvi. 1).—2. Son of Jonathan (1 Chr. ii. 33).

PEL'ETHITES (Heb. PELETHI, *courier*). Mentioned with the Cherethites: they were the body-guard of King David (2 Sam. viii. 18; xxii. 23). See CHERETHITES.

PELI'AS. BEDEIAH (1 Esd. ix. 34).

PEL'ICAN (Heb. KAATH, *to vomit*). The bird is supposed to be so named from its habit of emptying the pouch under the beak to feed its young. Cormorant, translated in Is. xxxiv. 11, and Zeph. ii. 14, means *pelican*. It is mentioned as among unclean birds in Lev. xi. 18, and Deut. xiv. 17. "A *pelican* in the wilderness" (Ps. cii. 6) as a sign of desolation for the solitary habits of the bird and its inhabiting desolated spots.

PEL'ONITE, THE. Two of David's strong men are called Pelonites; Helez and Ahijah (1 Chr. xi. 27, 36).

PELU'SIUM. A city of EGYPT (Ez. xxx. 15).

PEN'IEL, PENUEL (*face of El—God*). (Gen. xxxii. 30). Where Jacob wrestled with a man, who changed Jacob's name to ISRAEL. It does not appear again until after 500 yrs. when Gideon, on his way from Succoth, on the Jordan, chasing Zeba and Zalmunna, being faint from want of food, asked the people of this place for bread for his soldiers, and was denied (Judg. viii. 8). He destroyed the tower of the city on his return (ver. 17). Jeroboam rebuilt the place (1 K. xii. 25). It has never been mentioned since, and is now lost.

PENIN'NAH (*coral*). Wife of ELKANAH (1 Sam. i. 2). HANNAH.

PEN'NY, PENNY-WORTH. Refer to MONEY. Gr. *denarion;* Roman *denarius*.

PEN'TATEUCH. See HISTORY OF THE BOOKS.

PEN'TECOST. See FESTIVALS.

PENU'EL. PENIEL.

PENU'EL. 1. Founder of GEDOR (1 Chr. iv. 4). —2. A chief, son of Shashak (viii. 25).

PE'OR (*the opening*). A mountain in Moab, from the top of which Balaam saw Israel encamped in the plain below (Num. xxiii. 28). There was a

a *Beit Faghur*, 5 ms. S. W. of Bethlehem, in *Wady Biar*, which is included in the list of towns in Judah, in the Septuagint, as Phagor (Josh. xv. 59).

PERA'ZIM, MOUNT (*of divisions*). Isaiah refers to it in his warnings of the divine vengeance which was threatened (xxviii. 21). It must have been on some of the hights bordering the plain of Rephaim; and on its top a high place to Baal (Baal Perazim, 2 Sam. v. 20).

PERDI'TION. DAMNATION.

PE'RES (*a breach*), (Dan. v. 28). Phā'rez, a fragment.

PE'RESH (*dung*). Son of Machir (1 Chr. vii. 16)

PE'REZ. Son of Judah. The children of Perez were of importance for several centuries (1 Chr. xxvii. 3).

PEREZ-UZZAH (Uzzah—*broken*). (See NACHON'S threshing-floor).

PER'FECT. Ten different words are used. 1. Heb. CALIL, *perfect* in Ez. xvi. 14. *Perfection* in Lam. ii. 15. The verb CALAL translated "to perfect" (Ez. xxvii. 4).—2. Heb. SHALEM, "*perfect*" in Deut. xxv. 15; 1 Chr. xii. 38; "*perfected*" in 2 Chr. viii. 16; "*Whole*" in Deut. xxvii. 6; "*Just*" in Prov. xl. 1.—3. Heb. TACHLITH, *perfect* in Ps. cxxxix. 22; perfection in Job xi. 7.—4. Heb. TAM, perfect in Job i. 1, 8. "Upright" in Prov. xxix. 10.—5. Heb. TOM, translated *perfect* in Ps. c. 2. "Full" (Job xxi. 23). 6. Heb. TAMIM, corresponding to 4 and 5 (Gen. v. 9; Lev. xxii. 21, etc.).—7. Gr. *akribos* (Luke i. 3). *Perfectly* in 1 Thess. v. 2; "*diligently*" in Matt. ii. 8.—8. Gr. *artios* (2 Tim. iii. 17). The verb *katartizo*, to make perfect (Heb. xiii. 21).—9. Gr. participle, *peplêromenos.*—10. Gr. *teleios*, Matt. v. 48. "Of full age" (Heb. v. 14). "Men" in 1 Cor. xiv. 20.

PERFUMES. Were used freely by the Orientals (Prov. xxvii. 9). The Hebrews made their perfumes from SPICES imported from Arabia, and from aromatic plants of their own country. Perfumes were used in the Temple-service in INCENSE and OINTMENT (Ex. xxx. 22–38). They were used in private life both on the person and on garments (Ps. xlv. 8), and beds (Prov. vii. 17). When a royal person went abroad "pillars of smoke" were thrown about his path (Cant. iii. 6). Perfume was not used in times of mourning (Is. iii. 24). See OINTMENT.

PER'GA. The ancient capital of Pamphylia, on the river Cestrus, 7 ms. from the sea. Diana (Artemis) was worshiped there, in a fine temple near the town. The coins of the city bear figures of Diana and the temple. Paul landed here from Paphos (Acts xiii. 13), and visited the city a second time on his return from the interior (xiv. 25). When Pamphylia was divided, Perga was made the capital of one section, and Side of the other. Called by the Turks *Eski-Kalessi*.

PERGA'MOS. In Mysia 3 ms. N. of the ancient Caicus. (See SEVEN CHURCHES.)

PERI'DA (*kernel*). Ancestor of children of Solomon's servants who returned from captivity (Neh. vii. 57). PERUDA.

PER'IZZITE, THE (*rustic*). Ancient inhabitants of Canaan (Gen. xv. 20); of the six tribes (Canaanites, Hittites, Amor-

SNAIL.

shrine, or holy high-place, on the summit, and the town of Beth Peor at its foot (Deut. iii. 29). Baal Peor was named from this mountain.—2. There is

ites, Perizzites, Hivites, and Jebusites), who inhabited the lands west of Jordan previous to the conquest of Joshua (Josh. xvii. 15). They were scattered, not concentrating around cities. They were subdued by Joshua but not dispersed, as they appear in the history of Solomon (1 K. ix. 20, and in Ezr. ix. 1).

PERSEP′OLIS. The capital of Persia, and partly burnt by Alexander, the temples—built of stone—only escaping. Antiochus Epiphanes attempted to capture and rob the temples, but was defeated (1 Macc. vi. 1, 2; 2 Macc. ix. 2). This city has been supposed to be identical with Passargadæ, the capital of Cyrus; but that city was 42 ms. N. of Persepolis, at a place now called *Murgaub*, where there is shown a tomb of Cyrus. The site of Persepolis is called Chehl-Minar (*forty pillars*, or *minarets*), from the remaining pillars of the palace built by Darius and Xerxes. Nanea (Diana, Artemis, Aphrodite), was the moon-goddess of the Persians, and had a temple in her honor, rich in gold shields, breastplates, and coverings of gold, and great treasures. The ruins of the palace now cover the platform, which is 350 by 380, and 30 ft. above the plain. A stairway of marble leading up to this platform is peculiar in having the rise only 3 or 4 inches for each step, with a tread of 14 inches, and the side-approaches decorated with sculpture. The ruins here show such parts of buildings as have entirely disappeared from the remains in Assyria, such as gates, columns, window-frames, staircases, etc., and giving a new style of column—very tall and slender. Pasargadæ was the ancient, and Persepolis the latter capital of Persia.

PER′SEUS. Son of Philip V and last king of Macedonia. He continued the war with Rome after his father's death (B. C. 179). He was defeated B. C. 168 and died at Alba (1 Macc. viii. 5). See cut on p. 203.

PER′SIA (*pure*). The province of Fars—Farsistan; is now not very large; and north of the Persian Gulf. The ancient empire extended north to Media, south to the Persian Gulf, east to Caramania, and west to Susiana; and in its greatest prosperity, from India to Egypt and Thrace (Ez. xxxviii. 5). The north country is mountainous, with very few valleys or plains, but very picturesque, and generally fertile, among which is the famous Shiraz of Arabian poetry. That part bordering the Gulf is sandy, like Arabia, and not very productive.

KING AND QUEEN OF PERSIA.

The original religion was simple; required temples, but neither altars, images, nor priests, and was based on a belief in the double nature of the infinite power, good and evil (Ormuzd and Ahriman), which was symbolized by light and darkness. Sacrifice was not practiced. Magianism and fire-worship mingled with, and almost superseded the ancient faith (Gomates, a Magian, became emperor, or Shah, B. C. 522), and the worship grew more and more complicated until the empire was destroyed. The Ahasuerus of Esther is probably Xerxes, the son of Darius, by Atossa, the daughter

PERSEPOLIS.

of Cyrus, the founder of the empire. The marriage with Esther is supposed to have taken place in the seventh year of his reign, the year after his flight from defeat in Greece. Artaxerxes, his son, is mentioned by Ezra (vii. 11-28) and Nehemiah (who was the king's cup-bearer, ii. 1-9) as friendly to the Jews; and he is the last but one of the Persian kings mentioned in Scripture. The last was Darius the Persian (Neh. xii. 22).

PER′SIAN (Heb. PARSI). The Persians were probably of the same race as the Medes, both of the Aryan root. Their mention only occurs in the later periods of biblical history. In Daniel, Esther, Nehemiah and Ezra, a very complete idea of the Persian court and administration is presented. The vizier or secretary of state was invested with great power as illustrated in the cases of Haman and Mordecai. (See MORDECAI). The signet was the badge of this office. The remarkable influence which Esther and Mordecai exercised over Xerxes was the result of the noble qualities of mind and body, for which the Hebrew race was, and still is, conspicuous.

PER′SIS (Gr. *destroying*). A Christian woman at Rome (Rom. xvi. 12).

PERU′DA (*kernel*), (Ezr. ii. 55).

PES′TLE, PESTILS. MORTAR (2 Chr. xxvi. 14; Prov. xxvii. 22).

PE′TER. Originally SIMEON, or SIMON, *heard*. (Cephas, *a stone*—Peter, *a rock*). The son of Jonas, and a native of Bethsaida, in Galilee. He was married (his wife's name was Concordia?) at the time of his call to follow Jesus; and lived with his mother-in-law, at Capernaum. He was a fisherman, and was fishing with his father and brother, Andrew, when Jesus found him. Peter and his brother Andrew were, probably, disciples of John the Baptist. Peter, James, and John, only, of the twelve, were witnesses of the transfiguration and the agony in Gethsemane. It seems that Peter was more intimate than any of the other apostles with Jesus, for the tax-collector asked him if his Master paid tribute; and to him and John was given the duty of providing the lamb for the paschal supper, although Judas carried the purse. Peter walked on the Sea of Galilee, but his heart failed, and he cried for help. He frequently declared his faith in Jesus, although he was disappointed that the Christ was not the temporal prince that the Jews had looked for. He first refused to have Jesus wash his feet; but when he learned that it was a symbol, he wished to have his hands and head washed also. He boldly and vauntingly avowed his attachment to Jesus, and offered to lay down his life for Him, and then disgracefully denied Him the same day, and wept bitterly when conscious of what he had done. Jesus forgave him, accepted his renewed professions, and gave him a new commission to work in his cause. After this time his character changed. Instead of a hasty zeal, he showed a sober dignity. He first proclaimed salvation through a crucified Saviour, and, when arrested with the others, boldly declared his faith and purpose before the Sanhedrin. He, by a miracle, punished with death two who tried an experiment on the omniscience of the Holy Ghost; and rebuked Simon the magician, at Samaria, who wished to buy the secret of working miracles. At Joppa he was taught, in a vision, that the ancient ritual distinctions of clean and unclean were abolished. Herod put him in prison, at Jerusalem, and he was released by an angel. He first advocated an exemption from the ceremonial law of Moses. Paul rebuked him for timidly dissembling on the question of the equality of the Jews and Gentiles, at Antioch. Here the Gospel history ends, and we have tradition only for the rest of his life, which says that he traveled (as Paul did) among the cities and churches to which his epistles are addressed, in Pontus, Galatia, Bithynia, Cappadocia, and Asia; that he visited Rome, and was made bishop of the church there, and suffered martyrdom under Nero, being crucified with his head downward.

PETHAHI'AH (*Jah sets free*). 1. A priest of the nineteenth course (1 Chr. xxiv. 16).—2. A Levite (Neh. ix. 5).—3. Son of Meshezabeel (xi. 24).

PE'THOR (*a table*). A town where Balaam resided (Num. xxii. 5).

PETHU'EL (*man of God*). Father of Joel the prophet (Joel i. 1).

PE'TRA (Gr. *rock*). The Greek translation of Sela, a celebrated Edomite city (Is. xvi. 1).

PEUL'THAI (*wages of Jah*). Son of Obed-edom (1 Chr. xxvi. 5).

PHAC'ARETH. Pochereth of Zebaim (1 Esd. v. 34).

PHAI'SUR. Pashur 1 (1 Esd. ix. 22).

PHALDAI'US. Pedaiah 4 (1 Esd. ix. 44).

PHALE'AS. Padon (1 Esd. v. 29).

PHA'LEC. Peleg (Luke iii. 35).

PHAL'LU. Pallu (Gen. xlvi. 9).

PHAL'TI. Palti, son of Laish, to whom Saul gave Michal (1 Sam. xxv. 44).

PHANU'EL. Father of Anna (Luke ii. 36).

PHAR'ACIM. Ancestor of servants of the Temple who returned from captivity (1 Esd. v. 31).

PHA'RAOH (Heb. PAR'ÔH, *the king;* from PHRA, *the sun*). The title of the kings of Egypt. The Egyptian king represents the sun-god. 1. The earliest mention of *Pharaoh* is in the history of Abraham (Gen. xii. 10–20); probably one of the shepherd-kings.—2. The *Pharaoh* of Joseph (Gen. xxxvii. 36.)—3. The *Pharaoh* of the oppression, "who knew not Joseph."—4. The *Pharaoh* who enslaved the Israelites is supposed by some to have been Rameses II: by others, as of Assyrian descent, from Is. lii. 4. The Exodus is dated in his time. 5. *Pharaoh* the father-in-law of Mered (1 Chr. iv. 18).—6. *Pharaoh* the father-in-law of Hadad (1 K. xi. 18) (see HADAD); perhaps Osochor.—7. *Pharaoh* father-in-law of Solomon, Psusennes II (1 K. iii. 1).—8. *Pharaoh*, the ally of the Jews against Sennacherib (Is. xxxvi. 6)—9. PHARAOH-NECHO (Jer. xlvi. 2). This and the Pharaoh which follows are the only two mentioned with proper names. He appears to have been an enterprising king, and to have reigned 16 years. He opposed the Assyrians; defeating and fatally wounding Josiah, King of Judah (2 K. xxiii. 29, 30). See, also, 2 K. xxiii. 30–34; 2 Chr. xxxvi. 1–4. This battle lost to Pharaoh all his Asiatic domin-

ions (2 K. xxiv. 7).—10 PHARAOH-HOPHRA (*son of the sun*) was the second successor of Necho, and mounted the throne B. C. 589. Several kings of Egypt are mentioned by their titles only, and it is important to give some account of them by way of distinction:

1. The Pharaoh of Abraham's time, according to the best authors, was of the line called Shepherd-Kings of the XVth Dynasty. The presents made to Abraham argue that Pharaoh was an owner of flocks and herds, and *camels*, which are not drawn on the monuments, or possessed by any other of Egypt's kings besides the Shepherd line, and were regarded by the people as hateful animals. See ABRAHAM.

2. In the history of Joseph there are many particulars of the Pharaoh who made him his minister of state. In the account of the death of Jacob, Joseph is made to address a petition to the Pharaoh, in such a manner as to give the impression that it was a successor of the one who had advanced him to honor. Some discoveries at Zoan, Egypt, lately made, have determined the historical question, that the Pharaohs of Joseph's time were shepherds, who had become Egyptianized, and built many monuments, which are known for several peculiarities. A strong argument is, the supposition that a native Egyptian king would not have elevated a Hebrew slave as he did Joseph. In our day, the Oriental rulers make viziers of barbers, or of any one who has the requisite ability, without regard to rank, condition, or religion.

3. The "new king which knew not Joseph," may have been a successor in the Shepherd line, but it is possible, if not probable, that he was of a new dynasty which did not favor the Hebrews. He set them harder tasks, building store cities; and attempted to diminish them by the use of midwives, but neither plan succeeded. This Pharaoh has been supposed to have been of the XVIIth dynasty, but it is difficult to determine the matter since the names of the whole line are unknown. His residence was at Avaris, in the sandy district, as we learn from the fact that Moses buried the body of the Egyptian that he killed, in the sand. The kings whose names are found in the Turin Papyrus bear names which are Egyptian translations of Assyrian titles.

4. The Pharaoh of the Exodus is described to us as impious and superstitious, vascillating between right and wrong. He seems to have expected the same works from his magicians as from Moses and Aaron. He was ready to promise, and as ready to break his promise, a course of conduct that only ended when he and his army were destroyed in the Red Sea. A recently deciphered record of Thothmes III, contains many names bordering the Hebrew territory, and mentions the battle of Megiddo. The Egyptians were either friendly at that time, or deemed it prudent to remember the Red Sea, and not attack the Hebrews. The first king of Egypt after the Exodus who did attack them was SHISHAK, a foreigner in that country, and not acquainted with the Jews. The friendly Egyptians had certain privileges under the law (Deut. xxiii. 7).

5. Bithiah a Pharaoh's daughter married a Hebrew, Mered, not long after the Exodus. Mered had a sister Miriam, perhaps named after the sister of Moses. It is supposed that this Pharaoh's daughter was taken in a foray from some caravan (1 Chr. iv. 18).

6. A Pharaoh gave shelter to Hadad and his followers, enemies of Solomon, assigning them land and provisions, and married his wife's sister to him (1 K. xi. 18–20). Hadad returned to Palestine after the death of David and Joab. It is not known which this one was, any nearer than that he was probably the predecessor of the one who gave his daughter to Solomon for a wife.

7. Solomon married a Pharaoh's daughter not later than the 11th year of his reign. This king has not been identified. He made a raid into Philistia, took a city (Gezer), and gave it for a present to his daughter, Solomon's wife. This alliance to Egypt was distinctly forbidden in the law, and produced fearful disasters, both spiritual and temporal.

Then after him came the Pharaohs Shishak, Zerah, and So. See SHISHAK, ZERAH and So. Zerah (Userken), is called a Cushite (2 Chr. xiv. 9). These were not called Pharaohs because they were not Egyptians, and had foreign names.

8. The Pharaoh who opposed Sennacherib was Tirhakah of Cush, also called the king of Mizraim. The symbol of a broken reed used in the Scriptures suggests the title of the king of Upper Egypt, SU-TEN, *reed-king*, whose emblem was a bent reed. This Pharaoh was Sethos according to Herodotus, called Zet by Manetho.

9. The first Pharaoh whose proper name is given is Necho, on the monuments NEKU, who was of XXVIth dynasty, and reigned 16 years. His name is given to a part of the canal between the Nile and the Red Sea; and is credited with sending an expedition around Africa in ships; and a war against Assyria, in which he killed Josiah, king of Judah. In his account of this expedition, Herodotus calls Jerusalem Cadytis—almost the same in sound as its modern Arabic name El-Kuds (*the Holy*). Some suppose that Cadytis refers to Ketesh, on the Orontes, which was then the chief city in Syria. Necho at that time worshiped Apollo. On its return towards Egypt, at Carchemish, Nebuchadnezzar defeated this army, Necho probably not being with it. The Egyptian after that "came not again out of his land" towards Palestine (2 K. xxiv. 7).

11. Pharaoh Hophra was the second successor after Necho. He attacked Sidon, and fought a battle at sea with Tyre, and after losing an army in Cyrene, probably by Nebuchadnezzar, he was superseded by Amasis as Pharaoh, and he was strangled. He is supposed to have aided king Zedekiah in one of his wars (Jer. xxxvii. 5, 8). Ezekiel's prophesy, and the history of Herodotus agree as to the character of this Pharaoh, describing him as an arrogant crocodile (xxxix. 3). There is no other Pharaoh mentioned in the Scriptures after Hophra.

PHA'RAOH, WIFE OF. Named Tahpenes; wife of the 6th Pharaoh.

PHA'RAOH'S DAUGHTER. Three daughters of Pharaoh appear in the Scriptures: 1. As the discoverer of the infant Moses, daughter of 3d Pharaoh (Ex. ii. 5-10).—2. Daughter of 5th Pharaoh—named Bithiah; she was wife of Mered, an Israelite (1 Chr. iv. 18).—3. Daughter of 7th Pharaoh; married to Solomon (1 K. iii. 1, viii. 8, ix. 24). A house was built for her (1 K. vii. 8, ix. 24).

PHAR'ATHONI (1 Macc. ix. 50). In the S. of Judæa? Lost.

PHA'RES. Son of Judah (Matt. i. 3).

PHAREZ (*a breach*). 1. Twin son with ZERAH 1 of Judah. The first-born of the twin sons of Judah by his daughter-in-law Tamar (Gen. xxxviii. 29). 2. In the line of David. In Ruth iv. 12 occurs the passage—"Let thy house be like the house of *Pharez*, whom Tamar bare unto Judah!"—3. PHARAZITES (Num. xxvi. 60).

PHARI'RA (1 Esd. v. 33). PERUDA.

PHAR'ISEES (Heb. PERUSHIM). One of the three sects of Judaism in the time of Christ. The name means separated by special works. The sect included all Hebrews who separated themselves from every kind of Levitical impurity, following the Mosaic law of purity.

They are first noticed as a sect about 150 B. C., but their origin is not recorded.

Their influence was very great, ruling, beyond question, the Sanhedrin, and all Jewish society, except the slight opposition of the Sadducees, even overawing the civil courts; and as they had gathered to themselves all the worst features of Judaism in the time of Christ, and used this against any reform, and especially against the Messiah, it was needful that Jesus should protest against them; and the contest resulting from his protest grew fiercer and more relentless on the part of the Pharisees, ending only with the crucifixion.

The applicant for admission to the sect was required to promise in the presence of three members: 1. That he would not eat of anything which had not been tithed, nor if there was any doubt about it; and 2. That he would keep the law of purity in all matters, most especially in family affairs.

In this matter they made of the civil rule of tithes a religious obligation, and so set apart the tithe as a holy thing, and taught that the eating of a holy thing was a deadly sin; and that if the tithe was not taken out, set apart, and paid to the priest, the whole produce was unlawful for food.

The law of clean and unclean was also applied in the extreme.

Their doctrines and rules are the basis of the faith of the orthodox party of the Jews to this day. The Essenes were a kind of intensified Pharisees, and the Sadducees were never a large or influential sect.

The Pharisees made themselves the people's party by teaching that "God has given to all men alike the kingdom, the priesthood, and Holiness (2 Macc. ii. 17). They tried to realize that the Jews were *a people of priests, a holy nation*, by diligent study of the law, a preparation for the office and duties of Rabbi, and by arranging the concerns of life on the model of those who minister in holy things.

Their social meals were modeled after the paschal supper, with all its ablutions, blessings, and Levitical rules.

That Jesus did not overstate their peculiar defects their own account of themselves will show. The Talmud says:

"There are seven kinds of Pharisees;

1. Shechemites; who keep the law for what it will profit them.

2. Tumblers; always hanging down the head, and dragging the feet.

3. Bleeders; who to avoid looking at women shut their eyes and so bump their heads.

4. Mortars; wearing caps in the form of a mortar, covering the eyes from seeing impurities.

5. What-am-I-yet-to-doers; who as soon as one law is kept, ask what is next.

6. Fearers; who keep the law from fear of a judgment.

7. Lovers; who obey Jehovah because they love him with all the heart.

Surely this indicates that they were impartially divided among fanatics and worldly-minded hypocrites; and yet they had developed the ideas of a Messiah, of a kingdom of heaven, the immortality of the soul, the future life. Of them were the devout Simeon, who took the infant Jesus in his arms; and also Zacharias, and Gamaliel, and Saul of Tarsus, who never uttered a word against the sect.

Jesus described them as whited sepulchres, hidden graves, and in retaliation they were his most determined enemies.

The spirit of proselytism (Matt. xxiii. 15), which was so strong in the time of Christ, led the way for the spread of Christianity, as is plainly shown in Paul's life. Their peculiar doctrines also opened the minds of men for the new facts of the life and work of Jesus.

PHA'ROSH (PAROSH, Ezr. viii. 3).

PHAR'PAR (*swift*). One of the two rivers mentioned by Naaman as rivers of Damascus, better than all the waters of Israel (2 K. v. 12). The Awaj is divided from the Barada (see ABANA) by the ridge of the Jebel Aswad, which is no where less than 8 ms. wide. It has two sources in the S. E. slopes of Hermon—one near the village of Arny, and the other near Beit Jenn, the two streams uniting below Sasa—and empties into the Hijaneh, the most southerly of the lakes E. of Damascus. There are nearly 50 villages in its course, containing about 18,000 people (Porter, *Five Years in Damascus*).

PHAR'ZITES, THE. Descendants of PHAREZ (Num. xxvi. 20).

PHAZE'AN. PASEAH 2 (Neh. vii. 51).

PHASE'LIS. In Lycia, near Pamphylia, on the coast. It was a city of importance in the 6th century B. C., but became a resort of pirates. It was a convenient port, on account of the lofty mountain Solyma (8,000 ft.), which was only 4 ms. back of the city, affording a landmark for sailors. Homer mentions the Solyma range in the Odyssey. The Romans broke up the pirates' stronghold, under Publius Servilius Isauricus, B. C. 75, and Pompey. The Romans required all their allies to deliver up to Simon, the high-priest, all Jewish exiles, naming this city among others (1 Macc. xv. 23).

PHAS'IRON. An Arab tribe (1 Macc. ix. 66).

PHAS'SARON. PASHUR (1 Esd. v. 25).

PHE'BE (*pure, bright*). (Goddess of the moon). A servant of the church at CENCHREÆ (Rom. xvi. 1, 2). DEACONESS.

PHE'NICE (*the date-palm*). Town on the S. coast of Crete, now called Lutro. Paul was on the way there from Fair Havens when the storm drove the vessel into Adria (Acts xxvii. 12). The White Mountains rise 9,000 ft. near the bay which is a safe harbor in winter.

PHENIC'IANS. See PHŒNICIA.

PHER'ESITES. PERIZZITES (1 Esd. viii. 69).

PHIBE'SETH (Ez. xxx. 17).

Epistle Paul recommends the granting pardon to Onesimus, who conveyed the Epistle, with those to the Colossians and Ephesians, from Rome to Colossæ. See Philemon i. 2, iv. 7, 19, etc., and Col. iv. 9, 17. See ONESIMUS. Philemon was probably a man of wealth, influence and liberality.

PHILE'MON, EPISTLE TO. See HISTORY OF THE BOOKS.

PHILE'TUS. An apostate Christian, who joined with HYMENÆUS and ALEXANDER (1 Tim. i. 20, and 2 Tim. ii. 18).

PHIL'IP (*fond of horses*). 1. Father of Alexander the Great (1 Macc. i. 1, vi. 2). King of Macedonia, B. C. 359–336.—2. Governor at Jerusalem (B. C. 170). He was very cruel toward the Jews (2 Macc. v. 22).—3. The foster-brother (ix. 29) of Antiochus Epiphanes, regent of Syria and guardian of Antiochus V (B. C. 164), son of the king (1 Macc. vi. 14, 15, 55, 56, 63).—4. Philip V, king of Macedonia, B. C. 220–179 (1 Macc. viii. 5).

PHIL'IP. One of the twelve apostles. A native of Bethsaida, in Galilee (John i. 44). He became a disciple of John the Baptist, and was the fourth of the twelve in the order of his call. He introduced Nathanael, who was afterwards called Bartholomew, the fifth apostle. Jesus asked Philip where bread (vi. 5) was to be found for feeding the 5000, and Philip did not even suspect the real source; nor did he seem to know the spiritual character of Jesus and his teaching much later, when he said to him, "Lord, show us the Father," (xiv. 8), and he had heard the voice from heaven, which was sent for the special instruction of such as were so slow to perceive the light—although he was at Cana when the water was made wine. He consulted with Andrew before gratifying the request of the Jews from Greece to see Jesus (out of curiosity only?) Philip was with the other apostles in that "upper room" (Acts i. 13) at Jerusalem, after the ascension, and on the day of Pentecost.

Tradition says he preached in Phrygia. There is no account of his death.

PHILIPPIANS, EPISTLE TO. See HISTORY OF THE BOOKS.

PHILIP, THE EVANGELIST. A resident (in the latter part of his life) of Cæsarea, where he had a wife and family, of whom four daughters are mentioned as singers. He was one of the SEVEN DEACONS of the Church in Judæa (Acts vi. 5, viii. 29). After Stephen was stoned he went to Samaria, where he baptized the magician Simon. From there he was sent by Peter to Gaza, and on the way (at Ain Karem?) he baptized the Ethiopian eunuch (Acts viii. 26–40). His tour extended from Azotus to Cæsarea, where he settled, and was visited by Paul, Agabus, and others (xxi. 8, 9). His death is not recorded.

PHILIP'PI. In Macedonia, 9 miles from the sea, on the

ORIENTAL CART.

PHI'CHOL (*mighty*). Captain in the army of ABIMELECH (Gen. xxi. 22, 23).

PHILADEL'PHIA. In Lydia, near Phrygia. (See SEVEN CHURCHES). There is a village on the ancient site called *Allah Shehr*—"City of God."

PHILAR'CHES. The name of an office. *Commander of the cavalry* (2 Macc. viii. 32).

PHILE'MON (Gr. *affectionate*). A Christian, probably a native of Colossæ, to whom Paul addressed the Epistle. See HISTORY OF THE BOOKS. In this

banks of the deep, rapid stream Gangites (now *Angista*). Paul says: "On the Sabbath we went out of the city by the river side, where prayer was wont to be made" (Acts xvi. 13). The ancient walls can be traced along the course of the river; and there are remains of a gate leading to a bridge across the stream. Philippi was a Roman military colony, originally named Krenides (*springs*), or Datum; and the Jews were probably not permitted to worship inside of the walls.

A ridge, 1600 feet high, behind the city, divided a broad plain from the bay and town of Neapolis, in Thrace. The mines produced 1000 talents of gold a year, from which Philip's coins were made (see COIN OF MACEDONIA. p. 189). The Via Egnatia passed through it. The ruins of the city are very extensive, but the place is not inhabited.

The famous battle which ended the Roman Republic, was fought on this plain, near Philippi, between armies led by Octavius Cæsar and Marc Antony on one side, and on the other by Brutus and Cassius, who were defeated with their republican forces (B. C. 42).

Paul visited the city a third time (Acts xx. 6), where he remained, in company with Silas, for some time. The church at Philippi was friendly to Paul, and sent him help frequently (Phil. iv. 10, 15, 18; 2 Cor. xi. 9; 1 Thess. ii. 2), for which, and their other kindnesses, he wrote them an Epistle from Rome.

PHILIS'TIA (*emigrant*). PALESTINE (Ps. xl. 8). A region extending from Joppa, 40 miles south, to Gerar, being 10 miles wide at the north and 20 at the south, and generally called SHEFELAH in the Scriptures. The prophets describe the people as the Philistines from Caphtor (Amos ix. 7), the remnant of the maritime district (Jer. xlvii. 4); and Moses as the Caphtorim that came out of Caphtor (Deut. ii. 23) and drove out the Avim. This would require us to read Gen. x. 14, "and Caphtorim, whence came Philistim." (See CAPHTOR). The most reasonable supposition seems to be that Philistia was settled by emigrants from Egypt, dating from the time of Amenoph, B. C. 1970, up to the time of the Judges in Israel, B. C. 1200.

Since we have only ten or twelve words remaining out of their language, and these, it may be, affected by contact with the Hebrew forms, it is impossible to determine their origin as a race. They came after the Canaanites (Gen. x. 19), who once occupied as far as Gaza and Gerar. Abimelech was king of the Philistines in Abraham's time. Moses avoided them on account of their strength; and Joshua found a confederacy of five cities—Gaza, Gath, Askelon, Ashdod and Ekron—ruled by princes, with whom he did not go to war. The first victory over them is recorded of Shamgar, who killed 600 with an ox-goad. They carried off the sacred ark after the battle of Aphek, and only restored it in David's time, when their territory was added to the kingdom of Judah; and the great king made Ittai, a man of Gath, captain of his body-guard, who were Philistines (2 Sam. xv.). For the location of the chief city of Philistia see GATH.

Their religion was similar to that of Phœnicia—nature-worship. Their name for God was Elohim; but they had other special divinities, such as Dagon, Derketo, Baal Zebub, and Ashtoreth, whose images were carried with them on their campaigns, besides charms which they wore on their persons (2 Macc. xii. 40). Josephus speaks of a council of 500 rulers at Gaza (Ant. xiii. 13, 3). Baal was a union of human (the head) and fish-like forms. Oracles, priests, sorcerers, altars, temples, etc., were scattered all over the land.

PHIL'ISTINES (Heb. PELESHETH, *wandering*). See PHILISTIA.

PHILOL'OGUS (*learned*). A Christian at Rome (Rom. xvi. 15).

PHILOS'OPHY. There was no Hebrew system of philosophy. The divine law furnished the rule, about which no speculation was needed. Facts built upon a species of divine philosophy, which led from God to man. The Greek philosophy led the mind from man up towards God. The philosophy of the Hebrews was developed in their national life; their books recording acts and not thoughts. The two books, Job and Ecclesiastes,

have many philosophical thoughts. See HISTORY OF THE BOOKS.

The Kabbala, mystical and speculative philosophy, arose in the time of the Captivity, and flourished most during the decay of the nation, when it was subject to the influence of other people, especially the Greeks. The Kabbala in its two great divisions, "the chariot," which treated with the manifestation of God in Himself, and "the creation," with His manifestation in Nature. The influence of other philosophies resulted in the adopting the Persian idea of emanation, and of the Incarnation, afterwards a leading idea in the Christian Church. The books now known among Jews on these subjects do not claim an earlier date than A. D. 1000 to 1550, and are colored all through with Pantheism. There are diluted imitations of the teachings of Pythagoras; and are much affected with the mystery of numbers (see KABBALA). Numbers are used to express the idea of the Divine Wisdom, the universe being a harmonious thought of Divine Wisdom, which having been formed into letters becomes reflected into man's soul; and he represents the whole universe repeated in miniature. This mingling of many systems, without definite design, produced a school of interpreters of the supposed hidden meanings of Scripture texts, whose influence is still felt in some quarters of the Christian Church.

The Pharisees were Stoics in their philosophy (see PHARISEES). The Sadducees advocated human freedom in its purest and widest sense (see SADDUCEES). The Essenes taught a system of mystic asceticism (see ESSENES), which, with the other two sects, completed the cycle of doctrine.

Much interesting detail on these points may be found in the fourth book of Maccabees (see HIST. OF THE BOOKS).

In Proverbs there is a certain advance in the idea of wisdom as a philosophy, which was expanded in the WISDOM OF SOLOMON, and in ECCLESIASTICUS (see HISTORY OF THE BOOKS), in which there is an approach to the doctrine of the Word, the Divine Logos, which John stated so clearly and truthfully. Philo had treated the subject, but not plainly, and the Gnostics mystified it beyond all possibility of understanding beginning or end.

Ancient philosophy has been regarded as a kind of covenant between God and man, which stood to the pagan world as the Abrahamic covenant did to the Hebrews, and in a peculiar sense it was a preparation for Christianity, for which work the Greek philosophy was most fit.

Philosophy is a natural outgrowth of human thought in the west, as the promulgation of law is natural to the despotic character of the Oriental. Greek philosophy was based on simple reason, without reference to faith, which stood separate and distinct by itself. After the Christian Church was established, philosophy left Greece and renewed its vitality in Alexandria, Egypt (see ALEXANDRIA). But the grand questions of the creation, future life, and man's true relation to God were left unsettled by philosophy, and were only answered by the simple and sublime words of the Old Testament and the New.

The spirit of Christianity is independent of history and of persons, and concerns the immediate relation of the soul to God.

PHIN'EES. Gr. form of PHINEHAS. 1. PHINEHAS 1 (1 Esd. v. 5; viii. 2, 29).—2. PHINEHAS 2 (2 Esd. i. 2 a).—3. PHINEHAS 3 (1 Esd. viii. 63). —4. PASEAH 2 (v. 31).

PHINE'HAS (*mouth of brass*). 1. Son of ELEAZAR 1 (Ex. vi. 25) and grandson of Aaron (Ex. vi. 25). He was promised the priesthood in his family forever for his services during the plague in Egypt (Num. xxv. 7; 10–13).

PHŒ'BE. Referred to by Paul in Rom. xvi. 1, as "our sister which is a servant of the church at

Cenchreæ." She was probably the bearer of the Epistle to the Romans.

PHŒNIC'IA. Phœnice (*phoinix—palm tree*). Phoinos, *purple*, another derivation of the name. Phœnix, the son of Agenor, and brother of Cadmus, is also honored as the source. This was the Greek name, while the native name was KENAAN, as may be seen on a coin of Laodicea, of the time of Antiochus Epiphanes; and from them—the strongest race—the country was called by the Hebrews the Land of Canaan. The country extended from the Ladder of Tyre, or rather the Ras el Abyad (*White Cape*), to the *Nahr el Auly*, above Sidon, 28 miles; with a width at Sidon of two miles, and at Tyre of five; and was called by Josephus the great plain of Sidon (Ant. v. 3, 1). Sidon and Tyre were 20 miles apart. (See SIDON and TYRE). Sarepta was a colony of Sidon, 8 miles south; and Tyre was either a colony of Sidon or received the honor of a change of the chief rule to it, after the war with the Philistines, because it was a stronger place than Sidon. Perhaps, at this time, the island was fortified. There were also colonies in Cyprus, the Grecian Isles, Lybia, and in Spain. Phœnicia was extended, in later times, north to the island of Aradus, and Antaradus, the boundary being the river Eleutherus, making a

male and female powers; whose symbols were the sun, moon and planets (7), which has been said to have been the most complete and beautiful form of idolatry ever devised. This system always had an influence over the Hebrews, more or less in different ages, recommended to the simple, pastoral Jews by the wealth and polished manners of the commercial Phœnicians. Solomon paid his respect to King Hiram by making shrines to his gods on Olivet, and his successors permitted houses to be built near the Temple for idolatrous practices (2 K. xxiii. 7). The worst feature of the system was the sacrifice of children to the god Molech. The colonies of Phœnicia also inherited this dreadful superstition, and we read that when Carthage was besieged by Agathocles, there were offered as burnt sacrifices to the god Saturn (the planet), *at the public expense*, 200 boys of the aristocracy; and when they had gained a victory, the most beautiful captives were sacrificed in the same manner (Diod. xx. 14, 65). The worship of Astarte also tended to break down the restraints of virtue between the sexes, and to solemnize the most abominable practices. Twice were a large number of the priests of Baal destroyed by a reformer in Israel; by Elijah, who killed 450 on Mt. Carmel, and by Jehu, who gathered all the Baal worship-

TOMBS IN THE VALLEY OF JEHOSHAPHAT.

coast of 120 miles. Beirut is now the chief, and almost the only port of this region. Gebal was anciently famous for its ship-builders, sailors (Ez. xxvii. 9), and workers in stone. Tripolis (now *Tarabulus*) was colonized in three distinct districts a few rods apart, each walled in and named after the cities from whence the emigrants came—Tyre, Sidon and Aradus. Aradus (Arvad, Gen. x. 18) was on a small island, colonized from Sidon. Massive ruins are still standing there. Carthage, in Africa, was its most famous colony. (For rivers, etc., see LEBANON).

The language was Semitic (that is, from Shem), to which family belong the Arabic, Aramaic and the Hebrew, which are as nearly allied as are English and German. No other language was so widely spread, because of their mariners and colonists. The Greeks gave the honor of the invention of letters to the Phœnicians, having first received 16 letters from Cadmus (*eastern* or *olden*). (See ALPHABETS). The letters are supposed to have been originally rude pictures, in outline, of natural objects, as—Aleph, an ox's head; Beth, a house; Gimel, a camel (the hump-back); Daleth, the tent-door; Lamed, an ox-goad; Ajin, an eye; Caph, the back of the head; Reish, the head; and Tau, a cross. The Egyptian phonetic characters were made on the same principle. The names of the Greek letters which end in *a*, are Aramaic in form.

The religion was a nature-worship, recognizing

ers in Israel, and in true Oriental style gave each one a garment for the grand occasion, and then killed every one, and burned the images and destroyed the temple of Baal (2 K. x. 18–28). The Phœnicians believed in the development theory, that the first created beings were without intellect, and progressed from one stage to another up to man (Sanchoniathon). Melchisedec was of this race and faith, worshiping Elyon, called *their* most high god; but Abraham worshiped Jehovah, the Lord (Gen. xiv. 22).

The country has always had a great many tribes, each holding to its peculiar religion, and they now live together, but separate, without friendship or mutual trust, suspecting and hating every other faith but their own; and this want of common union is the great obstacle to their progress.

There is a hopeful future for this people, for which the American mission is preparing the way quickening a desire and taste for education among the young of all classes, and of every faith, and meeting these new demands with schools of the best grades, good books, and qualified, earnest teachers. The material progress of the country will follow the advance in its moral elevation, as is the case in all other lands. The population is stated by *Thompson* (Land and Book, i. 246) to be less than two millions, divided among Moslems, the rulers (800,000), Kurds (50,000), Nusariyeh (Arabs, 150,000), Yezidy and Gipsies (20,000),

Druses (100,000), Jews (25,000), Maronites (200,-000), Greeks (150,000), Armenians (20,000), Jacobites (15,000), Romanists (80,000), and a few Protestants from England, Scotland and America, besides the roving tribes of Arabs who cannot be counted, or even estimated. The cities have a population of all classes, numbering in Tripoli 18,000, Beirut 50,000, Tyre 35,000, Acre 5,000, Khaifa 3,000, and Deir el Kamar, the Druse capital, 7,000; besides which there are a great number of small villages.

PHI'SON. PISON (Ecclus. xxiv. 25).

PHLE'GON (*burning*). A Christian at Rome (Rom. xvi. 14).

PHO'ROS. PAROSH (1 Esd. v. 9).

PHRY'GIA (*parched*). Asia Minor. Inland, S. of Bithynia and Galatia, W. of Cappadocia and Lycaonia, N. of Lycia and Pisidia, and E. of Caria, Lydia, and Mysia. The empire once included nearly all Asia Minor. The surface is level, with few ridges, and very productive of corn, fruit, wine, cattle, sheep, and horses. Laodicea, Hierapolis, and Colossæ (and perhaps Antioch) were the chief cities, mentioned in the New Testament.

PHUD. PHUT (Judg. ii. 23).

PHU'RAH (*bough*). Servant of GIDEON on his visit to the camp of the Midianites (Judg. vii. 10, 11).

PHU'RIM. PURIM (Esth. xi. 1).

PHUT, PUT. Son of HAM (Gen. x. 6). For the country and people, see LEHABIM.

PHU'VAH (*mouth*). Son of Issachar (Gen. xlvi. 13). PUAH.

PHYGEL'LUS (*fugitive*). A Christian (2 Tim. i. 15), a native of Asia, who deserted Paul at Rome in a critical time.

PHYLAC'TERY (*safeguard*). FRONTLETS.

PHYSICIAN. MEDICINE.

PI-BES'ETH (Egyptian *bahest*). *Bubastis* is the Greek form. On the Pelusiac branch of the Nile. Called, also, Bubastite, and named from the goddess whom the Greeks identified with Artemis (Coptic *Pascht*). The city was built on an artificial elevation, raised by criminals (chiefly), from the mud taken from the canals leading from this place to Suez. Pascht was the goddess of fire, and had a grand temple in her honor, to which multitudes flocked yearly on pilgrimage. Herodotus describes the city very minutely (ii. 5–9). The only remains are a few stones of the finest red granite, and heaps of broken pottery, mud banks, etc. When Ezekiel prophesied its destruction it was in its period of greatest prosperity (xxx. 17).

PICTURE. Idolatrous representations, or images (Is. ii. 16).

PIECE OF GOLD (2 K. v. 5). See MONEY.

PIECE OF MONEY (Matt. xvii. 27). STATER.

PIECE OF SIL'VER. "The piece of money paid Judas is represented by the tetradrachm of Antiochus III, which was equal to a shekel. (See cut on page 13.) (Matt. xxv. 15). See MONEY.

PI'ETY (*L. pietas*). Dutiful conduct toward God, parents, etc., (1 Tim. v. 4).

PIG'EON. See DOVE.

PI-HAHI'ROTH (*mouth of the caverns*, or if Egyptian, *where sedge grows*). Near Suez, a camping-place during the Exodus (xiv. 2, 9). There is a

place there now called *Ghuweibet el boos* (*the bed of reeds*).

PI'LATE, PON'TIUS. (L. *Pilatus*, probably from *pilum*, armed with a javelin. Pontius—probably of Gens Pontia a plebeian clan of Samnite origin) The sixth Roman procurator of Judæa, the successor of Valerius Gratus, under Tiberius Cæsar (Luke iii. 1). Tacitus writes "The author of that name (Christian) or sect was Christ, who was capitally punished in the reign of Tiberius by Pontius Pilate." The early fathers, Justin Martyr, Eusebius, Tertullian and others, say that Pilate sent to Rome an official report of the trial of Christ. Pilate oppressed the Jews, and violated the Roman law which respected the Jewish religion; of this there is the especial evidence of Josephus (Ant. xviii. 3, 1). He disregarded the law in having brought into Jerusalem effigies upon the ensigns, and by an attempt to force their introduction. Also in appropriating sacred money or treasure for the construction of an aqueduct (Luke xiii. 1). During the feasts the Roman governors resided in Jerusalem to preserve order. Thus at the feast of the Passover, Pilate was in Jerusalem in his official residence, Herod's palace. It was to the gates of this palace that the Jews brought Christ in the early morning, they not entering the house of a Gentile at the period of Passover (John xviii. 28). Pilate therefore came out to hear the indictment. (See JESUS.) Pilate assumed his office about A. D. 25. After ten years an appeal from the Samaritans (whom he had oppressed) to Vitellius, the President of Syria, caused him to be sent to Rome, to answer the charges brought against him. Tiberius died ere he reached Rome. It is generally held that he committed suicide from mortification.

PIL'DASH (*flame of fire*). Son of Nahor (Gen. xxii. 22).

PILE'HA (*a slice*). A chief who sealed the covenant (Neh. x. 24).

PIL'LAR (Heb. AMMUD; Gr. *stulos*). Pillars were an important feature in Oriental architecture: 1. *For monuments* (Gen. xxviii. 18). 2. *In building* (Judg. xvi. 25). 3. *As objects of idolatrous worship*

BETHANY.

(Deut. xii. 3). 4. Figuratively or symbolically (Ex. xxxiii. 9–10).

PILL'ED (*peeled*), (Gen. xxx. 37, 38). PEELED.

PIL'LON (Heb. CEBIR, braided), (1 Sam. xix. 13, 16).—2. Heb. pl. CESATHOTH, cushions (Ez. xiii.

18, 20).—3. Heb. pl. MERAASHOTH, *under the head* (Gen. xxviii. 11, 18).—4. Gr. *proskephalaion, a cushion for the head* (Mark iv. 28).

PIL'TAI. The head of the priestly house of Modiah (Neh. xii. 17).

PINE, PINE'-TREE. 1. Heb. TIDHAR (Is. xli. 19). Several varieties of pine grew upon Mt. Lebanon. 2. SHEMEN (Neh. viii. 15), rendered "oil-tree." See CEDAR.

PIN'NACLE (Matt. iv. 5). Some high part of the Temple, or of the courts or wings belonging to it. Josephus says Herod built the royal gallery on the S. part, from the top of which, if any one looked down, he would become dizzy (Wars, v. 5, Ant. xv. 11, 5, xx. 9, 7). Late explorations have discovered the actual hight of the foundation wall to be about 150 ft., and the Temple buildings must have been 50 to 75 ft. more; making over 200 ft. (287 ft. —Barclay, *City of Great King*, 251). Eusebius says that James, brother of Jesus, was precipitated from this hight.

PI'NON (*darkness*). Founder of a tribe of Edom (Gen. xxxvi. 4).

PIPE (Heb. CHALIL). One of the simplest, but most prominent, of MUSICAL INSTRUMENTS.

PI'PER (Rev. xviii. 22). Music.

PI'RA (1 Esd. v. 19). Repetition of CAPHIRA.

PI'RAM (*indomitable*). King of Jarmuth (Josh. x. 3, 27).

PIR'ATHON (*chief*). Where Abdon was buried, in the land of Ephraim (Judg. xii. 13, 15). Benaiah, one of David's captains, was from this city (2 Sam. xxiii. 30). Now called Ferata, 6 ms. S. W. of Shechem, in Wada Aly, near the foot of the mountain Shekh Abraham (Rob. iii. 134).

PIRA'THONITE. Native of PIRATHON. 1. ABDON 1 (*the judge*), (Judg. xii. 13, 15).—2. BENAIAH 2 (2 Sam. xxiii. 30).

PIS'GAH (*to divide*—i. e., *isolated peak*). Mountain in Moab (Deut. iii. 17, xxxiv. 1; Josh. xii. 3, xiii. 20). Although minutely described in the Scriptures, yet it has been difficult to locate. The present explanation of the matter is, that Abarim was the name of the range; Nebo one of the peaks; and Pisgah the top of Nebo. The passage would then read, "Moses went up to Mount Nebo, to the top of the hill." (See NEBO). The name Ras el Feshkah (the same as Pisgah) must have been transferred across the Dead Sea, as well as the name of the Jebel Mousa, S. E. of Bethany.

PISID'IA. In Asia Minor, S. of Phrygia, E. of Lydia, W. of Cilicia, and N. of Pamphylia. It is mountainous, but has many fertile plains and valleys. The scenery is wild and grand (some cliffs rising 1000 ft. over a foaming torrent); hightened by forests of oak, pine, and other trees, orchards of fruit-trees, and vineyards. Its people, in the time that Paul traveled through it, were warlike highlanders, and probably exposed the Apostle to the "perils of robbers" that he mentions. Antioch was in Pisidia, though on the border of Phrygia.

PI'SON (*overflowing*). River in Eden (Gen. ii. 11).

PIS'PAH (*spreading*). Son of Jether (1 Chr. vii. 38).

PIT. Used with a figurative as well as literal meaning. Heb. 1. SHEOL (Num. xvi. 30, 33), hollow.—2. SHAHATH (Ps. ix. 15), a pit dug into the earth.—3. BOR (Gen. xxxvii. 30, ff), a pit for water.

PITCH. A mineral pitch or asphalt. Heb. 1. ZEPHETH (Ex. ii. 3), liquid.—2. HEMAR, solid.—3. KOFER, in reference to its use in overlaying woodwork. Its nature is mentioned in Is. xxxiv. 9.

PITCH'ER (Heb. KAD, *barrel*). Water-jars with one or two handles, used by women for carrying water (Gen. xxiv. 15-20). They are carried on the head or shoulder. The Bedawin women use skin-bottles (Gen. xxi. 14).

PIT'DAH. One of the precious stones in the breast plate of the high priest (Ex. xxviii. 17). See PRECIOUS STONES.

PI'THOM. One of the store-cities built by the Israelites in Egypt, for the first oppressor (Ex. i. 11.) *Patumus* of Herodotus (ii. 158). Now called *Abhaseh*, at the entrance of *Wady Fumilat*, on the line of the ancient canal to the Red Sea.

PI'THON. A descendant of Saul, son of Micah (1 Chr. viii. 35).

PLAGUES, THE, OF EGYPT. The so-called plagues of Egypt form the chief part of the miraculous side of the great deliverance of the Israelites from Egyptian bondage. These plagues will teach essentially the same lessons that the deliverance itself teaches. Indeed, the meaning of the deliverance from Egypt will be best learned from considering these miracles, which show it not to have been a mere symbolcal act—shadowing or foreshadowing by this temporal deliverance from worldly bondage a spiritual redemption from spiritual oppression—but to have been itself a conflict with the powers of evil, deep and various, and a victory over them, and so a real redemption from the oppression of spiritual wickedness. The Jewish people were not only oppressed with sore bondage in brick and mortar, but their spirits were led captive under Egyptian idolatries; and the sight and circumstances of this deliverance shook them clear of these enslaving influences, though not completely. The so-called plagues are *ten* in number: 1. The turning of the waters of the Nile into blood (Ex. vii. 15). 2. Bringing up frogs from the river (Ex. viii. 1). 3. The gnats or mosquitoes (Ex. viii. 16). 4. Of flies (Ex. viii. 20). 5. The murrain of beasts (Ex. ix. 6). 6. The boils upon men and beasts (Ex. ix. 8). 7. Hail, etc. (Ex. ix. 13). 8. The locusts (Ex. x.). 9. The darkness (Ex. x. 21). 10. The destruction of the first-born of man and beast (Ex. xi.). The number *ten* is significant, ending, as it does, with the terrible blow struck direct from heaven—the full outpouring on Egypt of the divine wrath. See EXODUS, in HISTORY OF THE BOOKS.

PLAIN. Eight different Hebrew words are translated by this one word *plain*, in our version. 1. ABEL (*meadow*—see ABEL).—2. BIKA (*to cleave, a valley*). The valley between the two ranges of Lebanon is now called Buka. (See LEBANON). The same word is used to describe the plain on which the image was set up in the *plain* of Dura (Dan. iii.).—3. HAK-KIKKAR (ciccar), (*to move in a circle, as a coin or a loaf*), the plain around Jericho (Gen. xiii. 10).—4. HAM-MISHOR (*even place, plain*), in Deut. iii. 10, it refers to the region now called *El Belka*, the high level table-lands (of Moab) east of the Dead Sea.—5. HA-ARABAH (*dry region*), the peculiar name of the valley of the Jordan.—6. HA-SHEFELAH (*a low plain*), the name of the Plain of Philistia.—7. ELON (*oak*, or *grove of oaks*). The mistranslation loses much of the beauty and force of the original, as may be seen by correcting the reading in Gen. x. 6, to oak or grove of Moreh; and the same in Deut. xi. 30; in Gen. xiii. 18, to oak grove of Mamre; in Judg. iv. 11, to grove of the wanderers (Zanaim—wanderers), (where Bedawins pitch their tents?); in Judg. ix. 6, to the oak of the covenant, or monumental oak (The Charter Oak, Boston Elm, and Penn's treaty Elm, are instances in our country); in ver. 37, to grove of Meonenim (magicians); and in 1 Sam. x. 3, to oak or grove of Tabor.—8. EMEK (*valley*), applied to the Plain of Esdraëlon and other valleys or plains, as Achor, Ajalon, Baca, Berachah, Bethrehob, Elah, Gibeon, Hebron, Jehoshaphat, Keziz, Rephaim, Shaveh, Siddim, and Succoth, besides the valley of "decision" in Joel iii. 14.

PLAIT'ING. Braiding the HAIR (1 Pet. iii. 3).

PLANES (Is. xliv. 13). Carving tools. HANDI-CRAFT.

PLANE'-TREE (Ecclus. xxiv. 14). CHESTNUT-TREE.

PLAN'ETS (2 K. xxiii. v.). ASTRONOMY.

PLAS'TER. 1. A house infected with LEPROSY was to be replastered (Lev. xiv. 42, 43, 48).—2. The law was to be engraved on Mount Ebal, on stones coated with plaster (Deut. xxvii. 2, 4).—3. (Dan. v. 5), the writing by the mystic hand was on the plaster of the wall.—4. A plaster of figs were applied to boils (Is. xxxviii. 21).

PLAT, TO (Gr. *pleko*). Interweaving (Matt. xxvii. 29).

PLE'IADES (Gr. *pleo, to sail*). A cluster of seven stars in the constellation Taurus. The sun enters Taurus about the middle of April; its appearance was a sign of Spring.

PLOW. See AGRICULTURE.

PLUMB'-LINE (Heb. ANAK). A line with a weight attached (Amos vii. 7, 8). HANDICRAFT.

PLUM'MET (Heb. MESHKELITH). Used in leveling (Is. xxvii. 17).

POCH'ERETH (*snaring*). The children of Pochereth were among those who returned from captivity (Ezr. ii. 57; Neh. vii. 59).

PO'ETRY. See PSALMS, in the HISTORY OF THE BOOKS.

POI'SON. References to poison in the Scripture are very rare and no death occurring through poison is recorded. The two Heb. words, 1. CHEMAH, feverish heat, 2. ROSH, applied to some poisonous herb. The crime of poisoning never prevailed among the Hebrews. It was studied as a science in the East, and common at Rome. There were many venomous snakes and insects in Palestine. The poison of snakes was used by the Scythians and Arabs to anoint their arrows; as also alluded to by Job (Job vi. 4). It is used figuratively in poetry for anger and hate (Ps. lviii. 4).

POLL. The head (Num. i. 2, 18).

POLL. To clip (2 Sam. xiv. 26). HAIR.

POLYG'AMY. See MARRIAGE.

POMEGRANATE.

POME'GRANATE. (Heb. RIMMON). A bush with dark geen foliage and crimson flowers. The fruit is red when ripe and very juicy. The rind is used in the manufacture of leather. It is a native of Asia. The pillars in Solomon's Temple were adorned with carved figures of this fruit (1 K. vii.

18, 20). A fragment of the fruit with its pearly seeds imbedded in ruby liquid, is very beautiful. "Thy cheeks are like a piece of pomegranate" is the allusion of the poet to the fine transparent tint (Ca. iv. 3).

POM'MELS (*little apples*), (2 Chr. iv. 12, 13). BOWL.

POND (Heb. AGAM). The ponds of Egypt (Ex. vii. 19) were doubtless water left by the inundation of the Nile. Ponds for fish are mentioned in Is. xix. 10.

PON'TIUS PI'LATE. PILATE.

PON'TUS. A district on the Black Sea (Acts. ii. 9, 10).

POOL. 1. Heb. AGAM, pond.—2. Heb. BERAKAH, blessing.—3. Heb. BEREKAH, a reservoir for water. These pools in many parts of Palestine and Syria are the only resource for water in a dry season (Is. xliii. 15). Those of Solomon, 3 miles S. W. of Bethlehem, and Bethesda in Jerusalem, are the most celebrated (Eccl. ii. 6). See JERUSALEM.

POOR. The poor received special favors from the law (Deut. xi. 7). 1. The right of GLEANING (Lev. xix. 9, 10). 2. Their portion from the produce of the land in the SABBATICAL YEAR (Ex. xxiii. 11). 3. Possession of land in the JUBILEE year (ver. 25, 30). 4. USURY and pledges (35, 37). 5. Permanent bondage forbidden (Deut. xv. 12, 15). 6. Portions of tithes (Deut. xiv. 28). 7. Their entertainments at feasts (xvi. 11, 14). 8. Payments of WAGES (Lev. xix. 13).

POP'LAR (Heb. LIBNEH). Poplar and storax trees are common in Palestine (Hos. iv. 13).

POR'ATHA (*favored*). Son of Haman (Esth. ix. 8).

PORCH. 1. ULAM, a vestibule, open in front and at the sides. Sometimes closed with awnings or curtains.—2. MISDRON, a corridor, connecting the principal rooms of the house (Matt. xvi. 71).

PORCIUS, FESTUS. FESTUS.

PORT (L. *Porta*). Gate (Neh. ii. 13).

POR'PHYRY (*purple*). A hard rock of various colors, greatly prized for its beauty when polished (Esth. i. 6). MARBLE.

POR'TER (SHOER, *a gate-keeper*), (1 Chr. ix. 21). LEVITES.

POSIDO'NIUS. An envoy sent to Judas (2 Macc. xiv. 19).

POST. The door-case of a door (Is. vi. 4). The posts of the Temple door were of olive-wood (1 K. vi. 33). 1. AJIL, door-case of a door (Ez. xl. 16). —2. AMMAH, *cubit*, a post (Is. vi. 4).—3. MEZUZAH, motion on a centre.—4. SAF, threshold (Ex. xxvi. 1).—5. RAZ, to run, posts (Esth. iii. 13); also guard; and a runner or carrier of messages in Job ix. 25.

Our word post means a fixed place—as a post, station, military or for travelers; also, the one who carries messages or travels by post (that is, with horses supplied at the post), and also the letter-carrier; and hence post-office.

POT. Is applied to many kinds of vessels, bowl, basin, cup, etc. 1. ASUK, an earthen jar, deep and without handles.—2. CHERES, an earthen jar, used for baking (Ez. iv. 9).—DUD, a kettle, used for cooking (1 Sam. ii. 14).—4. SIR, used for flesh (Ex. xvi. 3).—5. MAZREF, fining-pot (Prov. xxvi. 23. xxvii. 21).—6. GEBIYIM, bulging jars in Jer. xxxv. 5.

The water-pots of Cana were of stone or earthenware. They were also of precious metals for domestic or public use. The water-pot of the Samarian woman was either an earthen jar or a leather bottle. Pottery was a handicraft among the Hebrews, remains of which are found in the debris of the most ancient ruins.

POT'IPHAR (*belonging to the sun*). A captain of

the guard to whom Joseph was sold (Gen. xxxix. 1).

POTIPH'ERAH. A priest of On. Father of Asenath. Wife of Joseph (Gen. xli. 45, 50).

POT'SHERD (Heb. cheres). Earthen vessel or bottle. Anything mean and contemptible, or very dry (Is. xxx. 14, xlv. 9; Job. ii. 8).

POTTER'S FIELD. Bought by the priests with the bribe of 30 pieces given to Judas (Matt. xxvii. 7). Aceldama.

"THE GREAT CAMEO."
A Sardonyx, 13 ⋈ 11 inches; in five colored layers.

POT'TERY. Was one of the most common and ancient of all manufactures. The clay, when wet, was trodden by the feet to form a paste, then placed on the wheel, and shaped by the hands. The wheel consisted of a wooden disc, placed on another larger one, and turned by the hand, or by a treadle (Is. xlv. 9). The vessel was then smoothed, and coated with a glaze, and burnt in a furnace (Is. xli. 25).

POUND. 1. (Heb. maneh, *a weight*). See Weights and Measures.—2. A piece of money (Luke xix. 12–27). Money. Maneh.

PRÆTO'RIUM. The head-quarters of the Roman governor. Judgment-hall.

PRAYER (Heb. tehinnah, *supplication;* tefillah, *to bow down*). To ask God for a blessing. Men have believed in all ages that the Divine Being hears prayer (Deut. iv. 29; 1 Chr. xxviii. 9, etc.), and answers it graciously (Ps. cxlv. 18, 19; 2 Chr. vii. 1) and willingly. Prayer is also called "seeking the Lord" (1 Chr. xvi. 10), intreating the face of the Lord (see Face), pouring out the heart or soul before Him or before His face (Ps. lxii. 8 ; 1 Sam. i. 15), crying (1 K. viii. 28) or calling unto God, and a beseeching of God (Ps. lv. 16 ; Ex. xxxii. 11).

In the N. T. the approach of the soul unto God, with desire and request for help, is very distinctly stated in many passages (Matt. vi. 6, vii. 7 ; Luke x. 2; John xiv. 13; Eph. vi. 18; Phil. iv. 6; Col. iv. 2, 3, etc.). Nowhere in the Bible is there any word of explanation of the reason for prayer; the fact is dealt with as a fact, as plain as day and night.

The use of forms, in some cases, seems intended to secure the praise of men rather than of God (Matt. vi. 5). When the form is the most extensive and showy the true spirit is in danger of being lost.

The Lord's Prayer (Matt. vi. 9–13; Luke xi. 2–4) is the model for all Christian prayer.

Prayer is first distinctly mentioned in Abraham's time. Moses gave no special rules or laws for prayer, but we learn that it was considered as a privilege and a duty to which man's own nature prompted him. The altar was the place where prayer was believed to be most acceptable in the patriarchal age, and the tabernacle, under the Mosaic covenant (1 Sam. i. 10), which was changed for the Temple, was called "the house of prayer" (Is. lvi. 7). Those who could, prayed in the Temple; others at a distance turned their faces towards it—a custom which is still in practice. The Mohammedans also turn their faces towards the city of Mecca, which contains the holy house, the kaaba. See 1 K. viii. 30; 2 K. xix; 2 Chr. vii. 14; Dan. vi. 10; Jonah ii. 4; Zech. vii. 2; Luke ii. 37, xviii. 10; Acts xxii. 17. There is a certain power in outward symbols in helping men to realize the presence of God, in quickening their faith, and in carrying out the idea that sinful man can best approach his Maker by a sacrifice. These sentiments are as extensive as the human race. There are seven prayers recorded at their full length in the Scriptures (David, 2 Sam. vii. 19–29; Solomon, 2 Chr. vi.; Hezekiah, 2 K. xix.; Jeremiah, ch. xxxii.; Daniel, ch. ix. 3; Nehemiah, chs. i. ix.).

Nearly all of the prayers recorded in the O. T. were for temporal blessings—the Mosaic covenant promising no other; and many were intercessory, by priests or prophets, except, as may be learned from the Psalms, where there is shown a spirit of striving against sin and for help against temptation. The Hebrews prayed three times a day (Ps. lv. 17; Dan. vi. 10), and particular times or hours were thought to be more fit than others, when prayer was thought to be more acceptable (Ps. lxix. 13). Confession of sins to God was usual at the time of prayer as a part of the intercession.

In the Christian Church, Jesus the Christ takes the place of the temple and the altar and the priests and prophets in the old dispensation. He is the intercessor for His people, asking of God the Father blessings for His sake. The Christian form of prayer includes the Hebrew idea of intercession, pleading for benefits; and also adds the higher spiritual desires based on the idea of the brotherhood of all men (Matt. v. 44, ix. 38; 1 Tim. ii. 2, 8; 1 Col. iv. 13; Phil. iv. 6; James v. 14).

It is supposed that if certain rules are neglected in prayer that God will not answer prayer (Ps. lxvi. 18; Pet. xv. 29, xxviii. 9; James iv. 3; Is. i. 15), nor if one of God's commands is disobeyed (1 Sam. viii. 18), or the supplicant is proud and independent (Job xxxv. 12; Luke xviii. 20), or a hypocrite (Job xxvii. 9), or if he doubts, wavers, or is double-minded (James i. 6; Jer. xxix. 13; Mark xi. 24). Enmity in the heart and secret idolatry are also stumbling-blocks. For posture in prayer see Adoration.

Prayer is the free utterance of the soul's wants to God the Father, asking benefits in the name of our Saviour, and interceding for the good of others also. Faith is quickened by prayer; and it may be said that prayer is an indication of the spiritual condition of the soul—it being to the soul what breath is to the body.

PREACH, TO. 1. (Heb. basar, *to bring glad tidings* (Ps. xl.).—2. kara, *to call* (Gen. 1, 5).—3. Gr. dianggello, *to announce fully* (Luke ix. 60).—4. Gr. dialegomai, *to discourse* (Acts xx. 7).—5. Gr. euanggellizo, *good news* (Luke iii. 18).—6. Gr. katanggello, *to publish* (Acts iv. 2).—7. Kerusso, *to proclaim* (Matt. iii. 1).—8. Gr. laleo, *to speak* (Mark ii. 2).—9. Prokerusso, *beforehand* (Acts iii. 20).—10. Gr. Proeuanggellizomai, *to announce glad tidings beforehand* (Gal. iii. 8).—11. *Parrhesiazo-*

mai, to be free, in speech or action (Acts ix. 27).—12. Gr. *plero, to fulfil* (Rom. xv. 19).—13. Gr. *akoë, the hearing* (Heb. iv. 2).

PREACH'ER (Heb. KOHELETH). A public instructor of the Gospel (1 Tim. ii. 7).

PREACH'ING (Heb. KERIAH). Public discourse of the prophets (Matt. xii. 41).

PRE'CIOUS STONES. Alluded to very often in the Scriptures, and were known, used, and valued from the earliest times. Engraved gems worn in rings (Cant. v. 14), and used for private seals (Neh. x.), are mentioned in Genesis, and all through the Bible. The twelve stones of the high-priest's breastplate were engraved with the name of one of the 12 tribes (Ex. xxviii. 17–21), and the whole when in their proper position on the breast of the high-priest were called Urim and Thummim (*light and perfection*).

The figurative uses of precious stones are very many, and highly poetical and important for instruction, and signify value, beauty, durability, excellence.

1. ADAMANT (SHAMIR), the diamond, (Jer. xvii. 1; Ez. iii. 9; Zech. vii. 12), was known and used for its peculiar hardness in cutting other stones, and figuratively to describe the obduracy of the Israelites. The word is the same in all the texts, although rendered both diamond and adamant. The Greek *smiris* was a corundum, our emory.

2. AG'ATE (SHEBO), (Ex. xxviii. 19), the second stone in the high-priest's breastplate. Named from the river Achates, Sicily, where it was first found by the Greeks, It is a quartz in colored layers.

3. AM'ETHYST (AHLAMAH), 3d in the 3d row of the breastplate, and is alluded to in Rev. xxi. 20, as one of the stones of the heavenly Jerusalem.

4. BER'YL (TARSHISH) a yellow EMERALD. There is little or nothing to lead to any satisfactory conclusion as to its identity, except in Cant. v. 14. The streets of Jerusalem shall be paved with beryl (Rev. xxi. 20; Tob. xiii. 17).

5. CAR'BUNCLE. 1. (Heb. EKDAH,) bright, sparkling, gem.—2. (BAREKATH), the third stone in the first row of the breast-plate (Ex. xxviii. 17); also one of the treasures of the king (Ez. xxviii. 13). It is a precious stone of a deep red color, commonly called *garnet*.

6. CHAL'CEDONY, (Gr. *Chalkedon*), a precious stone (Rev. xxi. 19), resembling the agate; of various colors, but often light brown or blue, found in most parts of the world, named after Chalcedon.

7. CHRYS'OLITE (*golden stone*). A transparent precious stone, having the color of gold mixed with green. It has a fine lustre (Rev. xxi. 20). Many suppose it to be the topaz of the moderns.

8. CHRYSO'PRASUS. The tenth of those precious stones in the walls of the heavenly Jerusalem. Its color was golden green (Rev. xxi. 20).

9. CHRYS'OPRASE is the leek-green variety of agate.

10. EM'ERALD, (NOPHECH; Gr. *Smaragdos*). First in the second row on the breastplate of the high-priest (Ex. xxviii. 18). Used as a seal or signet (Ecclus. xxxii. 6), and spoken of as one of the foundations of Jerusalem (Rev. xxi. 19). It is of a fine green color, found anciently in Ethiopia, in modern times only in South America (Ex. xxviii. 18). It ranks next in value to the diamond.

11. JA'CINTH, (Gr. *huakinthos*), (*hyacinth*). A precious stone, of a dark purple color (Rev. xxi. 20). It loses its color when heated, and resembles the diamond.

12. O'NYX (SHOHAM, *a nail*). An agate colored like a finger nail (Ex. xxviii. 20; Gen. ii. 12).

13. RU'BY, (PENINIM). A red sapphire diamond, and more valuable than a diamond of the same weight (Is. liv. 12).

14. SAP'PHIRE (SAPPIR). Next in hardness and value to the diamond (Ex. xxviii. 18), of a blue

EGYPTIAN PRIESTS.

color and of various shades. Pliny described it as the lapis lazuli (Ultramarine), but that could not have been the kind in the breastplate.

15. SAR'DIUS, SARDINE (ODEM). Josephus says sardonyx (Ant. iii. 7, 6). Now called carnelian from its flesh color. The Hebrew name means red like flesh. The Sardius is a kind of flint, or chalcedony, and is valued more as it is deeper red. The name Sardius was given it at Sardis, where it was worked and engraved. It was in the high-priest's breastplate (Ex. xxviii. 17), and is alluded to by John in the Revelation (iv. 3).

16. SAR'DONYX (YAHALOM). A chalcedony with layers of several shades, much used in finger rings for the signet (Rev. xxi. 20). Rendered diamond in the A. V.

17. TO'PAZ (PITDAH, Gr. *topazion*). Second in the breastplate of the high-priest (Ex. xxviii. 17), and the ninth in the foundation of the heavenly Jerusalem (Rev. xxi. 20). Its color is wine yellow, of every degree of shade, from dark red, sometimes lilac, to pale grayish yellow, or celadon green. It was highly prized. Job says that wisdom is more valuable than the pètdah of Cush (xxviii. 19). There is a topaz island in the Red Sea, where it is found. See SEAL, SIGNET RING.

ENGRA'VER, HARASH, (Ex. xxviii. 11). Print, to HAKAK, *to cut in* (Job xix. 23, 24).

PREPARA'TION, THE. (Mark xv. 42). PASSOVER.

PRES'BYTERY (from Gr. meaning *old, elder*). A body of elders in the Christian Church (1 Tim. iv.). Also a body consisting of pastors, ruling elders, laymen, commissioned to represent the churches belonging to the presbytery. This work is subject to the revision of the synod.

PRESS (Joel iii. 13). WINE-PRESS.

PRETO'RIUM, or PRÆTO'RIUM (*leader*). The head-quarters of the Roman military governor. JUDGMENT-HALL (Mark xv. 16).

PREVENT, TO (Gr. *prævenio, to come before*). 1. (Heb. KADEM, *to anticipate*), (2 Sam. xxii. 6, 19). Gr. *prophthano, to precede* (1 Thess. iv. 15.)

PRICK (*goads*): "To kick against the pricks" (Acts ix. 5), should read, to kick against the goads; as an ox kicking against the goad in the hand of the driver.

PRIEST (Heb. KŌHEN, *to foretell?* or *a mediator, a messenger*), Job xxxiii. 23). The word priest means one who presides over things relating to God, or, as Paul says, "Every high-priest taken from among men, is constituted on the behalf of men, with respect to their concerns with God, that he may present both gifts and sacrifices for sins" (Heb. v. 1). Adam is the first recorded priest; Noah was the first after the deluge. It is probable that the patriarchs were priests, as in Job i. 5. The prophet differed from the priest in receiving supernatural communications of knowledge, of the past, present, and future. In the patriarchal system, the first-born male was the priest of the family, and succeeded his father. The Mosaic system substituted the tribe of Levi, instead of the first-born (Ex. xxviii.). The Hebrews were promised that, if they would keep the law of Moses, they should be "a peculiar treasure," "a kingdom of priests," "a holy nation" (Ex. xix. 5, 6). [For dress of the priest, see DRESS. See cuts of priests, on pps. 16, 69, 77, 131.] The age at which they were permitted to serve was not definitely fixed, as in the case of the Levites, but was, probably, at maturity—from 20 yrs. old. The support of the high-priest was, the tithe of 1-10th of the tithes assigned to the Levites (Num. xviii. 28; Neh. x. 38). The candidate for orders must prove his descent from Aaron; be free from bodily defects (Lev. xxi. 16–23); must not mourn outwardly; must marry only a young woman. They were to keep the sanctuary and altar (Num. xviii. 5); to keep the fire always burning on the altar (Lev. i. 7, vi. 13); to prepare the burnt offerings, and kill the passover (2 Chr. xxix. 34; Ezr. vi. 20); to do the work of a certain part of the sacrifices, generally (see OFFERING; SACRIFICE): to attend to the services of atonement; to blow the trumpets for all occasions; to prepare the ointment, or perfumed oil, and the water of separation; act as assessors in judicial matters; to assist in the work of organizing and encouraging the army; and to keep the books of the law (Deut. xx. 1–4, xxi. 5, xxxi. 9). They were permitted to eat, at the sanctuary, the flesh of the various offerings; and also to carry away—to be eaten in Jerusalem—certain parts of offerings; and had a right to the first-fruits of oil, wine, and grain, and certain parts of sacrifices (Deut. xviii); the price of redemption of man and of unclean beasts; restitutions, and all devoted things; the skins of the sacrificed animals (which was a very rich perquisite); donations; and might own land (1 K. ii. 26; Jer. xxxii. 7, 8). The total income is supposed to have been about 1-5th of the

entire national income (see Gen. xlvii. 24). The priesthood was a perpetual inheritance, transmitted from father to son. After the Captivity, those who could not prove their descent from Aaron lost their privileges as priests. The corruption of the priesthood, by making their office a means of amassing wealth, and intriguing, in politics, for political power, hastened the ruin of the Jewish nation. Christ is described in the N. T. as the first-born, the king, the anointed, a priest after the order of Melchizedek (Heb. vii., viii.). The priesthood in

the Christian Church is a spiritual matter, deriving its powers and privileges from the Holy Spirit.

PRINCE. Governor of districts or local magistrates. JESUS CHRIST is "the PRINCE OF LIFE" (Acts iii. 15). SATAN "the prince of this world" (John xii. 31). PROVINCE.

PRIN'CESS (*noble lady*). "Queen" (Is. xlix. 23). Lady (Judg. v. 29).

PRINCIPALITY (*rulers*). The dominion of a PRINCE (Jer. xiii. 18).

PRINT, TO. (Heb. MATHAN, *to give*), (Gen. i. 29). See ENGRAVER; WRITING. "Printed," in Job xix. 23, should be "written" or "marked down."

PRIS'CA (*ancient*). PRISCILLA (2 Tim. iv. 19)

PRISCIL'LA. The wife of AQUILA (Rom. xvi. 3). The position, in several ancient MSS., of the name of Priscilla before that of her husband, indicates that she was the more active of the two in the Church, as appears in her teaching of Apollos. She is the type of the married servant of the Church, as Phebe is of the unmarried. Her assistance was asked by Timothy as of the utmost value in pointing out the actual wants and condition of the needy members of the Church.

PRIS'ON. Special places used as prisons were under the custody of a military officer (Gen. xl. 3). Private houses now sometimes used as places of confinement (Jer. xxxvii. 15). See PUNISHMENTS.

PRIS'ON-GATE. A gate of the JERUSALEM wall enclosing the Temple.

PROCH'ORUS (*leader of the chorus*). A Deacon (Acts vi. 5). DEACON.

PROCON'SUL. (Gr. *anthupatos, to be deputy*). A division of conquered provinces not requiring military rule, was governed by the Roman Senate by proconsuls, civil officers, and their districts were called proconsular. The term was usually one year. A coin of Ephesus gives the title ANTHUPATOS (Acts xix. 38). They did not have the power of life and death.

PROC'URATOR. Is the Latin name of the Roman ruler, translated GOVERNOR in the N. T. See PILATE. Gr. *egemon.* They were similar in power to the proconsul, and were selected from among those who had been consuls or prætors, or senators. Their term of office depended on the will of the emperor. They wore a military dress and sword, and were attended by six lictors. They had the power of life and death. The head-quarters in Judæa were at Cæsarea, but held judicial wherever they were, as Pilate at Jerusalem. The high priest could be removed at will by him.

PROGEN'ITORS. Parents or ancestors (Gen. xlix. 26). GENEALOGY.

PROGNOS'TICATORS, MONTHLY (Is. xlvii. 13). MAGICIANS.

PROPH'ET (Heb. NABI). Signifies an inspired person, an announcer of the words of another, not from his own influence and will (Ex. vii. 1, iv. 16); to foretell the future and secret events, and who revealed the will of God.

The O. T. prophets were special agents of Jehovah, raised up and sent, as occasion required, to incite to duty, to convict of sin, to call to repentance and reformation, to instruct kings and denounce against nations the judgments of God (2 K. xvii. 13). The prophets received their messages from God in visions, trances and dreams (Num. xxiv. 2–16). The O. T. contains the inspired writings of sixteen of the Hebrew prophets, four of whom, Isaiah, Jeremiah, Ezekiel and Daniel, are called the greater, and the other twelve the minor prophets. Christ, of whom all the prophets bore witness (Luke xxiv. 27, 44), is THE PROPHET of His Church in all ages (Deut. xviii. 15), revealing to them by His inspired servants, by Himself and by His spirit all we know of God and immortality.

PTOLEMY I.

PROPH'ETESS (Heb. NEBIAH). A female PROPHET (Ex. xv. 20). MIRIAM; DEBORAH.

PROPITIA'TION. One who makes ATONEMENT (1 John ii. 2).

PRO'REX (*for the king*). Viceroy (2 K. i. 17).

PROS'ELYTE (Gr. *proselyti;* Heb. GERIM). This word is often used in the Septuagint as the rendering of the Heb. GER, *a sojourner*, translated "a stranger" (Ex. xii. 48, xx.10, xxii. 21, etc.). The word from meaning "one who comes to," means, also, one "who comes over" from one faith to another. The law was liberal to strangers (GERIM), ordaining that they should be treated with forbearance and kindness (Ex. xxii. 21, xxiii. 9; Lev. xix. 33, 34). "The stranger that dwelleth with you shall be unto you as one born among you, and thou shalt love him as thyself, for ye were strangers," etc. The stranger or sojourner was ordered to be welcomed to the Passover Feast upon his observance of certain regulations (Ex. xii. 43, 45). The word in the sense of convert appears in the history and the writings of the prophets in Is. lvi. 3–8, "the sons of the stranger that join themselves to the Lord. The conquests of Alexander, the wars between Egypt and Syria, the struggle under Maccabees, and the occupation by Rome, brought the Jews into wide notice, and gave opportunities for proselytism. Such proselytes attended the Jewish worship and made pilgrimages to the feasts at Jerusalem (Acts ii. 10). The admission into Judaism of a convert was by circumcision. Converts to Judaism were classed: 1. As love-proselytes. 2. Man-for-woman or woman-for-man proselytes; where the husband followed the wife's religion or the reverse. 3. Esther-proselytes, where conformity was assumed to escape danger (Esth. viii. 17). 4. King's-table-proselytes, converts for the hope of court favor—as under David and Solomon. 5. Lion-proselytes, converts in the fear of a divine judgment—as the Samaritans (2 K. xvii. 26). Proselytes became numerous during and immediately after Christ's period; many were converted in parts remote from Jerusalem (Acts ii. 10, viii. 27).

PROV'ERBS. See HISTORY OF THE BOOKS.

PROV'ENDER. Food for cattle (Gen. xxiv. 25). GRASS, CORN, HAY, etc.

PROV'IDENCE. Foresight (Acts xxiv. 2). GOD.

PROV'INCE. (Heb. MEDINAH). A small district ruled by a judge (1 K. xx. 14, 15, 19).

PROVIS'ION. FOOD. To lay up a supply of food, or what is desired (Rom. xiii. 14).

PRU'NING-HOOK (Is. xviii. 5). See KNIFE.

PSALM (Heb. MIZMOR, *a song of praise*), (1 Cor. xiv. 26). MUSIC.

PSALMS, PSAL'TER. See HISTORY OF BOOKS.

PSAL'TERY (Heb. NEBEL). See MUSICAL INSTRUMENTS.

PTOL'EMAIS (*Ptolemy's city*). Acho, Acre (1 Macc. v. 15, 55, x. 1, 58, 60, xii. 48; Acts xxi. 7).

PTOL'EMEE. 1. Son of Dorymenes (1 Macc. iii. 38). He was active in the expedition which Lysias organized (1 Macc. iii. 38). He had great influence with Antiochus Epiphanes.—2. Son of Agesarchus, governor of Cyprus (2 Macc. viii. 8).—3. Son of Abubus, who married Simon's daughter. He was governor of the district of Jericho. He murdered Simon and two of his sons (1 Macc. xvi. 11).—4. Father of LYSIMACHUS I, the Greek translator of ESTHER (Esth. xi. 1).—5. PTOLEMY VI, PHILOMETOR (1 Macc. i. 18).—6. Son of DOSITHEUS (Esth. xi. 1). PTOLEMY.

PTOL'EMY. PTOL'OMEE, PTOL'EMEE (*the warlike*). The Greek title of the king of Egypt, as Pharaoh was the Egyptian title: first known to history in the time of Alexander, B. C. 323.

TABLE OF THE PTOLEMIES.

1 Ptol.	1 Ptolemæus I. Soter. B. C. 323–285.
	2 Ptol. II. Philadelphus. 285–247.
"	3 Arsinoe.
2 Ptol.	4 Ptol. III. Euergetes I. 247–222.
"	5 Berenice, married Antiochus II.
4 Ptol.	6 Ptol. IV. Philopator. 222–205.
"	7 Arsinoe. [Cleopatra).
7 Arsin.	8 Ptol. V. Epiphanes. 205–181; (m.
8 P. & C.	9 Ptol. VI. Philometor. 181–146.
"	10 Ptol. VII. Euergetes II. Physcon.
"	11 Cleopatra. [171–146–117.
11 Cleop.	12 Cleopatra (Alex. Balas her son).
"	13 Ptol. Eupator.
"	14 Cleopatra.
14 Cleop.	15 Ptol. VIII. Soter II. 117–81.

PTOLEMY I.—SOTER. Was the son of Lagus, a Macedonian, a natural son of Philip the King. Alexander made him a ruler in Egypt, where he

PTOLEMY II.

made a strong government. Daniel alludes to him (xi. 5), as one who should receive a part of Alexander's kingdom, by the title "King of the South." He treacherously captured Jerusalem on a Sabbath. Having carried many Jews to Alexandria, he gave them the full privileges of citizens in the new city. (See ALEXANDRIA).

PTOLEMY III.

PTOLEMY II.—PHILADELPHUS. Youngest son of Ptol. I, and was made king two years before his father's death. His daughter Berenice married Antiochus II; (see p. 18). This reign was a trying time for Judaism, and for the intellectual development of the ancient world (ALEXANDRIA). Philadelphus was a patron of art and science, and collected famous men and a large library. Daniel alludes to him in ch. xi.

PTOLEMY III.—EUER′GETES.—B.C. 247–222. Oldest son of Ptolemy Philadelphus, brother of Berenice (5). His sister's murder gave him an occasion for invading Syria (B. C. 246), alluded to in Dan. xi. 7. He recovered the images stolen out of Egypt by Cambyses, and brought home a vast treasure, earning the title of Benefactor (euergetes), and almost miraculously escaped from the threatened attacks of Seleucus (Dan. xi. 9), and developed the resources of his country.

PTOLEMY IV.—PHILOP′ATOR.—B. C. 222–205. He was a sensual and effeminate man, but energetic ruler. Daniel alludes to him (xi. 10–12). He offered sacrifices at Jerusalem in honor of his victories; but on attempting to enter the Holy of Holies he was struck with paralysis, for which he attempted to take revenge on the Alexandrian Jews, but was turned from his purpose by certain strange signs, which are differently reported by various historians. See APOCRYPHA. He was succeeded by

PTOLEMY V.—EPIPHANES.—B. C. 205–181. It was during this reign that ONIAS, the rightful

PTOLEMY IV.

high-priest, who had been driven away from Jerusalem, built a temple at Leontopolis. Daniel again pictures the actual condition of affairs in the words: "The robbers of the people exalted themselves to establish the vision" (xi. 14). "Many stood up against the king of the South" (Egypt); "so the king of the North (Antiochus) came and cast up a mount, and took the most fenced city" (Sidon), to which Scopas, the general of Ptolemy, had fled,

PTOLEMY V.

"and the arms of the South did not withstand" (Antiochus defeated the Egyptians at Paneas, B. C. 198—Dan. xi. 14, 15). The Romans then came in to make peace; "gave him (Ptolemy, his, Antiochus's, daughter) a young maiden" (as his wife, Dan. xi. 18), who did "not stand on his side," but supported her husband against her father.

PTOLEMY VI.

PTOLEMY VI.—PHILOMETER.—B. C. 181–146. Was son of Ptolemy V and Cleopatra, and was a child when his father was poisoned, the government being managed by his mother, who preserved peace with Syria until she died, B. C. 173. Antio-

chus Epiphanes invaded Egypt, but was forced to retreat by the Roman power. (See Dan. xi. 25–30). In this prophesy the ships of Chittim are the Romans. PTOLEMY EUERGETES II was ruler of Cyrene (1 Macc. xi. 18). Philometor is the last of the line mentioned in the Scriptures. In his reign the Jews were divided by the temple at Leontopolis. Onias, son of Onias III (see ONIAS), fled to Egypt from the political and priestly corruption at Jerusalem, and entered the service of the Ptolemy, with another Jew, Dositheus, and rose to supreme command, rendering important services to the Egyptian cause, in favor of Ptolemy Physcon against his brother. This service he made the basis of a demand for a ruined temple of Diana at Leontopolis, which he proposed to rebuild in imitation of the Temple at Jerusalem, quoting as divine authority Isaiah xix. 18. The building was made the same, but the furniture was different. Instead of the seven-branched candlestick there was a single lamp, suspended by a gold chain (Jos. Wars, vii. 10, 3). The altar and offerings were the same, and the service was by priests and Levites of clear descent. The building of the temple is dated about B. C. 149, but cannot be definitely fixed. Priests who had served in Egypt were forbidden to serve in Jerusalem, and the temple never had any great favor in Palestine, being looked upon as a kind of idolatrous shrine.

There were many Jews in Egypt (Jer. xliii. 6, 7), and Ptolemy Soter increased the number by policy and by force (Ant. xii. ii. 1), and they had great influence in Egypt (Ant. xii. 4); and one ARISTOBULUS is mentioned as the tutor (counselor) of the Ptolemy.

The Romans, in B. C. 71, plundered and closed the temple at Leontopolis (Jos. Wars, vii. 10).

PU′A. PUAH 2. Son of Issachar (Num. xxvi. 23).

PU′AH (*mouth*). 1. Father of Tola (Judg. x. 1).—2. Son of Issachar (1 Chr. vii. 1).—3 (*splendid*). One of the mid-wives whom Pharaoh ordered to kill the Hebrew male children (Ex. i. 15).

PUBAS′TUM (Ez. xxx. 17). PI′BESETH.

PUB′LICAN (Lat. *publicanus*; Gr. *telones*). Collectors of the Roman revenue. The publicans of the N. T. were regarded as traitors and classed with sinners (Matt. ix. 11), harlots (xxi. 31, 32), and with the heathen (xviii. 17). No money received from them was permitted to go into the alms-box. They were not allowed to sit in judgment or give testimony. Some of them were the earliest disciples of John the Baptist and of Christ (Luke xviii. 13).

PUB′LIUS (*public*). Governor of MELITA (Acts xxviii. 7, 8).

PU′DENS (*bashful*). A Christian friend of Timothy (2 Tim. iv. 21), at Rome. Martial, the Spanish poet, who lived at Rome about A. D. 66, mentions two or three friends, Pudens, Claudia, and Linus, who were the same as the friends of Paul and Timothy.

PU′HITES (*Jah is revelation*). Descendants of the family of Kirjath-Jearim.

PUL. Error for Phut or Put.

PUL (*king*). An Assyrian king, the first mentioned in Scripture. He made an expedition against MENAHEM, king of Israel. But we learn from the Assyrian monuments that Jehu had already paid tribute to Shalmanezer II, as recorded on the black obelisk. It is difficult, if not impossible, to identify Pul with any known Assyrian king. None of the monuments have a name at all like Pul. The monuments tell us that Tiglath-pileser took tribute of Menahem, and they say nothing of Pul. He may have been a usurper holding power in Western Assyria, and able to descend into Palestine; or a Babylonian, who grew to great command in those days. The period of Pul's invasion may be thus fixed: Tiglath-pileser records that he took tribute from Menahem—a war which was carried on from his fourth to his eighth year, about B. C. 741 to 737.

Menahem reigned ten years, so that Pul's expedition could not be earlier than B. C. 751, or later than B. C. 745.

PUL'PIT (Heb. MIGDAL). An elevated stage, usually translated "tower" (Neh. viii. 4).

PULSE (Heb. ZEROHIM, ZERONIM, "to scatter, to sow"). A general name of peas, beans, and such kinds of garden sauce (Dan. i. 12, 16).

PUN'ISHMENTS. Were two fold, capital and secondary. 1. Stoning (Ex. xvii. 4). 2. Hanging (Num. xxv. 4). 3. Burning (Gen. xxxviii. 24). 4. By the sword (Ex. xix. 13). 5. Strangling (John xviii. 31). 6. Drowning (Matt. xviii. 6). 7. Sawing asunder (2 Sam. xii. 31). 8. Pounding in a mortar or beating to death (Prov. xxvii. 22). 9. Precipitation (2 Macc. vi. 10).

OF SECONDARY.—1. Retaliation (Ex. xxi. 24–25). 2. Compensation in money, or goods, or service (Ex. xxi. 18–36). 3. Stripes (Deut. xxv. 3). 4. Scourging (Judg. viii. 16).

PUNISHMENTS, for crime, or offense against the law, were inflicted directly on the person, or indirectly on his goods, or relatives. Capital punishment was instituted among the covenant people by Noah (Gen. ix. 5, 6), because murder was an offense against the image of God. The system of blood avenging was also set on foot by him, requiring the near relative to slay the murderer, even among near kinsmen. The patriarch of the family or tribe dispensed justice in the case (Gen. xxvi. 11, 29; xxxviii. 24). The mode was usually by stoning. Cutting off the head with the sword is not sanctioned in the Mosaic law, except that it might be a retaliation *in kind*, as in the case of Agag (1 Sam. xv. 33). Precipitation from a rock, or high place, was borrowed from other nations, as also cutting asunder (Dan. ii. 5; iii. 29; Luke xii. 46); and whipping or beating to death (Heb. x. 35). Casting into a den of lions is still practiced in Morocco. Moses permitted the hanging of the body on a tree after death, but it must be buried the same night (Deut. xxi. 22). Hanging alive was a Canaanite mode (2 Sam. xxi. 9). Stones were heaped over the body (buried or unburied), as a mark of contempt (Josh. vii. 25, 26), and "to make heaps" of a city was a peculiar ignominy (Is. xxv. 2; Jer. ix. 11), as also to burn a dead body, which was only permitted in two cases (Lev. xx. 14; xxi. 9). Crucifixion was practiced in the last days of the nation. Scourging (whipping on the bare back) was limited to 40 stripes (which were in later limited, by custom, to 39, lest by accident the number 40 be exceeded, 2 Cor. xl. 24). The soles of the feet were beaten with rods, or a lash, when the victim was lying on his face, and assistants held his feet in position (Lev. xix. 20; Deut. xxii. 18; xxv. 2, 3). Servants might be whipped (Ex. xxi. 20). Offenses against the rules of the church were punished by whipping (Matt. x. 17; Acts xxvi. 11) in the synagogue. The law of *retaliation* was regulated by rules,

so as to prevent mere revenge (Ex. xxi. 23–25; Lev. xxiv. 19–22), and a system of compensation was adopted (Ex. xxi.).

A false accuser suffered what he proposed to inflict wrongfuly on another (Deut. xix. 19). Imprisonment was practiced for convenience rather than punishment (Lev. xxiv. 12). Debtors were shut up until they paid (Matt. xviii. 30); stocks were used (xiii. 27). See ANATHEMA. There is no direct reference to rewards or punishments in the future life in the Old Testament. See HADES.

PU'NITES, THE. Descendants of PUA, son of Issachar, (Num. xxvi. 23).

PU'NON (*darkness*). Identified with Pinon, the site of the copper-mines (Num. xxxiii. 42, 43), between Petra and Zoar. *Kalaat Phênan* is a ruined castle on a spur of Mt. Seir, and probably marks the ancient site.

PUR (*a lot*), (Esth. iii. 7). PURIM.

PURIFICA'TION (L. *making clean*). In all cases consisted by the use of waters—by ablution or sprinkling.

PU'RIM. The annual feast in memory of Esther. See HISTORY OF THE BOOKS.

PURSE. A BAG, in which the Hebrews carried their money when on a journey (Gen. xliii. 35); and merchants carried their weights (Deut. xxv. 13). The GIRDLE was used as a purse (Matt. x. 9).

PUT (1 Chr. i. 8). See PHUT.

PUTE'OLI. 8 ms. N. W. of Naples, on the shore; once called the Bay of Cumæ (see Virgil), and also Puteolanus. It was a famous watering-place, on account of its many warm springs. Ships landed cargoes of corn, and also passengers from the Levant, at this, the best harbor near Rome. The harbor was protected by a mole, the ruins of which are still to be seen. Scipio sailed from this port to Spain; Cicero had a villa in the vicinity, and Hadrian was buried near. Now called Puzzuoli.

PU'TIEL (*afflicted by God*). Daughter of Putiel, and mother of Phinehas (Ex. vi. 25).

PY'GARG. A clean animal (Deut. xiv. 5), of the antelope species.

PY'THON. A serpent slain by Apollo (Acts xvi.

PUTEOLI. PUZZUOLI

16). DIVINATION. In the Greek and Roman myth. ology, Python was a huge serpent (darkness, or ignorance), which was born in the mud of Deucalion's Deluge, and killed near Delphi by Apollo (the sun or intelligence).

Q

QUAILS (Heb. SELAV). The quail is a bird of passage, about the size of a turtle-dove, and resembles the American partridge. They are plentiful near the shores of the Dead Sea, the Jordan, and in the deserts of Arabia. Its flight is very low, especially when fatigued, and it keeps

COIN OF HADRIAN.

close to the ground. They migrate in vast flocks, and at night, when they settle, they are so exhausted they may be captured by the hand (Ex. xvi. 13).

QUAR'RY (Heb. PESEL). In Judg. iii. 19, only, in 52 other places graven, or carved images. See IDOL—GEOLOGY IN PALESTINE.

QUAR'TUS (*four, fourth*). A disciple of Corinth (Rom. xvi. 23). Tradition says he became bishop of Berytus.

QUATER'NION (*four*). A guard of four soldiers, two were attached to the prisoner, and two kept watch outside the cell (Acts xii. 4).

QUEEN (Heb. MALCAH, *wife*), (Esth. i. 9). SHEGAL, *consort* (Neh. ii. 6), GEBIRAH, *powerful* (1 K. xv. 13). Queen is applied to the woman who exercises the highest authority; and this in the East, is not the wife but the mother of the master. The case of Esther is an exception.

QUEEN OF HEAV'EN (MELECHETH HASHSHAMA-YIM). See MOON and HERA.

QUICK. 1. (Heb. HAY or CHAY, *alive, living*) (Num. xvi. 30).—2. (Heb. MIHYAH or MICHYAH, *the quick*), (Lev. xiii. 10).—3. (Heb. HARIHO or HARICHO, *to breathe*), (Is. xi. 3). Gr. *zon*, "the quick and the dead" (Acts x. 42).

QUICK'EN, TO (Heb. HIYAH or CHIYAH, *to live*), to give spiritual or eternal LIFE (John vi. 63).

QUICK'SANDS (Gr. *surtis;* Lat. *syrtis*), (Acts xxvii. 17). The sand from the great desert of Sahara is carried by the wind into the sea, along the shore, where the sluggish currents in the Syrtis Minor and Syrtis Major (two great bays on the coast of Africa) allow it to settle and form quicksand—that is sand and water in such a state as to move with a current or be tossed into waves by a storm of wind—where a vessel is in great danger. This same sand, when carried by currents to the shore of Palestine, fills up the harbors there, and creeps up inland, destroying every green thing for miles, as at Gaza, Ascalon, Acre, Tyre, etc.

QUIN'TUS MEM'MIUS (Latin), (2 Macc. xi. 34). See MEM'MIUS, QUINTUS.

QUIV'ER. 1. Heb. TELI, *to hang* (Gen. xxvii. 3).—2. Heb. ASHPAH (Job xxxix. 23). A case or sheath for holding arrows. See ARMS.

R

RA'AMAH (*trembling*). Fourth son of Cush (Gen. x. 7). Settled on the Persian Gulf (probably where we find Sheba, on the island Bahreyn), and renowned in Ezekiel's time as trading with

Tyre (Ez. xxvii. 22) in spices, precious stones and gold.

RAAMI'AH. A chief who returned from captivity (Neh. vii. 7).

RAAM'SES. RAMESES (Ex. i. 10).

RAB'BAH (*greatness*). Several places of this name. 1. (Deut. iii. 11). A very strong place east of Jordan; almost the only city of the Ammonites. This may have been the city of the Zuzims, in Ham (Gen. xiv. 5). The sarcophagus of the giant Og was here (Deut. iii. 11). The extensive ruins of Rabbah, now called *Amman*, are found on both sides of a perennial stream, the banks and bed also being paved through the city, about 19 miles southeast of Es Salt, and 22 miles from the Jordan, in a long valley, a branch of the Wady Zerka. The theatre is very large and well preserved. Roman and Christian buildings are also found. Some of the columns are five feet in diameter. Ezekiel's prophesy is literally fulfilled, and the place has become a stable for camels and a couching place for flocks (xxv. 5). David took the city by his general, Joab, when Uriah the Hittite was killed (2 Sam. xi.). It was named Philadelphia by Ptolemy Philadelphus, B. C. 250. Coins of this city are extant, bearing the figure of Astarte. The Christian Church is still in excellent preservation.—2. The city of AR was also called Rabbath Moab.—3. A city of Judah (Josh. xv. 60). Lost.—4. In Josh. xi. 8, Zidon is called Zidon Rabbah, translated great Zidon.

RAB'BATH. Of the children of Ammon (Deut. iii. 11).

RAB'BI (*my master*). A title of respect which the Jews gave to their teachers and physicians, and especially to our Lord (Matt. xxiii. 7, 8). EDUCATION. SCRIBES.

RAB'BITH (*multitude*), (Josh. xix. 20). Issachar. Lost.

RABBO'NI (*great master*), (John xx. 16). RABBI.

RAB'MAG (*chief priest*). A title borne by the king, NERGAL-SHAREZER (Jer. xxxix. 3, 13).

RAB'SACES. RABSHAKEH (Ecclus. xlviii. 18).

RAB'SARIS. 1. An officer of the king of Assyria (2 K. xviii. 17).—2. A prince who was present at the capture of Jerusalem, B. C. 588 (Jer. xxxix. 3–13).

RAB'SHA-KEH (*chief cup-bearer*). An officer of the king of Assyria sent against Jerusalem (2 K. xviii., xix.).

RA'CA (Chal. *reyka, worthless*). A term of contempt used by the Jews in Christ's age (Matt. v. 22).

RACE. See GAMES.

RA'CHAB. RAHAB, the harlot (Matt. i. 5).

RA'CHAL (*traffic*), (1 Sam. xxx. 29). South, in Judah. "Haunted" by David. Lost.

RA'CHEL (*a ewe*). The youngest daughter of LABAN, wife of JACOB, mother of JOSEPH and BENJAMIN. The history of Rachel may be found in Gen. xxix., xxxiii., xxxv. See JACOB. The so-called tomb of Rachel is about half a mile from Bethlehem, near the Jerusalem road.

RAD'DAI (*treading down*). Brother of David, and son of Jesse (1 Chr. ii. 14).

RA'GAU (Judg. i. 5, 15). RAGES? Mts. of R. 2. REU, in the line of CHRIST, (2 K. iii. 35).

RA'GES (Tob. i. 14, v. 5; Jud. i. 5). In Media, 5 ms. S. E. of the modern Teheren. Mentioned in the ancient inscriptions of Darius. The Zendavesta records that "the earliest settlement of the Aryans" in Media was in this city, and district of the same name. It was near the celebrated Caspian Gates, which guarded the great highway between India, Bactria, etc., to Media. The ruins cover a space of 13,500 ft. long, by 10,500 ft. broad. The walls were of great thickness, and flanked by towers, and there are immense heaps of ruins. The modern city, Teheren, was built from the ancient ruins, which are now called Rhey.

RA'GUEL (*friend of God*). 1. A prince-priest of Midian, father of ZIPPORAH (Ex. ii. 18, 21).—2. A pious Jew, father of Sara (Tob. iii. 7, 17).

RA'HAB (*broad*). A woman of Jericho, who

name Ramah forms a part of several names, and means *hight.* 1. In Benjamin (Josh. xviii. 25). Five miles N. of Jerusalem, near Geba. The palm tree of Deborah (Judg. iv. 5) was near it, in a valley toward Bethel. It is now a poor village in the midst of columns, hewn stones, and other ruins of antiquity. Cirama (1 Esd. v. 20).—2. In Mt. Ephraim (1 Sam. i. 1). The home of El-kanah, Samuel's father; the birthplace of Samuel, his home and official residence, the station of his altar, and where he was buried (xv. 1). Supposed by some to be the same as the first, in Benj.—3.

ANCIENT PERGAMOS.

entertained the spies sent by JOSHUA, and was saved, with her family, when the city was destroyed (Josh. ii. 1–21). She became the wife of Salmon, a prince of Judah (Ruth iv. 21), and so a mother in the royal line of David and of Jesus.

RA'HAB (Ps. lxxxvii. 4). A poetical name for Egypt. The word in Hebrew means *fierceness, insolence, pride.*

RA'HAM (*womb*). Son of Shema (1 Chr. ii. 44).

RA'HEL (RACHEL), (Jer. xxxi. 15).

RAI'MENT. DRESS.

RAIN (Heb. MALKOSH, *violent rain*). The "early" and the "latter" rain of Palestine is mentioned in Deut. xi. 14. See CLIMATE.

RAIN'BOW (Heb. KESHETH), (Gen. ix. 13–16). The token of the COVENANT.

RAIS'ING FROM THE DEAD. RESURRECTION.

RAI'SIN. VINE.

RA'KEM. Son of Sheresh (1 Chr. vii. 16).

RAK'KATH (*shore*), (Josh. xix. 35). A fortified city in Naphtali, near Hammath and Chinnereth. There is a Kerak near the outlet of Jordan, from the sea of Galilee, which may mark the site.

RAK'KON (*thinness*), (Josh. xix. 46). Near Joppa. Me-jarkon? Lost.

RAM (*high*). 1. Son of Hezron (Ruth iv. 19).—2. First born of Jerahmeel (ii. 25, 27).—3. Son of Barachel (Job xxxii. 2).

RAM (Heb. AYIL). Male sheep (Ezr. vi. 9, 17).

RAM, BATTERING (CAR). See ARMS.

RA'MA (Matt. ii. 18). RAMAH (Jer. xxxi. 15). A city in Mt. Ephraim, or Benjamin. Matthew refers to the ancient massacre, and also at the same time to that of the innocents of Bethlehem. The

(Josh. xix. 29). Boundary of Asher, 1 mile N. E. of Ras el Ain, two and a half S. E. of Tyre. There is another *Rameh,* 10 miles S. E. of Tyre. 4. In Naphtali (ib. v. 39), one of the fortified cities, 7 miles S. E. of Safed on the way to Acre, on a lofty hill commanding one of the finest views in Palestine. 5. RAMOTH GILEAD (2 K. viii. 29; 2 Chr. xxii. 6).—6. Ramleh (Neh. xi. 33), near Joppa.

RA'MATH LEHI (Judg. xv. 17). Where Samson slew 1,000 men with a jawbone, and named the place *Wielding of the Jawbone.*

RA'MATH MIZ'PEH (*high place of the watch tower*). (Josh. xiii. 26). Boundary of Gad. Where Jacob and Laban set up a monument of stones. Lost. Dr. Eli Smith found many names of places on the east of Jordan, which, when more carefully examined and their sites explored, may result in settling many points of topography in that region now wholly uncertain. The Palestine Exploration has made several discoveries, and added much to our knowledge of this region, and are still at work.

RA'MATH OF THE SOUTH (Josh. xix. 8). In Simeon, in the extreme south. Baalath Beer? South Ramoth (1 Sam. xxx. 27), or Ramoth Negeb. Lost.

RAMATHA'IM ZOPHIM (*the double eminence*). (1 Sam. i. 1). Supposed to have been south of Jerusalem. The same as Ramah 2?

RAM'ATHEM. Error in 1 Macc. xi. 34, for RA-MATHAIM.

RAM'ATHITE, THE. Native of RAMAH. Shimei had charge of the royal vineyards of King David (1 Chr. xxvii. 27).

RAM'ESES, RAAM'SES (Gen. xlvii. 11). The

land of Goshen. A city in the same land, enlarged and fortified by the Jews (Ex. i. 11, xii. 37). There were (and now are) other places of this name in Egypt. Abu Kesheyd, a modern village, has an antique monolith, on which is carved a group, Rameses II, between Tum and Ra.

RAM'IAH (*Jah hath set*). Son of PAROSH (Ezr. x. 25).

RA'MOTH (*hights*), (1 Chr. vi. 73). ISSACHAR. JARMUTH? REMOTH?

RA'MOTH (*hights*). A layman (Ezr. x. 29).

RA'MOTH IN GILEAD (Deut. iv. 43; Josh. xx. 8). Now Es Salt. The site is on a high and picturesque hill, almost surrounded by deep ravines, and encompassed by mountains. Jebel Osha, the highest peak of Gilead, is only 2 ms. N. Vineyards and olive-groves beautify and enrich the place; the ruins are not extensive, being a square castle with towers, and a moat, on the hight, and a great number of tombs and grottos in the ravines.

RAM'S SKINS, DYED RED. Were presented, by the Israelites, as offerings for the making of the Tabernacle (Ex. xxv. 5). They served for the inner coverings.

RAN'GES FOR POTS (Lev. xi. 35). Rack or bed for holding the egg-shaped-bottom earthern jars (pots), which will not stand alone.

RAN'SOM. 1. (Heb. KOFER, *a cover*), (Ex. xxxi. 12).—2. (Heb. PIDYON), (Ex. xxi. 30). REDEMPTION. Gr. *lutron, a ransom* (Matt. xx. 28).

RA'PHA (*tall*). 1. A giant, and father of a family of tall men (2 Sam. xxi. 16, ff).—2. A descendant of Benjamin (1 Chr. viii. 2).—3. Son of Binea (1 Chr. viii. 37).

STORK.

RA'PHAEL (*the divine healer*). One of the 7 holy angels (Tob. xii. 15).

RAPH'AIM. Ancestor of Judith (Jud. viii. 1).

RA'PHON (1 Macc. i. 37). Raphana (?), one of the Decapolis. Er Rafe?

RA'PHU (*healed*). Father of Palti (Num. xiii. 9).

RAS'SUS, CHILDREN OF. A nation whose country was ravaged by Holofernes (Jud. ii. 23).

RATH'UMUS. The story-writer (1 Esd. ii. 16, 17, 25, 30).

RA'VEN (Heb. OREB). A bird similar to the crow, but larger. It feeds on dead bodies (Prov. xxx. 17). It drives away its young as soon as they can shift for themselves (Job xxxviii. 41). Elijah was fed by ravens (1 K. xvii. 6). The raven was sent from the Ark on the subsiding of the waters (Gen. viii. 7).

RA'ZIS (*destruction*). An elder of Jerusalem, who killed himself rather than fall into the hands of the wicked (2 Macc. xiv. 37–46). This is the only instance of a suicide in the whole range of Jewish history, unless the cases of Samson and Saul are so considered.

RA'ZOR. The razor was very little used by the Jews (Num. vi. 9, 18).

REAI'A. Son of Micah (1 Chr. v. 5).

REAI'AH (*whom Jah cares for*). 1. Son of Shobal (1 Chr. iv. 2).—2. Ancestor of Nethinim, who returned from captivity (Ezr. ii. 47).

RE'BA (*fourth part*). A king of the Midianites (Num. xxxi. 8).

REBEK'AH. REBECCA (*ensnarer*). Daughter of BETHUEL (Gen. xxii. 23). Sister of LABAN, married to ISAAC. There is a beautiful and touching incident of "Rebekah at the well." This bright little picture, with its conclusion, comprises all the circumstances of a perfect marriage. The sanction of parents, the favor of God, the domestic habits of the wife, her beauty, kindness, modest consent, and her successful hold on her husband's love (even in the same tent with her mother-in-law). The account in Genesis gives many allusions to manners and customs, purely Oriental and strictly peculiar to the Hebrews as distinct from the people around them. The drawing of water at the well by women, the very mode of carrying the pitcher *on her shoulder* instead of on the head, as other people do; her manner of giving drink from her pitcher *on her hand;* her respectful request, "Drink, my lord," and finally her watering the camels in the trough—all are true in every particular, and of Hebrews only. The ornaments she wore, the hospitality offered and given, the marriage contract, journey to Canaan, the manner in which she met and saluted her betrothed husband, all indicate the minute truth and accuracy of the Bible text. Rebekah was buried in Machpelah, where she is still honored with a tomb near her husband's.

RE'CHAB (*horseman*). 1. Ancestor of Jehonadab (2 K. x. 15, 23).—2. Captain of bands in the service of Ishbosheth (2 Sam. iv. 2).—3. Father of Malchiah (Neh. iii. 14).

RE'CHABITES (*descendants of* RECHAB). Ancestor of JEHONADAB (1 Chr. ii. 55). See JEHONADAB.

RE'CHAH (*side*). The founder of Ir-nahash (1 Chr. iv. 12).

RECORD'ER (Heb. MAZCIR). An officer of high rank of the privy council (2 Sam. viii. 16).

REDEEM'ER (Heb. GOEL). One who redeems a field by paying back what it had been sold for; this right belonged to the nearest kinsman (Lev. xxv. 25, 26); often applied to God as the redeemer of men, and especially Israel (Job xix. 25).

REDEEMER, JESUS, THE (Gal. iii. 13, iv. 5).

REDEMP'TION. 1. Heb. GEULLAH, the *redemption* or repurchase of a field (Lev. xxv. 24, 51, 52).—2. Heb. PEDUTH, PIDYOM, *ransom* (Num. iii. 49; Ps. xlix. 8). 3. Gr. *apolutrosis, letting off for a ransom* (2 K. xxi. 28). 4. Gr. *lutrosis, deliverance* (2 K. ii. 38).

RED HEIF'ER. PURIFICATION.

RED SEA (Num. xxi. 14). Called *the sea*, in Ex. xiv. 2, 9, 16, etc. The Gulf of Suez in the Exodus, and also the Gulf of Akabah later in the wandering. Called the *sea of suph* in Ex. x. 19, that is, the sea of *reeds*, or *flags*. A seaweed resembling *wool* (in whiteness) is thrown up in great quantities on the shores of the Red Sea (Diodorus iii. 19). The same word was used to name the weeds, or reeds, in which Moses was laid when an infant (Ex. ii. 3). It is thought the *papyrus* was meant. The Abyssinians now use papyrus boats. It is supposed that "the tongue of the Egyptian

Sea," the head of the Suez Gulf, has dried up, as predicted by Isaiah (xi. 15, xix. 5), for a distance of 50 ms. The ancient head would have been at *Aboo Kesheyd*, which has been identified with the ancient Hero. Necho's canal, which was wide enough for two triremes to row abreast (Herodotus ii. 158), once led from the gulf to the Nile, but it is now filled with sand. The Suez canal, just opened, leads to the Mediterranean. The sea is nearly 1400 ms. long by 100 to 200 ms. in its widest part. The deepest water is 6,324 feet, in lat. 22° 30'. It is filled with coral and other rocks and rocky islands for 40 or 50 ms. on each side, leaving a narrow and dangerous channel, which is narrowest opposite El Medeenah. The Suez Gulf is 130 ms. long and 18 wide. The Akabah Gulf is 100 ms. long by 15 wide. This is a continuation of the *Arabah*, and is bordered on both sides by steep and high mountains—Sinai on the west, and the spurs of Mt. Seir, Edom, on the east, from 3,000 to 6,000 feet high, the highest being to the south. The island of Graia, fortified by the crusaders, lies near the west shore, not far from the north end. The ruins of walls, castles, a church, etc., mostly of the middle ages, cover the whole rocky area. The straits at the south end of the sea are called Bab el Mandeb (*Gate of Tears*), from the many shipwrecks which have happened after passing them, either way.

REED. See PAPYRUS.

REELAI'AH (*Jah makes tremble*). One who went with Zerubbabel (Ezr. ii. 2).

REE'LIUS (1 Esd. v. 8). BIGVAI.

REESAI'AS. RAAMIAH (1 Esd. v. 8).

REFI'NER (Heb. ZOREF. MEZAREF). Refining being the separation of the pure metal from the dross, by means of fire, suggested an apt subject for illustration, as in Is. i. 25; Zech. xiii. 9; Mal. iii. 2, 3. A full, figurative allusion to the refiner's process is in Jer. vi. 29, 30. See METALS.

REFUGE, CITIES OF. 6 out of the 48 Levitical cities were set apart as a refuge for any one who should accidentally kill another, to stay there until the death of the high-priest (Num. xxxv. 6, 13, 15; Josh. xx. 2, 7, 9). There were 3 on each side of Jordan. On the E. side were Bezer, Ramoth in Gilead, and Golan, and on the W. side were Kedesh in Galilee, Shechem, and Hebron. The right of asylum of many cities, in ancient classic nations, and of sanctuary in Christian countries (the privilege of many churches in the middle ages especially), are parallel, and show the wisdom of the law-makers, in providing a means of abating the evils of the system of blood-revenge, which are peculiarly Oriental, and very wasteful of human life. Moses abolished the custom of allowing money to be paid as a compensation for a human life, as was the case in Athens and many eastern countries, and is now among the Arabs. The cities are each described under their respective names.

RE'GEM (*friend*). Son of Jahdai (1 Chr. ii. 47).

RE'GEM ME'LECH (*friend of the king*). He, with Sherezer, was sent on behalf of some of the Captivity, to make inquiries at the Temple concerning fasting (Zech. vii. 2).

REGENERA'TION (*born again*). Birth into new spiritual life (John iii. 3), and thus becoming a new creature (2 Cor. v. 17), and being made partakers of the Divine Nature (2 Pet. i. 4) by means of the Holy Spirit (John iii. 4). "The washing of regeneration" alludes to the purifying by the Holy Spirit (Titus iii. 5). The especial work of the Holy Spirit in restoring man to the original image of God.

RE'GION. 1. (Heb. HEBEL, *a rope*), (Deut. iii. 4, 13). Once translated "the country of Argob" (iii. 14). Coast, in Zeph. ii. 5-7.—2. NOPHAH (*hight*). The region of Dor (1 K. iv. 11).—4.

Gr. *klima*, climate (2 Cor. xi. 10).—4. Gr. *chora*, country (Matt. ii. 12).

RE'GION ROUND ABOUT, THE (Gr. *he perichoros*). The populous and flourishing country which contained JERICHO, in the Jordan valley, enclosed by the hills of *Quarantana* (Mark vi. 55).

REHABI'AH (*whom Jah enlarges*). Son of Eliezer (1 Chr. xxii. 17).

RE'HOB (*room*). 1. Father of Hadadezer, king of Zobah (2 Sam. viii. 3, 12).—2. A Levite, who sealed the covenant (Neh. x. 11).

RE'HOB. Several of this name. 1. The northern limit of the exploration of the spies (Num. xiii. 21). Toward Hamath. Dan was "by Beth-rehob." *Ruhaibeh*, 25 miles N. E. of Damascus, has been offered as the locality. Dr. Robinson favored *Hunin*, a village and castle west of Paneas.—2. In Asher (Josh. xix. 28), near Zidon.—3. Another in Asher, not identified.

REHOBO'AM (*he enlarges the people*). The son of Solomon, by the Ammonite princess Naamah (1 K. xiv. 21, 31), whom he succeeded. By neglecting his father's counselors he hastened the division of the tribes which had been restrained by the government of Solomon. Instead of forcing submission by military means, Rehoboam was advised by Shemaiah to fortify the cities against the Egyptians (2 Chr. xi. 6-10). But resistance was useless against Shishak, king of Egypt, who, after having forced the protecting line of fortresses, marched upon Jerusalem, and Rehoboam had to purchase his release by giving up the treasure accumulated by Solomon, including the golden shields. After this calamity he reigned peacefully. He was on the throne seventeen years.

REHO'BOTH (*room*). A well dug by Isaac (Gen. xxvi. 22). The wells Sitnah, Esek and Rehoboth were west or southwest of Beersheba. *Wady Ruhaibeh* is 20 miles S. W. of Beersheba, and is claimed as the place by Dr. Bonar (*Desert of Sinai*, 316).—2. Rehoboth by the River (Gen. xxxvi. 37). On the Euphrates, just below the Khabur, stands *Rahabah*, in the midst of extensive ancient ruins. —3. THE CITY. One of the four built by Nimrod. As the name means in our tongue, "to be wide," or "spacious," or "streets," the passage in Gen. x. 11, 12, may describe one city, Nineveh, which was spacious, and had several quarters, as Resen, Calah, altogether forming "a great city."

RE'HUM (*compassionate*). 1. One who returned from captivity (Ezr. ii. 2). NEHUM.—2. One of those who wrote to Artaxerxes to stop the rebuilding of the Temple (iv. 8, 9, 17, 23).—3. A Levite, who rebuilt the wall (Neh. iii. 17).—4. A chief who sealed the covenant (x. 25).—5. Head of a priestly house (xii. 3).

RE'I (*friendly*). A person mentioned as loyal to David, during the rebellion (1 K. i. 8).

REINS (Gr. *renes, kidneys*). 1. (Heb. KELAYOTH.) In ancient physiology the kidneys are believed to be the seat of desire, and are often coupled with the heart (Ps. vii. 9).—2. (Heb. HALATSAYIM, *loins*, Gen. xxxv. 11; Gr. *nephros*, Rev. ii. 23).

RE'KEM (Heb. *flower-garden*). 1. One of the kings of Midian (Num. xxxi. 8).—2. Son of Hebron (1 Chr. ii. 43, 44).

RE'KEM (Josh. xviii. 27). Ain Karem, W. of Jerusalem?

REMALI'AH (*Jah decks*). Father of PEKAH, king of Israel (2 K. xv. 25, 37).

REM'ETH (*hight*), (Josh. xix. 21). Wezar (Ar. for *hight*), a ruin on a hill 5 ms. N. of Jenin, at the foot of Mt. Gilboa.

REM'MON (Josh. xix. 7). In Simeon. RIMMON.

REM'MON METH'OAR (Rimmon, *which reaches*), (Josh. xix. 13.) Zebulon, 6 miles N. of Nazareth.

REM'PHAN. An error for CHI'UN (in Acts vii. 43, from Amos v. 26). The Hebrew name of the Greek god Saturn. See IDOLATRY. Saturn was a king of Latium, and was, after his death, deified, and worshiped as the god of agriculture. (Gr. *sotor, planter*).

REND'ING, RENT. DRESS; MOURNING.

REPENT'ANCE (Heb. NOHAM). (Hos. xiii. 14). (Gr. *metanoia, change of purpose*), (Heb. xii. 17).— (Gr. *ametameletos, unchangeable*), (Rom. xi. 29). A change of mind, with sorrow for something done, and a wish that it was undone (Matt. xxvii. 3). Esau found no repentance in his father (Heb. xii. 17). God is sometimes said to repent of something he had done (Gen. vi. 6). The true Gospel repentance is sorrow for sin (Matt. iv. 17).

RE'PHAEL (*God heals*). Son of Shemaiah (1 Chr. xxvi. 7).

RE'PHAH (*riches*). Son of Ephraim (1 Chr. vii. 25).

REPHAI'AH (*whom Jah healed*). 1. His sons are among the descendants of Zerubbabel (1 Chr. iii. 21).—2. A Simeonite chief (iv. 42).—3. Son of Tola (vii. 4).—4. Son of Binea (ix. 43).—5. Son of Hur and ruler of the half-part of Jerusalem (Neh. iii. 9).

REPH'AIM (Heb. REPHAIM). See GIANTS.

REPH'AIM, THE VALLEY OF (*valley of the stretched=giants*). On the south of a hill which borders the valley of Hinnom, on the west. David made it famous on two (or three) distinct occasions (2 Sam. v. 18, 22; Is. xvii. 5). The very interesting incident related in 2 Sam. xxiii. 13–17, took place on one of these invasions of the Philistines. This valley (or plain) is flat, fertile, is shut in on all sides by rocky hill-tops and ridges, and ends to the west of the valley of Roses (*Wady el Werd*).

REPHI'DIM (*rests, or stays*), (Ex. xvii. 1, 8, xix. 2). Station of the Exodus, between Egypt and Sinai. The people murmured for water, and Moses smote the rock in Horeb "before the people;" and therefore if Horeb and Sinai be located at Jebel Sufsafeh and its vicinity, then Rephidim would be in Wady es Sheikh. WILDERNESS.

REP'ROBATE (Heb. NIMAS, *worthless, rejected*), (Jer. vi. 30). Hardened in sin and unbelief (Rom. i. 28).

RE'SEN. The ruins called *Nimrud*, at Mosul, on the Euphrates, are understood to represent the ancient Calah, and those on the opposite side of the river are the remains of Nineveh; and there are remains between the two, at *Selamiyeh*, which answer to the locality of Resen.

RESH (Heb. REYSH). The twentieth letter of the Hebrew alphabet (Ps. cxix). WRITING.

RE'SHEPH (*flame*). Son of Ephraim (1 Chr. vii. 25).

RESURREC'TION, Gr. *anastasis*, uprising; *exanastasis*, a rising up out of (Phil. iii. 11); *egersis*, waking up; "resurrection" in John xi. 25; and several other words, or derivatives, are rendered resurrection.

The idea is the rising again of the body from death, or its return to life in two senses; 1, of those who have been brought back to this life after death, as Lazarus, the widow's son of Nain, etc., and 2, of all true Christains, who will be raised in the future world.

This is one of the vital points in the Christian's creed. If there is no resurrection then there is no hope beyond this life. The Old Testament history prefigures the doctrine, in its records of several instances of restoration to life after death, as by Elijah (1 K. xvii. 21–24), and Elisha (2 K. iv. 20, 32–36). The vision of the dry bones may be accepted as touching on the general belief, though not a case of practical proof; the translations of Enoch and Elijah cannot argue resurrection, because death did not take place, and they are simply evidence of a continued existence after this life (Gen. v. 22; 2 K. ii.).

The Hebrews believed in an underworld, where the spirits or souls of all who had lived were still living and recognizable, which they called Hell, and did not restrict it to the modern meaning of that word, which is that it is the place of the wicked only. To the Hebrews it was the place where all souls went—or the condition that all souls were in after death and separation from the body (Ps. xvi. 10; fulfilled in Acts ii. 25–31, xiii. 35). In Isaiah (xxvi. 19), there is a direct statement of the belief as a prophesy of the restoration of the Jewish nation; as though he founded his argument on a well known and undoubted belief. Daniel (xii. 1–3), gives exactly the Christian idea of the final resurrection.

"Life and immortality" are "brought to light by the gospel." The New Testament idea is that it is (1) to be universal (John v. 28, 29; 2 Cor. v. 10; Rev. xx. 13), (2) and that souls will be recognizable; but whether the identity will be from physical or spiritual sources we are not instructed, unless Paul means that it will be spiritual in his argument to the Romans (vi. viii.) and to the Corinthians (1 Cor. xv. 44), where we may possibly see evidence of a belief in the rising of the identical shapes of our bodies of flesh, but changed into a spiritual substance. (3). The belief in a future life for the saints only and a second death for the impenitent is held by many, who find in the life and works of Jesus, and in Paul and John's teaching much to confirm this view. (4). It is the work of Jesus that has secured the resurrection and life of all who believe on Him, and His voice will call them from the tomb, who prayed, "Father, I will that they also, whom thou hast given me, may be with me where I am." (5). The time of the resurrection is not determined. There may be two, or rather two objects or ends to be answered: one being the actual life, which is believed to have been already given to several, whose names are mentioned in the Bible; and the other the great day of judgment.

The judgment comes after death, which is the end of the world for each soul, without regard to the whole human race. It does not follow that there will be no judgment until the last soul is born, lives, and dies, for it may be understood as an Orientalism, meaning the end of this life for each soul, what will happen to each soul and all souls, without exception (small and great), who must stand before the great white throne (white—pure—the only perfectly just tribunal).

Jesus "the author and finisher of our faith" was "the first fruits of them that slept," and His was the same body that was crucified, as He convinced Thomas by actual touch, but He did not instruct His disciples what to expect, so it remains a matter of faith for all His followers to expect to be like Him (1 John iii. 2).

RE'U (*friend*). Son of Peleg (Gen. xi. 18, 21).

REU'BEN (REU, *behold*, and BEN, *a son*). Eldest son of Jacob (Gen. xxix. 32), son of Leah. The tribe of Reuben was located, at their own request, on the E. side of Jordan, and against the wishes of Moses (Num. xxxii. 19).

REU'BENITE. Descendants of REUBEN (Num. xxvi. 7).

REU'EL (*friend of God*). 1. Son of Esau (Gen. xxxvi. 4, 10, 13, 17).—2. One of the names given to Moses' father-in-law (Ex. ii. 18).—3. Father of Eliasaph (Num. ii. 14).—4. Ancestor of Elah (1 Chr. ix. 8).

REU'MAH (*raised*). Second wife of Nahor (Gen. xxii. 24).

REVELA'TION. Gr. *apokalupsis, unveiling,* or *manifestation,* from God, by dream or vision (2 Cor. xii. 1, 7).

REVELA'TION OF ST. JOHN. See HISTORY OF THE BOOKS.

REVEN'GER OF BLOOD. AVENGER OF BLOOD is a name given to a man who had the right (and whose duty it was), of taking revenge on him who had killed one of his relations.

RE'ZEPH (2 K. xix. 12; Is. xxxvii. 12). A day's march W. of the Euphrates, now called Rasapha. Another is mentioned as near Bagdad.

REZI'A (*delight*). Son of Ulla, a chief (1 Chr. vii. 39).

RE'ZIN (*friend*). 1. King of DAMASCUS who united with Pekah, king of Israel, to invade Judah, B. C. 742 (2 K. xv. 37).—2. Ancestor of Nethinim who returned from captivity (Neh. vii. 50).

RE'ZON (*prince*). Son of Eliadah, and the founder of a small kingdom in Syria-Damascus, and a great annoyance to Solomon (1 K. xi. 23, 25).

RHE'GIUM. In Italy, on the straits of Messina, opposite the city of Messina, in Sicily (Acts xxviii. 13).

RHE'SA. Father of Joanna in the genealogy of Jesus (Luke iii. 27). Supposed, by some, to be an error, the word meaning "prince," the title of Zerubbabel.

RHINOÇ'EROS (Heb. REEM, *wild ox*). The word is always rendered unicorn. See UNICORN.

RHO'DA (*rose*). A maid, in the house of Mary, who announced Peter's arrival (Acts xii. 13).

RHO'DES. An island 120 miles long, by 36 wide, opposite the S. W. extremity of Asia Minor, celebrated from remote antiquity for commerce, navigation, literature and the arts; and during the middle ages as the residence of the Knights of St. John. Its maritime code was adopted by the Romans. The soil is fertile and the climate delightful. There are two cities: Rhodes (built 482 B. C.), which was celebrated by its having erected over the entrance to its harbor a brass statue of Apollo, 105 feet high (built by Chares of Lindus, B. C. 290, and thrown down by an earthquake, 224 B. C.); and Lindus and a number of villages. Population 30,000. Paul visited the island on his way to Jerusalem (Acts xxi. 1).

RHOD'OCUS. A Jew who betrayed his countrymen (2 Macc. xiii. 21).

RHO'DUS. RHODES (1 Macc. xv. 33).

RI'BAI. Father of Ittai (2 Sam. xxiii. 29).

RIB'AND. RIBBON (Heb. PATHIL, Num. xv. 38). See HEM, THREAD.

RIB'LAH (*fertility*). In the land of Hamath (2 K. xxiii. 33), on the east side of Ain (Num. xxxiv. 11). Both places are located in the Orontes valley, 35 miles N. E. of Baalbek; Riblah lying on the banks of a mountain stream, in the midst of a vast and fertile plain. Mentioned as Diblath in Ez. vi. 14. At Riblah, Pharaoh Necho deposed king Jehoahaz (2 Chr. xxxvi.), and Nebuchadnezzar put out the eyes of Zedekiah after killing his sons (2 K. xxv. 7).

RID'DLE (Heb. HIDAH, *intricate*). Artifice (Dan. viii. 23); a proverb (Prov. i. 6); an oracle (Num. xii. 8); a PARABLE (Ez. xvii. 2); in general, any wise or intricate sentence (Hab. ii. 6). The queen of Sheba came to ask riddles of SOLOMON (1 K. x. 1). The ancients were fond of riddles. They were generally proposed in verse. The only mention of a riddle in the N. T. is in Rev. xiii. 16–18.

RIGHT'EOUS (Heb. ZADDIK; sometimes YASHAR; Gr. *dikaios*). One who pursues the *right* course (Ex. ix. 27).

RIGHT'EOUSNESS (Heb. ZEDEK, ZEDAKAH; Gr. *dikaioma*). Holiness, justice, rectitude; an attribute of God only (Job xxxvi. 3; Is. li. 5–8; John

xvii. 25). The righteousness of Christ includes His spotless holiness and His perfect obedience to the law while on earth, and His suffering its penalty in our stead. "For the kingdom of God is not meat and drink; but righteousness, and peace, and joy in the Holy Ghost" (Rom. xiv. 17).

RIGHT HAND. Signifies power; the most efficient member of the body (Matt. v. 30). Figuratively the power of the Almighty (Ex. xv. 6; Ps. xxi. 8); the place of honor (Ps. xlv. 9; Matt. xxv. 34), of special benediction, paternal love, etc. It was raised in act of taking an oath, and of prayer (Gen. xiv. 22). The right hand means south in 1 Sam. xxiii. 19, as the left means north, as when facing east.

RIM'MON (*pomegranate*). 1. Zebulon (1 Chr. vi. 77), belonging to the Levites, Merari family.—2. Judah, in the extreme south, near Ziklag (Josh. xv. 32); afterward given to Simeon (xix. 7). Occupied after the return from Babylon (Neh. xi. 29). EN-RIMMON. UM-ER-RUMMANIM (*mother of pomegranates*), is a village and ruin 15 miles S. E. of Hebron. Between two hills (both covered with ruins), a mile south of the village, is a large fountain, the chief watering-place in the region.—3. THE ROCK RIMMON. A high rock or hill, 10 miles north of Jerusalem and 4 east of Bethel, on which is a modern village. The remnant of the tribe of Benjamin held this rock for four months against their enemies (Judg. xx. 47).—4. RIMMON-PAREZ (*breach*). The second station after Hazeroth, in the Exodus (Num. xxx. 19). Lost.

RIM'MON. Father of Rechab (2 Sam. iv. 2, 5, 9).

RIM'MON. Correctly RAMAM (*exalted*). The name of some idol under which the sun was represented (2 K. v. 18) in Damascus.

RINGS.

RING (TABBA'ATH, GALIL; Gr. *daktulios*). The ring, besides being an ornament, was used as a signet, or sign-manual, when its setting was engraved with some device, with or without the name of the owner, which was recognized as his personal emblem (Neh. x.). Such rings or seals were used by all persons in authority, and when stamped upon the parchment, or on a piece of wax or clay attached, stood instead of the name of the person agreeing to the compact. See SEAL. Several ancient rings have been preserved to the present, among which are the rings of Thothmes III, and of Pharaoh (Suphis): [cuts on pps. 84, 12.] The Scriptures mention several instances of their use in important business matters, as in Esth. iii. 10, where Ahasuerus gives Haman his ring as a badge of supreme authority over the army, and the treasury, for a certain purpose, and in 1 Macc. vi. 15, where Antiochus gave Philip his ring as a mark of his appointment as guardian to his son. It was worn on the right hand,

RIN'NAH (*shout*). Son of Shimon (1 Chr. iv. 20).

RI'PHATH (Gen. x. 3; 1 Chr. i. 6). A northern people, descended from Gomer. We have several names derived from this source, as, the Riphæan mts.; the river Rhebas in Bithynia; the Rhibii, a people E. of the Caspian; and the Riphæans, the original Paphlagonians.

RIS'SAH (*worm*). Station in the wilderness (Num. xxxiii. 21). Lost.

RITH'MAH (*broom*, the shrub, *retam*). Desert station (ib. ver. 18). Lost.

RIVER. 7 distinct Hebrew words are translated by "river" in our version. By river we mean a large stream of water, flowing summer and winter, and we have names for smaller streams, as, stream, creek, brook, torrent, rill, rivulet, · etc. There are such differences in the original Hebrew, which were overlooked in the translation, and it may be interesting to notice them: 1. AUBAL, YUBAL (Jer. xviii. 8; Dan. viii. 2, 3, 6), *tumult, fulness.* The word used for the deluge is from the same root, and is HAMMABUL (only in Genesis, and Ps. xxix. 10).—NAHAR (Gen. ii. 10; Ex. vii. 19, etc.), *to flow.* This means a river, as we use the word. With the definite article HÁN-NAHAR, (*the* river), the Euphrates is meant (Gen. xxxi. 21; 2 Sam. x. 16, etc.).—Incorrectly rendered "flood" in Josh. xxiv. 2, where the Euphrates is meant; and in Job xiv. 11, Ps. lxvi. 6, where the Red Sea, or the Jordan, is referred to. The Arab name of river is *nahr;* now used for all perennial streams.—3. *Nakhal,* (*to receive*), as, a water-course, therefore, a torrent-bed, common in Palestine, having water only in winter. This is translated "valley" in Gen. xxvi. 17, Num. xxi. 12; "brook," Deut. ii. 13, 2 K. xxiii. 6–12; "river" in Amos vi. 14; "streams" in Ps. lxxviii. 20; and, in all these cases *valley* is the true meaning. The modern term is WADY for such valleys as are dry in summer.—4. PELEG (*to flow*, or *division*): "River," in Ps. i. 3, Is. xxx. 25, Job xx. 17; "stream," in Ps. xlvi. 4; "divisions," in Judg. v. 15, 16. The word means, artificial streams for irrigation.—5. APHIK (*force or hold*, as, the bank of a river): "River" in Cant. v. 12, Ez. vi. 3, xxxi. 12, and "streams" in Ps. cxxvi. 4; in which last passage it refers to the dry water-courses of the Negeb, or South. In 2 Sam. xxii. 16 it is translated "channels," and also in Ps. xviii. 15.—6. YEOR, (the *Nile*), a word adopted into the Hebrew from the Egyptian language. This is the word used for the Nile in Genesis and Exodus, and is mistranslated "flood" in Amos viii. 8, ix. 5. RIVER OF EGYPT. Two terms were used in the original—differing, as will be seen—both of which are translated "river of Egypt." 1. NAHAR MITZRAIM (Gen. xv. 18), meaning *The Nile* (probably before the name YEOR was known to the Hebrews). —2. NAKHAL MITZRAIM (Num. xxxiv. 5), meaning the dry water-course of El Arish. The Nile is also called SHIHOR (Josh. xiii. 3, etc.). The importance of these corrections is felt, when it is seen that we are able to prove by them that the original Hebrew text was true in every one of its references to the peculiar features of the countries referred to, even in minute particulars.

RIZ'PAH (*a coal*). Second wife of King Saul, memorable for the touching example of maternal affection which she displayed in watching the dead bodies of her sons (2 Sam. iii. 7, xxi. 8, 10, 11).

ROADS. There were no roads, in ancient times, in the East, only narrow tracks, which we would call bridle-paths (1 Sam. xxvii. 10). See HIGHWAY.

ROB'BERY. Has ever been one of the principal employments of the Bedawin tribes of the East (Gen. xvi. 12). For an instance of a truly Bedawin character, see 1 Sam. xxvi. 6–12.

RO'BOAM. REHOBOAM (Ecclus. xlvii. 23).

ROCK (SELA, TSUR). Rocks were used for fortresses and strongholds. The word denotes a place of security, and, figuratively, a refuge, defense or protection (Ps. xviii. 2, 31, 46).

ROD (HOTER, MATTEH, MAKKEL, SHEBET; Gr. *rhabdos*). A branch or stick, such as may be used for a whip (Prov. xiv. 3); also a shepherd's staff (Ex. iv. 2 ff). The badge of authority of a ruler or king (Ps. cx. 2). An instrument for punishment or correction (Prov. x. 13).

ROD'ANIM (1 Chr. i. 7). DODANIM.

ROE. Roebuck (Heb. ZEBI, masc., ZEBIYAH, fem.). The Oriental antelope or gazelle. It is about two and a half feet in hight, of a reddish brown color, with white feet and belly, has long naked ears, and a short erect tail. The horns are black, about twelve inches long and bent like a lyre. It inhabits Barbary, Egypt, Arabia and Syria, and is about half the size of the fallow-deer. It goes in large flocks; is easily tamed, though very timid; its flesh is considered excellent food (Deut. xii. 15, 22).

RO'GEL (*fuller*), (1 K. i. 9). EN-ROGEL.

RO'GELIM (*feet*). The residence of Barzillai, the Gileadite (2 Sam. xvii. 27). East of Jordan. Lost.

ROH'GAH (*outcry*). A chief of the sons of Shamer (1 Chr. vii. 34).

ROI'MUS. REHUM 1 (1 Esd. v. 8).

ROLL (Heb. and Chal. MEGILLAH.) See V........-ING.

ROMAM'TIE'ZER (*I have exalted his help*). Son of Heman, and chief in the twenty-fourth division (1 Chr. xxv. 4, 31).

RO'MAN. An inhabitant of Rome (John xi. 48); also one who had the rights of a citizen of Rome (Acts xvi. 37, 38).

ROMAN EMPIRE. Rome is first mentioned in 1 Macc. i. 10, in connection with Antiochus Epiphanes, who had been a hostage there, and was a "wicked root." Pompey made Syria a Roman province, B. C. 65, and took Jerusalem two years later (Ant. xiv. 2, 3, 4; Wars i. 6, 7). Herod was made the first king under Roman rule by Antony, B. C. 40, and was confirmed by Augustus, B. C. 30. The tribute paid to Cæsar (Julius) was a fourth part of their agricultural produce in addition to the tithes (Ant. xiv. 10, 6). After A. D. 6, Judæa was made a province of Syria at the request of the Jews, who were worn out by the cruelties of the Herods, with the capital at Cæsarea; Coponius was the first procurator, and Pilate was the fifth. Jesus was crucified during Pilate's reign (A. D. 25 to 35). The many complaints of the tyranny of Pilate caused him to be ordered to Rome for trial by Vitellius, president of Syria; but the Emperor Tiberius died before his arrival. (Ant. xviii. 4, 1–3). Justin Martyr, Tertullian, Eusebius and others say that Pilate made an official report to Tiberius of the crucifixion of Jesus; which account is also mentioned by Chrysostom. Eusebius says that Pilate killed himself, being "wearied with misfortunes,"—perhaps on account of remorse for his conduct in Jerusalem.

The Roman empire was but a narrow strip along the shores of the Mediterranean until Pompey added Asia Minor, Syria, and (Antony) Egypt; Cæsar conquered Gaul; the generals of Augustus, Spain, and from the Alps to the Danube. Its population in the time of Christ was 85 millions. Gibbon says it was 120 millions in the time of Claudius, who appointed Felix procurator (A. D. 52–60). Festus succeeded him, and heard Paul (Acts xxv., etc.). Vespasian was sent into Judæa in A. D. 67, with a large army. Nero died in 68, and Vespasian was elected emperor by the legions in Judæa. Titus was sent to conduct the war in Judæa by his father A. D. 70, when he took Jerusalem after a siege of four months. Julius Cæsar allowed the Jews to live after their own customs, even in Rome; which privileges were confirmed by Augustus, who also respected their Sabbath (Ant. xiv. 10, 11, 19), and exempted them from military service; but Tiberius and Claudius banished them from Rome, as Suetonius says, because they were continually raising disturbances under the impulse of Chrestus—*i. e.*, Christ.

All official acts were strictly carried out in the Latin language, even to the remotest limits of the empire, but the people were generally left to use their native tongue. Scholars and the wealthy classes spoke Greek besides Latin, and official edicts were translatad into Greek. The inscription that Pilate put on the cross was written in Hebrew, Latin, and Greek, the usual custom—Hebrew for the common people, Latin the official language, and Greek the polite language. The prophets mention Rome as the fourth kingdom (Dan. ii. 40, vii. 7, 17, 19, xi. 30–40; and Deut. xxviii. 49–57?). The empire proper began with Augustus, at the battle of Actium, B. C. 31, when he became sole master, and ended by the abdication of Augustus, A. D. 476.

ROME. The City of Rome was founded B. C. 753, on 7 hills, 15 ms. from the mouth of the Tiber (Rev. xvii. 9). The modern city lies to the N. W. of the ancient site, on what was the Campus Martius (Field of Mars), a plain north of the

ROME. THE FORUM.

seven hills. It is only mentioned in Maccabees, Acts, Epistle to the Romans, and 2d Timothy. The Jews first settled in Rome after Pompey's conquests, when the Jewish king, Aristobulus, and his son were led in triumph. At the time of Paul's visit (after Augustus had "found the city of brick and left it of marble") the population was one million two hundred thousand (*Gibbon*)—one-half being slaves, and a large part of the freemen dependent on the rich, and living like paupers on public gratuities. Rome became the greatest repository of architecture, pictures, and sculptures that the world ever saw. The luxury, profligacy, and crime of this age is beyond the descriptive power of letters. It is believed that Paul lived here "two whole years," in his own hired house, bound by a chain to a soldier, according to the then custom of keeping certain prisoners (Acts xii. 6, xxviii. 16, 20, 30). Five of Paul's epistles were written at Rome, one of them just before his death, as is believed by beheading.

The localities made interesting by Paul at Rome are: the Appian Way, by which he approached the city; Cæsar's Court, or Palace (Phil. i. 13); and the Palatine Hill, on which was Cæsar's household (ib. iv. 22), and probably Paul's residence. It is also said, traditionally, that Peter and Paul were fellow-prisoners, for nine months, in the Mamertine prison, which is now shown under the church of S. Giuseppe dei Falegnami; and that they separated on their way to martyrdom at a spot on the Ostian road, now marked by a chapel:

afid the church of St. Paolo marks the site of Paul's martyrdom. The spot where Peter suffered is also covered by the church of St. Pietro in Montorio, on the Janiculum. A chapel on the Appian Way locates the beautiful legend of Jesus appearing to Peter as he was escaping from martyrdom, who, ashamed, returned and submitted to his fate (Ambrose). The bodies of the two apostles were first laid in the catacombs, and were finally buried, Paul on the Ostian road, and Peter in the church of St. Peter. The ruins of the Coliseum are still standing, as a memorial of those early nameless Christians who were exposed to the wild beasts in its arena, for the gratification of the people, who, while witnessing these awful sights, were sprinkled with perfumed water, which was conveyed about the building in secret pipes. Nearly two-thirds of the ancient site (within Aurelian's walls) are covered with ruins, and a few churches and convents, or open waste-places. In Pliny's time the circuit of the city was 20 ms.; it is now about 15 ms.

The first Christian church in Rome was built by Constantine, who gave his own palace on the Cælian hill as a site. St. Peter's on the Vatican hill was built next, A. D. 324—the first edifice built on the site—out of the ruins of the temples of Apollo and Mars, and stood 1200 years, being superseded by the present magnificent structure.

Rome is called Babylon (on account of the special hate of the Jews for the tyranny of its rulers), in Rev. xiv. 8, xvi. 19, xvii. 5, xviii. 2,—as the centre of heathenism, in contrast to Jerusalem, the centre of Judaism. It is supposed that the first Church in Rome consisted mainly of Gentiles. (See *Conybeare* and *Howson's* Life of St. Paul, *Gibbon*, *Draper's* Hist. Int. Devel. of Europe).

RO'MANS, EPISTLE TO THE. See HISTORY OF THE BOOKS.

ROOM (Heb. MAKONA). Place (Gen. xxiv. 23); KEN. Nest (vi. 14). Gr. *anogeon* or *anagaion*. Any thing above ground; an upper room (Mark xiv. 15). Room is sometimes synonymous with seat or place (Luke xiv. 8, 50).

ROOT (Heb. SHORESH; Gr. *rhiza*). The part of a tree or plant under ground (Job viii. 17). In poetry persons and nations are often compared to a plant or tree (Is. v. 24); figuratively, the lowest part, bottom (Job xxviii. 9); metaphorically, descendant, offspring (Is. xi. 10).

ROSE. 1. Heb. CHABAZZELETH (Cant. ii. 1). I am the rose of Sharon. 2. Gr. *rhodon* (Wis. ii. 8). Roses are greatly prized in the East, for the rose-water, which is in much request. Several varieties are still found in Palestine. The "rose of Sharon" is sacredly associated with the heavenly bridegroom (Cant. ii. 1).

The Rose of Sharon is thought by some to have been the Cistus, Rock-rose, of which there are several varieties in Palestine, and is now chiefly found on the hills, and especially on Mount Carmel, where it almost covers whole districts, tinting entire hillsides, as seen from a distance, in April.

Others, as Tristram (*Nat. Hist.* 476), thinks it was the Sweet-scented Narcissus, a native of Palestine, growing on Sharon, and nearly all over the country. It is very fragrant, and an especial favorite of the people, who, men and women, carry them for their perfume and fine color, vast numbers being sold in the bazaars.

Dr. Thomson suggested the Mallow, marsh-mallows, which grows into a stout bush, and bears thousands of beautiful flowers. Others again suggest the asphodel or the lily.

ROSH. In Ez. xxxviii. 2, 3, xxxix. 1, this name is translated "chief," and should read, "Magog, the prince of Rosh, Meshech, and Tubal." The Russ, or Russians, are also mentioned in the Koran. The country of the children of RASSES (Jud. ii. 23) was ravaged by Holofernes. Meshech is said to be the original Muscovy, and Rosh, the original Russia.

ROS'IN. The *resin* of turpentine after distillation. 1. In Ez. xxvii. 17, BALM.—2. In the Song of the Three Holy Children (23) the servants of the king are said to have "ceased not to make the oven hot with rosin (properly *naphtha*).

RU'BIES. See PRECIOUS STONES.

RUE (Gr. *pegamon*, in Luke xi. 42, only). Is doubtless, the common garden-rue (*ruta graveolus*), having a strong odor and a bitter taste: a shrubby plant, about 2 ft. high, and used as a medicine. In the middle ages it was used by the priests to sprinkle holy water, and was called *herb of grace*.

RU'FUS (L. *red*). Son of Simon the Cyrenian, who carried the cross on which the Saviour was to be crucified (Mark xv. 21). He is supposed to be the same person whom Paul salutes in Rom. xvi. 13.

RUHA'MAH (*pitied*). See HOSEA in HISTORY OF THE BOOKS.

RU'MAH (*lofty*), (2 K. xxiii. 36). DUMAH (Josh. xv. 52).

RUSH (Heb. AGMON). See PAPYRUS.

RUST (Gr. *Brosis*, Matt. v. 19, 30). A destroying substance that attacks treasures of any kind long undisturbed. In James v. 3, "rust" is the translation of Gr. *ios*, the *tarnish* which spreads silver, rather than "rust."

RUTH. See HISTORY OF THE BOOKS.

RYE (KUSSEMETH), (Ex. ix. 32). Rye is not an Egyptian or Syrian grain, but rather a northern plant. It is closely allied to wheat, which it much resembles. The sheath is coarser, and rougher, and the beard long. It is of less value, and the flour is generally mixed with that of wheat. See HARVEST.

S

SABACTHA'NI (*hast thou forsaken me?*). A part of our Saviour's exclamation on the cross (Matt. xxvii. 46); the whole is taken from Ps. xx. 1, where it is used prophetically.

SAB'AOTH (ZEBOTH, *hosts or armies*), (Joel ii. 15; 2 Sam. vi. 2; Ps. xxiv. 10; Jas. v. 4).

SA'BAT. 1. Ancestor of sons of Solomon's servants, who returned from captivity (1 Esd. v. 34). —2. SEBAT (1 Macc. xvi. 14). MONTH.

SABATE'AS. SHABBETHAI (1 Esd. ix. 48).

SABATUS. ZABAD (1 Esd. ix. 28).

SAB'BAN. BINNUI 1 (1 Esd. viii. 63).

SAB'BATH (Heb. SHABBATH, *the [day of] rest*). The name given to the seventh day of the week under the old covenant. Division of time into weeks was the custom from the earliest recorded ages, among the rudest as well as the most cultivated people. (CHRONOLOGY.) It is the only ordinance besides marriage which dates from the Creation (Gen. ii. 3), and it is one of the subjects of the Decalogue (Ex. xxxiv. 21). In Leviticus the whole law is repeated (xxiii. 2, 3), and one of the finest of the Psalms was written in honor of the day (Ps. xcii.). The prophets also honor the Sabbath as a holy day (Is. lvi. 1, 2; Ez. xx. 12, xliv. 24, xlvi. 3).

The observance of the Sabbath indicated a prosperity of religion, and its neglect showed a decay of religion generally. The day of rest was a great boon to the laborer, and to animals (Ex. xxiii. 12), but the great importance of the institution was its spirital and religious meaning, and as a sign of the holiness of God, and the holiness required of His people. Its deliberate violation was punished with death (Num. xv. 32–36).

The special rites and services appointed for the day show that it was to be spent in thoughts and exercises on the character and ways of God. The services of the sanctuary were peculiar to the day (Num. xxviii. 9; Lev. xxiv. 3–9); and the laws of Moses were read (Acts xv. 21), "teaching Jacob God's judgments and Israel His law" (Deut. xxxiii. 10).

Josephus alludes to the origin, design, and observance of the day in his discourse against Apion (ii. 18).

Jesus instructed His disciples, by His example as well as words, to keep the law of the Sabbath, and to works of kindness and mercy, and exercise of piety (Matt. xii. 1–13; Mark iii. 1–5; Luke iv. 16, vi. 9), and to keep the day in its true spirit, as a day of personal privilege and benevolent usefulness, for "the Sabbath was made for man, and not man for the Sabbath."

In Colossians ii. 16, Paul argues from the fact of the Sabbath having been superseded by the Lord's day.

SABBATH DAY'S JOURNEY. The distance between the tents and the ark in the camp, which was 2000 cubits. The common cubit of 18 inches would be 3000 feet, and the sacred cubit of 19.05 inches would be 4,762 feet. The English mile is 5,280 feet.

SABBATHE'US. Shabbethai, the Levite (1 Esd. ix. 14).

SABBE'US. SHEMAIAH 14 (1 Esd. ix. 32).

SABE'ANS. People ef SEBA.

SA'BI. ZEBAIM (1 Esd. v. 34).

SAB'TAH. Third son of Cush (Gen. x. 7). Located in Arabia, along the southern coast. Pliny (vi. xxiii. 32) says the chief city of the region had 60 temples, and was the capital of king Elisarus.

SABTE'CAH. Fifth son of Cush (Gen. x. 7). Settled on the Persian Gulf, on the Persian shore.

SA'CAR (reward). 1. Father of Ahiam (1 Chr. xi. 35).—2. Fourth son of Obed-edom (xxvi. 4).

SACK'BUT (Chal. *sabbecha*). A musical instrument: a brass trumpet with a slide, like the modern trombone (Dan. xii. v. 7, 10, 15).

SACK'CLOTH (Heb. SAK; Gr. *sakkos*). A coarse stuff, of a dark color, often made of goats'-hair (Is. 1, 3), and the coarse, black hair of the camel. In great calamities—in penitence, in trouble—the Jews wore sackcloth about their bodies (Gen. xxxvii. 34); The robe resembled a sack, and was confined by a girdle of the same material (2 Sam. iii. 31). In times of joy those who were clad in sackcloth took it off, and put on their usual clothing (Is. xxxii. 11). See DRESS.

SAC'RIFICE (Heb. MINCHAH, *to give;* KORBAN, *to approach;* ZEBACH, *to slaughter animals;* OLAH, *whole burnt-offering;* SHELEM, *peace-offering;* CHATTATH, *sin-offering;* ASHAM, *trespass-offering;* Gr. *thusia* (Matt. ix. 13); *doron, gift* (Matt. ii. 11); *eidolothuton, idol-sacrifice* (Acts xv. 29); *prosphora, offering* (Acts xxi. 26). The first recorded sacrifices were those of Cain and Abel (Minchah). Of Noah, after the flood (Gen. viii. 20); a burnt-offering (olah). The sacrifice of Isaac (Gen. xxii. 1–13), the only instance of human sacrifice, having been commanded by God as a test of faith, but not actually offered. In the burnt-offerings of Job (Job i. 5, xlii. 8), the offering was accompanied by repentance and prayer. The sacrifices of the Mosaic period commenced with the offering of the Passover (Ex. xxiv.). The law prescribed five kinds of sacrifices: the burnt-offering, the meat-offering (unbloody), the peace-offering (bloody), the sin-offering and the trespass-offering. In the consecration of Aaron and his sons (Lev. viii.), there was first a *sin-offering*, as an approach to God; next, a *burnt-offering*, typical of dedication to His service, and the *meat-offering* of thanksgiving; and further, a peace-offering for the congregation, which was accepted by the miraculous descent of fire upon the altar. This was ever afterwards the order of the sacrifices. The sacrifices regularly offered in the Temple were of burnt-offerings: first, the daily burnt-offerings (Ex. xxix. 38–42); second, the double burnt-offerings on the Sabbath (Num. xxviii. 9, 10); third, the burnt-offerings at the great feasts (Num. xxviii. 11, xxix. 39).

OF MEAT-OFFERINGS.—The daily meat-offerings accompanying the daily burnt-offerings (flour, oil and wine), (Ex. xxix. 40, 40); second, the shewbread (twelve loaves, with frankincense), replaced every Sabbath (Lev. xxiv. 5–9); third, the special meat-offerings at the Sabbath—a great feast (Num. xxviii. and xxix.); fourth, *wave-offerings*—the first fruits of the Passover (Lev. xxiii. 10–14) and at Pentecost (xxiii. 17–20). *Peace-offerings* of the first fruits of the threshing-floor at the harvest-time (Num. xv. 20, 21).

OF SIN-OFFERINGS.—First, a *sin-offering* each new moon, of a kid (Num. xxviii. 15); second, *sin-offerings* at the Passover, Pentecost, Feast of Trumpets and Tabernacles (Num. xxviii. 22, 30, xxix.); third, the offering of the two goats (one the scape-goat) for the people, and of a bullock for the priest on the great day of ATONEMENT (Lev. xvi.). Incense was offered morning and evening (Ex. xxx. 7, 8), and on the Great Day of Atonement. There were also the individual offerings of the people. See PRIESTS.

SADAMI'AS. Shallam, ancestor of Ezra (2 Esd. i. 1).

SA'DAS. AZGAD (1 Esd. v. 13).

SADDE'US. IDDOL (1 Esd. viii. 45).

SAD'DUC. Zadok, the high-priest (1 Esd. viii. 2).

SAD'DUCEES (named from ZADOK, the high-priest). A religious sect of the Jews at the time of Christ, who refused to accept that the oral law was the revelation of God to the Israelites, and believed exclusively in the written law. They joined with the Pharisees in asking for a sign from heaven (Matt. xvi. 1, 4, 6), but opposed their doctrines otherwise. The Sadducees never exercised the influence that the Pharisees did, and were more tolerant. They rejected the belief in a resurrection (Matt. xxii. 23), nor did they believe in future rewards and punishments. The high-priest, at the time of Christ, was of this sect, and the doctrine of the resurrection preached by Christ rendered the Sadducees especially bitter against him (Acts iv. 1, v. 17), but he did not censure the Sadducees as much as the Pharisees.

SA'DOC. 1. ZADOK 1 (2 Esd. i. 1).—2. A descendant of Zerubbabel in the genealogy of Jesus Christ (Matt. i. 14).

SAF'FRON (Ar. *Zafran, yellow.* Heb. CARCOM). A small bluish flower, whose yellow stigma is pulled out and dried, having a peculiar aromatic and penetrating odor and a bitter taste. Used as a stimulant in medicine and highly valued in the East as a perfume (Cant. iv. 14).

SAINT (Heb. HASID, KADOSH. Gr. *Nagios, a holy one*), (Dan. viii. 13). A title by which the disciples were known. Originally including all members of the Church, afterward restricted to a few (Rom. i. 1; Acts ix. 32; 1 Thess. iii. 13).

SA'LA. SALAH (Luke iii. 35).

SA'LAH (*extension*), (Gen. x. 24). Father of Eber. Settled in N. Mesopotamia.

SAL'AMIS. City on the east end of the island of Cyprus. Visited by Paul and Barnabas on their first missionary journey (Acts xiii. 5). There were many Jews in Cyprus, attracted by the copper mines. The ancient city was near the modern *Fumagousta*, by the river Pediæus, on a plain.

SALASAD'AI. ZURISHADAI (Jud. viii. 1).

SALA'THIEL or SHEALTIEL. Father of Zerubbabel (Ezr. iii. 2). One of the ancestors of Christ (Matt. i. 14; Luke iii. 27).

SAL'CAH (Deut. iii. 10; Josh. xiii. 11). A city on the extreme east limit of Bashan and Gad (1 Chr. v. 11). There was a district of the same name (Josh. xiii. 5), belonging to Og. Now called *Sulkhad*, at the south end of Jebel Hauran. The great Euphrates desert begins near this city and extends to the Persian Gulf. About three miles in circuit. In it is a castle on a lofty (volcanic) hill, 400 feet high. An inscription on a gate is dated A. D. 246, and one on a tombstone, A. D. 196.

SA'LEM. SHALEM (*peace*). Jerome said Salem was 8 Roman miles from Scythopolis (Bethshean), and in his day contained the ruins of the palace of Melchizedek. Some have identified it with Jerusalem. The plain of Salem has the mountains Ebal and Gerizim, with Shechem, on its west end, and the hills on which Salem stands on its east end. In Psalm lxxvi. 2, Salem means Jerusalem.

SA'LIM (John iii. 23). Near Ænon. 6 miles south of Bethshean and 2 miles west of Jordan is a site of ruins on the *Tell Redghah*, with a Mohammedan tomb, called *Shekh Salim*. The brook in *Wady Chusneh* runs close by, and a copious fountain gushes out near the tomb, while rivulets wind about in all directions. "Here is much water."

SAL'LAI (*basket maker*). 1. One who settled in Jerusalem after the Captivity (Neh. xi. 8).—2. Head of a course of priests who went with Zerubbabel (xii. 20).

SAL'LU (*weighed*). Son of Meshullam (1 Chr. ix. 7).

SALLU'MUS. SHALLUM 2 (1 Esd. ix. 25).

SAL'MA (*garment*), or SALMON (*clothed*). Son of Nashon, prince of Judah, the husband of Rahab (Matt. i. 4, 5).

SAL'MAH. SALMA (Ruth iv. 20).

SALMANA'SER. SHALMANESER (2 Esd. xiii. 40).

SALMANAS'SER. SHALMANESER (Hos. xi. 5).

SAL'MON (Judg. ix. 48). A hill near Shechem, on which Abimelech and his men cut down boughs with which they burnt the tower of Shechem. ZALMON. White as snow in Salmon (Is. lxviii. 14).

SALMO'NE. The east point of the island of CRETE (Acts xxvii. 7).

SA'LOM. 1. SHALLUM, father of Hilkiah (Bar. i. 7).—2. SALU, father of Zimri (1 Macc. ii. 26).

SALO'ME (*pacific*). 1. Wife of ZEBEDEE, mother of the *Apostles* James and John. She was a most devout and faithful disciple (Matt. xx. 20; Acts xvi. 1).—2. Salome, the daughter of Herodias; she was the cause of John Baptist's death (Matt. xiv. 6; Mark vi. 22). She was the wife of Philip, Tetrarch of Trachonitis, and afterwards married Aristobulus, king of Chalcis (Jos. Ant. xviii. 5, 4).

SALT (MELAH; Gr. *nats*). See SODOM.

SALT, CITY OF (Josh. xv. 62). In the wilderness, near Engedi and the Dead Sea. It may be the site is found in the modern *Nahr Maleh*, which is near the *Wady Amreh*, which is believed to be *Gomorrah*. The *Valley of Salt*. Two memorable victories occurred here: that of David over the Edomites (2 Sam. viii. 13; Ps. lx.); and that of Amaziah over the same people (2 K. xiv. 7). The site is lost. It has been located by some in the plain at the south end of the Dead Sea.

SA'LUM. 1. SHALLUM 8 (1 Esd. v. 28).—2. SHALLUM 6 (viii. 1).

SALUTA'TION (Heb. SHALOM LEKHA). Peace be with thee (John xx. 19). By this term is meant the friendly greeting, which, in ancient as in modern times, takes place between persons when meeting or parting; also when sending letters.

At parting the form was much the same as at meeting. "Go in peace (Judg. xviii. 6). The letter of an Arab will be nearly filled with salutations; and should he come in to tell you your house is on fire, he would first give and receive the compliments of the day before saying your house is on fire. Salutations are also given by kissing the hand, the forehead, cheek, the beard of a superior. The long, ceremonious greeting which occupied so much time, was deemed unfit for the use of the preachers of the gospel, and they were directed to salute no one by the way. It is not unusual for two ceremonious gentlemen to inquire carefully after every male relative, especially ancestors, of each other, several times over, at each meeting; smoking and sipping coffee during the one or two hours required for this very friendly (?) greeting. Custom does not permit inquiries after each others' female relatives, it being equal to a decided insult to even allude to another man's wife. If a man speaks of his wife he apologizes for the discourtesy.

SAMARITAN PRIEST.

SALVA'TION (Heb. YESHAH, YESHA; Gr. *soteria*). Deliverance from temporal evils or earthly destruction (Ex. xiv. 13). GOD is figuratively called "salvation" (Ps. xxvii. 1). JESUS CHRIST has provided the salvation of the Gospel, and is preeminently "the SAVIOUR" (Matt. i. 21).

SAM'AEL. SALAMIEL (Jud. viii. 1).

SAMAI'AS. 1. Shemaiah 23 (1 Esd. i. 9).—2. Shemaiah 11 (viii. 39).—3. The "great Samaias," father of Ananias and Jonathas (Tob. v. 13).

SAMA'RIA (*watch mountain*). Six miles N. W. of Shechem, on a hill which is surrounded by a broad basin-shaped valley. Here OMRI built the capital of the kingdom of Israel, on the hill which he bought (B. C. 925) of SHEMER for two talents of silver (1 K. xvi. 24). The site is singularly beautiful, and is always admired by every visitor.

Ahab built a temple to Baal, with images; and that part of the city was called "the city of the house of Baal" (1 K. xvi. 22), which was destroyed by Jehu (2 K. x. 25).

The Syrians besieged it in 901 B. C. (1 K. xx. 1), and in 892 B. C. (ib. vi. 24, vii. 20), and in both cases without success.

Shalmanezer, king of Assyria, took it after a siege of 3 years, B. C. 721 (2 K. xviii. 9, 10), and carried the people away to Assyria. Esarhaddon repeopled the country from Assyria, and these citizens were called *Samaritans*. Josephus describes it as a very strong city in the time of John Hyrcanus, who took it (B. C. 109), after a year's siege (Ant. xiii. 10, 2). After this time the Jews inhabited the city, until the age of Alexander Jannæus, and until Pompey restored it to the descendants of the original inhabitants (probably the Syro-Macedonians).

Herod the Great rebuilt it with some splendor, and called it SEBASTE (Augustus), after his patron the Emperor Augustus. The wall was 20 stadia in circuit. A magnificent temple was dedicated to Cæsar. 6,000 veteran soldiers were colonized here, and a large district given them for their support (Ant. xv. 8, 5; B. J. i. 20, 3, etc.).

The remains of the ancient city are mostly colonnades of Herod's time, or older. There is a group of 16 in a recess near the bottom of the hill, another of 16 near the top, and a long line of columns running around the hill, on one side, on a broad terrace, of which 100 are now standing, and a great many others fallen. The whole hill is covered with rubbish, the remains of a large and well-built city.

The city is not mentioned in the New Testament, and it was commanded, "Into any city of the Samaritans enter ye not."

Septimus Severus planted a Roman colony there in the 3d century. Roman coins struck in the city are preserved of the ages extending from Nero to Geta. In A. D. 409 the Holy Land was divided into 3 districts, of which the country of Philistia, the northern part of Judæa and Samaria, formed Palestina Prima; with Cæsarea for its capital.

The bishop of Samaria was present at the Council of Nicea, A. D. 325, signing his name as Maximus Sebastenus.

The Mohammedans took Sebaste during their siege of Jerusalem.

The present village is called *Sebustiyeh*, and consists of a few houses scattered among the ruins of the past. The ruined church of St. John the Baptist bears traces of its former magnificence. A long avenue of columns, many fallen, still lines the upper terrace of the hill. The prophesies of Micah (i. 6), and Hosea (xiii. 16), are descriptive of its present condition.

SAMARIA, THE DISTRICT OF. Was so called before the city was named (1 K. xiii. 32), and included all the tribes who accepted Jeroboam as king, on both sides of the Jordan, and the royal residence was Shechem (1 K. xiii. 25). The name Samaritan became contracted, as the kingdom was divided from time to time. The first limitation was probably the losing of Simeon and Dan. The second, when Pul, king of Assyria (B. C. 771) carried away the Reubenites and Gadites, and the half tribe of Manasseh (1 Chr. v. 26); the third, when Galilee and Gilead were taken by the Assyrians (2 K. xv. 29); and the fourth, when just before the last king of Israel, Hoshea, was deposed, Asher, Issachar and Zebulon, and also Ephraim and Manasseh, sent men up to the Passover at Jerusalem (2 Chr. xxx. 1-26), in Hezekiah's reign. Thus, the kingdom which once extended from the sea to the desert of Syria, and from Bethel to Dan in the north, was divided, until only the city Samaria, with a few villages, remained to the name, and even these were wiped out by Shalmanezer (2 K.

xvii. 5–26), who placed other people there instead of the Jews (v. 24), B. C. 721.

These new-comers were idolaters, and brought their idols with them (2 K. xvii. 29), and although instructed by Jewish priests, never became pure worshipers of Israel's God. When Judah and Benjamin returned from the Captivity and began to build the Temple, the Samaritans asked permission to assist; and on being refused they petitioned the king of Assyria and had the work stopped (Ezr. iv.). From this time the "adversaries of Judah and Benjamin" became open enemies, and the feud grew year by year more bitter. In the year B. C. 409, Manasseh, a priest who was expelled from Jerusalem for an unlawful marriage, obtained permission from the Persian king to build a temple on Mt. Gerizim, and made a copy of the law, which was the 5 books of Moses only (called the Pentateuch), and they claimed for this copy the highest antiquity, even above any copy in possession of the Jews.

The Samaritans claimed from Alexander an exemption from taxes on the Sabbatical year, on the plea that they were Jews; but on examination their claim was found to be false. The woman of Samaria also claimed to be a descendant of Jacob, when talking with Jesus (John vi. 12).

The boundaries, according to Josephus, in the time of Christ were from Jenin to Acrabatta. (See MAP.) The soil, productions, etc., are described under EPHRAIM and ISSACHAR.

SAM'ATUS. Son of Ozora (1 Esd. ix. 34).

SA'MECH (Heb. *fulcrum, support*). The 15th letter of the Hebrew alphabet (Ps. cxix). WRITING.

SAMEI'US. SHEMAIAH 13 (1 Esd. ix. 21).

SAM'GAR-NE'BO (Jer. xxxix. 3). The whole name is SAMGAR-NEBO-SAMSECHIM, which is to say, The *Cupbearer*, Nebo-Sarsechim.

SA'MI. SHOBA 1 (1 Esd. v. 28).

SAM'IS. SHIMEI 13 (1 Esd. ix. 34).

SAM'LAH (*a garment*). A king of Edom (Gen. xxxvi. 36, 37).

SAM'MUS. SHEMA (1 Esd. ix 43).

SA'MOS (*hight*). An island opposite the boundary between Ionia and Caria. Paul anchored for a night at Trogyllium, in the narrow strait between Samos and Mycale. The ancient Greeks fought a naval battle against the Persians in this strait, B. C. 479. Herod the Great met Marcus Agrippa in Samos, and obtained many privileges for the Jews (Jos. Ant. xvi. 2, 2).

SAMOTHRA'CIA (Acts xvi. 11). Mentioned in Paul's first voyage. It is a lofty and conspicuous island, seen at a great distance, being visible from the shore at Troas (*Eothen*, p. 64; Homer, Il. xiii. 12, 13). Paul anchored for a night off the island. A strong current from the Dardanelles sets southward between the island and the mainland. The mysteries of the Cabeiri (pagan divinities) were practiced here.

SAMP'SAMES. Now Samsun, on the coast of the Black Sea, between Trebizond and Sinope.

SAM'SON (Heb. SHIMSHON, *strong*). Son of MANOAH, in the tribe of DAN (Josh. xv. 33). The account of his birth, life, and exploits, is given in Judg. xiii. xvi. He was the strongest man, and celebrated for his fearless and wonderful acts, for his moral infirmities, and his tragical end. His sins brought him in great disgrace and misery (Heb. xi. 32).

SAM'UEL. See HISTORY OF THE BOOKS.

SANABAS'SAR. SHESHBAZZAR (1 Esd. ii. 12, 15).

SANABAS'SARUS. SHESHBAZZAR (1 Esd. vi. 18, 20).

SAN'ASIB. Ancestor of certain priests said to have returned with Zerubbabel (1 Esd. v. 24).

SANBAL'LAT. A Moabite of HORONAIM, but a resident of Samaria (Neh. ii. 10, 19), and a great enemy of the Jews. He was an officer in the service of Artaxerxes (Neh. iv. 2). See Nehemiah in the HISTORY OF THE BOOKS. His daughter married Manasseh, the high-priest, Eliashib's grandson, son of Joiada (Tobiah, a companion of his, had "allied" himself to Eliashib's family in the same manner—Neh. xiii. 4), on account of a settled policy of Sanballat, Tobiah and Geshem, who concerted together for the injury of the Jews. Nehemiah expelled Manasseh for marrying a Gentile wife. Sanballat attempted to entice Nehemiah from Jerusalem to some village near Ono (vi.), but the scheme failed, for the Tirshatha suspected mischief. Nothing further is related of Sanballat in the Scripture, and Josephus continues the history in rather a fabulous manner.

SANCTIFICA'TION. SANCTIFY (KADASH, *to sanctify*), (Gen. ii. 3); (Gr. *hagiazo*), (Matt. xxii. 17, 19). To be holy. In the O. T. it denotes the consecration of a person to God (Ex. xxxi. 13). To make holy, or to set apart for God (Gen. ii. 3; Ex. xix. 23). The tabernacle, altar, priests, etc., were solemnly set apart and sanctified for divine service (Lev. viii. 10–12). A day was set apart for fasting and prayer (Joel i. 14), and the Sabbath was so regarded (Deut. v. 12). In the N. T. the doctrine is the making truly and perfectly holy what was before defiled and sinful, and is a progressive work of divine grace upon the soul justified by the love of Christ. After a gradual cleansing from sin the sinner is presented "unspotted before the throne of God," which is the work of the Holy Spirit (John xiv. 26, xvii. 17). The ultimate sanctification of every believer in Christ is a covenant of mercy, purchased on the cross.

SAND (Heb. HOL; Gr. *ammos*), (Gen. xxii. 17; Job vi. 3). See SINAI. The sand of the desert of Petra and Sinai is very light, easily carried with the wind, and penetrates even the cases of a watch so as to stop the wheels. Some of it is a whitish yellow, hard and shining, and some is red.

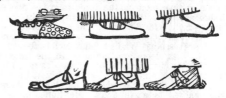

SANDALS.

SANDAL (Heb. NA'AL; Gr. *sandalon*, little sandal), (Mark vi. 9). See DRESS.

SAN'HEDRIM, correct **SANHEDRIN.** Gr. *sunedrion.* "COUNCIL." See HISTORY OF THE BOOKS.

SAN'HERIB. SENNACHERIB (2 K. xviii. 13).

SANSAN'NAH (*palm branch*). One of the towns in the S. of Judah (Josh. xv. 31). Lost, unless *Simsim* is the site.

SAPH (*threshold*). Son of "the Giant" slain by Sibbechai (2 Sam. xxi. 18), called SIPPAI in 1 Chr. xx. 4.

SA'PHAT. SHEPHATIAH 2 (1 Esd. v. 9).

SAPHATI'AS. SHEPHATIAH 2 (1 Esd. viii. 34).

SA'PHETH. SHEPHATIAH 3 (1 Esd. v. 33).

SA'PHIR (*fair*). (Micah i. 11). In the hill country, 8 miles N. E. of Ascalon. Now called *Es Sawafir.*

SAPPHI'RA (*beautiful*). Wife of ANANIAS 10, and the participator in his guilt and punishment (Acts v. 1–10).

SAP'PHIRE. See PRECIOUS STONES.

SA'RA. 1. Sarah, wife of Abraham (Heb. xi.

11). See ABRAHAM.—2. SERAH. Daughter of Asher (Num. xxvi. 46).

SARABI'AS. SHEREBIAH (1 Esd. ix. 48).

SARAI'AS. 1. SERAIAH, the high-priest (1 Esd. v. 5).—2. SERAIA, father of Ezra (viii. 1).

SAR'AMEL. Where Simon Maccabæus was made high-priest (1 Macc. xiv. 28). It is not certain whether this word means a place or a title of honor.

SA'RAPH (*fiery*). Descendant of Shelah, the son of Judah (1 Chr. iv. 22).

SARCHED'ONUS (Gr. *sacherdonos*). ESAR-HADDON (Tob. i. 21).

SAR'DIUS. AZIZA (1 Esd. ix. 28).

SAR'DINE. See PRECIOUS STONES.

SAR'DIS. A city on a spur of the mountain range Tmolus, about 2 ms. from the river Hermus, the ancient residence of the kings of Lydia. Its original name, in the time of Omphale, was HYDE'. It was naturally, from its convenient position and the fertile region surrounding it, a commercial mart of importance. Chestnuts were first made an article of commerce here, and called Nuts of Sardis. Pliny says the art of dyeing wool was invented here, and Phrygia furnished the material from its

 vast flocks. The carpets of Sardis were very celebrated. The Spartans sent to Sardis for gold to cover the face of Apollo at Amyclæ. The sands of the Pactolus, a brook from Tmolus running near Sardis, furnished the gold. Sardis was a slave mart, in very early times, and here traders first became stationary, as distinguished

CYBELE.

from traveling merchants. It was taken by Antiochus the Great, B. C. 214, and afterward became subject to Pergamus.

The city waned after the conquest of Alexander. The inscriptions remaining now visible are all of the Roman age, although there are remains of the earlier ages. The temple of Cybele still bears evidence to its former grandeur in its columns, two of which, with their capitals, "surpass any specimen of the Ionic in perfection of design and execution." There are remains of a theatre of 400 ft. diameter, and of a stadium of 1000 ft. The modern name is SERT KALESSI, and the river (Hermus) Wadis-tchai, which is about 180 ft. wide, 3 ft. deep, and muddy. In the time of Tiberius, the city, with 12 others, was destroyed by an earthquake, and suffered so much that its distress excited the compassion of its Roman rulers, who remitted its tax for 5 yrs. Mentioned in Rev. iii. 1-6. See SEVEN CHURCHES.

SAR'DITES, THE. Descendants of Sered, the son of Zebulun (Num. xxvi. 26).

SARDI'US. ODEM. Gr. *Sardios*. See PRECIOUS STONES.

SAR'DONYX. Gr. *Sardius and Onyx*. See PRECIOUS STONES.

SARE'A. An assistant secretary to Ezra (2 Esd. xiv. 24).

SAREP'TA. ZAREPHATH. E. of Sidon (Luke iv. 26).

SAR'GON (*king in fact*). One of the greatest Assyrian kings. He sent Tartan, his general, with an army against Ashdod, and took it. He built the palace at Nimroud. He was successor to Shalmanezer IV. The wars of Sargon were numerous, and he carried his victorious arms into many countries. A statue of Sargon, which is now in the Museum of Berlin, was discovered at Idalium, in Cyprus (Is. xx. 1, 4; 2 K. xviii. 9, 10).

SA'RID (Josh. xix. 10, 12). Zebulon, west of Chisloth Tabor. Lost.

SA'RON. The district in which Lydda stood (Acts ix. 25). The Sharon of the Old Testament.

SARO'THIC. One who returned from captivity; ancestor of sons of Solomon's servants (1 Esd. v. 34).

SAR'SECHIM (*chief of the eunuchs*). A general in Nebuchadnezzar's army (Jer. xxxix. 3). RABSARIS.

SA'RUCH. SERUG (Luke iii. 35).

SA'TAN. See DEVIL.

SATHRABUZA'NES. SHETHAR-BOZNAI (1 Esd. vi. 3, 7, 27).

SA'TYR (Heb. SAIR; pl. SEIRIM). "Hairy" in Gen. xxvii. 11, 23; "rough" (Dan. viii. 21); "devils" (Lev. vii. 7); "shaggy animals" (Is. xiii. 21). It is frequently applied *he-goats* (Lev. iv. 24). Satyrs, in Greek mythology, were imaginary demons, half men and half goats, believed by the superstitious to haunt forests and groves.

SAUL (Heb. SHAUL, *asked for*). 1. Saul of Rehoboth by the river; one of the early kings of Edom (Gen. xxxvi. 37, 38); called SHAUL in 1 Chr. i. 48.—2. Saul, the son of Kish, of the tribe of Benjamin; he was the first king of Israel; anointed by Samuel privately (1 Sam. ix., x.). Afterwards Saul was elected in a solemn assembly at Mizpah by the determination of the miraculous lot. Saul was remarkably tall, and of a courageous disposition (1 Sam. ix. 2, x. 23). His immediate act upon his election, was to head an army and oppose the invasion of the Ammonites. He found them, led by their king, Nahash, at Bezek, and totally routed them (1 Sam. xi. 11). After this triumph Saul was publicly anointed at Gilgal by Samuel (1 Sam. xii.). From this period Saul's reign was marked by a series of transgressions: he assumed upon the priestly office and disregarded God's injunction by ordering the offering up of sacrifices (1 Sam. xiii. 9) during his contest with the Philistines. He rebelled against Jehovah in regard to the destruction of the Amalekites (1 Sam. xiv. 48). Saul behaved with the utmost cruelty to David—twice attempting his life (1 Sam. xviii. 10, 11, xix. 10). He committed a great atrocity in the murder of Ahimelech, the priest (1 Sam. xxii.), and of eighty-five other priests of the house of Eli, as well as the inhabitants of Nob. He forced David into opposition, who twice mercifully spared his life (1 Sam. xxiv. 3-7, xxvi.).

Saul committed a further offense in consulting the witch of Endor (1 Sam. xxviii. 7), although he had previously expelled all practicers of magical arts (xxviii. 3). At this interview he was warned that he and his sons would die the following day. On that day he met the Philistines in Gilboa, on the plain of Esdraëlon, and after seeing the utter rout of his army and the death of his three sons (Jonathan of the number), he killed himself upon the battle-field. The bodies of Saul and his sons were exposed by the enemy upon the wall of Bethshan, but were secretly removed by the men of Jabesh-Gilead who in the remembrance of their former obligations to Saul (1 Sam. xi.), gave the bodies honorable burial. Their bones were afterwards removed by David to Zelah, and buried in the sepulchre of Kish. Saul was anointed B. C. 1791.

	KISH.	
	1 Saul.	
1 Saul,	2 Jonathan.	
"	3 Ishui.	
"	4 Malchi-Shua.	
"	5 Abinadab.	
"	6 Eshbaal.	
"	7 Merab.	
"	8 Michal, dau.	
"	9 Armoni.	
"	10 Mephibosheth.	
2 Jonathan,	11	Merib-baal.
"		Mephibosheth.
"	12 Micah.	
12 Micah,	13 Pithon.	
"	14 Melech.	
"	15 Tahrea.	
"	16 Ahaz.	

SAV'ARAN. An error for Avaran, borne by Eleazar 9 (1 Macc. vi. 43).

SAVI'AS. Uzzi, ancestor of Ezra (1 Esd. viii. 2).

SA'VIOR or **SA'VIOUR.** See JESUS.

SAW (Heb. MEGERAH, MASSOR). Egyptian saws were single-handed, the teeth usually inclining toward the handle, instead of away from it like ours. In most cases they have bronze blades, attached to the handles by leather thongs, but some of those in the British Museum have their blades let into them like our knives. A double-handed iron saw has been found at Nimroud. Double-handed saws were used (1 K. vii. 9; 2 Sam. xii. 31).

SCALES. Heb. PELES, *a balance*, (Is. xl. 12); also weight (Prov. xvi. 11). See WEIGHTS and MEASURES.

SCAPE'-GOAT. See ATONEMENT.

SCAR'LET. COLORS.

SCEP'TRE (Heb. SHEBET, Gr. *skeptron*). ROD or STAFF. A rod or decorated staff, sometimes six feet long, borne by kings and magistrates as a symbol of authority (Gen. xlix. 10).

SCE'VA (*prepared*). A Jew at Ephesus and leader among the priests (Acts xix. 14, 16). His seven sons pretended to practice exorcism.

SCHIN (Heb. SHIN, *a tooth*). The twenty-first letter of the Hebrew alphabet (Ps. cxix.).

SCHISM (Gr. *schisma*). Division (1 Cor. i. 10; rent, Matt. ix. 16). A rent or fissure, used in the N. T. to denote a division in the Church, by contentions.

SCHOOL (Gr. *schole*, *leisure*), (Acts xix. 9). A place where a teacher and his disciples met and held discussions. See EDUCATION.

The Arab school is primitive—a room with a smooth floor (often the bare ground) and one or two windows (generally without glass or any protection), a board and piece of chalk for each boy, and one for the teacher. The teacher also has a Koran from which he reads. The pupils learn to write by imitating the writing of their teacher. They spell by reciting the names of the letters as (n) NOON, (a) ALIF, (g) GAMEL, NAG (a colt). The rules of the Church are carefully taught, also grammar. Very few go beyond this in the schools. Those who are destined to the Church are educated specially for that end; and study theology, rhetoric, numbers, and other branches. Some of the priests (ulema) are very well educated, and have a good knowledge of their own and the literature of other people. Robert Morris, LL. D., in 1868, found the Pasha of Damascus able to converse in French and English, and to quote long passages from such poets as Shakespeare, Milton, Byron Longfellow, Bryant, and to give a sketch of our history as a people—in the United States. On geography he was not so well informed. The native maps are more amusing than instructive.

Every mosque must support one or more schools, according to its income. The best schools are now being conducted in a few places by the American missionaries; the principal one being the Seminary at Beirut. See PHŒNICIA.

SCI'ENCE (L. *scientia*, *knowledge;* Heb. MADDA; Gr. *gnosis*). In Dan. i. 4, and 1 Tim. vi. 20, the original means knowledge and not science.

In Wickliffe's Bible, in Luke i. 77, there is the sentence "science of health," instead of "knowledge of salvation," in the present edition. In Col. ii. 3, is "wisdom and science" for "wisdom and knowledge," as now written, and in 1 Tim. vi. 20, for science the old edition has "kunyinge" (cunning). See TIMOTHY, in HISTORY OF THE BOOKS.

SCOR'PION (Heb. AKRAB; Gr. *skorpios*). One of the largest and most malignant of all the insect tribes. It resembles the lobster. Those found in S. Europe seldom exceed 2 ins. in length, but, in tropical climates, they are 10 or 12. They live upon other insects, but kill and devour their own species also. When it is placed in danger, and sees no way of escape, it will sting itself to death. Their sting is very poisonous; it occasions great pain and inflammation, with alternate chills and burning. The scorpion of Judæa when curled up resembles an egg; hence the comparison in Luke xi. 11, 12; Rev. ix. 3–10.

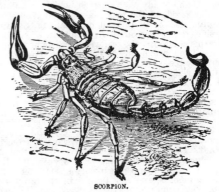

SCORPION.

SCOURG'ING. See PUNISHMENTS.

SCRIBE. See HISTORY OF THE BOOKS.

SCRIP (Heb. YALKUT—ZIKLON; Gr. *pera*). A bag or sack, in which travelers carried their food, or articles of convenience (1 K. xvii. 40; Matt. x. 10).

SCRIP'TURE. See HISTORY OF THE BOOKS.

SCROLL (Heb. SEPHER; Gr. *biblion*). MS. roll. See WRITING.

SCUR'VY. The diseases rendered "scab" and "scurvy," in Lev. xxi. 20, xxii. 22, and Deut. xxviii. 27, may be almost any skin–disease.

SCYTHE. See SICKLE (Jer. i. 16).

SCYTH'IAN (Col. iii. 11). Barbarians, living on the N. of the Black Sea and the Caspian. Herodotus (i. 103) says the Scythians made an incursion through Palestine, into Egypt, in the time of Josiah. This may account for the name *Scythopolis*, which may have been given by some of those people who settled at Bethshean.

SEA. This word is used in several ways: 1. Ocean (Gen. i. 10).—2. The Mediterranean Sea (Deut. xi. 24).—3. Any inland lake or sea (Ez. xlvii. 8).—4. Any great water-course, as the Nile or Euphrates (Is. xix. 5).

SALT SEA, THE. The most ancient name for the Dead Sea (Gen. xiv. 3; Num. xxxiv. 3; Deut. iii. 17; Josh. iii. 16). It is called the Sea of the Arabah (*plain*) in Deut. iii. 17, and the East Sea by Joel (ii. 20), Ezekiel (xlvii. 18), and by Zechariah (xiv. 8). In 2 Esd. (v. 7) it is called the Sodomitish Sea. Josephus calls it Lake Asphaltitis. The name Dead Sea was given by the Greeks (Pausanias, v. 7, and Galen, iv. 9); and by the Latins (Justin, xxxiv. 3). The Arabic name is Bahr Lut (*Sea of Lot*). The Dead Sea is the 3d of the lakes in the course of the Jordan, lying deepest in the valley at its S. end. It is 46 ms. long from N. to S., and 10 ms. wide, and its surface is 1317 ft. below the ocean level (Lynch). The depression was first noticed (in our day) in 1837. The great heat of the region carries off the water by evaporation. The Jordan flows into the N. end. 12 ms. (by the path) down the E. shore there enters the Zurka Main (the ancient Callirrhoë—the En Eglaim), and, 8 ms. further down the shore, the Mojib (Arnon); 10 ms. further, the Beni Hamad; 2 ms. beyond this, the Wady Kerak entering, by several channels, just above the peninsula; and just below it, in the lower bay of the lake, there are 10 or 12 streams, large and small: the largest being the Wady el Jeib, which drains ⅔ds of the Arabah. On the W. side, the first large stream is the Kedron (Wady el Nar), 5 to 6 ms. from the N. end of the lake; 8 ms. further S. is Wady Khureitum; 5 ms. beyond is Wady Sudeir, at Ain Jidy (Engedi); 2 ms. from this, Wady Areyeh, which, near Hebron, is called Wady Dibbeh; and beyond, at intervals of 3 or 4 ms., are, Birket Halil (Khuberah), Wady Seiyal, and Wady en Nemriyeh, which last flows by the N. side of the rock Masada, and Wady Zuweirah, just N. of the salt mountain of Usdum. Besides these, there are a great number of smaller streams all around the sea, with or without names. There is no visible outlet. The sea is divided into 2 parts by the peninsula of Lisan (*tongue*, Heb. LA-SHEN), which is about 9 ms. long, from N. E. to S. W., 4 to 6 ms. wide, and joined to the E. shore by a neck 5 ms. wide. The channel of the sea is 3 to 5 ms. wide opposite the Lisan, and is said to be fordable at the time of the lowest water, in October. The water of the main basin is 1300 ft. deep in the deepest part, opposite Ain Terabeh. The S. bay (Josh. xv. 2) is very shallow, varying from 12 to 3 ft. Careful observations have found that 20 million cubic ft. of water are poured, daily, into the sea, while its evaporating capacity is 24 million in the hottest months, and less than 20 in the rainy season. (See Humboldt.) It is believed that the level rises 10 to 15 ft. during the winter rains — falling again during the summer.

HELMETS.

The mountains come close to the shore on both the east and west sides, and are quite uniform in hight throughout the whole length, the eastern range being much the higher, and more broken by ravines. The general color is brown or reddish brown on the east (being sandstone, red and yellow, with porphyry), and gray, with whitish tints, on the west side (being limestone over sandstone). The only vegetation is found around the springs, and in the wadies, where palms, tamarisks, mimosa, osiers, oleanders, and a variety of trees and shrubs, besides grain and flowers, form a grateful relief to the general desolation. A plateau divides the mountains on the east side, half way up, extending from the head of the sea south as far as the Zurka Main, which is visible, near sunset, from Jerusalem. The western side is divided into several strata, which are quite distinct; and there are three parallel beaches, one above the other — the highest, 50 feet above the water, extending from *Wady Zuweirah* north to *Ain Jidy*, nearly 20 miles. Above *Ain Jidy* there is but one beach (covered with angular bits of flint, not rounded gravel), which skirts the mountains, being widest at the mouths of the largest brooks, as at the Kidron (*Wady Nar*) and *Ain Terabeh*, where it is more than half a mile wide. Many of the headlands come down steep into the water, cutting the beach in two, and therefore cannot be passed, except by climbing. There is a line of driftwood bordering the beach and marking the high-water line, all around the sea, brought down by the Jordan and other streams, gray and bleached, and some of it of great antiquity. On the west shore

of the south bay is the Salt Mountain of Sodom, called by the Arabs *Khasm Usdum*. (See GEOLOGY). There is an island in the sea, west of the Jordan, lying 300 feet from the shore at low water, circular and 400 feet in diameter. Stones and driftwood entirely cover the island. Some suppose the square stones found here are remains of ancient structures, because there are no similar stones on the shore. The plains at the north and south ends of the sea are flat, barren, stony, gently sloping up from the water, crusted with salt, soft and slimy to the foot, and destitute of vegetation, except a few reeds cluster round a spring. The eastern side of the south bay is an exception, where the vegetation, fed by copious streams of sweet water, is abundant, and with great variety of trees, plants, flowers and grasses.

The water of the sea is the heaviest known in all the world, being 12¼ lbs. to the gallon, distilled water weighing 9¾ lbs. This weight is due to the mineral salts held in solution. Eggs float with one-third exposed above the surface. The color is like the ocean, a greenish blue. The Jordan may be traced for several miles by its muddy color, as it flows into the clear water of the sea.

The analysis of the water of the Dead Sea by many scientific men, gives generally the same result, with but little variation, which is, that there are salts of magnesia, soda, lime, potass, manganese, ammonia, aluminum and iron; and of these there are chlorides, sulphates and bromides. The quantity averages from 13 to 26 parts in 100, according to the season of the year and the part of the sea from which the sample was taken.

Except the absence of vegetation, the appearance of the sea is that of savage and beautiful wildness. The presence of many kinds of birds and wild fowl enlivens the scenes. All along the shores, wherever a brook flows in, there the cane-brakes, trees and shrubs harbor partridges, snipe, ducks, doves, hawks, larks, quails, besides many kinds not yet named, or not identified, in great flocks. Frogs are also to be seen in the marshes (not the salt marshes) and hares in the thickets.

There has been no change in the size of the sea within the historic period; except the filling up of the south bay by silt from the rivers, and the destruction of the Cities of the Plain is believed to have been independent of the position or character of the sea, or the bed in which it lies. (See SODOM).

SEAL (Heb. HOTHAM; Gr. *sphragis*). The seal takes the place of our signature in the East. A name or device, well known as belonging to a certain person, was engraved on a seal of a ring, or on a small cylinder, and this was stamped on the papyrus, or parchment, with ink, or was pressed on a piece of clay, or wax, which was attached to the document. Many seals and cylinders of this kind have been found among the used by the ancient kings in signing or witnessing their treaties or decrees, and there is a piece of clay bearing the impression of both the Assyrian and Egyptian king's seals in the British Museum, deposited

SERAPIS.

MARRIAGE RING.

there by Layard, who found it in Assyria, and who thinks it the compact of Sabacho and of Sennacherib.

Doors of tombs, or houses, or treasuries, or any place that was to be guarded from intrusion, were closed, and a piece of clay stuck over the fastening, and this was impressed with the seal of the keeper or owner, so that the least meddling with the clay would break it (Job. xxxviii. 14). The ancient ruins in Assyria and Egypt. Seals were modern Orientals carry a seal hung by a string, or chain to the neck, or on the finger ring.

Specimens of engraved seals and gems are found in great numbers in the museums of antiquities, some of which are most valuable as confirmations of history. One in Alnwick museum bears the name of Osirtasen I, 3000 B. C. See the ring of Thothmes, and of Suphis, page 84. See seal of Haggai, p. 166, and Abraxas, p. 167.

SEA'MEN. See SHIP.

SEA'MONSTERS. See DRAGON.

SEASON. CLIMATE.

SE'BA. First son of Cush (Gen. x. 7). A nation in Africa included in Cush, and having a name and power in Solomon's time (Ps. lxxii. 10). Located in the island Meroe, which lies at the junction of the white and blue branches of the Nile. The chief city (Meroe) had an oracle of Jupiter Am-

SEIR (*rugged*). MOUNT (Gen. xiv. 6), and LAND OF (Gen. xxxii. 3, xxxvi. 30). The mountain and district on the east side of the Arabah, from Akabah to the Dead Sea (Deut. ii. 1, 8). Seir, the Horite, inhabited the land (ib. 20). Called GEBALA (*mountain*) by Josephus; and the northern section, from Petra, is still called JEBAIL by the Arabs. Its north border was probably Mt. Halak (*naked*), a range of white cliffs which run across the Arabah 8 ms. south of the Dead Sea (Josh. xi. 17). Esau drove out the Horites who dwelt in rock-hewn dwellings (Deut. ii. 12), probably such as are seen now in Petra, and changed its name to EDOM. Ezekiel prophesied the desolation of Mt. Seir, which seems to have been fulfilled in the present condition of the country (Ez. xxxv.).—2. SEIR (Josh. xv. 10). In Judah, between Kirjath-Jearim and Beth Shemesh. The village of SARIS, on the ridge between *Wady Aly* and *W. Ghurab*, is

EGYPTIAN CHARIOT.

mon (or the ram-headed Num), ruins of which are now visible, besides pyramids, and other indications of a great population. The great stature and beauty of this people was a theme of the ancients (Herod iii. 20, 114; Is. xliii. 3, xlv. 14; Ez. xxiii. 42). See Josephus, A. J. ii. 10, 2.

SEBAST'E. SAMARIA 1. Sebaste means in Greek the same as Augustus in Latin, which is "venerable," a title of the Roman Emperors.

SE'BAT. MONTH. SHEBET.

SECA'CAH. In the wilderness of Judah (Josh. xv. 61). Lost.

SECHENI'AS. 1. SCHECHANIAH 2 (1 Esd. viii. 29). 2. SHECHANIAH 3 (viii. 32).

SE'CHU (*eminence*), (1 Sam. xix. 22). Famous for a great well or cistern. Supposed to be *Bir Neballa* near *Neby Samwil*. Five ms. N. of Jerusalem.

SECUN'DUS (*second*). A disciple who went with Paul in some of his journeys (Acts xx. 4).

SEDECI'AS. 1. Father of Maaseiah (Bar. i. 1), apparently identified with the false prophet in Jer. xxix. 21, 22.—2. Zedekiah, king of Judah (Bar. i. 8).

SEED. Often used figuratively in Scripture (Dan. ix. 1). The Mosaic Law would not permit a field to be sown with mingled seed of several kinds (Lev. xix. 19). The precious seed is often committed to the ground with many fears, but the harvest is a season of joy (Ps. cxxvi. 5, 6).

SEED-TIME. See SOWING.

SEER. One who sees into the future. PROPHET.

SEETHE. To boil (Ex. xvi. 23). To prepare food in hot liquor.

SE'GUB (*elevated*). 1. Youngest son of Hiel (1 K. xvi. 34).—2. Son of Hezron (1 Chr. 21, 22).

probably near the ancient site, which is rugged enough to bear the name.

SEI'RATH (Judg. iii. 26). In Mt. Ephraim, where Ehud gathered the army with which he destroyed the Moabites who were with Eglon, the fat king, whom he killed in his tent. Lost.

SE'LA. SELAH (*the rock*). Petra. See EDOM, SEIR.

SE'LA-HAM-MAH'LEKOTH (*the cliff of divisions*). In the wilderness of Maon. Where David escaped from Saul (1 Sam. xxiii. 28). Lost.

SE'LAH. Pause. This word occurs 72 times in the Psalms, and 3 times in Habbakuk, and has given much trouble to translators; but it is now thought to mean a musical pause; when the choir rested, while the instruments played an interlude.

SE'LED (*exultation*). Son of Nadab (1 Chr. ii. 30).

SELEMI'A. An assistant of Ezra (2 Esd. xiv. 24).

SELAMI'AS. SHELEMIAH 1 (1 Esd. ix. 34).

SELEU'CIA. The seaport of Antioch in Syria. On the sea, near the mouth of the river Orontes. Paul (and Barnabas) sailed from here on his first journey (Acts xiii. 4), and probably landed there on his return (xiv. 26). Named after the first Seleucus, who built the fort and made the harbor, and was buried here, B. C. 175. It was a free city in Paul's time (Pliny, v. 18). The remains of the ancient works are still sound, and in use, especially the two piers of the harbor called Paul and Barnabas.

SELEU'CUS IV, PHILOP'ATOR (*loving his father*). King of ASIA (2 Macc. iii. 3), son and successor of ANTIOCHUS THE GREAT. After his father's death he ascended the throne. He was murdered after a reign of twelve years, B. C. 175, by HELIODORUS (Dan. xi. 20). His son gained the crown in 162 B. C. (1 Macc. vii. 1; 2 Macc. xiv. 1).

SEM. SHEM the patriarch (Luke iii. 36).

SEMACHI'AH (*Jah sustains*). Son of SHEMAIAH 9 (1 Chr. xxvi. 7).

SEM'EI. 1. SHIMEI 14 (1 Esd. ix. 32).—2. SHIMEI 16 (Esth. xi. 2).—3. Father of Mattathias, in the genealogy of Jesus (Luke iii. 26).

SEMEL'LIUS. SHIMSHAI (1 Esd. ii. 16, 17, 25, 30).

SE'MIS. SHIMEI 13 (1 Esd. ix. 23).

SEMIT'IC. SHEM. LANGUAGES. SHEMITIC.

SENA'AH (*thorny*). The "children of Senaah" were among the "people of Israel" who returned from captivity (Ezr. ii. 35; Neh. vii. 38).

SEN'ATE (Gr. *gerousia, the elders*), (Acts v. 21). ELDER.

SEN'EH (*thorn*), (1 Sam. xiv. 4). The south rock at the pass of Michmash, memorable in connection with the adventure of Jonathan and his armor-bearer.

SENIR' (*a coat of mail*). The Amorite name of MT. HERMON (1 Chr. v. 23; Ez. xxvii. 5; Deut. iii. 9); should be written without the "h," and also in Cant. iv. 8.

SENNACH'ERIB (Heb. TSIN–AKKI–IRIB, *the moon increases, brothers*). King of Assyria. He mounted the throne B. C. 702. In the fourteenth year of Hezekiah he attacked the fenced cities of Judah, and took them (2 K. xviii. 13–16) after having successfully made various war expeditions. He attacked Babylon B. C. 699, and then made a second invasion into Palestine Hezekiah had sought the protection of Egypt, upon which Sennacherib marched into Egypt and sent proposals to Hezekiah (2 K. ix. 7). Hezekiah not submitting, caused the king of Assyria to send him a

etc., at Koyunjik, and Khorsabad, record his exploits, and refer to the Hebrew nation as fallen from its proud station in the time of David and Solomon. The vessels drawn on the walls as trophies are of fine design, and it seems probable that they were from the Temple. The bas-relief on the rocks at Nahvel Kelb (Dog River), N. of Beirut, shows the king in the midst of six other kings, with a long inscription, in wedge-shaped characters, recording his exploits in Syria and Phœnicia. There are, also, inscriptions in Persian, Greek, Latin, and Arabic. On the monuments the amount of the tribute (2 K. xviii. 13–16), is stated differently from the amount in Kings; giving 800 talents of silver for the 300 talents in Kings. The probability is, that 800 talents was the value of the whole tribute, including the gold. There is in the British Musuem a clay impression from this king's seal. His attack on Lachish (see LACHISH) is, also, recorded in pictures and inscriptions. (See p. 175.) The iii. iv. and v. chapters of Isaiah, are most wonderfully fulfilled on the Assyrian monuments; where Jews appear as doing the work of horses, drawing the king's chariot, or carts and boats, loaded with sculptures. See the BLACK OBELISK, p. 220.

SEN'UAH (properly HASSENUAH, *bristling*). Father of Judah (Neh. xi. 9), who was over the second city.

SEO'RIM (*barley*). Chief of the fourth course of priests in David's time (1 Chr. xiv. 8).

SE'PHAR (Gen. x. 30). A mount in the East. Now called ZAFAR, an ancient seaport town in Yemen, in the province of Hadramawt (*Hazarmaveth*), Arabia, between Oman and Mirbat, on the shore of the Indian Ocean, at the foot of a lofty mountain. Frankincense is only found on the mountain of Zafar. It was the capital of the Himyerite kings. There was a Christian church there in A. D. 343

TYRE.

threatening written message. Whilst Sennacherib was awaiting the result his camp received a divine visitation, by which, in one night, one hundred and eighty-five thousand of his men were destroyed (2 K. xviii. 13), at which the king fled to his capital. He reigned for twenty-two years. He appears to have been the first king who fixed the seat of government permanently at Nineveh, which he adorned. Of his closing life we read in 2 K. xix. 37; Is. xxxvii. 38. The monuments, palaces,

SEPHA'RAD (Obad. v. 20). Where the Jews of Jerusalem were held captive. Most probably IONIA is meant.

SEPHARVA'IM (2 K. xix. 13; Is. xxxvii. 13; 2 K. xvii. 24). A city of Assyria, from which people were brought to repeople Samaria. Now SIPPARA, on the Euphrates, above Babylon (Ptol. v. 18). A tradition affirms that Noah buried near this city the records of the antediluvian world. It was a great seat of learning. The sun was the chief object of worship, and they burnt their children in the fire to Adramelech and Anamelech, the male and female powers of the sun (2 K. xvii. 31), which pagan worship they carried with them to Samaria.

SEPHAR'VITES. People from SEPHARVAIM.

SEPH'ELA. Greek form of the Hebrew HAS SHEFELAH, the ancient name for the plains between the hills of Samaria and Judæa and the Mediterranean Sea. Its northern part is called SHARON (Deut. i. 7; Josh. ix. 1, and in many other passages). Between Ekron and Gaza there were 47 cities besides their villages. It is one of the most productive districts of Palestine, and yearly produces fine crops of grain and fruit. It was anciently the grain-producing district, and was the subject of constant contention between the Israelites and Philistines.

SEP'TUAGINT (L. *septuaginta, the seventy*.) The most ancient Greek version of the O. T. See HISTORY OF THE BOOKS. So named from the sacred idea attached to the number 70.

SEP'ULCHRE (*a burial-place or tomb*). See TOMB.

SE'RAH (*abundance*). Daugnter of Asher (Gen. xlvi. 17).

SERAI'AH. The name of persons alluded to in the following passages: 2 Sam. viii. 17; 2 K. xxv. 18; Ezr. vii. 1; Jer. xxxvi. 26; xl. 8, li. 59. The last is termed "a quiet prince." He bore to the Jews a message from Jeremiah.

SER'APHIM (*burning ones*, or *angels of fire*). Two beings, each with 6 wings, seen by Isaiah in a vision (Is. vi. 2, 3).

SE'RED (*fear*). First-born of ZEBULUN, and ancestor of the SARDITES (Gen. xlvi. 14).

SER'GIUS PAU'LUS. Governor of the isle of Cyprus. He was converted under the teachings of Paul, A. D. 48 (Acts xiii. 7).

SER'JEANT (Gr. *rhabdouchos, a rod-holder*). An officer who attends on Roman magistrates of the higher class, and executes their orders (Acts xvi. 35, 38).

SE'RON. A general of Antiochus Epiphanes, defeated by Judas Maccabæus, B. C. 166 (1 Macc. iii., xiii. 24).

SER'PENT (Heb. NAHASH, any serpent, but especially the cobra). The serpent is alluded to in many passages in the Bible, and nearly always for its typical qualities, or habits, as intensifying similar things in the human family. Satan is called "The Old Serpent" (Rev. xii. 9; 2 Cor. xi. 1). See ADDER, ZAHAL, TANNIN, SARAF; Gr. *herpeton, ophis.* EPHEH, (*hisser*). A poisonous snake, about a foot long, called, by the Arabs, *el effah* (Gr. *echidna*). The viper that fastened on Paul's hand, in Malta (Acts xxviii. 3), and was either the common viper (*pelias veras*), or the *vipera aspis*—both found in the island. The Scriptural allusions are: To its subtilty (Gen. iii. 1); wisdom (Matt. x. 16); poison (Ps. lviii. 4; Prov. xxiii. 32); its forked, sharp, tongue (Ps. cxl. 3; Job. xx. 16); the bite (Num. xxi. 9); sly concealment, in hedges (Eccl. x. 8), in holes (Amos v. 19); living in dry, sandy places (Deut. viii. 15); crawling (Prov. xxx. 19); their birth alive (Is. lix. 5—"cockatrice"). The art of taming, or charming, is of great antiquity, and is alluded to in the Psalms lviii. 5; Eccles. x. 11; Jer. viii. 17, and, perhaps, James iii. 7. The Orientals believe the serpent to have a large share of sagacity, and they cite various reasons for it. They have, in all ages, been used as emblems of cunning and craftiness. There are two erroneous notions

that are popular regarding the serpent before the Fall, which are: 1. That they moved in an erect attitude, and 2. That they fed on dust. There is no reason to believe that the animal has been changed in form or habit; but it was set apart as a form to be hated, and avoided, with fear and disgust. And the eating of dust is only an accident, following wherever an animal eats its food from the ground. The expression means to do any dirty or dishonorable act; or also to speak offensive words. The serpent has been worshiped by several nations —as Phœnicians, Hindus, Chinese—as a beneficent

ASSYRIAN KING.

genius, of superior wisdom and power. The Egyptians used its form to represent KNEF, the author of all good, and also the god TYPHON, the author of all physical and moral evil; and in their symbolical alphabet the serpent stood for subtility, cunning, lust, sensual pleasure. The serpent coiled around a globe, winged, is a familiar emblem of eternity.

The Greeks used it as a sign of certain attributes in Ceres, Mercury, Æsculapius, in their best qualities, and in the terrible Furies, and the fearful monster, the Python, which was only destroyed by Apollo's arrows; and also as the legs of the impious giants who despise and blaspheme the power of heaven.

In Hindo mythology Krishna (the good spirit) contends with a serpent, and finally crushes his head.

The *fiery* serpents of Num. xxi. 6, 8, were so named from the burning sensation caused by their bite, or it may possibly also refer to their brilliant color. There is a small black snake, spotted with white, in the desert, whose bite is quickly fatal, causing great swelling of the body.

The Egyptians painted and sculptured monstrous serpents with wings, which may have been idealized from lizards.

BRAZEN SERPENT. The scene of the events was either Zalmonah or Punon; Zalmonah meaning the image's position, and Punon the origin of the material from which it was made, Punon the copper mines.

To some critics the brazen serpent is only the sign of the camp hospital—it really was the sign of the Great Physician. The serpent rod of Æsculapius was also a symbol of the supposed healing power of the god. It is difficult to account for the making of the image of the serpent, in the face of the 2d commandment; and yet it was probably made by the appointed artizan of the Tabernacle, Bezaleel or Aholiab. That it was a type of Christ does not explain how it acted as a healer at the time, because the faith in the Messiah never became a present reality, but was rather a future good to be expected. It has been interpreted as a symbol of wisdom, which left to itself leads the soul astray, but when guided by divine law, is the source of all healing, the serpent form would, in that light, be the symbol of health and deliverance.

The rod of Moses, that turned to a serpent, was a symbol to him of divine wisdom.

The brazen serpent was kept a long time after its proper work was done, and became an object of idolatry, in the reign of Hezekiah, who destroyed it (NEHUSHTAN).

The Church of St. Ambrose, Milan, has boasted of having the identical brazen image which Moses had made in the Wilderness, and which Hezekiah destroyed. It was probably the object of worship of some ancient serpent worshipers.

SMYRNA.

SERPENT CHARMING. From the earliest times in the East certain persons have exercised a remarkable power over poisonous snakes, and this is noticed in James iii. 7. The horned cerastes, and the hooded snakes are the kinds usually handled. They do not always take out the poison fangs. The secret of the power seems to be the simple courage and confidence of the men. They use shrill flutes and drums, which seem to attract the attention of the serpents.

SE'RUG (branch). Son of Reu, ancestor of Abraham (Gen. xi. 20–23). Jewish tradition says he was the first Idolater (Josh. xxiv. 2).

SER'VANT. 1. Heb. ENOSH, "man" (1 Sam. xxiv. 7).—2. Heb. NAAR (Num. xxii. 22), boy, lad, young man (Gen. xiv. 24).—3. Heb. MESHARETH, to wait on, serve (Ex. xxxiii. 11).—4. Heb.

EBED; found in the O. T. 800 times, and usually rendered servant, sometimes man-servant (Gen. ix. 25–27). This word often denotes a man who dedicates himself voluntarily to the service of another. Thus, Joshua was the servant of Moses. The servants of God are those who are devoted to His service. The word usually means in the Bible a hired servant, or one whose service was the property of his master. The households of the early patriarchs contained many servants, who were treated with kindness, justice, and they were trusted and confided in (Gen. xiv. 11–16). They shared the religious privileges of the family (Gen. xvii. 9–13), and were not transferred to other masters.

SE'SIS. SHASHAI (1 Esd. ix. 34).

SES'THEL. BEZALEEL, of the sons of Pahath-Moab (1 Esd. ix. 31).

SETH. First son of Adam after the death of Abel (Gen. iv. 25, 26).

SE'THUR (hidden). A spy and son of Michael (Num. xiii. 13).

SET'TLE (Heb. AZARAH), (Ez. xliii. 14). A port settled or sunk lower. Elsewhere "Court" in 2 Chr. iv. 9. Ledge in Fairbairn.

SEV'EN. See NUMBER.

SEVEN CHURCHES OF ASIA (Rev. i. 4). 1. EPH'ESUS was originally called Smyrna; and the orator Callinus, in an address to Jupiter, called the people Smyrnæans (Strabo xiv. 1, 4). Scattered over the site of Ephesus are now only heaps of shapeless ruins. The great Greek temples, in Athens, have come down to us so well preserved, although mutilated and ruined, that they are the admiration of the civilized world. But here, at the site of the temple which was the pride of all Asia, and one of the wonders of the world, we look in vain for even a relic of the multitude of columns; for they have been "removed," as well as the Christian Church. The most probable site is supposed to be that on which the artist stood to sketch for this picture, where the swamp fills the spaces among the piles of crumbling stones. The proudest title of an Ephesian was "a temple-sweeper" of the goddess Diana (NEOKOROS on the coins). The temple itself has been swept away. Its decay began in the 3d century, when Trajan sent the gates to Constantinople.

The Diana-worship was a mass of Oriental superstitions, weaving into itself magic, charms, amulets and the pretense of special miracles. The image of the tutelary divinity was of a great hight, carved in ebony wood, representing a woman with a great many full breasts, ending below in a pedestal ornamented with figures of lions, cows and stags; the whole decorated with gold and silver. The head was turreted, like that of Cybelè (see page 130); the moon was symbolized behind the head; on her bosom were the Zodiacal signs of the bulls, twins and crab, with two garlands below them of flowers and acorns. Her priests were women and eunuchs (Melissai and Megabyzi), with a high-priest (Esseen). There were no bloody sacrifices. Its image was adopted for use in private families, where it was more honored than any other, being carried into distant places. Games were celebrated at regular intervals in honor of the goddess, especially in May (the month of Diana), which attracted vast crowds of pilgrims, and gathered wealth from many countries.

The theatre of Ephesus is the only relic that is preserved so as to be recognizable. It is one of the largest in the world, ranking with the Coliseum of Rome and the theatre of El Djem, in Africa.

In 1869, J. T. Wood found what is supposed to be the monument (or part of it) of the tomb of Luke, on which there is a cross and a bull finely chiseled. About two miles N. of Ephesus, in Aisalik, is the great mosque, which was once the Church of St. John (rebuilt, on its original site, by Justinian); a peculiar building, having in it many carved marble slabs, with Arabic inscriptions, and four monolith granite columns, each four feet in diameter, which are supposed to have been in Diana's temple. (See EPHESUS).

2. SMYR′NA, the second of the "seven," is, unlike Ephesus, but once mentioned in the Scriptures; and yet that was an apocalyptic position which was given it in the apocalyptic message (Rev. ii. 8–11). It rejoiced in the proud title, "The Ornament of

temples generally built into walls as raw material. The citadel on the hight behind the town (Mt. Pagus), is built of the ruins of the ancient structure, whose massive foundations may still be traced. The theatre, in which Polycarp (who was bishop over the Church for seventy-four years), was burnt, was on the brow of the hill toward the sea; and it has almost entirely disappeared, except a few seats and the dens in which the wild beasts were kept. The ancient port was filled up by Taimour-Lang during his siege (A. D. 1400). The modern bay or harbor is about 33 ms. long, 15 ms. wide, and sheltered by high, steep, wooded hills on three sides; and the water is deep to the very shores, so that vessels may lie close to receive or discharge their cargoes. The "Two Brothers" (mountains near the head of the gulf) are 3,000 feet high, and are the weather-guage of the vicinity, giving the signal by their white-cloud cap.

The city is famous for its ample supply of fruit, vegetables, and its excellent wine. The suburbs

THYATIRA.

Asia." The great prosperity of the ancient city was the result of its policy in following the fortunes and securing the favor of each conqueror, in turn, who overran Asia. This was the reason why they gave to Antiochus the title "God and Saviour," and to his mother that of "Venus of Victory," and worshiped Tiberius, and stamped the head of Mithridates on their coins, and erected temples in honor of deified Rome. But the peculiar worship of the city was of the god Bacchus, the mysteries of which were solemnized with great pomp. Apollo was also honored; and there is a colossal head, in marble, now near the western gate of the city, which once crowned a statue of the god. The walls of the buildings in the upper part of the city are filled with fragments of columns, cornices, entablatures, and even busts, some of which were portraits of men or the ideals of the gods, built in with the common stone as so much rough material. The Turks have mutilated the features of these busts because of their hatred of images. It has been well said that the Moslem horror of all representations of the human form as idolatrous, has destroyed more Grecian statues than are now known to exist. There are many remains of the beautiful tesselated pavements of the ancient

are occupied by the summer residences of the merchants and the wealthy classes, whose fine gardens, shady groves, and fragrant orchards, are watered by many canals and branches of the river Meles. Population about 160,000; about one half of whom are Christians of the Greek rite. The mission here has succeeded in calling a studious attention to the Bible among both the Greeks and Armenians. 3 lines of railway have been built: 1 leading to Ephesus and Tralles (Aidin), 80 ms.; and another to Magnesia and Kassaba, 60 ms; and the third to the suburb of Bournabat, 6 ms., where there are many country-houses, which are also scattered along the sea-coast, N. W. and S. Not far from Smyrna, at Kara Bell, is the sculpture mentioned by Herodotus (ii. 106), cut in a panel in the limestone rock, perpendicular, and about 7 ft. high. It is an Egyptian figure, in profile, looking east, holding a spear in the left hand, and a bow in the right, with inscriptions in hieroglyphics near, and across the breast this one: "I conquered this country by the might of my arms." (See Daniel xi., and Van Lennep's *Asia Minor*.)

3. PER′GAMOS (correctly, Pergamum). This was the third Church addressed by the author of the Apocalypse; and it was commended for its fidelity

and firmness, in the midst of persecutions, in a city so eminently given to idolatry. It was the capital of a district of the same name, in Mysia, on the river Caicus, 20 ms. from the sea, and 60 from Smyrna. Its origin is lost in antiquity, dating beyond the Trojan war, when Pergamos, son of Pyrrhus, found King Arius here, and deposed him. The city was built on the lower slopes of two high and steep mountains. Eumenes founded the race of the Attalian kings of Pergamos, 200 yrs. B. C.; and his successors formed a large library, which rivaled the Alexandrian, besides making the city the equal of, or superior in importance to, all others in Asia Minor. Sheep and goat-skins were here first made into parchment (*pergamena*), and it is still the chief manufacture of the city. The library was removed to Alexandria by Cleopatra, to whom Antony gave the permission. The ruins of temples, a theatre, stadium, amphitheatre, and other buildings, are scattered over the ancient site. The great glory of the city was the grove Nicephorium—said to have been extremely beautiful—containing temples and statues of all the deities: Zeus, Athena (Minerva), Apollo, Æsculapius (its tutelary deity),

PTOLEMAIS.

ty), Dionysius, and Aphrodite. Pergamos had no rival in splendor, being a union of a cathedral city, a university town, and a royal residence. The Roman Senate recognized the right of sanctuary in the Grove of Æsculapius, which (with the others) was irrigated by many canals from the Caicus, and made very luxuriant in shade and fruit trees. It is called *Neokora* (*New City*) on the coins. This was probably the "throne of Satan," referred to by John (Rev. ii. 13); the idea having arisen from the title of *Soter*, which was given to Æsculapius on account of the *serpent* being his chief emblem (found on several coins of Pergamos), and also because charms and magic were a part of the worship. Nearly all of the pagan temples, and Christian churches (some of which were remodeled temples), are heaped alike in ruins. Their columns, capitals, cornices, and sculptures, of fine marble, have been carried away to rebuild other places, or burned into lime for mortar, or lie in heaps waiting such an inglorious end. The church of St. John (anciently a temple) is roofless, but still standing; and that of St. Sophia is remodeled into a mosque. The Acropolis (see cut on page 22) was the site of the temple of Minerva, built on an artificial platform, raised like that of Solomon's at Jerusalem. Some of the beautiful white-marble columns of this temple measure 4 ft. in diameter, and 40 feet long, as they lie prostrate. Half-way down the hill was the palace of the Attalian kings,

connected with the town by an aqueduct, which now crosses the river on its ancient and perfect masonry, the river Selinus passing under it through a double tunnel, 600 ft. long, each arch being 40 ft. wide and 20 high. Besides this work there are 5 ancient bridges. There are very perfect remains of theatres, and a vast Roman amphitheatre, in which Antipas was made the first martyr of Pergamos, followed by a long line. The present population of *Bergamah* is 30,000, only 4,000 of whom are Greek and Armenian Christians, the others being Moslems.

4. THYATIRA. On the river Lycus, N. E. of Smyrna 60 ms. It has been known as Pelopia, Semiramis, Euhippa, (Pliny), and is now called Ak Hissar (*white castle*). Apollo was worshiped under the name of Tyrimnas (a Macedonian king), also Artemis; and, besides these, there were several other gods. There was a curious worship of a certain Sambatha, a Chaldæan (or Jewish Sibyl; said to have been brought there by the Jews, and which is referred to in Rev. ii. 20, etc., under the name of Jezebel. Rome was also deified, as also Hadrian (see Coins, on pps. 29, 256), and other emperors. Games were celebrated in honor of Tyrimnas, Hercules, and of the ruling emperor. On the coins there are stamped the heads of Bacchus, Athene, Cybelè, and the emperors. There are many remains of antiquity, such as marble sculptures, generally in fragments built into modern walls, or used as troughs or well-covers, and a church of St. John, which was originally a pagan temple, and is now a mosque, with a tall minaret. Inscriptions are found which give an account of many corporate societies of different trades—bakers, potters, weavers, robe makers, and dyers, of which last Antonius Claudius Alphenus was at one time the honored leader, and of which Lydia, whom Paul met in Philippi, was a member. The distant view of the city is very beautiful, but, inside of the limits, there is little order, and less neatness. 2,000 houses pay taxes, and 500 hovels are exempt, sheltering, altogether, about 15,000 people. The railway from Smyrna now reaches Magnesia (30 ms. distant), and is to be continued to Thyatira, and perhaps beyond.

5. SAR'DIS. The capital of the ancient Lydia (which Homer called Mœonia), once "The Queen of Asia," was the famous valley of the classic Hermus, 2 ms. S. of the river, at the foot of Mt. Tmolus, on the river Pactolus. Its first king of whom we have a record was Candaules (716 B. C.); and the last was the renowned Crœsus, who enriched himself and the city by the golden sands of the Pactolus. But the real wealth of the city was derived from its commerce and manufactures (see SARDIS, on page 268). The invention of the art of dyeing, and of the system of trading in shops, is credited to it. (See Coin, p. 125). Not many years ago there were 6, and there are still standing 2, of the pillars of the temple of Cybele (60 ft. high), which are the oldest Greek monuments in the world, having been set up about 300 yrs. after Solomon's temple; the other 4 were made into lime by the Turks. The eminent author Melito was bishop of Sardis, in the 2d century; and the oldest catalogue of the books of the O. T. by any Christian writer, that has come down to us, was by his hand. The Council of Sardis was convened in 347, from a rule of which the Pope of Rome claims

his earliest authority; which was, that in case a bishop was deposed by the council, he might appeal to the bishop of Rome. (4th canon).

Julian the Apostate closed the churches and reopened the temples in Sardis in his endeavor to reestablish Pagan worship, A. D. 360.

The cemetery of the ancient kings of Lydia (of the dynasty of Crœsus) is on the top of a high plateau, 6 ms. north of Sardis, where there are mounds extending over a vast area. The monument of Alyattes, the father of Crœsus, so minutely described by Herodotus (i. 93), is still quite perfect. It is 3800 feet around and 1300 feet long, rising 300 feet above the plain. It has never been disturbed, and is supposed to contain many treasures valuable to the antiquary, illustrating the customs of a people whose civilization dates long before that of Greece, and second only to Egypt and Assyria.

Xerxes gathered his great army at Sardis when he marched to invade Greece by way of the Hellespont. Cyrus the Younger beautified the vicinity by making some fine gardens. Alexander left his general Pausanias here, and ordered the erection of a temple to Jupiter.

6. PHILADEL'PHIA was founded and named by Attalus Philadelphus, B. C. 140, as a mart for the great wine district, which is celebrated by Virgil. It is on the little river Cogamus, which joins the Hermus near Sardis, surrounded almost by an amphitheatre of hills, and bowered in orchards, in the midst of extensive gardens. The rock is basaltic, and streams of lava may be traced in several tracts, but covered by deep, black, rich soil. The great staple is opium, which is entirely monopolized by the government. Herodotus says the sugar-cane was anciently cultivated, and mentions a confection which was made of tamarisk and wheat, which is to-day the favorite sweetmeat of Philadelphia (called *halva*), after a continuance of over 2000 years. When Xerxes was on his way to Greece he rested under a great plane-tree near the city, and so much admired its beauty that he appointed a keeper for it, and adorned it with golden ornaments. Plane-trees still flourish here which surpass all others in the country.

Philadelphia was included in the message with Smyrna as deserving approbation and encouragement; and these two only out of the seven cities have continued to our day, and now possess a material prosperity somewhat equal to their ancient importance.

The present name is *Allah Shehr* (*city of God, or High town*). The site is a hill, with four flat summits, from which the view is very fine. The valley of the Hermus is here one of the most beautiful and extensive in Asia. There are fifteen churches in use, and about twenty in ruins. Of the ancient cathedral of St. John, all that is left are a few massive pilasters, which are shown in the engraving, towering above the modern buildings, and these are built up from fragments of more ancient pagan temples.

There are 15,000 people, one-third of whom are Greek Christians, who have a bishop, enjoy the free exercise of their religion in church, in processions in the streets, in the use of church bells (nowhere else allowed in the interior of Asia Minor), and their chief glory is in the honorable mention of their church in the Revelation.

7. LAODICE'A, an ancient city on the Lycus, in the valley of the Meander, forty miles east of Ephesus. Its site was on seven hills, which were drained by two brooks, the Asopus and Caprus. The ruins are of a stadium, in very complete preservation, three theatres (one of which was 450 feet in diameter), bridges, aqueducts, and a gymnasium, which testify to its ancient wealth and importance. Its original name was Diospolis (the city of Jupiter), which was changed to Rhoas, under which title it became the largest city in

Phrygia (Pliny). Antiochus II gave it the na me of his wife Laŏdīce.

The imagery in Rev. ii. 18, was suggested by the images of Apollo, the sun-god, on the coins. Sambatha had a fane there also (see THYATIRA). The emperors were also deified, especially Hadrian.

It became the seat of an archbishop, and in its cathedral church were gathered several councils; in one of which, a system of supplying the villages or small societies in the interior with church services by itinerating presbyters, was adopted (somewhat similar to the Methodist plan now in use), under the direction of the bishop of Laodicea. Here also was adopted a rule "that Christians should not Judaize by resting on the seventh day, but to work on it as usual, and rest on the Lord's day as far as possible, like Christians."

The city was utterly destroyed A. D. 1230, since when it has lain in shapeless ruins, only visited for its marble and other materials.

The aqueduct (which supplied the city, and is now almost perfect), which conveyed water *down* one hill, across the plain, and *up* another, in *stone pipes*, proves the Romans to have been acquainted with the hydrostatic law of water finding its level. The stone pipes have a diameter of two feet, and are fitted into each other at the ends, and the calcareous deposit from the water has incrusted them, forming almost a continuous pipe without a visible joint.

The seats in the stadium have letters and numbers, their owners' or the keeper's marks.

A recent visitor found a number of workmen sawing up the richly sculptured entablature of the ancient theatre, having been busy there for six years, cutting up the marble. Near them was a colossal statue, sawn into several pieces. In this manner have disappeared, during the past twenty years, two agate pillars, 18 inches in diameter; a great number of composite richly sculptured columns, adorned with busts and heads in relief, and vases with wreaths of leaves and fruits, and statues and busts and architectural ornaments without number (the tribute the art-world pays to Mohammed).

COLOSSÆ is about ten miles east from Laodicea, near the village of *Chonas*, but is without any interesting ruins, although it was an important city in the time of the expedition of Xerxes. (See view on page 62). Hierapolis has lately afforded a fine proof of the truth of an account of Strabo (xiii. iv. 14), who speaks of a deadly vapor (carbonic acid gas?) which killed any animal that approached the place. The experiment was tried by Svoboda recently on two fowls, and resulted fatally to both in a few seconds.

SEV'EN STARS, THE. See ASTRONOMY.

SEV'ENEH. SYENE (Ez. xxix. 10).

SEV'ENTY, THE. 1. The seventy disciples of Jesus sent out (Luke x. 17).—2. Is also used to denote the Septuagint.

SEXTA'RIUS (Gr. *xestes*). Nearly one pint English (Mark vii. 4). WEIGHTS, etc.

SHAAL'ABBIN (Josh. xix. 42). Dan, near Ajalon, probably the same as SHA'ALBIM (*city of foxes*), (Judg. i.). Now *Esalin*, near *Surâ*, (ZORAH). Eliahba was one of David's 37 heroes (2 Sam. xxiii. 32), and is called THE SHAALBONITE,

SHAAL'BONITE THE. One of David's 37 heroes (2 Sam. xxiii. 32), a native of Shaalbon.

SHA'APH (*division*). 1. Son of Jahdai (1 Chr. ii. 47).—2. Son of Caleb 1 (ii. 49).

SHAARA'IM (*two gateways*). Judah, in the Shefelah (Josh. xv. 36). On the way to Gath (1 Sam. xvii. 52), where the Philistines fled after Goliath's death, which was in the *Wady Sumt*.

SHAASH'GAZ (*beauty's servant*). Eunuch in charge of the women in Ahasuerus' Palace (Esth. ii. 14).

SHAB'BETHAI (*Sabbath-born*). 1. A Levite who assisted Ezra (Ezr. x. 15), and apparently the same who was with Jeshua (Neh. viii. 7).—2. A chief (xi. 16).

SHACHI'A (Heb. SHACHEYAH, *accusation*). Son of Shaharaim (1 Chr. viii. 10).

SHAD'DAI (Heb. SHADDAY). The Almighty. See JAH.

SHA'DRACH (*circuit of the sun*). The Chaldee name of Hananiah 7, one of the three friends of Daniel delivered from the burning furnace (Dan. i. 3). He was promoted to a high office after the appointment of Daniel as ruler of the province of Babylon. In refusing to worship the idols of Nebuchadnezzar, Shadrach, with Meshach and Abednego, were thrown into a furnace (Dan. iii.).

SHA'GE (*erring*). Father of Jonathan (1 Chr. xi. 34).

SHAHARA'IM (*the two dawns*). See 1 Chr. viii. 8. It has been proposed to remove the period from the end of verse 7, and read thus, "and Gera begat Uzza, Ahihud, and Shaharaim," etc.

SHAHAZI'MAH (*hights*). Issachar, between Tabor and the Jordan (Josh. xix. 22).

SHA'LEM (Gen. xxxiii. 18). The opinion seems to be that the text ought to read "Jacob came *safe* to the city of Shechem." If a proper name is meant, there is a place ready for it in the modern Salim. See ÆNON.

SHA'LIM, THE LAND OF. Benjamin. Between the "land of Shalisha," and the "land of Yemini," through which Saul passed on the way after his father's asses. Probably the land of *Shual*, 6 ms. north of Michmash (1 Sam. ix. 4).

SHAL'ISHA, THE LAND OF (1 Sam. ix. 4). Between Mt. Ephraim and the land of Shalim. Lost.

SHALLECH'ETH, THE GATE (*falling* or *casting down*). One of the gates of the house of Jehovah; now supposed to be the Bab. Silsileh, which enters the Haram wall 600 feet from the S. W. corner.

SHAL'LUM (*retribution*). 1. Son of Jabesh who killed Zachariah I, king of Israel, and usurped his kingdom, B. C. 772 (2 K. xv. 10–15).—2. See JEHOAHAZ 2.—3. The husband of Huldah, the prophetess (2 K. xxii. 14). Others of this name are alluded to in Num. xxvi. 49; 1 Chr. ii. 40, ix. 17, 19, 31; Ezr. ii. 42, vii. 2, x. 24, 42; Neh. iii. 12, vii. 45.

SHAL'LUN. Son of Col-hozeh. He was ruler of a district and repaired the fountain-gate and the wall (Neh. iii. 15).

SHAL'MAI (*my thanks*). Ancestor of Nethinim, who returned from captivity (Ezr. ii. 46).

SHAL'MAN. Shalmaneser, king of Assyria (Hos. x. 14).

SHALMANE'SER (*reverential toward fire*). King of Assyria. He ascended the throne, B. C. 730 (2 K. xvii. 3). He compelled Hoshea to pay tribute two years, but when he joined with So, king of Egypt, in rebellion, the Assyrian came again and took Samaria after a siege of three years, and carried Hoshea captive beyond the Euphrates, ending the kingdom of Israel. See ISRAEL and the BLACK OBELISK, page 220. He conquered Phœnicia, except the island part of the city of Tyre, which he besieged for five years in vain.

SHA'MA (*hearing*). Son of Hothan of Aroer (1 Chr. xi. 44). An assistant of David.

SHAMARI'AH. Son of Rehoboam (2 Chr. xi. 19).

SHAM'BLES (Gr. *makellon*). A meat market, or place for the sale of provisions (1 Cor. x. 25).

SHA'MED (*persecution*). Son of Elpaal (1 Chr. viii. 12).

SHA'MER. 1. A Levite (1 Chr. vi. 46).—2. Son of Heber (vii. 34).

SHAM'GAR (*cup-bearer*). Son of Anath, third Judge of Israel. It is recorded that he killed 600 Philistines with an ox-goad (Judg. iii. 31, v. 6).

SHAM'HUTH (*waste*). Captain in David's army (1 Chr. xxvii. 8).

SHA'MIR (*a thorn*), (Josh. xv. 48). In the mts. of Judah, S. of Hebron, near Jattir. Lost.—2. In Mt. Ephraim, the residence and burial-place of Tola, the judge (Judg. x. 1, 2). Supposed to be SAMMUR, a ruin 10 ms. N. E. of Shechem, on the edge of the Jordan valley.

SHA'MIR (*tried*). Son of Micah (1 Chr. xxiv. 24).

SHAM'MA (*desolation*). Son of Zophar (1 Chr. vii. 37).

SHAM'MAH. 1. One of the 3 chiefs of David's 30 heroes (2 Sam. xxiii. 11–17).—2. Brother of David (1 Sam. xvi. 9). Others of this name are mentioned in Gen. xxxvi. 13; 2 Sam. xxiii. 25, 33; 1 Chr. xi. 27, xxvii. 8.

SHAM'MAI (*desolated*). 1. Son of Onam, and brother of Jada (1 Chr. ii. 28, 32).—2. Son of Rekem (1 Chr. ii. 44, 45).—3. Brother of Miriam and Ishbah (1 Chr. iv. 17).

SHAM'MOTH (*desolations*). One of David's men (1 Chr. xi. 27).

SHAMMU'A. 1. Son of Zaccur (Num. xiii. 4).—2. Son of David by Bath-sheba (1 Chr. xiv. 4).—3. Father of Abda (Neh. xi. 17).—4. One of the priestly family of Bilgah (xii. 18).

SHAMMU'AH. Son of David (2 Sam. v. 14).

SHAM'SHERAI. Son of Jeroham (1 Chr. viii. 26).

SHA'PHAM (*cold*). A Gadite of Bashan (1 Chr. v. 12).

SHA'PHAN (*coney*). 1. Secretary of King Josiah, son of Azaliah (2 K. xxii. 3).—2. Father of Ahikam (2 K. xxiii. 12).

SHA'PHAT (*judge*). 1. Son of Hori (Num. xiii. 5).—2. Father of the prophet ELISHA (1 K. xix. 16, 19).—3. Son of Shemaiah, in the line of Judah (1 Chr. iii. 22.)—4. A Gadite (v. 12).—5. Son of Adlai (xxvii. 29). Keeper of David's oxen.

SHA'PHER, MT. (*mt. of pleasantness*), (Num. xxxiii. 23). A desert station. Lost.

SHA'RAI (*Jah frees him*). Son of Bani (Ezr. x. 40).

SHA'RAIM. SHAARAIM (Josh. xv. 36).

SHA'RAR (*twist*). Father of Ahiam (2 Sam. xxiii. 33). SACAR.

SHARE'ZER (*prince of fire*). Son and murderer of SENNACHERIB (2 K. xix. 37). ADRAMMELECH 2. 1. Son of Sennacherib, who assisted in killing his father (Is. xxxvii. 38).—2. A delegate sent to Jerusalem with Regemmelech and others soon after the return from captivity (Zech. vii. 2, viii. 19).

SHA'RON (Heb. HAS SHARON, *straight* or *even*). A broad, rich tract of land lying between the hills of Judæa and Samaria and the sea, and the northern part of the Shefelah. It was a place of pasture (1 Chr. xxvii. 29); beautiful as Carmel (Is. xxxv. 2). It was a simile for loveliness (Cant. ii. 1). The forest of Sharon was the scene of one of the most romantic exploits of Richard, the Crusader (*Michaud*, viii.). The Sharon of 1 Chr. v. 16 is supposed to have been on the east side of Jordan, in Gilead, but it has not been identified.

SHA'RONITE, THE. One from SHARON. Shitrai had charge of the royal herds (1 Chr. xxvii. 20).

SHARU'HEN (Josh. xix. 16). Given to Simeon. Tell Sheriah, in the Wady Sheriah, 10 miles west of Beersheba, may be the site.

SHA'SHAI (*whitish*). Son of Bani (Ezr. x. 40).

SHA'SHAK (*eagerness*). Son of Beriah (1 Chr. viii. 14, 25).

SHA'UL. 1. Son of Simeon (Gen. xlvi. 10).—2. A king of Edom (i. 48, 49).—3. Son of Uzziah (vi. 24).

SHA'ULITES. Descendants of SHAUL 1 (Num. xxvi. 13).

SHA'VEH, THE VALLEY OF (Gen. xiv. 17). A place on Abraham's route from Damascus, when he rescued his brother Lot. Lost.

SHA'VEH KIRIATHA'IM. Valley of K. (Gen. xiv. 5). Residence of the Emim. On the E. of Jordan. Lost.

SHAV'SHA (corruption of SERAIAH). Secretary in David's time (1 Chr. xviii. 16).

SHAWM. A musical instrument, resembling the clarionet (Ps. cxviii. 7).

SHEAF. The offering of the Omer or sheaf was to be brought to the priest on the 16th of the month, and waved before the altar in acknowledgment of the fruitfulness of the season (Lev. xxiii. 5, 6, 10, 12).

SHE'AL (*an asking*). Son of Bani (Ezr. x. 29).

SHEAL'TIEL (*I have asked him of God*). Father of Zerubbabel (Ezr. iii. 2, 8).

SHEARI'AH (*whom Jah estimates*). Son of Azel (1 Chr. viii. 38).

SHEARING-HOUSE, THE (2 K. x. 12). Near Mt. Gilboa, now Beth Kad. Where Jehu killed 42 members of the royal family of Judah.

Job (i. 15, vi. 19), with the robber habits that are peculiar to the Bedawin of our day.

SHE'BA (Josh. xix. 2). Simeon, near Beersheba. SHEMA.

SHE'BAH. Shibeah was the fourth well dug by Isaac's people (Gen. xxvi. 33). Abraham dug a well here also (Gen. xxi. 25–32). The name is one of the most ancient known, and is interpreted variously as "*seven*," "an oath," "abundance," and as "a lion." BEERSHEBA.

SHEBAM' (Num. xxxii. 3). East of Jordan. Given to Reuben. It was "a land for cattle." SHIBMAH or SIBMAH.

SHEBANI'AH (*Jah has made grow*). 1. A Levite who sealed the covenant (Neh. x. 10; ix. 4, 5).— 2. One of a priestly family who sealed the covenant (x. 4).—3. Another Levite who sealed the covenant (x. 12).—4. A priest (1 Chr. xv, 24).

SHEB'ARIM (*dividing*), (Josh. vii. 5). Near Ai. Lost.

SHE'BER (*breaking*). Son of CALEB 1 (1 Chr. ii. 48).

SHEB'NA (*youth*). A steward in king Hezekiah's palace (Is. xxii. 15).

SHEB'UEL (*captive of God*). 1. A descendant of

TEMPLE OF MINERVA.

SHE'AR JA'SHUB(*the remnant shall return*). Son of ISAIAH (Is. vii. 3).

SHE'BA (*red*), (Gen. x. 7). 1. Grandson of Cush; 2. Tenth son of Joktan (ver. 28); 3. Grandson of Keturah (ib. xxv. 3). 1. The name of the kingdom in South Arabia, before Himyer took its place, a few years before Christ (24—Strabo). Here were the Sabæans of Diodorus (iii. 38, 46). A queen of Sheba visited Solomon (1 K. x.), attended by a great train, camels loaded with spices, gold, and precious stones. The chief cities were Seba, Uzal (now *Sana*), Sephar (now *Zafar*), and Mariaba (now *Marib*). This district had the chief riches, best country, and greatest numbers of all the four peoples of Arabia. The local history is authentic only as far back as the first century A. D. Their ancient religion was pagan.—2. Settled on the Persian Gulf. On the island of Bahreyn, in the Gulf, are the ruins of an ancient city called Seba. Its merchants are mentioned in Ezekiel xxvii. 22.—3. The sons of Keturah are charged by

Gershom (1 Chr. xxiii. 16).—2. Chief in the thirteenth course in the Temple-choir (xxv. 4).

SHECANI'AH. 1. Chief of the tenth course of priests in David's time (1 Chr. xxiv. 11).—2. One who distributed portions to priests in Hezekiah's reign (2 Chr. xxxi. 15).

SHECHANI'AH (*families with Jah*). Seven of this name are mentioned in 1 Chr. iii. 21, 22; Ezr. viii. 3, 5, x. 2; Neh. iii. 29, vi. 18, xii. 3.

SHECH'EM (*ridge*). SICHEM (Gen. xxxiii. 18). It is not certain whether the city was named from Shechem, the son of Hamor, or that he was named after the city. It is on the top of the ridge between the waters of the Jordan and the Mediterranean Sea, between Ebal and Gerizim (Judg. ix. 7). Called Sychar in John iv. 5, in the story of the meeting of Jesus and the woman of Samaria. Now Nablus (Neapolis, so named by Vespasian—Jos., B. J., iv. 8, 1). Also known as Mabortha (Pliny v. 13). The situation is a favored one, and excites the admiration of all travelers, Dr. Clarke saying, that "there is nothing finer in all Palestine." The valley is sheltered by a high mountain on each side, and only about 1500 ft. wide, and elevated 1800 ft. above the sea. Water flows from the city E. and W. to the Jordan, and to the Mediterranean sea. The valley is full of gardens, orchards of all kinds of fruits, watered by fountains, and enlivened by the songs of birds. Abraham, on his first visit to the Land of Promise, pitched his tent under the oak of Moreh, at Shechem (Gen. xii. 6). Jacob bought a field of the children of Hamor (Gen. xxxiii. 19), where he dug a well, about a mile from the present town, and left it as a special patrimony to Joseph (Josh. xxiv. 32). Shechem was given to Ephraim (Josh. xx. 7), was assigned to the Le-

SHEEP-FOLD.

vites, and was made a City of Refuge (ib. xxi. 20, 21). The people assembled at Shechem to hear the law of Moses read, "half of them over against Mt. Gerizim, and half of them over against Mt. Ebal," the chief men and priests being around the ark in the midst (Josh. viii. 30-35); and again Joshua gathered all the tribes here just before his death (xxiv.), and delivered his last counsels. Abimelech raised a revolt in Shechem, and was made king (Judg. ix.); and Jotham denounced him and the men of Shechem in a parable, from the top of Gerizim (ver. 22), and after 3 yrs. he destroyed the city and the strong tower that was in the city, but lost his own life also (ver. 53). The 10 tribes made Jeroboam their king and Shechem their capital (1 K. xii. 20). When the people were carried away to Babylon the city was colonized from Assyria (2 K. xvii. 24), and again admitted strangers under Esar-haddon (Ezr. iv. 2). The present town of Nablus has about 5,000 people, living in stone houses of very ordinary style, except those of the wealthy sheikhs. There are no fine public buildings. There are not less than 80 springs of water in the valley. One of the largest, Ain Balata, rises in a chamber partly under ground, a few rods from Jacob's well. Olives, figs, almonds, walnuts, mulberries, pomegranates, oranges, apricots, and grapes, abound, besides vegetables of every sort. There are manufactories of wool, silk, and camel's-hair cloth, and especially of soap; and the district around it is rich in wool, grain and oil. As a confirmation of the truth and accuracy, even to minute detail, it is interesting to cite the words of the original Hebrew, describing this spot, on which Joseph's tomb stands, which are, CHELKAT HAS-SADE, meaning a *dead-level;* differing from SHEFELAH, (a *plain*), and EMEK (a *valley*), and this description is exactly correct—and besides, there is no other spot like it in all Palestine.

SHECH'INAH (*habitation*). Indwelling of God, is properly applied to visible manifestations of God's presence. Thus, Num. v. 3, *in the midst whereof I dwell* is rendered by the Targum "among whom *my shekinah* is dwelling." Difference of

opinion exists as to whether there was any continuous visible manifestations of God's presence in the Holy of Holies over the *cappereth* or mercy-seat. Jewish authorities hold there was, and that this shekinah did not return to the second temple. Many Christian writers deny its continuous visibility even in the first.

SHED'EUR (*darting of fire*). Father of Elizur (Num. i. 5).

SHEEP. Heb. AYIL, a ram (Gen. xv. 9); KAR, a lamb; KEBES, a he-lamb (xxx. 40); fem. KIBSAH, ewe-lamb (Gen. xxi. 28); ZON, ZONA, ZONAH, a flock of small cattle (Gen. iv. 4); RAHEL, RACHEL, fem. "ewe" (Gen. xxxi. 38; SEH, one of a flock, i. e. sheep or goat (Gen. xxii. 7); TALEH, a lamb, young and tender.

Of the Syrian sheep there are two varieties: the Bedaween, which have long and thick tails, but differ in no other respect from the larger kinds of sheep among us. The others have very large and broad tails, with a small end which turns back upon itself; they are of a substance between fat and marrow, which is not eaten separately, but mixed with the lean meat in many of their dishes, and also used instead of butter. A common sheep of this sort, without the head, feet, shin, and entrails, weighs from 60 to 80 pounds, of which the tail itself is usually 10 or 15 (see cut on page 89), and when fattened, twice or thrice that weight.

The sheep or lamb was the common sacrifice under the Mosaic law (Ex. xxix. 22). The innocence, mildness, submission and patience, of the lamb, render it suitable for a sacrifice (John i. 29).

There are frequent allusions in Scripture to sheep, and its proneness to go astray (Is. liii. 6). It is gregarious, and dependent on the protection and guidance of its master. Its name is often given to the people of God (2 K. xxii. 17). Sheep and goats are still found in Syria, feeding together, as in ancient times (Gen. xxx. 35). The season of sheep-shearing was one of great joy and festivity (1 Sam. xxv. 2, 8, 36). The Bedawins are compelled to move from place to place as their flocks and herds consume the pasture, and the supply of water is the one great question. The noon is the time for watering the animals (Ps. xxiii. 1, 2), when the tribe, or the shepherds gather to talk over the news.

Sheep-cotes or folds are generally open houses or enclosures, walled round (Num. xxxii. 16; 2 Sam. vii. 8).

SHEEP-MARKET, THE (John v. 2). Supposed to have been a GATE, and at present called St. Stephen's; and the great open ruined cistern near it is called the Pool of Bethesda.

SHEHARI'AH (*Jah seeks*). Son of Jeroham (1 Chr. viii. 26).

SHEK'EL. See MONEY.

SHE'LAH (*petition*). 1. Son of Judah 1 (Gen. xxxviii. 5, 11, 14, 26).—2. Heb. *missile, sprout.* Salah, son of Arphaxad (1 Chr. i. 18, 24).

SHE'LANITES, THE. Descendants of Shelah 1 (Num. xxvi. 20).

SHELEMI'AH. Nine of this name are alluded to in Ezr. x. 39; Neh. iii. 30, xiii. 13; Jer. xxxvii. 3, 13; 1 Chr. xxvi. 14; Ezr. x. 41; Jer. xxxvi. 14, 26).

SHEF'ELAH (see PHILISTIA). Low country; the plains below the hills of Judæa.

SHEL'EPH (*partridge chick*). Second son of Joktan, and father of a tribe who settled in Yemen, in Arabia, where there is now a district called Sulaf (Gen. x. 36).

SHE'LESH (*tried*). Son of Helem (1 Chr. vii. 35).

SHEL'OMI (*pacific*). Father of Ahihud (Num. xxxiv. 27).

SHEL'OMITH (*love of peace*). 1. Daughter of Dibri (Lev. xxiv. 11).—2. Daughter of Zerubbabel (1 Chr. iii. 19). Five others of the name are mentioned in 1 Chr. xxiii. 18, xxvi. 25, 26, 28, xxiii. 9; Ezr. viii. 10; 2 Chr. xi. 20.

SHEL'OMOTH (1 Chr. xxiv. 22). SHELOMITH.

SHEL'UMIEL (*friend of God*). Son of Rurishaddai (Num. i. 6).

SHEM. Eldest son of Noah (Gen. v. 32), settled between Japheth and Ham, the country from the Mediterranean Sea to the Indian Ocean, and from Lydia to the Red Sea, including Syria (Aram), Chaldæa (Arphaxad), Assyria (Asshur), Persia (Elam), and Arabia (Joktan). A special blessing is promised Shem in Gen. ix. 27.

SHEM'A. In Judah (Josh. xv. 26). SHEBA. Given to Simeon.

SHE'MA. 1. Ancestor of Bela (1 Chr. v. 8).—2. Son of Elpaal (viii. 13).—3. One who assisted Ezra (Neh. viii. 4).

SHEMAI'AH (*Jah hears*). Twenty-five of this name are alluded to in 1 K. xii. 22; 2 Chr. xi. 2, xii. 5, 7, 15; 1 Chr. iii. 22; Neh. iii. 29, iv. 37, v. 4, ix. 14; Neh. xi. 15; 1 Chr. ix. 16, xv. 8, 11, xxiv. 6, xxvi. 4, 6, 7; 2 Chr. xxix. 14; Ezr. viii. 13, 16, x. 21, 31; Neh. vi. 10, x. 8, xii. 6, 18, 34, 35, 36, 42; Jer. xxix. 24, 32; 2 Chr. xvii. 8, xxxi. 15, xxxv. 9; Jer. xxvi. 20, xxxvi. 12.

SHEMAI'AH (*Jah hears*). 1. A prophet of Israel (1 K. xii. 22–24). He is said to have written a history of Rehoboam's reign.—2. A Levite, who made a registry of 24 priestly classes (1 Chr. xv. 8).—3. A false prophet among the exiles in Babylon, opposed to Jeremiah (xxix. 24).—4. A false prophet in the pay of Sanballat and Tobiah (Num. iii. 8; Neh. vi. 10). 21 others were of no particular note.

SHEMARI'AH (*Jah keeps*). 1. A warrior who assisted David (1 Chr. xii. 5).—2. A layman (Ezr. x. 32).—3. One of the family of Bani (x. 41).

SHEME'BER (*lofty flight*). King of Zeboïm (Gen. xiv. 2).

SHE'MER (*preserved*). The owner of the hill on which the city of Samaria was built (1 K. xvi. 24).

SHEM'IDA (*farm of wisdom*). Son of Gilead (Num. xxvi. 32).

SHEM'IDAH (1 Chr. vii. 19).

SHEM'IDAITES, THE. Descendants of Shemida (Num. xxvi. 32).

SHEM'IMITH. The name of a melody in Ps. vi. xii.

SHEMIR'AMOTH (*Heaven most high*). 1. One in David's choir (1 Chr. xv. 18, 20).—2. A Levite, teacher of the law (2 Chr. xvii. 8).

SHEMIT'IC. The Shemitic languages (see Gen. x. 21), are also called Aryan, and Syro-Arabic. The extent of this family of languages may be indicated by the boundaries—the highlands of Armenia on the north, the Tigris and its mountain ranges on the east, the Red Sea, Levant, and Asia Minor on the west—the south is limited by the ocean. The uniform climate of this vast region has tended to keep the people to their unvarying customs from age to age, whether in the cities, or in the country, or on the trackless waste.

TABLE OF THE SHEMITIC LANGUAGES.

Living.	Dead.	Classic.
Arabic and its dialects }	Ethiopic	Arabic.
Amharic	Himyaritic.	
Hebrew	{ Biblical, Hebrew Samaritan Pentateuch Carthaginian } Inscrip'n Phœnician }	} Hebraic.
Neo. Syriac	{ Chaldee, Masora, Targum Biblical-Chaldee, Syriac Peshito of 2d cent. A. D. Cuneiform of Bab. & Nin. }	} Aramaic.

The Old Testament has traces of the changes in the languages of Palestine and Assyria, especially in the fragments of ancient poems, which contain many Aramaic words not used anywhere else in the Scriptures. The natural tendency of the Aryans has been, in all cases, to keep their language and customs free from any mixture from their neighbors; adopting very few words and very few habits from other people. Their language, religion, and manners were all unsocial, despotic, conservative; and what treasures they borrowed from the nations around them were not assimilated, but kept entire as when first found.

The peculiar character of these languages is that the original root words are nearly all of one syllable. The changes incident to growth have resulted in arranging the particles around the root words, or if making particles of these words, which become parts of the later form of words. There are no compound words—or very few. There are no logical arrangements, but the grouping of words which record facts, and carry forward the train of thought.

An instance:

> "Who is this, the King of Glory?
> Jehovah, strong and mighty;
> Jehovah, mighty in battle.
> Lift up your heads, ye gates,
> And lift up, ye everlasting doors
> That the King of Glory may come in,
> Who, then, is He, the King of Glory?
> Jehovah of hosts,
> He is the King of Glory." (Pause).
> .Ps. xxiv. 8–10

Here the mind is carried forward from one fact to another, in simple and sublime statement, without logic, except the irresistable logic of facts.

It appears to be beyond dispute, as can be proved from the ancient monuments, from tradition, and from dialects now spoken by their descendants, that a great Hamitic population must have overspread Europe, Asia and Africa, speaking languages more or less dissimilar in their vocabulary, but having almost a common grammar and construction. These people civilized Phœnicia, Babylonia, South Arabia and Egypt, and prepared the way for the Hebrew race, or the Shemitic races, who came after and benefited by their works.

The materials for a history of the Hebrew language are as few as for a history of a rock. The language from Abraham's time to this has not changed in one essential feature or element, except to decay. Very few words have been dropped, and not many added, and the greater number of the additions date from the Captivity. The language shows historic progress from Moses (the Pentateuch) to the Captivity (Ezra and Malachi), always degenerating, and every adopted word can be selected, even in its Hebrew dress, as YAVAN, from the Sanscrit yuvajana, young emigrants, meaning the Greeks. From the Captivity, pure Hebrew was confined by custom to the priests and the sanctuary, from which use it was never again separated, and with the passing away of the Temple worship, has become a dead language. It was even dead in the time of Christ, for the Scriptures were at that time known only in the Aramæan. The present Jewish speech is a combination of words Hebraized and borrowed from every quarter of the world.

It is argued that the Hebrew could not have been the one original source of languages for its oldest names, as Adam, Eve, etc., are derivatives, and may have been translated from other languages by Moses.

The language is rich in different terms for the same object, as 9 for "trust in God;" 14 for "inquire or ask;" 24 for "keep the law."

The Phœnician was so closely allied to the Hebrew as to be used in common; and it was more widely distributed (by sailors and merchants) than any other ancient speech, and from this very cause it went to pieces, after having become overloaded by adopted words. (The English language is being overloaded by Latinisms in the same manner).

The successor to Aramaic is Syriac, dating from the 2d century, A. D., in which there is a wealth of foreign words, especially Greek. The Aramaic after a career of eleven centuries as the sacred language of the Israelites, has, according to a law which works the same in all cases, passed away.

The remains of the ancient languages of Assyria are almost entirely found in the wedge-shaped and arrow-head characters; and the history of the language can be traced, quite distinctly, from the age of clay tablets to those of bricks and alabaster. It appears that the Babylonian alphabet was constructed on the more ancient syllabic alphabet of the wedge-shaped period. Some few remains of this speech are found in Daniel (see HISTORY OF THE BOOKS), but the originals of the Apocryphal books are lost, while the Gemaras are not free from mixture with other tongues, and the Zohar is peculiar in describing Gnostic atheism in Aramaic forms of speech, and so adds little to our knowledge of the Aramaic idiom. The peculiar idioms are better preserved in the Masora. Not much additional can be found in the Samaritan, which was the vulgar Aramaic and Hebrew mingled after the sacred dialect became the language of the sanctuary and Holy Books.

The dialect of Galilee was local, largely influenced and mingled with foreign elements, confused by the indifferent use of certain letters, as soft k and hard k, b and p, d for t final. The sacred dialect had but little influence, and was so little known in the time of Ezra and Nehemiah (viii. 8), as to need interpretation when read in public.

Eastern Aramaic is the language of the Targums, and of the Pharisees; while the Western branch is the language of the New Testament, of the Christians of the first century. As the sacred dialect disappeared from the popular mind, the work of the scholars arose to importance, in such works as the Targums. The Talmud was the growth of the ages dating from the Captivity to A. D. 426, but there are few additions to our knowledge of the languages used in the work.

Of the Palmyrene dialect the only remains are the inscriptions dating from A. D. 49 to A. D. 250, which contain words borrowed from the Arabic, Greek, and Latin.

The sacred dialect became classic, and confined to books, after the fall of Jerusalem, the chief seat of its schools being at Edessa until A. D. 440, when it was removed to Nisibis. Since the 8th century it has declined in interest, and was but partly restored to favor by the facilities afforded by the discovery of printing. (See CANON.) Chaldaic paraphrases of the Scriptures have thrown much light on manners and customs, and on certain difficult passages of the O. T., especially those claimed by Christians to be prophesies of the Messiah, which are proved beyond a question, by the paraphrases, to have been so regarded by the Jews, in all ages, before the appearance of Jesus the Christ.

The sacred language of Ethiopia, the Jeez (Ghez), has been traced to its relation with Arabic and Aramaic, and it is probably a relic of Himyarite emigration. Cush was on both sides of the Red Sea (see HAM). The alphabet is very curious; every consonant contains an r, and the vowels are made by adding a sound to a consonant. This system requires 202 letters.

The Arabic language shows by internal evidence its great antiquity, and its local habitation from the beginning in Arabia. Palgrave says that in Central Arabia, where very little or no foreign influence has ever been felt, that the Arabic is spoken now in the same purity as when Mohammed wrote the Koran, 1200 years ago. It is said in a legend that the language was formed by the union of several dialects, of which the Koreish was the leading one, and in which the Koran was written.

Arabian historians describe a golden age of poetry just preceding Mohammed, in which poets contended with each other for national honors, in grand public assemblies. Poetry and romance were the chief objects of attention, held in greater honor than trade or labor. These poets were either skeptical or voluptuaries, and their writings, as we now have them, give no idea of what their religion was before Mohammed. The Koran contains evidences of a change in Arabic literature, in progress at the time it was written; the closing chapters appearing to have been written earliest in point of time.

The Arabic is especially rich in words and in grammatical forms, and in greater number and variety than any other language.

The language was, as we know it, first the speech of robbers and herdsmen, without religion, superstitious, uncultivated; and afterwards that of a cultivated, self-satisfied, luxurious, licentious people, whose philosophy was borrowed, and religion invented and dogmatized in the most offensive and tiresome manner.

Its chief value to the Bible student is the vast mass of words that it furnishes in illustration of obscure Hebrew words, by which many obscure passages have been explained.

The question of the antiquity of the art of writing is settled in favor of a much earlier age than that of Moses, for he regulates a certain use of the art in Lev. xix. 28, and it is not probable that the Hebrew alphabet and system of writing was invented during the sojourn in the Wilderness. The theory most favored now is that the Egyptians had the art many years before the Hebrews were a people, or even before Phœnicia had its alphabet.

The oldest alphabet that is known is the Phœnician, and the oldest monument of it is the MOABITE STONE, recently discovered (see page 173). Coins are next in order of antiquity, and those struck by the Maccabæans are instances (see WRITING and MONEY).

The ancient relics exhibit the growth of the square Hebrew letter from age to age, having become settled in Ezra's time, and continuing without change from that to about 500 A. D. The letter became consecrated, and was preserved with superstitious care, especially after the fall of Jerusalem. The reverence of the Jews for their sacred writings would have been outraged by any attempt to introduce a system of interpretation different from the ancient one. To establish a uniform system was the object of the Masoretes (masters of tradition), by means of written vowels and accents, which dates from about the 6th century A. D. The Syriac adopted a similar system in the 1st or 2d century.

The ordinary Hebrew verb has 5 forms:

1. KAL. Simple form.

Causative.   *Reflective.*   *Intensive.*

2. HIPHIL.   3. NIPHAL.   4. PIEL.

Passive, HOPHAL. |_____| *Passive,* PUAL.

5. HITHPAEL.

There are no moods. In the Arabic there are 15 forms in the verb, by which ideas of time, place and action are conveyed as well as by our system of moods.

Names are intensified by prefixtures, as Ha-Arabah, *the* Arabah. There are dual names, as horse, meaning both horse and mare, or two horses, and there is a third class, meaning many, as attudim, *goats*, zōnē, *sheep*, as a flock. A fourth class represent many different individuals without distinction, as sand does in ours (many grains forming sand); Elohim (Gods) God.

There are no compound words. The great extent of the verb supplies this defect in some degree, some of the verb-forms indicating color, condition, etc.

The Arabic alphabet contains all the Hebrew letters; but in some cases there is not an exact parallel. The arrangement of the two alphabets was once the same, as is proved by the numbers expressed by each letter; but the order is now different. The earliest form of the letter is what is now called Himyarite.

SHEM'UEL. SAMUEL. 1. Son of Ammihud (Num. xxxiv. 20).—2. SAMUEL the prophet (1 Chr. vi. 33).—3. Son of Tola (vii. 2).

SHEN (1 Sam. vii. 12). Where Samuel set up the stone Ebenezer, between "the Mizpah and the Shen." Lost.

SHENA'ZAR (*fiery torch*). Son of SALATHIEL (1 Chr. iii. 18).

SHE'NIR (Deut. iii. 9; Cant. iv. 8). Senir, Mt. Hermon.

SHE'OL (Heb. SHEOL, *hell*). See HADES.

SHEPH'AM (Num. xxxiv. 10, 11). On the E. boundary of the land. Lost.

SHEPHATHI'AH. Father of Meshullam 6 (1 Chr. ix. 8).

SHEPHATI'AH. The name of 7 distinguished Jews, alluded to in the following passages: 2 Sam. iii. 34; 1 Chr. xii. 5, xxvii. 16, 2 Chr. xxi. 2; Ezr. ii. 4; 7 vii; Neh. xi. 4; Jer. xxxviii. 1.

SHEP'HERD (Heb. ROEH, *shepherd, pastor*). (Gen. xlix. 4; Jer. ii. 8). The wandering character of life, and the dependence upon flocks, rendered the care of sheep amongst the most important duties of life, from the earliest time in the East. (See SHEEP). "Abel was a keeper of sheep" (Gen. iv. 2). The employment of shepherd was not only followed by the chiefs (Gen. xxx. 29), but by their sons and daughters as well (Gen. xxix. 6; Ex. ii. 19). Extensive flocks fed in the wilderness of Judah (1 Sam. xxv. 2); at Bethlehem (1 Sam. xvi. 11; Luke ii. 8); at Gedor (1 Chr. iv.). As the people became more settled, agriculture became more general, and the care of sheep less important. Figurative allusion is continually made, both in the O. and N. T.: Christ applying the expression to himself, and frequently using the term figuratively (Ps. xxiii.; Is. xl. 11, xlix. 9, 10; Jer. xxiii. 3, 4; John x. 12, 14, 16; 1 Pet. v. 4; Luke ii. 8). It is the habit of the shepherd, in the East, to walk before his flock, leading by his voice (John x. 4); the dog following in the rear of it (1 Chr. xxx. 1). In leading to and from the pasturage, the mothers are led by the shepherd (Gen. xxxiii. 13), who *also* carries the tender lambs (Is. xi. 11). Tents and towers were erected for the shepherd as a point of observation: such was the tower of Eden (Gen. xxxv. 21). Shepherds used the sling (1 Sam. xvii. 40), both for defence and amusement; they also played upon a flute. The towers are still found in nearly every little district in Palestine. The shepherd follows the same customs of care, and watching of the flock, to-day, as in ancient times. In pleasant weather sleeping near them, in the field, under some rude hut, or under a tent; leading them to drink, and helping the young lambs, or lame sheep, by carrying or lifting them out of dangerous places by his crook. The custom of giving names to the members of the flock is still in use; the flock recognizing the shepherd's voice, and answering to their names. The shepherd is also exposed to danger of his life, in the protection of his flock against robbers and wild beasts. Many shepherds make a heavy cloak of sheep-skin, with the wool on; and others use the coarse goat's-hair, or camel's-hair cloth.

SHE'PHI (*wearing away*). Son of Shobal (1 Chr. i. 40), also written

SHE'PHO (*smoothness*), (Gen. xxxvi. 23).

SHEPHU'PHAN (*serpent*). A son of Bela (1 Chr. viii. 5).

SHE'RAH (*kinswoman*). Daughter of Ephraim (1 Chr. vii. 24).

SHERD. POTSHERD, fragment of an earthern vessel (Job ii. 8).

SHEREBI'AH (*heat of Jah*). An assistant of Ezra (Neh. viii. 7, ix. 4, 5; Ezr. viii. 18, 24).

SHE'RESH (*root*). Son of Machir (1 Chr. vii. 16).

SHERE'ZER. A messenger sent to inquire about the fasting (Zech. vii. 2).

SHER'IFFS (Heb. TIFTAYE, *lawyers*). The name of certain high officials among the Babylonians.

SHE'SHACH (Jer. xxv. 26, li. 41). Supposed to be Babylon by some. Others say it means Ur, the ancient capital of Babylonia, the city of Abraham.

SHE'SHAI (*whitish*). Son of Anak (Num. xiii. 22; Josh. xv. 14).

SHE'SHAN (*lily*). Descendant of Jerahmeel; father of AHLAI (1 Chr. ii. 31, 34, 35).

SHESHBAZ'ZAR (*fire-worshiper*). The Persian name given to ZERUBBABEL (Ezr. i. 8, 11).

SHETH. 1. SETH (1 Chr. i. 1).—2. The "Sons of Sheth" (Num. xxiv. 17).

SHE'THAR (*a star*). A prince of Persia and Media (Esth. i. 14).

SHETH'ARBOZ'NAI (*star of splendor*). A Persian officer of rank (Ezr. v. 3, 6).

SHE'VA. A corruption of SERAIAH. 1. Secretary of David (2 Sam. xx. 25).—2. Son of CALEB 1 (1 Chr. ii. 49).

SHEW-BREAD.

SHEW-BREAD (Heb. LEHEM, PANIM, *bread of the faces, of the presence of Jehovah*), (Ex. xxv. 30). On the north side in the holy place of the Tabernacle was the table of acacia wood, 3 feet 6 in. long, 1 foot 9 in. wide, and 2 feet 4 in. high; overlaid with gold; a rim and crown of gold encircling the top and another the bottom (Ex. xxv. 23-30). A figure of the table (removed by Titus from the Temple of Herod) is carved on the arch of Titus at Rome. Golden rings were attached to the corners of the table, through which poles could be passed for carrying it (as in the case of the ark). Upon it on every Sabbath were placed, in two piles, twelve freshly baked unleavened loaves of fine flour (typical of the twelve tribes), as an offering (Lev. xxiv. 7). See SACRIFICE. A golden pot filled with incense was placed on the top of each pile, and remained until the next Sabbath, when the incense was burned, the loaves were eaten by the priests in the Sanctuary, and twelve fresh ones laid for an offering (Lev. xxiv. 6, 7; 1 Chr. xxiii. 29). David, in extreme hunger, eat of the shew-bread (1 Sam. xxi. 4-6; Matt. xii. 4).

SHIB'BOLETH (*a stream*), (Judg. xii. 6). The

Hebrew word which the Gileadites made use of at the passage of the Jordan after their victory over the Ephraimites.

SHIB'MAH (Num. xxxii. 38). Shebam, east of Jordan.

SHIC'RON (Josh. xv. 11). Boundary of Judah, near Jabneel. Lost.

SHIGGAI'ON (Ps. vii. 1). Title of a melody.

SHI'HOR OF EGYPT (1 Chr. xiii. 5; Josh. xiii. 2, 3). *Wady el Arish*, Arabia Petræa. SHIHOR, the Nile. See SIHOR.

SHI'HOR LIBNATH (Josh. xix. 26). Boundary of Asher, below Mt Carmel. Lost.

SHIL'HI (*armed*). Father of Azubah (1 K. xxii. 42).

SHIL'HIM (Josh. xv. 32). Judah. Perhaps the same as SHARUHEN, which was given to Simeon (xix. 6).

SHIL'LEM (*requital*). Son of Naphtali (Gen. xlvi. 24).

TOMB OF EZRA.

SHIL'LEMITES, THE. Descendants of Shillem (Num. xxvi. 49).

SHILO'AH, THE WATERS OF (Jer. viii. 6). The prophet compares a quiet confidence in Jehovah with the waters of a brook, that "go softly," and contrasts this with the "waters of a river, strong and many, even the king of Assyria and all his glory: and he shall come up over all his channels, and go over all his banks." Supposed to refer to Siloam, near Jerusalem.

SHI'LOH (*rest*), (1 Sam. i. 24, iii. 21; Judg. xxi. 19). In Ephraim, north of Bethel, east of the road to Shechem, south of Lebonah. Now called *Seilun*. This was one of the earliest and most sacred of the Jews' sanctuaries. The ark was kept here (in a tent or tabernacle only), from the last days of Joshua (xviii. 1) to the time of Samuel (1 Sam. iv. 3). Here Joshua completed the division of the land among the tribes (xviii. 10, xix. 51). The Benjamites seized the "daughters of Shiloh," and preserved a tribe from extinction (Judg. xxi. 19), "at an annual feast of the Lord." Eli resided here as judge of Israel, and died of grief at the news that the ark of God was taken (1 Sam. iv. 11, 18). The story of Hannah, Samuel's mother, is an interesting incident, as illustrating the character and life of the Hebrews (1 Sam. i., etc.). Ahijah the prophet lived here when Jeroboam sent his wife to him to inquire what should become of their sick son (1 K. xiv.). The city was on a low hill, rising from an uneven plain surrounded by higher hills, except a narrow valley on the south. Very few, and not any important ruins are found here. An immense oak of great age grows among the ruins, and a few olive trees are scattered through the hollows The hills were once terraced and finely cultivated. A fine large fountain, half a mile away, flows out in a narrow vale, first into a pool, and then into a large reservoir, where flocks and herds are watered. There are rock-hewn sepulchres near, where perhaps some of Eli's "house" were laid.

SHILO'NI. Descendant of Shelah, the son of Judah (Neh. xi. 5).

SHI'LONITE, THE. Native of SHILOH (1 K. xi. 29).

SHI'LONITES, THE. Descendants of Judah, dwelling in Jerusalem (1 Chr. ix. 5).

SHIL'SHAH (*tried*). Son of Zophah (1 Chr. vii. 37).

SHIM'EA (*rumor*). 1. Son of David (1 Chr. iii. 5).—2. A Levite (vi. 30).—3. Ancestor of Asaph (vi. 39).—4. Brother of David (xx. 7).

SHIM'EAH. 1. Brother of David (2 Sam. xxi. 21).—2. A descendant of Jehiel (1 Chr. viii. 32).

SHIM'EAM (*fame*). Son of Mikloth (1 Chr. ix. 38).

SHIM'EATH. Mother of Jozachar (2 K. xii. 21).

SHIM'EATHITES (*descendants of Shimeath*). A family of scribes (1 Chr. ii. 55).

SHIM'EI. 1. A son of Gershom (Num. iii. 18).—2. Son of Gera; he insulted king David (2 Sam. xvi. 5–14).—3. An officer under David (1 K. i. 8). Others of this name are alluded to in the following passages: 1 K. iv. 18; 1 Chr. iii. 19, iv. 26–27, v. 4, vi. 42, xxv. 17, xxvii. 27; 2 Chr. xxix. 14, xxxi. 12, 13; Ezr. x. 23, x. 33, x. 38; Esth. ii. 5; 1 Chr. vi. 29, xxiii. 9.

SHIM'EON. A layman of the sons of Harim (Ezr. x. 31).

SHIM'HI. A Benjamite (1 Chr. viii. 21).

SHIM'I (Ex. vi. 17). SHIMEI.

SHIM'ITES, THE. Descendants of SHIMEI 1, the son of Gershom (Num. iii. 21).

SHIM'MA. Third son of Jesse (1 Chr. ii. 13).

SHI'MON (*desert*). The four sons of Shimon (1 Chr. iv. 20), are mentioned among the tribe of Judah.

SHIM'RATH (*watch*). Song of Shimhi (1 Chr. viii. 21).

SHIM'RI (*watchful*). Three of this name are mentioned in 1 Chr. iv, 37, xi. 45; 2 Chr. xxix. 13.

SHIM'RITH. Mother of Jehozabad (2 Chr. xxiv. 26).

SHIM'ROM. Son of Issachar (1 Chr. vii. 1).

SHIM'RON (*watch, guard*), (Josh. xix. 15). In Zebulon. Now *Simuniyeh*, west of Nazareth. The king of Shimron Meron was one of 31 vanquished by Joshua (xii. 20).

SHIM'RON. Fourth son of Issachar (Gen. xlvi. 13).

SHIM'RONITES, THE. The family of SHIMRON (Num xxvi. 24).

SHIM'SHAI (*sunny*). Secretary of Rehum (Ezr. iv. 8, 9, 17, 23).

SHI'NAB (*father's tooth*). King of ADMAH in Abraham's time (Gen. xiv. 2).

SHI'NAR, THE LAND OF (*country of the two rivers*), (Gen. xi. 2). Ancient name of Chaldæa and Babylonia. It is the Jewish name, and is not found in the native inscriptions. Abraham brought the name with him to Canaan.

SHIP (Heb. ONIYAH, SEFINAH; Gr. *ploion*). The fullest description of ships is in the narrative of Paul's voyage to Rome (Acts xxvii. xxviii.). Paul sailed first on an Adramyttian vessel from Cæsarea to Myra—a coasting ship of moderate size (Acts xxvii. 1-6), then in a large Alexandrian corn ship, in which he was wrecked on the coast of Malta (Acts xxvii. 6, xxviii. 1), and finally in a large Alexandrian corn ship, from Malta, by Syracuse, to Puteoli (xxviii. 11-13). The ship in which Paul was wrecked held 276 persons (Acts xxvii. 37), and was laden with wheat. From this it is estimated that such ships were between 500 and 1000 tons burden. Ships are often mentioned in the Old Testament, and figuratively in Job ix. 23; Ps. xlviii. 79, civ. 26, cvii. 23. Solomon built a fleet at EZION-GEBER (1 K. ix. 26). The fleet of Jehoshaphat, built in the same place, was destroyed (1 K. xxii. 48, 49; 2 Chr. xx. 36, 37). War ships are first alluded to in Dan. xi. 40. The ships' prows bore figure-heads or other insignia, called "sign" in Acts xxviii. 11.: "Whose sign was Castor and Pollux." When large, the ships were impelled by sails as well as oars, which were used alone in small craft. The sail was a large square one, attached to a long yard. The Gr. *artemon* mentioned in Acts xxvii. 40, was the foresail, useful in putting a large ship about. The anchors resembled those now in use. The ship in which Paul sailed had four anchors on board; they were anchored by the stern (Acts xxvii. 29). The ships were steered by two paddles at the stern, which are the rudders alluded to in the narrative of Paul's voyage. Anchoring by the stern necessitated the lashing up of these paddles to prevent interference. The build and rig of ancient ships caused a tendency in them to start their planks by their beams yielding; it was therefore necessary to provide under-girders or helps (Acts xxvii. 17) of chains or cables, to girth the frame of the ship in case of need. The ships also carried boats (Acts xxvii. 16, 32). The captains of these merchant ships were often the owners in part or whole. The steersman is called "the governor" in James iii. 4.

SHIPH'I (*abundant*). Father of Ziza, a prince in Hezekiah's time (1 Chr. iv. 37).

SHIPH'MITE, THE. One from Siphmoth (1 Chr. xxvii. 27).

SHIPH'RAH (*beauty*). One of two Hebrew women who disobeyed the command of Pharaoh (Ex. i. 15-21).

SHIPH'TAN (*judicial*). Father of Kemuel 2 (Num. xxxiv. 24).

SHI'SHA. Corruption of Seraiah, father of Elihoreph and Ahiah (1 K. iv. 3).

SHI'SHAK. A king of Egypt. He entered Judah, B. C. 971, and captured the strongest places in the country, and carried away the treasures. See EGYPT.

In the article on Egypt it is mentioned that Shishak invaded Judæa, and took several cities, and tribute from Rehoboam at Jerusalem, the account of which has lately been deciphered on the Egyptian monuments. Shishak's name is written SHE-SHONK, and he is said to have been an Ethiopian. He is shown as presenting to the gods of Thebes the prisoners taken by him in war, each name (of a king, or city, or nation) being in an oval shield. See page 84.

Here are some of the names as they stand on the walls of the great temple at Karnak. The first name recognized was Judæa, (see "king of Judah," page 84) by Champollion, which gave the clue to the others.

The names not yet identified are omitted. There were 133 in all.

Egyptian.	Hebrew.
13. Rebata.	Rabbith?
14. Taankau.	Taanach.
15. Shenema-aa.	Shunem.
16. Bat-shenraa.	Bethshan.
17. Rehabaa.	Rehob.
18. Hepurmaa.	Haphraim..
19. Aterma.	Adoraim.
22. Mahanma.	Mahanaim.
23. Kebaana.	Gibeon.
24. Bat-huaren.	Beth-horon.
25. Katmet.	Kedemoth.
26. Ayuren.	Ajalon.
27. Maketau.	Megiddo.
28. Ateera.	Edrei.
29. Yuteh-mark.	Judæa.
31. Haanem.	Anem?
32. Aarana.	Eglon?
33. Barma.	Bileam.
36. Bat-aarmet.	Alemeth.
37. Kakaree.	Kikkar (Jordan).
38. Shauka.	Shoco.
39. Bat-tepu.	Beth Tappuah.
40. Abaraa.	Abel?
56. Atmaa.	Edom?
66. Aa-aatemaa.	Azem, (great?)
68. Pehakraa.	Hagarites.
69. Fetyushaa.	Letushim?
72. Mersarama.	Salma?
73. Shebperet.	Shephelah.
78. Baabayt.	Nebaioth.
79. Aatetmaa.	Tema.
83. Kanaa.	Kenites?
84. Penakbu.	Negeb.
85. Atem-ketet-het.	Azem? (little?)
98. Mertmam.	Duma?
103. Heetbaa.	Abdeel?
107. Harekma.	Rekem (Petra).
108. Aarataa.	Eldaah.
109. Rabat.	Rabbah?
110. Aarataay.	Eldaa.
112. Yurahma.	Jurahmeelites?
117. Mertraaa.	Eddara.
119. Mahkaa.	Maachah?
124. Bataaat.	Beth-anoth?
127. Kernaa.	Golan?

This record of the conquest is peculiar to Egypt, and entirely independent of the Jews, or any of the writers of the Bible, or is a confirmation of the historical truth of 2 K. xxiii. 29, etc., and 2 Chr. xxxv. 20, etc.

SHIT'RAI (*Jah is arbitrator*). A Sharonite who had charge of David's herds (1 Chr. xxvii. 29).

SHIT'TAH-TREE. SHIT'TIM. Understood as the acacia tree, of which there are three or four species in the East, especially used in the construction of the tabernacle, ark, table of shew-bread, altars, etc. (Ex. xxv., xxvi., xxxvi., xxxvii., xxxviii.). "I will plant in the wilderness the cedar, the shittah-tree, and the myrtle, and the oil tree" (Is. xli. 19). It was probably the only available wood in the wilderness. This tree yields the gum arabic of commerce, from incisions cut deeply in the bark. Probably the burning-bush of Moses (Ex. iii. 2), called SENEH, was the shittim (or acacia) tree. The last camping ground of Israel was on the plains of Shittim. The Arabs use the gum for food. The bark is very astringent, and used in tanning leather. The wood is very hard, close-grained, of a fine brown color, excellent for cabinet-work. It grows in dry places, where no other tree can live. It is not the *acacia* of this country, which is a kind of locust. Tristram mentions trees on the Dead Sea shore at Engedi and other places, which are four feet in diameter.

SHIT′TIM (*acacia trees*), (Num. xxxiii. 49). Abel Has Shittim (*meadow of the acacias*). In the Arboth Moab, by Jordan. Jericho (Num. xxii. 1, xxvi. 3). Under the cool shade of the acacia groves the Israelites were led into the worship of Baal Peor by the Midianites, which sin Moses, by command, avenged (xxxi. 1). Joshua sent spies to Jericho from here (ii. 1).

ACACIA OR SHITTAH-TREE.

SHI′ZA (*loved*). Father of Adina (1 Chr. xi. 42).

SHO′A. A proper name which occurs only in Ezr. xxiii. 23, and signifies officer and ruler.

SHO′BAB (*rebellious*). 1. Son of David (2 Sam. v. 14).—2. Son of CALEB 1 (ii. 18).

SHO′BACH (*pouring*). A General of HADAREZER (2 Sam. x. 15–18).

SHO′BAI (*taking captive*). One who returned from captivity (Ezr. ii. 42; Neh. vii. 45).

SHO′BAL (*flowing*). 1. Son of Seir (Gen. xxxvi. 20).—2. Son of Caleb (1 Chr. ii. 50).—3. Descendant of Judah (iv. 1, 2).

SHO′BEK (*forsaking*). A chief who sealed the covenant (Neh. x. 24).

SHO′BI. Son of NAHASH (2 Sam. xvii. 27).

SHO′CO (2 Chr. xi. 7). See SOCOH.

SHO′CHO (2 Chr. xxviii. 18). See SOCOH.

SHO′CHOH (1 Sam. xvii. 1). See SOCOH.

SHO′HAM (*onyx*). Son of Jaaziah (1 Chr. xxiv. 27).

SHO′MER (*a keeper*). 1. An Asherite (1 Chr. vii. 32).—2. Mother of Jehozabad (2 K. xii. 21).

SHO′PHACH. SHOBACH (1 Chr. xix. 16, 18).

SHO′PHAN (Num. xxxii. 35). East of Jordan; fortified. Lost.

SHOSHAN′NIM. Title of a melody (Ps. xlv., lxix.).

SHOSHAN′NIM E′DUTH. Name of a melody called *lillies of testimony* (Ps. lxxx.).

SHU′A (*riches*). 1. Father of Judah's wife (1 Chr. ii. 3).—2. Daughter of Heber (vii. 32).

SHU′AH (*pit*). 1. Son of ABRAHAM by KETURAH (Gen. xxv. 2).—2. A Descendant of Judah (iv. 11).—3. SHUA, father of Judah's wife (Gen. xxxviii. 2, 12).

SHU′AL (*a fox or jackal*). Son of Zophah, a chief (1 Chr. vii. 36).

SHU′AL, THE LAND OF (*jackal*), (1 Sam. xiii. 17). North of Michmash. Lost.

SHU′BAEL. 1. Son of GERSHOM (1 Chr. xxiv. 20).—2. Son of HEMAN (xxv. 20).

SHU′HAM (*pit-digger*). Son of Dan (Num. xxvi. 42).

SHU′HAMITES, THE. Descendants of SHUHAM, the son of Dan (Num. xxvi. 42, 43).

SHU′HITE. Descendant of SHUAH 1. This name is frequent in the Book of Job.

SHU′LAMITE, THE (*peaceful*). The name given to the bride in Cant. vi. 13.

SHU′MATHITES (*native*). One of the 4 families who lived in Kirjath-Jearim (1 Chr. ii. 53).

SHU′NAMMITE, THE. Native of SHUNEM (2 K. iv. 1); applied to two persons: ABISHAG, the nurse of David (1 K. i. 3, 15), and the nameless hostess of Elisha (2 K. iv. 12, 25, 36).

SHU′NEM (*two resting-places*), (Josh. xix. 18). Issachar. Where the Philistines encamped before the battle of Gilboa (1 Sam. xxviii. 4). Here dwelt the good Shunammite, who welcomed Elisha the prophet, who oft passed by; and fitted up a little chamber for him (2 K. iv. 8), and was rewarded (ver. 36). This pleasant village was the native place of Abishag, David's attendant (1 K. i. 3), and possibly the heroine of Solomon's Song. The modern village is on the S. W. flank of Little Hermon, Jebel Duhy, 3 ms. from Jezreel, N., in full view of Mt. Carmel, and in the midst of the finest grain-fields in the land.

SHU′NI (*quiet*). Son of Gad (Gen. xlvi. 16).

SHU′NITES, THE. Descendants of SHUNI (Num. xxvi. 15).

SHU′PHAM (Heb. SHEPHUPHAM). SHUPPIM.

SHU′PHAMITES, THE. Descendants of SHUPHAM (Num. xxvi. 39).

SHUP′PIM (*serpents*). 1. He and HUPPIM, the children of Ir, are mentioned in 1 Chr. vii. 12.—2. A porter (xxvi. 16).

SHUR (*a wall*), (Gen. xvi. 7). Hagar sat by a fountain in the way to Shur, when the angel sent her back with a promise of a blessing. Abraham dwelt between Kadesh and Shur, in Gerar (xx. 1). Ishmael's descendants dwelt from Havilah unto Shur that is before Egypt (xxv. 18). Called, also, Etham (Ex. xv. 22; Num. xxxiii. 8).

SHU′SHAN (*lily*). Shushan the palace (Esth. i. 2). One of the most important towns in the whole East. Capital of ELAM, SUSIS, or SUSIANA. Inscriptions, dated 660 B. C., record the capture of the city by Asshur-bani-pal, giving, also, its plan. Daniel saw his vision of the ram and he-goat at Shushan the palace (Dan. viii. 2). Cyrus made it a Persian city, and its metropolis (Æschylus and Herodotus), although the building of the palace is credited to Darius. Alexander found there $60,-000,000, and all the regalia of the great king. After this, Susa was neglected for Babylon. Now called Sus, a vast ruin between the Eulæus and Shapur. E. and W. of the city, a few ms. were the rivers Coprates and Choaspes. The water of the Choaspes (now *Kerkhah*) was thought to be peculiarly healthful, and was the only water drank by the kings, at home or on journeys (Herod i. 188), and it is now prized above all other river-water by the people. The ruins cover a space 6,000 ft. E. to W. by 4,500 N. to S., being about 3 ms. in circuit. There are 4 artificial platforms. The smallest of these has an eminence 119 ft. high above the river, facing the E., and made of sun-dried brick, gravel, and earth. One platform has a surface of 60 acres. The remains of the Great Palace have been examined, and a plan made out, including 72 columns, some bearing tri-lingual inscriptions, having the names of Artaxerxes, Darius, Xerxes, Hystaspes, and crediting the building to Darius; besides naming the gods Ormazd, Tanaites, and Mithra. The number of columns is the same as in the Great Hall of Xerxes at Persepolis. It stood on a square platform, 1000 ft. each way, 60 ft. above the plain; itself being 120 ft. to the top of the roof, making a

Bered is a change of Becher, and Tahath becomes Tahan. The true genealogy is:

	1. Joseph.
1. Joseph.	2. Ephraim.
2. Ephraim.	3. Shuthelah.
3. Shuthelah.	4. Eran (Laadan).
4. Eran.	5. Ammihud.
5. Ammihud.	6. Elishama.
6. Elishama.	7. Nun.
7. Nun.	8. Joshua.

The story in 1 Chr. vii. 20, 21; viii. 13, belongs

SELLING THE CHILDREN OF JEWISH CAPTIVES.

hight in all of about 180 ft. The appearance must have been truly grand, rising as it did to such a great hight, amidst lower structures, beautified with trees and shrubs, reflected in the river at its base. Esther plead in this palace for her people, and saved them.

SHU'SHAN E'DUTH. The title of a melody; it denotes "the lily of testimony" (Ps. lx.).

SHU'THALHITES, THE. Descendants of SHU-THELAH (Num. xxvi. 35).

SHU'THELAH (*noise*). Head of an Ephraimite family (Num. xxvi. 35), and ancestor of Joshua (1 Chr. vii. 20–27).

The text in 1 Chr. vii. 20, is an error from careless copying, probably. The names Eran, Laadan, Eleadah, Elead, are repeated from one original.

to the history of the country after the passage of Jordan; the *descent* upon the Shefelah (Gath, etc.) agreeing with the topography of Palestine. This is probably a marginal gloss of some ancient scribe which has been adopted into the text.

SI'A (*congregation*). Ancestor of a family of Nethinim, who returned from captivity (Neh. vii. 47).

SI'AHA (Ezr. ii. 44). SIA.

SIB'BECAI. The Hushathite (2 Sam. xxi. 18).

SIB'BECHAI (*thicket of Jah*). A captain in David's army for the eighth month of 24,000 men (1 Chr. xi. 29). He belonged to one of the principal families of Judah.

SIB'BOLETH. The Ephraimite word for SHIB-BOLETH (Judg. xii. 6).

SIB'MAH (Josh. xiii. 19). East of Jordan, in Reuben. SHEBAM. Lost.

SIBRA'IM (Ez. xlvii. 16). A north boundary of the land. Lost.

SIC'CUTH (*a tabernacle* or *shrine*), (Amos v. 26).

SI'CHEM. SHECHEM.

SICK'LE (HERMESH, MAGGAL; Gr. *drepanon*). A curved knife for reaping; a reaping-hook or scythe (Deut. xvi. 9; Joel iii. 13).

SIC'YON (*market—weekly?*), (1 Macc. xv. 23). A later city built on the acropolis of an ancient city of the same name, near the eastern end of the Corinthian Gulf, about two miles from the sea, near a range of mountains, which were terraced, and rent with gorges. In the time of the Maccabees it was the most important Roman possession in Greece.

SID'DIM (*the vale of*), (Gen. xiv. 3, 8, 10). The Hebrew words *Emek has Siddim* mean a plain cut up by stony channels. Located by some scholars at the north end of the Dead Sea.

As an *emek* it resembled Jezreel; and therefore a suitable place for the combat mentioned in the text (ver. 8); but having a number of pitch-pits, or, as Josephus says, Wells of Asphalt (Ant. i. 9), and who says the site is under the Dead Sea (Asphaltitis). More probably near it. See GEOLOGY and SEA.

If the Salt Mountain, Usdum (see SODOM) is a recent elevation, then the cities may have been in the plain at the S. end of the Dead Sea, which would then have been the Vale of Siddim.

SI'DE (1 Macc. xv. 23). A colony of Cumæans on the coast of Pamphylia. The navy of Antiochus was made up of ships from Side and Aradus, Tyre and Sidon, and the fleet was stationed at Side on the eve of the battle with the fleet from Rhodes (Livy 37, 23). Its ruins indicate former wealth. The theater of the Roman time was one of the largest in Asia, seating 15,000. It was used as a fort in the middle ages. There was an AGORA (as at Athens), 180 ft. in diameter, surrounded by a double row of columns, and a pedestal for a statue in the centre, and a temple on the south side (mentioned by Strabo). The harbor was closed in, and was 1500 by 600 ft. in extent, with docks for unloading ships.

SI'DON (*fishing*). ZIDON (Phœnician *Tsidon*), (Gen. x. 15, 19). Great Zidon (Josh. xi. 8). Sidon (Matt. xi. 21; Mark iii. 8; Luke vi. 17). On the coast of the Mediterranean Sea, in the narrow Phœnician plain (2 miles), under the range of Lebanon, to which it once gave its own name (Jos. Ant. v. 3, 1). The city is built on the northern slope of a promontory that juts out into the sea, pointing S. W.; and the citadel is on the hight behind it. Zidon was the first-born of Canaan, and probably the city is an older one than Tyre, and the Phœnicians are (often) called Sidonians (never Tyrians) in Josh. xiii. 6; Judg. xviii. 7, etc. Skilled workmen were their special pride, not traders (1 K. v. 6). The prize given to the swiftest runner by Achilles was a large silver bowl, made at Sidon (Homer, Il. xxiii. 743). Menelaus gave Telemachus a most beautiful and valuable present, "a divine work, a bowl of silver with a gold rim, the work of Hephæstus, and a gift from king Phædimus of Sidon" (Od. iv. 614). Homer mentions the beautifully embroidered robes of Andromache, brought from Sidon. Pliny mentions the glass factories (v. 17).

Under the Persians, Sidon attained to great wealth and importance. To live carelessly, after their manner, became a proverb (Judg. xvii. 7). The prize in a boat-race, witnessed by Xerxes at Abydos, was won by Sidonians; and when he reviewed his fleet he sat under a golden canopy in a Sidonian galley; and when he assembled his officers in state the king of the Sidonians sat in the first seat. It was almost utterly destroyed by the Persians, B. C. 351. Being rebuilt, it opened its gates to Alexander. The Jews never conquered the city, and so far failed of the promise. Strabo said there was the best opportunity for acquiring a knowledge of the sciences of arithmetic and astronomy, and of all other branches of philosophy. At this time Greek was probably the language of the best society.

It is the most northern city visited by Jesus, and is about 50 miles from Nazareth. Now called *Saide*. The whole neighborhood is one great garden, filled with every kind of fruit-bearing trees, nourished by streams from Lebanon. Its chief exports are silk, cotton and nutgalls. A mission-station of Americans are working among 5000 people.

There are many ancient sepulchres in the rocks at the base of the mountain east of Sidon, and sepulchral caves in the plain. In one of these caves, in 1855, was discovered one of the most beautiful and interesting Phœnician monuments in existence. It is a sarcophagus of black syenite, with a lid carved in human form, bandaged like a mummy, the face being bare. There is an inscription in Phœnician on the lid, and another on the head. The king of the Sidonians is mentioned in them, and it is said that his mother was a priestess of Ashtoreth. It is supposed to belong to the 11th century B. C. It is now in the Louvre, Paris. See p. 192.

SIEVE (Is. xxx. 28). "To sift as wheat" (Luke xxii. 31); figuratively, to agitate and prove by trials and afflictions.

SI'HON (*sweeping away*). King of the Amorites (Num. xxi. 21).

SIHOR (*black*). Correctly Shihor. The Nile. (Sanscrit, *Nilah*, dark-blue). The water of the Nile is dark with mud, like our Ohio or Mississippi. The Egyptian name was Yeor. (The name of Egypt was *Kem*, black). The present name in Arabic is *Bahr el Azrak, dark-blue river*. Shihor is the name of the brook of Egypt (*Wady el Arish*), which is mentioned as the south boundary of David's kingdom (1 Chr. xiii. 5; Josh. xiii. 2, 3). See NILE.

SI'LAS. Contraction of SILVANUS, one of the chief men among the first disciples at Jerusalem (Acts xv. 22). He is mentioned in 2 Cor. ii. 9, i. 19; 1 Pet. x. 12; Acts xvi. 19, 25; Phil. iv. 10.

SILK (Heb. MESHI), (Ez. xvi. 10, 13). Silk in the time of the Ptolemies was sold for its weight in gold. It sometimes came in skeins, and was woven into a thin light gauze. It is not known how early or extensively the Jews used it (Rev. xviii. 12; Gen. xli. 42).

SIL'LA. Where Joash, the king, was killed (2 K. xii. 20). Lost.

SILO'AH (*dart*). SILOAM (*sent*), (Heb. SILOACH), (Neh. iii. 15). Arabic, *Silwan*. One of the few undisputed localities around Jerusalem. The water was "sweet and abundant" in Josephus day (B. J. v. 4, 1). It is in the Tyropœon valley, 200 ft. from the Kidron. There are no less than 40 natural springs within a circle of 10 miles around Jerusalem. The water flows out of a small artificial basin, under the cliff, into a reservoir 53 ft. long by 18 ft. wide and 19 ft. deep. It has been lately proved, by exploring, that the water flows from the Virgin's fountain to Siloam; and there is a remarkable ebb and flow, which varies in frequency with the season and supply of water (John ix. 7). The village of Siloam (*Silwan*) is not mentioned in Scripture, and is probably modern. It is poorly built, and occupies the site of Solomon's idol-shrines (1 K. xi. 7; 2 K. xxiii. 13).

SILOAM, TOWER IN. Mentioned by Jesus (Luke xiii. 4). Not located.

SILVER (Heb. KESEF, Chal. *kesaf*, Gr. *argurion*).

One of the precious metals, and the one used most as a coin among all nations. The ancient Hebrews weighed it out, instead of having coins. It is mentioned in Gen. xiii. 2, xx. 16, xxiii. 16, and Ex. xxvi. 19, 32; 1 Chr. xxix. 4. See MONEY.

SIL'VER-LINGS (*little silvers*). Pieces of silver or silver coins (Is. vii. 23).

SIMALCU'E (Heb. MELECH, *king*). An Arabian chief who had charge of ANTIOCHUS VI (1 Macc. xi. 39).

SIM'EON (*hearkening*). Second son of Jacob and Leah (Gen. xxix. 33).

The tribe of Simeon numbered six families (the head of one of which, Shaul, was a son of a Canaanite woman) when Jacob went down into Egypt (Gen. xlvi.), and at the Exode 59,300 men over 20, but only 22,000 at the last census by Moses.

A name of frequent occurrence in Jewish history. 1. Son of MATTATHIAS 2, and one of the famous MACCABEES (1 Macc. ii. 65).—2. Son of Onias, the high-priest.—3. A governor of the Temple (2 Macc. iii. 4).—4. SIMON, THE BROTHER OF JESUS (Matt. xiii. 55; Mark vi. 3).—5. Simon, the Canaanite, one of the twelve apostles (Matt. x. 4), otherwise described as Simon Zelotes (Luke vi. 15).—6. Simon of Cyre'ne. A Hellenistic Jew (Acts ii. 10), born in Cyrene, Africa.—7. Simon the Leper. A resident at Bethany, who had been miraculously cured of leprosy by Jesus (Matt. xxvi. 6).—8. Simon Mag'gnus, a sorcerer or magician (Acts viii. 9).—10. A Pharisee (Luke vii. 40).—11. The Tanner, a disciple living at Joppa (Acts ix. 43).—12. Father of JUDAS ISCARIOT (John vi. 71). Simon Chosame'us, error of the scribe in combining the last letters of Malluch ch with the first part of Shemariah. SHIMEON and the three following names in Ezr. x. 31, 32, are thus written in 1 Esd. ix. 32.

SIM'RI. Son of Hosah (1 Chr. xxvi. 10).

SIN (*mire*). Pelusium (*pelos*, Greek for *mire*), in Egypt. Sin, the strength of Egypt (Ez. xxx. 15). Probably a fortified city. Pompey was murdered here by order of Ptolemy, B. C. 48.

SIN, WILDERNESS OF. See WILDERNESS OF WANDERING.

SIN'AI. Mountain and desert forming a part of the peninsula between the gulfs of Suez and Akabah. The district of Sinai is near the center of the triangular space between the two arms of the Red Sea. (See maps, page 99). This peninsula is formed of granite, with dykes of porphyry and greenstone, without a trace of volcanic rocks. It is separated from the limestone district of Et Tyh (see WILDERNESS OF THE WANDERING), by the narrow plain of Er Ramleh, a desert of red sand. There are 3 mountain groups: Serbal on the W., Sinai in the center, and Katerin S. of Sinai; all nearly bare of foliage, but peculiarly beautiful in colors the most varied. A belt of sand borders the shore of the two arms of the Red Sea. The granite is the same kind as the red sienite, found at Assouan, on the Nile, of which the temples in Egypt were built. In Sinai, itself, the base is of a coarser quality than the peak, which has more quartz. Mt.

VIA DOLOROSA.

In the wilderness Simeon was on the south ide of the Tabernacle. The only great name of the tribe on record is that of the widow Judith, the heroine of the apocryphal Book of Judith, where she appears as an ideal type of piety, beauty, courage, and chastity. There were 18 cities, with their surroundings, given to Simeon out of the portion allotted to Judah, including the famous well of Beersheba, and one of which (Ziklag) became the private property of David, as a present from Achish the Philistine. A part of the tribe (500 men) took possession of a district in Mount Seir, where they were still living after the return from the Captivity (1 Chr. iv. 42, 43).

SI'MON. One of the twelve apostles. See PETER.

Katerin is nearly all porphyry. There is a difference of opinion as to which peak is the Sinai of Moses and the Law; some claiming Serbal with its ancient inscriptions, and others Sufsafa, with its convent, pit, and chapel. Both answer some of the requirements of the text, but neither all of the points. See EXODUS, WILDERNESS.

SINCERE' (Gr. *adolos, guileless, pure,* 1 Pet. ii. 2). Gr. *eilikrines,* judged of in sunlight (Phil. i. 10).

SIN'IM (Is. xlix. 12). The Chinese.

SIN'ITE (Gen. x. 17). The fortress of Sinna is mentioned by Strabo (xvi. 756) as in Mt. Lebanon. The ruins of Sini were known in the days of Jerome (Gen. loc. cit.).

SI'ON. A name of Mt. Hermon (Deut. iv. 48).

SIPH'MOTH (*bare-places*). Place in the S. of Judah, which David frequented during his wandering (1 Sam. xxx. 28). Site unknown.

SIP'PAI. Son of RAPHA, or "The Giant" (1 Chr. xx. 4).

SI'RACH. See HISTORY OF THE BOOKS.

SI'RAH (*a-going-off*) **THE WELL** (2 Sam. iii. 26), 1 m. out of Hebron.

SIRI'ON. The Sidonian name for Mt. Hermon (Deut. iii. 9; Ps. xxix. 6).

SIS'AMAI (*distinguished*). A descendant of Sheshan (1 Chr. ii. 40).

SIS'ERA (*battle-array*). 1. A general in the army of Jabin, king of Hazor (Judg. iv. 5).—2. One who returned from captivity (Ezr. ii. 53).

SISIN'NES. TATNAI (1 Esd. vi. 3).

SIS'TER (Heb. AHOTH, Gr. *adelphe*), used to denote one who is the daughter of the same parents (Gen. iv. 22), or the same parent (Lev. xviii. 9, 11); also, one of the same faith (Rom. xvi. 1).

SIT'NAH (*hatred*). The 2d of the two wells dug by Isaac (Gen. xxvi. 21). Site lost.

SI'VAN. MONTH.

in war (Gen. xvii. 13). Those born in the house often enjoyed the utmost confidence and privilege. This was illustrated in the case of Abraham commissioning his servant to select a wife for Isaac. Servitude under the law was much restricted (Ex. xxi. 16; Deut. xxiv). Debt, or poverty, were causes for servitude (Lev. xxv. 39, 40); also, it was the penalty for theft (Ex. xxii. 1–14), the servitude ceasing when an equivalent of labor had been paid. All Hebrew bondmen were released in the year of Jubilee (Lev. xxv. 47–54). Foreign slaves were not so treated. They could become the property of the Hebrews, as captives in war (Deut. xx. 14), or by purchase from the dealers (Lev. xxv. 44). The slave-trade is mentioned as being carried on with Tyre by Javan (Greeks), Tubal and Meshech (Ez. xxvii. 13). Joseph was the first person recorded as having been sold into slavery (Gen. xxxvii. 27, 28). Slaves were employed upon menial work (Lev. xxv. 39) in the household, and in attendance upon the master. It was a duty of female slaves to grind corn (Ex. xi. 5; Job xxxi. 10; Is. xlvii. 2).

SLEEP. Slumber or repose of the body (Gen. xxviii. 11). Used to denote DEATH (Jer. li. 39), or spiritual torpor (Rom. xiii. 11).

SLIME. Heb. HEMAR, *asphaltos and bitumen* (Gen. xi. 3). Found on and near the Dead Sea. It is commonly found in a solid state, but when heated and used as a mortar, it becomes hard as the rocks it cements together.

SLING. An instrument much used before the invention of fire-arms (Judg. xx. 16; 1 Sam. xvii. 48–50).

SMITH. An artificer in brass, iron, etc.; first mentioned in Gen. iv. 22. See HANDICRAFT.

SMYR'NA (Rev. ii. 8–11). Designed by Alexander the Great, and built by his successors Antigonus and Lysimachus, near the site of the ancient city of the same name (which had been destroyed by the Lydians 400 years before). It stood at the head of a gulf of the Ægean Sea, by the mouth of the river Meles, having a range of mountains on three sides of it. Tiberius granted the city permission to erect a temple in honor of the Roman emperor and senate. John (Rev. ii. 9) probably referred to the pagan rites in his letter to the church in Smyrna. See SEVEN CHURCHES.

The only ancient ruins are on the mountains, south. On the summit is a ruined castle. So convenient has it been to carry away antiquities that Smyrna has been nearly stripped. Van Lennep, the missionary, found a great number of small articles in the dirt-heap of the ancient city; rings, seals, lamps, household gods, and many other articles, more or less broken (except the seals), and probably thrown away as rubbish, or lost. In the time of Strabo it was one of the most beautiful cities in all Asia (Minor). There were a library and museum, with grand porticoes, dedicated to Homer (claimed as a native); an Odeum, and a temple to the Olympian Zeus. The Olympian games were celebrated. Polycarp was martyred here, being condemned by the Jews also.

SNAIL (Heb. SHABLUL). In Lev. xi. 30 a sort of lizard; and in Ps. lviii. 8 the common slug or snail without a shell, which

THEBAN STATUE.   EL MUMMY.

SLAVE (Heb. EBED, Gr. *somata*). Servitude, under the Mosaic law, was more that of bondman than slave. In the patriarchal period the servitude was of two kinds: those slaves or servants born in the house, and those who were purchased or taken

consumes away and dies by depositing its slime wherever it passes. 1. SHABLUL. The Septuagint says "melted wax" in Ps. liii. 9 (8 A. V).—2. CHOMET. The name of an unclean animal in Lev. xi. 30. Perhaps a lizard or a chameleon.

SNARE (Heb. MOKESH, *pah*). A noose for catching birds (Job xl. 24).

SNOW (Heb. SHELEG; Chal. *telag;* Gr. *chion*). Is often alluded to for its whiteness Ex. iv. 6; Num. xii. 10; in Prov. xxv. 13, "as the cold of snow in time of harvest" alludes to its use in cool drinks for the reapers. The snow lies deep in the ravines of Lebanon until late in the summer. The summit of Hermon perpetually glistens with snow. Snow, as actually falling, is alluded to but twice (2 Sam. xxiii. 20; 1 Macc. xiii. 22). Job refers to its supposed cleansing effects when melted (ix. 30), and to the rapid melting under the rays of the sun (xxiv. 19), and floods following (vi. 16). In Ps. lxviii. 14, thick-falling snow is alluded to as a synonyme for a host flying from defeat, probably with white dresses or turbans. Snow lies deep on Lebanon and Hermon late in the summer, from whence it is carried to the cities for cooling drinks. It never leaves the highest peaks of Lebanon or Hermon. (See HERMON, CLIMATE).

SNUFFERS. (Heb. 1. MEZAME-ROTH, *forceps*). Snuffers for lamps (1 K. vii. 50).—2. MELKAHAYIM (Ex. xxxvii. 23), tongs.

SO (Heb. SEVECH or SEVEC). A deity represented in the form of a crocodile. So, King of Egypt, made an alliance with Hosea, king of Israel, and promised him assistance, but was unable to prevent the king of Assyria from taking Samaria, B. C. 721 (2 K. xvii. 4). In the remains of Sennacherib's palace, recently disentombed, among the seals was found one of So, well known to students of Egyptian antiquities.

SOAP (Heb. BORITH), (Jer. ii. 22). A term for any substance of *cleansing* qualities. The soap familiar to us was unknown to the Egyptians, and probably to the ancients generally. They used certain vegetables and their ashes for cleansing linen, etc. Numerous plants, yielding alkalies, exist in Palestine, which, when pounded, serve as a substitute for soap. The *gilloo* or "soap-plant" of Egypt is used in the manufacture of soap at Joppa.

SO'CHO (1 Chr. iv. 18). SOCOH.

SO'CHOH (*branches*), (1 K. iv. 10).

SO'COH. 1. (Josh. xv. 35). In the Shefelah, now called *Esh Shuweikah*, in *Wady Sumt*, 3½ ms. S. W. of Jerusalem.—2. (ib. xv. 48). Judah, in the hill region. Now called *Esh Shuweikah* in *Wady Khalil*, 10 ms. S. W. of Hebron (1 Chr. iv. 18).

SOD. The preterite of seethe, to burn or cook.

SO'DI (*confident of Jah*). Father of Gaddiel (Num. xiii. 10).

SOD'OM (*vineyard* or *burning*). One of the most ancient cities of Canaan, in the Jordan valley, the chief of the five cities (Gen. x. 19). The plain was once like a garden, and was chosen by Lot, when Abram chose Canaan (ib. xiii. 10). As the two patriarchs were standing on a hight between Bethel and Ai they could see Jericho and the Jordan plain (called KIKKAR in the Hebrew, a term peculiar to this district alone); while they could not see the south end of the Dead Sea. But opposed to this is the event of Abraham looking toward the plain, and seeing the smoke go up as from a furnace (xix. 28). And that from no hight near Hebron can the Jordan plain near Jericho be seen, while the south end of the Dead

Sea and the Lisan are distinctly visible. There is a salt-mountain called Usdum (Sodom) on the S. W. shore of the Dead Sea, which may have inherited and preserved the name of the ancient city, but the site of that city is lost.

SOD'OMITE (*one from Sodom*). One of those who practiced their peculiar religious rite (Deut. xxiii. 17; 1 K. xiv. 24).

SOLDER. That the ancient Hebrews were acquainted with the use of solder is evident from Is. xli. 7. Nothing is known as to the composition of the solder, but, probably, lead was one of the materials used.

SOL'DIER. See ARMOR. Soldiers are first men-

DANDOUR.

tioned in 2 Chr. xxv. 13; and in Ezra (viii. 22), and Isaiah (xv. 4), and many times in the N. T. Paul alludes to fighting as a soldier (1 Cor. ix. 26), as also James (iv. 2), as well as nearly every writer in the Scriptures. The Christian's life is the life of a soldier, constantly in the armor of faith, fighting against evil.

SOL'OMON. In Hebrew, SHELOMOH (*the peaceful*). The youngest son of David and Bathsheba (1 Chr. iii. 5). He was educated under the care of Nathan, the prophet, in all that the priests, Levites, and prophets had to teach, and was named by him Jedidiah (*loved of Jah*), (2 Sam. xii. 25). He was only looked upon as the heir of the throne after Absalom's revolt and death; and only after Adonijah endeavored to seize the throne, Solomon was anointed by Nathan, and solemnly acknowledged as king, at the age of 19 or 20, 1015 B. C. (1

K. i. 5). David died soon after. From that time his history is nearly that of the nation. It is supposed by some that his personal appearance is the subject of the Shulamite's language in the Canticles (Cant. v. 10). His great wealth, which had been accumulated by David through many years, cannot be computed by our system, because the figures in the original accounts of the sum set apart for the Temple are uncertain, and vary in the two records: in 1 Chr. xxii. 14, the sum being stated at 100,000 talents of gold, and 1,000,000 of silver, and in chapter xxix. 4, at 3,000 talents of gold, and 7,000 of silver. The sources of this wealth were

HOUSE-TOPS.

many, for Solomon was a merchant as well as a monarch (2 Chr. viii. ix. 10). The exports were, wheat, barley, oil, wine, wool, silk, hides, fruit, and other articles. His ships (in care of or assisted by the Tyrians) navigated the Mediterranean and the Red Sea, and to the regions beyond; trading in gold, precious stones, ivory, apes, spice, and scented woods. Besides the ships, caravans of camels were, probably, used across the Syrian desert, and to the Red Sea and Egypt: which called for the building of Tadmor (Palmyra), and the fortifying of Thapsacus, on the Euphrates, and Eziongeber on the Red Sea.

The visit of the Queen of Sheba was one of the results of this commercial intercourse, and her very rich presents show the extreme value of their trade (1 K. x.)

Solomon's fame was established by the building of the great Temple at Jerusalem (1 K. vi.); but besides that he built his own palace, the queen's palace, the house of the forest of Lebanon, a grand porch, and the porch of judgment (law court). He had increased the walls of the city, and fortified Millo and other strongholds in different parts of the land (2 Chr. xxxii. 5, viii.).

In the work of building the Temple especially (and probably in all others) he employed slaves, of whom the Jews held at that time no less than 153,000, who were, it may be, Hittites (2 Chr. ii. 17). In this he followed the example of the Pharaohs, as he did also in state ceremony and display.

As soon as Nathan and Zadok, his father's counselors, were dead, he began to lower the standard of religious purity, by building shrines to heathen gods, although two sons of Nathan and a son of Zadok were among his advisers (1 K. xi. 33). (See JERUSALEM). This grant of indulgence to his heathen wives might have had a political motive (iii. 16). It is quite probable that Solomon himself was a believer in, if not an actual practicer of, the soothsayer's or magician's arts, for which he has, from his time to the present, had a reputation everywhere in the East.

It is in accordance with Eastern royalty that Solomon sometimes acted as a judge in cases of oppression, as in the case of the two children; and it may be that his porch of judgment contained his stated council and judicial chamber.

His harem was established on a magnificent scale; and he made a grand display of the chief luxury of wealth, in the number of his women, and especially in marrying an Egyptian princess (xi.). By these practices, and the idolatries which his foreign wives led him into, he lost the hearts of the prophets, and lost for his posterity the rule of the ten tribes. The most of this evil is charged by some to the influence of his mother, Bathsheba, who was grand-daughter to Ahithophel, who was renowned through all Israel for worldly wisdom and political sagacity.

It is to be regretted that we have not more of the writings of Solomon, and also that we do not even know certainly what he wrote of the books that are now attributed to him. After the return from the Captivity, the Rabbis of the Great Synagogue made extracts from the well-known books of law, history, poetry, and proverbs, accepting and preserving only a small part. These represent in the Canticles the young man, passionate but pure; in the Proverbs, the middle-aged man, with a practical, prudential thought, searching into the depths of man's heart, resting all duty on the fear of God; and in the Preacher, the old man, who had become a moralist, having passed through the stages of a philosopher and of a mystic, now made confession of his "crime of sense," and he could only realize that weariness which sees all earthly things only as vanity of vanities.

The immense influence which Solomon produced, on his own and later ages, is seen in the fact that men have claimed his great name for even the noblest thoughts of other authors—as in the Book of Wisdom, and possibly in Ecclesiastes—and have woven an endless fabric of fantastic fables, Jewish, Arabian, and Christian. Spells and charms of his invention (of which the famous *seal of Solomon* is an example) are supposed to have a power over disease, and evil spirits, which he conquered and cast into the sea; and magicians have "swarmed" in the Old World, who mingled his name in their incantations. His wisdom interpreted the speech of birds and beasts; and he knew the hidden virtues (mystic) of plants. His magic ring revealed to him the past, the present, and the future. And finally, all vast works, especially of architecture, of past time, whose history is lost, are credited to him.

The New Testament does not add to our knowledge of Solomon, but gives us his true measure as a man and a king, in a single sentence, which declares that in the humblest work of God, as a lily, there is a grace, and beauty, and purity, not equaled by all Solomon's glory (Matt. vi. 29).

SOL'OMON'S SER'VANTS, CHILDREN OF (Ezr. ii. 56, 58; Neh. vii. 57, 60). These appear in the lists of the exiles who returned from Captivity. They occupy almost the lowest places in those lists.

SOL'OMON'S SONG. See HISTORY OF THE BOOKS.

SOL'OMON, WISDOM OF. See HISTORY OF THE BOOKS.

SON (Heb. BEN; Gr. *huios*). A male child (Gen. xvii. 16, 19), or any remote descendant (Gen. xix. 5), or a son, by adoption (Gen. lxviii. 5), or by law (Ruth iv. 17), or education (1 Sam. iii. 6), or conversion (Tit. i. 4). And it also denotes a mental or moral resemblance (Judg. xix. 22). Men are sometimes called sons of God (Luke ii. 38) in a similar sense.

SON OF GOD. A peculiar appellation of Christ, expressing His eternal relationship to the Father (Ps. ii. 7). Christ always claimed to be the only begotten son of the Father (Matt. iv. 3, viii. 29, xxvii. 54); and the Jews rightly understood him as thus making himself equal with God (John v. 18, x. 30–33).

SON OF MAN. A title of Christ, assumed by Himself in His humiliation (John i. 51). It is applied to Him more than eighty times in the N. T. See HISTORY OF THE BOOKS.

SOP'ATOR (a contraction of SOSIPATOR). The son of Pyrrhus.

SOPH'ERETH (*scribe*). Ancestor of children of Solomon's servants, who returned from Captivity (Ezr. ii. 55).

SOPHONI'AS. ZEPHANIAH (2 Esd. i. 40).

SOUTH. Heb. DAROM, bright, sunny, region; NEGEB, dry, parched quarter; TEYMAN, on the right hand. "The South Country" is often used for the southern part of Judah (Gen. lxx. 1).

SOUTH RA'MOTH (*hights south*). One of the places David visited (1 Sam. xxx. 27).

SOW'ER. See AGRICULTURE.

SPAIN. The ancient name of both Spain and Portugal, and a Roman province in Paul's time, containing many Jews. It is not certain that Paul carried out his intention of visiting Spain (Rom. xx. 24, 28), since neither he nor any other writer of his time has left any evidence of such a visit.

SPAR'ROW (Heb. ZIPPOR; Gr. *strouthion*). (Ps. lxxxiv. 3; Matt. x. 29, 31). A small bird, with quill and tailfeathers brown; its body gray and black; resembling the small chirping-bird: it is bold and familiar in its habits. These birds are still numerous, troublesome, and cheap, in Jerusalem (Luke xii. 6).

SPAR'TA. A celebrated city of ancient GREECE, and the capital of Laconia. It was long the rival of ATHENS. Situated in a valley, on the Eurotas, 20 ms. from the sea. The remarkable correspondence related in 2 Macc. v. 9, probably had no foundation in history.

SO'REK (*noble vine*), **THE VALLEY OF.** Samson loved a woman in the valley of Sorek (Judg. xvi. 4). *Wady es Surar.*

SOSIP'ATER (*saving a father*). 1. A general of Judas Maccabæus (2 Macc. xii. 19–24).—2. Kinsman of Paul (Rom. xvi. 21).

SOS'THENES. Chief of the synagogue at Corinth (Acts xviii. 17).

SOS'TRATUS (*saving an army*). A commander of the Syrian garrison, B. C. 172 (2 Macc. iv. 27, 29).

SO'TAI (*one who turns aside*). Ancestor of a family of Solomon's servants who returned from Captivity (Ezr. ii. 55).

SPARROWS.

SOUL. Heb. 1. NEDIBAH (Job xxx. 15), elevated and happy state.—2. NEFESH, more than 500 times (Gen. ii. 7, xii. 5, 13). The meanings are: *a.* breath (Job. xli. 13); *b.* vital spirit, soul (Gen. xxxv. 18); *c.* life (Ex. iv. 19); *d.* ghost (Job xi. 20); *e.* pleasure (Ps. cv. 22).—3. NESHAMAH, breath; also blast (2 Sam. ii. 16; Job iv. 9); "spirit," "inspiration."—4. Gr. *psuche* (Matt. x. 28), the vital breath, life; properly, the soul.

The ancients supposed the soul, or rather the animating principle of life, to reside in the breath. Hence the Hebrew and Greek words where they refer to man are translated "soul" and rendered "life" or "breath" (Gen. ii. 7). The immortality of the soul is a fundamental doctrine of revealed religion. The ancient patriarchs lived and died persuaded of this truth, and it was in the hope of another life that they received the promises (Gen. l. 31; Num. xxiii. 10). To save the souls of men, Christ gave himself freely to death.

SPEAR'MEN (Gr. *dexiolaboi*, those taking the right). 200 formed part of the escort which accompanied PAUL in his march from Jerusalem to Cæsarea (Acts xxiii. 23).

SPICE, SPI'CERY, SPI'CES. 1. (Heb. BASAM, BESEM, Cant. v. 1). Sweet spices, incense, or spices; a general term to denote those aromatic substances which were used in the preparation of the anointing oil, the incense-offerings (Ex. xxv. 6, xxxi. 11).

SPI'DER (Heb. AKKABISH), (Job viii. 14; Is. lix. 5). Both passages allude to the fragile nature of the spider's web. They are found in every habitable portion of the globe, but are largest in warm climates.

SPIKE'NARD (Heb. NERD, Gr. *nardos*). A highly perfumed ointment, prepared from a plant in India growing in short spikes. Prized by the ancients, and was a favorite perfume at their baths and banquets. It was very costly (John xii. 3).

SPIN'NING. Is mentioned in Ex. xxxv. 25, 26; Matt. vi. 28; Luke xii. 27. The distaff round which the flax or wool for spinning was wound, and spindle on which the yarn or thread was wound in spinning. The spindle was held in one hand, while the other was employed in drawing out the thread.

SPIRIT. See SOUL.

SPIKENARD.

'SPIRIT, THE HOLY (Heb. NESHAMAH; L. *Spiritus*). The *Third person of the Trinity.* The *Spirit of God.* The character and influence of the Holy Spirit are chiefly shown in the N. T. That which was but imperfectly understood in patriarchal times became full of meaning to Christians. It is called the Holy Spirit of Jehovah in Ps. liii. 10, 11, the Good Spirit, Jehovah, in Ps. cxliii. 10. In the work of the creation the Holy Spirit is mentioned (Gen. i. 2). As the bestower and sustainer of life (Gen. ii. 7; Job xxvii. 3). From the epoch of Samuel, the work of the Spirit is manifest (1 Sam. x. 10, xvi. 14; 2 K. ii. 9; Neh. ix. 30; Is. xi. 27). In the N. T., both preceding and after the birth of Christ, the agency of the Holy Spirit was especially prominent in its manifestations. The presence of the Holy Spirit is constantly associated with the birth and life of Christ and the work of His disciples. The holy conception was of the Spirit (Matt. i. 18). The Holy Spirit openly appeared at Christ's baptism by John, and afterwards led Him into the wilderness (Luke iv. 1). In Christ's charge to the apostles are the words "For, it is not ye that speak, but the Spirit of your Father which speaketh in you" (Matt. x. 20; also in John xiv. 16; Acts i. 8). It was probably to correct the prevailing ignorance upon this subject that Christ condemned the blasphemers of the Holy Ghost (Matt. xii. 31). From the date of the Ascension commenced what is termed the "Dispensation of the Spirit" (Eph. iv. 8; John vii. 39). Christ ordained that Christians should be baptized in the name of the Holy Ghost (Matt. xxviii. 19). The rite of "laying on of hands" in its relation to the Holy Spirit is referred to in Acts vi. 6, etc.

SPONGE (Gr. *sponggos*). Belong to the animal kingdom. They have, when living, an apparently homogeneous jelly filling their pores and covering their surface. They come mostly from the Mediterranean and Bahama Islands. The value of the sponge was known from very early times, and was probably used by the Hebrews (Matt. xxvii. 48; Mark xv. 36).

SPOON. (Heb. CAPH, *palm* or *hollow*), (Ex. xxv. 29).

STA'CHYS (*an ear of grain*). A disciple at Rome saluted by Paul (Rom. xvi. 9).

STAC'TE (Heb. NATAF). One of the sweet spices in the holy incense (Ex. xxx. 34).. From the myrrh tree, the natural gum; myrrh being artificially produced by incisions. See MYRRH.

STARS (*Star of the Wise Men*). A general name for any of the heavenly bodies, except the Sun and Moon (Gen. i. 16). See ASTRONOMY.

STÄ'TER (*standard*). A piece of money. See MONEY.

STEEL. See METALS.

STEPH'ANAS (*crowned*). A convert of Corinth (1 Cor. i. 16, xvi. 15).

STE'PHEN (Syr. *Chelil*, a crown). The first Christian martyr; chief of the first seven deacons of the early Church of Jerusalem. He denounced the narrowness of Jewish worship (Acts vi. 13, 14). His continual attacks upon the Jewish ritual and worship caused his being charged with blasphemy before the Sanhedrin. In this tribunal the Pharisees were in the majority. In his defense he gave a critically just and true summary of the Jewish Church: denouncing the local worship, and bringing out clearly the spiritual element in its history; and he showed that in the previous Jewish history the presence of God was not limited to the Temple at Jerusalem; and that there was among the Jews, from the earliest, a spirit of intolerance. He addressed them with calmness (Acts vi. 15), but his words were received with anger. He was sentenced to be stoned to death, and the sentence was at once executed, Saul of Tarsus (Paul) consenting and assisting (Acts vii. 58, viii. 1). He died with the greatest firmness (Acts vii. 60).

The gate now called St. Stephen, at Jerusalem, is on the east side of the city. In the time of the Crusades it was on the north side, at what is now called Damascus Gate, near the probable site of the crucifixion on the hillock, over the so-called cave of Jeremiah, near which it is also probable that Stephen was stoned.

STOCKS (Heb. MAHPEKETH). In which the body was placed in a bent position; SAD, when the feet alone were confined. They consisted of two beams, the upper one movable, with grooves between them large enough to receive the ankles of the prisoner. They were often erected in market-places, that the insults of the people might be added to the pain of confinement (Job xiii. 27; Jer. xx. 2).

STOICS. A sect of fatalistic heathen philosophers, so named from the Greek word *stoa,* "*porch,*" or portico, because Zeno, its founder, held his school in a porch of the city, more than three centuries before Christ (Acts xvii. 18). See EPICUREANS.

STOM'ACHER. An ornament or support to the breast. Heb. PETHIGIL, a sort of girdle (Is. iii. 24). See DRESS.

STONES. Were used for building (Mark xiii. 1). Some were very large. Also for pavements (2 K. xvi. 17). Large stones were used for closing the entrances of caves (Josh. x. 18). Flint stones sometimes served for a *knife* (Ex. iv. 25). Stones were used in slings as ammunition of war (1 Sam. xvii. 40, 49), as weights for scales (Deut. xxv. 13), and for mills (2 Sam. xi. 21). Large stones were set up to commemorate any remarkable event (Gen. xxviii. 18). Such stones were occasionally consecrated by ANOINTING (Gen. xxviii. 18). The heathens worshiped stones (Is. lvii. 6). See JERUSALEM.

STONES, PRECIOUS. See PRECIOUS STONES

STORE. A quantity (Gen. xxvi. 14).

STORK (Heb. HASIDAH, *kindness* or *mercy*). It has the beak and legs long and red; it feeds on field-mice, lizards, snakes, frogs, and insects. Its plumage is white, with the tips of its wings, and some small part of its head and thighs black. Storks migrate to southern countries in August and return in Spring. They are still much venerated among the common people in Europe and Asia (Jer. viii. 7; Lev. xi. 19; Deut. xiv. 18). The Mohammedans allow them to make their nests on the roofs of their mosques, and feed them very generously, holding them in superstitious reverence.

STRAIN AT (Gr. *diulizo*, *strain out*). There can be little doubt that this obscure phrase is due to an error, and the true reading is "*strain out*" (Matt. xxiii. 24).

STRANGE WOMAN (Heb. ZONAH, KEDESHAH). Used for *foreign* in some passages, and as being the wife of another, or, at least, one who has no business with the person whom she tempts (Prov. ii. 16, 17). An adulteress.

STRANGER (Heb. GER, TOSHAB). A foreigner; one not an Israelite, living in the Promised Land. Explained by some to be all those not members of the Jewish Church; not the "foreigner" (Heb. NOCHRI) who was merely visiting the land as a traveler. The mixed multitude that went out of Egypt with the children of Israel (Ex. xii. 38); the original Canaanites, captives of war, fugitives, hired servants, etc., were all called foreigners. They equaled one-tenth of the whole population in Solomon's time (2 Chr. ii. 17). If the stranger was a bondman he had to be circumcised (Ex. xii. 44); and without this rite, if he were even independent, he could not be admitted to full privileges. The number of strangers who were slaves in Solomon's time were very great—probably 150,000.

STRAW (TEBEN). Both wheat and barley straw were used by the ancient Hebrews chiefly as fodder for their cattle (Gen. xxiv. 25). It was used by the Egyptians in making bricks (Ex. v. 7, 16). They reaped their corn close to the ear and cut the straw close to the ground. This was the straw that Pharaoh refused to give to the Israelites, and they were therefore compelled to gather STUBBLE (Heb. KASH), the short straw left standing (Is. v. 24).

STRAW, TO. To strew, to scatter (Ex. xxxii. 20).

STREAM OF EGYPT. See SIHOR, the RIVER OF EGYPT (Is. xxvii. 12).

STREET (Heb. HUZ, REHOB, SHUK; Gr. *plateia*, *rhume*). See JERUSALEM.

STRINGED IN'STRUMENTS. See MUSICAL INSTRUMENTS.

STRIPES. PUNISHMENTS.

STRONG DRINK. DRINK.

STUB'BLE (Heb. KASH). See STRAW.

SU'AH (*a sweeping*). Son of Zophah (1 Chr. vii. 36).

SU'BA. Ancestor of sons of Solomon's servants who returned from Captivity (1 Chr. vii. 36).

SU'BAI. SHALMAI (1 Esd. v. 30).

SUB'URBS (Heb. MIGRASH). A place where herds are driven to graze, *a pasture* (1 Chr. v. 16). Especially the open country round the Levitical cities (Lev. xxv. 34). According to the Talmud, and most English expositors, the space from the wall outward measured 1,500 feet (Num. xxx. v. 4), and was used as a common or suburb; and the space from without the city on the east side (ver. 5) was 3,000, and used for fields and vineyards.

SUC'COTH (*booths*), (Gen. xxxiii. 17). Where Jacob built booths (of reeds, long grass, branches of trees, etc.), and thus gave the place a name. *Sakut* is a ruin 10 miles S. of *Beisan*, on the W. bank of the Jordan, where there is a copious spring in a fertile plain. But this is on the wrong side of the Jordan, for it belonged to Gad (Josh. xiii. 27). The name may have been transferred across the

river. Succoth was mentioned as being near the clay ground where the metal work for Solomon's Temple was cast.—2. A station of the Wandering (Ex. xii. 37). Site lost.

SUC'COTH-BENOTH. Occurs only in 2 K. xvii. 30. It represents the Chaldæan goddess ZIRBANIT, the wife of MERODACH, who was especially worshiped at Babylon.

SU'CHATHITES (*descendants of a Suchah*). A family of Scribes at Jabez (1 Chr. ii. 5).

SUD. A river near Babylon, on whose banks the Jewish captives lived.

SUD. SIA or SIAHA (1 Esd. v. 29).

SU'DIAS. HODAVIAH 3 and HODEVAH (1 Esd v. 26).

SU'ET. FAT (Heb. YEKEB). Press-fat (Joel ii. 24).

SUK'KIIM (Heb. SUKKIYIM, *dwelling in booths*). A nation mentioned (2 Chr. xii. 3), as supplying part of the army which came out of Egypt with Shishak.

SUM'MER. CLIMATE.

SUM'MER FRUIT (KAYIZ, *fruit-harvest*). Fruit, especially figs, as harvested in summer (2 Sam. xvi. 1, 2).

There are many summer fruits in Palestine, and scarcely a month where there are not-fruits of some kind to be had.

SUN (Heb. SHEMESH; Gr. *helios*). The great luminary of the day, which furnishes so many similitudes to the Hebrew poets, as well as those of all nations (Judg. v. 31; Prov. iv. 18; Luke i. 78, 79; John viii. 12). For the idolatrous worship of the sun, see BAAL. ANNAM'MELECH.

INTERIOR OF HOUSE.

SUN'DIAL (Is. xxxviii. 8). DIAL.

SUPERSTI'TION (Gr. *deisidaimonia*, *fear of the gods*). Excessive exactness or rigor in religious opinions or practice; extreme and unnecessary scruples in the observance of religious rites not commanded (Acts xxv. 19, xvii. 22).

SU'PHAH. Translated Red Sea in Num. xxi. 14. The modern name is Yam Suf. See RED SEA.

SUR. One of the places on the seacoast of Palestine (Judg. ii. 28).

SUR, THE GATE OF (2 K. xi. 6). A gate of the Temple, called also "the gate of the foundation" (2 Chr. xxiii. 5).

SURETISHIP. One who makes himself responsible for the safe appearance of another (Gen. xliv. 32; Prov. xxii. 26), or the payment of his debts. Christ is the "surety of a better testament" (Heb. vii. 22).

SUSA. SHUSHAN (Esth. xi. 3).

SUSANCHITES, PEOPLE OF. SHUSHAN (Ezr. iv. 9).

SUSAN'NA (*a lily*). 1. The heroine of the Judgment of Daniel, or History of Susanna, in the Apocrypha.—2. One of the women who ministered to the Lord (Luke viii. 3).

SU'SI (*horseman*). Father of Gaddi (Num. xiii. 11).

SWAL'LOW (Heb. DEROR and AGUR, "swallow" "crane"). The well-known bird of passage, common in our country, Europe and the East (Is. xxxviii. 14).

SWAN. The translation of the Heb. TINSHEMETH in Lev. xi. 18, and Deut. xiv. 16. Some think it the purple hen or water fowl.

SWEARING. OATH.

SWEAT, BLOODY (Luke xxii. 44). A peculiar physical accompaniment of the agony in the garden.

SWEET. HONEY.

SWINE (Heb. HAZIR; Gr. *choiros, hus*). A well-known animal forbidden as food to the Hebrews, who held its flesh in such detestation that they would not pronounce its name (Lev. xi. 7; Deut. xiv. 8; Is. lxv. 4, lxvi. 3, 17; Matt. viii. 32; Luke v. 14, 16; 2 Pet. ii. 22; Matt. xvii. 6.)

KING OF EGYPT. (SEE PAGE 285.)

SYC'AMORE (Heb. SHIKMAH, Gr. *sukaminos*), (Luke xvii. 6). A tree of Egypt and Palestine, the fruit of which resembles the fig (1 K. x. 27). It grows to the size of a walnut tree, has wide spreading branches, and affords a delightful shade, and is planted by the way-sides. Its leaves are heart-shaped, downy on the under side and fragrant. The fruit grows from the trunk itself on little sprigs, and in clusters like the grape. To make the fruit eatable, three or four days before gathering it is punctured with a sharp instrument (Amos vii. 14). The wood is very durable; Egyptian mummy-coffins made of it being still perfectly sound. These trees were held in great value (1 Chr. xxvii. 28), and it was one of Egypt's calamities that her sycamores were destroyed (Ps. lxxviii. 47). The sycamore of America and of England are very different from those of the Scriptures.

SYC'AMINE TREE (Gr. *sukaminos*). A species of the mulberry tree (*morus*). Both black and white mulberry trees are common in Syria and Palestine, and are largely cultivated for supplying food to the silk-worm (Luke xvii. 6).

SY'CHAR (*falsehood*), (John iv. 5). A city of Samaria. (See SHECHEM.) Named so from the false worship on Mt. Gerizim (John iv. 22; Hab. ii. 18).

SY'CHEM. See SHECHEM.

SY'CHEMITE, THE. Inhabitants of SHECHEM (Jud. v. 16).

SYE'LUS. JEHIEL 3 (1 Esd. i. 8)

SYE'NE. Properly Sereneh (Ez xxix. 10, xxx. 6). From Migdol to Syene was a term for the whole extent of Egypt. Migdol was the last town in Egypt toward the E., and Syene was the last toward the S., and is now known by its ancient name. Its Egyptian name was SUN, which meant "to open," that is, the opening into Egypt from the south.

SYM'EON. SIMON (2 Pet. i. 1).

SYM'PHONY. A harmony of sounds (Dan. iii. 5).

SYN'AGOGUE. I. *History.*—The word *Synagogue* (συναγωγή), which means a "congregation," is used in the New Testament to signify a recognized place of worship. A knowledge of the history and worship of the synagogues is of great importance, since they are the characteristic institution of the later phase of Judaism. We cannot separate them from the most intimate connection with our Lord's life and ministry. In them he worshipped in his youth and in his manhood. They were the scenes, too, of no small portion of his work. We know too little of the life of Israel, both before and under the monarchy, to be able to say with certainty whether there was anything at all corresponding to the synagogues of later date. They appear to have arisen during the exile, in the abeyance of the temple-worship, and to have received their full development on the return of the Jews from captivity. The whole history of Ezra presupposes the habit of solemn, probably of periodic, meetings (Ezra viii. 15; Neh. viii. 2; ix. 1; Zech. vii. 5). The "ancient days" of which St. James speaks (Acts xv. 21) may, at least, go back so far. After the Maccabæan struggle for independence, we find almost every town of village had its one or more synagogues. II. *Structure.*—The size of a synagogue varied with the population. Its position was, however, determinate. It stood, if possible, on the highest ground, in or near the city to which it belonged. And its direction too was fixed. Jerusalem was the *Kibleh* of Jewish devotion. The synagogue was so constructed that the worshippers as they entered, and as they prayed, looked towards it. In the internal arrangement of the synagogue we trace an obvious analogy to the type of the Tabernacle. At the upper or Jerusalem end stood the ark, the chest which like the older and more sacred ark, contained the Book of the Law. Here were the "chief seats," after which Pharisees and Scribes strove so eagerly (Matt. xxiii. 6), to which the wealthy and honored worshipper was invited (James ii. 2, 3). III. *Officers.*—In smaller towns there was often but one Rabbi. The most prominent functionary in a large synagogue was known as the

Sheliach, the officiating minister who acted as the delegate of the congregation. The *Chazzan* or "minister" of the synagogue (Luke iv. 20) had duties of a lower kind, resembling those of the Christian deacon or sub-deacon. Besides these there were ten men attached to every synagogue, known as the *Batlanim*. IV. *Worship.*—It will be enough to notice in what way the ritual, no less than the organization, was connected with the facts of the N. T. history, and with the life and order of the Christian Church. From the synagogue came the use of fixed forms of prayer. To that the first disciples had been accustomed from their youth. They had asked their Master to give them a distinctive one, and he had complied with their request (Luke vi. 1), as the Baptist had done before for his disciples, as every Rabbi did for his. The large admixture of a didactic element in Christian worship, that by which it was distinguished from all Gentile forms of adoration, was derived from the older order. "Moses" was "read in the synagogues every Sabbath-day" (Acts xx. 21), the whole Law being read consecutively, so as to be completed, according to one cycle, in three years. The writings of the prophets were read as second lessons in a corresponding order. They were followed by the *Derash* (Acts xiii. 15), the exposition, the sermon of the synagogue. The conformity extends also to the times of prayer. In the hours of service this was obviously the case. The third, sixth, and ninth hours were in the times of the N. T. (Acts iii. 1; x. 3, 9), and had been probably for some time before (Ps. lv. 17; Dan. vi. 10), the fixed times of devotion. The same hours, it is well known, were recognized in the Church of the second, probably in that of the first century also. The solemn days of the synagogue were the second, the fifth, and the seventh, the last or Sabbath being the conclusion of the whole. The transfer of the sanctity of the Sabbath to the Lord's Day involved a corresponding change in the order of the week, and the first, the fourth, and the sixth became to the Christian society what the other days had been to the Jewish. From the synagogue, lastly, come many less conspicuous practices, which meet us in the liturgical life of the first three centuries: Ablution, entire or partial, before entering the place of meeting (Heb. x. 22; John xiii. 1–15); standing, and not kneeling, as the attitude of prayer (Luke xviii. 11); the arms stretched out; the face turned towards the Kibleh of the East; the responsive amen of the congregation to the prayers and benedictions of the elders (1 Cor. xiv. 16). V. *Judicial Functions.*—The language of the N. T. shows that the officers of the synagogue exercised in certain cases a judicial power. It is not quite so easy, however, to define the nature of the tribunal and the precise limits of its jurisdiction. In two of the passages referred to (Matt. x. 17; Mark xiii. 9) they are carefully distinguished from the councils. It seems probable that the council was the larger tribunal of 23, which sat in every city, and that under the term synagogue we are to understand a smaller court, probably that of the Ten judges mentioned in the Talmud. Here also we trace the outline of a Christian institution. The Church, either by itself or by appointed delegates, was

to act as a Court of Arbitration in all disputes among its members.

SYN'AGOGUE, THE GREAT. On the return of the Jews from Babylon, a great council was appointed, according to Rabbinic tradition, to reorganize the religious life of the people. It consist ⌐ of 120 members, and these were known as the men of the Great Synagogue, the successors of the prophets, themselves, in their turn, succeeded by scribes prominent, individually, as teachers. Ezra was recognized as president. Their aim was to restore again the *crown*, or *glory*, of Israel. To this end they collected all the sacred writings of former ages and their own, and so completed the canon of the O. T. They instituted the feast of Purim and organized the ritual of the synagogue. The narrative of Neh. viii. 13 implies the existence of a body of men acting as councillors under the presidency of Ezra; and these may have been an assembly of delegates from all provincial synagogues—a synod of the National Church.

SYN'TYCHE (*happy choice*). A woman, and a member of the Church of Philippi (Phil. iv. 2, 3).

SYR'ACUSE. On the E. coast of Sicily. A wealthy and populous place when visited by Paul (Acts xxviii. 12). Taken by the Romans 200 yrs. B. C.

SYR'IA (from TSUR, Tyre); ARAM (*high*) in the Hebrew. Aram was the fifth son of Shem (Gen. x. 22). Called Aram in Num. xxiii. 7. The country he settled is called Aram or Syria, and extended from the Mediterranean Sea to the Tigris, and from Canaan to Mt. Taurus, and had 6 names for its different sections, for which see ARAM. The country is divided into long, narrow sections, from N. to S. 1. Plains next to the sea, extending from the Ladder of Tyre to the Taurus, including the plains of Phœnicia, of Seleucia, and of the Issus.—2. The range of mountains called in the N. Amanus and Bargylus, and in the S. Lebanon.—3. The valley between Lebanon and Anti-Lebanon, Cœle, or Hollow Syria.—The mountain range rising N. of Aleppo, and ending at Mt. Hermon.—5. The Syrian desert, extending to the Euphrates. The principal rivers are the Orontes, (El Asy, *the rebellious*), and the Litany. The source of the Orontes is a little N. of Baalbek, where, within a few miles, a stream from both Lebanon and Anti-Lebanon unite to form the stream, flowing N. E.: It passes through a lake, 6 ms. long by 2 wide, near Emesa (HUMS); a little below Hamath it receives a branch; being turned W. by the Amanus, it receives the Kara Su (*Black river*), flows by Antioch, and empties into the sea; having a course of 200 ms. The Litany rises from a small lake, 6 ms. S. W. of Baalbek, and runs S. until it is turned W. by the hills of Galilee, when it reaches the sea 5 ms. N. of Tyre, having run about 80 ms. There are many other small streams, as the Eleutherus, Lycus, Adonis, the rivers of Damascus (Abana and Pharpar), which are lost in marshy lakes, the Koweik, near Aleppo, terminating in a marsh, and the Sajur, a branch of the Euphrates. The lakes are: The Lake of Antioch; the Salt Lake, near Aleppo; Kades, on the Orontes; and the Bahr el Merj, near Damascus. The cities are: Antioch, Damascus (150,000); Apameia, Aleppo (70,000); Beirut (50,000); Hamath (30,000), (Num. xiii. 21); Hums (20,000); Tripoli (13,000); Seleucia, Tadmor, (Palmyra), and many others, mentioned in their places. Syria was settled by Canaanites and Aramæans, descendants of Ham. Damascus and Zobah were the chief cities in David's time. Assyria made it a province, and Alexander conquered it (B. C. 323); and after him the Seleucid family governed it, one of them building Antioch, which was their only capital until 114 B. C. The Romans, under Pompey, captured it, B. C. 65. The Mohammedans succeeded the Romans A. D. 634, when, for 100 yrs. after, they made Damascus their capital.

SYR'IAC VER'SIONS. HISTORY OF THE BOOKS.

SYR'IA MA'ACHAH (1 Chr. xix. 6).

SYR'IAN. A native of Syria (Gen. xxv. 20).

SY'ROPHENI'CIAN. Is Phœnicia properly so-called, which was a part of Syria only when the Syrian kings governed Phœnicia. The Canaanitish woman is called a Syrophœnician (Mark vii. 26).

T

TA'ANACH (*sandy soil*), (Josh. xii. 21). An ancient city of Canaan, built on the end of a ridge which runs northward from the hills of Manasseh into the plains of Esdraëlon, at the base of which is the modern village of the same name (Ar. *Ta'annuk*). It was the headquarters of the army of Deborah and Barak, and Sisera's host was encamped between it and Megiddo (Judg. v. 19).

TA'ANATH-SHI'LOH (*approach to Shiloh*), (Josh. xvi. 6). Supposed to be Shiloh; Taanath being the Canaanite and Shiloh the Hebrew name of the same city.

TAB'AOTH. TABBAOTH (1 Esd. v. 29).

TAB'BAOTH (*rings*). Ancestor of a family of Nethinim, who returned from Captivity (Ezr. ii. 43).

TAB'BATH (Judg. vii. 22). In the Jordan valley, below and not far from Bethshean. It may be Tubakat Fahil (*Terrace of Fahil*).

TA'BEAL. The "son of Tabeal" was apparently a Syrian, whom the Syrians and Israelites intended to place on the throne (Is. vii. 6).

TA'BEEL (*God is good*). An officer of the Persian government (Ezr. iv. 7).

TABEL'LIUS. TABEEL (1 Esd. ii. 16).

TAB'ERAH (*burning*), (Num. xi. 3; Deut. ix. 22). In the Sinai district, but not identified.

TA'BERING. The obsolete word thus used in the A.V. of Nah. ii. 7 requires some explanation. The Hebrew word connects itself with *toph*, "a timbrel." The A.V. reproduces the original idea. The "tabour," or "tabor," was a musical instrument of the drum-type, which with the pipe formed the band of a country village. To "tabour," accordingly, is to beat with loud strokes as men beat upon such an instrument.

TAB'ERNACLE (*a tent*). See TEMPLE.

TAB'ERNACLES, THE FEAST OF. See FESTIVALS.

TAB'ITHA, also called Dorcas by St. Luke: a female disciple of Joppa, "full of good works," among which that of making clothes for the poor is specifically mentioned. While St. Peter was at the neighboring town of Lydda, Tabitha died; upon which the disciples at Joppa sent an urgent message to the apostle, begging him to come to them without delay. Upon his arrival, Peter found the deceased already prepared for burial, and laid out in an upper chamber, where she was surrounded by the recipients

and the tokens of her charity. After the example of our Saviour in the house of Jairus (Matt. ix. 25; Mark v. 40), "Peter put them all forth," prayed for the divine assistance, and then commanded Tabitha to arise (comp. Mark v. 41; Luke viii. 54). She opened her eyes and sat up, and then, assisted by the apostle, rose from her couch. This great miracle, as we are further told, produced an extraordinary effect in Joppa, and was the occasion of many conversions there (Acts ix. 36–42). The name of "Tabitha" is the Aramaic form, answering to the Hebrew *tsebiyah*, a "female gazelle." St. Luke gives "Dorcas" as the Greek equivalent of the name.

TA'BLE (Heb. LUAH, *a table* or *tablet*). Used especially of the tablets or slabs of stone on which were the TEN COMMANDMENTS (Ex. xxiv. 12). Also of other tablets for WRITING (Is. xxx. 8). Heb. MESAB (Cant. i. 12), "at his table." Heb. SHULHAN, *a table spread with food* (Ex. xxv. 23 ff.): Gr. *kline, a bed* (Mark vii. 4); also, a couch for resting or reclining at MEALS (Matt. ix. 2, 6).

TAB'LETS. 1. Heb. BOTTEYHAN-NEFESH, *houses of the soul; perfume-boxes.*—2. Heb. CUMAZ (Ex. xxxv. 22), (*a globule of gold*, or, rather, *a string of*

TABLE.

gold). Drops like beads were worn round the neck, or arm, by the Israelites in the desert.

TABOR, MT. (*hight*). (Josh. xix. 22). On the border of Issachar and Zebulon. It is of limestone, 1800 ft. high, rounded in form, and is studded with forests of oaks, pistachios, terebinths, mock-oranges, and other trees and bushes. Wolves, boars, lynxes, and other wild animals, besides reptiles, are found. It is now called *Jebel et Tur*, and is one of the most favorable points for beautiful and extensive views. The plain of Esdraëlon is seen, spread out like a carpet, between the hills of Samaria and those of Galilee, ending at Carmel. and in the season of early harvest (March and April) is diversified with the various colors of different fields in cultivation: some red from recent plowing—some yellow, white, or green, as the state of the crop may determine. The sea of Galilee and the Mediterranean are visible. The course of the Jordan can be traced for many miles. Lebanon and Hermon, with their snow-capped summits, and the hills of Galilee, including Hattin, the Mt. of Beatitudes, are on the N., and the countless hills and valleys of Bashan (*Hauran*), and Gilead, are to the E.; Little Hermon (Hill Mizar) and Gilboa to the S., while the mountains of Samaria fill up the view to the W., ending in the ridge of Carmel to the N. W., where we began. All around the top are foundations of a thick wall, built of large stones, some of which are beveled. There are ruins of towers and bastions. Toward the E. end of this enclosure are confused heaps of ruins of houses, churches, towers, and other buildings — some of hewn and others of beveled stones. One tall, pointed arch is standing, called the Gate of the Wind. The ruins are of different ages, from remote antiquity, the time of Josephus, the Crusades, and still later days. The early Christians adopted the legend of the Transfiguration of the Saviour on this mountain (Rob. ii. 358), but this is now located on Hermon, near Paneas.

TABOR, THE PLAIN OF. It has been already pointed out that this is an incorrect translation, and should be THE OAK OF TABOR. It is mentioned in 1 Sam. x. 3 only, as one of the points in the homeward journey of Saul after his anointing by Samuel. But unfortunately, like so many of the other spots named in this interesting passage, the position of the Oak of Tabor has not yet been fixed. Ewald seems to consider it certain that Tabor and Deborah are merely different modes of pronouncing the same name, and he accordingly identifies the Oak of Tabor with the tree under which Deborah, Rachael's nurse, was buried (Gen. xxv. 8). But this, though most ingenious, can only be received as a conjecture.

TAB'RET. [TIMBREL.]

TABRI'MON. Properly Tabrimmon, i. e. "good is Rimmon," the Syrian god. The father of Benhadad I., king of Syria in the reign of Asa (1 K. xv. 18).

TACHE. The word thus rendered occurs only in the description of the structure of the Tabernacle and its fittings (Ex. xxvi. 6, 11, 33; xxxv. 11; xxxvi. 13; xxxix. 33), and appears to indicate the small hooks by which a curtain is suspended to the rings from which it hangs, or connected vertically, as in the case of the veil of the Holy of Holies, with the loops of another curtain.

TACH'MONITE, THE. "The Tachmonite that sat in the seat," chief among David's captains (2 Sam. xxiii. 8), is in 1 Chr. xi. 11 called "Jashobeam an Hachmonite," or, as the margin gives it, "son of Hachmoni." Kennicott has shown that the words translated "he that sat in the seat" are a corruption of Jashobeam, and that "the Tachmonite" is a corruption of the "son of Hachmoni," which was the family or local name of Jashobeam. Therefore he concludes "Jashobeam the Hachmonite" to have been the true reading.

TAD'MOR, called "Tadmor in the wilderness" (2 Chr. viii. 4). There is no reasonable doubt that this city, said to have been built by Solomon, is the same as the one known to the Greeks and Romans and to modern Europe by the name, in some form or other, of Palmyra. The identity of the two cities results from the following circumstances: 1st, The same city is specially mentioned by Josephus (Ant. viii. 6, § 1) as bearing in his time the name of Tadmor among the Syrians, and Palmyra among the Greeks; and in his Latin translation of the Old Testament, Jerome translates Tadmor by Palmira (2 Chr. viii. 4). 2dly, The modern Arabic name of Palmyra is substantially the same as

the Hebrew word, being Tadmur or Tathmur. 3dly, The word Tadmor has nearly the same meaning as Palmyra, signifying probably the "City of Palms," from Tamar, a palm. 4thly, The name Tadmor or Tadmor actually occurs as the name of the city in Aramaic and Greek inscriptions which have been found there. 5thly, In the Chronicles, the city is mentioned as having been built by Solomon after his conquest of Hamath Zobah, and it is named in conjunction with "all the store-cities which he built in Hamath." This accords fully with the situation of Palmyra [HAMATH]; and there is no other known city, either in the desert or not in the desert, which can lay claim to the name of Tadmor. In addition to the passage in the Chronicles, there is a passage in the Book of Kings (1 K. ix. 18) in which, according to the marginal reading (Keri), the statement that Solomon built Tadmor likewise occurs. But on referring to the original te~t (Cethib), the word is found to be not Tadmor, but Tamar. Now, as all the other towns mentioned in this passage with Tamar are in Palestine (Gezer, Bethhoron, Baalath), as it is said of Tamar that it was "in the wilderness in the land," and as, in Ezekiel's prophetical description of the Holy Land, there is a Tamar mentioned as one of the borders of the land on the south (Ez. xlvii. 19), where, as is notorious, there is a desert, it is probable that the author of the Book of Kings did not really mean to refer to Palmyra, and that the marginal reading of "Tadmor" was founded on the passage in the Chronicles. If this is admitted, the suspicion naturally suggests itself, that the compiler of the Chronicles may have misapprehended the original passage in the Book of Kings, and may have incorrectly written "Tadmor" instead of "Tamar." On this hypothesis, there would have been a curious circle of mistakes; and the final result would be that any supposed connection between Solomon and the foundation of Palmyra must be regarded as purely imaginary. This conclusion is not necessarily incorrect or unreasonable; but there are not sufficient reasons for adopting it. As the city is nowhere else mentioned in the whole Bible, it would be out of place to enter into a long, detailed history of it on the present occasion. The following leading facts, however, may be mentioned: The first author of antiquity who mentions Palmyra is Pliny the Elder. Afterward it was mentioned by Appian, in connection with a design of Mark Antony to let his cavalry plunder it. In the second century A. D. it seems to have been beautified by the emperor Hadrian. In the beginning of the third century A. D. it became a Roman colony under Caracalla (211–217 A. D.), and received the jus Italicum. Subsequently, in the reign of Gallienus, the Roman senate invested Odenathus, a senator of Palmyra, with the regal dignity, on account of his services in defeating Sapor king of Persia. On the assassination of Odenathus, his celebrated wife Zenobia seems to have conceived the design of erecting Palmyra into an independent monarchy; and, in prosecution of this object, she for a while successfully resisted the Roman arms. She was at length defeated and taken captive by the emperor Aurelian (A. D. 273), who left a Roman garrison in Palmyra. This garrison was massacred in a revolt; and Aurelian punished the city by the execution not only of those who were taken in arms, but likewise of common peasants, of old men, women, and children. From this blow Palmyra never recovered, though there are proofs of its having continued to be inhabited until the downfall of the Roman Empire.

PALMYRA-TADMOR.

TA'HAN (*station*). Descendant of Ephraim (Num. xxvi. 35).

TA'HANITES, THE. Descendants of TAHAN (Num. xxvi. 35).

TAHAP'ANES. TAHPANHES.

TA'HATH (*below*). 1. Ancestor of Samuel and Heman (1 Chr. vi. 37).—2. Son of Bered (vii. 20).—3. Grandson of No. 2 (vii. 20).

TA'HATH (*lower*), (Num. xxxiii. 26). Desert station. Lost.

TAH'PANHES (*Daphne?*). An important town in Lower Egypt, in the land of Goshen, near Pelusium (Jer. xliii. 7). Located at *Tel Defenneh*, in the present Delta.

TAH'PENES. An Egyptian queen, wife of Pharaoh 6 (1 K. xi. 18–20).

TAHRE'A (*cunning*). Son of Micah (1 Chr. ix. 41).

TAH'TIM HOD'SHI, THE LAND OF (2 Sam. xxiv. 6). Lost. Supposed by some to be Harosheth (compare Judg. iv. 2).

TAL'ENT (Heb. KIKKAR; Gr. *talanton*). The greatest weight of the Hebrews. See MONEY, WEIGHTS AND MEASURES.

TALI'THA. CU'MI. Two Syriac words, meaning *damsel arise* (Mark v. 41). The Chaldee or Aramaic paraphrase on Prov. ix. 3, signifies a girl. Gesenius says the same word means a lamb.

TAL'MAI (*furrowed*). 1. Son of ANAK (Num. xiii. 22).—2. Son of Ammihud, and king of Geshur (2 Sam. iii. 3).

TAL'MON (*oppressed*). Head of the porters for the camps of the sons of Levi (1 Chr. ix. 17).

TAL'MUD. Is the work which embodies the canonical and civil law of the Jews. It contains those rules, precepts and interpretations by which the Jewish people profess to be guided, in addition to the O. T., and includes not merely religion, but philosophy, medicine, jurisprudence, history and the various branches of practical duty. The Jews have been accustomed to divide their law into written and unwritten: the written contained in the Pentateuch, the unwritten handed down orally, until it was found necessary to write it. Some

Jews have assigned the same antiquity to both, alleging that Moses received them on the Mount. *Midrashim*, or explanations of biblical topics, were of gradual growth. The system of interpretation which they exemplify and embody existed in the age of the so-called Sopherim (Scribes), who succeeded the prophets. The oldest Mishna is accredited to Hillel. It is divided into 6 orders or books, 63 treatises (MASSIKLOTH), and 525 chapters (PERAKIM). The first *Seder* treats of sowing, the productions of the earth, trees, and the uses of fruits, seeds, etc. The second *Seder* (MOED), the order of festivals. The third *Seder* (NASHIM) discusses the rights of men and women, marriage and divorce. The fourth *Seder* (NEZIKIN), consisting of ten treatises, with the losses and injuries w⁻ʿ°h one person may bring upon another. The fifth (KODASHIM) treats of sacrifices, oblations, etc. The sixth (TAHAROTH) relates to purifications of vessels, household furniture, etc. Rabbinical Jews have always set a high value on the Talmud, often placing it above the old Mosaic law. Hence we find in the Masseceth Soferim the saying, "The Biblical text is like water, and the Mishna like wine, and the six orders like aromatic wine." In another passage, "The law is like salt, the Mishna like pepper, but the six orders like fine spices." Again, "The words of the Scribes are lovely, above the words of the law; for the words of the law are weighty and light, but the words of the scribes are all weighty." These extravagant praises of the oral traditions agree with the Saviour's words: "Making the word of God of none effect, through your tradition, which ye have believed" (Mark vii. 13).

The first complete edition of the Babylonian Talmud was published at Venice in 1520–1523, in 12 vols. folio. This is the celebrated Bomberg edition now so rare, but not accurate.

The Jerusalem Talmud was first published by Bomberg about 1522–23, at Venice, folio; and subsequently at Cracow, 1609, folio.

The entire Talmud has not been translated into any language. The Mishna appeared in Latin in Surenhusius's edition, Amsterdam, 1698–1703, fol.

TAL'SAS. ELASAH (1 Esd. ix. 22).

TA'MAH (*laughter*). Ancestor of Nethinim, who returned from Captivity (Neh. vii. 55).

TA'MAR (Heb. THAMAR, *palm-tree*). 1. Wife of Er and Onan, the two sons of Judah (Gen. xxxviii. 6–30). She practiced a deception upon Judah, in retaliation for his neglect to give her his third son, Shelah, for a husband.—2. Daughter of David, mother of Absalom. She was badly treated by her brother Amnon (2 Sam. xiii. 1–32).—3. Daughter of Absalom (2 Sam. xiv. 7). The mother of Maachah 3, queen of Judah (1 K. xv. 3).

TA'MAR (*palm-tree*). (Ez. xlvii. 19). A town S. of Hebron, now called Kurnub.

TAM'MUZ. A Syrian idol mentioned in Ez. viii. 14, where the women are represented as weeping for it. It is generally supposed that Tammuz was the same deity as the Phœnician Adonis. The fabled death and restoration of Adonis, supposed to symbolize the departure and return of the sun, were celebrated at the summer solstice with lamentations first, and then rejoicings and obscene revels.

TA'NACH. TAANACH (Josh. xxi. 25).

TAN'HUMETH (*comfort*). Father of Seraiah (2 K. xxv. 23).

TA'NIS. Zoan, in Egypt (Jud i. 10).

TA'PESTRY (Heb. MARBADDIM). Cloth for hangings and bed-covers, ornamented with needle-work (Prov. vii. 16).

TA'PHATH (*drops*). Daughter of Solomon (1 K. iv. 11).

TAP'PUAH (*apple-region*). Son of Hebron (1 Chr. ii. 43).

TA'PHON (1 Macc. ix. 50). Beth Tappuah, near Hebron.

ix. 21, xx. 36). From these passages it seems that there was another Tarshish, which was in the direction of the Red Sea, and probably in India, judging from the articles brought from there, which were gold, silver, ivory, apes, and peacocks (1 K. x. 22). India was the native land of the peacock (Cuvier, viii. 136).

TAR'SUS. Chief town of CILICIA; the birthplace of Paul the Apostle (Acts ix. 11, xxi. 39). It was an important city in the time of the Greek kings. Alexander conquered it; and it was under the rule

MODERN TARSUS.

TAP'PUAH (Josh. xv. 34). In the Shefelah, 12 ms. W. of Jerusalem.—2. EN-TAPPUAH (Josh. xvi. 8, xvii. 7, 8). On the boundary of the children of Joseph—a city and a district of the same name. Supposed to be S. W. of Shechem. Perhaps in Wady Falaik.

TA'RAH. Desert station. Lost.

TAR'ALAH (Josh. xviii. 27). City of Benjamin. Site lost.

TARE'A. TAHREA (1 Chr. viii. 35).

TARES. A noxious plant, of the grass family, supposed to mean the darnel. It grows among the wheat everywhere in Palestine, and bears a great resemblance to it while growing—so closely that, before they head out, the two plants can hardly be distinguished. The grains are found, 2 or 3 together, in 12 small husks, scattered on a rather long head. The Arabs do not separate the darnel from the wheat, unless by means of a fan or sieve, after threshing (Matt. xiii. 25-30). If left to mingle with the bread, it occasions dizziness, and often acts as an emetic.

TAR'GET. A small, round shield (1 Sam. xvii. 6).

TAR'GUM. A translation of the Scriptures in the Chaldee language. Of these, the *Targum* of Jonathan, and that of Onkelos, are held in most esteem by the Jews.

TARPE'LITES (Ezr. iv. 9). Supposed to refer to the people of Tripolis, Phœnicia.

TAR'SHISH (Gen. x. 4; Ps. lxxii. 10; Jonah i. 3, etc.). Probably Tartassus, in Spain (Strabo, iii. 148). There was a city and a river in Spain of the same name; perhaps the same river is now called Guadalquiver. The articles brought to Tyre from Tarshish, such as silver, iron, lead, and tin (Ez. xxvii. 12), were productions of Spain.—2. (2 Chr.

of Antioch, and also that of the Ptolemies. Cæsar changed its name to Juliopolis. Augustus made it a free city. It was a celebrated seat of learning in the time of the early Roman emperors, and was compared by Strabo to Athens and Alexandria, and considered superior to them (xiv. 673). Among its famous citizens were Athenodorus, the tutor of Augustus, and Nestor, the tutor of Tiberius. Antony and Cleopatra met on the banks of the river Cydnus, which divides Tarsus in two.

TAR'TAK. One of the gods of the Avite (or Avvite) colonists of Samaria (2 K. xvii. 31). According to rabbinical tradition, Tartak is said to have been worshipped under the form of an ass. A Persian or Pehlvi origin has been suggested for the name, according to which it signifies either "intense darkness," or "hero of darkness," or the under-world, and so perhaps some planet of ill luck, as Saturn or Mars.

TAR'TAN, which occurs only in 2 K. xviii. 17 and Is. xx. 1, has been generally regarded as a proper name. Recent discoveries make it probable that in Tartan, as in Rabsaris and Rabshakeh, we have not a proper name at all, but a title or official designation, like Pharaoh or Surena. The Assyrian *Tartan* is a general or commander-in-chief.

TAT'NAI (*gift*), satrap of the province west of the Euphrates in the time of Darius Hystaspis (Ezr. v. 3, 6; vi. 6, 13). The name is thought to be Persian.

TAU (Heb. TAV. a mark or sign). The 23d letter of the Hebrew alphabet.

TAV'ERNS. Three Taverns. A station on the

Appian road between Puteoli and Rome, where Paul met brethren when on his way from Jerusalem. The modern Cisteran is probably near the site of the ancient place, which was about 30 miles from Rome.

TAX'ES. I. Under the Judges, according to the theocratic government contemplated by the law, the only payments incumbent upon the people as of permanent obligation were the TITHES, the FIRST-FRUITS, the REDEMPTION-MONEY of the first-born, and other offerings as belonging to special occasions. The payment by each Israelite of the half-shekel as "atonement-money," for the service of the Tabernacle, on taking the census of the people (Ex. xxx. 13), does not appear to have had the character of a recurring tax, but to have been supplementary to the freewill-offerings of Ex. xxv. 1–7, levied for the one purpose of the construction of the sacred tent. In later times, indeed, after the return from Babylon, there was an annual payment for maintaining the fabric and services of the Temple; but the fact that this begins by the voluntary compact to pay one-third of a shekel (Neh. x. 32) shows that till then there was no such payment recognized as necessary. A little later the third became a half, and under the name of the *didrachma* (Matt. xvii. 24) was paid by every Jew, in whatever part of the world he might be living.—II. The kingdom, with its centralized government and greater magnificence, involved, of course, a larger expenditure, and therefore a heavier taxation. The chief burdens appear to have been, (1) A tithe of the produce both of the soil and of live stock (1 Sam. viii. 15, 17). (2) Forced military service for a month every year (1 Sam. viii. 12; 1 K. ix. 22; 1 Chr. xxvii. 1). (3) Gifts to the king (1 Sam. x. 27; xvi. 20; xvii. 18). (4) Import duties (1 K. x. 15). (5) The monopoly of certain branches of commerce (1 K. ix. 28; x. 28, 29; xxii. 48). (6) The appropriation to the king's use of the early crop of hay (Am. vii. 1). At times, too, in the history of both the kingdoms, there were special burdens. A tribute of fifty shekels a head had to be paid by Menahem to the Assyrian king (2 K. xv. 20), and under his successor Hoshea this assumed the form of an annual tribute (2 K. xvii. 4).—III. Under the Persian Empire, the taxes paid by the Jews were, in their broad outlines, the same in kind as those of other subject races. The financial system which gained for Darius Hystaspis the name of the "shopkeeper-king" involved the payment by each satrap of a fixed sum as the tribute due from his province. In Judæa, as in other provinces, the inhabitants had to provide in kind for the maintenance of the governor's household, besides a money payment of forty shekels a day (Neh. v. 14, 15). In Ezr. iv. 13, 20; vii. 24, we get a formal enumeration of the three great branches of the revenue. The influence of Ezra secured for the whole ecclesiastical order, from the priests down to the Nethinim, an immunity from all three (Ezr. vii. 24); but the burden pressed heavily on the great body of the people.—IV. Under the Egyptian and Syrian kings, the taxes paid by the Jews became yet heavier. The "farming" system of finance was adopted in its worst form. The taxes were put up to auction. The contract sum for those of Phœnicia, Judæa, Samaria,

had been estimated at about 8000 talents. An unscrupulous adventurer would bid double that sum, and would then go down to the province, and by violence and cruelty, like that of Turkish or Hindoo collectors, squeeze out a large margin of profit for himself.—V. The pressure of Roman taxation, if not absolutely heavier, was probably more galling, as being more thorough and systematic, more distinctively a mark of bondage. The capture of Jerusalem by Pompey was followed immediately by the imposition of a tribute, and within a short time the sum thus taken from the resources of the country amounted to 10,000 talents. When Judæa became formally a Roman province, the whole financial system of the empire came as a natural consequence. The taxes were systematically farmed, and the publicans appeared as a new curse to the country. The Portoria were levied at harbors, piers, and the gates of cities (Matt. xvii. 24; Rom. xiii. 7). In addition to this, there was the poll-tax paid by every Jew, and looked upon, for that reason, as the special badge of servitude. United with this, as part of the same system, there was also, in all probability, a property-tax of some kind. In addition to these general taxes, the inhabitants of Jerusalem were subject to a special house-duty about this period

TAX'ING. The English word now conveys to us more distinctly the notion of a tax or tribute actually levied; but it appears to have been used in the 16th century for the simple assessment of a subsidy upon the property of a given county, or the registration of the people for the purpose of a poll-tax. Two distinct registrations, or taxings, are mentioned in the N. T., both of them by St. Luke. The first is said to have been the result of an edict of the emperor Augustus, that "all the world (*i. e.* the Roman Empire) should be taxed" (Luke ii. 1), and is connected by the evangelist with the name of Cyrenius, or Quirinus. [CYRENIUS.] The second, and more important (Acts v. 37), is distinctly associated, in point of time, with the revolt of Judas of Galilee.

TEACH'ER. One that imparts instruction, and communicates knowledge of religious truth or other things.

TEARS. Drops of water from the eye (2 K. xx. 5). The ancient Romans collected the tears of mourners for the dead, and preserved them in a bottle, of thin glass or simple pottery. They used to be placed in the sepulchres of the dead, in Rome and Palestine, where they are found in great numbers, on opening ancient tombs (Ps. lvi. 8).

TE'BAH (*slaughter*). Eldest son of NAHOR II (Gen. xxii. 24).

TEBALI'AH (*whom Jah has purified*). Third son of Hosah (1 Chr. xxvi. 11).

TE'BETH. The tenth month of the Hebrew sacred year, commencing with the new moon in January (Esth. ii. 16).

TEHAPH'NEHES. TAHPANHES.

TEHIN'NAH (*mercy*). Founder of IR-NAHASH, son of Eshton (1 Chr. iv. 12).

TEIL'-TREE. The lime-tree, or linden.

TEKO'A (*strikers*), (2 Chr. xi. 6). E. of Hebron; built by Ashur, son of Hezron (2 Chr. ii. 24). Residence of the wise woman who made peace between David and Absalom (2 Sam. xiv.). Ira, the Tekoite, was one of David's 30 "mighty men" (Ib. xxiii. 26). Rehoboam fortified it (2 Chr. xi. 6). Its people helped Nehemiah rebuild the walls of Jerusalem after the return from Babylon (Neh. iii. 5, 27). The prophet Amos was born here (Amos i., vii. 14). The modern name is Tekua, and it is a small village of Arab houses, on an elevated hill, from which there is an extensive view reaching to the mountains of Moab, Dead Sea, the hills around Jerusalem, and W. to Hebron, while toward the S. the mountains of Edom fill the horizon. There are ruins of walls of houses, cisterns, broken columns, and heaps of building-stones. Some of the stones have the peculiar Hebrew bevel, proving their antiquity. The ruins of Khureitun (possibly KERIOTH, the city of Judas) are near Tekua, on the brink of a frightful precipice.

TEKO'A. A name occurring in the genealogies of Judah (1 Chr. ii. 24; iv. 5) as the son of Ashur. There is little doubt that the town of Tekoa is meant.

TEKO'ITE, THE. IRA ben Ikkesh, one of David's warriors, is thus designated (2 Sam. xxiii. 26; 1 Chr. xi. 28; xxvii. 9). The common people among THE TEKOITES displayed great activity

the Assyrian inscriptions), all of which belong to the hill-country above the Upper Mesopotamian plain. Telassar, the chief city of a tribe known as the *Beni Eden*, must have been in Western Mesopotamia, in the neighborhood of Harran and Orfa.

TEL'EM (*oppression*). Judah (Josh. xv. 24). S. of Hebron. Now called Dhullam.

TEL'EM. A porter of the Temple (Ezr. x. 24).

TEL-HARSA. Tel-Haresha (*hill of the wood*). (Ezr. ii. 59; Neh. vii. 61). In the low country of Babylonia, near the Persian Gulf.

TELL HUM has recently been proved to be the site of the ancient CAPERNAUM. The original building of the synagogue, as appears by an inspection of the ruins, was 74 feet 9 inches long by 56 feet 9 inches wide; longer between north and south, with entrances at the south end. Many finely cut capitals were found in the interior, buried in the rubbish; and also several of the pedestals in their proper places. Epiphanius says there was a Christian church there A. D. 600, some of the ruins of

LIZARD.

in the repairs of the wall of Jerusalem under Nehemiah (Neh. iii. 5, 27).

TEL-A'BIB (*hill Abib*) was probably a city of Chaldæa or Babylonia, not of Upper Mesopotamia, as generally imagined (Ez. iii. 15). The whole scene of Ezekiel's preaching and visions seems to have been Chaldæa Proper.

TE'LAH (*breach*). A descendant of Ephraim, and ancestor of Joshua (1 Chr. vii. 25).

TEL'AIM. The place at which Saul collected and numbered his forces before his attack on Amalek (1 Sam. xv. 4, only). It may be identical with TELEM. On the other hand, the reading of the LXX. in 1 Sam. xv. 4, viz. Gilgal, is remarkable, and is almost sufficient to induce the belief that in this case the LXX. and Josephus have preserved the right name, and that, instead of Telaim, we should, with them, read Gilgal. The Targum renders it "lambs of the Passover," according to a curious fancy, mentioned elsewhere in the Jewish books, that the army met at the Passover, and that the census was taken by counting the lambs.

TELAS'SAR (*hill of Asshur*) is mentioned in 2 K. xix. 12 and in Is. xxxvii. 12 as a city inhabited by "the children of Eden," which had been conquered, and was held in the time of Sennacherib by the Assyrians. In both it is connected with Gozan (Gauzanitis), Haran (Carrhæ, now *Harran*), and Rezeph (the *Razappa* of

which are found near the synagogue. The plan of the synagogue was always peculiar, and different from that adopted by the Christians, or Pagans, or Mohammedans, so that there is no difficulty in determining the nature of certain ruins. This building may have been the one built by the centurion (Luke vii. 45), and that in which Jesus delivered the discourse recorded in John vi. One of the stones has a pot of manna sculptured on it.

At the north end of the town there are the remains of two very interesting tombs. One was built of limestone blocks, in a chamber cut from the basalt; and the other a building above ground, which had been whitewashed inside and out. (See Matt. xxii. 27).

TEL-ME'LAH (*hill of salt*). A city of the low district near the Persian Gulf. The city is called Thelme, by Ptolemy (v. 20).

TE'MA (*desert*), (Gen. xxv. 15; Is. xxi. 14.) A small town on the border of Syria, on the pilgrim route from Damascus to Mecca. It was once a stronghold.

TE'MAN (Gen. xxxvi. 11). A city or country named after one of the dukes of Edom, in the S. of the land of Edom. Eusebius and Jerome mention it as being 15 ms. from Petra.

TEM'ANI (Gen. xxxvi. 34). TEMANITE.

TEMAN'ITE. Descendant of TEMAN (1 Chr. i. 45). ELIPHA, the Temanite, was Job's friend, and one of the wise men of Edom (Job ii. 11).

TEM'ENI (*lucky*). Son of Ashur (1 Chr. iv. 6).

TEM'PLE (Heb. 1. MISH'KAN, *dwelling;* an open inclosed place, which can be dwelt in), (Ex. xxv. 9;

Lev. viii. 10, xvii. 13; Num. i. 50–53). It connects itself with the Jewish word SHECHINAH, as describing the dwelling-place of the Divine Glory.—2. OHEL, the tent, as a whole, or, perhaps, the covering, or roof only (Gen. iv. 20, ix. 21, etc.). This is used when applied to the Sacred Tent (Ex. xxvi. 9).—3. BAYITH, house (Ex. xxiii. 19).—4. KODESH, *holy.*—5. MIKDASH, sanctuary (Ex. xxv. 8); Heb. and

TEMPT TO, and **TEMPTA'TION.** These words denote the trying or putting one to the proof. (Heb. BAHAN MASSAH; Gr. *peirazo, ekpeirazo, peirasmos,* etc.). Designate the action of God or the course of His providence, or the earthly trial by which human character and feelings are brought out (Gen. xxii. 1). The Temptation may be used with reference to our first parents (Gen. iii.) or of the

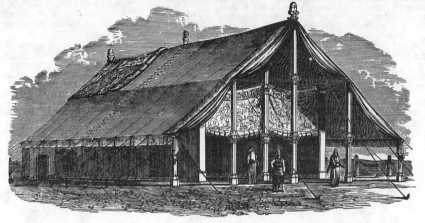

TEMPLE.

Chal. 6. HEY'KAL, temple, palace (2 K. xxiv. 13; 1 Sam. i. 9).—7. MO'ED, place of meeting (Ex. xxix. 42).—8. HA'EDUTH, place of a fixed meeting (Num. ix. 15).—9. OHEL HA'EDUTH, tabernacle of testimony (Num. xvii. 7); so named from the two tables of testimony. The tabernacle was a tent-like structure, adapted to the roving life of the desert, and made more important than the ordinary tent, or even than the best tents of the wealthiest skeikhs, which are lined with silk, or fine linen, or woolen, and very showy in form and color.

Its form was twice the length of its width, 30 cubits (45 feet) long by 10 cubits (15 feet) wide, and the side-walls were 10 cubits (15 feet) high. It stood in an inclosed place, 50 cubits (75 feet) wide by 100 cubits (150 feet) long, 15 feet from the west end. (See the plan on the map of the TWELVE TRIBES). The Holy of Holies, at the west end, was a cube of 10 cubits each way, and in it was the mercy-seat, on the lid of the ark, the cherubim, the ark and the Book of the Law. The room in front was 20 cubits long by 10 wide, and called the Holy Place. In it were the table of shew-bread and the seven-branched candlestick and the altar of incense (Ex. xxv.). The tent had a ridge, forming a right-angle, over which the roof coverings of cloth and skins were thrown. These extended 5 cubits beyond the walls all round the tent, like wide, projecting eaves. There were three coverings to the sides ; the inner of fine linen ; the next of badger-skins; the outer of ram-skins dyed red; and besides these, the roof had one of goats' hair. It was made under the direction of Bezaleel and Aholiab. Its place was in the centre of the camp (see ENCAMPMENT), where it was set up on the first day of the second year of the Exodus (Ex. xl. 2). It was the place where man met with God (Num. xi. 24, 25). It was moved from its place (a moving Bethel) in the Wilderness and in Canaan until the Temple was built, or rather until it lost its glory, when the ark was captured by the Philistines (1 Sam. iv. 22; Ps. lxxviii. 60). The form and size of the tent were symbolical; and to the Hebrews, who believed in the mystical and occult powers of numbers, it was peculiarly sacred because of its peculiar structure. On its altar of incense no strange fire must ever be used.

Jesus (Matt. iv. 1–11) in which Satan was the Tempter.

TEMPT'ER. One who tempts or entices another to sin (Matt. iv. 3).

TEN COMMANDMENTS. See DECALOGUE.

TENT (Heb. OHEL). Dwelling in tents was very general in ancient times among Eastern nations (Gen. iv. 20). The patriarchs, the Israelites from Egypt, dwelt in tents until they obtained the Promised Land, and to some extent afterwards (Judg. vii. 8; Heb. xi. 9). The people of the East live much in the open air. But those most remarkable for this unsettled and wandering life are the Arabs, who still live in tents. This kind of dwelling is not confined to the Arabs, but is used throughout Asia. Tents were usually made of canvas stretched out, and resting on poles, with cords secured to pegs driven into the ground (Is. xxxiii. 20). The house of God, and heaven, are spoken of in Scripture as the tent or tabernacle of Jah (Ps. xv. 1). Says Lord Lindsay: "There is something very melancholy in our morning flittings. The tent-pins are plucked up, and in a few minutes a dozen holes, a heap or two of ashes, and the marks of the camels' knees in the sand, soon to be obliterated, are the only traces left of what has been for a while our home. Often we found ourselves shelterless before being fully dressed." What a type of the tent of our body!

Tents are of various colors; black (Ps. cxx. 5), red, yellow, and white. They are also of various shapes; some circular, others of an oblong figure like the bottom of a ship turned upside down. In Syria the tents are generally made of cloth of goats' hair (Ex. xxxv. 26). Those of the Arabs are of black goats' hair. The Egyptian and Moorish inhabitants of Askalon use white tents. An Arab sheikh will have a number of tents (Gen. xxxi. 33). Usually one tent suffices for a family, being divided, if large, into apartments by curtains.

TENT'MAKERS (Acts xviii. 3).

TENTA'TION (Ex. xvii. 7). TEMPTATION.

TENTH. The tenth part of an ephah, probably the same as the Omer, about five pints (Lev. xxiii. 17).

TE'RAH (*station*). Son of Nahor, and father of

Abram (Gen. xi. 24–32). NAHOR 2, and HARAN 1, and through them the ancestor of the great families of the Israelites, Ishmaelites, Midianites, Moabites, and Amonites. He dwelt in Ur, and was an idolater (Josh. xxiv. 2). He lived 205 years, and died in Haran (xi. 31, 32).

TER'APHIM. This word is rendered "images," "idolatry," or the like. Now understood to represent small images, used as household gods.

Rachel is said to have stolen her father's teraphim (Gen. xxxi. 19). Laban calls them his gods (ver. 30). In the history of Micah of Mount Ephraim the teraphim appeared as objects of worship, and as part of the furniture which he provided for what is called "his house of Gods" (Judg. xvii. 5). Jacob pointed to the teraphim, when he called upon his household to put away "the strange gods" that were among them (Gen. xxxv. 2); to them also Josiah referred (2 Chr. xxxiv. 7; 2 K. xxii. 24). They are named by Hosea among the articles of false worship, and are among the objects of superstitious regard with the king of Babylon (Ez. xxi. 21).

TE'RESH (*severe*). One of the eunuchs who was discovered in his plot to assassinate Ahasuerus (Esth. ii. 21)

TER'TIUS. A disciple who assisted Paul (Rom. xvi. 22).

TENT.

TERTUL'LUS. A Roman orator, whom the Jews employed to bring forward their accusation against Paul (Acts xxiv. 1-2).

TES'TAMENT. See HISTORY OF THE BOOKS.

TES'TIMONY (Heb. EDAH, EDUTH, TEUDAH; Gr. *marturia, marturion*). Witness, evidence, proof (Matt. viii. 4; John iii. 32, 33, etc.). Applied also to the precepts, law, revelation of God (Ps. xix. 7), and especially to the TEN COMMANDMENTS, or DECALOGUE (Ex. xvi. 34).

TE'TA. HATITA (1 Esd. v. 28).

TETH (Heb. TEYTH, *a serpent*). The ninth letter of the Hebrew alphabet (Ps. cxix.).

TET'RARCH. Governor of the fourth part of a country. 1. HEROD ANTIPAS (Matt. xiv. 11), who is distinguished as "Herod the tetrarch;" also the title of king is assigned to him (Matt. xiv. 9).—2. HEROD PHILIP II is called tetrarch of ITUREA (Luke iii. 1); LYSANIAS (iii. 1), tetrarch of ABILENE. This title was probably applied to petty tributary princes also.

THAD'DEUS (Heb. TADDAY, *courageous*). JUDE.

JUDAS. Also called Lebbeus and Thaddeus (Matt. x.). One of the twelve. He is only mentioned as among those who could not see the spiritual kingdom of Jesus (John xiv. 22). Of his life, labors, and death, we know nothing. Tradition says he preached at Edessa, and died a martyr there (Mark iii. 18).

THA'HASH. BADGER. Son of NAHOR 2 by his second wife, Reumah (Gen. xxii. 24).

THA'MAH. Ancestor of a family of Nethinim (Ezr. ii. 53), who returned from Captivity.

THA'MAR. TAMAR 1 (Matt. i. 3).

THAM'NATHA. TIMNATH (1 Macc. ix. 50). Now called Tibneh, half way between Jerusalem and the Mediterranean.

THANK-OF'FERING. SACRIFICE.

THA'RA. TERAH (Luke iii. 34).

THAR'RA. TERESH (Esth. xii. 1).

THAR'SHISH. 1 (1 K. x. 22).—2. A Benjamite of the family of Bilhan (1 Chr. vii. 10).

THAS'SI (*debilitation*). The surname of Simon the son of Mattathias (1 Macc. ii. 3).

THE'ATER. For the general subject, see *Dict. of Ant.*, pp. 995–998. For the explanation of the biblical allusions, two or three points only require notice. The Greek term, like the corresponding English term, denotes the *place* where dramatic performances are exhibited, and also the *scene* itself, or *spectacle*, which is witnessed there. It occurs in the first or local sense in Acts xix. 29. It was in the theatre at Cæsarea that Herod Agrippa I. gave audience to the Tyrian deputies, and was himself struck with death, because he heard so gladly the impious acclamations of the people (Acts xii. 21–23). The other sense of the term "theatre" occurs in 1 Cor. iv. 9, where the Common Version renders, "God hath set forth us, the apostles, last, as it were appointed to death ; for we are made a *spectacle* unto the world, and to angels, and to men." Instead of "spectacle" (so also Wiclif and the Rhemish translators after the Vulgate) some might prefer the more energetic Saxon, "gazing-stock," as in Tyndale, Cranmer, and the Geneva Version.

THEBES (A. V., No, the multitude of No, populous No). A chief city of ancient Egypt, long the capital of the upper country, and the seat of the diospolitan dynasties that ruled over all Egypt at the era of its highest splendor. The sacred name of Thebes was *P-amen*, "the abode of Amon," which the Greeks reproduced in their *Diospolis*, especially with the addition *the Great*. No-Amon is the name of Thebes in the Hebrew Scriptures (Jer. xlvi. 25 ; Nah. iii. 8). Ezekiel uses *No* simply to designate the Egyptian seat of Ammon (Ez. xxx. 14, 16). The name of Thebes in the hieroglyphics is explained under No-AMON. The origin of the city is lost in antiquity. Niebuhr is of opinion that

Thebes was much older than Memphis, and that, "after the centre of Egyptian life was transferred to Lower Egypt, Memphis acquired its greatness through the ruin of Thebes." Other authorities assign priority to Memphis. But both cities date from our earliest authentic knowledge of Egyptian history. The first allusion to Thebes in classical literature is the familiar passage of the Iliad (ix. 381-385): "Egyptian Thebes, where are vast treasures laid up in the houses; where are a hundred gates, and from each two hundred men go forth with horses and chariots." It has been questioned whether Herodotus visited Upper Egypt; but he says, " I went to Heliopolis *and to Thebes*, expressly to try whether the priests of those places would agree in their accounts with the priests at Memphis" (ii. 3). Afterward he describes the features of the Nile Valley, and the chief points and distances upon the river, as only an eye-witness would be likely to record them. In the first century before Christ, Diodorus visited Thebes; and he devotes several sections of his general work to its history and appearance. Though he saw the city when it had sunk to quite secondary importance, he preserves the tradition of its early grandeur, its circuit of one hundred and forty stadia, the size of its public edifices, the magnificence of its temples, the number of its monuments, the dimensions of its private houses—some of them four or five stories high—all giving it an air of grandeur and beauty surpassing not only all other cities of Egypt, but of the world. Diodorus deplores the spoiling of its buildings and monuments by Cambyses (Diod. i. 45, 46). Strabo, who visited Egypt a little later, at about the beginning of the Christian era, describes (xvii. p. 816) the city under the name Diospolis.

But, in the uncertainty of these historical allusions, the *monuments* of Thebes are the most reliable witnesses for the ancient grandeur of the city. These are found in almost equal proportions upon both sides of the river. The parallel ridges which skirt the narrow Nile Valley upon the east and west from the northern limit of Upper Egypt, here sweep outward upon either side, forming a circular plain whose diameter is nearly ten miles. The plan of the city, as indicated by the principal monuments, was nearly quadrangular, measuring two miles from north to south, and four from east to west. Its four great landmarks were Karnak and Luxor upon the eastern or Arabian side, and Qoornah and Medeenet Haboo upon the western or Libyan side. There are indications that each of these temples may have been connected with those facing it upon two sides by grand *dromoi*, lined with sphinxes and other colossal figures. Upon the western bank there was almost a continuous line of temples and public edifices for a distance of two miles, from Qoornah to Medeenet Haboo; and Wilkinson conjectures that from a point near the latter, perhaps in the line of the colossi, the " Royal Street" ran down to the river, which was crossed by a ferry terminating at Luxor on the eastern side. Beginning at the northern extremity on the western bank, the first conspicuous ruins are those of the *Menephtheion*, a palace-temple of the nineteenth dynasty, and therefore belonging to the middle style of Egyptian architecture. Nearly a mile southward from the Menephtheion are the remains of the com-

bined palace and temple known since the days of Strabo as the Memnonium. An examination of its sculptures shows that this name was inaccurately applied, since the building was clearly erected by Rameses II. The general form of the Memnonium is that of a parallelogram in three main sections, the interior areas being successively narrower than the first court, and the whole terminating in a series of sacred chambers beautifully sculptured and ornamented. But the most remarkable feature of these ruins is the gigantic statue of Rameses II. Proceeding again toward the south for about the same distance, we find, at Medeenet Haboo, ruins upon a more stupendous scale than at any other point upon the western bank of Thebes. These consist of a temple founded by Thothmes I., which presents some of the grandest effects of the old Egyptian architecture, and its battle-scenes are a valuable contribution to the history of Rameses III. Behind this long range of temples and palaces are the Libyan hills, which, for a distance of five miles, are excavated to the depth of several hundred feet for sepulchral chambers. Some of these, in the number and variety of their chambers, the finish of their sculptures, and the beauty and freshness of their frescoes, are among the most remarkable monuments of Egyptian grandeur and skill. The eastern side of the river is distinguished by the remains of Luxor and Karnak, the latter being of itself a city of temples. The approach to Karnak from the south is marked by a series of majestic gateways and towers, which were the appendages of later times to the original structure. The temple properly faces the river—*i. e.* toward the north-west. The courts and propylæa connected with this structure occupy a space nearly 1800 feet square, and the buildings represent almost every dynasty of Egypt, from Sesortasen I. to Ptolemy Euergetes I. Courts, pylons, obelisks, statues, pillars, everything pertaining to Karnak, are on the grandest scale. The grandeur of Egypt is here in its architecture, and almost every pillar, obelisk, and stone tells its historic legend of her greatest monarchs. We have alluded to the debated question of the priority of Thebes to Memphis. As yet the data are not sufficient for its satisfactory solution, and Egyptologists are not agreed. When the Shepherds or Hyksos, a nomadic race from the East, invaded Egypt, and fixed their capital at Memphis, a native Egyptian dynasty was maintained at Thebes, at times tributary to the Hyksos, and at times in military alliance with Ethiopia against the invaders; until at length, by a general uprising of the Thebaid, the Hyksos were expelled, and Thebes became the capital of all Egypt under the resplendent eighteenth dynasty. This supremacy continued until the close of the nineteenth dynasty, or for a period of more than five hundred years; but under the twentieth dynasty the glory of Thebes began to decline, and after the close of that dynasty her name no more appears in the lists of kings. Still the city was retained as the capital, in whole or in part, and the achievements of Shishonk the Bubastite, of Tirhakah the Ethiopian, and other monarchs of celebrity, are recorded upon its walls. Ezekiel proclaims the destruction of Thebes by the arm of Babylon (Ez. xxx. 14-16). The Persian invader completed the destruction that the Babylonian had begun.

THE'BEZ (*brightness*), (Judg. ix. 50). A place 13 ms. N. E. of Shechem, now called Tubas, on a gentle hill, surrounded by large groves of olives, and well-cultivated fields (Rob. iii. 305). Abimelech was killed here by a piece of a millstone (2 Sam. xi. 21).

ARCH AT THESSALONICA.

THEC'OE (*the wilderness*). Thec'oe, the Greek form of TEKOA, which see.

THEFT. PUNISHMENTS.

THELA'SAR. TEL-ASSAR (2 K. xix. 12).

THELER'SAS. TEL-HARSA (1 Esd. v. 36).

THE'MAN. TEMAN (Bar. iii. 22, 23).

THEOCA'NUS. TIKVAH.

THEOD'OTUS (*God-given*). An envoy, sent by Nicanor to Judas Maccabæus, about B. C. 162 (2 Macc. xiv. 19).

THEOPH'ILUS (*friend of God*). 1. The person to whom Luke inscribes his Gospel and the Acts of the Apostles (Luke i. 3.—2. A Jewish HIGH-PRIEST, A. D. 37–41; the son of ANNAS.

THEOPH'YLACT (*God-guarded*). A native of Constantinople, and Archbishop of Acris, A. D. 1077 (Mark vii. 3).

THE'RAS. AHAVA (1 Esd. viii. 41, 61).

THER'MELETH. TEL-MELAH (1 Esd. v. 36).

THESSALO'NIANS. People of Thessalonica.

THESSALO'NIANS, FIRST AND SECOND EPIS-TLES TO THE. See HISTORY OF THE BOOKS.

THESSALONI'CA. Named after the sister of Alexander the Great. She was wife of ‧ Cassander, who rebuilt and enlarged the city. Its original name was Therma. In Macedonia, between the rivers of the Thermaic Gulf. It is still the most important town in European Turkey, after Constantinople, having a‧ population of 70,000, about one-third of whom are Jews. It was the residence of Cicero at one time, and the headquarters of Pompey and his Senate, and was made a free city by Octavius Cæsar. In the 1st century A. D., the time of Paul's visit and his two Epistles to the Thessa-

lonians, it was the most populous city in Macedonia. This was the chief station on the great Roman Road, the VIA EGNATIA, which led from Rome toward the whole country north of the seas, and therefore a most important centre for spreading the gospel. Its commerce was equal to Corinth and Ephesus. The first Christians of this city mentioned by name were Jason (Rom. xvi. 21), Demas (2 Tim. iv. 10), Gaius (Acts xix. 29), and Aristarchus and Secundus (Acts xx. 4). The truth and accuracy of the Scripture are confirmed in the mention of the fact of this being a free city and in giving the peculiar and correct term for the chief magistrate, who was called in Greek POLITARCH (Acts xvii. 6). This name is found nowhere else, and is preserved on an arch of the Imperial times, which spans the main street of the city (Aug. Beck. Insc. No. 1967). For several centuries after Christ this was called "The Orthodox City," and was the great center of Oriental Christianity.

THEU'DAS (*gift of God*). An insurgent Jew, mentioned by Gamaliel A. D. 33 (Acts v. 35–39), as of the preceding generation, and not to be confounded with a Theu'das of A. D. 44, mentioned by Josephus.

THIEVES, THE TWO (Gr. *lestai, robbery*). The men who appear in the history of the crucifixion (Matt. xxvii. 38, 44; Mark xv. 37, 42) were robbers, belonging to the lawless bands in Palestine. Against these brigands every Roman procurator had to wage war. They kept an armed police to encounter them (Luke xxii. 52).

THIMNA'THAH. Dan (Josh. xix. 43). Between Eglon and Ekron. The residence of Samson's wife. There must have been several towns of the same name. One is now known as Tibneh, ten miles south of Akir (Ekron).

THIS'BE. Naphtali (Tobit, i. 2). The birthplace of the prophet ELIJAH, THE TISHBITE (1 K. xvii. 1). The place has not been identified, but is looked for in the vicinity of Safed or Kadesh.

THIS'TLE, AND THORNS. There are nearly twenty Hebrew words which point to different

THESSALONICA.

kinds of prickly or thorny shrubs, and are variously rendered "thorns," "briers," "thistles," "brambles," etc. Thistles of various species are numerous in Palestine, and often of prodigious size, and in some parts the thorns and briers grow so luxuriantly that they must be burned off before the plow can operate (Thess. ii. 5, 28). They were a symbol of desolation (Prov. xxiv. 31); and were often used as fuel (Is. xxxiii. 12); also for hedges (Hos. ii. 6).

THOM'AS (*a twin;* Gr. *Dydimus, a twin.* Lydia

THRASE'AS. Father of Appollonius 1 (2 Macc. iii. 5).

THRESH'OLD (Heb. MIFTAN, SAF). A door-sill, a piece of timber or stone under a door or entrance (Judg. xix. 27).

SIDON FROM THE NORTH.

was his twin-sister). A native of Galilee. It has been suggested that he was a twin-brother of Jesus, but there is no proof that he was any relation to him. He was slow to believe, weighing the difficulties of the case, of a desponding heart, but ardently attached to his Master. He was ready to go with Jesus into any danger, but was incredulous about the unknown future; and after the resurrection, he would and he could only believe after he had seen and felt the very wounds made by the nails and the spear. He was one of the seven apostles who saw Jesus at the Sea of Galilee, and met with the others in the "upper room" after the ascension. Tradition says he preached in Parthia, was a martyr, and was buried at Edessa. The church in Malabar claims him as its founder, and shows a tomb as his.

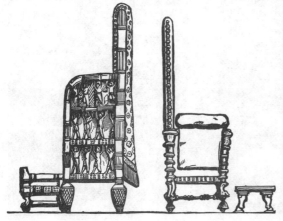

THRONE.

THRA'CIA (2 Macc. xii. 35). Thrace anciently included the whole country north of Macedonia and the Black Sea. It is supposed that TIRAS, in Gen. x. 2, means Thrace. It is also supposed that Tiras was the ancestor of the Tyrsi or Tyrseni, the Etruscans of Italy.

THRESH'OLDS, THE. (Heb. ASUPPEY) (Neh. xii 25). The thresholds of the gates. Heb. ASUPPEY HASH-SHEARIM, the store-chambers of the gates.

THRONE (Heb. CISSE; Gr. *thronos*). Any elevated seat occupied by a person in authority as high-priest (1 Sam. i. 9); judge (Ps. cxxii. 5); or a military chief (Jer. i. 15). The use of a chair in a country where squatting and reclining were the usual postures was regarded as a symbol of dignity (2 K. iv. 10). Solomon's throne was approached by six steps (1 K. x. 19), and Jehovah's throne was high and lifted up (Is. vi. 1). The materials and workmanship were costly (1 K. x. 18–20). Heaven is called God's throne, and the earth his footstool (Is. lxvi. 1).

THUM'MIN. URIM AND THUMMIN.

THUN'DER (Heb. RAAM, Gr. *bronte*), and LIGHTNING are extremely rare, during the summer, in Palestine; hence it was selected by Samuel as an expression of the divine displeasure toward the Israelites (1 Sam. xii. 17). As a symbol of God's power and majesty, thunder is frequently referred to in Scripture (Ex. xix. 16).

THYATI'RA. See PATMOS, and the SEVEN CHURCHES.

THY'INE-WOOD. An aromatic, evergreen tree, resembling the cedar, and found in Barbary, growing to the hight of 15 to 25 ft. The wood was used in burning incense, and, under the name of citron-wood, was highly prized by the Romans for ornamental wood-work. The rezin, known as sandarach is, the product of this tree (Rev. xviii. 12).

TIBE'RIAS. A city on the W. shore of the Sea of Galilee (John vi. 23). Some have supposed that it was built on the ruins (or near) of an ancient city, Rakkath, or Chinneroth (see *Land and Book*). Josephus says that it was built over an ancient cemetery, and was, therefore, unclean. Jesus never visited Tiberias, and it is scarcely mentioned in the Gospels. It was the capital of Galilee from its origin to the time of Herod Agrippa II. Celebrated schools of learning flourished here for several centuries. The MISHNA was compiled here by Rabbi Judah Hakkodesh, A. D. 190. That most important work, the MASORAH (*traditions*), originated here. By it has been preserved the vowel system and pronunciation of the Hebrew, and therefore the correct reading and understanding of the O. T. The Christians held it during the Crusades, and now it is under Turkish rule. Population about 4,000, ¼th being Jews. The Jews hold that 4 cities are holy, which are, Jerusalem, Hebron, Safed, and Tiberias. An earthquake, in 1837, nearly destroyed the city, and its effects are still seen, in walls tumbled down and houses in heaps.

TIBE'RIUS. The second emperor of Rome, successor of AUGUSTUS, A. D. 14–37. He was the son of Claudius Nero and Livia. He distinguished himself in various wars. At first he was moderate and just, but soon became infamous for his vices and crimes, and died A. D. 37, after a reign of 23 years. He is several times mentioned under the title of Cæsar (Luke xx. 22–25, xxiii. 22; John xix. 12). His subjects were commanded to worship his images.

TIB'HATH (*slaughter*). A city of Hardarezer, king of Zobah (1 Chr. xviii.). On the eastern skirts of Anti-Lebanon.

TIB'NI (*building of Jah*). An unsuccessful competitor with Omri, the general, for the throne of Israel (1 K. xvi. 18–23).

TI'DAL (*fear*). "A king of nations," under CHEDORLAOMER (Gen. xiv. 1–16).

TIG'LATH-PILE'SER (*lord of the Tigris*). King of Assyria; was invited by Ahaz, king of Judah, to assist him against the kings of Assyria and Israel (2 K. xvi. 7–10). He exacted a heavy tribute, so as to distress him without helping him (2 Chr. xxviii. 20–21). He made captive many of the inhabitants of Israel, and placed them in his kingdom, B. C. 740 (1 Chr. vi. 26), thus fulfilling unconsciously the predictions of Is. vii. 17, viii. 4).

POTTER.

bend of the Euphrates, in lat. 38° 10′, long. 39° 20′, and only 2 or 3 ms. from that river. The course is generally S. E. to its junction with the Euphrates at Kurnah, having traversed 1150 ms. 1000 ms.

of its course can be navigated by rafts. The river rises rapidly in March, from the melting snow of the Niphates mountains, and reaches the highest point in May, often flooding the country around Baghdad. Low water occurs again in July. In autumn the flood is much less in hight than in spring. The river has been purposely obstructed by dams at several places by the Persians for the uses of irrigation. The Tigris is mentioned by Daniel (x.) as the Great River, the Hiddekel. It traversed ancient Armenia, Assyria, and separated Babylonia from Susiana. The water is yellowish, runs in a rapid current, and abounds in fish. The banks are fringed with groves of palms, pomegranates, and jungles of reeds, the haunts of wild beasts.

TIK'VAH (*expectation*). 1. Father of Shallum 2 (2 K. xxii. 14).—2. Father of Jahaziah (Ezr. x. 15).

TIK'VATH (*obedience*). Tikvah 1 (2 Chr. xxxiv. 22).

TILE. A broad and thin brick, usually made of fine clay, and hardened in the fire. Such tiles were very common in Euphrates and Tigris (Ez. iv. 1). At Nineveh Layard found a large chamber stored full of inscribed tiles, like a collection of historical archives (Ezr. vi. 1). They are about 1 foot square and 3 inches thick.

TIL'GATH-PILNE'SER. Tiglath-pileser (1 Chr. v. 6, 26).

TI'LON (*gift*). Son of Shimon (1 Chr. iv. 20).

TIM'BREL, TAB'RET. (Heb. TOF, Gen. xxxi. 27); TOFETH (Job xvii. 6). See MUSICAL INSTRUMENTS, and cut on page 202.

TIME. Beside the ordinary uses of this word, the Bible sometimes employs it to denote a year, as in Dan. iv. 16, or a prophetic year, consisting of 360 natural years, a day being taken for a year. Thus in Dan. vii. 25, xii. 7, the phrase "a time, times, and the dividing of a time," is supposed to mean 3½ prophetic years, or 1,260 natural years. This period is elsewhere paralleled by the expression "forty-two months," each month including 30 years (Rev. xi. 2, 3, xii. 6, 14, xiii. 5).

TIME'US (*unclean*). Father of the blind Bartimeus (Mark x. 46).

TIM'NA (*one withheld*). 1. Second wife of Eliphaz, son of Esau (Gen. xxxvi. 12).—2. Son of Eliphaz (1 Chr. i. 36), a duke of Edom in the last list (1 Chr. i. 51).

CENCHREA.

TIG'RIS (*arrow*). River of Mesopotamia. Called Hiddekel in Hebrew. Like the Euphrates, it has two sources; the principal one is near the high mountain-lake Golenjik, which lies in the great

TIM'NAH (*divide*). 1. In the north of Judah (Josh. xv. 10), near Bethshemesh. It may be identical with Timnatha of Samson, a city of Dan (xix. 43). There is a modern village called Tibneh 2 ms. W. of Ain Shems (Bethshemesh), which is believed to be on the site of the ancient city.—2. In the mountain district of Judah (Josh. xv. 57), south of Hebron.

TIM'NATH. TIMNAH. 1. (Gen. xxxviii. 12). Where Judah kept his flocks.—2. The residence of Samson's wife (Judg. xiv. 1, 2, 5). In Philistia. There were vineyards; but as a lion was found in one, the place must have been thinly inhabited.

BLESSING.

TIM'NATH-HERES. The city and burial-place of Joshua (Judg. ii. 9). Also called *Timnath-serah* (Josh. xix. 50). In Mt. Ephraim, on the north side of Mt. Gaash. The site is lost, and with it the tombs of Joshu and Caleb. Dr. Eli Smith offered the ruins of a place 15 to 20 ms. N. W. from Jerusalem as the site in question, where there are, in a higher hill opposite, sepulchres hewn out of the rock, equal in size and decoration to the tombs of the kings at Jerusalem.

TI'MON (*honorable*). One of the seven deacons (Acts vi. 1-6).

TIMO'THEUS (*honoring God*). 1. A captain of the Ammonites, who was defeated by Judas Maccabæus, B. C. 164 (1 Macc. v. 6, 11, 34-44).—2. A leader in the invasion of Nicanor, B. C. 166 (2 Macc. viii. 30); killed at Gazara (x. 24-27).—3. The latin for Timothy (Acts xvi. 1).

TIM'OTHY. Is first mentioned in Acts xvi. 1, where he is described as the son of a Greek, by a Jewish mother. The father's name is unknown; his mother's was Eunice, and his grandmother's Lois (2 Tim. i. 5). The family resided either at Derbe or Lystra, which is uncertain (Acts xvi. 2). He became a disciple of Paul during his first visit to Lystra, A. D. 48, and was his friend and companion in his journeys, and shared for a time his imprisonment at Rome (Heb. xiii. 23), and left by him at Ephesus to continue his work (1 Tim. i. 3, iii. 14). He possessed the confidence and affection of Paul (Acts xvi. 1, xvii. 14).

TIMOTHY, FIRST EPISTLE TO. See HISTORY OF THE BOOKS.

TIN (Heb. BEDIL). A well-known white metal, easily melted, and very malleable. It was used at an early period (Num. xxxi. 22), and brought by the Tyrians from Tarshish (Zech. xxvii. 12). It was used for plummets (Zech. iv. 10), and it was known to the Hebrew metal-workers as one of the inferior metals. Tin is not found in Palestine. There can be little doubt that the mines of Britain were the chief source of supply to the ancient world.

TIPH'SAH (*ford*), (1 K. iv. 24). The outpost, toward the Euphrates, of Solomon's kingdom (2 K. xv. 16). Probably Thapsacus of the Greeks and Romans, and situated in Northern Syria, where the route eastward crossed the Euphrates. It was a great and important town in the time of Xenophon. A ford and a bridge supplied passage for caravans and armies. At the modern town of Suriyeh, on the Euphrates, there are paved causeways, visible on both sides of the river, which are the remains of the approaches to the ancient bridge; and a long line of mounds, arranged like those of Nineveh, in the form of a parallelogram.

TI'RAS (*longing*). The seventh son of Japheth. Tyrrhenians (?), in Italy.

TIRATH'ITES, THE (*people of Tira*) [*gate*]. One of the 3 families of Scribes residing at Jabez (1 Chr. ii. 55).

TIRE (PEER). An ornamental HEAD-DRESS, worn on festive occasions (Ez. xxiv. 17, 23).

TIR'HAKAH (*exalted*). King of ETHIOPIA, or Cush, and of Egypt, and the opponent of SENNACHERIB (2 K. xix. 9). He was a powerful monarch, ruling both Upper and Lower Egypt, and extending his conquests far into Asia.

TIR'HANAH (*inclination*). Son of Caleb 1 (1 Chr. ii. 48).

TIR'IA (*fear*). Son of Jehaleleel (1 Chr. iv. 16).

TIRSHA'THA (*stern*). It is added as a title after the name NEHEMIAH (Neh. viii. 9, x. 1), and usually rendered governor.

TIR'ZAH (*delight*). Youngest daughter of ZELOPHEHAD (Num. xxvi. 33).

TIR'ZAH. City of Canaan (Josh. xii. 24). After the separation of Israel and Judah it was the residence of Jeroboam (1 K. xiv. 17), and of his successors, Baasha, Elah and Zimri. The royal sepulchres (xvi. 6) of the first four kings of Israel were here. Omri destroyed Zimri in his palace by fire, and soon afterward removed the capital to Samaria (Shomron). Its beautiful situation is mentioned in Canticles (vi. 4) as equal to that of Jerusalem. There is a modern village called Telluzah, 4 or 5 mls. N. of Shechem, on a high hill, large and thriving, but without antiquities, which is supposed to be on the site of Tirzah.

TISH'BITE, THE (Heb. TISHBI). See THISBE.

TI'TANS (*avengers*). "The sons of Titans" stands parallel with giants.

WINDOW ON THE WALL.

TITHE (Heb. MA'ASER; Gr. *dekate, a tenth*). The proportion of a man's income devoted to sacred purposes (Gen. xiv. 20, xxviii. 22) prescribed by the Mosaic Law (Num. xxxi. 31). A twofold tithe was required of each Jewish citizen. The first consisted of one-tenth of the produce of his fields, trees, and herds, to be given to God (Lev. xxvii. 30-32). The Levites paid a tenth part of what they received to the priests (Num. xviii. 26-28). The second tithe required of each landholder one-tenth of the nine parts of his produce remaining after the first tithe, to be used at the Temple in entertaining the Levites (Deut. xii. 17-19, 22-29). Every third year a special provision was made for the poor, either out of this second tithe or in addition to it (Deut. xiv. 28, 29). The system of tithes was renewed both before and after the Captivity (2 Chr. xxxi. 5, 6, 12); but they were not always regularly paid, and then the Divine blessing was withheld (Mal. iii. 8–12).

TI′TUS (Gr. *Titus*). A Christian teacher of Greek origin (Gal. ii. 3), the companion of Paul, who converted him (Tit. i. 4; 2 Cor. viii. 23). He was one of those sent upon a mission to Jerusalem from the Church of Antioch (Acts v. 2; Gal. ii. 1). He was thence sent to Corinth, where he labored successfully (2 Cor. viii. 6; xii. 18). In his mission to collect for the poor of Judæa, he conveyed the Second Epistle of Paul to the Corinthians (2 Cor. viii. 16, 17, 23). Eight or ten years later he was at Crete, superintending the churches of the island (Tit. i. 5); he here received the epistle inscribed to him by Paul, then at Ephesus (Tit. iii. 12). This epistle is supposed to have been written A. D. 65.

TOBI′JAH. 1. A Levite, sent to teach the Law in Judah (2 Chr. xvii. 8).—2. One who returned from Captivity (Zech. vi. 10, 14).

TO′BIT (*my goodness*). Father of Tobias 1 (Tob. i. 1).

TO′BIT. See HISTORY OF THE BOOKS.

TO′CHEN. In Simeon (1 Chr. iv. 32).

TOGAR′MAH. A part of Armenia, named after Togarmah, a brother of Ashkenaz and son of Gomer (Gen. x. 3).

TO′HA. Ancestor of Samuel the prophet (1 Sam. i. 1).

TO′I (*error*). King of Hamath, in Syria, sent his son to rejoice with David (2 Sam. viii. 9–11).

TO′LA (*a worm*). 1. Eldest son of Issachar (Gen. xlvi. 13).—2. Judge of Israel after Abimelech (Judg. x. 1, 2); son of Puah, the son of Dodo.

TO′LAD. Simeon (1 Chr. iv. 29). EL-TOLAD.

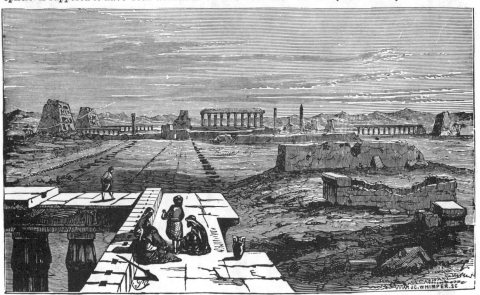

RUINS OF THEBES.

Paul therein desires him to meet him at Nicopolis. It is supposed that Titus accompanied Paul on his last journey to Rome. He is alluded to in 2 Tim. iv. 10, as being in Dalmatia.

TI′ZITE (Heb. TITSI). One from TAYITS (*extension*). One of David's heroes (1 Chr. xi. 45).

TO′AH (*inclined*). A Levite; ancestor of Samuel and Heman (1 Chr. vi. 34).

TOB, THE LAND OF (*good*). Jephthah's refuge (Judg. xi. 3), and residence, until invited to return by the sheikhs of Gilead (v. 5). Tob was somewhere in the Hauran, but is not identified.

TOB′ADONI′JAH (*God is my Lord Jah*). A Levite sent to teach the Law to the people of Judah (2 Chr. xvii. 8).

TOBI′AH (*pleasing to Jah*). 1. The children of Tobiah were a family who returned from Captivity, but were unable to prove their connection with Israel (Ezr. ii. 60).—2. A servant who took part in the opposition of SANBALLAT (Neh. ii. 10, 19) to the rebuilding the Temple.

TOBI′AS. 1. Son of TOBIT.—2. Ancestor of Hyrcanus, who was a man of great wealth (2 Macc. iii. 11).

TO′BIE. The seat of a colony of Jews (1 Macc. v. 13). The same as Tob.

TOBI′EL (*goodness of God*). Father of Tobit, and grandfather of Tobias 1 (Tob. i. 1).

TO′LAITES, THE. Descendants of Tola, son of Issachar (Num. xxvi. 26).

TOL′BANES. TELEM, a porter in Ezra's time (1 Esd. ix. 25).

TONGS (Heb. MELKAHAYIM, MAAZAD). Tongs with which burning coals and stones were handled (Is. vi. 6).

TONGUE (Heb. LASHON; Gr. *glossa dialektos*, *dialect* or *speech*). Literally the organ in the mouth, used by animals for tasting, licking, etc.; and by mankind for articulation (Ex. xi. 7); also language, nation or people, having their own language (Josh. vii. 21).

TOMB. The most extensive tombs were arranged as in the plan, cut in the solid rock (see pages 208, 213), and had many little places for the bodies, which were laid in the *loculi* (*places*) in their dress, with the ordinary costume of the living, or graveclothes, as in some cases. The *loculus* (*one place*) was closed up by a stone, or several small stones, cemented into place; and the entrance to the tomb was securely closed by a heavy stone door, or by a roller (round like a millstone, without the center hole), and a door also.

Eleven of the kings of Judah were buried in the Sepulchre of the Kings, in the City of David (City of the King), of two of whom only is there any special record (2 Chr. xvi. 14, xxxii. 33). Two other kings of the line were buried in the City of

David, but not in the Sepulchre of the Kings (xxi. 20, xxiv. 25); and one king (Uzziah), was buried in the field because he was a leper (xxvi. 23).

The Sepulchres of the Kings were probably on Zion, but have not yet been discovered, although some think they must have been near the Temple on Mt. Moriah (which is also supposed to have been the ancient Zion). The Mohammedans refuse to allow any explorations there at present. Ahaz was buried in Jerusalem, and not in the Sepulchre of the Kings.

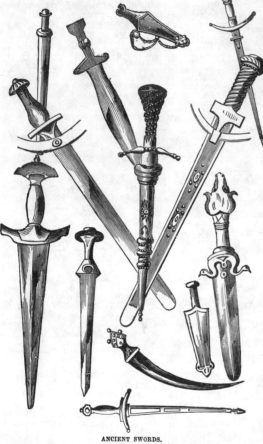

ANCIENT SWORDS.

There is not one tomb which can be traced beyond the Roman era. The so-called Tomb of Zechariah, in Kidron, is not a tomb, being cut in the solid rock, and only one side finished. There is no chamber or opening of any kind. The so-called Tomb of Absalom is also solid, and not a tomb. The Zechariah is 18 ft. 6 inches square, by 20 high; and the Absalom is 21 ft. square, by 24 high to the cornice, above which is a structure of stones cemented, and in the form of a bell or trumpet-shaped dome, making the whole 60 feet high. There is a chamber inside, with two very narrow loculi. Just behind this is an excavation, called the Tomb of Jehoshaphat, the plan of which is not known.

The most remarkable tomb is that of the "Judges," which has nearly 60 loculi, in double rows, the upper having a shelf or ledge in front. The "Tombs of the Kings," so called, north of Jerusalem (see map JERUSALEM). This tomb is also called Herod's, and in it, a few years

ago, there was discovered two sarcophagi, in the Roman style.

TONGUES, CONFUSION OF. The Jewish historians, who wrote the original records in Genesis, evidently intended to teach, in their two distinct accounts of the origin of the families of man, in which all are derived from a single family on the two occasions, Adam's and Noah's, that there was but one original pair, who were the first parents of the races of men, and also, that there was, originally, but one language, and that the Hebrew, or Aramaic, and that the great diversity of tongues was produced miraculously, at the building of the Tower of Babel, when the races were also distinctly separated from each other in color and feature. This appears to be the Scriptural view of the question; but it is received, now, with extreme caution by scholars. The whole question of the origin of language is beyond the possibility of proof, as to its history; and therefore theories about the origin of the substance of language cannot be sustained by historic facts. The Greeks held that reason was inward speech, and speech outward reason, and [both] independent of sound. The labors of scholars, during the present century, have resulted in a wonderful amount of interesting knowledge concerning the different languages of the world; arranging a large part of them into groups, or families, and showing, by a careful analysis, the affinities of many languages before this supposed to have nothing in common, as, Greek and Celtic, English and Sanscrit. The chain of historical evidence necessary to show any close connection between the great families of languages does not, at present, appear to be in existence. The original unity cannot be proved, and can only be supposed. Those who hold to a direct creation of distinct species of animals, trees, etc., see the same evidences of an original pair for each race of men, etc. It is asserted that there are certain "root-words," in all languages, from which the entire vocabulary is derived, by expansion or addition, and which are always of one syllable, of two or more letters (that is, a vowel-sound before or after, or between, two consonants). From these "roots" the languages are all formed in three modes: 1. By isolation. 2. By agglutination. 3. By inflection.

In the first group there is no such thing as grammar—that is, there is no difference between a noun (name) and a verb (a name and an action), and there are no adjectives, prepositions or pronouns. In the other two groups there are two kinds of "roots," one of which forms names, verbs, adjectives, and the other conjunctions, prepositions and particles. The terminations of names, verbs and adjectives are supplied by both kinds. An example is seen in the preposition *of*, which is traced to the German *ab*, the Greek *apo*, and the Sanscrit *apa*, the base of which was *a*.

The one-syllable form is not the only characteristic of the root of the Shemitic languages; there are many two-syllable forms also, if these are not single syllables joined by a consonant. Single syllables are found with two, three, and even four consonants. It is held by some scholars that purely one-syllable languages have never advanced beyond their primitive condition. The answer to this is that these languages have developed in a way peculiar to themselves.

The most apparent differences between the two kinds of languages are, that the agglutinating kind preserves the original root unchanged, although combined, while the inflectional join the roots, so as to lose the identity of the original roots. But it seems necessary that in all languages there should have been combination of roots—joining two or more simple words to make a more complete one—and also an isolation, when such compound words became familiar and useful, and were adopted for certain ideas or their uses, and so became stock words, of which every language has a number.

The ancient languages in America and Africa are distinct and peculiar, and can not be described in common with any in Asia or Europe. Their derivation is unknown, and there has not yet been traced any connection in root, structure or history with any other family.

An interesting inscription has been lately discovered in the East, and is interpreted by Dr. Oppert, in which it appears that the ancient Babylonians had a tradition of the confusion of tongues, preserved in the name Borsippa or Borsif, which means confusion in Chaldee. Borsippa is therefore Tongue-Tower, and was what is now called *Birs Nimroud* (see BABEL). Herodotus described the tower as dedicated to Jupiter Belus. The original name of the tower was BĬT-ZĬ-DA, *spirit-house* (the same as *Sarakh, tower, temple*). Nebuchadnezzar named it the Seven Lights of the Earth (7 planets). In the inscription there is the sentence, "Since the remote time people avoided the tower—cause unknown."

TONGUES, GIFT OF. The gift of tongues was the special work of the Holy Spirit on the Day of Pentecost; and the power was used as soon as received. "They were all filled with the Holy Ghost, and began to speak with other tongues as the spirit gave them utterance." At that time there were Jews from many nations in Jerusalem, speaking foreign tongues, and they heard and understood, every one in his native language. This power fulfilled the promise implied in the command "Go and teach all nations." It gave the teachers of the new religion access to the heart, while the priest of the old dispensation addressed the eye. Judaism had been local; Christianity was to "go" into all the world. Those who used the gift of tongues were also made to understand them; for if not, then he could not have increased his own knowledge and faith nor those of others. This gift was only for a short time. Even Paul did not long enjoy its benefits. It appears from the record that the gift on the Day of Pentecost fell on all alike, Apostles and hearers, men and women.

TOOTH (Heb. SHEN, Gr. *odous*), used mostly in respect to men and animals (Gen. xlix. 12). "Cleanness of teeth" indicates hunger and famine (Amos iv. 6); "gnashing of teeth" violent rage, anguish, or desperation (Ps. xxxv. 16): "tooth for tooth" was an instance of compensation (Ex. xxi. 24).

TO′PARCHY (Gr. *toparchia*). A district governed by a toparch, or governor (1 Macc. xi. 28).

TO′PAZ. See PRECIOUS STONES.

TO′PHEL. At the S. E. corner of the Dead Sea,

now called Tufileh. It is in a most fertile valley, having many springs and rivulets flowing into the Ghor, and large plantations of fruit-trees. Figs are exported. Partridges (katta) are found in great numbers, and deer (steinbock) in herds of 40 or 50 together.

TO′PHETH (*tabret-grove*). S. E. of Jerusalem, in the Valley of Hinnom (Jer. vii. 31, xix. 2). A music-grove of the king; a part of the royal gardens. After the sacrifices to the idol Moloch, it became a place of abomination (vii. 32).

POOL OF SILOAM.

TOR′MAH (Heb. BETORMAH); "privily" Judg. ix. 31).

TORMENT′OR (Gr. *basanisteo, a torturer, or prison-keeper*. Among the ancient Romans, a creditor might use certain legal tortures, as, a heavy chain, or of half-starvation, to extort from the debtor a confession of any concealed treasures (Matt. xviii. 34).

TOR′TOISE (Heb. ZAB). Various fresh-water tortoises, land-tortoises, and sea-tortoises, are found in Palestine and its neighborhood (Lev. xi. 29).

TO′U (TOI), (1 Chr. xviii. 9, 10).

TOW. 1. Heb. NE′ORETH; tow as shaken off from flax (Judg. xvi. 9.—2. PISHTAH, *a wick*, made of linen (Is. xliii. 17).

TOW′ER (Heb. MIGDAL, Gr. *purgos*). Towers were erected not only in the outer walls, and on the hights, within cities (Judg. ix. 47–49), but along the frontiers (Judg. ix. 17). A tower afforded refuge to the people in case of invasion (Prov. xviii. 10). They were built in vineyards for the watchmen, and on the hights, or along the side-hill, at convenient distances, so that the watchmen could see from one to another, and give signals of the approach of any danger, as of an enemy, or of wolves, bears, or other animals, destructive of the crops. Many of these are now in use all over the country. Some of them were very noted as Edar, Antonia, Migdol, Ophel, etc. The tower was a figure of God (Ps. lxi. 3), and of proud and powerful men (Is. ii. 15, xxx. 25).

TOWN. 1. Heb. BATH, *daughter;* in specifying small, dependent "towns" and "villages" (Josh. xv. 45, 47).—2. HAVVOTH, *villages*, properly places of *living* or dwelling (Josh. xiii. 30.—3. Heb. HAZER (Gen. xxv. 16), "court" or "village".—4. Heb. IR (Deut. iii. 5) translated "city" more than 1,000 times.—5. Heb. KIR, "wall" Josh. ii. 15).—6. PE-RAZOTH, *country regions, open country,* unwalled towns (Zech. ii. 4).—7. Gr. *kome,* a hamlet, country towns, without walls.—8. Gr. *komopolis,* a large village, without walls (Mark i. 38).

TOWN'-CLERK (Gr. *grammateus, a scribe, secretary—clerk*). The title of the magistrate at Ephesus who appeased the mob (Acts xix. 35), in the theater-tumult excited by Demetrius.

or rather lost to all outward impressions, and absorbed in the imagination; sometimes the result of religious impressions. Some persons can throw themselves into the state of religious trance at will (ecstasy of adoration). Mohammed was of this nature, and in that condition he made his (visionary) journey to heaven. Balaam sees the vision of God, *falling,* but with opened eyes (Num. xxiv. 4). Saul also prophesied and fell down (1 Sam. xix. 24).

Jeremiah was described as one that is mad and maketh himself a prophet (Jer. xxix. 26). Ezekiel sits motionless for seven days in stupor (Ez. iii. 15). He also sees the visions of God, lifted up between the earth and the heaven (viii. 3). Peter saw in a trance the vision of tolerance (Acts x. xi.). Paul received in a trance the command to preach to the Gentiles (Acts xxii. 17–21). In another he heard unspeakable words (2 Cor. xii. 1–4). The prophets received their messages from God in visions, trances, and dreams (Num. xxiv. 2–16; Joel ii. 28; Acts x. 11; Rev. i. 10–20).

The prophet is also called a SEER (Num. xii. 6; Lam. ii. 9); and received the word of the Lord (1 Sam. iii. 21). The spiritual man (Hos. ix. 7), is another term. The name

SANHEDRIN.

TRACHONI'TIS (*heap of stones*), (Luke iii. 1). The region also called ARGOB, GESHUR, and now EL-LEJAH, and is S. of Damascus, consisting of a plain and the W. slope of Jebel Hauran. On the N. border of this region are the extensive ruins of Mismiyeh, where there is an inscription on the door of a once beautiful temple, which contains the name of the ancient city, PHOCUS. On the E. are the ruins of Saccæa and Kenath, on the slope of Hauran. Josephus describes the inhabitants as having neither towns nor fields—dwelling in caves, and having cisterns of water and granaries; and the ground as almost a plain, covered with rugged rocks. See ARGOB, and GESHUR.

TRADI'TION (Gr. *paradosis, a precept, ordinance, instruction*). Applied, particularly, to the Oral Law of the Jews, or their doctrines, handed down from age to age (Matt. xv. 2, 3, 6). The Jews pay great regard to *tradition* in matters of religion, as do the Roman Catholics. Protestants reject the authority of *tradition* in sacred things, and rely, only, on the written word. *Traditions* may be good or bad—true or false (2 Thess. ii).

TRANCE (Heb. LOPAL, *falling;* Gr. *ekstasis;* Lat. *excessus*). The state in which a person has passed out of the usual order of its life, beyond the usual limits of consciousness and volition. The condition of seeming death. Loss of conscious perception. In medical terms, one form of catalepsy. A state in which there is a sudden suspension of thought, of sensibility, and of voluntary motion;

prophet (NABI) means *inspired person,* one whom God has qualified to impart consolation, light, and strength to others; a declarer and interpreter of the divine will respecting the past, the present, and the future. There are two elements in prophesy; the predicative and the moral. The moral or spiritual is always highest, although inseparable from the spoken word. Prophesy is the opposite of the miracle—miracles being evidences, signs, and prophesies being the word for edifying the church, comforting believers, and a sign to unbelievers, drawing their attention to Christ (1 Cor. xiv. 22). Miracles are addressed to unbelievers; prophesies to believers.

Three elements were essential: 1. Personal and direct communication from heaven. 2. The word to be consistent with the use of a supernatural agency. 3. And be delivered faithfully.

The Bible is a book of facts, and prophesy is based on history.

The *present* was (and is) the germ of the future, and a prophetic thread runs through the whole length of the history of the chosen people.

The theme entire was enunciated, at first, by Adam, Noah, Abraham and Moses; and was expanded as the world's history demanded. The first promise in the Garden of Eden contains, as in a seed, the whole of revelation and prophesy; and the growth of Christ's kingdom in the earth will restore the earth to the original state of Eden. All truly religious teaching is prophetical, as it always has been.

The line of prophets from Samuel to Malachi were the divinely accredited teachers of the Jewish people, and were supernaturally endowed with spiritual knowledge and genuine foresight to train them for the development of the future divine kingdom, and their succession during a period of 4000 years (Adam to Jesus), with their continual flow of divinations, perfect harmony of character, oneness of object, and sanctity of motive, is a greater mystery and miracle than any of their predictions. They were the witnesses for a divine kingdom among men, the commentators on its history, the exponents of its laws, and the heralds of its triumphs; directing the minds of the people to the person, the work, and the character of the King.

The Epistle to the Hebrews sets forth the doctrine that in person Jesus was joined to God in a mysterious union, and there are many references to the Old Testament in the New Testament throughout, touching on this theme, as in Malachi (iii. 1), quoted by Luke (vii. 27), where Jesus, in an allusion to himself, purposely changed the expression to avoid giving offense to the Jews; and also Psalms cx., alluded to in Matt. xxii. 42, 43, where his hearers distinctly understood him as making himself David's Son and Lord, in a spiritual sense, which was the same as God; and when he refers to the prophesy of Zechariah (xiii. 7), predicting his crucifixion (Matt. xxvi. 31).

The work of the Messiah was the foundation of his spiritual kingdom, the corner stone of the Church, as prophesied from the first, and especially promised to Abraham.

The prophesies prepared the minds of the Jews for the extinction of the national life at the appearance of the Messiah. The nation died that its spiritual life might be resurrected in the Gospel; a type of the experience of every disciple, prefiguring his entry upon a bright future when called away from this life. The polity and priesthood had served their end when it merged into the Church of Christ. In the new Church there is no local temple, no visible altar, no material offering, no sacrificing priesthood. It is a new earth and a new heaven. The whole world has now become a people of priests, where every soul may worship God in spirit and in truth (Ex. xix. 6).

TRANSFIGURA'TION. This event occurred in that period of the life of Christ between the temptation in the wilderness and the agony in Gethsemane. The incident is described in Matt. xvii. 1–9. It is supposed to have taken place on Mount Hermon, the highest of the Anti-Lebanon mountains. At the transfiguration Moses and Elijah appeared, representing the law and prophesy. The Apostles, Peter, James, and John, were the only witnesses (2 Pet. i. 16; John i. 14).

TREAS'URE (Heb. OZAR, HOZEN, MATMON; Chal. *ginzin;* Gr. *thesauros*), (Acts. viii. 27). Whatever is laid up in store—as provisions, gold, silver, etc. (Gen. xliii. 23).

TREASURE-CITIES (Ex. i. 11). Store-cities; that is, cities where were magazines or depôts of provision (Ezr. v. 17).

TREAS'URER (Heb. GIZBAR; Chal. *gedaberin*). One who has charge of royal treasures or a TREASURY (Ezr. i. 8).

TREAS'URY. 1. Heb. OZAR, *what is laid up;* a store or stock of produce or goods (Josh. vi. 19, 24).—2. Heb. GENAZIM, *treasure-chests* (Esth. iii. 9). —3. Heb. GANZACH, the *treasury* of the Temple (1 Chr. xxviii. 11), which, according to Rabbins,

was in chests (called *trumpets*), into which the Jews cast their offerings (Matt. xii. 41). Kings used to store their possessions, and guard what they most valued (Ex. i. 11).

TREES. Were frequently used as types of kings or men of wealth and power (Ps. xxxvii. 35; Dan. iv. x.). The "tree of knowledge of good and evil" (Gen. ii. 9, 17). The "tree of life," a seal of eternal holiness and bliss if man had not sinned (Rev. xxii. 2). The principal trees mentioned in Scripture are algum, or almug (1 K. v. 6; 2 Chr. ii. 8, ix. 10, 11; Rev. xviii. 12); Almond (Gen. xliii. 11; Ex. xxv. 33, 34, xxxvii. 19, 20; Num. xvii. 8; Eccles. xii. 5; Jer. i. 11); aloes (Ps. xlv. 8; Prov. vii. 17; Cant. iv. 14; John xix. 39); apple (Deut. xxxii. 10; Prov. xxv. 11; Cant. ii. 3, 5; Joel i. 12; Zech. ii. 8); bay (Ps. i. 3, xxxvii. 35; Dan. iv. 4); box (Is. xli. 19; lx. 13; 2 Esd. xiv. 24); cedar (Lev. xiv. 4, 6, 49, 51, 52; and about 60 other passages in the O. T., besides many in which it is called the glory of Lebanon); chestnut (Gen. xxx. 37; Ez.

SCRIBES.

xxxi. 8); fig (Gen. iii. 7; and in many passages all through the Bible); fir (2 Sam. vi. 5; and 20 other places in the O. T.); holm (Sus. ver. 58); juniper (1 K. xix. 4, 5; Job. xxx. 4; Ps. cxx. 4, 5); mastich (Sus. ver. 54); mulberry (2 Sam. v. 23, 24; 1 Chr. 14; 1 Macc. vi. 34; Luke xvii. 6); myrtle (Neh. viii. 15; Is. xli. 19, lv. 13; Zech. i. 8, 10, 11); oak (Gen. xxxv. 4, 8; and many times in the O. T. Several times the original word for oak (ELON, etc.) is rendered *plain);* oleaster, wild olive (Rom. xi. 17, 24); olive (Gen. viii. 11, and all through the Bible, in nearly every book); palm (Ex. xv. 27, and in nearly every book also); pine (Neh. viii. 15; Is. xli. 19, lx. 13); pomegranate (Ex. xxviii. 33, 34, xxxix., and nearly every other book of the O. T.); shittah-tree, acacia (Ex. xxv. 10, 23, and many other passages in Num., Deut., Is., and Micah); sycamine (Luke xvii. 6); sycamore (1 K. x. 27, and several others); willow (Lev. xxiii. 40; Job xl. 22; Ps. cxxxvii. 2; Is. xv. 7, xliv. 4; Ez. xvii. 5).

TRIAL. See JESUS CHRIST, PROCURATOR, SANHEDRIN, etc. The trial of Jesus Christ before Pilate was for an offense punishable by Roman law with death (Luke xxiii. 2, 28; John xix. 12, 15). Paul and Stephen were tried before the high-priest and Jewish rulers (Acts v. 27, vi. 12, etc.); the *decumviri* ("magistrates," A. V.). The trials of Paul at Cæsarea were conducted under Roman law. In that one held before Felix, the plaintiffs employed an advocate. In the second trial Paul appealed to Cæsar, as a Roman citizen, and the procurator conferred with the council or assessor who sat on the judicial bench (Acts xxv. 12). A judicial court held sessions in Ephesus (Acts xix. 38).

TRIBE (Heb. MALTEH, SHEBEH, Gr. *phule*). A race, people, or nation (Ps. lxxiv. 2). Usually a division, or branch of a people, especially one of the great divisions of the Israelites (Ex. xxxi. 2, 6). The 12 tribes continued united as one state, one people, till after the death of Solomon, when they revolted.

TRIB'UTE (Heb. MECHES, MAS). See TAXES.

TRI'POLIS. Possibly the ancient KADYTIS. On the coast N. of (Beirut), Sidon, and Tyre. The river that runs from Lebanon through the city is called Kadisha. Demetrius Soter landed here (B. C. 161), and made it his head-quarters while conquering Syria (2 Macc. xiv. 1). Pop. 16,000.

TOMB OF MORDECAI.

TRO'AS. Alexander Troas, in Asia Minor (Mysia), opposite the island of Tenedos. It was one of the most important towns in Asia. Paul made two voyages from here to Macedonia. (See LIFE OF PAUL.) It was connected, by good roads, with cities on the coast and in the interior. Constantine had, before he gave a just preference to the situation of Byzantium, conceived the design of erecting the seat of empire on this celebrated spot, from which the Romans derived their fabulous origin.

TROGYL'LIUM. Samos is exactly opposite this point of land, which lies at the boundary between Ionia and Caria. The channel is narrow (about 1 m.), and the current rapid, southward. E. of the point there is now an anchorage, called St. Paul's Port. (Acts xx. 15). In this bay there was a great naval battle between the Greeks and Persians, B. C. 479.

TROOP (Heb. GEDUD), is used, mostly, of light-armed troops engaged in plundering (Gen. xlix. 19). "Company," "band" (2 K. v. 2); "band of the rovers" (Hos. vi. 9).

TROPH'IMUS (*nourished*). A disciple of Paul, a Gentile, and an Ephesian by birth. He accompanied him in his journey to Jerusalem, A. D. 58 (Acts xx. 4). Paul left him sick at Miletus (2 Tim. iv. 20). He was the innocent cause of the tumult

in which Paul was apprehended (Acts xxi. 27, 29).

TRUM'PET. See MUSICAL INSTRUMENTS.

TRUM'PETS, FEAST OF (Num. xxix. 1). (See FESTIVALS).

TRYPHE'NA (*delicious*) and **TRYPHO'SA** (*living delicately*). Two women at Rome, saluted by Paul (Rom. xvi. 12): they were very useful and benevolent.

TRY'PHON (*reveler, glutton*). A usurper of the Syrian throne. His proper name was DIODOTUS (1 Macc. xiii.).

TUBAL (Heb. *to prepare*). Son of Japheth, who, with his brothers Javan and Meshech, traded in slaves and vessels of brass (Gen. x. 2; 1 Chr. i. 5). See SLAVES; also Ez. xxvii. 13).—2. Fifth son of Japheth. (See MESECH).

TUBAL-CAIN (Persian *tupal, iron;* Arabic *kainsmith*). Worker in metals. "A furbisher of every cutting instrument of copper and iron" (Gen. iv. 22). He was the son of Lamech. See METALS.

TUBIE'NI (Gr. *Toubienoi*). The Jews called Tubieni (2 Macc. xii. 17) those who were living in the towns of *Toubion*.

TUR'BANS (Dan. iii. 21). See HEAD-DRESS.

TUR'PENTINE-TREE (Gr. *tereminthos*). It is numbered among the choicest of trees, common in Palestine and the East. It grows to a large size. From incisions in the trunk a sort of balsam is said to flow, which constitutes a very pure and fragrant species of turpentine.

TUR'TLE-DOVE, or **TURTLE** (Heb. TOR). A name derived from the note of the bird. See DOVE. The migratory habits of this bird are alluded to in Cant. ii. 11, 12; Jer. viii. 7. It was allowed for a sin-offering by the poor (Lev. l. 14, v. 7; Matt. xxi. 22); also in purification, etc. (Lev. xii. 6–8). Before the giving of the law Abraham offered a turtle and a pigeon (Gen. xv. 9).

TWELVE, THE. The apostles of Jesus Christ, originally twelve in number (Matt. xxvi. 20, 47). See APOSTLE.

TYCH'ICUS (*fortunate*). A fellow-worker of Paul, accompanying him from Corinth to Jerusalem (Acts xx. 4). In Paul's first imprisonment he calls Tychicus "a beloved brother and a faithful minister and fellow-servant of the Lord" (Col. iv. 7, 8). With Onesimus, he was doubtlessly the bearer of the epistles to the Colossians, the Ephesians, and to Philemon.

TYPES (Gr. *tupoi, examples;* pl. of *tapos, type,* "print"), (John xx. 25); "figure" in Rom. iv. 15. Moses was to make the tabernacle according to the type he had seen in the mount (Acts vii. 44).

TYRAN'NUS (*a tyrant*). The name of a person at Ephesus in whose school Paul taught the Gospel (Acts xix. 9).

TYRE (*rock*). Ar. *Sur;* Heb. ZOR. On a rocky peninsula which was formerly an island (Ez. xxvii. 25), before the siege of Alexander. There was probably a city on the mainland, opposite the island city; but which was the more ancient is not decided. One of the places was called Palætyrus (Old Tyre). Hercules was worshiped under the name of Melkarth, and the temple in his honor on the island was said by Arrian (ii. 16) to have been the most ancient in the world.

The people were called Sidonians (Judg. xviii. 7; Josh. xiii. 6; Ez. xxxii. 30); Tyre and Sidon being inhabited by Phœnicians, and only 20 ms. apart (1 K. v. 6). Sidon (son of Canaan) is mentioned in the Pentateuch; Tyre is not (Gen. x. 15); it being mentioned first in Joshua (xix. 29), where it appears as a fortified city.

The Canaanites were not driven out of Tyre and Sidon, and other Phœnician cities (Judg. i. 31), as Moses directed, but the Jews lived among them. Hiram, king of Tyre, sent cedar-wood and workmen to build David a palace (2 Sam. v. 11); and afterward he also sent Hiram the widow's son, a Jew of the tribe of Naphtali, who cast the vessels of bronze for the temple, king Hiram furnishing the metal, besides also the cedar and fir trees; the Jews and Phœnicians working together. The friendship between the Jews and Phœnicians continued for at least a century, when King Ahab married a daughter of King Ethbaal of Sidon.

STREET OF COLUMNS, SYMARIA.

In the time of Joel (iii. 6-8) the Phœnicians sold Jewish children as slaves to the Greeks, and Joel threatened retaliation.

Carthage was planted as a colony of Tyre, 143 years after the building of Solomon's temple.

There is no record of a war between Jews and Phœnicians; and the reason why peace was so constant is, that Palestine furnished Phœnicia with grain, oil, grapes, and wine, besides cattle and sheep, as is the case now.

There was an altar in honor of Ashtoreth, the Tyrian goddess, "Queen of Heaven," built by Solomon on one of the summits of Olivet as a token of his friendship for Hiram, king of Tyre, which stood for 350 years, when it was destroyed by Josiah, only a few years before Jerusalem was taken by the Assyrians, under Nebuchadnezzar. Tyre was besieged for 13 years (B. C. 715) by the same king soon after, but it has never been settled whether he captured it or not. But Alexander did take the city after a siege of seven months (B. C. 332), when the island was connected to the mainland by a causeway built during the siege.

The dye called Tyrian purple was a source of great wealth. It was extracted from shell-fish found on the coast.

At the time of Christ, Tyre was equal in population to Jerusalem. Cassius, bishop of Tyre, attended the Council of Cæsarea. At the time of the Crusades (A. D. 1124) William was made archbishop, and his account of the city preserves the record of its wealth and strength. Glass and sugar are mentioned as articles of great value in trade. In June, 1291, Tyre was occupied by the Saracens (the Christians having abandoned it the night before), and from that day to this they have held it. It is now only a village of about 3,000 people; its strong walls have entirely disappeared, and the harbor is almost useless. The prophet Ezekiel (xxviii. 2) mentions the pride of Tyre—its boast that it was a god, and sat in the seat of God in the midst of the seas; and also describes its present desolation (xxvi. 3-5). The most complete fulfilment of his prophesies is felt in the silence and desolation of Tyre.

Almost the only relic of Tyre's great sea-wall, lies in the northern end of the island, and is a stone 17 ft. long, 6½ thick, and seems to lie in its original position, where it was placed 3000 yrs. ago. There are columns and floors of marble buried under rubbish or sunk in the sea, all over the site and along the sea border; and thousands of fine pieces of stone, wrought into columns, capitals, and panels, have been carried away to other cities— to Joppa, Acre, and Beirut. On the mainland are the ruins of the ancient Christian cathedral, 200 by 140, massive, and Byzantine in style. Paulinus was its bishop, and Eusebius wrote the consecration oration, which is still extant, for its opening. The historian, William of Tyre, held a priestly rank here, and the crusaders their last religious service in Palestine. In its dust lie the remains of the emperor Barbarossa, and of Origen, the Bible scholar. See cut, page 272.

TZAD'DI (Heb. ZADEY, *reaping-hook or scythe*). The 18th letter of the Hebrew alphabet (Ps. cxix.). WRITING.

TZI'DON. ZIDON (Gen. x. 15).

TZOR. TYRE (Josh. xix. 29).

U

U'CAL (Heb. *eaten up, consumed?*) Mentioned with the name of Ithiel in Prov. xxx. 1, who were disciples or SONS of Aguz, the son of Takeh. The reference is obscure.

U'EL (Heb. *will of God*). Of the family of Bani; he married a foreign wife during the Captivity (Ezr. x. 34).

UK'NAZ (Heb. KENAZ, *even*), (1 Chr. iv. 15). Probably a word is omitted before kenaz.

ULA'I (Dan. viii. 2, 16). A river near Susa. Called Eulæus by the Greeks and Romans. The river has changed its course since ancient days, and now has two branches—the Kerkha and the Kuran, by which its waters reach the Tigris. The Persian kings drank the water of this river only, when at home or on a journey, believing it to be lighter, and more wholesome and pleasant to the taste, than any other.

U'LAM (Heb. *front*). 1. Descendant of Gilead, the grandson of Manasseh (1 Chr. vii. 17).—2. Descendant of Saul; a Benjamite, and the first-born of Eshek (1 Chr. viii. 39, 40).

UL'LA (Heb. *yoke*). An Asherite chief (1 Chr. vii. 39).

UM'MAH (*gathering*). Asher (Josh. xix. 30). The modern site is called Alma, and is on the high land of the Ladder of Tyre, 5 ms. from the cape Ras en Nakura, in the midst of many ruins as yet without names.

UNCIRCUMCIS'ION. See CIRCUMCISION.

UNCLEAN MEATS. See CLEAN.

UNCLEANNESS. See CLEAN.

UNICORN. (Heb. REEM, REEYM, REYM). The name of some wild animal, not fabulous or one-horned (Deut. xxxiii. 17,) as it may be correctly translated: "His glory is like the firstling of his bullock, and his horns are like the horns of *unicorn''* (REEM). The unicorn is now believed to have been the Urus, an extinct species of Buffalo and not the rhinoceros. It is spoken of as a powerful and violent animal (Ps. xxii. 19, 21; Job xxxix. 9–12).

UNLEAV'ENED BREAD. See LEAVEN. PASSOVER.

UN'NI (Heb. *depressed*). 1. A musician and Levite doorkeeper (porter) in the time of David (1 Chr. xv. 18, 20).—2. A second Levite connected with the sacred office (Neh. xii. 9).

U'PHAZ (Jer. x. 9; Dan. x. 5). See OPHIR.

UR (Gen. xi. 28). The land of Haran, Ur of

BAZAAR IN JAFFA.

the Chaldees, from which Terah and Abraham came into the land of Canaan. Four localities are offered as the ancient site of Ur. 1. Now called Oorfah. The Greeks called it Edessa. The chief mosque is named Abraham's, and a pond in which some sacred fish are kept is called the Lake of Abraham the Beloved.—2. The second place is Warka, the Orchon of the Greeks, and Huruk in the Assyrian.—3. A place in eastern Mesopotamia, Ur, below Nineveh, on the Tigris.—4. Mugheir, or Om Mugheir (Mother of Bitumen), on the right bank of the Euphrates, 125 ms. from the sea. The ruins here are extensive and of the most ancient character, containing inscriptions. Once called Camarina. This was for ages the burial-place of the Assyrian kings.

UR. Father of Eliphal. One of David's strong men (1 Chr. xi. 35).

UR'BANE (L. *Urbanus, of the city, refined*). A disciple whom Paul saluted, in Rom. xvi. 9.

U'RI (Heb. *fiery*). 1. One of the tribe of Judah. Father of BEZALEEL 1, architect of the Tabernacle (Ex. xxxi. 2).—2. Father of Geber (1 K. iv. 19).—3. A doorkeeper in Ezra's time (Ezr. x. 24).

URI'AH (*flame of Jehovah*). 1. One of the "worthies" of king David; a captain in his army and a Hittite. He was the husband of Bathsheba, who became the object of David's criminal passion. When Uriah was commanding with the army before Rabbah, David directed Joab to place him in an exposed position in battle, where he was killed (2 Sam. xi. xxiii. 39). See DAVID, BATHSHEBA.—

2. A priest at the time of Ahaz, witness of Isaiah's prophesy concerning his son (Is. viii. 2). Probably Urijah (2 K. xvi. 18).—3. A priest of the family of Koz at the time of Ezra (Ezr. viii. 3). In Neh. iii. 4, 21, called Urijah.

URI'AS. 1. Husband of Bathsheba (Matt. i. 6).—2. URIJAH 3 (1 Esd. ix. 43).

U'RIEL (*fire of God*). The father of Michaiah, the mother of Abijah, king of Judah, according to 2. Chr. xiii. 2. Elsewhere the mother of Abijah appears as Maacah, the daughter of Absalom (1 K. xv. 2, 10, 13). Two Kohathites of the name of Uriel appear in 1 Chr. vi. 9, xv. 5–11.

URI'JAH (*flame of Jehovah*). 1. High-priest at the time of Ahaz. Without divine authority he had constructed and also made offerings upon an altar designed by Ahaz (2 K. xvi. 10–12). Notwithstanding the committal of this error, Urijah appears to have been a righteous man, and one of the "faithful witnesses" selected by Isaiah (Is. viii. 2) to attest his prophesy.—2. A prophet, son of Shemaiah : he uttered prophesies against Judæa and Jerusalem in the time of Jehoiakim. He was menaced with death by the king, and fled to Egypt, but was delivered up by Pharaoh-Necho to Jehoiakim, who had him executed and dishonorably buried (Jer. xxvi. 20–21).

U'RIM AND THUM'MIM (Heb. *light and perfections*). The twelve precious stones, when in position in the breast-plate of the high-priest, were consulted as an oracle. They were worn when the high-priest entered the Holy of Holies (Ex. xxviii. 30). The ceremony of placing the engraved gems in their proper positions in the breast-plate was very solemn and imposing, for it typified the presence of the twelve tribes before the altar of Jehovah. See PRECIOUS STONES.

U'SURY (Heb. NESEK). Interest for money or property loaned. Usury is forbidden by the laws, although it was permitted for the Israelites to take usury from any one not a Jew. This was used as a means of ruining the Canaanites. After the return of the Jews from Captivity they were ordered by Nehemiah "to leave off usury" (Neh. v. 10, 11), and to restore what had been exacted. Christ denounced all methods of extortion: "Give to every man that asketh of thee; and of him that taketh away thy goods ask them not again." "Love ye your enemies, and do good, and lend, hoping for nothing again" (Luke vi. 30–35; Ps. xv. 5).

U'TA. Ancestor of certain Nethinim (1 Esd. v. 30).

U'THAI (*Jah succors*). 1. Son of Ammihud (1 Chr. ix. 4).—2. Son of Bigvai, who returned from Captivity (Ezr. viii. 14).

U'THI. UTHAI 2 (1 Esd. viii. 40).

UZ. The land in which Job lived (Job i. 1), and evidently settled by a son of Aram, grandson of Shem (Gen. x. 23). Supposed to have been E. or S. E. of Palestine (Job i. 15, 17), in the vicinity of the Sabæans and the Chaldæans, and of Edom (Lam. iv. 21). The description of the people corresponds to that of the nomade tribes of Arabia Deserta.

U'ZAI (*strong*). Father of Palal, who assisted Nehemiah (Neh. iii. 25).

U'ZAL (*wanderer*), (Gen. x. 27; 1 Chr. i. 21; Ez. xxvii. 19). Javan. The capital city of Yemen,

Arabia; originally called Awzal, and now known as Sana. The city is better built than any other in Arabia, has many palaces, mosques, baths and khans, "resembling Damascus in the abundance of its trees or gardens, and the rippling of its waters."

UZ'ZA, GARDEN OF (2 K. xxi. 18, 26). Where Manasseh and his son Amon, kings of Judah, were buried. Supposed to have been in Jerusalem (2 Chr. xxxiii. 20). Lost.

UZ'ZA (*strength*). 1. A Benjamite of the sons of Ehud (1 Chr. viii. 7).—2. Uzzah (xiii. 7, 9–11). 3. One who returned from Captivity (Ezr. ii. 49). 4. A Levite, son of Shimei (1 Chr. vi. 29).

UZ'ZAH. Son of Abinadab, in whose house the Ark rested for twenty years, and who died while conducting the Ark from Kirjath-jearim (2 Sam. vi.; 1 Chr. xxiii.).

UZ'ZEN SHE'RAH (ozen, *ears*), (1 Chr. vii. 24). Built by Sherah, a daughter of Ephraim, near the Beth horons. Now Beit Sira in Wady Suleiman, 13 miles N. W. of Jerusalem.

UZ'ZI. 1. Son of Bukki, and father of Zerahiah (1 Chr. vi. 5, 51).—2. Son of Tola (1 Chr. vii. 2, 3).—3. Son of Bela, a chief (vii. 7).—4. Ancestor of the Elah, settled at Jerusalem after the Captivity (ix. 8).—5. Son of Bani, and overseer of the Levites at Jerusalem (Neh. xi. 22).—6. A priest (xii. 19).—7. A priest who assisted Ezra (xii. 42), also No. 6.

UZZI'A, the Ashterathite. One of David's men (1 Chr. xi. 44).

UZZIAH (*might of Jah*). 1. King of Judah; in some passages he is called Azariah. He began his reign at 16 yrs. of age, B. C. 806. This name was common among the Jews. He was afflicted with leprosy (2 Chr. xxvi. 16–23).—2. A Levite, ancestor of Samuel (1 Chr. vi. 24).—3. A priest of the sons of Harim (Ezr. x. 21).—4. Father of Athaiah (Neh. xi. 4):—5. Father of Jehonathan, one of David's overseers (1 Chr. xxvii. 25).

UZ'ZIEL (*might of God*). 1. The ancestor of the Uzzielites, the fourth son of Kohath, and one of the three families of the Kohathites (Ex. vi. 18, 22; Num. iii. 27).—2. Son of Ish; he was chief of an expedition against the remnants of the Amelekites left on Mount Seir (1 Sam. xiv. 48, xv. 7), he destroyed them and possessed their country (1 Chr. iv. 42, 43).—3. One of the goldsmiths who assisted in repairing the wall of Jerusalem (Neh. iii. 8).

V

VA'HEB (Heb. *a gift?*) An obscure word, translated "what he did." Only found in Num. xxi. 14. Probably a proper name of some place in Moab, on the Arnon.

VAIL. See Dress.

VAIL OF THE TABERNACLE. See Temple.

VA-JEZ'A-THA, or **VAJ-E-ZA'THA** (*white, pure*). One of Haman's ten sons killed in Shushan by the Jews (Esth. ix. 9).

VALE, VALLEY. Five Hebrew words are translated valley, each conveying a separate meaning. 1. Bikah (*to cleave*), generally a broad, open valley, enclosed by mountains or otherwise. The plain of Shinar is thus named (Gen. xi. 2). Palestine a "land of hills and valleys" (Deut. xi. 11).—2. Gai and ge (*to flow together*). A narrow valley or ravine. "Doves of the valleys" alluding to the rocks bordering the glens in Palestine being the resort of doves (Ez. vii. 16). The word ge often is used in combination with other words.—3. Nak-hal (*to receive*) signifies a torrent—bed, or a valley dry in summer but with a river or torrent flowing in winter. This word corresponds to the modern Arabic term for valley—*wady*. Used also to signify

a brook. "My brethren have dealt deceitfully as a *brook*, as the stream of *brooks* they pass away" (Job vi. 15–17). Also used for *valley* and for *stream*, as in 1 Kings xvii. 3, 4.—4. Erneh (*to be deep*), a low tract of land, surrounded by hills on high ground; as the wide "*valley* of Jezreel," lying between Gilboa and Moreh (Judg. vi. 35). Except in Josh. xix. 27, where the Hebrew word itself is used as Bath-emek, this word is translated valley or vale.—5. Shephelah (*a low plain*). With the exception, in Josh. xi. 16, where "*the valley of the same*" is used without the article denoting it a proper name, the word Shephelah means the plain of Philistia. See Plain.

MOSQUE OF OMAR.

VASH'NI. The eldest child of Samuel (1 Chr. vi. 28).

VASH'TI (*a beauty*). The queen of Persia, divorced by Ahasuerus, her husband, for refusing to appear unvailed before his reveling company (Esth. i.).

VAU (Heb. vav, *a peg, nail, hook*). The 6th letter of the Hebrew alphabet (Ps. cxix). Writing.

VER'SIONS, AN'CIENT, OF THE O. AND N. T. See History of the Books.

VES'SEL. See Cup.

VI'AL (Heb. pach, *a flask, bottle*), (1 Sam. x. 1). Gr. *phiale, a bowl, goblet*, broad and shallow (Rev. v. 8). Heb. mizrak, basin and bowl.

VIL'LAGE. See City and Town.

VINE (Heb. gefen, sorek). "The choicest vine" (Is. v. 2). Nazir "vine undressed" (Lev. xxv. 5, 11). See Vineyard.

VINE OF SODOM. "Their vine is the vine of Sodom" (Deut. xxxii. 32). This is generally supposed to allude to the apples of Sodom; but it is improbable, for a vine is distinctly mentioned. Probably it was used figuratively as in Ps. lxxx. 8, 14; Is. v. 2, 7. The enemies of Israel in this relation would be compared to the people of Sodom.

VINEYARDS, PLAIN OF THE (Judg. xi. 33). Beit el Kerm, 10 ms. N. of Kerak, on the ancient Roman road, where there are ruins of a temple.

VINEYARD. The vine, its fruit, the grape, and wine and vinegar produced from it, are frequently mentioned in the Scripture, as is natural from its being a native of the East (supposed to have originated in Margiana, S. of the Caspian Sea). It is mentioned in the earliest histories of all people, and has always been highly valued. Moses, Homer, and Herodotus wrote about it; and before their day, the Egyptians pictured it, and methods of preparing its products for use, on their monuments. Various preparations from the vine are in use, among which are: The juice of the unripe grape, for acid; in some parts the unripe grapes are dried and powdered, forming a pleasant acid; grapes, both fresh and dried, as raisins; the juice of grapes fresh pressed is valued as a pleasant beverage, called *must;* this juice is also boiled down into DIBS

ALABASTER BOXES.

(*molasses*), used at the table; wine, alcohol, and vinegar are made by fermentation; cream-tartar is made from the lees; a fragrant oil is pressed from the seeds; the ashes from the twigs and stalk yield carbonate of potash. A fruitful vine is often used as an emblem of the Hebrew nation, and a period of security, repose, peace, and prosperity is figured by every one sitting under his own vine and fig-tree; and the drinking of wine was also used as a symbol of the highest spiritual blessings (Is. lv. 1, 2). In fearful contrast to this is the desolation of the house of Israel, figured by the neglected, trodden-down, wasted vineyard, by Isaiah (v. 1–7); and by the vine brought out of Egypt, by Asaph (Ps. lxxx. 8–16). The first notice of wine in the Scriptures is when Noah planted a vineyard (Gen. ix. 20, 21), and suffered (himself and his posterity) from excess in its use. The next is in the story of Lot (xix.). When Isaac blessed Jacob, he prayed the Lord to give him, among other things, plenty of corn and wine (xxvii. 28). Pharaoh's chief butler made *must* for his king (xl. 11). Moses mentions wine (frequently in his laws, and) as a drink-offering (Num. xv. 5, 7, 10; see, also, Judg. ix. 13); but it was forbidden to the priests during their service in the tabernacle (Lev. x. 9); and it is thought that Nadab and Abihu transgressed because of an excess in its use. During a vow the Nazarite was not to drink wine or vinegar, to eat grapes, or touch any product of the vine: (as carbonate of potash enters into some kinds of bread, he may have been restricted to unleavened bread. Num. vi. 3, 4). The people drank wine at their sacred festivals (Deut. xiv. 22–26). The Rechab-

ites abstained from wine (and from living in houses) in obedience to the command of their ancestor. Wine was used in the ceremony of the Passover. There was a custom of giving medicated wine or vinegar to criminals who were condemned to death, to stupefy them, and thus lessen the pains of execution (Prov. xxi. 6, 7; Amos ii. 8), as in the case of the crucifixion, when the soldiers gave Jesus vinegar mixed with some drug, evidently with kind intentions (Matt. xxvii. 34; Mark xv. 23). Mixed wine is frequently mentioned. It was mixed with water (perhaps only to weaken it for common use, or it may be for deception (Is. v. 22), and with milk (Cant. v. 1), and with spices to increase its strength and flavor (Ps. lxxv. 8; Is. v. 22). The wine of Lebanon was peculiarly fine (Hosea xiv. 7), and had a grateful odor, and the Tyrians imported a famous quality from Helbon (Ezr. xxvii. 8). Wine (and other liquids) are kept in skins (bottles) made of goat-skins, or from the skins of other animals, especially of the ox for the largest, sewed and pitched, and stored, not generally in their houses, but in a wine-store, where it was fermented. Jesus sanctioned the use of wine, and made a supply at a marriage-feast (John ii.), and is charged with being a wine-bibber by his enemies, in contrast to John the Baptist, who abstained from both bread and wine (Luke vii. 33, 34). Paul advises Timothy to use *a little* wine for its expected relief from his "often infirmities" (1 Tim. iv. 23). The warnings against excess in its use as a beverage are frequent and severe in both the O. T. and the N. T. (Prov. xx. 1, xxiii. 29–35, xxxi. 4, 5; 1 Cor. vi. 10; Gal. v. 21). The wine-press was generally in the vineyard (Is. v. 2; Matt. xxi. 33), outside of the cities (Zech. xiv. 10; Rev. xiv. 20), where, in the vintage, they had a merry time treading the grapes (Judg. ix. 27; Is. xvi. 10; Jer. xxv. 30, xlviii. 33; Neh. xiii. 15; Is. lxiii. 2; Joel ii. 24), which custom furnished strong figures to the prophets of the judgments of the Lord upon Israel (Lam. i. 15; Joel iii. 13), and of his mercies and blessings also (Prov. iii. 10). The vineyards are generally planted on hill-sides, which are often terraced to the summit, far from the village, without hedge or fence, requiring constant watching. The strongest young men are set apart for this duty, and take their stand on the hill-tops or on towers; which custom Isaiah makes the subject of one of his finest figures of the prosperity of Zion (lii. 7, 8). The watchmen are stationed near each other (within sight and hearing of each other's voices), and have certain calls to use in case of danger, or in "publishing" peace and safety, now as in the olden time (*Land and Book*, ii. 412).

VIN'EGAR (Heb. HOMEZ). See VINEYARD.

VI'OL. A stringed instrument of music, resembling the psaltery (Is. v. 12; Amos vi. 5). See MUSICAL INSTRUMENTS.

VI'OLET. COLORS.

VI'PER. SERPENT.

VIRGIN (Heb. BATHULIA, ALMAH; Lat. *virgo*,

young woman), (Is. viii. 3, 4; Matt. i. 23; Prov. xxx. 19).

VIS'ION. A supernatural presentation of certain scenery or circumstances to the mind of a person either while awake or asleep (Is. vi.; Ez. l.; Dan. viii.; Acts xxvi. 13). See DREAM.

VOPH'SI (*my addition*). Father of Nahbi (Num. xiii. 14).

VOW (Heb. NEDER, *vow of devotion;* Heb. ESAR, *vow of abstinence;* and HEREM, *vow of destruction*). Vows, in general, are mentioned in Job xxii. 27, etc. (Gr. *anath'ema, devoted*). The earliest vow mentioned is Jacob's (Gen. xxviii. 18–22, xxxi. 13). The law regulated the practice of vows. A man might devote to sacred uses possessions or persons, but not the first-born either of man or beast (Lev. xxvii. 26). Moses enacted several laws for the regulation and execution of vows (Deut. xxiii. 21, 23). The vows of minors were not binding without the consent of the head of the family (Num. xxx.). These self-imposed services were more in keeping with the ancient dispensation—in which outward sacrifices had so large a share—than with enlightened Christianity.

VUL'GATE, THE. See HISTORY OF THE BOOKS.

VUL'TURE (Heb. DAAH), (Lev. xi. 14); (Heb. DAYYAH), (Deut. xiv. 13); AYYAH (Job. xxviii. 7). A large bird, belonging to the genus *hawks*, and including a great many species. It is pronounced unclean by Moses (Lev. xi. 14; Deut. xiv. 13). The vulture has a naked or downy head, a bare neck, and long wings. It is a carrion-bird, and is remarkable for its powers of vision, and the great hight at which it soars. It scents its prey from afar. Scarcely can an exhausted camel fall on its route, and die, before numbers of these filthy scavengers show themselves (Job. xxviii. 7).

W

WA'FER (Heb. RAKIK). A thin cake made of flour or leaf-like bread (Ex. xvi. 31), and used in various offerings, anointed with sweet oil.

WA'GES (Heb. MASKORETH, SACHAR; Gr. *misthos, opsonia*). The law was very strict in requiring daily payment of wages (Lev. xix. 13). The employer who refused to give his laborers sufficient food was censured (Job xxiv. 11), and the withholding wages was denounced (Jer. xxii. 13). The rich oppressed the poor in the later times, and called down Malachi's denunciation (iii. 5).

WAG'ON (Heb. AGALAH). See CART.

WALL. 1. Walls, supporting terraces on side-hills, are made from the loose stones gathered on the side-hill, either with or without mortar. These walls, ruined or entire, are found all over the hill-country, and are especially noticeable at Bethlehem and Gibeah, N. W. of Jerusalem. This custom doubled the capacity of the hill-sides in its power of producing grain or supporting trees, for the soil was washed down by the heavy rains, if not terraced. Walls were built around sheepcotes, in the open country, for the protection of the flock at night, and many such are still to be seen in the desert S. of Palestine. See GEDOR.

The ancient walls of temples and forts were sometimes built of very large stones, laid in a channel cut in the solid rock (see JERUSALEM). The style of rebated faces of blocks in a wall (called also beviled) is the mark of great antiquity, and almost always of Phœnician origin. The Hebrews followed this style in the temple-wall, and in some parts of the city wall of Jerusalem,

as appears in the remains of the temple-wall at the wailing-place, and underground, lately examined by the Palestine Exploration, and at the Damascus Gate, David's Tower, etc. Many other speci-

ROYAL EGYPTIAN ARCHER.

mens are found at Hebron, in the mosque over Machpelah, at Paneas, Tyre, etc.

The Assyrians often faced a wall of some coarse material (earth, loose stones, etc.) with slabs of marble, or bricks.

Walls of houses were made of dirt, clay, bricks (sunburnt or fire-kilned), and of stone, rough or dressed.

Where a common highway ran through a vineyard, it was often walled on both sides (Num. xxii. 24).

WAR. In war the custom of the Israelites resembled that of surrounding countries. See ARMY. Their first object in war was conquest; and then, when in Canaan, their defense against enemies. They consulted the Urim and Thummim, or the prophet, before going to war, or into battle. The Hebrews were almost always at war, with others or among themselves, generally on account of neglecting the true worship, when Jehovah punished the nation by the means of other people sent against them.

WASHING THE HANDS AND FEET. As no knives or forks were used at the table, washing of the hands before and after meals was necessary (Matt. xv. 2). Because of the dust and heat of the Eastern climate, washing the feet on entering a house was an act of respect to the company, and of refreshment to the traveler (Gen. xviii. 4). When done by the master of the house it was an especial mark of respect and honor to the guest.

WATCH. A division of the night. See CHRONOLOGY.

WATCH'ER. A figurative designation of heavenly things, apparently angels, as seen by Nebuchadnezzar in his dream (Dan. iv. 13, 17–23).

WATCH'MEN. Are of as early a date as cities, robbers, and wars (Ex. xiv. 24). Jerusalem and other cities had regular guards night and day (Cant. iii. 1–3, 5, 7). When danger is apprehended they are required to call to each other every few minutes. They were stationed at the gate of a city and in the adjacent tower (2 Sam. xviii. 24–27); and their responsible office required great vigilance and fidelity (Jer. vi. 17).

WA'TER (Heb. MAYIM; Gr. *hudor*). To the ancient Hebrews water was of inestimable value (Ex. xv. 22). It is an emblem of the spiritual blessings or SALVATION, which God bestows upon his people (Is. lv. 1). See JERUSALEM.

WA'TER-GATE (Neh. xii. 37). A gate of Jerusalem.

WATER OF JEALOUSY. Holy water mixed with dust from the floor of the Tabernacle, given in the case where a wife was suspected by the husband, on whom had fallen "the spirit of jealousy;" described in Num. v. 11–31. In such a case an offering had to be brought by the husband (Lev. ii. 2).

WA'TER-POT (Gr. *hudria*). A large vessel of stone in which water is kept standing, also for carrying water (John ii. 6, 7).

WAVE'-OF'FERING (Heb. TENUFAH). The breast of every PEACE-OFFERING, the Passover sheaf, loaves and lambs at Pentecost, etc., were to be "waved" before the Lord, and were hence called wave-offerings (Ex. xxix. 24–28).

WAX (Heb. DONAG). Mentioned in scripture as easily melted by heat (Ps. xxii. 14; Ex. xxii. 24).

WAY (Heb. DERECH, Gr. *hodos*). A road, track, path or HIGHWAY (Gen. xvi. 7); in Acts ix. 2 applied to the Christian religion.

WEA'SEL (Heb. CHOLED). Is identical with the Arabic *chuld* and the Syriac *chuldo*, both words signifying a mole; and therefore that the unclean animal mentioned in Lev. xi. 29, is not a weasel but a kind of mole. Several varieties of weasels and moles are found in Palestine.

WEAV'ING. Was practiced by the ancients, and exhibited on the ancient monuments of Egypt (Gen. xli. 42). It was usually performed by women (2 K. xxiii. 7). The distaff, the shuttle, and the weaver's beam and pin are mentioned in Judg. xvi. 14; 1 Sam. xvii. 7; Job vii. 6.

WEEK (Heb. SHABUA). See CHRONOLOGY.

WEIGHTS AND MEASURES. The notices of weights and measures in the Bible are few and incomplete, and we have to supply the wanting information from other sources; chiefly from the systems of ancient nations, following the chain from Rome up through Greece, Egypt, and Phœnicia, to Babylon, the origin. The system was nearly uniform everywhere, but varied from one age to another. Layard found at Nineveh the weights used by the Babylonians, which were in the form of lions and of ducks, with rings for handles, of different sizes, in a certain system, the lightest weighing about 4 oz., the heaviest about 40 lbs.

TABLE OF SILVER COIN WEIGHTS—PROPORTIONS AND VALUES.

	Paris grs	Prop.	lbs.	oz.	dwt.	grs.			
Gerah (*bean*)	13.7	60,000				13.7	1 Gerah =		2½ cts.
Bekah (*divided*)	137	6,000		6	17		10 Gerahs = 1 Bekah = 25		"
Shekel (*weight*)	274	3,000		13	14		2 Bekahs = 1 Shekel = 50		"
Maneh (*talent*)	13,700	60	2	3	2	12	50 Shekels = 1 Maneh = 25 dolls.		
Kikkar (*round*)	822,000	1	142	9	5	0	60 Manehs = 1 Kikkar = 1500 "		

Gold was reckoned at 10, 12 or 13 times the value of silver in different ages.

COPPER COINS.			GREEK COINS.		ROMAN COINS.	
	Grains.	Value.				
Mite (lepton)	15 to 20	2 mills.	Lepton = 2 mills.		As (farthing)	1¼ cents.
⅙ of a shekel	81 " 88	3 "	Drachm = 16 cents.		Quadrans	3¾ mills.
Quarter	125 " 132	5 "	Didrachm = 32 "		Denarius (penny)	15 cents.
Half (bekah)	235 " 264	1 cent.	Stater (tetr.) 64 "		Aureus (stater)	3 dollars.
Shekel	528	2 cents.	Mina (pound) 16 dollars.		Talent	961 "
Talent = 1500 shekels			Talent 960 "			

Silver was 60 to 80, and even once as high as 112 times the value of copper.

HEBREW COPPER COINS.			EGYPTIAN COPPER COINS.		
	Grains.	Value.		Grains.	
Gerah (1–20)	16 to 20	2 mills.	½ KeT	70	3 mills.
One-sixth	81 " 88	3 "	KeT	140	6 "
Zuzah (¼)	125 " 132	4 "	2 KeT	280	1 c. 2 "
Half (bekah)	235 " 264	8 "	5 KeT	700	3 c. 5 "
Shekel	528	1 c. 6 "	MeN (Maneh)	1400	7 c.
Talent = 1500 shekels = 25 dollars.					

The comparative weights of the talents of different nations may be seen in this table, each number standing for 1000 grains:

Hebrew gold,	1 320	Babylonian silver,	959	Egyptian silver,	840
" silver,	660	" lesser	479	Æginetan "	660
" copper,	792	Persian gold,	400	Attic	500

MEASURES OF LENGTH.

The names are derived from members of the human body—the CUBIT, the length of the forearm from the elbow po.nt to the third finger-tip, was the unit, a name and custom derived from Egypt, and recorded on the monuments. There is no record of the unit in the Bible, Josephus, nor in any ancient Hebrew building.

TABLE OF MEASURES OF LENGTH (Egyptian).

	Paris lines.	Inches.		Paris lines.	Inches.			
Cubit (*sacred*)	234.33	19.05	Cubit (*common*)	204.8	18	4 Fingers	=	1 Palm.
Span	117,166	9.52	Span	102.4	9	3 Palms	=	1 Span.
Palm (*wide*)	39.55	3.17	Palm	34.13	3	2 Spans	=	1 Cubit.
Finger "	9.76	0.79	Finger	8.53	¾	6 Cubits	=	1 Reed.

Land was measured by the cubit and reed, but never computed by square-measure, for they had no unit such as our acre.

MEASURES OF DISTANCE.

The ordinary day's journey for *one person*, was 30 ms.; for *a company*, 10. The Sabbath-day's journey was measured by the distance fixed between the tents and the ark in the wilderness, which was 2,000 cubits (*Smith's Dict.;* Kitto), which was also the limit outside of the Levitical cities. The moderns reckon by hours' travel, which vary from 4 to 2½ ms., as the length of the hour varies with the length of the day in summer and winter.[*]

MEASURES OF CAPACITY (Josephus).

There were two sets—one for dry, another for liquid things—both having a unit of the same value, the bath and the ephah (Ex. xlv. 11).

TABLE OF DRY AND LIQUID MEASURES.

									Equal to, in gallons, according to	
									JOSEPHUS.	RABBINS.
Homer									86.6	44.2
Bath of Ephah	10	1							8.6	4.4
Seah	30	3	1						2.8	1.4
Hin	60	6	2	1					1.4	0.7
Gomer	100	10	3⅓	1⅔	1				0.8	0.4
Cab	180	18	6	3	1 4-5	1			0.4	0.2
Log	720	72	24	12	7 1-5	4	1		0.1	0.6

The common cubit of 18 in. would give 3,000 ft. The sacred cubit of 19.05 in. would give 4,762 ft.
An English mile is 5,280 ft.

[*] Kitto, Sabbath-day's journey, v. iii., p. 722; Smith, do., v. iii., p. 1073.

WELL (Heb. BEER). The necessity and demand for water in a hot climate has rendered it a possession of the greatest importance (Judg. i. 15; Gen. xxi. 30, 31). So that, in war, the wells were often filled in by the enemy (2 K. iii. 19). Wells in Palestine have generally to be sunk through limestone; sometimes they are descended by steps (Gen. xxiv. 16). A curb or low parapet-wall encircles their mouths; sometimes they were furnished with stone covers (Ex. xxi. 33). Christ sat on the curb of the well when he conversed with the woman of Samaria (John iv. 6). The water was hoisted by a rope attached to a bucket, water-skin, or stone jar (Gen. xxiv. 14–20; John iv. 11). Also a wheel was used upon which was slung an endless belt, on which jars to hold the water were attached at intervals. The well-swing was of ancient use, being a beam balanced upon a pivot, with a rope and bucket at one end and a stone balance-weight at the other. Women were usually employed to fetch water. Many places are named in relation to wells, such as Beersheba, Beer-Elim, Rehoboth, etc.

WEN (Heb. YABBAL, *flowing*), (Lev. xxii. 22). A tumor which is movable, pulpy, and often elastic to the touch.

WENCH. Maid-servant (2 Sam. xvii. 17, only).

WEST (Heb. YAM (*sea*). MAARAB (Is. xlv. 6). MAARABAH. The place where the sun sets. Gr. *dusme, the setting* of the sun, the quarter of the heavens or earth which lies toward the setting sun, or opposite the east (Gen. xii. 8).

EAST (Heb. KEDEM, KADIM, KIDMAH, KADMON, KADMONI, *before*, or *in front of*, a person), (Job xxiii. 8, 9). Heb. MIZRAH, the place of the *sun's rising* (Ps. ciii. 12).

NORTH (Heb. ZAFON, Gr. *borrhas*). That quarter of the heavens or earth, or that direction which is at the left hand of a person who faces the east (Gen. xiii. 14).

SOUTH (Heb. DAROM, *bright, sunny.* TEYMAN. What is on the right hand of a person facing the east (Gen. xii. 9).

WHALE (Heb. TAN or TANNIN, *sea-monster, dragon*). "Even the sea-monsters (TANNIN) draw out the breast, they give suck to their young ones" (Lam. iv. 3). Here the whale is evidently alluded to. Probably the fish which swallowed Jonah was some large kind of shark, or a fish especially provided (John i. 17; Gen. i. 21; Matt. xii. 40).

WHEAT (Heb. DAGAN, RIFOTH, CHITTAH). In the account of Jacob's sojourn with Laban occurs the first mention of wheat (Gen. xxx. 14). Egypt was celebrated for wheat; of the bearded and also of the seven-eared kind (Gen. xli. 22),

WINDOW.

known now as mummy-wheat, from being found encased in the mummies: if such grain be planted it will yield. Wheat was plentiful in Syria and Palestine (Ps. lxxxi. 16, cxlvii. 14, etc.). The common kind would produce sometimes one hundred grains in the ear (Matt. xiii. 8). The wheat was planted in the winter, and reaping commenced towards the end of April, in May, and in June. See AGRICULTURE. HARVEST.

WHIRL'WIND (Heb. SUFAH), (Job. xxvii. 9). Storm (Job xxi. 18); SA'AR, *tempest* (Ps. lv. 8). A violent wind or hurricane. Sometimes the desert storms lift vast quantities of dry, hot sand into the air, darkening the sun at noon-day, and burying several feet deep any object in their course, even a whole caravan, with thousands of animals and travelers (Job i. 19). The Arabs name this sand-cloud "Efreet," *the bad one.* Houses, trees, and even great rocks, are moved by these terrible wind storms, which are sudden in coming, and are soon over.

WHITE (*purity*), (Is. i. 18). See COLORS.

WID'OW (Heb. ALMANAH; Gr. *chera*). The Mosaic dispensation made no provision for the maintenance of widows. They were left dependant upon their friends, especially the first-born or eldest son, whose birth-right or extra share of the property imposed such a duty upon him. The widow was commended to the care of the community (Ex. xxii. 22). The widow, when left childless, was to marry the brother of her deceased husband (Deut.

xxv. 5, 6). The high-priest was forbidden to marry a widow (Lev. xxi. 14). Poor widows were cared for, among others, in the early Church (Acts vi.; James i. 27).

WIL'DERNESS. 1. SIN. See EXODUS. 2. Of the Wandering. The district over which the Israelites wandered between the two visits to KADESH, for about 38 years is not certainly known. The probability is that it was what is now called Et Tyh, *the Wandering*. See PARAN. It is a high, limestone plateau, affording good pasture in the rainy season, and is not a desert at any time except in a few isolated patches. It may be divided into the sandy plain along the sea shore, the wadies (dry river vallies), and the high table-land. There are mountain peaks. The shore of the Mediteranean is bordered by a low sandy plain, grassy where watered, which extends, in the Wady El Arish and its branches, far inland, and is full of hills and shifting sand. The only really barren waste, like the Nefood, or the Dahna (*red waste*), of Arabia, occurs only here and there, where the springs have dried up from the loss of trees, and sand has been brought by the winds. Above the plain rise low table-lands, covered with a hard, white soil, which on the more elevated plateaus is displaced in places by gravel. Everywhere there are dry, treeless water-courses, green with herbage

where there are trees and plants, and evidences of a greater extent in the past. The remains of large trunks of trees scattered over this region indicate a more copious rain-fall, and the existence of groves, if not of forests, in some past age. Evidences of a former state of cultivation are found in stone walls all over the district, and, wherever there is water, flowers, herbs, grasses, and groves of acacia, tamarisk, and other trees. This region is now capable of supporting immense flocks and herds, and, under more favorable conditions of forest and rain, might have given support to the tribes of Israel for ages, independent of any miraculous supply. There are very few names even now, in the district, and none which can be traced to the time of the Exodus. See SINAI, GEOLOGY.

WILDERNESS OF THE WANDERING. See WILDERNESS AND EXODUS.

WIL'LOWS (Heb. ARABIM). Were used for making booths at the Feast of Tabernacles (Job xl. 22), also giving shade to BEHEMOTH (Is. xliv. 4); a common tree which grows in marshy places (Job xl. 22); with a leaf much like the olive (Lev. xxiii. 40). The "weeping willow" memorable in connection with the mourning Hebrew captives (Ps. cxxxvii. 2), is a native of Babylonia. The "Brook of the Willows," (Heb. NAHAL), (Is. xv. 7), on the S. border of Moab, flows into the S. E. extremity of the Dead Sea (Num. xxi. 19). NAHALIEL.

WILLS. Two instances are recorded in the O. T. under the Law, of testamentary disposition. 1. Effected in the case of Ahithophel (2 Sam. xvii. 23). 2. Recommended in the case of Hezekiah (2 K. xx. 1; Is. xxxviii. 1).

WIM'PLE (Heb. MITPAHATH). A mantle or shawl (Ruth iii. 15; Is. iii. 22).

WIND (Heb. RUAH or RUACH). Wind from the North, South, East, and West, was expressed as of the "four quarters" or "four winds" (Ez. xxxvii. 9; Dan. viii. 8; Matt. xxiv. 31). The cold wind of the N. is appealed to in Cant. iv. 16. The N. W. wind lasts from the autumnal equinox to the beginning of November, and the N. wind from June to the equinox. As the E. wind passes over the sandy wastes of the Arabian desert before arriving in Palestine, it was called the "wind of the wilderness" (Job i. 19; Jer. xiii. 24). The S. wind after passing over the Arabian peninsula acquires great heat (Job xxxvii. 17; Luke xii. 55). The W. and S. W. winds reach Palestine in a humid state acquired from the Mediterranean. The sea of Genesaret was subject to squalls of wind (Mark iv. 37; Luke viii. 23). The wind spoken of, figuratively, as in Jer. xviii. 17, typical of the waste of war; as transitory, in Job vii. 7; Ps. lxxviii. 39, etc. It represented the operations of the Holy Spirit in John iii. 8; Acts ii. 2.

WINDOW (Heb. HALLON or CHALLON). The windows were apertures closed in with lattice-work, called in Heb. ARUBBAH (Eccl. xii. 3). Although there were windows looking into the street they, for the most part, opened into the inner court (Judg. v. 28; Prov. vii. 6). See HOUSE.

WINE. The word wine is the translation of ten Hebrew and two Greek words. 1. Heb. YAYIN,

SHUSAN THE PALACE.

in the rainy season, furnishing good pastures but no tillage. The highest plateau is covered with a light, rich soil, with a few springs and wells, and brooks which are permanent for a mile or two only,

that which yields wine, in Micah vi. 15.—2. TI-ROSH, vintage-fruit (Micah vi. 15), new wine.—3. ASIS, grape-juice (Cant. viii. 2).—4. SOBE, or SOVE, boiled *must*, syrup (wine in Is. i. 22; literally, thy SOBE circumcised with water).—5. HEMER, pure red wine (Deut. xxxii. 14), or HAMAR (Ez. vi. 9, vii. 22), the pure blood of the grape, red wine in Is. xxvii. 2 (Ps. lxxv. 8, meaning desirable vineyard?).—6. MIMSACH, mixed wine; MEMSACH, mixed wine (Prov. xxiii. 30).—7. MESECH, mixture (mingled her wine, in Prov. ix. 2; wine is red, in Ps. lxxv. 8).—8. MEZEG, spiced wine, in Cant. viii. 2; liquor, in vii. 2.—9. SHEKAR, strong drink (strong wine in Num. xxviii. 7; "SHEKAR shall be bitter to them that drink it," in Is. xxiv. 9). Occurs 21 times in the N. T. (Arabic, *sukkar*, sugar).—10. HEMEZ, vinegar; vinegar (HOMEZ, in Num. vi. 3); (homez of yayin, and homez of shekar). Thine sour wine (Ruth ii. 14); as the *posca* (Greek), which the Roman soldiers gave to Jesus on the cross (John xix. 29, 30, etc.); ASHISHAH, a cake of dried raisins; flagons of wine, in 2 Sam. vi. 19; Cant. ii. 5, etc.; SHEMARIM, wine-lees.—1. Greek, *posca*.—2. *gleukos*, new wine in Acts. ii. 13, now called *must*. —3. *oinos*. Put young wine (*oinos neos*) into new skins (bottles in Matt. ix. 17); not to ferment, as that would burst the *bottles* or skins, new or old, but into new ones, to avoid the refuse of the old wine, which may be sour.

WINE-PRESS, THE (PURAH, GATH). Is of the highest antiquity, and is drawn on the walls of the Egyptian temples and tombs. Remains of wine-vats are found in many parts of Palestine, cut in the solid rock. Some were very large, as that in which Gideon threshed (Judg. vi. 11). Wine has always been in use, and the Scriptures only condemn its excessive use. Corn, wine, and oil are special gifts of Providence. It was the usual drink-offering (Ex. xxix. 40) to be presented among the first-fruits (Lev. xxiii. 13). The priests were prohibited from the use of wine and strong drink before service in the Temple (Lev. x. 9), and the Nazarite during his vow (Num. vi. 3). The wine-cup was handed round four times during the Paschal Feast, especially after the Captivity. Jesus speaks of the wine used as the *fruit* of the vine (Matt. xxvi. 29). Wine is generally mixed with water (warm; see Justin Martyr, *Apol.* i. 65). Those holding office in the Church were not to be given to wine (1 Tim. iii. 3), or to much wine (iii. 8), or a slave to much wine (Titus ii. 3). Paul once recommends its use (to Timothy, 1 Tim. v. 23).

WIT, TO. To know (Gen. xxiv. 21; 2 Cor. viii. 1).

WITH, WITHES (Heb. YETHARIM), (Judg. xvi. 7-9), a *cord* or *rope*. A *with* or *withe* is, probably, a flexible twig for binding.

WIS'DOM OF SOL'OMON, THE. See HISTORY OF THE BOOKS.

WITNESS. The law was very careful to provide and enforce evidence for all its infractions and all transactions bearing on them (Num. xv. 39, 40. Two witnesses, at least, are required to establish any charge (xxxv. 30). A false witness was punished. Women and slaves were not admitted to bear testimony (Josh. iv. 8).

In the N. T. the original notion of a witness is in the special form of one who attests his belief in the Gospel by personal suffering (Acts xxii. 20).

WOLF (Heb. ZEEB; Gr. *lukos*). A fierce and rapacious animal (Gen. xlix. 27) which prowls at night (Jer. v. 6), and especially destructive to sheep (Matt. x. 16; Luke x. 3). They were very plentiful in Palestine, but are now much less common. It closely resembles the dog. They are cruel but cowardly animals, swift of foot and strong enough to carry off a sheep at full speed, and is now, as of old, the dread of the shepherds of Palestine. They secrete themselves till dark

among the rocks, then leap into the fold and seize their victim by stealth. The wolf first tears out the entrails and devours the heart, liver and lungs before the muscular parts. His bite is vigorous and deadly; his mode of attack is by short, rapid snaps. A single wolf is far more destructive than a whole pack of jackals. The Syrian wolf is of lighter color than that of Europe, and larger and stronger.

TAMARISK.

WOM'AN, WOM'EN (Heb. ISHSHAH, *female; Gr. gume, theleia, female*), (Rom. i. 26, 27). Is mentioned in the Scriptures as the beloved and honored companion and helpmeet of man (Gen. xxii. 23, 24). In the East women have always lived in seclusion, not appearing in public unless closely vailed, not seeing the men who visit their husbands and brothers, nor even taking their meals with the men of their own family. They were chiefly engaged in domestic duties (Prov. xxxi.) The poor gleaned the remnants of the harvest (Gen. xxix. 9, xxiv. 15-20). Oriental women are never regarded or treated as equals by the men. This is seen on all occasions. They pronounce women to be weak and inferior in the most absolute terms. Even in polite society the gentlemen must be served first. So the husband and brothers sit down and eat, and the wife, mother, and sisters wait and take what is left. If they accompany their female relatives anywhere, they walk before, and the women follow at a respectful distance. It is very common to see small boys lord it over their mothers and sisters in the most insolent manner, and they are encouraged to do so by the father. They literally use the rod upon them. Instances are not rare in which the husband kills the wife outright, and no legal notice is taken of the murder. She is confined closely, watched with jealousy, and everything valuable is kept under lock and key; necessarily so, they say, for the wife will not hesitate to rob her husband if she gets an opportunity. The Arabs have a word—"*ajellack*"—by which they preface the mention of anything indelicate or unclean. Thus, ajellack, a donkey, or a dog, or my shoes; so, when compelled to speak of their women, they say "ajellack, my woman," or simply, "the woman is so and so." These and similar customs enable us to understand why it is that acquaintance before marriage is ordinarily out of the question. It is considered quite immodest for an unmarried lady to manifest any special regard for her future husband. The birth of a son is always a joyful event in a family; but that of a daughter is often looked upon as a calamity. If the first wife has no children the husband marries another or takes a slave. The whole system is productive of evil, and that only, to the individual, the family, and the community.

WOOL (Heb. ZEMER; Chal. *amar;* Gr. *erion*). Wool was an article of the highest value among the Jews (Lev. xiii. 47). The "fleece" (Heb. GEZ, GIZZAH), is mentioned in Deut. xviii. 4. The wool of Damascus was highly prized in Tyre (Ez. xxvii. 18). Wool is an image of purity (Is. i. 18; Dan. vii. 9). Garments made of woolen and linen were prohibited by the law; the cloth bore a peculiar name (Heb. SHAATRUZ), "thou shalt not wear a garment of divers sorts" (Deut. xxii. 11). Josephus (iv. 9, §11), says the reason for the law against wearing a garment woven of linen and wool was that such were worn by priests alone.

WORD (Heb. EMER, OMER, IMRAH, DABAR, MIL LAH, etc.; Gr. *logos* and *rema*. "Word" is applied to the Lord JESUS CHRIST. See HISTORY OF THE BOOKS.

WORLD (Heb. EREZ), (Is. xxiii. 17). Earth. Heb. HEDEL, *place of rest, region of the dead.* Heb. HELED, *this world.* Heb. OLAM (Ps. lxxiii. 12), "world without end." Heb. TEBEL, the earth fertile and inhabited. Gr. *aion, eternal* (Matt. xii. 32). See ALEXANDRIA.

FARLEIAN. JOHN I. 1, 2.

WORM (Heb. SAS), (Is. li. 8, only). Evidently denotes the caterpillar of the clothes-moth. Heb. RIMMAH and TOLEAH are used in various passages together, and more generally for the maggots or caterpillars of insects than for the earth-worm (Ex. xvi. 20–24). The worm is also named in the

O. and N. T. as a symbol of the gnawing pain of eternal punishment (Is. lxvi. 24; Mark ix. 44, etc.).

WORM/WOOD (Heb. LAANAH; Gr. *apsinthos*). A bitter plant, a symbol of whatever is nauseous and destructive (Deut. xxix. 18; Jer. ix. 15). Different species are found in Palestine. It was used by the Romans as a stomachic infusion in wine.

PALIMPSEST. SEVERUS, WRITTEN OVER LUKE XX. 9, 10

Diffused in alcohol, it is now used to an alarming extent in France and Switzerland. The Jews put it in their wines, probably for tonic purposes. The word occurs frequently in the Bible, and generally in a metaphorical sense (Amos v. 7).

WOR/SHIP, WOR/SHIPER. See ADORATION.

WORTH. Used as now to indicate value or equality in value (Gen. xxiii. 9, 15; Ez. xxx. 2).

WOT, TO. To know; to have knowledge (Gen. xxi. 26). WRITING.

WRITING (Heb. KATHAB, *to write;* SEFER, *a book;* SOFER, *a writer*). The Phœnician was the most ancient alphabet that is known to us. The Egyptian writing may have been more ancient, but that was not alphabetic, being both ideographic and phonetic. Pliny (vii. 56) says the Syrians (Phœnicians) invented writing, but gives the Assyrians credit for great antiquity in the use of the art. The discovery of the Moabite Stone (see p. 173) proves the origin of the Greek letters to have been Phœnician; and it is probable that the Hebrews used the alphabet in common with the Phœnicians, as may be inferred from their names; as Aleph, *ox;* Gimel, *camel*.

TABLE OF DERIVATION OF ALPHABETS.
1 Phœnician.
2 Greek (ancient), Persian (anc.), Numidian, Hebrew (anc.), Aramæan (anc.).
3 From Greek, Etruscan, Umbrian, Oscan, Samnite, Celtiberian, Roman, Runic; Later Greek, Coptic, Gothic, Slavonian.
4 From Persian, Sassanid, Zend, Pehlvi, Armenian?
5 From Aramæan, Palmyrene, Hebrew square, Estrangelo. Nestorian, Sabian, Cufic, Nischi, Peshito, Miguric or Old Turkish.
6 From Hebrew, Samaritan.

The English is the first pure alphabet, without double-letters.

The Hebrew alphabet has 22 letters. (See their names in the TABLE OF ALPHABETS).

the Ethiopic is like a round-top tent; 3. GIMEL, a camel, the Greek gamma—some say the camel's hump; 4. DALETH, a door, that is, a tent-door, a

ALPHABETS

		Hieroglyphic.	Hieratic.	Phœnician (Moabite Stone).	Phœnician (Siloam Inscription).	Hebrew (square character).
a	eagle		𝄢	𝋊𝋊	𝋊𝋊	א
b	crane			99	99	ב
g	bowl			ꓶ	ꓶ	ג
d	hand			◁△	◁◁	ד
h	plan of house?			⧢⧢	⧢⧢	ה
f,v	cerastes ..			YY	↑↑	וו
t (tch, z)	duck			⚊	⚊	ז
χ(kh)	sieve			ꓷꓮ	ꓷꓮ	ח
th	tongs; loop..					ט
i	leaves			⫟⫟⫟	⫟⫟	י
k	throne			ϒϒ	ϒϒ	ך
l	lioness			66	6	ל
m	owl			ϟϟ	ϟϟ	מם
n	water			ϟϟ	ϟϟ	נן
s	door bolt ..			⚏⚏		ס
ā	weapon ..			o	o	עy
p	door			♩♩	♩	פ
t(ts)	snake			ϻϻ	⚊	צ
q	knee?			ϙϙϙ	ϙϙ	ק
r	mouth			٩	٩٩	ר
š(sh)	field			w	⚍⚍	ש
t(tu)	arm with cake in hand			x	xx	ת

HEBREW AND PHENICIAN ALPHABETS, as derived from the Egyptian hieratic characters.

The Phœnicians, in order to form an alphabet, appear to have selected certain Egyptian letters from a type of the Hieratic character (a cursive form of Hieroglyphic), as found in papyri of about B.C. 2500.

names in the TABLE OF ALPHABETS). The arrangement of the letters is after the order as given in Psalm cxix. The meaning of each name as far as known is: 1. ALEPH, an OX; 2. BETH, a house;

triangle; Greek delta; 5. HE, no name; Greek ɛ, and also Phœnician turned round; 6. VAU (waw), a hook, or tent-peg, the Greek upsilon; 7. ZAIN (sajin), sword, ancient Greek san; 8. CHETH, a fence, Greek ETA; 9. TET (*teth*), a snake, or basket, Greek *theta;* 10. YOD, a hand, the Phœnician and Samaritan yod has a hint of fingers; 11. CAPH, the hollow of the hand, Greek *kappa;* 12. LAMED,

sigma; 16. AIN (*ajin*), an eye, O in Phœnician; 17. PE, a mouth, Greek *pi;* 18. ZADE, a fish-hook, Greek *zeta;* 19. KOF, back of the head (some say ear, others a pole, or eye of a needle); the old

ALPHABETS

	Cadmean.		GREEK.					LATIN.		
	Right to left.	Left to right.	Local forms.	Eastern.	Western.	Local forms.	Pelasgian.	Latin.		
alpha ..	A	A		A A	A A		A	A A A	a
beta ..	ያ	B	M Melos, etc. C Paros, Siphnos, Thasos, etc. ⌐ Corinth.	B B	B B		B	B B	b
gamma	∧	Γ	⟨ C Corinth, Megara, etc.	∧ Γ ∧	Γ Γ	⟨ C Chalcis, Phocis, Arcadia, Elis, Locris, etc.	⟨ C	⟨ C	c
delta ..	△	△		△ D	△ ▷ D		△ ▷ D	D	d
epsilon..	ጓ	℈	B Corinth, etc.	℞ E	℞ E		℞	E ‖	e
digamma	⅂	F		[℞]	℞ F		℞	F ᛁᛚ	f
zeta ..	⊥	⊥		⊥	⊥		⊥	[G a new letter formed from C.]	g
eta.. ..	⊟	⊟		⊟H(h,ē)	⊟H(h)		⊟	H	h
theta ..	⊗	⊗		⊗ ⊙	⊗ ⊙		⊗		
iota ..	⟩	⟨	⟨⟨ Crete, Thera, Melos, Corinth, etc.	I	I		⟩I	I	i
kappa ..	⋊	K		K	k		K	k	k
lambda ..	∧	∧	⌐ Attica, ⊦ Argos.	∧ ∧	∧ ∧	⌐ Chalcis, Bœotia, etc	∟	∟ ∟	l
mu ..	M	ᴍ		M M	M M		ᴍ	M	m
nu	ᴎ	N		ᴎ N	ᴎ N		ᴎ	N	n
xi	⊞	⊞	⧻ Later Argos [χσ, Attica, Naxos, Siphnos, Thasos, etc.]	王	[See below.]		⊞		
omikron	O	O	Ω Paros, Siphnos, etc. O C Melos.	O	O		O	O	o
pi	⌐	⌐		Γ Π	Γ Π		Γ	Γ P	p
san (ss)	M	M	⊤ Halicarnassus, Teos, Mesembria.				M		
koppa ..	ⵁ	ⵁ		[ⵁ]	ⵁ		ⵁ	Q	q
rho ..	⸠	P	M Crete, Thera, Melos, Argos, Corinth, etc.	P R	P R		P R	R R	r
sigma ..	⟩	⟨		⟨⟩	⟨⟩	M Phocis, etc.	⟨⟩	⟩ S	s
tau	T	T		T	T		T	T	t
upsilon..				V Y	V Y		V	V	uv
xi				[See above.]	X +		X	X	x
phi.. ..				Φ Φ	Φ Φ		Φ		
chi.. ..				X +	↓ Ψ		↓		
psi.. ..			[φσ, Attica, Naxos, Siphnos, Thasos, etc.]	↓ Ψ		X Ozol. Locris, Arcadia.			
omega ..			O Melos, Paros, Siphnos, etc. Ω [O used generally for o, ov, ω, except in Ionia.]				Adopted at a later period as foreign letters. } Y Z	y z

GREEK AND LATIN ALPHABETS.

The Greeks adopted for their alphabet twenty-two signs from the Phœnician. The letters which follow *tau* were afterwards added. Originally the letters were written from right to left; but afterwards from left to right. The early Greek alphabet may be arranged in two groups (with local varieties), viz. the Eastern or Ionian, used in Asia Minor and in certain islands and states of Greece; and the Western, used in other islands and states, and generally in the Greek colonies in Italy and Sicily. The two groups chiefly differed in the value to be attached to the letters χ and ψ. The early Italic alphabet, derived from the Western Greek alphabet, has been called the Pelasgian alphabet; of this the Latin alphabet rejected certain letters as superfluous, and at a later date it introduced others.

ox-goad, Greek *lambda;* the ancient Phœnician was curved like the modern Arabic; 13. MEM, water, or a trident and symbol of the sea; Greek *mu;* 14. NUN, a fish, Greek *nu;* 15. SAMECH, a prop, Greek

Hebrew P became the Greek *koppa*, and the Roman Q; 20. RESH, the head, Greek *ro;* 21. SHIN and SIN, a tooth, Greek *sigma;* 22. TAU, a mark, or sign, perhaps a cross ⋈, Greek *tau.*

The form of five of the Hebrew letters was changed when the letters were final (at the end of the word), a system which was useful when sentences were written without spaces between the words; for instance IwasGLADWHE*n*THEYSAID UNTOMELETUSGOU*p*TOTHEHOUSEOFTHELORD (Ps. cxxii. 1). This writing without division into words is a more close following of speech, which is a continuous flow of sound, the mind separating the words, or ideas. The Moabite Stone (page 94) is an instance from antiquity. The spaces there show where the stone has been broken or defaced, and letters lost.

Abbreviations were common both in books, and on coins, and also in inscriptions on the monuments, as ISR for ISRAEL, YAH for JEHOVAH.

Numbers were indicated by letters and figures. Figures are found on the Phœnician coins, and monuments in Palmyra, and Egypt. The Greeks also used letters in writing numbers. Differences in certain statements of numbers can be explained in this way; the scribe, or copyist mistaking a c for a G, c being 700, and G being 7,000.

The signs used by the Babylonian writers differed from those of Tiberias, and were nearly all above the letters. The present system is uniform everywhere and dates from about A. D. 1050.

Accents were also marked, for the purpose of noting the tone-syllable (directing the reader in the synagogue), and the chief words in the sentence. There were peculiar styles of recitation for each class of books, the law, prophets, and poets, which are still in use. The metrical chants have been lost. See MUSIC.

The materials which have come down to us from antiquity are, stone, bricks, papyrus, vellum, parchment. Embossed leather is still preserved, bearing the names and date of the Pharaohs 3,300 years ago. Papyrus is alluded to in 3 Macc. iv. 20, and 2 John 12 (Gr. *xartēs, chartes*); and in Josephus (Ant. iii. 11, 6, xii. 2, 10); and parchment in 2 Tim. iv. 13 (Gr. *membranai*). Skins of clean animals only could be used for the Scriptures; as KELEF (skin of the hairy side), for the tophillim, phylacteries; diksostos (Heb. DIKS), for the mezuzoth; and gëvil (of undivided skin, dressed). The ink (DEYO, Gr. *melan*, black), was of lampblack wet with gall-juice, sometimes diluted with vitriol. The inkstand (KESETH HASSOFER), was carried in a case (KALMARIN), with pens, knife, etc., by a strap over the shoulder, or fastened at the girdle.

The rolls were written in columns (DELA-THOTH), (one, two, or three, according to the width of the roll), with a margin above of 3 fingers, below of 4, and between the columns of an inch. The columns are about 2 fingers wide in the Herculaneum rolls; and others there are 3 in. (4 fingers).

WRITING MATERIALS.

The case in which the rolls were kept were called KEREK or KARKA.

Tablets of wood covered with wax were used for ordinary writing not intended for keeping a long time. On these the letters were impressed with a stylus (Job xix. 24), sometimes of iron (Ps. xlv. 2). For engraving on stone the point called CHE-RET (Ex. xxxii. 4; Is. viii. 1), and ZIPPOREN (Jer. xvii. 1), were used.

A reed pen (3 John 13; 3 Macc. iv. 20), was used on parchment and papyrus.

The oldest monument in alphabetical writing is the Moabite Stone (p. 173), which is dated as early as 900 B. C., if it does not belong to David's time (1025 B. C.). The ancient Phœnician monuments, dating later than the Moabite stone, are counted by hundreds.

No vowel points are found on the coins, in the Palmyrene inscriptions, or on the Phœnician monuments. It is probable that the vowel-points were first written by Ezra. The Arabic is the first in point of time to show the use of vowel-points, dating before A. D. 650. The present Arabic system of writing dates from about A. D. 930. Some scholars contend that the vowel-points were not in use before A. D. 550.

In the 8th century A. D., Moses the Punctator, followed by his son Judah the Corrector, used the

[Greek manuscript text]

A. D. 1044. ACTS XIII. 18-20.

points for the first time that is recorded, to assist his pupils.

TRANSLATION OF THE INSCRIPTION ON THE MOABITE STONE (p. 173).

1 I am Mesa, son of Chamos-nadab, the king of Moab (son of) Yabnis.

2 My father ruled over Moab (** years), and I have

3 reigned after my father. And I have built this high-place of sacrifice in Karkha, and platform for Chamos **.

4 (I call myself) Mesa, because he (Chamos) has saved me from (all who fought against Moab).

5 (Omri) the king of Israel joined (Moab's) haters, and oppressed Moab (many days). Chamos was angry.

6 The king's son succeeded him, and Moab was oppressed very sore.

7 ** And I saw him and his house (temple?). Israel was dispersed for ever. Omri took

8 Medeba, and remained there, and built forty **.

9 Chamos is our god. To him I built Baal Meon (walls and mounds), and sacrificed.

10 I took Kirjathaim, and men of Gad dwelt in the land from the days of their fathers.

11 The king of Israel built Kirjathaim. I fought against and took it, and

12 killed all the people that were in the city (as a sacrifice) to Chamos, god of Moab,

13 *** before the face of Chamos, in Kirjathaim; then I made prisoners the (old) men and the ****

14 * of the youth (morning). Chamos said: Go rule over Israel.

15 I went by night, and fought with him from the *** of the dawn to mid-day. I ***

16 **** entirely *****

17 **** who is for Astar Chamos ***

18 ** Jahveh (Jehovah) ** before the face of Chamos and the king of Israel (came to)

19 Yahas, and dwelt there (until?) my combat with him, and Chamos drove him from ****.

20 I took of Moab two hundred men in all, and I made them go up to Yahas, and I ******* (to annex it to)

21 **** on Dibon. It is I who built the esplanade(?) to the walls of Yearim(?) and the walls of

22 *** And it is I who have built its gates, and it is I who have built its fortress, and it is ***

23 I who have built Bet-Moloch, and it is I who have made the two ****
24 ** Kir and there were no wells in the interior of Kir on its esplanade. And I said to all the people
25 Make every man a well in his house. It is I who have offered the holocaust on the esplanade(?) in
26 ** Israel. It is I who have built Aroër(?) and it is I who who have made the road of Arnon.
27 It is I who have built Bet-Bamoth, which was destroyed(?) It is I who have built Bosor, which ***
28 *** Dibon, of the military chiefs, because all Dibon was subject, and I have
29 *** with the cities which I have added to the earth, and it is I who have built ***
30 *** Bet-Diblathaim and Bet-Baal Meon, and I have erected there the ***
31 ** the land. Horonaim, where resided **
32 ** Chamos said to me ** Fight at Horonaim, and I
33 ** Chamos ** on **
34 **

Some pieces of the broken stone have been lost.

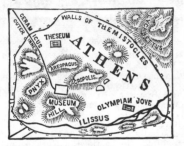

Translation of the inscriptions on the sarcophagus which was found at Sidon:

ON THE BODY.

1. In the month of Bul, year 14 of my reigning, I king Ashmanezer king of the Sidonians
2. Son of King Tabinth, king of the Sidonians: spake King Ashmanezer king of the Sidonians, saying: I have been stolen away
3. before my time—a son of the flood of days. The whilom great is dumb—the Son of God is dead. And I rest in this grave, even in thy tomb,
4. in the place which I have built. My adjuration to all the ruling powers, and all men. Let no one open this resting-place, and
5. not search with us for treasure, for there is no treasure with us, and *let him not bear away the couch of my rest*, and not trouble
6. us on this resting-place by disturbing the couch of my slumbers. Even if people should persuade thee, do not listen to their speech. For all the ruling powers and
7. all men who should open the tomb of this my rest, or any man who should *carry away the couch of my rest*, or any man who trouble me or
8. this my couch, unto them there shall be no rest with the departed; they shall not be buried in a grave, and there shall be to them neither son nor seed
9. in their stead, and the holy gods will send over them a mighty king who will rule over them, and
10. cut them off with their dynasty. If any human being should open this resting-place, and any man should carry away
11. this tomb—be he of royal seed or a man of the people; there shall be unto them, neither root below nor fruit above, nor honor among the living under the sun * * *

X—Y

XAN'THICUS. One of the Macedonian months (Neb. NISAN). MONTH.

YARN (Heb. MIKVEH, MIKVE). An error in 2 Chr. i. 16. The king's merchants from Coa took the horses from Coa at a price.

YEAR. CHRONOLOGY.

YELLOW. COLORS.

YOKE (Heb. MOT "bar"), (Nahum i. 13); MOTAH, "bands" (Ez. xxx. 18); Heb. ZEMED, a pair of oxen, so termed as being yoked together (1 Sam. xi. 7). A symbol of subjection and servitude (1 K. 12, 4). See AGRICULTURE.

YOKE-FELLOW (Gr. *suzugos*). A fellow-laborer (Phil. iv. 3).

Z

ZAAN'AIM, THE PLAIN OF, or probably the **OAK OF.** A sacred tree by Heber's tent, when Sisera took refuge in it (Judg. iv. 11). Near Kedesh Naphtali. Lost.

ZAAN'AN. In the Shefelah. ZENAN.

ZA'AVAN (*unquiet*). Son of Ezer (Gen. xxxvi. 27), a chief.

ZA'BAD (*whom God gave*). 1. Son of Nathan, son of Attai (1 Chr. ii. 31–37). He was one of David's men.—2. An Ephraimite (1 Chr. vii. 21).—3. Son of the Ammonitess Shimeath, and an assassin of King Joash (2 Chr. xxiv. 26).—4. The name of three Israelites in Ezra's time (Ezr. x. 27).—5. The second, one of the sons of Hashum (x. 33).—6. The third, one of the sons of Nebo (x. 43).

ZABADAI'AS. ZABAD 6. (1 Esd. ix. 35).

ZABADE'ANS (1 Macc. xii. 31). The modern *Zebedany* is a village, in a plain of the same name, high up on Anti-Lebanon, watered by the Barada. Pop. 3,000. Kefr Zabad is a small village near.

ZAB'BAI. A corruption of ZACCAI. 1. Son of Bebai (Ezr. x. 28).—2. Father of the BARUCH, who assisted Nehemiah (Neh. iii. 20).

ZAB'BUD. Son of Bigvai, and companion of Ezra (Ezr. viii. 14).

ZABDE'US. ZEBADIAH 6 (1 Esd. ix. 2).

ZAB'DI (*gift of Jah*). 1. Son of Zerah, and ancestor of Achan (Josh. vii. 1, 17).—2. Son of Shimhi (1 Chr. viii. 19).—3. David's officer over the wine-cellars (xxvii. 27), called the *shiphmite.*—4. Son of Asaph (Neh. xi. 17).

ZAB'DIEL (*gift of God*). 1. Father of JASHOBEAM (1 Chr. xxvii. 2).—2. An overseer, son of Haggedolim (Neh. xi. 14).—3. An Arabian chieftain who put ALEXANDER BALAS to death (1 Macc. xi. 17).

ZA'BUD (*given*). Son of NATHAN 1 (1 K. iv. 5) and confidential friend of Solomon.

ZAB'ULON. Gr. form of ZEBULUN (Matt. iv 13).

ZAC'CAI (*pure*). Ancestor of 760 who returned from Captivity (Ezr. ii. 9; Neh. vii. 14).

ZACCHÆ'US. The name of a tax-collector near Jericho, who, being short in stature, climbed up into a sycamore tree in order to obtain a sight of Jesus as he passed through that place. Luke only has related the incident (xix. 1–10). Zacchæus was a Jew, as may be inferred from his name, and from the fact that the Saviour speaks of him expressly as "a son of Abraham." The term which designates this office is unusual, but describes him, no doubt, as the superintendent of customs or tribute in the district of Jericho, where he lived, as one having a commission from his Roman principal (*manceps publicanus*) to collect the imposts levied on the Jews by the Romans, and who, in the execution of that trust, employed subalterns, who were accountable to him, as he in turn was accountable to his superior. The office must have been a lucrative one in such a region, and it is not strange that Zacchæus is mentioned by the evangelist as a rich man. The Saviour spent the night probably in the house of Zacchæus, and the next day pursued his journey to Jerusalem. He was in the caravan from Galilee which was going up thither to keep the Passover. We read in the rabbinic writings also of a Zacchæus who lived at Jericho at this same period, well known on his own account, and especially as the father of the celebrated Rabbi Jochanan ben Zachai.

ZACCHE'US. An officer of Judas Maccabæus (2 Macc. x. 19). Ap.

ZAC'CHUR. A Simeonite, of the family of Mishma (1 Chr. iv. 26).

ZAC'CUR (*mindful*). 1. Father of Shammua, the Reubenite spy (Num. xiii. 4).—2. A Merarite Levite, son of Jaaziah (1 Chr. xxiv. 27).—3. Son of Asaph the singer (1 Chr. xxv. 2, 10; Neh. xii. 35).—4. The son of Imri, who assisted Nehemiah in rebuilding the city wall (Neh. iii. 2). —5. A Levite, or family of Levites, who signed the covenant with Nehemiah (Neh. x. 12).—6. A Levite, whose son or descendant Hanan was one of the treasurers over the treasuries appointed by Nehemiah (Neh. xiii. 13).

ZACHARI'AH, or properly ZECHARIAH, was son of Jeroboam II., 14th king of Israel, and the last of the house of Jehu. There is a difficulty about the date of his reign. Most chronologers assume an interregnum of eleven years between Jeroboam's death and Zachariah's accession, during which the kingdom was suffering from the anarchy of a disputed succession; but this seems unlikely after the reign of a resolute ruler like Jeroboam, and does not solve the difference between 2 K. xiv. 17 and xv. 1. We are reduced to suppose that our present MSS. have here incorrect numbers, to substitute 15 for 27 in 2 K. xv. 1, and to believe that Jeroboam II. reigned 52 or 53 years. But whether we assume an interregnum, or an error in the MSS., we must place Zachariah's accession B. C. 771–72. His reign lasted only six months. He was killed in a conspiracy, of which Shallum was the head, and by which the prophecy in 2 K. x. 30 was accomplished.—2. The father of Abi, or Abijah, Hezekiah's mother (2 K. xviii. 2).

ZACHARIAS. 1. Zechariah the priest in the reign of Josiah (1 Esd. i. 8).—2. In 1 Esd. i. 15, Zacharias occupies the place of Heman in 2 Chr. xxxv. 15.—3.=SERAIAH 6, and AZARIAH (1 Esd. v. 8; comp. Ezr. ii. 2; Neh. vii. 7).—4. The prophet ZECHARIAH (1 Esd. vi. 1; vii. 3).—5. ZECHARIAH 8 (1 Esd. viii. 30).—6. ZECHARIAH 9 (1 Esd. viii. 37).—7. ZECHARIAH 10 (1 Esd. viii. 44). 8. ZECHARIAH 11 (1 Esd. ix. 27; comp. Ezr. x. 26).—9. Father of Joseph, a leader in the first campaign of the Maccabæan war (1 Macc. v. 18, 56–62).—10. Father of John the Baptist (Luke i. 5, etc.).—11. Son of Barachias, who, our Lord says, was slain by the Jews between the Altar and the Temple (Matt. xxiii. 35; Luke xi. 51). There has been much dispute who this Zacharias was. Many of the Greek Fathers have maintained that the father of John the Baptist is the person to whom our Lord alludes;

but there can be little or no doubt that the allusion is to Zechariah, the son of Jehoiada (2 Chr. xxiv. 20, 21). The name of the father of Zacharias is not mentioned by St. Luke; and we may suppose that the name of Barachias crept into the text of St. Matthew from a marginal gloss, a confusion having been made between Zechariah, the son of Jehoiada, and Zacharias, the son of Barachias (Berechiah) the prophet.

ZA'CHER (*remembrance*). Son of Jehiel (1 Chr. viii. 31).

THE GENEALOGY OF ZADOK.

1 Chr. vi. 3-14.	ix. 11.	Ezr. vii. 1-5.
1. Aaron.		1. Aaron.
2. Eleazar.		2. Eleazar.
3. Phinehas.		3. Phinehas.
4. Abishua.		4. Abishua.
5. Bukki.		5. Bukki.
6. Uzzi.		6. Uzzi.
7. Zerahiah.		7. Zerahiah.
8. Meraioth.		8. Meraioth.
9. Amariah.		
10. Ahitub.		
11. ZADOK.		
12. Ahimaaz.		
13. Azariah.		
14. Johanan.		
15. Azariah.		15. Azariah.
16. Amariah.		16. Amariah
17. Ahitub.		17. Ahitub.
	Meraioth.	
18. ZADOK.		18. Zadok.
19. Shallum (Meshullam).		19. Shallum.
20. Hilkiah.		20. Hilkiah.
21. Azariah.		21. Azariah.
22. Seraiah.		22. Seraiah.
23. Jehozadak.		* * *
		Ezra.

ZA'DOK (*righteous*). 1. Son of Ahitub, and one of the two chief priests in the time of David, Abiathar being the other. Zadok was of the house of Eleazar, the son of Aaron (1 Chr. xiv. 3), and eleventh in descent from Aaron. The first mention of him is in 1 Chr. xii. 28, where we are told that he joined David at Hebron after Saul's death with 22 captains of his father's house, and, apparently, with 900 men (4600–3700, ver. 26, 27). Up to this time, it may be concluded, he had adhered to the house of Saul. But henceforth his fidelity to David was inviolable. When Absalom revolted, and David fled from Jerusalem, Zadok and all the Levites bearing the Ark accompanied him, and it was only at the king's express command that they returned to Jerusalem, and became the medium of communication between the king and Hushai the Archite (2 Sam. xv., xvii.). When Absalom was dead, Zadok and Abiathar were the persons who persuaded the elders of Judah to invite David to return (2 Sam. xix. 11). When Adonijah, in David's old age, set up for king, and had persuaded Joab, and Abiathar the priest, to join his party, Zadok was unmoved, and was employed by David to anoint Solomon to be king in his room (1 K. i.). And for this fidelity he was rewarded by Solomon, who "thrust out Abiathar from being priest unto the Lord," and "put in Zadok the priest" in his room (1 K. ii. 27, 35). From this time, however, we hear little of him. It is said in general terms, in the enumeration of Solomon's officers of state, that Zadok was the priest (1 K. iv. 4; 1 Chr. xxix. 22) but no single act of his is mentioned. Zadok and Abiathar were of nearly equal dignity (2 Sam. xv. 35, 36; xix. 11). The duties of the office were divided. Zadok ministered before the Tabernacle at Gibeon (1 Chr. xvi. 39); Abiathar had the care of the Ark at Jerusalem. Not, however, exclusively, as appears from 1 Chr. xv. 11; 2 Sam. xv. 24, 25, 29. Hence, perhaps, it may be concluded that from the first there was a tendency to consider the office of the priesthood as somewhat of the nature of a corporate office, although some of its functions were necessarily confined to the chief member of that corporation.—2. According to the genealogy of the high priests in 2 Chr. vi. 12, there was a second Zadok, son of a second Ahitub, son of Amariah, about the time of King Ahaziah. It is probable that no such person as this second Zadok ever existed, but that the insertion of the two names is a copyist's error.—3. Father of Jerushah, the wife of King Uzziah and mother of King Jotham (2 K. xv. 33; 2 Chr. xxvii. 1).—4. Son of Baana, who repaired a portion of the wall in the time of Nehemiah (Neh. iii. 4). He is probably the same who is in the list of those that sealed the covenant in Neh. x. 21, as in both cases his name follows that of Meshezabeel.—5. Son of Immer, a priest who repaired a portion of the wall over against his own house (Neh. iii. 29).—6. In Neh. xi. 11 and 1 Chr. ix. 11 mention is made in a genealogy of Zadok, the son of Meraioth, the son of Ahitub. But it can hardly be doubtful that Meraioth is inserted by the error of a copyist, and that Zadok the son of Ahitub is meant.

ZA′HAM (*loathing*). Son of Rehoboam (2 Chr. xi. 19).

ZA′IN (*a weapon*). The seventh letter of the Hebrew alphabet (Ps. cxix.). WRITING.

ZA′IR (2 K. viii. 21). South of Kerek. Lost.

ZA′LAPH (*wound*). Father of Hanun (Neh. iii. 30).

ZAL′MON, MOUNT. Near Shechem (Judg. ix. 48).

ZALMO′NAH. Desert-station (Num. xxxiii. 41). Supposed to be Maan, a few ms. E. of Petra.

ZALMUN′NA (*shelter is denied him*). One of the two kings of *Midian* slain by GIDEON (Judg. viii. 5-21).

ZAM′BIS. AMARIAH 5 (1 Esd. ix. 34).

ZAM′BRI. ZIMRI 1 (1 Macc. ii. 26).

ZA′MOTH. ZATTU (1 Esd. ix. 28).

ZAMZUM′MIM (*noisy people*). A race of giants (Gen. xiv. 5). They were exterminated by the Ammonites (Deut. ii. 20, 21).

ZANO′AH. Two towns in Judah. 1. (Josh. xv. 34), in the Shefelah, now called Zunua, in Wady Ismail. Peopled after the return from Babylon (Neh. xi. 30).—2. (Josh. xv. 56), in the mountain district, 10 ms. S. of Hebron.

ZAPH′NATH-PA-A-NE′AH (Heb. ZAFENATH PA ANEAH). A name given by Pharaoh to JOSEPH 1 (Gen. xii. 45), meaning preserver of the age.

Egyptian titles of princes of high rank, in that age, were generally SUTEN-SA, Pharaoh's son, which was also given to the governor of Cush. Other titles were descriptive, as MERKETU, superintendent of buildings (or of public works). Some appear to have been nicknames, as MA, the shepherd (one of the Pharaohs); PE-MAY, the cat; S-NUFRE, good king; S-NUFRE ANKHEE, good worker; PET-AMEN-APT, belonging to Amen of Thebes; SHAFRA-SHA, Shafra rules; and AMEN-EM-HA, Amen in the front.

The original Egyptian name of Joseph has not yet been found on the monuments, where, indeed, but very few records of the age in which he lived have been found. It is expected that further discoveries will bring such records to light. The skilful suggestion of Mr. Poole gives Egyptian words PSENT-ANKHEE, meaning delight lives.

ZA′PHON (*northward*), (Josh. xiii. 27). On the E. side of Jordan. Lost.

ZA′RA. ZERHA 1 (Matt. i. 3).

ZARA′CES. Brother of Jehoiakim (1 Esd. i. 38).

ZA′RAH. ZERAH 1 (Gen. xxxviii. 30).

ZARAI′AS. 1. ZERAHIAH 1 (1 Esd. viii. 2).—2. ZERAHIAH 2 (viii. 31).—3. ZEBADIAH 5 (viii. 34).

ZA′REAH. ZORAH (Neh. xi. 29).

YA′REATHITES, THE. Inhabitants of ZAREAH (1 Ohr. ii. 53).

ZA′RED, THE VALLEY OF. Zered.

ZARE′PHATH. Sarepta, near Sidon (Ant. viii. 13, 2). The residence of the prophet Elijah. The miracle of the widow's cruse of oil was wrought here by Elijah (1 K. xvii. 9, 10; Luke iv. 26). There are remains of columns and slabs, and the Roman road is quite perfect here.

ZAR′ETAN. ZARTHAN (Josh. iii. 16). Supposed to be Kurn Surtabeh, N. of Jericho, in the Ghor.

ZA′RETH-SHA′HAR (Josh. xiii. 19). Reuben.

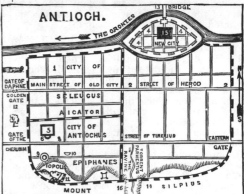

ANTIOCH.

Sara, near the Dead Sea, at the mouth of Wady Zerka Main.

ZAR′HITES, THE (*descendants of Zerah*). 1. A branch of the tribe of Judah (Num. xxvi. 20).—2. A family of Simeonites (Num. xxvi. 13).

ZART′ANAH (1 K. iv. 12). Near Bethshean. Zarthan?

ZAR′THAN. 1. Near Succoth (1 K. vii. 45).—2. The same as Zaretan in Josh. iii. 16.—3. In the upper part of the Jordan valley, near Bethshean.—4. Zeredathah, Zererah, Zererath, Zererathah.

ZATH′OE. Error for ZATTU in 1 Esd. viii. 32.

ZATHU′I. ZALTU (1 Esd. vi. 12).

ZAT′THU. ZALTU (Neh. x. 14).

ZAT′TU (*a sprout*). Ancestor of a family of laymen of Israel, who returned from captivity (Ezr. ii. 8; Neh. vii. 13).

ZA′VAN. ZAAVAN (1 Chr. i. 42).

ZA′ZA (*projection*). Son of Jonathan (1 Chr. ii. 33).

ZEAL (Heb. KINAH, Gr. *zelos*). May include warmth of feeling and vehemence of action, according to the good or bad motive, or the wisdom or folly, of the actor. Thus the zeal of Jehu (2 K. x. 16), of Saul (Phil. iii. 6), of the Israelites (Rom. x. 2), etc.

ZEBADI'AH (*Jah gave*). 9 of these persons mentioned, but none noted (1 Chr. viii. 15, viii. 17, xii. 7, xxvii. 7; Ezr. viii. 8, x. 20; 1 Chr. xxvi. 2; 2 Chr. xvii. 8, xix. 11.)

ZE'BAH (*sacrifice*). A king of MIDIAN, killed with ZALMUNNA (Judg. viii. 5–21).

ZEBA'IM (*antelopes*). The children of Pochereth, of Zeboim, are mentioned among those of Solomon's who returned from Captivity (Ezr. ii. 57; Neh. vii. 59).

22 others of this name are mentioned, but are of no particular account.

ZE'DAD (Num. xxxiv. 8; Ez. xlvii. 15). On the N. border of the land as promised by Moses. Passed through by the prophet Ezekiel on his way to Assyria as a captive. Sadud is on the N. end of Anti-Libanus, 50 ms. N. E. of Baalbek.

ZEDEKI'AH (*justice of Jah*) 1. The last king of Judah and Jerusalem. Son of JOSIAH and Hamutal (2 K. xxiv. 17, 19). His history is given in 2 K. xxv. 7, etc. Jer. xxxix. 1–7, lii. 1–11; and 2 Chr. xxxvi. 10, etc., also in Jer. xxi., xxiv., xxvii., xxix., xxxii., xxiv., xxxvii. — 2. A false prophet, exposed by Micaiah (2 K. xxii. 11–37).—3. Another false prophet denounced by Jeremiah (Jer. xxix. 21, 22)—4. Son of Hananiah, a prince of Judah (Jer. xxxvi. 12).

ZE'EB (*the wolf*), (Judg. vii. 25, viii. 3; Ps. lxxxiii. 11). One of the two princes (sheikhs) of Midian defeated by Gideon and the 300. He was killed at a winepress which was near the fords of Jordan, and his name given to the place.

ZE'LAH. In Benjamin (Josh. xviii. 28). Here was the residence and the family tomb of Kish, the father of Saul (2 Sam. xxi. 14), where Saul and Jonathan, and the two sons and five grandsons of Saul were buried. Probably Saul's residence before he was made king. Lost.

ZE'LEK (*fissure*). One of David's men (2 Sam. xxiii. 37).

ZEB'EDEE. The husband of Salome and father of James and John the apostles (Matt. iv. 21, xxvii. 56).

ZEBI'NA (*bought*). Son of Zebo (Ezr. x. 43).

ZEBO'IM (Gen. x. 19). One of the five cities of the plain. Shemeber was its king (xiv. 2). Lost.

ZEBO'IM, THE VALLEY OF (*ravine of the hyenas*), (1 Sam. xiii. 18). E. of Michmash.

ZEBU'DAH. Daughter of Pedaiah, wife of Josiah and mother of King Jehoiakim (2 K. xxiii. 36).

ZE'BUL (*habitation*). Governor of the Shechem (Judg. ix. 28).

ZEBU'LONITE. A member of the tribe of ZEBULUN (Judg. xii. 11, 12).

ZEB'ULUN (*dwelling*). 10th son of JACOB; 6th son of LEAH (Gen. xxx. 20, xxxv. 23). His tribe was respected for numbers (Num. i. 30, xxvi. 26). His posterity is often mentioned with Issachar, his nearest brother (Deut. xxxiii. 18).

ZEB'ULUNITES, THE. People of the tribe of ZEBULUN (Num. xxvi. 27 only).

ZECHARI'AH (*whom Jah remembers*). 1. The 11th in order of the 12 minor prophets. See HISTORY OF THE BOOKS.—2. Son of Shelemiah (1 Chr. ix. 21).—3. Son of Jehiel (ix. 37).—4. A Levite (xv. 18, 20).—5. A prince of Judah (2 Chr. xvii. 7).—6. Son of the high-priest Jehoiada (xxiv. 20).

ZELOPH'EHAD (*first-born*). Son of Hepher, son of Gilead (Josh. xvii. 3). He came out of Egypt with Moses, but died in the wilderness, leaving five daughters and no sons, which led to the establishment of a law that in such cases the daughters should inherit their father's patrimony, but they were not to marry out of their tribe (Num. xxvi. 33, xxvii. 1–11).

ZELO'TES. An epithet given to Simon 5 to distinguish him from Simon Peter (Luke vi. 15).

ZEL'ZAH (1 Sam. x. 2). Benjamin, near Rachel's sepulchre. Mentioned by Samuel the prophet, after anointing Saul king. Lost.

ZEMARA'IM (Josh. xviii. 22). Benjamin. Near Bethel, to the East. Es Sumrah is 4 ms. N. of Jericho, and is probably the place. There was also a Mount Zemaraim (2 Chr. xii. 4), which has not been identified, and may possibly mean the same locality. The Zemarite's tribe were sons of Canaan (Gen. x. 18), and belonged to this district, given to Benjamin.

ZEMI'RA (*song*). Son of Becher (1 Chr. vii. 8).

ZE'NAN (*flocks*), (Josh. xv. 37). Judah, in the Shefelah. The same as Zaanan (Micah i. 11). Placed by some travellers 2½ ms. S. E. of Mareshah, and now called *Zanabra*.

ZE'NAS (*given by Zeus*). A lawyer and a friend of Paul (Titus iii. 13).

ZEPHANI'AH. 1. A Kohathite, in the 7th generation from Levi (1 Chr. vi. 36).—2. A priest. He was among the captives slain by the king of Babylon (2 K. xxv. 18-21).—3. A prophet of the tribe of Simeon (2 Chr. xxiv. 3; Zeph. i. 4, 5).

ZE'PHATH (Judg. i. 17). A Canaanite city destroyed by Judah and Simeon, and its name changed to Hormah. Located in the pass Es Sufa, S. of the Dead Sea.

ZE'PHATHAH, THE VALLEY OF (2 Chr. xiv. 10). Near Mareshah, probably *Tell es Safieh*. Where Asa fought Zerah the Ethiopian and his host, and pursued them unto Gerar.

ZE'PHI. ZEPHO (1 Chr. i. 36).

ZE'PHO (*watch-tower*). Son of Eliphaz (Gen. xxxvi. 11), also a duke ver. 15.

ZE'PHON. Son of Gad (Num. xxvi. 15).

ZE'PHONITES, THE. A family of the tribe of Gad, descended from ZEPHON (Num. xxvi. 15).

ZER (Josh. xix. 35). Fortified town in Naphtali, S. W. of the lake of Gennesareth. May possibly be Hattin.

ZE'RAH (*a rising of light*). 1. Son of Reuel, and grandson of Esau (Gen. xxxvi. 13, 17).—2. Son of Judah and Tamar (Gen. xxxviii. 30); called Zara in Matt. i. 3.—3. Son of Simeon (Num. xxvi. 13); called Zohar in Gen. xlvi. 10.—4. Son of Iddo (1 Chr. vi. 21, 41).—5. A Cushite king who invaded Judah (2 Chr. xiv. 9-13): he was defeated by Asa.

ZERAHI'AH (*Jah caused to be born*). 1. Son of Uzzi, and ancestor of Ezra the scribe (1 Chr. vi. 6, 51). —2. Father of Elihœnai (Ezr. viii. 4).

ZE'RED, THE BROOK OF (*brook of willows*), (Deut. ii. 14). Now called Wady el Ahsy, and running into the S. E. corner of the Dead Sea. Here the wanderings of the Israelites ended; or it may be they continued to the time of the death of Moses.

ZER'EDA (*cooling*), (1 K. xi. 26). In Ephraim. The native city of Jeroboam, the first king of the kingdom of Israel, formed by the ten tribes that revolted. It was fortified for Solomon. The site has not been found, but is supposed by some to be the same as Tir'zah; and by others, Zeredatha.

ZERED'ATHA (2 Chr. iv. 17). Called *Zarthan* (1 K. vii. 46). The vessels for Solomon's temple were cast in the clay-ground between Succoth and this place, in the plain of Jordan. The finest clay is found on the banks of the Jordan, near Succoth, and is carried away for use in casting brass.

ZER'ERATH (Judg. vii. 22). In the Jordan valley. Zeredatha.

ZE'RESH (*gold*). Wife of HAMAN (Esth. vi. 10, 14).

ZE'RETH (*splendor*). Son of Ashur (1 Chr. iv. 7).

ZE'RI. IZRI, son of Jeduthun (1. Chr. xxv. 3).

ZE'ROR (*a bundle*). Ancestor of Kish, the father of Saul (1 Sam. ix. 1).

ZERU'AH (*leprous*). Mother of JEROBOAM 1 (1 K. xi. 26).

ZERUBB'ABEL (*sown in Babylon*). In N. T. and Apocrypha.

ZERU'IAH (*cleft*). Sister of David and mother of his famous generals Joab, Abishai, and Asahel (1 Chr. ii. 16).

ZE'THAM. Son or grandson of Laadan (1 Chr. xxiii. 8).

ZE'THAN (*olive tree*). Son of Bilhan (1 Chr. vii. 10).

ZE'THAR (*star*). One of the seven chamberlains of Ahasuerus (Esth. i. 10).

ZI'A (*motion*). A Gadite who dwelt in Bashan (1 Chr. v. 13).

ZI'BA (*statue*). A servant in Saul's house (2 Sam. ix. 2-12, xvi. 1-4, xix. 17, 29).

ZIB'EON (*dyed*). Father of ANAH (Gen. xxxvi. 2).

ZIBI'A (*roe*). Son of Shaharaim by his wife Hodesh (1 Chr. viii. 9).

ZIBI'AH (*roe*). Mother of King JOASH 1 (2 K. xii. 1).

ZICH'RI (*renowned*). 1. Son of Izhar the son of Kohath (Ex. vi. 21).—2. Son of Shimhi (1 Chr. viii. 19).—3. Son of Shashak (viii. 23).—4. Son of Jeroham (viii. 7).—5. Son of Asaph (ix. 15). 7 others of this name are mentioned in the following

WOMEN AT THE WELL.

passages: 1 Chr. xxvi. 25, xxvii. 16; 2 Chr. xvii. 16, xxiii. 1, xxviii. 7; Neh. xi. 9, xii. 17.

ZID'DIM (*the sides*). A town of Naphtali (Josh. xix. 35).

ZIDKI'JAH. ZEDEKIAH, one who sealed the Covenant (Neh. x. 1).

ZI'DON. See SIDON.

ZIF (*blooming*). MONTH.

ZI'HA (*dry*). 1. Ancestor of a family who returned from Captivity (Ezr. ii. 43).—2. Chief of the Nethinim in Ophel (xi. 21).

ZIK'LAG (Josh. xv. 31). Judah in the Negeb. It was the private property of David, and at one time his residence (1 Sam. xxx.). Supposed to be the site now called *Asluj*.

ZIL'LAH (*shade*). Wife of LAMECH 1 (Gen. iv. 19, 22, 23), the mother of Tubal-Cain and Naamah 1.

ZIL'PAH (*a dropping*). The maid of LEAH, who became the second wife of Jacob and mother of Gad and Asher (Gen. xxix. 24, xxx. 9–13).

ZIL'THAI (*shadow of Jah*). 1. A chief, son of Shimhi (1 Chr. viii. 20).—2. A captain who joined David (xii. 20).

ZIM'MAH (*mischief*). 1. Son of Jahath (1 Chr. vi. 20).—2. Son of Shimei, and grandson of Jahath (vi. 42).—3. Father of Joah (2 Chr. xxix. 12).

ZIM'RAN, (*sung*). Eldest son of ABRAHAM by KETURAH (Gen. xxv. 2).

AT LYSTRA.

ZIM'RI (*celebrated in song*). 1. A prince of the tribe of Simeon, slain by Phinehas (Num. xxv. 14). —2. A general of half the cavalry of Elah, king of Israel. He rebelled against his master, killed him, usurped his kingdom, and cut off the whole family, not sparing any of his relatives or friends. He reigned but seven days; for the army of Israel made their general, Omri, king, and took the city of Tirzah. Zimri burned himself in the palace, with all its riches (1 K. xvi. 1–20; 2 K. ix. 31). Others of this name are mentioned in 1 Chr. ii. 6; viii. 33–36.

ZI'NA. ZIZAH (1 Chr. iii. 10).

ZIN (*coldness*), **THE WILDERNESS OF.** A district between the Arabah and the Desert of Paran, or Tyh mountains, and consisting of three terraces, sloping toward the Dead Sea, by the *Wady Fikreh*, KADESH was in this. Josephus speaks of a hill called Sin, where Miriam was buried. This hill may be what is now *Moderah*, isolated, conical, and standing a little S. of Wady Fikreh.

ZI'OR. Judah (Josh. xv. 54), 6 ms. N. E. 'of Hebron. Now *Sair*.

ZI'PH (*mouthful*). 1. Judah, in the Negeb (Josh. xv. 24). Lost.—2. Judah, between Carmel and Juttah (Josh. xv. 55), about 3 ms. S. of Hebron. Some of David's greatest perils and most successful escapes belong to this district (1 Sam. xxiii. 14, 15, 24, xxvi. 2). Also called the Wilderness of Ziph. Rehoboam fortified Ziph (2 Chr. xi. 8).

ZIPH. Son of Jehaleleel (1 Chr. iv. 16).

ZI'PHAH. ZIPH (1 Chr. iv. 16).

ZIPH'IM, THE. Inhabitant of ZIPH 2 (title of Ps. liv).

ZIPH'ITES, THE. ZIPHIM (1 Sam. xxiii. 19).

ZIPH'ION (*a looking out*). Son of Gad (Gen. xlvi. 16).

ZIPH'RON (*sweet odor*), (Num. xxxiv. 9). In the N. boundary of the land. Now *Sudud*, near *Kurietein* (HATSAR ENAN).

ZIP'POR (*sparrow*). Father of BALAK, king of Moab (Num. xxii. 2, 4, 10, 16).

ZIP'PORAH. Daughter of JETHRO, wife of MOSES, and mother of GERSHOM 1 and ELIEZER 2 (Ex. ii. 21, iv. 25, xviii. 2).

ZITH'RI (*protection of Jah*). Son of Uzziel (Ex. vi. 22).

ZIZ, THE PASS OF (2 Chr. xx. 16). Pass of Ain Jidy.

ZI'ZA (*abundance*). 1. A Simeonite chief (1 Chr. iv. 37).—2. Son of Rehoboam (2 Chr. xi. 20).

ZI'ZAH. ZIZA. Second son of Shimei (1 Chr. xxiii. 11).

ZO'AN (*departure*). Tanis, Egypt, on the E. bank of the Tanitic branch of the Nile. It was an important post on the E. of the country, and chief town of a large district of pasture-lands. Called by the Egyptians HA-AWAR, and fortified by SALATIS, the first shepherd king, who stationed here 240,000 men as a protection against the Assyrians. Hebron was built 7 years before Zoan (Num. xiii. 22). There was a great temple here, dedicated to SET (Baal), embellished by Rameses II. The Pharaohs dwelt here, both in the time of Joseph and of the Exodus (Ps. lxxxviii. 12, 43). Mentioned by Isaiah, xix. 13, xxx. 4, 14. The ruins of the temple area show its size, 1250 by 1500 ft., and its remains prove its ancient grandeur. There were 10 or 12 obelisks, all now fallen; the stone for which was originally brought from Syene. The inscriptions and figures are of the age of the shepherd kings.

ZO'AR (*little*), (Gen. xiv. 2, 8). One of the oldest cities of Canaan. First called BELA. When the cities of the plain were destroyed, Zoar was spared as a refuge for Lot (ib. xix. 22, 30). Zoar was seen by Moses from the top of Pisgah (Deut. xxxiv. 3). Following Josephus (Ant. i. 11, § 4), the Crusaders, and later travelers, Zoar was on the LISAN, a promontory on the E. side of the Dead Sea, and now seen in extensive ruins in the lower end of Wady Kerak. Palms once flourished here so abundantly as to give it the name of City of Palms (William of Tyre, xxii. 30). Some have supposed Zoar to have been much nearer Jericho, and on the E. of Jordan, in the *Wady Seir*, near Nimrin.

ZO'BA or **ZO'BAH**, the name of a portion of Syria, which formed a separate kingdom in the times of the Jewish monarchs, Saul, David and Solomon. It probably was eastward of Cœle-Syria, and extended thence north-east and east toward, if not even to, the Euphrates. We first hear of Zobah in the time of Saul, when we find it mentioned as a separate country, governed, apparently, by a number of kings who owned no common head or chief (1 Sam. xiv. 47). Some forty years later than this, we find Zobah under a single ruler, Hadadezer, son of Rehob. He had wars with Toi, king of Hamath (2 Sam. viii. 10), and held various petty Syrian princes as vassals under his yoke (2 Sam. x. 19). David (2 Sam. viii. 3) attacked Hadadezer in the early part of his reign, defeated his army, and took from him a thousand chariots, seven hundred (seven thousand, 1 Chr. xviii. 4) horsemen and twenty thousand footmen. Hadadezer's allies, the Syrians of Damascus, were defeated in a great battle. The wealth of Zobah is very apparent in the narrative of this campaign. It is not clear whether the Syrians of Zobah submitted and became tributary on this occasion, or whether, although defeated, they were able to maintain their independence. At any rate, a few years later they were again in arms against David. The war was provoked by the Ammonites, who hired the services of the Syrians of Zobah. The allies were defeated in a great battle by Joab, who engaged the Syrians in person (2 Sam. x. 9). Hadadezer, upon this, made a last effort (1 Chr. xix. 16). A battle was fought near Helam, where the Syrians of Zobah and their new allies were defeated with great slaughter. Zobah, however, though subdued, continued to cause trouble to the Jewish kings. A man of Zobah, Rezon, son of Eliadah, made himself master of Damascus, where he proved a fierce adversary to Israel all through the reign of Solomon (1 K. xi. 23–25). Solomon also was, it would seem, engaged in a war with Zobah itself (2 Chr. viii. 3). This is the last that we hear of Zobah in Scripture. The name, however, is found at a later date in the Inscriptions of Assyria, where the kingdom of Zobah seems to intervene between Hamath and Damascus.

ZOBE'BAH (*slow-moving*). Son of Coz, of the tribe of Judah (1 Chr. iv. 8).

ZO'HAR (*whiteness*). 1. Father of Ephron the Hittite (Gen. xxiii. 8; xxv. 9).—2. One of the sons of Simeon (Gen. xlvi. 10; Ex. vi. 15); called ZERAH in 1 Chr. iv. 24.

ZO'HELETH (*serpent*) **THE STONE.** This was "by En-Rogel" (1 K. i. 9); and therefore, if En-Rogel be the modern *Um-ed-Deraj*, this stone, "where Adonijah slew sheep and oxen," was in all likelihood not far from the Well of the Virgin. The Targumists translate it "the rolling stone;" and Rashi affirms that it was a large stone on which the young men tried their strength in attempting to roll it. Others make it "the serpent stone." Others connect it with running water; but there is nothing strained in making it "the stone of the conduit" (*Mazchelah*), from its proximity to the great rock conduit or conduits that poured into Siloam.

ZO'HETH (*strong*). Son of Ishi of the tribe of Judah (1 Chr. iv. 20).

ZO'PAH (*a cruse*). Son of Helem, or Hotham, the son of Heber, an Asherite (1 Chr. vii. 35, 36).

ZOPHA'I. A Kohathite Levite, son of Elkanah, and ancestor of Samuel (1 Chr. vi. 26 [11]). In ver. 35 he is called ZUPH.

ZO'PHAR, ZIPPOR, one of the three friends of Job (Job ii. 11; xi. 1; xx. 1; xlii. 9).

ZO'PHIM (*watchers*), **THE FIELD OF.** A spot on or near the top of Pisgah, from which Balaam had his second view of the encampment of Israel (Num. xxiii. 14). If the word *sadeh* (rendered "field") may be taken in its usual sense, then the "field of Zophim" was a cultivated spot high up on the top of the range of Pisgah. But that word is the almost invariable term for a portion of the upper district of Moab. The position of the field of Zophim is not defined. May it not be the same place which, later in the history, is mentioned as MIZPAH-MOAB?

ZO'RAH (*hornets*). One of the towns in the allotment of the tribe of Dan. (Josh. xix. 41). It is previously mentioned (xv. 33), in the catalogue of Judah, among the places in the district of the Shefelah (A. V. ZOREAH). In both lists, it is in immediate proximity to ESHTAOL. Zorah was the residence of Manoah, and the native place of Samson. Zorah is mentioned amongst the places fortified by Rehoboam (2 Chr. xi. 10). In the *Onomasticon,* it is mentioned as lying some 10 miles north of Eleutheropolis on the road to Nicopolis. By the Jewish traveller happarchi, it is specified as three hours S.E. of Lydd. These notices agree in direction—though in neither is the distance nearly sufficient—with the modern village of *Sur'ah,* which has been visited by Dr. Robinson and Tobler. It lies just below the brow of a sharp-pointed conical hill, at the shoulder of the ranges which there

meet and form the north side of the *Wady Ghurab,* the northernmost of the two branches which unite just below *Sur'ah,* and form the great *Wady Surar.* In the A. V., the name appears also as ZEREAH and ZOREAH.

ZO'RATHITES, THE, *i.e.,* the people of ZORAH, mentioned in 1 Chr. iv. 2 as descended from Shobal.

ZO'REAH. Another form (Josh. xv. 33) of the name usually given in the A. V. as ZORAH.

ZO'RITES, THE, are named in the genealogies of Judah (1 Chr. ii. 54) apparently amongst the descendants of Salma and near connections of Joab.

ZOROB'ABEL (1 Esd. iv. 13; v. 5-70; vi. 2-29; Ecclus. xlix. 11; Matt. i. 12, 13; Luke iii. 27). [ZERUBBABEL.]

ZU'AR (*smallness*). Father of Nethaneel, the chief of the tribe of Issachar at the time of the Exodus (Num. i. 8: ii. 5; vii. 18, 23; x. 15).

ZUPH (*honey*), **THE LAND OF.** A district at which Saul and his servant arrived after passing through those of Shalisha, of Shalim, and of the Benjamites (1 Sam. ix. 5, only). It evidently contained the city in which they encountered Samuel (ver. 6), and that again was certainly not far from the "tomb of Rachel." The only trace of the name of Zuph in modern Palestine, in any suitable locality, is to be found in *Soba,* a well-known place about seven miles due west of Jerusalem, and five miles southwest of *Neby Samwil.* But this is at the best no more than conjecture; and, unless the land of Zuph extended a good distance east of *Soba,* the city in which the meeting with Samuel took place could hardly be sufficiently near to Rachel's sepulchre.

ZUPH. A Kohathite Levite, ancestor of Elkanah and Samuel (1 Sam. i. 1; 1 Chr. vi. 35 [20]). In 1 Chr. vi. 26 he is called ZOPHAI.

ZUR (*a rock*). 1. Father of Cozbi (Num. xxv. 15), and one of the five princes of Midian who were slain by the Israelites when Balaam fell (Num. xxxi. 8).—2. Son of Jehiel the founder of Gibeon (1 Chr. viii. 30; ix. 36).

ZU'RIEL. Son of Abihail, and chief of the Merarite Levites at the time of the Exodus (Num. iii. 35).

ZURISHAD'DAI (*my rock is the Almighty*). Father of Shelumiel, the chief of the tribe of Simeon at the time of the Exodus (Num. i. 6; ii. 12; vii. 36, 41; x. 19).

ZU'ZIMS, THE (*strong people*). The name of an ancient people who, lying in the path of Chedorlaomer and his allies, were attacked and overthrown by them (Gen. xiv. 5, only). Of the etymology or signification of the name nothing is known. Hardly more ascertainable is the situation which the Zuzim occupied. There is some plausibility in the suggestion of Ewald, that the Zuzim inhabited the country of the Ammonites, and were identical with the Zamzummim, who are known to have been exterminated and succeeded in their land by the Ammonites.

Four Thousand Questions and Answers

on the

Old and New Testaments.

INTENDED TO OPEN UP THE SCRIPTURES

FOR THE USE OF STUDENTS AND SUNDAY-SCHOOL TEACHERS.

THE FALL. (Gen. 2, 3.)

1. *Where did God place man when he had created him?*—In the garden of Eden, near the river Euphrates. Gen. 2: 8.

2. *What is a garden?*—A piece of ground enclosed and planted for the production of trees and flowers, of fruits and other food.

3. *What description have we given to us of this garden?*—That God made to grow in it the tree of life, the tree of knowledge of good and evil, and every tree that is pleasant to the sight and good for food. Gen. 2: 9.

4. *How was it watered?*—By a river, that flowed afterward in four rivers or channels to the sea. Gen. 2: 10-14.

5. *Can any of those rivers be now traced?*—The Euphrates only.

6. *Was man idle in the garden of Eden, or did God employ him there?*—He was put into the garden to dress it and keep it (Gen. 2: 15); so that it was a duty and a blessing, even in Paradise, to be employed.

7. *How was the garden refreshed, before man was placed there to tend it?*—By a mist from the earth. Gen. 2: 6.

8. *Did God permit man to pluck and eat the fruit of this garden?*—He was allowed freely to eat of every tree. Gen. 2: 16.

9. *Were there any restrictions to this permission?*—An exception was made of the tree of knowledge of good and evil, under the penalty of death. Gen. 2: 17. Thus was a trial made of obedience and love, and a gracious warning given.

10. *Were they forbidden to eat of the tree of life?*—They were not.

11. *What do we conclude from this?*—That they were intended to live forever.

12. *Did man obey God's command?*—He did not.

13. *What did he do?*—He ate the forbidden fruit.

14. *Who was the first transgressor?*—Eve.

15. *How came it about?*—The devil, in the form of a serpent, deceived her by a lie. Gen. 3: 1-6.

16. *What did the devil promise Eve?*—That they should not surely die, but be as gods, knowing good and evil. Gen. 3: 4, 5.

17. *Was she disappointed?*—Satan's words proved false, for there is no truth in him. They fell under sentence of death; and Satan showed himself a liar and a murderer from the beginning. John 8: 44.

18. *What foolish plan did they adopt to hide their shame?*—They hid themselves amongst the trees of the garden, knowing the evil they had done.

19. *Can any place conceal us from God's eye?*—None.

O Lord, thou hast searched me, and known me. Thou knowest my downsitting and mine uprising, thou understandest my thought afar off. Thou compassest my path and my lying down, and art acquainted with all my ways. For there is not a word in my tongue, but, lo, O Lord, thou knowest it altogether. Thou hast beset me behind and before, and laid thine hand upon me. Such knowledge is too wonderful for me; it is high, I cannot attain unto it. Whither shall I go from thy Spirit? or whither shall I flee from thy presence? If I ascend up into heaven, thou art there; if I make my bed in hell, behold, thou art there. If I take the wings of the morning, and dwell in the uttermost parts of the sea; even there shall thy hand lead me, and thy right hand shall hold me. If I say, Surely the darkness shall cover me; even the night shall be light about me. Yea, the darkness hideth not from thee: but the night shineth as the day: the darkness and the light are both alike to thee. Ps. 139: 1-12.

20. *What is it that makes us fear to meet God?*—The consciousness that we have sinned, and that he knows it.

21. *What do we do when we commit sin?*—We generally try to hide our wrong-doings even from ourselves.

22. *What ought we to do?*—To confess and be truly sorry for our sin; to come to God, through Christ, for the pardon of it, and to forsake it.

If we say that we have no sin, we deceive ourselves, and the truth is not in us. If we confess our sins, he is faithful and just to forgive us our sins, and to cleanse us from all unrighteousness. If we say that we have not sinned, we make him a liar, and his word is not in us. My little children, these things write I unto you that ye sin not. And if any man sin, we have an advocate with the Father, Jesus Christ the righteous, and he is the propitiation for our sins; and not for ours only, but also for the sins of the whole world. 1 John 1: 8-2: 2.

He that covereth his sins shall not prosper; but whoso confesseth and forsaketh them shall have mercy. Prov. 28: 13.

23. *Can we provide a covering for our sin?*—No: for our very best deeds are imperfect and defiled. We are all as an unclean thing, and all our righteousnesses are as filthy rags. Isa. 64: 6.

24. *Has God taken pity on us and given us a robe of righteousness?*—I will greatly rejoice in the Lord, my soul shall be joyful in my God; for he hath clothed me with the garments of salvation, he hath covered me with the robe of righteousness, as a bridegroom decketh himself with ornaments, and as a bride adorneth herself with her jewels. Isa. 61: 10 *Where is this further spoken of?*—Even the righteousness of God which is by faith of Jesus Christ unto all, and upon all them that believe. Rom. 3: 22.

25. *How was it made known to our first parents?*—It was included in the intimation of a Saviour, conveyed in the promise that the seed of the woman should bruise the serpent's head. Gen. 3: 15; and see No. 26.

26. *How did God cloths their bodies?*—In coats of skin. Gen. 3:21.

27. *What is it supposed was done with the bodies of the animals thus slain?*—That they were offered in sacrifice to God, as types or representations of the future sacrifice of Christ. Gen. 4:4.

28. *How did this represent the great atonement that Jesus afterward accomplished?*—By the shedding of blood, without which there is no remission of sins. Heb. 9:22.

29. *Did God give them any direct promise of this blessed Person?* See No. 25.

30. *Was the devil disappointed?*—Yes, he failed in ruining man for ever.

31. *Who got the curse?*—Satan, whose head or power was to be bruised or crushed. Gen. 3:15. Man also suffered, in a less degree, by being driven out of Eden, and condemned to laborious toil, and at last to bodily death. Gen. 3:17-19, 23, 24.

32. *For whose sake was the ground cursed?*—For man's sake. Gen. 3:17.

33. *How was man to feel this?*—By the weeds it brought forth, and the labor it required.

34. *Was there any special punishment to the woman for being first in the transgression?*—In personal suffering.

35. *Was there not also a special mercy granted to her?*—That she should be the ancestress of Christ. Gen. 3:15.

36. *Did they continue in the garden of Eden?*—No.

37. *Why not?*—Lest they should eat of the tree of life, and live for ever upon earth. Gen. 3:22.

38. *Is the tree of life ever mentioned again in Scripture? Where?*—In Rev. 22:1, 2, as standing by the river of the water of life, in the heavenly Jerusalem; Rev. 21:2, in the midst of the paradise of God. Rev. 2:7.

39. *Who will again eat of it?*—They that do God's commandments, and that overcome in the battle with Satan and with sin. Rev. 22:14; 2:7.

40. *How did God guard the gate of Eden?*—By cherubim or angels and a flaming sword. Gen. 3:24.

41. *Are the cherubim again mentioned in Scripture? Where?*—In the vision of Ezekiel, chapters 1 and 10, and in the account of the tabernacle and the temple, etc., twenty-one places altogether.

42. *Why did Adam name his wife Eve?*—Because she was the mother of all living, and the word means "living." Gen. 3:20.

CAIN AND ABEL. (Gen. 4.)

1. *What was the name of Adam's first child?*—Cain. Gen. 4:1.

2. *What is the meaning of the name?*—Got or obtained.

3. *Whom did Eve suppose him to be?*—The seed or child or Saviour promised.

4. *Was she disappointed?*—Yes; he became a wicked man and a murderer.

5. *What name did she give her second son?*—Abel, or Vanity.

6. *What did this show?*—That her expectations had declined.

7. *Did he prove as bad as his brother?*—No; his works were righteous. 1 John 3:12.

8. *What difference do we observe in the offerings of the two brothers?*—Cain offered of the fruit of the ground, and Abel the firstlings of his flock. Gen. 4:3, 4.

9. *How does this give us their characters?*—Cain showed indifference or self-will, and Abel obedience and faith.

By faith Abel offered unto God a more excellent sacrifice than Cain, by which he obtained witness that he was righteous, God testifying of his gifts and by it he being dead yet speaketh. Heb. 11:4.

10. *Will God receive us in any other way than the way he has appointed?*—He will not.

11. *How is that?*—Jesus saith, I am the way, the truth, and the life: no man cometh unto the Father, but by me. John 14:6.

12. *How did the slain lamb represent Jesus?*—In being without blemish and without spot (1 Pet. 1:19), and in having its blood shed; for without shedding of blood is no remission of sin. Heb. 9:22.

13. *What did John the Baptist say of Jesus?*—Behold! the Lamb of God, which taketh away the sin of the world. John 1:29.

14. *What proof did God give that the sacrifice was accepted?*—Probably the consuming it by fire from heaven, as Elijah's was consumed on Carmel. 1 Kings 18:38.

15. *How did Cain act when he found that his own way did not please God?*—He was very angry. Gen. 4:5.

16. *How should he have acted?*—He should have offered, in penitence and faith, the sacrifice that God required. Gen. 4:7.

17. *Did not sin lie at his own door, then, seeing God had provided a way to remove it?*—It did (Gen. 4:7), and led to greater guilt and sin.

18. *What awful act did Cain's jealousy of his brother lead to?*—The murder of his brother, his only brother.

19. *What fearful lie did he tell?*—He told the all-seeing God that he knew not where his murdered brother was.

20. *What did God say had cried to him?*—His brother's blood.

21. *In John 8:44 the devil is called a murderer. What is said of Cain in 1 John 3:10-12?*—In this the children of God are manifest, and the children of the devil: whosoever doeth not righteousness is not of God, neither he that loveth not his brother. For this is the message that ye heard from the beginning, that we should love one another. Not as Cain, who was of that wicked one and slew his brother. And wherefore slew he him? Because his own works were evil, and his brother's righteous.

22. *Did Cain procure for himself Satan's portion—a curse?*—See Gen. 4:11, 12.

23. *What did Cain feel when God's curse lighted on him?*—That his punishment was greater than he could bear, as any one might kill him.

24. *Did God in mercy mitigate Cain's punishment?*—He set a mark upon him to prevent his being killed.

25. *What is meant by Cain's going from God's presence?*—He perhaps never heard him again, or saw him in the form he used to take, or felt his Spirit within him. He left the place where his worship was held, and the place where his glory may have appeared. Gen. 3:24.

26. *When God takes vengeance into his own hand, will he let any one else perform it?*—God, to whom vengeance belongeth, says, Vengeance is mine; I will repay. Rom. 12:19; Ps. 94:1.

27. *Is there a day of reckoning coming?*—It is appointed unto men once to die, and after that the judgment. Heb. 9:27.

THE ANTEDILUVIAN PATRIARCHS. (Gen. 5.)

1. *What is the allotted age of man now?*—Threescore years and ten. Ps. 90:10.

2. *Could we then have imagined it possible for men to have lived so long as the patriarchs, if the Bible had not informed us?*—We could not.

3. *Place all these lives in a row, in long lines measured by 100 years, and say which lived the longest.*

	100	200	300	400	500	600	700	800	900
Adam									
Seth									
Enos									
Cainan									
Mahalaleel									
Jared									
Enoch									
Methuselah									
Lamech									
Noah									

4. *How is it that Enoch's is so much shorter than the others?*—Because God took him to himself before he had lived half the usual time. It is a blessing to us, in life and in death, to live near unto God.

5. *What does the apostle, in Heb. 11 : 5, say of Enoch?* —By faith Enoch was translated, that he should not see death.

6. *What remarkable prophecy of Enoch's does the apostle Jude repeat?*—Behold, the Lord cometh with ten thousands of his saints.

7. *To which coming of the Lord does it refer? To the first or second?*—The second.

8. *Is that second coming spoken of in other parts of the Bible? If so, where?*—In 1 Thess 4 : 16, 17, and fifty other places at least.

9. *When Jesus came the first time, was it to execute vengeance? If not, what was the object?*—God sent not his Son into the world to condemn the world; but that the world through him might be saved. John 3 : 17.

10. *What will be the design of the Lord's second coming?*—To judge the world.

11. *What remarkable likeness is there between the prophecy of God's first prophet and God's last prophet?* —Each foretold the coming of our Lord.

12. *What did John say?*—Behold, he cometh with clouds; and every eye shall see him, and they also which pierced him: and all kindreds of the earth shall wail because of him. Even so, Amen. Rev. 1 : 7.

13. *Who guided those who wrote the Bible?*—The Holy Ghost.

For the prophecy came not in old time by the will of man: but holy men of God spake as they were moved by the Holy Ghost. 2 Pet. 1 : 21.

14. *Do we know when the Lord Jesus is coming?*— Watch, therefore: for ye know not what hour your Lord doth come. Matt. 24 : 42.

15. *What effect should this uncertainty as to our knowledge have upon us?*—The day of the Lord will come as a thief in the night. Wherefore, beloved, seeing that ye look for such things, be diligent that ye may be found of him in peace, without spot and blameless. Pet. 3 : 10, 14.

16. *Was Enoch ready when he was caught up?*—Yes, quite.

17. *With whom was he walking in communion?*—With God. "Oh for a closer walk with God!"

18. *What is said in Amos 3 : 3?*—Can two walk together, except they be agreed?

19. *Who are our companions?*—We should choose, as often as we can, those whom we believe to be walking with God and who can help us to do so.

20. *Do we delight in being alone with him, or do we shrink from him?*—We *must* be alone with him in death; and it is our wisdom and comfort to be much alone with him in life.

21. *What solemn warning does God give in Heb. 3 : 7, 8?*—As the Holy Ghost saith, To-day if ye will hear his voice, harden not your hearts.

THE FLOOD. (Gen. 5, 6.)

1. *What do we read of Cain's descendants in Gen. 4 : 17–23?*—That Cain had a son Enoch, and built a city, etc.

2. *Were they as good as they were skillful?*—No, they shared the general corruption, and would probably be worse, from their ancestor's separation from the people of God and the presence of the Lord. Gen. 4 : 16; 6 : 5.

3. *What was the name of the son that God gave Adam in the place of Abel, whom Cain slew?*—Seth. Gen. 4 : 25.

4. *Did the children of Seth keep themselves separate from Cain's children?*—Yes. They called themselves by the name of the Lord. Gen. 4 : 26, margin.

5. *When God looked down from heaven, what did he see?*—The great wickedness of man. Gen. 6 : 5.

6. *What did he resolve to do?*—To destroy both man and beast. Gen. 6 : 7.

7. *Did he find one faithful family?*—Yes. Gen. 6 : 8, 18.

8. *Whose was that?*—Noah's.

9. *What is Noah said to be in 2 Pet. 2 : 5?*—A preacher of righteousness.

10. *When did Noah preach to these wicked people?* While the ark was preparing. 1 Pet. 3 : 20.

11. *What does the book of Jonah show us?*—That if man had repented, God would have spared.

God saw their works, that they turned from their evil way: and God repented of the evil, that he had said that he would do unto them; and he did it not. Jonah 3 : 10.

12. *Did these sinners repent at the preaching of Noah?* —No.

13. *What was the consequence?*—The flood came, and took them all away. Matt. 24 : 39; Gen. 7 : 21–23.

14. *How were Noah and his family preserved?*—In the ark, which Noah built at God's command.

15. *What is a type?*—A thing that represents another thing, or has some points of resemblance to it, or is intended to foreshow it.

16. *Of whom was the ark, in which Noah and his family were saved, a type?*—Of Christ.

17. *How?*—As an appointed means of saving man from destruction.

18. *Of what was the flood a type?*—Of the future destruction of the world.

The world that then was, being overflowed with water, perished: but the heavens and the earth, which are now, by the same word are kept in store, reserved unto fire against the day of judgment and perdition of ungodly men. 2 Pet. 3 : 6, 7.

19. *Does this concern us at all?*—Yes; as both living and dead will need a Saviour at that day.

20. *What opportunity does God give us of fleeing into a place of safety?*—He spares our lives, and gives us Bibles and preachers and teachers, to show us the way of salvation.

21. *Has he provided a secure place of dependence? What is it?*—God himself, in Christ, is our refuge.

A man shall be as an hiding-place from the wind, and a covert from the tempest; as rivers of water in a dry place, as the shadow of a great rock in a weary land. Isa. 32 : 2.

For this shall every one that is godly pray unto thee in a time when thou mayest be found: surely in the floods of great waters they shall not come nigh unto him. Thou art my hiding-place; thou shalt preserve me from trouble; thou shalt compass me about with songs of deliverance. Ps. 32 : 6, 7.

Thou art my hiding-place and my shield: I hope in thy word. Ps. 119 : 114.

22. *What does the Holy Spirit say to us in 2 Cor. 6 : 2?*—That now is the accepted time; now is the day of salvation.

23. *Can there be a time when even God shall forget to be gracious?*—Yes; as when, in the parable of the ten virgins, the door was shut. Matt. 25 : 10.

NOAH. (Gen. 7, 8, 9.)

1. *How long was the ark building?*—Perhaps a great part of the time that Noah was preaching, or of the one hundred and twenty years mentioned in Gen. 6 : 3.

2. *How old were Noah and his sons when they went into the ark?*—Noah, six hundred years (Gen. 7 : 6), and his sons about one hundred. Gen. 5 : 32 ; 11 : 10.

3. *Who shut them in?*—God himself. Gen. 7 : 16.

4. *What went into the ark with them?*—(Besides their wives) seven, or two, of every living creature. Gen. 7 : 2, 3, 7–9, 13–16.

5. *How long did it continue raining?*—Forty days and nights. Gen. 7 : 12.

6. *How long did the waters continue?*—One hundred and fifty days. Gen. 7 : 24.

7. *How did Noah ascertain when the waters had abated?*—By sending out a dove, which returned with an olive-leaf in its mouth; and which, when sent out again, did not return at all. Gen. 8 : 10–12.

8. *Why did not the raven return to the ark?*—It probably often went forth and returned, as the words "to and fro" are explained in the margin to mean. Gen. 8 : 7. But if it met with floating carcasses, it might not come in for food.

9. *Of what is that an emblem?*—Perhaps of the carnal heart, content with the corrupt enjoyments of the world.

10. *And is there anything to be learnt from the opposite conduct of the dove?*—The privilege of the soul, unsatisfied with the world, returning to Christ Jesus as its rest.

11. *What does the Lord Jesus say in Matt. 11 : 28–30?*—Come unto me, all ye that labor and are heavy laden, and I will give you rest. Take my yoke upon you, and learn of me; for I am meek and lowly in heart: and ye shall find rest unto your souls. For my yoke is easy, and my burden is light.

12. *What was Noah's first act when he came forth from the ark?*—He built an altar, and offered a sacrifice. Gen. 8 : 20.

13. *What was the burnt-offering?*—A bullock, sheep, goat, turtle-dove or young pigeon. Lev. 1.

14. *Did God accept it?*—It pleased him, as a sweet savor or smell. Gen. 8 : 21.

15. *What promise did God give Noah at that time?*—That he would not again curse the ground any more for man's sake, etc. Gen. 8 : 21–23 ; 9 : 2.

16, 17. *Did God condescend to give him a token? What was it?*—He said that the rainbow should be a token or remembrance of his covenant or promise. Gen. 9 : 8–17.

18. *Does it remain?*—Yes.

19. *When does it appear?*—Whenever the sun shines upon rain.

20. *Did God make any change in man's food at that time?*—He gave him animal food, in addition to his former vegetable food. Gen. 9 : 3.

21. *Under what restriction?*—That the blood should not be used with the flesh. Gen. 9 : 4.

22. *Why was not blood to be eaten?*—Because it was a type of the blood of Christ; and to restrain blood-thirsty cruelty to man or beast. Gen. 5 : 6.

23. *What evil use did Noah afterward make of the fruits of the earth?*—He once became drunk with wine. Gen. 9 : 21.

24. *Does the Bible cover up and hide the sins of God's people?*—No, it mentions them whenever it seemed to the wisdom of God to be desirable to do so.

25. *What does the Psalmist say of God's word in Ps.*

119 : 140?*—That it is "very pure." Many books and magazines and newspapers in our days are very impure, and are written to please the impure.

26. *Which of Noah's sons brought a curse on his posterity by his conduct to his father on this occasion?*—Ham.

27. *Do the effects of this curse continue to the present time? Where?*—Yes: in Africa, which was peopled by the descendants of Ham, and is the chief scene of the horrible traffic in slaves.

28. *Show the fulfillment of Shem's blessing?*—God's people, the Jews, and Christ himself descended from Shem.

29. *Describe how Japheth has been enlarged?*—By his descendants, the Greeks and Romans, and by many Gentile nations sprung from him.

30. *How old was Noah when he died?*—Nine hundred and fifty years. Gen. 9 : 29.

THE TOWER OF BABEL. (Gen. 10, 11.)

1. *What mighty nations have their origin given in these chapters?*—The Chaldeans, Assyrians, and Canaanites.

2. *Were the genealogies and histories of all these nations continued in the Bible?*—No.

3. *Why was one family singled out for this special honor?*—Because out of it came Jesus Christ.

4. *What great event happened in the days of Peleg?*—The scattering of mankind over all the earth. Gen. 11 : 9. Unto Eber were born two sons: the name of the one was Peleg—i. e., division (margin), because in his days the earth was divided. 1 Chron. 1 : 19.

5. *Why did God thus divide or scatter men?*—To restrain them from building the tower of Babel.

6. *What motive had these men in building the tower?*—To form a conspicuous gathering-point, in defiance of the divine intention.

7. *Of what did they compose it?*—Of bricks, joined together with mortar of slime or mud that dried hard.

8. *Are there any remains of the materials of which it was built yet in existence? Where?*—Yes, in the ruins of Babylon.

9. *Where did Shem's family remove to?*—Some of them from Upper and Middle Asia to Canaan.

10. *Which of Abraham's ancestors were alive when he was born?*—Nahor and Terah.

11. *How old was Shem when Abram was born?*—Four hundred and fifty-two years [B. C. 2448–1996]. Gen. 5 : 32; 11 : 27.

12. *How many years did Shem live after Abram was born?*—One hundred and forty-nine years [B. C. 1996–1847]. Gen. 11 : 10, 11.

13. *What was the name of Abram's father?*—Terah. Gen. 11 : 26.

14. *How many years had he lived with Noah?*—One hundred and twenty-eight years. Gen. 5 : 29 ; 11 : 24.

15. *Was Noah alive when Abram was born?*—No; he died two years before. Gen. 9 : 29.

16. *Was Adam alive when Noah was born?*—No; he died one hundred and twenty-six years before.

17. *Was Adam alive when Lamech was born?*—Yes.

18. *How many years did they live together?*—Fifty-six.

19. *How many years before Noah did Adam die?*—One hundred and twenty-six years before Noah was born.

20. *Do we not see by this how nearly Adam and Abram were contemporaries, although the world was nearly twenty hundred years old when Abram was born?*—There were only Lamech, Noah and Terah between them.

ABRAHAM. (Gen. 11–22.)

1. *What was the name of Abram's father?*—Terah. Gen. 11 : 26.

2. *Where was Abram born?*—In Ur of the Chaldees. Gen. 11 : 28.

3. *Did his father die there?*—No.

4. *To what land did his father remove?*—To Haran, on the way to Canaan.

5. *Which of Abram's brothers died before they left their native land?*—Haran. Gen. 11 : 28.

6. *Did he leave a son, and what was his name?*—Lot. Gen. 11 : 27.

7. *Did this grandson accompany Terah and Abram to Haran?*—Yes. Gen. 11 : 31.

8. *Where did Terah die?*—In Haran. Gen. 11 : 32.

CHAPTER 12.

9. *After his father's death, did Abram stay in Haran?*—No.

10. *Why did he remove?*—Because God told him so to do.

11. *Who went with him?*—Sarai his wife, and Lot and their servants.

12. *What relation was Lot to Abram?*—His nephew.

13. *Where are Ur, Haran and Canaan?*—Ur is in Chaldea, to the south-east of Babylon; Haran is in Mesopotamia, between Nineveh and Tarsus; and Canaan is on the eastern shore of the Mediterranean Sea, and is now called Palestine or the Holy Land.

14. *Where did Abram first settle, and what was his first act in the land of Canaan?*—At Sichem, in the plain of Moreh, near Samaria, where he built an altar to God, who appeared to him.

15. *What remarkable circumstance in the history of Jacob happened there?*—Jacob buried under an oak there the idols and earrings taken from his household. Gen. 35 : 4.

16. *What acts of Joshua's again distinguished this spot when he first subdued Canaan?*—His assembling of the tribes of Israel to renew their covenant with God; his appointing Shechem one of the cities of refuge; his reading the law between Mounts Gerizim and Ebal. Josh. 24 : 1, 25, 26 ; 20 : 7 ; 8 : 33.

17. *At what place did he rear the tabernacle, and at his death make a covenant with Israel?*—At *Shiloh*, near Sichem. Josh. 18 : 1. At Shechem. See No. 16.

18. *What event in the New Testament yet further endears the spot to us?*—Our Lord's conversation at Sychar with the woman of Samaria as he sat wearied upon Jacob's well. John 4 : 5–42.

19. *Did Abram continue to live at Sichem? Why?*—He removed to the neighborhood of Bethel, being doubtless directed by God to enter farther into the land. Gen. 12 : 8, 9 ; 13 : 17.

20. *What sin was Abram guilty of in Egypt?*—Of want of truthfulness and faith respecting Sarai his wife. Gen. 12 : 11–20.

21. *What does this teach us?* — We have before proved, both Jews and Gentiles, that they are all under sin; as it is written, There is none righteous, no, not one. Rom. 3 : 9, 10.

CHAPTER 13.

22. *Was Abram a rich or poor man?*—He was very rich. Gen. 13 : 2.

23. *How had Lot prospered?*—Very much. Gen. 13 : 5.

24. *What was the result?*—A quarrel between the herdmen of the two. Gen. 13 : 6, 7.

25. *How did Abram behave on this occasion?*—He proposed that they should part, and gave Lot the choice of the land. Gen. 13 : 8, 9.

26. *Do you think Lot behaved as well as Abram in this affair?*—He made no liberal offer in return, and thought more of the goodness of the pasture than of the character of the people. When choosing a family or place to reside in, we should know whether God is feared in it, and his truth faithfully taught.

27. *Had Lot cause to repent his choice?*—He suffered constant distress of mind, and at length narrowly escaped with his life, with the loss of his wife and of many of his family, and of most or all of his substance. Gen. 19 : 15–29.

Delivered just Lot, vexed with the filthy conversation of the wicked; for that righteous man dwelling among them, in seeing and hearing, vexed his righteous soul from day to day with their unlawful deeds. 2 Pet. 2 : 7, 8.

28. *Why? What kind of people did he go to sojourn amongst?*—Exceedingly wicked. Gen. 13 : 13.

29. *After this separation how did God manifest himself to Abram?*—He repeated to him his promises. Gen. 13 : 14–17.

CHAPTER 14.

30. *What doleful news did Abram soon hear of Lot?*—That Lot and his goods had been carried away in a war with Sodom and Gomorrah. Gen. 14 : 12, 13.

31. *How did Abram act?*—He armed his men and went in pursuit. Gen. 14 : 14.

32. *Was he successful? Give an account of the expedition?*—He divided his men, and attacked the enemy by night on several sides at once, routing them and recovering the prisoners and their goods. Gen. 14 : 15, 16.

33. *Who met Abram on his return?*—Melchizedek, king of Salem. Gen. 14 : 18.

34. *Where must Melchizedek have lived? Trace Abram's resting-place and the field of battle, and see what spot is between the two.*—At the present Jerusalem, which is between Dan and Mamre. Gen. 13 : 18.

35. *Is this mysterious person ever alluded to again in Scripture? Where?*—Heb. 6 : 20 ; 7 : 1–3.

36. *Of whom was he a type?*—Of Christ, in being both King and Priest; and also in his eternity, nothing being told us of his birth and death.

37. *What is a type?*—See page 2. Gen. 4 : 4.

38. *How did Abram behave after the battle, when urged by the king of Sodom to take part of the spoil?*—He declined taking anything but some food for his men. Gen. 14 : 21–24.

CHAPTER 15.

39. *What wonderful prophecy does this chapter record?*—That Abram's seed or descendants should be in number as the stars. Gen. 15 : 5.

40. *Had Abram at this time any children?*—No. Gen. 15 : 3.

41. *To what did God compare the number of his seed?*—See No. 39.

42. *Did Abram believe the Lord?*—Yes.

43. *What was his faith accounted or reckoned?*—For righteousness. Gen. 15 : 6.

44. *Is faith, then, very precious in the estimation of God?*—Yes, for his Son's sake.

45. *What is faith?*—That belief in Christ, as our own Saviour, which unites us to him, and makes us righteous before God in and through him.

46. *Does this account concern us?*—Now, it was not written for his sake alone, that it was imputed to him; but for us also, to whom it shall be imputed, if we believe on Him that raised up Jesus our Lord from the dead; who was delivered for our offences, and was raised again for our justification. Rom. 4 : 23–25.

47. *How much land did God promise to Abram?*—From a river in or near Egypt to the Euphrates. Gen. 15 : 18–21.

CHAPTER 16.

48. *Who was Hagar?* — One of Sarai's waiting-maids. Gen. 16 : 1.

49. *Why did Abram take her to be his wife?* — That Sarai might, by her, have children that would be reckoned as her own, and from whom the Messiah might come. Gen. 16 : 2.

50. *Did Sarai use her kindly?* — Hagar, when likely to have children, despised her mistress, and Sarai dealt hardly with her. Gen. 16 : 4-6.

51. *What did Hagar do?* — She ran away.

52. *Did the Lord approve of Hagar running away from her mistress?* — No; he ordered her to return and submit herself. Gen. 16 : 9.

Servants, be subject to your masters with all fear; not only to the good and gentle, but also to the froward. For this is thankworthy, if a man for conscience toward God endure grief, suffering wrongfully. For what glory is it, if, when ye be buffeted for your faults, ye shall take it patiently? but if, when ye do well, and suffer for it, ye take it patiently, this is acceptable with God. 1 Pet. 2 : 18-20.

53. *What did God promise her?* — That he would multiply her seed exceedingly; and the Arabians have sprung from her. Gen. 16 : 10.

54. *After she returned what event happened?* — She had a son.

55. *What name was given to Hagar's son?* — Abram called him Ishmael.

56. *How old was Abram when Ishmael was born?* — Eighty-six.

CHAPTER 17.

57. *When Abram was ninety-nine years of age, what further covenant did God enter into with him?* — He renewed his promise that he should have a great posterity, and covenanted to be his *God*, and to be *their* God. Gen. 17 : 1-8.

58. *How did Abram show his love to Ishmael?* — He prayed that he might live before God, or be favored by him. Gen. 17 : 18.

59. *Did God accept Abram's prayer?* — He blessed Ishmael, and promised to make him a great nation. Gen. 17 : 20.

60. *Who was to be the promised seed?* — Isaac, who was not yet born, and with whom God established his covenant. Gen. 17 : 19.

61. *How long did God fix for the fulfillment of his promise to Abram and his wife?* — A whole year. Gen. 17 : 21.

62. *How did the Lord alter their names?* — From Abram, or "high father," to Abraham, or, "multitude of nations;" and from Sarai, "*my* princess," to Sarah, or "princess of a multitude."

63. *What does the name Abraham signify?* — See No. 62.

64. *What does Sarah's name express?* — See No. 62.

65. *How old was Ishmael when he was circumcised?* — Thirteen.

CHAPTER 18.

66. *Where was Mamre?* — Near Hebron, in Judah. Gen. 13 : 18.

67. *What remarkable event happened to Abraham there?* — Three angels or heavenly visitors appeared to him in the form of men.

68. *What is said of this visit in Heb. 13 : 2?* — Be not forgetful to entertain strangers; for thereby some have entertained angels unawares.

69. *Did Abraham at first know whom he was entertaining? How did he find it out?* — He took them at first for ordinary travelers, but found out, by what one of them said, that they were angels and the Son of God. Gen. 18 : 10, 14.

70. *What is Abraham called in Isa. 41 : 8?* — The friend of God. James 2 : 23.

71. *How did Sarah displease the Lord at this time?* — By laughing within herself at the unlikelihood of what he said.

72. *What was she tempted to do when the Lord expressed his displeasure?* — To deny that she had laughed.

73. *When the three heavenly visitors had eaten with Abraham, did they all depart from him together?* — The Angel, Son of God, remained, and the other two angels went toward Sodom. Gen. 18 : 22.

74. *Who stayed, and who went?* — See No. 73.

75. *To what place did those who departed go?* — See No. 73.

76. *Why did they visit Sodom?* — To destroy it and to rescue Lot.

77. *How came Abraham to know the purpose of their visit to Sodom?* — From what the Lord said to him. Gen. 18 : 20, 21.

78. *Did Abraham venture to plead for the city? How?* — By six times asking the Lord to spare it if there were fifty, forty-five, forty, thirty, twenty, and even ten, righteous persons in it. Gen. 18 : 23-32.

79. *Did God permit him to go on as long as he would? How did the Lord reply?* — The Lord put no check upon his intercession, and consented to do all that he asked.

80. *What should this teach us?* — To persevere in prayer. Men ought always to pray, and not to faint. Luke 18 : 1.

Who can tell if God will turn and repent, and turn away from his fierce anger, that we perish not? And God saw their works, that they turned from their evil way; and God repented of the evil that he had said that he would do unto them; and he did it not. But it displeased Jonah exceedingly, and he was very angry. And he prayed unto the Lord, and said, I pray thee, O Lord, was not this my saying, when I was yet in my country? Therefore I fled before unto Tarshish: for I knew that thou art a gracious God, and merciful, slow to anger, and of great kindness, and repentest thee of the evil. Jonah 3 : 9, 10-4 : 1, 2.

81. *Who has turned away the righteous anger of God from us, and yet pleads our cause?* — If any man sin, we have an Advocate with the Father, Jesus Christ the righteous: and he is the propitiation for our sins: and not for ours only, but also for the sins of the whole world. 1 John 2 : 1, 2.

CHAPTER 19.

82. *Where did Lot dwell?* — In Sodom.

83. *What is said of him in 2 Pet. 2 : 9?* — The Lord knoweth how to deliver the godly out of temptations, and to reserve the unjust unto the day of judgment to be punished.

84. *What happened to him one evening as he sat in the gate of the city?* — Two angels came to him. Gen. 18 : 22; 19 : 1.

85. *Who did those persons prove to be?* — See No. 84.

86. *For what did they visit Sodom?* — To destroy it and to rescue Lot.

87. *Did they find it as wicked as they expected?* — It could hardly be worse than it was. Gen. 18 : 21.

88. *In what way did they punish the men who wished to get into Lot's house?* — They struck them blind. Gen. 19 : 11.

89. *How many of Lot's family believed the warning and fled with him?* — His wife and two daughters. Gen. 19 : 16.

90. *Did all these eventually escape? Describe the circumstances of Lot's wife?* — The daughters escaped, but his wife looked back and became a pillar of salt. Gen. 19 : 26.

91. *How are we reminded of this in the New Testament?* — In the days of Lot they did eat, they drank, they bought, they sold, they planted, they builded; but the same day that Lot went out of Sodom it rained

fire and brimstone from heaven and destroyed them all. Even thus shall it be in the day when the Son of man is revealed. In that day, he which shall be on the housetop, and his stuff in the house, let him not come down to take it away: and he that is in the field, let him likewise not return back. Remember Lot's wife. Luke 17 : 28–32.

92. *Does there remain any relic of this awful event at the present day?*—The Dead Sea, with its deadly waters.

93. *Of what is the overthrow of Sodom and Gomorrah a type?*—Of the future destruction of the world by fire.

94. *What did the angel say to Lot when he pleaded for Zoar?*—That he would not overthrow it. Gen. 19 : 20–22.

95. *What does that teach us?*—The Lord is not slack concerning his promise, as some men count slackness; but is long-suffering to us-ward, not willing that any should perish, but that all should come to repentance. 2 Pet. 3 : 9.

CHAPTER 20.

96. *Into what disgraceful fault were Abraham and Sarah again betrayed at Gerar?*—Untruthfulness and distrust, in concealing that they were man and wife.

97. *How did God preserve them?*—By warning Abimelech in a dream.

98. *How did Abimelech behave?*—He immediately restored to Abraham his wife (whom he had intended to marry) and made him a handsome present.

99. *Did not Sarah deserve the reproof which Abimelech gave her?*—She needed the reproof that her husband was her proper protector.

100. *How did the Lord put honor on Abraham?*—He heard his prayer for Abimelech and his family.

CHAPTER 21.

101. *When did God perform his promise to Sarah?*—At the end of the year, the time fixed. Gen. 21 : 2.

102. *By what name was this child of promise called?*—Isaac, meaning "laughter" or "joy."

103. *What circumstance occurred on the day Isaac was weaned?*—Abraham made a great feast. Gen. 21 : 8.

104. *What did Sarah wish Abraham to do?*—To send away Hagar and Ishmael. Gen. 21 : 9, 10.

105. *Who confirmed Sarah's wish?*—God himself, to carry out his purposes as to both Isaac and Ishmael. Gen. 21 : 12, 13.

106. *How did Abraham act?*—He sent them away provided with bread and water, and doubtless commended to the care of God. Gen. 21 : 14.

107. *What became of Hagar and Ishmael?*—They lived at last in the wilderness of Paran, in Arabia Petræa. Gen. 21 : 14–21.

108. *Who at the present day are the descendants of Ishmael?*—The Arabs.

109. *Who was Abraham's rightful heir and child of promise?*—Isaac. Gen. 21 : 1–3, 12.

110. *What testimony to Abraham's God, by a stranger, does this chapter record?*—King Abimelech said that God was with Abraham in all that he did. Gen. 21 : 22.

111. *What is the meaning of the word Beersheba?*—The "well of the oath." Gen. 21 : 31.

112. *Where was Abraham sojourning at this time?*—In the land of the Philistines. Gen. 21 : 34.

113. *Were the Philistines always friendly with Abraham's posterity, or the reverse? Is there any instance in Scripture?*—They were frequently at war with each other, as in the days of Samson and of David and Goliath.

CHAPTER 22.

114. *What was the greatest trial that Abraham's faith experienced?*—The command of God to make a burnt-offering of his only son Isaac, whom he loved.

115. *What is said of this act in Heb. 11 : 17–19?*—By faith Abraham, when he was tried, offered up Isaac; and he that had received the promises offered up his only begotten son, of whom it was said, That in Isaac shall thy seed be called: accounting that God was able to raise him up, even from the dead; from whence also he received him in a figure.

116. *What proof did Abraham give of his prompt obedience?*—He arose early in the morning and set out.

117. *Did he tell his son what he was about to do with him?*—No.

118. *When Isaac inquired for the lamb, what was Abraham's reply?*—That God would provide one. Gen. 22 : 8.

119. *To whom did Abraham allude?*—To Jesus Christ, the Lamb of God, which taketh away the sins of the world. "Your father Abraham rejoiced to see my day; he saw it, and was glad."—John 1 : 29; 8 : 56.

120. *When Isaac knew his father's intention, did he resist it?*—No.

121. *Was he able to have done so? How old was he at this time?*—Yes, as he was twenty-five years old.

122. *What is said of the Lord Jesus Christ when he was offered a sacrifice for sin?*—That he did it of himself.

Therefore doth my Father love me, because I lay down my life, that I might take it again. No man taketh it from me, but I lay it down of myself. I have power to lay it down, and I have power to take it again. This commandment have I received of my Father.—Let this mind be in you, which was also in Christ Jesus: who, being in the form of God, thought it not robbery to be equal with God: but made himself of no reputation, and took upon him the form of a servant, and was made in the likeness of men: and being found in fashion as a man, he humbled himself, and became obedient unto death, even the death of the cross. Wherefore God also hath highly exalted him, and given him a name which is above every name: that at the name of Jesus every knee should bow, of things in heaven, and things in earth, and things under the earth. John 10 : 17, 18; Phil. 2 : 5–10.

123. *Does the ram caught in the thicket and offered as a substitute for Isaac present a type?*—The ram would be without blemish, and Christ was without sin. He hath made Him to be sin for us who knew no sin, that we might be made the righteousness of God in him. 2 Cor. 5 : 21.

124. *By what name did Abraham call the place where this occurred? And what was the meaning of it?*—Jehovah-jireh, "the Lord will see or provide."

125. *Is Mount Moriah mentioned again in Scripture?*—Yes, in 2 Chron. 3 : 1. Then Solomon began to build the house of the Lord at Jerusalem in Mount Moriah, where the Lord appeared unto David, his father, in the place that David had prepared in the threshing-floor of Ornan the Jebusite. [But this is not now considered to be the same mountain.]

126. *What magnificent building stood on that mount?*—Solomon's temple.

127. *Give the account why this place was chosen for that building.*—See 125.

128. *What beautiful edifice now stands there?*—The mosque of Omar, a Mohammedan place of worship.

129. *What do the Jews feel when they see this?*—Doubtless deep grief, as they often visit a place near it called "the place of wailing."

130. *What special covenant did the Lord renew with Abraham at this time?*—That in Abraham's seed should all the nations of the earth be blessed. Gen. 22 : 15–18.

131 *Why is Nahor's posterity mentioned here?*—

Because one of them was Rebekah, Isaac's future wife.

ISAAC AND REBEKAH. (Gen. 23, 24.)

1. *How old was Sarah when she died?*—One hundred and twenty-seven years.

2. *Where did Abraham bury her?*—In the cave of Machpelah, near Mamre, Hebron or Kirjath-arba. Gen 23 : 2, 19.

3. *How did he obtain possession of this burying-place?*—By purchase from Ephron the Hittite. Gen. 23 : 3-18.

4. *What did that show?*—That Abraham had no land of his own. Gen. 23 : 4.

5. *How old was Isaac when his mother died?*—About thirty-seven.

6. *How many years did he live solitary and alone before he married?*—Forty years from his birth, and latterly near the well Lahai-roi, in the south country. Gen. 23 : 62.

7. *How did his father obtain a wife for him?*—He sent his steward to his own kindred in Mesoptamia for the purpose, after pledging him not to seek for one among the heathen around him. Gen. 24 : 2, 3, 4, 10. Be ye not unequally yoked together with unbelievers. Only in the Lord. 2 Cor. 6 : 14; 1 Cor. 7 : 39.

8. *Whom did Abraham send on this important mission?*—See No. 7.

9. *What was the name of this "eldest servant" of Abraham's house?*—Eliezer of Damascus. Gen. 15 : 2.

10. *How did this servant act?*—With prudence, prayerfulness, diligence and courtesy. Gen. 24 : 5-26.

11. *Did he succeed in his mission?*—He was led by God's providence to the house of Abraham's nephew, Bethuel, and obtained his daughter, Rebekah. Gen. 24 : 15, 51.

12. *Whom did he bring?*—See No. 11.

13. *What did he give to his young master's intended bride?*—Golden earrings, bracelets, jewels of silver and gold, and raiment, according to the custom of those lands and times. Gen. 24 : 22, 30, 53.

14. *How did he describe his master's possessions?*—That the Lord had greatly blessed him, and given him flocks and herds, silver and gold, etc. Gen. 24 : 35.

15. *Was she willing to leave her home on his report?*—She was. Gen. 24 : 58.

16. *Did she find it all true?*—Doubtless she did. Gen. 13 : 2.

17. *Who came out to meet her?*—Isaac himself. Gen. 24 : 62, 63.

18. *Where did he take her, and how did he feel toward her?*—To his mother's tent, and she became his wife, and he loved her. Gen. 24 : 67.

19. *Is this interesting account a type of spiritual things?*—Now all these things happened unto them for ensamples; and they are written for our admonition, upon whom the ends of the world are come. For whatsoever things were written aforetime were written for our learning, that we through patience and comfort of the Scriptures might have hope. 1 Cor. 10 : 11 : Rom. 15 : 4.

20. *Of whom is Abraham the type here?*—Of God the Father.

21. *Of whom is Rebekah the type?*—Of his Church and people.

22. *Of whom is Eliezer the type?*—Of God's Spirit, who finds those who are far from him, and brings them to him.

23. *Of whom is Isaac the type?*—Of Christ, the Bridegroom of the Church.

24. *And of what great event is the closing scene the type?*—Of the Church, the bride of Christ, being presented to him spotless at the last day

25. *How are we interested in this?*—We must each of us be found by him, and given to him, and adorned and sanctified by him, if we seek to live with him eternally.

JACOB AND ESAU. (Gen. 25, 26, 27.)

1. *Whom did Abraham marry after Sarah's death?* Keturah. Gen. 25 : 1.

2. *How many children had she?*—Six.

3. *How did he portion them?*—He made them gifts.

4. *To whom did he leave his great riches?*—To Isaac

5. *How old was Abraham when he died?*—One hundred and seventy-five years.

6. *Who buried him?*—Isaac and Ishmael.

7. *By what title are Ishmael's twelve sons called?*—Princes.

8. *What was Isaac's occupation, although his father's heir?*—That of a herdsman and shepherd.

9. *Of whom is he a type in this?*—Of Christ, who humbled himself, though Lord of all.

10. *How many sons had Isaac?*—Two—Esau and Jacob. Gen. 25 : 26.

11. *Were they born before Abraham's death?*—Yes, fifteen years. *Is there not a proof of this in the New Testament?*

By faith Abraham, when he was called to go out into a place which he should after receive for an inheritance, obeyed; and he went out, not knowing whither he went. By faith he sojourned in the land of promise, as in a strange country, dwelling in tabernacles with Isaac and Jacob, the heirs with him of the same promise. Heb. 11 : 8, 9.

12. *What was the difference personally between those two boys?*—Esau was red or hairy, and Jacob smooth. Gen. 25 : 25; 27 : 11.

13. *Did they grow up alike? Describe them?*—Esau was a skillful hunter, and Jacob a quiet man, fond of home. Gen. 25 : 27.

14. *Which was the first born?*—Esau.

15. *Did he value his birthright? The proof.*—He sold it, when hungry and faint, to Jacob for a dish of potted beans or other food. So thousands, for present pleasure, will risk or lose their souls.

16. *To whom did he sell it, and for what?*—See No. 15.

CHAPTER 26.

17. *What was Isaac's character?*—His conduct in this chapter entitles him to the character of a peacemaker. Gen. 26 : 14-31.

Blessed are the peacemakers : for they shall be called the children of God. Matt. 5 : 9.

18. *What covenant did God renew with Isaac?*—The covenant he had made with Abraham. Gen. 26 : 2-5

19. *What direction did God give Isaac as to his place of sojourn?*—That he should not go down into Egypt, but dwell among the Philistines at Gerar. Gen. 26 : 1, 2, 6.

20. *How did he act there?*—He was guilty of the same weakness and sin about his wife as Abraham was. Gen. 26 : 7-11.

21. *How did the Philistines behave toward Isaac?*—They envied his prosperity, and maliciously stopped up his old wells and claimed possession of his new ones. Gen. 26 : 14-21.

22. *Did he return evil for evil?*—No; he removed more than once out of their way.

23. *Whom did Esau choose as his wives?*—Judith and Bashemath, Hittites. Gen. 26 : 34.

24. *Did his parents approve his choice?*—No; they were grieved by it.

CHAPTER 27.

25. *What was it the custom of the ancient patriarchs to do before their death?*—To bless their children.

26. *Which son did Isaac consider his first-born?*—Esau. Gen. 27 : 1-4.

27. *How had he forfeited that honor?*—By selling it to his brother. Gen. 25 : 29–34.

28. *Did Jacob allow Esau to obtain the blessing of the birthright?*—No; he pretended to be Esau, to prevent it.

29. *Did he go the right way to work?*—No; he should have left it to God to secure him the blessing in his own time and way.

30. *Who shared his sin with him?*—His mother told him how to act.

31. *How did Esau feel when he found that he had lost his blessing?*—He was in great distress of mind.

32. *Had he not voluntarily sold it to Jacob some years before?*—Yes; about forty-five years before.

33. *Whom had he then to blame?*—Chiefly himself.

34. *Whom shall we have to blame if we, like Esau, despise God's blessing now?*—Ourselves alone.

35. *What lesson should Esau's bitter grief teach us?*—To earnestly seek God's blessing, and to carefully cherish it.

JACOB. (Gen. 28–35.)

1. *What was Jacob's general character?*—One of artifice and deceit.

2. *Did God then choose him for his natural goodness?*—No; there is no one whom he can choose on this account.

I will have compassion on whom I will have compassion. So then it is not of him that willeth, nor of him that runneth, but of God that showeth mercy. Rom. 9 : 15, 16.

3. *What should this teach us?*—That, as we all have sinned, it is only by the faith that unites us to Christ that we can be righteous before God.

For all have sinned, and come short of the glory of God; being justified freely by his grace through the redemption that is in Christ Jesus; whom God hath set forth to be a propitiation through faith in his blood, to declare his righteousness for the remission of sins that are past, through the forbearance of God; therefore being justified by faith, we have peace with God through our Lord Jesus Christ. Rom. 4 : 23–25 ; 5 : 1.

4. *How did Esau treat Jacob after Jacob had obtained the blessing?*—He hated him and determined to kill him. Gen. 27 : 41.

5. *What did Jacob's parents resolve to do?*—To send him to Haran out of Esau's way, and to get a wife among the daughters of Laban. Gen. 27 : 42–28 : 2.

6. *What remarkable thing occurred to Jacob on his way to Syria?*—He had a vision by night, and a renewal of God's promise and blessing. Gen. 28 : 10–15.

7. *Did he fully understand it? Can you explain his feelings?*—He could not fully understand what he saw, but seems to have felt that fear and awe which sinners must feel in the presence of a holy God.

8. *Can we see the meaning?*—We, happily, are taught to see Christ as the ladder of communication between heaven and earth.

Hereafter ye shall see heaven open, and the angels of God ascending and descending upon the Son of man. John 1 : 51.

9. *Whom did the latter typify?*—See No. 8.

10. *How did Jesus unite heaven and earth?*—By his birth, death, resurrection and ascension, as God and man in one.

11. *What promise did Jacob make at this place?*—That the Lord should be his God, and that he would devote to him a tenth of all that he should give him. Gen. 28 : 20–22.

CHAPTERS 29, 30, 31.

12. *Whom did Jacob first see when he got to Syria?*—The servants of Laban, and then Rachel his daughter. Gen. 29 : 3–5, 9.

13. *How did his uncle Laban receive him?*—With kindness and affection. Gen. 29 : 13, 14.

14. *What did he promise him?*—That he should have Rachel for his wife, in return for seven years' service.

15. *Did Laban afterward fulfill his promise?*—No; he gave him Leah instead.

16. *How many wives had Jacob?*—Both Rachel and Leah; and afterward their handmaids Bilhah and Zilpah by their mistresses' desire, and according to the custom of the time. See Gen. 16 : 2.

17. *How many years did Jacob serve Laban before he allowed him to have any cattle for his wages?*—Fourteen years. Gen. 30 : 26–30.

18. *Did Jacob succeed in obtaining large possessions of flocks and herds?*—Yes. Gen. 30 : 43.

19. *How did the sons of Laban feel when they observed this?*—They were displeased at the success of his plan.

20. *What did Jacob and his wives resolve to do?*—Jacob, at the command of God, resolved to return to Canaan, and Rachel and Leah resolved to go with him. Gen. 31 : 3, 14–16.

21. *What wicked act was Rachel guilty of?*—Of stealing her father's images. Gen. 31 : 19.

22. *What did it prove?*—That she and her father still worshiped heathen gods as well as the true God.

Joshua said unto all the people, Thus saith the Lord God of Israel, Your fathers dwelt on the other side of the flood in old time, even Terah, the father of Abraham, and the father of Nachor : and they served other gods. Josh. 24 : 2.

23. *What did Laban do when he found Jacob had left him?*—He pursued him.

24. *How did God protect Jacob from Laban's anger?*—By warning Laban in a dream.

25. *How did the interview between Laban and Jacob terminate?*—It ended peacefully and well. Gen. 31 : 44, 55.

CHAPTER 32.

26. *What is the meaning of the word Mahanaim?*—Two hosts or camps. Gen. 32 : 1, 2.

27. *Why was the place so called?*—Because a company of angels met Jacob there.

28. *How ought Jacob to have felt when he saw this angelic guard?*—That he was secure against all harm.

The angel of the Lord encampeth round about them that fear him, and delivereth them. Ps. 34 : 7.

29. *How did he feel when he heard his brother Esau was coming to meet him?*—He was greatly afraid and distressed. Gen. 32 : 7.

30. *How did Jacob act?*—He divided his people and flocks into two bands. Gen. 32 : 7, 8.

31. *What occurred to Jacob before he went over the brook?*—A heavenly Being wrestled with him during the night.

32. *How long did the Angel wrestle with Jacob?*—Until break of day.

33. *What name did Jacob give to the place where this occurred?*—Peniel, or "the face of God."

34. *Why did he so call it?*—Because he had seen God face to face. Gen. 32 : 30.

35. *Whom, then, may we suppose that wondrous Person to be with whom he wrestled?*—The Son of God; as no man hath seen God himself, who is a Spirit, at any time. John 4 : 24 ; 1 John 4 : 12.

36. *What spiritual act does this typify?*—Prayer, in which, if real, we have communion or intercourse of spirit with God.

37. *Are we interested in it?*—It encourages earnest perseverance in prayer.

He spake a parable unto them to this end, that men ought always to pray, and not to faint; saying, There was in a city a judge, which feared not God, neither regarded man; and there was a widow in that city, and she came unto him, saying, Avenge me of mine adversary. And he would not for a while; but afterward he said within himself, Though I fear not God, nor regard man; yet because this widow troubleth me, I will avenge her, lest by her continual coming she weary me. And the Lord said, Hear what the unjust judge saith. And shall not God avenge his own elect, which cry day and night unto him, though he bear long with them? I tell you that he will avenge them speedily. Luke 18 : 1-8.

So run, that ye may obtain. 1 Cor. 9 : 24.

CHAPTERS 33, 34, 35.

38. *How did Jacob and Esau meet?*—In brotherly affection and peace, in answer to Jacob's prayer.

39. *Where did Jacob pitch his tent and make booths for his cattle when he got into Canaan?*—At Succoth. Gen. 33 : 17.

40. *Name the two instances in Scripture where this purchase is afterward referred to?*—His purchase at Shalem, a city of Shechem, is referred to in John 4 : 5, 6, and Acts 7 : 15, 16. Gen. 33 : 18, 19.

Then cometh he to a city of Samaria, which is called Sychar, near to the parcel of ground that Jacob gave to his son Joseph. Now Jacob's well was there. So Jacob went down into Egypt, and died, he and our fathers, and were carried over into Sychem, and laid in the sepulchre that [he, like] Abraham bought for a sum of money of the sons of Emmor the father of Sychem.

41. *What two mountains was Shechem situate between?*—Gerizim and Ebal.

42. *Where was the tabernacle first reared in the land of Canaan?*—At Gilgal on the Jordan. (Not the Gilgal in Shechem.)

43. *Where did Joshua make his solemn covenant with Israel before his death?*—Joshua gathered all the tribes of Israel to Shechem, and called for the elders of Israel, and for their heads, and for their judges, and for their officers; and they presented themselves before God. Josh. 24 : 1.

44. *Where was the first idol temple built in Israel?*—In Shechem. 1 Kings 12 : 25-33.

45. *What act of treachery was Simeon and Levi guilty of to Shechem, the founder of this city?*—They slew him when, through their own contrivance, he was unprepared to resist them. Gen. 34 : 13, 25, 26.

46. *What did God at this time desire Jacob to do?*—To go and live at Bethel. Gen. 35 : 1.

47. *How did Jacob prepare for this journey?*—By calling upon his people to put away their idols, and be clean and change their garments.

48. *How did God preserve him from the anger of the inhabitants of the land? What proof is there that God's care of his people is the same now as then?*—By making the inhabitants afraid of him and of his God. He preserveth the souls of his saints; he delivereth them out of the hand of the wicked. Gen. 35 : 5; Ps. 97 : 10.

49. *What sorrowful event happened at Bethel?*—The death of Rebekah's nurse. Gen. 35 : 8.

50. *What peculiar name did God confirm, and what special blessing did he give, to Jacob at this place?*—The name of Israel and the gift of the land of Canaan. Gen. 35 : 9-12.

51. *What great loss did Jacob sustain when near Bethlehem?*—The death of Rachel. Gen. 35 : 19.

52. *How many children had Jacob at this time?*—Twelve. Gen. 35 : 22-26.

53. *How far south did Jacob travel?*—To Mamre, near Hebron.

54. *Who resided there?*—Isaac.

55. *How many years did Jacob live with his father before his father died?*—About three years.

56. *Who united together to bury Isaac?*—Esau and Jacob

JACOB AND HIS SONS. (Gen. 37.)

1. *To which son did Jacob show a great partiality?*—To Joseph. Gen. 37 : 3.

2. *Why did Jacob feel this, and how did he show it?*—Because he was the son of his old age. By making him a coat of many colors.

3. *What character did the other sons of Jacob display?*—An envious and malicious one.

4. *Why did they hate Joseph?*—Because of their father's special love to him.

5. *Did he deserve it? Had his dreams anything to do with it? What were they?*—No. Yes. That his brothers' sheaves made obeisance to his, and that the sun, moon and eleven stars did the same to him.

6. *How did Joseph's father feel when he heard one of the dreams?*—He was surprised at the dream, but doubtless felt it was from God. Gen. 37 : 11.

7. *How did Joseph get into his brethren's power?*—On Jacob sending him to them to see if they were well. Gen. 37 : 14.

8. *What did they do with him?*—They threw him into a pit. Gen. 37 : 24.

9. *How old was Joseph at this time?*—Sixteen.

10. *What story did they make up to their father?*—That they had found his coat bloody, and that he had been killed by a wild beast.

11. *What difference was there in Reuben's behavior toward Joseph to the rest of his brethren?*—He dissuaded them from killing him. Gen. 37 : 21, 22.

12. *How did Jacob receive the news?*—He mourned and refused to be comforted.

13. *How did the Midianites dispose of Joseph?*—They took him out of the pit and sold him to some Ishmaelites. Gen. 37 : 28.

14. *What connection was there between Abraham and the Midianites?*—Midian was a son of Keturah, his second wife. Gen. 25 : 1, 2.

15. *What connection was there between Moses and the Midianites?*—He lived among them and took his wife thence. Ex. 2 : 15, 21.

16. *What connection was there between Balaam and the Midianites?*—He lived among them and was killed in battle by the Israelites.

17. *What event in Gideon's history was connected with the Midianites?*—The appearance to him of the angel Son of God before he fought against and overthrew them. Judg. 6, 7.

JOSEPH IN EGYPT. (Gen. 39, 40, 41.)

1. *To whom did the Ishmaelites sell Joseph?*—To Potiphar, captain of Pharaoh's guard. Gen. 39 : 1.

2. *What office did Potiphar appoint Joseph to fill?*—Overseer of his house. Gen. 39 : 4.

3. *How was God's favor manifested to Joseph in this situation?*—By everything prospering under his care. Gen. 39 : 2-5.

4. *Was he not deprived of his situation by false accusation?*—Yes, through the wickedness of his master's wife, who was embittered against him by his virtue and his fear of God. Gen. 39 : 7-18.

5. *What unjust punishment was suffered by Joseph?*—He was put in prison.

6. *Did the Lord forsake him?*—He was with him and showed him mercy.

7. *How did the keeper of the prison behave to Joseph?*—He gave him the entire charge of the prison.

8. *What kind of prison was this? Who were principally confined there?*—A prison connected with Potiphar's house, and in which state prisoners were kept.

9. *What remarkable circumstance occurred to two of those prisoners?*—They had dreams which troubled them.

10. *How did Joseph assist them in their perplexity?*—He interpreted their dreams. Gen. 40.

11. *Were his words found true? Name the result.*—The chief butler was restored, and the chief baker was hanged, as Joseph had foretold.

12. *How did Pharaoh's butler behave to Joseph?*—He forgot his promise to get Joseph released.

13. *What brought his dream again to his mind?*—A dream which Pharaoh had. Gen. 41 : 1–13.

14. *Could the magicians of Egypt interpret Pharaoh's dream?*—They could not. Gen. 41 : 8.

15. *For whom did he send?*—For Joseph, whom the butler had named.

16. *Did Joseph take the honor of interpretation to himself, or confess God's power before the king?*—He said, It is not in me; *God* shall give Pharaoh an answer of peace. Gen. 41 : 16.

17. *Name a king who was smitten with worms and died because he gave* not *God the glory?*—Herod Agrippa, king of Judea. Acts 12 : 23.

18. *Name another king who was driven from men, and was for seven years like a beast, because he gave not glory to God?*—Nebuchadnezzar, who said, Is not this great Babylon, that I have built for the house of the kingdom by the might of my power, and for the honor of my majesty? While the word was in the king's mouth, there fell a voice from heaven, saying, O King Nebuchadnezzar, to thee it is spoken, The kingdom is departed from thee. And they shall drive thee from men, and thy dwelling shall be with the beasts of the field: they shall make thee to eat grass as oxen, and seven times shall pass over thee, until thou know that the Most High ruleth in the kingdom of men, and giveth it to whomsoever he will. Dan. 4 : 30–32.

19. *How was the latter part of verse 30 in 1 Sam. 2 fulfilled in Joseph's case?*—By his being made ruler over all Egypt. He had honored God by his resistance of temptation and his faithfulness to his duties, and now God honored *him*. Them that honor *me* I will honor. Gen. 41 : 43.

20. *How old was Joseph at this time?*—Thirty. Gen. 41 : 46.

21. *What name did Pharaoh give Joseph, and what is the meaning of it?*—Zaphnath-paanéah, a "revealer of secrets," or "the man to whom secrets are revealed."

22. *What were the names of Joseph's wife and his two sons?*—Asenath, Manasseh and Ephraim. 41 : 45, 51, 52.

23. *What did Joseph do during the seven years of plenty?*—He laid up the food in the cities. Gen. 41 : 48.

24. *When the people cried to Pharaoh for bread, to whom did he send them?*—To Joseph. Gen. 41 : 55.

25. *Was this great famine confined to the land of Egypt?*—It was over all the face of the earth, or all that part of it. Gen. 41 : 56, 57.

JACOB AND HIS SONS IN EGYPT. (Gen. 42–50.)

1. *Where was Jacob living at this time?*—In Canaan. Gen. 42 : 5.

2. *Did the famine extend to the land of Canaan?*—Yes. Gen. 42 : 5.

3. *How did they procure bread?*—Ten of Jacob's sons went to buy corn in Egypt. Gen. 42 : 3.

4. *How did Joseph behave to his brethren when he saw them?*—He made himself strange to them and spoke roughly to them, but not from a spirit of revenge. Gen. 42 : 7.

5. *Did they recognize him?*—No. Gen. 42 : 8.

6. *How did Jacob feel when they returned and told him the news?*—He felt that all things were against him, and that he should lose Benjamin also. But all things

work together for good to them that love God. Gen. 42 : 36, 38 ; Rom. 8 : 28.

7. *Whom did they take with them on their second journey?*—Benjamin. Gen. 43 : 15.

8. *What proof have we in this chapter of the truth of Num. 13 : 21–27?*—The fruits, honey and spices they took with them. Gen. 43 : 11.

They went up and searched the land. And they ascended by the south, and came unto Hebron. And they came unto the brook of Eshcol, and cut down from thence a branch with one cluster of grapes, and they bare it between two upon a staff: and they brought of the pomegranates and of the figs. And they went and came to Moses and to Aaron, and brought back word unto them and unto all the congregation, and showed them the fruit of the land. And they told him and said, We came unto the land whither thou sentest us, and surely it floweth with milk and honey ; and this is the fruit of it.

9. *How did Joseph feel when he saw Benjamin stand among his brethren?*—His love was greatly excited, and he retired to weep. Gen. 43 : 30, 31.

10. *What closer relationship was there between Joseph and Benjamin than between Joseph and his other brothers?*—They had the same mother, Rachel. Gen. 30: 22–24 ; 35 : 16–18.

11. *What effect did Joseph's kindness have on them?*—They wondered at it. Gen. 43 : 33.

12. *What was Joseph's intention in all this treatment?*—To make them conscious of their sin and sorry for it, and to better carry out his plans.

13. *Did it have the effect he desired?*—It had. Gen. 42 : 21 ; 44 : 16.

14. *How did Judah behave at this trying time?*—He begged that Benjamin might be allowed to go back with the rest, and offered to remain himself behind as surety for his return. Gen. 44 : 18, 33.

15. *Of whom was he a type in this?*—Of Jesus Christ, our Substitute, who suffered in our stead.

16. *How was Joseph's tender heart affected by all this?*—He could bear it no longer, but wept aloud, and told them he was Joseph their brother. Gen. 45 : 1–4.

17. *How did they feel when they knew this mighty prince was their own brother?*—They could not answer him for fear. Gen. 45 : 3.

18. *What proofs did he give them of it?*—He gave proofs of his love and power by the rich presents he made them and the promise of a home and plenty in Egypt. Gen. 45 : 17–23.

19. *Did Joseph and his father ever meet again?*—They met in Egypt, whither Jacob and all his family had come. Gen. 46 : 29.

20. *How?*—See No. 19.

21. *What proof have we in this of the truth of Rom. 8 : 28?*—What Jacob thought to be against him proved to be for his good. (See No. 6.)

22. *Where in the land of Egypt did Jacob and his family dwell?*—In the land of Goshen. Gen. 47 : 1.

23. *Had the Egyptians any particular antipathy to shepherds?*—They disliked shepherds and cattle-dealers from foreign lands for slaughtering their sacred animals, or from having formerly invaded and plundered their country.

24. *Why?*—See No. 23.

25. *Was Jacob introduced to Pharaoh?*—Yes, and gave him his blessing. Gen. 47 : 7.

26. *What proof have we in Jacob's remark to Pharaoh of the truth of Ps. 90?*—The longest life is but short to look back on.

For all our days are passed away in thy wrath : we spend our years as a tale that is told. The days of our years are threescore years and ten ; and if by reason of strength they be fourscore years, yet is their strength labor and sorrow ; for it is soon cut off, and we fly away. Ps. 90 : 9, 10.

27. *What peculiar blessing did Jacob give to the sons of Joseph?*—He placed his right hand on the younger instead of the elder. Gen. 48 : 17–19.

28. *In his prophetical blessing of his twelve sons, to whom did he give the birthright?*—Gen. 48 : 8.

Now the sons of Reuben the first-born of Israel (for he was the first-born; but, forasmuch as he defiled his father's bed, his birthright was given unto the sons of Joseph the son of Israel: and the genealogy is not to be reckoned after the birthright. For Judah prevailed above his brethren, and of him came the chief ruler; but the birthright was Joseph's). 1 Chron. 5 : 1, 2.

29. *What was the special blessing of Judah?*—That ut of his family the Messiah should come. Gen. 49 : 10.

30. *How was this fulfilled?*—Our Lord sprang out of Juda. Heb. 7 : 14.

The book of the generation of Jesus Christ, the son of David, the son of Abraham. Abraham begat Isaac; and Isaac begat Jacob; and Jacob begat Judas and his brethren; and Judas begat Phares. Matt. 1 : 1–3.

31. *To whom is allusion made in chap. 49, verse 24, in Joseph's blessing? Compare Num. 13 : 8, 16 with Num. 27 : 15–23.*—To Joshua.

Of the tribe of Ephraim, Oshea the son of Nun. And Moses called Oshea the son of Nun Jehoshua. And Moses spake unto the Lord, saying, Let the Lord, the God of the spirits of all flesh, set a man over the congregation, which may go out before them, and which may go in before them, and which may lead them out, and which may bring them in; that the congregation of the Lord be not as sheep which have no shepherd. And the Lord said unto Moses, Take thee Joshua the son of Nun, a man in whom is the spirit, and lay thine hand upon him: and set him before Eleazar the priest, and before all the congregation; and give him a charge in their sight. And thou shalt put some of thine honor upon him, that all the congregation of the children of Israel may be obedient. And he shall stand before Eleazar the priest, who shall ask counsel for him after the judgment of Urim before the Lord: at his word shall they go out, and at his word they shall come in, both he and all the children of Israel with him, even all the congregation. And Moses did as the Lord commanded him; and he took Joshua, and set him before Eleazar the priest, and before all the congregation; and he laid his hands upon him, and gave him a charge, as the Lord commanded by the hand of Moses.

32. *How was Joshua in this a type of Jesus?*—As Joshua led the Israelites in the wilderness and into the promised land, so Jesus is the guide of his people upon earth and the means of their entrance into heaven.

Then said Jesus unto them again, Verily, verily, I say unto you, I am the door of the sheep. All that ever came before me are thieves and robbers: but the sheep did not hear them. I am the door: by me if any man enter in, he shall be saved, and shall go in and out, and find pasture. My sheep hear my voice, and I know them, and they follow me. John 10 : 7–9, 27.

33. *What other Joshua was a type of Jesus under the double figure of a branch and a stone?*—And he showed me Joshua the high priest standing before the angel of the Lord. And the angel of the Lord protested unto Joshua, saying, Thus saith the Lord of hosts; If thou wilt walk in my ways, and if thou wilt keep my charge, then thou shalt also judge my house, and shalt also keep my courts, and I will give thee places to walk among these that stand by. Hear now, O Joshua the high priest, thou, and thy fellows that sit before thee: for they are men wondered at; for, behold, I will bring forth my servant the BRANCH. For behold the stone that I have laid before Joshua; upon one stone shall be seven eyes: behold, I will engrave the graving thereof, saith the Lord of hosts, and I will remove the iniquity of that land in one day. Zech. 3 : 1, 6–9.

34. *What does Isaiah prophesy of this stone?*—Thus saith the Lord God, Behold, I lay in Zion for a foundation a stone, a tried stone, a precious cornerstone, a sure foundation. Isa. 28 : 16.

35. *Give the texts in which the Lord Jesus speaks of himself under this figure?*—Jesus saith unto them, Did ye never read in the Scriptures, The stone which the builders rejected, the same is become the head of the corner: and whosoever shall fall on this stone shall be broken; but on whomsoever it shall fall, it will grind him to powder. Matt. 21 : 42, 44; Mark 12 : 10; Luke 20 : 17, 18.

36. *Find the text in which the apostle Peter speaks of the Lord Jesus under this figure?*—To whom coming, as unto a living stone, disallowed indeed of men, but chosen of God, and precious, ye also, as lively stones, are built up a spiritual house, an holy priesthood, to offer up spiritual sacrifices, acceptable to God by Jesus Christ. Wherefore also it is contained in the Scripture, Behold, I lay in Sion a chief cornerstone, elect, precious: and he that believeth on him shall not be confounded. Unto you therefore which believe he is precious: but unto them which be disobedient, the stone which the builders disallowed, the same is made the head of the corner, and a stone of stumbling, and a rock of offence, even to them which stumble at the word, being disobedient: whereunto also they were appointed. 1 Pet. 2 : 4–8.

37. *Where was Jacob buried?*—In the cave of Machpelah. Gen. 50 : 13.

38. *What fears had Joseph's brethren after their father's death?*—That Joseph would ill-treat them and punish them. Gen. 50 : 15.

39. *How did Joseph behave to them?*—He comforted them and spoke kindly to them.

40. *Of whom were Joseph and his brethren types in this transaction?*—Of Christ and his forgiving love.

41. *When was Joseph buried?*—Not until the Israelites reached Canaan, above two hundred years after his death. Gen. 50 : 26.

And the bones of Joseph, which the children of Israel brought up out of Egypt, buried they in Shechem, in a parcel of ground which Jacob bought of the sons of Hamor, the father of Shechem, for an hundred pieces of silver. Josh. 24 : 32.

JOSEPH'S HISTORY.

1. *What great peculiarity marks the Bible histories?*—Their reference to our Lord Jesus Christ.

2. *Of whose history can this pre-eminently be said?*—Of Joseph's.

3. *To whom must we look to enlighten our minds when studying God's word?*—To God the Holy Spirit; saying, Open thou mine eyes, that I may behold wondrous things out of thy law. Ps. 119 : 18; 2 Pet. 1 : 20, 21.

4. *What did Jesus say in John 5 : 39?*—Search the Scriptures; for in them ye think ye have eternal life: and they are they which testify of me.

5. *And how did he upbraid the two disciples whom he overtook going to Emmaus?*—O fools, and slow of heart to believe all that the prophets have spoken! Luke 24 : 26.

6. *Is it not, then, our duty to seek for Jesus even so far back as the writings of Moses?*—They drank of that spiritual Rock that followed them; and that Rock was Christ. 1 Cor. 10 : 4.

7. *Who wrote Genesis?*—Moses.

8. *How was Joseph a type of Jesus, when he was at home, clothed in a beautiful robe, the darling of his father?*—In that Jesus shared his Father's glory and enjoyed his love.

Thou lovedst me before the foundation of the world. John 17 : 24.

9. *How was Joseph a type in going out to see after the welfare of his brethren?*—In Jesus graciously visiting his brethren in human nature.

The Son of man is come to seek and to save that which was lost. Luke 19 : 10.

10. *How in their treatment of him?*—In being sold by Judas and delivered to death by the Jews.

He came unto his own, and his own received him not. John 1 : 11.

When the husbandmen saw the son, they said among themselves, This is the heir; come, let us kill him, and let us seize on his inheritance. Matt. 21 : 38.

11. *How in his dreams?*—In his prophecies of his future kingdom and glory. Matt. 25 : 31, 32.

12. *How in the false accusations brought against him?* —In his freedom from blame. Matt. 26 : 59, 60.

13. *How in being committed to prison?*—They laid hands on Jesus, and took him. Matt. 26 : 50.

14. *How in leaving that prison and being exalted?*— God hath made that same Jesus, whom ye have crucified, both Lord and Christ. Acts 2 : 36.

15. *How in his feeding and blessing his brethren and all who came to him?*—In being the Bread of life.

16. *How in Pharaoh transferring all his power to him?*—The Father committed all judgment unto the Son. John 5 : 22.

17. *How in his returning good for evil?*—Jesus died for his persecutors, and prayed for them to the last.

JOB.

1. *Who was Job?*—A very rich man in the north of Arabia who worshiped the true God. Job 1 : 3.

2. *When was he supposed to live?*—Probably about the time of Isaac.

3. *Why? Do we gather anything from his not mentioning God's wonders in Egypt and the Red Sea?*— From the age to which he lived, said to be two hundred years; from the very early customs alluded to in the book, as the worship of the sun, moon and stars, the use of engraving for writing, and the reckoning of riches by cattle, that they had not then occurred, or Job would certainly have heard of them and spoken of them. Job 21 : 26–28; 19 : 23, 24; 1 : 3.

4. *Can you give any proof from the fact that as head of the family he offered sacrifices?*—After God's appointment of priests he would not have done this.

5. *How is he supposed to have obtained his knowledge of the true God?*—By tradition, or knowledge passed down by word of mouth from one generation to another, and perhaps by direct revelation from God, like Adam and Moses.

6. *What proof of the truth of 1 Pet. 5 : 8 does the history of Job supply?*—Satan's plots against Job. Your adversary the devil, as a roaring lion, walketh about, seeking whom he may devour. Job 1 : 6–12; 2 : 1–7.

7. *Where is Satan called "the accuser of the brethren"?*—Rev. 12 : 10.

8. *What high terms of praise did the Lord use when speaking of Job to Satan?*—Job 1 : 8.

9. *And how did the Lord afterward, to Ezekiel, mention him?*—He classed him with Noah and Daniel.

Though these three men, Noah, Daniel, and Job, were in it, they should deliver but their own souls by their righteousness, saith the Lord God. Ezek. 14 : 14.

10. *In what way did the Lord first try this good man?* —By suffering him to be deprived in one day of his children, servants and goods. Job 1.

11. *Did he fail?*—He submitted to God's will, and blessed him in memorable words. Job 1 : 21.

12. *Did Satan again have permission to hurt him?*— Yes, by bodily suffering. Job 2 : 4–8.

13. *Did he continue steadfast?*—He seems to have uttered no complaint against God. Job 2 : 8.

14. *How did his wife afflict him?*—By tempting him to curse God, that he might die. Job 2 : 9.

15. *Did this prove too much for him?*—No; he again expressed his submission to the will of God. Job 2 : 10.

16. *Who came to comfort him?*—His three principal friends. Job 2 : 11.

17. *What relation is Eliphaz supposed to have been to Esau?*—These are the names of Esau's sons; Eliphaz the son of Adah the wife of Esau. . . . And the sons of Eliphaz were Teman, Omar, Zepho and Gatam, and Kenaz. Gen. 36 : 10, 11. Eliphaz seems to have been an Idumean or Arabian name.

18. *In what way did Job fail?*—He cursed his birth, though not his God, and sometimes showed a self-righteous spirit. Job 3.

My face is foul with weeping, and on my eyelids is the shadow of death; not for any injustice in mine hands: also my prayer is pure. Job 16 : 16, 17.

19. *Did not his friends suppose that all his misfortunes had come upon him in consequence of sin?*—They did. Job 4 : 7, 8.

20. *If Job, instead of justifying himself, had appealed unto God, would it not have shown a better knowledge?*— Yes, for it is easy to form a too favorable judgment of our own selves.

21. *How did the Lord Jesus Christ act when he was wrongfully accused?*—He answered not a word. Matt. 27 : 12–14.

22. *Who is the only perfect man that ever lived?*— The man Christ Jesus.

23. *How did Job feel when God himself spoke to him at last?*—Deeply humbled. *What did Job say?*—Then Job answered the Lord, and said, Behold I am vile; what shall I answer thee? I will lay my hand upon my mouth. Job 40 : 3, 4.

24. *Did the Lord condemn him?*—No; he accepted or forgave him. Job 42 : 9.

25. *How did the Lord pass over the error of Job's three friends in their condemnation of Job?*—In consideration of their sacrifice and of Job's prayer. Job 42 : 7–9.

26. *How did the Lord disappoint Satan and bless Job's latter end?*—He gave him a family again, and twice as much substance as he had before. Job 42 : 10, 12, 13.

27. *How old was Job when he died?*—About two hundred years. Job 42 : 16.

PHARAOH AND MOSES. (Ex. 1 : 2.)

1. *How did the Egyptians behave to the children of Israel after the death of Joseph?*—They enslaved and oppressed them. Ex. 1 : 8–14.

2. *Did the children of Israel multiply and increase very rapidly?*—They did. Ex. 1 : 12.

3. *Why should this have made the Egyptians afraid?* —Lest they should join their enemies. Ex. 1 : 10.

4. *How were the children of Israel employed by the Egyptians?*—In making bricks and other field-service. Ex. 1 : 14.

5. *What cruel device did Pharaoh resolve on to destroy the male children of Israel?*—To employ the Hebrew nurses to do so. Ex. 1 : 16.

6. *Who was Moses?*—The second son of Amram and Jochebed of the tribe of Levi. Ex. 2 : 1; 6 : 20.

7. *What plan did his mother adopt to spare his life?*— She hid him in a floating basket among the flags growing by a river-side. Ex. 2 : 2, 3.

8. *How did her design succeed?*—The child was found by Pharaoh's daughter, who took charge of it. Ex. 2 : 5–10.

9. *Whom had his mother set to watch the little ark?*—His sister Miriam. Ex. 2 : 4 ; 15 : 20.

10. *When the princess sought a nurse for the child, whom did Miriam fetch?*—His mother. Ex. 2 : 7–9.

11. *What blessing did this ensure to Moses?*—The tenderest care, and perhaps also the knowledge of the true God.

12. *What proof does this give us of the truth of Isa. 46 : 10?*—My counsel shall stand, and I will do all my pleasure.

There is no wisdom nor understanding nor counsel against the Lord. Prov. 21 : 30.

13. *With whom did Moses join himself—with the Egyptians or the Hebrews?*—By faith Moses, when he was come to years, refused to be called the son of Pharaoh's daughter; choosing rather to suffer affliction with the people of God. Heb. 11 : 24, 25.

14. *Did they receive him graciously?*—Who made thee a ruler and a judge over us? Wilt thou kill me as thou diddest the Egyptian yesterday? Acts 7 : 27, 28.

15. *What was Moses obliged to do?*—To leave Egypt. Ex. 2 : 11–15.

16. *To what land did he flee?*—To Midian.

17. *What occurred to him there?*—He married a daughter of the priest or prince of Midian. Ex. 2 : 16–21.

18. *How long did he stay there?*—Forty years. Acts 7 : 30.

19. *How many sons had he? What were their names and his wife's name?*—Two—Gershom and Eliezer; Zipporah. Ex. 2 : 22 ; 18 : 3, 4 ; 2 : 21.

THE BURNING BUSH. (Ex. 3, 4.)

1. *How was Moses employed when the Lord appeared to him?*—In keeping his father-in-law's flock. Ex. 3 : 1.

2. *What wondrous sight attracted the attention of Moses?*—A burning bush unconsumed. Ex. 3 : 2.

3. *Whose voice addressed him from the midst of the fire?*—The voice of the Son of God, God's messenger, and yet God himself. Ex. 3 : 2, 4.

4. *What commission did the Lord give to Moses?*—To go to Pharaoh and bring the Israelites out of Egypt. Ex. 3 : 10.

5. *Was Moses willing to undertake it?*—He said they would not believe that God had appeared to him. Ex. 4 : 1.

6. *What excuses did he make?*—See No. 5.

7. *How did the Lord show him that it was not his own might or power in which he was to go to Pharaoh?*—He changed Moses' rod into a serpent and made his hand leprous, and restored them again. Ex. 4 : 2–8.

8. *Did this remove his scruples?*—He then objected that he was too poor a speaker to deliver God's message. Ex. 4 : 10.

9. *How did the Lord graciously meet his weakness?*—He promised to teach him what to say. Ex. 4 : 12.

10. *Whom did the Lord appoint his helper?*—His brother Aaron, who could speak well. Ex. 4 : 14–16.

11. *What solemn rite had Moses neglected to perform on his sons in the land of Midian?*—Circumcision. Ex. 4 : 25.

12. *What punishment had God enjoined on those who neglected it?*—The uncircumcised man-child shall be cut off from his people ; he hath broken my covenant (by loss of privileges or by death). Gen. 17 : 14.

13. *Did not the sons of Moses narrowly escape?*—They were doubtless in imminent danger of punishment, with Moses himself. Ex. 4 : 24–26.

14. *Who met Moses on his return to Egypt?*—Aaron, by command of God. Ex. 4 : 27.

15. *How did the poor afflicted Israelites receive the message?*—They believed it, and worshiped God. Ex. 4 : 31.

THE PLAGUES OF EGYPT. (Ex. 5–11.)

1. *Who was the king of Egypt now?*—Pharaoh.

2. *Was it the same Pharaoh who had ordered the little children to be killed?*—No ; it was one who lived one hundred and forty years later.

3. *Did he treat the children of Israel more mercifully than the former king?*—Though he did not order their male offspring to death like the former king, he was very cruel to them.

4. *How did he receive Moses and Aaron when they went in to him?*—He abused them for interfering with the people's work. Ex. 5 : 2–4.

5. *What was the result?*—Heavier work was laid upon them. Ex. 5 : 6–9.

6. *Whom did the children of Israel blame for this?*—Moses and Aaron. Ex. 5 : 20, 21.

7. *Of whom was Pharaoh, in his daring rebellion, a type?*—Of the great rebel Satan. Jude 6.

8. *What was the first plague?*—The river Nile turned into blood. Ex. 7.

9. *In what respect was this a peculiar trial to the Egyptians?*—Because the yearly overflowing of the Nile was most valuable for their land, and they worshiped the river as a god, and much of their food was fish.

10. *What were the second and third plagues?*—Frogs and lice. Ex. 8.

11. *How far were the magicians permitted to follow Moses and Aaron?*—So far as to turn water into blood and to bring frogs. Ex. 7, 8.

12. *What did they say when they could go no farther?*—That the miracles of Moses were the finger of God. Ex. 8 : 19.

13. *What was the next plague?*—Swarms of flies or hurtful insects. Ex. 8 : 24.

14. *How did God mark the distinction between the Egyptians and Israelites in this?*—He suffered none in the land of Goshen, where the Israelites dwelt.

15. *Did this influence Pharaoh to let the Israelites go?*—No (Ex. 8 : 32), though he gave way a little at first. Ex. 8 : 28.

16. *What was the fifth plague?*—A murrain upon cattle, horses, asses, camels and sheep. Ex. 9.

17. *What painful attack on man and beast did God send next?*—Boils and blains, or sores. Ex. 9 : 9.

18. *Did any of these move the haughty king?*—No. Ex. 9 : 7, 12.

19. *What merciful provision did God make in the seventh plague for those who believed in his word?*—He warned them to remove their cattle to a place of shelter. Ex. 9 : 19.

20. *Why was this plague peculiarly terrible to the Egyptians?*—Because they were not accustomed to either hail or rain. Deut. 11 : 10, 11.

21. *Why was it that all these judgments had no effect on Pharaoh?*—Because his heart was hardened, or he hardened his own heart, as it is expressed in Ex. 8 : 15, 32 ; 9 : 34, 35, so that God gave him up to his own wicked heart, as he is said in Rom. 1 : 28, 21, 20 to have given up the Gentiles to a reprobate mind, their foolish heart being darkened, and they themselves without excuse.

Let no man say when he is tempted, I am tempted of God : for God cannot be tempted with evil, neither tempteth he any man. James 1 : 13.

22. *Is it not an awful thing when God gives a man over to his own hardened heart?*—If we sin willfully after that we have received the knowledge of the truth, there remaineth no more sacrifice for sins, but a certain fearful looking-for of judgment and fiery indignation, which shall devour the adversaries. Heb. 10 : 26, 27.

23. *What was the eighth plague?*—Locusts. Ex. 10.

24. *What appearance must the land of Egypt have presented at this time?*—The land was darkened by them, and every green thing eaten up. Ex. 10 : 15.

25. *What was the ninth plague?*—Thick darkness for three days. Ex. 10 : 21–23.

26. *What solemn interview had Moses with Pharaoh during this awful darkness?*—When Pharaoh bade Moses see his face no more. Ex. 10 : 28.

27. *What was the last plague?*—The destruction of first-born.

THE PASSOVER. (Ex. 12–14.)

1. *What did God command the Israelites to do before he brought the last plague on the Egyptians?*—To have the passover sacrifice and feast. Ex. 12.

2. *Of whom was the lamb a type?*—Of Christ the Lamb of God, slain from the foundation of the world. John 1 : 29; Rev. 13 : 8.

3. *In how many ways was the paschal lamb a type of Him whom it prefigured?*—In its gentleness and unblemished innocence, and in its being slain without a bone being broken; and in other respects besides.

4. *What divine ordinance in the Christian Church still commemorates the Passover?*—The Lord's Supper.

5. *When was it instituted?*—The evening before our blessed Saviour suffered.

6. *What does it set forth?*—The sacrifice of the death of Christ, and the benefits we receive thereby.

7. *Wherein does "the mass" of the Romish Church differ from "the Lord's Supper" in the Protestant churches?*—In the mass the priest professes every time to offer Christ himself as a sacrifice for sin, while the Lord's Supper is a remembrance of his perfect sacrifice made once for all.

8. *Which is most in harmony with the word of God?*—We are sanctified through the offering of the body of Jesus Christ once for all. For by one offering he hath perfected for ever them that are sanctified. Heb. 10 : 10, 14.

9. *What is the meaning of the word Passover?*—It refers to the destroying angel *passing over* the blood-sprinkled doorposts of the children of Israel. Ex. 12 : 23.

10. *How were the Israelites preserved from the destroying angel?*—By striking the lintels and doorposts of their houses with the blood of the slain lamb. Ex. 12 : 22.

11. *Why was not the blood sprinkled on the doorway?*—Lest any should trample on so sacred a thing.

Of how much sorer punishment, suppose ye, shall he be thought worthy who hath trodden under foot the Son of God, and hath counted the blood of the covenant, wherewith he was sanctified, an unholy thing, and hath done despite unto the Spirit of grace! Heb. 10 : 29.

12. *How was the bread to be prepared?*—Without leaven (or yeast or sour paste) to raise it. Ex. 12 : 15.

13. *What does the apostle Paul declare this to be a type of, in 1 Cor. 5 : 7, 8?*—Of purity and sincerity.

14. *What did the bitter herbs signify?*—The bitterness of Egyptian bondage, of true sorrow for sin and of Christ's cup of suffering. Ps. 69 : 20, 21.

15. *If any Israelite had despised the means of safety, what would have been the consequence?*—He would have lost his first-born child.

16. *And what will be our state if we despise the hiding-place which God has provided for us?*—We shall be destroyed by the storm of God's just wrath.

17. *Is God's salvation merely a safety from his wrath, or does he provide ample blessing for the soul that trusts in him?*—He provides not only escape from hell, but a home in heaven—eternal life begun below and perfected above.

18. *What part of this type is a proof of this?*—The feast upon the slaughtered lamb.

19. *Give some other parts of Scripture where the gospel provision is compared to a feast.*—Isa. 25 : 6; Rev 19 : 9.

20. *How did Pharaoh act when he found the threatened vengeance of God had descended on him?*—He ordered the Israelites to depart. Ex. 12 : 31, 32.

21. *How did God recompense the Israelites for all that they had suffered at the hands of the Egyptians?*—By disposing the Egyptians to give them gold and silver and raiment. Ex. 12 : 35, 36; Rom. 12 : 17–21.

22. *In what way did the Israelites obey the king's mandate?*—They hurried away with their flocks and herds and hastily-prepared food. Ex. 12 : 37–39.

23. *Did they remember Joseph's wish at this time?*—They took his bones with them. Ex. 13 : 19.

24. *Did Pharaoh quietly allow them to go?*—He pursued them to bring them back. Ex. 14 : 5–9.

25. *How did the children of Israel feel when they heard that Pharaoh was pursuing them?*—They were terribly afraid. Ex. 14 : 10.

26. *What had the Israelites to guide them as to the way they should take?*—A pillar of cloud and of fire. Ex. 14 : 19, 20, 24.

27. *What speech did Israel make to Moses when they saw the sea before them and the host of Pharaoh behind?*—That they had better have remained in Egypt. Ex. 14 : 11, 12.

28. *Did God reward them as they deserved for this wicked speech? What did he do?*—He made a way for them through the sea. Ex. 14 : 16.

29. *Which got on the fastest—Pharaoh in his chariots or Israel on foot?*—Israel on foot, as God took off the chariot-wheels. Ex. 14 : 25.

30. *How did the Lord hinder the Egyptians?*—See No. 29.

31. *How did God keep the hosts separate all the night?*—By the pillar of cloud, which kept the Egyptians in darkness and prevented them from moving on. Ex. 14 : 20.

32. *Ought we ever to doubt a God who can help his people in any difficulty?*—If God be for us, who can be against us? Rom. 8 : 31.

33. *What happened as soon as Israel was safely over the sea?*—The Egyptians were overwhelmed by the returning waters. Ex. 14 : 27, 28.

THE SONG OF MOSES. (Ex. 15 : 1–21.)

1. *What is the passage through the Red Sea a type of?*—The introduction of believers by baptism into covenant with God. 1 Cor. 10 : 1–4.

2. *What is baptism a type of?*—Of having done with sin on being given to God. Rom. 6 : 1–4.

3. *What did Jesus call his death?*—A baptism.

I have a baptism to be baptized with; and how am I straitened till it be accomplished! Luke 12 : 50.

4. *Is the song of Moses ever again mentioned in Scripture?*—Rev. 15 : 2, 3.

5. *Of whom is Pharaoh a type in these verses?*—Of the enemies of God.

6. *What is said of Pharaoh in Rom. 9 : 17?*—Even for this same purpose have I raised thee up, that I might show my power in thee.

7. *What will be the end of all God's enemies?*—To be subdued by Christ.

For David saith, The Lord said unto my Lord, Sit thou on my right hand, until I make thy foes thy footstool. Acts 2 : 34, 35.

8. *Which is the last enemy that is to be destroyed?*—Death. 1 Cor. 15 : 26.

9. *What song may the Christian sing even now in prospect of that victory?*—Death is swallowed up in victory. 1 Cor. 15 : 54–57.

10. *Through whom is the conquest obtained?*—Heb. 2: 14, 15; 1 Cor. 15: 57.

THEIR JOURNEY BEGUN. (Ex. 15: 22–27.)

1. *How many days did Israel travel in the wilderness before they found water?*—Three. Ex. 15: 22.

2. *And when they found water, of what kind was it?*—Bitter. Ex. 15: 23.

3. *How did the children of Israel bear this disappointment?*—They murmured against Moses. Ex. 15: 24.

4. *What is this world compared to?*—A wilderness.

5. *Are the journeyings of the children of Israel calculated to teach us any useful lessons?*—Not to expect perfect comfort in our pilgrimage here below—to follow God's guidance, and to cheerfully submit to all his dealings with us on our heavenward way.

6. *Are not young people apt to think that this world is a resting-place?*—They forget that youth and health may not last them long.

7. *What does God's word say in Mic. 2: 10?*—Arise ye, and depart; for this is not your rest: because it is polluted, it shall destroy you, even with a sore destruction.

8. *There is one thing that can turn the bitter waters of earthly sorrow into sweetness; what is it?*—Seeing a Father's hand overruling all our affairs.

9. *Where did Israel next encamp?*—At Elim. Ex. 15: 27.

10. *What blessing had the Lord in store for them there?*—Plenty of water.

11. *Is it not God's way ever to bring good out of evil?*—Who fed thee in the wilderness with manna, which thy fathers knew not, that he might humble thee, and that he might prove thee, to do thee good at thy latter end. Deut. 8: 16.

THE MANNA. (Ex. 16.)

1. *How were the Israelites fed in the wilderness?*—With manna.

2. *What was manna?*—A small round thing, like a frozen drop of dew, miraculously sent by God, and able to be made into bread. Ex. 16: 14, 15, 23, 31.

3. *How often were they to gather it?*—Every day except the Sabbath-day.

4. *What provision did the Lord make for sanctifying the Sabbath-day, and resting on it?*—A double quantity of manna the day before. Ex. 16: 22–30.

5. *Were the children of Israel obedient to the Lord in this arrangement? How did they act?*—Some of them went out to gather on the Sabbath-day. Ex. 16: 27.

6. *Who was it that declared himself to be the true bread that came down from heaven?*—I am the living bread which came down from heaven. John 6: 51.

7. *Were the Israelites satisfied with God's provision?*—Our soul loatheth this light bread. Num. 21: 5.

8. *What is said in 2 Tim. 3: 16?*—All Scripture is given by inspiration of God.

9. *What instruction ought we to gain from reading about the sins of Israel?*—To watch against falling into the same sins ourselves.

As in water face answereth to face, so the heart of man to man. Prov. 27: 19.

10. *What provision has God made for the life of our souls?*—His Son, his Spirit and his word.

11. *Are we satisfied with this, or do we prefer earthly pleasures?*—We are prone to love this present world.

12. *Compare Matt. 7: 1, 2 and 1 Cor. 10: 11, 12.*—Judge not, that ye be not judged. For with what judgment ye judge, ye shall be judged: and with what measure ye mete, it shall be measured to you again. All these things are written for our admonition. Wherefore let him that thinketh he standeth, take heed lest he fall.

THE SMITTEN ROCK. (Ex. 17: 1–7.)

1. *What are those who travel in deserts constantly liable to?*—The want of water.

2. *How were the Israelites supplied?*—From a stream that flowed from a rock in Horeb on Moses striking it with his rod. Ex. 17: 6.

3. *Of whom is the smitten rock a beautiful type?*—That rock was Christ. 1 Cor. 10: 4.

4. *What did Jesus say to the woman of Samaria?*—But whosoever drinketh of the water that I shall give him shall never thirst; but the water that I shall give him shall be in him a well of water springing up into everlasting life. John 4: 14.

5. *At the feast of tabernacles, which was a feast commemorative of the sojourn of Israel in the desert, they used to pour out water in remembrance of the smitten rock; when Jesus was present at this ceremony, what did he cry aloud?*—If any man thirst, let him come unto me and drink. John 7: 37.

6. *Have you obeyed that command?*—Let the conscience of each reply. If you have not yet come, come now.

7. *What excuse will you have to offer if you refuse to obey?*—None at all. Prov. 1: 20–31; Rev. 22: 17.

THE BATTLE WITH AMALEK. (Ex. 17: 8–16.)

1. *What is prayer?*—Prayer is the simplest words of the mouth and the earnest desire of the heart, taught by the Holy Spirit and presented through Jesus Christ.

2. *Why do we pray to God?*—Because he is willing to help us, and no one else can.

3. *How did God teach Israel this at Rephidim?*—By giving them victory over the Amalekites in answer to Moses' prayer. Ex. 17: 8–11.

4. *Who were the Amalekites?*—Descendants of Esau, to the south of Palestine.

5. *Was it not very cruel to come out and fight Israel when they were so weak?*—They thought now was their opportunity, but they forgot that God was on Israel's side.

6. *Was not God angry with them for this?*—God sentenced them to constant war, and at last to destruction. Ex. 17: 14, 16.

7. *Which army obtained victory?*—The Israelites'.

8. *How was this?*—By Moses' continued prayer. Ex. 17: 12.

9. *Of whom was Moses a type when he thus interceded for Israel?*—Of Christ, who ever lives to make intercession for us in heaven.

10. *Of whom was Joshua a type while leading on the battle?*—Of the great Captain of our salvation.

11. *What foes has the Christian to contend with?*—The temptations of his own evil heart, of Satan and of sinners around him.

12. *How can he overcome?*—In the strength of the Lord God.

13. *What is the meaning of Jehovah-nissi?*—"The Lord, my banner." Ex. 17: 15.

14. *If this be the banner of the Christian, what is his armor?*—Eph. 6: 10–18.

Be strong in the Lord, and in the power of his might. Put on the whole armor of God, that ye may be able to stand against the wiles of the devil. Eph. 6: 10, 11.

THE COVENANT OF WORKS. (Ex. 19–24.)

1. *What is the human heart most prone to?*—Sin.

2. *What does this show?*—The heart is deceitful above all things, and desperately wicked: who can know it? Jer. 17: 9.

3. *How did God teach this to Israel, and through them to us?*—By practical lessons which showed them their

weakness and wickedness, and their need of a better righteousness than their own, and of a greater sacrifice than the blood of bulls and goats. Gal. 3 : 24.

4. *What is the law?*—The term here refers to the Ten Commandments, and to others that immediately follow.

5. *Under what circumstances did God give the law?* —From the top of Mount Sinai, amidst thunder and lightning, clouds and darkness, trumpet-blast and earthquake. Ex. 19.

6. *Where is Sinai?*—In the wilderness, near the Red Sea.

7. *Could Israel bear the presence of God?*—They could not endure the light of God's presence in their consciences. Our God is a consuming fire. Heb. 12 : 20, 21, 29.

8. *Why not?*—See No. 7.

9. *Who went up into the thick darkness where God was?*—Moses. Ex. 19 : 20; 20 : 21.

10. *When he came forth with God's message to them, what did they promise to do?*—All the words which God had said. Ex. 24 : 3.

11. *Were they able to perform their promise?*—No.

12. *Why?*—From the sinfulness of their own hearts.

13. *Are we able to keep God's holy law now?*—No.

14. *What refuge, then, have we from God's wrath?*—Christ hath redeemed us from the curse of the law, being made a curse for us. Gal. 3 : 13.

THE COVENANT BROKEN. (Ex. 32.)

1. *How long was Moses upon the mount with God?*—Forty days and nights. Ex. 24 : 18.

2. *What awful proof did Israel give of their inability to keep the law, of their forgetfulness of God, and of their own evil hearts while Moses was on the mount?*—They made and worshiped a golden calf, probably after some idol in Egypt. Ex. 32 : 1–6.

3. *When was Moses made acquainted with their sin?* —God told him while he was on the mount. Ex. 32 : 7, 8.

4. *Did he plead for them with God?*—Yes, and his prayer was heard. Ex. 32 : 11–14.

5. *Who was waiting on the side of the mount for Moses when he came down?*—Joshua. Ex. 32 : 17.

6. *What sight did they see?*—The calf, and the people dancing about it. Ex. 32 : 19.

7. *What did Moses do?*—He broke the stone tables, as they had broken the law, and he destroyed the golden calf. Ex. 32 : 19, 20.

8. *Although Joshua was not in the transgression of making the calf, which of Israel's leaders was?*—Aaron. Ex. 32 : 2–5.

9. *Was not his excuse a vain one?*—Yes; and sinners now by silly falsehoods strive in vain to hide their sins.

10. *Why was this painful history recorded?*—For our instruction ; see 1 Cor. 10 : 1–12.

THE SECOND GIVING OF THE LAW. (Ex. 32 : 30–55; 33 and 34.)

1. *Who interceded for Israel at this awful time?*—Moses. Ex. 32 : 30–32.

2. *What testimony did Moses bear against them?*—That they had sinned a great sin. Ex. 32 : 30.

3. *Whom did Moses associate with himself in this act?* —Joshua, Abraham, Isaac and Jacob. Ex. 24 : 13; 32 : 13.

4. *What proof did the Lord give to Moses that he had accepted him?*—Allowing him to see something of his glory and proclaiming him his name. Ex. 33 : 16; 34 : 7.

5. *How was the law given the second time?*—By Moses taking two fresh tables of stone up the mount, and God's writing upon them the Ten Commandments. Ex. 34 : 1, 4, 28.

6. *How long was Moses in the mount this time?*—Forty days and forty nights. Deut. 10 : 10.

7. *What wonderful manifestation was there on the face of Moses that he had been with God, and had spoken to him face to face?*—His face shone brightly. Ex. 33 : 11; 34 : 29, 30.

And there arose not a prophet since in Israel like unto Moses, whom the Lord knew face to face. Deut. 34 : 10.

8. *How did the children of Israel feel when they saw this?*—They were afraid to come near him. Ex. 34 : 30.

9. *What was this a type of?*—Of the blindness of their minds, which prevented them from seeing the truth then, and which prevents them still.

Their minds were blinded : for until this day remaineth the same veil untaken away in the reading of the Old Testament; which veil is done away in Christ. 2 Cor. 3 : 14.

THE TABERNACLE. (Ex. 35–40.)

1. *How did Moses obtain the instruction to make the tabernacle?*—From God himself and a pattern shown him on the mount. Ex. 25 : 9, 40.

2. *What is a tabernacle?*—A tent.

3. *Whom did God specially endow with skill to perform this work?*—Bezaleel and Aholiab and other wise-hearted men. Ex. 36 : 1.

4. *Where did Moses get the materials?*—From the free offerings of the people. Ex. 35 : 21; 36 : 3–7.

5. *Did the women assist? In what?*—Yes. In spinning. Ex. 35 : 22, 25, 26.

6. *What solemn injunction did Moses receive?*—To make the tabernacle and its furniture according to the patterns God had shown him. Ex. 25 : 40; 26 : 30; Heb. 8 : 5.

7. *What expression, used eight times in the fortieth chapter of Exodus, shows that Moses fulfilled the work that God gave him to do?*—As the Lord commanded Moses.

8. *When was the tabernacle reared?*—On the first day (of the first month) of the second year of the sojourn in the wilderness. Ex. 40 : 17.

9. *Of whom is the tabernacle a type?*—Of Jesus Christ, the "true" and "perfect tabernacle." John 2 : 19–21; Heb. 8 : 2; 9 : 11.

10. *Are our bodies compared to a tabernacle and temple?*—Yes; to a tabernacle, to be taken down, in 2 Cor. 5 : 1, and to a temple of the Holy Ghost, to be kept holy, in 1 Cor. 6 : 19.

11. *In what respect was the tabernacle in the wilderness a type of Jesus?*—As the way to the Father's presence. Heb. 9 : 8, 9, 11, 12.

12. *What was its outward appearance?*—Plain, from its badger-skins covering. Ex. 26 : 14. As Christ had no outward beauty. Isa. 53 : 2, 3.

His visage was so marred more than any man, and his form more than the sons of men. Isa. 52 : 14.

13. *Was the inside different? How was this a type of Jesus?*—Yes; it was richly adorned with gold and silver and embroidery. Ex. 31 and 36. So He who was "altogether lovely" (Song of Sol. 5 : 16) pleased his heavenly Father.

Lo a voice from heaven, saying, This is my beloved Son, in whom I am well pleased. Matt. 3 : 17.

A cloud overshadowed them : and a voice came out of the cloud, saying, This is my beloved Son : hear him. Mark 9 : 7.

The centurion said, Truly this man was the Son of God. Mark 15 : 39.

The officers answered, Never man spake like this man. John 7 : 46.

14. To what did Jesus compare himself in John 10 and 14 : 6 ?—To the door of the sheepfold and to a road or way. (See No. 11.)

I am the way, the truth, and the life; no man cometh unto the Father, but by me.

15. How was the brazen altar a type of Jesus?—Because it bore the sacrificial fires which consumed the victims.

16. Who first kindled the fire on this altar?—God himself. Lev. 9 : 24.

17. What is fire a type of?—It is the element of urification Ezek. 21 : 31, 32; 22 : 31; Heb. 12 : 29.

18. What do we deserve?—We cannot possibly conceive the exceeding sinfulness of our estrangement from our Father.

19. Who was the Sin-bearer in our stead?—Christ Jesus.

He was wounded for our transgressions, he was bruised for our iniquities: the chastisement of our peace was upon him; and with his stripes we are healed. Isa. 53 : 5.

Even Jesus, which delivered us from the wrath to come. 1 Thess. 1 : 10.

20. Suppose any Israelite had refused to bring his offering to this altar, what would have been the consequence?—He would have remained unclean and deprived of the privilege of worshiping.

21. Suppose we refuse to lay our sins on Jesus, what will be the consequence?—They will remain upon ourselves, and the wrath of God will abide upon us.

22. What stood next to the brazen altar in the outer court?—The laver. Ex. 38 : 8.

23. What was its use?—For the priests to wash their feet. Ex. 30 : 18-21.

24. What was the laver a type of?—Of the word and Spirit of God, which cleanse and restore our souls.

25. Of what was the laver made?—Of brass, taken from the looking-glasses, or plates of polished metal, which the women used.

26. How does the apostle James allude to this in the first chapter of his Epistle?—Whoso looketh into the perfect law of liberty, and continueth therein, he being not a forgetful hearer, but a doer of the work, this man shall be blessed in his deed.

27. Is the word of God ever compared to water?—Christ also loved the Church, and gave himself for it, that he might sanctify and cleanse it with the washing of water by the word. Eph. 5 : 25, 26.

28. Where else is the word of God alluded to as a cleansing process?—Not by works of righteousness which we have done, but according to his mercy he saved us, by the washing of regeneration, and renewing of the Holy Ghost. Tit. 3 : 5. Except a man be born of water and of the Spirit, he cannot enter into the kingdom of God. John 3 : 5. Of his own will begat he us with the word of truth, that we should be kind of first-fruits of his creatures. James 1 : 18.

29. How did Jesus (the Word of God) declare we must be cleansed?—By himself.

If I wash thee not, thou hast no part with me. John 13 : 8.

30. What objects presented themselves when the doorway curtain of the tabernacle was drawn aside?—The altar of incense, the table of shewbread, the golden candlestick and the curtain or veil of the holy of holies.

31. What did Jesus say of himself in John 9 : 5 ?—As long as I am in the world, I am the light of the world.

32. What is said of the Lord's people in Matt. 5 : 14-16 ?—Ye are the light of the world. A city that is set on a hill cannot be hid.

33. Under what figure is prayer represented in Rev. 8 : 3, 4 ?—The smoke of burning incense.

34. What did the Lord Jesus style himself in John 6 : 35 ?—I am the bread of life: he that cometh to me shall never hunger; and he that believeth on me shall never thirst.

35. Who were permitted to go in and minister in this holy place?—The priests went always into the first tabernacle, accomplishing the service of God. Heb. 9 : 6.

36. Who alone might go into the most holy place?—But into the second went the high priest alone once every year, not without blood, which he offered for himself and for the errors of the people. Heb. 9 : 7.

37. How often might he go in?—See No. 36.

38. Of what is the most holy place a type?—Of the immediate presence of God.

39. Who has entered there?—Seeing then that we have a great High Priest, that is passed into the heavens, Jesus the Son of God, let us hold fast our profession. Heb. 4 : 14.

40. What happened to the beautiful veil of the temple when the Lord Jesus was crucified?—It was rent in twain from the top to the bottom.

41. If man had rent it, would it have been done in the same way? How?—It would have been rent from the bottom.

42. What did this show?—The rending of the veil showed that the way into heaven was now open. Heb. 10 : 19-22.

43. What stood in the most holy place?—The ark of the covenant.

44. Of what was the ark composed?—Of shittim-wood, overlaid with gold. Ex. 25 : 10, 11.

45. How did it represent the glory of Jesus?—By the mercy-seat and cherubim above it. Ex. 25 : 17-22.

46. What was preserved in the ark?—The golden pot that had manna, and Aaron's rod that budded, and the tables of the covenant. Heb. 9 : 4.

47. What was the budding rod a type of?—The resurrection of the dead. 1 Cor. 15 : 42.

48. What was this incorruptible manna a type of?—Being born again, not of corruptible seed, but of incorruptible, by the word of God, which liveth and abideth for ever. 1 Pet. 1 : 23; Acts 2 : 31, 32.

49. Where in the Revelation is this incorruptible manna alluded to?—To him that overcometh will I give to eat of the hidden manna. Rev. 2 : 17.

50. What proof have we that Jesus has gone into heaven with a human body?—Behold my hands and my feet, that it is I myself: handle me, and see; for a spirit hath not flesh and bones as ye see me have. And when he had thus spoken, he showed them his hands and his feet. And while they yet believed not for joy, and wondered, he said unto them, Have ye here any meat? And they gave him a piece of a broiled fish, and of an honeycomb. And he took it, and did eat before them. And he led them out as far as to Bethany, and he lifted up his hands, and blessed them. And it came to pass, while he blessed them, he was parted from them, and carried up into heaven. Luke 24 : 39-43, 50, 51.

51. What hope have we to rest on that we shall share that glory with him?—To him that overcometh will I grant to sit with me in my throne, even as I also overcame, and am set down with my Father in his throne Rev. 3. 21.

The Sacrifices and Offerings. (Lev. and Num. 19.)

1. What is the principal thing treated of in the book of Leviticus?—Access to God by a purified worshiper.

2. Name the four principal offerings.—The burnt-offering, the sin-offering, the trespass-offering and the peace-offering.

3. *What characterized the burnt-offering?*—It was a male without blemish from the herd or the flock, or a turtle-dove or young pigeon; the blood of the beast being sprinkled about, and its body cut up and burnt on the altar. Lev. 1.

4. *In what did the sin-offering and the trespass-offering differ from the burnt-offering?*—In the sin-offering having the blood sprinkled and poured out on and under the altar, and having the fat, and not the whole animal, burnt upon it; and in the trespass-offering being allowed to be of the female sex, and being on account of *special* rather than *general* sin. The sin-offering referred rather to atonement, and the burnt-offering to self-dedication. Lev. 4, 5, 6.

5. *What was there different to both these in the peace-offering?*—The peace-offering, whether from the herd or the flock, was an expression of thankfulness to God for his gifts. Lev. 3; 7 : 11–38.

6. *What difference was there between the meat- (or food-) and the burnt-offering?*—The meat-offering, of flour, oil and wine, was also a sacrifice of thanksgiving. Lev. 2.

7. *Who was prefigured by all these sacrifices?*—Jesus Christ, the *great* Atonement and the great self-devoted Sacrifice.

8. *What is said in Heb. 10 : 1–18 ?*—The sacrifice of Christ's body, once offered, hath for ever taken away sins.

9. *Where was Moses when God gave him the instruction about sacrifices?*—On Mount Sinai. Ex. 24 : 18; 32 : 15.

10. *What special type of Jesus was there in the cleansing of the leper?*—Christ brings near those who were far off, as the leper was obliged to be kept; and Christ was slain for us, like the one bird, and rose to heaven for us like the other. Lev. 14.

> But now in Christ Jesus ye who sometimes were far off are made nigh by the blood of Christ. Eph. 2 : 13.
> Who was delivered for our offences, and raised again for our justification. Rom. 4 : 25.

11. *What was the leprosy in the house a type of?*—Corruption. Lev. 14.

> Flesh and blood cannot inherit the kingdom of God; neither doth corruption inherit incorruption. 1 Cor. 15 : 50.

12. *Name some of the ceremonies which took place on the great day of atonement.*—Aaron the high priest made sin-offerings for himself and for the people, and sprinkled the blood upon the mercy-seat in the most holy place; confessed the sins of the people over the scapegoat, and sent it away into the wilderness; and offered burnt-offerings for himself and for the people. Lev. 16.

13. *What is the meaning of the word "atonement"?*—Reconciliation, or setting at one again, by a sacrifice in another's stead.

14. *Who atoned for our sins?*—Jesus Christ, who suffered in our place the punishment of our sins.

15. *How did the scapegoat set this forth?*—It bore the sins of Israel, as Christ bears ours.

16. *Have not you and I committed sin?*—Every day of our lives.

17. *Should we not ask ourselves where is our sin?*—It is the most important question we can ask ourselves.

18. *Where must it be—either by faith laid on Jesus, or where?*—Still resting on ourselves, with all its burden and its curse.

19. *What was the ceremony connected with the red heifer?*—The heifer was slain and burnt, and its blood was sprinkled before the tabernacle.

20. *What was the appointed use of the ashes of the red heifer?*—They were mixed with water and sprinkled upon persons who in various ways had become unclean, and as a token of purification for sin.

21. *Who was again prefigured in this type?*—How much more shall the blood of Christ, who through the eternal Spirit offered himself without spot to God, purge your conscience from dead works to serve the living God! Heb. 9 : 14.

THE FEASTS. (Lev. 23.)

1. *What is a type?*—A thing that represents another thing, or has some points of resemblance to it, or is intended to foreshow it.

2. *Why did God teach us so much truth in this way?*—To make it clearer to our minds.

3. *How do we teach little children?*—By pictures, imitations, comparisons and tales.

4. *What is God's way of pardoning sin?*—Accepting on behalf of every one who believes the punishment which Jesus bore in his stead.

5. *How has he shown this to us?*—By his accepting the sacrifices which referred to Christ.

6. *What is faith?*—Trusting in Christ as our own Saviour.

7. *How is faith in the Lord Jesus shown us in the typical sacrifices of the Old Testament?*—Because they could have no value in themselves, but only as referring to Him that was to come.

8. *What does this chapter especially describe to us?*—The Jewish feasts.

9. *Which is the first "feast" spoken of?*—The Sabbath.

10. *How often was it to be kept?*—Every seventh day

11. *When was the keeping of the Sabbath first enjoined?*—In the garden of Eden, when God first sanctified it or set it apart for holy use. (See also Ex. 16 and 20.)

> God blessed the seventh day, and sanctified it: because that in it he had rested from all his work which God created and made. Gen. 2 : 3.

12. *Why is it here called a "feast?"*—Because it is a day of sacred rest. (And see No. 14.)

13. *Does the word "feast" in this chapter mean a time of eating and drinking?*—No; but of meeting together for a holy, happy purpose. Lev. 23 : 4.

14. *What is the meaning of the word "festival?"*—A time of joyful worship.

15. *Does not God always unite happiness or joy with religion?*—He does.

> If thou turn away thy foot from the sabbath, from doing thy pleasure on my holy day; and call the sabbath a delight, the holy of the Lord, honorable; and shalt honor him, not doing thine own ways, nor finding thine own pleasure, nor speaking thine own words: then shalt thou delight thyself in the Lord; and I will cause thee to ride upon the high places of the earth, and feed thee with the heritage of Jacob thy father: for the mouth of the Lord hath spoken it. Isa. 58 : 13, 14,

16. *If it be not so to us, what is the cause?*—We have either no religion at all, or not enough to make us happy.

17. *Of what was the Jewish Sabbath a type?*—Of the rest of heaven. Heb. 4 : 8–11.

18. *How can our souls, even in this world, "enter into rest"?*—We may enjoy the rest of a steadfast faith, an anchored hope and an abiding peace.

19. *Which was the second feast or festival spoken of?*—The feast of the Passover or of unleavened bread. Lev 23 : 5, 6.

20. *When was that kept? How often?*—It began on the fifteenth day of the first month, about our March or April. Once a year.

21. *How was it kept?*—By the sacrifice of a lamb, the use of unleavened bread and offering the first-fruits of the early harvest. (But see No. 24.)

22. *When was this instituted?*—When the Israelites came out of Egypt.

23 *What did the Passover teach them, and what must it teach us?*--To remember their deliverance by blood, and to look for our own deliverance by the same means.

24. *What feast or festival came next?*—The offering of the first-fruits of the harvest at Pentecost.

25. *What ceremony were they to perform with the first sheaf?*—The priest was to wave it before the Lord. Lev. 23 : 10, 11.

26. *What did "waving" it mean?*—An act of worship of the Lord of the whole earth.

27. *Whom did that first sheaf represent?*—Now is Christ risen from the dead, and become the first-fruits of them that slept. 1 Cor. 15 : 20.

28. *Did Jesus compare himself to wheat when speaking of his death?*—The hour is come, that the Son of man should be glorified. Verily, verily, I say unto you, Except a corn of wheat fall into the ground and die, it abideth alone: but if it die, it bringeth forth much fruit.

29. *What were the Israelites to do fifty days after they had brought in the first-fruits?*—To offer a new meat-offering to the Lord. Lev. 15 : 15–21.

30. *Of what was this a type?*—This feast was a type of the outpouring of the Holy Ghost, fifty days after Christ our Passover was sacrificed for us, when the apostles received the first-fruits of the Spirit, and presented to God the first-fruit converts of the Christian Church. Acts 2.

31. *What festival was held on the first day of the seventh month?*—The feast of trumpets. Lev. 15 : 23–25.

32. *Of what was this a type?*—Of the call to repentance and of the preaching of the gospel.

Cry aloud, spare not, lift up thy voice like a trumpet, and show my people their transgression, and the house of Jacob their sins. Isa. 58 : 1.

Go ye into all the world, and preach the gospel to every creature. Mark 16 : 15.

33. *How many days after this festival of trumpets was the great day of atonement kept?*—Nine days.

34. *What remarkable ceremonies took place on this day?*—Aaron the high priest made sin-offerings for himself and for the people, and sprinkled the blood upon the mercy-seat in the most holy place; confessed the sins of the people over the scapegoat, and sent it away into the wilderness; and offered burnt-offerings for himself and for the people. Lev. 16.

35. *Are we not very prone to excuse ourselves when looking into our own sinful hearts?*—The heart is deceitful above all things, and desperately wicked: who can know it? Jer. 17 : 9.

36. *Where shall we best discover God's estimate of sin?*—In those parts of Scripture which contain his denunciations against it, his punishments of it, and (above all) his provision, in both the Old and New Testaments, for the pardon and removal of it.

37. *What other ceremony took place on this day, mentioned in this chapter and not in the sixteenth chapter?*—The blowing of a trumpet on the first day of the month. Lev. 23 : 24.

38. *Where is this more fully described?*—Lev. 25 : 9.

39. *Of what were the trumpets made?*—Of silver. Num. 10 : 2.

40. *Of what was the jubilee a type?*—It was typical of our redemption by Christ from the slavery of sin and Satan, and of our restoration to the glorious liberty of the children of God.

41. *How are we interested in it?*—See No. 40.

42. *How many days after the day of atonement did the feast of tabernacles occur?*—Five days. Lev. 23 : 34.

43. *What ceremonies marked this festival?*—The offering of sacrifices and the dwelling in booths.

44. *How many days did they keep it?*—Eight days.

45. *What is this festival a type of?*—Of heaven. Rev. 21 : 3, 4.

46. *What does the twenty-ninth chapter of Numbers tell of?*—Of the offerings at the feasts of trumpets and tabernacles and on the day of atonement.

47. *Is the feast of tabernacles ever mentioned in the New Testament?*—Now the Jews' feast of tabernacles was at hand. In the last day, that great day of the feast, Jesus stood and cried, saying, If any man thirst, let him come unto me and drink. John 7 : 2, 37.

48. *At what time of the year was King Solomon's temple dedicated?*—Solomon kept the feast seven days ii the seventh month, and all Israel with him, a very great congregation, from the entering in of Hamath unto the river of Egypt. 2 Chron. 7 : 8, 10.

49. *And when was the second temple dedicated?*—The children of the Captivity kept the Passover upon the fourteenth day of the first month. Ezra 6 : 19.

50. *Of what were those buildings a type?*—Of the Lord God Almighty and the Lamb, who are the temple of heaven. Rev, 21 : 22. (And see Rev. 21 : 3, 4, above—No. 45.)

THE NUMBERING OF THE ISRAELITES AND DEPARTURE FROM SINAI. (Num. 1–4, 7–10.)

1. *What do these chapters describe?*—The numbering of the people, the duties of the priests and Levites, the offerings for the tabernacle, the marchings of the Israelites, etc.

2. *How long had the children of Israel remained at Sinai?*—About eleven months.

3. *Tell me some of the most remarkable events that had occurred there?*—The giving of the law, the worship of the golden calf, the making of the tabernacle, and the punishment of Nadab and Abihu.

4. *How long was it after they left Egypt that the tabernacle was first set up?*—About ten months. Ex. 40 : 2.

5. *What rite did they celebrate on the fourteenth of the first month?*—The Passover. Num. 9 : 1–5.

6. *What did God command Moses to do on the first of the second month?*—To number the people. Num. 1 : 1–3.

7. *Whom did God accept for his service instead of the first-born?*—The Levites. Num. 3 : 12; 8 : 16.

8. *Did the numbers tell out exactly the same?*—The first-born were two hundred and seventy-three more. Num. 3 : 46.

9. *How was the difference arranged?*—Five shekels (or about $2.75) each was paid to Aaron for them. Num. 8.

10. *How were the children of Israel to encamp and to march on their journey?*—Each tribe was to march and encamp by itself, in a fixed order and place, the Levites in the midst. Num. 2.

11. *Who provided the wagons to carry the tabernacle?*—The princes or heads of the tribes. Num. 7 : 2, 3.

12. *Why had not the sons of Kohath any wagon allotted to them?*—Because their burdens were carrie on their shoulders.

13. *What part of the tabernacle did they carry?*—The holy things of the tabernacle. Num. 4 : 2–15.

14. *What did each of the princes of Israel offer as a gift to the service of the tabernacle?*—Gold and silver vessels and animals for sacrifice. Num. 7.

15. *What direction did the Lord give Moses as to making trumpets?*—That they should be of silver, and be used for assembling and for marching in journeys or in war. Num. 10 : 1–10.

16. *On which day did the cloud move?*— On the twentieth day of the second month of the second year. Num. 10 : 11.

17. *Of what was the moving of the cloud to inform the Israelites?*—That they were to proceed on their journey. Num. 9 : 17.

18. *When the first alarm of the trumpets was given,*

which tribes marched first?—Judah, Issachar and Zebulun.

19. *How many encamped on the east of the tabernacle?* The above three. Num. 2 : 3–9.

20. *What immediately followed these three tribes?*—The tabernacle. Num. 10 : 17 ; 7 : 7, 8.

21. *Which three tribes followed these wagons?*—Reuben, Simeon and Gad. Num. 10 : 18–20.

22. *What part of the tabernacle went next?*—The sanctuary. Num. 10 : 21.

23. *Name the six tribes that followed.*—Ephraim, Manasseh and Benjamin; Dan, Asher and Naphtali.

24. *Whom did Moses entreat to accompany them?*—Hobab, his father-in-law. Num. 10 : 29.

25. *Did he not at first refuse?*—He did. Num. 10 : 30.

26. *What proofs have we afterward that he changed his mind and went with the Israelites into the promised land?*—The children of the Kenite, Moses' father-in-law, went up out of the city of palm trees with the children of Judah into the wilderness of Judah, which lieth in the south of Arad; and they went and dwelt among the people. Judg. 1 : 16. Now Heber the Kenite, which was of the children of Hobab the father-in-law of Moses, had severed himself from the Kenites, and pitched his tent unto the plain of Zaanaim, which is by Kedesh. Judg. 4 : 11.

27. *To what family did Jonadab, mentioned in 2 Kings 10 and Jer. 35, belong?*—To the Kenites, that came of Hemath, the father of Rechab. 1 Chron. 2 : 55 ; 2 Kings 10 : 15.

28. *When all were ready for marching what beautiful prayer did Moses offer?*—Rise up, Lord, and let thine enemies be scattered; and let them that hate thee flee before thee. Num. 10 : 35.

29. *And what when the ark rested again?*—Return, O Lord, unto the many thousands of Israel. Num. 10 : 36.

TRANSGRESSIONS. (Num. 11.)

1. *By what were the children of Israel in the wilderness chiefly distinguished?* — By their repeated rebellions against God. Heb. 3 : 8–12 ; Ps. 106 : 7, 8, 13–46.

2. *Of what should their sad history warn us?*—Of the sad consequences of sin.

3. *On what did the Lord feed Israel while at Sinai?*—On manna.

4. *Ought they not, then, to have trusted God on their journey? Did they?*—They ungratefully and discontentedly desired a change of food. Num. 11 : 1–6.

5. *How were they punished?*—Many of them were destroyed by fire · and others were diseased by the quails that were sent in answer to their demand for *flesh* to eat.

6. *Did not Moses feel their continual provocation too much for him?*—He complained to God of the burden it was to him. Num. 11 : 11–15.

7. *How did the Lord assist him?*—He appointed seventy elders to assist him. Num. 11 : 16, 17.

8. *How did Joshua show his affection for his master and zeal for his honor?*—By telling him of two men who seemed to be unlawfully exercising the authority of Moses in the camp. Num. 11 : 26–28.

9. *What was Moses' beautiful reply?*—Enviest thou for my sake? Would God that all the Lord's people were prophets (or true teachers), and that the Lord would put his Spirit upon them!

10. *How did the people behave when they had got the food they coveted?*—They probably indulged in it to excess, forgetting the warning in Num. 11 : 20.

11. *How did the Lord punish them for their sin?*—The quails produced a disease or plague among them. Num. 11 : 19, 20, 33. See No. 5.

12. *What lessons should we reap from their trans-*

gressions?—With many of them God was not well pleased, for they were overthrown in the wilderness. Now these things were our examples, to the intent we should not lust after evil things, as they also lusted. 1 Cor. 10 : 5, 6.

MIRIAM'S SIN AND PUNISHMENT. (Num. 12.)

1. *What affecting proof have we here that Rom. 3 : 10 is true?*—The sin of Miriam and Aaron shows that there is none righteous, no, not one.

2. *What was the sin of Miriam and Aaron?*—They claimed equal authority with Moses himself. Num. 12 : 2.

3. *What special favor had God given to Moses?*—More friendly conversation with himself and a near view of his glory. Num. 12 : 8.

4. *Ought any one aspire to a station in which God has not placed him?*—St. Paul said: I have learned, in whatsoever state I am, therewith to be content; and, Godliness with contentment is great gain. For we brought nothing into this world, and it is certain we can carry nothing out. And having food and raiment, let us be therewith content. 1 Tim. 6 : 6–8.

5. *What special proof did God give of his displeasure?*—He made Miriam a leper. Num. 12 : 10.

6. *Who pleaded for Miriam?*—Aaron with Moses, and Moses with God. Num. 12 : 11, 13.

7. *How did the Lord mitigate her punishment?*—By removing her disease in seven days. Num. 12 : 14, 15.

8. *Of what was her punishment the type?*—Of the loathsomeness of sin in the eyes of God.

9. *In what way did the Lord permit the whole camp to sympathize with Miriam?*—By not requiring them to go on their way until she was restored.

THE REPORT OF THE SPIES.

1. *Where were the children of Israel at this time?*—In the wilderness of Paran. Ex. 12 : 16 ; 13 : 3.

2. *Was it far from the land of Canaan?*—One end of it was near to Judah.

3. *What did God command Moses to do?*—To send men to search the land of Canaan. Num. 13 : 2.

4. *Whom did Moses select for this errand?*—Heads of the tribes.

5. *What change did he make in the name of one of them?*—He called Oshea, the son of Nun, Jehoshua or Joshua. Num. 13 : 16.

6. *Give the meaning of the name before and after the change, and then say of whom he was the type.*—"Help" before, and "help of Jehovah" or "Saviour" after—a type of Christ the Saviour.

7. *To whom did Jacob refer in Gen. 49 : 24?*—To Joseph, another type of Christ.

8. *How long were they in searching the land?*—Forty days.

9. *What report did they bring?*—That the land flowed with milk and honey, but that the inhabitants were giants and the cities great and walled. Num. 13 : 26–28, 31–33.

10. *Did all the twelve join in the cowardly report?*—All but Caleb and Joshua. Num. 13 : 30; 14 : 6–9.

11. *What effect did this have on the people?*—They were in great distress, and proposed returning to Egypt. Num. 14 : 1–4.

12. *How did Moses and Aaron act?*—They fell on their faces in humiliation and intercessory prayer. Num. 14 : 5.

13. *What did Caleb and Joshua say?*—That the Lord was with Israel, and that they had nothing to fear from the inhabitants of the land. Num. 14 : 6–9.

14. *Who appeared at the moment when they were about to be stoned?*—God himself in his glory. Num. 14 : 10.

15. *What did he propose to Moses?*—To disinherit

Israel, and to make of Moses a mightier nation than theirs. Num. 14 : 11, 12.

16. *Did Moses accept this great honor?*—No; he pleaded for their pardon instead.

17. *What special mercy did the Lord promise to Caleb and Joshua?*—That they alone should enter the land of Canaan. Num. 14 : 30.

18. *How did he punish the ten rebels?*—They died of the plague. Num. 14: 37.

19. *What punishment did the Lord lay on the whole congregation?*—To wander forty years in the wilderness till they died. Num. 14 : 33.

20. *Of what foolish act were they guilty next day?*—They entered the land before the time.

21. *How were they punished?*—They were attacked and driven back. Num. 14 : 40–45.

THE SABBATH-BREAKER, THE SIN OF KORAH, AND THE BUDDING ROD. (Num. 15, 16, 17.)

1. *Of what sin was a man found guilty about this time?*—Of gathering sticks upon the Sabbath-day. Num. 15 : 32.

2. *What did they do with him?*—They brought him to Moses. Num. 15 : 33.

3. *How was he punished?*—He was stoned to death by God's command. Num. 15 : 35, 36.

4. *Had not God already declared his mind about this sin?*—Ye shall keep the sabbath therefore; for it is holy unto you: every one that defileth it shall surely be put to death; for whosoever doeth any work therein, that soul shall be cut off from among his people. Ex. 31 : 14.

5. *Had he here said* how *the man was to be put to death?*—He had not.

6. *Does this not show us that Moses acted in everything immediately under the Lord's direction?*—It does. Num. 15 : 34, 35.

7. *What did the Lord order the people to make, that they might keep in remembrance his commandments?*—A blue fringed ribbon on the borders of their garments. Num. 15 : 38–40.

8. *Who was Korah?*—A Levite. Num. 16 : 8.

9. *Who were Dathan and Abiram, On and Peleth?*—Of the tribe of Reuben. Num. 16 : 1.

10. *What sin did they commit?*—They rebelled against the authority of Moses and Aaron. Num. 16 : 3.

11. *Had they not lately had a warning of this very sin in Miriam's case?*—The very same. Num. 12.

12. *What did Moses propose for these men to do, to prove whether God accepted them as priests or not?*—That they should come to the tabernacle, burning incense, to see if God would accept them. Num. 16 : 7, 18.

13. *In what way did God at once manifest his displeasure?*—By commanding Moses and Aaron and the congregation to keep away from the rebellious company and their habitations (Num. 16 : 20–24), when the earth opened and swallowed them up. Num. 16 : 31–33.

14. *How did the two hundred and fifty men who had thus transgressed die?*—A fire from the Lord consumed them. Num. 15 : 38–40.

15. *Did this still the murmurings of the people?*—The people then charged Moses and Aaron with killing the people of the Lord. Num. 16 : 41.

16. *What happened the next day?*—See No. 15.

17. *How did God again appear to vindicate the honor of his own appointed priesthood?*—Above fourteen thousand were struck dead by the plague. Num. 16 : 49.

18. *What did Moses command Aaron to do to avert the judgment he felt was about to fall on the people?*—To burn incense and make an atonement. Num. 16 : 46.

19. *Did God accept the service and own the act?*—He immediately stopped the plague. Num. 16 : 47, 48.

20. *Of whom was Aaron the type?*—Of Christ, our ever-living Intercessor.

21. *And of what was incense the type?*—The prayers of saints. Rev. 5 : 8.

22. *What was done with the censers of the rebels?*—They were beaten into plates to cover the altar, as a memorial of their sin. Num. 16 : 38–40.

23. *How did the Lord himself show whom he had chosen?*—By causing Aaron's rod to bud. Ex. 17 : 1–10.

24. *And what proof has he given to us that Jesus " is able to save to the uttermost " all that put their trust in him?*—By raising him from the dead. Acts 17 : 31.

25. *Of what was the budding rod a type?*—Of the resurrection and eternal life of Christ.

26. *Why is resurrection a proof that Jesus is the Son of God?*—Because he laid down his life and took it again by his divine power. Acts 2.

27. *Could any one less than God atone for sin?*—No, for sin is against God. " Thanks be unto God for his unspeakable gift!"

THE SIN OF MOSES AND AARON; AARON AND MIRIAM'S DEATH. (Num. 20.)

1. *Where did Miriam die?*—At Kadesh, in the desert of Zin. Num. 20 : 1.

2. *What trial of their faith did the children of Israel have here?*—The want of water. Num. 20 : 2.

3. *How did they behave?*—They reproached Moses for it. Num. 20 : 2–5.

4. *What did the Lord command Moses to do?*—To speak to the rock before the people, and it should give forth water.

5. *How did Moses in this matter dishonor the Lord?*—He spoke as if he and Aaron, by their own power, would bring the water out; and he also struck the rock. Num. 20 : 10, 11.

6. *What punishment did he and Aaron bring upon themselves for this sin?*—They were not allowed to enter the promised land. Num. 20 : 12.

7. *How many times did Moses mention this in his after writings?*—Five times: Num. 27 : 14; Deut. 1 : 37 ; 3 : 26; 31 : 2; 32 : 51.

8. *Did the Lord alter his purpose?*—No.

9. *How did the Edomites behave at this time to the children of Israel?*—They ungraciously refused them a passage through their land. Num. 20 : 14–21.

10. *From whom had the Edomites descended?*—From " Esau, who was Edom." Gen. 36 : 1.

11. *Why were they called by this name?*—Esau was called Edom, or " red," from the red pottage he got from Jacob. Gen. 25 : 30.

12. *What event happened at Mount Hor?*—The death of Aaron. Num. 20 : 22–29.

13. *What solemnity attended it?*—The removal, first, of his priestly robes, and putting them on Eleazar his son.

14. *What mark of respect did the children of Israel pay to the memory of Aaron?*—They mourned for him thirty days.

15. *Of whom was Aaron a type?*—Of Jesus our great High Priest.

16. *What is the meaning of consecrated?*—Set apart for the service of God.

17. *How was Aaron a type of Jesus in this?*—Jesus was anointed by the Holy Ghost, sanctified or set apart for his atoning and interceding work.

18. *What is the meaning of the name Christ?*—Anointed.

19. *Where is Jesus spoken of as Intercessor?*—Jesus, ... because he continueth ever, hath an unchangeable priesthood. Wherefore he is able also to save them

to the uttermost that come unto God by him, seeing he ever liveth to make intercession for them. Heb. 7 : 22, 24. 25.

20. *Which of the apostles had a vision of Jesus dressed in priestly garments ?*—John, in Rev. 1 : 12, 13.

21. *How is the Lord Jesus described in Heb. 4 : 14 16 ?*—As a great High Priest. Seeing, then, that we have a great High Priest that is passed into the heavens, Jesus the Son of God.

22. *Read Ps. 89 : 15 and 119 : 103, and say what part of Aaron's robe set these forth ?*—The "golden bells and the pomegranates" "upon the hem" of it. Blessed is the people that know the joyful sound! they shall walk, O Lord, in the light of thy countenance. How sweet are thy words unto my taste! yea, sweeter than honey to my mouth. Ex. 28 : 34.

23. *Is the perfume of Aaron's garments ever spoken of in connection with the Lord Jesus ?*—All thy garments smell of myrrh, and aloes, and cassia, out of the ivory palaces, whereby they have made thee glad. Ps. 45 : 8.

24. *In how many respects does the priesthood of the Lord Jesus excel the priesthood of Aaron ?*—In its divinity and duration, Christ being God and a Priest for ever.

25. *What higher order of priesthood is compared to the priesthood of the Lord Jesus Christ ?*—The priesthood of Melchizedek, which *seemed* to be everlasting, nothing being said in Scripture of his birth and death. Heb. 5, 6, 7.

THE BRAZEN SERPENT. (Num. 21 : 1-9.)

1. *Who came and fought with Israel ?*—King Arad, the Canaanite.

2. *Which army was victorious ?*—The Israelites'.

3. *How came it about ?*—Because they made a vow unto God to destroy the Canaanites if he gave them the victory.

4. *Why were the people obliged to take such a long way round ?*—To avoid the land of Edom. Num. 20 : 21.

5. *How did they meet this trouble ?*—They were much discouraged, and complained of the want of bread and water.

6. *How did the Lord punish them ?*—By means of fiery serpents—fiery in their color or their bite.

7. *What remedy was Moses commanded to prepare ?*— A serpent of brass upon a pole, that the people might look upon it and live.

8. *Of whom was this a type ?*—Of Christ.

9. *How ?*—As the sinner may look upon him crucified, and live.

10. *Of what wicked spirit are the serpents a type ?*— Of that old serpent, the devil.

11. *Are we all in the same danger ?*—We are.

12. *What is our remedy ?*—To look unto Christ by faith.

13. *What is faith ?*—Faith in Christ is looking to him, fleeing to him, coming to him, apprehending or laying hold on him, trusting in him, leaning upon him.

BALAAM. (Num. 21 : 10-35; 22-26; and 31 : 1-8.)

1. *How far had the children of Israel got on their journey ?*—To the wilderness before Moab.

2. *Where was Moab ?*—On the east side on the Jordan.

3 *What interesting event had occurred at Beer ?*— A supply of water, followed by a song of praise.

4. *What two mighty kings did the children of Israel conquer and slay at this time ?*—Sihon, king of the Amorites, and Og, king of Bashan. Num. 21 : 23, 24, 33–35.

5. *What description is given of Og in Deuteronomy ?* That he was a giant.

For only Og king of Bashan remained of the remnant of giants; behold, his bedstead was a bedstead of iron; is it not in Rabbath of the children of Ammon? nine cubits was the length thereof, and four cubits the breadth of it, after the cubit of a man Deut. 3 : 11.

6. *How many times in the Psalms are these conquest spoken of ?*—Twice: Ps. 135 : 11 and 136 : 19, 20.

7. *What was the name of the king of Moab ?*—Balak Num. 22 : 4.

8. *How did he feel when he saw the host of Israel ?*— He was greatly alarmed. Num. 22 : 2-6.

9. *Who was Balaam ?*—A noted heathen soothsayer, or pretended prophet, who lived by the Euphrates in Mesopotamia, and who sometimes received revelations from God. Num. 22 : 5; 24 : 1, 2.

10. *Why did Balak desire so much to see him ?*—To get him to curse the Israelites, so that he might overcome them. Num. 22 : 6.

11. *Did Balaam desire to go ?*—Yes, as the rewards that were offered him tempted his covetousness.

12. *What hindered him ?*—The command of God Num. 22 : 12.

13. *Did God permit him to have his own way ?*—Yes. Num. 22 : 20.

14. *Did that show that God was pleased with the errand ?*—No; but it gave him an opportunity of showing his power over him in a more public and striking manner. Num. 23 : 7-12.

15. *How did God show his disapprobation ?*—By sending his angel to stop him on his way. Num. 22 : 22.

16. *Did God send Balaam back, or permit him to go on ?*—He let him go on. Num. 22 : 35.

17. *Had Balaam any power when he got there ?*—Only to say what God told him. Num. 22 : 38.

18. *Did he try by divination to accomplish Balak's wish ?*—Yes, while Balak offered sacrifice. Num. 23 : 3, 15, 23; 24 : 1.

19. *Did it succeed ?*—No; God made him utter a blessing instead of a curse. Num. 23 : 8–10, 20–24; 24 : 2–9.

20. *How did Balak feel when he found he had brought a blessing instead of a curse on his enemies ?*—He was angry with Balaam. Num. 24 : 10.

21. *When Balaam found that he could not prevail by enchantment, did he yield himself to the power of God ?*— Yes. Num. 24 : 13, 14.

22. *What beautiful prophecy did he utter of the glory of the Lord Jesus ?*—I see him, but not now (not as already come); I behold him, etc. Num. 24 : 17.

23. *How did he show he was a bad man ?*—By his infamous advice to Balak to tempt the children of Israel to sin.

24. *What was his end ?*—He was killed by the Israelites in battle with the Midianites. Num. 31 : 8.

25. *Of whom is he a type ?*—Of the enemies of God.

26. *Is he mentioned in the New Testament ?*—Woe unto them! for they have gone in the way of Cain, and run greedily after the error of Balaam for reward. Jude 11.

THE CITIES OF REFUGE. (Num. 26 and 27; 31-35.)

1. *What does chap. 26 record ?*—The numbering of the Israelites.

2. *After the numbering how many men were left of those who came out of Egypt with Moses ?*—Only two, Caleb and Joshua. Num. 26 : 65.

3. *How was this?*—God had said that all the rest should die in the wilderness. Num. 26 : 65.

4. *What lesson should it teach us?*—To beware of unbelief. Heb. 3 : 7–19.

5. *What kind arrangement did the Lord make for one family when all the men of it were dead?*—That the property of the father should go to his daughters. Num. 27 : 1–11.

6. *What petition did Moses present to the Lord at the end of chap. 27?*—That he would provide him a successor. Num. 27 : 15–17.

7. *Whom did the Lord appoint?*—Joshua.

8. *Of which tribe was Joshua?*—Ephraim. 1 Chron. 7 : 22–27.

9. *How does Jacob allude to him and to the Lord Jesus (of whom Joshua was a type) in Gen. 49 : 24?*—His bow abode in strength, and the arms of his hands were made strong by the hands of the mighty God of Jacob (from thence is the shepherd, the stone of Israel).

10. *What does chap. 31 describe?*—The defeat of the Midianites.

11. *How was the spoil to be purified?*—By fire or by water.

12. *To what is the judgment of the last day compared?*—1 Cor. 3 : 13–15.

13. *Which of the children of Israel had their inheritance on the east of the Jordan?*—Reuben, Gad and half the tribe of Manasseh. Num. 32.

14. *What do chaps. 33 and 34 describe?*—The forty-two stages of the journey through the wilderness, and the boundaries of Canaan, and the officers appointed to divide it.

15. *How many cities out of the tribes of Israel were to be given to the Levites?*—Forty-eight. Num. 35 : 7.

16. *For what purpose were six of these cities to be separated?*—For cities of refuge. Num. 35 : 6.

17. *Who had the privilege of fleeing thither?*—Any one who had accidentally killed another. Num. 35 : 11, 12, 24–28.

18. *Was there any protection to be afforded to the murderer?*—No. Num. 35 : 16–21.

19. *In what relationship did the "revenger of blood" stand to the slain person?*—Next of kin.

20. *How many witnesses were necessary to prove the wicked deed?*—Two.

21. *What event released the manslayer from the city of refuge, and permitted him to go at large again without fear of death?*—The death of the high priest. Num. 35 : 25.

22. *Of whom were those cities of refuge a type?*—Of Christ, the sinner's refuge from Satan and the wrath to come.

23. *Can you describe where those cities of refuge stood?*—Three on the east of Jordan, in the tribes of Reuben, Gad and Manasseh; and three on the west, in Galilee, Samaria and Judah. Deut. 4 : 41–43.
> And they appointed Kedesh in Galilee in Mount Naphtali, and Shechem in Mount Ephraim, and Kirjath-arba, which is Hebron, in the mountain of Judah. Josh. 20 : 7.

24. *Were they in valleys or on hills?*—On hills.

25. *Why was this?*—So as to be more easily seen.

26. *Of whom is the manslayer a type?*—Of Satan, the great enemy of souls.

27. *How can we be said to be manslayers?*—By the self-destruction of sin.
> O Israel, thou hast destroyed thyself; but in me is thine help. Hos. 13 : 9.

28. *Who is represented by the way to those cities?*—Jesus Christ.
> I am the way, the truth, and the life; no man cometh unto the Father, but by me. John 14 : 6.
> By a new and living way, which he hath consecrated for us, through the veil, that is to say, his flesh. Heb. 10 : 20.

29. *Of what is the avenger a type?*—Of the law, which requires us to do or die. Rom. 3 : 9–19; Gal. 3 : 22–24.

30. *Are we all conscious of our danger?*—Sinners are dead in sin, and both wise and foolish often slumber and sleep.

31. *Who must arouse us?*—Christ, by his awakening and enlightening Spirit. John 16 : 7–9; Eph. 5 : 13, 14.

32. *Are there any hinderances in the way?*—None from Christ himself.
> Come unto me, all ye that labor and are heavy laden, and I will give you rest. Matt. 11 : 28.

33. *To what is allusion made in Ps. 9 : 9; 57 : 1; 59 : 16; 61 : 4; 62 : 7, 8; 71 : 7; 91 : 1, 2; 142 : 4, 5?*—To the refuge we have in God, through Christ.
> The Lord also will be a refuge for the oppressed, a refuge in times of trouble. Ps. 9 : 9.
> Be merciful unto me, O God, be merciful unto me: for my soul trusteth in thee: yea, in the shadow of thy wings will I make my refuge, until these calamities be overpast. Ps. 57 : 1.

DEUTERONOMY. (Deuteronomy.)

1. *When was the book of Deuteronomy written?*—A little before Moses' death. Deut. 1 : 3.

2. *Where were Moses and the children of Israel at this time?*—In the land of Moab, on the east of Jordan. Deut. 1 : 1, 4, 5.

3. *Of what is the book of Deuteronomy a summary?*—Of much of the history and the laws contained in the three foregoing books.

4. *Of whom does Moses speak in Deut. 18 : 15–19 as "the prophet"?*—Of Jesus Christ. Acts 3 : 20–22.

5. *What beautiful ceremony does he bid them perform when they should get into the promised land?*—To bring a basket of first-fruits to the priest as a thank-offering to God. Deut. 26 : 1–11.

6. *What was the name of the two mountains on which the blessing and the curse were to be written?*—Gerizim and Ebal. Deut. 27 : 1–8, 11–13.

7. *What fearful prophecy and warning did Moses utter?*—Curses of pestilence, drought, war, famine and other evils for disobedience of God's law. Deut. 28–30.

8. *In what way (chap. 31) did the Lord signally set apart Joshua to the office of leader?*—By appearing to him in the tabernacle in the pillar of cloud. Deut. 31 : 14, 15.

9. *In what way did Moses preserve what he said to them?*—By writing it and delivering it to the priests (Deut. 31 : 9), to be put in the ark of the covenant. Deut. 31 : 24–26.

10. *What special song was he commanded to write and rehearse before them?*—That contained in Deut. 32 : 1–43; 31 : 19.

11. *Who assisted him in the task?*—Joshua. Deut. 32 : 44.

12. *What did the Lord command Moses to do immediately after he had finished this work?*—To go up Mount Nebo and die. Deut. 32 : 48–52.

13. *In pronouncing his dying blessing on the tribes of Israel which did he single out for peculiar honor?*—Levi and Ephraim and Manasseh.

14. *What spot on earth was appointed by God to be the place of the death of Moses?*—The top of Pisgah. Deut. 34 : 1.

15. *What splendid prospect did the Lord give him ere he died?*—A great part or the whole of the land of Canaan. Deut. 32 : 2–4.

16. *In what did Moses differ from any other prophet?*—In God's speaking to him (as if) face to face. Deut. 34 : 10.

17. *How old was Moses when he died?*—One hundred and twenty years. Deut. 34 : 7.

18. *What special power was manifested in the preservation of his bodily strength?*—The power of God, who

prolonged his life and strength so much beyond the usual seventy years.

JOSHUA. (Josh. 1–4.)

1. *Who was Joshua?*—The son of Nun, of the tribe of Ephraim.

2. *Of whom is he a type?*—Of Christ, the Leader and the Conqueror.

3. *Of what is Canaan a type?*—Of heaven.

4. *Of what is the wilderness a type?*—Of the world.

5. *Of what is the river Jordan a type?*—Of death.

6. *Of what was the ark a type?*—Of Christ, by whom we pass safely through the Jordan of death.

7. *Of what were the stones that they took from the river a type?*—Of memories in heaven, of mercies and deliverances on earth.

8. *When Jesus was born in Bethlehem, did he come as a warrior?*—No.

9. *To what coming, then, does this type refer?*—His coming to judgment.

10. *Where is the Lord's second coming spoken of as a day of terror to his enemies?*—Behold, he cometh with clouds; and every eye shall see him, and they also which pierced him: and all kindreds of the earth shall wail because of him. Rev. 1:7.

11. *To what glorious prospect have the followers of Jesus to look forward?*—The final triumph of Christ over all his and our enemies. Rev. 19:19–21.

THE TAKING OF JERICHO—THE SCARLET LINE. (Josh. 2, 5 and 6.)

1. *Where did the city of Jericho stand?*—Near the west side of the Jordan.

2. *How did Joshua endeavor to ascertain the strength of the city?*—By sending two spies.

3. *How were these men treated in Jericho?*—They were sheltered in the house of Rahab from the king of Jericho's messengers.

4. *What promise did they make to the woman who had sheltered them?*—To save the lives and property of her family on the taking of the city. Josh. 2:12–14.

5. *Did she avail herself of the token they gave?*—She did. Josh. 2:17–21.

6. *What effect had their report on the people?*—They were doubtless much encouraged.

7. *What remarkable events happened on the plains of Jericho?*—The keeping of the Passover, the ceasing of the manna, the appearance of a heavenly Being to Joshua.

8. *Who appeared to Joshua when he was under the walls of Jericho?*—The Son of God.

9. *Did Joshua perceive, at first, who it was?*—No; he merely saw an armed man.

10. *How did he find it out?*—By his saying he was Captain of the Lord's host.

11. *What directions did the Lord give him as to the taking of the city?*—To march round it with the ark and blowing of trumpets, and at last with a shout. Josh. 6:3–5.

12. *Did he and Israel obey the Lord?*—Yes. Josh. 6:8–16, 20.

13. *What was the result?*—The wall fell down flat, and the city was taken and destroyed. Josh. 6:20, 21, 24.

14. *Did Rahab perish with the slain?*—She was brought away safely. Josh. 6:23.

15. *What was her preservation?*—Her faith and the scarlet-cord token that she had been directed to use.

> By faith the harlot Rahab perished not with them that believed not, when she had received the spies with peace. Heb. 11:31.

16. *Of what is the destruction of Jericho a type?*—Of the destruction of all the enemies of God.

17. *Are we interested in this?*—Yes, as sinners.

18. *How?*—We are exposed to God's wrath, and deeply interested to know how we may be saved.

19. *What does the Bible tell us must be our safeguard in the day of wrath.* Rev. 7:13, 14.

20. *Can we trust that word?*—He is faithful that promised. Heb. 10:23.

21. *Had Rahab any reason to regret her faith in the word of the spies?*—No.

22. *Are there many ways of escape, or only one?*—There is none other Name under heaven given among men whereby we must be saved. Acts 4:12.

23. *Perhaps Rahab had been scoffed at for her scarlet line; did that deter her from trusting in it?*—No.

24. *Should the laugh and jeer of the world hinder us from trusting to the blood of Jesus for safety?*—The believer will enter into eternal joy, when the laughter ends in weeping and gnashing of teeth.

25. *Was Rahab alone saved?*—Her near relatives and her goods were saved with her. Josh. 6:22, 23.

26. *If we know a place of safety, should not we tell others of the same?*—It is our duty and privilege to do so.

27. *How can we do so?*—By telling them of Jesus Christ, and getting them to read and hear about him; and by living ourselves as those should do who know him and love him and enjoy him.

ACHAN'S SIN, AND THE TAKING OF AI. (Josh. 7 and 8.)

1. *What special command was given to Israel at the destruction of Jericho?*—To bring the silver and the gold into the treasury of the Lord. Josh. 6:18, 19.

2. *Who transgressed this command?*—Achan.

3. *What punishment did this sin bring on all Israel?*—A defeat by the men of Ai. Josh. 7.

4. *How was the offender discovered?*—By drawing lots under the guidance of God. Josh. 7:16–18.

5. *To what honored tribe did he belong?*—Judah. Josh. 7:1.

6. *Did this preserve him?*—No; honor and privilege often increase guilt.

7. *What awful punishment was necessary to cleanse Israel from the sin Achan had brought on them?*—The destruction of himself and his family and goods by stoning and by fire. Josh. 7:24, 25.

8. *What view of God's character does this history give us?*—His hatred of sin especially of "covetousness, which is idolatry;" and his severity to the impenitent sinner: "our God is a consuming fire." Heb. 12:29.

9. *Will the riches of the sinner avail when God brings him into judgment?*—Nothing at all.

10. *Can we hide our sins from God?*—O Lord, thou hast searched me, and know me. Thou knowest my downsitting and mine uprising, thou understandest my thought afar off. Thou compassest my path and my lying down, and art acquainted with all my ways. Ps. 139:1–3.

11. *When Achan's sin was wiped away, did God again give victory to Israel?*—The city of Ai was taken and destroyed. Josh. 8.

12. *Who bore the wrath of God and the punishment due to our sin?*—Our Lord Jesus Christ.

13. *Can God again smile on us?*—Yes, in Christ Jesus, in whom he is "well pleased."

14. *After the destruction of Ai what solemn act of obedience did Joshua perform?*—He wrote the law upon stone, and read its blessings and its curses on Mounts Gerizim and Ebal. Josh. 8:30–35.

15. *Where in the land of Canaan were these two mountains situated?*—Near Samaria.

16. *For what was Joshua remarkable as well as courage?*—For obedience to the will of God.

17. *Of whom was he a type in this?*—Of Christ. Heb. 10 : 7.

THE GIBEONITES. (Josh. 9.)

1. *How did the Gibeonites act when they saw the victories of the Israelites?*—They sent to Joshua messengers, who pretended that the Gibeonites did not live in Canaan, so that Joshua might be at liberty to spare them.

2. *Did they deceive Joshua and the elders of Israel?*—Yes. Josh. 9 : 15.

3. *How came Joshua to fail in this particular?*—Because he had not asked God's direction. Josh. 9 : 14.

4. *Who was the only Person who never failed?*—Christ, who knew the hearts of men.

5. *Were the Gibeonites spared?*—Yes.

6. *Why?*—Because of the league made with them, confirmed by oath. Josh. 9 : 16, 19.

7. *Was the Lord jealous when an oath was made in his name?*—Yes, very. Num. 30 : 2.

8. *What proof have we of this in the case of the Gibeonites in the after-history of Israel?*—2 Sam. 21 : 1, 2.

9. *To what service were the Gibeonites appointed?*—To be hewers of wood and drawers of water. Josh. 9 : 21.

THE BATTLE OF THE FIVE KINGS. (Josh. 10.)

1. *What did the rest of the kings of Canaan do when they found that the Gibeonites had made peace with Israel?*—Five of them joined in war against Gibeon.

2. *To whom did the Gibeonites appeal?*—To Joshua. Josh. 10 : 6.

3. *Who fought for and with Israel?*—God did. Josh. 10 : 10, 11.

4. *What signal proofs did the Lord give of this in the battle with those kings?*—Showering heavy hailstones upon their enemies, and miraculously prolonging the light of the sun and of the moon upon the scene of battle and pursuit. Josh. 10 : 11–14.

5. *Is this ever after referred to in Scripture?*—The sun and moon stood still in their habitation : at the light of thine arrows they went, and at the shining of thy glittering spear. Hab. 3 : 11.

6. *Of what battle is this the type?*—Of the spiritual warfare in every converted heart.

THE FINAL BATTLE WITH THE KINGS OF CANAAN. (Josh. 11.)

1. *What commandment had the Lord given relative to the destruction of the Canaanites?*—Ex. 34 : 11–13; Deut. 7 : 1, 2.

2. *Why did the Lord thus deal with these nations?*—Their wickedness had reached its height.

The iniquity of the Amorites is not yet full. Gen. 15 : 16.

Thou shalt not learn to do after the abominations of those nations. Deut. 18 : 9.

3. *How is the host that mustered against Joshua described?*—As being numerous as the sand upon the seashore. Josh. 11 : 4.

4. *What great advantage had they over Israel?*—The possession of chariots and horses.

5. *And yet which conquered?*—The Israelites, completely. Josh. 11 : 8.

6. *How was this?*—If God be for us, who can be against us? Rom. 8 : 31.

The Lord is on my side; I will not fear : what can man do unto me? Ps. 118 : 6–9.

7. *What did Joshua do with the city of Hazor?*—He burnt it with fire.

8. *Why Hazor in particular?*—Because it was the head of all the kingdoms he had fought with.

9. *Was this the last battle that Joshua fought?*—No;

he had a long war afterward, till he took the whole land. Josh. 11 : 15–23.

DIVIDING THE LAND, AND DEATH OF JOSHUA. (Josh. 12–24.)

1. *What did Joshua begin so soon as the land had rest from war?*—To divide it among the tribes.

2. *Where was the tabernacle set up?*—At Shiloh. Josh. 18 : 1.

3. *In which tribe was this?*—Ephraim.

4. *How many men did Joshua appoint to survey the land?*—Three men from each of the last seven tribes. Josh. 18 : 4.

5. *How was it divided?*—By lot before the Lord. Josh. 18 : 6.

6. *How were their portions registered?*—In a book. Josh. 18 : 9.

7. *Describe the position of all the tribes on the map.*—Asher, half-Manasseh, Ephraim and Dan down the west coast, but Ephraim reaching to the Jordan; Naphtali, Zebulon, Issachar, Benjamin and Judah by the west border of the sea of Chinnereth, the Jordan and the Dead Sea; and Simeon below; half-Manasseh, Gad and Reuben on the east borders.

8. *In which tribe had Joshua his inheritance?*—Ephraim.

9. *Why?*—Because of his own choice. Josh. 19 : 49, 50.

10. *What portion had Caleb?*—Hebron. Josh. 14 : 12–14.

11. *Why?*—Because he chose it; and as he had wholly followed the Lord, Joshua confirmed his choice.

12. *What was the next thing they did after dividing the land?*—They appointed the cities of refuge.

13. *Which tribe was it that had no portion of the land set apart for them?*—Levi.

14. *How were they provided for?*—Forty-eight cities were assigned to them by the tribes.

15. *How many tribes had their inheritance on the east of Jordan?*—Reuben, Gad and half-Manasseh. Num. 32 : 33.

16. *What part of these tribes passed over Jordan with their brethren?*—The armed men. Josh. 1 : 14.

17. *When did they return home to their families again?*—After the end of the war and the division of the land. Josh. 22.

18. *What unexpected act did they do which alarmed their brethren?*—They built an altar of their own to the Lord. Josh. 22 : 10.

19. *How did they explain it?*—They had not built it for burnt-offering or sacrifice, but to remind them, and their children after them, of their connection with the true altar. Josh. 22 : 26, 27.

20. *Was it satisfactory?*—Quite. Josh. 22 : 30–33.

21. *To what age had Joshua lived?*—About one hundred and nine years.

22. *What was the last act he performed?*—He gave the elders of Israel (Josh. 23) a short history of their nation, and a solemn exhortation to renew their covenant with God. Josh. 24.

23. *What solemn covenant did Israel enter into with him?*—That they would serve idols no more. (Josh. 24 : 16–24.

24. *Where did they make this covenant?*—At Shechem. Josh. 24 : 1.

25. *Where was Shechem?*—In Ephraim, or Samaria.

26. *What token of remembrance did Joshua set up there?*—A stone of witness. Josh. 24 : 26, 27.

27. *How old was Joshua when he died?*—One hundred and ten years.

28. *Where was he buried?*—In Mount Ephraim. Josh. 24 : 30.

29. *What other illustrious person was buried in Mount Ephraim?*—Eleazar. Josh. 24 : 33.

THE JUDGES.—BOCHIM, OR ISRAEL'S FAILURE. (Judg. 1, 2.)

1. *What is the meaning of the word Bochim?*—"Weepers." Judg. 2 : 5, marg.

2. *Why was the place so called?*—Because the Israelites wept there.

3. *What caused the weeping of Israel?*—Sorrow for the sin for which an angel had rebuked them. Judg. 2 : 1–4.

4. *How had they transgressed?*—By neglecting their covenant to make no league with the Canaanites, but to throw down their altars.

5. *Ought not the affecting history of Israel to lead us to look into our own hearts?*—That is what we should do whenever we read or hear of the sins or the faults of others.

6. *If we do, what shall we see there?*—The seeds of the same sins.

7. *Does God kindly admonish us as he did them?*—Take heed, brethren, lest there be in any of you an evil heart of unbelief, in departing from the living God. But exhort one another daily, while it is called to-day, lest any of you be hardened through the deceitfulness of sin. Heb. 3 : 12, 13.

8. *Where?*—See No. 7.

9. *When we try ourselves by God's standard are we justly condemned?*—We know that what things soever the law saith, it saith to them who are under the law : that every mouth may be stopped, and all the world may become guilty before God.

10. *To whom must we look for deliverance when the sins of our hearts, like the foes in Canaan, rise against us?*—To Christ our Saviour, whose blood and Spirit can remove the guilt and power of sin.

OTHNIEL, EHUD, SHAMGAR, DEBORAH AND BARAK. (Judg. 3–5.)

1. *Whom did the Lord first raise up as Israel's deliverer?*—Othniel. Judg. 3 : 9.

2. *To what great warrior was he related?*—To Caleb, who was probably his brother.

3. *How many years had the land rest?*—Forty. Judg. 3 : 11.

4. *When the children of Israel did evil again, to whom did the Lord deliver them?*—To Eglon, king of Moab, for eighteen years. Judg. 3 : 12–14.

5. *When they again repented, did God hear their prayer?*—Yes.

6. *Whom did he raise up to save them?*—Ehud, a Benjamite. Judg. 3 : 15.

7. *What was there remarkable about him?*—He was eft-handed.

8. *How did this bring about the king of Moab's death?*—It enabled Ehud to stab him in an unexpected manner. Judg. 3 : 21.

9. *Did Israel avail themselves of his death to go against the Moabites?*—Yes. Judg. 3 : 27, 28.

10. *How many did they slay?*—About ten thousand men. Judg. 3 : 29.

11. *Who was Israel's third deliverer?*—Shamgar. Judg. 3 : 31.

12. *What marvelous feat of strength is recorded of him?*—He slew six hundred Philistines with an ox-goad.

13. *What city was it in the north of Canaan that Joshua utterly destroyed?*—Hazor. Josh. 11 : 10, 11.

14. *By whom was it rebuilt?*—By Solomon. 1 Kings 9 : 15.

15. *Of what is this a proof?*—Of its importance as a fortress, and of disregard of the will of God.

16. *Who was judge at this time, and prophetess also?*—Deborah. Judg. 4 : 4.

17. *Who was Barak?*—A leader of the tribes of Zebulon and Naphtali. Judg. 4 : 6, 10.

18. *Which appeared to have the most courage, Deborah or Barak?*—Deborah, as Barak would not venture to fight without her. Judg. 4 : 8.

19. *How was Barak reproved for his faint-heartedness?*—By being told that the enemy's general would be given into the hands of a woman. Judg. 4 : 9.

20. *What kind of army did the Canaanitish general muster?*—Nine hundred chariots of iron formed part of it. Judg. 4 : 13.

21. *What was that general's name?*—Sisera. Judg. 4 : 7.

22. *How came it that Israel conquered such a host?*—The power of God was with them. Judg. 4 : 14, 15.

23. *Who was Jael?*—The wife of Heber. Judg. 4 : 17

24. *From what family had Heber, Jael's husband, descended?*—The Kenites and Hobab. Judg. 4 : 11.

25. *Was that an Israelitish family?*—No ; the Kenites were one of the families or nations promised to Abraham's seed, but *Hobab's* family was settled in Israel.

26. *Was this why Sisera took shelter in their tent?*—He took shelter with them because they were at peace with Jabin his master. Judg. 4 : 17.

27. *Which side of the battle did Heber favor?*—The Israelites'. Judg. 4 : 11.

28. *What proof did his wife give of this?*—She killed Sisera. Judg. 4 : 21.

29. *Which side did the Lord take?*—The Israelites'. Judg. 4 : 14, 15. (No. 22.)

30. *As this battle is a type of the spiritual warfare that goes on in the soul, what should we do with an enemy to God that we may find hiding in our bosoms?*—Overcome and destroy it.

31. *Who delivered Sisera into Jael's hand?*—The Lord himself. Judg. 4 : 9.

32. *Who helps us if we desire to conquer our evil passions?*—The grace of God is sufficient for us.

33. *To what evil in our hearts can we compare Sisera with his nine hundred chariots of iron?*—To our chief evil passion or temptation, whatever it may be.

34. *To whom did Deborah and Barak give the glory of the victory in their beautiful song?*—To God. Judg. 5 : 2.

35. *What fearful curse did they pronounce on those who would not assist in this battle?*—Read Judg. 5 : 23.

36. *And what will be our condemnation if we are indifferent to those momentous concerns?*—We shall suffer with the enemies of God, as those who are not with him are against him.

GIDEON. (Judg. 6–8.)

1. *How came it after this that Israel got into trouble again?*—They did evil in the sight of the Lord. Judg. 6 : 1.

2. *Whom did the Lord permit to be their scourge at this time?*—The Midianites and the Amalekites. Judg. 6 : 3.

3. *To what miserable plight were the Israelites reduced?*—They were left without food. Judg. 6 : 4.

4. *On which side of Israel did these two nations lie?*—The Midianites on the south-east, and the Amalekites on the south-west.

5. *Where was Gaza?*—In the land of the Philistines.

6. *What means did the children of Israel at last use*

to free themselves from their great affliction ?—They cried unto the Lord. Judg. 6 : 7.

7. *Did the Lord hear them ?*—He sent a prophet to them, and afterward a deliverer, Gideon. Judg. 6: 7–12.

8. *Who was Gideon? Of what tribe and family ?*—A warrior, of the tribe of Manasseh and family of the Abiezrites.

9. *Who appeared to him ?*—An angel (Judg. 6 : 11), or, rather, the Angel Son of God. Judg. 6 : 14.

10. *What was he doing ?*—Threshing wheat.

11. *Did he at first know who addressed him ?*—No ; he did not address his visitor at first as God. Judg. 6 : 13, 17.

12. *How did he find it out ?*—By the divine Angel's causing fire out of the rock to consume the food set before him (Judg. 6 : 21), and also by the language he used. Judg. 6 : 16.

13. *What were his feelings ?*—Those of deep humility and conscious sinfulness. Judg. 6 : 22.

14. *Had he any cause for fear ?*—Doubtless he was an Israelite indeed in whom was no guile, and as such he had nothing to fear.

15. *What makes man in general afraid of God ?*—The consciousness of unrepented sin. Gen. 3 : 9, 10.

16. *What has the Lord provided to remove our fear, of which Gideon's offering was a type ?*—The accepted sacrifice of Christ.

17. *Who has power to speak " peace " to the soul ?*—He who said to the sick of the palsy, " Thy sins be forgiven thee."

18. *What was Gideon's first act of faith ?*—To throw down the altar of Baal. Judg. 6 : 25–30.

19. *Did he get killed for fulfilling God's will ?*—No ; Joash his father prevented it by wisely saying that if Baal were a god he could punish him himself. Judg. 6 : 31, 32.

20. *How was his own father's heart influenced by the act ?*—See No. 19.

21. *How does God reward those who honor his word ?*—He says, " Them that honor me I will honor."

22. *What name of honor did Gideon get for this act ?*—Jerubbaal, or " let *Baal* plead " against him. Judg. 6 : 32.

23. *Describe the army that was at this time gathered against Israel ?*—The Midianites, Amalekites and other eastern nations. Judg. 6 : 33.

24. *What mighty power rested on Gideon at this time ?*—The Spirit of the Lord. Judg. 6 : 34.

25. *Was he entirely without fear ?*—No, for he asked God to give him a private token of his power. Judg. 6 : 36–40.

26. *How did he prove that God was a hearer and answerer of prayer ?*—By the sign of the wet fleece on the dry ground, and of the dry fleece on the wet ground.

27. *Does God change, or is he as near to us and as ready to hear us as he was near to Gideon and ready and willing to hear him ?*—Every good gift and every perfect gift is from above, and cometh down from the Father of lights, with whom is no variableness, neither shadow of turning. James 1 : 17. Jesus Christ, the same yesterday, and to-day, and for ever. Heb. 13 : 8.

28. *When Gideon blew his trumpet, how many came after him ?*—Thirty-two thousand. Judg. 6 : 34 ; 7 : 3.

29. *Did the Lord intend to use so many to destroy the enemy ?*—No, not even ten thousand.

30. *What sign did the Lord give to Gideon whereby he should know how many and which he had chosen ?*—Their two different ways of taking or drinking water on a particular occasion. Judg. 7 : 4, 5.

31. *How many remained with Gideon after this selection ?*—Three hundred men, who took the water in the quicker manner.

32. *How many were sent to their homes again ?*—Nine thousand seven hundred.

33. *Must this not have been a great trial to Gideon's faith ?*—No doubt it was. 1 Pet. 1 : 7.

34. *Did it fail ?*—No, for God strengthened it. Judg 7 : 7, 9, 14 ; Heb. 11 : 32–34.

35. *What great encouragement did the Lord give Gideon just before he and his three hundred men went down to battle ?*—A dream of one of the soldiers. Judg. 7 : 13, 14.

36. *What effect had this man's dream on Gideon ?*—He praised God, and immediately prepared his men. Judg. 7 : 15, 16.

37. *What effect did it have on his own people ?*—The same as on Gideon himself. Judg. 7 : 14, 20.

38. *Is the Lord ever at a loss for means to effect his purpose ?*—Never.

39. *What plan was adopted to surprise the enemy ?*—The unusual one of suddenly blowing trumpets and exposing a line of lights all round the enemy's camp in the middle of the night. Judg. 7 : 16–20.

40. *Did it answer? Why?*—Yes, because God was trusted in, and God blessed it.

41. *Of what were the lamps and pitchers a type ?*—Of God's faithful ministers, and the light of truth they possess and hold forth.

We have this treasure in earthen vessels, that the excellency of the power may be of God, and not of us. 2 Cor. 4 : 7.

42. *Does God always work by means ?*—He does, and we in our difficulties should use both prayer and means.

43. *Who tells us that he is " the light of the world " ?*—Jesus Christ, in John 8 : 12.

44. *Whom does God appoint to hold up that light ?*—His ministers especially, by their preaching and their example.

45. *Are not all Christians charged to do it ?*—They are in Christ's sermon on the mount.

Ye are the light of the world. Matt. 5 : 14.

46. *Whose mighty power is it that must accompany the word for it to be effectual ?*—The Spirit of truth. John 16 : 13.

47. *Why had Gideon's trumpets and his lamps such a wonderful effect on the enemy ?*—Because God worked with them and by them, and made the Midianites slay each other. Judg. 7 : 22.

48. *On whom must we depend if we are to overcome and conquer our spiritual foes ?*—On the same almighty power.

49. *Was Gideon conqueror ?*—Yes, completely. Judg. 7 : 22–25.

50. *Shall we be ?*—We certainly shall.

If God be for us, who can be against us ? Rom. 8 : 31 I can do all things through Christ which strengtheneth me. Phil. 4 : 13.

51. *How was Gideon treated after this victory by his fellow-countrymen when he was faint and weary ?*—They refused food to him and his men. Judg. 8 : 4–6.

52. *Did they afterward desire to honor him ?*—They wished him to be their king. Judg. 8 : 22.

53. *Would he accept the kingly office ?*—He declined it, as God had not yet appointed that form of government for Israel. Judg. 8 : 23.

54. *Yet what did he desire of them ?*—The golden earrings taken from their enemies. Judg. 8 : 24–26.

55. *What effect did this have on his family ?*—Gideon made the earrings into an ephod (an important part of the dress of the high priest as an intercessor with God. Ex. 28), and kept it in his city of Ophrah, where the people paid it some idolatrous worship, and brought temptation and punishment upon his family. Judg. 8 : 27.

ABIMELECH, OR THE CONTRAST. (Judg. 9.)

1. *Who was Abimelech?*—A son of Gideon. Judg. 9:1.

2. *Was his course an honorable one, like that of his father?*—No; he basely plotted to be made king. Judg. 9:2.

3. *Of what awful crime was he guilty?*—He slew his brethren. Judg. 9:5.

4. *Did either escape?*—Jotham alone.

5. *What parable did Jotham utter?*—He spoke of the useful trees, as the olive, the fig and the vine, refusing to be placed over the rest; and of the worthless bramble, as the only one that desired it. Judg. 9:8–15.

6. *Can you explain the meaning of this simile as it respects Abimelech?*—That part of it which speaks of the bramble represents the character and end of Abimelech. Judg. 9:52–57.

7. *Of what are the olive, vine and fig tree types?*—Together they are types of useful, amiable, wise and humble-minded men.

8. *Was it fulfilled? How?*—The parable was fulfilled in the foolish choice of Abimelech by the Shechemites, in the violent quarrels between them, and the destruction of both. Judg. 9:15, 20, 23, 49, 52, 54.

9. *Where did all this shameful scene take place?*—At Shechem.

10. *What remarkable events had rendered this spot peculiarly hallowed?*—The visit of Abraham on reaching Canaan, the reading of the law (Josh. 9), and the renewal of the covenant. Josh. 24.

11. *How did it stand with regard to the two mountains of blessing and cursing spoken of in Deut. 27 and in Josh. 8?*—In a narrow plain between them.

12. *How near was it to Shiloh, where the tabernacle was pitched?*—About twenty miles.

13. *What must an idol temple built on this spot be a proof of?*—That the Israelites had not yet conquered the whole country and destroyed its idols. Judg. 9:4–6.

14. *Has Jotham's parable anything to do with us?*—Yes, for all Scripture is given by inspiration of God. Tim. 3:16.

15. *Who in Scripture are compared to fruit trees?*—God's own people.

I am the vine, ye are the branches. John 15:5.

16. *Who are represented by the bramble?*—The wicked.

17. *What is expected of fruit trees?*—That they should bring forth fruit.

18. *What has the bramble or thorn to expect?*—To be burned. Isa. 30:12; 2 Sam. 23:6, 7.

19. *How is the hypocrite known from the true Christian?*—Ye shall know them by their fruits. Do men gather grapes of thorns, or figs of thistles? Matt. 7:16.

20. *What should our prayer be?*—Search me, O God, nd know my heart. Ps. 139:23.

TOLA, JAIR, JEPHTHAH, IBZAN, ELON AND ABDON. (Judg. 10–12.)

1. *Give me the name of the next judge of Israel.*—Tola. Judg. 10:1.

2. *How long did he judge Israel?*—Twenty-three years.

3. *Who succeeded him?*—Jair.

4. *How is his family described?*—As riding on ass-colts as deputy-judges. Judg. 5:10; 10:4.

5. *From whom did he get this inheritance?*—The children of Machir the son of Manasseh went to Gilead and took it, and dispossessed the Amorite which was in it. And Moses gave Gilead unto Machir the son of Manasseh; and he dwelt therein. And Jair the son of Manasseh went and took the small towns thereof, and called them Havoth-jair. Num. 32:39–41.

6. *How long did he judge Israel?*—Twenty-two years.

7. *How many idols are enumerated here which Israel at this time worshiped?*—Baalim and Ashtaroth, and the gods of five nations besides. Judg. 10:6.

8. *What had God commanded Israel with respect to this awful sin?*—Ye shall make you no idols nor graven image, neither rear you up a standing image, neither shall ye set up any image of stone in your land, to bow down unto it: for I am the Lord your God. Lev. 26:1, 14, 17.

9. *How did he punish them?*—By delivering them into the hands of the Philistines and Ammonites for eighteen years. Judg. 10:7, 8.

10. *When they prayed to the Lord did he hear them?*—No; he charged them with their ingratitude and idolatry. Judg. 10:10–14.

11. *Did he at once deliver them?*—See No. 10.

12. *Did he convince them of their sin?*—Yes; they confessed their guilt. Judg. 10:15.

13. *When God had convinced them of their sin, and they were humbled on account of it, did they forsake it?*—Yes; they put away their strange gods.

14. *How?*—See No. 13.

15. *What did the Lord then feel for them?*—His soul was grieved for their misery.

16. *Who was Jephthah?*—A great warrior of Gilead. Judg. 11:1.

17. *On which side of the land of Israel was the land of the Ammonites?*—On the east.

18. *Where was Gilead?*—In the neighboring tribe of Gad.

19. *Why did the men of Gilead choose Jephthah to be their captain?*—Because he was likely to lead them to victory.

20. *On what conditions did Jephthah accept the office?*—That he should be their head on his return. Judg. 11:9.

21. *What vow did Jephthah make before he went to battle?*—That if he were victorious, whoever came forth first out of his house to meet him on his return should be given up (like Samuel) to God's service for life, and that he would offer to the Lord a burnt-offering besides. Judg. 11:30, 31.

22. *Who came out first to meet him?*—His daughter and only child. Judg. 11:34.

23. *What did Jephthah feel and say when he saw his only child?*—He was deeply distressed, and told her of his vow. Judg. 11:35.

24. *What was her beautiful answer?*—That as God had given him victory he must do to her according to his vow. Judg. 11:36.

25. *What law of God was there to regulate what Jephthah said under these circumstances?*—That the subject of the vow might be redeemed by a payment in money. Lev. 27:2–5.

26. *What difference was there between "a vow" and a "devoted thing"?*—A thing devoted by some more solemn consecration than a vow could not be redeemed.

27. *For how much did Jephthah redeem his daughter if he did not slay her for an offering?*—About $5 or $15, according to her age.

28. *Why do we think he redeemed her?*—Because her friends went every year to lament her separation from them or to talk with her. Judg. 11:40, margin.

29. *Why was it a great grief for any woman in Israel to be childless?*—Because she might be the mother or ancestress of the Messiah, the promised seed of the woman that was to bruise the serpent's head. Gen. 3:15.

30. *Do you think that Jephthah valued the honor which he had sought, of being the head of his tribe, after this mournful event?*—Probably not, as it had cost him the

society of his only child; but he would still value the office of *judge* conferred on him by God.

31. *Can any honor or pleasure in this world give satisfaction in itself?*—No; nothing in the world that is passing away.

32. *What proof did Jephthah give of his knowledge of the Scripture history when he met the king of Ammon before the battle?*—He told him how it was that the Israelites became possessed of the land that the king was unlawfully claiming from them. Judg. 11 : 12–28.

33. *Where must our strength lie when we go against our spiritual foes?*—In the Lord and the power of his might. Eph. 6 : 10.

34. *What weapons did the Lord Jesus Christ use when he met Satan?*—The sword of the Spirit, the word of God. Eph. 6 : 17. It is written. Matt. 4 : 4, 7, 10.

35. *What is "the word of God" called in Heb. 4 : 12?*—Quick (or living) and powerful, and sharper than any two-edged sword.

36. *By what shall we be judged at the last day?*—The word that Christ has spoken.

37. *What painful circumstance arose from the jealousy of the Ephraimites?*—A quarrel with Jephthah, whom they had before unkindly treated, and a consequent defeat by him in battle with great slaughter. Judg. 12 : 1, 6.

38. *How long did Jephthah hold his honors?*—Six years.

39. *Who judged Israel after Jephthah?*—Ibzan.

40. *For how long?*—Seven years.

41. *Who succeeded Ibzan?*—Elon.

42. *How long did he judge Israel?*—Ten years.

43. *Who followed Elon?*—Abdon.

44. *How many sons and nephews had he?*—Seventy sons and nephews or grandsons.

45. *Was not this considered a great honor in Israel?*—Yes, as increasing the likelihood of being the ancestor of the Messiah.

46. *Why?*—See No. 45.

47. *What higher honor had Jephthah than even being the ancestor of the Messiah?*—The honor of being named with David and Samuel and the prophets in the roll of heroes and martyrs in the cause of God. Heb. 11 : 32.

SAMSON. (Judg. 13–17.)

1. *Who was Samson?*—One of the tribe of Dan. Judg. 13 : 1.

2. *What remarkable circumstance took place before his birth?*—The angel of the Lord appearing to his mother, and telling her that she should have a son, who should be a Nazarite unto God, and deliver Israel from the Philistines. Judg. 13 : 2–5.

3. *What was the name of Samson's father?*—Manoah. Judg. 13 : 2.

4. *Did he not seem to have some doubts lest his wife had been mistaken?*—Perhaps so, as he desired some further instruction. Judg. 13 : 8.

5. *Did the angel appear a second time?*—He did.

6. *Did he alter anything he had said before?*—He did not.

7. *What should this teach us?*—The truth: I am the Lord, I change not. Mal. 3 : 6.

8. *Which seemed to have the greatest faith, Manoah or his wife?*—His wife.

9. *How do you prove this?*—By Judg. 13 : 22, 23.

10. *How did Manoah and his wife know that their visitor was an angel?*—By the words he spoke, and by his ascending in the flame. Judg. 13 : 18–20.

11. *Did the angel ever appear to them again after the birth of Samson?*—No.

12. *What was there remarkable about Samson?*—His very great strength.

13. *What was a Nazarite?*—A person "separated unto the Lord." Num. 6 : 2–21.

14. *What special gift rested on Samson?*—The Spirit of the Lord. Judg. 13 : 25; 14 : 6.

15. *Where did Samson's strength lie? was it in his hair?*—No.

16. *Was it in his limbs?*—No.

17. *What was it that made the lamp and pitchers in Gideon's hand so effective?*—The power of God.

18. *What power rested on Deborah and Barak?*—See No. 17.

19. *What gave Jephthah the victory?*—See No. 17.

20. *Did the same power rest on Samson?*—Yes.

21. *Was Samson ever restored to the possession of his strength again?*—Yes, just before his death. Judg. 16 : 30.

22. *Name all his wonderful feats of strength, and say which was the greatest.*—He tore a young lion like a kid (Judg. 14 : 5, 6); he slew thirty Philistines (Judg. 14 : 19), and afterward one thousand (Judg. 15 : 15); he carried away the gates of Gaza (Judg. 16 : 3); he broke the green withs and new ropes with which he had been bound (Judg. 16 : 9); he carried away the beam of a weaving-machine to which his hair had been secured (Judg. 16 : 14); he pulled down a large building by its two pillars on the heads of the Philistines (Judg. 16 : 29, 30), the last and greatest feat of all.

23. *Does God still hear and answer prayer?*—He does, as every true Christian can bear witness.

24. *Of whom was Samson a type?*—Of Christ, in some of the special circumstances of his birth, and in his being devoted to God's service.

25. *In what respect particularly?*—As Christ triumphed in his death over Satan and his hosts.

26. *How did Samson, in type, show the resurrection of Jesus?*—In the recovery of his strength in spite of his enemies.

27. *Whom did the Lord Jesus meet single-handed? and who is called in Scripture a " roaring lion"?*—The devil. Matt. 4 and 1 Pet. 5–8.

28. *By what name is the Lord Jesus called in Isa. 9 : 6?*—"The mighty God."

29. *Where is the Lord Jesus, in prophecy, described as treading the wine-press of the wrath of God alone?*—In Isa. 63 : 3.

30. *Who is spoken of as bringing salvation alone?*—Jesus Christ.

He saw that there was no man, and wondered that there was no intercessor: therefore his arm brought salvation unto him; and his righteousness, it sustained him. Isa. 59 : 16.

31. *On whom must we then depend for salvation?*—Jesus Christ.

Neither is there salvation in any other: for there i none other Name under heaven given among men whereby we must be saved. Acts 4 : 12.

THE STORY OF MICAH, AND THE CLOSE OF THE JUDGES. (Judg. 17–21.)

1. *When a man does "that which is right in his own eyes" what is he sure to do?*—Wrong, for there is a way that seemeth right unto a man, but the end thereof are the ways of death. Prov. 16 : 25; Judg. 17 : 6.

2. *What standard has God given us by which we may judge ourselves?*—His holy word.

To the law and to the testimony: if they speak not according to this word, it is because there is no light in them. Isa. 8 : 20.

3. *What proof do Micah and his mother give that by doing "that which was right in their own eyes" they did wrong?*—They both committed idolatry, and Micah committed theft. Judg. 17 : 2, 3, 5.

4. Which commandments of God's law did Micah break?—The second and the eighth.

5. Why was it wrong to take a Levite for his priest?—The duties of the Levites were at the tabernacle in Shiloh; and none of them could be priests but those called by God.

He hath brought thee near to him, and all thy brethren the sons of Levi with thee; and seek ye the priesthood also? Num. 16 : 10.

6. Were Micah and his mother the only idolaters in Israel?—No; the Danites also. Judg. 18 : 30.

7. What relation had these Danites to Samson?—Some of them came from Zorah and Eshtaol, where Samson had been. Judg. 13 : 25.

8. To what part of Israel did they remove and settle?—To Laish, in the tribe of Naphtali.

9. Of what crimes were they guilty?—Of robbery, murder and idolatry. Judg. 18 : 17, 27, 30.

10. Do you think if you had lived in their days you would have done better?—Probably not.

Are we better than they? No, in no wise. Rom. 3 : 9.

11. Have we the same law to be our guide as they had?—The same law, and the teaching of the prophets, of our Lord and of his apostles besides.

12. What is the word of God compared to in Heb. 4 : 12?—A "two-edged sword;" so thoroughly does it pierce our hearts and expose our sin.

13. By what shall we be judged at the last day?—"The word that" Christ has "spoken," including the whole Bible spoken by his Spirit.

14. Is the Scripture our appointed rule, and is it sufficient?—Yes; it thoroughly furnishes all the instruction we need. 2 Tim. 3 : 16, 17.

15. What will be our condemnation if we neglect it?—Eternal punishment. Luke 16 : 20–31.

BOAZ, OR THE REDEEMER. (Ruth.)

1. Who was Elimelech?—A man of Bethlehem-judah. Ruth 1 : 1, 2.

2. What were the names of his wife and of his two sons?—Naomi, and Mahlon and Chilion.

3. Where did this family live?—In the country of Moab. Ruth 1 : 1, 2.

4. At what time did they live?—In the days of the judges. Ruth 1 : 1.

5. What event happened in Israel that drove them to sojourn in Moab?—A famine.

6. Of what was this a proof?—Of the disobedience and idolatry of the people. Deut. 28 : 15–18.

7. Whom did the sons marry?—Orpah and Ruth, women of Moab. Ruth 1 : 4.

8. Did they prosper and have long life?—Both the sons soon died. Ruth 1 : 5.

9. What became of Naomi after the death of her husband and sons?—She returned to Judah, as the famine had ceased. Ruth 1 : 6, 7.

10. What difference was there in the behavior of her daughters-in-law toward her?—Both were distressed at the idea of parting with her, and said they would go with her, but only Ruth went.

11. Did God accept this stranger who determined to forsake her people and her gods and trust in him?—He did, and showed her much favor.

12. And is God the same now as he was then?—Yes; he receives all who receive Christ.

Peter said, Of a truth I perceive that God is no respecter of persons. Acts 10 : 34.

13. What is the meaning of the name Naomi?—"Pleasant." Ruth 1 : 20, margin.

14. To what name did Naomi wish hers changed, and why?—To Mara, or "bitter," because of the sorrows she had suffered.

15. What rich and noble relative had the poor widow Naomi in her native place?—Boaz. Ruth 2 : 1.

16. Whose field did Ruth happen to glean in?—His field. Ruth 2 : 2.

17. Did Boaz notice Ruth? In what manner?—He told her to glean his fields until the end of harvest, and gave orders for her refreshment and protection, and for a plentiful gleaning. Ruth 2 : 4–17, 21.

18. What description can you give of Boaz, besides that he was rich and noble?—He was a kind-hearted and a good man who honored God. Ruth 2 : 8–12.

19. What effect did his kindness have on Naomi when she heard of it?—She blessed God for his goodness, and told Ruth how to claim Boaz as her kinsman in the manner which the custom of the country allowed. Ruth 2 : 19, 20; 3 : 1–4.

20. Did Ruth do as her mother-in-law bade her?—She did. Ruth 2 : 5–7.

Children, obey your parents in the Lord: for this is right. Honor thy father and mother; which is the first commandment with promise; that it may be well with thee, and thou mayest live long on the earth. Eph. 6 : 1–3.

21. What did this prove?—That she knew the privileges of filial obedience.

22. Did Boaz answer the high expectation that Naomi had of him?—Yes; he behaved both well and kindly to his virtuous relation, and promised to do a kinsman's duty to her according to the law. Ruth 2 : 8–17.

23. Was he the nearest relative that Naomi had?—He was not. Ruth 2 : 12; 4 : 1.

24. On whom did the duty of kinsman or redeemer fall?—If brethren dwell together, and one of them die, and have no child, the wife of the dead shall not marry without unto a stranger: her husband's brother shall go in unto her, and take her to him to wife, and perform the duty of an husband's brother unto her. And it shall be that the first-born which she beareth shall succeed in the name of his brother which is dead, that his name be not put out of Israel. And if the man like not to take his brother's wife, then let his brother's wife go up to the gate unto the elders, and say, My husband's brother refuseth to raise up to his brother a name in Israel, he will not perform the duty of my husband's brother. Then the elders of his city shall call him, and speak unto him: and if he stand to it, and say, I like not to take her; then shall his brother's wife come unto him in the presence of the elders, and loose his shoe from off his foot, and spit in his face, and shall answer and say, So shall it be done unto that man that will not build up his brother's house. And his name shall be called in Israel, The house of him that hath his shoe loosed. Deut. 25 : 5–10.

25. Did the nearest kinsman perform his duty to Naomi?—No; he declined doing it. Ruth 4 : 1–6.

26. What was the custom in such cases?—For the person who gave up his right to hand his shoe, as a token of such giving up, to the person who took his place. Ruth 4 : 7.

27. Who stepped in and took his place?—Boaz. Ruth 4 : 9, 10.

28. What blessing did the elders of Israel pronounce upon Ruth when she became the wife of Boaz?—They prayed that God would bless her with many children, that she might be an ancestress of the Messiah. Ruth 4 : 11, 12.

29. Do you think Naomi wished her name changed to Mara now?—Certainly not.

30. What should this teach us?—To trust God that all will at length be well.

Oh taste and see that the Lord is good: blessed is the man that trusteth in him. Many are the afflictions of the righteous; but the Lord delivereth him out of them all. Ps. 34 : 8, 19.

31. *What was the name of the son whom God gave to Ruth?*—Obed. Ruth 4 : 17.

32. *What were the names of his son and of his grandson?*—Jesse and David.

33. *What relation, then, was Ruth to David?*—Great-grandmother.

34. *Of what glorious Person was Ruth, then, the ancestress?*—Of Christ.

35. *What is the meaning of the name Boaz?*—Strength" or "Swiftness."

36. *Of whom was Boaz a type?*—Of Christ.

37. *In what particular character was Boaz the type of the Lord Jesus?*—In that of brother, kinsman and redeemer.

38. *Refer to some texts to show the Lord Jesus as a Redeemer.*—

1st. As being of the human family:
When the fullness of the time was come, God sent forth his Son, made of a woman, made under the law, to redeem them that were under the law, that we might receive the adoption of sons. Gal. 4 : 4, 5.

2d. That he is not ashamed to call us brethren:
Both He that sanctifieth and they who are sanctified are all of one; for which cause he is not ashamed to call them brethren. Heb. 2 : 11.

3d. The price paid for our redemption:
Ye know that ye were not redeemed with corruptible things, as silver and gold, from your vain conversation received by tradition from your fathers; but with the precious blood of Christ, as of a lamb without blemish and without spot. 1 Pet. 1 : 18, 19,

4th. Give a proof of our poverty:
Thou sayest, I am rich, and increased with goods, and have need of nothing; and knowest not that thou art wretched, and miserable, and poor, and blind, and naked: I counsel thee to buy of me gold tried in the fire, that thou mayest be rich; and white raiment, that thou mayest be clothed. Rev. 3 : 17, 18.

5th. Give a proof of the Lord's riches:
The unsearchable riches of Christ. Eph. 3 : 8.

6th. Give a proof that he is heir of all things:
God, who at sundry times and in divers manners spake in time past unto the fathers by the prophets, hath in these last days spoken unto us by his Son, whom he hath appointed heir of all things. Heb. 1 : 1, 2.

7th. That he hath taken the Church to be his Bride:
Christ loved the church, and gave himself for it: that he might sanctify and cleanse it with the washing of water by the word, that he might present it to himself a glorious church, not having spot, or wrinkle, or any such thing. Eph. 5 : 26, 27.

8th. That he has not only purchased her to himself, but that he is Lord of all creation:
Jesus Christ: he is Lord of all. Acts 10 : 36.

9th. That though now his people are poor and weak and despised, the great Redeemer will come and claim his and their rightful inheritance:
I go to prepare a place for you. And if I go and prepare a place for you, I will come again, and receive you unto myself; that where I am, there ye may be also. John 14 : 2, 3.

39. *Was the "Redeemer" also the "revenger of blood"?*—It was the nearest relation in both cases.

40. *Will the Lord Jesus, when he comes again, fulfill that double character?*—The Lord Jesus shall be revealed from heaven with his mighty angels, in flaming fire taking vengeance on them that know not God, and that obey not the gospel of our Lord Jesus Christ; who shall be punished with everlasting destruction from the presence of the Lord, and from the glory of his power; when he shall come to be glorified in his saints, and to be admired in all them that believe. 2 Thess. 1 : 7–10.

41. *On whom will he execute justice?*—See No. 40.

42. *What effect should this solemn truth have on our minds?*—It should stir us up to flee at once to Jesus, our Redeemer, from the wrath to come.

43. *In Rev. 5 : 5 the Lord Jesus is called "the root of David," to whom could that refer?*—As God, Christ was David's root or source; as man, he was his son. In Boaz, his type, he may also have been David's Redeemer or root.

44. *Why is the Lord Jesus called "the root of David," or Redeemer, in the same chapter as he is represented as the slain lamb?*—Because he redeemed us, not only as our kinsman in the human nature, but as the sacrificed Lamb of God.

Thou wast slain, and hast redeemed us to God by thy blood out of every kindred, and tongue, and people, and nation. Rev. 5 : 9.

45. *Compare Acts 20 : 28; Eph. 1 : 7; Heb. 9 : 11–14; 1 Pet. 1 : 18–25, and say if there be any excuse for those who neglect this great salvation.*—No, for redemption through the blood of Jesus is now plainly revealed and preached to us.

ELI AND SAMUEL. (1 Sam. 1–3.)

1. *Who was Eli?*—The priest—*i. e.* high priest. 1 Sam. 1 : 9.

2. *By whom was the priesthood in Israel appointed?*—By God himself.
This is the thing that thou shalt do unto them to hallow them, to minister unto me in the priest's office: Take one bullock, and two rams without blemish, etc. Ex. 29 : 1.

3. *Who was the first high priest?*—Aaron.

4. *Who ought to have succeeded him in the high priesthood?*—His sons Nadab and Abihu. Lev. 10.

5. *Which of Aaron's sons was high priest at his father's death?*—Eleazar.
Take Aaron and Eleazar his son, and bring them up unto Mount Hor; and strip Aaron of his garments, and put them upon Eleazar his son; and Aaron shall be gathered unto his people, and shall die there. Num. 20 : 25, 26.

6. *From whom had Eli descended?*—From Ithamar, Aaron's younger son.

7. *Did his sons walk in the way of their father Eli?*—No; they were very wicked. 1 Sam. 2 : 12–17.

8. *What sin was Eli guilty of that brought upon him God's anger?*—Only mildly reproving his wicked sons when he should have restrained them with the authority of a father. 1 Sam. 2 : 23, 24; 3 : 13, 14.

9. *Who was Elkanah?*—A Levite of Mount Ephraim. 1 Sam. 1 : 1.

10. *What were the names of his wives?*—Hannah and Peninnah.

11. *Which did he love the most?*—Hannah. 1 Sam. 1 : 5.

12. *What great trial had Hannah?*—Not having any child. 1 Sam. 1 : 10, 11.

13. *To whom did she tell her sorrow?*—To God in prayer.

14. *What did Eli suppose when he saw her lips moving in silent prayer?*—That she was drunken. 1 Sam. 1 : 13.

15. *When he found that he was mistaken, what did he say?*—Read 1 Sam. 1 : 17.

16. *Did this comfort Hannah's heart? and had she her desire?*—Her countenance was no more sad, and a child was born to her. 1 Sam. 1 : 18, 20.

17. *What name did she give the child?*—Samuel.

18. *What is the meaning of that name?*—"Asked of God."

19. *Why did she not go up with her husband to worship the next year?*—She preferred waiting until her child was old enough to remain altogether in the house of

the Lord to be his servant, according to her vow. 1 Sam. 1 : 22, 11.

20. *By whose command used the children of Israel to go up to Shiloh to worship?*—By God's command.

21. *How many times a year were all the men to appear before the Lord?*—Three times. Ex. 23 : 17.

22. *Which feast must this have been when the women met as well?*—The Passover, to which women sometimes went.

Now his parents went to Jerusalem every year at the feast of the passover. Luke 2 : 41.

23. *At what time of the year was this feast held?*—About the end of March or beginning of April.

24. *Did Hannah do with the child as she had promised?*—She did. 1 Sam. 1 : 24–28.

25. *How old was he when his mother took him up and dedicated him to the Lord?*—He "was young," perhaps six years old. 1 Sam. 1 : 24, margin.

26. *Why was it wrong of Eli's sons to take any part of the sacrifice they liked? Which part had God appointed for the priest's use?*—Because God had assigned them a particular part, the breast and the right shoulder. Lev. 7 : 31–34.

27. *What had God commanded relative to the fat of his sacrifices?*—Read Lev. 3 : 14–17.

28. *What condemnation did Eli's sons bring on themselves by eating the fat of the sacrifices?*—Whosoever eateth the fat of the beast, of which men offer an offering made by fire unto the Lord, even the soul that eateth it shall be cut off from his people. Lev. 7 : 25.

29. *Did the Lord send any messenger to warn Eli of the sin his sons were committing?*—He sent a man of God, a prophet. 1 Sam. 2 : 27–36.

30. *Is there any rule by which we may know if we are doing the will of God or not? What is it?*—Thy word is a lamp unto my feet and a light unto my path. Ps. 119 : 105.

31. *Did Eli regard this awful message?*—Perhaps not sufficiently, as another awful message was sent to him some years afterward; or it may have been too late and his sons become thoroughly hardened in sin. 1 Sam. 2 : 25.

32. *What manifest token did the Lord give that he had accepted the gift of Hannah and chosen her son as a prophet of his own?*—God gave him a special call and message. 1 Sam. 3 : 4–14, 20, 21.

33. *How old was Samuel when this occurred?*—About twelve, but some think he was much older.

34. *Had Eli instructed Samuel in the knowledge of God before this time?*—No doubt Eli had made him acquainted with God's law, and explained to him the tabernacle service; but Samuel had no experience yet of God's special way of making himself and his word or will known to his prophets. 1 Sam. 3 : 7.

35. *Are there any children now who, though often seen God's house, yet know him not?*—It is to be feared there are but very few of them who know God, so as to love and obey him, as Samuel did.

36. *When God called to Samuel, what did he answer?*—Speak, for thy servant heareth. 1 Sam. 3 : 10.

37. *Have you answered God's call to you?*—If not, he is calling to you now as you listen to his word—calling you to be his child, and to give him your heart. Ask him, for his dear Son's sake, to help you to obey the call. Give yourself to him now.

38. *What solemn message did the Lord give Samuel concerning Eli's house?*—That he would punish it for ever. 1 Sam. 3 : 11–14.

39. *Did the Lord continue to manifest himself to Samuel rather than to Eli?*—He did. 1 Sam. 3 : 19–21.

40. *What did this show?*—That God honors those who honor him, dishonors those who dishonor him. 1 Sam. 2 : 30.

THE TAKING OF THE ARK. (1 Sam. 4–7.)

1. *Who were Israel's greatest enemies at this time?*—The Philistines.

2. *What sinful act did Israel resort to when they found themselves smitten before the enemy?*—They brought the ark from its place at Shiloh. 1 Sam. 4 : 3–5.

3. *What effect did it have on the Philistines?*—They were afraid at first, but roused each other to a great effort. 1 Sam. 4 : 7–9.

4. *Of what was this a proof?*—That God was not with Israel, though the ark was.

Go not up, for the Lord is not among you; that ye be not smitten before your enemies. Num. 14 : 42.

5. *What was the fate of the ark, and of those who carried it?*—The ark was taken, and Eli's sons were slain. 1 Sam. 4 : 11.

6. *How did Eli bear the tidings?*—He fell back and died. 1 Sam. 4 : 18.

7. *What sorrowful event happened to the wife of Phinehas?*—She died in childbirth. 1 Sam. 4 : 19–22.

8. *What name did she give her son ere she died?*—Ichabod.

9. *What is the meaning of that name?*—"No glory."

10. *Why did she choose it?*—Because the glory had departed from Israel, the ark being taken.

11. *What did the Philistines do with the ark?*—They set it beside their idol Dagon. 1 Sam. 5 : 1, 2.

12. *What happened to their idol?*—It fell on its face before the ark. 1 Sam. 5 : 3, 4.

13. *Did this convince them of the sin of idolatry?*—Not at all.

14. *Whose office is it to open our minds to receive the truth?*—The Holy Spirit, who convinces of sin.

When he, the Spirit of truth, is come, he will guide you into all truth. John 16 : 13.

15. *Had they not full opportunity, living actually within the land of Israel, to know about the true God?*—Yes, but like thousands among ourselves now, they did not take advantage of it, and so they perished in their sins.

I said not unto the seed of Jacob, Seek ye me in vain: I the Lord speak righteousness, I declare things that are right. Look unto me, and be ye saved, all the ends of the earth : for I am God, and there is none else. Isa. 45 : 19, 22.

16. *What does David say about idols in Ps. 115?*—Their idols are silver and gold, the work of men's hands. They have mouths, but they speak not: eyes have they, but they see not: they have ears, but they hear not: noses have they, but they smell not: they have hands, but they handle not: feet have they, but they walk not: neither speak they through their throat. They that make them are like unto them; so is every one that trusteth in them.

17. *What proof did Dagon give of this in this history?*—He could not take care of himself. 1 Sam. 5 : 3, 4.

18. *What calamities did God's presence bring on his enemies?*—A painful disease and a plague of mice, and a deadly destruction besides. 1 Sam. 5 : 6, 9, 11, 12; 6 : 4, 5.

19. *What did they resolve to do?*—To send back the ark with a trespass-offering. 1 Sam. 6 : 2, 3.

20. *What test did they employ to ascertain if indeed the God of Israel had brought on them all these miseries?*—They yoked to the cart that carried the ark two cows, to see if they would go to the land of Israel without their calves. 1 Sam. 6 : 7–12.

21. *Who had power over the affections of these kine in making them go opposite to their natural feelings?*—God alone.

For every beast of the forest is mine, and the cattle upon a thousand hills. Ps. 50 : 10.

22. *How was the ark received?*—With joy (1 Sam. 6 :

13) and a sacrifice of thanksgiving to God. 1 Sam. 6: 14, 15.

23. *Of what act of impiety were the men of Beth-she-mesh guilty?*—Of looking into the ark (1 Sam. 6: 19), which caused God to slay fifty thousand and seventy men.

24. *Why was this act of theirs inexcusable?*—They shall not go in to see when the holy things are covered, lest they die. Num. 4: 20.

25. *Was the ark taken back again to Shiloh? If not, where was it taken?*—To Kirjath-jearim. 1 Sam. 7: 1.

26. *How long did it remain there?*—Twenty years (1 Sam. 7: 2), until the repentance of Israel.

27. *Who afterward removed it? and where did it go?*—David removed it to Mount Zion. 2 Sam. 6: 2–17.

28. *Did Israel repent of their sins?*—They did, at the call of Samuel. 1 Sam. 7: 3–6.

29. *To whom did they apply?*—To Samuel, to pray for their delivery from the Philistines. 1 Sam. 7: 8.

30. *What did he do for them?*—He offered a sacrifice and cried unto the Lord.

31. *What proof did the Lord give that he accepted their sacrifice and heard their prayer?*—He caused a great thunder-storm and a defeat of the Philistines. 1 Sam. 7: 10.

32. *Of what use could the offering of that lamb be to them?*—Because it typified or referred to Jesus, "the Lamb of God, which taketh away the sin of the world." John 1: 29.

33. *Is Samuel mentioned among those who had faith in Him who was to come?*—Yes, in Heb. 11: 32.

34. *Why is the Lord Jesus said (Rev. 13: 8) to be "the Lamb slain from the foundation of the world"?*—Because we are redeemed with the precious blood of Christ, as of a lamb without blemish and without spot: who verily was foreordained before the foundation of the world, but was manifest in these last times for you. 1 Pet. 1: 19, 20.

35. *Are there many ways by which we can be saved?*—There is one God, and one Mediator between God and men, the man Christ Jesus; who gave himself a ransom for all, to be testified in due time. 1 Tim. 2: 5, 6. Neither is there salvation in any other: for there is none other Name under heaven given among men, whereby we must be saved. Acts 14: 12.

36. *What memorial did Samuel set up in remembrance of this deliverance?*—A stone called Eben-ezer, or "the stone of help." 1 Sam. 7: 12.

37. *What three characters did Samuel unite in his person?*—Priest, prophet or teacher, and judge.

38. *Of whom was he thus a type?*—Of our Lord Jesus Christ. Deut. 18: 18, 19; 1 Sam. 2: 35; Gen. 18: 25; Rev. 19: 11; 20: 11, 12; Matt. 25: 31, etc.

39. *If we believe that Jesus will ere long be our Judge, as he was the Priest to atone for us and the Prophet and Advocate to pray for and instruct us, what ought we to do?*—Seek ye the Lord while he may be found, call ye upon him while he is near: let the wicked forsake his way, and the unrighteous man his thoughts: and let him return unto the Lord, and he will have mercy upon him; and to our God, for he will abundantly pardon Isa. 55: 6, 7.

SAUL. (1 Sam. 9–31.)

1. *Who was Saul?*—Son of Kish. 1 Sam. 9.

2. *Of which tribe was he?*—Benjamin.

3. *What was there remarkable about his person?*—He was very tall and very handsome. 1 Sam. 9: 2.

4. *What power did God allow to rest upon him?*—His Spirit, as he did to Balaam—in his gifts, but not his graces; in his enlightening, but not his converting power. 1 Sam. 10: 10.

5. *Are there not some characters more difficult to un-*

derstand than others?*—There are, as the tares of the East resemble the wheat, and the sheep the goats.

6. *What contradictions do there appear in Saul's character?*—In many things he honored Samuel and honored God, but he mixed his religion with superstition, and was proud, disobedient and self-willed.

7. *How can we come to a conclusion in so judging?*—No man can serve two masters; for either he will hate the one, and love the other; or else he will hold to the one, and despise the other. Ye cannot serve God and mammon. Matt. 6: 24.

8. *What made the children of Israel first think of having a king?*—Because Samuel was old, and his sons were unfit to help him or succeed him. 1 Sam. 8: 5, 20.

9. *How did Samuel feel about it?*—He was displeased with their so dishonoring and disobeying God. 1 Sam. 8: 6.

10. *How was he comforted?*—By prayer, and direction from God. 1 Sam. 8: 6, 7.

11. *In what spirit did the Lord give them a king?*—In anger: "I gave thee a king in mine anger." Hos. 13: 11.

12. *How did God establish the kingdom in his hand?*—By a victory over the Ammonites. 1 Sam. 11: 11–15.

13. *Did Saul follow up this victory?*—He next attacked the Philistines. 1 Sam. 13.

14. *Who was Jonathan?*—Saul's son.

15. *What marked difference was there between him and his father?*—He was of a modest and affectionate disposition, and loved David.

16. *Who obtained the victory recorded in 1 Sam. 13: 3?*—Jonathan.

17. *Who reaped the honor of it?*—Saul. 1 Sam. 13: 3, 4.

18. *Was it not unworthy of Saul to take the glory that did not belong to him?*—It was.

19. *How did Saul again show his mean spirit in this same chapter?*—By retiring to Gilgal, leaving Jonathan and his men exposed to the enemy. 1 Sam. 13: 2, 4.

20. *What did Samuel say to Saul when he came?*—He reproved him for offering a sacrifice to God without the high priest. 1 Sam. 13: 13.

21. *What proof does this chapter give us of the degraded state into which Israel had fallen?*—The Philistines did not allow them arms, or even a smith to sharpen their tools. 1 Sam. 13: 19, 20.

22. *What glorious victory does 1 Sam. 14: 4–23, 31 record?*—Over the Philistines between Michmash and Aijalon.

23. *Who was the brave warrior here?*—Jonathan. 1 Sam 14: 4–14.

24. *How did Saul nearly spoil the victory of that day?*—By pledging his people to eat nothing all day until the battle was won. 1 Sam. 14: 24.

25. *Was not an oath a very sacred thing?*—When thou shalt vow a vow unto the Lord thy God, thou shalt not be slack to pay it: for the Lord thy God will surely require it of thee; and it would be sin in thee. But if thou shalt forbear to vow, it shall be no sin in thee. Deut. 23: 21, 22.

26. *What proof can you give of this in 2 Sam. 21: 7?*—King David spared Mephibosheth, the son of Jonathan the son of Saul because of the Lord's oath that was between them, between David and Jonathan the son of Saul.

27. *Was not that transaction another proof of Saul's cowardly disposition? Who were the Gibeonites?*—It was cowardly of Saul to kill those who trusted to the Israelites' oath, and were not prepared to defend themselves. 2 Sam. 21: 2. They were Amorites who had

deceived the Israelites, but whom they had promised not to kill. Josh. 9.

28. *What great touchstone has God given to try man by?*—Not every one that saith unto me, Lord, Lord, shall enter into the kingdom of heaven; but he that doeth the will of my Father which is in heaven. Matt. 7 : 21.

29. *What test of* obedience *did God require from Saul?*—That in fighting with the Amalekites he should destroy their sheep and oxen also. 1 Sam. 15 : 3.

30. *How did he act?*—He spared the best of them. 1 Sam. 15 : 9.

31. *How did Samuel feel?*—He was grieved. 1 Sam. 15 : 11.

32. *How did Samuel act?*—He told Saul that he should be no longer king. 1 Sam. 15 : 23.

33. *How did Saul's real character come out in this transaction?*—He showed himself more anxious to please his people for his *own* honor than for the honor of God. 1 Sam. 15 : 30.

34. *What accident happened to Samuel's garment as he turned away from Saul?*—It was rent. 1 Sam. 15 : 27.

35. *What prophecy did Samuel utter in connection with it?*—That God had rent his kingdom from him, and had given it to a better man. 1 Sam. 15 : 28.

36. *When did Saul next see Samuel?*—When Saul prophesied before him in Ramah, whither Saul had gone to see *him* (1 Sam. 19 : 24), and afterward when Samuel came and appeared to *Saul*, by God's permission, at the summons of the witch of Endor. 1 Sam. 28 : 3–20.

37. *What proof does that transaction give us that God never alters the word that he has once spoken?*—Because Samuel repeated and confirmed God's former judgment against him. 1 Sam. 28 : 17.

38. *Was not the woman surprised at what she herself had been permitted to do?*—She cried out from fear. 1 Sam. 28 : 12.

39. *In whose keeping are the spirits of the departed dead?*—They are all in the keeping of God—the blessed in paradise with Christ, and the wicked with Satan in their own place.

40. *Suppose any could return to us again, could they add to the testimony of Scripture?*—They could only confirm it.

If they hear not Moses and the prophets, neither will they be persuaded, though one rose from the dead. Luke 16 : 31.

DAVID. (1 Sam. 16.)

1. *Who was David?*—The youngest son of Jesse, a Bethlehemite. 1 Sam. 16 : 1.

2. *What prophecy was spoken of the tribe of Judah by Jacob?*—Judah, thou art he whom thy brethren shall praise: thy hand shall be in the neck of thine enemies; thy father's children shall bow down before thee. Gen. 49 : 8.

3. *Why did the Lord reject Saul from being king?*—Because he had not obeyed his commands. 1 Sam. 15 : 11, 23.

4. *Whom did he choose in his place?*—David. 1 Sam. 16 : 1, 11–13.

5. *Who was appointed to anoint David?*—Samuel. 1 Sam. 16 : 1.

6. *Why had the Lord chosen Saul?*—On account merely of his being a tall and a noble-looking man; God being displeased with the Israelites' *asking* for a king. 1 Sam. 9 : 2.

7. *Did the same rule apply to David?*—No; he was chosen rather on account of his qualities of mind and heart. 1 Sam. 16 : 6, 7.

8. *How was Samuel taught this?*—By being told to reject Jesse's elder sons.

9. *What occupation was David following at this time?*—Keeping sheep. 1 Sam. 16 : 11.

10. *What deplorable loss did Saul sustain when the Spirit of the Lord rested upon David?*—The Spirit departed from himself. 1 Sam. 16 : 14.

11. *What evil power took possession of Saul?*—An evil spirit, by permission of God.

12. *In what way did he obtain comfort?*—By having some one to play to him on the harp. 1 Sam. 16 : 16.

13. *Who was selected as his minstrel?*—David. 1 Sam. 16 : 18–23.

14. *What did this prove?*—The guiding providence of God.

15. *As David was then a shepherd, what psalm may we suppose he sang on his harp to the king?*—Perhaps the twenty-third.

16. *What effect did David's sweet harp have on the king?*—He was soothed and refreshed, but Jesus Christ and his Spirit, alone, can give our troubled conscience peace.

DAVID AND GOLIATH. (1 Sam. 17.)

1. *Did David continue to live with Saul?*—No; he returned to his father's sheep. 1 Sam. 17 : 15.

2. *Did his intercourse with Saul's court unfit him for a shepherd life?*—By the grace of God, it seems not to have done so.

3. *Where were David's brothers at this time?*—The three eldest went with Saul to battle. 1 Sam. 17 : 13.

4. *What did Jesse desire David to do?*—To take his brothers a present, and see how they fared. 1 Sam. 17 : 17, 18.

5. *Who were Israel's greatest enemies at this time?*—The Philistines.

6. *What had these enemies particularly to encourage them to fight at this time?*—The giant Goliath was on their side. 1 Sam. 17 : 4–11.

7. *What did David do when he got to the camp?*—He asked who Goliath was, and what was to be the reward for killing him. 1 Sam. 17 : 26.

8. *What effect did David's questions have on his brothers?*—Eliab thought him proud and presumptuous, and was angry with him. 1 Sam. 17 : 28.

9. *How did David answer them?*—Meekly and calmly. 1 Sam. 17 : 29.

10. *For what pleasing traits of character was David always remarkable?*—Gentleness, patience and forbearance.

11. *What was he called?*—A man after God's own heart. Acts 13 : 22.

12. *Give some texts in which God commends a meek and gentle spirit?*—I therefore, the prisoner of the Lord, beseech you that ye walk worthy of the vocation wherewith ye are called, with all lowliness and meekness, with long-suffering, forbearing one another in love. Eph. 4 : 1, 2. Put on therefore, as the elect of God, holy and beloved, bowels of mercies, kindness, humbleness of mind, meekness, long-suffering; forbearing one another, and forgiving one another, if any man have a quarrel against any: even as Christ forgave you, so also do ye. Col. 3 : 12, 13.

13. *What is said to be "of great price" in the Lord's estimation?*—The ornament of a meek and quiet spirit. 1 Pet. 3 : 4.

14. *Who was the most meek and gentle Being who ever lived?*—Christ also suffered for us, leaving us an example, that ye should follow his steps: who did no sin, neither was guile found in his mouth: who, when he was reviled, reviled not again; when he suffered, he threatened not; but committed himself to Him that judgeth righteously. 1 Pet. 2 : 21–23.

15. *Of whom are we commanded to "learn"?*—Of Jesus Christ.

Take my yoke upon you, and learn of me; for I am meek and lowly in heart. Matt. 11 : 29.

16. *Did David gain the information that he sought?*—He did. 1 Sam. 17 : 25–27.

17. *What was the result?*—David undertook to fight with the Philistine. 1 Sam. 17 : 32.

18. *How did Saul wish to prepare David?*—With Saul's own armor. 1 Sam. 17 : 38.

19. *Did he use the armor?*—No, because he was unaccustomed to it.

20. *What preparation did David make?*—He only took his staff and sling and five stones in a bag. 1 Sam. 17 : 40.

21. *What was the result of the engagement?*—The giant was killed by the first stone slung. 1 Sam. 17 : 49.

22. *Was only the giant slain?*—The Philistines fled, and many of them were slain.

23. *What did David do with the head and armor of Goliath?*—He brought the head to Saul and to Jerusalem, and put the armor in his tent.

24. *How was it that David had such power?*—Because he trusted in the Lord his God.

25. *Is his act of faith mentioned in Heb. 11?*—Yes, in verse 32.

DAVID AND JONATHAN. (1 Sam. 17 : 55–58; 18, 19, 20.)

1. *What remarkable question did Saul ask Abner when David went to fight the giant?*—Whose son David was. 1 Sam. 17 : 55.

2. *Was Abner able to answer Saul's question?*—He was not.

3. *How did they ascertain who the young conqueror was?*—Saul ascertained it from David's own mouth.

4. *Which of Saul's sons standing by felt his soul knit to David?*—Jonathan. 1 Sam. 18 : 1.

5. *What touching proof did he give of his love?*—He gave him his robes and some of his arms, though the scarceness of arms had made them especially valuable. Compare 1 Sam. 18 : 4 with 1 Sam. 13 : 22.

6. *What joyful song did the women sing when they went to meet the conquerors after the battle?*—Saul has slain his thousands, and David his ten thousands. 1 Sam. 18 : 7.

7. *What effect did this have on Saul?*—It made him jealous and angry.

8. *How did David behave himself?*—Wisely. 1 Sam. 18 : 14.

9. *Did Saul remember his promise to give his daughter in marriage to the man who should slay Goliath?*—No; he gave her to another man. 1 Sam. 18 : 17–19.

10. *What artful design did he form to get David slain?*—He required him to kill one hundred Philistines as the price of his daughter Michal, hoping he would have been killed himself. 1 Sam. 18 : 25.

11. *Did it succeed?*—No; David slew two hundred, and was unhurt.

12. *What was Saul obliged to do?*—To give him his daughter Michal for his wife. 1 Sam. 18 : 27.

13. *Did Saul's daughter love David?*—Yes. 1 Sam. 18 : 20, 28.

14. *How did she prove this?*—By letting him down from a window, that he might escape her father's rage. 1 Sam. 19 : 12–17.

15. *Why was David obliged to flee?*—Because Saul designed to kill him. 1 Sam. 19 : 1, 15.

16. *Would Jonathan believe this?*—No. 1 Sam. 20 : 1, 2; 19 : 4–7.

17. *Where did David first escape to?*—To Samuel, in Ramah. 1 Sam. 19 : 18.

18. *What wonderful power did God exercise over the messengers sent to take David?*—The power of his Spirit, causing them to prophesy like Samuel's prophets. 1 Sam. 19 : 20, 21.

19. *Did David venture into Saul's presence again?*—He seems to have done so at Naioth in Ramah. 1 Sam. 19 : 22–24; 20 : 5.

20. *How did Jonathan assure himself that his father desired David's death?*—By what David said. 1 Sam. 20 : 3.

21. *When he discovered it, what course did he take?*—He promised to tell David of Saul's designs. 1 Sam. 20 : 9.

22. *What beautiful covenant did they make together?*—That Jonathan should warn David, and that David should be kind to Jonathan and his children. 1 Sam. 19 : 12–17, 23.

23. *Where did they each go afterward?*—David to his former hiding-place, and Jonathan to his father. 1 Sam 20 : 19; 19 : 2.

DAVID A FUGITIVE. (1 Sam. 21–31.)

1. *Whither did David flee?*—To Nob.

2. *What did he obtain there?*—Some bread.

3. *Did he do this honorably?*—No; he pretended he was on the king's business. 1 Sam. 21 : 2.

4. *What made him tell a lie?*—Want of food, and fear that the priest would not give it him.

5. *Did not this show a want of faith in the living God who had hitherto so wonderfully preserved him?*—It did.

6. *To what place did he next proceed?*—To Gath. 1 Sam. 21 : 10.

7. *Did he act more consistently there?*—No; he pretended to be mad, that he might escape being imprisoned. 1 Sam. 21 : 11–13.

8. *What does this show us?*—That even the best men often fall into weakness and sin through their forgetfulness of God.

9. *Where did he go when he left Achish?*—To the cave Adullam. 1 Sam. 22 : 1.

10. *Who came to him there?*—Every one that was discontented or in debt or distress. 1 Sam. 22 : 2.

11. *What kind care did he take of his father and his mother?*—He got the king of Moab to receive and protect them. 1 Sam. 22 : 3, 4.

12. *Why were they obliged to leave their native place, Bethlehem?*—Because the garrison of the Philistines was then in Bethlehem. 2 Sam. 23 : 14; 1 Chron. 11 : 15, 16.

13. *Who joined David here?*—Jonathan, in the wilderness of Ziph. 1 Sam. 23 : 15, 16.

14. *Is there any description given of his men?*—Three mighty chiefs are there mentioned who slew great numbers of the Philistines; and thirty other valiant men, among whom Abishai and Benaiah are especially noted for their exploits. 2 Sam. 23; 1 Chron. 11.

15. *What proof of love did his men give him at this time?*—Three of them broke through the host of the Philistines to fetch him water from a favorite well. 2 Sam. 23 : 16; 1 Chron. 11 : 18.

16. *How did he show the tenderness of his heart in return?*—By declining to drink what had been obtained at so great a risk of his men's lives, and by pouring out the water in thankfulness to God.

17. *What are courage and tenderness, united, a proof of?*—Of a truly manly character.

18. *What cowardly act was Saul again guilty of toward the priests who had helped David?*—He ordered them to be slain. 1 Sam. 22 : 17.

19. *How did David and his noble little band of warriors employ themselves?*—In fighting with the Philistines, and rescuing the inhabitants of Keilah. 1 Sam. 23 : 1–5.

20. *When Saul heard it, what did he resolve to do?*—

To besiege Keilah and take David prisoner. 1 Sam. 23 : 7, 8.

21. *How did the Lord deliver David when Saul had nearly taken him?*—By causing the Philistines to invade the land, David having first prayed for direction, and Jonathan having given him encouragement from God. 1 Sam. 23 : 27, 28, 10, 16.

22. *Did Saul again go after David?*—Yes, in the wilderness of Engedi. 1 Sam. 24 : 1, 2.

23. *How did David behave when the Lord put Saul in his power?*—He would not kill him nor allow his men to do so. 1 Sam. 24 : 4–7.

24. *What effect did this have on Saul?*—He wept and spoke kindly to David. 1 Sam. 24 : 8–22.

25. *What treatment did David at this time meet with from Nabal?*—He refused to give food to David and his men, though they had taken nothing from him all the time they had been hiding and in want of provisions near him. 1 Sam. 25 : 1–13.

26. *How did Nabal's wife act?*—She went to him with a supply of food. 1 Sam. 25 : 14–31.

27. *What proof did she give of the high honor in which she held David (though an exile) at her husband's death?* —She became his wife. 1 Sam. 25 : 39–42.

28. *Did Saul again seek after David?*—Yes, in the wilderness of Ziph. 1 Sam. 26 : 1, 2.

29. *How did David revenge himself?*—By again sparing Saul's life. 1 Sam. 26 : 7–12.

Dearly beloved, avenge not yourselves, but rather give place unto wrath: for it is written, Vengeance is mine; I will repay, saith the Lord. Therefore if thine enemy hunger, feed him; if he thirst, give him drink: for in so doing thou shalt heap coals of fire on his head. Be not overcome of evil, but overcome evil with good. Rom. 12 : 19–21.

30. *With what heathen did David again join himself?* —With Achish, king of Gath. 1 Sam. 27.

31. *Was this right?*—No; it was contrary to God's commandments to Moses and Joshua.

32. *What difficulties did David bring upon himself by this unholy alliance?*—He was invited by Achish to join him in fighting against the Israelites. 1 Sam. 28 : 1, 2.

33. *Where was David when the last decisive battle between Saul and the Philistines was fought?*—At Ziklag.

34. *To which side did David offer himself and his men?*—To Achish. 1 Sam. 29 : 8.

35. *Is it not likely he would have gone over to the side of Israel?*—No doubt.

36. *How did God preserve him from so very dangerous a position?*—By inducing the Philistine leaders to object to his being with them. 1 Sam. 29 : 4, 5.

37. *What event happened to him and his men while they were absent from Ziklag?*—The Amalekites burnt the city, and carried away the women and children captive. 1 Sam. 30 : 1, 2.

38. *Did they recover their treasures?*—Yes.

39. *How?*—They pursued and slew the Amalekites, and recovered all, after David had laid his trouble before God and obtained direction from him. 1 Sam. 30 : 6–20.

40. *What did he do with the spoil that they won?*—He divided it among all his men who had taken part in the pursuit or fight. 1 Sam. 30 : 21–25.

41. *What tremendous battle was happening in Israel while David and his men were thus employed?*—A battle with the Philistines in Mount Gilboa. 1 Sam. 31 : 1.

DAVID KING IN HEBRON. (2 Sam. 1–4.)

1. *How was David employed when the news came to him of the death of Saul and Jonathan?*—He was returned to Ziklag. 2 Sam. 1 : 1.

2. *What effect did the death of Saul have on David?*— He mourned for him and wept. 2 Sam. 1 : 12.

3. *How did Saul die?*—By his own hand, after being wounded by the Philistines. 1 Sam. 31 : 3, 4.

4. *What did David do to the young man who by his own confession had killed Saul?*—He ordered one of his soldiers to kill him. 2 Sam. 1 : 14–16.

5. *What touching record did David leave of his love to Saul and Jonathan?*—A song of lamentation. 2 Sam. 1 : 17–27.

6. *Did David at once go and possess the kingdom? How did he act?*—Yes; after seeking direction from God, he went up to Hebron, and was there anointed king. 2 Sam. 2 : 1–4.

7. *Which tribe first acknowledged David's claim?*— Judah.

8. *What act of unnecessary bloodshed took place at Gibeon?*—A battle between the men of Judah and the men of Israel, who had Ishbosheth, a son of Saul, for their king. 2 Sam. 2 : 8–17.

9. *Which were victorious, Joab's men or Abner's?*— Joab's.

10. *What happened to Asahel, Joab's brother?*—He was killed by Abner. 2 Sam. 2 : 18–23.

11. *How long did the war continue between the houses of Saul and David?*—About two years. 2 Sam. 2 : 10; 3 : 1.

12. *What event turned the scale on David's side?*— Abner's deserting Israel on account of a quarrel with Ishbosheth, and offering to make terms with David. 2 Sam. 3 : 6–20.

13. *Did David receive Abner?*—Yes, with hospitality and honor. 2 Sam. 3 : 20.

14. *How did Joab like this?*—He blamed David for it. 2 Sam. 3 : 24, 25.

15. *What did Joab do?*—He killed Abner in revenge for the death of Asahel. 2 Sam. 3 : 27.

16. *What course did David take when he heard this?* —He called upon all the people to mourn with him for Abner. 2 Sam. 3 : 31.

17. *What traits of character does David's conduct display?*—Tenderness of heart and readiness to forgive.

18. *Did David approve of Joab's conduct?*—No; as Abner was no longer a rebel, and as Joab had killed him deceitfully and revengefully in time of peace.

19. *Why did he not punish him?*—Because he had not the power. 2 Sam. 3 : 39.

20. *Who was Zeruiah?*—The mother of Abishai, Joab and Asahel.

21. *Of what act of treachery were the servants of Ishbosheth guilty?*—They killed their master. 2 Sam. 4 : 2, 5–8.

22. *Did not the death of Ishbosheth clear the way to David's ascent to the throne of Israel?*—It did, as no one else was seeking to be king.

23. *Did David on this account reward the murderers? How did he act toward them?*—So far from rewarding them for their treachery and infidelity, he ordered them to be slain.

DAVID AND THE ARK OF GOD. (2 Sam. 5 and 6, and 1 Chron. 14, 15, 16.)

1. *How old was David when all Israel came to anoint him king?*—Thirty. 2 Sam. 5 : 4.

2. *What was David's first conquest?*—The stronghold of Zion. Sam. 2 : 5, 7.

3. *What was there about this city that renders it so remarkable and makes it of peculiar interest to us?*—The temple in which our Lord so often taught was built there.

4. *What king made presents to David?*—Hiram, king of Tyre. 2 Sam. 5 : 11.

5. *Where was Tyre?*—To the north of Canaan, on the borders of the Mediterranean Sea.

6. *For what was Tyre remarkable?*—For its manufacture of purple dresses and for its commerce.

7. *Did the Philistines treat David as Hiram had? How did they act when they heard he was king?*—No; they went to fight against him. 2 Sam. 5 : 18.

8. *What did the Philistines take with them to battle?*—Images of their gods. 2 Sam. 5 : 21.

9. *How was David guided?*—By God, whose direction he had sought. 2 Sam. 5 : 19.

10. *Which host conquered?*—David's. 2 Sam. 5 : 20.

11. *What became of the gods of the Philistines?*—David burnt them. 2 Sam. 5 : 21.

12. *What was David's next act?*—To bring the ark from Kirjath-jearim. 2 Sam. 6 : 2, 3.

13. *How came the ark to be at Kirjath-jearim?*—Because God had not yet directed it to be removed thence.

14. *Where was the tabernacle at this time?*—In Gibeon. Scott on 2 Sam. 6 : 17.

15. *In whose house had the ark been kept?*—In the house of Abinadab. 1 Sam. 7 : 1.

16. *In what way did they bring it?*—In a new cart. 2 Sam. 6 : 3.

17. *What happened to Uzzah?*—He died by the hand of God for thoughtlessly and rashly taking hold of so sacred a thing as the ark when it seemed about to fall. 2 Sam. 6 : 6, 7.

18. *How did David feel?*—He was displeased, and afraid to go farther. 2 Sam. 6 : 8–10.

19. *What did he do with the ark then?*—He placed it in the house of Obed-edom the Gittite. 2 Sam. 6 : 10.

20. *How ought the ark to have been brought?*—By hand, with staves. Num. 4 : 15.

21. *How many months had elapsed before David had courage to fetch the ark?*—Three. 2 Sam. 6 : 11.

22. *What induced him then to do it?*—The blessing that rested upon those who had the charge of it. 2 Sam. 6 : 12.

23. *How was it accomplished this time?*—The Levites bore the ark with staves upon their shoulders. 1 Chron. 15 : 2, 15.

24. *Why was Michal, David's wife, offended with David?*—Because of his dancing to the music before the ark. 2 Sam. 6 : 20.

25. *What did David's manner really express?*—Religious joy and humble thankfulness.

26. *Of whom in his humility was David a type?*—Of Christ, the lowly one of heart.

27. *Where did David place the ark?*—In a tent on Mount Zion, in the city of David. 1 Sam. 7 : 1, 3; 16 : 1.

28. *Was he satisfied with this? What did he desire to do?*—No; he desired to build for the ark a house of cedar. 1 Sam. 17 : 1.

29. *Did the Lord permit him to do it?*—No.

30. *How did the Lord make his will known to David?*—By Nathan the prophet. 1 Sam. 7 : 3–15.

31. *What did David feel? and what did he say?*—He felt deeply humble and very unworthy of God's promised blessings, and prayed to God to confirm his word. 1 Sam. 7 : 16–27.

32. *In whom was David's house to be confirmed for ever?*—In Jesus Christ, as Zacharias declared in Luke 1 : 68–70.

33. *Was the claim of Jesus as "son of David" acknowledged when he was on earth? When?*—Yes, when he rode into Jerusalem.

And the multitudes that went before, and that followed, cried. saying, Hosanna to the son of David! Matt. 21 : 9.

34. *When does Jesus call* himself *"the offspring of David"?*—In Rev. 22 : 16.

35. *Has he yet sat on David's throne?*—No; we see not yet all things put under him. Heb. 2 : 8.

36. *Where is it said "I will give to him the throne of his father David"?*—The Lord God shall give unto him the throne of his father David: and he shall reign over the house of Jacob for ever; and of his kingdom there shall be no end. Luke 1 : 32, 33.

37. *When will this be fulfilled?*—When Christ returns to judge and reign.

DAVID'S CONQUEST—HIS SIN. (2 Sam. 8–12; 1 Chron. 18–20.)

1. *What had God's promise been of the boundary of Israel's possession?*—"From the river of Egypt unto the river Euphrates."

2. *What conquests did David make which fulfilled this?*—The conquest of the Philistines, Moabites, Ammonites and Syrians. 2 Sam. 8 : 1, 2, 6, 12, 14; 10 : 19.

3. *What splendid armor had the Syrians?*—Golden shields. 2 Sam. 8 : 7.

4. *What did David do with the spoil that he took in battle?*—He gave the gold and silver and brass for the ornament and service of the tabernacle. 2 Sam. 8 : 10, 11.

5. *How did he arrange his kingdom?*—He made Joab commander-in-chief; Jehoshaphat, historian; Zadok and Ahimelech, priests; and his own sons and others, judges and officers. 2 Sam. 8 : 15–18.

6. *Did he forget his friend Jonathan in this his prosperity? What proof did he give?*—No; he inquired after the family of Saul, and gave Saul's land and a place at his own table to Mephibosheth, son of Jonathan. 2 Sam. 9.

7. *How often was it customary for kings to go forth to battle?*—"At the return of the year," or in spring.

8. *Whom did David send to besiege Rabbah?*—Joab. 2 Sam. 11 : 1.

9. *Where was David?*—At Jerusalem.

10. *Why did David send Uriah with a letter to Joab, telling him to put him in the front of the battle?*—In order that he might be killed. 2 Sam. 11 : 15.

11. *Why did David wish the brave Uriah to die?*—That he might get possession of his wife, with whom he had committed adultery.

12. *Was not this a very awful sin?*—Yes; it was adding *murder* to his other shocking sin.

13. *Whom did the Lord send to convince David of his sin?*—Nathan the prophet. 2 Sam. 12 : 1.

14. *How did he do it?*—By a parable.

15. *Did the Lord pardon David?*—Yes, and said he should not die. 2 Sam. 12 : 13.

16. *Did he not say also that in his feelings as a father he would chastise him for it?*—Yes, by the death of his child; and he was also punished by Absalom's rebellion. 2 Sam. 12 : 14.

17. *How did David feel?*—It is believed that his deep sorrow for his sin is expressed in the fifty-first Psalm.

18. *Did the Israelites conquer Rabbah?*—Yes. 2 Sam. 12 : 26.

19. *What message did Joab send to David?*—That he should come and have the honor of completing the conquest of the city himself. 2 Sam. 12 : 27, 28.

20. *Although David got the honor of conquering Rabbah, and had the crown placed on his head, do you think he felt happy in it when the brave Uriah had died under the walls?*—No; he said his sin was ever before him. Ps. 51 : 3.

21. *What signal proof did the Lord give to David of his full and free forgiveness?*—By giving him another child. 2 Sam. 12 : 24.

22. *What was the name of this child?*—Solomon.

23. *What was the meaning of the name?*—"Peaceable."

24. *What name did Nathan the prophet add to this? and what did it mean?*—Jedidiah, "Beloved of the Lord." 2 Sam. 12 : 25.

25. *Through whom must we obtain forgiveness of our sins?*—Through Jesus Christ.

26. *Is there any limit to God's forgiving grace?*—No; he will abundantly pardon. Isa. 55 : 7.

27. *What did Jesus say to the woman whom he forgave when on earth?*—"Neither do I condemn thee: go and sin no more." John 8 : 11.

DAVID AND ABSALOM. (2 Sam. 13–22.)

1. *Who was Absalom?*—A son of David. 2 Sam. 13 : 1.

2. *Why did he flee away to Geshur?*—Because he had killed his half-brother Ammon for outraging his sister Tamar. 2 Sam. 13 : 28, 32, 37.

3. *How long did he stay there?*—Three years.

4. *Who brought him back again?*—Joab, who by a kind contrivance had gotten David's leave. 2 Sam. 14 : 23.

5. *How did he repay his father's kindness?*—By making a conspiracy against him. 2 Sam. 15.

6. *What punishment had the Lord said should spring from David's own house?*—The sword and other evils. 2 Sam. 12 : 10, 11.

7. *Why?*—Because of his taking Uriah's wife.

8. *How did Absalom steal away the people's affections from David?*—By artful speeches and promises and civilities. 2 Sam. 15 : 2–6.

9. *When David heard of the conspiracy, what did he do?*—He fled from Jerusalem. 2 Sam. 15 : 13–16.

10. *Who went with him?*—All his household and six hundred men from Gath. 2 Sam. 15 : 16–18.

11. *What famous counselor followed Absalom?*—Ahithophel. 2 Sam. 15 : 31.

12. *Who managed by an artifice to set his counsel aside?*—Hushai, David's friend. 2 Sam. 15 : 32–37; 17 : 1–14.

13. *Whose advice did Absalom follow?*—Hushai's. 2 Sam. 17 : 14.

14. *What effect did this have on Ahithophel?*—He hanged himself. 2 Sam. 17 : 23.

15. *Why did Hushai give this advice?*—That he might secure David's escape.

16. *Who slew Absalom?*—Joab.

17. *How was it done?*—As Absalom hung from an oak tree by his hair, which had become entangled as he rode under it. 2 Sam. 18 : 9–15.

18. *What command had David given about Absalom to his captains?*—That they should deal gently with him for his sake. 2 Sam. 18 : 5.

19. *Did Joab seem to care for this?*—Not at all. 2 Sam. 18 : 11, 14.

20. *How did David feel, and what did he say, when Absalom was slain?*—He was deeply distressed, and said, "Would God I had died for thee, O Absalom, my son, my son!" 2 Sam. 18 : 33; 19 : 1–4.

21. *Of what sin was Absalom guilty?*—Rebellion against his father and against his king.

22. *Of whom, in both these particulars, was he a type?*—Of Satan, the rebel against God, and the angel of light.

23. *Describe Absalom's person?*—He was the handsomest man in the country, and was remarkable for his long, flowing hair. 2 Sam. 14 : 25, 26.

24. *What does the Lord say about pride in Proverbs?*—Pride, and arrogancy, and the evil way, and the froward mouth, do I hate. 8 : 13. When pride cometh, then cometh shame: but with the lowly is wisdom. 11 : 2. Pride goeth before destruction, and an haughty spirit before a fall. 16 : 18.

25. *Was peace at once again restored to Israel?*—It was. 2 Sam. 19 : 9, 14.

26. *Whom had David appointed captain of his host instead of Joab?*—Amasa. 2 Sam. 19 : 13.

27. *How did Joab act on hearing this?*—He killed him. 2 Sam. 20 : 9, 10.

28. *What relation was Amasa to David?*—Nephew, as son of his sister Abigail.

29. *Did David again spare Joab from punishment?*—Yes; he continued to be commander-in-chief. 2 Sam. 20 : 23.

30. *Who quelled the insurrection?*—Joab. 2 Sam. 28 : 14.

31. *What was a famine in Israel a sign of?*—National guilt. Deut. 28.

Heaven is shut up, and there is no rain, because they have sinned against thee. 1 Kings 8 : 35.

32. *What were David's feelings when a famine of three years visited Israel?*—Doubtless he felt compassion for his suffering people, and believed that the famine was a visitation of God. 2 Sam. 21.

33. *Of whom did he inquire?*—Of the Lord. 2 Sam. 21 : 1.

34. *What was the Lord's reply?*—That the famine was in consequence of the guilt incurred by the nation when Saul and his people slew the Gibeonites. 2 Sam. 21 : 1, 2.

35. *What expiation did the Gibeonites require?*—The death of seven of Saul's sons. 2 Sam. 21 : 6.

36. *What touching proof of a mother's love did Rizpah give?*—She watched the bodies of her sons night and day, to prevent their being torn by birds or beasts. 2 Sam. 21 : 10.

37. *What old enemies of David's again showed themselves?*—The Philistines. 2 Sam. 21 : 15.

38. *What proof have we of David's declining strength and of the faithful love of his followers?*—He was faint in battle, and Abishai preserved his life, and his people said he should no longer go out with them to battle. 2 Sam. 21 : 15–17.

39. *What is the twenty-second chapter of 2 Samuel about?*—It is David's psalm of thanksgiving for deliverance from his enemies.

DAVID'S TRANSGRESSION, HIS LAST ARRANGEMENTS, AND DEATH. (2 Sam. 24; 1 Chron. 21–29; 1 Kings 1, 2.)

1. *By whom was David tempted to number Israel?*—Satan. 1 Chron. 21 : 1.

2. *What is Satan called in 1 Pet. 5 : 8?*—A roaring lion, walking about seeking whom he may devour.

3. *Who remonstrated with David?*—Joab. 2 Sam. 24 : 3.

4. *Did not David's heart smite him after he had don it?*—Yes; he said he had sinned greatly and don very foolishly. 2 Sam. 24 : 10.

5. *What was God's promise to Abraham as to the number of Israel?*—That it should be very great, like the number of the stars.

6. *Whom did the Lord commission to reprove David?*—The prophet Gad. 2 Sam. 24 : 11.

7. *What did he offer him?*—The choice of one of three punishments.

8. *Which did David choose? and why?*—Famine or pestilence, rather than war; the immediate hand of God, rather than the hand of man.

9. *At what spot did the destroying angel stop?*—The threshing-floor of Araunah. 2 Sam. 24 : 16.

10. *What event had occurred on that hill about eight hundred years before?*—The offering up of Isaac (in the opinion of some).

11. *Of what was that circumstance a type?*—Of the sacrifice of Christ as the atonement for sin.

12. *How did David know that the Lord had accepted his offering?*—By the plague being stayed. 2 Sam. 24 : 25.

13. *By whose authority did he consecrate the threshing-floor of Araunah?*—By the authority of the prophet Gad. 2 Sam. 24 : 18.

14. *Why did he not go up to the tabernacle at Gibeon?* —Because he was afraid of meeting the angel again at the place of God's special presence. 1 Chron. 21 : 29, 30.

15. *What preparations did he make for the future building of the temple?*—Hewn stone, gold, silver, iron, brass and cedar. 1 Chron. 22 : 2–5, 14–16.

16. *What solemn charge did David give to Solomon concerning the temple?*—To build it, as David himself had desired to do. 1 Chron. 22 : 6–16.

17. *What other arrangements did David make?*—He divided the priests and Levites and other officers into orders, and fixed their duties. 1 Chron. 23 : 23–27.

18. *Who showed David the pattern of the future temple?*—God himself, by his Spirit. 1 Chron. 28 : 12, 19.

19. *Did any one besides David contribute toward the future glory of the temple?*—The chiefs and the people. 1 Chron. 29 : 6–9.

20. *Whom did David make king over Israel before he died?*—Solomon. 1 Chron. 23 : 1.

21. *Who had aspired to be king?*—Adonijah, one of David's sons. 1 Kings 1 : 5, 6.

22. *What charge did David give to Solomon concerning Joab and Shimei?*—That they should receive the punishment due to their guilt. 1 Kings 2 : 5, 6, 8, 9.

23. *What were the last words of David?*—Now bless the Lord your God. 1 Chron. 29 : 20.

24. *How old was David when he died?*—Seventy.

25. *How many years had he reigned in Hebron? how many over all Israel?*—David was thirty years old when he began to reign, and he reigned forty years. In Hebron he reigned over Judah seven years and six months; and in Jerusalem he reigned thirty-and-three years over all Israel and Judah. 2 Sam. 5 : 4, 5.

26. *In what respect was David a man after God's own heart?*—In the general character of his life, and in his being a type of Christ, his own beloved Son.

DAVID A TYPE OF CHRIST.

1. *What is the meaning of the name Christ?*— "Anointed."

2. *Was David made king at the time he was anointed?* —He was not at the time of his first anointing by Samuel.

3. *Tell how this circumstance is typical of the Lord Jesus Christ?*—Because, though Christ's kingdom began when he was anointed with the Holy Ghost and commenced his ministry on earth, his great universal reign has not yet taken place.

4. *What was David before he was called from his father's house?*—A keeper of sheep.

5. *What wild beasts did he fight with and kill?*—A lion and a bear.

6. *Of whom are those beasts a type?*—Of Satan the roaring lion. 1 Pet. 5 : 8.

7. *Who is "the Good Shepherd" who gives "his life for the sheep"?*—Jesus Christ. John 10 : 11.

8. *What was David's conduct to his father?*—That of a faithful, devoted and obedient son. 1 Sam. 17 : 20, 34, 35.

9. *Of whom is it recorded, "This is my beloved Son in whom I am well pleased"?*—Of Jesus Christ. Matt. 3 : 17.

10. *In what relative position did David stand to Saul?* —In that of servant to a master.

11. *What ought a servant to be?*—Honest, diligent, faithful and zealous, as serving God as well as man.

12. *How did David behave himself while serving Saul?* —Faithfully in duty and forbearing under provocation.

13. *Of whom is it recorded "I delight to do thy will, O my God"?*—Of Christ in the name of David. Ps. 40 : 8.

14. *Did David bear any other characters? Was he a prophet?*—Many. Yes.

15. *Did he speak of Jesus in the Psalms?*—Constantly, but especially in Psalms 22 and 110.

All things must be fulfilled, which were written in the law of Moses, and in the prophets, and in the psalms, concerning me. Luke 24 : 44.

16. *When did the Lord Jesus quote from the Psalms?* —Jesus saith unto them, Yea, have ye never read, Out of the mouth of babes and sucklings thou hast perfected praise? (Matt. 21 : 16 ; Ps. 8 : 2) ; Jesus cried with a loud voice, saying, Eli, Eli, lama Sabacthani? that is to say, My God, my God, why hast thou forsaken me? (Matt. 27 : 46 ; Ps. 22 : 1); and in other places.

17. *Of whom, then, as Psalmist, is David a type?*— Of Christ.

18. *Was not David a warrior, a captain and a leader?* —He was.

19. *What Scriptures show that the Lord Jesus was all these?*—Behold, I have given him for a witness to the people, a leader and commander to the people. Isa. 55 : 4 ; Rev. 19 : 13–15. The Captain of . . . salvation. Heb. 2 : 10.

20. *Where was David born?*—Doubtless at Bethlehem, where Jesse his father lived. 1 Sam. 17 : 12–15.

21. *Where was Jesus born?*—At Bethlehem. Matt. 2 : 1.

22. *Was the kingship of David acknowledged at once?* —No; Saul and his son Ishbosheth opposed or rebelled against him.

23. *Were there not a few who did recognize David as the anointed of God, even in his adversity? Name them.*—Samuel, Jonathan, Ahimelech, Gad, the Adullamites, Abiathar, Abigail, Joab, Abishai, Asahel and others.

24. *Were there any who owned the glory of Jesus when he was here in abasement?*—There were his apostles and disciples, and many women who ministered unto him.

25. *Did not the followers of David dearly love him?*— They did.

26. *Did they not even risk their lives for his sake?*— Many of them did in battle, and three of them to only get him some water for his thirst.

27. *And what is the feeling of those who own Jesus as their Lord and Master?*—A feeling, more or less warm and strong, of devoted, self-denying love.

28. *What did David feel toward them?*—A tender and grateful love.

29. *How did Jesus testify his estimation of love shown to him?*—Whosoever shall give to drink unto one of these little ones a cup of cold water only in the name of a disciple, verily I say unto you, he shall in no wise lose his reward. Matt. 10 : 42. Inasmuch as ye have done it unto one of the least of these my brethren, ye have done it unto me. Matt. 25 : 40.

30. *Did David conquer other nations, and rule beyond the limits of the twelve tribes of Israel?*—He conquered the Syrians, Ammonites and others.

31. *By what name is Jesus called in Rev. 19 : 16?* —KING OF KINGS AND LORD OF LORDS.

32. *What earthly throne is said to be everlasting?*— David's.

Thine house and thy kingdom shall be established for ever before thee: thy throne shall be established for ever. 2 Sam. 7 : 16.

33. *Of whom must that be spoken?*—Of Christ, the King.

34. *To whom does the parable in Luke 19 : 12–27 refer?*—The parable of the returned nobleman calling his servants to account refers to Christ coming again in his kingdom.

35. *Ought we not, then, to examine our hearts to see who is reigning there?*—Yes; for if he is not ruling over our affections now, we shall not be partakers of his kingdom hereafter.

36. *Have we not each some talent we shall be called to an account for?*—Yes; we all have time and influence, and more or less of means and abilities, to use for God's glory.

37. *Will you not have to give an account of even this lesson?*—Yes, and of every sermon we hear.

38. *What should you, then, strive to do?*—To remember what we hear, and, by the grace of God, to live and act according to it.

39. *Was David's reign a type of the peaceful reign of the Lord Jesus?*—No; he had been a man of war.

40. *Which king's reign is a type of it?*—Solomon's.

41. *What is the meaning of the name Solomon?*—"Peaceable."

SOLOMON. (1 Kings 1–11; 1 Chron. 21–29; 2 Chron. 1–9.)

1. *Of whom was Solomon a type?*—Of Christ, his peaceful reign being like the final kingdom of the Prince of Peace.

2. *Whose son was he?*—David's.

3. *What did the children cry of Jesus in the temple when he was on earth?*—Hosanna to the son of David! Matt. 21 : 15.

4. *Read John 6 : 15, and say what temporal honor the people wished to force upon Jesus?*—Jesus perceived that they would come and take him by force, to make him a king.

5. *Was the Lord Jesus rightful heir to David's throne on earth?*—Yes.

6. *Would he consent to take it from their hands?*—No.

7. *From whom will the Lord Jesus receive his kingdom?*—From God the Father in the appointed time.

8. *What did these same people do to the Lord Jesus very soon afterward?*—They derided his claim to be king and clamored for his crucifixion.

9. *When will Jesus take to himself his great power and reign?*—At the day of judgment. Rev. 11 : 15–18.

10. *Is this coming glory prophesied of in Scripture?*—In 2 Thess. 1 : 7–10, and other places.

11. *What was the first thing that Solomon did when he came to the throne—that is, after his father's death?*—He put Joab and Shimei (among others) to death. 1 Kings 2 : 28–46.

12. *Who had previously condemned them?*—David. 1 Kings 2 : 5, 6, 8, 9.

13. *How will our final award be settled?*—He that believeth and is baptized shall be saved; but he that believeth not shall be damned. Mark 16 : 16. Look to yourselves, that we lose not those things which we have wrought, but that we receive a full reward. 2 John 8.

14. *Who will be our Judge?*—God, in Christ.

15. *How does the Lord judge?*—Man looketh on the outward appearance, but the Lord looketh on the heart. 1 Sam. 16 : 7.

16. *By what standard shall we be judged?*—He that rejecteth me, and receiveth not my words, hath one that judgeth him: the word that I have spoken, the same shall judge him in the last day. John 12 : 48.

17. *Did Jesus judge men when he was on earth?*—No. If any man hear my words, and believe not, I judge

24*

him not: for I came not to judge the world, but to save the world. John 12 : 47.

18. *To what time does the Lord Jesus defer the judgment?*—To the last day. John 12 : 48.

19. *Were not David in deferring the judgment, and Solomon in executing it, great types of this?*—Yes.

20. *Have sinners any hope from the circumstance that God delays judgment?*—None at all, if they remain impenitent.

21. *Say what merciful reason the apostle Peter gives for delay in the last chapter of his Second Epistle?*—The Lord is not slack concerning his promise, as some men count slackness; but is long-suffering to us-ward, not willing that any should perish, but that all should come to repentance.

22. *Can you give some texts where the certainty of the judgment-day is spoken of?*—Behold, the Lord cometh with ten thousands of his saints, to execute judgment upon all. Jude 14, 15. When the Son of man shall come in his glory, and all the holy angels with him, then shall he sit upon the throne of his glory; and before him shall be gathered all nations; and he shall separate them one from another, as a shepherd divideth his sheep from the goats; and he shall set the sheep on his right hand, but the goats on the left. And these shall go away into everlasting punishment; but the righteous into life eternal. Matt. 25 : 31–36, 46. Behold, he cometh with clouds; and every eye shall see him, and they also which pierced him; and all kindreds of the earth shall wail because of him. Rev. 1 : 7.

23. *Can you give a description of it?*—I saw a great white throne, and him that sat on it, from whose face the earth and the heaven fled away; and there was found no place for them. And I saw the dead, small and great, stand before God; and the books were opened; and another book was opened, which is the book of life; and the dead were judged out of those things which were written in the books, according to their works. And the sea gave up the dead which were in it; and death and hell delivered up the dead which were in them; and they were judged every man according to their works. And death and hell were cast into the lake of fire. This is the second death. And whosoever was not found written in the book of life was cast into the lake of fire. Rev. 20 : 11–15.

24. *Will it be of any use for us to run to "the altar" (as Joab did) then?*—No; the day of salvation will have past, there will remain no more sacrifice for sin, and the mountains and rocks will be no shelter from the wrath of the Lamb.

25. *Of whom is the altar a type?*—Of Christ, the refuge now from the wrath to come.

26. *When should we flee to Jesus and lay hold of his righteousness?*—"Now is the accepted time." 2 Cor 6 : 2.

27. *Who was Solomon's queen?*—Pharaoh's daughter. 1 Kings 3 : 1.

28. *Had Egypt been a friend or enemy to Israel in former time?*—An enemy and oppressor for a long time after Joseph's death.

29. *Was it not remarkable that Solomon should choose a bride from Egypt?*—Yes, but she is supposed to have embraced the Jewish religion.

30. *Of whom was Solomon's bride a type?*—Of the Church, the bride of Christ. Rev. 19 : 7, 8.

31. *For whom did the Lord Jesus die? Was it for angels?*—Forasmuch, then, as the children are partakers of flesh and blood, he also himself likewise took part of the same. Heb. 2 : 14.

32. *By taking on himself our nature, to what place of dignity has he raised his people?*—To be "heirs of God, and joint-heirs with Christ" (Rom. 8 : 17), and "to sit with" him "in" his "throne." Rev. 3 : 21.

33. *By whose command did Solomon build the temple?* —By command of God. 1 Kings 5 : 5.

34. *Who had prepared greatly for this before him?*— David. 1 Chron. 22.

35. *Why was not David permitted to build the temple?* —Because he had "been a man of war." 1 Chron. 28 : 3.

36. *To whom had the pattern been shown?*—To David "by the Spirit" of God. 1 Chron. 28 : 11, 12.

37. *Who selected the place on which the temple was to be built?*—David. 1 Chron. 21 : 28–22 : 2.

38. *On what mountain was it built?*—Moriah. 2 Chron. 3 : 1.

39. *What wondrous act of faith had taken place on that mountain about eight hundred years before?*—It has been supposed that Abraham offered up Isaac on this spot.

40. *What is on that mountain now?*—The Turkish mosque or church of Omar.

41. *Who provided Solomon with timber, etc.?*—Hiram, king of Tyre. 1 Kings 5 : 1, 8–10.

42. *Was this a gift to Solomon, or did he pay for it?* —Solomon paid wages and supplied food to Hiram's men (1 Kings 5 : 6, 9), and gave him twenty cities in Galilee. 1 Kings 9 : 11.

43. *Was anything done in Lebanon besides felling the trees?*—Stone was hewn from the quarries. 1 Kings 5 : 17.

44. *Was the stone also prepared before it came to the temple?*—Yes. 1 Kings 5 : 18.

45. *Of what was this a type?*—Of the preparation of God's people to be "the temple of the living God" (2 Cor. 6 : 16), built upon the foundation of the apostles and prophets, Jesus Christ himself being the chief corner-stone. Eph. 2 : 20.

46. *What is said in Matt. 25 : 10 about being ready?* —While they went to buy, the bridegroom came ; and they that were ready went in with him to the marriage ; and the door was shut.

47. *Can you see any resemblance between the state of these virgins in the parable and the trees of Lebanon in the time of Solomon?*—Both were fit and ready for the service for which they were required.

48. *What tree does the woodman select when he seeks timber?*—A tree of the proper kind of wood, straight, sound and of sufficient size.

49. *What becomes of small wood, brambles, brushwood, etc.?*—They are burned.

50. *What warning word should we allow to have influence over us?*—Be ye also ready, for in such an hour as ye think not the Son of man cometh. Matt. 24 : 44.

51. *How was Solomon's temple dedicated?*—There was a solemn feast, the bringing in of the ark, Solomon's prayer and blessing, and a sacrifice of peace-offerings. 1 Kings 8.

52. *Who was raised up above all the people?*—Solomon.

53. *Who blessed them?*—Solomon.

54. *Of whom was he a type in this?*—Of Christ.

55. *Who will be gathered together when God's spiritual temple, formed of living stones, is reared?*—God's holy people.

If any man defile the temple of God, him shall God destroy ; for the temple of God is holy, which temple ye are. 1 Cor. 3 : 17.

Ye also, as lively stones, are built up a spiritual house, an holy priesthood, to offer up spiritual sacrifices, acceptable to God by Jesus Christ. 1 Pet. 2 : 5.

56. *Who is the foundation and chief corner-stone of that glorious building?*—"Jesus Christ himself." Eph. 2 : 20.

57. *Will it do to build good works or human merit on this foundation?*—We cannot add to or extend the foundation ; we can only build upon it the spiritual house, the . . . holy temple.

58. *What are all such vain things compared to in 1 Cor. 3 : 11–17?*—To "wood, hay and stubble."

59. *What remarkable dream did Solomon have immediately after his father's death?*—That God asked him what he should give him. 1 Kings 3 : 5.

60. *What did he ask for?*—Wisdom to govern his people well. 1 Kings 3 : 9.

61. *What did God promise to give him that he did not ask for?*—Riches and honor. 1 Kings 3 : 13.

62. *Describe Solomon's grandeur?*—He had an immense daily provision for his household, and thousands of chariot-horses and riders. 1 Kings 4 : 22, 23, 26.

63. *What queen, having heard of it from afar, came to visit Solomon?*—The queen of Sheba in Arabia. 1 Kings 10.

64. *Was she disappointed?*—No ; she said that half had not been told her. 1 Kings 10 : 7.

65. *What testimony did she leave behind her?*—She testified to the blessedness of those who served the living God.

66. *Has the glory of the Lord Jesus been exaggerated?* —No ; it exceeds all that is revealed to us on earth.

Eye hath not seen, nor ear heard, neither have entered into the heart of man, the things which God hath prepared for them that love him. But God hath revealed them unto us by his Spirit. 1 Cor. 2 : 9, 10.

67. *When the Lord Jesus compared himself with Solomon, and spoke about the queen of Sheba, what did he say?*—The queen of the south shall rise up in the judgment with this generation, and shall condemn it ; for she came from the uttermost parts of the earth to hear the wisdom of Solomon ; and, behold, a greater than Solomon is here. Matt. 12 : 42.

68. *How and by what means may we hope to share that glory by and by?*—By giving him our faith and love and service now.

69. *What is the best proof we can give that we believe the Bible to be true?*—Believing in the Saviour it reveals to us, obeying the commands it gives us, and making it known, as far as we can, to every creature.

PROVERBS.

1. *Who wrote the book of Proverbs?*—Solomon. Prov. 1 : 1.

2. *To whom is the book addressed?*—To his son Rehoboam.

3. *How many chapters does Solomon take in addressing his son before the Proverbs begin?*—Nine.

CHAPTER 1.

4. *What does Solomon say is the beginning of wisdom?* —The fear of the Lord. Prov. 1 : 7.

5. *What does he say is an ornament of grace to the neck of a child?*—Obedience to the instructions of his father and mother. Prov. 1 : 8, 9.

6. *How does he warn his son against sinners?*—To keep out of their way. Prov. 1 : 10–19.

7. *Whom does Solomon mean when he says, "Wisdom crieth without"?*—Jesus Christ.

Of him are ye in Christ Jesus, who of God is made unto us wisdom, and righteousness, and sanctification, and redemption. 1 Cor. 1 : 30.

The Son of man came eating and drinking, and they say, Behold a man gluttonous, and a winebibber, a friend of publicans and sinners. But wisdom is justified of her children. Matt. 11 : 19.

8. *Which is the only book that can be said to be "wisdom"?*—The Book, the Bible.

Therefore also said the wisdom of God, I will send them prophets and apostles, and some of them they shall slay and persecute. Luke 11 : 49.

9. *What has the Lord Jesus promised to "pour out" on those who "turn at his reproof"?*—He has said that our heavenly Father will give the Holy Spirit to them that ask him. Luke 11 : 13.

10. *And what has he said will be the condemnation of those who refuse when he calls?*—To be judged by his word at the last day. John 12 : 48.

11. *What is written in 2 Cor. 6 : 2?*—Behold, now is the day of salvation.

CHAPTER 2.

12. *What reward is promised those who seek diligently after the Lord Jesus, the true "Wisdom"?*—That they shall find him.

13. *What blessings will they enjoy?*—Pardon, peace, grace, hope, joy.

14. *From what will it preserve them?*—True wisdom preserves from the ways and society of the wicked, from all folly and sin, and from all real evil.

15. *Who rejoices to do evil?*—The ungodly man. Prov. 2 : 12–14.

16. *Who has promised to be the "guide of youth"?* —God, who thus invites the young to come unto him:

Wilt thou not from this time cry unto me, My Father, thou art the guide of my youth? Jer. 2 : 4.

17. *What great contrast is there in this chapter between the upright and the wicked?*—The upright shall dwell in the land, and the perfect shall remain in it. But the wicked shall be cut off from the earth, and the trangressors shall be rooted out of it. Prov. 2 : 21, 22.

CHAPTER 3.

18. *How can we write anything on the tablets of our heart?*—By fixing it in our memory and our affections.

19. *How can we hope that God will direct our path?* —If we seek and trust his guidance rather than our own. Prov. 3 : 5, 6.

20. *Why should we not be weary of God's correction?* —Because it is a sure token of his wisdom and love. Prov. 3 : 11, 12.

21. *Can you tell me some of the ways in which God corrects us?*—By sickness, losses, disappointments, and many things that are called accidents or misfortunes.

22. *Which does it make us, "happy" or unhappy, to find Jesus (the true "Wisdom")?*—Happy, as we have then a treasure we can never lose.

23. *How did Solomon estimate wisdom?*—Above riches and honor.

24. *What does the apostle Peter say about the value of the blood shed by the Lord Jesus?*—That it is "precious." 1 Pet. 1 : 19.

25. *What is the Lord Jesus to those who believe in him?*—"Precious." 1 Pet. 2 : 7.

26. *What is the Lord Jesus called in Matt. 13 : 44–46?*—A treasure and a pearl of great price.

27. *What are "wisdom's" ways called?*—"Ways of pleasantness and peace." Prov. 3 : 17.

28. *What does the Lord Jesus himself say of those in Matt. 11 : 28–30?*—Come unto me, all ye that labor and are heavy laden, and I will give you rest. Take my yoke upon you, and learn of me; for I am meek and lowly in heart: and ye shall find rest unto your souls. For my yoke is easy, and my burden is light.

29. *Who is here spoken of as "the tree of life"?*— Jesus Christ, the true Wisdom. Prov. 3 : 18.

30. *Where was that tree first planted?*—In the garden of Eden. Gen. 2 : 8, 9.

31. *Will any one have a right to taste it again?*— Yes.

Blessed are they that do his commandments, that they may have right to the tree of life, and may enter in through the gates into the city. Rev. 22 : 14.

To him that overcometh will I give to eat of the tree of life, which is in the midst of the paradise of God. Rev. 2 : 7.

32. *By whom did the Lord create the heaven and the earth?*—By Jesus Christ.

In the beginning was the Word, and the Word was with God, and the Word was God. All things were made by him; and without him was not any thing made that was made. John 1 : 1, 3.

Who is the image of the invisible God, the first-born of every creature; for by him were all things created that are in heaven, and that are in earth, visible and invisible, whether they be thrones, or dominions, or principalities, or powers: all things were created by him, and for him. Col. 1 : 15, 16.

33. *Have those anything to fear who put their trust in the Lord? Why not?*—No. Because God has promised it. Prov. 3 : 21–26, 5, 6.

34. *Is there any charge in this chapter to be benevolent?* —Prov. 3 : 9, 10, 27, 28.

35. *Who is an abomination to the Lord?*—The froward or self-willed. Prov. 3 : 32.

36. *What will be the glorious destiny of "the wise"?* —To inherit glory. Prov. 3 : 35.

37. *Does this mean earthly or heavenly wisdom?*— Heavenly, as much of the wisdom of this world is really folly and ends in shame.

CHAPTER 4.

38. *What description does Solomon give of his father and mother in this chapter?*—That his father wisely instructed him, and his mother tenderly loved him Prov. 4 : 3, 4.

39. *Who was Solomon's father?*—David.

40. *What was his mother's name?*—Bathsheba.

41. *What instructions did David give him?*—Prov. 4 : 4–19.

42. *What great contrast is there in the eighteenth and nineteenth verses between "the just" and "the wicked"?* —The way of the just is light, and of the wicked dark.

43. *Can you give any examples from the New Testament where wickedness is compared to darkness?*—This is the condemnation, that light is come into the world, and men loved darkness rather than light, because their deeds were evil. John 3 : 19. Have no fellowship with the unfruitful works of darkness, but rather reprove them. Eph. 5 : 11. The night is far spent, the day is at hand: let us therefore cast off the works of darkness, and let us put on the armor of light. Rom. 13 : 12.

44. *What does the Lord Jesus call himself in John 8 : 12?*—The light of the world.

45. *What does Jesus command in Matt. 5 : 16?*—Let your light so shine before men, that they may see your good works, and glorify your Father which is in heaven.

46. *What does Solomon say of "wisdom" in the seventh and two following verses?*—(Read them.)

47. Who *is intended by wisdom? Who is it that shall give us the promised "crown of glory"?*—Jesus Christ.

Blessed is the man that endureth temptation; for when he is tried, he shall receive the crown of life, which the Lord hath promised to them that love him. James 1 : 12.

When the chief Shepherd shall appear, ye shall receive a crown of glory that fadeth not away. 1 Pet. 5 : 4.

Looking unto Jesus, the author and finisher of our faith. Heb. 12 : 2.

Henceforth there is laid up for me a crown of righteousness, which the Lord, the righteous judge, shall give me at that day; and not to me only, but unto all them also that love his appearing. 2 Tim. 4 : 8.

48. *What does Solomon say about the heart in this chapter at the twenty-third verse?*—(Read it.)

49. *What does the prophet Jeremiah say about the heart?*—The heart is deceitful above all things, and desperately wicked: who can know it? Jer. 17 : 9.

50. *What did the Lord Jesus say about the heart when he was on earth?*—Out of the heart proceed evil

thoughts, murders, adulteries, fornications, thefts, false witness, blasphemies. Matt. 15 : 19.

51. *Repeat David's prayer respecting his heart.*—Create in me a clean heart, O God; and renew a right spirit within me. Ps. 51 : 10.

52. *Whose office alone is it to search the heart?*—I the Lord search the heart, I try the reins, even to give every man according to his ways, and according to the fruit of his doings. Jer. 17 : 10. The Lord seeth not as man seeth; for man looketh on the outward appearance, but the Lord looketh on the heart. 1 Sam. 16 : 7. Shall not God search this out? for he knoweth the secrets of the heart. Ps. 44 : 21. If thou sayest, Behold, we knew it not; doth not he that pondereth the heart consider it? and he that keepeth thy soul, doth not he know it? and shall not he render to every man according to his works? Ps. 24 : 12. O Lord of hosts, that triest the righteous, and seest the reins and the heart. Jer. 20 : 12.

53. *Who promises to renew the heart?*—I will give them one heart, and I will put a new spirit within you; and I will take the stony heart out of their flesh, and will give them an heart of flesh. Ezek. 11 : 19. A new heart also will I give you, and a new spirit will I put within you; and I will take away the stony heart out of your flesh, and I will give you an heart of flesh. Ezek. 36 : 26.

CHAPTERS 5, 6, 7.

54. *By what endearing title does Solomon address the youth in these chapters?*—The title of "son."

55. *What encouragement have we to regard God as our Father in Heb. 12 : 5-7?*—Because he there speaks tenderly to his afflicted people as children.

Ye have forgotten the exhortation which speaketh unto you as unto children, My son, despise not thou the chastening of the Lord, nor faint when thou art rebuked of him; for whom the Lord loveth he chasteneth, and scourgeth every son whom he receiveth. If ye endure chastening, God dealeth with you as with sons; for what son is he whom the father chasteneth not?

56. *To what little insect are we referred as an example in Prov. 6 : 6-8?*—To the ant.

57. *What has a lazy person to expect?*—Poverty and want. Prov. 6 : 9-11.

58. *Name the seven things that the Lord hates?*—See Prov. 6 : 16-19.

59. *How can we bind a thing continually on our heart?*—By thinking earnestly or affectionately upon it. Prov. 6 : 20, 27; 7 : 2, 3.

60. *Is there any blessing attached to a child who is obedient to his parents?*—Guidance in life and preservation from sin and harm are here promised. Prov. 6 : 20, etc.

61. *Which is the only commandment among the Ten Commandments which has a promise joined with it?*—The fifth.

62. *To what are a parent's instructions compared in Prov. 6 : 23?*—To a lamp or light.

63. *Where else is the word of God compared, as in this sense, to a lamp?*—In Ps. 119 : 105.

Thy word is a lamp unto my feet, and a light unto my path.

CHAPTERS 8, 9.

64. *Whom does Solomon mean when he says, "Wisdom cries, she standeth"?*—Christ Jesus, who is wisdom for us and in us.

Of him are ye in Christ Jesus, who of God is made unto us wisdom, and righteousness, and sanctification, and redemption. 1 Cor. 1 : 30.

65. *What does "Wisdom" say in chap. 8 : 6?*—Hear.

66. *What did the Lord Jesus say, when on earth, in Matt. 11 : 15; 13 : 9?*—He that hath ears to hear, let him hear.

67. *What does "Wisdom" say in chap. 8 : 7?*—"My mouth shall speak truth."

68. *What does the Lord Jesus say in John 14 : 6?*—"I am the truth."

69. *To what does Solomon compare "wisdom"?*—To gold and rubies. Prov. 8 : 11, 19.

70. *What did St. Paul, in his letter to the Philippians, consider all things when compared with Christ Jesus?*—I count all things but loss for the excellency of the knowledge of Christ Jesus my Lord; for whom I have suffered the loss of all things, and do count them but dung, that I may win Christ. Phil. 3 : 8.

71. *Does "the fear of the Lord" (Prov. 8 : 13) mean hating God, or hating what he disapproves of?*—It means hating what he disapproves of through love to him, and consequent fear of offending him.

72. *What does the Lord hate?*—Pride and all other sin. Prov. 8 : 13.

73. *If God hates pride, how ought we to feel toward that sin in ourselves?*—We should hate it too.

74. *By whom do kings and princes rule?*—By the KING OF KINGS AND LORD OF LORDS. Rev. 19 : 16.

75. *What encouragement does Jesus give to the young to seek him?*—Prov. 8 : 32, 33. Suffer the little children to come unto me, and forbid them not: for of such is the kingdom of God. And he took them up in his arms, put his hands upon them, and blessed them. Mark 10 : 14, 16.

76. *What blessings are promised to those who choose him for their portion?*—Constant guidance upon earth and a lasting treasure in heaven.

77. *Where was the Lord Jesus when God created the world?*—With God, as being God himself. Prov. 8 : 27-31.

78. *Had the Lord Jesus existed before that time?*—Yes, from everlasting. Prov. 8 : 22-26.

79. *Did Jesus even then take pleasure in his people?*—He did.

We love him, because he first loved us. 1 John 4 : 19.

80. *How does Jesus invite us to him?*—Come unto me, all ye that labor and are heavy laden, and I will give you rest. Matt. 11 : 28.

81. *What remarkable comparison is there between Prov. 9 : 1-5 and Matt. 22 : 1-14?*—The sameness of the feast or provision of religious truth then and now, and of the welcome to it.

82. *Who spreads the feast? and who are invited to come?*—Christ in each case spreads the feast, and all the needy are invited to come.

83. *Is not religion a personal thing?*—Yes; the word in the singular number here betoken this. Prov. 8 : 34, 35; 9 : 12. No mere union, by sacraments or profession, with a Christian Church will save our souls. We should be able to say with St. Paul in Gal. 2 : 20, he "loved *me* and gave himself for *me*."

84. *Whose fault will it be if those who are thus invited, warned and counseled are lost at last?*—Their own; and this consciousness of willful *folly*, as well as sin, will be a gnawing worm of anguish that will never die.

ECCLESIASTES.

1. *By whom was Ecclesiastes written?*—By Solomon.

2. *What is the meaning of the term Ecclesiastes?*—The "Preacher."

3. *Had Solomon any means of knowing the subject on which he wrote? How?*—He had personal experience and divine teaching.

4. *What was the result of his great knowledge?*—That all is vanity under the sun. Eccles. 1 : 2, 3.

5. *Was there anything that Solomon found under the sun sufficient to satisfy his soul?*—Nothing.

6. *What is the meaning of that term, "under the sun"?* —Things that relate to *this* world alone.

7. *Where, then, must we look for solid happiness?*—To the world to come.

8. *What will be the end of " everything under the sun"?* —The day of the Lord will come as a thief in the ight; in the which the heavens shall pass away with great noise, and the elements shall melt with fervent heat, the earth also and the works that are therein shall be burned up. 2 Pet. 3 : 10. All the host of heaven shal' be dissolved, and the heavens shall be rolled together as a scroll: and all their host shall fall down, as the leaf falleth off from the vine, and as a falling fig from the fig tree. Isa. 34 : 4. And the heaven departed as a scroll when it is rolled together; and every mountain and island were moved out of their places. Rev. 6 : 14.

9. *Where should we then lay up our treasure?*—Lay up for yourselves treasures in heaven, where neither moth nor rust doth corrupt, and where thieves do not break through nor steal; for where your treasure is, there will your heart be also. Matt. 6 : 20, 21.

10. *Did Solomon wish to impress this truth on us?*—He did.

11. *What arguments does he use in Eccles. 12 to urge this in early life?*—The approach of old age and of death. Eccles. 12 : 1–7.

12. *What does he say is the conclusion of the whole matter?*—Let us hear the conclusion of the whole matter: Fear God, and keep his commandments; for this is the whole duty of man. For God shall bring every work into judgment, with every secret thing, whether it be good, or whether it be evil. Eccles. 12 : 13, 14.

13. *Which, then, is the wisest and happiest person— he who lives in pleasure or he who lives to God?*—He who lives to God.

14. *What was the apostle Paul's estimate of present things and things to come?*—I reckon that the sufferings of this present time are not worthy to be compared with the glory which shall be revealed in us. Rom. 8 : 18. For our light affliction, which is but for a moment, worketh for us a far more exceeding and eternal weight of glory; while we look not at the things which are seen, but at the things which are not seen: for the things which are seen are temporal; but the things which are not seen are eternal. 2 Cor. 4 : 17, 18.

15. *What does Luke 16 : 19–25 teach us?*—The parable of the rich man and Lazarus shows us the sad end of those who have only earthly riches when they come to die.

16. *Can we venture to have a little of this world first, and hope for heaven after?*--No. Luke 12 : 16–21.

17. *What was the apostle James's estimate of all that might be enjoyed " under the sun"?*—Go to now, ye rich men, weep and howl for your miseries that shall come upon you. Your riches are corrupted, and your garments are moth-eaten. Your gold and silver is cankered; and the rust of them shall be a witness against you, and shall eat your flesh as it were fire. Ye have heaped treasure together for the last days. James 5 : 1–3.

18. *Was it not the prospect of resurrection and the coming of the Lord that also sustained the apostle Paul?* —It was.

I protest by your rejoicing which I have in Christ Jesus our Lord, I die daily. If after the manner of men I have fought with beasts at Ephesus, what advantageth it me if the dead rise not? let us eat and drink, for to-morrow we die. 1 Cor. 15 : 31, 32.

19. *Seeing life is uncertain, and death sure, what ought we to do?*—Forsake our wicked way, and " seek the Lord while he may be found." Isa. 55 : 6, 7.

REHOBOAM. (1 Kings 11 and 12.)

1. *What great sin was Solomon guilty of in his latter days?*—Idolatry, through the influence of his wives. 1 Kings 11 : 4.

2. *What did the Lord say to Solomon about this?*— That he would take away the greater part of his kingdom from his family. 1 Kings 11 : 11–13.

3. *To what " covenant" did the Lord refer?*—When thy days be fulfilled, and thou shalt sleep with thy fathers, I will set up thy seed after thee, which shall proceed out of thy bowels, and I will establish his kingdom. He shall build an house for my name, and I will stablish the throne of his kingdom for ever. I will be his father, and he shall be my son. 2 Sam. 7 : 12–14.

4. *Had Solomon broken this covenant?*—Yes, by his idolatry.

5. *What were the consequences?*—The stirring up of enemies after a long reign of peace.

6. *How many adversaries did the Lord raise up against Solomon?*—Hadad the Edomite, Rezon the Syrian, and Jeroboam his servant.

7. *Whom had Solomon to blame for this?*—Himself alone, for his folly and sin.

8. *Whom have we to blame for punishment if we sin against God?*—Ourselves alone.

9. *How long did Solomon reign?*—Forty years.

10. *Who succeeded him?*—Rehoboam his son.

11. *Was he a wise or a foolish king?*—A foolish one. 1 Kings 12.

12. *What is the proof?*—His following the advice of young men instead of old and experienced ones. 1 Kings 12 : 6–14.

13. *What opinion do young people often form of their elders?*—They often and foolishly think that their elders are behind the times, and are not so wise as they are themselves.

14. *What ought Rehoboam's history teach us?*—To value and follow the advice of older and wiser relations and friends.

THE KINGS OF ISRAEL—JEROBOAM'S DYNASTY. (1 Kings 11 : 26–43 ; 12–16.)

1. *Who was Jeroboam?*—Son of Nebat and servant of Solomon. 1 Kings 11 : 26.

2. *What was the name of the prophet who foretold his honors?*—Ahijah. 1 Kings 11 : 29.

3. *How did he do this?*—By tearing Jeroboam's outer garment into twelve pieces and giving him ten.

4. *When was this prophecy fulfilled?*—At the revol of the ten tribes. 1 Kings 12 : 16.

5. *How was it brought about?*—Through Rehoboam's refusing to listen to his people's complaint, by the advice of his young and ignorant companions. 1 Kings 12 : 16.

6. *How much of Israel did Jeroboam reign over?*— Ten tribes. 1 Kings 12 : 21.

7. *What wicked means did he use to keep the ten tribes under his rule?*—Setting up idol-worship in Bethel and Dan. 1 Kings 12 : 28, 29.

8. *Where was Bethel?*—In the tribe of Benjamin.

9. *What remarkable circumstance happened to Jacob there before he went to Syria?*—His dream of the ladder between earth and heaven.

10. *How did Jacob distinguish the place when he returned from Syria? Who was buried there?*—He built there an altar. Gen. 35 : 7. Deborah, Rebekah's nurse. Gen. 25 : 8.

11. *Is Bethel mentioned before Jacob's time?*—Abra-

ham is said, in Gen. 12:8, to have encamped near Bethel.

12. *Was not Jeroboam very wickedly wise to choose a place of such interest for his idol?*—He was.

13. *What state must Israel have been in that Jeroboam could so easily turn them to idolatry?*—In a very ungodly state.

14. *How is it that Satan's temptations so easily prevail over us?*—Because we do not sufficiently "watch and pray."

15. *Had God's law forbidden idolatry?*—Repeatedly.

16. *Have we any excuse for sin?*—No, as we have the word of God to go to, and the voice of conscience and the striving of the Spirit within us.

17. *Is there any point on which God has left us in doubt of his mind and will?*—None at all, as, besides *particular* directions, we have *general* ones that include all cases.

18. *Where must we go to learn God's will?*—To his holy word.

19. *What will be our condemnation if we do not?*—Eternal punishment if we willfully and habitually neglect it.

20. *Had the Israelites any excuse for idolatry, even though their king commanded it, when they had God's written law?*—They had no excuse at all.

21. *There was one of Jeroboam's family, though young in years, who feared the Lord; who was he?*—Abijah. 1 Kings 14:13.

22. *What did his parents do when they feared he would die?*—His mother went to Ahijah the prophet to have him cured. 1 Kings 14:1-4.

23. *Why did they not go to the calf at Bethel to save the child?*—Because they had no real confidence in their idol-god.

24. *Was it of any use that Jeroboam's wife disguised herself to the prophet?*—No; God knew it, and made it known to him. 1 Kings 14:5.

25. *Can we hide anything from God?*—There is not a word in my tongue, but, lo, O Lord, thou knowest it altogether. Thou hast beset me behind and before, and laid thine hand upon me. Whither shall I go from thy spirit? or whither shall I flee from thy presence? Ps. 139:4, 5, 7, etc.

26. *What promises has God given to encourage little children to love him?*—I love them that love me; and those that seek me early shall find me. Prov. 8:17.

27. *Does not this show that even a little child in a wicked family who tries to serve God is not unnoticed by him?*—God's noticing Abijah shows this.

28. *How many of Jeroboam's race came to the crown of Israel?*—Only Nadab his son. 1 Kings 15:25-30.

29. *In what disgraceful state was Elah (the last of Jeroboam's family) when he was slain?*—He was drunk. 1 Kings 16:9.

30. *By whom was he slain?*—By his servant Zimri.

THE DISOBEDIENT PROPHET. (1 Kings 13 and 2 Kings 23:15-18.)

1. *Did God suffer the sinful idolatry of Israel to go unrebuked?*—No.

2. *Whom did the Lord send to them?*—A prophet. 1 Kings 13:2, 3.

3. *How far did he go obediently to the Lord?*—To Bethel only. 1 Kings 13:1, 9, 10.

4. *Who was standing by the altar at Bethel when he got there?*—Jeroboam.

5. *Was the prophet afraid to deliver his message?*—No. 1 Kings 13:2, 3.

6. *When the king heard it, what did he do?*—He put out his hand to seize the prophet. 1 Kings 13:4.

7. *Was not this a very daring act? How was it pun-*

ished?—It was defying God. His arm was stiffened and dried up.

8. *How was the king's arm recovered?*—By the prophet's prayer.

9. *Did the man of God go home with the king and take refreshment with him?*—No, for God had told him not to do so. 1 Kings 13:7-9.

10. *Who tempted the man of God to turn aside?*—An old prophet. 1 Kings 13:11-19.

11. *Ought he to have rested on God's word spoken to him, or believed this old prophet's word?*—If there arise among you a prophet, or a dreamer of dreams, and giveth thee a sign or a wonder, and the sign or the wonder come to pass, whereof he spake unto thee, saying, Let us go after other gods, which thou hast not known, and let us serve them; thou shalt not hearken unto the words of that prophet, or that dreamer of dreams: for the Lord your God proveth you, to know whether ye love the Lord your God with all your heart and with all your soul. Deut. 13:1-3.

12. *Did God use the lips of the old prophet again to really speak his word?*—Yes. 1 Kings 13:20-22.

13. *Must not this have been heavy tidings to the disobedient one?*—It must indeed. How careful should we be to exactly obey!

14. *How was the prophecy fulfilled?*—He was killed by a lion. 1 Kings 13:24.

15. *Did God quite cast off the man of God for this act of disobedience?*—No; he preserved his body for burial, and took care that his prophecy was fulfilled.

16. *How did the old prophet feel toward him?*—He mourned for him and buried him, and wished to be laid beside him. 1 Kings 13:29-31.

17. *What mark of respect also did Josiah, the king of Judah, pay to his memory in after years?*—He "let no man move his bones." 2 Kings 23:18.

THE KINGS OF ISRAEL—ZIMRI, OMRI AND AHAB. (1 Kings 16-22.)

1. *Who was Zimri?*—One of the captains of Elah, son of Baasha. 1 Kings 16:8, 9.

2. *What vengeance did he execute on the wicked family of Jeroboam?*—He killed Elah, the third successor of Jeroboam.

3. *How long did Zimri reign?*—About seven days. 1 Kings 16:15-19.

4. *What was his end?*—He burnt himself in his house when surrounded by his enemies.

5. *Who reigned over Israel next?*—Omri. 1 Kings 16:16.

6. *Who was he? and how long did he reign?*—He was commander of the army, and reigned twelve years. 1 Kings 16:23.

7. *What city did he purchase and make the chief cit of Israel?*—Samaria. 1 Kings 16:24.

8. *What was the name of his son?*—Ahab.

9. *How was Ahab distinguished above the kings that went before him?*—In wickedness. 1 Kings 16:30.

10. *What was the name of his wife? and whose daughter was she?*—Jezebel, daughter of the king of Zidon. 1 Kings 16:31.

11. *What new idol-worship was she the means of bringing in?*—The worship of Baal.

12. *What is recorded of Jericho in his reign?*—That it was rebuilt by Hiel. 1 Kings 16:34.

13. *Of what prophecy was this the fulfillment?*—Joshua adjured them at that time, saying, Cursed be the man before the Lord that riseth up and buildeth this city Jericho: he shall lay the foundation thereof in his first-born, and in his youngest son shall he set up the gates of it (Josh. 6:26)—*i. e.,* he should lose all his children during the building of it.

14. *Can God's word ever fall to the ground?*—No; all must come to pass.

15. *Are there any prophecies yet to be fulfilled?*—Many in the book of Revelation and elsewhere as to the conversion and restoration of the Jews, the second coming and kingdom of Christ, the last judgment and other events.

16. *Are we interested in them?*—We are eternally in many of them.

17. *In what state should we at all times be found?*—Watching and ready, as we "know not what hour" our "Lord doth come." Matt. 24: 42, 44.

ELIJAH DURING FAMINE. (1 Kings 17.)

1. *Who was Elijah?*—A prophet of Gilead.

2. *Where was Gilead?*—On the east of Jordan.

3. *What was Elijah commissioned to tell Ahab?*—That there should be neither dew nor rain.

4. *Why did God send a famine on the land?*—It shall come to pass, if thou wilt not hearken unto the voice of the Lord thy God, to observe to do all his commandments and his statutes which I command thee this day; that all these curses shall come upon thee, and overtake thee: cursed shalt thou be in the city, and cursed shalt thou be in the field. Cursed shall be thy basket and thy store. Cursed shall be the fruit of thy body, and the fruit of thy land, the increase of thy kine, and the flocks of thy sheep. Deut. 28: 15-18.

5. *Where did God promise to provide for Elijah? and how?*—By the brook Cherith, and by means of ravens.

6. *When the brook dried up, where did the Lord command Elijah to go?*—To Zarephath (1 Kings 17: 9), where a widow would sustain him.

7. *In what sorrowful employment did Elijah find the woman engaged?*—In gathering sticks to dress her last meal.

8. *Did she seem aware of the wonderful miracle that was wrought day by day?*—No.

9. *What should this teach us?*—To beware of not observing and not being thankful for the good providence of God.

10. *How did the Lord convince her that he was the living God?*—By Elijah's restoring her dead child to life.

11. *Did she confess it at last?*—Yes. 1 Kings 17: 24.

12. *What proof have we that God is the living God?*—His word by St. Paul that "he giveth to all life and breath and all things," and that "in him we live and move and have our being."

13. *Is not the written word of God to us now what the spoken word was by the prophets then?*—Yes; "we have a more sure word of prophecy," to which we should "take heed." 2 Pet. 1: 19.

ELIJAH ON CARMEL. (1 Kings 18.)

1. *Were Israel at this time idolaters, or worshipers of the true God?*—Idolaters—worshipers of Baal.

2. *Were all Israel worshipers of Baal?*—No; seven thousand of them were not.

3. *Who was Obadiah?*—Governor or steward of Ahab's house.

4. *What kind act had he performed when Jezebel, the wicked queen, slew the Lord's prophets?*—He had hid and fed them.

5. *How many years had the famine lasted when Elijah stood before Ahab?*—Above two years. 1 Kings 18: 1.

6. *What did Ahab accuse Elijah of doing?*—Of being the cause of Israel's trouble.

7. *Who was really to blame?*—Ahab himself and the other idolaters.

8. *How did Elijah propose to decide the point as to who was the living God?*—By observing upon whose sacrifice the fire came down from heaven. 1 Kings 18: 24.

9. *How does Isaiah describe idols?*—He heweth him down cedars, and taketh the cypress and the oak: he burneth part thereof in the fire; with part thereof he eateth flesh; he roasteth roast, and is satisfied: yea, he warmeth himself, and saith, Aha, I am warm, I have seen the fire: and the residue thereof he maketh a god, even his graven image: he falleth down unto it, and worshipeth it, and prayeth unto it, and saith, Deliver me; for thou art my god. Isa. 44: 14, 16, 17.

10. *How does the Psalmist describe them?*—Their idols are silver and gold, the work of men's hands. They have mouths, but they speak not: eyes have they, but they see not: they have ears, but they hear not: noses have they, but they smell not: they have hands, but they handle not: feet have they, but they walk not: neither speak they through their throat. They that make them are like unto them; so is every one that trusteth in them. Ps. 115: 4-8.

11. *Was it of any use for Baal's priests to cry to him?*—None at all.

12. *How did Elijah mock them?*—By telling them to cry aloud, as their god might be asleep. 1 Kings 18: 27.

13. *Did he give them time enough to make a fair trial?*—Yes, from morni g till evening. 1 Kings 18: 26, 29.

14. *About what time in the day was it when Elijah built his altar to the true God?*—About evening. 1 Kings 18: 29, 30.

15 *Of what use was the trench he had made round the altar?*—That the water might not escape.

16. *Why did he drench the sacrifice with water?*—To show the power of the fire.

17. *How was the power of God manifested?*—By the fire drying up the water and burning the wet bullock and wood and stone.

18. *What effect did it have on the people?*—They fell on their faces and cried out that Jehovah was the true God. 1 Kings 18: 39.

19. *What became of Baal's priests?*—They were taken and slain.

20. *What did Elijah venture to promise Ahab even before there was any appearance of it?*—Abundance of rain.

21. *On what did Elijah's faith rest?*—On the promise of God. 1 Kings 18: 1.

22. *What is faith?*—"The substance" or realizing "of things hoped for," "the evidence" or assurance "of things not seen." Heb. 11: 1.

23. *How many times had Elijah to ask ere the promised blessing came?*—Seven or eight times.

24. *What should this teach us?*—Always to pray, and not to faint. Luke 18. 1-7.

25. *How was the Lord's power again manifested on Elijah, although he had had a day of such extraordinary energy?*—In enabling him to run before Ahab's chariot.

26. *Was Elijah like one of us, or was he a supernatural being?*—Elias was a man subject to like passions (or infirmities) as we are (a human being like ourselves), and he prayed earnestly that it might not rain; and it rained not on the earth by the space of three years and six months. And he prayed again, and the heaven gave rain, and the earth brought forth her fruit. James 5: 17, 18.

27. *Is God as much the hearer and answerer of prayer now as he was then?*—He is always the same.

ELIJAH IN THE DESERT. (1 Kings 19.)

1. *What proof did Elijah give that he was "a man subject to like passions with us"?*—In his weakness of body and mind he requested that he might die. 1 Kings 19: 4.

2. *To what place did he flee for fear of Jezebel?*—To Beersheba. 1 Kings 19: 3.

3. *What kind care did the Lord take of him there?*—An angel brought him bread and water.

4. *Was he more than once invited to eat?*—Yes, twice. 1 Kings 19 : 7.

5. *For hòw long did that food sustain him?*—Forty days.

6. *When he was revived, to what place did he go?*—To Mount Horeb.

7. *Is it the Lord's will that his servants should be idle?*—No; he has always work for every one to do.

8. *What did the Lord say to Elijah?*—What doest thou here, Elijah?

9. *Is this not a striking proof that it is not the Lord's will that people should live shut up in monasteries or live as lonely hermits?*—It is.

10. *Can any former work excuse them from future service?*—Not while the means are in their power.

11. *What is God's way of speaking to his people? Is it in the fire, wind and earthquake, or how?*—He sometimes speaks in the louder voice of suffering and distress, but more frequently in the gentler one of his Spirit's whisper to the heart.

12. *Where can we hear his "still small voice"?*—All Scripture is given by inspiration of God, and is profitable for doctrine, for reproof, for correction, for instruction in righteousness: that the man of God may be perfect, thoroughly furnished unto all good works. 2 Tim. 3 : 16, 17. God, who at sundry times and in divers manners spake in time past unto the fathers by the prophets, hath in these last days spoken unto us by his Son. Heb. 1 : 1, 2. We have also a more sure word of prophecy; whereunto ye do well that ye take heed, as unto a light that shineth in a dark place. 2 Pet. 1 : 19.

13. *What effect should it have on us?*—It should dispose us to say, with Eli, "Speak, Lord, for thy servant heareth." 1 Sam. 3 : 9.

14. *Can any supposed mystery in the dealings of God be an excuse for neglect of duty?*—No; we must do our part, and leave God to explain in his own time.

15. *What further work did the Lord give Elijah to do?*—To anoint two kings and a prophet. 1 Kings 19 : 15, 16.

16. *What effect did the casting of Elijah's mantle on Elisha have?*—It made him leave his work and his home for the service to which God had called him.

17. *Did Elisha wait till Elijah was taken up? or did he follow him at once?*—He followed him at once.

18. *What does the Lord say in Prov. 8 : 17 to encourage young people to follow him?*—"Those that seek me early shall find me."

AHAB'S PUBLIC AND PRIVATE CHARACTER. (1 Kings 20 and 21.)

1. *What was Ahab's character in the sight of God?*—He did more to provoke him than all the kings of Israel before him. 1 Kings 16 : 33.

2. *Had God at this time given up Israel?*—No; he still warned them by his prophets.

3. *Were there other prophets at this time in Israel besides Elijah?*—Yes, there were false prophets, as well as true.

4. *Who were Israel's greatest enemies at this time?*—The Syrians.

5. *What was the capital city of Syria?*—Damascus.

6. *Who was king of Syria at this time?*—Benhadad.

7. *What did he purpose to do to Israel?*—To destroy Samaria. 1 Kings 20 : 10.

8. *How did the Lord frustrate his design?*—By means of the household servants of Ahab's princes when Benhadad and his royal allies were drunk.

9. *Was Ahab grateful for this?*—Probably not.

10. *How did the Lord show his displeasure?*—By bringing the Syrians to attack him again. 1 Kings 20 · 26, 42.

11. *Who was Naboth?*—The owner of a vineyard near Ahab's palace in Jezreel. 1 Kings 21.

12. *Why did he not like to let Ahab have his vineyard?*—Because he was forbidden by the law to part with what had come to him from his fathers.

> The land shall not be sold for ever; for the land is mine; for ye are strangers and sojourners with me. And in all the land of your possession ye shall grant a redemption for the land. Lev. 25 : 23, 24.

13. *What wicked act did Jezebel stir Ahab up to do?*—To kill Naboth and take his vineyard.

14. *Did God suffer this to go unpunished?*—No.

15. *Who was sent to Ahab?*—Elijah.

16. *How did Ahab salute him?*—As his enemy who had found him out, for his conscience pricked him. 1 Kings 21 : 20.

17. *What fearful prediction did he utter?*—That God would destroy Ahab's family, and that the dogs should eat the flesh of Jezebel and lick his own blood.

18. *How did Ahab receive the tidings?*—He showed the outward signs of repentance and humbled himself before God.

19. *What proof is there in this place of the truth of Jonah 4 : 2?*—God delayed the punishment.

> I knew that thou art a gracious God, and merciful, slow to anger, and of great kindness, and repentest thee of the evil.

THE KINGS OF JUDAH—ABIJAH, ASA AND JEHOSHAPHAT. (2 Chron. 13–17.)

1. *Who succeeded Rehoboam as king of Judah?*—Abijah his son. 2 Chron. 12 : 16.

2. *What was his mother's name? and whose daughter was she?*—Michaiah, daughter of Uriel.

3. *What beautiful testimony did he bear against Israel's idolatry?*—That they had forsaken God and his altars, and made themselves golden calves. 2 Chron. 13 : 8-11.

4. *To whom did the army of Judah cry when they were in danger?*—To God. 2 Chron. 13 : 14.

5. *What was the result?*—They gained the battle, because they relied upon God.

6. *Who followed Abijah on the throne of Judah?*—Asa his son. 2 Chron. 14 : 1.

7. *What was Asa's character in God's estimation?*—He did what was good and right.

8. *What proof did he give of his heart being right with God when he first came to the throne?*—He destroyed the idols and their places of worship.

9. *Was his early reign prosperous?*—Yes, his land was at peace.

10. *How did he behave when the vast army from Ethiopia came up against him?*—He prayed to God and fought in his name.

11. *What was the result?*—The Ethiopians fled.

12. *Is God the same as he was then?*—The same now and for ever.

13. *Does he hear and answer prayer now as he did then?*—Yes, as every one, whether young or old, can testify who really prays.

14. *What encouragement did the Lord give Asa by the mouth of Azariah the prophet?*—That God would be with him as long as he was with God, or obedient to him. 2 Chron. 15 : 1-7.

15. *What similar promise is given to us in Prov. 8?*—"I love them that love me." Prov. 8 : 17.

16. *What effect did it have on the king and people?*—He put down idolatry, and the people made a covenant to seek the Lord with all their heart (2 Chron. 15 : 8-15), and God gave them peace.

17. *Did this happy state of things continue to the end of Asa's reign? How did he behave when Baasha king of Israel came against him?*—It continued to the thirty-

fifth year of his reign, when, instead of going for help to God, he sent to the king of Syria. 2 Chron. 16: 1-4.

18. *Did the Lord suffer this to go unnoticed?*—No; he sent Hanani to reprove him.

19. *What did the prophet say to Asa?*—He reminded him of God's readiness to help his people, and told him that henceforth he should have wars.

20. *How did Asa receive the reproof?*—He was enraged, and put the prophet in prison.

21. *How was he punished?*—He suffered and died of a painful disease.

22. *Are any of our actions hidden from God?*—The ways of man are before the eyes of the Lord, and he pondereth all his goings. Prov. 5 : 21. The eyes of the Lord are in every place, beholding the evil and the good. Prov. 15 : 3. Mine eyes are upon all their ways: they are not hid from my face, neither is their iniquity hid from mine eyes. Jer. 16 : 17. If I say, Surely the darkness shall cover me; even the night shall be light about me. Yea, the darkness hideth not from thee; but the night shineth as the day: the darkness and the light are both alike to thee. Ps. 139 : 11, 12.

23. *Who succeeded Asa on the throne of Judah?*—Jehoshaphat his son. 2 Chron. 17 : 1.

24. *What character did he bear?*—He sought the God of his father and walked in his commandments.

25. *What beautiful testimony is continually given to David?*—That he was a pattern in his general conduct for others to imitate.

26. *Was Jehoshaphat's a prosperous reign?*—Yes, he was long without war, and became a very great king, and had riches and honor in abundance.

27. *Describe his army?*—(Read 2 Chron. 17 : 14-19.)

MICAIAH. (2 Chron. 18 and 1 Kings 22.)

1. *What was the great error of Jehoshaphat's life?*—Making an alliance with Ahab.

2. *Was Ahab glad to make the compact?*—Yes; he made a feast for Jehoshaphat and his servants.

3. *Who were the enemies that still fought against Israel?*—The Syrians.

4. *What place had they taken?*—Ramoth-gilead.

5. *Where was it?*—In the tribe of Gad on the east of Jordan.

6. *What did Jehoshaphat require before he would go up to fight?*—That the will of God should be known.

7. *What did all Ahab's prophets say?*—That he might go, and God would be with him. 2 Chron. 18 : 5.

8. *Was the king of Judah satisfied?*—No.

9. *Whom did he wish to consult?*—Micaiah.

10. *Why did not Ahab like Micaiah?*—Because he always prophesied evil unto him.

11. *Was it not very foolish of Ahab to be satisfied with lies?*—Very.

12. *When are we like Ahab in this?*—When we let our own ignorant, selfish and sinful wishes influence our conduct and our prayers.

13. *What is the only sure test of truth?*—God's word.

14. *What does the Psalmist say in Ps. 119 : 105, 140?*—"Thy word is a lamp unto my feet, and a light unto my path" . . . "is very pure."

15. *What did Jehoshaphat's love of truth prove him to be?*—A true servant of God.

16. *What wonderful vision did Micaiah describe?*—Of God upon his throne, and the host of heaven around him, and of an evil spirit going forth to entice Ahab to his fall.

17. *Is there in Scripture any other display of what occurs in the unseen world?*—In Job 1 and Isa. 6 etc.

18. *How did Ahab reward the faithful prophet?*—He put him in prison.

19. *What did Ahab do to prevent his prediction from coming true?*—He disguised himself, that he might not be known.

20. *What narrow escape had Jehoshaphat in the battle?*—The Syrians mistook him for Ahab, and surrounded him.

21. *By whom was he delivered?*—By God, who caused them to leave him.

22. *Can any circumstances be too difficult for the Lord to overrule?*—None.

23. *How was Ahab killed?*—By an arrow shot at random.

24. *How was Elijah's prediction in 1 Kings 21 : 19 fulfilled?*—The dogs licked up his blood in his chariot.

25. *Was it of any use that Ahab disguised himself in the battle?*—None at all.

26. *Can we hide ourselves from God?*—We cannot.

27. *What during his life did Ahab build?*—Some cities, an ivory house and a sepulchre.

28. *Have these works rendered his name honorable?*—No.

29. *What alone is true honor?*—That which comes from God.

ELIJAH AND THE LIVING GOD. (2 Kings 1 and 2.)

1. *Which of Ahab's sons succeeded his father?*—Ahaziah. 1 Kings 22 ; 40.

2. *What character did he bear?*—He was wicked and idolatrous. 1 Kings 22 : 52, 53.

3. *What accident befell him?*—He fell from an upper room. 2 Kings 1 : 2.

4. *What means did he take for his recovery?*—He sent to an idol-god. 2 Kings 1 : 2.

5. *What testimony did Elijah bear to this impiety?*—He said that he should not recover.

6. *What course did Ahaziah take?*—He sent soldiers to take him.

7. *What befell his messengers?*—They were consumed by fire from heaven.

8. *Did all share alike?*—The last party was spared in answer to their leader's prayer.

9. *Was Elijah induced to alter his denunciation against the king?*—No.

10. *Who reigned in Israel after Ahaziah? and what relation was he to that king?*—Jehoram. His brother. 2 Kings 1 : 17; 3 : 1.

11. *What peculiar testimony did Elijah bear all through his life?*—Against idolatry and for the honor of God.

12. *Was not Elijah privileged to manifest this in his departure from this world?*—God's glory was shown in the miracle wrought and in the translation to heaven.

13. *How did that event take place?*—In a whirlwind, by a chariot and horses of fire. 2 Kings 2 : 11.

14. *Who was permitted to witness it?*—Elisha.

15. *What favor was Elijah permitted to grant Elisha ere he was parted from him?*—To ask what he should do for him.

16. *What did Elisha request?*—A double portion of Elijah's spirit.

17. *How often in Elijah's history is his mantle mentioned?*—Three times. 1 Kings 19 : 13, 19 and 2 Kings 2 : 8.

18. *Of what is Elijah's mantle a type?*—Of the Holy Spirit.

19. *How did Elisha use it?*—To divide the waters of Jordan.

20. *Of what is the parting of Jordan a type?*—Of the opening of the way to heaven,

21. How many times before this had Jordan been miraculously divided?—Twice—when Israel entered Canaan, and when Elijah crossed before his death.

22. How did the other prophets recognize the superiority of Elisha?—By the spirit of Elijah resting upon him. 2 Kings 2:15.

23. How did they manifest their unbelief?—By proposing to send men to search for Elijah.

24. Did Elisha yield?—He did, at last.

25. What proof did Elisha at once give that he, like Elijah, was the prophet of the living God?—By healing he unwholesome water.

26. What proof of Israel's impiety did the little children give?—They mocked Elisha.

27. What did they mean by "Go up"?—Go up to heaven, like Elijah.

28. How were they punished?—They were killed by bears.

29. Does this not show that even the faults of little children are noticed by God?—It does. He sees and hates all sin.

30. How did Jesus when on earth manifest his love for little children?—By calling them to him and blessing them.

31. And what does the Lord say in Prov. 8:17?—Those that seek me early shall find me.

JEHOSHAPHAT. (2 Kings 3; 2 Chron. 19, 20.)

1. Did the Lord suffer the evil confederacy which Jehoshaphat had made with Ahab to go unnoticed?—No.

2. Whom did the Lord send to warn the king?—Hanani the seer.

3. How did the Lord show his displeasure when Jehoshaphat joined affinity with Ahaziah, Ahab's son, in sending ships to go to Tarshish?—The ships were wrecked. 1 Kings 22:48.

4. When Ahaziah afterward wished his servants to go with Jehoshaphat's, what was his conduct?—He refused. 1 Kings 22:49.

5. Was Joram (son of Ahab) a better man than either his brother Ahaziah or his father?—He was better in putting away the image of Baal, but in other respects he was very wicked. 2 Kings 3:2, 3.

6. Did Jehoshaphat consent to go to battle with him?—He did. 2 Kings 3:7.

7. Whom did they go to fight?—The Moabites.

8. What other king went with them?—The king of Edom. 2 Kings 3:9.

9. What signal honor did the prophet Elisha put upon Jehoshaphat?—He told Jehoram that he would not have noticed him but for Jehoshaphat's sake. 2 Kings 3:14.

10. Why had Elisha been sent for?—To know from him whether the Moabites would be defeated or not.

11. How did the Lord appear for them?—He deceived the Moabites, by the miraculous appearance of reddened water, with the belief that the armies of the three kings had destroyed one another. 2 Kings 3:16, 20-23.

12. What frightful sacrifice did the king of Moab offer to propitiate his gods?—His eldest son as a burnt-offering. 2 Kings 3:27.

13. How did the king of Moab soon after try to revenge this defeat?—By making war against Jehoshaphat. 2 Chron. 20:1.

14. What kings joined with him?—The Ammonites and others.

15. How did Jehoshaphat feel?—He was afraid. 2 Chron. 20:3.

16. What did he do?—He proclaimed a fast and prayed to God before the people.

17. Who was Jahaziel?—A Levite.

18. What gracious message did the Lord send by him?—That he would destroy their enemies without a battle.

19. Did Jehoshaphat and his people believe the message that thus came to them from God?—Yes, and united together in praising God.

20. Does not God always honor faith in himself?—He does.

21. What is said of faith in Heb. 11:1?—That it "is the substance of things hoped for, the evidence of things not seen."

22. What is the message that God has given us of his Son which it is necessary for us to believe if we would be saved?—That "the blood of Jesus Christ his Son cleanseth us from all sin." 1 John 1:7.

23. Did Jehoshaphat and his people wait till after the victory before they began to praise, or did they begin before the fight?—They praised God as soon as his promise was given.

24. How did this prove their faith in God's word?—It showed that they realized what would come to pass. Heb. 11:1.

25. What is said of praise in Ps. 50:23?—That it honors God.

Whoso offereth praise glorifieth me: and to him that ordereth his conversation aright will I show the salvation of God.

26. What spoils did they gain?—Abundance of riches and jewels. 2 Chron. 20:25.

27. Of what is this a type?—Of the treasure in heaven of those who conquer on earth in the victory of faith.

28. What effect did this great conquest have on the nations around?—The fear of God was upon them, and they troubled Jehoshaphat no more. 2 Chron. 20:29, 30.

29. With whom is Jehoshaphat compared as to goodness?—With Asa his father.

30. What great abomination did he, notwithstanding all his excellence, leave in the land?—The high places of the heathen gods.

31. Which of his sons did Jehoshaphat make king during his own life?—Jehoram.

32. How long did Jehoram enjoy this honor before his father's death?—About a year. Compare 2 Kings 1:17 with 2 Kings 3:1; 8:16; and 2 Chron. 20:31.

33. How old was Jehoshaphat when he died? and how long had he reigned?—Sixty years old, having reigned twenty-five.

ELISHA'S MIRACLES—THE WATERS OF JERICHO. (2 Kings 2.)

1. Which was the last city Elijah and Elisha visited ere Elijah ascended to heaven?—Jericho. 2 Kings 2:4.

2. Did Elijah ascend near this place?—Yes, by Jordan.

3. By whom was Jericho chiefly inhabited at this time?—By students in the schools of the prophets.

4. Did Elisha return there?—Yes. 2 Kings 2:18.

5. How long did he stay there?—Only a short time. 2 Kings 2:23, 25.

6. What caused the waters of this place to be barren?—The curse of God.

7. By whom, and when, had the curse on Jericho been pronounced?—By Joshua, after the taking of the city.

8. What was Elisha permitted to do?—To make the water good.

9. How did he do it?—By casting a little salt into it, accompanied by the healing power of God.

10. Of what was salt a type in Scripture?—Of divine grace in the heart and life. "Ye are the salt of the earth." Matt. 5:13.

11. What peculiar quality has salt besides its being savory?—Of preserving things from corruption.

12. Of what, then, is it a symbol?—Of divine grace.

13. Were not the children of Israel commanded to use salt with their sacrifices?—Every oblation of thy meat.

offering shalt thou season with salt; neither shalt thou suffer the salt of the covenant of thy God to be lacking from thy meat-offering: with all thine offerings thou shalt offer salt. Lev. 2 : 13.

14. *How was this salt, thus used in the sacrifices, a type of the Lord Jesus Christ?*—See 1 Tim. 3 : 16; Phil. 2 : 5–8.

15. *By whom must the curse pronounced on this earth be removed?*—Christ hath redeemed us from the curse of the law, being made a curse for us; for it is written, Cursed is every one that hangeth on a tree. Gal. 3 : 13.

THE WIDOW'S OIL. (2 Kings 4 : 1–7.)

1. *Who cried to Elisha?*—The wife of one of the sons of the prophets.

2. *Why did she cry to him?*—Because he was the chief of the prophets.

3. *What was her trouble?*—That a creditor of her late husband had taken her two sons for bondmen for the debt.

4. *What plea had she to offer?*—That her husband had been a servant of God.

5. *What did he command her to do?*—To borrow several empty vessels and fill them from her pot of oil.

6. *When did the oil stop running?*—Only when there were no more vessels to fill.

7. *Of what is oil in the Scripture a type?*—Of the Holy Spirit.

8. *What does the Lord promise us if we ask for this blessed gift?*—If ye then, being evil, know how to give good gifts unto your children, how much more shall your heavenly Father give the Holy Spirit to them that ask him! Luke 11 : 13.

9. *Is there any limit to God's supply? or can we receive this heavenly gift according to the empty vessel we bring to receive it?*—There is no limit in God, but only in ourselves. He says, "Open thy mouth wide, and I will fill it." Ps. 81 : 10.

10. *How must our debt be paid?*—By Jesus Christ, wholly and alone.

11. *After our "debt" is paid on whom must we depend for the life of our souls?*—On Jesus still.

12. *Where was Shunem?*—In the tribe of Issachar.

13. *How was Elisha entertained by a rich woman there?*—She and her husband set apart a room, to be for his use whenever he came that way, because she knew him to be a holy man of God. 2 Kings 4 : 8–10.

14. *What kind gift did the Lord bestow upon her for Elisha's sake?*—A child when she had none.

15. *What happened to this child?*—He died by a sunstroke.

16. *Where was Elisha at the time?*—At Mount Carmel. 2 Kings 4 : 25.

17. *How did the poor mother act?*—She set off quickly o Elisha.

18. *What was her reply when Elisha inquired after the welfare of her household?*—"It is well." 2 Kings 4 : 26.

19. *What did this prove?*—Her resignation to God's will and her assurance of her child being in heaven.

20. *What means did Elisha at first use to recover the child?*—His servant laid Elisha's staff upon the child. 2 Kings 4 : 31.

21. *Did the Lord permit it to be effectual?*—No.

22. *What did Elisha then do?*—Elisha prayed, and then stretched himself upon the child, and he revived.

23. *Can God work as well without means as with them?*—He can.

24. *How does the Lord usually act?*—By means.

25. *What did the restoration of this child prove Elisha to have been?*—A true prophet and servant of God.

THE MEAL AND THE CORN. (2 Ki. 4:38–44.)

1. *What was the Lord Jesus manifested to destroy?*—"The works of the devil." 1 John 3 : 8.

2. *What was Satan's first great work?*—Bringing sin and death into the world by Adam's fall.

3. *By what means did the Lord Jesus destroy it?*—By his own death.

As the children are partakers of flesh and blood, he also himself likewise took part of the same; that through death he might destroy him that had the power of death, that is, the devil; and deliver them who through fear of death were all their lifetime subject to bondage. Heb. 2 : 14, 15.

4. *In what respect were the miracles Elisha was allowed to perform similar to the mission of the Lord Jesus?*—In restoring or creating health and life.

5. *How did the miracle of the meal thrown into the pot of wild gourds show this?*—It was an instance of a cause of death being taken away.

6. *What great distinction was there between the idols Israel at this time worshiped and Jehovah?*—They were without power and without life, and were worshiped with unholy rites, and by the *sacrifice*, instead of the *service*, of human lives.

7. *Is not death Satan's greatest triumph?*—Yes, the death or ruin of the soul.

The wages of sin is death. Rom. 6 : 23.

In Adam all die. 1 Cor. 15 : 22.

8. *In what, then, will the power of the Lord Jesus be the most manifestly seen?*—In triumphing over death.

Death is swallowed up in victory. Thanks be to God, which giveth us the victory through our Lord Jesus Christ! 1 Cor. 15 : 54, 57.

9. *What other alone attribute of Jehovah is ascribed to the Lord Jesus?*—Creation.

Who is the image of the invisible God, the first-born of every creature: for by him were all things created, that are in heaven, and that are in earth, visible and invisible, whether they be thrones, or dominions, or principalities, or powers: all things were created by him, and for him: and he is before all things, and by him all things consist. Col. 1 : 15–17.

In the beginning was the Word, and the Word was with God, and the Word was God. The same was in the beginning with God. All things were made by him; and without him was not any thing made that was made. John 1 : 1–3.

When he prepared the heavens, I was there: when he set a compass upon the face of the depth: when he established the clouds above: when he strengthened the fountains of the deep: when he gave to the sea his decree, that the waters should not pass his commandment: when he appointed the foundations of the earth. Prov. 8 : 27–29.

By the word of the Lord were the heavens made; and all the host of them by the breath of his mouth. Ps. 33 : 6.

God . . . created all things by Jesus Christ. Eph. 3 : 9.

10. *How did Elisha attempt to teach Israel, by using this power given to him, that he was the prophet of the living God?*—By doing miracles connected with the preservation or restoration of life, and by praying to God as the living God.

11. *Were there any of the miracles that the Lord Jesus wrought when on earth similar to this?*—The turning the water into wine and healing various diseases.

12. *Had the miracles of Elisha the effect of winning Israel back from their fearful idolatry?*—No.

13. *What was the Lord's merciful design in sending Elisha with such signs and wonders to his people?*—To bring them back to himself, and save them from the punishment due to their guilt.

14. *Did the miracles of the Lord Jesus convince the children of Israel in his day that he was "God manifest in the flesh"?*—No; their hearts were so hardened in willful ignorance, self-righteousness and sin that they would not believe.

15. *Should not this check the feeling that may arise in our hearts that if we had seen a miracle we should cer-*

tainly have believed?*—Yes; it should make us deeply thankful if God has given us to believe.

Abraham saith unto him, They have Moses and the prophets; let them hear them. And he said, Nay, Father Abraham: but if one went unto them from the dead they will repent. And he said unto him, If they hear not Moses and the prophets, neither will they be persuaded, though one rose from the dead. Luke 16: 29–31.

16. *What does the apostle Peter call the word of God?* —"A more sure word of prophecy, . . . that came not in old time by the will of man; but" was spoken by "holy men of God, . . . moved by the Holy Ghost." 2 Pet. 1: 16–21.

NAAMAN. (2 Kings 5.)

1. *With what loathsome disease was Naaman afflicted?* —Leprosy.

2. *Who was he?*—Commander of the army of the king of Syria.

3. *What did the little captive maid recommend her master to do?*—She wished he was with Elisha, as he would cure him. 2 Kings 5: 3.

4. *Did he go?*—Yes.

5. *How did Elisha receive him?*—He sent a message to him to wash in Jordan and be clean. 2 Kings 5: 10.

6. *What had Naaman expected?*—That Elisha would come to him and in a solemn manner call upon God to heal him.

7. *Was he induced to try the remedy?*—Yes; his pride and anger yielded to the wise advice of those about him.

8. *What was the result?*—He was perfectly cured.

9. *Is there any lesson to be gained by us in this history?*—Yes, humbleness of mind.

10. *Of what is leprosy a type in Scripture?*—Of sin.

11. *How must sin be put away?*—There shall be a fountain opened to the house of David and to the inhabitants of Jerusalem for sin and for uncleanness (Zech. 13: 1)—the fountain of the cleansing blood of Christ, sprinkled on the heart by faith.

12. *To whom does the prophet in that verse refer?*—To Jesus Christ, who "washed us from our sins in his own blood." Rev. 1: 5.

These are they which came out of great tribulation, and have washed their robes, and made them white in the blood of the Lamb. Rev. 7: 14.

How much more shall the blood of Christ, who through the eternal Spirit offered himself without spot to God, purge your conscience from dead works to serve the living God! Heb. 9: 14.

13. *How do we get this good news?*—By the gospel.

14. *Are we, like Naaman, desiring some other way than God's appointed way?*—By nature we expect and try to wholly or partly save *ourselves.*

15. *If so, in what state must we still remain?*—Diseased and dead.

16. *Will God say any more to us than he has said—* "*Wash and be clean*"*?*—No; the gospel invitation is the same. Come, and rest. Believe, and live.

17. *If so, why do we hesitate?*—From unbelief, pride, sloth and love of sin and the world.

18. *What was the blessed result of Naaman's falling in with God's simple plan?*—A perfect cure.

19. *What will be the thrice-blessed result to us if we are washed and cleansed in the blood of Jesus?*—Complete salvation.

20. *Ought each of us to tell what we know of the efficacy of this precious fountain?*—We ought to do so, for the glory of God and the good of man.

21. *If a little captive maid could be the means of such blessing to an earthly master, is there not something that each of us can do to spread the knowledge of a Saviour's*

worth among the heathen of our day?*—Some can give themselves, and all a portion of their money and their time, their influence and their prayers.

GEHAZI. (2 Kings 5: 20–27.)

1. *What dreadful sins did covetousness lead Elisha's servant to commit?*—Lying and tempting God's Spirit.

2. *What is said of covetousness in 1 Tim. 6: 9, 10?*—They that will be rich fall into temptation and a snare, and into many foolish and hurtful lusts, which drown men in destruction and perdition. For the love of money is the root of all evil; which while some coveted after, they have erred from the faith, and pierced themselves through with many sorrows.

3. *What proof does Gehazi's example afford us of the truth of Rom. 2: 28, 29; Gal. 6: 15?*—He was evidently, amidst all his religious privileges, an unconverted man.

He is not a Jew, which is one outwardly; neither is that circumcision which is outward in the flesh: but he is a Jew, which is one inwardly; and circumcision is that of the heart, in the spirit, and not in the letter; whose praise is not of men, but of God. Rom. 2: 28, 29.

For in Christ Jesus neither circumcision availeth any thing, nor uncircumcision, but a new creature. Gal. 6: 15.

4. *Can any outward rite or ceremony, any family connection or outward recognition by the people of God, make us indeed and of a truth "a member of Christ, a child of God and an inheritor of the kingdom of heaven"?*—It cannot.

5. *What is necessary?*—Except a man be born again, he cannot see the kingdom of God. John 3: 3.

6. *How is this new birth described in 2 Cor. 5: 17?*—If any man be in Christ, he is a new creature; old things are passed away; behold, all things are become new.

7. *What is it called in James 1: 18?*—Of his own will begat he us with the word of truth, that we should be a kind of first-fruits of his creatures.

8. *What was Gehazi compelled from this day and forward to do?*—To live apart.

The leper in whom the plague is, his clothes shall be rent, and his head bare, and he shall put a covering upon his upper lip, and shall cry, Unclean, unclean! All the days wherein the plague shall be in him he shall be defiled; he is unclean; he shall dwell alone; without the camp shall his habitation be. Lev. 13: 45, 46.

9. *What blessed contrast to this had Naaman experienced?*—The being brought near.

At that time ye were without Christ, having no hope, and without God in the world: but now in Christ Jesus ye who sometimes were far off are made nigh by the blood of Christ. Eph. 2: 12, 13.

10. *Ought we not to examine ourselves, lest we should be deceived in so momentous a question?*—Yes, both as to our hearts and lives.

11. *How did David do this in Ps. 51: 10; 139: 23, 24?*—He prayed for "a clean heart;" and said, "Search me, O God, and know my heart: try me, and know my thoughts: and see if there be any wicked way in me, and lead me in the way everlasting."

12. *Can we do better than follow his example, seeing our Master is omniscient, and can see our most secret actions, even as Elisha was permitted to know Gehazi's secret sin?*—We cannot; and we should do it at once, before our heart gets hard.

13. *Why is God's estimate of us so much more correct than the estimate man forms of us?*—The Lord seeth not as man seeth; for man looketh on the outward appearance, but the Lord looketh on the heart. 1 Sam 16: 7.

ELISHA MANIFESTING THE LORD'S ATTRIBUTES. (2 Kings 6, 7, 8 : 1–6.)

1. *What signal proof did Elisha give of God's omnipotent power? What is the meaning of "omnipotent"?* —Making an iron axe-head to swim. 2 Kings 6. All-powerful, or able to do everything.

2. *Why was it remarkable that iron should swim?*— Because when not hollow it is much heavier than water.

3. *What proof did Elisha next give of God's omniscient power?*—By knowing from God and telling the king of Syria's designs. 2 Kings 6 : 9.

4. *What is the meaning of "omniscience"?*—Knowing everything.

5. *How was the king of Syria affected by this?*—He was much troubled, and suspected his own people of betraying him.

6. *What means did he use to prevent it?*—He sent a host of men to take him.

7. *Who was king of Israel at this time?*—Jehoram. 2 Kings 3 : 1.

8. *How did Elisha's servant feel when he saw the host of Syrians?*—He was greatly afraid.

9. *Why was not Elisha equally frightened?*—Because he had confidence in God.

10. *Are not the people of God always as safe as Elisha was, whether they see it or not?*—They are safe from all harm that God does not permit.

The angel of the Lord encampeth round about them that fear him, and delivereth them. Ps. 34 : 7.

The chariots of God are twenty thousand, even thousands of angels: the Lord is among them, as in Sinai, in the holy place. Ps. 68 : 17.

11. *How did this wonderful circumstance manifest God's omnipresence?*—Without that attribute he would not have known of Elisha's danger, or been ready to help him.

12. *By what means did Elisha lead this host from Dothan to Samaria?*—By blinding them.

13. *Did it quite baffle the Syrians at that time?*—Yes; they came no more.

14. *Was the king of Israel (Joram) taught by this the wondrous power that rested on his favored land? What course did he take toward Elisha when the Syrians came against him and besieged Samaria?*—It seems not. He threatened to kill him.

15. *How did Elisha receive the king's messenger?*— He ordered him to be shut out.

16. *Did Joram himself go down with the executioner?* —He did.

17. *How did Elisha receive the king? and what did he promise him?*—He called upon him to hear the word of the Lord, and promised him plenty.

18. *Who accompanied the king?*—One of his lords.

19. *What unbelieving speech did he make?*—That unless God were to make windows in heaven the promise could not be fulfilled.

20. *Was not this a very fearful famine?*—Yes, for a woman fed upon her own child. 2 Kings 6 : 29.

21. *Was that any reason why God could not do what he had promised?*—None at all.

22. *How was the wondrous change of events brought about?*—By making the Syrians fancy they heard the noise of a great host, God caused them to fly for their lives and leave all their provisions behind.

23. *Have we not here a proof of God's faithfulness and mercy?*—Yes—of his faithfulness to his promise, and of his mercy to his people.

24. *How was the prediction respecting the nobleman fulfilled?*—He was trodden to death by the crowd as they rushed out of the city for food.

25. *Have we not here a display of God's justice?*— We have—a striking one.

26. *How many attributes of God has this Scripture lesson displayed?*—Five—his omnipotence, omniscience, faithfulness, mercy and justice.

27. *How does the remaining history of the Shunammite woman show God's providence?*—She had the land that she had left restored to her on her return. 2 Kings 8 : 6.

JEHU. (2 Kings 8 : 7–15 ; 9, 10.)

1. *Of whom is it said, "He putteth down one and setteth up another" king?*—Of God. Ps. 77 : 7.

2. *Whom did Elisha anoint king of Syria?*—Elisha told Hazael that he should be king. 2 Kings 8 : 13.

3. *Was he chosen by God for his goodness?*—No.

4. *Was he not greatly shocked when Elisha told him what he would do?*—He was. 2 Kings 8 : 13.

5. *Ought not this exhibition of the evil of man's nature make us cry out as in Ps. 2 : 10, 11?*—It should.

Create in me a clean heart, O God; and renew a right spirit within me. Cast me not away from thy presence; and take not thy Holy Spirit from me.

6. *Whom had the Lord already appointed king of Israel?*—Jehu. 1 Kings 19 : 16.

7. *Who anointed him?*—A young prophet sent by Elisha. 1 Kings 9 : 1–6.

8. *Who was Jehu? and where was he at this time?*— A captain in the army, at Ramoth-gilead.

9. *Where was Joram (king of Israel) at this time?*— At Jezreel. 1 Kings 9 : 15.

10. *Who was visiting Joram?*—Ahaziah, king of Judah. 1 Kings 9 : 16.

11. *Was Jehu long in executing God's vengeance?*— No; he set about it instantly.

12. *Had not the time arrived to which God had postponed it?*—It had.

Seest thou how Ahab humbleth himself before me? because he humbleth himself before me, I will not bring the evil in his days; but in his son's days will I bring the evil upon his house. 1 Kings 21 : 29.

13. *What now delays God's threatened vengeance on this apostate earth?*—The long-suffering of God.

The Lord is not slack concerning his promise, as some men count slackness; but is long-suffering to usward, not willing that any should perish, but that all should come to repentance. 2 Pet. 3 : 9.

14. *Did Jezebel (Joram's mother), Ahab's wicked wife, escape? How was she slain?*—No. She was thrown down from a window and killed. 2 Kings 9 : 33.

15. *What had been predicted of her? and by whom?* —Elijah had prophesied (1 Kings 21 : 23) that the dogs should eat her flesh in Jezreel.

16. *Of whom is Jezebel the type?*—Of any wicked Church or people that has cast off the true love and worship of God. Rev. 2 : 20–22 ; 17, 18, 19 : 1–3.

17. *What did Ahaziah king of Judah get by being found in such company?*—He was killed also. 2 Kings 9 : 27.

18. *What warning does the Lord give his people now in Rev. 18 : 4?*—Come out of her, my people, that ye be not partakers of her sins, and that ye receive not of her plagues.

19. *What was Jehu's character?*—He showed great zeal for the outward worship of God, but was in other respects a wicked man.

20. *Having executed God's vengeance on the king and his mother, how did he act toward the rest of Ahab's family?*—He had them all beheaded.

21. *What family relationship did there exist at this time between the royal families of Judah and Israel?*— Jehoram was Ahaziah's uncle.

22. *In what calamity did this involve the former?*— Ahaziah's family were slain. 2 Kings 10 : 13, 14.

23. *How did Jehu treat Baal's worshipers?*—He had them all slain. 2 Kings 10 : 23–25.

24. *Whom did he meet on the way?*—Jehonadab, son of Rechab. 2 Kings 10 : 15.

25. *To what family did this man belong?*—The Kenites.

26. *Is he ever mentioned in Scripture again?*—In Jer. 35, where is also mentioned his command to his family and descendants to drink no wine.

27. *Did Jehu thoroughly destroy Baal-worship in Israel?*—Yes. 2 Kings 10 : 28.

28. *What promise did the Lord make to him for thus fulfilling his will?*—That his children for four generations should sit on the throne of Israel. 2 Kings 10 : 30.

29. *Did he destroy the calves of Bethel as well as Baal, or leave that cursed idolatry in the land?*—He left that idolatry still.

30. *Then Jehu, after all, fell short of the worship of the true God?*—Very far short.

31. *What fearful lesson does this teach us?*—To be thoroughly sound in our Christian profession, lest, like the fig tree with leaves but no fruit, we be discovered and destroyed at the last. Mark 11 : 13, 20.

32. *What does the Lord find on us? Are we bearing fruit, or is there nothing on us but the leaves of an empty profession?*—Let the conscience of each answer as in the sight of God.

33. *How long did Jehu reign? and who succeeded him?* —Twenty-eight years. 2 Kings 10 : 36. Jehoahaz, his son. 2 Kings 13 : 1.

JEHU'S DYNASTY; ELISHA'S DEATH. (2 Kings 13, 14, 15 : 1–12.)

1. *What character did Jehoahaz bear?*—He was a wicked man. 2 Kings 13 : 2.

2. *How did the Lord punish Israel?*—By delivering them into the hands of the king of Syria.

3. *What effect did this have upon the king?*—He prayed to God for relief, and was heard, but idolatry still continued in the land.

4. *How long did he reign? and who succeeded him?*—Seventeen years. Joash, his son.

5. *Was he a better king? Describe him.*—He was no better, but walked, like his father, in Jeroboam's sins.

6. *What sorrowful event happened in this reign?*—The death of Elisha.

7. *When Joash heard of the prophet's illness, what did he do?*—He came and wept over him, and praised him.

8. *What symbolical prophecy did the prophet cause the king to act at this interview?*—Shooting, and striking the ground with arrows, as a token of success against the Syrians.

9. *What miraculous event took place in connection with Elisha's remains?*—A dead man revived when his body touched them.

10. *Where was Moab situated?*—On the south-east of the Dead Sea.

11. *Where was Elisha's grave, supposing he was buried in the inheritance of his fathers?*—At Abel-meholah in Simeon, where his father lived.

12. *Was Elisha's prophecy fulfilled in the days of Joash (called also Jehoash)?*—Joash defeated the Syrians thrice, as Elisha had said.

13. *How came Israel and Judah to go to war in this reign?*—Because the king of Judah challenged the king of Israel to do so. 2 Kings 14 : 8.

14. *What insolent message did Joash send to Amasiah?*—He proudly replied that he would crush him as a wild beast does a thistle.

15. *On which side did victory turn?*—On Israel's side.

16. *How long did Joash (or Jehoash) reign?*—Sixteen years. 2 Kings 13 : 10.

17. *Who succeeded Joash on the throne of Israel?*—Jeroboam his son. 2 Kings 14 : 16.

18. *How many years did he reign?*—Forty-one. 2 Kings 14 : 23.

19. *Of what character was he, morally?*—He did evil in the sight of the Lord.

20. *What kind of king and warrior was he?*—He was successful in war, and recovered some border-lands which Israel had lost.

21. *How came it that Jeroboam was so victorious?*—Because of God's pity and promise. 2 Kings 14 : 25-27.

22. *How many prophets besides Jonah prophesied in this reign?*—Four—Isaiah, Hosea, Joel and Amos.

23. *Who succeeded Jeroboam II.?*—Zachariah his son.

24. *Was his a long or short reign?*—Only six months. 2 Kings 15 : 8.

25. *How did he come by his death?*—He was killed by Shallum. 2 Kings 15 : 10.

26. *What promise had the Lord given Jehu?*—That his sons should be kings of Israel for four generations.

27. *How was this fulfilled?*—In the succession of Jehoahaz, Joash, Jeroboam and Zachariah.

28. *What is said in Isa. 46 : 9, 10?*—I am God, and there is none like me, declaring the end from the beginning, and from ancient times the things that are not yet done, saying, My counsel shall stand, and I will do all my pleasure.

JONAH, HOSEA AND AMOS.
JONAH.

1. *Is there any prophesying of Jonah's recorded besides the book called by his name?*—The prophecy of the reconquest by Jeroboam. 2 Kings 14 : 25.

2. *Why is he generally styled "the disobedient prophet"?*—Because he fled away when ordered by God to go to Nineveh.

3. *Against whom was he commanded to prophesy?*—Against the Ninevites.

4. *How is Nineveh described in Scripture?*—An exceeding great city, of three days' journey (or sixty miles) round.

5. *Do the vast ruins lately discovered confirm or contradict this Scripture testimony?*—They strongly confirm it.

6. *Why did Jonah shrink from his errand?*—From fear of being killed, or of seeming to be a false prophet if God's threatenings were mercifully unfulfilled, or from a dislike to prophesy to a mere heathen nation.

7. *Is it of any use for man to refuse to fulfill the will of God?*—None.

Woe unto him that striveth with his Maker! Let the potsherd strive with the potsherds of the earth. Shall the clay say to him that fashioneth it, What makest thou? or thy work, He hath no hands? Isa. 45 : 9.

That saith of Cyrus, He is my shepherd, and shall perform all my pleasure. Isa. 44 : 28.

8. *How did the Lord overtake Jonah in his rebellion?* —By a storm at Sea.

9. *What did the mariners strive to do?*—To save their lives by calling on their gods and lightening the ship, and rowing hard to reach the land.

10. *Was it of any use?*—No.

11. *How did Jonah own God's righteous dealing?*—By telling them of his flight, and that the storm was on his account.

12. *When thrown overboard, how did God preserve him?*—By means of a great fish he had prepared.

13. *Is Jehovah God ever at a loss to fulfill his purposes?*—Never.

14. *How did Jonah feel when in the fish's belly?*—Cast out of God's sight.

15. *How was Jonah's case a fulfillment of Ps. 139?*—He found it impossible to flee from God's presence.

If I take the wings of the morning, and dwell in the uttermost parts of the sea; even there shall thy hand lead me, and thy right hand shall hold me. Ps. 139: 9, 10.

16. *If the Lord could hear Jonah from the depths of the sea, can we be in any circumstances beyond the reach of his arm to save?*—Never.

17. *When the Lord again commanded Jonah to go to Nineveh, did he obey?*—He did. Jonah 3.

18. *What was the result of his preaching?*—The king and people believed God, and repented and turned from their evil way.

19. *How did Jonah like this?*—He was very angry that his threatening was not fulfilled, fearing, perhaps, that he would not be considered a true prophet, and that the Israelites would not repent when they saw that Nineveh was spared.

20. *How did the Lord comfort and reprove Jonah?*—By giving him a shade from the heat, and by rebuking his anger at its loss.

21. *Is not God's mercy to the Ninevites a pledge to us of his mercy and his grace?*—It is, if our repentance is as deep and sincere.

22. *How may it be that these poor heathen may rise in condemnation against us at the last day?*—If we do not repent under the teaching and preaching of God's word.

23. *But how much are our privileges greater than theirs?*—God hath in these last days spoken unto us by his Son. Heb. 1: 2. Therefore we ought to give the more earnest heed to the things which we have heard, lest at any time we should let them slip. Heb. 2: 1.

24. *Where is Nineveh?*—On the river Tigris, in the ancient Assyria, and near the modern towns of Mosul and Bagdad.

25. *What attribute of the Lord's glorious character does his conduct toward Nineveh display?*—His wonderful mercy.

26. *Where is Nineveh first mentioned in Scripture?*—In Gen. 10: 11, where Asshur is said to have built it.

27. *How old must this great city have been when Jonah prophesied against it?*—About fifteen hundred years.

HOSEA.

28. *Who was Hosea?*—A prophet, son of Beeri.

29. *In whose reigns did he prophesy?*—In the reigns of Uzziah, Jotham, Ahaz and Hezekiah, kings of Judah, and in the reign of Jeroboam, son of Joash, king of Israel.

30. *What touching expostulation does the Lord address to Israel in Hos. 8?*—How shall I give thee up, Ephraim? how shall I deliver thee, Israel? how shall I make thee as Admah? how shall I set thee as Zeboim? mine heart is turned within me, my repentings are kindled together.

31. *Who is meant by Ephraim?*—Israel.

32. *Why is the name of Ephraim given to Israel?*—Because the tribe of Ephraim was the chief part of the kingdom of Israel.

33. *What idolatries of Israel are alluded to in Hos. 13?*—The worship of Baal and the golden calves.

34. *What beautiful invitation is given in Hos. 14: 1, 2?*—O Israel, return unto the Lord thy God; for thou hast fallen by thine iniquity. Take with you words, and turn to the Lord: say unto him, Take away all iniquity, and receive us graciously.

35. *Does the Lord only address such gracious words to Israel as a nation, or may we believe them spoken to us?*—"For our sakes, no doubt, this is written," as sinners in every age and of every country need the same mercy and the same invitation. 1 Cor. 9: 9, 10.

AMOS.

36. *Who was Amos?*—A native of Tekoah in Judah and a prophet.

37. *What was his occupation when the Lord called him to be a prophet?*—That of a herdsman or shepherd.

38. *Against how many nations does he prophesy before he utters his denunciations against Israel?*—Against six—Syria, Philistia, Tyre, Edom, Ammon and Moab.

39. *Into what two sins of Israel does Amos 2 : 12 give us an insight?*—Drunkenness and rejection of God' word and prophets.

40. *How does Amos 3 : 12 show us that according to our privileges so will our punishment be?*—You only have I known of all the families of the earth: therefore I will punish you for all your iniquities.

41. *Point out our Lord's parables that more fully explain this.*—The wicked husbandmen (Matt. 21 : 33), the marriage-feast (Matt. 22), and our Lord's denunciation against Capernaum. Matt. 11 : 23.

42. *What prophecy against the altar of Bethel does Amos 3 also contain?*—In the day that I shall visit the transgressions of Israel upon him I will also visit the altars of Bethel; and the horns of the altar shall be cut off, and fall to the ground.

43. *When was this fulfilled? and by whom?*—About one hundred and sixty years after, by Josiah.

The altar that was at Bethel, and the high place which Jeroboam the son of Nebat, who made Israel to sin, had made, both that altar and the high place he brake down, and burned the high place, and stamped it small to powder, and burned the grove. 2 Kings 23 : 15.

44. *What great similarity is there between Amos 4 and Deut. 28?*—Amos 4 seems to be a fulfillment of the curses of drought, famine and pestilence pronounced in Deut. 28 upon their national sins.

45. *What prophecy is there in the lamentation of Amos (chap. 5) that Stephen quotes in Acts 7?*—Vs. 25–27; Acts 7 : 42, 43.

46. *What proofs of Israel's luxury at this time (in the reign of Jeroboam II.) does Amos 6 give us?*—(Read vs. 4–6.)

47. *What did Amaziah the priest of Bethel send and say to Jeroboam when Amos had uttered these prophecies?*—That Amos was conspiring against him. Amos 7 : 10.

48. *What did he advise Amos to do? and why?*—To go into Judah to live and to prophesy, as Bethel was the king's court.

49. *What sins of Israel does Amos 8 set forth?*—Dishonesty, oppression and neglect of God's word. Vs. 5, 6, 11, 12.

50. *After the fearful denunciations of chaps. 8 and 9, what predictions of after glory does the last chapter close with?*—The restoration of Israel to their own land in plenty and peace.

51. *By whom must "the fallen tabernacle of David" be reared?*—By Jesus Christ.

He shall be great, and shall be called the Son of the Highest: and the Lord God shall give unto him the throne of his father David: and he shall reign over the house of Jacob for ever; and of his kingdom there shall be no end. Luke 1 : 32, 33.

THE LAST KINGS OF ISRAEL. (2 Kings 15–17.)

1. *Who slew Zachariah, the last of Jehu's dynasty?*—Shallum. 2 Kings 15 : 10.

2. *How long did he reign?*—A month.

3. *Who destroyed him?*—Menahem.

4. *How long did Menahem reign?*—Ten years. 2 Kings 15 : 17.

5. *What kind of king was he?*—A wicked one.

6. *Who fought against him?*—Pul, king of Assyria.

7. *Who succeeded Menahem?*—Pekahiah his son.

8. *How long did Pekahiah reign?*—Two years.

9. *Who slew him?*—Pekah, one of his captains.

10. *How long did Pekah reign?*—Twenty years.

11. *Which was the last king of Israel?*—Hoshea.

12. *How long did he reign?*—Nine years. 2 Kings 17 : 1.

13. *Which of the kings of Assyria came against him?*—Shalmaneser.

14. *Did Israel conquer, or the Assyrians?*—The Assyrians.

15. *How was this?*—The Lord shall bring thee, and thy king which thou shalt set over thee, unto a nation which neither thou nor thy fathers have known; and there shalt thou serve other gods, wood and stone. Moreover, all these curses shall come upon thee, and shall pursue thee, and overtake thee, till thou be destroyed; because thou hearkenedst not unto the voice of the Lord thy God, to keep his commandments and his statutes which he commanded thee. Deut. 28 : 36, 45.

16. *Had not God often warned them of their danger?*—Yes, by his prophets.

17. *Will not all God's threatenings be fulfilled, as well as his promises?*—They will.

18. *What has God said in his word shall be the punishment of impenitent sinners?*—" Except ye repent, ye shall all likewise perish." Luke 3 : 13.

19. *If we slight the word of God as Israel did of old, what must we expect?*—Punishment—as a nation, here; and as individuals, here and hereafter, now and for ever.

20. *Have we a remedy? What is it?*—To "return unto the Lord, and he will have mercy upon" us. Isa. 55 : 6, 7.

21. *To what places was Israel carried captive?*—To places in Media and Mesopotamia.

22. *Who were brought in to fill the depopulated cities?*—People from Babylon and the regions around it. 2 Kings 17 : 24.

23. *What was the result?*—A mixture of the worship of God and of idols. 2 Kings 17 : 33.

JORAM (OR JEHORAM) TO AMAZIAH, KINGS OF JUDAH. (2 Chron. 21–25.)

1. *Whose son was Joram (Jehoram) king of Judah?*—Son of Jehoshaphat. 2 Chron. 21 : 1.

2. *Which of Israel's kings reigned at the same time?*—Ahaziah, and afterward Jehoram. 2 Kings 1 : 17, 18.

3. *Whose daughter was Joram's wife?*—Ahab's. 2 Chron. 21 : 6.

4. *What effect did this unholy alliance have on the king?*—It led him into the sins of Ahab's house. 2 Chron. 21 : 6.

5. *How many years did Joram reign jointly with his father?*—About two. 2 Kings 8 : 16.

6. *What was the first wicked thing he did after his father was dead and he reigned alone?*—He killed his brothers. 2 Chron. 21 : 4.

7. *What kingdom revolted from under the sway of Judah in this reign?*—Edom, and the city of Libnah.

8. *What message came to him from God by the hand of Elijah the prophet?*—Of a great plague or affliction for his family and people, and a mortal disease for himself.

9. *By what death did he die?*—By a long and painful illness.

10. *How long had he reigned?*—Eight years.

11. *Who succeeded him?*—Ahaziah his son.

12. *By what three names is this king called?*—Ahaziah, Jehoahaz and Azariah. 2 Chron. 21 : 17; 22 : 1, 6.

13. *By which is he more generally called?*—Ahaziah. 2 Kings 9.

14. *Which of Joram's sons was he?*—The youngest.

15. *Why did not Joram's eldest son reign?*—Because he had been killed with his brothers.

16. *What did this prove?*—That Elijah's message had come true.

17. *To what untimely end did this king of Judah come?*—He was killed, with Joram, by order of Jehu.

18. *How did it happen?*—He had gone under the guidance of God to visit Joram. 2 Kings 8 : 29; 2 Chron. 22 : 7.

19. *What was the name of Ahaziah's mother?*—Athaliah.

20. *When she saw her son was dead, what cruel act did she exercise toward his children, her own grandchildren?*—She had them all but one destroyed.

21. *Name her father and mother.*—Ahab and Jezebel.

22. *When we see how much evil the good Jehoshaphat brought on his family by his alliance with Ahab, should it not make us most careful as to the company we keep?*—It should indeed.

Be not deceived: evil communications corrupt good manners. 1 Cor. 15 : 33.

Be not deceived: God is not mocked: for whatsoever a man soweth, that shall he also reap. For he that soweth to his flesh shall of the flesh reap corruption; but he that soweth to the Spirit shall of the Spirit reap life everlasting. Gal. 6 : 7, 8.

23. *How was one grandchild unexpectedly preserved?*—He was hid by Jehoshabeath. 2 Chron. 22 : 11.

24. *What relation was the good Jehoshabeath to the little boy?*—His aunt.

25. *How long did the wicked Athaliah keep the throne?*—Six years. 2 Chron. 22 : 12.

26. *What was her end?*—She was slain when Joash, the lawful king, was raised to the throne.

27. *How old was the young king when he began to reign?*—Seven.

28. *How long did he continue to do well?*—During the life of Jehoiada the priest, about twenty-eight years.

29. *What good service did he do the temple of God during Jehoiada's life?*—He repaired and refitted it. 2 Chron. 24 : 4–14.

30. *To what commandment by Moses did the king refer as to the contribution to the Lord's service?*—And the Lord spake unto Moses, saying, When thou takest the sum of the children of Israel after their number, then shall they give every man a ransom for his soul unto the Lord, when thou numberest them; that there be no plague among them, when thou numberest them. This they shall give, every one that passeth among them that are numbered, half a shekel after the shekel of the sanctuary (a shekel is twenty gerahs): an half shekel shall be the offering of the Lord. Every one that passeth among them that are numbered, from twenty years old and above, shall give an offering unto the Lord. The rich shall not give more, and the poor shall not give less than half a shekel, when they give an offering unto the Lord, to make an atonement for your souls. And thou shalt take the atonement money of the children of Israel, and shalt appoint it for the service of the tabernacle of the congregation; that it may be a memorial unto the children of Israel before the Lord, to make an atonement for your souls. Ex. 30 : 11–16.

31. *How old was the good Jehoiada when he died?*—One hundred and thirty years. 2 Chron. 24 : 15.

32. *What honor did they show his remains?*—They buried him among the kings.

33. *How did Joash behave after his uncle's death?*—He worshiped idols.

34. *Whom did the Lord send to warn him of his sins?*—Zechariah the son of Jehoiada.

35. *What did Joash cause to be done to him?*—To be stoned to death.

36. *What did Zechariah say in dying?*—"The Lord look upon it, and require it."

37. *Is his death alluded to in the New Testament?*—That upon you may come all the righteous blood shed upon the earth, from the blood of righteous Abel unto the blood of Zacharias son of Barachias, whom ye slew between the temple and the altar. Matt. 23 : 35.

38. *How did the Lord punish Judah for their idolatry?*—By the Syrian army.

39. *How did he punish this wicked king?*—By great diseases.

40. *In what way did he die?*—He was killed by his own servants.

41. *How long did he reign?*—Forty years. 2 Chron. 24 : 1.

42. *Who succeeded him?*—Amaziah his son.

43. *Was Amaziah a better man than his father?*—Probably not, as his heart was not right toward God, and as, after reigning well for some time, he fell into idolatry.

44. *How did God try his faith?*—By telling him to trust him to replace the loss of one hundred talents which he had paid for the hire of an Israelitish army. 2 Chron. 25 : 6–10.

45. *Did he continue to serve the Lord?*—No. 2 Chron. 25 : 14, 27.

46. *What new idolatry did he introduce?*—The gods of Edom. 2 Chron. 25 : 14, 20.

47. *How was he punished for this?*—By defeat in war and by conspiracy at home.

48. *How did he die?*—He was killed by his own people.

49. *How long did he reign?*—Twenty-nine years.

50. *Which king of Israel reigned at the same time?*—Joash or Jehoash.

51. *What battle did these two kings fight?*—The battle of Bethshemesh.

52. *Which was victorious? Why?*—Joash, because of Amaziah's idolatry.

53. *Does not this show us that all our actions are noticed by God?*—Yes, and that he punishes idolatry, boasting and all other sin.

UZZIAH, JOTHAM AND AHAZ, KINGS OF JUDAH. (2 Chron. 26–32.)

1. *Who was Uzziah?*—Amaziah's son.

2. *How old was he when he began to reign?*—Sixteen.

3. *By what other name is he called?*—Azariah. 2 Kings 15 : 1.

4. *What king was reigning in Israel at this time?*—Jeroboam II.

5. *How many prophets prophesied in the reign of Uzziah?*—Five—Isaiah, Hosea, Joel, Amos and Jonah.

6. *What is said of Uzziah in 2 Chron. 26 : 5?*—That while he sought the Lord he prospered.

7. *How was this manifested in the early part of his reign?*—By great success in war. 2 Chron. 26 : 6–15.

8. *By whose influence was he kept in the right way?*—By the influence of Zechariah, a man of God.

9. *What effect did prosperity have on him?*—It lifted up his heart.

10. *What does it mean by his heart being lifted up?*—That he was proud and presumptuous.

11. *What does the Lord say about pride in the Scripture?*—That it "goeth before destruction." Prov. 16 : 18.

12. *To what act of impiety did Uzziah's pride prompt him?*—To burn incense like a priest.

13. *How was it punished?*—By being smitten with leprosy.

14. *What effect did his punishment have on him?*—It made him go and live alone.

15. *Of what was leprosy a type?*—Of sin.

16. *How was leprosy under the Mosaic law cleansed?*—The priest shall go forth out of the camp; and the priest shall look, and, behold, if the plague of leprosy be healed in the leper, then shall the priest command to take for him that is to be cleansed two birds alive and clean, and cedar-wood, and scarlet, and hyssop; and the priest shall command that one of the birds be killed in an earthen vessel over running water: as for the living bird, he shall take it, and the cedar-wood, and the scarlet, and the hyssop, and shall dip them and the living bird in the blood of the bird that was killed over the running water; and he shall sprinkle upon him that is to be cleansed from the leprosy seven times, and shall pronounce him clean, and shall let the living bird loose into the open field. Lev. 14 : 3–7.

17. *Who was typified by the bird that was slain, and by the living bird?*—The Saviour and the sinner.

18. *How many instances are recorded in Scripture of persons being punished by leprosy?*—Three—those of Miriam, Gehazi and Uzziah.

19. *What great deprivations did Uzziah suffer in consequence of this malady?*—He was cut off from the house of the Lord, from the honors of a king and from all human society.

20. *How had Uzziah occupied himself?*—In war, in building cities and towers, in digging wells, and in keeping much cattle; also in cultivating fruitful fields. *How many years did he reign?*—Fifty-two years.

21. *Who shared the government with him when he was laid aside, and succeeded him on the throne of Judah?*—Jotham his son.

22. *How old was Jotham when he began to reign?*—Twenty-five. 2 Chron. 27 : 1.

23. *How is his character described?*—"He did that which was right in the sight of the Lord."

24. *How does 2 Chron. 27 : 6 give us the secret of his prosperity?*—It says that "he prepared (or established) his ways before God." So Joshua and David had a fixed purpose or plan to serve the Lord.

25. *How long did he reign?*—Sixteen years.

26. *Who followed Jotham?*—Ahaz his son.

27. *Was he not a very different king?*—Yes; "he did not right in the sight of the Lord."

28. *In whose ways did he walk?*—In those of the kings of Israel.

29. *Who was king of Israel at this time?*—Pekah.

30. *Did Ahaz go on in this sad career without warning?*—No; he was warned by the prophets.

31. *Which of the prophets prophesied in his reign?*—Isaiah, Hosea and Micah.

32. *How does Isaiah, in his first chapter, describe the state of Israel and Judah at this time?*—Ah sinful nation, a people laden with iniquity, a seed of evil-doers, children that are corrupters: they have forsaken the Lord, they have provoked the Holy One of Israel unto anger, they are gone away backward.

33. *How are the daughters of Judah described in the end of his third chapter?*—The daughters of Zion are haughty, and walk with stretched-forth necks and wanton eyes, walking and mincing as they go, and making a tinkling with their feet.

34. *What idol-worship did Ahaz again introduce?*—Of Baal and of the gods of Syria. 2 Chron. 28 : 2, 23

35. *What cruel heathen practice did he exercise on his son?*—He burnt his children in sacrifice. 2 Chron. 28 : 3.

36. *What enemies came against Judah as a punishment for their sins?*—Pekah and Rezin.

37. *Who was Pekah?*—King of Israel.

38. *Who was Rezin?*—King of Syria.

39. *What encouragement did the Lord give by his prophet Isaiah concerning these kings?*—Take heed, and be quiet; fear not, neither be faint-hearted for the two tails of these smoking fire-brands, for the fierce anger of Rezin with Syria, and of the son of Remaliah. Isa. 7 : 4.

40. *When Ahaz declared he would not ask a sign of God, was that from reverence or disregard?*—From disregard.

41. *How did his seeking aid from the king of Assyria against his foes, and not from the Lord, decide this?*—It showed he was determined to take his own course.

42. *What was the consequence of his seeking to the Assyrians?*—Embarrassment instead of support. 2 Chron. 28 : 20.

43. *How did he strip the temple of God to pay the Assyrian king?*—He took away much of its brass (or copper) work. 2 Kings 16 : 17, 18.

44. *Did he, after all, obtain the help he desired?*—He did not.

45. *Which were the most prosperous kings, those who served the Lord, or those who forsook him?*—Those who served the Lord.

46. *What effect had chastisement on him?*—He sinned yet more against the Lord. 2 Chron. 28 : 23.

47. *What did this prove him not to be?*—It proved him not to be a son of God, or he would have profited by his fatherly chastisement.

If ye endure chastening, God dealeth with you as with sons; for what son is he whom the father chasteneth not? Heb. 12 : 7.

48. *How many years did he reign?*—Sixteen years.

49. *Was he buried among the good kings of Judah?*—No 2 Chron. 28 : 27.

ISAIAH, MICAH AND NAHUM.

1. *Who was Isaiah?*—A prophet, the son of Amoz.

2. *In whose reigns did he prophesy?*—In those of "Uzziah, Jotham, Ahaz and Hezekiah, kings of Judah."

3. *Is any part of his book historical? how much?*—Yes, about four chapters, chaps. 36–39.

4. *What great and glorious Person was he privileged to announce?*—The Messiah.

Unto us a Child is born, unto us a Son is given: and the government shall be upon his shoulder: and his name shall be called Wonderful, Counsellor, The Mighty God, The Everlasting Father, The Prince of Peace. Of the increase of his government and peace there shall be no end, upon the throne of David, and upon his kingdom, to order it, and to establish it with judgment and with justice from henceforth even for ever. Isa. 9 : 6, 7.

5. *What prophecy of Isaiah's is quoted in Matt. 1 : 23?*—Therefore the Lord himself shall give you a sign: Behold, a virgin shall conceive, and bear a son, and shall call his name Immanuel. Isa. 7 : 14.

6. *How many titles does Isaiah attribute to the Lord Jesus in Isa. 9 : 6, 7?*—Five.

7. *To whom does Isaiah attribute the term "Wonderful" in Isa. 28 : 29?*—To Jehovah himself.

The Lord of hosts, which is wonderful in counsel, and excellent in working.

8. *Who, then, must the Lord Jesus Christ be?*—God.

9. *Are there any other texts of Scripture that plainly show him forth to be "the Mighty God"?*—"The great God and our Saviour Jesus Christ." Tit. 2 : 13.

I am Alpha and Omega, the beginning and the ending, saith the Lord, which is, and which was, and which is to come, the Almighty. Rev. 1 : 8.

10. *How does John 10 : 30 prove that the Lord Jesus is "the Everlasting Father"?*—God is called "the everlasting God" in Rom. 16 : 26, and Jesus says in John 10 : 30, "I and my Father are one."

11. *To which character of the Lord Jesus does the* apostle Paul allude in Eph. 2 : 14?—"He is our peace" —"The Prince of Peace."

12. *When will the "government be on the shoulder" of the Lord Jesus?*—When his reign of one thousand years begins. Rev. 19 : 11–16.

13. *Is there any earthly throne which he is promised?*—"The throne of David."

14. *What power does the Lord Jesus exercise now?*—The power which, as God, he exercises by the Holy Spirit. Matt. 28 : 18.

15. *Where is the Lord Jesus now?*—On the throne of God in heaven.

David is not ascended into the heavens: but he saith himself, The Lord said unto my Lord, Sit thou on my right hand, until I make thy foes thy footstool. Therefore let all the house of Israel know assuredly, that God hath made that same Jesus, whom ye have crucified, both Lord and Christ. Acts 2 : 34–36.

Behold, I see the heavens opened, and the Son of man standing on the right hand of God. Acts 7 : 56.

To him that overcometh will I grant to sit with me in my throne, even as I also overcame, and am set down with my Father in his throne. Rev. 3 : 21.

16. *Under what name is the Lord Jesus spoken of in Isa. 11 : 1?*—"A Rod out of the stem of Jesse, and a Branch . . . out of his roots."

17. *Who was Jesse?*—The father of David.

18. *Who was the root of Jesse (that is, his forefather)?*—Christ, as David's Lord.

19. *From what "stem of Jesse" did the Lord Jesus spring?*—From David, whose father was Jesse and great-grandfather Boaz. Ruth 4 : 16, 17.

20. *Where does the Lord Jesus call himself "the root and offspring of David"?*—Rev. 22 : 16.

21. *What is the Lord Jesus called in Rev. 5 : 5?*—The Lion of the tribe of Juda, the root of David.

22. *Of what is the lion expressive?*—Of strength.

23. *What is the meaning of the name Boaz?*—"In strength."

24. *What connection have all these passages together?*—They all unite in describing Christ.

25. *How does Isaiah describe the kingly power of the Lord Jesus in Isa. 32 : 1?*—"Behold, a King shall reign in righteousness."

26. *Under what character does he represent the Lord Jesus in the second verse of that chapter?*—A man shall be as an hiding-place from the wind, and a covert from the tempest; as rivers of water in a dry place, as the shadow of a great rock in a weary land.

27. *Can his kingly glory be a joy to us unless we know him first as a "hiding-place"?*—No.

28. *What part of Isaiah did the Lord Jesus read when he was on earth, when "the eyes of all in the synagogue were fastened on him"?*—Isa. 61 : 1, 2. The Spirit of the Lord is upon me, because he hath anointed me to preach the gospel to the poor; he hath sent me to heal the broken-hearted, to preach deliverance to the captives, and recovering of sight to the blind, to set at liberty them that are bruised, to preach the acceptable year of the Lord. Luke 4 : 18, 19.

29. *What did he say when he closed the book?*—This day is this scripture fulfilled in your ears. Luke 4 : 21.

30. *How often does the Lord (that is, Jehovah) call himself by the name of Jesus (that is, Saviour) in the book of Isaiah?*—Four times or more—as, "I am the Lord thy God, the Holy One of Israel, thy Saviour" (Isa. 43 : 3); "a just God and a Saviour." Isa. 45 : 21.

31. *How often does he speak of himself as "Redeemer"?*—Directly and indirectly, nine times or more—as, "I will help thee, saith the Lord, and thy Redeemer, the Holy One of Israel" (Isa. 41 : 14); "And all flesh shall know that I the Lord am thy Saviour and thy Redeemer, the mighty One of Jacob." Isa. 49 : 26.

32. *What part of Isaiah's prophecy was the eunuch reading when Philip overtook him?*—Isa. 53 : 7, 8. The

place of the scripture which he read was this, He was led as a lamb to the slaughter; and like a lamb dumb before his shearer, so opened he not his mouth: in his humiliation his judgment was taken away: and who shall declare his generation? for his life is taken from the earth. Acts 8 : 32, 33.

33. *Who was intended by the term "lamb"?*—Jesus Christ.

John seeth Jesus coming unto him, and saith, Behold the Lamb of God, which taketh away the sin of the world. John 1 : 29.

Worthy is the Lamb that was slain. Rev. 5 : 12.

The Lamb slain from the foundation of the world. Rev. 13 : 8.

A Lamb stood on the Mount Sion. Rev. 14 : 1.

The song of the Lamb. Rev. 15 : 3.

34. *Give the fulfillment of the prophecy (Isa. 53) in each particular.*—

Verse 1:

Though he had done so many miracles before them, yet they believed not on him. John 12 : 37.

Verse 2:

He made himself of no reputation, and took upon him the form of a servant, and was made in the likeness of men. Phil. 2 : 7.

Verse 3:

Is not this the carpenter, the son of Mary? Mark 6 : 3.

Out of Galilee ariseth no prophet. John 7 : 52.

Thou art a Samaritan, and hast a devil. John 8 : 48.

He came unto his own, and his own received him not. John 1 : 11.

Verse 4:

He cast out the spirits with his word, and healed all that were sick. Matt. 8 : 16.

Verses 5 and 6:

Christ died for our sins according to the Scriptures. 1 Cor. 15 : 3.

Verse 7:

When he was accused of the chief priests and elders, he answered nothing. Matt. 27 : 12.

Verse 8:

And when they had bound him, they led him away, and delivered him to Pontius Pilate the governor: and when he had scourged Jesus, he delivered him to be crucified. Matt. 27 : 2, 26.

Verse 9:

There were also two other, malefactors, led with him to be put to death.

There came a rich man of Arimathea, named Joseph: he went to Pilate, and begged the body of Jesus. Then Pilate commanded the body to be delivered. Matt. 27 : 57, 58.

Verses 10 and 11:

Lo, a Lamb stood on the mount Sion, and with him an hundred forty and four thousand, having his Father's name written in their foreheads. These were redeemed from among men, being the first-fruits unto God and to the Lamb. And in their mouth was found no guile: for they are without fault before the throne of God. Rev. 14 : 1, 4, 5.

Verse 12:

Forasmuch then as the children are partakers of flesh and blood, he also himself likewise took part of the same: that through death he might destroy him that had the power of death, that is, the devil. Heb. 2 : 14.

And with him they crucify two thieves: the one on his right hand, and the other on his left. And the scripture was fulfilled, which saith, And he was numbered with the transgressors. Mark 15 : 27, 28.

35. *Compare Isa. 63 : 1–3 with Rev. 19 : 13, 15, and tell of whom the prophecies speak.*—He was clothed with a vesture dipped in blood: and his name is called The Word of God. And he treadeth the winepress of the fierceness and wrath of Almighty God.

36. *Are we concerned in this?*—Yes, for as sinners we are enemies of God.

37. *Then what should we do now?*—We should come at once by faith to Christ our Saviour, and be cleansed by his atoning blood.

38. *Are there not many gracious invitations to sinners throughout the book of Isaiah?*—Come now, and let us reason together, saith the Lord: though your sins be as scarlet, they shall be as white as snow; though they be red like crimson, they shall be as wool. Isa. 1 : 18. Ho, every one that thirsteth, come ye to the waters, and he that hath no money; come ye, buy, and eat; yea, come, buy wine and milk without money and without price. Isa. 55 : 1.

39. *Were there not many special promises to the Gentiles?*—Yes, as in chaps. 9, 11, 35, 42, 49, 60, 65.

40. *Who are the Gentiles?*—All who are not Jews.

41. *To whom are the principal prophecies in this book addressed?*—To the Jews.

42. *How are the sins of Israel described in Isa. 1 and elsewhere?*—Thy princes are rebellious, and companions of thieves; every one loveth gifts, and followeth after rewards: they judge not the fatherless, neither doth the cause of the widow come unto them. Isa. 1 : 23. The vineyard of the Lord of hosts is the house of Israel, and the men of Judah his pleasant plant: and he looked for judgment, but behold oppression; for righteousness, but behold a cry. Isa. 5 : 7.

43. *What glorious promises are addressed to God's favored people?*—As for me, this is my covenant with them, saith the Lord; My spirit that is upon thee, and my words which I have put in thy mouth, shall not depart out of thy mouth, nor out of the mouth of thy seed, nor out of the mouth of thy seed's seed, saith the Lord, from henceforth and for ever. Isa. 59 : 21. The Lord shall comfort Zion: he will comfort all her waste places; and he will make her wilderness like Eden, and her desert like the garden of the Lord. Isa. 51 : 3. Awake, awake; put on thy strength, O Zion; put on thy beautiful garments, O Jerusalem, the holy city: for henceforth there shall no more come into thee the uncircumcised and the unclean. Isa. 52 : 1.

44. *How does Isaiah describe their idolatry in Isa. 44?*—He heweth him down cedars, and taketh the cypress and the oak, which he strengtheneth for himself among the trees of the forest: he planteth an ash, and the rain doth nourish it. Then shall it be for a man to burn: for he will take thereof, and warm himself; yea, he kindleth it, and baketh bread; yea, he maketh a god, and worshipeth it; he maketh it a graven image, and falleth down thereto. He burneth part thereof in the fire; with part thereof he eateth flesh; he roasteth roast, and is satisfied: yea, he warmeth himself, and saith, Aha, I am warm, I have seen the fire: and the residue thereof he maketh a god, even his graven image: he falleth down unto it, and worshipeth it, and prayeth unto it, and saith Deliver me; for thou art my god.

45. *Under what beautiful symbol does he describe God's care of Israel in chap. 5?*—A husbandman's care of his vineyard.

What could have been done more to my vineyard, that I have not done in it? wherefore, when I looked that it should bring forth grapes, brought it forth wild grapes?

46. *What touching images does he use to portray God's love to his people in chaps. 49 : 14, 16; 54 : 5–8; 66 : 13?*—As one whom his mother comforteth, so will I comfort you.

47. *Are there not many fearful denunciations against the wicked in this prophecy?*—There are, as in 1 : 28:

The destruction of the transgressors and of the sinners shall be together, and they that forsake the Lord shall be consumed. And the strong shall be as tow, and the maker of it as a spark, and they shall both burn together, and none shall quench them.

48. *What nations then flourishing did Isaiah specially prophesy against by name?*—Assyria, Babylon, Palestine, Moab, Israel, Ethiopia, Egypt, Arabia, Tyre, Jerusalem, the Jews.

49. *Take each in succession, and tell us as nearly as you can their present state.*—Assyria is now in a very low state, under Turkish rule.

Babylon is so utterly destroyed that travelers have passed over its place without knowing it.

Palestine, generally, is in an uncultivated, thinly-peopled, oppressed and half-barbarous state.

Moab is in the same condition.

Israel is described under Palestine, above.

Ethiopia is in the same condition.

Egypt is in an improving state, but probably far less populous and less richly cultivated than of old.

Arabia is still chiefly inhabited by wandering tribes, whose hand is against every man.

Tyre is reduced to a mere fishing-village.

Jerusalem is in the hands of Mohammedans, and shares the fate of Judah and Israel and Palestine at large.

50. *To what period does this wonderful prophecy extend?*—To the end of time.

Behold, I create new heavens and a new earth; and the former shall not be remembered, nor come into mind. Isa. 65 : 17.

51. *What glorious vision did Isaiah see which prepared him to do the Lord's service?*—In the year that King Uzziah died I saw also the Lord sitting upon a throne, high and lifted up, and his train filled the temple. Above it stood the seraphims. Then flew one of the seraphims unto me, having a live coal in his hand, which he had taken with the tongs from off the altar: and he laid it upon my mouth, and said, Lo, this hath touched thy lips; and thine iniquity is taken away, and thy sin purged. Also I heard the voice of the Lord, saying, Whom shall I send, and who will go for us? Isa. 6 : 1, 2, 6–8.

52. *In whose reign did he see that vision?*—In Uzziah's.

53. *Do you find anything similar to it in the book of Revelation?*—I was in the spirit: and, behold, a throne was set in heaven, and One sat on the throne. Rev. 4 : 2.

54. *What effect did the sight of God's glory have on Isaiah?*—He deeply felt his sinfulness.

Then said I, Woe is me! for I am undone; because I am a man of unclean lips, and I dwell in the midst of a people of unclean lips: for mine eyes have seen the King, the Lord of hosts. Isa. 6 : 5.

55. *What was Job's expression when God spoke to him?*—I have heard of thee by the hearing of the ear: bu. now mine eye seeth thee. Wherefore I abhor myself, and repent in dust and ashes. Job 42 : 5, 6.

56. *What alone can remove the terror which all men as sinners must feel in the presence of God?*—"The blood of Jesus Christ his Son, that cleanseth us from all sin." 1 John 1 : 7.

57. *What removed Isaiah's terror?*—The live coal touching his lips.

58. *How could a coal touching his lips remove sin?*—As a token of God's grace.

59. *What does "an altar" imply?*—A sacrifice.

60. *In the vision of the apostle John, Rev. 6 (which corresponds with Isaiah's), who is seen there as the slain sacrifice on the altar?*—Jesus Christ, the "Lamb as it had been slain." Rev. 5 : 6.

61. *What preparation, then, do we require ere we can dare to meet Jehovah's presence and glory?*—To be cleansed by the blood of Christ, and made one with him by a living faith.

62. *Is there any hinderance to our obtaining it?*—None whatever.

Ho, every one that thirsteth, come ye to the waters, and he that hath no money; come ye, buy, and eat; yea, come, buy wine and milk without money and without price. Seek ye the Lord while he may be found, call ye upon him while he is near: let the wicked forsake his way, and the unrighteous man his thoughts: and let him return unto the Lord, and he will have mercy upon him; and to our God, for he will abundantly pardon. Isa. 55 : 1, 6, 7.

The Spirit and the bride say, Come. And let him that heareth say, Come. And let him that is athirst come. And whosoever will, let him take the water of life freely. Rev. 22 : 17.

MICAH.

63. *In whose reigns did Micah prophesy?*—In the reigns of Jotham, Ahaz and Hezekiah, kings of Judah.

64. *What prophecy of his is referred to in Jer. 26 : 18?*—Micah the Morasthite prophesied in the days of Hezekiah king of Judah, and spake to all the people of Judah, saying, Thus saith the Lord of hosts: Zion shall be ploughed like a field, and Jerusalem shall become heaps, and the mountain of the house as the high places of a forest.

65. *Where is it found in his book? and how has it been fulfilled?*—Mic. 3 : 12. The site of the temple was really ploughed over by a Roman emperor; and Jerusalem has at different times been made heaps in the various sieges it has sustained.

66. *In what state does he declare Samaria will be?*—"As an heap of the field." Mic. 1 : 6.

67. *What sins of Israel are enumerated in Mic. 3, 6, 7?*—Cruelty, oppression and idolatry.

68. *What promises for the latter days does Mic. 4 : 1–4 record?*—The restoration of Zion and the reign of peace.

69. *What glorious Person is prophesied of in Mic. 5 : 2?*—Jesus Christ.

70. *Where was Jesus born?*—At Bethlehem.

71. *Where is Bethlehem first mentioned in the Bible?*—In Gen. 35 : 19: "Rachel died, and was buried in the way to Ephrath, which is Bethlehem."

72. *Where did Rahab (who was saved in Jericho) live?*—At Bethlehem after her marriage.

73. *Whose wife was she?*—Salmon's.

74. *Whose mother was she?*—Boaz's.

75. *Where did Ruth live?*—At Bethlehem. Ruth 1 : 1, 2, 19, 22.

76. *Where was David born?*—At Bethlehem.

77. *What striking proof of love did three of his mighty men give when David desired a draught of water from the well at Bethlehem?*—The three mighty men brake through the host of the Philistines, and drew water out of the well of Bethlehem that was by the gate, and took it, and brought it to David. 2 Sam. 23 : 16.

78. *To what glorious event did the prophet allude when he spoke of Bethlehem's glory?*—To the birth of Jesus.

79. *Read Prov. 8 : 22, 23; John 1 : 1; Col. 1 : 17, and say to whom they refer.*—The Lord possessed me in the beginning of his way, before his works of old. I was set up from everlasting, from the beginning, or ever the earth was. Prov. 8 : 23, 23. In the beginning was the Word. John 1 : 1. And he is before all things, and by him all things consist (Col. 1 : 17): viz., Jesus Christ.

80. *Of whom alone can it be said in the words of Micah, "Whose goings forth have been from of old, even from everlasting"?*—Of God.

81. *Who, then, must the Lord Jesus be?*—God.

NAHUM.

82. *Against whom did Nahum utter his prophecy?*—Against the inhabitants of Nineveh.

83. *Josephus says Nahum prophesied in the reign of Jotham king of Judah; how long was this after Jonah's prophecy?*—About sixty years.

84. *In which reign of the kings of Israel did Jonah preach at Nineveh?*—Jeroboam II.'s.

85. *In which tribe did Nahum live?*—Simeon, as some think.

86. *How long after Nahum's prophecy was his prediction fulfilled?*—About one hundred years.

HEZEKIAH, KING OF JUDAH. (2 Chron. 29–32.)

1. *Who reigned after Ahaz?*—Hezekiah.

2. *How old was Hezekiah when he began to reign?*—Twenty-five.

3. *Into what state of neglect does 2 Chron. 29 : 3, 7 show that the temple of God had fallen?*—Into even a filthy state. 2 Chron. 29 : 5.

4. *What did Hezekiah do to set up the worship of God again?*—He called upon the priests and Levites to assist.

5. *Did the priests, Levites and people respond to the call?*—Yes, very heartily. 2 Chron. 29 : 12-17, 28-35.

6. *What proof does the end of 2 Chron. 29 give that it was so?*—The abundance of the sacrifices and offerings that were made.

7. *Was his reformation confined to Judah, or did he desire to extend it to all Israel?*—He invited all Israel and Judah to join in a solemn Passover.

8. *In what state was the kingdom of Israel at this time?*—In a sad and idolatrous state under the reign of Hoshea. 2 Kings 17.

9. *How were Hezekiah's messengers received?*—They were laughed at and mocked. 2 Chron. 30 : 10.

10. *Were there any who responded to his appeal?*—Several came from Asher, Manasseh and Zebulun.

11. *What beautiful prayer did Hezekiah offer for these?*—That the good Lord would pardon every one who had prepared his heart to seek him, though he was not clean according to the temple laws.

12. *Did the Lord accept it?*—He did. 2 Chron. 30 : 20.

13. *What proof does 2 Chron. 30 : 23 give us that the service of God, when sincerely engaged in, and not as an empty form, is pleasant?*—They kept the holy feast a second week.

14. *How long had it been since there had been such a Passover as this?*—Not since the time of Solomon, three hundred years before.

15. *How does David describe his pleasure in the Lord's service?*—How amiable are thy tabernacles, O Lord of hosts! My soul longeth, yea, even fainteth for the courts of the Lord; my heart and my flesh crieth out for the living God. Ps. 84 : 1, 2. I was glad when they said unto me, Let us go into the house of the Lord. Ps. 122 : 1.

16. *What effect did this joy in the Lord have on the people with regard to the idols of the land?*—They destroyed them all. 2 Chron. 31.

17. *What is said in Prov. 27 : 19?*—As in water face answereth to face, so the heart of man to man.

18. *Can we not, then, try our hearts, and ascertain their state by knowing if the service of God is our joy?*—We can do so, and ought to do so.

19. *If not, in what condition are we?*—In a state of condemnation and death.

20. *What was the next proof the people gave that their hearts were right with God?*—The abundance of their offerings for the service of God. 2 Chron. 31 : 5-7.

21. *How did Zaccheus manifest the same feeling?*—Zaccheus said unto the Lord; Behold, Lord, the half of my goods I give to the poor; and if I have taken any thing from any man by false accusation, I restore him fourfold. Luke 19 : 8.

22. *How can we show our love to his service?*—By giving to it, as far as we can, our money and our time.

23. *Read Prov. 23 : 26, and say how Hezekiah, in the twenty-first verse of this chapter, fulfilled this.*—" My son, give me thine heart." He did every work for God with all his heart.

24. *Who was Hezekiah's father?*—Ahaz.

25. *What foolish compact had he made with the king of Assyria?*—He bought his help against his enemies by robbing God's house.

26. *Did it prosper?*—No; he was distressed by him, and not helped. 2 Chron. 28 : 19-21.

27. *How was Hezekiah made to feel this?*—Sennacherib, the succeeding king, was tempted to attack him.

28. *What did Hezekiah do when the king of Assyria came against him?*—He fortified Jerusalem and cut off the water from the enemy's camp.

29. *On whom did he depend for succor?*—On God alone. 2 Chron. 32 : 8.

30. *How did the people feel when Hezekiah cheered them?*—They rested on his words.

31. *What did Sennacherib do to endeavor to shake their confidence in God?*—He boasted of his victories in other lands.

32. *Did he succeed?*—No; the people held their peace. 2 Kings 18 : 36.

33. *Who was the exalted prophet of Israel at this time?*—Isaiah.

34. *To whom did Hezekiah send? and what did he himself do?*—He sent to Isaiah, and went into the temple for prayer to God. 2 Kings 19 : 1, 2.

35. *How did the Lord appear for his people at this time?*—He promised them the departure and death of Sennacherib. 2 Kings 19 : 6, 7.

36. *Was the king of Assyria aware that God was fighting against him? or did he make another attempt on Jerusalem?*—He made another attempt.

37. *Did he address Hezekiah by word of mouth, as before, or send a letter to him?*—He sent a letter.

38. *What did Hezekiah do with the letter?*—He spread it before the Lord in prayer.

39. *Where should we go when in trouble?*—Direct to God.

40. *Is God now the hearer and answerer of prayer, as he was then?*—He is, as every true child of God can testify.

41. *What was Hezekiah's prayer?*—That God would save them for his own glory. 2 Kings 19 : 15-19.

42. *By whom did the Lord answer his prayer?*—Isaiah.

43. *How was this wonderful deliverance effected?*—By means of an angel of God, who struck the Assyrian army with death.

44. *What was Sennacherib's miserable end?*—He was killed by his own sons.

45. *What mighty city was the capital of the Assyrian empire?*—Nineveh.

46. *Are there any proofs in the present day of this Assyrian king's conquests and final defeat?*—The ruins of Nineveh have lately been exposed to view, and letters and figures been met with, carved upon slabs of stone, which thoroughly confirm the Bible account.

47. *What is next recorded of Hezekiah?*—That he was " sick unto death." 2 Kings 20 : 1.

48. *Did he die of this illness? or was he restored? and how?*—He was restored to health in answer to prayer and by God's blessing on the means which Isaiah ordered to be used. 2 Kings 20 : 3-7.

49. *Was there any part of Hezekiah's history that was dishonorable to him?*—Yes; he made a display to the king of Babylon's messengers of all his treasures.

50. *Of what sin was he guilty?*—Of pride. "A proud heart is sin." Prov. 21 : 4.

51. *How does the Lord estimate pride of heart?*—Every one that is proud in heart is an abomination to the Lord; though hand join in hand, he shall not be unpunished. Prov. 16 : 5. Him that hath an high look and a proud heart will not I suffer. Ps. 101 : 5.

52. *What fearful prediction was Isaiah commissioned to take to him?*—That all his treasures should in a future age be carried away to Babylon. 2 Kings 20 : 17, 18.

53. *How did Hezekiah receive the reproof?*—He humbly submitted to the will of God.

54. *What did this prove him to be?*—A true son God.

Ye have forgotten the exhortation which speaketh unto you as unto children, My son, despise not thou the chastening of the Lord, nor faint when thou art rebuked of him: for whom the Lord loveth he chasteneth, and scourgeth every son whom he receiveth. If ye endure chastening, God dealeth with you as with sons; for what son is he whom the father chasteneth not? Heb. 12 : 5-7.

55. *Name the benefits in a domestic way that Hezekiah conferred on Jerusalem?*—He erected various public buildings and brought water from a distance.

56. *How much of Hezekiah's history is written in the book of Isaiah?*—Nearly the whole.

57. *How long did he reign?*—Twenty-nine years. 2 Kings 18 : 2.

58. *Where did they bury him?*—In the chief sepulchre of the kings.

MANASSEH AND AMON, KINGS OF JUDAH.
(2 Chron. 33.)

1. *Whose son was Manasseh?*—Hezekiah's.

2. *Was he a good king like his father? Describe his character as given in the first seven verses of this chapter.* —No; he restored idolatry and witchcraft, and set up idols even in the temple itself.

3. *How was he punished by the Lord for this?*—He was carried captive to Babylon.

4. *What effect did captivity have on him?*—It brought him, by the grace of God, to penitence and prayer.

5. *Did the Lord hear and answer his prayer?*—Yes; he restored him to his kingdom.

6. *How did Manasseh act on his return to his kingdom?*—He put away idolatry throughout all Judah.

7. *What encouragement does his history give to us?*—That if we confess and forsake our sins, he will abundantly pardon.

8. *Is God as compassionate now as he was then?*—Yes, as thousands of true penitents can thankfully declare.

9. *Are we to dare to sin because God is merciful?*—Shall we continue in sin, that grace may abound? God forbid. How shall we, that are dead to sin, live any longer therein? Rom. 6 : 1, 2.

10. *Are we to dare to postpone repentance because God is merciful?*—No.

Now is the accepted time; now is the day of salvation. 2 Cor. 6 : 2.

11. *How does the apostle Paul say that he obtained mercy?*—Through the free grace of Christ.

I thank Christ Jesus our Lord, who hath enabled me, for that he counted me faithful, putting me into the ministry; who was before a blasphemer, and a persecutor, and injurious: but I obtained mercy, because I did it ignorantly in unbelief. 1 Tim. 1 : 12, 13.

12. *Does the apostle give any other reason for this favor?*—That he might be a pattern for the encouragement of penitent sinners in all time,

This is a faithful saying, and worthy of all acceptation, that Christ Jesus came into the world to save sinners; of whom I am chief. Howbeit for this cause

I obtained mercy, that in me first Jesus Christ might show forth all long-suffering, for a pattern to them which should hereafter believe on him to life everlasting. 1 Tim 1 : 15, 16.

13. *Is not the invitation so free that none need doubt?* —It is to "every one"—"whosoever will."

Ho, every one that thirsteth, come ye to the waters, and he that hath no money; come ye, buy, and eat; yea, come, buy wine and milk without money and without price. Isa. 55 : 1.

And the Spirit and the bride say, Come. And let him that heareth say, Come. And let him that is athirst come. And whosoever will, let him take the water of life freely. Rev. 22 : 17.

14. *Will not Manasseh rise up in the judgment and condemn us if we should plead that we are too great sinners for God to save us?*—He may do so.

15. *How long did Manasseh reign?*—Fifty-five years.

16. *Who succeeded him?*—Amon his son.

17. *Did Amon follow his father's steps in the end or the beginning of his reign?*—He followed, throughout his reign, his father's steps in the *beginning* of his reign.

18. *How long did Amon reign?*—Two years.

19. *What was his melancholy end?*—He was killed by his own servants.

JOEL, HABAKKUK AND ZEPHANIAH.
JOEL.

1. *Is it known when Joel prophesied by his own writings?*—No, not at all distinctly.

2. *How do we gather from his prophecy that he wrote it in a time of famine?*—He speaks of the devourings by locusts and of the want of pasture, corn, wine and figs. Joel 1 : 4-20.

3. *Of what was a famine in Israel ever a proof?*—Of God's anger against sin.

4. *What does he call on the people to do?*—To fast, repent and pray.

5. *To what solemn event does he call attention in his second chapter?*—To the day of judgment.

6. *What does the apostle Peter say about "the day of the Lord"?*—The day of the Lord will come as a thief in the night; in the which the heavens shall pass away with a great noise, and the elements shall melt with fervent heat, the earth also and the works that are therein shall be burned up. Seeing then that all these things shall be dissolved, what manner of persons ought ye to be in all holy conversation and godliness? 2 Pet. 3 : 10, 11.

7. *Is this important "day" ever mentioned elsewhere in Scripture?*—As in the days that were before the flood they were eating and drinking, marrying and giving in marriage, until the day that Noe entered into the ark, and knew not until the flood came, and took them all away; so also shall the coming of the Son of man be. Matt. 24 : 38, 39.

8. *To what period does it refer?*—To the day of judgment.

9. *Are we at all interested in that solemn event?*—Yes.

10. *How?*—Because we shall all stand before the judgment-seat of Christ.

11. *Ought we not to be prepared for it?*—We ought indeed.

12. *How can we be?*—By being in Christ, and clothed with his righteousness by faith. Phil. 3 : 7-11.

13. *In what part of the book of the Acts does the apostle Peter quote this prophecy in reference to the miraculous gift of tongues?*—In Acts 2 : 16-21 he quotes Joel 2 : 28-32.

14. *What proof does Joel 3 give us that this prophet wrote after the days of Jehoshaphat, and probably very near the Captivity?*—Because he mentions the valley of Jehoshaphat, and because his referring to the cap-

tivity of *Judah* only (in v. 1) makes it probable that his prophecy was written *after* the captivity of *Israel.*

15. *With what glorious and consoling promises does the prophecy close?*—Those of the future glory of Jerusalem and of the Church in 3: 16–21.

HABAKKUK.

16. *What proof does Hab. 1: 6 give us that Habakkuk wrote before the Captivity?*—Because he there prophesies its coming.

17. *Who were the Chaldeans?*—The inhabitants of Babylon and the surrounding country.

18. *What threatenings respecting them had Isaiah given to Hezekiah?*—That they would come and carry away all his treasures.

19. *What prediction does Habakkuk record in Hab. 2?*—That in due time God would destroy the Chaldean power.

20. *What promise is given in verse 14 of this chapter?*—The earth shall be filled with the knowledge of the glory of the Lord, as the waters cover the sea.

21. *Which verse in this prophecy answers the important question, " How can man be justified before God"?*—Hab. 2: 4. "The just shall live by his faith."

22. *How many times, and where, is this emphatic verse quoted in the New Testament?*—Three times—Rom. 1: 17; Gal. 3: 11; Heb. 10: 38.

23. *Can you tell me what great Reformer was converted to God by it?*—Martin Luther.

24. *What contrast is displayed in verses 18–20 of this chapter?*—Between dumb idols and the true God.

25. *To what great event in past history does the opening of Hab. 3 refer?*—To the giving of the law on Mount Sinai.

26. *To what event is reference made in verses 8 and 15?*—To the passing of the Red Sea.

27. *To what event in verse 11?*—To Joshua's victory at Gibeon.

28. *How does the prophet express his confidence in God?*—In the beautiful words of verses 17, 18.

ZEPHANIAH.

29. *In whose reign did Zephaniah prophesy?*—Josiah's.

30. *How does the first chapter show the abominations of the land before Josiah's reformation?*—It speaks of the idolatry and indifference to God that prevailed. Zeph. 1: 5, 12.

31. *Against how many nations besides Judah is this prophecy uttered?*—Five others—Philistia, Moab, Ammon, Ethiopia and Assyria.

32. *What proof is there in this book that Nahum's prophecy against Nineveh had not been fulfilled in the early part of Josiah's reign?*—Its desolation is spoken of as yet to come. Zeph. 2: 13.

33. *With what glorious promises of Israel's restoration does the prophecy close?*—With those of Zeph. 3: 8–20, and especially verses 10–13, and the expression of God's joy and love in verse 17.

JOSIAH, KING OF JUDAH. (2 Chron. 34, 35, and 2 Kings 22, 23.)

1. *How old was Josiah when he ascended the throne of Judah?*—Eight.

2. *Whose son was he?*—Amon's.

3. *What character did he bear?*—He did that which was right in the sight of the Lord.

4. *How soon did he begin to manifest his piety?*—At the age of fifteen. 2 Chron. 34: 3.

5. *What was the first reformation he effected?*—The removal of everything connected with idol-worship.

6. *What wonderful discovery was made in cleansing the temple?*—A book of the law.

7. *What did this prove?*—That it had been neglected and despised.

8. *What effect did the reading of God's word have on the young king?*—He was shocked and alarmed by the national guilt and danger.

9. *To whom did he send to inquire the will of God concerning his people?*—To Huldah the prophetess.

10. *Did God alter the word that had gone forth out of his mouth?*—No. 2 Chron. 24: 24, 25.

11. *How did he comfort Josiah notwithstanding?*—B promising that his judgments should not take plac during Josiah's life.

12. *What effect did this message have on Josiah?*—He caused the book of the law to be publicly read, and induced the people to renew their covenant with God.

13. *How does 2 Chron. 35: 3 show us that the ark had been taken out of the temple?*—By relating Josiah's order that it should be put in again.

14. *What multiplied idolatries does 2 Kings 23 show had gained footing in Judah at this time?*—The worship of Baal and the abominations of Sidon, Moab and Ammon.

15. *How did Josiah deal with them all?*—He destroyed and defiled them.

16. *What remarkable prophecy had gone before of this young king?*—And, behold, there came a man of God out of Judah by the word of the Lord unto Bethel: and Jeroboam stood by the altar to burn incense. And he cried against the altar in the word of the Lord, and said, O altar, altar, thus saith the Lord; Behold, a child shall be born unto the house of David, Josiah by name; and upon thee shall he offer the priests of the high places that burn incense upon thee, and men's bones shall be burnt upon thee. 1 Kings 13: 1, 2.

17. *Did he fulfill it?*—Yes, exactly. 2 Chron. 34: 5.

18. *Could all Josiah's goodness turn away God's wrath from Judah?*—No. 2 Kings 24: 3, 4.

19. *What was Josiah's end?*—He was killed in battle.

20. *How did this come about?*—He had attacked the king of Egypt as he was going against the king of Assyria.

21. *Was not this the only failure recorded of this good and pious king?*—It was.

22. *Must not their transgressions have reached a fearful height, seeing even Josiah's reformation could not purge the land?*—They must indeed.

23. *How was the news of his death received by his people?*—With deep and universal mourning.

24. *Which famous prophet is named as mourning for him?*—Jeremiah. 2 Chron. 35: 25.

The breath of our nostrils, the anointed of the Lord, was taken in their pits, of whom we said, Under his shadow we shall live among the heathen. Lam. 4: 20

25. *Where was Josiah slain?*—At Megiddo.

26. *How does Zechariah the prophet, who lived above seventy years after this, refer to this grievous lamentation over Josiah?*—In that day shall there be a great mourning in Jerusalem, as the mourning of Hadadrimmon in the valley of Megiddon. Zech. 12: 11.

27. *How long had this good king reigned?*—Thirty-one years.

JEREMIAH AND THE LAST KINGS OF JUDAH. (Jer., 2 Kings 23 to 25 and 2 Chron. 36.)

1. *In whose reign is Jeremiah first mentioned?*—Josiah's.

2. *In which year of his reign did this prophecy commence?*—The thirteenth. Jer. 1: 2.

3. *Was this before or after Josiah's reformation?*—The fifth year after.

4. *How did Jeremiah at first feel when he found the Lord had appointed him to the prophet's office?*—Timid and unfitted, like a child.

5. *By what promises did the Lord comfort him?*—That he would be with him to deliver him. Jer. 1: 8, 19.

6. *What office did Jeremiah hold by birthright? and which was his native city?*—A priest. Anathoth, in Benjamin. Jer. 1: 1.

7. *How does Jer. 2 display Judah's sin at this time?*—It shows their worship of Baal and other gods. Jer. : 20–28.

8. *How does the prophet beautifully describe the contrast between God's service and idolatry in chap. 2: 13?*—My people have committed two evils; they have forsaken me the fountain of living waters, and hewed them out cisterns, broken cisterns, that can hold no water.

9. *May we not ask ourselves here, On which are we resting?*—Yes, for our deceitful hearts may have many Idols.

10. *Although there may be no open idolatry in the land, what objects can the heart set up and do homage to rather than God?*—Riches, pleasures, fame and many more.

11. *What is the result of this heart-idolatry?*—"Evil and bitter" in the end. Jer. 2: 19.

12. *Compare Jer. 2: 21 with Isa. 5 and Ps. 80, and describe God's people under this figure.*—Like a vineyard, or a vine, they are tenderly sheltered, nourished, and trained, are wisely instructed and restrained, and bear rich and abundant fruit.

13. *Who has revealed himself to us as the only "true Vine"?*—Jesus Christ.

I am the true vine, and my Father is the husbandman. John 15: 1.

14. *Have we any hope of participation in its blessings?*—We are all *invited* to partake; and if we have a true faith in Christ, we *do* partake *now.*

15. *How does chap. 3: 22 describe the reformation under Josiah? also chap. 4: 1–4?*—They speak of the return of the Jews from their evil ways.

16. *Name some of the sins of Judah set forth in chap. 5; also chap. 6: 13.*—Adultery, covetousness, fraud, corruption and oppression, and general rebellion against God.

17. *What coming judgment is foretold in chap. 6: 1–9?*—War and siege.

18. *Why?*—Because of their wickedness. Jer. 6: 7.

19. *Where did the Lord command Jeremiah to stand when he uttered this prophecy?*—In the gates or principal places of assembly. Jer. 17: 19.

20. *Was Jeremiah the only prophet whom the Lord had sent to warn Israel?*—No; they had constantly had warning prophets in time past. Jer. 7: 25, 26.

21. *Did the Lord at this time (the reign of Josiah) give the people any encouragement to obey him?*—Yes; another invitation was given, with promises of blessing. Jer. 17: 19–27.

22. *Which of Josiah's sons succeeded him on the throne?*—Jehoahaz. 2 Chron. 36.

23. *How old was he when he began to reign? and how long did he reign?*—Twenty-three. Three months.

24. *How was it that his reign was so short? and where did he die?*—He was put down from his throne by the king of Egypt, and carried away into Egypt, and died there. Jer. 22: 11, 12.

25. *Who reigned next?*—Eliakim.

26. *What relation was he to Josiah?*—Son.

27. *To what name did the king of Egypt change Eliakim's?*—Jehoiakim.

28. *How old was he when he began to reign? and how long did he reign?*—Twenty-five. Eleven years.

29. *What tax had he to pay Pharaoh-Nechoh?*—Silver and gold. 2 Kings 23: 35.

30. *What prophecy against Egypt and this king did Jeremiah utter (Jer. 46)? and when was it fulfilled?*—Their conquest, by Nebuchadnezzar (2 Kings 24: 7). About eight years after.

31. *What prophecy was Jeremiah commanded to utter in this (Jehoiakim's) reign?*—That the Jews should be punished for their guilt if they did not repent. Jer. 26; 7; 9.

32. *What special charge was given to the prophet as to where he was to stand and how he was to perform the mission?*—He was to stand in the court of the Lord's house, and to speak to all who came thither from all parts of Judah to worship. Jer. 26.

33. *How did the people receive the message?*—They gathered together against Jeremiah.

34. *What did they wish to do to Jeremiah?*—To put him to death.

35. *How was he rescued from them?*—By Ahikam.

36. *What wicked act of Jehoiakim's does the sixteenth chapter record?*—He killed the prophet Urijah.

37. *What pleasing contrast is given to this in Hezekiah's history?*—Hezekiah hearkened to the prophecy of Micah, and besought the Lord.

38. *Read Jer. 7, 8, 9, 10, and say where Jeremiah uttered the prophecies recorded in them.*—In the gateway of the temple.

39. *What sins of Israel do they reveal?*—Robbery, murder, adultery, false-swearing and idolatry.

40. *What coming judgments do they record?*—The captivity of the people and desolation of the land.

41. *How does the Lord plead with them?*—With tender reproach.

42. *To what does he compare them?*—To a horse rushing headlong into battle. Jer. 8: 6.

43. *What bitter lamentation does the prophet utter in chap. 8: 20?*—"The harvest is past, the summer is ended, and we are not saved."

44. *Has that word any warning to us?*—It solemnly applies to many of us year after year.

45. *How does the prophet bewail the state of things in chap. 9: 1, 2?*—In most pathetic words. Read them.

46. *Of what event which is not recorded either in the Kings or Chronicles does chap. 14 complain?*—Of dearth.

47. *Of what was a dearth in Israel always a sign?*—Of national guilt. Deut. 28.

48. *What honorable testimony does the Lord give to Moses and Samuel in chap. 15?*—That they were holy men of prayer.

49. *When was Moses intercessor for Israel?*—After they had made the golden calf.

50. *When was Samuel intercessor for Israel?*—When the Philistines were going to attack them. 1 Sam 7: 9.

51. *How did the Lord comfort Jeremiah in chap. 15?*—By promising him kind treatment and deliverance. Vs. 11, 21.

52. *How does the Lord describe the sin of Judah in chap. 17: 1?*—As graven deeply on their hearts.

53. *To what does the Lord in chap. 17 compare the man who trusts for salvation in his fellow-men?*—To the heath in the desert, that cannot thrive.

54. *What blessed contrast does the Lord give of the man who rests alone on Christ for salvation?*—He is like a tree by the water-side, fruitful and ever green. Jer. 17: 7, 8.

55. *Should we not ask ourselves, On what is our hope resting?*—We should, if we would be safe for a single hour.

Neither is there salvation in any other: for there is none other Name under heaven given among men, whereby we must be saved. Acts 4: 12.

56. *Is not the same simile used in Ps. 1 : 1–4?*—Yes. Blessed is the man that walketh not in the counsel of the ungodly, nor standeth in the way of sinners, nor sitteth in the seat of the scornful. But his delight is in the law of the Lord; and in his law doth he meditate day and night. And he shall be like a tree planted by the rivers of water, that bringeth forth his fruit in his season; his leaf also shall not wither; and whatsoever he doeth shall prosper. The ungodly are not so: but are like the chaff which the wind driveth away.

57. *Does not chap. 17 also supply a beautiful prayer for us to utter?*—"Heal me, O Lord, and I shall be ealed; save me, and I shall be saved." V. 14.

58. *To what does the Lord compare himself and Israel in chap. 18?*—To a potter moulding clay, and dealing with it as he wills.

59. *What sign did the Lord bid Jeremiah show them? and what was the meaning of it?*—The breaking of a potter's vessel as a token of the ruin of Israel. Chap. 19.

60. *What misery did Jeremiah bring on himself by thus faithfully proclaiming God's word?*—He was put in the stocks. Jer. 20.

61. *What did Pashur bring upon himself by this?*—Captivity in Babylon.

62. *Was not the good Jeremiah sometimes tempted to keep back God's word?*—Yes, when he saw it was so badly received. Jer. 20 : 8, 9.

63. *Was there not a mighty power over him that he could not withstand?*—Yes; God was stronger than he. Jer. 20 : 7.

64. *How did Jeremiah comfort himself in the Lord?*—By remembering that God was with him. Jer. 20 : 11–13.

65. *Of whom does Jeremiah speak in chap. 23 : 5, 6?*—Of Jesus Christ.

66. *How many other prophets spoke of Christ as a "Branch"?*—Two.

There shall come forth a rod out of the stem of Jesse, and a Branch shall grow out of his roots. Isa. 11 : 1.

Thus speaketh the Lord of hosts, saying, Behold the man whose name is The BRANCH; and he shall grow up out of his place, and he shall build the temple of the Lord. Zech. 6 : 12.

67. *Where, besides this place, is Jesus spoken of as "King"?*—

Yet have I set my king upon my holy hill of Zion. I will declare the decree: the Lord hath said unto me, Thou art my Son: this day have I begotten thee. Ps. 2 : 6, 7.

All this was done, that it might be fulfilled which was spoken by the prophet, saying, Tell ye the daughter of Sion, Behold, thy King cometh unto thee. Matt. 21 : 4, 5.

These shall make war with the Lamb, and the Lamb shall overcome them: for he is the Lord of lords, and King of kings. Rev. 17 : 14.

68. *By what name will Jesus be called when he comes again as King of Israel?*—"The Lord our Righteousness." Jer. 23 : 6.

69. *What does St. Paul say in 1 Cor. 1 : 31 and in Phil. 3 : 8?*—He that glorieth, let him glory in the Lord. "Christ Jesus my Lord."

70. *Read Jer. 35, and say what Jeremiah was commanded to do.*—To give the Rechabites wine.

71. *Who were the Rechabites?*—Descendants of Rechab.

When he (Jehu) was departed thence, he lighted on Jehonadab the son of Rechab coming to meet him. 2 Kings 10 : 15.

These are the Kenites that came of Hemath, the father of the house of Rechab. 1 Chron. 2 : 55.

72. *Who were the Kenites?*—The children of the Kenite, Moses' father-in-law, went up out of the city of palm trees with the children of Judah into the wilderness of Judah, which lieth in the south of Arad; and they went and dwelt among the people. Judg. 1 : 16.

73. *Is not this a proof that Moses's father-in-law did go with him after all?*—It is.

74. *How was this tribe distinguished from Israel?*—By separate origin and abode.

75. *What excellent virtue had they practiced?*—Abstinence from wine.

76. *What is said of drunkards in the Bible?*—

They shall say unto the elders of his city, This our son is stubborn and rebellious, he will not obey our voice; he is a glutton, and a drunkard. And all the men of his city shall stone him with stones, that he die. Deut. 21 : 20, 21.

Hear thou, my son, and be wise, and guide thine heart in the way. Be not among winebibbers; among riotous eaters of flesh: for the drunkard and the glutton shall come to poverty. Who hath woe? who hath sorrow? who hath contentions? who hath babbling? who hath wounds without cause? who hath redness of eyes? they that tarry long at the wine; they that go to seek mixed wine. Look not thou upon the wine when it is red, when it giveth his color in the cup, when it moveth itself aright. At the last it biteth like a serpent, and stingeth like an adder. Prov. 23 : 19–21, 29–32.

Nor thieves, nor covetous, nor drunkards, shall inherit the kingdom of God. 1 Cor. 6 : 10.

77. *What great honor did the Lord set on temperanc and obedience in chap. 35?*—The preservation of the family of the Rechabites when others were cut off.

78. *Who was the strongest man?*—Samson.

79. *Did he ever taste wine and strong drink?*—No.

80. *What was a Nazarite?*—One who devoted himself to the service of God, and also abstained from wine.

81. *What command did the Lord give to Aaron and his sons after the death of Nadab and Abihu?*—Do not drink wine nor strong drink, thou, nor thy sons with thee, when ye go into the tabernacle of the congregation, lest ye die: it shall be a statute for ever throughout your generations. Lev. 10 : 9.

82. *Is it not therefore supposed that Nadab and Abihu were drunk when they offered the strange fire?*—Yes.

83. *What does the apostle Paul say about drunkenness in Rom. 13 : 13; Gal. 5 : 21; Eph. 5 : 18?*—Let us walk honestly as in the day; not in rioting and drunkenness, envyings, murders, revellings, and such like: of the which I tell you before, as I have also told you in time past, that they which do such things shall not inherit the kingdom of God. Be not drunk with wine, wherein is excess.

84. *Read Jer. 25 : 9, and tell me who was to come up against Judah and take it.*—Nebuchadrezzar, king of Babylon.

85. *How long was the Captivity to last?*—Seventy years. Jer. 25 : 12.

86. *What was to happen at the end of it?*—Babylon was to be destroyed. Jer. 25 : 12–14.

87. *How long was this special prophecy uttered before it was fulfilled? In which year of Jehoiakim was it uttered?*—About eighteen years. The fourth.

88. *After Jeremiah had spoken these words, what did the Lord command him to do?*—To write them in a roll or book. Jer. 36.

89. *Whom did Jeremiah employ to write it?*—Baruch.

90. *Who read it to the people?*—Baruch.

91. *To whom did Michaiah desire the roll to be read?*—The princes.

92. *When the princes heard it, to whom did they wish it to be read?*—The king.

93. *Why did they tell Jeremiah and Baruch to go and hide themselves?*—Lest the king should seize them.

94. *How did King Jehoiakim receive the message? Did he allow it all to be read to him?*—With anger and contempt. Only three or four leaves.

95. *What did he do with it?*—He cut it and burnt it.

96. *Could he by this destroy the word of God?*—Certainly not.

97. *What was Jeremiah commanded to do?*—To write the words in another roll.

98. *What punishment did the king bring on himself by this act?*—His dead body was cast out unburied, and his family ceased to reign on the throne of Judah. Jer. 36 : 30; 22.

99. *Did his determination not to hear God's word hinder it from being fulfilled?*—No, not at all.

100. *Who was in that roll predicted, and who did come up against Judah and carry Jehoiakim's son captive to Babylon? And how was Jehoiakim himself to be disgraced?*—Nebuchadrezzar. Jer. 36 : 2; 22 : 25; 39 : 1. By being left without burial. Jer. 22 : 18, 19.

101. *What kind promise did the Lord give Baruch at this time of trouble because he had done the Lord's work?*—That he would save his life in the desolation of the land. Jer. 45.

102. *Who succeeded Jehoiakim?*—His son.

103. *By how many names is this king called?*—Jehoiachim (2 Kings 24 : 8), Jeconiah (1 Chron. 3 : 16) and Coniah. Jer. 22 : 24.

104. *How old was he when his father died?*—Eight years.

105. *How soon after was he carried to Babylon?*—About three months. 2 Chron. 36 : 9, 10.

106. *Had not the Lord foretold this in Jer. 36 : 30?*—Yes. Jer. 22 : 25.

107. *When Nebuchadrezzar carried this young prince captive to Babylon, whom did he make king over the remnant of Judah? and how did he change his name?*—His uncle, Mattaniah. Zedekiah.

108. *What relation was Zedekiah to the good Josiah?*—Brother.

109. *What did Nebuchadrezzar carry away with the young prince and his mother from Jerusalem?*—The treasures and ornaments of the temple.

110. *What character did he bear in the Lord's sight?*—He did evil in God's sight. 2 Chron. 36 : 12.

111. *What prediction did Jeremiah utter to King Zedekiah of the complete and entire destruction of Jerusalem?*—That by sword, famine and pestilence its people should be consumed. Jer. 24.

112. *How do chaps. 11 and 12 show the sins of Judah at this time?*—By describing their idolatry and their persecution of the prophet.

113. *Which was Jeremiah's native city?*—Anathoth.

114. *How was he treated there?*—They plotted to kill him.

115. *Read Jer. 24, and say to what the captives now in Babylon were compared, and to what Zedekiah and those left in Judah were compared, and why?*—The former to good figs, and the latter to bad, the one being penitent, and the other not.

116. *What comforting letter was Jeremiah commanded to write to the former?*—That they should seek God and nd him, and be restored to their own land. Jer. 29.

117. *Who withstood Jeremiah's words?*—Shemaiah.

118. *How did the Lord punish him?*—By shortening nis life and cutting off his seed.

119. *Read Jer. 27, and say by what beautiful simile did the Lord show that he had given the nations to the king of Babylon.*—By bonds and yokes upon the prophet's neck.

120. *Who prophesied in opposition to Jeremiah?*—Hananiah. Jer. 28.

121. *What symbol did he make with the yoke which was on the neck of Jeremiah?*—He broke it, as if God would break Nebuchadrezzar's yoke.

122. *Did the Lord suffer such impiety to pass? What message did he send to Hananiah by Jeremiah?*—No. That he should die the same year.

123. *When was it accomplished?*—In the seventh month.

124. *What should this teach us?*—All flesh is as grass, and all the glory of man as the flower of grass. The grass withereth, and the flower thereof falleth away : but the word of the Lord endureth for ever. 1 Pet. 1 : 24, 25.

125. *Did Zedekiah believe that it was God's will t bow Judah beneath the yoke of the king of Babylon?*—He sent to Jeremiah to know.

126. *What message did the Lord send to Zedekiah or this subject?*—That those who escaped the pestilence and famine should fall by the king of Babylon's sword. Jer. 21.

127. *Read Jer. 34, and say what transgression the people of Judah again fell into, which brought wrath upon them.*—They again enslaved their released bondservants, contrary to the law.

128. *What special prophecy against Zedekiah was there in chap. 34?*—That he should be carried captive to Babylon.

129. *What army did Zedekiah get to help him against the Chaldeans?*—The Egyptians. Jer. 37.

130. *Did it prosper, or was it only for a time that the Chaldeans withdrew?*—Only for a time.

131. *While they were away, what did Jeremiah desire to do?*—To return to his own land. Jer. 37 : 12.

132. *Why was he persecuted? and what did the princes do with him?*—Because they thought he was deserting to the Chaldeans. They put him into prison.

133. *Who released Jeremiah?*—Zedekiah.

134. *Did the kindness of the king tempt Jeremiah to alter God's word to him?*—No. Jer. 38 : 1, 3.

135. *How did the king permit the princes to treat the prophet?*—He allowed them to imprison him again.

136. *Who stood up and spoke for Jeremiah?*—Ebed-melech.

137. *How did he rescue him?*—He raised him by cords from the dungeon-pit.

138. *Did the king's kindness again to Jeremiah tempt him to swerve from the truth? What did he tell the king?*—No. That if he stayed in the city it would be taken and burnt. Jer. 38 : 18.

139. *Did the king believe him and obey the word of the Lord?*—No; he stayed till it was too late. Jer. 39 : 2, 4, 8.

140. *Where was Jeremiah when the city was taken?*—In the court of the prison. Jer. 38 : 28.

141. *What kind deliverance did the Lord grant to Ebed-melech in remembrance of his kindness to Jeremiah in the pit?*—From the Chaldeans. Jer. 39 : 16-18.

142. *What should this teach us?*—To always show special kindness to God's own people. Matt. 25 : 34-36.

He that receiveth you receiveth me, and he that receiveth me receiveth Him that sent me. And whoso-ever shall give to drink unto one of these little ones a cup of cold water only in the name of a disciple, verily I say unto you, he shall in no wise lose his reward. Matt. 10 : 40, 42.

143. *How did Nebuchadrezzar treat Zedekiah?*—He put out his eyes, after killing his sons in his sight, and imprisoned him in Babylon for life. Jer. 52 : 10, 11.

144. *How was the loss of Zedekiah's eyesight foretold by the prophet Ezekiel?*—This burden concerneth the prince in Jerusalem, and all the house of Israel that are among them. They shall remove and go into captivity. And the prince that is among them shall bear upon his shoulder in the twilight, and shall go

forth: he shall cover his face, that he see not the ground with his eyes. And I will bring him to Babylon to the land of the Chaldeans; yet shall he not see it, though he shall die there. Ezek. 12: 10-13.

145. *How did the Chaldeans treat Jeremiah?*—By order of the king he was kindly sent back, according to his wish, to his own land. Jer. 39, 40.

146. *What comforting promises did the Lord give his people ere they were carried away captive?*—Of return to their own land, and of the coming of the Messiah, the Lord our Righteousness. Jer. 32, 33.

147. *When were these uttered?*—About five hundred and ninety years before Christ.

148. *Whom did the king of Babylon leave as governor in Judah?*—Gedaliah. 2 Kings 25; Jer. 40.

149. *What happened to him?*—He was killed by Ishmael and others. Jer. 40, 41.

150. *What was the sad result of his death?*—The carrying away as prisoners those under his charge. Jer. 41: 10.

151. *Whither did the people purpose to bend their steps for fear the Chaldeans should revenge his death?*—Toward Egypt. Jer. 41: 17, 18.

152. *What did the people pretend to desire after they had made up their minds to go down into Egypt?*—Direction from God. Jer. 42: 2, 3; 43: 1-7.

153. *Did they not prove this by their conduct?*—Yes, they showed their hypocrisy by going into Egypt, notwithstanding Jeremiah's warning against it.

154. *Did they take Jeremiah and Baruch with them, or leave them behind?*—They took them with them. Jer. 43: 6, 7.

155. *Had Jeremiah any message from the Lord to his rebellious people in Egypt?*—He threatened them with destruction for their idolatry. Jer. 44.

156. *What abominable idolatry does this chapter reveal?*—Burning incense to the queen of heaven and to other gods. Jer. 44.

157. *Were the people better off in Egypt than in Judea?*—No, as its conquest by Nebuchadnezzar was foretold. Jer. 46.

158. *Against how many foreign countries did Jeremiah prophesy?*—Against ten or more, as Egypt, Philistia, Moab, Ammon, Edom, Damascus, Kedar, Hazor, Elam and Babylon. Jer. 50, 51.

159. *What other book did Jeremiah write besides his prophecy?*—The Lamentations.

160. *Where is it supposed Jeremiah died?*—In Egypt, by the hands of the Jews.

EZEKIEL.

1. *Who was Ezekiel?*—A priest and prophet.

2. *Where was he when he saw the wonderful vision his first chapter records?*—By the river Chebar.

3. *How came he there?*—With the Jews carried captive to Babylon.

4. *How old was he at this time?*—In his thirtieth year, according to some. Ezek. 1: 1.

5. *How long had he been in captivity?*—Above four years. Ezek. 1: 2.

6. *Who was the Jehoiachin whose captivity is here spoken of?*—King of Judah.

7. *Who had carried them captive?*—Nebuchadnezzar.

8. *Where was the river Chebar?*—In Mesopotamia.

9. *Where are the cherubim first spoken of in the Bible?*—In Gen. 3, in Eden.

10. *For what were they placed in Eden?*—To guard the tree of life.

11. *What was always associated with the cherubim?*—The glory of God. Ezek. 1: 28; 3: 23; 43: 2.

12. *Where is God said to dwell in Ps. 80: 1; 99: 1?*—Between the cherubim.

13. *Mention other texts to show that the cherubim are always symbols of God's promise?*—"He rode upon a cherub, and did fly." Ps. 18: 10.

14. *When it was said (Gen. 4: 16) "Cain went out from the presence of the Lord," from what symbol of his presence is it supposed he departed?*—From the cherubim.

15. *How were the carved cherubim in the tabernacle and Solomon's temple connected with the glory of the Lord?*—Because they were over the mercy-seat, where the glory of the Lord was seen.

16. *Where did God say he would meet his people?*—"Above the mercy-seat between the cherubim." Ezek. 25: 22.

17. *Have we any record of this?*—When Moses was gone into the tabernacle of the congregation to speak with him, then he heard the voice of one speaking unto him from off the mercy-seat that was upon the ark of testimony, from between the two cherubim: and he spake unto him. Num. 7: 89.

18. *Are the cherubim ever spoken of in the New Testament?*—Not by that name.

19. *Are not the seraphim seen by Isaiah (chap. 6) the same in appearance as the cherubim?*—Very much the same.

20. *In how many respects are the "cherubim" of Ezekiel, the "seraphim" of Isaiah and the "living creatures" (translated "beasts") in Rev. 4, alike?*—In having wings.

21. *Do we not learn by Isa. 6: 3 and Rev. 4: 8 that in God's presence all is holiness?*—Yes, as these winged beings are there described as saying, "Holy, holy, holy . . . Lord of hosts, . . . Lord God Almighty." "God sitteth upon the throne of his holiness." Ps. 47: 8.

22. *What is said in Heb. 12: 14 and Rev. 21: 27?*—"Without" "holiness" "no man shall see the Lord." "There shall in no wise enter into it any thing that defileth."

23. *How, then, can guilty sinners hope to be admitted there?*—By having their robes washed and made "white in the blood of the Lamb." Rev. 7: 9-17.

24. *Ought we not to be very anxious to know if we have on that spotless robe?*—We ought indeed.

25. *What became of that man who ventured into the feast without the wedding-garment?*—He was cast "into darkness," to "weeping and gnashing of teeth." Matt. 22.

26. *What was that garment meant to represent?*—"The righteousness of saints." Rev. 19: 7, 8.

27. *How does the Lord in Ezek. 2 describe the children of Israel to whom he sent Ezekiel to prophesy?*—As "most rebellious."

28. *How did the Lord prepare the prophet for his mission?*—By encouraging and warning him not to fear. Ezek. 3.

29. *How was the destruction of Jerusalem (which had not then taken place) described by Ezekiel?*—Under the figure of a siege, with tokens of severe famine. Ezek. 4.

30. *How long after Jehoiachin's captivity was Jerusalem taken by Nebuchadnezzar?*—About eleven years. 2 Kings 25.

31. *How was the utter dispersion of Israel described in Ezek. 5, 6, 7?*—God said they should be scattered "into all the winds."

32. *How was Ezekiel transported to Jerusalem?*—In a vision by the Spirit of God. Ezek. 8: 3.

33. *What abominations did the Lord reveal to him there?*—Those of the vilest idolatry. Ezek. 8-11.

34. *Whose captivity is predicted in Ezek. 12? and how is the loss of his eyesight foretold?*—Zedekiah's. When it is said that he should die at Babylon without seeing it.

35. *What great honor does the Lord put on Noah, Daniel and Job in Ezek. 14? and which of these three was living at this time?*—By distinguishing them as eminently righteous men.   Daniel.

36. *To what does the Lord compare the inhabitants of Jerusalem in Ezek. 15 and 16?*—To a useless vine-branch and to a neglected infant.

37. *To what is Nebuchadnezzar compared in Ezek. 17?*—To a great eagle.

38. *How does God show in Ezek. 18: 19, 20 that the son shall not be punished for his father's sins?*—"The son shall not bear the iniquity of the father."

39. *Which of the kings of Judah are spoken of under the figures of the young lions?*—Jehoahaz and Jehoia-kim. Ezek. 19; 2 Chron. 36.

40. *To what animal did Jacob, in blessing his sons, compare the tribe of Judah?*—"A lion's whelp." Gen. 49: 9.

41. *Is the Lord Jesus ever spoken of under this symbol?*—Yes, as the Lion of the tribe of Judah. Rev. 5: 5.

42. *How does Ezek. 21: 21, 22 show us the manner in which the ancient Chaldeans divined?*—By casting lots with arrows bearing the names of their enemies' cities to be attacked, and by observing the appearances of the entrails of their sacrifices.

43. *Against how many nations besides Israel did Ezekiel prophesy?*—Eight—Ammon, Moab, Edom, Philistia, Tyre, Zidon, Egypt and Assyria.

44. *Read Ezek. 33: 8, and say what is the "watchman's" duty.*—To warn the wicked to turn from his evil way.

45. *What is the duty of those who have the alarm sounded in their ears?*—To turn at once from their evil ways.

46. *Does this concern us?*—Quite as much as it concerned them.

47. *What will be our condemnation if warned to flee from the wrath to come, and we disregard it?*—The worm of remorse that never dies, and the fire that is never quenched.

48. *Against whom is the prophecy in Ezek. 34 uttered?* Against the priests, prophets or religious teachers.

49. *Who is the Good Shepherd?*—Jesus Christ. Ezek. 34: 23.

50. *By what name is that glorious Person spoken of in chap. 34: 29?*—A plant of renown.

51. *Are there any promises of future blessing in Ezekiel's prophecy?*—Yes, of the restoration of Israel to their own land, and of great spiritual blessings, like a resurrection of the dead. Ezek. 36: 37.

52. *What remarkable vision did the prophet see?*—A valley of dry bones revived into an army of living men.

53. *In what state are our souls by nature?*—Dead in sin. Eph. 2: 1.

54. *By what means is life imparted to them?*—By being "born again" "of the Spirit." John 3: 1-8.

55. *What means was the prophet to use to waken these dry bones?*—To prophesy or preach and pray.

56. *And what means are constantly being used to rouse us?*—The teaching and preaching of God's word and prayer for his blessing upon it.

57. *If "dry bones" can live, are we not without excuse?*—Yes, for our blessed Lord says, Ask, and it shall be given you; seek, and ye shall find; knock, and it shall be opened unto you.   For every one that asketh receiveth; and he that seeketh findeth; and to him that knocketh it shall be opened. Luke 11: 9, 10.

58. *What vision did Ezekiel see in the twenty-fifth year of the captivity of Judah?*—Of a glorious temple, and of healing waters issuing from it. Ezek. 40-48.

59. *To what place was he in vision transported to see it?*—To a mountain in the land of Israel.

60. *As Jerusalem has never been built by this pattern, to what must it refer?*—To the future spiritual glory of Israel and the Church.

61. *What great similarity is there between Ezek. 47 and Rev. 22?*—The waters issuing from the temple are like the pure river of water of life, clear as crystal, proceeding out of the throne of God and of the Lamb.   And as in Ezekiel's vision there were on the bank of the river fruitful and healing trees, so in John's vision.

62. *When and why was the "tree of life" prohibited?* —At Adam's fall and spiritual death, lest he should live again without the atoning and restoring blood of Christ.

63. *Will it ever be tasted again?*—It will.

64. *By whom?*—By "him that overcometh." Rev. 2: 7.

65. *How can we "overcome"?*—"By the blood of the Lamb." Rev. 12: 11.

66. *What beautiful ceremony ere the children of Israel left Egypt teaches us the value of the blood of Christ?*— The sprinkling about their doors of the blood of a lamb, to preserve them from the destroying angel's hand.

67. *Of what was the "scarlet line" which Rahab hung out from her window, when Jericho was taken and she was spared, a type?*—Of the saving blood of Christ.

68. *Shall not we be without excuse if we neglect to take refuge in Jesus?*—We shall indeed.

If ye know these things, happy are ye if ye do them. John 13: 17.

DANIEL DURING THE BABYLONIAN DYNASTY. (Dan. 1-4, 5, 7, 8.)

1. *When was Daniel taken to Babylon?* — With Jehoiakim, king of Judah.

2. *Where was Babylon?*—On the Euphrates, in Chaldea.

3. *What relationship did Jehoiakim bear to the good Josiah?*—He was his son.

4. *Was Daniel also of the royal family of Judah?*— He was. Dan 1: 3.

5. *How came he to Babylon?*—With the captives Nebuchadnezzar made.

6. *Who was Nebuchadnezzar?*—King of Babylon.

7. *What commandment did he give respecting the royal captives of Judah?*—That some of the choicest and cleverest of them should be specially prepared for the king's service.

8. *Why did Daniel object to eat the king's food?*— It shall be a perpetual statute for your generations throughout all your dwellings that ye eat neither fat nor blood. Lev. 3: 17.

9. *What was the result of the experiment that David requested might be tried on them?*—They looked better than those who ate the king's food. Dan. 1: 15.

10. *How does this prove the truth of 1 Sam. 2: 28-30?* It shows that God "will honor" those who obey and "honor" him.

11. *What astonishing proof did Daniel give Nebuchadnezzar in Dan. 2 that God had endowed him with divine knowledge?*—By telling him the dream that he had forgotten.

12. *What was the dream?*—That he had seen a great image, with a golden head, struck and destroyed by a stone, which became a great mountain. Dan. 2: 31.

13. *Did Daniel take the honor to himself, or give it to God?*—He gave it to God. Dan. 2: 19-23, 28.

14. *How did Daniel interpret this dream?—Who did he say was the "head of gold"?*—Nebuchadnezzar himself. Dan. 2: 38.

15. *In what position did Nebuchadnezzar stand to the*

other kingdoms of the earth at this time?—He was a king of kings in glory and power. Dan. 2: 37.

16. *What kingdom was represented by the "breast and arms of silver"?*—The kingdom of the Medes and Persians.

17. *In what respect were the two arms of the image a graphic representation of this kingdom?*—They showed their united power.

18. *What kingdom did "the belly and thighs" (or "sides," see margin) "of brass" represent?*—The Macedonian or Grecian kingdom.

19. *In what respect was "brass" an appropriate symbol for this power?*—It was gained and held by force of arms, and was less splendid than the other kingdoms before it in outward show.

20. *How did the fourth kingdom differ from the former ones?*—In strength.

21. *When might this kingdom be said to be an "iron" power?*—When it conquered the kingdom of Greece and other lands.

22. *When was it in an enfeebled state?*—When it joined the conquered nations to maintain its power.

23. *What power was to be greater than all these kingdoms, and crumble them into atoms?*—The kingdom of Christ.

24. *What does it mean when it says it was "cut out without hands"?*—Because it was formed by the power of God, without the help of man. Isa. 63: 1-6.

25. *When was this kingdom to be set up?*—In the days of one of these kingdoms or kings. Dan. 2: 44.

26. *At what time, as represented in this image, was Jesus born?*—Under the iron or Roman kingdom.

27. *What effect did the wonderful interpretation of this dream have on Nebuchadnezzar?*—He worshiped Daniel as the messenger of God.

28. *To what was Daniel promoted?*—To be ruler over the whole province of Babylon.

29. *About whom did he make request when himself in power?*—About Shadrach, Meshach and Abed-nego, that they should have a share in the government of the province.

30. *How was the faith of these three friends of Daniel tried? What did the king command them to do?*—By Nebuchadnezzar's setting up a great image of gold, to be worshiped by all his people. Dan. 3. To fall down and worship with the rest.

31. *Were they able to do this? Why not?*—No. Because they could worship only the one true God.

32. *What was the consequence?*—They were cast into a burning fiery furnace.

33. *Who walked with them in the furnace?*—The Son of God.

34. *What happened to the men that threw them in?*—They were killed by the flames.

35. *Were the three servants of God injured?*—Not at all, nor even their clothes touched.

36. *What effect did this wonderful deliverance have on Nebuchadnezzar?*—He blessed and honored God, and promoted his three faithful servants.

37. *What had been God's promise, by the mouth of his servant the prophet Jeremiah, to those who went down into Babylon?*—Seek the peace of the city whither I have caused you to be carried away captives, and pray unto the Lord for it: for in the peace thereof shall ye have peace. Jer. 29: 7.

38. *Was not this the fulfillment of it?*—Doubtless it was.

39. *And is not God as faithful to his word now as he was then?*—He is, as every day's experience of his people proves.

40. *Can God see into man's heart?*—Yes; "the Lord looketh on the heart." 1 Sam. 16: 7.

41. *Did the Lord see the heart of Nebuchadnezzar humbled by what he had beheld of the true God, or still proud?*—He saw the pride within.

42. *What dream did he give the king to warn him?*—A vision of a lofty and flourishing tree hewn down, with its stump left for seven years among the grass and beasts of the field. Dan. 4.

43. *Who interpreted this dream to Nebuchadnezzar?*—Daniel.

44. *Did the king take warning? How was his pride humbled?*—No. Dan. 4: 30. By his being deprived of reason and made a companion of beasts. Dan. 4: 33.

45. *What was the effect of this on the king?*—At the end of seven years his reason returned, and he acknowledged and praised God.

46. *Is there any account given in the book of Daniel of Evil-merodach, Nebuchadnezzar's son?*—No.

47. *Where must we turn to read about him?*—It came to pass in the seven and thirtieth year of the captivity of Jehoiachin king of Judah, that Evil-merodach king of Babylon in the first year of his reign lifted up the head of Jehoiachin king of Judah, and brought him forth out of prison, and spake kindly unto him, and set his throne above the throne of the kings that were with him in Babylon. Jer. 52: 31, 32.

48. *Who was this Jehoiachin? and when was he carried captive? Give his other names.*—King of Judah. In the first year of his reign. Jeconiah and Coniah.

49. *What wonderful vision does Dan. 7 record?*—Of four great beasts that came up from the sea.

50. *In which year of Belshazzar's reign did this happen?*—The first.

51. *Who was Belshazzar?*—King of Babylon.

52. *What kingdom was represented by the first of these four beasts?*—The kingdom of Babylon.

53. *Do we see anything similar to this on the Nineveh sculptures lately discovered?*—Yes; many winged lions are there portrayed.

54. *What was the second beast like?*—A bear.

55. *What kingdom did that symbolize?*—The kingdom of the Medes and Persians.

56. *What was the third beast like?*—A leopard.

57. *How did the "four wings" symbolize this power?*—Because the Grecian conquests were rapid as a bird's flight.

58. *Who were represented by these four wings?*—The kings of the four parts into which the Grecian kingdom was divided.

59. *What was the fourth beast like?*—It was terrible and strong, and had iron teeth and ten horns.

60. *In what respect was this kingdom "diverse" from the others?*—In having horns.

61. *Who is the representative of that fourth or final power now? What "wears out the saints of the Most High"?*—The pope of Rome. The popish system, as far as it has any remaining power.

62. *How long is it to continue?*—Till about the time when our Lord returns.

63. *Who is meant by "the Ancient of Days"?*—The eternal God.

64. *When will his throne of judgment be set?*—When the millennium begins and God puts down his enemies' power.

65. *What glorious Person, under the name "Son of man," is introduced in this chapter?*—Jesus Christ.

66. *What "kingdom" is spoken of that "the saints of God" are to take and possess for ever and for ever?*—The kingdom of Christ to the end of time.

67. *When the Lord Jesus came on the earth the first time, did he come as a conqueror?*—No, as a servant.

68. *When will he come to reign?*—When the number

of his people is complete, and the time has come "which the Father has put in his own power." Acts 1 : 7.

69. *What vision of Daniel's does Dan. 8 set forth?*—Of the ram and he-goat.

70. *In what year of Belshazzar's reign did this take place?*—The third.

71. *Do these two beasts represent any of the kingdoms of the former visions?*—Yes—the ram the Median and Persian, and the goat the Grecian.

72. *Whom do the two horns of the first of these two beasts symbolize?*—The separate Median and Persian powers.

73. *Do not the four horns of the second beast in this vision mean the same as the four wings of the fowl in the third beast of the former vision? In what respect are they similar?*—Yes. They both correspond in numbers to the four kingdoms into which the Grecian was divided.

74. *Is the "little horn" of this vision the same as "the little horn" of the former vision?*—No.

75. *What erroneous form of religion does "the little horn" of the first vision symbolize?*—The popish one.

76. *What other great error or false religion does "the little horn" of the second vision symbolize?*—The Mohammedan one.

77. *Is there any limit put to the rule of these false religions?*—Yes; in periods obscurely expressed, but which seem likely to end together about the present time. Dan. 7 : 25; 8 : 14.

78. *Has not God purposely hidden the time when they shall come to an end?*—He has, in order that all may watch in every age.

Heaven and earth shall pass away, but my words shall not pass away. But of that day and hour knoweth no man, no, not the angels of heaven, but my Father only. Matt. 24 : 35, 36.

79. *What effect did these visions have on Daniel?*—He fainted and was greatly distressed.

80. *How soon after this were they fulfilled?*—They began to be fulfilled by the overthrow of Babylon by the Medes and Persians in about sixteen years.

81. *What impious act of profanity was King Belshazzar guilty of the very night in which his kingdom was taken?*—Drinking out of the gold and silver vessels of the temple. Dan. 5.

82. *How was it that he did not know that destruction was so near?*—He was bent on sinful pleasure, and probably refused to know and understand.

83. *Who took the city? and how?*—Darius, the king of the Medes. By turning the river into another channel, and so entering the city by surprise through the open gates.

84. *Which of the beasts of Daniel's visions, and what part of Nebuchanezzar's image, were symbols of this conquering power?*—The bear and ram and the silver breast and arms.

85. *How did God reveal to Belshazzar his impending fate just before it fell on him?*—By an awful handwriting on the wall.

86. *Who came in and reminded the king of Daniel?*—The queen.

87. *What did the mystic handwriting on the wall predict? Mene? Tekel? Peres?*—MENE: God hath numbered thy kingdom, and finished it. TEKEL: Thou art weighed in the balances, and art found wanting. PERES: Thy kingdom is divided, and given to the Medes and Persians. Dan. 5 : 26–28.

88. *And if "Tekel" were said to us, what would be our hope, our refuge?*—Jesus Christ alone, in whom his people are complete.

89. *Who has satisfied God's justice, and whose righteousness must avail for us?*—Christ has fully paid our debt, and his righteousness is sufficient for us.

90. *Of whom alone can it be said, "Thou art weighed in the balances and not found wanting"?*—He "who did no sin" (1 Pet. 2 : 22), but "is holy, harmless, undefiled." Heb. 7 : 36.

91. *How will his righteousness avail for us?*—As perfect in itself, and performed and offered in our stead.

As by one man's disobedience many were made sinners, so by the obedience of one shall many be made righteous. Rom. 5 : 19.

The wages of sin is death; but the gift of God is eternal life through Jesus Christ our Lord. Rom. 6 : 23.

There is therefore now no condemnation to them which are in Christ Jesus, who walk not after the flesh, but after the Spirit. Rom. 8 : 1.

92. *What empty honor did Belshazzar put upon Daniel when he had interpreted the handwriting?*—A chain of gold and higher rank.

93. *How soon after it was Belshazzar slain?*—The same night.

94. *Who was associated with Darius in taking Babylon?*—Cyrus, his nephew and son-in-law.

95. *How long before this had his name been mentioned by the prophet Isaiah?*—About one hundred and seventy years.

That saith to the deep, Be dry, and I will dry up thy rivers. That saith of Cyrus, He is my shepherd, and shall perform all my pleasure. Thus saith the Lord to his anointed, to Cyrus, whose right hand I have holden, to subdue nations before him; and I will loose the loins of kings, to open before him the two-leaved gates; and the gates shall not be shut. Isa. 44 : 27, 28; 45 : 1.

96. *How does this prophecy describe the manner of taking Babylon?*—Compare No. 83 with Isa. 44 : 27, 28; 45 : 1.

97. *Of what spiritual power is Babylon the type?*—Of the popish or any other apostate, false and persecuting Church. Rev. 17, 18.

98. *By what majestic figure is the destruction of that spiritual power represented?*—A mighty angel took up a stone like a great millstone, and cast it into the sea, saying, Thus with violence shall that great city Babylon be thrown down, and shall be found no more at all. Rev. 18.

99. *Did not the prophet Jeremiah use a similar symbol when he predicted the fall of the natural Babylon?*—It shall be, when thou hast made an end of reading this book, that thou shalt bind a stone to it, and cast it into the middle of the Euphrates; and thou shalt say, Thus shall Babylon sink, and shall not rise from the evil that I will bring upon her. Jer. 51 : 63, 64.

100. *What is the present state of the natural Babylon?*—A huge mass of brick and stone and earth, so mingled together that travelers have passed over the site without knowing it.

101. *Are we not sure that God's word will be fulfilled on the spiritual Babylon as it has on the natural?*—We are, for Christ says, Heaven and earth shall pass away, but my words shall not pass away. Matt. 24 : 35.

102. *What command, then, should those who are in error take heed to?*—Come out of her, my people, that ye be not partakers of her sins, and that ye receive not of her plagues. Rev. 18 : 4.

103. *And how can we be preserved from error?*—Thy word is a lamp unto my feet, and a light unto my path. Psa. 119 : 105. From a child thou hast known the Holy Scriptures, which are able to make thee wise unto salvation through faith which is in Christ Jesus. 2 Tim. 3 : 15.

DANIEL UNDER THE MEDO-PERSIAN DYNASTY. (Dan. 6, 9–12.)

1. *What relationship was there between Darius and Cyrus?*—Cyrus was nephew and son-in-law to Darius.

2. *How are these two kings described in Daniel's vision, chap. 8?*—As the ram with two horns. Dan. 8: 3, 20.

3. *Which was the most powerful king?*—Cyrus the Persian.

4. *Which reigned over Babylon first?*—Darius. Dan. 5: 31; 6: 28.

5. *What feelings did Daniel's prosperity excite in the minds of the king's other princes?*—Jealousy, envy and malice.

6. *How did they try first to find an occasion against him?*—Out of his manner of performing the duties of his office.

7. *What unwilling testimony did they bear to his excellence of character and uprightness?*—That they could find in him no error or fault.

8. *What trap did they lay for him?*—They obtained a royal decree that no one should offer a petition or prayer for thirty days to any one but the king.

9. *Did he forsake the worship of his God when he knew the consequences?*—No.

10. *Why did Daniel pray so publicly, when Jesus said, "Enter thy closet and shut the door"?*—He desired in this case to show that he was not ashamed of his duty to God.

> If they return to thee with all their heart and with all their soul in the land of their captivity, whither they have carried them captives, and pray toward their land, which thou gavest unto their fathers, and toward the city which thou hast chosen, and toward the house which I have built for thy name: then hear thou from the heavens, even from thy dwelling-place, their prayer and their supplications, and maintain their cause, and forgive thy people which have sinned against thee. 2 Chron. 6: 38, 39.

11. *Had Daniel heard these words of the Lord Jesus?*—No; he lived many years before the Christian era.

12. *Under what dispensation did Daniel live?*—The old and strict one of the law.

13. *What was his act, then?—was it ostentation or devout prayer?*—Devout prayer.

14. *How did the king feel when he found what his edict had involved?*—He was much displeased with himself.

15. *Why would not the king alter the decree?*—Because of a foolish law of the Medes that no decree of the king could be changed.

16. *What became of Daniel in the den?*—He was unhurt.

17. *Was it because the lions were not hungry?*—No.

18. *How do you prove this?*—By the fury with which they devoured those who immediately after were cast into the den.

19. *How were Daniel's enemies punished by the king?*—With the same dreadful punishment they had intended for him.

20. *What effect had this wonderful deliverance on the king?*—He ordered reverence to be paid to the God of Daniel throughout his kingdom.

21. *Was not all this overruled of God for the benefit of the poor captive Jews in Babylon?*—It was.

22. *What was God's promise to those who went into captivity?*—That he would "bring" them "again into the place whence" he had "caused" them "to be carried away captive." Jer. 29: 14; 28.

23. *How long had the Lord declared the captivity in Babylon should last?*—"Seventy years." Dan. 29: 10.

24. *How did Daniel feel as he found the time drawing near for the return of the people to the land of their fathers?*—Anxious, probably, to hasten it on. Dan. 9.

25. *How did Daniel seek to obtain the Lord's mind?*—By prayer and fasting and confession of sin. Dan. 9.

26. *How soon was his prayer answered?*—Before it was finished. Dan. 9: 20.

27. *What remarkable contrast is there between the time of the answer to these petitions and the one recorded in Dan. 10?*—The one in Dan. 10 was not answered until twenty-one days after, though God had heard and accepted it. Ver. 2, 12, 13.

28. *In what gracious way does the Lord allude to Daniel's prayers in Ezekiel's prophecy?*—Son of man, when the land sinneth against me by trespassing grievously, then will I stretch out mine hand upon it, and will break the staff of the bread thereof, and will send famine upon it, and will cut off man and beast from it: though these three men, Noah, Daniel, and Job, were in it, they should deliver but their own souls by their righteousness, saith the Lord God. Ezek 14: 13, 14.

29. *Which three principal prophets were contemporaries?*—Jeremiah, Ezekiel and Daniel, for about ten years.

30. *It was at "the time of the evening sacrifice" that God answered Daniel's prayer. What other signal answer to prayer did God give at the same hour in Ahab's reign?*—The fire to consume Elijah's sacrifice. 1 Kings 18: 29, 38.

31. *What revelation of God's future will concerning Israel does chap. 9 give?*—The end of the Jewish sacrifices and the destruction of their city and temple. Ver. 24–27.

32. *Of what glorious Person does this chapter speak?*—Of the Messiah.

33. *Reckoning a day for a year, how soon might the Jews of that day anticipate his coming?*—In rather less than four hundred and ninety years.

34. *Did Jesus come exactly when he was by Daniel's prophecy expected?*—Yes, when Simeon and others were looking for him.

35. *What is the meaning of the name Messiah?*—"Anointed."

36. *How is the death of Christ set forth in this prophecy?*—He was to be cut off, but not for himself. Dan. 9: 26.

37. *If he was to be "cut off," but "not for himself," for whom did he die?*—Instead of fallen men, that they might not die for ever.

38. *Who was sent to Daniel to give him this revelation?*—Gabriel. Dan. 9: 21.

39. *In how many other places in Scripture is this angel spoken of?*—In Dan. 8: 16, and in Luke 1: 19, 26 as appearing to Zacharias and Mary.

40. *What is said of angels in Heb. 1: 13, 14 and in Ps. 103: 20?*—To which of the angels said he at any time, Sit on my right hand, until I make thine enemies thy footstool? Are they not all ministering spirits, sent forth to minister for them who shall be heirs of salvation?—Bless the Lord, ye his angels, that excel in strength, that do his commandments, hearkening unto the voice of his word.

41. *How was Daniel employed when the next heavenly messenger was sent to him?*—In fasting, humiliation and prayer. Dan. 10: 2, 3, 12.

42. *Is the Lord always the hearer and answerer of prayer?*—Always, but in his own good time and way.

43. *How long was Daniel kept without an answer to this prayer?*—Twenty-one days.

44. *Was it because God had not heard him?*—No, but because he had reason for delay. Dan. 10: 12.

45. *Who is said to be "the prince of the power of the air"?*—"The spirit that now worketh in the children of disobedience." Eph. 2: 2.

46. *Whom are we to resist?*—Put on the whole armor of God, that ye may be able to stand against the wiles of the devil. For we wrestle not against flesh and blood, but against principalities, against powers, against the rulers of the darkness of this world, against spiritual wickedness in high places. Eph. 6: 11, 12.

47. *Does not this chapter (Dan. 10) reveal to us the conflict that goes on unseen by us?*—Yes, in verse 13.

48. *What do Job 2, 1 Kings 22 and Rev. 12 : 7–9 also show?*—They show, by expressions about Job and Ahab and their tempters, and about Michael and Satan, that there is a perpetual conflict between the powers of good and evil for dominion over the soul of man.

49. *How do we also get a sight of angelic agency, good and bad, in Jude 9?*—Michael the archangel, when, contending with the devil, he disputed about the body of Moses.

50. *Who may we suppose was the glorious Being who appeared to Daniel, and strengthened him to receive this final revelation?*—The glorious Being who appeared to Daniel in chap. 10 : 5 was doubtless the Son of God, and his hand, or that of an angel, afterward gave him strength. Dan. 10 : 10.

51. *To what extended period did it reach?*—Until the second coming of Christ. Dan. 12.

52. *What blessed promise is given in Dan. 12 : 3?*—They that be wise shall shine as the brightness of the firmament; and they that turn many to righteousness as the stars for ever and ever.

53. *Although much of this prophecy is to be understood by history, may we not join with the prophet, chap. 12 : 8?*—We may indeed exclaim or humbly inquire, "What shall be the end of these things?"

54. *Where is Daniel supposed to have died?*—At Susa, in Persia, after having been previously governor of Judæa. Compare Dan. 10 : 1, 4 with Ezra 1.

55. *What solemn announcement does Dan. 12 : 2 give?*—Many of them that sleep in the dust of the earth shall awake, some to everlasting life, and some to shame and everlasting contempt.

56. *Will it not in the present life be decided on which side we shall stand?*—It will.

If the tree fall toward the south, or toward the north in the place where the tree falleth, there it shall be. Eccles. 11 : 3.

57. *What, then, ought we to do?*—We ought to come to Christ now, that we may be his in the hour of death and at the day of judgment.

Ezra, Haggai, Zechariah and Esther.

1. *In whose reign did the Jews return from their seventy years' captivity?*—In the reign of Cyrus, king of Persia.

2. *By which prophet had this captivity been foretold?*—By Jeremiah (chap. 25 : 11): "These nations shall serve the king of Babylon seventy years."

3. *Why had that exact time been fixed?*—See 2 Chron. 36 : 20, 21; Lev. 26 : 33–35.

Them that had escaped from the sword carried he away to Babylon: where they were servants to him and his sons until the reign of the kingdom of Persia: to fulfill the word of the Lord by the mouth of Jeremiah, until the land had enjoyed her sabbaths: for as long as she lay desolate she kept sabbath to fulfill threescore and ten years.

I will scatter you among the heathen, and will draw out a sword after you: and your land shall be desolate, and your cities waste. Then shall the land enjoy her sabbaths, as long as it lieth desolate, and ye be in your enemies' land; even then shall the land rest, and enjoy her sabbaths. As long as it lieth desolate it shall rest: because it did not rest in your sabbaths, when ye dwelt upon it.

4. *How often ought Israel, according to God's command, to have put aside a year for rest to the land?*—Every seventh year.

In the seventh year shall be a sabbath of rest unto the land, a sabbath for the Lord: thou shalt neither sow thy field, nor prune thy vineyard. Lev. 25 : 4.

5. *Of how many sabbatical years, or years of rest, had Israel robbed the Lord?*—About one hundred and twenty-three—from the entry into Canaan to the removal to Babylon.

6. *Which attribute of God does this display?*—His exact and unfailing justice.

7. *Ought the unerring justice of God (Eccles. 12 : 14) to make us afraid?*—Yes, for God shall bring every work into judgment, with every secret thing, whether it be good, or whether it be evil.

8. *What remedy is there for this fear?*—Refuge in Christ.

As it is appointed unto men once to die, but after this the judgment: so Christ was once offered to bear the sins of many. Heb. 9 : 27, 28.

9. *If Israel was judged by God's law, by what shall we be judged?*—This is the condemnation, that light is come into the world, but men loved darkness rather than light, because their deeds were evil.

He that rejecteth me, and receiveth not my words, hath one that judgeth him: the word that I have spoken, the same shall judge him in the last day. John 12 : 48.

10. *Ought we not, then, to study God's word, that we may know and do his will?*—Yes; it is as needful for us as our food, and happily always within our reach.

For this commandment which I command thee this day, it is not hidden from thee, neither is it far off. It is not in heaven, that thou shouldest say, Who shall go up for us to heaven, and bring it unto us, that we may hear it, and do it? Neither is it beyond the sea, that thou shouldest say, Who shall go over the sea for us, and bring it unto us, that we may hear it, and do it? But the word is very nigh unto thee, in thy mouth, and in thy heart, that thou mayest do it. Deut. 30 : 11–14.

11. *How did David esteem God's word?*—I rejoice at thy word, as one that findeth great spoil. How sweet are thy words unto my taste! yea, sweeter than honey to my mouth! Thy word is a lamp unto my feet, and a light unto my path. Therefore I love thy commandments above gold; yea, above fine gold. Mine eyes prevent the night watches, that I might meditate in thy word. Ps. 119 : 162, 103, 105, 127, 148.

12. *What proof was there in King Josiah's reign that the cause of Israel's apostasy was disregard of God's word?*—Great is the wrath of the Lord that is poured out upon us, because our fathers have not kept the word of the Lord, to do after all that is written in this book. 2 Chron. 34 : 21.

13. *What "books" did Daniel study (Dan. 9) when he found out God's will concerning Israel?*—Probably the books of Jeremiah, Chronicles, Deuteronomy, etc.

14. *What proof is there in Ezra 1 : 1 that God puts honor on his own word?*—The proclamation by Cyrus is there said to be owing to God's word by Jeremiah.

15. *Who was Cyrus?*—King of the Persians.

16. *Which prophet had prophesied of this king by name?*—Isaiah.

Thus saith the Lord to his anointed, to Cyrus, whose right hand I have holden, to subdue nations before him. Isa. 45 : 1.

17. *How long had that been uttered before the event?*—About one hundred and seventy years before the taking of Babylon.

18. *What edict concerning the captive Jews did Cyrus issue?*—That they should return to Judæa and rebuild the temple.

19. *Who was at this time prince of Judah?*—Shezbazzar.

20. *Who was the head of the tribe of Levi, and by birth high priest?*—Jeshua, or Joshua. Ez. 2 : 40; 3 : 2.

21. *How many returned to Judæa when this decree was published?*—42,360, besides 7337 servants. Ez. 2 : 1, 64, 65.

22. *What did they bring with them?*—The gold and silver vessels of the temple. Ez. 1 : 9–11.

23. *In which month of the year did they return?*—The seventh. Ez. 3 : 1.

24. *What feast fell on the fifteenth day of that month?*—The feast of tabernacles.

25. *Did they keep it?*—Yes. Ez. 3 : 4.

26. *What was there remarkable about this feast?*—The living in booths.

Ye shall take you on the first day the boughs of goodly trees, branches of palm trees, and the boughs of thick trees, and willows of the brook; and ye shall rejoice before the Lord your God seven days. Lev. 23 : 40.

27. *How far did they get in building the temple before they were interrupted?*—The foundation was laid. Ez. 3 : 11 ; 4 : 4.

28. *Who were their enemies?*—The Samaritans.

29. *By what means did the Lord rouse them to their duty?*—By Haggai and Zechariah, the prophets. Ez. 5.

30. *Who was Haggai?*—A prophet.

31. *How does his first chapter show us that the Jews were more anxious to build their own houses than the temple of the Lord?*—Is it time for you, O ye, to dwell in your ceiled houses, and this house lie waste? Hag. 1 : 4.

32. *Is not worldly ease our besetting sin also?*—It is.

33. *What effect ought the word of the Lord to have on us?*—To make us diligent and obedient.

34. *What effect had it on Zerubbabel the prince of Judah, and Joshua the high priest?*—The Lord stirred up the spirit of Zerubbabel the son of Shealtiel, governor of Judah, and the spirit of Joshua the son of Josedech, the high priest, and the spirit of all the remnant of the people; and they came and did work in the house of the Lord of hosts, their God. Hag. 1 : 14.

35. *To whom did the prophet refer in Hag. 2 : 6, 7?*—To Christ, as "the desire of all nations."

36. *When the foundation of this new temple was laid, the people who had seen the former temple wept, yet the Lord says (Hag. 2 : 9) that the glory of the latter house shall exceed the former. How was this to be?*—Because Christ would glorify it by his presence.

37. *What promises did the Lord give to the Jews in connection with the building of his house?*—That he would be with them, and give them glory and peace. Hag. 2 : 4, 9.

38. *And what blessing may we expect if we too work for him?*—Grace, mercy and peace, and as many other blessings as he sees good.

39. *To whom does the silver and the gold belong?*—To God, to give and to take away.

40. *What must we say if we offer of our substance to the Lord?*—Thine, O Lord, is the greatness, and the power, and the glory, and the victory, and the majesty; for all that is in the heaven and in the earth is thine; thine is the kingdom, O Lord, and thou art exalted as head above all. Both riches and honor come of thee, and thou reignest over all; and in thine hand is power and might: and in thine hand it is to make great, and to give strength unto all. Now therefore, our God, we thank thee, and praise thy glorious name. But whom am I, and what is my people, that we should be able to offer so willingly after this sort? for all things come of thee, and of thine own have we given thee. 1 Chron. 29 : 11–14.

41. *By what other prophet were they stirred up?*—By Zechariah.

42. *In which king's reign did these prophets utter their message?*—Darius's.

43. *Was this the same Darius who put Daniel into the den of lions?*—No.

44. *Whom does chap. 3 of this book (Zechariah) reveal to us as the hidden adversary of Israel?*—Satan.

45. *What does the apostle Paul tell us of this wily foe in Eph. 6 : 11–17?*—That he is a wicked spirit, ruling "the darkness of this world," working by "wiles" and casting "fiery darts."

46. *What is Satan called in Rev. 12 : 9, 10?*—The great dragon, that old serpent, called the devil, and Satan, which deceiveth the whole world: the accuser of our brethren, which accused them before our God day and night.

47. *What glorious Person did the Lord speak of to comfort his people under the name of "the Branch"?*—Jesus Christ. Zech. 3 : 8 ; 6 : 12.

48. *Who was destined to crush the head of "the old serpent"?*—The seed of Eve. Gen. 3 : 15.

49. *What special promises to Zerubbabel does Zech. 4 contain?*—The grace and help of the Holy Spirit and the providential care of God.

50. *What further prophecy of the Lord Jesus is there in Zech. 9 : 9?*—Rejoice greatly, O daughter of Zion; shout, O daughter of Jerusalem: behold, thy King cometh unto thee; he is just, and having salvation; lowly, and riding upon an ass, and upon a colt the foal of an ass.

51. *When was this fulfilled?*—When Jesus entered Jerusalem riding on an ass.

52. *To what fountain does Zech. 13 refer?*—To the blood of Jesus Christ, that cleanseth from all sin.

53. *To what does the Lord Jesus compare himself in John 10 : 11, etc.?*—To a good shepherd.

54. *Of whom does "the Lord of hosts" speak when he says (Zech. 13 : 7), "Awake, O sword, against my shepherd, against the man that is my fellow"?*—Of Jesus Christ.

55. *How was "the man" Christ Jesus God's fellow or equal?*—As himself also almighty and eternal God.

56. *When was this prophecy of the smitten shepherd and the scattered sheep fulfilled?*—When Jesus was crucified and his disciples fled.

57. *What prophecy is there in Zech. 14: 4 of the second coming of the Lord Jesus?*—"His feet shall stand in that day upon the Mount of Olives."

58. *From what part of Judea did the Lord Jesus ascend to heaven?*—"From the mount called Olivet." Acts 1 : 12.

59. *What did the angels say to his disciples who had seen him go into heaven?*—This same Jesus, which is taken up from you into heaven, shall so come in like manner as ye have seen him go into heaven. Acts 1 : 11.

60. *In verse 8 of this chapter (Zech. 14) living waters are spoken of; where else in Scripture are these described?*—In Ezek. 47 : 1–12, as issuing "out of the sanctuary;" in Joel 3 : 18, as coming "forth of the house of the Lord;" in Rev. 22 : 1, as "proceeding out of the throne of God and of the Lamb."

61. *What glorious promises does this prophecy contain of future blessings in store for Israel?*—That God would bring them again to their own land (Zech. 10 : 6–12), and would dwell among them (Zech. 2 : 10–12), and pour his Spirit upon them (Zech. 12 : 6–14), and that they should be holiness unto the Lord (Zech. 14 : 16–21), and be a blessing. Zech. 8 : 3–23.

62. *Must not these have been peculiarly comforting to the poor Jews in their impoverished state?*—They must indeed.

63. *What effect did it have on them?*—They began to build the house of God, and prospered and finished it. Ez. 5 : 2 ; 6 : 14.

64. *How did they withstand their adversaries?*—Through "the eye of their God" upon them. Ez. 5 : 5.

65. *What new edict did they obtain from the king?*—That the Persian governors should furnish them

supplies for the building and the sacrifices. Zech. 6: 6–12.

66. *How had this been brought about?*—Through the discovery of the former decree of Cyrus. Ez. 5: 3; 6: 5.

67. *When was the temple finished?*—In the sixth year of King Darius, and about the year 515. B. C.

68. *How was it dedicated?*—With special sacrifices and the keeping of the Passover. Ez. 6: 16–22.

69. *Who is the Artaxerxes mentioned in Ez. 6: 14, and again in Ez. 7: 1?*—Artaxerxes Longimanus, son of Xerxes.

70. *By what other name is he called in the book of Esther?*—Xerxes, or Artaxerxes; a previous one, of Ez. 4: 7, is in Esther called Ahasuerus.

71. *How came a Jewish damsel to be his wife?*—Ahasuerus's former wife had been divorced, and Esther had been chosen in her place from many who had been taken to the king by his command. Esth. 1: 9; 2: 1–17.

72. *What was the name of Esther's uncle?*—Mordecai.

73. *What kind of relationship had he sustained toward her?*—That of father since her parents' death.

74. *Where was the Persian court held at this time?*—At Shushan (or Susa) in Persia.

75. *Who was the Jews' great enemy at this time?*—Haman.

76. *From whom had he descended?*—From Agag, king of Amalek.

77. *Would not this account for his great antipathy to the Jews?*—Yes, as his ancestors had been almost destroyed by them. 1 Sam. 15.

78. *What had the Lord decreed concerning Amalek?*—The Lord said unto Moses, Write this for a memorial in a book, and rehearse it in the ears of Joshua; for I will utterly put out the remembrance of Amalek from under heaven. And Moses built an altar, and called the name of it Jehovah-nissi: for he said, Because the Lord hath sworn that the Lord will have war with Amalek from generation to generation. Ex. 17: 14–16.

79. *Would this not account for Mordecai refusing to bow down to him?*—It would, as he was thus numbered among the enemies of God.

80. *How did Haman attempt to wreak his vengeance on the Jews?*—By destroying all of them throughout the kingdom.

81. *How did the Lord prevent this?*—By means of Esther, the Jewish queen. Esth. 4.

82. *What did the king command to be read before him to amuse his waking hours?*—The history of his reign. Esth. 6: 1.

83. *Must not Haman have been woefully disappointed when the honor he intended for himself was placed on Mordecai?*—Yes; such is often the mortification of malice and pride.

84. *How did Esther obtain the deliverance of her kindred?*—By petitioning the king.

85. *Was it not likely that she was raised to the throne of Persia with this intent?*—Yes, extremely likely. Esth. 4: 14.

86. *Is the Lord ever at a loss for means to accomplish his purposes?*—Never.

87. *What feast was ever after celebrated among the Jews to commemorate this deliverance?*—The feast of Purim. Esth. 9: 26.

88. *Why was it so called?*—Because their enemies had cast Pur, or the lot, as to the time of destroying them. Esth. 9: 24: 3: 6, 7.

89. *To what dignity was Mordecai raised in the Persian court?*—The highest dignity under the king. Esth. 10: 3.

90. *Will not this account for the great favor shown to the Jews at Jerusalem by the Persian king?*—It will.

91. *Who was Ezra?*—A priestly descendant of Aaron and a writer of the law. Ez. 7: 1–5, 11.

92. *Is it supposed that he went up to Jerusalem in the reign of Cyrus, or not till that of Artaxerxes (Longimanus)?*—In that of Artaxerxes Longimanus.

93. *What was his object in going to Jerusalem?*—To carry back the treasures of the temple (Ez. 7: 19) and royal gifts for the temple service.

94. *What kind letter and munificent gift was he the bearer of from the Persian king?*—A letter empowering the Jews to return to Jerusalem, and exempting many of them from tribute and custom; and a gift of silver and gold and other needful things. Ez. 7: 11–26; 8: 26, 27.

95. *Whose unseen Hand is beheld here, and whom did Ezra acknowledge in the last verses of this chapter (Ez. 7)?*—The hand of God, God having put it into the king's heart.

96. *How does Ezra describe his journey from Babylon to Judea?*—That they set out with fasting and prayer, and arrived in safety. Ez. 8: 21–23, 31, 32.

97. *What proof have we in Ez. 8: 23 of the truth of 1 Kings 8: 46–49; 9: 3?*—The prayer of the penitent captives was heard.

98. *What did Ezra and his company take up with them?*—The royal gifts for the service of the temple.

99. *What act of worship did they perform when they arrived in Judæa?*—They offered a burnt-offering. Ez. 8: 35.

100. *What sinful act was Ezra made acquainted with by the princes of Judah?*—Of the Jews intermarrying with the people of the land. Ez. 9.

101. *How did Ezra receive this mournful information?*—He was greatly distressed.

102. *Did he justify these acts before the Lord, or confess the sin to him?*—He confessed it with the deepest humiliation.

103. *What effect did his faithfulness have on the people?*—They were truly penitent and distressed, and put away their wives. Ez. 10: 1, 19.

104. *How did they bring about the desired reformation?*—They made a covenant with God and with each other, and a public proclamation.

105. *Were there many in this trespass?*—Many. Ez. 10: 13.

106. *Were the priests included in the number?*—Yes. Ez. 10: 18.

107. *What had been the Lord's special command on this point?*—(See Ex. 34: 12–16.)

Take heed to thyself, lest thou make a covenant with the inhabitants of the land whither thou goest, lest it be for a snare in the midst of thee: but ye shall destroy their altars, break their images, and cut down their groves: for thou shalt worship no other god: for the Lord, whose name is Jealous, is a jealous God: lest thou make a covenant with the inhabitants of the land, and they go a-whoring after their gods, and do sacrifice unto their gods, and one call thee, and thou eat of his sacrifice; and thou take of their daughters unto thy sons, and their daughters go a-whoring after their gods, and make thy sons go a-whoring after their gods.

NEHEMIAH AND MALACHI.

1. *Was Ezra left alone to reform the people, or did he soon obtain a companion in the good work?*—God sent him a fellow-worker. Neh. 8: 9.

2. *Who was this?*—Nehemiah. Neh. 1.

3. *What office had he held in the Persian court?*—That of king's cupbearer. Neh. 1: 11.

4. *Why did he wish to give up so high an appointment?*—That he might return to Judæa to assist in the rebuilding of the temple.

5. *What means did he adopt to obtain his desire?*—Prayer to God. Neh. 1: 11; 2: 4.

6. *Can God, then, hear the desire of the heart, as well as the words of the mouth?*—He can, for he is a discerner of the thoughts and intents of the heart. Neither is there any creature that is not manifest in his sight: but all things are naked and opened unto the eyes of Him with whom we have to do. Heb. 4 : 12, 13. When Jesus perceived their thoughts, he answering said unto them, What reason ye in your hearts? Luke 5 : 22; 6 : 8; 9 : 47; 11 : 17.

7. *Did the king grant his request?*—He did. Neh. 2 : 6.

8. *Had Nehemiah gone unprepared into the king's presence, or had he sought the Lord by prayer?*—He had offered humble and earnest prayer.

9. *What promise had he pleaded in prayer?*—God's promise to his people by Moses, that if they returned in penitence and obedience to him, he would restore them to their land. Neh. 1 : 8, 9.

10. *May not we too depend on God, that what he has promised to us he will perform?*—We always and confidently may, for "He is faithful that promised."

11. *What does Nehemiah's example encourage us to do?* —To be "instant in prayer."

12. *What king was this before whom Nehemiah was so "sore afraid"?*—Artaxerxes Longimanus.

13. *What was the name of his queen?*—Uncertain—not Vashti or Esther.

14. *What was Nehemiah's particular request to the king?*—That he would send him into Judæa to rebuild his city. Neh. 2 : 5.

15. *Whom had the king sent with Nehemiah?*—Ezra. Ez. 7 : 12, 13.

16. *How did the Jews' enemies feel when they understood Nehemiah's errand?*—They were much displeased. Neh. 2 : 10, 19; 4 : 1, 7.

17. *What was Nehemiah's first act after he got to Jerusalem?*—He privately examined the ruins by night. Neh. 2 : 12-15.

18. *In what state did he find the wall?*—Everywhere broken down.

19. *Who assisted him in repairing it?*—The high priest, the priests and many of the rulers, merchants and others. Neh. 3.

20. *Were they all regular masons and builders?*—No; some were goldsmiths (ver. 32) and apothecaries (ver. 8).

21. *Who are spoken of in Neh. 3 : 12?*—The daughters of a ruler, as giving their help.

22. *Should not this teach us that in the Lord's work all can assist?*—Yes, and that all should feel glad and honored to do so.

23. *What did Paul say in Acts 9 : 6?*—"Lord, what wilt thou have me to do?"

24. *What honorable mention is made of a "ruler" and his daughters" assisting in the good work, contrasted with what is said of "the nobles of Tekoah" in Neh. 3 : ?*—The "nobles put not their necks to the work of their Lord." (See No. 21, ver. 12.)

25. *Is it not so in the present day?*—"Not many noble are called." 1 Cor. 1 : 26.

26. *When the enemies of the Jews saw the wall of Jerusalem progressing, what did they wish to do?*—To stop the work. Neh. 4 : 11.

27. *What reproachful thing did they say of the work?* —"If a fox go up, he shall even break down their stone wall." Neh. 4 : 3.

28. *Did they succeed in hindering the work?*—No.

29. *How did Nehemiah meet the danger?*—By prayer and faith, and by being armed and watchful. Neh. 4 : 9-23.

30. *What great zeal and self-denial does Neh. 23 record?*—Their not putting off their clothes at night.

31. *What great abuse did Nehemiah set himself to*

rectify?—The requiring usury, or excessive interest, for the loan of money to the famished and distressed. Neh. 5.

32. *Were the people willing to do as he said?*—Yes, and did it at once. Neh. 5 : 12, 13.

33. *What example did Nehemiah himself set them?*—He declined receiving his own allowance, to spare the poor.

34. *How was it that he was so disinterested?*—From "fear of God." Neh. 5 : 15.

35. *To whom did he look for recompense?*—From God. Neh. 5 : 19.

36. *Was not the eye of Moses fixed on the same blessed object?*—It was.

By faith Moses, when he was come to years, refused to be called the son of Pharaoh's daughter; choosing rather to suffer affliction with the people of God, than to enjoy the pleasures of sin for a season; esteeming the reproach of Christ greater riches than the treasures in Egypt: for he had respect unto the recompense of the reward. Heb. 11 : 24-26.

37. *What was the sustaining power that upheld the apostle Paul in his arduous course?*—His expectation of "a crown of righteousness" to be given him "at that day." 2 Tim. 4 : 6-8.

38. *Does not the apostle Peter remind us that it is that same blessed period to which we must look?*—When the chief Shepherd shall appear, ye shall receive a crown of glory that fadeth not away. 1 Pet. 5 : 4.

39. *What does Matt. 25 tell us about that time?*—That those who serve God and his people upon earth, shall, when Christ returns in his glory, enter into eternal life and the joy of their Lord. Vs. 19-23, 31-40, 46.

40. *Ought we not, then, to examine ourselves, to see whether we are getting our reward here or waiting for it hereafter?*—Yes, as it is of *hypocrites* that it is said (Matt. 6 : 2, 5, 16), "They *have* their reward," and have no other and better to come.

41. *What wicked device did Sanballat and his companions next try to put the good Nehemiah in fear?*—They invited him to a meeting in order to get him into their hands, and they sent him a false prophet to induce him to leave his work. Neh. 6.

42. *Did they succeed?*—No.

43. *On whom did Nehemiah depend?*—Upon God. Neh. 6 : 9.

44. *Was any one ever disappointed who put his trust in God?*—Never.

45. *How long was the wall building?*—Fifty-two days. Neh. 6 : 15.

46. *What prophecy of Daniel was connected with the building of this wall?*—Know therefore and understand, that from the going forth of the commandment to restore and to build Jerusalem unto the Messiah the Prince shall be seven weeks, and threescore and two weeks: the street shall be built again, and the wall, even in troublous times. Dan. 9 : 25.

47. *Whom did Nehemiah appoint to the charge of Jerusalem, and why?*—I gave my brother Hanani, and Hananiah the ruler of the palace, charge over Jerusalem: for he was a faithful man, and feared God above many. Neh. 7 : 2.

48. *What did God put into the heart of Nehemiah to do after this?*—To make a register of the families that returned from Babylon. Neh. 7 : 5.

49. *Why was the preservation of the genealogies of the children of Israel so important?*—To show the fulfillment in Christ of the promise to Abraham, that in his seed should all the nations of the earth be blessed (Dan. 22 : 18) and of the promise to David, that God would raise up a king to sit for ever on his throne. Acts 2 : 29, 30; Luke 1 : 30-33.

50. *What further arrangement was completed by the*

seventh month?—The settling of the Israelites in their cities. Neh. 7 : 73.

51. *What special feast was to be kept in that month?*—The feast of tabernacles. Neh. 8 : 14–18.

52. *Of what was it symbolical?*—The booths were in remembrance of the tents in the wilderness. Luke 23 : 43.

> Speak unto the children of Israel, saying, The fifteenth day of this seventh month shall be the feast of tabernacles for seven days unto the Lord. On the first day shall be an holy convocation: ye shall do no servile work therein. Seven days ye shall offer an offering made by fire unto the Lord: on the eighth day shall be an holy convocation unto you: and ye shall offer an offering made by fire unto the Lord: it is a solemn assembly; and ye shall do no servile work therein. Ye shall dwell in booths seven days. Lev. 23 : 34–36, 42.

53. *When will be its great antitype?*—I saw a new heaven and a new earth: for the first heaven and the first earth were passed away; and there was no more sea. And I John saw the holy city, new Jerusalem, coming down from God out of heaven, prepared as a bride adorned for her husband. And I heard a great voice out of heaven saying, Behold, the tabernacle of God is with men, and he will dwell with them, and they shall be his people, and God himself shall be with them, and be their God. Rev. 21 : 1–3.

54. *Who read the law to Israel at this solemn feast?*—Ezra himself.

55. *Does not Neh. 8 : 8 show that their seventy years' residence in a foreign land had made them forget their mother-tongue, Hebrew?*—Yes, as distinct reading and explanation were required.

56. *What effect did the reading of the law have on the people?*—They wept, from mingled feelings of sorrow and of joy. Neh. 8 : 9.

57. *How did Ezra encourage the people?*—He said the joy of the Lord was their strength. Neh. 8 : 10.

58. *What does Neh. 9 record?*—A solemn fast, with reading of the law and confession of sin.

59. *What further arrangements do Neh. 10 and 11 set forth?*—The entering into a covenant with God for obedience to his law and as to the offerings for his service, and the selecting the inhabitants of the city and country.

60. *How was the wall dedicated?*—With music and thanksgiving and great joy. Neh. 12 : 27–43.

61. *How long did this reformation last?*—During the days of Zerubbabel and Nehemiah. Neh. 12 : 47.

62. *When had Nehemiah returned to the king of Persia, his master?* (Neh. 13).—In the thirty-second year of Artaxerxes' reign. Neh. 5 : 14.

63. *When he returned to Jerusalem again, did he find the government going on prosperously?*—No.

64. *What evils did he discover?*—Abuse and neglect of the house of God, Sabbath-breaking and heathen marriages.

65. *How did he correct them?*—He cleansed the temple and made new treasurers of its funds, and closed the city gates against Sabbath traffic, and put an end to marriage of heathen wives.

66. *Had not the Sabbath-day been the great token of the covenant between the Lord and Israel?*—It had. Isa. 58 : 13, 14; Ezek. 20 : 12–20.

> Speak thou also unto the children of Israel, saying, Verily, my sabbaths ye shall keep: for it is a sign between me and you throughout your generations; that ye may know that I am the Lord that doth sanctify you. It is a sign between me and the children of Israel for ever: for in six days the Lord made heaven and earth, and on the seventh day he rested, and was refreshed. Ex. 31 : 13, 17.

67. *Will God suffer his laws to be trampled on without punishment?*—No, as we see in the case of the Jews' neglect to keep their seventh years of rest.

> Them that had escaped from the sword carried he away to Babylon; to fulfill the word of the Lord by the mouth of Jeremiah, until the land had enjoyed her sabbaths; for as long as she lay desolate she kept sabbath, to fulfill threescore and ten years. 2 Chron. 36 : 20, 21.

68. *What command did the Lord give about marrying heathen wives?*—Thou shalt smite them, and utterly destroy them; thou shalt make no covenant with them, nor show mercy unto them; neither shalt thou make marriages with them: thy daughter thou shalt not give unto his son, nor his daughter shalt thou take unto thy son. For they will turn away thy son from following me, that they may serve other gods. Deut. 7 : 2–4.

69. *Did not Nehemiah vigorously root out this evil?*—He did. Neh. 13 : 25, 28, 30.

70. *Where is Nehemiah supposed to have ended his days?*—At Babylon, as cupbearer to the king. Neh. 1 : 11; 13 : 6.

71. *After his death, what further evils does the prophecy of Malachi record?*—Scanty and mean sacrifices and offerings to God. Mal. 1.

72. *Does not chap. 2 : 1–11 of this prophecy show us that the sin which Nehemiah had with such zeal cleansed away a few years before, the priests had fallen into again?*—Yes; they seemed to have married heathen wives. Mal. 1 : 1–11.

73. *Had they not made it an excuse for putting away their wives?*—Yes. Mal. 2 : 14–16.

74. *Would God wink at this sin?*—No, for he hateth putting away.

75. *Of whom does Mal. 3 : 1 speak?*—Of John the Baptist.

76. *How is he described?*—As God's messenger, to prepare his way.

77. *Does not this chapter reveal yet further Israel's sin at that time?*—Yes, it speaks of their adultery, false swearing, oppression of the poor and robbery of God. Mal. 3 : 5–9.

78. *Were there any faithful ones left among this general corruption?*—Yes, some that feared God, and met together to speak about him for their mutual comfort and help, and who were all written down in his book of remembrance. Mal. 3 : 16, 17.

79. *What awful day does the prophet speak of in Mal. 4 : 1, 5?*—The great and dreadful day of judgment.

80. *Is this "day" mentioned in any other part of Scripture?*—Yes, in Joel 2 : 31 as "the great and terrible day of the Lord."

81. *Who have need to fear the terror of "that day"?*—"Scoffers" who walk "after their own lust." 2 Pet. 3 : 3.

> And the kings of the earth, and the great men, and the rich men, and the chief captains, and the mighty men, and every bondman, and every free man, hid themselves in the dens and in the rocks of the mountains; and said to the mountains and rocks, Fall on us, and hide us from the face of Him that sitteth on the throne, and from the wrath of the Lamb. Rev. 6 : 15, 16.
>
> For the great day of his wrath is come; and who shall be able to stand?

82. *With what feelings may those who "fear the Lord" look forward to it?*—With solemn awe, with humble hope, with calm peace and thankful joy.

83. *Who is spoken of under the figure of the "Sun of Righteousness"?*—Our Lord Jesus Christ.

84. *To whom does Deborah allude in her song in Judg. 5 : 31?*—To Jesus Christ, "the sun" going "forth in his might."

85. *Did not David look forward to the same blessed Person in his "last words"?*—Yes, as the light of the morning, when the sun riseth. 2 Sam. 23 : 4.

86. *Should we not ask ourselves, Are we ready for his appearing?*—Yes, day by day, knowing the time, that now it is high time to awake out of sleep: for now is our salvation nearer than when we believed. The night is far spent, the day is at hand: let us therefore cast off the works of darkness, and let us put on the armor of light. Rom. 13 : 11, 12.

87. *How can we know that we are ready?*—By knowing that we are in Christ by faith; for as it is appointed unto men once to die, but after this the judgment: so Christ was once offered to bear the sins of many; and unto them that look for him shall he appear the second time without sin unto salvation. Heb. 9 : 27, 28.

88. *What in Rev. 19 : 8 is the bride's dress said to be in which she appears to meet the Lord?*—To her was granted that she should be arrayed in fine linen, clean and white; for the fine linen is the righteousness of saints (even the righteousness of Christ).

89. *Whose righteousness must we be clothed in if we sit down at the marriage-supper of the Lamb?*—"Not" our "own righteousness, which is of the law, but that which is through the faith of Christ, the righteousness which is of God by faith." Phil. 3 : 9.

90. *How can we procure this?*—"Through Jesus Christ our Saviour." Tit. 3 : 5–7.

91. *What right have we to obtain it?*—A perfect righ through Christ by faith. "And the Spirit and the bride say, Come. And whosoever will" may come Rev. 22 : 17.

THE NEW TESTAMENT.

LUKE 1.

1. *Who was the evangelist Luke?*—The writer of a Gospel and of the Acts of the Apostles, a physician, and said to have been born at Antioch in Syria.

2. *Was he a personal disciple of our Lord?*—This is not known.

3. *Who was Theophilus?*—A Gentile of rather high rank, and a Christian. Acts 1 : 1.

4. *How much of Palestine was under Herod's jurisdiction?*—Judæa. Luke 1 : 5.

5. *What is meant by the courses of the priests?*—They were "divided by lot" "in the service of the house of the Lord." 1 Chron. 24 : 1–19.

6. *Does not the word "temple" in verse 9 signify rather the holy place?*—It does, for God says to Moses, "Thou shalt make an altar to burn incense upon," "and thou shalt put it" "before the mercy-seat." Ex. 30 : 1, 6–8.

7. *What was our Lord's testimony to John the Baptist at a later period?*—That "he was a burning and a shining light." John 5 : 35.

8. *What prophecy agrees with verse 17?*—Behold, I will send you Elijah the prophet before the coming of the great and dreadful day of the Lord: and he shall turn the heart of the fathers to the children, and the heart of the children to their fathers, lest I come and smite the earth with a curse. Mal. 4 : 5, 6.

9. *How much older was John the Baptist than our Lord?*—About six months. V. 36.

10. *Is there not a connection between verses 28 and 38?*—The angel said to Mary, "The Lord is with thee," and Mary replied, "Behold the handmaid of the Lord."

11. *Whom does Mary speak of as God my Saviour?*—Of God the Father who designed the salvation of man, and sent his Son to execute it.

12. *What was the oath unto Abraham?*—The angel of the Lord called unto Abraham out of heaven, and said, By myself have I sworn, saith the Lord, for because thou hast done this thing, and hast not withheld thy son, thine only son: that in blessing I will bless thee, and in multiplying I will multiply thy seed as the stars of the heaven, and as the sand which is upon the sea-shore; and thy seed shall possess the gate of his enemies: and in thy seed shall all the nations of the earth be blessed; because thou hast obeyed my voice. Gen. 22 : 15–18.

13. *To what do we owe the remission of our sins?*—To the righteousness and death of Christ, "through the tender mercy of our God." Vs. 77, 78.

14. *How do we know that the way of life is light and peace?*—By the word of God (v. 79), and by the experience of our own minds and hearts.

MATTHEW 1 : 18–25.

15. *How do we know it was the same angel as appeared to Mary?*—Because he is spoken of in v. 20 as "the angel of the Lord."

16. *What is the meaning of being saved from our sins?*—Being saved from the power and guilt and punishment of them, and made "holy and unblamable and unreprovable in" God's "sight." Col. 1 : 22.

LUKE 2.

17. *Who was Cæsar Augustus?*—The first emperor of Rome.

18. *What does the term "all the world" include?*—The Roman empire, which then included nearly all the known or civilized world.

19. *How do the angels speak of Jesus to the shepherds?*—As "a Saviour," "Christ the Lord." V. 11.

20. *Is there not a sign of the poverty of Joseph and Mary in the offering they presented?*—There is. When the days of her purifying are fulfilled, tor a son, or for a daughter, she shall bring a lamb of the first year for a burnt-offering, and a young pigeon, or a turtledove, for a sin-offering, unto the door of the tabernacle of the congregation, unto the priest: who shall offer it before the Lord, and make an atonement for her; and she shall be cleansed from the issue of her blood. This is the law for her that hath borne a male or a female. And if she be not able to bring a lamb, then she shall bring two turtles, or two young pigeons; the one for the burnt-offering, and the other for a sin-offering: and the priest shall make an atone ment for her, and she shall be clean. Lev. 12 : 6–8.

21. *Is Simeon of verse 25 the same person as in Acts 15 : 14?*—No; the Simeon of the Acts was Simon Peter.

22. *Who are the Gentiles?*—All nations but the Jews.

23. *How does the compulsory taxation of Luke 2 : 1 agree with the boast of the Jews in John 8 : 33?*—It does not agree at all, but shows the falseness of their boast.

24. *What was the feast of the Passover?*—Observe the month of Abib, and keep the passover unto the Lord thy God: for in the month of Abib the Lord thy God brought thee forth out of Egypt by night. Thou shalt therefore sacrifice the passover unto the Lord thy God, of the flock and the herd, in the place which the Lord shall choose to place his name there. Thou shalt eat no leavened bread with it. Deut. 16 : 1–3.

MATTHEW 2 : 1–12.

25. *Who were the wise men?*—Some Magi from the East, who studied the stars and the supposed influence of the stars on human affairs.

26. *Why was all Jerusalem troubled, instead of welcoming their promised King?*—Many were afraid lest he should overthrow the reigning king.

He came unto his own, and his own received him not. John 1 : 11.

27. *What proof of the overruling providence of God is there in verse 12?*—The special warning by a dream.

28. *Why was the term "Nazarene" a reproach?*—Because of the contempt in which Nazareth was held by the educated Jews.

LUKE 3 (MATTHEW 3, MARK 1).

29. *Who was Tiberius Cæsar?*—The second emperor of Rome.

30. *What was the Roman title of Pontius Pilate?*—Governor. Luke 3 : 1.

31. *What was the special feature of John's preaching?*—Repentance for remission or pardon of sin through the coming Messiah, and baptism as the outward sign and public profession.

32. *What is repentance?*—Not only sorrow for sin, but a total change of mind and heart.

33. *Who is addressed in Mark 1 : 2; Mal. 3 : 1; Isa. 40 : 3?*—Jesus Christ is addressed in Mark 1 : 2, and referred to in Mal. 3 : 1: "Behold, I will send my messenger, and he shall prepare the way before me;" and in Isa. 40 : 3: "The voice of him that crieth in the wilderness, Prepare ye the way of the Lord."

34. *Was John's preaching successful?*—Yes; people from all parts of Judæa confessed and were baptized. Matt. 3 : 5; Mark 1 : 5.

35. *Whither should we flee from the wrath to come?*—To Christ, our perfect and only Shield.

36. *What is the fruit of true repentance?*—Ceasing "to do evil," willfully and habitually, any more. Isa. 1 : 16.

37. *What solemn warning is contained in Luke 3 : 9?*—Now also the axe is laid unto the root of the trees: every tree therefore which bringeth not forth good fruit is hewn down and cast into the fire.

38. *How does John's reply in Luke 3 : 11 illustrate the second great commandment?*—By teaching kindness and self-denial for each other's good.

39. *What were the publicans?*—Jewish collectors of Roman taxes.

40. *Why were they so odious to their countrymen?*—Because they farmed the taxes, and made as much out of them as possible for their own benefit.

41. *What is the meaning of the word Christ?*—"Anointed." Luke 4 : 18.

42. *What was the difference between John's baptism and the Lord's?*—The baptism ordained by our Lord was "into the name of the Father, and of the Son, and of the Holy Ghost," and was accompanied by the grace of the Holy Spirit to those who believed. "John truly baptized with water; but ye shall be baptized with the Holy Ghost not many days hence." Acts 1 : 5. As took place at Pentecost and in the house of Cornelius. Acts 2 : 2–4; 11 : 15.

43. *What is the meaning of baptism with fire?*—The purifying fire of the Holy Spirit, or some searching and exposing power.

Every man's work shall be made manifest: for the day shall declare it, because it shall be revealed by fire: and the fire shall try every man's work of what sort it is. 1 Cor. 3 : 13.

44. *What is the allusion to the use of the fan?*—The final separation by Christ of the righteous and the wicked, as the winnowing-fan divides the chaff from the wheat.

45. *What proof of our Lord having no need of repentance is found in Luke 3 : 22?*—The approving voice of the holy and omniscient God.

LUKE 4 (MATTHEW 4, MARK 1).

46. *How did the Lord Jesus ascertain the will of God concerning himself from day to day?*—By constant filial communion with the Father.

47. *What is the devil called in Mark 1 : 13?*—Satan.

48. *What is the meaning of the two terms?*—Satan means "adversary" or "enemy," and devil, "accuser."

49. *What proof of the divine authority of the Pentateuch is in Luke 4 : 4?*—Its being quoted by Christ.

50. *What does "living by every word of God" signify?*—Trusting his promises and keeping his commands.

51. *What is the meaning of the word "tempt" in Luke 4 : 12?*—Presumptuously try or provoke.

52. *Was it an empty boast of the devil in Luke 4 : 6?*—Not altogether, as he is called "the god of this world" (Eph. 2 : 2) and "the prince of the power of the air." 2 Cor. 4 : 4.

53. *What relation is there between our Lord's temptation and John 2 : 16?*—They both show that there can be no fellowship between Christ and Satan, and between God's service and the world's.

JOHN 1.

54. *Why is our Lord called the Word?*—Because he is the revelation of God. V. 18.

55. *What proof of his divinity is there in verse 1, and again in verse 2, and again in verse 3?*—He is stated to be "God," and to have been "in the beginning," and to have "made" "all things."

56. *What is the glad hope of eternal life called in verse 4?*—"The light of men" in Christ.

57. *How do we know the gospel is free to all?*—Because Christ, like the light, reaches all, "that all through him might believe." Vs. 7, 9.

58. *Who are meant by "his own"?*—The Jews. V. 11.

59. *What great change takes place in us when we truly believe?*—We become new creatures in Christ, even "sons of God."

60. *Who effects this change?*—"God" himself through Christ, by the Holy Spirit. V. 13.

61. *Out of whose fullness do we receive every grace?*—Out of the fullness of Christ.

62. *Trace the connection between verses 18 and 1?*—Christ, as the word of God, declares him or makes him known.

63. *What was the difference between priests and Levites?*—The priests were descendants of Aaron, and the chief officers of the temple; the Levites, of other families of the tribe, and the assistants of the priests.

64. *Who was Elias?*—"Elijah the prophet."

65. *Why was he expected to reappear?*—Because Malachi prophesied that he should come. Mal. 4 : 5.

66. *Who was meant by "that prophet"?*—Christ, who, like Moses, was a mediator and teacher.

The Lord thy God will raise up unto thee a prophet from the midst of thee of thy brethren; like unto me Deut. 18 : 15.

67. *Why did John call Jesus the "Lamb of God"?*—Because he was the spotless sacrifice and gift of God.

68. *What further proof of the freeness of the gospel is there in verse 29?*—He "taketh away the sin of the world."

69. *What language is the word "rabbi"?*—Hebrew.

70. *In what estimation was Nazareth commonly held?*—It was much despised—more even than Galilee in general, whose inhabitants were looked down upon by the more civilized Jews.

71. *Can we too often use Philip's invitation?*—No. Having seen and known Jesus ourselves, we should say unto all who inquire, and all who doubt, and all who pass by, "Come and see."

72. *What is an "Israelite indeed"?*—One who sincerely inquires or believes.

Truly, God is good to Israel, even to such as are of a clean heart. Ps. 73 : 1.

For he is not a Jew, which is one outwardly; neither is that circumcision, which is outward in the flesh : but he is a Jew, which is one inwardly; and circumcision is that of the heart, in the spirit, and not in the letter; whose praise is not of men, but of God. Rom. 2 : 28, 29.

73. *What proof of our Lord's divinity does verse 48 contain?*—He saw Nathanael, by his all-seeing power, when he thought he was alone in prayer.

74. *What is the meaning of the word "Israel"?*—"A prince of God." Gen. 32: 28, margin.

Thy name shall be called no more Jacob, but Israel: for as a prince hast thou power with God and with men, and hast prevailed.

75. *Compare verse 51 with Gen. 28 : 12 and Heb. 1 : 14.*—Christ is the ladder of communication between heaven and earth, between earth and heaven; and angels were messengers and servants to Jacob of old and to Christ upon earth, and are "ministering spirits" "to the heirs of salvation" now.

JOHN 2.

76. *Is not the Passover generally called the Lord's Passover?*—It is, in many parts of the Old Testament.

77. *For what purpose were the animals brought to the temple?*—To be sold as offerings and sacrifices to God, and for the food of the priests and people.

78. *What temple did our Lord refer to in verse 19?*—The temple of his own body.

79. *How does this verse illustrate John 10 : 18?*—Each verse shows his "power to take again" the body or life he had laid down.

80. *Who built the temple that was then standing?*—Ezra and Nehemiah.

81. *What proof of the omniscience of Jesus is in verse 25?*—"He knew what was in man."

JOHN 3.

82. *Who were the Pharisees?*—A sect of the Jews who "trusted in themselves that they were righteous, and despised others." Luke 18 : 9, 10.

83. *What recent miracles does Nicodemus refer to?*—Those related or referred to in John 2 : 2, 7–11, 23.

84. *Is there any exception to the necessity for the new birth?*—None.

85. *By whom are we born again?*—By the Holy Spirit.

86. *Who are the "we" of verse 11?*—Jesus and the Father.

87. *What fresh proof of the freeness of the gospel is there in verses 15 and 16?*—Jesus saying, that " *whosoever* believeth in him" shall " have everlasting life."

88. *What proof of salvation being a present blessing is there in verse 18?*—The saying of Jesus, that "He that believeth on him is not condemned," but (v. 30) "*hath* everlasting life."

89. *Why do we reject the Light of life?*—Because we love sin, or darkness, better.

90. *Who is the great Example of verse 21?*—Jesus himself.

91. *Who is the "bride" of verse 29?*—The Church or people of Christ.

92. *What is the meaning of the expression "set to his seal"?*—Shown his belief.

93. *What are the terrible consequences of unbelief?*—Being "condemned already" and under the abiding "wrath of God." Vs. 18, 36.

MARK 6 (MATTHEW 14, LUKE 3).

94. *Why was John imprisoned?*—Because of his faithful boldness in respect to Herod's unlawful marriage with his brother's wife. Mark 6 : 17, 18.

95. *Did not Herod's respect for John greatly add to*

his criminality?—It did, as it showed that his conscience told him John was right.

JOHN 4.

96. *Why must Jesus "needs go through Samaria"?*—Because it lay between. Vs. 3, 4.

97. *When was the parcel of ground sold to Jacob?*—Jacob bought it on his return from Laban, and probably gave it to Joseph as part of his dying blessing. Josh. 24 : 32.

98. *Why had the Jews no dealings with the Samaritans?*—Because they did not come to Jerusalem to worship. V. 20.

99. *Who were the Samaritans?*—Colonists from Assyria who worshiped God, but not like the Jews.

100. *Is not the freeness of the gospel again brought out in verse 10?*—Yes; the Samaritan woman, living in open sin, was welcome to the living water of the Spirit if she asked.

101. *What are the soul-satisfying effects of faith?*—The grace and comfort of the Holy Spirit. Vs. 13, 14.

102. *What proof of omniscience is there in this narrative?*—Jesus knowing the history of the woman's life. V. 18.

103. *What is the true worship which alone is acceptable to God?*—The worship of the heart. Vs. 23, 24.

104. *Compare verses 31–34 with Matt. 4 : 4.*—God's word is the food of the soul.

105. *What simple act of faith is recorded in verse 50?*—The nobleman's instant belief that Jesus had cured his child.

LUKE 4 (MATTHEW 4, MARK 1).

106. *Who are the "broken-hearted," verse 18?*—Those whose hearts are broken or crushed under godly sorrow for sin.

107. *What is the captivity referred to?*—To Satan, who leads his victims captive at his will.

108. *What is it to be blind to the truth?*—To be unwilling, and so unable, to see and receive it.

109. *Why is it called "the acceptable year of the Lord"?*—The time of grace (compared to the jubilee year), when God is ready to hear and to forgive. Isa. 1 : 18, etc.

110. *Why did our Lord not read the remainder of the verse?*—Because "the day of vengeance" was not yet come.

111. *Will not the time come when the rest of the sentence will be fulfilled?*—The day of the Lord will come as a thief in the night: in the which the heavens shall pass away with a great noise, and the elements shall melt with fervent heat, the earth also and the works that are therein shall be burned up. Seeing then that all these things shall be dissolved, what manner of persons ought ye to be in all holy conversation and godliness, looking for and hasting unto the coming of the day of God? 2 Pet. 3 : 10–12.

112. *Why did they wonder in verse 22?*—Because they knew him only as a Nazarene carpenter's son.

113. *Why did our Lord's declaration in verses 24–27 so excite their wrath?*—Because of their Jewish pride and contempt for all other people.

114. *Was Sarepta a Jewish town?*—No, a city of Sidon, in Phœnicia.

115. *Was Naaman a Jew?*—No, a Syrian.

LUKE 5 (MATTHEW 4, MARK 1).

116. *What proof of the power of Jesus does the draught of fishes show?*—By bringing the fish in great numbers where there were none the night before.

117. *Did not Peter's exclamation show how much he realized the divinity of our Lord?*—Yes; it made him deeply feel his own sinfulness in the presence of Christ's holiness and power.

118. *In what sense was Peter henceforth to catch men?* —By drawing them out of the world to Christ in the gospel net.

119. *What act of faith is recorded of the disciples?*— Their letting down their net, after a night of fruitless toil, at Jesus' word.

MARK 1: 29 (MATTHEW 8, LUKE 4).

120. *How do we see the completeness of the cure of Peter's wife's mother?*—She was able to wait upon them immediately.

121. *Why did they wait for sunset?*—Because it was the Sabbath-day. Mark 1: 32.

122. *Why did not Jesus allow the devils to speak?*— Perhaps because (as in the case of Paul and the female soothsayer) they might make it appear he was in league with them. Acts 16: 16–18.

123. *Who is the great Example of fervent prayer?*— Jesus, whose long and earnest prayers by day or night, and especially before great duties and events, are often named.

124. *What is meant by "all Syria" in Matt. 4: 24?* —That part of it which adjoined the Holy Land.

125. *Was there any need for the "if" in the leper's appeal, Mark 1: 40?*—No; and Christ is as willing now, as he is able now, to cleanse us from all sin.

126. *How could Jesus touch the leper without being himself rendered unclean?*—By his divine purity.

Command the children of Israel, that they put out of the camp every leper; that they defile not their camps, in the midst whereof I dwell. Num. 5: 2, 3.

127. *Is it not a proof of the immaculate purity of our Lord?*—Yes; we may conclude that, as he could not be defiled without, he must have been equally undefiled within.

128. *What offering was required by the law?*—Two lambs, doves or pigeons, with flour and oil. Lev. 14: 10, 21, 22.

MARK 2 (LUKE 5, MATTHEW 9).

129. *What proof of the connection between sin and suffering is there in Mark 2: 5?*—Jesus saying to the sick of the palsy, "Thy sins be forgiven thee."

130. *Why was not our Lord's forgiveness of sins blasphemy?*—Because he was God himself. Isa. 43: 25.

131. *What other proof of his Godhead does Mark 2: 8 contain?*—His knowledge of the people's thoughts.

132. *Why does Matthew, in chap. 9, verse 9, call himself by his common name, while in Mark and Luke he is called Levi?*—He calls himself Matthew from humility: he is called by his new name of Levi from respect.

JOHN 5.

133. *What proof of the connection between sin and suffering is there in verse 14?*—The warning of Jesus to the sick man to sin no more, lest a worse disease or thing should happen unto him.

134. *Does not verse 17 show that God cannot rest until redemption is accomplished?*—Yes; all his works, in providence and grace, show him to have that end in view.

135. *Compare verse 18 with Phil. 2: 6.*—Christ Jesus is there said to be "in the form of God" and "to be equal with God."

136. *Who is to be the Judge of all? and why?*—Christ is to be the Judge, that he may have equal honor with God. V. 23.

137. *Why is the verb in the present tense before "everlasting life," and in the future tense before "condemnation"?*—Because the everlasting life of believers is already begun, while condemnation is reserved for those who will not believe.

138. *What is the terrible alternative of resurrection unto life?*—Resurrection to damnation, to "shame and everlasting contempt." Dan. 12: 2.

139. *What is a fatal stumbling-block to faith?*—The preference of honor from men to honor from God.

140. *What confirmation of the inspiration of the Pentateuch is there in verse 46?*—Jesus quoting it as written of himself.

141. *What is the abiding testimony against the Jews' unbelief?*—The writings of Moses and the prophets, which testify of Christ.

MATTHEW 12 (MARK 2, LUKE 6).

142. *Were the disciples justified in taking the growing corn?*—They were.

When thou comest into the standing corn of thy neighbor, then thou mayest pluck the ears with thine hand; but thou shalt not move a sickle unto thy neighbor's standing corn. Deut. 23.

143. *How did the priests profane the Sabbath and remain blameless?*—They *appeared* to do so by killing the sacrifices on that day as on other days.

In the first day shall be an holy convocation; ye shall do no manner of servile work therein: but ye shall off r a sacrifice made by fire for a burnt-offering unto the Lord; two young bullocks, and one ram, and seven lambs. Num. 28: 18, 19.

144. *What is taught of the nature of the Sabbath in Mark 2: 27?*—That "the sabbath was made for man, and not man for the sabbath;" the day being appointed, even in Paradise, as a day of rest; and being now a blessed season of rest of body and mind from earthly care and pleasure and toil—a time of special regard to the interests of our immortal souls, and of kind offices to the souls and bodies of our fellow-men.

145. *What was the shew-bread?*—An important offering.

Thou shalt take fine flour, and bake twelve cakes thereof. And thou shalt set them in two rows, six on a row, upon the pure table before the Lord. And thou shalt put pure frankincense upon each row, that it may be on the bread for a memorial, even an offering made by fire unto the Lord. Every sabbath he shall set it in order before the Lord continually, being taken from the children of Israel by an everlasting covenant. And it shall be Aaron's and his sons'; and they shall eat it in the holy place: for it is most holy unto him of the offerings of the Lord made by fire by a perpetual statute. Lev. 24: 5–9.

146. *What is meant by a "bruised reed" and "smoking flax"?*—The conscience-stricken and spiritually distressed and the weak in faith.

MATTHEW 5 (LUKE 6).

147. *To whom was the sermon on the mount addressed?* —To the disciples of Jesus.

148. *Who are "the poor in spirit"?*—The humble-minded.

149. *What is the "mourning" referred to?*—Mourning for sin and for the low state of the Church. Isa. 61: 2, 3.

150. *What is meekness?*—Patience under provocation, after the example of Christ, "who, when he was reviled, reviled not again." 1 Pet. 2: 23.

151. *What is it to hunger and thirst after anything?*— To greatly long for it and to seek and strive to obtain it.

152. *Who are the "merciful"?*—Those who are kind to the poor, the "hungry" and the "afflicted." Isa. 58: 10, 11.

153. *What is it to be "pure in heart"?*—To have that "holiness without which no man shall see the Lord." Heb. 12: 14.

154. *Why are the "peacemakers" so distinguished?*— Because of the difficulty of making and keeping peace, and as Christ is the Prince of peace.

If it be possible, as much as lieth in you, live peaceably with all men. Rom. 12 : 18.

155. *How does our Lord connect his disciples with himself in Matt. 5 : 11?*—By promising them a blessing upon all that they endured for his sake.

156. *What great lesson of mutual forgiveness does Matt. 5 : 23–26 contain?*—That we should come to the worship and service of God in peace and reconciliation with our fellow-men.

157. *What rule against trifling with evil is contained in Matt. 5 : 29, 30?*—That we should make any sacrifice to be free from sin.

158. *What lesson against procrastination is there in Matt. 5 : 25?*—We may learn, if we are living in enmity toward God, our Judge, to be earnest in seeking reconciliation with him, through Christ, while we have time.

159. *What lesson of the largeness of the love of God have we in Matt. 5 : 45 and Luke 6 : 35?*—"He is kind" to "the unthankful" and "evil," and pours his daily blessings alike upon the wicked and the good.

160. *Compare Matt. 5 : 48 with Luke 6 : 36.*—We should strive to be like our heavenly Father in holiness and mercy.

MATTHEW 6.

161. *Does not the first precept commend itsey ,o our consciences?*—It does, or should do. The eye and favor of God should be our chief thought and aim.

162. *Compare the reward of verse 2 with that of verse 4.*—The hypocrite's reward is the present and fleeting one of honor from men, while the true Christian's reward (besides peace and blessing upon earth) is the eternal one of glory in heaven.

163. *What encouragement for our imperfect petitions is there in verse 8?*—That our heavenly Father knows what we have need of before we ask.

164. *How do the first words of the Lord's Prayer adapt it to the whole family of man?*—They show that we have "all one Father."

165. *What is it to "hallow" anything?*—To treat it as holy.

166. *How are we taught that we must render practical obedience to the will of God?*—By the standard of the obedience of the angels in heaven. V. 10.

167. *Does not verse 11 refer to the daily supply of manna?*—It does, and teaches us not to be over-thoughtful about to-morrow's supply.

168. *What striking condition is added to the petition for forgiveness of our trespasses?*—That we should forgive those who have trespassed against us.

169. *Give an example of the sort of temptation intended here.*—The tempting or trying of the faith of Abraham by requiring Isaac's life. Gen. 22 : 1.

170. *How can we judge whether we love God?*—By thinking where our chief treasure is, whether on earth or in heaven. V. 21.

171. *Who takes care of our lives?*—Our heavenly Father. Vs. 26, 30, 32, 33.

MATTHEW 7 (LUKE 6).

172. *What lesson of self-examination do the first five verses convey?*—Lest we should condemn our neighbor, while we are worse ourselves.

173. *What is the meaning of the strait gate?*—The narrow entrance into heaven, which, "though wide enough for any sinner, is too strait for any sin."

174. *Is there any immediate sign of danger in the broad road?*—No, not to the eye of the thoughtless worldly man.

175. *Should not our Lord's declaration in Matt. 7 : 14 excite us to make diligent search?*—Yes, that we are among the few in the narrow way.

176. *What lesson do we learn about our conduct in Matt. 7 : 16 and following verses?*—That we shall be judged by our conduct, rather than our profession—by our fruits rather than our leaves.

LUKE 7 (MATTHEW 8).

177. *What was the particular feature of the centurion's faith?*—It was humble and strong, and was the faith of a Gentile, and not of a Jew.

178. *What practical answer did Jesus give to John the Baptist's messengers?*—That they were to conclude he was the Messiah from the miracles he did and the prophecies he fulfilled. Luke 7 : 21.

179. *How does our Lord sum up his reference to the greatness of John the Baptist?*—By saying that the least of those in the kingdom of Christ were greater even than John.

180. *What does Luke 7 : 35 refer to?*—To the wisdom of God, as shown in the conduct of Christ and of John, being seen and acknowledged by all God's people.

MATTHEW 11 : 20.

181. *May we not apply these woes to our own country and time?*—Yes, with still greater truth.

182. *What state of heart is specially inculcated in verses 25–30?*—Humility, teachableness and meekness.

183. *What blessing is vouchsafed to those who take Christ's yoke upon them?*—The blessing of rest in Christ from self-righteous and worldly labors and cares.

LUKE 7 : 36.

184. *In what manner did they sit at table?*—They reclined on sofas round it.

185. *What was the reason for the omission of providing water for his feet?*—Abraham offered water for his visitors' feet (Gen. 18 : 4), but Simon had invited Jesus from curiosity alone, and did not care to show him respect.

LUKE 12 : 14 (MATTHEW 12, MARK 3).

186. *What was Beelzebub?*—The fly-god of Ekron, in Philistia. 2 Kings 1 : 2.

187. *What proof of our Lord's omniscience is there in Luke 11 : 17–20?*—His knowing the people's thoughts.

MATTHEW 12 : 31–37 (MARK 3).

188. *Who will judge our words?*—Christ, at the day of judgment, even every idle word.

189. *How do we see that the closest family relationships are subordinate to discipleship?*—By Christ's saying that those who did his Father's will were to him as brother and sister and mother. Matt. 12 : 46–50.

LUKE 11 : 37.

190. *Who were the scribes and lawyers?*—Persons who copied and explained the law.

LUKE 12 : 1.

191. *What is "the leaven" of the Pharisees?*—Their bad principles and influence and hypocrisy. Matt. 16 : 6.

192. *Whom does Christ advise us to fear? and why?*—God, who has power to cast into hell. Luke 12 : 5.

193. *What proof of God's overruling providence have we in verse 6?*—Even sparrows not being forgotten by him.

194. *What blessing is promised to the confession of Christ?*—Those who are not afraid or ashamed to acknowledge Christ upon earth will be acknowledged by him before all the angels at the last day.

195. *Against what are we warned in verses 17–20?*—Against the love of the riches and pleasures of the world.

196. *What does the soul's "being required" mean?*—Being called away from earth to its great account.

197. *What is it to be "rich toward God"?*—To be full of love to him and of good works for his sake.

198. *What is it to have a treasure in the heavens?*—To have Christ there as our own Saviour, and all his riches as our own through him.

199. *What great event is involved in the exhortation to "watch"?*—The sudden coming of our Lord.

200. *What responsibility is attached to knowing the Lord's will?*—The doing it.

201. *What is the meaning of verse 49?*—It may refer to the "fire" of "the Holy Ghost," "the spirit of burning" (Isa. 4 : 4), and to the gospel of peace being made an occasion of burning hatred among the families and nations of men. Matt. 3 : 11.

LUKE 13.

202. *What is the call to repentance in verses 1–9?*—The sudden death of others and the gracious sparing of our own lives are solemn calls upon us to repent, lest we likewise perish.

MATTHEW 13 (MARK 4, LUKE 8).

203. *Who are they that receive the gospel?*—Those who truly receive it are those who receive it into their hearts, as seed into good ground, and show its effects in their lives. V. 8.

204. *What is the fate of the tares?*—To be burned.

205. *What is meant by the harvest?*—The judgment-day. V. 30.

206. *What is meant by the barn?*—The heavenly treasure-house and home.

207. *Who are the reapers?*—The angels.

208. *How are the tares described?*—As the children of the wicked one. V. 38.

MATTHEW 8 (MARK 4, LUKE 8).

209. *What proof have we in Matt 8 : 20 of the poverty of our Lord?*—He had not where to lay his head.

210. *What do we learn from our Lord's calling the conduct of the disciples before the stilling of the tempest an act of little faith?*—That we ought to have strong faith at all times in his goodness and power.

MARK 5 (MATTHEW 8, LUKE 8).

211. *Was it lawful for the Jews to trade in swine?*—It was not.

212. *How does Mark 5 : 17 illustrate John 3 : 19?*—It shows that they did not wish their evil deeds to be brought to light.

LUKE 5 : 29 (MATTHEW 9, MARK 2).

213. *Compare Luke 5 : 30 with 1 Tim 1 : 15.*—Jesus ate and drank with "sinners," because he came into the world to "seek" and "save" them.

214. *Of what material were the wine-bottles made?*—Of skins or leather.

MARK 5 : 22 (MATTHEW 9, LUKE 8).

215. *What was the reason of the poor woman's timid and almost stealthy manner of approaching Christ?*—Because a person with her disease was ordered to be kept separate, and was considered unclean.

216. *What was the difference between the touch of the thronging multitude and that of the woman?*—Hers was the touch of faith.

217. *Ought the death of the little girl to have made them give up hope after having applied to Jesus?*—No, for Jesus was coming, and He who could cure could also restore to life.

218. *What is death called in Mark 5 : 39?*—A "sleep," from which Jesus could "awake." John 11 : 11.

219. *Was the life thus miraculously restored independent of natural circumstances for its preservation?*—No; Jesus ordered her something to eat.

MATTHEW 9 : 27.

220. *What was the proof of the faith of the blind men?*—They acknowledged Jesus to be Christ, the Son of David; and they prayed and persevered.

221. *May we not secure the same blessing if we use the same means?*—We may.

MARK 6 (MATTHEW 13).

222. *Why did Jesus refrain from doing his mighty works?*—Because of their obstinate unbelief.

223. *What ought to be the effect of our Lord's miracles on us?*—To strengthen our faith. Mark 6 : 6.

224. *To what are sheep having no shepherd exposed?*—To be "scattered" and destroyed: and we, who are by nature as "sheep going astray," should be deeply thankful to Him who came to seek and to save. Matt. 9 : 36: Isa. 53 : 6.

225. *Is the harvest yet all gathered in?*—No; the invitation of the gospel is still, "Whosoever will, let him take the water of life freely."

MATTHEW 10 (MARK 6, LUKE 9).

226. *Compare Matt. 10 : 8 with Acts 20 : 33–35?*—The words, "Freely ye have received, freely give," and "It is more blessed to give than to receive," convey the same truth.

227. *Who would provide for the destitute disciples?*—Christ undertook to provide for them.

228. *Why are Sodom and Gomorrah used to point the terrors of the Lord's denunciation?*—Because the privileges and opportunities of Sodom and Gomorrah were not so great as those of cities of our Lord's time and of our own.

229. *What is the end spoken of in Matt. 10 : 22?*—The end of life.

230. *Compare Matt. 10 : 36 with Mic. 7 : 6.*—The words are almost exactly the same, showing the hostility to true religion in every age.

231. *Is taking the cross only the endurance of petty vexations, or does it represent the preliminary of ignominy and death?*—It includes every trial, small or great, that God appoints.

232. *What is the meaning of finding life in Matt. 10 : 39?*—Saving one's earthly life by giving up Christ.

233. *What encouragement have we for active love to the Lord's people?*—Christ's assurance that the giver of even a cup of cold water to one of his disciples shall not lose his reward.

MARK 6 : 14 (MATTHEW 14, LUKE 9).

234. *What was the testimony of Herod's conscience when he heard of our Lord's miracles?*—That they were done by John, whom he had beheaded, and who (he believed) had risen from the dead.

235. *Who was Herodias?*—His brother Philip's wife.

236. *Why does Herodias say "by and by"?*—Because she knew that John's prison was at some distance.

237. *Was John imprisoned at the place where these festivities were held?*—No—at Machærus, on the Dead Sea.

238. *Ought the disciples to have been so surprised at our Lord's walking on the water?*—No; they ought to have remembered his former miracles. Mark 6 : 52.

239. *What was the power that enabled Peter to walk on the water?*—The power of Christ, that gave him faith and help. Matt. 14 : 28–31.

240. *What was Peter's cause of failure?*—His faith being weak and giving way. Matt. 14 : 31.

241. *Was Jesus ready to save?*—Yes, immediately. Matt. 14:31.

JOHN 6:22.

242. *How did our Lord rebuke the insincerity of those who came seeking him?*—By telling them that they came for the sake of the loaves he had fed them with.

243. *What is the meaning of the "meat which perisheth"?*—Worldly comforts and riches.

244. *What is the meaning of the word "sealed" in verse 27?*—Stamped or approved as his own by the miracles he wrought.

245. *Does not verse 28 show how ready we are to bring our works before God?*—In verse 28 they asked what they should do.

246. *Does not verse 29 show the true simplicity of the way of life?*—Yes; it is only to "repent and believe" (Mark 1:15), when all good works will follow.

247. *What was the nature of the Jews' demand in verse 30 after beholding his mighty miracles?*—A dissatisfied and unbelieving one.

248. *What bread were the Jews willing to accept?*—Bread from heaven.

249. *Is there not in Jesus what will completely satisfy the soul?*—Yes; he is the bread of life, that satisfies all hunger and thirst. V. 35.

250. *What gracious assurance of acceptance have we in coming to Christ?*—That he "will in no wise cast out." V. 37.

251. *How many times does our Lord repeat the promise of the resurrection in this chapter?*—Four times. Vs. 39, 40, 44, 54.

252. *How do we know that everlasting life may be our present possession?*—From Jesus saying that "he that believeth on" him "hath everlasting life." Vs. 47–51.

253. *Do not many now fall into the same mistake as the Jews of old in supposing the Lord's literal body was intended?*—Yes; papists and their imitators believe that the consecrated bread they eat is the body of Christ, who is in heaven. The true Protestant feeds daily and hourly upon Christ himself, but only by faith. V. 53.

254. *What antidote have we to this error in verse 63?*—The lesson that it is the Spirit only that gives life to what is written.

MARK 7 (MATTHEW 15).

255. *Did the traditions of the elders always correspond with the law of God?*—No; they made it of no effect. Mark 7:7–13.

256. *What lesson of the necessity of sincerity in dealing with God do verses 6 and 7 contain?*—The warning that he knows the heart, and that all hypocritical worship is "vain."

257. *What is the sentence passed upon false teachers in Matt. 15:14?*—That they and their followers would perish together.

258. *Do we really believe that our hearts are the abodes of all these terrible evils?*—If we did, we should keep our hearts with more diligence than we do. Mark 7:21–23.

259. *Were Tyre and Sidon Jewish cities?*—No; they were on the sea-coast, to the north-west.

260. *Who were meant by the "children" in Mark 7:27?*—The Jews. Matt. 15:24, 26.

261. *Is there any limit to the power of faith?*—No; it takes hold of the power of God. Mark 7:29

262. *Why did Jesus sigh?*—He was oppressed with their unbelief. Mark 7:34.

263. *What does the word "Ephphatha" show us of the dialect in which our Lord usually conversed?*—That it was Syriac he spoke. Mark 5:41.

MARK 8 (MATTHEW 15 AND 16).

264. *Were not the doubts of the disciples wonderful after their experience of the previous miracles?*—They were indeed, but we do just the same.

265. *May we not learn a lesson from their unbelief?*—Yes, to trust God, at all times, to give us whatever is good for us.

266. *Compare Matt. 16:18, 19; 1 Cor. 3:11; Acts 4:11, 12; and Eph. 2:20.*—The true Church is built, not on Peter himself, as the papists suppose, but on the truth contained in what he had said about Christ, even upon the foundation of the apostles and prophets, Jesus Christ himself being the chief corner-stone. Neither is there salvation in any other: for there is none other Name under heaven given among men, whereby we must be saved. For other foundation can no man lay than that which is laid, which is Jesus Christ.

267. *What remarkable rebuke was addressed to Peter soon after his noble confession?*—"Get thee behind me, Satan!"

268. *What is the meaning of the word "savorest"?*—Likest or mindest.

269. *What explanation of Mark 8:36 is found in Luke 5:25?*—What is a man advantaged if he gain the whole world, and lose himself or be cast away.

MARK 9 (MATTHEW 17, LUKE 9).

270. *Is there any other testimony to Jesus as the "beloved Son," Mark 9:7?*—Yes, at his baptism. Matt. 3:17.

271. *What are we enjoined to do in Mark 9:7?*—To hear him.

272. *Whom did our Lord mean when he said, "Elias is indeed come"?*—John the Baptist.

273. *Why were the people amazed?*—Because of the remaining glory of his appearance. V. 15; compare v. 3.

274. *Why could not the disciples cure the demoniac?*—From want of faith and prayer. Mark 9:18, 19, 23, 24, 29.

275. *Compare Mark 9:19 with Num. 14:11, 27.*—They contain the same complaint of unbelief, notwithstanding "all the signs which" God had "showed among them."

276. *Did not the poor father's faith almost fail?*—Yes; he doubted Jesus' power. Mark 9:22.

277. *How did Jesus strengthen it?*—By telling him that "all things were possible to him that believeth."

278. *Where does Jesus foretell his death and resurrection besides Mark 9:31?*—In John 2:19, 21, when he spoke of raising up the temple of his body in three days.

MATTHEW 17:24 (MARK 9).

279. *What was this tribute-money?*—"Half a shekel," or about thirty cents, "for the offering of the Lord" or the service of the temple. Ex. 30:13; 2 Chron. 24:9.

280. *What is the meaning of "prevented"?*—"Anticipated" what Peter was going to say.

281. *What lesson of considerateness does the Lord of all teach us?*—Not to give needless offence, especially in little matters.

282. *What do we learn from the "piece of money" being the exact amount claimed for Peter and our Lord?*—Perhaps that Jesus had miraculously brought the exact coin required into the fish's mouth.

MARK 9:33 (MATTHEW 18, LUKE 9).

283. *What lesson did our Lord teach in Mark 9:35–37?*—Humility.

284. *What great reward is promised to those who learn this lesson?*—All the blessings that follow from receiving Christ and being his.

285. *Is not all intolerance discouraged in Mark 9 : 39?* —Yes; when we feel assured of any one that he is a true servant of Christ, we should not disown him because he does not agree on all religious subjects with ourselves.

286. *Are great deeds done for Christ the only ones accepted by him?*—No; even the giving of a cup of water for Christ's sake shall have its reward.

287. *What further lesson have we against all persecution?*—That any one who wilfully injures a young, weak or lowly believer in Jesus is liable to a greater punishment than even loss of life. Mark 9 : 42.

288. *How are we to deal with our sins?*—To give them up, and every help or temptation to them, at any cost.

289. *Are any of them to be tenderly dealt with?*—No; all of them firmly, promptly and decidedly.

MATTHEW 18 : 10.

290. *How do we see the care of our Lord over the least of his disciples?*—By his appointing angels to watch over them.

291. *Are there any exceptions to verse 11?*—No; all are lost, and all may be saved.

292. *What condition of the sheep led to the exercise of the Shepherd's love?*—Their being gone astray.

293. *How does our Lord inculcate the duty of mutual forbearance and forgiveness?*—By calling upon the injured to strive to gain over the offender by a quiet appeal to him when alone.

294. *To whom in another Gospel was the promise in verse 18 given?*—To the disciples generally, and not to Peter only. John 20 : 23; Matt. 16 : 19.

295. *Is there any limitation to the two blessed promises in verses 19, 20?*—Only that what we ask of God must be "according to his will." 1 John 5 : 14.

296. *What was the utmost extent of forgiveness that seemed possible to Peter?*—Forgiving seven times.

297. *Did the estimate of Jesus agree with him?*—No; he ordered us to forgive seventy times seven.

298. *In the parable, verse 23, what was the amount of the debt, at £187 10 each talent?*—Nearly ten million dollars.

299. *Does not this show the incalculable claims that God has upon us for breaches of only the first commandment?*—It may well do so.

300. *Do we not also see the entire freeness of the divine forgiveness:*—Yes, as compassion alone forgave the debt.

301. *Are we not called upon to imitate the long-suffering of God?*—We are indeed; and if we know ourselves forgiven by him, we shall certainly do so.

302. *Where do we learn that the merciful God is also a God of judgment?*—In the same parable, by his sentence on the ungrateful and unforgiving servant. V. 34.

JOHN 7.

303. *What was the "feast of tabernacles"?*—In the fifteenth day of the seventh month, when ye have gathered in the fruit of the land, ye shall keep a feast unto the Lord seven days: and ye shall take you on the first day the boughs of goodly trees, branches of palm trees, and the boughs of thick trees, and willows of the brook; and ye shall rejoice before the Lord your God seven days. Lev. 23 : 39, 40.

304. *What hidden motives influenced the relatives of Jesus in their advice to our Lord?*—To bring him into danger and expose him if he were a deceiver, and to cause him to proclaim himself as king for their worldly benefit if he were really the Messiah.

LUKE 9 : 51.

305. *Why is the term "steadfastly" used?*—Because Jesus knew all the sufferings that would come upon him.

306. *What example of meekness did our Lord show?*—By not punishing the Samaritans for their inhospitable conduct.

307. *Who are the dead that are to bury their dead?*-The dead in sin.

308. *Why is it particularly hurtful to look back while ploughing?*—Because you may lose the right course.

LUKE 10.

309. *Do not the directions to the Seventy show the daily and hourly care of the Master?*—Yes, for their bodily comfort as well as for their ministerial success.

310. *How was Capernaum exalted to heaven?*—As a prosperous city, that had enjoyed the privilege of Christ's preaching.

311. *What proof have we in verse 16 of the union between Christ and his people?*—His saying that the hearing or despising of his ministers was the hearing or despising of himself.

LUKE 17 : 11.

312. *Why did the lepers stand "afar off"?*—Because they were obliged by law to keep separate from others.

313. *Why were they to show themselves to the priests?*—First, to know if they were lepers; and afterward, to know if they were healed. Lev. 13 : 2.

314. *Was their cleansing previous to or after they had acted in faith?*—After they had showed their faith by calling upon Jesus for mercy.

315. *Did the ingratitude of the nine hinder their blessing?*—It did not make Jesus recall their cure.

JOHN 7 : 11.

316. *Why were the people afraid of the Jews?*—"Lest they should be put out of the synagogue," or excommunicated, if they confessed themselves followers of Christ. Acts 5 : 13.

317. *What remarkable connection is there between obedience and the knowledge of right doctrine?*—The man who really desires to do God's will shall understand the truth and meaning of his word. V. 17.

318. *Whom did the people mean by the "very Christ"?*—The true Messiah.

319. *What was the hinderance of verse 34?*—Insincerity and worldly motives.

320. *Who are the "dispersed"?*—The scattered Israelites. V. 35.

321. *Could the Jews bear to think that the gospel was to be preached to the Gentiles?*—No; they were too jealous, selfish and proud to think it.

322. *What is it to come to Jesus and drink?*—To receive him as our Saviour, and so to satisfy all the longings of the thirsty soul.

323. *Who was referred to as "the prophet"?*—The one that Moses said God would "raise up" like unto himself. Deut. 18 : 15, 18.

324. *What is meant by "the law" in verse 49?*—The law of Moses and the writings of the prophets.

325. *Had not the interview with Jesus strengthened the faith of Nicodemus?*—Yes, for he took Jesus' part. Vs. 50, 51.

326. *Was Galilee held in honor by the Jews?*—No; it was despised.

327. *Where was the search to be made?*—In the Scriptures, which spoke (Isa. 9 : 1, 2) of "Galilee" as a land of "darkness." V. 52.

JOHN 8.

328. *What striking instance of the power of conscience when under the eye of the Judge of all the earth is there in verse 9?*—The sinful accusers of the adulterous woman going out of his presence, every one.

329. *In what condition are they who walk without th*

Light of life?—In darkness now, and in the way to "blackness of darkness for ever."

330. *What is it to "judge after the flesh"?*—To judge by outward appearances and worldly notions.

331. *How are we to know God the Father?*—In and through Jesus Christ. V. 19.

332. *What does our Lord mean by being "lifted up"?*—Being raised on the cross.

333. *How is verse 29 full of blessing?*—It shows how completely our blessed Saviour is accepted by God, and what grace and help his people may have through him.

334. *How did verse 33 agree with the payment to the Roman emperor?*—Not at all, being an idle boast of the Jews.

335. *What were the works of Abraham?*—The "obedience of faith," which should have led the Jews to believe and obey Christ.

336. *Who alone can say, "Who convinceth me of sin"?*—Jesus only.

337. *What example of grace is there in verse 49?*—The gentleness of Jesus' reply to so shameful an accusation.

338. *Is death of the body referred to in verse 51?*—No—the death or ruin of the soul, "the second or everlasting death."

339. *How did Abraham see the "day of Christ"?*—By the far-seeing eye of faith, looking at the promises of God.

340. *Why did the Jews say "fifty years old"?*—Because "his visage was so marred" by privation and suffering that he looked older than he was. Isa. 52:14.

341. *What does our Lord mean by "I am"?*—That he was *always* in being, from all eternity; as God called himself to Moses, "I AM." Ex. 3:14.

342. *Why did he not say "I was"?*—Because "I am" is a stronger expression of eternal being, and also made him equal with God.

LUKE 10:20.

343. *Is anything to be reserved in obeying the two great commandments?*—No; they require the love of the whole heart.

344. *What is the lesson taught by the parable?*—How to reduce to practice God's commands, and how far we must always fall short of entire obedience to his will. We shall never *do* and live; we must *believe* and live.

345. *What is the "one thing needful"?*—To come to Christ for salvation of the soul. V. 42.

346. *What is the true cause of rejoicing?*—That we have found Christ, and have our names written in heaven. V. 20.

347. *What was the cause of our Lord's joy?*—The bringing of his humble disciples to the saving knowledge of the truth.

LUKE 11.

348. *Compare verses 2-4 with Matt. 6:9-13?*—We may use our Lord's Prayer, or pray in our own words after its manner, placing the concerns of God before our own.

349. *How should we use importunity in prayer?*—By feeling and speaking earnestly and perseveringly, as those who will not be denied whatever it may be God's will to grant.

JOHN 9.

350. *What did our Lord mean by verse 3.*—That the blindness gave an opportunity of showing the power of God.

351. *What does our Lord mean by day and night?*—Life as the time of working for God, and death as the rest from our labor.

352. *What is meant by expulsion from the synagogue?*—Not allowing attendance at the chief place of religious meeting, and so bringing disgrace and distress, and some social privations besides.

353. *What proof of our Lord's divine nature is there in verses 36-38?*—His allowing himself to be worshiped as the Son of God.

JOHN 10.

354. *What sort of sheepfolds were in use in Palestine?*—Uncovered enclosures in the pasture-grounds for the protection of the sheep at night.

355. *What is promised to those who enter in by the door?*—Those ministers and teachers who are called and qualified by the Holy Spirit may expect a blessing on their work.

356. *What was our Lord's solemn object in coming into the world?*—To lay down his life in order to give life. Vs. 15, 10.

357. *How is the atonement taught in verses 11, 15-18?*—By Jesus saying that he laid down his "life for the sheep," or in their stead, that they might live.

358. *What was the feast of the dedication?*—It was kept in memory of God's delivery of the temple from King Antiochus. 1 Mac. 4:52-59; 2 Mac. 10:5-8.

359. *What is the security of the Lord's true people?*—His own assurance that they shall never perish. Vs. 27, 28.

360. *Why cannot the Scripture be broken?*—Because it is the word of God.

361. *What is the special use of miracles?*—To prove a commission from God, and to give divine authority to what is spoken in his name. Vs. 22-42.

JOHN 11.

362. *What interesting fact about sickness do we learn in verse 4?*—That the sickness of God's people is for his glory.

363. *What is taught us about the right use of opportunity in verses 9, 10?*—That time and opportunity will soon be at an end.

364. *How is death spoken of?*—As a sleep in the case of the people of God, as they will awake and arise to a new and spiritual life.

365. *What does Thomas mean in verse 16?*—That he expected Jesus would be killed by the Jews.

366. *How was Jesus himself the resurrection and the life?*—Because his people, by their union with him, have a glorious resurrection to eternal life.

367. *Who are the dead spoken of in verse 25?*—"The dead in Christ." 1 Thess. 4:16.

368. *Who are the living who shall never die?*—Those who "are alive" at "the coming of the Lord." 1 Thess. 4:17.

369. *What proof of our Lord's true humanity is there in verse 35?*—His weeping at the grave.

370. *Are not Caiaphas and Balaam examples of unbelieving prophets?*—Yes; God merely "put a word in Balaam's mouth," for he "loved the wages of unrighteousness," and he afterward died in battle among the enemies of God. Num. 33:5, 16; 2 Pet. 2:15.

LUKE 13:10.

371. *Does not the readiness of the poor woman to glorify God after being healed account for the omission of any mention of her previous faith?*—No doubt it does.

372. *Who is said to be the author of such affliction?*—Satan. V. 16.

373. *What constitutes the inability of verse 24?*—No want of power or will on the part of God, but a want of will in man from long indulgence in sin—an inability from not casting off all sin or from coming too late.

374. *Is there not a limit to the day of grace?*—Yes;

"*now* is the accepted time." Every day's continuance in an unconverted state, every day's indulgence in a sinful world, only makes the heart more hard.

375. *Who are they that will be rejected?*—Those who neglect or refuse to be received and saved.

376. *What is the meaning of verse 30?*—The Jews, who were the first to receive the light of the truth, give place to the Gentiles, who were the last.

377. *What does our Lord mean in verse 33?*—That he would be safe for the short time he remained in Galilee.

378. *Compare verse 35 with Luke 19 : 38.*—The disciples used these words as Jesus afterward entered into Jerusalem. The whole verse (35) may also be a prophecy of the present unbelief and future conversion of the Jews.

LUKE 14.

379. *What might be lawfully done on the Sabbath-day?* —Works of necessity and mercy.

380. *How do we know that this lesson of humility may be applied to ourselves?*—By our consciousness of the natural pride of our own hearts. V. 11.

381. *Who are meant by the invited guests? and to whom was the offer of mercy conveyed on* their rejection *of it?*—The Jews. The Gentiles. Vs. 16–24.

382. *Were not the excuses made by the guests very hollow?*—Yes; they showed their worldly minds.

383. *What comforting assurance is there in verse 22?* —There is always room at the gospel feast and in the heavenly mansions for all who will come.

384. *Is it an easy thing to be a disciple of Jesus?* —No; it requires a readiness to sacrifice not only our sins, but our affections and our lives, to the love of God and the salvation of our souls. Vs. 26, 27.

LUKE 15.

385. *What important truth does verse 2 contain?*— That it is the blessed character of Christ that he receives sinners coming to him with the burden of their sins.

386. *How do we learn our preciousness in the sight of God?*—By the joy in heaven that a repenting sinner creates. Vs. 7, 10.

387. *To what extremity was the prodigal son reduced in the service of sin and Satan?*—He had spent all, and was perishing with hunger, and no man gave unto him.

388. *Can we be said to be in our right mind when we are afar off from God?*—No; our hearts and minds are willfully blinded and deceived, and the grace of God alone can bring us to ourselves. V. 17.

389. *What difference is there between what the prodigal intended to say and what he actually said?*—He intended, in the deep penitence of his heart, to have asked to be one of his father's servants.

390. *Did the father's love give him time to say the rest?*—No; and *so* ready is our *heavenly* Father to welcome his repenting and returning sons.

391. *How is the sinner returning to God described?*— As dead and lost, and then alive and found. V. 32.

LUKE 16.

392. *What principle did the unjust steward act upon?* —Upon the worldly and sinful one of making friends by any means, whether good or bad.

393. *What is meant by serving mammon?*—Seeking riches or the favor of the world.

394. *Does God's judgment of human affairs correspond with our judgment of them?*—No, for he judges by the heart. V. 15.

395. *What is the lesson to be learned from the parable of the rich man and Lazarus?*—To take care, if we are rich, to make a good use of our riches, and, whether rich or poor, to have a treasure in heaven.

396. *What responsibility is connected with the possession of the Scriptures?*—To "search" them, "receive" them and obey them, as "able to save" our "souls." V. 31.

LUKE 17.

397. *What measure of faith was required to do the mighty works mentioned in verse 6?*—A very small measure, as it takes hold of the omnipotence of God.

398. *Does obedience warrant self-exaltation?*—No; at the best we can but do our duty, and can never repay God's mercy. Vs. 9, 10.

399. *What is the meaning of the kingdom of God being "within" us?*—It means God's rule in the hearts of his people, producing "righteousness and peace and joy in the Holy Ghost." Rom. 14 : 17.

400. *Will there be any remarkable difference in the state of society at the time of the coming judgment?*— It will be still the same as in former judgments, though a larger proportion of persons (vs. 34–36) may now be in the number of the saved. Vs. 26, etc.

401. *What is the lesson of Lot's wife?*—To escape for our lives, and not to look back to the world.

LUKE 18.

402. *What does the parable of the importunate widow teach?*—That we should continue to pray and never faint.

403. *Notice the solemn observation at the end of verse 8.*—There will be such "a falling away first" that faith in Christ as a Saviour, or the faith that looks for his coming, will scarcely be found.

404. *What should we learn from the parable of the Pharisee and the publican?*—To be penitently humble, instead of self-righteously proud.

405. *What state of the heart is acceptable in God's sight?*—The sacrifices of God are a broken spirit; a broken and a contrite heart, O God, thou wilt not despise. Ps. 51 : 17. For thus saith the high and lofty One that inhabiteth eternity, whose name is Holy; I dwell in the high and holy place, with him also that is of a contrite and humble spirit, to revive the spirit of the humble, and to revive the heart of the contrite ones. Isa. 57 : 15. The Lord is nigh unto them that are of a broken heart; and saveth such as be of a contrite spirit. Ps. 34 : 18.

406. *What is the teaching in verse 17?*—To humbly accept God's way of salvation by faith, however lowering to human pride.

407. *Was not our Lord's question in verse 19 put with the hope of eliciting a confession of his personal Godhead?* —Yes, as the ruler does not seem to have looked upon Jesus as more than man.

408. *Is the possession of wealth always a blessing?*— No; it is always a temptation and snare, often our ruin, and very seldom a blessing. Vs. 22, 23.

409. *How do we learn the deep-rooted nature of covetousness?*—By our Lord's description of the extreme difficulty of a rich man's entering into the kingdom of God. Vs. 25, 26.

410. *What is to be understood by the "world to come"?* —The state or time after death. V. 30.

MATTHEW 20 (MARK 10, LUKE 18).

411. *What does the parable of the householder teach as to God's sovereignty?*—"That God is debtor unto no man," and gives to all as he thinks fit.

412. *What is true humility?*—Being ready to be last of all and servant of all. Matt. 20 : 26.

413. *How did the blind men prove the sincerity of their faith?*—By their persevering prayers to Jesus as the Christ, the son of David. Matt. 20 : 31.

LUKE 19.

414. *How did our Lord respond to the faith of Zaccheus?*—By noticing him and making himself a guest at his house. V. 5.

415. *What do we learn of the practices of the tax-gatherers?*—That they were in the habit of taking more than was due. V. 8.

416. *For what did Jesus come into the world?*—To seek and to save the lost. V. 10.

417. *What is the object of the parable of the nobleman?*—To impress upon us the duty of using our time and talents and opportunities to God's glory and in remembrance of our final account.

418. *How did our Lord assert his divine authority?*—By telling his disciples to say, concerning the colt, that the Lord had need of it. V. 31.

419. *What special miracle was the occasion of the exultation of the people?*—Vs. 37, 38. The people that was with him when he called Lazarus out of his grave, and raised him from the dead, bare record. For this cause the people also met him, for that .they heard that he had done this miracle. John 12 : 17, 18.

420. *How may we learn the convincing nature of the miracles of our Lord?*—By our Lord's assertion that if men did not acknowledge them, the very stones would cry out. V. 40.

421. *How was our Lord's prophecy about Jerusalem fulfilled?*—In its destruction by the Romans within forty years after.

422. *What remarkable act of authority is recorded in verse 45 and in Mark 11 : 15, 16?*—Jesus sending the buyers and sellers and money-changers out of the temple.

MARK 11 : 20 (MATTHEW 21).

423. *What is declared to be the power of faith?*—The obtaining whatever we desire that is according to God's will. Mark 11 : 22–24.

424. *Is a spirit of forgiveness important to our success in prayer?*—It is indispensable. Mark 11 : 25, 26.

MARK 12 (MATTHEW 21, LUKE 20).

425. *Who are the husbandmen, who are the servants, and who the son in this parable?*—The Jews generally, and especially their rulers and teachers; the prophets; and Christ himself.

426. *What was the snare laid for Jesus in Mark 12 : 14, 15?*—A question designed to bring an answer that would almost certainly offend against either the Jewish law or the Roman.

427. *Upon what single word in Mark 12 : 26 does the Lord's argument depend?*—The word "am," which signified that though dead they were still existing as departed spirits when he spoke.

428. *Who was the living example of the fulfillment of these two great commandments?*—Jesus himself. Mark 12 : 30, 31.

429. *What testimony to the inspiration of the Scriptures is in Mark 12 : 36?*—It is said that David spoke "by the Holy Ghost." Ps. 110 : 1.

MATTHEW 23 (MARK 12, LUKE 20).

430. *How does our Lord distinguish between profession and practice?*—By saying of the scribes and Pharisees, "they say, and do not."

431. *What are phylacteries?*—Slips of parchment, with texts of Scripture upon them, which the Pharisees wore as charms, or "preservatives," as the word means; probably taking the idea from Ex. 13 : 15, 16; Num. 15 : 38, 39.

432. *What is the difference between the long prayers of the Pharisees and the "pray without ceasing" of the apostle?*—The long prayers of the Pharisees were made for a pretence, to obtain the character of being holy men, while the injunction of the apostle was to encourage and maintain a constant *spirit* of prayer.

433. *What feature in the character of the scribes and Pharisees is most prominent in our Lord's denunciations?*—Their woeful hypocrisy.

MARK 12 : 41.

434. *How is the truth that the Lord looks on the heart illustrated by the widow's mite?*—Because he would not have commended the gift if he had not known the motive with which it was given.

JOHN 12 : 20.

435. *Who were the Greeks?*—Persons from Greece who had embraced the Jewish faith.

436. *What connection is there between their wish to see Jesus and his declaration in verse 23?*—Jesus meant that they must be prepared for his death and for any trials which that event might bring upon his followers.

437. *Why must a grain of wheat die before it can be fruitful?*—Because it contains the germ of life of the new plant, which it must yield up.

438. *For what cause did our Lord come to the hour of his self-sacrifice?*—Because he had willingly given himself up to die for the salvation of men and his own final glory. Vs. 27, 28; compare verses 24, 32.

439. *What is meant by "all men" in verse 32?*—People of all kinds and of all nations.

I beheld, and, lo, a great multitude, which no man could number, of all nations, and kindreds, and people, and tongues, stood before the throne, and before the Lamb, clothed with white robes, and palms in their hands. Rev. 7 : 9.

440. *What is the great sin of the human race?*—Not believing on Christ, and obstinately rejecting him. Vs. 37, etc.

MATTHEW 24 (MARK 13, LUKE 21).

441. *Who built the temple then standing?*—The Jews, under Ezra and Nehemiah.

442. *When was it destroyed?*—About forty years after Christ's death.

443. *By whom?*—By the Romans, under Titus.

444. *Is the universal success of the gospel promised in Matt. 24 : 14?*—No; only its universal *preaching* as a testimony of Christ; and this seems to be now nearly fulfilled.

445. *What was the "abomination of desolation"?*—The banners of the desolating and destroying Roman armies surrounding Jerusalem. Luke 21 : 20.

446. *Would not many who heard this prophecy be alive at its accomplishment thirty-seven years later?*—They would. Matt. 24 : 34.

447. *What are we enjoined to do while prophecy is fulfilling?*—To watch. Matt. 24 : 42, etc.; Mark 13 : 37.

MATTHEW 25.

448. *Is there any special lesson to be learnt from verse 5?*—That even the Lord's own people may slumber and sleep.

449. *Also from the time at which the cry breaks forth, "Behold, the Bridegroom cometh!"?*—That our Lord, instead of being faithfully and lovingly looked for, will be generally unexpected when he comes.

450. *What is the lesson taught by the parable of the talents?*—To impress upon us the duty of using our time and talents and opportunities to God's glory and in remembrance of our final account.

451. *Will any people be exempted from the final judgment?*—No; all nations will be assembled and judged. V. 32.

452. *What oneness of Christ and his disciples is there in verses 35, 40?*—His regarding what is done or undone to one of his least disciples as done or undone to himself.

453. *How may we judge whether we are serving Christ?* —By our feeling and conduct toward his humble disciples. V. 45.

MATTHEW 26 (MARK 14, LUKE 22).

454. *Where do we learn that the Jews at first proposed the private assassination of Jesus?*—From Matt. 26 : 4.

455. *What remarkable act of living faith is recorded in Matt. 26 : 7?*—The woman's pouring a box of precious ointment upon Jesus' head in anticipation, by faith, of his burial.

456. *Who was this woman?*—Mary, the sister of Lazarus. John 12 : 3.

457. *What is to be understood by Mary's " doing this for the burial of Jesus"?*—It was usual to anoint the dead, and Mary wished perhaps to do now what she might not be able to do after.

458. *Did not Judas show his estimate of his Master by the price he demanded for his betrayal?*—Yes; it was the compensation-money for a servant killed by an ox. Ex. 21 : 32.

459. *What had the disciples to prepare for the Passover?*—The lamb, with unleavened bread, bitter herbs, wine, and a sauce made of dates, raisins, and other things, from which Judas received the sop.

460. *What lesson of true humility do we learn from Luke 22 : 26–28 and John 13 : 1, etc.?*—To be as willing to serve as to rule, and to be ready to render any offices of kindness to our brethren and sisters in Christ.

JOHN 13 (MATTHEW 26, MARK 14, LUKE 22).

461. *What all-important declaration does Jesus make in John 13 : 8?*—He said to Peter, "If I wash thee not, thou hast no part with me."

462. *From what must we be washed before we can have part with Jesus?*—From all our sins in his own blood.

463. *Is not the reality of our complete forgiveness shown in John 13 : 10?*—Yes; all past guilt is washed away by a look of living faith, and our robes are clean and white.

464. *What is the meaning of leaning on Jesus' bosom?* —Being the nearest to him in the order of reclining at the feast.

465. *Did John ask Jesus so as to be heard by the rest or in a whisper?*—In a whisper.

466. *Compare John 13, verses 34 and 35, with verse 1.*—And learn to love as Christ did, and to love unto the end.

467. *What is the true test of discipleship?*—Love one to another. John 13 : 35.

468. *Was there not a wide difference between Peter's profession and his practice?*—Yes, a sad difference when he denied him in his hour of utmost need; but he repented under his Lord's forgiving look, and long afterward he died a martyr for his sake. John 13 : 38.

LUKE 22 : 19 (MATTHEW 26, MARK 14, 1 CORINTHIANS 11).

469. *What is the object of the Lord's Supper?*—That we may remember our Lord's death till he come, and that our souls may be strengthened and refreshed as we feed together upon him in loving fellowship and faith.

JOHN 14.

470. *What is meant by the Father's house?*—Our home in heaven.

471. *How must we come to the Father?*—By Christ, the only way.

472. *How do we know that our Lord was a perfect manifestation of the Father?*—By Christ's assertion to Philip that whoever had seen him had seen the Father. Vs. 7, etc.

473. *Who will answer our petitions?*—Our heavenly Father if we ask in Jesus' name. V. 14.

474. *Who was the promised Comforter?*—The Holy Ghost. V. 26.

475. *Was the Holy Ghost a temporary gift?*—No; to abide with us for ever.

476. *Why cannot the world receive him?*—Because it knows him not, nor Christ, through whom he comes.

477. *How can we judge whether we love Christ?*—By our prevailing obedience to his commands, by the witness of the Spirit within us that we love Him who first loved us. Vs. 21, 23.

478. *What enabled the evangelists to remember the sayings and doings of the Lord?*—The teaching of the Holy Ghost. V. 26.

479. *Does Christ mean that his disciples shall have peace on earth when he gave them his peace?*—No; he told them they should have tribulation without, but peace within. John 16 : 33.

480. *Who only could say with truth that he had yielded no allegiance to the prince of this world?*—Jesus Christ. V. 30.

481. *Who is the prince of this world?*—Satan, who rules over the evil spirits of the air and in the hearts of men.

JOHN 15.

482. *In what condition only can we bring forth fruit?* —By being united to Christ and abiding in him by a living faith. V. 5.

483. *What will be the consequence of our not bearing fruit?*—Eternal misery in separation from God and Christ, as dead leaves are cast forth and burned. V. 6.

484. *What is the token of being Christ's friends?*— The doing whatsoever he commands. V. 14.

485. *Are we to be surprised by the hatred of the world?* —No, for it first hated our Lord, who was perfect goodness and perfect love.

486. *Is love of the world compatible with love to our Lord?*—No; there can be no true love for a holy Saviour and an unholy world. V. 19.

487. *What sin is referred to in verses 22 and 24?*— The sin of seeing Christ's miracles and hearing his words, and yet rejecting both God and him.

JOHN 16.

488. *Compare verse 2 with Acts 26 : 9–11.*—Saul thought when in his unconverted state that he ought to persecute the followers of Christ.

489. *What was the " little while" in verse 16?*—Jesus was separated a little while from his disciples by his death, and was with them again a little while after his resurrection.

490. *What was the proof that satisfied the unbelieving disciples?*—Jesus knowing their wish or thought, and telling them plainly that he was going back to his Father. Vs. 19, 30.

491. *What is our consolation in trouble?*—That Christ has overcome the world, and that in him we may have peace. V. 33.

JOHN 17.

492. *What " hour" did Jesus refer to in verse 11?*— The time of his death upon the cross.

493. *What is " life eternal"?*—To truly know God as our reconciled Father in Jesus Christ. Union with Christ is life eternal already begun.

494. *Can we at the end of our life use the words of our Lord in verse 4?*—No; we all of us fall short of doing

the work for God, and so of bringing him the glory that we might.

495. *Must we not rather use the words of Isa. 53 : 6 ?* —Yes; we have indeed too much "turned every one to his own way."

496. *Who was the son of perdition ?*—Judas, who was fast falling into ruin and perdition.

497. *How do we know that believers of the present day were included in the Lord's petition ?*—Because they believe through the word of the apostles handed down in the New Testament, and through the preaching and teaching of a succession of Christ's people from that day to this. V. 20.

JOHN 18 : 19 (MATTHEW 26, MARK 14, LUKE 22).

498. *Why did the high priest question Jesus as to his disciples ?*—To know the number and rank of his followers.

499. *Does not John 18 : 28 contain an illustration of the parable of the mote and beam ?*—Yes; the people shrunk from entering a heathen court, as they thought it would defile them, and so unfit them to eat the Passover; and yet they did not shrink from the far greater guilt of causing Jesus' death. Matt. 7 : 5.

500. *Does John 18 : 30 show the hollowness of the accusations of the Jews ?*—Yes, as they did not dare to bring any particular charge against him.

501. *How did John 18, verses 31 and 32, show in what manner our Lord would be put to death ?*—The Jews put to death by stoning, but as they were now under Roman government, Jesus would suffer by the Roman form of crucifixion.

502. *To whom did our Lord appear first after his resurrection ?*—To Mary Magdalene and Mary the mother of James. Matt. 28 : 1, 5; 27 : 56.

503. *To whom was his second appearance ?*—To Mary Magdalene. John 20 : 11-18.

504. *To whom was his third appearance ?*—To Peter. 1 Cor. 15 : 5.

505. *To whom was Jesus' fourth appearance ?*—To two disciples on the way to Emmaus. Luke 14 : 13.

506. *To whom was the fifth appearance ?*—To an evening assembly of the apostles or disciples. John 20 : 19; 1 Cor. 15 : 5.

507. *What were the circumstances of the sixth ?*—Jesus appeared again to the disciples, and made himself especially known to Thomas. John 20 : 24.

508. *To whom was the seventh manifestation ?*—To some of the disciples and to Nathanael at the Sea of Tiberias. John 21 : 1.

509. *How many saw the Lord upon his eighth appearance ?*—The apostles and about five hundred brethren at once.

510. *Where ?*—On a mountain in Galilee.

511. *To whom was our Lord's ninth appearance ?*—To James. 1 Cor. 15 : 7.

512. *Who witnessed the final appearance ?*—"All the apostles," by whom he had been "seen forty days." 1 Cor. 15 : 7; Acts 1 : 4.

513. *What was our Lord's last act upon earth ?*—To give the disciples his blessing. Luke 24 : 50, 51.

ACTS 1.

514. *Who wrote the Acts ?*—St. Luke.

515. *What is the meaning of "passion" ?*—Suffering.

516. *What were some of the infallible proofs ?*—The wounds in his hands and his side, which he allowed Thomas to feel. John 20 : 26-28.

517. *What were the "things pertaining to the kingdom of God" ?*—The prophecies concerning himself, and the preaching the Gospel "among all nations, beginning at Jerusalem." Luke 24 : 45-49

518. *Find an example of baptism with the Holy Ghost.* —His descent upon the assembly in the house of Cornelius. Acts 11 : 15.

519. *How did the disciples understand the kingdom of God ?*—The restoring the kingdom to Israel, with Christ as king. Vs. 3, 6.

520. *What proof have we in verse 11 that Jesus is the "same yesterday, to-day and for ever" ?*—The testimony of the angels that he would come again "in like manner as" the disciples had seen him go.

521. *How far was the Mount of Olives from Jerusalem ?*—About a mile.

522. *What proof of the inspiration of the Psalms is there in verse 16 ?*—The assertion of Peter that the Holy Ghost spake by David.

523. *Compare verse 17 with Matt. 7 : 22, 23.*—"Many will say to me in that day, Lord, Lord, have we not prophesied in thy name? and in thy name have cast out devils? and in thy name done many wonderful works? and then will I profess unto them, I never knew you; depart from me, ye that work iniquity."

524. *What was this "reward of iniquity" ?*—Thirty pieces of silver. Matt. 26 : 15.

525. *Who are "these men" of verse 21 ?*—The seventy disciples. Luke 10 : 1.

526. *Compare verse 14 with the selection of David.*—David was chosen by "the Lord," who "looketh on the heart."

527. *What awful illustration of Ps. 17 is there in verse 15 ?*—The doom of Judas.

The wicked shall be turned into hell, and all the nations that forget God.

ACTS 2.

528. *What was the day of Pentecost ?*—"Seven Sabbaths," or "fifty days," from the Passover. Luke 18 : 15, 16.

529. *How was it that there were Jews "out of every nation" ?*—Because they were scattered "among all people," as God had said they should be, for their sins. Deut. 28 : 64.

530. *Compare verse 7 with chap. 1 : 11.*—In both verses the disciples are called Galileans.

531. *At what time was the "third hour of the day" ?*—At nine A. M. V. 15.

532. *What is probably the "day" referred to in verse 20 ?*—The destruction of Jerusalem.

533. *Why is it not likely to be the day of final judgment ?*—Because at that day it will be too late to call and be saved. V. 21.

534. *Why was it not possible Jesus should be holden of death ?*—Because of his divine power, and of the necessity of his body's rising again to prove his Godhead and complete his work.

535. *What blessed hope in connection with our Lord's resurrection is there in 1 Cor. 6 : 14 ?*—That "God" "will also raise up us by his own power."

536. *Can we learn anything of the pious dead from verse 34 ?*—That they are not yet "ascended into the heavens."

537. *What is the meaning of "pricked in their heart" ?* —Having the conscience convinced of sin, and being brought to say with the jailer, "What must I do to be saved?" Acts 16 : 30.

538. *What does "had all things common" mean ?*—Voluntarily brought all their goods into one common stock. V. 44.

539. *What is "singleness of heart" ?*—Sincerity.

ACTS 3.

540. *What time was the ninth hour ?*—Three P. M.

541. *Compare verse 12 with John 15 : 5 ; 2 Cor. 3 : 5.*—Peter knew that "without" Christ he could "do nothing," and that his "sufficiency" was "of God."

542. *Refer to Pilate's efforts to save Jesus.*—Pilate said more than once that he found no fault in Jesus. Luke 23 : 4, 14, 16, 20, 22; John 19 : 4, 6, 12, 15.

543. *Compare verse 15 with 2 Tim. 1 : 10.*—Christ, "the Prince of Life," "brought life and immortality to light."

544. *Was the "ignorance" excusable?*—No; it was *willful* ignorance that made them guilty. V. 17.

545. *How does verse 19 prove this?*—By showing that they had sin which needed to be blotted out.

546. *Who was the prophet predicted by Moses?*—Jesus Christ, to despise whom would be to despise God who sent him. Vs. 22, 23; Luke 10 : 16.

ACTS 4.

547. *Why were the Sadducees particularly grieved?*—Because they believed there was "no resurrection." Acts 23 : 8.

548. *How does verse 8 fulfill the promise in Luke 12 : 11, 12?*—Because Christ had promised that when brought before rulers "the Holy Ghost" should teach his disciples what to say.

549. *Compare verse 12 with 1 John 5 : 11, 12.*—This is the record, that God hath given to us eternal life, and this life is in his Son. He that hath the Son hath life; and he that hath not the Son of God hath not life.

550. *How does verse 13 explain 1 Cor. 1 : 27?*—It is an instance of God's choosing the "weak" and seemingly "foolish" things of the world to confound the "mighty" and "the wise."

551. *What general principle is laid down in verse 19?*—That "we ought to obey God, rather than men." Acts 5 : 29.

552. *How did Hezekiah act when he was overwhelmed with threatenings?*—Like the apostles (vs. 23–30), he brought his trouble before the Lord in prayer. Isa. 37 : 14–17.

ACTS 5.

553. *What was the heinousness of the sin of Ananias?*—His lying not only unto men, but unto God.

554. *What is the devil called in John 8 : 44?*—"A liar and the father of" lies.

555. *How did they tempt the Holy Spirit?*—By trying his knowledge, as if he might not know, and as if he were "altogether such an one as" themselves. Ps. 50 : 21.

556. *Compare verse 28 with Matt. 27 : 25.*—Then answered all the people, and said, His blood be on us and on our children.

557. *What examples of the principles laid down in verse 29 are there?*—When Shadrach, Meshach and Abed-nego refused to worship the image, and when Daniel persevered in prayer to God. Dan. 3 : 18; 6 : 10.

558. *Who was one of Gamaliel's pupils?*—Paul. Acts 22 : 3.

ACTS 6.

559. *What was the meaning of "serving tables"?*—Attending to the distribution of food.

560. *What did the laying on of the apostles' hands signify?*—The setting apart of the chosen men for their work.

561. *Compare verse 7 with Isa. 55 : 10, 11.*—In the latter place we read:

As the rain cometh down, and the snow from heaven, and returneth not thither, but watereth the earth, and maketh it bring forth and bud, that it may give seed to the sower, and bread to the eater: so shall my word be that goeth forth out of my mouth: it shall not return unto me void, but it shall accomplish that which I please, and it shall prosper in the thing whereto I sent it.

562. *What promise was fulfilled in verse 10?*—I will give you a mouth and wisdom, which all your adversaries shall not be able to gainsay nor resist. Luke 21 : 15.

ACTS 8.

563. *Who was Saul?*—A young Jew and bigoted Pharisee.

564. *To whose death was he consenting?*—Stephen's.

565. *Did the apostles leave Jerusalem at that time in consequence of the persecution?*—No; while others were scattered they remained.

566. *How did the persecution defeat its own object?*—The scattered ones everywhere preached the word. V. 4.

567. *What was Simon's intention in offering Peter money?*—That he might have the power of giving the Holy Ghost. V. 19.

568. *In what did Peter declare that Simon had no part?*—In the religion of Christ, which he professed to believe.

ACTS 9.

569. *What proof of the oneness of Christ and his disciples is there in verse 4?*—Christ's treating the persecution of his disciples as the persecution of himself.

570. *What proof of Saul's immediate conversion is there in verses 5, 6?*—His addressing Jesus as his Lord, and asking what he would have him to do.

571. *What was the most striking proof of the great change that had taken place in Saul?*—His praying.

572. *How did Ananias, in obedience to the vision, immediately address the persecutor Saul?*—As "Brother Saul."

573. *Where did Saul obtain the ability to preach with the power of verse 22?*—"By the revelation of Jesus Christ." Gal. 1 : 11, 12.

574. *Why had the churches rest at that time?*—The loss of the leadership of Saul had checked persecution for a while.

ACTS 10.

575. *What is a centurion?*—An officer in the Roman army.

576. *What assurance that God notices our actions and keeps account of them is there in verse 4?*—Cornelius' prayers and alms were remembered by God.

577. *What proof is there in verse 6 that the Lord knows where all his disciples are dwelling?*—The angel told Cornelius where Peter lodged.

578. *Why was the housetop convenient for prayer?*—The houses there have flat roofs surrounded by a parapet wall.

579. *What did the variety mentioned in verse 12 signify?*—The "redeemed" unto God "out of every kindred and tongue and people and nation." Rev. 5 : 9.

580. *What did Peter mean by "unclean"?*—Forbidden to be eaten by the law.

581. *Compare verse 15 with Eph. 2 : 14.*—Showing Christ, "our peace," making Jew and Gentile "one."

582. *Why was the vision thrice repeated?*—Because, like the subject of Pharaoh's dream, "the thing" referred to was "established by God," who would "shortly bring it to pass." Gen. 41 : 32.

583. *What proof of an overruling Providence is there in verse 20?*—The men who came to Peter were sent by God.

584. *Were not the Jews very slow to realize the calling in of the Gentiles?*—Yes; even believers in Jesus "were astonished" to find that "God also to the Gentiles" had "granted repentance unto life." V. 45, and Acts 11 : 18.

ACTS 11.

585. *What name was given to the disciples at Antioch?*—Christians. V. 26.

Acts 12.

586. *Which was strongest—the prison or the prayer of the Church?*—Prayer. V. 5.

587. *Was there any sign of hurry in Peter's deliverance?*—No; he had time to dress. V. 8.

588. *What other remarkable instance of the same deliberation is there in John 10 : 7?*—Our Lord's graveclothes being neatly folded up.

589. *Ought not the fact recorded in verse 12 to have prevented the unbelief of verse 15?*—Yes, but we are always slow in expecting answers to our prayers.

590. *What is the meaning of the word "examined" in verse 19?*—Scourged them to make them confess the truth. Acts 22 : 24.

591. *What example of pride is there in verses 21-23?* —Herod's being pleased with the gross flattery of his people, and being instantly and dreadfully punished by God.

592. *Compare verse 23 with Dan. 4 : 37.*—I Nebuchadnezzar praise and extol and honor the King of heaven, all whose works are truth, and his ways judgment: and those that walk in pride he is able to abase.

593. *What is the usual result of persecution?*—To defeat its own purpose. V. 24.

Acts 13.

594. *What illustration of the custom of the synagogue have we in verse 15?*—It was the custom for any one present to be allowed to read or speak, as Jesus did at Nazareth and Paul at Antioch. Luke 4 : 16.

595. *What is the gospel message called in verses 26, 32, 38?*—"The word" of "salvation," "glad tidings" and "forgiveness of sins."

596. *Was the gospel at this time preached only to the Jews?*—Yes; hitherto only to the Jews. Vs. 42-48.

597. *What should be the result of the reception of the gospel?*—The being "filled with joy and with the Holy Ghost." V. 52.

Acts 14.

598. *What was the condition of healing?*—The sufferer's faith, as Jesus elsewhere "did not many mighty works" "because of their unbelief." V. 9; Matt. 13 : 58.

599. *Should Christians expect to escape trouble?*—No; it is only "through much tribulation" that we can "enter into the kingdom of God." V. 22.

600. *How do we as Gentiles enter the family of God?* —By the door of faith. V. 27.

Acts 15.

601. *What was the effect upon Paul and Barnabas by the corruption of the gospel mentioned in verses 1, 5?*— They firmly withstood it. V. 2.

602. *What was the witness of God to the disciples?*— The giving them the Holy Ghost. V. 8.

603. *How is the Jewish ceremonial law spoken of?*— As "a yoke" that it was difficult "to bear." V. 10.

604. *Why did they so strenuously resist the rite of circumcision?*—For as many as are of the works of the law are under the curse: for it is written, Cursed is every one that continueth not in all things which are written in the book of the law to do them. Gal. 3 : 10. For whosoever shall keep the whole law, and yet offend in one point, he is guilty of all. James 2 : 10.

605. *Who was Simeon?*—Simon Peter. Vs. 14, 7.

606. *What conclusion did the apostles come to?*—To lay upon the disciples no greater burden of Jewish ceremonial law than the abstaining from some things that were chiefly connected with polluted idol-worship. V. 20.

Acts 16.

607. *Are our hearts naturally inclined to receive the gospel?*—No; God must open our hearts. V. 14.

608. *What is the meaning of "divination" and "soothsaying"?*—Pretended knowledge of future events and fortune-telling.

609. *Compare verse 17 with Luke 4 : 33, 34.*—There was a man which had a spirit of an unclean devil, and cried out with a loud voice, saying, Let us alone; what have we to do with thee, thou Jesus of Nazareth? art thou come to destroy us? I know thee who thou art; the Holy One of God.

610. *How does verse 19 show that the deliverance from the evil spirit was a reality?*—The "masters saw that the hope of their gains was gone."

611. *What did the keeper of the prison fear?*—Death, which Peter's keepers had suffered. V. 27; Acts 12 : 19.

612. *What was the privilege of being a Roman?*—Not to be bound or punished without a regular trial.

613. *Compare verse 40 with 2 Cor. 1 : 3-6?*—In the latter place we read:

Blessed be God, even the Father of our Lord Jesus Christ, the Father of mercies, and the God of all comfort: who comforteth us in all our tribulation, that we may be able to comfort them which are in any trouble, by the comfort wherewith we ourselves are comforted of God. For as the sufferings of Christ abound in us, so our consolation also aboundeth by Christ. And whether we be afflicted, it is for your consolation and salvation, which is effectual in the enduring of the same sufferings which we also suffer: or whether we be comforted, it is for your consolation and salvation.

Acts 17.

614. *What is the supreme authority in religious controversies?*—"The Scriptures." Vs. 2, 3, 11; Acts 18 : 28.

615. *What proof is there in verse 7 of the subjection of the Jews to the Gentile power?*—Their being under the decrees of the Roman emperor, Claudius Cæsar.

616. *And does not this same verse illustrate John 1 : 11?*—Yes; here, as in his native land, Christ's own people, the Jews, "received him not."

617. *What was it that distinguished the Bereans?*— Their readiness to receive the word preached, and their daily searching of the Scriptures respecting it.

618. *What was Athens remarkable for at that time?* —All the Athenians and strangers which were there spent their time in nothing else but either to tell or to hear some new thing.

619. *Who is to be the final Judge of all men?*—God, by Jesus Christ. V. 31.

620. *Who appoints the day of judgment?*—God himself.

621. *Did the Athenians believe in a future life?*— Very few of them did.

Acts 18.

622. *Were the Jews in favor with the Romans?*--No; they had been expelled from Rome. V. 2.

623. *Is manual labor necessarily undignified?*—No; Paul was obliged to work as a tentmaker for the support of himself and those that were with him. Acts 20 : 34.

624. *Was there not a limit to the apostle's forbearance?* —Yes; he was not bound to cast "pearls before swine." Vs. 5, 6.

625. *Why did the Greeks beat Sosthenes rather than Paul?*—Because Paul was a Roman citizen.

626. *Was the Mosaic economy superseded at this time?* —Yes, but Paul might have had reasons that are not mentioned for complying with the custom at that time. V. 21.

627. *What is the meaning of "mighty in the Scriptures," as distinguished from "eloquence"?*—Well acquainted with them, and enabled to understand them and to teach from them by the Holy Ghost.

ACTS 19.

628. *What example of practical repentance do verses 18, 19 show?*—The fortune-tellers and others burning the books that were the means of their profits and of their sin.

629. *Was the worship of Diana a costly service?*—Yes; her temple was filled with ornaments and gifts, and sin and error are usually more costly than holiness and truth. V. 27.

630. *Why did the disciples hinder Paul?*—Lest he should be injured by the crowd. V. 30.

631. *Were the Jews held in honor at Ephesus?*—No, as they despised all idolatry. V. 34.

632. *Was not the testimony of the Jews to the one God the cause of the uproar?*—Yes.

633. *What were the deputies?*—Judges appointed by the Romans. V. 38.

634. *By whom were the assembly in danger of being called to account?*—The Roman governor.

ACTS 20.

635. *How far was Miletus from Ephesus?*—Thirty-six miles.

636. *What country is meant by Asia?*—A part of Asia Minor or Turkey in Asia, about Ionia and Smyrna, was so called. V. 18.

637. *Notice the holy fortitude of verse 14.*—So Jesus steadfastly set his face to go up to Jerusalem. Acts 21:13.

638. *What did Paul mean by being "pure from the blood of all men"?*—That as he had faithfully taught the whole truth of God, his hearers had only themselves to blame if they rejected it and were lost. V. 27.

When I say unto the wicked, Thou shalt surely die; and thou givest him not warning, nor speakest to warn the wicked from his wicked way, to save his life; the same wicked man shall die in his iniquity; but his blood will I require at thine hand. Ezek. 3:18.

639. *Who appoints the ministry of the Church?*—Whatever human means are used, true ministers are made by the Holy Ghost alone. V. 28.

640. *Compare verse 33 with 1 Sam. 12:3.*—In the latter place we read:

Behold, here I am; witness against me before the Lord, and before his anointed: whose ox have I taken? or whose ass have I taken? or whom have I defrauded? whom have I oppressed? or of whose hand have I received any bribe to blind mine eyes therewith? and I will restore it you.

ACTS 21.

641. *What is the meaning of "took up our carriages"?*—Took our baggage or things carried. V. 15.

642. *Of what nation were the soldiers who rescued Paul?*—They were Romans.

643. *What was the nature of the double chain put upon Paul?*—Being chained to "two soldiers," as Peter was. Acts 12:6.

ACTS 22.

644. *What was it that so provoked the Jews?*—Paul's speaking of being sent to the Gentiles. Vs. 21, 22.

645. *How were the thongs used when not employed for binding prisoners?*—In scourging them to extort the truth. V. 24.

ACTS 23.

646. *What form of unbelief were Sadducees subject to?*—Denying the resurrection.

647. *Was the danger from the bigotry of the Jews unimportant?*—No; it was thought prudent to give Paul nearly five hundred soldiers as a guard. V. 23.

648. *How far was Cæsarea from Jerusalem?*—About sixty miles.

ACTS 24.

649. *Which address to Felix was the most truthful?*—The simpler words of Paul, as Felix's government was "a mean, cruel and profligate" one.

650. *Did Paul spare the conscience of Felix?*—No; he touched it till he trembled. V. 25.

651. *How does the effect of Paul's reasoning upon Felix illustrate Heb. 4:12?*—It shows that the word of God is quick and powerful, and sharper than any two-edged sword, piercing even to the dividing asunder of soul and spirit, and of the joints and marrow, and is a discerner of the thoughts and intents of the heart.

652. *What mercenary motive influenced Felix?*—The hope of a bribe from Paul to release him.

653. *In what did the two governors agree?*—In desiring to please the Jews, and so to keep them at peace. V. 27; Acts 25:9.

ACTS 25.

654. *To what privilege of Roman citizenship did Paul appeal?*—That of having his cause heard by Cæsar.

655. *Who was the Cæsar referred to?*—The Roman emperor Nero.

656. *Who was King Agrippa?*—The second Herod Agrippa, and Jewish king or viceroy of the country to the north and east of Galilee.

657. *What invaluable modern privilege does verse 27 foreshadow?*—The habeas corpus act, which prevents a long imprisonment without trial.

ACTS 26.

658. *What great results are to follow the preaching of the gospel?*—The turning the Gentiles "from darkness to light." V. 18.

659. *What must be added to repentance and turning to God?*—Works consistent with it. V. 20.

660. *Why did Festus accuse Paul of insanity?*—Because he had spoken of a resurrection of the dead.

ACTS 27.

661. *Why did the soldiers advise the killing of the prisoners?*—Lest, like Peter's keepers, they should be put to death if they escaped. V. 42; Acts 12:19.

ACTS 28.

662. *What is the meaning of the term "barbarous"?*—Strange.

663. *To what did the barbarians refer when they said, "Vengeance suffereth him not to live"?*—Vengeance is here a sort of proper name of a mythological deity.

664. *In what way did the soldier "keep" Paul?*—By a chain to himself. Vs. 16, 20.

LANGUAGES OF THE BIBLE.

OLD TESTAMENT.—The Old Testament, not including the Apocrypha, is written in Hebrew, with the exception of Dan. 2:4 to 7:28; Ezra 4:8 to 6:18, and 7:12-26, which are written in Aramaic, called also Chaldee. One verse of Jeremiah (10:11) is also written in Aramaic.

The Hebrew language is one of a large group of dialects embraced under the term Semitic—from Shem, the oldest son of Noah. The Semitic language, or languages, includes the Assyrian, Babylonian, Hebrew, Samaritan, Aramaic, Syriac, Phœnician, Punic or language of Carthage, Ethiopic, and a few other dialects known only from monumental inscriptions.

Old Testament Hebrew was closely related to the languages of the nations bordering on Palestine in early times, as is shown by the inscription on the Moabite stone, and by many Phœnician inscriptions. As a spoken language it was subject to certain provincialisms, as all languages are; but as a written language, and especially for sacred purposes, it remained comparatively unchanged from the time of Moses to the captivity. After the captivity the language was considerably affected by intercourse with foreign peoples. The Aramaic, in which portions of Ezra and Daniel are written, was the speech of Aram (Padan-Aram), or that part of Syria included between the rivers Euphrates and Tigris. But, being a trade language, it spread among many nations, and encroached upon the Hebrew in northern Palestine. Some have thought that the Jews brought back the Aramaic language with them from the captivity, and for this reason the Aramaic portions of the Bible are sometimes called Chaldee, but there is nothing in the language to connect it with Chaldea. In later times, two or three centuries before Christ, the Greek language threatened to displace both the Hebrew and Aramaic in Palestine, but this was prevented by a reaction brought about through the Rabbinic schools.

NEW TESTAMENT.—The language of the New Testament is Greek. It is not, however, the Greek of classical writers, but a mixed Greek, called Judæo-Greek or Hellenistic—a dialect aptly described as " Hebrew thought in Greek clothing." The Septuagint version was written in this language, and it was largely used in Egypt, Asia Minor and Palestine, though it varied greatly in the Asiatic and African provinces subject to Macedonian rule. We have but an imperfect knowledge of this language as spoken, but it seems to have been absorbed by contact with other languages better adapted for commerce.

THE CANON OF SCRIPTURE.

The word " canon " meant, in Greek, a " reed " or " rod," and was applied to a measuring rod or rule. Hence, when anything accorded with standard measure it was agreeable to the canon or established rule. In the sense of " a rule of life " it occurs in Gal. 6:16. Before the time of Origen, in the third century A. D., the truth recognized in the Church had come to be spoken of as a canon, or text of doctrine; but Origen extended the word to the books that were regarded as in accord with the rules of faith, and embodied them by calling them canonized or canonical. Since the Scriptures contain in written form the true standard of faith, they came to be spoken of as the Canon, or rule by which other books must be judged. Therefore the Canon, or Canonical Scripture, embraces the whole collection of books contained in the Bible. When a single book is spoken of, it is said to be in the Canon, or Canonical. There is also a division of the books into Old Testament Canon and New Testament Canon. Uncanonical books are those not included in the Canon. Apocryphal are those of doubtful origin and authority. They were not originally written in Hebrew, and are not counted genuine by the Hebrews.

OLD TESTAMENT CANON.—The formation of the Canon of the Old Testament was gradual, and out of writings covering many centuries. Moses ordered the " Book of the Law " to be put in the side of the Ark, Deut. 31:26. To this was afterwards added Joshua, Josh. 24:26, and later Proverbs and some of the prophecies, for Daniel refers to the " Books," Dan. 9:2; Zechariah to the " Law and Former Prophets," Zech. 7:12; and Isaiah to the " Book of the Lord," Isa. 29:18; 34:16. Ezra, with the aid of the " Great Council," no doubt collected and finally determined the Canon of the Law, after the return from captivity. In this work he was assisted by Nehemiah, who, according to 2 Macc. 2:13, " gathered together the acts of the kings and the prophets and those of David " when founding a library for the second temple.

Notice now began to be taken of the later prophets. Jesus Sirach, about B. C. 200, author of the apocryphal book Ecclesiasticus, speaks (49:10) of the twelve, or minor, prophets in such a way as to leave no doubt that these twelve writings were then, as now, classed together. After a time, about B. C. 132, the grandson of Jesus, who translated Ecclesiasticus into Greek, speaks of his grandfather as being familiar with "the Law and the Prophets, and the other books which follow them." The custom, dating probably back to the time of Ezra, was to read a part of the prophetical Scriptures in stated worship, in connection with the lesson of the law for the day.

It is impossible to fix an exact date for the closing of the O. T. Canon, for beside the "Law and the Prophets" there were other sacred writings, *Ketubim* of the Hebrews, *Hagiographa* of the Greeks, of an historic and poetic character, which had not been formally mentioned in connection with the Canon. The author, Philo Judæus, writing about B. C. 20, refers to the Pentateuch as the source of all the laws and teachings of his day, and refers to the constant use of the "laws and oracles produced by the prophets, and hymns and other writings." The Jewish historian, Josephus, writing about A. D. 70, enumerates twenty-two books as "divine"—five of Moses, thirteen of prophets, and four of "hymns and directions of life." He mentions all the books of the Old Testament as Canonical, except Job, Proverbs, Ecclesiastes and the Song of Solomon, and it may be that his omission of these was due to the fact that he had no occasion to refer to them in the preparation of his works. He also adds that since the death of Artaxerxes (B. C. 424) no one had dared, up to his day, "to add anything to them, to take anything from them, or to make any change in them."

The inference from all the data thus presented would be that from the time of Ezra and Nehemiah there was a general acceptance of what constituted the Jewish Canon, and that its contents were identical with the O. T. Canon of to-day, our thirty-nine books being grouped so as to accord with the twenty-two letters of the Hebrew alphabet. This grouping counted the two books of Samuel, Kings and Chronicles as one; Ruth was coupled with Judges, Ezra with Nehemiah, Jeremiah with Lamentations, while the twelve minor prophets were considered as one book. Jerome notices that the twenty-two books coincide with the letters of the Hebrew alphabet, and that the five double letters coincide with the five double books—Samuel, Kings, Chronicles, Ezra and Jeremiah. He gives the contents of the Law, Prophets and Hagiographa in exact accord with the Hebrew authorities, as mentioned above, classing Daniel with the last. The Talmud also agrees in the same list, and gives the names of the writers of the several books.

There are some authorities who, while accepting the three great divisions under which the Hebrew Canon took final form, to-wit: Law, Prophets, and Writings (Hagiographa), enumerate twenty-four original books, or minor divisions, for which reason, they say, the Hebrew Bible is sometimes spoken of as "the four and twenty." In this division and enumeration the authors of the historical books, Joshua, Judges, Samuel and Kings, are classed as "former prophets." The arrangement would be as follows:

		BOOKS.
(a) *Law:* Pentateuch, Genesis to Deuteronomy		5
(b) *Prophets, Former:* Joshua, Judges, Samuel, Kings		4
" Later: Isaiah, Jeremiah, Ezekiel, the Twelve		4
(c) *Writings, Poetry:* Job, Psalms, Proverbs		3
" Rolls: Song of Solomon, Ruth, Lamentations, Ecclesiastes, Esther		5
" Books: Daniel, Ezra, Nehemiah, Chronicles		3
		24

The New Testament furnishes abundant évidence that in the era, and among those who produced it, the Old Testament Canon was received not only as complete, but as of ancient date and undisputed authority. The New Testament references to "Scripture" are so frequent and positive as to dispel any uncertainty as to what writings were accepted as canonical. Nearly all the Old Testament books are referred to, and many quoted directly. Even the threefold division of the Canon is indicated in Christ's reference to what is written "in the law of Moses and the prophets and the psalms concerning Himself."

NEW TESTAMENT CANON.—The New Testament Canon was gradually added to the Old. But it was some time after the Lord's ascension before any of the books contained in it were actually written. The teaching of the apostles was at first oral, but in course of time it became necessary to commit the oral gospel to writing, and this necessity became paramount as the time drew near for the departure of the teachers from this life. Thus the Gospels came into existence, two by Apostles themselves, and two by friends and close companions of the Apostles.

But there had already arisen another kind of composition. The founders of churches, often unable to visit them personally, and anxious for harmony and the spread of true faith and doctrine, resorted to writings of epistles, which were sent forth from time to time to meet special wants and emergencies.

The existence and authority of the several writings which thus came to comprise the New Testament Canon are abundantly attested by quotations from a series of Christian authors, beginning with the immediate successors of the Apostles. Clement of Rome refers to 1 Corinthians as the work of Paul. Polycarp, who had heard St. John, refers to the Pastoral Epistles of St. Paul. Justin Martyr was so well acquainted with the writings of the first three Evangelists that it would be possible to reproduce from his works a considerable part of the life of Christ. Irenæus quotes almost every book of the New Testament and often names their authors. So do Tertullian and Clement in the next generation. Origen not only bears testimony to quotation, but speaks definitely on the subject of authorship.

But besides quotations there are lists or collections of books known to be Apostolic and authoritative, one specimen of which is the famous Muratorian Fragment of the Canon, published by Muratori in A. D. 1740 from a MS. in the Ambrosian Library at Milan, which had originally belonged to the Irish monastery at Bobbio. The date of this fragment is fixed at about A. D. 170. It was probably written at Rome, and may be taken to represent the Canon in use among the Western Churches at the date of its composition. Owing to its fragmentary state, the books of Matthew, Hebrews, James, 3 John and Peter are not found on the list. A similar list may be made out from the Peshito, the Bible of the Syrian Christians, which dates from the closing of the second century. It has all the books of our present Canon, except 2 Peter, 2 and 3 John, Jude and Revelation. Almost contemporary with it is the Old Italian Version, or Bible of the North African churches, which contains all of the New Testament, except Hebrews, 2 Peter and James.

The persecution of Diocletian, A. D. 303, demanded that the Scriptures be given up. The Christians refused to surrender them. The contest made it necessary to know exactly what books were Apostolic. Our New Testament as it stands was the result of the inquiry, lengthily carried on by the most eminent scholars of the time. The Council of Carthage, A. D. 397, issued a decree respecting the contents of the Sacred Books, and once for all the books of the New Testament as we now have them were settled by authority of the Christian Church.

BIBLE TEXTS AND ANCIENT VERSIONS.

OLD TESTAMENT TEXTS AND VERSIONS.

Notwithstanding the care exercised by the Hebrews, especially in the time of Ezra, to preserve the text of the Old Testament, after the Canon had become practically complete, there are no very ancient MSS. of the Old Testament extant. This may be accounted for by the fact that the Aramaic version of the Old Testament came into popular use in the synagogue, being read in connection with and as explanatory of the Hebrew text, and in time superseding it among a people who had dropped Hebrew as their spoken language. Again, it may be accounted for by the later Jewish custom of burying or destroying their worn-out MSS.

The earliest Hebrew text known is one in the British Museum, and it is not given a date beyond the ninth century A. D. It, with all others extant at or about that time, is traceable to a common ancestor which had an existence at a period not later than the second century A. D. But notwithstanding this poverty of early MSS., there are three important sources of evidence as to the integrity of the Old Testament text. And first—

THE TALMUD.—The Talmud is the body of Jewish civil and canonical law not comprised in the Pentateuch, and commonly including the Mishna and the Gemara, but sometimes limited to the latter. It is written in Aramaic, and consists of two great collections—the "Jerusalem Talmud," embodying the discussions on the Mishna of the Palestinian doctors, from the second to the fifth centuries A. D., and the "Babylonian Talmud," embodying those of the Jewish doctors in Babylonia, from about 190 A. D. to the seventh century. These Talmudists undertook a highly critical collation of many texts which, however, they interpreted by means of traditional testimony. Still, they collected all that was known and approved, oral and written, respecting the sacred books, rejecting what was not supported by a considerable weight of testimony. In the sixth century A. D. a school of Jewish doctors at Tiberias, known as the "Massoretes," began to extract from the Talmud such traditional comments, criticisms and grammatical emendations, as would, in their opinion, suffice to fix beyond question a standard Hebrew text. Their work, carried on to a period as late as the tenth century, became the Masora (Massorah), printed in 1525 at Venice. The Massoretic text soon became a standard from which others were multiplied. In the eleventh century a collation was made of the Massoretic text and Babylonian text, and while some eight hundred differences of reading were found, none of them affected materially the sense of the subject matter.

THE TARGUMS.—After the return of the Hebrews from captivity, and when the Aramaic speech had supplanted Hebrew for daily use, a Targum, or oral interpretation of the sacred books as read in Hebrew, became necessary, Neh. 8 : 8. This oral Targum was at first a simple repetition of the Hebrew text in Aramaic, together with such explanation of original meanings as sufficed to make them clear. But in process of time it became more elaborate, and in order to fix the limit of interpretation the Targum itself was reduced to writing. These written Targums, adapted to both Babylonian and Palestinian Jews, are among our most valuable aids for fixing the text as read in the Hebrew synagogues, and for the interpretation which the priests attached to difficult passages.

The most notable Targums are those of Onkelos on the Pentateuch, and of Jonathan Ben Uzziel on the Historical Books and Prophets. Their date is uncertain, but that of Onkelos is usually assigned to the second century A. D., while that of Jonathan Ben Uzziel is placed at two centuries later.

But while the Targums are thus valuable as helping to prove the integrity of the Hebrew text, still stronger aid is afforded by the translations made in early times from the Hebrew. These come under the head of "Ancient Versions," of which may be mentioned first—

THE SAMARITAN PENTATEUCH.—This is hardly a "version," for the Samaritans have preserved the Pentateuch, written in Samaritan, or Old Hebrew characters, independently of the orthodox Jews. It exists in MSS. supposably almost as ancient as the Hebrew, and its reading does not vary from that of the Hebrew as much as might be expected, considering the schism that existed between Hebrews and Samaritans.

SEPTUAGINT VERSION.—Outside of the Massoretic text, the chief authority for the primitive form of the Old Testament is the translation made into the Greek language at Alexandria, by seventy (seventy-two) Jewish scholars, and therefore called Septuagint, or Version of the Seventy. The story of this great undertaking is to the effect that Ptolemy Philadelphus, King of Egypt, B. C. 284-246, desiring to add to his library at Alexandria, sent, at the suggestion of his librarian, Demetrius Phalerus, an embassy to Eleazar, the high priest at Jerusalem, to obtain copies of the sacred books of the Hebrew law, and to make translations of the same. Eleazar sent the copies requested, together with a body of seventy (or seventy-two) translators, who were assigned quarters in the Island of Pharos (some say, were shut up in separate cells on the island, and that their translations when made tallied exactly), where they completed their translation. Whatever of legend there may be in all this, it is agreed that the Hebrew Pentateuch was translated into Greek at Alexandria as early as the time of Ptolemy Philadelphus. It would seem that the work of translating the other Old Testament books was carried on leisurely, and that it was not completed much before 150 B. C. The completed version was by no means a clear and satisfactory rendering of the Hebrew, as might well be expected from its having passed through so many hands. It shows many variations from the original, both in words and phrases, as well as some additions ; and it contains many Coptic words. Moreover, it has come down to us in a state of great corruption, which renders it difficult to ascertain what the first translators wrote. But as the Septuagint is the oldest translation of the Hebrew Bible, as it is constantly quoted by the writers of the New Testament, and as all the other translations are made from it, except the Peshito Syriac and Jerome's Vulgate, its importance as a source of study and means of verification cannot be overestimated.

VERSION OF AQUILA.—Aquila was a Jewish proselyte, of Pontus. At the instigation of Alexandrian Jews he sought to supply a literal rendering of the Hebrew text for the benefit of those who were more familiar with the Greek than the original and because the Septuagint had been appropriated by the Christians. His work dates about the beginning of the second century A. D., and it was so very literal as to be sometimes unintelligible. It was highly esteemed by the Jews, and is quoted in the Talmud, but early Christian writers did not rely upon it.

VERSION OF THEODOTION.—Theodotion was also a Jewish proselyte, of Ephesus. He did not so much translate as revise and reform the text of the Septuagint. As a result many of his emendations were introduced into the Septuagint, the entire Book of Daniel being given a place instead of the inexact version of the Seventy. His work is given a date somewhere in the latter half of the second century A. D.

VERSION OF SYMMACHUS.—Symmachus was an Ebionite of Samaria, about A. D. 200. He gave his name to a new translation of the Scriptures, which was paraphrastic like that of the Septuagint, but displays more purity and elegance of style and language.

THE HEXAPLA.—When the great Christian scholar Origen was engaged upon a study of the Greek Old Testament in Alexandria, in the early part of the third century, he arranged the extant translations side by side in parallel columns for the purpose of comparative study, and with them he placed the Hebrew text and a transliteration of the Hebrew text in Greek letters, the arrangement being shown somewhat as follows :

1. Hebrew Text.	2. Hebrew Text in Greek Letters.	3. Translation of Aquila.	4. Translation of Symmachus.	5. Translation of the Seventy.	6. Translation of Theodotion.

This work he called the Hexapla, or sixfold work, on account of the arrangement of columns. Had this work of Origen survived there would have been three Greek translations to compare with the Septuagint, but unfortunately nothing has been preserved except a few disjointed quotations.

THE SYRIAC VERSION.—There is a Syriac version of the Bible made directly from the Septuagint as it stood in the Hexapla of Origen. But the one to which most importance is attached is the Syriac version called the Peshito—that is, simple, common or vulgate version. The Old Testament portion was made direct from the Hebrew, with occasional references to the Septuagint, and much of the rendering is very exact. The Old Testament is given a date as early as the first century, and it is supposed to have been prepared at the instance and for the use of Jewish proselytes. The entire work bears evidence of long preparation by many hands. It contains all the Canonical Books of the Old Testament as well as of the New, except the second and third Epistles of John, 2 Peter, the Epistle of Jude and Revelation. It was in general use in Syria in the fourth century, and has always been accepted by the Syrian Church as authentic. Several Arabian translations have been made from it.

OLD LATIN VERSION.—Fragments of an old Latin version of the Bible are found in ancient Christian writings, but the history of its origin is lost. It was supposably prepared in northern Africa for the Latin-speaking element of the early Christian Church. It is merely a translation of the Greek Septuagint, and was an extant work during the closing period of the second century. In the New Testament it omitted the Epistle to the Hebrews, James and 2 Peter.

THE VULGATE.—The above-mentioned old Latin version had undergone some changes upon its general acceptance and use in Italy. This inspired Eusebius Hieronymus, better known as St. Jerome, one of the greatest Biblical scholars of his day, though he acquired Hebrew at a late period of his life, to undertake the task of revising the old Latin version. He translated the Gospels into Latin, then the vernacular or vulgar (hence *vulgate*) tongue, about A. D. 383, and the remainder of the New Testament somewhat later. Wishing to make his translation of the Old Testament with direct reference to the Hebrew, he withdrew to Bethlehem, where he completed the work between the years A. D. 390 and 405. By the ninth century the Vulgate version had entirely superseded the old Latin version of the second century, especially in the Western Church. The Vulgate edition of Pope Clement VIII., of 1592–93, is the source of the modern Douay version, and the accepted standard of the Roman Catholic Church. Though Jerome's work was unevenly done some books undergoing very little change, while others were carefully treated, his labors were very important, since he supposably had access to Hebrew MSS. of great antiquity. From the ninth to the fifteenth centuries the Vulgate edition of Jerome became corrupted by the intermixture of other Latin versions. The discordance in copies was noticed by a decree in the Council of Trent, and Sextus V. gave to the world a revised text in A. D. 1590, and three years afterwards Clement VIII. issued the present standard edition, as above stated.

OTHER VERSIONS.—Besides the versions mentioned there are many others, made at different times and in different countries. Among these are the famous Gothic version of Ulfilas, the Armenian version, Arabian version, Ethiopic version, and Coptic or Egyptian version, all having their value in elucidating the sacred text. The value of these ancient versions consists in the fact that for the most part they afford independent testimonies, and not mere copies of some common original, as their verbal differences sufficiently attest; yet their complete agreement in all essential points demonstrates the integrity of the texts of the Bible more satisfactorily than that of any other ancient book.

NEW TESTAMENT TEXT AND VERSIONS.

MANUSCRIPTS.—No work that has come down to us from classical writers presents so many valuable MSS. of ancient date by which to establish the text as the New Testament. A Virgil in the Vatican claims an antiquity as early as the fourth century, but generally the MSS. of the classics belong to periods between the tenth and fifteenth centuries.

The earliest MSS. of the New Testament are called Uncial MSS., from the Latin *uncia*, "inch," because the letters were large, closely resembling modern capitals. The writing was done on fine vellum, or the prepared skins of calves or kids. Later on came the Cursive MSS., so called because the writing was in a cursive or running hand. *See* Cursive, below. Of the Greek Uncial MSS. the most important are the following:

(*a*) **Sinaitic** (*Codex Sinaiticus*), written in Uncial Greek on three hundred and ninety leaves of fine vellum. A large portion of the Old Testament is wanting. The MS. belonged to the convent of St. Catherine on Mount Sinai, where, in 1844, it first came under the notice of Tischendorf, who at first got possession of forty-three leaves from the Old Testament, and in 1859 secured the rest. The New Testament is complete, and is followed by an Epistle of Barnabas, and part of the "Shepherd" of Hermas. It is referred to the fourth century A. D.

(*b*) **Alexandrian** (*Codex Alexandrinus*), written in Uncial Greek, and now in the British Museum. It originally belonged to the Patriarchal Chamber of Alexandria, whence it was probably carried by Cyral Lucar, Patriarch of Constantinople, A. D. 1621, who presented it to Charles I. of England in 1627. Some parts of the New Testament are missing. It ends with the first Epistle of Clement and part of the second.

(c) **Vatican** (*Codex Vaticanus*), written in Uncial Greek, and now in the Vatican at Rome, where it has been since the fifteenth century. Nothing is known of its previous history. The first and second Epistles to Timothy, and the Epistles to Titus and Philemon are wanting. Hebrews 9 : 14 to the end and Revelation have been supplied by a modern hand.

(d) **Ephrem's**, a palimpsest in Paris Library, containing fragments of the Septuagint, and parts of nearly every book in New Testament. The original was effaced in the twelfth century, and Greek translations from Ephrem Syrus' works were written over it.

(e) **Beza's**, in Cambridge Library. Found by Beza in monastery of St. Irenæus at Lyons in 1562. It is a Græco-Latin MS. of Gospels and Acts, with a small fragment of 3 John.

(f) **Clermont**, in Paris Library. It is a Græco-Latin MS. of Paul's Epistles.

(g) **Laudian**, in Bodleian Library. A Græco-Latin MS. of the Acts of the Apostles.

(h) **Parisian**, in Paris Library. Written in Uncial Greek, and containing parts of the four Gospels. It agrees in a remarkable manner with the quotations found in Origen, and with the Vatican MSS.

CURSIVE MSS.—The Cursive MSS. date from the tenth century onward. Whereas, of the Uncial MSS. there are more than a hundred, of the Cursive there are some two thousand eight hundred accessible to scholars. Of the Cursive MSS. few have been collated thoroughly, though some of them may have high value, if the copyists were in possession of old originals.

PATRISTIC QUOTATIONS.—Quotations of the fathers of the Christian Church from the early Bible MSS. and translations at their command afford corroborative evidence of the integrity of Scripture texts, especially those of the New Testament, from whose sources they were but little removed as to time. Standing alone, these quotations may not reflect more than an individual reading or the understanding of a particular time, but when several of them from different writers are found to agree, they become of great importance in support of textual integrity.

VERSIONS.—All the versions of the New Testament are not of critical value. The oldest of them have been handed down to us in MSS. as the Greek original has been, and in some languages we have a large number of versions, in others few. If an ancient version accords with the early Greek MSS. in some particular reading, we have important proof of the early prevalence of that reading. If a second version supports the reading in question, the weight of evidence in its favor becomes enormously greater. *See* VERSIONS under head of OLD TESTAMENT TEXTS AND VERSIONS.

ENGLISH VERSIONS OF THE BIBLE.

Translations of the Psalter, Gospels and other portions of the Scriptures were made into Anglo-Saxon as early as the eighth century, and into English of the thirteenth century. These translations had no traceable effect on the English Bible.

WYCLIF'S VERSION (1380).—Wyclif, with some of his followers, translated the entire Bible into English from the Latin Vulgate. Being accomplished before the days of printing, it existed only in MS. form up until 1848 or 1850, when it was published in type.

TINDALE'S NEW TESTAMENT (1525).—William Tindale began the publication of his translation of the New Testament in Cologne in 1525. Being compelled to flee, he finished the publication in Worms. Three thousand copies of quarto size were printed. These Testaments began to reach England in 1526, and were burned by order of the bishops. In making his translation, Tindale used the Greek Testament of Erasmus (1519), the German Testament of Luther (1523), and the Latin Vulgate.

TINDALE'S PENTATEUCH (1530).—Tindale's life being in danger at Worms, he went to Marburg, in Hesse, where he published his translation of the Pentateuch into English in 1530. It was a thick, small octavo of 768 pages, the type page measuring 5 inches by 2½. He used a Hebrew text as his original, and Luther and the Vulgate as aids.

TINDALE'S NEW TESTAMENT (1534).—Tindale's New Testament, carefully revised throughout by the translator, was printed at Antwerp in 1534. The work is a noble example of the translator's learning and care, and may be regarded as the true primary version of the English New Testament.

COVERDALE'S BIBLE (1535).—Miles Coverdale translated the Bible from the Zurich (Swiss-German) Bible and the Latin version of Pagninus. It was probably printed and published in Zurich. This was the first version of the entire Bible published in English.

MATTHEW'S BIBLE (1537).—This was made up of Tindale's Pentateuch and New Testament, and completed from Coverdale for the rest of the Old Testament and Apocrypha, the whole edited by John Rogers. It was probably printed at Antwerp, but was published in London with the license of King Henry VIII., thus becoming the first "authorized version."

TAVERNER'S BIBLE (1539).—This was simply an edition of Matthew's Bible, edited by Taverner

THE GREAT BIBLE (1539).—This was a new edition of Matthew's Bible, revised and compared with the Hebrew by Coverdale, and published in England under the sanction of Thomas Cromwell in 1539. Archbishop Cranmer wrote a prologue to the second of the seven editions through which it passed.

THE GENEVA BIBLE (1560).—Two years after the accession of Elizabeth an entirely new edition of the Bible was printed at Geneva. Three men out of a company of English refugees and reformers at Geneva began this work. Other men of that Christian church then under the care of John Knox found the money for it. The three men began work in January, 1558, and finished it in April, 1560. This was the most scholarly English Bible that had yet appeared. It was of handy size and clear Roman type. It became for a period of seventy-five years *the* Bible of the English people. Because of the rendering in Gen. 3 : 7, it became known as the " Breeches " Bible.

THE BISHOPS' BIBLE (1568).—The rapid popularity of the Geneva Bible was not acceptable to Elizabeth and her bishops, who did not sympathize with Genevan church views and polity. Therefore, a revision of the Great Bible was made, at the suggestion of Archbishop Parker, by fifteen theologians, eight of whom were bishops. A second edition of the Bishops' Bible appeared in 1572.

REIMS NEW TESTAMENT (1582).—This translation was made from the Latin Vulgate, and was published in 1583 at Reims. At the same time and place the New Testament portion of the Douay, or Roman Catholic, version appeared.

AUTHORIZED VERSION (1611).—There is no evidence that this version was authorized in any special way. It won its place, under royal and ecclesiastical patronage, by its merits. The work had its inception at Hampton Court Conference in 1604, and was promoted by James I., who approved a list of fifty-four scholars to be assigned to the undertaking. Of these but forty-seven appear to have taken part. These revisers were grouped into six companies, two meeting at Westminster, two at Oxford, and two at Cambridge. Genesis to 2 Kings and Romans to Jude were done at Westminster; 1 Chronicles to Ecclesiastes and the Apocrypha at Cambridge; Isaiah to Malachi, and the Gospels, Acts and Revelation at Oxford. There were fifteen regulations laid down for the guidance of the revisers, the two main ones being that the Bishops' Bible was to be followed and as little altered as the truth of the original permitted; second, that new translations were to be used only when they agreed better with the text than the Bishops' Bible, Tindale's, Matthew's, Coverdale's, Whitechurch's, Genevan. The central thought was " not to make a new translation, nor yet to make of a bad one a good one, but to make a good one better." The A. V. was, therefore, not a new translation, but a thorough and scholarly revision of an already good version. The revisers used the texts of Beza's Latin and Greek Testaments of 1598, and were largely influenced by the Geneva Bible of 1560 and the Reims New Testament of 1582.

THE REVISED VERSION (1881–85).—The King James or Authorized Version stood practically untouched for 270 years. True, many small changes had been introduced into the text by successive printers, but no authoritative revision had taken place. It began to be felt that revision was needed for three leading reasons: (1.) Many weak points had become evident in the A. V. of the New Testament through careful study of the Greek MSS. (2.) Because in the course of three centuries many words and phrases had become obsolete or changed their meanings. (3.) Because Greek and Hebrew scholarship had developed to a higher degree than in the seventeenth century. Accordingly, in 1870, the English Houses of Convocation appointed two bodies of revisers, consisting of twenty-five for the Old Testament and twenty-five for the New. Among other rules adopted for their guidance, they were to introduce as few changes as possible into the A. V. text; adopt no text except the evidence in favor of it greatly preponderated; make or retain no change in the text on final revision except two-thirds of those present approved.

Two similar companies of American scholars co-operated in the work. The Revised New Testament was issued in 1881, and the Revised Bible in 1885. The work as completed is a decidedly forward step in English Biblical scholarship. In the Old Testament, especially in the poetry and prophecies, many meanings are made clear which were otherwise obscure. In the New Testament, especially in the Epistles, texts which were provocative of doubt or clouded in expression have been rendered luminous and satisfactory. Yet with all the aid afforded by the Revised Version to the Bible reader and student, the Authorized Version still retains its wonted place in the popular heart.

To be more explicit as to the aim of the revisers, they strove to obtain a text which comported better with early MSS., with ancient versions, and with quotations from the Fathers, many of which might be regarded in the light of discoveries since the establishment of the A. V. text, and all of which were deemed a proper subject for modification in view of the progress made in Biblical learning and interpretation during a period of nearly three centuries of research and study. But just here it must be noted that there was a great difference between the Old and New Testaments in respect to the aim of the revisers. The Massoretic MS. of the Old Testament, which is of no very great antiquity, has been so unanimously accepted as the only authoritative basis, that little room was left to the revisers for originality or innovation. Yet they have clarified many points hitherto obscure or debatable. As an instance, the word " grove " in Judg. 3 : 7; 6 : 25, and elsewhere, is returned to its original, *Asherah, Asherim* or *Asheroth*, all significant of an actual idol or idols, and of place or places of worship. So in Lev. 16 the vague word " scapegoat " is left to its original, " goat for Azazel." In the rendition of technical terms greater uniformity has been introduced. The same must be said of the names of persons and places, which were variant and confusing in the A. V. As to the names of plants, animals and precious stones, the revisers have rendered a most valuable service in the line of greater accuracy in translation. Even where that two-third agreement necessary to effect a change of the A. V. reading was wanting, they have, by their marginal suggestions, put the reader on the track of thoughts, names and terms far more accurate and satisfactory than those previously in use.

While the changes above indicated are chiefly those of language, others, relating to forms, are interesting and important. The old divisions of chapters and verses are ignored for the sake of textual contiguity and straightforward reading. Yet by use of the old verse figures on the margins the ancient convenience of reference is preserved. The books are divided into paragraphs suited to the subjects under treatment, and where the change of subject is entire the fact is noted by a wide space between the lines. The difference between the prose and poetical texts is clearly defined by setting the latter forth according to the forms used in modern poetry. The New Testament quotations from the prophetical books are given in lines. The usual headings to chapters are omitted, as involving questions of interpretation beyond the design of the revisers. Only such titles are retained as already existed in the Hebrew, such as are found in some of the Psalms, the new translations of which, together with the marginal references, are full of interest and instruction. The entire Book of Psalms is subdivided into five books or collections corresponding to the ancient arrangement of the Hebrew Psalter.

Another interesting and satisfying feature of the R. V. text is the obliteration of mistranslations in so far as the same was possible and necessary. This feature is naturally more noticeable in the New than in the Old Testament, for the reason that the learning and discoveries which have affected original texts have been deeper and more frequent along the line of the Greek than the Hebrew. The instances are manifold, especially in the New Testament, where evident mistranslations have been corrected, where confusing words and expressions have been rendered clear, and where meaningless readings have been given force and vigor. A few samples will suffice to show what the revisers have accomplished by means of this class of improvement. In Luke 23:15 occurs the expression " for I sent you to him." This expression was not only a mistranslation but was without meaning till the revisers corrected it so as to read " for he sent him back unto us." This reading infuses new life and pith in Pilate's address to the priests and rulers, for why should he condemn Jesus when even Herod had found no fault in him, but had "sent him back unto us" as one not worthy to suffer condemnation and death. So, in Acts 26:28, the A. V. reading, "Almost thou persuadest me to be a Christian " takes on a new light and significance in the corrected rendering of the R. V., " With but little persuasion thou wouldst fain make me a Christian." Once more, in Acts 27:14, the A. V. rendering is, " But not long after there arose against it a tempestuous wind, called Euroclydon." This has given rise to both geographic and meteorological confusion, which the R. V. rendering corrects—" But after no long time there beat down from it a tempestuous wind called Euraquilo." This presents clearly the actual phenomenon of that stormy northeast wind of the Levant which passes over the island of Crete, gathering strength among its heights and chasms, and beating down from it upon the shipping that may happen to be skirting its shores or resting in its havens. But it is needless to multiply these instances of clearer and better renderings. However numerous they may be, and whatever excellent a purpose they may serve the reader and student, it can be said of them all that they disturb none of the doctrines that have found source and support in the old version of either Testament.

HISTORY

OF THE

BOOKS OF THE BIBLE.

OF THE BIBLE TITLES.

THE BIBLE is the only authentic source from which instruction can be derived, in relation to the knowledge of God; His various dispensations to mankind, and the duties required of men by their Creator. As it claims to be regarded as the book of God, a Divine authority, so it claims to be the only authority. It is not *a* rule, it is *the* rule both of faith and practice.

The names by which this volume is distinguished are not wanting in significance. It is called the BIBLE, or the *book*, from the Gr. word *biblos*, book, a name given originally (like *liber* in Latin) to the inner bark of the linden, or teil-tree, and afterwards to the bark of the papyrus, the materials of which early books were sometimes made. The terms: "The Scripture," "The Scriptures," and "The Word of God," are also applied in the Bible itself to the sacred books, as is the expression: "The Oracles of God," though this last is sometimes used to indicate the *place* where, under the old dispensation, the will of God was revealed (1 K. viii. 6; 2 Chr. 11, 20; Ps. xxviii. 2). "The Law" and "The Prophets" are each employed, and sometimes unitedly, by a common figure of speech, to designate the whole of the O. T. The sacred writings were sometimes called the *canon* of Scripture from a Gr. word signifying a straight rod, and hence a rule or law (Gal. vi. 16; Phil. iii. 16). This term was employed in the early age of Christianity with some indefiniteness, though generally denoting a standard of opinion and practice. From the time of Origen, however, it has been applied to the books which are regarded by Christians as of Divine authority. The Bible, therefore, is the canon; that is, the authoritative standard of religion and morality.

Of all these titles "The Word of God" is perhaps the most impressive and complete. It is sufficient to justify the faith of the feeblest Christian, and it gathers up all that the most earnest search can unfold. It teaches us to regard the Bible *as the utterance* of Divine wisdom and love.

OF THE BIBLE DIVISIONS.

The most common and general division of the canonical Scriptures is, into the OLD and NEW TESTAMENTS, the former containing those revelations of the Divine will which were communicated to the Hebrews, Israelites, or Jews, before the birth of Christ, the latter comprising the inspired writings of the Evangelists and Apostles. This distinction is founded on 2 Cor. iii. 6, 14; Matt. xxvi. 28; Gal. iii. 17; Heb. viii. 8, ix. 15-20); where the ancient Latin translators have rendered *diatheke* (which signifies both *a covenant* and *a testament*, but in Biblical usage always answers to the Hebrew, *berith*, *a covenant*), by *Testamentum, a testament*, "because," says Jerome (Comment. on Mal., ch. ii. 22), "they by a Græcism attributed to this word the sense of *fœdus, a covenant*." Were such the usage, therefore, there would be no impropriety in terming the two main portions of the Scriptures the *Old* and *New Covenant*, implying thereby not two distinct and unrelated covenants, but merely the *former* and the *latter* dispensation of the one grand covenant of mercy, of which the Prophet Jeremiah (xxxi. 31-34), as expounded by the apostles (Heb. viii. 6-13), gives so ample a description. The books of the O. T. are usually further subdivided by the Jews into the *Law*, the *Prophets*, and

437

Hagiographa, that is the *Holy Writings,* which latter division comprehended the Psalms, Proverbs, Job, Song of Solomon, Ruth, Lamentations of Jeremiah, Ecclesiastes, Esther, Daniel, Ezra, and Nehemiah (reckoned as 1), and the 2 books of Chronicles, also reckoned as 1. These were designated "Holy Writings," because they were not orally delivered as the law of Moses was, but the Jews affirm that they were composed by men divinely inspired.

The subordinate division into chapters and verses is of comparatively modern date. The former is attributed to Hugo de Sancto Caro, a Roman Catholic Cardinal, who flourished about A. D. 1240, the latter to Rabbi Mordecai Nathan, a celebrated Jewish teacher, who lived A. D. 1445. The author of the verse-division in the N. T. was Robert Stephens, a distinguished printer of Paris, who lived in the 16th century. "The verse-division of the O. T.," says Dr. Smith, "was adopted by Stephens in his edition of the Vulgate, 1555, and by Frellon in that of 1556; it appeared for the first time in an English translation, in the Geneva Bible of 1560, and was thence transferred to the Bishops' Bible of 1568, and the authorized version of 1611. With the N. T. the division into chapters, adopted by Hugh de St. Cher, superseded those that had been in use previously, appeared in the early editions of the Vulgate, was transferred to the English Bible by Coverdale, and so became universal. As to the division into verses, the absence of an authoritative standard left more scope to the individual discretion of editors or printers, and the activity of the two Stephenses caused that which they adopted in their numerous editions of the Greek Testament and Vulgate, to be generally received. In the Preface to the Concordance, published by Henry Stephens, 1594, he gives an account of the origin of this division. The whole work was accomplished 'inter equitandum' on his journey from Paris to Lyons. While it was in progress, men doubted of its success. No sooner was it known than it met with universal acceptance. The edition in which this division was first adopted, was published in 1551. It was used for the English version published in Geneva in 1560, and from that time, with slight variations in details, has been universally recognized."

GENUINENESS OF THE OLD TESTAMENT.

It is an inquiry of considerable importance, what books were contained in the canon of the Jews. The O. T., according to our Bibles, comprises 39 books, viz.: The Pentateuch, or 5 books of Moses, called Genesis, Exodus, Leviticus, Numbers, and Deuteronomy; the books of Joshua, Judges, Ruth, 1 and 2 Samuel, 1 and 2 Kings, 1 and 2 Chronicles, Ezra, Nehemiah, Esther, Job, Psalms, Proverbs, Ecclesiastes, the Song of Solomon, the Prophesies of Isaiah, Jeremiah with his Lamentations, Ezekiel, Daniel, Hosea, Joel, Amos, Obadiah, Jonah, Micah, Nahum, Habakkuk, Zephaniah, Haggai, Zechariah, and Malachi. But among the ancient Jews they formed only 22 books, according to the letters of their alphabet, which were 22 in number, reckoning Judges and Ruth, Ezra and Nehemiah, Jeremiah and his Lamentations, and the 12 minor prophets (so called from the comparative brevity of their compositions), respectively, as one book. Josephus says: "We have not thousands of books, discordant, and contradicting each other; but we have only *twenty-two,* which comprehend the history of all former ages, and are justly recognized as divine. *Five* of them proceed from Moses; they include as well the *laws* as an account of the creation of man, extending to the time of his (Moses) death. This period comprehends nearly 3000 years. From the death of Moses to that of Artaxerxes, who was king of Persia after Xerxes, the *prophets* who succeeded Moses committed to writing, in 13 books, what was done in their days. The remaining 4 books contain *hymns* to God (the Psalms) and instructions of life for man." The three-fold division of the O. T. into the Law, the Prophets, and the Psalms, mentioned by Josephus, was expressly recognized before his time by Jesus Christ, as well as by the subsequent writers of the N. T. We have, therefore, sufficient evidence that the O. T. existed at that time; and if it be only allowed that Jesus Christ was a teacher of a fearless and irreproachable character, it must be acknowledged that we draw a fair conclusion when we assert that the Scriptures were not corrupted in His time: for when He accused the Pharisees of making the law of no effect by their traditions, and when He enjoined His hearers to search the Scriptures, He could not have failed to mention the corruptions or forgeries of Scripture, if any had existed in that age. About 50 years before the time of Christ were written the Targums of Onkelos on the Pentateuch, and of Jonathan Ben-Uzziel on the Prophets (according to the Jewish classification of the books of the O. T.), which are evidence of the genuineness of these books at that time.

We have, however, unquestionable evidence of the genuineness of the O. T., in the *fact* that its canon was fixed some centuries before the birth of Jesus Christ. Jesus, the son of Sirach, author of the book of Ecclesiasticus, makes evident references to the prophesies of Isaiah, Jeremiah, and Ezekiel, and mentions these prophets by name: he speaks also of the 12 minor prophets. It likewise appears from the prologue to that book, that the law and the prophets, and other ancient books, were extant at the same period. The book of Ecclesiasticus, according to the best chronologers, was written in the Syro-Chaldaic dialect, A. M. 3772, that is, 232 years before the Christian era, and was translated by the grandson of Jesus into Greek, for the use of the Alexandrian Jews. The prologue was added by the translator; but this circumstance does not diminish the evidence for the antiquity of the O. T., for he informs us, that the Law and the Prophets, and the other books of their fathers, were studied by his grandfather; a sufficient proof that they were extant in his time. 50 years, indeed, before the age of the author of Ecclesiasticus, or 282 years before the Christian era, the Greek version of the O. T., usually called the Septuagint, was executed at Alexandria, the books of which are the same as in our Bibles, whence it is evident that we still have those identical books which the most ancient Jews attested to be genuine. The Christian fathers, too, Origen, Athanasius, Hilary, Gregory, Nazianzen, Epiphanius, and Jerome, speaking of the books that are allowed by the Jews as sacred and canonical, agree in saying that they are the same in number with the letters in the Hebrew alphabet, that is, 22, and reckon particularly those books which we have already mentioned. Nothing can be more satisfactory and conclusive than all the parts of the evidence for the authenticity and integrity of the canon of the O. T. Scriptures.

It may be added that the books of the O. T. have been always allowed, in every age and by every sect of the Hebrew church, to be the genuine works of those persons to whom they are usually ascribed, and they have also been universally and exclusively, without any addition or exception, considered by the Jews as written under the immediate influence of the Divine Spirit. Those who were contemporaries with the respective writers of these books, had the clearest evidence that they acted and spoke by the authority of God Himself; and this testimony, transmitted to all succeeding ages, was in many cases strengthened and confirmed by the gradual fulfilment of predictions contained in their writings. The Jews of the present day, dispersed all over the world, demonstrate the sincerity of their belief in the Authenticity of the Scriptures, by their inflexible adherence to the Law, and by the anxious expectation with which they wait for the accomplishment of the prophesies. "Blindness has happened to them" only "in part" (Rom. xi. 25), and the constancy with which they have endured persecution, and suffered hardships, rather than renounce the commands of their lawgiver, fully proves their firm conviction that these books were divinely inspired, and that they remain uninjured by time and transcription. Handed down, untainted by suspicion, from Moses to the present generation, they are naturally objects of their unshaken confidence and attachment. But suppose the case reversed: destroy the grounds of their faith, by admitting the possibility of the corruption of their Scriptures, and their whole history becomes utterly inexplicable. "A book of this nature," says Dr. Jenkin, speaking of the Bible, "which is so much the ancientest in the world, being constantly received as a Divine revelation, carries great evidence with it that it is authentic; for the first revelation is to be the criterion of all that follows, and God would not suffer the ancientest book of religion in the world to pass all along under the notion and title of a revelation, without causing some discovery to be made of the imposture, if there were any in it, much less would He preserve it by a particular and signal Providence for so many ages. It is a great argument for the truth of the Scriptures, that they have stood the test, and received the approbation, of so many ages, and still retain their authority, though so many ill men in all ages have made it their endeavor to disprove them; but it is a still further evidence in behalf of them, that God has been pleased to show so remarkable a providence in their preservation."

But the most decisive proof of the authenticity and inspiration of the ancient Scriptures is that (already hinted at) which is derived from the N. T. The Saviour of the world Himself, even He who came expressly "from the Father of Truth to bear witness to the Truth," in the last instructions which He gave to His Apostles just before His ascension, said: "These are the words which I spake unto you, while I was yet with you, that all things must be fulfilled which were written in the Law of Moses, and in the Prophets, and in the Psalms, concerning me" (Luke xxiv. 44). Our Lord, by thus adopting the common division of the Law, the Prophets, and the Psalms, which comprehended all the Hebrew Scriptures, ratified the canon of the O. T. as it was received by the Jews, and by declaring that these books contained prophesies which must be fulfilled; He established their divine inspiration, since God alone can enable men to foretell future events. At another time Christ told the Jews that they made "the word of God of none effect through their traditions" (Mark vii. 13). By thus calling the written rules which the Jews had received for the conduct of their lives, "the word of God," He declared that the Hebrew Scriptures proceeded from God Himself. Upon many other occasions Christ referred to the ancient Scriptures as books of divine authority; and both he and his Apostles constantly endeavored to prove that "Jesus was the Messiah" foretold in the writings of the Prophets. Paul bears strong testimony to the Divine authenticity of the Jewish Scriptures when he says to Timothy, "From a child thou hast known the Holy Scriptures, which are able to make thee wise unto salvation, through faith, which is in Christ Jesus" (2 Tim. iii. 15); this passage incontestably proves the importance of the ancient Scriptures, and the connection between the Mosaic and Christian dispensations; and in the next verse the Apostle expressly declares the inspiration of Scripture: "All Scripture is given by inspiration of God." To the same effect Luke says that "God spake by the mouth of his holy prophets" (i. 70). And Peter tells us that "prophesy came not in old time by the will of man, but holy men of God spake as they were moved by the Holy Ghost (2 Pet. i. 21). In addition to these passages, which refer to the ancient Scriptures collectively, we may observe that there is scarcely a book in the O. T. which is not repeatedly quoted in the N. T. as of Divine authority.

It appears from the different styles in which the books of Scripture are written, and from the different manner in which the same events are related, and predicted by different authors, that the sacred penmen were permitted to write as their several tempers, understandings, and habits of life, directed, and that the knowledge communicated to them by inspiration, upon the subject of their writings, was applied in the same manner as any knowledge acquired by ordinary means. In different parts of Scripture we perceive that there were different sorts and degrees of inspiration: God enabled Moses to give an account of the creation of the world. He enabled Joshua to record with exactness the settlement of the Israelites in the land of Canaan. He enabled David to mingle prophetic information with the varied effusions of gratitude, contrition, and piety. He enabled Solomon to deliver wise instructions for the regulation of human life. He enabled Isaiah to deliver predictions concerning the future Saviour of mankind, and Ezra to collect the sacred Scriptures into one authentic volume: "But all these worketh that one and the self-same Spirit, dividing to every man severally as He will" (1 Cor. xii. 11). In some cases inspiration only produced correctness and accuracy in relating past occurrences, as in writing the words of others; in other cases it communicated ideas, not only new and unknown before, but infinitely beyond the reach of unassisted human intellect; and sometimes inspired prophets delivered predictions for the use of future ages, which they did not themselves comprehend, and which can not be fully understood till they are accomplished. But whatever distinctions we may make with respect to the sorts, degrees, or modes of inspiration, we may rest assured that there is one property which belongs to every inspired writing, viz.: that it is free from error, and this property must be considered as extending to the whole of each of those writings, for we can not suppose that God would suffer any errors tending to mislead our faith or pervert our practice, to be mixed with those truths which He Himself has mercifully revealed to His rational creatures as the means of their eternal salvation. In this sense it may be confidently asserted, that the sacred writers always wrote under the influence, or guidance, or care of the Holy Spirit, which sufficiently establishes the truth and Divine authority of all Scripture.

THE PENTATEUCH.

The Pentateuch, the name by which the first five books of the Bible are designated, is derived from two Greek words, *pente*, *five*, and *teuchos*, a *volume*, thus signifying the five-fold volume. Originally these books formed one continuous work, as in the Hebrew manuscripts they are still connected in one unbroken roll. At what time they were divided into five portions, each having a separate title, is not known, but it is certain that the distinction dates at or before the time of the Septuagint translation. The names they bear in our English version are borrowed from the LXX, and they were applied by those Greek translators as descriptive of the principal subjects—the leading contents of the respective books. In the later Scriptures they are frequently comprehended under the general designation, *The Law, The Book of the Law*, since, to give a detailed account of the preparations for, and the delivery of, the Divine code, with all the civil and sacred institutions that were peculiar to the ancient economy, is the object to which they are exclusively devoted. They have been always placed at the beginning of the Bible, not only on account of their priority in point of time, but as forming an appropriate and indispensable introduction to the rest of the sacred books. The numerous and oft-recurring references made in the later Scriptures to the events, the ritual, and the doctrines of the ancient church, would have not only lost much of their point and significance, but have been absolutely unintelligible without the information which these five books contain. They constitute the groundwork or basis on which the whole fabric of revelation rests, and a knowledge of the authority and importance that is thus attached to them, will sufficiently account for the determined assaults that infidels have made on these books, as well as for the zeal and earnestness which the friends of the truth have displayed in their defense.

The books of the Pentateuch, of which Moses was the author, contain the history of the creation of the world and its inhabitants, the fall and curse of man, the destruction of all the human race save one family of eight souls, the dispersion of the nations, the deliverance of the chosen people of God from oppression, and the introduction of that wonderful dispensation of which the Divine Being Himself was the author and executor, and under which the civil and ecclesiastical government of these nations was administered for so many ages.

And whence did Moses receive the knowledge which philosophy has been so long in reaching through the paths of geology? Was the generation in which he lived more learned than any which succeeded for thousands of years? There is not the slightest shadow of evidence to sustain so incredible a position. It could not be through the slow processes of geological investigation, either of himself or his contemporaries, that Moses learned the sublime truths which were hidden from Aristotle and Pythagoras. The superior wisdom which distinguishes the Hebrew prophet from all his contemporaries, and renders his simple narrative a standard of truth in all ages, was from above. It was from Him who made the world that Moses learned the history of its creation; and in no other way could his successors on the inspired page be possessed of the truth and wisdom which shines as brightly in their pages as in his.

The inspiration of the author of the Pentateuch is one of "the things most surely believed among us." Messiah Himself was a prophet like unto Moses. The Pentateuch is the foundation of Scripture; all the subsequent books of revelation are full of allusions to these early documents. The books themselves claim Moses for their author, and there is no reason to doubt their statement. Their style and composition show them to have been written "at sundry times:" narrative and legislation are naturally interspersed. Laws are given in various forms; for, according to the growing exigencies of the time, did earlier statutes require modification. (Compare, for example, Ex. xxi. 2–6, with Deut. xv. 12–17, Num. iv. 24–33, with Num. vii. 1–9, Num. iv. 3, with Num. viii. 24, Lev. xvii. 3, 4, with Deut. xii. 5, 6, 21, Ex. xxii. 26, with Deut. xxiv. 6, 10-15, Ex. xxii. 16, 17, with Deut. xxii. 29). Had these books been a modern compilation, the laws would have been classified and arranged under separate heads; but they are given by Moses in the simple form in which they were originally enacted. The Hebrew nation has always received these treatises as the books of Moses, and they were read to the assembled tribes at stated periods. It is impossible that the nation could have received such publications at any period later than Moses. And so we find, from the time of Moses downwards uninterrupted witness to the existence and genuineness of the Pentateuch. (See Josh. i. 7, 8, xxiii. 6; compare Josh. xxiv. 26, with viii. 32, 34, 1 K. ii.3, 2 K. xxii. 8, 2 Chr. xxxiv. 14). To prove that these references are made to the very same books of Moses which we now possess, nothing more is necessary than to make a careful comparison of the passages in the historical books with the passages alluded in the Pentateuch (2 K. xiv. 6, with Deut. xxiv. 16, 2 K. xxiii. 2–25, and 2 Chr. xxxv. 1–19, with Lev. xxvi. 3–45 and Deut. vii. 11, xxviii. 68, Ezr. iii. 2–6, with Lev. vi. vii., Ezr. vi. 18, with Num. iii. 6–45, viii. 11, 14, Neh. i. 7–9, with Lev. xxvi. 41, and Deut. iv. 26, 27, xxviii. 64, xxx. 3–5). All these multiplied references may be verified by consulting the places referred to in the books of Moses.

The same thing occurs in the Prophets. Israel and Judah separated after the death of Solomon, but the 10 tribes preserved the law of Moses, the only religious book in circulation among them; and it is still known to the learned as the Samaritan Pentateuch. The prophets who labored among these 10 tribes often allude to the Pentateuch. (Compare Hos. ix. 10, with Num. xxv. 3, Hos. xi. 8, with Deut. xxix. 23, Hos. xii. 4, 5, with Gen. xxxii. 24, 25, Hos. xii. 12, with Gen. xxviii. 5, xxix. 20, Amos ii. 9, with Num. xxi. 21, 24, Amos. iv. 4, with Num. xxviii. 3, 4, Amos iv. 10, with Ex. vii.–xi., Amos iv. 11, with Gen. xix. 24, 25, Amos ix. 13, with Lev. xxvi. 5). The prophets, also, who flourished in Judah, are full of varied references to the law and early literature of their people. The history and character of the Jewish nation are a perpetual monument of the ancient existence, the veracity, and authenticity of the books of Moses, the man of God. The prophesies contained in the Pentateuch have also been strikingly and minutely fulfilled; and Jews, in their present condition, dispersion, and degradation, are living witnesses of their truth.

Let not the evidence adduced be deemed defective because we can not produce testimonies that Moses was the author of the Pentateuch from contemporary writers. If there were any at that remote period, their works and their memory have perished. "The Jews, as a nation," says Sumner, in his *Treatise on the Records of Creation*, "were always in obscurity, the certain consequence, not only of their situation, but of the peculiar constitution and jealous nature of their government. Can it, then, reasonably be expected that we should obtain positive testimony concerning this small and insulated nation from foreign historians, when the most ancient of these, whose works remain, lived more than 1000 yrs. posterior to Moses? Can we look for it from the Greeks, when Thucydides has declared that even respecting his own countrymen he could procure no authentic record prior to the Trojan war? or from the Romans, who had scarcely begun to be a people when the empire of Jerusalem was destroyed and the whole nation reduced to captivity? Such profane testimony as can be produced, serves only to show what was the prevailing opinion among heathens, and when we find them not only recording many of the facts in the narrative of Moses, but speaking of him by name, and referring to his law, we conclude that no doubt was entertained that he was the lawgiver of the Jews, or that his writings were genuine. Diodorus Siculus, Strabo, Tacitus, Juvenal and Longinus, make mention of him and his writings, in the same manner as we appeal to Cicero and his works. The truth is, no ancient book is surrounded with such evidence of its genuineness, authenticity, and inspiration, as the Pentateuch. Venerable in their age, sublime in their natural simplicity, overpowering in their evidence, and mighty in their results, are the five books of Moses.

GENESIS.

The first book of Moses is called "Genesis," because it gives an account of the "Generation," or origin of all things (ii. 4). It may be divided into two parts: the history of the world to the call of Abraham; and the history of 4 patriarchs. It is the record of a period of 2369 years:

	YEARS		YEARS
From the creation to the deluge	1656	From the death of Abraham to that of Isaac	105
– deluge to the call of Abraham	427	– – Isaac to that of Jacob . .	27
The remainder of the life of Abraham . . .	100	– – Jacob to that of Joseph .	54

This book records the history of the world from the commencement of time; the introduction of sin; the origin of the Church, and its state under the patriarchal dispensation. It may be viewed, indeed, as being in an especial manner the history of the Church. The Church and the world have always been distinct. The patriarchs were the heads of the ancient Church, who, surrounded with idolatry and iniquity, worshiped the true Jehovah, and adorned religion by their piety and virtue. We look with delight on Abel, Enoch, and Noah, on Abraham, Isaac, Jacob and Joseph, examples for the study and imitation of the good of all ages. Inspecting this sacred record more closely, we see that its great topics are: The creation, the first condition of man, the fall, the promise of a deliverer, the prevalence of sin in the world, the deluge, the preservation of Noah, the confusion of tongues, the call of Abraham, the destruction of Sodom and Gomorrah, the lives of Abraham, Isaac, Jacob, and, in part, of Joseph, and the descent into Egypt. Such is the general outline; but there are in this book subordinate agents and incidents which demand attention. In every page we see the wonderful works and ways of that God who, gracious and merciful, just and holy, rules over all things, and is especially mindful of his faithful people. The characters of the pious are here drawn with truth and impartiality; and while we behold in them that excellence which we ought to admire and to seek, we also behold in them those faults and defects which we ought to lament and shun. We look to the groves and bowers of Eden, but those only form a lovely vision that quickly fades from our view. Iniquity prevailed, and in the waters of an awful deluge we see the proof of the Divine displeasure on account of it. The earth is re-peopled by the descendants of Noah; but sin was soon the triumphant cause. Abraham is called to the knowledge and service of the true God; and in his history and in that of his descendants, we have the history of the Church then confined to narrow limits. Here we see the patriarchs in private as well as in public life; and while we contemplate with joy their faithfulness to God—their general excellence, we also contemplate with regret their display of weakness and folly, which was productive of much evil and misery. While, then, we see in this book the discovery of the character of God, and the nature and state of man, let every truth, character, and event; every development of sacred principle and of human passion and perverseness; be made the subject of close consideration, for we ought always to remember that all Scripture is given us "for doctrine, for reproof, for correction, for instruction in righteousness."

EXODUS.

This is the second book of the Pentateuch: the name by which we commonly distinguish it is that attached to it in the Septuagint version, being a Greek word significant of the principal transaction recorded, viz., the *departure* of Israel from Egypt. The Jews generally designate it by the two initial words, or, more shortly, by the second of them.

In Hebrew bibles it is divided into 11 *perashioth*, or *chapters*, and 29 *sedarim* or *sections*. In our own it is distributed into 40 chapters.

The contents of the book of Exodus may be regarded as compirsing (1) historical, and (2) legislative matter; the first may be considered as extending from i. 1 to xix. 2, the second from xix. 3 to xl. inclusive. But there is some legislation intermixed with the former, and some narrative with the latter part; we may, therefore, note some sub-divisions. I. In the first part we have (1) the condition of Israel in Egypt before their departure (i.) with the events preparatory to that deliverance, such as the birth of Moses and his settlement in Midian (ii.), the commission given him to liberate the people, and his announcement of this to them (iii. iv.), the negotiations with Pharaoh and infliction of the plagues, together with the institution of the Passover (v.-xii. 30); (2) the thrusting out of Israel by the Egyptians, the departure, the passage of the Red Sea, with the song of victory, and the march under the Divine protection to Sinai (xii. 31, xix. 2). II. In the second part we find the preparation for the establishment of the theocratic covenant (xix. 3-25), the promulgation of the moral law (xx.), ordinances chiefly of a judicial kind (xxi.-xxiii.), the ratification of the covenant, with the summoning of Moses to receive directions for ceremonial worship (xxiv.), the orders for the construction of a sanctuary with things pertaining to it, and the selection of a priestly caste (xxv.-xxxi.) interrupted by the apostasy of Israel, and Moses' intercession for them (xxxii., xxxiii.), with the resumption of the Divine directions, and the construction of the tabernacle in obedience thereto (xxxiv.-xl.).

The book of Exodus is closely connected with that of Genesis, yet it has a distinct character. Through the former book the large history of the human race was continually narrowing into that of a family to be separated from other nations as the chosen depository of Divine truth, whose fortunes should exhibit the outlines of the Divine dealings, to be filled up in the future trials and triumphs of the church. And branch after branch of that family is divided off, till a single nucleus is reached, to whom the promise of extended blessing was committed. The book of Exodus takes up the narrative of that family so circumscribed, and follows out its development in the increase of a household into a people, in the consolidation of vague promises into an orderly covenant, with its sanctions, and its regulations, and its priesthood, all pointing forward again to something still more substantial and more sufficient, when the teachings of a long minority should have ended, and the shadows of a tedious night have been succeeded by the bright rising of the Sun of Righteousness. Taken by itself, without reference to what preceded and what followed, the Book of Exodus would be a riddle, viewed in its right proportion as but a part of the great counsel of God, it is luminous with instruction and encouragement.

The time comprised in this book is generally believed to be about 145 yrs., from the death of Joseph to the erection of the tabernacle. This is of course on the supposition that the sojourn of Israel in Egypt was for 215 yrs., the 430 (Ex. xii. 40), being computed from the giving of the promise to Abraham (Gal. iii. 17). The authorship of Exodus has, through long ages, been ascribed to Moses. See on PENTATEUCH.

LEVITICUS.

This book is called "Leviticus" because it contains the laws respecting religion, or more particularly respecting the ceremonial ordinances, which were committed to Aaron and to his sons, who were of the tribe of "Levi." Strictly speaking, it is a continuation of the book of Exodus, in ch. xxv., of which book the ceremonial law begins, and it is continued through this book. Here we have an account of the different sorts of sacrifices and offerings: of the consecration of priests, of various sorts of uncleanness, with their purifications, of festivals, vows, tithes, and devoted things. ch. x. is historical, and xxvi. is hortatory. The period of time which the book comprises is about 1 month. Here, then, we have the Jewish ritual minutely unfolded to us. Such was the worship which God appointed for the descendants of Abraham until Shiloh should come, the subject of the prophesies and the substance of the types. In viewing the several sacrifices we do not pretend to assert in what particular or specific manner each of them referred to Christ. All of them, undeniably, did refer to Him. The burnt-offering was that which prevailed during the patriarchal period; and probably the eucharistic offerings existed under that part of the Divine economy. The burnt-offering and the peace-offering were of a general character, while the sin-offering and trespass-offering would seem to have been of a more particular nature; but all the sacrifices taught the great lesson that without the shedding of blood there is no remission of sin; and all of them pointed to Him who was to appear in the end of the world, "to put away sin by the sacrifice of himself" (Heb. ix. 26). The ritual sacrifices could not expiate sin as moral evil (Heb. x. 1-4). "They were commemorative acknowledgments of guilt, and typical pledges only of a sufficient sacrifice. They were ordained as an atonement of the breach of the ritual laws, and delivered the people from those civil and ecclesiastical punishments to which they were exposed from the wrath of God, considered as a political governor. They sanctified to the purifying of the flesh, washed away legal defilements, but were never intended to wipe off the stains of moral guilt, or to avert God's anger against sin, except as figurative of that perfect atonement, at the coming of which sacrifice and oblation should cease." On the subject of uncleanness and purification (xi.–xv.), it may be sufficient to observe, in general, that whatever other purposes it might have served (as restraining the Israelites from idolatry, keeping them a distinct people, and teaching them to revere God and to respect themselves), it undoubtedly had a reference to moral purity. Here material things, according to the genius of the whole economy, shadowed out immaterial things. The several offerings, the consecration of Aaron, the leprosy, the great day of atonement, the chief festivals, and the year of jubilee, will particularly arrest the attention of the serious mind, recollecting always, "that the whole service, like the vail on the face of Moses, concealed a spiritual radiance under an outward covering;" and taking from the Epistle to the Hebrews the true principle of interpreting this book, the reflecting reader cannot fail to compare the high-priest of the Jewish with the high-priest of the Christian dispensation, the sacrifices offered on the Jewish altar with the one sacrifice of Christ upon the cross, the Jewish leper with depraved and morally polluted man, the splendid festivals of the Jewish Church with the simple but expressive ordinances of the Gospel, and the Jewish jubilee with the whole period of evangelical constitution (Is. lxi. 1, 2). The Jewish ritual was "a yoke too heavy to be borne;" and we can not review it in a proper manner without seeing great cause of thankfulness that we live in a period when the shadows have past away, when the true light shines, and when we enjoy "the liberty with which Christ has made us free." But, still, we must view the Jewish ritual as being perfect in its kind, consider its design, to whom it was given, the state of the world when it was promulged, and the many purposes which it was to accomplish, and we may easily discover in it unnumbered proofs of the wisdom and goodness of God. If, then, we study the Jewish ritual in the light of the Gospel, we shall learn invaluable lessons of piety. God was once worshiped with a shadowy service; but the shadows exist no longer, and He is to be "worshiped in spirit and in truth." But religion is, substantially, always one and the same thing. We are polluted with sin; the leprosy of moral evil pervades our nature, and the just and holy God can only be approached by sacrifice, only served by holiness and obedience. Let us look, then, to our High-priest, to his blood and intercession; and let us implore the influences of his Spirit, and then we shall be justified, pardoned, sanctified, and made obedient; our Sabbaths will be days of holy rest, our festivals will be seasons of religious joy, and our life will be the jubilee of grace, preparatory to the jubilee of glory.

NUMBERS.

This book occupies the fourth place in the Pentateuch. It has several names among the Jews, the most common of which are the first and the fifth words in the first verse, which signify, respectively, "And he spake," and "In the wilderness." The name which we give it is taken from the fact that twice it records a numbering of Israel. By the Jews it is divided into ten *perashioth.*

There is no definite plan visible in the composition of this book, which contains both legal enactments and historical notices. It was probably written at different times during the period which it includes, that is, from the first day of the second month in the second year after the departure from Egypt, to the beginning of the eleventh month of the fortieth year (Num. i. 1, xxxvi. 13, compared with Deut. i. 3). But we may, for convenience, distribute its contents into three parts: I. Comprising the events and regulations during the continuance of the Israelites at Sinai (Num. i. 1, x. 10). In this we have the account of the first census. II. Transactions in the wilderness, from their quitting Sinai till the beginning of the fortieth year (x. 11, xix. 22). III. The occurrences and commands given in the first 10 or 11 months of the fortieth year (xx., xxxvi.). The second census is here detailed, also the deaths of Aaron and Miriam, and the arrival of the people in the plains of Moab, on the eastern bank of the Jordan. A list of their various stations through the whole of their wanderings is given in xxxiii.

It will be observed that most of the events narrated in Numbers occurred in the second and fortieth years of the wilderness-life of Israel. Little, and that not dated, is recorded of what happened in the interval. Exception has been taken to this fact. But it is in accordance with God's general plan in Scripture. Those events, only, He would have recorded for the permanent instruction of his Church, which were necessary to illustrate the covenant relationship in which. He designed to stand to them. Blanks, therefore, are often left in the history: much is omitted which it would have gratified our curiosity to know; all is related which is needful for our guidance and profit. One direct quotation, only, from this book (ch. xvi. 5), is made in the N. T. (2 Tim. ii. 19); but indirect references to it, by the later sacred writers, are very numerous.

DEUTERONOMY.

The Book of Deuteronomy (from *deuteros, second,* and *nomos, law*), as its name denotes, contains a repetition of the civil and moral law, which was a second time delivered by Moses, with some additions and explanations, as well as to impress it more forcibly upon the Israelites in general, as in particular for the benefit of those, who, being born in the wilderness, were not present at the first promulgation of the Law. It contains, also, a recapitulation of the several events which had befallen the Israelites since their departure from Egypt, with severe reproaches for their past misconduct, and earnest exhortations to future obedience. The Messiah is explicitly foretold in this book; and there are many predictions interspersed in different parts of it, particularly in chs. xxviii., xxx., xxxii., and xxxiii., relative to the future condition of the Jews. The Book of Deuteronomy includes only the short period of about 2 months, and finishes with an account of the death of Moses, which is supposed to have been added by his successor, Joshua.

As to the internal evidence that Moses wrote Deuteronomy, Rosenmueller argues it from very many places in the book, which show that *Canaan* was *not yet attacked,* but was *shortly to be occupied* by the Israelites: as vi. 1, 10, 11, 18, 19, vii. 1-5, 16-26, and xx. 16, 17. That this book is of Divine authority need not be questioned, when the several quotations out of it are observed as made by the Apostles of Christ, in Acts iii. 22; Rom. xii. 19; Heb. x. 30; Gal. iii. 10, out of chs. xviii. 15, and xxxii. 35, 36, and xxvii. 26, and by our Lord himself, Matt. xviii. 16, from ch. xix. 15. All Christ's answers to Satan's temptations are from this book; and the voice from heaven, directing the Apostles to hearken to Him, refers to a prophesy of Him in ch. xviii. 15.

The whole book may be considered as the last address of an aged parent to an undutiful race of children; and the earnestness and affection which prevail render it peculiarly interesting. It abounds with the finest models of oratory and poetry, which show that the mind of Moses, like his body, retained its full vigor. "This book and the Epistle to the Hebrews" (says Dr. A. Clarke), "contain the best comment on the nature, designs, and use of the law; the former may be considered as an evangelical commentary on the four preceding books, in which the spiritual reference and signification of the different parts of the law are given in such a manner as none could give who had not a clear discovery of the glory which was to be revealed. It may be safely asserted that very few parts of the O. T. can be read with greater profit by the genuine Christian than *Deuteronomy.*"

Deuteronomy has 7 parts, giving—

1. A summary of privileges and history of the Israelites (i.-iv. 40).
2. A summary of their laws, moral, civil, and ceremonial (iv. 40-26).
3. Directions as to what is to be done after crossing Jordan, including the blessings and curse (xxvii., xxviii.).
4. Exhortations to obedience (xxix., xxx.).
5. A narrative of events subsequent, with the song of Moses (xxxi., xxxii.).
6. The benediction of Moses (xxxiii.), and
7. An account of his death (xxxiv.), a period of 5 or 8 weeks.

JOSHUA.

This is the first book in the sacred canon called after the name of an individual. Of the books thus distinguished, some bear the names of their authors, as all the books of Prophesy; and others, those of persons who act a conspicuous part in the transactions recorded as Ruth, Job, and others. The present book might well be called "the Book of Joshua" on the latter ground, as it exclusively relates to the proceedings of that great leader, in fulfilment of the high commission entrusted to him, and terminates with his death. If, however, as many critics suppose, Joshua himself was the author of the book, it has a two-fold claim to be distinguished by his name. But the true authorship and date of the book have never been, and probably never can be, satisfactorily ascertained, and it would be to little profit to canvass the different hypotheses which have been advanced on the subject. The sum of the matter seems to be—(1). That the book was either written by Joshua towards the close of his life—the 5 last verses being added by a properly authorized person after his death—or, (2). That it was wholly written after his demise, from documents penned by him or under his direction. These are the substantial alternatives, and it cannot be very material which of them is adopted, as the genuineness and canonical authority of the book is in either case left entirely unaffected. If it were not written by Joshua himself, a comparison of ch. xv. 63, with 2 Sam. v. 6-8, respecting the capture of a part of Jerusalem, will make it quite evident that it must have been written before the 7th year of David's reign. But it may be safely admitted that even on the supposition that the substance of the book was indited by Joshua, there are in addition to the 5 last verses, several others interspersed which could not have been written by him, but were inserted by a later hand, and the above, for aught that appears, may have been of the number. But passages of this description are few and brief, and do not materially affect the plausibility of the opinion which ascribes the authorship of the book to the personage whose name it bears. This opinion is confirmed, though not established, by the fact that appears, the general voice of Jewish tradition assigns to the book the same author.

The book relates to the history of Israel while under the command and government of Joshua, the entrance of the Hebrews into Canaan, their conquest of the greater part of the country, the division of the territory by lot among the several tribes, and the provision made for the settlement and establishment of the Jewish Church in that country. The length of time embraced in this history is variously stated by chronologists, at 17, 27, and 30 yrs. Between 26 and 27 yrs. is the usually received and most probable period. The leading drift of the writer is to demonstrate the faithfulness of God in the perfect accomplishment of all his promises to the patriarchs, Abraham, Isaac, Jacob, and Joseph, and also to Moses, that the children of Israel should obtain possession of the land of Canana. Viewed in this light, it is an invaluable appendage to the preceding 5 Books of Moses, and indeed bears to them very much the same relation as does the Acts of the Apostles to the Gospels of the 4 Evangelists. The inspired historian relates, with all the animation of one who was an actual eye-witness and participator of the scenes described, the successive miracles that favored and secured the conquest of the country, the general zeal, activity, and obedience of Israel in prosecuting their wars, with the occasional lapses and transgressions that interrupted the career of their victories. We see the Divine power and faithfulness conspicuously displayed in guiding, cherishing, and defending the chosen people amidst all the trials to which they were exposed; and while the general tenor of the narrative affords a striking emblem of the warfare of the Christian in gaining possession of his heavenly inheritance, it ministers the most abundant encouragement to those who, in sincerity and faith, throw themselves upon the superintending care of that Being who keepeth covenant and mercy forever.

JUDGES.

This book contains the history of the Israelites from the death of Joshua to the days of Eli, under 13 Judges (men whom God raised in times of imminent danger for the deliverance of His people from their enemies). Samuel, probably, wrote it. Its chronology is very difficult; but it must comprise the period of about 300 yrs.

The latter part of the book, chs. xvii.-xxi., belongs, in chronological order, to a period not long after the death of Joshua; but it is put at the end in order that the regular narrative may not be interrupted.

As to the real character of several of the Judges, it is by no means easy to form a correct idea of it. Where our knowledge is so scanty and imperfect, our decisions ought to be cautious and modest. They were men raised up for especial purposes, and they acted by an especial commission. We are not, therefore, either to justify or condemn them with unreflecting promptitude. The clear and weighty instruction which the book is intended to convey is what demands our chief consideration. It furnishes, us then, with a striking picture of a country without magistracy; of the contest between true and false religion; of the judgments of God on impiety, and of his mercy to the penitent. The Israelites, now settled in Canaan, instead of improving their blessings, to the glory of God, and to their own happiness, plunged into idolatry, and brought on themselves the severe chastisements of Almighty God. They sinned, and were punished; they repented, and were delivered; renewed offense was followed by renewed chastisement; but, in the truth and forbearance of God, they were still preserved.

The 13 Judges were Othniel, Ehud, Shamgar, Deborah, Gideon, Tola, Jari, Jephtha, Ibzan, Elon, Abdon, Eli, and Samson; but it does not appear that they ruled in succession, but at intervals, and more than one of them at the same time, in different parts of the land.

RUTH.

Ruth is the 8th in order of the books of the O. T., and is regarded as a kind of supplement to the book of Judges. In the old Jewish canon, Judges and Ruth formed but one book. The precise period when the events related in it occurred cannot be accurately determined. The book itself refers in general to the epoch of the Judges; but it does not determine under what Judge these interesting scenes took place. Perhaps the government of Gideon may be regarded as an approximation to a correct chronology. Salmon, the father of Boaz, was married to Rahab. Between Salmon and David there were at least 300 yrs.; and yet Boaz, Obed, and Jesse are the only intervening individuals; so that if no other names are omitted from the catalogue, the progenitors of David are examples of remarkable longevity. Jesse went "among men for an old man in the days of Saul" (1 Sam. xvii. 12). If Samuel was the author of this book, the genealogy found at the conclusion may have been added by a later hand, as David's accession to the kingdom is evidently implied in it. The Jews now place it among the Hagiographa. The book contains a biography of the individual above named, and her family. It has only 4 chapters; and though there are at its close some highly important genealogical facts, its prominent design is to prove the watchful care of God's providence over such as fear and trust him. It showed that heathen blood was not unworthy at all times of a Hebrew alliance. The simplicity of rural life is beautifully depicted; not by a shadowy fiction, but in the homely records of affection and virtue. Ancient manners were frank, truthful, and undisguised. This prose idyl far excels those labored songs and artificial delineations which grace the pastoral poetry of Greece and Rome.

THE FIRST AND SECOND BOOKS OF SAMUEL.

The Books of Samuel contain a brief outline of the life and times of Samuel, Saul, and David. Being contemporaries, though unequal in age, and successors in the high office of chief ruler in Israel, their biographies are necessarily much entwined. The times to which the history relates were, in the highest sense, seasons of trouble. By the imbecility and wickedness of the later Judges, the nation had degenerated into a state of lawless confusion. Separated as they were, by the division of tribes, into distinct communities, each section had secured a degree of independence altogether incompatible with national subordination and prosperous tranquility. The annals, therefore, which record a transition from this state, and the chief persons who took part in the important changes, necessarily possess a large degree of interest. Samuel is first introduced by the sacred penman, who fills up the first 7 chapters by a notice of the extraordinary circumstances of his birth, a glimpse of the low state of religion and morals which character- ized both rulers, priests, and people, an account of Samuel's call and introduction to the prophetic office, the calamities which befell Israel in a warlike engagement with the Philistines, when the sons of Eli and much people were slain, and the ark of God taken captive, the election of Samuel to the office of Judge, his success in battle, his upright government, his peaceful reign, and his strict attention to religious duty. The sacred annalist goes on to tell of the regency of Samuel's sons, their misrule, the disaffection and fears of the people, their resolute demand for a king to reign over them, Samuel's fidelity to the theocracy, and reluctance to yield to the popular clamor, and the anointing, selection, and proclamation of Saul as the first monarch in Israel. These things fill up the next 5 chapters. Saul now occupies the foreground of the history for a considerable space. There are briefly noticed—his early degeneracy, the expostulation of the prophet, and his announcement that the kingdom would be wrested from the son of Kish, and given to another; the choice and consecration of David, the melancholy and distress of Saul, his frequent wars with his neighbors, his enmity against David and frequent attempts to take away his life, and the inglorious death of himself and Jonathan, his son, in Mt. Gilboa, where Israel had been vanquished by the Philistines. This last event is recorded at the end of book first. Much of the preceding annals, however, is taken up with the history of David, where he plays an extensive, though only a secondary part. The inspired historian tells of David's introduction at court as a skilful musician, for the purpose of soothing the troubled spirit of Saul; his encounter with Goliath; his consequent fame throughout all Israel; his subsequent exploits; his dangers, and his escapes while "hunted like a partridge" on the mountains by his inveterate persecutor. The sacred annalist proceeds in the second book to give the details of David's history. There are recorded his gradual progress to the summit of power; his taking of Jerusalem, and constituting it the capital of the kingdom; his bringing up the ark from Gilboah to the metropolis; his resolution and preparation to build a temple to Jehovah; his various wars and singular successes, and his enlargement and settling of all the borders of Israel. David's respect for the principles of the Divine government; his attachment to religious matters, and his eminent piety, are set forth with due prominence; and his faults and misfortunes are not overlooked. No attempt is made to conceal his distrustfulness in equivocating to Achish, his wickedness towards Uriah and Bathsheba, or his haughtiness in numbering the people. The domestic trials of the royal Psalmist, arising from polygamy (that bane of Oriental households), are noticed with sufficient minuteness; and the multifarious evils which accrued to the kingdom and the monarch from Absalom's unnatural rebellion, are preserved in graphic and striking colors. A specimen of the divine songs of David, corresponding almost entirely with the xviiith in the Book of Psalms, and the last inspired effusion which "the sweet singer" penned, are given towards the close; and the history terminates abruptly, after mentioning the numbering of the people, the judgment which followed, and the becoming penitence of the king and his smitten subjects. Throughout the narrative is varied and enlivened by fragments of Hebrew poetry; such as, Hannah's song (1 Sam. ii. 1–10); the "Song of the Bow" (2 Sam. i. 19–27), and David's thankgiving (2 Sam. ii. 17), poetry at once beautiful in composition, and interesting and elevated in the sentiments it breathes.

The authorship of the Books of Samuel, and the date of their compilation, are matters involved in considerable obscurity. An old opinion ascribes the work to the pen of Samuel; but it was impossible for him to have written it in its present form, otherwise he not only recorded his own death, but very much that occurred after that event. The notion is founded on the words in 1 Chr. xxix. 29: "Now, the acts of David, the king, first and last, behold, they are written in the Book of Samuel, the seer, and in the Book of Nathan, the prophet, and in the Book of Gad, the seer." These words, by no means, prove Samuel to be the author of the books which bear his name; but they are fitted to suggest a very probable solution of the difficulty. It was customary with the prophets to keep a register of all the leading events of the times in which they lived (1 Sam. x. 25); and to such records the passage quoted from Chronicles may refer. Samuel, Nathan, and Gad lived and occupied prominent stations as prophets during the most important periods of the time of David. In addition to the changes in the government, and events of Saul's reign, the register of Samuel would naturally contain the chief points of David's early history. The narrative of the prophet Gad, who attended the son of Jesse in his wanderings (1 Sam. xxii. 5), would embrace the leading points in this section of his life; and the writings of Nathan would fill up what was lacking of the events of David's reign, and the occurrences of his more advanced years. The works of these three seers, therefore, would contain all the materials of the Books of Samuel; and seeing that the history closes before the king's death, the conclusion is most probable that Gad was the person who put the compilation into its present form. Besides the manuscripts already mentioned, the compiler had before him the Book of Jasher, a collection of national odes, from which the "Song of the Bow," and, it may be, most of the other poetic fragments were extracted. It is impossible to say by what name Gad would designate his work when completed; but the great reason of the present appellation, "Books of Samuel," seems to be in the fact that the Son of Elkanah, the most prominent and interesting place is in the early parts of the history. If it be admitted that the prophet Gad compiled the books as they now stand, their authenticity and credibility will, of necessity, demand our assent. The production of an inspired prophet has no need of further witness to commend it to our faith. But, although the genuineness of the history be a doubtful point, its credibility rests on a most sure word of testimony. This is the authority of the N. T. Acts xiii. 22; Heb. i. 5, are respectively quoted from 1 Sam. xiii. 14, 2 Sam. vii. 14.

THE BOOKS OF KINGS.

The two Books of Kings follow and are closely connected with those of Samuel, carrying on the history of the chosen people from the point where the preceding record leaves it. They are not separate compositions; in fact, in the Hebrew canon, they formed but a single book, in which the author has exhibited the progressive development of the theocracy, according to the principle of God's promise to David (2 Sam. vii. 12–16). This promise is the connecting thread; and its fulfilment is illustrated in the way in which God preserved an inheritance to David's family. In the kingdom of the 10 tribes the sceptre is seen passing from one to another, seized by bold usurpers, whose descendants retained it rarely above 2 or 3 generations; but David wanted not a man to sit upon his throne continually, a pregnant fact, a gracious assurance being therein conveyed of that everlasting kingdom which should be fully established in the person of David's greater Son, who was to have the heathen for his inheritance, and the uttermost parts of the earth for his possession (Ps. ii. 8).

It is to the illustration of this great principle that the Books of Kings are dedicated. And they evince a sufficient unity to show that they were composed by a single author. They are compiled, no doubt, from various sources; yet they are not a bald compilation, but a perfect history, worked up on a definite plan, in method and in style giving ample proof of their independent completeness.

The sources from which the author drew his materials are exactly indicated. Thus at the close of Solomon's history he refers to *the Book of the Acts of Solomon* (1 K. xi. 41); for every king of Judah to *the Book of the Chronicles of the kings of Judah* (xiv. 29, xv. 7, 23, xxii. 45; 2 K. viii. 23, xii. 19; and elsewhere): and for every king of Israel to *the Book of the Chronicles of the kings of Israel* (1 K. xiv. 19, xv. 31, xvi. 5, 14, 20, 27, xxii. 19; 2 K. i. 18, x. 34, and elsewhere). The book of the Acts of Solomon has been thought identical with *the Book of Nathan the Prophet* (2 Chr. ix. 29): it was more probably a comprehensive history compiled from, or at all events comprehending all that was recorded in, the three books named in the same place. The Book of the Chronicles of the kings of Israel is cited for the last time in 2 K. xv. 31, that of the kings of Judah last in xxxiv. 5; possibly these Chronicles did not come down to a later point than the reigns of Pekah and Jehoiakim respectively. We can only conjecture that these works may have been part of a complete history cited as *the Book of the kings of Judah and Israel*, in 2 Chr. xxxii. 32, and with slight variations of title in xx. 34, xxiv. 27, xxxv. 27. Some have imagined that these were annals duly kept by the "recorders," of whom we frequently hear as officers of state, but this is very unlikely. It is more probable that prophetic men from time to time wrote the leading events of their own days (hence, may be, the full account of the acts of Elijah and Elisha), not perhaps in a regular succession, but still so as to furnish a number of memoirs from which the history of the nation might be compiled before the Exile. It is some corroboration of this conjecture that "the book of Jehu, the son of Hanani" is said to be incorporated (such is the meaning of the text) with "the book of the kings of Israel" (2 Chr. xx. 34).

The composition of the books of Kings may be dated between the death of Jehoiacin (the exact time of which we do not know) and the return from Captivity. The author can not be identified. These books have always had a place in the Jewish canon, and the history they contain is authenticated by the references we find in the N. T. (Luke iv. 25-27 ; Acts vii. 47 ; Rom. xi. 2-4 ; James v. 17, 18). Modern research is also adding fresh evidence to the truth of the narrative.

These books may properly be distributed into three different parts: I. The narrative of Solomon's reign (1 K. i.-xi.). II. The contemporary history of the two kingdoms of Israel and Judah from the division of the nation (xii. 2; K. xvii.). III. The account of the kingdom of Judah while it stood alone to the period of the Babylonish Captivity (xviii.-xxv.). The length of time embraced is about 453 years. It may be observed that the first book would end better at xxii. 50 than at 53, ver. 51-53 more properly belongs to 2 K. i.

CHRONICLES.

The 13th and 14th books of the O. T. are called the 1st and 2d books of Chronicles, or Annals. In the Hebrew, they are called *Books of Days*, that is, *diaries*. By the Septuagint translators, they are named *paraleipomena, things omitted*, or *supplements*, because they seem to be in some sense supplemental to the 2 books of Kings which precede them. They appear to have been compiled from the national diaries or journals, but it does not satisfactorily appear who compiled them.

The probability is that Ezra was the author, as the history is brought down to his period. The Books of Chronicles which we are now considering, are not to be confounded with these public records so often referred to as the Chronicles of the Kings of Israel and Judah. The compiler of the canonical books of Chronicles had before him all the available sources of Jewish history. He has made use of the Pentateuch, of the books of Samuel and Kings, and of many other public annals no longer in existence. He refers his readers to the book of Nathan, the vision of Iddo, the book of Gad the seer, and of Samuel the seer, the prophesy of Ahijah the Shilonite, the vision of Isaiah, book of Jehu and of Shemaiah the prophet, the Chronicles of King David, and the Lamentations for Josiah. All these were sources of information patent to the inspired compiler. None seem to be identical with any of our canonical books, but were in use and circulation when Ezra flourished. The style, too, in which the books of Chronicles are written, corresponds with the mixed and degenerate Hebrew in common currency after the Captivity. It employs many words peculiar to the language of that country in which the Jews had lived for 70 yrs. In the Hebrew Bibles the books of Chronicles are placed last, and form the conclusion of the inspired volume.

The principal object of the author of these books seems to have been, to point out, from the public records, the state of the different families before the Captivity, and the distribution of the lands among them, that each tribe might, as far as possible, obtain the ancient inheritance of their fathers at their return. So that this portion of the O. T. may be considered as an epitome of all the *sacred* history, but more especially from the origin of the Jewish nation to their return from the first Captivity; embracing a period of nearly 3,500 yrs. The 1st book traces the rise and propagation of the children of Israel, from Adam, together with a circumstantial account of the reign and transactions of David: the 2d continues the narrative, relates the progress and dissolution of the kingdom of Judea (apart from Israel), to the year of the return of the people from Babylon.

This book, (for both were originally reckoned but one in the Hebrew Scriptures), therefore, in its construction and design differs from Samuel and Kings. Samuel is more biographical in its nature, while Kings is a theocratic history—a history of the nation, as the people of God, and yet forming a human commonwealth. Chronicles is more ecclesiastic in its structure, is more concerned with the Jews as a church, than the Jews as a state. The order and arrangement of the public worship occupy a prominent place. David's wars and victories are in this book subordinate to the peculiar ordinances which he enacted for the national service of God. His preparations for building the Temple are minutely detailed and fully dwelt upon, and the only portions of Solomon's life rehearsed at length are those in connection with the erection and dedication of that magnificent sanctuary which formed the most glorious epoch of his reign. The brief accounts of the other sovereigns have generally some relation to the religious element of the government. This is continually kept in view. Under Rehoboam, and after the schism, we are told: "And the priests and the Levites that were in all Israel resorted to him out of all their coasts. For the Levites left their suburbs, and their possession, and came to Judah and Jerusalem, for Jeroboam and his sons had cast them off from executing the priest's office to the Lord " (2 Chr. xi. 13, 14). Again, when Ahijah and Jeroboam were met on the field of battle, the former is reported to have delivered this address: "And now ye think to withstand the kingdom of the Lord in the hand of the sons of David, and ye be a great multitude, and there are with you golden calves, which Jeroboam made you for gods. Have ye not cast out the priests of the Lord, the sons of Aaron, and the Levites, and have made you priests after the manner of the nations of other lands? so that whosoever cometh to consecrate himself with a young bullock and seven rams, the same may be a priest of them that are no gods. But as for us, the Lord is our God, and we have not forsaken him, and the priests, which minister unto the Lord, are the sons of Aaron, and the Levites wait upon their business; and they burn unto the Lord, every morning and every evening, burnt sacrifices and sweet incense ; the shew-bread also set they in order upon the pure table, and the candlestick of gold, with the lamps thereof, to burn every evening: for we keep the charge of the Lord our God, but ye have forsaken him" (1 Chr. xiii. 8-11). Asa's reformation is fully described, as well as his religious homage, and his gifts to the house of God : "And they offered unto the Lord the same time, of the spoil which they had brought, seven hundred oxen and seven thousand sheep; . . . . . And he brought into the house of God the things that his father had dedicated, and that he himself had dedicated, silver, and gold, and vessels " (2 Chr. xv. 11, 18). The ecclesiastical deeds of Jehoshaphat are also brought out : "Moreover, in Jerusalem, did Jehoshaphat set of the Levites, and of the priests, and of the chief of the fathers of Israel, for the judgment of the Lord, and for controversies, when they returned to Jerusalem: . . . . . . And, behold, Amariah the chief priest is over you in all matters of the Lord ; and Zebadiah the son of Ishmael, the ruler of the house of Judah, for all the king's matters; also the Levites shall be officers before you. Deal courageously, and the Lord shall be with the good" (2 Chr. xix. 8, 11). "And the Levites, of the children of the Kohathites, and of the children of the Korhites, stood up to praise the Lord God of Israel with a loud voice on high; . . . . . . And when he had consulted with the people, he appointed singers unto the Lord, and that should praise the beauty of holiness, as they went out before the army, and to say, Praise the Lord, for his mercy endureth for ever" (2 Chr. xx. 19, 21). The part which the priests and Levites took in the proclamation and coronation of Joash occupies a considerable space, and this king's desire to repair the Temple is almost the only incident of his life recorded, though he reigned 40 years. In Kings, it is told that God smote Uzziah or Azariah with leprosy, but the reason is not stated. In Chronicles, however, you find a full account of his sin and punishment. The crime which brought upon him this penalty was an invasion of the priest's office (2 Chr. xxvi. 16-19). A long account is given of the life of Hezekiah, who had much of David's spirit within him, in reforming and reinstituting the public worship, and in afterwards keeping a solemn passover. This period was a revival, not unlike the first dedication of the Temple, and so it is copiously and minutely narrated: "And thus did Hezekiah throughout all Judah, and wrought that which was good, and right, and truth, before the Lord his God. And in every work that he began in the service of the house of God, and in the law, and in the commandments, to seek his God, he did it with all his heart, and prospered" (2 Chr. xxxi. 20, 21). The reign of Josiah has, for similar reasons, a special prominence given to it: "So all the service of the Lord was prepared the same day, to keep the passover, and to offer burnt offerings upon the altar of the Lord, according to the commandment of king Josiah. And the children of Israel that were present kept the passover at that time, and the feast of unleavened bread seven days. And there was no passover like to that kept in Israel from the days of Samuel the Prophet: neither did all the kings of Israel keep such a passover as Josiah kept, and the priests and the Levites, and all Judah and Israel that were present, and the inhabitants of Jerusalem" (2 Chr. xxxv. 16-18). Now, these sections of Jewish history, are either omitted altogether, or but slightly referred to in the books of Kings; and this peculiar construction of the Book of Chronicles, this peculiar selection of materials proves, that it is to a great extent a Church history, and that it was meant to impress the Jews returning from Babylon with the necessity of establishing and organizing anew the national ritual. This purpose is kept constantly in view throughout the entire narrative, and gives it its distinctive form and aspect. Still Samuel, Kings, and Chronicles, should be read and compared together, as they relate substantially the same records, though with different degrees of particularity, and with different means of information: so that the whole contains but one history, and what is obscure or defective in one part may be explained or supplied in another.

The following useful table taken from De Wette's Introduction, may facilitate the study and collation of these 3 books:

TABLE OF PASSAGES PARALLEL WITH 1 CHR. X.—2 CHR. XXXVI.

1 Chr. x. 1-12 . . . . 1 Sam. xxxi.	2 Chr. xx. 31—xxi. 1 . 1 Kings xxii. 41-51.
- xi. 1-9 . . . . 2 Sam. v. 1-10.	- xxi. 5-10 . . . 2 Kings viii. 17-24.
- xi. 10-47 . . . - xxiii. 8-39.	- xxii. 1-9 . . { - viii. 25, 29, ix. 16-28, x. 12-14.
- xiii. 1-14 . . . - vi. 1-11.	
- xiv. 1-7 . . . . - v. 11-16.	- xxii. 10—xxiii. 21 - xi.
- xiv. 8-17 . . . - v. 17-25.	- xxiv. 1-14, 23-27 - xii.
- xv. xvi. . . . . - vi. 12-23.	- xxv. 1-4, 11, 17-28 - xiv. 1-14, 17-20.
- xvii. . . . . . - vii.	- xxvi. 1-4, 21, 23 { - xiv. 21, 22, xv. 2-5, 7.
- xviii. . . . . . - viii.	
- xix. . . . . . - x.	- xxvii. 1-3, 9 . . - xv. 33-35, 38.
- xx. 1-3 . . . . - xi. 1, xii. 26-31.	- xxviii. 1-4 . . . - xvi. 2-4.
- xx. 4-8 . . . - xxi. 18-22.	- xxix. 1, 2 . . . - xviii. 2, 3.
- xxi. . . . . . - xxiv.	- xxii. 9-21 . . { - xviii. 17-35, xix. 14, 15, 35-37.
2 Chr. i. 2-13 . . . . 1 Kings iii. 4-15.	
- i. 14-17 . . . . - x. 26-29.	- xxxii. 24, 25, 30-33 . . . { - xx. 1, 2, 8, 9, 12, sqq., 20, 21.
- ii. . . . . . - v. 15-32.	
- iii. 1—v. 1 . . - vi. vii. 13, 51.	- xxxiii. 1-10, 20 . - xxi. 1-10, 18.
- v. 2—vii. 10 . . - viii.	- xxxiii. 21-25 . . - xxi. 19-24.
- vii. 11-22 . . - ix. 1-9.	- xxxiv. 1, 2, 8-28 - xxii.
- viii. . . . . - ix. 10-28.	- xxxiv. 29-33 . . - xxiii. 1-20.
- ix. 1-12 . . . - x. 1-13.	- xxxv. 1, 18, 20, 24, xxxvi. 1. { - xxiii. 21-23, 28-30
- ix. 13-31 . . . - x. 14-29.	
- x. 1—xi. 4 . . . - xii. 1-24.	- xxxvi. 2-4 . . . - xxiii. 31-34.
- xii. 2, 9-11, 13-16 - xiv. 21-31.	- xxxvi. 5, 6, 8 . { - xxiii. 36-37, xxiv. 1, 6.
- xiii. 1, 2, 23 . - xv. 1, 2, 7, 8.	
- xiv. 1, xv. 16-19 . - xv. 11-24.	- xxxvi. 9, 10 . . - xxiv. 8-10, 14, 17.
- xv. 1—6, 11-14 .	- xxxvi. 11, 12 . . - xxiv. 18, 19.
- xviii . . . . . - xxii. 2-35.	- xxxvi. 22, 23. . Ezra, i. 1, 2.

The authenticity of the Chronicles is placed beyond dispute by a vast variety of collateral evidence. There are some discrepancies, it is true, especially in numbers, for as the letters of the Hebrew alphabet were employed in enumeration, and many of them are so like, the copyist was in such matters peculiarly liable to introduce variations. The Jewish history, though reaching back to so remote a period, is precise and minute, and the abundance of correct registers, preserved by families and tribes, and incorporated in these annals, leaves us in no doubt of the great truth that Jesus, according to prophesy, was the seed of Abraham and son of David.

The object of the writer of Chronicles can not be fully understood unless we bear in mind, that his purpose was to teach by writing history, to illustrate by the past experience of the nation, certain important and fundamental truths, connected with their progress and destiny. His grand theme is this, religion is the basis of national prosperity, a great fact, to the certainty and importance of which, the annals of a thousand years bear constant and thrilling testimony. If these books are read in the light of this idea, their wise and benignant aim will be warmly admired. Let the reader, as he studies them, prefix to them this motto, "righteousness exalteth a nation, but sin is the reproach of any people," and he will find them not a dry detail and dull catalogue, but verily, "profitable for doctrine, for reproof, for correction, and for instruction in righteousness."

EZRA.

Ezra, the author of the book which bears his name, was of the sacerdotal family, being a direct descendant from Aaron, and succeeded Zerubbabel in the government of Judea. This book begins with the repetition of the last two verses of the second book of Chronicles, and carries the Jewish history through a period of 79 yrs., commencing from the edict of Cyrus. It is to be observed, that between the dedication of the Temple and the departure of Ezra, that is, between the 6th and 7th chapters of this book, there was an interval of about 58 yrs., during which nothing is here related concerning the Jews, except that, contrary to God's command, they intermarried with Gentiles. This book is written in Chaldee from the 8th verse of the 4th chapter to the 27th verse of the 7th chapter. It is probable that the sacred historian used the Chaldean language in this part of his work, because it contains chiefly letters and decrees written in that language, the original words of which he might think it right to record, and indeed the people, who were recently returned from the Babylonian Captivity, were at least as familiar with the Chaldee as they were with the Hebrew tongue.

Till the arrival of Nehemiah, Ezra had the principal authority in Jerusalem. Josephus says that Ezra was buried at Jerusalem, but the Jews believe that he died in Persia, in a second journey to Artaxerxes. His tomb is shown there in the city of Tamura. He is said to nave lived nearly 120 yrs.

Ezra was the restorer and publisher of the Holy Scriptures, after the return of the Jews from the Babylonian Captivity. 1. He corrected the errors which had crept into the existing copies of the sacred writings by the negligence or mistake of transcribers. 2. He collected all the books of which the Holy Scriptures then consisted, disposed them in their proper order, and settled the canon of Scripture for his time. 3. He added throughout the books of his edition what appeared necessary for illustrating, connecting, or completing them, and of this we have an instance in the account of the death and burial of Moses, in the last chapter of Deuteronomy. In this work he was assisted by the same Spirit by which they were at first written. 4. He changed the ancient names of several places become obsolete, and substituted for them new names, by which they were at that time called. 5. He wrote out the whole in the Chaldee character, that language having grown into use after the Babylonish Captivity. The Jews have an extraordinary esteem for Ezra, and say that if the law had not been given by Moses, Ezra deserved to have been the legislator of the Hebrews.

NEHEMIAH.

Nehemiah professes himself the author of the book which bears his name, in the very beginning of it, and he uniformly writes in the first person. He was of the tribe of Judah, and was probably born at Babylon during the Captivity. He was so distinguished for his family and attainments, as to be selected for the office of cup-bearer to the king of Persia, a situation of great honor and emolument. He was made governor of Judea, upon his own application, by Artaxerxes Longimanus, and this book, which in the Hebrew Canon was joined to that of Ezra, gives an account of his appointment and administration, through a space of about 36 yrs. to A. M. 3595, at which time the Scripture history closes, and consequently these historical books, from Joshua to Nehemiah inclusive, contain the history of the Jewish people from the death of Moses, A. M. 2553, to the reformation established by Nehemiah, after the return from Captivity, being a period of 1042 yrs.

Nehemiah presents a noble example of true patriotism, founded on the fear of God (v. 15), and seeking the religious welfare of the state. His respect for the Divine law, his reverence for the Sabbath (xiii. 18), his devout acknowledgment of God in all things (i. ii. 2, 18), his practical perception of God's character (iv. 14, ix. 6-33), his union of watchfulness and prayer (iv. 9, 20), his humility in ascribing all good in himself to the grace of God (ii. 12, vii. 5), are all highly commendable. In the 9th chapter, we have an instructive summary of the history of the Jews, in its most important light, showing at once what God is, and what men are. Few books, indeed, of the Bible, contain a richer illustration of Divine philosophy—that is, of true religion taught by example.

ESTHER.

This book is so termed because Esther is the principal figure in it, not from any notion that she wrote it. It has generally been held in high esitmation among the Jews, who class it with Ruth, Ecclesiastes, Solomon's Song, and the Lamentations, as the five *megillath* or *rolls*, and solemnly read it at the feast of Purim.

With regard to the writer of this book nothing certain can be said. Some have ascribed it to Mordecai, or to Mordecai and Esther jointly, grounding their notion on Esther ix. 20, 23, 32. But the statements there made refer, not to the authorship of the book, but to the circular letter sent to the Jews. That it was written by a resident in Persia may very well be allowed. There is a thorough acquaintance evinced with Persian customs (see i. 1, 10, 14, 19, ii. 9, iii. 7, 12, 15, iv. 11, viii. 8). The diction closely resembles that of Ezra and Nehemiah, mixed with some Persisms, just such as we might suppose a contemporary of theirs likely to use. The arguments employed by some critics to bring the composition down to a late date, grounded on the language, are therefore of little weight. Neither is the alleged spirit of revenge pervading the narrative, nor the supposed formalism in religion, worth mentioning. The spirit of revenge is not in the writer, but, if anywhere, in the persons whose deeds are chronicled. And, as revengeful deeds have been committed in all ages, the occurrence of them can not be taken as a chronological mark. Neither is more stress laid on fasting than in other times of Hebrew history (comp. Judg. xx. 26; 2 Sam. xii. 16, 17, 21, 22). The composition, therefore, of the book may most reasonably be placed about or soon after the time when the facts occurred. But there is one great peculiarity of the history. The name of God does not occur in it. Various hypotheses have been devised to explain this fact. A very probable one is that, as the history of the reigns of Persian kings was duly chronicled (Esth. ii. 23, vi. 1, x. 2), and the events here narrated were of course recorded in the annals of the empire, this book may be a translated extract from those annals. There would be nothing more strange in such an extract's being preserved in the sacred canon than in Dan. iv., being, as it is, a decree of Nebuchadnezzar.

The contents of this book may be thus stated:

It relates to the royal feast of Ahasuerus, and the divorce of Vashti, ch. i. The elevation of Esther to the Persian throne, and the service rendered to the king by Mordecai, in detecting a plot against his life. 2. The promotion of Haman, and his purposed destruction of the Jews. 3. The consequent affliction of the Jews, and the measures taken by them. 4. The defeat of Haman's plot against Mordecai, through the instrumentality of Esther, the honor done to Mordecai, and the execution of Haman. 5, 6, 7. The defeat of Haman's general plot against the Jews, the institution of the festival of Purim, in commemoration of this deliverance, and Mordecai's advancement, 8, 9, 10.

The Book of Esther shows how these Jews, though scattered among the heathen, were preserved, even when doomed by others to destruction. Though the *name* of God is not found in the book, his hand is plainly seen, *anticipating* threatened evil, *defeating* and *overruling* it to the greater good of the Jews, and even of the heathen, i. 2, 4–10. Nor was it the safety of the Jews in Babylon only that was in peril; if Haman had succeeded, as the power of Persia was then supreme at Jerusalem, and throughout Asia, the Jews throughout the world, must have perished, and with them the whole of the visible Church of God.

Mark and admire the Providence of God, using what seems the most trifling circumstance to accomplish His will (6). Mark also the faith of Mordecai, whose fear of the unalterable Persian decree was less than his trust in the faithfulness of God (iv. 14). Though he knew not *how*, he foresaw indemnity to Israel, and he asks the aid of Esther, rather for *her* honor, than for *their* deliverance.

THE BOOK OF JOB.

It has been supposed by some, says the Rev. A. R. Fausset, that the Book of Job is an allegory, not a real narrative, on account of the artificial character of many of its statements. But the sacred numbers, *three* and *seven*, often occur. He had *seven* thousand sheep, *seven* sons, both before and after his trials; his *three* friends sit down with him *seven* days and *seven* nights; both before and after his trials he had *three* daughters. So also the number and form of the speeches of the several speakers seem to be artificial. The name of Job, too, is derived from an Arabic word signifying *repentance*.

But Ez. (xiv. 14) speaks of "Job" in conjunction with "Noah and Daniel," real persons. James (v. 11) also refers to Job as an example of "patience," which he would not have been likely to do had Job been only a fictitious person. Also the names of persons and places are specified with a particularity not to be looked for in an allegory. As to the exact *doubling* of his possessions after his restoration, no doubt the *round* number is given for the exact number, as the latter approached near the former: this is often done in undoubtedly *historical* books. As to the studied number and form of the speeches, it seems likely that the arguments were *substantially* those which appear in the Book, but that the *studied and poetic form* were given by Job himself guided by the Holy Spirit. He lived 140 yrs. after his trials, and nothing would be more natural, than that he should, at his leisure, mold into a perfect form the arguments used in the momentous debate, for the instruction of the Church in all ages. Probably, too, the debate itself occupied several sittings, and the number of speeches assigned to each was arranged by preconcerted agreement, and each was allowed the interval of a day or more to prepare carefully his speech and replies: this will account for the speakers bringing forward their arguments in regular series, no one speaking out of his turn. As to the name Job—*repentance*—(supposing the derivation correct) it was common in old times to give a name from circumstances which occurred at an advanced period of life, and this is no argument against the reality of the person.

Eusebius fixes the age when Job lived two ages before Moses, *i. e.* about the time of Isaac; 1800 yrs. before Christ, and 600 after the Deluge. Agreeing with this are the following considerations: 1. Job's length of life is patriarchal, 200 yrs. 2. He alludes only to the earliest form of idolatry, viz: the worship of the sun, moon, and heavenly hosts (called *Saba*, whence arises the title, Lord of *Sabaoth*, as opposed to Sabeanism), (ch. xxxi. 26–28). 3. The number of oxen and rams sacrificed, *seven*, as in the case of Balaam. God would not have sanctioned this *after* the giving of the Mosaic law, though He might graciously accommodate Himself to existing customs *before* the law. 4. The language of Job is Hebrew, interspersed occasionally with Syriac and Arabic expressions, implying a time when all the Shemitic tribes spoke one common tongue and had not branched into different dialects, Hebrew, Syriac, and Arabic. 5. He speaks of the most ancient kind of writing, viz., sculpture. Riches also are reckoned by cattle. The Hebrew word translated *a piece of money*, ought rather to be rendered *a lamb*. 6. There is no allusion to the Exodus from Egypt and to the miracles that accompanied it: nor to the destruction of Sodom and Gomorrah (*Patrick*, however, thinks there is); though there is to the flood (ch. xxii. 15); and these events, happening in Job's vicinity, would have been striking illustrations of the argument for God's interposition in destroying the wicked and vindicating the righteous, had Job and his friends known of them. Nor is there any *undoubted* reference to the Jewish law, ritual, and priesthood. 7. The religion of Job is that which prevailed among the patriarchs previous to the law; sacrifices performed by the head of each family; no officiating priesthood, temple, or consecrated altar.

Respecting the *author* of the book, a difference of opinion prevails. Some ascribe it to Job, others to Elihu, and others to Moses. Whoever was its author, its canonical authority is proved by its place in the Jewish Scriptures, and the recognition of the whole collection by our Lord and His Apostles.

The book may be divided into three parts:

I. The *historical introduction* in prose, 1, 2, giving a narrative of sudden and severe affliction, borne with exemplary patience.

II. The *argument or controversy*, in poetry, in five divisions.

1. The *first* series of discussions, comprising Job's complaint, 3; the speech of Eliphaz, 4, 5, and Job's answer, 6, 7; of Bildad, 8, and Job's answer, 9, 10; of Zophar, 11, and Job's answer, 12, 14.

2. The *second* series, comprising the speech of Eliphaz, 15; and Job's answer, 16, 17, of Bildad, 18, and Job's answer, 19, of Zophar, 20; and Job's answer, 21.

3. The *third* series, comprising the speech of Eliphaz, 22; and Job's answer, 23, 24, of Bildad, 25; and Job's answer, 26–31.

The question discussed thus far is, whether great suffering be not an evidence of great guilt. Job's friends affirm it, and exhort him to repent and reform. Job denies it, appeals to facts, and complains bitterly of his friends for aggravating his distress by false charges.

4. The speech of Elihu, 32–37. Elihu maintains that afflictions are meant for the good of the sufferer, even when not properly the consequences of sin, he reproves Job for justifying himself, rather than God, and vindicates the Divine character and government.

5. The close of the discussion, by the address of the Almighty (not condescending to explain his conduct, but) illustrating His power and wisdom, 38–41, and Job's response and penitential confession, 42, 1–6.

III. The *conclusion* in prose, 42, 7–17, giving an account of Job's acceptance and prosperity.

The exact meaning and design and object of this book has not always been clearly apprehended. Dr. Hengstenberg considers that the question is, "how the afflictions of the righteous and the prosperity of the wicked can be consistent with God's justice. But it should be observed," he proceeds, "that the direct problem exclusively refers to the first point, the second being only incidentally discussed on occasion of the leading theme. If this is overlooked, the author would appear to have solved only one-half of his problem: the case from which the whole discussion proceeds has reference merely to the leading problem." But he regards it as an error to refer the whole solution to the doctrine of retribution after death. God's moral government is always in exercise, not inactive at present to make up hereafter. It is to be shown not merely that the ultimate result of a good man's affliction is happy, but that, while these afflictions are needful, there is present consolation under them as they work their due effect. In the earlier dispensation, such consolations depended more on external circumstances; in the N. T. they have more of a spiritual cast. Dr. Kitto, in a sensible paper, takes substantially the same view, and observes that "the book is, in fact, engaged with the great problem regarding the distribution of good and evil in the world, especially as viewed in connection with the doctrine of a righteous retribution in the present life. It sets forth the struggle between faith in the perfect government of God, and the various doubts excited by what it sees and knows of the prosperity of the many among those who are despised of God. The subject thus appears to be one that comes home to men's business and bosoms. Even under the light of Christianity, there are perhaps few who have not at particular seasons felt the strife between faith in the perfect government of the world and the various feelings excited in the mind by what they have experienced of human suffering. The event showed that Job's friends had judged him too soon: had he been a righteous man, his troubles, they thought, would end. They did end, and very consolatory must have been the story to those who in times immediately subsequent to its composition, pondered this book. It has not lost its effect for us. We, as the Apostle James admonishes us, must see "the end of the Lord," and hold on in faith and patience accordingly.

Little need be said as to the nature of the poetry of this book. Some will have it an epic, some a dramatic poem, while others class it with lyric compositions. It matters not what name be given it: it is poetry of the highest order. There is a wonderful glow of fancy, and power of description so that even if it had no higher merit it must be regarded as one of the most admirable productions of the pen. The language, it may be added, has much in it of an archaic cast.

PSALMS.

The book of Psalms is a collection of hymns or sacred songs in praise of God, and consists of poems of various kinds. They are the productions of different persons, but are generally called the Psalms of David, because a great part of them was composed by him, and David himself is distinguished by the name of the Psalmist.

We can not now ascertain all the Psalms written by David, but their number probably exceeds 70: and much less are we able to discover the authors of the other Psalms, or the occasions upon which they were composed; a few of them were written after the return from the Babylonian Captivity. The titles prefixed to them are of very questionable authority; and in many cases they are not intended to denote the writer, but refer only to the person who was appointed to set them to music. David first introduced the practice of singing sacred hymns in the public service of God, and it was restored by Ezra, who is supposed to have selected these Psalms from a much greater number, and to have placed them in their present order. It is to be presumed, that those which he rejected were either not inspired, or not calculated for general use. The authority of those, however, which we now possess, is established not only by their rank among the Sacred Writings, and by the unvaried testimony of every age, but likewise by many intrinsic proofs of Inspiration. Not only do they breathe through every part a divine spirit of eloquence, but they contain numberless illustrious prophesies that were remarkably accomplished, and that are frequently appealed to by the evangelical writers. The sacred character of the whole book is established by the testimony of our Saviour and His Apostles, who, in various parts of the N. T., appropriate the predictions of the Psalms as obviously apposite to the circumstances of their lives, and as intentionally preconcerted to describe them.

The veneration of the Psalms has in all ages of the Church been considerable. The fathers assure us, that in the earliest times the whole book of Psalms was generally learnt by heart, and that all ministers were expected to be able to repeat them from memory. These invaluable Scriptures are daily repeated without weariness, though their beauties are often overlooked in families and habitual perusal. As hymns immediately addressed to the Deity, they reduce righteousness to practice, and while we acquire the sentiments, we perform the offices of piety, as while we supplicate for blessings, we celebrate the memorial of former mercies, and while in the exercise of devotion, faith is enlivened by the display of prophesy.

Josephus asserts, and most of the ancient writers maintain, that the Psalms were composed in metre. They have undoubtedly a peculiar conformation of sentences, and a measured distribution of parts. Many of them are elegiac, and most of David's are of the lyric kind. There is no sufficient reason, however, to believe, as some writers have imagined, that they were written in rhyme, or in any of the Grecian measures. Some of them are acrostic; and though the regulations of the Hebrew measure are now lost, there can be no doubt, from their harmonious modulation, that they were written with some kind of metrical order, and they must have been composed in accommodation to the measure to which they were set. The Masoretic writers have marked them in a manner different from the other sacred writings. The Hebrew copies, and the Septuagint version of this book, contains the same number of Psalms, only the Septuagint translators have, for some reason which does not appear, thrown the 9th and 10th into one, as also the 114th and 115th, and have divided the 116th and 147th each into two.

THE FOLLOWING TABLE, SHOWING THE PROBABLE OCCASION WHEN EACH PSALM WAS COMPOSED IS FOUNDED ON *"Townsend's Harmony of the Old Testament."*

PSALMS.	AFTER WHAT SCRIPTURE.	PROBABLE OCCASION ON WHICH EACH PSALM WAS COMPOSED.	B. C.
BOOK I., IN THE JEWISH DIVISION.			
1	Neh. 13, 3	Written by David or Ezra, and placed as a preface to the Psalms	444
2	1 Chr. 17, 27	On the delivery of the promise by Nathan to David—a prophesy of Christ's kingdom	1044
3	2 Sam. 15, 29	On David's flight from Absalom	
4	2 Sam. 17, 29	During the flight from Absalom	1023
5	2 Sam. 17, 29	During the flight from Absalom	
6	1 Chr. 28, 21	Inserted towards the end of David's life	1015
7	2 Sam. 16, 14	On the reproaches of Shimei	1023
8	1 Chr. 28, 21	Inserted towards the end of David's life	1015
9	1 Sam. 17, 4, or 1 Chr. 16, 43	On the victory over Goliath	1063
10	Dan. 7, 28	During the Babylonish Captivity	539
11	1 Sam. 19, 3	When David was advised to flee to the mountains	1062
12	1 Chr. 28, 1	Inserted towards the end of David's life	1015
13, 14, 15	Dan. 7, 28	During the Babylonish captivity	539
16	1 Chr. 17, 27, or 1 Sam. 27	On the delivery of the promise by Nathan to David	1044
17	1 Sam. 22, 19	On the murder of the priests by Doeg	1060
18	2 Sam. 22, 51	On the conclusion of David's wars	1019
19	1 Chr. 28, 21	Inserted towards the end of David's life	1015
20, 21	2 Sam. 10, 19	On the war with the Ammonites and Syrians	1036
22	1 Chr. 17, 27	On the delivery of the promise by Nathan; or in severe persecution	1044
23, 24	1 Chr. 28, 21, or 1 Chr. 16, 43	Inserted towards the end of David's life	1015
25, 26, 27	Dan. 17, 28	During the Babylonish captivity	539
28, 29	1 Chr. 28, 21	Inserted towards the end of David's life	1015
30	1 Chr. 21, 30	On the dedication of the threshing-floor of Araunah	1017
31	1 Sam. 23, 12	On David's persecution by Saul	1060
32, 33	2 Sam. 12, 15	On the pardon of David's adultery	1034
34	1 Sam. 21, 15	On David's leaving the city of Gath	1060
35	1 Sam. 22, 19	On David's persecution by Doeg	1060
36, 37	Dan. 7, 28	During the Babylonish captivity	539
38, 39, 40, 41	1 Chr. 28, 21	Inserted towards the end of David's life	1015
42	2 Sam. 17, 29	On David's flight from Absalom	1023
BOOK II.			
43	1 Sam. 17, 29	On David's flight from Absalom	1023
44	2 K. 19, 7	On the blasphemous message of Rabshekeh	710
45	1 Chr. 17, 27	On the delivery of the promise by Nathan	1044
46	2 Chr. 20, 26	On the victory of Jehoshaphat	890
47	2 Chr. 7, 10	On the removal of the ark into the temple	1004
48	Ezr. 6, 22	On the dedication of the second temple	515
49, 50	Dan. 7, 28	During the Babylonish captivity	539
51	2 Sam. 12, 15	Confession of David after his adultery	1034
52	1 Sam. 22, 19	On David's persecution by Doeg	1060
53	Dan. 7, 28	During the Babylonish captivity	539
54	1 Sam. 23, 23	On the treachery of the Ziphims to David	1060
55	2 Sam. 17, 29	During the flight from Absalom	1023
56	1 Sam. 21, 15	When David was with the Philistines in Gath	1060
57	1 Sam. 24, 22	On David's refusal to kill Saul in the cave	1058
58	1 Sam. 24, 22	Continuation of Ps. 57	1058
59	1 Sam. 19, 17	On Saul surrounding the town of David	1061
60	1 K. 11, 20	On the conquest of Edom by Joab	1040
61	1 Chr. 28, 21	Inserted towards the end of David's life	1015
62	2 Sam. 17, 29	In David's persecution by Absalom	1023
63	1 Sam. 24, 22	Prayer of David in the wilderness of Engedi	1058
64	1 Sam. 22, 19	On David's persecution by Saul	1060
65	1 Chr. 28, 21	Inserted towards the end of David's life	1015
66	Ezr. 3, 13	On laying the foundation of the second temple	535
67	Dan. 7, 28	During the Babylonish captivity	593
68	2 Sam. 6, 11	On the first removal of the ark	1045
69	1 Chr. 28, 21	Inserted towards the end of David's life	1015

[CONCLUDED FROM PREVIOUS PAGE.]

PSALMS.	AFTER WHAT SCRIPTURE.	PROBABLE OCCASION ON WHICH EACH PSALM WAS COMPOSED.	B. C.
70, 71	2 Sam. 17, 29	On Absalom's rebellion	1023
72	1 Chr. 29, 19	On Solomon being made king by his father	1015
BOOK III.			
73	2 K. 19, 19	On the Destruction of Sennacherib	710
74	Jer. 39, 10	On the destruction of the city and temple	588
75, 76	2 K. 19, 35	On the destruction of Sennacherib	710
77	Dan. 7, 28	During the Babylonish captivity	539
78	1 Chr. 28, 21, or 2 Chr. 19, 56	Inserted towards the end of David's life	1015
79	Jer. 39, 10	On the destruction of the city and temple	588
80	Dan. 7, 28	During the Babylonish captivity	539
81	Ezr. 6, 22	On the dedication of the second temple	515
82	2 Chr. 19, 7	On the appointment of Judges by Jehoshaphat	897
83	Jer. 39, 10, or 2 Chr. 20	On the desolation caused by the Assyrians	588
84	Ezr. 3, 13	On the foundation of the second temple	535
85	Ezr. 1, 4	On the decree of Cyrus	536
86	1 Chr. 28, 21	Inserted towards the end of David's life	1015
87	Ezr. 3, 7	On the return from the Babylonish captivity	536
88	Ex. 2, 25	During the affliction in Egypt	1531
89	Dan. 7, 28	During the Babylonish captivity	539
BOOK IV.			
90	Num. 14, 45	On the shortening of man's life, etc.	489
91	1 Chr. 28, 10	After the advice of David to Solomon	1015
92, 93	Dan. 7, 28	During the Babylonish captivity	539
94	Jer. 39, 10	On the destruction of the city and temple	588
95	1 Chr. 28, 21	Inserted towards the end of David's life	1015
96	1 Chr. 16, 43	On the removal of the ark from Obed-edom's house	1051
97, 98, 99, 100	2 Chr. 7, 10	On the removal of the ark into the temple	1004
101	1 Chr. 28, 21	Inserted towards the end of David's life	1015
102	Dan. 9, 27	On the near termination of the captivity	538
103	2 Sam. 12, 15	On the pardon of David's adultery	1034
104	1 Chr. 28, 21	Inserted towards the end of David's life	1015
105, 106	1 Chr. 16, 43	On the removal of the ark from Obed-edom's house	1051
BOOK V.			
107	Ezr. 3, 7	On the return from the captivity	536
108	1 K. 11, 20	On the conquest of Edom by Joab	1040
109	1 Sam. 22, 19	On David's persecution by Doeg	1060
110	1 Chr. 17, 27	On the promise by Nathan to David	1044
111, 112, 113, 114	Ezr. 3, 7	On the return from the captivity	536
115	2 Chr. 20, 26	On the victory of Jehoshaphat	896
116, 117	Ezr. 3, 7	On the return from the captivity	536
118	1 Chr. 17, 27	On the promise by Nathan to David	1044
119	Neh. 13, 3	Manual of devotion by Ezra	444
120, 121, 122	1 Chr. 28, 21	Inserted towards the end of David's life	1015
123	Dan. 7, 28	During the Babylonish captivity	539
124	1 Chr. 28, 21	Inserted towards the end of David's life	1015
125	Ezr. 3, 7	On the return from the captivity	536
126	Ezr. 1, 4	On the decree of Cyrus	536
127, 128	Ezr. 3, 7	On the return from the captivity	536
129	Ezr. 4, 24	On the opposition of the Samaritans	535
130	Dan. 7, 28	During the Babylonish captivity	539
131	1 Chr. 28, 21	Inserted towards the end of David's life	1015
132	1 Chr. 15, 14	On the second removal of the ark	1051
133	1 Chr. 28, 21	Inserted towards the end of David's life	1015
134	Ezr. 3, 7	On the return from the captivity	536
135, 136	2 Chr. 7, 10	On the removal of the ark into the temple	1004
137	Dan. 7, 28	During the Babylonish captivity	539
138	Ezr. 6, 13	On the rebuilding of the temple	519
139	1 Chr. 13, 4	Prayer of David when made king over all Israel	1048
140	1 Sam. 22, 19	On David's persecution by Doeg	1060
141	1 Sam. 27, 1	Prayer of David when driven from Judea	1055
142	1 Sam. 22, 1	Prayer of David in the cave of Adullam	1060
143	2 Sam. 17, 29	During the war with Absalom	1053
144	2 Sam. 17, 29	On the victory over Absalom	1053
145	1 Chr. 28, 10	David, when old, reviewing his past life	1015
146 to 150	Ezra 6, 22	On the dedication of the second temple	515

PROVERBS.

Proverbs are short aphorisms, and sententious moral and prudential maxims, usually expressed in numbers, rhythm, or antithesis, as being more easily remembered, and of more use, than abstruse and methodical discourses. This method of instruction appears to be peculiarly suited to the disposition and genius of the Asiatics, among whom it has prevailed from the earliest ages. The mode of conveying instruction by compendious maxims obtained among the Jews from the first dawn of their literature to its final extinction, in the East, through the power of the Mohammedan arms, and it was familiar to the inhabitants of Syria and Palestine, as we learn from the testimony of Jerome.

Proverbs, in the Hebrew language, are called *meshalim*, which is derived from a verb signifying both "to rule, to have dominion," and "to compare," "to liken," "to assimilate": hence the term denotes the highly figurative and poetical style in general, and likewise those compendious and authoritative sentences in particular which are commonly denominated proverbs. This term, which our translators have adopted after the Vulgate, denotes, "a short sentence frequently repeated by the people, a saw, an adage," and no other word can, perhaps, be substituted more accurately expressing the force of the Hebrew, or, if there could, it has been so long familiarized by constant use, that a change is wholly inadmissible.

The *Meshalim*, or Proverbs of Solomon, on account of their intrinsic merit, as well as of the rank and renown of their author, would be received with submissive deference, in consequence of which they would rapidly spread through every part of the Jewish territories. The pious instructions of the king would be listened to with the attention and respect they deserve, and, no doubt, would be carefully recorded by a people attached to his person, and holding his wisdom in the highest admiraton. These, either preserved in writing or handed down by oral communication, were subsequently collected into one volume, and constitute the book in the sacred canon, entitled, " The Proverbs of Solomon, the son of David, king of Israel."

The genuineness and authority of this title, and those in ch. x. 1, and xxv. 1, can not be disputed, not the smallest reason appears for calling them in question. One portion of the book, from the 25th chapter to the end of the 29th, was compiled by the men of Hezekiah, as appears from the title prefixed to it. Eliakim, Shebna, Joah, Isaiah, Hosea, and Micah, personages of eminence and worth, were contemporary with Hezekiah, but whether these or others executed the compilation, it is now impossible to determine. They were persons, however, as we may reasonably suppose, well qualified for the undertaking, who collected what were known to be the genuine proverbs of Solomon from the various writings in which they were dispersed, and arranged them in their present order. Whether the preceding 24 chapters, which, doubtless, existed in a combined form previous to the additional collection, were compiled by the author, or some other person, is quite uncertain. Both collections, however, being made at so early a period, is a satisfactory evidence that the Proverbs are the genuine production of Solomon, to whom they are ascribed, for, from the death of Solomon to the reign of Hezekiah, according to the Bible chronology, was a period of 249 yrs., or, according to Dr. Hales, 265 yrs., too short a space to admit of any forgery or material error, as either must have been immediately detected by the worthies who flourished during the virtuous reign of Hezekiah.

ECCLESIASTES.

The name of this book, Ecclesiastes, is derived from the Septuagint version, it being a Greek word signifying a preacher, one who addresses a public assembly. The Hebrew title *Koheleth* conveys nearly the same idea, intended to intimate preaching wisdom. The book has generally been ascribed to Solomon as the author.

The scope of Ecclesiastes is indicated in 1, 2, and xii. 13. It is an inquiry into the chief good of man, and is distributed by Keil into four discourses. The first (i. ii.), exhibits (1), the vanity of theoretical wisdom directed to the knowledge of things, and (2), the nothingness of practical wisdom which aimed at enjoying life; the result being that man with all his striving can attain no lasting good. The second (iii.-v.), following the idea thrown out in ii. 21, 26, begins with a description (iii. 1-8) of man's entire dependence on a higher unchangeable providence, and, in reply to the question of the chief good, shows that there can be no higher (iii. 9-22) than self-enjoyment and benevolence, which, however (iv.), it is not easy to attain, still one must, in the fear of God and a conscientious fulfilment of duty, seek trustingly and contentedly to use earthly goods. In the third discourse (vi. 1–viii. 15), is shown the vanity of grasping riches (vi.), practical wisdom is then described (vii. 1–22), and the mode of attaining it indicated, spite of the incongruities of earthly life (vii., 23, viii. 15). The last (viii. 16, xii. 7), further discusses these incongruities, lays down rules for the conduct of a happy life, which may please God, and brings us to the conclusion of the whole (xii. 8–14), that a future judgment will clear up all present uncertainties. This is the great object the author intends to develope, he argues at first on lower principles, to show their imperfection, not prematurely expressing the whole truth (comp. iii. 21), but reserving that till he has raised by degrees the view to that high tribunal where every wrong will be redressed. The style of this book is loose and unconnected, with little practical character. It was one of the *megilloth* read, we are told, by the Jews at the feast of tabernacles.

THE SONG OF SOLOMON.

"Few poems have excited more attention, or found more translators, than the Song of Songs; but the learned are not yet agreed respecting its arrangement and design. Whether the poem be strictly one piece, or whether, as some have supposed, it be composed of several poems, or idyls, it is certainly one as to its subject, and the speakers are the same from the beginning to the end."

As to this poem, "the whole of it," Dr. Gray remarks, "is a thin vail of allegory thrown over a spiritual alliance, and we discover everywhere, through the transparent types of Solomon and his Bride, the characters of Christ and his personified Church, portrayed with those graces and embellishments which are most lovely and engaging to the human eye."

"The scope of this Song," says Dr. Roberts, "is, under the allegory of lovers upon contract, and intending marriage, to shadow out to us that sublime, spiritual, and happy union and communion betwixt Christ and His Church, which is inchoate in this life, and shall be consummate in the life to come. This is carried on dialogue-wise betwixt Christ and his Church, his friend and her damsels, who are the chief speakers, especially the first."

The following quotation from Scott's preface to this book in his commentary, is all that we judge further necessary to advance respecting this divine and exquisitely beautiful poem: "This Song is a divine Allegory in the form of a pastoral, which represents the reciprocal love betwixt Christ and his Church, under figures taken from the relation and affection which subsist betwixt a Bridegroom and his espoused Bride; an emblem continually employed in Scripture. It has some reference to the state of the Jewish Church, as waiting for the coming of the promised Messiah; but it likewise accords to the fellowship betwixt Christ and the true believer in every age. In order properly to understand it, we must consider the Redeemer as loving and as being loved by his Church. The marriage contract is already ratified, but the completion of this blessed union is reserved for the heavenly state. Here on earth the believer loves and rejoices in an unseen Saviour, and seeks his happiness from His spiritual presence. Christ manifests Himself to him as he doth not to the world, and these visits are earnests and foretastes of heavenly joy. But they are interrupted, suspended, or varied on many accounts: they are often lost by negligence or other sins, and can only be recovered by humble repentance and renewed diligence; yet the love on both sides remains unchanged as to its principle, though varied in the expression of it." "The varying experience and corresponding duties of the believer are delineated in a very animating and edifying manner."

THE BOOK OF THE PROPHET ISAIAH.

Of Isaiah and his family we know nothing but what is said in the 1st verse. His name signifies "the salvation of God." He is supposed to have have been of royal descent. He prophesied at least during a period of 48 yrs. The tradition that he was put to death by Manasseh is very uncertain. He is a prophet of the highest dignity, and was contemporary with several other prophets.

The scope of Isaiah's prophesies is three-fold: 1. To detect, reprove, and condemn the sins of the Jews in particular, also those of Israel, and of several surrounding nations, denouncing the severest judgments on all offenders. 2. To invite persons of every rank and condition, Jews and Gentiles, to repentance and reformation. 3. To comfort all the truly pious with prophetic promises of the Messiah

His prophesies are supposed to have been written as follows: 1. In the reign of Uzziah, ch. i.–v. 2. Of Jotham, ch. vi. 3. Of Ahaz, ch. vii.–xiv. 4. Of Hezekiah, ch. xv. to the end.

Isaiah has been styled "the Evangelical Prophet," on account of the number and variety of his prophesies concerning the advent and character, the ministry and preaching, the sufferings and death of Messiah, and the extension, permanence, and glory of His kingdom.

"This prophet," says Bp. Lowth, "abounds in such transcendent excellencies, that he may be properly said to afford the most perfect model of prophetic poetry. He is at once elevated and sublime, forcible and ornamented: he unites energy with copiousness, and dignity with variety. In his sentiments there is uncommon elevation and majesty, in his imagery the utmost propriety and elegance, dignity and diversity; in his language uncommon energy and beauty, and, notwithstanding the obscurity of his subjects, a surprising degree of clearness and simplicity."

THE BOOK OF THE PROPHET JEREMIAH.

Jeremiah was the son of Hilkiah, a priest of Anathoth, in Benjamin. He was called to the prophetic office about 70 yrs. after the death of Isaiah, in the 13th year of king Josiah, whilst he was very young (i. 6), and still living at Anathoth. It would seem that he remained in his native place for several years; but at length, probably in consequence of the persecution of his fellow-townsmen and even of his own family (xi. 21, xii. 6), as well as under the Divine direction, to have wider field for his labors, he left Anathoth, and came to Jerusalem. He also visited the cities of Judah, and prophesied altogether upwards of 40 yrs. (xi. 6).

During the reign of Josiah, he was, doubtless, a valuable coadjutor to that pious monarch in the reformation of religion. From his notice of Jehoahaz (xxii. 10–12), he probably prophesied without hindrance during his reign. But when Jehoiakim came to the throne he was interrupted in his ministry, "the priests and prophets" becoming his accusers, and demanding, in conjunction with the populace, that he should be put to death (xxvi.). The princes did not dare to defy God thus openly; but Jeremiah was either placed under restraint, or deterred by his adversaries from appearing in public. Under these circumstances, he received a command from God to commit his predictions to writing; and having done so, sent Baruch to read them in the Temple on a fast-day. The princes were alarmed, and endeavored to rouse the king by reading out to him the prophetic roll. But it was in vain: the reckless monarch, after hearing three or four pages, cut the roll in pieces, and cast it into the fire, giving immediate orders for the apprehension of Jeremiah and Baruch. God, however, preserved them, and Jeremiah soon afterwards, by Divine direction, wrote the same messages again, with some additions (xxxvi.).

In the short reign of the next king, Jehoiachim, we find him still uttering the voice of warning (see xiii. 18, compare 2 Kings xxiv. 12 and ch. xxii. 24–30), though without effect.

In the reign of Zedekiah, when Nebuchadnezzar's army laid siege to Jerusalem, and then withdrew upon the report of help coming from Egypt, Jeremiah was commissioned by God to declare that the Chaldeans should come again, and take the city, and burn it with fire. Departing from Jerusalem, he was accused of deserting to the Chaldeans, and was cast into prison, where he remained until the city was taken. Nebuchadnezzar, who had formed a more just estimate of his character, gave a special charge to his captain, Nebuzar-adan, not only to provide for him, but to follow his advice. The choice being given to the prophet, either to go to Babylon, where doubtless he would have been held in honor at the royal court, or to remain with his own people, he preferred the latter. He subsequently endeavored to persuade the leaders of the people not to go to Egypt, but to remain in the land, assuring them, by a divine message, that if they did so God would build them up. The people refused to obey, and went to Egypt, taking Jeremiah and Baruch with them (xliii. 6). In Egypt he still sought to turn the people to the Lord (xliv.), but his writings give no information respecting his subsequent history. Ancient historians, however, assert that the Jews, offended by his faithful remonstrances, put him to death in Egypt; Jerome says at Tahpanhes.

Jeremiah was contemporary with Zephaniah, Habakkuk, Ezekiel, and Daniel. The style of Jeremiah is peculiarly marked by pathos. He delights in expressions of tenderness, and gives touching descriptions of the miseries of his people.

The prophesies of this book do not appear to stand in respect to time as they were delivered. Why they are not so arranged, and how they are to be reduced to chronological order, it is not easy to say. Blayney proposes the following arrangement: The prophesies delivered (1), in the reign of Josiah, comprising i.-xii.; (2), in the reign of Jehoiakim, xiii.-xx., xxii., xxiii., xxv., xxvi., xxxv., xxxvi., xlv.-xlviii., xlix., 1—xxxiii.; (3), in the time of Zedekiah, xxi., xxiv., xxvii.-xxxiv., xxxvii.-xxxix., xlix., xxxiv.-xxxix., l.-lii.; (4), during the administration of Gedaliah, and in Egypt, xl.-xliv., ch. lii., seems made up from the latter chs. of Kings (see xxiv., xviii.-xxv.), and repeats parts of chs. xxxix. and xl. From ch. li. 34, and the later date of some of the facts, the whole ch. may be regarded as the work of a later writer, nad probably of Ezra.

THE LAMENTATIONS OF JEREMIAH.

This book has generally among the Jews for an appellation its first word, signifying *how*. It is also called by a name implying, as that we use does, the nature of its contents. In the Hebrew canon it is one of the five *megilloth* usually placed between Ruth and Ecclesiastes.

The Lamentations are expressly ascribed to Jeremiah in a verse prefixed to the Septuagint translation. This has been adopted in some other versions, but there is no reason to suppose that it was ever in the Hebrew original. It may be taken, however, as a valuable witness to the early belief of the Jeremiah authorship; and this authorship there is no valid reason for doubting. The writer is evidently an eye-witness (see ii. 11, iv. 17-20, v.): the diction is very similar, characteristic words and expressions being found in Jeremiah's prophesies and also in this book. It is the deliberate judgment of Bleek that there is an observable relationship between the Lamentations and the prophetical book, not only in style but in entire character and spirit, in contents and in tone of thought. And he points out how exactly Lam. iii. 52, etc., answers to Jer. xxxviii. 6, etc.

The book comprises five separate poems, each distinct and complete in itself, but yet connected by the same leading idea. The third describes the personal sufferings of the writer; the others the fate of the city. It is a nice point to determine with exactness the time of the composition. But, as we learn from the history (comp. Jer. xxxix. 2 and lii. 12, 13), that an interval of about a month elapsed between the capture of the city and its actual destruction by fire, some have imagined that they see indications in i., ii., iv., v., pointing to that interval: the king and the nobles were in Captivity (ii. 9, iv. 20); the Temple was profaned and the observance of the ritual service at an end (i. 4, 10, ii. 6, 7, 20): but yet it is not distinctly said that the Temple was burned or the city quite destroyed. Still it can not be denied that there are expressions which can hardly be fully understood except as intending that final catastrophe (as ii. 2, 3, iv. 11, v. 18). Perhaps, therefore, the date may be more justly fixed to that time when Jeremiah appears to have been carried with the rest of the captives to Ramah, where Nebuzar-adan released him and sent him to Gedaliah (Jer. xl.). And no time would seem to suit better with the personal lamentation of ch. iii.

The composition of these elegies is remarkable. Each consists of 22 periods or stanzas, and in the first 4 every one of these periods begins with words the initials of which are letters of the Hebrew alphabet in order. In ch. iii. the 3 verses of each period commence with the same letter. In ii., iii., iv., the verses beginning with the letter *pe* precede those beginning with *ain*. In the Vulgate and some other versions ch. v. is entitled the Prayer of Jeremiah. It is only necessary to add that these elegies must not be considered the lament which (2 Chr. xxxv. 25) Jeremiah is said to have made for Josiah.

THE BOOK OF THE PROPHET EZEKIEL.

Ezekiel, like his contemporary Jeremiah, was of the sacerdotal race. He was carried away captive to Babylon with Jehoiachim, king of Judah B. C. 598, and was placed with many others of his countrymen upon the river Chebar, in Mesopotamia, where he was favored with the Divine revelations contained in his book. He began to prophesy in the 5th yr. of his captivity, and is supposed to have prophesied about 21 yrs.   The boldness with which he censured the idolatry and wickedness of his countrymen, is said to have cost him his life, but his memory was greatly revered, not only by the Jews, but also by the Medes and Persians.

The book which bears Ezekiel's name may be considered under the five following divisions: the first 3 chapters contain the glorious appearance of God to the prophet, and his solemn appointment to his office, with instructions and encouragements for the discharge of it. From the 4th to the 24th chapter inclusive, he describes, under a variety of visions and similitudes, the calamities impending over Judea, and the total destruction of the temple and city of Jerusalem, by Nebuchadnezzar; occasionally predicting another period of yet greater desolation, and more general dispersion.   From the beginning of the 25th to the end of the 32d chapter, the prophet foretells the conquest and ruin of many nations and cities, which had insulted the Jews in their affliction; of the Ammonites, the Moabites, the Edomites, and Philistines of Tyre, of Sidon, and Egypt, all of which were to be punished by the same mighty instrument of God's wrath against the wickedness of man; and in these prophesies he not only predicts events which were soon to take place, but he also describes the condition of these several countries in the remote periods of the world.   From the 32d to the 40th chapter, he inveighs against the accumulated sins of the Jews collectively, and the murmuring spirit of his captive brethren, exhorts them earnestly to repent of their hypocrisy and wickedness upon the assurance that God will accept sincere repentance, and comforts them with promises of approaching deliverance under Cyrus, subjoining intimations of one far more glorious, but distant, redemption under the Messiah, though the manner in which it is to be effected is deeply involved in mystery.   The last 9 chapters contain a remarkable vision of the structure of a new temple and a new polity, applicable in the first instance to the return from the Babylonian Captivity, but in its ultimate sense referring to the glory and prosperity of the universal Church of Christ.

Jerome observes that the visions of Ezekiel are among the things in Scripture hard to be understood.   This obscurity arises, in part at least, from the nature and design of the prophesies themselves: they were delivered amidst the gloom of Captivity; and though calculated to cheer the drooping spirits of the Jews, and to keep alive a watchful and submissive confidence in the mercy of God, yet they were intended to communicate only such a degree of encouragement as was consistent with a state of punishment, and to excite an indistinct expectation of future blessings, upon conditions of repentance and amendment.   It ought also to be observed, that the last 12 chapters of this book bear a very strong resemblance to the concluding chapters of the Revelation.   The style of this prophet is characterized by Bishop Lowth as bold, vehement, and tragical, as often worked up to a kind of tremendous dignity.   He is highly parabolical, and abounds in figures and metaphorical expressions.   He may be compared to the Grecian Æschylus: he displays a rough but majestic dignity, an unpolished though noble simplicity, inferior perhaps in originality and elegance to others of the prophets, but unequalled in that force and grandeur for which he is particularly celebrated.   He sometimes emphatically and indignantly repeats his sentiments, fully dilates his pictures, and describes the idolatrous manner of his countrymen, under the strongest and most exaggerated representations that the license of Eastern style would admit.   The middle part of the book is in some measure poetical, and contains even some perfect elegies, though his thoughts are in general too irregular and uncontrolled to be chained down to rule, or fettered by language.

THE BOOK OF DANIEL.

Daniel is said to have been a descendant from the family of David.   He was taken captive to Babylon, B. C. 606, probably about his 18th or 20th year.   In the vicissitudes of his life, and in the virtues which he displayed, he has been thought to have resembled Joseph.   Piety, wisdom, courage, and fidelity strongly mark his character, and he largely contributed to spread the knowledge of God among the Gentile nations.   His last prophesy was given B. C. 534, when he must have been above 90 yrs. old.   Of his death nothing is known; it is probable that he died in Persia.

Such is the order and nature of this wonderful book, that it can never be read by the wise and humble but with the highest interest and with the greatest benefit.   The character of Daniel and of his friends, their deliverance, the religious sentiments of the book, the prophetical development of the four empires, and especially the predictions respecting Christ and His kingdom, are subjects worthy of our closest meditation.

"What an amazing prophesy is this," says Bishop Newton, "comprehending so many various events, and extending through so many successive ages, from the first establishment of the Persian empire, upwards of 530 yrs. before Christ, to the general resurrection! What a proof of a Divine Providence and of a Divine revelation! For who could thus declare the things that shall be, with their times and seasons, but He only who has them in His own power, whose dominion is over all, and whose kingdom endureth from generation to generation."

This book is written in prose. We shall only add the chronological dates of the commencement and end of the four empires.

I. The Babylonian empire. Its symbol is a lion with eagle's wings (Dan. vii. 4). So far as the prophesies of Daniel are concerned, this empire began with Nebuchadnezzar, B. C. 606, and ended B. C. 538; its duration being 68 yrs.

II. The Persian empire. Its symbol (Dan. vii. 5) was a bear. This empire was founded by Cyrus, B. C. 538, and it continued until Alexander the Great defeated Darius at Arbela, B. C. 331. Its duration was 207 yrs.

III. The Grecian empire. Its symbol (Dan. vii. 6) was a leopard with four wings of a fowl. This empire continued from the battle of Arbela, B. C. 231, to the defeat of Perseus by the Romans in the battle of Pydna, B. C. 168. Its duration was 163 yrs.

IV. The Roman empire. Its symbol (Dan. vii. 7) is only stated in general terms as being "a beast dreadful and terrible, and strong exceedingly." If we date the Roman empire from the battle of Pydna, and proceed to the reign of Augustulus, A. D. 475, we have 643 yrs. for the duration of the western empire, and if we again proceed to A. D. 1453, when Constantinople was taken by Mahomet II, we have an additional period of 978 yrs. for the duration of the eastern empire; but if we date the eastern empire from the dedication of Constantinople by Constantine, A. D. 330, its duration was 1123 yrs.

To the four great empires we may add, since much is spoken of them in the book of Daniel,

1. The Syrian kingdom. This was founded after the death of Alexander the Great by Seleucus, B. C. 312, and it continued till B. C. 65. Antiochus Asiaticus was its last king. It then became a Roman province.

2. The Egyptian kingdom. This also was founded after the death of Alexander the Great by Ptolemy Lagus, B. C. 304, and it continued till B. C. 30, when it became a Roman province.

HOSEA.

Hosea, son of Beeri, was first of the minor prophets. The title of the book gives for the beginning of Hosea's ministry the reign of Uzziah, king of Judah, but limits this vague definition by reference to Jeroboam II, king of Israel; it therefore yields a date not later than B. C. 783. The pictures of social and political life which Hosea draws so forcibly are rather applicable to the interregnum which followed the death of Jeroboam (712–772), and to the reign of the succeeding kings. It seems almost certain that very few of his prophesies were written until after the death of Jeroboam (783) and probably the life, or rather the prophetic career of Hosea, extended from 784 to 725, a period of 59 yrs.

Most of Hosea's prophesies are directed against the people of Israel, whom he reproves and threatens for their idolatry and wickedness, and exhorts to repentance, with the greatest earnestness, as the only means of averting the evils impending over their country. The principal predictions contained in this book, are the captivity and dispersion of the kingdom of Israel, the deliverance of Judah from Sennacherib, the present state of the Jews, their future restoration, and union with the Gentiles, in the kingdom of the Messiah, the call of our Saviour out of Egypt, and His resurrection on the third day.

The style of Hosea is peculiarly obscure: it is sententious, concise, and abrupt, the transitions of persons are sudden, and the connexive and adversative particles are frequently omitted. The prophesies are in one continued series, without any distinction as to the times when they were delivered, or the different subjects to which they relate. They are not so clear and detailed as the predictions of those prophets who lived in succeeding ages. When, however, we have surmounted these difficulties, we shall see abundant reason to admire the force and energy with which this prophet writes, and the boldness of the figures and similitudes which he uses.

JOEL.

This prophet opens his commission by announcing an extraordinary plague of locusts, accompanied with extreme drought, which he depicts in a strain of animated and sublime poetry under the image of an invading army. The fidelity of his highly-wrought description is corroborated and illustrated by the testimonies of Shaw, Volney, Forbes and other eminent travelers, who have been eye-witnesses of the ravages committed by this most terrible of the insect tribe. It is also to be observed that locusts are named by Moses as instruments of Divine justice (Deut. xxviii. 38, 39), and by Solomon in his prayer at the dedication of the Temple (1 K. viii. 37). In the second ch., the formidable aspect of the locusts, their rapid progress; their sweeping devastation; the awful murmur of their countless throngs; their instinctive marshalling; the irresistible perseverance with which they make their way over every obstacle and through every aperture, are delineated with the utmost graphic force.

The prophet after describing the approaching judgments, calls on his countrymen to repent, assuring them of the Divine placability and readiness to forgive (ii. 12-17). He foretells the restoration of the land to its former fertility, and declares that Jehovah would still be their God (ii. 18-26). He then announces the spiritual blessings which would be poured forth in the Messianic age (ii. 28-32). This remarkable prediction is applied by the Apostle Peter to the events that transpired on the day of Pentecost (Acts ii. 16-21). In the last ch. (iii.), the Divine vengeance is denounced against the enemies and oppressors of the chosen people, of whom the Phœnicians, Egyptians, and Edomites, are especially named.

The style of Joel unites the strength of Micah with the tenderness of Jeremiah. In vividness of description he rivals Nahum, and in sublimity and majesty is scarcely inferior to Isaiah and Habakkuk.

AMOS.

Amos was a native of Tekoa in Judah, about 6 ms. S. of Bethlehem, and was originally a shepherd and dresser of sycamore trees. He was called by God's Spirit to be a prophet, although not trained in any of the regular prophetic schools (i. 1 vii. 14, 15). He traveled from Judah into the northern kingdom of Israel or Ephraim, and there exercised his ministry, apparently not for any long time. His date can not be later than the 15th year of Uzziah's reign (B. C. 808) for he tells us that he prophesies "in the reign of Uzziah king of Judah, and Jeroboam the son of Joash king of Israel, two years before the earthquake." But his ministry probably took place at an earlier period, perhaps about the middle of Jeroboam's reign.

The book of the prophesies of Amos seems divided into four principal portions closely connected together. (1.) From i. 1 to ii. 3 he denounces the sins of the nations bordering on Israel and Judah. as a preparation for (2), in which, from ii. 4 to vi. 14, he describes the state of those two kingdoms, especially the former. This is followed by (3) vii. 1—ix. 10, in which, after reflecting on the previous prophesy, he relates his visit to Bethel, and sketches the impending punishment of Israel which he predicts to Amaziah. After this era (4) he rises to a loftier and more evangelical strain, looking forward to the time when the hope of the Messiah's kingdom will be fulfilled and his people forgiven, and established in the enjoyment of God's blessings to all eternity.

The chief peculiarity of the style consists in the number of allusions to natural objects and agricultural occupations, as might be expected from the early life of the author. See i. 3, ii. 13, iii. 4, 5, iv. 2, 7, 9, v. 8, 19, vi. 12, vii. 1, ix. 3, 9, 13, 14. The references to it in the N. T. are two: v. 25, 26, 27 is quoted by Stephen in Acts vii. 42, 43, and ix. 11 by James in Acts xv. 16.

OBADIAH.

Of Obadiah's history nothing certain is known. Some have inferred, from verse 20th of his prophesy, that he lived and wrote while Jerusalem was under the power of the Chaldeans, and after the deportation of its inhabitants to Babylon, and that he was probably himself one of the exiles, but this inference rests on an assumption which is questionable.

The prophesy of Obadiah consists of *three* parts. In the *first* (1-9), the certainty of Edom's overthrow is asserted; in the *second* (10-16), the cause of this, in Edom's enmity and violence to his brother Jacob, is set forth: and in the *third* (11-21), the establishment of the kingdom of God, and its triumph over all opposition is announced. In the concluding words, "And the kingdom shall be Jehovah's," we have the dominant idea of the book, the key-note of the prophet's song And the assertion of this is made with peculiar force in contrast with the overthrow of Edom, because that people, though allied to Israel by natural ties, were among its bitterest and most inveterate enemies.

The style of Obadiah is animated, and his elocution rapid. He deals much in appeal and interrogation. The language is pure and idiomatic, and his utterances are often highly poetic.

JONAH.

Jonah, son of Amittai, the 5th of the minor prophets, was born at Gathhëpher, in Galilee. He is generally considered as the most ancient of the prophets; and is supposed to have lived B. C. 840. The book of Jonah is chiefly narrative.

Upon the repentance of the Ninevites under his preaching, God deferred the execution of his judgment till the increase of their iniquities made them ripe for destruction, about 150 yrs. afterwards. The last chapter gives an account of the murmuring of Jonah at this instance of Divine mercy, and of the gentle and condescending manner in which it pleased God to reprove the prophet for his unjust complaint.

The style of Jonah is simple and perspicuous, and his prayer, in the second chapter, is strongly descriptive of the feelings of a pious mind under a severe trial of faith. Our Saviour mentions Jonah in the Gospel (Matt. xii. 41, Luke xi. 32).

MICAH.

Micah was a native of Mareshah, hence called the *Marasthite*, a village in the south of the territory of Judah (Josh. xv. 44). It is supposed that a reference to one of his predictions saved the life of Jeremiah (Jer. xxvi. 18-24). Such a reference vouches for the genuineness of the oracles ascribed to Micah.

The prophesy of Micah is the 33d in the order of the books of the Bible. It was uttered within the space of 50 years, viz., from the commencement of the reign of Jotham, A. M. 3245, to the close of the reign of Hezekiah, A. M. 3306, or nearly contemporary with Isaiah. The prophesies of Micah, which are recorded in the sacred canon, make but 7 chapters, and are divided into 3 sections:

1. Prophesies in the reign of Jotham, full of denunciation for sin—sin for which there could be no apology in a land of Divine illumination—foreshowing also Samaria's overthrow and Sennacherib's march against Jerusalem, ch. i.

2. Prophesies in the reign of Ahaz, somewhat similar in texture and design, menacing Israel, and foretelling destruction to Judah, conveying heavy censure and woes to such as could not bear to have the truth spoken to them, and who, full of spiritual indolence themselves, exercised a hateful tyranny over the people, ending, however, with a glorious prediction of blessings and extension of Messiah's kingdom (ch. ii.-iv. 8).

3. Prophesies in the reign of Hezekiah, containing, among other oracles, one of great beauty and precision in reference to the Saviour's birth (ch. iv. 9, v. 1-5, vii.)

The remarkable feature of this last prophesy is that it is very explicit respecting the birth-place and prominent characteristics of the Messiah, and the blessings of his reign upon earth. The passage now referred to is found in the 5th chapter:

"And thou Bethlehem Ephrathah,
Art small to be among Judah's thousands,
Still out of thee shall He come to me
To be a Governor in Israel;
Whose goings forth have been from old—
From days of eternity.
Notwithstanding he will give thee up,
Till the period when SHE who is to bear

Hath brought forth.
And the rest of his brethren shall come back
To the sons of Israel.   [Jehovah,
And he shall stand and feed in the strength of
In the majesty of the name of Jehovah his God,
And they shall endure:
For now shall He be great to the ends of the earth,
And this very one shall be our PEACE," etc.

Christ's birth of a woman pointed out so specifically, its place so correctly named, and his pre-existent dignity, along with his functions and success as Messiah, so graphically marked, are, "without controversy," contained in this old prediction.

The style of Micah approaches in many sections to that of Isaiah, as in ch. vii. 18–20, and it also bears some resemblance to the rapid transitions of Hosea. The rythm is in general round and full, with an occasional play upon words. His use of figurative language is beautiful and appropriate, and his oracles sometimes assume the form of a dialogue. Micah was a contemporary of Isaiah, and their nearness of age and similarity of theme may account for the remarkable coincidences of thought and style to be found in various portions of their writings.

NAHUM.

The Book of Nahum is a striking illustration of the moral use of prophesy, of its fitness to console (so the *name* of the prophet implies) the believer, and strengthen him for present duties.

Of Nahum himself, nothing is known, except that he belonged to Elkosh, a place now unrecognised, but which Jerome (who lived a thousand years afterwards) asserts to have belonged to Galilee.

He probably phophesied in Judah, after the 10 tribes had been carried captive, and between the two invasions of Sennacherib. At this period of perplexity, when the overthrow of Samaria must have suggested to Judah many fears for her own safety, when Jerusalem had been drained of its treasure by Hezekiah, in the vain hope of turning away the fury of Sennacherib, and when distant rumors of the conquest of part of Egypt, added still more to the general dismay, the prophet is raised up to reveal the power and tenderness of Jehovah (i. 1–8), to foretell the subversion of the Assyrian empire (i. 9–12), the death of Sennacherib, and the deliverance of Hezekiah (i. 13–15). The destruction of Nineveh is then predicted in the most glowing colors, and with singular minuteness, and profane history tells us that these predictions have been literally fulfilled.

This book is surpassed by none in sublimity of description. It consists of a single poem, which opens with a solemn description of the attributes and operations of Jehovah (i. 2–8). Then follows (i. 9–14), an address to the Assyrians, describing their perplexity and overthrow, vs. 12 and 13 being thrown in parenthetically, to console the Israelites with promises of future rest and relief from oppression. Ch. ii. depicts the siege and capture of Nineveh, and the consternation of the inhabitants. Ch. iii. describes the utter ruin of the city, and the various causes contributing to it. The example of No-Ammon (or Thebes), a great and strong city of Egypt, which fell under the judgments of God, is introduced (iii. 8–10), to illustrate the similar punishments coming on the Assyrians.

HABAKKUK.

This prophet was of the tribe of Simeon. He is said to have prophesied about B. C. 605, and to have been alive at the time of the destruction of Jerusalem by Nebuchadnezzar. It is generally believed that he remained and died in Judea. The principal predictions contained in this book are, the destruction of Jerusalem, and the Captivity of the Jews by the Chaldeans or Babylonians, their deliverance from the oppressor "at the appointed time," and the total ruin of the Babylonian empire. The promise of the Messiah is confirmed, the overruling providence of God is asserted, and the concluding prayer, or rather hymn, recounts the wonders which God has wrought for His people, when He led them from Egypt into Canaan, and expresses the most perfect confidence in the fulfilment of His promises. The style of Habakkuk is highly poetical, and the hymn in ch. iii. is perhaps unrivalled for sublimity, simplicity and power.

ZEPHANIAH.

Of Zephaniah nothing is known but what is said in the 1st verse. He probably prophesied in the early part of Josiah's reign, or about the time when Jeremiah entered on the prophetical office, when those abuses prevailed in Judah which Josiah reformed. In method and subject the greatly resembles Jeremiah. He is poetical, but not characterized by any remarkable beauties He teaches, like the other prophets, the hateful and ruinous nature of sin, the righteous government of God, and His gracious purposes towards His Church. We find here, as in all other parts of Scripture, what may awake our fears, animate our hopes, and direct our steps. The following is an analysis of Zephaniah:

Sect. 1. Denunciations against Judah for idolatry, with exhortations to repentance...... i. 1–19, ii. 1–3.
  – 2. Prophesies against the Philistines, Moabites, Ammonites, Ethiopians, and
        Assyrians.. ii. 4–15.
  – 3. Reproof of the Jews for obstinate iniquity, with intimation of the Captivity...... iii. 1–7.
  – 4. The punishment of their enemies, their own restoration, prosperous state of
        the Church.. 8–20.

HAGGAI.

Haggai was the 10th of the minor prophets, and was probably born at Babylon, whence he accompanied Zerubbabel. The captives, immediately after their return to Judea, began with ardor to rebuild the Temple, but the work was suspended 14 yrs., till after the death of Cambyses. Darius Hystaspes succeeding to the empire, Haggai was excited by God to exhort Zerubbabel, prince of Judah, and the high-priest Joshua, to resume the work of the Temple, which had been so long interrupted (B. C. 521). The remonstrances of the prophet had their effect, and in the 2d yr. of Darius, and the 16th yr. after the return from Babylon, they resumed this work (Hag. i. 14, ii. 1). The Lord commanded Haggai to tell the people, that if any one recollected the Temple of Solomon, and did not think this to be so beautiful and magnificent as that structure was, he ought not to be discouraged, because God would render the new Temple much more august and venerable than the former had ever been, not in embellishments of gold or silver, but by the presence of the Messiah, the Desire of all nations, and by the glory which His coming would add to it.

We know nothing of Haggai's death. Epiphanius asserts, that he was buried at Jerusalem among the priests; which might induce us to believe, that he was of Aaron's family; but Haggai says nothing of himself to favor this opinion.

ZECHARIAH.

This prophet was the son of Barachia, and the grandson of Iddo (Zech. i. 1). The expression in Ezra (v. 1), is consonant to the Jewish usage of calling a descendant son or daughter, and an ancestor father or mother, though they might be removed two or three degrees from these relations. Zechariah returned from Babylon with Zerubbabel, and prophesied contemporaneously with Haggai.

The book of Zechariah has been variously divided into 2, 3, or 4 parts. Perhaps we may most conveniently distribute it into 2 principal sections, in each of which are some minor divisions. 1. The first comprises i.–viii., in which we have, after an introductory message (i. 1–6). A series of visions with which the prophet was favored on the night of the 24th day of the 11th month in the 2d year of Darius Hystaspes (7–vi. 15), closely connected with the then State of Jerusalem, symbolically describing the 4 great Gentile empires, and exhibiting with comfortable promises the establishment of a new theocracy, also pointing onward to the future glory of God's people under the great King and Priest, the Messiah, who would purge away iniquity, and rule His chosen. 2. A response of happy prediction delivered in the 4th year of Darius to certain inquirers, showing how times of mourning for past calamities should be turned into seasons of joyful praise (vii., viii). 3. In the second part (ix.-xiv.), there are far-reaching prophesies, which leaving present events stretch onward to Messianic times. Included here we have—1. The struggle of worldly powers with God's chosen people, while Messiah's office is foreshadowed (ix.-xi.); 2. The last onset of foes upon Jerusalem, the repentance of the Jewish nation for their rejection and murder of Messiah, with the final glory of that new kingdom of righteousness which shall never pass away (xii.-xiv). The style of Zechariah is for the most part prosaic, though in the later chapters the grandeur of the subject has given an elevation to the language which describes it. Several references to Zechariah occur in the New Testament (e, g., Matt. xxi. 4-5, xxv. 31; John xii. 15, xix. 37).

MALACHI.

Of the history of this prophet we know nothing. The time when he lived may be approached with tolerably certainty. It is highly probable that he was contemporary with Nehemiah, and it has been generally believed that his prophesy must have been delivered while that eminent person was a second time governor of the Jews.

The book of Malachi (B. C. 436–420), is rightly placed last of the productions of the minor prophets. Both chronologically considered and also from its contents, it appropriately closes the O. T. canon, and is the last solemn utterance of the prophetic Spirit under the earlier covenant. Thenceforward the voice of prophesy was heard no more till the forerunner of Messiah here predicted opened the second volume of revelation.

After the return from Babylon, when the Jews had re-peopled their city and re-built their Temple, abuses crept in. The priests were negligent; the people were worldly and complaining. Accordingly Malachi was commissioned to reprove both priest and people, and to invite them to reformation by promises of blessing and warnings of awful judgment. His book is not marked out into distinct messages or sections. It has been supposed, therefore, that the prophet has collected and compressed in it the substance of his various utterances. Be this as it may, we can properly separate it into three parts: in the first of which there is set forth the loving, fatherly, forbearing, and pitiful mind of God towards the covenant-people; the character of Jehovah in the second as the only God and Father; in the third as the just and final Judge of his people. More particularly in 1 (i. 2, ii. 9), the prophet, contrasting the state of Judah with that of Edom which then lay waste, shows how groundless were the murmurings of the Jews against the Lord, as though He loved them not. He next reproves them, priest and people, for their neglect of God's service, and for the blemished offerings they brought, and then, reminding the priests of the grace of their original appointment, he threatens them with shame and punishment. In 2 (ii. 10-16) he censures intermarriage with strangers, and divorce of lawful, i. e. Hebrew wives. In 3 (ii. 17, iv. 6), against complaints as if God did not regard men's conduct, and would never arise to judgment, the prophet fortells the coming of Messiah and his forerunner, to purify the sons of Levi, and inflict a curse unless they repented. Reproofs and consolatory promises are interspersed, for the day of the Lord would separate between the righteous and the wicked. He concludes with enjoining the strict observance of the law, since no fresh prophet should arise till the forerunner already spoken of, who should go before Messiah in the spirit and power of Elijah, to introduce a new dispensation.

This book is prosaic in style, but by no means destitute of force and elegance. Reference is made to it in the N. T. (Matt. xi. 10, xvii. 11. 12; Mark i. 2, ix. 12, 13; Luke i. 17, vii. 27: Romans ix. 13).

NEW TESTAMENT.

REMARKS ON THE FOUR GOSPELS.

The mere circumstance, that the four Gospels record the life and instructions of our blessed Lord, is sufficient to induce us to look upon them with the deepest veneration, and to study them with the most lively interest and diligent care. They reveal Evangelical Truth in a more general form. Such was the method which God was pleased to adopt. Our Lord can not be said to have made a full development of the Gospel; that was left for the Holy Spirit to accomplish after His ascension, after His redeeming work was finished. But the great truths, facts, and principles of religion; the lost state of man — repentance, faith in Christ, spiritual influence, obedience, the resurrection, final judgment, and eternal happiness or misery — were explicitly stated by our Lord.

The peculiar manner in which the Gospels are written demands our notice. We are here made familiar, to speak so, as far as such documents would admit, with our Saviour Himself. We hear His words, we see his actions, we know His conduct, we feel His spirit. His biographers seem only solicitous to set Him forth to our view. Other persons are brought forward, but it is only that His words may be related, and that His conduct may be described.

Two advantages, amongst others, arise from this mode of writing. In the first place, we are led to contemplate our Lord in His holy, peaceful, laborious, patient, and benevolent life, as our Example. This is the great practical lesson. He was holy, harmless, undefiled, separate from sinners, and went about doing good. In the second place, we see in Him the fulfilment of the prophesies of the O. T.: for let us compare His history, as it is recorded by the Evangelists, with the various predictions of the Prophets, and we behold in Him their exact accomplishment, and this our faith in Him as the Messiah, "as the only Mediator between God and man," is confirmed.

We may add a third advantage arising from this mode of recording the life of our Lord; we see how He conducted Himself in His ministry, addressing different sorts of people in different ways. He observed moral proportions. He taught doctrine, and He also taught practice. He descended to the particulars of the Christian character. He did not teach the higher doctrines of religion in a cold, speculative, and systematic manner. Whatever He taught, He brought it home to the heart and to the life of man.

The miracles of our Lord should always be viewed—1, as proofs of His Divine mission, and of His Deity, and, 2, as sources of spiritual instruction. As to the latter view of them, they may be considered as a visible delineation of the invisible operations of the Redeemer's power and grace on the souls of men. It is this spiritual application of them that gives them a peculiar and universal interest. They are, if we may speak so, redemption rendered visible.

The parables of our Lord will not be rightly understood, unless we view them in the universality of their meaning and application. Many of them refer to the whole counsel of God, to the whole history of the Church, to men collectively, while, at the same time, they are applicable to individuals. We put a parable before us: we admire the propriety of its imagery, and the simplicity of its language. This is comparatively nothing. Let us examine how it unfolds the purposes and proceedings of God, the nature and state of the Church, and the character and condition of each of its members, and then we shall find in it instruction of the highest order, both as to others and as to ourselves.

Human nature is accurately unfolded in the Gospels, not merely in the discourses of our Lord, but also in the various characters with which they make us more or less familiar. We see it in the perverseness of most of the Jews, and we see it in the mingled character of the disciples. Hence the proper study of these books will assist us in becoming acquainted with ourselves.

Let us read these sacred pages with such views, and we shall read them with reflection, intelligence, and ample benefit, provided that we implore, and rely upon, the sanctifying power of the Holy Spirit, without which all the rules that we can observe, and all the labor that we can employ in our study of sacred things will, as to our salvation, be vain and fruitless. When we read the discourses, the miracles, and the parables of our Lord, when we contemplate His devotion, humility, benevolence and unwearied labors, let us pray that we may believe in Him as our Saviour, hear Him as our Prophet, obey Him as our King, and follow Him as our Example.

TOPICS TO BE NOTICED IN READING THE GOSPELS.

In the study of the New Testament, and of the Gospels especially, we need to inquire and compare. The inspired writings are infinitely rich in truth, and each verse is so connected with the rest that an intelligent inquirer may easily extend his investigations from one passage over the whole of Scripture. Without attempting to exhaust topics of inquiry, we mention the following. The letters may be prefixed to each verse, or not, according to the taste of the reader:

A. What *analogies* between sensible and spiritual things may be here traced?

a. What prophesy is here *accomplished?* where found? when written? what rule of interpretation is illustrated?

B. What *blessing* is here sought or acknowledged, or promised, and why?

C. What *custom* is here referred to?

c. What trait of *character* is here given? good or bad? belonging to our natural or our renewed state? what advantages are connected with it?

D. What *doctrine* is here taught? how illustrated? what its practical influence?

d. What *duty* is here enforced, and how? from what motives?

D. What *difficulty* is here found in history or in doctrine? how explained?

E. What *evangelical* or other *experience* is here recorded?

e. What *example* is here placed before us? of sin or of holiness? lessons?

F. What *facts* are here related? what doctrine or duty do they illustrate? do you commend or blame them, and why?

G. What is the *geographical* position of this country, or place? and what its history?

H. What facts of *natural history* or of *general history* are here referred to or illustrated?

I. What *institution* or ordinance is here mentioned? on whom binding? what its design? what its connection with other institutions?

i. What *instructions* may be gathered from this fact, or parable, or miracle?

K. What *knowledge* of human nature, or want of knowledge, is here displayed?

L. What *lofty* expressions of devotional fervor?

l. What *Levitical* institute is here mentioned? why appointed?

M. What *miracle* is here recorded? by whom wrought? in whose name? what were its results? what taught?

N. What is worthy of notice in this *name?*

P. What *prohibition* is here given? is it word, or thought, or deed it condemns?

p. What is the meaning of the *parable* here given? what truth as to God, Christ, man, "the kingdom," is taught?

P. What *promise* is here given? to whom?

R. What prophesy is here *recorded?* is it fulfilled how? when?

S. What *sin* is here exposed?

s. What *sect* is here introduced? mention its tenets.

T. What *type* is here traced?

t. What *threatening?* when inflicted?

U. What *unjustifiable* action of a good man? what *unusual* excellence in one not pious?

W. What *woe* is here denounced? what *warning* given? against whom, and why?

X. What is here taught of the work, character. person of Christ?

x. What sublimity of thought or of language is here? what inference follows?

THE GOSPEL ACCORDING TO MATTHEW.

This Gospel was written by the Apostle, according to the testimony of all antiquity. There has been considerable discussion as to the language in which it was originally composed. Every early writer, however, who mentions that Matthew wrote a Gospel *at all* says that he wrote in Hebrew, that is, in the Syro-Chaldaic.

A characteristic of this Gospel is its constant citations from the O. T. They are about 65 in number. The time when the Gospel was written is uncertain. The most probable supposition is that it was written between 50 and 60. It was written for Jewish converts, to show them in Jesus of Nazareth the Messiah of the O. T. whom they expected.

There are traces in this Gospel of an occasional superseding of the chronological order. Its principal divisions are: I. The introduction of the ministry of Christ, i.-iv. II. The laying down of the new Law for the Church in the Sermon on the Mount, v.-vii. III. Events in historical order, showing Him as the worker of miracles, viii. and ix. IV. The appointment of Apostles to preach the Kingdom, x. V. The doubts and opposition excited by His activity in divers minds—in John's disciples, in sundry cities, in the Pharisees, xi. and xii. VI. A series of parallels on the nature of the Kingdom, xiii. VII. Similar to V. The effects of His ministry on His countrymen, on Herod, the people of Gennesaret, Scribes and Pharisees, and on multitudes, whom He feeds, xiii. 53, xvi. 12. VIII. Revelation to His disciples of His sufferings. His instructions to them thereupon, xvi. 13, xviii. 35. IX. Events of a journey to Jerusalem, xix., xx. X. Entrance into Jerusalem and resistance to him there, and denunciation of the Pharisees, xxi.-xxiii. XI. Last discourses; Jesus as Lord and Judge of Jerusalem, and also of the world, xxiv., xxv. XII. Passion and Resurrection, xxvi.-xxviii.

THE GOSPEL ACCORDING TO MARK.

Mark is generally supposed to be the same with "Marcus" (1 Pet. v. 13), but whether he was the same with John Mark (Acts xv. 37–39; Col. iv. 10; 2 Tim. iv. 11), is not clear. The identity is, however, probable. Perhaps he was converted by Peter. He labored ultimately in Egypt, and is said to have founded a church in Alexandria.

Mark's Gospel, the second in the order of the books of the N. T., is supposed to have been written between A. D. 56 and 65. Mark records chiefly the actions of our Saviour. It is Jesus acting and not Jesus discoursing that he portrays. His object is to show how He discharged the duties of the Messiahship. If it was written at Rome and for the Romans, its composition and selection of striking facts is wisely calculated to arrest the attention of such a people—it was suited to their taste and temperament. Fact and not argument most deeply impressed them. It is often supposed, and it has also been asserted, that Mark's Gospel is an abridgment of Matthew's. The idea has no foundation. Mark is shorter than Matthew as a whole, but is longer relatively. It omits many scenes in Matthew, but in detailing those which are found in the record of the first Evangelist, it is more minute, more graphic, a more circumstantial, and therefore longer in such sections. Had it been an abridgment, there would have been more appearance of harmony in arrangement and chronology.

The old tradition is, that Mark wrote this Gospel at Peter's request or dictation. Thus it is said by Papias, an early disciple: "Mark being the interpreter (amanuensis) of Peter, wrote exactly whatever he remembered, but he did not write in order. . . . . . . Mark committed no mistake when he wrote down circumstances as he recollected them." Irenæus says, "Mark, the disciple and interpreter of Peter, has given us, in writing, the things which had been preached by Peter." Origen and Clement agree in this opinion. So do Eusebius and Jerome.

The city of Rome was probably the place of this Gospel's composition. We find some Latin words in it, only disguised by being written in Greek characters. He explains several of the Jewish customs. The Jewish phrase "defiled hands," he explains by saying, "that is, unwashen hands." The Gospel of Mark is an independent, original publication. There are a sufficient number of important differences between this Gospel and the other three, to show that this is not an abridgment or compilation from them, or either of them, and among these we may mention two miracles which are not recorded in any other Gospel, and yet there are but 24 verses in Mark which contain any important fact not mentioned by some other evangelist.

THE GOSPEL ACCORDING TO LUKE.

The 3d Gospel is ascribed, by the general consent of ancient Christendom, to "the beloved physician," Luke, the friend and companion of the Apostle Paul. From Acts i. 1, it is clear that the Gospel described as "the former treatise" was written before the Acts of the Apostles, but how much earlier is uncertain. Perhaps it was written at Cæsarea during Paul's imprisonment there, A. D. 58–60. The preface, contained in the first 4 verses of the Gospel, describes the object of its writer.

The Evangelist professes to write that Theophilus "might know the certainty of those things wherein he had been instructed" (i. 4). This Theophilus was probably a native of Italy, and perhaps an inhabitant of Rome, for in tracing Paul's journey to Rome, places which an Italian might be supposed not to know are described minutely (Acts xxvii. 8, 12, 16), but when he comes to Sicily and Italy this is neglected. Hence it would appear that the person for whom Luke wrote in the first instance was a Gentile reader, and accordingly we find traces in the Gospel of a leaning towards Gentile rather than Jewish converts.

It has never been doubted that the Gospel was written in Greek. Whilst Hebraisms are frequent, classical idioms and Greek compound-words abound. The number of words used by Luke only is unusually great, and many of them are compound-words for which there is classical authority. On comparing the Gospel with the Acts it is found that the style of the latter is more pure and free from Hebrew idioms.

This Gospel contains: 1. A preface (i. 1–4). 2. An account of the time preceding the ministry of Jesus (i. 5 to ii. 52). 3. Several accounts of discourses and acts of our Lord, common to Luke, Matthew, and Mark, related for the most part in their order, and belonging to Capernaum and the neighborhood (iii. 1 to ix. 50). 4. A collection of similar accounts, referring to a certain journey to Jerusalem, most of them peculiar to Luke (ix. 51 to xviii. 14). 5. An account of the sufferings, death and resurrection of Jesus, common to Luke with the other Evangelists, except as to some of the accounts of what took place after the Resurrection (xviii. 15 to the end).

THE GOSPEL ACCORDING TO JOHN.

John, the Evangelist and the Apostle, was the son of Zebedee, a fisherman of the town of Bethsaida; his mother's name was Salome. He seems to have possessed a temper singulary mild, amiable and affectionate; and he was enmiently the object of our Lord's regard and confidence. Some learned men have viewed his Gospel as controversial, written against Corinthus and other heretics. He possibly may refer to these; but too much importance perhaps has been attached to this idea. His narrative is characterised by singular perspicuity, and the most unaffected simplicity and benevolence. The following quotations from Bp. Bloomfield's Lectures will give a just idea of this Gospel, when viewed with reference to the three preceding Gospels. The Gospel of John was written several years after those of the other evangelists, and evidently with a different object. They relate the principal incidents of our Saviour's life: John is more diligent in recording his discourses. The other evangelists enumerate a great variety of miracles; John describes only a few of the most remarkable, which had a more immediate reference to the object of his Gospel. They repeat the discourses which Jesus held with the people, mostly in Galilee, in the form of parables, and short moral sentences; John has preserved the longer and more argumentative conversations of our Saviour with the learned Jews, on the subject of the Messiah; and those in which he explained to his disciples the nature of his mission and office." "Whatever other objects John may have had in view, this was one—to convey to the Christian world just and adequate notions of the real nature, character, and office, of that great teacher who came to instruct and redeem mankind. For this purpose he studiously selected for his narrative those passages of our Saviour's life which most clearly displayed his Divine power and authority, and those of his discourses, in which he spoke most plainly of his own nature and of the efficacy of his death, as an atonement for the sins of the world." "The real difference between the other evangelists and John is, that they wrote a history of our Saviour's life; but John of his person and office." Whoever then desires to form a just notion of the real office and dignity of the Saviour of the world let him study the representations which Jesus has given of himself in the discourses recorded by John. The Apostles speak of him in their epistles, it is true, in noble and characteristic expressions; but *here* the Saviour speaks of himself, and in language which no ingenuity can pervert.

THE ACTS OF THE APOSTLES.

This book is an inspired history of the actions and sufferings of the Apostles at or after the ascension of their adored Master. It chiefly relates those of Peter, John, Paul, and Barnabas. It gives us a particular account of Christ's ascension, of the choice of Matthias in the place of Judas; of the effusion of the Holy Ghost at the feast of Pentecost, of the miraculous preaching of the Gospel by the Apostles, and the success thereof, and their persecutions on that account (ch. i. to v.), of the choice of the deacons, the persecution and murder of Stephen, one of them (ch. vi.-vii.), of a more general persecution and dispersion of the Christian preachers into Samaria, and places adjacent; of the baptism and baseness of Simon the Sorcerer, and the conversion and baptism of the Ethiopian eunuch (ch. viii.); of Peter's raising Dorcas to life, preaching to and baptizing the Gentiles of Cornelius' family, and vindication of his conduct herein (ch. ix. 32-43, x., xi. 1-18); of the spread of the Gospel among the Gentiles by the dispersed preachers, and the contributions for the saints at Jerusalem in the time of a dearth (ch. xi. 19-29); of Herod's murder of James, imprisonment of Peter, and fearful death (ch. xii.); of the council held at Jerusalem, which condemned the imposition of Jewish ceremonies, and advised to avoid offence of the weak, to forbear eating of meats offered to idols, or of things strangled, or blood (ch. xv.).

The rest of the book relates the conversion, labors, and sufferings of Paul (ch. ix. 1–31, xiii., xiv., xvi. to the end). It contains the history of the planting and regulation of the Christian church for about 30 yrs. Nor have we any other for 250 yrs. after, that deserves our belief. This large gap between inspired history and that of human authority, which deserves credit, Providence no doubt ordered, that our faith and practice relative to the concerns of the Church should stand, not in the wisdom of man, but in the truth and power of God.

THE EPISTLE OF PAUL THE APOSTLE TO THE ROMANS.

This epistle is put the 1st, though it is the 5th or 6th in the order of time, either from the prëeminence of Rome, as being then the mistress of the world, or because it is the largest and most comprehensive of Paul's epistles. It is not known by whom the Gospel was first preached at Rome. The Christians there being partly Jews, and partly Gentiles, the former had strong prejudices about their peculiar privileges, and the latter claimed equal privileges with them; hence contentions arose. Paul wrote this epistle to compose their differences, and in it he unfolds the nature of the Gospel, and shows the purposes and measures of God respecting the Jewish and Gentile world. He shows the guilty state of all men, confutes the objections of the Jews, explains the doctrines of Justification and Sanctification, dwells on the happiness of true believers, asserts the calling of the Gentiles into the Christian Church, and inculcates moral and civil obedience.

There are four portions of this epistle (ch. v. 12–21, vii., viii. 28–30 and ix.) which may with propriety be pointed out as being, in the present state of our knowledge, peculiarly difficult. The mere fact that very different views are taken of them by able men, and that systems of opinion directly opposed to each other have been built upon them, or supported by them, is a proof, to say the least, that they are not of easy interpretation. While this epistle contains the fullest and most systematic exposition of the Apostle's *teaching*, it is at the same time a very striking expression of his *character*. Nowhere do his earnest and affectionate nature, and his tact and delicacy in handling unwelcome topics appear more strongly than when he is dealing with the rejection of his fellow-countrymen, the Jews.

THE FIRST EPISTLE OF PAUL THE APOSTLE TO THE CORINTHIANS.

Corinth was the metropolis of Achaia proper. It abounded in riches and elegance, in luxury and voluptuousness, so that its inhabitants became infamous to a proverb. Christianity was planted there by Paul himself (Acts xviii. 1–11); and he was succeeded by Apollos (Acts xviii. 27, 28, xix. 1). The Church consisted partly of Jews and partly of Gentiles, but chiefly of the latter; hence, in this Epistle, Paul combats with Jewish superstition and heathen licentiousness. Soon after he had quitted the Church, its peace was disturbed by false teachers. Two parties were formed; the one contending for Jewish ceremonies, and the other misinterpreting Christian liberty, and indulging in shameful excesses. Hence his object in this Epistle is twofold: to apply suitable remedies to the disorders and abuses which had crept into the Church, and to answer those points in which (ch. vii. 1) they had requested his advice and information. This has been called "the most elegant of the Epistles." It undeniably is a most masterly and accomplished composition, displaying the great dexterity of the writer in a very difficult case; and though much refers to customs and practices no longer in existence, yet the whole is of universal application and of perpetual use.

THE SECOND EPISTLE OF PAUL THE APOSTLE TO THE CORINTHIANS.

The first Epistle produced different effects. Some of the Corinthian Christians had been brought to repentance, and to an amendment of their ways, to submission to the Apostle's orders, and to a good disposition towards him. Some still adhered to the false teacher, and denied the

Apostolical authority of Paul. He was charged with lenity and irresolution of conduct, with pride and severity on account of his treatment of the incestuous person, with arrogance and vain-glory in his ministry, in which he lessened the authority of the law, and with being personally contemptible. Hence he vindicates himself and his conduct against all the arguments of his adversaries; and the different circumstances of the Church account for the tenderness and severity which he exhibits. Conscious of the goodness of his cause, he speaks of himself more freely, and justifies himself more boldly, and confutes his opponents with solid arguments. The whole work is strongly impressed with meekness and modesty, decision and energy, firmness and kindness, with affection the most pure, and irony the most keen. He accounts for his not having come to them, he declares his sentence against the incestuous person to have been neither rigid nor tyrannical, but necessary and pious; he intimates his success in preaching the Gospel, and shows the superiority of the Gospel, the ministration of righteousness, to the law, the ministration of death; he stirs them up to a holy life; he excites them to finish their contribution for their poorer brethren in Judea, and he apologizes for himself with respect to the contemptibleness imputed to him, asserting his authority, enumerating his labors, and appealing to "visions and revelations." Though this Epistle was thus limited and temporary with respect to its primary object, yet it abounds throughout with invaluable instructions (whether it refers to the character of good or wicked men, or to the development of the nature and spirit of the Gospel), which will never be obsolete.

THE EPISTLE OF PAUL THE APOSTLE TO THE GALATIANS.

Galatia was a large province in the centre of Asia Minor. It derived its name from the Gauls, who conquered the country and settled in it, about 280 B. C.; it was called also Gallo-Græcia, on account of the Greek colonists who afterwards became intermingled with them. About 189 B. C. it fell under the power of Rome, and became a Roman province, 26 B. C. The inhabitants were but partially civilized, and their system of idolatry was extremely gross and debasing. Paul and Silas traveled through this region about A. D. 51, and formed Churches in it, which Paul visited again in his second journey, 3 yrs. afterwards. This epistle was probably written soon after his first visit: see Acts, xvi. 6, xviii. 23; Gal. i. 6, 8, iv. 13, 19.

The epistle may be divided into three parts:

1. After his usual salutation, Paul asserts his full and independent authority as an Apostle of Christ: he relates the history of his conversion and introduction into the ministry, showing that he had received his knowledge of christian truth, not by any human teaching, but by immediate revelations, and that the other Apostles had recognized his Divine commission, and treated him as their equal (i. 2).

2. In support of his doctrine, that men are accepted of God by faith alone, and not by the rites and ceremonies of the law, he appeals to the experience of the Galatians, since their conversion to Christianity, and to the case of Abraham, who had been justified and saved by faith, and shows that the design of the law was not to supersede the Divine covenant of promise previously made with Abraham, but to prepare the way, and to exhibit the necessity for the Gospel (iii). He draws a contrast between the state of pupilage and the subjection of the people of God under the law, and their happier condition under the Gospel, when, by the redemption of the Son of God, they were put into possession of the privileges and blessings of sonship; and addressing that portion of the Galatians that had been heathens, he reminds them that, having been rescued from the far more degrading bondage of idolatry, it was especially deplorable that they should fall back into the slavery of superstition (iv. 1-2). He tenderly appeals to them as his spiritual children, reminding them of their former attachment to him; and then, addressing those who relied upon the law and the letter of the O. T., shows them that the history of Abraham's two sons afforded an emphatic illustration of the relative position and spirit of the two contending parties, and of the rejection of the one, and the blessedness of the other (iv. 2-31).

3. He exhorts the believers to stand firm in their Christian liberty, but not to abuse it, shows them that holiness of heart and life is secured under the Gospel by the authority of Christ and the grace of the Holy Spirit (v.), and enjoins upon them mutual forbearance, tenderness, love, and liberality, and, after again condemning the doctrine of the false teachers, closes his epistle with a declaration which may be regarded as the sum of the whole.

THE EPISTLE OF PAUL THE APOSTLE TO THE EPHESIANS.

Ephesus was the chief city of Asia on this side Mt. Taurus, and was celebrated for the temple of Diana (Acts xix. 27). The Gospel was first planted here by Paul (Acts xviii. xix). He wrote this Epistle during his imprisonment at Rome. We may suppose him to have been apprehensive lest advantage should be taken of his confinement to unsettle the minds of the Ephesian converts, who were mostly Gentiles. He therefore wrote this Epistle to establish them in the faith, giving them the most exalted views of the love of God, of the dignity and excellency of Christ, and fortifying their minds against the scandal of the Cross. He shows that miserable as their state had been, they now had equal privileges with the Jews; and he urges them to walk in a manner becoming their profession. This has been pronounced the richest and noblest of the Epistles, and certainly in variety and depth of doctrine, sublimity of metaphor, and animated fervor of style, occasionally rising to what has been called rapture, and Apostolic earnestness and exhortation, both as to doctrine and as to a life becoming the Christian profession, it stands unrivalled. The Apostle had no rebukes to utter, no controversy to engage in, and therefore with a noble mind and a warm heart, he expatiates freely, with sublime thought and copious expressions, on his subject, the unsearchable wisdom of God in the redemption of man, and his love towards the Gentiles, in making them through faith partakers of the benefits of the death of Christ.

THE EPISTLE TO THE PHILIPPIANS.

A tie of peculiar affection seems to have existed between the Apostle Paul and the Philippian Church. In their city he had suffered grievous wrong at the hands of the heathen magistrates, and from the disciples there he had, contrary to the general custom, twice accepted gifts soon after his departure from them (Phil. iv. 15, 16; comp. 2 Cor. viii. 1-6). Nor, when the Apostle was far away a prisoner at Rome, did the Philippians forget him. They sent him a present by Epaphroditus (Phil. iv. 18), on whose return he dispatched this letter, pouring out his heart in warm affection towards those who had so tenderly shown their love to him.

We may arrange this epistle in three sections. I. After an affectionate introduction (i. 1-11), the Apostle gives an account of his condition at Rome (12-26), and then exhorts to unanimity and Christain humility (27-ii. 16), adding an expression of his hope of visiting them, with a notice of Epaphroditus's sickness and recovery (17-30). II. The Apostle cautions the Philippians against Judaizing teachers, and confirms his warning by a special reference to his own experience, and thence, having shown how he renounced all self-dependence, he takes occasion to exhort to heavenliness of mind (iii. 1-iv. 1). III. He gives various admonitions (2-9), then expresses his thanks for the present sent him (10-20), and concludes with salutation and a benediction (21-23).

This Epistle is referred to by Polycarp, and cited by Irenæus and Clement of Alexandria, and other early writers. The style is animated and affectionate, occasionally abrupt, but in a strain of almost unqualified commendation. By reason of the influence of certain Judaizers there, there were, indeed, some tokens of disagreement, and therefore the Apostle earnestly presses unity upon them, but his admonitions are conceived and expressed in the tenderest spirit. They were, we may trust, not ineffective.

THE EPISTLE TO THE COLOSSIANS.

Colosse was one of the chief cities of Phrygia, which, at the date of this Epistle, was a very rich and fertile country, though now under the Moslem yoke, and, in a great measure, uncultivated. Phrygia was twice visited by Paul (Acts xvi. 8, xviii. 23), but whether he reached Colosse is doubted. The tenor of the Epistle favors the conclusion that he did not (see especially ii. 1); but it is certain that he knew several of the Colossian Christians, of whom Archippus, their minister, and Philemon are expressly named. The Colossians, having heard of Paul's imprisonment, sent to him Epaphras, their minister, to comfort the Apostle, and to inform him of their state. Epaphras, shortly after reaching Rome, was also imprisoned (Philemon 24). This Epistle was written during Paul's first imprisonment at Rome (i. 24, iv. 18).

It is evident that there is a very close connection between this inspired treatise and the epistle to the Ephesians. They are twin productions, written about the same period. Many similar expressions occur in both, showing that the condition of both churches was somewhat alike Epaphras had come to Rome, and given the Apostle information as to the state of the Christian communities in Asia Minor, and seeing the immediate danger of the Colossian Church, Paul wrote this letter. The Apostle begins by a reference to his own high office, and to the character and destiny of the Christians whom he purposed to address. Then the mention of Christ's name suggested to him the exalted glory and Divine dignity of the Redeemer, who is Himself Creator, Preserver, and Lord of the physical and spiritual universe, whose death is our reconciliation, and the knowledge of which is the prime mystery at last revealed to the world. The writer then passes on to theories which are endangering the purity and stability of the Colossian Church, and warns the Colossians against the seduction of a proud philosophy and vain asceticism, which were selfish in their origin, and ruinous in their consequences. Then follow exhortations suited to their circumstances, and cautions against sins too prevalent in the ancient world. The epistle closes with many salutations, showing the deep interest which the writer cherished for their spiritual welfare.

The spirit of the great Apostle of the Gentiles breathes in every sentence of this pithy and earnest composition Ardor undamped by imprisonment, interest unchilled by distance, zeal for the purity and simplicity of the Gospel, uncompromising to all who introduce rash speculation or vile and unscriptural vagaries, whether under the shape of higher wisdom or superior sanctity. are indubitable traits of Paul's character, and unmistakable features of the epistle to the Colossians.

I. EPISTLE TO THE THESSALONIANS.
II. EPISTLE TO THE THESSALONIANS.

When Paul was obliged to quit Thessalonica he went to Athens. Anxious to visit the Thessalonians again, he found himself unable (1 Thess. ii. 18), and in consequence sent Timothy (iii. 1, 2). When Timothy rejoined him at Corinth (Acts xviii. 1-5; 1 Thess. iii. 6), he wrote the *first* epistle. It is distinctly cited by Irenæus, Clement of Alexandria, and Tertullian.

The epistle consists of two main parts. I. After an inscription (i. 1) Paul celebrates the grace of God in their conversion and advancement in the faith (2-ii. 16), and then expresses his desire to see them and his affectionate solicitude for them (17-iii. 13). II. In the hortatory part he calls to holiness and brotherly love (iv. 1-12) he speaks of Christ's advent (13-v. 11), and adds various admonitions (12-24). He then concludes with a charge that the Epistle be generally read, with greetings, and a benediction (25-28).

This is the earliest of Paul's letters, and may be dated at the end of 52 or beginning of 53 A. D.

The *second* Epistle was written not long after the first; for Silas and Timothy were still with him (2 Thess. i. 1), probably in 53 A. D., and from the same place, Corinth. The evidence for it is even yet more conclusive than for the first. It is alluded to by Polycarp, cited by Irenæus, Clement of Alexandria, and Tertullian. This letter is supplementary to the first. That had been in some measure misapprehended, and the coming of Christ was taken to be close at hand. Moreover, an unauthorized use had been made of the Apostle's name. He therefore wrote to correct the mistake, and to check the evil results which had flowed from it in disorderly conduct.

This Epistle comprises, besides the inscription and conclusion, three sections. I. A thanksgiving and prayer for the Thessalonians (i. 3-12). II. The rectification of their mistake, and the doctrine of the man of sin (ii). III. Sundry admonitions (1) to prayer, with a confident expression of his hope respecting them (iii. 1-5); (2) to correct the disorderly (6-15). He then concludes with salutation and apostolical benediction, adding a remarkable authentication of his letters (16-18).

The style of these Epistles is for the most part plain and quiet, save, as might be expected, in the prophetic section (iii. 1-12).

I. EPISTLE TO TIMOTHY.
II. EPISTLE TO TIMOTHY.

These are the 15th and 16th in order of the books of the N. T. The first is supposed to have been written about the year 60, and contains special instructions respecting the qualifications and the duties of sundry ecclesiastical officers, and other persons, and the most affectionate and pungent exhortations of faithfulness. The second Epistle was written a year or two later, and while Paul was in constant expectation of martyrdom (2 Tim. iv. 6–8), and may be regarded as the dying counsel of the venerable apostolic father to his son in the Lord. It contains a variety of injunctions as to the duties of Christians under trials and temptations, and concludes with expressions of a full and triumphant faith in the Lord Jesus Christ, and in all the glorious promises made to his true followers.

These two Epistles are full of interesting matter, not only to pastors of churches, but to all members of the Christian community. What peace, harmony, and spirituality would characterize the Church if the affectionate counsels of these Epistles were fully acted on!

In ch. iii. of the first Epistle, there is an appropriateness not always perceived in the last two verses. The church is styled by the Apostle, the *Pillar* of the Truth, and as inscriptions were written on pillars, so the last verse of the chapter is composed of *stichoi*, to suit such an inscription:

GREAT IS THE MYSTERY OF GODLINESS;

GOD.

WAS MANIFESTED IN THE FLESH,

JUSTIFIED IN THE SPIRIT,

SEEN BY THE ANGELS,

PROCLAIMED AMONG THE GENTILES,

BELIEVED ON IN THE WORLD,

RECEIVED UP INTO GLORY.

Ephesus was famous for its pillars and inscriptions. The reading, "God," in the above quotation, has been controverted and often examined. The MSS., versions and quotations, are all in favor of the reading God. If the reading "who was manifest," be adopted, the meaning is the same, for the antecedent is "God," in the preceding verse.

THE EPISTLE TO TITUS.

It is by no means certain from what place Paul wrote this Epistle. But as he desires Titus to come to him at Nicopolis (iii. 12), and declares his intention of passing the winter there, some have supposed that when he wrote it, he was in the neighborhood of that city, either in Greece or Macedonia, others have imagined that he wrote it from Colosse, but it is difficult to say upon what ground. It was probably written in the yr. 64, after Paul's first imprisonment at Rome.

The principal design of this Epistle was to give instructions to Titus concerning the management of the Churches in the different cities of the island of Crete, and it was probably intended to be read publicly to the Cretans, that they might know on what authority Titus acted. Paul, after his usual salutation, intimates that he was appointed an Apostle by the express command of God, and reminds Titus of the reason of his being left in Crete; he describes the qualifications for bishops, and cautions him against persons of bad principles, especially against Judaizing teachers, whom he directs Titus to reprove with severity (i.); he informs him what instructions he should give to people in different situations of life, and exhorts him to be exemplary in his own conduct; he points out the pure and practical nature of the Gospel (ii), and enumerates some particular virtues which he was to inculcate, avoiding foolish questions and frivolous disputes, he tells him how he is to behave towards heretics, and concludes with salutations (iii).

THE EPISTLE TO PHILEMON.

This Epistle was written by Paul from Rome, where he was detained as a prisoner. Onesimus, a servant of Philemon, had fled to that city, and was there converted to the faith of the Gospel. Paul had begotten him in his bonds. Being about to return to Philemon, Paul wrote this letter, chiefly with a design to conciliate the feelings of Philemon towards his penitent servant, and now fellow-disciple. The slave may have apprehended the infliction of such a penalty as in slave countries is usually inflicted on runaways. Paul sent him back, not because Philemon might claim him, but to show the altered position in which Christianity had placed him. The Apostle pleads for his reception (though he might have enjoined it), pleads from his old age and suffering, the personal friendship of Philemon, and his instrumentality in his conversion, and held himself bound for any debt which Onesimus might be owing his master. The letter has been regarded by learned critics as a master-piece of epistolary composition. An eminent critic of ancient days says of it: "The Apostle craves pardon in behalf of a fugitive and pilfering slave, whom he sends back to his master; but while pleading his cause, he discourses with so much weight respecting the rules of Christian kindness, that he seems to be consulting for the whole Church, rather than managing the business of a particular individual. He intercedes for the humble man so modestly and submissively, as to show, more clearly than almost anywhere else, the gentleness of his nature, which is here drawn to the life."

THE EPISTLE OF PAUL THE APOSTLE TO THE HEBREWS

Who the Hebrews were is not agreed among the learned; but most probably they were the Jewish Christians resident in Palestine. Though the author of the Epistle is not mentioned, the evidence of its having been written by Paul is so strong that we can not reasonably doubt of its being with justice ascribed to him. It is directly opposed to the peculiar errors and prejudices of the Jews, proving with great solidity of argument and by such arguments as were well understood by the Jews, that the religion of Jesus is far more excellent and perfect than that of Moses. Its object is to show the Deity of Jesus Christ, and the superior excellency of the Gospel when compared with the Mosaical institution, to prevent the Jewish converts from relapsing to abolished rites and ceremonies, and to exhort them to perseverance in the faith after the example of the ancient believers. The whole is interspersed with warnings and exhortations to different sorts of persons. This Epistle connects the Old and New Testaments in the most convincing manner, and elucidates both more fully than any other Epistle. There, too, the great doctrines of the New Testament are stated, proved, and adapted to practical purposes in the most impressive manner. We often speak of the offices of Christ, under a three-fold division of them, the kingly, prophetical, and sacerdotal offices. It is the last of these which is particularly unfolded in this Epistle, in which we are principally led to consider the Sacrifice and Atonement which He made, His dignity and sufficiency as priest, and the prevalence of His intercession. These matters are elucidated by being put in contrast with the Levitical ordinances, of which they were the antitype. It is by the careful study of this Epistle, with an immediate examination of the different facts to which Paul refers in the Old Testament, that we form a right view of the great doctrine of the Atonement, that we rightly understand the nature and design of the great dispensations of God, the ritual and the spiritual, and that we rightly estimate our privileges under the Christian Dispensation.

THE EPISTLE OF JAMES.

The author of this Epistle, if not James the son of Zebedee, which is very unlikely, must be that prominent James, who was most probably the son of Alpheus. He addressed it to Hebrew Christians of the dispersion (James i. 1), to those primarily that were scattered throughout Judea (Acts viii. 4), but with a further purpose of reaching generally those of Abraham's seed who anywhere had embraced the faith of Christ. His object was to fortify the minds of the disciples against the trials to which, for their faith, they were exposed, and to warn them against the sins of which, as Jews, they were especially in danger.

Bengel divides this Epistle into 3 parts: I. The inscription (i. 1). II. The exhortation (i. 2–v. 18), enforcing (1) patience against external trials and inward temptations (i. 2–15), (2) and then, from regard to the Divine goodness (16–18), the importance of being "swift to hear, slow to speak, slow to walk" (19–21); the special admonitions for each being that *hearing* must be accompanied by doing (22–25), in silence (26), with compassion and self-denial (27), without regard to persons in public assemblies (ii. 1–13), so that generally faith must not be separated from works (14–26), that *speech* must be bridled (iii. 1–12), that *wrath*, with other swelling passions, must be restrained (13–iv.

17); (3) patience again, which the coming of the Judge, with the consequent destruction of the wicked (v. 1–6), and the deliverance of the just (7–12) should encourage, and which prayer will cherish (13–18). III. The conclusion, in which the Apostle, having shown his care for the spiritual welfare of those he addresses, would have them diligent for the salvation of others (19, 20).

The time when this Epistle was composed is uncertain; some place it early, A. D. 45, others think its date later, perhaps 61 or 62, A. D. Some persons think that this Epistle does not harmonise with the Epistles of Paul. On this topic little can be here said. The two Apostles had each his own aspect of a cardinal truth, and their expressions have reference to the special need of those they respectively addressed. Paul vindicates the power of a living faith, James shows that if it be not a living faith it is worthless. The two are not at variance. The style of this Epistle is earnest, the Greek comparatively free from Hebraisms.

THE FIRST EPISTLE GENERAL OF PETER.

It is doubted whether this Epistle was written only to the dispersed Hebrew Christians, afflicted on their dispersion, or to Christians in general, whether Jews or Gentiles. It was written from Babylon, but whether by Babylon he meant Rome, figuratively so named, or ancient Babylon, or a city of that name in Egypt, does not seem to be a point of easy determination. The Christians, it seems, were exposed to severe persecutions, and the design of the Epistle is to support them under afflictions and trials, and to instruct them how to behave in the midst of opposition and cruelty, with which they were treated, submissive to civil authority, attentive to their duties in their several stations, and leading blameless and exemplary lives. It has been said of this Epistle, that it is sparing in words, but full of sense, majestic, and one of the finest books of the New Testament. Peter writes in it with such energy and rapidity of style that we can scarcely perceive the pause in his discourses, or the distinction of his periods. Little solicitous about the choice of words, or the harmonious disposition of them, his thought and his heart were absorbed in the grand truth which he was Divinely commissioned to proclaim, and the indispensable obligation of Christians to adorn their profession with a holy life.

THE SECOND GENERAL EPISTLE OF PETER.

I. Clement of Rome and Hermas refer to this Epistle; it is mentioned by Origen and Eusebius, and has been universally received since the 4th century, except by the Syriac Christians. II. It is addressed to the same persons as the former Epistle, and the design of it was to encourage them to adhere to the genuine faith and practice of the Gospel. It was written when the Apostle foresaw that his death was at no great distance, and he might hope that advice and instruction given under such circumstances would have the greater weight. As he is supposed to have suffered martyrdom in the year 65, we may place the date of this Epistle in the beginning of that year. It was probably written from Rome. III. Peter, after saluting the Christian converts and representing the glorious promises of the Gospel dispensation, exhorts them to cultivate those virtues and graces which would make their calling and election sure; he expresses his anxiety to remind them of their duty at a time when he was conscious of his approaching end; he declares the divine origin of the Christian faith, which was attested by a voice from heaven and by the sure words of prophesy; he foretells the sure rise of heresies and false doctrines, and denounces severe judgments against those who shall desert the truth, while they who adhere to it will be spared, as Noah and Lot were in former times; he assures his Christian brethren that the object of this, and of his former Epistle, was to urge them to observe the precepts which they had received; he cautions them against false teachers, represents the certainty of the Day of Judgment, reminds them of the doctrines which he and Paul had inculcated, and exhorts them to grow in grace, and in the knowledge of our Lord and Saviour Jesus Christ. Some learned men have thought that the style of the second chapter of this Epistle is materially different from that of the other two chapters, and have therefore suspected its genuineness. We must own that we observe no other difference than of the subjects. The subject of the second chapter may surely lead us to suppose that the pen of the Apostle was guided by a higher degree of Inspiration than when written in a didactic manner. It is written with the animation and energy of the prophetic style, but there does not appear to us to be anything, either in phrase or sentiment, inconsistent with the acknowledged writings of Peter. Bishop Sherlock was of opinion that in this chapter Peter adopted the sentiment and language of some Jewish author who had described the false teachers of his own times. This conjecture is entirely unsupported by ancient authority, and it is in itself very highly improbable.

THE FIRST EPISTLE GENERAL OF JOHN.

At what place the 3 Epistles of John were written, can not be accurately determined. The first of them is not, properly speaking, an Epistle, but rather a didactic discourse upon the principles of Christianity in doctrine and practice; opening sublimely with the fundamental topics of God's perfection, and man's depravity and Christ's propitiation; perspicuously propounding the deepest mysteries of our holy faith, maintaining the sanctity of its precepts with energy of argument, and exhibiting in all its parts the most dignified simplicity of language—artless simplicity and benevolence blended with singular ardor and modesty—together with a wonderful sublimity of sentiment, are the characteristics of this treatise. The sentences considered separately, are exceedingly clear, but when we search for the connection we frequently meet with difficulties. The principal object seems to be to inculcate brotherly love, and to caution Christians against erroneous and licentious tenets, principles, and conduct. An affectionate spirit pervades the whole, but when the writer exposes false teachers and hypocrites, we discern a Boanerges. This treatise abounds more than any other book of the N. T. with criteria, by which Christians may soberly examine themselves whether they be in the faith.

THE SECOND EPISTLE OF JOHN.

It is uncertain to whom this Epistle was addressed. The most probable opinion is that it was addressed to the Lady Electa, who is supposed to have been some eminent Christian matron. It is an epitome of the first Epistle. The lady Electa is commended for the religious education of her children, is exhorted to abide in the doctrine of Christ, and to avoid the delusion of false teachers and is urged to the practice of Christian love and charity.

THE THIRD EPISTLE OF JOHN.

This Epistle, probably written about the same time as the preceding, is addressed to a converted Gentile, but it is uncertain who Gaius was. The object of the Epistle was, to commend his steadfastness in the faith, and his hospitality, to caution him against the ambition and turbulent practices of Diotrephes, and to recommend Demetrius to his friendship. It is not known who Diotrephes and Demetrius were.

THE GENERAL EPISTLE OF JUDE.

Jude, or Judas, surnamed Thaddeus, or Lebbeus, was son of Alpheus, brother of James the Less, and one of the twelve Apostles. The only particular incident related of him is in John xiv. 21-23. The time when, and the place where this Epistle was written, is uncertain. The coincidence between it and ch. ii. of Peter's 2d Epistle, renders it likely that it was written soon after that Epistle. There is much diversity of opinion about the persons to whom it was addressed; it probably relates to all who had received the Gospel. The design of it was to guard believers against false teachers, of whom he gives an awful description, laboring for words and images to impart to the reader an adequate idea of that profligate character. His expressions are strong, his language animated, and his figures and comparisons bold, apt, and striking. The whole shows how deeply the Apostle was grieved at the scandalous immoralities of those wicked men, who, under the mask of religion, were most abandoned persons.

THE BOOK OF THE REVELATION.

This is the last in the order of the books of the Bible, and is commonly called the Apocalypse, from a Greek word which signifies *revelation*. It is supposed to have been written about the years 95–96. It is the design of this book to present a prophetic history of the Church. It is called the Revelation of St. John the Divine, because to him was more fully revealed the Divine counsels than to any other prophet under the Christian dispensation. It has been observed that hardly any one book has received more early, more authentic, and more lasting attestations to its genuineness than this. But its canonical authority has sometimes been called in question. The fanatical rhapsodies of the ancient millennarians led many to call in question the authority of that book on which their reveries were based. This was wrong. If the Chiliasts misinterpreted the Apocalypse their opponents should have shown the absurdities of their expositions, and not have thrown discredit on the Apocalypse itself. The current of external evidence is wholly in its favor. Ignatius, Polycarp, Melito, Origen, Clement, and Tertullian refer to it as a portion of inspiration. That John the Apostle was its author was fully believed in ancient times. There is a great similarity of style between the Apocalypse and the fourth Gospel.

It seems to have been written to comfort the early Churches under persecution, and its keynote is the success of the new religion over every opposition. It is but an expanded illustration of the first great promise, "The seed of the woman shall bruise the head of the serpent." Its figures and symbols are august and impressive, and remind us of Isaiah, Ezekiel and Daniel. It is full of prophetic grandeur, awful in hieroglyphics and mystic symbols: seven seals opened, seven trumpets sounded, seven vials poured out, mighty antagonists arrayed against Christianity; hostile powers, full of malignity, against the new religion, and, for a season, oppressing it, but at length defeated and annihilated; the darkened heaven, tempestuous sea, convulsed earth fighting against them, while the issue of the long combat is the universal reign of peace, and truth, and righteousness; the whole scene being relieved at intervals by a choral burst of praise to God the Creator, and Christ the Redeemer and Governor. The book must have been so far intelligible to the readers for whom it was first designed, or it could not have yielded them either hope or comfort. It is also full of Christ. It exhibits His glory as Redeemer and Governor, and describes that deep and universal homage and praise which the "Lamb that was slain" is forever receiving before the throne. Either Christ is God, or the saints and angels are guilty of idolatry. It would far exceed our space to recount the many and opposing interpretations that have been given of this book in ancient and modern times. Some are simple and some are complex; some looking upon it as almost fulfilled, and others regarding the greater portion of it as yet to be accomplished. Between Mede, Faber and Elliot on the one hand, and Lucke and Stuart on the other, there stretches a wide gulf. In the hands of its expositors it resembles a musical instrument, there being no variation or fantasia which may not be played upon it. Some authors find its fulfilment in Constantine's elevation, others in Luther's Reformation. One discerns its completion in the French Revolution, and another sees in it a portraiture of the principles and struggles of the voluntary controversy. Woodhouse and Mede, Bicheno and Croly, Faber and Elliot, Newton and Stuart, have constructed opposite systems with equal tenacity of purpose and ingenuity of conjecture. In the meantime, we can only add that the year-day theory requires defence; that the purpose of the Apocalypse needs to be more clearly defined, and that fortuitous similitude of events is not to mold our interpretation of prophetic symbols. We have only room to exhibit one of the simpler views of the Apocalypse:

Two cities are mentioned as overthrown, and a third is established on their ruins. By Sodom is meant Jerusalem, as is evident from the mention of the "Temple" and "Holy City." By Babylon is meant Rome. These two cities are overthrown, and the New Jerusalem is established. Jerusalem is the symbol of Judaism, and Babylon of Paganism, both of which systems are at length overthrown by the spread and power of Christianity. The whole prophesy may be arranged thus: 1. Introduction of the seven Epistles to the seven Churches. 2. Preparation for the great events to follow— seven seals. 3. Sodom, or Jerusalem, representing Judaism, destroyed by a series of calamities— seven trumpets. 4. Birth of Christianity, the child of uncorrupted Judaism, and preservation of the infant from destruction, by the special interposition of heaven. 5. Babylon or Rome (in its first form as a marine monster), *i. e.* persecuting Paganism, destroyed by a series of calamities—seven vials. Under this part there is a distinct allusion to Mohammedanism, a compound of Judaism and Paganism, which, under the Saracenic power, overthrew Christianity in the East, etc. **6**. Babylon in another form—the Papal despotism, a compound of Paganism and Christianity; Babylon finally and completely destroyed—conflicts and victories succeeding the Reformation. **7**. The millennium—another hostile power still future, or post-millennial—the last judgment and final victory. **8**. Final and complete triumph of Christianity, and the consummation of its glory in the heavenly world.

RULES FOR READING THE BIBLE.

I. RULES OF INTERPRETATION.

1. Put yourself, as it were, in the times, places, and circumstancesof the sacred writers.

2. Form as correct a view as you can of the geography of Scripture, of the simplicity of ancient manners, of the arts and habits that existed in those times. The Psalms abound with allusions to hunting wild beasts. Many passages in Job are clear to him who has a correct view of judicial matters.

3. Ascertain, as far as it is possible, the plain, literal and primary meaning of Scripture. Exercise sound common sense. A right use of reason will supersede much criticism, and prove a valuable substitute for it.

4. Beware of mystical and ingenious refinement; do not aim to spiritualise every passage. Real spirituality and fanciful spirituality are different things. The former is real, deep, sublime, and satisfactory, the latter is ideal, shallow, specious and delusive.

5. Seek the literal before the spiritual meaning.

6. The true spiritual sense of a passage is that which is to be most highly esteemed.

7. Avoid ingenious conceits and far-fetched interpretations.

8. Make all allowance for idiomatical and figurative diction, especially when an absurdity would follow from adhering to the literal sense.

9. Always distinguish between plain and figurative language.

10. Never press a metaphor too far.

11. Carefully consider the context before you draw a conclusion from a separate passage.

12. Consider the circumstances of a passage as far as you can; that is, the occasion of it, to whom it was written, by whom it was written, and with what design.

13. Compare spiritual things with spiritual. Never be weary of referring to what are called parallel passages; that is, to illustrate passages: for Scripture is the best interpreter of Scripture.

14. Explain what is difficult by what is plain and easy.

15. Never expect fully to understand all things in the Scriptures; yet remember that wise, humble, devout, and persevering study will be always adding something to our knowledge.

16. When words and phrases are of doubtful meaning consider them well.

17. Do not always fix the same meaning to the same word, for the same word is frequently used in Scripture in various senses.

18. Endeavor to form clear and distinct ideas of the great and peculiar words of Scripture, such are faith, repentance, redemption, justification, sanctification, grace, righteousness, etc. [N. B.—It is to be deeply lamented that there is so little agreement among serious Christians about the ideas to be attached to such words. In vain do we look for peace and unanimity among Christians, while the sacred vocabulary remains so undefined as it is at present.]

19. Consider (see 12) the character of a writer, the state and character of those to whom he wrote, the errors which he opposed, the truths which he inculcated and established.

20. The New Testament is the fulfilment of the Old. Carefully compare them with each other.

21. The historical and prophetical books of the Old Testament mutually illustrate each other.

22. The Epistles of the New Testament are the comment of the Holy Spirit on the four Gospels.

23. The Epistle to the Hebrews is the key to the Jewish ritual, as contained in the last four books of Moses.

24. In order to form a just view of any book of Scriptures, read the whole of it, consider its parts, their relation to each other, and their formation of a whole.

25. Never form opinions from detailed parts and passages.

26. Be content to remain in ignorance, rather than plunge into error, where difficulties are before you.

27. Admit no doctrine as part of the Gospel which is not agreeable to the general tenor of the whole.

28. Interpret all that is said concerning God, after the manner of men, in a way that is agreeable to the infinite perfection.

29. Make no types and allegories which Scripture does not directly warrant.

30. Do not compel the whole of a parable to bear a spiritual meaning.

31. The whole is sometimes put for a part, and a part for the whole.

32. General terms are to be sometimes limited, particular terms are sometimes put for general, definite numbers are often put for indefinite.

33. Sometimes things by the figure hyperbole are magnified or diminished beyond or below their limits.

34. Negatives are often put for a strong affirmation of the contrary as "not guiltless," *i. e.* exceedingly guilty "shall not be moved," *i. e.* shall be firmly established.

35. Questions are frequently put for strong affirmations or negations (Jer. v. 9; St. Mark viii. 36).

36. In reading the poetical books remember the nature of Hebrew verse.

37. Interpret Prophesy by History, not by speculation, conjecture, and fancy.

38. The sacred writers, and especially the prophets, often change persons and tenses.

39. Many truths, delivered in the form of absolute and universal propositions, are to be interpreted under certain limitations and conditions.

40. One principle, or one duty, is frequently spoken of as implying the presence of all religion, for where it is, there all other essential things co-exist with it.

41. Promises made to particular persons in Scripture may be applied to all true believers.

42. Never separate promises from duties. The mind, heart, and conduct of man—the truth, power and commands of Scripture—study them in their inseparable relations.

43. Though Scripture was primarily addressed to particular people, yet its truths, laws, and spirit are of universal extent and perpetual duration. Hence, whatever we read in the Bible, we read that which God addresses to us as individuals.

—

II. PRACTICAL RULES.

Read and search the Scriptures—

1. With the deepest reverence, as the Word of God.

2. With humility and teachableness, not to cavil, but to learn.

3. With a devout mind, with heartfelt dependence on the various influences of the Holy Spirit.

4. With reflection, as a creature endowed with intelligence and reason. Reading without reflection will communicate no solid knowledge; it can, at the most, only fill the mind with crude, superficial, partial, and unconnected notions.

5. With patience, not expecting to know in a day all that they reveal, or to be in a day all that they require.

6. With a direct reference to personal improvement in the universality of Christian godliness; in holiness of mind, or its effectual illumination in Christian doctrine; in holiness of heart, of purity of principles and affections; and in holiness of conduct, or walking with God, and before God, in obedience to His laws.

7. With a proper recollection of what we read; as whether it be a doctrine, command, promise, warning, character, event, etc.

8. With so much attention as at least to remember something. Let something, whenever the Bible is opened, be impressed on the mind for subsequent meditation.

9. With a freedom from all bias to systems of human device. Let the one and only desire of your soul be—to be taught of God, to be cast into the pure mold of the Gospel of Christ.

10. With a due recollection that you have always much to learn, much to correct, etc.

11. With constant interrogation and self-application; what do I know of this truth—feel of this principle or affection—enjoy of this promise—fear of this threat—perform of this duty—avoid of this evil?

12. With meek and fervent prayer to the Father of Light. Make what you read the ground-work of your supplication.

13. With a grateful heart. Always bless God for giving you the rich treasure of His Word.

14. With a just sense of responsibility. God demands of us a due improvement of his gifts.

15. With constancy; not by fits and starts, not at wide intervals of time, but habitually, daily, through the whole of life.

CHRONOLOGICAL INDEX TO THE BIBLE.

PERIOD I. FROM THE CREATION TO THE DELUGE, CONTAINING 1,656 YEARS.

A. M.	B. C.		
1	4004	The creation of the world..	Gen. 1:2
	"	Fall of our first parents, Adam and Eve, from holiness and happiness, by disobeying God. Promise of a Saviour....	" 3
2	4002	Cain born..	" 4:1
3	4001	Abel born...	" 4:2
129	3875	Abel murdered by his brother Cain..	" 4:8
130	3874	Seth born, his father, Adam, being 130 yrs. old................................	" 5:3
622	3382	Enoch born..	" 5:18, 19
687	3317	Methuselah born...	" 5:21
930	3074	Adam dies, aged 930 yrs...	" 5:5
987	3017	Enoch translated, aged 365 yrs...	" 5:24
1042	2962	Seth dies, aged 912 yrs...	" 5:8
1056	2948	Noah born...	" 5:28, 29
			} 6:3–22
1536	2468	The Deluge threatened, and Noah commissioned to preach repentance during 120 yrs......	1 Pet. 3:20
			2 Pet. 2:5
1656	2348	Methuselah dies, aged 969 yrs..	Gen. 5:27
		In the same yr. Noah enters into the ark, being 600 yrs. old.................	" 7:6, 7

PERIOD II. FROM THE DELUGE TO THE CALL OF ABRAHAM, CONTAINING 427 YEARS.

A. M.	B. C.		
1657	2347	Noah, with his family, leaves the ark after the deluge, and offering sacrifice, he receives the covenant of safety, of which the rainbow was the token...............	} Gen. 8:18, 19
			" 9:8, 17
1770	2234	Babel built...	" 11
1770	2234	The confusion of language, and dispersion of mankind.......................	" 11
1771	2233	Nimrod lays the first foundation of the Babylonian or Assyrian monarchy...	" 10:8–11
1816	2188	Mizraim lays the foundation of the Egyptian monarchy.......................	" 10:13
2006	1998	Noah dies, aged, 950 yrs...	" 9:29
2008	1996	Abraham born..	" 11:26

PERIOD III. FROM THE CALL OF ABRAHAM TO THE EXODUS OF ISRAEL FROM EGYPT, 430 YEARS.

A. M.	B. C.		
2068	1936	Abraham called from Chaldean idolatry, at 60 yrs. of age....................	Gen. 11:31
2083	1921	Abraham's second call to Canaan..	" 12:1–4
2091	1913	Abraham's victory over the kings, and rescue of Lot...........................	" 14:1–24
2094	1910	Ishmael born, Abraham being 86 yrs. old..	" 16
2107	1897	God's covenant with Abram, changing his name to *Abraham*; circumcission instituted; Lot delivered, and Sodom, Gomorrah,	

485

A.M.	B.C.		
2108	1896	Admah and Zeboim destroyed by fire on account of their abominations	" 17-19
2133	1871	Isaac born, Abraham being 100 yrs. old	" 21
		Abraham offers Isaac as a burnt-sacrifice to God	" 22 / Heb. 11:17-19 / James 2:21
2145	1859	Sarah, Abraham's wife, dies, aged 127 yrs	Gen. 23:1
2148	1856	Isaac marries Rebecca	" 24
2168	1836	Jacob and Esau born, Isaac being 60 yrs. old	" 25:26
2183	1821	Abraham dies, aged 175 yrs	" 25:7,8
2245	1759	Jacob goes to his uncle Laban in Syria, and marries his daughters, Leah and Rachel	" 28
2258	1746	Joseph born, Jacob being 90 yrs. old	" 30:23,24
2265	1739	Jacob returns to Canaan	" 31:32
2275	1729	Joseph sold as a slave by his brethren	" 37
2288	1716	He explains Pharaoh's dreams, and is made governor of Egypt	" 41
2298	1706	Joseph's brethren settle in Egypt	" 43;44
2315	1689	Jacob foretells the advent of Messiah, and dies in Egypt, aged 147 yrs	" 49
2368	1636	Joseph dies, aged 110 yrs	" 50;56
2430	1574	Aaron born	Ex. 6:20; 7:7
2433	1571	Moses born	" 2:1-10
2473	1531	Moses flees into Midian	" 2:11-13
2513	1491	Moses commissioned by God to deliver Israel	" 3:2

PERIOD IV. FROM THE EXODUS OF ISRAEL FROM EGYPT TO THE BUILDING OF SOLOMON'S TEMPLE, 487 YEARS.

A.M.	B.C.		
2513	1491	Miraculous passage of the Red Sea by the Israelites	Ex. 14;15
2514	1490	The law delivered on Sinai	" 19-40
2552	1452	Miriam, sister of Moses, dies, aged 130 yrs	Num. 20:1
"	"	Aaron dies, aged 123 yrs	" 20:28, 29
2553	1451	Moses dies, aged 120 yrs., Joshua being ordained his successor	Deut. 34
"	"	The Israelites pass the river Jordan, the manna ceases, and Jericho is taken	Josh. 1-6
2561	1443	Joshua dies, aged 110 yrs	" 24
2849	1155	Samuel born	1 Sam. 1:19
2888	1116	Eli, the high-priest, dies. Ark of God taken by the Philistines	" 4:1
2909	1095	Saul anointed king of Israel	" 10:11;12
2919	1085	David born	
2941	1063	David is anointed to be king, and slays Goliath	" 16:13 / " 17:4,9
2949	1055	Saul is defeated in battle, and, in despair, kills himself. David acknowledged king by Judah	" 31
2956	1048	Ishbosheth, king of Israel, assassinated, and the whole kingdom united under David	2 Sam. 1
2957	1047	Jerusalem taken from the Jebusites by David, and made the royal city	" 5
2969	1035	David commits adultery with Bathsheba, and contrives the death of her husband, Uriah	" 11
2970	1034	David brought to repentance for his sin by Nathan the prophet, sent to him by the Lord	" 12
2971	1033	Solomon is born	" 12-24
2981	1023	Absalom rebels against his father, and is slain by Joab	" 15;18
2989	1015	David causes Solomon to be proclaimed king, defeating the rebellion of Adonijah	1 K. 1
2990	1014	David dies, aged 70 yrs	" 2
3000	1004	Solomon's temple finished, after 7 yrs. building	" 6;7

B.C.	KINGS OF JUDAH BEGAN TO REIGN.	KINGS OF ISRAEL BEGAN TO REIGN.	PROPHETS.
975	Rehoboam	Jeroboam I	Ahijah, Shemaiah
958	Abijah, or Abijam		
955	Asa	Nadab, 954	Azariah
953	"	Baasha	Hanani
930	"	Elah	Jehu
929	"	Zimri	
"	"	Omri	
918	"	Ahab	Elijah, 910–896; Micaiah
914	Jehoshaphat		Elisha, 896–838
897	"	Ahaziah	Jahaziel
896	"	Jehoram, or Joram	
892	Jehoram	"	
885	Ahaziah		
884	Athaliah	Jehu	Jehoiada
878	Joash, or Jehoahaz	"	
857	"	Jehoahaz	Jonah, 862
839	"	Jehoash	
825	Amaziah	Jeroboam II	
810	Uzziah, or Azariah	"	Joel, 800
784	"	Anarchy, 11 years	Amos, 787
773	"	Zechariah	Hos. 785–725
772	"	Shallum; Menahem	
761	"	Pekahiah	
759	"	Pekah	
758	Jotham	"	Micah, 750–698
742	Ahaz	"	Obed
730	"	Hoshea	
726	Hezekiah	(Captivity, 721)	Nahum, 713
698	Manasseh	"	
643	Amon	"	Zeph. 680
641	Josiah	"	Jer. 628–586
610	Jehoahaz, or Shallum	"	Hab. 626
"	Jehoiakim	"	Dan. 606–534
599	Jehoiachin, or Coniah		
"	Zedekiah		
588	Babylonian Captivity		Obadiah, 587

PERIOD VI.   FROM THE DESTRUCTION OF JERUSALEM BY NEBUCHADNEZZAR TO THE BIRTH OF CHRIST, 588 YEARS.

B.C.	HISTORICAL EVENTS.	PROPHETS.
588	Destruction of Jerusalem by the Chaldeans, and captivity of the Jews.	Ez. 595-575.
538	Babylon taken by Cyrus.	
536	Proclamation of Cyrus; return of captives under Zerubbabel. Joshua the high-priest.	
534	Foundation of the second temple.	
529	Artaxerxes (Cambyses) forbids the work.	Hag. 520-518.
520	Favorable decree of Ahasuerus (Darius Hystaspes)	Zech. 520-518.
518	Esther made queen.	
515	The second temple finished.	
510	Haman's plot frustrated.	
484	Xerxes, king of Persia.	
464	Artaxerxes Longimanus.	
457	Ezra sent to govern Jerusalem.	
445	Nehemiah sent as governor.	
423	Darius Nothus.	Mal. 397.
335	Alexander the Great invades Persia, and establishes the Macedonian or Grecian empire.	
332	Jaddus high-priest.	
323	Alexander dies.	
320	Ptolemæus Lagus surprises Jerusalem.	
277	Septuagint ver. made by order of Ptolemæus Philadelphus.	
170	Antiochus Epiphanes takes Jerusalem.	
167	His persecution.	
166	Judas Maccabæus governor.	
161	Jonathan governor.	
152	He becomes high-priest.	
143	Simon: treaty with the Romans and Lacedemonians.	
135	John Hyrcanus.	
107	Judas (Aristobulus) high-priest and king.	
88	Anna the prophetess born.	
63	Jerusalem taken by Pompey, and Judea made a Roman province.	
40	Herod made king.	
28	Augustus Cæsar emperor of Rome.	
19	The poet Virgil dies.	
18	Herod begins to rebuild the temple.	
4	John the Baptist born.	
4	Christ born, 4 yrs. before the era known as A. D.	

FROM THE BIRTH OF JESUS CHRIST TO THE END OF THE FIRST CENTURY.

YEAR		
1	Nativity of Jesus Christ.	Luke 2:1-16.
12	Jesus visits Jerusalem.	— 2:41-52.
18	Augustus Cæsar followed by Tiberius.	
26	Pilate sent from Rome as governor of Judea.	— 3:1.
29	John the Baptist begins his ministry.	Matt. 3:1.
30	Jesus baptized by John.	— 3:1.
33	Jesus Christ was crucified, and rose from the dead.	27:28.

A.D.

34	Ananias and Sapphira struck dead.	Acts 5.
35	Stephen stoned, and the church persecuted.	— 6; 7.
36	Saul converted.	— 9; 13:9.
38	Conversion of the Gentiles.	— 10.
42	Herod Agrippa made king of Judea.	
44	James beheaded by Herod : Peter liberated by an angel	— 12:1-19.
54	Claudius Cæsar followed by Nero.	
63	Paul sent a prisoner to Rome.	— 26; 28.
65	The Jewish war begins.	
66	Paul suffers martyrdom at Rome by order of Nero.	2 Tim. 4:6,7.
67	The Roman general raises the siege of Jerusalem, by which an opportunity is afforded for the Christians to retire to Pella beyond Jordan, as admonished by Christ	Matt. 24:16-20.
70	Jerusalem besieged and taken by Titus Vespasian, according to the predictions of Christ, when 1,100,000 Jews perished by famine, sword, fire, and crucifixion; besides 97,000 who were sold as slaves, and vast multitudes who perished in other parts of Judea.	Luke 19:41-44.
71	Jerusalem and its temple razed to their foundations.	Matt. 24:2.
79	Vespasian dies, and is succeeded by Titus.	
81	Titus dies, and is succeeded by Domitian.	
95	John banished to the isle of Patmos, by Domitian.	Rev. 1:9.
96	John writes the Revelation.	
97	John liberated from exile.	
100	John, the last surviving apostle, dies, about 100 yrs. old.	

THE EXODUS

AND

ROUTE TO CANAAN.

The periods and events which mark the passage of the Israelites from Egypt to the borders of Canaan may be grouped under five heads, as set forth below:

I. THE EXODUS.

RAMESES:—The Exodus began at Rameses, Ex. 12: 37; Num. 33: 3, in the first month and fifteenth day, with "about six hundred thousand on foot that were men, beside children." Rameses, or Ramses, was a leading city of Goshen, probably centrally located, and had been built by the Israelites as a store-city for the pharaoh, named Ramses. Modern Egyptologists date the exode during the reign of Pharaoh Meneptah, B. C. 1317. Another date, B.C. 1491, was formerly used. After a march of one day, or about sixteen miles, they arrived at

SUCCOTH:—Ex. 12: 37-39. Succoth appears to have been the district of which Pithom was the capital. It was a region of pasturage, watered by a canal from the Nile, and therefore a proper halting place for a people with "flocks and herds, even much cattle."

ETHAM:—Ex. 13: 20. They journeyed from Succoth to Etham, "in the edge of the wilderness." This encampment was at the north end of the Red Sea, and they could have gone thence to Canaan by two regular routes without crossing the sea. But God ordered otherwise, and changed their route to the southeast

PI-HAHIROTH:—Ex. 14: 1-9. They encamped "before Pi-hahiroth, between Migdol and the sea, over against Baal-zephon." Migdol was evidently a watch-tower on a hill, and the place of encampment lay between Lake Timsah and the so-called Bitter Lakes, where the sea was narrow, shallow, and easily affected by strong, persistent winds. Here the Pharaoh overtook them, and thence they made their miraculous escape through the sea to the east side. Ex. 14: 21-31.

II. THE ROUTE TO SINAI.

MARAH:—Ex. 15: 22-26. After celebrating their escape with song, timbrel and dance, Moses led them a three-days' journey into the wilderness of Shur, when they reached Marah, or "place of bitter waters." Here Moses sweetened the waters for his murmuring followers. They then came to

ELIM:—Ex. 15-27. At Elim were "twelve wells of water, and threescore-and-ten palm trees; and they encamped there."

WILDERNESS OF SIN:—Ex. 16. After leaving Elim, they "came into the Wilderness of Sin, which is between Elim and Sinai, on the fifteenth day of the second month" after leaving Egypt. Here they were miraculously fed with quails and manna. After journeying from the Wilderness of Sin, they encamped at Dophkah and Alush, and then pitched at

REPHIDIM:—Ex. 17: 1-8. Here they murmured for water, and Moses smote the rock in Horeb, giving them a supply. He also called the place "Massah and Meribah, because of the chiding of the children of Israel." Here, too, a battle took place between the Israelites and Amalekites, in which the former were victorious. Leaving this encampment, they entered the

WILDERNESS OF SINAI:—Ex. 18: 5-27; 19-40. In this wilderness they "encamped before the mount" (Mt. Sinai). Jethro, the father-in-law of Moses, paid him a visit. Moses chose able men, and made them heads over the people, "and they judged the people at all seasons." God gave to Moses the Ten Commandments, Ex. 20. A portion of the law was promulgated, Ex. 21-23. The Tabernacle was fashioned and its ceremonies prescribed. Aaron and his sons were set apart for the priest's office. The worship of the Golden Calf took place, followed by a slaughter of the people, Ex. 32. The Tabernacle was completed and furnished, and received the approval of Moses, Ex. 39. Ceremonial dedication of the Tabernacle, Ex. 40. The completed law was given and promulgated, Lev. 1-27. The people were numbered, Num. 1-8, and the second passover celebrated, Num. 9.

III. FROM SINAI TO KADESH-BARNEA.

The stay at Sinai covered the period from the fifteenth day of the third month of the first year, after leaving Egypt, until the twentieth day of the second month in the second year, or nearly one of our years. Ex. 19: 1;

Num. 10: 11. Then, Num. 10: 12, 33, "they departed from the Mount of the Lord three-days' journey," and came to

TABERAH:—Here their complainings brought upon them a consuming fire, Num. 11: 1-3; and here the "seventy elders" seem to have been first chosen. The next encampment was at

KIBROTH-HATTAAVAH (*graves of lust*). Here the murmuring people were smitten with a plague, ere they could chew the food God had sent, Num. 11: 34.

HAZEROTH:—Num. 11: 35. They next journeyed to Hazeroth, and abode there. Here Aaron and Miriam sinned, and Miriam was stricken with leprosy, Num. 12: 1-15. They next moved to

KADESH-BARNEA:—Num. 12: 16; 13: 26. It appears from Deut. 1: 2 that they consumed eleven days in marching from Sinai to Kadesh-barnea, which place was in the wilderness of Paran, and near the southern borders of Canaan. From this place the twelve spies were sent out to view the "Land of Promise," Num. 13: 2-33, all but two of whom (Joshua and Caleb) returned with an evil report.

IV. THE WILDERNESS WANDERINGS.

Num. 14: 1-39. The adverse report of the spies threw the people into rebellion against Moses and Aaron, and God declared, Num. 14: 23, "Surely they shall not see the land which I swore unto their fathers, neither shall any of them that provoked me see it." So, Num. 14: 25, He commanded, "To-morrow turn you, and get you into the wilderness by the way of the Red Sea." This period of rebellion and judgment seems to have been characterized by the outbreak and punishment of Korah and his followers, and by fire and plague, which destroyed thousands, Num. 16. In Num. 33, a series of encampments of the Israelites during their wilderness wanderings is given. They indicate that the life of the wanderers was not unlike that of the nomadic tribes in whose midst they were moving from place to place in search of water and pasturage, giving and receiving battle, the elders gradually dying off, the younger men acquiring skill and bravery for the conquest of Canaan.

V. KADESH-BARNEA TO THE RIVER JORDAN.

The wilderness wandering covered a period approximating thirty-eight years, after which there was a return to

KADESH-BARNEA:—Num. 20: 1-21; 27: 14. Here Miriam died and was buried, and here Moses smote the rock. Edom refused to give Israel passage through his border, Num. 20: 21, 22, wherefore Israel turned away and marched by the borders of Edom to

MOUNT HOR:—Num. 20: 22-29; 34: 7, 8. Hor was on the borders of Edom. Here Aaron died and was buried. After leaving Mount Hor, they made a long detour by way of

THE ARABAH:—Num. 21: 5-9; Deut. 2: 8, (R.V.) This detour for the purpose of compassing Edom, carried them to Elath and to Ezion-geber on an arm of the Red Sea. The encampments are mentioned in Num. 33: 41-48. On their northward march they at length reached the brook

ZARED OR ZERED:—Num. 21: 12; Deut. 2: 13, 14. This brook or wady separated Moab from Edom. They next crossed the

ARNON:—Num. 21: 13-15. The Arnon formed the boundary between the Amorites and Moabites. The next encampment was at

BEER:—Num. 21: 16-18. Here they sang the song of the well. Their marches were now through Moab, Num. 21: 19-22, to

JAHAZ:—Num. 21: 23, 24. Here they defeated the Amorite army and took possession of the country between the Arnon and Jabbok. Thence they marched to

EDREI:—Num. 21: 33. Here they defeated Og, King of Bashan, and occupied his country. They next pitched at

ABEL-SHITTIM:—Num. 22: 36; Deut. 34. This was the "Meadow of Acacias" in the plains of Moab, on the east side of Jordan, opposite Jericho. Here, in sight of Canaan, they defeated the combined armies of Moab, Ammon and Midian. The people were again numbered. Moses repeated and confirmed the law to the new generation of Israel, delivered his last charge, recited his song, viewed the promised land from Nebo, and died. Joshua took charge of affairs, crossed the Jordan, and began the conquest of Canaan, Josh. 1.

489

TABULAR View of the Prophets, showing the

Passages chiefly	Jonah, B.C. 840-784.	Amos, 810-785.	Hosea, 800-725.	Isaiah, 765-698.	Joel, 810-785.	Micah, B.C. 758-699.
MORAL, DEVOTIONAL	.	.	. . .	25.-27. 11 . . .	.	
To Israel	.	2.-8.	4.-13.	9. 8-21: 28. . . .	.	} 2: 3.
To Judah	.	. .	4, 15, etc.: 12. 2	1.-5.: 22. 8, etc.: 29: 30.	1. 8- 2. 12	} 6.
HISTORICAL . . .	1.-4.	. .	. . .	36.-39.	.	.
PROPHETIC (A)—						
Israel	.	2.-9. 10	3. ⎰ ⎱ 5. 8-6. 3	7. 1-25: ⎰14. 24- 8: 9. 8:⎱28: 17. 15. 11	.	1.
Judah	.	1. 2, 4, 5	⎩	22. 1: 24: ⎩8. 5-9 52.	1: 2. 27	} 7.
Assyria, Nineveh	3. 4.	. .	. .	9: 14: 30: 31. . .	.	.
Babylon, Chaldæa	.	. .	. .	13: 14. 24-28: 21.	.	.
Egypt	.	. .	. .	19: 20.	.	.
Ethiopia	.	. .	. .	18.	.	.
Edom	.	1. 11	. .	21. 11 . . .	.	.
Moab	.	2. 1	. .	15: 16. . . .	.	.
Syrians	.	1. 1, 3, 5	. .	7. 1-9: 8: 17. . .	.	.
Tyre	.	1, 9	. .	23. . . .	.	.
Other Nations . .	.	Ammon, 1.; Philistia, 1.	. .	Arabia, 21. 13, etc.	.	.
PROPHETIC (B)—						
Our Lord's *first* coming.	1. 17	. .	11. 1: 13. 14	7. 14: 9: 40-63. .	2. 28	5.
Events subsequent, where—	.	. .	. .	. . . .	.	.
Israel is named .	.	9. 11-15	13. 14 ⎰1. 10: ⎱2. 14- 23	28.5:10. ⎰ 20, etc. ⎱ 8.	⎰10.- ⎱12.	⎰2.12
Judah "	.	. .	14. ⎩3. 5	22. 20: ⎩ 40. 24. 14, etc.: 9: ⎰ to 1.-5.: ⎱ 27.-35. ⎩	2.28- 3.	4. 5 and
Gentiles . .	.	9. 12 See Acts 15. 17	. . ⎱	⎩ 66. ⎩		7.
Egypt converted	.	. .	. .	19. 18-23.	.	.
Assyria "	.	. .	. .	19. 23-25.	.	.
Moab restored	.	. .	. .	. . . . .	.	.
Elam "	.	. .	. .	. . . . .	.	.

order and chief subjects of their prophecies.

Nahum, 720–698.	Zephaniah, 640–609.	Jeremiah, 628–585.	Habakkuk, 612–598.	Daniel, 606–534.	Obadiah, 588–583.	Ezekiel, B. C. 595–536.	Haggai, 520–518.	Zechariah, 520–510.	Malachi, 436–397; B. C. 420.
.	.	Lam. 1.-5.	3.						
.	.	. . . .	.	. . . .	.	. . . .	1: 2. 10-19	1. 1-7: 7.	1: 2 3. 7- 18.
.	.	28: 29: 32. 1-25: 36.- 43. 7: 52.	.	1. 6.					
.	.	30: 31.							
.	1.	1.-25.: 27: 29: 30-31. 26: 33: 34: 44: 46. 26: 50.	1.	9.		9.-24.: 33: 36: 37: 39.-48.?	.	1. 7-7.: 11.	
1.-3.	2. 13	. . . . 25. 12: 37: 50: 51.	2.	2. 36: 4. 19: 5. 25	.	31. 3-18.			
.	.	43: 44. 29: 46: 50.		. . . .	.	29.-31.			
.	2. 12	. . . .	.	. . . .	.	30. 4-6.			
.	.	49. 7: Lam. 4. 21	.	. . . .	1	25.-35.			
.	2. 9	48. . . .	.		.	25.			
.	.	49. 23	.	. . . .	.	26.-28.			
.	Ammon, 2.; Philistia, 2.	Ammon, 49: Phi- listia, 47: Arabia, Persia, 49.		Persia, Grecia, Rome, 11: the four kingd.7.		Ammon, 21. 28: 25: Philistia, do.: Gog. 38: 39.			
.	.	31. 22: 30.		9. 24-26: 7. 13.		34. 23, etc.	2. 7, 9	2. 10, 11: 9. 9: 11. 12: 12. 10: 6: 13: 1. 7	3: 4, 1-3.
.	.	. . . .	.	7: 12.					
.	{ 3. 8-20	{ 30: 33: 31. 23. 5 { 3.13	.	. . . . { 17.- 21.		{ 6. 10. 39. { 28: 29. 23, 21: 36. { etc. 25: 34. 20, 21: 40-48:	{ 2. 6, 7	{ 1. 7-7.: 8.-14.	3. 4.
.			.	. . . .	.				
.			.	7.-12.	. . .				
.	. . .	48. 47. 49. 39.							

MIRACLES OF THE OLD TESTAMENT.

THE MIRACLE.	THE OBJECT OR OCCASION.	THE PLACE.	THE TEXT.
The Multiplication of Languages...	To Defeat Wrong Ambition...	Babel...	Gen. xi. 7-9.
Certain Sodomites Smitten with Blindness...	To Punish them for Murderous Intent...	Sodom...	xix. 11.
Destruction of Sodom and Gomorrah...	As Punishment for their Great Wickedness...	Sodom and Gomorrah...	xix. 24, 25.
Lot's Wife Turned into a Pillar of Salt...	As Punishment for Disobedience in Looking Back...	On the road from Sodom	xix. 26.
The Burning Bush—not Consumed...	The Call of Moses...	Horeb...	Ex. iii. 2.
Moses' Rod Transformed into a Serpent...	To Confirm his Faith...	Horeb...	iv. 2-5.
Moses' Hand made Leprous and Healed...	To Confirm his Faith...	Horeb...	iv. 6, 7.
Aaron's Rod Transformed into a Serpent...	To convince Pharaoh of his and Moses' Divine mission	Egypt...	vii. 10-12.
The Ten Plagues...	To Compel Pharaoh to let the Israelites Go Forth...	Egypt...	vii.–xii.
The Pillar of Cloud by Day and of Fire by Night...	To Baffle the Egyptians and Guide the Israelites...	Near Egypt...	xiii. 20, 21.
The Red Sea Divided, and Returned to its Channel...	To make a road for the Israelites and Drown the Egyptians	Near Egypt...	xiv. 21, 22.
The Waters of Marah made Sweet...	To Supply Drinking Water for the Israelites...	Marah...	xiv. 24, 25.
Quails and Manna Sent...	To Supply the Israelites with Food...	The Wilderness	xvi. 13-35.
Water brought from the Rock...	To Supply the Israelites with Water...	Horeb and Meribah...	xvii. 5-7; Num. xx. 8-12.
Victory over the Amalekites...		Rephidim...	xvii. 8-16.
Aaron's Rod Buds, Blossoms and bears Almonds...	To Convince the Israelites of his Authority...	Kadesh...	Num. xvii. 1-8.
Korah and his party Destroyed...	As Punishment for their Rebellion...		xvi. 31-35.
Plague Sent and Stayed...	To Rebuke their Murmurings...		41-50.
Fiery Serpents Sent and some of Those Bitten Cured	To Rebuke their Murmurings...	Desert of Zin...	xxi. 7-9.
Balaam's Ass Speaks...	To Rebuke him for Going to Balak...	Pethor...	xxii. 28-31.
Aaron's Sons Consumed with Fire from Heaven...	For Offering Strange Fire...	Sinai...	Lev. x. 1, 2.
Miriam's Leprosy Cured...	In Answer to Moses' Prayer...	Hazeroth...	Num. xii. 10-15.
The Jordan Divided...	To Open Passage for Israelites and for Elijah and Elisha...	River Jordan...	Josh. iii. 14-17; 2 K. ii. 8, 14.
The Walls of Jericho Fall...	To Aid the Israelites in its Capture...	Jericho...	vi. 6-21.
The Sun and Moon Stand Still...	To Lengthen the Day for the Israelites...	Gibeon...	x. 12, 13.
Samson receives Water from En-hakkore...	To Slake his Thirst...	Lehi...	Judg. xv. 19.
Sacrifices Consumed by Fire from Heaven...	To Attest Divine Authority...	Several Places...	Judg. ix. 24; Judg. vi. 21; Judg. xiii. 19, 20; 1 K. xviii. 38; 2 Chr. vii. 1.
Dagon and many Philistines Fall before the Ark...	To Compel the Philistines to return it to its Rightful Keepers...	Ashdod...	1 Sam. v.
Beth-shemeshites Smitten...	To Punish Irreverence...	Beth-Shemesh...	vii. 19.
Thunder and Rain in Harvest-time, in answer to Samuel's prayer...	To Inspire Reverence...	Gilgal...	xii. 18.
Uzzah Struck Dead...	To Punish Presumption...	Perez Uzzah...	2 Sam. vi. 7.
Jeroboam's Hand Withered...	To Punish his Defiance of God's Messenger...	Beth-el...	1 K. xiii. 4, 6.
The Widow's Meal and Oil Multiplied...	To provide her and her Son and the Prophet with food	Zarephath...	1 K. xvii. 10-16.
Ahaziah's Captains and their Fifties Consumed...	To Rebuke Ahaziah's Defiance of God's Prophet...	Near Samaria...	2 K. i. 9-12.
The Chariot of Fire takes Elijah to Heaven...	To Show God's Especial Regard for Him...	Near the Jordan...	2 K. ii. 11.

MIRACLES OF THE OLD TESTAMENT.—(Concluded.)

THE MIRACLE.	THE OBJECT OR OCCASION.	THE PLACE.	THE TEXT.
The Waters of Jericho made fit to Drink.	In Answer to the Prayer of the People.	Jericho	ii. 19-22.
Water provided for a Large Army.		Moab	iii. 16-20.
The Widow's Oil Multiplied.	To Afford Means to Pay her Debts.		iv. 1-7.
The Shunammite's Son Raised.	As a Reward for her Regard for the Prophet.	Shunam	iv. 32-36.
Poisonous Pottage Cured.	To Supply Food for the Sons of the Prophets.	Gilgal	iv. 40, 41.
One Hundred Men fed with Twenty Loaves.	The Same Purpose as the last.	Gilgal	iv. 42-44.
Naaman's Leprosy Cured.	Because of his Faith.	River Jordan	v. 10-14.
Gehazi made Leprous.	As Punishment.	Samaria	v. 24-27.
Axe-head caused to Float.		Jordan	vi. 6.
A Syrian Band Smitten with Blindness.	To Rescue the Prophet.	Dothan	vi. 19.
The Syrian Army put to Flight.	To Deliver Samaria from Siege.	Samaria	vii. 6, 7.
The Dead Man Revived by Contact with Elisha's remains			xiii. 20, 21.
Sennacherib's Army Destroyed.	To deliver Jerusalem, in answer to Hezekiah's Prayer.	Jerusalem	xix. 35.
The Sun Made to go Back.	As a Proof of what the Prophet had Said.	Jerusalem	xx. 9-11.
Uzziah made Leprous.	To Punish him for Usurping the Priest's functions.	Jerusalem	2 Chr. xxvi. 19-21.
Saved in the Fiery Furnace.	To Attest God's Power and Providence.	Babylon	Dan. iii. 19-27.
Daniel Saved from Lions.	The Same Object.	Babylon	vi. 16-23.
Jonah in the Whale's belly.	To Punish his Attempt to escape Duty.	Mediterranean	John i. 17.
Jonah Delivered.	In Answer to his Repentant Prayer.	Mediterranean	ii.

PARABLES OF THE OLD TESTAMENT.

BY WHOM SPOKEN.	THE PARABLE.	WHERE SPOKEN.	THE TEXT.
BALAAM.	Concerning the Moabites and Israelites.	Mount Pisgah.	Num. xxiii. 24.
JOTHAM.	Trees making a King.	Mount Gerizim.	Judg. ix. 7-15.
SAMSON.	Strong Bringing forth Sweetness.	Timnath.	xiv. 14.
NATHAN.	Poor Man's Ewe Lamb.	Jerusalem.	2 Sam. xii. 1-4.
WOMAN OF TEKOAH.	Two Brothers Striving.	Jerusalem.	xiv. 1.
THE SMITTEN PROPHET.	The Escaped Prisoner.	Near Samaria.	1 K. xx. 35-40.
JEHOASH, KING OF ISRAEL.	The Thistle and Cedar.	Jerusalem.	2 K. xiv. 9.
DAVID.	Israel Compared to a Vine.	Jerusalem.	Ps. lxxx. 8-16.
ISAIAH.	Vineyard yielding Wild Grapes.	Jerusalem.	Is. v. 1-6.
EZEKIEL.	The Vine Tree.	Jerusalem.	Eze. xv.
EZEKIEL.	The Great Eagles and the Vine.	Babylon.	xvii. 3-10.
EZEKIEL.	Lion's Whelps.	Babylon.	xix. 2-9.
EZEKIEL.	The Wasted Vine.	Babylon.	xix. 10-14.
EZEKIEL.	The Boiling Pot.	Babylon.	xxiv. 3-5.
HAGGAI.	Holy Flesh.	Jerusalem.	Hag. ii. 11-14.

CHRONOLOGICAL TABLE.

THE CONNECTION OF THE OLD AND NEW TESTAMENTS.

(S signifies a Sabbatic year.)

TABLE I.

THE PERSIAN DOMINATION.

B. C.	JUDÆA.	PERSIA.	GREECE and MACEDONIA.	ROME.	A.U.C.
		Years.			
536	Return of first caravan under Zerubbabel, prince, and 1. JESHUA, High-priest.	CYRUS. 1 Edict for the return of the Jews.	....	....	218
535	Rebuilding of the Temple begun.	 2	Thespis first exhibits tragedy.	....	219
S 534	Opposition of Samaritans.	Daniel x.-xii. 3	....	TARQUINIUS SUPERBUS.	220
529	Letter to the Persian king from the adversaries.	CAMBYSES (the 1 Ahasuerus of Ezra iv. 6. Artaxerxes in Ezra iv. 7).	....	....	225
			527. Death of Pisistratus.		227
525	....	Conquest of 4 Egypt.			
522	The building stopped by a royal decree.	The PSEUDO-SMERDIS (the Magian Gomates).	Death of Polycrates of Samos.	....	229
521	*Haggai* and *Zechariah.*	DARIUS I., son of 1 Hystaspes, confirms the edict of Cyrus.	....	....	232
S 520	Building resumed.....	 2	....	....	233
515	Temple dedicated.....	 7	....	....	234
514	....	Attacks India and 8 European Scythia.	Hipparchus slain......	....	240
510	....	 12	Hippias expelled......	Kings expelled..........	244
			Republic of Athens.	*Republic of Rome.*	
499	....	Ionian revolt 23	....		255
495	....	 27		Patricians oppress Plebeians.	259
494	....			Secession to the Sacred Mt.	260
490	....	 32	Marathon.		
486	....	XERXES (the 1		Tribunes and Ædiles of Plebs.	
480	....	Ahasuerus of 7	Salamis.		
479	....	Esther). 8	Platæa and Mycale.	Wars with Italians.	
476	....	 11	Cimon..................	....	278
474	....	Esther and Mordecai			
466	....	 21	Battles of the Eurymedon.	....	288
465	2. ELIASHIB, H.-P. (date uncertain).	ARTAXERXES I. 1 LONGIMANUS.		....	289
460		Revolt of Inaros 6 in Egypt.	Athenians in Egypt	....	294
458	Commission of *Ezra*	 7		....	296
S 457	Great reformation.....	 8		....	297
454	....	Egypt conquered. 12	Pericles	Patricians yield to Plebs.	300

TABLE I.

The Persian Domination—*continued.*

B. C.	JUDÆA.	PERSIA.	GREECE AND MACEDONIA.	ROME.	A.U.C.
		Years.			
451	....	 15	....	Laws of the XII. Tables.	303
449	....	 17	....	Decemvirs deposed...	305
445	....	 21	....	Tribuni Militum......	309
444	Commission of *Ne-hemiah.*	......,............... 22	444. Herodotus.	....	310
to	The walls rebuilt. Reading of the Law.				
433	Opposition of San-ballat.	 33			
431	....	 35	431. Peloponnesian war.	....	323
428	Second commission	 38		426. War with Veii.	328
r423	of Nehemiah.	425. Xerxes II. Sogdianus.	....	....	329
424	3. Joiada, H.-P. (date uncertain.) Samaritan Temple on Mount Gerizim?	Darius II.: No- 1 thus.	....	....	330
405	....	Artaxerxes II. 1 (Mnemon.)	....	....	349
			404. End. of ditto.....	....	350
§ 401	....	Expedition of 5 Cyrus the Younger.	Xenophon.............	....	353
400 about	*Malachi*, Prophet. O. T. Canon fixed.	 6	Retreat of the 10,000	....	354
399	....	 7	Death of Socrates...	....	355
396	....	 10	Agesilaus in Asia.	Camillus takes Veii..	358
§ 394	....	 12	Battle of Coronea.....	....	360
390	....	 16	....	Gauls take Rome....	364
§ 387	....	 19	Peace of Antalcidas..	....	367
382	4. Johanan, H.-P. (or Jonathan.)	 24	Olynthian War....... *Demosthenes* born.	....	372
379	....	 27	Rise of Theban power.	....	375
367 about	Murder of Joshua.	 39	....	Licinian Rogations passed.	387
362	....	 44	Battle of Mantinea...	....	392
361	....	Revolt of Tachos in Egypt.	45 Agesilaus in Egypt...	Gallic Invasion........	393
§ 359	....	Artaxerxes dies	47 Accession of Philip II., king of Macedonia.	....	395
		Ochus 1			
357	....	 3	The Social War......	First Plebeian Dictator.	397
356	....	 4	Alexander born........	First Plebeian Censor.	398
351	Alleged captivity of Jews.	Revolt of the Sidonians.	9		399
350	5. Jaddua, H.-P. (last name in O.T.)	 10	....	....	404
343	....	 17	....	First Samnite War.	411
340	....	 20	....	Latin War. Decius.	414
§ 338	....	Arses 1 War declared by the Greeks.	Philip chosen general of the Greeks at Corinth.	....	416
336	....	Darius III. 1 (Codomanus.)	Murder of Philip..... Alexander the 1 Great.	....	418
834	....	Invasion of Alexander.	3 Battle of the 3 Granicus.	....	420
333	....	....	4 Battle of Issus 4	....	421
832	Interview with Alexander?	....	5 Taking of Tyre 5 Alexandria built.	Alexander, king of Epirus in Italy.	422
§ 331	Settlement of Jews at Alexandria.	....	6 Battle of Arbela 6	....	423
330	6. Onias I. H.-P.	Murder of Darius.	Demosthenes de 7 Corona?	....	424

TABLE II.

The Grecian Domination.

B. C.	JUDÆA.	EGYPT.	SYRIA.	ROME.	A.U.C.
330	6. Onias I. H.-P.	Empire of Alexander............ 7		....	424
326	....	Alexander returns from India............ 11	Second Samnite War		428
323		Death of Alexander at Babylon......... 14		....	431
320	Ptolemy takes Jerusalem.	Ptolemy I., Soter...	Contests of the Diadochi in Asia and Europe.		
	Settlements of Jews at Alexandria, in Egypt and Cyrene.				
314	Palestine under Antigonus.	....	....	....	440
312	[Era of the Seleucidæ]	....	1. Seleucus I. Nicator	Appius Claudius censor.	442
309	Death of Onias I. (Jos.)		....	....	445
301	War of the *Diadochi* ended by the *battle of Ipsus* in Phrygia.....	....			453
	Palestine subject to Egypt till A. D. 198.				
300	Death of Onias I. (Eus.)		Jews settle in Syria.	....	454
	7. Simon I., the Just, H.-P.				
298	Canon of SS. completed?	....	....	Third Samnite War	456
292	8. Eleazar, H.-P.	....	....	Defeat of the Samnites.	462
285	Progress of the Egyptian Jews.	2. Ptolemy II. Philadelphus (with his father.)	....	[Greece, Ætolian, and Achæan Leagues.]	469
283	*Version of the LXX?* [N.B. The dates of the High-Priests down to Onias III. are very doubtful.]	Ptolemy II. alone.....	....	Gauls and Etruscans defeated.	471
281	....	Splendor of Egypt.	Seleucus murdered.	Pyrrhus in Italy......	473
280	....	....	2. Antiochus I. Soter	War with Pyrrhus...	474
264	....		....	First Punic War......	490
§ 261	....	The historian Manetho fl.	3. Antiochus II. Theos.	[Greece: Growth of Achæan League.	493
251	9. Manasseh, H.-P.	....	Revolt of Parthia.....	Aratus and Philopœmen.]	503
250	....	....	Era of the *Arsacidæ*.	Metellus in Sicily.....	504
§ 247	....	3. Ptolemy III. Euergetes.	Berosus: historian of Babylon, fl.	Hamilcar Barca......	507
246	....	War with Syria.	4. Seleucus II. Callinicus.	....	508
241		Friendly relations with Judæa interrupted.	Disastrous wars with Egypt and Parthia.	Peace with Carthage.	513
§ 240	10. Onias II. H.-P. Refuses Tribute. Joseph, son of Tobias.	....	236. Seleucus taken prisoner by the Parthians.	....	514
§ 226	11. Simon II., H.-P.	....	5. Seleucus III. Ceraunus.	....	538
223	....		6. Antiochus III. the Great.	....	531
222	....	4. Ptolemy IV. Philopator.	Quells revolt in Media.	....	532
§ 219	Antiochus overruns Palestine.	....	Makes war in Egypt.	Second Punic War...	535
217	Ptolemy recovers Palestine, profanes the Temple, but is driven out supernaturally.	Victory over Antiochus. Persecutes the Jews of Alexandria.	Defeat at Raphia. ... The Jews incline towards Syria.	Battle of Trasimene..	537

TABLE II.

THE GRECIAN DOMINATION.—*Continued.*

B.C.	JUDÆA.	EGYPT.	SYRIA.	ROME.	A.U.C.
216				Battle of Cannæ......	538
205	The Jews submit to Antiochus the Great, and are at first well treated.	5. PTOLEMY V. Epiphanes (5 yrs old).	Renews the war against Egypt.	....	549
201	....	War with Syria........	Many Jews transplanted from Babylonia to Asia Minor.	204. Scipio in Africa Peace with Carthage	550 553
200	....	His general Scopas treats the Jews ill.	....	War with Philip V.	554
§ 198	12. ONIAS III. H.-P.	....	Victory at Panium over the Egyptians.	....	556
197	Palestine and Cœle-Syria conquered by Antiochus, and confirmed to him by the peace with Rome.	....	....	Ended by the Battle of Cynosce-Ahalæ.	557
§ 191	....	Ptolemy marries Cleopatra, the daughter of Antiochus.	Defeated at Thermopylæ.	War with Antiochus.	563
190	....	....	And at Magnesia in Asia.	The Scipios in Asia.	564
188	....	....	Peace with Rome.....	Antiochus retires within the Taurus.	566
187	Attempt of Heliodorus to plunder the Temple?	....	7. SELEUCUS IV. Philopator.	....	567
181	....	6. PTOLEMY VI. Philometor (a minor), under his mother and tutors.	Demetrius sent to Rome.	War in Spain...........	573
175	Onias III. deposed, and the priesthood sold to JASON (Joshua), H.-P.	Great internal dissensions.	8. ANTIOCHUS IV. Epiphanes (Epimanes). Onias at Antioch; murdered by the contrivance of Menelaus (171).	....	579
172	MENELAUS (Onias), H.-P.	....	....	....	582
171	Hellenism rampant.	Egypt invaded by Antiochus, who is ordered out by the Romans.	....	Macedonian War.....	583
168	Menelaus deposed. Massacre at Jerusalem. Martyrdom of Eleazar and others. Revolt of MATTATHIAS.	Joint reign of Ptolemy and his brother Physcon. The latter receives Cyrene and Libya (163).	Expulsion from Egypt. Persecution of the Jews. Judæa revolts under the Maccabees.	Battle of Pydna....... Perseus taken prisoner. End of the Macedonian Kingdom.	586
167	....	....	Defeats of Syrian generals by Judas.	Polybius at Rome....	587
166	JUDAS MACCABÆUS.	....	Antiochus in Babylonia. Dies (164).	Terence exhibits the *Andria.*	588

TABLE III.

THE MACCABEES, AND ASMONÆAN KINGS.

B.C.	JUDÆA.	EGYPT.	SYRIA.	ROME.	A.U.C.
168	Revolt of MATTA-THIAS. Onias IV. titular H.-P.	Ptolemy VI.—*continued.*	Antiochus IV.—*continued.*	Macedonia conquered.	586
167	War against Apostates.	Onias IV. flees to Egypt, and founds a temple at Leontopolis.	Judas defeats the Syrian generals.	....	587
166 (Dec.)	1. JUDAS MACCABÆUS. Rededication of the Temple.	....	Battle of Bethsura. Judas takes Jerusalem. Antiochus in Elymais. Death of Antiochus.		588
164	League of neighbouring nations defeated. Execution of Menelaus. End of line of Jozadak.	....	9. ANTIOCHUS V. Eupator takes Bethsura and besieges Jerusalem. Peace with the Jews.	....	590
S 163	Death of Eleazar Savaran.	Partition of the kingdom with Physcon.	....	....	591
162	ALCIMUS (Jacimus) H.-P. set up by the Syrians.	....	10. DEMETRIUS I. Soter.	....	592
161	Victory of *Adasa.* Embassy to Rome. Death of Judas. 2. JONATHAN APPHUS. Death of John, the Maccabee. Death of Alcimus.	....	Defeat of Nicanor. Bacchides in Syria. Battle of *Eleasa.* Bacchides retires to Syria on the death of Alcimus.	Philosophers expelled. Alliance with Judæa, inscribed on brass.	593
158	Peace with Syria.	....	Returns and is defeated.	....	590
153	Jonathan High-priest.	....	Revolt of Alexander Balas.	Celtiberian War.	601
150	Alliance with Balas.	Balas marries Ptolemy's daughter Cleopatra.	11. ALEXANDER BALAS seizes the throne.	Galba in Spain.	604
S 149	Favors to Jerusalem.	....	....	Third Punic War.	605
147	Defeat of Apollonius.	Ptolemy sides with Demetrius against Balas.	Demetrius returns.	....	607
146	Alliance with Demetrius, whose life Jonathan saves.	....	12. DEMETRIUS II. Nicator.	CARTHAGE and CORINTH destroyed.	608
145	....	7. PTOLEMY VI. Physcon, or Euergetes.	Tryphon sets up ANTIOCHUS VI., who overthrows Demetrius.	Africa and Greece become Roman Provinces.	609
144	Antiochus grants new honors to Jonathan and his brother Simon. Jonathan taken and put to death by Tryphon.	....	Tryphon at war with Jonathan.	War with Viriathus.	610
143	3. SIMON THASSI, H.-P.	Embassy of Scipio.	TRYPHON kills Antiochus.	Q. Metellus in Spain.	611
S 142	....	....	....	....	612

TABLE III.

THE MACCABEES, AND ASMONÆAN KINGS—*continued*.

B. C.	JUDÆA.	EGYPT.	SYRIA.	ROME.	A.U.C.
141	Tower of Zion taken. *First year of Jewish freedom.*				613
140	Simon made hereditary prince of the Jews.				614
138	Prosperity of Judæa.		Demetrius prisoner to the Parthians.	Numantine War.	616
137	Recognised by Rome. Receives from Antiochus VII. the privilege of coining money.		13. ANTIOCHUS VII. Sidetes.		617
§ 135	Murder of Simon. 4. JOHN HYRCANUS, H.-P.		Deposes Tryphon, and makes war on Simon.		619
133	Surrenders Jerusalem.		Grants peace to Hyrcanus.	Fall of Numantia.	621
128	Goes to Parthia with Antiochus. *Judæa independent.*		Antiochus killed in Parthia. DEMETRIUS II. released.	Death of Tib. Gracchus.	626
125	Hyrcanus conquers the land E. of Jordan, Idumæa and Samaria.		14. SELEUCUS V. 15. ANTIOCHUS VIII. Grypus, 16. And ANTIOCHUS IX. Cyzicenus, rival kings.	123. Caius Gracchus. 122. Tribune. 121. Death of C. Gracchus.	629 630 632 633
117		8. PTOLEMY VIII. Lathyrus (Soter.)		111. JugurthineWar.	643
109	Destroys the Temple on Mount Gerizim. Joins the Sadducees.	Cyrene finally separated from Egypt.			
107		Driven to Cyprus by his mother CLEOPATRA, who reigns with her second son.			
106	Death of Hyrcanus. 5. ARISTOBULUS I., H.-P. Assumes the title of king.	PTOLEMY IX. Alexander I. [Great confusion to the end of the dynasty.]		106. Jugurtha taken. Cicero and Pompey born.	648
105	6. ALEXANDER JANNÆUS. Conquest of Gaza, Moab, &c. Civil war.	Judæa invaded by Ptolemy Lathyrus, rescued by Cleopatra.	From B. C. 95 to 83. 17. SELEUCUS VI. 18. ANTIOCHUS X. Eusebes. 19. PHILIPPUS. 20. DEMETRIUS III. Eucærus. 21. ANTIOCHUS XI. Epiphanes.	102. Marius routs the Cimbri and Teutones. 100. C. Julius Cæsar born. 92. Sulla in Asia: receives a Parthian embassy. 90. Social War. 88. First Mithridatic War, and Civil War at Rome.	652 653 654 662 664 666
81		PTOLEMY X. Alexander II.	22. ANTIOCHUS XII. Dionysus.	86. Death of Marius. 82. Sulla Dictator. 74. Great Mithridatic War.	668 672 680
80		PTOLEMY XI. Dionysus, or Auletes.	A period of confusion.		
78	Dying reconciliation with the Pharisees. 7. ALEXANDRA (queen.) Hyrcanus II., H.-P.		83. TIGRANES, king of Armenia, reigns over Syria, till he is defeated by Lucullus, 69.	70. Mithridates flies to Armenia. 69. Lucullus defeats Tigranes.	684 685

TABLE III.

The Maccabees, and Asmonæan Kings—*continued*.

B. C.	JUDÆA.	EGYPT.	SYRIA.	ROME.	A.U.C.
69	8. Hyrcanus II. (about 40) king, deposed by his brother after 3 months. 9. Aristobulus II. Rise of Antipater.	....	23. AntiochusXIII. last (nominal) king under Roman protection.	....	685
68	Hyrcanus and Antipater fly to Aretas, king of Arabia.	....	....	68. Success of Mithridates. 67. War against the Pirates, Pompey general.	686 687
65	Civil War of Hyrcanus and Antipater, aided by Aretas, against Aristobulus. Scaurus in Judæa: hears the ambassadors of both brothers.	....	66. Scaurus at Damascus. Pompey deposes Antiochus. *Syria a Roman province.*	66. Mithridatic War committed to Pompey. Defeats Mithridates in Armenia, and subdues Tigranes. 65. Levee of kings in Pontus. Pompey in the Caucasian countries.	688 689
64	Arbitration of Pompey.	....	Pompey at Damascus.	Pompey returns to Syria.	690
63	He takes Jerusalem on the Day of Atonement (Sept. 22), and enters the Holy of Holies. Hyrcanus II. restored as H.-P. Antipater civil governor (procurator.) *Judæa subject to Rome from this time.*	....	Receives Jewish ambassadors. *Roman Governors of Syria.* 62. Æmilius Scaurus, *Quæstor pro Prætore.* 61. L. Marcius Philippus, *Proprætor.*	Cicero consul. Conspiracy of Cataline. Birth of Augustus. 62. Cæsar prætor. 61. Triumph of Pompey. 60. Cæsar in Spain. *First Triumvirate.*	691 692 693 694
59	....	Ptolemy Auletes bribes Cæsar to obtain his acknowledgment as king.	Lentulus Marcellinus, *Proprætor.*	Cæsar consul.	695
58	....	Ptolemy Auletes expelled by his subjects. Goes to Rome. Berenice and Tryphæna reign during his absence.	....	Cæsar in Gaul. Cicero banished.	696
57	Successes of Alexander, son of Aristobulus II, against Hyrcanus. Defeated by Gabinius, proconsul of Syria. New Constitution: the Five Great Sanhedrims.	....	Gabinius, *Proconsul.* Syria is henceforth a consular province.	Cicero recalled.	697

TABLE III.

THE MACCABEES, and ASMONÆAN KINGS—*continued.*

B.C.	JUDÆA.	EGYPT.	SYRIA.	ROME.	A.U.C.
55	Reappearance and defeat of Aristobulus II., and his son Antigonus. New Insurrection of Alexander: his defeat at Mt. Tabor.	Gabinius in Egypt. Restores Ptolemy Auletes.	Expedition of Gabinius into Parthia.	Cæsar's first descent on Britain.	699
54	Crassus at Jerusalem: plunders the Temple.	....	Crassus, *Proconsul.*	Cæsar in Britain, the second time.	700
53	....	....	Slain by the Parthians. Cassius, *Quæstor.*	....	701
52	Cassius enslaves 30,000 Jews—the partisans of Aristobulus.	....	....	Clodius slain by Milo	702
§ 51	....	CLEOPATRA, with PTOLEMY XII. and PTOLEMY XIII.	Bibulus, *Proconsul.*	Cæsar finishes the conquest of Gaul.	703
50	....	....	[Scipio, Pompeian Proconsul].	50. Measures of Pompey against Cæsar.	704
49	Cæsar releases Aristobulus, who is murdered by the Pompeians. Alexander put to death by Scipio at Antioch.	....	....	*Civil war begins.* Cæsar enters Italy. Flight of Pompey to Greece. Cæsar in Spain against the Pompeians.	705
48	Antipater aids Cæsar, who makes him a citizen and *1st Procurator of Judæa,* with Hyrcanus as Ethnarch.	Cæsar in Egypt. Alexandrine war—ends in Jan. B.C. 47 (March 27, Old Calendar).	....	Battle of Pharsalia. Pompey killed in Egypt.	706
47	Immunities granted to the Jews. Antipater escorts Cæsar to Pontus.	....	Sex. Julius Cæsar. C. J. Cæsar in Syria.	War with Pharnaces. Cæsar Dictator.	707
46	Appoints his sons, Phasael and Herod, captains of Judæa and Galilee.	....	Q. Cæcilius Bassus, *Prætor.*	African War. *The Calendar reformed.*	708
45	Herod hostile to Hyrcannus.	....	....	War in Spain.	709
§ 44	Decree of Cæsar for refortifying Jerusalem.	....	....	DEATH OF CÆSAR.	710
43	Cassius plunders Jerusalem. Antipater poisoned. Herod visits Jerusalem.	....	C. Cassius Longinus, *Proconsul,* arrives in Syria. [NOTE. All the subsequent governors are *Legati*].	War of Mutina. *Second Triumvirate*	711
42	Herod defeats Antigonus, and enters Jerusalem in triumph. Is reconciled to Hyrcanus and betrothed to Mariamne.	Antony in Asia. Meets Cleopatra at Tarsus, and goes to Egypt.	....	Battles of Philippi.	712

TABLE III.

The Maccabees, and Asmonæan Kings—*continued.*

B. C.	JUDÆA.	EGYPT.	SYRIA.	ROME.	A.U.C
41	Herod gains favour with Antony.	....	L. Decidius Saxa *Legatus.*	War of Perusia.	713
40	10. ANTIGONUS set up by the Parthians. Phasael put to death, and Hyrcanus mutilated. HEROD escapes to Rome, gains over the triumvirs, and is appointed by the Senate King of Judæa about the end of the year. [Hence to his death in B.C. 4, Josephus reckons his reign 37 years.]	Antony goes to Tyre on his way against the Parthians; thence to Athens. Leagues with Sex. Pompey, and besieges Brundisium. Receives the Eastern Provinces.	Invasion of the parthians under Pacorus and Labienus. The legate Saxa slain. P. Ventidius, Bassus, *Legatus,* sent against them by Antony.	Perusia taken. Agrippa sent against Antony. Death of Fulvia. Reconciliation of Octavian and Antony at Brundusium. The empire divided. Antony and Octavian at Rome.	714
39	Herod returns, collects an army, and unites with Silo, who deserts his cause. Conquers Galilee.	Antony marries Octavia, goes to Greece and spends the winter at Athens.	The Parthians are defeated, and Labienus slain. Ventidius recovers Syria. Is bribed by Antigonus.	Conference at Misenum between Octavian, Antony, and Sex. Pompey.	715
38	Silo joins Ventidius. Ventidius sends aid to Herod. Herod marches to join Antony. His brother Joseph slain by Antigonus. Heron at Acre.	Antony joins Ventidius after his victory and besieges Samosato; receives Herod there. thence returns to Athens, leaving Sosius as his legate.	Great victory of Ventidius over the Parthians; Pacorus slain. Ventidius returns to Rome and triumphs. C. Sosius, *Legatus,* sends aid to Herod.	War between Octavian and Sex. Pompey. Agrippa commands the fleet.	716
§ 37	Herod marches against Jesusalem in the Spring. Marries Mariamne. Is joined by Sosius, and takes Jerusalem on the day of Atonement, Oct. 5, and on a Sabbath. Death of Antigonus. *End of the Asmonæan line.*	Antony in Italy. Returns by way of Greece, parting from Octavia at Corcyra.	Antony at Antioch, at the close of the year, where he condemns Antigonus to death by scourging and beheading.	Renewal of the triumvirate for five years. Preparations of Octavian against Sextus Pompey.	717

TABLE IV.

KINGDOM OF HEROD THE GREAT, SUBJECT TO AND UNDER THE PROTECTION OF ROME.

B. C.	JUDÆA.	EGYPT.	SYRIA.	ROME.	A.U.C.
37	HEROD THE GREAT 1 His actual reign dates by Consular years from Jan. 1, or by Jewish sacred years from the 1st of Nisan. Ananel made H.-P.	....	....	See Table III.	717
36	Herod................. 2 Hyrcanus comes from Babylon to Jerusalem. His daughter Alexandra seeks the Highpriesthood from Cleopatra for her son Aristobulus. Herod deposes Ananel, and appoints ARISTOBULUS H.-P.	Antony sends for Cleopatra, and gives her Phœnicia, Crete, &c. Antony marches against the Parthians. Cleopatra meets Herod in Judæa. Antony retires to Egypt.	Antony in Syria.	Naval war against Sextus Pompey. The latter, defeated, retires to Lesbos, and seeks aid from Antony, but is disappointed.	718
35	Herod................. 3 Aristobulus (æt. 17) warmly received at the Feast of Tabernacles, and drowned soon after (Sept. 19.) ANANEL H.-P.	Cleopatra, at the solicitation of Alexandra, appeals to Antony against Herod.	L. MUNATIUS PLANCUS, Legatus.	Sex. Pompey put to death at Miletus by Antony's general Titius.	719
34	Herod................. 4 Goes to Antony, and appeases him by presents. Puts his uncle Joseph to death.	Antony summons Herod before him at Laodicea. Gives Cleopatra Cœle-Syria. Antony in Armenia. Returns to Egypt.	....	Octavian in Gaul. Astrologers and sorcerers expelled from Rome. Sosius triumphs for the capture of Jerusalem.	720
33	Herod................. 5 Quarrel with Malchus, King of Arabia.	Antony forbids Octavia from joining him. Antony in Media.	....	Agrippa ædile. Final rupture between Octavian and Antony.	721
32	Herod................. 6 Levies troops on the side of Antony, who sends him agaicst Malchus. Herod, at first victorious, defeated in Cœle-Syria.	Antony and Cleopatra join the fleet at Ephesus. Proceed ro Athens, and thence to Corcyra, and winter at Patræ.	....	Sosius and Domitius, the consuls, join Antony. Titius and Plancus go over to Octavian.	722
31	Herod................. 7 Dreadful earthquake in Judæa. Herod sues to Malchus for peace, which is refused. Defeats the Arabians. Puts Hyrcanus to death.	Flight of Cleopatra and Antony from Actium to Egypt. Herod advises Antony to put Cleopatra to death, and then deserts his cause.	L. CALPURNIUS BIBULUS, Legatus.	BATTLE OF ACTIUM (Sept. 2.) Octavian proceeds to Asia. Winters at Samos.	723
§ 30	Herod................. 8 Meets Octavian at Rhodes, and is confirmed in his kingdom (about April.) Escorts Octavian to Antioch and returns to Judæa.	Three embassies from Antony and Cleopatra to Octavian. *Egypt reduced to a Roman province.*	Q. DIDIUS, Legatus.	After a hasty visit to Italy, Octavian advances to Egypt. Death of Antony and Cleopatra.	724

[NOTE. Egypt still retains importance in Scripture History as a chief seat of the Jewish dipersion.]

TABLE IV.

KINGDOM OF HEROD THE GREAT—continued.

B.C.	JUDÆA.	EGYPT, ARABIA, etc.	SYRIA.	ROME.	A.U.C.
29	Herod.............. 9 Puts Mariamne to death, about the close of the year.	....	M. VALERIUS MESSALA, Legatus.	Three triumphs of Octavian. Temple of Janus shut.	725
28	Herod.............. 10 Alexandra, daughter of Hyrcanus, put to death.	....	(?) M. TULLIUS CICERO (son of the orator), Legatus.	Illness of Octavian. Census taken. No. of citizens 4,164,000.	726
27	Herod.............. 11	Egypt is among the imperial provinces.	Syria an imperial province, governed by a Prefect, as Legatus Cæsaris.	The name of AUGUSTUS conferred on Octavian, with supreme power for ten years. He divides the provinces with the Senate.	727
26	Herod.............. 12 Salome divorces Costabarus, and betrays the last of the family of Hyrcanus, who are put to death. Herod builds a theatre at Jerusalem and amphitheatre at Jericho, and founds games in honour of Augustus.	Disgrace and suicide of the prefect Cornelius Gallus.	....	Augustus in Gaul and Spain.	728
25	Herod.............. 13 Indignation at Herod's Romanizing. Conspiracy of the Ten Herod strengthens the Antonia and fortifies Samaria. Famine and Plague.	....	....	He falls sick at Tarraco. During his absence Julia is married to Marcellus. Temple of Janus again shut.	729
24	Herod.............. 14 Lends 500 auxiliaries to Ælius Gallus. Another famine in Judæa and Syria; relieved by Herod with corn from Egypt. His sons Alexander and Aristobulus sent to Rome. Trachonitis, Auranitis, and Batanea, added to his kingdom.	Expedition of the prefect ÆLIUS GALLUS into Arabia. The Ethiopians, under Candace, invade Egypt: defeated by Petronius	VARRO, Legatus.	Augustus returns to Rome, still ill.	730
§ 23	Herod.............. 15 Employs 50,000 men to gather the abundant harvest. [NOTE.—It seems that the practice now was to reap, though not to sow, on the Sabbatic year.] Visits Agrippa in the winter.	Ælius Gallus enters the country of Aretas, the relative of OBODAS, King of Petra; and returns to Egypt.	M. VIPSANIUS AGRIPPA, special Legatus, administers the province from Lesbos. Receives a visit from Herod at Mytilene.	Augustus again ill. Receives the Tribunitian power for life. Jealousy between Marcellus and Agrippa. Death of Marcellus.	731

TABLE IV.

KINGDOM OF HEROD THE GREAT—*continued.*

B.C.	JUDÆA.	EGYPT, ARABIA, ETC.	SYRIA.	ROME.	A.U.C.
22	Herod............... 16 Rebuilds his palace. Removes JESUS, the son of Phabi, H.-P., the successor of Anael, and appoints SIMON H.-P., whose daughter Mariamne he marries. Builds the fortress of Herodium 7½ m. from Jerusalem.	The Æthiopians repulsed by Petronius.	....	Plague and famine in Italy. Conspiracy of Muræna. Augustus visits Sicily.	732
21	Herod............... 17 Founds *Cæsarea,* probably in this year.	The Æthiopians send an embassy to Augustus at Samos.	Agrippa summoned from Asia to marry Julia.	Agrippa forbids Egyptian rites at Rome. Augustus in Greece. Winters at Samos.	733
20	Herod............... 18 Defends himself before Augustus, at Antioch, against a complaint of the Gadarenes. Augustus gives Paneas to Herod, and the Tetrarchy of Peræa to his brother Pheroras. Appoints Herod *perpetual joint Procurator of Syria.* Herod erects a temple of Augustus at Paneas. Remits one-third of the taxes. Proposes the scheme of rebuilding the Temple.	....	Augustus visits Suria; deprives the Tyrians and Sidonians of their freedom; settles the petty kingdoms. Tiberius sent to Armenia to place Tigranes on the throne.	Augustus in Asia Minor and Syria. The standards of Crassus restored by King Phraates. Escorted by Herod to the Syrian coast (probably at Seleucia). Augustus winters at Samos. Birth of CAIUS, the son of Agrippa and Julia.	734
19	Herod...............19 Preparations for rebuilding the Temple.	....	M. T. CICERO, *Legatus* (son of the orator), placed here by some writers.	Agrippa goes to Gaul and Spain. Augustus returns to Rome.	735
18	Herod............... 20 *Rebuilding of the Temple* (the *vaos,* or Holy Place) begun about Passover. Herod sails to Rome, and brings back his sons, Aristobulus and Alexander; and banishes Antipater, his son by Doris.	....	....	Supreme power renewed ro Augustus for five years; and Tribunitian power to Agrippa for five years.	736
17	Herod...............21 Marries Alexander to Glaphyra, daughter of Archelaus, King of Cappadocia, and Aristobulus to Berenice. The Holy Place finished.	....	....	*Ludi Sæculares,* 5th time Birth of Lucius Cæsar, son of Agrippa, whom Augustus adopts, with his brother Caius.	737

TABLE IV.

KINGDOM OF HEROD THE GREAT—*continued.*

B.C.	JUDÆA.	EGYPT, ARABIA, etc.	SYRIA.	ROME.	A.U.C.
16	Herod.............. 22 Goes to meet Agrippa, and invites him to Judæa.		AGRIPPA, again *Legatus*, sent to regulate the affairs of Syria, arrives in Asia.	Augustus goes to Gaul. Settles disturbances on all the European frontiers.	738
15	Herod.............. 23 Receives the visit of Agrippa.		Visits Judæa; sees Cæsarea, Alexandrium, Herodium, Hyrcania. Sacrifices in the Temple at Jerusalem, and returns to Ephesus.	The Rhætians conquered by Tiberius and Drusus.	739
14	Herod.............. 24 Sails to visit Agrippa. Follows him to the Euxine, and meets him at Sinope (see col. 3). Privileges of the Jews confirmed by Agrippa. Herod addresses the Jews, and remits one-fourth of the taxes. Intrigues of Salome and Pheroras against Aristobulus and Alexander. Antipater recalled.		Agrippa's expedition against Bosporus. Herod pleads with him for the Ilians. (NICOLAUS DAMASCENUS employed in this affair). Returns with Herod to Samos.	Augustus in Gaul.	740
13	Herod.............. 25 Advancement of Antipater. Herod takes him to visit Agrippa, who takes Antipater to Rome, whence he writes letters against Aristobulus and Alexander.		End of Agrippa's 10 years' administration of Asia and Syria. No special prefect during this interval. The government now falls to M. TITIUS, *Legatus*.	Augustus returns to Rome from Gaul, and Agrippa from the East. Tribunitian power to Agrippa for five years more. He goes to Pannonia.	741
12	Herod.............. 26 Refuses the hand of Salome to the Arabian Syllæus. Further intrigues against the sons of Mariamne.		Asia (the province) suffers from earthquakes.	Death of Lepidus. AUGUSTUS PONT. MAX. *Death of Agrippa.* Birth of Agrippa Postumus. Victories of Tiberius in Pannonia, and of Drusus in Germany.	742
11	Herod.............. 27 Herod sails to Rome with Aristobulus and Alexander, whom he accuses before Augustus at Aquileia. Augustus effects a reconciliation. Herod returns by way of Cilicia. Invests Antipater, Aristobulus, and Alexander with insignia of royalty. Birth of Agrippa, son of Aristobulus. The outer Temple finished.	During Herod's absence the Trachonites rebel, at the instigation of Syllæus.		Drusus in Germany. Augustus at Milan, Ravenna, and Aquileia; while Tiberius subdues the revolt of Dalmatia and Pannonia. Herod contributes 300 talents for the games (Augustalia?), and receives the copper mines of Cyprus. Marriage of Julia Tiberius. Death of Octavia	743

TABLE IV.

KINGDOM OF HEROD THE GREAT—*continued*.

B. C	JUDÆA.	EGYPT, ARABIA, ETC.	SYRIA.	ROME.	A.U.C.
10	Herod.............. 28 Building of Cæsarea finished. Herod opens David's tomb in search of treasure. New family dissensions appeased for the time.	Massacre of the Trachonites by Herod.	Parthian hostages delivered to the prefect Titus.	Augustus in Gaul. Tiberius subdues the Dalmatians and Dacæa, and Drusus subdues the Chatti—They return to Rome with Augustus. Aug. 1. CLAUDIUS born.	744
9	Herod.............. 29 New family dissensions, appeased by Archelaus, king of Cappadocia.	Continued disturbances in Trachonitis.	C. SENTIUS SATURNINUS, *Legatus* (probably in this or the next year.)	Death of Drusus. Tiberius again subdues the Dalmatians and Pannonians.	745
8	Herod.............. 30 Sails with Archelaus to Italy, to state his case against Syllæus. Visits Olympia on the way, and makes presents for the games (Midsummer, Ol.193–1.)	Syllæus engages to give up the Trachonite brigands, but sails for Rome without performing the engagement. Remains there, and accuses Herod to Augustus.	Herod complains to Saturninus of the Trachonites and Syllæus.	Augustus receives the supreme power for 10 years more. Proceeds to Gaul with Tiberius, who crosses the Rhine. Both return to Rome. Death of Mæcenas. Census of Roman citizens.	746
7	Herod.............. 31 In disgrace with Augustus about the Arabian war: henceforth to rank as a subject. He sends Nicolaus Damascenus to Rome; also another embassy to complain of Alexander and Aristobulus. Herod allowed to proceed against them in conjunction with a council.	Herod razes the Trachonite stronghold, and makes war on the Arabians. ARETAS succeeds Obodas as king of Arabia Petræa. Syllæus condemned to death by Augustus; but first sent to Arabia to make reparation. He plots against Herod. Augustus confirms Aretas, instead of giving Petra to Herod.	*Census of Palestine* under Saturninus, perhaps connected with the threat of Augustus to treat Herod as a subject. The census was ordered in this year and carried out in the next.	Tiberius goes to Germany. Augustus at Rome. Preparations for absorbing Judæa into the Empire	747
6	Herod.............. 32 The Council meets at Berytus and condemns Alexander and Aristobulus, who are strangled at Sebaste (Samaria). Agitation in Judæa. Antipater tries to gain partisans by gifts, and then by terror. Forms a plot with Pheroras, Doris, etc., against Herod. He procures a letter summoning him to Rome.	Complicated intrigues of Syllæus, Fabatus (Cæsar's procurator), and Herod. Herod settles Zamaris, a Babylonian Jew, in *Batanea.* [*Mr. Lewin's Dates.* Feb. 22 (about), Birth of John the Baptist. Aug. 1 (about), NATIVITY OF JESUS CHRIST. —See c. xii. p.301.]	Saturninus and the procurator Volumnius take part in the trial of the sons of Mariamne (an indication of Herod's subjection.) Saturninus receives presents from Antipater. P. QUINTILIUS VARUS (*Legatus*) succeeds Saturninus before Sept. 2.	Tiberius in Armenia. Retires to Rhodes, and remains there seven years.	748

TABLE IV.

KINGDOM OF HEROD THE GREAT—*continued.*

B. C.	JUDÆA.	EGYPT, ARABIA, ETC.	SYRIA.	ROME.	A.U.C.
6 *cont.*	The census commences about July. The Pharisees refuse the oath to Cæsar and Herod, and are fined. They spread the report that Messiah has come; and Herod puts their leaders to death.				748
5 *Apr.*	Herod.............. 33 Sends Antipater to Rome with his will, appointing him his heir, and recalls thence his sons Archelaus and Philip. Pheroras retires to Petræa. His death discovers Antipater's plot. Disgrace of Doris. Simon deposed, and MATTHIAS made H.-P. (*before the Fast*, Sept. 11.)	Syllæus goes to Rome.	Varus is present at Jerusalem at trial of Antipater, and returns next day to Antioch.	C. Cæsar receives the *Toga Virilis.*	749
Aug.	Bathyllus sent by Antipater to poison Herod.				
Nov.	Antipater lands at Cæsarea, goes to Jerusalem, and is condemned by a Council. Herod writes to Augustus. Falls ill, and alters his will, making Herod Antipas his successor.				
4	Herod.............. 34 Goes to Jericho. Pulling down of the eagle, the symbol of Roman power. Matthias deposed, and Joazar made H.-P. Herod harangues the chiefs of the nation at Jericho, and burns the Rabbis.	5 ends, or 4 begg. NATIVITY OF JESUS CHRIST, according to Sulpicius and most modern authorities. [NOTE. On this view of the Nativity, the events at Bethlehem; the arrival of the Magi at Jerusalem, their adoration at Bethlehem, and return home; the purification of Mary, and presentation of Jesus in the Temple; the flight of Joseph and Mary with Jesus to Egypt; and the massacre of the children at Bethlehem, must all be comprehended in the first three months of this year.]	The Census, still in progress (if begun in B. C. 6) was probably one cause of the disturbance at Jerusalem.		750
Mar. 12–13 15–18 19 20	*Eclipse of the Moon.* Goes to the springs of Callirhoe, but without effect, and is plunged in a bath of oil. Despairs of his life. Returns to Jericho; donation to the army. Jewish chiefs shut up in the Hippodrome.				

CHRONOLOGICAL COMPENDIUM

OF

EVENTS IN THE LIFE OF CHRIST

AND

HARMONY OF THE GOSPELS.

THE CHRISTIAN ERA.

The Christian Era is usually supposed to begin with the birth of Christ. But the exact date of this event has given rise to much controversy. Dionysius the Little, a Roman abbot, introduced into Italy, during the sixth century A. D., the epoch or commencement as on the first of January in the fourth year of the 194th Olympiad, the 753d from the foundation of Rome, and the 4714th of the Julian period. His epoch, which secured wide adoption in Christian countries, evidently places the birth of Christ at a period four years too late, for it seems to have happened very shortly before the death of Herod the Great, which occurred in the 750th year from the foundation of Rome, or about four years before the usual period fixed as the beginning of Christian chronology. Some authors make this difference as much as five or six years. The agreement is general that at least four years must be counted between the first year of the Christian Era and the birth of Christ; that is, that He was born about B. C. 4.

Fortunately there is no such uncertainty about the starting-point of Christ's ministry, since it is set forth very clearly in Luke 3. 1. Tiberius Cæsar reigned jointly with Cæsar Augustus from A. D. 11–14, when the latter died. Add fifteen years to the first year of Tiberius' reign and it brings us to A. D. 26, at which time Pilate was procurator of Judea, Herod Antipas tetrarch of Galilee, Caiaphas high priest, and Annas probably president of the Sanhedrim, as related by Luke. These historic facts, fitting so nicely together, support the conclusion that John the Baptist began his work of baptism A. D. 26. That work fixes the baptism of Christ and beginning of His ministry.

It would also fix the date of His crucifixion and resurrection in A. D. 29 or 30, but owing to diverse meanings placed on John 5. 1, there is doubt as to whether Christ's ministry extended over a period of two and a half or three and a half years. If the "feast" mentioned by John was the Passover, then His ministry must have been three and a half years in length. If, however, it was not the Passover, it could not have been over two years and a half in length. The larger body of critics incline to the conviction that it was not the Passover. In the R. V. of John 5. 1 it is suggested marginally that many ancient authorities read *the feast* without any qualifying words.

Events.	Date B. C.	Place.	Matthew.	Mark.	Luke.	John.
CHRIST'S NATIVITY AND YOUTH.						
And the Word was God						1. 1–5
Annunciation of birth of John the Baptist	5	Jerusalem			1. 5–25	
Espousal of Mary by Joseph		Nazareth	1. 18		1. 27	
Annunciation of the birth of Jesus		"			1. 26–38	
Visitation of Mary to Elizabeth		Hebron or Juttah			1. 39–55	
Mary's return to Nazareth					1. 56	
The angel appears unto Joseph		Nazareth	1. 20–25			
Birth and infancy of John the Baptist		Hebron			1. 57–80	
The birth of Jesus	4	Bethlehem	2. 1		2. 1–7	
Adoration by the shepherds		"			2. 8–16	
Circumcision of the child Jesus		"	1. 25		2. 21	
Presentation to the Lord		Jerusalem			2. 22–29	
The genealogies of Christ			1. 1–17		3. 23–38	
Adoration by the wise men	3	Bethlehem	2. 1–12			
Flight of Joseph and family into Egypt	A. D.	Egypt	2. 13–15			
Massacre of children by Herod		Bethlehem	2. 16–18			
Return of Joseph and family to Nazareth	1	Nazareth	2. 19–23		2. 39	
The childhood of Jesus		"			2. 40	
Jesus with the doctors in the Temple	7	Jerusalem			2. 46–50	
Youth and early manhood of Jesus	7–26	Nazareth			2. 51, 52	
MINISTRY OF JOHN THE BAPTIST.						
Coming and preaching of John	26	{ Bethabara { Bethany (R. V.) }	3. 1–4	1. 1–8	3. 1–6	1. 6–15
Baptisms by John in Jordan		"	3. 5, 6	1. 5	3. 7	
First testimony of John to Christ		"	3. 11, 12	1. 7, 8	3. 15–18	
The baptism of Jesus by John		"	3. 13–17	1. 9–11	3. 21, 22	
The temptation of Jesus in the Wilderness		Wilderness of Judea	4. 1–11	1. 12, 13	4. 1–13	
Second testimony of John to Christ		{ Bethabara { Bethany (R. V.) }				1. 19–35
Jesus calls his first five disciples		"				1. 37–51
PUBLIC APPEARANCE AND PREACHING OF JESUS.						
Working of His first miracle at Cana	27	Cana				2. 1–11
His visit to Capernaum		Capernaum				2. 12
First Passover and first cleansing of the Temple		Jerusalem				2. 13–23
Discourse of Jesus with Nicodemus		"				3. 1–21

Events.	Date A. D.	Place.	Matthew.	Mark.	Luke.	John.
Last testimony of John to Jesus	27	Ænon				3. 25–36
Visit of Jesus to Samaria		Sychar				4. 1–42
Return of Jesus to Cana		Cana				4. 43–46
Healing of the nobleman's son		"				4. 46–54
Jesus makes a visit to Jerusalem		Jerusalem				5. 1
Miracle at the pool of Bethesda		"				5. 2–47
John the Baptist cast into prison		Machærus	4. 12	1. 14		
Preaching of Jesus in Galilee		Galilee			4. 14, 15	
His appearance as teacher and preacher at Nazareth		Nazareth		6. 1	4. 15–30	
His teaching and preaching at Capernaum		Capernaum	4. 13		4. 31	
Call of Andrew, Peter, James and John		"	4. 18–22	1. 16–20	5. 1–11	
Miracle of healing the demoniac		"		1. 23–27	4. 33–36	
" " " Peter's mother-in-law		"	8. 14, 15	1. 29–31	4. 38, 39	
" " " many sick and diseased		"	8. 16, 17	1. 32–34	4. 40, 41	
Withdrawal from the multitude for solitary prayer		"		1. 35	4. 42	
First general circuit through Galilee		Galilee	4. 23–25	1. 35–39	4. 42–44	
Sermon on the mount		Hill near sea	5–7. 27			
Sermon in the boat; draught of fishes		Gennesaret			5. 1–11	
Healing of a leper		Galilee	8. 1–4	1. 40–45	5. 12–16	
Withdrawal to wilderness for solitary prayer		"		1. 45	5. 16	
Healing of a paralytic		Capernaum	9. 1–8	2. 1–12	5. 18–26	
Call of Matthew (Levi) and discourse at feast		"	9. 9–17	2. 13–22	5. 27–39	

SECOND YEAR'S MINISTRY.

Note.—Those who regard the feast mentioned in John 5. 1 as the Passover, begin here to date the events of the second year of Christ's ministry. Others throw a few of the last events above mentioned into the second year's ministry, beginning with the visit of Jesus to Jerusalem.

Events.	Date A. D.	Place.	Matthew.	Mark.	Luke.	John.
Disciples pluck the ears of corn	28	Galilee	12. 1–8	2. 23–28	6. 1–5	
Healing of man with withered hand		Capernaum	12. 9–14	3. 1–6	6. 6–11	
Retirement for solitary prayer		"		3. 13	6. 12	
Call of the Twelve Apostles		"	10. 2–4	3. 13–19	6. 13–16	
Sermon in plain of Gennesaret		Near to sea.			6. 17–49	
Healing of centurion's servant		"	8. 5–13		7. 1–10	
Raising the son of widow of Nain		Nain			7. 11–17	
Message from John the Baptist, and Christ's testimony		Capernaum	11. 2–19		7. 18–35	
The warning to Chorazin, etc.		"	11. 20–28			
The woman which was a sinner					7. 36–50	
Tour through Galilee with the twelve		Galilee			8. 1–3	
Healing of a demoniac		Capernaum	12. 22			
Blasphemy against the Holy Ghost		"	12. 24–37	3. 22–30		
The unclean spirit		"	12. 43–46			
The interruption of His relatives		"	12. 46	3. 31		
A series of Parables—The Sower		Plain of Gennesaret	13. 1–9, 18–23	4. 1, 14–20	8. 4, 11–15	
" Tares		" "	13. 24			
" Mustard seed		" "	13. 21	4. 30		
" Leaven		" "	13. 33			
" Candle		" "		4. 21	8. 16	
" Treasure		" "	13. 44			
" Pearl		" "	13. 45			
" Drawnet		" "	13. 47			
Jesus calms the storm on sea		Sea of Gennesaret	8. 24–27	4. 37–41	8. 23–25	
The Gergesene demoniacs and swine		Gadara	8. 28–34	5. 1–15	8. 27–35	
The parable of the bridegroom		Capernaum	9. 15			
" " " new cloth and new wine		"	9. 16, 17			
Series of Miracles—Woman with issue of blood		Gennesaret	9. 20–22	5. 25–34	8. 43–48	
Jairus' daughter		Capernaum	9. 18	5. 22–24	8. 41, 42	
Two blind men		"	9. 27–30			
The dumb spirit		"	9. 32, 33			
The mission of the twelve Apostles		"	10. 1	6. 7–12	9. 1–6	
Death of John the Baptist		Machærus	14. 1–12	6. 14–29	9. 7	
Miraculous feeding of five thousand		Bethsaida	14. 13–21	6. 30–44	9. 12–17	6. 1–13
Jesus walked on the water		Lake of Gennesaret	14. 25	6. 48		6. 19
Discourse on plain and in synagogue		Capernaum	14. 34			6. 26–70

FROM SECOND TO THIRD PASSOVER, OR THIRD YEAR'S MINISTRY.

Events.	Date A. D.	Place.	Matthew.	Mark.	Luke.	John.
Opposition of Scribes and Pharisees		Capernaum	15. 1			
Discourse on pollution		"	15. 2–20	7. 1–23		
Healing the Syrophœnician's daughter		Phœnicia	15. 21–29	7. 24–30		
Series of Miracles—Healing of deaf and dumb man		Decapolis		7. 32		
" " sick persons		"	15. 30, 31			
Feeding of four thousand		Gennesaret	15. 32–39	8. 1–9		
Parable of the leaven		"	16. 1–12	8. 14–22		
The healing of the blind man		Bethsaida		8. 22–27		
Peter's confession of Christ's divinity		Cæsarea Philippi.	16. 13–21	8. 27–30		
First prediction of the passion		Bethsaida	16. 21–28	8. 31–38	9. 22–27	
The transfiguration		Tabor or Hermon	17. 1–8	9. 2–8	9. 28–36	
Healing the demonized child		" "	17. 14–21	9. 14–27	9. 37–42	
Second prediction of the passion		" "	17. 22, 23	9. 31	9. 43, 44	
The stater in the fish's mouth		Capernaum	17. 27			
A lesson on docility		"	18. 1–14	9. 33–37	9. 46–48	
" " forgiveness		"	18. 15	9. 43		
" " self-denial		"	18. 18			
Parable of the unmerciful servant		"	18. 23–35			
Journey through Samaria to Jerusalem		Samaria			9. 51, 52	
Jealousy of the Samaritans		"			9. 53	

Events.	Date A.D.	Place.	Matthew.	Mark.	Luke.	John.
Anger of the "Sons of Thunder"	28	Samaria			9. 54–56	
Feast of Tabernacles at Jerusalem		Jerusalem				7. 2–10
A series of discourses		"				7. 10–46
Officers sent to arrest Jesus		"				7. 30–46
The incident of the adulteress		"				8. 3
Another series of discourses		"				8. 12–19
Jesus threatened with stoning		"				8. 59
Healing of blind man and discourses		"				9. 1–41
Christ the door of the sheepfold		"				10. 1
" " good shepherd		"				10. 11
Departure from Jerusalem: Mission of the Seventy		Judea			10. 1–16	
Return of the Seventy		"			10. 17–24	
Parable of the Good Samaritan		"			10. 30–37	
Visit to Mary and Martha		Bethany			10. 38–42	
Teaches His disciples how to pray		Judea	6. 9–13		11. 1–13	
Heals the mute and rebukes Pharisees		"	12. 22–45		11. 14	
A series of discourses—The repentant Ninevites		"	12. 41		11. 29–36	
God's providence to birds and flowers		"			12. 22–30	
The rich fool		"			12. 13–21	
The murdered Galileans		"			13. 1–5	
The barren fig-tree		"			13. 6–9	
Healing of the woman with an infirmity		"			13. 10–17	
Visit to Jerusalem at Feast of Dedication		Jerusalem				10. 22–30
An attempt to stone Jesus		"				10. 31
Retreat of Jesus across Jordan		Peræa				10. 40
Are there few that be saved		"			13. 23–30	
The message to Herod		"			13. 31–33	
Healing of the man with the dropsy		"			14. 1–6	
Parable of the Great supper		"			14. 15–24	
" " Lost sheep		"			15. 1–7	
" " Lost coin		"			15. 8–10	
" " Prodigal son		"			15. 11–32	
" " Unjust steward		"			16. 1–13	
" " Dives and Lazarus		"			16. 19–31	
The sickness of Lazarus		Bethany				11. 1–10
Return of Jesus from Peræa to Bethany		"				11. 11–16
Raising of Lazarus from the dead		"				11. 17–46
Caiaphas and council of Pharisees		Jerusalem				11. 47–53
Jesus retires to the town of Ephraim		Ephraim				11. 54
Jesus starts on last journey to Jerusalem		Samaria	19. 1	10. 1	17. 11	
Healing of the ten lepers		"			17. 12–19	
Parable of the unjust judge		"			18. 1–8	
Parable of the Pharisee and publican		"			18. 9–14	
The question of divorce		"	19. 3–12	10. 2–12		
Jesus blesses the little children		"	19. 13–15	10. 13–16	18. 15–17	
The rich young ruler		"	19. 16–22	10. 17–22	18. 18–23	
Parable of the laborers in the vineyard		"	20. 1–16			
Third prediction of the passion		"	20. 17–19	10. 32–34	18. 31–34	
The request of James and John		"	20. 20–28	10. 35–45		
Healing of blind Bartimæus		Near Jericho	20. 29–34	10. 46–52	18. 35–43	
Visit of Jesus to house of Zacchæus		Jericho			19. 1–10	
Parable of the pounds		"			19. 11–28	
THE EVENTS OF HOLY WEEK.						
The supper in Simon's house	29	Bethany	26. 6–13	14. 3–9		12. 1–9
Mary anoints Jesus		"	26. 7–13	14. 3–8		12. 3–8
Entry of Jesus into Jerusalem		Jerusalem	21. 1–11	11. 1–10	19. 29–44	12. 12–19
Jesus surveys the Temple		"		11. 11		
Retirement of Jesus to Bethany		Bethany		11. 11		
The withering of the barren fig-tree		Mount of Olives	21. 18–19	11. 12–14		
Second cleansing of the Temple		Jerusalem	21. 12–17	11. 15–19	19. 45–48	
Retirement of Jesus to Bethany		Bethany	21. 17	11. 19		
The lesson of the fig-tree		Mount of Olives	21. 20–22	11. 20–25		
Temple discourses—The ruler's question		Jerusalem	21. 23–27	11. 27–33	20. 1–8	
Parable of the two sons		"	21. 28–32			
The wicked husbandman		"	21. 3–46	12. 1–12	20. 9–19	
The wedding garment		"	22. 1–14			
Pharisaic question of tribute money		"	22. 15–22	12. 13–17	20. 20–26	
Sadducaic question of the resurrection		"	22. 23–33	12. 18–27	20. 27–39	
Lawyer's question as to the great commandment		"	22. 34–40	12. 28–34		
Answers and counter-questions of Jesus		"	22. 41–46	12. 35–37	20. 41–44	
Denunciation of Scribes and Pharisees		"	23. 13–33			
The widow's mite		"		12. 41–44	21. 1–4	
The coming of the Greeks		"				12. 20–36
Departure of Jesus to Mount of Olives		Olivet	24. 1–3	13. 1–3		
Predictions—Destruction of Jerusalem		"	24. 3–28	13. 3–23	21. 5–24	
Of the second coming		"	24. 28–51	13. 23–37	21. 24–36	
Parables—The ten virgins		"	25. 1–13			
The talents		"	25. 14–30			
The sheep and the goats		"	25. 31–46			
The session of the Sanhedrim		Jerusalem	26. 3–5	14. 1, 2	22. 1, 2	
The betrayal compact with Judas Iscariot		"	26. 14–16	14. 10, 11	22. 3–6	
THE CRUCIFIXION AND BURIAL.						
The preparation of the Passover		Jerusalem	26. 17–19	14. 12–16	22. 7–13	
Washing of the Apostles' feet		"				13. 1–17
Breaking and blessing of the bread		"	26. 26	14. 22	22. 19	
"One of you shall betray me"		"	26. 21	14. 18	22. 21	13. 21
The sorrowing question, "Lord, is it I?"		"	26. 22–25	14. 19		
The sop given to Judas Iscariot		"				13, 26, 27
The departure of Judas		"				13. 30.

Events.	Date A.D.	Place.	Matthew.	Mark.	Luke.	John.
Warning of Jesus to Peter	29	Jerusalem	26. 34	14. 30	22. 34	13. 38
Jesus blesses the cup		"	26. 27, 28	14. 23, 24		
Discourses after the supper		"				14. 16
Prayer of Jesus for His Apostles		"				17
The singing of an hymn		"	26. 30	14. 26		
The agony in the garden		Gethsemane	26. 37	14. 33	22. 39	18. 1
The thrice-repeated prayer		"	26. 39, 44	14. 36–39	22. 42	
The bloody sweat and comforting angel		"			22. 43, 44	
The waiting Apostles fall asleep		"	26. 40–45	14. 37–41	22. 45, 46	
The betrayal by Judas Iscariot		"	26. 47–50	14. 43, 44	22. 47	18. 2–5
Peter smites the ear of Malchus		"	26. 51	14. 47	22. 50	18. 10
Jesus heals the ear of Malchus		"			22. 51	
Jesus is forsaken by His disciples		"	26. 56	14. 50		
Jesus is led away to Annas		Jerusalem				18. 12, 13
Jesus is tried by Caiaphas		"	26. 57	14. 53	22. 54	18. 15
Peter follows after Jesus		"	26. 58	14. 54	22. 55	18. 15
The adjuration of the high priest		"	26. 63	14. 61		
Jesus is condemned, buffeted and mocked		"	26. 66, 67	14. 64, 65	22. 63–65	
Peter's denial of Jesus		"	26. 69–75	14. 66–72	22. 54–62	18. 17–27
Jesus is taken before Pilate		"	27. 1, 2	15. 1	23. 1	18. 28
Judas repents and returns the betrayal money		"	27, 3			
Pilate comes out before the people		"				18. 29
Pilate speaks to Jesus in private		"				18. 33
Pilate orders Jesus to be scourged		"	27. 26	15. 15		19. 1
Jesus is crowned with thorns		"	27. 29	15. 17		19. 2
Jesus is exhibited to the public by Pilate		"				19. 5
Jesus is formally accused by Pilate		"	27. 11	15. 2	23. 2	
Jesus is sent by Pilate to Herod		"			23. 6–11	
Pilate says, "Behold your king"		"				19. 14
Pilate desires to release Jesus		"	27, 15	15. 6	23. 17	19. 12
Pilate receives a message from his wife		"	27. 19			
Pilate washes his hands of the matter		"	27. 24			
Pilate releases Barabbas from prison		"	27. 26			
Pilate delivers Jesus to be crucified		"	27. 26	15. 15	23. 25	19. 16
Simon of Cyrene acts as cross-bearer		"	27. 32	15. 21	23. 26	
They give Jesus vinegar and gall to drink		Golgotha	27. 34	15. 23	23. 36	
Jesus is nailed to the cross		"	27. 35	15. 24, 25	23. 33	19. 18
The written superscription		"	27. 37	15. 26	23. 38	19. 19
"Father, forgive them"		"			23. 34	
Parting of His garments and allotment of vesture		"	27. 35	15. 24	23. 34	19. 23
Railing of passers-by and two thieves		"	27. 39–44	15. 29–32	23. 35	
The penitent thief		"			23. 40	
"To-day shalt thou be with me in Paradise"		"			23. 43	
"Woman, behold thy son"		"				19. 26, 27
Darkness spreads over the land		"	27. 45	15. 33	23. 44, 45	
"My God, why hast thou forsaken me?"		"	27. 46	15. 34		
Jesus saith, "I thirst"		"				19. 28
Jesus receives the offered vinegar		"	27. 48	15. 36		19. 29
"It is finished"		"				19. 30
"Father, into thy hands I commend my spirit"		"			23. 46	
Rending of the Temple's veil		Jerusalem	27. 51	15. 38	23. 45	
Opening of graves and resurrection of saints		"	27. 52			
Testimony of the centurion		Golgotha	27. 54	15. 39	23. 47	
The watching of the women		"	27. 55	15. 40	23. 49	
The piercing of Jesus' side		"				19. 34
Removal from cross and burial		"	27. 57–60	15. 46	23. 53	19. 38–42
The sealed tomb and the guard		The Garden	27. 65, 66			
THE RESURRECTION AND ASCENSION.						
Women bear spices to the tomb		The Garden	28. 1	16. 1, 2	24. 1	
The angel rolls away the stone		"	28. 2			
Women announce the resurrection		Jerusalem	28. 8		24. 9, 10	20, 1, 2
Peter and John run to the tomb		The Garden			24. 12	20. 3
The women return to the tomb		"			24. 1	
Report of guards to the chief priests		Jerusalem	28. 11–15			
Christ appears to Mary Magdalene		The Garden		16. 9, 10		20. 14
"All hail! Fear not. Touch me not"		"	28. 9			20. 17
Appearance to women returning home		"	28. 9			
"Go tell my brethren," etc.		"	28. 10			
Appearance to two disciples on the way		Emmaus		16. 12	24. 13	
" to Peter		Jerusalem			24. 34	
" to ten Apostles in upper room		"			24. 36	
"Peace be unto you"		"				20. 19
"Receive ye the Holy Ghost"		"				20. 21
Appearance of Christ to eleven Apostles		"		16. 14		20. 22, 23
Appearance to Thomas. "Reach hither thy finger"		"				20. 26
"Blessed are they that have not seen"		"				20. 27
Appearance to disciples at the sea		Tiberias				20. 29
" to Peter. "Feed my sheep"		"				21. 1–24
" to eleven disciples on a mountain		Galilee	28. 16			21. 15–17
"All power is given unto me"		"	28. 18			
"Go ye and teach all nations"		"	28. 19			
"Lo, I am with you alway"		"	28. 20			
Appearance to five hundred brethren, 1 Cor. 15. 6		"				
" to St. James, 1 Cor. 15. 7		"				
The Ascension		Bethany		16. 19	24. 50, 51	

THE DISCOURSES OF JESUS,
ARRANGED IN CHRONOLOGICAL ORDER.

DISCOURSES.	PLACES.	REFERENCES.
Conversation with Nicodemus.	Jerusalem.	John iii. 1–21.
Conversation with the woman of Samaria.	Sychar.	iv. 1–42.
Discourse in the Synagogue of Nazareth.	Nazareth.	Luke iv. 16–31.
Sermon upon the mount.	"	Matt. v., vii.
Instruction to the Apostles.	Galilee.	x.
Denunciation against Chorazin, etc.	"	xi. 20–24.
Discourse on occasion of healing the infirm man at Bethesda.	Jerusalem.	John v.
Discourse concerning the disciples plucking of corn on the Sabbath.	Judea.	Matt. xii. 1–8.
Reputation of his working Miracles by the agency of Beelzebub.	Capernaum.	22–37.
Discourse on the bread of life.	"	John vii.
Discourse about internal purity.	"	Matt. xv. 1–20.
Discourse against giving or taking offence, and concerning the forgiveness of injuries.	"	xviii.
Discourse at the feast of tabernacles.	Jerusalem.	John vii.
Discourse on occasion of woman taken in adultery.	"	viii., i. ii.
Discourse concerning the sheep.	"	x.
Denunciations against the Scribes and Pharisees.	Paræa.	Luke xi. 29–36.
Discourse concerning humility and prudence.	Galilee.	xiv. 7–14.
Direction how to obtain heaven.	Paræa.	Matt. xix. 16–30.
Discourse concerning his sufferings.	Jerusalem.	xx. 17–19.
Denunciations against the Pharisees.	"	xxiii.
Prediction of the destruction of Jerusalem.	"	xxiv.
The consolatory discourse.	"	John xv., xvii.
Discourse as he went to Gethsemane.	"	Matt. xxvi. 31–36.
Discourse to the disciples before his ascension.	"	xxviii. 16–23.

THE PARABLES OF JESUS,
ARRANGED IN CHRONOLOGICAL ORDER.

PARABLES.	PLACES	REFERENCES.
PARABLE OF THE		
Sower.	Capernaum.	Matt. xiii. 1–23.
Tares.	"	24–30–36–43.
Seed spring up imperfectly.	"	Mark iv. 26–29.
Grain of mustard-seed.	"	Matt. xii. 31, 32.
Leaven.	"	xiii. 33.
Found treasure.	"	44.
Precious pearl.	"	45–46.
Net.	"	47–50.
Two debtors.	"	Luke vii. 36–50.
Unmerciful servant.	"	Matt. xviii. 23–35.
Samaritan.	Near Jericho.	Luke x. 25–37.
Rich fool.	Galilee.	xii. 16–21.
Servants who waited for their Lord.	"	xii. 35–48.
Barren fig-tree.	"	xiii. 6–9.
Lost sheep,	"	xv. 3–7.
Lost piece of money.	"	8–10.
Prodigal son.	"	11–32.
Dishonest steward.	"	xvi. 1–12.
Rich man and Lazarus.	"	19–31.
Unjust judge.	Paræa.	xviii. 1–8.
Pharisee and Publican.	"	9–14.
Laborers in the vineyard.	"	Matt. xx. 1–16.
Pounds.	Jericho.	Luke xix. 12–27.
Two sons.	Jerusalem.	Matt. xxi. 28–32.
Vineyard.	"	33–46.
Marriage feast.	"	xxii. 1–14.
The virgins.	"	xxv. 1–13.
Talents.	"	14–30.
Sheep and the goats.	"	31–46.

THE MIRACLES OF CHRIST,
ARRANGED IN CHRONOLOGICAL ORDER.

MIRACLES.	PLACES	REFERENCES.
JESUS		
Turns water into wine.	Cana.	John ii. 1–11.
Cures the nobleman's son of Capernaum.	"	iv. 46–64.
Causes a miraculous draught of fishes.	Sea of Galilee.	Luke v. 1–11.
Cures a demoniac.	Capernaum.	Mark i. 22–28.
Heals Peter's wife's mother of a fever.	"	30–31.
Heals a leper.	"	40–45.
Heals the centurion's servant.	"	Matt. viii. 5–13.
Raises the widow's son.	Nain.	Luke vii. 11–17.
Calms the tempest.	Sea of Galilee.	Matt. viii. 23–27.
Cures the demoniacs of Gadara.	Gadara.	28–34.
Cures a man of the palsy.	Capernaum.	ix. 1–8.
Restores to life the daughter of Jairus.	"	18, 19, 23–26.
Cures a woman diseased with a flux of blood.	"	Luke viii. 43–48.
Restores to sight two blind men.	"	Matt. ix. 27–31.
Heals one possessed with a dumb spirit.	"	32, 33.
Cures an infirm man at Bethesda.	Jerusalem.	John v. 1–9.
Cures a man with a withered hand.	Judea.	Matt. xii. 10–13.
Cures a demoniac.	Capernaum.	22–23.
Feeds miraculously five thousand.	Decapolis.	xiv., xv. 21.
Heals the woman of Canaan's daughter.	Near Tyre.	xv. 22–28.
Heals a man who was dumb and deaf.	Decapolis.	Mark vii. 31–37.
Feeds miraculously four thousand.	"	Matt. xv. 32–39.
Gives sight to a blind man.	Bethsaida.	Mark xiii. 22–26.
Cures a boy possessed of a devil.	Tabor.	Matt. xvii. 14–21.
Restores to sight a man born blind.	Jerusalem.	John ix.
Heals a woman under an infirmity eighteen years.	Galilee.	Luke xiii. 11–17.
Cures a dropsy.	"	xiv. 1–6.
Cleanses ten lepers.	Samaria.	xvii. 11–19.
Raises Lazarus from the dead.	Bethany.	John xi.
Restores to sight two blind men.	Jericho.	Matt. xx. 30–34.
Blasts the fig-tree.	Olivet.	xxi. 18–22.
Heals the ear of Malchus.	Gethsemane.	Luke xxii. 50, 51.
Causes the miraculous draught of fishes.	Sea of Galilee.	John xxi. 1–14.

THE MIRACLES RECORDED IN THE ACTS OF THE APOSTLES.

MIRACLES.	WHERE WROUGHT.	RECORDED IN
Peter heals a lame man.	Jerusalem.	Acts iii. 1–11.
Ananias and Sapphira struck dead.	Jerusalem.	v. 1–10.
Apostles perform many wonders.	Jerusalem.	v. 12–16.
Peter and John communicate the Holy Ghost.	Samaria.	viii. 14–17.
Peter healeth Eneas of a palsy.	Lydda.	ix. 33, 34.
– raiseth Tabitha, or Dorcas, to life.	Joppa.	ix. 36–41.
– delivered out of prison by an angel.	Jerusalem.	xii. 7–17.
God smites Herod, so that he dies.	Jerusalem.	xii. 21–23.
Elymas, the sorcerer, smitten with blindness.	Paphos.	xiii. 6–11.
Paul converted.	Road to Damascus.	ix. 1–9.
– heals a cripple.	Lystra.	xiv. 8–10.
– casts out a spirit of divination.	Philippi.	xvi. 16–18.
– and Silas's prison doors opened by an earthquake.	"	xvi. 25, 26.
– communicates the Holy Ghost.	Corinth.	xix. 1–6.
– heals multitudes.	"	xix. 11, 12.
– restores Eutychus to life.	Troas.	xx. 9–12.
– shakes off a viper.	Melita.	xxviii. 3–6.
– heals the father of Publius, and others.	"	xxviii. 7–9.

PROPHECIES AND ALLUSIONS TO CHRIST IN THE OLD TESTAMENT,

FULFILLED OR APPLIED TO HIM IN THE NEW TESTAMENT.

FIRST SERIES.*

Describing Christ in his Human Nature as the Promised Seed of the Woman in the grand Charter of our Redemption (Gen. 3 : 15); and his Pedigree, Sufferings and Glory in his successive manifestations of Himself until the End of the World.

I. *The Seed of the Woman,* Gen. 3 : 15; *Gal.* 4 : 4; 1 *Tim.* 2 : 15; *Rev.* 12 : 5.
II. *Born of a Virgin,* Ps. 22 : 10; 69 : 8; 86 : 16; 116 : 16; *Isa.* 7 : 14; 49 : 1; *Mic.* 5 : 3; *Jer.* 31 : 22; *Matt.* 1 : 23; *Luke* 1 : 26–35.
III. *Of the Family of Shem,* Gen. 9 : 26.
IV. *Of the Race of the Hebrews,* Ex. 3 : 18; *Phil.* 3 : 5; 2 *Cor.* 11 : 22.
V. *Of the Seed of Abraham,* Gen. 12 : 3; 18 : 18; 22 : 18; *Matt.* 1 : 1; *John* 8 : 56; *Acts* 3 : 25.
VI. *Of the Line of Isaac,* Gen. 17 : 19; 21 : 12; 26 : 4; *Rom.* 9 : 7; *Gal.* 4 : 23–28; *Heb.* 11 : 18.
VII. *Of Jacob or Israel,* Gen. 28 : 4–14; *Ex.* 4 : 22; *Num.* 24 : 17; *Ps.* 135 : 4, etc.; *Isa.* 41 : 8; 49 : 6; *Jer.* 14 : 8; *Luke* 1 : 68; 2 : 30; *Acts* 28 : 20.
VIII. *Of the Tribe of Judah,* Gen. 49 : 10; 1 *Chron.* 5 : 2; *Mic.* 5 : 2; *Matt.* 2 : 6; *Heb.* 7 : 14; *Rev.* 5 : 5.
IX. *Of the House of David,* 2 *Sam.* 7 : 12–15; 1 *Chron.* 17 : 11–14; *Ps.* 89 : 4–36; 132 : 10–17; 2 *Chron.* 6 : 42; *Isa.* 9 : 7; 11 : 1; 55 : 3, 4; *Jer.* 23 : 5, 6; *Amos* 9 : 11; *Matt.* 1 : 1; *Luke* 1 . 69; 2 : 4; *John* 7 : 42; *Acts* 2 : 30; 13 : 23; *Rom.* 1 : 3; 2 *Tim.* 2 : 8; *Rev.* 22 : 16.
X. *Born at Bethlehem, the City of David,* Mic. 5 : 2; *Matt.* 2 : 6; *Luke* 2 : 4; *John* 7 : 42.
XI. *His Passion or Sufferings,* Gen. 3 : 15; *Ps.* 22 : 1–

18; 31 : 13; 86 : 38–45; *Isa.* 53 : 1–12; *Dan.* 9 : 26; *Zech.* 13 : 6, 7; *Matt.* 26 : 31; *Luke* 24 : 26; *John* 1 : 29; *Acts* 8 : 32–35; 26 : 23.
XII. *His Death on the Cross,* Num. 21 : 9; *Ps.* 16 : 10; 22 : 16; 31 : 22; 49 : 15; *Isa.* 53 : 8, 9; *Dan.* 9 : 26; *John* 3 : 14; 8 : 28; 12 : 32, 33; *Matt.* 20 : 19; 26 : 2; 1 *Cor.* 15 : 3; *Col.* 2 : 15; *Phil.* 2 : 8.
XIII. *His Entombment and Embalmment,* Isa. 53 : 9; *Matt.* 26 : 12; *Mark* 14 : 8; *John* 12 : 7; 19 : 40; 1 *Cor.* 15 : 4.
XIV. *His Resurrection on the Third Day,* Ps. 16 : 10; 17 : 15; 49 : 15; 73 : 24; *John* 1 : 17; *Matt.* 12 : 40; 16 : 4; 27 : 63; *John* 2 : 19; *Acts* 2 : 27–31; 13 : 35; 1 *Cor.* 15 : 4.
XV. *His Ascension into Heaven,* Ps. 8 : 5, 6 : 47 : 5; 68 : 18; 110 : 1; *Acts* 1 : 11; 2 : 33; *John* 20 : 17; *Eph.* 4 : 8–10; *Heb.* 1 : 3; 2 : 9; *Rev.* 12 : 5.
XVI. *His Second Appearance at the Regeneration,* Isa. 40 : 10; 62 : 11; *Jer.* 23 : 5, 6; *Hos.* 3 : 5; *Mic.* 5 : 3; *Hab.* 2 : 7; *Dan.* 7 : 13, 14; *Matt.* 24 : 3–30; 26 : 64; *John* 5 : 25; *Heb.* 9 : 28; *Rev.* 20 : 4; 22 : 20.
XVII. *His Last Appearance at the End of the World,* Ps. 1 : 1–6; *Job* 19 : 25–29; *Eccl.* 12 : 14; *Dan.* 12 : 2, 3; *Matt.* 25 : 31–46; *John* 5 : 28–30; *Acts* 17 : 31; 24 : 25; *Rev.* 20 : 11–15.

SECOND SERIES.*
Describing his Character and Offices, Human and Divine.

I. *The Son of God,* 2 *Sam.* 7 : 14; 1 *Chron.* 17 : 13; *Ps.* 2 : 7; 72 : 1; *Prov.* 30 : 4; *Dan.* 3 : 25; *Mark* 1 : 1; *Luke* 1 : 35; *Matt.* 3 : 17; 17 : 5; *John* 1 : 34–50; 3 : 16–18; 20 : 31; *Heb.* 1 : 1–5; *Rom.* 1 : 4; 1 *John* 4 : 14; *Rev.* 1 : 5, 6.
II. *The Son of Man,* Ps. 8 : 4, 5; *Dan.* 7 : 13; *John* 1 : 51; 3 : 13; 5 : 27; *Matt.* 16 : 13; 26 : 64; *Heb.* 2 : 7; *Rev.* 1 : 13; 14 : 14.
III. *The Holy One or Saint,* Deut. 33 : 8; *Ps.* 16 : 10; 89 : 19; *Isa.* 10 : 17; 29 : 23; 49 : 7; *Hos.* 11 : 9; *Hab.* 1 : 12; 3 : 3; *Mark* 1 : 24; *Luke* 1 : 35; 4 : 34; 1 *John* 2 : 20.
IV. *The Saint of Saints,* Dan. 9 : 24.
V. *The Just One or Righteous,* Zech. 9 : 9; *Jer.* 23 : 5; *Isa.* 41 : 2; *Ps.* 34 : 19, 21; *Luke* 1 : 17; *Matt.* 27 : 19–24; *Luke* 23 : 47; *Acts* 3 : 14; 7 : 52; 22 : 14; 1 *John* 2 : 1, 29; *James* 5 : 6.
VI. *The Wisdom of God,* Prov. 8 : 22–30; *Matt.* 11 : 19; *Luke* 11 : 49; 1 *Cor.* 1 : 24.
VII. *The Oracle (or Word) of the Lord, or of God,* Gen. 15 : 1–4; 1 *Sam.* 3 : 1–21; 2 *Sam.* 7 : 4; 1 *Kings* 17 : 8–24; *Ps.* 33 : 6; *Isa.* 40 : 8; *Mic.* 4 : 2; *Jer.* 25 : 3; *John* 1 : 14; 3 : 34; *Luke* 1 : 2; *Heb.* 11 : 3; 4 : 12; 1 *Pet.* 1 : 23; 2 *Pet.* 3 : 5; *Rev.* 19 : 13.
VIII. *The Redeemer or Saviour,* Job 19 : 25–27; Gen. 48 : 16; *Ps.* 19 : 14; *Isa.* 41 : 14; 44 : 6; 47 : 4; 59 : 20; 62 : 11; 63 : 1; *Jer.* 50 : 34; *Matt.* 1 : 21; *John* 1 : 29; 4 : 42; *Luke* 2 : 11; *Acts* 5 : 31; *Rom.* 11 : 26; *Rev.* 5 : 9.
IX. *The Lamb of God,* Gen. 22 : 8; *Isa.* 53 : 7; *John*

1 : 29; *Acts* 8 : 32–35; 1 *Pet.* 1 : 19; *Rev.* 5 : 6; 13 : 8; 15 : 3; 21 : 22; 22 : 1.
X. *The Mediator, Intercessor, or Advocate,* Job 33 : 23; *Isa.* 53 : 12; 59 : 19; *Luke* 23 : 34; 1 *Tim.* 2 : 5; *Heb.* 9 : 15; 1 *John* 2 : 1; *Rev.* 5 : 9.
XI. *Shiloh, the Apostle,* Gen. 49 : 10; *Ex.* 4 : 13; *Matt.* 15 : 24; *Luke* 4 : 18; *John* 9 : 7; 17 : 3; 20 : 21; *Heb.* 3 : 1.
XII. *The High Priest,* Ps. 110 : 4; *Isa.* 59 : 16; *Heb.* 3 : 1; 4 : 14; 5 : 10; 9 : 11.
XIII. *The Prophet like Moses,* Deut. 18 : 15–19; *Luke* 24 : 19; *Mark* 6 : 15; *John* 1 : 17–21; 6 : 14; *Acts* 3 : 22, 23.
XIV. *The Leader or Chief Captain,* John 5 : 14; 1 *Chron.* 5 : 2; *Isa.* 55 : 4; *Mic.* 5 : 2; *Dan.* 9 : 25; *Matt.* 2 : 6; *Heb.* 2 : 10.
XV. *The Messiah, Christ, King of Israel,* 1 *Sam.* 2 : 10; 2 *Sam.* 7 : 12; 1 *Chron.* 17 : 11; *Ps.* 2 : 2; 45 : 1, 6; 72 : 1; 89 : 38; *Isa.* 61 : 1; *Dan.* 9 : 26; *Matt.* 2 : 3, 4; 16 : 16; *Luke* 23 : 2; *John* 1 : 41–49; 6 : 69; *Acts* 4 : 26, 27; 10 : 38.
XVI. *The God of Israel,* Ex. 24 : 10, 11; *Josh.* 7 : 19; *Judg.* 11 : 23; 1 *Sam.* 5 : 11; 1 *Chron.* 17 : 24; *Ps.* 41 : 13; *Isa.* 45 : 3; *Ezek.* 8 : 4; *Matt.* 15 : 31; 22 : 32; *John* 20 : 28.
XVII. *The Lord of Hosts or the Lord,* 2 *Sam.* 7 : 26; 1 *Chron.* 17 : 24; *Ps.* 24 : 10; *Isa.* 6 : 1–5; *Mal.* 1 : 14; *Rom.* 12 : 19; *Phil.* 2 : 9–11.
XVIII. *King of Kings and Lord of Lords,* Ps. 89 : 27; 110 : 1; *Dan.* 7 : 13, 14; *Matt.* 28 : 18; *John* 3 : 35; 13 : 3; 1 *Cor.* 15 : 25; *Eph.* 1 : 20–22; *Col.* 3 : 1; *Rev.* 19 : 16.

---

* **For Biblical Students** we bring into one point of view all the great prophecies and allusions to *Christ* in the *Old Testament* which are expressly cited, either as predictions fulfilled in him or applied to him, in the *New Testament.*
The first series describes *Christ* in his human nature as the promised *Seed of the woman* in the grand charter of our redemption (Gen. 3 : 15), and his pedigree, sufferings and glory in his successive manifestations of himself until the end of the world.
The second series describes his character and offices, human and divine.
The combination of these in all their branches, representing him as *the Son of God* and *Son of man* conjointly, was altogether fulfilled to the utmost nicety in *Jesus of Nazareth,* and altogether in *no other person that ever appeared,* demonstrating that it was " he of whom Moses and the prophets did write," and that we Christians have not followed cunningly-devised fables, but many infallible proofs, in holding him for *our Lord and our God.*
Such is the sublime, magnificent and stupendous *scheme of prophecy,* connected, though scattered like the beauties of Nature, through the pages of *Holy Writ,* which *God* revealed to mankind by the mouth of all his prophets, in divers degrees and sundry modes of inspiration (Heb. 1 : 1), from the grand charter of our *redemption,* given in Paradise (Gen. 3 : 15), to the last appearance of *his Son* upon earth (Rev. 20 : 20). when that *Son* promised that he would come quickly to refresh the world at the regeneration or restitution of all things (Acts 3 : 19–21); and as surely as he appeared before in humiliation "a man of sorrows and acquainted with grief," to instruct and save mankind by his example and by his death as "*the Apostle* and *High Priest* of our profession" (Heb. 3 : 1), so surely will " he appear a second time, in glory, for salvation to them who expect him" (Heb. 9 · 28), but as a consuming fire for destruction to them who despise and reject his awful message. Heb. 12 : 25–29.
"And behold I come quickly ; and my reward is with me, to give every man according as his work shall be." Rev. 22 : 12.
May we, " hearts fixed and trusting in the Lord " (Ps. 107 : 12; John 14 : 1), be enabled to join in the apostle's **patient and humble wish,** not presuming to hasten the time, but "tarrying *the Lord's* leisure."

CHRONOLOGY OF ACTS

AND

PAUL'S EPISTLES.

NOTE 1.—Some chronologists date Paul's first missionary journey in A. D. 48, the Council at Jerusalem in A. D. 50, and Paul's second missionary journey in A. D. 51. They also introduce a journey to Spain in A. D. 66; date the First Epistle to Timothy and Titus in A. D. 67; and the second imprisonment, Second Epistle to Timothy and the martyrdom of the Apostle in A. D. 68.

NOTE 2.—Roman provinces were divided into Senatorial and Imperial. The former were presided over by Proconsuls, generally appointed by lot and for a year, and not endowed with military power. The Imperial province was ruled by a Propretor or Procurator, who was appointed by the Roman Emperor, held authority as long as the Emperor wished, and was endowed with military authority. Syria became an Imperial province, to which Judea with its Proconsul was attached.

A. D.	Events.	Roman Emperors and Procurators.
30	Pentecost and pouring out of the Spirit.	Tiberius, Emperor. Pontius Pilate, Procurator.
31	Spread of the Gospel at Jerusalem.	
35	The preaching of Stephen, the first elder.	
36	The martyrdom of Stephen by stoning.	Pilate deposed.
37	The conversion of Saul of Tarsus,	Death of Tiberius. Accession of Emperor Caligula.
38	Paul goes into Arabia, Gal. 1 : 17.	Release of Herod Agrippa I.
	Philip converts the Samaritans and Ethiopian Eunuch.	
39	Herod Antipas banished to Gaul.	Caligula orders his statue to be set up at Jerusalem.
	Dominions of Herod Antipas given to Herod Agrippa I.	
40	St. Peter goes on a missionary journey.	
	The conversion of Cornelius.	
41	Herod Agrippa I. King of Judea and Samaria.	Claudius succeeds Caligula.
42	Spread of the Church as far as Antioch.	
	Disciples first called Christians at Antioch.	
44	Persecution of Christians by Herod Agrippa.	
	The killing of St. James with the sword.	
	Herod Agrippa imprisons St. Peter.	
	The death of Herod Agrippa.	Cuspius Fadus, Procurator.
45	First missionary journey of Saul and Barnabas.	
46	Saul and Barnabas return to Antioch.	Tiberius Alexander, Procurator.
48	The Judaizing opponents of Paul at Antioch	Ventidius Cumanus, Procurator.
	The Council at Jerusalem.	
49	Paul's second missionary journey with Silas.	
51	Paul goes into Macedonia.	
52	Paul arrives at Corinth.	Felix, Procurator.
	Writing of Epistle to the Thessalonians.	
53	Gallio Proconsul of Achaia.	
	Paul leaves Corinth and sails to Ephesus.	
	Paul goes to Jerusalem to Feast of Tabernacles.	
54	Return of Paul to Antioch.	Death of Claudius. Accession of Nero.
	Paul starts on his third missionary journey.	
54–57	Residence and preaching of Paul at Ephesus.	
57	Writing of First Epistle to the Corinthians.	
	The riot at Ephesus.	
	Paul leaves Ephesus for Troas.	
	Arrival of Paul in Macedonia.	
	Writing of Second Epistle to the Corinthians.	
	Paul abides three months in Corinth.	
58	Writing of Epistle to the Galatians.	
	Writing of Epistle to the Romans.	
	Paul leaves Corinth for Jerusalem.	
	Paul is arrested in the Temple.	
	Paul is sent to Cæsarea for trial before Felix.	Nero murders Agrippina.
59	Paul is given an interview by Felix.	Recall of Felix.
60	Paul appears before Festus and Agrippa.	Porcius Festus, Procurator.
	Paul makes his appeal to Cæsar.	
	Paul sets sail for Rome.	
	Paul is shipwrecked at Malta.	
61	Paul reaches Rome and lives in his own house.	
62	Writing of Epistles to the Philippians, the Colossians,	Earthquake at Pompeii
	Philemon and the Ephesians.	
	Trial and acquittal of Paul.	Albinus, Procurator.
	Writing of Epistle to the Hebrews.	
	Paul goes to Asia by way of Macedonia.	
64	Paul goes to Crete with Titus, and returns to Ephesus.	Burning of Rome.
	Paul goes by way of Philippi to Corinth.	Gessius Florus, Procurator.
	Writing of First Epistle to Timothy.	
	Writing of Epistle to Titus.	
	Paul passes the winter at Nicapolis.	
65	Paul journeys through Macedonia to Troas.	
	Paul is arrested and sent to Rome.	
66	Paul is tried before the Emperor.	Jewish war begins.
	Writing of Second Epistle to Timothy.	Massacre at Jerusalem.
	Martyrdom of St. Paul.	Repulse of Cestius Gallus.

MISSIONARY JOURNEYS OF ST. PAUL

AND

HIS VOYAGE TO ROME.

FIRST MISSIONARY JOURNEY.

ANTIOCH. Antioch, on the Orontes, was capital of the Roman province of Syria. A mixed body of Jewish and Greek converts formed an early Christian congregation there, which attracted the attention of the church in Jerusalem. It sent Barnabas to Antioch to encourage the congregation. Barnabas went to Tarsus to seek Paul as a helper, whom he knew by experience in Jerusalem as a man with special qualification for missionary work in Gentile fields. They returned to Antioch together (A. D. 43), and that city soon became a center of interest and progress in the church, the brethren being first called Christians there. At Antioch the Holy Ghost said: "Separate me Barnabas and Saul for the work whereunto I have called them. And when they had fasted and prayed, and laid their hands on them, they sent them away." Acts, 13 : 1-5. Thus called, and in company with John Mark, they started (A. D. 45) down the valley of the Orontes to

SELEUCIA, the port of Antioch. Here they took ship and embarked for

CYPRUS, landing on the east side of the island at Salamis, then a flourishing city with a large Jewish population. At

SALAMIS they preached in the synagogue, and then made a missionary tour of the island, finally arriving at

PAPHOS. This was the capital city and residence of the Proconsul, Sergius Paulus. Here also resided one Elymas, skilled in lore and magic, who tried to refute the doctrine of the missionaries and was struck blind. Sergius was converted. Acts 13 : 11, 12. Saul (now Paul) and his companions set sail from Paphos to the southern shores of Asia, and, probably landing at Attalia, went to

PERGA, a coast town of the province of Pamphylia. Here John Mark left his companions and returned to Jerusalem, Acts 13 : 37-39. After leaving Perga they crossed the Taurus range and arrived at

ANTIOCH IN PISIDIA, situated on the Anthius. It was a strong Roman colony and bulwark, with a large Jewish population, and a center of commerce between Ephesus and the East. Here, on the first Sabbath after their arrival, Paul preached his first recorded sermon to Jews, Acts 13 : 16-41. On the next Sabbath he preached to Gentiles, Acts 13 : 46-48. He incurred the hostility of the Jews, who could not understand how he could preach the same gospel to Jew and Gentile. They raised a persecution against the apostles, who were expelled by the rulers of the city. Crossing the hills to

ICONIUM, a trading city on the commercial highway between Ephesus and the East, they preached in the synagogue for a time, making many converts, Acts 14 : 3. But here, as at Antioch in Pisidia, they found a divided multitude, which rose up against them and threatened to stone them. They fled into Lycaonia, crossed the plain and the ridge which separates the Phrygian from the Lycaonian region of Galatia, and arrived at

LYSTRA, a small town peopled by very superstitious inhabitants. Here Paul healed a cripple, and the people at once said the gods had come among them. They called Paul Mercury, and Barnabas Jupiter, and the apostles had to intercede with priests and people to prevent them from worshiping them. Shortly afterwards a mob, influenced by Jews from Antioch and Iconium, stoned Paul and dragged him out of the city, leaving him for dead, Acts 14 : 19. But he recovered and fled with his companion over the plain, a distance of twenty-seven miles, to

DERBE, a small town on the edge of the Roman province, away from the highway, and near a pass called the "Cilician Gates." Here they rested for a time, preaching the word and teaching many, Acts 14 : 21. Thence they returned through Lystra, Iconium and Antioch, evidently not preaching much, but giving their attention to the organization of new churches and the appointment of elders for the same, in whose charge they left them. They then recrossed the mountains to Perga, where they preached again. Proceeding thence, about sixteen miles westward, they reached the harbor of

ATTALIA, where they took ship and sailed away for

ANTIOCH, the Syrian capital, from which they started. Here they made a report of their work to a full assembly of the church, and abode there "no little time with the disciples," Acts 14 : 27, 28 (R. V.)

COUNCIL AT JERUSALEM. Soon after the return of Paul and Barnabas to Antioch a dispute arose among the brethren over the free admission of Gentiles to the church without subscribing to the Jewish laws and customs. Peter was a visitor there and ate with Gentiles, but he wavered when he heard certain teachers sent out by James advocating that circumcision was necessary to salvation. Acts 15 : 24; Gal. 2 : 12. Paul and Barnabas adhered to the doctrine that circumcision was not necessary to salvation. To relieve the strained situation at Antioch, the church there sent Paul and Barnabas as delegates to Jerusalem to consult with the elders and apostles respecting the vexed question. On their journey thither they passed through Phœnicia and Samaria, advocating, as opportunity occurred, their doctrine of free acceptance of Gentile converts. On arriving in Jerusalem a general meeting of the church was convened, before which Paul and Barnabas laid an account of their work and the cause and object of their mission. The disputed question was referred to a special Council, which finally decided that Gentile converts need not subscribe to the Jewish law of circumcision, provided they abstained from idolatry, fornication, strangled flesh and blood. This decision was promulgated in writing to the churches in Antioch, Syria and Cilicia. Judas Barnabas and Silas were sent to Antioch to explain and confirm it in person. After seeing that the decision was generally received as satisfactory, Judas went back to Jerusalem and Silas stayed in Antioch. The date of the Council at Jerusalem is fixed by some chronologists as A. D. 48, or three years after Paul started on his first missionary journey. Other chronologists fix the date of Paul's first journey at A. D. 48, and that of the Council at A. D. 50.

PAUL'S SECOND MISSIONARY JOURNEY.

ANTIOCH. In or about the year A. D. 49 (some say A. D. 51) Paul suggested to Barnabas at Antioch that they should revisit the brethren in the churches they had founded, Acts 15 : 36. Barnabas assented, but wished to take John Mark along. Paul objected, because Mark had deserted them in Pamphylia. Thereupon Barnabas and Mark set sail for Cyprus, while Paul took Silas (Silvanus) and began a journey by land, Acts 15 : 37–41. Their mission was to preach, teach, convert, reconfirm, and organize new churches, but they had a special object in acquainting all their hearers with the decision and decree of the Council at Jerusalem, which was a vindication of the doctrine of Paul and Barnabas respecting the free admission of Gentiles into the Christian communion. In their passage through Syria they did not read and explain the decree of the Council, because that work was attended to from the capital, Antioch. Neither did they read it in passing through Cilicia, because it was part of the province of Syria. Crossing the Taurus ranges, they came to

DERBE and **LYSTRA**, in Lycaonia. At the latter place Paul found a disciple and a probably previous convert, named Timothy, son of a Greek father and Jewish mother, whom he circumcised in order to satisfy Jewish prejudices, and took along with him as companion, Acts 16 : 1; 2 Tim. 1 : 5. Passing through

PHRYGIA and **GALATIA**, Acts 16 : 6, visiting churches and delivering the decree of the Jerusalem Council, they crossed the frontier of the province and entered Asia. Forbidden by the Holy Spirit to preach in Asia, they turned northward, intending to enter the province of Bithynia. But when they came to a point on their way opposite to

MYSIA, Acts 16 : 7 (R. V.), the Holy Spirit suffered them not to go on into Bithynia. They, therefore, passed westward through Mysia, not preaching in the province, and came to

ALEXANDRIA TROAS. This was an important port town and a Roman colony, upon the Ægean Sea. Here Paul first met Luke, "the beloved physician," and here he witnessed the vision of a man calling him to come over into Macedonia, Acts 16 : 9. Taking Luke along, they sailed for Macedonia, touching at

SAMOTHRACIA, a lofty island in the Ægean, at one of whose anchorages they spent a night. On the next day they sailed past Thasos and reached

NEAPOLIS, the seaport of Thrace, and now the port and town of Kavalla. Thence they proceeded across the Pharsalian plain to

PHILIPPI, which was a Roman colony of Macedonia, Acts 16 : 11, 12. Here, on the Sabbath, they preached by the river side, outside of the city, Acts 16 : 13. One Lydia, of Thyatira, a seller of purple, was here converted and baptized. Paul cast the divining spirit out of a slave girl whose owners, seeing their gains cut off, caught Paul and Silas and drew them into the market-place before the magistrates. The charge brought against them was that they were Jews teaching customs not lawful for Romans to receive and observe. Being condemned without hearing, the magistrates tore off their clothes and ordered them to be scourged and thrown into prison. During the night they were miraculously delivered, and the jailor and his household were converted and baptized, Acts 16 : 14–40. After staying awhile at Lydia's house, Paul and Silas and Timothy (Luke seems to have been left behind) journeyed to

AMPHIPOLIS, a small city of Macedonia, thirty-three miles southwest of Philippi, and three miles from the seacoast. Passing through this and Apollonia they came to

THESSALONICA. This city, still known as Salonika, was the metropolis of Macedonia. There was a synagogue there, and Paul remained some time preaching and teaching. He made many converts, male and female, among the Grecian inhabitants, and worked for his own living, receiving only urgent supplies from the brethren in Philippi. Acts 17 : 1–4; Phil. 4 : 15, 16. Paul's success here roused the unbelieving Jews and the rabble and precipitated a riot, during which the house of Jason, where Paul lodged, was assaulted. Jason and some of the brethren were dragged before the rulers (politarchs) on the charge of treason against the Emperor, and were put under bonds to keep the peace. The brethren sent Paul and Silas away by night, Acts 17 : 5–10, to

BEREA, a city of Macedonia, on the eastern slope of the Olympian range. Here Paul preached successfully to both Greeks and Jews. But when the Jews of Thessalonica heard of his success they came and stirred up the people, and compelled the brethren to send Paul away to the seacoast, supposedly to Dium. Silas and Timothy remained. Acts 17 : 10–14. Paul's escort from Berea brought him by sea to

ATHENS, then a free Roman city of Achaia. After a little time Silas and Timothy joined him here. At Athens Paul preached in the synagogue, reasoned much with the Jews, and was brought by the philosophers before the Areopagus council to be heard. When he came to speak of the resurrection he was interrupted and mocked, and he departed from among them, Acts 17 : 22–33. He next went to

CORINTH, capital of the Roman province of Achaia, and emporium of a rich commerce between the East and West. Here Paul lodged with Aquila, and wrought with him at the trade of tent-making, and here Silas and Timothy, who had been sent from Athens back to Macedonia, rejoined him. Paul resided at Corinth for a year and a half, preaching vigorously in the synagogue, making many notable converts, and writing his Epistles to the Thessalonians. Incurring the hostility of the Jews, they brought Paul before the Proconsul, Gallio, on the charge that he was persuading men to worship God contrary to the law. Gallio refused to hear the accusers on a question of words and names and their law, and drove them from the judgment seat. After this, Paul sailed with Aquila and Priscilla from

CENCHREA, which is the eastern port of Corinth, to

EPHESUS. He was now on his return journey, and his ship did but little more than touch at Ephesus. However, Paul preached in the synagogue there, and, leaving his traveling companions, sailed on to

CÆSAREA, the political capital of Palestine, on the shores of the Mediterranean. Thence he journeyed overland to

JERUSALEM, where he saluted the church, and probably joined in the Passover ceremonies, which fell on March 22d, A. D. 53. On leaving Jerusalem he went to

ANTIOCH, where he remained for some time, Acts 18 : 23. Some authors say that during this residence at Antioch Paul wrote the Epistle to the Galatians, but others place the date at four years later, or A. D. 58.

PAUL'S THIRD MISSIONARY JOURNEY.

ANTIOCH. After a sojourn of some length at Antioch, Paul, accompanied by Timothy and, probably, Titus, began his third missionary journey by visiting the churches of

GALATIA and **PHRYGIA**. No details of this visit are given, but the inference from 1 Cor. 16 : 1, 2 is that he exhorted the brethren to contribute to the wants of the poorer brethren in Judea. Leaving these regions, he went to

EPHESUS, the seat of government of Roman Asia, and remarkable for its wealth, beauty of architecture, learning, idolatries and superstitions. Here Paul re-baptized twelve men who had been baptized only unto John's baptism, Acts 19: 2-7. He then went into the synagogue and preached regularly for three months, after which he taught for two years in the school of one Tyrannus, refuting the many errors of idolatry, sorcery and paganism. It was probably during this period that churches were established at Collossæ, Laodicea, Pergamos and other places by Timothy and his helpers. Paul wrought many miracles at Ephesus, and his preaching so interfered with the trade of the image-makers that one Demetrius, who was at the head of his craft, called the tradesmen together in angry council. They rushed over into the theatre, where Alexander, the coppersmith, was called upon to harangue the crowd; but when it was found that he was a Jew his voice was drowned by shouts of "Great is Diana of the Ephesians." The town clerk succeeded in appeasing and dismissing the mob, though not until Paul had passed through great danger, Acts 19: 23-41; 2 Cor. 1: 8. In the end Paul was compelled to leave Ephesus after a stay of at least two years and three months, during which time he wrote his Epistle to the Corinthians. On leaving Ephesus he sailed along the coast to

TROAS, where he expected to meet Titus, but was disappointed, 2 Cor. 2: 12, 13. Being anxious to learn of the effect of his letter to the Corinthians, he hastened onward to Macedonia and to

PHILIPPI, where he met Titus, and was greatly relieved to find that the state of the church in Corinth was excellent, 2 Cor. 7: 4-13. He spent some time in Macedonia, during which he wrote his Second Epistle to the Corinthians, probably at Philippi, and made a short tour into Illyricum, on the eastern shore of the Adriatic, north of Macedonia, Rom. 15: 19. On the approach of the winter (perhaps that of A. D. 57) he went down to Achaia, and took up his abode at

CORINTH, where he spent three months, and where he was met by Luke. During his stay there he wrote his Epistles to the Galatians and Romans. His intention was to sail thence to Jerusalem with the offerings to the poor, but it was frustrated by the discovery of a plot to kill him, and by the need of a hasty escape overland through Macedonia to

PHILIPPI. At Philippi Paul sent most of his traveling companions in advance to Troas, while he remained behind with Luke to keep the Feast of the Passover, Acts 20: 6. Then they set sail, and in five days arrived at

TROAS, where they joined their companions. On the last Sabbath of their stay here, and while Paul was preaching at midnight in an upper room, one Eutychus fell from a window and was taken up dead. Paul miraculously restored him to life, and returned to the room and to the breaking of bread till daybreak, Acts 20: 6-12. Paul then left Troas on foot for

ASSOS, a seaport of Mysia, opposite Lesbos, whither his companions had preceded him by sea. Here they all took ship, and on the first day reached

MITYLENE, the chief town of the island of Lesbos. The next day they anchored off Chios, Acts 20: 15, and the day following put in at

TROGYLLIUM, a promontory on the main land opposite the island of Samos. The next day they touched at

MILETUS, the ancient capital of Ionia. Here he called together the Ephesian elders, and delivered to them a solemn parting address, Acts 20: 18-35. Sailing thence, they passed Coos and Rhodes, and reached

PATARA, a seaport of Lycia. Here they changed vessels, and took passage on one sailing direct to Syria. They then sailed past Cyprus and reached

TYRE, the famous seaport of Phœnicia. There the ship was bound to unload cargo, and Paul went ashore and spent seven days with the Christians of Tyre, Acts 21: 3, 4. After ex-changing prayerful farewells on the seashore, the voyage was continued to

PTOLEMAIS, now called Acre. Here the voyage came to an end, and after remaining one day they set out on foot for

CÆSAREA, to find shelter and rest in the house of Philip the Evangelist, Acts 21: 8. Here they tarried many days, and were visited by Agabus, a Judean prophet, who bound his feet and hands in Paul's girdle, and prophesied his imprisonment in Jerusalem, if he dared to go there, Acts 21: 10-14. Whereupon they all implored Paul not to go, but in vain. Accompanied by certain disciples of Cæsarea, and by one Mnason, of Cyprus, an old disciple with whom they were to lodge, they set out overland for

JERUSALEM. Here they were welcomed by the brethren, on their arrival, and on the next day were formally received by a full assembly of apostles and elders. Paul delivered an address, in which he recounted his missionary efforts since his last visit to Jerusalem. The address was well received by all but the Judaizing sect in the church. These advised him to prove his observance of the Jewish law by taking charge of four Jewish Christians, who were under a vow, by purifying himself with them in the Temple, and by paying their expenses, Acts 21: 20-25. This Paul undertook to do, but before the necessary seven days were ended the Asiatic Jews stirred up the mob against him, and he would have been torn to pieces but for the timely arrival of a body of soldiers under their captain, Claudius Lysias, who extricated him and eventually sent him to Cæsarea to Felix, the Governor. Acts 21: 27-40; 22, 23.

PAUL'S VOYAGE TO ROME AND SUBSEQUENT MISSIONARY WORK.

CÆSAREA. When Felix learned that Paul was a Cilician he ordered him to be kept in Herod's judgment hall. In a few days Ananias, the high priest, with some members of the Sanhedrim and Tertullus, a lawyer, came down to Cæsarea to charge Paul with being a leader of the Nazarenes and a profaner of the Temple. Paul defended himself, and Felix postponed judgment till he could send for the captain, Claudius Lysias, and hear the whole matter of the mob, the rescue and the arrest in Jerusalem from his own lips. Meanwhile, Felix had interviews with Paul of such a serious nature as to make the cruel Governor tremble. He delayed trial of Paul, and hoped to get a ransom for his release. Thus two years passed, when Felix was succeeded by Porcius Festus as Procurator.

On the accession of Festus, the Jews besought him to bring Paul to Jerusalem for trial, intending to kill him on the way. Festus said he would hear the case at Cæsarea, and went down there. Paul claimed the rights of a Roman citizen, refused to be heard before Festus, and made his appeal directly to Rome and the Emperor. Just after this Herod Agrippa II., King of Chalcis, arrived, and Festus consulted with him about Paul's case. They agreed that his appeal to Rome must be respected, and they sent Paul to Rome, at the first opportunity, in company with other prisoners, Acts 26; 27: 1. He embarked at Cæsarea in a ship of Adramytium. The prisoners were in charge of Julius, a Roman centurion. The ship first touched at

SIDON, where Paul was permitted to go on shore and see his friends. They then sailed under the lee (along the north side) of

CYPRUS, and then across the sea which is over (off) Cilicia and Pamphylia to

MYRA, then a flourishing seaport of Lycia. Here they took one of the large ships which carried corn from Alexandria to Rome, and after sailing slowly for many days, owing to adverse winds, they came over against

CNIDUS, a promontory of Caria, at the extreme southwest of Asia Minor. Here the wind checked their direct course, and they were driven southward to

SALMONE, the eastern promontory of the island of Crete. Rounding it, they worked their way slowly along under shelter of the southern coast of the island to the roadstead of

FAIR HAVENS, about five miles east of the town of Lasæa. Here Paul advised them to winter, but the harbor being incommodious, an effort was made to reach

PHŒNIX (R. V.), PHENICE (A. V.), another harbor of Crete, looking to the southwest and northwest, Acts 27:1-13. But when the ship rounded Cape Matala it was caught by the stormy northeast wind called Euroclydon, Acts 27:14, (Euraquilo, R. V.,) beating down from the Cretan mountains, and was driven under the lee of

CLAUDA (A. V.), CAUDA (R. V.), an island southwest of Crete. It was with great difficulty that they rescued the ship's boats, and the ship itself had to be stayed with ropes about its frame, Acts 27:16, 17. Fearing they should be driven into the

SYRTIS, or "great quicksands" north of Lybia, they lowered the gear and drifted slowly before the wind through

ADRIA, or the sea lying between Malta, Italy, Greece and Crete. On the first day they lightened ship by throwing the freight overboard, and on the next crew and passengers joined in ridding the ship of its spare gear. Then they drifted in despair, but for the promises of Paul that the ship would eventually be saved, until the fourteenth day at midnight, when the sound of breakers was heard. Four anchors were thrown out of the stern, and daylight was anxiously awaited. The ship was then further lightened of cargo and run aground on a creek, where two seas met, of the island of

MALTA, MELITA. The passengers escaped safely to land, and were treated kindly by the inhabitants. Paul, while placing a stick on a fire, was bitten by a viper. The venom had no effect on him, whereupon the inhabitants regarded him as a god. He requited the kindness of Publius, the chief man, by curing his father of a fever, and he healed many of diseases. After a three months' stay at Malta they sailed for Rome in a ship called The Twin Brothers (Castor and Pollux), and soon reached

SYRACUSE, the chief port and city of Sicily. Here they stayed for three days, and from thence shaped a course toward the straits of Messina. But the wind being adverse, they were compelled, after making a circuit, Acts 28:13, to put into

REGIUM, at the extreme southwest of Italy, where they remained one day. Next day they reached

PUTEOLI, on the northern shore of the Bay of Naples, and at that time the harbor for the corn fleets of Alexandria. Here Paul rested seven days with the Christian brethren he found. The journey was now overland and by the celebrated Appian Way to

APPII FORUM, which was about forty-three miles south of Rome, Here a company of brethren met Paul, whom, when he saw, "he thanked God and took courage," Acts 28:15. Ten miles further on they came to

THE THREE TAVERNS, where another company of brethren greeted him. Then they went on to

ROME, where the centurion delivered his prisoners to the chief of the guard. Paul was allowed to live in his own hired house, in company with a soldier who guarded him. He remained in Rome for two years, preaching the kingdom of God, and teaching the things concerning the Lord Jesus Christ with all confidence, Acts 28:31, and writing his Epistles to Philemon, Colossians and Ephesians. Near the end of A. D. 61 he was tried and acquitted.

After his acquittal, his career, for a time, is not distinct, but he probably passed through Macedonia to Philippi, Phil. 2:24, and then through Troas to Ephesus. From the latter place he may have visited the churches of Colossæ, Laodicea and Pergamum, Phile. 22. Some say he may even have gone to Spain, and then returned to Macedonia, where he wrote the First Epistle to Timothy, 1 Tim. 1:3, to whom he had committed the care of the Ephesian church. Coming back to Ephesus, he wrote the Epistle to Titus, in which, Tit. 3:12, he said he intended to winter in

NICOPOLIS. Whether he wintered at Nicopolis is not certainly known, but he went from Ephesus to Miletus, where Trophimus took sick, and thence to Corinth, where Erastus remained. 2 Tim. 4:20. He was placed under arrest a second time and carried to

ROME. This time he was treated more harshly than before, 2 Tim. 1:8; 2:9. During his imprisonment, and when deserted by all his companions except Luke, he wrote his last and most pathetic Epistle to Timothy, in which he gave up hope of acquittal and recognized that "the time of my departure is come." According to the traditions, he suffered martyrdom in the reign of Nero by being beheaded with the sword. The date, according to some authorities, was A. D. 66, and according to others A. D. 68.

HISTORICAL ILLUSTRATIONS

OF

BIBLE TEXT,

DERIVED FROM

ANCIENT COINS AND GEMS

OF THE PERIOD OF TIME FROM

Alexander the Great to the Destruction of Jerusalem,

336 B. C. to 70 A. D.,

INCLUDING GREEK, ROMAN, AND HEBREW MONEY, DRAWN FROM THE ORIGINAL
ANCIENT COINS IN THE BRITISH MUSEUM, LONDON; IN COLLECTIONS IN PARIS,
AMSTERDAM, BRUSSELS, BERLIN, ROME, AND IN THE UNITED STATES.

BY A. L. RAWSON, LL.D.

COINS OF ALEXANDER AND HIS SUCCESSORS.

Before the time of Alexander the Great of Macedonia there were no portraits on coins, except of Gelon and Hiero at Syracuse in Sicily (108). Philip, the father of Alexander, left no portrait, his coins bearing a head of Zeus (Jupiter) or Hercules. The local deity of the country was honored on the coins of each—as Minerva at Athens (84), Arethusa at Syracuse (107), the Minotaur in Crete (142), Apollo and Diana in

No. 1.—ALEXANDER (336–323 B. C.).

many cities, and nearly every other divinity, hero or heroine, or deified ruler, including also animal forms and mythical figures, mentioned in the ancient classics.

The Greeks were the earliest people to make

No. 2.—SELEUCUS I. (312–280 B. C.).

and use coins with an image stamped on them, and also to make them depositories of portraits and figures of persons and objects which have

become of great value to the historical student, adding much to our knowledge of antiquity.

No. 3.—ANTIOCHUS I. SOTER (280–261 B. C.).

The kingdom of Alexander was too vast to hold together under any other ruler, and his generals assumed royalty after his death, and each seized a portion. Seleucus, who had been made satrap of Babylonia, founded the Syrian monarchy; Ptolemy (see DICTIONARY, p. 253), a half-brother of Alexander, founded the dynasty of Greek Ptolemies in Egypt; Lysimachus obtained Thrace;

No. 4.—ANTIOCHUS II. THEOS.

Antipater and Craterus jointly had Macedonia and Greece. Antiochus I. was son and successor of Seleucus I., and was honored with the title Soter (savior) for his military successes. Antiochus II., his son, was called in flattery Theos (god), and was the first of the name mentioned in the Bible. (See DICTIONARY, p. 18.) The first Seleucus mentioned was the Fourth, who was called Patriot (philopator), although he is said to have greatly increased the already heavy taxes.

No. 5.—ANTIOCHUS III., THE GREAT (222–187 B. C.).

(Ptolemy IV., in Dict., p. 254.)

The third Antiochus earned the title the Great for his military genius, although defeated by the Roman general Glabrio at Thermopylæ in Greece,

No. 6.—SELEUCUS IV.

and again by Scipio at Magnesia in Asia Minor, when he lost a great territory and paid fifteen millions to the Romans for the expenses of the war. (See his coin in DICTIONARY, p. 168.)

The custom of the Seleucid kings of Syria was to adopt the names Seleucus or Anti-

No. 7.—ANTIOCHUS V. EUPATOR (164–162 B. C.).

ochus alternately in succession; so the son and successor of Antiochus the Great was called Seleucus IV., and his brother, who succeeded him, was Antiochus IV. Epiphanes (see his coin in DICTIONARY, p. 18); and the student will find

No. 8.—DEMETRIUS I. AND LAODICE (162–150 B. C.).

(A. Balas, Dict., p. 13

many incidents of the history of these kings in the Apocrypha, in Maccabees, and in Josephus.

The likeness of Antiochus V. is here, and of the Sixth in the Dictionary, p. 449, Demetrius I., son of Seleucus IV., was educated in Rome, and succeeded Antiochus IV., whom he deposed; he was killed in battle against Alexander I. Balas (Baal, Lord; see coin in DICTIONARY, p. 13), who claimed to be a son of Antiochus IV., and who succeeded to the hrone. This Cleopatra was the

No. 9.—ALEXANDER BALAS AND CLEOPATRA (144 B. C.).

third of the name among the Greek kings in Syria, was very talented, the wife of three successive kings of Syria, and mother of two others. (See coin 15.)

Mithridates VI. was the last of a line of kings of Pontus, said to have had a Persian origin,

No. 10.—MITHRIDATES VI. (135–63 B. C.).

about 337 B. C. He was the most powerful enemy the Romans had to contend with next to Hannibal, as estimated by Cicero. He was father-in-law to Tigranes.

Demetrius II., son of Demetrius I. (No. 8), was taken prisoner by Mithridates VI., and held nearly nine years, who gave him his daughter for a wife, during which time his brother, Antiochus

No. 11.—DEMETRIUS II. NIKATOR (146–125 B. C.).

VII., held the throne of Syria, and espoused Cleopatra, wife of Demetrius, but was deposed on his return. He is mentioned in Maccabees (1 Macc. x., xi., xii., xiv.) and in Josephus (Ant. xiii. 9, 3) as a friend to the Jews, reducing their tribute. He wore a beard after the Parthian fashion, while nearly every other Syrian king in that age shaved, as appears on their coins. Nearly all of ese kings were occupied in wars and intrigues to the exclusion of any measures for the improvement of the condition of their people.

Tryphon was a usurper named Diodotus, from near Apamea, and was an officer of the court of Alexander Balas, who pretended a friendship for

NO. 12.—TRYPHON (142–139 B. C.).

the young king Antiochus VI., son of Alexander, and who usurped the throne after killing him. He put his name on the coins of the young king, as seen in the DICTIONARY, p. 19. (See 1 Macc. xi., xiii., etc.)

Antiochus VII. expelled Tryphon and took his brother's wife. He made concessions to Simon, "high priest and prince of the Jews" (1 Macc. xv.; Jos. Ant. xiii. 7, 3). He after-

NO. 13.—ANTIOCHUS VII. SIDETES (138–129 B. C.).

ward besieged Jerusalem, but made honorable terms with John Hyrcanus (133 B. C.), who accompanied him against the Parthians, where he was killed. This coin was struck at Tarsus. The shrine on the reverse of this coin contained a figure of the Greek goddess Hera (Juno in Rome) standing on a lion, holding in the left hand two palm-branches; the right hand extended, holding a staff or sceptre. She was called "Queen of heaven" in Jeremiah (vii. 18; xliv. 17; etc.). On each side of the lion is a vase or cup for the drink-offerings mentioned by Diodorus; a star over her head refers to the planet which was sacred to her. She was called the "Goddess of Syria," and had a great statue in her honor at Hierapolis (Dan. xi. 38). Called also Astarte, Ashtaroth, Mylitta, and Alitta.

NO. 14.—ALEXANDER II. ZEBINA (128–123 B. C.).

Alexander II. was a purchased slave (zebina) and a pretender to the throne, favored by Ptol-

emy Physcon of Egypt for his own purposes, but was deposed by him after six years for refusing to pay tribute. He imitated the coins of Balas, putting a head of Zeus, or of Dionysus, instead of his own, and on the reverse Pallas, or an elephant, horn of plenty, tripod, eagle, anchor, etc.

The coin of Cleopatra and Antiochus VIII. presents the heads of mother and son. She is entitled "goddess" on the reverse (THEAS). See

NO. 15.—CLEOPATRA AND ANTIOCHUS VIII. (125–121 B. C.).

coin 9 for an earlier portrait of Cleopatra. This king does not appear in Scripture, but was an active man—sometimes called Illustrious (epiphanes), and also Grypus (hook-nose). He was a man of energetic character.

Antiochus IX. was named Cyzicenus from the city where he was educated (by Craterus), and his coins add the title Patriot (philopatoros). He was a son of Antiochus VII. (13), and born while Demetrius was a prisoner among the Parthians; his mother was a Cleopatra. He shared the kingdom with his brother, Grypus (15), having Cœle-Syria and Palestine, with his residence at Damascus. His wife had been repudiated by Ptolemy

NO. 16.—ANTIOCHUS IX. (116–95 B. C.).

Lathyrus of Egypt, and brought him an army as a dowry. She was killed by order of her sister, Tryphena, at the altar of a sanctuary in Antioch. Besides his own head, he put on the coins those of Hercules, Zeus, Eros, Pallas and Apollo, Tyche, Dionysus, and Artemis, besides the anchor and various emblematic figures. This coin was struck at Sidon.

Demetrius III. Philopator (patriot) was a son of Antiochus Grypus (15). He was also flattered on his coins with the titles "savior," "god," and "thunderer." On the reverse is a figure of Demeter, called Ceres by the Romans.

Tigranes (See Coin No. 10) was son-in-law to Mithridates VI. (10), and after some extensive conquests assumed the title "King of kings" in Armenia. In 83 B. C. he conquered Syria and founded Tigranocerta. After submitting to the Romans, he was kept by them on the throne of

Armenia until he died, 55 B. C. He made captive and tributary kings his house-servants.

NO. 17.—DEMETRIUS III. (95–88 B. C.).

Mark Antony, one of the famous Triumvirs (three men, Octavius Cæsar and Lepidus the other

NO. 18.—ANTONY AND CLEOPATRA. (30. B. C.).

two), was born 83 B. C. He was a successful cavalry officer in Egypt B. C. 53, was Cæsar's lieutenant in Gaul, chief of the army in Italy in Cæsar's absence, and consul in 44. After Cæsar's death, Asia and Egypt were allotted to Antony, and with the famous Cleopatra he indulged in luxury and repose, neglecting state affairs. He was defeated at Actium, when Octavius became sole emperor and augustus. Cleopatra, the last of the Greek dynasty in Egypt, was celebrated for her personal charms and various accomplish-

NO. 19.—ARSACES XII. (70–60 B. C.).

ments, which fill a large space in the history of that age. Born 69, died 30 B. C. She was in

NO. 20.—PHRAATES IV. (36 B. C.–4 A. D.).

Rome with Julius Cæsar until his death, 44 B. C., and with Antony in Egypt 41 B. C. A portrait

of her son by Cæsar is sculptured on the wall of a temple at Koom Ombos on the Nile.

Arsaces also assumed the title of "King of kings," and warred with the Romans after his father, Mithridates, died. His grandson, called Phraates IV., made a treaty with Augustus, under which he restored some Roman standards taken by the Parthians in former wars. (See No. 132.)

HEBREW MONEY.

Demetrius II. (No. 11), before his captivity in Parthia, granted the Jews the privilege of striking coins with their own devices and superscrip-

NO. 21.—SILVER SHEKEL, SIMON (139 B. C.).

tions, and during his absence his brother, Antiochus VII., confirmed the decree. The first coin was made by them 139 B. C. It is called the shekel, and was valued at sixty cents. The inscription is read "Shekel of Israel" around, and A for year 1 over a cup on one side, and on the other, "Jerusalem the Holy" around a triple lily. The half-shekel is on page 206 of the Dictionary, and the copper shekel on page 187. The next coins were by John Hyrcanus, son of Simon.

NO. 22.—JOHN HYRCANUS (135–106 B. C.).

He was with Antiochus in Parthia, conquered the Idumæans, destroyed Samaria, and built Arak el-Emir, east of Jordan. His coins were not called shekels, and the inscriptions and devices differed from the shekel. On this we read "Johanan the high priest and the Jews' Union" in an olive-wreath, and see two horns of plenty on the other side.

Judas Aristobulus struck coins only in bronze, with a similar inscription to that on his brother

NO. 23.—JUDAS ARISTOBULUS (106 B. C.).

John's, calling himself "high priest." He also assumed the title of "king," putting an end to the theocracy and establishing the monarchy (Jos. Ant. xiii. 11, 1) for one year.

Alexander Jannæus, his brother, succeeded, and reigned twenty-seven years, issuing many coins. Ptolemy Lathyrus, king of Cyprus, invaded Judæa, and was defeated by Jannæus, assisted by Cleopatra, queen of Egypt, mother of Lathyrus. His coins have for devices a rose, lily, palm, star, anchor, and horn of plenty. The inscriptions are in Hebrew and Greek let-

NO. 24.—ALEXANDER JANNÆUS (105-78 B. C.).

ters, and he first called himself "king" (of the Jews) on the coins.

Antigonus was king until Herod was placed

NO. 25.—ANTIGONUS (40-37 B. C.).

on the throne by the Romans, and he struck some curious coins.

With Herod the Great the monarchy became powerful, although under the Romans. All the bronze coins of Herod have Greek inscriptions, and no Hebrew, and for devices many symbols of temple-worship, etc., but no human figure or

NO. 26.—HEROD THE GREAT (37-4 B. C.).

(Mite, Dict., p. 558.)

portrait. We read on No. 26, "Of King Herod." The Macedonian helmet and shield on No. 27

NO. 27.—HEROD THE GREAT.

are said to indicate his descent from the Greek kings of that country.

Herod Archelaus, son of Herod, was made ethnarch and governor of Judæa, Samaria, and

NO. 28.—HEROD ARCHELAUS (4 B. C.-6 A. D.).

Idumæa, but after ten years' misrule Augustus banished him to Gaul. (See No. 59.)

Herod Philip II. was son of Herod and Cleopatra, and was made TETRARCH (governor of a

fourth part) of the Hauran, etc. (Luke iii. 1). He married Salome, daughter of Herod Philip I. and Herodias. He built Cæsarea Philippi (Paneas), and named Bethsaida Julias (Luke x. 10), where he was buried under a monument

NO. 29.—PHILIP.

built by himself. This coin is dated 33 A. D. (L A Z, year 37 of his reign).

Herod Agrippa I. was grandson of Herod I.,

NO. 30.—HEROD AGRIPPA I.

and was educated at Rome with Drusus and Claudius, who was afterward emperor. He was made king and successor to Philip, and afterward ruler of Judæa and Samaria. In earnest a Jew, he lived at Jerusalem, kept the laws, and improved the country by building or repairing public works and instituting games.

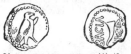

NO. 31.—HEROD OF CHALCIS (41-48 A. D.).

Herod of Chalcis was son of Aristobulus and Berenice, and brother of Agrippa. He was made king by Claudius (who at the same time gave Agrippa II. Judæa and Samaria), and resided at Chalcis in Cœle-Syria, and he was also given the appointment of the high priest, the superintendence of the temple, and regulation of the sacred treasury.

No. 32 is the only coin bearing a head of

NO. 32.—HEROD AGRIPPA II. (48-100 A. D.).

Agrippa II. or of any other of that family, and is dated 58 A. D. (See DICTIONARY, p. 129, for coins of Agrippa, with portrait of Titus.)

NO. 33.—CHALKOUS OF AGRIPPA.

The chalkous is supposed to have been the only money that the poor Jews were able to bring to the synagogue weekly in the year 73

A. D., as it is dated when the temple was in ruins.

Coponius was the first procurator of Judæa,

NO. 34.—COPONIUS (15 A. D.).

and was assigned to duty after Archelaus was banished, 6 A. D. He came with the prefect Quirinus (Cyrenius, No. 58). The procurator was the governor in Judæa, collector of revenue and general regulator of financial affairs, and in later times was supreme in both civil and military duties (Matt. xxvii.; Luke iii. 1; Acts xxii.; etc.). The second was Ambivius; the third, Marcus Rufus, in whose term the augustus died.

NO. 35.—VALERIUS GRATUS (16 A. D.).

Then Tiberius sent Valerius Gratus, who was eleven years in office, from 15 to 26 A. D., during whose term Joseph, called Caiaphas, was made high priest, who was also son-in-law of Annas. (John xviii. 13.)

Pontius Pilate succeeded Gratus, and the crucifixion of Jesus Christ is dated in the seventh

NO. 36.—PONTIUS PILATE (29 A. D.).

year of his term. He suspected a Samaritan impostor of plotting treason, and killed many people on Mount Gerizim, seized the sacred temple-treasure, built an aqueduct with it, and dedicated some Roman shields in the temple in honor of Tiberius.

Felix was a slave of Antonia, mother of Claudius, was advanced in the army and appointed to Judæa in 52 A. D. Tacitus says, "He wielded the sceptre of a monarch with the soul of a slave."

NO. 37.—FELIX, UNDER NERO (54–68 A. D.).

He married Drusilla, sister of Agrippa. His first wife was Drusilla, daughter of Juba; his third also a princess.

FIRST REVOLT OF THE JEWS.

The Jews were so oppressed by the Romans that they broke out into revolt several times, but were put down easily, except when, under Gessius Florus, they suffered unbearable tyranny. The first revolt began under the emperor Nero,

A. D 60, and one of the first war-measures was to issue money to pay soldiers and for the use

NO. 38.—ELÆAZAR (65 A. D.).

of the people, who detested the coins of the Romans as blasphemous and badges of servitude. The most capable leader was Eleazar, son of the high priest Ananias before whom Paul was tried. (Acts xxiii. 3.) His coins have the words "Eleazar the high priest" and "First year of the Re-

NO. 39.—ELEAZAR, BRONZE.
(Simon, Dict., p. 77.)

demption of Israel." The types he used were various, being vase, harp, treasury (for sacred books), fruit, palm tree, and others.

The only true shekels were those made by Simon the Maccabee (No. 21), all coins after his death having some other name, although writers usually call any piece of Hebrew money a shekel. The sizes of the various pieces were made to conform to those of the Greek and Roman standards. The stater (Nos. 9, 135, 140) was equal to sixty cents and Simon's shekel (No. 21); the double stater (Nos. 14, 10, 139, etc.) was equal to two shekels; the mite (Nos. 31, 33) of copper was about a quarter of a cent.

NO. 40.—SIMON, SON OF GAMALIEL.

Simon, son of Gamaliel, chief of the Sanhedrin, called "Nasi" (prince), struck coins after Eleazar's death, and also Ananus, son of Ananus. The Sanhedrin authorized bronze coins to be issued, with the legend "Year 2" around the vase, and "Deliverance of Zion" around the vine-leaf.

NO. 41.—SANHEDRIN.

On some coins the name Zion stands for Jerusalem. During the siege by Titus Cæsar (who was afterward the emperor Titus) the Jews used Greek or Roman coins to strike their own devices on, as appears on many coins of that time, as also on those of the second revolt. (Nos. 46, 47, 48.)

The Romans did not permit their provinces to strike coins of gold or silver; therefore, the only coins of Herod and his successors are in bronze. The tribute-money was of necessity a Roman coin, bearing the head of "Cæsar" or the emperor, and was valued at sixty cents, the sum required for two persons.

JERUSALEM CAPTURED.

The revolt was suppressed, and Jerusalem captured by the Romans under Titus, his father, Vespasian, being emperor. A great number was struck by the Romans to commemorate the event—by Vespasian, in gold, silver, and bronze, and also by Titus. One of Vespasian is shown on page 119 in the Dictionary. This bronze (42) coin of Titus is read, "The emperor Titus Cæsar

No. 42.—VESPASIAN (71 A. D.).
(See Dict., p. 119.)

Vespasian, Priest, Tribunal Power, Consul second time." On the reverse is a palm bearing dates, with a Roman soldier (Titus) armed, and a woman for Judæa weeping, seated on arms; S. C. for Decree of the Senate.

No. 43.—TITUS (73 A. D.).

No. 43 is described, "Titus standing, his right foot on the prow of a vessel, holding a 'Victory' and a spear; at his feet are two Jews in supplication, and near a palm." Dated 73 A. D. No. 44 is a coin in honor of a naval victory, and is supposed to refer to the one described by Josephus (Wars, iii. 9).

When the war began, Nero sent Vespasian with the army to Palestine, and he took his son, Titus, with him as his lieutenant; and when Nero died, A. D. 68, Vespasian became emperor, returned to Rome, and left Titus in command at Jerusalem. Vespasian was proclaimed emperor at Alexandria, Egypt, July 1, 69, and at Jerusalem, in the camp of Titus, July 3. Jerusalem was taken September 8, A. D. 70.

Titus was honored with the title of "emperor" (which was equal to commander-in-chief) on the fall of Jerusalem. He had served under his father in the siege and capture of the cities Tarichæa and Gamala, described by Josephus. In the triumphal procession of Vespasian at Rome, Titus was associated with his father and with his brother, Domitian; he was also nominated a cæsar—that is, an heir to the throne of Rome. A triumphal arch, the "Arch of Titus,"

No. 44.—TITUS.

was erected at Rome, and is still standing, bearing sculptures in memory of the trophies and victory over the Jews. It is the oldest arch of the kind in that city, and one of the most interesting monuments in the world. Besides the coins of Vespasian and Titus, those of Domitian bore devices recording the capture of Jerusalem. The Romans evidently regarded it as an important event, for they stamped it on their coins during twenty-six years.

THE SECOND REVOLT OF THE JEWS.

From the time of the first Cæsar, Julius, the Jews, when at peace, had a certain amount of

No. 45.—NERVA (115 A. D.).

liberty and many privileges. Some Jews had the Roman franchise at Ephesus and elsewhere, and Seneca said of them, "Though conquered, they gave laws to their conquerors." After the revolt which was put down by Titus, they paid tributes fixed by Vespasian, but under Nerva these were abolished, and coin No. 45 was struck to commemorate the event. But Jewish hatred

No. 46.—SIMON BARKOKAB.

to Rome could not so easily be quieted, and after a few years a second revolt broke out, in 115 A. D., in Cyrene, Egypt, Asia Minor, and Cyprus. In

117 A. D., Hadrian sent a colony of veteran soldiers to Jerusalem, and the revolt broke out there, aided by the cry, "The Messiah has come!" referring to the new leader, Simon Barkokab, called "Son of the Star" (Num. xxiv. 17–24), but the war did not begin until 131 A. D.

NO. 47.—SIMON BARKOKAB.

It was an ancient custom of the Syrian kings and Egyptian Ptolemies to honor a successful general or a patriotic king and general of the army with the title "SAVIOR"—in Greek, SOTER —as seen on coin No. 3; the first Ptolemy was a Soter, also the first Demetrius. The Romans honored their emperor or general with the title "Father of the Country" for similar services. The Hebrews were very jealous of permitting any human image on a coin, and therefore we read only the name of the high priest or other person in chief authority, and the pious sentence, "The Deliverance of Jerusalem," as on No. 47, and "The Deliverance of Zion" on others. These coins were issued at the mint under the authority of the Sanhedrin or senate, with a new device on the accession of each high priest, king, or ethnarch. The coin No. 48 is probably the last coined by the Jews as a people.

The leader Barkokab struck Hebrew devices over silver coins of Titus, as in this case, and over those of Trajan (No. 47) and of Domitian,

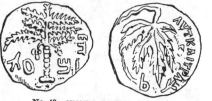

NO. 48.—SIMON BARKOKAB, BRONZE.

and of copper over various types, as in 48, where the letters on the margin show that the original coin was of Trajan.

The imperial coins struck at Jerusalem are preserved in great variety, and are of great value and interest. Hadrian rebuilt the city of Jeru-

NO. 49.—HADRIAN.

salem, and gave it the name of ÆLIA CAPITO-LINA, in honor of Jupiter of the Capitol at

Rome and of his own family, Ælius. This coin (49) is read, "Hadrian Augustus, Consul the third term, Father of the Country," around Ha-

NO. 50.—HADRIAN, COLONIAL COIN.

drian's bust; and on the reverse, "The advent of Augustus into Judæa:" a woman, as Judæa, standing with two children bearing palms, herself pouring incense on an altar: "By decree of the Senate." (See coin of Hadrian in DICTIONARY, p. 29.)   In No. 50 is shown a temple within which is a statue, probably of Jupiter, attended by two other divinities, perhaps Juno and Minerva. Coins were also struck by Antoninus Pius, Marcus Aurelius, Aurelius and Lu-

NO. 51.—AURELIUS AND VERUS.

cius Verus (51), by Julia Domna (which bears the title *Commodiana*, at the request of the em-

NO. 52.—JULIA DOMNA (173–217 A. D.).

peror Commodus), by Caracalla and Diadumenianus (on which a temple with a statue still ap-

NO. 53.—COIN OF DIADUMENIANUS (217 A. D.).

pears). The coin of Elagabalus records the ancient legend of the she-wolf suckling the twin-founders of Rome, Romulus and Remus. The series ended with Trajan, Ætruscus, and Hostilian. No other Roman coins of a later date struck at Jerusalem have been found. The next coinage of that city is of the Arabs, who made many varieties, No. 57 reading "Mohammed is the Apostle of God" in Cufic letters, and on the other side Palestine, on each side of the letter M, under a crescent. The coins and medals

NO. 54.—ELAGABALUS (218–222 A. D.).

on pages 153, 154, DICTIONARY, are of the crusaders after 1150 A. D.

Elagabalus was a Syrian, named Bassianus, but known by his title as priest of the sun-deity, which was worshiped at Emesa under that name. He was an Oriental in habits, tastes, and training, and had no sympathy for Roman laws, discipline, or its religion. His reign was cut short by the mob, his successor being Alexander Severus, his cousin.

NO. 55.—TRAJAN (249–251 A. D.).

Caius Messius Quintus Trajan Decius was urged to accept the throne of Rome much against his inclination. Under his rule the Goths first made their appearance in the empire as enemies. Decius entered the field against them, leaving Valerian in Rome to rule with the title of Censor. He was the first of all the Roman emperors to fall in battle with the enemy. The coins struck in Jerusalem with his head and titles were honorary, as it is not recorded that he ever visited the city. His wife, Herennia Ætruscilla, is honored on the coin with the title Augusta

NO. 56.—ÆTRUSCUS (249–251 A. D.).

gusta (the venerable), and with a fine bust-portrait, set in a crescent moon in reference to her purity of character. The figure on the other side of the coin is of the goddess Modesty, and is also in honor of the queen. These religious honors were decreed by the Senate, and have been the means of perpetuating the memory of the noble woman in the absence of other records.

The caliph Omar captured Jerusalem 637 A. D., and struck coins in honor of the event, one of a long series, during over 400 years, being given here. Their inscriptions are always in monogram, often artistically constructed. The soil in

and around the Holy City contains many buried treasures of coins, vast numbers of which are brought to light every year. The people in the villages of Palestine, in digging up old foundations or cellars for new houses, find deposits of ancient coins, mostly of bronze, a few silver, and only now and then gold. At Sidon three different deposits have been found of gold coins of

NO. 57.—ARABIAN.

Philip and Alexander the Great—in all over 20,000 pieces, of from $10 to $50 each in value.

NO. 58.—CYRENIUS, PREFECT OF SYRIA.

The coin of Cyrenius (Quirinus) recalls the mention of the census made for Cæsar Augustus in Luke (ii. 2), when "all the world" was taxed, about the time of the birth of Jesus. The portrait shows a character in accord with the accounts given by historians of the cruel and inhuman exactions of the tax-gatherers of that time. He was so detested that the Senate of Rome refused him the honors of a public funeral, although requested by the emperor Tiberius.

Herod Archelaus (59 and 28) was ruler in Palestine when, it is supposed, Paul was "at the foot of Gamaliel," Antipas governed Galilee and Peræa, and Philip (29) Trachonitis, Auranitis,

NO. 59.—ARCHELAUS.

and Batanæa. When Archelaus was banished, Judæa, etc. became a Roman province; Coponius was procurator when Cyrenius was prefect; he was succeeded by Ambivius, 10 A. D., and Annius Rufus, 13 A. D.; then Valerius Gratus, 14, and

NO. 60.—AMBIVIUS.

Pontius Pilate, 25; Marcellus, 35; Marullus, 37; and in 38 Agrippa I. was made governor of Judæa until 44; then Cuspius Fadus, Tiberius Alexander, 47, Felix, 52, and Festus, 60, Annas, 62, Albinus, 62; and the last one was Gessius Florus, in A. D. 65, who was the great cause of the first revolt.

The general policy of Augustus as to the government of Judæa was, as advised by Mæcenas, to continue the prefect in office three or five years. Augustus died 14 A. D., after a reign of fifty-seven years, at the age of seventy-seven, and was succeeded by his adopted son, Tiberius, son of his wife Livia, who was a less active and more luxurious ruler, and who adopted a new line of policy, which was to change the rulers of provinces as seldom as possible, so as to avoid plundering the people by new and hungry officials. In a reign of twenty-two years he changed the procurator of Judæa only once. The first procurator under Tiberius was Valerius Gratus, in whose time Joseph, also called Caiaphas, was made high

NO. 61.—ANNIUS RUFUS.

priest. After ruling eleven years he made way for Pontius Pilate, in the seventh year of whose rule (33 A. D., April 2d) the Gospel narrative makes Jesus of Nazareth appear before him for trial before crucifixion. Recent discoveries have enabled the student to follow the entire history of that age from one ruler to another, with nearly every detail supplied from antiquities.

Paul was a native of Tarsus, which was a metropolis, and had a famous idol-shrine (as shown here, and more distinctly on No. 13). These idol-shrines are scattered throughout Phœ-

NO. 62.—TARSUS.

nicia, and are now tumbling into ruins. Hera is standing on a lion, holding emblems in each hand, a conical object each side of the lion, and an eagle on the apex; garlands decorate the front and sides. The inscription is "(Money) of King Antiochus the Benefactor." Some of the coins of Tarsus have a figure of a woman as an emblem of the city, and of another for the river Cydnus, on which the famous Cleopatra made a magnificent display in entering the city. (See coin of Tarsus in DICTIONARY, p. 200.)

The coin of Antioch has an emblem of the river Orontes beneath the feet of a woman personifying the city, the inscription reading, "Of Antioch the Metropolis." This city was founded by Seleucus I., 300 B. C. (See DICTIONARY, p. 18.) The coinage includes many of the Greek kings and Roman governors of Syria. We have coins of the Roman governors—P. Q. Varus, dated B. C. 7–6, and Volusius Saturninus, prefect from

4–5 A. D.; and he was followed by Quirinus (Cyrenius; No. 58).

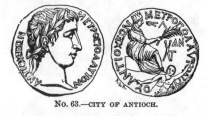

NO. 63.—CITY OF ANTIOCH.

The coin of Damascus is supposed to refer to the fountains or rivers that water its gardens in

NO. 64.—DAMASCUS.

the Greek word PEGAI. The device is an emblem of the city, a woman holding fruit and a horn of plenty, seated in a court surrounded by a market, a temple with a statue of a deity above, the sun and moon on either side. The head is of Julia Aquila Severa, wife of the emperor Elagabalus.

NO. 65.—ARETAS.

Aretas was the title of the rulers of the Nabatheans of Arabia, who built Petra and many other cities little known. There were several kings with this title, one of whom is here called "Bacchius the Jew," and on the other side of the coin is the name of a Roman general, Plautus. The head is an emblem of the city of Petra. (See No. 143.)

On coin 66 we read, "Tiberius Claudius Cæsar Augustus" around a grain-measure; and on the other side, "Elected Consul the second time, High Priest, Tribunal Power, Emperor," around S. C., for decreed by the Senate (of Rome); dated 41–42 A. D. This was once supposed to have been

NO. 66.—COIN OF CLAUDIUS.

struck to commemorate the great famine in Syria, relieved by Claudius.

Josephus says the great famine occurred under the procurators Fadus and Tiberius Alexander,

44 to 48 A. D. It was the custom of the Jews in all countries to send money to Jerusalem to relieve the distress of their brethren there. The custom is in full force now.

This Nicocles, king of Salamis, Cyprus, also on the coin "Of the Paphians," was son of Evagoras

No. 67.—NICOCLES, KING OF SALAMIS.

I., and ruled about 375 B. C. Isocrates, the orator of Athens, made a flattering eulogy on his life and deeds. The proconsul of Cyprus mentioned in Acts xiii. 7 was succeeded by the one named on the coin in the DICTIONARY, p. 55, whose inscription is "(Money) of the Cyprians,

No. 68.—PAPHOS IN CYPRUS.

(Cyprus, Dict., p. 55.)

under Cominius Proclus, Proconsul." The head is of the emperor Claudius. The coin of Paphos refers to a temple of Venus, now in ruins. The temple-ruins at Paphos have not yet been examined; but another temple to Venus—also called Aphrodite and Astarte—was exhumed at Golgos, near the centre of the island, when 1000 marble statues came to light, some colossal, others life-size, and many smaller. These are now in the Metropolitan Museum, New York. Pausanias says in his ancient history that Agapenor, a general of the Greeks under Agamemnon, returning after the close of the siege of Troy, was wrecked on the coast of Cyprus, landed, and built the town of Paphos and its temple to Venus, which was much later in time than the one at Golgos. The people of the island at that time are said to have numbered seven millions.

No. 69.—PERGA IN PAMPHYLIA.

Mark, the cousin of Barnabas, Paul's companion, left them at Perga, whose coin. shown

here, bears the image of the goddess Diana, a stag, and other religious emblems, with the inscription, "Of Diana of Perga." (See PERGA in the DICTIONARY.) Diana is named on this coin Artemis.

The coin of Iconium, shown here, is inscribed "Nero Cæsar Augustus" around a head of the young Nero; and on the reverse, "Poppæa Augusta of the Claud-Iconians," around a seated figure of Poppæa, wife of Nero. Iconium was

No. 70.—ICONIUM.

made a Roman colony by Claudius, and named Claudia. (See ICONIUM in the DICTIONARY.) Xenophon says it was a city in Phrygia, as in his history of the Expedition of Cyrus he says, "he came to Iconium, the last city of Phrygia," but Cicero, Strabo, and other ancients say it was in Pamphylia. It is a very ancient place, for Xenophon wrote about 360 B. C.

No. 71.—ATTALIA.

The coin of Attalia is of the emperor Commodus (180–192 A. D.), who required his subjects to salute him as Hercules the god. The place was originally called Corcyrus, and Attalus II. Philadelphus (see Nos. 127, 128), king of Pergamus, added a new town and built a wall around the whole, giving it his name.

The coin of Troas is of Alexander Severus, emperor of Rome, 222–237 A. D. The city was founded by Antigonus (No. 135), and named by him Antigonia, but enlarged by Lysimachus, who named it Antigonia Troas. It became a Roman

No. 72.—ALEXANDRIA TROAS.

colony under Augustus, and had many immunities and privileges. The port was artificial, with two basins, outer and inner, and it was an important commercial centre for many centuries. The antiquities found by Dr. Schliemann in his search for the Troy of Homer indicate great wealth and culture among the people in some early age. (See coin of Troas in DICTIONARY, p. 201.)

No. 73.—SAMOTHRACIA.

The island of Samothrace lies about halfway between Troas and Macedonia; it is eight miles long, six wide, and has lofty mountain-ranges, the highest being 5250 feet. From the top, or even high up on the sides, of the mountains of this island one can see the plains of Troy, as is said in Homer's *Iliad*. This is a very interesting confirmation of the accuracy of Homer as to geography and minute observation.

Macedonia under the Roman rule was divided into four districts for safety against a general rebellion, 167 A. D. A coin of the first division is

No. 74.—MACEDONIA, SECOND DIVISION.
(Mac. I., Dict., p. 189.)

on page 189 in the DICTIONARY; one of the second (74) is here; none is known of the third; but of the fourth there are several, besides this one, No. 75, which bears the mark of the emperor's legate (LEG). The chief cities were—

No. 75.—MACEDONIA UNDER ROMAN RULE.

Amphipolis, capital of the 1st district; Thessalonica, of the 2d; Pella, of the 3d; and Heraclea, of the 4th. The peoples of the several districts were kept wholly distinct, not even being allowed to marry those of another or have any dealings in houses or lands. The proconsul over the whole country resided at Thessalonica; the Roman roads were excellent throughout the country, uniting the capitals. The chief seaport eastward was Neapolis, the coin of which bears an archaic head of Diana with a peculiar style of hair-dressing, and the letters in Greek NEOP, for Neapolis; on the reverse a head of the fabu-

lous monster called Gorgon. The road from Neapolis to Philippi leads over the river Zygactes (break-pole), about which the Greeks tell this legend: Proserpine was gathering flowers by the river, when Pluto fell in love with her and

No. 76.—NEAPOLIS, MACEDONIA.

took her into his chariot, the pole of which broke as he tried to cross the river. The whole country is poetically dotted with similar legends and names.

The coin of Philippi shows that it was a Roman colony, the inscription being, "Tiberius Claudius Cæsar Augustus, High Priest, Tribunal Power, Emperor," around bust, and "Colony of Julia Augusta of Philippi" around statues of Julius Cæsar and Augustus, standing on a pedestal inscribed "The Deified Augustus." The city was first called Crenides, or Fountains, afterward Datum; but when Philip, father of Alex-

No 77.—PHILIPPI.

ander the Great, fortified it, he named it after himself. The gold-mines of the vicinity were very productive, yielding a million a year. The famous battle between Octavius (afterward Augustus) and Antony (No. 18) on one side, and Brutus and Cassius on the other, was fought here 36 B. C. The remains of the earthworks used on that day can be traced now for long distances, and there are remains of a triumphal arch near the modern city. (For Thyatira in Asia, where Lydia, found by Paul at Philippi, resided, see coin No. 123.)

No. 78.—BRUTUS AT PHILIPPI.

The coin of Brutus commemorates his victory at Philippi, showing trophies.

The scourging of Paul and Silas at Philippi is illustrated by this scene (No. 79) from an ancient gem, which leaves no doubt of the Roman manner. Livy (viii. 32) and Aulus Gellius (x. 3) describe the Roman manner of flogging in the public square or forum on the naked body.

No. 79.—FLOGGING IN SCHOOL.

Philippi was then the capital of the province, instead of Amphipolis (see under 75), and had the "Italian right," which included exemption from martial law and its hasty punishments, and from certain taxes, and also being favored with peculiar privileges. The Roman citizen, or any other person having the "Italian right," could not be condemned and punished without a trial, and he also had the right of appeal. The scourging was done in the public square of the city, before the assembled people. Some were tied to a post; others were stripped and had their hands tied behind the back.

No. 80.—THESSALONICA.

On the coin of Thessalonica, we find "Caius (Caligula), son of Augustus," around the portrait of Caius, and "Of the Thessalonians" (money) around a head of Augustus. Caius was an adopted son. He was one of the assessors when Archelaus and Herod Antipas and Philip were heard before Augustus prior to the death of Herod the Great. (Jos. Ant. xvii. 9, 5; see THESSALONICA in the DICTIONARY.)

The poetical allusions of Paul are cited as evidence of his acquaintance with, and keen relish for, their beauties. For instance, in his address to the Athenians there is an allusion to the poems of the Cilician poet Aratus in this line:

"For we are also his offspring" (Acts xvii. 28);

and when he rebukes the Cretans, he quotes from their own writer, Epimenides:

"The Cretans
Are always liars, evil beasts, slow bellies" (Tit. i. 12);

and for the Corinthians he selects a line from the comedy of "Thais," a word of the excellent writer Menander:

"Evil communications corrupt good manners."

The poet Aratus was a Cilician, born at Soli, and a fellow countryman with Paul. He was at the court of Antigonus Gonatas many years, where he wrote the astronomical Greek poem,

No. 81.—THE POET ARATUS (300–250 B. C.).

called "Phenomena," from which Paul quoted in Acts xvii. 28, on which Hipparchus wrote a commentary, and of which Cicero made a Latin version. Ovid said, "Aratus will always be associated with the sun and moon in the minds of men, for his excellent qualities."

No. 82.—MENANDER (b. 341 B. C.).

Menander, the Greek tragic poet, was the originator of the New Comedy, and had the highest reputation, being eulogized by Julius Cæsar, Plutarch, and other ancients. Paul quoted from

No. 83.—SOCRATES AND PLATO.

his comedy of Thais in 1 Cor. xiii. 33. The portraits of Socrates and Plato are from an ancient gem now in the possession of Mr. John Taylor

Johnston of New York City. They are introduced here because Socrates was accused of violating the laws by corrupting youth, and by acknowledging strange gods not sanctioned by the laws—accusations made against Paul. (On the subject of the accusations against Paul see Acts xxiii. and xvii. 22.)

The coin of Athens (84) is of the age of Pericles, 470 B. C. The purity of the silver and gold of the coinage of Athens after Solon's reform

NO. 84.—ATHENS.

made the type useful as late as the time of Alexander, who changed the standard in weight, and then new and better designs were adopted. The head is of Minerva, and the owl was sacred to that goddess; ATHE for Athens.

The coin of Cenchrea, the port of Corinth, is of the date of 138 A. D. or later, and shows a head of the emperor Antoninus Pius, the successor of Hadrian in that year. The reverse

NO. 85.—CENCHREA, PORT OF CORINTH.

has a plan of the port, where a circular row of warehouses end in an office, or perhaps a temple, on either side, and in the centre stands a statue of Neptune, while ships in full sail are in the harbor, with the initials of "Colonia Laus Julia Corinthos."

There are perhaps more coins of different types of Ephesus than of any other ancient city. The political and religious characteristics of the city and of the age are illustrated on them, which have many allusions to the Diana-worship, and bear the names and official titles

NO. 86.—EPHESUS.

of various public officers referred to in the New Testament. The one with the head of Nero

(No. 87), is dated about the time assigned to Paul's visit. We learn from the coins that there were many temples to Diana and other deities (117)—one of Apollo at the head of the port; one opposite the great theatre; another of Diana near the theatre. One of the Diana temples has four columns; another has columns all around

NO. 87.—EPHESUS.

it; a third (the great temple), eight columns in front (114). The theatre was the largest structure ever built by the Greeks, and would hold 50,000 spectators. In this were displayed the public games by the Asiarch—running, wrestling, feats of strength, boxing, horse-racing, gladiatorial contests, and fights with wild beasts (1 Cor. xv. 33); one of the latter is presented on the coin No. 88. (See 1 Cor. ix. 24, 25.) The emperor Claudius died during the time Paul was at Ephesus, 54 A. D.

The inscription on coin No. 87 is "Nero Cæsar," around a portrait of the emperor on one side, and on the other, "Of the Ephesians Neocori, Aichmocles Aviola, Proconsul," around a temple of Diana, on each side of which are EPH in Greek letters. The neokoros was a conductor of the public-worship; we have no such officer

NO. 88.—REGULUS.

now. The city also had the privilege of building a temple in honor of the reigning emperor; and on coin No. 117 the four temples suggest that one or more may have been of that class.

The inscriptions on the coins of Colossæ show that the name of the city was written differently in most ancient times. The place is now entirely deserted, while Xenophon says (Anab. ii. 2) it was a great, populous, and flourishing city; and Pliny says (v. 41) it was one of the most cele-

NO. 89.—COLOSSÆ.   NO. 90.—COLOSSÆ.

brated towns in Phrygia. Laodicea and Hierapolis were near, and were included in the circuit of labors of the apostle and his assistants (Col.

iv. 13). These three towns were all in the valley of the river Mæander, within a circuit of fifteen miles. Hierapolis is included among the illustrious cities of Asia by Tacitus. It has been shaken by earthquakes in successive ages, but is still a fine city, called by the Turks Pambook Kalessi. The hot springs near are the resort of invalids and curiosity-hunters, who examine the deposits of lime from the waters, which have formed vast masses in fantastic shapes. Among the ruins of the ancient city the theatre and the gymnasium are the most noted. The Stoic philosopher Epictetus was a native of Hierapolis, where he was sold in his youth as a slave to a freedman of the emperor Nero; which became the means of his good fortune, for he was taken to Rome, where he found means of gaining an education and his freedom.

No. 91.—NERO.

On coin No. 91 there is a front of a provision-market, called in Latin MACELLUM (MAC on the coin), which is interesting in connection with the text of 1 Cor. x. 25. The legend is, "Nero Claudius, Cæsar Augustus Germanicus, Tribunal Power, Emperor, Father of the Country," around a bust-portrait of Nero on one side, and on the other, "Provision-Market of Augustus, (struck by) Decree of the Senate."

The emperors supplied the poor people of Rome under Augustus, to the number of 200,000, with grain for bread. This free gift continued in practice until the time of Alexander Severus, 222 A.D., when it was abolished.

The island of Chios is named in Acts (xx. 15) as on Paul's route to Judæa, and coins Nos. 92, 93 are from it. On the larger one we read,

No. 92.—CHIOS.

"Under the Archonship of Quintus Valerius Primus, of the Chians," around an amphora (wine-bottle), and three asses around and below a sphinx. Three asses were equal to six cents.

No. 93.—CHIOS.

On the smaller we read, "Chios Æschines," on either side of a water-bottle. This was the far-

thing-piece or half a cent; two mites were equal to one of these.

Earthquakes have recently caused a great loss of life and a destruction of many houses in the cities and villages of Chios (now called Scio). The island is 32 miles long by 8 to 18 miles wide. Its fertility and the excellent quality of its wine, mastic, figs, and other products have been the theme of writers in all ages. This was one of the seven places that claimed the honor of Homer's nativity, the other six being Smyrna, Rhodes, Colophon, Salamis, Athens, and Argos. They show a sepulchre in Chios which is called Homer's, near the ruins of an ancient temple to Apollo.

No. 94.—SAMOS.

Samos was the capital of an island of the same name. We read on the coin No. 94, "Hegesianax, of the Samians," above a head and shoulders of an ox; the head of a lion is without inscription This is a very ancient place, and mentioned in the earliest history.

No. 95.—MILETUS.

The coin of Miletus has a head of Apollo bound with a wreath of laurel, and on the reverse a lion looking back at a star, with the monogram of Miletus and the name of Theodorus, who was a chief magistrate.

No. 96.—COS.

The island of Cos was called the garden of the Ægean Sea. It was mentioned in the book of Maccabees (1 Macc. xv. 23) and in Josephus (Ant. xiv. 7, 2) in connection with the war with Mithridates. Herod the Great conferred many favors on the Jews in Cos.

For coin of Rhodes, see DICTIONARY. It has a head of Apollo radiated as the sun on one side, and "Amynias (a magistrate) of the Rhodians" on the other, around an opening rose.

Patara was the port of Xanthus, the capital of Lycia, and stood eight miles east of the Yellow (xanthus) River. It is now a ruin, and its port is filled up with sand. On the coin a head of Apollo in a laurel-wreath is on one side, and a

No. 97.—PATARA.

(Rhodes, Dict., p. 232.)

head of Diana on the other, with the words "Of the Patareans." Ruins of a theatre, baths, and a triple arch which was once a city-gate mark the site.

Lycia was south of Asia, and had its Lysiarchs as Asia had its Asiarchs. It was a part of the

No. 98.—LYCIA.

Persian dominions before Alexander (Herodotus vii. 91, 92), then under the Greek kings to the time the Romans took it from Antiochus. It is mentioned in 1 Macc. xv. 23, and was made a Roman province under Claudius. On the coin is a head of Apollo and a lyre, with "Of the Lycians, Year 8."

No. 99.—ACRE PTOLEMAIS.

Acre was a city of Phœnicia, and was invested by the Romans with the privileges of a colony,

No. 100.—ADRAMYTTIUM.

as appears on this coin of Claudius, with the legend, "(Claudius) Cæsar, High Priest, Consul

4th time, Emperor 13th year." (47 A. D.), around a portrait, and "The Deified Claudius, Ptolemais, Claudian Colony, Citizens Saved," around two oxen and driver, with four standards of the legions—6, 9, 10, 11.

The coin of Adramyttium reads, "Antinous the Bacchus," around portrait of Antinous (who was deified in the reign of Hadrian), and "Dedicated by Egesias of the Adramyttians," around a figure of Ceres. This place was settled in the time of Crœsus by the Lydians, 590 B. C.

On the coin of Sidon we find a head of a king or emperor without name, and a group of the

No. 101.—SIDON.

fabled Europa and the bull, with the words "Of the Sidonians." This myth of Europa was recorded on many coins of different nations. (See SIDON in the DICTIONARY.) The name Europe means "the west" when applied to the country, but it means on this coin a deified daughter of Agenor, king of Phœnicia, of whom it is fabled that Jupiter was enamored, and she became the mother of the heroes Minos, Sarpedon, and Rhadamanthus, and after that married Asterius, the king of Crete; the Cretans deified her and built shrines for her worship.

No. 102.—CNIDUS.

Cnidus was known to the Jews in the second century B. C. (1 Macc. xv. 23), and was passed by Paul (Acts xxvii. 7). It must have been of great importance and magnificence. It was formerly on an island of the same name, but is now connected with the mainland by a causeway. The coin presents a head of Venus with many ornaments, and a lion's head, with Ethbolo, the name of a magistrate. This place has been named Triopia, Pegusia, and Stadia, because founded by Triopas. The chief deity worshiped there was Venus, whose temple was famed for its marble statue of that goddess, the work of Praxiteles. The mathematician Eudoxus, the philosopher Agatharcides, the historian Theopompus, and the physician Ctesias were natives of Cnidus. It is now a mass of ruins. The historian Theopompus is quoted by several ancient authors, and is favorably compared with Thucydides and Herodotus, but was more satirical and illiberal. His works are lost, only the passages quoted by others being extant. Ctesias wrote a history of Persia in twenty-three books.

Crete is rich in the early mythology of the Greeks; Cnossus was its chief city, and Gortyna

No. 103.—CNOSSUS.

second. (See DICTIONARY.) The famous Labyrinth is presented on this coin and on No. 142. The head of Diana has an ornamented cap, and she has earrings and necklace of pearls or hollow gold beads; the word is "Of the Knossians." The Cretans are named among those who witnessed the gift of tongues (Acts ii. 11). The strange fables of the Gnostics were received on the island. A natural cave is shown to travelers near Gortyna as the original Labyrinth; it has many rooms and passages, with stalactites, and may have suggested the poetic idea which the ancient poet crystallized in the tale of Theseus and the Minotaur.

Gaulos is a small island near Malta. The coin is Phœnician, and is described: Head of the governor of the island, with a caduceus in token of his good conduct in office; on the reverse a wreath of laurel around a vase, and the letters ALL, for alal, in Phœnician letters.

The coin of Malta was struck by the Greeks, and presents a head of the Egyptian goddess Isis with mystic head-dress and crown, a head of barley, and the words "Of the Maltese;" on the reverse a figure of the god Osiris, winged,

No. 104.—GAULOS.

crowned with the serpent, and holding the emblems of power in either hand. The knowledge and use of the Egyptian gods extended to Rome also in later times.

No. 105.—MELITA (MALTA).

The coin of Syracuse (No. 106) is of Gelon, 485–478 B. C., and presents the head of a girl, hair waved in front, one lock hanging over the ear, the rest braided and folded or gathered in

a net, bound with a wreath of olive; earring, with pendants and necklace; four dolphins swim around the head in the same direction, differing

No. 106.—SYRACUSE.

from the one below; on the other side was the chariot and four horses similar to that on the next coin.

No. 107.—SYRACUSE.

Coin No. 107 is of Hiero of Syracuse, 470 B. C., and bears a head of the goddess Arethusa, with earring, necklace, band, and hair in a net; four dolphins swim around, two meeting before the face, indicating, as is supposed, that the island on which the fountain of Arethusa is located was there united to the mainland by a causeway, built after the former coin was struck. The chariot and four horses commemorate victories won by King Hiero in the Olympic Games, which were celebrated by the poet Pindar in his Odes. Besides Pindar, his court was frequented by Æschylus, Simonides, and Epicharmus—all well-known authors of Greek literature. Hiero was a generous patron of the arts and sciences. This portrait of King Hiero on No. 108 is the oldest-known portrait on any coin, and is dated 480 B. C.

Nero was made emperor through the management of his mother, Agrippina, wife of Claudius, in 54 A. D., when he was seventeen years old. The portrait of the young man appears beardless on many coins (see 70), and his advancing years can be traced to the last (in 68 A. D.) on various specimens, No. 91 or 111 marking the greatest age. He was not old when he died (by his own hand), aged thirty-one. It is said his chief passion was to sing with a thin, shrill voice to the sound of a guitar, although he had talents in painting, sculpture, and poetry. It is said that he became a monster of crime and cruelty. Seneca, one of his advisers in state affairs, was the most elegant scholar of the age. He instituted games, called Juvenilia, in honor of his first beard. Coin No. 110 is inscribed, "Nero Claudius, Cæsar Augustus Germanicus," around a portrait with a radiated crown; on the reverse, "Freighted with (or by) Augustus," around a

NO. 108.—SYRACUSE.

grain-ship, in reference to the supplies obtained from Africa for the people of Rome.

NO. 109.—NERO (MUSICIAN).

Coin No. 109 has this legend: "Nero Claudius, Cæsar Augustus Germanicus, High Priest, Tri-

NO. 110.—NERO (GRAIN-SHIP).

bunal Power, Emperor, Father of the Country," around a youthful head of the emperor; and on the other side a figure of Nero playing on a lyre or cithara.

NO. 111.—NERO.

Coin No. 111 is inscribed, "Nero Claudius, Cæsar Augustus Germanicus, Tribunal Power, Father of the Country, Emperor;" and on the reverse, "Peace in the earth and on the sea, the temple of Janus closed," around a front of the temple of Janus hung with a garland over the door, the letters S C on either side for "Decree of the Senate."

THE SEVEN CHURCHES OF ASIA (Rev. i. 4).

Of Patmos there are no coins.

Of the cities of the seven churches in Asia, some are a heap of ruins, and others, like Ephesus, have been lost, and only recently restored by the explorer's shovel. The city was originally named Smyrna (Strabo xiv. 1, 4). The Diana-worship was peculiarly Oriental, and included magic, charms, amulets, soothsaying, and pretended miracles. The image of Diana in the great temple was of immense height, carved in ebony, ivory, and gold, and probably formed like those on the coins. The moon was symbolized behind the head and shoulders; the signs of the Zodiac were carved on the drapery of the breast, and animals or monstrous forms were distributed over the drapery of the lower limbs; in each hand was a tri-

NO. 112.—EPHESUS.   NO. 113.—EPHESUS.

dent. It was asserted that the image fell from heaven (or Jupiter) complete, as is also said of the Kaaba Stone in Mecca. Diana was worshiped in three characters — as the moon (Luna) in the heavens, Diana on earth, and Hecate in Hades. One month was named Artemisia from the annual festival in honor of the goddess (called Artemis), the record of which in a decree, engraved on a marble slab, was found near the temple, corroborating the text of Acts xix. 35. During the month of revels various scenes were enacted in which the gods were represented: a man as Jupiter the May King, who

NO. 114.—EPHESUS.

was appointed by the emperor or his legate; one as Apollo, and another as Mercury. The Jupiter wore a robe glittering with gold, white as snow, and a crown of carbuncles, pearls, and other precious stones (Malala, lib. xii.). Ephesus was the great market of the region, buyers and sellers flocking there in great numbers; thus religion, business, and pleasure combined to make the festival-month a success. It was in that month that Paul's visit was timed. The expenses of the games were paid, all or a part, by the Asiarch (see ASIARCH in the DICTIONARY), who superintended the exhibition. The great image was

No. 115.—EPHESUS.

copied in small sizes for use in private families, shops, etc., and for travelers.

No. 116.—EPHESUS.

On coin No. 115 are heads of Augustus and Livia joined, and on the reverse the legend,

No. 117.—EPHESUS.

"Aristion Menophantus, Recorder of the Ephesians," around a stag, the emblem of Diana of

No. 118.—APOLLO.

Ephesus. No. 116 presents the image of Diana the huntress, with bow, quiver, and a stag, from a

fine Greek model. No. 117 is a coin bearing the fronts of four temples, in one of which stands an image of Diana, the others having effigies of the emperors. The Apollo (118) was the male god, the sun, as the Diana was the female, the moon, and both are represented with bow and arrow. This Apollo is from the original marble in the Vatican, Rome; the Diana below, a chariot and two horses driven by the goddess, inside a

No. 119.—DIANA.

circle formed by a serpent with its tail in its mouth, the ancient symbol of eternity.

Smyrna, the second of the "seven," is mentioned only once in the Scriptures (Rev. ii. 8–11),

No. 120.—SMYRNA.

but honorably, and it enjoyed the proud title, "The Ornament of Asia." The most popular deity of the ancient city was the god Bacchus; other gods were Apollo, Diana, the Nemesis, the father of the gods (Zeus), the mother of the gods (Hera), the city of Rome as Roma, and peculiar-

No. 121.—SMYRNA.

ly, Dionysus, who was fabled to die by violence and be resuscitated every year. It had a large public library and a museum, dedicated to Homer, who was claimed as a countryman, an Odeum, and other public buildings, including a hall of justice, where appeals from other cities were heard under the Roman laws. It is now a city filled with ruins built into modern walls, which include many fragments of sculptures and other works of art. Herodotus described a statue which was near the city, cut on the face of a rock, seven feet high, Egyptian in style, with this inscription across the breast: "I conquered this country by the might of my arms." (See Dan. xi.) This city was founded by Alexander the Great after the battle of Granicus.

Pergamus, the third church in the list, was in a city which was the capital of a district of the same name. The city was founded before the Trojan war, when Pergamos, son of Pyrrhus, deposed

NO. 122.—PHILETAIRUS OF PERGAMUS.

King Arius there. Philetairus founded the race of Attalian kings of Pergamus, 280 B. C.; Eumenes, his nephew, succeeded him, 262 B. C. Eumenes II. was rewarded for services to the Romans by the addition to his kingdom of Mysia, Lydia, and Phrygia; he founded a library that became the rival of that at Alexandria. Attalus III. (133 B. C.) gave his kingdom to the Roman people and ended the monarchy of Pergamus.

NO. 123.—NERO AT THYATIRA.

Thyatira was mentioned fourth in the Apocalypse. (See in the DICTIONARY.) The coins bear the heads of Apollo (Tyrimnas), Hercules, Athene, Roma, Cybele, and the reigning emperors. The remains of antiquity are numerous, but ruinous, such as fragments of sculptures and inscribed stones giving an account of the various labor-guilds of that age. (Acts xvi. 14.)

NO. 124.—THYATIRA.

The city of Thyatira was founded by Seleucus (No. 2), as one of the many Macedonian col-

onies which were among the results of the partition of Persia by the successors of Alexander the Great. It had been a city from remote times, called Pelopia, Semiramis, and Euhippia, after various rulers in different ages, and under the Persian rule from the time of Cyrus the Great, 546 B. C. A very curious superstition is said to have been introduced there by the Jews in the worship of the sibyl Sambatha. (See Rev. ii. 20-24.)

NO. 125.—SARDIS.

Sardis was the fifth in the list, and the capital of ancient Lydia, which Homer called Mœonia, the "Queen of Asia," whose earliest king was Candaules, 716 B. C., and the last Crœsus, 560–546 B. C. The golden sands of the Pactolus furnished metal (electrum) for the money of that age, which assisted in developing the manufactures and trade of the city. (See in the DICTIONARY.) Two massive columns (6 feet 6 inches thick and 40 feet high) of the once magnificent temple of Cybele remain among a heap of ruins. It was of the same age as the temple of Zeus in

NO. 126.—SARDIS.

Ægina and of Hera in Samos. An earthquake in the time of Tiberius very much damaged the city, when its tribute to Rome was remitted for five years. Its theatre was nearly 400 feet in diameter, and the stadium adjoining it was 1000 feet long. The ancient name of the city was Hydè, under the rule of Omphale, a wife of Hercules. The modern name is Sart Kalessi, but the place is deserted; only heaps of ruins remain of the once famous city, which was full of temples, theatres, factories, and commodious dwellings, all of stone.

NO. 127.—ATTALUS II. PHILADELPHUS.

Philadelphia was a city on the border of Lydia and Phrygia, on the slopes of Mount Tmolus and on the banks of the Cogamus River.

Philadelphia was the sixth in the list of the churches in Asia. The city was founded by Attalus II., called Philadelphus, 140 B. C., as a mart for the famous wine-district celebrated by

NO. 128.—ATTALUS II. PHILADELPHUS (159–138 B. C.).

Virgil; and the coins of that period have a head of Bacchus or the figure of a Bacchante. Xerxes passed near the site of the city, and Herodotus speaks of the sorghum as in successful cultivation then (485–465 B. C.). The valley of the Hermus is one of the most extensive and fruitful in Asia. The coins of the later rulers are not very numerous. Attalus II. on coin No. 128 is repre-

NO. 129.—LAODICEA IN ASIA.

sented more or less ideally after the likeness of the progenitor of the dynasty of Pergamus (No. 122), whose descendant he was.

NO. 130.—LAODICEA.

The ruins of Laodicea are on seven hills, and comprise a stadium, three theatres (one 450 feet in diameter), a gymnasium, bridges, aqueducts, etc. The earliest name was Diospolis (city of Jupiter); after that, Rhoas, which was then the largest city in Phrygia; and finally Antiochus named it after his sister, Laodice. The aqueducts are constructed with a knowledge of hydraulics equal to ours, the theatres have seats numbered and lettered, and the place abounds in evidences of a high state of civilization. This city under the Roman rule was a place of importance for its trade and manufactures. In the Christian age it was a populous and wealthy city where the great councils of the Church met. The ruined site is called Denislu.

NO. 131.—LAODICEA.

PLACES MENTIONED IN THE ACCOUNT OF THE DAY OF PENTECOST, Acts ii. 9–11.

The Parthian kingdom was founded about 250 B. C. by Arsaces, a Scythian, and it extended over a large part of Asia. The Parthians were never wholly subdued by the Romans, their last king, Artabanus IV., being killed by the Persians 226 A. D. The Parthians captured many Roman

250 B. C.
NO. 132.—ARSACES, PARTHIA.

standards in battle, which were returned after a solemn treaty amid great rejoicing in Rome under Augustus, who struck several medals in commemoration of the event. The coin No. 132 is of Arsaces IX., Mithridates II., who was the first to make his nation known to the Romans under Sulla, 92 B. C.

Mesopotamia appears first in history as a country inhabited by many independent tribes, as Arabia is now, then as a part of the Assyrian empire, and after that divided between the

NO. 133.—MESOPOTAMIA.
(For Judæa, see No. 42.)

Medes and Babylonians. Cyrus added it to Persia, and Alexander made it a satrapy under his rule; it fell, after his death, to one of his generals, Seleucus I., and to the Parthians, B. C. 160. Trajan made it a Roman province A. D. 115.

Cappadocia was founded by Pharnaces 744 B. C.; conquered by Perdiccas of Macedonia 322. The Romans first encouraged the formation of cities The king Ariarathes mentioned in 1 Macc. xv. 22

was the sixth of that name. The last king of Cappadocia was Archelaus, who was favored by

No. 134.—ARIARATHES VII., CAPPADOCIA.

Augustus, but died at Rome A. D. 17, when the country was made a Roman province, under Tiberius.

No. 135.—PONTUS.

Pontus was originally a part of Cappadocia, near the Pontus Euxinus, and made an independent nation by Artabazus, under Darius of Persia, 487 B. C. Mithridates VI. (No. 10) conquered Scythia, Bosphorus, Colchis, and Cappadocia. The kingdom ended in the death of Mithridates, 63 B. C., and it became a Roman province under the emperors. Polemo was made king of Pontus by Antony, whom he attended in his expedition against Parthia. His son, whose head appears on this coin, was confirmed on the throne by Claudius.

Asia as a province dates from B. C. 133 (see Coin No. 122); before that it had been from the time of Alexander under the Seleucid kings, until it became a Roman province. The Greeks and Persians contended for centuries for supremacy in Asia until Alexander's time, since when it was under the Seleucid kings (except Pergamus, which was given to the Romans by will 133 B. C.), until it became a Roman province 15 A. D., under Tiberius.

No. 136.—SELEUCUS I.

Phrygia was made a part of the kingdom of Antigonus Cyclops after the death of Alexander, 323 B. C. It was made a Roman province 47 B. C. Phrygia was a vague term, including a

No. 137.—ANTIGONUS, PHRYGIA (333–301 B. C.).

large territory, from which portions were added to several Roman provinces at different times.

Iconium and Colosse were in Phrygia. Josephus says Antiochus the Great (No. 5) first introduced Jews to Phrygia about 200 B. C. (Ant. xii. 3, 4). Acts xiii. 14; xiv. 1, 19.

Pamphylia is mentioned by Herodotus (vii. 91, 92) as one of the lesser states. In Paul's time it was a Roman province, enlarged under

No. 138.—MYRA, IN PAMPHYLIA.

Claudius by Lycia and a part of Pisidia. Myra was the port where Paul changed ships on the way to Rome. It contains many relics of different ages: tombs with Lycian inscriptions, a theatre of the Greek age, a Byzantine church, and later remains. The Orthodox Greeks have a legend that St. Nicolas was born at Patara, buried

No. 139.—HADRIAN IN EGYPT (117–138 A. D.).

at Myra, and his bones now rest, having been moved to St. Petersburg recently. (See No. 69.)

The Egypt of the Bible, so far as the coins present it, dates from Alexander the Great, 332 B. C. (No. 1). The Ptolemies continued from 323 (see DICTIONARY) to Cleopatra, 30 B. C., when it became a Roman province. Hadrian spent the greater part of his reign in journeys throughout the provinces of his empire, displaying liberality, political wisdom, and love of the fine arts. On this coin appears the inscription, "Hadrian Augustus, Consul 3d time, Father of the Country," around head of the emperor; and an emblem of the Nile—a strong man surrounded by boys, representing the districts of Egypt, Sphinx and Crocodile, with S C for Decree of the Senate.

No. 140.—CYRENE, IN LIBYA.

Cyrenaica comprised five cities and their outlying districts (see DICTIONARY), was colonized by the Greeks as early as 600 B. C., and was named by Aristæus after his mother. After Alexander, it became a dependency of Egypt. The coin presents a head of Jupiter Ammon on one side, and on the other the sacred silphion plant, now extinct. The Romans received it as a legacy from Apion, son of Ptolemy Physcon, 97 B. C. It is now a desert.

This coin (141) is of the Roman people, and represents a young man with a staff and a horn

No. 141.—ROME.

of plenty. The people owned large districts in the provinces in the time of the emperors, and the taxes were derived for ages entirely from the countries subject to Rome outside of Italy. At one time, as Pliny says, six Roman proprietors owned half the land in Africa outside of Egypt, and Augustus owned all Egypt.

The Minotaur was fabled to have been shut in

the Cretan labyrinth and fed on young men and maids, supplied by Athens yearly, until Theseus (a king of Athens) killed the monster by the help of Ariadne, daughter of Minos, king of

No. 142.—GNOSSUS, IN CRETE.

Crete. Theseus was next to Hercules in success, killing the Minotaur, vanquishing the Centaurs, but was finally chained to a huge rock in Hades by Pluto for attempting the rescue of Proserpine. (See No. 103.)

The Aretas of Petra, king of the Nabatheans, was in alliance with the Greek kings of Syria, and inscribed his friendship on his coins, as on

No. 143.—ARETAS, ARABIA.

this: "Aretas, lover of the Greeks." He must have employed Greek architects in Petra, for the remains of the city, cut in the solid rock, are of their style. (See No. 65.)

COINS, MONEY AND WEIGHTS OF THE BIBLE.

BY F. W. MADDEN, M.R.A.S.

General Remarks.—Ancient money was of two kinds, uncoined and coined. By uncoined may be understood pieces not issued under an authority, though they may have borne some stamp or impress of their value. By coined may be understood ingots, of which the weight and fineness are certified by the integrity of designs impressed upon the surfaces of the metal (Prof. Jevons, *Money*, p. 57).

The first mention in the Bible, after the Flood, of uncoined money is when Abraham came up out of Egypt "very rich in cattle, in *silver*, and in *gold*" (Gen. xiii. 2; comp. Gen. xxiv. 35). Though this passage does not imply anything more than "bullion," yet we soon find a notice of the use of money (Heb. *silver*) as the *price* paid for a slave (Gen. xvii. 13). The first actual transaction of commerce is the purchase by Abraham of the cave of Machpelah for 400 shekels of silver, current [money] with the merchant (Gen. xxiii. 16); and silver as a medium of commerce appears to have been in general use among the nations of the Philistines (Gen. xx. 16; Judg. xvi. 5, 18; xvii. 2, seq.), the Midianites (Gen. xxxvii. 28), and the Syrians (2 Kings v. 5, 23). By the laws of Moses, men and cattle (Lev. xxvii. 3, seq.; Num.

iii. 45, seq.), the possessing houses and fields (Lev. xxvii. 14, seq.), provisions (Deut. ii. 6, 28; xiv. 26), all fines for offences (Exod. xxi., xxii.), the contributions to the Temple (Exod. xxx. 13; xxxviii. 26), the sacrifice of animals (Lev. v. 15), the redemption of the first-born (Num. iii. 47–50; xviii. 15), were estimated and regulated by money value. It is probable that a fixed weight was assigned to single pieces, so as to make them suitable for the various articles presented in trade. The system of weighing (though frequent mention is made of the balance and the weighing of money, Exod. xxii. 17; Lev. xix. 36; Deut. xxv. 13, 15; 2 Sam. xviii. 12; 1 Kings xx. 39; Jer. xxxii. 9, 10; Prov. xi. 1, etc.) is not likely to have been applied to every individual piece. In the large total of 603,550 half-shekels accumulated by the contributions of each Israelite (Exod. xxxviii. 26), each *individual half-shekel* could hardly have been weighed. Money was sometimes put into a chest, which when full was emptied by the high priest, and the money was bound up in bags, and then *told*, perhaps being weighed in the bags (2 Kings xii. 9, 10; comp. 2 Chron. xxiv. 8–11). That there were pieces of different denominations is evident from the passage in Exod. xxx. 13, where the *half-shekel* is to be paid as the atonement-money, and "the rich shall not give *more*, and the poor shall not give *less*" (Exod. xxx. 15). The *third part of the shekel* is mentioned in Persian times (Neh. x. 32), and the *fourth part* must have been an actual piece, for it was *all the silver* that the servant of Saul had to pay the seer (1 Sam. ix. 8, 9). Iron and lead bars of constant form and weight circulated in Egypt; in Greece, bars of iron; in Italy, bars of copper; in Britain, in the time of Julius Cæsar, bars of copper and iron; and from the earliest times gold and silver in the same shape were employed in general traffic in the East. This explains the mention of a wedge (Heb. *tongue*) of gold found by Achan at Jericho (Josh. vii. 21) [see *Talent* under WEIGHTS], as well as the different payments which are mentioned in the O. T., and which presuppose with certainty the currency of single pieces of metal according to weight.

It is also probable that a system of "jewel currency" or "ring-money" was in vogue. The case of Rebekah, to whom the servant of Abraham gave "a golden ear-ring of half a shekel weight, and two bracelets for her hands of ten shekels weight" (Gen. xxiv. 22), proves that the ancient Hebrews made their jewels of a specific weight, so as to know the value of these ornaments in employing them for money. That the Egyptians kept their bullion in jewels is evident from their monuments, where they are represented weighing rings of gold and silver, and is further illustrated by the fact of the Israelites having at their exodus from Egypt borrowed "jewels [vessels] of silver and jewels [vessels] of gold" (*Keli keseph, Keli zahab*), and "spoiled the Egyptians" (Exod. xii. 35, 36; comp. Exod. iii. 22; xi. 2). So too it would appear that the money used by the children of Jacob, when they went to purchase corn in Egypt, was an annular currency (Gen. xlii. 35). Their money is described as "bundles of money," and when returned to them was found to be "of [full] weight" (Gen. xliii. 21). It was therefore of a form capable of being tied up, which receives corroboration from the passage in Deuteronomy (xiv. 24–26), where directions are given as to the payment of the tithes to the sanctuary: "Then shalt thou turn it into money, and *bind up* the money in thy hand, and shalt go unto the place which the Lord thy God shall choose." The account of the sale of Joseph to the Midianites affords another instance of the employment of jewel ornaments as a medium of exchange (Gen. xxxvii. 28), as we gather from the account in Numbers (xxxi. 50, 51) of the spoiling of the Midianites, that they carried their whole wealth in the forms of chains, bracelets, ear-rings, and tablets. The friends of Job gave him, in addition to "a piece of money" [KESITAH], "an ear-ring of gold" (*nezem zahab*, LXX. *tetradrachmon chrusou kai asēmou*—tetradrachm of uncoined gold, Job xlii. 11). Now had these ear-rings of gold not been intended as representing money, all the friends of the patriarch would not have given him the same article, and that in conjunction with a piece of silver.

From these statements, it is evident, firstly, that if the Hebrews became learned in "all the wisdom of the Egyptians" (Acts vii. 22; comp. 1 Kings iv. 30), they did not learn from them the use of money; and secondly, that nowhere in the Pentateuch is there any mention of money that was *coined*. Nor do the passages in Joshua, Judges, and Job imply an actual coinage, any more than the "piece of silver" [AGORAH] mentioned at the time of Samuel (1 Sam. ii. 36). The reigns of David and Solomon were an era

of prosperity for Judæa—"Silver was in Jerusalem as stones; it was nothing accounted of in the days of Solomon" (1 Kings x. 21, 27: 2 Chron. ix. 20, 27): still, it is certain that there were no *real coins*—namely, pieces struck under an authority—before the Exile. On the other hand, the Hebrews, as I have shown, must have employed pieces of a definite weight; but the excavations in Palestine have never brought to light an example, any more than the excavations in Egypt, Assyria and Babylonia. It may, however, be observed that when the pieces of silver were collected for the treasury they were *melted down* before reissue. It is recorded (2 Kings xxii. 9; comp. 2 Chron. xxxiv. 17) that Shaphan the scribe came to King Josiah, and said, "Thy servants have gathered together (Heb. *melted*) the money that was found in the house;" and the same plan was also followed by the Persian king Darius (B. C. 521–485), who melted the gold and silver into earthen vessels, which when full were broken off, leaving the metal in a mass, from which pieces were broken off as necessity required.

The oldest coins extant are certain electrum staters of Lydia, probably about B. C. 720, which, issued on different standards, continued in circulation till the time of Crœsus, who, on his accession in B. C. 568, reorganized the Lydian coinage, abolished electrum, and issued instead pieces of gold and silver. Before the introduction of coined money into Greece, there was a currency of *obeliskoi*, "spits" or "skewers," probably of iron or copper, six of which made a handful (*drachmē*), and which were of a considerable size. The first Greek silver coins were struck at Ægina in B. c. 670–660.

The earliest coins mentioned in the Bible are the coins called *drams*, B. C. 538 [DRAM]. It is supposed by some that the Jewish silver shekels and half-shekels were introduced under Ezra, about B. C. 458 [SHEKEL]; but it is more probable that they were issued under Simon Maccabæus, B. C. 139 (1 Macc. xv. 6), and copper coins were struck by the Asmonæan and Herodian family.

The N. T. history falls within the reigns of Augustus, Tiberius, Caligula, Claudius, and Nero, but only Augustus (Luke ii. 1), Tiberius (Luke iii. 1), and Claudius (Acts xi. 28; xviii. 2), are mentioned; but Nero is alluded to in the Acts from chapter xxv. to the end, and in Phil. iv. 22. Coins of all these emperors would therefore be in circulation.

The following list embraces all the denominations of money mentioned in the Old and New Testaments:

Agorah. See *Piece of Silver*.

Bekah (Exod. xxxviii. 26). Literally "a half," "half a shekel," about 33 cts. Extant half-shekels weigh about 110 grains. [HALF A SHEKEL and SHEKEL.]

Brass [Money]. (1) In the O. T. a passage in Ezekiel (xvi. 36, Heb. *nechosheth*, LXX. *Chalkos*, Vulgate *œs*, A. V. *filthiness*) has been supposed to refer to *brass money*, but with no probability, as this was the latest metal introduced into Greece for money. The Hebrew word probably means something worthless, like "base metal" (comp. Jer. vi. 28; Ezek. xxii. 18). (2) *Chalkos, pecunia* (Matt. x. 9). The brass coins current in Palestine in the N. T. period consisted of Roman copper and Greek imperial coins, of the coins of Alexander Jannæus, of the Herodian family, and of the procurators of Judæa. See *Farthing* and *Mite*.

Daric. See *Dram*.

Denarius. See *Penny*.

Didrachm. See *Shekel* and *Tribute-money*.

Drachm, *Drachmē*, *drachma* (2 Macc. iv. 19; x. 20; xii. 43; Tobit v. 14). It is of various weights, according to the use of the different talents. The drachms here mentioned are of the Attic talent, which became almost universal on Alexander's succession (B. C. 338), and weighed about 67.2 grains. In later times (about B. C. 27), the drachm weighed only 61.3 grains, and thus became very nearly equal to the Roman *denarius* [PENNY], the average weight of which was 60 grains. The earliest Attic drachm contained about $\frac{1}{60}$ of the weight of alloy, and there remain 66.1 grains of silver to be valued. A dollar of the United States weighs 371.25 grains of pure silver. The earliest Attic drachm was therefore $\frac{66.1}{371.25}$ of a dollar, or a little less than 18 cents. The later Attic drachm, deducting $\frac{1}{60}$ of the weight for alloy, was worth $\frac{60}{371.25}$ of a dollar; hence its value would be about 16 cents, which was also the value of the Roman *denarius*. But these values, of course, changed with the value of silver. See *Piece of Silver* and *Penny*.

Dram. The translation in the A. V. of the Hebrew words *Adarkon* and *Darkemon* (Ezra ii. 69; viii. 27; Neh. vii. 70–72; 1 Chron. xxix. 7). Though there are several opinions concerning the origin of these words, it is agreed that by them a gold coin or *stater*—the Persian *daric*—is intended. The origin of the term has been sought in the name of Darius the Mede, but on no sure grounds, or of that of Darius, son of Hystaspes. In consequence of the type of the coins being "an archer" (by which name —*toxotai*—they were sometimes called), some have thought that the Hebrew words were derived from *darak*, "to bend the bow;" whilst others suggest a connection with the Persian words *dashtan*, "to have, to hold, to possess," or *dara*, "a king," which latter would be a likely derivation, as the figure represented is not any particular king, but the king of Persia in a general sense. Though the passages in Ezra and Nehemiah would seem to show that coins of similar name were current during the reigns of Cyrus, Cambyses, and Darius Hystaspes, it is a question if the coin called "daric" is intended by those mentioned during the reign of Cyrus, B. C. 530 (Ezra ii. 69). The daric proper was not in circulation till the reign of Darius, son of Hystaspes (B. C. 521–485), who issued a new coinage of pure gold, though the actual name of *daric stater* was not in vogue till the time of his successor, Xerxes (B. C. 485–465); and the *drams* mentioned under the reign of his son, Artaxerxes Longimanus (Ezra viii. 27; Neh. vii. 72), are certainly the coins called *darics*, which at this period extensively circulated in Persia. It is probable that the staters of Crœsus, king of Lydia, continued in circulation from after the capture of Sardis in B. C. 554 to the time when Darius reformed the coinage; and if so, the Lydian staters would be those alluded to during the reign of Cyrus. The ordinary Persian *daric* is a thick gold piece, bearing the figure of a king kneeling, holding in *left* hand a bow and in *right* a spear or a dagger (comp. Ezek. xxxix. 3; Isa. lxvi. 19), and has an average weight of 130 grains. A gold dollar of the United States contains 25.8 grains, or 23.22 grains, less the alloy. Reckoning the daric to contain 124.6 grains of pure gold, its value would therefore be about five dollars and thirty cents, which value fluctuated with the value of gold. Double *darics*, weighing about 260 grains — but rare — and perhaps half-darics, weighing sixty grains, are also in existence. With reference to the mention of *drams*, at the time of David (1 Chron. xxix. 7), it must be remembered

that the writer, who in all probability was Ezra, wished to express in language intelligible to his readers the value of the gold subscribed, and therefore translated the terms employed in his documents, whatever they were, into terms that were in use in his own day (*Speaker's Com.*, vol. iii., p. 271).

Farthing. This word occurs four times in the A. V. of the N. T. Two names of coins are rendered by it. (1) *Assarion* (Matt. x. 29; Luke xii. 6), the Greek name of the Roman *as* or *assarius*. From the fact that the Vulgate substitutes the word dipondius (= two *asses*) for the *two assaria* of the Greek text, it is more than probable that a single coin is intended by this latter expression—an idea fully borne out by the copper coins of Chios, on which are inscribed the words *assarion*, *assaria duō* or *duŏ*, and *assaria tria*. The *assarion* of the N. T. must be sought for among the Greek imperial coins, and the second brass coins of Antioch in Syria seem to furnish us with probable specimens. One of these coins, with the counter-mark GAD (in Greek letters), proves that it was lawfully current in Gadara of Decapolis. These coins, from the time of Augustus, consist of two series—(*a*) with Greek legends, and having the name of the town and the date of the era of Antioch; and (*b*) with the name of the emperor in Latin, and on the reverse the letters S. C. (*Senatus consulto*). After the reign of Vespasian (A. D. 79) the two sets became amalgamated, and form one series. The second brass coins of these series average in weight 143 grains, and are specimens of the *as*, which, at 10 to the *denarius* [PENNY], would be equivalent to 1½c. of our money. (2) *Kodrantēs* (Matt. v. 26; Mark xii. 42), or *quadrans*, the fourth part of the Roman *as*, originally equal to the *chalkous*, weighing 67.2 grains. The copper currency of Palestine in the time of Augustus and Tiberius consisted partly of Roman and Jewish coins and partly of Græco-Roman or Greek imperial. In consequence of the reduction of the weight of the *as*, the *quadrans* became reduced to just half the weight, or 33.6 grains, and the Roman coins and small copper coins of the Herodian family of this weight represent the *farthing* of the N. T. The *as* being equivalent, as we have shown above, to 1½ cent, the *quadrans* would be equal to about ⅜ of an American cent. According to St. Mark, "two mites make a farthing;" but on this question see *Mite*.

Fourth Part of a Shekel. *Rebah* (1 Sam. ix. 8), about 16 cents. [SHEKEL.]

Gerah (Exod. xxx. 13; Lev. xxvii. 25; Num. iii. 47; xviii. 16; Ezek. xlv. 12). The twentieth part of a shekel, about 3 cents. [SHEKEL.]

Gold [Money]. (1) There is no positive mention of the use of *gold money* among the Hebrews (see Isa. xlvi. 6; Job xxviii. 15) [PIECE OF GOLD; SHEKEL], though gold constituted part of the wealth of Abraham (Gen. xiii. 2), if we exclude the "600 shekels of gold" paid by David for the threshing-floor and oxen (1 Chron. xxi. 25; comp. 2 Sam. xxiv. 24, "shekels of silver"), and it was generally employed for personal ornaments and for objects in connection with the Temple (2 Chron. iii. 9, etc.). (2) *Chrusos*, *aurum* (Matt. x. 9; James v. 3); *Chrusion*, *aurum* (Acts iii. 6; xx. 33; 1 Pet. i. 18). The gold coinage current in Palestine in the N. T. period was the Roman imperial *aureus*, which passed for 25 denarii, and was worth about $4.00.

Half a Shekel (Exod. xxx. 13, 15), about 33 cents. [BEKAH; SHEKEL.]

Keseph. See *Money*, *Silver* and *Silverling*.

Kesitah. See *Piece of Money* and *Piece of Silver*.

Mite (Mark xii. 42; Luke xii. 59; xxi. 2). The rendering of the Greek word *lepton*, which was a small Greek copper coin $\frac{1}{15}$ of the obol, weighing 33.6 grains, and hence half of the original *chalkous* or *quadrans*. St. Mark states "two mites, which is a farthing;" but he probably meant "two small pieces of money," the smallest pieces then extant, and the words "which is a *quadrans*" have been added to show that the *quadrans*, weighing about 33.6 grains, was then the smallest piece struck. The mite alluded to was a Jewish coin, for the Jews were not permitted to bring any but Jewish money into the Holy Place, and for this cause money - changers [MONEY-CHANGERS] stood at the entrance to the Temple in order to give Jewish money in exchange for foreign ; and it is probable that the small coins of Alexander Jannæus, ranging in weight from 30 grains to 15 grains, are the pieces in question. Their value would be about $\frac{1}{5}$ of an American cent. If, however, the pieces of 15 grains are the half of those of 30, and not examples of the same coin of light weight, then two would equal a *quadrans*, and their value would be $\frac{1}{15}$ of an American cent. But this conjecture is by no means sure.

Money. (1) In the O. T. the general expression is *Keseph*. (2) In the N. T. *money* is rendered as follows :—(*a*) *Argurion, pecunia*, "silver" (Matt. xxv. 18, 27; xxviii. 12, 15; Mark xiv. 11; Luke ix. 3; xix. 15, 23; xxii. 5; Acts vii. 16 [*argentum*] ; viii. 20 [*pecunia*]. In Matt. xxvi. 9, the phrase is "much [money]"). (*b*) *Chalkos, æs*, "brass" (Mark vi. 8; xii. 41). (*c*) *Chrēma*, "a thing that one uses or needs," *pretium* (Acts iv. 37; *pecunia*, viii. 18, 20; xxiv. 26). (*d*) *Kerma*, "anything cut small," *æs* (John ii. 15). [SILVER and MONEY-CHANGERS.]

Penny. *Dēnarion, denarius* (Matt. xviii. 28; xx. 2, 9, 10, 13; xxii. 19; Mark vi. 37; xii. 15; xiv. 5; Luke vii. 41; x. 35; xx. 24; John vi. 7; xii. 5; Rev. vi. 6). Its standard weight in the reign of Augustus, and to the time of Nero, was 60 grains. Deducting $\frac{1}{30}$ of the weight for alloy, there remain 58 grs. of pure silver, and as the dollar of the United States contains 371.25 grains of pure silver, we have $\frac{58}{371.25}$ or about 16 cents. In the time of Nero the weight was reduced to 52.5; and applying to this the same method of reckoning, the penny of Nero's time would equal about 14 cents. There is no doubt that most of the silver currency in Palestine during the N. T. period consisted of *denarii*, and "a penny" was the tribute-money payable by the Jews to the Roman emperor [TRIBUTE (money), 2.] "A penny" was the day's pay for a laborer in Palestine at the time of our Lord (Matt. xx. 2, 9, 10, 13; comp. Tobit v. 13), as it was the pay of a field laborer in the Middle Ages; and the term *denarius* is still preserved in English £ *s. d.* [DRACHM and PIECE OF SILVER, 2.]

Piece of Gold. This phrase occurs only once in the O. T., in the passage respecting Naaman the Syrian (2 Kings v. 5). In several other passages of a similar kind in connection with gold, the A. V. supplies the word "shekels" [SHEKEL]; and as a similar expression is found in connection with silver, and as there is not much doubt that a weight is intended, the word understood in this passage would also probably be "shekels."

Piece of Money. (1) *Kesitah* (Gen. xxxiii. 19; "piece of silver," Josh. xxiv. 32; Job xlii. 11). From the translation by the LXX. of " lambs," it has been assumed that the *kesitah* was a coin bearing the impression of a lamb or a sheep, but the coins so frequently quoted as examples belong probably to Cyprus, and were not struck till after B. C. 450. The

real meaning of *kesitah* is "a portion," and it was in all probability a piece of rough silver of fixed weight. (2) *Stater* (Matt. xvii. 27). The word *stater* means a coin of a certain weight, and hence a standard (comp. *shekel* and *pondo*), and was a term applied by the Greeks to coins of gold, of electrum, and of silver. The name was applied first to the didrachm (two drachms), and then to the tetradrachm (four drachms). During the first and second centuries, the silver currency of Palestine consisted of tetradrachms of Antioch on Orontes, of Tyre, etc., and of Roman *denarii* of a quarter their weight. The Attic tetradrachm was called *stater*, as the standard coin of the system, and no other *stater* was current in Palestine at this time. The great cities of Syria and Phœnicia either ceased to strike tetradrachms, or debased their coinage before the close of the first century A. D. Antioch continued to strike tetradrachms to the third century, but gradually depreciated them, the commencement of which cannot be determined. It was carried so far as to destroy the correspondence of the *stater* to four *denarii* by the time of Hadrian (A. D. 117). Other cities, if they issued *staters* towards the close of the first century, struck them of such base metal as to render their separation from copper money impossible. On this evidence, the Gospel is of the first century. The tetradrachm of Antioch (*stater*) is a specimen of the "piece of money" that was found by St. Peter in the fish's mouth (Matt. xvii. 27). It represents the tax for two persons—for our Lord and for St. Peter [TRIBUTE (Money), 1.]. It is equivalent in weight to the shekel, averaging 220 grains, and to about 64 cents in value. [PIECE OF SILVER, 2.]

Piece of Silver. This phrase occurs in the A. V. of both the O. T. and N. T. (1) The word "pieces" has been supplied in the A. V. for a word understood in the Hebrew. The rendering is always "a thousand," or the like "of silver" (Gen. xx. 16; xxxvii. 28; xlv. 22; Judg. ix. 4; xvi. 5; 2 Kings vi. 25; Song of Solomon viii. 11; Hosea iii. 2; Zech. xi. 12, 13). In similar passages, the word "shekels" occurs in the Hebrew [SHEKEL], and there is no doubt that this is the word understood in all these cases. There are, however, some exceptional passages where a word equivalent to "piece" or "pieces" is found in the Hebrew. The first occurs in 1 Sam. ii. 36, *Agorah keseph*, "piece of silver," and the *agorah* may be the same as the *gerah* (*q. v.*). Both are translated in the LXX. by *obolos*. The second is in Ps. lxviii. 30 [*Heb.* 32], *Ratsee keseph*, "pieces of silver" (LXX. [lxvii. 30] *argurion*), and the word *ratz* from *ratsats*, "to break in pieces," must mean a fragment or piece broken off. The third, the *kesitah*, to which I have already alluded [PIECE OF MONEY, 1]. (2) Two words are rendered in the N. T. by "piece of silver." (*a*) *Drachmē, drachma* (Luke xv. 8), and here correctly rendered, as the Attic drachm was at the time of St. Luke equivalent to the Roman *denarius* [DRACHM; PENNY]. This accounts for the remark of Josephus (*Antiq.* iii. 8, 2), who says that "the shekel . . . . . equalled four Attic drachms," for in his time the drachm and *denarius* were almost equal to the quarter of a shekel [SHEKEL]. Value about 16 cents. (*b*) *Argurion, argenteus, denarius*. This word occurs in two passages—(A) the account of the betrayal of our Lord for "thirty pieces of silver" (Matt. xxvi. 15; xxvii. 3, 5, 6, 9). These have usually been considered to be *denarii*, but on no sufficient ground. The parallel passage in Zechariah (xi. 12, 13) is translated "thirty [*pieces*] of silver;" but which should doubtless be read, "thirty *shekels* of silver," whilst it is observable that "thirty *shekels* of silver" was the price of blood to be paid in the case of a servant accidentally killed (Exod. xxi. 32). The passage may therefore be explained as "thirty *shekels* of silver"—not current shekels, but tetradrachms of the Attic standard of the Greek cities of Syria and Phœnicia. These tetradrachms were common at the time of our Lord, and of them the *stater* was a specimen [PIECE OF MONEY, 2]. In the A. V. of St. Matthew the prophecy is ascribed to Jeremiah instead of to Zechariah. Many suggestions have been made on this question, but it may be observed that the Syriac version omits the proper name, and merely says "the prophet;" hence a copyist might have inserted the wrong name. (B) The price of the conjuring books that were burnt (Acts xix. 19). The Vulgate has accurately rendered the phrase *denarii*, as there is no doubt that these coins are intended. [MONEY and SILVER.]

Pound. Mnâ (Luke xix. 13–25)—money of account. At this time the Attic talent obtained in Palestine. Sixty *minæ* went to the talent (*q. v.*). The "pound" contained 100 drachms. The drachm of the Gospel period being equivalent to about 16 cents, the value of the pound would be 16 dollars. The Greek name *mnâ* was probably derived from the Hebrew *maneh* (*q. v.* under WEIGHTS).

Ratz. See *Piece of Silver*.

Rebah. See *Fourth Part of a Shekel*.

Shekel. A word signifying "weight," and also the name of a coin, either silver or copper. It only occurs in the O. T., where it signifies the weight of certain objects, or where it is employed for a piece of silver of fixed value. The word "shekel" occurs in the Hebrew and the A. V. in the following passages: Gen. xxiii. 15, 16; Exod. xxi. 22; xxx. 13, 15; xxxviii. 24–26; Lev. v. 15; xxvii. 3–7; Num. iii. 47, 50; vii. 13, 19, 25, 31, 37, 43, 49, 55, 61, 67, 73, 79, 85, 86; xviii. 16; Josh. vii. 21; 1 Sam. ix. 8; xvii. 5, 7; 2 Sam. xiv. 26; xxi. 16; xxiv. 24; 2 Kings xv. 1; xv. 20; 1 Chron. xxi. 25 (gold shekels); 2 Chron. iii. 9 (gold shekels); Neh. v. 15; x. 32; Jer. xxxii. 9; Ezek. iv. 10; xlv. 12; Amos viii. 5. It is supplied in the A. V. in connection with "silver" in Deut. xxii. 19, 29; Judg. xvii. 2–4, 10; 2 Sam. xviii. 11, 12; 1 Kings x. 29; 2 Chron. i. 17; and in connection with "gold" in Gen. xxiv. 22; Num. vii. 14, 20, 26, 32, 38, 44, 50, 56, 62, 68, 74, 80, 86; Judg. viii. 26; 1 Kings x. 16; 2 Chron. ix. 15, 16 [see *Maneh* under WEIGHTS]. Three kinds of shekels appear to be mentioned—(1) the shekel, (2) the shekel of the sanctuary, and (3) the shekel of the king's weight. The "shekel of the sanctuary," or "holy shekel," a term generally applied to the silver shekel, but once to the gold (Exod. xxxviii. 24), was probably the normal weight, and was kept by the priests. The "shekel of the king" was connected with the Assyrio-Babylonian *maneh* of the king, as marked on the monuments from Nineveh [*Talent* under WEIGHTS]. The LXX. translate the denominations in silver by *didrachmon* and *siklos*. The shekel as extant corresponds in weight to the tetradrachm or didrachm of the early Phœnician talent in use in the cities of Phœnicia under Persian rule. It is probable that the Alexandrian Jews adopted the term "didrachm" as the common name of the coin which was equal in weight to the shekel. The value of the silver shekel is about 64 cts. The gold shekel, as derived from a passage in Josephus, must have weighed about 253 grains [see *Pound* under WEIGHTS], a very little lower than the 60th of the Assyrian mina in gold, which weighed 260 grains; and when he says in another passage (*Antiq.* iii. 8. 10; comp. Num. vii. 14) that ten gold shekels equalled ten darics, he

must mean the double darics, weighing about 260 grains. The gold shekel was worth about $10. None have ever been discovered. (See *General Remarks.*) Fifteen shekels of silver, each weighing about 224 grains, were equal in value to one shekel of gold [*Talent* under WEIGHTS]. The divisions of the shekel mentioned in the O. T. are the half (*bekah*), the third part, the fourth part (*rebah*) and the twentieth part (*gerah*), *q. v.* In the reign of Artaxerxes Longimanus (B. C. 458) a special commission was granted to Ezra "to do what seems good with the rest of the silver and the gold" (Ezra vii. 18); and it has been suggested that this was virtually permission to the Jews to coin money; and the silver shekels extant, dated of the years 1 to 5, and the half-shekels of the years 1 to 4, weighing about 220 and 110 grains respectively, are considered to be of this period. As regards the "shekels of silver" mentioned in Nehemiah (v. 15; comp. x. 32), these may perhaps refer to the silver coin circulating in the Persian kingdom called *siglos*, of which 20 went to one gold daric, and weighing 84 grains, but having no connection with the *siklos* (weighing about 220 grains), excepting in name. These coins are, like the darics, impressed with the figure of an archer [DRAM]. In the year B. C. 139, Antiochus VII. (Sidetes) granted special permission to Simon Maccabæus to coin money *with his own stamp* (1 Macc. xv. 6), and the silver shekels and half-shekels most probably belong to Simon, and perhaps the copper pieces ($\frac{1}{2}$ shekel, $\frac{1}{4}$ shekel, and $\frac{1}{8}$ of shekel), dated in the fourth year; but there is great uncertainty as to the latter.

The Asmonæan dynasty continued to issue a copper coinage, gradually showing Greek tendencies, to the time of Antigonus, the last prince of the Asmonæan dynasty, (B. C. 40–37), and the numerous coinage of Alexander Jannæus (B. C. 105–78) doubtless circulated even to N. T. times [MITE]. The Idumæan princes, commencing with Herod I. (surnamed the Great), continued a copper coinage with only Greek legends, which circulated in Judæa (as well as a procuratorial coinage, A. D. 6–59) till the death of Agrippa II. (Acts xxv. 13; xxvi. 2, seq.) in A. D. 100. The national coinage, consisting of silver shekels and $\frac{1}{4}$ shekels, as well as of copper, with old Hebrew inscriptions, was revived during the first revolt (May, A. D. 66–September, A. D. 70), and during the second under Bar-cochab (A. D. 132–A. D. 135), at which time many of the Jewish $\frac{1}{4}$ shekels were struck over Roman *denarii*.

Silver [Money]. (1) *Keseph* in O. T. (*q. v.*); (2) in N. T. *arguros, argentum* (Matt. x. 9; James v. 3), or *argurion, argentum* (Acts iii. 6; xx. 33; 1 Pet. i. 18). The silver coins current in Palestine in N. T. period consisted of the tetradrachms and drachms of the Attic standard, and of the Roman *denarius*. [MONEY, 1 and 2, and PIECE OF SILVER, 2.]

Silverling. *Keseph* (Isa. vii. 23). The word *silverling* occurs in Tyndale's version of Acts xix. 19, and in Coverdale's of Judg. ix. 4; xvi. 5. The German *silberling* is found in Luther's version (*Bible Word-Book*). The same word is also used in Cranmer and Tyndale for the money stolen by Micah (Judg. xvii. 2, 3)—"the leuen hundredth *syluerlyngs*" (*Bible Educator*, vol. iv., p. 210).

Stater. See *Piece of Money*, 2, and *Tribute-money*, 1.

Sum [of Money]. (1) *Kephalaion* (Acts xxii. 28), *i. e.* in classical authors capital as opposed to interest or income (cp. "principal," Lev. vi. 5; Num. v. 7). In Mk. xii. 15 *epikephalaion*, "poll-tax," is used in the place of the ordinary word *kēnsos*. [TRIBUTE (Money), 2.] SUM OF MONEY. (2) *Timē arguriou*, *pretium argenti* (Acts vii. 16), *i. e.* price in silver. [MONEY.]

Talent. *Talanton, talentum,* a sum, not a coin. (1) In O. T. the rendering of the Hebrew *kiccar* [see *Talent* under WEIGHTS]; (2) in N. T. this word occurs—(*a*) in the parable of the unmerciful servant (Matt. xviii. 23–25); and (*b*) in the parable of the talents (Matt. xxv. 14–30). At this time the Attic talent obtained in Palestine; 60 *minæ* and 6000 *drachmæ* went to the talent. It was consequently worth about $970. [POUND.]

Third Part of the Shekel (Neh. x. 32), about 21c. See *Shekel* and *Tribute* [*Money*].

Tribute [Money]. (1) *The sacred tribute, didrachma* (Matt. xvii. 24). The sacred tribute or payment of the "atonement-money" was half a shekel (Exod. xxx. 13, 16), and was originally levied on every male of twenty years old and above when the Israelites were first numbered. In the reign of Joash the same sum was demanded for the repair of the Temple (2 Chron. xxiv. 4–14). After the return from the Captivity, the annual payment "for the service of the house of God" was one-third of the shekel (*q. v.*), and was voluntarily contributed (Neh. x. 32). The amount of tribute was again restored to the half-shekel (*q. v.*), which the Jews when dispersed throughout the world continued to pay toward the Temple. It is to this tribute that St. Matthew refers, and the *stater* found in the fish's mouth was an Attic tetradrachm, and at this time equal to a shekel [PIECE OF MONEY; SHEKEL]. Many commentators, both ancient and modern, have entirely missed the meaning of this miracle by interpreting the payment as a *civil* one. That it was the *sacred tribute* is plain from our Lord's reason for exemption: "Of whom do the kings of the earth take custom or tribute? of their own children or of strangers?" (Matt. xvii. 25, 26), and further, from His reason for payment, "lest we should offend them," which shows that the Jews *willingly* paid the tribute; indeed, it was not enforced by law even in the earliest times, being in this respect unlike the civil tribute. (2) *The civil tribute, nomisma tou kēnsou, kēnsos, phoros* (Matt. xxii. 17, 19; Mark xii. 14; Luke xx. 22; xxiii. 2). This was a tax paid to the Roman emperor, and was doubtless established when Judæa became a Roman province. The sum paid annually is not known; but after the capture of Jerusalem and destruction of the Temple, Vespasian ordered the Jews, in whatever country they might be, to pay the sum of *two drachmæ* to the temple of Jupiter Capitolinus, as they had previously paid to the Temple at Jerusalem. Under Domitian the tax was enforced with great severity, but upon the accession of Nerva it was abolished. Numismatic records establish this fact; coins are extant with the legend, *Fisci Judaici calumnia sublata* (comp. *sycophantia*—false accusation—Luke xix. 8). After the revolt of Bar-cochab, Hadrian renewed the tax, and in the reign of Alexander Severus (A. D. 226) the Jews continued to pay the didrachm. This civil tribute was paid in *denarii.* "Show me the tribute-money; and they brought unto Him a *penny*" (Matt. xxii. 19; comp. Mark xii. 15; Luke xx. 24). "And He saith unto them, Whose is this image and superscription? They say unto Him, Cæsar's." The title of Cæsar is common to all the Roman emperors, and the name of Tiberius, who was the Cæsar alluded to, is abbreviated on the coins, TI., while the title CÆSAR is at length. The answer may further be illustrated by the small brass coins issued under the procurators Coponius, Ambivius, and Rufus, circulating in Judæa at this time, on which is simply the legend *Kaisaros*—of Cæsar. [PENNY.]

Twentieth Part of the Shekel; about 3½c. See *Gerah* and *Shekel.*

The two following terms bear direct relation to money, and are worthy of illustration:

Money-Changers. Three distinct terms are employed in the N. T. to express this class—(1) *Trapezites, numularius,* A. V. "exchanger" (Matt. xxv. 27), from *trapeza,* "a table," a word employed for the "tables" (*mensæ*) of the money-changers in Matt. xxi. 12; Mark xi. 15; John ii. 15, and for the "bank" (*mensa*) in Luke xix. 23. *Trapezites* was the ordinary name for the banker at Athens. His principal occupation was that of changing money at an *agio.* He was a private banker, like the *argentarii* at Rome, who must be distinguished from the *mensarii* or *mensularii* and the *numularii,* who were public bankers appointed by the state on various emergencies, the latter of whom seem to have been permanently employed. Hence the Vulgate has rendered their name in all cases correctly. As the Greek word *trapezites* is from *trapeza,* "a table," so our English word "banker" (French, *banquier*) is derived from the French *banc,* "a bench," on which the person sat to do his business. (2) *Kollubistes, numularius,* A. V. "money-changer" (Matt. xxi. 12; Mark xi. 15); A. V. "changer" (John ii. 15), from *kollubos* or *kollubon,* sometimes designated as "the changing of money," or "rate of exchange," sometimes as "a small coin" or "a kind of money." A passage in Theophrastus shows us that the *kollubos* must have been a *silver* piece ranging between the *lepton* [MITE] and the ¼ obol, and therefore ⅛ of an obol, weighing about 1.4 grains. It would thus be the *silver equivalent* of the *chalkous,* which was the copper ⅛ of an obol. (3) *Kermatistes, numularius;* A. V. "changer of money" (John ii. 14), from a Greek word signifying "to cut small," which is from *kerma,* "money," John ii. 15 [MONEY]. Money-changing was called *kermatismos.* No coin was called by this name. The money-changers, of which perhaps the "goldsmiths" who repaired the vessels of the Temple (Neh. iii. 8) are prototypes, sat in the courts of the Temple on the 25th of Nizan for the purpose of exchanging foreign money for Jewish, as the Temple tax could only be paid in this latter coin. They also seem to have acted as bankers, money being placed in their hands for the purpose of increasing it, and on which interest was paid (Matt. xxv. 27; Luke xix. 23). Though the system of "lending" was not altogether objected to in the O. T. (Exod. xxii. 25; Lev. xxv. 36, 37; Deut. xxiii. 19, 20; Prov. vi. 1; Ps. xv. 5; Jer. xv. 10; Ezek. xxii. 12; xviii. 13, etc.), yet after the Captivity the Jews were compelled to leave off usury (Neh. v. 11, 12), whilst in the N. T. period it was sanctioned, provided it was done "hoping for nothing again" (Luke vi. 35; comp. Matt. v. 42). The system, however, pursued by the money-changers in the Temple must have been a vicious one, as is apparent from our Lord's denunciation of their doings (Matt. xxi. 13; Mark xi. 17; Luke xix. 46; comp. Isa. lvi. 7; Jer. vii. 11).

Treasury or **Treasure.** This term is used in the A. V. of the N. T. as the translation of three different words—(1) *Gazophulakion* (Mark xii. 41, 43; Luke xxi. 1; John viii. 20), from *gaza,* "a treasure," and *phulassō,* "to keep." The word *gaza* (Heb. *ganza*), which occurs in this sense in Acts viii. 27, is employed frequently in the O. T. for "treasures" or "treasure-house" (Ezra v. 17; vi. 1; vii. 20; Esth. iii. 9; iv. 7; Ezek. xxvii. 24; 1 Chron. xxviii. 11).

It is not a Hebrew word, but probably a Persian. The term *gazophulakion* or *gazophylacium* occurs in various passages of the Maccabees, and the Vulgate uses it as the term for the "chest" (Heb. *arun*, LXX. *kibōtos*) in which Jehoiada collected the money for the repairs of the Temple [see *General Remarks*]. The treasury-chamber appears to have been a place where people came to offer their charity-money for the repairs and other uses of the Temple, and consisted of 13 brazen chests (Heb. *trumpets*, because the mouths were wide at the top and narrow below), which stood in the women's court. (2) *Korbanas*, *corbōna* (Matt. xxvii. 6), the sacred treasure of the Jews, and explained in Mark vii. 11 as a *gift* (*dōron*), and by Josephus as "a gift to God." *Korban* in the O. T. is principally employed for unbloody sacrifices" (comp. Lev. ii. 1, 4, 5, 6). *Dōron* in the N. T. principally means "gifts in general" (Matt. ii. 11), "sacrificial gifts" (Matt. v. 23, 24; Heb. v. 1; xi. 4), "gifts of God to man" (Ephes. ii. 8), "of man to man" (Rev. xi. 10); but it is also used of gifts to the "treasury" (Luke xxi. 1), and in one case appears to mean the "treasury itself" (Luke xxi. 4). (3) *Thesauros, thesaurus.* (*a*) As the "treasure-house" (Matt. ii. 11; xiii. 52); (*b*) as the "treasure" (Matt. vi. 19, 20; xii. 35; xiii. 44; xix. 21; Mark x. 21; Luke vi. 45; xii. 33; xviii. 22; 2 Cor. iv. 7; Col. ii. 3; Heb. xi. 26). The word is used in the LXX. as the translation of the Hebrew *otsar*, meaning either "treasures of God," "store-house for corn," "treasury for gold and silver," etc. (Deut. xxviii. 12; xxxii. 34; 1 Chron. xxvii. 27; Josh. vi. 19; 1 Kings vii. 51, etc.).

WEIGHTS.

The following weights are mentioned in the Bible: *Bekah* (Gen. xxiv. 22), "half," "half a shekel." This word occurs only in the Pentateuch. See *Bekah* under MONEY.

Gerah. Properly a "grain" or "bean," the smallest silver weight, $\frac{1}{20}$th part of the shekel. See *Gerah* under MONEY and *Shekel*.

Litra. See *Pound*.

Maneh (LXX. *mnā*; Vulgate, *mina*). "A portion or part;" A. V. "pound," sometimes called *stater*—standard; a word owing its origin to Babylon, and which, as the weight was employed by the Egyptians, Phœnicians, Hebrews, and Greeks, has the same meaning in the language of all these nations. The weight of the golden targets made by Solomon for the Temple is stated to have been 300 [*shekels*] of gold each (2 Chron. ix. 16), whilst in the parallel passage the amount of gold employed for each shield is given as three *pounds* (*manehs*, 1 Kings x. 17). It would thus appear that the *maneh* of gold was equal to 100 shekels, but it must be observed that in the Chronicles the Hebrew is "300 of gold," the word *shekels* being supplied in the A. V.; and it has consequently been suggested by some that the Chronicles was written in the Macedonian period, and that consequently one should reckon what is here meant as "100 *drachms* to the *maneh*," as in use among the Greeks. The passage, however, is obscure, and in any case the calculation of 100 shekels to the *maneh* is not likely. That in Ezekiel (xlv. 12) relative to the *maneh* is also difficult of explanation [SHEKEL; TALENT]. The word *maneh* further occurs in Ezra ii. 69; Neh. vii. 71, 72; comp. 1 Esdras v. 45.

Pound. (1) *Mnā*, mina (1 Macc. xiv. 24; xv. 18). Here large sums are weighed by this standard, and it refers to the Attic talent. (2) *Litra*, a word used by the Greeks of Sicily in their system of weights

and money, sometimes called *stater*—standard—and equivalent to the Latin word *libra* or *as*, the unit of weight among the Romans. Josephus says that the Hebrew *maneh* of gold equalled 2½ *litræ*. The *libra* or Roman pound = 5059 grains, consequently 2½ Roman pounds = 12,647 grains; and as the Hebrew gold shekel was the fiftieth part of the *maneh*, it must have weighed about 253 grains [*Shekel* under MONEY]. The word *litra* occurs in the N. T. in John xii. 3 and xix. 39.

Shekel. A word signifying "weight," according to which numerous objects were weighed, especially the metals. The passage in Ezek. xlv. 12 is confusing, and cannot be satisfactorily explained, but it must be remembered that it is prophetical. 50 or 60 shekels equalled a *maneh* [MANEH; POUND]. 3600 or 3000 shekels equalled a talent [TALENT]. See *Shekel* under MONEY.

Talent. *Kikkar*, properly "a circle" or "globe;" hence *kuklos, circus.* The largest Hebrew weight for metals. First occurs in Exod. xxv. 39, "a talent of pure gold." It is also specially spoken of as "talent of silver" (2 Kings v. 22), "talent of lead" (Zech. v. 7), "talent of brass" (Exod. xxxviii. 29), and "talent of iron" (1 Chron. xxix. 7). A talent of silver bound up in a bag, and one change of garment, were about as much as one man could carry (2 Kings v. 23), and weighing was probably avoided by the sealed bags containing a certain weight of silver. The Hebrew talent was derived from Assyria and Babylonia. Of the talents current in these countries, the heavy or Assyrian talent passed through Mesopotamia and Syria to the Phœnician coast-towns, and to Palestine, where we find it in use among the Israelites. In Nineveh, as well as in Palestine, besides the weights talent of the king of 3600 sixtieths of the *maneh* for valuing precious metals, a special reckoning was made by talents of 3000 gold and silver units; but when it was found convenient to reckon 3000 shekels instead of 3600 to the talent is not known, nor when a deviation was made from the sexagesimal division of the *maneh*, and it was limited to 50 instead of to 60 units. The sum-total of the taxes to the sanctuary paid by the people is stated to be (Exod. xxxviii. 25) 100 talents, 1775 shekels, to which 603,550 men each contributed a half shekel, so that, according to this, 3000 shekels are reckoned to the talent; and as the talent is always divided into 60 *manehs*, 20 shekels went to the *maneh*; which is corroborated from the fact that the taxes for persons of various age and sex commence at a maximum point of 50 shekels (Lev. xxvii. 3, 16), and that Achan found a wedge of gold of just 50 shekels' weight, and not 60 (Josh. vii. 21). [See *General Remarks*.]

The shekels of the weight talent "of the king" and the gold talent are identical, the latter talent having been formed from the former, which appears to have been used for weighing other materials than the metals ("king's weight," 2 Sam. xiv. 26). [SHEKEL.] The weight of 9 "holy" silver shekels (224.7975×9) thus equals 8 sixteenths of the "weight" *maneh* (252.9165×8), and the *value* of 15 "holy" silver shekels equals that of 1 gold shekel—$9.70. Some, however, have taken the silver talent as weighing 660,000 grains [114$\frac{7}{12}$ lbs. troy], and, on the basis of the shekel being equivalent to 64 cents, equal to $2182, and the gold talent (with a shekel of about 132 grains) as weighing double the silver, 1,320,000 grains [229$\frac{1}{4}$ lbs. troy], and equalling, at $20 an ounce, $53,350 (Smith, *Student's O. T. Hist.*). As to the copper talent, which is supposed by some to have had a shekel of four times the weight of the gold shekel, though only 1500 to the talent, and therefore equalling 792,000 grains, it is impossible to speak with certainty; but in all probability the copper talent did not contain a fewer number of shekels than that of the silver.

The amounts of talents mentioned in the Bible during the reigns of David and Solomon are almost incredible (1 Chron. xxii. 14; xxix. 4, 7). The annual income of Solomon is said to have been 666 talents of gold (1 Kings x. 14; 2 Chron. ix. 13), which, taking the estimate of some, that the gold talent was double the silver, would be equivalent to $38,000,000—a sum more than the revenues of the whole Persian empire under Darius, which has been calculated at about seventeen million dollars. But if we take 15 shekels of silver as equalling one shekel of gold, and 15 talents of silver as equalling one talent of gold, then 666⅔ talents of gold were exactly 10,000 talents of silver, or $19,400,000. It is, however, difficult to hazard any safe conjecture, and most likely the figures in all these passages have been corrupted.

MINING AND METALLURGY OF THE BIBLE.

The graphic account in Job xxviii. is a striking description of mining operations in olden times: "Surely there is a source for the silver, and a place for the gold which they fine. Iron is taken out of the earth, and he [i. e. the miner or workman] poureth forth stone as copper. He hath made an end of darkness, and he searcheth to every extremity [i. e. to great depths and with diligent care] for the stone of darkness and of the shadow of death. He breaketh through a shaft away from those who tarry above; there, forgotten of every foot, they hang and swing far from men. The earth, from it cometh forth bread, and beneath it is upturned like fire: its stones are the place of the sapphire, which also hath dust of gold. A way that no bird of prey knoweth, and the eye of the hawk hath not seen it; which the proud beasts of prey have not trodden, nor the lion passed along. He layeth his hand upon the stone, he turneth up mountains from the root. He cutteth channels in the rocks, and his eye seeth all rare things. He bindeth fast the rivers that they leak not, and that which is hidden he bringeth to light" (Job xxviii. 1–11).

There are, as we have already seen, traces of ancient mining in Egypt, in the desert of Sinai, in Palestine, and in the adjoining lands, and this poetic description must be held as applying to some of these operations. The writer sketches the vast labor and dangerous enterprises which men will undertake in order to win from the earth its treasures, and then passes on to the question: "Where shall wisdom be found, and where is the place of understanding?" These shall baffle the skill of the miner, and are more difficult of attainment than the precious treasures of the earth. For "the fear of the Lord, that is wisdom; and to depart from evil is understanding" (vs. 12, 28).

It may be well here briefly to summarize what is known concerning the mines of biblical antiquity. Clearly, gold, silver, and tin were brought to the lands of the Bible mainly by commerce, though there are traces or records of gold-working in Egypt, and of both gold and silver in Arabia and Edom. Copper and iron were both native products of Palestine, and were worked also in the island of Meroë, at the mouth of the Nile and in the peninsula of Sinai. The island of Cyprus is also mentioned as a source of copper, and there is every probability that both iron and copper were worked in other districts likewise, though there is no distinct and ex-

plicit proof. There were lead-mines in Egypt, near the coast of the Red Sea, and also near Sinai, and it is not improbable that these lead-mines may have yielded small quantities of silver also.

Diodorus Siculus gives a minute description of the method of mining and refining gold. Shafts were sunk into what Diodorus calls veins of marble of excessive whiteness (evidently quartz-rock), from which day-and-night relays of convicts extracted the auriferous quartz. This was then broken up with picks and chisels, and further reduced by iron pestles in stone mortars to small fragments. Then it was ground to powder, spread upon a broad inclined table, and washed with water and fine sponges until the gold became pure from earthy matter. Finally, it was put, with a little lead, tin, salt and bran, into earthen crucibles closed with clay, and subjected for five days and nights to the fire of a furnace. From this description it may be seen that gold-mining in these ancient times did not radically differ from that of one hundred years ago.

Concerning the arts of *metallurgy* in ancient times we are left in much ignorance. These arts must have existed in considerable excellence amongst the Egyptians and Assyrians; and the accounts given in the Bible of the buildings of David and Solomon show that the Israelites, and especially the Phœnicians, were accomplished metal-workers. Situated between the great ancient empires of the East and West, Palestine was alternately the prey of each, and the carrying away of metal-workers into captivity shows the esteem in which they were then held. See 1 Sam. xiii. 19; 2 Kings xxiv. 14, 15; Jer. xxiv. 1; xxix. 2. The book of Ecclesiasticus (chap. xxxviii. 27, 28), in the Apocrypha, gives an account of a smith's workshop which those who are used to factories and foundries will fully appreciate: "So every carpenter and workmaster, that laboreth night and day; and they that cut and grave seals, and are diligent to make great variety, and give themselves to counterfeit imagery, and watch to finish a work: the smith also sitting by the anvil, and considering the iron-work, the vapor of the fire wasteth his flesh, and he fighteth with the heat of the furnace; the noise of the hammer and the anvil is ever in his ears, and his eyes look still upon the pattern of the thing that he maketh; he setteth his mind to finish his work, and watcheth to polish it perfectly."

In the Bible are references to casting (Ex. xxv. 12; xxvi. 37; 2 Chron. iv. 17; Isa. xl. 19); soldering and welding (Isa. xli. 7); hammering into sheets (Num. xvi. 38; Isa. xliv. 12; Jer. x. 4, 9); gilding and overlaying with metal (Ex. xxv. 11–24; xxvi. 37; 1 Kings vi. 20; 2 Chron. iii. 5; Isa. xl. 19; Zech. xiii. 9). But perhaps the most interesting of all such allusions are those to the melting and separation and refining of metals (Ps. xii. 6; Prov. xvii. 3, etc.; Isa. i. 25; Jer. vi. 29; Ezek. xxii. 18–20). Malachi (iii. 2, 3) makes use of a striking metaphor derived from the metallurgy of silver. Before the discovery of quicksilver, lead was used for the purification of the precious metals. How far the ancients were acquainted with what is now known as "Pattison's method" of obtaining silver from argentiferous lead-ore is uncertain, but Pliny apparently hints at something of the kind in these words: "When submitted to the action of fire, part of the ore precipitates itself in the form of lead, while the silver is left floating on the surface." Clearly, however, the passage from Malachi above named refers to the process of "cupellation:" "He [the Messiah] shall sit as a refiner and purifier of silver; and he shall purify the sons of Levi, and purge them as gold and silver, that they may offer unto the Lord an offering in righteousness."

REMARKABLE MOUNTAINS AND HILLS MENTIONED IN THE BIBLE,

ARRANGED GEOGRAPHICALLY FROM N. TO S.

I.—N. E. of the Promised Land—*i. e.* beyond the Euphrates. II.—Within the Land of Promise. III.—Within the Land of Possession.—E. of the Jordan.—W. of the Jordan, in three principal groups (Deut. xxxiv. 2):—(1) Of Naphtali; (2) of Ephraim; (3) of Judah. IV.—S. of the Land of Promise and Possession.

	MENTION.	NAME.	COUNTRY.	WHY REMARKABLE.	MODERN NAME.
I.	Gen. viii. 4. Jer. li. 27. 2 Kings xix. 37. Isa. xxxvii. 38. Ezek. xxvii. 14.	Ararat (= Araratia, or Arme-nia, or To-garmah).	Armenia (the cen-tral prov-ince of).	A mountain-district between the Black Sea and the Caspian, S. of the Caucasus Mts., the water-shed of the Araxes and of the Tigris and Eu-phrates—peopled by Togarmah, and famous for its horses. The resting-place of Noah's ark, etc. The refuge of Sennacherib's sons.	The range of Jebel Judi —(tradition),—or the cul-minating double peak (vol-canic) named Massis (Ar-menian), Agri Dagh (Turk-ish), Kuh-i-Nuh (Persian), 17,260 ft.
II.	1 Kings v. 6. Ps. xxix. 5. Isa. xiv. 8. Ezra iii. 7. Josh. xiii. 6.	Lebanon or Libanus.	Syria.	For its forests of oak, pine and cedar, which supplied timber for the Phœ-nician ships and the palaces and temple of David and Solomon. It was never conquered by the He-brews. The land of Hiram (the king and the artist) of Tyre and Sidon.	Jebel Liban, 7500–10,000 ft.
	Josh. xiii. 5. Judith i. 7.	Lebanon, "towards the sun-rising."	Do.	The source of the Abana.	Jebel Esh Shurky = *the East* Mountain. Average, 5000 ft.
	Num xxxiv. 7, 8.	Mount Hor.	Do.	A *northern* landmark of the Prom-ised Land (perhaps a summit of Leb-anon).	Awaits identification; but probably (*Gesenius*) only an archaic form of the Hebrew generic word for "mountain."
III. E. of J.	Sol. Song iv. 8. Deut. iii. 9. Ps. xxix. 6. Deut. iv. 48. Judg. iii. 3. 1 Chr. v. 23.	Hermon; or Sirion (Si-donian), Shenir, also prob-ably Senir (Amorite). Sion = (Gk. for) Zion (Hebrew). Baal-Her-mon.	Do. (Palestine).	The great landmark and N. bound-ary of the Hebrews, being a glistening (Shenir = breastplate) dome of nearly perennial snow. Famous for snow, abundant dews and as the sources of the Jordan and Pharpar. Probably (*Stanley*) the scene of the Transfigu-ration.	Jebel Esh Sheyk = the chief; Jebel Esh Thelj = the snowy mountain. 9000 ft.
	Ezek. xxvii. 6. Ezek. xxxix 18. Josh. xiii. 29–31. Luke iii. 1. Deut. iii. 13.	Bashan.	Do. Auranitis. Gaulanitis. Trachonitis Batanæa.	A mountain-district N. of Gilead, part of the kingdom of Og, in the N. E. of the Land of Possession. Fa-mous for its high hills and their oak forests, for its pasture and cattle. Allotted to half the tribe of Manasseh with "half Gilead."	The range of Jebel Hau-ran, 4000–6000 ft., and basin of river Yarmuk (Hieromax), or plain of the Hauran.
	Gen. xxxi. 25, 47–9. Deut. iii. 12–17.	Gilead (Ga-leed).	Syria (Pe-ræa).	A hill-country between Bashan and the Arnon, divided by the Jabbok; fa-mous for its downs, woods and park-like pastures, its balm, etc. The S. section (Sihon's kingdom) was allotted to Gad and Reuben. Scene of Laban's compact with Jacob, Jephthah's and Elijah's home and the refuge of He-brew exiles, *e.g.* David(2 Sam. xvii. 22).	Jebel Ajlun, to the N. of the Wady Zurka (Jabbok), and to the S. of it the con-spicuous range of Jebel Ji-lad, culminating in Jebel Osha, 3750 ft.
	Num. xxvii. 12. Deut. xxxii. 49; xxxiv. 1.	Abarim, the Pisgah, or Nebo (= head).	Syria.	The whole upland E. of Jordan = Peræa of the N. T., but especially the E. wall of the Jordan Valley and Dead Sea facing Jericho; of which "the Pis-gah" was a ridge from whose peak, dedicated to the god Nebo, Moses took his first and last view of the Land of Promise.	Pisgah and Nebo await identification, "in Moab, opposite Jericho."
	Gen. xiv. 6. Deut. ii. 12.	Seir of the Horites, and later Edom.	Arabia Pe-træa (*i. e.* of Petra).	The mountain-district of the Cave-dwellers (Horites or Troglodytes), dis-possessed by Esau (Edom), on the E. of the Arabah or "plain."	Jebâl to the N. and Esh Sherah to the S. of the Wady El Ahsy (brook Ze-red). Av. 2000 ft.
	Num. xx. 22, 23, 28.	Mount Hor.	Do.	The prominent peak of the range of Edom on its E. border, and the second halting-place of the Hebrews on their final journey(round Edom) to Canaan. There Aaron died.	Jebel Nebi-Harûn (= "the Mountain of the Prophet Aaron"), close above Petra. 4350 ft.

REMARKABLE MOUNTAINS AND HILLS MENTIONED IN THE BIBLE.

	MENTION.	NAME.	COUNTRY.	WHY REMARKABLE.	MODERN NAME.
	Josh. xi. 17. Josh. xii. 7.	Halak.	? Syria.	The S. limit of Joshua's conquests.	Awaits identification: "goeth up to Seir."
W. of J.	Josh. xix.22. Judg. iv. 6. Judg. viii. 18, 19.	Tabor.	Syria (Palestine), plain of Esdraëlon —i. e. Jezreel.	A wooded cone, a bound-mark between Issachar and Zebulun, near Nazareth; Barak's head-quarters (against Sisera); here Zebah and Zalmunna murdered Gideon's brethren.	Jebel-Et-Tûr. 2000 ft.
	Judg. vii. 1.	Moreh.	Do.	Hence Gideon attacked the Midianites. Distinguish the Oak (A. V. "plain") of Moreh.	Jebel-Ed-Duhy(orDahi), or "Little Hermon," of Jerome, 1800 ft.
	1 Sam. xxxi. 1.	Gilboa.	Do.	Scene of the Hebrews' defeat by the Philistines, of Jonathan's death and Saul's suicide.	Jebel Faku'a. 1700 ft.
	Isa. xxxiii. 9. Isa. xxxv. 2. Mic. vii. 14. Jer. xlvi. 18. 1 Kin. xviii. 19. 2 Kings ii. 25; iv. 25.	Carmel "by the sea."	Syria (Palestine).	For the "excellency" (i. e., above the rest of W. Palestine) of its evergreen trees and luxuriant copse-wood; for the reformation begun there by Elijah, and as the residence of Elisha.	Mar Elyas (= Eliseüs = Elisha). More rarely Kurmel. 1700 ft.
	1 Kings xvi. 24, 32. 1 Kin. xx. 1. 2 Kin. vi. 24. 2 Kin. xviii. 9, 10.	Samaria, or Shemer.	Syria, vale of Shechem.	Site of Omri's capital, Samaria, and of Ahab's great temple to Baal; twice ineffectually besieged by the Syrians, and taken after three years' siege by Shalmaneser.	Sebastiyeh. 1550 ft.
	Deut. xi. 26–30. John iv. 20.	Ebal and Gerizim.	Do., "beside the plain of Moreh" = Shechem, Judg.iv. 7.	A pair of mountain-ranges flanking the valley of Shechem, on which Moses bade Israel "put the curse and blessing" respectively. Gerizim, the later sacred "mountain" of the Samaritans.	Jebel Sulemiyeh. E.—2986 ft. G.—2855 ft.
	Judg. xx. 1. 1 Sam. x. 17. 1 Ki. xv. 22.	Mizpah, or Mizpeh.*	Do., hill-country of Benjamin.	The most commanding mountain near Jerusalem, the central place of assembly of the Hebrews; and later, the N. outpost of the kingdom of Judah.	Neby Samwil, 3000 ft. (or Mt. Scopus.—Grove).
	1 Sa. xxi. 1. 1 Sa. xxii. 1. Neh. xi. 32. Isa. x. 32.	Nob.	Do.	Scene of the massacre of the priests by Doeg the Edomite, by Saul's order.	? Bet Nuba, which overlooks Jerusalem from the N.—(Porter.)
	2 Chron. iii. 1 only.	Moriah.	Do., Jerusalem.	Site of Solomon's temple, but probably not (as tradition says it is) the "one of the mountains" in "the land of Moriah" where Isaac was offered (Gen. xxii. 2).	
	2 Sa. v. 7–9.	Zion.	Do.	The Acropolis of Jebus, later Jerusalem, taken by Joab and re-fortified by David, and called thereafter "the city of David."	Jerusalem. 2550 ft.
	Zech. xiv. 4. 2 Sa. xv. 30. 1 Kin. xi. 7. Ezek. xi. 23. Mark xiii. 3. 2 Kin. xxiii. 13. 1 Kin. xi. 7.	Olives or Olivet, or Mount of Corruption.	Do., facing ("before") Jerusalem on E.	The E. ascent from the ravine embraced Jerusalem toward Jericho, by which David fled from Absalom. The site of Solomon's idolatrous temples, and of the triumphal progress, agony and betrayal of Christ.	Jebel-Et-Tûr. 2700 ft. 2641 (Wilson, R. E.).
IV.	Ex. xix. 1, 11, etc. Lev. vii. 38. Deut. xxxiii 2. Judg. v. 5. Neh. ix. 13. Ps. lxviii. 8. Gal. iv. 25.	Sinai.	Arabia.	Place of Israel's encampment for ten months of the first year after leaving Egypt, and of the delivery of the Law.	Jebel Musa, 7375 ft. (the lower part of the Horeb range); Ras Sufsafeh (the special peak, 1500 ft. above the plain where the Wadies Esh-Sheikh and Er-Râhah meet).
	Ex. iii. 1. 1 Ki. xix. 8. Deut. i. 6. Deut. iv. 15. Deut. xviii. 16. Ps. cvi. 19. Ex.xxxiv.4.	Horeb, "the Mount of God."	Do.	Where Moses and Elijah, in exile (to save their lives), came into God's immediate presence; Moses hearing out of the burning bush, and Elijah after "the convulsion of nature" his "still small voice."	Jebel Tûr = the rock. See Sinai. The highest peak in the peninsula is Um Shaumer, 9300 ft.

* Gibeah = "hill," and Mizpeh = a hill, which is also a "watch-tower" or "beacon," are terms applied to various localities E. and W. of Jordan, and especially frequent in the land of Benjamin. Gibeah of Benjamin or of Saul is, probably, *Tuleil el Ful*, the only conspicuous peak N. of Jerusalem, Neby Samwil excepted.

N. B.—As to the height of these mountains, etc., authorities differ so greatly that it is here stated approximately, rather to indicate their relative elevation than their absolute height above the sea-level.

RIVERS AND WATERS OF SCRIPTURE.

ABANA. R. V. Abanah. Modern name Abanias. A river of Syria, whose waters were preferred to those of Jordan for healing purposes by Naaman. 2 K. 5:12. It was one of the channels of the main stream Barada, and was made to flow through the residential southwest portion of the city of Damascus. After flowing some eighteen miles eastward beyond the city it is lost in the "Meadow Lakes."

ARNON. Now the Wady Mojib. It is a tributary of the Dead Sea from the East. It formed the boundary between the Moabites and Amorites, Num. 21:13-15; Judg. 11:18. Scene of a great victory for the Israelites on their way to Canaan. A subsequent boundary between Israel and Moab. Josh. 12:1; Judg. 11:13.

BESOR. Now the Wady Sheriah, in south Judah, near Ziklag, where David's fainting soldiers remained while the rest marched on, 1 Sam. 30:9, 10, 21.

CEDRON. See KIDRON.

CHEBAR. Now Nahr Malcha. A river of Chaldea, and scene of Ezekiel's visions during his captivity in Babylon. Ezek. 1:3; 3:15, 23.

CHERITH. Supposedly one of the western tributaries of Jordan. Notes the place where Elijah was fed by ravens. 1 K. 17:5.

CHINNERETH, Sea of. Old name of the inland sea known as Lake Gennesareth, or Sea of Galilee. Probably so named from an ancient city which stood on or near its shores. Num. 34:11; Deut. 3:17; Josh. 13:27; 19:35. See GALILEE, SEA OF.

CHINNEROTH, Sea of. Another spelling of Chinnereth, which see. Josh. 11:2; 12:3; 1 K. 15:20.

EAST SEA. See SALT SEA.

EGYPT, River of. Now the wady or brook El-Arish. A southwest boundary of the Promised Land, Num. 34:5. Called "brook of Egypt" in R. V., 1 K. 8:65; Isa. 27:12. In A. V., Isa. 27:12, "stream of Egypt."

ESHCOL. Now Gadis. A wady or brook near Hebron. Here the spies found grapes, indicating the fertility of Canaan. Num. 13:22-27; 32:9; Deut. 1:24.

EUPHRATES. A great river of western Asia, rising in Armenia and emptying into the Persian Gulf. Called "the river" in R. V. 1 K. 4:21. One of the boundaries of Eden, Gen. 2:14; 15:18. A vague eastern limit of Promised land, Deut. 1:7; 11:24; Josh. 1:4; 1 Chr. 5:9. Limit of David's conquests, 2 Sam. 8:3; 1 Chr. 18:3. Babylon was situated on its banks. Jer. 13:2-7; 46:2-10; 51:63, 64.

GALILEE, Sea of. That expansion of the waters of the Jordan called anciently the sea of Chinnereth or Chinneroth. See CHINNERETH. Called "Lake of Gennesaret," Luke 5:1; "Sea of Tiberias," John; "the sea," Mat.

GENNESARET, Lake of. Sea of Galilee is so called in Luke 5:1, after the name of the district lying to the northwest of it.

GIHON. Second river of Eden, Gen. 2:13. It compassed Ethiopia, or, in R. V., Cush.

GREAT SEA. The Mediterranean Sea, Num. 34:6; Josh. 1:4; 9:1; 15:12, 47; Ezek. 47:15, 19, 20.

HIDDEKEL. Third river of Eden. Now generally associated with the Tigris. Gen. 2:14. Scene of one of Daniel's visions, Dan. 10:4.

JABBOK. Now the Wady Zerka. A tributary of Jordan on east side. Boundary between Ammon and Moab. Scene of Jacob's wrestling in prayer. Gen. 32:22; Deut. 2:37; 3:16; Josh. 12:2; Judg. 11:13.

JORDAN. Chief river of Palestine, forming its eastern boundary. Rises in Anti-Libanus range, flows southward, enlarges into Sea of Galilee, empties into Dead Sea. It is a swift, narrow, yet fordable stream, with a course of two hundred miles. Gen. 3:10; Josh. 2:7; Judg. 3:28; 2 Sam. 10:17; Mat. 3:13.

KANAH. In the R. V. "brook of Kanah." A boundary stream between Ephraim and Manasseh. Josh. 16:8; 17:9.

KIDRON. Now the Wady en-Nâr. The brook or ravine between Jerusalem and Olivet. Scene of Adonijah's rebellion, and of the burning of idols and of the grove which Josiah found erected in the house of the Lord. Crossed by Christ and his Apostles on the night of betrayal. 2 Sam. 15:23; 2 K. 23:6; 2 Chr. 29:16. Spelled Cedron in John 18:1.

KISHON. Now Nahr Mukutta. The brook or wady which drains the valley of Esdraelon. Scene of Sisera's defeat by Barak, and of Elijah's execution of the priests of Baal. Judg. 4:7, 13; 5:21; 1 K. 18:40. Spelled Kison in Ps. 83:9.

MEROM, Waters of. Now L. Huleh. The lake, or expansion of the waters of Jordan, above the Sea of Galilee. Scene of Joshua's victories over the Canaanitish kings. Josh. 11:5-7.

NILE. The great river of Egypt. Not mentioned directly in Scripture, but referred to as "the river," Gen. 41:1; Ex. 2:3; 7:21; "the river of Egypt," Gen. 15:8; "flood of Egypt," Am. 8:8; Sihor, "black," Josh. 13:3; Shihor, "dark blue," 1 Chr. 13:5; "Nachal of Egypt;" "river of Cush," etc.

PHARPAR. A river of Syria, now generally associated with the Taura, a diverted branch of the Barada, made to flow through the residential northwestern part of the city of Damascus. Like the Abana, it loses its waters in the "Meadow Lakes" beyond the city. Naaman thought its waters better than those of Jordan for healing purposes. 2 K. 5:12.

PISON. One of the four rivers of Eden. It bounded Harilah, a land of gold and precious stones. By many associated with the Indus or Ganges. Gen. 2:11, 12.

SALT SEA. The Dead Sea, or Bahr Lut (Lot's Sea). Known to classical writers as Lake Asphaltites. Receives waters of the Jordan. No outlet. About 1300 feet below the level of the Mediterranean. Called "Sea of the Plain" in Deut. 4:49; 2 K. 14:25; "Salt Sea," Deut. 3:17; Josh. 3:16; 12:3; "East Sea," Ezek. 47:18; Joel 2:20; Zech. 14:8; "The Sea," Ezek. 47:8; "Vale of Siddim," Gen. 14:3; "Sodomitish Sea," 1 Esdras 5:7.

SEA OF THE PLAIN. See SALT SEA.

TIBERIAS, Sea of. Sea of Galilee is so called in John 6:1, after the name of the city Tiberias, on its western shore.

ZARED. Now El-Hesi. A brook or wady separating Moab from Edom, Num. 21:12. Written Zered in Deut. 2:13, 14.

553

ZOOLOGY IN THE BIBLE.

PART I.

BIBLE MAMMALIA.

ANTELOPE. The R. V. introduces "antelope" into the text of Deut. 14 : 5 instead of "wild ox," and into Isa. 51 : 20 instead of "wild bull." The Lxx refer the Hebrew *teo* to the *Oryx*, which is the Greek word for the antelope or gazelle of Egypt and Libya. The species that best suits the above texts is the *Oryx beatrix*, found in southern Persia and Arabia. It is quite the counterpart of the African oryx or antelope in size, speed and habit, but its horns are nearly straight and very prominent.

APE. Imported into Palestine from the same countries which supplied ivory and peacocks, 1 K. 10 : 22; 2 Chr. 9 : 21. Apes are pictured on Egyptian monuments and represented in Assyrian sculptures.

ASS. A highly-prized beast for saddle and burden in the East from the earliest times, being pictured on Assyrian and Egyptian monuments. Five different Hebrew words serve to designate it in the Bible. The white ass was deemed a fitting palfrey for kings, priests and notables. Gen. 22 : 3; 1 Chr. 27 : 30; Job 1 : 3; Zech. 9 : 9; Mat. 21 : 1–9. *See* Bible Ill., O. T., p. 425.

ASS, Wild. Two Hebrew words, *pere* and *arod*, appear to discriminate between the wild ass of Syria and Arabia. Job 39 : 5–8; Jer. 2 : 24; 14 : 6. The wild ass is fleet, gregarious and hard to tame.

BADGER. Badgers are native to Arabia and Palestine, and are small, sly, burrowing animals, hard to catch. Their skins are mentioned in Ex. 25 : 5; 35 : 7 as for tent-coverings, and in Ezek. 16 : 10 as for shoes. As either of these uses was unlikely, if not impossible, the R. V. translates the original, *tachash*, as "sealskins," and marginally suggests "or porpoise." The Arabic word, *tucash*, is used to designate seals, dolphins, porpoises, dugongs, and similar aquatic animals, whose skins are adapted for coverings and shoes.

BAT. Bats abound in Palestine, in caves, temples, quarries and rocks. Though classed as an unclean fowl in Lev. 11 : 19; Deut. 14 : 18; it is a true mammal of the mouse species. A symbol of desolate loneliness, Isa. 2 : 20. *See* Bible Ill., O. T., p. 760.

BEAR. The Syrian bear, found in the forests of Galilee and Lebanon, is very like the brown bear of Europe in size and habit. Its color is somewhat lighter. 2 Sam. 17 : 8; 2 K. 2 : 24; Prov. 17 : 12. *See* Bible Ill., O. T., p. 367.

BEAST, Wild. Three Hebrew words refer to wild animals, or beasts, in general. Gen. 1 : 28; Ps. 50 : 11; Isa. 13 : 21.

BEHEMOTH. The A. V. margin of Job 40 : 15, suggests "elephant," while that of the R. V. suggests "hippopotamus." The Hebrew original, *behemah*, signifies a "great beast," but it is applied also to the hippopotamus, in a specific sense. Though the genus is African, it was once familiar in all the waters of the Nile, and may have extended to the marshes of Palestine. Job's description of the hippopotamus corresponds with the size, habits and chase of it as depicted on Egyptian monuments. *See* Bible Ill., O. T., p. 631.

BOAR. The wild boar is common in the sedgy fastnesses of the Jordan valley, and when driven out by high water proves destructive to fields, vineyards and gardens. Ps. 80 : 13.

BULL, BULLOCK. Terms applied somewhat generally to animals of the bovine kind, as in Ps. 22 : 12. Oxen in Gen. 12 : 6; bullock in Isa. 45 : 25; cow in Ezek. 4 : 15. The "wild ox" of Deut. 14 : 5 and "wild bull" of Isa. 51 : 20 become "antelope" in the R. V. *See* Antelope. *See* Bible Ill., O. T., p. 124.

CAMEL. The Arabian, or one-humped, camel generally meant. Used from most remote times, and throughout the East, for desert travel and traffic. A source of wealth, Gen. 12 : 16; Judg. 7 : 12; 2 Chr. 14 : 15; Job 1 : 3; Isa. 30 : 6. Flesh a prohibited food, though its milk was used, Lev. 11 : 4. Hair used for clothing, 2 K. 1 : 8; Zech. 13 : 4; Mat. 3 : 4. Figuratively for something beyond human power, Mat. 19 : 24; 23 : 24. The Bactrian, or two-humped, camel, is represented on Assyrian monuments. It was not known to western Asia. *See* Bible Ills., O. T., pp. 606, 814.

CAT. Mentioned only in Baruch 6 : 22. It was doubtless known to the Hebrews, as it was held sacred by the Egyptians, and was mummified and entombed the same as human beings.

CATTLE. Domestic bovine animals, as oxen, cows, bulls, calves; also any live stock. The main source of wealth among pastoral peoples. Bovine cattle were used for hauling, plowing, threshing, sacrifices and food. In the north of Palestine cattle grew larger than in the maritime plains and east of Jordan. Gen. 13 : 2; Ex. 12 : 29; 34 : 19; Num. 20 : 19; 32 : 16; Job 1 : 3; Ps. 50 : 10. *See* Bible Ill., O. T., p. 159.

CHAMELEON. A species of lizard, arborial in habit. The R. V. so renders the Hebrew *tinshemeth* in place of "mole" in the text of Lev. 11 : 30.

CHAMOIS. A food animal mentioned in Deut 14 : 5. The chamois is native only to the mountains of central Europe. The Hebrew original, *zemer*, implies a leaping animal, and must refer to some of the species of wild sheep, goats or other animal familiar to the ancient Hebrews. Three have been suggested as meeting the requirements of the text—the ibex, the wild sheep or moufflon of the Arabian desert, and the wild goat of Syria. *See* Bible Ill., O. T., p. 225.

CONEY. *Hyrax Syriacus*, or rock badger, in the R. V. margin of Lev. 11 : 5; Deut. 14 : 7; Ps. 104 : 18; Prov. 30 : 26. A small, timid animal somewhat resembling the rabbit in size, color and habit, but so different in structure as to be classed as another order of mammals. *See* Bible Ill., O. T., p. 128.

DEER. The fallow deer is mentioned in Deut. 14:5 as a food animal, and in 1 K. 4:23 as one of the provisions for Solomon's table. While it is reasonably certain that the fallow, or dappled, deer was found in Palestine, it is generally agreed that the Hebrew original, *yachmur*, refers to the *Bubalis buselaphus*, "wild-cow," of Arabia, the Arabic name of which is *yachmur*. It is of the size of the red deer, has a uniform ruddy color, and tail tipped with black. Its face is lengthy like a cow's, and its horns are light and slightly curved. Its flesh was considered the most savory of all desert game. The name "bubalis" has been transferred to the roebuck of northern Galilee and the Lebanon ranges, and in the R. V. of the texts above mentioned the word roebuck takes the place of fallow deer.

DOG. The dog is frequently mentioned in the Bible, and mostly with contempt. It seems to have been of very common breed, and used as a guard for flocks, house watch and street scavenger. Ex. 11:7; Deut. 23:18; 1 Sam. 17:43; 2 Sam. 9:8; 1 K. 14:11; Job 30:1; Ps. 22:16-20; Isa. 56:10; Mat. 7:6; Rev. 22:15.

DRAGON. The Hebrew *tan*, pl. *tannim*, translated "dragon," or "dragons," in the A. V. texts of Job 30:29; Ps. 44:19; Isa. 34:13; Jer. 9:11; Mic. 1:8, is rendered "jackals" in the R. V. *See* JACKAL.

DROMEDARY. The post camel of the East (*Camelus dromedarius*), usually the one-humped species, as distinguished from the Bactrian camel (*Camelus bactrianus*), or two-humped species. 1 K. 4:28; Isa. 60:6; Jer. 2:23; Mic. 1:13. *See* Bible Ill., O. T., p. 606.

ELEPHANT. The Hebrew *eleph* means an ox. Elephant not mentioned in canonical books of Bible and is not a part of Syrian fauna. But in the Books of Maccabees they are mentioned as part of the fighting force of Antiochus. "Elephant's teeth" is suggested as an A. V. marginal reading for "ivory" in 1 K. 10:22; 2 Chr. 9:21. *See* Bible Ill., N. T., p. 222.

EWE. *See* SHEEP.

FALLOW DEER. *See* DEER.

FERRET. An unclean domesticated animal of the weasel family, used for catching rats. But the R. V. of Lev. 9:30 renders the Hebrew *anâkah* as "gecko," which is thought to be correct, since the root of *anâkah* means to click, and the gecko, common to Palestine, is a lizard which gives forth a clicking sound. Moreover, the text seems to call for an animal of the creeping kind.

FOX. In the N. T., where fox is mentioned, the animal is that we understand by the name, Luke 9:58. On the contrary, the Hebrew, *shual*, implies the "jackal," as suggested in the R. V. margin of Judg. 15:4; Ps. 63:10. Only in S. of S. 2:5; Ezek. 13:4 is the word *shual* translated "foxes" without question.

GAZELLE. The word is introduced into the R. V. text of Deut. 14:5 and 1 K. 4:23 in place of roebuck. The gazelle abounds in Palestine. It is the smallest of the antelope family, gregarious, of fawn color, with white belly, and dark stripes down its face. Noted for its beauty, fleetness, timidity and affection.

GOAT. Several Hebrew words are used to designate the goat (*Capra hircus*) and its kinds, "he goat," "she goat," "kid," "leading goat," etc. The goat was an important part of the wealth of the pastoral East. It furnished both food and clothing, while its skin was used for wine, oil and water bottles. There were many varieties, wild and tame. Gen. 27:9; 1 Sam. 24:2; Job 39:1. The "scapegoat" was one of two

offered on the Day of Atonement, over which the priest confessed the sins of Israel, and then let it escape to the wilderness, Lev. 16:7-26. *See* Bible Ills., O. T., pp. 135, 163.

GOAT, Wild. It is agreed that the *Capra beden* or Sinaitic ibex is the animal meant by the Hebrew original. The ibex is common in the mountains of Palestine. It is of light fawn color, with long curved horns, and its flesh is highly prized for food. It is the "roe" of Prov. 5:19. Another word, *akko*, is translated "wild goat" in Deut. 14:5. *See* Bible Ill., O. T., p. 225.

GREYHOUND. The Hebrew original implies "one girt about the loins," as a wrestler. The A. V. margin of Prov. 30:31 suggests "horse," and the R. V. "war horse." This last would seem to be a suitable rendering, though the Persian greyhound may have been known to Solomon. It is pictured on the Assyrian sculptures in chasing the gazelle.

HARE. The hare, *arnebeth* in Hebrew, was a forbidden food to the Iraelites. Lev. 11:6; Deut. 14:7. It was wrongly supposed to chew the cud. Two kinds of hare are found in Palestine. One, *Lepus Syriacus*, inhabits the north and resembles the English hare. The other, *Lepus Ægypticus*, is found in Judea and along the Jordan. It resembles the American rabbit. The Lxx render the word "hedgehog."

HART. Is mentioned as food allowed by the Mosaic law, Deut. 12:15; 14:5, and as furnishing provision for Solomon's table, 1 K. 4:23. The Hebrew, *ayyal*, clearly implies a deer of some kind, possibly the red deer, now extinct in Palestine. The valley of *Ayyalon* (Ajalon) was the "place of deer or stags." Its traits are frequently referred to—panting after water, Ps. 42:1; leaping nimbly, Isa. 35:6; beautiful in form, S. of S. 2:9; fleetness, 2 Sam. 2:8; tender love, Prov. 5:19; fear of thunder, Ps. 29:9; concealment of young, Job 39:1. In Gen. 49:21 it is made a symbol of Naphtali. *See* Bible Ill., O. T., p. 654.

HEDGEHOG. This is the Lxx rendering of *arnebeth* in Lev. 11:6 for hare. It is also a Lxx rendering of *kippod*, which in the A. V. of Isa. 14:23; 34:11; Zeph. 2:14 is translated "bittern," and in the R. V. "porcupine." The hedgehog and porcupine are both common to Palestine.

HIND. Female of the hart or red deer. Gen. 49:21; Ps. 29:9; Prov. 5:19.

HIPPOPOTAMUS. *See* BEHEMOTH.

HORSE. The horse was not a favorite animal among early Hebrews, being forbidden to the kings, at least the horses of Egypt, Deut. 17:16. They were not used as beasts of burden, but chiefly in war. David and Solomon brought cavalry and chariots into use in time of war. Only once is the horse mentioned in connection with agriculture, Isa. 28:28. *See* Bible Ill., O. T., p. 516.

HYENA. The Lxx rendering of *tzabua* in Jer. 12:9, the "speckled bird" of the A. V. and R. V. Zeboim, in 1 Sam. 13:18, means "valley of hyenas." The hyena was, and is, common to Syria, living in caves, prowling in the night, and feeding on carrion and bones.

JACKAL. The R. V. suggests "jackals" as the proper rendering of *shual* in Judg. 15:4; Ps. 63:10, instead of "foxes." The Jackal (*Canis aureus*) was common in Palestine. They herd in packs and make night hideous with their howls. *See* Bible Ill., O. T., p. 770.

KID. Young goat. An offering, Num. 7:12-82. A favorite meat, Gen. 38:17; 1 Sam. 16:20. *See* Bible Ill., O. T., p. 118.

LAMB. Young of the sheep or goat. Favorite sacrifices, Ex. 29:38-41; Num. 28:9-29. *See* Bible Ill., O. T., p. 167.

LEOPARD. This fierce, spotted beast of the cat species must have been familiar to the Hebrew writers who so aptly allude to its color, cunning and ferocity. It gave name to Beth-Nimrah, "the home of leopards," east of Jordan, and the name is still preserved in the Arabic Beit-Neim'r. It is said that leopards may still be found in Moab and on Carmel. The cheetah, or hunting leopard, is also found east of Jordan. It is trained for hunting deer or antelope. Jer. 13 : 23; Dan. 7 : 6; S. of S. 4 : 8. *See* Bible Ill., O. T., p. 826.

LION. The lion was formerly well known to all countries east of the Mediterranean. It is represented by several Hebrew words, and finds frequent mention in the Bible, not only as to its real characteristics, but in a symbolical way. It is now rarely found west of the Euphrates. Gen. 49 : 9; Judg. 14 : 5, 6; 1 Sam. 17 : 34–36; Job 4 : 10; Dan. 6 : 16–24. *See* Bible Ills., O. T., pp. 307, 425, 688, 769, 959.

MOLE. The mole is not found in Palestine. *Tinshemeth* translated "mole" in Lev. 11 : 30, is rendered "chameleon" in the R. V. In Isa. 2 : 20, the Hebrew *chaphor-peroth*, translated "mole," is thought to refer to the mole-rat, a tailless, burrowing animal of silver-gray color, living on roots and very destructive in gardens. *See* Bible Ill., O. T., p. 760.

MOUSE. The Hebrew *achbar* is regarded as a generic name including rats, mice and the small rodents, all of which abounded in Palestine and were very destructive. Lev. 11 : 29; 1 Sam. 6 : 4; Isa. 46 : 17.

MULE. Not used by the Hebrews prior to David's time, when, with the horse, it supplanted the ass as the beast of royalty. Mules of a superior breed are represented on the Assyrian monuments. 2 Sam. 13 : 29; 1 K. 1 : 33; 2 Chr. 9 : 24. The Hebrew *yemen*, translated "mules" in the A. V. of Gen. 36 : 24, is rendered "warm springs" in the R. V.

OX. The Hebrew original, *bakar*, is of generic significance, and in modified forms embraces the bovine species. The ox of Palestine was a small, shaggy creature, both long and short-horned. Used for food, Deut. 14 : 4; plowing, Deut. 22 : 10; threshing, Deut. 25 : 4; draught, Num. 7 : 3; burden, 1 Chr. 12 : 40; sacrifices, 1 K. 1 : 9. *See* Bible Ills., O. T., pp. 338, 722, 929.

PORCUPINE. See HEDGEHOG.

PYGARG. The Hebrew *dishon*, translated "pygarg" in Deut. 14 : 5, is probably the *antelope addax*. The Greek of the Lxx has *pygargos*, meaning "white rumped." There were several species of white-rumped antelope common to the Saharah, Egypt and Arabia, most of them of large size, with long, twisted horns and flattened hoofs, so as to resist the sand.

RAM Male of the sheep, or of any of the ovine species. It was the prescribed sacrifice for the trespass offering, for new moon and Day of Atonement. The fat of its tail was part of the peace offering. Its dyed skins were highly esteemed. Gen. 15 : 9; 22 : 13; Ex. 25 : 5; Lev. 6 : 6.

ROE, ROEBUCK. In the R. V. of 2 Sam. 2 : 18 and 1 Chr. 12 : 8 the word "roe," as a translation of *tsebi*, is retained. In the texts of S. of S. 2 : 17; 8 : 14 the word "roe" is retained, with the marginal suggestion of "gazelle," while in the texts of Deut. 14 : 5 and 1 K. 4 : 23 the word "roebuck" becomes "gazelle." The consensus of opinion is that the *Gazella dorcas* is meant. *See* GAZELLE. *See* also Bible Ill., O. T., p. 224.

SATYRS Isa. 13 : 21; 34 : 14. Literally "hairy ones." The mythical creatures, half man and half goat, that inhabited woods and waste places.

SHEEP. An important animal among Hebrews and a main source of wealth. The common sheep of Syria and Palestine were of the broad-tailed variety, though in the mountainous portions a short-wooled breed existed, similar to the modern merino. Shepherd's occupation an honored one, Gen. 4 : 2; Ex. 3 : 1; 1 Sam. 16 : 11; Job 42 : 12, though odious to the Egyptians. Sheep were used largely in sacrifices. Lambs were slain for feasts and to entertain guests. Ewe's milk was valued for drink, seething and curds. Wool formed an important article of clothing. Sheep-shearing time was a jubilee, Ex. 20 : 24; Lev. 9 : 3; 1 Sam. 25 : 18. Sheep were paid as tribute, 2 K. 3 : 4. Sheep and shepherd employed much figuratively, 2 Chr. 18 : 16; Ps. 119 : 176; Mat. 9 : 36; John 10 : 11; Heb. 13 : 20. *See* Bible Ills., O. T., pp. 348, 482, 701, 808, 927.

SWINE. The hog was pronounced unclean for food, Lev. 11 : 7; Deut. 14 : 8. Priests and Arabians abstained from the meat for dietetic reasons. Swine-keeping a degrading business, Luke 15 : 15, yet swine were kept, Mat. 8 : 32. To cast "pearls before swine" was to waste truth on those who despised it, Mat 7 : 6. *See* Bible Ill., N. T., p. 101.

UNICORN. A fabulous animal pictured as having one horn on its forehead and the body of a horse. The Hebrew *reem*, translated "unicorn" in the A. V. of Num. 23 : 22; 24 : 8; Deut. 33 : 17; Job 39 : 9; Ps. 22 : 21; 29 : 6; Isa. 34 : 7, does not refer to the one-horned creature of fable, but evidently to a two-horned animal of strength and ferocity, as is plain from Deut. 33 : 17. The R. V. inserts "wild ox" in all of the above texts, with a marginal suggestion of "antelope" in the texts of Num. 23 : 22; 24 : 8; Deut. 33 : 17, and Job 39 : 9. From the similarity of the Assyrian *rimu* to the Hebrew *reem*, they are taken to refer to the same animal. The Assyrian *rimu* was the *Bos primigenus* of naturalists, the *auroch* of the ancient Germans, and the *urus* of Cæsar, which he describes as of great strength and speed, with immense size of horn, and sparing neither man nor beast when they have caught sight of them. The species is now extinct, but the caverns of Lebanon reveal bones, taken to be those of the auroch, or wild ox, above described. Its chase is represented on Assyrian monuments. *See* Bible Ill., O. T., p. 251.

WEASEL. The Hebrew *choled* is translated "weasel" in Lev. 11 : 29. Some refer it to the "mole," some to the "mole-rat," some to the "polecat." The two last, as well as the weasel, are found in Palestine. There does not seem to be any good reason for disputing the A. V. and R. V. rendering.

WOLF. The wolf (*Canis lupus*) is found throughout the northern hemisphere, and infests the hills and valleys of Palestine. It is everywhere known as the foe of sheep and dread of shepherds, and pictured as an emblem of ferocity and bloodthirstiness. Syrian wolves are larger and lighter in color than those of Europe. Owing to the milder climate and greater ease of obtaining food, they are not gregarious as in extreme northern countries, but sally forth at night singly to seize their prey. A wolf typed the rapacity of Benjamin, Gen. 49 : 27; cruelty of Israel's oppression, Ezek. 22 : 27; destruction of the wicked, Jer. 5 : 6; iniquity of false prophecy and shepherdhood, Mat. 7 : 15; 10 : 16; John 10 : 12; Acts 20 : 29. *See* Bible Ill., O. T., p. 819.

PART II.

BIRDS OF THE BIBLE.

BITTERN. A bird of the heron tribe, solitary in its habits, frequent in the marshes of Syria and the Tigris, and noted for the bellowing noise of the male in spring-time. Though the habits of the bird conform closely to the requirements of the texts of Isa. 14:23; 34:11; Zeph. 2:14, the R. V. translates the Hebrew word *kippoa*, in the above texts, as "porcupine," that being the translation or suggestion in the Lxx and Vulgate.

COCK. Male of the *Gallus ferrugineus*, East India jungle fowl, probably the original of the *Gallus domesticus*, or common domestic fowl. Though domestic fowls are but once alluded to in the O. T., and as a provision for Solomon's table, 1 K. 4:23, in N. T. times they were as common as they are now. The crowing of the cock, in Mat. 26:34; Mark 14:30; Luke 22:34, indicated the third watch of the night, from midnight to daylight.

CORMORANT. A large, greedy water bird, pronounced unclean in Lev. 11:17; Deut. 14:17. It is found on all the coasts, lakes and rivers of Palestine. In the texts of Isa. 34:11; Zeph. 2:14, another Hebrew word, *kaath*, is rendered "cormorant" in the A. V. with the marginal suggestion of "pelican." In the R. V. of these two texts the word "pelican" is inserted instead of cormorant. *See* Bible Ill., O. T., p. 685.

CRANE. A large, long-necked, heron-like bird, of gray plumage, noisy on the wing, and noted for migratory observance of times and seasons. Vast flocks of them pass over Palestine in March, returning southward in October. The Hebrew *agur*, translated "crane" in A. V. of Isa. 38:14; Jer. 8:7, is translated "swallow" in the R. V.; while the Hebrew *soos*, translated "swallow" in the same A. V. text, is rendered "crane" in the R. V., thus making a complete transposition of the words. *See* Bible Ill., O. T., p. 795.

CUCKOO. Though two species of cuckoo are common to Palestine, it is agreed that the *shachaph* of Lev. 11:16; Deut. 14:15, translated "cuckoo" in the A. V., is properly rendered "seamew" in the R. V. The seamew (*Larus canus*) is a general name for the different species of gull (sea-gull) which swarm in the waters of Palestine.

DOVE. The dove and pigeon belong to the family of *Columbæ*, of all parts of the world, though most abundant in the East. The Old-World rock-dove (*Columba livia*) is the original of the domestic pigeon, of which there are many breeds. The Hebrew *yonah* is pigeon or dove, while *tor-yonah* is turtle-dove. Pigeon and dove are so closely allied, and mentioned so frequently together in the Bible, that a description of one will answer for the other. They were the only birds used for sacrifices under the law. Four species of pigeon and three of dove are found in Palestine, the former being domesticated and very plentiful, the latter migratory and overspreading the wooded sections in spring-time. They were in request as offerings for the poor, Gen. 15:9; Lev. 5:7; 12:6-8; Luke 2:24; symbol of innocence, Mat. 10:16; harbinger of God, Gen. 8; emblem of Holy Spirit, Mat. 3:16. *See* Bible Ills., O. T., pp. 13, 119, 815.

EAGLE. This is the translation of the Hebrew *nesher* in the A. V. and R. V. of the O. T., and of the Greek *aetos* in the N. T. But in the R. V. margins of Lev. 11:13 and Deut. 14:12 "great vulture" is suggested, and in margins of Mic. 1:16; Mat. 24:28; Luke 17:37 "vulture" is suggested. The agreement is nearly unanimous that the bird meant by the above originals is the *Gyps fulvus*, or griffin vulture, seen everywhere in the East. This is the bird meant by the Arabic *niss'r*, which word is the same as the Hebrew *nesher*. The griffin vulture does not catch its food, but feeds on carcasses, by preference fresh ones. By its size, flight and stateliness it is associated with the lordly and noble throughout the East. Pronounced unclean, Lev. 11:13; Deut. 14:12; noted for height and rapidity of flight, Prov. 23:5; 2 Sam. 1:23; Job 9:26; Deut. 28:49; Jer. 4:13; great age, Ps. 103:5; care of young, Ex. 19:4; Mic. 1:16; Mat. 24:28; Luke 17:37. *See* Bible Ills., O. T., pp. 629, 906.

FALCON. R. V. translation of Hebrew *ayyah* in Job 28:7, instead of A. V. "vulture." Same word rendered "kite" in Lev. 11:14; Deut. 14:13. Falcon may mean any falconine bird, as the kestrel, duck-hawk, sparrow-hawk, buzzard, kite, or common hawk. It is also the diurnal bird of prey used by falconers in hunting, and noted for its keen eyesight and swift flight.

FOWLS. "Fowls of the air" in O. T. usually implies a limitation to the larger birds, as eagles and vultures, though the Hebrew original for fowl embraces birds in general, Gen. 1:20. The Greek original provides the domestic limitation, Luke 12:24. The "fatted fowl" of 1 K. 4:23 would seem to indicate that Solomon had introduced from India others of the domestic fowls, besides peacocks, though there is no positive evidence that the Hebrews reared poultry before the captivity.

GIER EAGLE. An unclean bird of prey, Lev. 11:18; Deut. 14:17. The R. V. renders the Hebrew *racham* as "vulture" in the above texts, and inserts "gier eagle" for "ossifrage." Since the Arabic name for the Egyptian vulture, or "Pharaoh's hen," is identical with the Hebrew *racham*, there can be but little doubt that this bird, familiar to the entire East, is the one meant.

GLEDE. An unclean bird mentioned in Deut. 14:13. The Hebrew *ra'ah* means the "far-seer." The modern glede, or "glider," is the European kite. But the term is also applied to the buzzard, and this may be the bird meant by *ra'ah*. Three species of buzzard are found in Palestine, the most common being a large kind, resembling a small eagle.

GRIFFIN-VULTURE. *See* EAGLE.

HAWK. The Hebrew *netz* is of generic significance, embracing the falcon family, at least the smaller members, as the kestrel, merlin and peregrine, all of which are found in Palestine. Lev. 11:16; Deut. 14:15; Job 39:26.

HEN. Female of the *Gallus domesticus*, common in Palestine during the N. T. period, Mat. 23:37; Luke 13:34. *See* COCK.

557

HERON. A. V. and R. V. translation of Hebrew *anaphah* in Lev. 11:19; Deut. 14:18; but the R. V. suggests "ibis" in margin of Lev. 11:19. Many varieties of heron exist in the swamps and marshy places of Palestine, some of which are migratory; but the common, or buff-backed, heron remains throughout the year. Another common variety, the *Ardea cinerea*, may be frequently seen with cattle in the pastures, associated with purple ibises. *See* Bible Ill., O. T., p. 513.

HOOPOE. *See* LAPWING.

IBIS. Suggested in R. V. margin of Lev. 11:19 instead of "heron." The ibis is a wading bird, with cylindrical bill, bent downward. It feeds on reptiles, fish, etc. The sacred ibis of the Egyptians was white, except the ornamental plumes over the hind quarters, the bill, feet and naked head, which were black.

KITE. A bird of the hawk species. Pronounced unclean in Lev. 11:14; Deut. 14:13. The same Hebrew original, *ayyah*, is translated "vulture" in A. V. of Job 28:7, and "falcon" in R. V. Three species of kite are found in Palestine, of which the red kite and black migratory kite are the most common. The European kite and glede are identical.

LAPWING. The Hebrew *dukipath* is rendered "lapwing" in A. V. of Lev. 11:19, and "hoopoe" in the R. V. The Coptic and Syriac names for hoopoe are identical with the Hebrew *dukipath*. The hoopoe is common in the East, and is noted for its beautiful shape and plumage. The Arabs call it the "doctor bird."

NIGHT-HAWK. The translation of *tachmas* in Lev. 11:16, though the R. V. suggests the uncertainty of it. Some suggest the nightjar or goatsucker as the bird meant, but the Lxx and Vulgate refer it to the owl. As there are no less than five species of owl common to Palestine, four of which are identified by other Hebrew names, the word *tachmas* may mean the barn or screech owl found throughout Palestine.

OSPREY. A widely-distributed pandionoid bird of prey, dark-brown above, with head, neck and lower parts mostly white. It preys upon fish, which it catches in its talons. Its flesh was forbidden food, Lev. 11:13; Deut. 14:12.

OSSIFRAGE. The unclean bird of Lev. 11:13; Deut. 14:12, which the R. V. calls "gier eagle." The Hebrew *peres* and English "ossifrage" mean "breaker," or bone-breaker. The bird is the lammer-geier or great bearded vulture *Gypaetus barbatus* of the lofty mountains of southern Europe, Asia and Africa. It forms a connecting link between the eagles and vultures, and measures about ten feet in expanse of wing. The top of its head is white, bounded with black, the beard black, the neck and under parts tawny, and the upper grayish-black. It feeds on both carrion and living prey, and is said to have the habit of carrying bones to a great height and dropping them on rocks to obtain pieces small enough to swallow.

OSTRICH. Three similar Hebrew words are in the A. V. variously rendered "ostrich," Lam. 4:3; "owl," Lev. 11:16; Deut. 14:15; Job 30:29; Isa. 13:21; 34:13; 43:20; Jer. 50:39; Mic. 1:8; "peacock," Job 39:13. In all of these passages the R. V. uses the word "ostrich" as the proper translation. The ostrich is the *Struthio camelus* of naturalists, the largest of living birds, found formerly in the Arabian deserts, but now limited to Africa. It is unable to fly, but runs with the speed of a horse. Chase of it is pictured on the Assyrian sculptures. Allusions to it in Job show that the author was familiar with its plumage and habits. The Hebrew types it as the "daughter of greediness." It is the "camel bird" of the Arabs and Greeks. *See* Bible Ill., O. T., p. 628.

OWL, Great. As will be seen under the title OSTRICH, many A. V. texts containing the word "owl," contain, in the R. V., the word "ostrich" instead. The "great owl" of Lev. 11:17; Deut.

14:16 was pronounced unclean. The "owl" of Isa. 34:11, for which the R. V. suggests "bittern," has the same Hebrew original as the above texts, but in Isa. 34:15 the original of "great owl" is *kippoz*, which the R. V. renders "arrow snake." It is thought that the *Bubo ascalaphus*, or eagle owl, a bird common to Egypt and Palestine, answers best to the intent of the original word *yanshuph*, and that *kippoz* is more surely a bird, perhaps of the owl species, than a snake, since the context speaks of it as "laying," "hatching," and "gathering under shadow." *See* Bible Ill., O. T., p. 770.

OWL, Screech. The Hebrew *lilith* is rendered "screech owl" in the A. V. of Isa. 34:14, and "night monster" in the R. V. The rabbis refer *lilith* to a ghoul or night spectre, fabled as carrying off children. As the text seems to imply a bird of gloomy, nocturnal habit, it has been suggested that the Syrian hooting owl, found throughout western Asia, is the one that best supplies the sense.

OWL, Little. Translation of the Hebrew *cos* in Lev. 11:17; Deut. 14:16, where it is an unclean bird. Same word translated "owl" (owl of the desert) in Ps. 102:6. The little owl, *Athene glaux*, is by far the most numerous species in Palestine, and is found in nearly all countries. It was the bird of wisdom of the Greeks, and was stamped on Athenian coins.

OWL, Horned. In the texts of Lev. 11:18; Deut. 14:16, where the A. V. has "swan," the R. V. has "horned owl," as a better rendering of the Hebrew *tinshemeth*. The only owl which zoologically warrants the title "horned" is the Virginian eared owl (*Bubo Virginianus*) common to North America.

PARTRIDGE. Two varieties of partridge are found in Palestine—one in the Jordan valley and wilderness stretches to the south, the other in the hills of the northern section. They are much hunted by Arabs for their flesh and eggs. The desert, or southern, partridge is smaller than ours, while the northern is nearly as large as a pheasant. 1 Sam. 26:20; Jer. 17:11.

PEACOCK. Peacocks, along with ivory and apes, were imported by Solomon in ships of Tarshish. The original word for peacock is not Hebrew, but Tamil, *tokei*, which is still the word for peacock in Ceylon and on the coasts of Malabar. 1 K. 10:22; 2 Chr. 9:21. The peacock of A. V. Job 39:13 becomes "ostrich" in R. V. *See* Bible Ill., O. T., p. 526.

PELICAN. The Hebrew *kaath* is translated "pelican" in A. V. of Lev. 11:18; Deut. 14:17; Ps. 102:6, and "cormorant" in Isa. 24:11; Zeph. 2:14. The R. V. rendering is "pelican" in all texts. A voracious water bird, large and strongbilled. The original word means "vomiter" from the habit of the bird in storing great quantities of fish in the pouch under its bill and disgorging them as food for its young. From the red appearance of its bill it was said to be feeding its young with its blood, and this error has been perpetuated in the Christian church by making the pelican the emblem of spiritual care, even to the extent of life's blood. Two species of pelican spend the winter in Palestine and migrate northward in summer. Pelicans grow to a height of four or five feet and have an expanse of wing of ten to twelve feet. They inhabit dense marshes and lonely sea wastes and subsist entirely on fish. *See* Bible Ill., O. T., p. 685.

PIGEON. *See* DOVE.

QUAIL. The Old-World perdicine bird of the *Coturnix* or other related genus, having a very short tail, limited flight and gregarious habit. The variety *Coturnix coturnix*, common to northern Africa and the Arabian peninsula, is believed to be the quail of Scripture. The annual migrations of the quail northward in spring-time, their exhaustive flights across the narrow arms of the Red Sea, their sudden appearance in countless numbers in the Arabian desert, where they afford a welcome food, quite comport with their appearance to the Hebrews in the wilderness, as mentioned in Ex. 16:13; Num. 11:31, 32; Ps. 105: 40. Their trail through Palestine is in the line of the Arabah and the Jordan valley. *See* Bible Ill., O. T., p. 85.

RAVEN. First bird definitely mentioned in the Bible, Gen. 8:7. Flesh prohibited food, Lev. 11:15. Type of the Lord's care for his creatures, 1 K. 17:6. Its glossy, dark plumage alluded to in S. of S. 5:11. The Hebrew *oreb* (*Corvus corax*) is the common raven of the northern hemisphere, of which eight varieties are found in Palestine. It is a large, omniverous, crow-like corvine, with the feathers of its throat elongated. It is noted for its intelligence when tamed. The American form of raven (*Corvus carnivora*) is now regarded as a sub-species of the *Corvus corax*. *See* Bible Ill., O. T., p. 429.

SPARROW. The Hebrew *tzippor* is a generic term, embracing all small birds, or "twitterers," and is generally rendered by "bird" or "fowl." Only twice in the O. T. is it rendered "sparrow," Ps. 84:3; 102:7. In N. T. the reference is directly to the sparrow species, used as a cheap food, Matt. 10:29; Luke 11:6, 7. The house sparrow abounds in all the towns and coasts of Palestine, as do hundreds of species of tree and field birds falling under the generic title *tzippor*. The allusion in Ps. 102:7 is thought to be to the thrush, a solitary bird with a peculiarly plaintive note. *See* Bible Ill., N. T., p. 48.

STORK. A large wading bird, very plentiful in Palestine at certain seasons, gregarious, migratory, nesting in trees and ruins, and noted for tenderness to its young. It frequently attains a height of four feet, and is of white plumage, with red legs and bill, and glossy black wings. Its food consists of fish, frogs and reptiles. It was forbidden food. Lev. 11:19; Deut. 14:18; Ps. 104:17; Jer. 8:7; Zech. 5:9. A black stork is also found in Palestine, but it is less frequent and far more wary than the white, or common stork. The stork is one of the few birds which has no note. *See* Bible Ill., O. T., p. 829.

SWALLOW. Translation of the Hebrew *derur* in Ps. 84:3; Prov. 26:2. Another word, *sis*, is translated "swallow" in Isa. 38:14; Jer. 8:7. It is thought by some that *sis* would be better rendered by "swift," which, though a species of swallow, is purely migratory, and has a harsh, shrill cry, not unlike that of the crane. There are many species of swallow in Palestine, most of them migratory. They have in general the habits we observe in the common swallow, as of building under eaves of houses, beneath temple cornices and porticoes, and in the sides of cliffs, and rapidly circling about their homes in search of their aerial food. *See* Bible Ill., O. T., p. 795.

SWAN. The Hebrew *tinshemeth*, rendered "swan" in the A. V. of Lev. 11:18; Deut. 14:16 is translated "horned owl" in the same texts of the R. V. The swan is very rarely seen in Palestine; and, as suggested under the title OWL (Horned), the existence of that bird there would be next to zoologically impossible. The LXX render the word "porphyrio" and "ibis." The former is the water-hen, common to Egypt; the latter was a large wading bird once found in lower Nile regions, and held sacred by the Egyptians. *See* IBIS and OWL (Horned).

TURTLE DOVE. *See* DOVE.

VULTURE. *See* EAGLE, FALCON, GIER EAGLE, KITE. *See* also Bible Ill., O. T., p. 128.

PART III.

FISHES, REPTILES, INSECTS.

ADDER. In Hebrew there are no less than eight words used to designate snakes. They are not to be taken as indicating snakes of a certain kind, for there is no evidence that Hebrew knowledge admitted of reptilian classes and distinctions. The best that can be done toward ascertaining kinds alluded to, or meant, is to consider the occasion and environment of the mention, and to conclude accordingly. The first mention of adder is in Gen. 49:17 in connection with the tribe of Dan, "an adder in the path, that biteth the horse-heels." Here the original is *shephiphon*, and the A. V. suggests marginally "arrow snake," and the R. V. "horned snake." In Ps. 58:4 the Hebrew *pethen* is translated "adder," and the A. V. margin suggests "asp." In Ps. 140:3 the Hebrew *acshub* is rendered "adder." In Prov. 23:32 the Hebrew *tziph'oni* is translated "adder," and the A. V. margin suggests "cockatrice," and the R. V. margin "basilisk." Of the above originals *pethen* is generic, meaning any snake. The other three imply a venomous snake, and may refer to both the horned viper (*Vipera cerastes*) and sand viper (*Echis carinata*), which are common to the desert districts within and about Palestine. They are short, thick snakes, which bask in the hot sun, coiling themselves in convenient hollows, awaiting the approach of their prey, and not hesitating to leap at the feet or limbs of passing men and animals. *See* SERPENT.

ANT. Palestine is the habitat of a great variety of ants, which there, as elsewhere, feed alike on animal and vegetable matter, and surpass most other insects in instinct and industry, Prov. 6:6; 30:25.

ASP. This is a translation of the Hebrew *pethen* in Isa. 11:8, and a suggestion in margin of Ps. 58:4. As *pethen* is generic, the snake meant must be left to conjecture; but the asp proper is a hooded, venomous snake, the African cobra (*Naja haje*), commonly assumed to have caused Cleopatra's death. Asp embraces also the European viper (*Vipera vulgaris*) or other venomous serpent. *See* SERPENT.

BASILISK. The R. V. rendering of the Hebrew *tziph'oni* in Isa. 11:8; 14:29; 59:5; Jer. 8:17, instead of cockatrice. From Isa. 59:5 something less general than *pethen* and more deadly is meant. Both cockatrice and basilisk signify a fabulous creature hatched by a cock from serpent's eggs, with four legs and a cock's comb. The above original is translated "adder" in Prov. 23:32, and in the R. V. margins of several of the above texts there are suggestions of "adder." *See* ADDER and SERPENT.

BEE. Honey bees and honey abounded in Palestine. The "banded bee," which is the chief honey-producing bee of Palestine, is somewhat smaller than the European or American honey bee. It is most prolific of honey in its wild state, and its home may be found in hollow trees and amid crevices of rocks. Honey entered largely into the ordinary diet of the Hebrews, was significant of the abundance of Canaan, and became an article of export to other countries. Gen. 43:11; Ex. 3:8, 17; Deut. 1:44; 1 K. 14:3; Ps. 81:16; Isa. 7:15, 18; Mat. 3:4.

BEETLE. The A. V. translation of *chargol* in Lev. 11:22, but "cricket" in the R. V., with the marginal note that the text and context calls for "four kinds of locusts or grasshoppers which are not certainly known." Beetles of many varieties are found in Palestine in great plentitude, but since they have not "legs above its feet to leap with," it is quite clear that some insect akin to the locust or grasshopper suits the sense better.

CANKERWORM. The cankerworm is a variety of caterpillar. The Hebrew, *yelek*, translated "cankerworm" in Joel 1:4; 2:25; Nahum 3:15, 16, is rendered "caterpillar" in the A. V. of Ps. 105:34; Jer. 51:14, 27, but "cankerworm" in the R. V. The R. V. margin of Joel 1:4 suggests, "Probably different kinds of locusts, or locusts in different stages of growth." The original seems to imply some insect pest destructive to leaves and grass. *See* LOCUST.

CATERPILLAR. Caterpillar is the larvæ of the butterfly. The Hebrew *chasil*, translated "caterpillar" in 1 K. 8:37; 2 Chr. 6:28; Ps. 78:46; Isa. 33:4; Joel 1:4, would seem rather to imply a locust in some stage of its destructive growth, as suggested in R. V. margin of Joel 1:4. *See* LOCUST.

CHAMELEON. A species of lizard, of arborial or climbing habit. It is made a rendering of Hebrew *tinshemeth* in place of "mole" in the R. V. text of Lev. 11:30.

COCKATRICE. The original, *tziph'oni*, is translated "adder" in Prov. 23:32, and "cockatrice" in the A. V. of Isa. 11:8; 14:29; 59:5; Jer. 8:17; but "basilisk" in the R. V. *See* BASILISK, ADDER, SERPENT.

CORAL. The red coral of commerce is found in the rocky bottoms of the Mediterranean. The black coral is found in the Red Sea. Coral is the skeleton or hard structure of marine zoophytes, and it assumes many fantastic forms while in process of growth. It was much used by Hebrews for beads and ornaments, and even ranked among the precious stones. Job 28:18; Ezek. 27:16.

CRICKET. R. V. rendering of *chargol* in Lev. 11:22, instead of A. V. "beetle." *See* BEETLE.

CRIMSON, Scarlet. The Hebrew *tola*, generally rendered "crimson" or "scarlet," is literally the "crimson worm" (*Coccus ilicis*) which attaches itself to the Syrian holm oak. It is similar to the cochineal insect, which yields a deeper and more expensive dye. It is dark red, of the size of a cherry pit, and when dried shrivels to the size of a wheat grain. It once had extensive use in Palestine as a dye, but has been largely superseded by foreign dyes.

DRAGON. The Hebrew *tan*, pl. *tannim*, translated "dragon" or "dragons," in the A. V. texts of Job 30:29; Ps. 44:19; Isa. 34:13; Jer. 9:11; Mic. 1:8, is no doubt correctly rendered "jackals" in the R. V. texts. But the Hebrew *tannin* is variably translated "dragon," "serpent," "sea monster," "great whale," etc., the allusion being to some huge creature, usually aquatic, of indefinite shape. In Gen. 1:21 sea monsters in general are meant. In Ex. 7:9–12; Deut. 32:33 some kind of a serpent is implied. In Ezek. 29:3 the "great dragon" might better read "crocodife."

FISH. Though some thirty-three different species of fish are found in the waters of Palestine, there are only two allusions in the Bible to a specific kind—that in Jonah 1:17, "a great fish," and in Mat. 12:40, to the same, under the name

560

of "whale," Greek *katos*, which last is really any huge fish or sea monster. Scaleless fish were forbidden food under the Mosaic law, Lev. 11 : 9–12. Their worship was prohibited, Deut. 4 : 18. Fishing was an important industry around the Sea of Galilee. They were caught with nets, hooks and spears, Job 41 : 7; Hab. 1 : 15; Luke 5 : 5–7. The fishes of Jordan waters, the most important of which belong to the carp family, are quite similar to those in the Nile. The briny waters of the Dead Sea are fatal to fish.

FLEA. Fleas are a pest in Palestine and throughout the East. The flea is mentioned only twice in Scripture, as an illustration of insignificance. 1 Sam. 24 : 14; 26 : 20.

FLY. Two Hebrew words are translated "fly," *arob* or *oreb*, in Ex. 8 : 21; Ps. 78 : 45. In Ex. 8 : 21 the R. V. suggests marginally "mixture of noisome beasts." Interpreters are not agreed whether a particular fly is meant, or whether *arob* is generic, embracing the entire family of Egyptian pests, as the fly, mosquito, sand-fly, gnat, etc. The other word is *zebub*, Eccl. 10 : 1; Isa. 7 : 18. In the former text (Eccl. 10 : 1), though some poisonous fly, "fly of death," seems to be meant, the majority opinion is that the common fly quite suits the conditions, since its presence in any numbers in an ointment would soon cause it to stink. In the latter text (Isa. 7 : 18) the reference is to the variety and plentitude of flies in Egypt; so abundant and pestiferous in fact as to symbolize the destructive attacks of Egypt on Israel, just as the bee, in the same text, symbolizes the attacks made by Assyria. The Lord will hiss for them both—that is, call them to definite account.

FROG. The Hebrew original for frog is of Arabic extraction, and only occurs in the O. T. in connection with the Egyptian plague. The *Rana esculenta*, edible frog, is found in abundance in both Egypt and Palestine. In Egypt the frog was held as a symbol of regeneration. Ex. 8 : 2; Ps. 78 : 45; 105 : 30. The frog of the N. T., *batrakos*, represents uncleanness, Rev. 16 : 13.

GECKO. The translation of *anakah* in the R. V. of Lev. 11 : 30 instead of "ferret." The gecko is a wall lizard found in Palestine and Egypt, and noted for the peculiar clicking sound it gives forth. *See* FERRET.

GNAT. Greek *konops*, gnat, or diminutive fly, is one of the multitudinous pests of Egypt and Palestine. The R. V. of Mat. 23 : 24, which strain out the gnat, is an allusion to the Jewish practice of straining wine infested by gnats and similar small insects. From its smallness the gnat furnishes a striking contrast with the bulky camel.

GRASSHOPPER. An insect of the locust species, having the hind legs much developed, with stout and powerful legs for leaping. There are many varieties of the grasshopper in Palestine, and very rightly described in Lev. 11 : 22 as having "legs above their feet to leap withal upon the earth." They were a permissive food under the Mosaic law. The Hebrew words, translated "grasshopper" in the A. V. of Judg. 6 : 5; 7 : 12; Job 39 : 20; Jer. 46 : 23, are rendered "locust" in R. V. of same texts; and no comprehensive or satisfactory distinction can be drawn from the Hebrew between the closely allied family of grasshoppers and locusts. *See* LOCUST.

HORNET. Hornets are common in Palestine, larger than ours, and more persistent and dangerous in attack. They are mentioned three times in the O. T. as an agency by which God helped the Israelites in the conquest of Canaan. Ex. 23 : 28; Deut. 7 : 20; Josh. 24 : 12.

HORSELEECH. Both the horseleech and medical leech are common to Palestine. They are found in stagnant waters and low, damp places. The horseleech, Prov. 30 : 15, symbolizes insatiate greed, from its habit of fastening itself to the nostrils of animals when drinking. The R. V. margin of above text suggests "vampire," an animal both mythical and real, whose mission is to suck the blood of men and animals when asleep.

LEVIATHAN. This is the Hebrew word which stands for itself in Job 41 : 1; Ps. 74 : 14; 104 : 26; Isa. 27 : 1. The R. V. margin of Job 41 : 1 suggests "crocodile," which is very clearly the animal intended in Job 41 : 1; Ps. 74 : 14. The crocodile was formerly found in the waters of the lower Nile, and must have been familiar to the Hebrews, at least to the author of Job 41 : 1, who so faithfully describes its size, strength, plated body and all-devouring mouth. The reference in Ps. 104 : 26 is to any large marine animal, and that in Isa. 27 : 1 to a great serpent, as the python, often seen on Egyptian monuments. In the A. V. text of Job 3 : 8 the word "leviathan" is marginally suggested, and fully adopted in the R. V. The probability is that "crocodile" was in the mind of the poet.

LICE. Hebrew *kinnim*, or lice, constituted the third Egyptian plague, Ex. 8 : 16–18; Ps. 105 : 31. The R. V. margins suggest "sand fleas or flies." The translation of *kinnim* has given rise to volumes of discussion. The pests meant arose from the dust, a source whence lice, fleas, and the innumerable parasitic hosts of the East readily spring.

LIZARD. The Hebrew *letaah*, lizard, is found only once in the O. T., where its flesh is a proscribed food, Lev. 11 : 30. In the R. V. margin is the statement as to "gecko," "land crocodile," "lizard" and "sand lizard," "words of uncertain meaning, but probably denoting four kinds of lizards." Lizards abound in Palestine, some forty species being known. The largest is the monitor lizard, frequently attaining three or four feet in length. It is of two species—one living on land, the other an amphibian. The more common lizards are found everywhere in wood, field and waste. The family of skinks is peculiar to desert places. They are thought to be meant by the Hebrew *chomet*, translated "snail" in A. V. of Lev. 11 : 30, and "sand lizard" in R. V. The gecko, or wall lizard, also abounds. *See* GECKO. The *spinipes* rank as among the larger species, and are armed with formidable tails. They are supposed to be represented by the Hebrew *tzab*, translated "tortoise" in the A. V. of Lev. 11 : 29, but "great lizard" in the R. V. The chameleon is found in the Jordan valley. It is the translation of the Hebrew *tinshemeth* in R. V. of Lev. 11 : 30, instead of "mole" in the A. V. *See* CHAMELEON.

LOCUST. Forty species of locust have been identified in Palestine. The Bible abounds in passages referring to them by different names, embracing the locust proper, beetle, cankerworm, caterpillar, grasshopper, bald locust, palmerworm, etc. Locusts constituted the eighth Egyptian plague, Ex. 10 : 1–15. They and their kind were a permitted food to the Israelites, Lev. 11 : 22. No less than nine Hebrew words, constituting a series of perplexing originals, are supposed to refer to the locust species, in some places with vigorous and accurate descriptive energy, frequently with allusion to their annoying and destructive qualities. The Hebrew *arbeh*, which is taken to mean the true locust, Ex. 10 : 1–15, begins a description of the habits of the insect, which modern knowledge verifies. They hatch in swarms, move in clouds before the winds, and utterly destroy vegetation where they light. Deut. 28 : 38, 42; 1 K. 8 : 37; Ps. 109 : 23. The same Hebrew original is translated "grasshopper" in A. V. of Judg. 6 : 5; 7 : 12; Job 39 : 20; Jer. 46 : 23. *See* GRASSHOPPER.

In Lev. 11 : 22 the Hebrew *sal'am* is rendered "bald locust." This is associated with the *truxalis*, a species of grasshopper having a smooth head and inhabiting rocks.

Chargol is rendered "beetle" in the A. V. of Lev. 21 : 22, and "cricket" in the R. V. *See* BEETLE and CRICKET.

Chagab is generally translated "grasshopper."

Lev. 11 : 22; Num. 13 : 33; Isa. 40 : 22, but in 2 Chr. 7 : 13 "locusts."

Gazam, rendered "palmerworm" in Joel 1 : 4; 2 : 25; Am. 4 : 9, is translated "caterpillar" in the Lxx and some other ancient versions. It is supposed to refer to the larvæ of locusts before developing wings, or to the larvæ of butterflies, moths or other insects destructive to plants.

Yelek is translated "caterpillar" in A. V. of Ps. 105 : 34; Jer. 51 : 14, 27, but "cankerworm" in R. V.; and "cankerworm" in Joel 1 : 4; 2 : 25; Nah. 3 : 15, 16. As the insect is described as "rough" like a caterpillar, Jer. 51 : 27, yet as having wings, Nah. 3 : 16, and as the original implies "a licker-up of grass," the insect really meant must be left to conjecture.

Tzelatzal, rendered "locust" in both A. V. and R. V. of Deut. 28 : 42, signifies a "tinkler," or cymbal. The reference may, therefore, well be to some chirping grasshopper, or to the cicada. The locust itself and the cricket make a stridulating sound.

Gob, translated "locust" in Isa. 33 : 4; "grasshopper" in A. V. of Am. 7 : 1, but "locust" in R. V., and "grasshopper" in Nah. 3 : 17. The A. V. margin of Am. 7 : 1 suggests "green worm."

Chasil is always translated "caterpillar," 1 K. 8 : 37; 2 Chr. 6 : 28; Ps. 78 : 46; Isa. 33 : 4; Joel 1 : 4; 2 : 25. The R. V. margin of Joel 1 : 4 suggests: "Probably different kinds of locusts, or locusts in different stages of growth." The original signifies "a consumer," and as *chasil* is generally mentioned together with locusts, the inference in the R. V. margin is plausible.

There can be no doubt about the identity of the insect in Mat. 3 : 4, where locusts constitute part of the food of John the Baptist; nor in Rev. 9 : 3, 7, where they are a noxious horde. *See* Bible Ill., O. T., p. 75.

MOTH. The Hebrew *ash* is no doubt the *tinea,* or clothes-moth, of which there are several species, all destructive to fur and woolen garments. It is the larva of a lepidopterous insect, but not a true butterfly. The Bible makes frequent allusions to its destructiveness. Job 13 : 28; 27 : 18; Ps. 39 : 11; Isa. 50 : 9; Mat. 6 : 19.

PALMERWORM. *See* LOCUST.

PEARLS. The pearl is the stony secretion of the pearl oyster. It is reckoned as a gem, and is highly prized for ornament. The A. V. "pearls" of Job 28 : 18 becomes "crystal" in the R. V., which is a better rendering of the original. In N. T. pearl becomes a frequent source of metaphor. Mat. 13 : 45; 1 Tim. 2 : 9; Rev. 17 : 4; 21 : 21.

PURPLE. A valuable dye, and a color significant of royalty. The art of obtaining and using the dye was a Tyrian secret, now lost. But tradition has it that it was an exudation from a species of whelk, or mollusk, found on the Phœnician coast. Trade in purple was an extensive one, wherever Phœnician ships went. Judg. 8 : 26; Luke 16 : 19; Acts 16 : 14.

SCARLET. *See* CRIMSON.

SCORPION. The Hebrew *agrab,* scorpion, is found in Palestine, and several different varieties exist. The scorpion belongs to the spider family, but resembles the lobster. Its sting is painful and often fatal. Deut. 8 : 15; 1 K. 12 : 11; 2 Chr. 10 : 11, 14; Ezek. 2 : 6; Luke 10 : 19; 11 : 12; Rev. 9 : 3, 5, 10.

SERPENT. More than thirty different kinds of serpents are common to Palestine, at least six of which are venomous and dangerous to man and beasts. The seven or eight Hebrew words used to designate snakes are translated indiscriminately, so that it is impossible to distinguish with accuracy the specific kind of serpent or snake meant. (*See* remarks under ADDER.)

Nachash is rendered serpent in Ps. 58 : 4; Prov. 30 : 19, and no particular species is denoted.

Tannin is rendered serpent in Ex. 7 : 9, 10, but in other places "dragon," and in Job 7 : 12, A. V. "whale," R. V. "sea monster." *See* DRAGON.

Pethen, in Ps. 58 : 4, is translated "adder," and the A. V. margin suggests "asp." It is translated "asp" in Isa. 11 : 8. *See* ADDER and ASP.

Shephiphon, in Gen. 49 : 17, is rendered "adder," with an A. V. marginal suggestion of "arrow snake," and an R. V. of "horned snake." *See* ADDER.

Eph'eh is rendered "viper" in Job 20 : 16; Isa. 30 : 6; 59 : 5, and the viper (*Vipera aspis*) is mentioned in Acts 28 : 3.

Achshub is found only in one passage, "adder's poison," Ps. 140 : 3.

Tziph'oni is translated "adder" in Prov. 23 : 32, with an A. V. marginal suggestion of "cockatrice" and an R. V. suggestion of "basilisk." The same original is translated "cockatrice" in the A. V. of Isa. 11 : 8; 14 : 29; 59 : 5; Jer. 8 : 17; and in the R. V. "basilisk." In both A. V. and R. V., however, there are marginal suggestions of "adder." *See* COCKATRICE, BASILISK, ADDER.

SERPENT, Fiery. The *saraph,* or fiery serpent, of Num. 21 : 6, 8; Deut. 8 : 15, is generally associated with the horned viper or sand viper of the desert (*see* ADDER), "fiery" being an allusion to the burning sensation of their bite. The "fiery flying serpent" of Isa. 14 : 29; 30 : 6 is a figure of speech duplicated, in substance, in Jer. 8 : 16, 17, the allusion being to furious visitation.

SNAKE. *See* SERPENT.

SNAIL. The Hebrew *chomet,* translated "snail" in the A. V. of Lev. 11 : 30, is rendered "sand lizard" in the R. V., with the noted margin, "Words of uncertain meaning, but probably denoting four kinds of lizards." The word *shablul* rendered "snail" in Ps. 58 : 8, refers to the common snail, slug, or slime snake, of which many varieties abound in Palestine, and are not eschewed as food.

SPIDER. The Hebrew *akkabish* is translated "spider" in Job 8 : 14; Isa. 59 : 5, and no doubt correctly, as the allusion to the fragility of its web shows. Another Hebrew word, *semamith,* is translated "spider" in the A. V. of Prov. 30 : 28, but "lizard" in the R. V. If the latter, probably the wall lizard or gecko. *See* LIZARD, GECKO. The species of spider in Palestine are numbered by the hundred.

TORTOISE. The rendering of the Hebrew *tzab* in A. V. of Lev. 11 : 29. The R. V. has "great lizard," and the Lxx "land crocodile." It is generally agreed that the A. V. rendering is faulty, though the land tortoise is found everywhere in Palestine. A water species also exists in the streams and marshes.

VAMPIRE. *See* HORSELEECH.

VIPER. A translation of *eph'eh* in Job 20 : 16; Isa. 30 : 6; 59 : 5. The original seems to imply a hissing, venomous serpent, as the common viper or adder, the horned viper of the *cerastes* genus, and the Indian vipers. A symbol of deceit and destruction, Mat. 3 : 7; 12 : 34; 23 : 33; Luke 3 : 7.

WHALE. The Hebrew *tannin,* "great whales" of A. V. Gen. 1 : 21, is more correctly rendered "great sea monsters" in the R. V., the original implying a monster of some kind. In Ex. 7 : 9–12; Deut. 32 : 33 the word is rendered serpent, and in Ezek. 29 : 3 great dragon. *See* DRAGON. The *katos,* or "whale," of Mat. 12 : 40 is equally any huge fish or sea monster. The true whale is not found in the Mediterranean, and is a very rare visitor in the Red Sea.

WORM. The Hebrew *sas,* translated "worm" in Isa. 51 : 8, is generally referred to the moth in its larval state. Two other Hebrew words, *rimmah* and *tole'ah,* are used many times in the O. T., and are apparently synonyms, both referring to the things embraced in the English word worm. If there be any distinction, *rimmah* refers the oftener to larval products dependent on putrid matter, while *tole'ah* refers to larval existence dependent on vegetation for food. The helplessness of the worm affords figures in Job 25 : 6; Ps. 22 : 6; Isa. 41 : 14.

VEGETABLE KINGDOM
IN THE BIBLE.

ACACIA. The R. V. rendering of "shittim" in Ex. 25:10-13; 26:15, 26, and of "shittah" in Isa. 41:19. The acacia grows in the valleys about the Dead Sea and in the desert southward, to the height of fifteen or twenty feet, and produces a hard, grained wood, which was used in making the tabernacle furniture.

ALGUM. ALMUG. Former in 2 Chr. 2:8; 9:10, 11; latter in 1 K. 10:11, 12. Supposably the red sandal wood of India. Used for temple furniture and musical instruments. See Bible Ills., O. T., pp. 420, 421.

ALMOND. Tree native to Palestine. Grows both wild and cultivated. Resembles the peach in height, form, blossom and fruit. Blossoms before it leaves. Covering of fruit downy and succulent. Chiefly valuable for its nut. Gen. 43:11; Ex. 25:33; Num. 17:8; Jer. 1:11. See Bible Ill., O. T., p. 748.

ALOES. Probably the gum or fragrant wood of an Indian tree called "eagle tree" (*Aquilaria agallocha*). It was used as one of the ingredients of spices and perfumes, Ps. 45:8; Prov. 7:17; S. of S. 4:14; John 19:39. The "lign (*wood*) aloes" of Num. 24:6 is evidently some native tree. See Bible Ill., O. T., p. 193.

AMOMUM. Suggested in R. V. margin as a substitute for "spice" in Rev. 18:13. Not known what plant is meant.

ANISE. A plant of the parsley family producing an aromatic seed used in cookery and medicine, and with which tithes were paid. Mat. 23:23. The R. V. margin suggests "dill" as the plant meant. See Bible Ill., N. T., p. 36.

APPLE. The Hebrew *tappuach* applies to both the apple tree and fruit. The tree grows in Palestine, but the fruit is inferior. Name applied to many places in Palestine, as in Josh. 12:17; 15:34, etc. Fruit alluded to in Prov. 25:11; S. of S. 2:5; 7:8. Tree mentioned in S. of S. 2:3; 8:5; Joel 1:12. For figurative use see Prov. 7:2; Zech. 2:8; Ps. 17:8; Lam. 2:18. For "Dead Sea apple" see Bible Ill., O. T., p. 24.

ASH. The ash does not grow in Palestine. The Lxx translate the Hebrew *oren* as *pitus*, pine or fir. In the R. V. it is also rendered "fir tree." Isa. 44:14.

BALM. The balm of Gilead, or Mecca balsam, exudes an agreeable balsamic resin, which was highly prized in the East as an unguent and cosmetic, as the crushed leaves were for their odor. Gen. 37:25; 43:11; Jer. 8:22; 46:11; Ezek. 27:17. See Bible Ill., O. T., p. 48.

BARLEY. Much cultivated by the Hebrews, Ex. 9:31; Lev. 27:16; Deut. 8:8; Ruth 2:7. Used for bread, especially among the poor, Judg. 7:13; 2 K. 4:42; John 6:9-13; and for cattle feed, 1 K. 4:28. Barley harvest preceded wheat harvest, Ruth 1:22; 2:23; 2 Sam. 21:9, 10.

BAY TREE. The Hebrew original, *ezrach*, does not refer to any particular tree, as to the laurel, as some suppose, but is best translated as in R. V., "green tree in its native soil." Ps. 37:35.

BDELLIUM. A gum resin of the *Balsamodendron Africanum* (African bdellium), and this may be meant in Gen. 2:12; Num. 11:7, where a precious stone is seemingly referred to.

BEAN. The common bean (*Faba vulgaris*) was much cultivated in Palestine, and used both as a vegetable and flour. 2 Sam. 17:28; Ezek. 4:9.

BOX TREE. This is the *Buxus longifolius*, or long-leaved box, which ranks as a forest tree in the Lebanon mountains, Isa. 41:19; 60:13. In the R. V. of Ezek. 27:6 the benches of Tyrian ships are said to be "of ivory inlaid with boxwood from the isles of Kittim."

BRAMBLE, BRIAR, THISTLE, THORN. Nine Hebrew and three Greek words in Scripture are translated into these titles, without reference to any particular plant, but with reference to the jagged, spiny flora peculiar to Palestine and desert surroundings. Gen. 3:18. Figurative for desolation, Prov. 24:31; Isa. 5:6; Hos. 2:6; providential visitation, Num. 33:55; Judg. 2:3; 2 Cor. 12:7; hindrance, Prov. 15:19; troubles, Prov. 22:5; derision and punishment, as "crown of thorns," Mat. 27:29.

BRIER. See BRAMBLE.

BROOM. The broom family embraces a wide variety of shrubs, grasses and canes. The word is made to take the place of "juniper" in R. V. of Job 30:4, and is suggested in margin of 1 K. 19:4; Ps. 120:4.

BULRUSH. Six Hebrew words are translated somewhat indiscriminately "rush" or "bulrush." The consensus of opinion is that the papyrus plant is meant. It formerly grew luxuriantly on the lower Nile, and still grows in the waters of Lake Merom, upon Jordan. The R. V. introduces "papyrus" into the text of Isa. 18:2, and suggests it in Ex. 2:3; Job 8:11. See Bible Ill., O. T., p. 775.

BUSH. As used of the "burning bush," supposably the thorny acacia of the Arabian peninsula, Ex. 3:2-6. A locality is referred to in Deut. 33:16; Mark. 12:26; Luke 20:37.

CALAMUS. A spice used as an ingredient of the anointing oil, Ex. 30:23. It was imported and sold in Tyrian markets, Ezek. 27:19. Usually identified with the lemon grass or sweet flag of India. "Sweet cane" in Isa. 43:24; Jer. 6:20.

CAMPHIRE. The gum of the camphor tree. But in R. V. of S. of S. 1:14; 4:13, "henna" is substituted. Henna is a small shrub bearing clusters of white, fragrant flowers, and famous as the source of the cosmetic used to stain lips, nails and hands.

CANE, Sweet. The R. V. margin of Isa. 43:24; Jer. 6:20 suggests "calamus," which see.

CAPER-BERRY. In R. V. of Eccl. 12:5 "caper-berry" is inserted for "desire," and "desire" carried into the margin. The caper is an abundant shrub in Palestine, found on walls and rocks. The bud, preserved in vinegar, is a favorite condiment.

CAROB TREE. In R. V. of Luke 15:16 "pods of the carob tree" is inserted for "husks." The carob, or locust, grows in Mediterranean countries, producing long, brown pods containing pulpy seeds, nutritious for animals. The pods are sometimes called locust beans and St. John's bread, from the erroneous notion that John the Baptist used them for food. See Bible Ill., N. T., p. 101.

CASSIA. An ingredient of the anointing oil, Ex. 30:24. The R. V. suggests "costus," an Indian plant, whose aromatic root is used as an ingredient of incense. In Ezek. 27:19 cassia is mentioned as an article of Syrian commerce. In Ps. 45:8 the plant is unidentified.

CEDAR. In the Pentateuch, Lev. 14:4, the cedar was probably the aromatic juniper. Elsewhere it is the cedar of Lebanon, the glory of the Palestinian forests, and the symbol of grandeur, might, loftiness and expansion. It produces a hard, durable, fragrant wood, prized for building purposes. 1 K. 7:2; Ps. 92:12; S. of S. 5:15; Isa. 2:13; Ezek. 31:6. See Bible Ills., O. T., pp. 410, 647.

CHESTNUT TREE. In the R. V. text of Gen. 30:37; Ezek. 31:8 "plane tree" is inserted, with universal consent. The plane tree, sycamore, or buttonwood, grows vigorously in Palestine near streams.

CINNAMON. Inner bark of the cinnamon tree, native of Ceylon. An ingredient of the anointing oil, Ex. 30:23; a perfume, Prov. 7:17; article of commerce, Rev. 18:13.

CITRON. "Boughs of goodly trees," in Lev. 23:40, is made to read by the Rabbis, "fruit of the citron trees." The citron was a native of India, but became the most common of the orange tribe in Palestine. It is used by the Rabbis in celebrating the Feast of the Tabernacles.

COCKLE. Doubtless some weed of the Arum family is meant in Job 31:40, but just which is not known. The same original is translated "wild grapes" in Isa. 5:2, 4. In A. V. and R. V. margins "noisome weeds" is suggested.

COPHER. The Hebrew word for camphire or henna is introduced into the R. V. margin of S. of S. 1:14.

CORIANDER (*Coriandrum sativum*). Cultivated in Egypt and Palestine for its aromatic seeds, which were used for flavoring bread and sauces. The plant is of the parsley family. Ex. 16:31; Num. 11:7. See Bible Ill., O. T., p. 85.

CORN. In Bible sense, grain of every kind, except maize, or Indian corn, and perhaps oats. The American revisers suggest "grain" in every case. Eleven different Hebrew words are used in the Bible for corn. They cover barley, millet, wheat, rye, spelt, etc., and apply to corn in various stages of cultivation, threshing and preparation for food. Corn supplies many figures of speech in Scripture. Gen. 41:22; Ex. 9:32; Deut. 11:14; 2 Chr. 2:15; Mat. 12:1. See Bible Ill., O. T., p. 617.

COSTUS. See CASSIA.

COTTON. Not mentioned in A. V., but the R. V. inserts it marginally in Esth. 1:6; Isa. 19:9, as it was cultivated in Egypt and India and woven into fabrics.

CROCUS. The R. V. margin of S. of S. 2:1 suggests "autumn crocus" as a substitute for "rose."

CUCUMBER. This fruit was largely cultivated in Egypt and Palestine, and much prized as a food. Num. 11:5; Isa. 1:8.

CUMMIN. An umbelliferous plant producing aromatic seeds used as a condiment. The seeds were threshed out with a rod, Isa. 28:25, and tithable, Mat. 23:23. See Bible Ill., N. T., p. 36.

CYPRESS. Though the cypress is common to the uplands of Palestine, and produces a hard wood, the R. V. of Isa. 44:14 introduces the "holm tree" as the tree meant by the Hebrew *tirzah*. The holm oak is an evergreen, resembling holly.

DARNEL. Introduced into the R. V. margin of Mat. 13:25 for the word "tares."

DESIRE. See CAPER-BERRY; also Bible Ill., O. T., p. 748.

DILL. See ANISE.

DOVE'S DUNG. Eaten as a last resort in time of famine, 2 K. 6:25. The thought that a plant is meant is not now contended for by critics.

EBONY. The hard, heavy, dark wood of the *Dyospyros* variety, growing in the East Indies, and used for furniture, instruments and ornaments. Ezek. 27:15.

ELM. Elm not found in Palestine. Same original, *elah*, translated, other than in Hos. 4:13,

as "oak" or teil tree. R. V. of Hos. 4:13 has "terebinth."

FIG. The fig (*Ficus carica*) is common in Palestine and frequently mentioned in Scripture. The fruit is a hollow, fleshy receptacle containing minute flowers lining its cavity. It appears in February, a month or six weeks before the leaves, and when the latter appear the fruit is ripe. The common and sycamore figs are the two leading varieties of Palestine. Deut. 8:8; 1 K. 4:25; Isa. 34:4; Mat. 21:19. Pressed figs are mentioned in 1 Sam. 25:18. See Bible Ill., O. T., p. 408.

FIR. A tree of the pine family. In the Lxx the original, *berosh*, is rendered "pine," "cypress" and "juniper." The R. V. marginally suggests "cypress." Several species of fir exist in Palestine. The wood is hard, and was used for making musical instruments, 2 Sam. 6:5; in building the temple, 1 K. 5:8; S. of S. 1:17. Often mentioned in connection with the cedar as a choice and goodly tree, Isa. 37:24; 60:13.

FITCHES. Fitch is an old form for vetch. Fitches, or vetches, represent two Hebrew words, meaning in Isa. 28:25-27 black cummin, and in Ezek. 4:9 spelt, which see.

FLAG. The two Hebrew words translated "flag" do not refer to particular plants, but to water plants in general, as rushes, reeds, sea and meadow weeds, etc. Ex. 2:3-5; Job 8:11; Isa. 19:6. See Bible Ill., O. T., p. 605.

FLAX. Earliest material known to have been manufactured into clothing. Grown and used largely in Egypt, Canaan and throughout the East. In spun and woven form it is called linen. Gen. 41:42; Ex. 9:31; Josh. 2:6; Isa. 19:9; 42:3; Hos. 2:9; Mat. 12:20. Spinning and weaving of linen was a female industry of honor, Prov. 31:13, 19, 24.

FRANKINCENSE. An ingredient of the holy incense, Ex. 30:34, 35. An offering of sweet savor, Lev. 2:2. A yellowish gum of some tree which cannot now be identified, but probably indigenous to Arabia, Jer. 6:20. The Hebrew originals clearly distinguish between "frankincense" and "incense," the former being an ingredient of the latter. Ex. 30:7, 9; Lev. 16:12, 13; Rev. 8:3. See Bible Ill., O. T., p. 489.

GALBANUM. A gum-resin of yellowish color, and pungent; disagreeable odor when burning. It was an ingredient of the holy incense, Ex. 30:34. Modern galbanum is medicinal, and a product of the *Ferula galbaniflua*.

GALL. The Hebrew *rosh* is "gall," Deut. 29:18; 32:32; Job 16:13, etc., but is also twice translated "poison," also "hemlock." It is often mentioned with wormwood, and may mean any bitter herb. Jer. 9:15; Hos. 10:4; Amos 6:12. Probably myrrh is meant in Mat. 27:34; Mark 15:23.

GARLIC. A bulbous plant similar to the onion and leek. Longed after by the Hebrews in the wilderness, Num. 11:5. Grows both cultivated and wild in Palestine.

GOPHER. The unknown wood used in the building of Noah's Ark. Gen. 6:14.

GOURD. The gourd that protected Jonah was evidently of the climbing variety. It grows rapidly in the East, and often perishes quickly under insect attack. It belongs to a large family, covering the melon, pumpkin, squash, calabash, etc. Jonah 4:6-10. The R. V. margin suggests *Palma Christi*, or castor-oil plant. The wild gourd of 2 K. 4:39, grows in Palestine, but the bitter apple, or bitter cucumber, a ground fruit resembling an orange and known as colocynth, is thought to be the variety meant. The "vine of Sodom," Deut. 32:32, may be the same plant. As suggested in the R. V. margin of 1 K. 6:18, the carved cedar knops of Solomon's Temple may have been fashioned after the fruit of the colocynth vine. See Bible Ill., O. T., p. 995.

GRAPE. See VINE, and Bible Ill., O. T., p. 175.

GRASS. The Hebrew *deshe* means the grass of pasture, Gen. 1 : 12; the word *yerek*, in Num. 22 : 4, means herbage in general; the word *chatzir*, in Isa. 35 : 7, means grass for hay. The grass lands of Palestine are confined to the valleys and lowlands. The uplands furnish only scanty grazing. Grass has a large figurative use, Ps. 90 : 5, 6; Isa. 40 : 6, 8; Jas. 1 : 10, 11; 1 Pet. 1 : 24.

GROVE. The Hebrew word *eshel*, translated "grove" in Gen. 21 : 33, is rendered "tamarisk tree" in the R. V. The other Hebrew word, *Asherah*, translated "grove" in Deut. 16 : 21; 1 K. 18 : 19; 2 K. 13 : 6, remains untranslated in R. V., as meaning an idol of that name.

HAY. The translation of Hebrew *chatzir*, meaning grass for hay or fodder. Ps. 72 : 6; Prov. 27 : 25; Isa. 15 : 6. *See* GRASS.

HAZEL. Rendered "almond" in R. V. of Gen. 30 : 37, the Hebrew *luz* being identical with the Arabic name of the almond tree.

HEATH. No heath in Palestine. The Hebrew *arar* is identical with the Arabic for juniper, which in the desert is but a stunted shrub. The R. V. margin of Jer. 17 : 6; 48 : 6 suggests "tamarisk."

HEMLOCK. The plant grows in Palestine, but is not thought to be the one alluded to in the Bible. The Hebrew *rosh*, translated "hemlock" in Hos. 10 : 4, is "gall" in Deut. 29 : 18, in both instances some bitter, poisonous herb being meant. In the R. V. of Am. 6 : 12 the word "wormwood" has been very properly substituted for hemlock.

HENNA. *See* CAMPHIRE.

HERB. Various Hebrew words are applied to herbs, *eseb* being herbs as opposite to grass; *yarak* being cultivated herbs; *oroth* herbs for food, though the latter, whose root is "light," is translated as "sunshine" in Isa. 18 : 4, and "light" is suggested for same word in Isa. 26 : 19. Bitter herbs, as lettuce, endive, chicory, nettles, etc., were eaten with the Paschal lamb, Ex. 12 : 8.

HUSKS. As in R. V. margin of Luke 15 : 16, "the pods of the carob tree." *See* CAROB TREE.

HYSSOP. An unidentified plant furnishing the twigs used in the Mosaic purification and sacrificial rites; thought by some to have been a species of marjoram (*Origanum maru*); by others the caper-bush. Some suggest the name of any common article in the form of a brush or broom. Ex. 12 : 22; Lev. 14 : 4, 6, 51; 1 K. 4 : 33; John 19 : 29. *See* Bible Ill., O. T., p. 409.

JUNIPER. Not the evergreen, but the desert broom-shrub, growing to a height of ten feet. It is capable of affording shelter to travelers, 1 K. 19 : 4, 5, and charcoal may be made of its large roots, Ps. 120 : 4. The R. V. of Job 30 : 4 treats the roots of the broom as edible, or, in the margin, as a source of warmth. *See* Bible Ill., O. T., p. 434.

KNOPS. The R. V. marginal reading of 1 K. 6 : 18, is "gourds," as if the knops were carved after the fashion of this fruit.

LADANUM. The Hebrew *lot* is translated "myrrh" in Gen. 37 : 25; 43 : 11. In the former instance, the substitute "ladanum" is suggested, as the equivalent of the Arabic *ladan*, a fragrant resinous gum of the *Cistus*, or rock rose, of which there are many varieties in Palestine.

LEEKS. The Hebrew *chatzir*, generally rendered "grass," is translated "leeks" in Num. 11 : 5. Leeks are allied to onion and garlic, and were a favorite vegetable among Egyptians and Hebrews.

LENTILS. Lentils are the small, dark, lens-like seeds of the *Ervum lens*, a vetch plant cultivated throughout the East. The seeds are still made into pottage as in the days of Jacob, Gen. 25 : 30. The flour of the seeds also makes a nutritious food. 2 Sam. 17 : 28. *See* Bible Ill., O. T., p. 32.

LIGN ALOES. *See* ALOES.

LILY. The white lily is a native of Palestine. So are many other flowers of garden and field that may answer to the Hebrew *shushan*, or even the Greek *krinon*. Hence much controversy is had over the flower mentioned as "lily" in Scripture. Whatever it may have been, it has proved a source of rich imagery. 1 K. 7 : 19; S. of S. 2 : 1, 2; 5 : 13; Mat. 6 : 28; Luke 12 : 27. *See* Bible Ill., N. T., p. 12.

LOCUST. *See* CAROB TREE.

LOVE APPLES. Suggested in R. V. margin of Gen. 30 : 14 as a reading for mandrakes. In America "love apple" applies only to the primitive tomato.

MALLOWS. The Jew's-mallow is an Asiatic plant used in Syria and Egypt as a pot-herb. But since the root of the Hebrew *malluach* implies saltness, the R. V. of Job 30 : 4 translates it "salt-wort," a maritime plant, succulent, bluish-green, brittle, bushy, prickly, and common to both hemispheres.

MALOBATHRON. Suggested as a reading for *Bether*, in the R. V. margin of S. of S. 2 : 17. Melobathron is a leaf or spice of Eastern origin, used in connection with oil or wine as a perfume or medicine.

MANDRAKE. A narcotic plant, resembling rhubarb, bearing a yellow, aromatic fruit about the size of a plum. It is common throughout Palestine, especially in deserted fields, and has been long famed for its virtues in love incantations. Gen. 30 : 14-1o; S. of S. 7 : 13. The R. V. marginally suggest "love apples." *See* Bible Ill., O. T., p. 38.

MANNA. Officinal manna is the dried, sweet juice of the tamarisk, manna ash, and other shrubs. This origin does not associate it with the *man-hu*, " What is it ? "—or miraculous bread substitute sent to the wandering Israelites—which was small and round like coriander seed, white, and with a taste like wafer and honey. Ex. 16 : 14-36; Num. 11 : 7-9; Deut. 8 : 3; Josh. 5 : 12.

MASTIC. Suggested in R. V. margin of Gen. 37 : 25 for "balm." Gum mastic is a West Indian tree of the myrrh variety.

MELON. Melons of many varieties were a favorite fruit in Egypt and Palestine, as they are to-day in most countries with a hot, dry summer. Num. 11 : 5.

MILLET. Here a grass. Abroad a cereal, ranking with wheat, barley, beans and lentils, as a food. It is a bristly-spiked grass with small, roundish, straw-colored seeds. Its cultivation in Egypt extends back to the earliest times. Ezek. 4 : 9.

MINT. An aromatic herb. Several species grow in Palestine. Hebrews ate it with their meat. One of the bitter herbs of the Paschal feast. The Pharisees tithed it, while they neglected more important things. Mat. 23 : 23; Luke 11 : 42.

MULBERRY. For the Hebrew *baca*, rendered "mulberry" in 2 Sam. 5 : 23, 24; 1 Chr. 14 : 14, the R. V. margin suggests "balsam tree;" but in Ps. 84 : 6 "valley of Baca" is made to read "valley of Weeping." As the poplar is a characteristic of the valleys and water-courses of Palestine, it has been suggested by critics that "poplar" be read in all of the above texts. The true black mulberry is meant in N. T. by the Greek *sycamine*. Luke 17 : 6.

MUSTARD. No doubt the annual herb from which the seeds used as a condiment are obtained. It grows larger in the East than in colder latitudes. Mat. 13 : 31, 32; 17 : 20; Mark 4 : 31, 32; Luke 17 : 6.

MYRRH. A gum resin obtained from a small, thorny Arabian tree, the *Balsamodendron myrrha*. It was used as an ingredient of the holy anointing oil, Ex. 30 : 23; as a domestic perfume, with "aloes, cassia and cinnamon," Prov. 7 : 17; in the purification of women, Esth. 2 : 12; and as a burial spice, John 19 : 39. The R. V. suggests *ladanum* in Gen. 37 : 25. *See* Bible Ill., O. T., p. 55.

MYRTLE. A small, bushy tree, native of Palestine, whose flowers, dark-green leaves and berries were much used by Hebrews for perfume, ornament and spicery. Still used in synagogues on Feast of Tabernacles. Neh. 8 : 15; Isa. 41 : 19; 55 : 13; Zech. 1 : 8–11.

NARD. See SPIKENARD.

NETTLES. The word *kimmosh*, translated "nettles" in Isa. 34 : 13, is supposed to mean the common stinging nettle, four varieties of which are found in Palestine. The word *charul*, translated "nettle" in Job 30 : 7; Prov. 24 : 3, and Zeph. 2 : 9, seems to apply better to weeds in general. The R. V. margin suggests "wild vetches."

NIGELLA SATIVA. This botanical name of "black cummin" has been introduced into R. V. margin of Isa. 28 : 25 as a substitute for "fitches" in the text.

NUTS. *Egoz*, translated "nuts" in S. of S. 6 : 11, is supposed to refer to the walnut, which is native to the higher parts of Palestine. The *botnim* of Gen. 43 : 11 is supposed to be the Arabic pistachio nut, cultivated in Palestine for its edible fruit. The R. V. margin suggests "pistachio nut."

OAK. Two Hebrew words, *allah* and *el*, are translated "oak" in the Bible. As there are nine species of oak in Palestine, most of them noted for girth and expanse, but not for height, it is impossible to fix the species meant in any particular text. The oak at Mamre, famed as "Abraham's Oak," was the *Quercus pseudo-coccifera*, an evergreen tree like the holm oak. Gen. 35 : 8; Judg. 6 : 11, 19; 2 Sam. 18 : 9–14. The word *el*, translated "oak" in Isa. 1 : 29, refers, as is generally agreed, to the teil tree, or terebinth. The R. V. margin suggests "terebinth" in all of the above references.

OIL TREE. The Hebrew *etz shemen*, rendered "oil tree" in Isa. 41 : 19, is rendered "olive tree" in the A. V. of 1 K. 6 : 23, and "olive wood" in the R. V. The same original is also rendered "pine branches" in Neh. 8 : 15, and in the R. V. "wild olive." In the R. V. margin of Isa. 41 : 19 the word "oleaster" is suggested, which is doubtless the tree meant, as it grows profusely in Palestine, producing a small fruit from which oil is extracted.

OLEASTER See OIL TREE.

OLIVE The olive is common to Palestine. It much resembles the apple tree in size and shape, and bears a plum-like fruit, prized for its oil. Gen. 8 : 11; Deut. 8 : 8; Job 24 : 11. Olive wood was used in building and furnishing the temple, 1 K. 6 : 23, 31–33. See Bible Ills., O. T., pp. 218, 237, 509.

ONION. A single-bulbed plant cultivated extensively in Egypt, and highly prized as a food. Num. 11 : 5.

ONYCHA. One of the ingredients of the sacred confection, Ex. 30 : 34. Some think it was burnt sea shell, but as a spice is clearly implied by the text, the gum ladanum has been suggested, that being the word used in the Arabic version of the O. T.

PALM. The date palm (*Phœnix dactylifera*) once grew generally and vigorously in Palestine. Its tall stem, frequently rising to a height of eighty feet, and tipped with feathery foliage, was a symbol of elegance and grace. The fruit grows in bunches clustered about the bases of the leaves. Ex. 15 : 27; Deut. 34 : 3; Judg. 1 : 16; 1 K. 6 : 32; S. of S. 7 : 7. See Bible Ill., O. T., p. 683.

PALMA CHRISTI. See GOURD.

PANNAG. The Lxx makes it "cassia," the Vulgate "balsam," the Syriac "millet," the R. V. margin of Ezek. 27 : 17 "perhaps a kind of confection." It is impossible to tell what it was.

PAPYRUS. See BULRUSH, and Bible Ill., O. T., p. 775.

PINE TREE. The Hebrew *tidhar* is twice rendered "pine tree" in Isa. 41 : 19; 60 : 13. The R. V. suggests "plane tree," which is probably correct. See Bible Ill., O. T., p. 816.

PISTACHIO. See NUTS.

PLANE TREE. See CHESTNUT and PINE TREE.

POMEGRANATE. A low, straight-stemmed tree, native of Persia, Syria, Egypt and Arabia, with blood-red flowers and globular fruit, containing numerous seeds, each enclosed in a red, juicy pulp from which a refreshing drink was made. Num. 13 : 23; Deut. 8 : 8; S. of S. 4 : 3; 6 : 7; 8 : 2. See Bible Ill., O. T., p. 113.

POPLAR. Three species of poplar grow in Palestine—the white poplar, the black poplar and Euphrates poplar. Hos. 4 : 13. The R. V. suggests "storax tree" as the proper rendering of *libneh* in Gen. 30 : 37. See MULBERRY.

PULSE. Pulse is inserted after the word "parched" in 2 Sam. 17 : 28, and, it may be, correctly. *Zeroim*, translated "pulse" in Dan. 1 : 12–16, means grain or seeds of any kind, a simple food being implied.

PURSLAIN. The R. V. of Job 6 : 6 suggests "the juice of purslain" as a reading for "the white of an egg." Purslain is common in Palestine in damp places, and is a prostrate annual, fleshy herb, used as a pot-herb. It is insipid, and a fit illustration of tastelessness.

REED. Usual translation of the Hebrew *kaneh*, and may refer to any one of the many tall rushes and grasses common to shallow and semi-tropical waters. The Greek *kalamos*, or reed of the N. T., has the same general meaning. Source of frequent metaphor. 2 K. 18 : 21; Job 40 : 24; Isa. 19 : 6; Ezek. 29 : 6; Mat. 11 : 7; 12 : 20; 27 : 29.

RIE, RYE. Rye is a grain of cold countries, and not cultivated in Egypt, Palestine or Syria. The A. V., therefore, suggests "spelt," for the Hebrew *cussemeth*, in the margins of Ex. 9 : 32; Isa. 28 : 25. In the R. V. the word "spelt" has been introduced into the text in both of the above instances.

ROSE. The rose is rare in Palestine, being found only in the Lebanon mountains. The root of the Hebrew *chabatzeleth*, rendered "rose" in S. of S. 2 : 1; Isa. 35 : 1 signifies "a bulb;" and some bulbous plant, as the lily, narcissus or crocus, must therefore be looked to as the one meant The R. V. suggests marginally "the autumn crocus."

RUE. A shrubby plant, two to three feet high, with divided leaves and small, yellowish flowers. The leaves emit a powerful, fetid odor, due to the presence of volatile oil. It was cultivated for its supposed medicinal properties, and was tithable. Luke 11 : 42.

RUSH. See BULRUSH and REED.

SAFFRON. A common plant in Palestine. It is a purple-flowered crocus, blooming in the autumn. Its yellow stamens and style yield an aromatic odor. It is used in cooking, as a flavoring and coloring, and is eaten raw. S. of S. 4 : 14.

SALT WORT. See MALLOWS.

SANDARAC. See THYINE WOOD.

SHITTAH TREE. See ACACIA.

SHITTIM WOOD. In R. V. of Ex. 25 : 10–13; 26 : 15, 26; 27 : 1, the rendering is "acacia wood," *i. e.* wood of the shittah tree. See ACACIA. Shittim, whence the spies were sent forth to Jericho, Josh. 2 : 1; 3 : 1, was called Abel-Shittim, "meadow of acacias."

SODOM, VINE OF. In Deut. 32 : 32 this vine bore "grapes of gall." It has been associated with the colocynth, see GOURD, and also with the *Solanum sanctum*, "thorny potato."

SPELT. Rendering of *cussemeth* in the R. V. text of Ex. 9 : 32; Isa. 28 : 25, instead of Rie. See RIE. Spelt is the cereal (*Triticum Spelta*) intermediate between wheat and barley, but usually considered a hard, grained variety of wheat. It was the chief cereal of ancient Egypt, being probably the rye of the time of Moses, Greece and the Roman Empire. It is still cultivated in southern Europe.

SPICERY. Spice-bearing trees not indigenous to Palestine. For "spicery" in Gen. 37 : 25 the R. V. suggests marginally "gum tragacanth," a resin of the milk vetch, which abounds in Asia. "Storax" is also suggested.

SPIKENARD. A plant of the valerian family, growing in the Himalayas, whose odoriferous roots yielded the costly spikenard, or nard, of Scripture. S. of S. 1 : 12 ; 4 : 13 ; Mark 14 : 3 ; John 12 : 3. The R. V. margin of Mark 14 : 3 ; John 12 : 3 suggests "pistic nard," the word "pistic" being, perhaps, a local name, taken by some to mean "genuine," by others "liquid."

STACTE. The Hebrew *nataph* is translated "stacte" in Ex. 30 : 24. It means a "drop," and is so translated in Job 36 : 27. It is not known precisely what was meant by "stacte," but the agreement is that it was a gum or spice. The R. V. margin suggests *opo-balsamum*, "juice of the balsam," but many insist that "storax" is meant, which is the gum of the storax tree, having the odor of vanilla, and formerly used as a medicine.

STORAX. *See* STACTE.

SYCAMINE. The black mulberry (*Morus nigra*), indigenous to Asiatic countries, and now cultivated everywhere. The white mulberry also grows in Palestine. Luke 17 : 6.

SYCAMORE. A medium-sized, bushy tree (*Ficus Sycomorus*) of Syria and Egypt, allied to the common fig. Its abundance of small fruit is still used in Egypt for food, and its light, soft, though durable, wood was used for mummy cases. 1 K. 10 : 27 ; 1 Chr. 27 : 28 ; Ps. 78 : 47 ; Am. 7 : 14 ; Luke 19 : 4. It should not be confounded with the American sycamore, or buttonwood, nor with the English sycamore-maple, which belong to the plane-tree family. *See* Bible Ills., O. T., p. 988 ; N. T., p. 107.

TAMARISK. Introduced into the R. V. text of Gen. 21 : 33 in the place of "grove," and into the text of 1 Sam. 22 : 6 in the place of "tree." Several species of tamarisk are found in Palestine and Arabia, the most common in the latter section being the *Tamarisk mannifera*, growing from five to ten feet high, with feathery branches, imbrecated leaves, white or pink flowers. When punctured, it exhudes a mucilaginous juice, which, on hardening, is gathered by the Arabs and made into cakes called "manna."

TARES. The R. V. margin of Mat. 13 : 25 suggests "darnel." Bearded darnel, *Lolium tumulentum*, is a noxious weed, once supposed to be poisonous. Common darnel is another species of the genus *Lolium*. It is sometimes called ray or rye grass, and is sown for grass or hay.

TEIL TREE. Old name of the European lime or linden. Teil tree occurs only in the text of Isa. 6 : 13, where the Hebrew *elah* is so translated. In other texts the same original is translated "oak," except in Hos. 4 : 13, where it is wrongly rendered "elm." In Isa. 6 : 13 and Hos. 4 : 13 the R. V. introduces "terebinth" instead of teil tree. In the other texts it suggests "terebinth" marginally. *See* Bible Ill., O. T., p. 763.

TEREBINTH. Introduced into the R. V. texts of Isa. 6 : 13 ; Hos. 4 : 13 instead of "teil tree" and "elm," and suggested in other texts as the proper rendering of *elah*, or "oak." The terebinth is a small tree with leaves resembling the ash, but smaller. It grows in southern Palestine, where it takes the place of the oak, being confounded with it from the resemblance in its branching. Called also turpentine tree. *See* Bible Ill., O. T., p. 763.

THISTLE. *See* BRAMBLE.

THORN. *See* BRAMBLE.

THYINE WOOD. A wood mentioned in Rev. 18 : 12, supposed to be wood of the sandarac tree, which is native to north Africa, of the pine family, yielding the pale-yellow gum sandarac, and a dark, hard, fragrant wood, called *alerce*, susceptible of a high polish and used in ornamental work.

VETCHES. *See* FITCHES and NETTLES.

VINE. A favorite Oriental plant of many varieties and cultivated from the earliest times for fruit, wine, etc. Source of frequent Scripture metaphor. Gen. 9 : 20 ; Num. 13 : 23 ; Deut. 32 : 32. Emblem of felicity, 1 K. 4 : 25 ; Israel compared to "wild grapes," Isa. 5 : 2 ; "strange vine," Jer. 2 · 21 ; "empty vine," Hos. 2 : 1 ; symbol of spiritual union, John 15 : 1–5. *See* Bible Ill., O. T., p. 408.

WHEAT. Cultivated as the chief food crop throughout Egypt, Palestine and Mesopotamia. Gen. 30 : 14 ; 41 : 22 ; Ps. 81 : 16 ; Mat. 13 : 8. Wheat-harvest (April to June) marked a division of the year. The double-headed variety of Egypt is still raised there. *See* Bible Ill., O. T., p. 978.

WILLOW. Eight species of willow are known to Palestine, and two different Hebrew words are translated willow, which fact leads some to suppose that one of the words could be better rendered "oleander," which flourishes abundantly along the water courses.

WORMWOOD. A bitter plant, bearing much-divided leaves and numerous small flowers. Five species are found in Palestine. Often used in Scripture in connection with gall, to denote what is offensive and nauseous. Deut. 29 : 18 ; Prov. 5 : 4 ; Jer. 9 : 15 ; 23 : 15 ; Lam. 3 : 15 ; Am. 5 : 7.

BIBLE MINERALS,
METALS AND PRECIOUS STONES.

ADAMANT. The Hebrew original, *shamir*, is translated "adamant" in Ezek. 3 : 9; Zech. 7 : 12, and "diamond" in Jer. 17 : 1. Some very hard substance, as steel or corundum, is meant, but precisely what is not known.

AGATE. A variety of quartz (crystallized silica) in which the colors are in bands or groups. The Hebrew original, *shebo*, is also translated "amethyst," and the Hebrew *kadkod* is also translated "agate." It was the second stone in third row of high priest's breastplate. Ex. 28 : 19; 39 : 12; Isa. 54 : 12; Ezek. 27 : 16.

ALABASTER. White or delicately tinted and fine-grained gypsum, used for making vases, statuettes and ornamental boxes. Mat. 26 : 7; Mark 14 : 3; Luke 7 : 37.

AMBER. A fossil gum, hard, brittle, translucent, yellow. The *elektron* of the Greeks. The Hebrew *chasmal*, translated "agate," is supposed to refer to the yellow metal known as *electrum*. Ezek. 1 : 4, 27; 8 : 2.

AMETHYST. A purplish quartz, ranking as a gem. Third stone in third row of high priest's breastplate, Ex. 28 : 19. Stone in foundation of the New Jerusalem, Rev. 21 : 20.

BERYL. An aluminum silicate of various colors. Ranks as a gem when white. First stone in fourth row of high priest's breastplate, Ex. 28 : 20.

BDELLIUM. A gem, perhaps pearl or amber, Gen. 2 : 12; Num. 11 : 7.

BITUMEN. Any mixture of hydrocarbons, as naphtha and asphalt. Found on shores of Dead Sea and in Euphrates valley.

BRASS. An alloy of copper and zinc. The Hebrew *necosheth*, translated "brass," is generally accepted as meaning "copper," or the alloy of copper and tin known as bronze. Gen. 4 : 22; Deut. 8 : 9; Judg. 16 : 21.

BRIMSTONE. Sulphur, Gen. 19 : 24. Of frequent figurative use, Job 18 : 15; Ps. 11 : 6; Isa. 34 : 9; Rev. 21 : 8.

CARBUNCLE. Anciently, any stone of fiery color, especially red, Isa. 54 : 12. A stone in high priest's breastplate, Ex. 28 : 17, where the translation should be "emerald."

CHALCEDONY. A many-colored precious stone of the agate variety. Rev. 21 : 19.

CHRYSOLITE. The yellow topaz is evidently meant, Rev. 21 : 20.

CHRYSOPRASUS. The chrysoprase, an apple-green variety of chalcedony. Rev. 21 : 20.

CLAY. Much used by Hebrews for houses, pottery, brick-making, sealing, tablets, etc.

COPPER. Supposably the "brass" of the Bible. Copper was well known to Egyptians and Israelites, being imported from Arabia and Cyprus. Largely used for temple vessels, ornaments, mirrors, helmets, spears, etc.

DIAMOND. Pure crystallized carbon. Third stone in second row of high priest's breastplate, Ex. 28 : 18. The Hebrew *gahalon* is supposed to be mistranslated "diamond." The R. V. suggests "sardonyx." Others suggest "onyx," "alabaster," or "jasper."

EMERALD. A bright-green variety of beryl. The emerald of Ex. 28 : 18; 39 : 1; Ezek. 27 : 16; 28 : 13; Rev. 4 : 3; 21 : 19, is supposably the carbuncle, a fiery red garnet.

GOLD. In O. T. six different Hebrew words are translated "gold," showing an early knowledge and extensive use of it, Gen. 2 : 11. Used for ornaments, Gen. 24 : 22; money, temple furniture and utensils, Ex. 36 : 34–38; 1 K. 7 : 48–50; emblem of purity and nobility, Job 23 : 10; Lam. 4 : 1. Obtained chiefly from Ophir, Job 28 : 16; Parvaim, 2 Chr. 3 : 6; Sheba and Raamah, Ezek. 27 : 22.

IRON. The Hebrew *barzel* may not always be correctly translated "iron," but the metal was early known among Semitic nations, Gen. 4 : 22. Prepared in furnaces, 1 K. 8 : 51; used for tools, Deut. 27 : 5; weapons, 1 Sam. 17 : 7; implements, 2 Sam. 12 : 31; war chariots, Josh. 17 : 16, etc.

JACINTH. The Greek *hyakinthos* was probably the sapphire, as suggested in R. V. margin. Modern jacinth is zircon, a vari-colored gem of great hardness. Rev. 9 : 17; 21 : 20.

JASPER. A colored quartz. Last stone in high priest's breastplate, and first in New Jerusalem foundation. Ex. 28 : 20; Rev. 21 : 19.

LEAD. Early known, imported and used variously by Hebrews. Ex. 15 : 10; Num. 31 : 22; Job 19 : 24; Ezek. 27 : 12.

LIGURE. In R. V. "jacinth," and in R. V. margin "amber." First stone in third row of high priest's breastplate. Ex. 28 : 19; 39 : 12.

MARBLE. A calcium or magnesium carbonate, of various colors. But in Scripture any white or shining stone may be meant. 1 K. 7 : 9–12; Esth. 1 : 6; Rev. 18 : 12.

NITRE. Modern nitre is the saltpetre of commerce. The Hebrew *nether* was carbonate of soda. Prov. 25 : 20. In R. V., Jer. 2 : 22, "lye."

ONYX. A veined and shelled quartz, of agate variety. R. V. margin suggests "beryl." Ex. 28 : 9; 1 Chr. 29 : 2.

ROCKS. Clay, dust, earth, flint, stone, sand, etc., occur often in the Bible, and are used in their ordinary sense.

RUBY. A ruddy, valuable gem. The Hebrew original, *peninim*, is thought to mean "coral," or "pearl." Job 28 : 18; Prov. 3 : 15.

SALT. Abundant in Palestine. Used with food, in sacrifical offerings, and gives rise to many emblems and figures of speech.

SAPPHIRE. A blue variety of corundum. Second stone in second row of high priest's breastplate, Ex. 24 : 10; 28 : 18. A foundation stone of New Jerusalem, Rev. 21 : 19.

SARDINE, SARDIUS. The sard or carnelian, a blood-red or flesh-colored stone, first in first row of high priest's breastplate, Ex. 28 : 17; Rev. 4 : 3.

SARDONYX. A precious stone combining the sard and onyx varieties, whence its name, Rev. 21 : 20.

SILVER. Known from earliest times, and much used by Hebrews for money, vessels and ornaments. After captivity used for coins. Supplied from Arabia and Tarshish. Gen. 13 : 2; 24 : 53; 44 : 2; 2 Chr. 9 : 14, 21; Job 28 : 1; Mat. 26 : 15; Acts 19 : 24.

SULPHUR. *See* BRIMSTONE.

TIN. Early known to Hebrews, and probably used in the making of bronze, Num. 31 : 22. R. V. margin suggests "alloy" in Isa. 1 : 25. Imported from Tarshish, Ezek. 27 : 12.

TOPAZ. A variously-hued gem, corresponding to modern chrysolite. Ex. 28 : 17; Job 28 : 19; Rev. 21 : 20.

VERMILION. A bright-red pigment, much used by Hebrews for painting of beams and ceilings. Jer. 22 : 14; Ezek. 23 : 14.

BIBLE MUSIC AND MUSICAL INSTRUMENTS.

MUSIC, Vocal and Instrumental. Music, vocal and instrumental, formed an important part of the festal and religious services of the Hebrews. It even entered into private social affairs, Gen. 31:27; Judg. 11:34; Isa. 5:1; 29:9. It was one of the earliest expressions of joy, Ex. 15:21, and was accompanied with dancing, 2 Sam. 6:16, and with clapping of hands, especially in the chorus, Ps. 47:1. In public rejoicing it was a popular feature, 1 Sam. 18:6. The annual pilgrimages to Jerusalem were enlivened by music, Isa. 30:29. Music also found a place in martial affairs, 2 Chr. 20:21. But it was in religious service that Hebrew music reached its widest use and greatest perfection. In accordance with David's plans for perfecting sacred choristry, the sons of Asaph, Heman and Jeduthun were set apart for the musical services, and they and their brethren that were instructed in the songs of the Lord numbered two hundred and eighty. They were divided, like the priests, into twenty-four courses, 1 Chr. 25. Of the thirty-eight thousand Levites four thousand praised the Lord with instruments. Each course or class had one hundred and fifty-four musicians and three leaders, and all were under the general direction of Asaph and his brethren. This regal direction of sacred music was kept up during the reigns of David and Solomon, the erection of the Temple giving to it its fullest effect. Under succeeding kings it fell into partial disuse, and, of course, was largely discontinued during the captivity. Yet the musical spirit of the Hebrews survived even this cruel blow, and we find that among the captives that returned to the Holy Land with Ezra there were two hundred musicians, Ez. 2:65.

MUSICAL INSTRUMENTS. Instruments of music are among the earliest recorded inventions, Gen. 4:21. The earliest kinds were the tabret, cymbal and pipe; or, since there is great obscurity about the Hebrew words denoting musical instruments, a better division would be into stringed instruments, blowing instruments, and such as gave sound by being struck. These were the germs of all others.

CORNET. Generally accepted as nearly identical with the Hebrew *shophar*, usually rendered "trumpet." The difference, if any, would be that the cornet had less flare, at the open end, than the trumpet. It was used in concert with regular instruments on festal and religious occasions, as well as for signals, 1 Chr. 15:28. The cornet of Dan. 3:5 was the Assyrian trumpet, straight and longer than the Egyptian. *See* Bible Ill., O. T., p. 84.

CYMBAL. Cymbals were of two kinds. The "loud cymbals" consisted of two metal plates, in either hand, which were struck together. The "high-sounding cymbals" consisted of two larger plates, one in each hand, which were struck together. Cymbals were used in the temple worship, for military purposes, and in accompaniment to songs and dances. 1 Chr. 13:8; 16:5; Ps. 150:5; 1 Cor. 13:1.

DULCIMER. Dan. 3:5. In the Greek of the Lxx, *sumphonia*, symphony. In Luther's Bible, "lute." In the A. V. margin, "singing" or "symphony." In the R. V. margin, "bagpipe." Rabbinic scholars and a large school of Bible critics incline to the suggestion made in the R. V. margin. Peasants in northwestern Asia still use a bagpipe, called by a name very similar to the Hebrew *sumphoniah*. It has no resemblance to the modern dulcimer, which is a stringed instrument.

FLUTE. A suggested reading for pipe in 1 K. 1:40, and a musical instrument mentioned among others in Dan. 3:5-15, where it is generally referred to the *syrinx*, a pipe or system of pipes in much vogue among ancients. In the third century B. C. the *syrinx* had as many as ten pipes, and in older sculptures it is represented with

seven or eight. It was blown like pipes of the present day. The flute, or instrument blown at the side, was the Greek *photinx*, while the flute blown at the end, like the modern clarionet, was so ancient that the Egyptians, in attributing it to Osiris, intimated that its origin was lost in antiquity.

HARP. This is the translation of the Hebrew *kinnor* in Gen. 4:21; 31:27; 1 Sam. 16:23; Job 21:12; 30:31; Ps. 137:2; Isa. 5:12. The harp in its most ancient form, being a triangular lyre with eight or nine strings. The word *nebel*, translated "harp" in 1 Sam. 10:5; Neh. 12:27; Ps. 33:2; 57:8; 92:3; 150:3; Isa. 5:12, is supposed to mean the harp in an improved Phœnician form, still triangular, but with one of its sides rounded, and with ten strings. The same word is sometimes rendered "psaltery," "lute" and "viol." The word *asor*, translated "harp" in Ps. 33:2, and "psaltery" in Ps. 144:9, is supposed to be a smaller instrument of Assyrian origin—the "instrument of ten strings." The harp was pre-eminently the instrument of the Jews, and was played with both fingers and plectrum. *See* Bible Ills., O. T., pp. 84, 348, 505.

LUTE. Rendering of the Hebrew *nebel* in R. V. of Isa. 5:12. The lute was an instrument of the guitar family. Whether the word *nebel*, so frequently rendered otherwise, is here properly translated "lute," is an open question.

ORGAN. In Gen. 4:21 the Hebrew original seems to imply all wind instruments. It is generally accepted that a pipe or perforated wind instrument is meant. Job 21:12; 30:31; Ps. 150:4. The R. V. has "pipe" in all of the above texts.

PIPE. Translation of Hebrew *chalil* in 1 Sam. 10:5; 1 K. 1:40; Isa. 5:12; 30:29; Jer. 48:36. In A. V. margin of 1 K. 1:40 flute is suggested. The pipe was the principal perforated wind instrument among Hebrews. It was made of reed, copper, bronze, etc., and was played on all occasions—in the choir, at feasts, weddings, and even at funerals, Mat. 9:23. *See* FLUTE.

PSALTERY. A translation of *nebel* in several texts, but "lute" in Isa. 5:12, and "viol" in Isa. 14:11; Am. 5:23; 6:5. Another word, *pesanterin*, is translated "psaltery" in Dan. 3:5, 10, 15. Some critics insist that only the harp is intended. Others, and perhaps the largest number, accept viol as the instrument intended. It was a guitar-shaped instrument, with six strings. The psalteries of David were made of cypress, 2 Sam. 6:5, those of Solomon of algum, 2 Chr. 9:11.

SACKBUT. A sackbut is a wind instrument, the trombone, but the Chaldee *sabbeca*, of Dan. 3:5, 7, 10, 15, is associated with the Greek *sambuke*, which was the name of several instruments, as the *trigon*, or small triangular harp, with four strings; the *barbitas*, or many-stringed harp; the *lyre-phœnix*, or Phœnician lyre; the dulcimer and pipe.

TABRET. The rendering of the Hebrew *toph* in A. V. of 1 Sam. 18:6. In the R. V. the word is rendered "timbrel," as in both A. V. and R. V. of Ex. 15:25; Judg. 11:34; Ps. 68.25. *See* TIMBREL.

TIMBREL. The rendering of Hebrew *toph* throughout the R. V. Timbrel or tabret was no doubt an instrument resembling the modern tambourine. It was played principally by women as an accompaniment to the song and dance. Ex. 15:20; Judg. 11:34; 1 Sam. 18:6; Ps. 68:25. *See* Bible Ill., O. T., p. 614.

TRUMPET. A wind instrument with a flaring mouth, made of horn or metal, curved or straight, and differing but little in the uses to which it was applied from the cornet. Ex. 19:16. *See* CORNET.

VIOL. A translation of the Hebrew *nebel* in Isa. 14:11; Am. 5:23; 6:5, but "lute" in the R. V. of Isa. 5:12. Supposably a stringed instrument resembling the psaltery in make, tone and use. *See* PSALTERY.

569

CORRESPONDING DATES FOR THREE YEARS.			JEWISH CALENDAR. (In the Sacred Order of the Months.)
A.M. 5623. A.D. 1863.	A.M. 5624. A.D. 1864.	A.M. 5625. A.D. 1865.	
			I. ABIB or NISAN. April
Mar. 21.............	Apr. 7.............	Mar. 28.............	1. New Moon.
Apr. 4,5,10,11.	Apr. 21,22,27,28	Apr. 11,12,17,18	15, 16, 21, 22. PASSOVER Days, 1, 2, 7, last.
Apr. 19.............	....	....	30. New Moon.
			II. JYAR (Yiah). May.
Apr. 20.............	May 7.............	Apr. 27.............	1. New Moon.
Apr. 29.............	May 24.............	May 14.............	10. Death of Elijah (Lag B' Omer). *Fast.*
May 1.............			12.
May 17.............			28. Death of Samuel. *Fast.*
May 19.............			30. New Moon.
			III. SIVAN. June.
May 19.............	June 5.............	May 26.............	1. New Moon.
May 24,25.......	June 10,11.......	May 31, June 1.	6, 7. PENTECOST or Sebuoth.
June 17.............	....	....	30. New Moon.
			IV. THAMMUZ. July.
June 18.............	July 5.............	June 25.............	1. New Moon.
July 5.............	July 21.............	July 11.............	17. Taking of Jerusalem by Titus. *Fast.*
			V. A B. August.
July 17.............	Aug. 3.............	July 24.............	1. New Moon.
July 26.............	Aug. 11.............	Aug. 1.............	9. Destrcution of Temple. *Fast.*
July 31.............			15. Tubeah. *Little Festival.*
Aug. 15.............	....	....	30. New Mooon.
			VI. ELUL. September.
Aug. 16.............	Sept. 2.............	Aug. 23.............	1. New Moon.
Aug. 22.............			7. Dedication of Walls by Nehemiah. *Feast.*
Sept. 1.............	....	....	17. Expulsion of the Greeks.

A.M. 5624. A.D. 1863–4.	A.M. 5625. A.D. 1864–5.	A.M. 5626. A.D. 1865–6.	Beginning of Civil Year.
			VII. TISRI. October.
Sept. 14, 15.......	Oct. 1, 2.............	Sept. 21, 22.......	1, 2. NEW YEAR and New Moon.
Sept. 16.............	Oct. 3.............	Sept. 24.............	3. Death of Gedaliah. *Fast.*
Sept. 23.............	Oct. 10.............	Sept. 30.............	10. Kipur. DAY OF ATONEMENT. *Fast.*
Sept. 28, 29.......	Oct. 15, 16.......	Oct. 5, 6.......	15, 16. FEAST OF TABERNACLES.
Oct. 1.............			18. Hosanna Rabba.
Oct. 4.............	Oct. 21.............	Oct. 11.............	21. Feast of Branches or of Palms.
Oct. 5.............	Oct. 22.............	Oct. 12.............	22. End of Feast of Tabernacles.
Oct. 6.............	Oct. 23.............	Oct. 13.............	23. Feast of the Law.
			VIII. CHESVAN (Marchesvan). November.
Oct. 14.............	Oct. 31.............	Oct. 21.............	1. New Moon.
			IX. CHISLEU. December.
Nov. 12.............	Nov. 30.............	Nov. 19.............	1. New Moon.
Dec. 6.............	Dec. 24.............	Dec. 13.............	25. Hanuca. Dedication of Temple.
			X. THEBET. January.
Dec. 11.............	Dec. 30.............	Dec. 19.............	1. New Moon.
Dee. 20.............	1865. Jan. 8.............	Dec. 28.............	10. Siege of Jerusalem. *Fast.*
1864. Jan. 9.............	Jan. 28.............	1866 Jan. 17.............	**XI. SEBAT. February.** 1. New Moon.
			XII. ADAR. March.
Feb. 8.............	Feb. 27.............		1. New Moon.
Feb. 21.............	....	....	14. Littla Purim.
			⎰XII.* VEADAR (Intercalary). Latter part
			⎱ of March and beginning of April.
Mar. 9.............			1. New Moon.
Mar. 21.............	Mar. 9.............		13. Feast of Esther.
Mar. 22, 23.......	Mar. 12, 13.......		14, 15. Feast of Purim and Shusham Purim.
Apr. 6.............	....		Last Day of the year.

MEM.—The Jewish year Contains 354 days, or 12 lunations of the moon; but in a cycle of 19 years an Intercalary month (*Veadar*) is seven times introduced to render the average length of the year nearly correct.

ANALYTICAL AND COMPARATIVE
CONCORDANCE
TO THE OLD AND NEW TESTAMENTS

EMBRACING THE SALIENT AND READY-WORKING FEATURES OF THE LARGER
CONCORDANCES OF CRUDEN, YOUNG, AND OTHERS.

By JAMES P. BOYD, A. M.

AUTHOR OF THE "ILLUSTRATED SELF-PRONOUNCING BIBLE DICTIONARY," "PEOPLE'S POCKET
DICTIONARY OF THE HOLY BIBLE," ETC.

NOTES.—References to proper names will be found in place in the accompanying dictionary.
In Scripture one original word is sometimes rendered by various English words; and so, one English
word is often used to translate various original words. Therefore, in its analytical feature, this Concordance
shows in Italics the different shades of meaning attached to the originals, where such are important.

In its comparative feature, this Concordance notes the word-changes made in the Revised Version,
wherever such are of moment. Words omitted in the R. V. are indicated by a ——.

Nouns and verbs spelled alike are indicated by (*n.*) and (*v.*).

Nouns plural are referred to under their singulars.

Past tenses of verbs and their participles are, as a rule, referred to under their present tenses.

Abase. *To make low, humble.*
Job 40. 11 Behold proud, and *a.*
Eze..21. 26 and *a.* him that is high
Dan. 4. 37 in pride is able to *a.*
To submit oneself.
Isa. 31. 4 he will not *a.* himself
Abased. *Made low, humbled.*
Matt. 23. 12 exalteth himself shall
be *a.*
Luke 14. 11; 18. 14
Phil. 4. 12 I know how to be *a.*
R. V. Matt. 23. 12; Luke 14. 11;
18. 14 humbled
Abasing. *Making low, humbling.*
2 Cor. 11. 7 offence in *a.* myself
Abated. *Cut off, diminished.*
Gen. 8. 3 waters were *a.* 8. 8, 11
Lev. 27. 18 it shall be *a.* from
Deut. 34. 7 nor his force *a.*
Judg. 8. 3 their anger was *a.*
R. V. Gen. 8. 3 decreased
Abba. *Father.*
Mark 14. 36 *A.* Father, all things
Rom. 8. 15 whereby we cry *A.*
Gal. 4. 6 crying *A.* Father
Abhor. *Despise, reject, loath.*
Lev. 26. 11 my soul shall not *a.*
26. 15, 30, 43, 44
Deut. 7. 26 shalt utterly *a.* it.
23. 7 not *a.* an Edomite
1 Sam. 27. 12 his people to *a.* him
Job 9. 31 clothes shall *a.* me
30. 10; 46. 2
Ps. 5. 6 the Lord will *a.*
Prov. 24. 24 nations shall *a.* him
Jer. 14. 21 do not *a.* us
Amos 5. 10 they *a.* him
Mic. 3. 9 ye that *a* judgment
Rom. 12. 9 *a.* that which is evil
Abhorred. *Made stinking, hated,
rejected.*
Ex. 5. 21 made our savor to be *a.*
Lev. 20. 23 and therefore I *a.*
Deut. 32. 19 he *a.* them
1 Sam. 2. 17 men *a.* the offering
2 Sam. 16. 21 art *a.* of thy father
2 K. 11. 25 he *a.* Israel
Job 19. 19 inward friends *a.* me
Ps. 22. 24 nor *a.* the affliction
28. 59; 89. 38; 106. 40

Prov. 22. 14 *a.* of the Lord
Lam. 2. 7 hath *a.* his sanct.
Ezek. 16. 25 beauty to be *a.*
Zech. 11. 8 their soul also *a.* me
R. V. Ps. 89. 38, rejected; Ezek. 16.
25 an abomination
Abhorrest.
Isa. 7. 16 land that thou *a.*
Rom. 2. 22 that thou *a.* idols
Abhorreth.
Job 33. 20 so life *a.* bread
Ps. 10. 3 whom the Lord *a.*
Isa. 49. 7 whom the nation *a.*
Abhorring.
Isa. 66. 24 an *a.* to all flesh
Abide. *Stay, sit, settle, dwell.*
Gen. 22. 5 *a.* you here with
Ex. 16. 29 *a.* every man in
Lev. 8. 35 *a.* at the door of
1 Sam. 5. 7 the ark shall not *a.*
2 Sam. 16. 18 with him shall I *a.*
Job 24. 13 nor *a.* in paths of light
Ps. 15. 1 shall *a.* in tabernacle
61. 4, 7; 91. 1
Prov. 7. 11 her feet *a.* not in
Ec. 8. 15 shall *a.* of his labor
Jer. 10. 10 to *a.* his indigna.
Joel 2. 11 who can *a.* it
Mic. 5. 4 they shall *a.* for now
Nah. 1. 6 can *a.* in his anger
Mal. 3. 2 who may *a.* the day
Matt. 10. 11 and there *a.* till
Mark 6. 10; Luke 9. 4; 19. 5
John 12. 46 not *a.* in darkness
Acts 27. 31 *a.* in the ship
1 Cor. 3. 14 if any man's work *a,*
Phil. 1. 24 to *a.* in the flesh
1 John 2. 24 let that *a.* in you
R. V. Ps. 15. 1 sojourn; Hos. 11. 6
fall upon; Rom. 11. 23 continue
Abideth. *Stayeth, remaineth, dwel-
leth.*
2 Sam. 16. 3 he *a.* at Jerus.
Ps. 49. 12 man in honor *a.* not
55. 19; 119. 90; 125. 1
Prov. 15. 31 *a.* among the wise
Ec. 1. 4 the earth *a.* forever
John 3. 36 wrath of God *a.* on
1 Cor. 13. 13 now *a.* faith, hope
2 Tim. 2. 13 yet he *a* faithful

Heb. 7. 3 Mel. *a.* a priest
1 Pet. 1. 23 word of G. which *a.*
1 John 2. 6 he *a.* in him ought
2 John 9 whoso *a.* not in the
Abiding. *Sitting, remaining, dwel-
ling.*
1 Sam. 26. 19 from *a.* in inherit.
1 Chr. 29. 15 there is none *a.*
Luke 2. 8 shepherds *a.* in the field
John 5. 28 his word *a.* in you
1 John 3. 15 hath eternal life *a.*
Ability. *Power, strength, wealth.*
Ez. 2. 69 gave after their *a.*
Neh. 5. 8 after our *a.* redeemed
Dan. 1. 4 had *a.* to stand in
Matt. 25. 15 each accord. to his *a.*
Acts 11. 29 according to *a.*
1 Pet. 4. 11 as of the *a.* which G.
R. V. 1 Pet. 4. 11 strength
Abjects. *Smitten, stricken.*
Ps. 35. 15 the *a.* gathered thems.
Able. *Sufficient, full.*
Lev. 5. 7 not *a.* to bring a lamb
12, 8; 25, 26; 25, 28
2 Tim. 2. 2 shall be *a.* to teach
Power, strength, ability.
Ex. 18. 21 provide *a.* men
Num. 1. 3 *a.* to go to war
Deut. 16. 17 give as he is *a.*
Josh. 23. 9 man been *a.* to stand
1 Sam. 6. 20 who is *a.* to stand
1 K. 3. 9 who is *a.* to judge
2 Chr. 2. 6 who is *a.* to build
Job 41. 10 who then is *a.* to
Prov. 27. 4 who is *a.* to stand
Dan. 3. 17 our God is *a.*
Mat. 3. 9 God is *a.* of these stones
9. 28; 19.12; 20. 22; 22. 46; Luke 3.8
Mark 4. 33 they were *a.* to hear
John 10. 29 no man is *a.* to pluck
Acts 15. 10 fathers nor we were *a.*
Rom. 4. 21 he was *a.* to perform
11. 23; 14. 4; 15. 14
1 Cor. 3. 2 ye were not *a.*
2 Cor. 3. 6 made us *a.* ministers
Eph. 3. 20 that is *a.* to do
Phil. 3. 21 he is *a.* to subdue
2 Tim. 1. 12 he is *a.* to keep
Heb. 2. 18 he is *a.* to succor
5. 7; 7. 25; 11. 19

Jam. 1. 21 which is *a.* to save
Jude 24 him that is *a.* to keep
Rev. 5. 3 no man was *a.* to open
  13. 4; 15. 18
R. V. Lev. 25. 26, waxen rich; Jos.
  23. 9 —; Acts 25. 5 are of power;
  2 Cor. 3. 6 sufficient as; Eph. 3
  18 strong.
Able, used negatively
  Num. 13. 31 we be not *a.* to go
  2 K. 18. 29 not be *a.* Is. 36. 14
  Ez. 10. 13 we are not *a.* to stand
  Neh. 4. 10 we are not *a.* to build
  Ps. 18. 38 not *a.* to rise
  21. 11; 36. 12; 40. 12
  Ec. 8. 17 not be *a.* to find
  Is. 47. 11 shall not be *a.* to put
  Jer. 11. 11 not *a.* to escape
  Ezek. 7. 19 gold shall not be *a.*
  Am. 7. 10 land is not *a.* to bear
  Luke 13. 24 and shall not be *a.*
  12. 26; 14. 29; 21. 15
  John 21. 6 not *a.* to draw for the m.
  Acts 6. 10 not *a.* to resist the w.
Aboard. *To go on or upon.*
  Acts 21. 2 went *a.* and set forth
Abode (*n.*). *Home, mansion, sitting.*
  2 K. 19. 27 I know thy *a.* Is. 37. 28
  John 14. 23 Come and make our *a.*
Abode (*v.*). *Stayed, sat, settled, dwelt.*
  Gen. 29. 14 Jacob *a.* with him
  Ex. 24. 16 glory of G. *a.* on Si.
  Num. 9. 17 where the cloud *a.*
  9. 18, 20; 20. 1; 22. 8
  Deut. 1. 46 ye *a.* in Kadesh
  Jos. 5. 8 they *a.* in their places
  Judg. 5. 17 Gilead *a.* beyond Jor.
  1 Sam. 1. 23 the woman *a.* and gave
  7. 2; 13. 16; 22. 6; 23. 14;
  2 Sam. 14. 12 Uriah *a.* in Jerus.
  1 K. 17. 19 a loft where he *a.*
  Jer. 38. 28 J. *a.* in the court
  Mat. 17. 22 they *a.* in Galilee
  Luke 1. 56 Mary *a.* with her
  John 1. 32 Spirit, and it *a.* on him
  7. 9; 8. 44; 11. 6
  Acts 1. 13 room where *a.* Peter
  14. 3; 18. 3; 21. 7
  Gal. 1. 18 and *a.* with Peter
Abodest
  Judg. 5. 16 why *a.* thou among the
Abolish. *Break down, blot out.*
  Isa. 2. 18 idols he shall utterly *a.*
Abolished. *Made inactive.*
  2 Cor. 3. 13 end of that which is *a.*
  Eph. 2. 15 having *a.* in the flesh
  2 Tim. 1. 10 who hath *a.* death
  Broken down, wiped away, blotted
  out.
  Isa. 51. 6 my right. shall not be *a.*
  Ezek. 6. 6 your works may be *a.*
  R. V. Is. 2. 18 pass away; 2 Cor
  3. 13, passing away.
Abominable. *Impure, detestable.*
  Lev. 7. 21 or an *a.* unclean thing
  11. 43; 18. 30; 19. 7; 20. 25
  Deut. 14. 3 not eat any *a.* thing
  1 Chr. 21. 6 king's word was *a.* to
  2 Chr. 15. 8 put away *a.* idols
  Job 15. 16 much more *a.* is man
  Ps. 14. 1 have done *a.* works
  Isa. 14. 19 like an *a.* branch
  Jer. 44. 4 this *a.* thing I hate
  Ezek. 4. 14 came *a.* flesh into my
  Mic. 6. 10 measure that is *a.*
  Nah. 3. 6 I will cast *a.* filth on
  Tit. 1. 16 deny him being *a.*
  1 Pet. 4. 3 walked in *a.* idolatries
  Rev. 21. 8 unbelieving and the *a.*
Abominably. *Detestably, unlaw-*
  fully.
  1 K. 21. 26 Ahab did very *a.*
Abomination. *Impure, detestable*
  thing.
  Lev. 7. 18 it shall be an *a.*
  Deut. 29. 17 ye have seen their *a.*
  1 K. 11. 5 S. went after the *a.* of
  2 K. 23. 13 the *a.* of the Zido.
  Isa. 66. 3 delighteth in their *a.*
  Isa. 44. 1 put away thine *a.*
  7. 30; 13. 27; 32. 34
  Ezek. 5. 11 and with all thine *a.*
  20. 7, 8, 30.
  Dan. 9. 27 the overspreading of *a.*
  Hos. 9. 10 and their *a.* were
  Abomination, detestation.

Lev. 11. 10 shall be an *a.* unto you
  11. 11, 12, 13, 20, 23, 41, 42
  That excites disgust, anger, loath-
  ing.
  Gen. 43. 32 that is an *a.* unto the
  46. 34 every shepherd is an *a.*
  Ex. 8. 26 we shall sacrifice the *a.*
  Lev. 18. 22 shalt not lie with man-
    kind, it is *a.*
  18. 26, 27, 29; 20, 13.
  Deut. 7. 25 it is an *a.* to the L.
  12, 31; 13. 14; 17. 1; 18. 9; 20. 18;
  32. 16.
  1 K. 14. 24 according to all the *a.*
  2 K. 16. 3 according to the *a.* of the
  2 Chr. 28. 3 after the *a.* of the hea.
  33. 2; 34. 33; 36. 8:
  Ez. 9. 1 according to their *a.*
  Ps. 88. 8 thou hast made me an *a.*
  Prov. 3. 32 the froward is *a.*
  6. 16; 8. 7; 11. 1; 12. 22; 13. 19;
  15. 8.
  Isa. 1. 13 incense is an *a.*
  Jer. 2. 7 mine heritage an *a.*
  6. 15; 7. 10; 8. 12; 32. 35; 44. 22
  Ezek. 5. 9 because of all thine *a.*
  6. 9; 7. 3; 8. 6; 9. 4; 11. 18; 12. 16
  Mal. 2. 11 an *a.* is committed
  Mat. 24. 15 see the *a.* of desolation
  Mark 13. 14 ye shall see the *a.*
  Luke 16. 15 among men is *a.*
  Rev. 17. 4 golden cup full of *a.*
Abound. *To be in great plenty.*
  Prov. 28. 20 faithful *a.* with
  Mat. 24. 12 iniquity shall *a.*
  Rom. 5. 20 the offence might *a*
  6. 1; 15. 13
  2 Cor. 1. 5 as suffering *a.* so
  8. 7; 9. 8
  Phil. 1. 9 that .. love may *a.* more
  4. 12, 17, 18
  1 Thes. 3. 12 make you to *a.* in love
  2 Pet. 1. 8 things be in you and *a.*
  R. V. Mat. 24. 12 multiplied
Abounded, eth, ing.
  Prov. 8. 24 no fountains *a.* with
  Rom. 3. 7 of G. hath more *a.*
  1. 10 Cor. 15. 58 always *a.* in the
  2 Cor. 8. 2 poverty *a.* to riches
  Eph. 1. 8 he hath *a.* toward
  Col. 2. 7 *a.* therein with thanksg.
  2 Thes. 1. 3 char. to each other *a*
About (*prep.*). *Around, on, upon.*
  Num. 2. 2 *a.* the tabernacle
  Deut. 17. 14 nations that are *a.*
  1 K. 18. 32 a trench *a.* the altar.
  Job 29. 5 my children were *a.*
  Jer. 17. 26 places *a.* Jerusalem
  Mat. 3. 4 girdle *a.* his loins
  Mark 1. 6 girdle of skin *a.*
  Luke 10. 40 Martha was cum-
    bered *a.*
  John 3. 25 and the Jews *a.*
About (*adv.*). *Around, nearly, as*
  if.
  2 K. 3. 25 slingers went *a.* it
  2 Chr. 17. 9 went *a.* throughout
  Eccl. 2. 20 therefore went I *a.*
  Is. 23. 16 go *a.* the city
  Mat. 14. 21 were *a.* five thousand
  Mark 5. 13; 6. 44; 8. 9.
  Luke 1. 56 with her *a.* three months
  John 4. 6 *a.* the sixth hour
  Acts 2. 41 added *a.* three thousand
  On the point of.
  Acts 3. 3 seeing P. & J. *a.* to go
  Heb. 8. 5 when he was *a.* to make
  Rev. 10. 4 I was *a.* to write.
Above. *On high, higher, over,*
  beyond.
  Gen. 6. 16 shalt thou finish *a.*
  Ex. 20. 4 that is in heaven *a.*
  Lev. 11. 21 which have legs *a.*
  Deut. 4. 39 God in heaven *a.*
  1 K. 7. 3 covered with cedar *a.*
  1 Chr. 23. 27 twenty years old and *a.*
  2 Chr. 4. 4 and the sea *a.* upon
  Job 18. 16 and *a.* shall his branch
  Prov. 8. 28 established the clouds *a.*
  Isa. 6. 2 *a.* it stood the seraphims
  Jer. 35. 4 which was *a.* the chamber
  Ezek. 1. 22 over their heads *a.*
  Mat. 10. 24 disciple is not *a.* ... master
  Luke 13. 2 sinners *a.* all the
  Acts 26. 13 *a.* the brightness of
  Rom. 14. 5 esteemeth one day *a.*

Heb. 1. 9 anointed thee *a.* thy
Jas. 5. 12 *a.* all things, swear not
1 Pet. 4. 8 *a.* all things have charity
Abroad. *Outside, without, far and*
  wide.
  Gen. 15. 5 brought him forth *a.*
  Ex. 21. 19 and walk *a.* upon
  Lev. 18. 9 born at home or *a.*
  Judg. 12. 9 daughters from *a.*
  2 K. 4. 3 borrow the vessels *a.*
  2 Chr. 31. 5 as com. came *a.*
  Job 15. 23 wandereth *a.* for bread
  Ps. 41. 6 he goeth *a.*
  Prov. 5. 16 be dispersed *a.*
  Jer. 6. 11 on children *a.*
  Mark 1. 45 blaze *a.* the matter
  Luke 1. 65 sayings were noised *a.*
  Acts 2. 6 noised *a.* the multitude
  Rom. 5. 5 love of God shed *a.*
Absence. *Off or away from.*
  Luke 22. 6 betray him in *a.* of mul.
  Phil. 2. 12 much more in my *a.*
Absent. *To be away from.*
  Gen. 31. 49 L. watch when we are *a.*
  1 Cor. 5. 3 verily as *a.* in body
  2 Cor. 5. 6 *a.* from the Lord
  5. 8, 9; 10. 1, 11; 13. 2, 10
  Phil. 1. 27 or else be *a.*
  Col. 2. 5 I be *a.* in the flesh
Abstain. *To hold off from.*
  Acts 15. 20 we write .. that they *a.*
  15. 29 that ye *a.* from meats
  1 Thes. 4. 3 that ye should *a.*
  1 Tim. 4. 3 to *a.* from meats
  1 Pet. 2. 11 *a.* from fleshly lusts
Abstinence. *Self-denial of food.*
  Acts 27. 21 after long *a.* Paul stood
Abundance. *Large supply or*
  number.
  Deut. 33. 19 suck of the *a.* of
  1 Sam. 1. 16 out of *a.* of my compl.
  1 K. 18. 41 sound of *a.* of rain
  2 Chr. 9. 9 of spices great *a.*
  Job 22. 11 and *a.* of waters
  Ps. 72. 7 shall be *a.* of peace
  Eccl. 5. 10 that loveth *a.*
  Isa. 15. 7 the *a.* they have
  47. 9; 60. 5; 66. 11
  Jer. 33. 6 reveal *a.* of peace
  Ezek. 16. 49 *a.* of idleness
  Zech. 14. 14 apparel in great *a.*
  Mat. 12. 34 out of the *a.* of
  13. 12; 25. 29; Luke 6. 45
  Luke 12. 15 consisteth not in *a.*
  Mark 12. 44 cast in of their *a.*
  Rom. 5. 17 receive *a.* of grace
  2 Cor. 8. 2 *a.* of their joy
  Rev. 8. 3 *a.* of delicacies
  R. V. 2 Cor. 8. 20 bounty
Abundant. *Much, many, plenteous.*
  Ex. 34. 6 and *a.* in goodness
  Isa. 56. 12 this day much more *a.*
  Jer. 51. 13 *a.* in treasures
  1 Cor. 12. 23 bestow more *a.*
  12. 24 having given more *a.*
  2 Cor. 4. 15 that the *a.* grace
  7. 15; 9. 12; 11. 23
  Phil. 1. 26 rejoicing be more *a.*
  1 Tim. 1. 14 was exceeding *a.*
  1 Pet. 1. 3 his *a.* mercy
  R. V. 2 Cor. 4. 15 multiplied; 1 Pet.
  1. 3 great
Abundantly. *Plenteously, richly.*
  Gen. 1. 20, 21 waters bring forth *a.*
  8. 17; 9. 7
  Ex. 1. 7 Israel increased *a.*
  Num. 20. 11 water came out *a.*
  1 Chr. 22. 5 David prepared *a.*
  Job 12. 6 into hand God bringeth *a.*
  Ps. 36. 8 *a.* satisfied with fatness
  6. 10; 132. 15; 145. 7
  S. of S. 5. 1 drink *a.* O beloved
  Isa. 15. 3 shall howl, weeping *a.*
  35. 2 blossom *a.* and rejoice
  55. 7 will *a.* pardon
  John 10. 10 have life more *a.*
  1 Cor. 15. 10 I laboured more *a.*
  2 Cor. 1. 12 and more *a.* to you
  2. 4; 10. 15; 12. 15
  Eph. 3. 20 to do exceeding *a.*
  1 Thes. 2. 17 more *a.* to see your
  Tit. 3. 6 he shed *a.* through
  Heb. 6. 17 G. willing more *a* to
  2 Pet. 1. 11 be ministered unto you *a.*
Abuse. *Misuse, wrong, malign.*
  Judg. 19. 25 *a.* her all the night

1 Sam. 31. 4 lest uncircum. *a.* me
1 Chr. 10. 4 come and *a.* me
1 Cor. 9. 18 I *a.* not my power
R. V. 1 Cor. 9. 18 not to us to the full
Abusers, ing.
1 Cor. 6. 9 nor *a.* of themselves
7. 31 use . . world as not *a.* it
Accept. *Receive, take hold of*
Ex. 2. 11 owner of it shall *a.*
Acts 24. 3 we *a.* it always
To lift up, be pleased.
Deut. 33. 11 and *a.* the work of
1 Sam. 26. 19 let him *a.* an offering
2 Sam. 24. 23 Lord thy God *a.*
Job 13. 8 will ye *a.* his person
Ps. 20. 3 *a.* thy burnt sacrifice
Prov. 18. 5 not good to *a.* the per.
Jer. 14. 10 L. doth not *a.* them
Ezek. 20. 40 there will I *a.* them
Mal. 1. 8 pleased, or *a.* thy person
Acts 24. 3 we *a.* it always
R. V. Job 13. 10 ; 32. 21 ; Ps. 82. 2
respect
Acceptable. *Pleasing, receivable.*
Deut. 33. 24 *a.* to his brethren
Ps. 19. 14 medita. of my heart be *a.*
Prov. 10. 32 know what is *a.*
Ec. 12. 10 sought *a.* words
Isa. 49. 8 in an *a.* time have I
Jer. 6. 20 offerings are not *a.*
Dan. 4. 27 let my counsel be *a.*
Luke 4. 19 preach the *a.* year
Rom. 12. 1 holy, *a.* to God
12. 2 ; 14. 18 ; 15. 16
Eph. 5. 10 proving what is *a.*
Phil. 4. 18 a sacrifice *a.* well pleas.
1 Tim. 2. 3 *a.* in sight of God
1 Pet. 2. 5 sacrifices *a.* to God
Acceptably. *Pleasingly.*
Heb. 12. 28 we may serve G. *a.*
Acceptance. *Good pleasure.*
Isa. 60. 7 with *a.* on mine altar
Acceptation. *Full reception.*
1 Tim. 1. 15 worthy of all *a.* 4. 9
Accepted. *Good in sight of.*
Gen. 4. 7 shalt thou not be *a.*
Lev. 10. 19 *a.* in the sight of L.
1 Sam. 18. 5 was *a.* in sight of
Jer. 37. 20 supplication be *a.* 42. 2
To be pleased with.
Ex. 28. 38 that they may be *a.*
Lev. 1. 4 it shall be *a.* 7. 18
Lev. 22. 21 ; 23. 11 to be *a.*
Esth. 10. 3 *a.* of the multitude
Isa. 56. 7 sacrifices shall be *a.*
Eph. 1. 6 hath made us *a.*
Receivable, well pleasing.
Luke 4. 24 no prophet is *a.*
Acts 10. 35 righteousness is *a.*
Rom. 15. 31 service may be *a.*
2 Cor. 6. 2 now is the *a.* time
5. 9 ; 8. 12, 17 ; 11. 4
Acceptest, eth.
Luke 20. 21 neither *a.* thou
Job 34. 19 *a.* not persons of
Eccl. 9. 7 G. now *a.* thy works
Hos. 8. 13 L. *a.* them not
Gal. 2. 6 G. *a.* no man's person
Access. *Leading unto.*
Rom. 5. 2. also we have *a.*
Eph. 2. 18 have *a.* to the F.
3. 12 and *a.* by faith
Accompany, nied. *Come, go with.*
Acts 10. 23 brethren from Joppa *a.*
11. 12 six brethren *a.* me
20. 4 Sopater *a.* Paul
20. 38 and they *a.* him
Accompanying. *Along with.*
2 Sam. 6. 4 *a.* the ark of God
R. V. 6. 4 with
Accomplish. *To complete, perfect.*
Job 14. 6 till he shall *a.*
Ps. 64. 6 *a.* a diligent search
Isa. 55. 11 shall *a.* that I please
Jer. 44. 25 surely *a.* your vows
Ezek. 6. 12 will I *a.* my fury
7. 8 ; 13. 15 ; 20. 8, 21
Dan. 9. 2 he would *a.* 70 yrs.
Luke 9. 31 should *a.* at Jerusalem
R. V. Jer. 44. 25 established
Accomplished. *Completed, finished.*
Est. 2. 12 purification of *a.* Luke 2. 22
Job 15. 32 shall be *a.* before
Prov. 13. 19 desire *a.* is sweet
Isa. 40. 2 her warfare is *a.*

Jer. 25. 12 seventy years are *a.*
Lam. 4. 11. L. hath *a.* his fury
Ezek. 5. 13 shall mine anger be *a.*
Dan. 11. 36 indignation be *a.*
Luke 1. 23 his ministrations *a.*
2. 6 ; 12. 50 ; 18. 31 ; 22. 37
John 19. 28 things are now *a.*
Acts 21. 5 had *a.* those days
1 Pet. 5. 9 afflictions are *a.*
R. V. Jer 25. 34 fully come
Luke 1. 23 ; 2. 6, 21,22 fulfilled
Accomplishment. *Fulfilled.*
Acts 21. 6 to signify the *a.* of the
Accord. *Like-minded, joint-souled*
Acts 1. 14 with one *a.* in prayer
2. 1 all with one *a.*
2. 46 daily with one *a.*
4. 24 voice with one *a.*
5. 12 were all with one *a.* in
7. 57 ; 8. 6 ; 12. 10, 20 ; 15. 25 ; 18. 12
Phil. 2. 2 love of one *a.*
Choosing of himself.
2 Cor. 8. 17 of his own *a.* he went
One mouth, spirit.
Josh. 9. 2 to fight with one *a.*
R. V. Lev. 25. 5 itself ; Acts 2. 1 tog.
According. *Just as, agreeably to.*
Gen. 43. 7 *a.* to the tenor of words
Ex. 12. 4 every man *a.* to . . eating
Lev. 25. 16 *a.* to the multitude
Num. 6. 21 *a.* to the vow . . vowed
Deut. 17. 10 shalt do *a.* to the
Jos 18. 4 describe it *a.* to the
1 K. 17. 1 but *a.* to my word
1 Chr. 12,23 *a.* to the word of L.
2 Chr. 31. 2 every man *a.* to his
Ez. 6. 14 and *a.* to the com.
Isa. 59. 18 *a.* to their deeds
Mat. 2. 16 *a.* to the time which
9. 29 ; 16. 27 ; 25. 15
Mark 7. 5 thy disciples *a.* to
Luke 1. 9 *a.* to the custom
2. 22, 24, 29, 39 ; 23. 56
John 7. 24 judge not *a.* to the
Acts 2. 30 *a.* to the flesh
7. 44 ; 13. 23 ; 22. 12
Rom. 1. 3 seed of D. *a.* to the
2. 2 ; 4. 18 ; 8. 27; 9. 3 ; 10. 2 ; 11. 5
1 Cor. 3. 8 *a.* to his own labor
2 Cor. 1. 7 *a.* to the flesh
Gal. 1. 4 *a.* to the will of God
Eph. 1. 5 *a.* to the good pleasure
Phil. 1. 20 *a.* to the working
Col. 1. 11 *a.* to his glories
1 Tim. 1. 11 *a.* to the glorious gos.
2 Tim. 1. 1 *a.* to the promise
Tit. 3. 7 heirs *a.* to the hope
Heb. 2. 4 gifts *a.* to his own
Jas. 2. 8 gifts *a.* to the scripture
1 Pet. 3. 7 *a.* to knowledge
Rev. 2. 23 *a.* to your works
Accordingly. *Just so*
Isa. 59. 18 *a.* he will repay
Account (*n.*), *Thought, device, reckoning.*
Job 33. 13 giveth not *a* of his
Ps. 144. 3 that thou makest *a.*
Eccl. 7. 27 to find out the *a.*
Dan. 6. 2 princes might give *a.*
Mat. 12. 36 *a.* thereof
Luke 16. 2 an *a.* of stewardship
Acts 19. 40 give an *a.* of this
Rom. 14. 12 give *a.* of himself
Phil. 4. 17 abound to your *a.*
Phile. 18 put that on mine *a.*
Heb. 13. 17 that must give *a.*
2 Pet. 4. 5 *a.* to him that judgeth
Accounted, ed, ing (*v.*). *Thought, reckoned.*
Deut. 2. 11 also were *a.* giants
1 K. 10. 21 it was nothing *a.* of
2 Chr. 9. 20 not anything *a.* of
Ps. 22. 30 *a.* to the Lord
Isa. 2. 22 wherein is he to be *a.*
Mark 10. 42 *a.* to rule over
Luke 20. 35 be *a.* worthy
Rom. 8. 36 we are *a.* as sheep
1 Cor. 4. 1 man so *a.* of us
Gal. 3. 6 *a.* to him for right
Heb. 11. 19 *a.* that God was able
2 Pet. 3. 15 *a.* that the long-suf.
R. V. 2 Chr. 26. 11 ; Mat. 18. 23
reckoning,
Accursed. *Devoted, doomed thing.*
Deut. 21. 23 is *a.* of God
Josh. 6. 17 the city shall be *a.*

7. 12 because they are *a.*
7. 15 with the *a.* thing
1 Chr. 2. 7 in the thing *a.*
Isa. 65. 20 100 yrs. old shall be *a.*
Devoted, put up, anathema
Rom. 9. 3 were *a.* from Christ
1 Cor. 12. 3 no man..calleth Jesus *a.*
Gal. 1. 8, 9 let him be *a.*
R. V. 1 Chr. 2. 7 devoted thing ;
Rom. 9. 3 ; 1 Cor. 12. 3 ; Gal. 1. 8,
anathema
Accusation. *Cause, charge, matter.*
Ez. 4. 6. an *a.* against Judah
Mat. 27. 37 over his head his *a.*
Mark 15. 26 snperscription of his *a.*
Luke 6. 7 find an *a.* against
John 18. 29 what *a.* bring ye
Acts 25. 18 they brought none *a.* as
1 Tim. 5. 19 receive not an *a.*
2 Pet. 2. 11 bring not a railing *a.*
Jude 9 not bring a railing *a.*
R. V. 2 Pet. 2. 11 ; Jude 9 judgment
Accuse. *Charge, complain, blame.*
Prov. 30. 10 *a.* not a servant
Mat. 12. 10 might *a.* him
Mark 3. 2 ; Luke 11. 54
Luke 3. 14 not *a.* any falsely
John 5. 45 that I will *a.* you
Acts 24. 2 Tertullus began to *a.*
25. 5, 11 ; 28, 19
1 Pet. 3. 16 falsely *a.* your good
R. V. Prov. 30. 10 slander
Accused. *Spoken down, charged.*
Dan. 3. 8 Chaldeans *a.* the Jews
Mat. 27. 12 *a.* answered nothing
Mark 15. 3 chief priests *a.* him
Luke 16. 1 the same was *a.* unto him
Acts 22. 30 certainty wherefore *a.*
23. 28, 29 ; 25. 16 ; 26. 2, 7
Tit. 1. 6 not *a.* of riot
Rev. 12. 10 who *a.* them before
Accuser. *Who speaks down.*
John 8. 10 those thine *a.*
Acts 23. 30 to his *a.* also
23. 35 when thine *a.* are come
24. 8 ; 25. 16, 18
2 Tim. 3. 3 without affection, false *a.*
Tit. 2. 3 not false *a.*
Rev. 12. 10 the *a.* of our brethren
R. V. 2 Tim. 3. 3 ; Tit. 2. 3 slanderers
Accuseth, ing.
John 5. 45 one that *a.* you, even M.
Rom. 2. 15 the mean while *a.*
Accustomed. *Taught, trained.*
Jer. 13. 23 that are *a.* to do evil.
Acknowledge, ed. *Make known.*
Deut. 21. 17 *a.* the son of the
33. 9 *a.* his brethren
Ps. 32. 5 ; 51. 3 I *a.* my sin
Prov. 3. 6 in all thy ways *a.*
Isa. 33. 13 *a.* my might
61. 9 ; 63. 16
Jer. 3. 13 *a.* thine iniquity
14. 20 *a.* our wickedness
Dan. 11. 39 whom he shall *a.*
Hos. 5. 15 they *a.* their offence
1 Cor. 14. 37 let him *a.* the things
2 Cor. 1. 13 what ye read or *a.*
Acknowledging, eth
2 Tim. 2. 25 repentance to the *a.*
Tit. 1. 1 the *a.* of the truth
Phile. 6 the *a.* every good
1 John 2. 23 he that *a.* the Son
R. V. 1 John 2. 23 confesseth
Acknowledgment. *Full knowledge.*
Col. 2. 2 *a.* of the mystery
Acquaint, ed, ing. *Make known.*
Job 22. 21 *a.* thyself with him
Ps. 139. 3 *a.* with all my ways
Eccl. 2. 3 *a.* my heart with
Isa. 53. 3 and *a.* with grief
Acquaintance. *Known.*
2 K. 12. 5 every man of his *a.*
Job 19. 13 mine *a.* are estranged
Ps. 31. 11 reproach to mine *a.*
55. 13 ; 88. 8, 18
Acts 24. 23 none of his *a.*
R. V. Acts 24. 23 friends
Acquit. *Declare innocent.*
Job 10. 14 not *a.* me from . . iniquity
Nah. 1. 3 will not at all *a.*
Acre. *Yoke, furrow.*
1 Sam. 14. 14 half *a.* of land
Isa. 5. 10 ten *a.* of vineyard

Act. *Word, thing, deed.*
Deut. 11. 3, 7 and his *a.* which
Judg. 5. 11 the righteous *a.*
1 Sam. 12. 7 all righteous *a.*
2 Sam. 23. 20 had done many *a.*
1 K. 10. 6 true report . . of thy *a.*
  11.41 the *a* of Solomon
2 K. 10. 34 the *a.* of Jehu
1 Chr. 11. 22 had done many *a.*
2 Chr. 16. 11 the *a.* of Asa
Esth. 10. 2. all the *a.* of his
Ps. 103. 7 his *a.* to the childr.
  106. 2 ; 145. 4 ; 150. 2
Isa. 28, 21 his strange *a.*
John 8. 4 in the very *a.*
Actions. *Acts, deeds.*
1 Sam. 2. 3 by him *a.* are weighed
Activity. *Strength, force.*
Gen. 47. 6 knowest men of *a.*
Adamant. *Brier, diamond.*
Ezek. 3. 9 as an *a.* have I made
Zech. 7. 12 heart as an *a.* **stone**
Adar. *Fire-god*
Ez. 6. 15 on third of A.
Esth. 3. 7 that is, the month A.
Add. *Give, increase, put to.*
Gen. 30. 24 L. shall *a.* to me
Deut. 4. 2 ye shall not *a.* unto
2 K. 20. 6 will *a.* unto thy days
1 Chr. 22. 14 mayest *a.* thereto
2 Chr. 28. 13 *a.* more to sins
Ps. 69. 27 *a.* iniquity to iniquity.
Prov. 3. 2 shall they *a.* to thee
Isa. 29. 1 *a.* ye year to year
  30. 1 may *a.* sin to sin
Mat. 6. 27 can *a.* one cubit
Luke 12. 25 can *a.* to his stat.
Phil. 1, 16 to *a.* affliction
2 Pet. 1 5 *a.* to your faith
Rev. 22. 18 (od shall *a.* to him
Added. *Increased, put to.*
Deut. 5. 22 and he *a.* no more
1 Sam. 12. 19 *a.* to all our sins
Jer. 36. 32 there were *a.* besides
Dan. 4. 36 majesty was *a.*
Mat. 6. 33 shall be *a.* to you
Luke 3. 20 Herod *a.* yet this
Acts 2. 41 were *a.* 3,000 souls
  2. 47 ; 5. 14 ; 11. 24
Gal. 2. 6 *a.* nothing to me
  3. 19 the law was *a.*
Adder. *Asp, basilisk, viper.*
Gen. 49. 17 Dan shall be an *a.*
Ps. 58. 4 like the deaf *a.*
  91. 13 shalt tread upon . . *a.*
  140. 3 *a.* poison is under . . lips
Prov. 23. 32 stingeth like an *a.*
Addeth. *Increaseth.*
Job 34. 37 he *a.* rebellion
Prov. 10. 22 he *a.* no sorrow
  16. 23 wise *a.* learning to lips
Gal. 3. 15 disannulleth or *a.*
Addicted. *Arranged, set.*
1 Cor. 16. 15 *a.* thems. to ministry
R. V. 1. Cor. 16. 15 set.
Additions. *Joinings, wreaths.*
1 K. 7. 29 certain *a* made of
  7. 30 side of every *a.*
  7, 36 every one, and *a.*
Adjure, ed. *Cause to take oath.*
Josh. 6. 26 Joshua *a.* them
1 Sam. 14. 24 Saul had *a.*
1 K. 22. 16 shall 1. *a.* thee
2 Chr. 18. 15 times shall I *a.*
Mat. 26. 63 I *a.* thee by liv. God
Mark 5, 7 I *a.* thee by God
Acts 19. 13 *a.* you by Jesus
Administered. *Ministered.*
2 Cor. 8, 19 *a.* by us to the glory
  8. 20 abundance which is *a.*
Administration. *Ministry.*
1 Cor. 12. 5 differences of *a.*
2 Cor. 9. 12 *a.* of the service
Admiration. *Wonder.*
Jude 16 men's persons in *a.*
Rev. 17. 6 with great *a.*
R. V. Rev. 17. 6 wonder ; Jude 16
respect of persons.
Admired. *Wonaered at.*
2 Thes. 1. 10 to be *a.* in all
R. V. marvelled at.
Admonish, ed. *Put in mind, warn.*
Eccl 4. 13 will no more be *a.*
Jer. 42. 19 that I have *a.*
Acts 27, 9 Paul *a.* them
Rom. 15. 14 to *a.* one another

1 Thes. 5. 12 over you and *a.* you
2 Thes. 3. 15 *a.* him as a brother
Heb. 8 5 as Moses was *a.*
R. V. Jer. 42. 19 testified unto ; Heb.
8. 5 warned.
Admonition. *Reminder, warning.*
1 Cor. 10, 11 written for our *a.*
Eph. 6. 4 *a* of the Lord
Tit. 3. 10 after the second *a.*
Ado. R. V. *Tumult.*
Mark 5. 39 why make ye this *a.*
Adoption. *Placing as a son.*
Rom. 8. 15 the Spirit of *a.*
  8. 23 waiting for the *a.*
  9. 4 pertaineth the *a.*
Gal. 4. 5 receive the *a.* of sons
Eph. 1. 5 predestinated us to *a.*
Adorn. *To polish, deck.*
1 Tim. 2. 9 women *a.* themselves
Tit. 2. 10 that they may *a.* the
Adorned, eth, ing.
Isa. 61. 10 as a bride *a.*
Jer. 31. 4 shalt again be *a.*
Luke 21. 5 *a.* with goodly stones
1 Pet. 3. 3 whose *a.* let it not be
  3. 5 holy women also *a.*
Rev. 21. 2 as a bride *a.*
Adulterer. *Debaucher.*
Lev. 20. 10 *a.* shall surely be **put**
Job. 24. 15 eye also of the *a.*
Ps. 50. 18 partaker with *a.*
Isa. 57. 3 the seed of the *a.*
Jer. 9. 2 for they be all *a.*
Hos. 7. 4 all *a.*, as oven heated
Mal. 3. 5 witness against the *a.*
Luke 18. 11 am not as others, *a.*
1 Cor. 6. 9 neither *a.* shall inherit
Heb. 13. 4 *a.* God will judge
Ja. 4. 4 ye *a.*, . . know ye not that
Adulteress.
Lev. 20. 10 *a.* shall be put to death
Prov. 6. 26 the *a.* will hunt . . life
Ezek. 23. 45 after the manner of *a.*
Hos. 3. 1 wom. belov. yet an *a.*
Rom. 7. 3 no *a.*, though married
Jas. 4. 4 and *a.*, know ye not that
Adulteries. *Adulterous acts.*
Ezek. 23. 43 her that was old in *a.*
Adulterous.
Prov. 30. 20 way of an *a.* woman
Mat. 12. 39 evil and *a.* genera.
  16. 4 wicked and *a.* genera.
Mark 8. 38 *a.* and sinful gen.
Adultery. *Illicit married intercourse.*
Ex. 20. 14 thou shalt not commit *a.*
Lev. 20. 10 that committeth *a.* shall
Deut. 5. 18 neither shalt thou c. *a.*
Mat. 5. 27 ; 19. 18 ; Rom. 13. 9
Prov. 6. 32 whoso committeth *a.*
Jer. 3. 8 Israel committed *a.*
  5. 7 ; 7. 9 ; 13. 27 ; 23. 14 ; 29. 23
Ezek. 16. 32 wife that com. *a.*
Hos. 2. 2 *a.* between her breasts
Mat. 5. 28 *a.* in his heart
Mark 10. 11 marry another com. *a.*
  Luke 16. 18 ; 18. 20 ; Jas. 2. 11
John 8. 3 woman taken in *a.*
Rom. 2. 22 shall not com. *a.*
Gal. 5. 19 flesh manifest *a.*
2 Pet. 2. 14 eyes full of *a.*
Rev. 2. 22 them that com. *a.*
Advanced. *Lifted up, made great.*
Est. 10. 2 ; 3. 1 ; 5. 11 *a.* him
1 Sam. 12. 6 L. that *a.* Moses
R. V. 1 Sam. 12. 6 appointed
Advantage (n.) *Profit, use.*
Job. 35. 3 what *a.* will it be
Rom. 3. 1 what *a.* then hath
2 Cor. 2. 11 lest Sat. should get *a.*
Advantaged, eth. *Profited.*
Luke 9. 25 what is a man *a.*
1 Cor. 15. 32 what *a.* it me
R. V. Luke 9. 25 profited
Adventure, ed. *Give, try, send forth.*
Deut. 28. 56 would not *a.* to set
Judg. 9. 17 fought for you, and *a.*
Acts 19. 31 not *a.* himself in theat.
Adversary. *Straitener, distresser*
Ex. 23. 22 an *a* unto thine *a.*
Deut. 32. 27 lest their *a.* should
Josh. 5. 13 for us, or for our *a.*
1 Sam. 1. 6 and her *a.* also
Ez. 4. 1 now when the *a.*
Neh. 4. 11 and our *a.* said

Est. 7. 6 Esther said, the *a.*
Ps. 74. 10 how long shall the *a.*
Isa. 1. 24 ease me of mine *a.*
Jer. 30. 16 all thine *a.* shall go
Lam. 1. 5 *a.* are the chief enemies
Amos 3. 11 an *a.* even round . . **land**
Mic. 5. 9 hand upon thine *a.*
Nah. 1. 2 vengeance on his *a.*
Accuser, opponent, enemy.
Num. 22. 22 L. stood an *a.* against
1 Sam. 29. 4 he be an *a.* to us
2 Sam. 19. 22 this day be *a.* unto **me**
1 K. 5. 4 is neither *a.* nor
Job. 31. 35 mine *a.* had written
Ps. 71. 13 consumed that are *a.*
Isa. 50. 8 who is mine *a.*
Mat. 5. 25 agree with thine *a.*
Luke 12. 58 goest with thine *a.* **to**
  13. 17 his *a.* were ashamed
1 Cor. 16. 9 and there are many *a.*
Phil. 1. 28 terrified by your *a.*
1 Tim. 5. 14 give no occasion to *a.*
Heb. 10. 27 devour the *a.*
1 Pet. 5. 8 your *a.* the devil
R. V. enemy, in most O. T. texts
Adversity. *Straitness, distress, evil.*
1 Sam. 10. 19 saved you of all *a.*
2 Sam. 4. 9 soul out of all *a.*
2 Chr. 15. 6 vex them with all *a.*
Ps. 10. 6 shall never be in *a.*
  31. 7 ; 35. 15 ; 94. 13
Prov. 17. 17 brother born for *a.*
Eccl. 7. 14 in the day of *a.*
Isa. 30. 20 L. give bread of *a.*
Heb. 13. 3 them which suffer *a.*
Advertise, *Counsel, uncover.*
Num. 24. 14 I will *a.* thee
Ruth 4. 4 thought to *a.* thee
Advice. *Word, counsel.*
Judg. 19. 30 take *a.* R. V. counsel
  20. 7 You *a.* and counsel
1 Sam. 25. 33 thy *a.* R. V. wisdom
2 Sam. 19. 43 our *a.* not be first
2 Chr. 10. 14 *a.* of. R. V. counsel
Prov. 20. 18 good *a.* R. V. guidance
2 Cor. 8. 10 my *a.* R. V. judgment
Advise, ed. *Counsel.*
2 Sam. 24. 13 now *a.*, and see
1 K. 12. 6 how do ye *a.*
1 Chr. 21. 12 *a.* thyself what
Prov. 13. 10 but with the well *a.*
Acts 27. 12 *a.* to depart thence
Advisement. *Counsel.*
1 Chr. 12. 19 Philist. upon *a.* sent
Advocate. *Called alongside.*
1 John 2. 1 we have an *a.* with F.
Afar. *Far off.*
Gen. 22. 4 the place *a.* off
Ex. 2. 4 sister stood *a.* off
Num. 9. 10 in a journey *a.* off
1 Sam. 26 13 top of a hill *a.* off
2 K. 2. 7 stood to view *a.* off
Ez. 3. 13 was heard *a.* off
Neh. 12. 4. 3 heard even *a.* off
Job 2. 12 up their eyes *a.* off
Ps. 10. 1 standest thou *a.* off
Isa. 23. 7 carry her *a.* off
Jer. 23. 23 not a God *a.* off
Mic. 4. 3 strong nations *a.* off
Mark 11. 13 a fig tree *a.* off
Luke 17. 12 which stood *a.* off
Acts 2. 39 all that are *a.* off
Eph. 2. 17 which were *a.* off.
Heb. 11. 13 having seen them *a.* off
Affair. *Thing, service. business.*
1 Chr. 26. 32 *a.* of the king
Ps. 112. 5 guide *a.* with discretion
Dan. 2. 49 *a.* of the province
Eph. 6. 22 might know our *a.*
Phil. 1. 27 hear of your *a.*
2 Tim. 2. 4 himself with the *a.*
Affect, ed, eth. *Move, impress.*
Lam. 3. 51 mine eye *a.* mine heart
Acts 14. 2 made their minds evil *a.*
Gal. 4. 17 zealously *a.* you
Affection. *Feeling, passion.*
1 Chr. 29. 3 have set my *a.*
Rom. 1. 31 without natural *a.*
2 Cor. 7. 15 his inward *a.* is more
Col. 3. 2 your *a.* on things above
Gal. 5. 24 crucified flesh with *a.*
R. V. Col. 3. 2 mind ; Rom. 1. 26 ;
Gal. 5. 24 passions
Affectionately. *Longing, yearning.*

1 Thes. 2. 8 so being *a*. desirous

Affectioned.
Rom. 12. 10 *a*. one to another

Affinity *Join oneself.*
1 K. 3. 1 Solomon made *a*. with
2 Chr. 18. 1 joined *a*. with Ahab
Ez. 9. 14 join in *a*. with people

Affirm, ed. *Assert, maintain.*
Luke 22. 59 hour after another *a*.
Acts 12. 15 Rhoda constantly *a*.
25. 19 whom Paul *a*. alive
Rom. 5. 8 and as some *a*.
1 Tim. 1. 7 whereof they *a*.
Tit. 3. 8 things *a*. constantly

Afflict. *Grieve, lower, press.*
Gen. 15. 13 *a*. them 400 years
Ex. 1. 11 taskmasters will *a*.
Lev. 16. 29 shall *a*. your souls
Num. 24. 24 ships shall *a*. Ashur
Judg. 16. 19 she began to *a*. him
2 Sam. 7. 10 wickedness *a*. them
1 K. 11. 39 *a*. seed of David
2 Chr. 6. 26 when thou dost *a*.
Ez. 8. 21 *a*. ourselves before God
Job 57. 23 he will not *a*.
Ps. 44. 2 did *a*. the people
Isa. 9. 1 grievously *a*. her
Jer. 31. 28 I watched to *a*.
Lam. 3. 33 L. not *a*. willingly
Am. 5. 12 they *a*. the just
Nah. 5. 12 I will *a*. thee
Zeph. 3. 19 undo all that *a*. thee
R. V. Ez. 8 21 humble; Ps. 55. 19
answer

Afflicted. *Bruised,* lowered,
pressed.
Ex. 1. 12 the more they *a*. them
2 Sam. 22. 28 *a*. people will save
1 K. 2. 26 my father was *a*.
Job 6. 14 him that i- *a*.
Ps. 18. 27 save the *a*. people
22.24; 25. 16; 82. 3; 88. 7; 90. 15
Prov. 15. 15 days of the *a*. are evil
22. 22. 26. 28; 31. 5
Isa. 9. 1 lightly *a*. the land
49. 13; 51. 21; 53. 4; 54. 11; 58. 3
Lam. 1. 12 wherewith L. *a*.
Mic. 4. 6 her that I have *a*.
Nah. 1. 12 *a*. . will afflict no more
Zeph. 3. 12 leave an *a*. people
Mat. 24. 9 del. you up to be *a*.
2 Cor. 1. 6 whether we be *a*.
1 Tim. 5. 10 relieved the *a*.
Heb. 11. 37 being destitute, *a*.
Jas. 4. 9 *a*. and mourn, and weep
R. V. Job 6. 14 ready to faint;
James 5. 13 suffering

Affliction. *Pressure, trouble, suf-*
fering.
Gen. 41. 52 in a land of *a*.
Ex. 3. 17 up out of the *a*.
Deut. 16. 3 eat bread of *a*.
2 Sam. 16. 12 L. look on my *a*.
2 K. 14. 26 saw *a*. of Israel
2 Chr. 20. 9 cry unto thee in our *a*.
Neh. 1. 3 are in great *a*.
Job 5. 6 *a*. cometh not forth
10. 15; 30. 16; 36. 8, 15, 21
Ps. 25. 18 my *a*. and pain
34. 19 the *a*. of righteousness
44. 24; 66. 11; 88. 9; 106. 44;
Isa. 30. 20 give water of *a*.
Jer. 16. 19 in days of *a*.
Lam. 1. 7 remembered in *a*.
Hos. 5. 15 in *a*. seek me early
Am. 6. 6 grieved for *a*.
Nah. 1. 9 *a*. not rise second time
Zech. 1. 15 helped forward the *a*.
Mark 4. 17 when *a*. ariseth
Acts 7. 11 dearth and great *a*.
20. 23 bonds and *a*.
2 Cor. 2. 4 out of much *a*.
6. 4 approving in *a*.
Phil. 1. 16 to add *a*. to my
1 Thes. 1. 6 word in much *a*.
3. 3 moved by these *a*.
2 Tim. 1. 8 *a*. of the gospel
Heb. 11. 25 rather to suffer *a*.
Jas. 1. 27 visit fatherless in *a*.
1 Pet. 5. 9 *a*. accomplished in

Affording. *Bring out.*
Ps. 144. 13 *a*. all manner of

Affright, ed. *Terrified.*
Deut. 7. 21 be not *a*. at them
Job 18. 20 that went before *a*.
Isa. 21. 4 fearfulness *a*. me

Jer. 51. 32 men of war are *a*.
Mark 16. 5 and they were *a*.
Rev. 11. 13 remnant were *a*.

Afoot. *On foot.*
Mark 6. 33 man ran *a*. thither
Acts 29. 13 P. minding to go *a*.

Afore. *Before.*
Isa. 18. 5 for *a*. the harvest
Ps. 129. 6 which withered *a*.
Ezek. 33. 22 *a*. he that was escaped
Rom. 1. 2 had promised *a*. by his
Eph. 3. 3 wrote *a*. in few words

Aforehand. *In advance.*
Mark 14. 8 she is come *a*.

Aforetime. *Former time.*
Neh. 13. 5 where *a*. they laid the
Job 17. 6 *a*. I was as a tabret
Jer. 30. 20 children as *a*.
Dan. 6. 10 prayed as he did *a*.
John 9. 13 him that *a*. was
Rom. 15. 4 things written *a*.

Afraid. *To fear.*
Gen. 18. 15 for she was *a*.
Ex. 3. 6 for he was *a*.
Lev. 26. 6 shall make you *a*.
Num. 12. 8 not *a*. to speak
Deut. 1. 29 neither be *a*. of them
Josh. 2. 9 we were sore *a*.
1 Sam. 4. 7 Philistines were *a*.
2 Sam. 1. 14 wast thou not *a*.
2 K. 1. 15 be not *a*. of him
1 Chr. 10. 4 for he was sore *a*.
2 Chr. 20. 15 be not *a*. nor dismayed
Neh. 2. 2 I was very sore *a*.
Job 5. 21 *a*. of destruction
Ps. 3. 6 I will not be *a*.
Prov. 3. 25 *a*. of sudden fear
Eccl. 12. 5 they shall be *a*.
Isa. 10. 24 be not *a*. of the Assyr.
Jer. 10. 5 be not *a*. of them
Ezek. 2. 6 be not *a*. of their word
Joel 2. 22 be not *a*. ye beasts
Jonah 1. 5 the mariners were *a*.
Hab. 3. 2 speech, and was *a*.
Mat. 2. 22 *a*. to go thither
Mark 5. 15 and they were *a*.
Luke 8. 25 and they being *a*.
John 6. 9 were all *a*. of him
Acts 18. 9 be not *a*., but speak
Rom. 13. 3 not be *a*. of the powers
Gal. 4. 11 I am *a*. of you
Heb. 11. 23 not *a*. of the king
1 Pet. 3. 14 not *a*. of their terror

Afresh. *Again, anew.*
Heb. 6. 6 crucify Son of God *a*.

After. *Subsequent to.*
Gen. 5. 4 days of Adam *a*.
Job 18. 20 they that come *a*.
Jer. 13. 6 *a*. many days
According, to.
Matt. 23. 3 *a*. their works
Luke 2. 27 *a*. the custom of
Acts 13. 22 a man *a*. mine own h.
Rom. 2. 5 but *a*. thy hardness

Afternoon. *Declining day.*
Judg. 19. 8 they tarried till *a*.

Afterward, s. *Next in order.*
Gen. 10. 18 *a*. were the families
Ex. 5. 1 and *a*. M. and A.
Lev. 14. 19 and *a*. he shall kill
Job. 18. 2 *a*. we will speak
Ps. 73. 24 *a*. receive me to glory
Prov. 20. 11 keepeth it in till *a*.
Mat. 4. 2 he was *a*. an hungered
Mark 16. 14 *a*. he appeared
John 13. 36 shall follow me *a*.

Again. *Once more.*
Gen. 4. 25 Adam knew his wife *a*.
Deut. 24. 20 go over the boughs *a*.
Ps. 71. 25 shalt quicken me *a*.
Mat. 4. 7 it is written *a*.
Mark 2. 1 *a*. he entered into Caper
John 1. 35 *a*. the next day after

Against. *Opposite.*
Josh. 8. 33 over against mt. Ger.
1 K. 7. 5 light *a*. light in ranks
In opposition to.
Mat. 10. 21 shall rise up *a*.
Mark 9. 40 he that is not *a*. us
In contact with.
Gen. 15. 10 each piece one *a*.
Judg. 7. 24 come down *a*. the

Agate. *Agate or ruby.*
Ex. 28. 19; 39. 12 third row an *a*.
Isa. 54. 12 windows of *a*. R. V. rubies

Ezek. 27. 16 and *a*. R. V. **rubies**

Age. *Period of existence.*
Num. 8. 25 *a*. of fifty years
Job 8. 17 of the former *a*.
Isa. 38. 12 mine *a*. is departed
State of being old.
Gen. 18. 11 well stricken in *a*.
1 K. 14. 4 by reason of his *a*.
Job. 5. 26 grave in full *a*.
John 9. 21, 23 he is of *a*.
R. V. Josh. 23. 1, 2 years; Job. 11.
17 life

Aged. *Old.*
2 Sam. 19. 32 a very *a*. man
Job 12. 20 understanding of the *a*.
Jer. 6. 11 the *a*., with full days
Tit. 2. 2 *a*. men be sober
Phile. 9 as Paul the *a*.
R. V. Job 12. 20 elders

Ages. *Periods of time.*
Eph. 2. 7 in the *a*. to come.
Col. 1. 26 hath been hid from *a*.
Generations.
Eph. 3. 5 which in other *a*.
3. 21 throughout all *a*.

Ago. *Agone, former time.*
1 Sam. 9. 20 lost three days *a*.
Ez. 5. 11 these many years *a*.
Acts 10. 30 four days *a*. I was
2 Cor. 8. 10 forward a year *a*.

Agone. *Ago, former time.*
1 Sam. 30. 13 three days *a*. I

Agony. *Intense suffering.*
Luke 22. 44 in *a*. he prayed

Agree, ed, eth. *Of one mind.*
Am. 3. 3 except they be *a*.
Mat. 5. 25 *a*. with thine adversary
Mark 14. 56 witness *a*. not together
Luke 5. 36 *a*. not with the old
John 9. 22 had *a*. already
Acts 5. 9 have *a*. to tempt
Rev. 17. 17 *a*., and give their k.

Agreement. *Accord, conformity.*
2 K. 18. 31 make an *a*. with me
Isa. 28. 15 with hell we are at *a*.
Dan. 11. 6 to make an *a*.
2 Cor. 6. 16 what *a*. hath the
R. V. 2 K. 18. 31; Isa. 36. 16 your
peace

Aground. *Grounded, stranded.*
Acts 27. 41 they ran the ship *a*.

Ague. *Fever.*
Lev. 26. 16 burning *a*. R. V. **fever**

Aha. *Joy, surprise, mockery.*
Ps. 35. 21 *A*., *a*., our eye hath seen
Isa. 44. 16 *A*., I am warm
Ezek. 25. 3 thou saidst *A*. against
26. 2 *A*., she is broken

Aid. *Help.*
Judg. 9. 24 *a*. him in the killing
R. V. strengthened his hands

Aileth. *Troubleth, disturbeth.*
Gen. 21. 17 what *a*. thee, Hagar?
Judg. 18. 23 Micah, What *a*. thee
1 Sam. 11. 5 what *a*. the people
Ps. 114. 5 what *a*. thee, O sea
Isa. 22. 1 what *a*. thee now, that

Air. *Wind, atmosphere.*
Job 41. 16 no *a*. can come between
Acts 22. 23 threw dust into the *a*.
1 Cor. 9. 26 one that beateth the *a*.
Eph. 2. 2 the power of the *a*.
1 Thes. 4. 17 Lord in the *a*.
Rev. 9. 2 the sun and the *a*.
Heaven.
Gen. 1. 26 the fowl of the *a*.
Deut. 4. 17 that flieth in the *a*.
2 Sam. 21. 10 the birds of the *a*.
Prov. 30. 19 an eagle in the *a*.
Mat. 6. 26 the fowls of the *a*.
Mark 4. 4; Luke 8. 5; Acts 10. 12
R. V. In Gos. and Acts, heaven

Alabaster Box. *Alabaster.*
Mat. 26. 7; Mark 14. 3; Luke 7. 37
an *a. b.* of ointment

Alarm. *Jubilee or battle shout.*
Num. 10. 5 when ye blow an *a*.
2 Chr. 13. 12 to cry an *a*.
Jer. 4. 19 the trumpet, the *a*.
Zeph. 1. 16 *a*. against fenced **cities**

Alas. *Aha! (complaint).*
Josh 7. 7 *A*., O Lord God.
Judg. 6. 22; 11. 35; 2 K. 3. 10; Joel
1. 15
Grief, threatening.

Num. 24. 23 *A*., who shall live
1 K. 13. 30 mourned over him, *A*.
Jer. 30. 7 *A*., for that day
Am. 5. 16 in all the highways, *A*.
Rev. 18. 10, 16, 19 *A*., *a*. great city
Albeit. *Even, if, though.*
Ezek. 13. 7 *a*. I have not spoken
Phile. 19 *a*. I do not say
Algum. *Costly wood.*
2 Chr. 2. 8 : 9. 10, 11 *a* trees
Alien. *Sojourner.*
Ex. 18. 3 *a*. in a strange land
Unknown, foreigner.
Deut. 14. 21 sell it unto an *a*.
Job 19. 15 an *a*. in thy sight
Ps. 69. 8 *a*. unto my mother's
Isa. 61. 5 sons of the *a*. shall
Lam. 5. 2 our houses to *a*.
Eph. 2. 12 being *a*. from the
Heb. 11. 34 armies of the *a*.
R. V. Ex. 18. 3 sojourner ; Deut. 14. 21 foreigner.
Alienate, ed. *To pass over.*
Ezek. 48. 14 not *a*. the first fruits
Give to others.
Eph. 4. 18 being *a*. from
Col. 1. 21 that were sometimes *a*.
Disjointed.
Ezek. 23. 17, 18, 22, 28 mind is *a*.
Alike. *Like. similar.*
Deut. 12. 22 shall eat them *a*.
1 Sam. 30, 24 they shall part *a*.
Job 21. 26 shall lie down *a*.
Ps. 33. 15 their hearts *a*.
Prov. 20. 10 *a*. abominations to
Eccl. 11. 6 both shall be *a*. good
Rom. 14. 5 Every day *a*.
Alive. *Living, to live.*
Gen. 7. 23 Noah remained *a*.
Ex. 4. 18 whether they be yet *a*.
Lev. 14. 4 cleansed two birds *a*.
Num. 16. 33 down *a*. into the pit
Deut. 5. 3 all of us here *a*.
Josh. 2. 13 save *a*. my father
Judg. 8. 19 had saved them *a*.
1 Sam. 15. 8 he took Agag *a*.
1 K. 20. 18 peace or war take *a*.
2 K. 5. 7 to kill and make *a*.
2 Chr. 25. 12 other 10, 000 left *a*.
Ps. 30. 3 thou hast kept me *a*.
Prov. 1. 12 swal. *a*. as the grave
Jer. 49. 11 I will preserve *a*.
Ezek. 13. 18 souls *a*. that come
Mark 16. 11 heard that he was *a*.
Luke 15. 24 dead and is *a*.
Acts 1. 3 *a*. after his passion
Rom. 6. 11 *a*. to God through C.
1 Cor. 15. 22 all be made *a*.
Rev. 1. 18 I am *a*. forevermore
R. V. Gen. 7. 23 ; Lev. 10. 16 ; 26. 36 —— ; Num. 21. 35 remaining
All. *Entire quantity or number.*
Gen. 3. 17 shalt thou eat it *a*.
Ez. 4. 20 have ruled over *a*.
Dan. 2. 12 to destroy *a*. the
Complete, wholly.
Ex. 28. 31 ephod *a*. of blue,
Multitude.
Deut. 28. 47 abundance of *a*.
Job. 4. 14 *a*. my bones to shake
All together.
Mat. 6. 32 after *a*. these things
Mark 5. 40 had put them *a*. out
Luke 3. 16 saying unto them *a*.
Acts 2. 1 *a*. with one accord
Eph. 6. 13 and having done *a*.
Jas. 3. 2 we offend *a*.
The whole.
Mat. 1. 22 *a*. this was done
Mark 1. 28 abroad throughout *a*.
Luke 1. 65 fear came on *a*.
Acts 2. 2 it filled *a*. the house
2 Cor. 1. 1 *a*. the saints which
Phil. 1. 13 are manifest in *a*.
1 Thes. 4. 10 toward *a*. the brethren
Heb. 3. 2 faithful in *a*. his house
Rev. 3. 10 upon *a*. the world
All, any, every one.
Mat. 2. 3 and *a*. Jerusalem with
Mark 1. 5 unto him *a*. the land
Luke 2. 1 that *a*. the world should
John 5. 22 *a*. judgment unto the S.
Acts 1. 8 and in *a*. Judea
Rom. 1. 18 against *a*. ungodliness
1 Cor. 1. 5 and in *a*. knowledge
2 Cor. 1. 3 and the God of *a*.

R. V. Gen. 35. 4 ; 41. 45 ; 47. **13**
Lev. 25. 10 ; Mat. 18. 29 ; Mark 12
29 , Luke 12. 31 ; John 18. 40 ——
Alleging. *Putting alongside.*
Acts 17. 3 opening and *a*. that *C*.
Allegory. *To speak otherwise*
Gal. 4. 24 which things are an *a*.
Alleluiah. *Praise.*
Rev. 19. 1, 3, 4, 6 voice saying A.
R. V. Rev. 19. 1, 3, 4, 6 Hallelujah
Allied. *Neared.*
Neh. 13. 4 our God was *a*.
Allow. *To know, recognize.*
Rom. 7. 15 which I do I *a*. not
Trial, test, proof.
Rom. 14. 22 thing which he *a*.
1 Thes. 2. 4 *a*. of God to be
Take to oneself.
Acts 24. 15 themselves also *a*. that
To think well of
Luke 11. 48 bear witness that ye *a*.
R. V. Luke 11. 48 consent unto ;
Acts 24. 15 look for ; Rom. 7. 15
know ; Rom 14. 22 approveth ; 1 Thes. 2. 4 approved.
Allowance. *Usual diet.*
2 K. 25. 30 a continual *a*.
Allure. *Persuade, entice.*
Hos. 2. 14 I will *a*. her
2 Pet. 2. 18 *a*. through the lusts
R. V. 2 Pet. 2. 18 entice.
Almighty. *Sufficient, all-powerful.*
Gen. 17. 1 am the *A*. God
Ex, 6. 3 the name of God *A*.
Num. 24. 4 vision of the *A*.
Ruth 1. 20 the *A*. hath dealt very
Job 5. 17 chastening of the *A*.
Ps. 68.14 the *A* scattered kings
Isa. 13. 6 ; Joel 1. 15 destr. from *A*.
Ezek. 1. 24 voice of the *A*.
2 Cor. 6. 18 saith the Lord *A*.
Rev. 4. 8 holy, holy L. G. *A*.
Almond. *Almond.*
Gen, 43. 11 honey, nuts and *a*.
Ex. 37. 19 the fashion of *a*.
Num. 17. 8 and yielded *a*.
Eccl. 12. 5 *a*. tree shall flourish
Jer. 1. 11 rod of an *a*. tree
R. V. Gen. 25, 33, 34 : 37. 19 *A*. blos.
Almost. *Few, little, nearly, about.*
Ex. 17. 4 *a*. ready to stone me
Ps. 73. 2 feet were *a*. gone
Prov. 5. 14 I was *a*. in all evil
Acts 26. 28 *a*. thou persuadest me
Heb. 9. 22 *a*. all things by the law
R. V. Ps. 94. 17 soon ; Prov. 5. 14 well nigh , Acts 26. 28 with but little
Alms. *Kind act, pity, mercy.*
Mat. 6. 1 that ye do not your *a*.
Luke 11. 41 rather give *a*. of things
Acts 3. 2, to ask *a*. of them
3. 3, 10 ; 10. 2, 4, 31 ; 24. 17
R. V. Mat. 6. 1 righteousness
Almsdeeds. *Kind acts.*
Acts 9. 36 woman was full of *a*.
Almug-tree. *Almug-tree*
1 K. 10. 11 plenty of *a*. t. 10. 12
Aloes. *Lign or wood aloes.*
Num. 24. 6 trees of lign *a*.
Ps. 45. 8 smell of myrrh and *a*.
Prov. 7. 17 perfum. my bed with *a*.
S. of S. 4. 14 frankincense and *a*.
John 19. 39 mixture of myrrh and *a*.
Alone. *One, only, separate.*
Gen. 2. 18 not good man . . be *a*.
Ex. 18. 18 not able thyself *a*.
Num. 11. 14 all this people *a*.
Deut. 32. 12 L. *a*. did lead him
2 Sam. 18. 24 a man running *a*.
1 K. 11. 29 two *a*. in field
2 K. 19. 15 art God, even thou *a*.
Job 1. 15 escaped *a*. to tell thee
Ps. 83. 18 name *a*. is Jehovah
Eccl. 4. 8 *a*. and not a second
Isa. 2. 11 L. *a*. shall be exalted
14. 31 ; 51. 2 ; 63. 3
Lam. 3. 28 sitteth *a*. and keepeth
Mat. 4. 4 not live by bread *a*.
Mark 4. 34 where *a*. he expected
Luke 6. 4 for the priests *a*.
John 6. 15 into a mountain *a*.
Acts 19. 26 not *a*. at Ephesus
Rom. 4. 23 for his sake *a*.
Gal. 6. 4 rejoicing in himself *a*.
Heb. 9. 7 the high priest *a*.

Jas. 2. 17 faith is dead, being *a*.
R. V. Mark 4. 34 privately
Along. *Way, go on, over, through.*
Judg. 9. 25 came *a*. that way
1 Sam. 6. 12 went *a*. the highway
2 Sam. 3. 16 with her *a*. weeping
Jer. 41. 6 forth weeping all *a*.
Aloof. *From before, off from.*
Ps. 38. 11 my friends stand *a*.
Aloud. *Great voice, shout.*
1 K. 18. 27 and said, Cry *a*.
Ez. 3. 12 shouted *a*. with joy
Ps. 132. 16 shout *a*. for joy
Isa. 58. 1 cry *a*., spare not
Dan. 3. 4 an herald cried *a*.
Mic. 4. 9 dost thou cry out *a*.
Alpha. *Greek A.*
Rev. 1. 8, 11 ; 21. 6 ; 22. 13 *A*. and O.
Already. *Now, by this time.*
Eccl. 1. 10 it hath been *a*.
Mat, 17. 12 Elias is come *a*.
John 3. 18 is condemned *a*.
Phil. 3. 16 we have *a*. attained
Rev. 2. 25 that ye have *a*. hold fast
Also. *Besides, as well, in addition.*
Gen. 6. 3 he *a*. is flesh
1 Sam. 14. 44 do so, and me *a*.
Ps. 68. 18 gifts . . for rebellious *a*.
Mat. 6. 21 will your heart be *a*.
John 5. 19 *a*. doth the Son
1 Cor. 15. 8 seen of me *a*.
2 Tim. 1. 5 persuaded in thee *a*.
Altar. *Hill, slaughter place.*
Gen. 8. 20 Noah builded an *a*.
Ex. 17. 15 Moses built an *a*.
Lev. 1. 5 blood upon the *a*.
Num. 3. 26 and by the *a*.
Deut. 7. 5 shall destroy their *a*.
Josh. 8. 30 Joshua built an *a*.
Judg. 2. 2 throw down their *a*.
1 Sam. 2. 28 offer upon mine *a*.
2 Sam. 24. 18 an *a*. unto the L.
1 K. 1. 50 caught horns of the *a*.
2 K. 11. 11 *a*. and the temple
1 Chr. 6. 49 offered upon the *a*.
2 Chr. 4. 1 made an *a*. of brass
Ez. 3. 2 the *a*. of the God of Is.
Neh. 10. 34 burn upon the *a*.
Ps. 26. 6 I compass thine *a*.
Isa. 6. 6 with tongs from the *a*.
Jer. 11. 13 set up *a*. to
Lam. 2. 7 cast off his *a*.
Ezek. 6. 4 *a*. shall be desolate
Hos. 8. 11 made many *a*. to sin
Joel 1. 13 ministers of the *a*.
Am. 2. 8 pledge by every *a*.
Mat. 5. 23 thy gift to the *a*.
Luke 1. 11 right side of the *a*.
Rom. 11. 3 digged down thine *a*.
1 Cor. 9. 13 partakers with the *a*.
Heb. 7. 13 attendance at the *a*.
Jas. 2. 21 off. his son upon the *a*.
Rev. 6. 9 saw under the *a*.
R. V. Isa. 65. 3 ——
Alter. *Change.*
Lev. 27. 10 shall not *a*. it
Ez. 6. 11 whosoever shall *a*. this
Ps. 89. 34 I will not break nor *a*.
Altered. *Changed.*
Esth. 1. 19 that it be not *a*.
Luke 9. 29 countenance was *a*.
Altereth. *Changeth.*
Dan. 6. 8, 12 Medes . . which *a*.
Although. *Even though.*
Ex. 13. 17 *a*. that was near
Job 35. 14 *a*. thou sayest thou
Mark 14. 29 *a*. it shall be
Heb. 4. 3 *a*. the works were
Altogether. *Wholly together.*
Ps. 14. 3 are *a*. become filthy
19. 9 ; 50. 21 ; 53. 3 ; 62. 9 ; 139. 4
Isa. 10. 8 my princes *a*. kings
Jer. 5. 5 *a*. broken the yoke
S. of S. 5. 16 he is *a*. lovely
John 9. 34 *a*. born in sins
Acts 26. 29 and *a*. such as I
Alway, s. *All time, continually.*
Gen. 6. 3 shall not *a*. strive
Ex. 27. 30 lamp to burn *a*.
Deut. 11. 12 are *a*. upon it
Job 7. 16 I would not live *a*.
Ps. 16. 8 the L. *a*. before me
Mat. 28. 20 I am with you *a*.
Mark 14. 7 ye have not *a*.
John 8. 29 do *a*. those things
R. V. Job 32. 0 ——

Am, I am.
Ex. 3. 14 I *a.* that I *a.*
Job 9. 32 not a man as I *a.*
Isa, 44. 6 I *a.* first, I *a.*last
Luke 22. 70 ye say that I *a.*
John 8. 58 before A. was I *a.*
1 Cor. 15. 10 I *a.* that I *a.*
Gal. 4. 12 be as I *a.*

Amazed. *Astonished.*
Ex. 15. 15 Edom shall be *a.*
Judg. 20. 41 men of B. were *a.*
Job 32. 15 they were *a.*
Isa. 13. 8 *a.* one at another
Ezek. 32. 10 many people *a.* at thee
Mat. 19. 25 the disciples were *a.*
Mark 2. 12 that they were all *a.*
Luke 4. 36 they were all *a.*
Acts 9. 21 that heard were *a.*
R. V. Mat. 19. 25 ; Luke 2. 48 ; 9. 43 astonished

Amazement. *Ecstasy, terror.*
Acts 3. 10 with wonder and *a.*
1 Pet. 3. 6 not afraid with any *a.*
R. V. 1 Pet. 3. 6 terror

Ambassador. *Messenger, elder.*
Josh. 9. 4 if they had been *a*
2 Chr. 35. 21 he sent *a.* to him
Isa. 30. 4 and his *a.* came
Ezek. 17. 15 in sending his *a.*
2 Cor. 5. 20 we are *a.* for Christ
Eph. 6. 20 I am an *a.* in bonds

Ambassage. *Embassy, eldership.*
Luke 14. 32 he sendeth an *a.*

Amber. *Amber, electrum.*
Ezek. 1. 4, 27 ; 8. 2 the color of *a.*

Ambush. *Plot, concealed.*
Josh. 8. 2, 7, 9, 12, 14, 19, 21 in *a.*
Jer. 51 12 *a.* for the Lord

Ambushment. *Woven plot.*
2 Chr. 13. 13 caused an *a.* to come
20. 22 Lord sent *a.* against Am.
R. V. 2 Chr. 20. 22 liers in wait

Amen. *So be it, steadfast.*
Num. 5. 22 woman shall say, *A.*
Deut. 27. 15 answer and say, *A.*
1 K. 1. 36 Benaiah answered, *A.*
1 Chr. 16. 36 people said, *A.*
Neh. 5. 13 congregation said, *A.*
Ps. 41. 13 blessed the Lord. *A.*
72. 19 ; 89. 52 ; 106. 48
Jer. 28. 6 Jeremiah said, *a.*
Mat. 6. 13 glory, forever. *A.*
Luke 24. 53 And blessing God. *A.*
John 21. 25 should be written. *A.*
Rom. 1. 25 blessed forever. *A.*
9. 5 ; 11. 36 ; 15. 33 ; 16. 20, 24, 27
1 Cor. 14. 16 say *A.* at thy giving
2 Cor. 1. 20 and in him *A.*
Gal. 1. 5 forever and ever. *A.*
Eph. 3. 21 world without end. *A.*
Phil. 4. 20 ever and ever. *A.*
Col. 4. 18 grace be with you. *A.*
1 Thes. 5. 28 ; 2 Thes. 3. 18 ; 1 Tim.
1. 17 ; Tit. 3. 15 ; Phile. 25 ; Heb.
13. 21 ; 1 Pet. 4. 11 ; Rev. 1. 6
R. V. *A.* is omitted in Mat. 6. 13 ;
28. 20 and many other places in N. T.

Amend (*v.*). *Repair, better.*
2 Chr. 34. 10 to repair and *a.* houses
Jer. 7. 3 *a.* your ways and doings
7. 5 ; 26. 13 ; 35. 15
John 4. 52 he began to *a.*

Amends (*n.*). *Recompenses.*
Lev. 5. 16 he shall make *a.*
R. V. restitution

Amerce. *To fine.*
Deut. 22. 19 they shall *a.* him

Amethyst. *Amethyst.*
Ex. 28. 19 ; 39. 12 and an *a.*
Rev. 21. 20 the twelfth an *a.*

Amiable. *Beloved.*
Ps. 84. 1 how *a.* are thy taber.

Amiss. *Out of place, error.*
2 Chr. 6. 37 we have done *a.*
Dan. 3. 29 which speak anything *a.*
Luke 23. 41 hath done nothing *a.*
Jas. 4. 3 because ye ask *a.*

Among. *In the midst of.*
Gen. 24. 3 *a.* whom I dwell
Ex. 17. 7 is the L. *a.* us
Lev. 17. 4 from *a.* his people
Mat. 2. 6 not the least *a.*
Mark 5. 3 *a.* the tombs
Luke 1. 1 are believed *a.*
John 1. 14 dwelt *a.*

Anathema. *Set up, consecrated.*
1 Cor. 16. 22 let him be *a.*

Ancestor. *First, former.*
Lev. 26. 45 covenant of their *a.*

Anchor. *Anchor.*
Acts 27, 29, 30, 40 cast *a.*
Heb. 6. 19 an *a.* of the soul

Ancient. *Aged, senior, elder, old.*
Deut. 33. 15 the *a.* mountains
1 Sam. 24, 13 proverb of the *a.*
2 K. 19. 25 heard of *a.* times
1 Chr. 4. 22 these are *a.* things
Ez. 3. 12 *a.* man that had seen
Job 12. 12 with the *a.* is wisdom
Isa. 3. 2 prudent, and the *a.*
Jer. 19. 1 *a.* of the people
Ezek. 7. 26 counsel from the *a.*
Dan. 7. 9 the *A.* of days

Angel. *Messenger, agent.*
Gen. 16. 7 the *a.* of the Lord
19. 1 ; 21. 17 ; 22. 11 ; 24. 7 ; 28. 12
Ex. 23. 20 I send an *a.*
Num. 22. 23 ass saw the *a.*
Judg. 13. 9 the *a.* of God came
1 Sam. 29. 9 as an *a.* of God
2 Sam. 14. 17 for as an *a.* of God
1 K. 13. 18 an *a.* spake unto me
2 K. 1. 3 the *a.* of the Lord
1 Chr. 21. 16 David saw the *a.*
Job. 4. 18 his *a.* he charged
Ps. 34. 7 the *a.* of the Lord
35. 5 ; 78. 49 ; 91. 11 ; 103. 20 ; 104. 4
Isa, 63. 9 the *a.* of his presence
Dan. 3. 28 hath sent his *a.*
Hos. 12. 4 power of the *a.*
Zech. 1. 9 the *a.* that talked
Mat. 1. 20 the *a.* of the Lord
Mark 1. 13 the *a.* ministered unto
Luke 1. 13 the *a.* said unto him
John 5. 4 an *a.* went down
Acts 6. 15 the face of an *a.*
Rom. 8. 38 that neither *a.* nor
1 Cor. 4. 9 a spectacle unto *a.*
2 Cor. 11 14 transformed into an *a.*
Gal. 1. 8 or an *a.* from heaven
Col. 2. 18 worshipping of *a.*
2 Thes. 1. 7 with his mighty *a.*
1 Tim. 3. 16 seen of *a.*, preached unto
Heb. 1. 4 better than the *a.*
1 Pet. 1. 12 the *a.* desire to look
2 Pet. 2. 4 G. spared not the *a.*
Rev. 1. 1 signified by his *a.*
2. 1 ; 3. 1 ; 5. 2 ; 7. 1 ; 8. 2 ; 9. 1
R. V. Rev. 8. 13 eagle ; Rev. 8. 7 ;
16. 3, 4, 8, 10, 11, 17 —

Anger (*v.*). *To make wroth.*
Ps. 106, 32 *a.* him at waters
Rom. 10. 19 nation I will *a.*

Anger (*n.*). *Indignation, wrath.*
Gen. 27. 45 until thy brother's *a.*
Ex. 4. 14. *a.* of the Lord
Num. 11. 1 his *a.* was kindled
Deut. 6. 15 lest the *a.* of the Lord
Josh. 7. 1 the *a.* of the Lord
Judg. 6. 39 let not thine *a.* be hot
1 Sam. 11. 6 his *a.* was kindled
2 Sam. 12. 5 David's *a.* was kindled
2 K. 13. 3 the *a.* of the Lord
2 Chr. 25. 10 home in great *a.*
Neh. 9. 17 slow to *a.*
Job 35. 15 visited in his *a.*
Ps. 6. 1 rebuke me not . . in *a.*
7. 6 ; 27. 9 ; 30. 5 ; 37. 8 ; 56. 7 ; 69. 24
Prov. 15. 1 grievous words stir up *a.*
Isa. 5. 25 *a.* of the L. kindled
Jer. 2. 35 his *a.* shall turn
Lam. 1. 12 in his fierce *a.*
Ezek. 5. 13 thus shall mine *a.*
Dan. 9. 16 let thine *a.* be
Hos. 8. 5 mine *a.* is kindled
Joel 2. 13 slow to *a.*
Am. 1. 11 and his *a.* did tear
Jonah 3. 9 from his fierce *a.*
Mic. 5. 15 vengeance in *a.*
Nah. 1. 3 the L. slow to *a.*
Mark 3. 5 looked on them with *a.*
Eph. 4. 31 and wrath and *a.*
Col. 3. 8 put off all these, *a.*
R. V. Ps. 38. 3 ; 85. 4 indignation ;
Prov. 22. 8 wrath ; Isa. 1. 4 —

Angle. *Angle, hook.*
Isa. 19. 8 they that cast *a.* into
Hab. 1. 15 with the *a.*

Angry. *Heated, wrathy.*
Gen. 18. 30 let not the L. be *a.*
Lev. 10. 16 he was *a.* with

Deut. 1. 37 L. was *a.* with me
Judg. 18. 25 lest *a.* fellows run
1 K. 8. 46 be *a.* with them
2 K. 17. 18 was *a.* with Israel
2 Chr. 6. 36 and thou be *a.* with
Ez. 9. 14 wouldst be *a.* with
Ps. 2. 12 lest he be *a.*
7. 11 ; 76. 7 ; 79. 5 ; 80. 4
Prov. 14. 17 soon *a.* dealeth
21. 19 ; 22. 24 ; 25. 23 ; 29. 22
Eccl. 5. 6 God be *a.* with
S. of S. 1. 6 children were *a.*
Isa. 12. 1 wast *a.* with me
Ezek. 16. 42 will be no more *a.*
Jonah. 4. 1 Jonah was very *a.*
Mat. 5. 22 whosoever is *a.*
Luke 14. 21 being *a.* said
John 7. 23 are ye *a.* at me
Eph. 4. 26 be *a.*, and sin not
Tit. 1. 7 be not soon *a.*
Rev. 11. 18 the nations were *a.*
R. V. S. of S. 1. 6 incensed ; John.
7. 23 ; Rev. 11. 18 wroth ; Prov.
21. 19 fretful ; 22. 24 given to anger

Anguish. *Straitness, distress.*
Gen. 42. 21 the *a.* of his soul
Ex. 6. 9 for *a.* of spirit
Deut. 2. 25 and be in *a.*
2 Sam. 1. 9 *a.* is come upon me
Job. 7. 11 will speak in *a.*
Ps. 119. 143 trouble and *a.* have
Prov. 1. 27 when distress and *a.*
Isa. 8. 22 behold dimness of *a.*
Jer. 4. 31 *a.* of her that
John 16. 21 no more the *a.*
Rom. 2. 9 tribulation and *a.*
2 Cor. 2. 4 out of *a.* of heart
R. V. Gen. 42. 21 distress

Anise. *Anise, dill.*
Mat. 23. 23 tithe of mint and *a.*

Ankle. *Ankle, end.*
Ezek 47. 3 waters were to the *a.*
Acts 3. 7 *a.* bones received strength

Anoint. *To fatten.*
Ps. 23. 5 thou *a* my head
To smear, anoint.
Gen. 31. 13 thou *a.* the pillar
Ex. 28. 41 and shall *a.* them
29. 7 ; 30 26 ; 40. 9, 10, 11, 13, 15
Lev. 7. 36 day that he *a.* them
Num. 7. 1 had *a.* it, and sanct.
Judg. 9. 8 to *a.* a king
1 Sam. 9. 16 thou shalt *a.* him
2 Sam. 2. 4 they *a.* David king
1 K. 1. 34 let Zadok *a.* him
2 K. 9. 3 I have *a.* thee king
1 Chr. 11. 3 they *a.* David king
2 Chr. 22. 7 the Lord had *a.*
Ps. 43. 7 God had *a.* thee
Isa. 21. 5 *a.* the shield
Dan. 9. 24 *a.* the most Holy
Mat. 6. 17 *a.* thine head
Mark. 6. 13 *a.* with oil many.
Luke 7. 38 and *a.* them with
John 11. 2 Mary which *a.* the
Jas. 5. 14 *a.* him with oil.
To pour out.
Deut. 28. 40 shalt not *a.* with oil
Ruth 3. 3 and *a.* thee, and
2 Chr. 28. 15 and *a.* them
Ezek. 16. 9 and I *a.* thee with
Mic. 6. 15 not *a.* thee with oil
To rub in or on.
Luke 4. 18 *a.* me to preach
John 9. 6 hath *a.* the eyes
Acts 4. 27 whom thou hast *a.*
2 Cor. 1. 21 hath *a.* us in God
Heb. 1. 9 hath *a.* thee with
Rev. 3. 18 *a.* thine eyes with
Anointed, smeared.
Lev. 4. 3 priest that is *a.*
Num. 7. 10 that it was *a.*
1 Sam, 2. 10 horn of his *a.*
12. 3 ; 16. 6 ; 24. 6 ; 26. 9
2 Sam. 1. 14 destroy the Lord's *a*
1 Chr. 16. 22 touch not mine *a.*
2 Chr. 6. 42 face of thine *a.*
Ps. 2. 2 and against his *a.*
18. 50 mercy to his *a.*
20. 6 Lord saveth his *a.*
28. 8 ; 84. 9 ; 89. 38 ; 105. 15
Zech. 4. 14 the two *a.* ones.

Anointing. *Smearing, anointing*
Ex. 25. 6 spices for *a.* oil
Lev. 7. 35 the *a.* of Aaron
Num. 4. 16 and the *a.* of oil

Isa. 10. 27 because of the *a.*
1 John 2. 27 the same *a.* teacheth

Anon. *Straightway, directly.*
Mat. 13. 20 *a.* with joy receive her
Mark 1. 30 and *a* they tell him
R. V. straightway

Another. *An, with other, different.*
Gen. 26. 31 sware one to *a.*
Ex. 26. 19 sockets under *a.* board
Lev. 7. 10 have one as much as *a.*
Deut. 21. 15 beloved, and *a.* hated
Judg. 9. 37 *a.* comp. came along
1 Sam. 10. 3 *a.* carrying three loaves
1 K. 18. 6 Obadiah went *a.* way
2 K. 7. 6 said one to *a.*
1 Chr. 26. 12 wards one against *a.*
Neh. 4. 19 one far from *a.*
Job. 41. 17 joined one to *a.*
Ezek. 10. 9 *a.* wheel by a cherub
Dan. 8. 13 saint speaking, and *a.*
Am. 4. 7 rain upon *a.* city
Mat. 11. 3 do we look for *a.*
Mark 14. 19 *a.* said. Is it I ?
Luke 16. 7 then said he to *a.*
John 19. 37 *a* scripture saith
Acts 1. 20 bishoprick let *a.* take
Rom. 2. 1 wherein thou judgest *a.*
1 Cor. 12. 8 to *a.* the word
2 Cor. 11. 4 preacheth *a.* Jesus
Gal. 1. 7 which is not *a.*
Heb. 4. 8 have spoken of *a.*
Rev. 6. 4 went out *a.* horse
R. V. Ex. 18. 16 his neighbor;
2 K. 3. 23 his fellow ; Rom. 7. 23
a different.

Answer(n). *Saying, word, response.*
Gen. 41. 16 an *a.* of peace
Deut. 20. 11 if city make *a.*
2 Sam. 24. 13 what *a.* I return
Job. 19. 16 he gave me no *a.*
Prov. 15. 1 soft *a.* turneth away w.
Mic. 3. 7 no *a.* of God
Luke 20. 26 marvelled at his *a.*
John 1. 22 that we may give *a.*
Rom. 11. 4 what saith *a.* of God.
1 Cor. 9. 3 mine *a.* is this
2 Tim. 4. 16 at my first *a.*
1 Pet. 3. 15 ready to give *a.*

Answer (v.). *Say, speak, respond.*
Gen. 18. 27 Abraham *a.* and said
Ex. 4. 1 Moses *a.* and said
Num. 11. 28 Joshua *a.* and said
Deut. 1. 14 ye *a.* me, and said
Josh. 1. 16 they *a.* Joshua, saying
Judg. 5. 29 wise ladies *a.* her
Ruth 2. 6 servant *a.* and said
1 Sam. 1. 15 Hannah *a.* and said
2 Sam. 4. 9 David *a.* Rechab
1 K. 1. 28 king D. *a* and said
2 K. 7. 2 *a.* the man of God
1 Chr. 21. 18 the Lord had *a.* him
2 Chr. 10. 13 *a.* them roughly
Ez. 10. 2 *a* and said unto
Neh. 8. 6 all the people *a.*
Esth. 5. 7 then *a.* Esther
Job 1. 7, 9 Satan *a.* the Lord
Ps. 18. 41 he *a.* them not
Prov. 1. 28 but I will not *a.*
Eccl. 10. 19 but money *a* all
Isa. 14. 32 what shall one then *a.*
Jer. 7. 13 but ye *a.* not
Joel 2. 19 Lord will *a.* and say
Am. 7. 14 then *a.* Amos
Mic. 6. 5 Beor *a.* him
Mat. 22. 46 no man was able to *a.*
Mark 14. 40 wist they what to *a.*
Luke 11. 7 from within shall *a.*
2 Cor. 5. 12 somewhat to *a.* them
Col. 4. 6 how to *a.* every man
R. V. 25. 16 to make defence ; 2
Tim. 4. 16 defence ; 1 Pet. 3. 21 interrogation.

Answerable. *Responsive*
Ex. 38. 18 *a.* to the hangings of

Ant. *Ant.*
Prov. 6. 6 go to the *a.* thou s.
30. 25 the *a.* are a people

Antichrist. *Opponent of Christ.*
1 John 2. 18 there are many *a.*
4. 3 spirit of *a.* whereof ye
2 John 7 deceiver and an *a.*

Antiquity. *Former, ancient state.*
Isa. 23. 7 joyous city, whose *a.*

Anvil. *Stroke, step, block.*
Isa. 41. 7 him that smote the *a.*

Any. *One, all, every, some.*

Gen. 24. 16 neither had *a.* man
Ex. 34. 24 neither shall *a.* man
Lev. 7. 8 that offereth *a.* man's
Num. 5. 10 *a.* man giveth the
Deut. 19. 11 if *a.* man hate his
1 K. 18. 26 *a.* that answered
Job 33. 27 if *a.* say, I have sinned
Ps. 4. 6 show us *a.* good
Isa. 44. 8 I know not *a.*
Am. 6. 10 is there yet *a.*
Mark 8. 26 nor tell it to *a.*
Acts 9. 2 if he found *a.*

Apace. *Rapid pace.*
2 Sam. 18. 25 and he came *a.*
Jer. 46. 5 and are fled *a.*
R. V. Ps. 68. 12 they flee

Apart. *Separate.*
Ex. 13. 12 shalt set *a.*
Lev. 15. 19 she shall be put *a.*
Ps. 4. 3 Lord shall set *a.*
Zech. 12. 12 every family *a.*
Mat. 14. 13 a desert place *a.*
Mark 6. 31 *a.* into a desert
Jas. 1. 21 lay *a.* filthiness
R. V. Jas. 1. 21 away

Ape, *Ape, marmoset.*
1 K. 10. 22 silver, ivory, and *a.*
2 Chr. 9. 21 and *a.*, and peacocks

Apiece. *Each one.*
Num. 7. 86 weighing ten shekels *v*
Luke 9. 3 have two coats *a.*
John 2. 6 or three firkins *a.*
R. V. Num. 17. 6; Luke 9. 3 —

Apostle. *One sent forth.*
Mat. 10. 2 names of the twelve *a.*
Mark 6. 30 the *a.* gathered
Luke 6. 13 whom he named *a.*
Acts 1. 26 with the eleven *a.*
Rom. 1. 1 called to be an *a.*
1 Cor. 9. 1 am I not an *a.*
2 Cor. 1. 1 Paul an *a.* of Jesus
Gal. 1. 1 other of the *a.*
Eph. 2. 20 foundations of the *a.*
Col. 1. 1 Paul an *a.* of Jesus
1 Thes. 2. 6 burdensome, as the *a.*
1 Tim. 2. 7 preacher and an *a.*
2 Tim. 1. 1 ; Tit. 1. 1
Heb. 3. 1 consider the *a.*
1 Pet. 1. 1 Peter, an *a.* of J. C.
2 Pet. 1. 1 a servant and *a.*
Jude 17 before of the *a.*
Rev. 2. 2 say they are *a.*
18. 20 ; 21. 14
R. V. Acts. 5. 34 men

Apostleship. *Sending forth.*
Acts 1. 25 this ministry and *a.*
Rom. 1. 5 received grace and *a.*
1 Cor. 9. 2 seal of mine *a.*
Gal. 2. 8 *a.* of the circumcision

Apothecary. *Mixer, perfumer.*
Ex. 30. 25 the art of the *a.*
2 Chr. 16. 14 by the *a's* art
Neh. 3. 8 son of the *a.*
Eccl. 10. 1 ointment of the *a.*
R. V. Ex. 30. 25, 35 ; 37. 29 ; Eccl.
10. 1 perfumer.

Apparel. *Raiment, clothing.*
Judg. 17. 10 a suit of *a.*
1 Sam. 27. 9 took away .. and the *a*
2 Sam. 14. 2 put on now mourn. *a.*
1 K. 10. 5 ministers and their *a.*
2 Chr. 9. 4 and their *a.*
Ez. 3. 10 priests in their *a.*
Isa. 3. 22 suits of *a.*
Zeph. 1. 8 clothed in strange *a.*
Acts 1. 10 stood in white *a.*
1 Tim. 2. 9 women in modest *a.*
Jas. 2. 2 come in goodly *a.*
1 Pet. 3. 3 or putting on *a.*
R. V. Isa. 3. 22 —— ; Jas. 2. 2 clothing

Apparelled. *Clothed.*
2 Sam. 13. 18 daughters were *a.*
Luke 7. 25 are gorgeously *a.*

Apparently. R. V. *Manifestly.*
Num. 12. 8 will I speak .. *a.*

Appeal. *Call upon.*
Acts 25. 11 I *a.* unto Cæsar
25. 12, 21, 25 ; 26. 32 ; 28. 19

Appear. *Come into view, seem.*
Gen. 1. 9. let the dry land *a.*
Ex. 23. 15 none *a.* before me
Lev. 9. 4 to day the L. will *a.*
Deut. 31. 11 Israel *a.* before L.
1 Sam. 2. 27 *a.* to the house
2 Chr. 1. 7 God *a.* to Solomon

Ps. 42. 2 shall I come and *a.*
S. of S. 2. 12 flowers *a.* on earth
Isa. 1. 12 ye come to *a.*
Jer. 13. 26 thy shame may *a.*
Ezek. 21. 24 doings your sins do *a*
Mat. 6. 16 may *a.* to men
Luke 11. 44 as graves which *a.*
Acts 26. 16 in which I will *a.*
Rom. 7. 13 that it might *a.*
2 Cor. 5. 10 *a.* before judgment
Col. 3. 4 our life shall *a.*
1 Tim. 4. 15 profiting may *a.*
Heb. 9. 24 *a.* in the presence
1 Pet. 4. 18 and the sinner *a.*
1 John 2. 28 when he shall *a.*
Rev. 3. 18 nakedness do not *a.*
R. V. 1 Sam. 2. 27 reveal myself;
S. of S. 4. 1 ; 6. 5 lie along the side;
Acts 22. 30 come together ; Rom.
7. 13 shewn to be : 2 Cor. 5. 10;
7. 12; Col. 3. 4; 1 Pet. 5. 4; 1 John
2. 28 manifested

Appearance. *Aspect, semblance*
Num. 9. 15 as the *a.* of fire
1 Sam. 16. 7 on the outward *a.*
Ezek. 1. 5 this was their *a.*
Dan. 8. 15 the *a.* of a man
John 7. 24 according to the *a.*
2 Cor. 5. 12 which glory in *a.*
1 Thes. 5. 22 abstain from all *a.*
R. V. 2 Cor. 10. 7 before your face ; 1 Thes. 5. 22 every form

Appearing. *Manifestation.*
1 Tim. 6. 14 *a.* of our Lord
2 Tim. 1. 10 *a.* of our Saviour
Tit. 2. 13 looking for a glorious *a.*
R. V. 1 Pet. 1. 7 revelation

Appease. *Quiet, pacify.*
Gen. 32. 20 I will *a.* him
Esth. 2. 1 wrath of king A. was *a.*
Prov. 15. 18 slow to anger ... strife
Acts 19. 35 had *a.* the people
R. V. Esth. 2. 1 pacified ; Acts 19.
35 quieted

Appertain. *Belong to.*
Num. 16. 30 with all that *a.*
Jer. 10. 7 to thee doth it *a.*

Appetite. *Craving.*
Job 38. 39 fill the *a.* of lions
Prov. 23. 2 a man given to *a.*
Eccl. 6. 7 yet *a.* not filled
Isa. 29. 8 his soul hath *a.*

Apple. *Apple, quince, pupil.*
Deut. 32. 10 the *a.* of his eye
Ps. 17. 8 keep me as the *a.*
Prov. 7. 2 as the *a.* of thine eye
S. of S. 2. 5 *a.* tree among trees
Lam. 2. 18 not *a.* of thine eye
Zech. 2. 8 *a.* of his eye
Joel 1. 12 *a.* tree is withered

Apply. *Set, incline, devote.*
Ps. 90. 12 *a.* hearts unto wisdom
Prov. 2. 2 *a.* thine heart to under
Eccl. 7. 25 I *a.* mine heart to
R. V. Eccl. 7 25 heart was set

Appoint. *Set, designate, decree.*
Lev. 26. 16 will *a.* over you
2 Sam. 6. 21 to *a.* me a ruler
Job 14. 13 *a.* me a set time
Isa. 26. 1 will G. *a.* for walls
Jer. 15. 3 *a.* over them four
Ezek. 21. 19 *a.* thee two ways
Hos. 1. 11 shall *a.* one head
Mat. 24. 51 *a.* him his portion
Luke 22. 29 I *a.* you a kingdom
Acts 6. 3 men whom we *a.*
R. V. Num. 35. 6 give ; 2 Sam. 15
15 choose; Ezek. 21. 22 set.

Appointed. *Set, decreed, chosen.*
Gen. 18. 14 at the time *a.*
Ex. 23. 15 time *a.* of the month
Num. 9. 2 at his *a.* season
Josh. 8. 14 at a time *a.*
1 Sam. 13. 11 within the days *a.*
2 Sam. 24. 15 to the time *a.*
1 K. 1. 35 *a.* him to be ruler
Neh. 6. 7 hast *a.* prophets
Job 7. 3 nights are *a.* to me
Ps. 44. 11 sheep *a.* for meat
Prov. 7. 20 home at a day *a.*
Isa. 1. 14 *a.* feasts my soul hateth
Jer. 5. 24 the *a.* weeks
Ezek. 4. 6 *a.* each day for
Mic. 6. 9 and who hath *a.*
Luke 3. 16 exact what is *a.*
Acts 1. 23 they *a.* two

1 Cor. 4. 9 as it were *a*.
1 Thes. 3. 3 we are *a*. thereto
2 Tim. 1. 11 I am *a*. a preacher
Heb. 9. 27 *a*. to men once to die
1 Pet. 2. 8 whereunto they were *a*.
R. V. 1 Sam. 19. 20 as head; 2 Chr.
  34. 22 commanded; Acts 1. 23 put
  forward

Appointment. *Set apart, fixed.*
Num. 4. 27 At the *a*. of Aaron
2 Sam. 13. 32 by the *a*. of Absalom
Ez. 6. 9 according to the *a*.
Job 2. 11 had made an *a*.
R. V. Num. 4. 27 commandment;
  Ez. 6. 9 word

Apprehend. *Receive thoroughly.*
Phil. 3. 12, 13 that I may *a*.
To press, seize.
Acts 12. 4 when he had *a*. him
2 Cor. 11. 32 desirous to *a*. me
R. V. Acts 12. 4 taken; 2 Cor. 11. 32
  take

Approach. *To draw near.*
Lev. 18. 6 none of you shall *a*.
Num. 4. 19 when they *a*. unto
Deut. 20. 3 ye *a*. this day
Josh. 8. 5 *a*. unto the city
2 K. 16. 12 *a*. to the altar
Job 40. 19 make his sword to *a*.
Jer. 30. 21 his heart to *a*.
Ezek. 42. 14 *a*. to those things
Luke 12. 33 where no thief *a*.
Heb. 10. 25 ye see the day *a*.
1 Tim. 6. 16 no man can *a*. unto
R. V. Ezek. 42. 13 ; 43. 19 are near

Apron. *Girded on.*
Gen. 3. 7 and made *a*.
Acts 19. 12 handkerchiefs or *a*.

Approve. *Test, sanction.*
Ps. 49. 13 *a*. their sayings
Lam. 3. 36 the Lord *a*.
Acts 2. 22 a man *a*. of God
Rom. 2. 18 *a*. things more excellent
1 Cor. 16. 3 whomsoever ye shall *a*.
Phil. 1. 10 that ye may *a*.

Approved. *Tested, tried.*
Rom. 14. 18 and *a*. of men
1 Cor. 11. 19 they which are *a*.
2 Cor. 13. 7 we should appear *a*.
2 Tim. 2. 15 *a*. unto God.

Apt. *Fitted, able.*
2 K. 24. 16 strong and *a*. for war
1 Tim. 3. 2 ; 2 Tim. 2. 24 *a*. to teach

Archangel. *Chief messenger.*
1 Thes. 4. 16 voice of the *a*.
Jude 9 Michael the *a*.

Archer. *Shooter with bow.*
Gen. 21. 20 and became an *a*.
Judg. 5. 11 the noise of the *a*.
1 Sam. 31. 3 wounded of the *a*.
1 Chr. 10. 3 the *a*. hit him
2 Chr. 35, 23 the *a*. shot at king **J.**
Job 16. 13 his *a*. compass me
Isa. 21. 17 the number of the *a*.
Jer. 51. 3 *a*. bend his bow

Arches. *Arches, porches.*
Ezek. 40. 16 windows to the *a*.
  40. 21, 22, 24, 25, 30, 31, 34, 36

Are. *Are or is.*
Num. 15. 15 as ye *a*., so
Job 38. 35 here we *a*.
Jer. 14. 22 *a*. there among the
Mic. 6. 10 *a*. there yet the treasures
Mat. 2. 18 because they *a*. not
Luke 13. 25 whence you *a*.
John 17. 11 one as we *a*.
1 Cor. 1. 28 things which *a*. not
Rev. 1. 19 the things which *a*.

Argue. *To reason.*
Job 6. 25 what doth your *a*. rep.

Argument. *Reasoning.*
Job 23. 4 fill my mouth with *a*.

Aright. *Right, rightly.*
Ps. 78. 8 set not their heart *a*.
Prov. 15. 2 useth knowledge *a*.
Jer. 8. 6 they spake not *a*.
R. V. Prov. 23. 31 smoothly

Arise. *Rise up, stand up.*
Gen. 13. 17 *a*., walk through the land
Deut. 9. 12 *a*., get thee down
Josh. 1. 2 *a*., go over this Jordan
Judg. 5. 12 *a*., Barak, lead
2 Sam. 2. 14 young men now *a*
1 K. 3. 12 any *a*. like thee
1 Chr. 22. 16 *a*., be doing
Job 7. 4 when shall I *a*.

Ps. 3. 7 *a*., O Lord, save me
Prov. 6. 9 *a*. out of thy sleep
S. of S. 2.13 *a*., my love, my fair one
Isa. 26. 19 dead body shall *a*.
Jer. 2. 27 in trouble will say, *A*.
Lam. 2. 19 *a*., cry out in the night
Dan. 2. 39 shall *a*. another king
Am. 7. 2 whom shall Jacob *a*.
Mic. 2. 10 *a*., this is not your
Hab. 2. 19 to the dumb stone, *A*.
Mal. 4. 2 Sun of righteousness *a*.
Mat. 9. 5 or to say, *A*., and walk
Mark 5. 41 damsel, *a*.
Luke 7. 14 young man, *A*.
John 14. 31 *a*., let us go hence
Acts 9. 40 said, Tabitha, *a*.
Eph. 5. 14 *a*. from the dead
2 Pet. 1. 19 till the day star *a*.

Ariseth. *Ariseth, standeth.*
1 K. 18. 44 *a*. little cloud
Ps. 112. 4 to the upright *a*.
Isa. 2. 19. *a*. to shake terribly
Mat. 13. 21 persecution *a*.
John 7. 52 out of Galilee *a*.
Heb. 7. 15 similitude of these *a*.

Ark. *Chest, coffin, vessel.*
Gen. 6. 14 an *a*. of gopher wood
Ex. 2. 3 an *a*. of bulrushes
Num. 3. 31 charge shall be the *a*.
Josh. 4. 11 the *a*. of the Lord
1 Sam. 6. 19 looked into the *a*.
2 Sam. 6. 2 from thence the *a*.
1 K. 2. 26 thou barest the *a*.
1 Chr. 6. 31 after that the *a*. had
2 Chr. 1. 4 but the *a*. of God
Ps. 132. 8 the *a*. of thy strength
Jer. 3. 16 the *a*. of the covenant
Mat. 24. 38 entered into the *a*.
Heb. 11. 7 Noah prepared an *a*.
1 Pet. 3. 20 while the *a*. was
Rev. 11. 19 in his temple the *a*.

Arm (*n*.). *Arm, upper limb.*
Gen. 49. 24 the *a*. of his hands
Ex. 6. 6 a stretched out *a*.
Deut. 4. 34 by a stretched out *a*.
Judg. 15. 14 that were upon his *a*.
1 Sam. 2. 31 cut off thine *a*.
2 Sam. 22. 35 broken by mine *a*.
1 K. 8. 42 thy stretched out *a*.
2 K. 9. 24 between his *a*.
2 Chr. 32. 8 an *a*. of flesh
Job 22. 9 *a*. of the fatherless
Ps. 10. 15 the *a*. of the wicked
Prov. 31. 17 strengtheneth her *a*.
S. of S. 8. 6 as seal upon thine *a*.
Isa. 9. 20 flesh of his own *a*.
  63. 12 with his glorious *a*.
Jer. 17. 5 maketh flesh his *a*.
Ezek. 4. 7 thine *a*. shall be
Dan. 10. 6 his *a*. and his feet
Hos. 7. 15 strengthened their . *a*
Zech. 11. 17 his *a*. shall be clean
Luke 1.51 strength with his *a*.
John 12. 38 the *a*. of the Lord
Acts 13. 17 with an high *a*.
R. V. Job 31. 22 shoulder

Arm (*v*.). *Furnish with weapons.*
Num. 31. 3 *a*. some of yourselves
1 Pet. 4. 1 *a*. yourselves likewise

Armed. *Weaponed, protected.*
Num. 31. 5 thousand *a*. for war
Deut. 3. 18 shall pass over *a*.
Josh. 6. 7 him that is *a*.
1 Chr. 12. 2 *a*. with bows
Ps. 78. 9 Ephraim being *a*.
Prov. 6. 11 want as an *a*. man
Luke 11. 21 a strong man *a*.

Armhole. *Armhole.*
Jer. 38. 12 under thine *a*.
Ezek. 13. 18 sew pillows to all *a*.
R. V. Ezek. 13. 18 elbows

Armour. *Defensive covering.*
1 Sam. 14. 1 man that bare his *a*.
2 Sam. 18. 15 that bare Joab's *a*.
1 K. 22. 38 they washed his *a*.
2 K. 20. 13 house of his *a*.
1 Chr. 10. 9 head, and his *a*.
Isa. 22. 8 to the *a*. of the
Luke 11. 22 all his *a*. wherein
Rom. 13. 12 put on *a*. of light
2 Cor. 6. 7 *a*. of righteousness
Eph. 6. 11 whole *a*. of God
R. V. 1 Sam. 17. 38, 39 apparel

Armourbearer. *Bearer of weapon.*
Judg. 9. 54 the young man his *a. b.*
1 Sam. 14. 7 his *a. b.* said

2 Sam. 23. 37 *a. b.* to Joab
1 Chr. 10. 4 said Saul to his *a. b.*

Armoury. *Place for arms, arsenal.*
Neh. 3. 19 going up to the *a*.
S. of S. 4. 4 like tower . . for an *a*.
Jer. 50. 25 hath opened his *a*.

Army. *Troop, host, armed force.*
Gen. 26. 26 captain of his *a*.
Ex. 6. 26 according to the *a*.
Num. 1. 3 number them by their *a*.
Deut. 11. 4 the *a*. of Egypt
Judg. 8. 6 bread unto thine *a*.
1 K. 20. 19 the *a*. which followed
2 K. 25. 5 *a*. of the Chaldees
1 Chr. 11. 26 men of the *a*.
2 Chr. 13. 3 *a*. of valiant men
Neh. 2. 9 sent capts. of the *a*.
Ps. 44. 9 forth with our *a*.
S. of S. 6. 13 company of two *a*.
Isa. 43. 17 bringeth forth the *a*.
Jer. 32. 2 king of B.'s army
Ezek. 17. 17 P. with his mighty *a*.
Dan. 11. 7 shall come with an *a*.
Mat. 22. 7 sent forth his *a*.
Luke 21. 20 compassed with *a*.
Acts 23. 27 came with an *a*.
Rev. 9. 16 *a*. of the horsemen
R. V. Gen. 26. 26 ; 1 Chr. 27. 34
  host ; Rev. 9. 16 armies

Arose. *Raised up, stood up.*
Gen. 37. 7 lo, my sheaf *a*.
Ex. 1. 8 *a*. a new king
Judg. 2. 10 *a*. a generation
1 Sam. 9. 26 and they *a*. early
2 K. 23. 25 neither after him *a*.
2 Chr. 36. 16 wrath of the Lord *a*.
Job 29. 8 *a*. and stood up
Ps. 79. 6 *a*. to judgment
Eccl. 1. 5 hasteth where he *a*.
Mat. 2. 14 *a*. and took the child
Mark 9. 27 and he *a*.
Luke 6. 48 when the flood *a*.
Acts 19. 23 *a*. no small stir
R. V. Mat. 26. 62 stood up ; Mar
  4. 39 awoke.

Array (*n*.). *Clothing, arrange-*
  ment.
2 Sam. 10. 17 set themselves in *a*.
Job. 6. 4 set themselves in *a*.
Isa. 22. 7 set themselves in *a*.
Jer. 50. 9 in *a*. against
1 Tim. 2. 9 pearls, or costly *a*.
R. V. 1 Tim. 2. 9 raiment

Array (*v*.). *Clothe, arrange.*
Gen. 41. 42 *a*. in vestures of
2 Chr. 28. 15 and *a*. them, and shod
Esth. 6. 10 may *a*. the man
Job. 40. 10 *a*. thyself with glory
Jer. 43. 12 *a*. himself with land
Mat. 6. 29 was not *a*. like one
Luke 23. 11 and *a*. him in a
Acts 12. 21 *a*. in royal apparel
Rev. 7. 13 these *a*. in white

Arrived. *Reached, touched.*
Luke 8. 26 *a*. at the country
Acts 20. 15 we *a*. at Samos
R. V. Acts 20. 15 touched

Arrogancy. *Overbearing pride.*
1 Sam. 2. 3 let not *a*. come
Prov. 8. 13 *a*. do I hate
Isa. 13. 11 *a*. of the proud
Jer. 48. 29 loftiness, and his *a*.

Arrow. *Arrow.*
Num. 24. 8 through with *a*.
Deut. 32. 23 will spend mine *a*.
1 Sam. 20. 20 will shoot three *a*.
2 Sam. 22. 15 he sent out *a*.
2 K. 13. 15 take bow and *a*.
1 Chr. 12. 2 *a*. out of a bow
2 Chr. 26. 15 *a*. and great stones
Job 6. 4 *a*. of the Almighty
Ps. 7. 13 ordaineth his *a*. against
  11. 2 ; 18. 14 ; 38. 2 ; 45. 5 ; 57. 4
Prov. 25. 18 and a sharp *a*.
Isa. 5. 28 whose *a*. are sharp
Jer. 9. 8 an *a*. shot out
Lam. 3. 12 a mark for the *a*.
Ezek. 5. 16 evil *a*. of famine
Hab. 3. 11 light of thine *a*.
Zech. 9. 14 his *a*. shall go forth
R. V. Lam. 3. 13 shafts

Art. *Work, skill.*
Ex. 30. 35 *a*. of the apothecary
2 Chr. 16. 14 by the apoths. *a*.
Acts 17. 29 graven by *a*.
19. 19 which used curious *a*.

Artificer. *Engraver, carver.*
Gen. 4. 22 instructor of every *a.*
1 Chr. 29. 5 work made by *a.*
2 Chr. 34. 11 *a.* and builders
Isa. 3. 3 and the cunning *a.*
R. V. Gen. 4. 22 cutting instrument;
 2 Chr. 34. 11 carpenters

Artillery. *Instrument, weapons.*
1 Sam. 20. 40 gave his *a.* unto.
R. V. weapons

Ascend. *Go, or come up.*
Gen. 28. 12 angels of God *a.*
Ex. 19. 18 *a.* as the smoke
Num. 13. 22 *a.* by the south
Josh. 6. 5 people shall *a.* up
Judge. 13. 20 the Lord *a.* in a flame
1 Sam. 28. 13 I saw gods *a.*
Ps. 24. 3 *a.* into a hill
Prov. 30. 4 who hath *a.* up
Isa. 14. 13 I will *a.* into heaven.
Ezek. 38. 9 thou shalt *a.*
Luke 19. 28 *a.* up to Jerusalem
John 1. 51 angels of God *a.*
Acts 2. 34 David is not *a.*
Rom. 10. 6 shall *a.* into heaven.
Eph. 4. 8 when he *a.* up
Rev. 7. 2 angel *a.* from the

Ascent. *Going up.*
Num. 34. 4 south to the *a.* of
2 Sam. 15. 30 by the *a.* of O.
1 K. 10. 5 his *a.* by which he
2 Chr. 9 4 *a.* by which he

Ascribe. *Give.*
Deut. 32. 3 *a.* ye greatness unto
1 Sam. 18. 8 *a.* unto David ten
Job 36. 3 will *a.* righteousness
Ps. 68. 34 *a.* ye strength unto

Ash. *Ash, pine.*
Isa. 44. 14 he planteth an *a.*

Ashamed. *Abashed, paled*
Gen. 2. 25 and were not *a.*
Num. 12. 14 be *a.* seven days
Judg. 3. 25 till they were *a.*
2 Sam. 10. 5 men were greatly *a.*
2 K. 2. 17 till he was *a.*
1 Chr. 19. 5 were greatly *a.*
2 Chr. 30. 15 Levites were *a.*
Ez. 8. 22 *a.* to require of the
Job 19. 3 ye are not *a.*
Ps. 6. 10 enemies be *a.*
 25. 2; 31. 1; 35. 26; 37. 19; 40 14
Isa. 1. 29 *a.* of the oaks
Jer. 2. 36 be *a.* of Egypt
Ezek. 32. 30 terror they are *a.* of
Hos. 4. 19 they shall be *a.*
Joel 2. 26 shall never be *a.*
Mic. 3. 7 the seers be *a.*
Zeph. 3. 11 thou not be *a.*
Zech. 13. 4 prophets shall be *a.*
Mark 8. 38 shall be *a.* of
Luke 16. 3 to beg I am *a.*
Rom. 1. 16 I am not *a.*
2 Cor. 7. 14 I am not *a.*
2 Tim. 2. 15 not to be *a.*
Heb. 2. 11 not *a.* to call
1 Pet. 4. 16 let him not be *a.*
1 John 2. 28 and not be *a.*
R. V. Job 6. 20 confounded; Luke
 13. 17; Rom. 9. 33; 10 11; 2 Cor.
 7. 14; 9. 4; 10. 8; Phil. 1. 20;
 Heb. 11. 16; 1 Pet. 3. 16 put to
 shame.

Ashes. *Bruised fine, dust.*
Gen. 18. 27 but dust and *a.*
Ex. 9. 10 *a.* of the furnace
Lev. 1. 16 place of the *a.*
Num. 19. 17 take of the *a.*
2 Sam. 13. 19 put *a.* on her head
1 K. 20. 38 disguised with *a.*
2. K. 23. 4 carried the *a.* of
Esth. 4. 1 sackcloth with *a.*
Job 2. 8 down among the *a.*
Ps. 102. 9 eaten *a.* like bread
Isa. 44. 20 he feedeth on *a.*
Jer. 6. 26 wallow thyself in *a.*
Lam. 3. 16 covered me with *a.*
Ezek. 28. 18 will bring thee to *a.*
Dan. 9. 3 prayer, fasting, and *a.*
Jonah 3. 6 and sat in *a.*
Mal. 4. 3 *a.* under the soles
Mat. 11. 21 in sackcloth and *a.*
Luke 10. 13 in sackcloth and *a.*
Heb. 9. 13 *a.* of an heifer
R. V. 1 K. 20. 38, 41 his headband

Aside. *Apart, away from.*
2 K. 4. 4 set *a.* that which

S. of S. 6. 1 turned *a.* R. V. him
Mat. 2. 22 he turned *a.* unto
Mark. 7. 33 took him *a.* from
John 13. 4 laid *a.* his garments
Acts 26. 31 when they were gone *a.*
Heb. 12. 1 lay *a.* every weight

Ask. *Inquire, solicit, crave.*
Gen. 24. 47 I *a.* her and said
Ex. 13. 14 thy son *a.* thee
Num. 27. 21 who shall *a.* counsel
Deut. 4. 32 *a* now of the days
Josh. 4. 6 when your children *a.*
Judges 1. 1 Israel *a.* the Lord
1 Sam. 1. 17 thou hast *a.* of him
2 Sam. 14. 18 that I shall *a.* thee
1 K. 2. 16 I *a.* one petition
2 K. 2. 9 what I shall do
2 Chr. 1. 7 *a.* what I shall give
Neh. 1. 2 I *a.* them concerning
Job 12. 7 *a.* now the beasts
Ps. 2. 8 *a.* of me, and I shall
Isa. 7. 11 *a.* thee a sign
Jer. 6. 16 *a.* for the old paths
Lam. 4. 4 young children *a.* bread
Mic. 7. 3 the prince *a.*
Hag. 2. 11 *a.* now the priests
Zech. 10. 1. *a.* ye of the Lord
Mat. 5. 42 give to him that *a.*
Mark 6. 22 *a.* of me whatsoever
Luke 1. 63 *a.* for a writing table
John 4. 9 being a Jew., *a.* drink
Acts 3. 2 *a.* alms of them
Rom. 10. 20 that *a.* not
Eph. 3. 20 that we *a.* or think
Jas. 1. 6 let him *a.* in faith
1 Pet. 3. 15 every man that *a.*
1 John 3. 22 whatsoever ye *a.*

Asleep. *Sleeping, dead*
Judg. 4. 21 fast *a.* and weary
1 Sam. 26. 12 for they were all *a.*
S. of S. 7. 9 those that are *a.*
Jonah 1. 5 Jonah was fast *a.*
Mat. 8. 24 but he was *a.*
 26. 40 and findeth them *a.*
Mark 14. 40 he found them *a.*
Acts 7. 60 said this, he fell *a.*
1 Cor. 15. 6 some are fallen *a.*
1 Thes. 4. 13 them which are *a.*
2 Pet. 3. 4 the fathers fell *a.*

Asp. *Asp, adder.*
Deut. 32. 33 cruel venom of *a.*
Job 20. 14 the gall of *a.*
Isa. 11. 8 hole of the *a.*
Rom. 3. 13 the poison of *a.*

Ass. *Ass of endurance.*
Gen. 49. 11 and his *a.* colt
Num. 22. 21 and saddled his *a.*
Judg. 5. 10 that ride on white *a.*
1 Sam. 9. 3 the *a.* of Kish
2. K. 4. 22 one of the *a.*
1 Chr. 27. 30 over the *a.*
Job 1. 14 and the *a.* feeding
Zech. 9. 9 the foal of an *a.*
Ass of ruddy color.
Gen. 22. 5 here with the *a.*
Ex. 4. 20 set them upon an *a.*
Num. 16. 15 not taken one *a.*
Deut. 5. 14 work . . nor thine *a.*
Josh. 6. 21 destroyed sheep and *a.*
Judg. 1. 14 lighted from off her *a.*
1 Sam. 8. 16 will take . . your *a.*
2 Sam. 16. 1 with a couple of *a.*
1 K. 2. 40 and saddled his *a.*
2 K. 6. 25 until an *a.* head
1 Chr. 5. 21 of *a.* two thousand
Job 24. 3 they drive away the *a.*
Prov. 26. 3 a bridle for the *a.*
Isa. 1. 3 the *a* his master's crib
Jer. 22. 19 the burial of an *a.*
Ezek. 23. 20 the flesh of *a.*
Zech. 9. 9 riding upon an *a*,
Ass of burden.
Mat. 21. 2 ye shall find an *a.*
 21. 5 sitting upon an *a.*
Luke 13. 15 his ox or his *a.*

Assault. *Attack, pressure.*
Esth. 8. 11 that would *a.* them
Acts 14. 5 there was an *a.* made
 17. 5 they *a.* the house.

Assay. *Try, attempt.*
Deut. 4. 34 hath God *a* to go
1 Sam. 17. 39 David *a.* to go
Job 4. 2 we *a.* to commune
Acts 9. 26 he *a.* to join himself
Heb. 11. 29 the Egyptians *a.* to

Assemble. *Gather together.*

Ex. 38. 8 *a.* at the door of tabernacle
Num. 1. 18 *a.* all the congregation
1 Sam. 2. 22 the women that *a.*
1 K. 8. 1 Solomon *a.* the elders
1 Chr. 28. 1 David *a.* all the princes
Esth. 9. 18 the Jews *a.* together
Ez. 9. 4 then were *a.* unto me
Neh. 9. 1 chil. of Israel were *a.*
Ps. 48. 4 kings were *a.*
Isa. 45. 20 *a.* yourselves and come
Ezek. 11. 17 I will . . *a.* you out
Mat. 26. 57 the elders were *a.*
John 20. 19 the disciples were *a.*
Acts 11. 26 they *a.* themselves
Heb. 10. 25 forsaking the *a.* of
R. V. Mat. 26. 3, 57; Acts, 4. 31 gathered

Assembly. *Gathering, meeting.*
Gen. 49. 6 their *a.*, mine honor
Ex. 12. 6 *a.* of the congregation
Lev. 4. 13 eyes of the *a.*
Num. 14. 5 before all the *a.*
Deut. 5. 22 unto all your *a.*
Judg. 20. 2 themselves in the *a.*
1 Sam. 17. 47 all this *a.* shall know
2 Chr. 30. 23 *a.* took counsel to keep
Ps. 89. 7 feared in the *a.*
Isa. 1. 13 the calling of *a.*
Jer. 15. 17 sat not in the *a.*
Ezek. 13. 9 not be in the *a.*
Acts 19. 32 the *a.* was confused
Heb. 12. 23 to the general *a.*
Jas. 2. 2 come unto your *a.*
R. V. Lev. 8, 4; Num. 8. 9; 10. 2.
 3; 16, 2; 2 Chr. 30, 23 congrega-
 tion; Ps. 89. 7; 111. 1; Ezek. 13.
 9 council; Jas. 2. 2 synagogue

Assent (*n.*). *Mouth.*
2 Chr. 18. 12 to the k. with one *a.*

Assent (*v.*). *Agree.*
Acts 24. 9 the Jews also *a*
R. V. joined in the charge

Assign. *Give, appoint.*
Josh. 20. 8 they *a.* Bezer in the w
2 Sam. 11. 16 *a.* U. unto a place

Assist. *Aid, help, succor.*
Rom. 16. 2 and that ye *a.* her

Associate. *Rage, do evil.*
Isa. 8. 9 *a.* yourselves, O ye people
R. V. make an uproar.

Assuage. *Abate, subside*
Gen. 8. 1 and the waters *a.*
Job 16. 5 mov. of lips should *a.*
 16. 6 my grief is not *a.*

Assurance. *Confidence, pledge.*
Deut. 28. 66 shalt have none *a.*
Isa. 32. 17 effect of righteous *a.*
Acts 17. 31 he hath given *a.*
Col. 2. 2 riches of the full *a.*
1 Thes. 1. 5 and in much *a.*
Heb. 6. 11 the full *a.* of hope
R. V. 6. 11; 10. 22 fulness

Assure. *Make certain*
Lev. 27. 19 and it shall be *a.*
Jer. 14. 13 give you *a.* peace
2 Tim. 3. 14 hast been *a.* of
1 John 3. 19 and shall *a.* our hearts

Assuredly. *Surely, certainly*
1 Sam. 28. 1 know thou *a.*, that
1 K. 1. 13 *a.* S. thy son shall
Jer. 32. 41 in this land *a.*
Acts 2. 36 house of Is. know *a.*
R. V. Jer. 38. 17 ——

Assuage. *see* Assuage.

Astonied. *Astounded, astonished*
Ez. 9. 3 and sat down *a.*
Job 18. 20 after him shall be *a.*
Jer. 14. 9 be as a man *a.*
Dan. 4. 19 was *a.* for one hour
R. V. Dan. 5. 9 perplexed

Astonished. *Greatly struck, amazed.*
Lev. 26. 32 shall be *a.* at it
1 K. 9. 8 by it shall be *a.*
Job 21. 5 mark me, and be *a.*
Jer. 2. 12 be *a.*, O ye heavens
Ezek. 27. 35 the isles shall be *a.*
Dan. 8. 27 and I was *a.*
Mat. 7. 28 the people were *a.*
Mark 1. 22 *a.* at his doctrine
Luke 4. 32 they were *a.* at
Acts 9. 6 he trembling and *a.*
R. V. In N. T. generally, amazed

Astonishment. *Wonder, amaze-ment.*
Deut. 28. 37 shalt become an *a.*

2 Chr. 7. 21 shall be an *a.*
Ps. 60. 3 drink the wine of *a.*
Jer. 8. 21 *a.* hath taken hold on
Ezek. 4. 16 drink water with *a.*
Zech. 12. 4 smite horse with *a.*
R. V. Ps. 60. 3 staggering ; Mark
 5. 42 amazement

Astray. *Err, wander.*
Jer. 50. 6 caused them to go *a.*

Astrologer. *Enchanter, magician.*
Isa. 47. 13 let now the *a.*
Dan. 1. 20 better than all the *a.*
 2. 27 ; 4. 7 ; 5. 11 ; 5. 15
R. V. In Dan. cnchanters

Asunder. *Between, apart.*
2 K. 2. 11 parted them both *a.*
Ezek. 30. 16 No shall be rent *a.*
Heb. 4. 12 dividing *a.* of soul
R. V. Heb. 4. 12 ——

Ate. *Did eat.*
Ps. 106. 28 and *a.* the sacrifices
Dan. 10. 3 *a.* no pleasant bread
Rev. 10. 10 book, and *a.* it up

Athirst. *Thirsty.*
Judg. 15. 18 he was sore *a.*
Ruth 2. 9 when thou art *a.*
Mat. 25. 44 unto him that is *a.*
Rev. 22. 17 let him that is *a.* come

Atonement. *Cover, reconciliation.*
Ex. 29. 36 sin offering for *a.*
Lev. 23. 27 a day of *a.*
Num. 5. 8 whereby an *a.* shall be
2 Sam. 21. 3 shall I make the *a.*
1 Chr. 6. 49 an *a.* for Israel
2 Chr. 29. 24 to make an *a.* for
Neh. 10. 33 an *a.* for Israel
Rom. 5. 11 we have received *a.*
R. V. Rom. 5. 11 reconciliation

Attain. *Reach, get, come.*
Gen. 47. 9 not *a.* unto the days
2 Sam. 23, 19 he *a.* not unto first
1 Chr. 11. 21 *a.* not to the first
Ps. 139. 6 I cannot *a.* unto it
Hos. 8. 5 they *a.* to innocency
Acts 27. 12 might *a.* to Phenice
Rom. 9. 30 have *a.* to right
Phil. 3. 12 I had already *a.*
1 Tim. 4. 6 whereto thou *a.*
R. V. Acts 27. 12 could reach

Attend. *Give attention.*
Job 32. 12 I *a.* unto you
Ps. 17. 1 *a.* to my cry
 55. 2 ; 61. 1 ; 66. 19 ; 86. 6 ; 142. 6
Prov. 4. 1 and *a.* to know
Acts 16. 14 *a.* unto the things
Rom. 13. 6 *a.* continually upon
1 Cor. 7. 35 that ye may *a.*
R. V. Ps. 86. 6. hearken ; Acts 16.
 14 to give heed

Attendance. *Standing.*
1 K. 10. 5 *a.* of his ministers
2 Chr. 9. 4 *a.* of his ministers
 Holding toward, heed, presence.
Heb. 7. 13 no man gave *a.*
1 Tim. 4. 13 give *a.* to. R. V. heed

Attent. *Attentive.*
2 Chr. 6. 40 *a.* unto the prayer
 7. 15 And mine ears *a.* unto

Attentive. *Observant, intent, mindful.*
Ps. 130. 2 let thine ears be *a.*
Neh. 1. 6, 11 ear be *a.* and
Luke 19. 48 people were very *a.*
R. V. Luke 19. 48 hung upon

Attentively. *Intently.*
Job 37. 2 hear *a.* the noise

Attire. *Thing put on.*
Jer. 2. 32 or a bride her *a.*
Prov. 7. 10 *a.* of an harlot

Attired. *Wrapped round.*
Lev. 16. 4 mitre shall be *a.*

Audience. *Ear, hearing.*
Gen. 23. 10 *a.* of the children
Ex. 24. 7 *a.* of the people
1 Sam. 25. 24 speak in thine *a.*
1 Chr. 28. 8 the *a.* of our God.
Neh. 13. 1 read in the *a.*
Luke 7. 1 sayings in the *a.*
Acts 13. 16 fear God, give *a.*
R. V. 1 Sam. 25. 24 ; Luke 7. 1 ears

Aught. *See* **Ought.**

Augment. *Add to.*
Num. 32. 14 *a.* yet the fierce anger

Aul. *Awl.*
Ex. 21. 6 ear through with an *a.*
Dent. 15. 17 thou shalt take an *a.*

Aunt. *Father's sister, uncle's wife.*
Lev. 18. 14 she is thine *a.*

Austere. *Rough, harsh.*
Luke 19. 21, 22 art an *a.* man

Author. *Cause, leader.*
1 Cor. 14. 33 God is not the *a.*
Heb. 5. 9 *a.* of eternal salvation
 12. 2 the *a.* and finisher
R. V. 1 Cor. 14. 33 a God

Authority. *Privilege, power.*
Esth. 9. 29 wrote with *a.*
Prov. 29. 2 righteous are in *a.*
Mat. 7. 29 as one having *a.*
Mark 1. 22 as one that had *a.*
Luke 4. 36 with *a.* and power
John 5. 27 hath given him *a.*
Acts 9. 14 he hath *a* from
1 Cor. 15. 24 put down all *a.*
2 Cor. 10. 8 more of our *a.*
1 Tim. 2. 12 to usurp *a.* over
Tit. 2. 15 rebuke with all *a.*
1 Pet. 3. 22 and *a.* made subject to
Rev. 13. 2 gave him great *a.*
R. V. 1 Tim 2. 2 high place ; 2. 12
 have dominion

Avail. *To equal, profit, strong.*
Esth. 5. 13 this *a.* me nothing
Gal. 5. 6 neither circumcision *a.*
Jas. 5. 16 prayer of righteous *a.*

Avenge. *Breathe out, give ease, retaliate, vindicate, judge.*
Gen. 4 24 Cain shall be *a,*
Lev. 19. 18 thou shalt not *a.*
Num. 31. 2 *a.* the childr. of Israel
Deut. 32. 43 he will *a.* the blood
Judg. 15. 7 yet will I be *a.*
1 Sam. 24. 12 the Lord *a.* me
2 Sam. 18. 19 Lord hath *a.* him
2 K. 9. 7 I may *a.* the blood
Ps. 18. 47 God that *a.* me
Isa. 1. 24 and *a.* me of mine ene.
Hos. 1. 4 and I will *a.* thee
Luke 18. 3 *a.* me of mine. ad.
Acts 7. 24 and *a.* him that
Rom. 12. 19 *a.* not yourselves.
Rev. 6. 10 and *a.* our blood
R. V. Lev. 19. 18 take vengeance ;
 26. 25 execute's ; Rev. 18. 20 judg-
 ed your judgment

Avenger. *Vindicator, judge.*
Num. 35. 12 for refuge from the *a.*
Deut. 19. 6 the *a.* of the blood
Josh. 20. 3 refuge from the *a.*
Ps. 8. 2 still the enemy and *a.*
1 Thes. 4. 6 Lord is the *a.* of all

Avenging. *Giving ease, freeing.*
Judge. 5. 2 for the *a.* of
1 Sam. 25. 26 from *a.* thyself with

Averse. *To turn back.*
Mic. 2. 8. as men *a.* from war

Avoid. *Go round, evade.*
1 Sam. 18. 11 David *a.* out of his
Prov. 4. 15 *a.* it, turn from it
Rom. 16. 17 and *a.* them
1 Cor. 7. 2 to *a.* fornication
2 Cor. 8. 20 *a.* this, that no man
1 Tim. 6. 20 *a.* profane babblings
2 Tim. 2. 23 unlearned questions *a.*
Tit. 3. 9 *a.* foolish questions
R. V. Rom. 16. 17 turn away from ;
 2 Tim. 2. 23 refuse ; Tit. 3. 9 shun

Avouch. *Say.*
Deut. 26. 17, 18 hast *a.* the Lord

Await. *Counsel against.*
Acts 9. 24 their laying *a.* was known
R. V. plot

Awake. *Wake, stir up.*
Judge. 5. 12 *a.*, *a.*, Deborah
Job. 8. 6 would *a.* for thee
Ps. 7. 6 *a.* for me to the judg.
Prov. 23. 35 when shall I *a.*
S. of S. 2. 7 nor *a.* my love
Isa. 26. 19 *a.* ye that dwell
Jer. 51. 57 sleep, and not *a.*
Dan. 12. 2 in the dust shall *a.*
Joel 1. 5 *a.* ye drunkards
Mark 4. 38 they *a.* him. and say
Luke 9. 32 when they were *a.*
John 11. 11 that I may *a.* him
1 Cor. 15. 34 *a.* to righteousness
Eph. 5 14 *a.* thou that sleepest

Awaked, est, eth, ing.
1 Sam. 26. 12 knew it, neither *a.*
1 K. 18. 27 and must be *a.*
2 K. 4. 31 the child is not *a.*
Ps. 73. 20 when thou *a.*, shalt

Prov. 6. 22 when thou *a.*, it shall
Isa. 29. 8 he *a.*, and his soul
Jer. 31. 26 I *a.*, and beheld
Acts 16. 27 keeper of the prison *a.*

Aware. *To know, conscious of*
S. of S 6. 12 or even I was *a.*
Jer. 50. 24 thou wast not *a.*
Mat. 24. 50 that he is not *a.* of
Luke 11. 44 over them not *a.*

Away. *Off, go off, be off*
Ex. 19. 24 *a.* get thee down
1 Sam. 24. 19 let him go well *a.*
2 Sam. 18. 3 if we flee *a.*
Job. 11. 14 put it far *a.*
Isa. 1 13 I cannot *a.* with
Zech. 7. 11 and pulled *a.* the
Mat. 13. 48 cast the bad *a.*
Luke 23. 18 *a.* with this man
John 19. 15 ; Acts 21. 36 ; 22. 22

Awe. *Shrinking fear, solemn dread*
Ps. 4. 4 stand in *a.* and sin not
 33. 8 the world stand in *a.*
 119. 161 in *a* of thy word

Awl. *See* **Aul**

Awoke. *Waked.*
Mat. 8 25 and *a.* him, saying
Luke 8. 24 came and *a.* him

Axe. *Axe, hatchet.*
Deut. 20 10 destroy trees by *a.*
Judg. 9. 4 Abim. took an *a.*
1 Sam. 13. 20 went to sharpen *a.*
1. K. 6. 7 neither hammer nor *a.*
2 K. 6. 5 *a.* head fell into water.
Isa. 10. 15 shall the *a.* brast
Jer. 10. 3 forest . . with an *a.*
Mat. 3. 10 also the *a.* is laid
R. V. Ps. 74. 6 hatchet

Axletree. *Iron*
1 K. 7. 32, 33 *a.* of the wheels

B.

Babbler. *Tongue-master, seed-picker.*
Eccl. 10. 11 and a *b.* is no better
Acts 17. 18 what will this *b.* say?
R. V. Eccl. 10. 11 charmer

Babbling. *Empty sound.*
Prov. 23. 29 who hath *b.* ?
1 Tim. 6. 20 avoiding vain *b.*
2 Tim. 2. 16 shun vain *b.*
R. V. Prov. 23. 29 complaining

Babe. *Suckling, infant, youth.*
Ex. 2. 6 behold the *b.* wept
Ps. 8. 2 out of mouth of *b.*
Isa. 3. 4 *b.* shall rule over them
Mat. 11. 25 revealed them unto *b.*
Luke 1. 41 that the *b.* leaped
Rom. 2. 20 a teacher of *b.*
1 Cor. 3. 1 unto *b.* in Christ
Heb. 5. 13 for he is a *b.*
1 Pet. 2. 2 as new born *b.*

Back. *Rear, behind.*
2 Sam. 1. 22 Jon. turned not *b.*
Ps. 9. 3 enemies are turned *b.*
Isa. 42. 17 shall be turned *b.*
Jer. 38. 22 are turned away *b.*
Lam. 1. 13 hath turned me *b.*
Mat. 24. 18 return *b.* to take
Mark 13. 16 field, turn not *b.*
Luke 9. 62 and looking *b.*, is fit
John 6. 66 many . . disciples went *b*
 Opposite the front, back part.
Ex. 23. 27 enemies turn their *b.*
Josh. 7. 8 Israel turneth their *b.*
2 Chr. 29. 6 fathers turned their *b*
1 K. 14. 9 behind thy *b.*
Neh. 9. 26 law behind their *b*
Ps. 129. 3 plowed upon my *b*
Prov. 10. 13 a rod for the *b.*
Isa. 50. 6 I give my *b.* to
Ezek. 23. 35 cast me behind thy *b.*

Backbite. *Bear tales.*
Ps. 15. he that *b.* not
R. V. slandereth.

Backbiter. *Who speaks against*
Rom. 1. 30 *b.*, haters of God

Backbiting. *Talking down.*
Prov. 25. 23 countenance a *b.*
2 Cor. 12. 20 wraths, strifes, *b.*

Backbone. *Spine, firm part.*
Lev. 3. 9 hard by the *b.*

Backside. *Back part.*
Ex. 3. 1 flock to the *b.*
Rev. 5. 1 within and on the *b.*
R. V. back.

Backslider. *A goer back.*

Prov. 14. 14 the *b.* in heart.
Backsliding. *Turning back.*
Jer. 2. 19 *b.* shall reprove thee
  3. 6 ; 5. 6 ; 8. 5 ; 31. 22 ; 49. 4.
Hos. 4. 16 as a *b.* heifer
R. V. Hos. 4. 16 stubborn
Backward. *Rearward.*
Gen. 49. 17 rider shall fall *b.*
1 Sam. 4. 18 fell off the seat *b.*
2 K. 20. 10 shadow return *b.*
Job 23. 8 and *b.,* but I cannot
Isa 1. 4 are gone away *b.*
Jer. 7. 24 went *b.,* and not forward
Lam. 1. 8 sigheth and turneth *b.*
John 18. 6 went *b.* and fell
Bad. *Base, evil, unfit.*
Gen. 24. 50 unto the *b.* or good
Lev. 27. 10 or a *b.* for a good
Num. 13. 19 whether good or *b.*
2 Sam. 13. 22 neither good nor *b.*
1 K. 3. 9 between good and *b.*
Jer. 24. 2 they were so *b.*
Mat. 13. 48 cast the *b.* away
2 Cor. 5. 10 whether good or *b.*
R. V. 1 K. 3. 9 evil
Bade. *See* **Bid.**
Badger. *Dark red color.*
Ex. 25. 5 and *b.* skins
Num. 4. 6 covering of *b.* skins
Ezek. 16. 10 shod thee with *b.* skin
R. V. sealskin
Badness. *Evil.*
Gen. 41. 19 never saw in . . for *b.*
Bag. *Bag, purse, bundle.*
Deut. 25. 13 have in thy *b.*
1 Sam. 17. 40 in a shepherd's *b.*
2 K. 5. 23 silver in two *b.*
Job 14. 17 sealed up in a *b.*
Prov. 7. 20 a *b.* of money
Isa. 46. 6 gold out of a *b.*
Mic. 6. 11 *b.* of deceitful weights ?
Luke 12. 33 provide yourselves *b.*
John 12. 6 and had the *b.*
R. V. Luke 12. 33 purses
Bake. *Bake, boil, cook.*
Gen. 19. 3 did *b.* unleavened bread
Ex. 12. 39 they *b.* unleavened cakes
Lev. 24. 5 and *b.* twelve cakes
1 Sam. 28. 24 did *b.* unleavened br.
2 Sam. 13. 8 and did *b.* the cakes
Isa. 44. 19 I have *b.* bread
R. V. Num. 11. 8 seethed
Bakemeats. *Food.*
Gen. 40. 17 all manners of *b.* meats
Baken. *Baken, dried, dipped.*
Lev. 6. 21 the *b.* pieces of meat
1 K. 19. 6 cake *b.* on the coals
R. V. Lev. 21 soaked
Baker. *Who bakes.*
Gen. 40. 1 his *b.* had offended
1 Sam. 8. 13 daughters to be *b.*
Jer. 37. 21 out of the *b.* street
Hos. 7. 4 oven heated by the *b.*
Balance. *Stalk, cross-bar, scales.*
Lev. 19. 36 just *b.,* just weights
Job 6. 2 calamity laid in the *b.*
Ps. 62. 9 to be laid in the *b.*
Prov. 16. 11 just weight and *b.*
Jer. 32. 10 money in the *b.*
Ezek. 5. 1 take thee *b.* to weigh
Dan. 5. 27 art weighed in the *b.*
Hos. 12. 7 *b.* of deceit in hand
Am. 8. 5 falsifying the *b.*
Mic. 6. 11 pure with the wicked *b.*
Rev. 6. 5 had a pair of *b.*
Balancing. *Poisings.*
Job 37. 16 *b.* the clouds of
Bald. *Without scalp hair.*
Lev. 13. 43 or in his *b.* forehead
2 K. 2. 23 thou *b.* head ; go up
Jer 48. 37 every head shall be *b.*
Ezek. 29. 18 every head . . made *b.*
Mic. 1. 6 make thee *b.,* and poll
Baldness. *Bald state.*
Lev. 21. 5 shall not make *b.*
Deut. 14. 1 nor make any *b.*
Isa. 3. 24 well set hair *b.*
Jer. 47. 5 *b.* is come upon Gaza
Ezek. 7. 18 *b.* upon all their heads
Amos. 8. 10 and *b.* on every head
Mic. 1. 16 enlarge thy *b.*
Ball. *Round thing.*
Isa. 22. 18 toss thee like a *b.*
Balm. *Balsam, gum.*
Gen. 37. 25 bearing spicery and *b.*
Jer. 8. 22 no *b.* in Gilead

Ezek. 27. 17 and oil, and *b.*
Band. *Fetter, bond.*
Lev. 26. 13 *b.* of your yoke
Judg. 15. 14 *b.* loosed off his h.
2 K. 23. 33 put Jehoahaz in *b.*
Job 38. 9 darkness a swaddling *b.*
Ps. 2. 3 break their *b.* asunder
Eccl. 7. 26 snares, hands as *b.*
Isa. 28. 22 let *b.* be made strong
Jer. 2. 20 I have burst thy *b.*
Ezek. 3. 25 put *b.* on thee
Dan. 4. 15 with a *b.* of iron
Hos. 11. 4 drew them with *b.*
Zech. 11. 7 the other I called *B.*
Luke 8. 29 and he brake the *b.*
Acts 16. 26 ev. one's *b.* were loosed
Col. 2. 19 the body by joints and *b.*
Troop, wing, company.
Gen. 32. 10 am become two *b.*
1 Sam. 10. 26 went with him a *b.*
2 K. 13. 21 spied a *b.* of men
1 Chr. 12. 18 captains of the *b.*
Job 1. 17 made out three *b.*
Ps. 119. 61 *b.* of wicked robbers
Prov. 30. 27 locusts go by *b.*
Ezek. 12. 14 scatter all his *b.*
Mat. 27. 27 unto him the whole *b.*
John 18. 12 the *b.* took Jesus
Acts 10. 1 *b,* called the Italian
R. V. Gen. 32. 7, 10 companies ;
  Lev. 26. 13 ; Ezek. 34. 27 bars ;
  1 K. 11. 24 troop ; Ps. 2, 3 ; 107.
  14 ; Isa. 28. 22 ; 52. 2 ; 58. 6 ; Jer.
  2. 20 bonds ; Ezek. 38. 6, 9, 22 ;
  39. 4 hordes
Banded. *Turned together.*
Acts 23. 12 the Jews *b.* together
Banished. *Driven away.*
2 Sam. 14. 13, 14 home again his *b.*
Banishment. *Exile, expulsion.*
Ez. 7. 26 death, or to *b.*
Lam. 2. 14 and causes of *b.*
Bank. *Edge, ridge, table.*
Gen. 41. 17 the *b.* of the river
Deut. 4. 48 *b.* of the river A.
Josh. 4. 18, 12. 2 ; 13. 9, 16
2 Sam. 20. 15 they cast up a *b.*
2 K. 2. 13 the *b.* of Jordan
1 Chr. 12. 15 overflown all the *b.*
Isa. 8. 7 over all his *b.*
Ezek. 47. 7 the *b.* of the river
Dan. 12. 5 this side of the *b.*
Luke 19. 23 money into the *b.*
R. V. Gen. 41. 17 brink ; Deut. 4.
  48 ; Josh. 12. 2 ; 13. 9, 16 edge ; 2
  Sam. 20. 15 ; 2 K. 19. 32 mount
Banner. *Sign, standard.*
Ps. 60. 4 hast given a *b.* to
S. of S. 2. 4 his *b.* over me
Isa. 13. 2 lift ye up a *b.*
R. V. Isa. 13. 2 ensign
Banquet. *A shouting, drinking.*
Esth. 5. 4 this day unto the *b.*
Job 4. 16 make a *b.* of him
Dan. 5. 10 came into the *b.* house
Am. 6. 7 the *b.* of them that
R. V. Job. 41. 6 traffic ; Am. 6. 7
  revelry
Banqueting. *Wine, drinking.*
S. of S. 2. 4 to the *b.* house
1 Pet. 4. 3 walked in lusts, *b.*
Baptism. *Baptism, baptism.*
Mat. 3. 7 Sad. came to his *b.*
Mark 1. 4 and preach the *b.*
Luke 7. 29 with the *b.* of John
Acts 1. 22 from the *b.* of John
  10. 37 ; 13. 24 ; 18. 25 ; 19. 3
Rom. 6. 4 buried with him by *b.*
Eph. 4. 5 one faith, one *b.*
1 Pet. 3. 21 *b.* doth now save
Baptist. *Who baptizes.*
Mat. 3. 1 came John the *B.*
  11. 11 ; 14. 2 ; 16. 14 ; 17. 13
Mark 6. 24 head of J. the *B.*
Luke 7. 20 J. *B.* hath sent
Baptize. *To consecrate by by pour-
  ing out on or putting into.*
Mat. 3. 11 I indeed *b.* you with w.
Mark 1. 4 John did *b.* in wilder.
Luke 3. 16 he shall *b.* you with H. G.
Acts 1. 5 John truly *b.* with water
1 Cor. 1. 14 I *b.* none of you
Baptized. *To baptize.*
Mat. 3. 6. were *b.* of him in Jordan
Mark 10. 38 and be *b.* with baptism
Luke 3. 21 the people were *b.*

John 3. 23 came, and were *b.*
Acts 1. 5 ye shall be *b.*
Rom. 6. 3 *b.* into Jesus Christ
1 Cor. 10. 2 *b.* unto Moses in the
Gal. 3. 27 as have been *b.* unto Christ
Baptizing. *To baptize.*
Mat. 28. 19 *b.* them in the name
John 1. 28 where John was *b.*
Bar (*n.*). *Shooting thing, barrier,
  lock.*
Ex. 26. 26 make *b.* of s. wood
  35. 11 ; 36. 31 ; 39. 33 ; 40. 18
Num. 3. 36 and the *b.* thereof
Deut. 3. 5 high walls . . and *b.*
Judg. 16. 3 with them, *b.* and all
1 Sam. 23. 7 hath gates and *b.*
1 K. 4. 13 walls and brazen *b.*
2 Chr. 8. 5 walls, gates, and *b.*
Neh. 3. 3 set up *b.* thereof
Job 38. 10 set *b.* and doors
Ps. 107. 16 cut the *b.* of iron
Prov. 18 19 *b.* of a castle
Isa. 45. 2 sunder the *b.* of iron
Jer. 49. 31 neither gates, nor *b.*
Lam. 2. 9 and broken her *b.*
Bar (*v.*). *Hold fast.*
Neh. 7. 3 shut the d. and *b.* them
Barbarian. *Bearded, foreigner.*
Acts 28. 4 when the *b.* saw
Rom. 1. 14 debtor to the *b.*
1 Cor. 14. 11 that speaketh a *b.*
Col. 3. 11 neither Greek nor *b.*
Barbarous. *Foreign, alien.*
Acts 28. 2 the *b.* people shewed
Barbed. *Pointed.*
Job 41. 7 fill his skin with *b.* irons
Barber. *Bearder.*
Ezek 5. 1 take thee a *b.* razor
Bare. *Uncovered.*
Lev. 13. 45 and his head *b.*
Ezek. 16. 7 wast naked and *b.*
1 Cor. 15. 37 *b.* grain, it may chance
Stripped or drawn off
Isa. 47. 2 make *b.* the leg
Jer. 49. 10 have made Esau *b.*
Joel 1. 7 made it clean *b.*
Bare (*v.*). *See* **Bear**
Barefoot. *Unshod.*
2 Sam. 15. 30 and he went *b.*
Isa. 20. 2, 3, 4 walked naked and *b.*
Bark. *Lift up the voice.*
Isa. 56. 10 dogs, they cannot *b.*
Cut or stripped off.
Joel 1. 7 and *b.* my fig-tree
Barley. *Barley, long beard.*
Ex. 9. 31 the *b.* was smitten
Lev. 27. 16 an homer of *b.* seed
Num. 5. 15 ephah of *b.* meal
Deut. 8. 8 land of wheat and *b.*
Judg. 7. 13 a cake of *b.* bread
Ruth 1. 22 begin. of the *b.* harvest
2 Sam. 14 30 and he hath *b.* there
1 K. 4. 28 *b.* also and straw for
2 K. 4. 22 twenty loaves of *b.*
1 Chr. 11. 13 ground full of *b.*
2 Chr. 2. 10 thousand measures of *b.*
Job. 31. 40 cockle instead of *b.*
Isa. 28. 25 the appointed *b.* and rie
Jer. 41. 8 have treasures of *b.*
Ezek. 4. 9 take thee wheat and *b.*
Hos. 3. 2 an homer of *b.*
Joel 1. 11 wheat and for the *b.*
John 6. 9 hath five *b.* loaves
Rev. 6. 6 three measures of *b.*
Barn. *Threshing floor*
2 K. 6. 27 out of the *b.* floor
Job 39. 12 gather it into thy *b.*
Hag. 2. 9 seed yet in the *b.*
Place for putting away.
Prov. 3. 10 shall thy *b.* be filled
Joel 1. 17 *b.* are broken down
Matt. 6. 26 nor gather in *b.*
Luke 12. 18 will pull down my *b.*
R. V. Job 39. 12 ; 2 K. 6. 27 thresh
  ing floor
Barrel. *Earthen jar.*
1 K. 17. 12, 14, 16 the *b.* of meal
  18. 33 fill four *b.* with water
Barren. *Sterile.*
Gen. 11. 30 but Sarai was *b.*
Ex. 23. 26 be *b.* in thy land
Deut. 7. 14 not be male or f. *b.*
Judg. 13. 2 his wife was *b.*
1 Sam. 2. 5 the *b.* hath born seven
2 K. 2 19 and the ground *b.*
Job. 39. 6 the *b.* land his dwelling

Ps. 113. 9 the *b.* woman to keep
Isa. 54. 1 Sing, O *b.*, thou that
Luke 1. 7 Elisabeth was *b.*
23. 29 blessed are the *b.*
Gal. 4. 27 *b.* that bearest not
R. V. 2 K. 2. 19 miscarrieth; Job
39. 6 salt; S. of S. 4. 2; 6. 6 be-
reaved; 2 Pet. 1. 8 idle
Barrenness. R. V. *Salt desert.*
Ps. 107. 34 fruitful land unto *b.*
Base. *Stand, pedestal*
1 K. 7. 31 the work of the *b.*
7. 27 to 7. 43
2 K. 16. 17 borders of the *b.*
2 Chr. 4. 14 *b.* and lavers made
Ez. 3. 3 altar upon the *b.*
Jer. 27. 19 concerning the *b.*
Zech. 5. 11 upon her own *b.*
Humble, low, abject.
2 Sam. 6. 22 *b.* in my own sight
Job 30. 8 children of *b.* men
Isa. 3. 5 *b.* against the honourable
Ezek. 17. 14 kingdom might be *b.*
Mal. 2. 9 contemptible and base
1 Cor. 1. 28 *b.* things of the world
2 Cor. 10. 1 am *b.* among you
Baser. R. V. *Rabble.*
Acts 17. 5 fellows of the *b.* sort
Basest. *Humblest.*
Ezek. 29. 15 *b.* of the kingdoms
Dan. 4. 17 setteth up the *b.* of men
Basin. *Cup, bowl, ewer.*
Ex. 24. 6 and put it in *b.*
Num. 4. 14 the vessels and the *b.*
2 Sam. 17. 28 brought beds and *b.*
1 K. 7. 40 lavers and the *b.*
2 K. 12. 13 bowls, snuffers, *b.*
1 Chr. 28. 17 for the golden *b.*
2 Chr. 4. 8 hundred *b.* of gold
Neh. 7. 70 Tirshatha gave fifty *b.*
Jer. 52. 19 the *b.* and fire pans
John 13. 5 poureth w. into a *b.*
R. V. 1 Chr. 28. 17; Ez. 1. 10 bowls;
Jer. 52. 19 cups
Basket. *Basket, hamper, kettle.*
Gen. 40. 16 I had three white *b.*
Ex. 29. 3 put them in one *b.*
Lev. 8. 2 a *b.* of unleavened bread
Num. 6. 19 take cake out of the *b.*
Judg. 6. 19 flesh he put in a *b.*
2 K. 10. 7 and put their heads in a *b.*
Jer. 24. 1 behold, two *b.* of figs
Mat. 14. 20 remained twelve *b.*
Mark 6. 43 took up twelve *b.*
Luke 9. 17 to them twelve *b.*
John 6. 13 *b.* with the fragments
Acts 9. 25 let down . . in a *b.*
2 Cor. 11. 33 in a *b.* was I let down
Bastard. *Spurious, mixed.*
Deut. 23. 2 a *b.* shall not enter
Zech. 9. 6 a *b.* shall not dwell
Heb 12. 8. then are ye *b.*
Bat. *Night bird.*
Lev. 11. 19 lapwing, and the *b.*
Deut. 14. 18 lapwing, and the *b.*
Isa. 2. 20 moles and to the *b.*
Bath. *A fluid measure.*
1 K. 7. 26 it con. two thousand *b.*
2 Chr. 2. 10 thousand *b.* of wine
Ez. 7. 22 hundred *b.* of wine
Isa. 5. 10 shall yield one *b.*
Ezek. 45. 10 just ephah, and just *b.*
Bathe. *Wash, rub.*
Lev. 15. 13 and *b.* his flesh in water
Num. 19. 7 *b.* his flesh in water
Isa. 34. 5 sword shall be *b.*
R. V. Isa. 34. 5 hath drunk its fill
Batter. *Destroy.*
2 Sam. 20. 15 Joab *b.* the wall
Battle. *Fight, struggle, arms.*
Gen. 14. 8 joined *b.* with them
Num. 31. 21 which went to the *b.*
Deut. 2. 9 con. with them in *b.*
Josh. 4. 13 passed bef. Lord unto *b.*
Judg. 8. 13 Gideon returned from *b.*
1 Sam. 4. 1 against the Philis. to *b.*
2 Sam. 1. 4 are fled from the *b.*
1 K. 8. 44 people go out to *b.*
2 K. 3. 7 against Moab to *b.*
1 Chr. 5. 20 cried to God in *b.*
2 Chr. 13. 3 set the *b.* in array
Job 39. 25 smelleth the *b.* afar
Ps. 24. 8 the Lord mighty in *b.*
Prov. 21. 31 against the day of *b.*
Eccl. 9. 11 nor the *b.* to the strong
Isa. 13. 4 the host of the *b.*

Jer. 8. 6 rusheth into the battle
Ezek. 7. 14 none goeth to the *b.*
Dan. 11. 25 stirred up in *b.*
Hos. 1. 7 by bow, nor by *b.*
Joel 2. 5 set in *b.* array
Am. 1. 14 in the day of *b.*
1 Cor. 14. 8 prepare himself to *b.*
Rev. 9. 7 horses prep. unto *b.*
R. V. Num. 31. 14; Josh. 22. 33;
2 Sam. 21. 18, 19, 20; 1 Cor. 14. 8;
Rev. 9. 7, 9; 28. 8 war
Battle-axe, bow.
Jer. 51. 20 *b. a.* and weapons
Zech. 9. 10 the *b. a.* shall be cut
Battlement. *Barrier.*
Deut. 22. 8 a *b.* for thy roof
Jer. 5. 10 take away her *b.*
R. V. Jer. 5. 10 branches
Bay. *Tongue.*
Josh. 15. 2 *b.* that looketh south
18. 19 were at the north *b.*
Strong, deep red.
Zech. 6. 3 chariot grisled and *b.*
Bay-tree. R. V. *Tree in its native soil.*
Ps. 37. 35 like a green *b. t.*
Bdellium. *Pearl, gum.*
Gen. 2. 12 *b.* and the onyx stone
Num. 11. 7 as the color of *b.*
Beacon. *Signal.*
Isa. 30. 17 a *b.* upon the top of
Beam. *Bar, rafter, joist, board.*
Judg. 16. 4 the pin of the *b.*
1 Sam. 17. 7 like a weaver's *b.*
1 K. 7. 3 above upon the *b.*
2 K. 6. 2 thence every man a a *b.*
1 Chr. 20. 5 like a weaver's *b.*
2 Chr. 3. 7 the *b.*, the posts, and
S. of S. 1. 17 the *b.* of our house
Mat. 7. 3 the *b.* that is in thine
Luke 6. 41 cast out first the *b.*
Bean. *Bean, pea.*
2 Sam. 17. 28 parched corn and *b.*
Ezek. 4. 9 wheat, and barley, and *b.*
Bear (*n.*). *Shaggy animal.*
1 Sam. 17. 34 came a lion and a *b.*
2 Sam. 17. 8 as a *b.* robbed of her
2 K. 2. 24 came forth two she *b.*
Prov. 17. 12 let *b.* robbed of whelps
Isa. 11. 7 and the cow and the *b.*
Lam. 3. 10 unto me as a *b.*
Dan. 7. 5 second, like to a *b.*
Hos. 13. 8 as a *b.* bereaved
Am. 5. 19 lion, and a *b.* met him
Rev. 3. 2 feet as of a *b.*
Bear (*v.*). *Bring forth, beget.*
Gen. 4. 1 and *b.* Cain and said
Ex. 2. 2 conceived and *b.* a son
Lev. 12. 2 and *b.* a man child
Num. 26. 59 she *b.* unto Amram
Deut. 21. 15 have *b.* him children
Judg. 8. 31 she also *b.* him a son
Ruth 1. 12 should also *b.* sons
2 Sam. 11. 27 and *b.* him a son
1 K. 1. 6 and his mother *b.* him
1 Chr. 1. 32 she *b.* Zimran
Job 24. 21 barren that *b.* not
Prov. 17. 25 to her that *b.* him
Eccl. 3. 2 a time to be *b.*
Luke 1. 13 E. shall *b.* thee a son
Jas. 3. 12 *b.* olive berries
Rev. 22. 2 *b.* twelve manner of f.
Lift up, carry, endure.
Gen. 4. 13 greater than I can *b.*
Ex. 18. 22 and they shall *b.*
Lev. 5. 17 and shall *b.* his iniquity
Num. 1. 5 the tabernacle
Deut. 1. 9 not able to *b.* you
Josh. 4. 16 priests that *b.* the ark
Judg. 3. 18 people that *b.* present
1 Sam. 14. 1 young man that *b.* his
2 Sam. 6. 13 they that *b.* the ark
1 K. 2. 26 thou *b.* the ark
1 Chr. 5. 18 *b.* buckler and sword
Ps. 55. 12 then I could have *b.*
Prov. 9. 12 thou alone shalt *b.*
Isa. 1. 14 I am weary to *b.*
Jer. 10. 5 must needs be *b.*
Lam. 3. 27 that he *b.* the yoke
Ezek. 14. 10 *b.* the punishment
Mat. 3. 11 am not worthy to *b.*
Luke 7. 14 they that *b.* him
John 12. 6 and *b.* what was put
Acts 9. 15 *b.* my name before me
Rom. 11. 18 thou *b.* not the root
Rev. 2. 2 canst not *b.* them

Beard. *Beard, face hair.*
Lev. 13. 29 plague upon . . the *b.*
1 Sam. 17. 35 caught him by his *b.*
2 Sam. 10. 4 shaved off . . their *b.*
1 Chr. 19. 5 until your *b.* be grown
Ez. 9. 3 hair of head and of my *b.*
Ps. 133. 2 ran down upon the *b.*
Isa. 7. 20 also consume the *b.*
Jer. 41. 5 having their *b.* shaven
Ezek. 5. 1 and upon they *b.*
Beast. *Cattle, quadruped*
Gen. 6. 7 both man and *b.*
Ex. 8. 17 lice in man, and in *b.*
Lev. 7. 21 or any unclean *b.*
Num. 3. 13 hallow. both man and *b.*
Deut. 4. 17 likeness of any *b.*
Judg. 20. 48 the men, as the *b.*
1 K. 4. 33 he spake also of *b.*
2 Ch. 32. 28 stalls for all . . *b.*
Ez. 1. 4 with goods and with *b.*
Neh. 2. 12 neither . . any *b.* with me
Job 12. 7. but ask now the *b.*
Ps. 8. 7 and the *b.* of the field
Prov. 12. 10 the life of his *b.*
Eccl. 3. 18 they themselves are *b.*
Isa. 18. 6 left to *b.* of the earth
Jer. 7 20 upon man and upon *b.*
Ezek. 8. 10 creeping things and *b.*
Joel 1. 18 how do *b.* groan
Jonah 3. 7 neither man nor *b.*
A living creature.
Gen. 1. 24 *b.* of the earth after
Ex. 23. 11 the *b.* of the field
Lev. 5. 2 carcase of an unclean *b.*
Num. 35. 3 suburbs be for their *b.*
1 Sam. 17. 46 wild *b.* of the earth
Job 5. 22 afraid of the *b.*
Ps. 50. 10 *b.* of the forest
Isa. 35. 9 nor any ravenous *b.* shall
Jer. 12. 9 assemble all the *b.*
Mark 1. 13 with the wild *b.*
Luke 10. 34 set him on his own *b*
Acts 28. 5 he shook off the *b.*
1 Cor. 15. 39 another flesh of *b.*
Tit. 1. 12 always liars, evil *b.*
Heb. 12. 20 so much as a *b.*
Jas. 3. 7 for every kind of *b.*
Rev. 6. 8 the *b.* of the earth
R. V. Ex. 11. 5; Num. 20. 8, Isa
63. 14 cattle; in Rev. generally, liv
ing creatures
Beat. *Pound, strike, smite*
Ex. 30. 36 shalt *b.* some of it
Num. 11. 8 *b.* it in a mortar
Deut. 24. 20 *b.* thine olive tree
Judg. 8. 17 *b.* down the tower
1 Sam. 14. 16 went on *b.* down
2 Sam. 22. 43 I *b.* them as small
2 K. 13. 25 did Joash *b.* him
Ps. 89. 23 will *b.* down his foes
Isa. 27. 12 the Lord shall *b.* off
Mat. 7. 27 *b.* upon that house
Mark 4. 37 waves *b.* into the ship
Luke 12. 45 begin to *b.* the men
Acts 18. 17 and *b.* him before the
1 Cor. 9. 26 one that *b.* the air
2 Cor. 11. 25 thrice was I *b.* with
R. V. Judg. 8. 17; 2 K. 13. 25 smite,
Mat. 7. 27 smote
Beaten. *Smitten, pounded.*
Ex. 5. 14 the officers . . were *b.*
Deut. 25. 2 worthy to be *b.*
Josh. 8. 15 they were *b.* before
2 Sam. 2. 17 and Abner was *b.*
Isa. 30. 31 shall the Assyrian be *b.*
Jer. 46. 5 mighty ones are *b.*
Mic. 1. 7 images . . shall be *b.*
Mark 13. 9 ye shall be *b.*
Luke 12. 47 *b.* with many stripes
Beating. *Thrashing, flaying.*
Mark 12. 5 *b.* some, killing some
Acts 21. 32 they left *b.* of Paul
Beautiful. *Fair, good form.*
Gen. 29. 17 Rachel was *b.*
Deut. 21. 11 seest . . a *b.* woman
1 Sam. 16. 12 a *b.* countenance
Esth. 2. 7 maid fair and *b.*
Isa. 4. 2 branch of the Lord be *b.*
Jer. 13. 20 the flock, . . thy *b.* flock
Ezek. 16. 12 a *b.* crown upon head
Mat. 23. 27 appear *b.* outward
Acts 3. 2 gate . . called *B.*
Rom. 10. 15 *b.* are the feet of
Beautify. *Make beautiful.*
Ezra 7. 27 to *b.* the house
Ps. 149. 4 will *b.* the meek

Isa. 60. 13 to *b*. the place of

Beauty. *Honor, fairness, majesty.*
Ex. 28. 2 for glory and for *b*.
2 Sam. 14. 25 as Absalom for *b*.
1 Chr. 16. 29 the Lord in the *b*. of
2 Chr. 20. 11 the *b*. of holiness
Esth. 1. 11 shew princes . . her *b*.
Ps. 45. 11 greatly desire thy *b*.
Prov. 6. 25 lust not after her *b*.
Isa. 3. 24 burning instead of *b*.
Lam. 2. 15 the perfection of *b*.
Ezek. 16. 15 trust in thine own *b*.
Zech. 9. 17 how great is his *b*.
R. V. 2 Sam. 1. 19 glory; Job 40.
10; Lam. 1. 6 majesty; Isa. 61. 3
garland

Beckon. *Nod or wave down.*
Luke 1. 22 he *b*. unto them
John 13. 24 Peter therefore *b*. to
Acts 19. 33 Alexr. *b*. with the hand
R. V. Luke 1. 22 continued making
signs

Beckoning. *Waving downward.*
Acts 12. 17 but he *b*. unto them
13. 16 Paul stood up, and *b*.

Become. *Befit, worthy of.*
Ps. 93. 5 holiness *b*. thine house
Mat. 3. 15 thus it *b*. us to
Eph. 5. 3 named . . as *b*. saints
1 Tim. 2. 10 *b*. women professing
Tit. 2. 1 the things which *b*.
Heb. 2. 10 for it *b*. him, for whom
Come to, grow to.
2 Sam. 7. 24 art *b*. their God
Job 30. 21 art *b*. cruel to me
Mat. 13. 22 and he *b*. unfruitful
Mark 1. 17 *b*. fishers of men
John 1. 12 gave he power to *b*.
Acts 7. 40 wot not what is *b*.
Rom. 3. 19 world may *b*. guilty
1 Cor. 3. 18 let him *b*. a fool
2 Cor. 5. 17 all things are *b*. new
Gal. 4. 16 therefore *b*. your enemy
Phil. 2. 8 and *b*. obedient
1 Thes. 1. 6 *b*. followers of us
Heb. 5. 9 *b*. author of eter. salv.
Jas. 2. 4 *b*. judges of evil thoughts
Rev. 6. 12 sun *b*. black as sackcloth

Bed. *Thing spread out, couch,*
mattress, reclining place.
Gen. 47. 31 bowed . . upon the *b*.
Ex. 8. 3 and come upon thy *b*.
Lev. 15. 4 *b*. whereon he lieth
1 Sam. 19. 13 and laid it in *b*.
2 Sam. 4. 7 he lay on his *b*.
1 K. 17. 19 laid him upon his *b*.
2 Chr. 24. 25 slew him on his *b*.
Esth. 1. 6 *b*. were gold and silver
Job 33. 15 slumberings upon the *b*
Ps. 6. 6 make I my b. to swim
Prov. 26. 14 slothful upon his *b*.
S. of S. 3. 1 by night on my *b*.
Isa. 57. 2 shall rest in their *b*.
Ezek. 23. 17 into the *b*. of love
Dan. 2. 29 came . . upon thy *b*.
Mat. 9. 6 Arise, take up thy *b*.
Mark 7. 30 daught. laid upon the **b.**
Luke 5. 18 men brought in a *b*.
John 5. 8 rise, take up thy *b*.
Acts 5. 15 on *b*. and couches
Heb. 13. 4 and the *b*. undefiled
Rev. 2. 22 cast her into a *b*.
R. V. many places in O. T., couch

Bedchamber. *Inner bedroom.*
Ex. 8. 3 and into thy *b. c.*
2 Sam. 4. 7 his bed in his *b. c.*
2 K. 6. 12 speakest in thy *b. c.*
2 Chr. 22. 11 put him in a *b. c.*

Bedstead. *Arched bed.*
Deut. 3. 11 his *b*. was a *b*. of iron

Bee. *Bee.*
Deut. 1. 44 chased you as *b*. do
Judg. 14. 8 swarm of *b*. and honey
Ps. 118. 12 com. me about like *b*.
Isa. 7. 18 for the *b*. that is in

Beetle. R. V. *Cricket.*
Lev. 11. 22 *b*. after its kind

Beeves. *Herd, ox, heifer.*
Lev. 22. 19 a male . . . of the *b*.
Num. 31. 28 offer male of the *b*.
R. V. Lev. 22. 21 of the herd

Befall. *Meet, come upon, occur.*
Gen. 42. 4 lest . . mischief *b*. him
Lev. 10. 19 things have *b*. me
Num. 20. 14 travail hath *b*. us
Deut. 31 29 evil will *b*. you

Josh. 2. 23 all that *b*. them
Judg. 6. 13 why is all this *b*. us?
Dan. 10. 14 what shall *b*. thy peo.
Mark 5. 16 how it *b*. to him
Acts 20. 19 tempt. which *b*. me

Before. *In front of, prior.*
Ps. 39. 13 spare me *b*. I go
Isa. 43. 13 *b*. the day was I am he
Mat. 24. 25 I have told you *b*.
John 13. 19 I tell you *b*. it come
Phil. 3. 13 things that are *b*.
Heb. 7. 18 command going *b*.
2 Pet. 3. 17 know these things *b*.
R. V. Rev. 13. 12; 19. 20 in his sight

Beforehand. *In advance.*
Mark 13. 11 take no thought *b*.
2 Cor. 9. 5 make up *b*. your bounty
1 Tim. 5. 24 some sins are open *b*.
1 Pet. 1. 11 when it testified *b*.
R. V. 1 Tim. 5. 24 evident

Beforetime. *In former time.*
Deut. 2. 12 Horims dwelt in Seir *b*.
Josh. 20. 5 hated him not *b*.
1 Sam. 10. 11 all that knew him *b*.
2 Sam. 7. 10 wickedness . . as *b*.
2 K. 13. 5 Israel dwelt . . as *b*.
Acts 8. 9 Simon, which *b*. in

Beg. *Ask, seek, entreat.*
Ps. 37. 25 his seed *b*. bread
Prov. 20. 4 shall he *b*. in harvest
Mat. 27. 58 and *b*. the body of Jesus
Mark 10. 46 sat by the highway *b*.
Luke 16. 3 to *b*. I am ashamed
John 9. 8 he that sat and *b*.
R. V. Mat. 27. 58, Luke 23. 52 asked
for

Began. See **Begin.**

Begat. See **Beget.**

Beget. *Generate, bring forth*
Gen. 5. 3 Adam *b*. a son to
Lev. 25. 45 they *b*. in your land
Num. 26. 29 and Machir *b*. Gilead
Deut. 32. 18 the rock that *b*. thee
Ruth 4. 22 and Jesse *b*. David
2 K. 20. 18 which thou shalt *b*.
1 Chr. 1. 34 Abraham *b*. Isaac
2 Chr. 11. 21 Rehoboam *b*. . . sons
Job 28. 38 *b*. the drops of dew
Eccl. 5. 14 and he *b*. a son
Isa. 39. 7 which thou shalt *b*.
Jer. 16. 3 fathers that *b*. them
Ezek. 18. 10 if he *b*. a son
Mat. 1. 2-16 A. *b*. Isaac, etc.
Acts 7. 8 so A. *b*. Isaac
1 Cor. 4. 15 I have *b*. you
Heb. 1. 5 this day have I *b*.
1 John 5. 1 him that *b*. loveth him

Beggar. *Needy, cringing.*
1 Sam. 2. 8 he . . lifteth up the *b*.
Luke 16. 20 there was a certain *b*.
R. V. 1 Sam. 2. 8 needy

Beggarly. *Cringingly.*
Gal. 4. 9 to the weak and *b*.

Begin. *Commence.*
Gen. 6. 1 men *b*. to multiply
Num. 16. 46 the plague is *b*.
Deut. 2. 24 *b*. to possess it
Josh. 3. 7 this day will I *b*.
Judg. 10. 18 that will *b*. to fight
1 Sam. 3. 2 eyes *b*. to wax dim
2 K. 10. 32 the Lord *b*. to cut
1 Chr. 1. 10 he *b*. to be mighty
2 Chr. 3. 1 S. *b*. to build the h.
Ez. 3. 6 *b*. they to offer
Neh. 4. 7 breaches *b*. to be stop.
Esth. 6. 13 thou hast *b*. to fall
Jer. 25. 29 I *b*. to bring evil
Mat. 4. 17 Jesus *b*. to preach
Mark 1. 45 and *b*. to publish
Luke 3. 8 *b*. not to say within
John 13. 5 *b*. to wash the disci.
Acts 1. 1 *b*. both to do and teach
2 Cor. 8. 6 as he had *b*., so finish
Gal. 3. 3 having *b*. in the Spirit
Phil. 1. 6 *b*. a good work in you
Rev. 10. 7 shall *b*. to sound

Beginning. *Commencement.*
Gen. 1. 1 in the *b*. God created
Ex. 12. 2 unto you the *b*. of
Num. 10. 10 in the *b*. of your mo.
Deut. 11. 12 from the *b*. of the y.
Judg. 7. 19 in the *b*. of the watch
2 Sam. 21. 9 in the *b*. of barley har
2 K. 17. 25 *b*. of their dwelling
Ez. 4. 6 the *b*. of his reign
Job 8. 7 thy *b*. was small

Ps. 111. 10 fear of the Lord is the *b*
Prov. 8. 22 L. possessed me in the *l*
Eccl. 3. 11 God maketh from the *b*
Isa. 40. 21 told you from the *b*.
Jer. 26. 1 *b*. of the reign of Jehoi.
Lam. 2. 19 *b*. of the watches
Ezek. 40. 1 *b*. of the year
Mat. 19. 4 at the *b*. made
Mark 1. 1 the *b*. of the gospel
Luke 1. 2 from the *b*. were
John 1. 1 in the *b*. was the Word
Acts 11. 15 as on us at the *b*.
Phil. 4. 15 *b*. of the gospel
Col. 1. 18 who is the *b*.
2 Thes. 2. 13 God hath from the *b*.
Heb. 1. 10 in the *b*. hast laid
1 John 1. 1 was from the *b*.
Rev. 1. 8 the *b* and end
R. V. 1 Chr. 17. 9; Acts 26. 5; 2
Pet. 2. 20 first

Begotten. *Generated, brought*
forth.
Lev. 18. 11 *b*. of thy father
Deut. 23. 8 children that are *b*.
Judg. 8. 30 sons of his body *b*.
John 1. 14 only *b*. of the Father
Heb. 11. 17 offered up his only *b*
1 John 4. 9 only *b*. Son
Rev. 1. 5 *b*. of the dead

Beguile. *Deceive, entrap.*
Gen. 3. 13 the serpent *b*. me
Num. 25. 18 they have *b*. you
Josh. 9. 22 ye *b*. us, saying
2 Cor. 11 3 serpent *b*. Eve
Col. 2. 4 lest any man *b*. you
2 Pet. 2. 14 *b*. unstable souls
R. V. Col. 2. 4 delude; 2. 18 rob
2 Pet. 2. 14 enticing

Begun. See **Begin.**

Behalf. *On the part of*
Ex. 27. 21 on *b*. of the children
2 Sam. 3. 12 Abner sent on his *b*.
2 Chr. 16. 9 strong in *b*. of them
Job 36. 2 speak on God's *b*.
Dan. 11. 18 for his own *b*.
Rom. 16. 19 glad on your *b*.
1 Cor. 1. 4 thank God on your *b*.
2 Cor. 1. 11 given on our *b*.
Phil. 1. 29 given in *b*. of Christ
1 Pet. 4. 16 glorify God on this *b*.
R. V. Dan. 11. 18 —— ; 1 Pet. 4. 16
name

Behave. *Act, comport.*
Deut. 32. 27 lest adversaries *b*.
1 Sam. 18. 5 David *b*. wisely
1 Chr. 19. 13 let us *b*. valiantly
Ps. 101. 2 I will *b*. wisely
Is. 3. 5 child shall *b*. proudly
Mic. 3. 4 they have *l*. ill
1 Cor. 7. 36 he *b*. uncomely
1 Thes. 2. 10 unblameably we *b*.
1 Tim. 3. 15 thou oughtest to *b*.

Behaviour. *Conduct, demeanour*
1 Sam. 21. 13 D. changed his *b*.
1 Tim. 3. 2 be of good *b*.
Tit. 2. 3 in *b*. as becometh
R. V. 1 Tim. 3. 2 orderly; Tit. 2. 3
reverent in demeanour.

Beheaded. *Head taken off.*
2 Sam. 4. 7 *b*. him and took his h.
Mat. 14. 10 and *b*. John in prison
Mark 16. 16 John, whom I *b*.
Luke 9. 9 John have I *b*.
Rev. 20. 4 them that were *b*.
R. V. Deut. 21. 6 whose neck was
broken.

Beheld. See **Behold.**

Behemoth. *Large beast.*
Job 40. 15 behold now *b*.

Behind. *Rearward, after, back of*
Gen. 18. 10 door, which was *b*.
Ex. 14. 19 a. of God . . went *b*.
Deut. 25. 18 smote all . . *b*. thee
Josh. 8. 14 ambush against him *b*.
Judg. 18. 12 *b*. Kirjath-jearim
1 Sam. 21. 9 cloth *b*. the ephod
2 Sam. 1. 7 when he looked *b*.
1 K. 14. 9 cast me *b* thy back
2 K. 9. 18 come about *b*.
1 Chr. 19. 10 battle . . before and *b*
2 Chr. 13. 13 to come about *b*.
Neh. 4. 16 *b*. all the house of Jud.
Ps. 50. 17 castest my word *b*.
S. of S. 2. 9 standeth *b*. our wall
Isa. 30. 21 hear a word *b*. thee
Ezek. 3. 12 heard *b*. me a voice

Mat. 16. 23 Get thee *b*. me, Satan
Mark. 5. 27 came in the press *b*.
Luke 8. 44 came *b*. and touched
1 Cor. 1. 7 come *b*. in no gift
2 Cor. 11. 5 was not a whit *b*.
Col. 1. 24 that which is *b*.
Phil. 3. 13 things which are *b*.
Rev. 1. 10 heard *b*. me a great voice
R. V. Col. 1. 24 lacking
Behold. *Lo, see, look.*
Gen. 28. 15 *b*.; I am with thee
Num. 12. 8 of Lord shall he *b*.
Deut. 3. 27 *b*. it with thine eyes
Job 1. 12 *b*., all he hath in thy pow.
Ps. 11. 4 his eyes *b*., his eyelids
Prov. 7. 7 *b*. among the simple
Eccl. 1. 14 *b*. all is vanity and vex.
S. of S. 3. 11 *b*. king Solomon
Isa. 26. 10 not *b*. the majesty of L.
Jer. 4. 23 I *b*. the earth, and, lo
Lam. 1. 1 *b*. my affliction
Ezek. 1. 15 *b*. the living creatures
Dan. 9. 18 *b*. our desolation
Am. 3. 9 *b*. the great tumults
Mic. 7. 9 *b*. his righteousness
Hab. 1. 13 than to *b*. evil
Mat. 19. 26 but Jesus . . . and said
Mark 1. 2 *b*. I send my messenger
Luke 20. 17 he *b*. them, and said
John 1. 42 when Jesus *b*. him
Acts 1. 10 *b*., two men stood by
Rom. 9. 33 *b*., I lay in Sion stum.bl.
2 Cor. 5. 17 *b*., all things are . . new
Heb. 2. 13 *b*. I and the children
Rev. 11. 12 their enemies *b*. them
Beholding. *Seeing, viewing.*
Ps. 119. 37 turn . . eyes from *b*.
Eccl. 5. 11 saving the *b*. of
Mat. 27. 55 women were there *b*.
Luke 23. 35 the people stood *b*.
Acts 8. 13 *b*. the miracles and signs
2 Cor. 3. 18 *b*. as in a glass
Col. 2. 5 joying and *b*. your order
Jas. 1. 23 *b*. his natural face
Beloved. *Needful for.*
Luke 24. 46 it *b*. Christ to suffer
Heb. 2. 17 it *b*. him to be made
Being. *Life, existence.*
Ps. 104. 33 while I have my *b*.
Acts 17. 28 move, and have our *b*.
Belch. *Utter, send forth.*
Ps. 59. 7 *b*. with their mouths
Belied. *Lied about.*
Jer. 5. 12 they have *b*. the Lord
Belief. *Confidence, trust.*
2 Thes. 2. 13 of the Spirit and *b*.
Believe. *To remain steadfast.*
Gen. 15. 6 he *b*. in the Lord
Ex. 4. 1 they will not *b*. me
Num. 14. 11 how long . . ere they *b*.
Deut. 1. 32 did not *b*. the Lord
1 Sam. 27. 12 Achish *b*. David
2 K. 17. 14 that did not *b*. in
2 Chr. 9. 6 I *b*. not their words
Job 9. 16 would I not *b*. that
Ps. 27. 13 unless I had *b*.
Prov. 14. 15 the simple *b*. ev. word
Isa. 7. 9 if ye will not *b*.
Jer. 12. 6 *b*. them not, though
Dan. 6. 23 because he *b*. in his God
Jonah 3. 5 peo. of Nineveh *b*. God
To be persuaded.
Acts 17. 4 some of them *b*.
27. 11 the centurion *b*.
To adhere to, trust, rely on.
Mat. 8. 13 as thou hast *b*.
Mark 5. 36 be not afraid, only *b*.
Luke 1. 20 because thou *b*. not
John 1. 7 through him might *b*.
Acts 2. 44 all that *b*. were together
Rom. 1. 6 every one that *b*.
1 Cor. 1. 21 to save them that *b*.
2 Cor. 4. 15 I *b*. . . we also *b*.
Gal. 2. 16 we have *b*. in Jesus Christ
Eph. 1. 13 after that ye *b*.
Phil. 1. 29 only to *b*. in him
1 Thes. 1. 7 to all that *b*.
1 Tim. 1. 16 which should . . *b*. on him
2 Tim. 1. 12 whom I have *b*.
Tit. 3. 8 which have *b*. in God
Heb. 4. 3 *b*. do enter into rest
Jas. 2. 19 the devils also *b*.
1 Pet. 1. 8 yet *b*., ye rejoice with joy
Jude 5 destroyed them that *b*. not

R. V. Acts 19. 9; Heb. 3. 18, dis-
obedient
Believer. *Trust, rely on*
Acts 5. 14 *b*. were the more added
1 Tim. 4. 12 example of the *b*.
Bell. *Clock, little bell.*
Ex. 28. 33 *b*. of gold between
28. 34; 39. 25; 39. 26
Zech. 14. 20 be upon the *b*. of hors.
Bellow. *Sound, R. V. neigh.*
Jer. 50. 11 and *b*. as bulls
Bellows. *Bellows, skin-bag.*
Jer. 6. 29 the *b*. are burnt
Belly. *Belly, paunch, inward part.*
Gen. 3. 14 upon thy *b*. shalt thou go
Lev. 11. 42 goeth upon the *b*.
Num. 5. 21 and thy *b*. to swell
Judg. 3. 21 thrust it into his *b*.
1 K. 7. 20 over against the *b*.
Job 3. 11 I came out of the *b*.
Ps. 17. 14 whose *b*. thou fillest
Prov. 13. 25 *b*. of the wicked want
S. of S. 7. 2 *b*. like . . heap of wheat
Isa. 46. 3 borne . . from the *b*.
Jer. 1. 5 formed thee in the *b*.
Ezek. 3. 3 cause thy *b*. to eat
Jonah 1. 17 in *b*. of fish three days
Hab. 3. 16 my *b*. trembled
Mat. 12. 40 three days in whale's *b*.
Mark 7. 19 not into h., but into the *b*.
Luke 15. 16 fain have filled his *b*.
John 7. 38 out of his *b*. flow rivers
Rom. 16. 18 serve their own *b*.
1 Cor. 6. 13 meats for the *b*.
Phil. 3. 19 whose God is their *b*.
Rev. 10. 9 make thy *b*. bitter
R. V. Job. 20. 20 within him; 31. 9
body; S. of S. 5. 14 body; Jer. 51.
34 maw; Tit. 1. 12 gluttons
Belong. *Appertain, part of.*
Gen. 40. 8 interpretations *b*. to God
Lev. 27. 24 the possession . . did *b*.
Deut. 29. 29 the secret things *b*.
Judg. 19. 14 which *b*. to Benjamin
1 K. 1. 8 which *b*. to David
Ez. 10. 4 for this matter *b*. to thee
Esth. 2. 9 such things as *b*. to her
Mark 9. 41 because ye *b*. to Christ
Luke 23. 7 knew that he *b*. unto Her.
Heb. 5. 14 meat *b*. to them of age
See also Ps. 3. 8; 47. 9; 62. 11; 68.
20; Prov. 24. 23 Dan. 9. 7, 8, 9;
Heb. 10. 30
Beloved. *Loved dearly.*
Deut. 21. 15 have two wives, one *b*.
Neh. 13. 26 Sol. was *b*. of his God
Ps. 60. 5 thy *b*. may be delivered
S. of S. 1. 16 thou art fair, my *b*.
Jer. 11. 15 what hath my *b*. to do in h.
Hos. 3. 1 love a woman *b*. of friend
Mat. 3. 17; 17. 5; Mark 1. 11; 9. 7;
Luke 3. 22; 9. 35; This is my *b*.
Son
Acts 15. 25 chosen men . . with our *b*.
Rom. 1. 7 To all in Rome, *b*. of God
1 Cor. 4. 14 *b*. sons, I warn you
1 Tim. 6. 2 are faithful and *b*.
Phile. 2 to our *b*. Apphia
Heb. 6. 9 *b*. . we are persuaded
1 Pet. 4. 12 *b*., think it not strange
2 Pet. 1. 17; 1 John 3. 2; 3 John 2;
Jude 3
R. V. Luke 9. 35 my chosen ; Phile.
2 sister
Bemoan. *Nod, moan, lament.*
Job 42. 11 they *b*. him, and comfort
Jer. 15. 5 or who shall *b*. thee
16. 5; 22. 10; 31. 18; 48. 17
Nah. 3. 7 who will *b*. her?
Bench. *Board, bench.*
Ezek. 27. 6 the A. have made . . *b*.
Bend. *Tread, curve, crook.*
Ps. 7. 12 he hath *b*. his bow
Isa. 5. 28 ar. sharp, their bows *b*.
Jer. 46. 9 handle and *b*. the bow
Lam. 2. 4 he hath *b*. his bow
Zech. 17. 7 vine did *b*. her roots
Ezek. 19. 3 I have *b*. Judah
R. V. Ps. 58. 7 aimeth
Beneath. *Below, under, down.*
Ex. 26. 24 coupled together *b*.
Deut. 4. 18 in the waters *b*.
Job 18. 16 shall be dried up *b*.
Prov. 15. 24 depart from hell *b*.
Jer. 31. 37 earth searched out *b*.
Mark 14. 66 as Peter was *b*. in pal.

John 8. 23 ye are from *b*.
Acts 2. 19 signs in the earth *b*.
Benefactor. *Well-doer.*
Luke 22. 25 ex. auth. are called *b*
Benefit (*v*.). *To do good.*
Jer. 18. 10 I said I would *b*. them
Benefit (*n*.). *Deed, good work.*
2 Chr. 32. 25 according to the *b*-
Ps. 103. 2 forget not all his *b*.
2 Cor. 1. 15 have a second *b*.
1 Tim. 6. 2 partakers of the *b*.
R. V. Phile. 14 goodness.
Benevolence. *Good mind, deed.*
1 Cor. 7. 3 render . . wife due *b*.
R. V. her due
Bent. *Hang to.*
Hos. 11. 7 *b*. to blacksliding
See **Bend**
Bereave. *Make childless, deprive*
Gen. 42. 36 me have ye *b*.
Eccl. 4. 8 *b*. my soul of good
Jer. 18. 21 let their wives be *b*.
Lam. 1. 20 abroad the sword *b*.
Ezek. 5. 17 and they shall *b*. thee
Hos. 9. 12 yet will I. *b*. them
R. V. Jer. 18. 21 ch'ldless
Berries. *Berry, fruit.*
Isa. 17. 6 two or three *b*. in top
Jas. 3. 12 can the fig bear olive *b*.
R. V. Jas. 3. 12 olives
Beryl. *Beryl, green gem.*
Ex. 28. 20 fourth row a *b*.
S. of S. 5. 14 rings set with a *b*.
Ezek. 1. 16 the color of a *b*.
Dan. 10. 6 body . . like the *b*.
Rev. 21. 20 the eighth, *b*.
Beseech. *Seek, inquire.*
Gen. 42. 21 guilty, when he *b*. us
Deut. 3. 23 I *b*. the Lord, saying
2 Sam. 12. 16 D. therefore *b*. God
1 K. 13. 6 man of God *b*. the Lord
2 K. 13. 4 Jehoahaz. *b*. the Lord
2 Chr. 33. 12 he *b*. the Lord
Ez. 8. 23 fasted, and *b*. our God
Esth. 8. 3 *b*. him with tears
Jer. 26. 19 and *b*. the Lord
Mal. 1. 9 *b*. God that he will
Question, petition, pray.
2 K. 20. 3 I *b*. thee, O Lord
Neh. 1. 5 ; Ps. 116. 1 ; Isa. 38. 3 ;
Jonah 1. 14
Mat. 8. 5 a centurion *b*. him
Mark 7. 26 she *b*. him that he
Luke 4. 38 they *b*. him for her
John 4. 40 *b*. him that he . . tarry
Acts 13. 42 the Gentiles *b*. that
Rom. 12. 1 I *b*. you therefore
1 Cor. 1. 10 ; 2 Cor. 2. 8; Eph. 4. 1;
Phil. 4. 2 ; 1 Thes. 4. 10; 1 Tim. 1.
3; Phile. 9; Heb. 13. 19; 1 Pet. 2. 11
R. V. In O. T. mostly changed to
pray; Phil. 4. 2 ; 1 Thes. 4. 10;
Heb. 13. 22 exhort
Beset. *Surround, bind.*
Judg. 20. 5 *b*. the house round
Ps. 22. 12 bulls of B. have *b*. me
Hos. 7. 2 doings have *b*. them
Heb. 12. 1 sin which doth easily *b*.
Beside. *By the side of.*
Ex. 29. 12 pour all the blood *b*.
Lev. 1. 16 cast it *b*. the altar
Deut. 11. 30 *b*. the plains of Moreh
1 K. 10. 19 two lions stood *b*. stays
2 K. 12. 9 set it *b*. the altar
Neh. 8. 4 *b*. him stood Mattithiah,
Ezek. 9. 2 stood *b*. the brazen altar
Apart from, save, except.
Gen. 26. 1 *b*. the first famine
Lev. 9. 17 *b*. the burnt sacrifice
Num. 6. 21 *b*. that his hand get
Deut. 4. 35 is God ; . . none else *b*.
Josh. 22. 29 *b*. the altar of the Lord
1 K. 10. 13 asked *b*. that which
1 Chr. 17. 20 neither . . God *b*. thee
Isa. 26. 13 lords *b*. thee have
Mal. 25. 20 have gained *b*. them
Mark 3. 21 he is *b*. himself
Luke 24. 21 *b*. all this, to day
Acts 26. 24 thou art *b*. thyself
2 Cor. 5. 13 we be *b*. ourselves
2 Pet. 1. 5 *b*. this, giving all dil.
R. V. Judg. 20. 36 against ; **Mat.**
25. 20——: Acts 26. 24 mad;
Pet. 1. 5 for this very cause
Besiege. *Press, straiten.*
Deut. 20. 12 then thou shalt *b*. it

BESOM

1 Sam. 23. 8 to *b.* David and his **men**
2 Sam. 20. 15 came and *b.* him in Ab.
1 K. 16. 17 and they *b.* Tirzah
2 K. 24. 10 and the city was *b.*
1 Chr. 20. 1 came and *b.* Rabbah
Isa. 21. 2 *b.*, O Media, all the
Jer. 21. 4 which *b.* you without
Ezek. 6. 12 *b.* shall die by famine

Besom. *Broom.*
Isa. 14. 23 the *b.* of destruction

Besought. *See* **Beseech.**

Best. *Most excellent.*
Gen. 47. 6 the *b.* of land make dwell
Ex. 22. 5 *b.* of his own field
Num. 18. 12 the *b.* of the oil and wine
Deut. 23. 16 where it liketh him *b.*
2 K. 10. 3 *b.*, and meetest of sons
S. of S. 7. 9 like the *b.* wine
Luke 15. 22 bring . . the *b.* robe
1 Cor. 12. 31 covet . . the *b.* gifts
R. V. 1 Cor. 12. 31 greater

Bestead. *Beset, distressed.*
Isa. 8. 21 hardly *b.* and hungry

Bestir. *Move sharply.*
2 Sam. 5. 24 thou shalt *b.* thyself

Bestow. *Put, place.*
1 K. 10. 26 *b.* in the cities for **char.**
2 Chr. 9. 25 *b.* in the chariot cities
To give, lay up
Ex. 32. 29 may *b.* upon you
Deut. 14. 26 shalt *b.* that money
2 K. 12. 15 be *b.* on workmen
1 Chr. 29. 25 *b.* on him royal maj.
Ez. 7. 20 have occasion to *b.*
Luke 12. 18 I *b.* all my fruits
John 4. 38 whereon ye *b.* no labor
Rom. 16. 6 who *b.* much labor
2 Cor. 8. 1 *b.* on the churches
1 John 3. 1 what love Fath. hath *b.*
R. V. 2 Cor. 8. 1 which hath been
given in; John 4. 38 ye have not
laboured

Bethink. *Turn to heart.*
1 K. 8. 47 shall *b.* themselves in
1 Chr. 6. 37 yet if they *b.* them.

Betimes. *With the dawn.*
Gen. 26. 31 they rose up *b.* and
2 Chr. 36. 15 rising up *b.* and
Job. 8. 5 seek unto God *b.*
Prov. 13. 24 chastenest him *b.*
R. V. 2 Chr. 36. 15 early; Job 8. 5;
24. 5 diligently

Betray. *Give up another.*
1 Chr. 12. 17 to *b.* me to enemies
Mat. 10. 4 who also *b.* him
17. 22; 20. 18; 24. 10; 26. 2; 27. 3
Mark. 3. 19 which also *b* him
Luke 21. 16 *b.* both by parents
John 6. 64 who should *b.* him
1 Cor. 11. 23 night . . he was *b.*
R. V. in N. T. mostly, delivered up

Betrayers. *Who betray.*
Acts 7. 52 ye have been *b.* and murd

Betroth. *Espouse.*
Ex. 21. 8 who hath *b.* her
Lev. 19. 20 a bondmaid *b.* to
Deut. 20. 7 hath *b.* a wife
Hos. 2. 19 I will *b.* thee

Better. *Preferable, more excellent*
Gen. 29. 19 *b.* that I give her
Ex. 14. 12 *b.* for us to serve
Num. 14. 3 *b.* for us to return
Judg. 8. 2 *b.* than the vintage of Abi.
Ruth 4. 15 which is *b.* to thee
1 Sam. 1. 8 am not I *b.* to thee
2 Sam. 18. 3 *b.* that thou succour
1 K. 2. 32 more righteous and *b.*
2 K. 5. 12 *b.* than all . . waters
2 Chr. 21. 13 *b.* than thyself
Ps. 63. 3 kindness . . *b.* than life
Prov. 8. 11 wisdom *b.* than rubies
Eccl. 4. 9 two are *b.* than one
S. of S. 1. 2 love . . *b.* than wine
Isa. 56. 5 name *b.* than of sons or d
Mat. 18. 8 *b.* . . to enter life halt
Mark 9. 42 *b.* . . that a millstone
Luke 5. 39 he saith, The old is *b.*
Rom. 3. 9 what then? are we *b.*
1 Cor. 8. 8 nei. if we eat, are we *b.*
Heb. 6. 9 persuaded *b.* things of
R. V. Mat. 12. 12 of more value
Mark 9. 43; Luke 5. 39; 1 Cor.
15 good

Bettered. *Profited.*
Mark 5. 26 and was nothing *b.*

Between. *Middle, midst, in*

John 2. 3 thy *b.* . . . passed **over me**

Bind. *Tie, fasten, fetter.*
Gen. 37. 7 *b.* sheaves in the field
Ex. 28. 28 shall *b.* the breastplate
Num. 30. 2 oath to *b.* his soul
Deut. 6. 8 *b.* them for a sign
Josh. 2. 18 *b.* this line of scarlet
Judg. 15. 10 to *b.* Samson are we
2 K. 17. 4 *b.* him in prison
2 Chron. 33. 11 and *b.* him with fet
Job 39. 10 cans't thou *b.* the unic.
Ps. 105. 22 to *b.* his princes
Prov. 26. 8 that *b.* stone in sling
Isa. 49. 18 shalt surely *b.* them
Ezek. 3. 25 shall *b.* thee with them
24. 17 *b.* the tire of thine head
Mat. 12. 29 first *b.* the strong man
Mark 5. 3 no man could *b.* him
Luke 13. 16 whom Satan hath *b.*
John 11. 44 *b.* hand and foot with
Acts 9. 2 bring them *b.* unto Jerus.
Rom. 7. 2 woman . . is *b.* by law
1 Cor. 7. 27 Art *b.* unto a wife?
2 Tim. 2. 9 word of God is not *b.*
Heb. 13. 3 bonds as *b.* with them
Rev. 9. 14 *b.* in the great river

Binding. *Binding, edge.*
Ex. 28. 32 a *b.* of woven work
Num. 30. 13 every *b.* oath to afflict

Bird. *Fowl, winged animal.*
Gen. 7. 14 every *b.* of every sort
Lev. 14. 4 cleansed two *b.* alive
Deut. 14. 11 clean *b.* ye shall eat
Job 41. 5 play with him as a *b.*
Ps. 11. 1 Flee as a *b.* to mountain
Prov. 6. 5 as a *b.* from the hand
Eccl. 12. 4 as *b.* that are caught
Isa. 16. 2 as a wandering *b.*
Jer. 4. 25 *b.* of the heavens
Ezek. 39. 4 unto the ravenous *b.*
Hos. 9. 11 fly away like a *b.*
Mat. 8. 20 birds of . . air have **nests**
13. 22; Luke 9. 58
Rom. 1. 23 *b.* and four f. beasts
1 Cor. 15. 39 and another of *b.*
Jas. 3. 7 beasts and of *b.*
Rev. 18. 2 every unclean *b.*

Birth. *Being born, nativity.*
Ex. 28. 10 according to their *b.*
2 K. 19. 3 children are come to . . *b.*
Job 3. 16 hidden . . *b.* I had not
Ps. 58. 8 like untimely *b.* of wom.
Isa. 66. 9 shall I bring to the *b.*
Eccl. 7. 1 than day of one's *b.*
Hos. 9. 11 shall fly from the *b.*
Mat. 1. 18 the *b.* of Jesus Christ
Luke 1. 14 shall rejoice at his *b.*
John 9. 1 which was blind from *b.*
Gal. 4. 19 I travail in *b.*
Rev. 12. 2 cried, travailing in *b.*

Birthday. *Day of birth.*
Gen.40.20 third day . . Pharaoh's *b.d.*
Mat. 14. 6 Herod's *b. d.* was kept
Mark 6. 21 Herod on his *b. d.*

Birthright. *Right of firstborn.*
Gen. 25. 31 sell me . . thy *b. r.*
25; 32; 33, 34; 36; 43. 33
1 Chr. his *b. r.* was given . . sons
Heb. 12. 16 for meat sold his *b. r.*

Bishop. *Overseer.*
Phil. 1. 1 the *b.* and deacons
1 Tim. 3. 1 the office of a *b.*
Tit. 1. 7 *b.* must be blameless
1 Pet. 2. 25 the *b.* of your souls

Bishopric. *Oversight.*
Acts 1. 20 his *b.* let another take
R. V. office

Bit (*n.*). *Bridle, curb.*
Ps. 32. 9 held in with *b.* and bridle
Jas. 3. 3 put *b.* in horses' mouths

Bit (*v.*). *See* **Bite.**

Bite. *Seize with teeth.*
Gen. 49. 17 a serpent that *b.*
Num. 21. 9 serpent had *b.* any **man**
Prov. 23. 32 it *b.* like a serpent
Eccl. 10. 8 a serpent shall *b.*
Jer. 8. 17 and they shall *b.* you
Am. 5. 19 and a serpent *b.* him
Mic. 3. 5 that *b.* with their teeth
Gal. 5. 15 if ye *b.* and devour

Bitten. *Bitten.*
Num. 21. 8 every one that is *b.*
Job 18. 12 his strength . . hunger *b.*

Bitter. *Bitter, acrid.*
Gen. 27. 34 cried with . . *b.* cry
Ex. 1. 14 made their lives *b*

BETWIXT

Gen. 15. 17 lamp that passed *b.*
Ex. 28. 33 bells of gold *b.*
1 K. 18. 21 halt *b.* two opinions
Ezek. 10. 2 go in *b.* the wheels
Mat. 18. 15 *b.* thee and him
Luke 11. 51 perished *b.* the altar
John 3. 25 *b.* some of John's dis.
Acts 12. 6 Peter was sleeping *b.*
Rom. 1. 24 dishonor . . bodies *b.*
1 Cor. 6. 5 able to judge *b.*

Betwixt. *Between.*
Gen. 31. 37 judge *b.* us both
Job. 36. 32 cloud that cometh *b.*
Phil. 1. 23 I am in a strait *b.* two
R. V. Job 36. 32 strike the mark

Bewail. *Weep, wail, lament.*
Lev. 10. 6 *b.* the burning which
Deut. 21. 13 *b.* her father and mother
Judg. 11. 37 *b.* my virginity
Isa. 16. 9 *b.* with weeping
Jer. 4. 31 daughter of Zion *b.*
Luke 8. 52 wept, and *b.* her
2 Cor. 12. 21 I shall *b.* many
Rev. 18. 9 kings . . shall *b.* her
R. V. Rev. 18. 9 weep; 2 Cor. 12. 21
should mourn for.

Beware. *Watch, take heed.*
Gen. 24. 6 *b.* thou that . . bring
Ex. 23. 21 *b.* of him, and obey
Deut. 6. 12 *b.* lest thou forget
Judg. 13. 4 *b.* I pray thee
2 Sam. 18.12 *b.* that none touch
2 K. 6. 9 *b.* that thou pass
Mat. 7. 15 *b.* of false prophets
Mark 8. 15 *b.* of the leaven of Phar.
Luke 12. 15 *b.* of covetousness
Acts 13. 40 *b.* therefore, lest that
Col. 2. 8 *b.* lest any . . spoil you
2 Pet. 3. 17 *b.* lest ye also fall
R. V. Ex. 23. 21; Col. 2. 8 take
heed; Luke 12. 15 keep yourselves
from.

Bewitched. *Eye-smitten, charmed.*
Acts 8. 9 *b.* the people of Samaria
8. 11 *b.* them with sorceries
Gal. 3. 1 who hath *b.* you

Bewray. *Reveal, betray.*
Isa. 16. 3 *b.* not him that wandereth
Prov. 27. 16 hand which *b.* itself
Mat. 26. 73 thy speech *b.* thee
R. V. Prov. 27. 16 encountereth
Prov. 29. 24 uttereth

Beyond. *Over, other side.*
Gen. 35. 21 spread his tent *b.* Edar
Deut. 3. 20 given them *b.* Jordan
Josh 9. 10 the two kings . . *b.*
Judg. 5. 17 Gilead abode *b.* Jordan
1 Sam. 20. 22 arrows are *b.* thee
2 Sam. 10. 16 that were *b.* the river
1 K. 4. 12 the place that is *b.* Jokne.
2 Chr. 20. 2 from *b.* the sea
Neh. 2. 7 governors *b.* the river
Isa. 9. 1 by way of sea, *b.* Jordan
Jer. 22. 19 forth *b.* the gates
Mat. 19. 1 coasts . . *b.* Jordan
Mark 3. 8 Jer., and . . *b.* Jordan
John 1. 28 Bethabara *b.* Jordan
Acts 7. 43 carry away, *b.* Babylon
2 Cor. 8. 3 their power of
R. V. 1 Thes. 4. 6 transgress

Bid. *Say, invite, command.*
Gen. 43. 17 did as Joseph *b.*
Ex. 16. 24 till morn., as Moses *b.*
Num. 14. 10 *b.* stone them with st.
Josh. 6. 10 until I *b.* you shout
1 Sam. 9. 27. *b.* the servant pass
2 Sam. 1. 18 *b.* them teach the chil.
2 K. 4. 24 except I *b.* thee
Esth. 4. 15 Esther *b.* them return
Mat. 22. 3 call them that were *b.*
Luke 7. 39 the Pharisee which *b.*
Acts 18. 21 *b.* them farewell
2 John 10 *b.* him God speed

Bidding. *R. V. Council.*
1 Sam. 22. 14 David goeth at thy *b.*

Bier. *Bier.*
2 Sam. 3. 31 David . . followed the *b.*
Luke 7. 14 he . . touched the *b.*

Bill. *Book, writing.*
Deut. 24. 1 a *b.* of divorcement
Isa. 50. 1 where is the *b.* of divorce
Jer. 3. 8 given her a *b.* of divorce
Luke 16. 6 take thy *b.*, and sit down
R. V. Luke 16. 6 bond

Billow. *Heap, breaker.*
Ps. 42. 7 thy *b.* are gone

Num. 5. 18 *b.* water that causeth
Deut. 32. 32 their clusters are *b.*
2 K. 14. 26 that it was very *b.*
Esth. 4. 1 a loud and *b.* cry
Job 3. 20 and life unto the *b.* soul
Ps. 64. 3 arrows, even *b.* words
Prov. 5. 4 is *b.* as wormwood
Eccl. 7. 26 more *b.* than death
Isa. 5. 20 put *b.* for sweet
Jer. 2. 19 an evil thing and *b.*
Ezek. 27. 31 *b.* of h. and *b.* wailing
Am. 8. 10 the end thereof as a *b.* day
Hab. 1. 6 that *b.* and hasty nation
Col. 3. 19 love .. wives, and be not *b.*
Jas. 3. 11 sweet water and *b.*
Rev. 10. 9 make thy belly *b.*
R. V. Job 23. 2 rebellious

Bitterly. *Sharply, mournfully.*
Judg. 5. 23 curse ye *b.* the inhab.
Ruth. 1. 20 A. hath dealt very *b.*
Isa. 22. 4 I will weep *b.*
Ezek. 27. 30 shall cry *b.*, cast dust
Hos. 12. 14 E. provoked him *b.*
Mat. 26. 75 went out and wept *b.*
Luke 22. 62 Pet. went out and w. *b.*

Bittern. R. V. *Porcupine.*
Isa. 14. 23 possession for a *b.*
34. 11 the *b.* shall possess it
Zeph. 2. 14 the *b.* shall lodge

Bitterness. *Being bitter.*
1 Sam. 1. 10 she was in *b.* of soul
2 Sam. 2. 26 it will be *b.* in end
Job 9. 18 filleth me with *b.*
Prov. 14. 10 the heart knoweth .. *b.*
Isa. 38. 15 the *b.* of my soul
Lam. 3. 15 filled me with *b.*
Ezek. 3. 14 I went in *b.* of spirit
Zech. 12. 10 shall be in *b.* for him
Acts 8. 23 in the gall of *b.*
Rom. 3. 14 full of cursing and *b.*
Eph. 4. 31 let all *b.* be put away
Heb. 12. 15 lest any root of *b.*

Black. *Dark, swarthy, not white.*
Lev. 13. 31 no *b.* hair in it
1 K. 18. 45 the heaven was *b.*
Esth. 1. 6 pavement of .. *b.* marble
Job 30. 30 skin is *b.* upon me
Prov. 7. 9 in the *b.* and dark
S. of S. 1. 5 I am *b.*, but comely
Jer. 4. 28 shall the heavens be *b.*
Lam. 5. 10 our skin was *b.*
Mat. 5. 36 one hair white or *b.*
Rev. 6. 5 and lo a *b.* horse
R. V. S. of S. 1. 6 swarthy

Blackish. *Dark.*
Job 6. 16 *b.* by reason of ice

Blackness. *Darkness.*
Job 3. 5 let the *b.* of the day terrify it
Isa. 50. 3 clothe the heavens with *b.*
Joel 2. 6 faces shall gather *b.*
Nah. 2. 10 the faces .. gather *b.*
Heb. 12. 18 are not come to *b.*
Jude 13 to whom is reserved *b.*

Blade. *Stalk, cutting part.*
Judg. 3. 22 fat closed upon the *b.*
Job 31. 22 from my shoulder *b.*
Mat. 13. 26 when the *b.* was sprung
Mark. 4. 28 first the *b.*, then the ear.

Blains. *Swellings.*
Ex. 9. 9, 10 breaking forth with *b.*

Blame (*n.*). *Censure.*
Gen. 43. 9 let me bear the *b.*
44. 32 bear the *b.* to my father
Eph. 1. 4 be holy and without *b.*
R. V. Eph. 1. 4 blemish

Blame (*v.*). *Censure.*
2 Cor. 6. 3 ministry be not *b.*
Gal. 2. 11 he was to be *b.*

Blameless. *Without blame.*
Gen. 44. 10 and ye shall be *b.*
Josh. 2. 17 will be *b.* of thine oath
Judg. 15. 3 shall I be more *b.*
Mat. 12. 5 profane sab. and are *b.*
Luke 1. 6 walking in all .. *b.*
1 Cor. 1. 8 *b.* in the day of L. J. C.
Phil. 2. 15 be *b.* and harmless
1 Thes. 5. 23 be preserved *b.*
1 Tim. 3. 2 bishop must be *b.*
Tit. 1. 6 if any be *b.*
2 Pet. 3. 14 ye may be found *b.*
R. V. Mat. 12. 5 guiltless; 1 Tim.
3. 2; 5. 7 without reproach

Blaspheme. *Revile, speak impiously.*
Lev. 24. 11 woman's son *b.* Lord
1 K. 21. 10 *b.* God and the king

---

2 K. 19. 6 servants of k. have *b.* me
Ps. 44. 16 reproacheth and *b.*
Isa. 37. 6 wherewith .. servants *b.*
Ezek. 20. 27 your fathers have *b.*
Mat. 9. 3 scribes said, This man *b.*
Mark 3. 28 wherewith they shall *b.*
Luke 12. 10 unto him that *b.* Hol. G.
John 10. 36 thou *b.* because I said
Acts 13. 45 contradicting and *b.*
Rom. 2. 24 the name of God is *b.*
1 Tim. 1. 20 learn not to *b.*
Tit. 2. 5 that word of G. be not *b.*
Jas. 2. 7 opened his mouth to *b.*
Rev. 16. 11 *b.* the God of heaven

Blasphemer. *Who speaks impiously.*
Acts 19. 37 not yet *b.* of your god.
1 Tim. 1. 13 who was before a *b.*
2 Tim. 3. 2 lovers of selves, *b.*
R. V. 2 Tim. 3. 2 railers

Blasphemies. *Impious speakings.*
Ezek. 35. 12 heard all thy *b.*
Mat. 15. 19 out of heart proceed *b.*
Mark 2. 7 this man thus speak *b.*
Luke 5. 21 who .. speaketh *b.*
Rev. 13. 5 speaking gr. things and *b.*

Blasphemous. *Speaking impiously.*
Acts 6. 11 speak *b.* words against M.

Blasphemously. *Impiously.*
Luke 22. 65 other things *b.* spake

Blasphemy. *Impious speakings.*
2 K. 19. 3 day of trouble and *b.*
Mat. 12. 31 all manner of sin and *b.*
Mark. 7. 22 out of heart .. pro. *b.*
John 10. 33 we stone thee for *b.*
Col. 3. 8 also put off malice, *b.*, and
Rev. 2. 9 the *b.* of them which say
R. V. 2 K. 19. 3; Isa. 37. 3 contumely; Mark 7. 22 ; Col. 3. 8 railing

Blast. *Breath, wind.*
Ex. 15. 8 the *b.* of thy nostrils
2 Sam. 22. 16 the *b.* of the breath of
2 K. 19. 7 send a *b.* upon him
Job 4. 9 by *b.* of God they perish
Ps. 18. 15 *b.* of the breath of nostrils
Isa. 25. 4 *b.* of the terrible ones

Blasted. *Blighted.*
Gen. 41. 6 *b.* with the east wind
2 K. 19. 26 *b.* before it be grown up
Isa. 37. 27 *b.* before it be grown up

Blasting. *Blighting.*
Deut. 28. 22 with the sword and *b.*
1 K. 8. 37 pestilence, *b.*, mildew
2 Chr. 6. 28 if there be *b.* or mildew
Am. 4. 9 smitten you with *b.*
Hag. 2. 17 smote you with *b.*

Blaze. R. V. *Spread.*
Mark 1. 45 *b.* abroad the matter

Bleating. *Voice, sound.*
Judg. 5. 16 the *b.* of the flocks
1 Sam. 15. 14 this *b.* of the sheep
R. V. Judg. 5. 16 pipings for

Blemish. *Spot, defect.*
Ex. 12. 5 lamb shall be without *b.*
Lev. 1. 3 offer male without *b.*
Num. 6. 14 one he lamb without *b.*
Deut. 15. 21 if there be *b.* therein
2 Sam. 14. 25 no *b.* in Absalom
Ezek. 43. 22 a kid without *b.*
Dan. 1. 4 children in whom no *b.*
Eph. 5. 27 be holy and without *b.*
1 Pet. 1. 19 of lamb without *b.*
2 Pet. 2. 13 spots they are and *b.*

Bless. *Bestow favour, prosper, invoke.*
Gen. 1. 22 God *b.* them, saying
Ex. 12. 32 begone ; and *b.* me also
Lev. 9. 23 Aaron . . *b.* the people
Num. 6. 23 ye shall *b.* the children
Deut. 1. 11 the Lord *b.* you
Josh. 8. 33 *b.* the people of Israel
Judg. 5. 9 *b.* ye the Lord
Ruth 2. 4 the Lord *b.* thee
1 Sam. 2. 20 Eli *b.* Elkanah
2 Sam. 6. 11 the Lord *b.* Obed-edom
1 K. 1. 47 servants came to *b.*
1 Chr. 4. 10 thou wouldest *b.* me
2 Chr. 6. 3 and *b.* the whole cong.
Neh. 8. 6 Ezra *b.* the Lord
Job 1. 10 thou hast *b.* the work
Ps. 5. 12 Lord wilt *b.* the righteous
10. 3; 16. 7; 26. 12; 28. 9; 29. 11
Prov. 3. 33 but he *b.* the habitation
Isa. 19. 25 the Lord shall *b.*, saying
Jer. 31. 23 the Lord *b.* thee. O hab.

Hag. 2. 19 this day will I *b.* you
To speak well of.
Mat. 5. 44 *b.* them that hate you
Mark 6. 41 *b.*, and brake the loaves
Luke 2. 28 and *b.* God, and said
Acts 3. 26 sent him to *b.* you
Rom. 12. 14 *b.* them which per. you
1 Cor. 4. 12 being reviled, we *b.*
Gal. 3. 9 are *b.* with faithful Abrah.
Eph. 1. 3 Father .. who hath *b.* us
Heb. 6. 14 b. I will *b.* thee
Jas. 3. 9 therewith *b.* we God
1 Pet. 3. 9 but contrariwise *b.*

Blessed. *Happy, blessed.*
Gen. 9. 26 *b.* be the Lord God
Ex. 18. 10 *b.* be the Lord
Num. 22. 12 for they are *b.*
Deut. 7. 14 *b.* above all people
Judg. 17. 2 *b.* be thou of the Lord
Ruth 2. 20 *b.* be he of the Lord
1 Sam. 15. 13 *b.* be thou of the Lord
2 Sam. 2. 5 ; 1 K. 1. 48 ; 1 Chr. 16.
36 ; 2 Chr. 2. 12
Ps. 18. 46 the Lord liveth and *b.*
Prov. 5. 18 thy fountain be *b.*
Isa. 19. 25 *b.* be Egypt my people
Jer. 17. 7 *b.* is the man that trusteth
Ezek. 3. 12 *b.* be the glory of Lord
Mat. 5. 3. *b.* . are the poor in spirit
Mark 11. 9 *b.* is he that cometh
Luke 1. 45 *b.* is she that believed
John 20. 29 *b.* they that have not seen
Acts 20. 35 more *b.* to give than re.
Rom. 4. 7 *b.* they whose iniquities
1 Tim. 1. 11 gospel of the *b.* God
2 Cor. 1. 3 *b.* be God, even the F.
Eph. 1. 3 *b.* be the God and Father
Tit. 2. 13 looking for that *b.* hope
Jas. 1. 12 *b.* is the man that endureth
1 Pet. 1. 3 *b.* be the God and Father
Rev. 1. 3 *b.* is he that readeth

Blessedness. *Blessed state.*
Rom. 4. 6 the *b.* of the man unto
Gal. 4. 15 where is then the *b.* that

Blessing. *Divine favor, mercy.*
Gen. 12. 2 and thou shalt be a *b.*
Ex. 32. 29 bestow upon you a *b.*
Lev. 25. 21 command my *b.* upon
Deut. 11. 26 I set before you .. a *b.*
Josh. 15. 19 answered, Give me a *b.*
1 Sam. 25. 27 this *b.* brought be given
2 Sam. 7. 29 with thy *b.* let be bles.
2 K. 5. 15 therefore take a *b.*
Neh. 9. 5 exalted above all *b.*
Job 29. 13 *b.* of him .. ready to per.
Ps. 3. 8 Lord, thy *b.* is upon thy peo.
Prov. 10. 6 *b.* are upon head of just
Isa. 19. 24 a *b.* in the midst of land
Ezek. 34. 26 shall be showers of *b.*
Joel 2. 14 leave a *b.* behind
Zech. 8. 13 ye shall be a *b.*
Mal. 2. 2 I will curse your *b.*
Rom. 15. 29 fulness of the *b.* of gosp.
1 Cor. 10. 16 the cup of *b.* we bless
Gal. 3. 14 the *b.* of Abraham
Eph. 1. 3 blessed with all spiritual *b.*
Heb. 6. 7 earth receiveth *b.*
Jas. 3. 10 proceedeth *b.* and cursing
1 Pet. 3. 9 that ye should inherit a *b.*
Rev. 5. 12 receive honor, .. and *b.*

Blew. *See* **Blow**

Blind. *Closed, contracted.*
Ex. 4. 11 or who maketh the.. *b.*
Lev. 19. 14 put s. block before the *b.*
Deut. 28. 29 as the *b.* gropeth
2 Sam. 5. 6 take away the *b.* and l.
Job. 29. 15 I was eyes to the *b.*
Ps. 146. 8 openeth the eyes of the *b.*
Isa. 29. 18 the *b.* shall see out
Jer. 31. 8 gath. the *b.* and the lame
Lam. 4. 14 wandered as *b.* men
Mal. 1. 8 offer the *b.* for sacrifice
Destitute of sight, blind.
Mat. 9. 27 two *b.* men followed
11. 5; 12. 22; 15. 14; 21. 14; 23 16
Mark 8. 22 they bring a *b.* man
Luke 18. 35 a certain *b.* man sat
John 9. 17 say unto the *b.* man
Acts 13. 11 and thou shalt be *b.*
Rom. 2. 19 a guide of the *b.*
2 Pet. 1. 9 he that lacketh .. is *b.*
Rev. 3. 17 poor, and *b.*, and naked

Blind (*v.*). *Make blind.*
Ex. 23. 8 for the gift *b.* the wise
Deut. 16. 19 gift doth *b.* the eyes
1 Sam. 12. 3 bribe to *b.* mine eyes

587

John 12. 40 he hath *b.* their **eyes**
Rom. 11. 7 the rest were *b.*
2 Cor. 3. 14 their minds were *b.*
1 John 2. 11 darkness hath *b.* . . eyes
R. V. Rom. 11. 7 ; 2 Cor. 3. 14 hardened

Blindfold. *Cover round.*
Luke 22. 64 when they had *b.* him

Blindness. *Sightlessness.*
Gen. 19. 11 smote the men . . with *b.*
Deut. 28. 28 smite thee with *b.*
2 K. 6. 18 smote them with *b.*
Zech. 12. 4 smite every horse with *b.*
Rom. 11. 25 ; *b.* . . is happen. to Is.
Eph. 4. 18 because of the *b.* of
R. V. Rom. 11. 25 ; Eph. 4. 18 hardening

Blood. *Blood.*
Gen. 4. 10 thy brother's *b.* crieth
Ex. 4. 9 water shall become *b.*
Lev. 1. 5 and sprinkle the *b.*
Num. 18. 17 shalt sprinkle their *b.*
Deut. 12. 16 shalt not eat the *b.*
Josh. 2. 19 his *b.* be upon his head
Judg. 9. 24 their *b.* be upon Abim.
1 Sam. 14. 33 they eat with the *b.*
2 Sam. 1. 22 the *b.* of the slain
1 K. 2. 5 shed the *b.* of war
2 K. 3. 22 water red as *b.*
1 Chr. 11. 19 shall I drink the *b.*
2 Chr. 19. 10 between *b.* and *b.*
Job 16. 18 cover not thou my *b.*
Ps. 9. 12 maketh inquisition for *b.*
Prov. 1. 11 let us lay wait for *b.*
Isa. 1. 11 I delight not in *b.*
Jer. 2. 34 *b.* found of the souls of in.
Lam. 4. 13 shed the *b.* of the just
Ezek. 3. 18 *b.* will I require
Hos. 1. 4 will avenge the *b.* of
Joel. 2. 30 earth, *b.*, and fire
Mic. 3. 10 build up Zion with *b.*
Hab. 2. 8 because of men's *b.*
Zeph. 1. 7 *b.* shall be poured out
Zech. 9. 7 will take away his *b.*
Mat. 16. 17 *b.* hath not revealed
Mark 5. 25 which had an issue of *b.*
Luke 11. 50 *b.* of all the prophets
John 1. 13 born not of *b.* nor flesh
Acts 1. 19 Aceldama, the field of *b.*
Rom. 3. 15 feet swift to shed *b.*
1 Cor. 10. 16 communion of the *b.*
Gal. 1. 16 conferred not with f. and *b.*
Eph. 1. 7 redemption through his *b.*
Col. 1. 20 peace through the *b.* of
Heb. 2. 14 partakers of flesh and *b.*
1 Pet. 1. 2 *b.* of Jesus Christ
1 John 1. 7. *b.* of J. C. cleanseth
Rev. 1. 5 washed us in his own *b.*

Bloodguiltiness.
Ps. 51. 14 deliver me from *b. g.*

Bloodthirsty.
Prov. 29. 10 *b. t.* hate the upright

Bloody. *Blood-stained, sanguinary.*
Ex. 4. 25 a *b.* husband art thou
2 Sam. 16. 8 thou art a *b.* man
Ps. 5. 6 Lord will abhor the *b.*
Ezek. 7. 23 land full of *b.* crimes
Nah. 3. 1 Woe to the *b.* city
Acts 28. 8 Pub., lay sick of a *b.* flux
R. V. Ps. 5. 6 ; 55. 23 ; 59. 2 ; 139. 19 bloodthirsty ; Acts 28. 8 dysentery.

Bloom. *Shine, sprout.*
Num. 17. 8 A's rod *b.* blossoms

Blossom (n). *Flower, sprout*
Gen. 40. 10 her *b.* shot forth
Num. 17. 8 A's rod bloomed *b.*
Isa. 5. 24 their *b.* shall go up

Blossom (*v.*). *Shine, break forth.*
Num. 17. 5 man's rod . . shall *b.*
Isa. 27. 6 Israel. shall *b.* and bud
Ezek. 7. 10 the rod hath *b.*
Hab. 3. 17 fig tree shall not *b.*
R. V. Num. 17. 5 bud.

Blot (n). *Spot.*
Job 31. 7 if any *b.* hath cleaved to h.
Prov. 9. 7 that rebuke wick. get. *b.*
R. V. Job 31. 7 spot

Blot (*v.*). *Rub or wipe off.*
Ex. 32. 32 *b.* me, I pray thee, out of
Num. 5. 23 shall *b.* them out
Deut. 9. 14 des. and *b.* out their name
2 K. 14. 27 would *b.* out the name
Neh. 4. 5 let not their sin be *b.* out
Ps. 51. 1 *b.* out my transgressions
Isa. 43. 25 I am he that *b.* out

Acts 3. 19 your sins may be *b.* out
Col. 2. 14 *b.* out the handwriting of
Rev. 3. 5 not *b.* out his name out of
Blow (n). *Stroke, smiting.*
Ps. 39. 10 consumed by the *b.*
Jer. 14. 17 broken with a grievous *b.*
Blow (*v.*). *Blow, breathe.*
Ex. 15. 10 didst *b.* with thy wind
S. of S. 4. 16 *b.* upon my garden
Isa. 54. 16 the smith that *b.* coals
Ezek. 22. 20 *b.* the fire upon it
Hag. 1. 9 I did *b.* upon it
Mat. 7. 25 floods came, and winds *b.*
Luke 12. 55 see the south wind *b.*
John 3. 8 wind *b.* where it listeth
Acts 27. 13 south wind *b.* softly
Rev. 7. 1 wind should not *b.* on earth
To strike, strike up
Num. 20. 5 when ye *b.* an alarm
Josh. 6. 4 *b.* with the trumpets
Judg. 3. 27 he *b.* a trumpet
1 Sam. 13. 3 Saul *b.* the trumpet
2 Sam. 2. 28 Joab *b.* a trumpet
1 K. 1. 34 *b.* ye with the trumpet
2 K. 9. 13 *b.* with trumpets, **saying**
Ps. 81. 3 *b.* up the trumpet in
Isa. 18. 3 when he *b.* a trumpet
Jer. 4. 5 *b.* ye the trumpet
Ezek. 7. 14 they have *b.* the **trumpet**
Hos. 5. 8 *b.* ye the cornet in Gib.
Zech. 9. 14 Lord God shall *b.* **trum.**
Blowing. *Striking, shouting.*
Lev. 23. 24 a memorial of *b.*
Num. 29. 1 it is a day of *b.*
Josh. 6. 9 *b.* with the trumpets
Blown. *Breathed on, struck.*
Job 20. 26 fire not *b.* shall **consume**
Isa. 27. 13 trumpet shall be *b.*
Amos. 3. 6 shall a trumpet be *b.*
Blue. *Blue or violet.*
Ex. 25. 4 *b.*, and purple, and **scar.**
Num. 4. 7 spread a cloth of *b.*
2 Chr. 2. 7 and crimson, and *b.*
Esth. 1. 6 green and *b.* hangings
Jer. 10. 9 *b.* and purple their **cloth.**
Ezek. 23. 6 were clothed with *b.*
Blueness. R. V. *Stripes.*
Prov. 20. 30 the *b.* of a wound
Blunt. *Weak, dull.*
Eccl. 10. 10 if the iron be *b.*
Blush. *Cut in, flush.*
Ez. 9. 6 am ashamed and *b.*
Jer. 6. 15 neither could they *b.*
Boar. *Boar, swine.*
Ps. 80. 13 *b.* out of the wood
Board. *Board, plank, rib.*
Ex. 26. 15 thou shalt make *b.*
  26. 16–29 ; 35. 11 ; 36. 20–34 ; 40. 18
Num. 4. 31 *b.* of the tabernacle
1 K. 6. 9 with beams and *b.*
S. of S. 8. 9 enclose her with *b.*
Ezek. 27. 5 ship *b.* of fir trees
Acts 27. 44 and the rest, some on *b.*
R. V. Ex. 27. 8 ; 38. 7 ; 1 K. 6. 9 ; Ezek. 27. 5 ; Acts 27. 44 planks
Boast (n). *Proud speech, brag.*
Ps. 32. 4 shall make her *b.*
Rom. 2. 17 maketh thy *b.* of God
Boast (*v.*). *Brag about, vaunt.*
1 K. 20. 11 let not him . . *b.*
2 Chr. 25. 19 lifteth thee up to *b.*
Ps. 10. 3 the wicked *b.* of desire
Prov. 27. 1 *b.* not of to morrow
Isa. 10. 15 shall the axe *b.* itself
Acts 5. 36 Theudas *b.* himself
Rom. 11. 18 *b.* not against the **bran.**
2 Cor. 7. 14 if I have *b.* any thing
Eph. 2. 9 lest any man should *b.*
Jas. 3. 5 and *b.* great things
R. V. Rom. 11. 18 ; 2 Cor. **9. 2 ;** 10. 8 glory
Boaster. R. V. *Boastful.*
Rom. 1. 30 *b.*, inventors of **evil**
2 Tim. 3. 2 covetous, *b.*, proud
Boasting. R. V. *Glorying.*
Rom. 3. 27 where is *b.* then
2 Cor. 7. 14 even so our *b.*
  8. 24 ; 9. 4 ; 11. 10, 17
Jas. 4. 16 rejoice in your *b.*
Boat. *Skiff, water-craft.*
2 Sam. 19. 8 went over a ferry *b.*
John 6. 22 none other *b.* there
Acts 27. 16 to come by the *b.*
Bodily. *In person, in flesh.*
Luke 3. 22 in *b.* shape like dove
2 Cor. 10. 10 *b.* presence is weak

1 Tim. 4. 8 *b.* exercise prof. little
Col. 2. 9 fulness of the Godhead *b.*
Body. *Belly, back, flesh.*
Gen. 47. 18 nought left but their *b.*
Deut. 28. 4 the fruit of thy *b.*
1 Sam. 31. 10 they fastened his *b.*
1 Chr. 10. 12 took away *b.* of Saul
Neh. 9. 37 dominion over our *b.*
Job 13. 12 your *b.* to *b.* of clay
Ps. 132. 11 of the fruit of thy *b.* will
Prov. 5. 11 thy flesh and thy *b.*
Isa. 10. 18 consu. both soul and *b.*
Ezek. 10. 12 *b.* and their backs
Dan. 10. 6 *b.* like the beryl
Carcase, fallen thing.
Lev. 21. 11 nei. go to any dead *b.*
Num. 6. 6 come at no dead *b.*
Ps. 79. 2 dead *b.* of thy servants.
Isa. 26. 19 with my dead *b.* arise
Jer. 26. 23 dead *b.* into graves
Rev. 11. 8 dead *b.* in the streets
Entire physical part.
Mat. 5. 29 whole *b.* shall be cast
  6. 22 ; 10. 28 ; 14. 12 ; 26. 12 ; 27. 52
Mark 5. 29 felt in her *b.* that
Luke 11. 34 the light of the *b.*
  11. 36 ; 12. 4 ; 17. 37 ; 22. 19 ; 23. 52
John 2. 21 the temple of the *b.*
Acts 9. 40 turning to the *b.* said
Rom. 1. 24 dishonour their own *b.*
1 Cor. 5. 3 as absent in *b.*
2 Cor. 4. 10 bearing about in the *b.*
Gal. 6. 17 I bear in my *b.* marks of
Eph. 1. 23 which is his *b.*
Phil. 1. 20 magnified in my *b.*
Col. 1. 18 the head of the *b.*, the ch.
1 Thes. 5. 23 whole *b.* be preserved
Heb. 10. 5 *b.* hast thou prepared
Jas. 2. 16 things needful to the *b.*
1 Pet. 2. 24 sins in his own *b.*
Jude 9 disputed about the *b.*
R. V. Isa. 51. 23 back ; Mat. 14. 12
  15. 45 corpse
Boil (n.). *Burning, inflammation*
Ex. 9. 9 a *b.* breaking forth
Lev. 13. 18 in which was a *b.*
2 K. 20. 7 and laid it on the *b.*
Job 2. 7 smote Job with sore *b.*
Isa. 38. 21 lay plaister upon the *b.*
Boil (*v.*). *Bubble, seethe.*
Lev. 8. 31 *b.* the flesh at door of tab.
1 K. 19. 21 *b.* their flesh with instr.
2 K. 6. 29 we *b.* my son and eat him
Job 30. 27 my bowels *b.*
Isa. 64. 2 causeth waters to *b.*
Ezek. 46. 20 where priests shall *b.*
Boisterous. *Strong.*
Mat. 14. 30 saw the wind *b.*
R. V. ——
Bold. *Brave, courageous.*
Prov. 28. 1 righteous are *b.* as a lion
Acts 13. 46 and Barnabas waxed *b.*
Rom. 10. 20 Esaias is very *b.*
2 Cor. 10. 1 being absent am *b.*
Phil. 1. 14 more *b.* to speak
1 Thes. 2. 2 *b.* in our God to speak
Phile. 8 be much *b.* in Christ
R. V. 2 Cor. 10. 1 good courage
Boldly. *Freely, bravely.*
Gen. 34. 25 came upon the city *b.*
Mark 15. 43 Joseph went in *b.*
John 7. 26 But, lo, he speaketh *b.*
Acts 9. 27 preached *b.* at Damascus
Rom. 15. 15 written the more *b.*
Eph. 6. 19 open my mouth *b.*
Heb. 4. 16 come *b.* unto the throne
R. V. 7. 26 openly ; Eph. 6. 19 ——;
  Heb. 13. 6 with good courage
Boldness. *Free utterance.*
Acts 4. 13 the *b.* of Peter and John
2 Cor. 7. 4 great is my *b.* of speech
Eph. 3. 12 in whom we have *b.*
Phil. 1. 20 that with all *b.*
1 Tim. 3. 13 great *b.* in the faith
Heb. 10. 19 having therefore . . *b.*
1 John 4. 17 *b.* in the day of judg.
R. V. Eccl. 8. 1 hardness
Bolled. *Calix of flowers.*
Ex. 9. 31 the flax was *b.*
Bolster. *Place of the head.*
1 Sam. 19. 13 a pillow . . for his *b.*
  19. 10 ; 26. 7, 11, 12, 16
R. V. head, at the head
Bolt. *Bind up.*
2 Sam. 13. 17, 18 and *b.* the door
Bond. *Slave, servant.*

1 Cor. 12. 13 whether *b.* or free
Gal. 3. 28 neither *b.* nor free
Eph. 6. 8 whether he be *b.* or free
Col. 3. 11 Scythian *b.* nor free
Rev. 13. 16 both free and *b.* to rec.
Band, bond, fetter.
Num. 30. 2 bind . . with a *b.*
Job 12. 18 he looseth the *b.*
Ps. 116. 16 hast loosened thy *b.*
Jer. 5. 5 have . . burst the *b.*
Ezek. 20. 37 bring you into *b.*
Nah. 1. 13 I burst thy *b.*
Luke 13. 16 loosed from this *b.*
Acts 8. 23 thou art in the *b.*
Eph. 6. 20 ambassador in *b.*
Phil. 1. 7 as both in my *b.*
Col. 4. 18 remember my *b.*
2 Tim. 2. 9 suff. trouble even to *b.*
Phile. 10 begotten in my *b.*
Heb. 10. 34 compassion . . in my *b.*
Bondage. *Service, servitude.*
Ex. 1. 14 bitter with hard *b.*
  2. 23; 6. 6; 13. 3; 20. 2
Deut. 5. 6 from the house of *b.*
Josh. 24. 17; Judg. 6. 8
Neh. 5. 18 the *b.* was heavy
Isa. 14. 3 rest from the hard *b.*
John 8. 33 were never in *b.* to man
Acts 7. 7 they shall be in *b.*
1 Cor. 7. 15 brother is not under *b.*
2 Cor. 11. 20 bring you into *b.*
Gal. 4. 24 which gendereth to *b.*
2 Pet. 2. 19 is he brought in *b.*
R. V. Ex. 1. 14; Isa. 14. 3; service
Bondmaid. *Handmaid.*
Lev. 19. 20 whoso lieth with *b. m.*
Gal. 4. 22 R. V. handmaid
Bondman. *Slave, servant.*
Gen. 43. 18 take us for *b. m.*
Lev. 25. 42 not be sold as *b. m.*
Deut. 6. 21 Pharaoh's *b. m.* in E.
Josh. 9. 23 freed from being *b. m.*
1 K. 9. 22 Solomon make no *b. m.*
2 K. 4. 1 take . . sons to be *b. m.*
2 Chr. 28. 10 keep for *b. m.*
Ez. 9. 9 for we were *b. m.*
Esth. 7. 4 been sold for *b. m.*
Jer. 34. 13 out of the house of *b. m.*
Rev. 6. 15 every *b. m.* and *f. m.*
R. V. Deut. 7. 8; Jer. 34. 13 bondage; 1 K. 9. 22 bondservants
Bondservant. *Servant-service.*
Lev. 25. 39 serve as a *b. s.*
Bondservice. *Slave-service.*
1 K. 9. 21 levy tribute of *b. s.*
Bondwoman. *Handmaid, slave.*
Gen. 21. 10 cast out this *b. w.*
Deut. 28. 68 sold for *b. w.*
2 Chr. 28. 10 to keep *b. m.* and *b. w.*
Esth. 7. 4 been sold for *b. w.*
Gal. 4. 23 he who was of the *b. w.*
R. V. Gal. 4. 23, 30, 31, handmaid
Bone. *Body, substance, bone.*
Gen. 2. 23 now *b.* of my *b.*
Ex. 12. 46 neither . . break a *b.*
Num. 12 nor break any *b.*
Josh. 24. 32 the *b.* of Joseph buried
Judg. 9. 2 I am your *b.* and flesh
1 Sam. 31. 13 they took their *b.*
2 Sam. 5. 1 thy *b.* and flesh
1 K. 13. 2 men's *b.* shall be burnt
2 K. 13. 21 touched the *b.* of Elisha
1 Chr. 10. 12 they buried their *b.*
2 Chr. 34. 5 he burnt the *b.* of priests
Job 2. 5 touch his *b.* and flesh
Ps. 6. 2 for my *b.* are vexed
  22. 14; 31. 10; 32. 3; 34. 20; 35. 10
Prov. 3. 8 and marrow to thy *b.*
Eccl. 11. 5 nor how *b.* do grow
Isa. 38. 13 he break all my *b.*
Jer. 8. 1 the *b.* of the kings
Lam. 1. 13 he sent fire into my *b.*
Ezek. 6. 5 will scatter your *b.*
Am. 2. 1 he burned the *b.* of king
Mic. 3. 2 pluck flesh from off their *b.*
Hab. 3. 16 rottenness entered my *b.*
Mat. 23. 27 full of dead men's *b.*
Luke 24. 39 spirit hath not fl. and *b.*
John 19. 36 *b.* . . shall not be broken
Eph. 5. 30 members of . . his *b.*
Heb. 11. 22 gave com. con. his *b.*
Bonnet. R. V. *headtire.*
Ex. 28. 40 make for them . . *b.*
Lev. 8. 13 Moses put *b.* on them
Isa. 3. 20 will take away the *b.*
Ezek. 44. 18 *b.* upon their heads

Book. *Word.*
1 Chr. 29. 29 in the *b.* of Samuel
2 Chr. 9. 29 in the *b.* of Nathan
Writing, book.
Gen. 5. 1 the *b.* of the generations
Ex. 17. 14 write memorial in a *b.*
Num. 5. 23 write . . curses in a *b.*
Deut. 17. 18 write . . law in a *b.*
Josh. 1. 8 this *b.* of the law
1 Sam. 10. 25 Samuel wrote in a *b.*
2 Sam. 1. 18 in the *b.* of Jasher.
1 K. 11. 41 written in the *b.* of the
2 K. 1. 18 in the *b.* of chronicles
1 Chr. 9. 1 in *b.* of the kings
2 Chr. 17. 9 had the *b.* of the law
Ez. 4. 15 search in the *b.* of records
Neh. 8. 1 bring the *b.* of the law
Esth. 2. 23 was written in the *b.*
Job. 31. 35 mine adver. had wr. a *b.*
Ps. 40. 7 in vol. of *b.* it is written
Eccl. 12. 12 making *b.* . . is no end
Isa. 29. 11 vision as words of a *b.*
Jer. 25. 13 is written in this *b.*
Ezek. 2. 9 roll of a *b.* was therein
Dan. 9. 2 Daniel understood by *b.*
Nah. 1. 1 *b.* of vision of Nahum
Mal. 3. 16 *b.* of remembrance
Little book, roll, scroll.
Mat. 1. 1 the *b.* of the generations
Mark 12. 26 *b.* of Moses
Luke 4. 17 delivered to him the *b.*
John 20. 30 not written in this *b.*
Acts 1. 20 in the *b.* of Psalms
Gal. 3. 10 in all things . . in the *b.*
2 Tim. 4. 13 bring with thee, . . the *b.*
Phil. 4. 3 names in the *b.* of life
Heb. 9. 19 sprinkled both the *b.*
Rev. 1. 11 write in a *b.* and send it
R. V. 1 Chr. 29. 29; 2 Chr. 9. 29;
  12. 15; 20. 34 history; Jer. 32. 12
  deed; Rev. 21. 19 tree
Booth. *Shelter, stall.*
Gen. 33. 17 made *b.* for his cattle
Lev. 23. 42 ye shall dwell in *b.*
Neh. 8. 14 Israel should dwell in *b.*
Job 27. 18 build. house . . as a *b.* that
Jonah 4. 5 Jonah made him a *b.*
Booty. *Prey, spoil.*
Num. 31. 32 *b.,* the rest of the prey
Jer. 40. 32 camels shall be a *b.*
Hab. 2. 7 thou shalt be for *b.*
Zeph. 1. 13 their goods shall bec. *b.*
Border (*v.*). *Bound, enclose.*
Zech. 9. 2 Hamath also shall *b.*
Border (*n.*). *Lip, edge, hem.*
Ex. 25. 25 make unto it a *b.*
1 K. 7. 28 the *b.* were between
2 K. 16. 17 Ahaz cut off the *b.*
S. of S. 1. 11 make *b.* of gold
Mat. 23. 5 *b.* of their garments
Mark. 6. 56 might touch but the *b.*
Luke 8. 44 and touched the *b.*
Enclosure, boundary.
Gen. 10. 19 *b.* of the Canaanites
Ex. 8. 2 will smite thy *b.* with frogs
Num. 20. 16 in uttermost of thy *b.*
Deut. 12. 20 God shall enlarge thy *b.*
Josh. 12. 2 *b.* of the children of Am.
Judg. 2. 9 *b.* of his inheritance
1 Sam. 6. 12 the *b.* of Beth-shemesh
1 K. 4. 21 unto the *b.* of Egypt
2 K. 3. 21 and stood in the *b.*
1 Chr. 7. 29 by the *b.* of Manasseh
2 Chr. 26 reigned . . to *b.* of Egypt
Ps. 78. 54 *b.* of his sanctuary
Prov. 15. 25 the *b.* of the widow
Isa. 15. 8 round about *b.* of Moab
Jer. 15. 13 even in all thy *b.*
Ezek. 11. 10 judge in *b.* of Israel
Joel 3. 6 remove far from their *b.*
Am. 1. 13 might enlarge their *b.*
Mal. 1. 4 call them *b.* of wickedness
Bore. *Pierce, perforate.*
Ex. 21. 6 shall *b.* his ear through
2 K. 12. 9 and *b.* a hole in lid
Job 41. 2 *b.* his jaw through
Born. *Begotten, brought forth.*
Gen. 21. 5 Isaac was *b.* unto him
Ex. 12. 19 or *b.* in the land
Lev. 23. 42 Israelites *b.* shall dwell
Num. 26. 60 unto A. was *b.* Nadab,
Josh. 8. 33 as he that was *b.* among
Judg. 18. 29 who was *b.* unto Israel.
2 Sam. 3. 2 unto David were sons *b.*
Ruth 4. 17 is a son *b.* to Naomi
1 K. 13. 2 a child shall be *b.*

1 Chr. 2. 3 three were *b.* unto him
Ez. 10. 3 and such as are *b.*
Job 1. 2 *b.* unto him seven sons
  3. 3; 5. 7; 11. 12; 15. 7; 38. 21
Ps. 22. 31 people that shall be *b.*
Prov. 17. 17 brother is *b.* for ad.
Eccl. 4. 14 also he that is *b.*
Isa. 66. 8 nation be *b.* at once?
Jer. 20. 14 cursed . . day I was *b.*
Mat. 1. 16 of whom was *b.* Jesus
Mark 14. 21 had never been *b.*
Luke 1. 35 thing which shall be *b.*
John 1. 13 *b.,* not of blood, but God
Acts 2. 8 wherein we were *b.*
Rom. 9. 11 children being not yet *b.*
1 Cor. 15. 8 *b.* out of due time
Gal. 4. 23 was *b.* after the flesh
Heb. 11. 23 Moses, when he was *b.*
1 Pet. 2. 2 as new *b.* babes
1 John 2. 29 right. is *b.* of him
Rev. 12. 4 devour child as soon as *b.*
Borne. *See* **Bear.**
Borrow. *Ask, obtain.*
Ex. 3. 2 every woman shall *b.*
Deut. 15. 6 thou shalt not *b.*
2 K. 4. 3 go, *b.* thee vessels
Neh. 3. 4 we have *b.* money
Ps. 37. 21 wicked *b.* and payeth not
Mat. 5. 42 him that would *b.*
R. V. Ex. 3. 22; 11. 2; 12. 35 ask
Borrower. *Who borrows.*
Prov. 22. 7 *b.* is servant to lender
Isa. 24. 2 with lender, so with the *b.*
Bosom. *Hollow place, inlet.*
Gen. 16. 5 given maid into thy *b.*
Ex. 4. 6 Put thine hand into thy *b.*
Num. 11. 12 Carry them in thy *b.*
Deut. 13. 6 if wife of thy *b.* entice
Ruth 4. 16 child, laid it in her *b.*
2 Sam. 12. 3 and lay in his *b.*
1 K. 1. 2 and let her lie in thy *b.*
Ps. 89. 50 do bear in my *b.* reproach
Prov. 5. 20 embrace the *b.* of
Eccl. 7. 9 in the *b.* of fools
Isa. 40. 11 carry lambs in his *b.*
Jer. 32. 18 *b.* of their children
Lam. 2. 12 into their mother's *b.*
Mic. 7. 5 that lieth in thy *b.*
Luke 6. 38 men give into your *b.*
  16. 22, 23 carried into A's *b.*
John 1. 18 in the *b.* of the Father
R. V. Prov. 19. 24; 26. 15 dish
Boss. *Protuberance.*
Job 15. 26 *b.* of his bucklers
Botch. R. V. *boil.*
Deut. 28. 27, 35 smite with a *b.*
Bottle. *Hollow thing, leathern bag*
Gen. 21. 14 and a *b.* of water
Josh. 9. 13 these *b.* of wine were new
Judg. 4. 19 opened a *b.* of milk
1 Sam. 16. 20 a *b.* of wine, and a kid
Job 38. 37 stay the *b.* of heaven
Ps. 56. 8 put . . my tears into thy *b.*
Jer. 48. 12 and break their *b.*
Hab. 2. 15 thatt puttest thy *b.*
Mat. 9. 17 new wine into old *b.*
Mark. 2. 22 wine doth burst the *b.*
Luke 5. 37 the *b.* shall perish
R. V. generally, skins or wine skins
Bottom. *Lowest part, base, depth*
Ex. 15. 5 sank into the *b.*
Lev. 4. 7 *b.* of the altar
Job 36. 30 the *b.* of the sea
S. of S. 3. 10 *b.* thereof of gold
Ezek. 43. 13 even the *b.* a cubit
Dan. 6. 24 came at the *b.*
Am. 9. 3 the *b.* of the sea
Jonah 2. 6 *b.* of the mountains
Zech. 1. 8 trees that were in the *b.*
Mat. 27. 51 rent from top to *b.*
Mark 15. 38 in twain from top to *b.*
Bottomless. R. V. *abyss.*
Rev. 9. 1 key of the *b.* pit
  9. 2, 11; 11. 7; 17. 8; 20. 1, 3.
Bough. *Branch.*
Gen. 49. 22 Joseph . . a fruitful *b.*
Lev. 23. 40 take *b.* of thick trees
Deut. 24. 20 not go over the *b.*
Judg. 9. 48 cut down *b.* from trees
2 Sam. 18. 9 under the thick *b.*
Job 14. 9 bring forth *b.* like a plant
Ps. 80. 11 she sent out her *b.*
S. of S. 7. 8 take hold of the *b.*
Isa. 10. 33 Lord shall lop the *b.*
Ezek. 17. 23 shall bring forth *b.*
Dan. 4. 12 fowls . . dwelt in *b.*

R. V. Lev. 23. 40 fruit: Ps. 80. 11 ;
S. of S. 7. 8 ; Dan. 4. 12 ; branches
Bought. *See* **Buy.**
Bound. *See* **Bind.**
Bound (*n.*).   *Enclosure, limit.*
Gen. 49. 26 *b.* of the everlasting
Ex. 19. 23 *b.* about the mount
Deut. 32. 8 *b.* of the people
Job 14. 15 *b.* he cannot pass
Ps. 104. 9 waters set a *b.*
Isa. 10. 13 removed *b.* of the people
Jer. 5. 22 sand for *b.* of the sea
Hos. 5. 10 them that remove *b.*
Acts 17. 26 hast determined the *b.*
Bountiful.   *Good, rich, free.*
Prov. 22. 9 hath *b.* eye .. be blessed
Isa. 32. 5 churl said to be *b.*
Bountifully.   *Freely, liberally.*
Ps. 13. 6 L. hath dealt *b.* with me
116. 7 ; 119. 17 ; 142. 7
2 Cor. 9. 6 soweth *b.* shall reap *b.*
Bountifulness.   R.V. *liberality*
2 Cor. 9. 11 enriched .. to all *b.*
Bounty.   *Gift, blessing, favor.*
1 K. 10. 13 Solomon gave .. royal *b.*
2 Cor. 9. 5 ready, as a matter of *b.*
Bow (*n.*).   *Bent, curved.*
Gen. 9. 13 set my *b.* in the cloud
Josh. 24. 12 sword, nor with thy *b.*
1 Sam. 2. 4 *b.* of .. men are broken
2 Sam. 1. 18 teach c of Judah the *b.*
1 K. 22. 34 a man drew a *b.*
2 K. 6. 22 smite with sword and *b.*
1 Chr. 5. 18 able to shoot with *b.*
2 Chr. 14. 8 bare shields and drew *b.*
Neh. 4. 13 set the people with *b.*
Job. 20. 24 the *b.* .. shall strike
Ps. 7. 12 he hath bent his *b.*
Isa. 5. 28 arrows .. sharp .. and *b.*
Jer. 6. 23 lay hold on *b.* and spear
Lam. 2. 4 he hath bent his *b.*
Ezek. 1. 28 *b.* that is in the cloud
Hos. 1. 5 break the *b.* of Israel
Am. 2. 15 that handleth the *b.*
Hab. 3. 9 thy *b.* was made naked
Zech. 9. 10 *b.* shall be cut off
Rev. 6. 2 he that sat on him had a *b.*
Bow (*v.*).   *Bend, stoop.*
Gen. 18. 2 and *b.* himself toward gr.
Ex. 11. 8 *b.* down .. unto me
Lev. 26. 1 nor *b.* down to it.
Num. 25. 2 *b.* down to their gods
Deut. 5. 6 thou shalt not *b.* down
Josh. 23. 7 not serve them, nor *b.*
Judg. 2. 12 and *b.* themselves unto
Ruth 2. 10 herself to the ground
1 Sam. 20. 41 *b.* himself three times
2 Sam. 22. 10 he *b.* the heavens
1 K. 19. 18 knees which have not *b.*
2 K. 19. 16 Lord, *b.* down thine ear
1 Chr. 21. 21 *b.* himself to David
2 Chr. 7. 3 *b.* .. with their faces
Job 39. 3 they *b.* themselves
Ps. 44. 25 our soul is *b.* down
Prov. 5. 1 *b* thine ear to understand
Isa. 45. 23 every knee shall *b.*
Eccl. 12. 3 strong men shall *b.*
Mic. 6. 6 *b.* myself before God.
Mat. 27. 29 *b.* the knee before him
Mark 15. 19 and *b.* knees, worship
Luke 13. 11 and was *b.* together
John 19. 30 Jesus *b.* his head
Rom. 11. 4 not *b.* the knee to Baal.
Eph. 3. 14 I *b.* .. unto the Father
Phil. 2. 10 every knee should *b.*
Bowels.   *Inner parts, heart.*
Gen. 15. 4 out of thine own *b.*
43. 30 his *b.* did yearn upon bro.
Num. 5. 22 shall go into thy *b.*
2 Sam. 7. 12 proceed out of thy *b.*
1 K. 3. 26 her *b.* yearned upon son
2 Chr. 21. 15 until thy *b.* fall out
Job 20. 14 meat in his *b.* is turned
Ps. 22. 14 heart melted in .. my *b.*
S. of S. 5. 4 my *b.* moved for him
Isa. 16. 11 my *b.* shall sound
Jer. 4. 19 my *b.* ! I am pained
Lam. 1. 20 my *b.* are troubled
Ezek. 3. 3 fill thy *b.* with this roll
Acts 1. 18 his *b.* gushed out
2 Cor. 6. 12 straitened in your own *b.*
Phil. 1. 8 you are in the *b.* of Jesus
Col. 3. 12 put on *b.* of mercies
Phile. 7 *b.* of saints are refreshed
R. V. Ps. 109. 18 inward parts ; 2
Cor. 6. 12 affections ; Phil. 1. 8 ;

2. 1 tender mercies ; Col. 3. 12 ;
Phile. 7, 20 heart
Bowl.   *Calix, cruse, cup.*
Ex. 25. 31 his *b.*, his knops of same
25. 33, 34 ; 37. 17, 19, 20
Judg. 6. 38 wringed *b.* full of water
1 K. 7. 41 two *b.* of the chapiters
Eccl. 12. 6 golden *b.* be broken
Zech. 4. 2 *b.* on top of it
Pan, basin, dish.
Num. 7. 13 *b.* of seventy shekels
7. 19, 25, 31, 37, 43, 49, 55. 61, 67
1 K. 7. 50 *b.*, and the snuffers
2 K. 25. 15 fire pans and *b.*
1 Chr. 28. 17 *b.* and the cups
Jer. 52. 18 *b.* and the spoons
Am. 6. 6 drink wine in *b.*
Zech. 9. 15 shall be filled like *b.*
Bowls.   *Sacrificial bowls.*
Ex. 25. 29 shalt make the *b.*
Num. 4. 7 the *b.* and covers
R. V. Ex. 25. 31, 33, 34 ; 37. 17, 19,
20 ; 1 K. 7. 50 ; 2 K. 12. 13 cups ;
2 K. 25. 15 ; 1 Chr. 28. 17 ; Jer.
52. 18 basons
Bowman.   *Who casts with bow.*
Jer. 4. 29 noise of the .. *b. m.*
Bowshot.   *Bow stretching.*
Gen. 21. 16 as it were a *b. s.*
Box.   *Cruet, flask, box.*
2 K. 9. 1 take this *b.* of oil
Mat. 26. 7 wom. having alabaster *b.*
Mark 14. 3 she brake the *b.*
Luke 7. 37 alabaster *b.* of ointment
R. V. 2 K. 9. 1 vial ; Mat. 26. 7 ;
Mark 14. 3 ; Luke 7. 37 cruse
Box-tree.   *Sherbin cedar.*
Isa. 41. 19 I will set .. the *b. t.*
60. 13 pine tree, and the *b.* together
Boy.   *One born, youth.*
Gen. 25. 27 And the *b.* grew
Joel 3. 3 have given a *b.* for
Zech. 8. 5 streets .. be full of *b.*
Bracelet.   *Arm band.*
Gen. 24. 22 two *b.* for her hand
Ex. 35. 22 brought *b.*, and earrings
Num. 31. 50 chains, and *b.*
2 Sam. 1. 10 the *b.* .. on her arm
Isa. 3. 19 chains and the *b.*
Ezek. 16. 11 *b.* upon thy hands
R. V. Gen. 38. 18, 25 cord ; Ex.
35. 22 brooches
Brake.   *See* **Break.**
Bramble.   *Thistle, thorn.*
Judg. 9. 14 said .. trees unto the *b.*
Isa. 34. 13 *b.* in the fortresses
Luke 6. 44 nor of a *b.* gather grapes
R. V. Isa. 34. 13 thistles
Branch.   *Reed, cane.*
Ex. 25. 31 *b.*, his bowls, his knops
25. 32–36 ; 37. 17–22
Bough, twig, shoot.
Gen. 40. 10 in the vine were three *b.*
Lev. 23. 40 take *b.* of palm
Job 15. 32 *b* shall be green
Ps. 80. 11 she sent out her *b.*
Prov. 11. 28 flourish as a *b.*
Isa. 4. 2 shall the *b.* of the Lord
Jer. 23. 5 David a righteous *B.*
Ezek. 8. 17 put *b.* to their nose
Dan. 4. 14 hew tree, cut off his *b.*
Hos. 11. 6 consume Ephraim's *b.*
Zech. 3. 8 forth my servant the *B.*
Joel. 1. 7 *b.* thereof are made white
Nah. 2. 2 marred their vine *b.*
Mat. 13. 32 birds lodge in the *b.*
Mark 4. 32 shooteth out great *b.*
Luke 13. 19 fowls lodged in the *b.*
John 15. 5 I am the vine, ye are the *b.*
Rom. 11. 16 root holy, so are the *b.*
11. 17 if some *b.* be broken
Brand.   *Torch, brand.*
Judg. 15. 5 set the *b.* on fire
Zech. 3. 2 *b.* plucked out of fire
Brandish.   *Move swiftly.*
Ezek. 32. 10 I shall *b.* my sword
Brasen.   *Brass, copper, bronze.*
Ex. 27. 4 make four *b.* rings
Lev. 6. 28 sodden in a *b.* pot
Num. 26. 39 E. took the *b.* censers
1 K. 4. 13 walls and *b.* bars
2 K. 16. 14 brought .. the *b.* altar
1 Chr. 18. 8 Sol. made the *b.* sea
Jer. 1. 18 *b.* walls against the land
Ezek. 9. 2 stood beside the *b.* altar
Mark 7. 4 cups, pots, *b.* vessels

Brass.   *Brass, copper.*
Gen. 4. 22 every artificer in *b.*
Ex. 25. 3 gold, silver, and *b.*
26. 11 ; 27. 2 ; 30. 18 ; 31. 4 ; 35. 5
Lev. 26. 19 and your earth as *b.*
Num. 21. 9 M. made a serpent of *b.*
Deut. 8. 9 thou mayest dig *b.*
Josh. 6. 19 vessels of *b.* and iron
Judg. 16. 21 bound with fetters of *b.*
1 Sam. 17. 5 an helmet of *b.* on head
2 Sam. 8. 8 David took .. much *b.*
1 K. 7. 14 to work all works in *b.*
2 K. 25. 13 the pillars of *b.*
1 Chr. 15. 19 sound cymbals of *b.*
2 Chr. 2. 7 gold, silver, and *b.*
Job 28. 2 and *b.* is molten of stone
Isa. 45. 2 break .. the gates of *b.*
Jer. 6. 28 *b.* and iron .. all corrupters
Ezek. 1. 7 sparkled like burnished *b.*
Dan. 10. 6 feet like .. polished *b.*
Zech. 6. 1 the mountains of *b.*
Mic. 4. 13 make thy hoofs *b.*
Copper, bronze.
Mat. 10. 9 provide neither g. s. nor *b*
1 Cor. 13. 1 become as sounding *b.*
Rev. 1. 15 feet like unto fine *b.*
9. 20 idols of gold and silver and *b.*
Bravery.   *Beauty.*
Isa. 3. 18 *b.* of .. tinkling ornaments
Brawler.   *Without battle, wrangler.*
1 Tim. 3. 3 not a *b.*, not covetous
Tit. 3. 2 to be no *b.*, but gentle
R. V. 1 Tim. 3. 3 contentious
Brawling.   *Wrangling.*
Prov. 21. 9 than with a *b.* woman
25. 24 *b.* woman in a .. house
Bray.   *Bray, pound.*
Job. 6. 5 doth the wild ass *b.*
Prov. 27. 22 *b.* a fool in a mortar
Breach.   *Break, rent, gulf.*
Gen. 38. 29 this *b.* be upon thee
Lev. 24. 20 *b.* for *b.*, eye for eye
Num. 14. 34 my *b.* of promise
Judg. 21. 15 a *b.* in the tribes
2 Sam. 5. 20 as the *b.* of waters
1 K. 11. 27 Solomon repaired the *b.*
2 K. 12. 5 repair the *b.* of the house
1 Chr. 13. 11 Lord made a *b.* upon
Neh. 6. 1 no *b.* left therein
Job 16. 14 with *b.* upon *b.*
Ps. 106. 23 Moses stood .. in the *b.*
Prov. 15. 4 perverseness is *b.* in sp.
Isa. 30. 26 Lord bindeth up the *b.*
Jer. 14. 17. broken with a great *b.*
Lam. 2. 13 for thy *b.* is great
Ezek. 26. 10 city wherein is a *b.*
Am. 4. 3 ye shall go out at the *b.*
R. V. Num. 14. 34 alienation ; Judg.
5. 17 creeks ; Isa. 30. 26 hurt
Bread.   *Food, sustenance, loaf.*
Gen. 3. 19 sweat of .. f. shalt eat *b.*
14. 18 ; 18. 5 ; 21. 14 ; 25 ; 34 ; 27. 17 ;
Ex. 2. 20 that he may eat *b.*
16. 3 ; 23. 25 ; 29. 2 ; 34. 28 ; 40. 23
Lev. 7. 13 his offering leavened *b.*
8. 26 ; 21. 6 ; 22. 25 ; 23. 14 ; 24. 7 ;
Num. 4. 7 const. *b.* shall be thereon
Deut. 8. 3 not live by *b.* alone
Josh. 9. 5 all the *b.* .. was dry
Judg. 7. 13 cake of barley *b.* tumbled
Ruth 1. 6 people in giving them *b.*
1 Sam. 2. 5 hired out .. for *b.*
2. 36 ; 9. 7 ; 10. 3 ; 16. 20 ; 21. 3 ;
2 Sam. 3. 29 or that lacketh *b.*
1 K. 13. 8 neither will I eat *b.*
2 K. 4. 8 he turned in to eat *b.*
1 Chr. 12. 40 brought *b.* on asses
2 Chr. 18. 26 feed with *b.* of affl.
Ez. 10. 6 he did eat no *b.*
Neh. 5. 14 not eaten *b.* of governor
Job 15. 23 he wandereth .. for *b.*
Ps. 37. 25 nor his seed begging *b.*
41. 9 ; 53. 4 ; 78. 20 ; 80. 5 ; 102. 4
Prov. 4. 17 eat the *b.* of wickedness
6. 26 ; 9. 5 ; 12. 9 ; 20. 13 ; 23. 6 ;
Eccl. 9. 7 eat thy *b.* with joy
Isa. 3. 1 the whole stay of *b.*, and wat.
Jer. 5. 17 eat thine harvest and *b.*
Lam. 4. 4 young children ask *b.*
Ezek. 4. 9. make thee *b.* thereof
Dan. 10. 3 ate no pleasant *b.*
Hos. 2. 5 give me *b.* and water.
Am. 4. 6 want of *b.* in all places
Mal. 1. 7 ye offer polluted *b.*
Mat. 4. 3 that stones be made *b.*
4. 4 ; 6. 11 ; 7. 9 ; 15. 2 ; 16. 5

Mark. 3. 20 could not .. eat *b*.
6. 8 ; 7. 2 ; 8. 4 ; 14. 22
Luke 4. 3 command this s .. be *b*.
7. 33 ; 9. 3 : 11. 3 ; 14. 1 ; 15. 17
John 6. 5 whence shall we buy *b*.
6. 7–58 ; 13. 18 ; 21. 9 ; 21. 13
Acts 2. 42 in breaking of *b*.
1 Cor. 10. 16 *b*. which we break
2 Cor. 9. 10 both minister *b*. for
2 Thes. 3. 8 neither .. e. any man's *b*.
Thing squeezed together, unleav-
ened bread.
Gen. 19. 3 bake unleavened b.
Ex. 12. 8 flesh and unleavened *b*.
Lev. 6. 16 with unleavened *b*.
Num. 6. 15 basket of unleavened *b*.
Deut. 16. 3 shalt thou eat unleav. *b*.
1 Sam. 28. 24 did bake unleavened *b*.
2 K. 23. 9 did eat of unleavened *b*.
2 Chr. 8. 13 feast of unleavened *b*.
Ez. 6. 22 kept the feast of unleav. *b*.
Ezek. 45. 21 unleav. *b*. shall be eaten
Mat. 26. 17 feast of unleavened *b*.
Mark 14. 1 two days .. of unl. *b*.
Luke 22. 1 feast of unl. *b*. drew
Acts 12. 3 days of unleavened *b*.
1 Cor. 5. 9 unl. *b*. of sincerity
Breadth. *Width.*
Gen. 6. 15 *b*. of it fifty cubits
Ex. 25. 10 cubit and a half the *b*
25. 23 ; 26. 2 ; 27. 12 : 28. 16 ; 30. 2
Deut. 3. 11 four cubits the *b*. of it
1 K. 6. 3 *b*. thereof twenty cubits
2 Chr. 3. 3 the *b*. twenty cubits
Job 37. 10 the *b*. of the waters
Isa. 8. 8 the *b*. of the land
Ezek. 40. 5 he measured the *b*.
41. 1 ; 42. 2 ; 43. 13 ; 45. 1 ; 48. 8
Dan. 3. 1 *b*. thereof six cubits
Hab. 1. 6 the *b*. of the land
Zech. 2. 2 see the *b*. thereof
Eph. 3. 18 what is the *b*., and length
Rev. 20. 9 the *b*. of the earth
Break (*n*.). *Breaking forth.*
2 Sam. 2. 32 Joab came at *b*. of day
Acts 20. 11 talked even till *b*. of day
Break (*v*.). *Crush, beat, fracture*
Gen. 19. 9 came .. to *b*. the door
Ex. 12. 46 neither *b*. a bone
Lev. 11. 33 and ye shall *b*. it
Num. 9. 12 nor *b*. any bone of it
Deut. 31. 16 people *b*. my covenant
Judg. 2. 1 will never *b*. my cov.
1 K. 15. 19 *b*. thy league with B.
2 K. 11. 18 *b*. in pieces .. rocks
1 Chr. 11. 18 the three *b*. through
2 Chr. 23. 17 *b*. his altars and images
Ez. 9. 14 again *b*. thy command.
Neh. 4. 3 shall *b*. down stone wall
Job 13. 25 wilt *b*. a leaf driven
Ps. 10. 15 *b*. .. arm of .. wicked
Prov. 25. 15 soft tongue .. the bone
S. of S. 2. 17 until the day *b*.
Isa. 28. 28 nor *b*. the wheel
Jer. 2. 20 I have *b*. thy yoke
Ezek. 4. 16 I will *b*. the staff
Dan. 8. 7 and *b*. his two horns
Zech. 11. 10 I might *b*. my covenant
Mat. 12. 20 reed shall he not *b*.
14. 19 blessed, and *b*., and gave
Mark 8. 6 gave thanks, and *b*.
Luke 5. 6 and their net *b*.
John 19. 31 that .. legs might be *b*.
Acts 2. 46 *b*. bread from house to h.
1 Cor. 10. 16 bread which we *b*.
Gal. 4. 27 *b*. forth and cry
R. V. Gen. 27. 40 shake ; Ex. 34. 13
Deut. 7. 5 ; 12. 3 dash in pieces ;
Job 13. 25 harass ; 39. 15 trample ;
S. of S. 2. 17 ; 4. 5 be cool ; Isa. 54.
3 spread ; Ezek. 23. 34 gnaw ;
Mat. 9. 17 burst
Breaker. *Transgressor.*
Mic. 2. 13 the *b*. is come up
Rom. 1. 31 covenant *b*., unmerciful
2. 25 a *b*. of the law
2 Tim. 3. 3 truce *b*., false accusers
R. V. Rom. 2. 25 transgressors
Breaking. *Going up, fracturing.*
Gen. 32. 24 until the *b*. of morn
Ex. 22. 2 If a thief be found *b*.
1 Chr. 14. 11 *b*. forth of waters
Job 41. 25 by reason of *b*.
Ps. 144. 14 no breaking in, nor
Isa. 30. 13 whose *b*. cometh sud.
Ezek. 21. 6 the *b*. of thy loins

Hos. 13. 13 the *b*. forth of children
Luke 24. 35 Known .. in *b*. of bread
Acts 2. 42 in *b*. of bread, and prayer
Rom. 2. 23 through *b*. the law
R. V. Job 41. 25 consternation ;
Rom. 2. 23 thy transgression of
Breast. *Chest, teat.*
Gen. 49. 25 blessings of the *b*.
Ex. 29. 26 take .. *b*. of the ram
Lev. 7. 30 the fat with the *b*.
Num. 6. 20 with the wave *b*.
Job 24. 9 pluck .. fatherless from .. *b*.
Ps. 22. 9 *b*. that I should suck
Prov. 5. 19 let her *b*. satisfy thee
S. of S. 1. 13 lie .. betwixt my *b*.
4. 5 ; 7. 3 ; 8. 1 ; 8. 10
Isa. 28. 9 milk drawn from .. *b*.
Lam. 4. 3 monsters draw out the *b*.
Ezek. 16. 7 thy *b*. are fashioned
Hos. 2. 2 from between her *b*.
Joel 2. 16 that suck the *b*.
Nah. 2. 7 doves tabering on .. *b*.
Luke 18. 13 smote upon his *b*.
John 13. 25 lying on Jesus' *b*.
Rev. 15. 6 having their *b*. girded
Breastplate. *Breast-cover, cuirass.*
Ex. 25. 7 stones set in the *b. p*.
28. 4, 15, 22—30 ; 29. 5 ; 35. 9 ; 39. 8
Lev. 8. 8 he put the *b. p*. on him
Isa. 59. 17 put on right. as a *b. p*.
Eph. 6. 14 *b. p*. of righteousness
1 Thes. 5. 8 putting on *b. p*. of faith
Rev. 9. 9 they had *b. p*.
Breath. *Air, wind, spirit.*
Gen. 2. 7. nostrils the *b*. of life
2 Sam. 22. 16 *b*. of his nostrils
1 K. 17. 17 no *b*. left in him
Job 15. 30 by *b*. of his mouth
41. 21 his *b*. kindleth coals
Ps. 18. 15 the blast of the *b*.
Eccl. 3. 19 they have all one *b*.
Isa. 11. 4 the *b*. of his lips
Jer. 10. 14 is no *b*. in them
Lam. 4. 20 *b*. of our nostrils taken
Ezek. 37. 5 cause *b*. to enter .. you
Dan. 5. 23 whose hand thy *b*. is
Hab. 2. 19 no *b*. in the midst
Acts 17. 25 giveth to all .. *b*.
R. V. Job 4. 9 blast ; 17. 1 spirit
Breathe. *Respire.*
Gen. 2. 7 *b*. into his nostrils
Deut. 20. 16 save .. nothing that *b*.
Josh. 11. 11 not any left to *b*.
1 K. 15. 29 left not .. any that *b*.
Ps. 27. 12 such as *b*. out cruelty
Lam. 3. 56 hide not .. at my *b*.
Ezek. 37. 9 come, *b*. upon these
John 20. 22 he *b*. on them
Acts 9. 1 *b*. out threatenings
Bred. *See* Breed.
Breeches. *Breech covers, trousers.*
Ex. 28. 42 linen *b*. to cover
Lev. 6. 10. linen *b*. shall he put on
Ezek. 44. 18 shall have linen *b*.
Breed. *Progeny.*
Deut. 32. 14 rams of the *b*. of
Breed (*v*.). *Beget.*
Gen. 8. 17 that they may *b*. abund.
Ex. 16. 20 it *b*. worms and stank
Zeph. 2. 9 even the *b*. of nettles
R. V. Zeph. 2. 9 a possession
Brethren. *Brothers.*
Gen. 9. 22 and told his two *b*.
9. 25 ; 13. 8 ; 16. 12 ; 19. 7 ; 24. 27 ;
Ex. 1. 6 Joseph died, and all his *b*.
Lev. 10. 4 carry your *b*. bef. sanct.
Num. 8. 26 minister with their *b*.
Deut. 1. 16 hear .. between your *b*.
Josh. 1. 14 pass before your *b*.
Judg. 8. 19 they were my *b*.
Ruth 4. 10. not cut off .. among .. *b*.
1 Sam. 16. 13 in .. midst of his *b*.
2 Sam. 15. 20 take back thy *b*.
1 K. 1. 9 Adonijah called all his *b*.
2 K. 9. 2 arise from among his *b*.
1 Chr. 5. 7 *b*. by their families
2 Chr. 5. 12 *b*. arrayed in white
Ez. 3. 2 son of Jozadak and his *b*.
Neh. 1. 2 Hanani one of my *b*.
Esth. 10. 3 multitude of his *b*.
Job. 6. 15 My *b*. have dealt deceit.
Ps. 22. 22 declare name unto my *b*.
133. 1 how pl. for *b*. to dwell
Prov. 6. 19 soweth dis. among *b*.
Isa. 66. 5 *b*. that hated you
Jer. 7 15 have cast out all your *b*.

Ezek. 11. 15 Son of man, thy *b*.
Hos. 2. 1 Say ye unto your *b*.
Mic. 5. 3 remnant of his *b*. return
Mat. 1. 2 J. begat J. and his *b*.
4. 18 ; 5. 47 ; 12. 46 ; 13. 55 ; 19. 29
Mark 3. 31 then came his *b*.
Luke 8. 20 Thy mother and thy *b*.
John 7. 3 his *b*. said unto him, Dep.
Acts 1. 16 *b*. this scripture must
2. 29 ; 3. 17 ; 6. 3 ; 7. 2 ; 9. 30 ; 10. 23
Rom. 7. 1 Know ye not, *b*. how law
1 Cor. 1. 10 I beseech you, *b*.
2 Cor. 1. 8 we would not, *b*.
Gal. 1. 2 all the *b*. which are with
Eph. 6. 10 *b*., be strong in the Lord
Phil. 1. 12 ye should understand, *b*.
Col. 1. 2 faithful *b*. in Christ
1 Thes. 1. 4 Knowing, *b*. your elec.
2 Thes. 1. 3 thank G. .. for you, *b*.
1 Tim. 4. 6 put the *b*. in remem.
2 Tim. 4. 21 Claudia, and all the *b*.
Heb. 2. 11 not ash. to call them *b*.
Jas. 1. 2 my *b*., count it all joy
2 Pet. 1. 10 *b*., make your call. sure
1 John 2. 7 *b*., I write no new com.
Rev. 6. 11 ; 12. 10 ; 19. 10 ; 22. 9
R. V. Acts 20. 32 ; Rom. 15. 15 ;
1 Cor. 11. 2— ; 1 John 2. 7 beloved
Bribe. *Cover, reward, bribe.*
1 Sam. 8. 3 took *b*. and perverted j.
12. 3 have I received *b*.
Ps. 26. 10 right hand is full of *b*.
Isa. 33. 15 hands from holding of *b*.
R. V. 1 Sam. 12. 3 ransom
Bribery. *Bribe.*
Job. 15. 34 consume the tab. of *b*.
Brick. *Brick.*
Gen. 11. 3 let us make *b*.
Ex. 1. 14 bondage, in morter and *b*.
5. 7 give straw to make *b*.
Isa. 9. 10 *b*. are fallen down
Brickkiln. *Brickmaking place.*
2 Sam. 12. 31 pass through the *b. k*.
Jer. 43. 9 hide them .. in the *b. k*.
Nah. 3. 14 make strong the *b. k*.
R. V. Jer. 43. 9 brickwork
Bride. *Perfect one.*
Isa. 49. 18 bind them as a *b*.
61. 10 as the *b*. adorneth herself
62. 5 as the *b*. rejoiceth
Jer. 2. 32 or a *b*. her attire
7. 34 ; 16. 9 ; 25. 10 ; 33. 11
Joel 2. 16 *b*. go out of her closet
Newly-married woman.
John 3. 29 hath the *b*. is the *b. g*.
Rev 18. 23 voice of the *b. g*. and *b*.
21. 2, 9 ; 22. 17
Bridechamber. *Nuptial cham.*
Mat. 9. 15 children of the *b. c*.
Mark 2. 19 ; Luke 3. 24
Bridegroom. *Bridesman.*
Ps. 19. 5 as *b. g*. coming out of cham.
Isa. 61. 10 as a *b. g*. decketh hims.
Jer. 7. 34 the *b. g*. and voice of bri.
16. 9 ; 25. 10 ; 33. 11
Joel 2. 16 let the *b. g*. go forth
Mat. 9. 15 as the *b. g*. is with them
9. 15 ; 25. 1, 5, 6, 10
Mark 2. 19, 20 ; Luke 5. 34, 35
John 2. 9 gov. called the *b. g*.
Rev. 18. 23 voice of the *b. g*. heard
Bridle (*n*). *Bit, rein.*
2 K. 19. 28 put my *b*. in thy lips
Job 30. 11 also let loose the *b*.
Ps. 32. 9 mouth must be held with *b*
Prov. 26. 3 a *b*. for the ass
Isa. 30. 28 *b*. in the jaws of people
Rev. 14. 20 unto the horse *b*.
Bridle (*v*.). *Check, curb.*
Jas. 1. 26 *b*. not his tongue
Briefly. *Concisely.*
Rom. 13. 9 *b*. comprehended in
1 Pet. 5. 12 I have written *b*.
R. V. Rom. 13. 9 summed up
Brier. *Prickly shrub.*
Judg. 8. 7, 16 tear flesh with *b*.
Isa. 5. 6 shall come up *b*.
7. 23–25 ; 9. 18 ; 10. 17 ; 27. 4 ; 32. 13
Ezek. 28. 24 no more a pricking *b*.
Mic. 7. 4 the best of them is as a *b*.
Heb. 6. 8 beareth thorns and *b*.
R. V. Heb. 6. 8 thistles
Brigandine. R. V. *coat of mail.*
Jer. 46. 4 ; 51. 3 put on the *b*.
Bright. *Freckled.*
Lev. 13. 2–39 scab, or *b*. spot

Light, shining.
1 K. 7. 45 vessels .. of *b.* brass
Job. 37. 21 see not the *b.* light
S. of S. 5. 14 as *b.* ivory overlaid
Ezek. 1. 3 the fire was *b.*
Zech. 10. 1 shall make *b.* clouds
Nah. 3. 3 horsem. lifted .. *b.* swords
Mat. 17. 5 behold a *b.* cloud
Acts 10. 30 man stood in *b.* array
Rev. 22. 16 *b.* and morning star
R. V. 1 K. 7. 45 burnished; Jer.
51. 11 sharp; Ezek. 21. 15 light-
ning; Nah. 3. 3 flashing
Cleanse, sharpen.
Jer. 51. 11 make *b.* the arrows
Ezek. 21. 21 made his arrows *b.*
Brightness. *Shining, brilliant.*
2 Sam. 22. 13 the *b.* before him
Job. 31. 26 or moon walking in *b.*
Ps. 18. 12 at *b.* . . clouds passed
Isa. 60. 3 kings to *b.* of thy rising
Ezek. 28. 7 shall defile thy *b.*
Dan. 2. 31 great image whose *b.*
Am. 5. 20 even very dark, and no *b.*
Hab. 3. 4 his *b.* was as the light
Acts 26. 13 above the *b.* of the sun
2 Thes. 2. 8 with *b.* of his coming
Heb. 1. 3 who being *b.* of his glory
R. V. Heb. 1. 3 effulgence
Brim. *Edge, upper part.*
Josh. 3. 15 dipped in *b.* of the water
John. 2. 7 filled them to the *b.*
R. V. Josh. 3. 15 brink
Brimstone. *Bitumen, pitch.*
Gen. 19. 24 the Lord rained *b.*
Deut. 29. 23 land thereof is *b.*
Job 18. 15 *b.* shall be scattered
Ps. 11. 6 on wicked he shall rain *b.*
Isa. 30. 33 like a stream of *b.*
Ezek. 38. 22 hailstones, fire, and *b.*
Divine fire, sulphur.
Luke 17. 29 rained *b.* from heaven
Rev. 9. 17 issued fire and *b.*
9. 18; 14. 10; 19. 20; 20. 10; 21. 8
Bring. *Cause to come.*
Gen. 2. 19 *b.* them unto Adam
4. 3; 6. 17; 18. 19; 20. 9; 24. 67
Ex. 2. 10 *b.* him unto Pharaoh's d.
Lev. 2. 2 shall *b.* it to Aaron's sons
Num. 5 15 shall man *b.* his wife
Deut. 6. 10 when L. shall have *b.*
Josh. 23. 15 shall the Lord *b.*
Judg. 1. 7 *b.* him to Jerusalem
1 Sam. 1. 22 I will *b.* him before L.
2 Sam. 1. 10 have *b.* them hither
1 K. 1. 3 her to the king
2 K. 4. 20 taken him and *b.* to moth.
1 Chr. 5. 26 *b.* them unto Halah
2 Chr. 2. 16 *b.* it to thee in floats
Ez. 3. 7 *b.* cedar trees from Leb.
Neh. 8. 1 *b.* the book of the law
Esth. 1. 11 to *b.* Vashti bef. king
Job 12. 6 into hand G. *b.* abundantly
Ps. 43. 3 let them *b.* me to holy hill
Prov. 21. 27 *b.* with wicked mind
Eccl. 3. 22 who shall *b.* him to see
S. of S. 1. 4 the king hath *b.* me
Isa. 1. 13 *b.* no more oblations
Jer. 4. 6 I will *b.* evil from north
Lam. 1. 21 thou wilt *b.* the day that
Ezek. 5. 17 will *b.* the sword on thee
Dan. 1. 2 he *b.* the vessels
Amos 4. 1 *b.*, and let us drink
Mic. 1. 15 I *b.* an heir unto thee
Zeph. 3. 20 will I *b.* you again
Hag. 1. 8 go . . and *b.* wood
Zech. 8. 8 I will *b.* them, and they
Mal. 1. 13 ye *b.* an offering
Mat. 14. 11 his head was *b.* in char.
Mark 1. 32 they *b.* him all diseased
Luke 5. 18 men *b.* in a bed
John 4. 33 hath man *b.* ought to eat
Acts 4. 37 having *b.* the money
Rom. 7. 4 *b.* forth fruit unto God
1 Cor. 1. 19 will *b.* to nothing
2 Cor. 11. 20 if man *b.* you into bond.
Gal. 3. 24 *b.* us to Christ
1 Thes. 4. 14 sleep will God *b.*
1 Pet. 3. 18 *b.* us to God
2 John 10 if any *b.* not this doctrine
Rev. 21. 24 do *b.* their glory
Bringer. *That brings.*
2 K. 10. 5 *b.* up thy children
Bringing. *Bearing, carrying.*
2 Chr. 9. 21 ships *b.* gold, and ivory
Ps. 126. 6 *b.* his sheaves with him

Mark 2. 3 *b.* one sick of the palsy
Luke 24. 1 they came *b.* the spices
Acts 5. 16 a multitude *b.* sick folks
Heb. 2. 10 in *b.* many sons
Brink. *Lip, edge.*
Gen. 41. 3 stood . . upon the *b.*
Ex. 2. 3 flags by the river's *b.*
Deut. 2. 36 *b.* of the river Arnon
Josh. 3. 8 come to *b.* of the water
R. V. Deut. 2. 36 edge; Ezek. 47. 6
bank
Broad. *Wide.*
Ex. 27. 1 make altar five cubits *b.*
1 K. 6. 6 chamber was six cubits *b.*
Neh. 3. 8 fortified unto the *b.* wall
Job 36. 16 removed into a *b.* place
Ps. 119. 96 thy command. is . . *b.*
S. of S. 3. 2 in *b.* ways . . I seek
Isa. 33. 21 place of *b.* rivers
Jer. 5. 1 seek in *b.* places thereof
Nah. 2. 4 justle in *b.* ways
Mat. 7. 13 *b.* is the way to destr.
R. V. Num. 16. 38 beaten
Broidered. *Plaited, variegated.*
Ex. 28. 4 a. broidered coat, a mitre
Ezek. 16. 10 clothed . . with *b.* work
16. 13, 18; 26. 16; 27. 7, 16, 24
1 Tim. 2. 9 adorn not with *b.* hair
R. V. Ex. 28. 4 checker; 1 Tim. 2. 9
braided
Broiled. *Seethed.*
Luke 24. 42 gave piece of *b.* fish
Broken. *Shivered, shattered.*
Gen. 7. 11 fountains of g. d. *b.*
Lev. 22. 22 blind, or *b.* or maimed
1 Sam. 2. 4 bows of . . men are *b.*
1 K. 22. 48 ships were *b.* at Ezion
2 K. 25, 4 the city was *b.* up
2 Chr. 25. 12 all were *b.* in pieces
Job 17. 11 my purposes are *b.*
Ps. 37. 15 their bows shall be *b.*
Prov. 6. 15 shall he be *b.* without
Eccl. 12. 6 or the pitcher be *b.*
Isa. 30. 14 potter's vessel that is *b.*
Jer. 37. 11 army of the C. was *b.*
Mat. 15. 37 took up of the *b.* meat
Luke 20. 18 stone shall be *b.*
John 21. 11 was not the net *b.*
1 Cor. 11. 24 my body *b.* for you
See also **Break.**
Broken-footed.
Lev. 21. 19 or a man *b., f.*
Broken-hearted.
Isa. 61. 1 sent me to bind . . *b. h.*
Luke 4. 18 sent me to heal . . *b. h.*
Brood. *Nest, brood.*
Luke 13. 34 as a hen gather her *b.*
Brook. *Small stream.*
Gen. 32. 23 sent them over . . *b.*
Lev. 23. 40 willows of the *b.*
Num. 13. 23 came unto the *b.* Esch.
Deut. 2. 13 get you over the *b.*
1 Sam. 17. 40 stones out of the *b.*
2 Sam. 15. 23 over the *b.* Kidron
1 K. 1. 37 passest over the *b.*
2 K. 23. 6 unto the *b.* Kidron
1 Chr. 11. 32 the *b.* of Gaash
2 Chr. 20. 16 at the end of . . *b.*
Neh. 2. 15 went up . . by the *b.*
Job 6. 15 dealt deceitfully as a *b.*
Ps. 83. 9 as to Jabin at the *b.*
Prov. 18. 4 wisdom as a flowing *b.*
Isa. 15. 7 carry away to the *b.*
Jer. 31. 40 unto the *b.* of Kidron
John 18. 1 went . . over the *b.* Ced.
R. V. Num. 21. 14, 15 valleys
Broth. *Thin soup.*
Judg. 6. 19 put . . *b.* in a pot
Isa. 65. 4 *b.* of abominable things
Brother. *Brother.*
Gen. 4. 2 she . . bare his *b.* Abel
9. 5; 10. 21; 25. 5; 14. 12, 20. 5
Ex. 4. 14 is not Aaron thy *b.*
Lev. 16. 2 speak unto Aaron thy *b.*
Num. 20. 14 saith thy *b.* Israel
Deut. 1. 16 judge right. between *b.*
Josh. 15. 17 Othniel . . *b.* of Caleb
Judg. 9. 21 for fear of A. his *b.*
Ruth 4. 3 was our *b.* Elimelech's
1 Sam. 14. 3 Ahitub, Ichabod's *b.*
2 Sam. 1. 26 distressed for . . *b.* Jon.
1 K. 1. 10 and Solomon his *b.*
1 Chr. 1. 19 *b's* name was Joktan
2 Chr. 31. 12 his *b.* was next
Neh. 5. 7 exact usury ev. one of his *b.*
Job 30. 29 I am a *b.* to dragons

Ps. 35. 14 behaved as my *b.*
Prov. 17. 17 a *b.* for adversity
Eccl. 4. 8 hath neither child nor *b.*
S. S. 8. 1 thou wert as my *b.*
Isa. 3. 6 take hold of his *b.*
Jer. 9. 4 trust ye not in any *b.*
Ezek. 18. 18 spoiled his *b.* by vio.
Hos. 12. 3 took his *b.* by the heel
Amos 1. 11. did pursue his *b.*
Obad. 10 violence against thy *b.*
Mic. 7. 2 hunt every man his *b.*
Hag. 2. 22 the sword of his *b.*
Zech. 7. 9 shew mercy . . to his *b.*
Mal. 1. 2 Was not Esau Jacob's *b.?*
Brother, relative, friend.
Mat. 4. 18 Simon and Andrew his *b.*
5. 22; 7. 3; 10. 2; 12. 50; 14. 3
Mark 3. 17 John the *b.* of James
Luke 6. 14 mote . . in thy *b's* eye
John 1. 41 findeth his *b.* Simon
Acts 12. 2 killed James *b.* of John.
Rom. 14. 10 why . . judge thy *b.?*
1 Cor. 6. 6. goeth to law with *b.*
2 Cor. 1. 1 and Timothy our *b.*
Gal. 1. 19 James the Lord's *b.*
Eph. 6. 21 Tychicus, a beloved *b.*
Phil. 2. 25 my *b.* and companion
Col. 4. 9 faithful and beloved *b.*
1 Thes. 3. 2 Timotheus, our *b.*
2 Thes. 3. 6 withdraw . . from ev. *b.*
Phile. 7 refreshed by thee, *b.*
Heb. 8. 11 shall not teach . . his *b.*
Jas. 1. 9 let the *b.* . . rejoice
1 Pet. 5. 12 Silvanus, a faithful *b.*
2 Pet. 3. 15 our beloved *b.* Paul
1 John 2. 9 that hateth his *b.* is
Jude 1 Jude . . *b.* of James
Rev. 1. 9 I John, . . am your *b.*
R. V. Luke 6. 16; Acts 1. 13 son
Brotherhood. *Brothership.*
Zech. 11. 14 might break the *b. h.*
1 Pet. 2. 17 love the *b. h.*
Brotherly. *Fraternal.*
Am. 1. 9 the *b.* covenant
Rom. 12. 10 one to ano. with *b.* love
1 Thes. 4. 9 as touching *b.* love
Heb. 13. 1 let *b.* love continue
2 Pet. 1. 7 godliness and *b.* kind.
Brought. *See* **Bring.**
Brow, *Forehead, summit.*
Isa. 48. 4 and thy *b.* brass
Luke 4. 29 the *b.* of the hill
Brown. *Dusky.* R. V. *black.*
Gen. 30. 32—40 all the *b.* cattle
Bruise (*n.*). *Stripe, breach.*
Isa. 1. 6 but wounds, and *b.*, and sores
Jer. 30. 12 thy *b.* is incurable
Nah. 3. 19 no healing of thy *b.*
R. V. Jer. 30. 12; Nah. 3. 19 hurt.
Bruise, *Crush, batter, dent.*
Gen. 3. 15 it shall *b.* thy head
Lev. 22. 24 not offer . . which is *b*
2 K. 18. 21 staff of this *b*, reed
Isa. 53. 5 *b.* for our iniquities
Ezek. 23. 21 in *b.* thy teats
Dan. 2. 40 break in pieces and *b.*
Mat. 12. 20 *b.* reed shall he not br.
Luke 9. 39 *b.* him hardly departeth
Rom. 16. 20 God . . shall *b.* Satan
R. V. Dan. 2. 40 crush; Isa. 28. 28
ground
Bruit. *Report.*
Jer. 10. 22 the noise of the *b.*
Nah. 3. 19 hear the *b.* of thee
Brute. *Speechless animal.*
2 Pet. 2. 12 as natural *b.* beasts ·
Jude 10 know naturally as *b.* beasts
R. V. creatures without reason
Brutish. *Brute-like.*
Ps. 49. 10 fool and *b.* person perish
Prov. 12. 1 that hateth reproof is *b*
Isa. 19. 11 wise . . is become *b.*
Jer. 10. 21 pastors are become *b.*
Ezek. 21. 31 into the hand of *b.* men
Bucket. *Pail.*
Num. 24. 7 pour water out of his *b*
Isa. 40. 15 nations are as drop of *b.*
Buckler. *Shield.*
2 Sam. 22. 31 *b.* to all that trust
1 Chr. 5. 18 men able to bear *b.*
2 Chr. 23. 9 delivered *b.* and shield
Job 15. 26 run. upon bosses of his *b.*
Ps. 18. 2 my *b.* and the horn
Prov. 2. 7 he is a *b.* to them that
S. of S. 4. 4 hang a thousand *b.*
Jer. 46. 3 order ye the *b.* and shield

Ezek. 23. 24 set against thee *b*.
R. V. 2 Sam. 22. 31; Ps. 18. 2;
  Prov. 2. 7 shield; 1 Chr. 12. 8
  spear.
Bud (*n*). *Blossom, shoot.*
Num. 17. 8 and brought forth *b*.
Job 38. 27 to cause the *b*. to spring
  61. 11 earth bringeth forth her *b*.
Ezek. 16. 7 multiply as the *b*.
Hos. 8. 7 *b*. shall yield no meal
Bud (*v*.). *Break forth, bloom.*
Gen. 40. 10 as though it *b*.
Num. 17. 8 rod of Aaron was *b*.
Job 14. 9 scent of water it will *b*.
Ps. 132. 17 make horn of David to *b*.
S. of S. 7. 12 let promegr. *b*. forth.
Ezek. 7. 10 behold, pride hath *b*.
Heb. 9. 4 and Aaron's rod that *b*.
R. V. S. of S. 6. 11 were in flower
Buffet. *Smite with fist.*
Mat. 26. 67 to spit in face and *b*. him
Mark 14. 65 spit . . and to *b*. him
1 Cor. 4. 11 naked, and are *b*.
2 Cor. 12. 7 mes. of Satan to *b*. me
1 Pet. 2. 20 *b*. for your faults
Build. *Construct, erect.*
Gen. 4. 17 and Cain, he *b*. a city
Ex. 1. 11 they *b*. . . treasure cities
Num. 23. 1 *b*. me here seven altars
Deut. 6. 10 cities which thou *b*.
Josh. 6. 26 riseth up and *b*. a city
Judg. 6. 24 Gideon *b*. an altar
Ruth 4. 11 *b*. the house of Israel
1 Sam. 2. 35 *b*. him a sure house
2 Sam. 5. 9 David *b*. round about
1 K. 2. 36 *b*. thee an house in Jer.
2 K. 14. 22 Azariah, he *b*. Elath
1 Chr. 6. 10 temple of S. *b*. in Jer.
2 Chr. 2. 1 S. deter. to *b*. an house
Ez. 1. 2 hath charged me to *b*.
Neh. 2. 5 that I may *b*. it
Job 3. 14 which *b*. desolate places
Ps. 28. 5 he shall destroy and not *b*.
Prov. 9. 1 wisdom hath *b*. her house
Eccl. 2. 4 I *b*. me houses
S. of S. 8. 9 *b*. . . palace of silver
Isa. 5. 2 and *b*. a tower in midst
Jer. 1. 10 to *b*. and to plant
Lam. 3. 5 hath *b*. against me
Ezek. 4. 2 *b*. a fort against it
Dan. 9. 25 com. to *b*. Jerusalem
Hos. 8. 14 Israel . . *b*. temples
Am. 5. 11 *b*. houses of hewn stone
Mic. 3. 10 *b*. up Zion with blood
Hab. 2. 12 woe to him that *b*.
Zeph. 1. 13 shall also *b*. houses
Hag. 1. 8 bring wood, *b*. the house
Zech. 6. 12 *b*. the temple of the Lord
Mal. 1. 4 *b*. the desolate places
Mat. 7. 24 *b*. his house upon a rock
Mark 15. 29 *b*. it in three days
Luke 4. 29 whereon their city was *b*.
Acts 15. 16 *b*. again the tabernacle
Rom. 15. 20 *b*. upon another found.
1 Cor. 3. 12 *b*. on this foundation
Gal. 2. 18 if I *b*. again the things
Eph. 2. 22 in whom ye are *b*.
Heb. 3. 3 who hath *b*. the house
Builder. *Who builds.*
1 K. 5. 18 Sol.'s *b*. and H.'s b.
2 K. 12. 11 laid it out to *b*.
2 Chr. 34. 11 to *b*. gave they it
Ez. 3. 10 *b*. laid the foundation
Ps. 118. 22 stone the *b*. refused.
Mat. 21. 42 stone which the *b*. rejec.
Mark 12. 10; Luke 20. 17; 1 Pet. 2. 7
Acts 4. 11 stone set at nought of b.
Heb. 11. 10 whose *b*. . . is God
Building (*n*.). *Structure.*
1 K. 9. 1 Solomon finished the *b*.
1 Chr. 28. 2 made ready for the *b*.
2 Chr. 33. 3 instructed for the *b*.
Eccl. 10. 18 slothful *b*. decayeth
Ezek. 40. 5 breadth of *b*. one reed
Mat. 24. 1 show . . *b*. of the temple
1 Cor. 3. 9 ye are God's *b*.
2 Cor. 5. 1 we have a *b*. of God
Eph. 2. 21 *b*. fitly framed . . groweth
Heb. 9. 11 tabernacle not of this *b*.
Rev. 21. 18 *b*. of wall was jasper
Built. *See* Build.
Bull. *Bull, ox, bullock.*
Gen. 32. 15 forty kine and ten *b*.
Job 21. 10 their *b*. genderth
Ps. 50. 13 eat the flesh of *b*.
Isa. 34. 7 and the bullock with the *b*.

Jer. 50. 11 and bellow as *b*.
Heb. 9. 13 blood of *b*. and goats
R. V. Isa. 51. 20 antelope
Bullock. *Bull, steer, ox.*
Ex. 29. 1 take one young *b*.
Lev. 4. 4 bring the *b*. to the door
Num. 7. 87 burnt off. were twelve *b*.
Deut. 15. 19 the firstlings of thy *b*.
Judg. 6. 25 take thy father's young *b*.
1 Sam. 1. 25 they slew a *b*.
1 K. 18. 23 Let them give us two *b*.
1 Chr. 15. 26 they offered seven *b*.
2 Chr. 29. 21 they brought seven *b*.
Ez. 8. 35 twelve *b*. for all Israel
Job 42. 8 take unto you now seven *b*.
Ps. 69. 31 better than ox or *b*.
Isa. 1. 11 delight not in blood of *b*.
Jer. 50. 27 slay all her *b*.
Ezek. 39. 18 eat flesh of . . *b*.
Hos. 12. 11 sacrifice *b*. in Gilgal
R. V. Lev. 4. 10; 9. 18; Deut 17. 1
  ox; Jer. 31. 18 calf; Jer. 50. 11
  strong horses
Bulrush. *Rush, papyrus.*
Ex. 2. 3 took for him an ark of *b*.
Isa. 18. 2 in vessels of *b*. upon water
  58. 5 bow down his head as a *b*.
R. V. Isa. 58. 5 rush; 18. 2 papyrus
Bulwark. *Fort, defence.*
Deut. 20. 20 shalt build *b*. against
2 Chr. 26. 15 on the towers and *b*.
Ps. 48. 13 mark well her *b*.
Eccl. 9. 14 and built great *b*.
Isa. 26. 1 appoint walls and *b*.
R. V. 2 Chr. 26. 15 battlements
Bunch. *Bundle, cluster, hump.*
Ex. 12. 22 take a *b*. of hyssop
2 Sam. 16. 1 met him with *b*. of raisins
1 Chr. 12. 40 figs and *b*. of raisins
Isa. 30. 6 treasures on *b*. of camels
R. V. 2 Sam. 16. 1; 1 Chr. 12. 40
  clusters
Bundle. *Compressed thing.*
Gen. 42. 35 every man's *b*. of money
1 Sam. 25. 29 bound in the *b*. of life
S. of S. 1. 13 *b*. of myrrh is my belov.
Mat. 13. 30 bind them in *b*. to burn
Acts 28. 3 Paul had gathered a *b*.
Burden (*n*.). *Load.*
Ex. 23. 5 see ass lying under his *b*.
Num. 4. 15 the *b*. of the sons of K.
Deut. 1. 12 How can I bear your *b*.
2 Sam. 15. 33 shalt be a *b*. to me
2 K. 8. 9 took forty camels' *b*.
2 Chr. 24. 27 concr. *b*. laid upon him
Neh. 13. 15 all manner of *b*. which
Job 7. 20 I am a *b*. to myself
Ps. 55. 22 Cast thy *b*. upon the Lord
Isa. 13. 1 the *b*. of Babylon
Jer. 17. 21 bear no *b*. on the sab. d.
Ezek. 12. 10 this *b*. concerneth the
Hos. 8. 10 sorrow for *b*. of the king
Nah. 1. 1 the *b*. of Nineveh
Hab. 1. 1 the *b*. which Habakkuk
Zech. 9. 1 the *b*. of the word of the L.
Mat. 20. 12 which have borne the *b*.
Luke 11. 46 lade men with *b*.
Acts 21. 3 ship was to unlade her *b*.
Gal. 6. 5 man shall bear his own *b*.
Rev. 2. 24 put . . none other *b*.
R. V. Gen. 49. 14 sheepfolds; Am.
  5. 11 exactions
Burden. (*v*.). *To load, oppress.*
Eccl. 12. 5 grasshop. shall be a *b*.
Zech. 12. 3 all that *b*. themselves
2 Cor. 12. 16 I did not *b*. you
R. V. 2 Cor. 8. 13 distressed
Burdensome. *Oppressive, irksome.*
Zech. 12. 3 make Jerus. a *b*. stone
2 Cor. 11. 9 kept . . from being *b*.
1 Thes. 2. 6 we might have been *b*.
Burial. *Sepulture.*
2 Chr. 26. 23 the *b*. belonged to k.
Eccl. 6. 3 that he have no *b*.
Isa. 14. 20 not joined with them in *b*.
Jer. 22. 19 buried with the *b*. of
Mat. 26. 12 she did it for my *b*.
R. V. Acts 8. 2 buried
Buried. *See* Bury.
Burier. *Who buries.*
Ezek. 39. 15 till *b*. have buried it
Burn. *Consume by fire.*
Gen. 11. 3 make brick and *b*. them
Ex. 3. 2 the bush *b*. with fire
Lev. 4. 12 *b*. him on the wood
Num. 11. 1 fire of the Lord *b*.

Deut. 4. 11 mount. *b*. with fire
Josh. 6. 24 *b*. the city with fire
Judg. 15. 6 *b*. her and her father
1 Sam. 30. 14 and we *b*. Ziklag
1 K. 9. 16 taken Gezer, and *b*. it
2 K. 10. 26 im. of Baal, and *b*. them
1 Chr. 14. 12 com., and they were *b*.
2 Chr. 15. 16 *b*. it at . . Kidron
Esth. 1. 12 and his anger *b*.
Job 1. 16 hath *b*. up the sheep
Ps. 79. 5 jealousy *b*. like fire
Isa. 1. 31 shall both *b*. together
Jer. 4. 4 *b*. that none can quench
Lam. 2. 3 he *b*. against Jacob.
Ezek. 1. 13 appearance like *b*. coals
Hos. 7. 6 in morning it *b*. as fire
Mal. 4. 1 shall *b*. as an oven
Mat. 13. 30 bind them . . to *b*. them
Luke 3. 17 the chaff he will *b*.
John 5. 35 *b*. and shining light
Acts 19. 19 brought . . books and *b*.
Rom. 1. 27 woman, *b*. in their lust
1 Cor. 7. 9 better to marry than *b*.
2 Cor. 11. 29 offended, and I *b*. not
Heb. 13. 11 those beasts are *b*.
Rev. 21. 8 lake which *b*. with fire
Burning. *Flaming, consuming.*
Gen. 15. 17 a *b*. lamp that passed
Lev. 26. 16 will appoint *b*. ague
Deut. 28. 22 smite with extreme *b*.
Job 41. 19 out of his mouth go *b*.
Ps. 140. 10 *b*. coals fall upon them
Prov. 16. 27 his lips as *b*. fire
Isa. 34. 9 land . . become *b*. pitch
Jer. 20. 9 word in heart as *b*. fire
Ezek. 1. 13 appearance like *b*. coals
Dan. 3. 6 cast into *b*. furnace
Luke 12. 35 loins girded, lights *b*.
John 5. 35 *b*. and shining light
Rev. 4. 5 lamps *b*. before throne
Burning (*n*.).
Ex. 21. 25 *b*. for *b*., wound for w.
Lev. 10. 6 bewail *b*. which . . Lord
Deut. 29. 23 brimstone, . . salt . . *b*.
2 Chr. 16. 14 made great *b*. for him
Isa. 3. 24 and *b*. instead of beauty
Jer. 34. 5 and with *b*. of thy fathers
Am. 4. 11 firebrand pluck. out of *b*.
Rev. 18. 9 see smoke of her *b*.
Burnished. *Polished.*
Ezek. 1. 7 like colour of *b*. brass
Burnt. *See* Burn.
Burnt Offering.
Gen. 8. 20 and offered *b*. *o*.
Ex. 10. 25 sacrifices and *b*. *o*.
Lev. 1. 4 hand on head of *b*. *o*.
Num. 6. 11 sin offering . . *b*. *o*.
Deut. 12. 6 shall bring your *b*. *o*.
Josh. 8. 31; Judg. 11. 31; 1 Sam.
  6. 14; 2 Sam. 6. 17; 1 K. 3. 4; 2
  K. 3. 27; 1 Chr. 6. 49; 2 Chr. 1. 6;
  Ez. 3. 2; Neh. 10. 33; Job 1. 5,
  Ps. 40. 6; Isa. 1. 11; Jer. 6. 20;
  Ezek. 40. 42; Mark 12. 33; Heb.
  10. 6
Burnt Sacrifice.
Ex. 30. 9 offer no strange *b*. *s*.
Lev. 1. 3; Num. 23. 6; Deut. 33.
  10; Judg 6. 26; 2 Sam. 24. 22; 1
  K. 18. 33; 2 K. 16. 15; 1 Chr.
  16. 1; 2 Chr. 13. 11; Ps. 20. 3
Burst. *Break, rend.*
Job 32. 19 *b*. like new bottles
Prov. 3. 10 thy presses shall *b*.
Isa. 30. 14 not found in the *b*. of it
Jer. 2. 20 I have . . *b*. thy bands
Nah. 1. 13 and will *b*. thy bonds
Mark 2. 22 wine doth *b*. the bottles
Acts 1. 18 headlong, he *b*. asunder
R. V. Prov. 3. 10 overflow; Isa.
  30. 14 pieces
Bury. *Inter, entomb.*
Gen. 23. 4 I may *b*. my dead
Num. 11. 34 *b*. people that lusted
Deut. 21. 23 thou shalt . . *b*. him
Josh. 24. 30 *b*. him in the border
Judg. 16. 31 *b*. him between Z. & E.
1 Sam. 2. 1 *b*. him in his house
2 Sam. 2. 4 men of Jabesh-g. *b*. Saul
1 K. 2. 31 Do as he said, . . and *b*.
2 K. 9. 10 and . . none to *b*. her
1 Chr. 10. 12 *b*. their bones under
2 Chr. 9. 31 was *b*. in city of David
Ps. 79. 3 was none to *b*. them
Jer. 7. 32 they shall *b*. in Tophet
Ezek. 39. 11 there shall they *b*. Gog

Hos. 9. 6 Memphis shall *b.* them
Mat. 8. 21 suffer me to *b* my father
  8. 22 ; 14. 12 ; 27. 7 ; Luke 9. 59 ;
  9. 60 ; 16. 22 ; Acts 5. 6, 9, 10 ; 1
  Cor. 15. 4

Burying. *Entombment.*
Gen. 23. 4 give poss. of . . *b.* place
Judg. 16. 31 in the *b.* place of M.
Mark 14. 8 anoint my body to the *b.*
John 12. 7 against the day of my *b.*

Bush. *Shrub, bramble.*
Ex. 3. 2 flame . . out of . . a *b.*
Deut. 33. 16 that dwelt in the *b.*
Job 30. 4 cut up mallows by the *b.*
Isa. 7. 19 shall rest upon all *b.*
Mark 12. 26 in the *b.* God spake
Luke 20. 37 Moses showed at the *b.*
Acts 7. 30 in flame of fire in a *b.*
R. V. Isa. 7. 19 pastures

Bushel. *Measure.*
Mat. 5. 15 Mark 4. 21 ; Luke 11. 33
is candle to be put under a *b.*

Bushy. *Flowing.*
S. of S. 5. 11 his locks are *b.*

Business. *Work, matter, calling.*
Gen. 39. 11 went . . to do his *b.*
Deut. 24. 5 neither be charged with *b.*
Josh. 2. 14 utter not this our *b.*
Judg. 18. 7 had no *b.* with . . man.
1 Sam. 21. 2 king hath com. me a *b.*
1 Chr. 26. 30 in the *b.* of the Lord
2 Chr. 13. 10 Levites wait their *b,*
Neh. 11. 16 oversight of the . . *b.*
Esth. 3. 9 have charge of . . *b.*
Ps. 107. 23 do *b.* in great waters
Prov. 22. 29 man diligent in *b.*
Eccl. 5. 3 through multitude of *b.*
Dan. 8. 27 Dan. did the king's *b.*
Luke 2. 49 be about my Father's *b.*
Acts 6. 3 may appoint over this *b.*
Rom. 12. 11 Be not slothful in *b.*
1 Thes. 4. 11 study to do your *b.*
R. V. Luke 2. 49 house ; Rom. 12.
  11 diligence ; 16. 2 matter

Busy. *Engaged.*
1 K. 20. 40 thy servant was *b.*

Busybody. R. V. *meddler.*
1 Tim. 5. 13 but tattlers and . . *b.* s
2 Thes. 3. 11 working not, but . . *b. b.*
1 Pet. 4. 15 *b. b.* in . . men's matters

Butler. *Who gives drink.*
Gen. 40. 1 *b.* of the king of Egypt
  40. 2, 5, 9, 13, 20, 23 ; 41. 9

Butlership. *Butler's office.*
Gen. 40. 21 restored chief b. to *b.*

Butter. *Curdled milk, cheese*
Gen. 18. 8 took *b.* and milk
Deut. 32. 14 *b.* of kine, and milk
Judg. 5. 25 she brought forth *b.*
2 Sam. 17. 29 honey, and *b.* and sheep
Job. 20. 17 brooks of honey and *b.*
Ps. 55. 21 words . . smoother than *b.*
Prov. 30. 33 churning . . bringeth *b.*
Isa. 7. 15 *b.* and honey shall he eat

Buttocks. *Hip, bottom.*
2 Sam. 10. 4 cut off gar. to . . *b.*
1 Chr. 19. 4 cut off garments by . . *b.*
Isa. 20. 4 even with *b.* uncovered

Buy. *Acquire, purchase.*
Gen. 33. 19 he *b.* a parcel of a field
Ex. 21. 2 if thou *b.* an Hebrew ser.
Lev. 22. 11 if . . priest *b.* any soul
Deut. 2. 6 ye shall *b.* meat of
Josh. 24. 32 in ground which J. *b.*
Ruth 4. 4 *b.* it before the inhab.
2 Sam. 12. 3 which he *b.* and nour.
1 K. 16. 24 *b.* the hill Samaria
2 K. 12. 12 *b.* timber and . . stone
1 Chr. 21. 24 I will verily *b.* it
2 Chr. 34. 11 *b.* hewn stone and t.
Neh. 5. 16 neither *b.* we any land
Prov. 23. 23 *b.* truth, sell it not
Isa. 43. 24 hath *b.* no sweet cane
Jer. 32. 8 *b.* my field, I pray
Am. 8. 6 that we may *b.* the poor
Mat. 13. 44 selleth all . . and *b.*
  13. 46 ; 14. 15 ; 21. 12 ; 25. 9 ; 27. 7
Mark 6. 36 may go and *b.* themselves
Luke 9. 13 go and *b.* meat for
John 4. 8 gone away . . to *b.* meat
Acts 7. 16 sepulchre that Abrah. *b.*
1 Cor. 6. 20 ye are *b.* with a price
Jas. 4. 13 continue there . . and *b.*
2 Pet. 2. 1 denying the Lord that *b.*
Rev. 3. 18 *b.* of me gold tried

Buyer. *Who buys.*

Prov. 20. 14 naught, sayeth the *o.*
Isa. 24. 2 as with the *b.,* so
Ezek. 7. 12 let not the *b.* rejoice

By and By. *Straightway.*
Mat. 13. 21 *b. and b.* he is off
Mark 6. 25 give me *b. and b.*
Luke 17. 7 *b. and b.* sit down

Byways. *Crooked ways.*
Judg. 5. 6 trav. walked through *b. w.*

Byword. *Reproach.*
Deut. 28. 37 a *b.* among nations
1 K. 9. 7 *b.* among all people
2 Chr. 7. 20 make this house a *b.*
Job 17. 6 made me a *b.* of people
Ps. 44. 14 mak. us *b.* among heathen

<h1 style="text-align:center">C.</h1>

Cab. *About three pints.*
2 K. 6. 25 fourth *c.* of dove's dung

Cabins. R. V. *cells.*
Jer. 37. 16 Jer. . . entered into the *c.*

Cage. *Basket, guard.*
Jer. 5. 27 *c.* is full of birds
Rev. 18. 2 *c.* of every unclean . . b.
R. V. Rev. 18. 2 hold

Cake. *Perforated mass.*
Ex. 29. 2 *c.* . . tempered with oil
Lev. 2. 4 bring *c.* of fine flour
Num. 6. 15 *c.* . . mingled with oil
2 Sam. 6. 19 every one a *c.* of b.
Mass baked on hot stones.
Gen. 18. 6 made *c.* on the hearth
Ex. 12. 39 they baked unleavened *c.*
Num. 11. 8 and made *c.* of it
Josh. 5. 11 unleavened *c.* and . . corn
Judg. 7. 13 *c.* of barley bread
2 Sam. 13. 8 and did bake the *c.*
1 K. 17. 13 make me . . a little *c.*
Jer. 7. 18 knead dough to make *c.*
Ezek. 4. 12 eat it as barley *c.*
Hos. 7. 8 Ephraim is *c.* not turned
Mass, lump, tract.
1 Sam. 25. 18 two hun. *c.* of figs
1 Chr. 12. 40 knead . . and make *c.*
R. V. 1 Chr. 23. 29 wafers

Calamity. *Mist, distress.*
Deut. 32. 35 day of *c.* is at hand
2 Sam. 22. 19 in the day of my *c.*
Ps. 141. 5 prayer also . . in their *c.*
Prov. 1. 26 will laugh at your *c.*
Jer. 46. 21 day of their *c.* was come
Ezek. 35. 5 shed blood in . . their *c.*
Obad. 13 in the day of their *c.*
Accident, misfortune.
Job 6. 2 *c.* laid in the balances
Ps. 57. 1 my refuge until these *c.*
Prov. 19. 13 foolish son is the *c.* of
R. V. Ps. 141. 5 wickedness

Calamus. *Reed, cane.*
Ex. 30. 23 sweet *c.* two hun. and
S. of S. 4. 14 saffron, *c.* and cin.
Ezek. 27. 19 *c.* were in thy market

Caldron. *Kettle, pot.*
1 Sam. 2. 14 struck it into the . . *c.*
2 Chr. 35. 13 in *c.* and in pans
Job 41. 20 as of seething pot or *c.*
Jer. 52. 19 the bowls and the *c.*
Ezek. 11. 3 this city is the *c.*
Mic. 3. 3 as flesh within the *c.*
R. V. Job 41. 20 burning rushes ;
  Jer. 52. 18, 19 pots

Calf. *Calf, bullock.*
Gen. 18. 7 fetch *c.* tender and good
Ex. 32. 4 made it a molten *c.*
Lev. 9. 3 take a *c.* and lamb
Deut. 9. 21 the *c.* which ye had
1 Sam. 14. 32 took . . oxen and *c.*
1 K. 12. 28 made two *c.* of gold
2 K. 10. 29 the golden *c.* that were
2 Chr. 11. 15 *c.* which he had made
Neh. 9. 18 made them a molten *c.*
Ps. 29. 6 mak. th. to skip like a *c.*
Isa. 11. 6 *c.* and young lion togeth.
Jer. 34. 18 cut the *c.* in twain
Ezek. 1. 7 feet like sole of . . *c.*
Hos. 8. 5 thy *c.,* O Samaria
Am. 6. 4 *c.* eat out of . . the stall
Mal. 4. 2 grow up as *c.* of stall
Luke 15. 23 bring . . the fatted *c.*
Acts 7. 41 and they made a *c.*
Heb. 9. 19 took the blood of *c.*
Rev. 4. 7 second beast like a *c.*

Calker. *Repairer.*
Ezek. 27. 9 wise men were thy *c.*

Call. *Name, bid, cry out.*
Gen. 1. 5 God *c.* the light Day

---

  2. 19 ; 3. 9 ; 4. 17 ; 5. 2 ; 11. 9 ; 12. 8
Ex. 1. 18 king . . *c.* for midwives
  2. 7 ; 3. 4 ; 7. 11 ; 8. 8 ; 9. 27 ; 10. 16
Lev. 1. 1 Lord *c.* unto Moses
Num. 11. 3 he *c.* . . the place Tab.
  12. 5 ; 13. 16 ; 16. 12 ; 21. 3 ; 22. 5
Deut. 2. 11 M. call them Emims
Josh. 4. 4 Joshua *c.* the twelve mer.
Judg. 1. 26 *c.* the name . . Luz
Ruth 1. 20 *c.* me not Naomi
1 Sam. 3. 4 the Lord *c.* Samuel
2 Sam. 1. 7 saw me, and *c.* unto me
1 K. 1. 9 Adoni. *c.* all his brethren
2 K. 3. 10 the Lord hath *c.* these
1 Chr. 4. 9 *c.* his name Jabez
2 Chr. 3. 17 *c.* the . . name Jachin
Neh. 5. 12 Then I *c.* the priests
Esth. 4. 5 Then *c.* Esther for H.
Job 1. 4 *c.* their three sisters
Ps. 4. 1 hear me when I *c.,* O God
  14. 4 ; 17. 6 ; 18. 3 ; 20. 9 ; 31. 17
Prov. 1. 24 I have *c.,* ye refused
S. of S. 5. 6 I *c.,* he gave no answer
Isa. 7. 14 *c.* his name Immanuel
  8. 3 ; 12. 4 ; 13. 3 ; 21. 11 ; 22. 12
Jer. 1. 15 *c.* all the families
  3. 17 ; 6. 30 ; 7. 13 ; 9. 17 ; 10. 25
Lam. 1. 15 *c.* an assembly against
Ezek. 36. 29 will *c.* for the corn
Dan. 2. 2 k. com. to *c.* the mag.
Hos. 1. 4 *c.* his name Jezreel
Joel 1. 14 *c.* a solemn assembly
Amos 5. 8 *c.* for the waters of sea
Jonah 1. 6 arise, *c.* upon God
Zeph. 3. 9 all *c.* upon name of L.
Hag. 1. 11 I *c.* for a drought
Zech. 3. 10 *c.* every man his neighb
Mal. 1. 4 *c.* them . . bor. of wick.
Mat. 1. 21 *c.* his name Jesus
  10. 1 *c.* unto him his twelve
  20. 8 ; 22. 3 ; 23. 9 ; 25. 14
Mark 1. 20 straightway he *c.* them
  6. 7 ; 7. 14 ; 8. 1 ; 12. 43 ; 15. 44
Luke 1. 13 *c.* his name John
  7. 19 ; 16. 5 ; 18. 16 ; 19. 13 ; 20. 44
John 10. 3 *c.* his . . sheep by name
Acts 6. 2 the twelve *c.* the multi.
Rom. 4. 17 quickeneth the d. and *c*
1 Cor. 7. 15 hath *c.* us to peace
Gal. 5. 13 been *c.* to liberty
Eph. 4. 4 as ye are *c.* in hope
Col. 3. 15 are *c.* in one body
1 Tim. 6. 12 whereunto ye are *c.*
Heb. 3. 13 while it is *c.* to day
Jas. 2. 23 *c.* the friend of God
1 Pet. 2. 21 hereunto were we *c.*
1 John 3. 1 *c.* the sons of God
Rev. 1. 9 the isle *c.* Patmos

Calling. *Vocation, summons.*
Rom. 11. 29 gifts and *c.* of God
1 Cor. 1. 26 ye see your *c.,* brethren
Eph. 1. 18 the hope of his *c.*
Phil. 3. 14 press tow. high *c.* of. God
2 Thes. 1. 11 worthy of this *c.*
2 Tim. 1. 9 *c.* us with an holy *c.*
Heb. 3. 1 partakers of . . heavenly *c*
2 Pet. 1. 10 make . . *c.* and e. sure

Calm (*n.*). *Silence, stillness.*
Ps. 107. 29 maketh the storm a *c.*
Mat. 8. 26 there was a great *c.*
Mark 4. 39 ; Luke 8. 24

Calm (*a.*). *Quiet, serene.*
Jonah 1. 11, 12 the sea may be *c.*

Calvary. R. V. *The skull.*
Luke 23. 33 the place ·called C.

Calve. *Yield, bring forth.*
Job 21. 10 the cow *c.* and casteth
  39. 1 mark when hinds do *c.*
Ps. 29. 9 L. maketh hinds to *c.*
Jer. 14. 5 the hinds also *c.*

Came. *See* **Come.**

Camel. *Camel.*
Gen. 12. 16 she asses and *c.*
  24. 10–64 ; 30. 43 ; 31. 17 ; 32. 7 ;
Ex. 9. 3 hand of Lord is upon *c.*
Lev. 11. 4 *c.* because he cheweth
Deut. 14. 7 the *c.* and . . hare
Judg. 6. 5 *c.* were without numbe.
1 Sam. 15. 3 ox and sheep and *c.*
1 K. 10. 2 *c.* that bare spices
2 K. 8. 9 forty *c.* burden
1 Chr. 5. 21 took away their *c.*
2 Chr. 14. 15 car. away sheep and *c*
Ez. 2. 67 their *c.,* four hundred
Esth. 8. 14 post rode upon *c.*
Job 1. 3 sub. was . . three thousand *c*

Isa. 21. 7 saw a chariot of *c.*
Jer. 49. 29 vessels, and their *c.*
Ezek. 25. 5 make R. a stable for *c.*
Zech. 14. 15 the plague of the *c.*
Mat. 3. 4 had his raiment of *c.* hair
Mark 10. 25 *c.* to go through the e.
Luke 18. 25 easier for a *c.* to go

Camp (*n.*).   *Encampment.*
Ex. 14. 20 *c.* of the Egyptians
16. 13; 19. 16; 29. 14; 32. 17; 33. 7
Lev. 4. 12 forth without the *c.*
6. 11; 8. 17; 9. 11; 10. 4; 13. 46; 14. 3
Num. 1. 52 every man to his *c.*
4. 5; 5. 2; 10. 2; 11. 1; 12. 14; 14. 44
Josh. 5. 8 they abode in . . the *c.*
Judg. 7. 17 I come outside the *c.*
1 **Sam.** 4. 3 people were come into *c.*
4. 5; 13. 17; 14. 21; 17. 4; 26. 6
2 **Sam.** 1. 2 man came out of *c.*
1 **K.** 16. 16 made Omri king in . . *c.*
2 **K.** 3. 24 came to *c.* of Israel
2 **Chr.** 22. 1 the Arabians to the *c.*
Ps. 78. 28 the midst of their *c.*
Isa. 37. 36 angel . . and smote the *c.*
Ezek. 4. 2 set the *c.* against it
Joel 2. 11 his *c.* is very great
Am. 4. 10 stink of your *c.* to come
Heb. 13. 11 bodies burnt without *c.*
Rev. 20. 9 compassed the *c.* of

Camp (*v.*).   *Settle down, encamp.*
Ex. 19. 12 *c.* before the mount
Isa. 29. 3 I will *c.* against thee
Jer. 50. 29 *c.* against it, round
Nah. 3. 17 which *c.* in the hedges

Camphire.   R. V.   *Henna.*
S. of S. 1. 14 as a cluster of *c.*
4. 13 fruits, *c.* with spikenard

Can, Cannot.
Gen. 3. 16 if man *c.* number dust
19. 19 I *c. n.* escape to mount
Ex. 10. 5 *c. n.* be able to see
Num. 22. 18 I *c. n.* go beyond
Deut. 7. 17 *c.* I dispossess them
Josh. 24. 19 ye *c. n.* serve the Lord
Ruth 4. 6 *c. n.* redeem for myself
1 **Sam.** 17. 39 I *c. n.* go with you
2 **Sam.** 12. 23 *c.* I bring him back
Neh. 6. 3 I *c. n.* come down
Esth. 8. 6 how *c.* I endure
Job 4. 2 who *c.* withhold himself
Ps. 78. 19 *c.* God furnish a table
Prov. 30. 21 four it *c. n.* bear
Eccl. 1. 15 *c. n.* be made straight
S. of S. 8. 7 waters *c. n.* quench love
Isa. 59. 14 and equity *c. n.* enter
Dan. 2. 10 not a man *c.* show
Mat. 5. 14 city on hill *c. n.* be hid
Mark 1. 4 thou *c.* make me clean
Luke 1. 22 he *c. n.* speak to them
John 3. 5 he *c. n.* enter the kingdom
Acts 10. 47 *c* any man forbid water,
1 **Cor.** 2. 14 neither *c.* he know them
2 **Cor.** 3. 7 Israel *c.* not . . behold
Gal. 3. 21 which *c.* have given life
1 **Thes.** 3. 9 thanks *c.* we render
1 **Tim.** 6. 7 *c.* carry nothing out
Heb. 3. 19 they *c.* not enter in
Jas. 2. 14 *c.* faith save him
1 **John** 4. 20 how *c.* he love God
Rev. 2. 2 thou *c.* not bear them

Candle.   R. V.   *Lamp.*
Job 18. 6 *c.* shall he put out
Ps. 18. 28 thou wilt light my *c.*
Prov. 20. 27 spirit of man is the *c.*
Jer. 25. 10 take . . light of the *c.*
Zeph. 1. 12 search Jerusalem with *c.*
Mat. 5. 15 neither do men light a *c.*
Mark 4. 21 is a *c.* brought to
Luke 11. 36 a *c.* doth give light
Rev. 22. 5 they need no *c.*

Candlestick.   *Lamp-stand.*
Ex. 25. 31 make a *c.* of pure gold
26. 35; 30. 27; 31. 8; 35. 14; 37. 17
Lev. 24. 4 order the pure *c.*
Num. 3. 31 *c.* and the altars
1 **K.** 7. 49 S. made *c.* of pure gold
2 **K.** 4. 10 table, stool and *c.*
1 **Chr.** 28. 15 the weight for the *c.*
2 **Chr.** 4. 7 he made ten *c.* of gold
Jer. 52. 19 the caldrons and *c.*
Dan. 5. 5 wrote over against the *c.*
Zech. 4. 2 and, behold, *c.* of gold
Mat. 5. 15 put it on a *c.*
Mark 4. 21 is *c.* . . not . . set on *c.*
Luke 8. 16; 11. 33
Heb. 9. 2 tabernacle wherein the *c.*

Rev. 1. 12 saw seven golden *c.*
1. 13, 20; 2. 1, 5; 11. 4
R. V. **Mat.** 5. 15; **Mark** 4. 21;
Luke 8. 16 stand

Cane.   *Reed, cane.*
Isa. 43. 24 brought me no sweet *c.*
Jer. 6. 20 *c.* from a far country

Canker.   *Gangrene.*
2 **Tim.** 2. 17 word will eat as a *c.*

Cankered.   *Eaten, rusted.*
Jas. 5. 3 your gold and silver is *c.*

Cankerworm.   *Chafer, locust.*
Joel 1. 4 which the *c. w.* hath left
Nah. 3. 15 eat thee like the *c. w.*

Captain.   *Leader, chief.*
Gen. 37. 36 sold him to Pharaoh's *c.*
Num. 2. 3–29 *c.* of the sons
Deut. 1. 15 *c.* over thousande
Josh. 5. 14 as *c.* of the host
Judg. 4. 2 *c.* of whose host was Sis.
1 **Sam.** 9. 16 shalt anoint him *c.*
2 **Sam.** 2. 8 Abner . . *c.* of Saul's
1 **K.** 1. 19 Joab *c.* of the host
2 **K.** 1. 9 king sent unto him a *c.*
1 **Chr.** 11. 6 shall be chief and *c.*
2 **Chr.** 1. 2 to the *c.* of thousands
Job 39. 25 the thunder of the *c.*
Isa. 3. 3 take away the *c.* of fifty
Jer. 13. 21 taught them to be *c.*
Ezek. 23. 6 clothed . . *c.* and rulers
Dan. 3. 2 governors and *c.* gath.
Nah. 3. 17 thy *c.* as grasshoppers
Mark 6. 21 lords, high *c.*, and
Luke 22. 4 communed with the *c.*
John 18. 12 *c.* and officers took J.
Acts 21. 31 tidings came to the *c.*
Rev. 19. 18 may eat the flesh of *c.*
R. V. 1 **Sam.** 9. 16; 10. 1; 13. 4
prince; **Jer.** 51. 23, 28, 57; **Dan.**
3. 2, 3, 37; 6. 7 governors

Captive.   *Exile, prisoner.*
Gen. 31. 26 carried . . daughters as *c.*
Ex. 12. 29 firstborn of the *c.*
Deut. 21. 10 hast taken them *c.*
Judg. 5. 12 and lead thy captivity *c.*
1 **K.** 8. 46 carry them away *c.*
2 **K.** 24. 16 king of Bab. brought *c.*
1 **Chr.** 5. 6 king of Assyria carried *c.*
2 **Chr.** 28. 5 carried mul. of them *c.*
Ps. 68. 18 hast led captivity *c.*
Isa. 49. 24 shall . . *c.* be delivered
Jer. 28. 4 with all the *c.* of Judah
Ezek. 1. 1 I was among the *c.*
Dan. 2. 25 found a man of the *c.*
Am. 6. 7 carried away *c.* the
Obad. 11. strangers carried away *c.*
Luke 21. 24 shall be led away *c.*
2 **Tim.** 2. 26 taken *c.* by him at will
Eph. 4. 8 he led captivity *c.*
R. V. **Isa.** 20. 4; 45. 13; 49. 21 exile

Captivity.   *Exile, bondage.*
Num. 21. 29 into *c.* unto Sihon
Deut. 21. 13 put raiment of her *c.* off
Judg. 18. 30 until the day of *c.*
2 **K.** 24. 15 those carried he into *c.*
1 **Chr.** 5. 22 dwelt . . until the *c.*
2 **Chr.** 6. 37 pray in land of their *c.*
Ez. 2. 1 went up out of *c.*
Neh. 1. 2 which were left of the *c.*
Esth. 2. 6 carried away with . . *c.*
Job 42. 10 turned the *c.* of Job
Ps. 68. 18 hast led *c.* captive
Isa. 5. 13 people are gone into *c.*
Jer. 15. 2 for the *c.* to the *c.*
Lam. 1. 5 children . . gone into *c.*
Ezek. 12. 11 shall go into *c.*
Dan. 11. 33 shall fall by *c.* and spoil
Hos. 6. 11 the *c.* of my people
Obad. 20 *c.* of this host of children
Mic. 1. 16 gone into *c.* from
Nah. 3. 10 they went into *c.*
Hab. 1. 9 shall gather the *c.*
Zeph. 2. 7 shall turn away their *c.*
Zech. 6. 10 Take of them of the *c.*
Rom. 7. 23 to the law of sin
2 **Cor.** 10. 5 bring. into *c.* . . thought
Eph. 4. 8 he led *c.* captive
Rev. 13. 10 he that leadeth into *c.*

Carbuncle.   *Bright stone.*
Ex. 28. 17 a topaz and *c.*
Isa. 54. 12 make thy gates of *c.*
Ezek. 28. 13 the emerald, the *c.*

Carcase.   *Dead body.*
Gen. 15. 11 fowls came upon the *c.*
Lev. 5. 2 *c.* of unclean cattle
Num. 14. 29 thy *c.* shall fall in

Deut. 28. 26 thy *c.* shall be meat
Josh. 8. 29 take his *c.* down from
Judg. 14. 8 bees and honey in the *c.*
1 **Sam.** 17. 46 give *c.* . . unto the fowls
1 **K.** 13. 22 thy *c.* shall not come
2 **K.** 9. 37 *c.* . . shall be as dung
Isa. 14. 19 as a *c.* trodden under feet
Jer. 7. 33 the *c.* of the people
Ezek. 43. 7 nor by the *c.* of their kings
Nah. 3. 3 and a great number of *c.*
Mat. 24. 28 wheresoever the *c.* is
Heb. 3. 17 *c.* fell in wilderness
R. V. **Lev.** 11. 26–; **Judg.** 14. 8 body

Care (*n.*).   *Anxiety, oversight.*
1 **Sam.** 10. 2 left *c.* of the asses
2 **K.** 4. 13 careful . . with all this *c.*
Jer. 49. 21 the nation without *c.*
Ezek. 4. 16 shall eat bread with *c.*
Luke 10. 34 he took *c.* of him
1 **Cor.** 9. 9 doth God take *c.* for oxen ?
2 **Cor.** 11. 28 *c.* of all the churches
1 **Tim.** 3. 5 take *c.* of the church
1 **Pet.** 5. 7 casting all your *c.* upon him
R. V. **Ezek.** 4. 16 carefulness; 1
Pet. 5. 7 anxiety

Care (*v.*).   *Regard, concern.*
Deut. 11. 12 land thy God *c.* for
2 **Sam.** 18. 3 they will not *c.* for us
Ps. 142. 4 no man *c.* for my soul
Mat. 22. 16 neither *c.* thou for any
Mark 4. 38 Master, *c.* thou not
Luke 10. 40 dost thou not *c.* that
John 12. 6 he *c.* for the poor
Acts 18. 17 Gallio *c.* for none
1 **Cor.** 7. 34 she that is married *c.*
Phil. 2. 20 who will naturally *c.*
1 **Pet.** 5. 7 God, for he *c.* for you

Careful.   *Mindful.*
2 **K.** 4. 13 thou hast been *c.* for us
Jer. 17. 8 *c.* in year of drought
Dan. 3. 16 not *c.* to answer thee
Luke 10. 41 art *c.* and troubled
Phil. 4. 6 be *c.* for nothing
Tit. 3. 8 *c.* to maintain good works
R. V. **Phil.** 4. 10 did take thought

Carefully.   *Anxiously.*
Deut. 15. 5 if thou *c.* hearken
Mic. 1. 12 inhab. waited *c.* for good
Phil. 2. 28 sent him the more *c.*
Heb. 12. 17 sought it *c.* with tears
R. V. **Deut.** 15. 5; **Phil.** 2. 28;
Heb. 12. 17 dilligently; **Mic.** 1. 12
anxiously

Carefulness.   *Cautiousness.*
Ezek. 12. 18 drink . . water with *c.*
1 **Cor.** 7. 32 have you without *c.*
2 **Cor.** 7. 11 what *c.* it wrought
R. V. 1 **Cor.** 7. 32 be free from
cares; 2 **Cor.** 7. 11 earnest care

Careless.   *Confident.*
Judg. 18. 7 the people . . dwelt *c.*
Isa. 32. 9 *c.* daughters; give ear
Ezek. 30. 9 make the *c.* . . afraid
R. V. **Judg.** 18. 7 in security

Carelessly.   *Confidently.*
Isa. 47. 8 thou that dwellest *c.*
Ezek. 39. 6 dwell *c.* in the isles
Zeph. 2. 15 city that dwelt *c.*
R. V. **Ezek.** 39. 6 securely

Carnal.   *Fleshly.*
Rom. 7. 14 but I am *c.*, sold unto sin
1 **Cor.** 3. 1 speak but as unto *c.*
2 **Cor.** 10. 4 weapons . . are not *c.*
Heb. 7. 16 law of a *c.* commandm.
R. V. 1 **Cor.** 3. 4 men; 2 **Cor.** 10. 4
of the flesh; **Rom.** 8. 7 mind of
the flesh

Carnally.   *Lustfully.*
Lev. 18. 20 shalt not lie *c.* with
Num. 5. 13 man lie with her *c.*
Rom. 8. 6 to be *c.* minded is death
R. V. **Rom.** 8. 6 mind of the flesh

Carpenter.   *Wood artificer.*
2 **Sam.** 5. 11 cedar trees, and *c.*
2 **K.** 12. 11 laid it out to the *c.*
1 **Chr.** 14. 1 and *c.* to build him
Isa. 44. 13 *c.* stretcheth his rule
Jer. 24. 1 with the *c.* and smiths
Zech. 1. 20 Lord shewed me four *c.*
Mat. 13. 55; **Mark** 6. 3 the *c.'s* son
R. V. **Jer.** 24. 1; 29. 2 craftsmen;
Zech. 1. 20 smiths

Carriage.   R. V.   *Baggage, goods.*
Judg. 18. 21 put the *c.* before them
1 **Sam.** 17. 22 in hand of keeper of *c.*
Isa. 10. 28 at Mic. hath laid up his *c.*

Acts 21 15 we took up our *c.*
Carried. *See* **Carry.**
Carry. *Bear, convey.*
Gen. 42. 19 *c.* corn for the famine
Ex. 12. 46 shalt not *c.* forth ought
Lev. 6. 11 *c.* forth the ashes
Num. 11. 12 *c.* them in thy bosom
Deut. 14. 24 not able to *c.* it
Josh. 4. 3 ye shall *c.* them over
Judg. 16. 3 Samson *c.* them up
1 Sam. 5. 8 let the ark be *c.*
2 Sam 19. 18 *c.* king's household
1 K. 21. 13 then they *c.* him forth
2 K. 4. 19 *c.* him to his mother
1 Chr. 6. 15 Lord *c.* away Judah
2 Chr. 36. 20 *c.* he away to Babylon
Ez. 2. 1 king of Babylon had *c.* away
Neh. 7. 6 k. of Babylon had *c.* away
Job 5. 13 forward is *c.* headlong
Ps. 49. 17 shall *c.* nothing away
Eccl. 10. 20 bird .. shall *c.* the voice
Isa. 41. 16 wind shall *c.* them away
Jer. 20. 5 *c.* them to Babylon
Lam. 4. 22 will no more *c.* thee away
Ezek. 22. 9 are men that *c.* tales
Dan. 1. 2 *c.* into land of Shinar
Hos. 10. 6 shall be *c.* unto Assyria
Joel 3. 5 have *c.* into your temples
Mat. 1. 17 until the *c.* away into Bab.
Mark 15. 1 Jesus, and *c.* him away
Luke 10. 4 *c.* neither purse, nor scrip
John 5. 10 not lawful to *c.* thy bed
Acts 7. 43 I will *c.* you away
1 Cor. 12. 2 *c.* away dumb idols
Eph. 4. 14 *c.* about with every wind
1 Tim. 6. 7 we can *c.* nothing out
Heb. 13. 9 *c.* with divers doctrines
2 Pet. 2. 17 clouds *c.* with a tempest
Rev. 12. 15 *c.* away of the flood
Cart. *Two-wheeled wagon.*
1 Sam. 6. 7 make a new *c.*
2 Sam. 6. 3 set ark upon a new *c.*
1 Chr. 13. 7 Ahio drave the *c.*
Isa. 5. 18 sin as it were with a *c.* rope
Am. 2. 13 as a *c.* is pressed.
Cartwheel.
Isa. 28. 27 nor is *c. w.* turned about
Carve. *Cut in.*
Ex. 31. 5 in *c.* of timber to work
1 K. 6. 29. 32, 35 and he *c.* all walls
Carved. R. V. *Graven.*
Judg. 18. 18 fetched the *c.* image
1 K. 6. 29 *c.* figures of cherubims
2 Chr. 33. 7 And he set a *c.* image
Ps. 74. 6 break down the *c.* work
Prov. 7. 16 decked bed with *c.* work
Case. *Matter. condition.*
Ex. 5. 19 see they were in evil *c.*
Deut. 19. 4 the *c.* of the slayer
Ps. 144. 15 people that is in such a *c.*
Mat. 5. 20 shall in no *c.* enter into
John 5. 6 been long time in that *c.*
1 Cor. 7. 15 bondage in such *c.*
R. V. Deut. 22. 1 ; 24. 13 surely
Casement. R. V. *Lattice.*
Prov. 7. 6 I looked through my *c.*
Cassia. *Coarse cinnamon.*
Ex. 30. 24 of *c.* five hundred shekels
Ps. 45. 8 all thy garments smell of *c.*
Ezek. 27. 19 *c.* and cal. in thy market
Cast. *Throw, fling, hurl.*
Gen. 21. 15 she *c.* the child under
Ex. 1. 22 ye shall *c.* into the river
Lev. 1. 16 *c.* it beside the altar
Num. 19. 6 the priest shall *c.* it
Deut. 9. 21 *c.* the dust into brook
Josh. 10. 27 *c.* them into the cave
Judg. 9. 53 *c.* a piece of millstone
1 Sam. 18. 11 And Saul *c.* the javelin
2 Sam. 18. 17 *c.* him into a pit
1 K. 14. 9 hast *c.* me behind thy back
2 K. 2. 21 and *c.* the salt in there
1 Chr. 24. 31 these likewise *c.* lots
2 Chr. 24. 10 and *c.* into the chest
Neh. 9. 26 *c.* thy law behind
Esth. 3. 7 *c.* Pur, the lot, before H.
Job 27. 22 God shall *c.* upon him
Ps. 43. 2 why dost thou *c.* me off
Prov. 16. 33 lot *c.* into the lap
Isa. 14. 19 art *c.* out of thy grave
Jer. 22. 28 are *c.* into a land which
Ezek. 7. 19 *c.* silver in the streets
Dan. 7. 9 thrones were *c.* down
Joel 1. 7 barked fig t. and *c.* it away
Am. 4. 3 shall *c.* them into the palace
Jonah 2. 3 *c.* me into the deep

Mic. 7. 19 *c.* all sins into the depths
Nah. 3. 6 *c.* abominable filth upon
Zech. 5. 8 *c.* the weight of lead
Mat. 3. 10 every tree is *c.* into fire
4. 6 ; 5. 13 ; 6. 30 ; 7. 6 ; 13. 42
Mark 1. 16 saw Andrew *c.* a net
4. 26 ; 7. 27 ; 9. 22 ; 11. 23 ; 12. 41
Luke 12. 28 grass is *c.* into the oven
John 3. 24 not yet *c.* into prison
Acts 16. 23 they *c.* them into prison
1 Cor. 7. 35 that I *c.* a snare on you
Rom. 13. 12 let us *c.* off works
Gal. 4. 30 *c.* out the bondwoman
3 John 10 *c.* them out of the church
Rev. 2. 10 devil shall *c.* some of you
4. 10 ; 6. 13 ; 8. 5 ; 12. 4 : 18. 19
Castaway. R. V. *rejected.*
1 Cor. 9. 27 I myself should be a *c.*
Casting. *Fused.*
1 K. 7. 37 all of them had one *c.*
Castle. *Palace, fortress.*
Gen. 25. 16 their names by their *c.*
Num. 31. 10 burnt all their .. *c.*
1 Chr. 11. 5 David took *c.* of Zion
2 Chr. 17. 12 he built in Judah *c.*
Prov. 18. 19 like bars of a *c.*
Acts 21. 34 to be carried into the *c.*
21. 37 ; 22. 24 ; 23. 10 ; 23. 16, 32
Catch. *Lay hold, seize.*
Gen. 39. 12 *c.* him by his garment
Ex. 4. 4 forth his hand, and *c.* it
Lev. 17. 13 and *c.* any beast
Num. 31. 32 prey which men .. had *c.*
Judg. 21. 21 *c.* every man his wife
1 Sam. 17. 35 when he arose .. I *c.*
2 Sam. 2. 16 *c.* every one his fellow
1 K. 11. 30 Ahijah *c.* the new gar.
2 K. 7. 12 we shall *c.* them alive
2 Chr. 22. 9 and they *c.* him
Ps. 10. 9 he doth *c.* the poor
Prov. 7. 13 *c.* him and kissed him
Jer. 5. 26 set a trap, they *c.* men
Ezek. 19. 3 learned to *c.* prey
Hab. 1. 15 *c.* them in their net
Mat. 21. 39 *c.* him, and cast him out
Mark 12. 13 *c.* him in his words
Luke 5. 10 thou shalt *c.* men
John 10. 12 and the wolf *c.* them
Acts 16. 19 they *c.* Paul and Silas
2 Cor. 12. 16 being crafty, I *c.* you
1 Thes. 4. 17 shall be *c.* up together
Rev. 12. 5 her child was *c.* up
R. V. Mat. 13. 19 ; John 10. 12 snatcheth
Caterpillar. *Devourer.*
1 K. 8. 37 locust, if there be *c.*
2 Chr. 6. 28 if there be dearth or *c.*
Ps. 78. 46 gave increase unto *c.*
Isa. 33. 4 gathered like the *c.*
Joel. 1. 4 left hath the *c.* eaten
A cankerworm.
Ps. 105. 34 locusts came and *c.*
Jer. 51. 14 fill thee as with *c.*
R. V. Jer. 51. 14, 27 cankerworm
Cattle. *Beasts.*
Gen. 1. 24 *c.* and creeping things
Ex. 12. 29 smote .. firstborn of *c.*
Lev. 1. 2 bring offerings of *c.*
Num. 3. 41 take *c.* of the Levites
Deut. 2. 35 only the *c.* we took
Josh. 8. 2 only the spoil .. and *c.*
2 K. 3. 9 *c.* that followed them
Neh. 10. 36 firstborn .. of our *c.*
Ps. 50. 10 *c.* upon a thousand hills
Isa. 46. 1 idols were upon .. *c.*
Jonah 4. 11 wherein are much *c.*
Hag. 1. 11 upon men and .. *c.*
Zech. 2. 4 multitude of men and *c.*
Wealth, substance, possession.
Gen. 4. 20 of such as have *c.*
Ex. 9. 3 hand .. is upon thy *c.*
Num. 20. 19 if I and my *c.* drink
Deut. 3. 19 your *c.* shall abide
Josh. 1. 14 your little ones, your *c.*
Judg. 6. 5 they came up with .. *c.*
1 Sam. 23. 5 brought away their *c.*
2 K. 3. 17 ye and your *c.* and beasts
1 Chr. 5. 9 their *c.* were multiplied
Job 36. 33 *c.* also concerning
Isa. 30. 23 in that day thy *c.* feed
Jer. 9. 10 neither hear voice of the *c.*
Ezek. 38. 13 take away *c.* and goods
Domesticated bovine animals
Gen. 30. 39 brought forth *c.* ringst.
1 K. 1. 9 slew .. oxen and fat *c.*
Eccl. 2. 7 pos. of gr. and sm. *c.*

Isa. 7. 25 for treading of lesser *c.*
Luke 17. 7 plowing or feeding *c.*
John 4. 12 drank thereof, chil., .. *c.*
R. V. Gen. 30. 40–43 flock
Caught. *See* **Catch.**
Caul. *Diaphragm.*
Ex. 29. 13 the *c.* above the liver
Lev. 3. 4 ; 4. 9 ; 7. 4 ; 8. 16 ; 9. 10
Pericardium.
Hos. 13. 8 the *c.* of their hearts
Netted caps.
Isa. 3. 18 L. will take away .. *c.*
Cause (*n.*). *Reason, agency, suit.*
Ex. 18. 19 bring the *c.* unto God
Num. 16. 11 *c.* of thee and
Deut. 1. 17 *c.* too hard for you
Josh. 5. 4 *c.* why Joshua did circum.
1 Sam. 24. 15 Lord plead my *c.*
2 Sam. 13. 16 she said, There is no *c.*
1 K. 8. 45 and maintain their *c.*
1 Chr. 21. 3 why be a *c.* of trespass
2 Chr. 19. 10 what *c.* shall come
Job 5. 8 would I commit my *c.*
Ps. 9. 4 thou hast maintained my *c.*
Prov. 18. 17 first in his own *c.*
Eccl. 7. 10 say not, What is the *c.*
Isa. 1. 23 nei. *c.* of the widow come
Jer. 5. 28 they judge not the *c.*
Lam. 3. 59 Lord, .. judge my *c.*
Ezek. 14. 23 not done without *c.*
Mic. 7. 9 until he plead my *c.*
Mat. 5. 32 for *c.* of fornication
Luke 22. 22 no *c.* of death in him
John 15. 25 hated me without *c.*
Acts 10. 21 what is the *c.* wherefore
Rom. 1. 26 for this *c.* God gave
1 Cor. 4. 17 for this *c.* have I sent
2 Cor. 4. 16 which *c.* we faint not
Eph. 3. 14 for this *c.* I bow knees
1 Thes. 2. 13 for this *c.* thank we
1 Tim. 1. 16 ; Heb. 9. 15 ; 1 Pet. 4. 6
R. V. 2 Chr. 19. 10 controversy ;
Prov. 31. 9 judgement ; John 18. 37 to this end.
Cause (*v.*). *Make, do.*
Gen. 45. 1 *c.* every man to go
Num. 16. 5 will *c.* him to come
Deut. 1. 38 *c.* Israel to inherit
2 Sam. 7. 11 *c.* thee to rest from en
2 Chr. 34. 32 *c.* all to stand to it
Ez. 6. 12 *c.* his name to dwell
Esth. 3. 13 and to *c.* to perish
Job 31. 16 *c.* eyes of widow to fail
Ps. 135. 7 *c.* vapors to ascend
Prov. 4. 16 they *c.* some to fall
Eccl. 5. 6 *c.* thy flesh to sin
S. of S. 7. 1 *c.* lips of those asleep
Isa. 19. 14 have *c.* Egypt to err
Jer. 3. 12 not *c.* mine anger to fall
Lam. 3. 32 though he *c.* grief
Ezek. 34. 15 *c.* them to lie down
Dan. 9. 17 *c.* thy face to shine
Joel 3. 11 *c.* mighty ones to come
Hab. 1. 3 *c.* me to behold griev.
Zech. 3. 4 *c.* iniquity to pass
Mal. 2. 8 have *c.* many to stumble
Mat. 5. 32 *c.* her to commit ad.
John 11. 37 *c.* that even this man
Acts 15. 3 *c.* great joy unto brethren
Rom. 16. 17 which *c.* divisions and
2 Cor. 2. 5 if any have *c.* grief
Col. 4. 16 *c.* that it be read
Rev. 12. 15 *c.* her to be carried
R. V. Mat. 5. 32 ; Rev. 13. 12 maketh: 2 Cor. 9. 11 worketh
Causeless. *Without cause.*
1 Sam. 25. 31 hast shed blood *c.*
Prov. 26. 2 curse *c.* shall not come
Causeway. *Cast up way.*
1 Chr. 26. 16, 18 *c.* of the going up
Cave. *Hole, cavity.*
Gen. 19. 30 Lot, he dwelt in a *c.*
23. 9 ; 25. 9 ; 49. 29 ; 50. 13
Josh. 10. 16 hid .. in a *c.* at Mak.
Judg. 6. 2 and *c.* and strong holds
1 Sam. 13. 6 people hide .. in *c.*
2 Sam. 23. 13 unto the *c.* of Adul.
1 K. 18. 4 hid them .. in a *c.*
1 Chr. 11. 15 captains went into *c.*
Job 30. 6 dwell in *c.* of the earth
Isa. 2. 19 go into the *c.* of the earth
Ezek. 33. 27 forts and in the *c.*
John 11. 38 it was a *c.*, and stone lay
Heb. 11. 38 wandered in dens and *c.*
R. V. Job 30. 6 ; Heb. 11. 38 holes
Cease. *Leave off, pause.*

Gen. 18. 11 it *c.* to be with Sarah
Num. 17. 5 I will make to *c.* mur.
Ex. 9. 29 the thunder shall *c.*
Deut. 15. 11 poor shall never *c.*
Josh. 22. 25 make our children *c.*
Judg. 5. 7 they *c.* in Israel, until
1 Sam 2. 5 that were hungry *c.*
2 Chr. 16. 5 and let his work *c.*
Ez. 4. 23 made them to *c.* by force
Neh. 4. 11 cause the work to *c.*
Job 3. 17 wicked *c.* from troubling
Ps. 46. 9 maketh war to *c.* unto end
Prov. 18. 18 causeth contentions to *c.*
Isa. 1. 16 *c.* to do evil
Jer. 14. 17 tears, let them not *c.*
Lam. 3. 49 eye trickleth and *c.* not
Ezek. 7. 24 make pomp of str. to *c.*
Dan. 9. 27 cause oblations to *c.*
Hos. 1. 4 *c.* the kingdom
Am. 7. 5 *c.*, I beseech thee
Mat. 14. 32 into ship, the wind *c.*
Mark 4. 39 ; 6. 51 ; Luke 8. 24 ; 11. 1
Acts 5. 42 *c.* not to teach and preach
1 Cor. 13. 8 tongues, they shall *c.*
Eph. 1. 16 *c.* not to give thanks
Col. 1. 9 do not *c.* to pray
Heb. 10. 2 they would not have *c.*
1 Pet. 4. 1 that suf. hath *c.* from sin
2 Pet. 2. 14 that cannot *c.* from sin

Ceasing.
Rom. 1. 9 without *c.* I make ment.
2 Tim. 1. 3 without *c.* I have remem.
1 Thes. 1. 3 remembering without *c.*
5. 17 Pray without *c.*
R. V. Rom. 1. 9 ; 2 Tim. 1. 3 unceasingly ; Acts 12. 5 earnestly

Cedar. *Firm wood.*
Lev. 14. 4 *c.* wood, and scarlet
Num. 24. 6 as *c.* trees beside waters
Judg. 9. 15 and devour the *c.* of Leb.
2 Sam. 5. 11 Hiram sent *c.* trees
1 K. 5. 10 H. gave Sol. *c.* trees
2 K. 14. 9 thistle . . sent to the *c.*
1 Chr. 17. 1 dwell in house of *c.*
2 Chr. 2. 8 send also *c.* trees
Ez. 3. 7 *c.* trees from Lebanon
Job. 40. 17 moveth . . like a *c.*
Ps. 29. 5 the Lord breaketh the *c.*
S. of S. 1. 17 beams of house are *c.*
Isa. 2. 13 all the *c.* of Lebanon
Jer. 22. 7 cut down choice *c.*
Ezek. 17. 3 highest branch of the *c.*
Am. 2. 9 the height of the *c.*
Zech. 11. 2 for the *c.* is fallen
Zeph. 2. 14 uncover the *c.* work

Ceil. *Line, roof.*
2 Chr. 3. 5 *c.* the greater house
Jer. 22. 14 house is *c.* with cedar
Hag. 1. 4 dwell in *c.* houses

Ceiling. *Lining.*
1 K. 6. 15 cedar, the walls of the *c.*

Celebrate. *Observe.*
Lev. 23. 32 shall ye *c.* your sabbath
Isa. 38. 18 death cannot *c.* thee
R. V. Lev. 23. 32 keep

Celestial. *Heavenly.*
1 Cor. 15. 40 there are . . *c.* bodies

Cellar. *Treasury.*
1 Chr. 27. 27, 28 for the wine *c.*

Censer. *Incense pan.*
Lev. 10. 1 sons of Aaron took . . *c.*
Num. 4. 14 the *c.* and fleshhooks
1 K. 7. 50 the *c.* of pure gold
2 Chr. 4. 22 spoons and the *c.*
Ezek. 8. 11 with every man his *c.*
Rev. 8. 3 having a golden *c.*
R. V. Num. 4. 14 ; 1 K. 7. 50 ; 2
Chr. 4. 22 firepans

Centurion. *Leader of a hundred men.*
Mat. 8. 5 there came to him a *c.*
Mark 15. 39 when the *c.* saw that
Luke 7. 2 *c*'s servant was sick
Acts 10. 1 a *c.* of the band called
10. 22 ; 21. 32 ; 24. 23 ; 27. 1, 31
R. V. Acts 28. 16

Ceremonies. R. V. *ordinances.*
Num. 9. 3 according to the *c.*

Certain. *A man.*
Num. 9. 6 there was *c.* men
Judg. 19. 22 *c.* sons of Belial
1 K. 11. 17 he and *c.* Edomites
2 Chr. 28. 12 *c.* of the heads of
Ez. 10. 16 priest with *c.* chief of
Neh. 13. 25 smote *c.* of them
Jer. 26. 17 rose *c.* of the elders

Ezek. 14. 1 came *c.* of the elders
Any one, any thing, some.
Judg. 9. 53 a *c.* woman cast piece
1 Sam. 1. 1 a *c.* man of Ramath.
2 Sam. 18. 10 a *c.* man saw it
1 K. 20. 35 a *c.* man of the sons
2 K. 4. 1 there cried a *c.* woman
Esth. 3. 8 is a *c.* people scattered
Dan. 10. 5 behold, *c.* man clothed
Mat. 9. 3 *c.* of the scribes said
Mark. 12. 13 send *c.* of Pharisees
Luke 20. 27 came *c.* of the Sad.
John 12. 20 *c.* Greeks among them
Acts 6. 9 *c.* of the synagogue
9. 19 ; 10. 23 ; 12. 1 ; 13. 1 ; 15. 1
Sure, stated, evident.
Deut. 13. 14 behold . . the thing *c.*
Dan. 2. 45 the dream is *c.*
Neh. 11. 23 *c.* portion should be
Acts 25. 26 no *c.* thing to write
1 Tim. 6. 7 *c.* we can carry nothing
The word is largely omitted in R. V.

Certainly. R. V. *surely.*
Gen. 43. 7 could we *c.* know
Ex. 3. 12 and he said, *C.*
1 Sam. 20. 3 thy father *c.* knoweth
Jer. 13. 12 do we not *c.* know
Lam. 2. 16 *c.* this is day looked for
Luke 23. 47 saying, *C.* this was

Certainty. *Surely known.*
Josh. 23. 13 know for a *c.* that
1 Sam. 23. 23 come . . with the *c.*
Prov. 22. 21 *c.* of words of truth
Dan. 2. 8 *c.* ye would gain . . time
Luke 1. 4 mightest know the *c.* of
Acts 21. 34 could not know the *c.*

Certify. *Cause to know.*
2 Sam. 15. 28 come word . . to *c.* me
Esth. 2. 22 Esther *c.* the king
Ez. 4. 14 we sent and *c.* the king
Gal. 1. 11 I *c.* you, brethren
R. V. Esth. 2. 22 told ; Gal. 1. 11
make known to

Chafed. *Bitten.*
2 Sam. 17. 8 they *c.* in their minds

Chaff. *Husk, straw, hay.*
Job 21. 18 as *c.* that the storm car.
Ps. 1. 4 *c.* which wind driveth
Isa. 5. 24 flame consumeth the *c.*
Jer. 23. 28 what is *c.* to the wheat.
Dan. 2. 35 like *c.* of the summer
Hos. 13. 3 as *c.* is driven by whirlw.
Zeph. 2. 2 before day pass as the *c.*
Mat. 3. 12 will burn up *c.* with fire
Luke 3. 17 but the *c.* he will burn
R. V. Isa. 5. 24 dry grass ; Jer.
23. 28 straw

Chain. *Links, bond.*
Gen. 41. 42 put gold *c.* about neck
Ex. 28. 14 make two *c.* of pure gold
Num. 31. 50 jewels of gold, *c.*
Judg. 8. 26 beside the *c.* that were
1 K. 6. 21 by *c.* of gold bef. oracle
2 Chr. 3. 5 set palm trees and *c.*
Ps. 45. 14 bind the kings with *c.*
Prov. 1. 9 ornament . . and *c.*
S. of S. 4. 9 with one *c.* of thy neck
Isa. 45. 14 in *c.* they shall come
Jer. 39. 7 and bound him with *c.*
Lam. 3. 7 hath made my *c.* heavy
Ezek. 16. 11 put a *c.* on thy neck
Dan. 5. 7 and have a *c.* of gold
Nah. 3. 10 men were bound in *c.*
Mark 5. 3 bind him, no, not with *c.*
Luke 8. 29 was kept bound with *c.*
Acts 28. 20 I am bound with th s *c.*
2. Tim. 1. 16 not ashamed of my *c.*
Jude 6 reserved in everlasting *c.*
2 Pet. 2. 4 del. into *c.* of darkness
Rev. 20. 1 having . . a great *c.*
R. V. Num. 31. 50 ankle chains ;
S. of S. 1. 10 strings ; Isa. 3. 19
pendants ; Jer. 39. 7 ; 52. 11 fetters ;
Ezek. 19. 4 hooks ; Jude 6 bonds

Chalcedony. *Carnelian.*
Rev. 21. 19 stones, the third a *c.*

Chalkstone. *Limestone.*
Isa. 27. 9 stones of the altar as *c. s.*

Challenge. *Say.*
Ex. 22. 9 which another *c.* to be his

Chamber. *Enclosed place.*
Gen. 43. 30 he entered into his *c.*
Judg. 3. 24 in his summer *c.*
2 Sam. 13. 10 bring meat into the *c.*
1 K. 1. 15 went . . into the *c.*
2 K. 4. 10 Let us make a little *c.*

1 Chr. 9. 26 Levites were over the *c.*
2 Chr. 12. 11 brought . . into guard *c.*
Ez. 8. 29 *c.* of the house of Lord
Neh. 13. 8 cast . . out of the *c.*
Job. 9. 9 maketh *c.* of the south
Ps. 104. 3 layeth beams of his *c.*
Prov. 7. 27 to the *c.* of death
S. of S. 1. 4 brough* me into his *c*
Isa. 26. 20 enter thou into thy *c.*
Jer. 35. 2 bring into one of the *c.*
Ezek. 8. 12 every man in the *c.* of
Dan. 6. 10 windows open in his *c.*
Joel 2. 16 go forth of his *c.*
Mat 24. 26 he is in the secret *c.*
Acts 9. 37 laid her in an upper *c.*
R. V. 1. K. 6.6 story ; Ezek. 40. 7
lodge

Chambering. *Couching.*
Rom. 13. 13 walk . . not in *c.* and

Chamberlain. *Eunuch, couch officer, steward.*
2 K. 23. 11 by chamber of the *c.*
Esth. 2. 3 ; 4. 4 ; 6. 2 ; 7. 9
Acts 12. 20 made Blastus king's *c.*
Rom. 16. 23 Eras. the *c.* of the city
R. V. Rom. 16. 23 treasurer

Chameleon. *Lizard.*
Lev. 11. 30 *c.* and the lizard.

Chamois. *Giraffe.*
Deut. 14. 5 wild ox, and the *c.*

Champaign. R. V. *Arabah.*
Deut. 11. 30 which dwell in the *c.*

Champion. *Mighty one.*
1 Sam. 17. 4 there went out a *c.*

Chance (*v.*). *Happen.*
Deut. 22. 6 if a bird's nest *c.*
1 Cor. 15. 37 it may *c.* of wheat

Chance (*n.*). *Happening.*
1 Sam. 6. 9 a *c.* that happened
2 Sam. 1. 6 I happened by *c.*
Eccl. 9. 11 time and *c.* happeneth
Luke 10. 31 by *c.* there came down

Chancellor. *Master.*
Ez. 4. 8, 9, 17 Rehum the *c.*

Change (*n.*). *Substitute.*
Gen. 45. 22 gave each *c.* of raiment
Lev. 27. 33 the *c.* shall be holy
Judg. 14. 12 thirty *c.* of garments
2 K. 5. 5 took ten *c.* of raiment
Job 14. 14 wait till my *c.* come
Ps. 55. 19 Because they have no *c.*
Heb. 7. 12 of necessity a *c.* of law

Change (*v.*). *Alter, turn.*
Gen. 31. 7 hath *c.* my wages ten t.
Lev. 27. 10 shall not alter it, nor *c.*
1 Sam. 21. 13 *c.* behaviour bef. them
2 Sam. 12 20 David *c.* his apparel
2 K. 24. 17 *c.* name to Zedekiah
Job 17. 12 they *c.* night into day
Ps. 15. 4 sweareth and *c.* not
Prov. 24. 21 that are given to *c.*
Eccl. 8. 1 bold. of face shall be *c.*
Isa. 9. 10 we will *c.* them to cedars
Jer. 2. 11 my people have *c.*
Lam. 4. 1 how is the most fine gold *c*
Ezek. 5. 6 hath *c.* my judgments
Dan. 2. 21 he *c.* the times
Hos. 4. 7 will I *c.* their glory
Mic. 2. 4 hath *c.* the portion
Acts 6. 14 and *c.* the customs
Rom. 1. 23 *c.* the glory of uncor.
1 Cor. 15. 51 we shall all be *c.*
2 Cor. 3. 18 are *c.* into same image
Gal. 4. 20 I desire to *c.* my voice
Phil. 3. 21 who shall *c.* our vile body
Heb. 7. 12 priesthood being *c.*
R. V. Job 30. 18 disfigured

Changeable. R. V. *festival.*
Isa. 3. 22 *c.* suits of apparel

Changer. *Coin dealer.*
Mat. 21. 12 overthrew tab. of mon. *c.*
Mark. 11. 15 ; John 2. 14, 15

Changing. R. V. *exchanging.*
Ruth 4. 7 manner concerning *c.*

Channel. *Trough, stream.*
2 Sam. 22. 16 the *c.* of the sea
Ps. 18. 15 *c.* of waters were seen
Isa. 8. 7 shall come over all his *c.*
R. V. Isa. 27. 12 flood

Chant. R. V. *sing idle songs.*
Am. 6. 5 *c.* to sound of viol

Chapel. R. V. *sanctuary.*
Am. 7. 13 it is the king's *c.*

Chapiter. *Capital, top.*
Ex. 36. 38 overlaid their *c.* with g.
1 K. 7. 16 made two *c.* of . . brass

2 K. 25. 17 the c. upon it was brass
2 Chr. 4. 12 the c. which .. on the top
Jer. 52. 22 the c. of brass was

Chapman. *Travelling merchant.*
2 Chr. 9. 14 c. and merchants

Chapt. *Cracked.*
Jer. 14. 4 because the ground is c.

Charge (*n.*). *Thing watched.*
Gen. 26. 5 Abraham kept my c
Lev. 8. 35 keep the c. of the Lord
Num. 1. 53 keep c. of the tabernacle
3. 7; 4. 27; 8. 26; 9. 19; 18. 3
Deut. 11. 1 keep his c. and statutes,
Josh. 22. 3 kept c. of the command.
1 K. 2. 3 keep the c. of the Lord
1 Chr. 9. 27 the c. was on them
2 Chr. 8. 14 appointed L. to .. c.
Ezek. 40. 45 keepers of the c.
Zech. 3. 7 if thou wilt keep my c.
Provision, expense.
Acts 21. 24 be at c. with them
1 Cor. 9. 7 who goeth at his own c.?
Oversight.
Job 34. 13 given him a c. over earth
2 K. 7. 17 to have the c. of the gate
Exek. 44. 11 having c. at the gates
Acts 8. 27 c. of all her treasures
Command.
Gen. 28. 6 he gave him a c.
Ex. 6. 13 gave them a c., saying
Num. 27. 19 Moses gave him a c.
Deut. 31. 33 he gave Joshua a c.
1 Chr. 22. 12 I give thee charge
2 Sam. 14. 8 I will give a c. con. thee
Neh. 7. 2 gave my brother c.
Ps. 91. 11 give his angels c.
Isa. 10. 6 I give him a c.
Jer. 47. 7 Lord hath given it a c.

Charge (*v.*). *Command, adjure.*
Gen. 26. 11 Abimelech c. his people
Ex. 1. 16 I c. your judges
Deut. 1. 16 I c. your judges
Josh. 18. 8 Joshua c. them that
Ruth 2. 9 have I not c. the men
2 Sam. 11. 19 and c. the messenger
1 K. 2. 1 David c. Solomon
2 K. 17. 15 whom the Lord had c.
1 Chr. 22. 6 David c. him to build
2 Chr. 19. 9 he c. them, saying
Esth. 2. 10 Mordecai had c. her
Job 4. 18 his angels he c. with folly
S. of S. 2. 7 I c. you, O ye daughters
Mat. 12. 16 c. them that they
Mark 5. 43 he c. them straitly
Luke 9. 21 he straitly c. them
Acts 16. 23 c. the jailor to keep them
1 Tim. 6. 17 c. them that are rich
1 Thes. 2. 11 comforted and c. every

Chargeable. *Weighted.*
2 Sam. 13. 25 lest we be c. unto thee
Neh. 5. 15 governors were c.
2 Cor. 11. 9 I was c. to no man
1 Thes. 2. 9 would not be c. unto
2 Thes. 3. 8 might not be c. to any
R. V. 1 Thes. 2. 9; 2 Thes. 3. 8
burden

Charger. *Dish, trencher.*
Num. 7. 13 offering was one .. c.
7. 19-79; 7. 84-85
Ez. 1. 9 thirty c. of gold
Mat. 14. 8., 11 give me .. head in a c.
Mark 6. 25, 28 brought head in .. c.

Chariot. *Riding cart.*
Gen. 41. 43 made him ride in .. c.
Ez. 14. 25 took off their c. wheels
Deut. 11. 4 to horses and their c.
Josh. 11. 6 burn their c. with fire
Judg. 4. 15 Sisera lighted off his c.
1 Sam. 8. 11 some run before his c.
2 Sam. 15. 1 Absalom prepared .. c.
1 K. 7. 33 like work of a c. wheel
2 K. 5. 21 Naam. lighted from his c.
1 Chr. 28. 18 gold for pattern of c.
2. Chr. 1. 17 brought forth .. a c.
S. of S. 6. 12 make me like the c.
Isa. 2. 7 neither any of their c.
Jer. 4. 13 c. shall be as whirlwind
Joel 2. 5 like noise of c. on mount.
Mic. 5. 10 Lord will destroy thy c.
Nah. 3. 2 horses and jumping c.
Hab. 3. 8 ride .. horses and c.
Hag. 2. 22 I will overthrow the c.
Zech. 6. 1 there came four c.
War wagon or cart.
Gen. 50. 9 went up c. and horsemen
Ex. 14. 6 Pharaoh made ready his c.

Deut. 20. 1 and seest horses and c.
Josh. 11. 4 with horses and c. many
Judg. 1. 19 bec. they had c. of iron
1 Sam. 8. 12 instruments of his c.
2 Sam. 1. 6 c. and horsemen fol.
1 K. 1. 5 Adonijah prepared him c.
2 K. 2. 12 Elij. cried, The c. of Israel
1 Chr. 18. 4 David took thousand c.
2 Chr. 1. 14 Solomon gathered c.
Ps. 20. 7 some trust in c.
S. of S. 1. 9 horses in Pharaoh's c.
Isa. 21. 7 saw a c. with horsemen
Jer. 17. 25 riding in c. and on hors.
Ezek. 26. 7 with horses and .. c.
Dan. 11. 40 like whirlwind with c.
Nah. 2. 3 c. with flaming torches
Zech. 9. 10 will cut off the c. from E.
Acts 8. 28 sit. in his c. read Esaias
Rev. 9. 9 sound was as sound of c.
R. V. S. of S. 3. 9 palanquin; Isa.
21. 7, 9 troop; 2 Sam. 8. 4 ——

Charitably. R. V. *In love.*
Rom. 14. 15 walkest thou not c.

Charity. R. V. *love.*
1 Cor. 8. 1 knowl. puf., but c. edifieth
13. 1-13; 14. 1; 16. 14
Col. 3. 14 above all .. things put cn c.
1 Thes. 3. 6 bro. tidings of your c.
2 Thes. 1. 3 c. of every one abound.
1 Tim. 1. 5 end of the com. is c.
2 Tim. 2. 22 follow .. faith, c., peace
Tit. 2. 2 sound in faith, in c.
1 Pet. 4. 8 have fervent c.
2 Pet. 1. 7 to brotherly kindness c.
3 John 6 witness of thy c. bef. church
Jude 12 spots in your feasts of c.
Rev. 2. 19 know thy works and c.

Charmed.
Jer. 8. 17 which will not be c.

Charmer. *Juggler.*
Deut. 18. 11 or a c. or consulter
Ps. 58. 5 not hearken to voice of c.
Isa. 19. 3 seek to the idols and to c.

Charming. *Enchanting.*
Ps. 58. 5 voice of charmers, c.

Chase. *Pursue.*
Lev. 26. 7 ye shall c. your enemies
Deut. 1. 44 Am. came out .. and c.
Josh. 7. 5 they c. them from gate
Judg. 9. 4 Abimelech c. him
1 Sam. 17. 53 Isra. returned from c.
Neh. 13. 28 therefore I c. him
Job. 18. 18 and c. out of the world
Ps. 35. 5. let the angels .. c. them
Prov. 19. 26 wasteth .. and c. away
Isa. 17. 13 shall be c. as the chaff
Lam. 3. 52 mine enemies c. me sore
R. V. Josh. 8. 24 pursued; Ps. 35.
5 driving

Chaste. *Consecrated.*
2 Cor. 11. 2 present you as a c. virgin
Tit. 2. 5 To be c. keepers at home
1 Pet. 3. 2 your c. conversation
R. V. 2 Cor. 11. 2 pure

Chasten. *Chastise, discipline.*
Deut. 8. 5 as a man c. his son
2 Sam. 7. 14 c. him with a rod
Job. 33. 19 he is c. also with pain
Ps. 6. 1 neither c. me in thy displ.
38. 1; 73. 14; 94. 12; 118. 18
Prov. 19. 18 c. thy son while .. hope
Dan. 10. 12 c. thyself before God
1 Cor. 11. 32 we are c. of the Lord
2 Cor. 6. 9 we live, as c., not killed
Heb. 12. 6 whom Lord loveth he c.
Rev. 3. 19 as I love, I rebuke and c.
R. V. Dan. 10. 12 humble

Chastening. *Instruction.*
Job. 5. 17 despise not .. the c.
Prov. 3. 11 despise not .. the c.
Isa. 26. 16 c. was upon them
Heb. 12. 5, 7, 11 despise not c. of L.

Chastise. *Instruct, punish.*
Lev. 26. 28 will c. you seven times
Deut. 22. 18 elders shall .. c. him
1 K. 12. 11 my father hath c. you
2 Chr. 10. 11 c. you with whips
Hos. 7. 12 I will c. them
Ps. 94. 10 he that c. the heathen
Jer. 31. 18 I was c. as bullock
Luke 23. 16 I will therefore c. him

Chastisement. *Chastening.*
Deut. 11. 2 not seen the c. of Lord
Isa. 53. 5 the c. of our peace on him
Jer. 30. 14 with the c. of a cruel one
Heb. 12. 8 if ye be without c.

R. V. Heb. 12. 8 chastening

Chatter. *Chirp.*
Isa. 38. 14 like swallow .. I c.

Check. R. V. *reproof.*
Job 20. 3 the c. of my reproach

Checker. *Lattice work.*
1 K. 7. 17 nets of c. work

Cheek. *Chap, jowl, jaw.*
Deut. 18. 3 shoulder, and two c.
1 K. 22. 24 smote Micaiah on the c.
2 Chr. 18. 23 smote Micaiah on the c.
Job. 16. 10 smitten me upon the c.
Ps. 3. 7 smitten .. upon the c bone
S. of S. 1. 10 thy c. are comely
Isa. 50. 6 c. to them that plucked
Lam. 1. 2 tears are on her c.
Mic. 5. 1 smite judge upon the c.
Joel 1. 6 has c. teeth of a great lion
R. V. Joel 1. 6 jaw

Cheer (*n.*). *Courage, cheerful*
Mat. 9. 2 son, be of good c.
Mark 6. 50 saith .. Be of good c.
John 16. 33 but be of good c.
Acts 23. 11 said, Be of good c.

Cheer (*v.*). *Rejoice.*
Deut. 24. 5 shall c. up his wife
Judg. 9. 13 which c. God and man
Eccl. 11. 9 let thy heart c. thee

Cheerful. *Good, glad.*
Prov. 15. 13 mer. h. mak. c. count.
Zech. 8. 19 to Judah shall be c. feasts
2 Cor. 9. 7 Lord loveth a c. giver
R. V. Zech. 9. 17 flourish

Cheerfully. *Gladly.*
Acts 24. 10 I .. the more c. ans.

Cheerfulness. *Gladness.*
Rom. 12. 8 showeth mercy with c.

Cheese. *Curdled milk.*
1 Sam. 17. 18 carry these ten c.
2 Sam. 17. 29 c. of kine for David
Job 10. 10 and curdled me like c.

Cherish. *Foster, care for.*
1 K. 1. 2 let her c. him
Eph. 5. 29 nourisheth and c. it
1 Thes. 2. 7 nurse c. her children

Cherub. *Grasped thing.*
Ex. 25. 19 c. on the one end
1 K. 6. 24 five c. one wing of the c.
2 Chr. 3. 11 wing of the other c.
Ps. 18. 10 rode upon a c. and did fly
Ezek. 9. 3 glory was gone from c.
10. 2-14; 28. 14; 42. 18

Cherubim. *Things grasped*
Gen. 3. 24 placed east of .. E. c.
Ex. 25. 18 make two c. of gold
25. 19-22; 26. 1; 36. 8: 37. 7-9
Num. 7. 89 between the two c.
1 Sam. 4. 4 dwelleth between the c.
2 Sam. 6. 2 1 K. 6. 23-35; 7. 36; 8. 6
2 K. 19. 15; 1 Chr. 13. 6; 28. 18
2 Chr. 3. 7 graved c. on walls
Ps. 80. 1 dwellest between the c.
Isa. 37. 16; Ezek. 10. 1-20; 41. 18
Heb. 9. 5 over it the c. of glory
R. V. cherubim

Chestnut. *Plane-tree.*
Gen. 30. 37 rods of hazel and c. tree
Ezek. 31. 8 c. trees were not like

Chest. *Ark, box.*
2 K. 12. 9 Jehoiada took a c.
2 Chr. 24. 8-11 they made a c.
Ezek. 27. 24 c. of rich apparel

Chew. *Masticate.*
Lev. 11. 7 he c. not the cud
Num. 11. 33 flesh, ere it was c.
Deut. 14. 6-7 beast that c. the cud

Chicken. *Nestling.*
Mat. 23. 37 as a hen gathereth her c.

Chide. *Strive, contend.*
Gen. 31. 36 and c. with Laban
Ex. 17. 2 the people did c.
Num. 20. 3 people c. with Moses
Judg. 8. 1 c. with him sharply
Ps. 103. 9 he will not always c.
R. V. Ex. 17. 2 strive, strove.

Chiding. R. V. *striving.*
Ex. 17. 7 the c. of the children of Is

Chief. *Father.*
Num. 1. 16 prince of the c. house
Josh. 22. 14 each c. house a prince
One exalted, a head.
Num. 3. 24, 30, 35 c. of the house
Judg. 20. 2 c. of all the people
1 Sam. 14. 38 c. of the people
1 K 8. 1 Solomon assembled the c.
1 Chr. 9. 26 the four c. porters

2 Chr. 5. 2 c. of the fathers of Is.
Head.
Num. 31. 26 c. fathers of the cong.
Deut. 1. 15 took c. of your tribes
2 K. 25. 18 Seraiah the c. priest
1 Chr. 5. 7 c., Jeiel and Zechariah
  8. 28; 9. 17; 11. 6; 15. 12; 16. 5;
  23. 8; 24. 4; 26.10; 27. 1
2 Chr. 1. 2 the c. of the fathers
Ez. 1. 5 then rose up the c. .. fathers
Neh. 7. 70 some .. c. of the fathers
  8. 13; 10. 14; 11. 3, 13, 16; 12. 7-46
Job 12. 24 taketh away heart of c.
Ps. 137. 6 prefer Jerus. above my c
Jer. 52. 24 Seraiah the c. priest
Lam. 1. 5 her adversaries are the c.
Ezek. 27. 22 with c. of all spices
Prince, head.
Gen. 40. 2 the c. of the butlers.
  40. 9-23; 41. 9-10
1 K. 5. 16 c. of Solomon's officers
1 Chr. 15. 5 Uriel the c. and his breth.
2 Chr. 8. 9 and c. of his captains
Ez. 8. 24 separated twelve of the c.
Beginning.
1 Sam. 15. 21 took c. of the things
Job 40. 19 c. of the ways of God
Ps. 78. 51 smote c. of their stength
Jer. 49. 35 the c. of their might
Dan. 11. 41 c. of the children of Am.
Am. 6. 1 named c. of the nations
First, foremost.
Lev. 21. 4 being a c. man am'g peo.
Deut. 33. 15 for the c. things of
1 Chr. 7. 3 all of them c. men
Ez. 7. 28 gathered .. c. men
Prov. 16. 28 separateth c. friends
Mat. 20. 27 will be c. among you
Mark 6. 21 c. estates of Galilee
Luke. 11. 15 Beelz. c. of the devils
Acts 16. 12 Philippi is the c. city
1 Tim. 1. 15 of whom I am c.
R. V. In O. T. frequently, prince,
  head, captain; Mat. 20. 27 first;
  Luke 11. 15 prince; 14. 1 rulers;
  Acts 18. 8-17——; Luke 19. 47;
  Acts 25. 2 principal men
Chiefest. *First, foremost.*
1 Sam. 9. 22 sit in the c. places
2 Chr. 32. 33 in c. of sepulchres
S. of S. 5. 10 c. of ten thousand
Mark 10. 44 whosoever will be c.
R. V. Mark 10. 44 first
Chiefly. *Most of all.*
Rom. 3. 2 c. because that unto th.
Phil. 4. 22 c. they of Cæsar's house.
2 Pet. 2. 10 c. them that walk aft. fl.
R. V. Rom. 3. 2 first of all; Phil.
  4. 22 especially.
Child *Little one, young one.*
Gen. 11. 30 Sarai had no c.
  21. 8; 37. 30; 45. 22; 44. 20
Ex. 2. 3 ark, and put the c. therein
Lev. 22. 13 widow, and have no c.
Judg. 11. 34 she was his only c.
Ruth 4. 16 Naomi took the c.
Judg. 13. 5 c. shall be a Nazarite
1 Sam. 1. 11 wilt give a man c.
2 Sam. 12. 15 Lord struck the c.
1 K. 3. 7 I am but a little c.
2 K. 4. 18 when the c. was grown
Job 33. 25 flesh fresher than a c.
Eccl. 4. 13 better is a wise c. than
Prov.20. 11 c. is known by .. doings
  22. 6; 23. 13; 29. 15
Isa. 3. 5 the c. shall behave himself
Jer. 1. 6 cannot speak, for I am a c.
Hos. 11. 1 when Israel was a c.
Mat. 18. 2 Jesus called a little c.
Mark 10. 15 as a little c., shall not
Luke 1. 7 they had no c., because
John 4. 49 come down ere my c. die
Acts 4. 27 against thy holy c. Jesus
1 Cor. 13. 11 when I was a c., I spake
1 Tim. 2. 15 be saved as a c.
2 Tim. 3. 15 from a c. .. hast known
Gal. 4. 1 long as he is a c.
Heb. 11. 23 Moses was a proper c.
Rev. 12. 4 devour her c. as soon as b.
Conceive, in travail.
Gen. 16. 11 thou art with c.
Ex. 21. 22 hurt a woman with c.
2 Sam. 11. 5 woman said, I am with c.
2 K. 8. 12 rip women with c.
Eccl. 11. 5 womb of her that is with c
Isa. 26. 17 like woman with c. that

Jer. 31. 8 lame, the woman with c.
Hos. 12. 16 with c. shall be ripped
Am. 1. 13 ripped women with c.
Mat. 1. 18 with c. of the Holy Ghost
Mark 13. 17 woe .. that are with c.
Luke 21. 13; 1 Thes. 5. 3
Rev. 12. 2 being with c. cried
Childhood. *R. V. youth.*
1 Sam. 12. 2 walk. bef. y. from my c
Eccl. 11. 10 remove sorrow for c.
Childish. *Babyish.*
Hos. 13. 11 put away c. things
Childless. *Without child.*
Gen. 15. 2 seeing I go c.
Lev. 20. 20 they shall die c.
1 Sam. 15. 33 sword made women c.
Jer. 22. 30 write ye this man c.
Luke 20. 30 to wife, and he died c.
R. V. Luke 20. 30 ——
Children. *Sons.*
Gen. 3. 16 in sor. shalt bring forth c.
  10. 21; 11. 5; 18. 19; 19. 38; 21. 7
Ex. 1. 1 these are names of c. of Is.
  2. 23; 3. 9; 4. 29; 5. 14; 6. 5; 7. 2
Lev. 1. 2 Speak unto the c. of Israel
  4. 2; 6. 18; 7. 23; 9. 3; 10. 11; 11.2
Num. 1. 2 congregation of the c.
  2. 2; 3. 4; 5. 2; 6. 2; 7. 24; 8. 9
Deut. 1. 3 Moses spake unto the c.
Josh. 1. 2 give to them, even to the c.
Judg. 1. 1 c. of Israel asked Lord
1 Sam. 2. 5 that hath many c.
2 Sam. 1. 18 bade them teach the c.
1 K. 2. 4 if thy c. take heed
2 K. 4. 7 live thou and thy c.
1 Chr. 1. 43 king reigned over c.
2 Chr. 5. 2 fathers of the c. of Is.
Ez. 2. 1 these are the c. of the prov.
Neh. 1. 6 I pray for the c. of Israel
Job. 5. 4 her c. are far from safety
Ps. 11. 4 behold .. the c. of men
Prov. 5. 7 hear, O ye c., depart not
S. of S. 1. 6 mother's c. were angry
Isa. 1. 2 nourish. and brought up c.
Jer. 2. 9 with c. will I plead
Ezek. 2. 3 send thee to the c. of Is.
Dan. 1. 3 bring certain of the c. of Is.
Hos. 1. 10 number of c. be as sand
Joel 1. 3 tell your c. of it
Am. 2. 11 transgression of the c.
Obad. 12 rejoiced over the c. of Jud.
Mic. 1. 16 poll thee for delicate c.
Zeph. 1. 8 punish the king's c.
Zech. 10. 7 yea, their c. shall see it
Mal. 4. 6 turn heart of the c. to fath.
One born, offspring.
Mat. 2. 18 Rachel weeping for her c.
  3. 9. 7. 11; 10. 21; 11. 19; 15. 26
Mark 7. 27 let the c. first be filled
  10. 24, 29; 12. 19; 13. 12
Luke 1. 7 turn hearts .. to the c.
  3. 8; 7. 35; 11. 13; 13. 34; 14. 26
John 8. 39 if ye were Abraham's c.
Acts 2. 39 promise is .. to your c.
Rom. 8. 16 we are the c. of God
1 Cor. 7. 14 were your c. unclean
2 Cor. 6. 13 I speak as unto my c.
Gal. 4. 25 is in bondage with her c.
Eph. 2. 3 the c. of disobedience
Col. 3. 20 c., obey your parents
1 Thes. 2. 7 provoke not your c.
1 Tim. 3. 4 hav. his c. in subjection
Tit. 1. 6 having faithful c. not accus.
1 Pet. 1. 14 hope .. as obedient c.
2 Pet. 2. 14 having .. cursed c.
1 John 3. 10 c. of God are manifest
2 John 1 elect lady and her c.
3 John 4 hear that my c. walk in tr.
Rev. 2. 24 I will kill her c.
People, inhabitants.
Judg. 6. 3 c. of the east came up
2 K. 19. 12 c. of Eden in Thelasar
Isa. 37. 12 c. of Eden which were
R. V. frequently, sons
Chimney. *Outlet.*
Hos. 13. 3 smoke out of the c.
Chode. see **Chide.**
Choice. *Chosen, select.*
Gen. 23. 6 c. of our sepulchres
Deut. 12. 11 all your c vows
1 Sam. 9. 2 Saul, a c. young man
2 Sam. 10. 9 chose all the c. men
2 K. 3. 19 smite every c. city
1 Chr. 19. 10 chose .. the c of Israel
2 Chr. 25. 5 found three h. t. c. men
Neh. 5. 18 prep. daily, six c. sheep

Prov. 8. 10 knowledge rather than c
S. of S. 6. 9 she is the c. one
Isa. 37. 24 cut down c. fir trees
Jer. 22. 7 cut down c. cedars
Ezek. 24. 5 take the c. of the flock
Acts 15. 7 God made c. among us
R. V. 1 Sam. 9. 2 ——; 2 Chr. 25. 5
  chosen
Choke. *Hinder, strangle.*
Mat. 13. 7 thorns sprung up, and c
Mark 4. 19 lusts c. the word, and
Luke 8. 14 c. with cares and rich.
Choler. *Anger, bitter.*
Dan. 8. 7 and he was moved with c.
Choose. *Select, pick.*
Gen. 6. 2 wives which they c.
Ex. 17. 9 c. us out men, and go
Num. 16. 5 him whom he hath c.
Deut. 4. 37 therefore he c. their seed
Josh. 8. 3 Joshua c. out thirty thous.
1 Sam. 2. 28 did I c. him out of all
2 Sam. 6. 21 Lord which c. me
1 K. 3. 8 people which thou hast c.
2 K. 21. 7 have c. out of all tribes
1 Chr. 15 2 them hath the Lord c.
2 Chr. 6. 5 I c. no city among all
Neh. 1. 9 place I have c. to set name
Job 7. 15 my soul c. strangling
  9. 14; 15. 5; 29. 25: 34. 4; 36. 21
Ps. 25. 12 teach in way he shall c.
  33. 12; 47. 4; 65. 4; 78. 67
Prov. 1. 29 c. fear of the Lord
Isa. 1. 29 for gardens ye have c.
  7. 15; 14. 1; 40. 20; 41. 8; 43. 10
Jer. 33. 24 which the Lord has c
Ezek. 20. 5 when I c. Israel
Hag. 2. 23 for I have c. thee
Zech. 1. 17 shall yet c. Jerusalem
Mat. 12. 18 servant whom I have c.
Mark 13. 20 whom he haih c.
Luke 10. 42 Mary hath c. good part
John 6. 70 have not I c. you
Acts 1. 2 apostles whom he had c.
1 Cor. 1. 27 c. the foolish things
2 Cor. 8. 19 c. of the churches
Eph. 1. 4 as he hath c. us
2 Tim. 2. 4 c. him to be a soldier
Jas. 2. 5 hath not God c. the poor
Phil. 1. 22 yet what shall I c.
2 Thes. 2. 13 God .. hath c. you
Heb. 11. 25 c. rather to suffer affl.
R. V. Acts 22. 14: 2 Cor. 8. 19 ap-
  pointed
Chop. *Spread out.*
Mic. 3. 3 c. them in pieces, for pot
Chose See **Choose.**
Chosen. *Selected, choice.*
Ex. 14. 7 six hundred c. chariots
Judg. 20. 15 seven hundred c. men
1 Sam. 24. 2 three thousand c. men
2 Sam. 6. 1 Dav. gathered all the c.
1 K. 12. 21 c. men which were war.
1 Chr. 16. 13 seed of Is., his c. ones
2 Chr. 11. 1 score thousand c. men
Ps. 89. 19 have exalted one c.
Prov. 22. 1 name is rather to be c.
Isa. 43. 20 give drink to my ...c
Jer. 8. 3 death shall be c. rather
Mat. 20. 16 many called, but few c.
Luke 23. 35 if he be Christ the c.
Acts 15. 22 apost's to send c. men
Rom. 16. 13 Rufus c. in the Lord
1 Pet. 2. 4 but c. of God, and prec.
Rev. 17. 14 with Him called and c.
Christian. *Belonging to Christ.*
Acts 11. 26 called c. .. in Antioch
  26. 28 persuadest me to be a c.
1 Pet. 4. 16 if any man suffer as a c
Chronicles. *Day matters.*
1 K. 14. 19 writ. in book of the c.
1 Chr. 27. 24 number put in c.
Esth. 2. 23 written in book of c.
Chrysolite. *Topaz.*
Rev. 21. 20 the seventh, c.
Chrysoprasus. *Golden leek.*
Rev. 21. 20 the tenth, a c
Church, *Called out, assembly.*
Mat. 16. 18 on this rock build my c.
  18. 17 tell it unto the c.
Acts 2. 47 added to the c. daily
  5. 11; 7. 38; 8. 1; 9. 31; 11. 22; 12
  1; 13. 1; 14. 23; 15. 3; 16. 5; 18. 22
Rom. 16. 1 Phebe, servant of the c.
1 Cor. 1. 2 unto the c. of God
  4. 17; 6. 4; 7. 17; 10. 32; 11. 16
2 Cor. 1. 1 c. of God at Corinth

Gal. 1. 2 unto the c. of Galatia
Eph. 1. 22 head over all to the c.
Phil. 3. 6 persecuting the c.
Col. 1. 18 head of the body, the c.
1 Thes. 1. 1 c. of the Thessalonians
1 Tim. 3. 5 take care of the c.
Phile. 2 and to the c. in thy house
Heb. 2. 12 in midst of the c.
Jas. 5. 14 call for elders of the c.
3 John 6 thy charity before the c.
Rev. 1. 4 John to the seven c.
  2. 1-23 ; 3. 1-14 ; 22. 16
Churl. *Miser, niggard.*
Isa. 32. 5, 7 nor the c. said to be b.
Churlish. *Hard, harsh.*
1 Sam. 25. 3 the man was c.
Churning. *Pressing, shaking.*
Prov. 30. 33 c. of milk bringeth b.
Ciel *See Ceil.*
Cieling. *See* **Ceiling.**
Cinnamon. *Cinnamon.*
Ex. 30. 23 take . . of sweet c.
Prov. 7. 17 perfumed my bed with c.
S. of S. 4. 14 pl. are calamus and c.
Rev. 18. 13 c., and odors, and oint.
Circle. *Arch, vault.*
Isa. 40. 22 he sitteth upon the c.
Circuit. *Circle, arch, vault.*
1 Sam. 7. 16 year to year in c.
Job 22. 14 walketh in the c. of heav.
Ps. 19. 6 his c. unto the ends of h.
Eccl. 1. 6 wind . . according to his c.
Circumcise. *Cut around.*
Gen. 17. 10 man child shall be c.
  21. 4 Abraham c. his son Isaac
Ex. 12. 48 let all males be c.
Lev. 12. 3 the flesh . . shall be c.
Deut. 10. 16 c. therefore the foreskin
Josh. 5. 2 c. again the children
Jer. 9. 25 c. with the uncircumcised
Luke 1. 59 they came to c. him
John 7. 22 on the sabbath day c.
Acts 15. 1 said, Except ye be c.
Rom. 4. 11 though they be not c.
1 Cor. 7. 18 let him not be c.
Gal. 2. 3 neither compelled to be c.
  5. 2 ; 6. 12, 13 ; Col. 2. 11
Circumcising.
Josh. 5. 8 when they had done c.
Luke 2. 21 accomplished for the c.
Circumcision. *Cutting around.*
Ex. 4. 26 because of the c.
John 7. 22 Moses gave unto you c.
Acts 7. 8 gave . . covenant of c.
Rom. 2. 25 c. verily profiteth, if
  2. 26-29 ; 31, 30 ; 4. 9-12 ; 15. 8
1 Cor. 7. 19 c. is nothing, but keep
Gal. 2. 7 as gospel of the c. to Peter
Eph. 2. 11 is called the c. in flesh
Phil. 3. 3 for we are the c.
Col. 2. 11 c. made without hands
Tit. 1. 10 specially they of the c.
Circumspect. *Watchful.*
Ex. 23. 13 I have said . . be c.
R. V. take ye heed
Circumspectly. R. V. *carefully.*
Eph. 5. 15 see then that ye walk c.
Cistern. *Well, pit.*
2 K. 18. 31 drink ye . . waters of his c.
Prov. 5. 15 drink . . of thine own c.
Eccl. 12. 6 wheel broken at the c.
Isa. 36. 16 drink waters of his own c.
Jer. 2. 13 hewed c., broken c.
Citizen. *Citizen.*
Luke 15. 15 joined himself to a c.
Acts 21. 39 c. of no mean city
Eph. 2. 19 fellow c. with saints
City. *Enclosed place.*
Gen. 4. 17 Enoch, he builded a c.
  13. 12 Lot dwelt in the c.
Ex. 1. 11 built for Phar'h treasure c.
  9. 29 gone out of the c. of plain
Lev. 14. 40 cast them without . . c.
  25. 32 the c. of the Levites
Num. 13. 19 what c. they dwelt in
  21. 26 c. of Sihon the king of Am.
Deut. 1. 28 c. great and walled
  2. 36 from c. that is by the river
Josh. 3. 16 far from the c. Adam
  9. 17 c. were Gibeon,and Chephirah,
Judg. 1. 8 set the c. on fire
  10. 4 they had thirty c.
Ruth 1. 19 all the c. was moved
1 Sam. 1. 3 out of his c. yearly
  6. 18 lords both of fenced c.
2 Sam. 2. 1 go into any of the c.

5. 7 same is the c. of David
1 K. 2. 10 D. was buried in the c. of
  4. 13 great c. with walls and bars
2 K. 3. 25 they beat down the c.
  7. 4 then the famine is in the c.
1 Chr. 1. 43 name of his c. was Din.
  2. 22 Jair had three and twenty c.
2 Chr. 5. 2 bring ark . . out of c.
  8. 6 store c. that Solomon had
Ez. 2. 70 Nethinims dwelt in their c.
  10. 14 with them elders of every c.
Neh. 2. 3 the c. lieth waste
  7. 73 and all Israel, dwelt in . . c.
Esth. 3. 15 c. Shushan was perplexed
  9. 2 Jews gathered in their c.
Job 15. 28 dwelleth in desolate c.
  24. 12 men groan from out of the c.
Ps. 31. 21 kindness in strong c.
  69. 35 God will . . build c. of Judah
Prov. 1. 21 in the c. she uttereth
Eccl. 7. 19 mighty men . . in the c.
S. of S. 3. 2 and go about the c.
Isa. 1. 8 Zion is left as a besieged c.
  6. 11 until the c. be wasted
Jer. 1. 15 against all the c. of Judah
  4. 29 whole c. shall flee for noise
Lam. 1. 1 doth the c. sit solitary
  5. 11 ravished . . maids in the c.
Ezek. 6. 6 dwellingplaces in c.
  7. 23 chain for c. full of violence
Dan. 9. 24 upon thy holy c.
  11. 15 k. shall take the fenced c.
Hos. 8. 14 send fire upon his c.
Joel 2. 9 run to and fro in c.
Am. 9. 14 shall build the waste c.
Jonah 3. 2 Nineveh, that great c.
Obad. 20 captivity possess the c.
Mic. 7. 12 Assyr. and from forti. c.
Nah. 3. 1 woe to the bloody c.
Zeph. 2. 15 this is the rejoicing c.
Zech. 14. 2 the c. shall be taken
Mat. 2. 23 a c. called Nazareth
  4. 5 ; 5. 14 ; 8. 33 ; 9. 1 ; 10. 5
Mark 1. 33 all the c. was gathered
  5. 14 ; 6. 11 ; 11. 19 ; 14. 13
Luke 1. 26 angel . . sent into a c.
  2. 3 ; 4. 29 ; 5. 12 ; 7. 11 ; 8. 27 ; 9. 5
John 1. 44 Bethsaida, c. of Andrew
Acts 7. 58 cast him out of the c.
  8. 40 ; 9. 6 ; 11. 9 ; 12. 10 ; 14. 6
Rom; 16. 23 chamberlain of the c.
2 Cor. 11. 26 in perils in the c.
Tit. 1. 5 and order elders in every c.
Heb. 11. 10 looked for a c. which
Jas. 4. 13 we will go into such a c.
2 Pet. 2. 6 c. of Sodom and Gomor.
Rev. 3. 12 the name of the c. of God
  11. 2 ; 14. 8 ; 16. 19 ; 17. 18 ; 18. rc
Clad. *Cover, wrap.*
1 K. 11. 29 c. hi self with . . new g.
Isa. 59. 17 was c. with zeal as cloke
Clamour. *Outcry.*
Eph. 4. 31 let all c. be put away
Clamorous. *Make noise.*
Prov. 9. 13 foolish woman is c.
Clap. *Strike hands.*
2 K. 11. 12 they c. their hands
Job 34. 37 he c. his hands among us
Ps. 98. 8 let floods c. their hands
Isa. 55. 12 trees . . shall c. hands
Lam. 2. 15 all that pass by c. hands
Ezek. 25. 6 hast c. thy hands
Nah. 3. 19 shall c. hands over thee
Clave. *See* **Cleave.**
Claw. *Parted hoof.*
Deut. 14. 6 cleav. cleft into two c.
Zech. 11. 16 tear their c. in pieces
R. V. Deut. 14. 6 —— ; Zech. 11. 16 hoofs
Clay. *Mire, mud.*
Ps. 40. 2 brought me out of miry c.
Isa. 41. 25 as potter treadeth c.
Nah. 3. 14 go into c., and tread
Hab. 2. 6 ladeth hims. with thick c.
Heavy soil.
1 K. 7. 46 c. ground between Suc.
2 Chr. 4. 17 in the c. ground bet. S.
Potter's clay.
Dan. 2. 33-45 of iron, and part of c.
Mortar, clay.
Job 4. 19 that dwell in houses of c.
  10. 9 ; 13. 12 ; 27. 16 ; 33. 6 ; 38. 14
Isa. 29. 16 esteemed as potter's c.
Jer. 18. 4 vessel made of c. was mar.
John 9. 6 he spat on gr. and made c.
Rom. 9. 21 potter power over the c.

R. V. Jer. 43. 9 mortar ; Hab. 2. 6 pledges.
Clean (a.). *Pure, clear.*
Gen. 7. 2 Of every c. beast take
Lev. 4. 12 carry forth into a c. place
Num. 9. 13 the man that is c.
Deut. 12. 15 c. may eat thereof
Josh. 3. 17 passed c. over Jordan
1 Sam. 20. 26 S. spake not.. he is not c.
2 K. 5. 10 thou shalt be c.
2 Chr. 30. 17 one that was not c.
Job 14, 4 who can bring c. thing
Ps. 19. 9 fear of the Lord is c.
Prov. 20. 9 I have made my heart c.
Eccl. 9. 2 to good and to the c.
Isa. 66. 20 bring offer. in a c. vessel
Jer. 13. 27 wilt not be made c.
Ezek. 36. 25 I sprinkle c. water
Zech. 11. 17 arm shall be c. dried up
Mat. 8. 3 saying, I will ; be thou c.
Mark 1. 41 ; Luke 5. 13
John 13. 10 but is c. every whit
Acts 18. 6 own heads, I am c.
2 Pet. 2. 18 that were c. escaped
Rev. 19. 8 fine linen, c. and white
R. V. Mat. 23. 25 ; Luke 11. 39 cleanse
Cleanness. *Cleanliness.*
2 Sam. 2. 21 the c. of my hands
Ps. 18. 20 according to c. of hands
Am. 4. 6 have given you c. of teeth
Cleanse. *Make clean.*
Ex. 29. 36 thou shalt c. the altar
Lev. 16. 19 c. it, and hallow it
Num. 8. 6 take Levites and c. them
2 Chr. 29. 15 c. the house of Lord
Neh. 13. 9 they c. the chambers
Job 37. 21 wind passeth, and c.
Ps. 51. 2 wash me, . . and c. me
Prov. 20. 30 blueness . . c. away evil
Jer. 4. 11 not to fan, nor to c.
Ezek. 36. 25 from idols . . I c. you
Dan. 8. 14 shall the sanctuary be c.
Joel 3. 21 will c. blood, I have not c.
Mat. 8. 3 his leprosy was c.
Mark 1. 42 and he was c.
Luke 4. 27 none of them was c.
Acts 10. 15 what God hath c.
2 Cor. 7. 1 let us c. ourselves
Eph. 5. 26 sanctify and c. it
Jas. 4. 8 c. your hands, ye sinners
1 John 1. 7 blood of Jesus Christ c.
R. V. Neh. 13. 22 purify ; Ps. 19. 12 clear
Cleansing. *Purifying.*
Lev. 13. 7 seen of the priest for his c.
Num. 6. 9 shave head day of his c.
Mark 1. 44 offer for thy c. those th.
Luke 5. 14 offer for thy c.
Clear. *Declare innocent.*
Ex. 34. 7 by no means c. the guilty
Clear. *Innocent, free.*
Gen. 24. 8 shall be c. from oath
Bright, pure, clean.
Job 11. 17 be c. than the noonday
Ps. 51. 4 be c. when thou judgest
S. of S. 6. 10 Who is she, c.as the sun
Isa. 18. 4 like a c. heat upon herbs
Am. 8. 9 darken . . earth in the c. day
Zech. 14. 6 light shall not be c.
2 Cor. 7. 11 approved yourselves c.
Rev. 21. 18 gold, like unto c. glass
R. V. Zech. 14. 6 with brightness ;
  2 Cor. 7. 11 Rev. 21. 18 pure ; 22. 1 bright
Clearing. *Making free.*
Num. 14. 18 no means c. the guilty
2 Cor. 7. 11 what r. of yourselves
Clearly. *Distinctly*
Job 33. 3 lips utter knowledge c.
Mark 8. 25 and saw every man c.
R. V. Job. 33. 3 sincerely
Clearness. *Brightness.*
Ex. 24. 10 body of heaven in his c.
Cleave. *Adhere.*
Gen. 2. 24 shall c. unto his wife
Deut. 10. 20 c. unto him shalt thou c.
Josh. 22. 5 c. unto him and serve
Ruth 1. 14 Ruth c. to her
2 Sam. 20. 2 men c. unto their king
1 K. 11. 2 Solomon c. unto these
2 K. 3. 3 he c. unto the sins
Neh. 10. 29 c. to their brethren
Job 19. 20 my bone c. to my skin
Ps. 44. 25 belly c. to earth
Jer. 13. 11 girdle c. to loins

Lam. 4. 4 tongue *c.* to roof of mo.
Dan. 2. 43 not *c.* one to another
Mat. 19. 5 shall a man . . *c.* to his wife
Luke 10. 11 very dust which *c.*
Acts 17. 34 men *c.* unto him
Rom. 12. 9 *c.* to that which is good
Dig, *rend asunder.*
Gen. 22. 3 *c.* the wood for offering
Lev. 1. 17 *c.* it with wings thereof
Num. 16. 31 ground *c.* asunder
Deut. 14. 6 *c.* the cleft into claws
1 Sam. 6. 14 *c* wood of the cart
Ps. 74. 15 didst *c.* the fountain
Eccl. 10. 9 he that *c.* wood endang.
Isa. 48. 21 he *c.* the rock also
Zech. 14. 4 mount of Olives shall *c.*
Hab. 3. 9 thou didst *c.* the earth
Mic. 1. 4 valleys shall be *c.*
Cleft. *See* **Cleave.**
Cleft. *Recess, hollow place.*
Deut. 14. 6 cleaveth the *c.* into cl.
Isa. 2. 21 go into the *c.* of rocks
S. of S. 2. 14 thou art in the *c.*
Jer. 49. 16 that dwelleth in the *c.*
Am. 6. 11 the little house with *c.*
Obad. 3 that dwel. in *c.* of the rocks
R. V. Isa. 2. 21 caverns
Clemency. *Pliability.*
Acts 24. 4 hear us of thy *c.* a few **w.**
Clerk. *Writer, scribe.*
Acts 19. 35 when the *c.* had appeased
Cliff. *Ascent, steep.*
2 Chr. 20. 16 up by *c.* of Ziz
Job 30. 6 to dwell in the *c.* of **val.**
Clift. R. V. *cleft.*
Ex. 33. 22 put thee in a *c.*
Isa. 57. 5 children . . under the *c.*
Climb. *Go up.*
1 Sam. 14. 13 Jonathan *c.* up on h'**ds**
Jer. 4. 29 they *c.* upon the rocks
Joel 2. 9 *c.* upon the houses
Am. 9. 2 *c.* up to heaven
Luke 19. 4 Z. *c.* up a sycomore **tree**
John 10. 1 *c.* up some other way
Clip. *Diminish.*
Jer. 48. 37 and every beard *c.*
Cloak. *Veil, outer garment.*
Mat. 5. 40 let him have thy *c.* **also**
Luke 6. 29 that taketh away thy *c.*
John 15. 22 no *c.* for their sins
2 Tim. 4. 13 *c* that I left at Troas
1 Pet. 2. 16 for a *c.* of maliciousness
Clod. *Lump, soil.*
Job. 7. 5 flesh clothed with . . *c.*
21. 33 *c.* of the valley sh. be **sweet**
Joel 1. 17 seed is rotten under *c.*
Cloke. *Robe.*
Isa. 59. 17 clad with zeal as a *c.*
Close (*a*). *Near, tight, shut.*
Num. 5. 13 and be kept *c.* fr. **husb.**
2 Sam. 22. 46 out of their *c.* places
Job 41. 15 shut as with a *c.* seal
Ps. 18. 45 afraid out of *c.* places
Luke 9. 36 they kept it *c.*, told no **m.**
Acts 27. 13 they sailed *c.* by Crete
Close (*v.*). *Shut.*
Num. 16. 33 earth *c.* upon them
Judg. 3. 22 fat *c.* upon the blade
Isa. 29. 10 Lord hath *c.* your eyes
Jer. 22. 15 reign, because thou *c.*
Dan. 12. 9 words are *c.* up and sea**l.**
Am. 9. 11 *c.* up the breaches
Mat. 13. 15 their eyes they have *c.*
Luke 4. 20 he *c.* the book
Acts 28. 27 their eyes have they *c.*
R. V. Jer. 22. 15 strivest to excel
Closet. *Inner chamber.*
Joel 2. 16 let bride go out of her *c.*
Mat. 6. 6. enter into thy *c.*, pray to **F.**
Luke 12. 3 have spoken in ear in *c.*
R. V. Luke 12. 3 inner chamber
Cloth. *Woven fabric.*
Ex. 31. 10 the *c.* of service and hol.
Num. 4. 6 spread over it a *c.*
Deut. 22. 17 spread the *c.* before
1 Sam. 19. 13 covered it with a *c.*
2 Sam. 20. 12 cast a *c.* upon him
2 K. 8. 15 took a thick *c.* and dipped
Mat. 9. 16 no man putteth . . new *c.*
Mark 2. 21 seweth a piece of new *c.*
Luke 24. 12 linen *c.* laid by them
John 19. 40 wound it in a linen *c.*
R. V. Ex. 31. 10; 35. 19; 39. 1;
Deut. 22. 17; 2 Sam. 20. 12 gar-
ment; 2 K. 8. 15 coverlet
Clothe. *Dress, invest.*

Gen. 3. 21 Lord God . . *c.* them
Ex. 40. 14 bring . . sons and *c.* them
Lev. 8. 7 *c.* him with a robe
2 Sam. 1. 24 *c.* you in scarlet
1 Chr. 15. 27 D. was *c.* with . . robe
2 Chr. 28. 15 *c.* all that were naked
Esth. 4. 4 raiment to *c.* Mordecai
Job. 10. 11 *c.* me with skin and fl.
Ps. 35. 26 let them be *c.* with shame
Prov. 23. 21 *c.* a man with rags
Isa. 22. 21 *c.* him with thy robe
Jer. 4. 30 *c.* thyself with crimson
Ezek. 7. 27 shall be *c.* with des.
Dan. 5. 7 shall be *c.* with scarlet
Zeph. 1. 8 *c.* with strange apparel
Zech. 3. 3 *c.* with filthy garments
Mat. 25. 36 naked, and ye *c.* me
Mark 16. 5 sitting on right side, *c.*
Luke 16. 19 rich man who was *c.*
2 Cor. 5. 2 earnest. desiring to be *c.*
Rev. 1. 13 Son of man *c.* with gar.
7. 9; 10. 1; 12. 1; 19. 13
Clothes. *Garments.*
Gen. 37. 29 he rent his *c.*
Ex. 12. 34 bound up in their *c.*
Lev. 10. 6 neither rend your *c.*
Num. 8. 7 let them wash their *c.*
Josh. 7. 6 Joshua rent his *c.*, and said
Judg. 11. 35 he rent his *c.*
1 Sam. 19. 24 S. stripped off his *c.*
2 Sam. 3. 31 rend your *c.*, and gird
1 K. 1. 1 they covered him with *c.*
2 K. 5. 7 he rent his *c.*, and said
2 Chr. 34. 27 rend thy *c.* and weep
Neh 4. 23 none of us put off our *c.*
Esth. 4. 1 Mordecai rent his *c.*
Prov. 6. 27 his *c.* not be burnt
Isa. 36. 22 came with their *c.* rent
Jer. 41. 5 heads shaven and *c.* rent
Ezek. 16. 39 strip thee of thy *c.*
Am. 2. 8 lay thems. down upon *c.*
Mat. 21. 7 put on them their *c.*
Mark 5. 28 if I may touch but his *c.*
Luke 8. 27 certain man ware no *c.*
John 11. 44 bound . . with grave *c.*
Acts 7. 58 witnesses laid down . . *c.*
R. V. Gen. 37. 34; Ex. 19. 14; Lev.
16. 32; Mat. 21. 7; 26. 65; Mark
5. 28; 15. 20; Luke 19. 36; Acts
7. 58; 14. 14; 22. 23; garments;
Ezek. 27. 20; John 19. 40; 20. 5, 7
cloths
Clothing. *Raiment, apparel.*
Job 22. 6 stripped . . naked of *c.*
Ps. 35. 13 my *c.* was sackcloth
Prov. 27. 26 lambs are for thy *c.*
Isa. 59. 17 gar. of vengeance for *c.*
Jer. 10. 9 purple is their *c.*
Mat. 7. 15 come to you in sheep's *c.*
Mark 12. 38 love to go in long *c.*
Acts 10. 30 man stood . . in bright *c.*
Jas. 2. 3 that weareth the gay *c.*
R. V. Mat. 11. 8 raiment; Mark 12.
38 robes; Acts 10. 30 apparel
Cloud. *Cloud.*
Gen. 9. 13 see my bow in the *c.*
Ex. 13. 21 went bef. in a pillar of *c.*
14. 19; 16. 10; 19. 9; 24. 15; 34. 5
Lev. 16. 2 I will appear in the *c.*
Num. 9. 15 *c.* covered the tabernacle
10. 11; 15. 25; 2. 5; 14. 14; 16. 42
Deut. 1. 33 went . . before you in a *c.*
2 Sam. 22. 12 waters, and thick *c.*
1 K. 8. 10 *c.* filled the house
2 Chr. 5. 13 house . . filled with a *c.*
Neh. 9. 19 pillar of *c.* departed
Job 7. 9 the *c.* is consumed
38. 37 who can number the *c.*
Ps. 78. 14 led them with a *c.*
Prov. 3. 20 *c.* drop down the dew
Jer. 4. 13 shall come up as *c.*
Lam. 3. 44 cover thyself with a *c.*
Ezek. 1. 4 a great *c.* and fire
Dan. 7. 13 S. of man came with *c.*
Hos. 6. 4 goodness is as a morning *c.*
Joel 2. 2 day of *c.* and darkness
Nah. 1. 3 *c.* are the dust of his feet
Zeph. 1. 15 day of *c.* and darkness
Mat. 17. 5 a bright *c.* overshadowed
Mark 9. 7 *c.* that overshadowed
Luke 9. 35 came voice out of the *c.*
Acts 1. 9 a *c.* received him out of
1 Cor. 10. 1 fathers were under a *c.*
1 Thes. 4. 17 caught up in a *c.*
2 Pet. 2. 17 *c.* that are carried
Jude 12 *c.* they are without water

Rev. 1. 7 he cometh with *c.*
10. 1; 11. 12; 14. 14, 15, 16
R. V. In Job and Ps. mostly skies
Cloudy. R. V. *of cloud.*
Ex. 33. 9 *c.* pillar descended
Neh. 9. 12 leddest them . . by *c.* pil,
Ps. 99. 7 spake unto them in *c.* pillar
Ezek. 30. 3 day is near, . . a *c.* day
Clouted. *Spotted, patched.*
Josh. 9. 5 shoes *c.* upon their feet
Cloven. *Split.*
Lev. 11. 3 hoof, and is *c.* footed
Deut. 14. 7 or divide the *c.* hoof
Acts 2. 3 appeared . . them *c.* tongues
R. V. Acts 2. 3 parting asunder
Cluster. *Stem, bunch.*
Gen. 40. 10 *c.* . . brought forth ripe
Num. 13. 23 a branch with one *c.*
Deut. 32. 32 their *c.* are bitter
1 Sam. 25. 18 hundred *c.* of raisins
S. of S. 1. 14 unto me as a *c.*
Isa. 65. 8 wine found in the *c.*
Mic. 7. 1 is no *c.* to eat
Rev. 14. 18 gather the *c.* of vine
Coal. *Ember.*
Lev. 16. 12 censer full of burning *c*
2 Sam. 14. 7 shall quench my *c.*
Job 41. 12 his breath kindleth *c.*
Ps. 18. 8 *c.* were kindled by it
Prov. 6. 28 can one go on hot *c.*
Isa. 44. 19 baked bread upon *c.*
Ezek. 1. 13 appearance like . . *c.*
John 18. 18 serv. made a fire of *c.*
Rom. 12. 20 heap *c.* of fire on head
Hot or burning stone
1 K. 19. 6 cake baken on the *c.*
S. of S. 8. 6 *c.* thereof are *c.* of fire
Heb. 3. 5 burning *c.* went forth
R. V. Prov. 26. 21 embers; S. of S.
8. 6 flashes; Hab. 3. 5 bolts
Coast. *Border.*
Ex. 10. 4 bring locusts unto thy *c.*
Num. 20. 23 *c.* of land of Edom
Deut. 2. 4 pass through the *c.* of
Josh. 12. 4 *c.* of Og and Bashan
Judg. 1. 8 took Gaza with the *c.*
1 Sam. 5. 6 smote Ashdod and the *c.*
2 Sam. 21. 5 from remaining in . . *c.*
1 K. 1. 3 throughout all the *c.* of Is.
2 K. 10. 32 smote them in all . . *c.*
1 Chr. 4. 10 and enlarge my *c.*
2 Chr. 11. 13 out of all their *c.*
Ps. 105. 31 came lice in all their *c.*
Ezek. 47. 16 which is by the *c.* of H.
Joel 3. 4 O Tyre, . . the *c.* of Pales.
Boundary, part, end.
Jer. 25. 32 raised up from the *c.*
Mat. 2. 16 and in all the *c.* thereof
15. 21. *c.* of Tyre and Sidon
Mark 5. 17 depart out of their *c.*
Acts 19. 1 passed through . . upper *c.*
Edge, shore.
Num. 34. 3 *c.* of the salt sea
Josh. 19. 29 from the *c.* to Achzib
Ezek. 25. 16 destroy the . . sea *c.*
Zeph. 2. 6 sea *c.* shall be dwellings
Luke 6. 17 peo. from sea *c.* of Tyre
Acts 27. 2 sail by *c.* of Asia
R. V. border, with very few excep-
tions
Coat. *Tunic, long robe.*
Gen. 3. 21 God make *c.* of skins
Ex. 28. 4 broidered *c.*, a mitre
Lev. 8. 7 and he put on him the *c.*
1 Sam. 2. 19 mother made him a . . *c.*
2 Sam. 15. 32 came . . with his *c.* rent
Job 30. 18 as . . collar of my *c.*
S. of S. 5. 3 I have put off my *c.*
Dan. 3. 21 were bound in their *c.*
Mat. 5. 40 take away thy *c.*
Mark 6. 9 and not put on two *c.*
Luke 3. 11 he that hath two *c.*
John 19. 23 the *c.* was without seam
Acts 9. 39 shewing the *c.* and gar.
Coat of mail, breastplate.
1 Sam. 17. 5 armed with a *c.* of mail
R. V. 1 Sam. 2. 19 robe; Dan. 3. 21,
27 hosen
Cock. *Male fowl.*
Mat. 26. 34 before the *c.* crow
Mark 14. 68 porch; and the *c.* crew
Luke 22. 34 *c.* shall not crow this
John 18. 27 immediately the *c.* crew
Cockatrice. *Basilisk, adder.*
Isa. 11. 8 hand on the *c.'s* den
Jer. 8. 17 I will send serpents, *c.*

Cockle. *Weed, darnel.*
Job 31. 40 thistles instead of . . c.
Coffer. *Box, chest.*
1 Sam. 6. 8, 11, 15 put jew. in . . c.
Coffin. *Ark, chest.*
Gen. 50. 26 Joseph was put in a c.
Cogitations. R. V. *thoughts.*
Dan. 7. 28 c. much troubled me
Cold. *Cold.*
Gen. 8. 22 c. and heat, sum. and w.
Job 24. 7 no covering in the c.
Ps. 147. 17 who stand before his c. ?
Prov. 25. 20 taketh . . gar. in c. wea.
Jer. 18. 14 the c. flowing waters
Nah. 3. 17 camp . . in the c. day
Mat. 10. 42 give a cup of c. water
John 18. 18 made fire, for it was c.
Acts 28. 2 and because of the c.
2 Cor. 11. 27 in c. and nakedness
Rev. 3. 15 art neither c. nor hot
R. V. Prov. 20 4 winter
Collar. *Mouth, drop.*
Judg. 8. 26 beside ornaments, and c.
Job 30. 18 bindeth me about as the c.
R. V. Judg. 8. 26 pendants
Collection. *Burden, gathering.*
2 Chr. 24. 6 bring out of J. the c.
1 Cor. 16. 1 concerning the c.
R. V. 2 Chr. 24. 6, 9 tax
College. R. V. *second quarter.*
2 K. 22. 14 she dwelt in Jer. in the c.
2 Chr. 34. 22 in Jer. in the c.
Collops. *Folds.*
Job 15. 27 maketh c. of fat
Colony. R. V. *Roman colony.*
Acts 16. 12 chief city, and a c.
Color. *Aspect, eye.*
Lev. 13. 55 not changed his c.
Num. 11. 7 as the c. of bdellium
Prov. 23. 31 giveth c. in the cup
Ezek. 1. 4 as the c. of amber
Pieces, ends.
Gen. 37. 3 made him coat of many c.
2 Sam. 13. 18 garment of divers c.
Showing, pretence.
Acts 27. 30 under c. as though
Paint, spot.
Isa. 54. 11 lay stones with fair c.
Ezek. 16. 16 deckest . . with divers c.
R. V. Num. 11. 7 appearance
Colt. *Son, foal.*
Gen. 32. 15 camels with their c.
Judg. 10. 4 rode on thirty ass c.
Job 11. 12 like a wild ass's c.
Zech. 9. 9 c. the foal of an ass
Mat. 21. 2 ass tied, and c. with her
Mark 11. 2 ye shall find a c. tied
Luke 19. 33 were loosing the c.
John 12. 15 sitting on an ass's c.
Come. *Arrive, come.*
Gen. 6. 18 thou shalt c. into the ark
Ex. 1. 1 which c. into Egypt
Lev. 11. 34 on which such water c.
Num. 4. 5 Aaron shall c. and
Deut. 1. 22 c. near unto me
Josh. 2. 1 c. into an harlot's house
Judg. 3. 20 Ehud c. unto him
Ruth 1. 2 c. into country of Moab
1 Sam. 1. 19 c. to their house to Ram,
2 Sam. 1. 2 behold a man c. out of c.
1 K. 1. 28 came into the king's pres.
2 K. 2. 4 they c. to Jericho
1 Chr. 2. 25 the Kenites that c.
2 Chr. 5. 4 elders of Israel c.
Ez. 3. 8 second year of their c.
Neh. 2. 7 till I c. to Judah
Esth. 1. 12 Vashti refused to c.
Job 1. 6 the sons of God c. to pres.
Ps. 5. 7 will c. into thy house in mer.
Prov. 1. 26 mock when your fear c.
Eccl. 1. 4 gen. passeth, another c.
S. of S. 2. 8 behold he c. leaping
Isa. 1. 12 ye c. to appear before me
Jer. 1. 15 I call, and they c.
Lam. 1. 4 none c. to the . . feasts
Ezek. 1. 4 behold, whirlwind c.
Dan. 11. third year c. Nebuchad.
Hos. 4. 15 c. not unto Gilgal
Joel 1. 13 c. lie all night in sackcloth
Am. 4. 2 lo, the days shall c.
Obad. 5 if thieves c. to thee
Jonah 1. 8 and whence c. thou ?
Mic. 1. 15 he shall c. unto Adullam
Hab. 1. 8 their horsemen shall c.
Zeph. 2. 2 anger of the Lord c.
Hag. 1. 14 c. and did work in house

Zech. 1. 21 what c. these to do ?
Mal. 3. 1 Lord shall suddenly c.
Mat. 2. 2 seen his star, and are c.
Mark 1. 7 there c. one mightier
Luke 1. 43 my Lord should c. to me
John 1. 7 same c. for a witness
Acts 1. 11 this Jesus shall so c.
Rom. 1. 10 will of God to c. to you
1 Cor. 2. 1 when I c. to you
2 Cor. 1. 15 I was minded to c.
Gal. 2. 11 Pet. was c. to A...tioch
Eph. 2. 17 c. and preached peace
Phil. 1. 27 whether I c. and see
Col. 3. 6 wrath of God c. on childr.
1 Thes. 1. 10 del. from wrath to c.
2 Thes. 1. 10 c. to be glorified
1 Tim. 1. 15 Jesus c. into the world
2 Tim. 4. 21 do thy diligence to c.
Tit. 3. 12 be diligent to c.
Heb. 6. 7 rain that c. oft upon it
2 Pet. 3. 3 c. in . . last days scoffers
1 John 2. 18 antichrist shall c.
2 John 7 Jesus Christ is c. in flesh
3 John 3 rejoiced when brethren c.
Jude 14 the Lord c. with . . his saints
Rev. 1. 7 Behold, he c. with clouds
Coming. *Arriving, coming.*
Gen. 30. 30 blessed thee since my c.
1 Sam. 16. 4 elders trem. at his c.
2 Sam. 3. 25 going out, and c. in
Isa. 32. 19 c. down on the forest
Ezek. 43. 11 and the c. in thereof
Mat. 24. 48 lord delayeth his c.
Luke 9. 42 as he was yet a c.
John 1. 27 who c. after me is pref.
Acts 7. 52 c. of the Just One
1 Cor. 15. 23 are Christ's at the c.
2 Cor. 7. 6 not by his c. only
Phil. 1. 26 by my c. to you
1 Thes. 2. 19 not even ye at his c.
Jas. 5. 7 be patient unto the c. of L
1 Pet. 1. 16 c. of our Lord Jesus
1 John 2. 28 ashamed c. at his c.
Comeliness. *Honor, beauty.*
Isa. 53. 2 he hath no form nor c.
Ezek. 16. 14 perfect through my c.
Dan. 10. 8 my c. was turned
1 Cor. 12. 23 have more abundant c.
R. V. Ezek. 16. 14 majesty
Comely. *Becoming, stately.*
1 Sam. 16. 18 Jesse . . a c. person
Job 41. 12 not conc. his c. proportion
Ps. 33. 1 rejoice, praise is c.
Prov. 30. 29 four are c. in going
Eccl. 5. 18 good and c. to eat and d.
S. of S. 1. 10 thy cheeks are c.
Isa. 4. 2 the fruit of earth shall be c.
Jer. 6. 2 c. and delicate woman
1 Cor. 11. 13 c. that a woman pray
R. V. Prov. 30. 29 stately ; 1 Cor.
7. 35 ; 11. 13 seemly
Comer. *Who comes.*
Heb. 10. 1 make the c. . . perfect
Comfort. (n.). *Cheer, courage.*
Job 6. 10 then should I . . have c.
Ps. 119. 76 kindness be for my c.
Isa. 57. 6 I receive c. in these
Ezek. 16. 54 art a c. unto them
Mat. 9. 22 Daughter, be of good c.
Mark 10. 49 Be of good c., rise
Luke 8. 43 Daugh., be of good c.
Acts 9. 31 c. of the Holy Ghost
Rom. 15. 4 c. of the scriptures
1 Cor. 14. 3 speak. exhortation and c.
2 Cor. 1. 3 the God of all c.
Phil. 2. 1 if there be any c. of love
R. V. Mal. 9. 22 ; Mark 10. 49 cheer ;
1 Cor. 14. 3 ; Phil. 2. 1 consolation
Comfort (v.). *Cheer, encourage,
solace, brighten, refresh.*
Gen. 5. 29 this same shall c. us
Judg. 19. 8 c. thine heart, I pray
Ruth 2. 13 for thou hast c. me
2 Sam. 10. 2 David sent to c. him
1 Chr. 7. 22 breth. came to c. him
Job 2. 11 mourn with and c. him
Ps. 23. 4 thy rod and staff . . c. me
S. of S. 2. 5 c. me with apples
Isa. 12. 1 praise thee, thou c. me
Jer. 8. 18 I would c. myself
Lam 1. 2 city hath none to c. her
Ezek. 14. 23 they shall c. you
Zech. 1. 17 L. shall . . c. Zion
John 11. 9 c. them concerning bro.
Acts 16. 40 c. them, and departed
2 Cor. 1. 4 who c. us, that we . . c.

Eph. 6. 22 might c. your hearts
Col. 4. 8 that he might c. your hearts
1 Thes. 2. 11 c. and charged . . you
2 Thes. 2. 17 c. your hearts and
R. V. 1 Thes. 2. 11 encouraging ;
5. 11 exhort one another
Comfortable. *Restful.*
2 Sam. 14. 17 word shall . . be c.
Zech. 1. 13 good words and c. wor.
Comfortably. *Heartfully.*
2 Sam. 19. 7 speak c. unto thy ser.
2 Chr. 30. 22 Hezekiah spake c.
Isa. 40. 2 speak . . c. to Jerusalem
Hos. 2. 14 speak c. unto her
Comforter. *Consoler, helper.*
2 Sam. 10. 3 hath sent c. unto thee
Job 16. 2 miserable c. are ye
Ps. 69. 20 looked for c. . . found
Eccl. 4. 1 they had no c.
Lam. 1. 9 she had no c.
Nah. 3. 7 whence shall I seek c.
John 14. 16 give you another C.
14. 26 ; 15. 26 ; 16. 7
Comfortless. R. V. *desolate.*
John 14. 18 he will not leave you c.
Command (n.). *Mouth, order.*
Job 39. 37 eagles mount at thy c.
Command (v.). *Say, charge, en-
join.*
Gen. 18. 19 he will c. his children
Ex. 4. 28 signs which he had c.
Lev. 6. 9 c. Aaron and his sons
Num. 1. 19 as the Lord c. Moses
Deut. 1. 18 I c. you at that time
Josh. 1. 7 which Moses my ser. c.
Judg. 2. 20 which I c. their father
Ruth 2. 15 Boaz c. his young men
1 Sam. 2. 29 have c. in my hab.
2 Sam. 4. 12 D. c. his young men
1 K. 2. 46 so the king c. Benaiah
2 K. 11. 5 And he c. them, saying
1 Chr. 6. 49 all that Moses had c.
2 Chr. 7. 13 if I c. the locusts
Ez. 4. 3 king Cyrus . . hath c. us
Neh. 1. 7 c. thy servant Moses
Esth. 3. 2 for the king had so c.
Job 36. 32 light, c. it not to shine
Ps. 7. 5 judgment thou hast c.
Isa. 5. 6 will also c. the clouds
Jer. 1. 7 whatsoever I c. thee speak
Lam. 1. 17 Lord hath c. concerning
Ezek. 9. 11 done as thou hast c.
Am. 2. 12 ye c. the prophets
Zech. 1. 6 I c. my servants
Mal. 4. 4 which I c. unto him
Mat. 10. 5 Jesus sent forth and c.
Mark 1. 27 for with authority c. he
Luke 4. 3 if thou be Son of God c.
John 8. 5 Moses in the law c.
Acts 4. 18 c. them not to speak
1 Cor. 7. 10 unto the married I c.
1 Thes. 4. 11 work . . as we c. you
2 Thes. 3. 4 do things which we c.
1 Tim. 4. 11 these things c. and teach
Rev. 9. 4 and it was c. them
R. V. very frequently, especially in
N. T., charged or enjoined
Commander. *Who sets up.*
Isa. 55. 4 given him c. for people
Commandment. *Saying, precept,
charge, law, order.*
Gen. 26. 5 Abraham kept my c.
Ex. 15. 26 give ear to his c.
Lev. 4. 2 If soul sin against any c.
Num. 15. 22 not obs. all these c.
Deut. 4. 13 ten c., and he wrote
Josh. 8. 8 according to the c.
Judg. 2. 17 obeying the c. of Lord
1 Sam. 13. 13 hast not kept the c.
2 Sam. 12. 9 thou despised the c.
1 K. 2. 3 keep his stat. and c.
2 K. 17. 19 Judah kept not the c.
1 Chr. 28. 7 if constant to do my c.
2 Chr. 7. 19 if ye forsake my c.
Ez. 7. 11 a scribe of the . . c.
Neh. 1. 5 that observe his c.
Esth. 3. 3 transgress the king's c.
Job 23. 12 gone back from the c.
Ps. 19. 8 the c. of Lord is pure
78. 7 ; 89. 31 ; 112. 1 ; 119. 6 ;
Prov. 2. 1 not, if thou hide my c.
Eccl. 8. 5 whoso keepeth the c.
Isa. 36. 21 king's c. was, Ans. not
Jer. 35. 14 obey their father's c.
Dan. 9. 23 the c. came forth
Hos. 5. 11 Ephr. walked after the c.

Am. 2. 4 have not kept his *c.*
Mal. 2. 1 this *c.* is for you
Mat. 5. 19 break one of these least *c.*
Mark 7. 8 laying aside the *c.* of God
Luke 1. 6 walking in all the *c.*
John 10. 18 this *c.* have I received
Acts 17. 15 received a *c.* unto Silas
Rom. 7. 12 *c.* holy and just, good
1 Cor. 7. 19 keeping of the *c.*
2 Cor. 8. 8 I speak not by *c.*
Eph. 2. 15 even the law of *c.*
Col. 4. 10 whom ye received *c.*
1 Tim. 6. 14 keep this *c.* without s.
Tit. 1. 14 not giving heed to *c.*
Heb. 7. 5 they have a *c.* to take
2 Pet. 2. 21 turn from the holy *c.*
1 John 2. 3 if we keep his *c.*
2 John 4 have received a *c.* from F.
Rev. 12. 17 keep the *c.* of God
R. V. Frequently, word, decree, precept, charge, statute.

Commend. *Praise, recommend.*
Gen. 12. 15 princes of Pharaoh *c.*
Eccl. 8. 15 I *c.* mirth, because
Luke 16. 8 *c.* the unjust steward
Acts 14. 23 *c.* them to the Lord
Rom. 3. 5 if unrighteousness *c.*
1 Cor. 8. 8 meat *c.* us not to God
2 Cor. 3. 1 begin .. to *c.* ourselves
Commendation. *Recommendation.*
2 Cor. 3. 1 epistles of *c.* to you
Commission. *Trust, authority.*
Ez. 8. 36 delivered the king's *c.*
Acts 26. 12 with authority and *c.*
Commit. *Do, give over, trust.*
Gen. 39. 8 hath *c.* all he hath
Lev. 5. 17 if a soul sin and *c.*
Num. 5. 6 when man or wo. shall *c.*
Deut. 17. 5 *c.* that wicked thing
Josh. 7. 1 ch. of Israel *c.* a trespass
Judg. 20. 6 *c.* lewdness and folly
1 K. 14. 27 *c.* them unto .. hands of
1 Chr. 10. 13 transgres. which he *c.*
2 Chr. 12. 10 them to the hands
Job. 5. 8 unto God .. I *c.* my cause
Ps. 37. 5 *c.* thy way unto .. L.
Prov. 16. 3 *c.* thy works unto .. L.
Isa. 22. 21 will *c.* thy government
Jer. 39. 14 *c.* him unto God.
Ezek. 3. 20 when right. m. doth *c.*
Hos. 6. 9 for they *c.* lewdness
Mal. 2. 11 an abomination is *c.*
Mark 15. 7 who had *c.* murder
Luke 12. 48 and did *c.* things wor.
John 8. 34 whosoever *c.* sin, is
Acts 8, 3 haling m. and w. *c.* them
Rom. 1. 32 which *c.* such things
1 Cor. 10. 8 as some of them *c.*
2 Cor. 5. 19 *c.* unto us the word
Gal. 2. 7 gospel .. was *c.* unto uncir.
1 Tim. 6. 20 keep that which is *c.*
2 Tim. 1. 14 good thing which was *c.*
Tit. 1. 3 which is *c.* unto me
Jas. 2. 9 ye *c.* sin, and are conv.
1 Pet. 2. 23 he *c.* himself to him
Commodious. *Convenient, spacious.*
Acts 27. 12 haven was not *c.*
Common. *Ordinary, jointly.*
Lev. 4. 27 any of the *c.* people
Num. 16. 29 men die the *c.* death
1 Sam. 21. 4 no *c.* bread under
Eccl. 6. 1 There is evil, and it is *c.*
Jer. 31. 5 eat them as *c.* things
Ezek. 23. 42 men of the *c.* sort
Acts 2. 44 and had all things in *c.*
Tit. 1. 4 own son after the *c.* faith
Jude 3 write .. of the *c.* salvation
R. V. Eccl. 6. 1 heavy upon; Jer. 31. 5 enjoy the fruits thereof; Acts 5. 18 public; 1 Cor. 10. 13 can bear.
Commonly. *Generally.*
Mat. 28. 15 saying is *c.* reported
1 Cor. 5. 1 it is reported *c.*
R. V. Mat. 28. 15 was spread abroad; 1 Cor. 5. 1 actually
Commonwealth. *Community.*
Eph. 2. 12 aliens from the *c.*
Commotion. *Shaking, tumult.*
Jer. 10. 22 *c.* out of the north
Luke 21. 9 ye hear of wars and *c.*
R. V. Luke 21. 9 tumults
Commune. *Speak, talk.*
Gen. 18. 33 had left .. *c.* with Abraham
23. 8 · 34. 6; 42. 24; 43. 19

Ex. 25. 22 I will *c.* with thee
Judg. 9. 1 Abim. went and *c.* with
1 Sam. 9. 25 Samuel *c.* with Saul
1 K. 10. 2 she *c.* with him
2 K. 22. 14 and they *c.* with her
2 Chr. 9. 1 she *c.* with him
Job 4. 2 assay. to *c.* with thee
Ps. 64. 5 *c.* of laying snares
Eccl. 1. 16 *c.* with mine heart
Dan. 1. 19 king *c.* with them
Zech. 1. 14 angel that *c.* with me
Luke 6. 11 *c.* with one another
Acts 24. 26 sent .. and *c.* with him
R. V. Gen. 42. 24; 43. 19; Judg. 9. 1; 1 Sam. 25. 39, spake; Zech. 1. 14 talked
Communicate. *Impart, partake*
Gal. 2. 2 I *c.* unto them that gospel
Phil. 4. 15 no church *c.* with me
1 Tim. 6. 18 be willing to *c.*
Heb. 13. 16 and to *c.* forget not
R. V. Gal. 2. 2 laid before them; Phil. 4. 14, 15 had fellowship
Communication. *Speech, talk.*
2 Sam. 3. 17 Abner had *c.* with eld.
2 K; 9. 11 the man and his *c.*
Mat. 5. 37 let your *c.* be Yea; Nay
Luke 24. 17 what manner of *c.*
1 Cor. 15. 33 evil *c.* corrupt good m.
Eph. 4. 29 no corrupt *c.* proceed
Phile. 6. the *c.* of thy faith
R. V. 2 K. 9. 11 talk; Mat. 5. 37; Eph. 4. 29 speech; Col. 3. 8 speaking; Phile. 6 fellowship
Communion. *Fellowship, interchange.*
1 Cor. 10. 16 the *c.* of the blood
2 Cor. 6. 14 what *c.* hath light
13. 14 love of God, and the *c.*
Compact. *Joined.*
Ps. 122. 3 as a city that is *c.*
Compacted. R. V. *knit together.*
Eph. 4. 16 whole body fitly *c.*
Companies. *Parties.*
Mark 6. 39 to make sit down by *c.*
R. V. 2 K. 5. 2 bands
Companion. *Friend, associate.*
Ex. 32. 27 every man has his *c.*
Judg. 11. 38 she went with her *c.*
1 Chr. 27. 33 H. was the king's *c.*
Ez. 4. 7 the rest of their *c.*
Job. 30. 29 and a *c.* to owls
Ps. 45. 14 her *c.* that follow her
Prov. 13. 20 a *c.* of fools be destr.
S. of S. 1. 7 turneth .. flocks of thy *c.*
Isa. 1. 23 and *c.* of thieves
Ezek. 37. 16 *c.* of Israel his *c.*
Dan. 2. 17 M. and Azariah his *c.*
Mal. 2. 14 yet is she thy *c.*
Acts 19. 29 having caught Paul's *c.*
Phil. 2. 25 Epaphro. my *c.* in labour
Heb. 10. 33 ye became *c.* of them
Rev. 1. 9 am your brother and *c.*
R. V. Job 41. 6 bands of fishermen; 1 Chr. 27. 33 friend; Phil. 2. 25 fellow-worker; Rev. 1. 9 partaker with you
Company. *Camp.*
Gen. 32. 8 then the other *c.* escape
2 K 5. 15 returned he and all his *c*
1 Chr. 9. 18 were porters in the *c.*
Adherents.
Num. 14. 7 spake unto all the *c.*
16. 5–40; 26. 9, 10; 27. 3
Job 16. 7 made desolate all my *c.*
Ps. 106. 17, 18 *c.* of Abiram
Troop.
1 Sam. 30. 15 bring me down to this *c.*
2 K. 5. 2 Syrians had gone out by *c.*
Ps. 68. 30 rebuke the *c.* of spearmen
S. of S. 6. 13 the *c.* of two armies
Congregation.
Gen. 35. 11 a *c.* of nations be of thee
Num. 22. 4 now shall this *c.* lick
1 Sam. 19. 20 when they saw the *c.*
Jer. 31. 8 great *c.* shall return
Ezek. 16. 40 also bring upon *c.*
17. 17; 23. 46; 26. 7; 27. 27; 32. 3
Detachment.
Judg. 7. 16 divided .. into three *c.*
7. 20; 9. 34–44; 1 Sam. 11. 11;
Crowd, multitude.
Gen. 37. 25 a *c.* of Ishmaelites
1 Sam. 10. 5 meet a *c.* of prophets
2 Chr. 20. 12 great *c.* that cometh
Ps. 55. 14 walked unto house in *c.*

Luke 5. 29 great *c.* of publicans
John 6. 5 Jesus saw a great *c.*
Acts 6. 7 great *c.* of priests were
Heb. 12. 22 innumerab. *c.* of angels
Party, companions.
Judg. 18. 23 comest with such a *c.*
Isa. 21. 13 traveling *c.* of Dedanim
Luke 9. 14 sit down by fifty in a *c.*
Acts 4. 23 went to their own *c.*
Mix with, accompany.
Prov. 29. 3 keepeth *c.* with harlots
Acts 1. 21 men which have *c.* with us
10. 28 a Jew to keep *c.* with him
1 Cor. 5. 9 not to *c.* with fornicators
2 Thes. 3. 4 have no *c.* with him
R. V. Num. 14. 7; 16. 16; 22. 4 congregation; Luke 5. 29; 23. 27 multitude; Acts 17. 5 crowd; Heb. 12. 22 hosts
Comparable. *Weighed with.*
Lam. 4. 2 sons of Zion, *c.* to gold
Compare. *Liken, weigh.*
Ps. 89. 6 who .. can be *c.* unto Lord
Prov. 3. 15 are not to be *c.* to her
S. of S. 1. 9 *c.* thee, O my love
Isa. 46. 5 to whom will ye *c.* me
Mark 4. 30 what com. shall we *c.* it
1 Cor. 2. 13 *c.* spiritual things
2 Cor. 10. 12 *c.* ourselves with some
R. V. Mark 4. 30 set it forth
Comparison. *Compared with.*
Judg. 8. 2 done now in *c.* of
Hag. 2. 3 in your eyes in *c.*
Mark 4. 30 with what *c.* shall we *c.*
Compass (*n.*). *Circle, compass.*
Ex. 27. 5 put it under the *c.*
Josh. 15. 3 and fetched a *c.* to Kar.
2 Sam. 5. 23 but fetch a *c.* behind th.
1 K. 7. 35 *c.* of half a cubit high
Prov. 8. 27 set a *c.* upon depths
Isa. 44. 13 marketh it with a *c.*
Acts 28. 13 thence we fetched a *c.*
R. V. Prov. 8. 27 circle; Isa. 44. 13 compasses; 2 K. 3. 9; Acts 28. 13 made circuit
Compass (*v.*). *Go round, gird.*
Gen. 2. 11 *c.* the whole land
Num. 21. 4 to *c.* the land of Edom
Deut. 2. 1 we *c.* mount Seir
Josh. 6. 3 ye shall *c.* the city
Judg. 11. 18 went along and *c.* the
1 Sam. 23. 26 Saul .. *c.* David
1 K. 7. 15 twelve cubits did *c.*
2 K. 6. 15 host *c.* the city
2 Chr. 4. 3 oxen, *c.* the sea round
Job 19. 6 God hath *c.* me
Ps. 17. 11 have *c.* us in our steps
Isa. 50. 11 *c.* yourselves about
Jer. 52. 21 twelve cubits did *c.* us
Lam. 3. 5 hath *c.* me with gall
Hos. 11. 12 Ephraim *c.* me wi. lies
Jonah 2. 5 waters *c.* me about
Hab. 1. 4 wicked doth *c.* about
Mat. 23. 15 ye *c.* sea and land
Luke 21. 20 shall see Jerusalem *c.*
Heb. 11. 30 after they were *c.*
Rev. 20. 9 *c.* the camp of the saints
R. V. Frequently in O. T., turned about
Compassion. *Mercy, pity.*
Ex. 2. 6 she had *c.* on him
Deut. 13. 17 show mercy and have *c.*
1 Sam. 23. 21 for ye have *c.*
1 K. 8. 50 give them *c.* before
2 K. 13. 23 the Lord had *c.* them
2 Chr. 30. 9 your children .. find *c.*
Ps. 78. 38 being full of *c.*, forgave
86. 15; 111. 4; 112. 4; 145. 8
Isa. 49. 15 she should not have *c.*
Jer. 12. 15 return, and have *c.*
Lam. 3. 22 because his *c.* fail not
Ezek. 16. 5 to have *c.* on thee
Zech. 7. 9 show mercy and *c.*
Mat. 15. 32 have *c.* on the multitude
Mark 9. 22 have *c.* on us, and help
Luke 7. 13 he had *c.* on her
Rom. 9. 15 will have *c.* on whom
Heb. 5. 2 who can have *c.* on
Jude 22 and of some have *c.*
1 Pet. 3. 8 *c.* one of another
R. V. Mat. 18. 33; Mark 5. 19; Jude 22 mercy; Heb. 5. 2 bear gently with.
Compel. *Drive, force.*
Lev. 25. 39 not *c.* him to serve
1 Sam. 28. 23 his servants *c.* him

2 Chr. 21. 11 and c. Judah thereto
Esth. 1. 8 none did c., for so
Mat. 5. 41 c. thee to go a mile
Mark 15. 21 they c. one Simon
Luke 14. 23 c. them to come in
Acts 26. 11 punished and c. them
2 Cor. 2. 11 ye have c. me
Gal. 2. 3 c. to be circumcised
R. V. 1 Sam. 28. 23; Luke 14. 23 constrain

Complain. *Murmur, find fault.*
Num. 11. 1 when the people c.
Judg. 21. 22 brethren came..to c.
Job 7. 11 c. in the bitterness of
Ps. 77. 3 I c., and my spirit was
Lam. 3. 39 wherefore doth..man c.

Complainer. *Fault-finder.*
Jude 16 murmurers, c., walking

Complaining. R. V. *outcry.*
Ps. 144. 14 no c. in our streets

Complaint. *Talk, murmur.*
1 Sam. 1. 16 abundance of my c.
Job 7. 13 couch shall ease my c.
9. 27; 10. 1; 21. 4; 23. 2
Ps. 55. 2 I mourn in my c.
Acts 25. 7 laid many grievous c.
R. V. Acts 25. 7 bringing charges

Complete. *Full, perfect.*
Lev. 23. 15 sabbaths shall be c.
Col. 2. 10 ye are c. in him
4. 12 stand perfect and c
R. V. Col. 2. 10 made full; 4. 12 fully assured

Composition. *Proposition.*
Ex. 30. 32, 37 after the c. of it

Compound. *Perfume, spice.*
Ex. 30. 25, 33 ointment c. after art

Comprehend. *Know.*
Job 37. 5 things we cannot c.
Embrace, contain.
Isa. 40. 12 who c. the dust of earth
Receive fully.
John 1. 5 and the darkness c. it not
Rom. 13. 9 is briefly c. in this say.
Eph. 3. 18 be able to c. with saints
R. V. John 1. 5; Eph. 3. 18 apprehend; Rom. 3. 9 summed up

Conceal. *Cover, hide.*
Gen. 37. 26 slay our brother, and c.
Deut. 13. 8 neither shalt thou c. him
Job 6. 10 c. the words of .. Holy One
Ps. 40. 10 not c. thy lovingkindness
Prov. 11. 13 a faithful spirit c. mat.
Jer. 50. 2 publish and c. not
R. V. Job 6. 10 denied; 4. 12 keep silence concerning

Conceit. *Eye, imagination.*
Prov. 18. 11 as a .. wall in his own c.
26. 5 wise in his own c.
Rom. 11. 25 wise in your own c.
R. V. Prov. 18. 11 imagination

Conceive. *Become pregnant.*
Gen. 4. 1 she c., and said
16. 4; 21. 2; 25. 21; 29. 32; 30. 5
Ex. 2. 2 and the woman c.
Lev. 12. 2 if a woman have c.
Num. 11. 12 all this people
Judg. 13. 3 shalt c., and bear a son
1 Sam. 1. 20 after Hannah had c.
2 Sam. 11. 5 woman c., and sent
2 K. 4. 17 wom. c., and bare a son
1 Chr. 7. 23 she c., and bare a son
Job 15. 35 they c. mischief
Ps. 7. 14 travaileth and hath c
S. of S. 3. 4 chamber of her that c.
Isa. 7. 14 Behold, a virgin shall c.
Hos. 2. 5 she that c. them
Mat. 1. 20 that which is c. is of H G.
Luke 1. 24 after those days E c.
Think, devise, reckon.
Jer. 49. 30 hath c. purpose ag. you
Acts 5. 4 why hast thou c. this

Conception. *Impregnation.*
Gen. 3. 16 will multiply thy c.
Ruth 4. 13 the Lord gave her c.
Hos. 9. 11 womb, and from the c.

Concern. *Engage, occupy.*
Acts 28. 31 things which c. the L.
2 Cor. 11. 30 glory of things which c.

Concerning. *In relation to.*
Gen. 24. 9 sware to him c. matter
Josh. 14. 6 the man of God c.
2 Sam. 18. 5 king gave charge c.
Ez. 5. 5 answer by letter c.
Jer. 7. 22 spake not c. burnt off.
Dan. 2. 18 mercies of God c.

Mat. 4. 6 give angels charge c.
Mark 5. 16 told them . . c. the swine
Luke 2. 17 which was told them c.
John 7. 12 much murmuring c.
Acts 1. 16 H. G. spake before c.
19. 39; 21. 24; 22. 18; 23. 15;
Rom. 1. 3 c. his Son Jesus Christ
1 Cor. 7. 25 c. virgins I have no co.
2 Cor. 11. 21 speak as c. reproach
1 Thes. 3. 2 comfort you c. . . faith
1 Tim. 1. 19 having put away c. faith
2 Tim. 2. 18 c. truth have erred
Heb. 7. 14 Moses spake nothing c.
1 John 2. 26 have written you c.
R. V. Luke 2. 17; Acts 19. 39 about; 1 Cor. 5. 3 judged; Phil. 36 touching

Concision. *Cutting down.*
Phil. 3. 2 beware of the c.

Conclude. *Decide, reckon.*
Acts 21. 25 have written and c.
Rom. 3 28 c. that a man is justified
Embrace, shut together.
Rom. 11. 32 God hath c. them all
Gal. 3. 22 scripture hath c. all
R. V. Rom. 11. 32 shut up; Acts 21. 25 given judgment

Conclusion. R. V. *end.*
Eccl. 12. 13 let us hear the c.

Concord. *Harmony.*
2 Cor. 6. 15 what c. hath C. with B.

Concourse. *Gathering.*
Prov. 1. 21 crieth in the place of c.
Acts 19. 4 an account of this c.

Concubine. *Half-wife.*
Gen. 22. 24 c. whose name was R.
Judg. 8. 31 his c. . . in Shechem
2 Sam. 3. 7 Saul had a c , Rizpah
1 K. 11. 3 Sol. had three hundred c.
1 Chr. 1. 32 sons of Ketu. A's. c.
2 Chr. 11. 21 all his wives and c.
Esth. 2. 14 which kept the c.
S. of S. 6. 8 queens, and fourscore c.
Dan. 5. 2 his wives and his c.

Concupiscence. *Over-desire.*
Rom. 7. 8 wrought . . all manner of c.
Col. 3. 5 inordinate aff., evil c.
1 Thes. 4. 5 not in lust of c.
R. V. Rom. 7. 8 coveting; Col. 3. 5 desire; 1 Thes. 4. 5 lust

Condemn. *Judge against.*
Ex. 22. 9 whom judges shall c.
Deut. 25. 1 justify the right, and c.
2 Chr. 36. 3 c. the land in hun. tal.
Job. 9. 20 mine own mouth shall c.
Ps. 37. 33 Lord will not c. him
Prov. 12. 2 wicked devices will he c.
Isa. 50. 9 who . . shall c. me
Am. 2. 8 drink . . wine of the c.
Mat. 12. 41 rise . . and shall c. it
Mark 10. 33 shall c. him to death
Luke 11. 32 men of N. shall c. it
John 8. 10 hath no man c. thee?
Rom. 14. 22 he that c. not himself
1 Cor. 11. 32 we should not be c.
Tit. 2. 8 speech that cannot be c.
Heb. 11. 7 he c. the world
Jas. 5. 9 grudge not . . lest ye be c.
2 Pet. 2. 6 c. them with overthrow
R. V. Ps. 109. 31; John 3. 17 judge

Condemnation. *Judgment against.*
Luke 23. 40 art in the same c.
John 3. 19 this is the c., that light
Rom. 5. 16 judgment by one to c.
1 Cor. 11. 34 come not . . unto c.
1 Tim. 3. 6 the c. of the devil
Jas. 3. 1 receive the greater c.
Jude 4 ordained to this c. cer. men
R. V. John 3. 19; 5. 24; 1 Cor. 11. 34; Jas. 5. 12 judgment

Condescend. *Led away by.*
Rom. 12. 16 c. to men of low estate

Condition. *Terms.*
1 Sam. 11 2 on this c. will I make
Luke 14. 32 and desireth c. of peace

Conduct. *Lead, escort.*
2 Sam. 19. 31 to c. him over Jordan
Acts 17. 15 they that c. Paul
1 Cor. 16. 11 c. him forth in peace
R. V. 2 Sam. 19. 15 bring

Conduit. *Aqueduct.*
2 K. 18. 17 c. of the upper pool
Isa. 7. 3 at the end of the c.

Coney. *Hare, hedgehog.*
Lev. 11. 5 c., because he cheweth
Deut. 14. 7 camel, hare, and c.

Ps. 104. 18 the rocks for the c.
Prov. 30. 26 c. are but a feeble folk

Confection. *Perfume, spice.*
Ex. 30. 35 c. after the art of apoth.

Confectionary. *Perfumer.*
1 Sam. 8. 13 daughters to be c.

Confederacy. R. V. *conspiracy.*
Isa. 8. 12 say ye not, a c.
Covenant, agreement.
Obad. 7 men of thy c. have brought

Confederate. *Ally.*
Gen. 14. 13 these were c. with Abr.
Isa. 7. 2 Syria is c. with Ephraim.
R. V. Ps. 83. 5 make a covenant

Confer. *Talk together.*
1 K. 1. 7 he c. with Joab
Acts 4. 15 c. among themselves
Gal. 1. 16 I c. not with flesh

Conference. *Consultation.*
Gal. 2. 6 in c. added nothing
R. V. who were of repute

Confess. *Admit, acknowledge.*
Lev. 5. 5 c. that he hath sinned
Num. 5. 7 shall c. their sin
1 K. 8. 33 turn again to thee, and c.
2 Chr. 6. 24 return and c. thy name
Ez. 10. 1 when he had c., weeping
Neh. 1. 6 c. the sins of the children
Job 40. 14 then will I also c.
Ps. 32. 5 will c my transgressions
Prov. 28. 13 who c. and forsaketh
Dan. 9. 20 c. my sin and s. of my peo.
Mat. 3. 6 baptized . . in Jordan, c.
Mark 1. 5 all baptized of him c.
Acts 19. 18 c. and shewed their deeds
Rom. 14. 11 every tongue shall c.
Phil. 2. 11 should c. that Jesus
Jas. 5. 16 c. your faults one to ano.
Rev. 3. 5 c. his name before my F
Speak as another, profess.
Mat. 10. 32 whosoever . . shall c. me
Luke 12. 8 him shall Son of man c.
John 1. 20 c. and denied not
Acts 23. 8 the Pharisees c. both
Rom. 10. 9 shalt c. with thy mouth
1 John 1. 9 if we c. our sins
2 John 7 who c. not that Jesus C.
R. V. Rom. 15. 9 give praise to

Confession. *Admission, profession.*
Josh. 7. 19 make c. unto him
Ez. 10. 11 c. unto the Lord God
1 Tim. 6. 13 P. witnessed a good c.

Confidence. *Trust reliance.*
Judg. 9. 26 men of Shechem put c. in
2 K. 18. 19 what c. is there wherein
Job 4. 6 is this thy fear, thy c.
Ps. 65. 5 c. of all the ends of . . earth
Isa. 30. 15 in quietness and c.
Prov. 3. 26 Lord shall be thy c.
Jer. 2. 37 hath rejected thy c.
Ezek. 29. 16 be no more the c.
Mic. 7. 5 put ye not c. in a guide
Acts 28. 31 all c., no man forbidding
2 Cor. 1. 15 in this c. I was minded
Gal. 5. 10 I have c. in you
Eph. 3. 12 gave access with c.
Phil. 1. 25 having this c., I know
2 Thes. 3. 4 have c. in the Lord
Phile, 21 c. in thy obedience
Heb. 6. 14 beginning of our c.
R. V. Judg. 9. 26 trust; Acts 28. 31; Heb. 3. 6; 10. 35; 1 John. 2. 28; 3. 21 boldness

Confident. *Trustful, courageous.*
Ps. 27. 3 in this will I be c.
Prov. 14. 16 fool rageth and is c.
Rom. 2. 19 art c. that thou art c.
2 Cor. 5. 6 we are always c. guide
Phil. 1. 6 being c. of this thing
R. V. 2 Cor. 5. 6, 8 of good courage

Confirm. *Establish, ratify.*
Num. 30. 14 he c. them, because
Deut. 27. 26 cursed be he that c. not
2 Sam. 7. 24 thou hast c. thy people
Ruth 4. 7 for to c. all things
1 K. 1. 14 will come and c. thy
2 K. 15. 19 be with him to c.
1 Chr. 14. 2 Lord had c. him king
Esth. 9. 29 c. this second letter
Ps. 68. 9 whereby thou didst c.
Isa. 35. 3 c. the feeble knees
Ezek. 13. 6 they would c. the word
Dan. 9. 27 shall c. the covenant
Mark. 16. 20 c. the word with signs
Acts 14. 22 c. souls of the disciples
Rom. 15. 8 to c. the promises

1 Cor. 1. 6 testimony of Christ was c.
2 Cor. 2. 8 c. your love toward
Gal. 3. 15 covenant, if it be c.
Heb. 2. 3 was c. unto us
R. V. 2 K. 14. 5; 1 Chr. 14. 2 established; Dan. 9. 27 made firm;
Heb. 6. 17 interposed with
Confirmation. *Firmly established.*
Phil. 1. 7 the defence and c. of gos.
Heb. 6. 16 an oath for c. is to them
Confiscation. *Fine, oppression.*
Ez. 7. 26 or to c. of goods
Conflict. *Contest, struggle.*
Phil. 1. 30 same c. which ye saw
Col. 2. 1 knew what great c. for you
Conformable. *Same form.*
Phil. 3. 10 made c. unto his death
Conformed. *Same form or way*
Rom. 8. 29 did predestinate to be c.
12. 2 be not c. to this world
R. V. Rom. 12. 2 fashioned according
Confound. *Mix, dismay, shame.*
Gen. 11. 7 there c. their language
Jer. 1. 17 lest I c. thee before them
1 Cor. 1. 27 fool. things .. to c...w.
1 Pet. 2. 6 believeth, shall not be c.
R. V. Jer. 1. 17 dismay; 1 Cor. 1. 27 that he might put to shame
Confounded. *Shamed, confused.*
2 K. 19. 26 were dismayed and c.
Job 6. 20 they were c. because
Ps. 35. 4 let them be c.
Isa. 1. 29 be c. for the gardens
Jer. 15. 19 she hath been a. and c.
Ezek. 16. 52 be thou c. also
Mic. 3. 7 and the diviners c.
Zech. 10. 5 riders .. shall be c.
R. V. Ps. 66. 6 brought to dishonour; 83. 17; Ezek. 16. 54; Mic. 7. 16 ashamed; Jer. 10. 14; 46. 24; 50. 2 put to shame
Confuse. R. V. *in confusion*
Acts 19. 32 the assembly was c.
Confused. *Shaking, trembling.*
Isa. 9. 5 battle with c. noise
Confusion. *Shame, embarrassment.*
1 Sam. 20. 30 chosen to thine own c.
Ez. 9. 7 to spoil, and to c. of face
Job 10. 15 I a.m full of c.
Ps. 44. 15 my c. is .. before me
Isa. 30. 3 the shadow of your c.
Jer. 3. 25 lie down in .. our c.
Dan. 9. 7 unto us c. of faces
Tumult, perplexity.
Lev. 18. 23 stand before a beast is c.
Isa. 24. 10 city of c. is broken
Acts 19. 29 city was filled with c.
1 Cor. 14. 33 God is not author of c.
Jas. 3. 16 c. and every evil work
R. V. 1 Sam. 20. 30; Ps. 109. 29 shame; Job 10. 15 ignominy; Ps. 44. 15; 70. 2 dishonour
Congealed. *Hardened, frozen.*
Ex. 15. 8 depths were c. in .. sea
Congratulate. *Declare blessed.*
1 Chr. 18. 10 enquire .. and c. him
Congregation. *Meeting, assembly.*
Ex. ،2. 3 speak unto all the c.
Lev. 4. 13 if whole c. of Israel sin
Num. 1. 2 take .. sum of all the c.
Deut. 31. 14 tabernacle of the c.
Josh. 9. 15 princes of the c. sware
Judg. 20. 1 c. was gathered together
1 Sam. 2. 22 assembled at door .. of c.
1 K. 8. 5 Solomon and all the c.
1 Chr. 6. 32 minis. before the .. c.
2 Chr. 5. 6 c. of Israel were assem.
Ez. 2. 64 whole c. together was for.
Neh. 5. 13 all the c. said, Amen
Job 15. 34 the c. of hypocrites
Ps. 1. 5 stand, nor sinners in the c.
Prov. 5. 14 in the midst of the c.
Jer. 6. 18 hear, nations, and know c.
Lam. 1. 10 should not enter thy c.
Hos. 7. 12 chastise them, as their c.
Joel 2. 16 gath. peo., sanctify the c.
Mic. 2. 5 cast cord by lot in c.
Acts 13. 43 when c. was broken up
R. V. in O. T. generally, assembly, meeting; Acts 13. 43 synagogue
Conquer. *Subdue.*
Rev. 6. 2 went forth c. and to c.
Conqueror. *Victor.*
Rom.٠ 8. 37 we are more than c.

Conscience. *Knowing with self.*
John 8. 9 convicted by their own c.
Acts 23. 1 lived in all good c.
Rom. 2. 15 c. also bearing witness
1 Cor. 8. 7 with c of the idol
2 Cor. 1. 12 testimony of our c.
1 Tim. 1. 5 good c., and faith unfei.
2 Tim. 1. 3 serve with pure c.
Tit. 1. 15 mind and c. is defiled
Heb. 9. 9 as pertaining to the c.
1 Pet. 2. 19 for c. toward G. endure
R. V. John 8. 9 ——
Consecrate. *Set apart, devote.*
Ex. 28. 41 anoint and c. them
Lev. 8. 33 till days of your c.
Num. 6. 12 shall c. unto the Lord
Josh. 6. 19 vessels .. are c. unto L.
Judg. 17. 5 Mic. c. one of his sons
1 K. 13. 33 whoso. would, he c. him
1 Chr. 29. 5 is willing to c. his
2 Chr. 13. 9 cometh to c. himself
Ez. 3. 5 feasts .. that were c.
Ezek. 43. 26 they shall c. themselves
Heb. 7. 28 maketh the c. for ever.
R. V. Ex. 28. 3; 30. 30 sanctify; Num. 6. 12 separate; Josh. 6. 19 holy; Heb. 7. 28 perfected; 10. 20; dedicated   [*tion.*
Consecration. *Filling in, separa-*
Ex. 29. 22 it is a ram of c.
Lev. 7. 37 offering, and of the c.
Num. 6. 7 the c. of his God
R. V. Num. 6. 9 separation
Consent (n.). *United voice.*
1 Sam. 11. 7 came with one c.
Ps. 83. 5 consulted .. with one c.
Hos. 6. 9 priests murder .. by c.
Zeph. 3. 9 serve him with one c.
1 Cor. 7. 5 except with c. for a time
R. V. 1 Sam. 11. 7 as one man
Consent (v.). *Be willing, say with.*
Gen. 34. 15 will we c. unto you
Deut. 13. 8 thou shalt not c.
1 K. 20. 8 hearken not, nor c.
2 K. 12. 8 priests c. to receive
Ps. 50. 18 then thou c. with him
Prov. 1. 10 if sinners entice .. c. not
Dan. 1. 14 he c. to them in matter
Luke 23. 51 the same had not c.
Acts 8. 1 Saul was c. to his death
Rom. 7. 16 I c. unto the law
1 Tim. 6. 3 if a man c. not
R. V. Dan. 1. 14 hearkened unto
Consider. *Know, regard, behold.*
Ex. 33. 13 c. that this nation is
Lev. 13. 13 the priest shall c.
Deut. 32. 7 c. the years of .. gen.
Judg. 18. 14 now therefore c. what
1 Sam. 12. 24 c. how great things
1 K. 3. 21 when I had c. it
2 K. 5. 7 wherefore I c. I pray
Ps. 5. 1 Lord, c. my meditation
Prov. 23. 1 to eat, c. diligently what
Eccl. 5. 1 for they c. not that
Isa. 1. 3 my people doth not c.
Jer. 2. 10 send unto Kedar and c.
Lam. 1. 11 see, O Lord, and c.
Ezek. 12. 3 they will c., though
Dan. 7. 8 I c. the horns, and, behold
Hag. 1. 5 thus saith the Lord, C.
Mat. 7. 3 not the beam that
Mark 6. 52 c. not the miracle
Luke 12. 24 c. the ravens : for they
John 11. 50 c. that it is expedient
Acts 15. 6 elders came together to c.
Rom. 4. 19 c. not his own body
Gal. 6. 1 c thyself, lest .. be tempted
2 Tim. 2. 7 c. what I say, and Lord
Heb. 7. 4 c. how great this man
R. V. Jer. 23. 20; 32. 24 understand; Lam. 1. 11; 2. 20; 5. 1 behold; Mark 6. 52 understood
Consist. *Be, put together.*
Luke 12. 15 man's life c. not in ab.
Col. 1. 17 by him all things c.
Consolation. *Comfort.*
Job 15. 11 are the c. of God small
Isa. 66. 11 the breasts of her c.
Jer. 16. 7 give them the cup of c.
Luke 2. 25 waiting for the c. of Is.
Acts 4. 36 Barnabas, the son of c.
Rom. 15. 5 God of patience and c.
2 Cor. 1. 5 c. also aboundeth
Phil. 2. 1 there be therefore any c.
2 Thes. 2. 16 given us everlasting c.
Phile. 7 have great joy and c.

Heb. 6. 18 might have strong c.
R. V. Acts 4. 36 exhortation; Rom. 15. 5; 2 Cor. 1. 5; 7. 7; 2 Thes. 2. 16; Phile. 7 comfort; Heb. 6. 18 encouragement
Consort. *Associate.*
Acts 17. 4 believed and c. with
Conspiracy. *Sworn together.*
2 Sam. 15. 12 and the c. was strong
2 K. 17. 4 king of Assyria found c.
2 Chr. 25. 27 they made a c.
Jer. 11. 9 Lord said, A c. is found
Ezek. 22. 25 c. of her prophets
Acts 23. 13 forty which made this c.
Conspirator. *Who conspires.*
2 Sam. 15. 31 Ahitho. among the c،
Conspire. *Bind, swear together.*
Gen. 37. 8 they c. against him
1 Sam. 22. 8 all have c. against me
1 K. 15. 27 Baasha, son of Ahijah, c.
2 K. 10. 9 I c. against my master
2 Chr. 24. 21 they c. against him
Neh. 4. 8 all c. together to come
Am. 7. 10 Amos c. against thee
Constant. *Keep hold.*
1 Chr. 28. 7 c. to do my command.
Constantly. *Perpetually.*
Prov. 21. 28 man .. speaketh c.
R. V. Acts 12. 15; Tit. 3. 8 confidently.
Constellation. *Thick, firm.*
Isa. 13. 10 stars of heaven and the c.
Constrain. *Press, compel.*
2 K. 4. 8 she c. him to eat bread
Job 32. 18 spirit within me c. me
Mat. 14. 22 Jesus c. his disciples
Mark 6. 45 he c. his disciples
Luke 24. 29 they c. him, saying
Acts 28. 19 was c. to appeal to Cæs
2 Cor. 5. 14 the love of Christ c. us
Gal. 6. 12 c. you to be circumcised
R. V. Gal 6. 12 compel
Constraint. *Necessity.*
1 Pet. 5. 2 not by c., but willingly
Consult. *Inquire, take counsel.*
1 K. 12. 6 Rehoboam c. with old men
1 Chr. 13. 1 D. c. with the captains
2 Chr. 20. 21 when he had c. with
Neh. 5. 7 Then I c. with myself
Ps. 62. 4 only c. to cast him down
Ezek. 21. 21 he c. with images
Dan. 6. 7 captains have c. together
Mat. 26. 4 c. that they .. take Jesus
Luke 14. 31 c. whether he be able
John 12. 10 chief priests c. that
R. V. 1 K. 12. 6, 8; 2 Chr. 20. 21; Mat. 26. 4; Luke 14. 31; John 12. 10 took counsel
Consultation. *Counsel.*
Mark 15. 1 priests held a c.
Consulter. *Inquirer.*
Deut. 18. 11 c. with familiar spirits
Consume. *Devour, finish.*
Gen. 41. 30 day of drought c. me
Ex. 15. 7 wrath which c. them
Lev. 6. 10 which the fire hath c.
Num. 16. 21 that I may c. them
Deut. 4. 24 L. thy God is a c. fire
Josh. 24. 20 he will turn and c. you
Judg. 6. 21 c. flesh and unlea. bread
1 Sam. 2. 33 man .. shall be to c.
2 Sam. 21. 5 man that c. us, and dev.
1 K. 18. 38 then fire of the Lord c.
2 K. 1. 10 let fire come .. and c.
2 Chr. 8. 8 whom chil. of Israel c.
Ez. 9. 14 till thou hadst c. us
Esth. 9. 24 to c. and destroy them
Job 1. 16 fire hath burnt and c.
Ps. 59. 13 c. them in wrath, c. them
Prov. 5. 11 when thy f. and b. are c.
Isa. 10. 18 c. the glory of his forest
Jer. 49. 27 c. palaces of Ben-hadad
Lam. 2. 22 hath mine enemy c.
Ezek. 13. 13 great hailstones to c.
Dan. 2. 44 break in pieces and c. all
Hos. 11. 6 sword shall c. .. branches
Zech. 14. 12 their flesh shall c. away
Zeph. 1. 2 I will utterly c. all things
Mal. 3. 6 sons of Jacob are not c.
Luke 9. 54 c. them even as Elias
Gal. 5. 15 take heed that ye be not c.
2 Thes. 2. 8 whom the Lord shall c.
Jas. 4. 3 that ye may c. it upon lusts
Heb. 12. 29 For our God is a c. fire
R. V. Frequently in O. T. devour;
2 Thes. 2. 8 Jesus shall slay

Consummation. *Completion.*
Dan. 9. 27 desolate, even until the *c.*
Consumption. *Completion.*
Isa. 10. 22, 23 God .. shall make *c.*
R. V. consummation
Wasting away, consumption.
Lev. 26. 16 appoint over you, *c.*, ague
Deut. 28. 22 Lord smite thee with *c.*
Contain. *Embrace.*
John 21. 25 world itself could not *c.*
Rom. 2. 14 do .. things *c.* in the law
1 Pet. 2. 6 it is *c.* in the scripture
Retain.
1 Cor. 7. 9 cannot *c.*, let them marry
R. V. 1 Cor. 7. 9 have not conti-
nency
Contemn. *Despise, reject.*
Ps. 15. 4 In wh. eyes a vile person is *c.*
S. of S. 8. 7 it would utterly be *c.*
Isa. 16. 14 glory of Moab shall be *c.*
Ezek. 21. 10 it *c.* the rod of my son
R. V. Ps. 15. 4 despised
Contempt. *Loathing, despising.*
Esth. 1. 18 too much *c.* and wrath
Job. 12. 21 poureth *c.* on princes
Ps. 119. 22 remove from me .. *c.*
Prov. 18. 3 cometh also *c.* wi. ignom
Dan. 12. 2 some to everlasting *c..*
Contemptible. *Loathed.*
Mal. 1. 7 table of the Lord is *c.*
2 Cor. 10. 10 presence weak, speech *c.*
R. V. 2 Cor. 10. 10 of no account
Contemptuously. R. V. *contempt.*
Ps. 31. 18 speak grievous things *c.*
Contend. *Strive.*
Deut. 2. 9 distress not .. neither *c.*
Neh. 13. 11 *c.* I with the rulers
Job. 9. 3 if he will *c.* with, not answ.
Prov. 29. 9 If a wise man *c.* wi. fool.
Eccl. 6. 10 neither may he *c.*
Isa. 49. 25 for I will *c.* with him
Jer. 18. 19 voice of them that *c.*
Am. 7. 4 God called to *c.* by fire
Mic. 6. 1 Arise, *c.* thou before mts.
Acts 11. 2 were of the circum. *c.*
Jude 9. the archangel when *c.*
R. V. Prov. 29. 9 hath controversy
Content. *Pleased, satisfied.*
Gen. 32. 27 his brethren were *c.*
Ex. 2. 21 Moses was *c.* to dwell
Lev. 10. 20 Moses heard, he was *c.*
Josh. 7. 7 would .. we had been *c.*
Judg. 17. 11 Levite was *c.* to dwell
2 K. 5. 23 Naaman said, Be *c.*, take
Job 6. 28 therefore be *c.*, look on me
Mark 15. 15 willing to *c.* the people
Luke 3. 14 be *c.* with your wages
1 Tim. 6. 8 having food .. let us be *c.*
Phil. 4. 11 state I am, .. to be *c.*
Heb. 13. 5 be *c.* with such things
3 John 10 and not *c.* therewith
Contention. *Strife.*
Prov. 18. 18 causeth *c.* to cease
Jer. 15. 10 and a man of *c.* to earth
Hab. 1. 3 that raise up strife and *c.*
Acts 15. 39 the *c.* was sharp bet. th.
1 Cor. 1. 11 there are *c.* among you
1 Thes. 2. 2 speak .. with much *c.*
Phil. 1. 16 one preach Christ of *c.*
Tit. 3. 9 avoid foolish *c.*, and, striv.
R. V. Phil. 1. 16 faction ; 1 Thes.
2. 2 in conflict ; Tit. 3. 9 strifes
Contentious. *Loving strife.*
Prov. 21. 19 with *c.* and angry wom.
Rom. 2. 8 them that are *c.*, indignat.
1 Cor. 11. 16 if any man seem to be *c.*
R. V. Rom. 2. 8 factious
Contentment. *Self-sufficiency.*
1 Tim. 6. 6 godli. with *c.* is gr. gain
Continual. *Unremitting.*
Ex. 29. 42 a *c.* burnt offering
Num. 4. 7 *c.* bread shall be thereon
2 K. 25. 30 his allowance was *c.*
2 Chr. 2. 4 for the *c.* shewbread
Ez. 3. 5 offered the *c.* burnt offering
Neh. 10. 33 shewbread for the *c.* off.
Prov. 15. 15 merry heart .. a *c.* feast
Isa. 14. 6 smote peo. with *c.* stroke
Jer. 52. 34 was *c.* diet given him
Ezek. 39. 14 men of *c.* employment
Luke 18. 5 lest by her *c.* coming
Rom. 9. 2 have *c.* sorrow in heart
R. V. Rom. 9. 2 unceasing
Continually. *Unceasingly.*
Gen. 6. 5 heart was only evil *c.*
Ex. 28. 29 mem. before the Lord *c.*

Lev. 24. 2 cause lamps to burn *c.*
1 Sam. 8. 29 became D's enemy *c.*
2 Sam. 9. 7 eat bread at my table *c.*
1 K. 10. 8 happy .. which stand *c.*
2 K. 4. 9 holy man .. passeth .. *c.*
1 Ch. 16. 6 priests with trumpets *c.*
2 Chr. 9. 7 thy men which stand *c.*
Job 1. 5 Thus did Job *c.*
Ps. 34. 1 praise shall *c.* be in mouth
Prov. 6. 21 bind them *c.* upon heart
Isa. 21. 8 I stand *c.* on watchtower
Jer. 6. 7 before me *c.* is grief
Ezek. 46. 14 prep. a meat offering *c.*
Hos. 12. 6 wait on thy God *c.*
Obad 16 the heathen drink *c.*
Nah. 3. 19 wickedness passed *c.*
Hab. 1. 17 not spare *c.* to slay nat.
Luke 24. 53 were *c.* in the temple
Acts 10. 7 soldier .. waited on him *c.*
Rom. 13. 6 attending *c.* upon this
Heb. 13. 15 sacrifice of praise to
God *c.*
R. V. 1 Chr. 16. 11 evermore ; Ps.
44. 15 all day long ; 58. 7 apace ;
109. 10 —
Continuance. *Days, holding on.*
Ps. 139. 16 which in *c.* were fash.
Isa. 64. 5 in those is *c.*, we be saved
Rom. 2. 7 who by patient *c.* in well
R. V. Ps. 139. 16 day by day ; Isa.
64. 5 them have we been of long
time ; Rom. 2. 7 patience
Continue. *Tarry, remain.*
Ex. 21. 21 if he *c.* a day or two
Lev. 12. 4 shall then *c.* in the blood
Judg. 5. 17 Asher *c.* on the sea
1 Sam. 1. 12 as she *c.* praying bef. L.
2 Sam. 6. 11 ark of the Lord *c.* in ho.
Ruth 2. 7 *c.* even from the morning
1 K. 22. 1 they *c.* three years
Job 14. 2 fleeth as a shadow and *c.*
Ps. 36. 10 O *c.* thy lovingkindness
Isa. 5. 11 that *c.* until night till wine
Jer. 30. 23 with fury, a *c.* whirlwind
Dan. 11. 8 he shall *c.* more years
Mat. 15. 32 because they *c.* with me
Luke 22. 28 they which have *c.* with
John 2. 12 *c.* there not many days
Acts 19. 10 *c.* .. space of two years
Rom. 6. 1 shall we *c.* in sin, that
Gal. 3. 10 cursed is every one that *c.*
Col. 1. 23 if ye *c.* in faith, grounded
Phil. 1. 25 shall .. *c.* with you all
1 Tim. 4. 16 take heed .. *c.* in them
2 Tim. 3. 24 *c.* thou in the things
Heb. 7. 24 because he *c.* ever, hath
1 John 2. 19 would have *c.* with us
Rev. 17. 10 he must *c.* a short space
R. V. John 2. 12 ; 8. 31 ; 15. 9 abide,
abode ; Acts 15. 35 tarried ; 18. 11
dwelt ; 20. 7 prolonged ; in O. T.
frequent changes to, abide
Contradict. *Speak against.*
Acts 13. 45 things spoken by Paul *c.*
Contradiction. *Speaking against.*
Heb. 7. 7 without all *c.*, less is bless.
R. V. Heb. 7. 7 any dispute ; 12. 3
gainsaying
Contrariwise. *On the contrary.*
2 Cor. 2. 7 *c.* ye ought rather forgive
Gal. 2. 7 but *c.*, when they saw gos.
1 Pet. 3. 9 *c.* blessing, knowing that
Contrary. *Opposite, perverse.*
Lev. 26. 21 if ye walk *c.* unto me
Ezek. 16. 34 And the *c.* is in thee
Mat. 14. 24 for the wind was *c.*
Mark 6. 48 wind was *c.* unto them
Acts 18. 13 to worship God *c.* to
Rom. 11. 24 graffed *c.* to nature
Gal. 5. 17 th. are *c.* one to the other
Col. 2. 14 which was *c.* to us
1 Thes 2. 15 please not G. and are *c.*
1 Tim. 1. 10 other thing that is *c.*
Tit. 2. 8 is of the *c.* part be asham.
Contribution. *Common use.*
Rom. 15. 26 make a certain *c.* for
Contrite. *Bruised.*
Ps. 34. 18 saveth such as be of *c.* spirit
Isa. 57. 15 wi. him that is of *c.* spirit
Controversy. *Strife, contention.*
Deut. 17. 8 of *c.* within thy gates
2 Sam. 15. 2 any man that had a *c.*
2 Chr. 19. 8 judg. of Lord and for *c.*
Isa. 34. 8 recompense for the *c.*
Jer. 25. 31 Lord has *c.* with nations
Ezek. 44. 24 in *c.* thy shall stand

Hos. 4. 1 Lord hath *c.* with inhab-
itants
Mic. 6. 2 Hear ye .. the Lord's *c.*
1 Tim. 3. 16 without *c.* great is mys
R. V. 2 Sam. 15. 2 suit
Convenient. *Timely, suitable.*
Prov. 30. 8 feed me with food *c.*
Jer. 40. 4 seemeth good and *c.* for
Mark 6. 21 a *c.* day was come
Acts 24. 24 when I have *c.* season
Rom. 1. 28 do those things .. not *c.*
1 Cor. 16. 12 he shall have *c.* time
Eph. 5. 4 nor jesting, which are not *c.*
Phile. 8 enjoin thee that which is *c.*
R. V. Prov. 30. 8 that is needful
Rom. 1. 28 fitting ; Eph. 5. 4
Phile. 8 befitting ; 1 Cor. 16. 12
opportunity
Conveniently. *Seasonably.*
Mark 14. 11 sought how he might *c.*
Conversant. *Acquainted, versed.*
1 Sam. 25. 15 we were *c.* with them
Josh. 8. 35 strangers that were *c.*
Conversation. *Way.*
Ps. 37. 14 such as be of upright *c.*
50. 23 that ordereth his *c.* aright
Turn, manner, behaviour, life.
2 Cor. 1. 12 we have had our *c.*
Gal. 1. 13 ye have heard of my *c.*
Eph. 2. 3 we all had our *c.* in times
Phil. 3. 20 our *c.* is in heaven
1 Tim. 4. 12 an example of .. in *c.*
Heb. 13. 7 consid'g the end of their *c.*
Jas. 3. 13 show out of a good *c.*
1 Pet. 1. 15 holy in all manner of *c.*
2 Pet. 2. 7 vexed with filthy *c.*
R. V. Ps. 37. 14 in the way ; Gal.
1. 13 ; Phil. 1. 27 ; 1 Tim. 4. 12 ;
1 Pet. 3. 16 manner of life ; 1 Pet.
2. 12 ; 3. 1 behaviour, Heb. 13. 7 ;
2 Pet. 2. 7 life ; 2 Pet. 3. 11 living
Conversion. *Turning of, or upon.*
Acts 15. 3 declaring *c.* of Gentiles
Convert. *Turn about, or upon.*
Ps. 51. 13 sinners shall be *c.*
Isa. 6. 10 understand .. nd *c.*
Mat. 13. 15 they .. should be *c.*
Mark 4. 12 lest .. they should be *c.*
Luke 22. 32 and when thou art *c.*
Acts 3. 19 repent ye, and be *c.*
Jas. 5. 19 do err from truth, and are *c.*
R. V. Ps. 19. 7 restoring ; Isa. 6o. 5
turned ; Mat. 13. 15 ; 18. 3 ; Mark
4. 12 ; Luke 22. 32 ; John 12. 40 ;
Acts 3. 19 ; 28. 27 turn, or turn
again
Converts. *Turned back.*
Isa. 1. 27 and her *c.* with righteous.
Convey. *Move, carry.*
1 K. 5. 9 and I will *c.* them by sea
Neh. 2. 7 that they may *c.* me over
John 5. 13 Jesus *c.* himself away
R. V. K. 5. 9 make ; Neh. 2. 7
let .. pass
Convict. *Awaken to sin.*
John 8. 9 *c.* by their own conscience
Convince. *Make plain.*
Job 32. 12 none of you *c.* Job
Convict.
John. 8. 46 which of you *c.* me
Acts 18. 28 he mightily *c.* the Jews
1 Cor. 14. 24 he is *c.* of all, is judg.
Tit. 1. 9 to *c.* the gainsayers
Jas. 2. 9 are *c.* of the law as transg.
Jude 15 *c.* all that are ungodly
R. V. 1 Cor. 14. 24 reproved by ;
Acts 18. 28 comforted ; John 8. 46 ;
Tit. 1. 9 ; Jas. 2. 9 ; Jude 15 con-
vict
Convocation. *Calling together,*
assembly.
Ex. 12. 16 there shall be an holy *c.*
Lev. 23. 2–37 ye sh. proclaim holy *c.*
Num. 28. 18 first day .. an holy *c.*
Cook. *Who cooks.*
1 Sam. 8. 13 take daughters to be *c.*
9. 23, 25 Samuel said to the *c.*
Cool (*n.*). *Wind.*
Gen. 3. 8 walk. in the *c.* of the day
Cool (*v.*). *Make cool.*
Luke 16. 24 water, and *c.* my tongue
Coping. *Projecting stone.*
1 K. 7. 9 from foundation to *c.*
Copper. R. V. *bright brass.*
Ez. 8. 27 weighed vessels of fine *c.*

Coppersmith. *Brazier.*
2 Tim. 4. 14 Alexander the *c.* did me
Copulation. *Coition, effusion.*
Lev. 15. 16 if seed of *c.* go out
Copy (*n.*). *Double, transcript.*
Deut. 17. 18 write *c.* of this law
Josh. 8. 32 he wrote on stones a *c.*
Ez. 4. 11 this is the *c.* of the letter
Esth. 3. 14 the *c.* of the writing
Copy (*v.*). *Transcribe.*
Prov. 25. 1 men of Hezekiah *c.* out
Cor. *A dry and liquid measure.*
Esek. 45. 14 a bath out of the *c.*
Coral. *Red coral.*
Job 28. 18 no mention be made of *c.*
Ezek. 27. 16 occupied fairs with *c.*
Corban. *Vow, offering.*
Mark 7. 11 if man shall say, it is *c.*
Cord. *Rope, twine, string.*
Ex. 35. 18 the p s .. and their *c.*
Num. 3. 26 and the *c.* of it for
Josh. 2. 15 let them down by a *c.*
Judg. 15. 13 bound him with .. *c.*
Esth. 1. 6 fastened with *c.* of linen
Job 36. 8 holden in *c.* of affliction
Ps. 140. 5 hid snare for me and *c.*
Prov. 5. 22 holden with *c.* of his sins
Eccl. 12. 6 or ever the *c.* be loosed
Isa. 5. 18 draw iniquity with *c.*
Jer. 38. 6 let down Jeremiah with *c.*
Ezek. 27. 24 chests .. bound with *c.*
Hos. 11. 4 I drew them with *c.*
Mic. 2. 5 cast a *c.* by lot in the cong.
John 2. 15 made scourge of small *c.*
R. V. Judg. 15. 13 ropes; Mic. 2.
5 the line
Coriander. *Aromatic seed.*
Ex. 16. 31 it was like *c.* seed
Num. 11. 7 manna was as *c.* seed
Cormorant. R. V. *pelican.*
Isa. 34. 11 *c.* and bittern possess it
Zeph. 2. 14 *c.* and b. shall lodge
Corn. *Wheat, grain.*
Gen. 41. 35 lay up *c.* under .. Phar.
Ex. 22. 6 that standing *c.* be consu.
Lev. 23. 14 eat neither bread nor .. *c.*
Num. 18. 27 *c.* of the threshingfloor
Deut. 7. 13 bless thy *c.* and wine
Josh. 5. 11 did eat of the old *c.*
Judg. 15. 5 go into the standing *c.*
Ruth 2. 2 glean ears of *c.* after him
1 Sam. 17. 17 take .. of parched *c.*
2 Sam. 17. 28 brought flour and *c.*
2 K. 18. 32 take you to land of *c.*
2 Chr. 31. 5 first fruits of *c.*, wine
Neh. 5. 2 we take up *c.* for them
Job 24. 6 they reap his *c.* in field
P . 4. 7 their *c.* and w. increased
Isa. 36. 17 land of *c.* and wine
Lam. 2. 12 they say .. Where is *c.*
Ezek. 36. 29 I will call for the *c.*
Hos. 2. 8 not know that I gave her *c.*
Joel 1. 10 for the *c.* is wasted
Hag. 1. 11 upon *c.* and new wine
Zech. 9. 17 *c.* sh. make men cheerful
Mat. 12. 1 began to pluck ears of *c.*
Mark 4. 28 after that the full *c.*
Luke 6. 1 he went through the *c.*
John 12. 24 except *c.* of wheat fall
Acts 7. 12 Jacob heard there was *c.*
R. V. Mat. 12. 1 cornfield; John
12. 24 grain
Corner. *Wing, angle.*
Ex. 25. 26 put rings in the four *c.*
Lev. 19. 9 shalt not reap .. the *c.*
Num. 24. 17 smite *c.* of Moab
Josh. 18. 4 compassed .. *c.* of sea
1 K. 7. 34 undersetters to the .. *c.*
2 K. 14. 13 gate of E. unto the *c.*
2 Chr. 26. 9 built towers at *c.* gate
Neh. 3. 24 from house of A. to *c.*
Job 1. 19 wind smote four *c.* of hou.
Ps. 118. 22 become head⁺.. of the *c.*
Prov. 7. 12 lieth in wait at every *c.*
Isa. 28. 16 lay .. precious *c.* stone
Jer. 31. 38 unto gate of the *c.*
Ezek. 43. 20 four *c.* of the settle
Zech. 10. 4 out of him came .. *c.*
Mat. 6. 5 love to pray, stand. in *c.*
Mark 12. 10 become head of the *c.*
Luke 20. 17 same is become head of *c.*
Acts 10. 11 sheet knit at the four *c.*
1 Pet. 2. 6 lay in Zion a chief *c.* stone
Rev. 7. 1 angels standing on four *c.*
R. V. Ex. 25. 12; 37. 3; 1 K. 7. 30
feet; Ex. 30. 4; 37. 27 ribs; Ex.

---

36. 25; 2 K. 11. 11 side; Zech. 10.
4 corner stone
Cornet. *Horn, trumpet.*
2 Sam. 6. 5 house of Is. played .. *c.*
1 Chr. 15. 28 with sound of the *c.*
2 Chr. 15. 14 sware unto Lord with *c.*
Ps. 98. 6 with .. sound of *c.* make
Dan. 3. 15 what time ye hear .. *c.*
Hos. 5. 8 blow ye the *c.* in Gibeah
Cornfloor. *Grainfloor.*
Hos. 9. 1 lov. reward on every *c. f.*
Corpse. *Dead body.*
2 K. 19. 35 they were all dead *c.*
Isa. 37. 36 they were all dead *c.*
Nah. 3. 3 is none end of their *c.*
Correct. *Reprove, instruct.*
Job 5. 17 happy .. man whom G. *c.*
Ps. 94. 10 chastis., shall not he *c.*?
Prov. 3. 12 whom Lord loveth he *c.*
Jer. 2. 19 thy wick. shall *c.* thee
Heb. 12. 9 had fathers .. which *c.*
R. V. Prov. 3. 12 reproveth; Heb.
12. 9 to chasten
Correction. *Reproof, instruction.*
Job 37. 13 whether for *c.* or for
Prov. 7. 22 as fool to *c.* of stocks
Jer. 2. 30 chil., they received no *c.*
Zeph. 3. 2 she receiveth not *c.*
Hab. 1. 12 hast estab. them for *c.*
2 Tim. 3. 16 scrip. is profitable for *c.*
R. V. Prov. 3. 11 reproof; Jer. 7. 28;
instruction
Corrupt (*a.*). *Bad, putrid, rotten.*
Job 17. 1 my breath is *c.*, days ex.
Ps. 38. 5 wounds stink and are *c.*
Prov. 25 26 man fall. is a *c.* spring
Ezek. 20. 44 accor. to your *c.* doings
Dan. 2. 9 prepar. lying and *c.* words
Mat. 7. 17 *c.* tree bringeth evil fruit
Luke 6. 43 doth *c.* tree bring good f.
Eph. 4. 29 let no *c.* com. proceed
1 Tim. 6. 5 disputings of men of *c.*
2 Tim. 3. 8 men of *c.* minds rep.
Corrupt. *Deprave, pollute, consume.*
Gen. 6. 12 all flesh had *c.* his way
Ex. 32. 7 the people have *c.* them
Deut. 4. 16 lest ye *c.* yourselves
Judg. 2. 9 *c.* themselves more than
Ezek. 28. 17 th. hast *c.* thy wisdom
Dan. 11. 32 shall he *c.* by flatteries
Hos. 9. 9 they have *c.* themselves
Zeph. 3. 7 th. rose early, and *c.* all
Mal. 2. 8 ye have *c.* the covenant
Mat. 6. 19 moth and rust doth *c.*
Luke 12. 33 steal, neither moth *c.*
1 Cor. 15. 33 evil com. *c.* good man.
2 Cor. 2. 17 not as many which *c.*
Jas. 5. 2 your riches are *c.*
Rev. 19. 2 which did *c.* the earth
R. V. Job. 17. 4. consumed; Ps.
73. 8 scoff; Dan. 11. 32 pervert;
Mal. 1. 14 blemished; Mat. 6. 19
consume; Jude 10 destroyed
Corrupter. *Who corrupts.*
Isa. 1. 4 ev. doers, children that are *c.*
Jer. 6. 28 revolters, they are all *c.*
Corruptible. *Pervertible.*
Rom. 1. 23 image made like *c.* man
1 Cor. 9. 25 do it to obtain *c.* crown
1 Pet. 1. 23 born again, not of *c.* seed
Corruption. *Depravity, decay.*
Lev. 22. 25 their *c.* is in them
2 K. 23. 13 hand of the mount of *c.*
Job. 17. 14 I have said to *c.*, Thou
Ps. 16. 10 will suffer H. O. to see *c.*
Isa. 38. 17 soul del. from pit of *c.*
Dan. 10. 8 comeliness turned to *c.*
Jonah 2. 6 brought up life from *c.*
Acts 2. 27 nei. suffer H. O. to see *c.*
Rom. 8. 21 delivered from bon. of *c.*
1 Cor. 15. 42 it is sown in *c.*
Gal. 6. 8 shall of the flesh reap *c.*
2 Pet. 1. 4 the *c.* that is in the world
R. V. Jonah 2. 6 pit; 2 Pet. 2. 12
destroying
Corruptly. *Wickedly.*
2 Chr. 27. 2 the people did yet *c.*
Neh. 1. 7 We have dealt very *c.*
Cost. *Expense, outlay.*
2 Sam. 24. 24 which *c.* me nothing
1 Chr. 21. 24 offer b. off. without *c.*
Luke 14. 28 sit., and counteth the *c.*
Costliness. *Preciousness.*
Rev. 8. 19 by reason of her *c.*
Costly. *High priced.*

---

1 K. 5. 17 brought great *c.* stones
John 12. 3 ointment of spik. very *c.*
R. V. John 12. 3 precious
Cotes. R. V *folds.*
2 Chr. 32. 28 stalls, and *c.* for flocks
Cottage. *Lodge, booth.*
Isa. 1. 8 daugh. of Zion left as a *c.* in
24. 20 earth be removed like a *c.*
Zeph. 2. 6 dwellings and *c.* for shep
R. V. Isa. 1. 8 booth; 24. 20 hut
Couch. *Mattress, bed.*
Gen. 49. 4 thou wentest up to my *c*
Job. 7. 13 *c.* shall ease my complaint
Ps. 6. 6 water my *c.* with tears.
Am. 3. 12 dwell in Damascus in a *c*
Luke 5. 19 let his *c.* into the midst
Acts 5. 15 laid them on beds and *c.*
Couched. *Crouch.*
Gen. 49. 9 Judah, he *c.* as a lion
Num. 24. 9 he *c.*, he lay down as lion
Deut. 33. 13 deep that *c.* beneath
Job 38. 40 they *c.* in their dens
Couching. *Resting, herding.*
Ezek. 25. 5 ma. R. *c.* place for flocks
Could. *See Can.*
Coulter. *Cutter.*
1 Sam. 13. 20, 21 his *c.* and axe
Council. *Assembly, sanhedrim.*
Ps. 68. 27 princes of Judah and .. *c.*
Mat. 5. 22 shall be in danger of the *c.*
Mark 13. 9 deliver you up to *c.*
Luke 22. 66 led him into their *c.*
John 11. 47 gath. chief priests in *c.*
Acts 4. 15 commanded to go out of *c.*
5. 21; 6. 12; 22. 30; 23. 1; 24. 20
Counsel (*n.*). *Consultation, advice.*
Ex. 18. 19 I will give thee *c.*, and G.
Deut. 32. 28 are a nation void of *c.*
Judg. 20. 7 give .. your advice and *c.*
2 Sam. 15. 31 turn the *c.* Ahithophel
1 K. 1. 12 let me .. give thee *c.*
2 K. 18. 20 I have *c.* and strength
2 Chr. 10. 8 R. forsook the *c.* which
Ez. 10. 3 according to the *c.* of lord
Neh. 4. 15 brought their *c.* to nought
Job 5. 13 *c.* of froward is carried
Ps. 1. 1 walketh not in *c.* of ungod.
13. 2; 14. 6; 20. 4; 33. 10; 73. 24
Prov. 1. 25 set at nought all my *c.*
8. 14; 12. 15; 19. 20; 20. 5; 21. 30
Isa. 5. 19 let the *c.* of the Holy One
8. 10; 11. 2; 16. 3; 19. 3; 25. 1
Jer. 18. 18 nor *c.* from the wise
Ezek. 7. 26 law shall perish and *c.*
Hos. 10. 6 ashamed of his own *c.*
Mic. 4. 12 neither understand his *c.*
Zech. 6. 13 *c.* of peace shall be bet.
Mat. 22. 15 took *c.* how they might
Mark 3. 6 went forth and took *c.*
Luke 7. 30 Phar. .. rejected the *c.*
John 18. 14 Caiaphas gave *c.* to Jews
Acts 2. 23 delivered by the deter. *c.*
1 Cor. 4. 5 make manifest the *c.*
Eph. 1. 11 things after the *c.* of will
Heb. 6. 17 immutability of his *c.*
R. V. Num. 27. 21; Judg. 20. 23 —
Prov. 11. 14; 24. 6 guidance; Isa.
19. 17 purpose; Acts. 5. 33 were
minded
Counsel (*v.*). *Give counsel.*
2 Sam. 16. 23 wh. A. *c.* in those days
17. 11–21 *c.* that all Is. be gathered
Job 26. 3 how hast thou *c.* him that
Counsellor. *Adviser.*
2 Sam. 15. 12 Absalom sent for D's *c.*
1 Chr. 26. 14 Zech. his son, a wise *c.*
2 Chr. 22. 3 his mother was his *c.*
Ez. 4. 5 people hired *c.* against them
Job 3. 14 with king and *c.* of earth?
Ps. 119. 24 thy testimonies are my *c.*
Prov. 11. 14 in multitude of *c.* is saf.
Isa. 1. 26 restore thy judge and *c.*
Dan. 3. 24 Neb. said unto his *c.*
Mic. 4. 9 no king? is thy *c.* perished?
Nah. 1. 11 There is one .. a wicked *c.*
Mark 15. 43 Joseph an honourable *c.*
Luke 23. 50 behold, Joseph, a *c.*
Rom. 11. 34 who hath been his *c.*
Count. *Think, devise, reckon.*
Gen. 15. 6 he *c.* it for righteousness
Ex. 38. 21 testimony as it was *c.*
Lev. 25. 27 let him *c.* the years
Num. 23. 10 who can *c.* the dust
1 Sam. 1. 16 *c.* not thine handmaid for
1 Chr. 21. 6 Levi and Benj. *c.* he not
Job. 19. 11 he *c.* me unto him as one

Ps. 87. 6 The Lord shall *c.*, when he
Isa. 33. 18 he that *c.* the towers
Mat. 14. 5 they *c.* him as a prophet
Mark 11. 32 all men *c.* John proph.
Luke 14. 28 sitteth, and *c.* the cost
Acts 20. 24 neither *c.* I my life
Rom. 2. 26 shall not his uncir. be *c.*
Phil. 3. 8 and I *c.* all things but loss
2 Thes. 3. 15 *c.* him not an enemy
1 Tim. 1. 12 for that he *c.* me faithful
Phile. 17 If thou *c.* me a partner
Heb. 10. 29 hath *c.* the blood of c.
Jas. 1. 2 *c.* it all joy when ye fall
2 Pet. 2. 13 that *c.* it pleasure to riot
R. V. Mark 11. 32 verily held ; Rom.
2. 26 ; 4. 3, 5 ; 9. 8 reckoned

Countenance. *Face, appearance.*
Gen. 4. 5 Cain was wroth, his *c.* fell
Num. 6. 26 the Lord lift up his *c.*
Judg. 13. 6 his *c.* was like . . angel
1 Sam. 1. 18 her *c.* was no more sad
2 Sam. 14. 27 Tamar ; wom. of fair *c.*
2 K. 8. 11 settled his *c.* stedfastly
Neh. 2. 2 Why is thy *c.* sad . ?
Job 14. 20 changest his *c.* and send.
Ps. 4. 6 lift thou up the light of thy *c.*
11. 7 ; 21. 6 ; 42. 5 ; 43. 5 ; 44. 3
Prov. 15. 13 merry h. make cheer. *c.*
Eccl. 7. 3 by sadness of *c.* the heart
S. of S. 2. 14 let me see thy *c.*
Isa. 3. 9 The show of their *c.* doth
Ezek. 27. 35 be troubled in their *c.*
Dan. 8. 23 a king of fierce *c.* shall
Mat. 28. 3 his *c.* was like lightning
Luke 9. 29 fashion of his *c.* was al.
Acts 2. 28 make . . full of joy with . . *c.*
2 Cor. 3. 7 M . . . the glory of his *c.*
Rev. 1. 16 *c.* was as the sun shineth
R. V. Ex. 23. 3 favour ; Ps. 11. 7 ; 2
Cor. 3. 7 face ; Ps. 21. 6 presence ;
S. of S. 5. 15 aspect ; Mat. 28. 3
appearance

Countervail. R. V. *compensated for.*
Esth. 7. 4 enemy could not *c.*

Country. *Land, domain.*
Gen. 10. 20 in their *c.* and nations
Lev. 25. 31 counted as fields of *c.*
Num. 21. 20 valley in *c.* of Moab
Deut. 4. 43 Bezer . . in the plain *c.*
Josh. 2. 2 came men to search . . *c.*
Judg. 8. 28 the *c.* was in quietness
Ruth 1. 1 went . . in *c.* of Moab
1 Sam. 6. 1 ark of L. was in the *c.*
2 Sam. 15. 23 and all the *c.* wept
1 K. 4. 19 the *c.* of Sihon king
2 K. 3. 20 *c.* was filled with water
1 Chr. 20. 1 Joab wasted the *c.*
2 Chr. 6. 32 strang. come from far *c.*
Ez. 3. 3 fear bec. people of those *c.*
Ps. 110. 6 wound heads over many *c.*
Prov. 25. 25 good news from far *c.*
Isa. 1. 7 your *c.* is desolate
Jer. 22. 7 brought you into plen. *c.*
Ezek. 5. 5 and *c.* round about her
Dan. 9. 7 though all *c.* whither
Hos. 12. 12 Jacob fled into the *c.*
Zech. 6. 10 go forth into the north *c.*
Mat. 2. 12 departed into their own *c.*
Mark 5. 1 came into *c.* of Gadarenes
Luke 2. 8 were in same *c.* shepherds
John 11. 54 Jesus went unto a *c.*
Acts 12. 20 their *c.* was nourished
Heb. 11. 14 declare . . they seek a *c.*
R. V. Mat. 9. 31 ; Acts 7. 3 land ;
Mat. 14. 35 ; Luke 3. 3 ; 4. 37
region ; in O. T. mostly land,
region, inheritance

Countryman. *Same tribe, race.*
1 Thes 2. 14 suffered like . . own *c.*
2 Cor. 11. 26 perils by mine own *c.*

Couple (*n.*). *Pair, yoke.*
Judg. 19. 3 servant, and a *c.* of asses
2 Sam. 13. 6 make a *c.* of cakes
Isa. 21. 7 chariot with *c.* horses
R. V. Isa. 21. 7, 9 in pairs

Couple (*v.*). *Join together.*
Ex. 26. 3 five curtains *c.* together
26. 24 ; 36. 17, 29 ; 39. 4
R. V. double, join

Coupling. *Joining.*
Ex. 26. 4 from selvage in the *c.*
26. 5 ; 28. 27 ; 36. 11, 12, 17 ; 39. 20
2 Chr. 34. 11 buy . . timber for *c.*

Courage. *Strength, fortitude.*
Num. 13. 20 be ye of good *c.*

Deut. 31. 6, 7, 23 be strong, of . . *c.*
Josh. 1. 6, 9, 18 ; 10. 25 ; 2 Sam.
10. 12 ; 1 Chr. 22. 13 ; Ez. 10. 4 ;
Ps. 27. 14 ; 31. 24 ; Isa. 41. 6

Courageous. *Valiant.*
Josh. 1. 7 be thou strong and very *c.*
2 Sam. 13. 28 I commanded you ? be *c.*
2 Chr. 32. 7 be strong and *c.*, not afr.
Am. 2. 16 he that is *c.* among migh.

Courageously. *Valiantly.*
2 Chr. 19. 11 deal *c.*, and the Lord

Course. *Portion, division.*
1 K.'5. 14 sent t. thous. a month by *c.*
1 Chr. 23. 6 D. divided them into *c.*
27. 1–21 ; 2 Chr. 5. 11 ; 8. 14 ; 23. 8
Luke 1. 5 Zach., priest of *c.* of Abia
Way, career, direction.
Judg. 5. 20 stars in their *c.* fought
Ps. 82. 5 foundation are out of *c.*
Jer. 8. 6 every one turned his *c.*
Acts. 13. 25 John fulfilled his *c.*
1 Cor. 14. 27 by three, and that by *c.*
Eph. 2. 2 walked according to the *c.*
2 Thes. 3. 1 word may have free *c.*
Jas. 3. 6 tongue setteth on fire the *c.*
R. V. Acts 21. 7 voyage ; 1 Cor.
17. 27 in turn ; 2 Thes. 3. 1 run ;
Jas. 3. 6 wheel

Court. *Enclosed place.*
Ex. 27. 9 make the *c.* of the taber.
27. 12–19 ; 35. 17 ; 38. 9–31 ; 40. 8
Lev. 6. 16 in *c.* of the tabernacle
Num. 3. 26 the hangings of the *c.*
2 Sam. 17. 18 house had a well in *c.*
1 K. 6. 36 built the inner *c.* wi. stone
2 K. 21. 5 he built altars in two *c.*
1 Chr. 23. 28 office was to wait in *c.*
2 Chr. 4. 9 he made *c.* of the priests
Neh. 3. 25 King's house by the *c.*
Esth. 1. 5 feast in *c.* of the garden
Ps. 65. 4 that he may dwell in thy *c.*
84. 2 ; 92 13 ; 96. 8 ; 100. 4 ; 116. 16
Isa. 1. 12 ye come to tread my *c.* ?
Jer. 19. 14 he stood in the *c.*
26. 2 ; 32. 2 ; 33. 1 ; 36. 10 ; 37. 21
Ezek. 8. 7 brought me to door of *c.*
9. 7 ; 10. 3 ; 40. 14 ; 41. 15 ; 42. 1
Rev. 11. 2 *c.* without the temple
R. V. 2 K. 20. 4 part of the city
Am. 7. 13 royal house

Courteous. *Friendly minded.*
1 Pet. 3. 8 love, be pitiful, be *c.*
R. V. humble minded

Courteously. *Friendly.*
Acts 27. 3, 7 Julius *c.* entreated P.
R. V. 27. 3 treated kindly

Cousin. R. V. *kinswoman*
Luke 1. 36, 58 behold thy *c.* Eliz.

Covenant (*n.*). *League, compact.*
Gen. 6. 18 will I establish my *c.*
9. 9 ; 15. 18. 17. 2 ; 21. 27 ; 26. 28.
Ex. 2. 24 and God remember. his *c.*
Lev. 2. 13 suffer the salt of the *c.*
Num. 10. 33 the ark of *c.* . . . went
Deut. 4. 13 declared unto you his *c.*
Josh. 3. 6 take up the ark of the *c.*
Judg. 2. 1 will never break my *c.*
1 Sam. 4. 3 fetch the ark of the *c.*
2 Sam. 15. 24 bearing the ark of . . *c.*
1 K. 3. 15 before the ark of . . *c.*
2 K. 11. 4 made . . *c.* with them
1 Chr. 11. 3 David made a *c.* with
2 Chr. 5. 2. 7 ark of . . *c.* of . . Lord
Ez. 10. 3 let us make a *c.* with our
Neh. 1. 5 keepeth *c.* and mercy
Job. 31. 1 make *c.* with mine eyes
Ps. 25. 10 unto such as keep his *c.*
44. 17 ; 50. 5 ; 55. 20 ; 74. 20 ; 78. 10
Prov. 2. 17 and forgetteth the *c.*
Isa. 24. 5 broken the everlasting *c.*
Jer. 3. 16 ark of the *c.* of the Lord
11. 2 ; 14. 21 ; 22. 9 ; 31. 31 ; 32. 40
Ezek. 16. 8 entered into a *c.* with
Dan. 9. 4 keeping the *c.* and mercy
Hos. 2. 18 I make a *c.* for them
Am. 1. 9 rememb. not the broth. *c.*
Zech. 9. 11 by blood of thy *c.* I sent
Mal. 2. 4 that thy *c.* might be with
Luke 1. 72 to remember his holy *c.*
Acts 3. 25 *c.* which God made with
Rom. 9. 4 the *c.* and giving of law
Gal. 3. 15 though but a man's *c.*
Eph. 2. 12 strangers from the *c.*
Heb. 8. 6 is mediator of a better *c.*
8. 8–10 ; 9. 4 ; 10. 16, 29 ; 12. 24 ;

Covenant (*v.*). *Set, establish.*

2 Chr. 7. 28 as I have *c.* with D.
Hag. 2. 5 the word that I *c.* with
Mat. 26. 15 *c.* with him for thirty p.
Luke 22. 5 glad, and *c.* to give
R. V. Mat. 26. 15 weighed unto

Cover (*n.*). *Cup, jug, can.*
Ex. 25. 29 spoons thereof, and *c.*
Num. 4. 7 and the bowls, and *c.*

Cover (*v.*). *Overlay, enwrap, hide.*
Gen. 9. 23 and *c.* the nakedness of
Ex. 8. 6 frogs came, and *c.* the land
10. 5 ; 14. 28 ; 15. 8 ; 16. 13 ; 21. 33
Lev. 3. 3, 9, 14 fat that *c.* . . inwards
Num. 4. 5 and *c.* the ark of testimony
Deut. 22. 12 ves. wherewith thou *c.*
Josh. 24. 7 brought the sea . . and *c.*
Judg. 4. 18 turned in, she *c.* him
1 Sam. 19. 13 took image, and *c.* it
2 Sam. 19. 4 the king *c.* his face
1 K. 1. 1 they *c.* him with clothes
2 K. 19. 2 sent E. *c.* with sackcloth
1 Chr. 28. 18 *c.* the ark of the cov.
2 Chr. 4. 12 two wreaths to *c.* two
Neh. 3. 15 Shal. built it, and *c.* it
Esth. 7 8 they *c.* Haman's face
Job. 9. 24 *c.* faces of the judges
Ps. 32. 1 blessed he whose sin is *c.*
44. 15 ; 69. 7 ; 85. 2 ; 104. 6 ; 106. 11
Prov. 10. 6 violence *c.* the mouth
Isa. 6. 2 with twain he *c.* his face
Jer. 3. 25 our confusion *c.* us
Lam. 3. 43 thou hast *c.* with anger
Ezek. 1. 11 two were joined, two *c.*
7. 18 ; 12. 6 ; 16. 8 ; 18. 7 ; 24. 7 ;
Hos. 1. 9 flax to *c.* her nakedness
Obad. 10. violence, shame shall *c.*
Mic. 7. 10 shame shall *c.* her
Hab. 2. 14 as the waters *c.* the sea
Mal. 2. 13 *c.* altar of L. with tears
Mat. 8. 24 ship was *c.* with waves
Mark 14. 65 *c.* his face and to buffet
Luke 8. 16 no man *c.* it with a ves.
Rom. 4. 7 bless. . whose sins are *c.*
1 Cor. 11. 7 man . . ought not to *c.*
1 Pet. 4. 8 char. *c.* mul. of sins
R. V. Ex. 40. 21 screened ; 1 K.
6. 35 ; Prov. 26. 23 overlaid ; 1
Cor. 11. 6 veiled

Covering. *Cover, curtain.*
Gen. 8. 13 Noah removed *c.* of ark
Ex. 26. 14 make *c.* for the tent
Lev. 13. 45 put *c.* on upper lip
Num. 3. 25 *c.* thereof and hangings
2 Sam. 17. 19 woman . . spread a *c.*
Job 22. 14 clouds are a *c.* to him
Ps. 105. 39 spread a cloud for *c.*
S. of S. 3. 10 the *c.* of it of purple
Isa. 25. 7 destroy face of the *c.* cast
Ezek. 28. 13 precious stone . . thy *c.*
1 Cor. 11. 15 hair given her for *c.*
R. V. Ex. 35. 12 ; 39. 34 ; 40. 21
screen ; Prov. 7. 16 ; 31. 22 car-
pets ; Isa. 30. 22 overlaying ; S. of
S. 3. 10 seat

Covert, *Secret hiding place.*
1 Sam. 25. 20 came . . by *c.* of . . hill
2 K. 16. 18 the *c.* for the sabbath
Job 40. 21 lieth . . in the *c.* of reed
Ps. 61. 4 trust in *c.* of thy wings
Isa. 16. 4 *c.* to them from face of
Jer. 25. 38 He hath forsaken his *c.*
R. V. 2 K. 16. 8 covered way

Covet. *Desire, crave, lust after.*
Ex. 20. 17 shalt not *c.* thy neighbor's
Deut. 5. 21 neither *c.* thy neighbor's
Josh. 7. 21 I *c.* them, and took
Prov. 21 26 he *c.* greedily all day
Mic. 2. 2 they *c.* fields and take
Hab. 2. 9 Woe to him that *c.* evil *c.*
Acts 20. 33 have *c.* no man's silver
Rom. 7. 7 Thou shalt not *c.*
1 Cor. 12. 31 *c.* earnestly best gifts
1 Tim. 6. 10 while some *c.* after
R. V. Hab. 2. 9 getteth ; 1 Cor. 12.
31 desire ; 14. 39 desire earnestly ;
1 Tim. 6. 10 reaching

Covetous. *Eagerly desirous.*
Ps. 10. 3 *c.* the Lord abhorreth
Luke 6. 14 Pharisees who were *c.*
1 Cor. 5. 10 wi. the *c.* or extortioners
Eph. 5. 5 nor unclean person, nor *c.*
2 Tim. 3. 2 lovers of selves, *c.*
2 Pet. 2. 14 exer. with *c.* practices
R. V. Luke 6. 14 ; 1 Tim. 3. 3 ; 2
Tim. 3. 2 lovers of money.

Covetousness. *Avariciousness.*

Ex. 18. 21 provide truth, hating *c.*
Ps. 119. 36 incline my heart not to *c.*
Prov. 28. 16 that hateth *c.* shall pro.
Isa. 57. 17 the iniquity of his *c.* was
Jer. 6. 13 every one is given to *c.*
Ezek. 33. 31 heart goeth after *c.*
Hab. 2. 9 that coveteth an evil *c.*
Mark 7. 22 thefts, *c.*, wickedness
Luke 12. 15 heed, and beware of *c.*
Rom. 1. 29 fornica., wickedness, *c.*
2 Cor. 9. 5 bounty, not as of *c.*
Eph. 5. 3 *c.*, let it not be named
Col. 3. 5 evil concupiscence and *c.*
1 Thes. 2. 5 neither used cloak of *c.*
Heb. 13. 5 let . . con. be without *c.*
2 Pet. 2. 3 through *c.* make merch.
R. V. Ex. 18. 21 unjust gain; Ezek.
33. 31; Hab. 2. 9 gain; Mark
7. 22 covetings; 2 Cor. 9. 5 extor-
tions; Heb. 13. 5 free from love
of money

Cow. *Heifer, young cow.*
Job 21. 10 *c.* calveth and casteth not
Isa. 7. 21 man shall nourish young *c.*
11. 7 and the *c.* and bear shall feed
Bullock, ox.
Lev. 22. 28 whether it be *c.* or ewe
Num. 18. 17 firstling of *c.* not redeem
Cattle, herd.
Ezek. 4. 15 have given the *c.'s* dung
R. V. Num. 18. 17 ox; Am. 4. 3
one straight

Crackling. *Voice, sharp sound.*
Eccl. 7. 6 *c.* of thorns under a pot
Cracknels. *Small dry cakes.*
1 K. 14. 3 take ten loaves and *c.*
Craft. *Guile, deceit.*
Dan. 8. 25 shall cause *c.* to prosper
Mark 14. 1 might take him by *c.*
Work, trade, business.
Acts. 19. 25 by this *c.* we have wealth
19. 27 our *c.* is in danger to be set
Rev. 18. 22 of whatever *c.* he be
R. V. Mark 14. 1 with subtilty;
Acts 18. 3; 19. 27 trade; 19. 25
business
Craftiness. *Cunning, subtilty.*
Job 5. 13 taketh the wise in own *c.*
Luke 20. 23 But he perceived their *c.*
1 Cor. 3. 19 taketh wise in own *c.*
2 Cor. 4. 2 not walking in *c.*
Eph. 4. 14 sleight . . and cunning *c.*
Craftsman. *Artificer, artisan.*
Deut. 27. 15 work . . hands of the *c.*
2 K. 24. 14 carried away all the *c.*
1 Chr. 4. 14 for they were *c.*
Neh. 11. 35 Ono, the valley of *c.*
Hos. 13. 2 all of it work of the *c.*
Acts 19. 24 brought . . gain unto . . *c.*
Rev. 18. 22 no *c.* of whatso. craft
Crafty. *Subtile, cunning.*
Job 5. 12 disap. the devices of the *c.*
Ps. 83. 3 they have taken *c.* counsel
2 Cor. 12. 16 being *c.*, I caught you
Crag. *Tooth, cliff.*
Job 39. 28 abide. upon *c.* of the rock
Crashing. *Breaking.*
Zeph. 1. 10 great *c.* from the hills
Crave. *Entreat, long for.*
Prov. 16. 26 his mouth *c.* it of him
Mark 15. 43 *c.* the body of Jesus
R. V. Mark 15. 43 asked for
Create. *Make, form, fashion.*
Gen. 1. 1 God *c.* the heaven and e.
1. 27; 2. 3; 5. 1, 2; 6. 7
Deut. 4. 32 day that God *c.* man
Ps. 51. 10 *c.* in me a clean heart
Isa. 4. 5 Lord will *c.* upon ev. dwel.
40. 26; 41. 20; 42. 5; 43. 1; 45. 7
Jer. 31. 22 Lord hath *c.* a new thing
Ezek 21. 30 pl. where thou wast *c.*
Mal. 2. 10 hath not one God *c.* us
Mark 13. 19 creation which God *c.*
1 Cor. 11. 9 neither was the man *c.*
Eph. 2. 10 *c.* in Christ Jesus to good
Col. 1. 16 by him were all things *c.*
1 Tim. 4. 3 which God hath *c.*
Rev. 4. 11 thou hast *c.* all things
Creation. *A making, thing made.*
Mark 10. 6 from beginning of the *c.*
Rom. 1. 20 of him from the *c.* of wor.
8. 22 whole *c.* groaneth in pain
2 Pet. 3. 4 from the beginning of *c.*
Rev. 3. 14 witness, the begin. of *c.*
Creator. *Who creates.*
Eccl. 12. 1 remember now thy *C.*

Isa. 40. 28 the Lord the *C.* faint. not
Rom. 1. 25 served crea. more than *C.*
1 Pet. 4. 19 doing unto a faithful *C.*
Creature. *Thing created.*
Gen. 1. 21 G. created every living *c.*
Lev. 11. 46 every . . *c.* that moveth
Ezek. 1. 5 likeness of four living *c.*
1. 13–22; 3. 13; 10. 15, 17
Mark 16. 15 preach gos. to every *c.*
Rom. 1. 25 wor. and served the *c.*
2 Cor. 5. 17 in Christ, he is a new *c.*
Gal. 6. 15 not uncircum., but new *c.*
Col. 1. 15 God, firstborn of every *c.*
1 Tim 4. 4 every *c.* of God is good
Heb. 4. 13 nei. and *c.* that is not
Jas. 1. 18 th. we be firstfruits of his *c.*
Rev. 5. 13 every *c.* heard I saying
R. V. Mark 16. 15 whole creation;
Col. 1. 15 all creation
Creditor. *Lender.*
Deut. 15. 2 every *c.* that lendeth
2 K. 4. 1 *c.* is come to take my sons
Isa. 50. 1 which of my *c.* is it
Luke 7. 41 there was a certain *c.*
R. V. Luke 7. 41 lender
Creek. *R. V. bay.*
Acts 27. 39 they discov. a certain *c.*
Creep. *Crawl.*
Gen. 1. 26 dom. over ev. thing that *c.*
1. 30; 7. 8, 14; 8. 17, 19
Lev. 11. 29 creeping things that *c.*
Deut. 4. 18 likeness of thing that *c.*
Ps. 104. 20 beasts . . do *c.* forth
2 Tim. 3. 6 sort which *c.* into houses
Jude 4 certain men *c.* in unawares
R. V. Gen. 8. 19; Lev. 11. 44 moveth
Creeping. *Crawling.*
Gen. 1. 24 Let earth br. fo. . *c.* things
Lev. 5. 2 touch unclean *c.* things
Deut. 14. 19 thing . . is unclean
1 K. 4. 32 *c.* things and fishes
Ps. 104. 25 wherein are things *c.*
Ezek. 8. 10 every form of *c.* thing
Hos. 2. 18 *c.* things of the ground
Hab. 1. 14 *c.* things that have no
Acts 10. 12 beasts, *c.* things and fowls
Rom. 1. 23 beasts and *c.* things
Crew. *See Crow.*
Crib. *Feeding-place.*
Job 39. 9 unicorn abide by thy *c.*
Prov. 14. 4 Wh. no ox., the *c.* is clean
Isa. 1. 3 and ass his master's *c.*
Cried. *See Cry.*
Crime. *Cause, indictment.*
Acts 25. 16 conc. *c.*, laid against him
25. 27 and not to signify the *c.* laid
Judgment, iniquity.
Ezek. 7. 23 land full of bloody *c.*
Crimson. *Carmine, scarlet.*
2 Chr. 2. 7 purple, *c.*, and blue
Jer. 4. 30 clothe thyself in *c.*
Isa. 1. 18 though they be red like *c.*
R. V. Jer. 4. 30 scarlet
Cripple. *Lame, halt.*
Acts 14. 8 *c.* from his mother's womb
Crisping-pin. *R. V. satchels.*
Isa. 3. 22 whimples and *c.* pins
Crookbacked. *Humpbacked.*
Lev. 21. 20 or a *c. b.* or a dwarf
Crooked. *Perverse, twisted.*
Deut. 32. 5 perverse and *c.* genera.
Job 26. 13 hath formed the *c.* scr.
Ps. 125. 5 turn aside unto *c.* ways
Prov. 2. 15 whose ways are *c.*
Eccl. 1. 15 *c.* cannot be made st.
Isa. 27. 1 leviathan, that *c.* serpent
Lam. 3. 9 he hath made my path *c.*
Luke 3. 5 *c.* shall be made straight
Phil. 2. 15 *c.* and perverse nation
R. V. Job 26. 13 swift; Isa. 45. 2
rugged
Crop (n.). *Craw.*
Lev. 1. 16 shall pluck away his *c.*
Crop (v.). *Cut, pluck.*
Ezek. 17. 14 he *c.* off the top of twigs
17. 22 I will *c.* off from the top
Cross. *Stake.*
Mat. 10. 38 that taketh not the *c.*
16. 24; 27. 32, 40, 42.
Mark 8. 34 take up his *c.* and fol.
10. 21; 15. 21; 15. 30; 15. 32
Luke 9. 23 take up his *c.* daily
John 19. 17 he bearing his *c.* went
1 Cor. 1. 17 lest the *c.* of Christ
Gal. 5. 11 offence of the *c.* ceased

Eph. 2. 16 one body by the *c.*
Phil. 2. 8 even the death of the *c.*
Col. 1. 20 through blood of the *c.*
Heb. 12. 2 endured the *c.*, despising
Crossway. *Crossway.*
Obad. 14 neith. have stood in the *c.*
Crouch. *Bow down.*
1 Sam. 2. 36 *c.* to him for . . silver
Ps. 10. 10 *c.* and humbleth himself
R. V. 1 Sam. 2. 36 bow down
Crow. *Sound, crow.*
Mat. 26. 34 night, before the cock *c.*
26. 74 immediately the cock *c.*
Mark 17. 30 before . . cock *c.* twice
Luke 22. 34 cock shall not *c.* this
22. 60 while he spake the cock *c.*
John 13. 38 cock shall not *c.* till
Crown (n.). *Border, ring.*
Ex. 25. 11 make . . *c.* of gold around
25. 24; 30. 3; 37. 2, 11, 12, 26, 27
Chaplet
Ex. 29. 6 put . . *c.* upon the mitre
Lev. 8. 9 put golden plate, holy *c.*
2 Sam. 1. 10 I took the *c.* that
2 K. 11. 12 Je. put the *c.* upon him
Ps. 89. 39 thou hast profaned his *c.*
Prov. 27. 24 doth the *c.* endure
Zech. 9. 16 shall be as stones of a *c.*
Diadem, crown.
2 Sam. 12. 30 took their king's *c.*
1 Chr. 20. 2 took the *c.* of their king
Esth. 8. 15 with a great *c.* of
Job 19. 9 taken *c.* from my head
Ps. 21. 3 settest a *c.* of pure gold
Prov. 4. 9 a *c.* of glory shall she del.
S. of S. 3. 11 behold Sol. with the *c.*
Isa. 28. 1 woe to *c.* of pride which
Jer. 13. 18 even the *c.* of your glory
Lam. 5. 16 *c.* is fallen from our head
Ezek. 16. 12 put beautiful *c.* upon
Zech. 6. 14 *c.* shall be to Helem
Mat. 29. 29 platted a *c.* of thorns
Mark 15. 17 *c.* of thorns and put it
John 19. 5 came Jesus, wearing *c.*
1 Cor. 9. 25 do it to obtain a *c.*
Phil. 4. 1 longed for my joy and *c.*
1 Thes. 2. 19 or *c.* of rejoicing
2 Tim. 4. 8 laid up for me a *c.*
Jas. 1. 12 shall receive the *c.* of life
1 Pet. 5. 4 receive the *c.* of glory
Rev. 2. 10 will give thee a *c.* ot life
3. 11; 4. 4; 6. 2; 9. 7; 12. 1; 14. 14
R. V. Rev. 12. 3; 13. 1; 19. 12 dia.
Top of head.
Gen. 49. 26 bless. be on *c.* of head
Deut. 33. 20 teareth arm with *c.* of h.
2 Sam. 14. 25 foot even to *c.* of him
Isa. 3. 17 smite with scab the *c.*
Jer. 2. 16 have broken the *c.* of head
Crown (v.). *Compass, crown.*
Ps. 8. 5 hast *c.* him with glory
Prov. 14. 18 prudent *c.* with knowl.
S. of S. 3. 11 his mother *c.* him
Isa. 23. 8 *c.* city whose merchants
Nah. 3. 17 thy *c.* are as the locusts
2 Tim. 2. 5 mastery, yet he is not *c.*
Heb. 2. 7 *c.* him with glory and hon.
Crucify. *To put to death on a cross*
Mat. 20. 19 to scourge and *c.* him
23. 34; 26. 2; 27. 22; 28. 5
Mark 15. 13 they cried out, *c.* him
15. 14, 15, 20, 24, 25, 27; 16. 6
Luke 23. 21 cried, saying, *C.* him
John 19. 6 cried, saying, *C.* him, *c.*
Acts 2. 36 Jesus whom ye have *c.*
Rom. 6. 6 our old man is *c.* wi. him
1 Cor. 1. 13 was Paul *c.* for you?
2 Cor. 13. 4 *c.* through weakness
Gal. 3. 1 Jesus Christ hath been *c.*
Heb. 6. 6 *c.* to them. Son of God
Rev. 11. 8 where our Lord was *c.*
Cruel. *Fierce, hard.*
Gen. 49. 7 cur. be wrath, for it was *c.*
Ex. 6. 9 heark. not for *c.* bondage
Deut. 32. 33 wine is *c.* venom
Job 30. 21 art become *c.* to me
Ps. 25. 19 hate me with *c.* hatred
Prov. 5. 9 give thy years unto the *c.*
Isa. 19. 4 give to hand of a *c.* lord
Jer. 6. 23 *c.*, and have no mercy
Lam. 4. 3 daughter . . is become *c.*
Heb. 11. 36 had trial of *c.* mockings.
R. V. Heb. 11. 36 ——
Cruelly. *Hardly.*
Ezek. 18. 18 becau. he *c.* oppressed
Cruelty. *Violence, rigour.*

Gen. 49. 5 instruments of *c.* are
Judg. 9. 24 the *c.* done to the sons
Ps. 27. 12 such as breathe out *c.*
Ezek. 34. 4 with *c.* have ye ruled
R. V. Gen. 49. 5 ; Judg. 9. 24 ; Ps.
74. 20; violence; Ezek. 34. 4 rigour

Crumb. *Bit.*
Mat. 15. 27 *c.* which fall from table
Mark 7. 28 eat of the chilldren's *c.*
Luke 16. 21 fed with the *c.* which

Cruse. *Dish, pan.*
2 K. 2. 20 bring .. *c.*, put salt therein
Bottle, flask.
1 Sam. 26. 11 take .. the *c.* of water
1 K. 17. 12 ha. but a little oil in a *c.*

Crush. *Break, bruise, oppress.*
Lev. 22. 24 which is bruised or *c.*
Num. 22. 25 and *c.* Baalam's foot
Deut. 28. 33 oppressed and *c.* alway
Job 4. 19 are *c.* before the moth
Isa. 59. 5 which is *c.*, breaketh
Jer. 51. 34 Nebuchadrez. hath *c.* me
Lam. 3. 34 *c.* under his feet all the

Cry (*n.*(. *Call, shout, groan.*
Gen. 18. 20 *c.* of Sodom and Go.
Ex. 2. 23 *c.* came up unto God
1 Sam. 5. 12 *c.* of the city went up
2 Sam. 22. 7 my *c.* did enter ears
1 K. 8. 28 hearken unto the *c.*
2 Chr. 6. 19 hearken unto *c.* and p.
Neh. 5. 6 when I heard their *c.*
Esth. 4. 1 Mor. cried with a loud *c.*
Job 16. 18 let my *c.* have no place
Ps. 9. 12 forgetteth not *c.* of humble
Prov. 21. 13 stopped his ears at *c.*
Eccl. 9. 17 more than in *c.* of him
Isa. 15. 5 raise *c.* of destruction
Jer. 18. 22 let thy *c.* be heard
Lam. 3. 56 hide not thine ear at my *c.*
Ezek. 27. 28 shake at sound of *c.*
Zeph. 1. 10 the noise of *c.* at gate
Mat. 25. 6 at midnight there was a *c.*
Acts 23. 9 there arose a great *c.*
Rev. 14. 18 cried with a loud *c.* to
R. V. Rev. 14. 18 great voice

Cry (*v.*). *Call, groan, shout.*
Gen. 4. 10 brother's blood *c.* to me
Ex. 5. 8 they *c.*, saying, Let us go
Lev. 13. 45 upper lip, and shall *c.*
Num. 1. 2 people *c.* unto Moses
Deut. 22. 24 because she *c.* not
Josh. 24. 7 they *c.* unto the Lord
Judg. 4. 3 children of Israel *c.* to L.
1 Sam. 17. 8 Gol. *c.* unto the armies
2 Sam. 18. 25 and the watchman *c.*
1 K. 13. 2 he *c.* against the altar
2 K. 11. 14 Ath. rent her clo. and *c.*
1 Chr. 5. 20 they *c.* to God in battle
2 Chr. 14. 11 Asa *c.* unto the Lord
Neh. 9. 4 Levi. *c.* with a loud voice
Esth. 4. 1 Mordec. *c.* with bitter cry
Job 31. 38 if my land *c.* against
Ps. 22. 5 thy *c.* unto thee were del.
27. 7; 28. 1; 30. 8; 34. 6; 56. 9; 57. 2
Prov. 1. 21 she *c.* in the chief place
Isa. 6. 3 one *c.* unto another, said
Jer. 2. 2 go *c.* in the ears of Jerus.
Lam. 4. 15 *c.* unto them, Depart
Ezek. 8. 18 thy *c.* in mine ears
Dan. 6. 20 *c.* with lamentable voice
Hos. 8. 2 Israel shall *c.* unto me
Joel 1. 14 *c.*, unto the Lord
Am. 3. 4 will a young lion *c.*
Jonah 1. 2 go to Nineveh and *c.*
Mic. 3. 5 that bite .. teeth and *c.*
Hab. 1. 2 *c.* out unto thee of violence
Zech. 1. 4 former prophets have *c.*
Mat. 9. 27 blind men followed, *c.*
Mark 1. 26 spir. *c.* with a loud voice
Luke 18. 39 *c.* so much the more
John 1. 15 John bare witness and *c.*
Acts 8. 7 unclean spirits *c.* with voi.
Rom. 8. 15 adoption whereby we *c.*
Gal. 4. 27 break forth and *c.*
Jas. 5. 4 the hire of the labourers *c.*
Rev. 6. 10 *c.* with a loud voice
7. 2; 10. 3; 12. 2; 14. 15; 18. 2; 19. 17

Crying. *Calling, groaning.*
1 Sam. 4. 14 when Eli heard .. the *c.*
Job 39. 7 neither regardeth the *c.*
Ps. 69. 3 I am weary of my *c.*
Prov. 19. 18 soul spare for his *c.*
Isa. 22. 5 it is a day of *c.*
Jer. 48. 3 voice of *c.* from Horonaim
Mal. 2. 13 with weeping and *c.*
Heb. 5. 7 offering prayer with .. *c.*

Rev. 21. 4 no more death, nor *c.*

Crystal. *Ice, glass.*
Job 28. 17 gold and *c.* cannot equal
Ezek. 1. 22 colour of the terrible *c.*
Rev. 4. 6 sea of glass like *c.*
R. V. Job 28. 17 glass

Cubit. *Measure, forearm.*
Gen. 6. 15 length of ark th. hun. *c.*
Ex. 25. 10 two *c.* and half shall be l.
25. 17; 26. 2; 27. 1; 30. 2; 36. 9
Num. 11. 31 two *c.* upon face
Deut. 3. 11 nine *c.* the length
Josh. 3. 4 two thousand *c.* by mea.
Judge. 3. 16 dagger, *c.* in length
1 Sam. 17. 4 Goli., height was six *c.*
1 K. 6. 2 length was three sc. *c.*
2 K. 14. 13 unto .. gate five hun. *c.*
1 Chr. 11. 23 Egyptian five *c.* high
2 Chr. 3. 3 length was three sc. *c.*
Ez. 6. 3 breadth was threescore *c.*
Neh. 3. 13 thous. *c.* on the wall
Esth. 5. 14 gallows be fifty *c.* high
Jer. 52. 21 pillar was eighteen *c.*
Ezek. 40. 5 chambers were five *c.*
40. 9-49; 41. 1-22; 42. 2-8; 43. 13
Dan. 3. 1 height was threescore *c.*
Mat. 6. 17 which .. can add one *c.*
Luke 12. 25 add to stature one *c.*
John 21. 8 as it were two hun. *c.*
Rev. 21. 17 hun. forty and four *c.*

Cuckoo. *R. V. seamew.*
Lev. 11. 16 the *c.* and hawk
Deut. 14. 15 *c.* and hawk after

Cucumber. *Melon, gourd.*
Isa. 1. 8 as a lodge in garden of *c.*

Cud. *Chewed food.*
Lev. 11. 3–26 whatso. cheweth .. *c.*
Deut. 14. 6 chew. *c.* among beasts

Cumber. *Trouble, clog.*
Luke 10. 40 Martha was *c.* about
13. 7 fig tree, why *c.* it the ground?

Cumbrance. *Burden, pressure.*
Deut. 1. 12 can I .. bear your *c.*

Cumi. *Arise.*
Mark 5. 41 *c.*; which is, Damsel, arise

Cummin. *Sharp smelling.*
Isa. 28. 25, 27 doth not scatter *c.*
Mat. 23. 23 pay tithe of mint and *c.*

Cunning. *Wise, skilful.*
Ex. 26. 1 cherubims of *c.* work
1 K. 7. 14 *c.* to work all works
1 Chr. 22. 15 all manner of *c.* men
2 Chr. 2. 7 man *c.* to work in gold
S. of S. 7. 1 hands of a *c.* workman
Isa. 3. 3 a *c.* artificer, and orator
Jer. 9. 17 send for *c.* women
Dan. 1. 4 *c.* in knowledge and sci.

Cup. *Dish. bowl, cup.*
Gen. 40. 11 Phar's *c.* was in hand
1 Sam. 12. 3 drank of his own *c.*
1 K. 7. 26 like the brim of a *c.*
1 Chr. 28. 17 pure gold for .. the *c.*
2 Chr. 4. 5 brim like brim of *c.*
Ps. 11. 6 the portion of their *c.*
Isa. 51. 17 drunk .. *c.* of his fury
Jer. 16. 7 neither .. give them the *c.*
Lam. 4. 21 the *c.* also shall pass
Ezek. 23. 31 theref. will I give her *c.*
Hab. 2. 16 *c.* of L's right hand
Zech. 12. 2 make Jer. a *c.* of tremb.
Mat. 10. 42 *c.* of cold water only
20. 22; 23. 25; 26. 27, 39, 42
Mark. 7. 4 washing of *c.* and pots
9. 41; 10. 38, 14. 23; 14. 36
Luke 11. 39 make clean outside of *c.*
John 18. 11 *c.* my F. hath given
1 Cor. 10. 16 *c.* of blessing which
Rev. 14. 10 poured out .. into *c.*

Cupbearer. *Give to drink.*
1 K. 10. 5 attendance of his *c. b.*
2 Chr. 9. 4 his *c. b.* also, and
Neh. 1. 11 he was the king's *c. b.*

Curdle. *Harden, curdle.*
Job 10. 10 hast *c.* me like cheese

Cure (*n.*). *Healing.*
Jer. 33. 6 bring it health and *c.*
Luke 13. 32 and I do cures to-day

Cure. *Heal.*
Jer. 33. 6 I will *c.* them, and reveal
Hos. 5. 13 saw *c.* he not .. *c.*
Mat. 7. 16 and they could not *c.*
Luke 7. 21 *c.* many of their infir.
John 5. 10 said unto him that was *c.*

Curious. *Cunning.*
Ex. 35. 32 to devise *c.* works
Acts 19. 19 many which used *c.* arts

Curiously. *Dexterously.*
Ps. 139. 15 *c.* wrought in .. parts

Current. *Passable.*
Gen. 23. 16 *c.* money with .. mer.

Curse (*n.*). *Oath, imprecation.*
Num. 5. 21 Lord make thee a *c.*
Deut. 29. 19 he heareth .. of this *c.*
2 Chr. 34. 24 all the *c.* are written
Neh. 10. 29 they entered into a *c.*
Job 31. 30 wishing a *c.* to his soul
Isa. 24. 6 the *c.* devoured thee
Jer. 29. 18 to be a *c.* and astonish.
Dan. 9. 11 *c.* is poured upon us
Zech. 5. 3 thisis *c.* that goeth forth
A devoted thing.
Josh. 6. 18 make camp of Israel a *c.*
Isa. 34. 5 upon the people of my *c.*
Mal. 4. 6 smite earth with a *c.*
Acts 23. 12 bound them .. under a *c.*
Gal. 3. 10 works .. are under .. *c.*
Rev. 22. 3 there shall be no more *c.*
R. V. Josh. 6. 18 accursed; Jer.
29. 18 execration

Curse (*v.*). *Execrate, swear.*
Gen. 12. 3 bless them that *c.* you
Ex. 21. 17 he that *c.* his father
Lev. 19. 14 shall not *c.* the deaf
Deut. 23. 4 they hired Balaam to *c.*
Josh. 24. 9 Balak call. Balaam to *c.*
Judg. 9. 27 eat and drink, and *c.*
1 Sam. 17. 43 the Phil. *c.* David
2 Sam. 16. 5 Shim. came forth and *c.*
1 K. 2. 8 Shimei .. which *c.* me
2 K. 2. 24 Elisha *c.* them in name of
Neh. 13. 2 hired Bal. that he *c.*
Job 3. 1 op. Job his mouth and *c.*
Ps. 37. 22 that be *c.* of him be cut off
Prov. 20. 20 whoso *c.* father or mo.
Eccl. 7. 21 hear thy ser. *c.* thee
Isa. 8. 21 *c.* their king and God
Jer. 15. 10 every one .. doth *c.* me
Mal. 1. 14 *c.* be the deceiver
Mat. 5. 44 bless them that *c.* you
Mark 11. 21 fig tree which thou *c.*
Luke 6. 28 bless them that *c.* you
John 7. 49 who know not law are *c.*
Rom. 12. 14 bless them which .. *c.*
Gal. 3. 10 *C.* every one that contin.
Jas. 3. 9 therewith *c.* we men
2 Pet. 2. 14 unstable souls, *c.* chil.
R. V. Deut. 7. 26; 13. 17; de-
voted; Job. 1. 5 renounced;
John 7. 49 accursed

Cursing. *Execration.*
Num. 5. 21 charge .. with oath of *c.*
Deut. 28. 20 send upon the *c.*
Josh. 8. 34 read all blessings and *c.*
2 Sam. 16. 12 requite me .. for his *c.*
Ps. 10. 7 mouth is full of *c.*
Prov. 29. 24 he heareth *c.* and
Rom. 3. 14 mouth is full of *c.*
Heb. 6. 8 rejected, is nigh unto *c.*
Jas. 3. 10 out of mouth proceed. *c.*
R. V. Prov. 29. 24 adjuration

Curtain. *Veil, hanging.*
Ex. 26. 1 make tab. with ten *c.*
26. 2–13; 36. 8–17.
Num. 3. 26 and *c.* for the door
2 Sam. 7. 2 ark .. dwel. within *c.*
1 Chr. 17. 1 ark .. remain, under *c.*
Ps. 104. 2 stretchest heavens like *c.*
S. of S. 1. 5 as the *c.* of Solomon
Isa. 54. 2 let them stretch forth .. *c.*
Jer. 4. 20 tents spoiled and my *c.*
Hab. 3. 7 the *c.* of the land of Mid.

Custody. *Hand, keeping, charge.*
Num. 2. 36 the *c.* and charge of
Esth. 2. 3–14 *c.* of .. king's cham.

Custom. *Way, usage.*
Gen. 31. 35 for the *c.* of women
1 Sam. 2. 13 priest's *c.* with people
Ez. 3. 4 feast, according to the *c.*
Luke 4. 16 as his *c.* was, went .. syna.
John 18. 39 ye have a *c.* that
1 Cor. 11. 16 we have no such *c.*
Statute, judgment
Lev. 18. 30 one of these abom. *c.*
Judg. 11. 39 it was a *c.* in Israel
Jer. 32. 11. sealed according to *c.*
Toll, tax.
Ez. 4. 13 pay toll, tribute and *c.*
Mat. 9. 9 sitting at the receipt of *c.*
Mark 2. 14 sitting at the receipt of *c.*
Luke 5. 27 sitting at receipt of *c.*
Rom. 13. 7 *c.* to whom *c.*, fear to f.
R. V. Gen. 31. 35 manner : Ex. 3. 4

ordinance ; Mat. 9. 9; Mark 2. 14;
Luke 5. 27 place of toll ; Mat. 17.
25 receive toll.
Cut. *Hew, carve, sever.*
Gen. 17. 14 soul shall be *c.* off
Ex. 34. 13 sh. *c.* down their groves
Lev. 7. 20 shall be *c.* off from people
Num. 4. 18 *c.* ye not off the tribe
Deut. 12. 29 thy God shall *c.* off
Josh. 7. 9 *c.* off our name fr. earth
Judg. 6. 25 and *c.* down the grove
1 Sam. 17. 51 and *c.* off his head
2 Sam. 10. 4 *c.* off their garments
1 K. 18. 23 and *c.* it in pieces.
2 K. 9. 8 I will *c.* off from Ahab
1 Chr. 17. 8 *c.* off all thine enemies
2 Chr. 22. 7 had anoint. to *c.* off
Job 28. 10 he *c.* out rivers am. rocks
Ps. 12. 3 *c.* off all flattering lips
Prov. 2. 2 wicked shall he *c.* off
Isa. 37. 24 *c.* down tall cedars
Jer. 9. 21 to *c.* off the children
Ezek. 6. 6 your images may be *c.*
Dan. 9. 26 shall Messiah be *c.* off
Hos. 8. 4 that they may be *c.* off
Joel 1. 5 *c.* off from your mouth
Am. 1. 5 *c.* off the inhabitants
Mic. 5. 10 will *c.* off thy horses
Nah. 1. 14 *c.* off graven images
Obad 14 to *c.* off those that escape
Zeph. 1. 3 I will *c.* off man
Zech. 9. 6 will *c.* off the pride
Mal. 2. 12 Lord will *c.* off man
Mat. 24. 51 shall *c.* him asunder
Mark 11. 8 others *c.* down branches
Luke 12. 46 will *c.* him in sunder
John 18. 10 Pet. *c.* off his right ear
Acts 27. 32 soldiers *c.* off the ropes
Rom. 11. 22 thou shalt be *c.* off
2 Cor. 11. 12 may *c.* off occasion
Gal. 5. 12 would they were *c.* off
Cutting. *Carving, cutting.*
Ex. 31. 5 cun. to work in *c.* of stones
Lev. 19. 28 shall not make any *c.*
Isa. 38. 10 in the *c.* off of my days
Jer. 48. 37 upon .. hands shall be *c.*
Hab. 2. 10 consulted shame by *c.*
R. V. Isa. 38. 10 noontide
Cymbal. *Cymbal.*
2 Sam. 6. 5 played on cornets and *c.*
1 Chr. 13 8 with timbrels and *c.*
2 Chr. 5. 12 arrayed in linen, hav. *c.*
Ez. 3. 10 with *c.* to praise the Lord
Neh. 12. 27 with singing, with *c.*
Ps. 150. 5 praise him upon .. *c.*
1 Cor. 13. 1 I am .. as a tinkling *c.*
Cypress. R. V. *holm-tree.*
Isa. 44. 14 taketh *c.* and oak

D.

Dagger. *Short weapon.*
Judg. 3. 16, 21, 22 Ehud made .. a *d*
Daily. *Day by day.*
Ex. 5. 13 fulfil your *d.* tasks
Num. 28. 24 ye shall offer *d.*
Judg. 16. 16 she pressed him *d.* with
2 K. 25. 30 *d.* rate for every day
2 Chr. 31. 16 every one his *d.* por.
Ez. 3. 4 offer *d.* burnt offerings
Esth. 3. 4 they spake *d.* unto him
Ps. 42. 10 they say *d.* unto me
Prov. 8. 30 was *d.* his delight
Isa. 58. 2 they seek me *d* and delight
Jer. 7. 25 *d.* rising up early
Ezek. 45. 23 rams without blem. *d.*
Dan. 1. 5 *d.* increaseth lies and
Mat. 6. 11 give us this day . . *d.* bread
Mark 14. 49 I was *d.* with you
Luke 9. 23 and take up his cross *d.*
Acts 2. 46 *d.* with one accord
1. Cor. 15. 31 I protest, I die *d.*
2 Cor. 11. 28 cometh upon me *d.*
Heb. 7. 27 who needeth not *d.*
Jas. 2. 15 if bro. destitute of *d.* food
R. V. In O. T. largely, continual
Dainties. *Tasteful things.*
Gen. 49. 20 shall yield royal *d.*
Job. 33. 20 and his soul *d.* meat
Ps. 141. 4 let me not eat of their *d.*
Prov. 23. 3 not desirous of . . *d.*
Rev. 18. 14 things . . *d.* and goodly
Dale. *Valley.*
Gen. 14. 17 which the king's d.
2 Sma. 18. 18 pillar, in . . king's d.
Dam. *Mother.*
Ex. 22. 30 seven days . . with his *d.*

Lev. 22. 27 seven days under the *d.*
Deut. 22. 6 *d.* sitting upon . . young
Damage. *Hurt, loss.*
Ez. 4. 22 why should *d.* grow
Esth. 7. 4 counterva. the king's *d.*
Prov. 26. 6 cutteth .. and drinketh *d.*
Dan. 6. 2 king should have no *d.*
Acts 27. 10 with hurt and much *d.*
2 Cor. 7. 9 that ye might receive *d.*
Damnable. R. V. *Destructive.*
2 Pet. 2. 1 who bring in *d.* heresies
Damnation. *Condemnation.*
Mat. 23. 14 shall rec. the greater *d.*
Mark 3. 29 in danger of eternal *d.*
Luke 20. 47 shall receive greater *d.*
John 5. 29 unto the resurrec. of *d.*
Rom. 3. 8 whose *d.* is just
1 Cor. 11. 29 eateth and drinketh *d.*
1 Tim. 5. 12 having *d.*, because they
R. V. Mat. 23. 14 ——; 22.33 ; John
  5. 29; Rom. 13. 2 judgment ;
  Mark 3. 29 sin; 12. 40; Luke
  20. 47 ; Rom. 3. 8 ; 1 Tim. 5. 12
  condemnation
Damned. *Judged down.*
Mark 16. 16 that bel. not shall be *d.*
Rom. 14. 23 that doubteth is *d.*
2 Thes. 2. 12 all *d.* who believe not
R. V. Mark 16. 16; Rom. 14. 23
  condemned ; 2 Thes. 2. 12 judged
Damsel. *Lass, girl.*
Gen. 24. 14 *d.* to whom I shall say
Deut. 22. 15 shall .. farther of the *d.*
Judg. 19. 3 father of the *d.* saw
Ruth 2. 5 said Boaz, Whose *d.* is this
1 Sam. 25. 42 with five *d.* of hers
1 K. 1. 3 they sought for a fair *d.*
Ps. 68. 25 among them . . *d.* playing
Mat. 14. 11 his head was given to *d.*
Mark 5. 41 D., I say unto thee, arise
John 18. 17 then saith the *d.* that
Acts 12. 13 a *d.* came to hearken
R. V. Mat. 26. 69 ; Acts 12. 13 maid ;
  Mark 5. 39, 40, 41 child
Dance (*n.*). *Dance, chorus.*
Ex. 15. 20 with timbrels and with *d.*
Judg. 11. 34 meet him with t. and *d.*
1 Sam. 21. 11 sing . . of him in *d.*
Ps. 149. 3 praise his name in *d.*
Jer. 31. 13 virgin rejoice in the *d.*
Lam. 5. 15 *d.* is turned into mourn.
Dance (*v.*). *Leap, turn, skip.*
Judg. 21. 21 daugh. of Shi. come *d.*
1 Sam. 30. 16 were drinking and *d.*
2 Sam. 6. 14 D. *d.* before the Lord
1 Chr. 15. 29 saw king David *d.*
Job 21. 11 and their children *d.*
Eccl. 3. 4 time to mourn, time to *d.*
Isa. 13. 21 satyrs shall *d.* there
Mat. 11. 17 and ye have not *d.*
Mark 6. 22 daughter of Herodias *d.*
Luke 7. 32 and ye have not *d.*
Dancing. *Moving round, leaping.*
Ex. 32. 19 Mos. saw the calf and *d.*
1 Sam. 18. 6 singing and *d.* to meet
2 Sam. 6. 16 saw D. leaping and *d.*
Ps. 30. 11 turned my mourn. into *d.*
Luke 15. 25 he heard music and *d.*
Dandled. *Fondle.*
Isa. 66. 12 sh. be borne, and be *d.*
Danger. *Liable to.*
Mat. 5. 21 in *d.* of the judgment
Mark 3. 29 of eternal damnation
R. V. Mark. 3. 29 guilty
Dangerous. *Perilous.*
Acts 27. 9 when sailing was now *d.*
Dare. *Adventure, defy.*
Mat. 22. 46 neither *d.* any man
Mark 12. 34 no man .. *d.* ask him
Luke 20. 40 they *d.* not ask him
John 21. 12 none of the dis. *d.* ask
Acts 5. 13 of the rest *d.* no man
Rom. 5. 7 some even would not *d.*
1 Cor. 6. 1 *d.* any of you, having
2 Cor. 10. 12 *d.* not make ourselves
Jude 9 *d.* not bring against him
R. V. 2 Cor. 10. 12 not bold to
Dark. *Without light, obscure.*
Gen. 15. 17 sun down, and it was *d.*
Lev. 13. 6 if plague be somewhat *d.*
Num. 12. 8 speak not in *d.* speeches
Josh. 2. 5 when it was *d.*, that
2 Sam. 22. 12 *d.* w. and thick clouds
Neh. 13. 19 g. of J. began to be *d.*
Job 12. 25 they grope in the *d.*
Ps. 18. 11 pavilion about were *d.*

Prov. 1. 6 and their *d.* sayings
Isa. 29. 15 their works are in the *d.*
Jer. 13. 16 stumble upon the *d.* m.
Lam. 3. 6 hath set me in *d.* places
Ezek. 32. 7 make the stars thereof *d.*
Dan. 8. 23 understanding *d.* sent.
Am. 5. 8 that maketh the day *d.*
Joel 2. 10 s. and m. shall be *d.*
Mic. 3. 6 it shall be *d.* unto you
Zech. 14. 6 shall not be cl. nor *d.*
Luke 11. 36 having no part *d.*
John 6. 17 it was now *d.* and J.
R. V. Zech. 14. 6 with gloom
Darken. *Make dark.*
Ex. 10. 15 so that the land was *d.*
Job 38. 2 who is this that *d.*
Ps. 69. 23 let their eyes be *d.*
Eccl. 12. 2 while stars be not *d.*
Isa. 5. 30 the light is *d.* in heavens
Ezek. 30. 18 the day shall be *d.*
Joel. 3. 15 sun and moon shall be *d.*
Am. 8. 9 I will *d.* the earth
Zech. 11. 17 eye shall be utterly *d.*
Mat. 24. 29 days, shall the sun be *d.*
Mark 13. 24 the sun shall be *d.*
Luke 23. 45 the sun was *d.* and
Rom. 1. 21 their foolish heart was *d.*
Eph. 4. 18 having the understand. *d.*
Rev. 8. 12 third part of them was *d.*
R. V. Luke 23. 45 failing
Darkly. *In an enigma.*
1 Cor. 13. 12 see through a glass *d.*
Darkness. *Obscurity, gloom.*
Gen. 1. 2 *d.* .. upon face of the deep
Ex. 10. 21 that there may be *d.*
Deut. 4. 11 with *d.* cloud and th. *d.*
1 Sam. 2. 9 wicked . . be silent in *d.*
2 Sam. 22. 12 made *d.* pavili. round
1 K. 8. 12 he would dwell in thick *d.*
2 Chr. 6. 1 he wo. dwell in thick *d.*
Job 3. 4 let that day be *d.*
Ps. 18. 11 Made *d.* his secret place
Prov. 2. 13 walk in the ways of *d.*
Eccl. 2. 13 as light excelleth *d.*
Isa. 5. 20 *d.* for light, and light for *d.*
Jer. 2. 31 have I been a land of *d.*
Lam. 3. 2 brought me into *d.* not li.
Ezek. 32. 8 set *d.* upon thy land
Dan. 2. 22 knoweth what is in *d.*
Joel 2. 2 day of *d.* and gloominess
Am. 5. 18 day of the Lord is *d.*
Mic. 7. 8 wh. I sit in *d.*, L., be light
Nah. 1. 8 and *d.* shall pursue enem.
Zeph. 1. 15 day of *d.* and gloom
Mat. 4. 16 people which sat in *d.*
Mark 15. 33 *d.* over the whole land
Luke 1. 79 light to them that sit in *d.*
John 3. 19 men loved *d.* rather than
Acts 2. 20 sun shall be turned into *d.*
Rom. 2. 19 light of them . . in *d.*
1 Cor. 4. 5 light hidden things of *d.*
2 Cor. 4. 6 light to shine out of *d.*
Eph. 5. 8 ye were sometimes *d.*
Col. 1. 13 delivered from power of *d.*
1 Thes. 5. 4 ye, brethren, are not in *d.*
Heb. 12. 18 nor unto black. and *d.*
1 Pet. 2. 9 who called you out of *d.*
2 Pet. 2. 17 midst of *d.* is reserved
1 John 1. 6 if we . . walk in *d.*
Jude 13 reserved the blackness of *d.*
Darling. *Only, favorite.*
Ps. 22. 20 deliver my *d.* from power
  35. 17 rescue my *d.* from the lions
Dart. *Arrow, spear, missile.*
2 Sam. 18. 14 took three *d.* in hand
2 Chr. 32. 5 made *d.* and shields
Job 41. 29 *d.* counted as stubble
Prov. 7. 23 till a *d.* strike through
Eph. 6. 16 quench all the fiery *d.*
Heb. 12. 20 thrust through with a *d.*
R. V. Job 41. 29 clubs ; 2 Chr. 32.
  5 weapons; Prov. 7. 23 arrow ;
  Heb. 12. 20 ——
Dash. *Smite, break, beat.*
Ex. 15. 6 hand . . hath *d.* in pieces
2 K. 18. 12 wilt *d.* their children
Ps. 2. 9 shalt *d.* them in pieces
Isa. 13. 16 children also shall be *d.* in
Jer. 13. 14 *d.* them one ag. anoth.
Hos. 10. 14 mother was *d.* in pieces
Nah. 3. 10 young chil. were *d.* in
Mat. 4. 6 lest . . thou *d.* thy foot
Daub. *Plaster, overlay.*
Ex. 2. 3 *d.* took ark and *d.* it wi. slime
Ezek. 13. 10-15 *d.* it with morter
  22. 28 prophets have *d.* them with

Daughter. *Female child, descendant.*
Gen. 11. 29 Milcah, the *d.* of Haran
Ex. 1. 16 if it be a *d.*, then live
Lev. 12. 6 for a son, or for a *d.*
Num. 25. 15 Cozbi, *d.* of Zur
Deut. 5. 14 nor thy son, nor thy *d.*
Josh. 15. 16 to him I give A. my *d.*
Judg. 11. 34 *d.* came .. to meet him
Ruth 2. 2 said unto her, Go, my *d.*
1 Sam. 1. 16 count not thy h. m. for *d.*
2 Sam. 3. 3 son of Maacah *d.* of Tal.
1 K. 3. 1 Sol. took Pharaoh's *d.* and
2 K. 8. 18 *d.* of Ahab was his wife
1 Chr. 1. 50 *d.* of Ma., *d.* of Mez.
2 Chr. 8. 11 Sol. brought up the *d.* of
Ez. 2. 61 took wife of *d.* of Barzillai
Neh. 3. 12 Shallum he and his *d.*
Esth. 2. 7 Esther his uncle's *d.*
Job 1. 2 seven sons and three *d.*
Ps. 9. 14 praise in gates of *d.* of Zion
Prov. 30. 15 horse leach hath two *d.*
Eccl. 12. 4 *d.* of music .. be brought
S. of S. 1. 5 but comely, O ye *d.*
Isa. 3. 16 *d.* of Zion are haughty
Jer. 3. 24 devour. flocks, sons and *d.*
Lam. 3. 51 all the *d.* of my city
Ezek. 13. 17 set thy face against *d.*
Dan. 11. 6 king's *d.* of the south
Hos. 4. 13 *d.* shall com. whoredom
Joel 2. 28 your *d.* shall prophesy
Am. 7. 17 thy *d.* shall fall by sword
Mic. 1. 13 beginning of sin to the *d.*
Zeph. 3. 10 *d.* of my dispersed
Zech. 2. 7 dwellest with *d.* of Bab.
Mal. 2. 11 married the *d.* of strange
Mat. 9. 18 my *d.* is even now dead
Mark 5. 34 *D.*, thy faith made thee
Luke 1. 5 Zac. wife was *d.* of Aaron
John 12. 15 fear not, *d.* of Zion
Acts 7. 21 Pharaoh's *d.* took him up
2 Cor. 6. 18 ye shall be sons and *d.*
Heb. 11. 24 called son of Phar.'s *d.*
1 Pet. 3. 6 whose *d.* ye are, as long
R. V. Mark. 7. 30 child ; 1 Pet. 3. 6 children
Dawn. *Shine through.*
Mat. 28. 1 as it began to *d.* toward
2 Pet. 1. 19 until the day *d.*
Dawning. *Shining through.*
Josh. 6. 15 rose early about the *d.*
Judg. 19. 26 came the wom. in the *d.*
Job 3. 9 neither let it see the *d.*
Ps. 119. 147 I prevented the *d.*
R. V. Job 3. 9 eyelids
Day. *Day, daylight, time.*
Gen. 1. 5 God called the light *d.*
Ex. 2. 13 he went out the second *d.*
Lev. 6. 5 in the *d.* of trespass off.
Num. 3. 1 *d.* I smote the firstborn
Deut. 1. 10 are this *d.* as stars of h.
Josh. 3. 7 this *d.* will I begin to
Judg. 1. 21 dwell with .. unto this *d.*
Ruth 3. 18 finished the thing this *d.*
1 Sam. 2. 34 one *d.* they shall die
2 Sam. 1. 2 came to pass on third *d.*
1 K. 1. 25 he is gone down this *d.*
2 K. 2. 22 waters healed unto this *d.*
1 Chr. 4. 43 dwelt there unto this *d.*
2 Chr. 5. 9 there it is unto this *d.*
Ez. 3. 6 from first *d.* of seventh mo.
Neh. 1. 11 prosper .. thy ser. this *d.*
Esth. 1. 10 on the seventh *d.*, when
Job 1. 4 feasted .. every one his *d.*
Ps. 2. 7 this *d.* have I begotten thee
7. 11 ; 18. 18 ; 19. 2 ; 20. 1 ; 25. 5
Prov. 4. 18 shineth .. unto the per. *d.*
Eccl. 7. 1 *d.* of death than *d.* of b.
S. of S. 2. 17 until the *d.* break
Isa. 2. 11 shall be exalted in that *d.*
3. 7 ; 4. 1 ; 5. 30 ; 7. 17 ; 9. 4 ; 10. 3
Jer. 1. 10 I have this *d.* set thee
Lam. 1. 12 *d.* of his fierce anger
Ezek. 1. 28 cloud in the *d.* of rain
Dan. 6. 10 kneeled three times a *d.*
Hos. 1. 5 come to pass at that *d.*
Joel 1. 15 alas for the *d.* ! for the day
Am. 1. 14 shouting in *d.* of battle
Obad. 8 shall I not in that *d.*
Jonah 3. 4 enter city a *d's* journey
Mic. 2. 4 in that *d.* shall one take
Nah. 1. 7 stronghold in *d.* of trouble
Hab. 3. 16 rest in *d.* of trouble
Zeph. 1. 7 *d.* of Lord is at hand
Hag. 1. 1 sixth month, in first *d.* *d.*
Zech. 1. 7 on four and twentieth

Mal. 3. 2 who may abide the *d.*
Mat. 6. 34 suf. unto .. *d.* is the evil
Mark 4. 35 same *d.* wh. even .. co.
Luke 1. 59 on eighth *d.* they came
2. 37 ; 4. 16 ; 6. 13 ; 9. 12 ; 10. 12
John 1. 39 abode with him that *d.*
Acts 1. 2 *d.* he was taken up
Rom. 2. 5 against the *d.* of wrath
1 Cor. 1. 8 blameless in the *d.* of
2 Cor. 1. 14 ours in the *d.* of L. J.
Eph. 4. 30 unto the *d.* of redem.
Phil. 1. 5 fellowship from first *d.*
Col. 1. 6 since the *d.* ye heard
1 Thes. 2. 9 laboring night and *d.*
2 Thes. 1. 10 that believe in that *d.*
1 Tim. 5. 5 prayers night and *d.*
2 Tim. 1. 3 remembrance n. and *d.*
Heb. 3. 8 in the *d.* of temptation
Jas. 5. 5 as in a *d.* of slaughter
1 Pet. 2. 12 glorify God in *d.* of vis.
2 Pet. 1. 19 dark pl. until *d.* dawn
1 John 4. 17 have boldness in *d.* of
Jude 6 judgment of the great *d.*
Rev. 4. 8 rest not *d.* and night
R. V. Mat. 27. 62 ; John 1. 29 ;
Acts 14. 20 ; 21. 8 ; 25. 6 on the mor.
Daysman. *Umpire.*
Job 9. 33 neither .. any *d.* betwixt
Deacon. *Ministrant.*
Phil. 1. 1 with the bishops and *d.*
1 Tim. 3. 8, 10, 12, 13 *d.* be grave
Dead. *Lifeless.*
Gen. 23. 3 A. stood .. before his *d.*
Ex. 12. 33 we be all *d.* men
Lev. 21. 11 nei. go to any *d.* body
Num. 6. 6 shall come at no *d*.bod.
Deut. 2. 16 men were con. and *d.*
Josh. 1. 2 Moses my servant is *d.*
Judg. 1. 1 did evil when E. was *d.*
1 Sam. 4. 17 Hoph. and Phin. are *d.*
2 Sam. 1. 4 many people are *d.* and
1 K. 3. 21 behold it was *d.* : but
2 K. 4. 1 thy servant my hus. is *d.*
1 Chr. 10. 7 S. and his sons were *d.*
2 Chr. 22. 10 Ath. saw .. son was *d.*
Job 1. 19 young men .. they are *d.*
Ps. 88. 5 free among the *d.* like the
Eccl. 4. 2 I praised the *d.* which
Isa. 8. 19 for the living to the *d.*?
Jer. 16. 7 comfort them for the *d.*
Lam. 3. 6 a2 they that be *d.* of old
Ezek. 24. 17 make no mourn. for *d.*
Mat. 8. 22 let the *d.* bury their *d.*
Mark 6. 14 John was risen from d.
Luke 7. 22 deaf hear, *d.* are raised
John 5. 21 Father raised up the *d.*
Acts 3. 15 G. hath raised from .. *d.*
Rom. 1. 4 resurrection from the *d.*
1 Cor. 15. 12 he rose from the *d.*
2 Cor. 1. 9 G. which raiseth the *d.*
Gal. 1. 1 raised him from the *d.*
Eph. 5. 14 arise from the *d.*, and
Phil. 3. 11 attain unto res. of the *d.*
Col. 1. 18 firstborn from the *d.*
1 Thes. 1. 10 he raised from the *d.*
2 Tim. 2. 8 J. C. was raised .. *d.*
Heb. 6. 2 and of resur. of the *d.*
1 Pet. 1. 3 res. of Jesus from the *d.*
Rev. 1. 5 first begotten of the *d.*
Deadly. *Death producing.*
1 Sam. 5. 11 there was a *d.* des.
Ps. 17. 9 *d.* enemies who compass
Mark 16. 18 if they drink .. *d.* thing
Jas. 3. 8 tongue is full of *d.* poison
Rev. 13. 3 *d.* wound was healed
R. V. Rev. 13. 3, 12 death stroke
Deadness. *State of death.*
Rom. 4. 19 *d.* of Sarah's womb
Deaf. *Silent, dull, dumb.*
Ex. 4. 11 maketh the dumb or *d.*
Lev. 19. 14 shalt not cause the *d.*
Ps. 38. 13 I as a *d.* man, heard not
Isa. 29. 18 that day shall .. *d.* hear
Mic. 7. 16 their ears shall be *d.*
Mat. 11. 5 and the *d.* hear, the
Mark 7. 32 bring .. one that was *d.*
Luke 7. 22 lame walk .. the *d.* hear
Deal. *Do, apportion.*
Gen. 24. 49 if ye will *d.* kindly and
Ex. 5. 15 wherefore *d.* thou thus
Num. 11. 15 if thou *d.* thus with
Josh. 2. 14 *d.* kindly and truly with
Judg. 9. 16 if ye have *d.* well with
Ruth 1. 8 *d.* kindly with you, as
1 Sam. 20. 8 thou shalt *d.* kindly wi.
2 Sam. 6. 19 he *d.* among all people

2 K. 12. 15 for they *d.* faithfully
1 Chr. 20. 3 even so *d.* David with
2 Chr. 2. 3 as thou didst *d.* with D
Job. 42. 8 lest I *d.* with you after
Ps. 103. 10 he hath not *d.* with us
Prov. 10. 4 becometh poor that *d.*
Jer. 6. 13 prophet .. every one *d.*
Ezek. 8. 18 will I also *d.* in fury
Dan. 1. 13 *d.* with thy servants
Zech. 1. 6 so hath he *d.* with us
Luke 1. 25 thus Lord *d.* with me
Acts 7. 19 the same *d.* subtilly with
Rom. 12. 3 as God *d.* to every man
Heb. 12. 7 God *d.* with you as sons
R. V. Acts 25. 24 made suit to
Dealer. *Who deals.*
Isa. 21. 2 treach. *d.* dealeth treach.
24. 16 *d.* dealt treacherously
Dealings. *Doings.*
John 4. 9 Jews have no *d.* with S.
Dealt. *See Deal.*
Dear. *Precious, loved.*
Jer. 31. 20 is Ephraim my *d.* son
Luke 7. 2 centu. ser. who was *d.*
Acts 20. 24 neither count I life *d.*
Eph. 5. 1 followers of G. as *d.* chil.
Col. 1. 7 learned of our *d.* .. ser.
1 Thes. 2. 8 because we are *d.*
R. V. Eph. 5. 1 ; Col. 1. 7 beloved
Dearth. *Want, famine.*
Gen. 41. 54 seven years of *d.* began
2 K. 4. 38 was a *d.* in the land
2 Chr. 6. 28 if there be *d.* in land
Jer. 14. 1 came to Jer. con. the *d.*
Neh. 5. 3 buy corn, because of .. *d.*
Acts 7. 11 now there came a *d.*
R. V. Jer. 14. 1 drought ; Gen. 41.
54 ; 2 Chr. 6. 28 ; Acts 7. 11 famine
Death. *Death.*
Gen. 2. 16 let me not see the *d.*
Ex. 10. 17 take away .. this *d.*
Lev. 16. 1 after *d.* of the two sons
Num. 16. 29 die the common *d.* of
Deut. 22. 26 no sin worthy of *d.*
Josh. 1. 1 after the *d.* of Moses
Judg. 1. 1 after the *d.* of Joshua
Ruth. 1. 17 if ought but *d.* part
1 Sam. 15. 32 bitter. of *d.* is past
2 Sam. 1. 1 after the *d.* of Saul
1 K. 11. 40 until the *d.* of Solomon
1 Chr. 22. 5 D. pre. .. before his *d.*
2 Chr. 22. 4 after *d.* of his father
Job 3. 21 which long for *d.*, but
Ps. 6. 5 in *d.* .. is no remembrance
7. 13 ; 9. 13 ; 13. 3 ; 18. 4 ; 22. 5
Prov. 2. 18 her house incli. unto *d.*
5. 5 ; 7. 27 ; 8. 36 ; 10. 2 ; 11. 4 ;
Eccl. 7. 1 day of *d.* their day of
S. of S. 8. 6 love is strong as *d.*
Isa. 25. 8 he will swallow up *d.*
Jer. 8. 3 *d.* .. cho. rather than life
Lam. 1. 20 at home there is *d.*
Ezek. 18. 32 no pleas. in *d.* of him
Hos. 13. 14 will re. them from *d.*
Jonah 4. 9 angry even unto *d.*
Hab. 2. 5 desire as hell, and is as *d.*
Mat. 4. 16 sat in .. shadow of *d.*
10. 21 ; 15. 4 ; 16. 28 ; 20. 18 ;
Mark 7. 10 let him die the *d.*
9 1 ; 11. 33 ; 13. 12 ; 14. 34 ; 14. 64
Luke 1. 79 that sit in shadow of *d.*
John 5. 24 passed from *d.* unto life
Acts 2. 24 loosed the pains of *d.*
Rom. 1. 32 com. such, are wor. of *d.*
5. 10 ; 6. 3 ; 7. 5 ; 8. 2, 6, 38
1 Cor. 3. 22 or of things present
2 Cor. 1. 9 sen. of *d.* in ourselves
Phil. 1. 20 whether by l. or by *d.*
Col. 1. 22 body of, flesh through *d.*
1 Tim. 1. 10 J. C. .. hath abolish.
Heb. 2. 9. for the sufferings of *d.*
Jas. 1. 15 fin., bringeth forth *d.*
1 John 3. 14 we have passed from *d.*
Rev. 1. 18 keys of hell and *d.*
2. 10 ; 6. 8 ; 9. 6 ; 12. 11 ; 13. 3
R. V. Mark 14. 1 ; Luke 18. 33 kill him
Debase. *Make low.*
Isa. 57. 9 *d.* thyself .. unto hell
Debate (n). *Controversy, strife.*
Isa. 58. 4 ye fast for strife and *d.*
Rom. 1. 29 full of *d.*, deceit, malig.
2 Cor. 12. 20 lest there be *d.*
R. V. Isa. 58. 4 contention, Rom.
1. 29 strife ; 2 Cor. 12. 20 should be strife

Debate (*n*.).   *Strive, plead.*
Prov. 25. 9 *d*. thy cause with neigh.
Isa. 27. 8 shoot. forth thou wilt *d*. it
R. V. Isa. 27. 8 dost contend

Debt.   *Loan, indebtedness.*
1 Sam. 22. 2 every one that was .. *d*.
2 K. 4. 7 sell oil, and pay thy *d*.
Neh. 10. 31 exaction of every *d*.
Prov. 22. 26 that are sureties for *d*.
Mat. 6. 12 forgive us our *d*., as
Rom. 4. 4 not reck. of gr. but of *d*.
R. V. Mat. 18. 30 which was due

Debtor.   *One bound, indebted.*
Ezek. 18. 7 res to *d*. his pledge
Mat. 6. 12 as we forgive our *d*.
Luke 7. 41 cr. which had two *d*.
Rom. 1. 14 I am *d*. . . to Greek
Gal. 5. 3 *d*. to the whole law

Decay.   *Waste, impair, rot.*
Lev. 25. 35 bro. be fallen in *d*. with
Neh. 4. 10 strength of bear. is *d*.
Job 14. 11 flood *d*. and drieth up
Eccl. 10. 18 by sloth. building *d*.
Isa. 44. 26 raise up *d*. places
Heb. 8. 13 now that which *d*.
R. V. Heb. 8. 13 becoming old.

Decease.   *Outgoing.*
Luke 9. 31 *d*. which he should ac.
2 Pet. 1. 15 be able after my *d*.

Deceased.   *Ended, dead.*
Isa. 26. 14 thy are *d*.. they shall
Mat. 22. 25 married a wife, *d*.

Deceit.   *Deception. fraud.*
Job 15. 35 their belly prepareth *d*.
Ps. 10. 7 mouth full of c. and *d*.
Prov. 12. 5 coun. of wicked are *d*.
Isa. 53. 9 neither *d*. in his mouth
Jer. 5. 27 their houses full of *d*.
Hos. 11. 12 house of Is. with *d*.
Am. 8. 5 falsifying balances by *d*.
Zeph. 1. 9 fill mas. house with *d*.
Mark 7. 22 cov., wickedness, *d*.
Rom. 1. 29 full of . . debate, *d*.
1 Thes. 2. 3 our exhor. was not *d*.
R. V. Ps. 55. 11; 72. 14; oppres-
sion; Prov. 20. 17 falsehood; 1
Thes. 2. 3 error

Deceitful.   *Guileful, false.*
Ps. 5. 6. abhor the .. *d* man
Prov. 27. 6 kisses of an en. are *d*.
Mic. 6. 12 their tongue is *d*.
Zeph. 3. 13 nei. shall *d*. tongue be
2 Cor. 11. 13 such are false apos., *d*.
Eph. 4. 22 according to *d*. lusts
R. V. Prov. 27. 6 profuse; 29. 13
oppressor; Eph. 4. 22 deceit

Deceitfully.   *With deceit.*
Gen. 34. 13 sons of J. answered *d*.
Ex. 21. 8 he hath dealt *d*. with her
Lev. 6. 4 things he hath *d*. got
Job 13. 7 will ye speak and talk *d*.
Ps. 52. 2 like .. razor, working *d*.
Jer. 48. 10 doeth work of L. *d*.
Dan. 11. 23 he shall work *d*.
2 Cor. 4. 2 handl. word of God *d*.
R. V. Gen. 34. 13 with guile

Deceitfulness.   *Deceit.*
Mat. 13. 22 *d*. of riches choke word
Mark 4. 19 *d*. of riches choke word
Heb. 3. 13 hardened through *d*. of sin

Deceivableness.   *Deceit.*
Isa. 30. 10 speak unto us, proph. *d*.

Deceive.   *Mock, play upon.*
Gen. 31. 7 your father has *d*. me
Jer. 9. 5 *d*. every man his neighbour
Entice, persuade, deceive.
1 Sam. 19. 17 why hast thou *d*. me
2 Sam. 3. 25 Abner came to *d*. thee
2 K. 4. 28 say, do not *d*. me.
Prov. 24. 28 and *d*. not with lips
Jer. 20. 7 Lord, thou hast *d*. me
Lam. 1. 19 lovers, but they *d*. me
Rom. 7. 11 for sin *d*. me, and
1 Cor. 3. 18 let no man *d*. himself
2 Thes. 2. 3 let no man *d*. you
1 Tim. 2. 14 Adam was not *d*., but
Jas. 1. 26 brid. not tongue, but *d*.
To lead astray.
2 K. 18. 29 let not Hezekiah *d*.
2 Chr. 32. 15 let not Hezek. *d*. you
Isa. 37. 10 God whom thou trust, *d*.
Jer. 4. 10 hast greatly *d*. this people
Obad. 3 pride of thine heart hath *d*.
Mat. 24. 4 heed that no man *d*.
Mark 13. 5 lest any man *d*. you
Luke 21. 8 heed that ye be not *d*.

John 7. 12 nay, but he *d*. the peo.
1 Cor. 6. 9 be not *d*.; neither forn.
Gal. 6. 7 be not *d*., G. is not mocked
2 Tim. 3. 13 deceiving, and being *d*.
Tit. 3. 3 foolish, disobedient, *d*.
1 John 1. 8 no sin, we *d*. ourselves
Rev. 12. 9 Satan, which *d*. whole
R. V. Mat. 24. 4, 5, 11, 24; Mark
13. 5, 6; 1 John 3. 7 lead astray;
Rom. 16. 18; 2 Thes. 2. 3 beguile.

Deceived.   *Persuaded, beguiled.*
Deut. 11. 16 heed, heart be not *d*.
Job. 12. 16 *d*. and deceiver are
Prov. 20. 1 whosoever is *d*. thereby
Isa. 44. 20 a *d*. heart hath turned
Jer. 20. 7 I was *d*., thou art stronger
Ezek. 14. 9 if the prophets be *d*.
R. V. Lev. 6. 2 oppressed; Job 31.
9 enticed; Prov. 20. 1 erreth;
Luke 21. 8; John 7. 47 led astray;
Rom. 7. 11 1 Tim. 2. 14 beguiled.

Deceiver.   *Who deceives.*
Gen. 27. 12 I shall seem to him a *d*.
Job. 12. 16 the deceiver and *d*.
Mal. 1. 14 cursed be the *d*.
Mat. 27. 63 we rem. that *d*. said
2 Cor. 6. 8 hon. and dishon. as *d*.
Tit. 1. 10 many vain talkers and *d*.
2 John 7 many *d*. are entered into

Deceiving.   *Deceit.*
Jas. 1. 22 *d*. your own selves
2 Pet. 2. 13 sporting with own *d*.
R. V. Jas. 1. 22 deluding

Decently.   *Becomingly.*
1 Cor. 14. 40 all things be done *d*.

Decide.   *Determine.*
1 K. 20. 40 judg. be; thou hast *d*.

Decision.   *Determination.*
Joel 3. 14 multitudes in valley of *d*.

Deck.   *Adorn.*
Job. 40. 10 *d*. thyself with majesty
Prov. 7. 16 *d*. my bed with coverings
Isa. 61. 10 as bridegroom *d*. himself
Jer. 10. 4 they *d*. it with silver
Ezek. 16. 3 wast thou *d*. with gold
Hos. 2. 13 *d*. herself with earrings
Rev. 17. 4 *d*. with gold and pr. stones

Declaration.   *Statement.*
Esth. 10. 2 *d*. of greatness of Mor.
Job. 13. 17 hear diligently, my *d*.
Luke 1. 1 set forth in order a *d*. of
R. V. Esth. 10. 2 full account;
Luke 1. 1 narrative.

Declare.   *Speak, make known.*
Gen. 41. 24 none that could *d*. it
Ex. 9. 16 name be *d*. throughout
Lev. 23. 44 Moses *d*. unto children
Num. 15. 34 it was not *d*. what
Deut. 4. 13 *d*. unto you his coven.
Josh. 20. 4 *d*. his cause in ears of
Judg. 14. 12 if ye can certainly *d*. it
2 Sam. 19. 6 thou hast *d*. this day
1 Chr. 16. 24 *d*. his glory among h.
Esth. 4. 8 *d*. it unto her, to charge
Job 12. 8 fishes of sea shall *d*.
Ps. 2. 7 I will *d*. the decree
19. 1; 22. 22; 50. 16; 66. 16; 73. 28
Isa. 3. 9 *d*. their sin as Sodom
Jer. 4. 5 ye in Judah and publish
Ezek. 23. 36 *d*. to them their abom.
Dan. 4. 18 *d*. their interpretation
Hos. 4. 12 their staff *d*. unto them
Am. 4. 13 *d*. unto man what is
Mic. 1. 10 *d*. it not in Gath
Zech. 9. 12 I *d*. I will render
Mat. 13. 36 *d*. unto us the parable
Luke 8. 47 she *d*. unto him before
John 1. 18 only begot. S. hath *d*.
Acts 10. 8 when he had *d*. these
Rom. 9. 17 my name might be *d*.
1 Cor. 1. 11 hath been *d*. unto me
2 Cor. 3. 3 *d*. to be the epistle of C.
Col. 4. 7 my state shall Tychicus *d*.
Heb. 11. 14 *d*. . . that they seek a
1 John 1. 3 that we have seen . . *d*.
Rev. 10. 7 hath *d*. to his servant
R. V. Ps. 2. 7; 73. 28; 75. 1; 78. 6
tell of; Eccl. 9. 1 explore; Isa. 43.
26 set forth thy cause; Mat. 13. 36
explain; Rom. 3. 25 shew; John
17. 26; Col. 4. 7 make known; 1
John 1. 5 announce; Acts 15. 4, 14
rehearsed, Rom. 9. 17 published

Decline.   *Incline.*
Ex. 23. 2 neither speak in cause to *d*.
Job. 23. 11 ways I kept and not *d*.

Ps. 44. 18 neither have our steps *d*.
Prov. 4 5 neither *d*. from the word
Turn aside.
Deut. 17. 11 shalt not *d*. from
2 Chr. 34. 2 *d*. neither to right nor left
Prov. 7. 25 let not thine heart *d*.
Rev. Ex. 23. 2; Deut. 17. 11; 2
Chr. 34. 2; Job 23. 11 turn aside;
Ps. 119. 51, 157 swerved

Decrease.   *Lessen.*
Gen. 8. 5 the waters *d*. continually
Ps. 107. 38 suffereth not .. cattle to *d*.
John 3. 30 He increase, but I must *d*.

Decree (*n*.).   *Bond, order, law.*
2 Chr. 30. 5 so they established a *d*.
Ez. 5. 13 Cyrus made a *d*. to. build
Esth. 2. 8 when k.'s *d*. was heard
Job 28. 26 he made a *d*. for rain
Ps. 2. 7 I will declare the *d*.
Prov. 8. 29 gave to the sea his *d*.
Isa. 10. 1 unrighteous *d*. and
Jer. 5. 22 bound sea by perpetual *d*.
Dan. 2. 9 there is but one *d*. for you
Jonah 3. 7 by *d*. of the king
Mic. 7. 11 shall *d*. be far removed
Zeph. 2. 2 before the *d*. bring forth
Luke 2. 1 there went out a *d*. from
Acts 16. 4 delivered them the *d*.
R. V. Dan. 2. 9 law; 6. 7, 8, 9, 12,
13, 15 interdict; Esth. 9. 32 com-
mandment

Decree (*v*.).   *Order, determine.*
Esth. 2. 1 remembered what was *d*.
Job 22. 28 shalt also *d*. a thing
Prov. 8. 15 kings reign, princes *d*.
Isa. 10. 1 woe . . that *d*. unrighteous.
1 Cor. 7. 37 and hath so *d*. in heart
Esth. 9. 31 ordained; Isa. 10. 22;
1 Cor. 7. 37 determined

Dedicate.   *Separate, hallow.*
Deut. 20. 5 man hath not *d*. it
Judg. 17. 3 I wholly *d*. the silver
2 Sam. 8. 11 which .. David did *d*.
1 K. 5. 71 which David had *d*.
2 K. 12. 18 his fathers .. had *d*.
1 Chr. 18. 11 them also .. David *d*.
2 Chr. 7. 5 Sol. the house of God
Ezek. 44. 29 every *d*. thing in Is.
Heb. 9. 18 neither first test. was *d*.
R. V. 2 K. 12. 4 hallowed; Ezek.
44. 29 devoted

Dedicating.   *Separating, hallow-*
ing.
Num. 7. 10, 11 offered for *d*. of

Dedication.   *Separating, hallow-*
ing.
Num. 7. 84 was the *d*. of the altar
Ez. 6. 16 kept the *d*. of this house
Neh. 12. 27 *d*. of the wall of Jer.
Dan. 3. 2 to come to *d*. of the image
John. 10. 22 at Jerusalem feast of *d*.

Deed.   *Act, work, doing.*
Gen. 20. 9 hast done *d*. unto me
1 Chr. 16. 8 make known his *d*.
2 Chr. 35. 27 his *d*. . . are written
Ez. 9. 13 is come upon us for evil *d*.
Esth. 1. 17 *d*. of the queen shall
Ps. 28. 4 give them accor. to their *d*.
Isa. 59. 18 according to their *d*.
Jer. 5. 28 overpass *d*. of the wicked
Luke 23. 41 due reward of our *d*.
John 3. 19 because their *d*. were evil
Acts 7. 22 mighty in words and *d*.
Rom. 2. 6 render according to his *d*.
1 Cor. 5. 2 hath done this *d*. might
2 Cor. 10. 11 also in *d*. when we
Col. 3. 17 what. ye do in word or *d*.
2 Pet. 2. 8 with their unlawful *d*.
1 John 3. 18 nei. tongue, but in *d*.
2 John 11 partaker of his evil *d*.
3 John 10 will remember his *d*.
Jude 15 of all their ungodly *d*.
Rev. 2. 6 hatest the *d*. of the Nic.
R. V. In N. T. mostly, works

Deem.   R. V. *Surmise.*
Acts 27. 27 shipmen *d*. they drew

Deep (*n*.).   *Shaded place.*
Neh. 9. 11 throwest into the *d*.
Job. 41. 31 maketh the *d*. to boil
Ps. 69. 15 nei. let the *d*. swal. me
Isa. 44. 27 saith to the *d*., be dry
Depth, having depth, abyss.
Gen. 1. 2 darkness on face of the *d*.
Deut. 33. 13 the *d*. that coucheth
Job. 38. 30 face of the *d*. is frozen
Ps. 36. 6 judgments are a great *d*.

Prov. 8. 28 strength. fountains of *d.*
Eccl. 7. 24 far off, and exceed. *d.*
Isa.. 51. 10 waters of the great *d.*
Ezek. 26. 19 bring the *d.* upon thee
Am. 7. 4 devoured the great *d.*
Jonah 2. 3 cast me into the *d.*
Zech. 10. 11 *d.* of the riv. shall dry
Hab. 3. 10 *d.* uttered his voice
Luke 8. 31 to go out into the *d.*
Rom. 10. 7 shall descend into the *d.*
2 Cor. 11. 25 have been in the *d.*
R. V. Isa. 63. 13 Jonah 2. 3 depth;
    Luke 8. 31; Rom. 2. 7 abyss

Deep, Deeper (*adj.*). *Far down, sound.*
Gen. 2. 21 L. caused *d.* sleep to fall
Lev. 13. 3 if plague in sight be *d.* in
1 Sam. 26. 12 *d.* .. sleep was fallen
Job 4. 13 *d.* sleep falleth on men
Ps. 80. 9 cause to take *d.* root
Prov. 19. 15 slothful. cast. *d.* sleep
Eccl. 7. 24 far off, and exceeding *d.*
Isa. 30. 33 he hath made it *d.*
Jer. 49. 8 dwell *d.* O inhabitants
Ezek. 32. 14 make their waters *d.*
Dan. 2. 22 revealeth the *d.* things
Luke 6. 48 built house and dig. *d.*
John 4. 11 and the well is *d.*
Acts 20. 9 being fall. into *d.* sleep
1 Cor. 2. 10 the *d.* things of God
R. V. Ps. 135. 6 deeps; Ezek.
    32. 14; 34. 18 clear

Deeply. *With depth.*
Isa. 31. 6 chil. of Is. have *d.* revolt.
Hos. 9. 9 have *d.* corrupted thems.

Deepness. *Depth.*
Mat. 13. 5 they had no *d.* of earth

Defame. *Speak injuriously.*
1 Cor. 4. 13 being *d.* we entreat

Defaming. *Slandering.*
Jer. 20. 10 heard the *d.* of many

Defeat. *Frustrate, make void.*
2 Sam. 15. 34 then mayest thou .. *d.*
    17. 14 Lord had appointed to *d.*

Defence. *Cover, tower, fortress.*
Num. 14. 9 their *d.* is departed
2 Chr. 11. 5 and built cities for *d.*
Job. 22. 25 Almighty shall be thy *d.*
Ps. 7. 10 my *d.* is of God which sav.
Eccl. 7. 12 wisdom is a *d.*
Isa. 4. 5 upon all glory shall be a *d.*
Nah. 2. 5 *d.* shall be prepared
Apology, plea, answer.
Acts 22. 1 hear ye my *d.* which
Phil. 1. 7 in the *d.* and confirmation
R. V. Job 22 25 treasure ; Ps. 7. 10
    89. 18 shield; 59. 9, 16; 62. 2, 6;
    94. 22 high tower; Isa. 4. 5 canopy;
    19. 6 Egypt; Nah. 2. 5 mantelet

Defenced. *Fenced off.*
Isa. 25. 2 made of a *d.* city a ruin
    27. 10; 36. 1; 37. 26
Jer. 1. 18 have made thee .. a *d.* c.
Ezek. 21. 20.in Jerusalem the *d.*

Defend. *Protect, uphold.*
Judg. 10. 1 th. arose to *d.* Is. Tola
2 Sam. 23. 12 stood in .. ground, *d.*
2 K. 19. 34 I will *d.* this city
Ps. 20. 1 God of Jacob *d.* thee
Isa. 31. 5 *d.* also he will deliver it
Zech. 9. 15 Lord of hosts shall *d.*
Acts 7. 24 he *d.* him, and avenged
R. V. Judg. 10. 1 save ; Ps. 20. 1 ;
    59. 1 set up on high; 82. 3 judge;
    Isa. 31. 5 protect

Defer. *Postpone, delay.*
Gen. 34. 19 the young man *d.* not
Prov. 13. 12 hope *d.* maketh h. sick
Eccl. 5. 4 who vow... *d.* not to pay
Isa. 48. 9 for name's sake will I *d.*
Dan. 9. 19 *d.* not, .. O my God
Acts 24. 22 heard. .things, he *d.* them
R. V. Prov. 19. 11 maketh him slow

Defied *see* **Defy.**

Defile. *Pollute, make unclean.*
Gen. 34. 5 that he has *d.* Dinah
Ex. 31. 14 that *d.* it shall surely be
Lev. 11. 44 neither shall ye *d.* yours.
Num. 5. 3 *d.* not their camps in
Deut. 24. 4 after that she is *d.*
1 Chr. 5. 1 he *d.* his father's bed
2 K. 23. 8 *d.* king the high places
Job 16. 15 *d.* my horn in the dust
Ps. 79. 1 holy temple have they *d.*
S. of S. 5. 3 how shall I *d.* them
Isa. 59. 3 hands are *d.* with blood

Jer. 2. 7 when ye ent. ye *d.* my land
Ezek. 5. 11 hast *d.* my sanctuary
Dan. 1. 8 Dan. would not *d.* himself
Hos. 5. 3 and Israel is *d.*
Mat. 15. 11 which goeth into m. *d.*
Mark 7. 15 entering into him, *d.*
John 18. 28 lest they should be *d.*
1 Cor. 8. 7 con. being weak is *d.*
1 Tim. 1. 10 them that *d.* themselves
Jas. 3. 6 tongue *d.* the whole body
Heb. 12. 15 thereby many be *d.*
Jude 8 dreams *d.* the flesh
Rev. 3. 4 have not *d.* their garments
R. V. Ex. 31. 14; Ezek. 7. 24; 28.
    18 profaned; Num. 35. 33; Isa.
    24. 5; Jer. 3. 9; 16. 18 polluted;
    Gen. 34. 2 humbled; Deut. 22. 9;
    forfeited; Lev. 13. 14; 15. 32;
    Num. 5. 2; Ezek. 4. 13; Rev. 21.
    27 unclean

Defraud. *Oppress.*
Lev. 19. 13 shalt not *d.* thy neigh.
1 Sam. 12. 3 whom have I *d.*
Deprive of, overclaim.
Mark 10. 19 *d.* not, honour thy fath.
2 Cor. 7. 2 we have *d.* no man
1 Thes. 4. 6 no man .. *d.* his brother
R. V. Lev. 19. 13 oppress; 2 Cor.
    7. 2 took advantage of; 1 Thes. 4.
    6 wrong

Defy. *Challenge, reproach.*
Num. 23. 7 and come, *d.* Israel
1 Sam. 17. 10 I *d.* the armies of Is.
2 Sam. 21. 21 when he *d.* Israel
1 Chr. 20. 7 when he *d.* Israel

Degenerate. *Turned, inferior.*
Jer. 2. 21 art turned into *d.* plant

Degree. *Ascent, grade, step.*
2 K. 20. 9 for ten *d.*, or go back
1 Chr. 17. 17 a man of high *d.*
Ps. 120—134 *titles.* A Song of *d.*
Isa. 38. 8 bring shadow of the *d.*
Luke 1. 52 exalted them of low *d.*
1 Tim. 3. 13 purchase ..a good *d.*
Jas. 1. 9 brother of low *d.* rejoice
R. V. 2 K. 20. 9, 10, 11 steps;
    Tim. 3. 13 standing

Delay (*n.*). *Casting back.*
Acts 25. 17 without .. *d.* on the mor.

Delay (*v.*). *Tarry, postpone.*
Ex. 22. 29 shalt not *d.* to offer
Ps. 119. 60 *d.* not to keep thy com.
Mat. 24. 48 My lord *d.* his coming
Luke 12. 45 servant say, My lord *d.*
Acts 9. 38 would not *d.* to come
R. V. Mat. 24. 48 tarrieth

Delectable. *Desirable.*
Isa. 44. 9 *d.* things shall profit not

Delicacy. R. V. *wantonness.*
Rev. 18. 3 through abund. of her *d.*

Delicate. *Dainty, luxurious.*
Deut. 28. 54 man that is .. very *d.*
Isa. 47. 1 no more called tender, *d.*
Jer. 6. 2 likened daughter to a *d.*
Mic. 1. 16 poll thee for thy *d.* chil.
R. V. Mic. 1. 16 of .. delight

Delicately. *Daintily.*
1 Sam. 15. 32 Agag came to him *d.*
Lam. 4. 5 they that did feed *d.*
Luke 7. 25 gor. appar., and live *d.*

Delicateness. *Delicate.*
Deut. 28. 56 her foot on gr. for *d.*

Deliciously. R. V. *wantonly.*
Rev. 18. 7, 9 glor. herself and lived *d.*

Delight (*n.*). *Pleasure, gratification.*
Gen. 34. 19 had *d.* in Jacob's daugh.
Deut. 21. 14 if thou have no *d.*
1 Sam. 18. 22 king hath *d.* in thee
2 Sam. 15. 26 I have no *d.* in thee
Job 22. 26 have *d.* in the Almighty
Ps. 1. 2 his *d.* is in the law
Prov. 29. 17 give *d.* unto thy soul
Eccl. 2. 8 *d.* of the son of man
S. of S. 7. 6 pleas., O love, for *d.*
Isa. 58. 13 call the sabbath a *d.*
Jer. 6. 10 they have no *d.* in it
R. V. Prov. 19. 10 delicate living

Delight (*v.*). *Please, gratify, charm.*
Num. 14. 8 if the Lord *d.* in us
1 Sam. 19. 2 Jonathan .. *d.* much in
2 Sam. 22. 20 because he *d.* in me
1 K. 10. 9 God which *d.* in thee
2 Chr. 9. 8 Lord thy God, which *d.*
Neh. 9. 25 *d.* them. in .. goodness

Esth. 2. 14 the king *d.* in her
Job 27. 10 *d.* himself in the Almi.
Ps. 18. 19 delivered me because he *d.*
Prov. 1. 22 scorners *d.* in scorning
Isa. 1. 11 I *d.* not in blood of bull.
Jer. 9. 24 I *d.*, saith the Lord
Mic. 7. 18 because he *d.* in mercy
Mal. 2. 17 and he *d.* in them
Rom. 7. 22 I *d.* in the law of God

Delightsome. *Delightful.*
Mal. 3. 12 for ye shall be a *d.* land

Deliver. *Gave, give, free.*
Gen. 32. 11 *d.* me, I pray thee
Ex. 2. 19 an Egyptian *d.* us out of
Lev. 26. 26 they shall *d.* your bread
Num. 21. 2 if thou *d.* this people
Deut. 1. 27 *d.* us into hand of Amor.
Josh. 2. 24 hath *d.* into our hands
Judg. 1. 2 have *d.* the land into
1 Sam. 14. 10 Lord hath *d.* them
2 Sam. 3. 14 *d.* me my wife Michel
1 K. 8. 46 *d.* them to the enemy
2 K. 3. 10 *d.* them into hand of Moa.
1 Chr. 14. 10 and wilt thou *d.* them
2 Chr. 6. 36 *d.* them over before en.
Ez. 8. 36 *d.* the king's commission
Neh. 9. 27 thou *d.* them into hand
Esth. 6. 9 let appar. and horse be *d.*
Job 5. 4 neither is th. any to *d.* them
Ps. 7. 1 that persecute me, and *d.*
    18. 17; 22. 8; 25.20; 31.2; 33.19
Prov. 2. 12 *d.* thee from way of evil
Isa. 5. 29 and none shall *d.* it
Jer. 1. 8 I am with thee to *d.* thee
Lam. 1. 14 Lord hath *d.* me into
Ezek. 3. 19 thou hast *d.* thy soul
Hos. 2. 10 none shall *d.* her out
Am. 2. 14 nei. shall the mighty *d.*
Jonah 4. 6 to *d.* him from grief
Mic. 5. 6 thus shall he *d.* us
Zeph. 1. 18 nei. be able to *d.* them
Zech. 11. 6 I will *d.* the men ev. one
Mat. 5. 25 adver. *d.* thee to *d.* judge
    11. 27; 18. 34; 20. 19; 25. 14; 26. 15
Mark 7. 13 trad. which ye have *d.*
    9. 31; 10. 33; 15. 1, 10, 15
Luke 1. 2 even as *d.* them unto us
John 18. 30 we would not have *d.*
Acts 6. 14 customs which Moses *d.*
Rom. 4. 25 *d.* for our offences
1 Cor. 5. 5 to *d.* such .. unto Satan
2 Cor. 4. 11 we .. are alway *d.* unto
1 Thes. 1. 10 Jesus, which *d.* us
2 Thes. 3. 2 th. we may be *d.* from
2 Tim. 3. 11 out of all the L. *d.* me
Heb. 11. 11 through faith Sah. was *d.*
2 Pet. 2. 7 and *d.* just Lot, vexed
R. V. Lev. 6. 4; 2 Sam. 10. 10; 1
    Chr. 19. 11 committed; Deut. 5.
    22 gave; Judg. 2. 16, 18; 3. 9, 31;
    8. 22; 10. 12; 12. 2, 3 saved; 2
    K. 18. 30; 19. 10; Isa. 36. 15
    given; 1 Chr. 11. 14 defended;
    Ps. 55. 18; 78. 42 redeemed; 81.
    6 freed; Ezek. 6. 21; Mark 9. 31;
    15. 1, 10 delivered up; Mic. 4. 10
    rescued

Deliverance. *Escape, safety.*
Gen. 45. 7 to save .. by a great *d.*
Judg. 15. 18 hast given this gr. *d.*
2 K. 5. 1 Lord hath given *d.*
1 Chr. 11. 14 L. saved by a great *d.*
Ez. 9. 13 hast given such *d.* as this
Esth. 4. 14 *d.* arise to the Jews
Ps. 18. 50 great *d.* giveth he to k.
Isa. 26. 18 not wrought any *d.* in
Joel 2. 32 in Jerusalem shall be *d.*
Obad. 17 mount Zion shall be *d.*
Luke 4. 18 preach *d.* to captives.
Heb. 11. 35 tortured, not accep. *d.*
R. V. 2 K. 5. 1; 13. 17; 1 Chr. 11.
    14 victory; Joel 2. 32; Obad. 17
    those that escape; Luke 4. 18 re-
    lease

Deliverer. *Who delivers.*
Judg. 3. 9 Lord raised up a *d.*
2 Sam. 22. 2 L. is my rock and *d.*
Ps. 18. 2; 40. 17; 70. 5: 144. 2
Acts 7. 35 did God send to be a *d.*
Rom. 11. 26 shall come of Sion .. *D.*
R. V. Judg. 3. 9, 15 saviour

Delivery. *Bringing forth.*
Isa. 26. 17 wom. near time of her *d.*

Delusion. *Error, vexation.*
Isa. 66. 4 I will choose their *d.*
2 Thes. 2. 11 G. shall send strong *d.*

R. V. 2 Thes. 2. 11 working of
error
Demand (*n*.). *Requirement.*
Dan. 4. 17 and the *d*. by the word
Demand. *Ask, require.*
Ex. 5. 14 officers over them *d*.
2 Sam. 11. 7 David *d*. of him how
Job 38. 3 I will *d*. of thee, and ans.
Dan. 2. 27 secret which the king *d*.
Mat. 2. 4 *d*. of them where Christ
Luke 17. 20 when he was *d*. of Phar.
Acts 21. 33 chief capt. *d*. who he was
R. V. 2 Sam. 11. 7; Luke 3. 14
asked; Mat. 2. 4; Acts 21. 33 in-
quired
Demonstration. *Showing out.*
1 Cor. 2. 4.*d*. of the Spirit and pow.
Den. *Cave, pit, lair, haunt.*
Judg. 6. 2 chil. of Israel made *d*.
Job 37. 8 beasts go into their *d*.
Ps. 104. 22 lay them down in *d*.
S. of S. 4. 8 from the lion's *d*.
Isa. 11. 8 on the cockatrice's *d*.
Jer 9. 11 make Jerusalem a *d*. of
Dan. 6. 7–24 cast into *d*. of lions
Am. 3. 4 will .. lion cry out of *d*.
Nah. 2. 12 filled .. *d*. with ravin
Mat. 21. 13 made it a *d*. of thieves
Mark 11. 17; Luke 19. 46
Heb. 11. 38 *d*. and caves of earth
Rev. 6. 15 in *d*. and rocks of mount.
R. V. Jer. 9. 11; 10. 22 dwelling
place; Job 37. 8 coverts; Rev. 6.
15 caves
Denied. *See* DENY.
Denounce. *Put before, declare.*
Deut. 30. 18 I *d*. unto you this day
Deny. *Lie, feign.*
Gen. 18. 15 Sarah denied, saying, I
Josh. 24. 27 lest ye *d*. your God
Job 8. 18 it shall *d*. him, saying
Prov. 30. 9 lest I be full, and *d*.
Withhold, keep back.
1 K. 20. 7 and I *d*. him not
Prov. 30. 7 *d*. me them not before
Withhold, refuse, reject.
Mat. 10. 33 whosoever shall *d*. me
16. 24; 26. 35, 70, 72, 75;
Mark 8. 34 let him *d*. himself
14. 30, 31, 7, 72
Luke 8. 45 when all *d*., Peter and
John 1. 20 he confessed, and *d*. not
Acts 3. 13 *d*. him in the presence
1 Tim. 5. 8 he hath *d*. the faith
2 Tim. 2. 12 if we *d*. him, he also
Tit. 1. 16 in works they *d*. him
2 Pet. 2. 1 *d*. the Lord that bought th.
1 John 2. 22 that *d*. that Jesus is C.
Jude 4 *d*. the only Lord God
Rev. 2. 13 and hast not *d*. my faith
Depart. *Go away, remove, with-*
draw.
Gen. 12. 4 Abram *d*., as the Lord
14. 12; 21. 14; 24. 10; 26. 17;
Ex. 19. 2 for they were *d*. from
Lev. 25. 41 then shall he *d*. from thee
Num. 10. 33 they *d*. from .. mount
Deut. 1. 19 when we *d*. from Horeb
Josh. 2. 21 and they *d*., and she
Judg. 9. 55 *d*. every man unto his pl.
1 Sam. 6. 6 let peo. go, and they *d*.
2 Sam. 6. 19 peo. .. every one
1 K. 12. 5 *d*. yet for three days
2 K. 1. 4 surely die, and Elijah *d*.
1 Chr. 16. 43 all the people *d*.
2 Chr. 10. 5 and the people *d*.
Ez. 8. 31 then we *d*. from the river
Neh. 9. 19 pillar of cloud *d*. not
Job. 15. 30 he shall not *d*. out of *d*.
Ps. 6. 8. *d*. from me, all ye work.
Prov. 3. 7 feared L. and *d*. from e.
Isa. 7. 17 that day that Ephraim *d*.
Jer. 17. 5 and whose heart *d*. from
Lam. 4. 15 *d*. ye, it is unclean
Dan. 9. 5 by *d*. from thy precepts
Hos. 10. 5 glory thereof is *d*.
Zech. 10. 11 sceptre of E. shall *d*.
Mal. 2. 8 but we are *d*. out of the
Mat. 8. 18 gave com. to *d*. unto oth.
Mark 1. 35 *d*. into a solitary place
Luke 1. 23 he *d*. to his own house
John 4. 3 left Judea and *d*. again
Acts 10. 7 an. which spake .. was *d*.
1 Cor. 7. 10 let not the wife *d*.
2 Cor. 12. 8 besought that it might *d*.
Phil. 4. 15 I *d*. from Macedonia

1 Tim. 4. 1 lat. times some shall *d*.
2 Tim. 2. 19 ev. one *d*. from iniq.
Phile. 15 he . . *d*. for a season
Jas. 2. 16 *D*. in peace, be warned
Heb. 3. 12 take heed, in *d*. from
R. V. very largely, go, went away,
withdrew.
Departure. *Going out.*
Ezek. 26. 18 sea troubled at thy *d*.
2 Tim. 4. 6 my *d*. is at hand
Deposed. *Put down or out.*
Dan. 5. 20 *d*. from his kingly throne
Deprive. *Bereave, dispossess.*
Gen. 27. 45 why should I be *d*.
Job. 39. 17 God hath *d*. her of wisd.
Isa. 38. 10 I am *d*. of . . years
R. V. Gen. 27. 45 bereaved
Depth. *Deep.*
Ex. 15. 5 *d*. have covered them
Deut. 8. 7 *d*. that spring out of val.
Job 28. 14 *d*. sayeth, It is not in me
Ps. 33. 7 layeth . . *d*. in storehouses
Prov. 3. 20 by knowl. *d*. are broken
Isa. 7. 11 ask it in *d*. or in height
Jonah 2. 5 *d*. closed around me
Mic. 7. 19 sins into *d*. of the sea
Mat. 18. 6 drowned in the *d*. of
Mark 4. 5 bec. it had no *d*. of earth
Rom. 8. 39 nor height, nor *d*., nor
Eph. 3. 18 breadth, length, and *d*.
Rev. 2. 24 not known the, *d*. of S.
R. V. Ex. 15. 5, 8; Ps. 33. 7 deeps;
Job 28. 14; 38. 16; Prov. 8. 27
deep; Mark 4. 5 deepness
Deputy. *Governor, pro-consul.*
1 K. 22. 47 in Edom; a *d*. was king
Esth. 8. 9; 9. 3 *d*. and rulers
Acts 13. 7, 8, 12 *d*. of the country
18. 12 Gallio was the *d*. of Achaia,
19. 38 and there are *d*.; let them
R. V. Esth. 8. 9; 9. 3 governors;
Acts 13. 7, 8, 12; 18. 12; 19. 38
pro-consul
Deride. *Laugh at, scoff.*
Hab. 1. 10 sh. *d*. every stronghold
Luke 16. 14 Pharisees also *d*. him
23. 35 rulers also . . *d*. him, saying
R. V. Luke 16. 14; 23. 35 scoffed at
Derision. *Scorn.*
Job 30. 1 younger . . have me in *d*.
Ps. 2. 4 Lord shall have them in *d*.
Jer. 20. 7 I am in *d*. daily, every
Lam. 3. 14 I was *d*. to all my people
Ezek. 23, 32 be . . and had in *d*.
Hos. 7. 16 this shall be their *d*.
R. V. Jer. 20. 7 laughing stock
Descend. *Go or come down.*
Gen. 28. 12 angels . . ascend. and *d*.
Ex. 19. 18 because the Lord *d*.
Num. 34. 11 the border shall *d*.
Deut. 9. 21 the brook that *d*. out of
Josh. 2. 23 *d*. from the mountain
1 Sam. 26. 10 shall *d*. into battle
Ps. 49. 17 his glory shall not *d*.
Prov. 30. 4 hath asc. into hea. or *d*.?
Isa. 5. 14 that rejoiceth, shall *d*.
Ezek. 26. 20 down with them that *d*.
Mat. 3. 16 he saw Spirit of God *d*.
Mark 1. 10 saw Spirit like a dove *d*.
Luke 3. 22 the Holy Ghost *d*.
John 1. 32 Spirit *d*. from heaven
Acts 10. 11 a certain vessel *d*.
Rom. 10. 7 Who shall *d*. into deep
Eph. 4. 9 that he also *d*. first into
1 Thes. 4. 16 Lord himself shall *d*.
Jas. 3. 15 this wisdom *d*. not fr. ab.
Rev. 21. 10 Jerus. *d*. out of heaven
R. V. Num. 34. 11; 1 Sam. 26. 10
go down; Mark 15. 32; Ps. 133. 3;
Acts 24. 1; Jas. 3. 15; Rev. 21 10
come or came down; Josh. 17. 9;
18. 13. 16, 17 went down
Descent. *Coming down.*
Luke 19. 37 *d*. of mount of Olives
Genealogy.
Heb. 7. 3, 6 without *d*., nei. begin.
R. V. Heb. 7. 3, 6 genealogy
Describe. *Write out, say out.*
Josh. 18. 4–9 *d*. it according to
Rom. 4. 6 David . . *d*. the blessed.
10. 5 Moses *d*. the righteousness
R. V. Rom. 4. 6 pronounceth bless-
ing upon; 10. 5 writeth
Descry. R. V. *spy out.*
Judg. 1. 23 Joseph sent to *d*. Bethel
Desert. *Deserving.*

Ps. 28. 4 render to them their *d*.
Ezek. 7. 27 according to their *d*.
Desert. *Waste place, wilderness.*
Ex. 3. 1 flock to back side of the *d*.
Num. 20. 1 whole cong. into *d*. of
Deut. 32. 10 found him in a *d*. land
2 Chr. 26. 10 built towers in the *d*.
Job 24. 5 wild asses in the *d*. go **th.**
Ps. 102. 6 like an owl of the *d*.
Isa. 48. 21 led him through the *d*.
Jer. 25. 24 people that dwell in *d*.
Ezek. 47. 8 go down into the *d*.
Mat. 24. 26 Behold, he is in the *d*.
Mark 1. 45 was without in *d*. places
Luke 4. 42 went into a *d*. place
John 6. 31 did eat manna in the *d*.
Acts 8. 26 unto Gaza, which is *d*.
Heb. 11. 38 they wandered in *d*.
R. V. Ps. 102. 6 waste places; Ezek.
47. 8 Arabah; Ex. 3. 1; 5. 3; 19.
2; 23. 31; Num. 21. 1; 27. 14; 33
16; 2 Chr. 26. 10; Isa. 21. 1; Jer.
25. 24; Mat. 24. 26; John 6. 31
wilderness.
Deserving. *Deed, desert.*
Judg. 9. 17 according to the *d*. of
Desirable. *Worthy.*
Ezek. 23. 6, 12, 23 *d*. young men
Desire (*n*.). *Longing, delight,*
wish.
Gen. 3. 16 thy *d*. be to thy husband
Deut. 18. 6 come with all *d*. of mind
1 Sam. 9. 20 all the *d*. of Israel
2 Sam. 23. 5 all my salvation and *d*.
1 K. 5. 8 I will do all thy *d*.
2 Chr. 9. 12 gave to queen .. her *d*.
Job 31. 16 withheld poor from .. *d*.
34. 36 my *d*. is that Job be tried
Ps. 37. 4 give thee the *d*. of thine h.
Prov. 10. 24 *d*. of right. . . be grant.
Eccl. 12. 5 burden, and *d*. shall fail
S. of S. 7. 10 and his *d*. is tow. me
Isa. 26. 8 *d*. of our soul is to thy na.
Dan. 11. 37 nor the *d*. of women
Hos. 10. 10 *d*. that I should chastise
Mic. 7. 3 uttereth mischievous *d*.
Hab. 2. 5 enlargeth his *d*. as hell
Hag. 2. 7 the *d*. of all nations shall
Luke 22. 15 with *d*. I have desired
Rom. 15. 23 having a great *d*.
2 Cor. 7. 11 yea, what vehement *d*.
Eph. 2. 3 fulfilling *d*. of the flesh
Phil. 1. 23 having *d*. to depart
1 Thes. 2. 17 see your face with .. *d*.
R. V. Job 31. 35 signature; 2 Cor.
7. 7; Rom. 15. 23 longing; Ps. 78.
29 lusteth after
Desire (*v*.). *Ask, wish, crave.*
Ex. 10. 11 serve L.; that ye did *d*.
Deut. 5. 21 nei. . . . *d*. neighbor's wife
Judg. 8. 24 I would *d*. a request
1 Sam. 12. 13 behold the king ye *d*.
2 Sam. 3. 21 all that thine heart *d*.
1 K. 11. 37 all that thy soul *d*.
2 K. 4. 28 did I *d*. a son of my lord
2 Chr. 11. 23 he *d*. many wives
Neh. 1, 11 servants who *d*. to fear
Esth. 2. 13 what she *d*. was given
Job 13. 2 to reason with God
Ps. 19. 10 more to be *d*. than gold
Prov. 13. 4 soul of the sluggard *d*.
Eccl. 6. 2 nothing of all he *d*.
Isa. 26. 9 with my soul have I *d*.
Jer. 17. 16 nei. have I. *d*. the .. day
Dan. 2. 16 *d*. of the king that
Hos. 6. 6 I *d*. mercy, not sacrifice
Am. 5. 18 Woe unto you that *d*.
Mic. 7. 1 my soul *d*. the . . fruit
Zeph. 2. 1 gather, O nation not *d*.
Mat. 20. 20 worshipping him and *d*.
Mark 10. 35 do whatsoever we .. *d*.
Luke 23. 25 released . . whom they *d*.
John 12. 21 *d*. him, saying, Sir, we
Acts 16. 39 *d*. them to de. out of c.
1 Cor. 14. 1 *d*. spiritual gifts
2 Cor. 5. 2 *d*. to be clothed upon
Gal. 4. 9 *d*. again to be born
Eph. 3. 13 *d*. that ye faint not
Phil. 4. 17 but I *d*. fruit that may ab.
Col. 1. 9 *d*. that ye might be filled
1 Tim. 3. 1 he *d*. a good work
2 Tim. 1. 4 greatly *d*. to see thee
Heb. 6. 11 we *d*. that every one
1 Pet. 12 the angels *d*. to look into
Rev. 9. 6 shall *d*. to die, and death
R. V. Job 20, 20 delighteth; Ps. 27. 4

Mat. 16. 1 ; Mark 15. 6 ; John 12.
21 ; Acts 3. 14 ; 7.46 ; 9. 2 ; 13.21,
28 ; 18. 20 ; 1 John 5. 15 asked ;
Hos. 6. 6 ; Mic. 7. 1 desire ; Luke
9. 9 ; Acts 3. 7 sought ; 2 Cor. 8. 6 ;
12. 18 exhorted

Desirous. *Wishful.*
Prov. 23. 3 be not d. of dainties
Luke 23. 8 Herod was d. to see him
John 16. 19 they were d. to ask
2 Cor. 11. 32 gov. kept the city d.
Gal. 5. 26 not be d. of vain glory
1 Thes. 2. 8 affectionately d. of you

Desolate. *Lonely, bare, forlorn.*
Gen. 47. 19 that the land be not d.
Ex. 23. 29 lest the land become d.
Lev. 26. 33 your land shall be d.
2 Sam. 13. 20 Tamar remained d.
2 Chr. 36. 21 long as she lay d.
Job 3. 14 which built d. places of e.
Ps. 25. 16 have mercy, I am d.
Isa. 1. 7 your country is d., cit. burn.
Jer. 10. 25 made his habitation d.
Lam. 1. 4 Zion, all her gates are d.
Ezek. 26. 19 make thee a d. city
Dan. 9. 27 be poured upon the d.
Hos. 5. 9 Ephraim shall be d.
Joel 2. 3 behind them a d. wilderness
Am. 7. 9 high places of I. shall be d.
Mic. 6. 13 making thee d. because
Zeph. 3. 6 their towers are d.
Zech. 7. 14 land was d. after them
Mal. 1. 4 and build the d. places
Mat. 23. 38 your house is left d.
Luke 13. 35 house .. left unto you d.
Acts 1. 20 let his habitation be d.
Gal. 4. 27 the d. hath many children
1 Tim. 5. 5 she is a widow, and d.
Rev. 17. 16 make her d. and naked

Desolation. *Loneliness, forlorn-*
ness,dreariness, sadness, affliction.
Lev. 26. 31 bring your sanc. unto d.
Josh. 8. 28 made it an heap, a d.
2 K. 22. 19 they should become a d.
2 Chr. 30. 7 gave them up to d.
Ez. 9. 9 repair the d. thereof
Job 30. 14 in the d. they rolled
Ps. 46. 8 L., what d. he hath made
Prov. 1. 27 your fear cometh as d.
Isa. 51. 19 two things are come .. d.
Jer. 22. 5 house shall become a d.
Lam. 3. 47 fear is come, d. and destr.
Ezek. 7. 27 prince .. clothed with d.
Dan. 9. 2 seventy years in d.
Hos. 12. 1 increaseth lies and d.
Joel 3. 19 Egypt snall be a d.
Mic. 6. 16 should make thee a d.
Zeph. 2. 14 d. shall be in the thresh.
Mat. 24. 15 see the abomination of d.
Mark 13. 14 shall the .. abom. of d.
Luke 21. 20 the d. thereof is nigh
R. V. Jer. 49. 13, 17 astonishment ;
Prov. 1. 27 storm ; Lam. 3. 47 de-
vastation ; Job 30. 14 ; Ez. 9. 9 ; Ps.
74. 31 ruins

Despair (n.). *Hopelessness.*
2 Cor. 4. 8 perplexed. but not in d.
Despair (v.). *Give up hope.*
1 Sam. 27. 1 Saul shall d. of me
Eccl. 2. 20 cause my heart to d.
2 Cor. 1. 8 we d. even of life
Desperate. *Hopeless, despairing.*
Job 6. 26 speeches of one that is d.
Isa. 17. 11 the day of .. d. sorrow
Desperately. *Sickly, furiously.*
Jer. 17. 9 above all .. and d. wicked
Despise. *Loathe, contemn, reject.*
Genesis 25. 34 Esau d. his birthright
Lev. 26. 15 shall d. my statutes
Num. 15. 31 he hath d. the word
Judg. 9. 38 people thou hast d.
1 Sam. 2. 30 they that d. me shall
2 Sam. 6. 16 she d. him in .. heart
2 K. 19. 21 daughter of Zion hath d.
1 Chr. 15. 29 d. him in her heart
2 Chr. 36. 16 d. his word, and mis.
Neh. 2. 19 laughed to scorn, and d.
Esth. 1. 17 they shall d. .. husbands
Job. 5. 17 d. not the chastening of
Ps. 22. 24 hath not d. nor abhorred
Prov. 14. 2 he that is perverse .. d.
Eccl. 9. 16 poor man's wisdom is d.
S. of S. 8. 1 I should not be d.
Isa. 37. 22 daughter of Zion hath d.
Jer 4. 30 lovers will d. thee
Lam. 2. 6. d. in the indignation of

Ezek. 16. 57 daugh. of Phil. which d.
Am. 2. 4 they have d. the law
Obad. 2 Behold .. thou art greatly d.
Zech. 4. 10 d. day of small things?
Mal. 1. 6 priests that d. my name
Mat. 6. 24 hold .. one, d. the other
Luke 10. that d. you, d. me
Acts 19. 27 temple of Diana .. be d.
Rom. 2. 4 Or d. thou the riches of
1 Cor. 11. 22 d. ye the church of God
Gal. 4. 14 tempt. in flesh ye d. not
1 Thes. 5. 20 d. not prophesyings
1 Tim. 4. 12 no man d. thy youth
Tit. 2. 15 let no man d. thee
Heb. 12. 5 d. not the chastening of
Jas. 2. 6 ye have d. the poor
2 Pet. 2. 10 and d. government
R. V. Lev. 26. 15 reject ; 26. 43 ;
Num. 11. 20. 14. 31 ; Ps. 53. 5 ;
Ezek. 20. 13, 16,24 ; Am. 2. 4 re-
jected ; Luke 18. 9 Heb. 10. 28 set
at nought : Jas. 2. 6 ; 1 Cor. 4. 10
dishonour ; Acts 19. 27 made of no
account : Prov. 19. 16 careless of ;
Luke 10. 16 ; 1 Thes. 4. 8 rejecteth

Despiser. *Who despises.*
Acts 13. 41 behold, ye d. and wonder
2 Tim. 3. 3 d. of those .. good
R. V. 2 Tim. 3. 3 no lovers of

Despite. *Spite, malice.*
Ezek. 25. 6 rejoice .. with all thy d.
Heb. 10. 29 done d. unto Sp. of gr.

Despiteful. *Spiteful.*
Ezek. 25. 15 take ven. with d. heart
Rom. 1. 30 d., proud, boasters
R. T. Rom. 1. 30 insolent

Despitefully. *Spitefully.*
Mat. 5. 44 pray for .. wh. d. use you
Luke 6. 28 pray for .. which d. use
Acts 14. 5 to use them d., to stone th.
R. V. Acts 14. 5 shamefully

Destitute. *Lacking, devoid,*
naked.
Gen. 24. 27 not left d. my master
Ps. 102. 17 regard prayer of the d.
Prov. 15. 21 joy to him that is d.
1 Tim. 6. 5 cor. minds, d. of truth
Heb. 11. 37 being d., afflicted, tor.
Jas. 2. 15 sister d. of daily food
R. V. Gen. 24. 27 forsaken ; Prov.
15. 21 void ; 1 Tim. 6. 5 bereft ;
Jas. 2. 15 in lack

Destroy. *Blot out, cut off, kill.*
Gen. 6. 13 will d. them with thee
Ex. 10. 7 knowest that Egypt is d?
Lev. 26. 30 will d. your high pl.
Num. 21. 2 will ut. d. their cities
Deut. 2. 34 d. men and women
Josh. 2. 10 Og, whom ye utterly d.
Judg. 1. 17 Zeph., and utterly d. it
1 Sam. 15. 3 d. all that they have
2 Sam. 14. 7 will d. the heir also
1 K. 13. 34 d. it from off .. earth
2 K. 10. 17 Ahab, till he had d. him
1 Chr. 5. 25 whom God d. before
2 Chr. 20. 10 turn. from them and d.
Ez. 4. 15 which cause was city d.
Esth. 3. 9 written that they be d.
Job 12. 23 increas. nations, and d.
Ps. 78. 38 forgave .. and d. them not
Prov. 6. 32 doeth it d. his own soul
Eccl. 7. 16 why shouldest .. d. thy.
Isa. 10. 7 in his heart to d. nations
Jer. 5. 9 will utterly d. them
Lam. 3. 66 and d. them in anger
Dan. 8. 24 shall d. wonderfully
Hos. 2. 12 I will d. her vines
Am. 2. 9 yet d. I the Amorites
Obad. 8 d. the wise men of Edom
Mic. 5. 10 I will d. thy chariots
Zeph. 2. 5 Can., I will even d. thee
Mal. 3. 11 shall not d. the fruits
Mat. 2. 13 seek the young child to d.
10. 28 ; 12. 14 ; 21. 41 ; 22. 7 ; 27. 20
Mark 1. 24 art thou come to d.
Luke 6. 9 to save life, or to d. it?
6. 9 ; 9. 56 ; 17. 27 ; 19. 47 ; 20. 16
John 10. 10 steal, kill, and to d.
Acts 3. 23 every soul shall be d.
Rom. 14. 15 d. not him with .. meat
1 Cor. 1. 19 will d. the wisdom of
2 Cor. 4. 9 cast down, but not d.
Gal. 2. 18 build again .. which I d.
2 Thes. 2. 8 d. with the brightness of
Heb. 2. 14 through d. he might d.
2 Pet. 2. 12 made to be taken and d.

1 John 3. 8 d. works of the devil
Rev. 8. 9 third part of ships were d.
11. 18 d. them which d. the earth
R. V. Gen. 18. 23, 24 ; 1 Chr. 21. 12
consume ; Ex. 23. 27 ; Deut. 7. 23 ;
Ps. 144. 6 discomfit ; Ex. 34. 13 ;
Num. 24. 17 ; Deut. 7. 5 ; Ps. 28.
5 break down ; Deut. 7. 24 ; 9. 3 ;
28. 51 ; Josh. 7. 7 perish ; 2 Sam.
22. 41 ; Ps. 18. 40 ; 54. 5 ; 69. 4 ;
101. 5 ; 1 K. 15. 13 cut off, or down ;
Ps. 5. 10 hold guilty ; Prov. 15. 25
root up ; Acts 9. 21 ; Gal. 1. 23
made havoc ; Rom. 14. 20 overthrow ; 1 Cor. 6. 13 ; Heb. 2. 14 ;
2 Thes. 2. 8 bring to nought ; Rom.
6. 6 done away ; 1 Cor. 10. 5. 26 abolished ; 1 Cor. 10. 9, 10 ; 2 Pet. 2. 12
perish ; Acts 19. 27 despised

Destroyer. *Who destroys.*
Ex. 12. 23 Lord will not suffer .. d.
Judg. 16. 24 the d. of our country
Job 33. 22 Yea .. and his life to the d.
Ps. 17. 4 kept me from path of d.
Prov. 28. 24 rob. fa. is comp. of a d.
Isa. 49. 27 thy d. and they that
Jer. 4. 7 d. of the Gentiles on his way
R. V. Jer. 50. 11 that plunder ; Job
15. 21 ; spoiler ; Ps. 17. 4 violent

Destroying. *Destructive.*
Isa. 28. 2 hail, a d. storm, as a flood
Jer. 51. 25 against thee, O d. mount.
Ezek. 9. 1 man with d. weapon

Destruction. *Ruin, calamity.*
Deut. 7. 23 destroy with a mighty d.
1 Sam. 5. 9 with very great d.
1 K. 20. 42 appointed to utter d.
2 Chr. 22. 4 counsellors to his d.
Esth. 8. 6 see d. of my kindred
Job 5. 21 neither be afraid of d.
18. 12 ; 21. 17 ; 26. 6 ; 28. 22 ; 30. 12
Ps. 35. 8 let d. come unawares
55. 23 ; 73. 18 ; 88. 11 ; 90. 3 ; 91. 6
Prov. 1. 27 d. come. as a whirlwind
10. 14 ; 13. 3 ; 14. 28 ; 15. 11 ; 16. 18
Isa. 1. 28 d. of transgressions
Jer. 4. 6 from the north, a great d.
Lam. 2. 11 d. of daughter of people
Ezek. 7. 25 d. cometh, seek peace
Hos. 9. 6 are gone, because of d.
Joel 1. 15 as d. from the Almighty
Obad. 12 in d. the day of their
Mic. 2. 10 destroy .. with sore d.
Zech. 14. 11 sh. be no more utter d.
Mat. 7. 13 broad the way .. to d.
Rom. 3. 16 d. and misery in ways
1 Cor. 5. 5 Satan for d. of flesh
2 Cor. 10. 8 for edi. not for your d.
Phil. 3. 19 walk, whose end is d.
1 Thes. 5. 3 sudden d. cometh on th.
1 Tim. 6. 9 drown men in d. and per.
2 Pet. 2. 1 and bring upon th. swift d.
R. V. Deut. 7. 23 ; 1 Sam. 5. 9, 11
discomfiture ; Job 18. 12 ; 21. 17,
30 ; 31. 3, 23 ; Prov. 1. 17 calamity ;
Job 26. 6 ; Prov. 15. 11 ; 27. 20
Abaddon ; Prov. 24.2 oppression ;
Phil. 3. 19 perdition ; 2 Cor. 10. 8 ;
13. 10, casting down

Detain. *Keep in, restrain.*
1 Sam. 21. 7 serv. d. before the Lord
Judg. 13. 15 let us d. thee, until
Determinate. *Specific, distinct.*
Acts 2. 23 del. by the d. counsel
Determination. *Judgment.*
Zeph. 3. 8 my d. is to gather nations
Determine. *Say, decide, resolve.*
1 Sam. 20. 7 this evil is d. by him
2 Sam. 13. 32 this hath been d.
2 Chr. 2. 1 S. d. to build .. hous
Esth. 7. 7 was evil d. against him
Job 14. 5 Seeing his days are d.
Isa. 19. 17 which he hath d. against
Dan. 9. 24 seventy weeks are d.
Luke 22. 22 Son .. goeth, as was d.
Acts 3. 13 Pilate, d. to let him go
11. 29 ; 15. 2 ; 17. 26 ; 12. 39 ; 20. 16
1 Cor. 2. 2 I d. not to know thing
2 Cor. 2. 1 d. this with myself, that I
Tit. 3. 12 for I have d. there to winter
R. V. 2 Chr. 2. 1 ; Isa. 19. 17 ; Acts
20. 3 purposed ; Dan. 9. 24 decreed ; Acts 15. 37 was minded ;
19. 39 settled in the regular ; 15. 2
the brethren appointed.

Detest. *Hold in abomination.*

Deut. 7. 26 thou shalt utterly *d*. it
Detestable. *Abominable.*
Jer. 16. 18 carcases of their *d*. things
Ezek. 5. 11 defiled with thy *d*. things
7. 20; 11. 18, 21; 37. 23
Device. *Thought, design, plot.*
2 Chr. 2. 14 find out every *d*. which
Esth. 8. 3 *d*. he had devised ag. Jews
Job 5. 12 disap. the *d*. of the crafty
Ps. 33. 10 maketh *d*. of the people
Prov. 19. 21 many *d*. in man's heart
Eccl. 9. 10 no work, nor *d*., nor know.
Jer. 11. 19 devised *d*. against me
Lam. 3. 62 their *d*. against me all
Dan. 11. 24 forecast his *d*. against
Acts 17. 29 by art and man's *d*.
2 Cor. 2. 11 not ignorant of his *d*.
R. V. Ps. 33. 10 thoughts; Lam. 3.
62 imagination
Devil. *Hairy one, goat.*
Lev. 17. 7 no more offer .. unto *d*.
2 Chr. 11. 15 for high pl. and .. *d*.
Spoiler, destroyer.
Deut. 32. 17 they sacrificed unto *d*.
Ps. 106. 37 sons and daugh. unto *d*.
Demon, shade.
Mat. 7. 22 name have cast out *d*.
9. 33; 10. 8; 11. 18; 12. 24; 17. 18
Mark 1. 34 and cast out many *d*.
3. 15; 6. 13; 7. 26; 9. 38; 16. 17
Luke 4. 33 spirit of an unclean *d*.
7. 33; 8. 2; 9. 1; 10. 17; 11. 14
John 7. 20 said, Thou hast a *d*. who
1 Cor. 10. 20 they sacrifice to *d*.
1 Tim. 4. 1 and doctrines of *d*.
Jas. 2. 19 the *d*. also believe, and **tr.**
Rev. 9. 20 should not worship *d*.
Accuser, tempter, adversary.
Mat. 4. 1 to be tempted of the *d*.
4. 5, 8, 11; 13. 39; 25. 41
Luke 4. 2 forty days tempted of .. *d*.
John 6. 70 and one of you is a *d*.
Acts 10. 38 were oppressed of the *d*.
Eph. 4. 27 Neither give place to .. *d*.
1 Tim. 3. 6 fall into con. of the *d*.
Heb. 2. 14 death, that is, the *d*.
Jas. 4. 7 resist the *d*., and he will flee
1 Pet 5. 8 your adversary the *d*.
1 John 3. 8 that com. sin is of the *d*.
Jude 9 when contending with the *d*.
Rev. 2. 10 *d*. shall cast some into pr.
12. 9, 12; 20. 2, 10
R. V. Lev. 17. 7; 2 Chr. 11. 15 he
goats, Deut. 32. 17; Ps. 106. 37
demons
Devise. *Think, design, invent.*
Ex. 31. 4 to *d*. cunning works
2 Sam. 14. 14 yet doth he *d*. means
1 K. 12. 33 *d*. of his own heart
Esth. 8. 3 *d*. against the Jews
Ps. 35. 4 brought to confu. that *d*.
Prov. 3. 29 *d*. not evil against neig.
Isa. 32. 7 he *d*. wicked devices
Jer. 11. 19 knew not they had *d*.
Lam. 2. 17 L. hath done .. which .. *d*.
Ezek. 11. 2 men that *d*. mischief
Mic. 2. 1 Woe to them that *d*. iniq.
2. Pet. 1. 16 not fol. cunning. *d*. fables
Devote. *Vow, set apart, consecrate.*
Lev. 27. 21 be holy .. as a field *d*.
27. 28 every *d*. thing is holy
Num. 18. 14 every thing *d*. in Israel
Devotions. R. V. *objects of worship.*
Acts 17. 23 and beheld your *d*.
Devour. *Eat, consume.*
Gen. 31. 15 hath *d*. also our money
Ex. 24. 17 glory of L. .. like *d*. fire
Lev. 10. 2 fire from Lord *d*. them
Deut. 32. 17 they shall be *d*., and
Judg. 9. 15 fire *d*. cedars of Lebanon
2 Sam. 2. 26 shall .. sword *d*. forever
2 Chr. 7. 13 command locusts to *d*.
Job 18. 13 *d*. strength of his skin
Ps. 18. 8 fire out of his mouth *d*.
Prov. 30. 14 *d*. the poor from .. e.
Isa. 1. 7 your land, strangers *d*. it
Jer. 2. 3 that *d*. him shall offend
3. 24; 5. 14; 8. 16; 10. 25; 12. 12
Lam. 2. 3 flaming fire which *d*.
Ezek. 7. 15 fam. and pest. shall *d*.
Dan. 7. 5 said, Arise, *d*. much flesh
Hos. 5. 7 now shall a mouth *d*. th.
Joel 1. 19 fire hath *d*. the pastures
Am. 1. 4 *d*. the palaces of Ben-hadad
Obad. 18 Esau, kindle in them and *d*.

Nah. 2. 13 sword shall *d*. thy .. lions
Hab. 3. 14 to. *d*. the poor secretly
Zech. 9. 15 L. .. *d*. and subdue with
Mat. 23. 14 ye *d*. widow's houses
Mark 4. 4 fowls .. air came and *d*. it
Luke 15. 30 *d*. thy living with harlots
2 Cor. 11. 20 suffer, if a man *d*. you
Gal. 5. 15 if ye bite and *d*. one ano.
Heb. 10. 27 shall *d*. the adversaries
Rev. 11. 5 fire proceedeth and *d*.
R. V. Ps. 80. 13 feed on; Isa. 42. 14
pant together; Prov. 19. 28; Hab.
1. 13; swalloweth up; Pr. 20. 25
rashly to say; Mat. 23. 14 ——
Devourer. *Who devours.*
Mal. 3. 11 I will rebuke the *d*.
Devouring. *Consuming.*
Ps. 52. 4 Thou lovest all *d*. words
Isa. 29. 6 the flame of *d*. fire
Devout. *Religious, reverent.*
Luke 2. 25 the man was just and *d*.
Acts 2. 5 *d*. men, of every nation
8. 2; 10. 2; 13. 50; 17. 4; 22. 12
Dew. *Dew, moisture.*
Gen. 27. 28 God give .. *d*. of heaven
Ex. 16. 13 the *d*. lay round about
Num. 11. 9 *d*. fell upon the camp
Deut. 32. 2 speech .. distil as the *d*.
Judg. 6. 37 if *d*. be on the fleece
2 Sam. 1. 21 let there be no *d*.
1 K. 17. 1 not be *d*. nor rain
Job. 29. 19 the *d*. lay all night
Ps. 110. 3 hast the *d*. of thy youth
Prov. 3. 20 clouds drop down the *d*.
S. of S. 5. 2 head is filled with *d*.
Isa. 18. 4 like a cloud of *d*. in heat
Dan. 4. 15 wet with *d*. of heaven
Hos. 6. 4 goodness is as .. early *d*.
Mic. 5. 7 in midst of people as *d*.
Hag. 1. 10 heaven is stayed from *d*.
Zech. 8. 12 heavens shall give *d*.
R. V. Ps. 133. 3 ——
Diadem. *Crown, mitre, tiara.*
Job 29. 14 judgment as robe and *d*.
Isa. 28. 5 Lord he, for a *d*. of beauty
Ezek. 21. 26 remove the *d*. and take
R. V. Ezek. 21. 26 mitre
Dial. *Ascent, step.*
2 K. 20. 11 gone down in the *d*. of
Isa. 38. 8 gone down in *d*. of Ahaz
Diamond. *Diamond, adamant.*
Ex. 28. 18 second row .. a *d*.
Ezek. 28. 13 sardius, topaz, and *d*.
Jer. 17. 1 written with point of *d*.
Did. *See Do.*
Die. *Breathe out, expire.*
Gen. 2. 17 eatest thereof shalt .. *d*.
Ex. 1. 6 Jos. *d*., and all his brethren
Lev. 8. 35 keep charge .. that ye *d*.
Num. 3. 4 N. and A. *d*. before the L.
Deut. 5. 25 why should we *d*.?
Josh. 5. 4 the men of war *d*. in wil.
Judg. 1. 7 Jerusalem, and there he *d*.
Ruth 1. 5 and Elimelech *d*. and was
1 Sam. 2. 33 all .. thine h. shall *d*.
2 Sam. 1. 15 smote him that he *d*.
1 K. 1. 52 if wicked .. he shall *d*.
2 K. 1. 4 shalt not come, but .. *d*.
1 Chr. 1. 51 Hadad *d*. also, and
2 Chr. 10. 18 stoned him .. that he *d*.
Job 2. 9 curse God and *d*.
Ps. 41. 5 when shall he *d*. and
Prov. 5. 23 shall *d*. without instruc.
Eccl. 2. 16 how *d*. the wise man?
Isa. 22. 13 to morrow we shall *d*.
Jer. 11. 21 prophesy not that thou *d*.
Ezek. 3. 18 thou shalt surely *d*.
Hos. 13. 1 when he offended, he *d*.
Jonah 4. 8 wished in himself to *d*.
Zech. 11. 9 said I, .. that *d*., let it *d*.
Mat. 22. 24 Moses said, if a man *d*.
Mark 12. 19 if man's brother *d*.
Luke 16. 22 the beggar *d*. and was
John 4. 49 come .. ere my child *d*.
6. 50; 8. 21; 11. 16; 12. 24; 18. 32
Acts 9. 37 she was sick and *d*.
Rom. 5. 6 Christ *d*. for the ungodly
1 Cor. 15. 22 as in Adam all *d*., so
2 Cor. 5. 14 judge, .. if one *d*. for all
Phil. 1. 21 to live is C., to die is gain
1 Thes. 4. 14 if we believe that J. *d*.
Heb. 7. 8 men that *d*. receive tithes
Rev. 3. 2 that are ready to *d*.
Diet. *Allowance.*
Jer. 52. 34 for his *d*., was con. *d*.
Differ. *Bear diversely.*

Rom. 12. 6 gifts *d*. according to
1 Cor. 4. 7 who maketh thee to *d*.
Gal. 4. 1 *d*. nothing from a servant
Difference. *Separation, distinction.*
Ex. 11. 7 Lord put a *d*. between
Lev. 10. 10 may put *d*. between holy
Acts 15. 9 put no *d*. between us
Rom. 3. 22 on all, there is no *d*.
1 Cor. 12. 5 are *d*. of administration
Jude 22 have compas. making a *d*.
R. V. 20. 25 separate; Acts 15. 9;
Rom. 3. 22; 10. 12 distinction;
Ezek. 22. 26 discern; 1 Cor. 12. 5
diversities; Jude 22 who are in
doubt
Dig. *Break earth, excavate.*
Gen. 21. 30 I have *d*. this well
Ex. 7. 24 all Egyptians *d*. round
Num. 21. 18 the princes *d*. the well
Deut. 23. 13 thou shalt *d*. therewith
2 Chr. 26. 10 and *d*. many wells
Neh. 9. 25 houses full .. wells *d*.
Job 3. 21 *d*. for it more than for
Ps. 7. 15 made a pit; and *d*. it
Prov. 16. 27 ungodly man *d*. up evil
Eccl. 10. 8 that *d*. a pit shall fall
Isa. 5. 6 not be pruned nor *d*.
Jer. 13. 7 went to Euphrates and *d*
Ezek. 8. 8 *d*. now in the wall
Am. 9. 2 though they *d*. into hell
Mat. 21. 33 *d*. a wine press in it
Mark 12. 1 *d*. .. the winefat, and
Luke 6. 48 man .. built an house, *d*.
Rom. 11. 3 killed the proph. and *d*.
R. V. Gen. 49. 6 houghed; Job 11.
8 search; 6. 27 make merchandise
of; Num. 21. 18 delved; Prov. 16.
27 deviseth; Isa. 5. 6 hoed; Deut.
6. 11; 2 Chr. 26. 10; Neh. 9. 25;
hewn, or hewed out, Deut. 6. 11
hewedst
Dignity. *Greatness, exaltation.*
Gen. 49. 3 excellency of *d*. and
Esth. 6. 3 what honor and *d*. hath
Eccl. 10. 6 folly is set in great *d*.
Hab. 1. 7 their *d*. shall proceed
2 Pet. 2. 10 not afr. to sp. ev. of *d*.
Jude 8 despise dom. speak evil of *d*.
Diligence. *Guard, work, haste.*
Prov. 4. 23 keep thy heart with all *d*.
Luke 12. 58 give *d*. that thou may
Rom. 12. 8 that ruleth with *d*.
2 Cor. 8. 7 in all *d*. and love to us
2 Tim. 4. 9 do thy *d*. to come shortly
Heb. 6. 11 do show the same *d*.
2 Pet. 1. 5 giving all *d*., add to faith
Jude 3 I gave all *d*. to write unto
R. V. Cor. 8. 7 earnestness
Diligent. *Assiduous, painstaking.*
Deut. 19. 8 judges .. make *d*. in.
Josh. 22. 5 take *d*. heed to do
Prov. 10.4 hand of the *d*. maketh rich
2 Cor. 8. 22 we have .. proved *d*. in
Tit. 3. 12 be *d*. to come unto me
2 Pet. 3. 14 be *d*. that ye may
R. V. 2 Cor. 8. 22 earnest; Tit. 3
12; 2 Pet. 3. 14 give diligence
Diligently. *Carefully, attentively.*
Deut. 4. 9 keep thy soul *d*.
Ez. 7. 23 let it be *d*. done
Isa. 21. 7 he hearkened *d*. with
Jer. 2. 10 send .. and consider *d*.
Mat. 2. 8 search *d*. for the child
Luke 15. 8 seek *d*. till she find
2 Tim. 1. 17 sought me out *d*.
Tit. 3. 13 bring Zenas and Apollos *d*.
R. V. Ez. 7. 23 exactly; Mat. 2. 7,
8, 16; Acts 18. 25; Heb. 12. 15
carefully; Heb. 11. 6. after
Dim. *Weak, darkened, obscure.*
Gen. 27. 1 old, and his eyes were *d*.
Deut. 34. 7 his eye was not *d*., nor
1 Sam. 3. 2 eyes began to wax *d*.
Job 17. 7 mine eye also is *d*.
Isa. 32. 3 eyes .. shall not be *d*.
Lam. 4. 1 how is the gold become *d*.
R. V. 1 Sam. 4. 15 set
Diminish. *Make small, decrease.*
Ex. 5. 8 ye shall not *d*. ought
Lev. 25. 16 shalt *d*. the price of it
Deut. 4. 2 neither shall ye *d*. ought
Prov. 13. 11 wealth .. by v. .. be *d*.
Isa. 21. 17 mighty men shall be *d*.
Jer. 29. 6 increased there, not *d*.
Ezek. 29. 15 for I will *d*. them

Rom. 11. 12 *d.* of them the riches
R. V. Isa. 21. 17 few; Rom. 11. 12 their loss

Dimness. R. V. *gloom.*
Isa. 8. 22 darkness, *d.* of anguish
9. 1 the *d.* shall not be such as was

Dine. *Eat.*
Gen. 43. 16 men shall *d.* with me
Breakfast.
Luke 11. 37 Phar. besought him to *d.*
John 21. 12 Jesus saith, Come and *d.*
R. V. John 21. 12 break your fast;
21. 15 broken their fast

Dinner. *Dish, allowance.*
Prov. 15. 17 better .. a *d.* of herbs
Breakfast.
Mat. 22. 4 I have prepared my *d.*
Luke 11. 38 had not washed bef. *d.*

Dip. *Moisten, besprinkle.*
Gen. 37. 31 *d.* the coat in .. blood
Ex. 12. 22 *d.* it in the blood in bas.
Lev. 4. 6 *d.* his finger in .. blood
Num. 19. 18 *d.* it in the water
Deut. 33. 24 *d.* his foot in oil
Josh. 3. 15 *d.* in brim of .. water
Ruth 2. 14 *d.* thy mor. in vinegar
1 Sam. 14. 27 *d.* it in a honeycomb
2 K. 5. 14 *d.* himself .. in Jordan
Ps. 68. 23 foot may be *d.* in blood
Dip, dip in.
Mat. 26. 23 he that *d.* his hand
Mark 14. 20 one .. that *d.* with me
Luke 16. 24 *d.* the tip of his finger
John 13. 26 when I have *d.* it
Rev. 19. 13 vesture *d.* in blood
R. V. Rev. 19. 13 sprinkled with

Direct. *Make straight, guide.*
Gen. 46. 28 *d.* his face unto Gosh.
Job 32. 14 not *d.* his words against
Ps. 5. 3 will I *d.* my prayer to thee
Prov. 3. 6 he shall *d.* thy paths
Eccl. 10. 10 wisdom is prof. to *d.*
Jer. 10. 23 not in man .. to *d.*
1 Thes. 3. 11. L. J. C. *d.* our way
2 Thes. 3. 5 Lord *d.* our hearts
R. V. Gen. 46. 28 shew; Ps. 5. 3;
Prov. 21. 29 order; Ps. 119. 5 established; Isa. 45. 13 make straight; 61. 8 give them

Directly. *Straightly, at once.*
Num. 19. 4 sprinkle .. blood *d.* bef.
Ezek. 42. 12 way *d.* before the wall
R. V. Num. 19. 4 toward front of

Dirt. *Mire, mud, dung.*
Judg. 3. 22 and the *d.* came out
Ps. 18. 42 cast them out as *d.*
Isa. 57. 20 waters cast .. mire and *d.*
R. V. Ps. 18. 42 mire of

Disallow. *Disavow, reject.*
Num. 30. 5 if her husband *d.* her
1 Pet. 2. 4 *d.* indeed of men, but
R. V. 1 Pet. 2. 4, 7 rejected

Disannul. *Break, make void.*
Job 40. 8 wilt thou *d.* my judg.
Isa. 14. 27 and who shall *d.*
Gal. 3. 15 no man *d.* or addeth
Heb. 7. 18 a *d.* of the command.
R. V. Gal. 3. 15 maketh it void

Disappoint. *Make void, defeat.*
Job 5. 12 *d.* devices of the crafty
Ps. 17. 13 Arise, O Lord, *d.* him
Prov. 15. 22 without c. purp. are *d.*
R. V. Job 5. 12 frustrateth; Ps. 17. 13 confront

Discern. *Know or judge thoroughly, distinguish, interpret.*
Gen. 27. 23 he *d.* him not, because
2 Sam. 14. 17 so is my k., to *d.* good
1 K. 3. 9 *d.* between good and bad
Ez. 3. 13 could not *d.* the noise
Job 4. 16 but I could not *d.* form
Prov. 7. 7 I *d.* among the youths
Eccl. 8. 5 a wise man's heart *d.*
Ezek. 43. 23 cause them to *d.* be.
Mal. 3. 18 *d.* between the righteous
Mat. 16. 3 *d.* the face of the sky
Luke 12. 56 ye do not *d.* this time
1 Cor. 12. 10 to another *d.* of spirits
Heb. 5. 14 *d.* both good and evil
R. V. Luke 12. 56 know how to interpret; 1 Cor. 2. 14 judge

Discerner. R. V. *quick to discern.*
Heb. 4. 12 a *d.* of the thoughts

Discharge. *Send away.*
1 K. 5. 9 cause them to be *d.*
Eccl. 8. 8 there is no *d.* in that war

R. V. 1 K. 5. 9 broken up

Disciple. *Taught or trained one.*
Isa. 8. 16 seal the law among my *d.*
Mat. 5. 1 his *d.* came unto him
8. 21 another of his *d.* said
9. 10 and sat down with .. his *d*
10. 1 had called .. his twelve *d*
11. 1 end of com. his twelve *d.*
13. 10 the *d.* came and said
14. 12 *d.* .. took up the body
15. 2 why do thy *d.* transgress
16. 5 when his *d.* were come
17. 6 when the *d.* heard it
18. 1 at same time came the *d.*
19. 10 his *d.* say unto him
20. 17 took the twelve *d.* apart
21. 1 then sent Jesus two *d.*
22. 16 sent .. unto him their *d.*
23. 1 to the multitude, and .. *d.*
24. 1 his *d.* came to him
26. 1 he said unto his *d.*
27. 64 his *d.* come by night
28. 7 go quickly, and tell his *d.*
Mark 2. 15 sat with Jesus and his *d.*
3. 7; 4. 34; 5. 31; 6. 1; 7. 2; 8. 1;
9 14; 10. 10; 11. 1; 12. 43; 13. 1;
14. 12; 16. 7
Luke 5. 30 Phar. mur. against his *d.*
6. 1; 7. 11; 8. 9; 9. 10, 23;
11. 1; 12. 1; 14. 26; 16. 1; 17. 1;
18. 15; 19. 29; 20. 45; 22. 11
John 1. 35 John stood, and two *d.*
2. 2; 3. 22; 4. 1; 6. 3; 7. 3; 8. 31;
9. 2; 11. 7; 12. 4; 13. 5; 15. 8;
16. 17; 18. 1; 19. 26; 20. 2; 21. 1
Acts 1. 15 stood in midst of *d.* 6. 1;
9. 1; 11. 26; 13. 52; 14. 20; 15. 10;
16. 1; 18. 23; 19. 1; 20. 1
R. V. Mat. 26. 20; 28. 9; Mark 2.
18; Luke 9. 11; John 6. 11 ——;
Acts 1. 15 brethren

Discipline. R. V. *instruction*
Job 36. 10 openeth their ear to *d.*

Disclose. *Reveal.*
Isa. 26. 21 earth shall *d.* her blood

Discomfit. *Trouble, crush, destroy.*
Ex. 17. 13 Joshua *d.* Amalek and
Num. 14. 45 smote them and *d.*
Josh. 10. 10 Lord *d.* them before Is.
Judg. 4. 15 the Lord *d.* Sisera and
1 Sam. 7. 10 upon the Phil. and *d.*
2 Sam. 22. 15 sent lightning and *d.*
Ps. 18. 14 shot .. lightnings and *d.*
Isa. 31. 8 young men shall be *d.*
R. V. Num. 14. 45 beat down; Isa. 31. 8 tributary   [*tion.*

Discomfiture. *Trouble, destruc-*
1 Sam. 14. 20 was a very great *d.*

Discontented. *Bitter of soul.*
1 Sam. 22. 2 every one .. *d.* gathered

Discontinue. *Let. go, release.*
Jer. 17. 4 shalt *d.* from thine heri.

Discord. *Strife, contention.*
Prov. 6. 14 dev. mischief .. soweth *d.*
6. 19 that soweth *d.* among breth.

Discourage. *Break, dishearten.*
Num. 21. 4 soul of peo. was .. *d.*
Deut. 1. 21 fear not .. neither be *d.*
Isa. 42. 4 not fail nor be *d.*
Col. 3. 21 chil., lest they be *d.*

Discover. *Uncover, reveal.*
Ex. 20. 26 thy nakedness be not *d.*
Lev. 20. 18 hath *d.* her fountain
Deut. 22. 30 not *d.* his father's skirt
1 Sam. 14. 8 *d.* ourselves unto them
2 Sam. 22. 16 found. of world were *d.*
Job 12. 22 he *d.* deep things out
Ps. 29. 9 voice of the Lord *d.* forests
Prov. 25. 9 *d.* not a secret to anoth.
Isa. 22. 8 *d.* .. covering of Judah
Jer. 13. 26 will I *d.* thy skirts
Lam. 2. 14 have not *d.* thine iniq.
Ezek. 16. 37 will *d.* thy nakedness
Hos. 2. 10 will I *d.* her lewdness
Mic. 1. 6 will *d.* the foundations
Nah. 3. 5 I will *d.* thy skirts upon
Hab. 3. 13 by *d.* the foundation
Acts 21. 3 when we have *d.* Cyprus
R. V. 2 Sam. 2. 22; Ps. 18. 15;
Isa. 3. 17; Hab. 3. 13 lay bare;
Lev. 20. 18 made naked; Deut.
22. 30 uncover; Job 41. 13 strip off;
Prov. 18. 2 reveal; 25. 9 disclose;
Isa. 22. 8 took away; Ps. 29. 9
strippeth bare; Act. 21. 3 come in
sight of; 27. 39 perceived

Discreet. *Intelligent, sound-minded.*
Gen. 41. 33 look out a man *d.* and
Tit. 2. 5 *d.*, chaste, keepers at home
R. V. Tit. 2. 5 sober-minded

Discreetly. *Understandingly.*
Mark 12. 34 J. saw .. he answered *d.*

Discretion. *Judgment, thoughtfulness.*
Prov. 1. 4 to young man kn. and *d.*
2. 11; 3. 21; 5. 2; 11. 22; 19. 11
Ps. 112. 5 guide his affairs with *d.*
Isa. 28. 26 God .. instruct him to *d.*
Jer. 10. 12 stretc. .. heav. by his *d.*
R. V. Ps. 112. 5 in judgment; Isa.
28. 26 aright

Disdain. *Despise, contempt.*
1 Sam. 17. 42 saw David, he *d.* him
Job 30. 1 wh. fathers I would have *d.*

Disease. *Sickness, weakness.*
Ex. 15. 26 put none of these *d.* upon
Deut. 28. 60 bring upon thee all *d.*
2 K. 1. 2 shall recover of this *d.*
2 Chr. 16. 12 his *d.* was exceed. great
Ps. 41. 8 evil *d.* cleaveth fast unto
Eccl. 6. 2 vanity, and it is an evil *d.*
Mat. 4. 23 and all manner of *d.*
Mark 1. 34 healed .. sick of div. *d.*
Luke 4. 40 had .. sick of divers *d.*
John 5. 4 whatsoever *d.* he had
Acts 19. 12 *d.* departed from them
R. V. 2 K. 1. 2; 8. 8, 9; Mat. 9. 35
sickness; John 5. 4 ——

Diseased. *Ill, sick.*
1 K. 15. 23 in .. old age he was *d.*
2 Chr. 16. 12 Asa was *d.* in his feet
Ezek. 34. 4 *d.* have ye not strength.
Mat. 14. 45 brou. .. all that were *d.*
Mark 1. 32 him all that were *d.*
John 6. 2 he did on th. that were *d.*
R. V. Mat. 14. 35; Mark 1. 32;
John 6. 2 sick

Disfigure. *Hide, deform.*
Mat. 6. 16 for they *d.* their faces

Disgrace. *Dishonor.*
Jer. 14. 21 do not *d.* the throne of

Disguise. *Hide, change.*
1 Sam. 28. 8 Saul *d.* himself, and
1 K. 20. 38 *d.* himself with ashes
2 Chr. 18. 29 I will *d.* myself, and
Job 24. 15 No eye .. and *d.* his face

Dish. *Cup, bowl.*
Judg. 5. 25 brought .. butter in a *d.*
Pan, cruse.
2 K. 21. 13 as a man wipeth a *d.*
Flatdish, saucer.
Ex. 25. 29 shall make .. *d.* thereof
Num. 4. 7 table .. put thereon the *d.*
Dish, tureen.
Mat. 26. 23 dip. .. with me in .. *d.*
Mark 14. 20 dip. with me the *d.*

Dishonest. *Not honest.*
Ezek. 22. 13 thy *d.* gain which thou
22. 27 destroy souls to get *d.* gain

Dishonesty. R. V. *shame.*
2 Cor. 4. 2 renounced .. things of *d.*

Dishonour (*n.*). *Shame, without honour.*
Ez. 4. 14 not meet to seek .. k's *d.*
Ps. 35. 26 clothed with *d.* that
Prov. 6. 33 and *d.* shall he get
Rom. 9. 21 honour .. another unto *d.*
1 Cor. 15. 43 it is sown in *d.*, raised
2 Cor. 6. 8 by honour and *d.*, by ev.
2 Tim. 2. 20 some to h., some to *d.*

Dishonour (*v.*). *Put to shame.*
Mic. 7. 6 son *d.* the father, the dau.
John 8. 49 I h. my F., ye do *d.* me
Rom. 1. 24 to *d.* their own bodies
1 Cor. 11. 4 having .. head cov. *d.*

Disinherit. *Take possession.*
Num. 14. 12 *d.* them, and will make

Dismayed. *Troubled, cast down.*
Deut. 31. 8 fear not, neither be *d.*
Josh. 1. 9 neither be thou *d.*
1 Sam. 17. 11 *d.* and greatly afraid
2 K. 19. 26 were *d.* and confounded
1 Chr. 22. 13 dread not, nor be *d.*
2 Chr. 20. 15 be not afraid nor *d.*
Jer. 1. 17 be not *d.* at their faces
Isa. 21. 3 I was *d.* at seeing of it
Ezek. 2. 6 nor be *d.* at their looks
Obad. 9 mighty men shall be *d.*
R. V. Jer. 48. 1 broken down

Dismaying. *Casting down, terror.*
Jer. 48. 39 shall Moab be a *d.*

Dismiss. *Loose away.*
2 Chr. 23. 8 for Jehoiada *d.* not
Acts. 15. 30 when they were *d.* they
Disobedience. *Insubordination.*
Eph. 2. 2 worketh in children of *d.*
Col. 3. 6 cometh on children of *d.*
Lack of attention.
Rom. 5. 19 by one man's *d.* were
2 Cor. 10. 6 to revenge all *d.*
Heb. 2. 2 *d.* rec. just recompence
Disobedient. *Insubordinate.*
1 K. 13. 26 who was *d.* unto word
Neh. 9. 26 and rebelled
Luke 1. 17 *d.* to the wisdom of
Acts 26. 19 I was not *d.* unto vis.
Rom. 1. 30 Backbiters, . . *d.* to par.
1 Tim. 1. 9 for the lawless and *d.*
2 Tim. 3. 2 blasphemers, *d.* to par.
Tit. 1. 16 being abominable and *d.*
1 Pet. 2. 7 unto them which be *d.*
R. V. Pet. 2. 7 such as disbelieve
Disobey. *Rebel, become bitter.*
1 K. 13. 21 *d.* . . mouth of the Lord
R. V. been disobedient unto
Disorderly. *Not in order.*
1 Thes. 3. 6, 7, bro. that walketh *d.*
Dispatch. *Cut down.*
Ezek. 23. 47 company shall *d.* them
Dispensation. R. V. *steward-ship.*
1 Cor. 9. 17 a *d.* of gospel is com.
House law or arrangement.
Eph. 1. 10 *d.* of the fulness of
Col. 1. 25 accor. to of God
Disperse. *Spread out, scatter.*
1 Sam. 14 *d.* yourselves . . peo.
2 Chr. 11. 23 *d.* of all his children
Esth. 3. 8 *d.* among the people
Prov. 5. 16 let thy fountains be *d.*
Isa. 11. 12 gather . . the *d.* of Judah
Ezek. 36. 19 *d.* through the countries
Zeph. 3. 10 the daughter of my *d.*
John 7. 35 will he go unto the *d.*
Acts 5. 37 as obeyed him, were *d.*
2 Cor. 9. 9 writ., He hath *d.* abroad
R. V. John 7. 35 Dispersion; Acts
5. 37; 2 Cor. 9. 9 scattered
Dispersion. *Scattering.*
Jer. 25. 34 days of . . *d.* are accom.
R. V. Jer. 25. 34 I will break you
in pieces
Displayed. *Shown.*
Ps. 60. 4 it may be *d.* because
Displease. *Grieve.*
Gen. 38. 10 which he did *d.* the L.
Num. 11. 1 peo. complained, it *d.*
1 Sam. 8. 6 the thing *d.* Samuel
2 Sam. 11. 25 let not this . . *d.* thee
1 K. 1. 6 his fath. had not *d.* him
Isa. 59. 15 *d.* him that there was
Jonah 4. 1 *d.* Jonah exceedingly
To be angry, weighed down.
Num. 11. 10 Moses also was *d.*
2 Sam. 6. 8 David was *d.*, because
1 K. 20. 43 went to his house . . *d.*
1 Chr. 21. 7 God was *d.* with . . king
Ps. 60. 1 O God, . . thou hast been *d.*
Prov. 24. 18 lest . . L. see . . and it *d.*
Dan. 6. 14 the king . . was sore *d.*
Hab. 3. 8 was the Lord *d.* against
Zech. 1. 2 Lord hath been sore *d.*
Mat. 21. 15 they were sore *d.*
Mark 10. 14 Jesus saw . . he was *d.*
Acts 12. 20 Herod was highly *d.*
R. V. Gen. 31. 35; Ps. 60. 1 angry;
Gen. 38. 10 evil in sight of; Num.
11. 1 speak evil in ears of; Mat.
21. 15; Mark 10. 14, 41 moved with
indignation
Displeasure. *Heat, wrath, fury.*
Deut. 9. 19 afraid of . . anger and *d.*
Judg. 15. 3 though I do them a *d.*
Ps. 6. 1 neither chasten me in . . *d.*
R. V. Judg. 15. 3 mischief
Dispose. *Put, set, place.*
Job 34. 13 hath *d.* the whole world
37. 15 dost know when G. *d.* them
To wish, desire.
Acts 18. 27 *d.* to pass unto Achaia
1 Cor. 10. 27 bid you . . and ye be *d.*
R. V. Job 37. 15 layeth his charge
upon; Acts 18. 27 minded
Disposing. *Judgment.*
Prov. 16. 33 whole *d.* . . is of the L.
Disposition. *Arrangement.*
Acts 7. 53 received . . law by . . *d.*

R. V. As if ordained by
Dispossess. *Take possession.*
Num. 32. 39 *d.* the Amorite which
Deut. 7. 17 how can I *d.* them
Judg. 11. 23 God of Israel hath *d.*
R. V. Num. 33. 53 take possession
Disputation. *Argumentation.*
Rom. 14. 1 but not to doubtful *d.*
Acts 15. 2 had no small dissen. and *d.*
R. V. Acts 15. 2 questioning
Dispute. *Argue, controvert.*
Job 23. 7 the righteous might *d.*
Mark 9. 34 had *d.* among themselves
Acts 17. 17 *d.* he in the synagogue
Jude 9 contend with . . devil, he *d.*
R. V. Job 23. 7 reason; Mark 9.
33 were ye reasoning; Acts 17. 17
reasoned
Disputer. *Arguer, joint seeker.*
1 Cor. 1. 20 where is . . *d.* of this
Disputing. *Reasoning, contention.*
Acts 19. 8 space of three months, *d.*
19. 9 *d.* daily in the schools
Phil. 2. 14 do all things without *d.*
1 Tim. 6. 5 *d.* of men of corrupt
R. V. Acts 19. 8, 9 reasoning;
1 Tim. 6. 5 wranglings
Disquiet. *To trouble, anger.*
1 Sam. 28. 15 why hast thou *d.* me
Prov. 30. 21 three things earth is *d.*
Roar, sound, make noise.
Ps. 39. 6 surely they are *d.* in vain
42. 5; 42. 11; 43. 5
R. V. Prov. 30. 21 doth tremble
Disquietness. *Howling, dis-quietude.*
Ps. 38. 8 roared by reason of the *d.*
Dissemble. *Lie, deny, feign.*
Josh. 7. 11 *d.* also, and have put
Prov. 26. 24 he that hateth *d.* with
Jer. 42. 20 ye *d.* in your hearts
Gal. 2. 13 other Jews *d.* likewise
R. V. Jer. 42. 20 dealt deceitfully
Dissembler. *Hypocrite.*
Ps. 26. 4 neither will I go in with *d.*
Dissension. *Controversy.*
Acts 15. 2 P. and B. had no small *d.*
23. 7, 10 there arose a *d.* between
Dissimulation. *Hypocrisy.*
Rom. 12. 9 let love be without *d.*
Gal. 2. 13 carried away with their *d.*
R. V. Rom. 12. 9 hypocrisy
Dissolve. *Melt, loose, solve.*
Job 30. 22 liftest me up and *d.* sub.
Ps. 75. 3 inhabitants thereof are *d.*
Isa. 14. 31 whole Palestina, art *d.*
Dan. 5. 16 make interpret. and *d.*
Nah. 2, 6 the palace shall be *d.*
2 Cor. 5. 1 if . . earthly house were *d.*
2 Pet. 3. 11 all . . things shall be *d.*
R. V. Isa. 14. 31 melted away
Distaff. *Circuit, staff.*
Prov. 31. 19 her hands hold the *d.*
Distant. R. V. *joined to.*
Ex. 36. 22 two tenons, equally *d.*
Distil. *Flow, drop.*
Deut. 32. 2 speech shall *d.* as . . dew
Job 36. 28 which clouds . . drop . . *d.*
R. V. 36. 28 drop.
Distinction. *Difference.*
1 Cor. 14. 7 give a *d.* in the sounds
Distinctly. *Understandingly.*
Neh. 8. 8 they read in the book *d.*
Distracted. *Disturbed, confused.*
Ps. 88. 15 suffer terror, I am *d.*
Distraction. *Drawn to and fro.*
1 Cor. 7. 35 attend upon L. with. *d.*
Distress (n.). *Straitness, calamity.*
Gen. 35. 3 ans. me in . . day of my *d.*
Judg. 11. 7 come, when ye are in *d.*
1 Sam. 22. 2 every one . . in *d.* gath.
2 Sam. 22. 7 in my *d.* I called upon
1 K. 1. 29 redeemed . . soul out of *d.*
2 Chr. 28. 22 in the time of his *d.*
Neh. 9. 37 and we are in great *d.*
Ps. 4. 1 God enlarged me when in *d.*
Prov. 1. 27 when *d.* and ang. come
Isa. 25. 4 strength to needy . . *d.*
Lam. 1. 20 behold, Lord, I am in *d.*
Ezek. 30. 16 Noph sh. have *d.* daily
Obad. 12 spoken proudly in . . of *d.*
Zeph. 1. 15 a day of trouble and *d.*
Luke 21. 23 there shall be great *d.*
Rom. 8. 35 shall trib., or *d.*, or per.
1 Cor. 7. 26 good for the present *d.*
2 Cor. 6. 4 patience in afflict., in *d.*

1 Thes. 3. 7 comforted in all our *d.*
R. V. Ezek. 30. 16 adversaries; 1
K. 1. 20 adversity; Neh. 2. 17 evil
ease; Rom. 8. 35 anguish
Distress. (v.). *Straiten, oppress.*
Gen. 32. 7 Jacob was . . afraid and *d.*
Num. 22. 3 Moab was, *d.* because
Deut. 2. 9 Lord said, *D.* not the Mo.
Judg. 2. 15 and they were greatly *d.*
1 Sam. 13. 6 for the people were *d.*
2 Sam. 1. 26 I am *d.* for thee, bro.
2 Chr. 28. 20 king of As. came and *d.*
Isa. 29. 2 Yet I will *d.* Ariel, and
Jer. 10. 18 will *d.* them, that they
2 Cor. 4. 8 troubled . . yet not *d.*
R. V. Deut. 2. 9, 19 vex; 2 Cor. 4. 8
straitened.
Distribute. *Apportion, share.*
1 Chr. 24. 3 David *d.* them, both Za.
2 Chr. 23. 18 D. had *d.* in the house
Neh. 13. 13 their office was to *d.*
Job. 21. 17 God *d.* sorrows . . anger
Luke 18. 22 sell all thou hast, and *d.*
John. 6. 11 had given thanks, he *d.*
Rom. 12. 13 *d.* to the neces. of saints
1 Cor. 7. 17 but as God hath *d.*
2 Cor. 10. 13 rule which God hath *d.*
1 Tim. 6. 18 rich . . works, ready . . *d.*
R. V. 1 Chr. 24. 3 divided; Rom.
12. 13 communicating; 2 Cor. 10.
13 apportioned
Distribution. *Dealing out.*
Acts 4. 35 *d.* was made to every man
2 Cor. 9. 13 and for your lib. *d.* unto
Ditch. *Trench, pit.*
2 K. 3. 16 make . . valley full of *d.*
Job 9. 31 shalt . . plunge me into . . *d.*
Ps. 7. 15 is fallen into the *d.* he made
Prov. 23. 27 a whore is a deep *d.*
Isa. 22. 11 ye made . . a *d.* between
Mat. 15. 14 both shall fall into . . *d.*
Luke 6. 39 both fall into the *d.*
R. V. 2 K. 3. 16 trenches; Isa. 22.
11 reservoir; Mat. 15. 14; Luke
6. 39 pit
Divers. *Some, different, several.*
Deut. 25. 13 shalt not have *d.* weigh.
Judg. 5. 30 a prey of *d.* colors
1 Chr. 29. 2 *d.* colors, and all mank.
2 Chr. 30. 11 *d.* of Asher and Man.
Prov. 20. 10 *d.* weights, and *d.* meas.
Ezek. 17. 3 feathers, which had *d.*
Mat. 4. 24 peo. . . taken with *d.* dis.
Mark 13. 8 earthquakes in *d.* places
Luke 4. 40 that . . sick with *d.* dis.
Acts 19. 9 when *d.* were hardened
2 Tim. 3. 6 led away with *d.* lusts
Tit. 3. 3 deceived, serving *d.* lusts
Heb. 2. 4 and with *d.* miracles
Jas. 1. 2 fall into *d.* temptations
R. V. Deut. 22. 11 mingled stuff;
22. 9 two kinds of; Ps. 78. 45; 105.
31 swarms; Mark 8. 3; Acts 19. 9
some; Heb. 2. 4 manifold power;
Jas. 1. 2 manifold
Diverse. *Different.*
Lev. 19. 19 gender with a *d.* kind
Esth. 1. 7 vessels . . of one from an.
Dan. 7. 3 beasts *d.* one from anoth.
Diversity. *Sort, variety.*
1 Cor. 12. 4 there are *d.* of gifts
12. 28 governments, *d.* of tongues
R. V. 1 Cor. 12. 28 divers kinds
Divide. *Separate, apportion.*
Gen. 1. 4 and God *d.* the light
Ex. 15. 9 I will *d.* the spoil
Lev. 1. 17 shall not *d.* it asunder
Num. 31. 27 *d.* . . prey into two parts
Deut. 14. 7 that *d.* the cloven hoof
Josh. 13. 7 *d.* this land for . . inher.
Judg. 5. 30 have th. not *d.* the prey
2 Sam. 1. 23 in death . . were not *d.*
1 K. 3. 25 *d.* the living child in two
2 K. 2. 8 were *d.* hither and thither
1 Chr. 24. 4 and thus they were *d.*
2 Chr. 35. 13 *d.* them speedily amo.
Neh. 9. 11 thou didst *d.* the sea
Job 27. 17 innocent shall *d.* . . silver
Ps. 78. 13 he *d.* the sea. and caused
Prov. 16. 19 *d.* the spoil with . . proud
Isa. 9. 3 men rejoice when they *d.*
Jer. 31. 35 which *d.* the sea when
Lam. 4. 16 anger of . . L. hath *d.* them
Ezek. 45. 1 ye shall *d.* by lot
Dan. 2. 41 the kingdom shall be *d*
Hos. 10. 2 their heart is *d.*

Am. 7. 17 thy land shall be d.
Mic. 2. 4 he hath d. our fields
Zech. 14. 1 thy spoil shall be d.
Mat. 12. 25 kingdom d. against itself
Mark 3. 25 if house be d. against its.
Luke 12. 13 that he d. the inherit.
Acts 13. 19 d. their land to them
1 Cor. 1. 13 is Christ d.? was Paul
2 Tim. 2. 15 rightly d. the word of
Rev. 16. 19 the great city was d.
R. V. Lev. 11. 4, 7; Deut. 14. 7. 8
part; Num. 33. 54 inherit; Josh.
19. 45 distributing; 23. 4; Neh. 9.
22 allot; Mat. 25. 32 separateth;
Acts 13. 19 gave them their land
for an inheritance; 2 Tim. 2. 13
handling aright

Dividing. *Separating.*
Dan. 7. 25 times and the d. of time
Heb. 4. 12 d. asunder of soul and sp.
R. V. Dan. 7. 25 half a

Divination. *Art of divining.*
Num. 23. 23 neither is there any d.
Deut. 18. 10 that useth d. or an ob.
2 K. 17. 17 used d. and enchant.
Jer. 14. 14 a false vision and d.
Ezek. 13. 6 seen van. and lying d.
Python.
Acts 16. 16 possessed with spir. of d.

Divine *(adj.).* *Godly, god-like.*
Prov. 16. 10 a d. sentence is in
Heb. 9. 1 had ordinan. of d. service
2 Pet. 1. 3 as his d. power hath

Divine *(v.)* *Practice, divination,
solve, invent.*
Gen. 44. 5 whereby indeed he d.
1 Sam. 28. 8 d. unto me the .. spirit
Ezek. 22. 28 and d. lies unto them
Mic. 3. 6 dark ..that ye shall not d.

Diviner. *Who practices divina-
tion.*
Deut. 18. 14 hearkened unto .. d.
1 Sam. 6. 2 Philistines called for .. d.
Isa. 44. 25 frustrateth and maketh d.
Jer. 27. 9 hearken not to your d.
Mic. 3. 7 seers be ashamed, and .. d.
Zech. 10. 2 the n. have seen a lie

Division. *Cause, separation.*
Ex. 8. 23 a d. between my people
Josh. 11. 23 according to their d.
Judg. 5. 15 the d. of Reuben were
1 Chr. 24. 1 the d. of the sons of A.
2 Chr. 35. 5 d. of the families of Lev.
Ez. 6. 18 set priests in their d.
Neh. 11. 36 of Lev. were d. in Jud.
Luke 12. 51 nay, but rather d.
John 7. 43 was d. among the people
Rom. 16. 17 mark .. which cause d.
1 Cor. 3. 3 among you env. and d.
R. V. Judg. 5. 15, 16 watercourses;
1 Cor. 3. 3 ——

Divorce. *Cutting off.*
Jer. 3. 8 I had given her a bill of d.
R. V. divorcement

Divorced. *Cut or cast off.*
Lev. 21. 14 a d. woman or profane
Num. 30. 9 of her that is d.
Mat. 5. 32 shall marry her that is d.
R. V. Mat. 5. 32 put away

Divorcement. *Casting off.*
Deut. 24. 1 write her a bill of d.
Isa. 50. 1 bill of your mother's d.
Mat. 5. 31 give her a writing of d
Mark 10. 4 suf. to write a bill of d.

Do. *Act, execute, transact.*
Gen. 3. 13 what is this thou hast d.
Ex. 1. 17 d. not as the k. command.
Lev. 4. 2 which ought not to be d.
Num. 1. 54 chil. of Israel d. accord.
Deut. 1. 14 spoken is good to d.
Josh. 1. 8 mayest observe to d.
Judg. 1. 7 as I have d., so G. hath
Ruth 1. 17 the Lord d. so to me
1 Sam. 1. 7 he d. so year by year
2 Sam. 2. 6 ye have d. this thing
1 K. 1. 6 Why hast thou d. so?
2 K. 1. 18 acts of Ahaz. which he d.
1 Chr. 10. 11 heard all the Phil. had d.
2 Chr. 6. 23 d., and judge thy ser.
Ez. 7. 10 seek the law of L. and d. it
Neh. 1. 9 keep thy command. and d.
Esth. 1. 8 should d. according to
Job. 1. 5 thus d. Job continually
Ps. 1. 3 what. he d. shall prosper
Prov. 2. 14 who rejoice to d. evil
Eccl. 2. 2 said of mirth, What d. it

S. of S. 8. 8 what shall we d. for
Isa. 5. 4 that I have not d. in it
Jer. 2. 23 know what thou hast d.
Lam. 1. 21 glad thou hast d. it
Ezek. 3. 20 right. which he has d.
Dan. 8. 4 d. according to his will
Hos. 6. 4 what shall I d. to thee
Joel 2. 20 he hath d. great things
Am. 3. 6 and the Lord hath not d. it
Obad. 15 it shall be d. unto you
Jonah 1. 10 why hast thou d. this
Mic. 6. 3 what have I d. unto thee
Zeph. 3. 5 he will not d. iniquity
Hag. 1. 14 they came and d. work
Zech. 1. 6 d. they not take hold
Mal. 2. 12 cut off the man that d.
Mat. 1. 24 d. as the angel of the L.
Mark 2. 24 why d. they on sab. day
Luke 1. 49 hath d. me great things
John 2. 5 whatso. he saith .. d. it
Acts 1. 1 Jesus began both to d.
Rom. 1. 28 to d. those things which
1 Cor. 5. 2 he that hath d. this
2 Cor. 8. 10 not only to d., but also
Gal. 2. 10 I .. was forward to d.
Eph. 3. 20 him that is able to d.
Phil. 2. 14 d. all .. without murmur.
Col. 3. 17 whatso. ye d. in word
1 Thes. 4. 10 ye d. it toward all
2 Thes. 3. 4 both d. and will d. the
1 Tim. 1. 13 because I d. it ignor.
2 Tim. 4. 5 d. work of an evang.
Tit. 3. 5 works which we have d.
Phile. 14 without .. mind I d. noth.
Heb. 6. 3 and this will we d.
Jas. 2. 7 d. not they blaspheme
1 Pet. 2. 22 who d. no sin, neither
2 Pet. 1. 10 if ye d. these things
1 John 1. 6 and d. not the truth
3 John 5 d. faithfully what thou d.
Rev. 2. 5 d. the first works, or

Doctor. *Teacher.*
Luke 2. 46 sitting in midst of d.
Acts 5. 34 Gamaliel, a d. of law

Doctrine. *Thing taught, instruc-
tion.*
Deut. 32. 2 d. shall drop as rain
Job 11. 4 my d. is pure, and
Prov. 4. 2 I give you good d.
Isa. 29. 4 that mur. shall learn d.
Jer. 10. 8 stock is a d. of vanities
Mat. 7. 28 peo. were aston. at his d.
Mark 7. 7 teaching for d. the com.
Luke 4. 32 were astonished at his d.
John 7. 16 my d. is not mine
Acts 2. 42 con. .. in the apostles' d.
Rom. 6. 17 obeyed .. that form of d.
1 Cor. 14. 6 speak to you by d.
Eph. 4. 14 car... with ev. wind of d.
Col. 2. 22 after the com. and d.
1 Tim. 1. 10 contrary to sound d.
2 Tim. 4. 2 with long suf. and d.
Heb. 6. 2 of the d. of baptism
2 John 9 abideth not in d. of C.
Rev. 2. 14 them that hold the d.
R. V. in N. T. generally, teaching

Doer. *Actor, worker.*
Gen. 39. 22 Joseph .. he was the d.
2 K. 22. 5 the d. of the work that
Ps. 101. 8 I may cut off all wicked d.
Rom. 2. 13 d. of the law sh. be justif.
2 Tim. 2. 9 I suf. troub. as an evil d.
Jas. 1. 22 be ye d. of the word
R. V. 2 K. 22. 5 workmen; Ps. 101.
8 workers of iniquity; 2 Tim. 2. 9
malefactor

Dog. *Dog.*
Ex. 11. 7 shall not a d. move ..tong.
Deut. 23. 18 bring .. the price of a d.
Judg. 7. 5 lappeth as a d. lappeth
1 Sam. 17. 43 am I a d., that thou
2 Sam. 3. 8 am I a d's head which
1 K. 14. 11 in the city shall the d.
2 K. 8. 13 is thy servant a d.
Job 30. 1 set with the d. of my fl'k
Ps. 22. 16 d. have compassed me
Prov. 26. 11 as a d. returneth to
Eccl. 9. 4 living d. is better than
Isa. 56. 10 they are all dumb d.
Jer. 15. 3 d. to tear, and the fowls
Mat. 7. 6 gi. which is holy unto d.
Mark 7. 27 to cast it unto d.
Luke 16. 21 d. came and licked
Phil. 3. 2 beware of d., beware
2 Pet. 2. 22 d. is turned to his v.
Rev. 22. 15 without are d. and sor.

Doing.
Ex. 15. 11 fearful in pr., d. wonders
Lev. 18. 3 after the d. of l. of Egypt
Deut. 28. 20 wickedness of thy d.
Judg. 2. 19 ceas. not from .. own d.
1 Sam. 25. 3 man was evil in his d.
2 Chr. 17. 4 walked not after the d.
Ps. 9. 11 declare among peo. his d.
Prov. 20. 11 child is known by .. d.
Isa. 1. 16 put away evil of your d.
Jer. 4. 4 because of evil of your d.
7. 3; 11. 18; 17. 10; 18. 11; 21. 12
Ezek. 36. 31 ye remember your d.
Hos. 4. 9 reward them their d.
Mic. 2. 7 Lord .. are these his d.?
Zech. 1. 6 according to their d.
Zeph. 3. 7 corrupted all their d.
Mat. 21. 42 this is the Lord's d.
Mark 12. 11 L's d., and is marv.
2 Cor. 8. 11 perform the d. of it
Gal. 6. 9 not .. weary in well d.
1 Tim. 4. 16 d. this thou shalt save

Doleful. *Wailing, howling.*
Isa. 13. 21 houses .. full of d. crea.
Mic. 2. 4 lament with d. lamenta.

Dominion. *Rule, power.*
Gen. 27. 40 thou shalt have the d.
Num. 24. 19 he that shall have d.
Judg. 14. 4 Phil. had d. over Israel
1 K. 4. 24 he had d. over all
2 K. 20. 13 nothing in all his d.
1 Chr. 4. 22 who had the d. in Moab
2 Chr. 8. 6 all the land of his d.
Neh. 9. 28 had the d. over them
Job. 25. 2 d. and fear are with him
Ps. 49. 14 upright shall have d.
Isa. 26. 13 lords .. have had d.
Jer. 34. 1 all .. kingdoms .. of his d.
Dan. 11. 5 his d. shall be great
Mic. 4. 8 O tower .. even the first d.
Zech. 9. 10 d. shall be from sea
Mat. 20. 25 Gent. exercise d. over
Rom. 6. 9 death hath no more d.
2 Cor. 1. 24 have d. over your faith
Eph. 1. 21 might, and d., and name
1 Pet. 4. 11 praise, and d. for ever
Jude 25 d. and power, both now
Rev. 1. 6 glory, and d. for ever
R. V. Judg. 14. 4 rule; 2 Chr. 21.
8 hand; Neh. 9. 37 power; 2 Cor.
1. 24 lordship; Mat. 20. 25 lord it

Done. See. Do.

Door. *Door, opening.*
Gen. 4. 7 not well, sin lieth at the d.
Ex. 12. 22 none shall go out at d.
Lev. 1. 3 offer it .. in the d.
Num 3. 25 the hanging for the d.
Deut. 22. 21 bring .. damsel to d.
Josh. 19. 51 at the d. of the tab.
Judg. 4. 20 stand in d. of the tent
1 Sam. 2. 22 women assem. at .. d.
2 Sam. 11. 9 Uriah slept at the d.
1 K. 6. 8 d. for the middle chamber
2 K. 4. 15 she stood in the d.
1 Chr. 9. 21 porter of the d of tab.
3 Chr. 3. 7 He overlaid also the d.
Neh. 3. 1 and set up the d. of it
Esth. 2. 21 those which kept the d.
Job 3. 10 shut not up the d. of
Ps. 24. 7 lift up, ye everlasting d.
Prov. 5. 8 come not nigh the d.
Eccl. 12. 4 the d. shall be shut
S. of S. 8. 9 if she be a d., we incl.
Isa. 26. 20 my people shut thy d.
Jer. 35. 4 Shal., the keeper of the d.
Ezek. 8. 3 to the d. of the inner gate
Hos. 2. 15 Achor for d. of hope
Mic. 7. 5 keep the d. of thy mouth
Mat. 6. 6 hast shut thy d., pray
Mark 1. 33 city was gath. at the door
Luke 11. 7 the d. is now shut
John 10. 1 that enter not by the d.
Acts 5. 9 are at the d., and sh. carry
12. 6; 14. 27; 16. 26; 21. 30
1 Cor. 16. 9 a great d. .. is opened
2 Cor. 2. 12 a d. was opened to me
Col. 4. 3 God would open .. a d.
Jas. 5. 9 judge standeth before .. d.
Rev. 3. 8 set before thee .. open d.
R. V. Am. 9. 11 chapters; Ezek.
41. 2, 3 entranc ; 41. 16 thresh-
olds ; 1 K. 14. 17 house

Dote. *Be foolish.*
Jer. 50. 36 and they shall d.

Dote, love.
Ezek. 13. 5, 7, 9, 12, 16, 20 d. on lov

To be sick.
1 Tim. 6. 4 but *d.* about questions
Double (*a.*). *Twofold.*
Gen. 43. 12 take *d.* money in . . hand
Ex. 22. 4 or ass, shall restore *d.*
Deut. 21. 17 giving him a *d.* portion
2 K. 2. 9 *d.* portion of thy spirit
Chr. 12. 33 forth . . not of *d.* heart
Job 11. 6 they are *d.* to that wh. is
Ps. 12. 2 and with a *d.* heart speak
Isa. 40. 2 *d.* rec'd for all her sins
Jer. 16. 18 recompense their sin *d.*
Zech. 9. 12 will render *d.* unto thee
1 Tim. 5. 17 be counted worthy of *d.*
Jas. 1. 8 *d.* minded man is unstable
Rev. 18. 6 *d.* according to her works
R. V. Job 11. 6 manifold
Double (*v.*). *Make double.*
Gen. 41. 32 dream was *d.* unto Phar.
Ex. 26. 9 shalt *d.* the sixth curtain
Exek. 21. 14 let the sword be *d.*
Doubt (*n.*). *Question, uncertainty.*
Gen. 37. 33 Jos. is without *d.* rent
Job 12. 2 no *d.* ye are the people
Dan. 5. 12 dissolving of *d.* were
Luke 11. 20 no *d.* kg. of G. has come
Acts 2. 12 amazed, and were in *d.*
1 Cor. 9. 10 No *d.* this is written
Gal. 4. 20 for I stand in *d.* of you
R. V. Luke 11. 20 then ; 1 Cor. 9. 10
yea ; Gal. 4. 20 perplexed
Doubt (*v.*). *To question.*
Mat. 14. 31 wherefore didst thou *d.*
Mark 11. 23 shall not *d.* in his heart
John 13. 22 dis. looked . . *d.* of whom
Acts 10. 20 go with them . . *d.* nothing
Rom. 14. 23 he that *d.* is damned
1 Tim. 2. 8 lift. hol. h'ds without *d.*
R. V. John 10. 24 hold us in sus-
pense ; Acts 5 24 ; 10. 17 ; 25. 20
much perplexed ; 1 Tim. 2. 8 dis-
puting
Doubtful. *Wavering.*
Luke 12. 29 neither be . . of *d.* mind
Rom. 14. 1 not to *d.* disputation
Doubtless. *Without doubt.*
Num. 14. 30 *d.* ye shall not come
Ps. 126. 6 He shall *d.* come again
Isa. 63. 16 *d.* thou art our Father
1 Cor. 9. 2 apostle, *d.* I am to you
2 Cor. 12. 1 not ex. for me *d.* to glory
Phil. 3. 8 yea *d.*, and I count all
R. V. Num. 14. 30 surely ; Ps. 126. 6
——; Isa. 63. 16 for ; 1 Cor. 9. 2
at least ; 2 Cor. 12. 1 I must needs
glory though ; Phil. 3. 8 verily
Dough. *Swollen, dough.*
Ex. 12. 34 *d.* before it was leavened
Num. 15. 20 offer . . cake of first . . *d.*
Neh. 10. 37 bri. firstfruits of our *d.*
Jer. 7. 18 women knead their *d.*
Ezek. 44. 30 unto priest first of . . *d.*
Hos. 7. 4 he hath kneaded the *d.*
Dove. *Dove, pigeon.*
Gen. 8. 8 he sent forth a *d.*
Ps. 55. 6 had wings like a *d.* from
S. of S. 1. 15 thou hast *d's* eyes
Isa. 38. 14 I did mourn as a *d.*
Jer. 48. 28 be like a *d.* that ma. nest
Ezek. 7. 16 on . . mountains like *d.*
Hos. 7. 11 Ephraim is like a silly *d.*
Nah. 2. 7 lead her with voice of *d.*
Mat. 3. 16 Spir. . . descend. like a *d.*
10. 16 serpents, and harmless as *d.*
Mark 11. 15 of them that sold *d.*
Luke 3. 22 descended . . like a *d.*
John 2. 14 sold ox, sheep, and *d.*
Dove's dung. *Roasted chick pea.*
2 K. 6. 25 a cab of *d. d.* for silver
Down. *Beneath, low.*
2 Chr. 32. 30 brought it straight *d.*
Mat. 4. 6 S. of God. cast thyself *d.*
Mark 5. 13 herd ran violently *d.*
Luke 8. 33 ran vio. *d.* a steep place
John 8. 6 Jesus stooped *d.* and wo.
Acts 20. 9 fell *d.* from the third loft
Downsitting. *Sit down.*
Ps. 139. 2 thou knowest my *d. s.*
Downward. *Beneath, low.*
2 K. 19. 30 Judah shall take root *d.*
Eccl. 3. 21 the beast that goeth *d.*
Isa. 37. 31 Judah shall take root *d.*
Ezek. 1. 27 of his loins even *d.*
Dowry. *Portion.*
Gen. 30. 20 endued me with a good *d.*
Ex. 22. 17 pay . . according to the *d.*

1 Sam. 18. 25 k. desireth not any *d.*
Drag (*n.*). *Net, drag.*
Hab. 1. 15, 16 gather them in the *d.*
Drag (*v.*).
John 21. 8 came in ship, *d.* the net
Dragon. *Howler, jackal.*
Job 30. 29 I am a brother to *d.*
Ps. 44. 19 broken us in place of *d.*
Isa. 13 22 *d.* in pleasant palaces
Jer. 9. 11 Make Jerusa. a den of *d.*
Ezek. 29. 3 Pharaoh . . the great *d.*
Mic. 1. 8 make a wailing like the *d.*
Mal. 1. 3 herit. waste for the *d.* of
Sea Serpent.
Deut. 32. 33 wine is poison of *d.*
Ps. 74. 13 breakest the heads of *d.*
Isa. 27. 1 he shall slay the *d.*
Jer. 51. 34 swallowed me like a *d.*
Lizard, serpent, monster.
Rev. 12. 3 *d.* having seven heads
12. 4–17 ; 13. 2, 4 ; 16. 13 ; 20. 2
R. V. Job 30. 29 ; Ps. 44. 19 ; Isa.
13. 22 ; 34. 13 ; 35. 7 ; 43. 20 ; Jer.
9. 11 ; 10. 22 ; 14. 6 49. 33 ; 51. 37 ;
Mic. 1. 8 ; Mal 1. 3 jackals
Dragon Well. *Fountain of Jackals.*
Neh. 2. 13 went even before the *d. w.*
Drams. *Darics.*
1 Chr. 29. 7 and ten thousand *d.*
Ez. 2. 69 ; 8. 27 ; Neh. 7. 70, 71, 72
Drank. *See* **Drink.**
Draught. *Catch, haul.*
Luke 5. 4, 9 let down . . nets for a *d.*
Privy, cess-pool.
2 K. 10. 27 and made it a *d.* house
Mat. 15. 17 is cast out into the *d.*
Mark 7. 19 goeth out into the *d.*
Drave. *See* **Drive.**
Draw. *Move, pull, come.*
Gen. 24. 13 men . . come out to *d.* w.
Ex. 2. 10 *d.* him out of the water
Lev. 9. 5 congregation *d.* near
Num. 22. 23 saw a. and his sword *d.*
Deut. 21. 3 hath not *d.* in the yoke
Josh. 8. 6 till we have *d.* them from
Judg. 19. 13 let us *d.* near to place
Ruth 2. 9 which young men have *d.*
1 Sam. 7. 6 they gath. . . and *d.* water
2 Sam. 23. 16 *d.* water out of . . well
1 K. 8. 8 they *d.* out the staves
2 K. 3. 26 sev. hun. men that *d.* bow
1 Chr. 10. 4 thy sword, and
2 Chr. 18. 33 certain man *d.* a bow
Esth. 5. 2 Esther *d.* near and touch.
Job 21. 33 every man shall *d.* after
Ps. 10. 9 *d.* him into his net
Prov. 20. 5 man of unders. will *d.* it
S. of S. 1. 4 *d.* me, we will run after
Isa. 5. 18 woe to them that *d.* iniq.
Jer. 31. 3 with . . kindness have I *d.*
Lam. 3. 57 thou *d.* near in the day
Ezek. 21. 3 *d.* forth my sword out
Hos. 11. 4 I *d.* them with cords
Zeph. 3. 2 she *d.* not near to her G.
Mat. 13. 48 when it was full, they *d.*
Mark 14. 47 that stood by *d.* a sword
Luke 15. 25 *d.* nigh to the house
John 6. 44 Father which sent *d.* him
Acts 5. 37 and *d.* away much people
Heb. 10. 39 not of them who *d.* back
Jas. 4. 8 *d.* nigh to God, and he will
Rev. 12. 4 his tail *d.* the third part
Drawer. *Who draws.*
Deut. 29. 11 unto the *d.* of thy water
Josh. 9. 21, 23, 27 *d.* of water
Drawn. *Pulled, carried, marked.*
Num. 22. 31 and his sword *d.* in
Deut. 30. 17 but shalt be *d.* away
Josh. 8. 16 people were *d.* away from
Judg. 20. 31 chil. of Benj. were *d.*
1 Chr. 21. 16 angel . . hav. a *d.* sword
Job 20. 35 it is *d.* and cometh out
Prov. 24. 11 that one *d.* unto death
Isa. 21. 15 fled . . from the *d.* sword
Jer. 22. 19 *d.* and cast forth beyond
Ezek. 21. 28 the sword is *d.* for the
Jas. 1. 14 *d.* away of his own lust
R. V. Mark 6. 53 moved ; Luke 15.
1 ; Acts 27. 27 were drawing ;
Acts 19. 33 drew out ; Acts 14. 19 ;
17. 6 ; 21. 30 dragged
Dread (*n.*). *Fear, terror.*
Gen. 9. 2 *d.* of you . . be on every
Ex. 15. 16 fear and *d.* shall fall
Deut. 2. 25 I begin to put the *d.*
Job 13. 11 shall not his *d.* fall on

Isa 8. 13 fear, . . let him be your *d.*
Dread (*v.*). *Fear.*
Deut. 1. 29 *d.* not, neither be afraid
1 Chr. 22. 13 . . of good cour., *d.* not
Dreadful. *Fearful, terrible.*
Gen. 28. 17 said, How *d.* is this pla
Job 15. 21 *d.* sound is in his ears
Ezek. 1. 18 so high . . they were *d.*
Dan. 7. 7 beast *d.* and terrible
Hab. 1. 7 They are terrible and *d.*
Mal. 1. 14 my name is *d.* among
R. V. Dan. 7. 7, 19 ; Mal. 1. 14 ; 4
5 terrible
Dream (*n.*). *Dream, fantasy.*
Gen. 20. 3 God came to A. in a *d.*
31. 10 : 37. 5 ; 40. 5 ; 41. 7 ; 42. 9
Num. 12. 6 speak unto him in a *d.*
Deut. 13. 1 or a dreamer of *d.*
Judg. 7. 13 a man that told a *d.*
1 Sam. 28. 6 L. ans. him not . . by *d.*
1 K. 3. 5 L. appeared to S. in a *d.*
Job 7. 14 thou scarest me with *d.*
Ps. 73. 20 as *d.* when one awaketh
Eccl. 5. 3 *d.* com. through the mul
Isa. 29. 7 be as a *d.* of a night visior
Jer. 23. 27 forget my name by . . *d.*
Dan. 1. 17 understanding in all . . *d*
2. 4–45 ; 4. 5–19 ; 5. 10 ; 7. 1
Joel 2. 28 old men shall dream *d.*
Zech. 10. 2 and have told a false *d.*
Mat. 1. 20 appeared to him in a *d.*
2. 12, 13, 19 ; 2. 22 ; 27. 19
Acts 2. 17 old men shall dream *d.*
Dream (*v.*). *Dream.*
Gen. 28. 12 *d.*, and behold a ladder
37. 5, 9, 10 ; 40. 5 ; 41. 1–15 ; 42. 9
Judg. 17. 13 *d.* a dream, and, lo
Ps. 126. 1 were like them that *d.*
Isa. 29. 8 as when hungry man *d.*
Jer. 23. 25 pro. lies, saying, I have *d.*
Joel 2. 28 old men shall *d.* dreams
Acts 2. 17 old men shall *d.* dreams
Dreamer. *Who dreams.*
Gen. 37. 19 Behold, this *d.* cometh
Deut. 13. 1 arise among you p. or *d.*
Jer. 27. 9 nor to your div. nor *d.*
Jude 8 filthy *d* defile the flesh
Dregs. *Lees, grounds.*
Ps. 75. 8 *d.* . . all . . wicked sh. drink
Isa. 51. 17 hast drunken the *d.* of
Dress. *Make right, trim.*
Ex. 30. 7 when he *d.* the lamps
Till, serve.
Gen. 2. 15 put him in gar. to *d.* it
Deut. 28. 39 plant vineyards . . and *d.*
Heb. 6. 7 for them by whom it is *d.*
Do, make, prepare.
Gen. 18. 7 and he hasted to *d.* it
Lev. 7. 9 that is *d.* in frying pan
1 Sam. 25. 18 took five sheep ready *d.*
2 Sam. 12. 4 *d.* for . . wayfaring mar
1 K. 17. 12 that I may . . *d.* it for
R. V. Heb. 6. 7 tilled
Drew. *See* **Draw.**
Dried (*a.*). *Made dry.*
Num. 6. 3 nei. eat moist grapes nor *d.*
Dried (*v.*). *See* **Dry.**
Drink (*n.*). *Juice, beverage.*
Lev. 11. 34 *d.* that may be drunk
Ez. 3. 7 gave . . meat, *d.*, and oil
Ps. 102. 9 mingled . . *d.* wi. weeping
Isa. 32. 6 cause *d.* of . . thirsty to
Dan. 1. 10 appoint. your m. and *d.*
Hos. 4. 18 their *d.* is sour
John 6. 55 my . . blood is *d.* indeed
Rom. 14. 17 king. of G. is not . . *d.*
1 Cor. 10. 4 all drink same spir. *d.*
Col. 2. 16 let no man judge you in *d*
Give to drink.
Gen. 21. 19 and gave the lad *d.*
Num. 20. 8 give cong. and beasts *d.*
Judg. 4. 19 milk, and gave him *d.*
2 Sam. 23. 15 give me *d.* of the w.
1 Chr. 11. 17 give me *d.* of the w.
Esth. 1. 7 gave them *d.* in vessels
Ps. 78. 15 gave them *d.* out of dep.
Isa. 43. 20 give *d.* to my people
Mat. 25. 35 and ye gave me *d.*
Rom. 12. 20 if he thirst, give him *d.*
Drink (*v.*). *Banquet, take liquid.*
Gen. 9. 21 Noah . . *d.* of the wine
24. 14 ; 25. 34 ; 26. 30 ; 27. 25
Ex. 7. 18 Egyptians . . lothe to *d.* of
15. 23 ; 17. 1 ; 24. 11 ; 32. 6 ; 34. 28
Lev. 10. 9 do not *d.* wine nor str. dr.
Num. 6. 3 *d.* no vinegar of wine

Deut. 2. 6 buy w. that ye may *d.*
Judg. 7. 5 that bow. down .. to *d.*
Ruth 3. 7 when Boaz had e. and *d.*
1 Sam. 1. 9 Han. rose .. after they *d.*
2 Sam. 11. 13 did e. and *d.* be. him
1 K. 1. 25 they e. and *d.* before him
2 K. 6. 22 they may eat and *d.*
1 Chr. 11. 18 D. would not *d.* of it
Ez. 10. 6 did eat no br. nor *d.* w.
Neh. 8. 10 eat .. fat, and *d.* . sweet
Esth. 3. 15 Haman sat down to *d.*
Job 1. 4 called .. three sisters to *d.*
Ps. 50. 13 *d.* the blood of goats
Prov. 4. 17 *d.* the wine of violence
Eccl. 2. 24 eat and *d.* and enjoy
S. of S. 5. 1 I have *d.* my wine
Isa. 5. 22 mighty to *d.* wine, and
Jer. 2. 18 *d.* the waters of the river?
Lam. 5. 4 we have *d.* our water
Ezek. 4. 11 *d.* also water by measure
Dan. 1. 12 give us .. water to *d.*
Joel 3. 3 sold a girl, that th. might *d.*
Am. 2. 8 *d.* the wine of the condem'd
Obad 16 have *d.* upon my holy mt.
Jonah 3. 7 not feed nor *d.* water
Mic. 6. 15 but shalt not *d.* wine
Hab. 2. 16 *d.* thou also, and let
Zeph. 1. 13 plant vineyards but not *d.*
Hag. 1. 6 ye *d.* but are not filled
Zech. 7. 6 eat, and when ye did *d.*
Mat. 11. 18 John came nei. e. nor *d.*
6. 25; 24. 38; 26. 27; 27. 34
Mark 2. :6 *d.* with pub. and sinners
Luke 1. 15 *d.* neither wine nor str. d.
5. 30; 7. 33; 10. 7; 12. 19; 13. 26
John 4. 7 Jesus saith, Give me to *d.*
Acts 9. 9 and neither did eat nor *d.*
Rom. 14. 21 nei. eat fl. nor *d.* wine
1 Cor. 9. 4 not power to eat and *d.*
Heb. 6. 7 earth which *d.* in rain
Rev. 14. 10 shall *d.* of the wine of

Drinker. *Who drinks.*
Joel 1. 5 howl, all ye *d.* of wine

Drinking. *Drinking.*
Gen. 24. 19 until they have done *d.*
Ruth 3. 3 have done eating and *d.*
1 Sam. 30. 16 eating and *d.*, and danc.
1 K. 4. 20 *d.* and making merry
1 Chr. 12. 39 three days eating and *d.*
2 Chr. 9. 20 *d.* ves. of king Solomon
Esth. 1. 8 *d.* was according to law
Job 1. 13 eating and *d.* wine in ho.
Isa. 22. 13 eating flesh and *d.* water

Drink-offering.
Gen. 35. 14 poured a *d.* off. therein
Ex. 29. 40; Lev. 23. 13; Num. 6.
15; 2 K. 16. 13; 1 Chr. 29. 21; 2
Chr. 29. 35; Ps. 16. 4; Isa. 57. 6;
Jer. 7. 18; Ezek. 20. 28; Joel 1. 9

Drive. *Thrust away, cast out, com-*
pel, impel, guide.
Gen. 3. 24 So he *d.* out the man
Ex. 6. 1 shall he *d.* them out of land
Num. 22. 6 that I may *d.* them out
Deut. 30. 1 whither the L. G. hath *d.*
Josh. 24. 12 which *d.* them out from
Judg. 2. 3 I will not *d.* them out
1 Sam. 26. 19 they have *d.* me out
2 Sam. 6. 2 Abinadab *d.* the new cart
2 K. 4. 24 said, D. and go forward
1 Chr. 13. 7 U. and A. *d.* the cart
2 Chr. 20. 7 didst *d.* out the inhab.
Job 6. 13 is wisdom *d.* quite from me
Ps. 68. 2 as smoke is *d.* so drive
Prov. 14. 32 the wicked is *d.* away
Isa. 8. 22 shall be *d.* to darkness
Jer. 46. 15 because the Lord had *d.*
Ezek. 4. 13 whither I will *d.* them
Dan. 9. 7 whither thou has *d.* them
Hos. 9. 15 I will *d.* them out of
Joel 2. 20 *d.* him into a land barren
Mic. 4. 6 gather her that is *d.* out
Hab. 3. 6 *d.* asunder the nations
Zeph. 3. 19 gather her that was *d.*
Mark 1. 12 spirit *d.* him into the wil.
Luke 8. 29 he was *d.* of the devil
John 2. 15 *d.* them all out of temple
Acts 18. 16 *d.* them from the judg.
Jas. 3. 4 ships .. *d.* of fierce winds
R. V. Job 18. 11 chase; Isa. 22. 19
thrust; Judg. 11. 24 dispossessed;
Deut. 30. 4 outcasts for

Driver. *Charioteer.*
1 K. 22. 34 said unto *d.* of his char.

Driving. *Impelling, dispossessing.*
Judg. 9. 23 left those na. without *d.*

---

2 K. 9. 20 *d.* is like the *d.* of Jehu

Dromedary. *Swift beast, courser.*
1 K. 4. 28 straw for horses and *d.*
Esth. 8. 10 riders on m. c. and .. *d.*
Isa. 60. 6 the *d.* of Midian and Ep.
Jer. 2. 23 a swift *d.* traversing
R. V. 1 K. 4. 28 swift steeds; Esth.
8. 10 bred of the stud

Drop (*n.*). *Drop, clot.*
Job 36. 27 maketh small the *d.* of w.
S. of S. 5. 2 locks with *d.* of .. night
Isa. 40. 15 behold nations as a *d.* of
Luke 22. 44 sweat was as *d.* of blo.

Drop (*v.*). *Drop, distil.*
Deut. 32. 2 doctrine shall *d.* as rain
Judg. 5. 4 the clouds also *d.* water
1 Sam. 14. 26 behold, the honey *d.*
2 Sam. 21. 10 harvest until water *d.*
Job 29. 22 and my speech *d.* upon
Ps. 65. 11 and thy paths *d.* fatness
Prov. 3. 20 clouds *d.* down the dew
Eccl. 10. 18 the house *d.* through
S. of S. 4. 11 lips .. *d.* as the honey
Isa. 45. 8 D. down, ye heavens
Ezek. 20. 46 *d.* thy word toward .. s.
Joel 3. 18 mts. shall *d.* new wine
Am. 7. 16 *d.* not thy word against

Dropsy. *Full of water.*
Luke 14. 2 man .. which had a *d.*

Dross. *Refuse, scum, slag.*
Ps. 119. 119 put away .. wicked .. *d.*
Prov. 25. 4 take away the *d.* from **s.**
Isa. 1. 22 thy silver is become *d.*
Ezek. 22. 18 Israel is to me become *d*

Drought. *Want of rain, dearth.*
Gen. 31. 40 day the *d.* consumed me
Deut. 8. 15 and scorpions, and *d.*
Job 24. 19 D. and heat consume
Ps. 32. 4 turned into *d.* of summer
Isa. 58. 11 satisfy thy soul in *d.*
Jer. 2. 6 led us through a land of *d.*
Hos. 13. 5 in the land of great *d.*
Hag. 1. 11 called for a *d.* upon land
R. V. Deut. 8. 15 thirsty ground;
Isa. 58. 11 dry places

Drove (*v.*). see **Drive.**

Drove (*n.*) *Flock, herd, company.*
Gen. 32. 16, 19 every *d.* by thems.
33, 8 all this *d.* which I met
R. V. Gen. 33. 8 company

Drown. *Wash away, sink, drown.*
Ex. 15. 4 chosen captains also are *d.*
S. of S. 8. 7 neither can floods *d.* it
Am. 8. 8 shall be cast out and *d.*
Mat. 18. 6 were *d.* in the depths
1 Tim. 6. 9 *d.* men in destruction
Heb. 11. 29 Egyptians .. were *d.*
R. V. Ex. 15. 4 sunk; Am. 8. 8; 9.
5 sink again; Heb. 11. 29 swal-
lowed up

Drowsiness. *Somnolence.*
Prov. 23. 21 *d.*:. clo. man with rags

Drunk (*v.*) see **Drink.**

Drunk (*a.*). *Satiated, intoxicated.*
Lev. 11. 34 that may be *d.* in every
Deut. 32. 42 make mine arrows *d.*
2 Sam. 11. 13 and he made him *d.*
Isa. 63. 6 made them *d.* in the fury
Jer. 46. 10 be satiate and made *d.*
John 2. 10 when men have well *d.*
Eph. 5. 18 be not *d.* with wine
Rev. 17. 2 have been made *d.* with

Drunken. *Satiated, merry.*
Gen. 9. 21 drank wine, and was *d.*
1 Sam. 1. 13 thought she had been *d.*
Job 12. 25 stagger like a *d.* man
Ps, 107. 27 stagger like a *d.* man
Isa. 19. 14 err .. as a *d.* man staggers
Jer. 23. 9 I am like a *d.* man
Lam. 41. 21 shall be *d.* and shalt
Ezek. 39. 19 drink bl. till ye be *d.*
Hab. 2. 15 makest him *d.* also
Nah. 3. 11 thou also shalt be *d.*
Mat. 24. 49 eat and drink with the *d.*
Luke 12. 45 eat, drink, and be *d.*
Acts 2. 15 for these are not *d.* as ye
1 Cor. 11. 21 one hungry, another *d.*
1 Thes. 5. 7 that are *d.* in the night
Rev. 17. 6 woman *d.* with the blood

Drunkenness. *Satiety.*
Deut. 29. 19 to add *d.* to thirst
Eccl. 10. 17 for strength and not *d.*
Jer. 13. 13 fill all .. Jerusa. with *d.*
Ezek. 23. 33 shalt be filled with *d.*
Luke 21. 34 overcharged with .. *d.*
Rom. 13. 13 walk .. not in .. *d.*

Gal. 5. 21 *d.*, revellings and such

Dry (*a.*). *Waterless, withered.*
Gen. 1. 9 let the *d.* land appear
Ex. 4. 9 pour it upon the *d.* land
Lev. 7. 10 mingled with oil and *d.*
Josh. 3. 17 priests .. stood .. on *d.* g
Judg. 6. 37 be *d.* upon the earth
2 K. 2. 8 went over on *d.* ground
Neh. 9. 11 through .. sea on *d.* land
Job 13. 25 will .. pursue the *d.* stub.
Ps. 66. 6 turned the sea unto *d.* land
Prov. 17. 1 better is a *d.* morsel, and
Jer. 4. 11 *d.* wind of the high places
Ezek. 30. 12 will make the rivers *d.*
Hos. 2. 3 and set her like a *d.* land
Jonah 1. 9 made the sea and the *d.*
Nah. 1. 4 rebu. sea, and maketh it *d.*
Zeph. 2. 13 will make Nineveh .. *d.*
Hag. 2. 6 will shake .. the *d.* land
Mat. 12. 43 walketh through *d.* pl.
Luke 23. 31 what .. be done in .. *d.*
Heb. 11. 29 passed .. sea as by *d.* l.

Dry (*v.*). *Parch, wither, exhaust.*
Josh. 2. 10 Lord *d.* up the water
1 K. 13. 4 Jerobo. .. his hand .. *d.* up
2 K. 19. 24 with .. feet have I *d.* up
Job 15. 30 flame shall *d.* his branch
Ps. 74. 15 thou *d.* up mighty rivers
Prov. 17. 22 broken spir. *d.* the bones
Isa. 42. 15 *d.* up all their herbs
Ezek. 17. 24 have *d.* .. the green tr.
Nah. 1. 4 sea, .. *d.* up all the rivers
Zech. 10. 11 the deeps .. shall *d.* up
Mark 5. 29 fount. of her blood was *d.*
Rev. 16. 12 water thereof was *d.*
R. V. Lev. 2. 14; Isa. 5. 13 parched;
Joel 1. 12; Mark 11. 20 withered

Dryshod. *Sandaled.*
Isa. 11. 15 make men go over *d. s.*

Due. *Portion, proper, owing.*
Lev. 10. 13 it is thy *d.*, and thy son's
Deut. 11. 14 rain .. in his *d.* season
Neh. 11. 23 portion *d.* for every day
Ps. 104. 27 give .. meat in *d.* season
Prov. 15. 23 word spoken in *d.* sea.
Mat. 18. 34 pay all that was *d.*
Luke 23. 41 receive the *d.* reward
Rom. 13. 7 render .. to all their *d.*
1 Cor. 7. 3 render to wf. *d.* benev.
1 Tim. 2. 6 to be test. in *d.* time
Tit. 1. 3 hath in *d.* times manifested
R. V. 1 Tim. 2. 6 its own; Tit. 1. 3
his own

Duke. *Leader, Prince.*
Gen. 36. 15-43 these were *d.* of Es.
Ex. 15. 15 *d.* of E. shall be amazed
Josh. 13. 21 *d.* of Sihon, dwelling
1 Chr. 1. 51-54 *d.* were *d.* Timnah
R. V. Josh. 13. 21 princes

Dulcimer. *Double-pipe, bagpipe.*
Dan. 3. 5, 10, 15 ye hear the .. *d.*

Dull. *Slothful.*
Mat. 13. 15 ears are *d.* of hearing
Acts 28. 27 and their ears are *d.*
Heb. 5. 11 seeing ye are *d.* of hear.

Dumb. *Tied, speechless, blunted.*
Ex. 4. 11 or who maketh the *d.*
Ps. 39. 2 I was *d.* with silence
Prov. 31. 8 open thy mouth for .. *d.*
Isa. 35. 6 shall tongue of the *d.* sing
Ezek. 3. 26 that thou shalt be *d.*
Dan. 10. 15 had spok .. I became *d.*
Hab. 2. 18 trusteth therein to m. *d.*
Mat. 9. 32 brought to him a *d.* man
9. 33; 12. 22; 15. 30, 31
Mark 7. 37 maketh .. the *d.* to speak
Luke 11. 14 devil, and it was *d.*
Acts 8. 32 lamb *d.* before .. shearers
1 Cor. 12. 2 carried .. unto .. *d.* idols
2 Pet. 2. 16 the *d.* ass speaking with
R. V. Luke 1. 20 silent

Dung (*n.*). *Excrement, dirt.*
Ex. 29. 14 flesh of bull.. .and.. *d.*
Lev. 4. 11 skin of bullock and .. *d.*
Num. 19. 5 her *d.* shall be burned
1 K. 14. 10 as a man taketh away *d.*
2 K. 9. 37 car. of J. shall be as *d.*
Neh. 2. 13 and to the *d.* port
Job 20. 7 perish .. lik.: his own *d.*
Ps. 83. 10 they became as *d.* for the e.
Isa. 36. 12 may eat their own *d.*
Ezek. 4. 15 have given the cow's *d.*
Zeph. 1. 17 and their flesh as the *d.*
Mal. 2. 3 Behold, I will .. spread *d.*
Phil. 3. 8. and do count them but *d.*

Dung (*v.*). *To manure.*

Luke 13. 8 sh. dig about it and *d.* it
Dungeon. *Pit, chamber.*
Gen. 40. 15 should put me into the *d.*
Ex. 12. 29 captive that was in the *d.*
Jer. 37. 16 Jer. was ent. into the *d.*
38. 6, 7, 9, 10, 11, 13
Lam. 3. 53 cut off my life in the *d*
Dunghill. *Dung heap.*
1 Sam. 2. 8 lifteth . . beggar from *d. h.*
Ez. 6. 11 house be made a *d. h.*
Ps. 113. 7 lift. needy out of the *d. h.*
Isa. 25. 10 as straw trodden for *d. h.*
Lam. 4. 5 in scarlet, embrace a *d. h.*
Luke 14. 35 nor yet for the *d. h.*
Dan. 2. 5 houses shall be made *d. h.*
Durable. *Lasting.*
Prov. 8. 18 *d.* riches and righteous.
Isa. 23. 18 to eat, and for *d.* clothing
Durst. *See* **Dare.**
Dust. *Ashes, clay, powdered matter.*
Gen. 2. 7 God formed man of *d.*
3. 14, 19; 13. 16; 18. 27; 28. 14
Ex. 8. 17 *d.* of the land became lice
Lev. 14. 41 pour out the *d.* that
Num. 23. 10 Who can count . . *d.* of J.
Deut. 9. 21 was as small as *d.*
Josh. 7. 6 put *d.* upon their heads
1 Sam. 2. 8 raiseth . . poor out of . . *d.*
2 Sam. 16. 13 threw stones . . cast *d.*
1 K. 16. 2 exalted thee out of the *d.*
2 K. 13. 7 made them like the *d.*
2 Chr. 1. 9 like the *d.* of the earth
Job 2. 12 sprinkled *d.* upon . . heads
4. 19; 5. 6; 7. 5; 10. 9; 14. 19;
Ps. 7. 5 lay mine honour in the *d.*
18. 42; 22. 15; 30. 9; 44. 25; 72. 9
Prov. 8. 26 nor . . *d.* of the world
Eccl. 3. 20 all are of the *d.*, and
Isa. 2. 10 hide thee in the *d.*, for fear
25. 12; 26. 5; 29. 4; 34. 7; 40. 12
Lam. 2. 10 cast . . *d.* upon their heads
Ezek. 24. 7 to cover it with *d.*
Dan. 12. 2 many . . that sleep in . . *d.*
Am. 2. 7 that pant after the *d.*
Mic. 1. 10 house of Aphrah roll in *d.*
Hab. 1. 10 for they shall heap *d.*
Zeph. 1. 17 blood . . poured out as *d.*
Zech. 9. 3 heaped up silver as . . *d.*
Mat. 10. 14 shake off the *d.* of
Mark 6. 11 shake off the *d.* under
Luke 10. 11 even . . *d.* of your city
Acts 13. 51 they shook off the *d.*
Rev. 18. 19 cast *d.* on their heads
R. V. Lev. 14. 41 mortar
Duty. *Matter, owing, obligation.*
Ex. 21. 10 to her *d.* of marriage
2 Chr. 8. 14 as *d.* of ev. day required
Ez. 3. 4 *d.* of every day required
Luke 17. 10 done . . which was our *d.*
Rom. 15. 27 their *d.* is . . to minist.
R. V. Rom. 15. 27 owe it to them
Dwarf. *Small, lean.*
Lev. 21. 20 or crookbackt, or *d.*
Dwell. *Sit down, sojourn, live.*
Gen. 4. 16 Cain . . *d.* in land of N.
11. 2; 13. 6; 14. 7; 16. 3; 19. 29
Ex. 2. 15 Moses . . *d.* in land of Mi.
Lev. 13. 46 uncl., he shall *d.* alone
Num. 13. 18 people that *d.* therein
Deut. 1. 6 *d.* long enough in . . mt.
Josh. 2. 15 she *d.* upon the wall
Judg. 1. 9 the Canaanites that *d.*
Ruth 1. 4 *d.* there about ten years
1 Sam. 4. 4 Lord of Hosts which *d.*
2 Sam. 2. 3 *d.* in city of Hebron
1 K. 2. 36 build . . house and *d.* there.
2 K. 4. 13 I *d.* among mine own
1 Chr. 2. 55 scribes which *d.* at Jab.
2 Chr. 2. 3 build . . house to *d.* there.
Ez. 2. 70 Nethinims *d* in their cities
Neh. 3. 26 Nethinims *d.* in Ophel
Esth. 9. 19 *d.* in unwalled towns
Job 22. 8 honourable man *d.* in it
Ps. 9. 11 sing pr. to the L. which *d.*
23. 6; 24. 1; 27. 4; 65. 8; 68. 10
Prov. 3. 29 seeing thy *d.* securely
S. of S. 8. 13 that *d.* in the gardens
Isa. 6. 5 *d.* in midst of a people
9. 2; 10. 24; 23. 18; 24. 6; 26. 5
Jer. 2. 6 land . . where no man *d.*
4. 29; 8. 16; 9. 26; 12. 4; 20. 6
Lam. 1. 3 she *d.* among the heathen
Ezek. 2. 6 dost *d.* among scorpions
3. 15; 7. 7; 12. 2; 16. 46; 28. 25;
Hos. 4. 3 every one that *d.* therein

Joel 3. 20 Judah shall *d.* forever
Am. 3. 12 chil. of Is. . . *d.* in Samaria
Mic. 7. 13 because of them that *d.*
Nah. 1. 5 world, all that *d.* therein
Hab. 2. 8 city and all that *d.* there
Zeph. 1. 18 riddance of all that *d.*
Hag. 1. 4 *d.* in your cieled houses
Zech. 2. 7 *d.* with daughter of Bab.
Mat. 2. 23 *d.* in city called Nazareth
Luke 11. 26 enter in, and *d.* there
John 1. 38 said, where *d.* thou?
Acts 4. 16 mani. to all that *d.* in J.
Rom. 8. 11 his Spirit that *d.* in you
1 Cor. 3. 16 Spirit of God *d.* in you
2 Cor. 6. 16 said, I will *d.* in them
Eph. 3. 17 C. may *d.* in your hearts
Col. 1. 19 in him should . . fulness *d.*
1 Tim. 6. 16 *d.* in the light which
2 Tim. 1. 14 Holy Ghost that *d.* in
Heb. 11. 9 *d.* in taberna. with Isaac
James 4. 5 the spirit that *d.* in us
1 John 3. 17 how *d.* the love of God
2 John 2 truth's sake, which *d.* in
Rev. 2. 13 was slain . . where Satan *d.*
3. 10; 6. 10; 11. 10; 13. 8; 14. 6;
R. V. frequently in O. T., sit, sojourn
Dwellers. *Settlers, inhabitants.*
Isa. 18. 3 all *d.* on the earth, see ye
Acts 1. 19 known to all *d.* at Jeru.
Dwelling. *Habitation, home.*
Gen. 10. 30 their *d.* was from Mes.
Ex. 10. 23 had light in their *d.*
Lev. 3. 17 statute . . throughout . . *d.*
Num. 35. 29 statute in all your *d.*
1 K. 8. 30 hear . . in heaven thy *d.*
2 K. 17. 25 beginning of their *d.*
2 Chr. 6. 2 place for thy *d.* forever
Job. 18. 19 nor any remain. in his *d.*
Ps. 55. 15 wickedness is in their *d.*
Prov. 21. 20 oil in the *d.* of the wise
Isa. 32. 18 my peo. dwell . . in sure *d.*
Jer. 9. 19 our *d.* have cast us out
Ezek. 25. 4 make their *d.* in thee
Dan. 4. 25 *d.* shall be with beasts
Zeph. 2. 6 sea coast shall be *d.*
Mark 5. 3 had . . *d.* among the tombs
Dwelling-place. *Seat, habitation.*
Num. 24. 21 strong is thy *d. p.*
1 Chr. 6. 32 ; 2 Chr. 30. 27 ; Job 8.
22 ; Ps. 52. 5 ; Jer. 30. 18 ; Ezek.
6. 6 ; Hab. 1. 6 ; 1 Cor. 4. 11
R. V. 1 Chr. 6. 32 tabernacle ; 2 Chr.
30. 27 ; Ps. 79. 7 ; Isa. 4. 5 habitation ; Job 8. 22 ; Ps. 52. 5 tent
Dwelt. *See* **Dwell.**
Dyed. *Colored, brightened.*
Ex. 25. 5 offer., ram's skins *d.* red
Isa. 63. 1 cometh . . with *d.* garments
Ezek. 23. 15 exceeding in *d.* attire
Dying. *Expiring.*
Luke 8. 42 daugh. . . . and she lay a *d*
2 Cor. 4. 10 the *d.* of the L. Jesus
Heb. 11. 21 Jacob when he was a *d*

E.

Each. *One by one, part by part.*
Gen. 15. 10 laid *e.* piece one against,
Ex. 30. 34 of *e.* shall there be alike
Num. 7. 11 *e.* prince on his day
Josh. 22. 14 ten princes of *e.* . . ho.
Judg. 21. 22 to *e.* man his wife
Ruth 1. 8 return *e.* to . . mother's h.
1 K. 4. 7 *e.* man his month in year
2 K. 15. 20 *e.* man fif. shek. of sil.
2 Chr. 4. 13 two rows of pom. on *e.*
Isa. 6. 2 stood the seraph.; *e.* one
Luke 13. 15 doth not *e.* one of you
Acts 2. 3 clo. tongues . . sat on *e.*
Rev. 4. 8 the four beasts had *e.*
R. V. Num. 14. 34 ; Josh. 22. 14
every
Eagle. *Eagle, vulture.*
Ex. 19. 4 bear you on *e's* wings
Lev. 11. 13 the *e.* and the ossifrage
Deut. 32. 11 as *e.* stirreth . . her ne.
2 Sam. 1. 23 swifter than *e.* they
Job 9. 26 as . . *e.* that hasteth to
Ps. 103. 5 youth renew. like the *e's*
Prov. 23. 5 riches fly away as an *e.*
Isa. 40. 31 mount with wings as *e.*
Jer. 4. 13 horses are swifter than *e.*
Lam. 4. 19 per. are swifter than *e' s*
Ezek. 1. 10 had the face of an *e.*
Dan. 4. 33 hairs were grown like *e's.*
Hos. 8. 1 as an *e.* against the house

Obad. 4 exalt thyself as the *e.*
Mic. 1. 16 enlarge . . bald. as the *e.*
Hab. 1. 8 shall fly as the *e.* that
Mat. 24. 28 there will *e.* be gathered
Luke 17. 37 will *e.* be gathered tog.
Rev. 4. 7 beasts like a flying *e.*
R. V. Lev. 11. 18 ; Deut. 14. 17
vulture
Ear (*v.*). *Plough, sieve.*
Deut. 21. 4 valley which is nei. *e.*
1 Sam. 8. 12 set them to *e.* his grou.
Isa. 30. 24 asses that *e.* the ground
R. V. 1 Sam. 8. 12 plow ; Isa. 30.
24 till
Ear. *Organ of hearing.*
Gen. 20. 8 told . . things in their *e.*
Ex. 10. 2 tell in *e.* of thy son, and
Lev. 8. 23 tip of Aaron's right *e.*
Num. 11. 18 wept in . . *e.* of the L.
Deut. 5. 1 judg. . . I spk. in your *e.*
Josh. 20. 4 declare. . . cause in *e.* of
1 Sam. 3. 11 *e.* of . . one that hear.
2 Sam. 3. 19 A. spake in *e.* of B.
2 K. 18. 26 in the *e.* of the people
1 Chr. 17. 20 have heard with our *e.*
2 Chr. 6. 40 let thine *e.* attend to
Neh. 1. 6 let thine *e.* be attentive
Job 4. 12 and mine *e.* received a
12. 11 ; 13. 1 ; 15. 21 ; 28. 22 ; 29. 11
Ps. 10. 17 cause thine *e.* to hear
17. 6 ; 18. 6 ; 31. 2 ; 34. 15 ; 40. 6
Prov. 2. 2 incline thine *e.* to wisdom
5. 1 ; 15. 31 ; 18. 15 ; 20. 12 ; 21. 13
Eccl. 1. 8 eye not sat., nor *e.* filled
Isa. 5. 9 in mine *e.*, said L. of H.
6. 10 ; 11. 3 ; 22. 14 ; 30. 21 ; 32. 3
Jer. 2. 2 cry in *e.* of Jerusalem
6. 10 ; 7. 24 ; 9. 20 ; 11. 8 ; 17. 23 ;
Lam. 3. 56 hide not thine *e.* at
Ezek. 3. 10 w. . . hear with thine *e.*
Dan. 9. 18 my God, incline thine *e.*
Am. 3. 12 taketh . . a piece of . . *e.*
Mic. 7. 16 their *e.* shall be deaf
Zech. 7. 11 they . . stopped their *e.*
Mat. 10. 27 what ye hear in the *e.*
Mark 4. 9 that hath *e.* . . let him h.
Luke 1. 44 sal. sounded in mine *e.*
John 18. 10 Pet. cut off his right *e.*
Acts 7. 51 uncir. in heart and *e.*
Rom. 11. 8 given . . *e.* that they may
1 Cor. 2. 9 eye hath not seen, nor *e.*
2 Tim. 4. 3 teachers, hav. itching *e.*
Jas. 5. 4 cries . . ent. into their *e.*
1 Pet. 3. 12 *e.* not open to prayer
Rev. 2. 7 that hath *e.* . . let him hear
Fruit-spike, head, sprout
Gen. 41. 5 seven *e.* of corn came up
Lev. 2. 14 *e.* of corn dried by the
Ex. 9. 31 the barley was in the *e.*
Ruth 2. 2 and glean *e.* of corn
2 K. 4. 42 *e.* of corn in the husk
Job 24. 24 cut off as . . *e.* of corn
Isa. 17. 5 reapeth the *e.* with his a.
Mat. 12. 1 began to pluck the *e.*
Mark 2. 23 dis. began to pluck . . *e.*
Luke 6. 1 disciples plucked the *e.*
Earing. *Plowing, cutting.*
Gen. 45. 6 neither be *e.* nor harvest
Ex. 34. 21 in *e.* time and harvest
Early. *Betimes, first, morning.*
Gen. 19. 27 Abraham gat up *e.* in
Judg. 19. 9 get you *e.* on your way
1 Sam. 29. 10 be up *e.* in the morn.
Ps. 46. 5 help her, and that right *e.*
S. of S. 7. 12 up *e.* to the vineyards
Dan. 6. 19 the king arose very *e.*
Hos. 6. 4 as *e.* dew it goeth away
Mark 16. 9 when Jesus was risen *e.*
Luke 24. 22 women . . were *e.* at se.
John 20. 1 first day . . cometh M. *e.*
Jas. 5. 7 receive *e.* and latter rain
R. V. Judg. 7. 3 ; Ps. 57. 8 right
early ; 9. 14 in the morning ; 101.
8 morning by morning ; Ps. 1. 28 ;
8. 17 diligently ; Hos. 5. 15 earnestly ; Mark 16. 2 early in the
morning ; Acts 5. 21 about daybreak
Earn. *Gain, hire out.*
Hag. 1. 6 he that *e.* wages *e.* wages
Earnest. *Surety, pledge.*
2 Cor. 1. 22 the *e.* of the Spirit in
Eph. 1. 14 *e.* of our inheritance
Earnestly. *Steadfastly, fervently.*
Luke 22. 56 and *e.* looked upon him
Acts 3. 12 why look ye so *e.* on

Jas. 5. 17 prayed *e.* that it might
R. V. Mic. 7. 3 diligently ; Luke 22
56 ; Acts 23. 1 stedfastly ; Acts
3. 12 fasten your eyes ; Jas. 5. 17
fervently

Ear-ring. *Amulet, ear or nose ring.*
Gen. 24. 22 man took a golden *e.*
Ex. 32. 2 break off the gold. *e.r.*
Num. 31. 50 w. ev. man hath . . *e.r.*
Judg. 8. 24 give . . every man the *e.r.*
Job 42. 11 ev. man . . g. him . . *e.r.*
Prov. 25. 12 as an *e.r.* of gold
Ezek. 16. 12 put . . *e. r.* in thine *e.*
R. V. Gen. 24. 22, 47 ; 35. 4 ; Ex.
32. 2, 3 ; Job 42. 11 ring, rings ;
Isa. 3. 20 amulets

Earth. *Ground, soil, land*
Gen. 1. 25 ev. thing that creep. on *e.*
4. 1 ; 6. 1 ; 7. 4 ; 9. 2 ; 12. 3 ; 28. 14
Ex. 10. 6 day they were upon . . *e.*
Num. 12. 3 all the men . . upon . . *e.*
Deut. 4. 10 days . . they sh. live on *e.*
1 Sam. 4. 12 man . . wi. *e.* on his head
2 Sam. 1. 2 and *e.* upon his head
1 K. 13. 34 destroy from face of . . *e.*
2 K. 5. 17 two mules' burden of *e.*
Neh. 9. 1 sackclothes and *e.* upon
Ps. 83. 10 became as dung for . . *e.*
Isa. 23. 17 all kingdoms upon . . *e.*
Jer. 16. 4 be as dung upon the *e.*
Ezek. 38. 20 things . . creep upon . . *e.*
Dan. 12. 2 sleep in . . dust of the *e.*
Am. 3. 2 known of all . . the *e.*
Mat. 5. 5 they shall inherit the *e.*
5. 13 ; 6. 10 ; 9. 6 ; 10. 34 ; 11. 25 ;
12. 40 ; 13. 5 ; 16. 19 ; 17. 25 ; 18. 18
Mark 2. 10 S. of m. hath power on *e.*
Luke 2. 14 on *e.* peace, good will
5. 24 ; 6. 49 ; 10. 21 ; 11. 2 ; 12. 49
John 3. 31 that is of *e.* is earthly
Acts 1. 8 uttermost part of the *e.*
2. 19 ; 3. 25 ; 4. 24 ; 7. 49 ; 8. 33
Rom. 9. 17 declar. through all the *e.*
1 Cor. 8. 5 whether in heaven or *e.*
Eph. 1. 10 in C., and which are on *e.*
Col. 1. 16 and that are in *e.*, visible
2 Tim. 2. 20 also of wood and *e.*
Phil. 2. 10 and things under the *e.*
Heb. 1. 10 laid . . foundation of . . *e.*
Jas. 5. 5 lived in pleasure on *e.*
2 Pet. 3. 5 *e.* standing out of water
1 John 5. 8 three . . bear wit. on *e.*
Rev. 1. 5 prince of kings of the *e.*
3. 10 ; 5. 3 ; 6. 4 ; 7. 1 ; 8. 5 ; 9. 1

Land, the planet.
Gen. 1. 1 God created heaven and *e.*
1. 2-30 ; 2. 1-6 ; 4. 12 ; 6. 5-17 ; 7.
3-24 ; 8. 1-22 ; 9. 1-19 ; 10. 8 ; 11. 1
Ex. 9. 14 none like me in all the *e.*
Lev. 11. 2 among all beasts on the *e.*
Num. 14. 21 all *e.* . . be filled wi. glo.
Deut. 3. 24 what G. is there in . . *e.*
4. 17 ; 5. 8 ; 10. 14 ; 12. 16 ; 13. 7
Josh. 2. 11 God in heaven and in *e.*
Judg. 5. 4 *e.* trembled, and the h.
1 Sam. 2. 10 judge the ends of the *e.*
2 Sam. 1. 2 fell to the *e.* and did ob.
1 K. 1. 31 bowed her face to the *e.*
2 K. 5. 15 no God in all the *e.*
1 Chr. 1. 10 began to be m. upon *e.*
2 Chr. 1. 9 like dust of *e.* in multi.
Ez. 1. 2 given me . . kingds. of the *e.*
Neh. 9. 6 hast made heav., . . the *e.*
Job 1. 7 going to and fro in the *e.*
2. 2 ; 3. 14 ; 5. 10 ; 7. 1 ; 8. 9 ; 9. 6
Ps. 2. 2 kings of the *e.* set thems.
7. 5 ; 8. 1 ; 10. 18 ; 12. 6 ; 16. 3 ;
17. 11 ; 18. 7 ; 19. 4 ; 21. 10 ; 22. 29
Prov. 2. 22 wicked . . be cut . . from *e.*
Eccl. 1. 4 *e.* abideth forever
S. of S. 2. 12 flowers appear on the *e.*
Isa. 1. 2 Hear, . . and give ear, O *e.*
2. 19 ; 4. 2 ; 5. 8 ; 6. 3 ; 8. 22 ; 10.
14 ; 11. 4 ; 12. 5 ; 13. 13 ; 14. 7
Jer. 6. 19 *e.*, behold I will bring
7. 33 ; 9. 3 ; 10. 10 ; 14. 4 ; 15. 3
Lam. 2. 1 cast . . from h. unto the *e.*
Ezek. 1. 15 one wheel upon the *e.*
Dan. 8. 5 on face of the whole *e.*
Hos. 2. 21 they shall hear the *e.*
Joel 2. 30 wonders in h. and in *e.*
Am. 2. 7 pant after the d. of the *e.*
Jonah 2. 6 *e.* with her bars was
Mic. 4. 13 unto the Lord of the *e.*
Nah. 1. 5 *e.* is burned at his pres.

Hab. 2. 14 *e.* shall be filled with
Zeph. 2. 3 seek . . L. all . . meek of *e.*
Hag. 1. 10 *e.* is stayed from . . fruit
Zech. 1. 10 walk to and fro thro' . *e.*
Mal. 4. 6 smite *e.* with a curse
R. V. very frequently in O. T.,
land

Earthen. *Made of earth.*
Lev. 6. 28 the *e.* vessel wherein it
Num. 5. 17 take . . w. in an *e.* ves.
2 Sam. 17. 28 bro. . . basons and *e.* v.
Jer. 19. 1 get a potter's *e.* bottle
Lam 4. 2 esteemed as *e.* pitchers
2 Cor. 4. 7 have . . treas. in *e.* ves.

Earthly. *Of the earth.*
John 3. 31 that is of earth is *e.*
2 Cor. 5. 1 know . . if our *e.* house
Phil. 3. 19 who mind *e.* things
Jas. 3. 15 descendeth not . . but is *e.*
R. V. John 3. 31 of the earth

Earthquake. *Shaking, trembling.*
1 K. 19. 11 after the wind an *e. q.*
Isa. 29. 6 with *e. q.* and great noise
Am. 1. 1 two years before the *e. q.*
Zech. 14. 5 fled from before the *e. q.*
Mat. 24. 7 shall be fam. . . and *e. q.*
Mark 13. 8 shall be *e. q.* in div. pl.
Luke 21. 11 great *e. q.* shall be in
Acts 16. 26 suddenly there was . . *e. q.*
Rev. 6. 12 sixth s., . . was a great *e. q.*
8. 5 ; 11. 13, 19 ; 16. 18

Earthy. *Made of earth.*
1 Cor. 15. 47 man is of earth, *e.*
25. 48, 49

Ease (*v.*). *Make light, relieve.*
Deut. 23. 13 when thou wilt *e.* thy.
2 Chr. 10. 4 *e.* . . the grievous servi.
Job 7. 13 couch shall *e.* my com.
Isa. 1. 24 *e.* me of mine adversaries
2 Cor. 8. 13 that other men be *e.*
R. V. Deut. 23. 13 sitteth down ; 2
Chr. 10. 4, 9 wake

Ease (*n.*). *Quiet, comfort.*
Deut. 28. 65 among na. . . find no *e.*
Judg. 20. 43 trod them down wi. *e.*
Job 12. 5 thought of him . . at *e.*
Ps. 25. 13 His soul shall dwell at *e.*
Isa. 32. 9 rise, ye women . . at *e.*
Jer. 46. 27 be in rest and at *e.*
Ezek. 23. 42 voice of mul. being at *e.*
Am. 6. 1 woe to them . . at *e.* in Z.
Zech. 1. 15 heathen that are at *e.*
Luke 12. 19 take thine *e.*, eat, dr.

Easier. *Less hard or heavy.*
Ex. 18. 22 so shall it be *e.* for self
Mat. 9. 5 for whether is *e.* to say
Mark 10. 25 *e.* for a camel to go
Luke 16. 17 *e.* for h. and e. to pass

East. *Rising of the sun, east.*
Gen. 3. 24 at *e.* gate of the garden
10. 30 ; 11. 2 ; 12. 8 ; 13. 11 ; 25. 6
Ex. 10. 13 Lord brought an *e.* wind
Lev. 1. 16 beside . . the altar on *e.*
Num. 10. 5 camps that lie on *e.*
Josh. 4. 19 in *e.* border of Jericho
Judg. 6. 3 the children of the *e.*
1 K. 7. 25 three looking toward . . *e.*
1 Chr. 5. 10 throughout all the *e.*
2 Chr. 5. 12 stood at *e.* . . of altar
Neh. 3. 26 against . . gate to. . . *e.*
Job 1. 3 greatest of . . men of . . *e.*
Ps. 48. 7 breakest ships wi. *e.* wind
Isa. 2. 6 replenished from the *e.*
Jer. 19. 2 Hin., entry of the *e.* gate
Ezek. 17. 10 when *e.* wind touch. it
19. 12 ; 27. 26 ; 40. 6 ; 41. 14 ; 42. 10
43. 1 ; 44. 1 ; 45. 7 ; 46. 1 ; 47. 18
Dan. 8. 9 great, toward the *e.*, and
Hos. 12. 1 followed after the *e.* wind
Joel 2. 20 face toward the *e.* sea
Am. 8. 12 from north, even to the *e.*
Jonah 4. 5 sat on *e.* side of the cit.
Hab. 1. 9 faces sup . . as the *e.* wind
Zech. 8. 7 save my peo. from the *e.*
Mat. 2. 1 came wise men from the *e.*
2. 2, 9 ; 8. 11 ; 24. 27
Luke 13. 29 they . . come from the *e.*
Rev. 7. 2 angel ascendeth from the *e.*
21. 13 on the *e.*, three gates
R. V. Jer. 19. 2 Harsith ; Rev. 7. 2 ;
16. 12 sunrising

Easter. R. V. *The Passover.*
Acts 12. 4 intending after *E.* to

Eastward. *Sun's rising.*
Gen. 13. 14 and southward, and *e.*

Ex. 27. 13 courts on east side *e.*
Lev. 16. 14 finger on mer. seat *e.*
Num. 3. 38 taber. of . . congrega. *e.*
Deut. 3. 17 salt sea, under Ash., *e.*
Josh. 11. 8 unto val. of Mizpeh *e.*
1 Sam. 13. 5 Micmash, *e.* from Beth
1 K. 7. 39 right side of the house *e.*
2 K. 10. 33 from Jordan *e.*, all
1 Chr. 5. 9 *e.* ye inhabited unto
Neh. 12. 37 into the water gate *e.*
Ezek. 11. 1 gate . . which looketh *e.*
R. V. Gen. 2. 14 in front ; Num.
3. 38 toward the sunrising.

Easy. *Good, kind, light.*
Prov. 14. 6 knowl. is *e.* unto him
Mat. 11. 30 my yoke is *e.*, and my

Eat. *Chew, partake, consume.*
Gen. 2. 16 tree . . thou may. freely *e.*
3. 1-22 ; 9. 4 ; 14. 24 ; 18. 8 ; 19. 3
Ex. 2. 20 call him, that he may *e.*
Lev. 3. 17 *e.* neither fat nor blood
Num. 6. 3 neither . . *e.* moist grapes
Deut. 2. 28 sell me m. . . that I may *e.*
Josh. 5. 11 did *e.* of the old corn
Judg. 9. 27 did *e.* and drink, and cur.
Ruth 2. 14 *e.* of the bread, and dip
1 Sam. 1. 7 she wept, and did *e.*
2 Sam. 9. 7 *e.* bread at my table
1 K. 1. 25 *e.* and drink before him
2 K. 4. 8 she constr. him to *e.* brd.
1 Chr. 12. 39 were wi. D. . . *e.* and dr.
2 Chr. 30. 18 did they *e.* the passov.
Ex. 12. 8 said . . they should not *e.*
Neh. 5. 2 take . . corn . . th. we may *e.*
Esth. 4. 16 nei. . . nor dr. three days
Job 1. 4 called . . three sisters to *e.*
Ps. 14. 4 who *e.* up my people
22. 26 ; 27. 2 ; 41. 9 ; 50. 13 ; 78. 24
Prov. 1. 31 of the fruit of . . own w.
Eccl. 2. 24 he should not *e.* and dr.
S. of S. 4. 16 *e.* his pleasant fruits
Isa. 1. 19 ye shall *e.* the good of land
3. 10 ; 4. 1 ; 5. 17 ; 7. 15 ; 9. 20 11. 7
Jer. 2. 7 to *e.* the fruit thereof
Lam. 2. 20 shall wom. *e.* their fruit
Ezek. 2. 8 open thy mouth and *e.*
Dan. 1. 12 let th. give us pulse to *e.*
Hos. 2. 12 beasts of the field shall *e.*
Joel 1. 4 locust *e.*, cankerworm *e.*
Am. 6. 4 *e.* lambs out of the flock
Mic. 3. 3 *e.* the flesh of my people
Nah. 3. 15 *e.* thee . . like cankerw.
Hab. 1. 8 eagle that hasteth to *e.*
Hag. 1. 6 ye *e.*, but have not enough
Zech. 7. 6 when ye did *e.*, and when
Mat. 9. 11 why *e.* your Mas. with
11. 18 ; 12. 1 ; 14. 21 ; 15. 2 ; 24. 49
Mark 1. 6 and he did *e.* locusts
2. 16 ; 7. 2 ; 14. 18, 22
Luke 6. 1 dis. plucked . . and did *e.*
7. 33 ; 10. 7 ; 12. 45 ; 15. 16 ; 17. 27
John 4. 31 dis. prayed, saying, M. *e.*
Acts 9. 9 neither did *e.* nor drink
Rom. 14. 2 who is weak *e.* herbs
1 Cor. 8. 8 if we *e.*, are we better
Gal. 2. 12 did *e.* with the Gentiles
2 Thes. 3. 8 nei. *e.* we any man's b.
Heb. 13. 10 they have no right to *e.*
Jas. 5. 3 *e.* your flesh as it were fire
Rev. 2. 14 *e.* things sacrifi. to idols

Eaten. *Partaken of.*
Gen. 6. 21 take . . all food that is *e.*
Ex. 13. 7 unleav. bread shall be *e.*
Lev. 6. 30 no sin offer. . . shall be *e.*
Num. 28. 17 sev. d. shall unl. br. *e.*
Deut. 12. 22 as the . . hart is *e.*
Job 6. 6 can that . . unsavoury be *e.*
Isa. 6. 13 shall return and sh. be *e.*
Jer. 24. 2 which could not be *e.*
Ezek. 45. 21 unl. bread shall be *e.*

Eater. *Who eats.*
Judg. 14. 14 out of . . *e.* cometh . . m.
Isa. 55. 10 seed to . . sower, . . br. to *e.*
Nah. 3. 12 fall into the mouth of . . *e.*

Eating. *Chewing, partaking.*
Ex. 12. 4 ev. man according to his *e.*
Job. 20. 23 rain it on him while . . *e.*
Mat. 26. 26 were *e.* Jesus took bread
1 Cor. 8. 4 concerning . . the *e.* of

Ebony. *Heavy, dark wood.*
Ezek. 27. 15 horns of *e.* and ivory

Edge. *Mouth, sharpness.*
Gen. 34. 26 slew H. with *e.* of sword
Ex. 17. 13 dis. A. with *e.* of sword
Num. 21. 24 smote . . with *e.* of s.
Deut. 13. 15 smite with *e.* of sword

Josh. 6. 21 destroyed all with *e.* of
Judg. 1. 8 smitten it with *e.* of swd.
1 Sam. 15. 8; 2 Sam. 15. 14; 2 K.
10. 25; Job 1. 15; Ps. 89. 43; Jer.
21. 7; Luke 21. 24; Heb. 11. 34;
Rev. 2. 12
To be blunt.
Jer. 31. 29 chil's teeth are set on *e.*
31. 30; Ezek. 18. 2
End, lip, border, hem.
Ex. 26. 4 loops . . on *e.* of the one
26. 10; 36. 11, 17
Num. 38. 6 *e.* of the wilderness
Josh. 13. 27 *e.* of sea of Chinnereth
R. V. Ex. 28. 7; 39. 4 ends; Josh.
13. 27 uttermost part
Edification. *Building up.*
1 Cor. 14. 3 speaketh unto men to *e.*
2 Cor. 10. 8 Lord hath giv. us for *e.*
R. V. Rom 15. 2 unto edifying; 2
Cor. 10. 8; 13. 10 building up
Edify. *Build up.*
Acts 9. 31 had ch. rest .. and were *e.*
Rom. 14. 16 things where. one may *e.*
1 Cor. 8. 1 knowl. puff. . . but char. *e.*
1 Thes. 5. 11 and *e.* one another
R. V. 1 Thes. 5. 11 build each .. up
Edifying. *Building up.*
1 Cor. 14. 5 that ch. may receive *e.*
2 Cor. 12. 19 do all . . for your *e.*
Eph. 4. 12 for *e.* of the body of C.
1 Tim. 1. 4 rather than godly *e.*
R. V. Eph. 4. 12; 4. 16 building up;
1 Tim. 1. 4 a dispensation of God
Effect (*n.*). *Outcome, result.*
Num. 30. 8 make .. vow.. of none *e.*
Ps. 33. 10 make. devices .. of none *e.*
Isa. 32. 17 the *e.* of righteousness
Ezek. 12. 23 *e.* of every vision
Mat 15. 6 made com. of none *e.*
Mark 7. 13 mak. . . word . . of no. *e.*
Rom. 4. 14 promise made of none *e.*
1 Cor. 1. 17 lest cross .. be .. none *e.*
Gal. 5. 4 Christ is become of no *e.*
R. V. Num. 30. 8; Mat. 15. 6;
Mark 7. 13; 1 Cor. 1. 17 void;
Rom. 9. 6 come to nought; Gal.
5. 4 severed from Christ
Effect (*v.*). *Do, bring about.*
Jer. 48. 30 his lies shall not so *e.*
2 Chr. 7. 11 came .. he prosperously *e.*
R. V. Jer. 48. 30 have wrought noth.
Effectual. *Efficacious.*
1 Cor. 16. 9 great door and *e.* is op.
2 Cor. 1. 6 *e.* in the enduring of
Eph. 3. 7 given . . by the *e.* working
Phile. 6 that .. com. . . may become *e.*
Jas 5. 16 the *e.* fervent prayer of
R. V. 2 Cor. 1. 6 worketh patient;
Eph, 3. 7 according to; 4. 16 work-
ing in due measure; Jas. 5. 16
supplication
Effectually. *With effect.*
Gal. 2. 8 he that wrought *e.*
1 Thes 2. 13 which *e.* worketh also
R. V. Gal. 2. 8 for; 1 Thes. 2. 13 ——
Effeminate. *Soft.*
1 Cor. 6. 9 nor *e.*, nor abusers of
Egg. *Egg, yolk.*
Deut. 22. 6 young ones, or *e.*, or
Job. 6. 6 is .. taste in white of .. *e.*
Isa. 10. 14 as one gathered *e.*
Jer. 17. 11 as the partridge sitteth
on *e.* and hatcheth
Luke 11. 12 if one shall ask an *e.*
Eight. *Eight.*
Gen. 5. 4 days of Ad. .. were *e.* hun.
Ex. 26. 2 length of one curtain .. *e.*
Num. 2. 24; Deut. 2. 14; Josh. 21.
41; Judg. 3. 8; 1 Sam. 4. 15; 2
Sam. 23. 8; 1 K. 7. 10; Luke 2.
21; John 5. 5; Acts 9. 33; 1 Pet.
3. 20
Eighteen. *Eight and ten.*
Gen. 14. 14 own house, three hun. .. *e.*
Judg. 3. 14; 2 Sam. 8. 13; 1 K.
7. 15; 2 K. 24. 8
Luke 13. 4 those *e.* upon whom fell
Eighteenth.
1 K. 15. 1; 2 K. 3. 1; 1 Chr. 24. 15;
2 Chr. 13. 1
Jer. 32. 1 *e.* year of Nebuchadrezzar
Eighth.
Ex. 22. 30 *e.* day thou shalt give;
Num. 6. 10; 2 K. 6. 38; 1 Chr. 12.

12; 2 Chr. 7. 9; Luke 1. 59; Acts
7. 8; 2 Pet. 2. 5; Rev. 17. 11
Eightieth. *Eighty.*
1 K. 6. 1 four hun. and *e.* year
Eighty.
Gen. 5. 25 M. lived hun. and . . *e.*
Either. *Or, one or other.*
Lev. 10. 1 took *e.* of them his censer
Deut. 17. 3 *e.* the sun or moon
1 K. 7. 15 did compass *e.* of them
1 Chr. 21. 12 *e.* three years of fam.
Mat. 6. 24 *e.* he will hate the one
Luke 6. 42 *e.* how canst thou say
John 19. 18 two other .. on *e.* side
Acts 17. 21 *e.* to tell, or to hear
1 Cor. 14. 6 speak to you *e.* by rev.
Phil. 3. 12 had already attained, *e.*
Jas.. 3. 12 *e.* a vine figs? so can no
Rev. 22. 2 on *e.* side of the river
Elder. *Great.*
Gen. 10. 21 bro. of Japh. the *e.*
1 Sam. 18. 17 behold my *e.* daughter
1 K. 2. 22 he is mine *e.* brother
Ezek. 16. 46 *e.* sister is Samaria
Old, aged, bearded.
Gen. 50. 7 *e.* of his house, and
Ex. 3. 16 gather the *e.* of Israel
Lev. 4. 15 *e.* of the congregation
Num. 11. 16 seventy men of the *e.*
Deut. 5. 23 heads . . tribes, and . . *e.*
Josh. 7. 6 he and the *e.* that outli.
Judg. 2. 7 days of the *e.* that outli.
Ruth 4. 2 took ten men of the *e.*
1 Sam. 4. 3 *e.* of Israel said, Where.
2 Sam. 3. 17 communicatton with *e.*
1 K. 8. 1 Solomon assembled the *e.*
2 K. 6. 32 the *e.* sat with him
1 Chr. 11. 3 therefore came all the *e.*
2 Chr. 5. 4 the *e.* of Israel came
Ez. 10. 8 counsel of princes and *e.*
Ps. 107. 32 praise him in assem. of *e.*
Prov. 31. 23 sitteth among the *e.*
Isa. 37. 2 and the *e.* of the priests
Jer. 26. 17 rose up certain of the *e.*
Lam. 1. 19 my priests and *e.* gave
Ezek. 8. 1 *e.* of Judah sat before me
Joel 1. 14 gather the *e.* and all inha-
Elder, aged person.
Mat. 15. 2 transgress the trad. of *e.*
16. 21; 21. 23; 26. 3; 27. 1; 28. 12
Mark 7. 3 holding the trad. of .. *e.*
8. 31; 11. 27; 14. 43, 53; 15. 1
Luke 7. 3 sent to him the *e.* of Jew.
Acts 4. 5 rulers and *e.* and scribes
6. 12; 11. 30; 14. 23; 15. 2; 16. 4
1 Tim. 5. 1 rebuke not an *e.*, but
Tit. 1. 5 ordain *e.* in every city
Heb. 11. 2 by it the *e.* obtained
Jas. 5. 14 call for .. *e.* of the church
1 Pet. 5. 1 *e.* which are among you
2 John 1 *e.* unto the elect lady
3 John 1 *e.* unto the . . well beloved
Rev. 4. 4 saw four and twenty *e.*
5. 5; 7. 11; 11. 16; 14. 3; 19. 4
R. V. Joel 1. 14; 2. 16 old men;
Mat. 26. 59 ——
Eldest. *First born.*
Num. 1. 20 Reuben, Israel's *e.* son
2 K. 3. 27 he took his *e.* son, that
Job 1. 13 drinking . . in .. *e.* bro's **h.**
Great.
Gen. 27. 1 called Esau his *e.* son
1 Sam. 17. 13 *e.* of sons of Jesse
First.
2 Chr. 22. 1 had slain all the *e.*
Oldest.
John 8. 9 beginning at the *e.*
R. V. Num. 1. 20; 26. 5 first born
Elect. *Chosen, choice.*
Isa. 45. 4 and for Israel mine *e.*
65. 9 and mine *e.* shall inherit it
Mat. 24. 22 for the *e.'s* sake those
24. 24 shall deceive the very *e.*
Mark 13. 20 be saved; but for the *e.*
Luke 18. 7 shall not G. avenge his *e.*
Rom. 8. 33 to charge of God's *e.*
Col. 3. 12 as the *e.* of God, holy
1 Tim. 5. 21 charge .. before G. and *e.*
2 Tim. 2. 10 endure all . . for *e.* sake
Tit. 1. 1 accord. to faith of God's *e.*
1 Pet. 1. 2 *e.* accord. to foreknowl.
2 John 1 unto the . lady and
R. V. Isa. 42. 1; 45. 4; 65. 9, 22 **my**
chosen
Elected. *Chosen.* R. V. *elect.*
1 Pet. 5. 13 at Babylon, *e.* together

Election. *Choice, laying out.*
Rom. 9. 11 according to *e.* might **s.**
11. 7 *e.* hath obtained it
1 Thes. 1. 4 k., breth. belov. your *e.*
2 Pet. 1. 10 make .. calling and *e.*
Elements. *First step or things.*
Gal 4. 3 in bondage under the *e.*
4. 9 turn to the weak and beggarly *e.*
2 Pet. 3. 10 *e.* shall melt wi. fer. heat
R. V. Gal. 4. 3, 9 rudiments
Eleven. *One and ten.*
Gen. 32. 22 women servants, and *e.*
2 K. 23. 36; 2 Chr. 36. 5; Jer. 52.
1; Mat. 28. 16; Mark 16. 14;
Luke 24. 9; Acts 1. 26
Eleventh. *Eleven.*
Num. 7. 72 on the *e.* day Pagiel
Deut. 1. 3; 1 K. 6. 38; 2 K. 9. 29;
1 Chr. 12. 13; Jer. 1. 3; Ezek. 26.
1; Zech. 1. 7; Mat. 20. 6; Rev.
21. 20
R. V. *terebinth.*
Elm. R. V. *terebinth.*
Hos. 4. 13 under oaks, poplars and *e.*
Eloquent. *Intelligent, wordy.*
Ex. 4. 10 I am not *e.*, neither
Isa. 3. 3 hon. man and the *e.* orator
Acts 18. 24 an *e.* man and mighty
R. V. Isa. 3. 3 skilful; Acts 18. 24
learned
Else. *Other, besides, instead.*
Deut. 4. 35 none *e.* beside him
1 K. 8. 60; Isa. 45. 5; Joel 2. 27
Judg. 7. 14 noth. *e.* save .. sword of
1 Chr. 21. 12 or *e.* three days the
Ps. 51. 16 de. not sac.,*e.* would I give
Isa.. 47. 8 I am, none *e.* beside me
John 14. 11 *e.* believe me for wks'
Rom. 2. 15 accusing or *e.* excusing
Rev. 2. 5 *e.* I will come quickly
R. V. 2 Chr. 23. 7; Eccl. 2. 25;
Mat. 29, 33; Phil. 1. 27 ——
Embalm. *Perfume, preserve.*
Gen. 50. 2, 3, 26 com. to *e.* his father
Embolden. *Build or brace up.*
Job 16. 3 what *e.* that thou answerest
1 Cor. 8. 10 weak be *e.* to eat
R. V. Job 16. 3 provoketh
Embrace. *Clasp, cleave.*
Gen. 29 13 *e.* him, and kissed him
2 K. 4. 16 this season . . thou shalt *e.*
Job 24. 8 *e.* the rock for want of
Prov. 4. 8 when thou dost *e.* her
Eccl. 3. 5 a time to *e.*, and a time
S. of S. 2. 6 right hand doth *e.* me
Lam. 4. 5 brought up in purple *e.*
Acts 20. 1 called .. the dis. and *e.*
Heb. 11. 13 persuaded of them, and *e.*
R. V. Acts 20. 1 exhorted; Heb. 11
13 greeted them from afar
Embroider. R. V. *weave.*
Ex. 28. 39 shalt *e.* the coat of lin.
Embroiderer. *Who embroiders.*
Ex. 35. 35 *e.* in blue and purple
Emerald. *Carbuncle, ruby.*
Ex. 28. 18 second row shall be an *e.*
Ezek. 27. 16 occupied .. fairs with *e.*
Green stone.
Rev. 4. 3 rainbow, in sight like an *e.*
21. 19 the fourth an *e.*
Emerods. *Tumor, boil, plague*
spot.
Deut. 28. 27 L. will smite .. with *e.*
1 Sam. 5. 6 smote them with *e.*
5. 9, 12; 6. 4, 5, 11, 17
R. V. 1 Sam. 5. 6, 12; 6. 4, 5, 11;
1 Sam. 5. 6, 12; 6. 4, 5, 11 tumors
Eminent. *Arched, lofty.*
Ezek. 16. 24 built to thee an *e.* pl.
16. 31, 39; 17. 22
Empire. R. V. *kingdom.*
Esth. 1. 20 pub. through. all his *e.*
Employed. R. V. *stood up.*
Ez. 10. 15 Jon. and Jah. . . were *e.*
Emptied. *See* **Empty** (*v.*).
Emptier. *Who empties.*
Nah. 2. 2 *e.* have emptied them
Emptiness. *Vainness, voidness.*
Isa. 34. 11 confus., and stones of *e.*
Empty (*a.*). *Void, vacant, vain.*
Gen. 31. 42 sent me away now *e.*
Ex. 3. 21 wh ye go, ye shall not go *e.*
Deut. 15. 13 not let him go away *e.*
Judg. 7. 16 *e.* pitchers and lamps
Ruth 1. 21 brought me home again *e.*
1 Sam. 6. 3 ark of G.,.. send it not *e.*
2 Sam. 1. 22 sword of S. returned *e.*

2 K. 4. 3 borrow..e. vessels; borrow
Job 22. 9 sent widows away e.
Isa. 29. 8 awaketh, and his soul is e.
Jer. 14. 3 returned with vessels e.
Ezek. 24. 11 set it e. upon the coals
Hos. 10. 1 Israel is an e. vine
Nah. 2. 10 she is e. and void
Mat. 12. 44 is come, he findeth it e.
Mark 12. 3 and sent him away e.
Luke 1. 53 he hath sent e. away
R. V. Hos. 10. 1 luxuriant

Empty (v.). *Make vacant, void.*
Gen. 24. 20 e. her pitcher into trough
Lev. 4. 36 that they e. the house
2 Chr. 24. 11 officer came and e.
Eccl. 11. 3 if clouds be full..they e.
Isa. 24. 1 L. maketh the earth e.
Jer. 48. 12 and shall e. his vessels
Hab. 1. 17 shall they .. e. their net
Nah. 2. 2 emptiers have e. them
Zech. 4. 12 thro' .. golden pipes e.

Emulation. R. V. *jealousy.*
Rom. 11. 14 I may provoke to e.
Gal. 5. 20 hatred, variance,e.,wrath

Enable. *Put strength in.*
1 Tim. 1. 12 thank C... who e. me

Encamp. *Settle down, camp.*
Ex. 13. 20 took th. journey ..and e.
14. 2, 9; 15. 27; 18. 5
Num. 1. 50 e. round about the tab.
2. 17; 3. 38; 10. 31; 33. 10-46
Josh. 4. 19 peo. came .. and e. in Gil.
Judg. 6. 4 they e. against them
1 Sam. 11. 1; 2 Sam. 11. 11; 1 K.
16. 15; 1 Chr. 11. 15; 2 Chr. 32.
1; Job. 19. 12
Ps. 27. 3 though an host should e.
Zech. 9. 8 will e. about mine house

Enchanter. *Charmer, whisperer.*
Deut. 18. 10 or an e., or a witch
Jer. 27. 9 hearken not .. to your e.
R. V. Jer. 27. 9 soothsayers

Enchantment. *Charm.*
Ex. 7. 11 did in iike man. with .. e.
Lev. 19. 26 neither shall ye use e.
Num. 23. 23 surely there is no e.
2 K. 21. 6 obser. times and used e.
2 Chr. 33. 6 obser. times and used e.
Eccl. 10. 11 serp. will bite .. e.
Isa. 47. 9 great abund. of thine e.
R. V. Eccl. 10. 11 charmed

Encounter. *Throw together.*
Acts 17. 18 cer. philosophers ..e.

Encourage. *Strengthen, harden.*
Deut. 1. 38 e. him; for he shall
Judg. 20. 22 men of Is. e. themselves
1 Sam. 30. 6 David e. himself in
2 Sam. 11. 25 over. it, and e. .. him
2 Chr. 31. 4 might be e. in the law
Ps. 64. 5 e. themselves in evil
Isa. 41. 7 carpenter e. the goldsmith
R. V. 1 Sam. 30. 6 strengthened

End (n.). *Extremity, close, far-*
thest port, purpose in view, border.
Gen. 6. 13 e. of all flesh is come
Ex. 12. 41 at e. of'the four hundred
Deut. 11. 12 from begin. .. unto e.
Josh. 9. 16 pass, at e. of three days
Judg. 6. 21 ang. of L. put forth the e.
Ruth 3. 7 lie down at e. of heap
1 Sam. 9. 27 going down the e.
2 Sam. 24. 8 came to Jer. at e. of
1 K. 9. 10 pass at e. of twenty years
2 K. 8. 3 pass at e. of seven years
2 Chr. 5. 9 e. of the staves were seen
Ez. 9. 11 from one e. to another
Neh. 3. 21 e. of house of Eliashib
Job 6. 11 what is mine e., that
Ps. 39. 4 L. make me .. know m. e.
Prov. 30. 4 established all the e.
Eccl. 7. 14 to the e. that man sh'ld
Isa. 45. 22 saved, all ..e. of earth
Jer. 3. 5 will he keep it to the e.
Lam. 4. 18 for our e. is come
Ezek. 7. 2 an e., the e. is come upon
Dan. 8. 17 at .. time of the e. shall
Amos. 8. 10 make .. e. thereof bit.
Mic. 5. 4 great unto e. of earth
Hab. 2. 3 at the e. it shall speak
Nah. 2. 9 none e. of the store
Zech. 9. 10 to the e. of the earth
Mat. 10. 22 that endureth to the e.
Mark 3. 26 cannot stand, but hath e.
Luke 1. 33 k. there shall be no e.
John 13. 1 loved them unto the e.
Acts 7. 19 to the e. they might not

Rom. 6. 21 e. of .. things is death
1 Cor. 1. 8 confirm you unto the e.
2 Cor. 1. 13 acknowl. even to the e
Phil. 3. 19 whose e. is destruction
1 Thes. 3. 13 to the e. he may stab.
1 Tim. 1. 5 e. of the command. is
Heb. 3. 6 hope firm unto the e.
Jas. 5. 11 seen the e. of the Lord
1 Pet. 1. 9 receive. e. of your faith
2 Pet. 2. 20 latter e. is worse than
Rev. 2. 26 keep. .. works unto the e.
R. V. Josh. 15. 8; 18. 15; Isa. 13.
5: Acts 13. 47 uttermost part;
Dan. 12. 8; Heb. 13. 7 issue;
Luke 22. 37 hath fulfilment; Mat.
28. 1 now late on; 1 Pet. 1. 13
perfectly on; 2 Pet. 2. 20 last
state .. become

End (v.). *Leave off, finish.*
Gen. 2. 2 sev. day God e. his work
Ruth 2. 21 have e. all my harvest
2 Sam. 20. 18 so they e. the matter
Isa. 24. 8 noise of them that rej. e.
Ezek. 4. 8 e. days of thy siege
Mat. 7. 28 pass, when Jesus had e.
Luke 4. 2 when they were e., he
Aots 21. 27 when .. days were al. e.
R. V. Gen. 2. 2; Deut. 31. 30; 1 K.
7. 51 finished; Ezek. 4. 8 accom-
plished; Luke 4. 2, 13; Acts 21.
27 completed; John 13. 2——

Endamage. *Cause loss.*
Ez. 4. 13 shalt e. the revenue of k.

Endanger. *Put in danger.*
Eccl. 10. 9 that cleav. wood sh. be e.
Dan. 1. 10 make me e. my head

Endeavour (v.). *Seek, strive.*
Acts 16. 10 we e. to go unto Maced.
Eph. 4. 3 e. to keep the unity
1 Thes. 2. 17 e. the more .. to see
2 Pet. 1. 15 I will e. that ye be able
R. V. Acts 16. 10 sought; Eph. 4.
3; 2 Pet. 1. 15 give diligence

Endeavours. R. V. *doings.*
Pъ. 28. 4 accor. to wick. of their e.

Endless. *Without end.*
Heb. 7. 16 after .. power of ..e. life
1 Tim. 1. 4 nei. give head to .. e. gen.

Endow. *Bestow, purchase.*
Ex. 22. 16 e. her to be his wife

Endue. *Endow, clothe.*
Gen. 30. 20 e. me wi. .. good dowry
2 Chr. 2. 12 e. with prudence and
Luke 24. 49 until ye be e. wi. power
R. V. Gen. 30. 20 endowed; Luke
24. 49 clothed.

Endure. *Be, exist, undergo, suffer,*
continue, bear up under.
Gen. 33. 14 children be able to e.
Ex. 18. 23 thou shalt be able to e.
Esth. 8. 6 how can I e. to see
Job 8. 15 fast, but it shall not e.
Ps. 9. 7 Lord shall e. forever
Ezek. 22. 14 can thine heart e., or
Mat. 10. 22 that e. to the end shall
Mark 13. 13 he that shall e.
John 6. 27 meat which e. unto life
Rom. 9. 22 e. with .. long suffering
1 Cor. 13. 7 hopeth all things, e. all
2 Cor. 1. 6 effectual in the e. of
2 Thes. 1. 4 tribulations that ye e.
2 Tim. 4. 3 will not e. sound doctr.
Heb. 10. 34 better and e substance
1 Pet. 1. 25 word of .. L. e. forever
R. V. Gen. 33. 14 according to the
pace; Job 31. 23 do nothing; Ps.
9. 7 sitteth; 30. 5 tarry; John
6. 27; 1 Pet. 1. 25 abideth; Heb.
10. 34 abiding

Enemy. *Opponent, adversary foe.*
Gen. 14. 20 delivered thine e. into
Ex. 15. 6 dashed in pieces the e.
Lev. 26. 7 ye shall chase your e.
Num. 10. 9 go to war ..against the e.
Deut. 1. 42 be smitten before your e.
Josh. 7. 8 Is. turn.. backs bef. .. e.
Judg. 2. 14 sold them in. hands of e.
1 Sam. 2. 1 mouth enlarged over ..e.
2 Sam. 4. 8 Saul thine e., which
1 K. 21. 20 asked the life of thine e.
2 K. 17. 39 del. you out of ..your e.
1 Chr. 14. 11 broken in upon mine e.
2 Chr. 6. 28 e. besiege them in cities
Ez. 8. 22 help us against the e.
Neh. 4. 15 when our e. heard that
Esth. 7. 6 adver. and e. is this wick.

Job 13. 24 holdest me for thine e.
Ps. 3. 7 hast smitten all mine e.
6. 10 let all mine e. be ashamed
7. 5 let e. persecute my soul
8. 2 thou mightest still the e.
9. 3 when mine e. are turned back
13. 2 shall mine e. be exalted
17. 9 deadly e. who compass me
18. 37 I have pursued mine e.
21. 8 hand shall find out all thine e.
41. 5 mine e. speak evil of me
72. 9 his e. shall lick the dust
Prov. 16. 7 maketh e. to be at peace
Isa. 1. 24 will avenge me of mine e.
Jer. 6. 25 e. and fear is on every side
Lam. 1. 2 friends ..are become as e.
Ezek. 36. 2 e. hath said against you
Hos. 8. 3 the e. shall pursue him
Am. 9. 6 go into cap. before the e.
Mic. 2. 8 my people is risen as .. e.
Nah. 1. 2 reserveth wrath for e.
Zeph. 3. 15 hath cast out thine e.
Mat. 5. 43 love .. neig., and hate ..e.
5. 44 love your e. and bless
Mark 12. 36 make thine e. my foot.
Luke 1. 71 that we be sav. from ..e.
Acts 13. 10 child of d. .. e. of .. rig.
Kom. 5. 10 if when ye were e.
1 Cor. 15. 25 hath put all e. under
Gal. 4. 16 and I .. become your e.
Phil. 3. 18 are e. of the cross of C.
Col. 1. 21 e. .. now hath he recon.
2 Thes. 3. 15 ye count .. not as an e.
Heb. 1. 13 make thine e. my foots.
Jas. 4. 4 friend of .. world is e. of
Rev. 11. 5 five .. devoureth their e.
R. V. Very frequently in O. T., es-
pecially in Ps., adversary

Enflame. *Excite, inflame.*
Isa. 57. 5 e. yourselves with idols

Engage. *Pledge.*
Jer. 30. 21 who is this th. e. .. heart
R. V. He that hath had

Engines. *Inventions, rams.*
2 Chr. 26. 15 he made in Jerusa.
Ezek. 26. 9 he set e. of war against

Engrafted. R. V. *implanted.*
Jas. 21 rec. with meekness the e.

Engrave. *Open up, carve.*
Ex. 28. 11 e. the two stones with
Zech. 3. 1 will e. the graving
2 Cor. 3. 7 ministrations of death e.

Engraver. *Opener up, carver.*
Ex. 28. 11 work of an e. in stone
35. 35 all manner of work of the e.

Engraving. *Graving, Carving.*
Ex. 28. 11 like the e. of a signet
39. 14 like .. e. of a signet

Enjoin. *Charge, command, urge.*
Esth. 9. 31 and Esther .. had e. th.
Job 36. 23 who hath e. him his way
Phile. 8 e. thee that which is conv.
Heb. 9. 20 test. which God hath e.
R. V. Heb. 9. 20 commanded to you-
ward

Enjoy. *Possess, delight in.*
Lev. 26. 34 shall .. land e. her sab.
Num. 36. 8 children of Is. may e.
Deut. 28. 41 thou shalt not e. them
Josh. 1. 15 return to the land and e.
2 Chr. 36. 21 until the land had e.
Eccl. 2. 1 prove .. wi. m ..there. e.
Isa. 65. 22 mine elect shall long e.
Acts 24. 2 seeing .. by thee we e.
1 Tim. 6. 17 giveth us .. all th. to e.
Heb. 11. 25 e. the pleasures of sin
R. V. Num. 36. 8; Josh. 1. 15
possess

Enlarge. *Open, make broad.*
Gen. 9. 27 God shall e. Japheth
Ex. 34. 24 I will .. e. their borders
Deut. 12. 20 when L. thy G. shall e.
1 Sam. 2. 1 my mouth is e. over
2 Sam. 22. 37 thou has e. my steps
1 Chr. 4. 10 thou wouldst e. my c.
Job 12. 25 he e. the nations. and
Ps. 4. 1 hast e. me .. in distress
Isa. 5. 14 hell hath e. herself
Am. 1. 13 that they might e. their
Mic. 1. 16 e. thy baldness as the e.
Hab. 2. 5 man .. who e. his desires
Mat. 23. 5 e. the borders of their g.
2 Cor. 6. 11 our heart is e.
R. V. Ps. 4. 1 set me at large; 2
Cor. 10. 15 magnified in

Enlargement. R. V. *relief.*

Esth. 4. 14 shall their *e.* and deliv.

Enlargening. *Making broad.*
Ezek. 41. 7 was an *e.* in the wind

Enlighten. *Make to shine.*
1 Sam. 14. 27 and his eyes were *e.*
Job 33. 30 *e.* with the light of liv.
Ps. 18. 28 God will *e.* my darkness
Eph. 1. 18 your understand. being *e.*
Heb. 6. 4 impos. for those .. once *e.*
R. V. Ps. 18. 28 lighten

Enmity. *Hatred, hostility.*
Gen. 3. 15 I will put *e.* bet. thee
Num. 35. 21 or in *e.* smite him.
Luke 23. 12 before they were at *e.*
Rom. 8. 7 carnal mind is *e.* against
Eph. 2. 15 abolished in flesh all *e.*
Jas. 4. 4 friend. of world is *e.* with G.

Enough. *Sufficiency.*
Gen. 24. 25 both straw and prov. *e.*
Ex. 9. 28 entreat the Lord, it is *e.*
Josh. 17. 16 the hill is not *e.* for us
2 Sam. 24. 16 it is *e. ;* stay thy hand
1 K. 19. 4 it is *e.*; now, O Lord
1 Chr. 21. 15 said to .. angel, It is *e.*
2 Chr. 31. 10 we have had *e.* to eat
Prov. 27. 27 milk *e.* for thy food
Isa. 56. 11 dogs .. can never have *e.*
Hos. 4. 10 eat, and not have *e.*
Obad. 5 not stolen till they had *e.?*
Nah. 2. 12 lion did tear .. *e.* for
Hag. 1. 6 but ye have not *e.*
Mal. 3. 10 shall not be room *e.*
Mat. 10. 25 it is *e.* for the disciple
Mark 14. 41 take your rest; it is *e.*
Luke 22. 38 said unto them, It is *e.*
R. V. Ex. 2. 19 ──

Enquire. *Seek, request, ask, search.*
Gen. 25. 22 went to *e.* of the Lord
Ex. 18. 15 people came to me to *e.*
Deut. 12. 30 heed .. that thou *e.* not
Judg. 4. 20 man doth come and *e.*
1 Sam. 9. 9 man went to *e.* of God
2 Sam. 2. 1 David *e.* of the Lord
1 K. 22. 5 *E.*, I pray thee, at
2 K. 1. 2, 3, 6, 16 *e.* of Baal-zebub
1 Chr. 10. 13 a familiar spirit, to *e.*
2 Chr. 18. 7 by whom we may *e.*
Ez. 7. 14 to *e.* concerning Judah
Job 10. 6 *e.* after mine iniquity
Ps. 27. 4 beauty of the L., and to *e.*
Eccl. 7. 10 thou dost not *e.* wisely
Isa. 21. 12 if ye will *e.*, *e.* ye
Jer. 21. 2 *e.*, I pray thee, of the L.
Ezek. 14. 7 cometh to prophet to *e.*
Dan. 1. 20 the king *e.* of them
Zeph. 1. 6 have not sought .. nor *e.*
Mat. 2. 7 Herod .. *e.* of them dilig.
Luke 22. 23 began to *e.* among them.
John 4. 52 *e.* he of them the hour
Acts 9. 11 *e.* in house of Judas
1 Pet. 1. 11 prophets have *e.* and
R. V. Almost always changed to in-
  quire; Mat. 27. 7, 16 learned; 1
  Pet. 1. 10 sought

Enquiry. R. V. *inquiry.*
Prov. 25. 25 after vows to make *e.*
Acts 10. 17 men .. sent, made *e.* for

Enrich. *Make rich.*
1 Sam. 17. 25 the king will *e.* him
Ps. 65. 9 thou greatly *e.* it with
Ezek. 27. 33 didst *e.* the kings of E'
1 Cor. 1. 5 in everything ye are *e.*
2 Cor. 9. 11 being *e.* in everything

Ensample. *Type, secret, example.*
1 Cor. 10. 11 things happened .. for *e.*
Phil. 3. 17 so ye have us for *e.*
1 Thes. 1. 7 were *e.* to all that
2 Thes. 3. 9 make ourselves an *e.* to
1 Pet. 5. 3 nei. as lords.. but being *e.*
2 Pet. 2. 6 an *e.* unto those that
R. V. 1 Cor. 10. 11 by way of example; 2 Pet. 2. 6 example

Ensign. *Sign, banner, signal.*
Num. 2. 2 *e.* of their father's house
Ps. 74. 4 enemies .. set up their *e.*
Isa. 5. 26 lift up an *e.* to the nations
11. 10, 12; 18. 3; 30. 17; 31. 9
Zech. 9. 16 shall be .. lift.. up as an *e.*
R. V. Zech. 9. 16 on high

Ensnared. *Snared.*
Job 34. 30 lest the people be *e.*

Ensue. R. V. *pursue.*
1 Pet. 3. 11 seek peace, and *e.* it

Entangle. *Perplex, ensnare, hamper.*
Ex. 14. 3 chil. of Is. *e.* in the land

Enter. *Go in, or into.*
Gen. 7. 13 selfsame day *e.* Noah
Ex. 33. 9 Moses *e.* into the taberna.
Num. 4. 3 all that *e.* into the host
Deut. 23. 1 not *e.* into .. congrega.
Josh. 2. 3 bring .. men .. which are *e.*
Judg. 6. 5 *e.* the land to destroy it
2 Sam. 10. 14 children of Ammon .. *e.*
1 K. 14. 12 thy feet *e.* into the city
2 K. 7. 4 we will *e.* into the city
1 Chr. 19. 15 fled .. and *e.* in. the city
2 Chr. 7. 2 priest could not *e.* into h.
Neh. 2. 8 house that I shall *e.*
Esth. 4. 2 none *e.* the king's gate
Job 22. 4 *e.* with thee into judgment
Ps. 37. 15 sword shall *e.* .. their own
Prov. 2. 10 when wisdom *e.* thine h.
Isa. 2. 10 *e.* into the rock and hide
Jer. 2. 7 when ye *e.*, ye defiled
Lam. 1. 10 the heathen *e.* into
Ezek. 2. 2 spirit *e.* into me wh. he sp.
Dan. 11. 7 *e.* into the fortress
Hos. 11. 9 I will not *e.* into the city
Am. 5. 5 Beth-el. nor *e.* into Gilgal
Obad. 13 shouldst not have *e.*
Jonah 3. 4 Jonah began to *e.* .. city
Hab. 3. 16 rottenness *e.* my bones
Zech. 5. 4 *e.* house of the thief
Mat. 5. 20 no case *e.* into kingdom
  6. 6; 7. 21; 8. 5; 10. 5; 12. 4; 18. 3
Mark 1. 21 *e.* into the synagogue
  2. 1; 3. 1; 5. 12; 6. 10; 7. 17; 9. 25
Luke 1. 40 *e.* the house of Zacharias
  4. 38; 6. 6; 7. 1; 8. 30; 10. 5; 17. 12
John 3. 4 can he *e.* the second time
Acts 3. 8 *e.* with them into temp.
Rom. 5. 12 by one man sin *e.* .. world
1 Cor. 2. 9 nei. have *e.* the heart of m
Heb. 9. 25 as priest *e.* holy place
Jas. 5. 4 cries .. are *e.* into ears of L.
2 John 7 deceivers are *e.* into the w.
Rev. 11. 11 Spirit of life .. *e.* into
R. V. Mark 5. 40; 7. 18 goeth. The
  same change is frequent in O. T.

Entering. *Going in, entrance.*
Ex. 35. 15 door at *e.* of the taberna.
Josh. 8. 29 cast it at *e.* of the gate
Judg. 9. 25 Gaal. stood at *e.* of gate
2 Sam. 11. 23 upon them even un. *e.*
1 K. 6. 31 for the *e.* of the oracle
2 K. 7. 3 were .. lep. men at the *e.*
1 Chr. 5. 9 inhabited unto the *e.* in
2 Chr. 7. 8 from *e.* in of Hamath
Isa. 23. 1 no house, no *e.* in
Jer. 1. 15 *e.* of gates of Jerusalem
Am. 6. 14 afflict you from the *e.*
1 Thes. 1. 9 manner of *e.* we had
R. V. Ex. 35. 15 door; 2 Chr. 18. 9;
  23. 13 entrance; Mark 7. 15 going;
  Acts 27. 2 embarking

Enterprise. *Wisdom, project.*
Job 5. 12 hands cannot perform .. *e.*

Entertain. *Receive strangers.*
Heb. 13. 2 have *e.* angels unawares
R. V. Show love unto

Entice. *Persuade, allure, bait.*
Ex. 22. 16 if a man *e.* a maid
Deut. 13. 6 if thy bro. .. *e.* thee se.
Judg. 14. 15 *e.* thy husband, that
2 Chr. 18. 19 who shall *e.* Ahab
Job 31. 27 heart hath been secretly *e.*
Prov. 1. 10 son, if sinners *e.* thee
Jer. 20. 10 he will be *e.*, and we
Jas. 1. 14 drawn of own lust, and *e.*

Enticing. *Persuasive, alluring.*
1 Cor. 2. 4 not with *e.* words of
Col. 2. 4 beguile .. with *e.* words
R. V. 1 Cor. 2. 4 persuasive; Col.
  2. 4 persuasiveness of

Entire. *Whole.*
Jas. 4. 1 may be perfect and *e.*

Entrance. *Opening, way in.*
Num. 34. 8 unto the *e.* of Hamath
Judg. 1. 24 show us .. the *e.* into
1 K. 22. 10 in the *e.* of the gate
1 Chr. 4. 39 went to .. *e.* of Gedor
2 Chr. 12. 10 guard that kept the *e.*
Ps. 119. 130 *e.* of thy words giv. l.
Ezek. 40. 15 the gate of the *e.*
Mic. 5. 6 land of Nim. in the *e.*
1 Thes. 2. 1 know our *e.* unto you

2 Pet. 1. 11 *e.* shall be ministered
R. V. Num. 34. 8; 1 Chr. 4. 39; 1
  Thes. 2. 1 entering; 2 Chr. 12. 10
  door; Ps. 119. 130 opening

Entreat, Intreat. *Meet, ask, im-plore.*
Gen. 23. 8 *e.* for me to Ephron
Jer. 15. 11 cause .. enemy to *e.* thee
Luke 15. 28 came his father and *e.*
Acts 27. 3 and Julius .. *e.* Paul
1 Cor. 4. 13 being defamed, we *e.*
Phil. 4. 3 and I *e.* thee also
1 Tim. 5. 1 rebuke not an el. but *e.*
Jas. 3. 17 gentle, and easy to be *e.*
R. V. Jer. 15. 11 make supplication;
  Luke 20. 11 handled; Acts 27. 3
  treated .. kindly

Entreaty. *Call for help.*
Prov. 18. 23 poor useth *e.*, but rich
2 Cor. 8. 4 praying .. with much *e.*

Entry. *Going in, opening.*
2 K. 16. 18 kings *e.* without, turned
1 Chr. 9. 19 were keepers of the *e.*
2 Chr. 4. 22 the *e.* of the house
Prov. 8. 3 she crieth at .. *e.* of city
Jer. 19. 2 by the *e.* of the east gate
Ezek. 40. 11 measured breadth of *e.*
R. V. Ezek. 40. 11 opening; 40. 38
  door

Envious. *Jealous.*
Ps. 37. 1 nei. be thou *e.* against the
Prov. 24. 1 be not .. *e.* against the

Environ. R. V. *compass.*
Josh. 7. 9 hear of it, and *e.* us

Envy (n.). *Zeal, jealousy.*
Job 5. 2 *e.* slayeth the silly one
Prov. 14. 30 *e.* the rotten. of bones
Eccl. 9. 6 their *e.* is now perished
Isa. 11. 13 *e.* of Eph. shall depart
Ezek. 35. 11 according to thine *e.*
Mat. 27. 18 for *e.* they had delivered
Mark 15. 10 had deliv. him for *e.*
Acts 7. 9 patri. mov. with *e.* sold J.
Rom. 1. 29 full of *e.*, murder, debate
Phil. 1. 15 some preach C. ev. of *e.*
1 Tim. 6. 4 whereof cometh *e.*, strife
Tit. 3. 3 living in malice and *e.*
Jas. 4. 5 the spirit .. lusteth to *e.?*
1 Pet. 2. 1 laying aside all *e.*
R. V. Isa. 26. 11 see thy zeal for
  the people; Job 5. 2; Prov. 27. 4;
  Acts 7. 9; 13. 45; 17. 5 jealousy

Envy (v.). *To be zealous, jealous.*
Gen. 26. 14 the Philistines *e.* him
Num. 11. 29 *e.* thou for my sake
Ps. 106. 16 they *e.* Moses also
Prov. 3. 31 *e.* thou not the oppressor
Isa. 11. 13 Eph. shall not *e.* Judah
Ezek. 31. 9 trees, in the garden .. *e.*
1 Cor. 13. 4 charity *e.* not
Gal. 5. 26 provoking .. *e.* one ano.

Envying. *Zeal, jealousy.*
Rom. 13. 13 walk .. in strife and *e.*
1 Cor. 3. 3 there is among you *e.*
2 Cor. 12. 20 lest there be debates, *e.*
Gal. 5. 21 *e.*, murders, drunkenness
Jas. 3. 14 if ye have bitter *e.* and
R. V. Rom. 13. 13; 1 Cor. 3. 3; 2
  Cor. 12. 20; Jas. 3. 14, 16 jealousy

Ephah. *Measure, three seah.*
Ex. 16. 36 omer is tenth part of *e.*
Lev. 5. 11 part of *e.* of .. flour
Num. 5. 15 part of *e.* of barley
Judg. 6. 19 cakes of *e.* of flour
Ruth 2. 17 about an *e.* of barley
1 Sam. 1. 24; Isa. 5. 10; Ezek. 45.
  10; 46. 5; Am. 8. 5; Zech. 5. 6

Ephod. *Priestly garment.*
Ex. 25. 7 stones .. set in the *e.*
  28. 4-31; 29. 5; 35. 9; 39. 2-22
Lev. 8. 7 put the *e.* upon him
Judg. 8. 27 Gideon made an *e.*
1 Sam. 2. 18 girded with a linen *e.*
2 Sam. 6. 14 D. was gird. with .. *e.*
1 Chr. 15. 27 had upon him an *e.*
Hos. 3. 4 without an *e.* and teraph.

Epistle. *Writing, letter.*
Acts 15. 30 they delivered the *e.*
Rom. 16. 22 Ter. who wrote this *e.*
1 Cor. 5. 9 wrote .. you in an *e.*
2 Cor. 3. 1 need we .. *e.* of com.
Col. 4. 16 when this *e.* is read
1 Thes. 5. 27 charge you .. that th. *e.*
2 Thes. 2. 15 been tau. .. by w. or *e.*
2 Pet. 3. 1 this .. *e.* .. I now write
R. V. Acts 23. 33 letter

Equal (v.). *To match, array.*
Job 28. 17, 19 crystal cannot *e.* it
Equal (a.) (n.). *Same degree, equality.*
Ps. 55. 13 thou, a man mine *e.*
Prov. 26. 7 legs of lame are not *e.*
Isa. 46. 5 liken me, and make me *e.*
Lam. 2. 13 what shall I *e.* to thee
Ezek. 18. 25 way of L. is not *e.*
Mat. 20. 12 made them *e.* to us
John 5. 18 Father, making himself *e.*
Gal. 1. 14 above my *e.* in mine own
Phil.. 2. 6 not robbery to be *e.* with
Col. 4. 1 give . . that which is *e.*
Rev. 21. 16 br. and height . . are *e.*
R. V. Ps. 17. 2 equity; Prov. 26.
7 hang loose; Gal. 1. 14 of mine
own age
Equality. *Being equal.*
2 Cor. 8. 14 *e.*, that there may be *e.*
Equity. *Rightness, fairness.*
Ps. 98. 9 judge the . . people with *e.*
Prov. 1. 3 receive the instr. of *e.*
Eccl. 2. 21 wis., in knowl., and in *e.*
Isa. 11. 4 reprove with *e.* for meek
Mic. 3. 9 abhor and pervert all *e.*
Mal. 2. 6 walked . . in peace and *e.*
R. V. Prov. 17. 26; Isa. 59. 14;
Mal. 2. 6 uprightness; Eccl. 2. 21
with skilfulness.
Ere. *Before.*
Ex. 1. 19 del. *e.* the mid w. come
Num. 11. 33 *e.* it was chewed, the
Jer. 47. 6 how long *e.* thou be quiet
Hos. 8. 5 *e.* they attain to innocency
John 4. 49 saith . . Sir, come down *e.*
Erect. *Set up.*
Gen. 33. 20 he *e.* there an altar
Err. *Wander, go astray.*
Lev. 5. 18 ignorance wherein he *e.*
Num. 15. 22 if yc have *e.* and not
1 Sam. 26. 21 played the fool and *e.*
2 Chr. 33. 9 Manas. made Judah to *e.*
Job 6. 24 underst. where. I have *e.*
Ps. 95. 10 a people that do *e.*
Prov. 10. 17 that refuseth reproof *e.*
Isa. 28. 7 also have *e.* through wine
Jer. 23. 13 caused my people . . to *e.*
Ezek. 45. 20 for every one that *e.*
Hos. 4. 12 whoredoms have c. . . *e.*
Am. 2. 4 lies caused them to *e.*
Mic. 3. 5 prophets . . make my p. *e.*
Mat. 22. 29 ye do *e.*, not knowing
Mark 12. 24 do ye not therefore *e.*
1 Tim. 6. 10 have *e.* from the faith
Heb. 3. 10 do always *e.* in heart
Jas. 1. 16 do not *e.*, beloved breth.
R. V. 1 Tim. 6. 10 been led astray;
Jas. 1. 16 be not deceived
Errand. *Word, matter.*
Gen. 24. 33 till I have told mine *e.*
Judg. 3. 19 I have a secret . ., O king
2 K. 9. 5 I have an *e.* to thee, O cap.
Error. *Wandering, oversight, mistake.*
2 Sam. 6. 7 God smote him for . . *e.*
Job 19. 4 mine *e.* remaineth with
Ps. 19. 12 who can underst. his *e.* ?
Eccl. 5. 6 neither say . . it was an *e.*
Isa. 32. 6 iniquity . . to utter *e.*
Jer. 10. 15 vanity, and work of *e.*
Dan. 6. 4 neither was any *e.* . . found
Mat. 27. 64 last *e.* shall be worse
Rom. 1. 27 that recomp. of their *e.*
Heb. 9. 7 offered himself for the *e.* of
Jas. 5. 20 converted sinner from *e.*
2 Pet. 2. 18 them who live in *e.*
1 John 4. 6 and the spirit of *e.*
Jude 11 ran . . after *e.* of Balaam
R. V. Jer. 10. 15; 51. 18 delusion
Escape (n.). *Deliverance.*
Ps. 55. 8 hasten my *e.* from storm
Escape (v.). *Flee forth, slip away, evade, avoid, elude.*
Gen. 19. 17 *e.* for thy life; look not
Ex. 10. 5 eat . . that which is *e.*
Num. 21. 29 given his sons that *e.*
Deut. 23. 15 servant which is *e.*
Josh. 8. 22 let none remain or *e.*
Judg. 21. 17 inherit for them that *e.*
1 Sam. 14. 41 but the people *e.*
2 Sam. 4. 6 Baanah his brother *e.*
1 K. 18. 40 said, let not one *e.*
2 K. 10. 24 if any of the men . . *e.*
1 Chr. 4. 43 Amalekites that were *e.*
2 Chr. 16. 7 king of Syria *e.* out of

Ez. 9. 14 sh. be no remnant nor *e.*?
Neh. 1. 2 asked . . con. J. that had *e.*
Esth. 4. 13 *e.* in the king's house
Job 11. 20 wicked . . shall *e.* not
Ps. 56. 7 shall they *e.* by iniquity
Prov. 19. 5 that . . lies shall not *e.*
Eccl. 7. 26 who pleaseth God shall *e.*
Isa. 4. 2 comely for them that are *e.*
Jer. 11. 11 they sh. not be able to *e.*
Ezek. 17. 15 shall he *e.* that doeth
Dan. 11. 42 Egypt shall not *e.*
Joel 2. 3 nothing shall *e.* them
Am. 9. 1 that *e.* of them shall not
Mat. 23. 33 how can ye *e.* damna.
Luke 21. 36 be account. worthy to *e.*
John 10. 39 *e.* out of their hands
Acts 27. 42 should swim out and *e.*
Rom. 2. 3 shalt *e.* the judg. of God
1 Cor. 10. 13 also make a way to *e.*
2 Cor. 11. 33 was I let down . . and *e.*
1 Thes. 5. 3 and they shall not *e.*
Heb. 2. 3 how shall we *e.* if we neg.
2 Pet. 1. 4 having *e.* the corruption
Eschew. *Turn aside, avoid.*
Job 1. 1 feared God and *e.* evil
1 Pet. 3. 11 *e.* evil and do good
R. V. 1 Pet. 3. 11 turn away from
Especially. *Most of all.*
Ps. 31. 11 reproach . . *e.* among my
Acts 26. 3 *e.* because I know thee
Gal. 6. 10 good, . . *e.* unto them who
1 Tim. 5. 17 *e.* they who labor
2 Tim. 4. 13 but *e.* the parchments
R. V. Ps. 31. 11 exceedingly
Espousal. *Betrothal.*
S. of S. 3. 11 crowned him in day of *e.*
Jer. 2. 2 I rem. . . the love of thine *e.*
Espouse. *Betroth, marry.*
2 Sam. 3. 14 wife Michal which I *e.*
Mat. 1. 18 his mother Mary was *e.*
Luke 1. 27 virgin *e.* to a man
2 Cor. 11. 2 for I have *e.* you to
R. V. 2 Sam. 3. 14; Mat. 1. 18;
Luke 1. 27 betrothed
Espy. *See, look, spy out.*
Gen. 42. 27 he *e.* his money, for
Josh. 14. 7 sent me to *e.* . . the land
Jer. 48. 19 stand by the way and *e.*
Ezek. 20. 6 land that I had *e.* for th.
R. V. Josh. 14. 7 spy
Establish. *Found, raise up, confirm.*
Gen. 6. 18 with thee I *e.* my cov.
Ex. 6. 4 have *e.* my covenant with
Lev. 26. 9 *e.* my covenant with you
Num. 30. 13 her husband may *e.* it
Deut. 8. 18 may *e.* his cov. which
1 Sam. 1. 23 the Lord *e.* his word
2 Sam. 5. 12 Lord had *e.* him king
1 K. 2. 24 L. liveth, which hath *e.*
1 Chr. 17. 11 I will *e.* his kingdom
2 Chr. 12. 1 Reho. had *e.* his kingdom
Job 22. 28 shall be *e.* unto thee
Ps. 24. 2 *e.* it upon the floods
Prov. 3. 19 by understand. hath he *e.*
Isa. 7. 9 not believe, ye sh. not be *e.*
Jer. 10. 12 he hath *e.* the world
Ezek. 16. 60 I will *e.* unto thee
Dan. 6. 7 to *e.* a royal statute
Am. 5. 15 love . . good, and *e.* judg.
Mic. 4. 1 mountain . . shall be *e.* in
Zech. 5. 11 shall be *e.* and set
Mat. 18. 16 that . . word may be *e.*
Acts 16. 5 so were the churches *e.*
Rom. 1. 11 to the end ye may be *e.*
2 Cor. 13. 1 mouth . . every word be *e*
1 Thes. 3. 2 to *e.* you, and comfort
Heb. 8. 6 cov. which was *e.* upon
2 Pet. 1. 12 *e.* in the present truth
R. V. 2 Sam. 7. 25 confirm; Isa.
49. 8 raise up; Lev. 25. 30; 2 Sam.
7. 16 made sure; Prov. 8. 28 made
firm; Zech. 5. 11 prepared; Heb.
8. 6 hath been enacted; Acts 16. 5
strengthened
Establishment. R. V. *faithfulness.*
2 Chr. 32. 1 things, and the *e.* thereof
Estate. *Station, condition, property.*
1 Chr. 17. 17 accord. to the *e.* of a
Esth. 1. 19 give her . . *e.* to another
Eccl. 3. 18 *e.* of the sons of men
Ezek. 16. 55 return to former *e.*
Dan. 11. 7 sh. one stand up in his *e.*
Luke 1. 48 low *e.* of his handmaiden

Rom. 12. 16 con. to men of low *e.*
Col. 4. 8 he might know your *e.*
Jude 6 angels which kept not first *e.*
R. V. Dan. 11. 7, 20, 21, 38 place;
Mark 6. 21 chief men; Rom. 12.
16 things lowly; Jude 6 own principality
Esteem. *Think, hold, reckon.*
1 Sam. 2. 30 that de. . . be lightly *e.*
Job 23. 12 *e.* the words of his mouth
Isa. 29. 16 *e.* as the potter's clay
Lam. 4. 2 *e.* as earthen pitchers
Luke 16. 15 wh. is . . *e.* among men
Rom. 14. 5 *e.* one day above anoth.
1 Cor. 6. 4 are least *e.* in the church
Phil. 2. 3 let each *e.* other better
1 Thes. 5. 13 *e.* them . . in love for
Heb. 11. 26 *e.* . . reproach of C. great.
R. V. Job 23. 12 treasured up; 41. 27;
Isa. 27. 17 counted; Luke 16. 15
exalted; Rom. 14. 14 accounteth;
Heb. 11. 26 accounting
Estimate. *Array, value.*
Lev. 27. 14 the priest shall *e.* it
Estimation. *Array, valuation.*
Lev. 5. 15 with thy *e.* by shekels
5. 18; 6. 6; 27. 2-27; Num. 18. 20
Estrange. *Make unknown, strange.*
Job 19. 13 mine acquaint. are . . *e.*
Ps. 58. 3 the wicked are *e.* from
Jer. 19. 4 they have *e.* this place
Ezek. 14. 5 they are all *e.* from me
Eternal. *Everlasting.*
Deut. 33. 27 *e.* God is thy refuge
Isa. 60. 15 make . . an *e.* excellency
Mat. 19. 16 that I may have *e.* life
Mark 3. 29 in danger of *e.* damna.
Luke 10. 25 what . . do to in. *e.* life
John 3. 15 not per. but have *e.* life
Acts 13. 48 were ordained to *e.* life
Rom. 2. 7 seek for glory . . *e.* life
2 Cor. 4. 17 and *e.* weight of glory
1 Tim. 6. 12 lay hold on *e.* life
2 Tim. 2. 10 salva. . . with *e.* glory
Tit. 1. 2 in hope of *e.* life, which
Heb. 5. 9 author of *e.* salvation
1 Pet. 5. 10 called us unto *e.* glory
1 John 1. 2 show . . you that *e.* life
Jude 7 suffered vengeance of *e.* fire
R. V. Rom. 1. 20 everlasting
Eternity. *Duration.*
Isa. 57. 15 One that inhabiteth *e.*
Eunuch. *Castrate, officer.*
2 K. 9. 32 looked out him three *e*
Isa. 39. 7 shall be *e.* in palace of k
Jer. 29. 2 king, and queen, and *e.*
Dan. 1. 3 Ash. the master of his *e.*
Mat. 19. 12 some *e.* . . were made *e.*
Acts 8. 27 an *e.* of great authority
R. V. Jer. 52. 35 officer
Evangelist. *Bearer of good news.*
Acts 21. 8 house of Philip the *e.*
Eph. 4. 11 some proph. and some *e.*
2 Tim. 4. 5 do the work of an *e.*
Even. *Evening.*
Gen. 19. 1 came two angels . . at *e*
Ex. 12. 18 fourteenth day . . at *e*
Lev. 11. 24 shall be unclean till *e.*
Num. 9. 3 at *e.*, ye shall keep it
Deut. 28. 67 would God it were *e.*
Josh. 5. 10 day of the month at *e.*
Judg. 19. 16 out of the field at *e.*
Ruth 2. 17 she gleaned . . till *e.*
1 Sam. 20. 5 unto . . third day at *e.*
2 Sam. 1. 12 and fasted until *e.*
Ezek. 12. 7 in the *e.* I digged
Mat. 8. 16 when the *e.* was come
Mark 13. 35 at *e.*, or midnight
John 6. 16 when *e.* was now come
R. V. Mark 11. 19 every evening
Even (ad.). *Also.*
1 K. 1. 48 mine eyes *e.* seeing it
Prov. 22. 19 made known *e.* to thee
Even (a.). *Level.*
Job 31. 6 weighed in *e.* balance
Ps. 26. 12 standeth in *e.* place
S. of S. 4. 2 flock of sheep. *e.* shorn
Luke 19. 44 lay thee *e.* with the gr'd.
Evening. *Evening.*
Gen. 1. 5, 8 13 *e.* and morning were
8. 11; 24. 11; 29. 23; 30. 16
Ex. 12. 6 shall kill it in the *e.*
Lev. 24. 3 order it from *e.* to morn.
Deut. 23. 11 when *e.* cometh on, he
Josh. 10. 26 hanging on trees till *e.*

Judg. 19. 9 day draweth toward *e*.
1 Sam. 14. 24 that eat. . food till *e*.
1 K. 17. 6 bread and flesh in the *e*.
2 K. 16. 15 the *e*. meat offering
1 Chr. 16. 40 offering . . morn. and *e*.
2 Chr. 2. 4 burnt off. morning and *e*.
Ez. 9. 4 astonied until the *e*. sacrifice
Esth. 2. 14 in the *e*. she went
Job 4. 20 destr. from morning till *e*.
Ps. 55. 17 *e*., and morning, and noon
Prov. 7. 9 *e*. in the black and dark
Eccl. 11. 6 in the *e*. with hold not
Jer. 6. 4 shadows of *e*. are stretched
Ezek. 33. 22 h. of Lord on me in *e*.
Dan. 8. 26 vision of *e*. and morning
Hab. 1. 8 more fierce than *e*. wolves
Zeph. 2. 7 shall they lie down in *e*.
Zech. 14. 7 *e*. time it shall be light
Mat. 14. 15 when it was *e*., his dis.
Mark 14. 17 in the *e*. he cometh
Luke 24. 29 for it is toward *e*., and
John 20. 19 the same day at *e*.
Acts 28. 23 persua. from mor. till *e*.

Event. *Occurrence.*
Eccl. 2. 14 one *e*. happened to all
9. 2, 3 one *e*. to the righteous

Eventide. *Evening time.*
Gen. 24. 63 to meditate in . . at *e. t.*
Josh. 7. 6 fell to earth . . until *e. t.*
8. 29 hanged on tree until *e. t.*
R. V. Josh. 7. 6 evening

Ever. *Perpetual.*
Isa. 28. 28 not *e*. be threshing it
At any time.
Isa. 33. 20 stakes . . *e*. be removed
Eph. 5. 29 no man *e*. hated his own
Before.
Acts 23. 15 or *e*. he come near
Age-lasting.
Gen. 8. 22 taste of tree . . live for *e*
Ex. 3. 15 this is my name for *e*.
Lev. 6. 18 be my statute for *e*.
Num. 10. 8 be . . an ordinance for *e*.
Deut. 12. 28 child. after thee for *e*.
Josh. 4. 7 unto c. of Israel for *e*.
Judg. 11. 25 *e*. strive against Israel
1 Sam. 1. 22 and there abide for *e*.
2 Sam. 3. 28 guiltless before L. for *e*.
1 K. 2. 33 peace for *e*. from Lord
2 K. 5. 27 unto thy seed for *e*.
1 Chr. 15. 2 minister unto him for *e*.
2 Chr. 6. 2 pl. for thy dwelling for *e*.
Ez. 9. 12 nor seek peace . . for *e*.
Neh. 9. 5 bless the Lord . . for *e*.
Job 19. 24 graven . . in rock for *e*.
Ps. 9. 7 Lord shall endure for *e*.
Prov. 12. 19 truth . . be estab. for *e*.
Eccl. 1. 4 but earth abideth for *e*.
Isa. 34. 10 smoke shall go up for *e*.
Jer. 3. 5 reserve his anger for *e*. ?
Lam. 3. 31 L. will not cast off for *e*.
Ezek. 37. 25 children's chil. for *e*.
Dan. 12. 7 him that liveth for *e*.
Hos. 2. 19 will betroth thee . . for *e*.
Joel 3. 20 Judah shall dwell for *e*.
Obad. 10 shall be cut off for *e*.
Jonah 2. 6 e. . . was about me for *e*.
Mic. 2. 9 taken . . my glory for *e*.
Zech. 1. 5 pro., do they live for *e*.?
Mat. 6. 13 power and glory for *e*.
Mark 11. 14 eat fruit of thee . . for *e*.
Luke 1. 33 reign over . . Jacob for *e*.
John 6. 51 eat, he shall live for *e*.
Rom. 1. 25 who is blessed for *e*.
2 Cor. 9. 9 right. remaineth for *e*.
1 Thes. 4. 17 *e*. be with the Lord
2 Tim. 3. 7 *e*. learning, never able
Heb. 5. 6 priest for *e*. after the
1 Pet. 1. 23 liv. and abideth for *e*.
2 Pet. 2. 17 mist of d. reser. for *e*.
1 John 2. 17 doeth will . . abid. for *e*.
2 John 2 and shall be with us for *e*.
Jude 13 blackness of darkness for *e*.

Everlasting. *Age-lasting.*
Gen. 9. 16 remem. the *e*. covenant
Ex. 40. 15 sh. be an *e*. priesthood
Lev. 16. 34 shall be an *e*. statute
Num. 25. 13 cov. of *e*. priesthood
Deut. 33. 27 under. are the *e*. arms
2 Sam. 23. 5 made an *e*. covenant
1 Chr. 16. 17 to Is. for an *e*. cov.
Ps. 24. 7 be ye lift up, ye *e*. doors
41. 13; 90. 2 93. 2; 100. 5; 103. 17
Prov. 8. 23 I was set up from *e*.
Isa. 24. 5 broken the *e*. covenant
26. 4; 33. 14; 35. 10; 40. 28; 45. 17

Jer. 10. 10 living God and *e*. king
Ezek. 16. 60 establish . . an *e*. cov.
Dan. 9. 24 bring in *e*. righteousness
Mic. 5. 2 goings fr. of old, from *e*.
Hab. 3. 6 He stood .. his ways are *e*.
Mat. 18. 8 than . . be cast into *e*. fire
Luke 16. 9 receive . . *e*. habitations
John 3. 16 not perish, but have *e*. life
Acts 13. 46 unworthy of *e*. life, lo
Rom. 6. 22 and the end *e*. life
Gal. 6. 8 shall of Spirit reap *e*, life
2 Thes. 1. 9 punished with *e*. destr.
1 Tim. 1. 16 believe on him to *e*. life
Heb. 13. 20 blood of the *e*. covenant
2 Pet. 1. 11 unto the *e*. kingdom
Rev. 14. 6 having the *e*. gospel
R. V. 1 Chr. 16. 36; Ps. 100. 5;
119. 44 for ever; Hab. 3. 6; Mat.
18. 8; 19. 29; 25. 41, 46; Luke
16. 9; 18. 30; John 3. 16, 36; 5.
24; 6. 27, 40, 47; 12. 50; Acts 13.
46; Rom. 6. 22; 16. 26; Gal. 6.
8; 2 Thes. 1. 9; 2. 16; 1 Tim. 1.
16; 6. 16; Heb. 3. 20; 2 Pet. 1. 11
eternal

Evermore. *Age-lasting, alway.*
Deut. 28. 29 op. and spoiled *e*. *m*.
2 Sam. 22. 51 to his seed for *e*. *m*.
1 Chr. 17. 14 throne. . be es. for *e*. *m*.
Ps. 16. 11 there are pleas. for *e*. *m*.
Ezek. 37. 26 sanc. in m. . . for *e*. *m*.
John 6. 34 Lord, *e*. *m*. give us bread
2 Cor. 11. 31 J.C. . . blessed for *e. m.*
1 Thes. 5. 16 Rejoice *e*.
Heb. 7. 28 is consecrated for *e*. *m*.
R. V. 1 Thes. 5. 16 always

Every. *Each.*
Gen. 9. 5 at hand of *e*. man's bro.
Ex. 1. 1 *e*. man and his household
Lev. 19. 3 fear *e*. man his m. and f.
Num. 1. 52 *e*. man by his own camp
Deut. 1. 41 girded *e*. man his weap,
Josh. 6. 5 ascend . . *e*. man straigh,
Judg. 2. 6 *e*. man to his inher.
1 Sam. 4. 10 fled *e*. man to his tent
2 Sam. 3. 2 *e*. man with his h. hold
2 K. 4. 25 *e*. man under his vine
1 K. 3. 25 cast *e*. man his stone, and
2 Chr. 16. 43 *e*. man to his house
1 Chr. 6. 30 render unto *e*. man ac.
Neh. 5. 13 God shake out *e*. man
Esth. 1. 8 accor. to *e*. man's pleas.
Job 34. 11 a man to find his ways
Ps. 39. 6. *e*. man walketh in vain
Isa. 9. 20 eat *e*. man the flesh of arm
Jer. 12. 15 *e*. man to his heritage
Ezek. 8. 11 with *e*. man his censer
Jonah 1. 5 cried *e*. man to his god
Mic. 4. 4 *e*. man under his vine
Hag. 1. 9 ye run *e*. man unto house
Zech. 3. 10 call *e*. man his neighbor
Mal. 2. 10 *e*. man against his bro.
Mat. 16. 27 reward *e*. man accor.
Mark 13. 34 *e*. man to his work
John 7. 53 *e*. man went unto his own
Acts 2. 8 how hear we *e*. man
Rom. 2. 6 render to *e*. man accord.
1 Cor. 3. 5 as Lord gave *e*. man
2 Cor. 9. 7 *e*. man . . as he purpos.
Gal. 6. 4 let *e*. man prove . . work
Eph. 4. 25 speak *e*. man truth with
Phil. 2. 4 look . . *e*. man on his . . things
Heb. 8. 11 tea. *e*. man his neighbour
Jas. 1. 14 but *e*. man is tempted
1 Pet. 1. 17 accor. to *e*. man's work
Rev. 20. 13 judged *e*. man accor.
All, every one.
Mat. 3. 10 *e*. tree which bringeth
Mark 9. 49 *e*. sac. shall be salt
Luke 4. 23 *e*. male that openeth the
John 1. 9 which lighteth *e*. man
Acts 2. 5 men. out of *e*. nation under
Rom. 2. 9 upon *e*. soul of man
1 Cor. 1. 2 all that in *e*. place call
2 Cor. 2. 14 knowl. by us in *e*. place
Gal. 5. 3 testify . . to *e*. man that is
Eph. 1. 21 name that is named,
Phil. 1. 9 upon *e*. remembrance
Col. 1. 10 fruitful in *e*. work, and
1 Thes. 1. 8 in *e*. place your faith
2 Thes. 2. 17 *e*. good word and work
1 Tim. 4. 4 *e*. creature . . is good
2 Tim. 2. 21 prep. unto *e*. good work
Tit. 1. 16 unto *e*. . . work reprobate
Heb. 2. 2 and *e*. transgression recei.
Jas. 1. 17 *e*. good gift and ev. perfect

1 Pet. 2. 13 submit . . to *e*. ordinance
1 John 4. 1 believe not *e*. spirit
Rev. 1. 7 *e*. eye shall see him, and

Evidence. *Letter, book.*
Jer. 32. 10 I subscribed the *e*.
32. 11, 12, 14, 16, 44
Conviction.
Heb. 11. 1 *e*. of things not seen
R. V. Jer. 32. 10, 11, 12, 14, 16, 44
deed.

Evident. *Manifest.*
Job 6. 28 for it is *e*. unto you if I lie.
Gal. 3. 11 no man is justified . . is *e*.
Heb. 7. 14 *e*. our Lord sprang . . J.

Evidently. *Openly.*
Acts 10. 3 saw in a vision *e*. about
Gal. 3. 1 been *e*. set forth, crucified

Evil (n.). *Badness, affliction.*
Gen. 2. 9 the tree . . of good and *e*.
3. 5; 6. 5: 8. 21; 19. 19; 37. 2
Ex. 10. 10 look . . for *e*. is before you
Lev. 5. 4 pronouncing . . to do *e*.
Num. 32. 13 done *e*. in sight of L.
Deut. 17. 12 put away *e*. from Is.
Josh. 23. 15 L. bring upon you *e*.
Judg. 2. 11 children of Is. did *e*.
1 Sam. 6. 9 done us this great *e*.
2 Sam. 12. 11 raise up *e*. against thee
1 K. 11. 6 Sol. did *e*. in sight of L.
2 K. 6. 33 this *e*. is of the Lord
1 Chr. 7. 23 went *e*. with his house
2 Chr. 7. 22 he brought all this *e*.
Neh. 9. 28 they did *e*. again before
Esth. 7. 7 there was *e*. determined
Job 1. 1 feared G. and eschewed *e*.
Ps. 5. 4 nei. shall *e*. dwell with thee
Prov. 1. 16 their feet run to *e*.
Eccl. 2. 21 is vanity and a great *e*.
Isa. 3. 9 rewarded *e*. unto thems.
Jer. 1. 14 an *e*. shall break forth
Lam. 3. 38 out of m. proceed. not *e*.
Ezek. 5. 16 send upon them the *e*.
Dan. 9. 12 bringing . . a great *e*.
Joel 2. 13 repenteth him of . . *e*.
Am. 3. 6 shall there be *e*. in city
Jonah 1. 7 for whose cause this *e*.
Mic. 1. 12 *e*. came down from the L.
Nah. 1. 11 imagin. *e*. against the L.
Hab. 1. 13 purer eyes than to beh. *e*.
Zeph. 3. 15 not see *e*. any more
Zech. 7. 10 imagine *e*. against . bro.
Mal. 1. 8 is it not *e*.? and if ye offer
Mat. 6. 34 suf. unto . . day is the *e*.
27. 23 Why, what *e*. hath he done?
Mark 3. 4 lawful to do good, or *e*.?
Luke 6. 45 bringeth . . which is *e*.
John 18. 23 bear witness of the *e*.
Acts 9. 13 how much *e*. he hath d.
Rom. 3. 8 do *e*. that good may co.
1 Cor. 13. 5 not *e*. prov., think. no *e*.
2 Cor. 13. 7 pray G. . . ye do no *e*.
1 Thes. 5. 15 none render *e*. for *e*.
1 Tim. 6. 10 Love of mon. . . r. of . . *e*.
2 Tim. 4. 14 cop. sm. did me much *e*.
Heb. 5. 14 discern both good and *e*.
Jas. 1. 13 G. cannot be tempt. w. *e*.
1 Pet. 3. 9 not rendering *e*. for *e*.
Rev. 2. 2 not bear . . which are *e*.
R. V. Judg. 9. 5 wickedness; 2 Sam.
13. 16 great wrong; 1 Chr. 2. 3;
21. 17 wickedly; Ps. 40. 17 hurt;
Prov. 16. 27 mischief; Jer. 24. 3,
8; 29. 17 bad; Mat. 5. 37; 6. 13;
John 17. 15; 2 Thes. 3. 3 evil one;
Jas. 3. 16 vile; Jas. 4. 11; 1 Pet.
3. 16 ——

Evil (a.). *Bad, sinful, wicked.*
Gen. 37. 2 brought to fath. . . *e*. rep.
Ex. 5. 19 they were in *e*. case
Lev. 26. 6 rid *e*. beasts out of land,
Deut. 1. 35 men of this *e*. genera.
Num. 13. 32 brought up an *e*. report
Judg. 9. 23 God sent an *e*. spirit
1 Sam. 2. 23 hear of your *e*. dealings
1 K. 13. 33 ret. not from his *e*. way
2 K. 17. 13 turn from your *e*. ways
Ez. 9. 13 is come . . for our *e*. deeds
Neh. 13. 17 matter for an *e*. report
Job 8. 20 nei. will he help *e*. doers
Ps. 10. 15 break . . arm of . . *e*. man
Prov. 6. 24 keep thee from *e*. wom.
Eccl. 12 riches per. by *e*. travail
Isa. 7. 5 have taken *e*. counsel agai.
Jer. 3. 17 imagina. of . . *e*. heart
Ezek. 6. 11 abominations of
Am. 5. 13 for it is an *e*. time

Jonah 3. 10 turned from their *e.* **way**
Hab. 2. 9 that covet an *e.* covetous.
Zech. 1. 4 turn now from *e.* ways
Mat. 24. 48 if that *e.* servant shall
Mark 7. 21 fr. within proc. *e.* th'ts
Luke 6. 45 *e.* man out of *e.* treas.
Acts 19. 12 *e.* spirits went out of
Rom. 1. 30 inventors of *e.* things
1 Cor. 15. 33 *e.* com. cor. good ma.
Gal. 1. 4 del. us from . . *e.* world
Phil. 3. 2 beware of *e.* workers
Col 3. 5 *e.* concupis. and **covetous.**
1 Tim. 6. 4 comleth . . *e.* surmisings
2 Tim. 3. 13 *e.* men and seducers
Tit. 1. 12 Cretians are . . *e.* beasts
Heb. 3. 12 lest there be . . an *e.* h.
Jas. 2. 4 become judg. of *e.* hearts
1 Pet. 3. 17 suf. for . . than for *e.* d.
R. V. Eph. 4. 31 railing ; 1 Pet. 3.
16 ——

Ewe. *Female sheep.*
Gen. 31. 38 *e.* . . have not cast . . y.
Lev. 22. 28 whether . . cow or *e.*
Ps. 78. 71 the *e.* great with young

Ewe Lamb. *Ewe lamb.*
Gen. 21. 28 Abra. set seven *e.* lamb
Lev. 14. 10 one *e. l.* of . . first year
Num. 6. 14 ; 2 Sam. 12. 3

Exact. *Compel, extort, require.*
Deut. 15. 2 not *e.* it of his neighbour
2 K. 15. 20 Menah. *e.* money of Is.
Neh. 5. 7. ye *e.* usury of . . brother
Job 11. 6 know . . God *e.* of thee
Ps. 89. 22 enemy shall not *e.* upon
Isa. 58. 3 and *e.* all your labours
Luke 3. 13 *e.* no more than that
Neh. 5. 10 lend ; Luke 3. 13 extort

Exaction. *Compulsion, extortion.*
Neh. 10. 31 the *e.* of every debt
Ezek. 45. 9 take away your *e.* from

Exactor. *Who exacts.*
Isa. 60. 17 make . . *e.* righteousness

Exalt. *Make high, lift up.*
Ex. 15. 2 L. my strength, I will *e.*
Num. 24. 7 his kingdom shall be *e.*
1 Sam. 2. 1 my horn is *e.* in . . L.
2 Sam. 5. 12 he had *e.* his kingdom
1 K. 1. 5 son of Hag. *e.* himself
2 K. 19. 22 hast thou *e.* thy voice
1 Chr. 29. 11 art *e.* as head above
Neh. 9. 5 is *e.* above all blessing
Job 24. 24 are *e.* but a little while
Ps. 99. 5 ye the Lord our God
Prov. 14. 34 righteous. a nation
Isa. 25. 1 O Lord . . I will *e.* thee
Ezek. 17. 24 I the Lord . . have *e.*
Dan. 11. 14 robbers . . shall *e.* them.
Hos. 11. 7 none at all would *e.* him
Obad. 4 *e.* thou thyself as the eagle
Mic. 5. 1 shall¹¹ be *e.* above the hills
Mat. 11. 23 which are *e.* unto heav.
Luke 1. 52 put down . . mi. . . and *e.*
10. 15 ; 14. 11 ; 18. 14
Acts 2. 33 by right hand of God *e.*
2 Cor. 11. 7 abasing . . that ye be *e.*
Phil. 2. 9 God hath highly *e.* him
2 Thes. 2. 4 opposeth and *e.* him.
Jas. 1. 9 bro. . rejoice in that he is *e.*
1 Pet. 5. 6 that he may *e.* you
R. V. Job 36. 22 doeth loftily ; Ps.
148. 14 ; Ezek. 31. 10 hath lifted
up ; Prov. 17. 19 raiseth high ;
Jas. 1. 9 his high estate

Examination. *Investigation.*
Acts 25. 26 after *e.* had, I might

Examine. *Try, prove, investi-*
gate.
Ez. 10. 16 sat down . . to *e.* matter
Ps. 26. 2 *E.* me, O L., and prove me
Luke 23. 14 having *e.* him before
Acts 4. 9 if we this day be *e.* of the
1 Cor. 9. 3 ans. to them that *e.* is this
2 Cor. 13. 5 *e.* yourselves, whether
R. V. 1 Cor. 11. 28 prove ; 2 Cor.
13. 5 try your ownselves

Example. *Sample, type, model.*
Mat. 1. 19 make her a publick *e.*
John 13. 15 I have given you an *e.*
1 Cor. 10. 6 these things were our *e.*
1 Tim. 4. 12 be thou an *e.* of the
Heb. 8. 5 serve . . the *e.* and shadow
Jas. 5. 10 *e.* of suffering afflic., and
1 Pet. 2. 21 Christ, . . leaving us an *e.*
Jude 7 cities . . are set forth for an *e.*
suffering the vengeance
R. V. 1 Tim. 4. 12 example to

those that believe ; Heb. 8. 5 that
which is a copy

Exceed. *Go beyond, surpass, ex-*
cel
Deut. 25. 3 lest if he should *e.*, and
1 Sam. 20. 41 and wept . . until D. *e.*
1 K. 10. 7 thy wisdom and pros. *e.*
2 Chr. 9. 6 *e.* the fame . . I heard
Job 36. 9 transgress. . . they have *e.*
Mat. 5. 20 except . . righteous. sh. *e.*
2 Cor. 3. 9 minis. of righteous. *e.* in
R. V. Job 36. 9 behave themselves
proudly

Exceeding. *Very great, surpass-*
ing.
Gen. 15. 1 shield, and *e.* . . reward
Ex. 1. 7 Israel . . waxed *e.* mighty
Num. 14. 7 it is an *e.* good land
1 Sam. 2. 3 talk no more so *e.* proud.
2 Sam. 8. 8 D. took *e.* much brass
1 K. 4. 29 G. gave Sol. wisdom . . *e.*
1 Chr. 20. 2 he br. . . *e.* much spoil
2 Chr. 11. 12 made them *e.* strong
Ps. 119. 96 thy command, is *e.* broad
Prov. 30. 24 but they are *e.* wise
Jer. 48. 29 Moab, he is *e.* proud
Ezek. 9. 9 iniquity of Is. is *e.* great
Dan. 3. 22 and the furnace *e.* hot
Jonah 4. 6 was *e.* glad of the gourd
Mat. 2. 16 Herod . . was *e.* wroth
Mark 9. 3 shin. *e.* white as snow
Luke 23. 8 Her. saw J. he was *e.*
Acts 7. 20 born, and was *e.* fair
Rom. 7. 13 might become *e.* sinful
2 Cor. 4. 17 more *e.* . . weight of g.
Eph. 1. 19 *e.* greatness of his power
R. V. 2 Chr. 14. 14—— ; 2 Cor. 7.
4 overflow with joy ; 1 Tim. 1. 14
abounded exceedingly

Exceedingly. *Greatly, vehem-*
ently.
Gen. 7. 19 waters prevailed *e.* upon
1 Sam. 26. 21 fool, and have erred *e.*
2 Sam 13. 15 Amnon hated her *e.*
2 K. 10. 4 But they were *e.* afraid
1 Chr. 29. 25 L. magnified Sol. *e.*
2 Chr. 1. 1 God . . magnified him *e.*
Neh. 2. 10 it grieved them *e.* that
Esth. 4. 4 was the queen *e.* grieved
Job 3. 22 rejoice *e.* and are glad
Ps. 68. 3 yea, let them *e.*, rejoice
Isa. 24. 19 the earth is moved *e.*
Dan. 7. 7 terrible and strong *e.*
Jonah 1. 10 were the men *e.* afraid
Mat. 19. 25 they were *e.* amazed
Mark 4. 41 they feared *e.*, and said
Acts 16. 20 these . . *e.* trouble our city
2 Cor. 7. 13 and *e.* the more joyed
Gal. 1. 14 being more *e.* zealous
1 Thes. 3. 10 night and day pray. *e.*
2 Thes. 1. 3 that your faith grow. *e.*
Heb. 12. 21 Moses said, I *e.* fear
R. V. Gen. 16. 10 greatly ; Ps. 68.
3 with gladness ; 2 Chr. 28. 6
waxed exceeding strong

Excel. *Go up, be over, surpass.*
Gen. 49. 4 un. . . thou shalt not *e.*
1 K. 4. 30 Sol's wisdom *e.* the wis.
1 Chr. 15. 21 wi. harps on Shem. to *e.*
Ps. 103. 20 angels that *e.* in strength
Prov. 31. 29 but thou *e.* them all
Eccl. 2. 13 *e.* folly, as light *e.* dark.
1 Cor. 14. 12 seek that ye may *e.*
2 Cor. 3. 10 by reas. of glor. that *e.*
R. V. 1 Chr. 15. 21 lead ; Ps. 103.
20 ye mighty ; 1 Cor. 14. 12
abound unto

Excellency. *Majesty, superiority.*
Gen. 49. 3 *e.* of dignity, and *e.* cf
Ex. 15. 7 in greatness of thine *e.*
Deut. 33. 26 ride. . . in . . *e.* on sky
Job 37. 4 thunder, wi. voice of . . *e.*
Ps. 47. 4 the *e.* of Jacob, whom
Eccl. 7. 12 *e.* of knowl. is wisdom
Isa. 13. 19 beauty of Chaldees' *e.*
Ezek. 24. 21 *e.* of your strength, the
Am. 6. 8 abhor the *e.* of Jacob
Nah. 2. 2 *e.* of Jacob, as the *e.* of
1 Cor. 2. 1 with *e.* of speech or wis.
2 Cor. 4. 7 *e.* of power may be of G.
Phil. 3. 8 *e.* of knowledge of Christ
R. V. Gen. 37. 4 majesty ; Isa. 13.
19 ; Ezek. 24. 21 pride

Excellent. *Honorable, abundant,*
precious, surpassing, pre-eminent,
preferable.

Esth. 1. 4 honor of his *e.* majesty
Job 37. 23 Almi., he is *e.* in power
Ps. 8. 1, 9 O L., how *e.* is thy name
Prov. 17. 7 *e.* speech becom. not a f.
S. of S. 5. 15 as Leb. *e.* as the cedars
Isa. 12. 5 he hath done *e.* things
Ezek. 16. 7 come to *e.* ornaments
Dan. 2. 3 whose brightness was *e.*
Luke 1. 3 write . . most *e.* Theophilus
Acts 23. 26 Lysias unto the most *e.*
Rom. 2. 18 things that are most *e.*
1 Cor. 12. 31 show I . . a more *e.* way
Phil. 1. 10 approve things that are *e.*
Heb. 1. 4 obtained a more *e.* name
2 Pet. 1. 17 voice . . from more *e.* g.
R. V. Ps. 36. 7 precious ; 141. 5 as
upon the head ; 148. 13 exalted ;
Prov. 17. 27 cool ; 12. 26 guide to

Except. *If not, omitting, but, un-*
less.
Gen. 43. 10 For *e.* we had lingered
Num. 16. 13 *e.* thou make thyself
Deut. 32. 30 *e.* their Rock had sold
Josh. 7. 12 *e.* ye destroy the accursed
1 Sam. 25. 34 *e.* thou hadst hasted
Esth. 4. 11 *e.* such to whom the k.
Isa. 1. 9 *e.* the Lord of hosts had
Dan. 2. 11 *e.* the gods, whose dwell.
Am. 3. 3 walk tog. *e.* they be agreed ?
Mat. 5. 20 *e.* your righteousness shall
Mark 3. 27 *e.* he will first bind
Luke 9. 13 *e.* we should . . buy meat
John 3. 2 *e.* God be with him
4. 48 ; 6. 44 ; 12. 24 ; 15. 4
Acts 8. 31 *e.* some man should gui.
Rom. 10. 15 how shall they preach *e.*
1 Cor. 14. 6 *e.* ⁷ shall speak to you
2 Cor. 13. 5 *e.* ye be reprobates
2 Thes. 2. 3 there came a failing
2 Tim. 2. 5 *e.* he strive lawfully
Rev. 2. 22 *e.* they repent of their d.
R. V. Gen. 47. 26 only ; Num. 16.
13 but ; 2 Sam. 3. 9 ; 1 Cor. 14. 17
if ; 14. 6, 9 ; 2 Cor. 13. 5 unless

Excepted. *Without, outside.*
1 Cor. 15. 27 he is *e.* which did put

Excess. *Incontinence, prodigality.*
Mat. 23. 25 full of extortion and *e.*
Eph. 5. 18 dr. with wine, where. is *e.*
1 Pet. 4. 3 lasc., lusts, *e.* of wine
R. V. Eph. 5. 18 riot ; 1 Pet. 4.
wine bibbings

Exchange (*n.*). *Change, inter-*
change.
Lev. 27. 10 it and the *e.* thereof hol.
Job 28. 17 *e.* of it shall not be for
Mat. 16. 26 what shall man give in *e.*
Mark 8. 37 what . . give in *e.* for his s.

Exchange (*v.*). *Change.*
Job 28. 17 the *e.* of it shall not be
Ezek. 48. 14 neither *e.* nor alienate

Exchangers. R. V. *bankers.*
Mat. 25. 27 put my money to the *e.*

Exclude. *Shut out.*
Rom. 3. 27 Wh. is boasting ? It is *e.*
Gal. 4. 17 yea they would *e.* you

Excuse (*n.*). *Apology.*
Luke 14. 18 all . . began to make *e.*
Rom. 1. 20 they were without *e.*

Excuse. *Ask off, apologize.*
Luke 14. 18 I pray thee have me *e.*
Rom. 2. 15 accusing or else *e.* one
2 Cor. 12. 19 think . . we *e.* ourselves
R. V. 2 Cor. 12. 19 are excusing

Execration. *Imprecation, curse.*
Jer. 42. 18 shall be an *e.* and aston.

Execute. *Do.*
Ex. 12. 12 ag. Eg. I will *e.* judgment
Num. 5. 30 priests shall *e.* upon her
Deut. 10. 18 *e.* the judgment of the
1 Sam. 28. 18 his fierce wrath
2 Sam. 8. 15 David *e.* judgment and
1 K. 6. 12 *e.* my judgments, then I
2 K. 10. 30 *e.* that which is right
1 Chr. 18. 14 *e.* judgment and justice
2 Chr. 24. 24 so they *e.* judgment
Ez. 7. 26 let judgment be *e.* speedily
Ps. 9. 16 known by judg. which hee.
Eccl. 18. 11 evil work . . not *e.* speed.
Jer. 5. 1 if be any that *e.* judgment
Ezek. 5. 8 will *e.* judgment in nat.
11. 9 ; 16. 41 ; 18. 8 ; 20. 24 ; 23. 10
Hos. 11. 9 the fierceness of
Joel 2. 11 strong that *e.* his word
Mic. 5. 15 will *e.* vengeance in ang
Zech. 7. 9 *e.* true judgment, and

John 5. 27 authority to *e.* judgment
Jude 15 *e.* judgment upon all
R. V. Num. 8. 11 be to do; Jer. 5. 1
 doeth; Isa. 46. 11 of; Rom. 13. 4
 for

Execution. *To be done.*
Esth. 9. 1 drew near to be put in *e.*

Executioner. *Spearman.*
Mark 6. 27 king sent an *e.*, and
R. V. Mark 6. 27 soldier of the guard

Exempted. *Freed.*
1 K. 15. 22 throughout J. none was *e.*

Exercise (*n.*). *Exertion.*
1 Tim. 4. 8 bod. *e.* profiteth little

Exercise (*v.*). *Do, work up, train.*
Job 9. 24 which *e.* lovingkindness
Ps. 131. 1 neither do I *e.* myself
Eccl. 1. 13 hath G. given . . to be *e.*
Jer. 9. 24 Lord . . *e.* lovingkindness
Ezek. 22. 29 *e.* robbery, and vexed
Acts 24. 16 herein do I *e.* myself
1 Tim. 4. 7 *e.* thyself unto godliness
Heb. 5. 14 *e.* to discern both g. and e.
2 Pet. 2. 14 *e.* with cov. practices
Rev. 13. 12 he *e.* all the power of
R. V. Mat. 20. 25; Mark 10. 42 lord
 it; Luke 22. 25 have

Exhort. *Call near, advise, urge.*
Acts 2. 40 other words did he . . *e.*
Rom. 12. 8 he that *e.*, on exhorta.
2 Cor. 9. 5 necessary to *e.* . . breth.
1 Thes. 2. 11 ye know how we *e.*
2 Thes. 3. 12 *e.* by our Lord J. C.
1 Tim. 2. 1 I *e.* therefore that first
2 Tim. 4. 2 *e.*, with longsuffering
Tit. 1. 9 to *e.* and to convince
Heb. 3. 13 *e.* one another daily
1 Pet. 5. 1 elders . . among you I *e.*
Jude 3. *e.* you that ye should earn.
R. V. 2 Cor. 9. 5 entreat

Exhortation. *Calling near.*
Luke 3. 18 other things in his *e.*
Acts 13. 15 if ye have . . word of *e.*
Rom. 12. 8 that exhorteth, on *e.*
1 Cor. 14. 3 edifi. ation and *e.*, and
2 Cor. 8. 17 he accepted the *e.*
1 Thes. 2. 3 our *e.* was not of deceit
1 Tim. 4. 13 to reading, to *e.*, to doc.
Heb. 12. 5 ye have forgotten the *e.*

Exile. *Removed, wanderer.*
2 Sam. 15. 19 stranger, also an *e.*
Isa. 51. 14 the captive *e.* hasteneth

Exorcist. *Adjurer out of demons.*
Acts 19. 13 certain of the . . Jews, *e.*

Expect. *Look for, wait.*
Acts 3. 5 *e.* to receive something
Heb. 10. 13 *e.* till his enemies be m.

Expectation. *Hope, looking for.*
Ps. 9. 18 *e.* of . . poor shall not per.
Prov. 10. 28 *e.* of . . wicked shall per.
Isa. 20. 5 ashamed of Eth. their *e.*
Zech. 9. 5 for her *e.*, shall be asha.
Luke 3. 15 as the peo. were in *e*
Rom. 8. 19 the earnest *e.* of the
Phil. 1. 20 accord. to my earnest *e.*
R. V. Prov. 23. 18; 24. 14 thy hope

Expected. *Hoped.*
Jer. 29. 11 to give you an *e.* end
R. V. Hope in your latter.

Expedient. *Bear together, advisable.*
John 11. 50 it is *e.* for us that one
1 Cor. 6. 12 all things are not *e.*
2 Cor. 8. 10 this is *e.* for you, who

Expel. *Cast out, dispossess.*
Josh. 13. 13 Is. *e.* not the Geshurites
Judg. 1. 20 Mos. *e.* the sons of Anak
2 Sam. 14. 14 his banished be not *e.*
Acts 13. 50 *e.* them out of . . coasts
R. V. 2 Sam. 14. 14 an outcast;
 Acts 13. 50 cast

Expenses. *Outgoings.*
Ez. 6. 4, 8 let the *e.* be given out of

Experience. *Seeing, observation.*
Gen. 30. 27 I have learned by *e.*
Eccl. 1. 16 had great *e.* of wisdom
Rom. 5. 4 patience *e.*, and *e.* hope
R. V. Gen. 30. 27 divined; Rom.
 5. 4 probation

Experiment. *Proof.*
2 Cor. 9. 13 *e.* of this ministration
R. V. seeing that the proving of
 you by

Expert. *Taught, skilful.*
1 Chr. 12. 33 *e.* in war, with all ins.
S. of S. 3. 8 all hold swords. being *e.*

Jer. 50. 9 arrows . . as of a mighty *e.*
Acts 26. 3 *e.* in all customs and ques.

Expire. *End, fill out.*
1 Sam. 18. 26 the days were not *e*
2 Sam. 11. 1 after the year was *e.*
1 Chr. 17. 11 when thy days be *e.*
2 Chr. 36. 10 when the year was *e.*
Esth. 1. 5 when these days were *e.*
Ezek. 43. 27 when these days are *e.*
Acts 7. 30 when forty years were *e.*
Rev. 20. 7 when thous. years w. *e.*
R. V. 1 Chr. 17. 11; Esth. 1. 5;
 Acts 7. 30 fulfillled; Rev. 20 7
 finished; 2 Sam. 11. 1; 1 Chr. 2. 1:
 2 Chr. 36. 10 at the return of the
 year.

Exploits. R. V. *his pleasure.*
Dan. 11. 28, 32 shall do *e.* and return

Expound. *Put before, solve.*
Judg. 14. 14 could not . . *e.* the riddle
Mark 4. 34 *e.* all things to his dis.
Luke 24. 27 *e.* unto them in . . scrip.
Acts 11. 4 *e.* it by order unto them
R. V. Judg. 14. 14 declare; Luke
 24. 27 interpreted.

Express (*v.*). *Defined, marked out.*
Num. 1. 17 men . . *e.* by their names
1 Chr. 12. 31 which were *e.* by name
2 Chr. 28. 15 men . . *e.* by name rose
Ez. 8. 20 all of them were *e.* by name

Express (*a.*). R. V. *very.*
Heb. 1. 3 *e.* image of his person

Expressly. *Definitely, exactly.*
1 Sam. 20. 21 if I *e.* say unto lad
Ezek. 1. 3 word came *e.* to Ezek.
1 Tim. 4. 1 the Spirit speaketh *e.*
R. V. 1 Sam. 20. 21 ——

Extend. *Stretch out.*
Ez. 7. 28 *e.* mercy unto me
Ps. 109. 12 none to *e.* mercy unto
Isa. 66. 12 I will *e.* peace to her

Extinct. *Extinguished.*
Job 17. 1 My days are *e.*, graves
Isa. 43. 17 they are *e.*, they are

Extol. *Lift up, exalt.*
Ps. 66. 17 was *e.* with my tongue
Isa. 52. 13 shall be exalted and *e.*
Dan. 4. 37 *e.* and hon. K. of heav.
R. V. Ps. 68. 4 cast up a highway
 for; Isa. 52. 13 lifted up.

Extortion. *Oppression, snatching.*
Ezek. 22. 12 hast greed. gained by *e.*
Mat. 23. 25 within . . full of *e.*
R. V. Ezek. 22. 12 oppression

Extortioner. *Biter, usurer.*
Ps. 109. 11 let the *e.* catch all
Wringer out.
Isa. 16. 4 the *e.* is at an end
Snatcher away.
Luke 18. 11 not as other men, *e.*
1 Cor. 5. 10 with covetous or *e.*

Extreme. R. V. *fiery heat.*
Deut. 28. 22 L. smite with *e.* burn.

Extremity. *Last degree.*
Job 35. 15 knoweth it not in gr. *e.*
R. V. neither doth he greatly regard
 arrogance

Eye. *Eye, organ of vision.*
Gen. 3. 5 your *e.* shall be opened
 6. 8; 13. 10; 16. 4; 18. 2; 19. 8;
 20. 16; 21. 19; 22. 4; 24. 63; 27. 1
Ex. 5. 21 in the *e.* of Pharaoh, and
Lev. 4. 13 thing be hid from *e.* of
Num. 5. 13 hid from *e.* of . . husb.
Deut. 1. 30 all he did before your *e.*
Josh. 5. 13 lifted up his *e.* and
Judg. 16. 21 and put out his *e.*
Ruth 2. 9 let thine *e.* be on the field
1 Sam. 2. 33 be to consume thine *e.*
2 Sam. 6. 20 uncov. himself in *e.* of
1 K. 1. 20 *e.* of . . Is. are upon thee
2 K. 4. 34 upon *e.*, and his hand
1 Chr. 13. 4 right in *e.* of all the peo.
2 Chr. 6. 20 thine *e.* may be open
Ez. 3. 12 foundations . . laid be. . . *e.*
Neh. 1. 6 let thine . . *e.* be open that
Esth. 1. 17 despise husb. in their *e.*
Job 2. 12 they lifted up their *e.* afar
 3. 10; 4. 16; 7. 7; 10. 4; 11. 4;
Ps. 6. 7 mine *e.* is consumed because
 10 8; 11. 4; 13. 3; 15. 4; 17. 8;
Prov. 3. 7 be not wise in thine own *e.*
 4. 21; 5. 21; 6. 4; 10. 10; 12. 6;
Eccl. 1. 8 *e.* not satisfied with seeing
S. of S. 1. 15 thou hast doves' *e.*
Isa. 1. 15 I will hide mine *e.* fr. you

3. 8; 5. 15; 6. 5; 11. 3; 13. 16;
Jer. 3. 2 lift up thine *e.* unto high pl.
Lam. 1. 16 mine *e.* runneth down
Ezek. 1. 18 full of *e.* round about
Dan. 4. 34 Nebuch. lift. up mine *e.*
Hos. 13. 14 repentance . . hid from *e.*
Joel 1. 16 cut off before our *e.*
Am. 9. 4 will set mine *e.* upon them
Mic. 4. 11 and let our *e.* look on Z.
Hab. 1. 13 of purer *e.* than to behold
Zeph. 3. 10 turn back cap. . . before *e.*
Hag. 2. 3 *e.* in comparison of is
Zech. 1. 18 lifted I up mine *e.*, saw
Mal. 1. 5 and your *e.* shall see
Mat. 5. 29 . . right *e.* offend, pluck
 6. 22; 7. 3; 9. 29; 13. 15, 17. 8
Mark 7. 22 evil *e.*, blasph., pride
Luke 2. 30 *e.* have seen thy salvation
 4. 20; 6. 20; 10. 23; 11. 34; 16. 23
John 4. 35 lift up your *e.*, look
 6. 5; 9. 6; 10. 21; 11. 37; 12. 40
Acts 9. 8 when his *e.* were opened
Rom. 3. 18 no fear of G. before . . *e.*
1 Cor. 2. 9 *e.* hath not seen, nor ear
Gal. 3. 1 before whose *e.* J. C. hath
Eph. 1. 18 *e.* of understand. being en.
Col. 3. 22 not with *e.* service, as men
Heb. 4. 13 unto the *e.* of him whom
1 Pet. 3. 12 *e.* of Lord are over the
2 Pet. 2. 14 having *e.* full of adultery
1 John 1. 1 we have seen with our *e.*
Rev. 1. 7 every *e.* shall see him
 2. 18; 3. 18; 4. 6; 5. 6; 19. 12;
R. V. 1 K. 16. 25; 2 Chr. 21. 6; 29.
 6; Jer. 52. 2 sight; Ruth 2. 10 thy
 sight

Eyesight. *Eye.*
2 Sam. 22. 25 accor. to clean. in his *e.*
Ps. 18. 24 clean. of hands in his *e.*

F.

Fable. *Tale, legend, myth.*
1 Tim. 1. 4 nei. give heed to *f.* and
2 Tim. 4. 4 shall be turned unto *f.*
Tit. 1. 14 not giving heed to Jew. *f.*
2 Pet. 1. 16 not fol. cunning. devis. *f.*

Face. *Face, visage, surface.*
Gen. 1. 2 darkness . . upon the *f.* of
3. 19 in sweat of . . *f.* shall eat br.
Ex. 10. 5 locus. cover *f.* of the earth
Lev. 9. 24 shouted, and fell on . . *f.*
Num. 6. 25 Lord make his *f.* shine
Deut. 1. 17 not be afraid of *f.* of m.
Josh. 5. 14 Joshua fell on his *f.*
Judg. 6. 22 seen an angel . . *f.* to *f.*
Ruth 2. 10 then she fell on her *f.*
1 Sam. 5. 3, 4 Dagon was fall. on . . *f.*
2 Sam. 2. 22 I hold up my *f.* to Joab
1 K. 2. 15 set their *f.* on me, that
2 K. 4. 29 lay staff on *f.* of child
1 Chr. 12. 8 *f.* like *f.* of lions
2 Chr. 3. 13 and their *f.* were inwa.
Ez. 9. 6 and I blush to lift my face
Esth. 7. 8 they covered Haman's *f.*
Job 1. 11 he will curse thee to thy *f.*
 4. 15; 9. 24; 11. 15; 13. 24; 16. 8;
Ps. 5. 8 way straight before thy *f.*
 10. 11; 13. 1; 17. 15; 21. 12; 22. 24
Prov. 7. 15 diligently to seek thy *f.*
Eccl. 8. 1 wisdom make *f.* to shine
Isa. 3. 15 grind the *f.* of the poor
 6. 2; 8. 17; 13. 8; 14. 21; 16. 4
Jer. 1. 8 be not afraid of their *f.*
Lam. 2. 19 like water before . . *f.* of
Ezek. 1. 6 every one had four *f.*
 1. 8—28; 3. 8; 4. 3; 6. 2; 7. 18;
 8. 16; 9. 8; 10. 14; 11. 13; 12. 6;
Dan. 1. 10 see your *f.* worse liking
 8. 5; 9. 3; 10. 6; 11. 17, 18, 19
Hos. 5. 5 doth testify to his *f.*
Joel 2. 6 before their *f.* the people
Am. 5. 8 poureth . . out upon . . *f.* of
Mic. 3. 4 will even hide his *f.* from
Nah. 2. 1 is come up before thy *f.*
Hab. 1. 9 their *f.* shall sup up as
Zech. 5. 3 curse . . goeth . . over *f.* of
Mal. 2. 3 spread dung upon your *f.*
Mat. 6. 16 they disfigure their *f.*
 11. 10; 16. 3; 17. 2; 18. 10; 26. 39
Mark 1. 2 send mess. before thy *f.*
Luke 1. 76 go before the *f.* of Lord
 2. 31; 5. 12; 7. 27; 9. 51; 10 1
Acts 6. 15 saw his *f.* as . . *f.* of angel
1 Cor. 13. 12 through glass . . *f.* to *f.*
2 Cor. 3. 7 could not . . behold *f.* of M
Gal. 1. 22 unknown by *f.* unto . . ch

Col. 2. 1 as have not seen my *f.*
1 Thes. 2. 17 see your *f.* with .. des.
Jas. 1. 23 behold. .. nat. *f.* in .. glass
1 Pet. 3. 12 *f.* of L. is against them
Rev. 4. 7 beast had *f.* as a man
R. V. Gen. 24. 47 nose; 46. 28 way;
  1 Sam. 26. 20: Luke 22. 64——

Fade. *Lose color, wear away.*
2 Sam. 22. 46 strangers sh. *f.* away
Ps. 18. 45 *f.* away, and be afraid of
Isa. 1. 30 as an oak whose leaf *f.*
  24. 4; 28. 1; 40. 7. 8
  64. 6 all do *f.* as a leaf, and our
Jer. 8. 13 leaf shall *f.*, and .. things
Ezek. 47. 12 whose leaf shall not *f.*
Jas. 1. 11 so .. the rich man *f.* away
1 Pet. 1. 4 inher. .. that *f.* not away
R. V. Ezek. 47. 12 wither

Fail (*n.*). *Default.*
Josh. 3. 10 will without *f.* drive
Judg. 11. 30 without *f.* deliv. Am.
Ez. 6. 9 given day by day without *f.*
R. V. Judg. 11. 30 indeed

Fail (*v.*). *Give out, waste away,*
prove deficient or wanting, turn
out badly.
Gen. 42. 28 heart *f.*, they were afraid
Deut. 28. 32 eyes *f.* with longing
Josh. 1. 5 I will not *f.* thee, nor for.
1 Sam. 17. 32 let no man's heart *f.*
2 Sam. 3. 29 not *f.* from h. of Joab
1 K. 2. 4 shall not *f.* thee .. a man
1 Chr. 28. 20 not *f.* thee, nor forsake
2 Chr. 6. 16 not *f.* thee a man .. to
Ez. 4. 22 take heed that ye *f.* not
Esth. 9. 28 days of Pur. sh. not *f.*
Job. 14. 11 as .. waters *f.* from the sea
Ps. 12. 1 the faithful *f.* among men
Prov. 22. 8 rod of .. anger shall *f.*
Eccl. 12. 5 burden,and desire shall *f.*
S. of S. 5. 6 soul *f.* when he spake
Isa. 44. 12 hun., and his strength *f.*
Jer. 14. 6 their eyes did *f.*, because
Lam. 2. 11 eyes do *f.* with tears
Ezek. 12. 22 and every vision *f.*
Hos. 9. 2 new wine shall *f.* in her
Am. 8. 4 make .. poor of .. land to *f.*
Hab. 3. 17 labor of the olive shall *f.*
Zeph. 3. 5 he *f.* not, but the unjust
Luke 16. 17 than one tit. of law to *f.*
1 Cor. 13. 8 prophecies, they sh. *f.*
Heb. 1. 12 thy years shall not *f.*
R. V. Gen. 47. 15 was all spent;
  Josh. 3. 16 wholly; Ez. 4. 22 be
  slack; Ps. 40. 26; 59. 15 is lack-
  ing; Isa. 19. 3 make void; 34. 16
  be missing; Ver. 48. 33 cease;
  Luke 16. 17 fall; 1 Cor. 13. 8 be
  done away; Heb. 12. 15 that fall-
  eth short

Failing. *Wasting, fainting.*
Deut. 28. 65 and *f.* of eyes, and sor.
Luke 21. 26 men's hearts *f.* th. for
R. V. Luke 21. 26 fainting

Faint (*a.*). *Sick, weary, timid,*
feeble.
Deut. 20. 8 man .. fear. and *f.* heart.
Gen. 25. 29 Esau came .. he was *f.*
Judg. 8. 4 Gid. .. *f.* yet pur. them
1 Sam. 14. 28 and the peo. were *f.*
2 Sam. 21. 15 and David waxed *f.*
Isa. 1. 5 head sick, and the heart *f.*
Jer. 8. 18 my heart is *f.* in me
Lam. 1. 22 sighs many .. heart is *f.*
R. V. Isa. 13. 7 feeble

Faint (*v.*). *To be weary.*
Job. 4. 5 upon thee, and thou *f.*
Isa. 40. 28 Creator .. *f.* not, neither
Jer. 45. 3 I *f.* in my sighing .. no rest
Rev. 2. 3 borne .. and hast not *f.*
Become weak, feeble.
Gen. 47. 13 *f.* by reason of famine
Ps. 107. 5 thirsty, their soul *f.*
Prov. 24. 10 *f.* in day of adversity
Lam. 2. 19 child. that *f.* for hunger
Ezek. 21. 7 every spirit shall *f.*
Dan. 8. 27 And I Daniel *f.* and was
Jonah 2. 8 my soul *f.* within me
Consume, melt.
Deut. 20. 8 lest his breth. heart *f.*
Josh. 2. 24 inhab. of country do *f*

Ps. 84. 2 soul longeth, yea, even *f.*
Ezek. 21. 15 that their heart may *f.*
Isa. 10. 18 when standard bear. *f.*
Wrap up, swoon.
Isa. 51. 20 Thy sons have *f.*, they lie
Amos 8. 13 sh. the fair virgins .. *f.*
Jonah 4. 18 *f.* .. and wished .. to die
To be soft, tender, timid.
Deut. 20. 3 let not your hearts *f.*
Jer. 51. 46 lest your heart *f.* and ye
Turn out badly, shrink.
Luke 18. 1 always pray, and not *f.*
2 Cor. 4. 1 received mercy, we *f.* not
Eph. 3. 13 I desire that ye *f.* not
Loosen, relax.
Mat. 9. 36 *f.* and were scattered
Mark 8. 3 they will *f.* by the way
Gal. 6. 9 we shall reap, if we *f.* not
Heb. 12. 3 wearied, and *f.* in ..m.
R. V. Deut. 20. 8; Ezek. 21. 15
  melt; Josh. 2. 9, 24 melt away;
  Isa. 13. 7 feeble; Jer. 45. 3; Rev.
  2. 3 weary; Mat. 9. 36 distressed

Fainthearted. *Melted.*
Isa. 7. 4 neither be *f. h.* for the two
Jer. 49. 23 H. and Arpad are *f. h.*
R. V. Isa. 7 4 faint; Jer. 49. 23
  melted away

Faintness. *Fainting.*
Lev. 26. 36 send *f.* into their hearts

Fair. *Beautiful.*
Gen. 12. 11 thou art a *f.* woman
1 Sam. 17. 42 ruddy, and of *f.* coun.
2 Sam. 13. 1 Absalom .. had *f.* sis.
1 K. 1. 3 sought for a *f.* damsel
Esth. 2. 2 let .. *f.* virgins be sought
Job 42. 15 no woman found so *f.*
Prov. 11. 22 *f.* woman .. without dis.
S. of S. 1. 15 thou art *f.*, my love
Jer. 11. 16 a green olive tree, *f.*, and
Ezek. 31. 3 cedar .. wi. *f.* branches
Dan. 4. 12 leaves thereof were *f.*
Am. 8. 13 shall *f.* virgins .. faint
Acts 7. 20 Moses .. was exceed. *f.*
Gal. 6. 12 desire to make *f.* show
Clean, pure, good.
Gen. 6. 2 daugh. of men .. were *f.*
Judg. 15. 2 her .. sister *f.* than she
Esth. 1. 11 for she was *f.* to look on
Ps. 45. 2 *f.* than children of men
Isa. 5. 9 houses great and *f.* without
Dan. 1. 15 countenances appeared *f.*
Hos. 10. 11 passed .. up. her *f.* neck
Zech. 3. 5 *f.* mitre upon his head
Agreeable, shining.
Prov. 7. 21 with *f.* speech she cause.
Isa. 54. 11 lay .. stone wi. *f.* colors
Jer. 12. 6 speak *f.* words unto thee
Mat. 16. 2 it will be *f.* weather, sky
Rom. 16. 18 and *f.* speeches deceive
Traffic, market.
Ezek. 27. 12–27 traded in thy *f.*
R. V. Ezek. 27. 12–17 wares; Job
  37. 22 golden.

Faith. *Steadiness, trust, faith.*
Deut. 32. 20 child. in whom is no *f.*
Hab. 2. 4 just shall live by his *f.*
Mat. 8. 10 ha. not found so great *f.*
  9. 2; 15. 28; 17. 20; 21. 21; 23. 23
Mark 2. 5 Jesus saw their *f.*, he
Luke 7. 50 *f.* hath made thee whole
  8. 25; 17. 5; 18. 8, 42; 22. 32
Acts 3. 16 through *f.* in his name
  6. 5; 11. 24; 13. 8; 14. 9; 15. 9
Rom. 1. 5 obedience to *f.* among
  3. 3; 4. 5; 5. 1; 9. 30; 10. 6; 11. 20
1 Cor. 2. 5 *f.* should not stand in
  12. 9; 13. 2; 15. 14; 16. 13
2 Cor. 1. 24 have dominion over y. *f.*
Gal. 1. 23 preacheth the *f.* which
  2. 16; 3. 2–26; 5. 5; 6. 10
Eph. 1. 15 heard of your *f.* in the
Phil. 1. 25 furtherance and joy of *f.*
Col. 1. 4 heard of your *f.* in Christ
1 Thes. 3. 1 remember. .. work of *f.*
2 Thes. 1. 3 your *f.* growing exceed.
1 Tim. 1. 2 my own son in the *f.*
  2. 15; 3. 9; 4. 1; 5. 8; 6. 10
2 Tim. 1. 5 unfei. *f.* that is in thee
Tit. 1. 1 accor. to *f.* of God's elect
Phile. 5 hearing of thy love and *f.*
Heb. 4. 2 mixed with *f.* in them
  6. 1; 10. 22; 11. 1–39; 12. 2; 13. 7.
Jas. 1. 3 trying of your *f.* worketh
1 Pet. 1. 5 through *f.* unto salvation
2 Pet. 1. 1 obtained like precious *f.*

1 John 5. 4 overc. .. world, e. our *f.*
Jude 3. *f.* .. once del. unto saints
Rev. 2. 13 and has not denied my *f.*
R. V. Acts 6. 8 grace; Rom. 3. 3;
  Gal. 5. 22 faithfulness.

Faithful. *Steady, truthful faith-*
fulness.
Num. 12. 7 Moses, who is *f.* in all
Deut. 7. 9 he is God, the *f.* God
1 Sam. 2. 35 raise me up a *f.* priest
2 Sam. 20. 19 peaceable and *f.* in Is.
Neh. 7. 2 he was a *f.* man, and f. G.
Ps. 89. 37 a *f.* witness in heaven
Prov. 27. 6 *f.* are wounds of a friend
Isa. 1. 21 *f.* city become an harlot
Jer. 42. 5 true and *f.* witness bet. us
Dan. 6. 4 forasmuch as he was *f.*
Hos. 11. 12 Judah .. is *f.* with .. s.
Mat. 24. 15 who then is a *f.* .. ser.
Luke 12. 42 that *f.* and wise steward
Acts 16. 15 judged me to be *f.* to
1 Cor. 1. 9 God is *f.* by whom ye
Gal. 3. 9 blessed with *f.* Abraham
Eph. 1. 1 to the *f.* in Jesus Christ
Col. 1. 2 and *f.* brethren in Christ
1 Thes. 5. 24 *f.* is he that calleth
2 Thes. 3. 3 the Lord is *f.*, who
1 Tim. 1. 12 he counted me *f.*, put.
2 Tim. 2. 2 commit thou to *f.* men
Tit. 1. 6 having *f.* children, not
Heb. 2. 17 and *f.* high priest in
1 Pet. 4. 19 as unto a *f.* Creator
1 John 1. 9 he is *f.* and just to
Rev. 1. 5 who is the *f.* witness
R. V. 1 Tim. 6. 2 believing; Tit. 1.
  6 that believe who are

Faithfully. *Faithfulness, stability.*
2 K. 12. 15 for they dealt *f.*
2 Chr. 19. 9 *f.* and with per. heart
3 John 5 thou doest *f.* whatsoever

Faithfulness. *Fidelity, stability.*
1 Sam. 26. 23 render to ev m. .. *f.*
Ps. 36. 5 thy *f.* reacheth unto .. cl.
Isa. 11. 5 *f.* the girdle of .. reins
Lam. 3. 23 new ev. m. great is thy *f.*
Hos. 2. 20 betroth .. into me in *f.*

Faithless. *Unsteadfast, unfaith-*
ful.
Mat. 17. 17 O *f.* and perverse gene.
Mark 9. 19; Luke 9. 41
John 20. 27 be not *f.* but believing

Fall (*n.*). *Stumbling, downfall.*
Prov. 16. 18 haughty spirit before a *f.*
Ezek. 26. 15 isles shake at sound .. *f.*
Jer. 49. 21 e. moved at noise of .. *f.*
Mat. 7. 27 great was the *f.* of it
Luke 2. 34 child is set for the *f.*
Rom. 11. 11 though .. *f.* salva. is co.

Fall (*v.*). *Fall.*
Gen. 4. 5 and his countenance *f.*
Ex. 15. 16 dread shall *f.* upon them
Lev. 9. 24 and *f.* on their faces
Num. 14. 3 to *f.* by the sword
Deut. 22. 8 if any man *f.* .. thence
Josh. 5. 14 Joshua *f.* on his face
Judg. 4. 16 Sisera *f.* upon the edge
Ruth 2. 10 she *f.* on her face, and
1 Sam. 14. 52 not an hair of him *f.* to e.
2 Sam. 1. 2 he *f.* to the earth, and
1 K. 1. 52 not an hair of him *f.* to e.
2 K. 2. 13 took .. the mantle .. *f.*
1 Chr. 5. 10 who *f.* by their hand
2 Chr. 15. 9 *f.* to him out of Is.
Esth. 6. 13 shalt surely *f.* before him
Job 1. 16 fire of G. *f.* from heaven
Ps. 5. 10 *f.* by their own counsels
Prov. 11. 5 *f.* by his own wickedness
Eccl. 10. 8 that diggeth pit, shall *f*
Isa. 3. 25 shall *f.* by the sword
Jer. 6. 15 *f.* among them that *f.*
Lam. 1. 7 peo. *f.* into hand of end.
Ezek. 1. 28 *f.* upon my face and
Dan. 10. 7 great quaking *f.* upon th.
Hos. 7. 16 princes .. *f.* by the sword
Joel 2. 8 they *f.* upon the sword
Am. 3. 5 Can a bird *f.* in snare
Jonah 1. 7 the lot *f.* upon Jonah
Mic. 7. 8 when I *f.*, I shall arise
Nah. 3. 12 *f.* into the mouth of the
Mat. 7. 25 house, and it *f.* not
Mark 4. 4 some *f.* by the way side
Luke 6. 39 both *f.* into the ditch
John 12. 24 except a corn of wheat *f.*
Acts 1. 26 the lot *f.* upon Matthias
Rom. 11. 11 stumb. that they .. *f.*
1 Cor. 10. 8 *f.* in one day .. thousand

Heb. 3. 17 carcases *f.* in . . wilder.
Jas. 5. 12 lest ye *f.* into condemna.
Rev. 1. 17 *f.* at his feet as dead
Stumble, fall.
Lev. 26. 37 *f.* upon one another
2 Chr. 25. 8 God shall make thee *f.*
Ps. 9. 3 they shall *f.* and perish
Prov. 10. 8 a prating fool shall *f.*
16. 18 and haughty spir. before a *f.*
Isa. 28. 30 *f.* backwards and be brok.
Jer. 6. 21 sons . . shall *f.* upon them
Lam. 1. 14 made my strength to *f.*
Ezek. 36. 15 cause thy nations to *f.*
Dan. 11. 14 robbers, they shall *f.*
Hos. 5. 5 therefore shall Israel *f.*
R. V. Lev. 26. 37; Ps. 64. 8; Isa.
31. 3; Jer. 6. 21; 46. 16; Ezek.
36. 15; Hos. 4. 5; 5. 5; 2 Pet. 1.
10 stumble: Acts 27. 17 cast; 27. 34
perish

Fallen. *Fall, stumble.*
Gen. 4. 6 why is thy countenance *f.*
Num. 32. 19 our inheritance is *f.*
Josh. 2. 9 terror is *f.* upon us
Judg. 3. 25 their l. was *f.* . . dead
1 Sam. 5. 3, 4 Dagon was *f.* upon
2 Sam. 1. 4 many people are *f.*
1 Chr. 10. 8 found S. and his sons *f.*
2 Chr. 20. 24 bodies *f.* to the earth
Esth. 7. 8 Ham. was *f.* upon . . bed
Job 1. 16 fire of God is *f.* from h.
Ps. 7. 15 is *f.* into the ditch which
Isa. 3. 8 and Judah is *f.* because
Jer. 38. 19 afraid of Jews that are *f.*
Lam. 2. 21 my young men are *f.*
Ezek. 13. 12 when the wall is *f.*
Hos. 7. 7: Am. 5. 2; Zech. 11. 2
Rev. 2. 5 rem. . . whence thou art *f.*

Falling. *Falling, stumbling.*
Num. 24. 4, 16 *f.* into a trance
Job 4. 4 upholden him that was *f.*
Ps. 56. 13 deliver my feet from *f.*
Prov. 25. 26 righteous man *f.* down
Isa. 34. 4 as *f.* fig from the tree
2 Thes. 2. 3 except there come a *f.*
Jude 24 able to keep you from *f.*
R. V. Isa. 34. 4 fading; Acts 27. 41
lighting upon; Jude 24 stumbling;

Fallow. *Yellowish-brown.*
Deut. 14. 5 roebuck and *f.* deer
1 K. 4. 23 harts .. roe. and *f.* deer
Unseeded, uncultivated.
Jer. 4. 3 break up your *f.* ground
Hos. 10. 12 break up your *f.* ground
R. V. Deut. 14. 5; 1 K. 4. 23 roe-
buck

False. *Deceitful, lying.*
Ex. 23. 1 shalt not raise *f.* report
Deut. 5. 20 nei. .. thou bear *f.* wit.
2 K. 9. 12 they said, It is *f.*; tell us
Job 36. 4 my words shall not be *f.*
Ps. 27. 12 *f.* witnesses are risen up
Prov. 11. 1 *f.* balance is abomination
Jer. 14. 14 they prophesy . . a vision
Lam. 2. 14 seen for thee *f.* burdens
Ezek. 21. 23 be . . as a *f.* divination
Zech. 8. 17 and love no *f.* oath
Mal. 3. 5. come near to .. *f.* swearers
Mat. 7. 15 *f.* proph. in sheep's clo.
Mark 13. 22; Luke 6. 26
Acts 6. 13 and set up *f.* witnesses
1 Cor. 15. 15 are found *f.* witnesses
2 Cor. 11. 13 such are *f.* apostles
Gal. 2. 4 because of *f.* brethren
Tit. 2. 3 they be not *f.* accusers
2 Pet. 2. 1 should be *f.* teachers
1 John 4. 1 *f.* prophets gone out
R. V. Ps. 35. 11 unrighteous; 120. 3
deceitful; Prov. 17. 4 wicked; Jer.
14. 14; 23. 32 lying; Lam. 2. 14
vanity; Mat. 26. 60——; Luke 19.
8 wrongfully; Rom. 13. 9 covet;
Tit. 2. 3 slanderers

Falsehood. *Lie, deceit, error.*
2 Sam. 18. 13 should have wrought *f.*
Job 21. 34 in .. ans. there remain *f.*
Ps. 7. 14 he .. and brought forth *f.*
Isa. 28. 15 under *f.* have we hid
Jer. 10. 14 his molten image is *f.*
Hos. 7. 1 for they commit *f.*, and
Mic. 2. 11 walketh in spirit and *f.*

Falsely. *Lyingly, deceitfully.*
Gen. 21. 23 not deal *f.* with me
Lev. 6. 5 which he hath sworn *f.*
Deut. 19. 18 hath testified *f.* against
Ps. 44. 17 neither have we dealt *f.*

Jer. 5. 2 L. liv., surely they swear *f.*
Hos. 10 4 swearing *f.* in mak. cov.
Zech. 5. 4 house of him that swear *f.*
Mat. 5. 11 say . . evil against you *f.*
1 Tim. 6. 20 science *f.* so called
R. V. Luke 3. 14 wrongfully; 1 Pet.
3. 16 ——

Falsifying. *Perverting.*
Am. 8. 5 *f.* the balances by deceit

Fame. *Hearing, wide report.*
Gen. 45. 16 the *f.* thereof was heard
Num. 14. 15 nations .. ha. heard . .*f.*
Josh. 6. 27 and his *f.* was noised
1 K. 4. 31 his *f.* was in all nations
1 Chr. 14. 17 *f.* of David went out
2 Chr. 9. 1 of Sheb. heard of the *f.*
Esth. 9. 4 Mor. was great, and his *f.*
Job 28. 22 we have heard the *f.*
Isa. 66. 19 th. have not heard my *f.*
Jer. 6. 24 we have heard the *f.*
Zeph. 3. 19 get them praise and *f.*
Mat. 4. 24 his *f.* went through. Syr.
Mark 1. 28 his *f.* spread abroad
Luke 4. 37 *f.* of him went out
R. V. Job 28. 22 rumor; Zeph. 3.
19 name; Mat. 4. 24; 14. 1; Luke
5. 15 report; Luke 4. 37 went
forth rumor.

Familiar. *Known, acquainted.*
Job 19. 14 *f.* friends have forgot. me
Ps. 41. 9 Yea, mine own *f.* friend
Jer. 20. 10 all my *f.* watched for my
Necromantic.
Lev. 19. 31 them that have *f.* spirits
Deut. 18. 11 consulter with *f.* spirits
1 Sam. 28. 3 put away . . had *f.* spir.
2 K. 21. 6 dealt with *f.* spirits
1 Chr. 10. 13 asking counsel of *f.* sp.
2 Chr. 33. 6 dealt with *f.* spirits
Isa. 8. 19 seek . . that have *f.* spirits
R. V. Jer. 20. 10 familiar friends

Family. *House, household.*
Gen. 10. 5 everyone . . after their *f.*
Ex. 6. 14 these be the *f.* of Reuben
Lev. 20. 5 set my face . . against h. *f.*
Num. 1. 2 take sum of their *f.*
2. 34; 3. 15-39; 4. 2-46; 26. 5-58.
Deut. 29. 18 lest there should . . *f.*
Josh. 7. 14 come according to the *f.*
Judg. 1. 25 let go man and all his *f.*
Ruth 2. 1 man . . of *f.* of Elimelech
1 Sam. 9. 21 my *f.* least of all *f.*
2 Sam. 14. 7 the whole *f.* is risen
1 Chr. 2. 53 *f.* of Kirjath-jearim
Neh. 4. 13 set people after their *f.*
Esth. 9. 28 every *f.*, every province
Job 31. 34 or did contempt of *f.* ter.
Ps. 107. 41 maketh *f.* like a flock
Jer. 1. 15 will call all the *f.* of north
Ezek. 20. 32 as the heathen, as the *f.*
Am. 3. 1 against the whole *f.* which I
Mic. 2. 3 behold, against this *f.*
Nah. 3. 4 *f.* through her witchcrafts
Zech. 12. 12 the *f.* of David apart
Eph. 3. 15 the whole *f.* in heaven
R. V. 2 Chr. 35. 5 father's houses

Famine. *Hunger, extreme dearth.*
Gen. 12. 10 there was a *f.* in the land
Ruth 1. 1 there was a *f.* in the land
2 Sam. 21. 1 *f.* in the days of David
1 K. 8. 37 if there be in the land a *f.*
2 K. 6. 25 there was a great *f.* in Samaria
1 Chr. 21. 12 either three years' *f.* or
2 Chr. 20. 9 evil cometh upon us or *f.*
Job 5. 20 in *f.* he shall redeem
Ps. 33. 19 and keep them alive in *f.*
Isa. 14. 30 I will kill thy root with *f.*
Jer. 5. 12 neither see sword nor *f.*
Lam. 5. 10 skin black, because of *f.*
Ezek. 5. 12 with *f.* shall they be con.
Am. 8. 11 I will send *f.* in the land
Mat. 24. 7 shall be *f.* and pestilence
Mark 13. 8 shall be *f.* and troubles
Luke 4. 25 when gr. *f.* was throughout
Rom. 8. 35 *f.*, or nakedness, or peril
Rev. 18. 8 death, mourning, and *f.*
R. V. Job 5. 22 dearth

Famish. *Make lean, hunger.*
Gen. 41. 55 land of Egypt was *f.*
Prov. 10. 3 will not suffer soul to *f.*
Isa. 5. 13 honorable men are *f.*
Zeph. 2. 11 Lord will *f.* all the gods

Famous. *Known, called, honour-
able.*
Num. 16. 2 *f.* in the congregation
Ruth 4. 11 and be *f.* in Bethlehem

1 Chr. 5. 24 men of valour, *f.* men
Ps. 136. 18 and slew *f.* kings, for his
Ezek. 23. 10 she became *f.* among w
R. V. Num. 16. 2; 26. 9 called; Ps
74. 5 seemed as men that; Ezek
23. 10 a byword

Fan. *Scatter winnow.*
Isa. 30. 24 w. with the shovel and *f.*
Jer. 15. 7 will *f.* them with a *f.*
Mat. 3. 12 whose *f.* is in his hand
Luke 3. 17 *f.* in his hand, and he

Fanners. R. V. *strangers.*
Jer. 51. 2 will send unto Babylon *f.*

Far. *Afar, distant, very greatly.*
Gen. 18. 25 That be *f.* from thee
Num. 2. 2 *f.* off about the taber.
Deut. 13 7 nigh unto thee or *f.*
Josh. 9. 6 come from a *f.* country
Judg. 18 7 *f.* from the Zidonians
1 Sam. 2. 30 saith, Be it *f.* from me
2 Sam. 15. 17 tarried in place *f.* off
1 K. 8. 41 cometh out of a *f.* country
2 K. 20. 14 they are come from a *f.*
2 Chr. 26. 15 his name spread *f.* ab.
Neh. 4. 19 one *f.* from another
Esth. 9. 20 sent letters, nigh and *f.*
Job 5. 4 children are *f.* from safety
Ps. 22. 11 be not *f.* from me tor tro.
Prov. 22. 5 keep his soul shall be *f.*
Eccl. 7. 23 but it was *f.* from me
Isa. 54. 14 be *f.* from oppression
Jer. 12. 2 near in their mouth and *f.*
Lam. 1. 16 comforter is *f.* from me
Ezek. 22. 5 and those that be *f.*
Dan. 9. 7 unto all Israel, that are *f.*
Joel 3. 8 sell . . to a people *f.* off
Hab. 1. 8 horse. shall come from *f.*
Zech. 10. 9 remember me in *f.* count.
Mat. 15. 8 but their heart is *f.* fr. me
Mark 12. 34 not *f.* from k. of God
Luke 7. 6 not *f.* from the house
John 21. 8 were not *f.* from land
Acts 17. 27 though they be not *f.*
Rom. 13. 12 the night is *f.* spent
2 Cor. 4. 17 *f.* more exceed. weight
Eph. 1. 21 *f.* above all principalit.
Phil. 1. 23 with C. .. is *f.* between
Heb. 7. 15 yet *f.* more evident
R. V. Job 30. 10 aloof; Judg. 9. 17;
Ps. 27. 9; Isa. 19. 6; 26. 15; Ezek.
7. 20; Mark 13. 34 ——; Mat. 21.
33; 25. 14; Mark 12. 1 another;
2 Cor. 4. 17 more and more

Fare (*n*.). *Hire, reward.*
Jonah 1. 3 so he paid the *f.* thereof
Fare (*v*.). *Live, get on.*
1 Sam. 17. 18 look how thy breth. *f.*
Luke 16. 19. and *f.* sumpt. every day

Farewell. *Go ye well, rejoice.*
Luke 9. 61 bid them *f.*, which are
Acts 15. 29 do well. *F.* ye well
2 Cor. 13. 11 Finally, brethren *f.*,
R. V. Acts 18. 21 taking his leave,
23. 30 ——

Farm. *Cultivated field.*
Mat. 22. 5 one to his *f.*, another to
Farther. *Other side.*
Mark 10. 1 by the *f.* side of Jordan
Farthing. *Tenth of a denarius.*
Mat. 10. 29 two spar. sold for a *f.*
Luke 12. 6 five spar. sold for two *f.*
Fourth of an as.
Mat. 5. 26 till paid the uttermost *f.*
Mark 12. 42 two mites . . make a *f.*
Luke 12. 6 five spar. sold for two *f.*

Fashion (*n*.). *Thus.*
Mark 2. 12 we never saw it on this *f.*
Type, model.
Acts 7. 44 make according to the *f.*
1 Cor. 7. 31 *f.* of this world passeth
Phil. 2. 3 being found in *f.* as a man
Judgment, rule.
Ex. 26. 30 tab. according to the *f.*
1 K. 6. 38 according to the *f.* of it
Ezek. 42. 11 according to their *f.*
Likeness, appearance.
2 K. 16. 10 k. sent the *f.* of the altar
Ezek. 43. 11 house, and the *f.* thereof
Luke 9. 29 *f.* of his counte. altered
Jas. 1. 11 the *f.* of it perisheth
R. V. Acts 7. 44 figure

Fashion (*v*.). *Do, form, frame.*
Ex. 32. 4 *f.* he it with graving tool
Job 10. 8 hands have made me and *f.*
Ps. 33. 15 he *f.* their hearts alike
Isa. 22. 11 respect unto him that *f.*

Ezek. 16. 7 thy breasts are *f.* and
Phil. 3. 21 *f.* like unto his glo. body
1 Pet. 1. 14 not *f.* yourselves ac. to
R. V. Phil. 3. 21 conformed to

Fast (*n.*).   *Abstinence.*
1 K. 21. 9 Proclaim a *f.* and set Na.
2 Chr. 20. 3 pro. *f.* throughout . . J.
Ez. 8. 21 I proclaimed a *f.* there
Isa. 58. 3 in the day of your *f.* ye find
Jer. 36. 9 pro. a *f.* before the Lord
Joel 1. 14 sanctify ye a *f.*, a solemn
Jonah 3. 5 *f.*, and put on sackcloth
Zech. 8. 19 the *f.* of the seventh

Fast (*a. adv.*).   *Speedy, tight.*
Gen. 20. 18 Lord had *f.* closed up
Ez. 5. 8 and this work goeth *f.* on
Judg. 15. 13 we will bind thee *f.*
Jer. 48. 16 his affliction hasteth *f.*
Acts 16. 24 made . . feet *f.* in stocks

Fast (*v.*).   *Abstain.*
Judg. 20. 26 and *f.* th. d. until even
1 Sam. 7. 6 *f.* on that day, and said
2 Sam. 1. 12 mourn. and wept, and *f.*
1 K. 21. 27 *f.*, and lay in sackcloth
1 Chr. 10. 12 and *f.* seven days
Ez. 8. 23 so we *f.* and besought
Neh. 1. 4 and mourned cer. d. and *f.*
Esth. 4. 16 gather all Jews, and *f.*
Isa. 58. 3 wherefore have we *f.*
Jer. 14. 12 when they *f.*, I will not h.
Zech. 7. 5 When ye *f.* and mourned
Mat. 4. 2 wh. he had *f.* forty days and
Mark 2. 18 Phar., but thy dis. *f.*
Luke 5. 33 Why do the disciples *f.*
Acts 10. 34 four days ago I was *f.*

Fasten.   *Lay hold, fix, strengthen.*
Ex. 28. 14 *f.* the wrea. chains to the
Judg. 16. 14 and she *f.* it with a pin
1 Sam. 31. 10 *f.* his body to the wall
2 Sam. 20. 8 girdle with a sword *f.*
1 K. 6. 6 beams should not be *f.*
1 Chr. 10. 10 *f.* his head in . . temple
2 Chr. 9. 18 six steps . . which were *f.*
Esth. 1. 6 *f.* with cords of fine linen
Job 38. 6 the foundations thereof *f.*
Eccl. 12. 11 goads, and as nails *f.* by
Isa. 22. 23 *f.* him as a nail in sure
Jer. 10. 4 they *f.* it with nails and
Ezek. 40. 43 within were hooks . . *f.*
Luke 4. 20 eyes . . in synag. were *f.*
Acts 3. 4 Peter *f.* his eyes upon
R. V. Ex. 28. 14 shalt put; 28. 25
put on; 40. 18 laid; Judg. 4. 21
pierced through; 1 K. 6. 6 have
hold

Fasting.   *Not eating, abstaining.*
Neh. 9. 1 chil. of Is. assem. with *f.*
Esth. 4. 3 mourn. among Jews, . . *f.*
Ps. 35. 13 humbled my soul with *f.*
Jer. 36. 6 in Lord's h. upon *f.* day
Dan. 6. 18 k. passed the night *f.*
Joel 2. 12 turn ye to me with *f.*
Mat. 15. 32 not send them away *f.*
Mark. 9. 29 come by noth. but by *f.*
Luke 2. 37 served God with *f.* and
Acts 14. 23 had prayed with *f.* they.
1 Cor. 7. 5 may give yourselves to *f.*
2 Cor. 6. 5 in labours, watchings, *f.*
R. V. Mat. 17. 21; Mark 9. 29 ——

Fat.   *Fat, oil, grease, best part*
Gen. 4. 4 and of the *f.* thereof
Ex. 23. 18 nei. shall *f.* of my sac. r.
Lev. 3. 16 all the *f.* is the Lord's
Num. 18. 17 *f.* for an offering made
Deut. 32. 14 with *f.* of lambs and
Judg. 3. 22 *f.* closed upon the blade
1 Sam. 2. 15 before they burnt the *f.*
2 Sam. 1. 22 from . . *f.* of the mighty
1 K. 8. 64 *f.* of the peace offering
2 Chr. 7. 7 *f.* of the peace offerings
Neh. 8. 10 go your way, eat the *f.*
Ps. 17. 10 inclosed in their own *f.*
Prov. 11. 25 liberal soul shall be . . *f.*
Isa. 1. 11 full of *f.* . . of fed beasts
Jer. 5. 28 they are waxen *f.*, th. shine
Ezek. 34. 3 ye eat the *f.*, and clcthe
Am. 5. 22 regard peace off. of . . fat
Hab. 1.16 because their portion is *f.*
Zech. 11. 16 eat the flesh of the *f.*
R. V. Ps. 92. 14 full of sap; Isa.
58. 11 strong; Jer. 50. 11 wanton
as an

Father.   *Father, ancestor, source.*
Gen. 2. 24 a man shall leave his *f.*
Ex. 3. 6 I am the God of thy *f.*
Lev. 20. 9 he hath cursed his *f.* or

Num. 27. 3 our *f.* died in the wild.
Deut. 5. 16 honour thy *f.* and mother
Josh. 2. 12 show kindness to my *f.*
Judg. 6. 15 am least in my *f.* house
Ruth 2. 15 hast left thy *f.* and moth.
1 Sam. 2. 25 hearkened not unto . . *f.*
2 Sam. 2. 32 buried him in sep. of *f.*
1 K. 1. 6 *f.* had not displeased him
2 K. 2. 12 My *f.*, the char. of Israel
1 Chr. 2. 17 *f.* of Amasa was Jether
2 Chr. 1. 8 showed mercy to . . my *f.*
Neh. 1. 6 my *f*'s house have sinned
Esth. 2. 7 had neither *f.* nor moth.
Job 15. 10 much elder than thy *f.*
Ps. 27. 10 when *f.* and moth. forsake
Prov. 1. 8 hear the instr. of thy *f.*
Isa. 9. 6 God, the everlasting *F.*
Jer. 3. 19 thou shalt call me, My *f.*
Ezek. 16. 3 thy *f.* was an Amorite
Dan. 5. 2 silver vessels which his *f.*
Am. 2. 7 a man and his *f.* will go in
Mic. 7. 6 son dishonoureth his *f.*
Zech. 13. 3 *f.* and m. that begat him
Mal. 1. 6 A son honoureth his *f.* and
Mat. 2. 22 reign . . in room of his *f.*
3. 9 We have Abraham to our *f.*
4. 21 in ship with Zebedee their *f.*
5. 16 glorify your *F.* which is in h.
6. 4 thy *F.* which seeth in secret
7. 21 he that doeth the will of my *F.*
8. 21 suffer me to bury my *f.*
10. 29 not fall . . without your *F.*
11. 29 *F.*, Lord of heaven and earth
12. 50 whoso. shall do . . w. of . . *F.*
13. 43 sun in kingdom of their *F.*
15. 4 honour thy *f.* and thy mother
16. 17 my *F.* which is in heaven
18. 10 behold the face of my *F.*
19. 5 this cause shall a m. leave *f.*
20. 23 it is prepared of my *F.*
23. 9 call no m. your *f.* upon earth
25. 34 Come, ye blessed of my *F.*
26. 39 O my *F.*, if it be possible
28. 19 baptizing in name of the *F.*
Mark 7. 10 whoso curseth *f.* or m.
Luke 1. 32 give . . the throne of his *f.*
John 1. 14 only begotten of the *F.*
Acts 1. 4 wait for promise of . . *F.*
Rom. 1. 7 peace from God our *F.*
1 Cor. 8. 6 be to us God, the *F.*
2 Cor. 11. 31 *F.* of our Lord J. C.
Gal. 1. 3 peace from God the *F.*
Eph. 3. 14 bow . . knees unto the *F.*
Phil. 4. 20 unto . . our *F.* be glory
Col. 1. 12 giving thanks unto the *F.*
1 Thes. 1. 3 in sight of G. and our *F.*
2 Thes. 1. 1 our *F.* and the L. J. C.
1 Tim. 1. 2 peace, from God our *F.*
2 Tim. 1. 2 God the *F.* and Christ
Tit. 1. 4; Phile. 3; Heb. 1. 5; Jas.
1. 17; 1 Pet. 1. 2; 2 Pet. 1. 17; 1
John 1. 2; 2 John 3; Jude 1; Rev.
1. 6

Fatherless.   *Without father.*
Deut. 14. 29 stranger, *f.*, and widow
Ps. 94. 6 slay . . and murder the *f.*
Jer. 7. 6 if ye oppress not . . the *f.*
Zech. 7. 10 oppress not . . nor the *f.*

Fathom.   *Fathom (six feet).*
Acts 27. 28 and fcund it twenty *f.*

Fatling.   *Fat one, fed one.*
1 Sam. 15. 9 spared . . of the *f.* and
2 Sam. 6. 13 sacrificed oxen and *f.*
Ps. 66. 15 offer burnt sacrifices of *f.*
Isa. 11. 6 lion and the *f.* together
Ezek. 39. 18 all of them *f.* of Bashan
Mat. 22. 4 my ox and *f.* are killed

Fatness.   *Fatliness, best part, fulness.*
Gen. 27. 28 and the *f.* of the earth
Judg. 9. 9 should I leave my *f.*
Job. 15. 27 cov. his face with his *f.*
Ps. 36. 8 be . . satisfied with the *f.*
Isa. 34. 6 it is made fat with *f.*
Jer. 31. 14 satiate the soul with *f.*
Rom. 11. 17 partakest of . . root and *f.*
R. V. Deut. 32. 15 become sleek

Fats.   R. V. *vats.*
Joel 2. 24; 3. 13 *f.* shall overflow

Fatted.   *Fed, fattened.*
1 K. 4. 23 fallow deer and *f.* fowl
Jer. 46. 21 men are like *f.* bullocks
Luke 15. 23 bring hither the *f.* calf
R. V. Jer. 46. 21 calves of the stall

Fatter.   *Fat, firm.*
Dan. 1. 15 countenances appear . . *f.*

Fattest.   *Fatness, fat one.*
Ps. 78. 31 and slew the *f.* of them
Dan. 11. 24 enter upon the *f.* pl.

Fault.   *Blame, error, sin.*
Gen. 41. 9 I do remember my *f.*
Ex. 5. 16 *f.* is in thine own people
Deut. 25. 2 beaten . . accord. to his *f.*
1 Sam. 29. 3 I found no *f.* in him
2 Sam. 3. 8 chargest me . . with a *f.*
Ps. 59. 4 prepare . . without my *f.*
Dan. 6. 4 find none occa. nor *f.*
Mat. 18. 15 bro., go tell him his *f.*
Mark 7. 2 with . . hands they found *f.*
Luke 23. 4 I find no *f.* in this m.
John 19. 4 know I find no *f.* in him
Rom. 9. 19 Why doth he find *f.?*
1 Cor. 6. 7 now . . there is utterly a *f.*
Gal. 6. 1 if a man be overtak. in a *f.*
Heb. 8. 8 for, finding *f.* with them
Jas. 5. 16 confess . . *f.* one to anoth.
1 Pet. 2. 20 ye be buffeted for your *f.*
Rev. 14. 5 without *f.* before . . throne
R. V. Deut. 25. 2 wickedness; Mark
7. 2 ——; John 18. 38; 19. 4, 6
crime; 1 Cor. 6. 7 defect; Gal. 6. 1
any trespass; Jas. 5. 16 sins; Rev.
14. 5 blemish

Faultless.   *Without blame.*
Heb. 8. 7. if th. first cov. had been *f.*
Jude 24 *f.* before the presence of his
R. V. Jude 24 blemish in.

Faulty.   R. V. *guilty.*
2 Sam. 14. 13 as one which is *f.*
Hos. 10. 2 now . . they be found *f.*

Favour (*n.*).   *Grace, good will.*
Gen. 18. 3 now I have found *f.*
Ex. 3. 21 I will give this people *f.*
Num. 11. 11 have I not found *f.*
Deut. 24. 1 that she find no *f.* in
Josh. 11.20 that they . . have no *f.*
Ruth 2. 13 let me find *f.* in thy sight
1 Sam. 2. 26 S. was in *f.* with the L.
2 Sam. 15. 25 if I shall find *f.* in
1 K. 11. 19 Hadad found great *f.*
Neh. 2. 5 if thy ser. have found *f.*
Esth. 2.17 Es. obtained grace and *f.*
Job 10. 12 granted me life and *f.*
Ps. 5. 12 with *f.* wilt thou compass
Prov. 8. 35 obtain *f.* of the Lord
Eccl. 9. 11 nor *f.* to men of skill
S. of S. 8. 10 as one that found *f.*
Isa. 27. 11 he will shew them no *f.*
Jer. 16. 13 I will not shew you *f.*
Dan. 1. 9 brought Daniel into *f.*
Luke 1. 30 for thou hast found *f.*
Acts 2. 47 and having *f.* with all
R. V. Ps. 112. 5 that dealeth graciously; Prov. 14. 9 good will; S.
of S. 8. 10 peace

Favour (*v.*).   *Be gracious, delight in*
2 Sam. 20. 11 said, He that *f.* Joab
Ps. 41. 11 I know that thou *f.* me
102, 13 Zion, ti. to *f.* her is come
Lam. 4. 16 they *f.* not the elders
R. V. Ps. 102. 13, 14 have pity;
41. 11 delighted in

Favourable.   *Gracious, pleased with.*
Judg. 21. 22 be *f.* unto them for
Job 33. 26 and he will be *f.* unto him.
Ps. 77. 7 and will he be *f.* no more?
R. V. Judg. 21. 22 grant them graciously

Favoured.   *Fair to sight, gracegiven.*
Gen. 29. 17 Rachel was . . well *f.*
41. 18 kine, . . fleshed and well *f.*
Luke 1. 28 highly *f.* Lord is with

Fear (*n.*).   *Dread, terror, reverence.*
Gen. 20. 11 *f.* of God is not in th. pl.
Ex. 20. 20 his *f.* be before . . faces
Deut. 2. 25 begin to put *f.* upon nat.
Josh 22. 24 done it for *f.* of th. thing
Judg. 9. 21 Jotham ran, for *f.* of A.
1 Sam. 11. 7 *f.* of L. fell on . . peo.
2 Sam. 23. 3 ruling in the *f.* of God
1 Chr. 14. 17 L. brought *f.* of him
2 Chr. 14. 14 *f.* of the Lord came
Ez. 3. 3 was upon them because
Neh. 5. 9 walk in *f.* of our God
Esth. 8. 17 *f.* of the Jews fell upon
Job 4. 14 *f.* came upon me, and
Ps. 2. 11 serve the Lord with *f.*
Prov. 1. 7 *f.* of L . . begin. of knowl.
S. of S. 3. 8 because of *f.* in . . night
Isa. 7. 25 shall not come thither *f.*

Jer. 30. 5 have heard a voice of *f.*
Lam. 3. 47 *f.* and a snare is come
Ezek. 30. 13 will put a *f.* in the land
Mat. 14. 26 they cried out for *f.*
Luke 1. 12 when Zach. saw, *f.* fell
John 7. 13 no man spake .. for *f.* of
Acts 2. 43 *f.* came upon every soul
Rom. 3. 18 no *f.* of. G. before .. eyes
1 Cor. 2. 3 I was with you .. in *f.*
2 Cor. 7. 1 holiness in *f.* of God
Eph. 5. 21 submit. .. in *f.* of God
Phil. 2. 12 work out .. salva. with *f.*
Heb. 2. 15 who through *f.* of death
1 Pet. 1. 17 pass the time of .. in *f.*
1 John 4. 18 there is no *f.* in love
Jude 23 others save with *f.*, pulling
Rev. 11. 11 great *f.* fell upon them
R. V. very often in O. T., terror

Fear (*v.*). *To fear, dread, reverence.*
Gen. 15. 1 F. not, Abram, I am
Ex. 1. 17 the midwives *f.* God
Lev. 19. 3 *f.* every man his mother
Num. 14. 9 neither *f.* .. ye the peo.
Deut. 1. 21 *f.* not, nei. be discour.
Josh. 4. 14 *f.* him, as they *f.* Moses
Judg. 4. 18 turn into me, *f.* not
Ruth 3. 11 my daughter. *f.* not
1 Sam. 3. 15 Sam. *f.* to show El!
2 Sam. 3. 11 not ans., because he *f.*
1 K. 1. 50 Ad. *f.* because of Sol.
2 K. 6. 16 he answered, F. not; for
1 Chr. 28. 20 *f.* not, nor be dismayed
2 Chr. 6. 31 that they may *f.* thee
Neh. 1. 11 who desire to *f.* thy na.
Job 1. 9 Doth Job *f.* God for n't ?
Ps. 23. 4 I will *f.* no evil : for thou
33. 8 let all earth *f.* the Lord
112. 1 bless. man that *f.* the Lord
Prov. 3. 7 *f.* the Lord, dep. from ev.
Eccl. 3. 14 G. doeth .. that men .. *f.*
Isa. 7. 4 heed, be quiet, *f.* not
Jer. 3. 8 her .. sister Judah *f.* not
Lam. 3. 57 called .. thou saidst, *f.* not
Ezek. 3. 9 *f.* them not, neither
Dan. 10. 12 said he .. F. not, Daniel
Hos. 10. 3 no k. because we *f.* not
Joel 2. 21 F. not, O land, be glad
Am. 3. 8 lion roar., who will not *f.*
Jonah 1. 16 men *f.* the L. exceed.
Mic. 7. 17 God, and shall *f.* bec.
Zeph. 3. 7 surely thou wilt *f.* me
Hag. 1. 12 peo. *f.* before the Lord
Zech. 8. 13 *f.* not, let hands be str.
Mal. 2. 5 wherewith he *f.* me
Mat. 1. 20 Joseph .., *f.* not to take
Mark 4. 41 *f.* exceedingly, and said
Luke 1. 13 angel said to him, F. not
John 9. 22 parents, because they *f.*
Acts 5. 26 for they *f.* the people
Rom. 11. 20 be not highmind., but *f.*
2 Cor. 11. 3 I *f.* lest .. as the serp
Gal. 2. 12 and separated himself, *f.*
Col. 3. 22 singleness of heart, *f.* G.
1 Tim. 5. 20 that others also may *f.*
Heb. 4. 1 Let us therefore *f.*, lest, a
1 Pet. 1. 17 Honour all men. *f.* God
1 John 4. 18 that *f.* is not .. perfect
Rev. 1. 17 *f.* not, I am the first

Fearful. *Timid, terrible, reverential.*
Ex. 15. 11 Lord,,. *f.* in praises
Deut. 28. 58 this glorious and *f.* na.
Judg. 7. 3 whoso. is *f.* and afraid
Isa. 35. 4 of *f.* heart, be strong
Mat. 8. 26 why are ye *f.*, O ye
Mark 4. 40 said, Why are ye so *f.*
Luke 21. 11 *f.* sights .. great signs
Heb. 10. 27 *f.* looking for of judg.
Rev. 21. 8 the *f.*, and unbelieving
R. V. Luke 21. 11 terrors

Fearfully. *Awfully, reverentially.*
Ps. 139. 14 am *f.* and wonder. made

Fearfulness. *Fear, trembling, horror.*
Ps. 55. 5 *f.* and trembling are come
Isa. 21. 4 heart panted, *f.* affrighted
33. 14 *f.* hath surprised hypoc.
R. V. Isa. 21. 4 horror hath ; 33. 14 trembling

Feast (*n.*). *Festival, sumptuous repast.*
Gen. 19. 3 he made them a *f.* and
Ex. 10. 9 hold a *f.* unto the Lord
12. 14 ; 13. 6 ; 23. 15 ; 32. 5 ; 34. 18
Lev. 23. 6 is the *f.* of unleav. bread

Num. 29. 12 keep *f.* unto the Lord
Deut. 16. 10 keep the *f.* of weeks
Judg. 14. 10 Samson made there a *f.*
1 Sam. 25. 36 held *f.* in his house
2 Sam. 3. 20 David made Abner a *f.*
1 K. 3. 15 Solomon .. made a *f.*
1 Chr. 23. 31 burnt sac. on the set *f.*
2 Chr. 5. 3 Is. assembled .. in *f.*
Ez. 3. 4 they kept *f.* of tabernacles
Neh. 8. 14 dwell in booths in *f.* of
Esth. 1. 3 third year .. he made a *f.*
Ps. 81. 3 blow trump. on our sol. *f.*
Prov. 15. 15 merry heart hath con. *f.*
Isa. 5. 12 and wine, are in their *f.*
Jer. 51. 39 I will make their *f.*, and
Lam. 1. 4 none come to the sol. *f.*
Ezek. 36. 38 flock of Jeru. in sol. *f.*
Hos. 2. 11 cause to cease her .. *f.*
Am. 8. 10 turn *f.* into mourning
Nah. 1. 15 keep thy solemn *f.*
Zech. 8. 19 gladness and cheerful *f.*
Mal. 2. 3 dung of your solemn *f.*
Mat. 23. 6 love upper. rooms at *f.*
Mark 15. 6 at *f.* he released .. one
Luke 2. 41 every year at *f.* of pass.
John 4. 45 they went unto the *f.*
5. 1 ; 6. 4 ; 7. 2 ; 11. 56 ; 12. 12
Acts 18. 1 I must .. keep this *f.*
1 Cor. 5. 8 let us keep the *f.*, not wi.
R. V. Lam. 1. 4 ; 2. 6, 7 ; Hos. 2.
11 assembly ; Mat. 26. 17 ; Luke
23. 17 ; Acts 18. 21 ——

Feast (*v.*). *Feed sumptuously, banquet.*
Job 1. 4 his sons went and *f.*
2 Pet. 2. 13 while they *f.* with you
Jude 12 feeding *f.* with you, feeding
R. V. Jude 12 love feasts

Feasting. *Banqueting, drinking.*
Esth. 9. 17, 18 day of *f.* and glad.
Job 1. 5 days of their *f.* were gone
Eccl. 7. 2 mour. than to house of *f.*
Jer. 16 8 not also go into house of *f.*

Feather. *Wing, feather.*
Lev. 1. 16 pluck .. crop with his *f.*
Job 39. 13 wings and *f.* unto .. os.
Ps. 68. 13 her *f.* with yellow gold
Ezek. 17. 3 full of *f.*, .. divers colors
R. V. Lev. 1. 16 the filth thereof ;
Ps. 68. 13 ; 91. 4 pinions

Feathered. *Winged.*
Ps. 78. 27 He rained .. *f.* fowls like
Ezek. 39. 17 speak to every *f.* fowl
R. V. Ps. 78. 27 winged ; Ezek. 39.
17 the birds of every sort

Fed (*a.*). *Fatted.*
Isa. 1. 11 full of fat of *f.* beasts
Jer. 5. 8 they were as *f.* horses

Fed. *See Feed.*

Feeble. *Weak.*
Gen. 30. 42 when the cattle were *f.*
Deut. 25. 18 smote .. all .. *f.* behind
1 Sam. 2. 5 hath .. child. is waxed *f.*
2 Sam. 4. 1 his hands were *f.*, and
2 Chr. 28. 15 carried .. *f.* upon asses
Neh. 4. 2 what do these *f.* Jews
Job 4. 4 strengthened the *f.* knees
Ps. 38. 8 am *f.* and sore broken
Prov. 30. 26 the conies .. a *f.* folk
Isa. 16. 14 remnant .. very small .. *f.*
Jer. 49. 24 Damascus has waxed *f.*
Ezek. 7. 17 all hands shall be *f.*
Zech. 12. 8 he that is *f.* among them
1 Cor. 12. 22 members .. seem more *f.*
1 Thes. 5. 14 comfort the *f.* minded
Heb. 12. 12 lift up .. the *f.* knees
R. V. 1 Sam. 2. 5 languisheth ; Ps.
38. 8 faint ; Isa. 16. 14 of no ac-
count ; 1 Thes. 5. 14 fainthearted ;
Heb. 12. 12 palsied

Feebleness. *Weakness.*
Jer. 47. 3 back .. for *f.* of hands

Feebler. *Weaker.*
Gen. 30. 42 so the *f.* were Laban's

Feed. *Give food, tend, nourish.*
Gen. 29. 7 sheep, go and *f.* them
Ex. 16. 32 see.. bread ..I have *f.* you
Deut. 8. 3 I *f.* thee with manna
1 Sam. 17. 15 David went .. *f.*
2 Sam. 5. 2 shalt *f.* my people Is.
1 K. 22. 27 *f.* him with br. of afflic.
1 Chr. 17. 6 com. to *f.* my people
2 Chr. 18. 26 *f.* him with the bread of
Job 24. 2 take away flocks and *f.*
Ps. 28. 9 save thy people .. *f.* them
Prov. 10. 21 lips of right. *f.* many

S. of S. 1. 7 tell me .. where thou *f.*
Isa. 5 17 lambs *f.* after their man.
Jer. 3. 15 shall *f.* you with knowl.
Lam. 4. 5 that *f.* delicately are des.
Ezek. 16. 19 oil and honey .. I *f.* thee
Dan. 5. 21 *f.* him with grass like
Hos. 4. 16 the Lord will *f.* them
Jonah 3. 7 let them not *f.* nor drink
Mic. 5. 4 and *f.* in the strength of L.
Zeph. 2. 7 they shall *f.* thereupon
Zech. 11. 4 *f.* the flock of the slaugh.
Mat. 6. 26 heavenly Father *f.* them
Mark 5. 11 great herd of swine *f.*
Luke 12. 24 consid. .. ravens, G. *f.*
John 21. 15 he saith .. *f.* my lambs
Rom. 12. 20 if .. enemy hung.,*f.* him
1 Cor. 13. 3 bestow all .. goods to *f.*
1 Pet. 5. 2 F. the flock of God
Jude 12 *f.* themselves without fear
Rev. 7. 17 the Lamb .. shall *f.* them
R. V. Gen. 46. 32 keepers of ; John
21. 16 ; 1 Pet. 5. 2 tend ; 2 Sam.
19. 33 sustain ; Ps. 49. 14 ; Rev.
7. 17 be their shepherd ; Rev. 12.
6 may nourish

Feeding. *Giving food, tending.*
Gen. 37. 2 Joseph .. was *f.* the flock
Job 1. 14 and the asses *f.* beside th.
Nah. 2. 11 *f.* place of the young

Feel. *Know, perceive, suffer.*
Job 20. 20 shall not *f.* quietness
Ps. 58. 9 before .. pots can *f.* thorns
Prov. 23. 35 beaten me .. I *f.* it not
Eccl. 8. 5 keepeth the com. shall *f.*
Mark 5. 29 she *f.* .. she was healed
Acts 28. 5 beast, and *f.* no harm
Touch, grope, feel after.
Gen. 27. 21 near, that I may *f.* thee
Judg. 16. 26 suffer .. that I .. *f.* the
Acts 17. 27 if .. they might *f.* after
R. V. Job 20. 20 knew no ; Eccl. 8.
5 know

Feeling. *Suffering, sensation.*
Eph. 4. 19 who being past *f.* have
Heb. 4. 15 cannot be touched with *f.*

Feet. *Feet.*
Gen. 18. 4 wash your *f.* and rest
Ex. 3. 5 put off shoes from off thy *f.*
Lev.. 8. 24 toes of their right *f.*
Num. 20. 19 go through on my *f.*
Deut. 33. 3 they sat down at thy *f.*
Josh. 3. 13 *f.* of the priests that
Judg. 3. 24 cover. his *f.* in summer
Ruth 3. 4 go in and uncover his *f.*
1 Sam. 2. 9 keep the *f.* of his saints
2 Sam. 3. 34 hands not bound, nor *f.*
1 K. 5. 3 L. put them under .. *f.*
2 K. 4. 27 she caught him by the *f.*
1 Chr. 28. 2 David .. stood upon his *f.*
2 Chr. 3. 13 they stood on their *f.*
Neh. 9. 21 and their *f.* swelled not
Esth. 8. 3 Esther fell at his *f.*
Job 29. 15 *f.* was I to the lame
Ps. 8. 6 put all things under his *f.*
18. 9 ; 22. 16 ; 25. 15 ; 31. 8 ; 40. 2
Prov. 1. 16 their *f.* run to evil
S. of S. 5. 3 I have washed my *f.*
Isa. 3. 16 make. tinkling with their *f.*
Jer. 13. 16 before your *f.* stumble
Lam. 1. 3 spread net for my *f.*
Ezek. 1. 7 their *f.* were straight *f.*
Nah. 1. 3 clouds are dust of his *f.*
Hab. 3. 5 coals went forth at his *f.*
Zech. 14. 4 *f.* shall stand that day
Mal. 4. 3 ashes under .. your *f.*
Mat. 15. 30 cast them at Jesus' *f.*
Mark 6. 11 shake off dust under .. *f.*
Luke 1. 79 guide our *f.* into .. peace
John 11. 2 wiped his *f.* with her hair
Acts 4. 35 laid them .. at apost.. *f.*
Rom. 3. 15 *f.* swift to shed blood
1 Cor. 15. 25 put all en. under his *f.*
Eph. 6. 15 *f.* shod with the prepara.
1 Tim. 5. 10 if she washed saints' *f.*
Heb. 2. 8 in subjection under his *f.*
Rev. 1. 15 *f.* like unto fine brass
R. V. Isa. 3. 18 ; Mat. 18. 29——

Feign. *Devise, pretend.*
2 Sam. 14. 2 *f.* .. to be a mourner
1 K. 14. 5 *f.* to be another woman
Neh. 6. 8 *f.* them out of the heart
Luke 20. 20 *f.* themselves just men

Feigned. *Deceitful.*
Ps. 17 1 prayer.. not out of *f.* lips
2 Pet. 2. 3 *f.* words make merchand

Feignedly. *With falsehood.*

Jer. 3. 10 not with .. heart but *f.*
Fell. *See* **Fall.**
Feller. *Cutter off.*
Isa. 14. 8 no *f.* is come up against us
Felling. *Cause to fall.*
2 K. 6. 5 one was *f.* a beam, the axe
Felloes. *Rims, spokes.*
1 K. 7. 33 *f.* and spokes were molten
Fellow. *Man, friend, companion.*
Ex. 2. 13 Wherefore smit. thou thy *f.*
Judg. 7. 13 told a dream unto .. *f.*
1 Sam. 14. 20 ev. .. sw. against h. *f.*
2 Sam. 2. 16 caught .. his *f.* by .. h.
Ps. 45. 7 anointed thee above .. *f.*
Eccl. 4. 10 one will lift up his *f.*
Isa. 34. 14 satyr shall cry to his *f.*
Ezek. 37. 19 tribes of Israel his *f.*
Dan. 2. 13 sought Daniel and his *f.*
Jonah 1. 7 said every one to his *f.*
Zech. 3. 8 thy *f.* that sit before
Mat. 11. 16 like chil. calling to *f.*
Acts. 17 5 lewd *f.* of the baser sort
Heb. 1. 9 anointed thee above .. *f.*
R. V. Judg. 11. 37 ; Ezek. 37. 19 ;
Dan. 2. 13 companions ; 1 Sam. 29.
4 ; Mat. 12. 24 ; 26. 61 ; Luke 22. 59 ;
23. 2 ; John 9. 29 ; Acts 18. 13 man
Fellow-citizen.
Eph. 2. 19 but *f. c.* with the saints
Fellow-heirs.
Eph. 3. 6 Gentiles should be *f. h.*
Fellow-helper.
2 Cor. 8. 23 Titus, he is my *f. h.*
3 John 8 be *f. h.* to the truth
Fellow-labourer.
1 Thes. 3. 2 sent Timothy our *f. l.*
Phil. 4. 3 Clement, .. with other *f. l.*
Phile. 1 Paul.to Phile. our *f. l.*
Fellow-prisoner.
Rom. 16. 7 And. and Junia, my *f. p.*
Col. 4. 10 Aristarch. *f. p.* saluteth
Phile. 23 Epaphras my *f. p.* in Chr.
Fellow-servant.
Mat. 18. 28 *f. s.* who owed him
Col. 1. 7 Epaphras our dear *f. s.*
Rev. 6. 11 *f. s.* should be fulfilled
Fellowship. *Communion.*
Acts 2. 42 apostles' doctrine and *f.*
1 Cor. 1. 9 called unto the *f.* of .. Son
2 Cor. 8. 4 *f.* of the ministering
Gal. 2. 9 gave .. the right hands of *f.*
Eph. 3. 9 the *f.* of the mystery
Phil. 1. 5 your *f.* in the Gospel
1 John 1. 3 that ye may have *f.*
Partakership, partnership.
Lev. 6. 2 commit trespass in .. *f.*
Ps. 94. 20 shall .. iniq. have *f.* with
1 Cor. 10. 20 not have *f.* with devils
2 Cor. 6. 14 what *f.* hath right. with
Eph. 5. 11 have no *f.* with .. unfruit.
R. V. Lev. 6. 2 bargain ; 1 Cor.
10. 20 communion ; Eph. 3. 9 dispensation.
Fellow-soldier.
Phil. 2. 25 Epaphroditus my *f. s.*
Phile. 2 Paul, .. to Archippus our *f. s*
Fellow-worker.
Col. 4. 11 these only are my *f. w.*
Felt. *See* **Feel.**
Female. *Female.*
Gen. 1. 27 created man .. male and *f.*
Lev. 3. 1 male or *f.*, he shall offer
Num. 5. 3 m. and *f.* shall be put
Deut. 4. 16 likeness of male or *f.*
Mat. 19. 4 he .. made them m. and *f.*
Mark 10. 6 God made th. m. and *f.*
Gal. 3. 28 there is neither m. nor *f.*
Fen. *Mire, swamp.*
Job 40. 21 lieth in covert of .. *f.*
Fence (*n.*). *Hedge, wall.*
Ps. 62. 3 wall, and as a tottering *f.*
Fence (*v.*). *Hedge, wall up, surround.*
2 Sam. 23. 7 must be *f.* with iron
Job 10. 11 hast *f.* me with bones
Isa. 5. 2 *f.* it, and gath. out stones
R. V. Job 10. 11 knit together
Fenced. *Walled, fortified.*
Num. 32. 17 shall dwell in *f.* cities
Deut. 3. 5 these cities were *f.* with
Josh. 14. 12 cities were great and *f.*
1 Sam. 6. 18 *f.* cities, and .. villages
2 Sam. 20. 6 lest he get .. *f.* cities
2 K. 18. 13 come up against . . *f.* cit.
2 Chr. 12. 4 he took the *f.* cities
Isa. 2. 15 every tower and *f.* wall

Jer. 5. 17 impoverish thy *f.* cities
Ezek. 36. 35 ruined c. are become *f.*
Hos. 8. 14 Judah hath mul. *f.* c.
Zeph. 1. 16 alarm against *f.* cities
Ferret. R. V. *gecko.*
Lev. 11. 30 the *f.* and chameleon
Ferry-boat. *Ferry-boat.*
2 Sam. 19. 18 a *f. b.* to carry over
Fervent. *Zealous, extended, fervid.*
Acts 18. 25 being *f.* in spirit, he spk.
Rom. 12. 11 not slothful, .. *f.* in spir.
2 Cor. 7. 7 told us .. your *f.* mind
Jas. 5. 16 *f.* prayer availeth much
1 Pet. 4. 8 above all .. have *f.* char.
R. V. 2 Cor. 7. 7 zeal for ; Jas. 5. 16
much in its workings
Fervently. *Extended, outstretched.*
Col. 4. 12 labouring *f.* in prayers
1 Pet. 1. 22 love .. with pure heart *f.*
R. V. Col. 4. 12 striving
Fetch. *Bring, convey, turn about.*
Gen. 18. 5 *f.* a morsel of bread
Ex. 2. 5 she sent her maid to *f.* it
Num. 20. 10 *f.* you w. out of rock
Deut. 19. 5 *f.* stroke with .. axe
Judg. 11. 5 elders .. went to *f.* Jeph.
1 Sam. 4. 3 *f.* the ark of the cov.
2 Sam. 4. 6 as though they w. .. *f.*
1 K. 7. 13 Solomon .. *f.* Hiram
2 K. 6. 13 spy, that I may *f.* her
2 Chr. 1. 17 *f.* up, and brought forth
Neh. 8. 15 go forth .. and *f.* olive
Job 36. 3 *f.* my knowl. from afar
Isa. 56. 12 I will *f.* wine, and we
Jer. 36. 21 sent Jehu. to *f.* the roll
Acts 28. 13 thence we *f.* .. compass
R. V. Num. 20. 10 bring forth ;
Acts 16. 37 bring ; 2 Sam. 14. 20
change ; Num. 34. 5 ; Josh. 15. 3 ;
turn about ; 2 K. 3. 9 ; Acts 28. 13
made a circuit.
Fetter. *Chain, shackle.*
Judg. 16. 21 bound him with *f.* of
2 Sam. 3. 34 nor .. feet put into *f.*
2 K. 25. 7 bound .. with *f.* of brass
2 Chr. 33. 11 and bound him with *f.*
Job 36. 8 and if they be bound in *f.*
Ps. 105. 18 feet they hurt with *f.*
Mark 5. 4 been often bound with *f.*
Luke 8. 29 was kept bound .. in *f.*
Fever. *Burning warmth, fever.*
Deut. 28. 22 smite thee .. with a *f.*
Mat. 8. 15 and the *f.* left her, and
Mark 1. 30 wife's mo. lay sick of *f.*
Luke 4. 39 and he rebuked the *f.*
John 4. 52 the hour, the *f.* left him
Aets 28. 8 Publius lay sick of *f.*
Few. *Not many.*
Gen. 27. 44 tarry .. a *f.* days, until
Lev. 25. 52 remain but *f.* days unto
Num. 13. 18 whether .. *f.* or many
Deut. 33. 6 let not his men be *f.*
Josh. 7. 3 people, for they are but *f.*
1 Sam. 14. 6 to save by many or *f.*
2 K. 4. 3 borrow vessels .. not a *f.*
1 Chr. 16. 19 a *f.* .. and strangers in
2 Chr. 29. 34 the priests were too *f.*
Neh. 7. 4 people *f.* therein
Job 10. 20 are not my days *f.* ? cease
Ps. 109. 8 let his days be *f.* ; and let
Eccl. 12. 3 grinders cease .. are *f.*
Isa. 10. 7 cut off nat. not a few
Jer. 42. 2 are left .. a *f.* of many
Ezek. 5. 3 bake a *f.* in number
Dan. 11. 20 in *f.* days he .. be des.
Mat. 7. 14 *f.* there be that find it
20. 16 many .. called, but *f.* chosen
Mark 8. 7 had a *f.* small fishes : and
Luke 10. 2 but .. labourers are *f.*
Acts 17. 4 of chief women not a *f.*
Eph. 3. 3 as I wrote .. in *f.* words
Heb. 12. 10 for *f.* days chastened
1 Pet. 3. 20 *f.* .. were saved by wa.
Rev. 3. 4 *f.* names even in Sardis
Fewer. *Lesser number.*
Num. 33. 54 to *f.* give less inherit.
Fewest. *Least number.*
Deut. 7. 7 ye were *f.* of all people
Fewness. *To be few.*
Lev. 25. 16 accord. to *f.* of years
Fidelity. *Faith, steadfastness.*
Tit. 2. 10 but showing all good *f.*
Field. *Earth, land, soil, level spot, cultivated space, open country.*

Gen. 2. 5 every plant of the *f.* bef.
23. 9 cave in end of his field
36. 35 smote Midian in *f.* of Moab.
Ex. 8. 13 frogs died .. out of *f.*
9. 25 hail brake every tree of *f.*
Lev. 14. 7 let .. bird loose in .. *f.*
26. 4 trees of *f.* shall yield fruit
Num. 16. 14 inheritance of *f.* and
Deut. 5. 21 nor cov. .. neighbour's *f.*
Josh. 8. 24 inhab. of Ai in the *f.*
Judg. 1. 14 moved him to ask a *f.*
Ruth 2. 2 Let me now go to the *f.*
1 Sam. 4. 2 slew of army in *f.* about
2 Sam. 1. 21 nei. .. rain upon, nor *f.*
1 K. 2. 26 Get .. unto thine own *f.*
2 K. 4. 39 one went .. into the *f.*
1 Chr. 16. 32 let the *f.* rejoice
2 Chr. 26. 23 buried him in *f.* of bur.
Neh. 11. 25 villages with their *f.*
Job 5. 23 in league with stones of *f.*
Ps. 78. 43 wrought wond. in *f.* of Z.
Prov. 23. 10 enter not *f.* of .. father.
Eccl. 5. 9 the k. is served by .. *f.*
S. of S. 2. 7 charge you .. by h. of *f.*
Isa. 5. 8 woe .. that lay *f.* to *f.*
Jer. 6. 12 with *f.* and wives togeth.
Ezek. 7. 15 that is in *f.* shall die
Dan. 2. 38 b. of *f.* hath he given
Hos. 2. 12 b. of *f.* shall eat them
Joel 1. 10 *f.* is wasted, land mourn.
Obad. 19 possess the *f.* of Ephraim
Mic. 1. 6 make Sama. as heap of *f.*
Zech. 10. 1 Lord .. give grass in *f.*
Mal. 3. 11 vine cast fruit .. in field
Mat. 6. 28 Consider lilies of the *f.*
13. 24 sowed good seed in his *f.*
27. 7 bought with them .. potter's *f.*
Mark 13. 16 in the *f.* not turn back
Luke 12. 28 grass, which is .. in *f.*
John 4. 35 lift .. eyes, look on the *f.*
Acts 1. 18 man purchased a *f.* with
Jas. 5. 4 who reaped down your *f.*
R. V. Gen. 33. 19 ground ; Jer. 12.
4 the whole country ; Ezek. 17. 5
soil ; 29. 5 earth.
Fierce. *Strong.*
Gen. 49. 7 Curs. anger, for it was *f.*
Deut. 28. 50 nation of *f.* counten.
Isa. 19. 4 *f.* king shall rule .. them
Dan. 8. 23 king of *f.* countenance
Heated, violent.
Ex. 32. 12 turn from thy *f.* wrath
Num. 25. 4 *f.* anger of the Lord
1 Sam. 28. 18 nor execut. his *f.* wrath
2 Chr. 28. 11 ; Ps. 88. 16 ; Isa. 13. 9 ;
Jer. 4. 8 ; Lam. 2. 3 ; Jonah 3. 9 ;
Zeph. 2. 2.
Roaring, strong, ferocious.
Job 4. 10 voice of the *f.* lion, broken
Isa. 33. 19 shall not see a *f.* people
Hab. 1. 8 horses, more *f.* than wol.
Mat. 8. 28 exceeding *f.*, so that no
Luke 23. 5 they were the more *f.*
2 Tim. 3. 3 incontinent, *f.*, desperate
Jas. 3. 4 ships .. driven of *f.* winds
R. V. Job 10. 16 — ; Luke 23. 5 urgent ; Jas. 3. 4 rough
Fierceness. *Heatedness, wrathiness.*
Deut. 13. 17 Lord may turn from *f.*
Josh. 7. 26 so Lord turned from *f.*
2 K. 23. 26 Lord turned not from *f.*
2 Chr. 30. 8 *f.* of his wrath may turn
Job 39. 24 He swal. the ground w. *f.*
Ps. 78. 49 cast upon them .. *f.* of
Jer. 25. 38 desolate because of *f.*
Hos. 11. 9 will not ex. the *f.* of
Nah. 1. 6 abide in the *f.* of .. anger
Rev. 16. 19 wine of the *f.* of .. wrath
Fiercer. *Sharper.*
2 Sam. 19. 43 words of .. Judah w. *f.*
Fiery. *Burning.*
Num. 21. 6. Lord sent *f.* serpents.
Deut. 8. 15 *f.* serpents and scorpions
Ps. 21. 9 make them as a *f.* oven
Isa. 14. 29 fruit shall be a *f.* serpent
Dan. 3 6, 11, 15 in midst of *f.* fur.
Eph. 6. 16 to quench all the *f.* dart.
Heb. 10. 27 looking for of *f.* indig.
1 Pet. 4. 12 concerning the *f.* trial
R. V. Heb. 10. 27 fierceness of fire
Fifteen. *Five and ten.*
John 11. 18 Beth. was .. *f.* fur. off
Acts 7. 14 kindred .. threescore a. *f.*
Gal. 1. 18 abode with him *f* d.
Fifteenth. *Fifth and tenth.*

Ex. 16. 1 f. day of second month
Lev. 23. 6; Num. 28. 17; 1 K. 12. 13;
2 K. 14. 23; 1 Chr. 24. 14; 2 Chr.
15. 10; Esth. 9. 18; Ezek. 32. 17;
Luke 3. 1 f. year of reign of Tib.

Fifth. *Fifth.*
Gen. 1. 23 E. and m. were f. day
Lev. 19. 25 f. year shall ye eat of fr.
Num. 5. 7; Josh. 19. 24; Judg. 19. 8;
2 Sam. 3. 4; 1 K. 14. 25; 2 K. 25. 8;
1 Chr. 2. 14; Ez. 7. 8; Jer. 1. 3;
Ezek. 1. 2; Zech. 7. 3;
Rev. 6. 9 had opened the f. seal

Fifties. *By fifty.*
Mark 6. 40 sat .. in ranks by f.
Luke 9. 14 by f. in a company
R. V. Luke 9. 14 in companies about
fifty each

Fiftieth. *Fiftieth.*
Lev. 25. 10 shall hallow the f. year
2 K. 15. 23 in f. year of Azariah

Fifty. *Fifty.*
Gen. 6. 15 breadth of it f. cubits
Ex. 18. 21 rulers of f. and tens
Lev. 23. 16; Deut. 1. 15
Josh. 7. 21 gold f shekels weight
1 Sam. 6. 19; 2 Sam. 15. 1; 1 K.
1. 5; 2 K. 1. 9
Luke 7. 41 hun. pence, the other f.
John 8. 57 art not yet f. years old
Acts 13. 20 space of four h. and f.

Fig. *Fig, fig-tree.*
Gen. 3. 7 sewed f. leaves together
Num. 13. 23 of pomegranates and f.
Deut. 8. 8. land of wheat and f. t.
Judg. 9. 10 trees said to the f. t.
1 K. 4. 25 man under his vine a. f. t.
2 K. 18. 31 eat .. ev. one of his f. t.
Neh. 13. 15 wine, grapes, and f.
Ps. 105. 33 smote their vines and f. t.
Prov. 27. 18 who keep. f. t. shall e. f.
S. of S. 2. 13 f. tree put forth .. f.
Isa. 34. 4 as falling f. from f. t.
Jer. 5. 17 eat thy vines and f. t.
Hos. 2. 12 destroy her v. and f. t.
Joel 1. 7 He hath barked my f. t.
Am. 4. 9 your f. t. .. increased
Mic. 4. 4; Nah. 3. 12; Hab. 3. 17;
Hag. 2. 19; Zech. 3. 10
Mat. 7. 16 do men gath. .. f. of thist.
Mark 11. 13 time of f. is not yet
Luke 13. 6 certain man had f. t.
John 1. 50 I saw thee under f. t.
Jas. 3. 12 can f. t. bare olive ber.
Rev. 6. 13 as f. t. casteth her f.
R. V. Isa. 34. 4 fading leaf

Fight (*n.*). *War, battle, conflict.*
1 Sam. 17. 20 host going forth to f.
1 Tim. 6. 12 f. good f. of faith
2 Tim. 4. 7 have fought a good f.
Heb. 10. 32 endured .. f. of afflic.
R. V. Heb. 10. 32 conflict of suffer'g.

Fight (*v.*). *War, battle, strive, oppose.*
Ex. 1. 10 join .. en. and f. against us
Num. 21. 1 he f. against Israel
Deut. 1. 30 G. .. shall f. for you
Josh. 9. 2 gathered .. together to f.
Judg. 1. 1 who shall go .. to f.
1 Sam. 4. 9 quit .. like men, and f.
2 Sam. 2. 28 peo. stood still, nei. f.
1 K. 12.21 f. against house of Is.
2 K. 3. 21 Kings were come up to f.
1 Chr. 10. 1 Philistines f. .. Israel
2 Chr. 13. 12 f. not against the L. G.
Neh. 4. 8 to f. against Jerusalem
Ps. 109. 3 f. against me without c.
Isa. 19. 2 f. ev. one against .. bro.
Jer. 1. 19 they shall f. against thee
Dan. 10. 20 will I return to f. with
Zech. 10. 5 they shall f., because
John 18. 36 then would my ser. f.
Acts 5. 39 lest ye be found to f. ag.
1 Cor. 9. 26 so f. I, not as one
1 Tim. 6. 12 f. the good f. of faith
2 Tim. 4. 7 I have f. a good f. fight
Heb. 10. 32 endured a .. f. of afflic.
Jas. 4. 2 ye f. and war, yet ye have
Rev. 12. 7 M. and his angels f.

Fighting. *Striving, warring.*
2 Chr. 26. 11 Uz. had host of f. m.
2 Cor. 7. 5 without were f., within
Jas. 4. 1 whence come wars and f.

Figure. *Parable.*
Heb. 9. 9; 11. 19 a f. for the time
Form, type, image

Deut. 4. 16 the similitude of any f.
1 K. 6. 29 carved walls with c. f.
Isa. 44. 13 mak. it after f. of man
Acts 7. 43 took up f. .. ye .. made
Rom. 5. 14 f. of him that is to come
Heb. 9. 24 which .. the f. of the true
1 Pet. 3. 21 f. whereunto .. baptism
R. V. Heb. 9. 24 like in pattern to;
1 Pet. 3. 21 after a true likeness

File. *Notched edge.*
1 Sam. 13. 21 had f. for mattocks

Fill (*n.*). *Full.*
Lev. 25. 19 and ye shall eat your f.
Deut. 23. 24 mayest eat grapes thy f.
Prov. 7. 18 take thy f. of love

Fill (*v.*). *Make full, load, satisfy.*
Gen. 1. 22 f. the waters in the seas
Ex. 2. 16 f. the troughs to water
Num. 14. 21 earth shall be f. with
Deut. 6. 11 houses which thou f. not
Josh. 9. 13 bottles .. which we f.
1 Sam. 16. 1 f. thine horn with oil
1 K. 7. 14 f. with wis. and underst.
2 K. 3. 17 valley shall be f. with w.
2 Chr. 5. 13 house was f. with a cloud
Ez. 9. 11 abominations which have f.
Neh. 9. 25 they did eat, and were f.
Job 3. 15 princes .. who f. .. houses
Ps. 17. 14 whose belly thou f. with
Prov. 1. 13 f. our house with spoils
Eccl. 6. 3 soul be not f. with good
S. of S. 5. 2 my head is f. with dew
Isa. 33. 5 f. Zion with judgment
Jer. 13. 13 f. all the inhabitants
Lam. 3. 30 is f. full with reproach
Ezek. 3. 3 f. .. bowels with this roll
Dan. 2. 35 stone .. f. the whole earth
Hos. 13. 6 so .. they were f. and
Nah. 2. 12 lion.. f. .. holes with p.
Hab. 2. 16 f. with shame for glory
Zeph. 1. 9 f. their masters' houses
Hag. 2. 7 f. this house with glory
Zech. 9. 13 f. the bow with Ephr.
Mat. 27. 48 spunge f. it with vinegar
Mark 6. 42 did all eat and were f.
Luke 1. 53 f. hungry with good th.
John 2. 7 f. the waterpots .. and they
Acts 2. 4 were all f. with H. G.
Rom. 1. 29 f. with all unrighteous.
2 Cor. 7. 4 I am f. with comfort
Eph. 1. 23 fulness of him that f.
Phil. 1. 11 being f. with fruits of
Col. 1. 9 f. with the knowledge of
1 Thes. 2. 16 to f. up their sins
2 Tim. 1. 4 see .. that I may be f.
Rev. 18. 6 cup which she hath f.
R. V. Job 38. 39; Ezek. 32. 4 satisfy; Ps. 104. 28; Prov. 18. 20; 30.
16 satisfied; Mat. 9. 16; Mark 2.
21 should fill; Rev. 15. 1 finished;
18. 6 mingle unto; Rom. 15. 24 in
some measure I shall have been
satisfied

Fillet (*n.*). *Thread, cord.*
Ex. 27. 10 their f. shall be of silver
Jer. 52. 21 f. of twelve cubits did
R. V. Jer. 52. 21 line

Fillet (*v.*). *Bind, fasten.*
Ex. 27. 17 shall be f. with silver
38. 28 overlaid chap. and f. them

Filth. *Dirt, excrement.*
Isa. 4. 4 Lord .. washed away the f.
1 Cor. 4. 13 are made as f. of world
1 Pet. 3. 21 put. away .. f. of flesh

Filthiness. *Uncleanness, impurity.*
2 Chr. 29. 5 carry forth the f. out of
Ez. 6. 21 from f. of the heathen
Prov. 30. 12 yet not washed from f.
Isa. 28. 8 tables are full of vomit, f.
Lam. 1. 9 Her f. is in her skirts
Ezek. 16. 36 thy f. was poured out
2 Cor. 7. 1 cleanse ourselves from f.
Eph. 5. 4 neither f. nor foolish talk.
Jas. 1. 21 lay apart all f. and superfl.
Rev. 17. 4 golden cup .. full of .. f.
R. V. Ez. 9. 11 through the uncleanness; 2 Cor. 7. 1 defilement of;
Rev. 17. 4 even the unclean things

Filthy. *Dirty, shameful, polluted.*
Job 15. 16 more abominable and f. is
Ps. 14. 3 all together become f.
Isa. 64. 6 righteousness are as f. rags
Zeph. 3. 1 Woe to her that is f.
Zech. 3. 4 take away the f. garments
Col. 3. 8 put off .. f. communications

Tit. 1. 11 teaching .. for f. lucre's
2 Pet. 2. 7 vexed with f. communica.
Rev. 22. 11 is f., let him be f. still
R. V. Job 15. 16 corrupt; Isa. 64. 6
polluted; Zeph. 3. 11 rebellious;
Col. 3. 8 shameful; 1 Tim. 3. 3
money; 2 Pet. 2. 7 lascivious;
Jude 8 ——

Fin. *Fin.*
Lev. 11. 9 whatsoever hath f. and s.
Deut. 14. 9 all that have f. and scal.

Finally. *End, lastly.*
2 Cor. 13. 11 F., brethren, farewell
Eph. 6. 10; Phil. 3. 1; 2 Thes. 3. 1
1 Pet. 3. 8 F., be all of one mind

Find. *Fall in with, discover, learn.*
Gen. 4. 14 that f. me shall slay me
6. 8 Noah f. grace in eyes of Lord
Ex. 5. 11 get straw, where ye can f
Lev. 6. 3 or have f. which was lost
Num. 11. 11 have I not f. favor
Deut. 4. 29 thou shalt f. him, if
Josh. 2. 22 sought, but f. them not
Judg. 6. 17 if now I have f. grace
Ruth 1. 9 L. grant .. ye may f. rest
1 Sam. 1. 18 let thine h. m. f. grace
2 Sam. 7. 27 hath thy servant f. in
1 K. 11. 19 Hadad f. great favour
2 K. 4. 39 f. a wild vine and gath.
1 Chr. 4. 40 they f. fat pasture
2 Chr. 20. 16 f. them at .. brook
Ez. 8. 15 f. there none of sons of L.
Neh. 5. 8 and f. nothing to answer
Esth. 5. 8 f. favour in sight of king
Job 3. 22 glad when they f. .. grave
Ps. 10. 15 seek wicked. till thou f.
Prov. 1. 13 f. all precious substance
Eccl. 7. 14 man should f. nothing
S. of S. 3. 1 but f. him nought
Isa. 10. 10 hath f. kingdom of idols
Jer. 6. 16 f. rest for your souls
Lam. 1. 3 Judah .. she f. no rest
Ezek. 3. 1 S. of man, eat that thou f.
Dan. 1. 20 f. them ten times better
Hos. 9. 10 I f. Israel like grapes in
Am. 8. 12 word, and shall not f.
Jonah 1. 3 f. a ship going to Tarsh.
Mat. 1. 18 f. with child of Holy G.
Mark 7. 30 f. the devil gone out
Luke 1. 30 hast f. favour with God
John 1. 41 He f. his brother Simon
Acts 5. 22 f. them not in prison
Rom. 7. 10 I f. to be unto death
1 Cor. 15. 15 f. false witn. of God
2 Cor. 2. 13 f. not Titus my brother
Gal. 2. 17 we also are f. sinners
Phil. 2. 8 being f. in fashion as man
2 Tim. 1. 17 sought .. dili. and f.
Heb. 4. 16 f. grace to help in time
1 Pet. 2. 22 neither was guile f. in
2 Pet. 3. 14 be f. of him in peace
2 John 4 f. children walk. in truth
Rev. 2. 2 and hast f. them liars

Fine (*v.*). R. V. *refine.*
Job 28. 1 gold, where they f. it

Fine (*a.*). *Pure, delicate, no. coarse.*
Lev. 2. 1 offering shall be of f. flour
Num. 6. 15 cakes of f. flour ming.
1 K. 4. 22 was thirty meas. of f. flour
2 K. 7. 1; 1 Chr. 9. 29
2 Chr. 2. 14 wor. in blue and f. liner
Ez. 8. 27 two vessels of f. copper
Esth. 1. 6 with cords of f. linen
Ps. 147. 14 fill thee with f. wheat
Prov. 3. 14 gain thereof than f. gold
Isa. 19. 9 that work in f. flax, and
Ezek. 16. 13 thou didst eat f. flour
Dan. 2. 32 head was of f. gold, his
Zech. 9. 3 and f. gold as mire of the
Mark 15. 46 and he bought f. linen
Luke 16. 19 clothed in .. and f. lin.
Rev. 1. 15 feet like unto f. brass
R. V. Isa. 19. 9 combed; Lam. 4.
1; Dan. 10. 5 pure; Mark 15. 46
linen cloth; Rev. 1. 15; 2. 18
burnished.

Finer. *Refiner.*
Prov. 25. 4 come .. vessel for the f.

Finger. *Finger.*
Ex. 8. 19 this is the f. of God: and
Lev. 4. 6 priest shall dip his f. in bl.
Num. 19. 4 take .. blood with .. f.
Deut. 9. 10 written with f. of God
2 Sam. 21. 20 on every hand six f.

1 Chr. 20. 6 *f.* and toes .. four and
Ps. 8. 3 heavens, the work of thy *f.*
Prov. 6. 13 he teacheth with his *f.*
S. of S. 5. 5 *f.* with sweet smelling
Isa. 2. 8 their own *f.* have made
Jer. 52. 21 thickness .. was four *f.*
Dan. 5. 5 came forth *f.* of a hand
Mat. 23. 4 not move .. with their *f.*
Mark 7. 33 put his *f.* into his ears
Luke 11. 20 with *f.* of G. cast out d.
John 8. 6 with *f.* wrote on ground
20. 25 put *f.* in print of nail
20. 27 reach hither thy *f.* and
Fining-pot. *Refining vessel.*
Prov. 17. 3 the *f. p.* is for silver
Finish. *Complete, end fully.*
Gen. 6. 16 cubit shalt .. *f.* it above
Ex. 40. 38 so Moses *f.* the work
Ruth 3. 18 *f.* the thing this day
1 K. 6. 9 built the house and *f.* it
1 Chr. 27. 24 *f.* not, bec. wrath fell
2 Chr. 7. 11 Sol. *f.* the h. of the L.
Ez. 5. 16 building, and yet it is not *f.*
Neh. 6. 15 the wall was *f.* in the
Dan. 5. 26 numbered thy k. and *f.* it
Zech. 4. 9 his hands shall also *f.* it
Mat. 13. 53 when J. had *f.* .. para.
Luke 14. 29 and is not able to *f.* it
John 4. 34 will .. and to *f.* his work
Acts 21. 7 we had *f.* our course
Rom. 9. 28 he will *f.* the work, and
2 Tim. 4. 7 I have *f.* my course
Heb. 4. 3 works were *f.* from found.
Jas. 1. 15 when it is *f.*, bringeth
Rev. 10. 7 myst. of G. should be *f.*
R. V. Luke 14. 28; 2 Cor. 8. 6
complete; John 3. 34; 5. 36; 17.
4 accomplish; Acts 20. 24 may
accomplish; Jas. 1. 15 full-grown
Finisher. R. V. *perfecter.*
Heb. 12. 2 author and *f.* of our faith
Fir. *Fir, cypress, pine.*
2 Sam. 6. 5 instru. .. of *f.* wood
1 K. 5. 8 concerning timber of *f.*
2 K. 19. 23 cut .. the choice *f.* tree
2 Chr. 3. 5 gr. h. he cieled with *f.* t.
Ps. 104. 17 stork, *f.* tree are her h.
S. of S. 1. 17 and our rafters of *f.*
Isa. 14. 8 the *f.* tree rejoice at thee
Ezek. 27. 5 boards of *f.* of Senir
Hos. 14. 8 I am like a green *f.* tree
Nah. 2. 3 *f.* tree shall be .. shaken
Zech. 11. 2 howl, *f.* t., .. ced. has fal.
R. V. Nah. 2. 3 spears are
Fire. *Fire, light.*
Gen. 19. 24 *f.* from Lord out of h.
Ex. 3. 2 *f.* out of midst of bush
Lev. 1. 7 put *f.* upon the altar
Num. 3; 4 off. strange *f.* before **L.**
Deut. 1. 33 *f.* by night to show
Josh. 6. 24 burnt the city with *f.*
Judg. 6. 21 rose *f.* out of the rock
1 Sam. 3. 1 Ziklag, and b. it with *f.*
2 Sam. 14. 30 go and set it on *f.*
1 K. 19. 12 after .. earthquake a *f.*
2 K. 1. 10 came .. *f.* from heaven
1 Chr. 14. 12 gods .. were b. with *f.*
2 Chr. 7. 3 Is. saw how the *f.* came
Neh. 1. 3 gates .. are burnt with *f.*
Job 1. 16 *f.* of God is fallen from
Ps. 11. 6 he sh. rain *f.* and brimstone
Prov. 6. 27 can man take *f.* in bos.
S. of S. 8. 6 coals .. are coals of *f.*
Isa. 1. 7 yo. cities are burnt with *f.*
5. 24 as *f.* devoureth stubble
9. 18 wickedness burneth as *f.*
Jer. 4. 4 lest my fury come as *f.*
Lam. 1. 13 sent *f.* into my bosom
Ezek. 1. 4 cloud, and *f.* enfold. it
10. 2; 15. 4; 16. 41; 19. 12; 20. 31
Dan. 10. 6 his eyes as lamps of *f.*
Hos. 7. 6 it burneth as a flaming *f.*
Joel 1. 19 *f.* hath dev. the pastures
Am. 1. 4 send *f.* into house of Haz.
Obad 18 house of Jac. shall be a *f.*
Mic. 1. 4 as wax before the *f.*, and
Nah. 1. 6 fury poured out like *f.*
Hab. 2. 13 labour in the very *f.*
Zeph. 1. 18 dev. by *f.* of his jeal.
Zech. 2. 5 a wall of *f.* round about
Mal. 3. 2 like a refiner's *f.*, and like
Mat. 3. 10 every tree cast into the *f.*
5. 22 fool, in danger of hell *f.*
Mark 9. 43 *f.* .. shall nev. be quen.
Luke 3. 16 bap. with H. G. and .. *f.*
John 15. 6 men .. cast .. into *f.* and

Acts 2. 3 cloven tongues .. as of *f.*
Rom. 12. 20 heap .. of *f.* on his head
1 Cor. 3. 13 shall be revealed by *f.*
2 Thes. 1. 8 in *f.* taking vengeance
Heb. 1. 7 ministers a flame of *f.*
Jas. 3. 5 gr. mat. a little *f.* kindleth
1 Pet. 1. 7 faith, though tried with *f.*
2 Pet. 3. 7. reserved unto *f.* against
Jude 7 suff. vengeance of eternal *f.*
Rev. 1. 14 eyes as a flame of *f.*
3. 18 buy of me gold tried in the *f.*
19. 20 cast into a lake of *f.*
R. V. Mat. 5. 22; 18. 9 the hell of
fire; Mark 9. 44, 46, 47
Firebrand. *Brand, spark, lamp.*
Judg. 15. 4 took *f. b.*, and turned tail
Prov. 26. 18 mad man who cast *f. b.*
Isa. 7. 4 two tails of smoking *f. b.*
Am. 4. 11 as *f. b.* plucked out of
R. V. Am. 4. 11 brand
Firepan. *Censer, snuffdish.*
Ex. 27. 3 his flesh-hooks and *f. p.*
2 K. 25. 15 *f. p.* and the bowls and
Jer. 52. 19 *f. p.* and the candlestick
Firkin. *Measure.*
John 2. 6 two or three *f.* apiece
Firm. *Strong, steadfast, binding.*
Josh. 3. 17 stood *f.* on dry ground
Job 41. 23 they are *f.* in themselves
Ps. 73. 4 but their strength is *f.*
Dan. 6. 7 to make a *f.* decree, that
Heb. 3. 6 of hope *f.* unto the end
R. V. Dan. 6. 7 strong
Firmament. *Expanse.*
Gen. 1. 6 Let there be a *f.* in waters
1. 7, 8, 14, 15, 17, 20
Ps. 19. 1 *f.* showeth his handywork
Ezek. 1. 22 likeness of *f.* upon heads
Dan. 12. 3 as brightness of the *f.*
First. *One.*
Gen. 1. 5 e. and m. were the *f.* day
Ex. 40. 2 on *f.* day of .. mo. shalt
Lev. 23. 24 seventh mo., in the *f.*
Num. 1. 1 *f.* .. of the second month
Deut. 1. 3 eleven. month, on the *f.*
1 K. 16. 23 thirty *f.* year of Asa
2 Chr. 29. 17 they began on the *f.*
Ez. 1. 1 in *f.* year of Cyrus king of P.
Neh. 8. 2 *f.* day of seventh month
Job 42. 14 name of the *f.* Jemima
Ezek. 26. 1 eleventh year, in the *f.*
Dan. 9. 1 in the *f.* year of Darius
Hag. 1. 1 sixth month, *f.* day of mo.
Mat. 28. 1 dawn toward the *f.* day
Mark 16. 2 *f.* day of week, they
Luke 24. 1 upon *f.* day of week
John 20. 1 *f.* day of w. cometh M.
Acts 20. 7 *f.* day of week, when
Former, foremost.
Ex. 23. 19 *f.* of the firstfruits bring
Num. 15. 20 offer cake of the *f.*
Deut. 18. 4 *f.* of the fleece of sheep
Ezek. 44. 30 give to priest the *f.*
Dan. 7. 4 beast, the *f.* .. like a lion
Mat. 10. 2 *f.* .. who is called Peter
Mark 9. 35 if any .. desire to be *f.*
Luke 2. 2 this taxing was *f.* made
John 1. 41 *f.* findeth his own bro.
Acts 12. 10 were past the *f.* ward
Rom. 10. 19 *f.* Moses saith, I will
1 Cor. 15. 45 *f.* man A. was made
Eph. 6. 2 which is the *f.* command.
Phil. 1. 5 fellowship from *f.* day
1 Tim. 1. 16 in me *f.* J. C. might s.
2 Tim. 2. 6 that laboureth must be *f.*
Heb. 8. 7 if that *f.* coven. had been
1 John 4. 19 because he *f.* loved us
Rev. 1. 11 A. and O. *f.* and last
Chief, principle.
Josh. 21. 10 theirs was the *f.* lot
1 Chr. 12. 9 Ezer the *f.*, Ob. second
Job 15. 7 *f.* man that was born?
Am. 6. 7 go captive with the *f.* th.
Head, first.
Gen. 8. 13 *f.* mo. the w. were dr.
Ex. 4. 8 nei. hearken to voice of *f.*
Lev. 4. 21 as he burned *f.* bullock
Num. 2. 9 these shall *f.* set forth
Deut. 9. 18 at the *f.*, forty days
Josh. 8. 5 come to pass .. at the *f.*
Judg. 18. 29 name .. was Laish, at *f.*
1 Sam. 14. 14 *f.* slaughter was about
2 Sam. 19. 43 advice should not be *f.*
1 Chr. 11. 6 so Joab .. went *f.* up
2 Chr. 3. 3 cubits after the *f.* meas.
Ez. 3. 12 that had seen the *f.* house

Neh. 7. 5 which came up at *f.* and,
Esth. 1. 14 sat *f.* in the kingdom
Prov. 18. 17 is *f.* in his own cause
Isa. 1. 26 will restore judges as at *f.*
Jer. 7. 12 I set my name at the *f.*
Ezek. 29. 17 in *f.* m. the word of
Dan. 8. 21 gr. horn .. is the *f.* king
Hos. 2. 7 will go .. to my *f.* husb.
Joel 2. 23 latter rain in the *f.* month
Mic. 4. 8 shall it come, even the *f.*
Hag. 2. 3 saw house in her *f.* glory
Zech. 6. 2 in *f.* chariot were red h.
Mat. 5. 24 *f.* be reconciled to bro.
Mark 3. 27 except he will *f.* bind.
Luke 6. 42 cast out *f.* the beam.
John 18. 13 led him away to Annas *f.*
Acts 3. 26 Unto you *f.* God, having
Rom. 1. 8 *F.*, I thank my God thro.
1 Cor. 12. 28 *f.* apostles, sec. proph.
2 Cor. 8. 5 *f.* give ourselves to Lord
Eph. 4. 9 he .. descend *f.* into the
1 Thes. 4. 16 dead in C. shall rise *f.*
2 Thes. 2. 3 except .. a fal. away *f.*
1 Tim. 2. 1 I exhort .. that *f.* of all
2 Tim. 1. 5 *f.* in thy grand mo. Lois
Heb. 7. 2 *f.* being by interpretation
Jas. 3. 17 wisdom .. is *f.* pure, then
1 Pet. 4. 17 and if it *f.* begin at us
Firstbegotten. *Firstborn.*
Heb. 1. 6 he bringeth in the *f. b.*
Rev. 1. 5 Jesus Christ .. *f. b.* of d.
R. V. Heb. 1. 6 firstborn
Firstborn. *Firstling, eldest.*
Gen. 10. 15 Can. begat Sid. his *f. b.*
Ex. 4. 22; Num. 3. 2; Deut. 21. 15;
Josh. 6. 26; Judg. 8. 20; 1 Sam
8. 2; 2 Sam. 2. 3; 1 Chr. 1. 13
Mat. 1. 25 brought forth her *f. b.*
Luke 2. 7; Rom. 8. 29; Col. 1. 15;
Heb. 11. 28
Heb. 12. 23 to general assem. of *f. b.*
Firstfruits. *Earliest fruits.*
Ex. 23. 16 *f. f.* of thy labors, which
Lev. 2. 14; Num. 28. 26; 2 K. 4.
42; Neh. 10. 35; Ezek. 44. 30
Rom. 8. 23 have *f. f.* of the spirit
1 Cor. 15. 20 *f. f.* of them that slept
Jas. 1. 18 should be a kind of *f. f.*
Rev. 14. 4 *f. f.* unto God and Lamb
Firstling. *Firstborn.*
Gen. 4. 4 Abel .. brought of the *f.*
Ex. 13. 12 set every *f.* that cometh
Lev. 27. 26 only the *f.* of .. beasts
Num. 3. 41 instead of all the *f.*
Deut. 15. 19 all the *f.* males that co.
Neh. 10. 36 *f.* of our herds and flo.
Fish (*v.*). *To fish.*
Jer. 16. 16 and they shall *f.* them
Fish (*n.*). *Fish.*
Gen. 1. 26, 28 have domin. over the *f.*
Ex. 7. 18 *f.* .. in river shall die
Num. 11. 5. we remem. *f.* we did e.
Deut. 4. 18 the likeness of any *f.*
1 K. 4. 33 he spake also .. of *f.*
2 Chr. 33. 14 entering at the *f.* gate
Neh. 3. 3 *f.* gate did the sons of H.
Job 12. 8 *f.* of the sea shall declare
Ps. 8. 8 *f.* of the sea, and whatso.
Eccl. 9. 12 as the *f.* that are taken
Isa. 50. 2 *f.* stinketh, because no w.
Ezek. 29. 4 will cause *f.* .. to stick
Jonah 2. 1 prayed .. out of *f* s belly
Mat. 7. 10 if he ask a *f.*, will he
Mark 6. 3 they say, Five, and two *f.*
Luke 5. 6 inclosed a gr. mul. of *f.*
John 21. 8 dragging the net with *f.*
1 Cor. 15. 39 another of *f.*, another
R. V. Isa. 19. 10 hire
Fisher. *Who fishes.*
Isa. 19. 8 the *f.* also shall mourn
Jer. 16. 16 will send for many *f.*
Ezek. 47. 10 *f.* shall stand upon it
Mat. 4. 19 will make you *f.* of m.
Mark 1. 16 sea, for they were *f.*
John 21. 7 he girt his *f's* coat unto
R. V. Job 41. 1; John 21. 7 ——
Fisherman. *Fisher.*
Luke 5. 2 but the *f.* were gone out
Fishing. *To fish.*
John 21. 3 Peter saith .. I go a *f.*
Fish-gate. *Fishmarket gate.*
2 Chr. 33. 14 ent. in at the *f. g.*
Neh. 3. *f. g.* did sons of H. build
Zeph. 1. 10 noise of cry from *f. g.*
Fish-hook. *Hook for catching fish.*

Am. 4. 2 take . . posterity with *f. h.*
Fish-pools. R. V. *pools.*
S. of S. 7. 4 eyes . . the *f. p.* in H.
Fish-spears. *Fishgigs.*
Job 41. 7 fill . . his head with *f's*
Fist. *Clenched hand.*
Ex. 21. 18 smite another . . with *f.*
Prov. 30. 4 gath. the wind in . . *f.*
Isa. 58. 4 smite with *f.* of wickedness
Fit (*a.*). *Ready, suitable.*
Lev. 16. 21 by . . hand of a *f.* man
1 Chr. 7. 11 *f.* to go out for war and
Prov. 24. 27 make it *f.* for thy self
Luke 9. 62 no man . . look. is *f.*
Acts 22. 22 not *f.* . . he should live
Col. 3. 18 submit . . as is *f.* in the L.
R. V. Lev. 16. 21 that is in readi.
1 Chr. 7. 11 that were able; 12. 8
trained; Prov. 24. 27 ready; Col.
3. 18 is fitting
Fit (*v.*). *Make ready, shape.*
1 K. 6. 35 gold *f.* upon carved work
Prov. 22. 18 they sh. be *f.* in thy lips
Isa. 44. 13 carp., he *f.* it with planes
Rom. 9. 22 ves. of wrath *f.* to destr.
R. V. Isa. 44. 13 shapeth; Prov. 22
18 established together upon
Fitches. *Spelt.*
Ezek. 4. 9 take thou also barley, *f.*
Black cummin.
Isa. 28. 25, 27 cast abroad the *f.*
R. V. Ezek. 4. 9 spelt
Fitly. *Properly.*
Prov. 25. 11 word *f.* spoken is like
S. of S. 5. 12 eyes washed and *f.* set
Five. *Five.*
Gen. 5. 6 Seth lived hun. and *f.* y'rs
Ex. 22. 1 restore *f.* ox for an ass
Lev. 26. 8 *f.* shall chase an hundred
Num. 1. 21; Josh. 8. 12; Judg. 3.
3; 1 Sam. 6. 4; 2 Sam. 4. 4; 1 K.
4. 32; 2 K. 6. 25; 1 Chr. 2. 4;
2 Chr. 3. 11; Ez. 1. 11; Neh. 7.
13; Esth. 9. 6; Job 1. 3; Isa. 7.
8; Jer. 52. 22; Ezek. 8. 16; Dan.
12. 12
Mat. 14. 17 have here but *f.* loaves
Mark 8. 19 brake the *f.* loaves
Luke 12. 6 are not *f.* spar. sold for
John 4. 18 thou hast had *f.* husb.
Acts 24. 1 number . . *f.* thous.
1 Cor. 14. 19 had rather speak *f.*
Rev. 9. 5 be tormented *f.* months
Fix. *Set, set up, establish.*
Ps. 57. 7 my heart is *f.*, O God
108. 1; 112. 7
Luke 16. 26 between us . . is . . gulf *f.*
Flag. *Reed, weed.*
Ex. 2. 3 ark of bul., she laid it in *f.*
Job 8. 11 can *f.* grow without w.?
Isa. 19. 6 reeds and *f.* shall wither
Flagon. *Cake, layer, bottle.*
2 Sam. 6. 19 he dealt . . a *f.* of wine
1 Chr. 16. 3 dealt every one a *f.* of
S. of S. 2. 5 stay me with *f.*, comfort
Isa. 22. 24 even all the vessels of *f.*
Hos. 3. 1 Is. . . love *f.* of wine
R. V. 1 Sam. 8. 13 confect.; S. of
Hos. 3. 1. cake; S. of S. 2. 5
raisins.
Flakes. *Folds, flecks.*
Job 41. 23 *f.* of his flesh are join.
Flame. *Fire, blaze, glow.*
Ex. 3. 2 angel of L. appeared in a *f.*
Num. 21. 28 *f.* from city of Sihon
Judg. 13. 20 angel . . ascended in *f.*
Job 15. 30 *f.* shall dry his branches
Ps. 29. 7 voi. of L. divideth *f.* of fire.
S. of S. 8. 6 hath a most vehement *f.*
Isa. 5. 24 as *f.* consumeth the chaff
Jer. 48. 45 *f.* from midst of Sihon
Dan. 7. 11 given to the burning *f.*
Joel 1. 19 *f.* hath burnt all the trees
Obad. 18 the house of Joseph a *f.*
Luke 16. 24 am tormented in this *f.*
Acts 7. 30 angel of L. in *f.* of fire
Heb. 1. 7 maketh . . ministers a *f.*
Rev. 1. 14 and his eyes were as a *f.*
R. V. Judg. 20. 38, 40 cloud; Dan.
7. 11 with fire; Isa. 13. 8 faces of
flame
Flaming. *Fiery, flashing.*
Gen. 3. 24 a *f.* sword which turned
Ps. 104. 4 his ministers a *f.* fire
Isa. 4. 5 shining of a *f.* fire by night
Lam. 2. 3 against Jacob like a *f.* fire

Ezek. 20. 47 *f.* flame . not be quen.
Hos. 7. 6 it burneth as a *f.* fire
Nah. 2. 3 chariots with *f.* torches
2 Thes. 1. 8 in *f.* fire taking veng.
R. V. Nah. 2. 3 flash in the steel
Flanks. *Loins, sides.*
Lev. 3. 4, 10, 15 fat wh. is by the *f.*
Job 15. 27 collops of fat on *f.*
R. V. 3. 4, 10, 15; 4. 9; 7. 4 loins
Flat. *Level, prostrate, compressed.*
Lev. 21. 18 he that hath *f.* nose
Num. 22. 31 Balaam fell *f.* on face
Josh. 6. 5 wall . . shall fall down *f.*
R. V. Num. 22. 31 ——
Flatter. *Make smooth, entice.*
Ps. 5. 9 they *f.* with their tongues
78. 36 they *f.* with their mouth
Prov. 2. 16 stranger, *f.* with . . words
25. 9 man that *f.* his neighbour
R. V. Prov. 20. 19 openeth wide
Flatteries. *Smoothnesses.*
Dan. 11. 21, 32, 34 he corrupt by *f.*
Flattering. *Smoothing, adulating.*
Job 32. 21 neither . . give *f.* titles
Ps. 12. 2 *f.* lips, with double heart
Prov. 26. 28 *f.* mouth worketh ruin
Ezek. 12. 24 nor *f.* divination within
1 Thes. 2. 5 neither . . use we *f.* words
Flattery. *Smoothness, adulation.*
Job 17. 5 speaketh *f.* to friends
Prov. 6. 24 from *f.* of tongues of
R. V. Job 17. 5 for a prey
Flax. *Flax, wick, linen.*
Ex. 9. 31 the *f.* . . was smitten
Josh. 2. 6 hid them with stalks of *f.*
Judg. 15. 14 as *f.* burnt with fire
Prov. 31. 13 she seeketh wool and *f.*
Isa. 19. 9 they that work in fine *f.*
Ezek. 40. 3 line of *f.* in his hand
Hos. 2. 5 my wool and my *f.*
Mat. 12. 20 smok. *f.* shall he not qu.
Flay. *Strip off.*
Lev. 1. 6 shall *f.* the burnt offering
2 Chr. 29. 34 they could not *f.* all
Mic. 3. 3 who also . . *f.* their skin
Flea. *Flea.*
1 Sam. 24. 14 whom pursue., after a *f.*
26. 20 king is come out to seek a *f.*
Fled *see* Flee.
Flee. *Run away from, escape.*
Gen. 16. 8 I *f.* from the face of my
Ex. 2. 15 Moses *f.* from . . Pharaoh
Lev. 26. 17 *f.* when none pursueth
Num. 10. 35 let them that hate. . *f.*
Deut. 4. 42 the slayer might *f.* thither
Josh. 7. 4 they *f.* before the men of Ai
Judg. 9. 21 Jotham ran away and *f.*
1 Sam. 4. 10 *f.* every man to . . tent
2 Sam. 4. 4 nurse took him . . and *f.*
1 K. 2. 28 Joab *f.* into the taberna.
2 K. 7. 7 and *f.* in the twilight
1 Chr. 10 1 men of Israel *f.* bef. Ph.
2 Chr. 10. 18 Reho. made speed to *f.*
Neh. 6. 11 should such a man as I *f.*
Job 14. 2 he *f.* also as a shadow
Ps. 68. 1 let them also that hate him *f*
Prov. 28. 1 wick. *f.* when no m. pur.
Isa. 10. 3 to whom . . *f.* for help?
Jer. 4. 25 all the birds . . were *f.*
Dan. 10. 7 th. *f.* to hide themselves
Hos. 12. 12 Jacob *f.* into . . Syria
Am. 5. 19 as if a m. did *f.* from lion
Nah. 3. 7 all that look . . shall *f.*
Zech. 2. 6 *f.* from land of the north
Mat. 2. 13 take . . child . . and *f.* to E.
Mark 5. 14 that fed the swine *f.*
Luke 3. 7 warned you to *f.* from
John 10. 5 will not follow, but *f.*
Acts 27. 30 shipmen were about to *f.*
1 Cor. 6. 18 *f.* fornication. Ev. sin
1 Tim. 6. 11 O man . . *f.* these things
2 Tim. 2. 22 *f.* also youthful lusts
Jas. 4. 7 resist the devil, he will *f.*
Rev. 9. 6 death shall *f.* from them
R. V. Job 30. 10 stand; 30. 3 gnaw
the dry ground; Ps. 64. 8 wag the
head; Jer. 48. 9 fly; Hos. 7. 13
wandered; Acts 16. 27 escaped
Fleece. *Fleece, mowings.*
Deut. 18. 4 first of the *f.* of . . sheep
Judg. 6. 37 put *f.* of wool in floor
6. 38, 39, 40
Job 31. 20 not warmed with the *f.*
Fleeing. *Flight.*
Lev. 26. 36 as *f.* from a sword

Deut. 4. 42 and that *f.* unto one
Job 30. 3 *f.* into the wilderness in
Flesh. *Flesh.*
Gen. 2. 21 closed up the *f.* instead
2. 23 this is now *f.* of my *f.*
Ex. 4. 7 turned again as his other *f.*
Lev. 11. 8 their *f.* shall ye not eat
Num. 8. 7 let them shave all their *f.*
Deut. 12. 15 eat *f.* in all thy gates
Judg. 6. 19 *f.* he put in a basket
1 Sam. 2. 13 while . . *f.* was seething
2 Sam. 5. 1 thy bone and thy *f.*
1 K. 17. 6 ravens brought him . . *f.*
2 K. 4. 34 *f.* of child waxed warm
1 Chr. 11. 1 we are thy bone and *f.*
2 Chr. 32. 8 with him is arm of *f.*
Neh. 5. 5 *f.* is as flesh of brethren
Job 2. 5 touch his bone and *f.*
Ps. 16. 9 my *f.* shall rest in hope
Prov. 14. 30 sound heart is life of *f.*
Eccl. 4. 5 fool . . eateth his own *f.*
Isa. 9. 20 they shall eat *f.* of his arm
40. 6 all *f.* is grass, and the godli.
Jer. 12. 12 no *f.* shall have peace
Lam. 3. 4 my *f.* hath he made old
Ezek. 4. 14 neither came abomina. *f.*
Dan. 1. 15 fatter in *f.* than children
Hos. 8. 13 sacrifice *f.* for the sac.
Joel 2. 28 pour out my s. on all *f.*
Mic. 3. 3 as *f.* within the caldron
Hag. 2. 12 if one bear holy *f.*
Zeph. 1. 17 their *f.* as the dung
Zech. 2. 13 be silent, O all *f.*
Mat. 16. 17 *f.* and bl. hath not sev.
Mark 10. 8 twain shall be one *f.*
Luke 3. 6 all *f.* shall see the sal.
John 1. 13 nor of will of the *f.*
1. 14 the Word was made *f.*
6. 54 who. e. my *f.* hath eter. life
Acts 2. 17 pour my Spirit on all *f.*
Rom. 1. 3 seed of D. accor. to the *f.*
1 Cor. 1. 26 wise men after the *f.*
2 Cor. 1. 17 purpose accord. to the *f.*
Gal. 1. 16 conferred not with *f.*
Eph. 2. 3 conversa. in lusts of . . *f.*
Phil. 1. 22 But if I live in the *f.*
Col. 1. 22 body of his *f.* through
1 Tim. 3. 16 G. was manif. in the *f.*
Phile. 16 bro. in *f.* and in the Lord
Heb. 2. 14 chil. are partakers of *f.*
Jas. 5. 3 eat your *f.* as it were fire
1 Pet. 1. 24 for all *f.* is grass
2 Pet. 2. 10 that walk after the *f.*
1 John 2. 16 the lusts of the *f.*
2 John 7 Jesus C. is come in the *f.*
Jude 7 cities . . going after the . . *f.*
Rev. 17. 16 eat her *f.*, and burn her
R. V. Acts 2. 30; Rom. 8. 1; Eph.
5. 30
Flesh-hook. *Flesh-fork.*
Ex. 27. 3. and his *f. h.* and firepans
Num. 4. 14; 1 Sam. 2. 13; 1 Chr.
28. 17; 2 Chr. 4. 16
Fleshly. *Fleshlike.*
2 Cor. 1. 12 not with *f.* wisdom, but
Col. 2. 18 vain. puffed up by *f.* mind
1 Pet. 2. 11 abstain from *f.* lusts
R. V. 2 Cor. 3. 3 tables that are
hearts of flesh
Flew. *See* Fly.
Flies. *Beetles, flies.*
Ps. 78. 45 sent divers sorts of *f.*
105. 31 divers sorts of *f.* and lice
Flieth. *See* Fly.
Flight. *Cause to flee.*
Lev. 26. 8 shall put ten thous. to *f.*
Deut. 32. 30 two put ten thous. to *f.*
1 Chr. 12. 15 put to *f.* all them
Isa. 52. 12 with haste, nor go by *f.*
Am. 2. 14 *f.* shall not per. from sw.
Mat. 24. 20 that *f.* be not in winter
Heb. 11. 34 who turned to *f.* armies
R. V. Lev. 26. 8 chase; Mark
13. 18 it
Flint. *Flint, rock.*
Deut. 8. 15 water out of rock of *f.*
Ps. 114. 8 turned the *f.* into a fount.
Isa. 50. 7 have I set my face like a *f.*
Ezek. 3. 9 harder th. *f.* made forehead
Flinty. *Flint.*
Deut. 32. 13 oil out of the *f.* rock
Floats. *Rafts.*
1 K. 5. 9 convey them by sea in *f.*
R. V. Make them into rafts to go
to sea
Flock. *Drove, herd.*

Gen. 4. 4 brought firstlings of his *f.*
Ex. 2. 16 to water their father's *f.*
Lev. 1. 2 the cattle of . . and of the *f.*
Num. 11. 22 shall the *f.* be slain
Deut. 8. 13 and . . thy *f.* multiply
1 Sam. 30. 20 David took all the *f.*
2 Sam. 12. 2 had exceeding many *f.*
1 Chr. 4. 39 to seek past. for their *f.*
2 Chr. 17. 11 Arabians brought . . *f.*
Ez. 10. 19 a ram of the *f.* for . . tres.
Neh. 10. 36 firstlings of our . . *f.*
Job. 21. 11 send . . little ones like a *f.*
Ps. 65. 13 pastures are clo. with *f.*
Prov. 27. 23 know the state of thy *f.*
S. of S. 1. 8 go . . by footstep of . . *f.*
Isa. 60. 7 *f.* shall be gathered togeth.
Jer. 5. 17 shall eat up thy *f.* and th. h.
Ezek. 24. 5 take the choice of the *f.*
Hos. 5. 6 They shall go with their *f.*
Am. 6. 4 and eat lambs out of the *f.*
Mic. 7. 14 feed . . *f.* of thine heritage
Hab. 3. 17 *f.* shall be cut off fr. fold
Zeph. 2. 6. coast . . be folds for *f.*
Zech. 9. 16 save . . as *f.* of his people
Mat. 25. 31 sheep of *f.* shall be scat.
Luke 2. 8 keeping watch over . . *f.*
Acts 20. 28 take heed . . to all the *f.*
1 Cor. 9. 7 eateth not of . . the *f.*
1 Pet. 5. 2 feed the *f.* of God
R. V. Ezek. 34. 3, 8, 10, 15, 19, 31 sheep

Flood. *Deluge.*
Gen. 6. 17 I bring a *f.* of water
7. 6, 7, 10, 17; 9. 11, 15, 28; 10. 1
Ps. 29. 10 Lord sitteth upon the *f.*
Mat. 24. 38 in days . . before the *f.*
Luke 17. 27 *f.* came and destroy. all
2 Pet. 2. 5 bringing . . *f.* upon . . w.
River.
Josh. 24. 2 on other side of the *f.*
Job 14. 11 the *f.* decay and drieth up
Ps. 24. 2 established it upon the *f.*
S. of S. 8. 7 neither can *f.* drown it
Isa. 59. 19 en. shall come like *f.*
Ezek. 31. 15 I restrained the *f.*
Jonah 2. 3 *f.* compassed me about
Flowing, overflowing inundation.
Ex. 15. 8 *f.* stood upright as heap
2 Sam. 22. 5 *f.* of ungodly m. made
Job 28. 4 *f.* breaketh out from inh.
Ps. 32. 6 in *f.* of great waters shall
Isa. 28. 2 as *f.* of mighty waters
Jer. 46. 7 that cometh up as a *f.*
Dan. 9. 26 end thereof . . with a *f.*
Am. 8. 8 drowned, as by the *f.*
Nah. 1. 8 with . . overrunning *f.* he
Mat. 7. 25 and the *f.* came, and w.
Luke 6. 48 when the *f.* arose, the
Rev. 12. 15 cast out . . water as a *f.*
R. V. Josh. 24. 2, 3, 14, 15 beyond the river; Job 14. 1; Ps. 66. 5; Ezek. 31. 15; Rev. 12. 15, 16 river; Job 22. 16; 28. 11; Ps. 78. 44; Isa. 44. 3; Jer. 47. 2; Rev. 12. 15 stream, streams; Job 24. 8 breaketh open a shaftway; Isa. 28. 2 tempest; 59. 19 rushing stream; Jer. 46. 7, 8 Nile; Jonah 2. 3 flood; Ps. 32. 6 when the great waters overflow; Am. 8. 8; 9. 5 river

Floor (v.). *Join, cause to meet.*
2 Chr. 34. 11 and to *f.* the houses
R. V. make beams for

Floor (n.). *Place for threshing.*
Gen. 50. 11 mourning in *f.* of Atad
Deut. 15. 14 furnish . . out of thy *f.*
Judg. 6. 37 put fleece . . in the *f.*
Ruth 3. 3 get thee down to the *f.*
Isa. 21. 10 and the corn of my *f.*
Hos. 9. 1 reward upon ev. corn *f.*
Joel 2. 24 *f.* shall be full of wheat
Mic. 4. 12 gather them into the *f.*
Bottom surface.
Num. 5. 17 dust that is in the *f.*
1 K. 6. 15 built the *f.* of the house
6. 16, 30; 7. 7
Bottom surface, barn.
Mat. 3. 12 throughly purge his *f.*
Luke 3. 17 he will . . purge his *f.*
R. V. 1 K. 7. 7 floor to floor;
Deut. 15. 14; Judg. 6. 37; Ruth 3. 14; Hos. 9. 2; 13. 3; Mic. 4. 12; Mat. 3. 12; Luke 3. 17 threshing-floor

Flotes. *Floats, rafts.*
2 Chr. 2. 16 bring it to thee in *f*

Flour. *Dough.*
2 Sam. 13. 8 took *f.* and kneaded it
Crushed grain, meal.
Ex. 29. 2 of wheaten *f.* . . make them
Lev. 2. 2 take of the *f.* thereof
Num. 15. 4 deal of *f.* mingled with
Judg. 6. 19 cakes of an eph. of *f.*
1 Sam. 1. 24 one ephah of *f.,* and
2 Sam. 17. 28 brought barley and *f.*
Rev. 18 13 fine *f.,* and wheat and
R. V. 2 Sam. 13. 8 dough; Judg. 6. 19; 1 Sam. 1. 24; 2 Sam. 17. 28 meal

Flourish. *Grow, thrive, bloom.*
Ps. 72. 7 days shall the righteous *f.*
72. 16; 90. 6; 92. 7; 103. 15 132. 18
Prov. 11. 28 righteous shall *f.* as
Eccl. 12. 5 the almond tree shall *f.*
S. of S. 6. 11 see whether . . vine *f.*
Isa. 17. 11 thou make thy seed to *f.*
Ezek. 17. 24 made . . dry tree to *f.*
Phil. 4. 10 your care of me hath *f.*
R. V. Isa. 17. 11; Eccl. 12. 5 blossom; S. of S. 6. 11; 7. 12 budded; Phil. 4. 10 ye have revived

Flourishing. *Fresh, flourishing.*
Ps. 92. 14 they shall be fat and *f.*
Dan. 4. 4 Nebuchadnezzar was *f.*
R. V. Ps. 92. 14 green

Flow. *Abound, issue.*
Ex. 3. 8, 17 land *f.* with m. and h.
Lev. 20. 24; Num. 13. 27; Deut. 6 3;
Josh. 5. 6; Jer. 11. 5; Ezek. 20. 6
Move, run, pour out or over.
Josh. 4. 18 w. . . *f.* over . . his banks
Job 20. 28 *f.* away in day of wrath
Ps. 147. 18 causeth the waters to *f.*
S. of S. 4. 16 that spices . . may *f.*
Isa. 2. 2 and all nations shall *f.*
Jer. 31. 12 come . . and *f.* together
Lam. 3. 54 waters *f.* over mine head
Joel 3. 18 hills shall *f.* with milk
Mic. 4. 1 and people shall *f.* unto
John 7. 38 *f.* rivers of living waters
R. V. Josh. 4. 18 went; Isa. 60. 5 be lightened

Flower. *Blossom, head, bloom.*
Ex. 25. 31 *f.* shall be of the same
25. 33; 34; 37. 19, 20
Num. 8. 4 *f.* thereof, was beaten
1 K. 7. 26 wrought . . wi. *f.* of lilies
2 Chr. 4. 5 brim . . with *f.* of lilies
Job 14. 2 he cometh forth like a *f.*
Ps. 103. 15 as *f.* of the fields, he
S. of S. 2. 13 his cheeks are as . . *f.*
Isa. 18. 5 grape is ripening in the *f.*
28. 1 glorious beauty is a fading *f.*
Nah. 1. 4 *f.* of Leb. languisheth
Jas. 1. 10 as *f.* . . he sh. pass away
1 Pet. 1. 24 glory of man is as *f.*
Best point, brightest period.
1 Sam. 2. 33 die in *f.* of their age
1 Cor. 7. 36 pass *f.* of her age, and

Flowers. R. V. *impurity.*
Lev. 15. 24, 33 sick of her *f.*

Flowing. *Sending forth, overflowing.*
Prov. 18. 4 wisdom as a *f.* brook
Isa. 66. 12 glory of Gen. like *f.*
Jer. 18. 14 shall the . . *f.* waters that
R. V. Isa. 66. 12 overflowing

Flute. *Pipe, reed, flute.*
Dan. 3. 5, 7, 10, 15 sound of the *f.*

Flutter. *Move, shake, vibrate.*
Deut. 32. 11 as eagle *f.* over . . young

Flux. *Dysentery.*
Acts 28. 8 lay sick . . of bloody *f.*

Fly (n.). *Fly.*
Eccl. 10. 1 *f.* cause the ointment to
Isa. 17. 18 L. shall hiss for the *f.*

Fly (v.). *Fly with wings, soar, hasten, retreat, flee, escape.*
Gen. 1. 20 fowl . . may *f.* above earth
Deut. 4. 17 fowl that *f.* in the air
1 Sam. 14. 32 peo. *f.* upon . . spoils
2 Sam. 22. 11 rode on cher. and did *f.*
Job 5. 7 unto troub. as sparks *f.* up.
20. 8 shall *f.* away as a dream
Ps. 55. 6 then would I *f.* away
Prov. 23. 5 *f.* away as an eagle
Isa. 6. 6 then *f.* one of . . seraph.
Ezek. 13. 20 souls to make them *f.*
Dan. 9. 21 being caused to *f.* swiftly
Hos. 9. 11 their glory shall *f.* away
Hab. 1. 8 shall *f.* as the eagle that

Rev. 4. 7 beast . . like a *f.* eagle
12. 14 might *f.* into wilderness
R. V. Job 39. 26 soar; Ps. 18. 10 flew swiftly; Isa. 11. 14 fly down

Flying. *Winging, winged, floating.*
Lev. 11. 21 ev. *f.* and creep. thing
Ps. 148. 10 creep. things, and *f.* fowls
Prov. 26. 2 as swallow by *f.,* so
Isa. 14. 29 fruit . . a fiery *f.* serpent
Zech. 5. 1 and behold, a *f.* roll
R. V. Lev. 11. 21, 23 winged

Foal. *Son, colt.*
Gen. 32. 15 twenty asses, and ten *f.*
Zech. 9. 9 riding on colt, the *f.* of
Mat. 21. 5 and a colt the *f.* of an ass

Foam (v.). *To froth, rage.*
Luke 9. 39 teareth him that he *f.*
Mark 9. 18, 20 he *f.,* and gnasheth
Jude 13 waves *f.* out their shame

Foam. (n.) *Froth, foam.*
Hos. 10. 7 her king is cut off as *f.*

Fodder. *Provender.*
Job 6. 5 loweth the ox over his *f.?*

Foe. *Enemy, oppressor.*
1 Chr. 21. 12 destroyed before thy *f.*
Esth. 9. 16 Jews . . slew of their *f.*
Ps. 27. 2 mine enemies and my *f.*
Mat. 10. 36 man's *f.* be of own hous.
Acts 2. 35 make thy *f.* thy footstool
R. V. Esth. 9. 16 them that hated them; Ps. 89. 23 adversaries; Acts 2. 35 thine enemies.

Fold. (n) *Fenced place, pen.*
Num. 32. 16 build sheep *f.* here
Ps. 50. 9 nor the goats out of thy *f.*
Isa. 13. 20 shep. make their *f.* there
Jer. 23. 3 bring them . . to their *f.*
Ezek. 34. 14 shall th.lie in a good *f.*
Mic. 2. 12 as flock in midst of *f.*
Hab. 3. 17 flock . . be cut off from . . *f.*
Zeph. 2. 6 sea coast shall be . . *f.*
John 10. 16 sheep . . not of this *f.*
The flock.
John 10. 16 there shall be one *f.*
R. V. Mic. 2. 12 pasture; John 10. 16 flock.

Fold (v.). *Clasp, roll up, wrap.*
1 K. 6. 34 leaves of the door . . *f.*
Prov. 6. 10 little *f.* of the hands
Eccl. 4. 5 fool *f.* his hands together
Nah. 1. 10 *f.* together as thorns
Heb. 1. 12 as vesture shalt thou *f.*
R. V. Heb. 1. 12 roll

Folk. *Nation, people.*
Gen. 33. 15 the *f.* that are with me
Prov. 30. 26 conies are a feeble *f.*
Jer. 51. 58 and the *f.* in the fire
Mark 6. 5 laid hands on few sick *f.*
John 5. 3 multitude of impotent *f.*
Acts 5. 16 about, bringing sick *f.*
R. V. Jer. 51. 58 nations for; John 5. 3 them that were sick.

Follow. *Go or come after, attend, pursue, pattern after, strive after,*
Gen. 24. 5, 8 not be willing to *f.*
Ex. 14. 4 he shall *f.* after them
Num. 14. 24 he hath *f.* me fully
Deut. 1. 36 hath wholly *f.* the Lord
Josh. 6. 8 ark of the covenant . . *f.*
Judg. 2. 12 forsook . . and *f.* other g.
Ruth 3. 10 as thou *f.* not young m.
1 Sam. 13. 7 people *f.* him trembling
2 Sam. 3. 31 David himself *f.* the
1 K. 18. 18 thou hast *f.* Baalim
2 K. 5. 21 Geh. *f.* after Naaman
1 Chr. 10. 2 Phil. *f.* hard after S.
2 Chr. 23. 14 who. *f.* . . let him be sl.
Neh. 4. 23 nor the men . . which *f.*
Ps. 23. 6 good. and mercy shall *f.*
Prov. 21. 21 he that *f.* after right.
Isa. 1. 23 and *f.* after rewards
Jer. 17. 16 not hastened to *f.* thee
Ezek. 16. 34 none *f.* to commit wh.
Hos. 2. 7 she sh. *f.* after her lovers
Am. 7. 15 Lord took me as I *f.*
Mat. 4. 20 they straightway *f.* him
16. 24 take . . cross, and *f.* me
Mark 1. 18 forsook their nets, and *f.*
Luke 5. 27 said unto him, *F.* me
9. 57 Lord, I will *f.* thee whitherso
John 1. 37 heard and they *f.* Jesus
Acts 12. 8 cast thy gar., and *f.* me
Rom. 9. 30 *f.* not after righteousn.
1 Cor. 14. 1 *f.* after charity, and
Phil. 3. 12 I *f.* after, if that I may

1 Thes. 5. 15 ever *f.* . . which is good
2 Thes. 3. 7 know . . ye ought to *f.*
1 Tim. 5. 10 if she have diligently *f.*
2 Tim. 2. 22 *f.* righteousness, faith
Heb. 13. 7 whose faith *f.*, consider.
1 Pet. 2. 21 ye should *f.* his steps
2 Pet. 1. 16 not *f.* cunning . . . fables
3 John 11 *f.* not that which is evil
Rev. 6. 8 and Hell *f.* with him
R. V. Ex. 14. 17 go in after; Mat.
4. 19 come ye after; 27. 62 the day
after; 2 Thes. 3. 7; Heb. 13. 7;
3 John 11 imitate; Phil. 3. 12,
press on.

Followers. R. V. *imitators.*
1 Cor. 4. 16 beseech, be ye *f.* of me
Eph. 5. 1 be ye. . *f.* of God, childr.
Phil. 3. 17 be *f.* together of me
1 Thes. 1. 6 ye became *f.* of us, and
Heb. 6. 12 be not slothful, but *f.*
1 Pet. 3. 13 *f.* of that which is good

Following. *Succeeding day, morrow.*
Luke 13. 33 to day . . and the day *f.*
Acts 21. 1 came the day *f.* unto Rho.
John 1. 43 day *f.* Jesus would go
R. V. John 1. 43; 6. 22 on the mor.

Folly. *Emptiness, senselessness.*
Gen. 34. 7 he had wrought *f.* in Is.
Deut. 22. 21; Josh. 7. 15
Judg. 19. 23 brethren, do not this *f.*
1 Sam. 25. 25 and *f.* is with him
2 Sam. 13. 12 do not thou this *f.*
Job 4. 18 angels he charged with *f.*
Ps. 49. 13 their way is their *f.*
Prov. 5. 13 in . . his *f.* he shall go
13. 16; 14. 8; 16. 22; 26. 4, 5, 11
Eccl. 7. 25 know . . wickedness of *f.*
Isa. 9. 17 every mouth speaketh *f.*
Jer. 23. 13 seen *f.* in the prophets
2 Cor. 11. 1 bear with me . . in my *f.*
2 Tim. 3. 9 their *f.* shall be manif.
R. V. 2 Cor. 11. 1 foolishness

Food. *Food, aliment.*
Gen. 41. 35 let them gather . . *f.*
47. 2; 43. 2; 44. 1; 47. 24
Ex. 21. 10 her *f.* sh. not diminish
Lev. 3. 11, 16 the *f.* of the offering
Deut. 10. 18 giving him *f.* and rai.
1 Sam. 14. 24 cursed . . man that eat *f.*
2 Sam. 9. 10 son may have *f.* to e.
1 K. 5. 9 in giving *f.* for my househ.
Job 38. 41 provide for raven his *f.*
Ps. 78. 25 man did eat angel's *f.*
Prov. 27. 27 goat's milk for thy *f.*
Ezek. 48. 18 *f.* unto them that serve
Acts 14. 17 filling our hearts with *f.*
2 Cor. 9. 10 minister bread for yo. *f.*
1 Tim. 6. 8 having . . *f.* let us be con.
Jas. 2. 15 if brother be dest. of . . *f.*
R. V. Gen. 42. 33 corn; Lev. 22. 7
2 Sam. 9. 10 bread; Ps. 78. 25 bread
of the mighty

Fool. *Self-confident one.*
Ps. 49. 10 *f.* and the brutish . . perish
Prov. 1. 22 and *f.* hate knowledge
3. 35; 8. 5; 10. 18; 12. 23; 13. 16;
14. 8; 15. 2; 17. 10; 18. 2; 19. 1;
23. 9; 26. 1
Eccl. 2. 14 *f.* walketh in darkness
4. 5; 5. 1; 6. 8; 7. 4; 9. 17; 10. 12
Empty person, witless, foolish.
1 Sam. 26. 21 I have played the *f.*
2 Sam. 3. 33 died Abner as a *f.*
Job 30. 8 they were children of *f.*
Ps. 14. 1 *f.* hath said in . . heart
Prov. 1. 7 *f.* despise wisdom and
10. 8; 11. 29; 14. 9; 24. 7; 27. 22
Eccl. 10. 14 *f.* is full of words
Isa. 19. 11 princes of Zoan are *f.*
Jer. 17. 11 at his end shall be a *f.*
Hos. 9. 7 the prophet is a *f.*
Mat. 5. 22 whoso. shall say, Thou *f.*
Luke 12. 20 *f.*, this night thy soul
Rom. 1. 22 wise, they became *f.*
1 Cor. 3. 18 let him become a *f.*
2 Cor. 11. 23 (I speak as a *f.*) I am m.
Eph. 5. 15 ye walk circum. not as *f.*
R. V. 2 Cor. 11. 23 one beside himself; Prov. 11. 29; 12. 15; Luke
12. 20; 1 Cor. 15. 36; 2 Cor. 11. 16;
12. 6, 11 foolish; Ps. 75. 4 arrogant;
Eph. 5. 15 unwise

Foolish. *Self-confident, empty, senseless.*
Deut. 32. 6 O *f.* people and unwise

Job 2. 10 as *f.* women speaketh
Ps. 39. 8 make me not reproach of *f.*
Prov. 9. 13 *f.* woman is clamorous
Eccl. 4. 13 than an old and *f.* king
Isa. 44. 25 maketh their knowl. *f.*
Jer. 10. 8 they are brutish and *f.*
Lam 2. 14 proph. have seen *f.* things
Zech. 11. 15 instru. of *f.* shepherd
Mat. 7. 26 likened unto a *f.* man
25. 2 five . . wise, and five were *f.*
Rom. 1. 21 *f.* heart was darkened
1 Cor. 1. 20 God made *f.* the wisdom
Gal. 3. 1 O *f.* Gal., who hath bewi.
Eph. 5. 4 neither filth. nor *f.* talk.
1 Tim. 6. 9 *f.* and hurtful lusts
2 Tim. 2. 23 *f.* and unlearned ques.
Tit. 3. 3 we also were . . *f.*, dis.
1 Pet. 2. 15 silence the ignorant of *f.*
R. V. Ps. 5. 5; 73. 3 arrogant; 73.
22 brutish; Prov. 9. 6 ye simple
ones; Rom. 1. 21 senseless; 10. 19
void of understanding

Foolishly. *With folly, without sense.*
Gen. 31. 28 thou hast now done *f.*
Num. 12. 11 wherein we have done *f.*
1 Sam. 13. 13 thou hast done *f.*
2 Sam. 24. 10 for I have done very *f.*
1 Chr. 21. 8; 2 Chr. 16. 9
Job 1. 22 sin. not, nor charged God *f.*
Ps. 75. 4 said to fools deal not *f.*
Prov. 14. 17 soon angry dealeth *f.*
2 Cor. 11. 17 which I spk., I spk. *f.*
R. V. Ps. 75. 4 arrogantly

Foolishness. *Folly, senselessness.*
2 Sam. 15. 31 turn coun. of A. into *f.*
Ps. 38. 5 corrupt because of my *f.*
Prov. 12. 23 heart of f. proclaim *f.*
14. 24; 15. 2; 19. 3; 22. 15; 24. 9
Eccl. 7. 25 even of *f.* and madness
Mark 7. 22 blasphemy, pride, *f.*
1 Cor. 1. 18 preach. of the cross is . . *f.*
1. 21, 23, 25; 2. 14; 3. 19
R. V. Prov. 14. 24; 15. 2, 14 folly

Foot. *Base, pedestal.*
Ex. 30. 18 make his *f.* of brass
31. 9; 35. 16; 38. 8; 39. 39; 40. 11
Lev. 8. 11 the laver and his *f.*
Foot.
Gen. 8. 9 no rest for sole of her *f.*
Ex. 21. 24 hand for hand, *f.* for *f.*
Lev. 8. 23 great toe of his right *f.*
Num. 22. 25 crushed Balaam's *f.*
Deut. 2. 5 no, not . . *f.'s* breadth
Josh. 1. 3 sole of your *f.* shall tread
Judg. 5. 15 sent on *f.* into valley
2 Sam. 2. 18 light of *f.* as a roe
2 K. 19. 24 s. of my *f.* have I dried
2 Chr. 33. 8 nei. will I . . remove . . *f.*
Job 2 from sole of *f.* unto crown
Ps. 9. 15 net, . . is their own *f.* taken
91. 12 dash thy *f.* against a stone
Prov. 1. 15 refrain thy *f.* from . . path
Eccl. 5. 1 keep thy *f.* when . . goest
S. of S. 7. 1 how beautiful are thy *f.*
Isa. 20. 2 put off shoe from thy *f.*
Jer. 2. 25 withhold thy *f.* from
Ezek. 6. 11 stamp with thy *f.*, say
Am. 2. 15 swift of *f.* shall not del.
Mat. 4. 6 lest . . dash thy *f.* against
Mark 9. 45 if thy *f.* offend, cut it off
Luke 4. 11 dash *f.* against a stone
John 11. 44 b. hand and *f.* with g. c.
Acts 7. 5 as to set his *f.* on : yet he
1 Cor. 12. 15 if the *f.* shall say
Rev. 1. 13 clothed . . down to the *f.*
R. V. Ex. 31. 9; 35. 16; 38. 8; 39.
39; 41. 11; Lev. 8. 11 base; Isa.
18. 7 down; Lam. 1. 15 set at
nonght

Footman. *Man on foot, infantry.*
Num. 11. 21 six hund. thousand *f.*
Judg. 20. 2 1 Sam. 4. 10; 2 Sam.
10. 6; 1 K. 20. 29; K. 13. 7; 1 Chr.
8. 4; Jer. 12. 5
R. V. 1 Sam. 22. 17 guard

Footstep. *Foot.*
Tread, footprint.
Ps. 17. 5 paths, that my *f.* slip not
Ps. 77. 19 thy *f.* are not known
89. 51 reproached the *f.* of thine an.
S. of S. 1. 8 go . . forth by the *f.* of
R. V. Ps. 17. 5 feet

Footstool. *Stool for the foot.*
1 Chr. 28. 2 for the *f.* of our God
2 Chr. 9. 18 throne, with a *f.* of gold

Ps. 99. 5 and worship at his *f.*
110. 1 make thine enemies thy *f.*
Isa. 66. 1 s . . L . . the earth is my *f.*
Lam. 2. 1 remembered not his *f.*
Mat. 5. 35 nor by earth, for it is his *f.*
Mark 12. 36 make thine en. thy *f.*
Luke 20. 43 ; Aets 2. 35 ; Heb. 1. 13
R. V. In N. T. footstool of thy feet

Forbade. See **Forbid.**
Forbare. See **Forbear.**
Forbear. *Refrain or abstain from, cease, spare, patiently, indulge.*
Ex. 23. 5 wouldst *f.* to help him
Num. 9. 13 *f.* to keep the passover
Deut. 23. 22 if thou *f.* to vow
1 Sam. 23. 13 told S., . . he *f.* to go
1 K. 22. 6 go to battle, or shall I *f.*
25. 6 then the prophet *f.*, and said
Neh. 9. 30 many yrs. didst thou *f.*
Job 16. 6 though I *f.*, what am
Prov. 24. 11 if thou *f.* to deliver
Jer. 41. 8 so he *f.* and slew . . not
Ezek. 2. 5 hear, or whether they . . *f.*
Zech. 11. 12 my price; and if not, *f.*
1 Cor. 9. 6 power to *f.* working
2 Cor. 12. 6 I *f.*, lest any man
Eph. 4. 2 long. suf. *f.* one another
Col. 3. 11 *f.* . . and forgiving one a.
1 Thes. 3. 1 could no longer *f.*
R. V. Neh. 9. 30 bear with ; Prov.
24. 11 hold not back ; Ezek. 24. 17
sigh but not aloud.

Forbearance. *Holding back, refraining.*
Rom. 2. 4 riches of his good. and *f.*
3. 25 through the *f.* of God

Forbearing. *Sparing, indulging.*
Prov. 25. 15 by long *f.* is a prince
Bearing up, sustaining.
Jer. 20. 9 I was weary with *f.*

Forbid. *Command against, prohibit, interdict.*
Gen. 44. 7 God *f.* that thy servant
Lev. 5. 17 any . . things which are
Num. 11. 28 my lord Moses, *f.* the
Deut. 2. 37 whatsoever the L. G. *f.*
Josh. 22. 29 God *f.* that we . . rebel
1 Sam. 12. 23 God *f.* that I . . sin
1 K. 21. 3 N. said to A., the L. *f.*
1 Chr. 11. 19 My God *f.* it me
Job 27. 5 God *f.* that I . . justify
Mat. 3. 14 John *f.* him, saying
19. 14 and *f.* them not to come
Mark 9. 38 fol. not us, and we *f.*
Luke 6. 29 *f.* not to take . . coat also
Acts 10. 47 can any man *f.* water
Rom. 3. 4 God *f.*, yea, let God be
3. 6 ; 6. 2 ; 7. 7 ; 9 14 ; 11. 1, 11
1 Cor. 14. 39 *f.* not to speak with t.
Gal. 2. 17 minister of sin, God *f.*
1 Thes. 2. 16 *f.* us to speak to Gen.
1 Tim. 4. 3 *f.* to marry, to abstain
2 Pet. 2. 16 voice *f.* the madness
3 John 10 and *f.* them that would
R. V. Mat. 3. 14 would have hindered; Luke 6. 29 withhold not;
Gal. 6. 14 far be it from me; 2
Pet. 2. 16 and stayed

Force (*v.*). *Drive, press, crush, compel.*
Deut. 20. 19 by *f.* an axe against
Judg. 1. 34 Amor. *f.* the chil. of D.
1 Sam. 13. 12 I *f.* myself therefore
2 Sam. 13. 12 nay, bro., do not *f.* me
Esth. 7. 8 Will he *f.* the queen also
Prov. 30. 33 *f.* of wrath bring. strife
R. V. Deut. 20. 19 wielding

Force (*n.*). *Might, strength, army.*
1 Sam. 2. 16 if not . . will take it by *f.*
2 Chr. 17. 2 placed *f.* in . . fenced cit.
Ez. 4. 23 made them cease by *f.*
Job 36. 19 nor all the *f.* of strength
Isa. 60. 5, 11 *f.* of Gentiles come
Jer. 18. 21 blood by *f.* of sword
Ezek. 34. 4 with *f.* . . have ye ruled
Dan. 11. 38 honour the God of *f.*
Am. 2. 14 shall not strength. his *f.*
Obad. 11 carried away captive his *f.*
Mat. 11. 12 the violent take it by *f.*
John 6. 15 came . . take him by *f.*
Acts 23. 10 to take him by *f.* from
Heb. 9. 17 a testament is of *f.* after
R. V. Isa. 60. 5. 11 wealth; Ezek.
35. 5 power; Dan. 11. 38 fortresses; Obad. 11 substance

Forcible. *Powerful.*

Job 6. 25 how *f.* are right words
Ford. *Passage.*
Gen. 32. 22 pass. over the *f.* Jabbok
Josh. 2. 7 to Jordan unto the *f.*
Judg. 3. 28 took the *f.* of Jordan
Isa. 16. 2 shall be at *f.* of Arnon
Forecast. R. V. *devise.*
Dan. 11. 24. 25 *f.* devices against h.
Forefather *First father, pro-*
   genitor.
Jer. 11. 10 iniquities of their *f.*
2 Tim. 1. 3 I serve from my *f.*
Forefront. *Face, front, head.*
Ex. 26. 9 the *f.* of the tabernacle
Lev. 8. 9 upon *f.* he put the .. plate
1 Sam. 14. 5 *f.* of the one was situ
2 Sam. 11. 15 set Uriah in the *f.*
2 K. 16. 14 from: the *f.* of the house
2 Chr. 20. 27 Jehoshaphat in the *f.*
Ezek. 40. 19 *f.* of the lower gate
R. V. Lev. 8. 9 in front; 1 Sam. 14. 5
   one crag
Forehead. *Front, brow.*
Ex. 28. 38 shall be upon Aaron's *f.*
Lev. 13. 41 fallen off .. he is *f.* bald
1 Sam. 17. 49 smote the Philis. in *f.*
2 Chr. 26. 19 leprosy rose .. in his *f.*
Jer. 3. 3 thou hadst a whore's *f.*
Ezek. 3. 8 *f.* strong against their *f.*
Rev. 7. 3 sealed servants in their *f.*
   9. 4; 13. 16; 14. 1; 17. 5; 20. 4; 22. 4
R. V. Ezek. 16. 12 nose
Foreigner. *Stranger, settler, so-*
   journer.
Ex. 12. 45 a *f.* and .. servant shall
Deut. 15. 3 of a *f.* thou may exalt
Obad. 11 *f.* entered into his gates
Eph. 2. 19 no more strangers and *f.*
R. V. Ex. 12. 45 sojourner; Eph.
   2. 19 sojourners.
Foreknow. *Know beforehand.*
Rom. 8. 29 whom he did *f.*, he
   11. 2 cast away his peo. which he *f.*
Foreknowledge. *Knowing be-*
   forehand.
Acts 2. 23 determined counsel and *f.*
1 Pet. 1. 2 elect according to the *f.*
Foremost. *First, chief.*
Gen. 32. 17 he commanded the *f.*
2 Sam. 18. 27 running of .. is like
Foreordain. *Know beforehand.*
1 Pet. 1. 20 who .. was *f.* before
Forepart. *Face, front, prow.*
Ex. 28. 27 toward the *f.* thereof
1 K. 6. 20 the oracle in the *f.* was
Ezek. 42. 7 outer court on the *f.*
Acts 27. 41 ship .. the *f.* stuck fast
R. V. 1 K. 6. 20 within; Ezek. 42. 7
   before; Acts 27. 41 fore ship.
Forerunner *Runner before.*
Heb. 6. 20 *f.* is for us entered
Foresaw. *See* **Foresee.**
Foresee. *See Before.*
Prov. 22. 3 prudent man *f.* the evil
Acts 2. 25 I *f.* the Lord always bef.
Gal. 3. 8 scripture, *f.* that God would
R. V. Prov. 22. 3; 27. 12 seeth;
   Acts 2. 25 beheld
Foreship. *Bow, prow.*
Acts 27. 30 cast anchors out of *f.*
Foreskin. *Prepuce.*
Gen. 17. 11 circum. flesh of your *f.*
Ex. 4. 25; Lev. 12. 3; Deut. 10. 16;
   Josh. 5. 3; 1 Sam. 18. 25; 2 Sam.
   3. 14; Jer. 4. 4; Hab. 2. 16
Forest. *Spread-out-place, thicket,*
   wood.
1 Sam. 22. 5 David came to *f.* of H.
1 K. 7. 2 built also the house of the *f.*
2 K. 19. 23 enter into *f.* of Carmel
2 Chr. 9. 16 house of *f.* of Lebanon
Neh. 5. 8 keeper of the king's *f.*
Ps. 50. 10 every beast of *f.* is mine
Isa. 9. 18 shall kindle in thickets of *f.*
Jer. 5. 6 lion out of the *f.* shall slay
Ezek. 15. 2 vine tree .. among tr. of *f.*
Hos. 2. 12 and I will make them a *f.*
Am. 3. 4 Will a lion roar in the *f.*
Mic. 3. 12 high places of the *f.*
Zech. 11. 2 *f.* of vintage has come
Foretell. *Say beforehand.*
Mark 13. 23 behold, I have *f.* you all
Acts 3. 24 have likew. *f.* of these days
2 Cor. 13. 2 and *f.* you, as if present
R. V. 2 Cor. 13. 2 say beforehand
Foretold. *See* **Foretell.**

Forewarn. *Say or show before.*
Luke 12. 5 I will *f.* you whom
1 Thes. 4. 6 as we have *f.* you
R. V. Luke 12. 5 warn
Forfeited. *Devoted, lost.*
Ez. 10. 8 substance should be *f.*
Forgat. *See* **Forget.**
Forgave. *See* **Forgive.**
Forge. *Sew on, invent.*
Ps. 119. 69 The proud have *f.* a lie
Forger. *Stitcher, inventor.*
Job 13. 4 ye are *f.* of lies, ye are all
Forget. *Lose from memory ne-*
   glect.
Gen. 41. 51 God .. made me *f.* .. toil
Deut. 4. 9 keep thy soul .. lest thou *f.*
Judg. 3. 7 *f.* the Lord their God
1 Sam. 1. 11 remember me, and not *f.*
2 K. 17. 38 covenant .. ye shall not *f.*
Job 8. 13 the paths of all that *f.* God
Ps. 9. 12 *f.* not the cry of the humble
   103. 2 and *f.* not all his benefits
Prov. 2. 17 *f.* the covenant of .. God
Isa. 17. 10 hast *f.* the God of thy s.
Jer. 2. 42 can maid *f.* her ornaments
Lam. 3. 17 removed my soul .. I *f.*
Ezek. 22. 12 *f.* me, saith the Lord
Hos. 2. 13 went aft. lovers, and *f.* me
Am. 8. 7 will never *f.* .. their works
Mat. 16. 5 they had *f.* to take bread
Mark 8. 14 the disciples had *f.* br.
Luke 12. 6 not one of them is *f.*
Phil. 3. 13 *f.* those things which
Heb. 6. 10 God is not unright. to *f.*
Jas. 1. 24 *f.* what manner of man
2 Pet. 1. 9 hath *f.* he was purged
Forgetful. *Neglectful.*
Heb. 13. 2 be not *f.* to entertain str.
Jas. 1. 25 being not a *f.* hearer
Forgetfulness. *Forgetfulness.*
Ps. 88. 12 righteousness in land of *f.*
Forgive. *Gracious to.*
Luke 7. 43 he, to whom he *f.* most
2 Cor. 2. 7 ye ought rather to *f.*
Eph. 4. 32 tender-hearted, *f.* one an.
Col. 2. 13 having *f.* you all trespass
Cover up.
Ps. 78. 38 he, full of comp., *f.* their
Jer. 18. 23 L. .. *f.* not their iniquity
Lift-off, loose away, pardon.
Gen. 50. 17 *f.* .. trespas. of thy breth.
Ex. 10. 17 *f.*, I pray thee, my sin
Num. 14. 19 as thou hast *f.* this peo.
Josh. 24. 19 will not *f.* your transg.
1 Sam. 25. 28 *f.* the trespass of thine
1 K. 8. 30 when thou hearest, *f.*
2 Chr. 6. 39 *f.* and thy people which
Ps. 25. 18 my pain; and *f.* all my sins
Isa. 2. 9 therefore *f.* them not
Jer. 31. 34 for I will *f.* their iniquity
Dan. 9. 19 O Lord, *f.*, .. hearken
Am. 7. 2 O Lord, .. *f.*, I beseech thee
Mat. 6. 12 *f.* us our debts, as we
   6. 16; 9. 2; 12. 31; 1821
Mark 2. 5 Son, thy sins be *f.* thee
Luke 5. 21 who can *f.* sins, but G.
Acts 8. 22 the thought .. may be *f.*
Rom. 4. 7 whose iniquities are *f.*
Jas. 5. 15 sins, they shall be *f.*
1 John 1. 9 faithful and just to *f.* us
R. V. Luke 6. 37 release; Mark 11.
26 ——
Forgiven. *Lifted away, let go.*
Lev. 4. 20 and it shall be *f.* them
   Num. 15. 25 Deut. 21. 8
Ps. 32. 1 whose transgression is *f.*
Isa. 33. 24 the people shall be *f.*
Forgiveness. *Sending away, let-*
   ting go.
Ps. 130. 4 *f.* with thee, that thou
Dan. 9. 9 to the L. our God, *f.*
Mark 3. 29 hath never *f.*, but is in
Acts 5. 31 a Saviour to give .. *f.* of
Eph. 1. 7 in whom we have .. *f.*
Col. 1. 14 have .. the *f.* of sins
R. V. Acts 5. 31; 13. 38; 26. 18 re-
   mission.
Forgiving. *Lifting up or off.*
Ex. 34. 7 *f.* iniquity and transgres.
Num. 14. 18 *f.* iniquity and transg.
Being gracious to.
Eph. 4. 52 tender-hearted *f.* one an.
Col. 3. 13 forbearing .. and *f.* one an.
Forgotten. *Cease to know or*
   think of.
Gen. 41. 30 the plenty shall be *f.*

Deut. 31. 21 shall not be *f.* out of
Job 28. 4 waters *f.* of the foot, they
Ps. 9. 18 needy shall not .. be *f.*
Eccl. 8. 10 they were *f.* in the city
Isa. 23. 15 Tyre shall be *f.* seventy
Jer. 20. 11 confus. shall nev. be *f.*
Lam. 2. 6 caused .. sabbaths to be *f.*
See also **Forget.**
Fork. *Triple tined.*
1 Sam. 13. 21 countless, and for .. *f.*
Form (n.). *Appearance, shape,*
   kind.
Gen. 1. 2 the earth was without *f.*
1 Sam. 28. 14 said, what *f.* is he of
2 Sam. 14. 20 fetch .. this *f.* of speech
2 Chr. 4. 7 candlesticks .. ac. to .. *f.*
Job 4. 16 could not discern the *f.*
Isa. 52. 14 *f.* more than sons of m.
Jer. 4. 23 lo, it was without *f.*, void
Ezek. 43. 11 show .. this *f.* of the h.
Dan. 2. 31 the *f.* thereof was terri.
Mark 16. 12 appear. in another *f.* to
Rom. 2. 20 hast .. *f.* of knowledge
Phil. 2. 6 being in the *f.* of God
2 Tim. 1. 13 hold .. *f.* sound words
R. V. Gen. 1. 2; Jer. 4. 23 waste;
   Job 4. 16 appearance; Dan. 2. 31;
   3. 25 aspect; 2 Tim. 1. 13 pattern
Form (v.). *Make, mould, shape.*
Gen. 2. 7 the Lord God *f.* man of
Deut. 32. 18 hast forgot. G. that *f.*
2 K. 19. 25 times that I .. *f.* it
Job 26. 13 hand .. *f.* the crooked s.
Ps. 90. 2 or ev. thou hadst *f.* the e.
Prov. 26. 10 great God that *f.* all
Isa. 27. 11 that *f.* them will show
   37. 26; 43. 1; 44. 2; 45. 7; 49. 5
Jer. 1. 5 before I *f.* thee in .. belly
Am. 4. 13 he that *f.* the mountains
Zech. 12. 1 and *f.* the spirit of man
Rom. 9. 20 say to him that *f.* it
Gal. 4. 19 travail .. until C. be *f.* in
1 Tim. 2. 13 for Adam was first *f.*
R. V. Deut. 32. 18 gave birth; Job
   26. 5 tremble; 26. 13 pierced
Prov. 26. 10 wounded; Isa. 44. 10
   fashioned
Former (n.). *Maker, shaper,*
   framer.
Jer. 51. 19 he is *f.* of all things
Former (a.). *Eastern, ancient.*
Zech. 14. 8 half .. toward the *f.* sea
Mal. 3. 4 pleasant .. as in *f.* years
First, foremost, antecedent.
Gen. 40. 13 cup, after the *f.* manner
Num. 21. 16 fought against *f.* king
Deut. 24. 4 her *f.* husband which
Ruth 4. 7 was the manner in *f.* time
1 Sam. 17. 30 answered .. after *f.* m.
2 K. 1. 14 captains of *f.* fifties
Neh. 5. 15 but the *f.* governors
Job 30. 3 wilder. in *f.* time desolate
Ps. 79. 8 remem not .. *f.* iniquities
Eccl. 1. 11 no remem. of .. *f.* things
Isa. 41. 22 let them show .. *f.* things
Jer. 5. 24 rain, both *f.* and latter
Ezek. 16. 55 return to .. *f.* estate
Dan. 11. 29 built it not as the *f.*
Hos. 6. 3 come as latter and *f.* rain
Joel 2. 23 hath given you the *f.* rain
Zech. 1. 4 *f.* prophets have cried
Acts 1. 1 *f.* treatise have I made
Eph. 4. 22 concern. *f.* conversation
Heb. 10. 32 call to remem. *f.* days
1 Pet. 1. 14 accord. to the *f.* lusts
Rev. 21. 4 *f.* things are pass. away
R. V. Zech. 14. 8 eastern; Mal. 3.
   4 ancient; Job 30. 3 gloom of;
   Hos. 6. 3 rain that watereth; Rev.
   21. 4 the first
Fornication. *Illicit sexual inter-*
   course, whoredom, harlotry.
Chr. 21. 11 caused inhab. to com. *f.*
Isa. 23. 17 Tyre .. commit *f.* with all
Ezek. 16. 15 pour. out thy *f.* on
Mat. 5. 32 saving for cause of *f.*
Mat 7. 21 from within .. pro. .. *f.*
John 8. 41 we be not born of *f.*
1 Cor. 5. 1 there is *f.* among you
   6. 13, 18; 7. 2
2 Cor. 12. 21 not repented of .. *f.*
Gal. 5. 19 works of flesh .. are *f.*
Eph. 5. 3 *f.* .. let it not be named
Col. 3. 5 *f.* .. inordinate affec., evil
1 Thes. 4. 3 that ye .. abstain from *f.*
Jude 7. giving themselves over to *f.*

Rev. 2. 21 space to repent of her *f*.
R. V. 2 Chr. 21. 11 go a whoring;
Isa. 23. 17 play the harlot; Ezek.
16. 15, 29 whoredom, Rom. 1.
29

Fornicator. *Who fornicates.*
1 Cor. 5. 9 not to company with *f*.
5. 10, 11 ; 6. 9
Heb. 12. 16 lest there be any *f*. or
Forsake. *Leave off, abandon, desert.*
Deut. 12. 19 heed .. that thou *f*. not
14. 27 ; 28. 20 ; 29. 35 ; 31. 6 ; 32. 15
Josh. 1. 5 I will not fail, nor *f*. thee
Judg. 2. 12 *f*. the L. G. of .. fathers
1 Sam. 8. 8 they have *f*. me, and
1 K. 6. 13 I will not *f*. my people
2 K. 21. 22 he *f*. the Lord God of
1 Chr. 10. 7 *f*. their cities and fled
2 Chr. 7. 19 ye turn away and *f*. stat.
Ez. 9. 10 we have *f*. thy commandm.
Neh. 9. 19 *f*. them not in wildern.
Job 6. 14 *f*. fear of the Almighty
Ps. 22. 1 God, why hast thou *f*. me
Prov. 2. 17 *f*. the guide of .. youth
Isa. 1. 4 *f*. the L., .. have provoked
Jer. 5. 7 thy children have *f*. me
Lam. 5. 20 wherefore dost thou *f*. us
Ezek. 8. 12 the Lord has *f*. the earth
Dan. 11. 30 intel. with them that *f*.
Am. 5. 2 virgin is *f*. upon her land
Jonah 2. 8 that observe vanity *f*.
Zeph. 2. 4 for Gaza shall be *f*. and
Mat. 27. 46 my G.. why hast thou *f*.
Mark 1. 18 and .. they *f*. their nets
Luke 5. 11 *f*. all, and followed him
Acts 21. 21 teach. Jews to *f*. Moses
2 Cor. 4. 9 persecuted, but not *f*.
2 Tim. 4. 10 For Demas hath *f*. me
Heb. 10. 25 not *f*. the assembling of
2 Pet. 2. 15 have *f*. the right way
R. V. Deut. 4. 31 fail; Judg. 9. 11
leave; 6. 13 ; 2 K. 21. 14 ; Jer. 23.
33. 39 cast off ; Job 20. 13 will not
let it go; Jer. 15. 6 rejected; 18.
14 dried up; Am. 5. 2 cast down;
Mat. 19. 27 ; 26. 56 ; Mark 14.
50 ; Luke 5. 11 left; Luke 14. 33
renounceth
Forsook. *See* Forsake.
Forsomuch. R. V. *forasmuch.*
Luke 19. 9 *f*. as he is the son of A.
Forswear. *Swear falsely, perjure.*
Mat. 5. 33 Thou shalt not *f*. thyself
Fort. *Fortress, bulwark, tower.*
2 Sam. 5. 9 David dwelt in the *f*.
2 K. 25. 1 they built *f*. against it
Isa. 25. 12 fortress of the high *f*.
32. 14 *f*. and tow. shall be .. dens
Jer. 52. 4 and built *f*. against it
Ezek. 21. 22 mount, and to build *f*.
Dan. 11. 19 turn.. face toward the *f*.
R. V. 2 Sam. 5. 9 ; Ezek. 33. 27
stronghold ; Isa. 29. 3 siege works;
32. 14 hills ; Dan. 11. 19 fortresses;
Ezek. 4. 2 ; 26. 8 forts
Forth. *Out, without, away.*
Gen. 39. 13 saw that he was fled *f*.
Judg. 19. 25 took .. and .. her *f*.
2 K. 11. 13 her body *f*. without
2 Chr. 23. 14 ha. her *f*. of the ranges
Ps. 126. 6 He goeth *f*. and weepeth
Am. 7. 17 Is. sh. go into captivity *f*.
Mark 3. 3 and he saith .. Stand *f*.
John 11. 43 cried .. Lazarus, come *f*.
15. 6 ; 19. 4, 5, 13
Forth has very frequent Scriptural
use in connection with such verbs
as break, bring, call, cast, go, pour,
put, show, shoot, spread, stretch,
etc. ; and in R. V. is often changed
to *out*, or else is omitted
Forthwith. *Straightway, immediately.*
Ez. 6. 8 *f*. expenses be given unto
Mat. 13. 5 and *f*. they sprung up
Mark 1. 29 *f*., when they were come
John 19. 34 *f*. came thereout blood
Acts 9. 18 and he received sight *f*.
R. V. Ez. 6. 8 with all diligence;
Mat. 13. 5 ; 26. 49 ; Mark 1. 29,
43 ; John 19. 34 ; Acts 12. 10 ; 21.
30 straightway ; Mark 5. 13 ; Acts
9. 18—
Fortieth. *Fortieth.*
Num. 33. 38 died .. in *f*. year after

Deut. 1. 3 ; 1 Chr. 26. 31 ; 2 Chr.
16. 13
Fortify. *Fence, bind, strengthen.*
Judg. 9. 31 they *f*. the city against
2 Chr. 11. 11 he *f*. the strongholds
Neh. 3. 8 and they *f*. Jerusalem un.
Isa. 22. 10 houses .. broke. down to *f*.
Jer. 51. 53 though she should *f*. the
Mic. 7. 12 the *f*. cities, and from
Nah. 3. 14 siege, *f*. thy strongholds
R. V. Judg. 9. 31 constrain ; Mic.
7. 12 of Egypt; Nah. 3. 14
strengthen
Fortress. *Fenced place, stronghold.*
2 Sam. 22. 2 L. is my rock and *f*.
Ps. 18. 2 L. is my rock and my *f*.
31. 3 ; 71. 3 ; 91. 2 ; 144. 2
Isa. 17. 3 *f*. shall cease from Eph.
Jer. 6. 27 set thee .. a tower .. a *f*.
Dan. 11. 7 one shall enter into the *f*.
Hos. 10. 14 thy *f*. shall be spoiled
Am. 5. 9 shall come against the *f*.
Mic. 7. 12 and from *f*. even to river
R. V. Jer. 10. 17 siege ; 16. 19
stronghold ; Mic. 7. 12 Egypt
Forty. *Forty.*
Gen. 5. 13 Cainan lived e. h. and *f*.
Ex. 16. 35 ; Lev. 25. 8 ; Num. 1.
21 ; Deut. 2. 7 ; Josh. 4. 13 ;
Judg. 3. 11 ; 1 Sam. 4. 18 ; 2 Sam.
2. 10 ; 1 K. 2. 11 ; 2 K. 2. 24 ; 1
Chr. 5. 18 ; 2 Chr. 9. 30 ; Ez. 2.
8 ; Neh. 5. 15 ; Job 42. 16 ; Ps.
95. 10 ; Jer. 52. 30 ; Ezek. 4. 6 ;
Am. 2. 10 ; Jonah 3. 4
Mat. 4. 2 had fasted *f*. days and ni.
Mark 1. 13 ; Luke 4. 2 ; John 4.
20 ; Acts 1. 3 ; 2 Cor. 11. 24 ;
Heb. 3. 9 ; Rev. 7. 4
Forward. *Frontward, ahead, onward.*
Gen. 26. 13 and went *f*. and grew
Ex. 14. 15 chil. of Is., that they go *f*.
Num. 1. 51 when tab. setteth *f*.
2. 17 ; 4. 5 ; 10. 17–28 ; 21. 10
1 Sam. 10. 3 shall thou go on *f*.
1 Chr. 23. 4 set *f*. the work of house
Job. 23. 8 behold, I go *f*., but he
Jer. 7. 24 went backward, not *f*.
Ezek. 39. 22 from that day and *f*.
2 Cor. 8. 10 but also to be *f*. a year
Gal. 2. 10 which I also was *f*. to
3 John 6 bring *f*. on their journey
R. V. Gen. 26. 13 more and more ;
Num. 10. 5 take their journey ; 2.
24 ; 1 Cor. 6. 11 forth; Num. 21.
10 ; 22. 1 journeyed ; 1 Chr 23. 4
oversee ; Ez. 3. 8, 9 have over-
sight; Gal. 2 10 zealous; 2 Chr.
8. 10 will; 8. 17 himself very
earnest
Forwardness. R. V. *earnestness.*
2 Cor. 8. 8 by occasion of the *f*. of
R. V. *readiness.*
2 Cor. 9. 2 know the *f*. of your mind
Fought. *See* **Fight.**
Foul (a.). *Unclean, disagreeable.*
Job 16. 16 face is *f*. with weeping
Mat. 16. 3 *f*. weather to day, sky red
Mark 9. 25 Je. rebuked the *f*. spirit
Rev. 18. 2 the hold of every *f*. spirit
R. V. Mark 9. 25 ; Rev. 18. 2 un-
clean
Foul (v.). *Trample, dirty.*
Ezek. 32. 2 and thou *f*. their rivers
34. 18, 19 drink that which ye have *f*.
Found. *See* **Find.**
Found. *Found, lay foundation.*
Ps. 24. 2 he hath *f*. it upon the seas
Prov. 3. 19 the Lord .. has *f*. the ear
Isa. 14. 32 the Lord hath *f*. Zion
Am. 9. 6 and hath *f*. his troop in the
Mat. 7. 25 for it was *f*. upon a rock
Luke 6. 48 for it was *f*. upon a rock
R. V. Luke 6. 48 because it had been
well builded
Foundation. *Thing laid, substructure, base.*
Ex. 9. 18 not in E. since the *f*. thereof
Deut. 32. 22 shall set on fire the *f*.
Josh. 6. 26 lay the *f*. thereof
2 Sam. 22. 8 *f*. of heaven moved
1 K. 5. 17 bro. stones, to lay the *f*.
2 Chr. 8. 16 unto day of the *f*. of ho.
Ez. 3. 6 the *f*. .. was not yet laid
Job 4. 19 whose *f*. is in the dust

Ps. 11. 3 If the *f*. be destroyed, what
Prov. 8. 29 he appointed the *f*. of
Isa. 24. 18 *f*. of earth do shake
Jer. 50. 15 Babyl. .. her *f*. are fallen
Lam. 4. 11 it hath devoured the *f*.
Ezek. 30. 4 her *f*. shall be broken
Mic. 1. 6 discover the *f*. ther. of
Hab. 3. 13 by discovering the *f*.
Hag. 2. 18 day *f*. of temple was laid
Zech. 4. 9 Zerub. laid *f*. of this house
Mat. 13. 35 kept secret from the *f*. of
Luke 6. 48 digged deep, and laid *f*.
John 17. 24 lovedst me before the *f*.
Acts 16. 26 so that *f*. of prison shak.
Rom. 15. 20 build on anoth. man's *f*.
1 Cor. 3. 10 I have laid the *f*., and an.
Eph. 1. 4 before the *f*. of the world
1 Tim. 6. 19 laying up a good *f*. ag.
2 Tim. 2. 19 *f*. of God standeth sure
Heb. 1. 10 hast laid the *f*. of the e.
1 Pet. 1. 20 foreordained before the *f*
Rev. 13. 8 slain from *f*. of the world
R. V. Isa. 16. 7 raisin cakes ; Jer. 50.
15 bulwarks
Founder. *Refiner.*
Judg. 17. 4 mo. gave them to the *f*.
Jer. 6. 29 the *f*. melteth in vain
10. 9, 14 ; 51. 17
R. V. Jer. 6. 29 do they go on refin-
ing ; 10. 9, 14 ; 51. 17 goldsmith
Fountain. *Spring, well, cistern, source.*
Gen. 16. 7 angel .. found her by a *f*.
Lev. 11. 36 a *f*. or pit wherein water
Num. 33. 9 in E. twelve *f*. of water
Deut. 8. 7 land of brooks of wa. of *f*.
Josh. 15. 9 unto the *f*. of the water
1 Sam. 29. 1 Israelites pitched by a *f*.
1 K. 18. 5 go .. unto all *f*. of water
2 Chr. 32. 3 stop the waters of the *f*.
Neh. 2. 14 went to gate of the *f*.
Ps. 74. 15 didst cleave the *f*. and
Prov. 5. 16 let thy *f*. be dispersed
Eccl. 12. 6 pitcher be broken at *f*.
S. of S. 4. 12 spring shut up.. *f*. sealed
Isa. 41. 18 op. *f*. in midst of valleys
Hos. 13. 15 his *f*. shall be dried up
Joel 3. 18 *f*. shall come forth of h.
Zech. 13. 1 there shall be a *f*. opened
Mark 5. 29 *f*. of her blood was dried
Jas. 3. 11 doth a *f*. send forth water
Rev. 7. 17 lead them to living *f*.
8. 10 ; 14. 7 ; 16. 4 ; 21. 6
R. V. Num. 33. 9 ; Prov. 5. 16
springs ; Jer. 6. 7 well
Four. *Four.*
Gen. 2. 10 riv. became into *f*. heads
Ex. 12. 40 ; Lev. 11. 20 ; Num. 1.
29 ; Deut. 3. 11 ; Josh. 19. 7 ; Judg.
9. 34 ; Job 1. 19 ; Ps. 30. 15 ; Prov.
30. 15 ; Isa. 11. 12 ; Jer. 15. 3 ;
Ezek. 1. 5
Mat. 24. 31 gather .. from *f*. winds
Mark 2. 3 ; Luke 2. 37 ; John 11. 17
Acts 10. 11 sheet knit at *f*. corners
Rev. 4. 4 ; 5. 6 ; 6. 1 ; 7. 1 ; 9. 13
Fourfold. *Four times.*
2 Sam. 12. 6 restore the lamb *f*.
Luke 19. 8 if I ha. tak., I restore *f*.
Four-footed. *Quadruped.*
Acts 10. 12 all manner of *f*. beasts
Rom. 1. 23 *f*. beasts, and creeping
Fourscore. *Eighty.*
Gen. 16. 16 Abram was *f*. and six
Ex. 7. 7 Moses was *f*. years old,
Num. 2. 9 ; Josh. 14. 10 ; Judg. 3.
20 ; 1 Sam. 22. 18 ; 2 Sam. 19. 32 ;
1 K. 5. 15 ; 2 K. 6. 25 ; 1 Chr. 7. 5 ;
2 Chr. 2. 2 ; Ez. 8. 8 ; Neh. 7. 26 ;
Esth. 1. 4 ; Ps. 90. 10 ; S. of S. 6.
8 ; Isa. 37. 36 ; Jer. 41. 5 ; Luke 2.
37 ; 16. 7
Foursquare. *Four-sided or cornered.*
Ex. 27. 1 altar shall be *f*., th. height
28. 16 ; 30. 2 ; 37. 25 ; 38. 1 ; 39. 9
1 K. 7. 31 with their borders, *f*.
Ezek. 40. 47 ; 48. 20 ; Rev. 21. 16
Fourteen. *Four and ten.*
Gen. 31. 41 served thee *f*. years for
Num. 1. 27 ; Josh. 15. 36 ; 1 K. 8.
65 ; 1 Chr. 25. 5 ; 2 Chr. 13. 21 ; Job
42. 12 ; Ezek. 43. 17 ; Mat. 1. 7 ; 2
Cor. 12. 2 ; Gal. 2. 1
Fourteenth. *Fourth and tenth.*
Gen. 14. 5 in *f*. year came Ched.

Ex. 12. 6; Lev. 23. 5; Num. 9. 3;
Josh. 5. 10; 2 K. 18. 13; 1 Chr. 24.
13; 2 Chr. 30. 15; Ez. 6. 19; Esth.
9. 15; Isa. 36. 1; Ezek. 40. 1; Acts
27. 27

Fourth. *Four.*
Gen. 1. 19 even. and mo. were *f.* day
Ex. 20. 5; Lev. 23. 13; Num. 15. 4;
Josh. 19. 17; Judg. 19. 5; 1 K. 6.
1; 2 K. 10. 30; 1 Chr. 2. 14; Ez. 8.
33; Jer. 25. 1; Ezek. 1. 1; Dan. 2.
40; Zech. 6. 3
Mat. 14. 25 *f.* watch of the night
Mark 6. 48; Rev. 4. 7; 16. 18

Fowl. *Feathered creature.*
Gen. 1. 20 wat. bring *f.* that may fly
1. 21, 22, 26, 30; 2. 19; 6. 7; 7. 3
Lev. 1. 14 if sacrifice . . be of *f.*
Deut. 14. 20 clean *f.* may ye eat
1 Sam. 17. 44 will give thy flesh to *f.*
1 K. 4. 33 spake of beasts and *f.*
Job 12. 7 ask . . *f.* of the air, sh. tell
Ps. 50. 11 I know all the *f.* of the m.
Jer. 7. 33 shall be meat for *f.* of heav.
Ezek. 29. 5 given thee for meat . . to *f.*
Dan. 2. 38 *f.* of heaven hath . . given
Mat. 6. 26 behold the *f.* of the air
Mark 4. 4 *f.* of air came and dev. it
Luke 8. 5 *f.* of air devoured it
Acts 10. 12 creeping things and *f.* of
Rev. 19. 17 to all the *f.* that fly
R. V. Gen. 15. 11; Job 28. 7 bird of
prey; Lev. 11. 20 winged; Isa. 18.
19 ravenous birds; Mat. 6. 26; 13.
4; Mark 4. 4, 32; Luke 8. 5; 12.
24; 13. 19; Rev. 19. 17. 21 birds

Fowler. *Catcher, ensnarer.*
Ps. 91. 3 deliver thee from . . the *f.*
Prov. 6. 5 as bird from hand of *f.*
Hos. 9. 8 prophet is a snare of a *f.*

Fox. *Fox, jackal.*
Judg. 15. 4 Sam. caught three h. *f.*
Neh. 4. 3 if *f.* go up, he shall even
Ps. 63. 10 shall be a portion for *f.*
S. of S. 2. 15 Take us the *f.*, the
Lam. 5. 18 Zion, the *f.* walk upon it
Ezek. 13. 4 prophets are like the *f.*
Mat. 8. 20 *f.* have holes, and birds
Luke 13. 32 go ye, and tell that *f.*

Fragments. R. V. *broken pieces.*
Mat. 14. 20 took up of the *f.* that
Mark 6. 43 twelve baskets of *f.*
Luke 9. 17 there was taken up of *f.*
John 6. 12 gathered up the *f.* that

Frail. *Short-lived, feeble.*
Ps. 39. 4 may know how *f.* I am

Frame (n.). *Formation, fabric.*
Ps. 103. 14 for he knoweth our *f.*
Ezek. 40. 2 wh. was as the *f.* of a city

Frame (v.). *Join together, construct.*
Judg. 12. 6 could not *f.* to pronounce
Ps. 50. 19 thy tongue *f.* deceit
Isa. 29. 16 shall the thing *f.* say of
Jer. 18. 11 Beho., I *f.* evil against you
Hos. 5. 4 will not *f.* their doings
Eph. 2. 21 building fitly *f.* together
Heb. 11. 3 worlds were *f.* by . . word
R. V. Hos. 5. 4 their doings will not
suffer them

Frankincense. *Free-incense.*
Ex. 30. 34 Take spices with pure *f.*
Lev. 2. 1 and shall . . put *f.* thereon
Num. 5. 15 no oil, nor put *f.* thereon
1 Chr. 9. 29 and the *f.* and the spices
Neh. 13. 5 laid the *f.* and the vessels
S. of S. 3. 6 perfumed with . . *f.*
Mat. 2. 11 presented . . him . . gold, *f.*
Rev. 18. 13 no man buyeth their *f.*

Frankly. *Freely.*
Luke 7. 42 he *f.* forgave them both
R. V.

Fraud. *Oppression, deception.*
Ps. 10. 7 his mouth is full of . . *f.*
Jas. 5. 4 which is . . kept back by *f.*
R. V. Ps. 10. 7 oppression

Fray. *Affright, terrify.*
Deut. 28. 26 no man shall *f.* away
Jer. 7. 33 and none shall *f.* away
Zech. 1. 21 these are come to *f.* them
Freckled. R. V. *tetter.*
Lev. 13. 39 it is a *f.* spot that grow.

Free (a.). *Gratis.*
Ex. 21. 11 go out *f.* without money
Willing, noble, liberal.
Ex. 36. 3 brought to him *f.* offering

---

2 Chr. 29. 31 as were of a *f.* heart
Ps. 51. 12 uphold me with thy *f.* spir.
Am. 4. 5 publish the *f.* offerings
Rom. 5. 15 so also is the *f.* gift
At liberty, independent.
Ex. 21. 2 he shall go out *f.* for noth.
Lev. 19. 20 because she was not *f.*
Num. 5. 19 *f.* from this bitter water
Deut. 15. 12 thou shalt let him go *f.*
1 Sam. 17. 25 make his father's h. *f.*
1 Chr. 9. 33 in the chambers were *f.*
Job 3. 19 ser. is *f.* from his master
Ps. 88. 5 *f.* from the dead, like
Isa. 58. 6 let the oppressed go *f.*
Jer. 34. 9 let his maidservant go *f.*
Mat. 17. 26 then are the children *f.*
John 8. 33 ye shall be made *f.*
Acts 22. 28 Paul said, I was *f.* born
Rom. 6. 18 being made *f.* from sin
1 Cor. 7. 21 thou mayest be made *f.*
Gal. 3. 28 neither bond nor *f.*, all one
Eph. 6. 8 receive of Lord, bond or *f.*
Col. 3. 11 Bar., Scyth., bond or *f.*
1 Pet. 2. 16 as *f.* and not using lib.
Rev. 13. 16 causeth all, *f.* and bond
R. V. Ex. 21. 11 for nothing; 36. 3
free will; 2 Chr. 29. 31; Am. 4. 5
willing; Ps. 88. 5 cast off; Acts 22.
28 am a Roman; Col. 3. 11 free-
man; 2 Thes. 3. 1 run; Mat. 15. 6;
Mark 7. 11 —

Freed. *Made free.*
Josh. 9. 23 none of you be *f.* from
Rom. 6. 7 is dead, is *f.* from sin
R. V. Rom. 6. 7 justified

Freedom. *Liberty, exemption.*
Lev. 19. 20 not all red. nor *f.* given
Immunity. R. V. *citizenship.*
Acts 22. 28 gr. sum obtained I this *f.*

Freely. *Willingly.*
Ps. 54. 6 will *f.* sacrifice unto thee
Hos. 14. 4 I will love them *f.*, for
Gratis, liberally.
Num. 11. 5 wh. we did eat in Egypt *f.*
Mat. 10. 8 *f.* ye have received, *f.* gi.
Rom. 3. 24 justified *f.* by grace
2 Cor. 11. 7 have pr. to you gospel *f.*
Rev. 21. 6 athirst . . the water of life *f.*
Easily, with full speech.
Acts 2. 29 let me *f.* speak to you
26. 26 before whom . . I speak *f.*

Freeman. *Free person.*
1 Cor. 7. 22 called in L. is L.'s *f.*
Rev. 6. 15 every b. me and every *f.* m.
R. V. 1 Cor. 7. 22 freedman

Frequent. R. V. *abundantly.*
2 Cor. 11. 23 in prisons more *f.*

Freewill. *Willing.*
Lev. 22. 18 all his *f.* offerings which
Num. 15. 3; Deut. 12. 6; 2 Chr. 31.
14; Ez. 1. 4; Ps. 119. 108
Ez. 7. 16 minded of their own *f.* will

Freewoman. *Free person.*
Gal. 4. 22, 23, 24 other by a *f. w.*

Fresh. *Unspoiled, sweet, refresh-
ing.*
Num. 11. 8 manna . . as taste of *f.* il
Job 29. 20 My glory was *f.* in me
33. 25 flesh shall be *f.* than a child's
Ps. 92. 10 be anointed with *f.* oil
Jas. 3. 12 no *f.* yields salt w. and *f.*
R. V. Jas. 3. 12 sweet

Fret. *Irritate, worry, anger.*
1 Sam. 1. 6 provok . . . to make her *f.*
Ps. 37. 1 *f.* not . . bec. of ev. doers
Prov. 19. 3 heart *f.* against the Lord
Isa. 8. 21 they shall *f.* themselves
Ezek. 16. 43 hast *f.* me in all things
Rub, chafe, corrode.
Lev. 13. 51, 52 for it is a *f.* leprosy
13. 55 it is *f.* inward, whether it be
Fried. R. V. *soaked.*
Lev. 7. 12 offer cakes of fine flour, *f.*
1 Chr. 23. 29 for that which is *f.*

Friend *Beloved one, intimate and
trusted one, adherent, ally.*
Gen. 38. 12 Jud., he and his *f.* Hirah
Ex. 33. 11 as man speaketh to *f.*
Deut. 13. 6 if thy *f.* entice thee
Judg. 14. 20 he had used as his *f.*
1 Sam. 30. 26 sent spoil to . . his *f.*
2 Sam. 13. 3 but Ammon had a *f.*
1 K. 16. 11 neith. of kinsfolks nor *f.*
2 Chr. 20. 7 seed of Abraham thy *f.*
Esth. 5. 10 Haman . . called for his *f.*
Job 2. 11 when Job's three *f.* heard

---

6. 14; 16. 20; 17. 5; 19. 21; 32. 3
Ps. 35. 14 he had been my *f.* or bro
Prov. 6. 1 if thou be surety for *f.*
17. 17; 18. 24; 19. 4; 22. 11; 27. 9
S. of S. 5. 1 eat, O *f.*; drink, yea
Jer. 6. 21 neigh. and *f.* shall perish
Lam. 1. 2 *f.* have dealt treacherou.
Hos. 3. 1 woman beloved of her *f.*
Mic. 7. 5 Trust ye not in a *f.*, put ye
Mat. 11. 19 *f.* of publicans and sin.
Mark 3. 21 when his *f.* heard, they
Luke 7. 6 centurion sent *f.* to him
11. 5; 12. 4; 14. 10; 15. 6; 16. 9
John 3. 39 the *f.* of the bridegroom
Acts 10. 24 Cor. called together his *f.*
Jas. 2. 23 was called the F. of God
3 John 14 Our *f.* salute thee. Greet
R. V. 2 Sam. 19. 6 them that love
thee; Prov. 6. 1; 17. 18 neighbour

Friendly. *Kindly, favourably in-
clined.*
Judg. 19. 3 after her. to speak *f.*
Ruth 2. 13 thou hast spoken *f.* unto
Prov. 18. 24 man must show him. *f.*
R. V. Judg. 19. 3; Ruth 2. 13
kindly; Prov. 18. 24 doth it to his
own destruction

Friendship. *Friendship.*
Prov. 22. 24 make no *f.* wi. angry m.
Jas. 4. 4 know ye not that *f.* of worl.

Fringe. *Border, wreath.*
Num. 15. 38 bid them make *f.* in
Deut. 22. 12 thou shalt make thee *f.*

Fro. *Turn back.*
Gen. 8. 7 raven went forth to and *f.*
Fro is used mostly in connection
with *to*, after such verbs as driven,
go, run, toss, walk, etc.

Frog. *Frog.*
Ex. 8. 2–13 smite thy borders with *f.*
Ps. 78. 45 he sent *f.* . . which destr.
Rev. 16. 13 saw . . unclean sp. like *f.*

From. *Out of.*
Gen. 2. 6 went up a mist *f.* the earth
Mat. 3. 17 a voice *f.* heaven, saying
etc., etc.

Front. *Face, forward part, before.*
2 Sam. 10. 9 saw that *f.* of the bat.
2 Chr. 3. 4 porch that was in *f.* of
R. V. 2 Chr. 3. 4 before

Frontier. *End, extremity, border.*
Ezek. 25. 9 his cities wh. are on his *f.*

Frontlets. *Brow-bands.*
Ex. 13. 16 *f.* between their eyes
Deut. 6. 8 and they shall be as *f.*

Frost. *Rime, ice, cold.*
Gen. 31. 40 day, and the. *f.* by night
Job 37. 10 by br. of G. *f.* is given.
Ps. 78. 47 their sycomore trees with *f.*
Jer. 36. 30 cast . . in night to the *f.*
R. V. Job 37. 10 ice

Froward. *Tortuous, perverse,
wayward.*
Deut. 32. 20 they are a *f.* generation
2 Sam. 22. 27 with *f.* thou wilt show
Job 1. 13 counsel of the *f.* is carried
Ps. 101. 4 *f.* heart shalt depart fr. me
Prov. 3. 32 the *f.* is abomination
4. 24 put away from thee a *f.* mouth
1 Pet. 2. 18 to the good, also to *f.*
R. V. 2 8am. 22. 27; Ps. 18. 26;
Prov. 3. 32. 11. 20 perverse; 21. 8
him that is laden with guilt is exceeding crooked.

Frowardly. *With back-turning.*
Isa. 57. 17 went *f.* in the way of

Frowardness. *Perverseness.*
Prov. 2. 14 delight in *f.* of the wicked
6. 14; 10. 32

Frozen. *Struck together.*
Job 38. 30 and face of the deep is *f.*

Fruit. *Fruit.*
Gen. 1. 11 the *f.* tree yielding *f.* after
Ex. 10. 15 did eat of *f.* of the tree
Lev. 19. 23 shall count the *f.* thereof
Num. 13. 20 bring of *f.* of the land
Deut. 7. 13 bless *f.* of the womb
Josh. 5. 12 did eat *f.* of the land of C.
Judg. 9. 11 should I forsake . . my *f.*
2 K. 19. 29 plant vineyards and eat *f.*
Neh. 9. 36 land, to eat the *f.* thereof
Ps. 1. 3 bringeth forth *f.* in season
Prov. 8. 19 my *f.* is better than gold
Eccl. 2. 5 trees . . of all kind of *f.*
S. of S. 2. 3 and his *f.* was sweet
Isa. 3. 10 they eat *f.* of their doings

Jer. 11. 16 tree, fair and of goodly *f.*
Lam. 2. 20 shall .. women e. their *f.*
Ezek. 17. 8 that it might bear *f.*
Hos. 9. 16 they shall bear no *f.*, tho.
Joel 2. 22 the tree beareth her *f.*
Am. 2. 9 I destroyed his *f.* fr. above
Mic. 6. 7 *f.* of my body for the sin
Zech. 8. 12 the vine shall give her *f.*
Mal. 3. 11 not destroy *f.* of your gr.
Mat. 3. 8 bring .. *f.* meet for repen.
  7. 16; 12. 33; 13. 8; 21. 19, 34, 43
Mark 4. 7 cho., and it yielded no *f.*
Luke 1. 42 blessed be *f.* of thy w.
  3. 8; 6. 43; 8. 8; 12. 17; 13. 6
John 4. 36 gath *f.* unto life eternal
  12. 24; 15. 2, 4, 5, 8, 16
Acts 2. 30 the *f.* of his loins, accor.
Rom. 1. 13 that I might have .. *f.*
1 Cor. 9. 7 and eat. not of *f.* thereof
2 Cor. 9. 10 incr. *f.* of your right.
Gal. 5. 22 the *f.* of Spirit is love
Eph. 5. 9 *f.* of Spirit is .. goodness
Phil. 1. 11 filled with *f.* of right.
Col. 1. 6 and bringeth forth *f.* as
2 Tim. 2. 6 be .. partakers of the *f.*
Heb. 12. 11 yield. the .. *f.* of right.
Jas. 3. 17 full of mercy and good *f.*
Jude 12 trees whose *f.* withereth
Rev. 22. 2 bare twelve man. of *f.*
R. V. Ex. 23. 10; Deut. 22. 9 in-
  crease; Lev. 25. 15 crops; Isa.
  28. 4; S. of S. 6. 11 green plant;
  Mic. 7. 1 fig'; Am. 7. 14 trees;
  Luke 12. 18 corn; Jude 12
  autumn trees

Fruitful. *Bearing fruit, pro-*
ductive.
Gen. 1. 22 be *f.* and multiply and f.
Ex. 1. 7 children of Israel were *f.*
Lev. 26. 9 I will make you *f.*, and
Ps. 128. 3 wife shall be as a *f.* vine
Isa. 5. 1 vineyard in a very *f.* hill
Jer. 4. 26 *f.* place was a wilderness
Ezek. 17. 5 planted it in a *f.* field
Hos. 13. 15 be *f.* among .. brethren
Acts 14. 17 give us rain .. and *f.* sea.
Col. 1. 10 *f.* in every good work, and

Frustrate. *Make void, put aside.*
Ez. 4. 5 to *f.* their purpose, all the
Isa. 44. 25 *f.* the tokens of liars
Gal. 2. 21 not *f.* the grace of God
R. V. Gal. 2. 21 make void

Fryingpan. *Pan, kettle.*
Lev. 2. 7; 7. 9 offer. baken in *f.* p.

Fuel. *Good, matter for burning.*
Isa. 9. 5 with burn. and *f.* of fire
Ezek. 15. 4 cast into the fire for *f.*

Fugitive. *One fleeing, wanderer.*
Gen. 4. 12 a *f.* and vag. .. thou be
Judg. 12. 4 ye Gileadites are *f.* of E.
2 K. 25. 11 the *f.* that fell away
Isa. 15. 5 *f.* shall flee unto Zoar
Ezek. 17. 21 *f.* with all his bands
R. V. 2 K. 25. 11 those; Isa. 15. 5
  nobles

Fulfil. *Fill in, up or out, complete,*
finish, end, accomplish, make full.
Gen. 25. 24 when her days .. were *f.*
  29. 27 *f.* her week, and we will
Ex. 23. 26 num. of thy days I will *f.*
Lev. 12. 4 days of her purif. be *f.*
Num. 6. 5 until days be *f.* in which
2 Sam. 14. 22 k. hath *f.* the request
1 K. 2. 27 *f.* the word of the Lord
1 Chr. 22. 13 heed to *f.* the statutes
2 Chr. 6. 4 hath with his hands *f.*
Ez. 1. 1 that the word .. might be *f.*
Job 36. 17 hast *f.* the judgment of
Ps. 20. 5 Lord *f.* all thy petitions
Jer. 44. 25 and *f.* with your hand
Lam. 2. 17 he hath *f.* his word
Ezek. 5. 2 when days of .. siege are *f.*
Dan. 10. 3 till three weeks were *f.*
Mat. 1. 22 that it might be *f.* which
  2. 15; 8. 17; 12. 17; 13. 35; 21. 4
Mark 1. 15 the time is *f.*, and the
Luke 4. 21 this day is this scrip. *f.*
John 3. 29 this my joy theref. is *f.*
Acts 1. 16 scrip. must have been *f.*
Rom. 2. 27 if it *f.* the law, judge
2 Cor. 10. 6 when your obed. is *f.*
Gal. 5. 14 all the law is *f.* in one
Eph. 2. 3 *f.* the desires of the flesh
Phil. 2. 2 *F.* ye my joy, that ye be
Col. 1. 25 ma. minister. to *f.* the word
2 Thes. 1. 11 *f.* all the good pleas.

Jas. 2. 8 if ye *f.* the royal law ac.
Rev. 15. 8 till .. sev. plagues were *f.*
R. V. 2 Sam. 14. 22 performed; 1
  Chr. 22. 13 observe to do; Job.
  36 17 art full of; Ezek. 1. 1; Mat.
  5. 18; 24. 34; Mark 13. 4; Luke
  21. 32; Rev. 17. 17 accomplished;
  Mat. 27. 35; 15. 28 ——; Acts 13.
  22 who shall do; Rev. 15. 8: 20.
  3 finished

Full. *Filled, plentifnl, satiated.*
Gen. 41. 7 thine ears dev. .. the *f.*
Ex. 8. 21 h. of Egypt. .. be *f.* of fl.
Lev. 16. 12 take censer *f.* of burn.
Num. 22. 18 give me his house *f.*
Deut. 6. 11 houses *f.* of all good th.
Judg. 6. 38 winged .. bowl *f.* of w.
Ruth 1. 21 I went out *f.* and the L.
1 Sam. 2. 5 that were *f.* have hired
2 Sam. 8. 2 with one *f.* line to keep
2 K. 4. 6 when the vessels were *f.*
1 Chr. 11. 13 parcel of gr. *f.* of bar.
2 Chr. 24. 15 Jehoiada was *f.* of days
Neh. 9. 25 houses *f.* of all goods
Esth. 3. 5 then was H. *f.* of wrath
Job 7. 4 and I am *f.* of tossings
Ps. 17. 14 they are *f.* of children
Prov. 17. 1 than an h. *f.* of sacrif.
Eccl. 1. 7 in sea, yet the sea is not *f.*
Isa. 1. 21 city .. was *f.* of judgment
Jer. 4. 12 a *f.* wind from those plac.
Lam. 1. 1 city solitary that was *f.*
Ezek. 1. 18 rings .. *f.* of eyes round
Dan. 10. 2 mourning three *f.* weeks
Joel 2. 24 floors .. be *f.* of wheat
Mic. 3. 8 I am *f.* of power by spirit
Hab. 3. 3 earth was *f.* of .. praise
Zech. 8. 5 streets .. be *f.* of boys
Mat. 14. 20 took up .. twelve bas. *f.*
Mark 4. 28 after that the *f.* corn
Luke 4. 1 Jesus, being *f.* of H. G.
John 1. 14 *f.* of grace and truth
Acts 6. 3 men *f.* of the Holy Ghost
Rom. 1. 29 *f.* of envy, murder, deb.
1 Cor. 4. 8 ye are *f.*, now ye are rich
Phil. 4. 18 I am *f.*, having received
Jas. 3. 8 tong. is *f.* of deadly poison
2 Pet. 2. 14 eyes *f.* of adultery be *f.*
1 John 1. 4 Hav. that your joy may
2 John 8 that we receive *f.* reward
Rev. 4. 6 four beasts *f.* of eyes
R. V. Lev. 2. 2 a; 2 K. 4. 2 fresh;
  Prov. 27. 20 satisfied: Acts 7. 23
  well nigh; Heb. 10. 22 ful-
  ness; Rev. 16. 10 darkened

Fuller. *Washer, cloth-dresser.*
2 K. 18. 17 way of the *f*'s field
Isa. 7. 3 highway of the *f*'s field
Mal. 3. 2 fire, and fuller *f*'s sope
Mark 9. 3 as no *f.* on earth can

Fully. *Completely.*
Num. 7. 1 day that M. had *f.* set
Ruth 2. 11 hath been *f.* showed me
1 K. 11 6 S. went not *f.* after .. L.
Eccl. 81. 11 heart .. of men is *f.* set
Nah. 1. 10 devoured as stubble *f.*
Acts 2. 1 day of Pent. was *f.* come
Rom. 15. 19 *f.* preached the gos. of
2 Tim. 3. 10 hast *f.* known my doc.
Rev. 14. 18 her grapes are *f.* ripe
R. V. Acts 2. 1 now; 2 Tim. 3.
  10 ——

Fulness. *Being full.*
Num. 18. 27 *f.* of the winepress
Deut. 33. 16 things of earth and *f.*
1 Chr. 16. 32 sea .. and the *f.* thereof
Job 20. 22 in *f.* of his sufficiency
Ps. 24. 1 e. is the Lord's, and the *f.*
Ez. 16. 49 *f.* of bread, and abund.
John 1. 16 and of his *f.* have we rec.
Rom. 11. 12 how much more their *f.*
1 Cor. 10. 26 e. is the L's. and .. *f.*
Gal. 4. 4 when *f.* of time was come
Eph. 1. 10 in dispensation of the *f.*
Col. 1. 19 in him should all *f.* dwell
R. V. 1 Cor. 10. 28 ——

Furbish. *Scour, polish.*
Jer. 46. 4 *f.* the spears, put on brig.
Ezek. 21. 9–11, 28 a sword is also *f.*

Furious. *Heated, wrathful.*
Prov. 22. 24 with *f.* man .. not go
Ezek. 5. 15 ex. judg. in *f.* rebukes
Dan. 2. 12 the king was very *f.*
Nah. 1. 2 L. revengeth and is *f.*
R. V. Prov. 22. 24 wrathful; Nah.
  1. 2 full of wrath

Furiously. *Madly, heatedly.*
2 K. 9. 20 Jehu .. for he driveth *f.*
Ezek. 23. 25 shall deal *f.* with thee

Furlong. *Stade, eighth of a mile.*
Luke 24. 13 from Jer. threescore *f.*
John 6. 19 about five and twenty ... *f.*
Rev. 14. 20 space of a thousand .. *f.*

Furnace. *Oven, smelting pot or*
place.
Gen. 15. 17 a smoking *f.*, and burn.
Ex. 9. 8 take to you ashes of the *f.*
Deut. 4. 20 brought you out of .. *f.*
1 K 8. 51 bro. fr. midst of *f.* of iron
Neh. 3. 11 Hash. repaired the .. *f.*
Ps. 12. 6 silver tried in a *f.* of earth
Prov. 17. 3 pot for sil., *f.* for gold
Isa. 48. 10 chosen thee in *f.* of afflic.
Jer. 11. 4 brot. them .. from iron *f.*
Ezek. 22. 18 brass .. in midst of *f.*
Dan. 3. 6, 11, 15 in midst of fiery *f.*
Mat. 13. 42 shall cast them into a *f.*
Rev. 1. 15 as if they burned in *f.*

Furnish. *Fit out. equip, supply.*
Deut. 15. 14 shalt *f.* him liberally
1 K. 9. 11 Hir. .. *f.* Sol. with cedar
Ps. 78. 19 can G. *f.* tab. in wilder.
Prov. 9. 2 she hath also *f.* her table
Isa. 65. 11 th. *f.* the drink offering
Jer. 46. 19 *f.* thyself to go into
Mat. 22. 10 wedding was *f.* with
Mark 14. 15 a large upper room *f.*
Luke 22. 12 show .. upper room *f.*
2 Tim. 3. 17 *f.* unto all good works
R. V. Ps. 78. 19 prepare; Isa. 65.
  11 fill up; Mat. 22. 10 filled

Furniture. *Bolster.*
Gen. 31. 34 put them in .. camel's *f.*
Vessel, implement.
Ex. 31. 7 the *f.* of the tabernacle
  31. 8, 9, 14; 39. 33.
Nah. 2. 9. glory out of all pleas. *f.*
R. V. Ex. 31. 8, 9; 35. 14 vessels.

Furrow. *Trench, groove.*
Job 31. 38 *f.* likewise .. complain
Ps. 65. 10 thou settlest the *f.* thereof
Ezek. 17. 7 water it by the *f.* plant.
Hos. 10. 4 spring. as hemlock in *f.*
  10. 10 build themselves in two *f.*
R. V. Ezek. 17. 7, 10 beds; Hos.
  10. 10 transgressions

Further. *(v.)* *Lift up, prosper.*
Ez. 8. 36 they *f.* the people and how
Bring out, encourage.
Ps. 140. 8 *f.* not his wicked device

Further. *(adv.)* *Moreover.*
Eccl. 12. 12 and *f.*, by these, my son
More, yet, again.
Deut. 20. 8 officers shall speak *f.*
Esth. 9. 12 what is thy request *f.*
Mat. 26. 65 what *f.* need have we
Mark 5. 35 why tr. the Master *f.*
Luke 22. 71 what need we *f.* wit.
Acts 21. 28 and *f.* brought Greeks
Heb. 7. 11 what *f.* need that ano.
Farther.
Num. 22. 26 angel of L. went *f.*
Job 38. 11 hitherto .. come, but no *f.*
Luke 24. 28 he would have gone *f.*
Acts 4. 17 But that it spread no *f.*
R. V. Acts 12. 5 ——; 21. 28 more-
  over; 27. 28 after a little space;
  Eccl. 12. 12 furthermore

Furtherance. R. V. *progress.*
Phil. 1. 12, 25 fallen .. unto the *f.*

Furthermore. *Moreover, also,*
again.
Ex. 4. 6 L. said *f.* unto him, Put now
Ezek. 8. 6 he said *f.* unto me, Son
1 Thes. 4. 1 *f.* then we beseech you
Heb. 12. 9 *f.* we have had fathers
R. V. 1 Sam. 26. 10; 1 Chr. 29. 1;
  Ezek. 8. 6 and; 1 Chr. 17. 10; Job
  34. 1 moreover; 2 Cor. 2. 12 now;
  1 Thes. 4. 1 finally

Fury. *Heat, wrath, fierceness.*
Gen. 27. 44 until thy bro's. *f.* turn
Lev. 26. 28 walk contrary .. in *f.*
Job 20. 23 cast the *f.* .. upon him
Isa. 27. 4 *f.* is not in me; who wo. set
  34. 2; 42. 25; 51. 13; 63. 3; 66. 15
Jer 4. 4 lest *f.* come forth like fire
  6. 11; 7. 20; 10. 25; 23. 19; 44. 6
Lam. 2. 4 poured out his *f.* like fi.
Ezek. 5. 13 will cause my *f.* to rest
  6. 12; 7. 8; 8. 18; 13. 13; 16. 38
Dan. 8. 6 he goat ran unto him in *f.*

G.

Gain (*n.*). *Price, increase, profit.*
Judg. 5. 19 kings of C. took no *g.*
Job 22. 3. is it *g.* to him, that thou
Prov. 1. 19 one that is greedy of *g.*
Isa. 33. 15 despiseth . . *g.* of oppres.
Ezek. 22. 13 smitten . . at dishon. *g.*
Dan. 11. 39 divide the land for *g.*
Acts 16. 16 brought masters much *g.*
2 Cor. 12. 17 did I make a *g.* of you
Phil. 1. 21 to l. is C., and to die is *g.*
1 Tim. 6. 5 suppos. that *g.* is godli.
Jas. 4. 13 buy and sell, and get *g.*
R. V. Prov. 28. 8; Dan. 11. 39 price;
   Acts 19. 24 little business ; 2 Cor.
   12. 17, 18 take advantage

Gain (*v.*). *Get, inquire, profit.*
Job 27. 8 what hope . . tho. he h. *g.*
Ezek. 22. 12 thou hast greedily *g.*
Dan. 2. 8 that ye would *g.* the time
Mat. 16. 26 if ye . . *g.* whole world
   18. 25 ; 25. 17, 20, 22
Mark 8. 36 *g.* whole world, and lose
Luke 9. 25 ; 19. 15, 16, 18
Acts 27. 21 *g.* this harm and loss
1 Cor. 9. 19 ser. . . that I might *g.*
R. V. Luke 19. 16, 18 made ; Acts
   27. 21 gotten . . injury.

Gainsay. *Say against.*
Luke 21. 15 shall not be able to *g.*
Rom. 10. 21 disobedient and *g.* peo.

Gainsayer. *Speaker against.*
Tit. 1. 9 and to convince the *g.*

Gainsaying. *Speaking against.*
Acts 10. 29 came I . . without *g.*
Jude 11 perished in the *g.* of Core

Galbanum. *Bitter gum.*
Ex. 30. 34 take . . thee s. spices . . *g.*

Gall. *Bitter thing, venom.*
Deut. 29. 18 a root that beareth *g.*
Job 16. 13 he poureth out my *g.*
   20. 14 it is the *g.* of asps within him
Ps. 69. 21 gave me . . *g.* for . . meat
Jer. 8. 14 given us w. of *g.* to drink
Lam. 3. 5 compassed me with *g.* and
Am. 6. 12 turned judgment into *g.*
Mat. 27. 34 vinegar . . mingled w. *g.*
Acts 8. 22 art in the *g.* of bitterness

Gallant. *Honorable, glorious.*
Isa. 33. 21 neither shall *g.* ship pass

Gallery. *Portico, corridor.*
Ezek. 41. 15, 16 *g.* round about on
   42. 3, 5 *g.* against *g.*, three stories
Ringlet, tress.
S. of S. 7. 5 king is held in the *g.*
R. V. S. of S. 7. 5 tresses.

Galley. *Oar-ship.*
Isa. 33. 21 shall go no *g.* with oars

Gallows. *Wood, tree.*
Esth. 5. 14 let *g.* be made fifty c.
   6. 4 ; 7. 9 ; 8. 7 ; 9. 13, 25

Gap. *Breach.*
Ezek. 13. 5 have not gone . . into *g.*
   22. 30 stand in *g.* before me for the l.

Gape. *Open wide, yawn.*
Job 16. 10 they have *g.* upon me
Ps. 22. 13 *g.* on me with . . mouths

Garden. *Planted place, orchard.*
Gen. 2. 8 God planted a *g.* east.
   2. 9, 10, 15, 16 ; 3. 1, 3, 8, 10 ; 13. 10
Num. 24. 6 as *g.* by the river side
Deut. 11. 10 waterest it . . as a *g.*
1 K. 21. 2 have it for *g.* of herbs
2 K. 9. 27 fled by way of *g.* house
Neh. 3. 15 pool of S. by king's *g.*
Esth. 1. 5 *g.* of the king's palace
Job 8. 16 branch shooteth . . in *g.*
S. of S. 4. 12 *g.* inclo. is . . sister's s.
   4. 15 ; 5. 1 ; 6. 2, 11 ; 8. 13
Eccl. 2. 5 made me *g.* and orchard.
Isa. 1. 29 be confounded for the *g.*
   1. 30 ; 51. 3 ; 58. 11 ; 61. 11 ; 65. 3
Jer. 29. 5 plant *g.* . . and eat fruit
Lam. 2. 6 tabernacle as if it were *g.*
Ezek. 28. 13 been in E. the *g.* of G.
Am. 4. 9 when your *g.* and viney.
Luke 13. 19 took, and cast into . . *g.*
John 18. 1 over . . Cedron, w. was *g.*
   18. 26 ; 19. 41

Gardener. *Who gardens.*
John 20. 15 sup. him to be the *g.*

Garland. *Wreath, chaplet.*
Acts 14. 13 brought oxen and *g.* unto

Garlick. *Garlic.*
Num. 11. 5 the leeks, onions, and *g.*

Garment. *Mantle, cloak, clothing*
Gen. 25. 25 red . . like an hairy *g.*
Ex. 28. 2 make holy *g.* for Aaron
Lev. 6. 11 he shall put off his *g.*
Num. 20. 26 strip Aaron of his *g.*
Deut. 22. 5 nei. m. put on wom. *g.*
Josh. 9. 5 and old *g.* upon them
Judg. 8. 25 spread *g.* and . . cast her
1 Sam. 18. 4 stripped himself of . . *g.*
2 Sam. 13. 31 the king . . tare his *g.*
1 K. 10. 25 brought *g.* and armor
2 K. 5. 22 give . . two changes of *g.*
1 Chr. 19. 4 cut off . . *g.* in midst of
Ex. 2. 69 gave . . hund. priests' *g.*
Neh. 7. 70 fiv. . . hun. . . priests' *g.*
Esth. 8. 15 *g.* of fine lin. and purple
Job 13. 28 consum. as *g.* . . mo. eaten
Ps. 22. 18 they part my *g.* among th.
Prov. 20. 16 take . . *g.* that is surety
Eccl. 9. 8 let thy *g.* be always white
Isa. 50. 9 th. all shall wax old as a *g.*
   51. 8 ; 52. 1 ; 59. 6 ; 61. 10 ; 63. 1
Jer. 36. 24 not afr. nor rent their *g.*
Lam. 4. 14 men could not touch . *g.*
Ezek. 16. 18 took thy broidered *g.*
Dan. 3. 21 bound in . . hats and *g.*
Joel 2. 13 rend you hearts, not . . *g.*
Mic. 2. 8 ye pull off robe with *g.*
Hag. 2. 12 bear . . flesh in skirt of *g.*
Zech. 3. 3 J. was clo. with filthy *g.*
Mat. 9. 16 put. new cloth unto old *g.*
   9. 20 ; 14. 36 ; 21. 8 ; 22. 12 ; 23. 5
Mark 10. 50 cast. away his *g.*, rose
Luke 19. 35 cast their *g.* upon . . colt
John 19. 23 soldiers . . took his *g.*
Acts 9. 39 showing the . .*g.* which D.
Heb. 1. 11 shall wax old as doth *g.*
Jas 5. 2 riches are corrupt., and *g.*
Jude 23 hating . . the *g.* spotted
Rev. 3. 4 few . . have not defiled . *g.*
R. V. Deut. 22. 11 mingled stuff;
   Judg. 14. 12, 13, 19 ; 1 K. 10. 25 ;
   2 K. 5. 22, 23 ; Ps. 109. 19 ; Dan.
   11. 9 raiment; Josh. 7. 21 ; Zech.
   13. 4 mantle; Esth. 8. 15 ; Mark
   16. 5 robe ; 1 Sam. 18. 4 ; 2 Sam.
   20. 8 ; Luke 24. 4 apparel ; Mark
   13. 16 ; Luke 22. 36 cloak ; Ps. 69
   11 clothing ; 104. 6 vesture; Mat.
   27. 31

Garner. *Granary, barn.*
Ps. 144. 13 That our *g.* may be full
Joel 1. 17 the *g.* are laid desolate
Mat. 3. 12 gather his wheat into *g.*
Luke 3. 17 will gath. wheat into . . *g.*

Garnish. *Adorn, put in order.*
2 Chr. 3. 6 *g.* . . house with prec. s.
Job 26. 13 he hath *g.* the heavens
Mat. 12. 44 house emp., swept and *g.*
Luke 11. 25 cometh, he findeth it *g.*
Rev. 21. 19 *g.* with . . precious stones
R. V. Rev. 21. 19 adorned

Garrison. *Station, armed force.*
1 Sam. 10. 5 where the *g.* of . Phil.
2 Sam. 23. 14 *g.* of the Phil. was in
1 Chr. 11. 16 Phil. *g.* was then at B.
2 Chr. 17. 2 set *g.* in land of Judah
Ezek. 26. 11 *g.* shall go down to gr.
2 Cor. 11. 32 kept the city . . with *g.*
R. V. Ezek. 26. 11 thy pillars of
   strength; 2 Cor. 11. 32 guarded

Gat. *See* **Get.**

Gate. *Door, opening, entrance.*
Gen. 19. 1 Lot sat in *g.* of Sodom
Ex. 20. 10 nor stranger within thy *g.*
Num. 4. 26 hanging for door of *g.*
Deut. 3. 5 fenced with high walls, *g.*
Josh. 2. 5 time of shutting the *g.*
Judg. 5. 8 then was war in the *g.*
Ruth 4. 1 went Boaz up to the *g.*
1 Sam. 4. 18 fell . . by side of the *g.*
2 Sam. 3. 27 Joab took him . . in *g.*
1 K. 22. 10 entrance of *g.* of Sama.
2 K. 7. 1 for shekel in *g.* of Samaria
1 Chr. 9. 18 in in the king's *g.* eastw.
2 Chr. 8. 14 porters . . at every *g.*
Neh. 1. 3 the *g.* thereof are burned
Esth. 2. 19 Mordecai sat in king's *g.*
Job. 5. 4 children one crushed in *g.*
Ps 9. 13 lifted me from *g.* of death
Prov. 1. 21 crieth in opening of *g.*
S. of S. 7. 4 by *g.* of Bath-rabbim

Isa. 14. 31 howl, O *g.*, cry, O city
Jer. 1. 15 at ent. of *g.* of Jerusalen
Lam. 1. 4 all her *g.* are desolate
Ezek. 8. 3 to door of inner *g.* that
   40. 3-48 ; 44. 1-17 ; 46. 1-19
Dan. 2. 49 Daniel sat in *g.* of king
Am. 5. 10 hate him that rebuk. in *g.*
Obad. 11 foreigners ent. into his *g.*
Mic. 1. 9 come unto *g.* of my people
Nah. 2. 6 *g.* of rivers shall be open.
Zeph. 1. 10 noise from the fish *g.*
Zech. 8. 16 and peace in your *g.*
Mat. 7. 13 enter ye in at the strait *g.*
   16. 18 *g.* of hell shall not prevail
Luke 7. 12 came nigh to *g.* of city
Acts 3. 10 sat for alms at Beautiful *g.*
Heb. 13. 12 Jesus suf. without the *g.*
Rev. 21. 12 great wall . . and twel. *g.*
R. V. Esth. 5. 1 entrance ; Ezek.
   40. 6——; Neh. 13. 19 ; Isa. 45. 1,
   2 ; S. of S. 7. 13 ; Luke 13. 24 ;
   Acts. 4. 2 door, doors

Gather. *Bring together, assemble,*
collect.
Gen. 6. 21 food . . thou shalt *g.* in
Ex. 15. 8 waters were *g.* together
Lev. 25. 3 prune . . and *g.* in fruit
Num. 11. 16 *g.* me seventy men
Deut. 4. 10 *g.* me the people togeth.
Josh. 24. 1 Joshua *g.* tribes of Israel
Judg. 3. 13 he *g.* the children of A.
Ruth 2. 7 let me . . *g.* after reapers
1 Sam. 5. 8 *g.* all the lords of Phil.
2 Sam. 21. 13 *g.* bones of them that
1 K. 10. 26 Solomon *g.* chariots and
2 K. 22. 20 *g.* thee unto thy fathers
1 Chr. 19. 17 he *g.* all Israel and
2 Chr. 24. 11 *g.* money in abundance
Ez. 3. 1 *g.* themselves . . as one m.
Neh. 7. 5 *g.* the nobles and rulers
Esth. 2. 8 when . . maidens were *g.*
Job 34. 14 if he *g.* . . his spirit and
Ps. 26. 9 *g.* not my soul with sin.
Prov. 30. 4 who *g.* . . wind in his fists
Eccl. 2. 26 to *g.* and to heap up
S. of S. 5. 1 have *g.* my myrrh with
Isa. 10. 14 as one *g.* eggs . . have I
Jer. 10. 17 *g.* up thy wares out of la
Ezek. 24. 4 *g.* the pieces thereof
Dan. 3. 3 *g.* unto the dedication
Hos. 1. 11 the children of Is. be *g.*
Joel 1. 14 *g.* the elders and all inh.
Mic. 1. 7 *g.* it of the hire of an har.
Nah. 2. 10 faces of all *g.* blackness
Zeph. 3. 19 *g.* her that was driven
Zech. 10. 8 will hiss for them and *g.*
Mat. 7. 16 do men *g.* gr. of thorns
Mark 5. 21 much people *g.* to him
Luke 3. 17 *g.* wheat into the garner
John 4. 36 *g.* fruit unto eternal life
Acts 28. 3 Paul *g.* bundle of sticks
1 Cor. 5. 4 when ye are *g.* together
Eph. 1. 10 he might *g.* togeth. in one
Rev. 14. 18 *g.* clusters of the vine
R. V. Gen. 49. 2 ; Ex. 35. 1 ; Lev.
   8. 3 ; Num. 8. 9 ; 16. 3 ; 19. 42 ;
   20. 2, 8 ; Deut. 4. 10 ; 31. 12, 18 ;
   Judg. 9. 6 ; 20. 1 ; 1 Chr. 13. 5 ;
   Ezek. 38. 13 ; Mic. 4. 11 assembled ;
   Ex. 9. 19 hasten in ; Job 11. 10
   call unto judgment; Isa. 62. 9 gar-
   nered ; Jer. 6. 1 flee for safety;
   51. 11 hold firm; Joel 2. 6 ; Nah.
   2. 10 waxed pale ; Eph. 1. 10 sum
   up.

Gatherer. *Who gathers.*
Am. 7. 14 was *g.* of sycamore fruit

Gathering. *Assembling, collect-*
ing.
Gen. 1. 10 *g.* together of the waters
Num. 15. 33 that found him *g.* sticks
1 K. 17. 10 woman was there *g.* st'ks
Isa. 32. 10 the *g.* shall not come
1 Cor. 16. 2 be no *g.* when I come
2 Thes. 2. 1 and by our *g.* unto him
R. V. Gen. 49. 10 obedience ; 2 Chr.
   20. 25 taking ; Isa. 32. 10 ingathering ; 1 Cor. 16. 2 collections

Gave. *See* **Give.**

Gay. R. V. *fine.*
Jas. 2. 3 that weareth *g.* clothing

Gaze. *See, look, behold.*
Ex. 19. 21 break through . . to *g.*
Acts 1. 11 why stand ye *g.* up int
R. V. Acts 1. 11 looking

Gazing. *Make a spectacle.*

Nah. 3. 6 will set thee as a *g*. stock
Heb. 10. 33 ye were made a *g*. stock

Gender. *To beget.*
Lev. 19. 19 shall not let thy cattle *g*.
Job 38. 29 frost .. who hath *g*. it
Gal. 4. 24 one which *g*. to bondage
2 Tim. 2. 23 knowing .. they *g*. strife.
R. V. Gal. 4. 24 bearing children

Genealogy. *Family record. pedigree.*
1 Chr. 5. 1 *g*. is not to be reckoned
2 Chr. 12. 15 in book .. concern *g*.
Ez. 2. 62 that were reckoned by *g*.
Neh. 7. 5 might be reckoned by *g*.
1 Tim. 1. 4 neither heed endless *g*.
Tit. 3. 9 avoid *g*. and contentions

General. R. V. *captain.*
1 Chr. 27. 34 *g*. of k.'s army was J.
Common to all.
Heb. 12. 23 *g*. assembly and church

Generally. *In general.*
2 Sam. 17. 11 Is. be *g*. gathered unto
Jer. 48. 38 lamenta. *g*. on house-top
R. V. Jer. 48. 38 everywhere

Generation. *Circle, period.*
Gen. 6. 9 Noah, man perfect in his *g*.
Ex. 1. 6 Joseph died, and all that *g*.
Lev. 3. 17 per. statute for your *g*.
Num. 10. 8 ord. for. through. your *g*.
Deut. 1. 35 men of this evil *g*. see
Josh. 22. 27 you, and our *g*. after us
Judg. 2. 10 all that *g*. were gathered
1 Chr. 16. 15 com. to a thousand *g*.
Esth. 9. 28 kept throughout every *g*.
Job 42. 16 Job saw .. even four *g*.
Ps. 12. 7 preserve them from this *g*.
Prov. 27. 24 crown endure to ev. *g*.
Eccl. 1. 4 one *g*. passeth away, and
Isa. 13. 20 dwelt in from *g*. to *g*.
Jer. 2. 31 O *g*., see ye the word
Lam. 5. 19 thy throne from *g*. to *g*.
Dan. 4. 3 dominion is from *g*. to *g*.
Joel 1. 3 their childʳⁱⁿ another *g*.
Mat. 1. 17 all the *g*. are fourteen *g*.
Mark 8. 12 why doth .. *g*. seek .. sign
Luke 1. 48 all *g*. shall call me bless.
21. 32 this *g*. shall not pass away
Acts 2. 40 save your. from this *g*.
Col. 1. 26 hid from ages and .. *g*.
Heb. 3. 10 grieved with that *g*.
1 Pet. 2. 9 But ye are a chosen *g*.
Births.
Gen. 2. 4 the *g*. of the heavens
Ex. 6. 16 according to their *g*.
Num. 1. 20 by their *g*., after fam.
Ruth 4. 18 these are *g*. of Pharez
1 Chr. 1. 29 These are their *g*.
R. V. Mat. 3. 7; 23. 33; 12. 34;
Luke 3. 7 ye offspring; 1 Pet. 2. 9
an elect race

Gentle. *Yielding, mild.*
1 Thes. 2. 7 we were *g*. among you
2 Tim. 2. 24 be *g*. .. apt to teach
Tit. 3. 2 *g*., showing all meekness
Jas. 3. 17. *g*., easy to be intreated
1 Pet. 2. 18 not only to the *g*., but

Gentleness. *Humility, kindness.*
2 Sam. 22. 36 thy *g*. hath made me
Ps. 18. 35 *g*. hath made me great
2 Cor. 10. 1 beseech you by *g*. of C.
Gal. 5. 22 fruit of the Spirit is *g*.
R. V. Gal. 5. 22 kindness

Gently. *Kindly, patiently.*
2 Sam. 18. 5 *g*. .. with .. young man

Get. *Go, betake, obtain.*
Gen. 12. 1 *g*. thee out fs my country
Ex. 5. 11 Go ye, *g*. you straw where
Lev. 14. 32 hand is not able to *g*.
Num. 14. 40 *g*. them up into mount
Deut. 3. 27 *g*. thee up into Pisgah
Josh. 2. 16 *g*. you to the mountain
Judg. 7. 9 *g*. thee down unto the host
Ruth 3. 3 *g*. thee down .. to field
1 Sam. 15. 6 *g*. you down from .. A.
2 Sam. 19. 3 peo. *g*. them by stealth
1 K. 1. 13 *g*. thee unto king David
2 K. 7. 12 and shall *g*. into the city
2 Chr. 10. 18 speed to *g*. him up
Neh. 9. 10 so didst thou *g*. .. name
Job 31. 25 because mine hand had *g*.
Ps. 116. 3 pains of hell *g*. hold on
Prov. 6. 33 dishonour shall he *g*.
Eccl. 3. 6 time to *g*., time to lose
Isa. 22. 15 *g*. thee to this treasurer
Jer. 5. 5 *g*. me unto the great men
Lam. 5. 9 we *g*. our bread with per.

Ezek. 3. 4 *g*. thee to house of Israel
Dan. 9. 15 God hast *g*. thee renown
Joel 3. 13 come, *g*. you down, for
Zech. 6. 7 G. you hence, walk to and
Mat. 14. 22 his dis. to *g*. into a ship
Mark 8. 33 G. thee behind me, Sat.
Luke 9. 12 may go .. and *g*. victuals
Acts 7. 3 *g*. thee out of thy country
2 Cor. 2. 11 lest Sat. *g*. an advant.
Jas. 4. 13 buy, sell, and *g*. gain
R. V. Deut. 28 43 mount; Prov.
17. 16; Jer. 13. 1; 19. 1 buy; Eccl.
3. 6 seek; Zeph. 3. 19 make; Mat.
14. 22; Mark 6. 45 enter

Getting. *Acquiring, obtaining.*
Gen. 31. 18 car. away cattle of his *g*.
Prov. 4. 7 with *g*. get understanding
21. 6 *g*. of treas. by lying tongue

Ghost. *Soul, breath, spirit.*
Gen. 25. 8 Abraham gave up the *g*.
Job 3. 11 why did I not give up the *g*.
Jer. 15. 9 she hath given up the *g*.
Lam. 1. 19 elders gave up the *g*.
Mat. 27. 50 cried .. yielded up the *g*.
Mark 15. 37; Luke 23. 46; John
19. 30
Acts 5. 5 Ananias .. gave up the *g*.
R. V. Mat. 27. 50; John 19. 30 his
spirit

Giant. *Mighty, strong, fearful one.*
Gen. 6. 4 there were *g*. in the earth
Num. 13. 33 there we saw the *g*.
Deut. 2. 11 were accounted *g*., as A.
Josh. 12. 4 Og .. of the remnant of *g*.
2 Sam. 21. 16 of the sons of the *g*.
1 Chr. 20. 6 also was a son of the *g*.
Job 16. 14 run, upon me like *g*.
R. V. Gen. 6. 4; Num. 13. 33 Nephilim; Deut. 2. 11, 20; 3. 11, 13;
Josh. 12. 4; 13. 12; 15. 8; 17. 15;
18. 16 Rephaim

Gier-eagle. R. V. *vulture.*
Lev. 11. 18 swan, pelican, and *g. e*.
Deut. 14. 17 the *g. e*. and cormorant

Gift. *Offering, present, reward,
grace, favour.*
Gen. 25. 6 Abraham gave *g*. and
Ex. 28. 38 hallow in all .. holy *g*.
Lev. 23. 38 be. your *g*. .. and vows
Num. 18. 6 a *g*. for the Lord, to do
Deut. 16. 19 for a *g*. doth blind
2 Sam. 19. 42 hath he given us .. *g*.
1 Chr. 18. 2 be. D's. ser. and br. *g*.
2 Chr. 26. 8 Ammon. gave *g*. to Uz.
Esth. 9. 22 days .. of *g*. to the poor
Ps. 72. 10 She. and Seba shall offer *g*.
Prov. 18. 16 man's *g*. maketh room
Eccl. 7. 7 *g*. destroyeth the heart
Isa. 1. 23 every one loveth *g*., and
Ezek. 16. 33 they give *g*. to whores
Dan. 2. 6 ye shall receive .. *g*. and
Mat. 2. 11 th. presented unto him *g*.
5. 23; 7. 11; 8. 4; 15. 5; 23. 18
Mark 7. 11 Corban, that is, *g*.
Luke 21. 1 saw men casting their *g*.
John 4. 10 knewest the *g*. of God
Acts 2. 38 sh. receive *g*. of Holy G.
Rom. 5. 15 and the *g*. by grace, wh.
1 Cor. 1. 7 come behind in no *g*.
2 Cor. 1. 11 bestowed on us by *g*.
Eph. 3. 7 *g*. of grace of God to me
Phil. 4. 17 not because I desire *g*.
1 Tim. 4. 14 neglect not the *g*. that
2 Tim. 1. 6 stir up the *g*. of God
Heb. 2. 4 and *g*. of the Holy G.
Heb. 6. 4 tasted of the heavenly *g*.
Jas. 1. 17 every per. *g*. is from ab.
1 Pet. 4. 10 man hath received *g*.
Rev. 11. 10 send *g*. one to another
R. V. 2 Sam. 8. 2, 6; 1 Chr. 18. 2,
6 presents; Ezek. 22. 12 bribes;
Luke 21. 5 offerings; 2 Cor. 8. 4
this grace

Gin. *Snare.*
Job 18. 9 *g*. shalt take him by heel
Ps. 140. 5 they have set *g*. for me
Isa. 8. 14 for a *g*. and snare to inhab.
Am. 3. 5 can bird fall where no *g*.

Gird. *Girdle, bind around.*
Ex. 12. 11 your loins *g*., your shoes
Lev. 16. 4 *g*. with a linen girdle
Deut. 1. 41 when ye had *g*. on weap.
Judg. 3. 16 *g*. it under his raiment
1 Sam. 17. 39 David *g*. his sword
2 Sam. 3. 31 *g*. you with sackcloth
1 K. 20. 32 so they *g*. sackcloth on

2 K. 4. 29 *g*. up thy loins and take
Neh. 4. 18 had his sword *g*. by si.
Job. 12. 18 *g*. their loins with gird.
Ps. 18. 32 God *g*. me with strength
Prov. 31. 17 she *g*. loins wi. strength
Isa. 22. 12 and to *g*. with sackcloth
Jer. 4. 8 for this *g*. you with sackc.
Lam. 2. 10 *g*. themselves with s. c.
Ezek. 44. 18 shall not *g*. thems.
Dan. 10. 5 loins *g*. with .. gold
Joel 1.8 lament like virgin *g*. wi. s. c.
Luke 12. 35 let your loins be *g*.
John 21. 7 Peter *g*. his fisher's coat
Acts 12. 8 *g*. thyself, and bind sand.
Rev. 15. 6 breasts *g*. with gold. g.
R. V. Job 12. 18 bindeth

Girding. *Girdle.*
Isa. 3. 34 instead of stom. *g*. of s. c.

Girdle. *Sash, belt, band.*
Ex. 28. 4 make coat, mitre, and a *g*.
Lev. 8. 7 he girded him with the *g*.
1 Sam. 18. 4 stripped .. ev. to .. *g*.
2 Sam. 20. 8 upon it a *g*. with s.
1 K. 2. 5 put blood .. upon his *g*.
2 K. 1. 8 *g*. of leather about loins
Job 12. 18 girded loins with a *g*.
Ps. 109. 19 *g*. wherewith he is *g*.
Prov. 31. 24 deliver. *g*. unto merch.
Isa. 3. 24 instead of *g*. a rent, and
Jer. 13. 1 Go and get thee a linen *g*.
Ezek. 23. 15 girded with *g*. upon l.
Mat. 3. 4 leath. *g*. about his loins
Mark 1. 6 *g*. of skin about .. loins
Acts 21. 11 took P's *g*. and bound
Rev. 1. 13 girt about .. wi. gold. *g*.
R. V. Ex. 28. 8, 27, 28; 29. 5; 39.
5, 20, 21; Lev. 8. 7 band

Girl. *Child, lass, female.*
Joel 3. 3 have .. sold *g*. for wine
Zech. 8. 5 *g*. playing in the streets

Girt. *Girded.*
2 K. 1. 8 hairy, and *g*. with a girdle
Eph. 6. 14 loins *g*. .. with truth
Rev. 1. 13 *g*. .. with golden girdle
See also **Gird.**

Give. *To give.*
Gen. 1. 29 I have *g*. .. every herb
Ex. 2. 9 I will. *g*. thee thy wages
Lev. 5. 16 *g*. it unto the priest
Num. 3. 9 *g*. the Levites unto A.
Deut. 1. 8 *g*. to them and .. seed
Josh. 1. 2 go unto land which I *g*.
Judg. 1. 13 *g*. him Achsah, his d.
Ruth 3. 17 meas. of barley *g*. he me
1 Sam. 1. 4 he *g*. to Penin. his wife
2 Sam. 4. 10 have *g*. him reward for
1 K. 1. 48 *g*. to sit on my throne
2 K. 4. 43 *g*. peo. that they .. eat
1 Chr. 2. 35 Shesh. *g*. daugh. to J.
2 Chr. 1. 7 ask what I shall *g*. thee
Ez. 1. 2 Lord God .. hath *g*. me
Neh. 2. 1 took wine, and *g*. it king
Esth. 1. 19 let k. *g*. her .. estate
Job 1. 21 L. *g*., and L. hath taken
Ps. 2. 8 ask .. and I shall *g*. thee
Prov. 1. 4 *g*. subtilty to .. simple
Eccl. 1. 13 *g*. my heart to seek and
S. of S. 2. 13 vines .. *g*. a g. smell
Isa. 3. 4 *g*. chil. to be .. princes
Jer. 3. 8 had *g*. her bill of divorce
Lam. 1. 11 *g*. their pleasant things
Ezek. 2. 8 and eat that I *g*. thee
Dan. 1. 12 *g*. us pulse to eat and
Hos. 2. 5 that *g*. me bread and w.
Joel 2. 17 *g*. not .. her. to reproach
Am. 4. 6 I have *g*. you cleanness
Mic. 1. 14 shalt thou *g*. presents to
Hag. 2. 9 in this place .. I *g*. peace
Zech. 3. 7 will *g*. thee places to walk
Mal. 2. 2 *g*. glory unto my name
Mat. 4. 9 all these things will I *g*.
Mark 8. 37 what shall man *g*. in ex.
Luke 1. 32 Lord G. shall *g*. to him
John 1. 17 the law was *g*. by Moses
Acts 2. 4 as sp. *g*. them utterance
Rom. 4. 20 faith, *g*. glory to God
1 Cor. 1. 4 grace .. *g*. you by J. C.
2 Cor. 1. 22 *g*. the earnest of spirit
Gal. 1. 4 *g*. himself for our sins
Eph. 1. 17 *g*. you the sp. of wis.
Col. 1. 25 dispen. of G. which is *g*.
1 Thes. 4. 2 what com. we *g*. you
2 Thes. 2. 16 hath *g*. .. everlast. c
1 Tim. 6. 17 who *g*. us richly all
2 Tim. 1. 9 grace .. *g*. us in C. J
Tit. 2. 14 who *g*. himself for us

Heb. 2. 13 chil. which G. hath *g*.
Jas. 1. 5 ask of G. . . that *g*. all
1 Pet. 1. 21 *g*. him glory, that faith
2 Pet. 3. 15 accor. to the wisdom *g*.
1 John 3. 23 as he *g*. us command.
Rev. 1. 1 Rev. which God *g*. to him

Giver. *Who gives.*
Isa. 24. 2 so with *g*. of usury to him
2 Cor. 9. 7 G. loveth a cheerful *g*.

Giving. *Giving.*
Deut. 10. 18 in *g*. food and raiment
Ruth. 1. 6 peo., in *g*. them bread
1 K. 5. 9 my desire, in *g*. food for h.
2 Chr. 6. 23 *g*. him according to ri.
Phil. 4. 15 concerning *g*. and rec.
See also **Give.**

Glad. *Joyful, pleased, cheerful.*
Ex. 4. 14 he will be *g*. in his heart
Judg. 18. 20 priest's heart was *g*.
1 Sam. 11. 9 men of J., they were *g*.
1 Chr. 16. 31 let the heavens be *g*.
Job 22. 19 righteous see . . and be *g*.
Ps. 9. 2 I be *g*. and rejoice in thee
Prov. 23. 25 thy mother shall be *g*.
10. 1 A wise son maketh a *g*. father
S. of S. 1. 4 will be *g*., and rejoice
Isa. 35. 1 Solomon pl. shall be *g*.
Jer. 20. 15 is born, making him *g*.
Lam. 1. 21 are *g*. thou hast done it
Dan. 6. 23 then was k. exceeding *g*.
Hos. 7. 3 they made the k. glad
Joel 2. 21 be *g*. and rejoice : for the
Jonah 4. 6 so Jonah was . . *g*. of
Hab. 1. 15 they rejoice and are *g*.
Zeph. 3. 14 O Isra., be *g*. and rejoice
Zech. 10. 7 chil. . . see, and be *g*.
Mat. 5. 12 rejoice and be ex. *g*.
Mark 14. 11 heard and . . were *g*.
Luke 15. 32 meet . . we should be *g*.
John 8. 56 he saw it and was *g*.
Acts 11. 23 was *g*., and exhorted all
Rom. 16. 19 I am *g*. therefore on yo.
1 Cor. 16. 17 *g*. of the coming of S.
2 Cor. 13. 9 *g*. when we are weak
1 Pet. 4. 13 ye may be *g*. also in joy.
Rev. 19. 7 let us be *g*. and rejoice
R. V. Ps. 48. 11 ; 104. 34 ; Acts 2.
  26 ; 1 Cor. 16. 17 ; 2 Cor. 13. 9 ; 1
  Pet. 4. 13 ; Rev. 19. 7 rejoice ;
  Luke 1. 19 ; 8. 1 ; Acts 13. 32 good

Gladly. *Joyfully.*
Mark 6. 20 did . . things, and h . . *g*.
Acts 2. 41 that *g*. received his word
2 Cor. 11. 19 for ye suffer fools *g*.
R. V. Luke 8. 40 ; Acts 2. 41 —

Gladness. *Joy, rejoicing, mirth.*
Num. 10. 10 in day of your *g*. blow
Deut. 28. 47 with *g*. of heart for
2 Sam. 6. 12 ark . . into city . . w. *g*.
1 Chr. 16. 27 strength and *g*. are in
2 Chr. 29. 30 sang praises with *g*.
Neh. 8. 17 there was very great *g*.
Esth. 8. 16 Jews had light and *g*.
Ps. 4. 7 hast put *g*. in my heart
Prov. 10. 28 hope of right. is *g*.
S. of S. 3. 11 in the day of the *g*.
Isa. 16. 10 *g*. is taken away, and
Jer. 31. 7 sing with *g*. for Jacob
Joel 1. 16 *g*. from the house of God
Zech. 8. 19 ho. of Judah joy and *g*.
Mark 4. 16 imme. receive it with *g*.
Luke 1. 14 shalt have joy and *g*.
Acts 2. 46 did eat meat with *g*. and
Phil. 2. 29 in the Lord with all *g*.
Heb. 1. 9 with the oil of *g*. above
R. V. Ps. 105. 43 singing ; 2 Sam.
  6. 12 ; Mark 4. 16 ; Acts 12. 14 ;
  Phil. 2. 29 joy

Glass. *Tablet, mirror.*
Ex. 38. 8 looking *g*. of the women
Job 37. 18 as a molten looking *g*.
Isa. 3. 23 the *g*., and fine linen
1 Cor. 13. 12 we see through *g*. dark.
Jas. 1. 23 behold. nat. face in *g*.
Something transparent.
Rev. 4. 6 a sea of *g*. like ; 15. 2 ;
  21, 18, 21 city like unto clear *g*.
R. V. Job 37. 18 mirror ; Isa. 3. 23
  hand mirrors ; Jas. 1. 23 mirror ;
  Rev. 4. 6 ; 15. 2 glassy sea.

Glean. *Gather.*
Lev. 19. 10 shall not *g*. thy vineyard
Deut. 24. 21 not *g*. it afterwards
Judg. 20. 45 *g*. of them in highway
Jer. 6. 9 shall . . *g*. the remnant of Is.
Ruth 2. 2–23 *g*. ears . . after him

Gleaning. *Gathering, gleaning.*
Lev. 19. 9 neither gather the *g*.
Judg. 8. 2 *g*. of grapes of Ephraim
Isa. 17. 6 *g*. grapes shall be left on
Jer. 49. 9 would not leave . . *g*. gr.
Mic. 7. 1 as grape *g*. of the vine

Glede. *Vulture, hawk.*
Deut. 14. 13 *g*., kite, and vulture

Glistering. R. V. *dazzling.*
Luke 9. 29 rai. was white and *g*.
R. V. *inlaid work.*
1 Chr. 29. 2 stones . . set, *g*. stones

Glitter. R. V. *be as lightning.*
Ezek. 21. 10 furbished that it may *g*.

Glittering. *Shining, flashing.*
Deut. 32. 41 whet my *g*. sword
Job 39. 23 the *g*. spear and shield
Ezek. 21. 28 consume bec. of the *g*.
Nah. 3. 3 bright s. and *g*. spear
Hab. 3. 11 at shining of thy *g*. spear
R. V. Job 39. 23 flashing ; Ezek.
  21. 28 may be as lightning

Gloominess. *Darkness, dimness.*
Joel 2. 2 day of . . *g*. Zeph. 1. 15

Glorified. *Beautified.*
Isa. 49. 3 in whom I will be *g*.
  60. 21 ; 61. 3
Honored, magnified, exalted.
Lev. 10. 3 bef. people I will be *g*.
Isa. 26. 15 O Lord, thou art *g*.
Ezek. 28. 22 I will be *g*. in midst of
Hag. 1. 8 and I will be *g*., saith Lord
Rom. 8. 17 th we may be *g*. together
2 Thes. 1. 10, 12 shall come to be *g*.

Glorify. *Beautify.*
Isa. 55. 5 Holy One . . he hath *g*.
  44. 23 ; 60. 7 ; 60. 9
Honor, magnify, exalt.
Dan. 5. 23 God . . hast thou not *g*.
Ps. 22. 23 all seed of Jacob, *g*. him
  50. 15 ; 50. 23 ; 86. 9 ; 86. 12
Isa. 24. 15 *g*. ye the Lord in fires
Jer. 30. 19 I will also *g*. them
Mat. 5. 16 *g*. your F. . . in heaven
Mark 2. 12 amazed, and *g*. God
Luke 2. 20 shepherds returned *g*.
  4. 15 ; 5. 25 ; 7. 16 ; 13. 13 ; 18 43
John 7. 39 Jesus was not yet *g*.
  11. 4 ; 12. 16 ; 13. 31 ; 14. 13 ; 16. 14
Acts 3. 13 God . . hath *g*. . . Jesus
  4. 21 ; 11. 18 ; 13. 48 ; 21. 20
Rom. 1. 21 they *g*. him not as God
  8. 30 ; 15. 6 ; 15. 9
1 Cor. 6. 20 *g*. G. in your body
2 Cor. 9. 13 they *g*. God for your
Gal. 1. 24 And they *g*. God in me
2 Thes. 3. 1 be *g*., even as it is with
Heb. 5. 5 so C. *g*. not himself
1 Pet. 2. 12 *g*. G. in day of visita.
Rev. 15. 4 not fear thee . . and *g*. thy
R. V. 1 Pet. 4. 14 —

Glorious. *Honorable, beautiful, exalted, majestic, resplendent.*
Ex. 15. 6 right hand . . is become *g*.
Deut. 28. 58 fear this *g*. . name
2 Sam. 6. 20 how *g*. was king of Is.
1 Chr. 29. 13 praise thy *g*. name
Neh. 9. 5 blessed be thy *g*. name
Esth. 1. 4 riches of his *g*. kingdom
Ps. 66. 2 sing, make his praise *g*.
  87. 3 *g*. things are spoken of thee
Isa. 4. 2 branch of Lord be . . *g*.
Jer. 17. 12 *g*. throne from begin.
Ezek. 27. 25 made *g*. in midst of
Dan. 11. 16 shall stand in *g*. land
Luke 13. 17 rejoice for all *g*. things
Rom. 8. 21 *g*. liberty of the childr.
2 Cor. 4. 4 light of *g*. gospel of C.
Eph. 5. 27 present it . . a *g*. church
Phil. 3. 21 fash. like . . his *g*. body
Col. 1. 11 accor. to his *g*. power
1 Tim. 1. 11 accor. to the *g*. gospel
Tit. 2. 13 looking for *g*. appearing
R. V. Ps. 111. 3 majesty ; Isa. 49. 5
  honourable

Gloriously. *Honorably, trium-phantly.*
Ex. 15. 1, 21 he hath triumphed *g*.
Isa. 24. 23 reign . . before ancients *g*.

Glory. (*n*.) *Honor, beauty, maj-esty, renown, exaltation, adora-tion.*
Gen. 31. 1 of fath. he got. all this *g*.
Ex. 16. 7 then ye shall see *g*. of L.
Lev. 9. 6 *g*. of the L. shall appear
Num. 14. 10 *g*. of the L. appeared

Deut. 5. 24 G. hath showed . . his *g*.
Josh. 7. 19 give . . *g*. to the L. G.
1 Sam. 2. 8 inherit a throne of *g*.
1 K. 8. 11 *g*. of L. had filled house
1 Chr. 16. 24 declare his *g*. among
2 Chr. 5. 14 *g*. of L. had filled house
Esth. 5. 11 H. told of *g*. of . . riches
Job 19. 9 hath strip. me of my *g*.
Ps. 8. 5 crowned him with *g*. and h.
  19. 1 heavens declare . of God
  24. 7, 9 King of *g*. shall come in
  62. 7 God is my salvation and *g*.
  104. 31 *g*. of L. shall endure f. ev
Prov. 3. 35 the wise shall inherit *g*.
Isa. 3. 8 provoke eyes of his *g*.
Jer. 13. 16 give *g*. to the L. . . G.
Ezek. 1. 28 likeness of *g*. of Lord
  42. 3 and the earth shined with *g*.
Dan. 2. 37 king., power, strength *g*.
Hos. 4. 7 change . . *g*. into shame
Mic. 2. 9 taken away my *g*. for ev.
Nah. 2. 9 none end of *g*. out of all
Hab. 2. 14 knowl. of *g*. of Lord
Hag. 2. 7 will fill this h. with *g*.
Zech. 2. 5 I will be a *g*. in midst of
Mal. 2. 5 give *g*. unto my name
Mat. 4. 8 kingdoms . . and *g*. of th.
  6. 13 power and the *g*. for ever
  6. 29 Sol. in all . . *g*. was not array
  16. 27 Son. of m. shall come in *g*.
Mark 8. 28 he com. in *g*. of his F.
Luke 2. 9 *g*. of the L. shone round
  2. 14 *g*. to God in the highest
John 1. 14 we beheld his *g*., the *g*.
  8. 50 I seek not mine own *g*.
Acts 7. 2 God of *g*. appeared unto
  22. 11 could not see for the *g*.
Rom. 1. 23 changed *g*. of uncorrupti.
  2. 7 seek for *g*., hon. and immort.
1 Cor. 2. 7 which G. ordain. to our *g*.
  10. 31 do all to the *g*. of God
  11. 7 ; 15. 40, 41, 43
2 Cor. 1. 20 Amen, unto *g*. of God
Gal. 1. 5 to whom be *g*. for ever
Eph. 1. 6 praise of *g*. of . . grace
Phil. 1. 11 unto *g*. and praise of God
Col. 1. 27 make known . . riches of *g*.
1 Thes. 2. 20 ye are our *g*. and joy
2 Thes. 2. 14 obtain. of *g*. of Lord
1 Tim. 1. 17 be hon. and *g*. forever
2 Tim. 2. 10 in C. J. with eter. *g*.
Heb. 1. 3 being bright. of his *g*.
Jas. 2. 1 L. J. C., the Lord of *g*.
1 Pet. 1. 7 found unto praise and *g*.
  5. 4 shall receive a crown of *g*;
2 Pet. 1. 3 called us to *g*. and vir.
Jude 24 faultless before . . his *g*.
Rev. 1. 6 be *g*. and dominion for e
  4. 11 ; 5. 12 ; 7. 12 ; 11. 13 ; 14. 7
R. V. 1 Chr. 16. 27 ; Job 40. 10
  honour ; 1 Chr. 16. 35 triumph ; Ps.
  89. 44 brightness ; Prov. 4. 9 ; Isa.
  62. 3 beauty ; Mat. 6. 13 —

Glory (*v*.) *Boast, exult, rejoice.*
Ex. 8. 9 Mos. said to P., G. over me
2 K. 14. 10 *g*. . . and tarry at home
1 Chr. 16. 10 *g*. in his holy name
Ps. 63. 11 that swear. by him shall *g*.
  105. 3 *g*. ye in his holy name
Isa. 41. 16 shalt *g*. in the Holy One
Jer. 4. 2 and in him shall they *g*.
  9. 23 let not the rich *g*. in riches
  49. 4 Wheref. *g*. thou in the valleys
Rom. 5. 3 but we *g*. in tribulation
1 Cor. 1. 29 no flesh *g*. in his pres.
2 Cor. 5. 12 them which *g*. in appear.
  10. 17 ; 11. 12, 18, 30 ; 12. 1, 5, 6, 9
Gal. 6. 13 may *g*. in your flesh
2 Thes. 1. 4 *g*. in you in the churches
Jas. 3. 14 *g*. not, and lie not ag. truth

Glorying. *Boasting, exulting.*
1 Cor. 5. 6 your *g*. is not good
2 Cor. 7. 4 great is my *g*. of you
R. V. 2 Cor. 12. 11 —

Glutton. *Who gluts, gormand.*
Deut. 21. 20 this our son is a *g*.
Prov. 23. 21 the drunk. and *g*. shall
R. V. Deut. 21. 20 riotous liver

Gluttonous. *Eating, gormand izing.*
Mat. 11. 19 behold a man *g*. Luke 7

Gnash. *Bite, grind, grate.*
Job 16. 9 *g*. on me with his teeth
Ps. 35. 16 ; 37. 12 ; 112. 10
Lam. 2. 16 hiss and *g*. the teeth
Mat. 8. 12 weeping and *g*. of teeth

13. 42; 22. 13; 24. 51; 25. 30
Mark 9. 18 and g. with his teeth
Luke 13. 28 shall be weeping and g.
Acts 7. 54 and they g. on him with
  R. V. Mark 9. 18 grindeth

Gnat. *Gnat, mosquito.*
Mat. 23. 24 which strain at a g. and

Gnaw. *Chew, tear, scrape.*
Zeph. 3. 3 they g. not the bones
Rev. 16. 10 g. their tongues for pain
  R. V. Zeph. 3. 3 leave nothing

Go, Went, Gone. *Move.*
The inherent idea of motion in **Go**,
and its parts, is often modified by the
preceding and following words.
Gen. 3. 14 upon belly shalt thou g.
7. 18 ark *went* on face of water
Ex. 2. 1 *went* man of house of Levi
4. 18 J. said to M. *G.* in peace
Lev. 9. 23 M. and A. *went* into tab.
Num. 10. 30 he said, I will not g.
Deut. 17. 3 hath g. and s. other g.
Josh. 1. 7 may. prosp. whith. th. g.
Judg. 1. 3 Simon *went* with him
Ruth 1. 1 g. . . to . . mother's house
1 Sam. 1. 17 Eli said, *G.* in peace
2 Sam. 3. 16 her hus. *went* with her
1 K. 1. 13 g. get thee unto . . David
2 K. 1. 2 said, . . *G.*, enquire of Baal
1 Chr. 4. 39 *went* to entra. of Gedor
2 Chr. 1. 3 Sol. *went* to high place
Ez. 8. 31 to g. unto Jerusalem
Neh. 8. 12 peo. *went* their way to
Esth. 4. 16 g. gather all the Jews
Job 42. 8 g. to my servant Job
Ps. 32. 8 way which thou shalt g.
Prov. 25. 8 g. not forth hastily to st.
Eccl. 1. 1 g. to now, I will prove
S. of S. 6. 6 as .. sheep which g. up
Isa. 2. 3 let us g. to mountain of L.
Jer. 5. 10 g. ye upon her walls
Lam. 4. 18 cannot g. in our streets
Ezek. 1. 9 *went* straight forward
Dan. 11. 44 g. forth with great fury
Hos. 6. 5 as light that g. forth
Joel 2 16 let bridegroom g. forth
Am. 4. 3 g. out at the breaches
Jonah 4. 5 Jonah *went* out of city
Mic. 4. 2 g. up mountain of th. Lord
Hab. 3. 5 burning coals *went* forth
Zech. 2. 3 the angel . . *went* forth
Mal. 4. 2 and ye shall g. forth
Mat. 2. 22 was afraid to g. thither
4. 24 his fame *went* through. Syr.
Mark 1. 20 left f. . . and *went* after
Luke 9. 57 will fol. whither thou g.
John 4. 47 he *went* unto him and
Acts 5. 20 g. stand .. speak in temple
Rom. 15. 25 now I g. to Jerusalem
1 Cor. 5. 10 then must we needs g.
1 Tim. 1. 3 when I *went* unto Mac.
Heb. 11. 8 he was called to g. into
Jas. 4. 13 we will g. into such a city
1 Pet. 3. 19 he *went* and preached
1 John 2. 19 they *went* out from us
Jude 11 have g. in way of Cain
Rev. 3. 12 he shall g. no more out
The R. V. changes are frequent, but
chiefly those relating to words be-
fore and after *go*.

Goad. *Prick, spur.*
Judg. 3. 31 slew six hun. with ox g.
1 Sam. 13. 21 to sharpen the g.
Eccl. 12. 11 words of wise are as g.

Goat. *Goat.*
Gen. 27. 9 go to flock, and fetch g.
Ex. 12. 5 take it out from . . the g.
Lev. 1. 10 if his offering be of g.
Num. 7. 16 kid of g. for sin offering
Deut. 14. 4 eat ox, sheep, and g.
1 Sam. 19. 13 pillow of g's hair for
2 Chr. 29. 21 lambs, and sev. he g.
Ez. 6. 17 twelve g. accor. to num.
Job 39. 1 when wild g. .. bring
Ps. 50. 13 will I eat .. blood of g.
Prov. 27. 27 g's milk enough .. food
S. of S. 4. 1 hair is as flock of g.
Isa. 1. 11 delight not in blood of g.
Jer. 50. 8 be as the he g. before the
Ezek. 43. 25 prepare every day a g.
Dan. 8. 8 the he g. waxed very great
Zech. 10. 3 and I punished the g.
Mat. 25. 32 divideth sheep from g.
Heb. 9. 12 neither by blood of g.

Goat-skin.
Heb 11. 37 wandered about in g. s.

Goblet. *Basin.*
S. of S. 7. 2 navel .. g. wanteth not

God. *Mighty one, Jehovah, object
of worship.*
See DIC. OF PROPER NAMES

Goddess. *Object of worship.*
1 K. 11. 5, 33 Ashtoreth g. of Zido.
Acts 19. 27 temple of the g. Diana
  R. V. Acts 19. 35 ——

Godhead. *Divine thing, deity.*
Acts 17. 29 G. is like unto gold
Rom. 1. 20 his eternal power and *G.*
Col. 2. 9 all the fulness of the *G.*
  R. V. Rom. 1. 20 divinity

Godliness. *Piety, reverence.*
1 Tim. 2. 2 peaceful life is all g.
2. 10; 3. 16; 4. 7; 6. 3, 5, 6, 11
2. Tim. 3. 5 having a form of g.
Tit. 1. 1 truth which is after g.
2 Pet. 1. 3 things that pertain to g.
  1. 6 and to patience, g.

Godly. *Kind, pious, reverential.*
Ps. 4. 3 set apart him that is g.
Mal. 2. 15 might seek a g. seed
2 Cor. 1. 12 in simp. and g. sincer.
1 Tim. 1. 4 rather than g. edifying
2 Tim. 3. 12 live g. in Jesus Christ
Tit. 2. 12 live soberly, right., and g.
Heb. 12. 28 with rever. and g. fear
2 Pet. 2. 9 L. know. how to del. g.
3 John 6 forward . . after g. sort
  R. V. 2 Cor. 1. 12 sincerity; 1 Tim.
  1. 4 dispensation of God; Heb. 12.
  28 awe; 3 John 6 worthily of God

Goeth. *See* **Go.**

Going. *Moving, going.*
Gen. 15. 12 when sun was g. down
Ex. 17. 12 steady until the g. down
Num. 34. 4 g. thereof shall be fr. s.
Deut. 33. 18 rejoice, Zeb., in thy g.
Josh. 7. 5 smote them in g. down
Judg. 1. 36 coast . . was from g. up
1 Sam. 29. 6 thy g. out and com. in
2 Sam. 3. 25 to know thy g. out
1 K. 22. 36 about g. down of sun
2 K. 9. 27 at g. up to Gur, which is
2 Chr. 18. 34 time of sun g. down
Neh. 12. 37 at g. up of the wall
Job 1. 7 g. to and fro in the earth
Ps. 104. 19 sun know. his g. down
Isa. 37. 28 g. out, and coming in
Jer. 48. 5 the g. down of Horonaim
Ezek. 44. 5 g. forth of sanctuary
Dan. 9. 25 from g. forth of com.
Mic. 5. 2 whose g. forth have been
Mal. 1. 11 unto g. down of same
Mat. 28. 11 when they were g. beho.
  R. V. Goings in O. T. is generally,
  steps or paths

Gold. *Shining metal, gold.*
Gen. 2. 11 Havilah, where is g.
Ex. 3. 22 silver and jewels of g.
Num. 7. 14 spoon . . ten shek. of g.
Deut. 8. 13 thy s. and g. is multiplied
Josh. 6. 19 g. and vessels of brass
Judg. 8. 26 t. sev. hun. shekels of g.
1 Sam. 6. 11 coffer with mice of g.
2 Sam. 8. 7 David took shields of g.
1 K. 6. 20 overlaid it with pure g.
2 K. 16. 8 Ahaz took silver and g.
1 Chr. 18. 10 vessels of g. and silver
2 Chr. 3. 4 overlaid it with pure g.
Ez. 1. 4 with g., and with goods
Neh. 7. 70 thousand drams of g.
Esth. 1. 6 the beds were of g. and s.
Job 23. 10 I shall come forth as g.
Ps. 19. 10 more to be desired than g.
Prov. 17. 3 pot for silver, fur. for g.
Eccl. 2. 8 gathered me silver and g.
S. of S. 1. 11 make the borders of g.
Isa. 2. 7 land is full of silver and g.
Jer. 4. 30 deck. thee with or. of g.
Lam. 4. 1 how is g. become dim
Ezek. 7. 19 their g. shall be remov.
Dan. 11. 38 shall he honour with g.
Hos. 2. 8 multiplied her s. and g.
Joel 3. 5 ha. taken my silver and g.
Nah. 2. 9 take ye the spoil of g.
Hab. 2. 19 it is laid over with g.
Zeph. 1. 18 nei. theirs s. nor g. shall
Hag. 2. 8 silver and the g. is mine
Zech. 4. 2 be. candlestick all of g.
Mal. 3. 3 purge them as g.
Mat. 2. 11 gifts; g., frankincense
Acts 3. 6 Silver and g. have I none
1 Cor. 3. 12 g. silver, precious stones

1 Tim. 2. 9 not with .. hair, nor g.
2 Tim. 2. 20 not only ves. of g. and
Jas. 5. 3 your g. and s. is cankered
Rev. 4. 4 they had .. crowns of g.

Golden. *Of gold.*
Gen. 24. 22 man took g. earring of
Ex. 25. 25 make a g. crown round
Lev. 8. 9 Moses did he put g. plate
Num. 7. 86 g. spoons were twelve
Judg. 8. 24 they have g. earrings of
1 Sam. 6. 4 g. emerods, and g. mice
2 K. 10. 29 g. calves that were in B.
1 Chr. 28. 17 g. basins .. by weight
2 Chr. 4. 19 the g. altar also S. made
Esth. 5. 2 k. held out the g. sceptre
Eccl. 12. 6 or g. bowl be broken
Isa. 13. 12 than g. wedge of Ophir
Jer. 51. 7 g. cup in Lord's house
Zech. 4. 12 two g. pipes empty g. oil
Heb. 9. 4 had the g. censer, and ark
Rev. 1. 12 saw seven g. candlest'ks
  1. 13; 2. 1; 5. 8; 8. 3; 9. 13; 14. 14

Goldsmith. *Refiner, purifier.*
Neh. 3. 32 repaired the g. and mer.
Isa. 40. 19; 41. 7; 46. 6.

Gone. *See* **Go.**

Good (*n.*). *Good.*
Gen. 1. 4 G. saw light, that it was g.
Num. 10. 29 Lord hath spoken g.
Josh. 24. 20 after he hath done g.
1 Sam. 24. 17 rewarded me g. for e.
2 Sam. 14. 32 g. for me to have been
1 K. 22. 13 words of proph. decl. g.
1 Chr. 29. 3 I prepared of my g.
2 Chr. 24. 16 had done g. in Israel
Ez. 9. 12 and eat the g. of the land
Est. 7. 9 had spoken g. for the king
Job. 2. 10 rec. g. at hand of God
Ps. 4. 6 Who will shew us any g. ?
Prov. 3. 27 withhold not g. from
Eccl. 3. 12 there is no g. in them
Isa. 1. 19 shall eat g. of the land
Jer. 8. 15 peace, but no g. came
Ezek. 16. 50 took them as I saw g.
Mic. 1. 12 Maroth waited for g.
Zech. 11. 12 if g., give me my price
Mat. 26. 24 been g. for that man if
John 4. 29 forth; that have done g.
Acts 10. 38 who went about doing g.
Rom. 8. 28 all things work for g.
1 Thes. 3. 1 g. to be left at Athens
1 John 3. 17 who hath this world's g.

Good (*a.*). *Kind, excellent, virtu-
ous, competent, valid, great.*
Gen. 2. 9 sight, and g. for food
Ex. 3. 8 unto a g. land and a large
Num. 14. 7 The land is exceeding g.
Deut. 1. 25 g. land which L. G. giv.
Josh. 21. 45 failed not of g. thing
Judg. 8. 32 Gid. died in a g. old age
1 Sam. 2. 24 no g. report I hear
1 K. 8. 36 teach them the g. way
2 K. 3. 19 ye shall fell ev. g. tree
1 Chr. 4. 40 found fat past. and g.
2 Chr. 10. 7 and speak g. words to
Ez. 7. 9 the g. hand of his God
Neh. 9. 13 g. ga. statutes and com.
Esth. 8. 17 Jews .. feast and a g. day
Job 22. 18 filled house with g. thi.
Ps. 25. 8. g. and upright is Lord
Prov. 4. 2 I give you g. doctrine
Eccl. 4. 9 g. reward for their labour
S. of S. 1. 3 savour of thy g. oint.
Isa. 39. 8 said, G. is word of Lord
Jer. 6. 16 ask .. where is the g. way
Ezek. 17. 8 g. soil by great waters
Hos. 4. 13 the shadow thereof is g.
Nah. 1. 7 the Lord is g., a strong h.
Zech. 1. 13 with g. words and com.
Mat. 7. 17 g. tree bringeth . . g. fr.
Mark 10. 17 G. Master what shall I.
Luke 6. 45 g. man . ut of g. treas.
  8. 8 other fell on g. ground, spr. up
John 7. 12 said, He is a g. man
Acts 9. 36 woman full of g. works
Rom. 10. 11 nei. having done g. nor
2 Cor. 9. 8 abound to ev. g. work
Eph. 2. 10 created . . unto g. works
Phil. 1. 6 he hath begun a g. work
Col. 10 fruitful in every g. work
1 Thes. 3. 6 ye have g. remembr.
2 Thes. 2. 16 g. hope through grace
1 Tim. 1. 5 and of a g. conscience
2 Tim. 2. 21 prepared unto g. work
Tit. 1. 16 unto .. g. work reprobate
Heb. 13. 21 make you per. in g. work

Jas. 1. 17 every g. and perfect gift
1 Pet. 3. 10 love life and see g. days
R. V. changes are frequent, but nearly all based on words before or after the word *good.*

Good-will. *Kindliness, benevolence.*
Deut. 33. 16 g. w. of him that dwelt
Mal. 2. 13; receiveth it with g. w.
Luke 2. 14 on e. peace, g. w. to men
Phil. 1. 15 preach Christ of g. w.
Eph. 6. 7 with g. w. doing service

Goodlier. *Likelier.*
1 Sam. 9. 2 not among chil. of. Is. a g.

Goodliest. *Likeliest.*
1 Sam. 8. 16 your g. young men, and
1 K. 20. 3 chil., ev. the g. are mine

Goodliness. *Kindliness.*
Isa. 40. 6 the g. thereof is as flower

Goodly. *Honorable, beautiful, agreeable, well-favored*
Gen. 27. 15 Rebekah took g. raim.
Ex. 2. 2 she saw he was a g. child
Lev. 23. 40 take boughs of g. trees
Num. 24. 5 How g. are thy tents
Deut. 3. 25 that g. mount. and Leb.
Josh. 7. 21 saw . . a g. Bab. garment
1 Sam. 9. 2 Saul, choice y. m. and g.
2 Sam. 23. 21 slew an E., a g. man
1 K. 1. 6 he was a very g. man
2 Chr. 36. 10 with g. ves. of house
Job 39. 13 gav. . . g. wings unto the
Ps. 16. 6 yea, I have a g. heritage
Jer. 11. 16 tree . . and of g. fruit
Ezek. 17. 23 fruit, and be g. cedar
Hos. 10. 1 have made g. images
Joel 3. 5 car. into temp. g things
Zech. 10. 3 made .. as his g. horse
Mat. 13. 45 man seeking g. pearls
Luke 21. 5 adorned with g. stones
Jas. 2. 2 a man .. in g. apparel
Rev. 18. 14 all things .. dainty and g.
R. V. Gen. 39. 6 comely; Num. 31. 10 encampments; Job 39. 13 —; Jas. 2. 2 fine; Rev. 18. 14 sumptuous

Good-man. *Master.*
Prov. 7. 19 the g. m. is not at home
Mat. 20. 11 mur. against g. m. of h.
Mark 14. 14 say to g. m. of house
Luke 12. 39 if g. m. of h. had known
R. V. Mat. 20. 11 householder; 24. 43; Luke 12. 39 master

Goodness. *Kindness, benignity, virtue, excellence.*
Ex. 18. 9 Jethro rejoice. for the g.
Num. 10. 32 what g. Lord shall do
Judg. 8. 35 according to all the g.
2 Sam. 7. 28 hast promise. . . g. unto
1 K. 8. 66 for all the g. that Lord
1 Chr. 17. 26 hast prom. this g. unto
2 Chr. 6. 41 let saints rejoice in g.
Ps. 16. 2 thou art my Lord, my g.
Prov. 20. 6 proclaim ev. one .. own g.
Isa. 63. 7 great g. toward house of
Jer. 2. 7 fruit thereof and g. thereof
Hos. 3. 5 fear the Lord and his g.
Zech. 9. 17 how great is his g.
Rom. 2. 4 g. of God leadeth thee
Gal. 5. 22 joy, gentleness, g., faith
Eph. 5. 9 g., and right., and truth
2 Thes. 1. 11 good pleasure of the g.
R. V. 2 Sam. 7. 28; 1 Chr. 17. 26 good thing; 2 Chr. 32. 32; 35. 26 good deeds; Ps. 33. 5; 144. 2 lovingkindness; Prov. 20. 6 kindness

Goods. *Substance, possessions.*
Gen. 24. 10 g. . . were in his hand
Ex. 22. 8, 11 put . hand to neigh's g.
Num. 16. 32 unto Kor. and all . . g.
Deut. 28. 11 L. . . make plent. in g.
2 Chr. 21. 14 wives, and all thy g.
Ez. 6. 8. of king's g., even tribute
Neh. 9. 25 poss. houses full of g.
Job 20. 10 hands shall resto. their g.
Eccl. 5. 11 when g. increase, they
Ezek. 38..12 ha. gotten cattle and g.
Zeph. 1. 13 g. shall become booty
Mat. 24. 47 make him ruler over . . g
Mark 3. 27 enter . . and spoil his g.
Luke 12. 18 I bestow all . . my g.
Acts 2. 45 and sold their pos. and g.
1 Cor. 13. 3 bestow . . g. to feed poor
Heb. 10. 34 the spoiling of your g.
R. V. Gen. 31. 18; Num. 35. 3; 2 Chr. 21. 14; Luke 15. 12 substance;

Neh. 9. 25 good things; Job 20. 21 prosperity; 20. 10; Zeph. 1. 13 wealth; Heb. 10. 34 possessions

Gopher. *Cedar, cypress, fir.*
Gen. 6. 14 make ark of g. wood

Gore. *Push, pierce.*
Ex. 21. 28, 31 ox g. man or woman

Gorgeous. *Bright, shining.*
Luke 23. 11 arrayed him in g. robe

Gorgeously. *Splendidly.*
Ezek. 23. 12 rulers clothed most g.
Luke 7. 25 which are g. apparreled

Gospel. *Good news, tidings, word.*
Mat. 4. 23 preaching of kingdom
9. 35; 11. 5; 24. 14; 26. 13
Mark 1. 1 beginning of g. of J. C.
1. 14; 8. 35; 10. 29; 13. 10; 14. 9
Luke 4. 18 hath anoint. me to pr. g.
7. 22; 9. 6; 20. 1
Acts 8. 25 pr. g. in many villages
Rom. 1. 1 Paul . . separa. unto the g.
2. 16; 10. 16; 11. 28; 15. 16; 16. 25
1 Cor. 4. 15 begot. you through g.
2 Cor. 4. 4 light of the g. of Christ
Gal. 1. 7 would pervert g. of Christ
Eph. 1. 13 after that ye heard . . g.
Phil. 1. 5 fellowship in g. from
Col. 1. 5 in the word of . . the g.
1 Thes. 1. 5 our g. came not to you
2 Thes. 1. 8 that obey not the g.
1 Tim. 1. 11 according to glor. g.
2 Tim. 1. 8 partakers of affl. of g.
Phile. 13. min. in bonds of the g.
Heb. 4. 2 unto us was g. preached
1 Pet. 4. 6 for this . . was g. preach.
Rev. 14. 6 having everl. g. to preach
R. V. Luke 4. 18; 7. 29; 1 Pet. 1. 25 good tidings; Rom. 10. 16 glad tidings; Rom. 10. 15 ——

Got, Gotten. See **Get.**

Gourd. *Gourd, melon.*
Jonah 4. 6, 7, 9, 10 L. G. prepar. g.
Knobs, wild cucumbers.
2 K. 4. 39 gathered .. wild g., lap full

Govern. *Bind up, lead, rule.*
1 K. 21. 7 g. the kingdom of Israel
Job 34. 17 shall he that hateth . . g.
Ps. 67. 4 g. nations upon earth

Government. *Rule, power.*
Isa. 9. 6 g. shall be on his shoulder
1 Cor. 12. 28 helps, g., div. of tong.
2 Pet. 2. 10 them that despise g.
R. V. 2 Pet. 2. 10 dominion

Governor. *Manager, leader, steward.*
2 Chr. 28. 7 Az. the g. of the house
Jer. 20. 1 Pas. chief g. in the house
Gal. 4. 2 but is under tutors and g.
John 2 8, 9 and bear to g. of feast
Ruler, prince, captain, viceroy.
Gen. 42. 6 Joseph was g. over land
Judg. 5. 9 heart toward g. of Israel
1 K. 10. 15 and of g. of the country
2 K. 23. 8 of gate of Joshua the g.
1 Chr. 24. 5 for g. of the sanctuary
2 Chr. 9. 14 and g. of the country
Ez. 8. 36 to g. on this side the river
Neh. 2. 7 to g. beyond the river
Esth. 3. 12 g. over every province
Ps. 22. 28 is g. among the nations
Jer. 30. 21 g. shall proceed from
Dan. 2. 48 chief of the g. of Babylon
Hag. 1. 1, 14 son of S. g. of Judah
Zech. 9. 7 shall be as a g. in Judah
Mal. 1. 8 offer it now unto thy g.
Leader, guide, superior, ethnarch.
Mat. 10. 18 be brought before g.
27. 2, 11, 14, 15, 21, 23, 27; 28. 14
Luke 2. 2 when Cyre. was g. of S.
3. 1 Pont. Pil. being g. of Judea
Acts 7. 10 made him g. over Egypt
23. 24 bring . . unto Felix the g.
23. 26, 33, 34; 24. 1, 10; 26. 30
2 Cor. 11. 32 unto Aretas the g.
Jas. 3. 4 turned . . whither g. list
1 Pet. 2. 14 unto g. as sent from th.
R. V. Gen. 45. 26; 2 Chr. 28. 7; Ps. 22. 28; Jer. 30. 21; John 2. 8, 9 ruler; 1 Chr. 24. 5; 29. 22; 2 Chr. 1.. 2 prince, or princes; Jer. 20. 1 officer; Zech. 9. 7; 12. 5, 6 chieftain; Mat. 27.23; Acts 23. 34 he; Gal. 4. 2 stewards; Jas. 3. 4 steersman

Grace. *Favor, clemency.*
Gen. 6. 8 Noah found g. in e. of L.

19. 19 servant found g. in thy sight
33. 8; 34. 11; 39. 4; 47. 25; 47. 29
Ex. 33. 12 thou hast found g. in si.
Num. 32. 5 if we have found g. in
Judg. 6. 17; Ruth. 2. 2; 1 Sam. 1. 18; 2 Sam. 14.22; Ez. 9. 8; Esth. 2. 17
Ps. 45. 2 g. is poured into thy lips
Prov. 1. 9 an ornament of g. unto
Jer. 31. 2 people found g. in wilder.
Zech. 4. 7 crying, G., g. unto it
Favor, graciousness, grace.
Luke 2. 40 g. of G. was upon him
John 1. 14 Word, full of g. and truth
Acts 4. 33 great g. was upon them
11. 23; 13. 43; 14. 3; 15. 11; 18. 27
Rom. 1. 5 we have received g. and
1. 7 g. to you, and peace from God
3. 24 being justified freely by g.
4. 4; 5. 2; 6. 1; 11. 5; 12. 3
16. 20 g. of our Lord Jesus Christ
1 Cor. 1. 3 g. be unto you, and p.
2 Cor. 8. 6 finish in you same. g.
Gal. 1. 3 g. be to you, and peace
Eph. 1. 7 accord. to riches of his g.
Phil. 1. 7 ye are partakers of my g.
Col. 1. 6 knew the g. of God in tru.
1 Thes. 1. 1 g. be unto you, and
2 Thes. 2. 16 good hope through g.
1 Tim. 1. 14 g. of L. was . . abund.
2 Tim. 2. 1 be strong in the g. that
Tit. 2. 11 g. . . that bringeth sal.
Phile. 3 g. to you, and peace fr. God
Heb. 4. 16 come . . to throne of g.
4. 16; 10. 29; 12. 15; 13. 9
Jas. 4. 6 but he giveth more g.
1 Pet. 1. 13 hope . . for the g. that
2 Pet. 1. 2 g. and p. be multipl.
2 John 3. g. be with you, mercy, and
Jude 4 turning g. in to lascivious.
Rev. 1. 4 g. be unto you, and p.
R. V. 2 Sam. 16. 4 favour; Rom. 11. 6; 16. 24 ——

Gracious. *Kind, benignant, affable.*
Gen. 43. 29 God be g. unto thee
Ex. 33. 19 g. to whom I . . be g.
Num. 6. 25 and be g. unto thee
2 Sam. 12. 22 G. will be g. to me
2 K. 13. 23 L. was g. unto them
2 Chr. 30. 9 L. your G. is g. and
Neh. 9. 17 g. and mer., slow to a.
Job 33. 24 Then he is g. unto him
Ps. 77. 9 hath G. forgot. to be g.
86. 15; 103. 8; 111. 4; 112. 4; 116. 5
Prov. 11. 16 g. woman retain. hon
Eccl. 10. 12 words of wise . . are g.
Isa. 33. 2 O Lord, be g. unto us
Jer. 22. 23 how g. shalt thou be
Joel 2. 13 for he is g. and merciful
Am. 5. 15 L. G. will be g. unto
Jonah 4. 2 I knew thou art a g. God
Mal. 1. 9 beseech God that he be g.
Luke 4. 22 wondered at g. words
1 Pet. 2. 3 tasted that Lord is g.
R. V. Jer. 22. 23 to be pitied

Graciously. *Benignantly.*
Gen. 33. 5 chil. God hath g. given
Ps. 119. 29 grant me thy law g.
Hos. 14. 2 receive us g., so will we
R. V. Hos. 14. 2 accept . . good

Graff. *R. V. graft.*
Rom. 11. 17 wert g. in among them
11. 19, 23; 24

Grain. *Kernel, seed, corn.*
Am. 9. 9 shall not the least g. fall
Mat. 13. 31 kingdom of heav. is . . g
17, 20 faith as g. of mustard seed
Mark 4. 31; Luke 13. 19; 17. 6
1 Cor. 15. 37 g., may chance of whe

Grandmother. *Mother, grandmother.*
2 Tim. 1. 5 dwelt first in thy g. Lois

Grant (n.). *Permission.*
Ez. 3. 7 g. they had of Cyrus

Grant (v.). *Give, bestow, concede*
Lev. 25. 24 g. a redemp. for land
Ruth 1. 9 L. g. ye may find rest
1 Sam. 1. 17 g. . . g. thy petition
1 Chr. 4. 10 G. g. him that which
2 Chr. 12. 7 g. them some deliv.
Ez. 7. 6 the king g. . . his request
Neh. 1. 11 him mercy in sight
Esth. 8. 11 the king g. the Jews
Job 6. 8 that God would g. the th
Ps. 85. 7 and g. us thy salvation

Prov. 10. 24 des. of right. shall be *g*.
Mat. 20. 21 *g*. . . my . . sons may sit
Mark 10. 37 *g*. us that we may sit
Luke 1. 74 that he would *g*. us
Acts 3. 14 desir. a mur. to be *g*.
   4. 29; 11. 18; 14. 3
Rom. 15. 5 *g*. you to be likeminded
Eph. 3. 16 would *g*. you accord. to
2 Tim. 1. 18 L. *g*. unto him that
Rev. 19. 8 and to her was *g*. that
   R. V. 1 Chr. 21. 22; Rev. 3. 21
   give; Mat. 20. 21 command; Rev.
   19. 8 given unto

Grape. *Grape, single berry.*
Gen. 40. 10 clusters brought ripe *g*.
Lev. 19. 10 nei. gather every *g*. of
Num. 6. 3 nor eat moist *g*., or dried
Deut. 23. 24 eat *g*. thy fill at thine
Judg. 8. 29 gleaning of *g*. of Ephr.
Neh. 13. 15 also wine, *g*., and figs
S. of S. 2. 13 vines with tender *g*.
Isa. 5. 2, 4 it should bring forth *g*.
Jer. 6. 9 turn . . hand as *g*. gather.
Hos. 9. 10 I found Israel like *g*.
Am. 9. 13 treader of *g*., him that
Obad. 5. if *g*. gatherer came to thee
Mic. 7. 1 I am . . as *g*. gleanings
Mat. 7. 16 do m. gath. *g*. of thorns
Luke 6. 44 nor of . . bush *g*. . . *g*.
Rev. 14. 18 her *g*. are fully ripe
   R. V. Lev. 19. 10 fallen fruit; S. of
   S. 2. 13; 7. 12 in blossom

Grass. *Herbage, hay, fodder, grass.*
Gen. 1. 11 let earth bring forth *g*.
Num. 22. 4 as ox licketh up the *g*.
Deut. 11. 15 I will send *g*. in field
2 Sam. 23. 4 the tender *g*. springeth
1 K. 18. 5 find *g*. to save the horses
2 K. 19. 26 the *g*. on the house tops
Job 6. 5 ass bray, when he hath *g*.?
Ps. 37. 2 soon be cut down like *g*.
   90. 5; 103. 15; 104. 14; 129. 6;
Prov. 19. 12 favour is as dew on *g*.
Isa. 15. 6 *g*. faileth, there is no green
Jer. 14. 5 forsook . . there was no *g*.
Dan. 4. 25 sh. make thee to eat *g*.
Am. 7. 2 made an end of eating *g*.
Mic. 5. 7 sh. be as showers upon *g*.
Zech. 10. 1 give . . to ev. one *g*. in f.
Mat. 6. 30 if God so clothe the *g*.
Mark 6. 39 make all sit . . on gr. *g*.
Luke 12. 28 if God so clothe the *g*.
John 6. 10 was much *g*. in the place
Jas. 1. 10 as the flower of the *g*.
1 Pet. 1. 24 all flesh is *g*., and all
Rev. 8. 7 all green *g*. was burnt up
   9. 4 should not hurt the g. of earth
   R. V. Isa. 15. 6 hay; Jer. 14. 6
   herbage; Jer. 50. 11 treadeth out
   the corn

Grasshopper. *Locust.*
Lev. 11. 22 ye may eat . . the *g*.
Num. 13. 33 we are . . as *g*., and
Judg. 6. 5 came as *g*. for multitude
Job 39. 20 make him afraid as *g*.
Eccl. 12. 5 and *g*. shall be a burden
Isa. 40. 22 inhabitants . . are as *g*.
Jer. 46. 23 they are more than the *g*.
Am. 7. 1 he formed *g*. in beginning
Nah. 3. 17 thy captains as great *g*.
   R. V. Judg. 6. 5; 7 12; Job. 39.
   20; Jer. 46. 23; Am. 7. 1 locusts

Grate. *Twisted, crossed, woven.*
Ex. 27. 4 make for it a *g*. of brass
   35. 16; 38. 4, 5, 30; 39. 39
   R. V. grating

Grave (*n*.). *The unseen state.*
Gen. 37. 34 I will go down into *g*.
   42. 38 gray hairs in sorrow to *g*.
1 Sam. 2. 6 bringeth down to the *g*.
1 K. 2. 6 not head go to *g*. in peace
Job 7. 9 he that goeth down to *g*.
   14. 13; 17. 13; 21. 13; 24. 19
Ps. 6. 5 in *g*. who . . give . . thanks
   30. 3; 31. 17; 49. 14; 88. 3; 141. 7
Prov. 1. 12 swallow them . . as *g*.
Eccl. 9. 10 no work . . in *g*. whither
S. of S. 8. 6 jealousy is cruel as *g*.
Isa. 14. 11 pomp is brought . . to *g*.
Ezek. 31. 15 he went down into *g*.
Hos. 13. 14 ransom . . fr. pow. of *g*.
1 Cor. 15. 55 O *g*., where is thy vic.
   Burial place.
Gen. 50. 5 *g*. which I have digged
Ex. 14. 11 no *g*. in Egypt hast thou

Num. 19. 16 toucheth .. bone .. or a *g*.
2 Sam. 3. 32 k. .. wept at *g*. of A.
1 K. 13. 30 laid .. carcase in his .. *g*.
2 K. 22. 20 be gathered unto thy *g*.
2 Chr. 34. 4 strowed it upon the *g*.
Job 3. 22 glad, when they find *g*.
   5. 26; 10. 19; 17. 1; 21. 32
Ps. 88. 5 like slain that lie in *g*.
Isa. 14. 19 thou art cast out of thy *g*.
Jer. 8. 1 bring bones . . out of *g*.
Ezek. 32. 22 his *g*. are about him
   32. 23, 25; 37. 12, 13; 39. 11
Nah. 1. 14 I will make my *g*., for
Mat. 27. 52 And the *g*. were opened
Luke 11. 44 for ye are as *g*. which
John 5. 28 all . . in the *g*. shall hear
   11. 17, 31, 38, 44; 12. 17
Rev. 11. 9 not suffer b. he put in *g*.
   R. V. Job 33. 22 pit; Mat. 27. 52;
   Luke 11. 44; John 5. 28; 11. 17
   31; Rev. 11. 9 tombs; 1 Cor. 15.
   55 death; Isa. 14. 19 sepulchre;
   Job 30. 24 ruinous heap; Job 7.
   9; 17. 13; Ps. 6. 5; 30. 3; 31. 17;
   49. 14, 15; 88. 3; 89. 48; Prov.
   1. 12; Hos. 13. 14 Sheol

Grave (*a*.). *Venerable, reverend.*
1 Tim. 3. 8. 11 deacons . . *g*., not d.
Tit. 2. 2 aged men be sober, *g*.

Grave (*v*.). *Cut, carve, hew out.*
Ex. 28. 9 *g*. on them the names of
1 K. 7. 36 he *g*. cherubims, lions
2 Chr. 2. 7 skill to *g*. with cunning
Job 19. 24 *g*. with iron pen . . in rock
Isa. 22. 16 *g*. an hab. for himself
Jer. 17. 1 *g*. on table of their heart
Hab. 2. 18 maker thereof hath *g*. it
Acts 17. 29 *g*. by . . man's device

Gravel. *Halved stone, pebbles*
Prov. 20. 17 mouth be filled with *g*.
Isa. 48. 19 offspring of bow. like *g*.
Lam. 3. 16 broken teeth with *g*. st.
   R. V. Isa. 48. 19 grains

Graven (*a*.). *Carved, cut, hewn.*
Ex. 20. 4 not make any *g*. image
Lev. 26. 1 make no idols nor *g*. im.
Dent. 4. 16; Judg. 17. 13; 2 K.
   21. 7; Isa. 40. 19; Jer. 10. 14;
   Nah. 1. 14; Hab. 2. 18; Hos. 11.
   12; Mic. 1. 7

Graving. *Carving.*
Ex. 32. 4 fashion it with *g*. tool
1 K. 7. 31 on mouth of it were *g*.
2 Chr. 2. 14 grave any manner of *g*.
Zech. 3. 9 I will engrave the *g*.

Gravity. *Sedateness.*
1 Tim. 3. 4 in subjec. with all *g*.
Tit. 2. 7 uncorruptness, *g*., sincer.

Gray. *Gray, hoary.*
Gen. 42. 38 bring my *g*. h. wi. sor.
Deut. 32. 25 with man of *g*. hairs
1 Sam. 12. 2 am old and *g*. headed
Job 15. 10 *g*. headed, and very aged
Ps. 71. 18 when I am old and *g*. h.
Prov. 20. 29 beaut. of old m. is *g*. h.
Hos. 7. 9 *g*. hairs are here and there
   R. V. Prov. 20. 29 hoary

Grease. *Fat.*
Ps. 119. 70 Their heart is as fat as *g*.

Great. *Large, big, immense, vast, important, noble, grand.*
Gen. 1. 16 G. made two *g*. lights
Ex. 3. 3 I will . . see this *g*. sight
Num. 13. 28 c. are walled, and .. *g*.
Deut. 1. 7 unto the *g*. river, Eu.
Josh. 1. 4 unto the *g*. sea toward
Judg. 2. 7 J. had seen all *g*. works
1 Sam. 2. 17 sin of young m. was .. *g*.
2 Sam. 5. 10 David . . grew *g*. and
1 K. 1. 40 peop. rejoiced with *g*. joy
2 K. 3. 27 *g*. indig. against Israel
1 Chr. 11. 14 L. saved . . by *g*. deliv.
Ez. 3. 11 peo. shouted with *g*. sho.
Neh. 1. 3 remnant are in *g*. afflic.
Esth. 1. 5 feast, unto *g*. and small
Job 1 19 came a *g*. wind from wil.
Ps. 21. 5 His glory is *g*. in thy salv.
Prov. 19. 19 *g*. wrath sh. suf. pun.
Eccl. 9. 13 and it seemed *g*. to me
Isa. 8. 1 take thee a *g*. roll and
Jer. 6. 22 *g*. nat. shall be raised fr.
Lam. 2. 13 thy breach is *g*. like sea
Ezek. 1. 4 *g*. cloud, and a fire infold
Dan. 8. 21 *g*. horn . . bet. his eyes
Hos. 1. 11 *g*. . . the day of Jezreel
Joel 2. 11 day of Lord is *g*. and ter.

Am. 6. 11 will smite the *g*. house
Jonah 1. 2 go to Nineveh . . *g*. city
Mic. 7. 3 *g*. man, he uttereth his
Nah. 1. 3 Lord slow to ang. and *g*.
Zeph. 1. 10 *g*. crashing from hills
Zech. 1. 14 jealous . . with a *g*. jeal.
Mal. 1. 11 name shall be *g*. among
Mat. 2. 10 rejoiced with excee. *g*. joy.
   4. 16 peo. in dark. saw *g*. light
   5. 19 be called *g*. in the kingdom
   7. 27 fell, *g*. was the fall thereof
   8. 24 there arose a *g*. tempest
   15. 28 O woman, *g*. is thy faith
   20. 26 whoso. will be *g*. among you
   22. 36 which is the *g*. command.
   24. 21 then shall be *g*. tribulation
   27. 60 rolled *g*. stone to door of sep.
   28. 2 there was *g*. earthquake, for
Mark 4. 32 shooteth out *g*. branches
Luke 1. 15 sh. be *g*. in sight of Lord
John 6. 18 by reason of *g*. wind
Acts 2. 20 before that *g*. notable day
   19. 28 *g*. is Diana of the Ephesians
Rom. 9. 2 That I have *g*. heaviness
1 Cor. 16. 9 *g*. door and ef. is open.
2 Cor. 3. 12 we use *g*. plain. of sp.
Eph. 5. 32 this is a *g*. mystery, but
Col. 4. 13 he hath a *g*. zeal for you
1 Thes. 2. 17 see . . face with *g*. desire
1 Tim. 3. 13 ha. *g*. boldness in faith
2 Tim. 2. 20 in *g*. house there are
Tit. 2. 13 appear. of the *g*. God
Phile. 7 we have *g*. joy and conso.
Heb. 10. 32 endur. *g*. fight of affl.
Jude 6 unto judgment of the *g*. day
Rev. 8. 10 fell *g*. star from heaven
   The R. V. changes, which are fre-
   quent, mostly turn on antecedent
   and consequent words

Greater. *Greater.*
Gen. 1. 16 *g*. light to rule the day
Ex. 18. 11 Lord is *g*. than all gods
Num. 14. 12 *g*. nation and mightier
Deut. 1. 28 people is *g*. and taller
Josh. 10. 2 Gibeon . . was *g*. than Ai
1 Sam. 14. 30 had there not been a *g*.
2 Sam. 13. 15 *g*. than the love wher.
1 Chr. 11. 9 David waxed *g*. and *g*.
2 Chr. 3. 5 *g*. house he cieled with
Esth. 9. 4 Morde. waxed *g*. and *g*.
Job 33. 12 ans, thee, that God is *g*.
Lam. 4. 6 *g*. than punishm. of sin.
Ezek. 8. 6 shalt see *g*. abomina.
Hag. 2. 9 glo. of this house . . be *g*.
Mat. 11. 11 hath not risen a *g*. than
Mark 4. 32 groweth and becom. *g*.
Luke 7. 28 not *g*. proph. than John
John 4. 12 *g*. than our father Jacob
Acts 15. 28 lay . . no *g*. burden than
1 Cor. 14. 5 *g*. is he that proph. th.
Heb. 6. 16 men . . swear by the *g*.
Jas. 3. 1 receive the *g*. condemna.
2 Pet. 2. 11 angels, which are *g*. in
1 John 3. 20 G. is *g*. than our heart

Greatest. *Greatest.*
1 Chr. 12. 14 *g*. over a thousand
Job 1. 3 *g*. of all the men of the east
Jer. 6. 13 from least even to the *g*.
Jonah 3. 5 from *g*. of them even to
Mat. 13. 32 mus. s. *g*. among herbs
   18. 4 same is *g*. in kingdom of heav.
Mark 9. 34 dis. who should be *g*.
Luke 22. 26 he that is *g*. . . let him
Acts 8. 10 ga. heed, from least to *g*.
1 Cor. 13. 13 but the *g*. of these is
Heb. 8. 11 know me from l. to *g*.

Greatly. *Mightily, much.*
Gen. 7. 18 and were increased *g*.
Ex. 19. 18 whole mount quaked *g*.
Num. 11. 10 ang. of L. was kindl. *g*.
Deut. 17. 17 nei. shall he *g*. multipl.
Josh. 10. 2 feared *g*. bec. Gib. was
Judg. 2. 15 they were *g*. distressed
1 Sam. 11. 6 anger was kindled *g*.
2 Sam. 12. 5 D's. ang. was *g*. kind.
1 K. 5. 7 Hiram heard, rejoiced *g*.
1 Chr. 16. 25 L.. and *g*. to be prai.
2 Chr. 33. 12 M. humbled himself *g*.
Job 8. 7 lat. end should *g*. increase
Ps. 38. 6 I am bowed down *g*. ; I go
Jer. 9. 19 we are *g*. confounded
Ezek. 20. 13 sab. they *g*. polluted
Dan. 5. 9 then was Bel. *g*. troubled
Obad. 2 small, thou art *g*. despised
Zeph. 1. 14 day near, and hasteth *g*.
Zech. 9. 9 rejoice *g*.. O daughters

Mat. 27. 14 the gov. marvelled *g.*
Mark 5. 23 besought him *g.* saying
John 3. 29 rejoice *g.* because of voi.
Acts 6. 7 disciples multiplied . . *g.*
1 Cor. 16. 12 I *g.* desired him to co.
Phil. 4. 10 I rejoice in the Lord *g.*
2 Tim. 4. 15 *g.* withstood my word
2 John 4 I rejoiced *g.* that I found
3 John. 3. For I rejoiced *g.* when

Greatness. *Greatness.*
Ex. 15. 7 in *g.* of thine excellency
Num. 14. 19 accord. unto the *g.* of
Deut. 3. 24 begun to show . . thy *g.*
1 Chr. 17. 19 hast . . done all this *g.*
2 Chr. 9. 6 *g.* of thy wisdom was not
Neh. 13. 22 spare . . accord. to *g.* of
Esth. 10. 2 declaration of *g.* of Mor.
Ps. 66. 3 through *g.* of thy power
Prov. 5. 23 sh. die in *g.* of his folly
Isa. 40. 26 names by the *g.* of his
Jer. 13. 22 *g.* of thine iniquity are sk.
Ezek. 31. 2 whom art thou like in *g.*
Dan. 4. 22 for thy *g.* is grown, and
Eph. 1. 19 what is the exceeding *g.*

Greaves. *Frontlets.*
1 Sam. 17. 6 had *g.* of brass on legs

Greedily. *Avariciously.*
Prov. 21. 26 he coveteth *g.* all day
Ezek. 22. 12 hast *g.* gained of neigh.
Jude 11 ran *g.* after error of Balaam

Greediness. *Avariciousness.*
Eph. 4. 19 work unclean. with *g.*

Greedy. *Avaricious, voracious.*
Prov. 1. 19 one that is *g.* of gain
Ps. 17. 12 like as lion *g.* of his prey
Isa. 56. 11 *g.* dogs . . nev. have eno.

Green. *Verdant, fresh, flourishing.*
Gen. 30. 37 took rods of *g.* poplar
Ex. 10. 15 remain, not any *g.* thing
Deut. 12. 2 and under every *g.* tree
Judg. 16. 7 bind me with *g.* withs
1 K. 14. 23 built . . under ev. *g.* tree
2 K. 17. 10 set im. under ev. *g.* tree
Esth. 1. 6 white, *g.*, and blue hang.
Job 15. 32 his branch sh. not be *g.*
Ps. 23. 2 maketh . . to lie in *g.* past.
    37. 35 spread. . . like *g.* bay tree
S. of S. 1. 16 also our bed is *g.*
Isa. 57. 5 idols under every *g.* tree
Jer. 2. 20 under . . *g.* t. thou wander.
Ezek. 6. 13 under every *g.* tree, and
Hos. 14. 8 I am like a *g.* fir tree
Mark 6. 39 sit down . . on *g.* grass
Rev. 8. 7 and all *g.* grass was burnt
R. V. Gen. 30. 37; Lev. 23. 14
   fresh: Lev. 2. 14 corn in the ear

Greenish. *Green, yellow.*
Lev. 13. 49 if plague be *g.* or red.
   14. 37 hollow strakes *g.* or reddish

Greenness. *Freshness, budding.*
Job 8. 12 whilst it is yet in 'his *g.*

Greet. R. V. *salute.*
Rom. 16. 13 *g.* Priscilla and Aquila
1 Cor. 16. 20 all the brethren *g.* you
2 Cor. 13. 12 *g.* on anoth. with kiss
Phil. 4. 21 the brethren with me *g.*
Col. 4. 14 Luke . . and Demas *g.*
1 Thes. 5. 26 *g.* all breth. with kiss
2 Tim. 4. 21 Ebulus *g.* thee, and P.
Tit. 3. 15 *g.* them that love us in fai.
1 Pet. 5. 14 *g.* one another with . . c.
2 John 13 chil. of el. sist. *g.* thee
3 John 14 *g.* the friends by name
To ask in peace.
1 Sam. 25. 5 *g.* him in my name

Greeting. *Rejoicing, good cheer.*
Acts 15. 23 elders . . send *g.* to breth.
Jas. 1. 1 Jas. to twelve tribes, *g.*
R. V. *salutation.*
Mat. 23. 7 *g.* in the markets and
Luke 11. 43 love . . *g.* in markets
   26. 24 which love *g.* in markets

Grew. *See* Grow.

Grey. *Gray, hoary.*
Ps. 71. 18 I am old and *g.* headed
Prov. 20. 29 beauty of o. m. is *g.* head

Greyhound. *Girt in the loins, stag.*
Prov. 30. 31 a *g.* and he goat also

Grief. *Sorrow, affliction, sadness.*
Gen. 26. 35 *g.* of mind unto Isaac
1 Sam. 1. 16 out of abund. of my *g.*
2 Chr. 6. 29 ev. one shall know . . *g.*
Job 2. 13 his *g.* was very great
Ps. 6. 7 mine eye is consum. . . of *g.*
Prov. 17. 25 foolish son is *g.* to fath.

Eccl. 1. 18 in much wis. is much *g.*
Isa. 53. 3 sorrows, acquaint. with *g.*
Jer. 6. 7 before me continuall. is *g.*
Lam. 3. 32 though he cause *g.*, yet
Jonah 4. 6 to deliver him from *g.*
2 Cor. 2. 5 if any have caused *g.*
Heb. 13. 17 with joy, and not . . *g.*
R. V. 1 Sam. 1. 16 provocation; 2
   Chr. 6. 29; Ps. 31. 10; 69. 29; Jer.
   45. 3; 2 Cor. 2. 5 sorrow; Joh 6. 2
   vexation; Jer. 6. 7 sickness; Jonah
   4. 6 evil case

Grievance. R. V. *perverseness.*
Hab. 1. 3 cause me to behold *g.*

Grieve. *Inflict sorrow, afflict, pain.*
Gen. 6. 6 and it *g.* him at his heart
Ex. 1. 12 were *g.* because of child.
Deut. 15. 10 heart shall not be *g.*
Judg. 10. 16 soul was *g.* for . . Is.
Ruth 1. 13 *g.* me much for your sakes
1 Sam. 1. 8 and why is thy heart *g.*?
2 Sam. 19. 2 k. was *g.* for his son
1 Chr. 4. 10 that it may not *g.* me
Neh. 8. 11 holy, neither be ye *g.*
Esth. 4. 4 queen was exceedingly *g.*
Job 30. 25 my soul was *g.* for poor
Ps. 95. 10 forty years long was I *g.*
Prov. 26. 15 it *g.* him to bring it ag.
Isa. 54. 6 woman forsaken and *g.*
Jer. 5. 3 stricken . . but have not *g.*
Lam. 3. 33 doth not afflict . . nor *g.*
Ezek. 28. 24 shall be no more *g.*
Dan. 7. 15 Daniel was *g.* in spirit
Amos. 6. 6 not *g.* for affliction of
Mark 3. 5 being *g.* for the hardness
John 21. 17 Peter was *g.* because
Acts 4. 2 *g.* that they taught people
Rom. 14. 15 if bro. be *g.* with . . meat
2 Cor. 2. 4 not that ye should be *g.*
Eph. 4. 30 *g.* not the Holy Spirit
Heb. 3. 10 was *g.* with that genera.
R. V. 1 Sam. 15. 11 was wroth; 1
   Chr. 4. 10 not to my sorrow; Prov.
   26. 15 wearieth; Isa. 57. 10 faint;
   Mark 10. 22 sorrowful; Acts 4. 2
   16. 18 sore troubled; 2 Cor. 2. 4
   made sorry; 2. 5 caused sorrow;
   Heb. 3. 10, 17 displeased

Grievous. *Distressing, heavy, hurtful.*
Gen. 12. 10 famine was *g.* in land
Ex. 8. 24 came *g.* swarm of flies
1 K. 2. 8 cursed me with *g.* curse
2 Chr. 10. 4 ease thou . . *g.* servitude
Ps. 31. 18 speak *g.* things proudly
Prov. 15. 10 correction is *g.* to him
Eccl. 2. 17 work th. is *g.* unto me
Isa. 21. 2 a *g.* vision is declared
Jer. 10. 19 woe . . my wound is *g.*
Nah. 3. 19 no healing . . wound is *g.*
Mat. 23. 4 burden *g.* to be borne
Luke 11. 46 lade . . with burdens *g.*
Acts 20. 29 shall *g.* wolves enter a.
Phil. 3. 1 to write me is not *g.*
Heb. 12. 11 seemeth . . joyous, but *g.*
1 John 5. 3 his comman. are not *g.*
Rev. 16. 2 there fell . . a *g.* sore
R. V. Gen. 12. 10 sore; Ps. 10. 5
   firm; 31. 18 insolently; Isa. 15. 4
   trembleth within; Jer. 23. 19
   whirling; Phil. 3. 1 perilous

Grievously. *Painfully, distressingly.*
Isa. 9. 1 afterwards did *g.* afflict
Jer. 23. 19 fall *g.* on head of wicked
Lam. 1. 20 for I have *g.* rebelled
Ezek. 14. 13 sinneth . . by tres. *g.*
Mat. 8. 6 sick of palsy, *g.* tormented
   15. 22 my daughter is *g.* vexed
R. V. Isa. 9. 1 hath made it glorious; Jer. 23. 19 burst; Ezek. 14.
   13 committing a trespass.

Grievousness. *Weightiness, misery.*
Isa. 10. 1 woe to them that write *g.*
   21. 15 they fled . . from *g.* of war
R. V. Isa. 10. 1 perverseness

Grind. *Make fine, rub.*
Ex. 32. 20 calf . . and *g.* it to pow.
Num. 11. 8 gath. it, and *g.* it, in a m.
Deut. 9. 21 took . . calf . . and *g.* it
Judg. 16. 21 he did *g.* in the prison
Job 31. 10 let . . wife *g.* unto anoth.
Lam. 5. 13 took young men to *g.*
Isa. 3. 15 *g.* faces of the poor? saith

Mat. 21. 44 it will *g.* him to powder
Luke 17. 35 two women thall be *g.*
R. V. Lam. 5. 13 young men bare
   the mill; Mat. 21. 44; Luke 20.
   18 scatter.

Grinder. *Who grinds.*
Eccl. 12. 3 the *g.* shall cease, bec.

Grinding. *Making fine, milling.*
Eccl. 12. 4 when sound of *g.* is low

Grisled. *Grizzled, gray.*
Gen. 31. 10 rams . . speckled and *g.*
Zech. 6. 3 in fourth char. . . *g.* horses

Groan. *Sigh.*
Joel 1. 18 How do the beasts *g.*! the
   Make dismal sound.
Job 24. 12 men *g.* from out of city
Jer. 51. 52 through . . l. wounded *g.*
Ezek. 30. 24 he shall *g.* before him
John 11. 33 he *g.* in the spirit, and
Rom. 8. 22 whole creation . . *g.* in
2 Cor. 5. 2 in this we *g.*, earnestly

Groaning. *Groaning, sighing.*
Ex. 2. 24 God heard their *g.* and
Judg. 2. 18 it repent. L. bec. of . . *g.*
Job 23. 2 stroke is heav. than . . *g.*
Ps. 6. 6 am weary with my *g.*; all
Ezek. 30. 24 groan . . with *g.* of a
Acts 7. 34 and I have heard their *g.*
Rom. 8. 26 for us with *g.* which

Grope. *Feel, search.*
Deut. 28. 29 shall *g.* at noon day
Job 12. 25 *g.* in dark without light
Isa. 59. 10 we *g.* . . like the blind

Gross. *Fat, thick, coarse.*
Mat. 13. 15 peo's heart is waxed *g.*
Acts 28. 27 heart of peo. is waxed *g.*

Ground. *Earth, soil, land, field.*
Gen. 2. 5 was not a man to till *g.*
   18. 2 Abr. bowed himself toward *g.*
Ex. 3. 5 where thou stand. is h. *g.*
   9. 23 and the fire ran along the *g.*
Lev. 20. 25 thing that creepeth on *g.*
Num. 16. 31 the *g.* clave asunder
Deut. 4. 18 anything that creep. on *g.*
Josh. 24. 32 *g.* which Jacob bought
Judg. 4. 21 nail, fastened it into *g.*
Ruth 2. 10 she bowed herself to *g.*
1 Sam. 3. 19 let none . . words fall *g.*
2 Sam. 2. 22 I smite thee to the *g.*
1 K. 7. 46 king cast them in clay *g.*
2 K. 2. 15 bowed themsel. to the *g.*
1 Chr. 27. 26 for tillage of the *g.*
2 Chr. 4. 17 in clay *g.* bet. S. & Z.
Neh. 10. 35 bring firstfruits of *g.*
Job 16. 13 poureth out gall on *g.*
Ps. 105. 35 devoureth fruit of *g.*
Isa. 3. 26 desolate, shall sit on *g.*
Jer. 14. 2 gates . . are black as *g.*
Lam. 2. 9 Her gates are sunk in *g.*
Ezek. 12. 12 see not *g.* with eyes
Dan. 8. 12 it cast . . truth to the *g.*
Hos. 2. 18 with creeping things of *g.*
Am. 3. 14 horns . . shall fall to *g.*
Hag. 1. 11 which *g.* bringeth forth
Zech. 8. 12 *g.* shall give . . increase
Mat. 10. 29 one . . shall not fall on *g.*
Mark 4. 8 and other fell on good *g.*
Luke 8. 15 that on good *g.* are they
John 8. 6 with finger wrote on *g.*
Acts 22. 7 fell unto *g.* and heard
1 Tim. 3. 15 pillar and *g.* of truth
R. V. Gen. 18. 2; 19. 1; Jer. 27. 5;
   Mark 4. 26; John 12. 24 earth;
   2 K. 2. 19; Ps. 107. 35; Ezek. 19.
   13 land; 2 Sam. 23. 12 plot; Isa.
   35. 7 sand; Mark 4. 16 rocky
   places; Luke 14. 18 field.

Grounded. *Founded.*
Isa. 30. 32 where *g.* staff shall pass
Eph. 3. 17 rooted and *g.* in love
Col. 1. 23 in faith *g.* and settled
R. V. Isa. 30. 32 appointed

Grove. R. V. *tamarisk trees.*
Gen. 21. 33 planted *g.* in Beer-she.
R. V. *Asherah, Asherim*
Asherah (pl. Asherim) was the Semitic goddess, consort of Bel. Her
images, pillars and shrines on hill
and in groves, typed her; and
hence, by figure, the *grove* came to
do the same.
Ex. 34. 13 shall . . cut down their *g.*
Deut. 12. 3 break pillars, and burn *g.*
Judg. 3. 7 serve Baalim and the *g.*
1 K. 14. 23 built h. pl., im. and *g.*
2 K. 13. 6 there remained the *g.*

2 Chr. 14. 3 break im. and cut .. *g.*
Isa. 27. 9 *g.* and im. shall not stand
Jer. 17. 2 remem. . . altars and *g.*
Mic. 5. 14 I will pluck up thy *g.*

Grow. *Go up, increase, thrive, become, come.*

Gen. 21. 8 and the child *g.,* and
Ex. 10. 5 eat every tree which *g.*
Lev. 13. 39 it is a freck. spot that *g.*
Deut. 29. 23 nor any grass *g.* therein
Judg. 19. 9 the day *g.* to an end
Ruth. 1. 13 tarry till they were *g.*
1 Sam. 2. 21 the child Samuel *g.*
2 Sam. 10. 5 tarry at Jer. till b. be *g.*
1 K. 12. 8, 10 young men . . *g.* up
2 K. 19. 29 as *g.* of themselves
1 Chr. 19. 5 tarry till beards be *g.*
Ez. 4. 22 why should damage *g.*
Job 38. 38 the dust *g.* into hardness
Ps. 104. 14 causeth grass to *g.* for cat.
Prov. 24. 31 all *g.* over with thorns
Eccl. 11. 5 know not how bones *g.*
Isa. 37. 30 eat .. such as *g.* of itself
Jer. 12. 2 *g.* yea, bring forth fruit
Ezek. 44. 29 nor suffer locks to *g.*
Dan. 4. 22 thou, O k., that art *g.*
Hos. 14. 5 he shall *g.* as the lily
Jonah 4. 10 neither madest it *g.*
Zech. 6. 12 he sh. *g.* out of his place
Mal. 4. 2 ye shall up *g.* as calves
Mat. 6. 28 lilies of field, how they *g.*
Mark 5. 26 noth. better. but rath. *g.*
Luke 1. 80 child *g.,* and wax. strong
Acts 7. 17 people *g.* and multiplied
Eph. 2. 21 *g.* unto an holy temple
1 Pet. 2. 2 that ye may *g.* thereby
2 Pet. 3. 18 *g.* in grace and knowl.
R. V. Lev. 13. 39 hath broken out ;
Job 14. 19 overflowings ; 18. 18
spring ; 38. 38 runneth ; Isa. 11. 1
bear fruit ; Hos. 14. 5, 7 blossom ;
Mal. 4. 2 gambol ; Mat. 21. 19 no
fruit from

Grown. *See Grow.*

Growth. *Product.*
Am. 7. 1 shooting up of latter *g.*

Grudge (n.). *Anger, hatred.*
Lev. 19. 18 shalt not .. bear any *g.*

Grudge (v.). *Murmur.*
Ps. 59. 15 *g.* if .. be not satisfied.
1 Pet. 4. 9 use hospital .. without *g.*

Groan, *sigh*
Jas. 5. 9 *g.* not one ag. another
R. V. Ps. 38. 8 all night ; Jas.
5. 9 ; 1 Pet. 4. 9 murmur

Grudgingly. *Out of grief.*
2 Cor. 9. 7 not *g.,* or of necessity

Guard. *Butcher, slaughterer.*
Gen. 37. 36 Potiphar, captain of *g.*
2 K. 25. 8 ; Jer. 39. 9 ; Dan. 2. 14
Defence, protection
2 Sam. 23. 23 D. set him over .. *g.*
1 Chr. 11. 25 D. set him over his *g.*
Watch
Neh. 4. 22 that th. may be a. g. to us
Ezek. 38. 7 be .. a *g.* unto them
Runner
1 K. 14. 27 unto hands of chief of *g.*
2 K. 10. 25 Jehu said to the *g.*
2 Chr. 12. 11 *g.* came and fetched

Guard-chamber. *Place of the guard.*
1 K. 14. 28 brought them into *g. c.*
2 Chr. 12. 11 brought them ag. to *g. c.*

Guest. *Invited one, sitter down.*
1 K. 1. 41, 49 Ado. and all the *g.* that
Prov. 9. 18 *g.* are in depths of hell
Zeph. 1. 7 sacrif., he hath bid his *g.*
Mat. 22. 10 wed. was furnish. w. *g.*
Luke 19. 7 *g.* with m. that is sin.
R. V. Luke 19. 7 gone in to lodge

Guest-chamber. *Place for resting.*
Mark 14. 14 saith, Where is the *g.* c.
Luke 22. 11 Where is the *g. c.* where

Guide (n.). *Leader, conductor.*
Ps. 48. 14 God .. will be our *g.*
Prov. 2. 17 forsak. *g.* of her youth
Jer. 3. 4. My father, thou art *g.* of
Mic. 7. 5 put not confidence in *g.*
Mat. 23. 16 Woe unto you, blind *g.*
Acts 1. 16 *g.* to them that took J.
Rom. 2. 19 thou art *g.* of blind
R. V. Ps. 55. 13 companion ; Prov.
2. 17 friend ; 6. 7 chief

Guide (v.). *Lead, show, tend*

Gen. 48. 14 *g.* his hands wittingly
Ex. 15. 13 hast *g.* . . in thy strength
2 Chr. 52. 22 L. saved .. and *g.* them
Job 38. 32 canst thou *g* Arcturus
Ps. 25. 9 meek will he *g.* in judg.
31. 3 for thy name's sake .. *g.*
32. 8 I will *g.* thee with mine eye.
Prov. 11. 3 integ. of upright shall *g.*
Isa. 49. 10 by springs .. shall he *g.*
Luke 1. 79 *g.* feet in way of peace
John 16. 13 will *g.* you to .. truth
Acts 8. 31 except some man *g.* me
1 Tim. 5. 14 younger wom. *g.* house
R. V. Ps. 32. 8 counsel ; 112. 5
shall maintain ; 1 Tim. 5. 14 rule

Guile. *Deceit, craftiness.*
Ex. 21. 14 if man .. slays .. with *g.*
Ps. 32. 2 in whose spirit is no *g.*
34. 13 keep lips from speaking *g.*
John 1. 47 Israel in whom is no *g.*
2 Cor. 12. 16 I caught you with *g.*
1 Thes. 2. 3 our ex. was not in *g.*
1 Pet. 2. 1 laying aside .. all *g.* and
Rev. 14. 5 mouth was found no *g.*
R. V. Rev. 14. 5 lie

Guilt. *Condemnation.*
Deut. 19. 13 *g.* of innocent blood
R. V. ——

Guiltiness. *Guilt.*
Gen. 26. 10 have brought *g.* upon
Ps. 51. 14 deliver me from blood *g.*

Guiltless. *Innocent, free.*
Ex. 20. 7 L. will not hold him *g.*
Num. 32. 22 and be *g.* before the
Deut. 5. 11 not hold him *g.* that
1 Sam. 26. 9 L's anoint. and be *g.*
2 Sam. 14. 9 k. and his throne be *g.*
1 K. 2. 9 therefore hold him not *g.*
Mat. 12. 7 not have cond. the *g.*
R. V. Num. 5. 31 free

Guilty. *Held in, subject to*
Mat .26. 66 said, He is *g.* of death
Mark 14. 64 condemn. him to be *g.*
1 Cor. 11. 27 *g.* of body and blood
Jas. 2. 10 offend in one .. *g.* of all
In or under guilt
Gen. 42. 21 *g.* concerning our br.
Lev. 4. 13 not be done, and are *g.*
Num. 35. 31 murderer which is *g.*
Judg. 21. 22 that ye should be *g.*
Prov. 30. 10 and thou be found *g.*
Ezek. 22. 4 art become *g.* in blood
Zech. 11. 5 hold themselves not *g.*
Mat. 23. 18 sweareth by gift he is *g.*
Rom. 3. 19 world may bec. *g.* bef. G
R. V. Mat. 23. 18 debtor ; 26. 66 ;
Mark 14. 64 worthy ; Rom. 3. 19
brought under judgment of

Gulf. *Chasm, rent.*
Luke 16. 26 bet. us is great *g.* fixed

Gush. *Flow, pour out.*
1 K. 18. 28 cut .. till the blood *g.*
Ps. 78. 20 smote rock that waters *g.*
Isa. 48. 21 clave rock .. waters *g.* out
Jer. 9. 18 our eyelids *g.* with waters
Acts 1. 18 and all his bowels *g.* out

Gutter. R. V. *watercourse.*
2 Sam. 5. 8 whoso. get. up to the *g.*
Gutter, trough.
Gen. 30. 38 set rods in the *g.* bef. flo.
30. 41 Jacob laid rods in the *g.*

H

Ha. *He-ah.*
Job 39. 25 saith among trumpe. *h. h.*

Habergeon. *Coat of mail.*
Ex. 28. 32 as it w. the hole of an *h.*
2 Chr. 26. 14 spears, helmets, and *h.*
Neh. 4. 16 shields, bows, and the *h.*
Job 41. 26 spear, the dart nor the *h.*
R. V. Ex. 28. 32 ; 39. 23 ; 2 Chr. 26.
14 ; Neh. 4. 16 coat, or coats, of
mail ; Job 41. 27 pointed shaft

Habitable. *Inhabitable.*
Prov. 8. 31 rejoi. in *h.* part of earth

Habitation. *Seat, dwelling place.*
Gen. 36. 43 according to their *h.*
Ex. 15. 13 guided .. unto thy holy *h.*
Lev. 13. 46 without camp .. his *h.* be
Num. 15. 2 come into l. of your *h.*
Deut. 26. 15 look .. from thy holy *h.*
1 Sam. 2. 29 have comman. in my *h.*
2 Sam. 15. 25 show me it .. his *h.*
2 Chr. 29. 6 turned .. faces from *h.*
Ez. 7. 15 God .. whose *h.* is in Jer.

Job 4. 3 suddenly I cursed his *h.*
Ps. 26. 8 I ha. loved *h.* of thy house
Prov. 3. 33 blesseth *h.,* of the just
Isa. 27. 10 the *h.* forsaken and left
Jer. 10. 25 ha. made his *h.* desolat
Lam. 2. 2 Lord hath swallow. all *h.*
Ezek. 6. 14 desolate in all their *h.*
Dan. 4. 21 the fowls .. had their *h.*
Am. 1. 2 *h.* of shepherds shall mourn
Obad. 3 in rock, whose *h.* is high
Hab. 3. 11 sun, moon stood .. in . *h.*
Zech 2. 13 raised out of .. holy *h.*
Luke 16. 9 receiv. . . . into everlast. *h.*
Acts 1. 20 let his *h.* be desolate, and
Eph. 2. 22 builded tog. for *h.* of G.
Jude 6. angels .. left their own *h.*
Rev. 18. 2 Bab. is become *h.* of dev.
R. V. Gen. 49. 5 their swords ; Ex.
15. 2 praise him ; Lev. 13. 46 dwelling ; 1 Chr. 4. 41 Meunim (Mehunim) ; Job 5. 24 ; Jer. 25. 30, 37
fold ; 41. 17 Geruth ; Ps. 89. 14 ;
97. 2 foundation ; Jer. 9. 10 ; 50. 19 ;
Am. 1. 2 pasture ; Luke 16. 9 eternal tabernacles

Had. *See Have.*

Haft. *Shaft, handle.*
Judg. 3. 22 *h.* went in after blade

Hail (n.). *Hail.*
Ex. 9. 18 cause it to rain a grievous *h.*
9. 19–34 ; 10. 5–12, 15
Job 38. 22 hast seen treas. of the *h.*
Ps. 18. 12, 13 *h.* s. and coals of fire
Isa. 28. 2 as a tempest of *h* and s.
Hag. 2. 17 I smote you with .. *h.*
Rev. 8. 7 there followed *h.* and fire
11. 19 ; 16. 21

Hail (v.). *To hail.*
Isa. 32. 19 quiet pl., when it shall *h.*

Hail (intj.).
Mat. 26. 49 said, *H,* Master and
Mark 15. 18 *H.* King of the Jews !
Luke 1. 28 *H.* ! highly favored, thou
John 19. 3 said, *H.* King of Jews !

Hailstones. *Stones of hail.*
Josh. 10. 11 more .. died of *h. s.* than
Isa. 30. 30 with tempest and *h. s.*

Hair. *Hair (of head or body.)*
Lev. 13. 3 *h.* in pla. is turned white
13. 4–37 ; 14. 8, 9
Num. 6. 5 let .. *h.* of his head grow
Judg. 16. 22 *h.* began to grow ag.
1 Sam. 14. 45 not *h.* of head fall to
2 Sam. 14. 11 not *h.* of thy son fall
1 K. 1. 52 not *h.* of him fall to earth
Ez. 9. 3 plucked .. the *h.* of my head
Neh. 13. 25 and plucked off their *h.*
Job 4. 15 the *h.* of my flesh stood up
Ps. 40. 12 more than *h.* of my head
S. of S. 4. 1 *h.* is as a flock of goats
Isa. 7. 20 L. sh. shave . . *h.* of the feet
Jer. 7. 29 cut off thine *h.,* O Jerusa.
Ezek. 16. 7 and thine *h.* is grown
Dan. 3. 27 nor was *h.* of head singed
Hos. 7. 9 gray *h.* here and there
Mat. 10. 30 *h.* of head are number.
Luke 7. 38 wipe .. with *h.* of her h'd
John 11. 2 wiped his f. with her *h.*
Acts 27. 34 not *h.* fall from head
1 Cor. 11. 14 m. have l. *h.* .. shame
11. 15 wom. have l. *h.* . . . glory
Rev. 1. 14 *h.* white like wool, as s.
Braided hair, curled wool.
Isa. 3. 24 instead of .. *h.* baldness
1 Tim. 2. 9 not with broided *h.,* or *g.*
1 Pet. 3. 3 not adorn. of plaiting *h.*
Hair of animals, wool.
Mat. 3. 4 John had rai. of cam. *h.*
Mark 1. 6 clothed with camel's *h.*
Rev. 6. 12 black as sackcloth of *h.*

Hairy. *Hirsute.*
Gen. 27. 11 Esau .. is a *h.* man
2 K. 1. 8 *h.* man, girt with girdle
Ps. 68. 21 *h.* scalp of such as go

Hale. *Draw, drag, haul.*
Luke 12. 58 lest he *h.* to the judge
Acts 8. 3 *h.* men and women, com.

Half. *Half, middle.*
Ex. 24. 6 Moses took *h.* of blood
Num. 12. 12 flesh is *h.* consumed
Deut. 3. 13 gave *h.* tribe of Man.
Josh. 1. 12 ; 1 Sam. 14. 14 ; 2 Sam.
10. 4 ; 1 K. 3. 25 ; 1 Chr. 2. 52 ; 2
Chr. 9. 6 ; Neh. 3. 9 ; Esth. 5. 3 ;
Ezek. 16. 51 ; Dan. 12. 7 ; Zeph.
14. 2

Mark 6. 23 will give, unto the *h.*
Luke 19. 8 *h.* my g. I give to poor
Rev. 8. 1 silence .. about *h.* hour
Hall. *Court, Prætor's office.*
Mat. 27. 27 took J. into common *h.*
Mark 15. 16 soldiers led him into *h.*
Luke 22. 55 had kind. fire in .. *h.*
R. V. Mark 15. 16; Luke 22. 55
   court
Hallow. *Set apart.*
Ex. 20. 11 blessed sab. day and *h.* it
Lev. 12. 4 touch no *h.* thing, nor
Num. 6. 11 sh. *h.* his head that day
Deut. 26. 13 brought .. the *h.* things
1 Sam. 21. 4 but there is *h.* bread
1 K. 9. 3 have *h.* this house which
2 K. 12. 18 Jehoash took all *h.* things
2 Chr. 7. 7 Solomon *h.* the .. court
Jer. 17. 22 but *h.* the sabbath day
Ezek. 20. 20 *h.* my sabbaths; and
Set apart, sanctify.
Mat. 6. 9 Fath .. *h.* be thy name
Luke 11. 2 say .. *h.* be thy name
R. V. Lev. 19. 8; Num. 16. 37, 38;
1 Sam. 21. 4, 6 holy
Halt. *Lame, crippled.*
Mat. 18. 8 better .. enter life *h.* than
Mark 9. 45 better .. ent. *h.* into life
Luke 14. 21 bring in .. poor and *h.*
John 5. 3 lay multitude of blind, *h.*
R. V. Luke 14. 21 lame
Halt (*v.*). *Stop, hesitate.*
Gen. 32. 31 the sun rose, and he *h.*
1 K. 18. 21 how long *h.* bet. two op.
Ps. 38. 17 For I am ready to *h.* and
Mic. 4. 6 will assemble her that *h*
Zeph. 3. 19 I will save her that *h.*
Halting. *Stopping, hesitating.*
Jer. 20. 10 familiars watch. my *h.*
Hammer. *Hammer.*
Judg. 4. 21 Jael .. took *h.* in hand
1 K. 6. 7 neither *h.* nor axe .. heard
Ps. 74. 6 break down wi. axe and *h.*
Isa. 41. 7 smootheth with the *h.*
Jer. 10. 4 fasten .. with nails and *h.*
Hand. *Hand.*
Gen. 3. 22 lest he put forth his *h.*
Ex. 4. 6 put his *h.* into his bosom
Lev. 7. 30 *h.* shall bring offerings
Num. 4. 45 word .. by *h.* of Moses
Deut. 1. 25 took fruit .. in their *h.*
Josh. 2. 24 L. hath del. into our *h.*
Judg. 1. 2 deliver. land into his *h.*
Ruth 4. 9 bought .. of *h.* of Naomi
1 Sam. 2. 13 with fleshhook .. in *h.*
2 Sam. 1. 14 stretch .. *h.* to destroy
1 K. 2. 25 Solomon sent by *h.* of B.
2 K. 3. 10 deliver. into *h.* of Moab
1 Chr. 4. 10 thine *h.* .. be with me
2 Chr. 6. 4 with .. *h.* fulfilled that
Ez. 1. 6 strengthened their *h.* with
Neh. 1. 10 redeemed .. by thy *h.*
Esth. 3. 10 k. took ring from .. *h.*
Job 1. 10 blessed work of his *h.*
Ps. 10. 12 L., O God, lift up thine *h.*
Prov. 6. 10 little folding of *h.* to sleep
Eccl. 4. 5 fool foldeth his *h.* togeth.
S. of S. 5. 5 *h.* dropped with myrrh
Isa. 1. 12 ha. required this at your *h.*
Jer. 1. 9 Lord put forth his *h.* and
Lam. 1. 14 yoke .. bound by his *h.*
Ezek. 1. 3 *h.* of the Lord was there
Dan. 1. 2 L. gave Jehoiak. into his *h.*
Hos. 7. 5 stretched .. *h.* wi. scorners
Joel 3. 8 *h.* of children of Judah
Am. 1. 8 turn .. *h.* against Ekron
Mic. 5. 9 *h.* shall be lifted upon adv.
Hab. 3. 4 horns coming out of *h.*
Zeph. 1. 4 stretch *h.* upon Judah
Hag. 2. 14 so every work of their *h.*
Zech. 2. 1 with measur. line in *h.*
Mal. 1. 10 nei. accept off. at .. *h.*
Mat. 3. 12 fan is in his *h.*, and he
   5. 30 if .. *h.* offend thee cut it off
   8. 3 Jesus put forth .. *h.* and touch.
   22. 13 said k. Bind him *h.* and foot
Mark 1. 31 and took her by the *h.*
   14. 41 is betrayed into *h.* of sinners
Luke 1. 66 *h.* of L. was with him
John 3. 35 given all .. into his *h.*
Acts 2. 23 wicked *h.* have crucified
Rom. 10. 21 stretched .. my *h.* unto
1 Cor. 4. 12 working with our .. *h.*
2 Cor. 11. 33 wall, and escaped his *h.*
Gal. 3. 19 ordain. by angels in *h.*
Eph. 4. 28 lab., working with his *h.*

Col. 4. 18 salutation by *h.* of P.
1 Thes. 4. 11 work wi. your own *h.*
2 Thes. 3. 17 salut. of P. ... own *h.*
1 Tim. 2. 8 pray, lifting up holy *h.*
2 Tim. 1. 6 by putting on of .. *h.*
Phile. 19 written with mine own *h.*
Heb. 1. 10 heav. are .. of thine *h.*
Jas. 4. 8 cleanse your *h.*, sinners
1 Pet. 5. 6 humble .. under migh. *h.*
1 John 1. 1 our *h.* have handled of
Rev. 1. 16 had in .. *h.* seven stars
Hand=breadth. *Hand-broad.*
Ex. 25. 25 make a border of an *h. b.*
1 K. 7. 26; 2 Chr. 4. 5; Ps. 39. 5;
   Ezek. 40. 5
Handful. *Handful, fistful.*
Gen. 41. 47 earth brought .. by *h.*
Ex. 9. 8 Take *h.* of ashes of furnace
Lev. 6. 15 shall take of it his *h.*
Num. 5. 26 priest shall take *h.* of
Ruth 2. 16 let fall some of the *h.*
1 K. 17. 12 but *h.* of meal in barrel
Ps. 72. 16 be an *h.* of corn in earth
Eccl. 4. 6 better is *h.* with quietness
Jer. 9. 22 as *h.* after harvest, and
Ezek. 13. 19 *h.* of barley, and for
R. V. Ruth 2. 16 for her from the
   bundles . Ps. 72. 16 abundance
Handkerchiefs. *Sweat-cloths,*
napkins.
Acts 19. 12 brought unto the sick *h.*
Handle (*n.*). *Haft, helve, hilt.*
S. of S. 5. 12 dropped .. myrrh upon *h*
Handle (*v.*). *Touch, use, ply.*
Gen. 4. 21 father of such as *h.* harp
Judg. 5. 14 they that *h.* pen of writ.
1 Chr. 12. 7 *h.* shield and buckler
2 Chr. 25. 5 that could *h.* spear and
Ps. 115. 7 hands, but they *h.* not
Jer. 2. 8 that *h.* law knew me not
Ezek. 21. 11 furb., that it may be *h.*
Am. 2. 15 neither sh. he stand that *h.*
Luke 24. 39 *h.* me .. sp. hath not fl.
2 Cor. 4. 2 nor *h.* word of G. deceit.
Col. 2. 21 touch not, taste not, *h.* not
1 John 1. 1 and our hands have *h.*
Handmaid. *Female servant, slave.*
Gen. 16. 1 Sarai, and she had an *h.*
Ex. 23. 12 son of thy *h.* and stranger
Judg. 19. 19 wine for me, and thy *h.*
Ruth 3. 9 answ., I am Ruth thine *h.*
1 Sam. 1. 18 let thine *h.* find grace in
2 Sam. 14. 6 thy *h.* had two sons
1 K. 1. 13 didst not swear unto *h.*
2 K. 4. 2 *h.* hath not any thing in ho.
Ps. 86. 16 and save son of thine *h.*
Prov. 30. 23 *h.* that is heir to mistr.
Isa. 14. 2 possess them for s. and *h.*
Jer. 34. 11 caused the servants and *h.*
Joel 2. 29 upon the servants and *h.*
Luke 1. 38 behold *h.* of the Lord
Acts 2. 18 on my *h.* I will pour out
R. V. 1 Sam. 1. 18; 25. 27; 2 Sam.
   14. 15 servant
Handstaves. *Handstaffs, javelins.*
Ezek. 39. 9 shall burn *h.* and spears
Handwriting. *Writing of hand.*
Col. 2. 14 blotting out the *h.* of ord.
R. V. bond written in
Handy-work. *Work of hands.*
Ps. 19. 1 firm. showeth thy *h. w.*
Hang. *Suspend, fasten.*
Gen. 40. 19 Pharaoh .. shall *h.* thee
Ex. 26. 13 it shall *h.* over .. tab.
Num. 25. 4 heads .. and *h.* them up
Deut. 28. 66 life shall *h.* in doubt
Josh. 8. 29 the king of Ai he *h.* on t.
2 Sam. 4. 12 *h.* them up over pool
Ez. 6. 11 and let him be *h.* thereon
Esth. 2. 23 they were both *h.* on t.
Job 26. 7 He 7 *h.* earth upon nothing
Ps. 137. 2 *h.* our harps on willows
S. of S. 4. 4 there *h.* thous. bucklers
Isa. 22. 24 shall *h.* on him all glory
Lam. 2. 10 virgins .. *h.* down heads
Ezek. 15. 3 pin of it to *h.* vessel on
Mat. 27. 5 Jud. went and *h.* himself
Mark 9. 42 millstone were *h.* about
Luke 23. 30 malef. which were *h.*
Acts 5. 30 Jesus, whom ye *h.* on t.
Gal. 3. 13 cursed every one that *h.*
Heb. 12. 12 lift hands which *h.* down
Hanging. *Suspended.*
Josh. 10. 26 *h.* on trees till evening
Curtain, drapery, screen.
Ex. 26. 36 sh. make *h.* for the door

27. 16; 35. 15; 36. 37; 37. 18; 39. 40
Num. 3. 25 *h.* for door of tabernacle
2 K. 27. 7 women wove *h.* for grove
R. V. mostly in Ex. and Num.,
   screen
Hap. *Chance.*
Ruth 2. 3 and her *h.* was to light on
Haply. *By chance, perchance, per-*
haps.
1 Sam. 14. 30 if *h.* people had eaten
Mark 11. 13 if *h.* he might find any
Luke 14. 29 lest *h.* after he laid fou.
Acts 5. 39 lest *h.* ye be found to fi.
2 Cor. 9. 4 lest *h.* they of Macedo.
R. V. 2 Cor. 9. 4 by any means
Happen. *Occur, befall, chance.*
1 Sam. 6. 9 chance that *h.* to us
2 Sam. 1. 6 I *h.* .. upon .. Gilboa
Esth. 4. 7 told him all that *h.* to
Prov. 12. 21 shall no evil *h.* to just
Eccl. 2. 14 that one event *h.* to all
Isa. 41. 22 show us what shall *h.*
Jer. 44. 23 evil is *h.* unto you th. day
Mark 10. 32 tell .. what .. should *h.*
Luke 24. 14 of all .. which had *h.*
Acts 3. 10 all which had *h.* unto
Rom. 11. 25 blindness .. is *h.* to Is.
1 Pet. 4. 12 strange thing *h.* .. you
2 Pet. 2. 22 *h.* unto them according
R. V. Rom. 11. 25 hath befallen
Happy. *Joyous, blessed, satisfied.*
Gen. 30. 13 *h.* am I, for daugh. will
Deut. 33. 29 *H.* art thou, O Israel
1 K. 10. 8 *h.* are these thy servants
Job 5. 17 *h.* man whom G. correct.
Ps. 127. 5 *h.* man that hath quiver
   128. 2; 137. 8; 144. 15; 146. 5
Prov. 3. 13 *h.* man that findeth wis.
   14. 21; 16. 20; 28. 14; 29. 18
Jer. 12. 1 wherefore are all they *h.*
Mal. 3. 14 we call the proud *h.*
John 13. 17 *h.* are ye if ye do them
Acts 26. 2 I think myself *h.*, k. Ag.
Rom. 14. 22 *h.* he that condem. not
1 Cor. 7. 40 she is *h.* if she so abide
Jas. 5. 11 we count them *h.* which
1 Pet. 3. 14 if ye suffer .. *h.* are ye
R. V. Jer. 12. 1 at ease; John 13.
   17; Jas. 5. 11; 1 Pet. 3. 14, 4. 14
   blessed
Hard. *Wonderful.*
Gen. 18. 14 is anything too *h.* for L.
Deut. 17. 8 matter too *h.* for thee
2 Sam. 13. 2 Ammon thought it *h.*
Jer. 32. 17 nothing too *h.* for thee
Stiff, sharp.
Ps. 60. 3 showed thy peo. *h.* things
Mar. 25. 24 knew thou art *h.* man
John 6. 60 this is an *h.* saying ; who
Acts 9. 5 *h.* to kick against pricks
Jude 15 *h.* speeches which ungod.
Near.
Lev. 3. 9 take off *h.* by backbone
1 K. 21. 1 *h.* by palace of Ahab
Acute, hidden.
1 K. 10. 1 prove with *h.* questions
2 Chr. 9. 1 prove Sol. with *h.* quest.
Dan. 5. 12 showing *h.* sentences
Difficult, weighty, firm, sharp.
Gen. 35. 16 Rachel .. had *h.* labor
Ex. 1. 14 bitter with *h.* bondage
Deut. 26. 6 laid on us *h.* bondage
2 Sam. 3. 39 sons of Zeru. be too *h.*
2 K. 2. 10 Thou hast asked a *h.* thing
Job 41. 24 *h.* as nether millstone
Prov. 13. 15 the way of transg. is *h.*
Ezek. 3. 5, 6 speech of *h.* language
Mark 10. 24 *h.* .. for them that trust
2 Pet. 3. 16 things *h.* to be underst.
Heb. 5. 11 things .. *h.* to be uttered,
R. V. Job 41. 24 firm ; Ps. 94. 4 ar-
   rogantly ; Prov. 13. 15 rugged
   Acts 9. 5 ———
Harden. *Strengthen, make heavy,*
stiff.
Ex. 4. 21 I will *h.* his heart, that he
   9. 12; 10. 20; 11. 10; 14. 4
Deut. 2. 30 Lord thy G. *h.* his spirit
Josh. 11. 20 it was of the Lord to *h.*
1 Sam. 6. 6 wherefore .. *h.* .. hearts
2 K. 17. 14 but *h.* their necks like
2 Chr. 36. 13 *h.* his heart from turn.
Neh. 9. 16 and *h.* their necks, and
Job 6. 10 I wo. *h.* myself in sorrow
Ps. 95. 8 *H.* not your heart, as in the
Prov. 21. 29 wicked m. *h.* his face

Isa. 63. 17 *h.* our heart from thy fear
Jer. 7. 26 *h.* their neck; did worse
Dan. 5. 20 his mind *h.* in pride
Mark 6. 52 for their heart was *h.*
John 12. 40 hath . . *h.* their heart
Acts 19. 9 But when divers were *h.*
Rom. 9. 18 and whom he will he *h.*
Heb. 3. 13 lest any of you be *h.*
R. V. Job 6. 10 exult; Ex. 7. 14;
9. 7 stubborn; Jer. 7. 26; 19. 15
made stiff

Harder. *Stronger.*
Jer. 5. 3 made . . faces *h.* than rock
Ezek. 3. 9 adamant *h.* than flint
Hardly. *Not, not wholly, with difficulty.*
Ex. 13. 15 Pha. would *h.* let us go
Isa. 8. 21 pass through it, *h.* bestead
Mat. 19. 23 rich m. shall *h.* enter
Mark 10. 23 how *h.* shall they that
Luke 9. 39 bruising him, *h.* depart.
Acts 27. 8 *h.* passing it, came unto
R. V. Mat. 19. 23 it is hard; Acts
27. 8 with difficulty
Hardness. *Stiffness, dryness.*
Job 38. 38 dust groweth into *h.*
Mat. 19. 8 bec. of *h.* of your hearts
Mark 10. 5 for the *h.* of your hearts
Rom. 2. 5 after thy *h.* and im. heart
2 Tim. 2. 3 endure *h.* as good sold.
R. V. Job 38. 38 mass; Mark. 3. 5
hardening; 2 Tim. 2. 3 suffer hard-
ship
Hare. *Hare.*
Lev. 11. 6 *h.*, because he cheweth
Deut. 14. 7 *h.* and c., for they chew
Harlot. *Fornicator.*
Gen. 38. 15 Judah thought her an *h.*
Lev. 21. 14 widow . . or *h.* these sh.
Josh. 2. 1 men came into *h's* house
Judg. 11. 1 Jephthah was son of *h.*
1 K. 3. 16 came women that were *h.*
Prov. 7. 10 wom. with attire of *h.*
Isa. 1. 21 how is . . cit. become an *h*
Jer. 5. 7 assembled in *h's* houses
Hos. 2. 5 mother . . played the *h.*
Joel 3. 3 given boy for an *h.*, and
Mic. 1. 7 gath. it of hire of an *h.*
Nah. 3. 4 whoredoms of fav. *h.*
Mat. 21. 31 that publicans and *h.* go
Luke 15. 30 devoured living with *h.*
1 Cor. 6. 15 make . . members of an *h.*
Heb. 11. 31 *h.* Rahab perished not
Jas. 2. 25 was not R., the *h.* just.
Rev. 17. 5 mother of *h.* and abom.
Harm (v.). *Wrong.*
1 Pet. 3. 13 who . . will *h.* you, if
Harm (n.). *Evil, injury, damage.*
Gen. 31. 52 shalt not pass . . for *h.*
Lev. 5. 16 the *h.* that he hath done
Num. 35. 23 neither sought his *h.*
1 Sam. 26. 21 no more do thee *h.*
2 Sam. 20. 6 Sheba . . do us more *h.*
2 K. 4. 41 there was no *h.* in the pot
1 Chr. 16. 22 do my prophets no *h.*
Ps. 105. 15 do . . prophets no *h.*
Prov. 3. 30 if he have done . . no *h.*
Jer. 39. 12 Take . . and do him no *h.*
Acts 16. 28 Do thyself no *h.*, for we
R. V. Acts 27. 21 injury; 28. 6
nothing amiss
Harmless. *Not bad, guileless.*
Mat. 10. 16 be wise, and *h.* as doves
Phil. 2. 15 th. ye be blameless and *h.*
Heb. 7. 26 *h.*, undefiled, separate
R. V. Heb. 7. 26 guileless
Harness (n.). *Armor, mail.*
1 K. 22. 34 smote between joi. of *h.*
2 Chr. 9. 24; 18. 33
R. V. 1 K. 20. 11; 2 Chr. 9. 24
armour
Harness (v). *Bind, arm.*
Ex. 13. 18 children of Is. went *h.*
Jer. 46. 4 *h.* horses, and get up ye
R. V. Ex. 13. 18 armed
Harp (n.). *Harp, zithern.*
Gen. 4. 21 fath. of such as handle *h.*
1 Sam. 10. 5 tabret, pipe, and *h.*
2 Sam. 6. 5 *h.*, psalteries, and cym.
1 K. 10. 12 *h.* and psalt. for sing.
1 Chr. 15. 28 making noise with . . *h.*
2 Chr. 5. 12 having cym. . . and *h.*
Neh. 12. 27 with cymbals and *h.*
Job 21. 12 they take tim. and *h.*
Ps. 33. 2 praise Lord with *h.*, sing
43, 4; 49. 4; 57. 8; 71. 22; 81. 2

Isa. 5. 12 *h.*, viol, the tab., and pipe
Ezek. 26. 13 sound of *h.* . . no more
Dan. 3. 5 hear sound of the . . *h.*
1 Cor. 14. 7 giving sound, p. or *h.*
Rev. 5. 8 having every one of th. *h.*
Harp (v.). *Play harp.*
1 Cor. 14. 7 how known what is *h.*
Rev. 14. 2 heard voi. of harpers *h.*
Harper. *Who plays harp.*
Rev. 14. 2 I heard the voice of *h.*
18. 22 voice of *h.* and musicians
Harrow (n.). *Pike, spike.*
2 Sam. 12. 31 put them under . . *h.*
1 Chr. 20. 30 cut . . with saws and *h.*
Harrow. *Level, harrow.*
Job 39. 10 will he *h.* the valleys
Hart. *Male red deer.*
Deut. 12. 15 may eat, and as of the *h.*
1 K. 4. 23 sheep, beside *h.* and
Ps. 42. 1 as *h.* panteth after brook
S. of S. 2. 9 my beloved is like . . *h.*
Isa. 35. 6 shall lame man leap as *h.*
Lam. 1. 6 become like *h.* that find
Harvest. *Reaping time.*
Gen. 8. 22 *h.* . . shall not cease
Ex. 23. 16 feast of *h.*, first fruits
Lev. 19. 9 and when ye reap the *h.*
Deut. 24. 19 when thou cuttest . . *h.*
Josh. 3. 15 Jor. overflow. time of *h.*
Judg. 15. 1 time of *h.* that Samson
Ruth 1. 22 came to Beth. in barley *h.*
1 Sam. 6. 13 reaping their wheat *h.*
2 Sam. 21. 9 put to death in . . *h.*
Job 5. 5. whose *h.* hungry eateth up
Prov. 6. 8 gathereth her food in *h.*
Isa. 9. 3 according to the joy in *h.*
Jer. 5, 17 they shall eat up thine *h.*
Hos. 6. 11 he hath set an *h.* for thee
Joel 1. 11 because the *h.* is perished
Am. 4. 7 yet three months to the *h.*
Mat. 9. 37 the *h.* truly is plenteous
9. 38; 13. 30, 39
Mark 4. 29 because the *h.* is come
Luke 10. 2 the *h.* truly is great, but
John 4. 35 and then cometh *h.*? beh.
Rev. 14. 15 reap, for *h.* of earth
Hast. *There is, there are.*
2 K. 4. 2 what *h.* thou in the house?
Job 33. 32 if thou *h.* any thing to say
Prov. 3. 28 go . . when thou *h.* it wi.
See also **Have.**
Haste (n.). *Speed, dispatch.*
Gen. 24. 46 she made *h.* and let
Ex. 34. 8 And Moses made *h.*, and
Deut. 16. 3 comest out of E. in *h.*
Judg. 9. 48 make *h.*, and do as I ha.
1 Sam. 23. 26 David made *h.* to get
2 Sam. 4. 4 she made *h.* to flee
2 K. 7. 15 Syr. cast away in . . *h.*
2 Chr. 26. 20 Uzzi. *h.* also to go out
Ez. 4. 23 went . . in *h.* to Jerusalem
Esth. 6. 10 make *h.*, take apparel
Job 20. 2 answer, for this I make *h.*
Ps. 38. 22 make *h.* to help, O Lord
Prov. 1. 16 make *h.* to shed blood
S. of S. 8. 14 Make *h.*, my beloved
Isa. 49. 17 chil. shall not make *h.*
Jer. 9. 18 let them make *h.* and
Dan. 2. 25 brought . . Daniel . . in *h.*
Nah. 2. 5 mak. *h.* to the wall thereof
Mark. 6. 25 came in . . with gr. *h.*
Luke 2. 16 with *h.*, and found Mary
Acts 22. 18 make *h.*, get thee quick.
Haste (v.). *Urge, push on, hurry.*
Gen. 18. 7 a calf . . he *h.* to dress it
Ex. 5. 13 the taskmasters *h.* them
Josh. 10. 13 sun *h.* not to go down
Judg. 20. 37 and liers in wait *h.*
1 Sam. 17. 48 David *h.* and ran tow.
2 Sam. 19. 16 Shimei *h.* and came
1 K. 20. 41 he *h.* and took the ash.
2 K. 9. 13 *h.*, and took ev. m. gar.
2 Chr. 26. 20 yea, himself *h.* also
Esth. 6. 12 Haman *h.* to his house
Job. 9. 26 as eagle *h.* to the prey
Ps. 48. 5 were troubled and *h.* away
Prov. 7. 23 as bird *h.* to the snare
Eccl. 1. 5 sun . . *h.* to his place where
Jer. 48. 16 evil his affliction *h.* fast
Hab. 1. 8 fly as eagle that *h.* to eat
Zeph. 1. 14 day of the Lord . . *h.*
Acts 20. 16 for he *h.*, if it were pos.
2 Pet. 3. 12 *h.* unto coming of day
R. V. Job 9. 26 swoopeth; 40. 23
trembleth
Hastened. *Speeded, hurried.*

Gen. 18. 6 Abraham *h.* into tent
2 Chr. 24. 5 the Levites *h.* it not
Esth. 3. 15 *h.* by k's. command.
Isa. 51. 14 The captive exile *h.* that
Jer. 17. 16 I have not *h.* from being
Hastily. *Speedily, quickly.*
Gen. 41. 14 brought him *h.* out
Judg. 2. 23 without driving . . out *h.*
1 Sam. 4. 14 the man came in *h.*
1 K. 20. 33 men . . did *h.* catch it
Prov. 20. 21 inherit. may be got *h.*
John 11. 31 that she rose np *h.* and
R. V. John 11. 31 quickly.
Hasty. *Sudden, quick, speedy.*
Prov. 14. 29 *h.* of spirit exalt. folly
Eccl. 7. 9 not *h.* in spir. to be angry
Isa. 28. 4 *h.* fruit before summer
Dan. 2. 15 why is the decree so *h.*
Hab. 1. 6 Chaldeans . . *h.* nation
R. V. Isa. 28. 4 first ripe; Dan.
2. 15 urgent
Hat. R. V. *mantle.*
Dan. 3. 21 men bound in their . . *h.*
Hatch. *Cleave, rend, bring forth.*
Isa. 34. 15 there shall the . . owl *h.*
59. 5 they *h.* cockatrice eggs
Jer. 17. 11 partridge sitteth . . and *h.*
Hate. *Oppose, dislike, detest.*
Gen. 27. 41 E. *h.* Jacob because of
Ex. 18. 21 men of truth, *h.* covet.
Lev. 19. 17 shalt not *h.* thy brother
Num. 10. 35 let them that *h.* flee
Deut. 5. 9 generation of them that *h.*
Josh. 20. 5 *h.* him not beforetime
Judg. 11. 7 *h.* me, and expel me
2 Sam. 22. 41 destroy them that *h.*
1 K. 22. 8 I *h.* him, he doth not
2 Chr. 19. 2 love them that hate L.
Esth. 9. 1 rule over them that *h.*
Job 8. 22 that *h.* . . shall be clothed
Ps. 5. 5 *h.* workers of iniquity
9. 13; 11. 5; 18. 17; 21. 8; 25, 19
Prov. 1. 12 how have I *h.* instr.
6. 16; 8. 13; 9. 8; 11. 15; 12. 1
Eccl. 3, 8 time to love, and to *h.*
Isa. 1. 14 your . . feasts my soul *h.*
Jer. 12. 8 therefore have I *h.* it
Ezek. 35. 6 thou hast not *h.* blood
Dan. 4. 19 dream to them that *h.*
Hos. 9. 15 I *h.* them, for wicked.
Am. 5. 15 *h.* evil and love good
Mic. 3. 2 who *h.* good, and love evil
Zech. 8. 17 these are things I *h.*
Mal. 1. 3 I *h.* Esau, and laid his mo.
Mat. 5. 43 love neigh. .. *h.* enemy
5. 44; 6. 24; 10. 22; 24. 9; 24. 10
Mark 13. 13 *h.* men for my . . sake
Luke 6. 22 blessed . . when men *h.*
14. 26; 16. 13; 19. 14; 21. 17
John 3. 20 that doeth evil *h.* light
7. 7; 12. 25; 15. 18; 17. 14
Rom. 7. 15 but what I *h.* that I do
Eph. 5. 29 no man . . *h.* his own flesh
Tit. 3. 3 hateful, and *h.* one another
1 John 2. 9 that *h.* bro. is in dang.
Jude 23 *h.* even the garment spotted
Rev. 2. 6 *h.* deeds of Nicol., I also *h.*
R. V. Gen. 49. 23; Ps. 55. 3 perse-
cute; Mat. 5. 44
Hateful. *Odious, abominable.*
Ps. 36. 2 until his iniq. be found *h.*
Tit. 3. 3 living in malice, envy, *h.*
Rev. 18. 2 cage of every . . *h.* bird
Hatefully. *With hatred.*
Ezek. 23. 29 they . . deal with thee *h.*
Hater. *Who hates.*
Ps. 81. 15 *h.* of Lord should have
Hath. *See* **Have.**
Hatred. *Enmity.*
Num. 35. 20 if he thrust him of *h.*
2 Sam. 13. 15 *h.* wherewith he hated
Ps. 25. 19 en. hate me with cruel *h.*
Prov. 10. 12 *h.* stirreth up strifes
Eccl. 9. 1 no man know. love or *h.*
Ezek. 35. 5 hast had perpetual *h.*
Hos. 9. 7 for . . iniq. and great *h.*
Gal. 5. 20 witchcraft, *h.*, variance
Haughtily. *Loftily.*
Mic. 2. 3 neither shall ye go *h.*
Haughtiness. *Loftiness, arro-
gance.*
Isa. 2. 11 *h.* of men shall be bowed
13. 11 will lay low *h.* of terrible
Jer. 48. 29 heard the *h.* of his heart
R. V. Isa. 16. 6 arrogancy
Haughty. *Lofty, arrogant.*

2 Sam. 22. 28 eyes are upon the *h.*
Ps. 131. 1 Lord, my heart is not *h.*
Prov. 16. 18 and *k.* spirit before fall
Isa. 10. 33 the *h.* shall be humbled
Ezek. 16. 50 *h.*, and com. abomina.
Zeph. 3. 11 shalt no more be *h.* bec.
R. V. Isa. 10. 33 ; 24. 4 lofty

Haunt (*n.*).   *Foot, resort.*
1 Sam. 23. 22 see .. where his *h.* is

Haunt (*v.*).   *To frequent.*
1 Sam. 30. 31 men were wont to *h.*
Ezek. 26. 17 terror . . on all that *h.* it

Have.   *Hold, own, possess.*
Gen. 33, 9 Esau said, I *h.* enough
Num. 18. 23 they *h.* no inheritance
Deut. 21. 17 portion of all he *h.*
2 Sam. 19. 28 wh. right . . *h.* I to cry
1 K. 17. 12 I *h.* not a cake, but an
1 Chr. 29. 3 I *h.* mine own good
2 Chr. 16. 9 thou shalt *h.* wars
Ez. 4. 16 thou shalt *h.* no portion
Neh. 13. 4 priest *h.* the oversight
Job 6. 8 th. I might *h.* my request
Eccl. 4. 9 *h.* a good reward for labor
Isa. 43. 8 Bring . . deaf that *h.* ears
Jer. 41. 3 we *h.* treasures in the field
Dan. 8. 20 ram *h.* two horns are k's
Mat. 3. 4 John *h.* raiment of . . hair
Mark 2. 10 Son of man *h.* power on
Luke 3. 11 he that *h.* two coats, let
John 3. 29 that *h.* bride is bridegr.
Acts 2. 44 *h.* all things common
Rom. 2. 14 *h.* not law, one law unto
1 Cor. 2. 16 but we *h.* mind of Chr.
2 Cor. 1. 9 we *h.* sentence of death
Gal. 2. 4 liberty we *h.* in Christ J.
Eph. 1. 7 in whom we *h.* redemp.
Phil. 1. 7 bec. I *h.* you in my heart
Col. 3. 13 if any man *h.* quarrel
1 Thes. 3. 6 ye *h.* good rememb.
2 Thes. 3. 9 not be. we *h.* not power
1 Tim. 3. 4 *h.* his children in subj.
2 Tim. 2. 19 *h.* this seal, The Lord
Tit. 1. 6 *h.* faithful children not ac-
Phile. 5 thou *h.* toward Lord Jesus
Heb. 3. 3 *h.* more hon. than house
Jas. 1. 4 let patience *h.* perfect work
1 Pet. 2. 12 *h.* your conv. honest
2 Pet. 1. 19 we *h.* a more sure word
1 John 1. 3 ve may *h.* fellowship
2 John 5 we *h.* from the beginning
3 John 4 I *h.* no greater joy than
Jude 19 sensual, *h.* not the Spirit
Rev. 1. 6 *h.* in hand seven stars
R. V. changes are frequent, but
chiefly in tenses, to other auxili-
aries, or in connection with preceding and succeeding words; the
same general sense being preserved. *See* also the often use of
have, had, hath, hast, having,
with words in other references.

Haven.   *Shore, shelter, port.*
Gen. 49. 13 Zebulun shall dwell at *h.*
Ps. 107. 30 bringeth them to desir. *h.*
Acts 27. 12 Phenice . . *h.* of Crete

Havens, Fair.   Acts 27. 8 called *F. H.*

Havoc.   R. V. *laid waste.*
Acts 8. 3 Saul made *h.* of church

Hawk.   *Hawk.*
Lev. 11. 16 and *h.* after his kind
Deut. 14. 16 the cuckow and the *h.*
Job 39. 26 doth *h.* fly by wisdom
Owl, cuckoo, swallow.
Lev. 11. 16 owl, and the night *h.*
Deut. 14. 15 night *h.* and cuckoo

Hay.   *Grass, fodder.*
Prov. 27. 25 *h.* appeareth, and grass
Isa. 15. 6 for the *h.* is withered away
1 Cor. 3. 12 stones, wood, *h.*, stubble
R. V. Isa. 15. 6 grass

Hazard.   *Give over, risk.*
Acts 15. 26 men have *h.* their lives

Hazel.   R. V. *almond.*
Gen. 30. 37 Jacob took of the *h.* tr.

He.   *That one. See* this word as
frequent nominative to blessed,
did, although, etc., and as pronom-
inal substitute for God, Jesus, Jacob, etc.

He.   *Male.*
Num. 7. 17 five *h.* goats, five lambs
2 Chr. 29. 21 ; Ez. 8. 35 ; Isa. 1. 11 ;
Jer. 50. 8 ; Ezek. 34. 17 ; Dan. 8. 8

Head.   *Head, top, chief, leader.*

Gen. 2. 10 river became into four *h.*
Ex. 6. 14 *h.* of their father's house
Lev. 1. 4 put his hand on *h.* of off.
Num. 1. 16 *h.* thousands in Israel
Deut. 1. 15 made them *h.* over you
Josh. 2. 19 his blood sh. be on his *h.*
Judg. 5. 26 Jael smote off Siser's *h.*
1 Sam. 1. 11 no razor come on his *h.*
2 Sam. 1. 2 and earth upon his *h.*
1 K. 2. 32 return blood on our *h.*
2 K. 4. 19 said . . my *h.* ! my *h.* !
1 Chr. 7. 2, 40 *h.* of . . father's ho.
2 Chr. 3. 16 put on *h.* of pillars
Ez. 9. 3 plucked off hair of my *h.*
Neh. 4. 4. tur. reproach on own *h.*
Esth. 2. 17 he set crown on her *h.*
Job 1. 20 then Job . . shaved his *h.*
Ps. 3. 3 glory, and lifter of my *h.*
24. 7 lift up your *h.*, O ye gates
Prov. 1. 9 ornament .. unto thy *h.*
Eccl. 2. 14 wise man's eyes . . in *h.*
S. of S. 2. 6 is filled with dew
Isa. 1. 5 whole *h.* is sick, heart faint
Jer. 2. 37 thine hands upon thine *h.*
Lam. 2. 10 th. cast dust on their *h.*
Ezek. 1. 25 firmament over their *h.*
Dan. 1. 10 endanger my *h.* to king
Hos. 1. 11 appoint thems. one *h.*
Joel 3. 4 recompense on your *h.*
Am. 2. 7 the dust on *h.* of the poor
Obad. 15 reward .. on thine own *h.*
Jonah 2. 5 weeds wrapped about *h.*
Mic. 3. 1 hear, pray, O *h.* of Jacob
Hab. 3. 13 thou woundest *h.* out of
Zech. 1. 21 no man did lift up his *h.*
Mat. 5. 3 neither .. swear by thy *h.*
8. 20 hath not where to lay his *h.*
27. 39 reviled .. wagging their *h.*
Mark 6. 24 said, *h.* of John Bap.
Luke 12. 7 hairs of . . *h.* are num.
John 19. 2 crown of thorns.. on .. *h.*
19. 30 bowed . . *h.*, gave up ghost
Acts 4. 11 become *h.* of the corner
27. 34 not hair fall from *h.* of any
Rom. 12. 20 heap coals . . on his *h.*
1 Cor. 11. 3 *h.* of ev. man is C.
Eph. 1. 22 gave him to be *h.* over all
5. 32 the husband is *h.* of the wife
Col. 1. 18 and he is *h.* of the body
1 Pet. 2. 7 same is . . *h.* of corner
Rev. 1. 14 *h.* and hair were white

Head-bands.   R. V. *sashes.*
Isa. 3. 20 *h.* and tablets, and earr.

Headlong.   *Precipitately, sheer.*
Luke 4. 29 might cast him down *h.*
Acts 1. 18 falling *h.*, he burst asun.

Headstone.   *Principal stone.*
Zech. 4. 7 he shall bring *h.* thereof

Heady.   R. V. *headstrong.*
2 Tim. 3. 4 *h.*, highminded, lov. of

Heal.   *Repair, make sound, cure.*
Gen. 20. 17 God *h.* Abimelech, and
Ex. 15. 26 I am Lord that *h.* thee
Lev. 13. 18 was boil . . and is *h.*
Num. 12. 13 *h.* her now, O God
Deut. 28. 27 itch . . can not be *h.*
1 Sam. 6. 3 then ye shall be *h.* and
2 K. 8. 29 Joram went to be *h.*
2 Chr. 7. 14 then will *h.* their land
Ps. 6. 2 O Lord, *h.* me, for bones
147. 3 he *h.* the broken in heart
Eccl. 3. 3 ti. to kill, and time to *h.*
Isa. 19. 22 L. shall smite it and *h.* it
53. 5 with his stripes we are *h.*,
Jer. 3. 22 will *h.* your backslidings
Lam. 2. 13 virgin, who can *h.* thee
Ezek. 47. 8 the waters shall be *h.*
Hos. 5. 13 yet could he not *h.* you
Mat. 4. 23 *h.* all man. of sickness
10. 8 *h.* sick, cleanse the lepers
Mark 1. 34 *h.* sick of div. disease
Luke 4. 23 Physician, *h.* thyself
Acts 4. 30 stretching . . hand to *h.*
Heb. 12. 13 lame . . let it be *h.*
Jas. 5. 16 pray .. that ye may be *h.*
1 Pet. 2. 24 by .. stripes ye were *h.*
Rev. 13. 3 his deadly wound was *h.*
R. V. Mark 5. 23 ; Luke 8. 36 ;
Acts 14. 9 made whole ; 28. 9
cured.

Healer.   *Who heals, biuder up.*
Isa. 3. 7 I will not be an *h.* ; for in

Healing.   *Making whole, curing.*
Jer. 14. 19 there is no *h.* for us
Nah. 3. 19 th. is no *h.* of thy bruise
Mal. 4. 2 Sun . . with *h.* in . . wings

Luke 9. 11 *h.* that had need of *h.*
Acts 4. 22 miracle of *h.* was showed
1 Cor. 12. 9 gifts of *h.* by the Spirit
Rev. 22. 2 for *h.* of the nations
R. V. Nah. 3. 19 assuaging

Health.   *Healing, soundness, safety.*
2 Sam. 20. 9 Art thou in *h.*, bro.
Ps. 42. 11 the *h.* of my countenance
Prov. 12. 18 tongue of wise is *h.*
Isa. 58. 8 *h.* shall spring forth speedi.
Jer. 33. 6 I bring it *h.* and cure
Acts 27. 34 meat, this is for your *h.*
3 John 2 mayest prosper, be in *h.*
R. V. 2 Sam. 20. 9 Is it well with t.

Heap (*n.*).   *Mass, wall.*
Ex. 15. 8 floods stood . . as an *h.*
Josh. 3. 13 they shall stand upon *h.*
Ps. 33. 7 waters together as an *h.*
Isa. 17. 11 harvest shall be a *h.* in
Hab. 3. 15 walk through *h.* of . . w.
Mound, pile, hillock.
Gen. 31. 46 did eat there upon *h.*
Ex. 8. 14 gath. them togeth. upon *h.*
Deut. 13. 16 it sh. be an *h.* for ever
Josh. 7. 26 *h.* of stones . . this day
Judg. 15. 16 *h.* upon *h.* with jaw of
Ruth 3. 7 lie down at end of the *h.*
2 Sam. 18. 17 laid . . *h.* of stones on
2 K. 10. 8 lay them in two *h.* at gate
2 Chr. 31. 6 and laid them by *h.*
Neh. 4. 2 revive stones out of *h.*
Job 8. 17 roots wrapped about *h.*
Ps. 79. 1 have laid Jerusalem on *h.*
S. of S. 7. 2 *h.* of wheat set about
Isa. 25. 2 hast made of city an *h.*
Jer. 9. 11 I will make Jerusalem *h.*
Hos. 12. 11 are as *h.* in the furrows
Mic. 1. 6 I will make Samaria as *h.*
Hag. 2. 16 *h.* of twenty measures
R. V. Isa. 17. 11 fleeth away ; Jer.
31. 21 guide posts

Heap (*v.*).   *Pile up, amass.*
Deut. 32. 23 *h.* mischiefs on them
Job 16. 4 I co. *h.* words against you
Ps. 39. 6 *h.*, riches, and knoweth not
Prov. 25. 22 *h.* coals of fire on head
Eccl. 2. 26 to gather and to *h.* up
Ezek. 24. 10 *h.*, wood, kindle fire
Hab. 1. 10 for they shall *h.* dust
Zech. 9. 3 Tyrus . . *h.* sil. as dust
Rom. 12. 20 thou shalt *h.* coals of
2 Tim. 4. 3 *h.* to themsel. teachers
Jas. 5. 3 ye have *h.* togeth. treasure

Hear.   *Give ear, listen to.*
Gen. 3. 8 *h.* the voice of Lord God
Ex. 2. 15 When Pharaoh *h.* this
Lev. 5. 1 *h.* the voice of swearing
Num. 7. 89 *h.* voice of . . speaking
Deut. 1. 34 Lord *h.* your words
Josh. 2. 10 *h.* how Lord dried up
Judg. 5. 3 *H.*, O ye kings, give ear
Ruth 1. 6 she had *h.* in . . Moab
1 Sam. 2. 22 *h.* . . that his sons did
2 Sam. 3. 28 when David *h.* it, he
1 K. 1. 11 hast not thou *h.* that
2 K. 3. 21 when all Moabites *h.* th.
1 Chr. 14. 8 *h.* David was anointed
2 Chr. 6. 23 *h.* thou from heaven
Ez. 4. 1 *h.* that children of captivity
Neh. 1. 4 when I *h.* these words
Esth. 1. 18 *h.* of deed of the queen
Job 2. 11 when Job's friends *h.*
Ps. 4. 1 *H.* when call, O God of my
Prov. 1. 5 a wise man will *h.*, and
Eccl. 5. 1 more ready to g. than *h.*
Isa. 1. 2 *H.*, O heaven, give ear
Jer. 2. 4 *H.* ye the word of the Lord
Lam. 1. 18 *h.*, I pray, all people
Ezek. 1. 24 I *h.* the voice of wings
Dan. 8. 13 I *h.* one saint speaking
Hos. 4. 1 *H.* word of the Lord ye
Joel 1. 2 *H.* this, ye old men, and
Am. 3. 1 *H.* word . . L. hath spoken
Obad. 1 We ha. *h.* rumor of the Lord
Jonah 2. 2 cried, and thou *h.* voice
Mic. 1. 2 *H.*, all ye people, hearken
Nah. 3. 19 all that *h.* .. shall clap
Hab. 1. 2 cry, and thou wilt not *h.*
Zeph. 2. 8 I have *h.* the reproach
Zech. 1. 4 did not *h.*, nor hearken
Mal. 2. 2 if ye will not *h.* and if
Mat. 2. 3 when Herod .. *h.* these
Mark 2. 1 when Jesus *h.* it, he
Luke 7. 22 lepers cleansed, deaf *h.*
John 1. 37 two dis. *h.* him speak

Acts 2. 8 *h.* every man in own tong.
Rom. 10. 14 how *h.* without preach.
1 Cor. 2. 9 eye not seen, nor ear *h.*
2 Cor. 12. 4 *h.* unspeakable words
Gal. 1. 13 ye *h.* of my conversation
Eph. 1. 13 after ye *h.* word of truth
Phil. 1. 27 may *h.* of your affliction
Col. 1. 4 *h.* of your faith in Christ
2 Thes. 3. 11 *h.* there are some wh.
1 Tim. 4. 16 save . . and them that *h.*
2 Tim. 1. 13 sound words . . thou . . *h.*
Phile. 5 *h.* of thy love and faith, wh.
Heb. 2. 1 heed things we have *h.*
Jas. 1. 19 every man be swift to *h.*
1 Pet. 1. 18 voice from heaven we *h.*
1 John 4. 6 that knoweth God *h.*
2 John 6 have *h.* from beginning
3 John 4 no greater joy than to *h.*
Rev. 1. 10 and I *h.* a great voice
Answer, respond.
1 Sam. 7. 9 Samuel cried, and L. *h.*
1 K. 18. 26 called on Baal, O . . *h.*
Job 30. 20 and thou dost not *h.*
Ps. 3. 4 he *h.* me out of . . holy hill
4. 1 *H.* me when I call, O God of
13. 3; 17. 6; 20. 1; 22. 2; 34. 4
Isa. 41. 17 I the Lord' will *h.* them
Hos. 2. 21 I will *h.,* saith, the Lord
Jonah 2. 2 I cried to L. and he *h.*
Mic. 3. 4 L., but he will not *h.* them
Zech. 10. 6 I am L. G. and will *h.*
R. V. The O. T. changes, which
are numerous, are chiefly to, *an-*
swer.

Heard. *See* **Hear.**
Hearing. *Ear, audition, audience.*
Deut. 31. 11 read this in their *h.*
2 Sam. 18. 12 in . . *h.* king charged
2 K. 4. 31 was neither voice nor *h.*
Job 33. 8 hath spoken in mine *h.*
Prov. 28. 9 turneth . . ear from *h.*
Eccl. 1. 8 nor the ear filled with *h.*
Isa. 21. 3 I was bowed . . at *h.* of it
Ezek. 9. 5 said in mine *h* , Go ye
Am. 8. 11 but of *h.* words of Lord
Mat. 13. 14 by *h.* ye shall hear, and
Acts 25. 21 entered into place of *h.*
Rom. 10. 17 So faith cometh by *h.*
1 Cor. 12. 17 eye, where were *h.*
Gal. 3. 2. law, or by *h.* of faith?
Heb. 5. 11 seeing ye are dull of *h.*
2 Pet. 2. 8 in seeing and *h.* vexed
Hearken. *Give ear, attend, heed.*
Gen. 3. 17 hast *h.* unto the voice of
Ex. 3. 18 they shall *h.* to thy voice
Lev. 26. 14 if ye will not *h.* unto me
Num. 14. 22 have not *h.* to my voice
Deut. 4. 1 now therefore *h.* O Israel
Josh. 1. 17 as we *h.* to Moses in all
Judg. 2. 17 would not *h.* to judg.
1 Sam. 2. 25 *h.* not unto voice of
2 Sam. 12. 18 would not *h.* unto our
1 K. 8. 28 *h.* unto the cry . . prayer
2 K. 13. 4 and the Lord *h.* unto him
2 Chr. 6. 20 *h.* unto prayer which
Neh. 9. 16 *h.* not to thy command.
Esth. 3. 4 and he *h.* not unto them
Job 32. 10 I said, *H.* to me ; I also
Ps. 45. 10 *H.* O daughter and consid.
Prov. 1. 33 whoso *h.* shall dwell
Isa. 46. 3 *H.* unto me O . . Jacob
Jer. 7. 24 but they *h.* not, nor incli.
Ezek. 3. 7 house of Israel will not *h.*
Dan. 9. 6 nei. *h.* unto . . the prophet
Hos. 9. 17 they did not *h.* unto him
Zech. 1. 4 they did not hear, nor *h.*
Mark 4. 3 *h.,* there went out sower
Acts 2. 14 men of I. *h.* to my words
Jas. 2. 5 *H.,* my beloved brethren
Heart. *Heart, soul.*
Gen. 6. 6 and it grieved him at *h.*
Ex. 4. 14 he will be glad in his *h.*
Num. 32. 9 discouraged *h.* of chil.
Deut. 28. 65 give thee trembling *h.*
Josh. 11. 20 was of L. to hard. . . *h.*
Judg. 5. 16 great searchings of *h.*
Ruth 3. 7 his *h.* was merry, he went
1 Sam. 1. 13 Han. spake in her *h.*
2 Sam. 6. 16 she despised him in . . *h.*
1 K. 3. 9 give serv. understanding *h.*
2 K. 9. 24 arrow went out at his *h.*
1 Chr. 12. 33 were not of double *h.*
2 Chr. 7. 10 glad and merry in *h.*
Ez. 36. 9 *h.* of the king of As.
Neh. 2. 2 nothing but sorrow of *h.*
Esth. 1. 10 when *h.* of k. was mer.

Job 7. 17 shouldst set *h.* upon him
Ps. 4. 7 Thou .. put gladness in my *h.*
51. 10 Create in me a clean *h.*
Prov. 2. 2 apply . . *h.* to understand.
15. 13 mer. *h.* mak. cheerful count.
Eccl. 1. 13 I gave my *h.* to seek
S. of S. 5. 2 sleep, but my *h.* wak.
Isa. 15. 5 *h.* shall cry for Moab
Jer. 4. 19 am pained at my very *h.*
Lam. 5. 17 for this our *h.* is faint
Ezek. 18. 31 make . . new *h.* and sp.
Dan. 1. 8 Daniel purposed in *h.*
Hos. 4. 11 wine . . take away the *h.*
Obad. 3 pride of *h.* deceived thee
Nah. 2. 10 and the *h.* melteth, and
Zeph. 3. 14 rejoice with all the *h.*
Zech. 7. 12 made . . *h.* as adamant
Mal. 2. 2 if ye will not lay it to *h.*
Mat. 5. 8 blessed are the pure in *h.*
11. 29 I am meek and lowly in *h.*
22. 37 love Lord God with all thy *h.*
Mark 3. 5 griev. for hardness of *h.*
7. 21 out of *h.* proc. evil thoughts
Luke 2. 19 Mary . pondered in *h.*
John 12. 40 hath . . hardened their *h.*
14. 27 Let not your *h.* be troubled
Acts 2. 26 theref. did my *h.* rejoice
Rom. 1. 21 their foolish *h.* was dark.
1 Cor. 2. 9 nei. ent. into *h.* of man
2 Cor. 1. 22 earnest of Spirit in *h.*
Gal. 4. 6 send Spirit . . into your *h.*
Eph. 3. 17 C. may dwell in your *h.*
Phil. 1. 7 becau. I have you in my *h.*
Col' 2. 2 that . . *h.* might be comfort.
1 Thes. 2. 4 G., which trieth our *h.*
2 Thes. 2. 17 comfort your *h.* and
1 Tim. 1 5 charity out of pure *h.*
2 Tim. 2. 22 call on L. out of pure *h.*
Heb. 3. 8, 15 harden not your *h.,* as
Jas. 1. 26 but deceiv. his own *h.*
1 Pet. 1. 22 love one . . with pure *h.*
2 Pet. 1. 19 day star arise in your *h.*
1 John 3. 19 assure our *h.* before
Rev. 2. 23 wh. searcheth reins and *h.*
R V. 2 Sam. 3. 21 ; Ezek. 25. 15 ;
27. 31 ; Lam. 3. 51 soul ; Job
38. 36 ; Jer. 7. 31 mind
Hearted. *Of heart.*
Ex. 28. 3 sh. speak unto all wise *h.*
Deut. 20. 8 what man . . faint *h.*
Ps. 76. 5 The stout *h.* are spoiled
Isa. 24. 7 all the merry *h.* do sigh
Ezek. 2. 4 impud. chil. and stiff *h.*
Luke 4. 18 sent . . to heal brok. *h.*
Hearth. *Stove, pan, hearth.*
Ps. 102. 3 bones are burned as an *h.*
Isa. 30. 14 to take fire from the *h.*
Jer. 36. 22 a fire on the *h.* burning
Zech. 12. 6 like an *h.* of fire among
R. V. Ps. 102. 3 firebrand ; Jer.
36. 22, 23 brazier ; Zech. 12. 6 pan
Heartily. *Out of the heart.*
Col. 3. 23 do it *h.,* as to the Lord
Hearty. *Earnest.*
Prov. 27. 9 man's friend by *h.* com.
Heat (*n.*). *Heat, warmth.*
Gen. 8. 22 cold and *h.,* summer and
Deut. 29. 24 what meaneth *h.* of
1 Sam. 11. 11 slew Am. until *h.* of
2 Sam. 4. 5 came about *h.* of day
1 K. 1. 1 covered . . but he gat no *h.*
Job 24. 19 *h.* consume snow and w.
Ps. 19. 6 nothing hid from the *h.*
Eccl. 4. 11 if two . . then they have *h.*
Isa. 4. 6 shadow in daytime from *h.*
Jer. 17. 8 shall not see when *h.* com.
Mat. 20. 12 borne . . *h.* of the day
Luke 12. 55 say, There will be *h.*
Acts 28. 3 came a viper out of *h.*
Jas. 1. 11 risen with a burning *h.*
2 Pet. 3. 10, 12 elem. melt with . . *h.*
Rev. 7. 16 neither sun . . nor any *h.*
16. 9 men scorched with great *h.*
R. V. Eccl. 4. 11 warmth ; Jas. 1. 11
scorching wind
Heat (*v.*). *Heat, warm.*
Dan. 3. 19 *h.* fur. sev. times more
Hos. 7. 4 as oven *h.* by baker, who
Heath. *Bare, naked.*
Jer. 17. 6 he shall be like *h.* in desert
48. 6 be like *h.* in the wilderness
Heathen. R. V. O. T. *nations.*
N. T. *Gentiles.*
Lev. 25. 44 of *h.* round about yo'
Deut. 4. 27 left few in num. among *h.*
2 Sam. 22. 44 to be head of the *h.*

2 K. 16. 3 abomination of the *h.*
1 Chr. 16. 24 decl. glor. among *h.*
2 Chr. 20. 6 over the kingdom of *h.*
Ez. 6. 21 from filthiness of the *h.* of
Neh. 5. 8 Jews wh. .. sold unto the *h.*
Ps. 2. 1 why do the *h.* rage, and peo.
Isa. 16. 8 lords of *h.* have broken
Jer. 9. 16 I scatter them among *h.*
Lam. 1. 3 she dwelleth among *h.*
Ezek. 11. 12 done after man. of *h.*
Joel 2. 19 make . . reproach among *h,*
Am. 9. 12 *h.,* which are called by na,
Obad. 1 ambassador sent among *h.*
Mic. 5. 15 anger and fury upon *h.*
Hab. 1. 5 Behold ye among the *h.*
Zeph. 2. 11 all the isles of the *h.*
Hag. 2. 22 strength of king. of *h.*
Zech. 11. 15 sore displeased with *h.*
Mal. 1. 11 name .. be gr. among *h.*
Mat. 6. 7 use not vain repeti. as *h.*
Acts 4. 25 Why did the *h.* rage, and
2 Cor. 11. 26 oft. in perils by the *h.*
Gal. 1. 16 mi. preach him among *h.*
3. 8 G. wo. justify *h.* through faith
Heave. *Make high, lift up.*
Ex. 29. 27 offeri. which is *h.* up of
Num. 15. 20 the . . off . . shall ye *h.*
18. 30 ye have *h.* the best thereof
Heave-offering. *Lifted off.*
Ex. 29. 27 sanctify. shoulder of *h. o.*
Lev. 7. 14 ; Num. 15. 19–21 ; 18. 8,
29 ; Der 12. 6, 11, 17
Heave-shoulder. *Lifted up*
shoulder.
Lev. 7. 34 *h. s.* have I taken of the
Num. 6. 20 wave breast and *h. s.*
Heaven. *Heaved up thing.*
Gen. 1. 1 God creates the *h.* and
1. 8 God called the firma. *H.*
Ex. 9. 10 M. sprinkled it tow. *h.*
Lev. 26. 19 make your *h.* as iron
Deut. 1. 10 ye are . . as stars of *h.*
Josh. 2. 11 God in *h.* . . and earth
Judg. 5. 20 fought from *h.,* the stars
1 Sam. 2. 10 out of *h.* be thunder
2 Sam. 18. 9 was taken up bet. *h.*
1 K. 8. 22 spread . . hands tow. *h.*
2 K. 1. 10, 12 let fire come from *h.*
1 Chr. 21. 16 stand bet. e. and *h.*
2 Chr. 2. 6 *h.* and *h.* of *h.* cannot
Ez. 1. 2 Lord God of *h.* hath given
Neh. 1. 4 prayed before God of *h.*
Job 1. 16 fire of G. is fal. from *h.*
Ps. 11. 4 the Lord's throne is in *h.*
134. 3 Lord made *h.* and earth
Prov. 23. 5 fly . . as eag. toward *h.*
Eccl. 5. 2 for God is in *h.,* and thou
Jer. 7. 18 make cakes to queen of *h.*
Lam. 4. 19 swifter than eag. of *h.*
Ezek. 31. 6 fowls of *h.* made nests
Dan. 8. 8 toward four winds of *h.*
Hos. 4. 3 with the fowls of *h.,* yea
Am. 9. 2 though they climb to *h.*
Jonah 1. 9 God of *h.* which hath
Nah. 3. 16 multipl. above stars of *h.*
Zeph. 1. 3 will consume fowls of *h*
Hag. 1. 10 *h.* over you is stayed
Zech. 2. 6 spread as f. winds of *h.*
Mal. 3. 10 not op. windows of *h.*
Mat. 3. 2 kingdom of *h.* is at hand
5. 3, 10 theirs is the kingdom of *h.*
5. 16 glorify your Father . . in *h.*
6. 9 our Father which art in *h.*
6. 10 Thy will be done as in *h.*
24. 35 *h.* and e. shall pass away
Mark 1. 11 came voice from *h.* say.
8. 11 seeking . . a sign from *h.*
Luke 6. 23 yo. reward is great in *h.*
John 1. 32. Sp. descend, from *h.* like
Acts 1. 10 stedf. tow. *h.* as he went
7. 49 *h.* is my throne, e. my foots.
22. 6 shone from *h.* a gr. light
Rom. 1. 18 wrath of G. rev. from *h.*
1 Cor. 15. 47 sec. man is L. from *h.*
2 Cor. 12. 2 caught up to third *h.*
Gal. 1. 8 or angel from *h.* preach
Eph. 6. 9 knowing . . Mas. is in *h.*
Phil. 3. 20 our conversation is in *h.*
Col. 1. 5 hope laid . . for you in *h.*
1 Thes. 1. 10 wait for . . Son from *h.*
2 Thes. 1. 7 L. J. be reveal. from *h.*
Heb. 9. 24 into *h.,* now to appear
Jas. 5. 12 nei. by *h.,* nei. by earth
1 Pet. 1. 4 inherit. reserved in *h.*
2 Pet. 1. 18 voice .. came from *h.*
1 John 5. 7 three bear record in *h*

Rev. 4. 1 door was opened in *h.*
R. V. Mark 11. 26; Luke 11. 2;
Heb. 10. 34; 1 John 5. 7; Rev.
16. 17 ——

Heavenly. *Of heaven.*
Mat. 18. 35 shall my *h.* Father do
Luke 2. 13 mul. of *h.* host praised
John 3. 12 I tell you of *h.* things
Acts 26. 19 not dis. unto *h.* vision
1 Cor. 15. 48 *h.*, such are they also
Eph. 1. 3 all blessings in *h.* places
2 Tim. 4. 18 preserve .. unto *h.* kind.
Heb. 3. 1 partakers of *h.* calling

Heavens. *Heaved up things, skies.*
Gen. 2. 1 thus *h.* and e. were fin.
Deut. 10. 14 *h.* of *h.* is the Lord's
Judg. 5. 4 *h.* dropped, clouds also
2 Sam. 22. 10 he bowed the *h.* also
1 K. 8. 27 *h.* of *h.* cannot contain
1 Chr. 16.26 but Lord made the *h.*
2 Chr. 6. 25 hear thou from the *h.*
Ez. 9. 6 our tresp. is grown to *h.*
Neh. 9. 6 *h.* of *h.* with all .. hosts
Job 9. 8 which .. spreadeth out *h.*
Ps. 18. 9 bowed *h.* and came down
19. 1 The *h.* declare thy glory
Prov. 8. 27 when he prep. the *h.*
Isa. 1. 2 Hear, O *h.*, give ear, O e.
65. 17 For, behold I create new *h.*
Jer. 2. 12 be astonished, O ye *h.*
Lam. 3. 66 destroy .. from nnder *h.*
Ezek. 1. 1 *h.* opened, I saw visions
Dan. 4.26 known that the *h.* do rule
Hos. 2. 21 saith L., I will hear the *h.*
Joel 2. 10 the *h.* shall tremble, sun
Hab. 3. 3 his glory covered the *h.*
Hag. 2. 6 I will shake the *h.* and ear.
Zech. 6. 5 are the four spirits of *h.*
Mat. 3. 16 lo, the *h.* were opened
Mark 1. 10 he saw the *h.* opened
Luke 12. 33 treas. in *h.* that fail not
Acts 2. 34 D. is not ascended to *h.*
2 Cor. 5. 1 house .. eternal in *h.*
Eph. 4. 10 ascend. far above all *h.*
Heb. 1. 10 *h.* are work of thine *h.*
2 Pet. 3. 5 by word of God *h.* were
Rev. 12. 12 rejoice ye *h.*, and ye th.

Heavier. *Weightier.*
Job 6. 3 *h.* than the sand of the sea
23. 2 stroke is *h.* than my groani.
Prov. 27. 3 fool's wrath is *h.* than

Heavily. *Weightily.*
Ex. 14. 25 that they drave them *h.*
Ps. 35. 14 I am bowed down *h.*
Isa. 47. 6 hast thou *h.* laid .. yoke
R. V. Ps. 35. 14 mourning

Heaviness. *Despondency, grief.*
Ez. 9.5 at sacri., I arose from my *h.*
Job. 9.27 I will leave off my *h.* and
Ps. 119. 28 my soul melteth for *h.*
Prov. 12. 25 *h.* in heart .. maketh it
Isa. 29. 2 shall be *h.* and sorrow
Rom. 9. 2. I have great *h.* and sor.
2 Cor. 2. 1 not come .. to you in *h.*
Phil. 2. 26 longed, and was full of *h.*
Jas. 4. 9 let your joy be turned to *h.*
1 Pet. 1. 6 ye are in *h.* through tem.
R. V. Ez. 9. 5 humiliation; Job
9. 27 sad countenance; Isa. 29 2
mourning; 2 Cor. 2. 1 with sor-
row; Phil. 2. 26 sore troubled;
Pet. 1. 6 have been put in grief

Heavy. *Weighty, burdensome*
Ex. 17. 12 Moses' hands were *h.*
Num. 11. 14 because it is too *h.* for
1 Sam. 4. 18 E. was old man, and *h.*
2 Sam. 14. 26 hair was *h.* on him
1 K. 12. 10 fath. made our yoke *h.*
2 Chr. 10. 4 *h.* yoke he put on us
Neh. 5. 18 bondage was *h.* on this
Job 33. 7 nei. shall .. hand be *h.*
Ps. 32. 4 thy hand was *h.* upon me
Lam. 3. 7 he hath made my chain *h.*
Prov. 27. 3 stone is *h.*, and sand w.
Isa. 30. 27 the burden thereof is *h.*
Mat. 23. 4 For they bind *h.* burdens
Bitter, sharp, evil, sour
1 K. 14. 6 sent .. with *h.* tidings
20. 43 went .. *h.* and displeased
Prov. 25. 20 sing. songs to *h.* heart
31. 6 to those that be of *h.* hearts
Heavy, weary, troubled, faint.
Mat. 26. 37 began to be .. very *h.*
26. 43 again, for their eyes were *h.*
Mark 14. 33 amazed, and to be .. *h.*
14. 40; Luke 9. 22

R. V. Prov. 31. 6 bitter; Isa. 30. 27
rising smoke; 46. 1 made a load;
58. 6 bands of the yoke; Mat. 26.
37; Mark 14. 33 troubled

Hedge (*d.*). *Fence, barrier, fold.*
1 Chr. 4. 23 dwelt am. plants and *h.*
Job 1. 10 hast not .. made *h.* about
Ps. 89. 40 hast broken down his *h.*
Prov. 15. 19 sloth. man is *h.* of th.
Eccl. 10. 8 whoso breaketh an *h.*
Isa. 5. 5 I will take away the *h.*
Jer. 49. 3 run to and fro by the *h.*
Ezek. 13. 5 neither made up the *h.*
Nah. 3. 17 which camp in the *h.*
Mark 12. 1 and set an *h.* about it
Luke 14. 23 go .. into h. ways and *h.*
R. V. 1 Chr. 4. 23 Gederah; Ps.
80. 12; Eccl. 10. 8; Jer. 49. 3 fences

Hedge (*v.*). *Inclose, fence about.*
Job 3. 23 and whom God hath *h.* in
Lam. 3. 7 he hath *h.* me about
Hos. 2. 6 *h.* thy way with thorns
Mat. 21. 33 and *h.* it round about, th.
R. V. Lam. 3. 7 fenced; Mat. 21. 33
set a hedge about

Heed. *Attention, regard, notice,
care.*
Gen. 31. 24 take *h.* .. speak not to J.
Ex 10. 28 fr. me, take *h.* to thyself
Num. 23. 12 must I not take *h.* to
Deut 27. 9 Take *h.*, hearken, O Is.
Josh. 23. 11 take *h.* to yourselves
1 Sam. 19. 2 *h.* to thyself until mor.
2 Sam. 20. 10 Amasa took no *h.* to
1 K. 2. 4 if thy children take *h.*
2 K. 10. 31 but Jehu took no *h.* to
1 Chr. 22. 13 tak. *h.* to fulfil statutes
2 Chr. 19. 6 take *h.* what ye do, for
Job 36. 21 *h.*, regard not iniquities,
Ps. 39. 1 I will take *h.* to my ways
Prov. 17. 4 giveth *h.* to false lips
Eccl. 7. 21 tak. no *h.* unto all words
Isa. 7. 4 *h.*, be quiet, fear not, neither
Jer. 9. 4 take *h.* .. of his neighbour
Hos. 4. 10 left off to take *h.* of Lord
Mal. 2. 15 take *h.* to your spirit
Mat. 16. 6 *h.* and beware of leav.
Mark 4. 24 take *h.* what ye hear
Luke 21. 8 *h.* th. ye be not deceived
Acts 8. 6 people .. gave *h.* unto
1 Cor. 3. 10 man .. *h.* how he build.
Gal. 5. 15 *h.* ye be not consumed
1 Tim. 1. 4 nei. give *h.* to fables
Tit. 1. 14 not giving *h.* to fables
Heb. 3. 12 *h.*, lest there be any of
R. V. Deut. 27. 9 silence; 2 Chr.
19. 6 consider; 33. 8 observe; Eccl.
12. 9 pondered; Mat. 18. 10 see;
Luke 11. 35 look; Acts 8. 11 re-
gard; 22. 18; Rom. 11. 21 ——

Heel. *Heel.*
Gen. 3. 15 thou shalt bruise his *h.*
25. 26 Jac. took hold on Esau's *h.*
Job 18. 9 gin shall take him by *h.*
Ps. 41. 9 lifted his *h.* against me
Jer. 13. 22 and thy *h.* made bare
Hos. 12. 3 took his brother by *h.*
John 13. 18 lifted up .. *h.* against me
R. V. Job 13. 27 soles

Heifer. *Heifer, cow, kine.*
Gen. 15. 9 take *h.* three years old
Num. 19. 2 bri. red *h.* without spot
Deut. 21. 3 elders .. shall take *h.*
Judg. 14. 18 not plough. with my *h.*
1 Sam. 16. 2 take *h.* .. thee and say
Isa. 15. 5 unto Zoar, an *h.* of three y.
Jer. 46. 20 Egypt is like very fair *h.*
Hos. 4. 16 slideth back as backsl. *h.*
Heb. 9. 13 ashes of *h.* sprinkling

Height. *Highness, altitude, stat-
ure.*
Gen. 6. 15 *h.* of it thirty cubits
Ex. 25. 10 cubits and half *h.* thereof
1 Sam. 17. 4 *h.* was six c. and span
1 K. 6. 2 *h.* thereof thirty cubits
2 K. 25. 17 *h.* of one pillar eighteen
2 Chr. 4. 1 ten cub. the *h.* thereof
Ez. 6. 3 *h.* was threescore cubits
Job 22. 12 God in the *h.* of heaven
Ps. 102. 19 from *h.* of his sanctuary
Prov. 25. 3 the heaven for *h.*, and
Isa. 37. 24 come up to *h.* of mount.
Jer. 31. 12 come sing in *h.* of Zion
Ezek. 17. 23 mount. of *h.* of Israel
Dan. 3. 1 whose *h.* was threescore c.
Am. 2. 9 *h.*was like *h.* of the cedars

Rom. 8. 39 nor *h.*, nor depth, nor
Eph. 3. 18 what is br., depth, and *h.*
Rev. 21. 16 breadth and *h.* are equal
R. V. Ezek. 31, 5, 10, 14 stature;

Heinous. *Wicked.*
Job. 31. 11 For this is an *h.* crime

Heir. *Possessor, successor.*
Gen. 15. 3 lo, one born .. is mine *h.*
2 Sam. 14. 7 will destroy the *h.* also
Prov. 30. 23 handmaid that is *h.* to
Jer. 49. 1 hath Israel no sons, no *h.*
Mic. 1. 15 yet will I bring an *h.* to
Who receives a lot or portion.
Mat. 21. 38 the *h.*; let us kill him
Mark 12. 7; Luke 20. 14
Rom. 4. 13 should be *h.* of world
8. 17 *h.* of G., joint *h.* with Christ
Gal. 3. 29 *h.* according to promise
Eph. 3. 6 Gent. should be fellow *h.*
Tit. 3. 7 made *h.* according to hope
Heb. 1. 2 whom he hath app. *h.*
Jas. 2. 5 *h.* of kingdom which he ha,
1 Pet. 3. 7 *h.* together of grace of l.
R. V. Jer. 49.2; Mic. 1. 15 possess;
Gal. 4. 30 inherit

Held. *See Hold.*

Hell. *Sheol, unseen state.*
Deut. 32. 22 burn unto lowest *h.*
2 Sam. 22.6 sorrows of *h.* comp. me
Job 11. 8 deeper than *h.*, what kn.
Ps. 9. 17 wick. shall be turn. into *h.*
139. 8 if I make my bed in *h.*, beho.
Prov. 5. 5 her steps take hold on *h.*
7. 27 her house is the way to *h.*
27. 20 *h.* and destruc. are never full
Isa. 5. 14 *h.* hath enlarged herself
Ezek. 31. 16 cast him down to *h.*
Am. 9. 2 though they dig into *h.*
Jonah 2. 2 out of the .. of *h.* cried I
Hab. 2. 5 enlargeth his desire as *h.*
Hades, unseen world.
Mat. 11. 23 be brought down to *h.*
16. 18 gates of *h.* shall not prevail
Luke 10. 15 be thrust down to *h.*
16. 23 in *h.* he lifted up his eyes
Acts 2. 27, 31 not leave .. soul in *h.*
Rev. 1. 18 have keys of *h.* and d.
6. 8; 20. 13, 14
Gehenna, valley of Hinnom.
Mat. 5. 22 sh. be in danger of *h.* fire
5. 29; 10. 28; 18. 9; 23. 15, 33
Mark 9. 43 two hands to go into *h.*
Luke 12. 5 ha. power to cast into *h.*
Jas. 3. 6 and it is set on fire of *h.*
Tartarus, dark abyss.
2 Pet. 2. 4 cast them down to *h.*
R. V. 2 Sam. 22. 6; Job 11. 8; 26.
6; Ps. 16. 10; 18. 5; 116. 3; 139. 8;
Prov. 5. 5; 7. 27; 9. 18; 15. 11,
24; 23. 14; 27. 30 Sheol; Mat. 11.
23; 16. 18; Luke 10. 15; 16. 23;
Acts 2. 27, 31; Rev. 1. 18; 6. 8;
20. 13, 14 Hades; Mat. 5. 22; 18. 9
hell of fire

Helm. R. V. *rudder.*
Jas. 3. 4 turned about with small *h.*

Helmet. *Head-armor.*
1 Sam. 17. 5 *h.* of brass on head
2 Chr. 26. 14 Uzziah prepared .. *h.*
Isa. 59. 17 *h.* of salvation on head
Jer. 46. 4 stand forth with your *h.*
Ezek. 23. 24 set shield and *h.* round
Eph. 6. 17 take the *h.* of salvation
1 Thes. 5. 8 for *h.* hope of salva.

Help (*n.*). *Assistance, succor.*
Gen. 2. 18 will make him *h.* meet
Ex. 18. 4 G. .. said he was mine *h.*
Deut. 33. 7 be thou *h.* to him fr. en.
Judg. 5. 23 to the *h.* of the Lord
1 Sam. 11. 9 hot, ye shall have *h.*
Ps. 108. 12 give us *h.* from trouble
Acts 26. 22 hav. obtain. *h.* of God
1 Cor. 12. 28 God hath set .. *h.*
R. V. 1 Sam. 11. 9 deliverance

Help (*v.*). *Strengthen, save, assist.*
Gen. 49. 25 God .. who shall *h.* thee
Ex. 2. 17 Moses stood up and *h.*
Deut. 22. 4 sh. *h.* him lift them up
Josh. 1. 14 men of valour, and *h.*
1 Sam. 7. 12 hitherto hath Lord *h.*
2 Sam. 10. 19 the Syrians feared to *h.*
1 K. 1. 7 they fol. Adonijah *h.* him
2 K. 6. 26 cried woman saying *h.*
1 Chr. 19. 12 then will I *h.* thee
2 Chr. 20. 9 cry, then thou wilt *h.*
Ez. 1. 4 let the men .. *h.* him w. sil

Esth. 9. 3 offi. of. king *h*. the Jews
Job. 8. 20 neither will he *h*. the evil
Ps. 22. 11 for there is none to *h*.
  109. 26 *h*. me, O Lord, O save
Eccl. 4. 10 not anoth. k. to *h*. him.
Isa. 30. 7 Egypt, shall not *h*. in *v*.
Lam. 1. 7 people fell .. none did *h*.
Ezek. 32. 21 hell with them that *h*.
Dan. 11. 34 be *h*. with a little *h*.
Zech. 1. 15 *h*. forward the affliction
Mat. 15. 25 worshipping saying, L. *h*
Mark 9. 29 have comp. .. and *h*. us
Luke 1. 54 hath *h*. his servant Israel
Acts 16. 9 come to Macedon. and *h*.
1 Cor. 16. 16 to every one that *h*.
2 Cor. 1. 11 ye also *h*. together by pr.
Phil. 4. 3 *h*. women which laboured
Heb. 4. 16 find grace to *h*. in .. need
R. V. 1 Chr. 18. 5 succor ; 2 Chr.
  20. 9. save ; Job 8. 20 uphold ; Ps.
  116. 6 saved ; Eccl. 4. 10 lift

Helper. *Who helps.*
2 K. 14. 26 nor any *h*. for Israel
1 Chr. 12. 1 mighty men, *h*. of war
Job 9. 13 proud *h*. do stoop under
Ps. 10. 14 thou art *h*. of fatherless
Jer 47. 4 cut off from Tyrus ev. *h*.
Ezek 30. 8 *h*. shall be destroyed
Nah. 3. 9 Put and Lub. were .. *h*.
Rom. 16. 3 greet P. and A. my *h*.
2 Cor. 1. 24 but are *h*. of your joy
Heb. 13. 6 say, The Lord is my *h*.

Helve. *Wood, handle.*
Deut. 19. 5 head slippeth from *h*.

Hem. *Border, skirt.*
Ex. 28. 33 beneath, upon the *h*. of it
  28. 34 ; 39. 24, 25, 26
Mat. 9. 20 touched *h*. of his garment
  14. 36 might only touch the *h*. of
R. V. Ex. 28. 33, 34 ; 39. 24, 25, 26
  skirts ; Mat. 9. 20 ; 14. 36 border

Hemlock. *Wormwood, poison plant.*
Hos. 10. 4 judgment spring. as *h*. in
Am. 6. 12 fruit of righteous into *h*.
R. V. Am. 6. 12 wormwood

Hen. *Fowl, hen.*
Mat. 23. 37 as *h*. gath. her chickens
Luke 13. 34 as *h*.doth gath. her brood

Hence. *From this.*
Gen. 37. 17 they are departed *h*.
Ex. 33. 15 go not, carry us not up *h*.
Ps. 39. 13 before I go *h*. and be no
Mat. 17. 20 shall say .. remove *h*.
Luke 13. 31 get thee out, depart *h*.
John 2. 16 said, Take these things *h*.
Acts 1. 5 H. G. not many days *h*.
Jas. 4. 1 come they not *h*., even of

Henceforth. *From now on.*
John 15. 15 *h*., I call you not ser.
Rom. 6. 6 *h*. we should serve not sin
2 Cor. 5. 15 *h*. live unto themselves
Gal. 6. 17 *h*. let no man trouble me
Eph. 4. 17 *h*. walk not as oth. Gent.
Heb. 10. 13 *h*. expecting till his en.
R. V. Rom. 6. 6 ; 2 Cor. 5. 16 so ;
  Eph. 4. 14 may ; Gal. 6. 17 15 ; 2
  Cor. 5. 15 ; Eph. 4. 17 no longer

Henceforward. *From now on.*
Num. 15. 23 *h*. among your genera.
Mat. 21. 19 no fruit grow on thee *h*.
R. V. Num. 15. 23 onward

Herald. *Messenger, crier.*
Dan. 3. 4 then *h*. cried aloud, To you

Herb. *Herbage, aromatic plant.*
Gen. 1. 11 the *h*. yielding seed
Ex. 9. 22 upon every *h*. of field
Deut. 11. 10 seed .. as garden of *h*.
2 K. 21. 2 have it for garden of *h*.
2 K. 4. 39 went out .. to gather *h*.
Job 8. 12 with. before any other *h*.
Ps. 37. 2 and wither as the green *h*.
Prov. 15. 17 better is a dinner of *h*
Isa. 18. 4 like a clear heat upon *h*.
Jer. 12. 4 how long shall *h*. with.
Mat. 13. 32 is the greatest among *h*.
Mark4. 32 becom. greater than all *h*.
Luke 11. 42 and all manner of *h*.
Rom. 14. 2 who is weak, eateth *h*.
Heb. 6. 7 bringeth forth *h*. meet
R. V. Job 38. 27 ; Isa. 66. 14 grass

Herd. *Oxen, cattle, drove, flock.*
Gen. 13. 5 Lot had flocks and *h*.
Ex. 10. 9 with our flocks and *h*.
Lev. 1. 2 bring offering of the *h*.
Num. 11·22 shall f. and *h*. be slain

Deut. 8. 13 thy *h*. and f. multiply
1 Sam. 11. 5 Saul came after *h*. out
2 Sam. 12. 2 rich man had exceed. *h*.
1 Chr. 27. 29 over the *h*. that fed in
2 Chr. 32. 29 provided .. *h*. in abund.
Prov. 27. 23 and look well to thy *h*.
Isa. 65. 10 Achor, place for *h*. to lie
Jer. 5. 17 shall eat up thy fl. and *h*.
Hos. 5. 6 shall go with their .. *h*.
Joel 1. 18 the *h*. .. are perplexed
Jonah 3. 7 let neither *h*. nor fl. taste
Hab. 3. 18 shall be no *h*. in stall
Mat. 8. 30 way off from them an *h*.
Mark 5. 11 a great *h*. of swine feed.
Luke 8. 32 an *h*. of many swine fee.
  8. 33 *h*. ran .. down steep place
R. V. 1 Sam. 11. 5 oxen

Herdman. *Feeder, sheep-master.*
Gen. 13. 7 the *h*. of Abram's .. and
1 Sam. 21. 7 Doeg, chiefest of the *h*.
Am. 1. 1 Amos, among *h*. of Tekoa

Here. *This place, hither.*
Gen. 16. 13 I *h*. looked after him
Ex. 24. 14 tarry ye *h*. for us, until
Num. 22. 15 stand here by thy off.
Judg. 20. 7 give *h*. your advice and
1 Sam. 16. 11 are *h*. all thy children
2 Sam. 18. 30 turn aside and stand *h*.
Job 38. 11 *h*... proud waves be stay.
Hos. 7. 9 gray hairs are *h*. and ther.
Mat. 12. 41 greater than Jonas is *h*.
Mark 6. 3 are not his sisters *h*. with
Luke 9. 33 it is good for us to be *h*.
John 6. 9 lad *h*. hath five bar. loa.
Acts 9. 14 and *h*. he hath authority
Col. 4. 9 make known to you .. *h*.
Heb. 7. 8 *h*. men .. receive tithes
Jas. 2. 3 sit thou *h*. in good place
Rev. 13. 10 *h*. is the patience and

Hereafter. *After this, from now.*
Isa. 41. 23 show things to come *h*.
Ezek. 20. 39 serve ye his idols and *h*.
Dan. 2. 29 what .. come to pass *h*.
Mat. 26. 64 *h*. shall ye see the Son
Mark 11. 14 no man eat fruit .. *h*.
Luke 22. 69 *h*. shall Son of m. sit
John 13. 7 but thou shalt know *h*.
Rev. 1. 19 things which shall be *h*.

Hereby. *In this, by this.*
Gen. 42. 15 *h*. ye shall be proved
1 Cor. 4. 4 yet am I not *h*. justified
1 John 2. 3 And *h*. we do know that
  2. 5 ; 3. 16 ; 4. 2, 6, 13

Herein. *In this.*
Gen. 34. 22 only *h*. will men cons.
John 4. 37 *h*. is that saying true
Acts 24. 16 *h*. do I exerc. myself
2 Cor. 8. 10 And *h*. I give my advice
1 John 4. 10 *h*. is love, not that we
R. V. Gen. 34. 22 on this condition

Hereof. *Of this.*
Mat. 9. 26 fame *h*. went abroad into
Heb. 5. 3 by reason *h*. he ought, as

Heresy. *Opinion, sentiment.*
Acts 24. 14 after way .. they call *h*.
1 Cor. 11. 19 must be *h*. among you
Gal. 5. 20 wrath, strife, sedition *h*.
2 Pet. 2. 1 who bring in damnable *h*.
R. V. Acts 24. 14 a sect

Heretic. *Heretical person.*
Tit. 3. 10 man that is an *h*. aft. admo

Heretofore. *Before this, yesterday*
Ex. 4. 10 not eloquent, neither *h*.
Josh. 3. 4 not passed this way *h*.
1 Sam. 4. 7 not seen such thing *h*.
Ruth 2. 11 peo. thou knew. not *h*.

Hereunto. *For this.*
1 Pet. 2. 21 even *h*. were we called

Herewith. *In, by, with this.*
Ezek. 16. 29 yet was not satisfied *h*.
Mal. 3. 10 and prove me now *h*.

Heritage. *Possession, inheritance.*
Ex. 6. 8 I will give it you for an *h*.
Job 20. 29 *h*. appointed .. by God
Ps. 94. 5 Lord, and afflict thine *h*.
Isa. 49. 8 cause to inherit desolate *h*.
Jer. 2. 7 made .. *h*. an abomination
Joel 2. 17 give not .. *h*. to reproach
Mic. 2. 2 oppress .. man and .. *h*.
Mal. 1. 3 and laid his .. *h*. waste
1 Pet. 5. 3 nei. .. lords over G's. *h*.
R. V. 1 Pet. 5. 3 charge allotted

Heron. *Heron.*
Lev. 11. 19 the *h*. after her kind
Deut. 14. 18 the *h*. .. and lapwing

Hew. *Cut, chop, hack, dress*

Ex. 34. 1 *h*. thee two tables of
Deut. 12. 3 *h*. down graven images
1 Sam. 11. 7 and *h*. them to pieces
1 K. 5. 17 brought great .. *h*. stones
2 K. 12. 12 buy timb. and *h*. stones
1 Chr. 22. 2 set masons to *h*. stones
2 Chr. 2. 2 to. men to *h*. in mountain
Prov. 9. 1 she hath *h*. out her pillars
Isa. 10. 33 high .. shall be *h*. down
Jer. 2. 13 *h*. them out cisterns, brok.
Dan. 4. 14 *h*. down tree, and cut
Hos. 6. 5 therefore have I *h*. them
Mat. 3. 10 not good fr. is *h*. down
Mark 15. 46 laid him in sepulch. *h*.
Luke 3. 9 not good fruit is *h*. down
R. V. 1 K. 5. 18 fashion ; 1 Sam.
  11. 7 cut

Hewn. *Cut, dressed, wrought.*
Ex. 20. 25 build it of *h*. stones, for
1 K. 6. 36 built .. court .. of *h*. sto.
2 K. 22. 6 buy .. *h*. stones to rep.
2 Chr. 34. 11 buy *h*. stone and tim.
Isa. 9. 10 we build with *h*. stones
Lam. 3. 9 inclosed ways with *h*. s.
Ezek. 40. 42 four tables .. of *h*. sto.
Am. 5. 11 built houses of *h*. stone
Luke 23. 53 in sepulchre *h*. in stone

Hewer. *Who cuts, hews, carves.*
Deut. 29. 11 from *h*. of wood unto
Josh. 9. 21 but let them be *h*. of wo
1 K. 5. 15 thous. *h*. in mountains
2 K. 12. 12 ; 1 Chr. 22. 15 ; 2 Chr.
  2. 18
Jer. 46. 22 come against her .. as *h*.

Hid. *See* **Aide.**

Hidden. *Concealed.*
Lev. 5. 2 if and it be *h*. from him
Deut. 30. 11 this command. is not *h*.
Job 3. 16 or as an *h*. untimely birth
Ps. 51. 6 in the *h*. part thou shalt
Prov. 28. 12 wick. rise, man is *h*.
Obad. 6 how are *h*. things sought
1 Cor. 4. 5 bring to light *h* things
2 Cor. 4. 2 renounced the *h*. things
1 Pet. 3. 4 be the *h*.man of the heart

Hide (*n*.). *Skin.*
Lev. 8. 17 the bullock and his *h*. be
  9. 11 and the *h*. he burnt with fire

Hide (*v*.). *Cover, secrete, conceal.*
Gen. 35. 4 Jac. *h*. them under oak
Ex. 2. 12 and *h*. him in the sand
Lev. 20. 4 if peo. ... do any ways *h*.
Deut. 31. 17 I will *h*. my face from
Josh. 6. 17, 25 bec. she *h*. the mess.
Judg. 6. 11 Gid. thresh. wheat .. to *h*
1 Sam. 3. 17 pray *h*. it not from me
2 Sam. 14. 18 H. not fr. me, I pray
1 K. 22. 25 go into .. to *h*. thyself
2 K. 11. 12 *h*. him .. and his nurse
1 Chr. 21. 20 sons .. *h*. themselves
2 Chr. 22. 11 Jehosh. *h*. from Ath.
Job. 10. 13 hast thou *h*. in .. heart.
Ps. 32. 5 mine iniq. have I not *h*.
Prov. 19. 24 slothful man *h*. hand
Isa. 2. 10 *h*. thee in dust, for fear
Jer. 13. 5 and *h*. it by Euphrates
Lam. 3. 56 *h*. not ear at my breath.
Ezek. 22. 26 *h*. eyes from my sab.
Dan. 10. 7 th. fled to *h*. themselves
Am. 9. 3 *h*. themselves in Carmel
Mic. 3. 4 he will *h*. his face from
Mat. 5. 14 c. on hill cannot be *h*.
Luke 18. 34 this saying was *h*. from
John 8. 59 Jesus *h*. himself, and
2 Cor. 4. 3 But if our gospel be *h*.
Eph. 3. 9 from begin. hath been *h*.
Col. 3. 3 life is *h*. with Christ in G.
1 Tim. 5. 25 otherwise cannot be *h*.
Heb. 11. 23 Moses .. w. *h*. three mo.
Jas. 5. 20 shall *h*. multitude of sins
Rev. 2. 17 him will I give *h*. manna
R. V. Deut. 30. 11 too hard for ;
  Job 15. 20 ; 20. 26 ; 24. 1 ; Prov.
  2. 1 laid up ; Prov. 19. 24 ; 26. 15
  burieth ; 27. 16 restraineth ; Jer.
  16. 17 ; Luke 9. 45 concealed ;
  Luke 8. 17 secret ; 2 Cor. 4. 3, 13
  is veiled ; Jas. 5. 20 cover

Hiding. *Secreting, secret.*
Ps 32. 7 thou art my *h*. place, thou
Isa. 32. 2 man .. be as an *h*. place
Hab. 3. 4 was the *h*. of his power

High. *Lofty, tall, above, pre-eminent, head, i. e. chief, haughty*
Gen. 7. 19 all *h*., hills were .. cover.
Ex. 14. 8 Is. went out with *h*. hand

Lev. 26. 30 will destroy .. *h.* places
Num. 21. 28 lords of *h.* place of A.
Deut. 3. 5 cit. fenced with *h.* walls
Josh. 20. 6 until death of *h.* priest
1 Sam. 9. 12 sac. .. in the *h.* place
2 Sam. 22. 14 most *H.* utter... voice
1 K. 14. 23 on every *h.* hill, and
2 K. 17. 10 groves in every *h.* hill
1 Chr. 19. 39 in *h.* place at Gibeon
2 Chr. 11. 15 ordain. priests for *h.* pl.
Neh. 3. 1 the *h.* priest rose up with
Esth. 5. 14 gallows fifty cubits *h.*
Job 41. 34 He beholdeth all things *h.*
Ps. 68. 18 thou hast ascended on *h.*
   113. 4 Lord is *h.* above nations
Prov. 18. 11 wealth .. is as *h.* wall
Eccl. 12. 5 sh. be afraid of which is *h.*
Isa. 2. 15 upon every *h.* tower, and
Jer. 25. 30 L. shall roar from on *h.*
Lam. 3. 35 before face of most *H.*
Ezek. 17. 22 plant .. on *h.* mounts.
Dan. 7. 18 saints of most *H.* shall
Hos. 7. 16 return .. not to most *H.*
Am. 4. 13 treadeth upon *h.* places
Mic. 1. 5 what are *h.* places of Jud.
Hab. 3. 19 walk upon mine *h.* pl.
Hag. 1. 1 son of Josed. the *h.* priest
Zech. 3. 8 hear Joshua the *h.* priest
Zeph. 1. 16 against the *h.* towers
Mat. 4. 8 dev. tak. him to .. *h.* mt.
Mark 14. 47 smote ser. of *h.* priest
Luke 1. 78 day spring from on *h.*
John 18. 13 Caiaph. .. was *h.* priest
Acts 13. 17 with *h.* arm brought he
Rom. 12. 16 mind not *h.* things, but
2 Cor. 10. 5 cast. down .. ev. *h.* th.
Eph. 4. 8 he ascended up on *h.*, he
Heb 1. 3 r. hand of Majesty on *h.*
Rev. 21. 10 carr. me to .. *h.* mount.
Higher. *More high, upper.*
1 Sam. 9. 2 *h.* than any of people
2 K. 15. 35 built *h.* gate of house
Neh. 4. 13 on *h.* pl. I set people
Job 35. 5 clouds wh. are *h.* than thou
Ps. 61. 2 lead me to rock that is *h.*
Eccl. 5. 8 he th. is *h.* than the highest
Isa. 55. 9 as heavens are *h.* than e.
Jer. 36. 10 read Baruch in *h.* court
Ezek. 43. 13 sh. be *h.* place of altar
Dan. 8. 3 one .. *h.* than the other
Luke 14. 10 say, Friend, go up *h.*
Rom. 13. 1 subject unto *h.* power
Heb. 7. 26 priest .. made *h.* than
Highest. *Most high, uppermost.*
Ps. 18. 13 and the *H.* gave his voice
Prov. 9. 3 she crieth upon *h.* places
Ezek. 17. 3 took *h.* branch of ced.
Mat. 21. 9 Lord; Hosanna in the *h.*
Mark 11. 10 bless. .. he, Hos. in *h.*
Luke 1. 32 be called Son of the *H.*
   2. 14 glory to God in the *h.*, and on
   14. 8 not sit down in *h.* room, lest
Highly. *Very abundantly*
1 Thes. 5. 13 esteem them very *h.*
See also its frequent connections
   with displeased, esteemed, think,
   etc.
High-minded. *Puffed up.*
Rom. 11. 20 be not *h. m.* but fear
1 Tim. 6. 17 charge th. .. be not *h. m.*
2 Tim. 3. 4 *h. m.*, lovers of pleas.
R. V. 2 Tim. 3. 4 puffed up.
Highness. *Excellency, pride.*
Job 31. 23 and by reason of his *h.* I
Isa. 13. 3 them that rejoice in my *h.*
R. V. Isa. 13. 3 proudly exulting
Highway. *Public way, road, path.*
Num. 20. 19 we will go by the *h.*
Deut. 2. 27 will go along by the *h.*
Judg. 5. 6 *h.* were unoccupied, and
1 Sam. 6. 12 went along *h.* lowing
2 Sam. 20. 12 Am. wallowed .. in *h.*
2 K. 18. 17 pool in *h.* of fuller's field
Prov. 16. 17 *h.* of upright is to depar.
Isa. 7. 3 pool in *h.* of fuller's field
Jer. 31. 21 set thine heart toward *h.*
Am. 5. 16 say in all *h.*, Alas! alas!
Mat. 22. 9 go ye .. into the *h.* and as
Mark 10. 46 Barti .. sat by *h.* beg.
Luke 14. 23 go into *h.* and hedges
R. V. Am. 5. 16 streets; Mat. 22. 9
   partings of highways; Mark 10.
   46 way
Hill. *Height, hillock, mount.*
Gen. 49. 26 bound of everlast. *h.*
Ex. 17. 9 stand on top of the *h.* with rod

Num. 23. 9 from *h.* I behold him
Deut. 12. 2 upon *h.* and und... tree
Josh. 24. 33 they buried him in a *h.*
Judg. 16. 3 car. them to top of *h.*
1 Sam. 26. 23 D. stood on top of *h.*
2 Sam. 21. 9 hanged them in the *h.*
1 K. 11. 7 did Sol. build in *h.* bef. Jer.
2 K. 16. 4 he sacrificed on the *h.*
2 Chr. 28. 4 sac. on the *h.* and under
Job 15. 7 wast thou made before *h.*
Ps. 2. 6 set my king on my holy *h.*
   95. 4 strength of the *h.* is his also
Prov. 8. 25 before *h.* was I br. forth
S. of S. 2. 8 come. skipping upon *h.*
Isa. 2. 2 sh. be exalted above the *h.*
Jer. 4. 24 and all the *h.* moved ligh.
Ezek. 6. 3 saith L. God .. to the *h.*
Hos. 4. 13 they sacrifice .. upon *h.*
Joel 3. 18 *h.* shall flow with milk
Am. 9. 13 and all the *h.* shall melt
Mic. 4. 1 it sh. be exalted above *h.*
Nah. 1. 5 *h.* melt, earth is burned
Hab. 3. 6 the perpetual *h.* did bow
Zeph. 1. 10 and gr. crash. from *h,*
Mat. 5. 14 c. on *h.* cannot be hid
Luke 3. 5 ev. .. *h,* shall be brought
   23. 20 they shall say to *h.*, Cover us
Acts 17. 22 Paul stood on Mars' *h.*
R. V. Ex. 24. 4; 1 K. 11. 7 mount;
   Gen. 7. 19; Num. 14. 44, 45; Deut.
   1. 41, 43; Josh. 15. 9; 18. 13, 14;
   24. 30; Judg. 2. 9; 16. 3; 1 Sam.
   25. 20; 26. 13; 2 Sam. 21. 9; 1 K.
   22. 17; Ps. 18. 7; 68. 15, 16; 80.
   10; 95. 4; 97. 5; 104. 10, 13, 18,
   32; 121. 1; Luke 9. 37 mountain,
   or mountains; Deut. 1. 7; Josh.
   9. 1; 11. 16; 17. 6 hill country;
   1 Sam. 9. 11; 2 Sam. 16. 1 ascent;
   Acts 17. 22 the Areopagus.
Hill-Country. *Hilly, mountain-ous.*
Josh. 13. 6 inhabitants of the *h c.*
Luke 1. 39 Mary .. went into *h. c.*
Him, Himself. *See* nouns for which
   they stand, as
Mat. 8. 18 J. saw gr. mul. about *h.*
Job 18. 4 He teareth *h.* in his anger
Hin. *Liquid measure,* 280 *cub. in.*
Ex. 29. 40 fourth of *h.* of oil for off.
Lev. 19. 36; Num. 15. 4; Ezek.
   4. 11
Hind. *Female red deer.*
Gen. 49. 21 Naph. is *h.* let loose
2 Sam. 22. 34 mak. my feet like *h's.*
Job 39. 1 canst mark when *h's* cal.
Ps. 29. 9 voice of L. mak. *h.* to calve
S. of S. 2. 7 charge .. by *h.* of field
Hab. 3. 19 make my feet like *h's.*
Hinder (*v.*). *Rear, stern, back part.*
2 Sam. 2. 23 with *h.* end of spear
1 K. 7. 25 h. all parts were inward
2 Chr. 4. 4; Ps. 78 66
Joel 2. 20 and *h.* part toward .. sea
Zech. 14. 8 half .. toward *h.* sea
Mark 4. 38 in *h.* part of ship asleep
Acts 27. 41 but *h.* part was broken
R. V. Ps. 78. 66 backward; Zech.
   14. 8 western; Mark 4. 38; Acts
   27. 41 stern
Hinder (*v.*). *Keep back, delay, obstruct, impede, check.*
Gen. 24. 56 he said .. *h.* me not
Num. 22. 16 let nothing .. *h.* thee
Ez. 6. 8 I decree that they be not *h.*
Neh. 4. 8 fight .. Jerus., and *h.* it
Job 9. 12 he tak. away, who can *h.*
Isa. 14. 6 persecuted, and none *h.*
Luke 11. 52 were entering in ye *h.*
Acts 8. 36 See .. what doth *h.* me
Rom. 15. 22 *h.* from com. to you
1 Cor. 9. 12 h. lest the gospel of C.
Gal. 5. 7 who did *h.* you that ye sho.
1 Thes. 2. 18 have come .. but S. *h.*
1 Pet. 3. 7 that .. prayers be not *h.*
Hindermost, Hindmost. *Behind, last, furthest, rear.*
Gen. 33. 2 he put .. R. and J. *h.*
Num. 2. 31 go *h.* with .. standards
Deut. 25. 18 How he smote *h.* of thee
Josh. 10. 19 and smite *h.* of them
Jer. 50. 12 *h.* of nat. shall be wild.
Hinge. *Hanging, opening.*
1 K. 7. 50 *h.* of gold .. for doors
Prov. 26. 14 as door turneth on *h.*
Hip. *Leg, limb, thigh.*

Judg. 15. 8 smote them *h.* and th.
Hire (*n.*). *Wage, prize, reward.*
Gen. 30. 18 G. hath giv. me my *h.*
Ex. 22. 15 hired, it came for his *h.*
Deut. 33. 18 not bring *h.* of whore
1 K. 5. 6 I give *h.* for thy servants
Isa. 23. 17 Tyre shalt turn to her *h.*
Ezek. 16. 31 in that thou scornest *h.*
Mic. 1. 7 *h.* thereof shall be burned
Zech. 8. 10 no *h.* for man, nor beast
Mat. 20. 8. give them their *h.*, begin.
Luke 10. 7 lab. is worthy .. his *h.*
Jas. 5. 4 *h.* of laborers which reaped
R. V. Gen. 31. 8 wages
Hire. (*v.*). *Contract for or with, reward, bribe.*
Gen. 30. 16 I have *h.* thee with my
Lev. 19. 13 wages of him *h.* .. not
Deut. 23. 4 *h.* against thee Balaam
Judg. 9. 4 Abime. *h.* vain persons
1 Sam. 2. 5 *h.* themselves for bread
2 Sam. 10. 6 *h.* the Syrians of Beth.
2 K. 7. 6 ls. hath *h.* against us Hit.
1 Chr. 19. 6 to *h.* chariots and hors.
2 Chr. 24. 12 *h.* masons and carpent.
Ez. 4. *h.* counsellors against them
Neh. 13. 2 *h.* Balaam against them
Isa. 46. 6 and they *h.* a goldsmith
Ezek. 16. 33 *h.* them, that they may
Hos. 8. 9 Ephraim hath *h.* lovers
Mat. 20. 1 went .. to *h.* lab. in v. y.
   20. 7 Th. say, Bec. no man hath *h.* us
Hired. *Hired, hireling.*
Ex. 12. 45 *h.* servant not eat thereof
Lev. 25. 6 *h.* servants and for stran.
Deut. 15. 18 worth a double *h.* ser.
Jer. 46. 21 *h.* men are in midst of her
Mark 1. 20 in ship with *h.* servants
Luke 15. 19 make me .. thy *h.* s.
Acts 28. 30 two y. in own *h.* house
Hireling. *One hired.*
Job 7. 1 his days like days of an *h.*
Isa. 16. 14 as the years of an *h.*, and
Mal. 3. 5 oppress *h.* in his wages
John 10. 13 *h.* fleeteth, bec. he is *h.*
His. *Of him.*
See the nouns for which it stands.
Hiss. R. V. *Overlook.*
1 K. 9. 8 be astonished, and shall *h.*
Job 27. 23 *h.* him out of his place
Isa. 5. 26 *h.* unto them from end
Lam. 2. 15 *h.* .. at daugh. of Jerus.
Ezek. 27. 36 merchants .. *h.* at thee
Zeph. 2. 15 that pass. her shall *h.*
Zech. 10. 8 I will *h.* for them, and
Hissing. *Hissing.*
2 Chr. 29. 8 to astonish. and to *h.*
Jer. 18. 16 land des. .. a perpetual *h.*
Mic. 6. 16 inhabitants thereof a *h.*
Hit. R. V. *Overlook.*
1 Sam. 31. 3 archers *h.* him, and
1 Chr. 10. 3 archers *h.*, and w. him
Hither *Hereward, this way.*
Gen. 15. 16 they shall come *h.* again
Ex. 3. 5 draw not nigh *h.*, put off
Judg. 18. 3 said, who brought thee *h.*
Ruth 2. 14 at meal time come *h.*
1 Sam. 14. 36 let us draw *h.* unto
2 K. 8. 7 man of God is come *h.*
Ps. 73. 10 his people return *h.*, and
Mat. 8. 29 art thou come *h.* to tor.
   17. 17 Jesus answered, bring him *h.*
Mark 11. 3 and he will send him *h.*
Luke 14. 21 bring *h.* poor and mai.
John 6. 25 Rabbi, when ca.. thou *h.*
Acts 9. 21 came *h.* for that intent.
Rev. 4. 1 come up *h.*, I will show
R. V. Judg. 19. 12; 1 Sam. 17. 28;
   Luke 15. 23; 19. 30 ——; 1 K. 22. 9
   quickly; Acts 10. 32 unto thee
Hitherto. *Until now.*
Ex. 7. 16 *h.* thou wouldest not hear
Josh. 17. 14 Lord hath blessed me *h.*
Judg. 16. 13 *h* thou has mocked me
2 Sam. 15. 34 thy father's servant *h.*
1 Chr. 17. 16 th. hast brought me *h.*
Isa. 18. 7 terrible from their begin. *h.*
Dan. 7. 28 *h.* is end of matter. As
John 5. 17 my Father worketh *h.*
Rom. 1. 13 to come, but was let *h.*
1 Cor. 3. 2 *h.* ye were not able to
R. V. Sam. 7. 18; 1 Chr. .. 16
   thus far; 2 Sam. 15. 34 in time
   past; Isa. 18. 2, 7 onward; Dan. 7.
   28 here; John 5. 17 even until now;
   1 Cor. 3. 2 yet

Ho. *Call, hail.*
Isa. 55. 1 *H.*, every one that thirst.
Zech. 2. 6 *H.*, *h.*, come forth, flee

Hoar. *White, gray, hoary.*
Ex. 16. 14 small as *h.* frost on gr.
1 K. 2. 6 let not his *h.* head go
Ps. 147. 16 scat. *h.* frost like ashes
Isa. 46. 4 ev. to *h.* hairs will I carry

Hoary. *White, gray.*
Lev, 19. 32 rise up before *h.* head
Job. 38. 29 *h.* frost, who hath gen.
Prov. 16. 31 *h.* head is crown of glo.

Hoise. R. V. *hoisted.*
Acts 27. 40 *h.* up mainsail to wind

Hold (*n.*). *Fortified place.*
1 Sam. 22. 4 while David was in *h.*
2 Sam. 5. 17 D... went down to *h.*
1 Chr. 11. 16 David was then in *h.*
Ezek. 19. 9 they brought him into *h*
Jer. 51. 30 have remained in their *h.*
Pit, cellar, hole.
Judg. 9. 46, 49 entered *h.* of house
Watch, ward.
Acts 4. 3 and put them in *h.* unto
Rev. 18. 2 *h.* of every foul spirit
Grasp, grip, seizure.
Gen. 25. 26 took *h.* on Esau's heel
Ex. 15. 14 take *h.* on inhab. of P.
Deut. 32. 41 hand take *h.* on judg.
Judg. 16. 27 Sam. took *h.* of .. pillars
1 Sam. 15. 27 laid *h.* upon skirt of
2 Sam. 4. 10 took *h.* of .. slew him
1 K. 13. 4 saying, Lay *h.* on him
2 K. 2. 12 took *h.* of his own clothes
Job 21. 6 trembling tak. *h.* my flesh
Ps. 48. 6 fear took *h.* on them there
Prov. 5. 5 her .. steps take *h.* on hell
Eccl. 7. 18 good that thou take *h.* of
S. of S. 7. 8 will take *h.* of boughs
Isa. 3. 6 when man take *h.* of bro.
Jer. 6. 23 lay *h.* on bow and spear
Ezek. 29. 7 took *h.*.. by thy hand
Mic. 6. 14 take *h.*.. but not deliver
Zech. 8. 23 take *h.* of skirt of a Jew
Mat. 12. 11 will he not lay *h.* on
Mark 3. 21 went to lay *h.* on him
Luke 20. 20 might take *h.* of .. words
1 Tim. 6. 12 lay *h.* on eternal life
Heb. 6. 18 lay *h.* on the hope set b.
Rev. 20. 2 he laid *h.* on the dragon
R. V. Jer. 51. 30 strong holds; Dan.
11. 39; Nah. 3. 12, 14 fortresses;
Acts 4. 3 ward

Hold. *Have, possess, keep.*
Gen. 21. 18 *h.* him in thine hand
Ex. 9. 2 and wilt *h.* them still, the L.
Num. 30. 4 father shall *h.* his peace
Judg. 7. 20 *h.* lamps in left hands
Ruth 3. 15 bring the vail .. and *h.* it
1 Sam. 10. 27 but he *h.* his peace
2 Sam. 13. 20 but *h.* now thy peace
1 K. 8. 65 Solomon *h.* a feast, and Is.
2 K. 18. 36 people *h.* their peace
1 Chr. 13. 9 Uzza put .. *h.* to *h.* ark
2 Chr. 4. 5 *h.* three thousand baths
Neh. 5. 8 Then *h.* they their peace
Esth. 4. 11 k. *h.* out golden sceptre
Job 2. 3 and he *h.* fast his integrity
Ps. 9 which *h.* our soul in life
Prov. 11. 12 m. of unders. *h.* his p.
31. 19 her hands *h.* the distaff
Eccl. 2. 3 and to lay *h.* on folly till I
S. of S. 3. 4 I *h.* him, and would not
Isa. 5. 29 and lay *h.* of the prey, and
Ezek. 30. 21 make strong to *h.* sw
Dan. 10. 21 none that *h.* with me in
Am. 1. 5, 8 him that *h.* sceptre from
Mat. 21. 26 J. John as a prophet
Mark 7. 3 *h.* tradition of the elders
Luke 20. 26 not take *h.* of his words
Acts 3. 11 as lame man .. *h.* Peter
Rom. 14. 4 he shall be *h.* up, for God
Col. 2. 19 and not *h.* the Head, from
Phil. 2. 16 *h.* forth word of life that
1 Thes. 5. 21 *h.* fast which is good
2 Thes. 2. 15 *h.* the traditions which
2 Tim. 1. 13 *h.* fast .. sound words
Tit. 1. 9 *h.* fast the faithful word as
Heb. 3. 6 if we *h.* confidence and
Rev. 2. 13 remember there. and .. *h.*
The R. V. changes are based on
words before and after *hold*

Holden. *Held.*
2 K. 23. 22 not *h.* such a passover
Job 36. 8 be *h.* in cords of affliction
Ps. 71. 6 by thee have I been *h.*

Hole. *Hollowed out place, open-ing, pit, cave, den.*
Ex. 28. 32 shall be an *h.* in top of it
1 Sam. 14. 11 Hebrews come out of *h*
2 K. 12. 9 Jehoiada .. bored *h.* in lid
S. of S. 5. 4 put in hand by *h.* of door
Isa. 2. 19 sh. go into *h.* of the rocks
Jer. 13. 4 hide it there in *h.* of rock
Ezek. 8. 7 behold *h.* in the wall
Mic. 7. 17 move out of *h.* like worms
Nah. 2. 12 and filled his *h.* with prey
Hag. 1. 6 wages put in bag in *h.*
Zech. 14. 12 eyes consume in their *h.*
Mat. 8. 20 foxes have *h.*, and birds
Luke 9. 58 *h.* and birds .. have nests
R. V. Mic. 7. 17 close places; Nah.
2. 12 caves; Zech. 14. 12 sockets

Holier. *More holy.*
Isa. 65. 5 for I am *h.* than thou

Holiest. *Most holy.*
Heb. 9. 3 tab. is called *H.* of all
9. 8; 10. 19
R. V. Heb. 10. 19 Holy of holies

Holily. *Graciously.*
1 Thes. 2. 10 how *h.*.. we have beh.

Holiness. *Separation, the setting apart, the person place or thing set apart.*
Ex. 15. 11 glorious in *h.*, fearful in
39. 30 wrote on it .. *H.* to Lord
1 Chr. 16. 29 wor. L. in beauty of *h.*
2 Chr. 20. 21 praise the beauty of *h.*
Ps. 29. 2. wor. L. in beauty of *h.*
Isa. 23. 18 hire shall be *h.* to Lord
Jer. 2. 3 Israel was *h.* to Lord, and
Am. 4. 2 L. G. hath sworn by his *h.*
Obad. 17 on Zion .. shall be *h.*
Zech. 14. 20 on bells .. *H.* unto L.
Mal. 2. 11 Judah hath profaned *h.*
Rom. 1. 4 according to spirit of *h.*
6. 19, 22 servants to righ. unto *h.*
2 Cor. 7. 1 perfecting *h.* in fear of G.
1 Thes. 3. 13 unblame. in *h.* bef. G.
1 Tim. 2. 15 if they continue in .. *h.*
Heb. 12. 10 be partakers of his *h.*
Graciousness, kindness.
Luke 1. 75 in *h.* and righ. before *h.*
Eph. 4. 24 created in righte. and *h.*
Reverence.
Acts 3. 12 by our own power or *h.*
Tit. 2. 3 in behavior as becometh *h.*
R. V. Ex. 28. 36; 39. 30; Zech. 14
20, 21 Holy; Isa. 62. 9 sanctuary;
Acts 3. 12 godliness; Rom. 6. 19,
22; 1 Thes. 4. 7; 1 Tim. 2. 15;
Heb. 12. 14 sanctification

Hollow. *Depression, cavity, grove.*
Gen. 32. 25 touched *h.* of thigh
Ex. 27. 8 *h.* with boards .. make it
Lev. 14. 37 walls .. with *h.* strakes
Judg. 15. 19 God clave an *h.* place
Isa. 40. 12 water in *h.* of his hand
Jer. 52. 21 and fillet .. it was *h.*

Holy. *Set apart, dedicated.* Said
of things, *sacred*; said of
persons, *pious, pure, holy.*
Ex. 3. 5 thou standest is *h.* ground
19. 6 priests, and an *h.* nation
Lev. 6. 16 be eaten in *h.* place
Num. 5. 17 take *h.* water in .. ves.
Deut. 7. 6 *h.* people unto Lord G.
Josh. 24. 19 for he is an *h.* God
1 Sam. 2. 2 none *h.* as the Lord
1 K. 8. 4 all the *h.* vessels in tab.
2 K. 4. 9 this is an *h.* man of God
1 Chr. 16. 10 glory in his *h.* name
2 Chr. 8. 11 bec. the places are *h.*
Ez 8. 28 and the vessels are *h.* also
Neh. 9. 14 made known thy *h.* sab.
Ps. 2. 6 Yet .. I set my k. on my *h.*
11. 4 The Lord is in his *h.* temple
103. 1 me, bless his *h.* name
Prov. 9. 10 knowl. of *h.* is unders.
Eccl. 8. 10 gone from place of *h.*
Isa. 6. 3 *H.*, *h.*, *h.* is L. of hosts
Jer. 11. 15 *h.* flesh is passed from
Ezek. 20. 39 pollute *h.* name no m.
Dan. 9. 16 Jerus., thy *h.* mount.
Hos. 11. 9 *H.* One in midst of thee
Joel 2. 1 alarm in my *h.* mount.
Obad. 16 drunk on my *h.* mount.
Jonah 2. 4 look tow. thy *h.* temple
Mic. 1. 2 L. from his *h.* temple
Hab. 2. 20 L. is in his *h.* temple
Zeph. 3. 11 haughty bec. of *h* mount.

Hag. 2. 12 if one bear *h.* flesh in sk.
Zech. 2. 12 his portion in *h.* land
Mat. 4. 5 devil tak. him into *h.* city
Mark 6. 20 he was just man and *h.*
Luke 1. 49 and *h.* is his name
John 17. 11 *H.* Fath., keep .. th. wh.
Acts 3. 21 by mouth of *h.* prophet.
Rom. 7. 12 the law is *h.*, and just
1 Cor. 3. 17 the temple of God is *h.*
2 Cor. 13. 12 greet .. with *h.* kiss
Eph. 3. 5 reveal to his *h.* apostles
1 Thes. 5. 27 read unto .. *h.* breth.
2 Tim. 1. 9 called .. with *h.* calling
Heb. 3. 1 *h.* breth., partakers of
1 Pet. 1. 15 is *h.*, so be ye *h.* in all
2 Pet. 1. 18 with him in *h.* mount.
Rev. 3. 7; 4. 8; 6. 10; 11. 2
R. V. Ex. 38. 24; Lev. 10. 17, 18;
14. 13; Ps. 68. 17; Ezek. 21. 2
sanctuary

Holy Ghost. *Holy Spirit.*
Mat. 1. 18 found with child of *H. G.*
Mark 1. 8 baptize you with *H. G.*
Luke 1. 15; John 1. 33; Acts 1. 2;
Rom. 5. 5; 1 Cor. 6. 19; 2 Cor.
6. 6; 1 Thes. 1. 5; 2 Tim. 1. 14;
Tit. 3. 5; Heb. 2. 4; 1 Pet. 1. 12;
2 Pet. 1. 21; Jude 20
R. V. Mat. 12.31, 32; Mark 3. 29;
Luke 2. 25, 26; John. 1. 33; 7.39;
Acts 2. 4; 6. 5; 1 Cor. 2. 13 Holy
Spirit

Home. *Tent, house, abode.*
Gen. 39. 16 until his lord came *h.*
Ex. 9. 19 shall be not brought *h.*
Lev. 18. 9 born at *h.* or abroad
Deut. 24. 5 sh.free at *h.* one year
Josh 2. 18 bring f. .. *h.* unto thee
Judg. 11. 9 bring me *h.* to fight
Ruth 1. 21 L. hath brought me *h.*
1 Sam. 2. 20 went unto .. their *h.*
2 Sam. 13. 7 D. sent *h.* to Tamar
1 K. 5. 14 Leb. .. two months at *h.*
2 K. 14. 10 glory .. and tarry at *h.*
2 Chr. 25. 10 to go *h.* .. they ret.
Esth. 5. 10 when we came *h.*, he
Job. 39. 12 will bring home thy seed
Ps. 68. 12 she that tarried at *h.*
Prov. 7. 19 good man is not at *h.*
Eccl. 12. 5 man go. to his long *h.*
Jer. 39. 14 he should carry him *h.*
Lam. 1. 20 at *h.* there is as death
Hab. 2. 5 proud m. nei. keep. at *h.*
Hag. 1. 9 when ye brought it *h.*
Mat. 8. 6 servant lieth at *h.* sick
Mark 5. 19 go *h.* to thy friends
Luke 15. 6 when he cometh *h.*, he
John 20. 10 disc. went to their *h.*
Acts 21. 6 and they returned *h.* ag.
1 Cor. 11. 34 let him eat at *h.* that
2 Cor. 5, 6 we are at *h.* in the body
1 Tim. 5. 4 learn. . show piety at *h.*
Tit. 2. 5 keepers at *h.*, good, obedi.
R. V. Gen 43. 16; Josh. 2. 18; 1
Sam. 10. 26; Mat. 8. 6; Mark
5. 19 house; Luke 9. 61 ——; 1
Tim. 5. 4 family

Home-born. *Native, house-born.*
Ex. 12. 49 one law .. to him *h. b.*
Jer. 2. 14 Israel, .. is he *h. b.* slave?

Homer. *Dry measure, 10 ephahs.*
Lev. 27. 16 *h.* of barley seed shall
Num. 11. 32 gath. least gath. ten *h.*
Isa. 5. 10 seed of *h.* shall yield ephah
Ezek. 45. 11 bath contain tenth of *h.*
Hos. 3. 2 and half *h.* of barley

Honest. *Excellent, upright.*
Luke 8. 15 is an *h.* and good heart
Rom. 12. 17 provide things *h.* in
2 Cor. 8. 21 providing for *h.* things
Phil. 4. 8 whatsoever things are *h.*
1 Pet. 2. 12 convers. *h.* among Gen.
R. V. Acts 6. 3 good; Rom. 12. 17;
1 Cor. 8. 21; 2 Cor. 13. 7; Phil.
4. 8 honourable; 1 Pet. 2. 12 behaviour seemly

Honestly. *Decently, uprightly.*
Rom. 13. 13 let us walk *h.* as in day
1 Thes. 4. 12 ye may walk *h.* tow.
Heb. 13. 18 willing to live honestly

Honesty. R. V. *gravity.*
1 Tim. 2. 2 in .. godliness and *h.*

Honey. *Honey.*
Gen. 43. 11 *h.*, spices, and myrrh
Ex. 3. 8, 17 land flowing with .. *h.*
Lev. 2. 11 nor *h.* in any offerings

Num. 13. 27 flow. with milk and *h.*
Deut. 8. 8. land of . . olive and *h.*
Josh. 5. 6 land that floweth with . . *h.*
Judg. 14. 8 bees and *h.* in carcase
1 Sam. 14. 25 was *h.* upon ground
2 Sam. 17. 29 *h.*, butter, and sheep
1 K. 14. 3 take . . cruse of *h.*, and
2 K. 18. 32 land of oil olive and *h.*
2. Chr. 31. 5 *h.* and of all the increase
Job 20. 17 brooks of *h.*, and butter
Ps. 19. 10. sweeter than *h.* and *h.*
Prov. 24. 13 My son, eat thou *h.*
S. of S. 4. 11 *h.* and milk . . under
Isa. 7. 15 *h.* shall he eat, that he
Jer. 11. 5 flow. with milk and *h.*
Ezek. 3. 3 in mo. as *h.* for sweetness
Mat. 3. 4 meat was locusts .. wild *h.*
Mark 1. 6 eat locusts and wild *h.*
Rev. 10. 9 thy mouth sweet as *h.*
Honeycomb. *Comb of honey.*
1 Sam. 14. 27 dipped it in an *h. c.*
Ps. 19. 10 sweeter than *h.* and *h. c.*
Prov. 16. 24 pleasant words .. as *h. c.*
S. of S. 4. 11 lips .. drop as the *h. c.*
Luke 24. 42 broiled fish, and *h. c.*
Honour (*n.*). *Consideration, regard, esteem, approbation, veneration, majesty, beauty.*
Gen. 49. 6 their assembly, mine *h.*
Num. 22. 17 promote thee to great *h.*
Deut. 26. 19 in praise, name and *h.*
Judg. 4. 9 shall not be for thine *h.*
1 K. 3. 13 given .. both *h.* and riches
1 Chr. 17. 18 for *h.* of thy servant
2 Chr. 1. 11 not asked .. wealth *h.*
Esth. 1. 4 *h.* of his excel majesty
Ps. 7. 5 and lay mine *h.* in the dust
Prov. 3. 16 and in her left hand .. *h.*
Eccl. 6. 2 God hath given.. *h.*
Dan. 11. 21 not give *h.* of kingdom
Mat. 13. 57 proph. is not without *h.*
Mark 6. 4 prophet .. not without *h.*
John 5. 41 I rec. not *h.* from men
Rom. 2. 7 seek glo., *h.* and immor.
1 Cor. 12. 23 on these we bestow .. *h.*
2 Cor. 6. 8 by *h.* and dishonour, by
Col. 2. 23 not in any *h.* to satis. of fl.
1 Thes. 4. 4 in sanctification and *h.*
1 Tim. 1. 17 be *h.* and glory forever
2 Tim. 2. 20 some to *h.*, some to dis.
Heb. 2. 7 crownedst him with .. *h.*
1 Pet. 1. 7 found unto .. *h.* and glory
2 Pet. 1. 17 receiv. from God .. *h.*
Rev. 4. 9 give glory and *h.* and tha.
R. V. Gen. 49. 6; Ps. 7. 5; 26. 8; 66.
  2; Prov. 14. 28; 25. 2; Dan. 4. 30;
John 5. 41, 44; 8. 54; 2 Cor. 6. 8
glory; Ps. 31. 25 dignity; Dan. 4.
36 majesty; Rev. 19. 1; 21. 24 ——
Honour (*v.*). *Esteem, respect, revere, glorify.*
Ex. 20. 12 *h.* thy father and mother
Dev. 19. 15 nor *h.* person of mighty
Deut. 5. 16 *h.* thy fath. and mother
Judg. 9. 9 by me they *h.* God and m.
1 Sam. 2. 29 and *h.* thy sons above
2 Sam. 10. 3 think. that D. doth *h.*
1 Chr. 19. 3 thinkest that D. doth *h.*
Ps. 15. 4 he *h.* them that fear the L.
Prov. 3. 9 *h.* L. with thy substance
Isa. 29. 13 this people .. do *h.* me
Lam. 1. 8 that *h.* her despise her
Dan. 11. 38 shall he *h.* God of forces
Mal. 1. 6. A son *h.* his father, and a
Mat. 15. 4 *h.* thy father and mother
Mark 7. 6 people *h.* me with lips
Luke 18. 20 *h.* thy father and moth.
John 5. 23 should *h.* Son, even as
Acts 28. 10 who also *h.* us with h.
Eph. 6. 2 *h.* thy father and mother
1 Tim. 5. 3 *h.* widows that are wid.
1 Pet. 2. 17 *h'* all men. Love the br.
R. V. John 8. 54 glorify
Honourable. *Held in honor.*
Gen. 34. 19 more *h.* than all the
Num. 22. 15 sent princes more *h.*
1 Sam. 9. 6 man of G., he is *h.* man
2. Sam. 23. 19 was he not most *h.* of
2 K. 5. 1 Naaman was gr. and *h.*
1 Chr. 4. 9 more *h.* than his breth.
Job 22. 8 the *h.* man dwelt in it
Ps. 45. 9 were among thy *h.* wom.
Isa. 3. 3 *h.* man and counsellor
Nah. 3. 10 cast lots for *h.* men
Mark 15. 43 Joseph .. an *h.* counsel.
Luke 14. 8 lest a more *h.* man than

Acts 13. 50 stirred devout and *h.*
1 Cor. 4. 10 ye are *h.*, but we desp.
Heb. 13. 4 marriage is *h.* in all
Hood. *Head-cover.*
Isa. 3. 23 the fine linen, and *h.*
Hoof. *Hoof.*
Ex. 10. 26 sh. not *h.* be left behind
Lev. 11. 3 what soever parteth *h.*
Deut. 14. 6 beast that parteth *h.*
Ps. 69. 31 ox or bul. that hath . . *h.*
Isa. 9. 28 horses' *h.* shall be count.
Jer. 47. 3 stamping of *h.* of horses
Ezek. 26. 11 with *h.* of his horses
Mic. 4. 13 will make thy *h.* brass
Hook. *Reed, spear.*
Job 41. 2 canst put *v.* into nose of
Peg, catch, hook, ring.
Ex. 26. 32 their *h.* shall be of gold
2 K. 19. 28 I will put *h.* in thy nose
Isa. 37. 29 put my *h.* in thy nose
Ezek. 29. 4 I will put *h.* in thy jaws
Angle, hook for fishing.
Job 41. 1 canst draw lev. with *h.*
Am. 4. 2 will take you away with *h.*
Mat. 17. 27 east *h.*, and take up fish
R. V. Job 41. 1 fishhook; 2 rope
Hope (*n.*). *Confidence, expectation.*
Ruth 1. 12 I have *h.*, if I should
Ez. 10. 2 there is no *h.* in Israel
Job 7. 6 days .. spent without *h.*
Ps. 71. 5 thou art mine *h.*, O Lord
Prov. 13. 12 *h.* def. make. heart sick
  19. 18 Chasten., while there is *h.*
Eccl. 9. 4 for to all living there is *h.*
Isa. 57. 10 saidst .. There is no *h.*
Jer. 31. 17 there is *h.* in thine end
Lam. 3. 18 my *h.* is perished from L.
Ezek. 19. 5 her *h.* was lost, then
Hos. 2. 15 gi. Achor, for door of *h.*
Joel 3. 16 Lord will be *h.* of people
Zech. 9. 12 Turn .. ye prisoners of *h.*
Acts 2. 26 my flesh shall rest in *h.*
Rom. 5. 5 *h.* maketh not ashamed
1 Cor 9. 10 that pl. should pl. in *h.*
  13. 13 abideth faith, *h.*, 2nd charity
2 Cor. 1. 7 our *h.* of you is stedfast
Gal. 5. 5 wait for *h.* of righteousness
Eph. 1. 18 may know what is the *h.*
Phil. 1. 20 my expectation and *h.*
Col. 1. 5 *h.* . . is laid up . . in heaven
1 Thes. 1. 3 patience of *h.* in L. J. C.
2 Thes. 2. 16 good *h.* through grace
1 Tim. 1. 1 L. J. C., which is our *h.*
Tit. 1. 2 in *h* of eternal life which G.
Heb. 6. 11 full assurance of *h.* unto
1 Pet. 1. 3 begot. us unto lively *h.*
1 John 3. 3 ev. man that has this *h.*
R. V. Job 8. 14 confidence; Ps. 16.
  9 safety; Jer. 17. 17 refuge; Lam.
  3. 18 expectation
Hope (*v.*). *Expect, trust.*
Esth. 9. 1 enemies of Jews *h.* to ha.
Job 6. 11 what . . that I should *h.*?
Ps. 31. 24 ye that *h.* in the Lord
  71. 14 I will *h.* continually, and pr.
  119. 81 My soul fainteth, but I *h.*
  130. 7 let Israel *h.* in the Lord
Prov. 14. 32 righteous hath *h.* in
Isa. 38. 18 cannot *h.* for thy truth
Lam. 3. 26 both *h.* and quietly wait
Ezek. 13. 6 have made others to *h.*
Luke 6. 34 whom ye *h.* to receive
Acts 24. 26 he *h.* that money should
Rom. 8. 24 why doth he yet *h.* for?
1 Cor. 13. 7 *h.* all things, endureth
2 Cor. 8. 5 not as we *h.*, but first
Phil. 2. 23 him therefore I *h.* to send
Heb. 11. 1 faith is sub. of things *h.*
1 Pet. 1. 13 *h.* to and for grace that
R. V. Jer. 3. 23 looked
Horn. *Horn.*
Gen. 22. 13 ram caught .. by his *h.*
Ex. 29. 12 put it on *h.* of the altar
Lev. 4. 7 put bl. upon *h.* of the altar
Deut. 33. 17 *h.* like *h.* of unicorn
Josh. 6. 5 a long blast with ram's *h.*
1 Sam. 2. 1 *h.* is exalted in Lord
2 Sam. 22. 3 the *h.* of my salvation
1 K. 1. 39 Zadok .. took *h.* of oil out
1 Chr. 25. 5 were sons to lift up *h.*
2 Chr. 18. 10 Zed . . made *h.* of iron
Job. 16. 15 I have .. defiled my *h.*
Ps. 18. 2 *h.* of my salvation, and
  75. 5 Lift not up your *h.* on high
Jer. 7. 1 graven .. upon *h.* of fath.
Lam. 2. 3 cut off .. all *h.* of Israel

Ezek. 27. 15 *h.* of ivory and ebony
Dan. 8. 3 a ram which had two *h.*
Am. 3. 14 *h.* of altar shall be cut
Mic. 4. 13 will make thine *h.* iron
Hab. 3. 4 *h.* coming out of hand
Zech. 1. 18 lifted eyes .. behold .. *h.*
Luke 1. 69 raised *h.* of salvation for
Rev. 5. 6 lamb .. having seven *h.*
  9. 13; 12. 3; 13. 1; 17. 3, 7, 12
Ink horn or vessel.
Ezek. 9. 2 with a writer's ink *h.*
R. V. Ex. 21. 29 ——; Hab. 3. 4
rays
Hornet. *Hornet, wasp.*
Ex. 23. 28 will send *h.* before thee
Deut. 7. 20 Lord .. will send thee *h.*
Josh. 24. 12 I sent *h.* before you
Horrible. *Desolating, vile.*
Ps. 11. 6 rain fire . . and *h.* tempest
Jer. 23. 14 have seen . . an *h.* thing
Hos. 6. 10 seen *h.* thing in Israel
R. V. Ps. 11. 6 burning
Horribly. *Frightfully.*
Jer. 2. 12 be *h.* afraid, be ye desola.
Ezek. 32. 10 kings shall be *h.* afraid
Horror. *Terror, fright.*
Gen. 15. 12 an *h.* of great darkness
Ps. 55. 5 *h.* hath overwhelmed me
Ezek. 7. 18 and *h.* shall cover them
R. V. Ps. 119. 53 hot indignation
Horse. *Horse.*
Gen. 47. 17 bread in exchange for *h.*
  49. 18 adder . . biteth *h.* heels
Ex. 14. 9 all *h.* and char. of Ph.
Deut. 17. 16 shall not multiply *h.*
2 Sam. 15. 1 Ab. prep. *h.* and char
1 K. 4. 28 barley and straw for *h.*
2 K. 2. 11 chariot, and *h.* of fire
2 Chr. 1. 16 *h.* brought of Egypt
Ez. 2. 66 *h.* were seven hun. thirty
Neh. 3. 28 above *h.* gate repaired
Esth. 6. 11 took H. the appar. and *h.*
Job 39. 18 scorneth the *h.* and rider
  39. 19 hast thou given *h.* strength
Ps. 20. 7 some trust in ch., some in *h.*
  32. 9 be not as *h.* nor as mule
Prov. 26. 3 whip for *h.*, bri. for ass
Eccl. 10. 7 I have seen ser. on *h.*
S. of S. 1. 9 comp. of *h.* in . . chariots
Isa. 2. 7 their land is also full of *h.*
Jer. 4. 13 his *h.* are swifter than ea.
  8. 6 as the *h.* rusheth into battle
Ezek. 17. 15 might give *h.* and peo.
Hos. 1. 7 will not save by *h.*, nor
Joel 2. 4 appearance of th. is as of *h.*
Am. 6. 12 shall *h.* run on the rock.
Mic. 5. 10 I will cut off thy *h.* out
Nah. 3. 2 noise . . of prancing *h.*
Hab. 1. 8 *h.* are swifter than leop.
Hag. 2. 22 *h.* and r. shall come down
Zech. 1. 8 behold man riding red *h.*
Jas. 3. 3 we put bits in *h's* mouths
Rev. 6. 2 and behold a white *h.*, and
  6. 4, 5, 8; 9. 7; 14. 20; 18. 13
Horseback. *Riding on horse.*
2 K. 9. 18 there went one on *h.*
Esth. 6. 9 bring him on *h.* through
  8. 10 sent letters by post on *h.*
R. V. Esth. 6. 11 to ride
Horse-hoof. *Horse's heel.*
Judg. 5. 22 then were *h. h.* broken
Horseleach. *Leech.*
Prov. 30. 15 *h. l.* hath two daugh.
Horseman. *Rider, driver, cavalryman.*
Gen. 50. 9 went up .. chariots and *h.*
Ex. 14. 9 *h.* and ar. overtook them
Josh. 24. 6 Egyptians pur. .. with *h.*
1 Sam. 8. 11 take sons .. to be his *h.*
2 Sam. 1. 6 char. and *h.* fol. after
1 K. 4. 26 Sol. had twelve thous. *h.*
2 K. 2. 12 chariot of Is., and the *h.*
1 Chr. 18. 4 D. took .. sev. thous. *h.*
2 Chr. 1. 4 Sol. gath. char. and *h.*
Ez. 8. 22 *h.* to keep against enemy
Neh. 2. 9 sent captains of a. and *h.*
Isa. 21. 7 he saw a chariot with *h.*
Jer. 4. 29 noise of *h.* and bowmen
Ezek. 23. 6 captains and *h.* riding
Dan. 11. 40 with *h.* and many ships
Hos. 1. 7 not save by bow . . nor *h.*
Joel 2. 4 as *h.*, so they shall run
Nah. 3. 3 *h.* lifteth up . . sword and
Hab. 1. 8 their *h.* shall spread them.
Acts 23. 23 *h.* threescore and ten
Rev. 9. 16 num. of army of the *h.*

R. V. Ezek. 27. 14 war-horses
Hosanna. *Save, we pray thee.*
Mat. 21. 9, 15 saying, *H.* to s. of D.
Mark 11. 9 *H.*! Blessed is he that
John 12. 13 *H.*: Blessed is K. of Is.
Hosen. *Upper garment.*
Dan. 3. 21 bound in coats, *h.*, and
Hospitality. *Love of stranger.*
Rom. 12. 13 distribut. . given to *h.*
1 Tim. 3. 2 good behav., given to *h.*
Tit. 1. 8 lover of *h.*, lov. of g. men
1 Pet. 4. 9 use *h.* one to another
Host. *Camp, encampment.*
Gen. 3. 2 this is God's *h.*; and
Ex. 14. 24 looked unto *h.* . . troub.
Deut. 2. 14 wasted from among *h.*
Josh. 1. 11 pass through *h.* and
Judg. 4. 15 L. discomf. Sis . . . and *h.*
1 Sam. 11. 11 came into midst of *h.*
2 Sam. 5. 24 go . . smite *h.* of Phil.
1 K. 22. 34 carry me out of *h.*, for
2 K. 3. 9 th. was no water for the *h.*
1 Chr. 9. 19 fathers, over *h.* of the L.
2 Chr. 14. 13 destroyed bef. L . . *h.*
Ps. 27. 3 though *h.* should encamp
Ezek. 1. 24 voice . . as a noise of *h.*
Entertainer, innkeeper.
Luke 10. 35 pence, and ga. them *h.*
Rom 16. 23 Gaius mine *h.*, and of
Multitude, army, warfare, service.
Gen. 2. 1 finished, and all *h.* of the
Ex. 12. 41 *h.* of L. went out from
Num. 1. 52 ev. man . . throughout *h.*
Deut. 4. 19 stars, all *h.* of heaven
Judg. 4. 2 cap. of whose *h.* was Sis.
1 Sam. 1. 3 sac. unto Lord of *h.*
2 Sam. 2. 8 Ner, capt. of Saul's *h.*
1 K. 1. 19 Joab the capt. of the *h.*
2 K. 3. 14 As the L. of *h.* liveth
1 Chr. 11. 9 L. of *h.* was with him
2 Ch. 18. 18 *h.* of heav. stand. on
Neh. 9. 6 heav. of heav., with . . *h.*
Ps. 24. 10 L. of *h.*, is k. of glory
84. 1 amiable thy tab., L. of *h.*
Isa. 1. 9 ex. L. of *h.* hath left us
6. 3 holy, holy is the Lord of *h.*
Jer. 3. 19 heritage of *h.* of nations
10. 16 The Lord of *h.* is his name
Dan. 8. 10 waxed gr., ev. to *h.* of
Hos. 12. 5 even Lord God of *h.*
Am. 5. 4 God of *h.* be with you
Mic. 4. 4 mouth of L. of *h.* . . spok.
Nah. 2. 13 against thee, saith L. of *h.*
Hab. 2. 13 not of the Lord of *h.*
Zeph. 1. 5 that worship *h.* of heav.
Hag. 1. 2 thus speaketh L. of *h.*
Zech. 1. 3 Turn to me, saith L. of *h.*
Mal. 1. 6 saith L. of *h.* to priests
Luke 2. 13 mul. of heav. *h.* singing
Acts 7. 42 to worship *h.* of heaven
Strength, wealth, army, force.
Ex. 14. 4 honour. . . upon his *h.*
Num. 31. 14 wroth with officers of *h.*
1 Sam. 14. 48 gath. *h.*, and smote
2 Sam. 8. 9 smitten *h.* of Hadad.
1 K. 15. 20 captains of *h.* which
2 K. 6. 14 sent thither . . a gr. *h.*
1 Chr. 18. 9 D. had smitten all *h.*
2 Chr. 14. 9 *h.* of thous. thous.
Ps. 33. 16 no k. saved by mul. of *h.*
Obad. 20 captivity of this *h.* of ch.
R. V. 16. 13; Deut. 2. 14, 15; Josh.
.1. 11; 3. 2; 18. 9; Judg. 7. 8, 10,
13, 15; 1 Sam. 11. 11; 14. 15, 19;
1 Chr. 9. 19 camp; 2 K. 18. 17;
25. 1; 2 Chr. 14. 9; 24. 23; 26. 11
army
Hostage. *Surety, pledge.*
2 K. 14. 14 took . . *h.*, and returned
2 Chr. 25. 24 *h.*, and ret. to Samar.
Hot. *Heated, burning, fervent,
vehement, fierce.*
Ex. 16. 21 when the sun waxed *h.*
22. 24 my wrath shall wax *h.*
Lev. 13. 24 in skin . . a *h.* burning
Deut. 19. 6 slayer, while heart is *h.*
Josh. 9. 12 our bread we took *h.* for
Judg. 2. 14 ang. of L. was *h.* ag'nst
1 Sam. 11. 9 to morrow . . , sun be *h.*
Neh. 7. 3 opened until sun be *h.*
Job 6. 17 *h.*, they are consumed
Ps. 6. 1 nei. chast. in *h.* displeas.
Ezek. 24. 11 brass . . may be *h.*, and
Dan. 3. 22 furnace excee ding *h.*
Hos. 7. 7 They are all *h.* as an oven
1 Tim. 4. 2 consc seared wi. *h.* iron

Rev. 3. 15 art neither cold nor *h.*
R. V. Judg. 2. 14; 3. 8; 6. 39; 10.
7 kindled.
Hotly. *Fiercely.*
Gen. 31. 36 thou hast so *h.* pursued
Hottest. *Fiercest.*
2 Sam. 11. 15 forefront of *h.* battle
Hough. *Hock, hamstring.*
Josh. 11. 6 shalt *h.* their horses, and
2 Sam. 8. 4 D. *h.* all the ch. horses
1 Chr. 18. 4 D. also *h.* char. horses
Hour. *Hour, time.*
Dan. 3. 6 same *h.* be cast into furn.
Mat. 8. 13 was healed in . . same *h.*
9. 22; 10. 19; 15. 28; 17. 18; 20. 3
27. 46 ninth *h.*, Jesus cried, Eli, Eli,
Mark 13. 32 that *h.* knoweth no m.
15. 25 third *h.*, they crucified him
Luke 7. 21 same *h.* he cured many
John 2. 4 woman *h.* . mine . is not
12. 23 *h.* is come, that Son of man
Acts 2. 15 it is but third *h.* of day
1 Cor. 4. 11 even unto present *h.*
Gal. 2. 5 gave place . . not for *h.*
Rev. 3. 3 not know what *h.* I come
R. V. Mat. 24. 42 on what day; 1
Cor. 8. 7 until now.
House. *House, household, family.*
Gen. 7. 1 come thou, and all thy *h.*
Ex. 2. 1 went a man of *h.* of Levi
Lev. 10. 6 whole *h.* of Israel bewail
Num. 1. 2 by *h.* of their fathers
Deut. 5. 6 land . . from *h.* of bond.
Josh. 2. 1 they came unto harlot's *h.*
Judg. 1. 22 *h.* of Joseph went up ag.
Ruth 1. 8 ret. each to mother's *h.*
1 Sam. 1. 7 went up to *h.* of Lord
2 Sam. 2. 4 D. k. over *h.* of Judah
1 K. 1. 53 Sol. said, Go to thine *h.*
2 K. 4. 2 what hast thou in the *h.*?
1 Chr. 4. 38 *h.* of fathers increased
2 Chr. 2. 1 build *h.* for . . the Lord
Ez. 1. 2 charged . . to build him *h.*
Neh. 1. 6 I and . . *h.* have sinned
Esth. 1. 8 appointed . . officers of *h.*
Job 1. 4 and sons feasted in their *h.*
17. 13 I wait, the grave is mine *h.*
Ps. 23. 6 dwell in *h.* of Lord forev.
69. 9 zeal of . . *h.* . . eaten me up
Prov. 1. 13 fill our *h.* with spoil
Eccl. 7. 2 *h.* of mourn. th. *h.* of feast
S. of S. 1. 17 beams of *h.* are cedar
Isa. 2. 5 O *h.* of Jacob, come ye
Jer. 2. 26 *h.* of Israel is ashamed
Lam. 2. 7 make noise in *h.* of L.
Ezek. 2. 5 th. are rebellious *h.* yet
Dan. 1. 2 part of vessels of *h.* of God
Hos. 1. 4 blood of Jez. on *h.* of J.
Joel 1. 9 cut off from *h.* of Lord
Am. 1. 4 send fire to *h.* of Hazael
Obad. 18 *h.* of Jacob shall be fire
Mic. 2. 9 wom. cast from pleasant *h.*
Nah. 1. 14 out of *h.* of thy gods
Hab. 2. 9 coveteth evil . . to his *h.*
Zeph. 1. 13 their *h.* a desolation
Hag. 1. 4 dwell in your cieled *h.*
Zech. 3. 7 then thou . . judge my *h.*
Mal. 3. 10 may be meat in mine *h.*
Mat. 2. 11 were come into the *h.*
7. 24 a wise man which built *h.*
8. 14 Jesus came to Peter's *h.*
23. 14 for ye devour widows' *h.*
Mark 3. 25 if *h.* be divided against
Luke 4. 38 arose and ent. Simon's *h.*
10. 7 Go not from *h.* to *h.*
John 4. 53 believed, and his whole *h.*
14. 2 in Father's *h.* are many man.
Acts 4. 34 posses. . of *h.* sold them
Rom. 16. 5 church that is their *h.*
1 Cor. 11. 22 have ye not *h.* to eat
2 Cor. 5. 1 earthly *h.* of this taber.
1 Tim. 3. 4 ruleth well his own *h.*
2 Tim. 2. 20 gr. *h.* there are vessels
Tit. 1. 11 who subvert whole *h.*
Phile. 2 and to the church in thy *h.*
Heb. 3. 2 Moses faithful in his *h.*
1 Pet. 2. 5; 2 John 10
R. V. Mat. 7. 25; 2 K. 7. 11; 10. 5,
12; 15. 5; Isa. 36. 3; 1 Cor. 1. 11;
1 Tim. 5. 14 household · 2 Cor. 5.
2 habitation
Household. *House, family.*
Gen. 35. 2 Then Jacob said to his *h.*
Ex. 1. 1 every man and his *h.* came
Lev. 16. 17 atonement . . for his *h.*
Num. 18. 31 eat it .. ye and vour *h.*

Deut. 6. 22 and upon all his *h.*, bef,
Josh. 7. 14 family shall come by *h.*
Judg. 6. 27 feared his father's *h.*
1 Sam. 25. 7 and against all his *h.*
2 Sam. 2. 3 bring ev. man with *h.*
1 K. 4. 6 victuals for king and *h.*
2 K. 7. 9 go and tell the king's *h.*
1 Chr. 24. 6 one . . *h.* being taken for
Neh. 13. 8 cast forth all the *h.* stuff
Job 1. 3 a very great *h.*; so that
Prov. 27. 27 milk for food of thy *h.*
Isa. 36. 22 Elia. that was over the *h.*
Mat. 24. 45 made ruler over his *h.*
Luke 12. 42 make ruler over his *h.*
Acts 16. 15 was baptized, and her *h.*
1 Cor. 1. 16 baptized . . *h.* of Steph.
Gal. 6. 10 especially to them of *h.*
Eph. 2. 19 citizens . . of *h.* of God
Phil. 4. 22 chief. they of Cæsar's *h.*
2 Tim. 4. 19 salute P. and A. and *h.*
R. V. Deut. 6. 22; 1 Sam. 25. 17;
2 Sam. 6. 11; 17. 23; 1 K. 11. 20;
2 Tim. 4. 19 house
Householder. *House-ruler.*
Mat. 13. 27 ser. of the *h.* camels
13. 52 like unto a man . . an *h.*
20. 1; 21. 33
Housetop. *Roof, top.*
2 K. 19. 26 as grass on the *h. t.*, and
Ps. 102. 7 as sparrow on the *h. t.*
Prov. 21. 9 dwell in a corner of *h. t.*
Isa. 22. 1 thou art gone up to *h. t.*
Jer. 48. 38 lamenta. . . on all *h. t.*
Zeph. 1. 5 worship host . . upon *h. t.*
Mat. 10. 27 preach ye upon the *h. t.*
Mark 13. 15 that is on *h. t.* not go
Luke 5. 19 went on *h. t.*, and let
Acts 10. 9 P. went on *h. t.* to pray
How. *In what way.*
Gen. 44. 34 *h.* shall I go up to my
Esth. 8. 6 *h.* can I endure to see
Mat. 6. 28 lilies, *h.* they grow; they
Mark 3. 23 g. can Satan cast out
Wherefore, why.
Mat. 18. 12 *h.* think ye? If man
Mark 2. 16 *h.* is it that he eateth
Luke 2. 4 *h.* is it ye sought me?
John 14. 22 *h.* is it thou wilt manif.
1 Cor. 7. 16 *h.* knowest thou, O m.
Eph. 6. 21 know my affairs, and *h.*
That.
Luke 1. 58 heard *h.* the Lord had
John 4. 1 Lord knew *h.* Phar. had
Acts 14. 27 he had open. door
Gal. 4. 13 *h.* through infirmity of fl.
Phile. 19 not say *h.* thou owest me
Jas. 2. 22 seest *h.* faith wrought
Rev. 2. 2 and *h.* thou canst not bear
Till when.
Mat. 17. 17 *h.* long shall I be with
Mark 9. 19; Luke 9. 41; John 10.
24; Rev. 6. 10
How great.
Mark 5. 19 tell them *h.* gr. things
Luke 8. 39; Acts 9. 16; Gal. 6. 11;
Heb. 7. 4
How many.
1 K. 22. 16 *h.* many times shall I.
2 Chr. 18. 15; Mat. 15. 34; Mark
6. 38; Luke 15. 17; Acts 21. 20.
How much.
Mat. 7. 11 *h.*much more shall yo. F
Luke 11. 13; Acts 9. 13; Rom. 11.
12; Phile. 16. Heb. 9. 14
How oft.
Ps. 78. 40 *h.* oft did they provoke
Mat. 18. 21 *h.* oft shall brother sin
Luke 13. 34 *h.* oft would I . . gath.
How that.
Mat. 12. 5 *h.* that on Sabbath days
Luke 7. 22; Acts 7. 25; Rom. 7. 1;
1 Cor. 1. 26; 2 Cor. 8. 2; Gal. 1.
13; Eph. 3. 3; Heb. 12. 17; Jas.
2. 24; Jude 5.
Howbeit. *But, although, be it as
it may.*
Judg. 18. 29 *h.* name of city was
1 Sam. 8. 9 *h.* yet protest solemnly
2 Sam. 12. 14 *h.*, bec. by this deed
1 K. 11. 13 *h.* I will not rend away
2 Chr. 32. 31 *h.* in bus. of ambassa.
John 6. 23 *h.* there came oth. boats
Acts 7. 48 *h.* most High dwelleth
1 Cor. 8. 7 *h.* . . . not in ev. man that
R, V. Mark 7. 7; Acts 4. 4; 14. 20;
17. 34; 28. 6; 1 Cor. 14. 2 but

Howl.   *Howl, wail.*
Isa. 13. 6 *H*. . . day of Lord is near
Jer. 25. 34 *H*., ye shepherds, cry
Ezek. 21. 12 cry and *h*., son of man
Hos. 7. 14 wh. th. *h*. upon their beds
Joel 1. 5 *h*., all ye drinkers of wine
Mic. 1. 8 I will wail and *h*.,I will go
Zech. 11. 2. *H*., fir tree, cedar has f.

Howling.   *Howling, wailing.*
Deut. 32. 10 found him . . in *h*. wild
Isa. 15. 8 the *h*. thereof unto Eglaim
Jer. 25. 36 an *h*. of principal of flock
Zeph. 1. 10 an *h*. from the second
Zech. 11. 3 voice of *h*. of shepherds
Am. 8. 3 songs of temple . . be *h*.

Howsoever.   *Come what may.*
Judg. 19. 20 *h*., let all my wants lie
2 Sam. 18. 22 *h*., let me, I pray thee
Zeph. 3. 7 *h*. I punished them
R. V. 2 Sam 18. 22, 23 come what
   may ; Zeph. 3. 7 according to all
   that

Huge.   *Great, abundant.*
2 Chr. 16. 8 were not Ethiop. . . *h*.

Humble (*a*.).   *Meek, afflicted,*
   lowly.
Job 22. 29 he shall save the *h*. pers.
Ps. 9. 12 he forget. not cry of *h*.
Prov. 16. 19 better . . *h*. spirit with
Isa. 57. 15 *h*. spirit, to revive the
Jas. 4. 6 G . . giveth grace to *h*.
1 Pet. 5. 6 G . . giveth gr. to *h*.
R. V. Ps. 9. 12 ; 10. 12 poor ; Ps.
   10. 17 ; 34. 2 ; 69. 32 ; Prov. 16.
   19 ; 29. 23 lowly.

Humble (*v*.).   *Afflict, make meek*
   or lowly, humiliate.
Ex. 10. 3 how long . . refuse to *h*.
Lev. 26. 41 if . . uncir. hearts be *h*.
Deut. 8. 2 to *h*. thee . .to prove thee
Judg. 19. 24 *h*. ye them, and do
1 K. 21. 29 how Ahab *h*. himself
2 K. 22. 19 hast *h*. thyself before L.
2 Chr. 7. 14 if peo . . shall *h*. them.
Ps. 35. 13 *h*. my soul with fasting
Prov. 6. 3 *h*. thyself, . .make friend
Isa. 2. 9 the great man *h*. himself
Jer. 13. 18 *h*. yourselves, sit down
Lam. 3. 20 soul . . is *h*. in me
Ezek. 22. 10 have they *h*. her that
Dan. 5. 22 hast not *h*. thine heart
Mat. 18. 4 whoso shall *h*. himself
Luke 14. 11 that *h*. him. . . be ex.
2 Cor. 12. 21 G. will *h*. me among
Phil. 2. 8 he *h*. himself, and became
Jas. 4. 10 *h*. yours. in sight of L.
1 Pet. 5. 6 *h*. yours. therefore under
R. V. Ps. 35. 13 afflicted ; Isa. 2.
   11 ; 10. 33 brought low ; Lam. 3.
   20 brought down

Humbleness.   R. V. *humility.*
Col. 3. 12 Put on . . *h*. of mind

Humbly.   *Meekly, lowly.*
2 Sam. 16. 4 I *h*. beseech thee that
Mic. 6. 8 to love mercy, to walk *h*.
R. V. 2 Sam. 16. 4 do.

Humiliation.   *Lowliness.*
Acts 8. 33 in his *h*. his judg. was

Humility.   *Lowliness, meekness.*
Prov. 15. 33 and before honour is *h*.
Acts 20. 19 serving L. with all *h*.
Col. 2. 18 in vol. *h*. and worship.
1 Pet. 5. 5 all . . be clothed with *h*.
R. V. Acts 20. 19 lowliness

Hundred.   *Hundred.*
Gen. 5. 3 A. lived *h*. thirty years
Ex. 18. 21 rulers of *h*., and . . fifties
Lev. 26. 8 five . . shall chase an *h*.
Deut. 1. 15 captains over *h*. and
Josh. 24. 29 Josh. died . . *h*. and t.
Judg. 3. 31 slew of Philis. six *h*.
1 Sam. 11. 8 c. of Is. were thr. *h*. t.
2 Sam. 2. 31 thr. *h*. threesc. m. died
1 K. 4. 23 *h*. sheep, besides harts
2 K. 3. 4 *h*. thousand lambs, and
1 Chr. 4. 42 five *h*. m. went to S.
2 Chr. 1. 2 captains of thous. and *h*.
Ez. 1. 10 of second sort four *h*. and
Neh. 5. 17 my table *h*. and fifty
Esth. 1. 1 *h*. twenty sev. provinces
Job 1. 3 five *h*. yoke of oxen, and
Prov. 17. 10 *h*. stripes into a fool
Eccl. 6. 3 if man beget *h*. children
S. of S. 8. 12 keep fruit thereof t. *h*.
Isa. 65. 20 child shall die *h*. y'rs old
Jer. 52. 23 pomegran. . .an *h*. round

Ezek. 40. 19 *h*. cubits east. and n.
Dan. 8. 14 two thous. three *h*. days
Am. 5. 3 thous. shall leave an *h*.
Mat. 18. 12 if man have *h*. sheep
Mark 4. 8 some sixty, some *h*. fold
Luke 16. 6 an *h*. meas. of oil
John 19. 39 aloes, an *h*. pound wei.
Acts 1. 15 about an *h*. and twenty
Rom. 4. 19 about an *h*. years old
1 Cor. 15. 6 seen of . . five *h*. breth.
Gal. 3. 17 law, was from *h*. thirty
Rev. 7. 4 *h*. forty and four thous.

Hundred-fold.   *Hundred times.*
Gen. 26. 12 in same year an *h*. f.
2 Sam. 24. 3 how many th. be, an *h*.f.
Mat. 13. 8 23 some *h*.f. some s. . f.
Mark 10. 30 shall receive an *h*. f.
Luke 8.8 sp. up and bare fruit an *h*.f.

Hundredth.   *Hundredth.*
Gen. 7. 11 six *h*. year of Noah's life
Neh. 5. 11 the *h*. part of the money

Hundreds.   *Hundred each.*
Mark 6. 40 sat down in ranks by *h*.

Hunger (*n*.),   *Craving, famine.*
Ex. 16. 3 kill this assembly with *h*.
Deut. 28. 48 in *h*. and in thirst
Neh. 9. 15 bread from heav. fr. th. *h*.
Ps. 34. 10 young lions . . suffer *h*.
Prov. 19. 15 idle soul shall suffer *h*.
Jer. 38. 9 Jer. . . is like to die for *h*.
Lam. 2. 19 children, that faint for *h*.
Ezek. 34. 29 no more con. with *h*.
Luke 15. 17 and I perish with *h*.
2 Cor. 11. 27 *h*. and thirst, in fastings
Rev. 6. 8 kill with sword, and *h*.
R. V. Jer. 38. 9 : Ezek. 34. 29 ; Rev.
   6. 8 famine

Hunger (*v*.).   *Crave, long for, fam-*
   ish.
Deut. 8. 3 suffered thee to *h*., and
Isa. 49. 10 shall not *h*. nor thirst
Mat. 5. 6 blessed are they which *h*.
Luke 4. 2 ended, he afterwards *h*.
John 6. 35 com. to me, shall nev. *h*.
Rom. 12. 20 if thine en. *h*., feed him
1 Cor. 4. 11 we both *h*. and thirst
Rev. 7. 16 They shall *h*. no more

Hunger-bitten.   *Famished.*
Job 18. 12 his strength . . be *h*. b.

Hungered.   *To hunger.*
Mat. 4. 2 he was afterward an *h*.
   12. 1 and his disciples were an *h*.
   25. 35 I was *h*., ye gave me meat
Mark 2. 25 need, he was an *h*., he and
Luke 6. 3 when himself was an *h*.

Hungry.   *Craving, famished.*
1 Sam. 2. 5 and that were *h*. ceased
2 Sam. 17. 29 people is *h*. and weary
2 K. 7. 12 They know that we be *h*.
Job 5. 5 Whose harvest *h*. eateth up
Ps. 107. 5 *h*. and . . their soul fainted
Prov. 25. 21 if . . en. be *h*., give br.
Isa. 8. 21 passed through it . . *h*.
Ezek. 18. 7 given his bread to the *h*.
Mark 11. 2 come from B., he was *h*.
Luke 1. 53 filled *h*. with g. things
Acts 10. 10 became very *h*., and
1 Cor. 11. 21 one is *h*., anoth. dru.
Phil. 4. 12 both to be full and be *h*.

Hunt.   *Lie in wait, pursue.*
Gen. 27. 5 Esau went . . to *h*. venison
Lev. 17. 13 *h*. . . any beast or fowl
1 Sam. 26. 20 one doth *h*. partridge
Job 10. 16 Thou *h*. me as fierce lion
Ps. 140. 11 evil shall *h*. violent man
Prov. 6. 26 adulteress will *h*. for
Jer. 16. 16 shall *h*. them from mt.
Lam. 4. 18 *h*. our steps, that we
Ezek. 13. 21 be no more . . in *h*.
Mic. 7. 2 *h*. every man his brother

Hunter.   *Who hunts.*
Gen. 10. 9 mighty *h*. before Lord
   25. 27 and Esau was a cunning *h*.
Jer. 16 16 will I send for many *h*.

Hunting.   *Lying in wait, pur-*
   suing.
Gen. 27. 30 Esau . . came in from *h*.
Prov. 12. 27 roast. not he took in *h*.

Hurl.   *Cast, sling.*
Num. 35. 20 *h*. at him by laying
1 Chr. 12. 2 in *h*. stones and shoot.
Job 27. 21 a4 as a storm *h*. him out
R. V. 1 Chr. 12. 2 slinging ; Job
   27. 21 sweepeth

Hurt (*n*.).   *Evil.*
Gen. 26. 29 thou wilt do us no *h*.

Josh. 24. 20 will turn and do you *h*.
1 Sam. 24. 9 David seeketh thy *h*.
2 Sam. 18. 32 rise . . to do thee *h*.
2 Chr. 25. 19 why . . meddle to thy *h*.
Esth. 9. 2 such as sought their *h*.
Ps. 35. 4 bro. to .. that devise my *h*.
Eccl. 5. 18 the owners . . to their *h*.
Jer. 7. 6 neither walk .. to your *h*.

Injury, damage, loss.
Gen. 4. 23 I ha. slain a man to my *h*.
1 Sam. 20. 21 peace to thee, and no *h*.
Ez. 4. 22 damage gr. to the *h*.of k. ?
Ps. 15. 4 sweareth to his own *h*.
Jer. 6. 14 they have healed the *h*.
Dan. 6. 23 no man of *h*. was found
Acts 27. 10 voyage will be with *h*.
R. V. Josh. 24. 20 evil ; Acts 27. 10
   injury

Hurt.   *Injure, harm.*
Gen. 31. 7 God suffer. him not to *h*.
Ex. 22. 10 if it die or be *h*., or driv.
Num. 16. 15 neither have I *h*. one
1 Sam. 25. 15 we are not *h*., neither
Ps. 105. 18 feet they *h*. with fetters
Eccl. 10. 9 who. remov. stones .. be *h*.
Isa. 11. 9 shall not *h*. nor destroy
Jer. 25. 6 and I will do you no *h*.
Dan. 6. 22 they have not *h*., me
Mark 16. 18 it shall not *h*. them
Luke 4. 35 out, and *h*. him not
Acts 18. 10 no man set on thee to *h*.
Rev. 6. 6 see thou *h*. not the oil
R. V. Acts 18. 10 harm

Hurtful.   *Evil, injurious.*
Ez. 4. 15 *h*. unto kings and prov.
Ps. 144. 10 del. .. ser. from *h*. sword
1 Tim. 6. 9 foolish and *h*. lusts

Husband.   *A man.*
Gen. 3. 6 and gave also unto her *h*.
   30. 20 now will my *h*. dwell with
Lev. 19. 20 maid, betrothed to *h*.
Num. 5. 13 hid from eyes of *h*.
Deut. 22. 23 if damsel . be betr. to *h*.
Judg. 13. 6 woman . . told her *h*.
Ruth 1. 3 Naomi's *h*. died, and
1 Sam. 1. 23 Elkanah her *h*. said
2 Sam. 3. 16 her *h*. went with her
2 K. 4. 1 thy servant my *h*. is dead
Jer. 6. 11 *h*. wi. wife shall be taken
Ezek. 16. 45 loath. her *h*. and chil.
Hos. 2. 2 wife, neither am I her *h*.
Mat. 1. 16 Joseph the *h*. of Mary
Mark 10. 12 if woman put away *h*.
Luke 2. 36 had liv. with *h*. sev. yr's.
John 4. 16 saith .. , Go, call thy *h*.
Acts 5. 10 and buried her by her *h*.
Rom. 7. 2 bound by law to her *h*.
1 Cor. 7. 2 ev. wom. have .. own *h*.
2 Cor. 11. 2 espouse you to one *h*.
Gal. 4. 27 than she which hath *h*.
Eph. 5. 23 submit your. unto your *h*.
   5. 23 For the *h*. is head of the wife
Col. 3. 19 *h*., love your wives, and
Tit. 2. 5 obedient to their own *h*.
1 Pet. 3. 1 in subjection to your *h*.
Rev. 21. 2 as bride adorned for *h*.

Lord, master, owner.
Ex. 21. 22 as the woman's *h*. will
Deut. 24. 4 her former *h*. which.
2 Sam. 11. 26 mourned for her *h*.
Esth. 1. 17 they shall despise their *h*.
Prov. 12. 4 vir. woman is crown to *h*.
Isa. 54. 5 For thy Maker is thine *h*,
Jer. 31. 32 although I was *h*. unto
Joel 1. 8 lament like virgin . . for *h*.

Son-in-law, bridegroom.
Ex. 4. 25 Surely a bloody *h*. art thou

Friend.
Jer. 3. 20 my *h*. . . depart. from her *h*.
R. V. 1 Cor. 7. 14 brother

Husbandman.   *Cultivator.*
Gen. 9. 20 Noah began to be an *h*.
2 K. 25. 12 to be vinedressers and *h*.
2 Chr. 26. 10 *h*. . . and vinedressers
Jer. 31. 24 shall dwell in Judah . .*h*.
Joel 1. 11 Be ye ashamed, O, ye *h*.
Am. 5. 16 shall call *h*. to mourning
Zech. 13. 5 am no prophet, I am *h*.
Mat. 21. 33 vine. and let it out to *h*.
Mark 12. 7 those *h*. said among them.
Luke 20. 10 but the *h*. beat him and
John 15. 1 and my Father is the *h*.
2 Tim. 2. 6 The *h*. that laboureth
Jas. 5. 7 *h*. waiteth for prec. fruits

Husbandry.   *Soil cultivation.*
2 Chr. 26. 10 built tow. . . he loved *h*.

1 Cor. 3. 9 for .. ye are God's *h.*
Husk. *Rind, hull, pod.*
Num. 6. 4 from kernel even to *h.*
2 K. 4. 42 full ears of corn in the *h.*
Luke 15. 16 with *h.* that swine did e.
Hymn. *Song of praise.*
Mat. 26. 30 when they had sung *h.*
Mark 14. 26 sung *h.*, they went out
Eph. 5. 19 in psalms and *h.* and sp.
Col. 3. 16 *h.*and spiritual songs, sing.
Hypocrisy. *Dissimulation.*
Isa. 32. 6 to vile per. practice *h.*, and
Mat. 23. 28 within ye are full of *h.*
Mark. 12. 15 he, know. their *h.*, said,
Luke 12. 1 leav. of Phar., which is *h.*
1 Tim. 4. 2 Speaking lies in *h.* ; hav.
Jas. 3. 17 without partiality and *h.*
1 Pet. 2. 1 *h.*, and envies, and all
R. V. Isa. 32. 6 profaneness
Hypocrite. *Who profanes.*
Job 8. 13 the *h's* hope shall perish
Prov. 11. 9 *h.* with mouth destroy.
Isa. 9. 17 is a *h.* and an evil doer
Who simulates, actor.
Mat. 6. 2 as *h.* do in the synagogues
6. 5 thou shalt not be as the *h.* are
7. 5 Thou *h.*, first cast the beam out
23. 14 woe unto you, Phar. and *h.*
Mark 7. 6 well hath E. proph. to *h.*
Luke 12. 56 *h.*, ye can discern face
R. V. Job 8. 13 ; 13. 16; 17. 8;
20. 5; 27. 8; 34. 30; 36. 13; Prov.
11. 9; Isa. 33. 14 godless; Isa.
9. 17 profane ; Mat. 16. 3 ; 23. 14;
Luke 11. 44—
Hypocritical. R. V. *profane.*
Ps. 35. 16 with *h.* mockers in feasts
Isa. 10. 6 send him against *h.* nat.
Hyssop. *Marjoram (supposably.)*
Ex. 12. 22 take bunch of *h.*, and
Lev. 14. 4, 49 take cedar, *h.* and sc.
Num. 19. 6 take cedar wood and *h.*
1 K. 4. 33 *h.* that spring. out of wall
Ps. 51. 7 purge me with *h.*, and
John 19. 29 sponge . . and put it on *h.*
Heb. 9. 19 took *h.* . . sprinkled . . b.

I.

I. *Myself.*
Gen. 6. 17 *I* .. do bring flood of w.
Ex. 3. 14 G. said . *I* am that I am
2 Sam. 5. 15 *I*, also, and Elishua
1 Chr. 3. 6 *I*, also, and Elishama
Ez. 6. 12 *I* Darius made a decree
Dan. 4. 4 *I* Nebuchad, was at rest
Mat. 3. 11 *I* indeed baptize you with
16. 13 say that *I* the Son of man
Mark 8. 27 ; Luke 24. 9; John 10. 16
Acts 3. 6 sil. and gold have *I* none
Rom. 3. 7 ; 2 Cor; 11. 18; Eph.
1. 15; Phil. 1. 7; Col. 4. 4;
Rev. 2. 6
Ice. *Frost, crystal, ice.*
Job 6. 16 blackish by reason of *i.*
38. 29 out of . . womb came *i.*
Ps. 147. 17 he casteth . . his *i.* like
Idle. *Slothful.*
Prov. 19. 15 *i.* soul . . suffer hunger
Remiss, indolent.
Ex. 5. 8 th. be *i.* ; therefore they cry
5. 17 ye are *i.* ; therefore ye say
Idle, unprofitable.
Mat. 12. 36 *i.* words that men sp'k
20. 3 saw others standing *i.* in the
20. 6 Why stand ye here all day *i.*?
Luke 24. 11 words seemed . . as *i.* t.
1 Tim. 5. 13 And they learn to be *i.*
R. V. Mat. 20. 6 —
Idleness. *Slothfulness.*
Prov. 31. 27 see . . eat. not bread of *i.*
Not occupied, laziness.
Eccl. 10. 18 thr. *i.* of hands the h.
Restfulness, spare time.
Ezek. 16. 49 abund. of *i.*, was in h.
R. V. Ezek. 16. 49 ease
Idol. *Vain, empty thing.*
Lev. 19. 4 Turn ye not unto *i.*, nor
26. 1 Ye shall make you no *i.* nor
1 Chr. 16. 26 gods of people are *i.*
Ps. 97. 7 that boast themselves of *i.*
Isa. 2. 8 Their land is also full of *i.*
2. 20 his *i.* of silver and *i.* of gold
Hab. 2. 18 trust. . . to make dumb *i.*
Zech. 11. 17 woe to the *i.* shepherd
Carved image.
1 Sam. 31. 9 publish it in house of *i.*
42*

1 Chr. 10. 9 carry tidings to their *i.*
2 Chr. 24. 18 served groves and *i.*
Ps. 106. 36 they served their *i.* which
115. 4 their *i.* are silver and gold
Isa. 10. 11 do to Jerusa. and her *i.*
46. 1 their *i.* were upon the beasts
Jer. 50. 2 her *i.* were confounded
Hos. 4, 17 Ephraim is joined to *i.*
Mic. 1. 7 *i.* will I lay desolate
Zech. 13. 2 will cut off names of *i.*
A terror, source of fright or grief.
1 K. 15. 3 because she had made *i.*
2 Chr. 15. 16 Asa cut down her *i.*
Isa. 45. 16 that are makers of *i.*
48. 5 Mine *i.* hath done them, and
57. 5 enflamed yourselves with *i.*
66. 3 he that .. as if he blessed an *i.*
Jer. 22. 28 Coniah a despised . . *i.*
Image, god.
Acts 7. 41 offered sac. unto the *i.*
15. 29 abstain from meats offer. *i.*
Rom. 2. 22 thou that abhorrest *i.*
1 Cor. 8. 1 touching things offered *i.*
12. 2 carried away unto dumb *i.*
2 Cor. 6. 16 what . . hath t . . . with *i.*
1 Thes. 1. 9 turned to G. from *i.*
1 John 5. 21 chil., keep yours. from *i.*
Rev. 2. 14 eat things sacrificed to *i.*
9. 20 should not worship d. and *i.*
R. V. 1 K. 15. 13 ; 2 Chr. 15. 16;
Jer. 50. 2 image, and images ; 2
Chr. 15. 18 abominations; Isa. 57.
5 among oaks; Jer. 22. 28 vessel;
Zech. 2. 10 teraphim ; 11. 17 worthless ; 1 Cor. 12. 28 —
Idolater. *Idol worshipper.*
1 Cor. 5. 10 extortioners, or with *i.*
6. 9 neither fornicators, nor *i.*, nor
10. 7 neither be ye *i.*, as some
Rev. 21. 8 *i.*, and all liars, shall
22. 15 without . . are dogs and *i.*
Idolatrous. *Idol worshipping.*
2 K. 25. 3 she put down *i.* priests
Idolatry. *Worship of idols.*
1 Sam. 15. 23 stubbornness is as .. *i.*
Acts 17. 16 saw city . . given to *i.*
1 Cor. 10.14 dearly beloved, fl. from *i*
Gal. 5. 20 *i.*, witchcraft, hatred, va.
Col. 3. 5 covetousness, which is *i.*
1 Pet. 4. 3 banquet, and abomina. *i.*
R. V. 1 Sam. 15. 23 teraphim ; Acts
17. 16 full of idols
Idol's Temple. *Place of idol.*
1 Cor. 8. 10 if man sit at meat in *i. t.*
Idols. *Logs, hence idol.*
Lev. 26. 30 cast . . on carcases of *i.*
Deut. 29. 17 seen their abom. and *i.*
1 K. 15. 12 Asa removed all *i.* that
2 K. 17. 12 they served *i.*, wheref.
21. 11 made Judah to sin with *i.*
2 Chr. 15. 8 put away abominable *i.*
Jer. 50. 2 her *i.* are confounded
Ezek. 6. 4 cast. . slain . . bef. your *i.*
14. 6 repent, turn from your *i.*
House gods, healers.
Zech. 10. 2 for *i.* have spoken vanity
R. V. *sun images.*
2 Chr. 34. 7 cut down all *i.* through
If. This particle renders conditional
the clause it introduces. *Suppos-
ing, provided.*
Mat. 4. 3 If thou be Son of God
Luke 11. 18 if Satan be divided,
Etc., etc.
Ignominy. *Shame, confusion.*
Prov. 18. 3 and with *i.* reproach
Ignorance. *Error, led astray.*
Lev. 4. 2 If a soul sin through *i.*
5. 18 concerning his *i.* wherein
Num. 15. 24 if ought be com. by *i.*
15. 25 be forgiven them for it is *i.*
Lack of knowledge.
Acts 3. 17 I wot. .. through *i.* ye did
17. 30 times of this *i.* God winked
Eph. 4. 18 alienated . . through *i.*
1 Pet. 1. 14 according to . . lusts in *i.*
R. V. Lev. 4. 2, 22, 27 ; 5. 18; Num.
15, 24, 26, 27, 28, 29 unwittingly ;
Lev. 4. 13 shall err; Num. 15. 25
was an error
Ignorant. *Without knowledge.*
Ps. 73. 22 so foolish was I, and *i.*
Isa. 56. 10 they are all *i.*, all dumb
63. 16 though Abraham be *i.* of us
Rom. 1. 13 would not have you *i.*
10. 3 being *i.* of God's righteous.

1 Cor. 14. 38 if any man be *i.*, let
2 Cor. 1. 8 would not have you *i.*
2. 11 for we are not *i.* of his devi.
1 Thes. 4. 13 would not have you *i.*
Heb. 5. 2 who . . have compass. on *i.*
Plebeian,
Acts 4. 13 that are unlearned and *i*
R. V. *forget.*
2 Pet. 3. 5 they willingly are *i.* of
. 8 be not *i.* of this one thing
R. V. Isa. 56. 10 without knowl
edge ; 63. 16 knoweth not
Ignorantly. *Without knowledge*
Num. 15. 28 atone. for s. that sin. *i*
Deut. 19. 4 whoso killeth neighbor *i*
Acts 17. 23 whom . . ye *i.* worship
1 Tim. 1. 13 because I did it *i.* in
R. V. Num. 15. 28 erreth ; Deut
19. 4 unawares
Ill. *Evil, evilly.*
Gen. 41. 3 kine . . *i.* fav. and lean
Deut. 15. 21 or have an *i.* blemish
Job 20. 26 it shall go *i.* with him
Ps. 106. 32 it went *i.* with Moses
Isa. 3. 11 Woe . . ! it shall be *i.* with
Jer. 40. 4 but if it seem *i.* to come
Mic. 3. 4 have behaved themselves *i*
Joel 2. 20 *i.* savour shall come up
Rom. 13. 10 love work. no *i.* to neig.
R. V. Mic. 3. 4 evil
Illuminated. R. V. *enlightened.*
Heb. 10. 32 after ye were *i.*, ye en.
Image. *Graven thing, thing set
up ; figure, likeness, idol.*
Gen. 1. 26 Let us make man in our *i.*
9. 6 in the *i.* of God made he man
Ex. 23. 24 shalt . . break down their *i*
Lev. 26. 1 nei. rear up standing *i.*
Deut. 16. 22 neither . . set up any *i.*
Judg. 18. 18 fetched the carved *i.*
1 Sam. 6. 5 sh. make *i.* of emerods
2 Sam. 5. 21 they left their *i.*, and
1 K. 14. 23 built high places, and *i*
2 K. 3. 2 he put away *i.* of Beth.
2 Chr. 14. 3 brake down the *i.* and
Job 4. 16 *i.* was before mine eyes
Ps. 73. 20 O Lord . . despise their *i.*
Jer. 43. 13 He shall break . . the *i.* of
Ezek. 8. 3 seat of the *i.* of jealousy
Dan. 2. 31 and behold a great *i.*
2. 31-35 ; 3. 1-15
Hos. 3. 4 without *i.* . . . and ephod
Am. 5. 26 *i.*, the star of your god, wh.
Mic. 5. 13 *i.* cut off out of the midst
Mat. 22. 20 whose *i.* and superscr. ?
Mark 12. 16 ; Luke 20. 24
Rom. 1. 23 *i.* like to corrup. man
8. 29 conformed to the *i.* of his Son
1 Cor. 11. 7 he is *i.* and glory of G.
2 Cor. 4. 4 Christ, who is *i.* of God
Col. 3. 10 after *i.* of him that creat.
Heb. 1. 3 express *i.* of his person
10. 1 not the very *i.* of the things,
Rev. 13. 14 make *i.* to the beast
13. 15 ; 14. 9 ; 15. 2 ; 16. 2 ; 19. 20
R. V. Lev. 26. 1 figured stones ;
Ex. 23. 24 ; 34. 13 ; Lev. 26. 1 ;
Deut. 7. 5 ; 16. 22 ; 1 K. 14. 23 ; 2
K. 17. 10 ; 18. 4 ; 23. 14 ; 2 Chr.
14. 3 ; 31. 1 ; Jer. 43. 13 ; Hos. 1.
2 ; Mic. 5. 13 pillar, and pillars ;
Job 4. 16 form ; Rom. 11. 4 —
Imagery. *Imagery.*
Ezek. 8. 12 in chambers of his *i.*
Images. R. V. *teraphim.*
Gen. 31. 19 Rach. had stolen the *i.*
1 Sam. 19. 13 Michal took *i.* and
19. 16 behold, was an *i.* in the bed
2 K. 23. 24 the *i.*, and the idols
Ezek. 21. 21 he consulted with *i.*
R. V. *sun-images.*
Lev. 26. 30 will cut down your *i.*
2 Chr. 14. 5 took .. high places and *i.*
34. 4 *i.* that were on high above
Isa. 17. 8 made, either groves or *i.*
27. 9 groves . . *i.* shall not stand up
Ezek. 6. 4 your *i.* shall be broken
6. 6 *i.* may be cut down, and your
Imagination. R. V. *stubbornness.*
Deut. 29. 19 walk in *i.* of my heart
Jer. 3. 17 walk after *i.* of evil hearts
7. 24; 9. 14; 11. 8; 13. 10; 16.
12; 18. 12; 23. 17
Conceit, device, reasoning.
Gen. 6. 5 every *i.* of the thoughts
8. 21 *i.* of man's heart is evil

Deut. 31. 21 I know their *i.* which
1 Chr. 28. 9 understandeth all *i.*
29. 18 keep this forever in *i.* of the
Prov. 6. 18 heart that deviseth .. *i.*
Lam. 3. 60, 61 all their *i.* against me
Luke 1. 51 scattered proud in the *i.*
Rom. 1. 21 become vain in their *i.*
2 Cor. 10. 5 casting down *i.*, and
R. V. Lam. 3. 60,61 devices; Rom.
   1. 21 reasonings

Imagine. *Think, conceive, devise,*
Gen. 11. 6 which they have *i.* to do
Job 6. 26 Do ye *i.* to reprove words
Ps. 2. 1 Why .. *i.* a vain thing?
10. 2 taken in devices they have *i.*
21. 11 they *i.* mischievous device
140. 2 which *i.* mischiefs in heart
Prov. 12. 30 deceit .. in heart .. that *i.*
Hos. 7. 15 *i.* mischief against me
Nah. 1. 9 what .. against the L.?
Zech. 7. 10 none .. *i.* evil against bro.
Acts 4. 25 why .. peo. *i.* vain things?
R. V. Gen. 11. 6 purpose

Immediately. R. V. *straight-
way, or forthwith.*
Mat. 4. 22 they *i.* left the ship and
8. 3 *i.* his leprosy was cleansed
14. 31 *i.* J. stretched forth hand
Mark 1. 31 *i.* fever left her, and she
4. 15 Satan cometh *i.* and taketh
Luke 6. 49 *i.* it fell; and the ruin
John 5. 9 *i.* man was made whole
Acts 9. 18 *i.* .. fell from his eyes
16. 26 and *i.* all doors opened, and
Gal. 1. 16 *i.* I conferred not with
Rev. 4. 2 And *i.* I was in the Spirit

Immortal. R. V. *incorruptible.*
1 Tim. 1. 17 K. eter , *i.*, invisible

Immortality. *Deathlessness.*
1 Cor. 15. 53 mortal must put on *i.*
1 Tim. 6. 16 who only hath *i.* dwel.
2 Tim. 1. 10 brought .. *i.* to light
R. V. *incorruption*
Rom. 2. 7 seek for glory .. and *i.*

Immutability. *Unchangeable-
ness.*
Heb. 6. 17 show .. of his counsel

Immutable. *Unchangeable.*
Heb. 6. 18 that by two *i.* things

Impart. *Give part, share, make
known.*
Job 39. 17 nei. .. *i.* to her underst.
Luke 3. 11 let him *i.* to him that
Rom. 1. 11 *i.* to you spiritual gift
1 Thes. 2. 8 willing to have *i.* unto

Impediment. *That impedes.*
Mark 7. 32 one had an *i.* in speech

Impenitent. *Without mental
change.*
Rom. 2. 5 after .. hardness and *i.* h.

Imperious. *Domineering.*
Ezek. 16. 30 work of *i.* whor. wom.

Implacable· *Unforgiving.*
Rom. 1. 31 without nat. affec., *i.*
R. V. Rom. 1. 31 —

Implead. R. V. *accuse.*
Acts 19. 28 craftsmen .. let them *i.*

Importunity. *Boldness, persist-
ence.*
Luke 11. 8 bec. of *i.* he will rise

Impose. *Lay, levy, cast.*
Ez. 7. 24 *i.* toll, tribute or custom
Heb. 9. 10 carnal ordinances *i.* on

Impossible. *Not possible.*
Mat. 19. 26 with men this is *i.*
Mark 10. 27 *i.*, but not with God
Luke 17. 2 *i.* but that offences will
Heb. 6. 4 it is *i.* for those who were
   11. 6 without faith it is *i.* to please
R. V. Luke 1. 37 void of power;
   Heb. 6. 4 as touching

Impotent. *Without strength.*
Acts 4. 9 good deed done to *i.* man
14. 18 sat a certain man *i.* in feet
R. V. *sick.*
John 5. 3 lay multitude of *i.* folk
5. 7 the *i.* man answered him, Sir,

Impoverish. *Make poor.*
Judg. 6. 6 Israel was greatly *i.* bec.
Isa. 40. 20 he that is so *i.* that he
Jer. 5. 17 shall *i.* thy fenced cities
Mal. 1. 4 Edom saith. we are *i.*
R. V. Judg. 6. 6 brought low;
   Jer. 5. 17; Mal. 1. 4 beat down

Imprison. *To prison, confine.*
Acts 22. 19 they know that I *i.* and

Imprisonment. *Band, fetter.*
Ez. 7. 26 confiscation of goods, or *i.*
Watch, confinement.
2 Cor. 6. 5 in stripes, *i.*, tumults
Heb. 11. 36 yea, .. of bonds and *i.*

Impudent. *Hard, sharp.*
Prov. 7. 13 with *i.* face said unto
Ezek. 2. 4 *i.* chil., and stiff hearted
3. 7 all house of Israel are *i.*
R. V. Ezek. 3. 7 of hard forehead

Impute. *Reckon, place, account.*
Lev. 7. 18 neither shall it be *i.* to
17. 4 blood shall be *i.* unto th, man
1 Sam. 22. 15 let not the king *i.* any
2 Sam. 19. 19 let not lord *i.* iniq.
Ps. 32. 2 unto whom Lord *i.* not
Rom. 4. 6 whom God *i.* righteous.
   4. 8-24; 5. 13
2 Cor. 5. 19 not *i.* their trespasses
Jas. 2. 23 *i.* to him for righteous.
R. V. Hab. 1. 11 even; Rom. 4, 6,
   8, 11, 22, 23, 24 reckon ; 2 Cor 5.
   19 reckoning ; Jas. 2. 23, reckoned

In. *Within, there, etc.*
Gen. 1. 20 fly .. *i.* open firmament
Mat. 2. 23 and dwelt *i.* a city . Naza.

Inasmuch. *In so much.*
Deut. 19. 6 *i.* as he hated him
Ruth 3. 10 *i.* as thou follow. not
Mat. 25. 40 *i.* as ye have done it to
Rom. 11. 13 *i.* as I am apos. of God
Heb. 3, 3 *i.* as he who should be the h.
1 Pet. 4. 13 *i.* as ye are partakers
R. V. Heb. 3. 3 by so much; 9.
   27 ——; 1 Pet. 4. 13 insomuch.

Incense. *Perfume.*
Ex. 25. 6 spices for anoint ... and *i.*
30. 1 ; 31. 8 ; 35. 8 ; 37. 25 ; 39. 38
Lev. 10. 1 put *i.* thereon, and off.
Num. 4. 16 sweet *i.* and meat off.
   7. 14 ; 16. 7, 17, 18, 35, 40, 46, 47
Deut. 33. 10 shall put *i.* before thee
1 Sam. 2. 28 to burn *i.*, wear ephod
1 Chr. 6. 49 off . . . on altar of *i.*
2 Chr. 2. 4 to burn before him .. *i.*
Ps. 66. 15 will offer unto thee . . *i.*
Isa. 1. 13 *i.* is an abom. unto me
Jer. 6. 20 what purpose cometh .. *i.*
Ezek. 8. 11 thick cloud of *i.* went
Mal. 1. 11 ev. pl. *i.* shall be off.
Luke 1. 10 praying .. at time of *i.*
Rev. 8. 3 was given him much *i.*
   8. 4 smoke of *i.* ascended bef. God
R. V. Ex. 30. 7, 8 —— ; Isa. 43.
   23 ; 60. 6 ; 66. 3 ; Jer. 6. 20 ; 17.
   26 ; 41. 5 frankincense

Incensed. *Heated, displeased.*
Isa. 41. 11 all that were *i.* against
45. 24 all *i.* against him shall be

Incline. *Stretch out, bow down,
lend.*
Josh. 24. 23 *i.* your heart unto L.
Judg. 9. 3 h. *i.* to follow Abimelech
1 K. 8. 58 may *i.* our hearts unto
Ps. 17. 6 hear me, O God, *i.* thine
7. 8. 1 *i.* your ears to the words
Prov. 2. 2 *i.* thine ear to wisdom
Isa. 37. 17 *i.* thine ear, Lord, and h.
Jer. 7. 24 hearkened not, nor *i.* ear
Dan. 9. 18 O God, *i.* thine ear
R. V. Ps. 71. 2 bow down

Inclose. *Surround, shut in.*
Ex. 39. 6 onyx stones, *i.* in ouches
Judg. 20. 43 *i.* the Benjamins round
Ps. 22. 16 assem. of wicked have *i.*
S. of S. 4. 12 garden *i.* is my sister
Lam. 3. 9 he hath *i.* my ways wi. st.
Luke 5. 6 net *i.* multitude of fishes
R. V. S. of S. 4. 12 shut up; Lam.
   3. 9 fenced up

Inclosings. R. V. *settings.*
Ex. 28. 20 be set in gold in their *i.*
39. 13 in ouches of gold in their *i.*

Incontinency. *No self-control.*
1 Cor. 7. 5 Sat. tempt . not for *i.*

Incontinent. R. V. *without self-
control*
2 Tim. 3. 3 tr. break,, false accu., *i.*

Incorruptible. *Not corruptible.*
1 Cor. 9. 25 cor. crown, but we an *i.*
15. 52 and the dead shall be raised *i.*
1 Pet. 1. 4 to an inheritance *i.* and
   1. 23 not of corruptible seed, but *i.*

Incorruption. *Not corrupt.*
1 Cor. 15. 42 sown in cor raised in *i.*

15. 50 neither doth cor. inherit *i.*
15. 53 this corrupt. must put on *i.*
15. 54 cor. shall have put on *i.*

Increase. (*n.*). *Product, fruit.*
Gen. 47. 24 come to pass in the i.
Lev. 19. 25 it yield unto you the i.
25. 12 ye shall eat *i.* thereof out of
25. 36 take no usury of him or *i.*
Num. 18. 30 as the *i.* of the floor
Deut. 14. 22 shalt tithe all the *i.*
   16. 15 God shall bless .. thine *i.*
Judg. 6. 4 destroyed *i.* of the earth
1 Sam. 2. 33 *i.* of thy h. shall die
2 Chr. 31. 5 firstfruits .. of all the *i.*
   32. 28 storehouses for the *i.* of corn
Neh. 9. 36 yieldeth much *i.* to kings
Job. 20. 28 *i.* of house shall depart
Ps. 67. 6 shall earth yield her *i.*
Prov. 3. 9 with firstfruits of .. *i*
   14. 4 much *i.* is by strength of ox
Eccl. 5. 10 that lov. abund. with *i.*
Isa. 9. 7 of the *i.* of his government
30. 23 bread of the *i.* of the earth
Jer. 2. 3 Is. was . . fruit of his *i.*
Ezek. 34. 27 earth shall yield her *i.*
Zech. 8. 12 gr. shall give her *i.*
1 Cor. 3. 6 wat., but God gave the *i.*
Eph. 4. 16 *i.* of body unto edifica.
Col. 2 19 body increaseth with *i.* of
R. V. Gen. 47. 34 ingathering

Increase (*v.*). *Strengthen, enlarge, multiply, add to, grow, become many.*
Gen. 7. 17 waters *i.*, and bare ark
30. 30 now *i.* unto a multitude, and
Ex. 1. 7 chil. of Is. .. *i.* abundantly
Lev. 25. 16 shalt *i.* price thereof
Deut. 6. 3 that ye may *i.* mightily
1 Sam. 14. 19 noise .. went on and *i.*
2 Sam. 15. 12 peo. *i.* continually
1 K. 22, 35 the battle *i.* that day
1 Chr. 4. 38 h. of their fathers *i.*
2 Chr. 18. 34 the battle *i.* that day
Ez. 10. 10 to *i.* trespass of Israel
Job 10. 16 it *i.* Thou huntest me
Ps. 62. 10 if riches *i.* set not heart
71. 21 Thou shalt *i.* my greatness
115. 14 Lord shall *i.* you more and
Prov. 13. 11 that gath. by lab. shall *i.*
Eccl. 6. 11 many things *i.* vanity
Isa. 9. 3 and hast not *i.* the joy
Jer. 5. 6 their backslidings are *i.*
   30. 15 thy sins are *i.*, I have done
Lam. 2. 5 hath *i.* in daugh. of Judah
Ezek. 5. 16 I will *i.* the famine upon
Dan. 12. 4 and knowledge shall be *i.*
Hos. 10. 1 Is., he hath *i.* the altars
Am. 4. 9 your fig and olive trees *i.*
Hab. 2. 6 Woe to him that *i.* that
Zech. 10. 8 shall *i.* as they have *i.*
Mark 4. 8 fruit that sprang and *i.*
Luke 2. 52 Jesus *i* in wisdom and
   17. 5 apostles said .. *I.* our faith
John 3. 30 he must *i.*, I must decr.
Acts 6. 7 the word of God *i.* ; and
9. 22 Saul *i.* the more in strength
2 Cor. 9. 10 *i.* the fruits of right.
Col. 1. 10 *i.* in knowledge of God
   2. 19 body *i.* with increase of God
1 Thes. 4. 10 beseech .. that ye *i.*
2 Tim. 2. 16 will *i.* to more ungodli.
Rev. 3. 17 I am rich, and *i.* in goods
R. V. Job 10. 16 exalteth; Prov.
   28. 8 augmenteth; Ps. 7. 23 ascendeth; Isa. 52. 1 made many; Jer.
   29. 16; Lam. 2. 5; Ezek. 16. 26;
   Hos. 4, 7; 10. 1; 12. 1 multiplied;
   Luke 2. 52 advanced; 2 Cor. 2. 15
   groweth; Rev. 3. 17 have gotten

Incredible. *Not to be believed.*
Acts 26. 8 why .. thought thing *i.*

Incurable. *Not curable.*
2 Chr. 21. 18 L smote .. with *i.* dis.
Job 34. 6 my wound is *i.* without tr.
Jer. 15. 18 why .. is my wound *i.*
   30. 12 Thy bruise is *i.*, thy wound
30. 15 thy sorrow is *i.* for the multi.
Mic. 1. 9 her wound is *i.*, for it is

Indebted. *Owing.*
Luke 11. 4 forgive ev. one that is *i.*

Indeed. *Verily, surely, truly.*
Gen. 17. 19 Sarah .. bear thee son *i.*
20. 12 yet *i.* she is my sister
Num. 22. 37 able *i.* to promote thee
Josh. 7. 20 *I.* I have sinned ag. the L
2 Sam. 14. 5 am *i.* a widow woman

1 K. 8. 27 will G. *i.* dwell on earth
Job. 19. 4 be it *i.* that I have erred
Ps. 58. 1 do ye *i.* speak righteous.
Mat. 3. 11 I *i.* bap. you with water
20. 23 Ye shall drink *i.* of my cup
26. 41 sp. *i.* is wil. but fl. . . weak
Mark 14. 21 Son of man *i.* goeth
Luke 11. 48 for they *i.* killed them
John 1. 47 Behold an Israelite *i.*
4. 42 we know this is *i.* the Christ
Acts 4. 16 *i.* a notable miracle hath
Rom. 14, 20 all things *i.* are pure
1 Cor. 11. 7 m. *i.* ought not cover
2 Cor. 8. 17 *i.* he accepted exhorta.
Phil. 1. 15 some *i.* preach Christ
1 Thes. 4. 9 ye do *i.* toward all
1 Tim. 5. 3 hon. wid. . . are wid. *i.*

Indignation. *Wrath, rage, fury.*
Deut. 29. 28 root. them out . . in gr. *i.*
2 K. 3. 27 great *i.* against Israel
Neh. 4. 1 wroth, and took great *i.*
Esth. 5. 9 full of *i.* against Mord.
Job 10. 17 increase thine *i.* on me
Ps. 69. 24 pour out thine *i.* on th.
Isa. 10. 5 staff *i.* . hand is my *i.*
30. 27 his lips are full of *i.*, tongue
Jer. 10. 10 nations not . . abide his *i.*
Lam. 2. 6 despised in *i.* of his anger
Ezek. 21. 31 pour out mine *i.* upon
Dan. 8. 19 shall be in . . end of *i.*
Mic. 7. 9 I will bear *i.* of the Lord
Zeph. 3. 8 pour on them mine *i.*
Mat. 20. 24 moved with *i.* against
Mark 14. 4 were some that had *i.*
Luke 13. 14 ruler . . answered with *i.*
Acts 5. 17 rose up . . filled with *i.*
Rom. 2. 8 obey unrighteousness, *i.*
2 Cor. 7. 11 *i.* yea . . fear, yea . . veh.
Heb. 10. 27 *i.*, which shall devour
Rev. 14. 10 poured . . cup of his *i.*
R. V. 2 K. 3. 27; Esth. 5. 9 wrath;
Acts 5. 17 jealousy; Heb. 10. 27
fierceness of fire; Rev. 14. 10
anger

Indite. R. V. *overflowing with.*
Ps. 45. 1 My heart is *i.* good mattter

Industrious. *Worker.*
1 K. 11. 28 seeing young man was *i*

Inexcusable. R. V. *without excuse.*
Rom 2. 1 thou art *i.*, O man, who

Infallible. R. V. ——
Acts 1. 3 showed . . by *i.* proof

Infamous. *Of unclean name.*
Ezek. 22. 5 mock thee which art *i.*

Infamy. *Evil account.*
Prov. 25. 10 and thine *i.* turn not
Ezek. 36. 3 lips . . and are in *i.*
R. V. Ezek. 36. 3 evil report

Infant. *Suckling, babe.*
1 Sam. 15. 3 slay man, woman, and *i.*
Job 3. 16 as *i.* which never saw li.
Isa. 65. 20 be no more thence an *i.*
Hos. 13. 16 *i.* . . be dashed in pieces
Luke 18. 15 brought unto him *i.*
R. V. Luke 18. 15 their babes

Inferior. *Less, worse.*
Job 12. 3 I am not *i.* to you; yea,
Dan. 2. 39 arise anoth. kingdom *i.*
2 Cor. 12. 13 wherein ye were *i.* to

Infidel. R. V. *unbeliever.*
2 Cor. 6. 15 that believeth with *i.*
1 Tim. 5. 8 denied faith, worse than *i*

Infinite. *Without end or nnmber.*
Job 22. 5 and thine iniquities *i.*?
Ps. 147. 5 his understanding is *i.*
Nah. 3. 9 strength, and it was *i.*
R. V. Job 22. 5 end

Infirmity. *Sickness, disease.*
Lev. 12. 2 days of sep. for her *i.*
Ps. 77. 10 And I said, This is my *i.*
Luke 7. 21 cured many of their *i.*
Weakness.
Mat. 8. 17 himself took our *i.*, and
Luke 5. 15 to be healed by him of *i.*
11. 13 wom. which had spirit of *i.*
John 5. 5 had *i.* thirty eight years
Rom. 6. 19 bec. of *i.* of your flesh
2 Cor. 11. 30 things which concern *i.*
Gal. 4. 13 Ye know how through *i.*
1 Tim. 5. 23 stom's sake and . . oft *i.*
Heb. 4. 15 touched with feeling of *i.*
5. 2 himself is compassed with *i.*
R. V. Lev. 12. 2 her sickness;
Luke 7. 21; 2 Cor. 12. 5, 9, 10
weaknesses

Inflame. *Make burn, excite.*

Isa. 5. 11 night, till wine *i.* them

Inflammation. *Burning, swelling.*
Lev. 13. 28 an *i.* of the burning
Deut. 28. 22 L. smite thee with . . *i.*
R. V. Lev. 13. 28 scar

Influences. R. V. *clusters.*
Job 38. 31 canst bind . . *i.* of Pleiades

Inflict. *Lay on, apply.*
2 Cor. 2. 6 punishment which was *i.*

Infolding. *Wrap up, involve.*
Ezek. 1. 4 cloud, and a fire *i.* itself

Inform. *Show, teach.*
Deut. 17. 10 do accord. to all they *i.*
Dan. 9. 22 he *i.* me, and talked
Acts 21. 21 they are *i.* of thee, that
24. 1 Tertullus, who *i.* the gov.
R. V. Deut. 17. 10 shall teach; Dan.
9 22 instructed

Ingathering. *Gathering in.*
Ex. 23. 16 feast of *i.* . . in end of
34. 22 *i.* feast of at the year's end

Inhabit. *Sit down, sojourn, dwell.*
Gen. 36. 20 sons of Seir, who *i.*
Num. 35. 34 defile not the land ye *i.*
Judg. 1. 17 slew Canaanites that *i.*
1 Chr. 5. 9 eastward he *i.* unto wil.
Ps. 22. 3 that *i.* praises of Israel
Prov. 10. 30 wicked shall not *i.* earth
Isa. 57. 15 saith . . lofty One that *i.*
Jer. 17. 6 shall *i.* parched places
Ezek. 33. 24 they that *i.* the wastes
Am. 9. 14 build waste cities and *i.*
Zech. 7. 7 when Jerusalem was *i.*
R. V. Prov. 10. 30; Jer. 48. 18 dwell in

Inhabitant. *Settler down, dweller, sojourner.*
Gen. 19. 25 overthrew . . all *i.* of
Lev. 18. 25 land vomiteth out her *i.*
25. 10 proclaim liberty . . to all *i.*
Num. 13. 32 land that eat. up the *i.*
Deut. 13. 15 thou shalt smite the *i.*
Josh. 2. 9 and that all *i.* of land faint
8. 26 utterly destroyed all *i.* of Ai
13. 6 all *i.* of the hill country
Judg. 1. 11 went against *i.* of Debir
2. 2 make no league with *i.* of
Ruth 4. 4 Buy it before the *i.* and
1 K. 21. 11 were *i.* in his city did as J.
2 K. 19. 26 *i.* were of small power
1 Chr. 8. 13 drove away *i.* of Gath
2 Chr. 20. 20 Hear, O Judah, and ye *i.*
Ez. 4. 6 accusation against *i.* of Ju.
Neh. 7. 3 appoint watchers of *i.*
Job 26. 5 under waters, and the *i.*
Ps. 33. 8 let all the *i.* of world stand
75. 3 earth and all *i.* thereof are
Isa. 5. 3 now, O *i.* of Jerusalem
12. 6 Cry . . and shout, thou *i.* of Zion
24. 6 *i.* of the earth are burned
Jer. 1. 14 evil . . break forth on all *i.*
10. 18 will sling out *i.* of land
Lam. 4. 12 all *i.* of world, would
Ezek. 12. 19 thus saith L. G. of *i.*
27. 35 All *i.* of isles shall be aston.
Dan. 9. 7 to men of Judah, and *i.*
Hos. 8. 4 L. hath controv. with *i.*
Joel 1. 2 give ear, all ye *i.* of land
Am. 1. 5 will cut off *i.* from . . Aven
Mic. 1. 11 pass away, thou *i.* of Sa.
Zeph. 2. 5 woe to *i.* of sea coast
Zech. 11. 6 will no more pity *i.* of
Rev. 17. 2 *i.* of earth have been ma.
R. V. Num. 33. 53 ——; Judg. 5.
7; 11 rulers; Ruth 4. 4 them that
sit here; 1 K. 2. 11 dwelt; 17. 1
sojourners; Job 28. 4 where men
sojourn; Jer. 10. 17 that abidest;
Ezek. 7. 7; Rev. 17. 2 that dwellest

Inhabited. *Settled in, dwelt in, peopled.*
Ex. 16. 35 till they came to land *i.*
Lev. 16. 22 iniqui. unto land not *i.*
Isa. 13. 20 Bab. It shall never be *i.*
Jer. 17. 6 in a salt land and not *i.*
Ezek. 26. 20 that thou be not *i.*
34. 13 in *i.* places of country
Zech. 2. 4 Jerusalem shall be *i.* as
R. V. Num. 16. 22 solitary land;
1 Chr. 5. 9; Zech. 12. 6; 14. 10, 11
dwell

Inhabiters. *Dwellers.*
Rev. 8. 13 woe, to *i.* of the earth
R. V. 8. 13 for them that dwell on;
12. 12 for

Inhabiting. *Dwelling in.*
Ps. 74. 14 meat to people *i.* wilder.

Inherit. *Occupy, possess.*
Gen. 15. 7 give thee this land to *i.*
Lev. 20. 24 ye shall *i.* their land
Deut. 2. 31 that thou mayest *i.* land
Ps. 25. 13 his seed shall *i.* the earth
37. 11 But the meek shall *i.* earth
37. 29 The righteous shall *i.* land
Isa. 54. 3 thy seed shall *i.* Gentiles
65. 9 mount., mine elect shall *i.* it
Jer. 8. 10 give fields to them that *i.*
Ezek. 33. 24 Ab. was one, and he *i.*
Receive or give as heir.
Ex. 23. 23. 30 until thou . . *i.* the land
Num. 26. 55 accor. to names . . they *i*
Deut. 1. 38 Joshua . . cause Is. to *i*
Josh. 14. 1 which chil. of Israel *i.*
Judg. 11. 2 not *i.* . . our father's h.
Ps. 69. 36 seed of servants shall *i.*
82. 8 thou shalt *i.* all nations
Prov. 3. 35 the wise shall *i.* glory
14. 18 the simple *i.* folly, but
Jer. 16. 19 our fathers have *i.* lies
Ezek. 47. 14 ye shall *i.* it, one anoth.
Zech. 2. 12 L. shall *i.* Jud. portion
Inheritance by allotment.
Mat. 5. 5 meek, they shall *i.* earth
19. 29 and shall *i* everlasting life
25. 34 *i.* kingdom prepared for you
Mark 10. 17 what do . . *i.* eter. life
Luke 10. 25; 18. 18
1 Cor. 6. 9 unrighteous shall not *i.*
6. 10 nor thieves nor . . *i.* kingdom
15. 50 fl. and bl. cannot *i.* king.
15. 50 nei. doth corrup. *i.* incor.
Gal. 5. 21 shall not *i.* king. of God
Heb. 6. 12 who through faith . . *i.*
1 Pet. 3. 9 ye should *i.* blessing
Rev. 21. 7 that overcometh shall *i.*
R. V. Isa. 54. 3; Jer. 8. 10; 49. 1
possess

Inheritance. *Heritage, thing inherited.*
Gen. 31. 14 yet any por. or *i.* for us
Ex. 15. 17 plant in mountain of *i.*
Num. 16. 14 or given us *i.* of fields
18. 20 I am thy part and *i.*
26. 53; 27. 7; 35. 2; 36. 2-12
Deut. 4. 20 be unto him a people of *i.*
10. 9 Levi hath no part nor *i.* with
Josh. 13. 6 divide it by lot . . for *i.*
14. 2; 15. 20; 16. 5; 17. 4; 18. 2
Judg. 2. 6 ev. man went to his *i.*
18. 1 Danites sought them *i.* to dw.
Ruth 4. 5 rais. name of dead upon *i.*
1 Sam. 10. 1 anoint. capt. ov. his *i.*
2 Sam. 14. 16 destroy me . . out of *i.*
1 K. 8. 36 given to thy people for *i.*
2 K. 21. 14 forsake rem. of mine *i.*
1 Chr. 16. 18 Can., the lot of your *i.*
2 Chr. 10. 16 none *i.* in son of Jesse
Neh. 11. 20 every one in his *i.*
Job 31. 2 what *i.* of Almighty from
Ps. 2. 8 shall give heathen thine *i.*
28. 9 save people, bless thine *i.*
Prov. 17. 2 ser. shall have part of *i.*
19. 14 house and riches are *i.* of
Eccl. 7. 11 wisdom is good with *i.*
Isa. 19. 25 blessed be Israel mine *i.*
Jer. 10. 16 Israel is rod of his *i.*
Lam. 5. 2 our *i.* is turned to strang.
Ezek. 44. 28 shall be to them for *i.*
Heritage, allotment.
Mat. 21. 38 and let us seize on his *i.*
Mark 12. 7 kill him, and *i.* shall
Luke 12. 13 that he divide *i.* with me
Acts 7. 5 gave him none *i.* in it
Gal. 3. 18 For if the *i.* be of the law
Eph. 1. 14 is earnest of our *i.* until
Col. 1. 12 to be partakers of *i.* of sa.
Heb. 9. 15 rec. promise of eternal *i.*
1 Pet. 1. 4 to an *i.* incorruptible
R. V. Josh. 13. 15, 24, 32 ——; Job
31. 2 Eph. 1. 11 heritage; Ezek.
22. 16 be profaned

Inheritor. *Possessor.*
Isa. 65. 9 out of Judah *i.* of my mts.

Iniquity. *Perversity.*
Gen. 15. 16 *i.* of Amor not yet full
44. 16 God hath found out *i.* of
Ex. 20. 5 visit. *i.* of fathers upon
34. 9 pardon our *i.* and our sin
Lev. 5. 1 then he shall bear his *i.*
Num. 5. 15 bringing *i.* to remem.
Deut. 32. 4 God of truth, without *i.*
Josh. 22. 17 is *i.* of Peor too little
1 Sam. 3. 13 will judge . . for *i.* wh.

20. 1 what .. done? what mine *i.?*
2 Sam. 14. 9 O king, *i.* be on me
1 Chr. 21. 8 do away *i.* of thy ser.
Ez. 9. 6 our *i.* are increased ov. head
Neh. 4. 5 and cover not their *i.*
Job 7. 21 why .. take away mine *i.?*
Ps. 25. 11 Lord, pardon mine *i.*
51. 2 wash me from mine *i.* cleanse
51. 5 I was shapen in *i.*, and in sin
51. 9 Hide face, blot out all mine *i.*
103. 3 who forgiveth all thine *i.*
Prov. 16. 6 by .. truth *i.* is purged
Isa. 1. 4 people laden with *i.*, a seed
53. 5 he was bruised for our *i.*
Jer. 2. 22 *i.* is marked before me
Lam. 4. 22 he will visit thine *i.*
Ezek 3. 19 he shall die in his *i.*
Dan. 9. 13 might turn from our *i.*
Hos. 4. 8 they set their heart on *i.*
Am. 3. 2 will punish you for all *i.*
Zech. 3. 4 I caused your *i.* to pass
Mal. 2. 6 he did turn many from *i.*
Vanity, wrong.
Num. 23. 21 not beheld *i.* in Jacob
1 Sam. 15. 23 stubbornness is as *i.*
Job 4. 8 they that plow *i.*, reap same
Ps. 5. 5 thou hatest workers of *i.*
6. 8 depart from me all work. of *i.*
Prov. 10. 29 destruc. to workers of *i.*
Isa. 29. 20 watch for *i.* are cut off
Hos. 6. 8 city of them that work *i.*
Mic. 2. 1 woe to them that devise *i.*
Hab. 1. 3 why dost thou show me *i.*
Wrong doing, lawlessness.
Mat. 7. 23 depart .. ye that work *i.*
23. 28 are full of hypocrisy and *i.*
24. 12 because *i.* shall abound
Luke 13. 27 depart .. ye workers of *i.*
Acts 1. 18 pur. field with reward of *i.*
8. 23 thou art in the bond of *i.*
Rom. 4. 7 blessed .. whose *i.* are
1 Cor. 13. 6 rejoiceth not in *i.* but in
2 Thes. 2. 7 mystery of *i.* doth work
2 Tim. 2. 19 ev. one depart from *i.*
Tit. 2. 14 th. he mi. redeem us from *i.*
Heb. 1. 9 loved right. and hated *i.*
Jas. 3. 6 tongue is a fire, a world of *i.*
2 Pet. 2. 16 was rebuked for his *i.*
R. V. 1 Sam. 15. 23 idolatry ; Job
6. 29, 30 injustice ; Job 22. 23 ; 36.
23 ; Ps. 37. 1 , 119. 13 ; Jer. 2. 5 ;
Ezek. 28. 15, 18 ; Mal. 2. 6 ; 1 Cor.
13. 6 : 2 Tim. 2. 19 unrighteousness ; Ps. 94. 20 ; Eccl. 3. 16 wickedness ; Dan. 9. 5 perversely ; Hab.
1. 13 perverseness ; 2 Thes. 2. 7
lawlessness ; Heb. 8. 12 —— ; 2
Pet. 2. 16 transgression

Injoin. *Change, impress, urge.*
Heb. 9. 20 testament wh. G. hath *i.*
Phile. 8 *i.* that which is convenient

Injure. R. V. *wrong.*
Gal. 4. 12 ye have not *i.* me at all

Injurious. *Spiteful, insulting.*
1 Tim. 1. 13 who was before .. *i.*

Injustice. R. V. *violence.*
Job 16. 17 not for .. *i.* in my hands

Ink. *Ink.*
Jer. 36. 18 I wrote them with *i.* in
2 Cor. 3. 3 not with *i.*, but .. spirit
2 John 12. would not write with . *i.*
3 John 13. not with *i.* and pen write

Ink-horn. *Ink vessel.*
Ezek. 9. 2, 3, 11 with writer's *i. h.*

Inn. R. V. *lodging place.*
Gen. 42. 27 give . . provender in *i.*
43. 21 when we came to the *i.* we o.
Ex. 4. 24 by the way in the *i.*, the L.
Guest chamber.
Luke 2. 7 no room for them in *i.*
Public house, inn.
Luke 10. 34 he brought him to an *i.*

Inner. *Within, innermost.*
1 K. 6. 27 set cherub within *i.*
20. 30 came to city, into *i.* chamber
2 K. 9. 2 carry him to *i.* chamber
1 Chr. 28. 11 pattern . . of *i.* parlors
2 Chr. 4. 22 *i.* doors thereof for the
Esth. 4. 11 come to king in *i.* court
Ezek. 8. 3 door of *i.* gate that look.
10. 3 and the cloud filled *i.* court
Acts 16. 24 thrust . . into *i.* prison
Eph. 3. 16 strengthened . . in *i.* man
R. V. Eph. 3. 16 inward

Innermost. *Inner part.*
Prov. 18. 8 into *i.* part of the belly

---

26. 22 down into *i.* parts of belly

Innocency. *Purity, cleanness.*
Gen. 20. 5 and *i.* of my hands have
Ps. 26. 6 I wi. wash mine hands in *i.*
Dan. 6. 22 as bef. him *i.* was found
Hos. 8. 5 ere they attain to *i.*

Innocent. *Clean, free, guiltless.*
Ex. 23. 7 *i.* and right slay thou not
Deut. 19. 10 *i.* blood be not shed
1 Sam. 19. 5 sin against *i.* blood
1 K. 2. 31 mayest take away *i.* blood
2 K. 21. 16 Manass. shed *i.* blood
Job 4. 7 who ev. perish. being *i.?*
Ps. 10. 8 in secret . . he murder *i.*
Prov. 1. 11 lurk privily for the *i.*
Isa. 59. 7 haste to shed *i.* blood
Jer. 2. 34 blo. of souls of the poor *i.*
Joel 3. 19 they have shed *i.* blood
Jonah 1. 14 lay not upon us *i.* blood
Mat. 27. 4 have betrayed *i.* blood
27. 24 I am *i.* of blood of this pers.
R. V. Ps. 19. 3 clear ; Prov. 6. 29 ;
28. 20 unpunished

Innumerable. *Without number.*
Job. 21. 33 draw . . as they are *i.*
Ps. 40. 12 *i.* evils encompass me
Jer. 46. 23 more than grassh., and *i.*
Luke 12. 1. an *i.* multitude gath.
Heb. 11. 12 as sand . . which is *i.*

Inordinate. R. V. *doting.*
Ezek. 23. 11 more corrupt in *i.* love
R. V, *passion.*
Col. 3. 5 uncleanness, *i.* affection

Inquisition. *Inquiry, search.*
Deut. 19. 18 judges shall make . . *i.*
Esth. 2. 23 when *i.* was made of
Ps. 9. 12 he maketh *i.* for blood

Inscription. *Writing above.*
Acts 17. 23 I found altar with this *i.*

Inside. *Within.*
1 K. 6. 15 covered . . *i.* with wood

Insomuch. *So that.*
Mat. 8. 24 *i.* that ship was covered
12. 22 *i.* that the blind and dumb
Mark 1. 27 *i.* that they question.
Luke 12. 1 *i.* that they trode one up.
Acts 1. 19 *i.* that field is called Acel.
2 Cor. 1. 8 *i.* we despairing of life
Gal. 2. 13 *i.* that Barnabas was car.
R. V. Mat. 24. 24 so as ; Mark 2. 2
so

Inspiration. *Breath, G. breathed.*
Job. 32. 8 the *i.* of Almighty giveth
2 Tim. 3. 16 s. is given by *i.* of God
R. V. Job 32. 8 breath ; 2 Tim. 3.
16 inspired.

Instant. *Moment, hour.*
Isa. 29. 5 shall be at an *i.* suddenly
Jer. 18. 7, 9 at what *i.* I shall speak
Luke 2. 38 she in that *i.* gave thanks
Eager, active, earnest.
Luke 23. 23 were *i.* with loud voices
Rom. 12. 12 continuing *i.* in prayer
2 Tim. 4. 2 be *i.* in season, out of sea.
R. V. Luke 2. 38 very hour ; Rom.
12. 12 earnestly.

Instantly. R. V. *earnestly.*
Luke 7. 4 they besought him *i.*
Acts 26. 7 unto which . . tribes *i.*

Instead. *In place of.*
Gen. 2. 21 and closed up the flesh *i.*
Num. 3. 12 of all firstborn that *i.*
Judg. 15. 2 take her I pray, *i.* of her
2 Sam. 17. 25 Amasa cap. *i.* of Joab
1 K. 3. 7 servant king *i.* of David
Esth. 2. 17 Esth. queen *i.* of Vashti
Job 31. 40 thistles grow *i.* of wheat
Ps. 45. 16 *i.* of thy fathers shall thy
Isa. 3. 24 *i.* of sweet smells, stink
Ezek. 16. 32 tak. strang. *i.* of husb.

Instruct. *Show, direct, teach.*
Deut. 4. 36 voice, that he might *i.*
2 K. 12. 2 days wherein Jehoi. . . *i.*
1 Chr. 25. 7 breth. that were *i.* in
2 Chr. 3. 3 Sol. was *i.* for building
Neh. 9. 20 gavest . . good spirit to *i.*
Job 40. 2 shall he that contend . . *i.*
Ps. 2. 10 be *i.*, ye judges of earth
16. 7 my reins *i.* me in night sea.
32. 8 I will *i.* thee and teach thee
Prov. 5. 13 nor inclin. ear to . . that *i.*
S. of S. 8. 2 house, who would *i.*
Isa. 8. 11 *i.* me that I should not wa.
28. 26 G. . . *i.* him to discretion
Jer. 6. 8 be thou *i.*, O Jerusalem
Dan. 11. 33 that understand shall *i.*

Mat. 13. 52 *i.* unto king. of heaven
Luke 11. 3 thou hast been *i.*
Acts 18. 25 this m. was *i.* in w. of L.
Rom. 2. 18 being *i.* out of the law
1 Cor. 2. 16 Lord, that he may *i.*
Phil. 4. 12 in all things I am *i.* both
2 Tim. 2. 25 in meekness *i.* those
R. V. Deut. 32. 10 cared for ; 2 Chr.
3. 3 laid ; Job 40. 2 contend with
Almighty ; Mat. 13. 52 hath been
made a disciple ; 14. 8 put forward
by ; Phil. 4. 12 learned the secret ;
2 Tim. 2. 25 correcting.   [*ing.*

Instructing. *Correction teach-*
Job 33 16 men, and sealeth their *i.*
Ps. 50. 17 seeing thou hatest *i.*
Prov. 1. 2 to know wisdom and *i.*
1. 7 fools despise wisdom and *i.*
1. 8 son, hear *i.* of thy father
10. 17 way of life that keepeth *i.*
12. 1 who loveth *i.* loveth knowl.
15. 5 fool despiseth father's *i.*
19. 20 hear counsel and receive *i.*
23. 12 apply thy heart to *i.*, and ear
Jer. 17. 23 not hear, nor receive *i.*
Ezek. 5. 15 an *i.* and astonishment
Zeph. 3. 7 thou wilt not receive *i.*
2 Tim. 3. 16 for *i.* is righteousness
R. V. Prov. 10. 17 ; 12. 1 ; 13. 18 ;
15. 5, 32 ; 16. 22 ; Zeph. 3. 7 correction.

Instructor. *Who instructs,*
teacher.
Gen. 4. 22 *i.* of ev. artificer in brass
Rom. 2. 20 art an *i.* of the foolish
1 Cor. 4. 15 though ye have t. th. *i.*
R. V. Gen. 4. 22 forger ; Rom. 2.
20 corrector ; 1 Cor. 4. 15 tutors.

Instrument. *Implement, contri-*
vance, vessel, weapon.
Gen. 49. 5 *i.* of cruelty . . their hab.
Ex. 25. 9 pattern of all *i.* thereof
Num. 3. 8 keep all *i.* of tabernacle
4. 32 by name shall reckon the *i.*
35. 16 and if he smite with *i.* of iron
1 Sam. 18. 6 came . . with *i.* of mus.
8. 12 *i.* of war, and *i.* of his char.
2 Sam. 24. 22 other *i.* of the oxen
1 K. 19. 21 boiled flesh with *i.* of
1 Chr. 9. 29 oversee vessels and *i.*
12. 33 expect in war with all *i.*
2 Chr. 4. 16 fleshhooks, and all *i.*
30. 21 singing with loud *i.* unto L.
Neh. 12. 36 with music. *i.* of David
Ps. 7. 13 prepared for him the *i.*
68. 25 players on *i.* followed
Isa. 32. 7 *i.*, also ot the churl are evil
Ezek. 40. 42 they laid *i.* wherewith
Dan. 6. 18 nei. were *i.* of m. brou.
Am. 6. 5 invent . . *i.* of music like D.
Hab. 3. 19 to . . singer on string. *i.*
Rom. 6. 13 *i.* of unrighteousness
R. V. Gen. 49. 5 ; Isa. 54. 16 wea-
pon ; Ex. 25. 9 ; Num. 3. 8 ; 7. 1 ;
2 Sam. 24. 22 furniture ; Num. 4.
12 ; 31. 6 ; 1 Chr. 9. 20 ; 28. 14 ; 2
Chr. 4. 16 ; 5. 1 vessels ; Ps. 68.
25 minstrels ; 87. 7 that dance ;
33. 2 ; 144. 9 ——

Insurrection. *Uprising, tumult.*
Ez. 4. 19 city hath made *i.* against
Ps. 64. 2 from *i.* of the workers of in.
Mark 15. 7 commit. murder in *i.*
Acts 18. 12 Jews made *i.* against
R. V. Ps. 64. 2 tumult, Acts 18. 12
rose up

Integrity. *Uprightness.*
Gen. 20. 5 in *i.* of my heart have I
1 K. 9. 14 in *i.* of h., and upright.
Job 2. 3 still he holdeth fast his *i.*
Ps. 7. 8 according to mine *i.* in me
25. 21 let *i.* and upright. preserve
Prov. 19. 1 better .. poor that .. in. *i.*
11. 3 *i.* of upright shall guide them

Intelligence. R. V. *regard unto.*
Dan. 11. 30 *i.* with them that for.

Intend. *Think, purpose.*
Ex. 2. 14 *i.* thou to kill me, as thou
Josh. 22. 33 Is. did not *i.* to go up
2 Chr. 28. 13 ye *i.* to add .. sins
Ps. 21. 11 they *i.* evil against thee
Luke 14. 28 which . . *i.* to build
Acts 5. 28 *i.* to bring . . man's blood
5. 35 take heed .. what ye *i.* to do
R. V. Ex. 2. 14 thinkest ; 2 Chr.
28. 13 —— ; Josh. 22. 33 spake

Luke 14. 28 desiring; Acts 5. 35 are about.
Intent. *Intention, purpose.*
2 Sam. 17. 14 to *i.* that Lord might
Jer. 30. 24 perfor. *i.* of his heart
Ezek. 40. 4 *i.* that I might show
Dan. 4. 17 to the *i.* that living
John 11. 15 to *i.* ye may believe
13. 28 for what *i.* he spake this unto
Acts 9. 21 came hither for that *i.*
1 Cor. 10. 6 *i.* we should not lust
Eph. 3. 10 to the *i.* that now unto
Heb. 4. 12 a discerner of the . . *i.*
R. V. 2 Chr. 16. 1 —
Intercession. *Meeting, coming between, mediation.*
Isa. 53. 12 made *i.* for transgressor
Jer. 7. 16 neither make *i.* to me
27. 18 now make *i.* to the Lord
36. 25 made *i.* to king that he wo.
Rom. 8. 26 the Spirit itself make. *i.*
8. 27 because he maketh *i.* for
8. 34 C . . . who also maketh *i.*
1 Tim. 2. 1 . . be made for all men
Heb. 7. 25 ever liveth to make *i.*
R. V. Rom. 11. 2 pleadeth with
Intercessor. *Who causes to meet.*
Isa. 59. 16 wond. there was no *i.*
Intermeddle. *Mix self with.*
Prov. 14. 10 stranger doth not *i.*
18. 1 seeketh and *i.* with wisdom
R. V. Prov. 18. 1 rageth against
Intermission. *Cessation.*
Lam. 3. 49 ceaseth not, without *i.*
Interpret. *Unfold, explain.*
Gen. 40. 22 as Jos had *i.* to them
41. 8, 12, 13, 15
Ez. 4. 7 written . . and *i.* in Syrian
Dan. 5. 12 *i.* of dreams and showing
Mat. 1. 23 Emman., . . *i.*, is God with
Mark 15. 22 Golgotha, *i.*, pl. of sk.
John 1. 38 to say, (being *i.*, Master)
Acts 4. 36 Barnabas (*i.*) son of con.
1 Cor. 12 30 with tongues? do all *i*?
14. 5 except he *i.*,... the church
R. V. Ez. 4. 7 set forth
Interpretation. *Explanation, unfolding.*
Gen. 40. 5 each . . accord. to the *i.*
40. 8, 12, 16; 41. 11
Judg. 7. 15 heard the. . dream, and *i.*
Prov. 1. 6 underst. proverb, and *i.*
Eccl. 8. 1 who knoweth *i.* of thing
Dan. 2. 4 dream, we will show *i.*
2. 5-45; 4. 6-24; 5. 7-26
John 1. 42 Cephas, by *i.*, a stone
Act 9. 36 Tabitha, by *i.*, . . Dorcas
13. 8 sorcerer, so his name by *i.*
1 Cor. 12. 10 another *i.* of tongues
Heb. 7. 2 being by *i.* K. of right.
2 Pet. 1. 20 no proph. is of priv. *i.*
R. V. 1. 6 a figure
Interpreter. *Who interprets.*
Gen. 40. 8 dream, and is no *i.* of it
Job 33. 23 an *i.*, one among thous.
1 Cor. 14. 28 if there be no *i.*, let
Into. *To and in. inside of.*
Gen. 6. 18 shalt come *i.* the ark
Mat. 2. 11 were come *i.* the house
Etc., etc.
Intreat or **Entreat.** *Beseech, pray, implore, ask, crave, exhort.*
Gen. 25. 21 the Lord was *i.* of him
Ex. 8. 30 Moses went out . . and *i.*
Judg. 13. 8 then Manoah *i.* the L.
Ruth 1. 16 *i.* me not to leave thee
1 Sam. 2. 25 who shall *i.* for him?
2 Sam. 21. 14 God was *i.* for land
1 K. 13. 6 *i.* now face of Lord God
1 Chr. 5. 20 God, he was *i.* of them
2 Chr. 33. 19 how G. was *i.* of him
Ez. 8. 23 God . . and he was *i.* of us
Job 19. 16 *i.* him with my mouth
Ps. 45. 12 rich among peo. shall *i.*
Prov. 19. 6 many will *i.* favor of pr.
Isa. 19. 22 Lord shall be *i.* of them
Jer. 15. 11 will cause enemy to *e.*
Luke 15. 28 came his father, and *i.*
1 Cor. 4. 13 being defamed, we *i.*
Phil. 4. 3 I *i.* thee . . yokefellow
1 Tim. 5. 1 rebuke not elder, but *i.*
Heb. 12. 19 they that heard *i.* that
Jas. 3. 17 easy to be *i.*, full of mercy
R. V. Job 19. 17 my supplication;
Phil. 4. 3 beseech; 1 Tim. 5. 1
exhort

Intreaty. *Supplication, entreaty.*
Prov. 18. 23 poor useth *i.*, but rich
2 Cor. 8. 4 praying . . with much *i.*
Intrude. R. V. *dwelling in the.*
Col. 2. 18 *i.* into those things which
Invade. *Strip, plunder, raid.*
1 Sam. 23. 27 Philis. have *i.* land
27. 8 David *i.* Geshurites, and the
2 Chr. 28. 18 Philist. had *i.* cities
Cut, assault.
Hab. 3. 16 he will *i.* them with his
Enter into, raid.
2 K. 13. 20 the Moabites *i.* the land
2 Chr. 20. 10 would not let Israel *i.*
R. V. 1 Sam. 23. 27; 27. 8; 30. 1
made a raid upon
Invasion. R. V. *raid.*
1 Sam. 30. 14 we made *i.* on south
Invent. R. V. *devise.*
Am. 6. 5 *i.* . . instruments of musick
Invented. *Devised, designed.*
2 Chr. 26. 15 engines *i.* by cun. m.
Inventions. *Doings, deeds.*
Ps. 99. 8 took vengeance of . . *i.*
106. 29 provoked . . with their *i.*
106. 39 whoring with their . . *i.*
Devices, designs.
Prov. 8. 12 find out knowl. . . witty *i.*
Eccl. 7. 29 have sought out many *i.*
R. V. Ps. 99. 8 ; 106. 29, 39 doings ;
Prov. 8. 12 and discretion.
Inventor. *Who finds out.*
Rom. 1. 30 *i.* of evil things, disob.
Invisible. *Unseen.*
Rom. 1. 20 the *i.* thing of him from
Col. 1. 15 who is image of the *i.* God
1. 16 vis. and *i.* whether . . thrones
1 Tim. 1. 17 unto K. eter., immor., *i.*
Heb. 11. 27 seeing him who is *i.*
Invite. *Call.*
1 Sam. 9. 24 I have *i.* the people
2 Sam. 13. 23 Absalom *i.* king's sons
Esth. 5. 12 to morrow and I *i.* unto
Inward. *Within, inner, toward inside, secret.*
Ex. 28. 26 in the side of the ephod *i.*
Lev. 13. 55 burn it . . it is fret *i.*
2 Sam. 5. 9 built wall from Millo *i.*
1 K. 7. 25 oxen . . hinder parts *i.*
2 Chr. 3. 13 stood . . their faces *i.*
Job. 19. 19 *i.* friends abhorred me
38. 36 hath put wisdom in *i.* parts
Ps. 51. 6 desirest truth in *i.* parts
Prov. 20. 27 searching all *i.* parts
Isa. 16. 11 and mine *i.* parts for Kir.
Jer. 31. 33 put law in their *i.* parts
Ezek. 40. 16 windows . . about *i.*
Luke 11. 39 *i.* part full of ravening
2 Cor. 4. 16 *i.* man is renewed day by
7. 15 *i.* affec. is more abundant
Inwards. *Middle parts, entrails.*
Ex. 29. 13 fat that covereth *i.* parts
Lev. 1. 9 his *i.* and his legs sh. wash
3. 3; 4. 8; 7. 3; 8. 16; 9. 14
Ps. 64, 6 *i.* . . of ev. one . . and heart
Inwardly. *within, inner part.*
Ps. 62. 4 with mou., but they curse *i.*
Mat. 7. 15 . . ravening wolves
Rom. 2. 29 Jew, which is one *i.*
Iron. *Iron.*
Gen. 4. 22 instructor of artif. in *i.*
Lev. 26. 19 make your heav. as *i.*
Num. 31. 22 only brass, *i.*, tin, lead
35. 16 smite with instrument of *i.*
Deut. 3. 11 his bedstead was of *i.*
4. 20; 8. 9; 27. 5; 28. 23; 33. 25
Josh. 6. 19 vessels of brass and *i.*
17. 16 Canaanites have char. of *i*
Judg. 1. 19 bec. had chariots of *i.*
1 Sam. 17. 7 six hun. shekels of *i.*
2 Sam. 12. 31 under harrows of *i.*
1 K. 6. 7 nor tool of *i.* heard in
2 K. 6. 6 thither, and the *i.* did swim
1 Ch. 2. 3 saws and harrows of *i.*
2 Chr. 2. 7 in silver, in brass, in *i.*
Job. 19. 24 were graven with *i.* pen
20. 24 flee from *i.* wea. and bow of
Ps. 2. 9 Thou sh. break with rod of *i.*
Prov. 27. 17 *i.* sharpeneth *i.* so man
Eccl. 10. 10 if *i.* be bl., and he do not
Isa. 10. 34 cut down thickets with *i.*
48. 4 thy neck is an *i.* sinew
Jer. 17. 1 written with pen of *i.* and
Ezek. 4. 3 set wall of *i.* between th.
Dan. 2. 33 His legs of *i.* feet part *i*
2. 34-45 ; 4. 15; 5. 4; 7. 7

Am. 1. 3 threshing instrument of *i.*
Mic. 4. 13 will make thine horn of *i.*
Acts 12. 10 they came unto *i.* gate
Rev. 2. 27 rule them with rod of *i.*
9. 9; 12. 5; 18. 12; 19. 15
Irons. *Weapon, dart.*
Job. 41. 7 canst fill skin with . . *i.*
Is. *Be.*
Gen. 28. 16 Lord *i.* in this place
Mark 7. 11 Corban, that *i.* to say
Etc. etc.
Island, Isle. *Isle, sea-coast.*
Gen. 10. 5 were *i.* of Gentiles div.
Esth. 10. 1 land . . and *i.* of sea
Job 22. 30 delivered *i.* of innocent
Ps. 72. 10 kings of Tarsh. and *i.*
Isa. 11. 11 Hamath, and *i.* of sea
23. 6 howl, ye inhab. of the *i.*
Jer. 2. 10 pass over *i.* of Chittim
Dan. 11. 18 shall return . . unto *i.*
Zeph. 2. 11 his place . . all the *i.*
Acts 27. 16 running under cert. *i.*
Rev. 1. 9 was in isle called Patmos
R. V. Isa. 13.22; 34. 14; Jer. 50.
39 —— ; Isa 20. 6 coast-land
Issue. (n). *A flow, or flowing*
Lev. 12. 7 cleansed from *i.* of blood
15. 2-30 bec. of his *i.* he is unclea.
Num. 5. 2 every one that hath *i.*
2 Sam. 3. 29 one that hath an *i.*, or
Ezek. 23. 20 *i.* is like *i* of horses
Running.
Mat. 9. 20 diseased with *i.* of blood
Mark 5. 25 woman which had an *i.*
Luke 8. 44 immed. her *i.* stanched
Birth, produce, seed.
Gen. 48. 6 *i.*, which thou begettest
Mat. 22. 25 having no *i.*, left wife
Outgoing, outcome.
Ps. 68. 20 for God belong the *i.*
Prov. 4. 23 out of it are *i.* of life
Isa. 22. 24 offspring and *i.* of all
R. V. Lev. 12. 7 fountain ; Mat.
22. 23 seed
Issue (v,). *Go forth.*
Josh. 8. 22 other *i.* out of city agai.
2 K. 20. 18 of thy sons that shall *i.*
Job 38. 8 as if it had *i.* out of womb
Isa. 39. 7 of sons that *i.* from thee
Ezek. 47. 1 waters *i.* out from und.
Dan. 7. 10 fiery stream *i.* forth bef.
Rev. 9. 17 mouths *i.* fire and smoke
R. V. Josh. 8. 22 came forth; Rev.
9. 17, 18 proceedeth
It. *Thing.*
Gen. 3. 6 *i.* was pleasant to eyes
Mat. 12. 11 if *i.* fall into pit on sab.
Etc, etc.
Itch. *Heat, itch.*
Deut. 28. 27 scab, and with the *t.*
Itching. *To itch.*
2 Tim. 4. 3 teachers having *i.* ears
Itself. *Its self.*
Ps. 68. 8 Sinai *i.*, in presence of
Mat. 12. 25 king. divided against *i.*
Etc., etc.
Ivory. *Tooth, ivory.*
1 K. 10. 18 king made throne of *i.*
2 Chr. 9. 17 made great throne of *i.*
9. 21 bringing gold, silver, *i.*, apes
Ps. 45. 8 out of *i.* palaces, whereby
S. of S. 5. 14 *i.* overlaid with sapph.
7. 4 Thy neck is as a tower of *i.*
Ezek. 27. 6 made thy benches of *i.*
27. 15 for a present horns of *i.*
Am. 3. 15 houses of *i.* shall perish
6. 4 lie upon b. of *i.*, and stretch
Rev. 18. 12 buy vessels of *i.*, and all

J.

Jacinth. R. V. *hyacinth.*
Rev. 9. 17 breastplates of fire, and *j.*
21. 20 prec. stones, the eleventh, a *j*
Jailor. *Prison guard, jailor.*
Acts 16. 23 charging the *j.* to keep
Jangling. R. V. *talking.*
1 Tim. 1. 6 some . . turned to vain *j.*
Jasper. *Jasper.*
Ex. 28. 20 fourth row, . . onyx, and *j.*
Ezek. 28. 13 *j.*, sapphire, emerald
Rev. 4. 3 was to look upon like *j.*
21. 11, 18, 19
Javelin. R. V. *spear.*
Num. 25. 7 Phin. . . use . . and took *j.*
1 Sam. 18. 10 was *j.* in Saul's hand
18. 11; 19. 9, 10; 20. 33

Jaw. *Cheek bone, jaw.*
Judg. 15. 15 found *j*. bone of ass
  15. 16, 17, 19
Job 29. 17 I brake *j*. of the wicked
  41. 2 canst bore *j*. with a thorn?
Ps. 22. 15 my tongue cleaveth to *j*.
Prov. 30. 14 their *j*. teeth as knives
Isa. 30. 28 be a bridle in *j*. of people
Ezek. 29. 4 will put hooks in thy *j*.
Hos 11. 4 take off yoke on their *j*.
R. V. Judg. 15. 16 jawbone; 15. 19
  Lehi

Jealous. *Zealous, jealous.*
Ex. 20. 5 Lord thy God am *j*. God
  34. 14 Lord, whose name is J., is
Num. 5. 14 he be *j*. of his wife
Deut. 4. 24 consuming fire . . *j*. God
  5. 9; 6. 15
Josh. 24. 19 is *j*. God; he will forg.
1 K. 19. 10 I have been *j*. for Lord
Ezek. 39. 25 *j*. for my holy name
Joel 2. 18 then will Lord be *j*. for
Nah. 1. 2 G. is *j*., and L. revengeth
Zech. 1. 14 I am *j*. for Jerusalem
  8. 2 I was *j*. for Zion . . I was *j*.
2 Cor. 11. 2 I am *j*. over you with

Jealousy. *Zeal, jealousy.*
Num. 5. 14 sp. of *j*. came upon him
  5. 15 for it is an offering of *j*.
  5. 18, 25, 29, 30; 25. 11
Deut. 29. 20 his *j*. shall smoke ag.
  32. 16, 21 provoked him to *j*. with
1 K. 14. 22 they provoked him to *j*
Ps. 79. 5 how long . . thy *j*. burn
Prov. 6. 34 *j*. is the rage of a man
S. of S. 8. 6 *j*. is cruel as the grave
Isa. 42. 13 he shall stir *j*. like man of
Ezek. 8. 3 seat of the image of *j*.
  16. 38 will give thee blood in . . *j*.
  16. 42; 23. 25; 36. 5, 6; 38. 19
Zeph. 1. 18 devoured by fire of his *j*.
Zech. 1. 14 jealous for Z. with gr. *j*.
Rom. 10. 19 will provoke you to *j*.
1 Cor. 10. 22 do we provoke L. to *j* ?
2 Cor. 11. 2 am jealous with godly *j*.

Jeopard. *Endanger, imperil.*
Judg. 5. 18 *j*. their lives to death

Jeopardy. *Danger, peril.*
2 Sam. 23. 17 men that went in *j*.
1 Chr. 11. 19 put their lives in *j*.
Luke 8. 23 filled . . and were in *j*.
1 Cor. 15. 30 why stand we in *j*.

Jesting. *Pleasantry.*
Eph. 5. 4 *j*., which is not convenient

Jewel. *Vessel, instrument.*
Gen. 24. 53 *j*. of sil., and *j*. of gold
Ex. 35. 22 brought . . tablets, all *j*. of
Num. 31. 50 *j*. of gold, chains, br.
1 Sam. 6. 8 put the *j*. of gold, which
2 Chr. 20. 25 *j*., they stripped off
  32. 27 treasuries . . for pleasant *j*.
Job 28. 17 exchange . . not be for *j*.
Prov. 20. 15 lips of knowl. are prec. *j*
Isa. 61. 10 as bride adorn . . with *j*.
Ezek. 16. 17 hast taken thy fair *j*.
  16. 39; 23. 26
Treasure, property.
Mal. 3. 17 th. day wh. I make up my *j*
Earrings, nose rings.
Prov 11. 22 as *j*. . . in swine's snout
Isa. 3. 21 take the rings, and nose *j*.
Ezek. 16. 12 I put *j*. on thy forehead
Ornament.
S. of S. 7. 1 joints of thighs like *j*.
Hos. 2. 13 she decked herself with *j*.
R. V. 2 Chr. 32. 27 vessels; S. of S.
  1. 10 hair; Ezek. 16. 12 ring

Join. *Unite, connect, combine,
couple, be adjacent to.*
Ex. 1. 10 they *j*. also unto our ene.
Num. 25. 3 Is. *j*. himself to Baal.
1 Sam. 4. 2 *j*. battle, Is. was smit.
2 Chr. 20. 35 *j*. himself with Ahaziah
Ez. 4. 12 walls, and *j*. foundations
  9. 14 and *j*. in affinity with people
Esth. 9. 27 all such as *j*. . . unto
Ps. 106. 28 *j*. thems. unto Baal-peor
Eccl. 9. 4 is *j*. to all living, is hope
Isa. 5. 8 Woe . . that *j*. house to h.
Jer. 50. 5 let us *j*. oursel. to the L.
Ezek. 37. 17 *j*. them one to another
Dan. 11. 6 shall *j*. thems. together
Mat. 19. 6 what . . G. hath *j*. together
  Mark 10. 6
Luke 15. 15 *j*. himself to citizen of
Acts 5. 13 durst no man *j*. himself

---

  8. 29 *j*. thyself to this chariot
  18. 7 house *j*. hard to synagogue
1 Cor. 1. 10 ye 6e perf. *j*. together
R. V. Ez. 4. 12 repaired; Isa. 9. 11
  stir up

Joined. *United, coupled.*
Gen. 14. 3 these were *j*. together
  29. 34 will . . husband be *j*. unto me
Ex. 28. 7 shoulder pieces thereof *j*.
Num. 18. 2 may be *j*. unto thee, and
  25. 5 that were *j*. unto Baal-peor
1 K. 20. 29 day the battle was *j*.
Neh. 4. 6 all wall was *j*. together
Job 3. 6 let it not be *j*. unto days
  41. 23 flakes of his flesh *j*. together
Ps. 83. 8 Assur also is *j*. with them
Eccl. 9. 4 for to him that is *j*. to all
Isa. 13. 15 every . . *j* . . shall fall by
Ezek. 1. 9 wings . . *j*. to one another
  46. 22 courts *j*. of forty cubits long
Hos. 4. 17 Ephraim is *j*. to idols
Zech. 2. 11 many nations be *j*. to L.
1 Cor. 6. 16 he which is *j*. to harlot
  6. 17 he that is *j*. unto Lord in sp.
Eph. 4. 16 whole body fitly *j*. tog.
  5. 31 sh. a man . . be *j*. unto his wife
R. V. Gen. 14. 8 set in array; Ez.
  4. 12 repaired; Job 3. 6 rejoice;
  Ezek. 46. 22 inclosed; 1 Cor. 1. 10
  perfected; Eph. 4. 16 framed; 5.
  31 cleave to

Joining. *Cleaving, coupling.*
1 Chr. 22. 3 prepared nails . . for *j*.
2 Chr. 3. 12 *j*. to wing of oth. cher.
R. V. 1 Chr. 22. 3 couplings

Joint. *Joining, coupling, fitting.*
Gen. 32. 25 Jacob's th. was out of *j*.
1 K. 22. 34 smote . . bet. *j*. of harness
  2 Chr. 18. 33
Ps. 22. 14 all my bones are out of *j*.
Prov. 25. 19 like . . a foot out of *j*.
S. of S. 7. 1 *j*. of thy th. like jewels
Dan. 5. 6 *j*. of his loins were loosed
Eph. 4. 16 that which ev. *j*. suppl.
Col. 2. 19 all body by *j*. and bands
Heb. 4. 12 asunder . . of *j*. and mar.
United with, sharing.
Rom. 8. 17 and *j*. heirs with Christ
R. V. Gen. 32. 25 strained

Jot. *Iota, i.*
The smallest letter in Gr. and Heb.
  alphabets.
Mat. 5. 18 *j*. or tit . . . no wise pass

Journey. *Way, travel, trip, passage, tour, pilgrimage.*
Gen. 13. 3 went on his *j*. from south
  24. 21 Lord had made his *j*. prosp.
  33. 12 Let us take our *j*., and . . go
Ex. 13. 20 th. took *j*. from Succoth
  40. 36 Israel went onward in all *j*.
Num. 9. 10 or be in a *j*. afar off, yet
  10. 6 blow an alarm for their *j*.
Deut. 1. 7 turn, and take your *j*.
Josh. 9. 11 take victuals . . for the *j*.
Judg. 4. 9 *j*. . . not be for thine hon.
1 Sam. 15. 18 Lord sent thee on *j*.
2 Sam. 11. 10 came. thou not from *j*.
1 K. 18. 27 or he is in a *j*. . . or sleep.
2 K. 3. 9 compass of seven days' *j*.
Neh. 2. 6 for how long thy *j*. be?
Prov. 7. 19 good man . . gone long *j*.
Jonah 3. 3 a city or three days' *j*.
Mat. 10. 10 nor scrip for . . *j*., nei.
  25. 15 and straightway took his *j*.
Mark 6. 8 should take noth. for . . *j*.
  13. 34 is as a man taking a far *j*.
Luke 2. 44 went a days' *j*., and
  15. 13 son took *j*. into far country
Acts 1. 12 from Jer. sab. day's *j*.
  10. 9 as they went on their *j*. and
  22. 6 th. as I m. my *j*., and was co.
Rom. 1. 10 might have prosper. *j*.
  15. 24 Wh. I take my *j*. into Spain
3 John 6 bring forward on their *j*.
R. V. Num. 33. 12; Deut. 10. 6
  journeyed; Mark 13. 34 sojourning in another country; Rom.
  1. 10 ——

Journeyed. *Travailed, moved,
passed.*
Gen. 11. 2 as they *j*. from the east
  12. 9; 13. 11; 20. 1; 33. 17; 35. 5
Ex. 12. 37 chil. of Israel *j*. from R.
  17. 1 Israel *j*. from wilderness
Num. 9. 17 after that chil. of Is. *j*.
  9. 18–23; 10. 29; 11. 35; 12. 15

Deut. 10. 7 thence they *j*. unto G.
Josh. 9. 17 chil. of Is. *j*., and came
Judg. 17. 8 to h. of Micah. as he *j*.
Luke 10. 33 Samar., as he *j*., came
Acts 9. 3 as he *j*., came near Dam.
  26. 13 and them which *j*. with me

Journeying. *Travelling, passing.*
Num. 10. 2 and for *j*. of the camps
Luke 13. 22 teaching, and *j*. tow. J.
2 Cor. 11. 26 in *j*. often, in perils

Joy (n.). *Rejoicing, gladness, delight.*
1 Sam. 18. 6 to meet Saul . . with *j*.
1 K. 1. 40 rejoiced with great *j*.
1 Chr. 12. 40 for there was *j*. in Is.
2 Chr. 30. 26 was great *j*. in Jerusa.
Ez. 3. 12 wept, many shouted for *j*.
Neh. 12. 43 *j*. of Jerus. was heard f.
Esth. 8. 17 Jews had *j*. and gladness
Job 20. 5 *j*. of hypoc. but for mom.
Ps. 16. 11 thy pres. is fulness of *j*.
  48. 2 *j*. of the whole earth is Zion
  51. 8 make me to hear *j*. and glad.
Prov. 12. 20 to couns. of peace is *j*.
  17. 21 father of fool hath no *j*.
  23. 24 beget. wise child have *j*.
Eccl. 2. 26 G. giv. man kn. and *j*.
  9. 7 go . . eat thy bread with *j*.
Isa. 29. 19 meek shall increase . . *j*.
Jer. 15. 16 thy word was unto me *j*.
  31. 13 turn their mourning to *j*.
Lam. 5. 15 *j*. of our hearts ceased
Ezek. 24. 25 *j*. of their glory, desire
Hos. 9. 1 rejoice not, O Is. for *j*.
Joel 1. 16 *j*. . . . from house of God
Zeph. 3. 17 rejoice over thee with *j*.
Zech. 8. 19 be to Judah *j*. and glad.
Mat. 2. 10 rejoiced with . . great *j*.
  13. 44 for *j*. goeth and selleth all
  25. 21 enter into *j*. of thy Lord
Luke 1. 44 babe leap. in w. for *j*.
  15. 7 *j*. shall be in heaven over
John 3. 29 this my *j*. is fulfilled
  16. 24 ask, that your *j*. may be full
Acts 8 was great *j*. in that city
  13. 52 disciples were filled with *j*.
Rom. 14. 17 peace and *j*. in Holy G.
2 Cor. 1. 24 are helpers of your *j*.
Gal. 5. 22. fr. of sp. is love, *j*., peace
Phil. 1. 4 making request with *j*.
1 Thes. 1. 6 with *j*. of Holy Ghost
  2. 19 what is our hope or *j*. or cro.
  2. 20 For ye are our glory and *j*.
2 Tim. 1. 4 that I be filled with *j*.
Phile. 7 ye have gr. *j*. and consol.
Jas. 1. 2 brethren, count it all *j*.
1 Pet. 1. 8 ye rejoice with *j*. unspeak.
1 John 1. 4 that your *j*. may be full
  2. John 12 that our *j*. may be full
3 John 4 I have no greater *j*. than
R. V. Job 41. 22 terror danceth;
  Jer. 48. 27 the head; Acts 2. 28
  gladness.

Joy (v.). *Leap, rejoice, be glad.*
Ps. 21. 1 k. shall *j*. in thy strength
Isa. 9. 3 they *j*. before thee accord.
  65. 19 and I will *j*. in my people
Hab. 3. 18 will *j*. in G. of my sal.
Zeph. 3. 17 L., he will *j*. over thee
Rom. 5. 11 but we also *j*. in God
2 Cor. 7. 13 the more *j*. we for the
Phil. 2. 17 I *j*. and rejoice with
Col. 2. 5 *j*. and beholding our or.
1 Thes. 3. 9 we *j*. for your sakes
R. V. Rom. 5. 11 rejoice

Joyful. *Full of joy.*
1 K. 8. 66 went unto their tents *j*.
Ez. 6. 22 Lord had made them *j*.
Esth. 5. 9 went Haman forth *j*.
Job 3. 7 let no *j*. voice come therein
Ps. 35. 9 my soul be *j*. in the Lord
  66. 1 make *j*. noise unto God, all
  81. 1; 95. 1; 98. 4; 100. 1
Eccl. 7. 14 in . . prosperity be *j*.
Isa. 49. 13 Sing. O heav.; be *j*., O e.
2 Cor. 7. 4 I am exceeding *j*. in
R. V. Ps. 96. 12; 149. 5 exult;
  98. 8 sing for

Joyfully. *With joy.*
Eccl. 9. 9 live *j*. with the wife wh.
Luke 19. 6 and he received him *j*.
Heb. 19. 34 took *j*. spoil. of goods

Joyfulness. *Rejoicing, gladness*
Deut. 28. 47 servedst not G. with *j*

Col. 1. 11 and long suffering with *j*.
R. V. Col. 1. 11 joy
Joyous. *Rejoicing, exulting.*
Isa. 22. 2 tumultuous, *j*. city ; thy
23. 7 is this your *j*. city whose
32. 13 the houses of joy in *j*. city
Jubilee. *Time of shouting.*
Lev. 25. 10 it shall be *j*. unto you
25. 11–54 ; 27. 17–24
Num. 36. 4 when *j*. of chil. of Is.
Judge (*n*.). *Discerner. sifter, magistrate, judge.*
Gen. 18. 25 shall not *j*. of all earth
Ex. 2. 14 who made thee pr. and *j*.
21. 22 shall pay as *j*. determine
Num. 25. 5 Mos. said unto *j*. of Is.
Deut. 1. 16 I charg. your *j*. at time
Josh. 8. 33 Israel .. and their *j*. st.
Judg. 2. 16 L. raised up *j*., which
11. 27 L. the Judge be *j*. this day
Ruth 1. 1 pass in days when *j*. rule
1 Sam. 8. 1 made sons *j*. over Is.
2 Sam. 15. 4 O that I were made *j*.
2 K. 23. 22 from the days of *j*. that
1 Chr. 23. 4 six thous. were off. and *j*.
2 Chr. 19. 5 he set *j*. in the land
Ez. 10. 14 elders of ev. city, and *j*.
Job 9. 15 would make sup. to my *j*.
12. 17 and maketh the *j*. fools
Ps. 2. 10 be instructed .. *j*. of earth
75. 7 God is *j*. ; he putteth down
Prov. 8. 16 even all *j*. of the earth
Isa. 1. 26 I will restore thy *j*. as at
33. 22 Lord is our *j*., Lord is our
Dan. 9. 12 spake . . against our *j*.
Hos. 7. 7 have devoured their *j*.
Am. 2. 3 I will cut off the *j*. from
Mic. 5. 1 they shall smite *j*. of Israel
Zeph. 3. 3 her *j*. are evening wolves
Mat. 5. 25 deliver thee to *j*., and
Luke 12. 58 we hale thee to the *j*.
18. 6 Hear what the unjust *j*. saith
Acts 10. 42 J. of quick and dead
24. 10 hast been many years *j*.
2 Tim. 4. 8 Lord, the righteous *j*,
Heb. 12. 23 to God the *J*. of all
Jas. 2. 4 bec. *j*. of evil thoughts?
R. V. 1 Sam. 2. 25 God ; Job 9. 15 mine adversary ;
Judge. (*v*.). *Discern, sift, decide.*
Gen. 16. 5 L. *j*. betw. me and thee
49. 16 Dan shall *j*. his people
Ex. 5. 21 L. look upon you, and *j*.
18. 13 Moses sat to *j*. the people
Lev. 19. 15 in right. shalt thou *j*.
Num. 35. 24 congrega. shall *j*. bet.
Deut. 1. 16 *j*. right. bet. every man
Judg. 3. 10 and he *j*. Israel, and
4. 4 ; 10. 2 ; 11. 27 ; 12. 7 ; 15. 20
1 Sam. 3. 13 that I will *j*. his house
4. 18 ; 7. 6 ; 8. 5 ; 24. 12
1 K. 3. 9 und. heart to *j*. thy people,
2 K. 15. 5 *j*. the people of the land
1 Chr. 16. 33 because he cometh to *j*.
2 Chr. 1. 10 for who can *j*. this peo.
Job 22. 13 can he *j*. through dark
Ps. 7. 11 God *j*. the righteous, and
43. 1 *J*. me, O God, and plead my
Prov. 29. 14 king that faithfully *j*.
Eccl. 3. 17 God shall *j*. righteous
Isa. 1. 17 *j*. fatherless, plead for w.
Jer. 11. 20 L. of hosts, that *j*. right.
Lam. 3. 59 O Lord . . *j*. my cause
Ezek. 7. 3, 8 *j*. thee accor. to thy w.
Dan. 9. 12 spake. . against *j*. that *j*.
Joel. 3. 12 will I sit to *j*. all heathen
Obad. 21 come up on Z. to *j*. moun.
Mic. 3. 11 The heads *j*. for reward
Zech. 3. 7 shalt also *j*. my house
Mat. 7. 1 *J*. not, that ye be not *j*.
7. 2 what judgment ye *j*, ye be *j*.
Luke 7. 43 said, Thou hast *j*. right.
19. 22 out of . . mouth will I *j*.
John 5. 22 for the Father *j*. no man
8. 15 Ye *j*. after the flesh ; I *j*. no m.
12. 47 I came not to *j*. the world
Acts 7. 7 nat. . . will I *j*., said God
Rom. 2. 1 wherein thou *j*. another
14. 13 let us not *j*. one another
1 Cor. 4. 5 *j*. nothing before time
11. 32 when *j*., we are chastened
2 Cor. 5. 14 we thus *j*.. that if one
Col. 2. 16 let no man *j*. you in meat
2 Tim. 4. 1 shall *j*. quick and dead
Heb. 10. 30 L. shall *j*. his people
Jas. 2. 12 be *j*. by the law of liberty

1 Pet. 1. 17 *j*. accord. to every man
Rev. 6. 10 dost thou not *j*. .. blood
R. V. 1 Sam. 24. 15 give sentence ;
Jer. 5, 28 plead ; Ezek. 28. 23 fall ;
1 Cor. 6. 5 decide ; 11. 31 ; 14. 29 discern ; Heb. 11. 11 counted ;
Acts 24. 6 ; Jas. 4. 12 ——.
Judgment. *Act* (of judging). *faculty* (of judging), *decision, visitation.*
Gen. 18. 19 shall . . do justice and *f*.
Ex. 21. 1 these are thee *j*. thou shalt
Lev. 18. 4 Ye shall do my *j*. and
26. 46 these are the statutes and *f*.
Num. 27. 21 after the *j*. of Urim
Deut. 1. 17 not respect persons in *j*.
16. 19 thou shalt not wrest *j*., thou
27. 19 cursed be he that pervert. *j*.
Josh. 20. 6 stand bef. congre. for *j*.
Judg. 4. 5 Is. came up to her for *j*.
1 Sam. 8. 3 took bribes, and perv. *j*.
2 Sam. 8. 15 David executed *j*. and
1 K. 2. 3 his commandments and *j*.
7. 7 Sol. made porch . . porch of j.
2 K. 25. 6 they gave *j*. upon him
1 Chr. 6. 12 wonders, and *j*. of his
2 Chr. 9. 8 made the king, to do *j*.
Ez. 7. 10 to teach in Is. stat. and *j*.
Neh. 1. 7 nor stat., nor *j*, which
Job 7. 3 doth God pervert *j*. ? or doth
34. 5 God hath taken away my j.
Ps. 1. 5 ungodly .. not stand in *j*.
19. 9 The *j*. of the Lord are true
25. 9 The meek will he guide in *j*.
89. 4 justice and *j*. are habitations
101. 1 I will sing of mercy and *j*.
146. 7 executeth *j*. for the oppres.
Prov. 2. 8 he keepeth the paths of *j*.
19. 28 ungodly witness scorneth *j*.
28. 5 evil men understand not *j*.
Eccl. 8. 6 to ev. purpose there is *j*.
Isa. 1. 17 learn to do well ; seek *j*.
28. 17 *j*. also will I lay to the line
61. 8 Lord love *j*. ; I hate robbery
Jer. 4. 2 Lord liveth in truth, in *j*.
10. 24 L., correct me, but with *j*.
Ezek. 5. 6 changed my *j*. into wick
Dan. 9. 5 from thy precepts and *j*.
Hos. 2. 19 betroth thee .. and in *j*.
Am. 5. 7 who turn *j*. to wormwood
Mic. 3. 8 I am full of *j*. and might
Hab. 1. 4 *j*. never go forth . . wrong
Zeph. 3. 15 Lord hath taken . . thy *j*.
Zech. 7. 9 ex. true *j*., and show mer.
Mal. 2. 17 where is the God of *j*. ?
Mat. 5. 21 shall be in danger of *j*.
7. 2 *j*. ye judge, ye shall be *j*.
Mark 6. 11 more tol. . . in day of *j*.
Luke 11. 42 pass over *j*. and love
John 5. 22 commit all *j*. unto Son
18. 28 then led J . . . unto hall of *j*.
7. 24 but judge righteous *j*.
Acts 24. 25 he reas. of temper. and *j*.
Rom. 14. 10 stand bef. *j*. seat of C.
1 Cor. 1. 10 in same mind and *j*.
2 Cor. 5. 10 must appear bef. *j*. seat
2 Thes. 1. 5 token of the righteous *j*.
1 Tim. 5. 24 sins, going before to *j*.
Heb. 9. 27 to die, but after this the *j*.
Jas. 2. 13 have *j*. without mercy
2 Pet. 2. 4 angels, be reserved unto *j*.
1 John 4. 17 have bold. in day of *j*.
Jude 15 to execute *j*. upon all, and
Rev. 14. 7 hour of his *j*. is come
R. V. Job 29. 14 justice ; Ps. 76. 3 ;
Acts 25. 15 ; 2 Pet 2. 3 sentence ;
Judg. 5. 10 on rich carpets ; Phil.
1. 9 discernment ; Mark 6. 11 ——
Juice. *Juice.*
S. of S. 8. 2 wine of *j*. of pomegr.
Jump. *Skip, dance.*
Nah. 3. 2 horses, and of *j*. chariots
Juniper. *Broom, juniper.*
1 K. 19. 4 sat down under *j*. tree
Job 30. 4 cut . . *j*. roots for meat
Ps. 120. 4 arrows . . with coals of *j*.
R. V. Job 30. 4 broom.
Jurisdiction. *Authority.*
Luke 23. 7 belonged to Herod's *j*.
Just. *Right, straight, upright, righteousness.*
Gen. 6. 9 Noah was a *j*. man, and
Lev. 19. 36 *j*. balances, *j*. weights
Deut. 16. 20 which is *j*. shalt thou
2 Sam. 23. 3 that ruleth . . must be *j*.
Neh. 9. 33 Howbe. thou art *j*. in all

Job 12. 4 *j*. man is laughed to scorn
Ps. 7. 9 estab. *j*. . . for right. God
37. 12 wicked plotteth against *j*.
Prov. 3. 33 blesseth habitations of *j*.
4. 18 path of *j*. is shining light
10. 6 blessings are on head of *j*.
20. 7 *j*. man walketh in integrity
Eccl. 7. 15 *j*. man that perisheth in
Isa. 26. 7 way of *j*. is uprightness
Lam. 4. 13 shed blood of *j*. in midst
Ezek. 18. 9 *j*., he shall surely live
Hos. 14. 9 *j*. shall walk in them
Am. 5. 12 your sins : they afflict the *j*.
Hab. 2. 4 but *j*. shall live by his
Zeph. 3. 5 The *j*. Lord is in midst
Zech. 9. 9 he is *j*. and having salva.
Mat. 1. 19 Joseph . . being a *j*. man
5. 45 sendeth rain on *j*. and unjust
Mark 6. 20 knowing he was *j*. man
Luke 15. 7 over ninety nine *j*. pers.
John 5. 30 my judgment is *j*., bec.
Acts 3. 14 denied Holy One and *j*.
Rom. 1. 17 The *j*. shall live by faith
Gal. 3. 11 The *j*. shall live by faith
Phil. 4. 8 whatsoever things are *j*.
Col. 4. 1. give . . that which is *j*.
Tit. 1. 8 But a lover of good men . . *j*.
Heb. 12. 23 sp. of *j*. men made per.
Jas. 5. 6 ye have . . killed the *j*.
1 Pet. 3. 18 suffered . . , *j*. for unjust
2 Pet. 2. 7 delivered *j*. Lot, vexed
1 John 1. 9 faithful and *j*. to forgive
Rev. 15. 3 *j*. and true are thy ways
R. V. For most part, righteous.
Justice. *Judgment, rightness.*
Gen. 18. 19 to do *j*. and judgment
Deut. 33. 21 he executed *j*. of Lord
2 Sam. 8. 15 *j*. unto all his people
1 K. 10. 9 made the king, to do . . *j*.
1 Chr. 18. 14 ex. . . *j*. among all peo.
2 Chr. 9. 8 king . . to do judg. and *j*.
Job. 8. 3 doth Almighty pervert *j*. ?
Ps. 82. 3 do *j*. to the afflicted and n.
Prov. 1. 3 receive instru. of wisd., *j*
Eccl. 5. 8 violent perverting of . . *j*.
Isa. 59. 14 they ask . . ordinances of *j*.
Jer. 31. 23 L. bless, O habitation of *j*
Ezek. 45. 9 and ex. judgment and *j*.
R. V. Ps. 89. 14, Isa. 9. 7 ; 56. 1 ;
59. 9, 14 righteousness.
Justification. *Setting right.*
Rom. 4. 25 raised again for our *j*.
5. 16 but the free gift is . . unto *j*.
5. 18 gift ca. upon all men unto *j*.
Justified. *Made right.*
Job. 11. 2 should man of talk be *j*.
25. 4 how then can man be *j*.,
Ps. 143. 2 in thy sight no man be *j*.
Isa. 43. 9 that they may be *j*.
R. V. Job 13. 18 am righteous 25. 4 just
Justifier. *Who justifies.*
Rom. 3. 26 *j*. of him which believ.
Justify. *Make right.*
Ex. 23. 7 I will not *j*. the wicked
Deut. 25. 1 they shall *j*. righteous
1 K. 8. 32 *j*. the righteous, to give
2 Chr. 6. 23 and by *j*. the righteous
Job 27. 5 God forbid I sho. *j*. you
Prov. 17. 15 he that *j*. wicked, and he
Isa. 5. 23 which *j*. wick. for reward
Jer. 3. 11 Israel hath *j*. herself more
Ezek. 16. 51 *j*. thy sisters in abom.
Mat. 11. 19 wisdom is *j*. of her chil.
Luke 16. 15 which *j*. yourselves bef.
18. 14 this man went to his house *j*.
Acts 13. 39 all that believe are *j*.
Rom. 2. 13 doers of law shall be *j*.
3. 24 being *j*. freely by grace thro.
5. 1 being *j*. by faith, we have pea.
8. 33 it is God that is *j*.
1 Cor. 4. 4 yet am I not hereby *j*.
Gal. 2. 16 knowing .. man is not *j*.
1 Tim. 3. 16 *j*. in Sp., seen of ang.
Tit. 3. 7 That being *j*. by his grace
Jas. 2. 21 was not Abraham *j*. by w.
R. V. Job 9. 20 ; 3. 18 righteous.
Justle. *Rush to and fro.*
Nah. 2. 4 *j*. one against another
Justly. *Rightly, righteously.*
Mic. 6. 8 do *j*., and love mercy
Luke 23. 41 and we indeed *j*. for we receive
1 Thes. 2. 10 holily *j*. and unblameably
R. V. 1 Thes. 2. 10 righteously

K.

Keep. *Watch, observe, hold, guard.*

Gen. 2. 15 Eden to dress and *k.* it
Ex. 13. 10 shalt *k.* this ordinance
31. 13 mv sabbaths ye shall *k.*
Lev. 8. 35 *k.* the charge of Lord
20. 8 ye shall *k.* my statutes and
Num. 6. 24 L. bless thee, and *k.* thee
Deui. 4. 2 that ye *k.* the command.
Josh. 10. 18 set men by it for to *k.*
Judg. 2. 22 their fathers did *k.* it not
1 Sam. 2. 9 will *k.* feet of his saints
2 Sam. 22. 22 have *k.* ways of Lord
1 K. 2. 43 hast thou not *k.* oath
2 K. 17. 19 Judah *k.* not command.
1 Chr. 10. 13 word .. which he *k.* not
2 Chr. 6. 14 which *k.* cov. .. and m.
Ez. 8, 29 watch ye, and *k.* them
Neh. 1. 9 *k.* my com. and do them
Esth. 2. 14 which *k.* the concubines
Job 23. 11 his way have I *k.*; and
Ps. 12. 7 thou shalt *k.* them, O L.
17. 8 *k.* me as the apple of the eye
25. 20 *k.* my soul, and deliver me
Prov. 2. 20 *k.* paths of righteous
7. 1 *k.* my words, and lay up my
Eccl. 3. 6 time to *k.*, time to cast aw.
Isa. 56. 1 *K.* judgment, do justice
Jer. 35. 18 *k.* all his precepts, and
Ezek. 18. 19 hath *k.* all my statutes
Dan. 9. 4 them that *k.* his command.
Hos. 12. 6 *k.* mercy and judgment
Am. 1. 11 he *k.* his wrath forever
Zech. 3. 7 shalt *k.* my courts, and
Mal. 2. 7 priest's lips should *k.* k.
Mat. 8. 33 they that *k.* them fled
14. 6 when Herod's birthday was *k.*
Mark 7. 9 that ye *k.*, sour traditions
Luke 2. 51 his moth. *k.* these sayings
John 2. 10 hast *k.* good wine till now
Acts 12. 5 Peter'wss *k.* in prison
Rom. 2. 26 if uncircum. *k.* right. of
1 Cor. 7. 37 decreed .. that he will *k.*
2 Cor. 11. 9 I have *k.* myself .. and
Gal. 6. 13 who are circum. *k.* law
Eph. 4. 3 endeav. to *k.* unity of spirit
2 Thes. 3. 3 and *k.* you from evil
1 Tim. 6. 20 *k.* which is committed to
2 Tim. 1. 14 *k.* by H. G. which dwel.
Heb. 11. 28 through faith he *k.* pass.
Jas. 1. 27 *k.* himself unspotted from
1 John 2. 3 know him, if we *k.* his c.
Jude 6 angels *k.* not first estate
Rev. 1. 3 *k.* things which are written
R. V. Deut. 5. 1, 12; 23. 23; 1 Chr.
28. 8; Ps. 105. 45; 119. 5. 8, 44, 57,
60. 63, 88 observe; Acts 12. 4;
Phil. 4. 7; 2 Thes. 3. 3; 1 Tim. 6.
20; 2 Tim. 1. 12; 1 John 5. 21;
Jude 24 guard

Keeper. *Guard, watcher, preserver, stayer.*

Gen. 4. 9 Am I my brother's *k.?*
39. 21 ga. him favour in sight of *k.*
1 Sam. 17. 20 left sheep with a *k.*
2 K. 11. 6 shall be *k.* of the wa,ch
1 Chr. 9. 19 *k.* of gates of taberna.
2 Chr. 34. 22 son of H., *k.* of ward.
Neh. 2. 8 Asaph *k.* of king's forest
Esth. 2. 3 chamberlain, *k.* of women
Job 27. 18 as booth that *k.* maketh
Ps. 121. 5 L.. is my *k.*; the Lord is
Eccl. 12. 3 day when *k.* of house
S. of S. 5. 7 *k.* of wails took my veil
Jer. 4. 17 as *k.* of a field, are they
Ezek. 40. 45, 46 priests *k.* of charge
Mat. 28. 4 for fear .. *k.* did shake
Acts 5. 23 *k.* standing .. bef. doors
16. 27 *k.* of prison awaking out of s.
Tit. 2. 3 discreet, chaste, *k.* at home
R. V. Mat. 28. 4 watchers; Acts
12. 6; 12. 19 guards; 16. 27 jailor;
Tit. 2. 5 workers

Keeping. *Watching, preserving holding.*

Ex. 34. 7 *k.* mercy for thousands
Num. 3. 28, 38 *k.* charge of sanc.
Neh. 12. 25 *k.* ward at threshold
Dan. 9. 4 *k.* covenant and mercy
2 Cor. 7. 19 *k.* of comman. of God

Kept. *See* **Keep.**

Kerchiefs. *Veils, kerchiefs.*
Ezek. 13. 18, 21 *k.* upon the head

Kernels. *Seeds. grains.*

Num. 6. 4 from *k.* even to husks

Kettle. *Vessel, basket.*
1 Sam. 2. 14 struck into pan, or *k.*

Key. *Opener, key.*
Judg. 3. 25 they took *k.*, and opened
Isa. 22. 22 *k.* of house of D. will
Mat. 16. 19 give thee *k.* of kingdom
Luke 11. 52 taken away *k.* of knowl.
Rev. 18 have *k.* of hell and death
3. 7; 9. 1; 20. 1.

Kick. *Kick, resist.*
1 Sam. 2. 29 wherefore *k.* at my sac.
Acts 9. 5 hard .. to *k.* against pricks
26. 14

Kid. *Young goat, he-goat.*
Gen. 27. 9 fetch me .. two good *k.*
37. 31 killed *k.* of goats, and dip.
Ez. 23. 19 not seethe *k.* in moth. m.
Lev. 4. 23 *k.* of g., male without b.
Num. 7. 16 *k.* of g. for sin offering
7. 87; 15. 24; 28. 15, 26. 5
Deut. 13. 21 not seethe *k.* in m. milk
Judg. 6. 19 Gideon .. make ready *k.*
1 Sam. 16. 20 bread, bot. of w., and *k*
1 K. 20. 27 like two lit. flocks of *k.*
2 Chr.35. 7 of flocks, lambs, and *k.*
S. of S. 1. 8 feed thy *k.* beside .. tents
Isa. 11. 6 leopard .. lie down with *k.*
Ezek. 43. 22 shalt offer *k.* of goats
Luke 15. 29 thou nev. gavest me *k.*
R. V. In Gen. Lev. Num. and Ezek.
mostly he-goat, or goat

Kidneys. *Reins, kidneys.*
Ex. 29. 13, 22 the two *k.*, and fat
Lev. 3. 10, 15 caul ab. liver with *k.*
4. 9; 7. 4; 8. 16; 9. 10, 19
Deut. 32. 14 goats, with fat of *k.*
Isa. 34. 6. with fat of *k.* of rams

Kill. *Slay, slaughter.*
Gen. 4. 15 lest finding him should *k.*
Ex. 2. 14 intendest thou to *k.* me
Lev. 1. 5 shall *k.* bullock before L.
Num. 14. 15 *k.* .. this peo. as one m.
Deut. 32. 39 I *k.*, and I make alive
Josh. 20. 3 slayer that *k.* .. unawares
Judg. 13. 23 if L. were pleas. to *k.* us
1 Sam. 2. 6 L. *k.*, and maketh alive
2 Sam. 21. 17 smote P. and *k.* him
1 K. 11. 40 Sol. sought to *k.* Jero.
2 K. 5. 7 am I G., to *k.*, and make al.
1 Chr. 19. 18 *k.* Shop. capt. of host
2 Chr. 30. 15 then they *k.* passover
Ez. 6. 26 *k.* the passover for all
Esth. 8. 13 to *k.*, and cause to per.
Job 24. 14 murder. ris. wi. light *k.*
Ps. 44. 22 for thy sake are we *k.*
Prov. 9. 2 she hath *k.* her beasts
Eccl. 3. 3 time to *k.*, time to heal
Isa. 14. 30 *k.* thy root with famine
Lam. 2. 21 thou hast *k.* .. not pitied
Ezek. 34. 3 ye *k.* them that are fed
Hos. 4. 2 by swearing, lying, and *k.*
Mat. 16. 21 *k.*, and be raised again
Mark 3. 4 lawful .. to save .. or to *k.?*
12. 7 the heir; come, let us *k.* him
Luke 13. 34 which *k.* proph. and s.
John 5. 18 J. sought more to *k.* him
Acts 3. 15 *k.* Prince of life, whom G.
Rom. 8. 36 for thy sake we are *k.*
2 Cor. 3. 6 letter *k.*, bu. sp. giveth
1 Thes. 2. 15 both *k.* L. J. and their
Jas. 2. 11 said also, Do not *k.* Now
Rev. 2. 23 I will *k.* her children
R. V. Ex. 20. 13; Deut. 5. 17; Mat.
19. 18 do no murder; Num. 35.
27; 1 Sam. 19. 2 K. 11. 15
Acts 23. 15; Rev. 6. 4 slay; Mark
14. 12; Luke 22. 7 sacrificed

Killing. *Murdering, slaughtering.*
2 Chr. 30. 17 Lev. had charge of *k.*
Isa. 22. 13 slay. oxen and *k.* sheep
Hos. 4. 2 swearing, lying, and *k.*
See also **Kill.**

Kin. *Relation, same race.*
Lev. 18. 6 approach any near of *k.*
20. 19; 21. 2; 25. 49
Ruth 2. 20 man is near of *k.* to us
2 Sam. 19. 42 king is near *k.* to us
Mark 6. 4 among his own *k.*, and

Kind (*a.*). *Humane, tender.*
2 Chr. 10. 7 if thou be *k.* to people
Luke 6. 35 he is *k.* to the unthankful
1 Cor. 13. 4 char. suffer. long .. is *k.*
Eph. 4. 32 be ye *k.* one to another

Kind (*n.*). *Species, race, family.*
Gen. 1. 11 yield. fruit after his *k.*

---

6. 20 of fowls after their *k.*
Lev. 11. 14 and the kite after his *k.*
Deut. 14. 13 the vulture after his *k,*
2 Chr. 16. 14 divers *k.* .. prepared by
Jer. 15. 3 And I will appoint four *k.*
Ezek. 47. 10 fish .. accord. to their *k.*
Dan. 3. 5 and all *k.* of musick, ye
Mat. 13. 47 sea, and gath. of ev. *k.*
Mark 9. 29 this *k.* can come forth.
1 Cor. 12. 10 anoth. divers *k.* of tong
Jas. 1. 18 be a *k.* of firstfruits of his
R. V. Mat. 17. 21 ——

Kindle. *Make to burn, burn.*
Gen. 30. 2 Jacob's anger was *k.*
Ex. 4. 14 anger of L. was *k.* against
Lev. 10. 6 burning wh. L. hath *k.*
Num. 22. 27 Balaam's anger was *k.*
Deut. 32. 22 fire is k. in mine anger
Josh. 7. 1 anger of L. was. *k.* against
Judg. 9. 30 heard, his anger was *k.*
1 Sam. 20. 30 then Saul's anger . *k.*
2 Sam. 12. 5 David's anger was *k.*
2 K. 23. 26 his ang. was *k.* ag. Judah
1 Chr. 13. 10 anger of Lord was *k.*
2 Chr. 25. 10 their anger was grea. *k.*
Job 32. 2 was *k.* wrath of Elihu
Ps. 18. 8 fire, coals were *k.* by it
Prov. 26. 21 contentious man *k.* str.
Isa. 30. 33 breath of L. doth *k.* it
Jer. 11. 16 tree, he hath *k.* fire on it
Lam. 4. 11 L. hath *k.* fire in Zion
Ezek. 20. 47 I will *k.* fire in thee
Hos. 8. 5 mine anger is *k.* against
Am. 1. 14 *k.* fire in walls of Rab.
Obad. 18 *k.* in them, and devour
Zech. 10. 3 mine anger was *k.* agai.
Mal. 1. 10 nei. do ye *k.* fire on
Luke 12. 49 what, if it be already *k?*
Acts 28. 2 *k.* fire, and received us
Jas. 3. 5 great matter, little fire *k?*
R. V. Prov. 26. 21 inflame; Jer. 33.
18 burn; Jas. 3. 5 much wood is
kindled by how small a fire.

Kindly. *Tenderly, with kindness.*
Gen. 24. 49 if ye will deal *k.* and
34. 3 damsel, and spake *k.* to her
Josh. 2. 14 will deal *k.* and truly
Ruth 1. 8 the Lord deal *k.* with you
1 Sam. 20. 8 thou shalt deal *k.* with
2 K. 25. 28 he spake *k.* to him, and
Jer. 52. 32 and spake *k.* to him, and
Rom. 12. 10 affectioned one to
R. V. Rom. 12. 10 tenderly

Kindness. *Tenderness, favor, affection.*
Gen. 20. 13 this is thy *k.* which
Josh. 2. 12 I have showed you *k.*
Judg. 8. 35 nei. showed they *k.* to
Ruth 2. 20 who hath not left off *k.*
1 Sam. 20. 14 show me *k.* of Lord
2 Sam. 2. 6 L. show *k.* and truth
1 K. 2. 7 show *k.* to sons of Bar.
1 Chr. 19. 2 will show *k.* unto Han.
2 Chr. 24. 22 *k.* remembered not *k.*
Neh. 9. 17 G. slow to ang., of gr., *k.*
Esth. 2. 9 and she obtained *k.* o. him
Ps. 31. 21 hath showed me his *k.*
Prov. 19. 22 desire of man in his *k.*
31. 26 in her tongue is the law of *k.*
Isa. 54. to my *k.* shall not depart
Jer. 2. 2 remember *k.* of thy youth
Joel 2. 13 slow to ang, of gr. *k.*
Acts 28. 2 peo. showed no little *k.*
2 Chr. 6. 6 by *k.*, by the Hoiy G.
Eph. 2. 7 *k.* toward us throuhh J. C.
Col. 4. 12 *k.* humb. of mind, meek.
Tit. 3. 4 *k.* and love of G. our Sav.
2 Pet. 1. 7 and to godliness bro. *k.*

Kindred. *Relation, family, tribe, race.*
Gen. 12. 1 out of country, from *k.*
24. 41 when thou come, to my *k.*
Num. 10. 30 will depart to my *k.*
Josh. 6. 23 brought out all her *k.*
Ruth 3. 2 is not Boaz of our *k.*
1 Chr. 16. 28 give unto Lord, ye *k.*
Esth. 2. 10 not showed her peo ... *k.*
Job. 32. 2 Barachel, of *k.* of Ram
Ps. 22. 27 all *k.* of nat. shall worship
96. 7 Give unto Lord, O ye *k.* of p.
Ezek. 11. 15 brethren, men of thy *k.*
Luke 1. 61 none of thy *k.* is called
Acts 4. 6 as many as were of the *k,*
7. 3 out of country, and from *k.*
Rev. 1. 7 all *k.* of earth shall wail
5. 9 out of every *k.*, and tongue

11. 9; 13. 7; 14.; 6
R. V. Gen. 24. 7; 31. 23 nativity;
 Ruth 2. 3; Job 32. 2; Acts 3. 25
 family; Ruth 3. 2 kinswoman; 1
 Chr. 12. 29 brethren; Acts 7. 13, 19
 race; Rev. 1. 7; 5. 6; 7. 9; 11. 9;
 13. 7; 54. 6 tribe or tribes

Kine. *Cow, heifer.*
Gen. 32. 15 forty *k*., and ten bulls
 41. 2 came up seven well favored *k*.
 41. 3–27
1 Sam. 6. 6 cart, take two milch *k*.
 6. 7, 10, 12, 14
Am. 4. 1 hear word, ye *k*. of Bash.
Horned cattle, herd.
Deut. 32. 14 butter of *k*., milk of s.
2 Sam. 17. 29 sheep, and cheese of *k*.
Ox. steer.
Deut. 8. 13 increase of *k*. and flocks
 28. 4. 18, 51

King. *Ruler, counsellor.*
Gen. 14. 1 days of Amragh. *k*. of Shi
 14. 10 *k*. of Sod. and Gom. fled
Ex. 1. 8 arose new *k*. over Egypt
Num. 20. 17 will go by *k*. highway
 31. 8 they slew the *k*. of Midian
Deut. 1. 4 Og *k*. of Bashan, which
Josh. 2. 2 it was told *k*. of Jericho
 12. 1 now these are the *k*. of land
 12. 9–24; 13. 10; 24. 9
Judg. 1. 7 threescore and ten *k*. hav.
 5. 3 hear, O *k*.; give ear, O princes
1 Sam. 2. 10 give strength unto his *k*.
 12. 13 Lord hath set a *k*. over you
 21. 11 is not this D. *k*. of land?
2 Sam. 2. 4 they anointed David k.
1 K. 1. 1 *k*. David was old and str.
 1. 34 say, God save *k*. Solomon
 4. 10 Sol. was *k*. over all Israel
 16. 5, 14 book of Chronicles of the *k*.
2 K. 1. 9. *k*. hath said, Come down
1 Chr. 1. 43 *k*. that reigned in Edom
2 Chr. 1. 12 such as none of *k*. had
 2. 3 Sol. sent to Hur. *k*. of Tyre
 36. 23 thus saith Cyrus *k*. of Per.
Ez. 1. 1 first year of Cy. *k*. of Per.
Neh. 1. 11 for I was *k*.'s cupbearer
Esth. 1. 2 *k*. Ahazuer, sat on throne
Job 3. 14 with *k*., and counsel. of e.
 12. 18 he looseth the bond of *k*.
Ps. 2. 10 Be wise now, O ye *k*.
 10. 16 Lord is *k*. for ever and ever
 24. 8, 10 who is this *K*. of glory?
 48. 2 mount Zion, city of great *k*.
Prov. 1. 1 Sol. son of D., *k*. of Israel
Eccl. 1. 12 Preacher was *k*. over Is.
S. of S. 7. 5 *k*. is held in galleries
Isa. 6. 5 mine eyes have seen th. *K*.
 43. 15 Creator of Israel, your *K*.
Jer. 3. 6 unto me in days of Jos. *k*.
Lam. 2. 6 hath despised *k*. and pr.
Ezek. 30. 21 have brok. arm of P. *k*.
Dan. 1. 1 reign. Jehoiak. *k*. of Jud.
Hos. 5. 1 give ear, O house of *k*.
Am. 1. 1 in days of Uz. *k*. of Jud.
Jonah 3. 6 word came to *k*. of Nin.
Mic. 4. 9 is there no *k*. in thee?
Nah. 3. 18 sheph. slum., O. *k*. of A.
Hab. 1. 10 shall scoff at *k*. and pr.
Zeph. 3. 15 *K*. of Is., even the Lord.
Hag. 1. 1, 15 second year of Dar. *k*.
Zech. 9. 5 *k*. shall per. from Gaza.
Mal. 1. 14 I am gr. *K*., saith Lord.
Mat. 1. 6 begat David the *k*., and
 5. 35 it is the city of the great *K*.
 18. 23 likened unto a certain *k*.
 27. 11 Art thou the *K*. of the Jews ?
Mark 6. 14 *k*. said unto damsel, Ask
 15. 18 salute him, Hail, *K*. of Jews !
Luke 1. 5 in days of H. *k*. of Judea.
 23. 37 if thou be *k*. of Jews, save
John 1. 49 Son of God ; art *k*. of Is.
 18. 37 Thou sayest that I am a *k*.
Acts 4. 26 *k*. of earth stood up, and
 17. 7 there is another *k*., one Jesus
2 Cor. 11. 32 gov. under Aretas *k*.
1 Tim. 1. 17 unto *K*. eter., im., invis.
Heb. 7. 1 *k*. of Salem, priest of G.
1 Pet. 2. 17 love brotherh., honor *k*.
Rev. 1. 5 prince of the *k*. of earth
 19. 16 *K*. of *k*., Lord of lords

Kingdom. *King's realm.*
Gen. 10. 10 begin. of his *k*. was B.
Ex. 19. 6 be unto me *k*. of priests
Num. 32. 33 *k*. of Og king of B.
Deut 3. 4 the *k*. of Og in Bashan

Josh. 11. 10 H. was head of those *k*.
1 Sam. 13. 13 established thy *k*. on I.
2 Sam. 3. 28 I and my *k*. are guilt.
1 K. 4. 21 Sol. reigned over all *k*.
2 K. 19. 15 thou art God of all *k*.
1 Chr. 29. 11 thine is the *k*. O, Lord
2 Chr. 9. 19 not like made in any *k*.
Ez. 1. 2 Lord hath given me all *k*.
Neh. 9. 22 gavest them *k*. and nat.
Ps. 68. 32 Sing unto God, ye *k*. of e.
Eccl. 4. 14 born in his *k*. becometh
Isa. 19. 2 city against c., *k*. against *k*.
 47. 5 no more called lady of *k*.
Jer. 1. 10 over nations and over *k*.
Lam. 2. 2 polluted *k*. and princes
Ezek. 17. 14 that *k*. might be base
Dan. 8. 22 four *k*. shall stand up
Hos. 1. 4 cause to cease *k*. of . . Is.
Am. 6. 2 be they bet. than these *k*. ?
Mic. 4. 8 *k*. shall come to daugh.
Nah. 3. 5 and the *k*. thy shame
Zeph. 3. 8 that I may assemble *k*.
Hag. 2. 22 I will overthrow . . *k*.
Mat. 3. 2 Repent: *k*. of heaven is
 5. 3 for theirs is *k*. of heaven
 6. 10 Thy *k*. come. Thy will be d.
 6. 13 thine is *k*., and power, and g.
Mark 3. 24 if a *k*. be divided ag'st
 10. 14 for of such is the *k*. of God
 14. 25 drink it new in *k*. of God.
Luke 4. 5 showed unto him all *k*.
 6. 20 poor; for yours is *k*. of God
 7. 28 he that is least in *k*. of God
 17. 21 *k*. of God is within you
 21. 31 *k*. of God is nigh at hand
John 18. 36 my *k*. is not of this world
Acts 1. 3 things per. to *k*. of God
 28. 31 preach. *k*. of G., and teach.
Rom. 17. 14 *k*. of God is not meat
1 Cor. 4. 20 *k*. of God not in word
Gal. 5. 21 shall not inherit the *k*.
Eph. 5. 5 hath inher. in *k*. of Christ
Col. 1. 13 translated us unto *k*. of S.
1 Thes. 2. 12 hath called you unto *k*.
2 Tim. 4. 18 preserve me unto h. *k*.
Heb. 11. 33 through faith subd. *k*.
Jas. 2. 5 rich in faith, heirs of *k*.
2 Pet. 1. 11 unto everlast. *k*. of L.
Rev. 1. 9 in *k*. of patience of Jesus

King's Country.
Acts 12. 20 was nourished by *k's c*.

King's Court.
Luke 7. 25 live delicate. are in *k's c*.

Kingly. *Regal.*
Dan. 5. 20 deposed from his *k*. th.

Kinsfolk. *Kinsmen.*
1 K. 16. 11 neither of his *k*. nor
2 K. 10. 11 his great men, and his *k*.
Job 19. 14 my *k*. have failed, and
Luke 2. 44 sought him among . . *k*.
 21. 16 parents, and brethren, and *k*.
R. V. 2 K. 10. 11 familiar friends

Kinsman. *Relation, of same race.*
Num. 5. 8 if the man have no *k*. to
Ruth 2. 1 Naomi hath *k*. of her hus.
 3. 9, 12, 13 ; 4. 1, 3, 6, 8, 14
Ps. 38. 11 lovers and *k*. stand afar
Luke 14. 12 nei. my *k*., nor neigh.
John 18. 26 *k*. whose ear Peter cut
Acts 10. 24 called together his *k*.
Rom. 9. 3 my *k*. according to flesh
 16. 7, 11, 21

Kinswoman. *Relation.*
Lev. 18. 12 she is thy father's *k*.
Prov. 7. 4 call understanding thy *k*.

Kiss (n.). *Kiss, greeting.*
Prov. 27. 6 *k*. of enemy are deceit.
S. of S. 1. 2 let him kiss me with *k*.
Luke 7. 45 thou gavest me no *k*.
 22. 48 betrayest Son of man wi. *k*.
Rom. 16. 16 salute one anoth. wi. *k*.
1 Cor. 16. 20 greet one anoth. wi. *k*.
2 Cor. 13. 12 ; 1 Thes. 5. 26 ; 1 Pet.
 5. 14

Kiss (v.). *To kiss. touch, greet.*
Gen. 27. 26 Come near, and *k*. me
 45. 15 *k*. his brethren, and wept.
Ex. 4. 27 he met him, and *k*. him
Ruth 1. 14 Orpah *k*. her mother-in-l.
1 Sam. 20. 41 *k*. one anoth., and wept
2 Sam. 14. 33 the king *k*. Absalom
1 K. 19. 20 let me . . *k*. my father
Job 31. 27 mouth hath *k*. my hand
Ps. 2. 12 *k*. Son, lest he be angry
 85. 10 righteous. and peace have *k*.
Prov. 7. 13 she caught him, and *k*. h.

S. of S. 1. 2 let him *k*. me wi. kisses
Hos. 13. 2 that sacrifice *k*. th. calves
Mat. 26. 48 whomsoever I *k*., that
Mark 14. 45 saith, Master ; and *k*.
Luke 7. 38 *k*. his feet, and anointed
 15. 20 fell on his neck, and *k*. him
Acts 20. 37 fell on Paul's neck . . *k*.

Kite. R. V. *falcon.*
Lev. 11. 14 and *k*. after his kind
Deut. 14. 13 glede, and *k*., and vul.

Knead. *Mix, work.*
Gen. 18. 6 *k*. it, and make cakes
1 Sam. 28. 24 took flour, and *k*. it
2 Sam. 13. 8 *k*. it, and made cakes
Jer. 7. 18 and women *k*. their dough
Hos. 7. 4 after he hath *k*. dough

Kneading-trough.
Ex. 8. 3 ovens, and into thy *k. t.*
 12. 34 their *k. t.* being bound up

Knee. *Knee.*
Gen. 30. 3 she shall bear upon my *k*.
Deut. 28. 35 L. shall smite thee in *k*.
Judg. 7. 5 that boweth upon his *k*.
1 K. 8. 54 from kneeling on his *k*.
2 K. 4. 20 sat on her *k*. till noon
2 Chr. 6. 13 Sol. kneeled upon his *k*.
Ez. 9. 5 I fell upon my *k*., and
Job 3. 12 why did *k*. prevent me ?
Ps. 109. 24 *k*. are weak through fast.
Isa. 35. 3 and confirm the feeble *k*.
 45. 23 unto me every *k*. shall bow
Ezek. 7. 17 and all *k*. shall be weak
Dan. 5. 6 *k*. smote one aginst anoth.
Nah. 2. 10 the *k*. smite together
Mark 15. 19 bowing their *k*. wor.
Luke 5. 8 fell at Jesus' *k*., saying
Rom. 14. 11 every *k*. shall bow to
Eph. 3. 14 I bow my *k*. unto Father
Phil. 2. 10 at name of J. ev. *k*. sho.
Heb. 12. 12 wherefore lift up . . . *k*.

Kneel. *Bow or bend knee.*
Gen. 24. 11 made his camels to *k*.
1 K. 8. 54 Sol. arose from *k*. on kn.
2 Chr. 6. 13 *k*. down upon his knees
Ps. 95. 6 let us *k*. before the Lord
Dan. 6. 10 *k*. on knees three times
Mat. 17. 14 man, *k*. down to him,
Mark 1. 40 beseeching him, and *k*.
Luke 22. 41 and *k*. down, and pray.
Acts 7. 60 he *k*. down, and cried
 9. 40 ; 20. 36 ; 21. 5

Knew. See **Know.**

Knife. *Knife, sword.*
Gen. 22. 6 took fire in hand, and *k*.
Josh. 5. 2 make thee sharp *k*. and
Judg. 19. 29 took *k*., and laid hold
1 K. 18. 28 cut themselves with *k*.
Ez. 1. 9 silver, nine and twenty *k*.
Prov. 23. 2 and put a *k*. to thy throat
 30. 14 genera., their jaw teeth as *k*.
Ezek. 5. 1 take the sharp *k*. caus. it
R. V. Ezek. 5. 1, 2 sword

Knit. *Bind, tie, knit.*
Judg. 20. 11 *k*. together as one man
1 Sam. 18. 1 soul of Jonathan was *k*.
1 Chr. 12. 17 heart shall be *k*. unto
Acts 10. 11 sheet *k*. at four corners
Col. 2. 2, 19 being *k*. together in love

Knock. *Beat, give blow.*
S. of S. 5. 2 voice of my beloved *k*.
Mat. 7. 7 *k*., and it shall be opened
Luke 13. 25 to *k*. at door, saying, L.
Acts. 12. 13 Peter *k*. at door of gate
Rev. 3. 20 I stand at door and *k*.

Knop *Gourd, cucumber.*
1 K. 6. 18 carved with *k*. and flowers
 7. 24 the *k*. were cast in two rows
Capital, chapter.
Ex. 25. 31 his *k*. and his flowers
 25. 33–36 ; 37. 17–22

Know. *Have knowledge, under-*
stand.
Gen. 3. 5 *k*. that in the day ye eat
 8. 11 Noah *k*. waters were abated
Ex. 1. 8 new king. which *k*. not J.
Lev. 5. 1 wheth. he hath seen or *k*.
Num. 10. 31 thou *k*. how we encamp
Deut. 7. 9 *k*. therefore that L. God
Josh. 2. 9 I *k*. that Lord hath given
Judg. 2. 10 which *k*. not L., nor
Ruth 2. 11 peo. which thou *k*. not
1 Sam. 3. 7 Sam. did not yet *k*. L.
2 Sam. 1. 5 how *k*. thou S. and Jon.
1 K. 2. 15 thou *k*. kingdom was mine
2 K. 2. 3 *k*. thou that L. will take
1 Chr. 28. 9 *k*. thou G. of thy fathers

2 Chr. 2. 8 *k.* that thy servant can
Neh. 2. 16 *k.* not whither I went
Esth. 1. 13 said to wise men which *k.*
Job 9. 2 I *k.* it is so of a truth
19. 25 I *k.* that my redeemer liveth
37 16 dost *k.* balancing of clouds
38. 33 *k.* thou ordinances of heaven
Ps. 1. 6 Lord *k.* the way of righteous
94. 11 Lord *k.* the thoughts of men
Prov. 1. 2 *k.* wisdom and instruction
14. 10 heart *k.* his own bitterness
27. 1 *k.* not what a day may bring
Eccl. 9. 12 man also *k.* not his time
S. of S. 1. 8 if thou *k.* not, O fairest
Isa. 1. 3 The ox *k.* his owner, and
Jer. 2 8 that handle law *k.* me not
Ezek. 2. 5 *k.* there has been prophet
Dan. 2. 3 sp. was troub. to *k.* dream
Hos. 8. 2 shall cry, My G., we *k.* thee
Joel 3. 17 ye *k.* that I am the Lord
Jonah 1. 10 the men *k.* that he fled
Mic. 4. 12 *k.* not tnoughts of Lord
Nah. 1. 7 he *k.* them that trust in h.
Zeph. 3. 5 the unjust *k.* no shame
Zech. 2. 9 *k.* that Lord hath sent
Mal. 2. 4 *k.* I sent this command.
Mat. 6. 3 let not left hand *k.* what
12. 33 for the tree is *k.* by his fruit
Mark 4. 11 I *k.* mystery of kingdom
Luke 1. 18 whereby shall I *k.* this
10. 22 no man *k.* who the Son is
John 1. 10 and the world *k.* him not
Acts 1. 7 to *k.* the times or seasons
Rom. 1. 21 when *k.* God, they glori.
1 Cor. 1. 21 world by wis. *k.* not G.
2 Cor. 2. 4 ye might *k.* love which
Gal. 4. 9 now, after ye have *k.* God
Eph. 3. 19 *k.* love of C , which pas.
Phil. 2. 19 good comfort, when I *k.*
Col. 4. 8 he might *k.* your estate
1 Thes. 3. 5 I sent to *k.* your faith
1 Tim. 1. 8 we *k.* that the law is good
2 Tim. 3. 15 from child thon hast *k.*
Tit. 1. 16 They profess they *k.* God
Phile. 21 *k.* thou wilt do more than
Heb. 8. 11 for all shall *k.* me, from
Jas. 2. 20 wilt thou *k.*, O vain man
1 Pet. 1. 18 *k.* ye were not redeem.
2 Pet. 2. 9 Lord *k.* how to deliver
1 John 2. 11 *k.* not whither he goeth
2 John 1 but all that have *k.* truth
3 John 12 ye *k.* our record is true
Jude 5 ye once *k.* this, how Lord
Rev. 2. 2 I *k.* thy works, and labour
R. V. Many changes to, perceive, understand, learn, discern, etc, but none affecting general meaning.

Knowledge. *Understanding, discernment, information.*
Gen. 2. 9 tree of *k.* of good and e.
Ex. 31. 3 in understanding, and *k.*
Lev. 4. 23 or if his sin come to his *k.*
Num. 24. 16 knew *k.* of most High
Ruth 2. 10 shouldst take *k.* of ms
1 Sam. 2. 3 the Lord is a God of *k.*
1 K. 9. 27 shipmen that had *k.* of sea
2 Chr. 8. 18 ser. that had *k.* of sea
Neh. 10. 28 every one having *k.* and
Job 36. 4 he that is perfect in *k.* is
Ps. 73 11 is there *k.* in most High?
Prov. 1. 7 fear of L. is begin. of *k.*
2. 10 *k.* is pleasant'unto thy soul
10. 14 Wise men lay up *k.* but fool.
Eccl. 2. 21 labour is in wis., and *k.*
9. 10 no device. nor *k.*, in grave
Isa. 33. 6 wis. and *k.* shall be stabl.
Jer. 11. 18 Lord hath giveu me *k.*
Dan. 1. 4 cunning in *k.* and underst.
Hos. 4. 1 no truth, nor mer., nor *k.*
Hab. 2. 14 earth be filled with *k.*
Mal. 2. 7 priest's lips should keep *k.*
Mat. 14. 35 men of that pl. had *k.*
Luke 1. 77 to give *k.* of salvation
Acts 4. 13 and they took *k.* of them
Rom. 3. 20 for by the law is *k.* of sin
1 Cor. 8. 1 *k.* puff., but char. edifi.
2 Cor. 2. 14 manifest savour of h .. *k.*
Eph. 3. 19 love of C., which pass. *k.*
Phil. 1. 9 may abound yet more in *k.*
Col. 1. 10 increasing in *k.* of God
1 Tim. 2. 4 come unto *k.* of truth
2 Tim. 3. 7 nev. able to come to *k.*
Heb. 10. 26 we have received *k.*
Jas. 3. 13 wise man endued with *k.*
1 Pet. 3. 7 dwell .. according to *k.*
2 Pet. 1. 5 virtue ; and to virtue *k.*

R. V. Prov. 2. 3 discernment;
Eph. 3. 4 understanding
Known. *Understood, acquainted with, cause to know.*
Cen. 41. 21 it could not be *k.* that
Ex. 2. 14 surely this thing is *k.*
Lev. 4. 14 when the sin is *k.* then
Num. 12. 6 L. will make myself *k.*
Deut. 1. 13 men *k.* among your tri.
Judg. 16. 9 his strength was not *k.*
Ruth 3. 3 make not thyself *k.* unto
1 Sam. 6. 3 it shall be *k.* to you why
2 Sam. 17. 19 the thing was not *k.*
1 K. 18. 36 let it be *k.* this day that
1 Chr. 16. 8 make *k.* his deeds amo.
Ez. 4. 12 Be it *k.* unto the king
Neh. 4. 15 heard that it was *k.*
Esth. 2. 22 thing was *k.* to Morde.
Ps. 9. 16 Lord. is *k.* by judgment
Prov. 12. 16 fool's wrath is pres. *k.*
Eccl. 6. 10 and it is *k.* that it is man
Isa. 19. 21 L. shall be *k.* to Egypt.
Jer. 28. 9 prophet be *k.* that L. hath
Lam. 4. 8 are not *k.* in the streets
Ezek. 39. 7 I make my holy name *k.*
Dan. 2. 15 Ar. made thing *k.* to D.
Hos. 5. 9 made *k.* which shall be
Hab. 3. 2 midst of years make *k.*
Nah. 3. 17 the place is not *k.* where
Zech. 14. 7 shall be *k.* to the Lord
Mat. 12. 16 should not make him *k.*
Luke 2. 15 which Lord hath made *k.*
John 18. 15 that disc. was *k.* to pr.
Act 1. 19 *k.* to all dwellers at Jer.
Rom. 1. 19 which may be *k.* of God
Eph. 1. 9 having made *k* .. mystery
Phil. 4. 6 requests be made *k.* to G.
Col. 1. 27 whom G. would make *k.*
2 Tim. 4. 17 preaching might be *k.*
2 Pet. 1. 16 we made *k.* the power

L.

Labour (*n.*).   *To bear child.*
Gen. 35. 16, 17 Rachel had hard *l.*
Perverseness, misery, burden.
Deut. 26. 7 look. on our afflic. and *l.*
Ps. 90. 10 yet is their strength *l.*
Prov. 14. 23 in all *l.* there is profit
Eccl. 1. 3 what profit hath man of *l.*
10. 15 *l.* of foolish wearieth ev. one
Isa. 58. 3 pleas., and ex. all your *l.*
Jer. 20. 18 out of womb to see *l.*
Work, doing, service, weariness, wearing out work, toil.
Gen. 31. 42 seen my affliction and *l.*
Ex. 23. 16 firstfruits of thy *l.*, which
Deut. 28. 33 fruit of thy land, and *l.*
Neh. 5. 13 house, and from my *l.*
Job. 39. 11 wilt thou leave thy *l.*
Ps. 78. 46 gave their *l.* unto locust
Prov. 10. 16 *l.* of righteous tendeth
13. 11 that gath. by *l.* shall incr.
Isa. 45. 14 *l.* of Egypt and merch.
Jer. 3. 24 For shame devoured *l.* of
Ezek. 23. 29 take away all thy *l.*
Hos. 12. 8 in my *l.* they find none
Hab. 3. 17 the *l.* of olive shall fail
Hag. 2. 17 hail in all *l.* of hands
John 4. 38 are entered into their *l.*
Rom. 16. 6 Mary, who bes. much *l.*
Gal. 4. 11 lest .. bestow. *l.* in vain
1 Cor 3. 8 according to his own *l.*
2 Cor. 6. 5 tumults, in *l.*, in watch
Phil. 1 22 this is the fruit of my *l.*
1 Thes. 1. 3 *l.* of love, and patience
2 Thes. 3. 8 wrought with *l.* and trav.
Heb. 6. 10 your work and *l.* of love
Rev. 14 13 I know thy works and *l.*
R. V. Deut. 26. 7 ; Rev. 2. 2 toil,
Eccl. 1. 8 weariness ; Phil. 1. 22
work
Labour (*v.*).   *Work, toil, serve, strive.*
Ex. 5. 9 that they may *l.* therein
20. 9 six days shalt thou *l.* and do
Deut. 5. 13 six days shalt thou *l.*
Josh. 7. 3 make not all people to *l.*
Job 9. 29 if I be wicked, why *l.*
Ps. 144. 14 our oxen be strong to *l.*
Prov. 23. 4 *l.* not to be rich ; ce. **fr.**
Eccl. 4. 8 for whom do I *l.*, and
Isa. 65. 23 they shall not *l.* in vain
Jer. 51. 58 people shall *l.* in vain
Lam. 5. 5 necks under persec., we *l*
Dan. 6. 14 *l.* till going down of sun
Jonah 4. 10 for which thou hast not *l.*

Hab. 2. 13 that people shall *l.* in
Mat. 11. 28 come .. all ye that *l.*
John 6. 27 *l.* not for meat which per.
Acts 20. 35 so *l.* ye ought to sup.
Rom. 16. 12 which *l.* much in Lord
1 Cor. 4. 12 *l.*, working with own h.
Eph. 4. 28 steal, but rather let him *l.*
Phil. 2 16 not run .. neither *l.* in vain
Col. 1. 29 whereunto I also *l.*, striv.
1 Thes. 2. 9 *l.* night and day, becau.
1 Tim. 4. 10 both *l.* and suffer re.
2 Tim. 2. 6 husbandman that *l.* must
Heb. 4 11 *l.* therefore to enter into
Rev. 2 3 for name's sake hast *l.*
R. V. Josh. 7. 3 ; 1 Cor. 4. 12 toil ;
Neh. 4. 21 wrought ; Lam. 5. 5 are
weary, 2 Cor. 5. 9 make it our
aim; Col. 4. 12 striving; 1 Thes.
2. 9 working; Heb. 4 11 give dili-
gence; Rev. 2. 3 ——.
Labouring.   *Doing, serving.*
Eccl. 5. 12 sleep of *l.* man is sweet
Labourer.   *Worker, labourer.*
Mat. 9. 37 plenteous, but *l.* are few
9. 38; 20. 1, 2, 8
Luke 10. 2 would send *l.* into harv.
1 Tim. 5. 18: Jas. 5. 4
1 Cor. 3. 9 are *l.* together with God
1 Thes. 3. 2 our fellow *l.* in gospel
Phile. 1. 24 Mar. .. Lucas, my fel. *l.*
Lace.   *Thread, ribbon, wire.*
Ex. 28. 28 unto rings of ephod with *l*
28. 37; 39. 21, 31
Lack (*n.*).   *Need, want.*
Ex. 16. 18 that gath. lit. had no *l.*
Job 4. 11 lion perish. for *l.* of prey
38. 41 they wander for *l.* of meat
Hos. 4. 6 peo. destroy for *l.* of kn.
2 Cor. 8. 15 that gath. lit. had no *l.*
Phil. 2. 30 supply your *l.* of service
1 Thes. 4. 12 may have *l.* of nothing
R. V. 1 Thes. 4. 12 need
Lack (*v.*).   *Want, need, be destitute.*
Gen. 18. 28 *l.* five of the righteous
Num. 31. 49 there *l.* not one man
Deut. 8. 9 shalt not *l.* any thing
Judg. 21. 3 one tribe *l.* in Israel?
2 Sam. 2. 30 *l.* of D's ser. nineteen
1 K. 4. 27 officers .. they *l.* nothing
Neh. 9. 21 they *l.* nothing ; their clo.
Ps. 34. 10 lions *l.*, and suf. hunger
Prov. 6. 32 adultery .. *l.* understand.
28. 27 that giv. to poor shall not *l.*
Eccl. 9. 8 let head *l.* no ointment
Jer. 23. 4 neither shall they be *l.*
Mat. 19. 20 youth up ; what *l.* I get?
Mark 10. 21 one thing thou *l.*; go
Luke 8. 6 away, bec. it *l.* moisture
Acts 4. 34 neither any that *l.* ; for
1 Cor. 12. 24 honour to part which *l.*
Jas. 1. 5 if any of you *l.* wisdom
2 Pet. 1. 9 he that *l.* these is blind
Lacking.   *Wanting.*
Lev. 2. 13 salt lacking from thy meat
1 Sam. 30. 19 was nothing *l.* to them
1 Cor. 16. 17 which was *l.* on your p.
2 Cor. 11. 9 for which was *l.* to me
1 Thes. 3. 10 perfect that which is *l.*
Lad.   *Child, young person, boy.*
Gen. 21. 12 grievous .. because of *l.*
21. 17-20; 22. 5; 37. 2; 43. 8
Judg. 16. 26 Samson said unto *l.*
1 Sam. 20. 21 and I will send a *l.*
20. 35-41
2 Sam. 17. 18 *l.* saw them, and told A
2 K. 4. 19 said to *l.*, Carry him to
John 6. 9 *l.* here, hath bar. loaves
R. V. 2 K. 4. 19 servant
Ladder.   *Ladder.*
Gen. 28. 12 and behold a *l.* set up
Lade, Load.   *Lay on, load.*
Gen. 42. 26 *l.* their asses with corn
1 K. 12. 11 my father did *l.* you
Neh. 4. 17 burdens, with those th. *l.*
Ps. 68. 19 blessed L., who daily *l.*
Isa. 46. 1 carriages were heavy *l.*
Hab. 2. 6 that *l.* himself with clay
Mat. 11. 28 labour and are heavy *l.*
Luke 11. 46 ye *l.* men with burdens
Acts 28. 10 *l.* us with such things
2 Tim. 3. 6 silly women *l.* wi. sins
R. V. Acts 28. 10 put on board
Lading.   *Bnrden, freight, cargo.*
Acts 27. 10 not only of *l.* and ship
Lady.   *Princess.*
Judg. 5. 29 her wise *l.* answered her

Esth. 1. 18 shall *l.* of P. and M. say
Mistress.
Isa. 47. 5, 7 no more called, *l.* of k.
Woman, lady.
2 John 1 The elder unto elect *l.* and
  5 now I beseech thee, *l.*, not as
R. V. Esth. 1. 18 princesses

Laid. *See* **Lay.**

Lain. *See* **Lie.**

Lake. *Lake.*
Luke 5. 1 he stood by *l.* of Gennes.
  8. 33 ran .. down steep place into *l.*
Rev. 19. 20 into *l.* of fire burning
  29. 10, 14, 15 ; 21. 8

Lamb. *Young sheep.*
Gen. 22. 7 where is *l.* for burnt off. ?
Ex. 12. 3 shall take every man a *l.*
Lev. 4. 32 if he bring *l.* for sin off.
Num. 6. 12 *l.* of first yr. for tr. off.
Deut 32. 14 with fat of *l.*, and rams
1 Sam. 7. 9 Sam. took suckling *l.*
2 Sam. 12. 3 noth. save one ewe *l.*
2 K. 3. 4 an hundred thousand *l.*
1 Chr. 29. 21 thous. rams, and thou. *l.*
2 Chr. 29. 22 killed also *l.*, and s.
Ez. 8. 35 offer. seventy and seven *l.*
Ps. 37. 20 as fat of *l.* ; they consume
Prov. 27. 26 *l.* are for thy clothing
Isa. 1. 11 I delight not in blood of *l.*
Jer. 11. 19 I was like *l.* or ox that
Ezek. 46. 15 thus shall they pre. *l.*
Hos. 4. 16 L. will feed them as *l.*
Am. 6. 4 eat *l.* out of the flock, and
Luke 10. 3 I send you forth as *l.*
John 1. 29 L. of God, which taketh
  21. 15 saith unto him, Feed my *l.*
Acts 8. 32 like *l.* dumb bef. shearers
1 Pet. 1. 19 as a *l.* without blemish
Rev. 5. 6 *L.* as it had been slain
  6. 1 ; 7. 9 ; 12. 11 ; 13. 8 ; 14. 1
•R. V. In Num., he-lamb

Lame. *Smitten, limping, crippled.*
Lev. 21. 18 blind m., or *l.*, or he that
Deut. 15. 21 if *l.* .. shalt not sac.
2 Sam. 4. 4 he fell, and became *l.*
Job. 29. 15 eyes to blind, feet to *l.*
Prov. 26. 7 legs of *l.* are not equal
Isa. 35. 6 the *l.* shall leap as hart
Jer. 31. 8 with them blind and *l.*
Mal. 1. 8 and if ye offer *l.* and sick
Mat. 11. 5 *l.* walk, lepers are cleans.
  21. 4 and blind and *l.* came to him
Luke 14. 13 call poor, maimed, *l.*
Acts 3. 2 man *l.* from moth. womb
Heb. 12. 13 lest *l.* be turned out

Lament. *Mourn, wail, grieve.*
Judg. 11. 40 went yearly to *l.* daugh.
1 Sam. 6. 19 peo. *l.*, because Lord
2 Sam. 1. 17 David *l.* with this lam.
2 Chr. 35. 25 Jeremiah *l.* for Josiah
Isa. 3. 26 and her gates shall *l.* and
Jer. 4. 8 gird with sackcloth, and *l.*
Lam. 2. 8 he made rampart . . to *l.*
Ezek. 27. 32 *l.*, saying, What city like
Joel 1. 13 gird yourselves, and *l.*
Mic. 2. 4 take up parable . . and *l.*
Mat. 11. 17 mourned, ye have not *l.*
Luke 23. 27 women, bewailed and *l.*
John 16. 20 ye shall weep and *l.*
Rev. 18. 9 bewail, and *l.* for her
R. V. Judg. 11. 40 celebrate ; Isa.
  19. 8 ; Mat. 11. 17 mourn ; 32. 12
smite upon ; Rev. 18. 9 wail over.

Lamentable. *Grievous.*
Dan. 6. 20 cried with *l.* voice unto

Lamentation. *Mourning, wailing.*
Gen. 50. 10 mourned with sore *l.*
2 Sam. 1. 17 D. lamented with this *l.*
2 Chr. 35. 25 they are written in *l.*
Ps. 78. 64 their widows made no *l.*
Jer. 7. 29 take up *l.* on high places
Lam. 2. 5 increased mourning and *l.*
Ezek. 2. 10 written *l.* and mourning
Am. 5. 1 Hear ye this wors. . a *l.*
Mic. 2. 4 one lament with doleful *l.*
Mat. 2. 18 In R. was voice heard, *l.*
Acts 8. 2 made great *l.* over him

Lamp. *Torch flame, light.*
R. V. Mat. 2. 18 ——.
Gen. 15. 17 burning *l.* that passed
Ex. 25. 37 shalt make the seven *l.*
Lev. 24. 2 cause *l.* to burn contin.
Num. 8. 2 And Aaron lighted the *l*
Judg. 7. 16 *l.* within the pitchers
1 Sam. 3. 3 ere *l.* of God went out

2 Sam. 22. 29 thou art my *l.*, O L.
1 K. 15. 4 give him *l.* in Jerusalem
1 Chr. 28. 15 for *l.* of gold, by weig.
2 Chr. 4. 20 candlesticks with their *l.*
Ps. 119. 105 word is *l.* unto my feet
Prov. 6. 23 commandment is a *l.*
Zech. 4. 2 seven pipes to seven *l.*
Mat. 25. 1 virgins, which took *l.* and
Rev. 4. 5 seven *l.* of fire burning
R. V. Gen. 15. 17 ; Rev. 8. 10 torch ;
  Judg. 7. 16, 20 ; Job 41. 19 ; Ezek.
  1. 13 torches.

Lance. R. V. *spear.*
Jer. 50. 42 shall hold bow and *l.*

Lancet. R. V. *lances.*
1 K. 18. 28 cut th. with knives and *l.*

Land. (n.). *Earth, ground, soil,*
  country, field, level place, region.
Gen. 2. 11 compasseth the whole *l.*
  28. 15 I will bring thee into this *l.*
Ex. 2. 15 and dwelt in *l.* of Midian
  20. 12 thy days may be long upon *l.*
Lev. 14. 34 come into *l.* of Canaan
  20. 24 ye shall inherit their *l.*, and
Num. 1. 1 were come out of *l.* of E.
  11. 12 *l.* which thou swarest unto
Deut. 1. 5 Jordan, in *l.* of Moab
  5. 16 *l.* which Lord G. giveth thee
Josh. 1. 2 unto the *l.* which I give
  23. 13 perish from off this good *l.*
Judg. 1. 2 I have delivered the *l.* to
Ruth 1. 1 there was famine in the *l.*
1 Sam. 6. 5 im. of m. that mar the *l.*
2 Sam. 9. 10 ser. shall till *l.* for him
1 K. 8. 21 brought th. out cf *l.* of E.
2 K. 3. 27 returned to their own *l.*
1 Chr. 1. 43 kings that reigned in *l*
2 Chr. 2. 17 strangers that were in *l.*
Ez. 4. 4 people of the land weakened
Neh. 4. 4 give them for prey in *l.*
Esth. 8. 17 peo. of *l.* became Jews
Job 1. 1 There a was man in *l.* of Uz
Ps. 10. 16 heath. per. out of his *l.*
Prov. 2. 21 upright shall dwell in *l.*
Eccl. 10. 17 Blessed art thou, O *l.*
S. of S. 2. 12 voice of turtle . . in *l.*
Isa. 1. 19 ye shall eat of good of *l.*
Jer. 4. 5 blow ye the trumpet in *l.*
Lam. 4. 21 that dwelleth in *l.* of Uz
Ezek. 1. 3 *l.* of Chaldeans by river
Dan. 1. 2 carried into *l.* of Shinar
Hos. 1. 2 *l.* committed whoredoms
Joel 1. 2 give ear, all inhab. of *l.*
Am. 2. 19 brought you from *l.* of E.
Mic. 5. 5 Assyrians sh. come into *l.*
Nah. 3. 13 gates of *l.* be set open
Hab. 1. 6 march thro. breadth of *l.*
Zeph. 1. 18 the *l.* shall be devoured
Hag. 1. 11 called for drought on *l.*
Zech. 2. 6 flee from *l.* of the north
Mal. 3. 12 shall be delightsome *l.*
Mat. 9. 26 fame went abroad into *l.*
Mark 6. 47 and he alone on the *l.*
Luke 4. 25 famine throughout all *l.*
John 21. 8 they were not far from *l.*
Acts 4. 37 having *l.*, sold it, and
  13. 19 he divided their *l.* by lot
Heb. 8. 9 to lead them out of the *l.*
Jude 5. saved peeple out of the *l.*
R. V. Many changes in O. T. to
  earth, ground, country, etc.

Land (v.). *Bring to land.*
Acts 18. 22 when he *l.* at Cæsarea
  28. 12 *l.* at Syracuse, we tarried

Landmark. *Border, boundary.*
Deut. 14. 19 not remove neigh. *l.*
Job 24. 2 some remove the *l.* ; they
Prov. 22. 28 remove not ancient *l.*
  23. 10 remove not the old *l.*, ent not

Lane. *Narrow way.*
Luke 14. 21 go into streets and *l.*

Language. *Word, tongue, speech.*
Gen. 11. 1 whole earth was of one *l.*
  11. 9 Lord did there confound *l.*
Neh. 13. 24 according to *l.* of each
Esth. 1. 22 to people after their *l.*
Ps. 81. 5 I understood not *l.*
Isa. 19. 18 speak the *l.* of Canaan
Jer. 5. 15 nat. whose *l.* thou know.
Ezek. 3. 5 strange. speech and . . *l.*
Dan. 3. 29 ev. people, nation, and *l.*
Zeph. 3. 9 turn to people a pure *l.*
Zech. 8. 23 out of all *l.* of nations
Acts 2. 6 heard speak in his own *l.*

Languish. *Become weak, sick.*
Isa. 16. 8 For the fields of Hesh. *l.*

  24. 4 the world *l.* and fadeth away
Jer. 14. 2 the gates thereof *l.*, they
Lam. 2. 8 rampart and wall *l.* togeth.
Hos. 4. 3 that dwel. therein shall *l.*
Joel 1. 10 new wine is dried, oil *l.*
Nah. 1. 4 Bashan *l.*, and Carmel

Languishing. *Sickness.*
Ps. 41. 3 strengthen him on bed of *l*

Lantern. *Light, torch.*
John 18. 3 cometh thither with *l.*

Lap. (n). *Cloak, bosom, lap.*
2 K. 4. 39 gath. gourds his *l.* full
Neh. 5. 13 I shook my *l.* and said
Prov. 16. 33 The lot is cast in the *l.*

Lap. (v.). *Lick, lap.*
Judg. 7. 5, 6, 7 that *l.* as dog *l.* him

Lapwing. R. V. *hoopoe.*
Lev. 11. 19 ; Deut. 14. 18 stork, the *l.*

Large. *Broad, wide, spacious.*
Gen. 34. 21 land, it is *l.* enough
Ex. 3. 8 unto a good land and a *l.*
Judg. 18. 10 peo. secure, and *l.* land
2 Sam. 22. 20 brought me into *l.* p.
Neh. 4. 19 the work is great and *l.*
Ps. 31. 8 ha. set my feet in *l.* room
Isa. 30. 33 hath made it deep and *l.*
Jer. 22. 14 wide house and *l.* cham.
Ezek. 23. 32 drink of cup deep and *l.*
Hos. 4. 16 feed as lamb in *l.* place
Mat. 28. 12 gave *l.* mon. to soldiers
Mark. 14. 15 show you *l.* up. room
  Luke 22. 12.
Gal. 6. 11 *l.* letter I have written
Rev. 21. 16 length *l.* as the breadth
  R. V. Neh. 7. 4 wide ; Jer. 22. 14
  spacious ; Rev. 21. 16 great

Largeness. *Greatness.*
1 K. 4. 29 *l.* of heart, ev. as sand

Lasciviousness. *Licentiousness.*
Mark 7. 22 *l.*, evil eye, blasphemy
2 Cor. 12. 21 *l.* they have committed
Gal. 5. 19 fornication, uncleanness *l.*
Eph. 4. 19 giv. thems. over unto *l.*
1 Pet. 4. 3 when we walked in *l.*
Jude 4 turning grace of G. into *l.*

Last. *At the end, latest, hind-*
  most, finally.
Gen. 49. 1 befall you in the *l.* days
  49. 19 shall overcome you at *l.*
Num. 23. 10 let *l.* end be like his
2 Sam. 19. 11 why are ye *l.* to bring
1 Chr. 23. 27 For by *l.* words of D.
2 Chr. 9. 29 acts of Sol., first and *l.*
Ez. 8. 13 A. of *l.* sons of Adonikam
Neh. 8. 18 from first day unto *l.*
Prov. 5. 11 and thou mourn at the *l.*
Isa. 2. 2 sh. come to pass in *l.* days
Jer. 12. 4 shall not see our *l.* end
Lam. 1. 9 remember not her *l.* end
Dan. 4. 8 at *l.* Daniel came in bef.
Am. 9. 1 I will slay the *l.* of them
Mic. 4. 1 in the *l.* days it shall come
Mat. 19. 30 first shall be *l.* ; *l.* first
Mark. 12. 22 *l.* of all woman died
Luke 12. 59 till hast paid *l.* mite
John 6. 40 raise him up at *l.* day
Acts 2. 17 come to pass in *l.* days
1 Cor. 15. 8 *l.* of all he was seen
2 Tim. 3. 1 *l.* days per. times come
Heb 1. 2 hath in *l.* days spoken
Jas. 5. 3 heaped treas. for *l.* days
1 Pet. 1 20 was manifest in *l.* times
1 John 2. 18 children, it is *l.* time
Jude 18 sho. be mockers in *l.* time
Rev. 11 Alph. and Om., first and *l.*
  R. V. Gen. 49. 1 ; Isa. 2. 2 ; Jer.
  12. 4 ; Lam. 1. 9 ; Dan. 8. 19 ; Mic.
  4. 1 latter ; Mat. 21. 37 ; Luke
  20. 32 afterward

Last (v.). *Endure, continue.*
Deut. 13. 15 precious things of *l.* hills
Judg. 14. 17 days while their feast *l.*

Latchet. *Thong, strap, buckle.*
Gen. 14. 23 thread even to a shoe *l.*
Isa. 5. 27 nor *l.* of shoes be broken
Mark 1. 7 *l.* .. not worthy to unloose
Luke 3. 16 *l.* of whose shoes I am
John 1. 27 *l.* I am not worthy to un.

Late. *Tarry, after delay.*
Ps. 127. 2 to sit up *l.*, to eat the br.
Mic. 2. 8 of *l.* my people is risen up
John 11. 8 Jews of *l.* sought to stone

Lately. *Recently.*
Acts 18. 2 *l.* come from Italy, with

Latin. *Roman language.*
Luke 23. 38 written in letters of **L.**

John 19. 20 writ. in Heb., Gr., and L.

Latter. *After first, late, recent.*
Ex. 4. 8 will believe voice of *l.* sign
Deut. 11. 14 first rain, and the *l.* rain
Ruth 3. 10 kindness in *l.* end than
2 Sam. 2. 26 be bitterness in *l.* end
Job 19. 25 shall stand at *l.* day upon
Prov. 16. 15 as a cloud of the *l.* rain
Jer. 3. 3 there hath been no *l.* rain
Ezek. 38. 16 shall be in the *l.* days
Dan. 10. 14 befall people in *l.* days
Hos. 3. 5 fear the Lord .. in *l.* days
Joel 2. 23 former rain, and the *l.* rain
Am. 7. 1 shooting up of *l.* growth
Hag. 2. 9 The glory of this *l.* house
Zech. 10. 1 rain in time of the *l.* rain
1 Tim. 4. 1 in *l.* times some depart
Jas. 5. 7 receive early and the *l.* rain
2 Pet. 2. 20 *l.* end worse than begin.

Lattice. *Casement, network.*
Judg. 5. 28 cried through *l.,* Why
2 K. 1. 2 Ahaziah fell through *l.* in
S. of S. 2. 9 showing himself thr. *l.*

Laud. *Applaud.*
Rom. 15. 11 Praise L., *l.* him, all peo.

Laugh. *Mock, scoff, deride.*
2 K. 19. 21 Zion .. *l.* thee to scorn
2 Chr. 30. 10 they *l.* us to scorn, and
Neh. 2. 19 they *l.* us to scorn, and
Job. 5. 22 at famine thou shalt *l.*
9. 23 *l.* at the trial of the innocent
Ps. 2. 4 that sitteth in heav. shall l.
80. 6 enemies *l.* among themselves
Prov. 1. 26 I will *l.* at your calamity
Isa. 37. 22 of Zion .. *l.* thee to scorn
Ezek. 23. 32 thou shalt be *l.* to scorn
Mat. 9. 24 And they *l.* him to scorn
Mark 5. 40; Luke 8. 53
Express joy.
Gen. 17. 17 Ab. fell on face, and *l.*
21. 6 said, God hath made me to *l.*
Eccl. 3. 4 A time to weep, time to *l.*
Luke 6. 21 that weep; ye shall *l.*

Laughing. *Laughter.*
Job. 8. 21 fill my mouth with *l.* and

Laughter. *Laughter.*
Ps. 126. 2 our mouth filled with *l.*
Prov. 14. 13 ev. in *l.* heart is sorrowf.
Eccl. 2. 2 I said of *l.,* It is mad
10. 19 feast is made for *l.,* and wine
Jas. 4. 9 let *l.* be turned to mourn.

Launch. *Send forth.*
Luke 5. 4 *L.* out unto the deep
Acts 27. 2 we *l.,* meaning to sail
R. V. Luke 5. 4 put; Acts 21. 1 set
sail; 27. 2, 4 put to sea

Laver. *Pan, laver.*
Ex. 30. 18 shalt make *l.* of brass
31. 9; 35. 16; 38. 8; 40. 7, 11, 30
Lev. 8. 11 anoi. both *l.* and his foot
1 K. 7. 38 Sol. made ten *l.* of brass
2 K. 16. 17 removed the *l.* from off
2 Chr. 4. 6 Sol., he made also ten *l.*

Lavish. *Pour forth.*
Isa. 46. 6 They *l.* gold out of .. bag

Law. *Statute, direction.*
Gen. 26. 5 Abraham obeyed my l.
Ex. 18. 16 know stat. of G., and his *l.*
Lev. 6. 9 this is *l.* of burnt offering
Num. 5. 29 this is *l.* of jealousies
Deut. 1. 5 began Moses to declare *l.*
Josh. 1. 8 book of *l.* shall not dep.
1 K. 2. 3 as written in *l.* of Moses
2 K. 22. 8 I have found book of *l.*
1 Chr. 16. 40 according to .. the *l.*
2 Chr. 12. 1 forsook *l.* of the Lord
Ez. 3. 2 as is written in *l.* of Moses
Neh. 8. 1 bring book of *l.* of Moses
Job 22. 22 Receive, I pray, the *l.*
Ps. 1. 2 del. is in the *l.* of the Lord
119. 97 O how I love thy *l.* ; it is
Prov. 3. 1 My son, forget not my *l.*
6. 20 forsake not *l.* of thy mother
28. 7 whoso keepeth the *l.* is wise
Isa. 1. 10 give ear to the *l.* of God
42. 21 magnify *l.* make it honour.
Jer. 8. 8 and the *l.* of Lord is with us
Lam. 2. 9 *l.* is more; her proph. also
Ezek. 7. 26 *l.* shall per. from priest
Dan. 9. 11 Is. have transgressed *l.*
Hos. 4. 6 hast forgotten *l.* of God
Am. 2. 4 have despised *l.* of Lord
Mic. 4. 2 *l.* shall go forth to Zion
Hab. 1. 5 therefore the *l.* is slacked
Zeph. 3. 4 ha. done violence to the *l.*
Hag. 2. 11 ask priest concerning *l.*

Zech. 7. 12 thou should hear the *l.*
Mal. 2. 6 *l.* of tr. was in his mouth
Mat. 5. 17 not I come to destroy *l.*
22. 40 on these two hang all the *l.*
Luke 2. 23 is written in *l.* of Lord
John 1. 17 for *l.* was giv. by Moses
Acts 6. 13 blasphem. words against *l*
Rom. 2. 12 in *l.* shall be judged by *l.*
10. 4 Christ is end of *l.* for right.
1 Cor. 7. 39 wife is bound by the *l.*
Gal. 3. 11 no man is justified by *l.*
Eph. 2. 15 even *l.* of commandments
Phil. 3. 9 righteous., which is of *l.*
Tit. 3. 9 avoid strivings about the *l.*
Heb. 7. 5 tithes .. according to *l.*
Jas. 1. 25 looketh into perfect *l.*
1 John 3. 4 sin is transgression of *l.*
R. V. Gen. 47. 26 ; 1 Chr. 16. 17 ;
Ps. 94. 20 ; 105. 10 statute ; Acts
15. 24 ; 24. 6 ; Rom. 9. 32 ; 1 Cor.
7. 39 ; 9. 20 ——

Lawful. *According to law.*
Ez. 7. 24 not *l.* to impose toll, trib.
Isa. 49. 24 or *l.* captive delivered?
Ezek. 18. 5 if man do which is *l.*
Mat. 12. 10 is it *l.* to heal on sab.
Mark 2. 26 which is not *l.* to eat
Luke 6. 2 why do which is not *l.*
John 5. 10 not *l.* to carry thy bed
Acts 22. 25 is it *l.* to scourge man
1 Cor. 10. 23 all things are *l.* for me
2 Cor. 12. 4 not *l.* for man to utter
R. V. Acts 19. 39 regular

Lawfully. *According to law.*
1 Tim. 1. 8 good. if man use it *l.*
2. Tim., 2. 5 except he strive *l.*

Lawgiver. *Who gives law.*
Gen. 49. 10 nor a *l.* from bet. feet
Num. 21. 18 digged by direction of *l.*
Deut. 33. 21 in portion of *l.,* was
Ps. 60. 7 G. is mine, Judah is my *l.*
Isa. 33. 22 Lord is our *l.,* . . our king
Jas. 4. 12 one *l.,* who is able to save
R. V. Gen. 49. 10. ruler's staff ; Num.
21. 18 ; Ps. 60. 7 ; 108. 8 sceptre

Lawless. *Unruly.*
1 Tim. 1. 9. for *l.* and disobedient

Lawyer. *Belonging to law.*
Mat. 22. 5 on of them, which was *l.*
Luke 7. 30 But Phar. and *l.* rejected
11. 46 woe unto you, ye *l.,* for ye
Tit. 3. 13 bring Zenas the *l.* and

Lay. *Put, place.*
Gen. 9. 23 and *l.* it upon shoulders
Ex. 2. 3 *l.* it in flags by river's br'k
Lev. 2. 15 put oil, and *l.* frankinc.
Num. 11. 11 *l.* burden of this people
Deut. 14. 28 shalt *l.* it up within
Josh. 8. 2 *l.* thee an ambush for
Judg. 18. 19 *l.* hand upon thy mouth
1 Sam. 6. 11 *l.* ark of L. upon cart
2 Sam. 13. 19 *l.* hand on her head
1 K. 18. 23 pieces, and *l.* it on wood,
2 K. 20. 17 fathers have *l.* up in store
2 Chr. 23. 15 they *l.* hands on her
Ez. 5. 16 *l.* found. of house of G.
Neh. 13. 5 where they *l.* meat off.
Esth. 2. 21 sought to *l.* hand on
Job 24. 12 yet God *l.* not folly to
Ps. 66. 11 *l.* affliction upon loins
Prov. 31. 19 *l.* her hands to spindle
Eccl. 7. 2 living will *l.* it to his hear.
Isa. 13. 9 L. com. to *l.* land desolate
Jer. 9. 8 but in heart he *l.* his wait
Lam. 4. 19 persecutors *l.* wait for
Ezek. 26. 12 *l.* thy stones and timber
Hos. 11. 4 and I *l.* meat upon them
Joel 1. 7 He hath *l.* my vine waste
Am. 2. 8 *l.* themselves down upon
Obad. 7 have *l.* wound under thee
Jonah 3. 6 he *l.* his robe from him
Mic. 1. 7 idols will I *l.* desolate
Zech. 3. 9 stone I *l.* before Joshua
Mal. 1. 3 Esau, and *l.* his mount's
Mat. 9. 18 *l.* thy hand upon her, and
Mark 6. 5 *l.* his hands upon a few
Luke 4. 40 *l.* his hands on ev. one
John 7. 30 no man *l.* hands on him
Acts 5. 18 *l.* hands on the apostles
Rom. 16. 4 for my life *l.* down own
1 Cor. 3. 10 I have *l.* the foundation
2 Cor. 12. 14 not to *l.* up for parents
1 Tim. 5. 22 *l.* hands on no man, nei.
2 Tim. 4. 8 is *l.* up for me a crown
Heb. 12. 1 let *l.* aside every weight
1 John 3. 16 he *l.* down his life for us

1 Pet. 2. 6 *l.* in Sion corner stone
Rev. 1. 17 *l.* right hand upon me
R. V. The frequent changes do not
modify general meaning.
See also the *v. i.* **Lie, lay, lain.**

Laying. *Putting upon.*
Acts 8. 18 through *l.* on of hands
1 Tim. 4. 14 with the *l.* on of hands
Heb. 6. 2 baptisms, and *l.* on of h.
Lying in wait.
Num. 35. 20 hurl at .. by *l.* of wait
Acts 9. 24 their *l.* await was known

Leach. *Leech.*
Prov. 30. 15 horse *l.* hath two daug.

Lead (*n.*). *Lead, metal.*
Ex. 15. 10 sank as *l.* in the m. waters
Num. 31. 22 brass, iron, tin, and *l.*
Job 19. 24 pen and *l.* in rock forev.
Jer. 6. 29 burnt, the *l.* is consumed
Ezek. 22. 18 *l.,* in midst of furnace
Zech. 5. 7 was lifted up talent of *l.*

Lead (*v.*). *Guide, conduct, tend.*
Gen. 24. 27 L. *l.* me to house of
Ex. 13. 21 pillar of cloud, to *l.* them
Num. 27. 17 which may *l.* them ou.
Deut. 32. 12 the L. alone did *l.* him
Josh. 24. 3 *l.* him throughout Cant
Judg. 5. 12 *l.* thy captivity captive
1 Sam. 30. 22 they may *l.* them away
2 Sam. 2. 2 *l.* out and brought in Is.
2. K. 6. 19 he *l.* them to Samaria
1 Chr. 20. 1 Joab *l.* power of army
2 Chr. 25. 11 Amaziah *l.* his people
Neh. 9. 12 *l.* them in day by cloud.
Job 12. 19 *l.* princes away spoiled
Ps. 25. 5 *l.* me in truth, and teach
Prov. 4. 11 have *l.* thee in right pa.
S. of S. 3. 2 I would *l.* thee, and
Isa. 3. 12 which *l.* cause thee to err
Jer. 2. 6 *l.* us through wilderness
Lam. 3. 2 *l.* me, and brought dark.
Ezek. 17. 12 and *l.* them to Babylon
Am. 2. 10 *l.* you forty years through
Nah. 2. 7 her maids shall *l.* her as
Mat. 7. 13 br. is way, that *l.* to destr.
Mark 8. 23 *l.* him out of the town
Luke 4. 1 *l.* by Spirit into wilder.
John 10. 3 sheep by name, and *l.*
Acts 8. 32 was *l.* as sheep to slaugh.
Rom. 2. 4 knowing goodness of G. *l.*
1 Cor. 9. 5 have we not power to *l.*
Gal. 5. 18 if ye be *l.* of the Spirit
1 Tim. 2. 2 we may *l.* peaceable life
Heb. 8. 9 *l.* them out of land of E.
Rev. 7. 17 *l.* them unto living foun.
R. V. Ps. 25. 5 ; Mat. 15. 14 ; Luke
6. 39 ; Rev. 7. 17 guide

Leader. *Who leads.*
1 Chr. 12. 27 Jehoiada *l.* of Aaron.
2 Chr. 32. 21 *l.* and captains in camp
Isa. 55. 4 I have given him for a *l.*
Mat. 15. 14 they be blind *l.* of bl.

Leaf. *Leaf, fold.*
Gen. 3. 7 sewed fig *l.* together, and
Lev. 26. 36 shak. *l.* shall chase them
1 K. 6. 34 two *l.* of door for folding
Job 13. 25 wilt thou break *l.* driven
Ps. 1. 3 his *l.* also shall not wither
Isa. 1. 30 as oak whose *l.* fadeth
Jer. 8. 13 tree, and the *l.* sh. fade
Ezek. 47. 12 and *l.* thereof for medi.
Mat. 21. 19 found noth. there., but *l.*
Mark 11. 13 fig tree afar having *l.*
Rev. 22. 2 the *l.* of tree for healing

League. *Covenant, alliance.*
Josh. 9. 6, 11 now .. make *l.* wi. us
Judg. 2. 2 make no *l.* with inhabit.
1 Sam. 22. 8 my son hath made *l.*
2 Sam. 5. 3 David made *l.* wi. them
1 K. 5. 12 they two made *l.* togeth.
2 Chr. 16. 3 is *l.* bet. me and thee
Job. 5. 23 be in *l.* with stones of
Ezek. 30. 5 men .. land that is in *l.*
Dan. 11. 23 and after the *l.* made
R. V. Josh. 9. 6, 7, 11, 15, 16 ;
Judg. 2. 2 ; 2 Sam. 3. 21 ; 5. 3
covenant

Lean (*a.*). *Weak, poor, thin.*
Gen. 41. 3 kine, ill favored and *l.*
Num. 13. 20 whether it be fat or *l.*
2 Sam. 13. 4 why .. *l.* fr. day to d. ?
Ezek. 34. 20 judge bet. fat cat. and *l.*

Lean (*v.*). *Incline, bend, rest, depend.*
Judg. 16. 26 pillars that I may *l.* up
2 Sam. 1. 6 Saul *l.* upon his spear

2 K. 5. 18 he *l.* upon my hand, and
Job 8. 15 He shall *l.* upon his house
Prov. 3. 5 *l.* not on own understand.
Isa. 36. 6 whereon if man *l.*, it wilf
Ezek. 29. 7 when they *l.* upon thee
Am. 5. 19 and *l.* his hand on wall
Mic. 3. 11 they *l.* upon the Lord
John 13. 23 was *l.* on Jesus' bosom
21. 20 *l.* on his breast at supper
R. V. John 13. 23 reclining

Leanness. *Thinness, weakness.*
Job 16. 8 and my *l.* rising up in me
Ps. 106. 15 sent *l.* into their soul
Isa. 24. 16 My *l.*, my *l.*, woe un. me!
R. V. Isa. 24. 16 I pine away

Leap. *Jump, skip, bound, dance.*
Gen. 31. 10 rams which *l.* on cattle
Lev. 11. 21 have legs to *l.* on earth
Deut. 33. 22 he shall *l.* from Bashan
2 Sam. 6. 16 saw D. *l.* and dancing
1 K. 18. 26 they *l.* upon the altar
Job 41. 19 and sparks of fire *l.* out
Ps. 18. 29 by my G. have I *l.* over
S. of S. 2. 8 cometh *l.* upon moun.
Isa. 35. 6 lame . . shall *l.* as hart
Joel 2. 5 shall *l.*, like noise of flame
Zeph. 1. 9 punish that *l.* on thresh.
Luke 1. 41 the babe *l.* in her womb
Acts 3. 8 *l.* up, stood, and walked
14. 10 and he *l.* and walked

Learn. *Get knowledge, be instructed.*
Gen. 30. 27 have *l.* by experience
Deut. 4. 10 *l.* to fear me all days
Ps. 106. 35 heath., and *l.* their ways
Prov. 22. 25 lest thou *l.* his ways
Isa. 1. 17 *l.* to do well; seek judg.
Jer. 10. 2 *l.* not way of the heathen
Ezek. 19. 3 lion *l.* to catch the prey
Mic. 4. 3 neither shall they *l.* war
Mat. 9. 13 But go ye and *l.* what
Mark 13. 28 *l.* parable of fig tree
John 6. 45 hath heard, and hath *l.*
Rom. 16. 17 doctrine which I have *l.*
1 Cor. 4. 6 that ye might *l.* in us
Gal. 3. 2 this only would I *l.* of you
Eph. 4. 20 ye have not so *l.* Christ
Phil. 4. 9 have both *l.*, and received
Col. 1. 7 as ye also *l.* of Epaphras
1 Tim. 2. 11 let woman *l.* in silence
2 Tim. 3. 7 ever *l.*, never able to co.
Tit. 3. 14 *l.* to maintain good works
Heb. 5. 8 tho. S., yet *l.* he obedi.
Rev. 14. 3 no man could *l.* the song

Learned. *Instructed, knowing.*
Isa. 29. 11 deliv. to one that is *l.*
50. 4 hath giv. thee tongue of *l.*
Acts 7. 22 Moses was *l.* in wisdom
R. V. Isa. 50. 4 are taught; Acts
7. 22 instructed

Learning. *Instruction.*
Prov. 1. 5 wise man will increase *l.*
Dan. 1. 17 knowledge and skill in *l.*
Acts 26. 24 doth make thee mad
Rom. 15. 4 were written for our *l.*

Leasing. *Lying.*
Ps. 4. 2 will ye love . . seek after *l.*?
5. 6 destroy them that speak *l.*
R. V. Ps. 4. 2 falsehood; 5. 6 lies

Least. *Smallest.*
Gen. 24. 55 abide few days at *l.* ten
Num. 11. 32 gath. *l.* gath. ten hom.
Judg. 6. 15 *l.* in my father's house
1 Sam. 9. 21 fam. *l.* of all families
2 K. 18. 24 *l.* of my master's servts.
1 Chr. 12. 14 *l.* was over a hundred
Isa. 36. 9 *l.* of my master's servants
Jer. 6. 13 from *l.* even unto greatest
Jonah 3. 5 greatest of them to the *l.*
Mat. 2. 6 not *l.* among princes of Ju.
5. 19 called *l.* in kingdom of heaven
Luke 7. 28 that is *l.* in king. of God
Acts 5. 15 at *l.* shadow of P. passing
1 Cor. 15. 9 I am the *l.* of apostles
Heb. 8. 11 know me, from *l.* to gr.
R. V. 1 Sam. 21. 4 only; Mat. 13. 22
less than; 11. 11; Luke 7. 28 but
little; Luke 16. 10 a very little; 1
Cor. 6. 4 of no account

Leather. *Skin.*
2 K. 1. 8 wi. girdle of *l.* about loins
Leathern. *Of skin.*
Mat. 3. 4 *l.* girdle about his loins
Leave (*v.*). *Cease, finish.*
Gen. 18. 33 *l.* communing wi. Aaron
41. 49 until he *l.* numbering, for it

Judg. 9. 9 should I *l.* my fatness
Ruth 1. 18 she *l.* speaking to her
1 Sam. 9. 5 lest my father *l.* caring
1 K. 15. 21 *l.* off building Ramah
2 Chr. 16. 5
Neh. 5. 10 I pray, let us *l.* off usury
Job 9. 27 will *l.* off this heaviness
Ps. 36. 3 he hath *l.* off to be wise
Prov. 17. 14 *l.* off conten., bef. it be
Jer. 38. 27 so they *l.* off speaking
Forsake, abandon.
Gen. 2. 24 therefore shall man *l.* f.
Ex. 9. 21 *l.* his servants and cattle
Lev. 19. 10 shalt *l.* them for poor
Num. 10. 31 *l.* us not, I pray thee
Josh. 8. 17 *l.* city open, and pursued
Judg. 2. 21 nations which Joshua *l.*
Ruth 1. 16 entreat me not to *l.* thee
1 Sam. 30. 13 my master *l.* me bec.
2 Sam. 5. 21 they *l.* their images, and
1 K. 19. 20 he *l.* the oxen and ran
2 K. 7. 7 *l.* their tents and horses
1 Chr. 14. 12 when they had *l.* gods
2 Chr. 11. 14 Levites *l.* their suburbs
Neh. 9. 28 therefore *l.* thou them
Job 10. 1 I will *l.* my complaint on
Ps. 16. 10 wilt not *l.* my soul in hell
Prov. 2. 13 who *l.* paths of unright.
Isa. 10. 3 where will ye *l.* glory?
Jer. 49. 11 *l.* thy fatherless children
Ezek. 23. 8 nei. *l.* she her whored.
Zech. 11. 17 Woe to shepherd that *l.*
Mal. 4. 1 *l.* them nei. root nor branch
Let go, go from, quit.
Mat. 4. 11 then the devil *l.* him
Mark 1. 20 *l.* Zebedee in the ship
13. 2 not be *l.* one stone on anoth.
Luke 13. 35 house is *l.* you desolate
18. 28 we have *l.* all and followed
John 4. 28 woman *l.* her water pot
Acts 14. 17 *l.* not himself without w.
Rom. 1. 27 *l.* nat. use of the woman
1 Cor. 7. 13 wi. her, let her not *l.* him
Eph. 5. 31 for this cause man sh. *l.*
1 Thes. 3. 1 good to be *l.* at Athens
2 Tim. 4. 13 the cloke I *l.* at Troas
Tit. 1. 5 this cause I *l.* thee in Crete
Heb. 4. 1 promise being *l.* us of ent.
1 Pet. 2. 21 called, *l.* us an example
Rev. 2. 4 thou hast *l.* thy first love
R. V. Changes frequent, but usual
meanings retained

Leave (*n.*). *Permission, departure.*
Num. 22. 13 L. refuseth to give *l.*
1 Sam. 20. 6 David asked *l.* of me
Neh. 13. 6 obtained I *l.* of the king
Mark 5. 13 And Jesus gave them *l.*
John. 19. 38 *l.* to take away body
Acts 18. 18 Paul took *l.* of brethren
2 Cor. 2. 13 taking my *l.* of them

Leaved. *Having leaves or folds.*
Isa. 45. 1 to open the two *l.* gates
Leaven. *Fermenting dough.*
Ex. 12. 15 ye sh. put away *l.* out of
Lev. 6. 17 shall not be baken with *l.*
Am. 4. 5 And offer a sacri. with *l.*
Mat. 13. 33 king. of heav. is like *l.*
Mark 8. 15 beware of *l.* of Pharis.
Luke 13. 21 like *l.*, which wom. took
1 Cor. 5. 7 purge out theref. old *l.*
Gal. 5. 9 little *l.* leaven. who. lump
Leavened. *Fermented.*
Ex. 13. 3 shall no *l.* bread be eaten
Lev. 7. 13 off. *l.* bread with sacrifice
Deut. 16. 4 sh. be no *l.* bread seen
Hos. 7. 4 kneaded dough, until *l.*
Mat. 13. 33 hid, till the whole was *l.*
Luke 13. 21
Leaveneth. *Fermenteth.*
1 Cor. 5. 6 lit. leaven *l.* whole lump
Gal. 5. 9
Leaves. *Folds, hangings.*
1 K. 6. 34 two *l.* of other door fold.
Isa. 45. 1 open the two *l.* gate; and
Jer. 36. 23 had read three or four *l.*
Ezek. 41. 24 two *l.* for the one door
Tree leaves or flowers.
Dan. 4. 12, 14, 21 The *l.* were fair
Led. *See* Lead.
Ledge. *Projection, molding.*
1 K. 7. 35 on top of the base the *l.*
7. 36, 28, 29
R. V. 1 K. 7. 35, 36 stays
Leek. *Herb, leek.*
Num. 11. 5 melons, and *l.*, and on.
Lees. *Dregs, preserves.*

Isa. 25. 6 a feast of wine on the *l.*
Jer. 48. 11 he hath settled on his *l.*
Zeph. 1. 12 punish men settled on *l.*
Left. *Opposite to right.*
Gen. 13. 9 then I will go to the *l.*
Ex. 14. 22 right hand, and on the *l.*
Lev. 14. 15 into palm of the *l.* hand
Num. 20. 17 not turn to right nor *l.*
Deut. 2. 27 neither turn right nor *l.*
Josh. 19. 27 goeth out to Cabul on *l.*
Judg. 7. 20 held the lamps in *l.* hand
1 Sam. 6. 12 turned not to right nor *l.*
2 Sam. 14. 19 or to the *l.* from ought
1 K. 7. 39 five on *l.* side of the house
2 K. 23. 8 were on man's *l.* at gate
1 Chr. 6. 44 sons of M. stood on *l.*
2 Chr. 4. 6 right hand, and five on *l.*
Neh. 8. 4 on *l.*, Peda. and Mishael
Job 23. 9 On *l.*, where he doth work
Prov. 3. 16 in *l.* hand riches and h.
Eccl. 10. 2 but a fool's heart at his *l.*
S. of S. 2. 6 *l.* h. is under my head
Isa. 9. 20 and he shall eat on *l.* hand
Ezek. 1. 10 had face of ox on *l.* side
Dan. 12. 7 held up right hand and *l.*
Jonah 4. 11 bet. their r. hand and *l.*
Zech. 4. 3 other upon *l.* side thereof
Mat. 20. 21 other on *l.*, in kingdom
Mark 10. 37 other on *l.* h., in glory
Acts 21. 3 we left it on the *l.* hand
Rev. 10. 2 he set his *l.* foot on earth
Left (*v.*). *See* Leave.
Left-handed. *Bound of right hand.*
Judg. 3. 15 Son of Gera, man *l. h.*
20. 16 seven hun. chosen men *l. h.*
Leg. *Lower limb.*
Ex. 12. 9 roast . . his head with his *l.*
Lev. 1. 9 his *l.* shall ye wash in wa.
Deut. 28. 35 in *l.*, with sore botch
1 Sam. 17. 6 greaves of brass on *l.*
Ps. 147. 10 taketh not pleasure in *l.*
Prov. 26. 7 *l.* of lame are not equal
S. of S. 5. 15. *l.* as pillars of marble
Isa. 47. 2 uncov. locks, make bare *l.*
Dan. 2. 33 his *l.* of iron, his feet part
Am. 3. 12 the mouth of lion two *l.*
John 19. 31 that *l.* might be broken
19. 32, 33
R. V. Isa. 47. 2 train
Legion. *Multitude.*
Mat. 26. 53 more than twelve *l.* ang.
Mark 5. 9 saying, my name is Legion
Luke 8. 30 thy name? He said, L.
Leisure. *Opportunity.*
Mark 6. 31 no *l.* so much as to eat
Lend. *Give, grant, make loan.*
Ex. 22. 25 if thou *l.* money to peo.
Lev. 25. 37 not *l.* him thy victuals
Deut. 15. 6 shalt *l.* unto many nat.
1 Sam. 1. 28 I have *l.* him to Lord
Ps. 37. 26 is ever merciful, and *l.*
Prov. 19. 17 pity on poor *l.* to Lord
Jer. 15. 10 I have nei. *l.* on usury
Luke 6. 34 sinners also *l.* to sinners
11. 5 Friend, *l.* me three loaves
R. V. Lev. 25. 37 give; 1 Sam. 1
28 granted
Lender. *Who lends.*
Prov. 22. 7 borrower is servant to *l.*
Isa. 24. 2 as with *l.*, so with borr.
Length. *At last, finally.*
Prov. 29. 21 become his son at the *l.*
At any time.
Rom. 1. 10 if by any means at *l.* I
From end to end, extent.
Gen. 6. 15 *l.* of ark was th. hun. c.
Ex. 26. 2 *l.* of one curtain shall be
Deut. 30. 20 life, and *l.* of thy days
Judg. 3. 16 ma. dagger, of a cubit *l.*
1 K. 6. 2 *l.* thereof threescore c.
2 Chr. 3. 3 *l.* . . after first measure
Job 12. 12 in *l.* of days understand.
Ps. 21. 4 gravest *l.* of days forever
Prov. 3. 16 *l.* of days in right hand
Ezek. 31. 7 in. the *l.* of his branches
Zech. 5. 2 *l.* thereof twenty cubits
Eph. 3. 18 what is breadth, and *l.*
Rev. 21. 16 *l.* as large as breadth
R. V. Prov. 29. 21 last
Lengthen. *Make long.*
Deut. 25. 15 that thy days may be *l.*
1 K. 3. 14 then I will *l.* thy days
Isa. 54. 2 *l.* thy cords, and strength.
Dan. 4. 27 a. *l.* of thy tranquillity
R. V. Deut. 25. 15 long upon

Lent. *See Lend.*

Lentiles. *Lentiles.*
Gen. 25. 34 bread and pottage of *l.*
2 Sam. 17. 28 beans, *l.*, and par. corn
Ezek. 4. 9 Take beans, *l.*, and millet

Leopard. *Leopard, panther.*
S. of S. 4. 8 from mountains of *l.*
Isa. 11. 6 *l.* shall lie down with kid
Jer. 5. 6 *l.* watch over their cities
13. 23 change skin, or *l.* his spots?
Dan. 7. 6 another, like *l.*, which
Hos. 13. 7 I will be as a *l.* by the way
Hab. 1. 8 horses are swifter than *l.*
Rev. 13. 2 beast .. was like unto *l.*

Leper. *Leprous one.*
Lev. 13. 45 and *l.* in whom plague is
Num. 5. 2 put out of camp every *l.*
2 Sam. 3. 29 hath issue, or that is *l.*
2 K. 5. 27 went from his pres. a *l.*
2 Chr. 26. 21 Uzziah the king was *l.*
Mat. 8. 2 came a *l.* and worshipped
Mark 14. 3 in house of Simon the *l.*
Luke 4. 27 many *l.* were in Israel

Leprosy. *Leprosy, scourge.*
Lev. 13. 3 it is plague of *l.*, priest sh.
Deut. 24. 8 take heed in plague of *l.*
2 K. 5. 3 would recover him of *l.*
2 Chr. 26. 19 *l.* rose in his forehead
Mat. 8. 3 and im. his *l.* was cleansed
Mark 1. 42 immediately *l.* departed
Luke 5. 12 behold man full of *l.*

Leprous. *With leprosy, scaly.*
Ex. 4. 6 his hand was *l.* as snow
Lev. 13. 44 He is a *l.* man, unclean
Num. 12. 10 behold, Miriam bec. *l.*
2 K. 7. 3 four *l.* man at entering
2 Chr. 26. 20 he was *l.* in forehead

Less. *Smaller, little.*
Ex. 16. 17 gath. some more, some *l.*
Num, 26. 54 to few give *l.* inherit
1 Sam. 25. 36 told nothing, *l.* or mo.
Ez. 9, 13 hath punished us *l.* than
Isa. 40. 17 counted to him *l.* than n.
Mark 4. 31 *l.* than all seeds that be
15. 40 Mary, mother of James the *l.*
2 Cor. 12. 15 mo. I love *l.* I be loved
Heb. 7. 7 *l.* is blessed of the better

Lesser. *Smaller, little.*
Gen. 1. 16 *l.* light to rule the night
Isa. 7. 25 for treading of *l.* cattle
Ezek. 43. 14 from *l.* settle to greater
R. V. Isa. 7. 25 sheep

Lest. *In order that, for fear that.*
Gen. 4. 15 *l.* any finding should kill
Mat. 17. 27 *l.* we offend them, go
Etc., etc.

Let. *Give, let, suffer, permit.*
Gen. 32. 26 I will not *l.* thee go
Ex. 3. 19 king will not *l.* you go
Lev. 14. 53 shall *l.* go living bird
Deut. 15. 12 shalt *l.* him go free
Josh. 8. 22 *l.* none of them remain
Judg 11. 37 *l.* me alone two months
1 Sam. 6. 6 did they not *l.* people go
2 Sam. 16. 11 *l.* him alone, *l.* him c.
1 K. 20. 42 *l.* him go out of thy hand
2 K. 23. 18 he said, *l.* him alone
2 Chr. 16, 1 *l.* none go out or come
Ez. 6. 7 *l.* the work of house alone
Job. 7. 16 *l.* me alone ; days are v.
Ps. 69. 6 *l.* not those be ashamed
Prov. 4. 13 *l.* her not go; keep her
S. of S. 8. 11 *l.* vineyard to keepers
Isa. 45. 13 shall *l.* go my captives
Jer. 34. 9 *l.* his manservant, go free
Ezek. 13. 20 and will *l.* the souls go
Mat. 7. 4 *l.* me pull out the mote
Mark 7. 27 *l.* children first be filled
Luke 9. 60 *l.* dead bury their dead
John 11. 44 Loose him, and *l.* him
Acts 2. 29 *l.* me speak unto you
Rom. 1. 13 come, but was *l.* hitherto
2 Thes. 2. 7 only he who *l.* will *l.*
Heb. 2. 1 lest we *l.* them sleep
R V. Many changes to shall, suffer, etc. but nearly all contingent on consequent word

Letter. *Epistle, book, account, anything written.*
2 Sam. 11. 14 David wrote *l.* to Joab
1 K. 21. 8 she wrote *l.* in A's name
2 Chr. 32. 17 he wrote *l.* to rail L.
Ez. 4. 7 writing of *l.* was written
Neh. 2 let *l.* be giv. to governors
Esth. 3. 13 *l.* were sent by posts
Isa. 37. 14 Hezekiah received *l.* fr

Jer. 29. 1 these are words of the *l.*
Luke 23. 38 written in *l.* of Greek
John 7. 15 How knoweth this man *l.*
Acts 9. 2 S. desired *l.* to Damascus
Rom. 2. 29 in spirit, and not in *l.*
1 Cor. 16. 3 shall approve by your *l.*
2 Cor. 7. 8 I made you sorry with *l.*
Gal. 6. 11 see . . *l.* I have written
2 Thes. 2. 2 nor by word, nor by *l.*
R. V. 2 Cor. 7. 8; 2 Thes. 2. 2 epistle; Luke 23. 38; 2 Cor. 3. 1 : Heb. 13. 22 ——.

Leviathan. *Great water animal.*
Job 41. 1 canst thou draw out *l.*
Ps. 74. 14 breakest the heads of *l.*
Isa. 27. 1 *l.* the piercing serpent

Levy (*n.*). *Burden, tribute.*
1 K. 5. 13 Sol. raised *l.* out of Is.
5. 14; 9. 15

Levy (*v.*). *Lift up, raise.*
Num. 31. 28 *l.* tribute unto Lord
1 K. 9. 21 on those did Sol. *l.* tribute
R. V. 1 K. 9. 21 raise.

Lewd, ly. *Wicked thought, vile.*
Ezek. 16. 27 are ashamed of thy *l.*
22. 11 hath *l.* defiled his daughter
Acts 17. 5 *l.* fellows of baser sort
R. V. Acts 17. 5 vile

Lewdness. *Wicked thought, vileness.*
Judge. 20. 6 they have committed *l.*
Jer. 11. 15 she hath wrought *l.* wi.
Ezek. 16. 43 shalt not commit this *l.*
Hos. 2. 10 now will I discover her *l.*
Acts 18. 14 matter of wrong or *l.*
R. V. Acts 18. 14 villany

Liar. *Who lies, deceiver.*
Deut. 33. 29 enemies be found *l.*
Job 24. 25 now who will make me *l.*
Ps. 116. 11 I said.., All men are *l.*
Prov. 19. 22 poor man is bet. than *l.*
Jer. 15. 18 wilt thou be to me as *l.*
John 8. 44 he is a *l.*, and father of it
Rom. 3. 4 true, but every man a *l.*
1 Tim. 1. 10 for *l.*, for perjured per.
Tit. 1. 12 Cretians are always *l.*
1 John 1. 10 we make him a *l.*, and
2. 4 is a *l.*, the truth is not in him
Rev. 2. 2 and hast found them *l.*
R. V. Jer. 15. 18 deceitful brook ;
50. 36 boasters ; Rev. 2. 2 false.

Liberal. *Free, generous, princely.*
Prov. 11. 25 *l.* soul sh. be made fat
Isa. 32. 5 vile . . be no more called *l.*
32. 8 *l.* deviseth *l.* things, and by *l.*
2 Cor. 9. 13 for *l.* distribution to th.

Liberality. *Simplicity, benevolence.*
1 Cor. 16. 3 bring your *l.* unto Jerus.
2 Cor. 8. 2 unto riches of their *l.*
R. V. 1 Cor. 16. 3 bounty.

Liberally. *Generously.*
Deut. 15. 14 shalt furnish him *l.*
Jas. 1. 5 God, that giveth to all *l.*

Libertines. *Freedmen.*
Acts 6. 9 called synagogue of the L.

Liberty. *Freedom, permission.*
Lev. 25. 10 proclaim *l.* throughout l.
Ps. 119. 45 I will walk at *l.*, for I
Isa. 61 1 proclaim *l.* to captives
Jer. 34. 8 to proclaim *l.* unto them
Ezek. 46. 17 his to the year of *l.*
Luke 4. 18 to set at *l.* them that
Acts 24. 23 to let him have *l.*, and
Rom. 8. 21 *l.* of children of God
1 Cor. 10. 29 why is my *l.* judged
2 Cor. 3. 17 wh. Lord is, there is *l.*
Gal. 2. 4 ca. to spy out our *l.* which
Heb. 13. 23 bro. Timothy is set at *l.*
Jas. 1. 25 who. looketh into law of *l.*
1 Pet. 2. 16 not using your *l.* for
2 Pet. 2. 19 while they promise *l.*
R. V. Acts 27. 3 leave ; 1 Cor. 7. 39 free ; Gal. 5. 13 freedom

Lice. *Gnats, lice.*
Ex. 8. 16 dust, that it may become *l.*
Ps. 105. 31 came *l.* in all their coasts

License. *Turn over upon, permit.*
Acts 21. 40 when he had given *l.*
25. 16 and *l.* to answer for himself
R. V. Acts 21. 40 leave ; 25. 16 opportunity

Lick. *Take by tongue, lap.*
Num. 22. 4 as ox *l.* up grass of the
1 K. 21. 19 shall dogs *l.* thy blood
Ps. 72. 9 and his enemies shall *l.*

Isa. 49. 23 *l.* up dust of feet; and
Mic. 7. 17 shall *l.* dust like serpent
Luke 16 21 the dogs *l.* his sores

Lid. *Leaf, door, cover.*
2 K. 12. 9 bored hole in *l.* of it

Lie (*n.*). *Device, deceit, falsehood.*
Judg. 16. 10 mocked me, and told *l.*
Job 13. 4 But ye are forgers of *l.*
Ps. 62 9 men of high degree are *l.*
Prov. 30. 8 remove far vanity and *l.*
Isa. 9. 15 prophet that teacheth *l.*
Jer. 9. 3 bend tong. like bow for *l.*
Ezek. 13. 8 spoken vanity, and . . *l.*
Dan. 11. 27 speak *l.* at one table
Hos. 7. 13 yet they have spoken *l.*
Am. 2. 4 their *l.* caused them to err
Nah. 3. 1 cit. full of *l.* and robbery
Zeph. 3. 13 Israel shall not speak *l.*
John 8. 44 when he speaketh a *l.*
Rom. 1. 25 who changed truth into *l.*
1 Tim. 4. 2 speaking *l.* in hypocrisy
2 Thes. 2. 11 that they sh. believe *l.*
1 John 2. 27 is truth, and is no *l.*
Rev. 21. 17 work. abom. or mak. *l.*
R. V. Job 11. 3 ; Jer. 48. 30 boastings ; Ezek.24. 12 toil ; Ps. 101. 7
Prov. 29. 12 ; Jer. 9. 3 ; Hos. 11. 12 falsehood

Lie (*v.*). *Feign, deceive.*
Lev. 6. 2 *l.* unto his neighbour in
Num. 23. 19 G. not m., that he .. *l.*
1 Sam. 15. 29 str. of Is. will not *l.*
1 K. 13. 18 But he *l.* unto them
2 K. 4. 16 not *l.* unto thine hand
Job 6. 28 is evident unto you *l.*
Ps. 78. 36 *l.* unto him with tongues
Prov. 14. 5 faithful wit. will not *l.*
Isa. 63. 8 my people .. will not *l.*
Mic. 2. 11 if man do *l.* ; saying I
Acts 5. 3 Satan filled heart to *l.* to
Rom. 9. 1 I say the truth, I *l.* not
2 Cor. 11. 31 God .. knoweth I *l.* not
Gal. 1. 20 before God, I *l.* not
Col. 3. 9 *l.* not one to another, seeing
1 Tim. 2. 7 I speak truth, and *l.* not
Heb. 6. 18 impossible for God to *l.*
Jas. 3. 14 and *l.* not against truth
1 John 1. 6 we *l.*, and do not truth
Rev. 3. 9 say they are Jews, but *l.*

Lie (*v.*). *Crouch, recline, lay prone.*
Gen. 29. 2 flocks of sheep *l.* by it
Ex. 22. 19 who. *l.* with beast shall
Lev. 26. 6 *l.*, and none make afraid
Num. 24. 9 he *l.* down as a lion
Deut. 11. 19 when *l.* down, when r.
Josh. 2. 8 before they were *l.* down
Judg. 16. 3 Samson *l.* till midnight
Ruth 3. 13 *l.* down until morning
1 Sam. 3. 5 he went and *l.* down
2 Sam. 4. 7 1 *l.* on bed in chamber
1 K. 1. 2 let her *l.* in thy bosom
2 K. 4. 34 went, and *l.* upon child
Ez. 8. 31 su. as *l.* in wait by the way
Neh. 3. 25 tower which *l.* out from
Esth. 4. 3 and many *l.* in sackcloth
Job 40. 21 he *l.* under shady trees
Ps. 3. 5 I *l.* me down and slept
68. 13 tho. ye have *l.* among pots
Prov. 23. 34 be as he that *l.* down
Eccl. 4. 11 if two *l.* tog. . . have heat
S. of S. 1. 13 *l.* betwixt my breasts
Isa. 14. 8 since thou art *l.* down
Jer. 3. 25 we *l.* down in our shame
Lam. 2. 21 young and old *l.* on gr.
Ezek. 4. 4 *l.* thou upon left side
Joel 1. 13 *l.* all night in sackcloth
Am. 6. 4 that *l.* on beds of ivory
Jonah 1. 5 *l.* and was fast asleep
Mic. 7. 5 keep doors from her that *l.*
Zeph. 2. 7 they *l.* down in evening
Mat. 8. 6 my servant *l.* sick of palsy
Mark 5. 40 ent. where damsel was *l.*
Luke 2. 12 find babe *l.* in manger
John 2. 5 saw the linen clothes *l.*
Acts 27. 20 no small tempest *l.* on
Eph. 4. 14 they *l.* in wait to deceive
1 John 5. 19 world *l.* in wickedness
Rev. 21. 16 the city *l.* four square
R. V. Gen. 4. 7 ; 49. 25 coucheth

Lien. *See Lie.*

Lier. *Who lies in wait.*
Josh. 8. 14 *l.* in ambush against
Judg. 16. 12 *l.* in wait in chamber

Lieutenants. R. V. *satraps.*
Ex. 8. 36 commission unto kings *l.*
Esth. 8. 9 written to *l.* and deputies

Life. *Being alive, breath, spirit, existence, living.*
Gen. 2. 7 breath. into nos. br. of *l.*
Ex. 1. 14 they made their *l.* bitter
Lev. 17. 1 the *l.* of the flesh is blood
Num. 35. 31 no sat. for *l* of murder.
Deut. 19. 21 *l.* for *l.* eye for an eye
Josh. 2. 14 our *l.* for yours, if ye
Judg. 12. 3 I put my *l.* in my hands
Ruth 4. 15 shall be restorer of thy *l.*
1 Sam. 19. 5 put his *l.* in his hand,
2 Sam. 1. 9 my *l.* is yet whole in me
1 K. 19. 4 O Lord, take away my *l.*
2 K. 1. 14 let now my *l.* be precious
1 Chr. 11. 19 have put their *l.* in je.
2 Chr. 1. 11 nor *l.* of thine enemies
Ez. 6. 10 and pray for *l.* of the king
Esth. 7. 3 let my *l.* be given me at my
Job 2. 4 all .. will he give for his *l.*
Ps. 16. 11 wilt shew me path of *l.*
Prov. 13. 3 that keepeth mouth .. *l.*
Eccl. 3. 12 to do good in his *l.*
Isa. 38. 12 cut off like weaver my *l.*
Jer. 8. 3 death chos. rather than *l.*
Lam. 3. 54 cut off my *l.* in dungeon
Ezek. 33. 15 walk in statutes of *l.*
Dan. 7. 12 *l.* were prolonged for sea.
Jonah 2. 6 brought my *l.* from cor.
Mal. 2. 5 cov. was of *l.* and peace
Mat. 6. 25 take no thought for *l.*
Mark 9. 43 bet. to enter *l.* maimed
Luke 10. 25 what do to inher. eter. *l.*
John 1. 4 In him was *l.*; *l.* was light
6. 35 I am the bread of *l.*
Acts 2. 28 made known ways of *l.*
Rom. 6. 23 eternal *l.* through J. C.
1 Cor. 3. 22 or *l.*, or death, or th. p.
2 Cor. 2. 16 other savour of *l.* unto *l.*
Gal. 6. 8 of spirit reap *l.* everlasting
Eph. 4. 18 alienated from *l.* of God
Phil. 2. 16 holding forth word of *l.*
Col. 3. 3 *l.* is hid with Christ in G.
1 Tim. 6. 12 lay hold on eternal *l.*
2 Tim. 1. 1 accord. to promise of *l.*
Tit. 1. 2 in hope of eternal *l.* which
Heb. 7. 16 after power of endless *l.*
Jas. 1. 12 shall receive crown of *l.*
1 Pet. 3. 7 being heirs of grace of *l.*
2 Pet. 1. 3 pertain unto *l.* and godli.
1 John 3. 14 passed from death to *l.*
Jude 21 of L. J. C. unto eternal *l.*
Rev. 2. 7 give to eat of tree of *l.*
22. 1 pure river of water of *l.*

Lifetime. *Living time.*
2 Sam. 18. 18 Absalom in his *l.* had
Luke 16. 25 thou in thy *l.* received
Heb. 2. 15 were all their *l.* subject

Lift. *Raise, make high, bear.*
Gen. 13. 10 Lot *l.* up his eyes and
Ex. 7. 20 he *l.* up the rod, and smo.
Lev. 9. 22 Aaron *l.* up his hand and
Num. 6. 26 L. *l.* up his countenance
Deut. 3. 27 *l.* up thine eyes west.
Josh. 4. 18 priest's feet were *l.* up
Judg. 2. 4 people *l.* up their voice
Ruth 1. 9 *l.* up th. voice, and wept
1 Sam. 24. 16 Saul *l.* voice, and wept
2 Sam. 23. 18 *l.* spear against three h.
1 K. 11. 26 *l.* hand against the king
2 K. 9. 32 Jehu *l.* face to window
1 Chr. 21. 16 David *l.* up his eyes
2 Chr. 17. 6 and his heart was *l.* up
Ez. 9. 6 blush to *l.* face to thee
Neh. 8. 6 Amen, with *l.* up hands
Job 30. 22 thou *l.* me up to wind
Ps. 24. 7 *l.* up heads, O ye gates
Prov. 30. 13 their eyelids are *l.* up
Isa. 2. 4 nat. not *l.* sword against n·
Jer. 3. 2 *l.* eyes unto high places
Lam. 3. 41 let us *l.* up our heart wi.
Ezek. 3. 14 so the spirit *l.* me up and
Dan. 8. 3 then I *l.* mine eyes, and
Mic. 4. 3 nat. not *l.* I sword against
Hab. 3. 10 deep *l.* hands on high
Zech. 5. 9 *l.* ephah between earth
Mat. 12. 11 will he not *l.* it out?
Mark 1. 31 took hand, and *l.* her up
Luke 16. 23 in hell he *l.* up his eyes
John 4. 35 *l.* eyes, look on the fields
Acts 4. 24 *l.* up their voice to God
1 Tim. 2. 8 *l.* holy hands, without w.
Heb. 12. 12 *l.* hands which hang d.
Jas. 4. 10 and he shall *l.* you up
Rev. 10. 6 angel *l.* hand to heaven
R. V. Ps. 30. 1; Mark 1. 31; 9. 27;
Acts 3. 7; 9. 41 raised.

Lifter. - *Who lifts.*
Ps. 3. 3 and the *l.* up of my head

Light (*n.*). *Radiance, shining, lamp.*
Gen. 1. 3 Let there be *l.*: was *l.*
Ex. 10. 23 children of Israel had *l.*
Lev' 24. 2 olive oil beaten for *l.*
Num. 4. 9 cover candlestick for *l.*
Judg. 19. 26 at door .. till it was *l.*
1 Sam. 14. 36 spoil them until m. *l.*
2 Sam. 23. 4 as *l.* of morning when
1 K. 7. 4 and *l.* was against *l.* in
2 K. 7. 9 tarry till the morning *l.*
Esth. 8. 16 Jews had *l.* and gladness
Job 12. 25 grope in dark without *l.*
Ps. 27. 1 L. is my *l.* and my salva.
Prov. 4. 18 as *l.*, that shineth more
Eccl. 2. 13 as far as *l.* excelleth dark.
Isa. 2. 5 let us walk in *l.* of Lord
Jer. 31. 35 L.. which giv. sun for *l.*
Lam. 3. 2 brought dark. but not *l.*
Ezek. 32. 7 moon shall not give *l.*
Hos. 6. 5 thy judgments are as *l.*
Am. 5. 18 day of L. is dark. not *l.*
Mic. 7. 9 he will bring me to *l.*
Hab. 3. 4 his brightness was as *l.*
Zeph. 3. 5 both bring judgment to *l.*
Zech. 14. 6 the *l.* shall not be clear
Mat. 4. 16 the people saw great *l.*
Mark 13. 24 moon shall not give *l.*
Luke 2. 32 *l.* to lighten Gentiles
John 1. 4 life, and life was the *l.*
8. 12 I am the *l.* of the world
Acts 9. 3 shined about him a *l.* from
Rom. 13. 12 put on the armour of *l.*
1 Cor. 4. 5 bring to *l.* hidden things
2 Cor. 4. 6 God command. *l.* to shine
Eph. 5. 8 walk as children of *l.*
Phil. 2. 15 shine as *l.* in the world
Col. 1. 12 inheritance of saints in *l.*
1 Thes. 5. 5 ye are all children of *l.*
1 Tim. 6. 16 *l.* no man can appr.
Jas. 1. 17 cometh from Father of *l.*
1 Pet. 2. 9 into his marvellous *l.*
1 John 1. 5 declare .. that God is *l.*
Rev. 18. 23 *l.* of candle .. shine no
R. V. 2 Sam. 21. 17; 1 K. 11. 36;
2 K. 8. 19; 2 Ch. 21. 7; Mat.
6. 22; Luke 11. 34 lamp

Light (*a.*). *Not heavy, unstable.*
Num. 21. 5 soul loatheth *l.* bread
Judg. 9. 4 hired vain and *l.* persons
1 Sam. 18. 23 seemeth it a *l.* thing
2 Sam. 2. 18 Asahel was *l.* of foot
1 K. 16. 31 as if a *l.* thing for him
2 K. 3. 18 *l.* thing in sight of the
Isa. 49. 6; Ezek. 8. 17
Zeph. 3. 4 her prophets are *l.* and
Mat. 11. 30 easy, and my burden *l.*
2 Cor. 4. 17 *l.* afflic., but for moment

Light (*v.*). *Light, kindle, illuminate, come down upon or from, fall upon.*
Gen. 24. 64 Rebekah *l.* off the camel
Ex. 25. 37 shall *l.* the lamps thereof
Num. 8. 2 when thou *l.* the lamps
Deut. 19. 5 *l.* upon neighbour, that he
Josh. 15. 18 and she *l.* off her ass
Judg. 4. 15 Sisera *l.* off his chariot
1 Sam. 25. 23 hasted, and *l.* off the a.
2 K. 10 15 he *l.* on Jehonadab the
Mat. 3. 16 descend. like dove, and *l.*
5. 15 Neither do men *l.* a candle
Luke 15. 8 doth not *l.* candle, and
John 1. 9 *l.* every man that cometh
Rev. 7. 16 nei. shall sun *l.* on them

Lighten. *Enlighten.*
Ps. 34. 5 looked on him, and were *l.*
Luke 2. 32 light to *l.* Gentiles, and
Rev. 18. 1 earth was *l.* with glory
To make lighter.
1 Sam. 6. 5 will *l.* his hand off you
Jonah 1. 5 cast for the wares to *l.* it
Acts 27. 38 they *l.* the ship and cast
Make to shine, illuminate.
2 Sam. 22. 29 L. will *l.* my darkness
Ez. 9. 8 that God may *l.* our eyes
Ps. 13. 3 O Lord, *l.* mine eyes, lest
Prov. 29. 13 Lord *l.* both their eyes
Luke 17. 24 as lightning that *l.* out

Lighter *Less heavy.*
1 K. 12. 4 make grievous service *l.*
3 Chr. 10. 10 but make it *l.* for us

Lighting. *Coming down.*
Isa. 30. 30 show *l.* down of his arm
Mat. 3. 16 like a dove, and *l.* upon him

Lightly. *Of little weight, carelessly.*
Gen. 26. 10 peo. might *l.* have lien
Deut. 32. 15 *l.* esteemed Rock of Sal.
Mark 9. 39 no man .. *l.* speak evil of

Lightness. *Levity, instability.*
Jer. 3. 9 came to pass through *l.*
23. 32 err by their lies, and their *l.*
2 Cor. 1. 17 minded, did I use *l.*?
R. V. Jer. 23 32 vain boasting; 2
Cor. 1. 17 fickleness

Lightning. *Sudden light, brightness, brightening.*
Ex. 19. 6 there were thunders and *l.*
2 Sam. 22. 15 sent *l.* and discom. th.
Job 37. 3 *l.* unto the ends of the earth
Ps. 97. 4 his *l.* enlightened world
135. 7 he maketh *l.* for the rain
Jer. 10. 13 he maketh *l.* with rain
Ezek. 1. 13 out of fire went forth *l.*
Dan. 10. 6 face as appearance of *l.*
Nah. 2. 4 chariots .. run like the *l.*
Zech. 9. 1 his arrow .. go forth as *l.*
Mat. 28. 3 countenance was like *l.*
Luke 10. 18 beheld Satan as *l.* fall
Rev. 4. 5 *l.* and thunder. and voices

Lign Aloes. *Wood of aloes, aloestree.*
Num. 24. 6 as trees of *l.* aloes plant.

Ligure. R. V. *jacinth.*
Ex. 28. 19 third row a *l.*, an agate
39. 12

Like. (*v.*). *Prefer, choose, please.*
Deut. 25. 7 if man *l.* not to take
1 Chr. 28. 4 *l.* me to make me king
Esth. 8. 8 write ye .. as it *l.* you
Am. 4. 5 for this *l.* you, O children
Rom. 1. 28 did not *l.* to retain G. in
R. V. Rom. 1. 28 refused

Like (*a.*). *Similar to, as, as if, so, alike, likely, same.*
Ex. 7. 11 did *l.* man. with enchant.
Deut. 22. 3 *l.* man. shalt thou do
1 Sam. 10. 24 none llke h. among p.
2 Sam. 22. 34 maketh feet *l.* hind's f.
1 K. 10. 20 not *l.* made in any king.
2 K. 18. 5 was none *l.* Hezekiah
2 Chr. 35. 18 no passover *l.* to that
Job 3 `. 19 I am become *l.* dust
Ps. 58. 4 poison is *l.* poi. of serpents
Prov. 26. 4 lest thou also be *l.* him
S. of S. 2. 9 my beloved is *l.* roe
Isa. 1. 9 been *l.* unto Gomorrah
Jer. 23. 29 not my word *l.* as a fire?
Lam. 1. 21 they shall be *l.* unto me
Ezek. 18. 10 doeth the *l.* to any one
Dan. 3. 25 fourth is *l.* Son of God
Hos. 4. 9 be, *l.* people *l.* priest
Jonah 1. 4 ship was *l.* to be broken
Mat. 6. 29 not arrayed *l.* one of these
Mark 4. 31 *l.* gr. of mustard seed
Luke 6. 48 *l.* man which built h.
John 9. 9 others said, He is *l.* him
Acts 17. 29 Godhead is *l* unto gold
Rom. 9. 29 made *l.* unto Gomorrah
1 Thes. 2. 14 have suffered *l.* things
1 Tim. 2. 9 in *l.* manner, also, that
Heb. 7. 3 made *l.* unto Son of God
Jas. 1. 6 that wavereth is *l.* wave
Rev. 18. 21 took stone *l.* millstone
R. V. Frequent changes to, as

Like-minded. R. V. *same mind.*
Rom. 15. 5 be *l. m* one toward an.
Phil. 2. 2 fulfil joy, that ye be *l. m.*

Liken. *Compare.*
Ps. 89. 6 who .. can be *l.* unto Lord
Isa. 40. 18 to whom will ye *l.* God
Jer. 6. 2 have *l.* daugh. of Zion to
Lam. 2. 13 what shall I *l.* to thee
Mat. 7. 24 will *l.* him to wise man
13 24 kingdom of heaven is *l.* to

Likeness. *Image, similitude, pattern, form.*
Gen. 1. 26 make man .. after our *l.*
Ex. 20. 4 or *l.* of any thing in h.
Deut. 5. 8 not make thee .. any *l.*
Ps. 17. 15 wh. I awake, with thy *l.*
Isa. 40. 18 what *l.* comp. unto him?
Ezek. 1. 5 out of midst .. came *l.*
Acts 14. 11 gods come in *l.* of men
Rom. 8. 3 sending Son in *l.* of fl.
Phil. 2. 7 was made in *l.* of men

Liketh. *Pleaseth, is good.*
Deut. 23. 16 dwell .. where it *l.* him
Esth. 8. 8 write Jews as it *l.* you, in the king's name

Likewise. *In like manner, also, moreover.*
Ex. 22. 30 *l.* do with thine oxen
Deut. 12. 30 even so will I do *l.*
Judg. 8. 8 Gid. spake unto them *l.*
Job 31. 38 furrows *l.* thereof com.
Mat. 17. 12 *l.* shall S. of man suffer
Mark 12. 21 second took .. and th. *l.*
Luke 20. 20 *l.* also cup after supper
John 6. 11 *l.* of fishes as much as
Rom. 8. 26 *l.* spirit also helpeth our
1 Cor. 7. 3 *l.* wife unto husband and
1 Tim. 3. 8 *l.* .. deacons be grave
Tit. 2. 6 young men *l.* exhort to be
Heb. 2. 14 himself *l.* took part of
Jas. 2. 25 *l.* also, was not Rahab
1 Pet. 3. 1 *l.*, wives, be in subjection
Jude 8 *l.* .. dreamers defile the flesh
Rev. 8. 12 day shone not .. night *l.*
R. V. very frequent changes, especially in N. T., to, in like manner, also, so, and.

Liking. *Sadder, looking.*
Dan. 1. 10 why see faces worse *l.*
Keeping, sound.
Job 39. 4 Their young are in good *l.*

Lily. *Lily.*
1 K. 7. 19 chapiters .. of *l.* work in
2 Chr. 4. 5 cup, with flowers of *l.*
S. of S. 2. 1 rose of Shar. .. *l.* of val.
Hos. 14. 5 he shall grow up as *l.*
Mat. 6. 28; Luke 12. 27 Consider *l.*

Lime. *Plaster, lime.*
Isa. 33. 12 peo. be as burnings of *l.*
Am. 2. 1 burned bones of k. into *l.*

Limit (n.). *Border, boundary,*
Ezek. 43. 12 *l.* thereof round about

Limit (v.). *Mark off, bound.*
Ps. 78. 41 Yea, they .. *l.* Holy One
Heb. 4. 7 he *l.* a certain day, saying
R. V. Ps. 78. 41 provoked; Heb. 4. 7 defineth

Line. *Cord, line, rope, thread.*
Josh. 2. 18 bind this *l.* of scar. thread
2 Sam. 8. 2 measured them with *l.*
Ps. 16. 6 *l.* are fallen .. in pleas. pl.
Ezek. 40. 3 with *l.* of flax in hand
Am. 7. 17 land be divided by *l.*
Zech. 2. 1 man measuring with *l.*
Cutting instrument, ochre,
Isa. 44. 13 marketh it out with *l.*
A line, a rule.
1 K. 7. 23 *l.* .. did compass it round
2 K. 21. 13 over Jeru. *l.* of Samaria
2 Chr. 4. 2 *l.* of thir. c. did com. it
Job 38. 5 who stretched *l.* upon it?
Ps. 19. 4 their *l.* is gone out through
Isa. 28. 10, 13 *l.* upon *l.*, *l.* upon *l.*
Sphere, scope, rule.
2 Cor. 10. 16 anoth. man's *l.* of th.
R, V. Isa. 44. 13 pencil; 2 Cor. 10. 16 province

Lineage. R. V. *family.*
Luke 2. 4 he was of the *l.* of David

Linen. *Woven flax.*
Gen. 41. 2 arrayed him in fine *l.*
Ex. 28. 42 make them *l.* breeches
Lev. 6. 10 priest put on *l.* garment
Deut. 22. 11 sorts, as of wool. and *l.*
1 Sam. 2. 18 child, gird. wi. *l.* eph.
2 Sam. 6. 14 D. was gird. wi. *l.* eph.
1 Chr. 15. 27 D. had ephod of *l.*
Prov. 31. 24 she maketh fine *l.*, and
Isa. 3. 23 The glasses, and the fine *l.*
Ezek. 9. 2 one man .. clothed wi. *l.*
Dan. 10. 5 certain man clothed in *l.*
Mat. 27. 59 wrapped it in *l.* cloth
Mark 14. 51 hav. *l.* cloth cast about
Luke 24. 12 *l.* cloths laid by thems.
John 19. 40 wound it in *l.* clothes
Rev. 15. 6 angels clothed in white *l.*
Spun flax, yarn.
1 K. 10. 28 Sol. had brought *l.* yarn
2 Chr. 1. 16 mer. received *l.* yarn
R. V. Prov. 7. 16 striped cloths;
Mark 15. 46 linen cloth; Rev. 15. 6 with precious stone

Linger. *Tarry, delay.*
Gen. 19. 16 while he *l.*, men laid
2 Pet. 2. 3 whose judgment .. *l.* not

Lintel. *Post, head-piece, top piece of door.*
Ex. 12. 22 strike *l.* and two posts
1 K. 6. 31 *l.* and posts were fifth
Am. 9. 1 smite *l.* of door, that posts
Zeph. 2. 14 bittern shall lodge in *l.*

R. V. Am. 9. 1; Zeph. 2. 14 chapiters

Lion. *Lion.*
Gen. 49. 9 Judah is a *l.*'s whelp
Num. 24. 9 he lay down as a *l.*
Deut. 33. 22 Dan is a *l.*'s whelp
Judg. 14. 5 young *l.* roared ag. him
1 Sam. 17. 34 came a *l.* and a bear
2 Sam. 1. 23 they were strong. th. *l.*
1 K. 7. 29 bor. were *l.*, oxen, cher.
2 K. 17. 25 L. sent *l.* among them
1 Chr. 11. 22 he .. slew *l.* in pit in
2 Chr. 9. 18 two *l.* stand. by stays
Job 4. 10 teeth of *l.* are broken
Ps. 7. 2 lest he tear my soul like *l.*
Prov. 28. 15 as roar. *l.* and rang. bear
Eccl. 9. 4 liv. dog bet. than dead *l.*
S. of S. from *l.*'s dens, fr. mount's
Isa. 11. 7 the *l.* eat straw like ox
Jer. 5. 6 *l.* out of forest shall slay
Lam. 3. 10 like *l.* in secret place
Ezek. 1. 10 face of *l.* on right side
Dan. 6. 7 be cast into den of *l.*
Hos. 11. 10 he shall roar like *l.*
Joel 1. 6 teeth as teeth of *l.*, and
Am. 3. 4 will *l.* roar in forest
Mic. 5. 8 as *l.* among beasts of for.
Nah. 2. 11 feeding place of young *l.*
Zeph. 3. 3 princes are as roaring *l.*
2 Tim. 4. 17 del. out of mouth of *l.*
Heb. 11. 33 faith .. stop. mouths of *l.*
1 Pet. 5. 8 as roaring *l.* .. seeking
Rev. 4. 7 first beast was like a *l.*
R. V. Gen. 49. 9; Num. 23. 24; 24. 9; Deut. 33. 20; Job 38. 39 lioness

Lioness. *Female lion.*
Ezek. 19. 2 What is thy moth.? A *l.*
Nah. 2. 12 lion strangled for his *l.*

Lion-like. R. V. *sons of Ariel.*
2 Sam. 23. 20 slew *l. l.* men of Moab
1 Chr. 11. 22 Benaiah .. slew *l. l.* m.

Lip. *Edge, lip, mouth, speech.*
Ex. 6. 12 hear me, of uncircumc. *l.*
Lev. 13. 45 put covering on upper *l.*
Num. 30. 6 uttered ought out of *l.*
Deut. 23. 23 gone out of thy *l.* keep
1 Sam. 1. 3 *l.* moved, voice was not
2 K. 19. 28 put my bridle in thy *l.*
Job 2. 10 not Job sin with his *l.*
Ps. 12. 3 Lord cnt off flattering *l.*
51. 15 O Lord, open thou my *l.*
Prov. 4. 24 perverse *l.* put far from
15. 7 *l.* of wise disperse knowledge
Eccl. 10. 12 *l.* of fool will swallow
S. of S. 4. 3 *l.* like thread of scarlet
Isa. 6. 5 I am a man of unclean *l.*
Jer. 17. 16 out of my *l.* was right
Lam. 3. 62 *l.* of those that rose
Ezek. 36. 3 taken up in *l.* of talkers
Dan. 10. 16 sons of men touched .. *l.*
Hos. 14. 2 so render calves of our *l.*
Mic. 3. 7 they shall cover their *l.*
Hab. 3. 16 heard .. my *l.* grieved
Mal. 2. 6 iniq. not found in his *l.*
Mat. 15. 8 peo. honoureth me with *l.*
Mark 7. 6 peo. hon. me with their *l.*
Rom. 3. 13 poison of asps is under *l.*
1 Cor. 14. 21 with other *l.* I speak
Heb. 13. 15 fruit of *l.* giving thanks
1 Pet. 3. 10 let him refrain his *l.*

Liquor. *Tear, liquid, wine.*
Ex. 22. 29 to offer first of thy *l.*
Num. 6. 3 nei. drink *l.* of grapes
S. of S. 7. 2 goblet, which want.. *l.*
R. V. S. of S. 7. 2 mingled wine

List. *Wish, please, will.*
Mat. 17. 12; Mark 9. 13 whatso.. *l.*
John 3. 8 wind blow. where it *l.*
Jas. 3. 4 whither. the governor *l.*
R. V. Jas. 3. 4 impulse of steersman willeth

Listen. *Hear, harken.*
Isa. 49. 1 *l.*, O isles, unto me

Litter. *Coach, shaft couch.*
Isa. 66. 20 upon horses, .. and in *l.*

Little. *Short, small, few, not large, petty.*
Gen. 18. 4 let *l.* water .. be fetched
Ex. 23. 30 *l.* by *l.* I will drive them
Lev. 11. 17 *l.* owl, and cormorant
Num. 31. 9 took women and *l.* ones
Deut. 1. 39 *l.* ones, which ye said
Josh. 22. 17 is iniq. of Peor too *l.*
Judg. 4. 19 give me *l.* water to dr.
Ruth 2. 7 she tarried a *l.* in house

1 Sam. 14. 43 did but taste *l.* honey
2 Sam. 16 1 when D. was *l.* past
1 K. 17. 12 not cake, but a *l.* oil
2 K. 5. 14 flesh came .. like *l.* child
2 Chr. 10. 10 my *l.* finger be thicker
Ez. 9. 8 give us a *l.* reviving
Neh. 9. 32 let all trouble seem *l.*
Esth. 8. 11 cause to perish *l.* ones
Job 24. 24 are exalted for *l.* while
Ps. 8. 5 made *l.* lower than angels
Prov. 6. 10 *l.* fold. of hands to sleep
Eccl. 9. 14 *l.* city, few men in it
S. of S. 2. 15 *l.* foxes th. spoil vines
Isa. 11. 6 *l.* child shall lead them
Jer. 14. 3 nobles have sent *l.* ones
Ezek. 11. 16 be as a *l.* sanctuary
Dan. 11. 34 holpen with a *l.* help
Hos. 8. 10 sorrow a *l.* for burden
Mic. 5. 2 be *l.* among thousand
Hag. 1. 6 sown, much, bring in *l.*
Zech. 1. 15 was but a *l.* displeased
Mat. 10. 42 unto .. *l.* ones cup of w.
Mark 14. 35 went forward *l.*, and fell
Luke 12. 32 Fear not, *l.* flock, for
John 6. 7 every one may take a *l.*
Acts 28. 2 peo. showed no *l.* kindness
1 Cor. 5. 6 *l.* leaven leaveneth lump
2 Cor. 8. 15 that gath *l.* had no lack
Gal. 5. 9 *l.* leav. leaven. whole lump
1 Tim. 5. 23 use *l.* wine for stom.
Jas. 3. 5 so tongue is *l.* member
Rev. 6. 11 rest yet for a *l.* season

Live (v.), *Be alive, exist.*
Gen. 5. 3 Adam *l.* h. and thir. years
Ex. 19. 13 or man, it shall not *l.*
Lev. 25. 35 that he may *l.* with thee
Num. 14. 21 I *l.*, all the earth shall
Deut. 32. 40 and say, I *l.* forever
Josh. 6. 17 only Rahab .. shall *l.*
Judg. 8. 19 as L. *l.*, if ye had saved
Ruth 3. 13 do part of kins., as L. *l.*
1 Sam. 1. 26 soul *l.*, I am the woman
2 Sam. 19. 34 How long have I to *l.*
1 K. 3. 23 This is my son that *l.*
2 K. 2. 2 and as thy soul *l.* I will not
2 Chr. 10 6 Sol... while he yet *l.*
Neh. 2. 3 let the king *l.* forever
Esth. 4. 11 sceptre, that he may *l.*
Job 7. 16 I would not *l.* alway
19. 25 I know that my redeemer *l.*
Ps. 18. 46 L. *l.*, blessed be my rock
Prov. 4. 4 keep my command. and *l.*
Eccl. 9. 9 joyfully with the wife
Isa. 55. 3 hear, and your soul shall *l.*
Jer. 4. 2 L. *l.*, in truth, in judgment
Lam. 4. 20 under shadow we shall *l.*
Ezek. 5. 11 As I *l.*, saith Lord God
Dan. 6. 21 said Dan., O k., *l.* forev.
Hos. 6. 2 and we shall *l.* in his sight
Am. 5. 6 seek Lord, and ye shall *l.*
Hab. 2. 4 the just shall *l.* by faith
Zech. 1. 5 prophets, do they *l.* forev.?
Mat. 4. 4 man not *l.* by bread alone
Mark 5. 23 lay hands .. she shall *l.*
Luke 10. 28 this do, and thou shalt *l.*
John 4. 50 Go thy way; thy son *l.*
Acts 17. 28 in him we *l.*, and move
Rom. 6. 10 in that he *l.*, he *l.* unto G.
1 Cor. 7. 39 law as long as husb. *l.*
2 Cor. 6. 9 as dying, behold, we *l.*
Gal. 2. 20 not I, but Christ *l.* in me
Phil. 1. 21 to me to *l.* is Christ
Col. 3. 7 walked, when ye *l.* in them
1 Thes. 5. 10 or sleep, we should *l.*
1 Tim. 5. 6 that *l.* in pleas. is dead
2 Tim. 3. 12 will *l.* godly in Christ
Tit. 2. 12 we should *l.* soberly
Heb. 7. 25 he *l.* to make intercess.
Jas. 4. 15 If Lord will, we shall *l.*
1 Pet. 1. 23 by word of G. which *l.*
1 John 4. 9 might L. through him
Rev. 1. 18 I am he that *l.* and was d.
R. V. 1 Cor. 9. 13 eat; Rev. 18. 7 waxed

Living. *Being alive, to live, life.*
Gen. 1. 21 God created .. ev *l.* creat.
Lev. 11. 10 any *l.* thing in waters
Num. 16. 48 stood bet. dead and *l.*
Deut. 5. 26 heard the voice of *l.* God
Josh. 3. 10 know *l.* G. is among you
Ruth 2. 20 not left off kind. to *l.*
1 Sam. 17. 26 defy armies of *l.* God
2 Sam. 20. 3 shut up *l.* in widow.
1 K. 3. 22 Nay; but the *l.* is my son
2 K. 19. 4 sent to reproach *l.* God
Job 30. 23 house appoint. for all *l.*

Ps. 42. 2 soul thirsteth for *l.* God
Eccl. 4. 2 praised dead more than *l.*
S. of S. 4. 15 well of *l.* waters, and
Isa. 39. 8 the *l.*, the *l.*, he shall pr.
Jer. 2. 13 forsaken, fount. of *l.* wat.
Lam. 3. 39 wheref. doth *l.* man co.
Ezek. 1. 5 likeness of *l.* creatures
Dan. 6. 20 Dan., servant of *l.* God
Hos. 1. 10 Ye are sons of *l.* God
Zech. 14. 8 *l.* waters go out of Jerus.
Mat. 16. 16 art C., Son of *l.* God
Mark 12. 27 not G of dead, but of *l.*
Luke 15. 13 wasted sub. in riotous *l.*
John 6. 51 I am the *l.* bread which
Acts 14. 15 should turn unto *l.* God
Rom. 9. 26 be called chil. of *l.* God
1 Cor. 15. 45 Adam was made *l.* soul
2 Cor. 3. 3 written with Spir. of *l.* G.
Col. 2. 20 as though *l.* in world
1 Thes. 1. 9 turned .. to serve *l.* God
1 Tim. 3. 15 is church of *l.* God
Tit. 3. 3 *l.* in malice and envy
Heb. 10. 20 by a new and *l.* way
1 Pet. 2. 4 coming as to *l.* stone
Rev. 7. 2 having seal of *l.* God

Live (*a.*). *Burning, hot.*
Isa. 6. 6 having *l.* coal in his hand
Living, alive.
Ex. 21. 35 sell *l.* ox, and divide
Lev. 16. 20 he shall bring *l.* goat

Lively. *Living, spirited.*
Ex. 1. 19 they are *l.*, and delivered
Ps. 38. 19 But mine enemies are *l.*
Acts 7. 38 received the *l.* oracles
1 Pet. 1. 3 begotten us unto *l.* hope

Liver. *Liver.*
Ex. 29. 13 caul above *l.*, and two kid.
Lev. 3. 4; 4. 9; 7. 4; 8. 16; 9. 10
Prov. 7 23 dart strike through his *l.*
Lam. 2. 11 my *l.* is poured upon e.
Ezek. 21. 21 k. of Bab. .. looked in *l.*

Lizard. *Lizard.*
Lev. 11. 30 and the *l.*, and the snail

Lo. *Behold.*
Gen. 29. 7 *L.*, it is yet high day
Mat. 2. 9 *l.*, the star, they saw in east
Etc., etc.

Load. *Lay on, lade.*
Ps. 68. 19 blessed L., who daily *l.*
2 Tim. 3. 6 silly wom. *l.* with sins
See also **Lade.**

Loaf. *Bread, cake, food.*
Ex. 29. 23 one *l.* of break, one cake
Lev. 23. 17 bring two wave *l.* of
Judg. 8. 5 give .. *l.* of bread unto
1 Sam. 17. 17 Take .. these *l.* and
1 K. 14. 3 take ten *l.*, and cracknels
2 K. 4. 42 twenty *l.* of barley, and
1 Chr. 16. 3 every one *l.* of bread
Mat. 14. 17 We have here but five *l.*
Mark 6. 38 How many *l.* have ye?
Luke 9. 16 he took the five *l.* and
John 6. 26 because ye did eat of *l.*

Loan. *Asking, lending.*
1 Sam. 2. 20 *l.* which is lent to Lord

Loathe. *Despise, abhor, reject.*
Num. 21. 5 soul *l.* this light bread
Job 7. 16 *l.* it; I would not live alw.
Prov. 27. 7 full soul *l.* honey comb
See also **Lothe.**

Loathsome. *Despised, abhorrent.*
Num. 11. 20 it be *l.* unto you
Job 7. 5 my skin is broken, and *l.*
Ps. 38. 7 lions filled with *l.* disease
Prov. 13. 5 but a wicked man is *l.*
R. V. Job 7. 5 out afresh; Ps. 38. 7
burning

Lock (*n.*). *Bolt, fastening.*
Judg. 3. 23. 24 shut doors .. and *l.* th.
Neh. 3. 3, 6, 13, 14, 15 *l.* thereof
S. of S. 5. 5 myrrh on handles of *l.*
Tuft of hair, braided hair.
Num. 6. 5 let *l.* of hair of head grow
Judg. 16. 19 caused him to sh. off *l.*
S. of S. 6. 11 *l.* bushy, black as raven
Isa. 47. 2 uncover *l.*, make bare legs
Ezek. 8. 3 took me by a *l.* of head
R. V. Num. 3. 5, 6, 13, 14, 15;
S. of S. 5. 5 bolt, or bolts; S. of S.
4. 1; 6. 7; Isa. 47. 2 veil

Locust. *Grasshopper.*
2 Chr. 7. 13 if I com. *l.* to devour
Isa. 33. 4 as running to and fro of *l.*
Locust.
Ex. 10 4 to morrow will I bring *l.*
Lev. 11. 22 may eat; *l.* after its kind

Deut. 28. 38 for *l.* shall consume it
1 K. 8. 37 if there be .. mildew, *l.*, or
Ps. 78. 46 gave their labour unto *l.*
Prov. 30. 27 The *l.* have no king, yet
Joel 1. 4 worm left hath *l.* eaten
Nah. 3. 17 Thy crowned are as *l.*
Mat. 3. 4 meat was *l.* and wild honey
Mark 1. 6 John .. did eat *l.* and w. h.
Rev. 9. 3 came out of smoke *l.* upon

Lodge (*n.*). *Place for passing
night.*
Isa. 1. 8 as *l.* in garden of cucumb.

Lodge (*v.*). *Pass night, abide, dwell.*
Gen. 24. 23 is there room .. *l.* in?
Num. 22. 8 *L.* here this night, and
Josh. 3. 1 *l.* there before they passed
Judg. 19. 4 eat and drink, and *l.* th.
Ruth 1. 16 where thou *l.*, I will *l.*
2 Sam. 17. 8 will not *l.* with people
1 K. 19. 9 he came to cave and *l.*
1 Chr. 9. 27 about house of God
Job. 31. 32 strang. did not *l.* in str.
S. of S. 7. 11 let us *l.* in villages
Isa. 1. 21 righteousness *l.* in it, but
Jer. 4. 14 how long vain thoughts *l.*
Zeph. 2. 14 bittern shall *l.* in lintels
Mat. 13. 32 birds .. *l.* in the branches
Mark 4. 32; Luke 13. 19
Acts 10. 6 he *l.* with one Simon a
1 Tim. 5. 10 if she have *l.* strangers
R. V. Josh. 2. 1 lay; Acts 28. 7 en-
tertained

Lodging. *Place for passing night,
inn, temporary, stopping place.*
Josh. 4. 3 in *l.*, where he lodged
2 K. 19. 23 enter *l.* of his borders
Isa. 10. 29 taken up *l.* at Geba
Jer. 9. 2 *l.* place of wayfar. men
Acts 28. 23 came many into his *l.*
Phile. 22. prepare me also a *l.*

Loft. *Upper chamber, story.*
1 K. 17. 19 carried him up into *l.*
Acts 20. 9 fell down from upper *l.*
R. V. 1 K. 17. 19 chamber; Acts.
20. 9 story.

Loftily. *Haughtily.*
Ps. 73. 8 are corrupt, and speak *l.*

Loftiness. *Height, haughtiness.*
Isa. 2. 17 *l.* of man shall be bowed
Jer. 48. 29 pride of Moab, his *l.*

Lofty. *Lifted up, high, haughty.*
Ps. 131. 1 haughty, nor mine eyes *l.*
Prov. 30. 13 O how *l.* are their eyes!
Isa. 2. 11 *l.* looks shall be humbled
5. 15; 26. 5; 57. 7, 15
R. V. Isa. 2. 12 haughty; **57.** 7 high

Log. *Liquid measure.*
Lev. 14. 10, 12, 15, 21, 24 *l.* of oil

Loin. *Lower part of back, gen-
erative power.*
Gen. 35. 11 kings come out thy *l.*
Ex. 12. 11 *l.* girded, shoes on feet
Deut. 33. 11 smite thro. *l.* of them
2 Sam. 20. 8 sword fastened upon *l.*
1 K. 2. 5. blood upon gird. about *l.*
2. K. 4. 29 Gird *l.*, and take staff
2 Chr. 6. 9 son, come out of thy *l.*
Job 31. 20 if *l.* have not blessed me
Ps. 66. 11 laidst afflic. upon our *l.*
Prov. 31. 17 She girdeth *l.* with s.
Isa. 11. 5 righteous. be gird. of *l.*
45. 1 I will loose the *l.* of kings
Jer. 1. 17 thou gird up thy *l.* and
Ezek. 8. 2 from his *l.* even upward
Dan. 10. 5. *l.* girded with gold of
Am. 8. 10 bring sackc. upon all *l.*
Nah. 2. 10 much pain is in all *l.*
Mat. 3. 4 leathern girdle about *l.*
Mark 1. 6 girdle of skin about *l.*
Luke 12. 35 Let your *l.* be girded
Acts 2. 30 fruit of *l.*, according to
Eph. 6 14 *l.* girt about with truth
Heb. 7. 5 come out of *l.* of Abrah.
1 Pet. 1. 13 gird up *l.* of thy mind

Long (*v.*). *Desire for, yearn.*
Gen. 31. 30 *l.* after father's house
Deut. 12. 20 thy soul *l.* to eat flesh
2 Sam. 13. 39 D. *l.* to go to Abs.
1 Chr. 11. 17 D. *l.*, and said, Oh that
Job 3. 21 *l.* for death, but com. not
Ps. 84. 2 My soul *l.*, even fainteth
Rom. 1. 11 I *l.* to see you, that
2 Cor. 9. 14 which *l.* after you for
Phil. 1. 8 how I *l.* after you in the

Long (*a.*). *Extended, length, afar,
lasting.*

Gen. 26. 8 had been there *l.* time
Ex. 20. 12 days may be *l.* upon land
Lev. 26. 34 as *l.* as it lieth desolate
Num. 20. 15 dwelt in Egypt *l.* time
Deut. 2. 3 compass. mount. *l.* enough
Josh. 6. 5 when they make *l.* blast
Judg. 5. 28 why char. so *l.* coming?
1 Sam. 20. 2 time was *l.*, twent. yr's
2 Sam. 14. 2 woman had *l.* mourned
1 K. 3. 11 hast not asked *l.* life
2 K. 19. 25 Hast not heard *l.* ago
2 Chr. 3. 11 wings of cher., twen. c. *l*
Esth. 5. 13 so *l.* as I see Mordecai
Ps. 91. 16 with *l.* life, I satisfy him
Prov. 3. 2 length of days, and *l.* life
Isa. 42. 14 have *l.* time holden peace
Jer. 29. 28 saying, This captivity is *l.*
Lam. 5. 20 Wheref. forsake us so *l.*?
Ezek. 40. 7 little chamber one reed *l*
Dan. 10. 1 time appointed was *l.*
Hos. 13. 13 he should not stay. *l.*
Mat. 23. 14 for pret. make *l.* prayers
Mark 12. 40; Luke 20. 47
John 5. 6 been a *l.* time in that case
Acts 14. 28 abode *l.* time with disci.
Rom. 7. 1 law hath dom. as *l.* as
1 Cor. 7. 39 wife is bound .. as *l.* as
Gal. 4. 1 the h. as *l.* as he is a child
Eph. 6. 3 mayest live *l.* on earth
1 Tim. 3. 15 if I tarry *l.* that thou
Jas. 5. 7 hath *l.* patience for it
1 Pet. 3. 6 as *l.* as ye do well, and
2 Pet. 1. 13 *l.* as I am in this tab.
Heb. 4. 7 To day, after so *l.* a time
R. V. Num. 9. 19; Deut. 28. 32;
Ps. 94. 4; Mat. 23. 14; Mark 16.
5; Luke 1. 20 ——

Longer. *Greater length, yet, still.*
Ex. 2. 3 she could not *l.* hide him
Judg. 2. 14 they could not *l.* stand
2 K. 6. 33 what wait for L. any *l.*?
Job 11. 9 the measure thereof is *l.*
Jer. 44. 22 Lord could no *l.* bear
Luke 16. 2 mayest be no *l.* steward
Acts 18. 20 desired him to tarry *l.*
Rom. 6. 2 how live they *l.* therein
2 Thes. 3. 1 could not *l.* forbear
1 Pet. 4. 2 he no *l.* should live
Rev. 10. 6 should be time no *l.*

Long-suffering.
Ex. 34. 6 merciful and gracious, *l. s.*
Num. 14. 18 The Lord is *l. s.*, and
Ps. 86. 15 *l. s.*, plenteous in mercy
Jer. 15. 15 take not away in thy *l. s.*
Rom. 2. 4 goodness, forbear., and *l. s*
2 Cor. 6. 6 by *l.* s., by kindness, by
Gal. 5. 22 fruit of Spirit is *l. s.*
Eph. 4. 2 with *l. s.*, forb. one anoth.
Col. 1. 11 unto all patience, and *l. s.*
1 Tim. 1. 16; 2 Tim. 3. 10; 1 Pet.
3. 20; 2 Pet. 3. 9
R. V. Ex. 34 6; Num. 14. 18; Ps.
86. 15 slow to anger

Look (*n.*). *Vision, sight, appear-
ance.*
Ps. 18. 27 will bring down high *l.*
Prov. 6. 17 A proud *l.*, lying tongue
Isa. 2. 11 lofty *l.* shall be humbled
Ezek. 2. 6 nor be dismayed at *l.*
Dan. 7. 20 *l.* more stout than fellows

Look (*v.*). *Gaze, see, attend, seem,
care for, expect.*
Gen. 6. 12 And God *l.* upon earth
Ex. 2. 12 And he *l.* this way and that
Lev. 13. 3 priest shall *l.* on plague
Num. 12. 10 Aaron *l.* upon Miriam
Deut. 9. 27 *l.* not to stubbornness
Josh. 8. 20 men of Ai *l.* behind
Judg. 6. 14 Lord *l.* on him, and said
1 Sam. 16. 7 *L.* not on his counten.
2 Sam. 16. 12 may be Lord will *l.*
1 K. 19. 6 he *l.*, behold, cake baken
2 K. 6. 32 *L.*, when messenger com.
1 Chr. 17 God of our fathers *l.*
2 Chr. 24. 22 Lord *l.* upon it, and
Neh. 4. 14 *l.*, rose up, and said
Esth. 1. 11 for she was fair to *l.* on
Job 6. 28 be content, *l.* upon me
Ps. 25. 18 *l.* upon mine afflictions
Prov. 23. 31 *l.* not on wine when red
Eccl. 12. 3 *l.* out windows be destr.
S. of S. 1. 6 *l.* not on me I am .. bl'k
Isa. 45. 22 *L.* unto me, be ye saved
Jer. 8. 15 *l.* for peace, but no good
Lam. 2. 16 this is the day we *l.* for
Ezek. 8. 3 gate that *l.* toward north

Dan. 12. 5 Dan. *l.*, there stood two
Hos. 3. 1 Isra., who *l.* to other gods
Obad. 3 shouldest not have *l.* on
Jonah 2. 4 *l.* toward thy holy temple
Mic. 7. 7 I will *l.* unto the Lord
Nah. 2. 8 stand, none shall *l.* back
Hab. 1. 13 canst not *l.* on iniquity
Hag. 1. 9 *l.* for much, lo, ca. to little
Zech. 2. 1 I lifted up eyes, and *l.*
Mat. 14. 19 *l.* to heaven, he blessed
Mark 10. 23 Jesus *l.* round about
Luke 21. 28 *l.* up, and lift up heads
John 13. 22 disc. *l.* one to another
Acts 1. 10 *l.* stedfastly toward hea.
1 Cor. 16. 11 *l.* for him with breth.
2 Cor. 4. 18 *l.* not at things seen
Phil. 3. 20 we. *l.* for the Saviour
Tit. 2. 13 *l.* for that blessed hope
Heb. 12. 2 *l.* unto Jesus, author
1 John 1. 1 which we have *l.* upon
2 John 8 *L.* to yourselves, that
1 Pet. 1. 12 angels desire to *l.* into
2 Pet. 3. 13 *l.* for new heav. and e.
Rev. 4. 3 to *l.* upon like jasper
   R. V. The changes are chiefly
those brought about by subsequent
words, and do not affect meanings.
Looking-glass. *Appearance,
   mirror.*
Ex. 38. 8 *l. g.* of women assembling
Job. 37. 18 spread sky as molten *l. g.*
   R. V. Job 37. 18 mirror
Loops. *Folds, links.*
Ex. 26. 4 make *l.* of blue upon cur.
26. 5, 10, 11 ; 36. 12, 17.
Loose. (*a.*). *Not fastened, untied.*
Gen. 49. 21 Naphtali is hind let *l.*
Lev. 14. 7 let bird *l.* into open field
Job 6. 9 would let *l.* his hand, and
Dan. 3. 25 Lo, I see four men *l.*
Loose. (*v.*). *Open, free from, re-
   lease. unbind, let go.*
Ex. 28. 28 breastplate be not *l.*
Deut. 25. 9 *l.* his shoes from foot
Josh. 5. 15 *L.* shoe from off foot
Judg. 15. 14 bands *l.* from hands
Job 38. 31 Canst *l.* bands of Orion?
Ps. 116. 16 thou hast *l.* my bonds
Eccl. 12. 6 or ever silver cord be *l.*
Isa. 45. 1 I will *l.* loins of kings
Jer. 40. 1 I thee from chains
Dan. 5. 6. joints of loins were *l.*
Mat. 18. 27 *l.* him, and forgave him
Mark 7. 35 string of tongue was *l.*
Luke 13. 15 on sab. day *l.* his ox
John 11. 44 Jesus saith, *L.* him, and
Acts 2. 24 having *l.* pains of death
13. 25 shoes, I am not wor. to *l.*
1 Cor. 7. 27 Art thou *l.* from wife?
Rev. 9. 14 *L.* angels which are b.
   R. V. Judg. 15. 14 dropped ; Mat.
18. 27 released ; Acts 13. 13 ; 16.
11 ; 27. 21 set sail ; 27. 13 weighed
anchor ; Rom. 7. 2 discharged
Lop. *Cut off.*
Isa. 10. 33 Lord shall *l.* the bough
Lord. *Sir, master, prince, owner.*
Gen. 19. 18 Lot said, not so, my *l.*
Ex. 32. 22 not ang. of my *l.* wax hot
Num. 11. 28 said, My *l.* Moses, for.
Josh. 13. 3 five *l.* of Philistines
Judg. 3. 25 their *l.* was fall. dead
Ruth 2. 13 Let me find fav., my *l.*
1 Sam. 1. 15 *l.*; I am wom. of sor.
2 Sam. 1. 10 brought him unto my *l.*
1 K. 1. 2 sought for my *l.* the king
2. K. 4. 16 my *l.* thou man of God
1 Chr. 21. 3 why doth my *l.* require
2 Chr. 2. 14 men of my *l.* David
Ez. 8. 25 *l.* and all Israel present
Isa. 19. 4 give into hand of a cruel *l.*
Jer. 34. 5 lament thee, saying, Ah *l.*
Ezek. 23. 23 great *l.* and renowned
Dan. 1. 10 fear my *l.* the King
Zech. 4. 4 what are these my *l.*?
Mat. 10. 25 and servant as his *l.*
Mark 12. 9 what *l.* of vineyard do?
Luke 12. 47 ser. which know *l.* will
John 13. 16 ser. not greater than *l.*
1 Tim. 6. 15 K. of k., and Lord of *l.*
1 Pet. 5. 3 being *l.* over God's herit.
Lordly. *Regal.*
Judg. 5. 25 brought butter in *l.* dish
Lordship. *Authority of lord.*
Mark 10. 42 exercise *l.* over them
Luke 22. 25 k. of Gent. exercise *l.*

R. V. Mark 10. 42 lord it
Lose. *Part with, let slip, fail.*
Deut. 22. 3 hath *l.*, thou hast found
Judg. 18. 25 *l.* thy life, with lives of
1 K. 18. 5 that we *l.* not all beasts
Job 31. 39 caused the owners to *l.*
Prov. 23. 8 and *l.* thy sweet words
Eccl. 3. 6 time to get, and time to *l.*
Isa. 49. 21 seeing I have *l.* children
Mat. 10. 39 shall *l.* it ; and he that *l.*
Mark 9. 41 he shall not *l.* reward
Luke 15. 9 found the piece I had *l.*
John 12. 25 loveth his life shall *l.* it
2 John 8 that we *l.* not those things
   R. V. Mat. 16. 26 ; Mark 8. 36 for-
feit : John 17. 12 perished
Loss. *Bereavement, privation,
   destruction, waste.*
Gen. 31. 39 torn I bare the *l.* of it
Isa. 47. 8 neither know *l.* of children
Acts 27. 21 gained this harm and *l.*
1 Cor. 3. 15 he shall not suffer *l.*
Phil. 3. 7 gain, those I counted *l.*
Lost. *Parted with, destroyed
   wasted.*
Ex. 22. 9 any manner of *l.* thing
Lev. 6. 3 or found which was *l.*
Num. 6. 12 day before shall be *l.*
Deut. 22. 3 *l.* thing of thy brother
1 Sam. 9. 3 asses of Kish were *l.*
Ps. 119. 176 astray like *l.* sheep
Jer. 50. 6 people hath been *l.* sheep
Ezek. 19. 5 saw that, her hope was *l.*
Mat. 10. 6 go to *l.* sheep of house
Luke 15. 24 for this my son was *l.*
John 6. 12 gath. frag. that noth. be *l.*
2 Cor. 4. 3 hid to them that are *l.*
Lot. *Chance, portion.*
Lev. 16. 8 and Aaron shall cast *l.*
Num. 26. 25 land be divided by *l.*
Josh. 14. 2 By *l.* was their inherit.
Judg. 1. 3 Come up wi. me into my *l.*
1 Chr. 25. 9 first *l.* came for Asaph
Neh. 10. 34 cast *l.* among priests
Esth. 3. 7 they cast Pur, this is *l.*
Ps. 22. 18 cast *l.* upon my vesture
Prov. 1. 14 Cast thy *l.* among us
Isa. 17. 14 the *l.* of them that rob us
Jer. 13. 25 *l.*, portion of thy meas.
Ezek. 24. 6 let no *l.* fall upon it
Dan. 12. 13 stand in thy *l.* at end of
Joel 3. 3 they cast *l.* for my people
Obad. 11 cast *l.* upon Jerusalem
Jonah 1. 7 Come, and let us cast *l.*
Mic. 2. 5 cast cord by *l.* in congreg.
Nah. 3. 10 cast *l.* for honourable men
Mat. 27. 35 parted gar., casting *l.*
Mark 15. 14 ; Luke 23. 34 ; John
   19. 24
Acts 1. 26 they gave forth their *l.*
   R. V. Mat. 27. 35 —
Lothe. *Cast away, abhor.*
Ex. 7. 18 the Egyptians *l.* to drink
Jer. 14. 19 hath thy soul *l.* Zion?
Ezek. 6. 9 *l.* themselves for the evils
16. 5 to the *l.* of thy person in the
Zech. 11. 8 and my soul *l.* them,
   R. V. Zech. 11. 8 weary of
Loud. *Great, strong, high.*
Gen. 39. 14 I cried with *l.* voice
Ex. 19. 16 voice of tr. exceeding *l.*
Deut. 27. 14 ; 1 Sam. 28, 12 ; 2
   Sam. 15. 23 ; 1 K. 8. 55 ; 2 K.
   18. 28 ; 2 Chr. 15. 14 ; 30. 21
Neh. 12. 42 And the singers sang *l.*
Esth. 4. 1 cried with *l.* and bit. cry
Ps. 150. 5 praise him on *l.* cymb.
Prov. 7. 11 she is *l.* and stubborn
Isa. 36. 13 *l.* voice in Jews' language
Ezek. 8. 18 cry in ears with *l.* voice
Mat. 27. 46 Jesus cried with *l.* voice
Mark 15. 37 ; Luke 23. 46
John 11. 43 with *l.* voice, Laz., come
Acts 16. 28 Paul cried with *l.* voice
Rev. 12. 10 heard with *l.* voice, saying
   R. V. Prov. 7. 11 clamorous ; Rev.
5. 2, 12 ; 6. 10 ; 7. 2, 10 ; 8. 13 ; 10. 3 ;
   12. 10 ; 14. 7, 9, 15, 18 great
Louder. *Mightier.*
Ex. 19. 19 long, and waxed *l.* and *l.*
Love (*n.*). *Love, affection.*
Gen. 29. 20 for *l.* he had for her
Deut. 7. 7 Lord set his *l.* upon you
2 Sam. 1. 26 thy *l.* was wonderful
1 K. 11. 2 Sol. clave to these in *l.*
Ps. 109. 5 rewarded hatred for *l.*

Prov. 10. 12 but *l.* covereth sins
Eccl. 9. 1 no man knoweth *l.* by
S. of S. 2. 4 banner over me was *l.*
Isa. 63. 9 in his *l.* . . he redeemed
Jer. 2. 2 *l.* of thine espousals, when
Ezek. 16. 8 time was time of *l.*
Hos. 3. 1 according to *l.* of Lord
Zeph. 3. 17 he will rest in his *l.*
Dan. 1. 9 into favour and *l.* with
Rom. 12. 10 one to anoth. with br. *l.*
1 Thes. 4. 9 as touch.bro. *l.* ye need
1 Tim. 6. 10 *l.* of mon. root of evil
Tit. 3. 4 the *l.* of God our Saviour
Heb. 13. 1 let bro. *l.* continue
1 Pet. 1. 22 unfeigned *l.* of breth.
Love (*v.*). *To love.*
Gen. 22. 2 son Isaac, whom thou *l.*
Ex. 20. 6 that *l.* me, and keep my c.
Lev. 19. 18 *l.* neighbor as thyself
Deut. 6. 5 *l.* Lord with all thy heart
Josh. 22. 5 charged you, to *l.* Lord
Judg. 16. 4 *l.* wom. in val. of Sorek
Ruth 4. 15 daughter . . which *l.* thee
1 Sam. 18. 16 all Is. and Jud. *l.* Dav.
2 Sam. 12. 24 son Sol., and L. *l.* him
1 K. 3. 3 Solomon *l.* the Lord
2 Chr. 11. 21 Rehoboam *l.* Maachah
Neh. 1. 5 mer. for them that *l.* him
Esth. 2. 17 k. *l.* Es. abov. all. wom.
Job 19. 19 whom I *l.* are turned
Ps. 97. 10 that *l.* Lord hate evil
Prov. 3. 12 whom L. *l.* he correcteth
Eccl. 3. 8 time to *l.*, time to hate
S. of S. 1. 7 thou whom my soul *l.*
Isa. 1. 23 every one *l.* gifts, and fol.
Jer. 5. 31 people *l.* to have it so
Ezek. 16. 37 all that thou hast *l.*
Dan. 9. 4 mer. to them that *l.* him
Hos. 3. 1 woman beloved of friend
Am. 5. 15 Hate evil, *l.* the good
Mic. 6. 8 to do justly, to *l.* mercy
Zech. 8. 19 *l.* the truth and peace
Mal. 2. 11 hol. of Lord which he *l.*
Mat' 19. 19 neighbour as thyself
Mark 10. 21 Jesus, beholding, *l.* him
Luke 6. 27 *l.* your enemies, do good
John 3. 16 God so *l.* world, that he
Rom. 8. 28 good to them that *l.* G.
1 Cor. 16. 22 if man *l.* not L. J. C.
2 Cor. 9. 7 for God *l.* cheerful giver
Gal. 2. 20 Son of God, who *l.* me
Eph. 5. 2 walk in *l.*, as Christ *l.* us
Col. 3. 19 Husbands, *l.* your wives
1 Thes. 4. 9 ye are taught of G. to *l.*
2 Thes. 2. 16 Father, which hath *l.* us
2 Tim. 4. 10 Demas *l.* pres. world
Tit. 3. 15 Greet them that *l.* us
Heb. 12. 6 whom L. *l.*, he chasten.
Jas. 2. 8 *l.* neighbour as thyself
1 Pet. 2. 17 Honour men, *l.* brother.
2 Pet. 2. 15 *l.* wages of unrighteous.
1 John 2. 10 that *l.* bro. abideth in
2 John 1 whom I *l.* in the truth
3 John 1 beloved Gaius whom I *l.*
Rev. 1. 5 Unto him that *l.* us
Lovely. *Lovable.*
2 Sam. 1. 23 Saul and Jon. were *l.*
S. of S. 5. 16 he is altogether *l.*
Ezek. 33. 32 very *l.* song of one
Phil. 4. 8 whatsoever things are *l.*
Lover. *Who loves.*
1 K. 5. 1 Hiram was *l.* of David
Ps. 38. 11 My *l.* . . stand aloof from
Jer. 3. 1 played harlot with many *l.*
Lam. 1. 19 I called for my *l.* but
Ezek. 16. 33 givest gifts to all *l.*
Hos. 2. 5 said I will go after my *l.*
2 Tim. 3. 4 *l.* of pleas. more than G.
Tit. 1. 8 of good men, sober, just
   R. V. Tit. 1. 8 given to
Lovingkindness. *Mercy.*
Ps. 17. 7 show thy marvellous *l. k.*
25. 6 ; 26. 3 ; 36. 7 ; 40. 10 ; 42. 8 ;
48. 9 ; 51. 1 ; 63. 3 ; 69. 16 ; 88. 11 ;
89. 33 ; 92. 2 ; 119. 88 ; 138. 2
Isa. 63. 7 will mention *l. k.* of Lord
Jer. 9. 24 Lord which exercise *l. k.*
Hos. 2. 19 in *l. k.*, and in mercy
Low. (*v.*). *Bellow.*
1 Sam. 6. 12 highway, *l.* as they wt.
15. 14 *l.* of oxen which I hear
Job 6. 5 *l.* as ox over fodder?
Low. *Humble, bowed down, deep.*
Deut. 28. 43 thou shalt come *l.*
1 Sam. 2. 7 *L.* bringeth *l.*, and lift
1 Chr. 27. 28 sycamore trees in *l.* pl

2 Chr. 26. 10 cattle, in *l.* country
Job 5. 11 set on high that be *l.*
Ps. 49. 2 *l.* and high, rich and poor
Prov. 29. 23 pride shall bring him *l.*
Eccl. 12. 4 sound of grinding is *l.*
Isa. 13. 11 will lay *l.* haughtiness
Lam. 3. 55 I called . . out of *l.* dung.
Ezek. 17. 6 became vine of *l.* stature
Luke 1. 52 exalted them of *l.* degree
Rom. 12. 16 con. to men of *l.* estate
Jas. 1. 9 Let bro. of *l.* deg. rejoice
R. V. 2 Chr. 26. 10; 28. 18 low-
land; Ps. 107. 39 bowed down;
Ezek. 26. 20 nether

Lower. *More low, below.*
Gen. 6. 16 with *l.* sec. and third sto.
Lev. 13. 20 in sight *l.* than skin
Neh. 4. 13 set I in *l.* places behind
Ps. 8. 5 made him lit. *l.* than angels
Prov. 25. 7 *l.* in presence of prince
Isa. 22. 9 gath. waters of *l.* pool
Eph. 4. 9 descended into *l.* parts
Heb. 2. 7 made him lit. *l.* than ang.

Lower (v.). *Lour, be gloomy.*
Mat. 16. 3 for the sky is red and *l.*

Lowest. *End, furthest down.*
Deut. 32. 22 burn unto *l.* hell, and
1 K. 12. 31 made priests of *l.* peo.
2 K. 17. 32 made of *l.* priests of
Ps. 86. 13 deliv. soul from *l.* hell
Ezek. 41. 7 so increased from *l.* to
Luke 14. 9 begin to take *l.* room

Lowliness. *Humility.*
Eph. 4. 2 with all *l.* and meekness
Phil. 2. 3 in *l.* of mind, esteem oth.

Lowly. *Humble.*
Ps. 138. 6 hath he respect unto *l.*
Prov. 3. 34 he giveth grace unto *l.*
Zech. 9. 9 *l.*, and riding on an ass
Mat. 11. 29 am meek and *l.* in heart

Lucre. *Unworthy gain.*
1 Sam. 8. 3 but turned aside after *l.*
1 Tim. 3. 3 not greedy of filthy *l.*
Tit. 1. 7 bish., not given to filthy *l.*
1 Pet. 5. 2 not for filthy *l.*, but

Lukewarm. *Little warm.*
Rev. 3. 16 So because thou art *l.*

Lump. *Bunch, cake, mass.*
2 K. 20. 7 Isaiah said, Take *l.* of figs
Isa. 38. 21 Let them take *l.* of figs
Rom. 9. 21 same *l.* to make vessel
1 Cor. 5. 6 lit. leav. leav. whole *l.*
Gal. 5. 9
R. V. 2 K. 20. 7; Isa. 38. 21 cake

Lunatick. R. V. *epileptic.*
Mat. 4. 24 those which were *l.*, and
17. 15 he is *l.*, and sore vexed

Lurk. *Hide, watch secretly.*
Ps. 17. 12 as lion *l.* in secret places
Prov. 1. 11 *l.* privily for innocent

Lurking-place. *Hiding-place.*
1 Sam. 23. 23 take knowl. of *l. p.*
Ps. 10. 8 He sitteth in *l. p.* of vil.

Lust (a.). *Inordinate desire.*
Ex. 15. 9 my *l.* shall be satisfied
Ps. 78. 18 asking meat for their *l.*
Mark 4. 19 *l.* of other things, choke
John 8. 44 *l.* of father ye will do
Rom. 7. 7 for I had not known *l.*
Gal. 5. 16 shall not fulfil *l.* of flesh
1 Thes. 4. 5 not in *l.* of concupisc.
1 Tim. 6. 9 many foolish and hurt.*l.*
2 Tim. 2. 22 Flee also youthful *l.*
Tit. 3. 3 serving div. *l.* and pleas.
Jas. 1. 14 drawn away of own *l.*
1 Pet. 2. 11 abstain from fleshly *l.*
2 Pet. 2. 10 walk after flesh in *l.*
1 John 2. 16 *l.* of flesh, *l.* of eyes
Jude 16 walking after their own *l.*
R. V. Ps. 81. 12 stubbornness; Rom.
7. 7 coveting; Jas. 4. 1, 3 pleasures

Lust. (v.). *Desire eagerly, long for.*
Num. 11. 4 mixed multitude fell *l.*
Deut. 12. 15 whatso. thy soul *l.* af.
Ps. 106. 14 *l.* exceedingly in wild.
Prov. 6. 25 *L.* not after her beauty
Mat. 5. 28 whoso. look. on wom. to *l.*
1. Cor. 10. 6 not *l.* after evil things
Gal. 5. 17 flesh *l.* against the Spirit
Jas. 4. 2 Ye *l.*, and have not: ye
Rev. 18. 14 fruits *l.* after are dead
R. V. Deut. 14. 26 desireth; Jas.
4. 5 long.

Lusty. *Stout, strong.*

Judg. 3. 29 ten thous. men, all *l.*

Lying. *Feigning, deceiving.*
1 K. 22. 22 I will be a *l.* spirit in
2 Chr. 18. 21 *l.* sp. in mouth of peo.
Ps. 31. 18 let. *l.* lips be put to sil.
119. 163 I hate and abhor *l.* but law
Prov. 6. 17 proud look, a *l* tongue
12. 22 *l.* lips are abomination
Isa. 59. 13 transgr. and *l.* against L.
Jer. 7. 4 Trust ye not in *l.* words
Ezek. 13. 6 have seen *l.* divination
Dan. 2. 9 ye have prep. *l.* words
Hos. 4. 2 By swearing, *l.* and kill.
Jonah 2. 8 that obser. *l.* forsake
Eph. 4. 25 Wherefore putt. away *l.*
2 Thes. 2. 9 with all power and *l.* w.

Recline, couch.
Gen. 34. 7 *l.* with Jacob's daughter
Ex. 23. 5 hateth thee *l.* under burd.
Num. 31. 17 known man by *l.* with
Deut. 22. 22 man found *l.* with wo.
Judg. 9. 35 rose up from *l.* in wait
Ps. 139. 3 compassed my *l.* down
Isa. 56. 10 *l.* down loving to slum.
John 13. 25 then *l.* on Jesus' breast
Acts 23. 16 heard of their *l.* in wait
R. V. Ps. Ps. 119. 29, 163; Eph.
4. 25 falsehood; Isa. 59. 13 deny-
ing; John 13. 25 leaning back;
Acts 20. 19 plots

M.

Mad. *Foolish, inflamed.*
Deut. 28. 34 *m.* for sight of eyes
1 Sam. 21. 13 feigned himself *m.* in
2 K. 9. 11 wheref. came this *m.* fel.
Ps. 102. 8 that are *m.* against me
Prov. 26. 18 As *m.* man, who cast.
Eccl. 2. 2 said of laughter, It is *m.*
Isa. 44. 25 L. that mak. diviners *m.*
Jer. 50. 38 are *m.* upon their idols
Hos. 9. 7 the spiritual man is *m.*
Acts 26. 11 exceed. *m.* against them
Insane, crazy.
John 10. 20 Hath devil, and is *m.*
Acts 12. 15 said to her, Thou art *m.*
26. 24 much *l.* doth make thee *m.*
26. 25 I am not *m.*, noble Festus
1 Cor. 14. 23 they not say ye are *m.*
R. V. Eccl. 7. 7 foolish

Made. *Caused to exist, created, induced, compelled.*
Ex. 25. 31 of beat. work c. s. be *m.*
Lev. 13. 48 or in anything *m.* of sk.
Num. 4. 26 all that is *m.* for them
2 Sam. 15. 4 that I were *m.* judge
1 K. 10. 20 not like *m.* in any king.
2 K. 12. 13 not *m.* for house of L.
1 Chr. 9. 31 things were *m.* in pans
2 Chr. 9. 19 not like *m.* in any king.
Ez. 5. 17 that decree was *m.* of Cyr.
Neh. 4. 7 walls of Jerusalem were *m.*
Job 15. 7 Art first, or wast thou *m.*
Ps. 33. 6 By word of L. were h. *m.*
139. 15 when I was *m.* in secret
Isa. 51. 12 son of man be *m.* as grass
Dan. 2. 5 houses be *m.* as dunghills
Mat. 4. 3 these stones be *m.* bread
9. 16 and the rent is *m.* worse
Mark 2. 27 sabbath was *m.* for man
Luke 23. 12 Pil and Her. .. *m.* friend
John 1. 3 All things were *m.* by him
1. 14 the Word was *m.* flesh, and
5. 6 Wilt thou be *m.* whole?
Acts 12. 5 prayer was *m.* with. ceas.
26. 6 promise *m.* of G. unto fathers
Rom. 1. 3 was *m.* of seed of David
11. 9 Let their table be *m.* snare
1 Cor. 1. 30 is *m.* unto us wisdom
4. 13 we are *m.* as filth of world
9. 22 I am *m.* all things to all men
2 Cor. 5. 21 might be *m.* righteous.
Gal. 3. 13 C., being *m.* curse for us
Eph. 2. 13 *m.* nigh by blood of C.
Phil. 2. 7 *m.* in likeness of men
Col. 1. 23 I Paul was *m.* minister
1 Tim. 1. 9 law not *m.* for right. m.
Tit. 3. 7 be *m.* heirs according to
Heb. 3. 14 are *m.* partakers of Christ
6. 20 an high priest forever
Jas. 3. 9 *m.* after similitude of God
1 Pet. 2. 7 same is *m.* head of cor.
R. V. The changes are mostly to
such words as, created, wrought,
become, manifested, etc.
See also **Make.**

Mad Man. *Erring, foolish.*
1 Sam. 21. 15 play *m. m.* in my pres.

Madness. *Folly, error, lunacy.*
Deut. 28. 28 L. smite thee with *m.*
Eccl. 1. 17 gave my heart to know *m.*
2. 12 behold wisdom, *m.*, and folly
10. 13 end of his talk is misch. *m.*
Zech. 12. 4 will smite rider with *m.*
Luke 6. 11 they were filled with *m.*
2 Pet. 2. 16 ass forbad *m.* of proph.

Magician. *Scribe, sorcerer.*
Gen. 41. 8 called for all *m.* of Egypt
Ex. 7. 22 *m.* of E. did so with their
Dan. 1. 20 ten times bet. than all *m.*
2. 20 asked such things at any *m.*

Magistrate. *Judge, ruler.*
Judg. 18. 7 no *m.* in the land, that
Ez. 7. 25 set *m.* and judges, which
Luke 12. 11 when they br. you to *m.*
Acts 16. 20 brought them to the *m.*
16. 22 *m.* rent off their clothes
Tit. 3. 1 put them in mi. to obe. *m.*
R. V. Judg. 18. 7 possessing author-
ity; Luke 12. 11 rulers; Tit. 3. 1
be obedient

Magnifical. *Make great.*
1 Chr. 22. 5 house must be exceed. *m.*

Magnificence. *Greatness.*
Acts 19. 27 her *m.* should be destroy.

Magnified. *Become great.*
2 Sam. 7. 26 let thy name be *m.* for.
1 Chr. 17. 24 thy name be *m.* forever
2 Chr. 32. 23 was *m.* in sight of na.
Ps. 35. 27 Let the Lord be *m.*
70. 4 say contin., Let God be *m.*
Zech. 12. 7 not *m.* thems. against J.
Mal. 1. 5 Lord will be *m.* from
R. V. 2 Chr. 32. 23 exalted
See also **Magnify.**

Magnify. *Make great, exalt.*
Gen. 19. 19 thou hast *m.* thy mercy
Josh. 3. 7 I begin to *m.* thee in Is.
4. 14 that day the Lord *m.* Joshua
1 Chr. 29. 25 L. *m.* Sol. exceedingly
2 Chr. 1. 1 G. was with him, and *m.*
Job 7. 17 man, that thou shouldst *m.*
Ps. 34. 3 O *m.* the Lord with me
138. 2 hast *m.* thy word above all
Isa. 10. 15 shall saw *m.* itself against
42. 21 he will *m.* the law, and
Jer. 48. 26 drunken, for he *m.* him.
Lam. 1. 9 enemy hath *m.* himself
Ezek. 38. 23 Thus will I *m.* myself
Dan. 11. 36 *m.* himself above ev. god
Zeph. 2. 8, 10 *m.* thems. against bor.
Luke 1. 46 My soul doth *m.* Lord
Acts 5. 13 but the people *m.* them
Rom. 11. 13 speak, I *m.* my office
Phil. 1. 20 also Christ shall be *m.*
R. V. Rom. 11. 13 glorify my min.

Maid. *Handmaid.*
Gen. 30. 3 Behold my *m.* Bilhah
Ex. 2. 5 she sent her *m.* to fetch
Lev. 25. 6 for thy servant, and *m.*
Ez. 2. 65 Besides their ser. and *m.*
Job 19. 15 my *m.* count me for str.
Nah. 2. 7 and her *m.* shall lead her
Maid-servant.
Gen. 16. 3 Sarai took Hagar her *m.*
16. 5, 6, 8; 29. 24; 30. 7, 9, 10, 12
Isa. 24. 2 as with *m.*, so with mistr.
Deut. 22. 14 I found her not a *m.*
2 K. 5. 2 brought captive a little *m.*
Esth. 2. 7 *m.* was fair and beautiful
Job 31. 1 why should I think on *m.*
Prov. 30. 19 and way of man wi. *m.*
Jer. 2. 32 can *m.* forget her orna.
Lam. 5. 11 ravished *m.* in cities
Ezek. 9. 6 both *m.*, and lit. children
Zech. 9. 17 cheerful, and new w. *m.*
Mat. 9. 24 Give place, *m.* is not dead
Mark 14. 66 cometh one of *m.* of
Luke 22. 56 beheld him as he sat
R. V. Gen. 16. 2; 29. 24; 30. 7;
Ex. 2. 5 handmaid; Mat. 9. 24
damsel

Maid-child. *Female.*
Lev. 12. 5 if she bear *m. c.*, then

Maiden. *Virgin, damsel, young woman.*
Gen. 30. 18 given *m.* to my husb.
Ex. 2. 5 her *m.* walked along by
Judg. 19. 24 Behold my daugh., a *m.*
1 Sam. 9. 11 *m.* going to draw w.
2 Chr. 36. 17 no compassion up. *m.*

Esth. 2. 4 let *m.* which pleaseth k.
Job 41. 5 wilt bind him for thy *m.*
Ps. 78. 63 *m.* not giv. to marriage
148. 12 Both young men and *m.*
Prov. 9. 3 She hath sent forth h. *m.*
Eccl. 2. 7 I got servants and *m.*
Ezek. 44. 22 take *m.* of seed of Is.
Luke 8. 51 father and mother of *m.*
12. 45 beat men servants and *m.*

Maid-servant. *Handmaid.*
Gen. 20. 17 G. heal. his w. and *m. s.*
Ex. 20. 10 thy man ser. nor thy *m. s.*
Deut. 5. 14 *m. s.* may rest well as th.
Judg. 9. 18 Abim. son of his *m. s.*
2 Sam. 6. 22 *m. s.* wh. thou hast sp.
Neh. 7. 67 their man ser. and *m. s.*
Job 31. 13 if I did despise my *m. s.*
Woman servant.
Gen. 12. 16 men ser. and *m. s.,* and
Ex. 11. 5 unto firstborn of *m. s.*
2 K. 5. 26 oxen, men ser., and *m. s.*
Jer. 34. 9 ev. man let *m. s.* go free

Mail. *Scales, armor.*
1 Sam. 17. 5 was armed wi. coat of *m.*

Maimed. *Disabled, injured.*
Lev. 22. 22 Blind, or broken, or *m.*
Mat. 15. 30 lame, bl., dumb, *m.,* and
Mark 9. 43 bet. to ent. life *m.* than
Luke 14. 13 call the poor, *m.,* lame
R. V. Mat. 18. 8 halt

Mainsail. R. V. *foresail.*
Acts 27. 40 hoisted up *m.* to wind

Maintain. *Uphold, sustain.*
1 K. 8. 45 hear, and *m.* their cause
1 Chr. 26. 27 out of sp. to *m.* house
2 Chr. 6. 35 hear, and *m.* th. cause
Job 13. 15 will *m.* mine own ways
Ps. 9. 4 For thou hast *m.* my right
16. 5 Lord, thou *m.* my lot
140. 12 I know the Lord will *m.*
Tit. 3. 8 careful to *m.* good works
3. 14 let ours also learn to *m.*
R. V. 1 Chr. 26. 27 repair

Maintenance. *Support.*
Ez. 4. 14 because we have *m.* from
Prov. 27. 27 for *m.* of thy maidens
R. V. Ez. 4. 14 eat salt of

Majesty. *Greatness, dignity, ex-cellence.*
1 Chr. 29. 11 glory, victory, and *m.*
29. 25 bestowed on him royal *m.*
Esth. 1. 4 hon. of his excellent *m.*
Job 37. 22 with God is terrible *m.*
40. 10 Deck thyself with *m.* and
Ps. 21. 5 *m.* hast thou laid upon
29. 4 voice of Lord is full of *m.*
96. 6 Honour and *m.* are bef. him
Isa. 2. 10, 19, 21 the glory of his *m.*
Ezek. 7. 20 he set it in *m.,* but
Dan. 4. 36 excellent *m.* was added
Mic. 5. 4 in *m.* of name of Lord
Heb. 1. 3 on right hand of *m.* on h.
8. 1 on right hand of throne of *m.*
2 Pet. 1. 16 eyewitnesses of his *m.*
Jude 25 glory and *m.,* dom. and p.
R. V. Dan. 4. 36; 5. 18, 19 greatness

Make. *Create, form, produce, construct, compel.*
Gen. 1. 7 God *m.* the firmament
2. 4 God *m.* the earth and heavens
2. 18 will *m.* him an helpmeet for
17. 6 will *m.* nations of thee, and
Ex. 20. 4 not *m.* any grav. image
Lev. 26. 1 Ye shall *m.* no idols nor
Num. 8. 4 so he *m.* the candlestick
Deut. 10. 3 I *m.* ark of shittim w.
Josh. 5. 2 *M.* thee sharp knives, and
Judg. 3. 16 Ehud *m.* him dagger
1 Sam. 2. 19 mother *m.* him . . coat
2 Sam. 7. 9 have *m.* thee gr. name
1 K. 3. 15 Sol. *m.* feast to servants
9. 26 Solomon. *m.* navy of ships
2 K. 4. 10 let us *m.* a little chamber
1 Chr. 15. 1 *m.* him houses in city
2 Chr. 3. 8 he *m.* most holy house
Ez. 10. 11 *m.* confession to Lord
Neh. 8. 4 pulpit, which they had *m.*
Esth. 1. 3 *m.* feast unto his princes
Job 9. 9 *m.* Arcturus, Orion, and P.
Ps. 95. 5 the sea is his, and he *m.* it
135. 7 he *m.* lightnings for the rain
Prov. 23. 5 riches *m.* thems. wings
Eccl. 2. 5 I *m.* me gardens and orch.
7. 29 God hath *m.* man upright
S. of S. 1. 11 *m.* thee borders of gold
Isa. 36. 16 *M.* agreement with me

Jer. 2. 28 gods which thou hast *m.*
46. 28 will *m.* a full end of nations
Ezek. 13. 18 Woe to wom. that *m.*
Dan. 3. 10 Thou hast *m.* a decree
Hos. 13. 2 *m.* them molten images
Joel 2. 19 no more *m.* you repro.
Am. 4. 13 that *m.* morning darkness
Jonah 4. 5 *m.* him booth, and sat
Mic. 1. 8 *m.* wailing like dragons
Nah. 1. 8 will *m.* end of the place
Hab. 1. 14 *m.* men as fishes of sea
Zeph. 2. 13 *m.* Nin. a desolation
Hag. 2. 23 I will *m.* thee as signet
Zech. 10. 1 L. shall *m.* bright clouds
Mal. 3. 17 when I *m.* up my jewels
Mat. 4. 19 I *m.* you fishers of men
Mark 7. 37 he *m.* both deaf to hear
Luke 3. 4 L., *m.* his paths straight
John 2. 15 he *m.* scourge of cords
12. 2 There they *m.* him a supper
Acts 1. 1 former treatise have I *m.*
Rom. 9. 21 to *m.* one ves. unto hon.
1 Cor. 6. 15 *m.* them members of
2 Cor. 5. 21 *m.* him to be sin for us
Gal. 2. 18 I *m.* myself transgressor
Eph. 1. 16 *m.* mention of you in pr.
Phil. 1. 4 for you all *m.* request
1 Thes. 1. 2 always *m.* ment. of you
1 Tim. 2. 1 prayer be *m.* for all men
Phile. 4 *m.* mention of thee always
Heb. 12. 13 *m.* straight paths for feet
Jas. 3. 18 of them that *m.* peace
2 Pet. 1. 10 *m.* calling and elec. sure
1 John 1. 10 we *m.* him a liar, and
Rev. 1. 6 *m.* us kings and priests

Maker. *Who fashions, forms, makes.*
Job. 4. 17 *m.* be more pure than *m.* ?
36. 3 ascribe right. to my *M.*
Ps. 95. 6 kneel before Lord our *M.*
Prov. 14. 31 oppress. poor re. his *M.*
22. 2 the Lord is *m.* of them all
Isa. 1. 31 and the *m.* of it as spark
54. 5 thy *M.* is thine husband
Jer. 33. 2 Thus saith L., *m.* thereof
Hos. 8. 14 Is. hath forgot. his *M.*
Hab. 2. 18 *m.* thereof hath grav. it
Heb. 11. 10 wh. build. and *m.* is G.

Making. *Doing, producing.*
Eccl. 12. 12 of *m.* of books no end
Ezek. 27. 16 mul. of wares of thy *m.*
See also **Make.**

Male. *Male, man.*
Gen. 1. 27 *m.* and female created he
34. 22 every. *m.* be circumcised
Ex. 12. 5 *m.* of the first year, take
Lev. 1. 3 offer *m.* without blemish
Num. 3. 40 num. all firstborn of *m.*
Deut. 4. 16 any figure, likeness of *m.*
Josh. 5. 4 *m.* even all men of war
Judg. 21. 11 Ye shall destroy ev. *m.*
1 K. 11. 15 had smitten ev. *m.* in E.
2 Chr. 31. 16 their genealogy of *m.,*
Ez. 8. 14 and with them seventy *m.*
Mal. 1. 14 which hath in flock *m.*
Mat. 19. 4 made them *m.* and fem.
Mark 10. 6 God made them *m.* and f.
Luke 2. 23 ev. *m.* that openeth wo.
Gal. 3. 28 there is nei. *m.* nor fema.

Malefactor. *Evil doer.*
Luke 23. 32 th. were two others, *m.*
John 18. 30 If he were not a *m.*

Malice. *Evil, badness.*
1 Cor. 5. 8 nei. with leaven of *m.*
14. 20 in *m.* be ye children, but in
Eph. 4. 31 be put away, with all *m.*
Col. 3. 8 put off these, ang., wr., *m.*
Tit. 3. 3 living in *m.* and envy
1 Pet. 2. 1 laying aside all *m.,* and
R. V. 1 Pet. 2. 1 wickedness

Malicious. R. V. *wicked.*
3 John 10 prating with *m.* words

Maliciousness. *Evil, badness*
Rom. 1. 29 Being filled with all *m.*
1 Pet. 2. 16 for a cloke of *m.,* but
R. V. 1 Pet. 2. 16 wickedness

Malignity. *Evil disposition.*
Rom. 1. 29 full of envy, deceit, *m.*

Mallows. R. V. *salt wort.*
Job 30. 4 Who cut up *m.* by bushes

Mammon. *Wealth, riches.*
Mat. 6. 24 Ye cannot ser. G. and *m.*
Luke 16. 9 Make to yours. fr. of *m.*

Man. *Man, human being.*
Gen. 1. 26 make *m.* in our image
r. 27 God created *m.* in own im.

Ex. 8. 17 became lice in *m.* and b.
Lev. 1. 2 If any *m.* bring offering
Num. 3. 13 hallow. both *m.* and bea.
Deut. 4. 32 since day G. created *m.*
Josh. 11. 14 ev. *m.* they smote with s.
Judg. 16. 7, weak, and as another *m.*
1 Sam. 17. 32 Let no *m's* heart fail
2 Sam. 7. 19 is this the man. of *m.*
1 K. 4. 31 Sol. was wiser than all *m.*
2 K. 23. 20 and burned *m.* bones on
1 Chr. 17. 17 accord. to estate of *m.*
2 Chr. 6. 18 will God dwell with *m.*
Neh. 2. 12 neither told I any *m.*
Job 5. 7 *m.* is born unto trouble
14. 1 *M.* . . is of few days, and
Ps. 8. 4 What is *m.,* that thou art
108. 12 for vain is help of *m.*
Prov. 3. 13 Happy is *m.* that findeth w.
Eccl. 6. 7 labour of *m.* is for mouth
Isa. 45. 12 made earth, and crea. *m.*
Jer. 2. 6 land where no *m.* dwelt
Lam. 3. 39 wherefore doth *m.* com.
Ezek. 1. 5 they had likeness of *m.*
Dan. 8. 16 I heard a *m's* voice
Hos. 9. 12 shall not be a *m.* left
Joel 1. 12 joy is withered from *m.*
Am. 4. 13 declareth unto *m.* what
Jonah 3. 8 But let *m.* be covered
Mic. 7. 2 none upright among *m.*
Hab. 1. 14 makest *m.* as fishes of
Zeph. 1. 3 will consume *m.* and be.
Hag. 1. 11 upon *m.,* and upon cattle
Zech. 2. 4 speak to this young *m.*
Mal. 3. 8 will a *m.* rob God? Yet
Mat. 4. 4 *m.* not live by br. alone
Mark 1. 17 make you fishers of m.
Luke 2. 14 peace, good will tow. *m.*
John 1. 4 the life was light of *m.*
Acts 4. 12 under heav. given am. *m.*
Rom. 12. 18 live peaceably with all *m.*
1 Cor. 15. 21 since by *m.* came death
2 Cor. 3. 2 known and read of all *m.*
Gal. 1. 1 not of *m.* neither by *m.*
Eph. 4. 24 that ye put on new *m.*
Phil. 2. 7 made in likeness of *m.*
Col. 1. 28 warning every *m.,* and
1 Thes. 2. 4 not as pleas. *m.,* but G.
2 Thes. 2. 3 that *m.* of sin be reveal.
1 Tim. 2. 4 will have all *m.* saved
2 Tim. 3. 17 *m.* of G. may be per.
Tit. 3. 2 to speak evil of no *m.*
Heb. 9. 27 appoint. unto *m.* to die
Jas. 2. 24 by works *m.* is justified
1 Pet. 1. 24 glory of *m.* as flower
2 Pet. 1. 21 but holy *m.* of G. spake
1 John 5. 9 If we rec. witness of *m.*
Jude 4. certain *m.* crept in unawares
Rev. 9. 7 faces were as faces of *m.*
Man as individual.
Gen. 2. 24 Therefore shall *m.* leave
6. 9 Noah was just *m.* and perfect
Ex. 15. 3 The Lord is *m.* of war
Lev. 13. 29 if *m.* or wom. have pla.
Num. 12. 3 *m.* Moses was very meek
Deut. 1 16. judge right, bet. every *m.*
Josh. 4. 4 Josh. called the twelve *m.*
Judg ,1. 4 spies saw *m.* come forth
Ruth 1. 2 name of *m.* was Elimel.
1 Sam. 1. 1 was certain *m.* of Ram.
2 Sam. 18. 27 He is good *m.,* and c.
1 K. 1. 42 for thou art a valiant *m.*
2 K. 1. 6 came *m.* up to meet us
1 Chr. 10. 1 *m.* of Is. fled bef. Philist.
2 Chr. 2. 13 I have sent cunning *m.*
Ez. 3. 1 gath. themselves as one *m.*
Neh. 7. 2 he was faithful *m.,* and
Esth. 9. 4 *m.* Mordecai waxed great
Job 2. 4 all *m.* hath will he give
Ps. 22. 6 I am a worm, and no *m.*
112. 1 Blessed *m.* that feareth Lord
Prov. 6. 27 can *m.* take fire in bos.
16. 28 A forward *m.* soweth strife
Eccl. 1. 8 labour, *m.* cannot utter it
S of S. 3. 8 ev. *m.* hath sword on t.
Isa. 2. 9 great *m.* humbleth himself
Jer. 18. 11 go speak to *m.* of Judah
Lam. 3. 33 not grieve children of *m.*
Ezek. 8. 11 seventy *m.* of ancients of
Dan. 10. 11 Dan., *m.* greatly beloved
Hos. 3. 3 shalt not be for anoth. *m.*
Am. 5. 19 *m.* did flee from lion
Jonah 1. 14 not per. for this *m.'s* life
Mic. 2. 2 oppress *m.* and his heritage
Nah. 2. 3 valiant *m.* are in scarlet
Zech. 1. 8 a *m.* riding on red horse
Mal. 2. 12 L. will cut off *m.* that

Mat. 7. 24 liken him unto wise *m.*
Mark 6. 20 knowing he was just *m.*
Luke 1. 27 virgin espoused to a *m.*
John 1. 30 After me cometh *m.* wh.
Acts 1. 10 two *m.* stood by them in
Rom. 7. 3 she be mar. to anoth. *m.*
1 Cor. 11. 3 head of every *m.* is C.
Eph. 4. 13 unto per. *m.*, unto meas.
1 Tim. 2. 8 will theref. that *m.* pray
Jas. 1. 12 Blessed *m.* that endur.
R. V. Numerous changes in N. T.
to, one

Mandrakes. *Love apples.*
Gen. 3. 14, 15, 16 found *m.* in field
S. of S. 7. 13 The *m.* give a smell,
Manger. *Crib, feeding trough.*
Luke 2. 7 laid him in a *m.*, because
2. 12 Ye shall find the babe in a *m.*
Manifest (*a.*). *Evident, plain.*
Mark 4. 22 hid, wh. shall not be *m.*
Luke 8. 17 that shall not be *m.*
John 1. 31 should be made *m.* to Is.
Rom. 1. 19 is *m.* in them, for God
1 Cor. 4. 5 make *m.* counsels of h.
2 Cor. 5. 11 we are made *m.* unto G.
Gal. 5. 19 now works of fl. are *m.*
Eph. 5. 13 things are *m.* by light
Phil. 1. 13 my bonds in C. are *m.*
Col. 1. 26 now made *m.* to saints
1 Tim. 3. 16 God was *m.* in flesh
2 Tim. 3. 9 their folly shall be *m.*
Heb. 9. 8 way was not yet made *m.*
1 Pet. 1. 20 *m.* in these last times
1 John 3. 10 children of God are *m.*
Rev. 15. 4 judgments are made *m.*
R. V. 1 Cor. 15. 27; 1 Tim. 5. 25;
2 Tim. 3. 9 evident
Manifest (*v.*). *Make plain, show forth.*
Eccl. 3. 18 that God might *m.* them
John 2. 11 and *m.* forth his glory
Rom. 3. 21 without the law is *m.*
Tit. 1. 3 but hath *m.* his word thro.
1 John 1. 2 life was *m.*, and we
3. 8 the Son of God was *m.* that
4. 9 was *m.* the love of God toward
Manifestation. *Making plain.*
Rom. 8. 19 waiteth for *m.* of sons
1 Cor. 12. 7 the *m.* of Spirit is given
2 Cor. 4. 2 *m.* of truth commending
R. V. Rom. 8. 19 revealing
Manifestly. R. V. *made manifest.*
2 Cor. 3. 3 *m.* declared to be epis.
Manifold. *Many fold.*
Neh. 9. 19 in thy *m.* mercies forsook
Ps. 104. 24 how *m.* are thy works
Am. 5. 12 I know your *m.* transgres.
Luke 18. 30 who sh. not receive *m.*
Eph. 3. 10 by ch. wisdom of God
1 Pet. 1. 6 heaviness thro. *m.* tempt.
4. 10 stewards of the *m.* grace
Mankind. *Human kind.*
Job 12. 10 and breath of all *m.*
1 Cor. 6. 9 nor abusers with *m.*
1 Tim. 1. 10 law of them defile *m.*
Jas. 3. 7 hath been tamed of *m.*
Male kind.
Lev. 18. 22 shalt not lie with *m.*
20. 13 if man also lie with *m.*
R. V. 1 Cor. 6. 9; 1 Tim. 1. 10 *m.*
Manna. *Sweet resin, gum.*
Ex. 16. 15 said one to anoth., It is *m.*
16. 35 children of Is. did eat *m.*
Num. 11. 6 nothing at all, besides *m.*
Deut. 8. 16 fed thee in wild. with *m.*
Josh. 5. 12 *m.* ceased on the morrow
Neh. 9. 20 withheldest not thy *m.*
Ps. 78. 24 had rained down *m.* upon
John 6. 31 Our fathers did eat *m.*
Heb. 9. 4 golden pot that had *m.*
Rev. 2. 17 give to eat of hidden *m.*
R. V. Ex. 16. 15 what is it; John
6. 58 ——
Manner. *Mode, habit, custom, way, sort, kind.*
Gen. 19. 31 after *m.* of all earth
32. 19 On this *m.* speak to Esau
Ex. 21. 9 deal with her after *m.*
Lev. 24. 22 shall have one *m.* of law
Num. 15. 16 one *m.* shall be for you
Deut. 15. 2 this is *m.* of release
Josh. 6. 1 comp. city after same *m.*
Judg. 18. 7 after *m.* of Zidonians
1 Sam. 8. 9 show them *m.* of king
2 Sam. 14. 3 speak on this *m.* to him
1 K. 18. 28 cut thems. after their *m.*

2 K. 1. 7 What *m.* of man was he
1 Chr. 24. 19 according to their *m.*
2 Chr. 4. 20 born after *m.* before
Neh. 6. 4 ans. them after same *m.*
Esth. 1. 13 so kings *m.* toward all
Ps. 144. 13 afford. all *m.* of store
Isa. 5. 17 lambs feed after their *m.*
Jer. 22. 21 this thy *m.* from youth
Ezek. 11. 12 done after *m.* of heath.
Am. 4. 10 pestilence after *m.* of E.
Mat. 6. 9 After this *m.* pray ye
Mark 13. 29 So ye, in like *m.*, when
John. 19. 40 spices, as *m.* of Jews
Acts 1. 11 shall come in like *m.*
13. 18 for years suff. he their *m.*
17. 2 Paul, as his *m.* was, went
1 Cor. 15. 33 evil com. cor. good *m.*
2 Tim. 3. 10 known my *m.* of life
Heb. 10. 25 not forsak. as *m.* of so.
1 Pet. 3. 5 after this *m.* in old time
Jude 7 in like *m.* giving themselves
Rev. 11. 5 must in this *m.* be killed
R. V. Numerous changes to cus-
tom, ordinance, from, etc.; and
frequent omissions of the word
Man-servant. *Male-servant.*
Gen. 12. 16 asses, and *m. s.*, and *m.*
Ex. 20. 17 nor his *m. s.* nor maids
Deut. 5. 14; 1 Sam. 8. 16; 2 K. 5.
26; Neh. 7. 67; Job 31. 13; Jer.
34. 9
Luke 12. 45 to beat *m. s.* and mai.
Mansion. *Abode.*
John 14. 2 in F's house many *m.*
Manslayer. *Murderer.*
Num. 35. 6 which ye ap. for *m. s.*
1 Tim. 1. 9 law not for right., *m. s.*
Mantle. *Robe, wrap.*
Judg. 4. 18 she cov. him with *m.*
1 Sam. 15. 27 laid hold upon his *m.*
1 K. 19. 13 wrapped his face in *m.*
2 K. 2. 8 Elijah took his *m.*, and
Ez. 9. 3 I rent my gar. and *m.*,
Job 1. 20 Then Job rent his *m.*
Ps. 109. 29 confusion, as with *m.*
Isa. 3. 22 suits of apparel, and *m.*
Many. *Numerous.*
Gen. 17. 4 be father of *m.* nations
Ex. 5. 5 the people of land are *m.*
Lev. 25. 51 If yet *m.* years behind
Num. 13. 18 strong or weak, few. *m.*
Deut. 1. 46 abode in Kadesh *m.*
Josh. 11. 4 horses and char. very *m.*
1 Sam. 25. 10 There be *m.* servants
2 Sam. 22. 17 drew me out of *m.* w.
1 K. 4. 20 Judah and Is. were *m.*
2 K. 9. 22 her witchcrafts are so *m.*
1 Chr. 5. 22 For there fell *m.* slain
2 Chr. 30. 17 were *m.* in congrega.
Ez. 3. 12 *m.* wept, and *m.* shouted
Neh. 5. 2 our sons and daugh. are *m.*
Esth. 2. 8 *m.* maidens were gathered
Job 4. 3 thou hast instructed *m.*
Ps. 22. 12 *m.* bulls have compass.
Prov. 10. 21 lips of righteous feed *m.*
19. 4 Wealth maketh *m.* friends
Eccl. 6. 3 days of his years be *m.*
S. of S. 8. 7 *M.* wat. cannot quench
Isa. 2. 4 shall rebuke *m.* people
Jer. 16. 16 send for *m.* fishers, *m.* h.
Lam. 1. 22 for my sighs are *m.*
Ezek. 12. 27 vision he seeth for *m.* d.
Dan. 8. 25 my peace shall dest. *m.*
Hos. 3. 3 abide for me *m.* days
Am. 8. 3 shall be *m.* dead bodies
Mic. 4. 2 *m.* nations shall come
Nah. 1. 12 though quiet, likewise *m.*
Hab. 2. 8 hast spoiled *m.* nations
Zech. 2. 11 *m.* nat. be joined to L.
Mal. 2. 6 did turn *m.* from iniquity
Mat. 7. 13 *m.* there be which go in
19. 30 *m.* that are first shall be last
22. 14 *m.* called, but few chosen
Mark 1. 34 and cast out *m.* devils
14. 24 blood, which is shed for *m.*
Luke 1. 14 *m.* shall rejoice at his
John 2. 23 *m.* believed in his name
14. 2 in F's house are *m.* mansions
Acts 8. 25 preached in *m.* villages
Rom. 12. 4 *m.* made the f. of *m.* nati.
1 Cor. 10. 17 being *m.* are one bread
2 Cor. 2. 4 wrote you with *m.* tears
Gal. 1. 14 above *m.* my equals in
Phil. 3. 18 *m.* walk, enemies of C.
1 Tim. 6. 9 into *m.* foolish lusts
2 Tim. 2. 2 heard among *m.* wit.

Tit. 1. 10 are *m.* unruly talkers
Heb. 2. 10 bringing *m.* sons to glory
Jas. 3. 2 in *m.* things we offend
1 John 2. 18 now are *m.* antichrists
2 John 12 having *m.* things to write
3 John 13 had *m.* things to write
Rev. 1. 15 voice as sound of *m* wat.
19. 12 on head were *m.* crowns
R. V. Gen. 17. 4. 5; Ex. 23. 2 mul-
titude; 2 Sam. 23. 20; 1 Chr. 11.
22 mighty.
Mar. *Injure, deface, spoil.*
Lev. 19. 27 nei. *m.* corner of beard
Ruth 4. 6 lest I *m.* inheritance
1 Sam. 6. 5 mice that *m.* the land
2 K. 3. 19 *m.* every good piece of l.
Job 30. 13 They *m.* my path, they
Jer. 13. 9 will I *m.* pride of Judah
Marble. *Marble.*
1 Chr. 29. 2 *m.* stones in abundance
Esth. 1. 6 rings and pillars of *m.*
S. of S. 5. 15 legs are as pillars of *m.*
Rev. 18. 12 vessels of brass, iron, *m.*
March. *Move in order, journey.*
Ex. 14. 10 Egyptians *m.* after them
Judg. 5. 4 when thou *m.* out of field
Ps. 68. 7 didst *m.* through wildern.
Jer. 46. 22 shall *m.* with an army
Joel 2. 2 *m* every one his ways
Hab. 1. 6 shall *m.* through land to
Mariner. *Rower, sailor.*
Ex. 27. 9 ships of sea with their *m.*
27. 27 thy *m.*, and pilots, and calk,
Jonah 1. 5 Then the *m.* were afraid
R. V. Ezek. 27. 8 rowers
Marish. *Ditch, marsh.*
Ezek. 47. 11 *m.* shall not be healed
Mark (*n.*). *Sign, stamp, target.*
Gen. 4. 15 Lord set *m.* upon Cain
Lev. 19. 28 not print *m.* upon you
1 Sam. 20. 20 as though I shot at *m.*
Job 7. 20 why set me as *m.* against
16. 12 shak. me, and set me for *m*
Lam. 3. 12 bow, and set me as *m.*
Ezek. 9. 4 set *m.* upon foreheads of
Phil. 3. 14 I press toward the *m.*
Gal. 6. 17 I bear *m.* of Lord Jesus
Rev. 13. 16 to receive *m.* in right h.
13. 17; 14. 9; 15. 2; 16. 2; 19. 20
R. V. Gen. 4. 15 sign; Phil. 3. 14
goal; Rev. 15. 2 ——
Mark (*v.*) *Make mark, heed, set. place, observe, watch.*
Ruth 3. 4 shalt *m.* the place where
1 Sam. 1. 12 that Eli *m.* her mouth
2 Sam. 13. 28 *M.* ye when Am's h.
1 K. 20. 7 *M.*, and see how this *m.*
Job 10. 14 If I sin thou hast *m.* me
21. 5 *M.* me, and be astonished
33. 31 *M.* well, O Job; and heark.
Ps. 37. 37 *M.* perf. man, and behold
48. 13 *M.* ye well her bulwarks
Isa. 44. 13 he *m.* it out with line
Jer. 2. 22 iniquity is *m.* before ne
23. 18 who hath *m.* his word?
Ezek. 44. 5 Son of man, *m.* well, and
Luke 14. 7 he *m.* how they chose
Rom. 16. 17 *m.* them wh. cause div.
Phil. 3. 17 *m.* them which walk so
R. V. Job 18. 2 consider; 22. 15
keep; 24. 16 shut themselves up
Market. *Assembly place, mer-chandise place.*
Ezek. 27. 13 ves. of brass in thy *m.*
27. 17 traded in thy *m.* wheat
27. 19; 27. 25
Mat. 11. 16 unto chil. sitting in *m.*
20. 3 standing idle in *m.* place
Mark 7. 4 when they come from *m.*
12. 38 love saluta. in *m.* places
Luke 20. 46 love greetings in the *m.*
John 5. 2 a pool by the sheep *m.*
Acts 16. 19 drew them into *m.* place
17. 17 in *m.* daily with them
R. V. Ezek. 27. 13, 17, 19, 25 mer-
chandise; Mat. 11. 16; 23. 7;
Luke 11. 43; 20. 46 market places;
John 5. 2 gate
Marred. *Injured, spoiled, ruined.*
Isa. 52. 14 his visage was so *m.*
Jer. 13. 7 behold, the girdle was *m.*
18. 4 vessel made of clay was *m.*
Mark 2. 22 and bottles will be *m.*
R. V. Mark 2. 22 ——
Marriage. *Wedding, nuptial es-tate.*

Gen. 39. 4 make ye *m*. with us.
Ex. 21. 10 her raim., and duty of *m*.
Deut. 7. 3 nei. make *m*. with them
Josh. 23. 12 shall make *m*. with them
Mat. 22. 2 k., which made *m*. for s.
24. 38 marrying and giving in *m*.
Mark 12 25 nor are given in *m*.
Luke 17. 27 they were given in *m*.
John 2. 1 there was in Cana
2. 2 called, and his discip. to *m*.
1 Cor. 7. 38 he hath giv. her in *m*.
Heb. 13. 4 *M*. is honourable in all
Rev. 19. 7 for *m*. of lamb is come
R. V. Mat. 22. 2, 4. 9; 25. 10 marriage feast
Married. *United in matrimony.*
Ex. 21. 3 were *m*., then wife sh. go
Num. 36. 3 if they be *m*. to sons of
Deut. 22. 22 with wom. *m*. to husb.
Prov. 30. 23 od. wom. when she is *m*.
Isa. 62. 4 and thy land shall be *m*.
Jer. 3. 14 for I am *m*. unto you
Mark 10. 12 if wom. *m*. to another
Rom. 7. 3 no adult, thongh she be *m*
1 Cor. 7. 10 unto *m*. I command
7. 33; 34; 39
See also **Marry.**
Marrow. *Fat, essence.*
Job 21. 24 bones moistened with *m*.
Ps. 63. 5 soul be satisfi., as with *m*.
Prov. 3. 8 and *m*. to thy bones
Isa. 25. 6 of fat things full of *m*.
Heb. 4. 12 and of joints and *m*.
Marry. *Espouse, take wife.*
Gen. 19. 14 s.in l., wh. *m*. his daugh.
38. 8 unto bro.'s wife, and *m*. her
Num. 12. 1 E. wom. whom he had *m*
Deut. 24. 1 hath tak. wif. and *m*. her
1 Chr. 2. 21 whom he *m*. when he
2 Chr. 13. 21 and *m*. fourteen wives
Neh. 13. 23 had *m*. wives of Ashdod
13. 27 trans. in *m*. strange wives
Mal. 2. 11 *m*. daught. of strange god
Mat. 5. 32 whoso. *m*. her that is div.
19. 9, 10; 22. 25, 30; 24. 38
Mark 6. 17 wife, for he had *m*. her
10. 11; 12. 25
Luke 14. 20 said, I have *m*. wife
16. 18; 17. 27; 20. 34, 35
1 Cor. 7. 9 better to *m*. than burn
7. 28, 36
1 Tim. 4. 3 Forbid. to *m*., and com.
Marsh. *See* **Marise.**
Mart. *Market, trading point.*
Isa. 23. 3 she is a *m*. of nations
Martyr. R. V. *witness.*
Acts 22. 20 blood of thy *m*. Stephen
Rev. 2. 13 Antipas was my faith. *m*.
17. 6 with blood of *m*. of Jesus
Marvel (*n*.). *Wonder, prodigy.*
Ex. 34. 10 before peo. I will do *m*.
2 Cor. 11. 14 And no *m*.; for Satan
Marvel (*v*.). *To wonder.*
Gen. 43. 33 men *m*. at one another
Ps. 48. 5 they *m*.; they were troub.
Eccl. 5. 8 *m*. not the matter, for he
Mat. 8. 10 Je. *m*., and said to them
9. 8 they *m*., and glorified God
Mark 5. 20 and all men did *m*.
12.17 are God's; and they *m*. at him
Luke 1. 63 name is John. And th. *m*.
20. 26 they *m*. at his answer
John 5. 28 *M*. not, for hour is com.
Acts 2. 7 *m*., saying one to another
Gal. 1. 6 *m*. that ye are so soon re.
1 John 3. 13 *M*. not, if world hate
Rev. 17. 7 Wherefore didst thou *m*.?
R. V. Ps. 48. 5 amazed; Mat. 9. 8
were afraid; Rev. 17. 7 wonder
Marvellous. *Wonderful.*
1 Chr. 16. 12 *m*. w. he hath done
Job 5. 9 *m*. things without number
10 16 showest thyself *m*. upon me
Ps. 9. 1 show all thy *m*. works
98. 1 for he hath done *m*. things
118. 23 L's doing; it is *m*. in our eyes
Isa. 29. 14 do *m*. works among peo.
Dan. 11. 36 spake *m*. things against
Mic. 7. 15 will show him *m*. things
Zech. 8. 6 If it be *m*. in eyes of
Mat. 21. 42 it is *m*. in our eyes?
Mark 12. 11
John 9. 30 herein is *m*. things that
1 Pet. 2. 9 out of dark. into *m*. light
Rev. 15. 1 saw anoth. sign, gr. .. *m*.
15. 3 *m*. are thy works, L. G. A.

R. V. Ps. 139. 14 wonderful; John
9. 30 the marvel
Marvellously. *Wonderfully.*
2 Chr. 26. 15 he was *m*. helped
Job 37. 5 God thunder. *m*. with v.
Hab. 1. 5 wonder *m*.,for I will work
Mason. *Stone-dresser,wall-builder.*
2 Sam. 5. 11 *m*.; they built D. house
2 K. 12. 12 to *m*., and hewers of st.
1 Chr. 14. 1 *m*. to build him house
22. 2 set *m*, to hew wrought stones
2 Chr. 24. 12 hired *m*. to repair h.
Ez. 3. 7 gave money unto the *m*.
Mast. *Pole, spar.*
Prov. 23. 34 that lieth on top of *m*.
Isa. 33. 23 could not well streng. *m*.
Ezek. 27. 5 tak. cedars to make *m*.
Master. *Lord, sir,*
Gen. 24. 9 under thigh of A. his *m*.
39. 20 Joseph's *m*. took him, and
Ex. 21. 5 I love my *m*., my wife
Deut. 23. 15 which is escap. from *m*.
Judg. 19. 11 serv. said unto his *m*.
1 Sam. 24. 6 do this unto my *m*.
2 Sam. 2. 7 your *m*. Saul is dead
1 K. 22. 17 L. said, These have no *m*.
2 K. 2. 3 L. will take away thy *m*.
1 Chr. 12. 19 will fall to his *m*. Saul
2 Chr. 18. 16 said, These have no *m*.
Job 3. 19 servant is free from *m*.
Ps. 123. 2 look unto the hand of *m*.
Prov. 30. 10 accuse not ser. unto *m*.
Isa. 24. 2 as with serv., so with *m*.
Jer. 27. 4 Thus shall ye say to *m*.
Am. 4. 1 which say to *m*., Bring
Zeph. 1. 9 fill *m's* houses with vio.
Mal. 1. 6 if I be *m*., where is fear?
Mat. 6. 24 No man can serve two *m*.
Mark 13. 25 not when *m*.of h. com.
Luke 14. 21 *m*. of h., being angry
Acts 16. 16 brought her *m*. much g.
Rom. 14. 4 to *m*. he stand. or falleth
Eph. 6. 5 *m*. according to the flesh
6. 9 knowing your *m*. is in heaven
Col. 4. 1 know. ye have *m*. in heav.
Rabbi, my teacher.
Mat. 26. 25 Judas said *M*., is it I?
26. 49 Hail, *M*., and kissed him
Mark 9. 5 *M*, it is good to be here
John 4. 31 disc. prayed, saying, *M*.
9. 2 *M*., who did sin, this man
Superintendent.
Luke 5. 5 *M*., we have toil. all night
8. 24 awoke him, saying, *M*., *m*.
Ruler, leader, owner.
Ex. 22. 8 *m*. of house be brought
Judg. 19. 22 spake to *m*. of house
Eccl. 12. 11 fastened by *m*. of assem.
Isa. 1. 3 ass his *m's* crib; but Israel
Dan. 1. 3 unto Aph. *m*. of eunuchs
Jonah 1. 6 the ship *m*. came to him
Despot, sovereign.
1 Tim. 6. 1 count their own *m*. w. of
2 Tim. 2. 21 and meet for the *m's* use
Tit. 2. 9 obedient unto their own *m*.
1 Pet. 2. 18 subject to *m*. with fear
Teacher.
Mal. 2. 12 cut off *m*. and scholar
Mat. 8. 19 *M*., I will follow thee
9. 11 Why eat. your *M*. with public.
10. 24 discip. is not above his *m*.
17. 24 Doth your *m*. pay tribute
26. 18 *M*. saith, My time is at hand
Mark 4. 38 *M*., carest thou not that
12. 19 *M*., Moses wrote unto us
14. 14 *M*. saith, Where is guest c.
Luke 3. 12 *M*., what shall we do?
10. 25 *M*., what do to inh. eter. life
John 1. 38 say, being interpreted, *M*.
3. 10 Art thou a *m*. of Israel, and
Jas. 3. 1 My breth. be not many *m*.
Prince, head, chief, captain.
Ex. 1. 11 did set over them task *m*.
1 Chr. 15. 27 *m*. of song with singers
Acts 27. 11 centurion believed the *m*
1 Cor. 3. 10 as a wise *m*. builder, I
Rev. 18. 17 And every ship *m*., all
See also **Sheep-master, taskmaster, ship-master.**
R. V. 1 Sam. 24. 6; 26. 16; 29. 4,
10; 2 Sam. 2. 7; Am. 4. 1; Mark
13. 39; Rom. 14. 4; 2 Pet. 2. 1
lord; Mat. 26. 25, 49; Mark 9. 5;
11. 21; 14. 45; John 4. 31; 9. 2;
11. 8 Rabbi; Mat. 23. 8; John 3.
10; Jas. 3. 1 teacher

Mastery. *Rule, power.*
Ex. 32. 18 them that shout for *m*.
Dan. 6. 24 lions had *m*. of them
1 Cor. 9. 25 every man striv. for *m*.
2 Tim. 2. 5 if man strive for *m*.
R. V. 1. Cor. 9. 25 in the games
Mate. *Friend, companion.*
Isa. 34. 15, 16 ev. one with her *m*.
Matrix. R. V. *womb.*
Ex. 13. 12 all that openeth the *m*.
13. 15; 34. 19; Num. 3. 12; 18. 15
Matter. *Thing, affair, speech.*
Gen. 24. 9 sware concern. that *m*.
Ex. 18. 16 When they have *m*., they
23. 7 keep thee far from false *m*.
Num. 16. 49 them that died about *m*.
Deut. 3. 26 spk. no more of this m.
Ruth 3. 18 how the *m*. will fall, for
1 Sam. 10. 16 But of *m*. of kingdom
16.18 man of war, and prudent in *m*.
2 Sam. 1. 4 How went *m*.? I pray t.
1 K. 8. 59 times, as *m*. shall require
1 Chr. 26. 32 for ev. *m*. pertain to G.
Ez. 5. 5 till the *m*. came to Darius
Neh. 11. 24 at k's hand in all *m*.
Esth. 2. 23 when in. was made of *m*.
Job 19. 28 root of *m*. is found in
32. 18 For I am full of *m*., the spirit
Ps. 45. 1 heart is inditing good m.
Prov. 11. 13 faith. spir. conceal. *m*.
Eccl. 5. 8 marvel not at the *m*.
Jer. 38. 27 for *m*. was not perceived
Ezek. 9. 11 reported the *m*., saying
Dan. 1. 14 he consented in this *m*.
Mark 1. 55 to blaze abroad the *m*.
Acts 8. 21 neither part nor lot in *m*.
1 Cor. 6. 1 dare any having *m*. ag.
2 Cor. 7. 11 approv. yours. in this *m*.
Gal. 2. 6 it maketh no *m*. to me
Jas. 3. 5 Behold how great *m*.
1 Pet. 4. 15 busybody in men's *m*.
R. V. Job 32. 18; Ps. 35. 20 words;
1 Sam. 16. 18 speech; Ps. 64. 5
purpose; Dan. 4. 17 sentence;
Jas. 3. 5 much wood
Mattock. *Axe, digging tool.*
1 Sam. 13. 20 coulter, axe, and his *m*.
13. 21 they had file for the *m*.
2 Chr. 34. 6 even un. Naph., wi. *m*.
Isa. 7. 25 shall be digged with *m*.
R. V. 2 Chr. 34. 6 in ruins
Maul. *Wooden hammer, beetle.*
Prov. 25. 18 that bear. false wit. is *m*.
Maw. *Stomach.*
Deut. 18. 3 shall give to priests *m*.
May, Night. *Be able, possibly.*
Gen. 43. 32 Egypt. *m*. not eat bread
Deut. 7. 22 *m*. not consume them
Josh. 9. 19 we *m*. not touch them
Judg. 21. 18 *m*. not give them wives
2 Sam. 17. 17 for they *m*. not be seen
1 K. 20. 9 this thing I *m*. not do
Job 1. 5 *m*. be my sons have sinned
Eccl. 6. 10 nei. *m*. he contend with
Jer. 13. 23 *m*. ye also do good
Mst. 26. 9 oint. *m*. have been sold
26. 42 if cup *m*. not pass away
Mark 4. 32 fowls *m*. lodge un. bran.
Luke 16. 2 *m*. be no longer steward
Acts 17. 19 *M*. we know new doct.
1 Cor. 14. 10 are, it *m*. be, m. voices
Eph. 3. 4 read, ye *m*. understand
1 Thes. 2. 6 *m*. have been burdens.
Rev. 13. 17 no man *m*. buy or sell
Me. *I (obj.)*
Gen. 24. 12 send *m*. good speed
Mat. 11. 29 take yoke, and learn .. *m*.
Etc., etc.
Meadow. R. V. *reed grass.*
Gen. 41. 2, 18 and they fed in *m*.
R. V. *Maareh-geba.*
Judg. 20. 33 forth out of *m*. of Gi.
Meal. *Ground grain. flour.*
Gen. 18. 6 Make three meas. of *m*.
Num. 5. 15 an ephah of barley *m*.
1 K. 17. 12 handful of *m*. in barrel
2 K. 4. 41 he said, Then bring *m*.
1 Chr. 12. 40 brought bread, meat,*m*.
Isa. 47. 2 Take mills. and grind *m*.
Hos. 8. 7 bud shall yield no *m*.
Mat. 13. 33 hid in three meas. of *m*.
Luke 13. 21
Meal Time. *Time of eating.*
Ruth 2. 14 At *m. t.* come thou hith.
Mean (*a*.). *Low, humble, obscure.*
Prov. 22. 29 not stand before *m*

Isa. 2. 9 the *m.* man boweth down
5. 15 *m.* man shall be br. down
31. 8 sword, not of *m.* man, devour
Acts 21. 39 citizen of no *m.* city
Mean (*v.*). *Intend, signify, design.*
Gen. 50. 20 G. *m.* it unto good
Ex. 12. 26 What *m.* ye by this ser.?
Deut. 6. 20 what *m.* testimonies?
Josh. 4. 6 What *m.* by these stones
Isa. 10. 7 he *m.* not so; neither
Ezek. 17. 12 what these things *m.*?
Mat. 9. 13 go learn what that *m.*
Mark 9. 10 what ris. from dead *m.*
Luke 15. 26 asked what these . .*m.*
Acts 2. 12 saying, What *m.* this?
21. 13 *m.* ye to weep and break my
27. 2 *m.* to sail by coasts of A.
2 Cor. 8. 13 I *m.* not that oth. men
R. V. Acts 21. 13 do; 2 Cor. 8. 13
say not this Acts 27. 2 which was
about; Luke 15. 26 might be
Meaning. *Intent, understanding.*
Dan. 8. 15 sought for *m.*, then
1 Cor. 14. 11 known not *m.* of voice
Means. *Agency, power, every way.*
Ex.34. 7 will by no *m.* clear guilty
2 Sam. 14. 14 yet doth he devise *m.*
1 K. 10. 29 bring out by their *m.*
2 Chr. 1. 17 kings of Syr., by . . *m.*
Ez. 4. 16 by this *m*. . . no portion
Prov. 6.26 by *m.* of whorish woman
Jer. 5. 31 priests bear rule by *m.*
Mal. 1. 9 this hath been by your *m.*
Mat. 5. 26 shalt by no *m.* come out
Luke 8. 36 *m.* he that was possessed
John 9. 21 by what *m.* he now seeth
Acts 18. 21 by all *m.* keep this feast
27. 12 if by any *m.* they might atta.
Rom. 1. 10; 2 Cor. 8. 9; Gal. 2. 2;
Phil. 3. 11; 1 Thes. 3. 5
1 Cor. 9. 22 might by all *m.* save
2 Cor. 11. 11 by *m.* of many persons
2 Thes. 2. 3 no man deceive by . . *m.*
Heb. 9. 15 that by *m.* of death, for
R. V. Prov. 6.26 on account; Luke
5. 18—; 8. 36; John 9. 21 how;
Luke 10. 19; 2 Thes. 2. 3 in any
wise; Judg. 5. 22 Rev. 13. 14
reason
Meant. *See Mean* (*v.*).
Meantime. *Between time.*
Luke 12. 1 *m. t.* gath. multitude
Meanwhile. *Between while.*
1 K. 18. 45 came to pass in *m. w.*
John 4. 31 *m. w.* his discip. prayed
Rom. 2. 15 thoughts *m.w.*accusing
Measure (*n.*). *Standard, limit, measurement, allotted part, judgment.*
Gen. 18. 6 three *m.* (*seah*) of meal
Ex. 26. 2 curtains have one *m.*
Lev. 19. 35 yard, in weight, or *m.*
Deut.25. 14 sh. not have divers *m.*
Josh. 3. 4 two thous. cubits by *m.*
1 Sam. 25. 18 five *m.* (*seah*) of corn
1 K. 18. 32 two *m.* (*seah*) of seed
2 K. 7. 1 *m.* (*seah*) oi fine flour
1 Chr. 23. 29 and for all manner of *m.*
2 Chr. 3. 3 length after first *m.*
Ez. 7. 22 hund. *m.* (*cor*) of wheat
Job 28. 25 weigheth waters by *m.*
38. 5 Who hath laid the *m.* thereof
Ps. 39. 4 know the *m.* of my days
80. 5 tears to drink in great *m.*
Prov. 20. 10 weights, and divers *m.*
Isa. 5. 14 op. her mouth without *m.*
27. 8 in *m.*(*seah*) when shoot. forth
Jer. 30. 11 will correct thee in *m.*
Ezek. 4. 11 shalt drink water by *m.*
Mich. 6. 10 scant *m.* is abomination
Mat. 7. 2 *m.* ye mete, it shall be *m.*
Mark 6. 51 were amazed beyond *m.*
Luke 6. 38 good *m.*, pressed down
16. 7 hundred *m.* (*cor*) of wheat
John 3. 34 God giv. not spirit by *m.*
Rom 12. 3 to every *m.* of faith
2 Cor. 10. 13 of rule which God
Gal. 1. 13 beyond *m.* I persecuted
Eph. 4. 13 *m.* of stat. of fulness
Rev. 21. 17 according to *m.* of man
R. V. Mark 10. 26; 2 cor. 1. 8 ex-
ceedingly; Mark 6. 51; Rev. 21.
15 —; 2 Cor. 10. 14; 12. 7 over
much.
Measure. (*v*). *Make measurement.*

Num. 35. *m.* from without city on
Deut. 21. 2 shall *m.* unto the cities
Ruth 3. 15 he *m.* six meas. of bar.
2 Sam. 8. 2 Moab, *m.* them with line
Isa. 40. 12 Who hath *m.* the waters
Ezek. 40, 5 *m.* breadth of building
Jer. 31. 37 If heaven ab. can be *m.*
Hos. 1. 10 cannot be *m.* or num.
Hab. 3. 6 stood, and *m.* the earth
Zech. 2. 2 said, To *m.* Jerusalem
Mat. 7. 2 shall be *m.* to you again
Mark 4. 24; Luke 6. 38
2 Cor. 10. 12 *m.* thems. by thems.
Rev. 11. 1 Rise, *m.* temple of God
Measuring. *Making measure.*
Jer. 31. 39 *m.* line shall go forth
Ezek 40. 3 flax in hand, and *m.* reed
Zech. 2. 1 behold, man with *m.* line
Meat. *Food, nourishment, meal.*
Gen. 1. 29 to you it shall be for *m.*
40. 17 all manner of baked *m.*
Lev. 11. 34 *m.* which may be eaten
22. 11 they shall eat of his *m.*
Num. 28. 24 *m.* of sac. made by fire
Deut. 2. 6 shall buy *m.* for money
Judg. 14. 14 Out of eater came *m.*
1 Sam. 20. 34 the king sat to eat *m*
2 Sam. 13. 5 come and give me *m.*
1 K. 10. 5 *m.* of his table, and sit.
1 Chr. 12. 40 mules, oxen, and *m.*
2 Chr. 9. 4 *m.* of his table, and sit.
Ez. 3. 7 *m.*, drink, and oil to them
Job 12. 11 and mouth taste his *m.*
20. 21 shall none of his *m.* be left
38. 41 they wander for lack of *m.*
Ps. 42. 3 tears have been my *m.*
44. 11 like sheep appoint. for *m.*
Prov. 6. 8 provideth her *m.* in sum.
31. 15 giv. *m.* to her household
Isa. 65. 25 dust be serpent's *m.*
Jer. 7. 33 meat for fowls of heaven
Lam. 4. 10 th. were their *m.* in dest.
Ezek. 47. 12 grow all trees for m.
Dan. 1. 10 who hath appoint. your *m*
Joel 1. 16 Is not *m.* cut off before
Hab. 3. 17 fields shall yield no *m.*
Hag. 2. 12 or wine, or oil, or any *m*
Mal. 1. 12 fruit thereof, even his *m.*
Mat. 3. 4 his *m.* was loc. and honey
25. 35 hung.. and ye gave me no *m*
Mark 7. 19 into draught purging *m.*
Luke 8. 55 command. to give her *m.*
12. 23 the life is more than *m.*
John 6. 55 my flesh is *m.* indeed
Acts 2. 46 eat their *m.* with gladness
16. 34 he set *m.* before them, and
Rom. 14. 17 king. of God is not *m.*
1 Cor. 3. 2 milk, and not with *m.*
8. 8 *m.* commend. is not to God
Col. 2. 16 no man judge you in *m.*
1 Tim. 4. 3 com. to abstain from *m.*
Heb. 5. 12 need of m., not strong *m.*
12. 16 for *m.* sold his birthright
R. V. very frequent changes to,
food, meat, etc.
Meat-offering. *An offering.*
Ex. 29. 41 according to the *m.*
Lev. 2. 1; Num. 4. 16; Josh. 22. 23;
Judg. 13. 19; 1 K. 8. 64; 2 K. 3.
20; 1 Chr. 21. 23; 2 Chr. 7. 7; Ez.
7. 17; Neh. 10. 33; Isa. 57. 6; Jer.
17. 26; Ezek. 42. 13; Joel 1. 19;
Am. 5. 22
Meddle. *Stir or mix up self with.*
Deut. 2. 5 *M.* not with them, for
2 K. 14. 10 why *m.* to thy hurt
2 Chr. 25. 19
Prov. 17. 14 before it be *m.* with
20. 3, 19 . 24. 21; 26. 17
R. V. Deut. 2. 5, 19 contend;
Prov. 17. 4; 20. 3 quarrelling; 26.
17 vexeth himself.
Mediator. *Middle man, interces-sor.*
Gal. 3. 19 angels in the hand of a *m.*
1 Tim. 2. 5 one *m.* bet. G. and man
Heb. 8. 6 he is *m.* of better coven.
12. 24 Jesus *m.* of new covenant
Medicine. *Remedy, healing.*
Prov. 17. 22 mer. h. do. good like *m*
Jer. 30. 13 thou hast no healing *m.*
46. 11 in vain shalt thou use *m.*
Ezek. 47. 12 for meat, and leaf for *m*
R. V. Ezek. 47. 12 healing
Meditate. *Fix mind, dwell, muse.*
Gen. 24. 63 Isaac went out to *m.*

Josh. 1. 8 *m.* therein day and night
Ps. 1. 2 and in his law doth he *m.*
63. 6 *m.* on thee in night watch
77. 12 will *m.* also of all thy work
119. 15 I will *m.* in thy precepts
143. 5 I *m.* on all thy works
Isa. 33. 18 Thine h. shall *m.* terror
Luke 21. 14 not *m.* what ye answer
1 Tim. 4. 15 *M.* upon these things
R. V. Isa. 33. 18 muse; 1 Tim. 4. 15
be diligent in
Meditation. *Revolve, move.*
Ps. 5. 1 O Lord; consider my *m.*
19. 14 Let the *m.* of my heart, be
49. 3 and the *m.* of my heart shall be
104. 34 *m.* of him shall be sweet
119. 97 thy law! it is my *m.* all day
Meek. *Humble, easy, mild*
Num. 12. 3 man Moses was very *m.*
Ps. 22. 26 *m.* shall eat and be sat.
37. 11 *m.* shall inherit the earth
147. 6 The Lord lifteth up the *m.*
149.4 will beautify *m.* with salva.
Isa. 29. 19 *m.* also shall increase
Am. 2. 7 turn aside way of *m.*
Zeph. 2. 3 seek Lord ye *m.* of earth
Mat. 5. 5 Blessed are the *m.*, for
11. 29 I am *m.* and lowly in heart
21. 5 King cometh unto thee, *m.*
1 Pet. 3. 4 of *m.* and quiet spirit
Meekness. *Humility, mildness.*
Ps. 45. 4 because of truth, and *m.*
Zeph. 2. 3 seek. righteous., seek *m.*
1 Cor. 4. 21 and in the spirit of *m.*
2 Cor. 10. 1 by *m.* and gentle. of C.
Gal. 5. 23 *m.*, temp., against such
Eph. 4. 2 With all lowliness and *m.*
Col. 3. 12 Put on *m.*, long suffering
1 Tim. 6. 11 follow love, patien., *m.*
2 Tim. 2. 25 In *m.* instructing those
Tit. 3. 2 gentle, showing all *m.*
Jas. 1. 21 receive with *m.* eng. word
1 Pet. 3. 15 hope is in you with *m.*
Meet (*a.*). *Fit, right, proper.*
Ex. 8. 26 It is not *m.* to do so
Deut. 3. 18 pass ov., all *m.* for war
Judg. 5. 30 *m.* for necks of them
Ez. 4. 14 not *m.* to see king's dis.
Esth. 2. 9 *m.* to be given her, out
Job 34. 31 *m.* to be said unto God
Prov. 11. 24 withhold. more th. is *m.*
Jer. 27. 5 giv. to whom it seem. *m.*
Ezek. 15. 4 Is it *m.* for any work?
Mat. 3. 8 fruits *m.* for repentance
Mark 7. 27 not *m.* to take chil. br.
Luke 15. 32 *m.* that we make merry
Acts 26. 20 do works *m.* for repent.
1 Rom. 1. 27 recom. of error was *m.*
1 Cor. 16. 4 if it be *m.* that I go
Phil. 1. 7 Even as it is *m.* for me
Col. 1. 12 us *m.* to be partakers of
2 Thes. 1. 3 thank God, as it is *m.*
2 Tim. 2. 21 and *m.* for master's use
Heb. 6. 7 and bringeth herbs *m.* for
2 Pet. 1. 13 Yea. I think it is *m.*
R. V. Deut. 3. 18 men of valor;
Jer. 26. 14; 27. 5; Phil. 1. 7; 2 Pet.
1. 13 right; Judg. 5. 30 on; Ezek.
15. 4 profitable; Mat. 3. 8; Acts
26. 20 worthy of; Rom. 1. 27 due
Meet (*v.*). *Come together.*
Gen. 18. 2 he ran to *m.* them from
Ex. 4. 14 cometh forth to *m.* thee
Num. 22. 36 he went out to *m.* him
Deut. 25. 18 he *m.* thee by the way
Josh. 11. 5 when kings were *m.* to.
Judg. 4. 18 Jael went to *m.* Sisera
Ruth 2. 22 *m.* thee not in the field
1 Sam. 13. 10 Saul went to *m.* him
2 Sam. 6. 20 Mic. came to *m.* David
1 K. 2. 19 king rose up to *m.* her
2 K. 1. 3 go up to *m.* messengers
1 Chr. 19. 5 and he sent to *m.* them
2 Chr. 15. 2 he went out to *m.* Asa
Neh. 8. 2 Come, let us *m.* together
Job 5. 14 They *m.* with darkness
Ps. 85. 10 Mercy and truth are *m.*
Prov. 22. 2 rich and poor *m.* toget.
Isa. 7. 3 Go forth now to *m.* Ahaz
Jer. 41. 6 as he *m.* them, he said
Hos. 13. 8 I will *m.* them as bear
Am. 4. 12 prepare to *m.* thy God
Zech. 2. 3 angel went to *m.* him
Mat. 8. 28 *m.* him two possessed
28. 9 Jesus *m.* them, saying, All h
Mark 5 2 *m.* him out of the tombs

Luke 8. 27 *m.* him a certain man
John 11. 30 pl. where Martha *m.* h.
12. 13 people went forth to *m.* him
Acts 10. 25 C. *m.* him, and fell down
1 Thes. 4. 17 caught up to *m.* Lord
Heb. 7. 1 who *m.* Abr. returning
R. V. Josh. 2. 16 light upon

Meetest. *Fittest.*
2 K. 10. 3 Look out best and *m.*

Meeting. *Coming together.*
1 Sam. 21. 1 Ahim. was afraid at *m.*
Mark 11. 4 place where two ways *m.*
See also **Meet** (*v.*).

Melody. *Song, sweet sound.*
Isa. 23. 16 make sweet *m.*, sing songs
51. 3 thanksgiv., and voice of *m.*
Am. 5. 23 not hear the *m.* of viols
Eph. 5. 19 making *m.* in h. to Lord

Melons. *Melons.*
Num. 11. 5 remem. cucum. and *m.*

Melt. *Dissolve, waste.*
Ex. 15. 15 inhabitants of Canaan *m.*
16. 21 when sun waxed hot, it *m.*
Josh. 2. 11 our hearts did *m.*, nei.
Judg. 5. 5 mountains *m.* bef. them
1 Sam. 14. 16 the multitude *m.* away
2 Sam. 17. 10 he shall utterly *m.*
Ps. 22. 14 *m.* in midst of bowels
46. 6 uttered his voice, earth *m.*
58. 8 As a snail which *m.*, let ev.
97. 5 hill *m.* like wax at the pres.
119. 28 My soul *m.* with heaviness
Isa. 13. 7 every man's heart shall *m.*
40. 19 workman *m.* graven image
Jer. 6. 29 The founder *m.* in vain
9. 7 will *m.* them, and try them
Ezek. 22. 20 blow the fire, to *m.* it
22. 22 As silver is *m.* in furnace
Am. 9. 13 and all the hills shall *m.*
Mic. 1. 4 the mountains shall be *m.*
Nah. 1. 5 hills *m.*, earth is burned
2. 10 heart *m.* and knees smite
2 Pet. 3. 10 elements *m.* with fer. h.
R. V. Judg. 5. 5 flowed down ; Jer.
6. 29 go on refining

Melting. *Dissolving.*
Isa. 64. 2 As when *m.* fire burneth
R. V. Fire kindleth brushwood

Member. *Limb, part of body.*
Job 17. 7 my *m.* are as a shadow
Ps. 139. 16 all my *m.* were written
Mat. 5. 29 that thy *m.* should per.
Rom. 6. 13 Nei. yield *m.* as instru.
7. 23 see another law in my *m.*
1 Cor. 6. 15 bodies are *m.* of Christ
12. 14 For the body is not one *m.*
Eph. 4. 25 we are *m.* one of anoth.
Col. 3. 5 Mortify your *m.* which
Jas. 3. 5 the tongue is a little *m.*
4. 1 your lusts that war in your *m.*
R. V. 1 Cor. 12. 23 parts

Memorial. *Remembrance.*
Ex. 3. 15 my *m.* unto all genera.
Lev. 2. 2 priest shall burn *m.* of
Num. 5. 26 *m.* thereof. and burn it
Josh. 4. 7 these stones shall be *m.*
Neh. 2. 20 no por., nor right, nor *m.*
Esth. 9. 28 nor *m.* of them that per.
Ps. 9. 6 their *m.* is perished with th.
Hos. 12. 5 hosts, the Lord is his *m.*
Zech. 6. 14 for *m.* in temp. of Lord
Mat. 26. 13 be told for a *m.* of her
Mark 14. 9 be spoken of for a *m.*
Acts 10. 4 come for *m.* before God

Memory. *Remembrance.*
Ps. 109. 15 that he may cut off *m.*
145. 7 shall abundantly utter *m.*
Prov. 10. 7 *m.* of the just is blessed
Eccl. 9. 5 *m.* of them is forgotten
Isa. 26. 14 made their *m.* to perish
1 Cor. 15. 2 keep in *m.* what I pre.

Men. *Man* (*pl.*)
Num. 9. 6 *m.*, who were defiled
Deut. 2. 34 utterly destroyed the *m.*
Judg. 20. 48 as well *m.* of ev. city
2 Sam. 10. 12 play *m.* for our peo.
Job 11. 11 For he knoweth vain *m.*
Ps. 17. 14 *m.* which are thy hand
Isa. 3. 25 *m.* shall fall by sword
Rom. 1. 27 *m.* with *m.* work. that
6. 19 I speak aft. manner of *m.*
1 Cor. 16. 13 Watch, quit you like *m.*
Jude 16 having *m's.* persons in ad.
See also **Man.**

Mend. *Strengthen, make fit.*
2 Chr. 24. 12 brass to *m.* h. of Lord

Mat. 4. 21 two breth. *m.* their nets
Mark 1. 19 in the ship *m.* their nets
R. V 2 Chr. 24. 12 repair

Mene. *Number.*
Dan. 5. 26 *M.*, G. hath num. thy k.

Menpleasers. *Pleasing men.*
Eph. 6. 6 Not with eye ser. as *m.p.*
Col. 3. 22

Menstealer. *Men enslaver.*
1 Tim. 1. 10 for *m.* s., liars perj. per.

Menstruous. *Sick, unclean.*
Lam. 1. 17 Jerus. is as *m.* woman
Isa. 30. 22 cast away as *m.* cloth.
Ezek. 18. 6 nei. come near *m.* wo.
R. V. Lam. 1. 17 ; Isa. 30. 22 un-
clean thing

Mention (*n.*). *Mentioning, allu-
sion.*
Gen. 40. 14 make *m.* of me to Phar.
Ex 23. 13 make no *m.* of oth. gods
Josh. 23. 7 nei. make *m.* of name of
1 Sam. 4. 18 when he made *m.* of ark
Job 28. 18 No *m.* be made of coral
Ps. 71. 16 I will *m.* thy righteous.
87. 4 will *m.* Rahab and Babylon
Isa. 12. 4 *m.* his name is exalted
48. 1 make *m.* of God of Israel
Jer. 20. 9 will not make *m.* of him
Am. 6. 10 may not *m.* name of L.
Rom. 1. 9 mk. *m.* of you in prayers
Eph. 1. 16 ; 1 Thes. 1. 2 ; Phile. 4
Heb. 11. 22 made *m.* of depart. of

Mention (*v.*). *Refer to, remember.*
Josh. 21. 9 cities here *m.* by name
1 Chr. 4. 38 these *m.* by names were
2 Chr. 20. 34 *m.* in book of kings
Isa. 63. 7 *m.* lovingkindness of L.
Jer. 23. 36 burd. of L. shall ye *m.*
Ezek. 18. 22 shall not be *m.* to him
R. V. 2 Chr. 20. 34 inserted ; Ezek.
18. 22, 24 ; 33. 16 remembered

Merchandise. *Trade, traffic,
wares*
Deut. 21. 14 not make *m.* of her
24. 7 If man maketh *m.* of him, or
Prov. 3. 14 better than *m.* of silver
31. 13 perceiveth her *m.* is good
Isa. 23. 18 her *m.* shall be holiness
45. 14 *m.* of Ethiop. and Sabeans
Ezek. 27. 9 ships to occupy thy *m.*
27. 33 mul. of riches, and thy *m.*
Mat. 22. 5 one to farm, anoth. to *m.*
John 2. 16 not my F's house h. of *m.*
2 Pet. 2. 3 wi. feigned words *m.* of
Rev. 18. 11 no man buyeth their *m.*
18. 12 *m.* of gold and silver, stones
R. V. Deut. 21. 14 ; 24. 7 deal
with ; Ezek. 27. 15 mart ; 28. 16
traffic

Merchant. *Buyer and seller,
trader.*
Gen. 23. 16 silver current with *m.*
37. 28 passed Midianite *m.* men
1 K. 10. 15 traffic of the spice *m.*
10. 28 k's *m.* received the linen
2 Chr. 9. 14 which chap. and *m.* br't
Neh. 3. 31 unto place of *m.*, over
Job 41. 6 shall part him among *m.*
Prov. 31. 14 She is like *m's* ship
31. 24 delivereth girdles unto *m.*
S. of S. 3. 6 per. with powders of *m.*
Isa. 23. 11 given command ag. *m.*
47. 15 thy *m.*, from thy youth
Ezek. 27. 12 Tarshish was thy *m.*
38. 13 Sheba, Dedan, and *m.* of
Hos. 12. 7 He is a *m.*, the balances
Nah. 3. 16 hast multiplied thy *m.*
Zeph. 1. 11 all *m.* peo. are cut down
Mat. 13. 45 like unto *m.* man seek.
Rev. 18. 3 *m.* of earth waxed rich
18. 11 the *m.* of earth shall weep
18. 23 thy *m.* were great men of ear.
R. V. Isa. 23. 11 concerning
Canaan ; 47. 15 that trafficked
with thee ; Ezek. 27. 20 ; Hos.
12. 7 trafficker ; Ezek. 27. 13, 15,
17 ; 22. 23, 24 traffickers

Mercies. *Compassions, forbear-
ances, benevolences, kindnesses.*
2 Sam. 24. 14 his *m.* are very great
1 Chr. 21. 13 very great are his *m.*
Neh. 9. 19 thou in thy *m.* forsook
Ps. 25. 6 Rem. L., thy tender *m.*
40. 11 Withhold not thy tender *m.*
119. 156 Great are thy tender *m.*, L.
Prov. 12. 10 *m.* of wicked are cruel

Isa. 54. 7 with *m.* will I gath. thee
Jer. 42. 12 will show *m.* unto you
Dan. 9. 9 To the L. God belong *m.*
Hos. 2. 19 me, in lov. kind. and *m.*
Zech. 1. 16 am ret. to Jerus, with *m.*
Acts 13. 34 give you sure *m.* of Dav.
See also **Mercy,** for other plural**s**
and R. V. changes

Merciful. *Kind, compassionate.*
Gen. 19. 6 L. being *m.* unto him
Ex. 34. 6 Lord God, *m.* and grac.
Deut. 21. 8 Be *m.* L., unto thy peo.
2 Sam. 22. 26 th. wilt shew thys. *m.*
1 K. 20. 31 kings of Israel are *m.*
2 Chr. 30. 9 L. your G. is gr. and *m.*
Neh. 9. 17 God .. gracious and *m.*
Ps. 26. 11 redeem me, and be *m.*
37. 26 He is ever *m.*, and lendeth
67. 1 G. be *m.* unto us, and bless
117. 2 his *m.* kindness is great
Prov. 11. 17 *m.* man doeth good to
Isa. 57. 1 *m.* men are taken away
Jer. 3. 12 I am *m.*, saith the Lord
Joel 2. 13 he is gracious and *m.*
Jonah 4. 2 art gracious God, and *m.*
Mat. 5. 7 Blessed are *m.*, for they
Luke 6. 36 Be *m.*, as your F. is *m.*
18. 13 G. be *m.* to me a sinner
Heb. 2. 17 be *m.* and faith. priest
8. 12 be *m.* to their unrighteous
R. V. Ex. 34. 6 ; Neh. 9. 17 ; Ps.
103. 8 ; Joel 2. 13 ; Jonah 4. 2 full
of compassion ; Ps. 41. 4 ; 41. 10 ;
119. 132 have mercy ; 37. 26 deal-
eth graciously

Mercy. *Lovingkindness.*
Gen. 19. 19 hast magnified thy *m.*
39. 21 showed him *m.*, gave favour
Ex. 15. 13 in *m.* led forth people
20. 6 showing *m.* unto thousands
Num. 14. 19 accord. to gr. of thy *m.*
Deut. 7. 9 which keep. cov. and *m.*
Judg. 1. 24 we will show thee *m.*
2 Sam. 7. 15 my *m.* shall not depart
1 K. 3. 6 showed *m.* according to
1 Chr. 16. 34 his *m.* endure for ever
2 Chr. 1. 8 showed gr. *m.* unto Dav.
Ez. 7. 28 hath extended *m.* to me
Neh. 1. 5 keepeth cov. and *m.*
Job 37. 13 for his land, or for *m.*
Ps. 6. 4 save me for *m's* sake
23. 6 goodness and *m.* shall follow
33. 22 Let *m.*, Lord, be upon us
103. 8 show to ang., plenteous in *m.*
106. 1 his *m.* endureth forever
Prov. 3. 3 Let not *m.* forsake thee
Isa. 16. 5 in *m.* the throne be estab.
Jer. 33. 11 his *m.* endureth forever
Lam. 3. 32 accord. to mul. of his *m.*
Dan. 9. 4 keeping cov. and *m.* to
Hos. 6. 6 desired *m.*, not sacrifi.
Jonah 2. 8 observe, forsake own *m.*
Mic. 6. 8 to do justly, and to love *m.*
Zech. 7. 9 show *m.* and compassion
Graciously inclined.
Deut. 7. 2 m. no cov., nor show *m.*
Ps. 4. 1 have *m.* and hear prayer
30. 10 Hear, O L., and have *m.*
Prov. 14. 31 that hon. him hath *m.*
Dan. 4. 27 br. offering., by show. *m.*
Love, pity, compassion.
Ex. 33. 19 will shew *m.* on whom I
Ps. 102. 13 arise, and have *m.* upon
Prov. 28. 13 confess., shall have *m.*
Isa. 14. 1 L. have *m.* upon Jacob
Jer. 6. 23 cruel, and have no *m.*
13. 14 not pity, spare nor have *m.*
Ezek. 39. 25 have *m.* on ho. of Is.
Hos. 2. 4 not have *m.* upon child.
Rom. 12. 1 beseech, by *m.* of God
2 Cor. 1. 3 Father of *m.*, and G. of
Phil. 2. 1 if any bowels and *m.*
Col. 3. 12 Put on bowels of *m.*
Heb. 10. 28 died without *m.* under
Kindness, beneficence.
Mat. 5. 7 for they shall obtain *m.*
9. 13 will have *m.*, not sacrifice
17. 15 Lord, have *m.* on my son
Mark 10. 47 S. of D., have *m.* on me
Luke 1. 50 *m.* on them that fear
10. 37 he that showed *m.* on him
Rom. 9. 16 of God that showeth *m.*
1 Cor. 7. 25 as one that obtain. *m.*
2 Cor. 4. 1 as we have received *m.*
Gal. 6. 16 peace on them, and *m.*
Eph. 2. 4 God, who is rich in *m.*

Phil. 2. 27 God had *m.* on him
1 Tim 1. 2 grace, *m.* and peace
2 Tim. 1. 18 may find *m.* of Lord
Tit. 3. 5 accord. to *m.* he saved
Heb. 4. 16 that we may obtain *m.*
Jas. 2. 13 that hath shewed no *m.*
1 Pet. 1. 3 accord. to his abund. *m.*
2 John 3 Grace be with you, *m.*
Jude 21 looking for *m.* of L. Jesus
R. V. Gen. 39. 21 ; 2 Sam. 22. 51 ;
  1 K. 3. 6 ; 2 Chr. 1. 8 ; Ps. 5. 7 ;
  18. 50 ; 21. 7 ; 25. 7, 10 ; 36. 5 ;
  61. 7 ; 143. 12 ; Isa. 16. 5 kindness, or lovingkindness ; Prov.
  14. 21 pity ; Isa. 9. 17 ; 14. 1 ; 27.
  11 ; 49. 13 ; Jer. 13. 14 ; 30. 18 ;
  Heb. 10. 28 compassion

Mercy Seat. *Lid, cover for sin,*
place of propitiation.
Ex. 25. 17 make *m. s.* of pure gold
  25. 18–22 ; 26. 34 ; 30. 6 ; 35. 12
Lev. 16. 2 within veil before *m. s.*
  16. 13–15 ; Num. 7. 89 ; 1 Chr. 28. 11
Heb. 9. 5 cherubim shadowing *m. s.*

Merry. *Cheerful, jovial, mirthful.*
Gen. 43. 32 drank, and were *m.*
Judg. 9. 27 trode grapes, made *m.*
  19. 22 as they were making *m.*
Ruth 3. 7 Boaz's heart was *m.*
1 Sam. 25. 36 Nabal's heart was *m.*
2 Sam. 13. 28 Amnon's heart is *m.*
1 K. 21. 7 let thine heart be *m.*
2 Chr. 7. 10 glad and *m.* in heart
Esth. 1. 10 when heart of k. was *m.*
Pro. 15. 13 *m.* heart mak. cheer. c.
  17. 22 a *m.* heart doeth good like
Eccl. 8. 15 to eat, drink, and be *m.*
  10. 19 wine maketh *m.*, but mon.
Isa. 24. 7 the *m.* hearted do sigh
Jer. 30. 19 voice . . that make *m.*
Luke 12. 19 ease, eat, drink, be *m.*
  15. 23 and let us eat, and be *m.*
  15. 32 was meet we should make *m.*
Jas. 5. 13 Is any *m?* let him sing
Rev. 11. 10 shall rej., and make *m.*
R. V. Judg. 9. 27 festival ; Prov.
  15. 15 ; Jas. 5. 13 cheerful ; 2 Chr.
  7. 10 joyful ; Eccl. 10. 19 glad in
  life

Merrily. *Rejoicingly.*
Esth. 5. 14 go thou in *m.* with king

Mess. *Burden, mass of food.*
Gen. 43. 34 he sent *m.* to them from
2 Sam. 11. 8 there followed him *m.*

Message. *Thing, matter, word.*
Judg. 3. 20 I have *m.* a from God
1 K. 20. 12 wh. Ben-hadad heard *m.*
Prov. 26. 6 that sendeth *m.* by fool
Hag. 1. 13 spake Hag. in Lord's *m.*
Luke 19. 14 sent *m.* after him, say.
1 John 1. 5 This is the *m.* which
  3. 11 this is *m.* ye heard from beg.
R. V. Luke 19. 14 ambassage

Messenger. *Ambassador.*
Prov. 25. 13 is a faithful *m.* to them
Isa. 57. 9 didst send thy *m.* far off
Apostle.
2 Cor. 8. 23 the *m.* of the churches
Phil. 2. 25 *m.*, he that is ministered
One sent.
Gen. 32. 3 Jacob sent *m.* before
Num. 14. 36 M. sent *m.* from Kad.
Deut. 2. 26 sent *m.* out of wilder.
Josh. 6. 17 because she hid the *m.*
Judg. 6. 35 Gid. sent *m.* unto Asher
1 Sam. 11. 4 came the *m.* to Gibeah
2 Sam. 3. 12 Ab. sent *m.* to David
1 K. 19. 2 Jezebel sent *m.* to Elijah
2 K. 1. 3 go up to meet the *m.* of k.
1 Chr. 14. 1 Hiram sent *m.* to David
2 Chr. 36. 16 but mocked *m.* of God
Neh. 6. 3 I sent *m.* unto them, say.
Job 1. 14 there came *m.* unto Job
Prov. 16. 14 wrath of a king is as *m.*
Isa. 18. 2 Go, swift *m.*, to a nation
Jer. 51. 31 one *m.* to meet another
Ezek. 23. 16 sent *m.* into Chaldea
Nah. 2. 13 voice of *m.* no more heard
Hag. 1. 13 spake Hag. Lord's *m.*
Mal. 2. 7 he is *m.* from Lord of hosts
Mat. 11. 10 I send my *m.* before thy
  Mark 1. 2 ; Luke 7. 27
2 Cor. 12. 7 of Sat. to buffet me
Jas. 2. 25 when she received the *m.*
R. V. Gen. 50. 16 message ; 1 Sam.
  4. 17 that brought tidings ; Job 33.

23 angel ; Isa. 57. 9 ambassador

Met. *See Meet (v.).*

Mete. *Measure.*
Ex. 16. 18 did *m.* it with an omer
Ps. 60. 6 *m.* out valley of Succoth
Isa. 18. 2, 7 nat. *m.* out and trodden
  40. 12 Who hath *m.* out heaven wi.
Mat. 7. 2 with what measure ye *m.*
  Mark 4. 24 ; Luke 6. 38

Mete Yard. *Yardstick.*
Lev. 19. 35 in *m. y.*, in weight, or

Mice. *See Mouse.*

Mid Day, *Middle of day.*
1 K. 18. 29 when *m. d.* was past
Neh. 8. 3 from morning until *m. d.*
Acts 26. 13 At *m. d.*, O. k., I saw

Middle. *Midst, mean between.*
Judg. 16. 29 took hold of *m.* pillars
1 K. 8. 64 did k. hallow *m.* of court
2 Chr. 7. 7 hallowed *m.* of the court
2 K. 20. 4 Isaiah gone . . to *m.* court
Jer. 39. 3 the princes sat in *m.* gate
Eph. 2. 14 ha. broken down *m.* wall

Middlemost. *Nearest to middle.*
Ezek. 42. 5 higher than *m.* of build.

Midnight. *Middle of night.*
Ex. 11. 4 About *m. n.* will I go out
Judg. 16. 3 Samson lay till *m. n.*
Ruth 3. 8 it came to pass at *m. n.*
1 K. 3. 20 she arose at *m. n* , and
Job 34. 20 peo. be troubled at *m. n.*
Ps. 119. 62 At *m. n.* I will rise to g.
Mat. 25. 6 at *m. n.* there was a cry
Mark 13. 35 cometh, at ev. or *m. n.*
Luke 11. 5 go unto him at *m. n.*
Acts 16. 25 at *m. n.* Paul prayed
  20. 7 continued speech until *m. n.*

Midst. *Central part, middle.*
Gen. 1. 6 Let there be fir. in *m.*
Ex. 8. 22 I am . . Lord in *m.* of earth
Lev. 16. 16 among them in *m.* of
Num. 2. 17 camp of Levites in *m.*
Deut. 4. 12 Lord spake out of *m.*
Josh. 3. 17 stood on ground in *m.*
Judg. 15. 4 and put firebrand in *m.*
1 Sam. 11. 11 came into *m.* of host
2 Sam. 23. 20 slew a lion *m.* of a pit
1 K. 3. 8 servant is in *m.* of people
2 K. 6. 20 behold, in *m.* of Samaria
1 Chr. 16. 1 ark . . and set in *m.* of tent
2 Chr. 6. 13 set it in *m.* of the court
Neh. 3. 11 so they went through *m.*
Esth. 4. 1 Mord. went into *m.* of city
Ps. 22. 14 melted in *m.* of bowels
  138. 7 Tho. I walk in *m.* of trouble
Prov. 8. 20 *m.* of paths of judgment
S. of S. 3. 10 the *m.* paved with love
Isa. 6. 5 I dwell in *m.* of a people
Jer. 6. 1 flee out of *m.* of Jerusalem
Lam. 1. 15 mighty men in *m.* of me
Ezek. 5. 5 set in *m.* of the nations
Dan. 3. 15 be cast in *m.* of burning
Hos. 11. 9 Holy One in *m.* of thee
Joel 2. 27 know I am in *m.* of Isr.
Am. 3. 9 the great tumults in *m.* of
Mic. 2. 12 as the flock in *m.* of fold
Jonah 2. 3 thou cast me in *m.* of seas
Nah. 3. 13 people in *m.* of thee
Hab. 2. 19 no breath at all in *m.* of
Zeph. 2. 14 flocks lie down in the *m.*
Zech. 2. 5 will be glory in *m.* of her
Mat. 10. 16 forth as sheep in *m.* of
  18. 20 there am I in the *m.* of thee
Mark 6. 47 ship was in *m.* of sea
Luke 2. 46 sitting in *m.* of doctors
  23. 45 veil of temple was rent in *m.*
John 8. 3 when they set her in *m.*
Acts 1. 15 Peter stood up in the *m.*
Phil. 2. 15 *m.* of . . perverse nation
Heb. 2. 12 *m.* of church will I sing
Rev. 5. 6 *m.* of elders, stood Lamb

Midwife. *Helper to bear.*
Gen. 35. 17 *m.* said, ,Fear not ; thou
Ex. 1. 15 king spake to Hebrew *m.*
  1. 16–21

Might (v.). *See May.*
Might (n.). *Strength, power.*
Gen. 49. 3 Reub., firstborn, my *m.*
Num. 14. 13 brought this peo. in *m.*
Deut. 3. 24 do according to thy *m.*
Judg. 5. 31 sun goeth forth in *m.*
2 Sam. 6. 14 Dav. danced with *m.*
1 K. 15. 23 his *m.* and all he did
2 K. 23. 25 with *m.*, accord. to law
1 Chr. 12. 8 men of *m.* came to D.
2 Chr. 20. 12 we have no *m.* against

Esth. 10. 2 acts of his power and *m.*
Ps. 76. 5 none men of *m.* have found
Eccl. 9. 10 to do, do it with thy *m.*
Isa. 11. 2 spirit of counsel and *m.*
Jer. 10. 6 thy name is great in *m.*
Ezek. 32. 30 ashamed of their *m.*
Dau. 2. 20 wisdom and *m.* are his
Mic. 3. 8 full of judgment and *m.*
Zech. 4. 6 Not by *m.*, nor by power
Eph. 1. 21 Far above all . . *m.*, and
Col. 1. 11 strengthened with all *m.*
2 Pet. 2. 11 angels, greater in *m.*
Rev. 7. 12 hon., power, *m.*, unto G.

Mightier. *More mighty.*
Gen. 26. 16 for thou art *m.* than we
Ex. 1. 9 chil. of Is. are *m.* than we
Num. 14. 12 make thee *m.* than they
Deut. 4. 38 drive nat. *m.* than thou
Ps. 93. 4 L. *m.* than noise of waters
Eccl. 6. 10 nei. may contend with *m.*
Mat. 3. 11 he that cometh after is *m.*
  Mark 1. 7 ; Luke 3. 16

Mighties. *Powerful.*
1 Chr. 11. 12 Eleazar was one of *m.*
  11. 24 Benaiah had name among *m*

Mightiest. *Most mighty.*
1 Chr. 11. 19 these did the three *m.*

Mightily. *Greatly, with might.*
Deut. 6. 3 that ye may increase *m.*
Judg. 4. 3 Jabin *m.* oppressed Is.
Jer. 25. 30 Lord shall *m.* roar from
Jonah 3. 8 man and beast cry *m.*
Nah. 2. 1 watch, fortify thy power *m.*
Acts 18. 28 he *m.* convinced Jews
  19. 20 So *m.* grew the word of God
Col. 1. 29 work., worketh in me *m.*
Rev. 18. 2 cried *m.*, saying, Babylon

Mighty. *Strong, great, powerful.*
Gen. 10. 9 Nimrod was a *m.* hunter
  49. 24 the hands of *m.* G. of Jacob
Ex. 16. 10 sank as lead in *m.* w.
Lev. 19. 15 nor hon. person of *m.*
Deut. 10. 17 God, *m.* and terrible
Josh. 10. 2 the men thereof were *m.*
Judg. 5. 13 have dominion over *m.*
1 Sam. 4. 8 out of land of *m.* gods.
2 Sam. 1. 19 how are the *m.* fallen
2 K. 11. 28 Jeroboam was *m.* man
2 K. 15. 20 all *m.* men of wealth
1 Chr. 7. 9 of fathers, *m.* of valor
2 Chr. 13. 3 chosen men, being *m.*
Ez. 4. 20 *m.* king over Jerusalem
Neh. 9. 32 *m.*, and terrible God
Job. 5. 15 he saveth poor from *m.*
Ps. 24. 8 strong and *m.* in battle
Prov. 16. 32 slow to ang. bet. than *m*
S. of S. 4. 4. all shields of *m.* men
Isa. 3. 2 take *m.* man, man of war
Jer. 5. 15 it is *m.* and ancient nation
Ezek. 17. 13 hath taken *m.* of land
Dan. 4. 3 how *m.* are his wonders
Am. 2. 14 neither shall *m.* deliver
Jonah 1. 4 there was a *m.* tempest
Zech. 11. 2 howl, the *m.* are spoiled
Mat. 11. 20 wherein *m.* works were
Mark 6. 2 *m.* works are wrought
Luke 19. 37 pr. God for *m.* works
Acts 7. 22 Moses was *m.* in words
Rom. 15. 19 Through *m.* s. and w.
1 Cor. 1. 26 after fl., not many *m.*
2 Cor. 13. 3 not weak, but *m.* in
Gal. 2. 8 same was *m.* in me tow. G.
Eph. 1. 19 working of *m.* power
2 Thes. 1. 7 reveal. with *m.* angels
Rev. 6. 13 . . tree shaken of *m.* wind
R. V. changes chiefly to **great,**
strong, etc.

Milch. *Suckling.*
Gen. 32. 15 *m.* camels with colts
1 Sam. 6. 7, 10 take two *m.* kine

Mildew. *Fungus, rust.*
Deut. 28. 22 sh. smite thee with *m*
1 K. 8. 37 if there be *m.*, locust
2 Chr. 6. 28 if be blasting, or *m.*, or
Am. 4. 9 have smitten you with *m*
Hag. 2. 17 I smote you with *m.*

Mile. *Mile.*
Mat. 5. 41 compel thee to go a *m.*

Milk (n.). *Milk.*
Gen. 18. 8 he took butter and *m.*
Ex. 3. 8 good land flowing with *m.*
Lev. 20. 24. Num. 14. 8 ; Deut. 6. 3
Judg. 4. 19 she opened bottle of *m.*
Job 10. 10 not poured me out as *m.*
  21. 24 His breasts are full of *m.*
Prov. 27. 27 goat's *m.* for thy food

S. of S. 5. 1 drunk wine with *m*.
Isa. 55. 1 buy *m*. without money
Lam. 4. 7 they were whiter than *m*.
Ezek. 25. 4 they shall drink thy *m*.
Joel 3. 18 hills shall flow with *m*.
1 Cor. 3. 2 have fed you with *m*.
Heb. 5. 12 such as have need of *m*.
1 Pet. 2. 2 desire the sincere *m*. of
Milk (*v*.). *Wring, suck.*
Isa. 66. 11 that ye may *m*. out and
Mill. *Millstones*
Ex. 11. 5 servant that is behind *m*.
Num. 11. 8 ground it in *m*., or
Mat. 24. 41 two wom. grind. at *m*.
Millet. *Corn, millet.*
Ezek. 49. 9 beans. lentiles, and *m*.
Millions. R. V. *ten thousands.*
Gen. 24. 60 be thou mother of *m*.
Millstone. *Stone of mill.*
Deut. 24 6 no man take *m*. to pl'g.
Judg. 9. 53 woman cast piece of *m*.
2 Sam. 11. 21
Job 41. 24 heart as hard as neth. *m*.
Isa. 47. 2 take . . *m*., and grind meal
Jer. 25. 10 take away sound of *m*.
Mat. 18. 6 bet. *m*. hang. about neck
Mark 9. 42 , Luke 17. 2
Rev. 18. 21 took stone like a gr. *m*.
Mincing. *Tripping nicely.*
Isa. 3. 16 walk. and *m*. as they go
Mind (*n*.). *Intellect, feeling and will, soul or spirit.*
Gen. 26. 35 grief of *m*, to Isaac and
Lev. 24. 12 *m*. of L. mi. be shewed
Num. 16. 28 not done of own *m*.
Deut. 30. 1 shalt call them to *m*.
1 Sam. 2. 35 in mine heart and *m*.
2 Sam. 17. 8 be chafed in their *m*.
2 K. 9. 15 If it be your *m*., then
1 Chr. 28. 9 per. heart and will. *m*.
Neh. 4. 6 for the people had a *m*. to
Job 34. 33 be according to thy *m*.?
Ps. 31. 12 as dead man ont of *m*.
Prov. 29. 11 fool uttereth all his *m*.
Isa. 26. 3 peace, whose. is stayed
Jer. 3. 16 neither shall it come to *m*.
Lam. 3. 21 This I recall to my *m*.
Ezek. 11. 5 things that come into *m*.
Dan. 5. 20 his *m*. hardened in pride
Hab. 1. 11 Then shall *m*. change
Mat. 22. 37 love L., with all thy *m*.
Mark 13. 30 ; Luke 10. 27
Mark 5. 15 clo., and in right *m*.
Acts 14. 2 made their *m*. evil affec.
20. 19 Serv. L. with humility of *m*.
Rom. 1. 28 gave over to reprob. *m*.
7. 23 warring against law of *m*.
8. 7 carnal *m*. is enmity against G.
1 Cor. 1. 10 joined togeth. in same *m*.
2. 16 But we have the *m*. of Christ
2 Cor. 16. 11 perfect, be of one *m*.
Eph. 4. 17 walk not in van. of *m*.
4. 23 renewed in spirit of your *m*.
Phil. 1. 27 one *m*. striving togeth.
Col. 2. 18 puffed up by . . fleshly *m*.
2 Thes. 2. 2 be not shaken in *m*.
1 Tim. 6. 5 disput. of corrupt *m*.
2 Tim. 3. 8 men of corrupt *m*. repro.
Tit. 1. 15 but even their *m*. defiled
Heb. 8. 10 put my laws into *m*.
12. 3 lest ye be wearied in your *m*.
1 Pet. 1. 13 gird up loins of your *m*.
3. 8 Finally, be ye all of one *m*.
2 Pet. 3. 1 stir up your pure *m*.
Rev. 17. 9 here is *m*. wh. hath wis.
Mind (*v*.). *Attend to, will.*
Acts 20. 13 *m*. himself to go afoot
Rom. 8. 5 that are after the flesh *m*.
12. 16 *m*. not high things, but con.
Phil. 3. 16 shame, who *m*. earthly
R. V. Acts 20. 13 intending
Minded. *Wished, willed, inclined, of mind.*
Ruth 1. 18 she was stedfastly *m*.
2 Chr. 24. 4 was *m*. to repair house
Mat. 1. 19 J. was *m*. to put her away
Acts 27. 39 to which they were *m*.
Rom. 8. 6 to be car. *m*. is death
2 Cor. 1. 15 I was *m*. to come unto
1. 17 When I therefore was thus *m*.
Gal. 5. 10 ye be none otherwise *m*.
Phil. 3. 15 as many as be perfect *m*.
1 Thes. 5. 14 comfort the feeble *m*.
2 Tim. 3. 4 be trai., heady, high *m*.
Tit. 2. 6 exhort to be sober *m*.
Ias. 1. 8 doub. *m*. man is unstable

Mindful. *Keeping in mind, heedful, observant.*
1 Chr. 16. 15 Be *m*. of his covenant
Neh. 9. 17 nei. *m*. of thy wonders
Ps. 8. 4 man, that thou art *m*. of h.
111. 5 ever be *m*. of his covenant
115. 12 Lord hath been *m*. of us
Isa. 17. 10 hast not been *m*. of Rock
2 Tim. 1. 4 being *m*. of thy tears
Heb. 2. 6 is man, that thou art *m*. of
11. 15 if they had been *m*. of that
2 Pet. 3. 2 be *m*. of words which
Mine. *Of me, my.*
Gen. 31. 43 all that thou seest is *m*.
Ex. 19. 5 for all the earth is *m*.
2 Sam. 14. 30 Joab's field is near *m*.
Ps. 50. 11 beasts of the field are *m*.
Prov. 23. 15 my heart rejoice, ev. *m*.
Mat. 7. 24 heareth sayings of *m*.
20. 23 is not *m*. to give, but it shall
Luke 11. 6 friend of *m*. in journey.
18. 3 Avenge me of *m*. adversary
John 7. 16 My doctrine is not *m*. but
10. 14 sheep, and am known of *m*.
17. 10 and all *m*. are thine, and
Acts 13. 22 man after *m*. own heart
Rom. 11. 13 I magnify *m*. office
12. 19 Vengeance is *m*. ; I repay
1 Cor. 1. 15 bap. in *m*. own name
9. 2 the seal of *m*. apostleship are
2 Cor. 12. 5 but in *m*. infirmities
Phil. 1. 4 in every prayer of *m*. for
2 Thes. 3. 17 saluta. of Paul with *m*.
Phile. 12 receive that is *m*. own
Mingle. *Mix, blend.*
Ex. 29. 40 deal of flour *m*. with oil
Lev. 9. 4 meat off. *m*. with oil
Num. 6. 15 cakes *m*. with oil, and
Ez. 9. 2 seed have *m*. themselves
Ps. 109. 2 *m*. drink with weeping
106. 35 were *m*. among the heathen
Prov. 9. 2 She hath *m*. her wine
9. 5 and drink of the wine I have *m*.
Isa. 5. 22 men to *m*. strong drink
19. 14 L. hath *m*. perverse spirit
Dan. 2. 43 *m*. themselves with seed
Mat. 27. 34 ga. vinegar *m*. with gall
Luke 13. 1 blood Pilate had *m*. with
Rev. 8. 7 fire *m*. with blood, and
15. 2 saw a sea of glass *m*. with fire
Mingled. *Mixed.*
Ex. 9. 24 and fire *m*. with the hail
Lev. 19. 19 not sow with*m* . seed
Jer. 25. 20 all *m*. peo., and kings
Ezek. 30. 5 Lydia, and all *m*. peo.
See also **Mingle.**
Minish. *Diminish.*
Ex. 5. 19 shall not *m*. aught of task
Ps. 107. 39 are *m*. and brought low
Minister (*n*.). *Server, assistant.*
Ex. 24. 13 Moses rose, and *m*. Josh.
Josh. 1. 1 spake to Josh. Moses' *m*.
1 K. 10. 5 the attendance of his *m*.
2 Chr. 9. 4 *m*., and their apparel
Ez. 7. 24 or *m*. of the house of God
Ps. 103. 21 *m*. that do his pleasure
104. 4 maketh his *m*. flaming fire
Isa. 61. 6 men call you *m*. of God
Jer. 33. 21 Levites, priests, my *m*.
Ezek. 44. 11 be *m*. in my sanct.
45. 5 also Levites, *m*. of the house
Joel 1. 9 the priests, the Lord's *m*.
Deacon, laborer, ministrant.
Mat. 20. 26 let him be your *m*.
Mark 10. 43 gr. am. you, be your *m*.
Rom. 13. 4 For he is *m*. of God
13. 6 pay tri., for they are God's *m*.
15. 8 C. was *m*. of circumcision
15. 16 should be *m*. of Jesus Christ
1 Cor. 3. 5 *m*. by whom ye believed
2 Cor. 3. 6 hath made us able *m*.
6. 4 approving ourselves as the *m*.
11. 15 transformed as *m*. of right.
11. 23 Are they *m*. of Christ?
Gal. 2. 17 is Christ the *m*. of sin?
Eph. 3. 7 Whereof I was made *m*.
Col. 1. 7 who is for you faithful *m*.
4. 7 belov. bro., and faithful *m*.
1 Thes. 3. 2 our bro., and *m*. of God
1 Tim. 4. 6 be good *m*. of Jesus C.
Heb. 1. 7 maketh *m*. flame of fire
8. 2 A *m*. of the sanctuary, and of
Under rower, assistant.
Luke 1. 2 eyewitnesses, and *m*.of w.
4. 20 he give it again to the *m*.
Acts 13. 5 had John to their *m*.

26. 16 make thee *m*. and witness
1 Cor. 4. 1 account of us as the *m*.
R. V. Ez. 7. 24 servants ; Luke 4. 24 attendant
Minister (*v*.). *Serve, assist, work, supply, furnish.*
Ex. 28. 35 be it sh. upon Aaron to *m*.
Num. 1. 50 they shall *m*. unto it
Deut. 10. 8 stand before Lord to *m*.
1 Sam. 2. 11 child did *m*. unto Lord
2 Sam. 13. 17 called his ser. that *m*.
1 K. 1. 4 cher. k., and *m*. unto him
2 K. 25. 14 ves. wherewith they *m*.
1 Chr. 6. 32 *m*. bef. dwelling place
16. 4 *m*. before the ark of the Lord
2 Chr. 5. 14 priests not stand to *m*.
Neh. 10. 36 priests that *m*. in house
Esth. 2. 2 said k's servants that *m*.
Ps. 9. 8 shall *m*. judgment to people
Isa. 60. 10 kings shall *m*. unto thee
Jer. 33. 22 Levites that *m*. unto me
Ezek. 40. 46 come near Lord to *m*.
Mat. 4. 11 angels came and *m*. to
8. 15 she arose, and *m*. unto them
20. 28 not to be *m*. unto but to *m*.
Mark 15. 41 fol. him, and *m*. to him
Luke 8. 3 *m*. unto him of substance
Acts 13. 2 As they *m*. to the Lord
19. 22 sent two that *m*. unto him
20. 34 have *m*. unto my necessities
24. 23 forbid none to *m*. or come
Rom. 15. 25 I go to Jerusalem to *m*.
15. 27 their duty is to *m*. unto them
1 Cor. 9. 13 which *m*. about ho. th.
2 Cor. 3. 3 epistle of Christ *m*. by
9. 10 both *m*. bread for your food
Gal. 3. 5 He that *m*. to you the Sp.
Eph. 4. 29 that it may *m*. grace unto
Phil. 2. 25 messenger, he that *m*.
Col. 2. 19 having nourishment *m*.,
1 Tim. 1. 4 Nei. heed which *m*. ques·
2 Tim. 1. 18 in things he *m*. unto
Phile. 13 he might have *m*. to me
Heb. 6. 10 ye have *m*. to the saints
10. 11 priest standeth daily *m*. and
1 Pet. 1. 12 did *m*. things which are
2 Pet. 1. 11 an entrance shall be *m*.
R. V. 1 Chr. 28. 1 served ; 2 Cor. 9. 10 ; Gal. 3. 5 supplieth
Ministering. *Serving.*
1 Chr. 9. 28 had charge of *m*. ves.
Rom. 12. 7 let us wait on our *m* , or
2 Cor. 8. 4 fellowship of the *m*. to
9. 1 as touching the *m*. to saints
Heb. 1. 14 Are they not *m*. spirits
R. V. 1 Chr. 9. 28 vessels of service ; Rom. 12. 7 ministry
Ministration. *Work, service.*
Luke 1. 23 as days of *m*. were end.
Acts 6. 1 wid. were neglected in *m*.
2 Cor. 3. 7 But if *m*. of death, writ. 3. 8, 9 ; 9. 13
Ministry. *Ministration, service.*
Num. 4. 47 to do service of the *m*.
2 Chr. 7. 6 D. praised by their *m*.
Hos. 12. 10 I have spoken by *m*.
Acts 1. 17 obtained part of this *m*.
6. 4 to prayer, to *m*. of the word
12. 25 when they fulfilled their *m*.
20. 24 mi., finish my course, and *m*.
21. 19 wrought among Gent. by *m*.
Rom. 12. 7 Or *m*., let us wait on our
1 Cor. 16. 15 addict. thems. to *m*.
2 Cor. 4. 1 seeing we have this *m*.
5. 18 given us *m*. of reconciliation
6. 3 offence, that *m*. be not blamed
Eph. 4. 12 for the work of *m*., for
Col. 4. 17 Take heed to the *m*. wh
1 Tim. 1. 12 putting me into the *m*.
2 Tim. 4. 5 make proof of thy *m*
4. 11 is profitable to me for my *m*
Heb. 8. 6 obtained more excel. *m*.
9. 21 sprinkled all vessels of *m*.
R. V. Acts 12. 25 ; 2 Cor. 6. 3 ministration ; Eph. 4. 12 ; 2. Tim. 4. 11 ministering ; 1 Tim. 1. 12 his service
Minstrel. *Player on instrument.*
2 K. 3. 15 now bring me a *m*. And
Mat. 9. 23 saw *m*. and peo. making
R. V. Mat. 9. 23 flute-players
Mint. *Aromatic herb.*
Mat. 23. 23 ye pay tithe of *m*. and
Luke 11. 42 ye tithe *m*. and rue
Miracle. *Sign, wonder.*
Ex. 7. 9 Show a *m*. for you, then

Num. 14. 22 my *m*. I did in Egypt
Deut. 11. 3 his *m*. which he did
29. 3 eyes have seen those great *m*.
Judg. 6. 13 and where be all his *m*.?
Mark 6. 52 consid. not *m*. of loaves
9. 39 no man which shall do *m*.
Luke 23. 8 hoped to have seen *m*.
John 2. 11 This begin. of mid J.
3. 2 ; 4. 54 ; 6. 2 ; 7. 31 ; 9. 16
Acts 4. 16 not *m*. hath been done
6. 8 did great wonders and *m*.
1 Cor. 12. 10 To anoth. work. of *m*.
12. 29 are all workers of *m*.?
Gal. 3. 5 he that worketh *m*. am. y.
Heb. 2. 4 with *m*., and gifts of H. G.
Rev. 13. 14 decei. by means of *m*.
16. 14 spir. of devils working *m*.
19. 20 false proph. that wrought *m*.
R. V. Heb. 2. 4 manifold powers.
Elsewhere, for most part, changed
to sign or signs

Mire.   *Wet earth, mud, dirt.*
2 Sam. 22. 43 did stamp them as *m*.
Job 8. 11 Can rush gr. without *m*.?
30. 19 He hath cast me into the *m*.
41. 30 spread. pointed things on *m*.
Ps. 69. 2 I sink in deep *m*., where
69. 14 Deliver me out of *m*., and
Isa. 57. 20 wat. cast up *m*. and filth
Jer. 38. 6 so Jeremiah sunk in *m*.
38. 22 thy feet are sunk in the *m*.
Mic. 7. 10 be trodden down as *m*.
Zech. 9. 3 and find gold as *m*. of the
10. 5 tread down enemies in *m*. of
2 Pet. 2. 22 sow to wallowing in *m*.

Mirth.   *Joy, merriment.*
Gen. 31. 27 sent thee away with *m*.
Neh. 8. 12 and to make great *m*.
Ps. 137. 3 that wasted, required *m*.
Prov. 14. 13 end of *m*. is heaviness
Eccl. 2. 1 will prove thee with *m*.
2. 2 I said of laughter and of *m*.
7. 4 heart of fools is in house of *m*.
8. 15 Then I commended *m*. be.
Isa. 24. 8 The *m*. of tabrets ceaseth
24. 11 darkened, *m*. of land is gone
Jer. 7. 34 voice of *m*., voice of glad.
16. 9 ; 25. 10
Ezek. 21. 10 should we th. make *m*.?
Hos. 2. 11 will cause *m*. to cease

Miry.   *Muddy.*
Ps. 40. 2 brought me out of *m*. clay
Ezek. 47. 11 *m*. places not be healed
Dan. 2. 41 iron mixed with *m*. clay

Miscarry.   *Fail.*
Hos. 9. 14 give them *m*. womb and

Mischief.   *Evil, harm, damage, hurtful agency.*
Gen. 42. 4 Lest pera. *m*. befall him
Ex. 21. 22 fruit depart, yet no *m*.
Deut. 32. 23 will heap *m*. up. them
1 Sam. 23. 9 Saul secretly pract. *m*.
2 Sam. 16. 8 art taken in thy *m*., bec.
1 K. 11. 25 the *m*. that Hadad did
2 K. 7. 9 some *m*. will come upon us
Neh. 6. 2 they thought to do me *m*.
Esth. 8. 3 put away *m*. of Haman
Job 15. 35 conceiv. *m*., br. forth van.
Ps. 7. 14 con. *m*., brought falsehood
10. 7 under his tongue is *m*. and v.
28. 3 but *m*. is in their hearts
52. 1 Why boasted thou in *m*.
94. 20 which frameth *m*. by a law
140. 9 let the *m*. of their lips cover
Prov. 6. 14 he devis. *m*. continual.
6. 18 that be swift in running to *m*.
10. 23 sport to fool to do *m*., but
12. 21 wicked sh. be filled with *m*.
17. 20 perv. tongue falleth into *m*.
24. 2 and their lips talk of *m*.
Isa. 47. 11 *m*. shall fall on thee
59. 4 conc. *m*.. bring forth iniquity
Ezek. 7. 26 *M*. shall come upon *m*.
11. 2 these men devise *m*., and
Dan. 11. 27 ks.' hearts shall do *m*.
Hos. 7. 15 imagine *m*. against me
Acts 13. 10 full of subtilty and *m*.
R. V. Ex. 32. 12 ; Prov. 6. 14 ; 13.
17 evil ; Ps. 52. 2 ; 119. 150 ; Prov.
10. 23 wickedness ; 2 K. 7. 9 punishment ; Ps. 36. 4 iniquity ; Pr.
24. 16 calamity ; Acts 13. 10 villany

Mischievous.   *Given to mischief.*
Ps. 21. 11 they imagined *m*. device
38. 12 seek hurt speak *m*. things

Prov. 24. 8 do evil shall be called *m*.
Eccl. 10. 13 end of his talk is *m*.
Mic. 7. 3 he uttereth his *m*. desire
R. V. Ps. 21. 11 ——.

Miserable.   *Wretched, distressed.*
Job 16. 2 Job said, *m*. comforters
1 Cor. 15. 19 we are of men most *m*.
Rev. 3. 17 thou art wretched, and *m*.
R. V. 1 Cor. 15. 19 pitiable

Miserably.   *Evilly.*
Mat. 21. 41 He will *m*. destroy wick.

Misery.   *Wretchedness, evil.*
Judg. 10. 16 grieved for *m*. of Is.
Job 11. 16 thou shalt forget thy *m*.
Prov. 31. 7 forget pov., remem. *m*.
Eccl. 8. 6 *m*. of man is great upon
Lam. 1. 7 remem. in days of *m*.
3. 19 remem. mine afflic. and *m*.
Rom. 3. 16 Dest. and *m*. in their
Jas. 5. 1 howl for your *m*. that shall

Miss.   *Fail, feel loss.*
Judg. 20. 16 sling stones and not *m*.
1 Sam. 20. 6 If thy father *m*. me
20. 18 thou shalt be *m*. because
25. 7 nei. was there ought *m*. unto
25. 15 not hurt nei. *m*. we anything
25. 21 so that nothing was *m*. of all
1 K. 20. 39 if he be *m*., then shall

Mist.   *Vapor, fog, darkness.*
Gen. 2. 6 there went *m*. from earth
Acts 13. 11 there fell on him *m*.
2 Pet. 2. 17 *m*. of dark. is reserved
R. V. 2 Pet. 2. 17 blackness

Mistress.   *Superior, mighty one.*
Gen. 16. 4 her *m*. was despised
16. 9 Return to thy *m*., and subm.
2 K. 5. 3 she said unto her *m*.
Ps. 123. 2 maid. unto hand of her *m*.
Prov. 30. 23 handmaid heir to *m*.
Isa. 24. 2 as with maid, so with *m*.

Lady, owner.
1 K. 17. 17 son of *m*. of the house
Nah. 3. 4 *m*. of witchcrafts, that

Misuse.   R. V. *scoff at.*
2 Chr. 36. 16 *m*. . his prophets, until

Mite.   *Tenth of penny.*
Mark 12. 42 she threw in two *m*.
Luke 12. 59 till thou hast paid *m*.
21. 2 saw widow casting in two *m*.

Mitre.   *Diadem, hood.*
Ex. 28. 4 make coat, *m*., and girdle
28. 37 ; 29. 6 ; 39. 28, 31
Lev. 8. 9 and he put *m*. on his head
16. 4 with lii. *m*. be attired
Zech. 3. 5 set a fair *m*. on his head

Mix.   *Mingle.*
Hos. 7. 8 Ephraim hath *m*. hims.

Mixed.   *Mingled.*
Ex. 12. 38 *m*. multitude went up
Num. 11. 4 *m*. mult. fell to lusting
Neh. 13. 3 Sep. from Is. *m*. mul.
Isa. 1. 22 thy wine *m*. with water
Dan. 2. 41 sawest iron *m*. with clay.
Heb. 4. 2 not being *m*. with faith

Mixture.   *Thing mixed.*
Ps. 75. 8 it is of full *m*., and he po.
John 19. 39 brought *m*. of myrrh
Rev. 14. 10 poured out without *m*.
R. V. Rev. 14. 10 prepared un-
mixed

Mock.   (*n*.) *Scorn.*
Prov. 14. 9. fools make a *m*. at sin

Mock.   (*v*.) *Scorn, scoff, deride.*
Gen. 19. 14 seemed as one that *m*.
21. 9 Sar. saw son of Hag. *m*.
39. 14 brought Hebrew to *m*. us.
Num. 22. 29 Bec. thou hast *m*. me
Judg. 16. 10 Beh., thou hast *m*. me
16. 15 hast *m*. me three times
1 K. 18. 27 Elijah *m*. them, and
2 K. 2. 23 *m*. him, said, Go up
2 Chr. 30. 10 laughed, and *m*. them
36. 16 they *m*. messenger of God
Neh. 4. 1 Sanballat . . *m*. the Jews
Job 11. 3 and when thou *m*., shall
12. 4 I am as one *m*. of h. neighbor
13. 9 as one man *:m*. anoth. ye so *m*.
39. 22 he *m*. at fear, and is not af.
Prov. 1. 26 will *m*. when fear com.
17. 5 Who *m*. poor reproach. his M.
30. 17 the eye that *m*. at his father
Jer. 20. 7 daily, every one *m*. me
Lam. 1. 7 did *m*. at her sabbaths
Mat. 2. 16 when he saw he was *m*.
20. 19 to *m*., scourge, and crucify
27. 29 *m*. him, saying, Hail, King

27. 31 after they had *m*. him they
27. 41 Likewise chief priests *m*.
Mark 10. 34 they shall *m*. him, and
15. 20 when they had *m*. him
Luke 14. 29 that behold, begin to *m*.
18. 32 *m*., and spitefully entreated
23. 36 And the soldiers also *m*. him
Acts 2. 13 Others *m*., said, These are
17. 32 of resurrection, some *m*.
Gal. 6. 7 be not dec. ; G. is not *m*.
R. V. Job 13. 9 deceiveth ; 12. 4
laughing stock

Mocker.   *Scorner, deceiver.*
Job 17. 2 Are there not *m*. with me
Ps. 35. 16 with hypocritical *m*.
Prov. 20. 1 Wine is a *m*. str., drk.
Isa. 28. 22. Now be ye not *m*., lest
Jer. 15. 17 sat not in assem. of *m*.
Jude 18 they told you there be *m*.
R. V. Isa. 28. 22 scorners ; Jer.
15. 17 them that made merry

Mocking.   *Scoffing, sporting.*
Ezek. 22. 4 made thee a *m*. to all
Heb. 11. 36 others had trial of *m*.
See also Mock.

Moderately.   R. V. *Just measure.*
Joel 2. 23 giv. you form. rain in *m*.

Moderation.   R. V. *forbearance.*
Phil. 4. 5 Let *m*. be known to all

Modest.   *Becoming.*
1 Tim. 2. 9 wom. adorn. in *m*. appar.

Moist.   R. V. *fresh.*
Num. 6. 3 neither eat *m*. grapes

Moistened.   *Dampened.*
Job 21. 24 bones are *m*. with mar.

Moisture.   *Freshness, sap.*
Ps. 32. 4 my *m*. is turned to droug.
Luke 8. 6 with., bec. it lacketh *m*.

Mole.   R. V. *chameleon.*
Lev. 11. 30 the lizard, snail, and *m*.

Mole.
Isa. 2. 20 shall cast idols to the *m*.

Mollified.   *Made tender, soft.*
Isa. 1. 6 neither *m*. with ointment

Molten.   *Melted, poured out, cast.*
Ex. 32. 4 he had made it a *m*. calf
34. 17 shalt make thee no *m*. gods
Lev. 19. 4 nor make yours. *m*. gods
Num. 33. 52 destroyed their *m*. im.
Deut. 9. 12 made them *m*. image
Judg. 17. 3, 4 graven, and *m*. image
1 K. 7. 16 made chap. of *m*. brass
7. 23 he made *m*. sea, ten cubits
7. 30 under l. were undersetters *m*.
7. 33 their felloes and spokes all *m*.
2 Chr. 4. 2 made *m*. sea, ten cubits
28. 2 made also *m*. images for B.
Neh. 9. 18 they had made *m*. calf
Job 28. 2 brass is *m*. out of stone
37. 18 and as *m*. looking glass
Ps. 106. 19 worshipped the *m*. im.
Isa. 30. 22 orna. of thy *m*. images
41. 29 *m*. images are wind and con.
Jer. 10. 14 *m*. image is falsehood
Ezek. 24. 11 filthiness be *m*. in it
Hos. 13. 2 made them *m*. images
Mic. 1. 4 mountains shall be *m*.
Nah. 1. 14 graven and *m*. images
Hab. 2. 18 *m*. im., teacher of lies

Moment.   *Point of time, instant.*
Ex. 33. 5 come into midst in *m*.
Num. 16. 21 may cons. them in *m*.
Job 7. 18 and try him every *m*.
20. 5 joy of hypocrite but for *m*.
21. 13 in *m*. go down to the grave
34. 20 In a *m*. shall they die
Ps. 30. 5 his ang. endur. but for *m*.
73. 19 unto desolation as in a *m*.
Prov. 12. 19 lying tongue is for *m*.
Isa. 26. 20 hide thyself for little *m*.
27. 3 I will water it every *m*.
47. 9 shall come to thee in a *m*.
54. 8 in w. I hid my face for a *m*.
Jer. 4. 20 spoiled curtains in *m*.
Lam. 4. 6 was overthrown as in *m*.
Ezek. 26. 16 tremble at every *m*.
Luke 4. 5 kingdoms of world in *m*.
1 Cor. 15. 52 In *m*., in twink. of e.
2 Cor. 4. 17 which is but for *m*.

Money.   *Money, silver.*
Gen. 17. 12 bought with *m*. of str.
23. 13 I will give thee *m*. for field
43. 12 take double *m*. in your hana
44. 8 *m*. we found in our sacks
Ex. 21. 11 then go free without *m*.
30. 16 thou shalt take atonement *m*.

Lev. 22. 11 if pr. sell soul for *m.*
Num. 3. 49 M. took redemption *m.*
Deut. 2. 6 buy water of them for *m.*
2. 28 and give me water for *m.*
Judg. 5. 19 they took no gain of *m.*
1 K. 21. 2 give thee worth in *m.*
2 K. 5. 26 Is it a time to receive *m.*
15. 20 Menahem exacted *m.* of Is.
23. 35 taxed the land to give *m.*
2 Chr. 24. 5 gath. of all Israel *m.*
Ez. 3. 7 gave *m.* unto masons
Neh. 5. 4 We have bor. *m.* for king's
Esth. 4. 7 of. *m* that Haman had
Job 31. 39 eaten fruits without *m.*
Ps. 15. 5 put. not his *m.* to usury
Prov. 7. 20 hath taken bag of *m.*
Eccl. 7. 12 and *m.* is a defense: but
10. 19 *m.* answereth all things
Isa. 43. 24 bought no cane with *m.*
52. 3 be redeemed without *m.*
55. 1 buy milk without *m.* and
Jer. 32. 9 and weighed him the *m.*
32. 44 men buy fields for *m.* and
Lam. 5. 4 have drunk. water for *m.*
Mic. 3. 11 prophets divine fot *m.*
Mat. 25. 18 and hid his lord's *m.*
28. 12 they gave *m.* unto soldiers
28. 15 So they took the *m.*, and
Mark 14. 11 prom. to give him *m.*
Luke 9. 3 Take nei. scrip, nei. *m.*
22. 5 covenanted to give him *m.*
Acts 7. 16 that Ab. bought for *m.*
8. 20 Thy *m.* perish with thee
Substance, value.
Acts 4. 37 sold it, and brought *m.*
8. 18 given, he offered them *m.*
24. 26 hoped . . *m.* sh. have been
Coin, piece of money.
Gen. 33. 19 for hun. pieces of *m.*
Job 42. 11 every man gave him *m.*
Mat. 17. 27 shalt find pieces of *m.*
22. 19 Shew me the tribute *m.*
Mark 6. 8 take no *m.* in thy purse
12. 41 beheld how peo. cast *m.* in.
John 2. 14 found chang. of *m.* sit.
2. 15 poured out the changers' *m.*
R. V. Gen. 23. 9, 13; Ex. 21. 35
price of; Ex. 21. 30 ransom; Mat.
17. 24 half-shekel; 17. 27 shekel;
Acts 7. 16 price in silver; 8. 20
silver
Money-changer. *Changer of coin.*
Mat. 21. 12 overthrew tab. of *m. c.*
Mark 11. 15
Monsters. R. V. *jackals.*
Lam. 4. 3 sea *m.* draw out breast
Month. *New moon, moon, month.*
Gen. 7. 11 sec. *m.*, founts. bro. up
38. 24 pass, three *m.* after, that it
Ex. 2. 2 child, she hid him three *m.*
12. 2 This *m.* be beginning of *m.*
Lev. 23. 41 cel. it in seventh *m.*
Num. 1. 1, 18 first day of sec. *m.*
Deut. 16. 1 Obser. *m.* of Abib, and
Josh. 4. 19 come on ten. of first *m.*
Judg. 11. 37 let me alone two *m.*
20. 47 abode in rock R. four *m.*
1 Sam. 20. 34 eat no *m.* sec. of *m.*
2 Sam. 2. 11 of Jud. sev. yr's six *m.*
1 K. 4. 7 each man his *m.* in year
2 K. 15. 8 reign over Israel six *m.*
1 Chr. 12. 15 went to Jor. first *m.*
2 Chr. 31. 7 fin. them in seventh *m.*
Ez. 3. 1 when seventh *m.* was come
Neh. 1. 1 to pass in *m.* Chisleu
Esth. 2. 12 after six *m.* with oil
Job 7. 3 ma. to possess *m.* of vanity
29. 2 that I were as in *m.* past, as
39. 2 Canst thou number *m.* that th.
Jer. 1. 3 car. Jerus. cap. fifth *m.*
Ezek. 8. 1 fifth of *m.*, as I sat in hou.
Dan. 4. 29 end of twelve *m.* he walk.
Hos. 5. 7 now shall *m.* devour them
Am. 4. 7 yet three *m.* to harvest
Hag. 1. 1 sixth *m.*, first day of *m.*
Zech. 7. 3 Should weep in fifth *m.*
A month.
Luke 1. 24 and hid herself five *m.*
1. 56 And Mary abode three *m.*
Acts 19. 8 spake boldly for three *m.*
28. 11 after three *m.* we departed
Gal. 4. 10 Ye obser. days and *m.*
Jas. 5. 17 by three years and six *m.*
Rev. 9. 5 be tormented five *m.*
22. 2 and yielded her fruit ev. *m.*
R. V. Num. 29. 6; 1 Sam. 20. 27;

Hos. 5. 7 new moon
Monthly. *New moon.*
Isa. 47. 13 the *m.* prognosticators
Monuments. R. V. *secret-places.*
Isa. 65. 4 peo. which lodge in *m.*
Moon. *Moon.*
Gen. 37. 9 behold, sun, *m.*, stars
Deut. 4. 19 when thou seest the *m.*
Josh. 10. 12 *m.*, in val. of Ajalon
10. 13 *m.* stayed, until the people
1 Sam. 20. 5 to morrow is new *m.*
2 K. 4. 23 nei. new *m.* nor sab.
1 Chr. 23. 31 in sab., in new *m.*
2 Chr. 2. 4 on sabbath, on new *m.*
Ez. 3. 5 burnt offering, of new *m.*
Neh. 10. 33 of sabbaths, of new *m.*
Job 25. 5 ev. to. *m.*, and it shineth
31. 26 *m.* walking in brightness
Ps. 8. 3 the *m.* thou hast ordained
81. 3 blow trumpet in the new *m.*
104. 19 He appoint. *m.* for seasons
136. 9 the *m.* to rule by night
148. 3 Praise him, sun and *m.*
Eccl. 12. 2 while sun, *m.* or stars
S. of S. 6. 10 fair as *m.* cl. as sun
Isa. 3. 18 round tires like the *m.*
24. 23 the *m.* shall be confounded
60. 20 neither shall *m.* withdraw
Jer. 8. 2 *m.*, and host of heaven
31. 35 ordinances of *m.*, and stars
Ezek. 32. 7 *m.* not give her light
46. 6 and in the day of the new *m.*
Hos. 2. 11 her feast days, her new *m.*
Joel 2. 10 sun and *m.* shall be dark
Am. 8. 5 When will the *m.* be gone
Hab. 3. 11 sun and *m.* stood still
Mat. 24. 29 *m.* sh. not give her light
Mark 13. 2
Luke 21. 25 shall be signs in the *m.*
Acts 2. 20 *m.* be turn into blood
1 Cor. 15. 41. another glory of *m.*
Col. 2. 16 holy day, of the new *m.*
Rev. 6. 12 the *m.* became as blood
21. 23 the city had no need of *m.*
R. V. Isa. 1. 13 new moon; 3. 18
crescents; Rev. 6. 12 whole moon
More. *Greater, additional, fur-ther, again.*
Gen. 8. 12 the dove returned not *m.*
36. 7. their riches were *m.* than
Ex. 1. 9 children of Is. are *m.* and
Lev. 11. 42 whatso. hath *m.* feet
Num. 26. 54 give the *m.* inheritance
Deut. 7. 17 nations are *m.* than I
Josh. 7. 12 nev. be with you any *m.*
Judg. 8. 28 lifted up heads no *m.*
1 Sam. 27. 4 sought no *m.* for him
2 Sam. 2. 28 nei. fought they any *m.*
2 K. 6. 23 bands of S, came no *m.*
1 Chr. 24. 4 *m.* chief men found
2 Chr. 32. 7 *m.* with us than him
Ez. 7. 20 whatsoever *m.* be needful
Neh. 13. 18 bring *m.* wrath on Is.
Esth. 6. 6 to do honour *m.* than
Job. 7. 7 eye shall no *m.* see good
Ps. 40. 12 *m.* than hairs of head
Prov. 4. 18 showeth *m.* and *m.* un.
Eccl. 2. 16 remem. of wise *m.* than
Isa. 1. 5 ye will revolt *m.* and *m.*
Ezek. 5. 9 I will not do any *m.*
Dan. 3. 19 heat fur. sev. times *m.*
Hos. 13. 2 they sin *m.* and *m.*
Mat. 5. 30 whatso. is *m.* than these
Mark 12. 43 poor wid. cast *m.* in
Luke 9, 13 no *m.* but five loaves
John 4. 1 bap. *m.* disc. than John
Acts 20. 35 *m.* blessed to give than
Rom. 5. 15 much *m.* grace of God
1 Cor. 14. 18 I speak *m.* than all
2 Cor. 10. 8 should boast some. *m.*
Gal. 4. 27 desolate hath *m.* children
Phil. 1. 14 *m.* bold to speak word
1 Thes. 4. 1 would abound *m.* and *m.*
2 Tim. 3. 4 lovers of pleas. *m.* than
Phile. 1. 16 how much *m.* unto thee
Heb. 3. 3 counted wor. of *m.* glo.
Rev. 2. 19 last be *m.* than the first
R. V. Mat. 27. 23; Mark 14. 31
exceedingly; Mark 15. 14; Acts
24. 10 ——.
Moreover. *Also, yet, still, and if.*
Gen. 32. 20 say ye *m.*, Behold, thy
Ex. 3. 15 God said *m.* unto Moses
Num. 16. 14 *m.* thou hast not bro't
2 Sam. 17. 13 *m.* if he be gotten
1 Chr. 11. 2 *m.* in time past, even

Eccl. 12. 9 *m.*, because Preacher
Luke 16. 21 *m.* dogs came and lick
Acts 2. 26 *m.* my flesh shall rest
1 Cor. 4. 2 *m.* it is required in ste.
Heb. 11. 36 *m.* bonds and imprison
R. V. very frequent changes to, and
Morning. *Light, dawn, daybreak.*
Cen. 1. 5. 8 e. and *m.* were first d.
Ex. 8. 20 Rise up early in the *m.*
Lev. 6. 12 burn wood on it ev. *m.*
Num. 9. 12 leave none of it unto *m*
Deut. 28. 67 Would God it were *m*
Josh. 3. 1 Josh. rose early in the *m.*
Judg. 6. 28 the men rose early in *m.*
Ruth. 3. 13 lie down until the *m.*
1 Sam. 3. 15 Samuel lay until *m.*
2 Sam. 2. 27 in the *m.* people had
1 K. 3. 21 I rose in the *m.* to give
2 K. 3. 20 it came to pass in the *m.*
1 Chr. 16. 40 offer *m.* and evening
2 Chr. 13. 11 burn unto Lord. ev *m.*
Ez. 2. 3 offerings *m.* and evening
Neh. 4. 11 from rising of the *m.* till
Job 4. 20 destroyed from *m.* to eve.
38. 7 When *m.* stars sang together
Ps. 59. 16 will sing aloud in the *m.*
90. 5 in the *m.* like grass which
Prov. 7. 18 t. our fill of love till *m.*
Eccl. 11. 6 In the *m.* sow thy seed
Isa. 17. 14 and before *m.* he is not
33. 2 be thou their arm every *m.*
Jer. 20. 16 let him hear cry in *m.*
Lam. 3. 23 They are new every *m.*
Ezek. 12. 8 in *m.* came word of L.
Dan. 8. 26 vision of *m.* and evening
Hos. 6. 4 your goodness is as *m.*
Joel 2. 2 *m.* spread upon mount's
Am. 4. 13 that maketh *m.* darkness
Jonah 4. 7 prepared worm when *m.*
Mic. 2. 1 when *m.* is light, they
Zeph. 3. 5 ev. *m.* he bring judgment
Mat. 20. 1. went out early in *m.*
Mark 11. 20 in *m.*, as they passed
Luke 21. 38 people came early in *m.*
John 8. 2 early in the *m.* he came
Acts 5. 21 ent. temp. early in the *m.*
Rev. 2. 28 will give him *m.* star
22. 16 I am the bright and *m.* star
R. V. Job 7. 21 diligently; Hos. 10.
15; Acts 5. 21 daybreak; Joel 2.
2 dawn; Mark 16. 2 early; John
21. 4 day
Morrow. *See* **To-morrow.**
Morsel. *Piece, bit, small meal.*
Gen. 18. 5 will fetch *m.* of bread
Judg. 19. 5 Com. h. with *m.* of br.
Ruth 2. 14 dip thy *m.* in vinegar
1 Sam. 2. 36 crouch to him for *m.*
1 K. 17. 11 Bring *m.* of bread in ha.
Job 31. 17 ha. eaten my *m.* myself
Ps. 147. 17 casteth his ice like *m.*
Prov. 17. 1 Bet. *m.*, and quietness
Heb. 12. 16 for *m.* sold his birth'.
R. V. 1 Sam. 2. 36 loaf; Heb. 12.
16 mess
Mortal. *Subject to death, human.*
Job 4. 17 *m.* be more just than G.
Rom. 6. 12 not sin reign in *m.* bod.
8. 11 quicken your *m.* bodies
1 Cor. 15. 53 *m.* must put on immor.
15. 54 *m.* shall have put on in.
2 Cor. 4. 11 made man. in. *m.* flesh
Mortality. R. V. *what is mortal.*
2 Cor. 5. 4 *m.* might be swal. up
Mortally. *Fatally.* R. V. —.
Deut. 19. 11 smite *m.* that he die
Mortar, Morter. R. V. *mortar.*
Gen. 11. 3 slime had they for *m.*
Ex. 1. 14 bondage, in *m.* and brick
Lev. 14. 42 he shall take other *m.*
Isa. 41. 25 come upon princes as *m.*
Nah. 3. 14 clay, and tread the *m.*
Hollow vessel.
Num. 11. 8 or beat it in a *m.*
Prov. 27. 22 should bray a fool in *m.*
Mortgage. *Pledge.*
Neh. 5. 3 We have *m.* our lands
Mortify. *Deaden, kill.*
Rom. 8. 13 if yɔ do *m.* deeds of bod.
Col. 3. 5 M. your members which
Most. *Greater, larger, utmost.*
Job 34. 17 wilt condemn *m.* just?
Prov. 20. 6 M. men will proclaim
S. of S. 5. 11 head is *m.* fine gold
Lam. 4. 1 is *m.* fine gold changed
Ezek. 35. 7 make Seir *m.* desol.

Dan. 3. 20 com. *m*. mighty men
Mark 5. 7 Son of the *m*. high God
Luke 8. 28 ; Acts 7. 48 ; Heb. 7. 1
Acts 20. 38 sorrowing *m*. of all for
Mote. *Particle, speck, chaff.*
Mat. 7. 3 why beholdest thou *m*.
7. 4 pull out the *m*. out of thine eye
Luke 6. 41, 42
Moth. *Insect, worm.*
Job 4. 19 houses crushed before *m*.
13. 28 as garment that is *m*. eaten
27. 18 buildeth his house as *m*.
Ps. 39. 11 beauty to cons. like *m*.
Isa. 50. 9 the *m*. shall eat them up
Hos. 5. 12 I be unto Ephraim as *m*.
Mat. 6. 19 where *m*, doth corrupt
6. 20 neither *m*. nor rust corrupt
Luke 12. 33
Moth-eaten. *Eaten by moth.*
Jas. 5. 2 your garments are *m. e.*
Mother. *Female parent, mother.*
Gen. 2. 24 shall man leave f. and *m*.
3. 20 Eve, she was *m*. of all living
Ex. 20. 12 Honour thy father and *m*.
Lev. 10. 3 fear every man his *m*.
Num. 6. 7 for his father or his *m*.
Deut. 5. 16 Hon. thy father and *m*.
Josh. 2. 13 will save alive my m.
Judg. 5. 28 *m*. of Sis. looked out
Ruth 1. 8 return to each *m's* house
1 Sam. 2. 19 *m*. made him lit. coat
2 Sam. 19. 37 by grave of my *m*.
1 K. 2. 19 seat set for king's *m*.
2 K. 4. 19 lad, Carry him to his *m*.
1 Chr. 4. 9 *m*. called name Jabez
2 Chr. 12. 13 *m's* name was Naam.
Esth. 2. 7 had neither father nor *m*.
Job 1. 21 naked .. I out of *m's* womb
Ps. 27. 10 When f. and *m*. forsake
51. 5 in sin did my *m*. conceive me
Prov. 1. 8 forsake not law of thy *m*.
Eccl. 5. 15 came forth of *m's* womb
S. of S. 1. 6 *m's* child. were angry
Isa. 66. 13 As one whom *m*. comf.
Jer. 15. 10 Woe is me, my *m*., that
Lam. 5. 3 our *m*. are as widows
Ezek. 16. 44 As *m*., so is daughter
Hos. 2. 2 Plead with your *m*., plead
10. 14 *m*. was dashed in pieces
Mic. 7. 6 daugh. riseth against *m*.
Zech. 13. 3 father and *m*. that begat
Mat. 1. 18 as *m*. Mary was espous.
2. 13 take the young child and *m*.
10. 37 that lov. father or *m*. more
12. 48 Who is my *m*? and who is
15. 4 that curs. fath. or *m*., let him
Mark 3. 32 thy *m*. and breth. seek
3. 34 Behold my *m*. and brethren
Luke 2. 33 Jos. and his *m*. marvel
John 2. 1 *m*. of Jesus was there
19. 25 there stood by cross his *m*.
Acts 3. 2 lame from his *m's* womb
Rom. 16. 13 Salute Rufus and his *m*.
Gal. 4. 26 Jerusalem, *m*. of us all
Eph. 5. 31 cause, sh. a man leave *m*.
1 Tim. 5. 2 The elder women as *m*.
2 Tim. 1. 5 dwelt in thy *m*. Eunice
Rev. 17. 5 *m*. of harlots and abom.
R. V. Luke 2. 43 his parents
Motions. R. V. *sinful passions.*
Rom. 7. 5 the *m*. of sins did work
Mouldy. *Moldy, musty.*
Josh. 9. 5 the bread was dry and *m*.
9. 12 now behold, it is dry and *m*.
Mount (*v*.), *Go up.*
Job 20. 6 Though excell. *m*. to heav.
39. 27 Doth eagle *m*. at command
Ps. 107. 26 They *m*. up to heaven
Isa. 15. 5 by the *m*. up of Luhith
40. 31 *m*. with wings of eagles
Jer. 51. 53 Though Bab. should *m*.
Ezek. 10. 16 lifted wings to *m*. up
R. V. Isa. 15. 5 ascent
Mount (*n*.). *Hill, height, moun-*
tain.
Gen. 31. 54 Jac. offered sac. on *m*.
Ex. 18. 5 encamped at *m*. of God
19. 14 Mos. went down from *m*.
24. 16 glo. of L. upon *m*. Sinai
Num. 10. 33 they departed from *m*.
Deut. 1. 16 dw. long enough in *m*.
Josh. 8. 30 altar to L. in *m*. Ebal
Judg. 4. 6 draw toward *m*. Tabor
2 Sam. 15. 30 D. went up *m*. Olivet
1 K. 19. 8 Elijah went to *m*. of G.
3 K. 23. 13 the *m*. of corruption

2 Chr. 3. 1 house of L. in *m*. M.
Neh. 9. 13 cam. down on *m*. Sinai
Isa. 14. 13 will sit on *m*. of cong.
Jer. 6. 6 cast *m*. against Jerusalem
Ezek. 17. 17 war, by casting up *m*.
Dan. 11. 15 k. of north cast up *m*.
Obad 8 destr. underst. out of *m*.
Zech. 14. 4 feet shall stand on *m*.
Mat. 21. 1 were come to *m*. of Ol.
Mark 13. 3 ; Luke 19. 29
Acts 7. 30 in wilder. of *m*. Sina
Gal. 4. 24 the one from *m*. of Sinai
Heb. 12. 18 are not come to the *m*.
R. V. In Josh., Judg., Sam., Kings,
Chron., mostly to, hill country
Mountain. *Mount, raised up.*
Gen. 7. 20 and *m*. were covered
8. 4 the ark rested on *m*. of Ararat
Ex. 3. 1 came to the *m*. of God
Num. 13. 17 and go up into the *m*.
Deut. 2. 37 unto cities in the *m*.
Josh. 2. 16 Get you to the *m*., lest
Judg. 1. 19 drave out inhab. of *m*.
1 Sam. 17. 3 Philistines stood on *m*.
2 Sam. 1. 21 Ye *m*. of Gilboa, let
1 K. 5. 15 four sc. th. hewers in *m*.
2 K. 2. 16 cast him upon some *m*.
1 Chr. 12. 8 swift as roes on the *m*.
2 Chr. 21. 11 made high pl. in *m*.
Job 9. 5 Which removeth the *m*.
Ps. 11. 1 Flee as bird to your *m*.
90. 2 bef. *m*. were brought forth
114. 4 the *m*. skipped like rams
Prov. 8. 25 Bef. *m*. were settled
S. of S. 2. 8 cometh leap. upon *m*.
Isa. 2. 2 established in top of *m*.
13. 2 Lift up a banner on high *m*.
34. 3 *m*. shall be melted with blood
52. 7 How beautiful upon the *m*.
66. 20 to my holy *m*. Jerusalem
Jer. 3. 6 gone up every high *m*.
46. 18 as Tabor is among the *m*.
Lam. 4. 19 pursued us upon *m*.
Ezek. 6. 3 Ye *m*. of Israel, hear
32. 5 and I will lay thy flesh on *m*.
38. 20 *m*. shall be thrown down
Dan. 9. 16 from Jerus., thy holy *m*.
Hos. 10. 8 say to *m*., Cover us
Joel 2. 2 as morning spread on *m*.
Am. 4. 13 lo, he that formeth *m*.
Jonah 2. 6 went to bottom of *m*.
Mic. 1. 4 *m*. shall be molten un. him
Nah. 1. 5 The *m*. quake at him, and
Hab. 3. 10 *m*. saw thee, they tremb.
Zeph. 1. 10 haughty bec. of my *m*.
Hag. 1. 8 Go to the *m*., bring word
Zech. 4. 7 Who are thou, O gr. *m*.?
Mal. 1. 3 hated Esau, laid his *m*.
Mat. 5. 1 he went up into a *m*., and
Mark 3. 13 and he goeth up into *m*.
11. 23 whoso. shall say unto *m*.
Luke 4. 5 taking him up high *m*.
John 4. 20 fath. worsh. in this *m*.
1 Cor. 13. 2 so I could remove *m*.
Heb. 11. 38 wand. in deserts and *m*.
Rev. 6. 14 *m*. and isl. w. removed.
6. 16 said to *m*., Fall on us and hi.
Mourn. *Weep, lament, bewail,*
grieve.
Gen. 23. 2 Ab. came to *m*. for Sar.
Ex. 35. 4 heard evil tid., they *m*.
Num. 20. 29 *m*. for Aaron thir. d.
1 Sam. 15. 35 Sam. *m*. for Saul, and
2 Sam. 13. 37 David *m*. for his son
1 K. 13. 29 proph. came to c., to *m*.
1 Chr. 7. 22 and Eph. *m*. many days
2 Chr. 35. 24 Judah *m*. for Josiah
Ez. 10. 6 bec. of transgression
Neh. 1. 4 wept, and *m*. certain days
Job. 5. 11 which *m*. may be exalted
14. 22 soul within him shall *m*.
30. 28 went *m*. without sun, I stood
Ps. 35. 14 bowed, as one that *m*.
38. 6 I go *m*. all the day long
55. 2 I *m*. in my complaint, I make
Prov. 29. 2 wicked rule, people *m*.
Eccl. 3. 4 time to *m*., time to dance
Isa. 38. 14 chatter, I did *m*. as dove
59. 11 we like bears, roar and *m*.
Jer. 4. 28 for this shall the earth *m*.
12. 4 How long shall the land *m*.
Lam. 1. 4 ways of Zion do *m*. becau.
Ezek. 7. 16 all of them *m*. everyone
24. 23 ye shall not *m*. nor weep
31. 15 I caused Lebanon to *m*.
Dan. 10. 2 th. days I Daniel was *m*.

Hos. 10. 5 people thereof shall *m*.
Joel 1. 10 field is wasted, land *m*.
Am. 1. 2 hab. of shep's shall *m*.
Mat. 5. 4 Blessed are they that *m*.
11. 17 we have *m*. unto you, and
Mark 16. 10 with him, as they *m*.
Luke 6. 25 Woe th. laugh, ye sh. *m*.
1 Cor. 5. 2 have not rather *m*., that
Jas. 4. 9 Be afflicted, and *m*., weep
Rev. 18. 11 mer. of earth shall *m*.
R. V. Gen. 50. 3 ; Num. 20. 29 wept ;
2 Sam. 11. 26 made lamentation ;
Job 2. 11 bemoan ; Gen. 50. 10 ;
Isa. 19. 8 lament ; Ps. 35. 14 be-
waileth ; 55. 2 am restless ; 88. 9
wasteth away ; Prov. 29. 2 sigh ;
Ezek. 24. 23 moan ; Mat. 11. 17 ;
Luke 7. 32 wailed.
Mourner. *Who mourns.*
2 Sam. 14. 2 feign thyself to be *m*.
Job 29. 25 as one that comf. the *m*.
Eccl. 12. 5 *m*. go about the streets
Isa. 57. 18 restore comforts to *m*.
Hos. 9. 4 sac. be as bread of *m*.
Mourning. *Weeping, grieving,*
lamenting, bewailing.
Gen. 37. 35 go down into grave *m*.
Deut. 26. 14 have not eaten in *m*.
2 Sam. 11. 27 when the *m*. was past
Esth. 4. 3 was great *m*. among Jews
Job 3. 8 ready to raise their *m*.
Ps. 30. 11 turned my *m*. into danc.
Eccl. 7. 2 bet. to go to house of *m*.
Isa. 51. 11 sor. and *m*. shall flee away
61. 3 to give the oil of joy for *m*.
Jer. 6. 26 make *m*., as for only son
31. 13 turn their *m*. into joy
Lam. 5. 15 dance is turned to *m*.
Ezek. 2. 10 lamentation, and *m*.
24. 17 make no *m*. for the dead
Joel 2. 12 Turn, with weep. and *m*.
Am. 8. 10 will turn your feasts to *m*.
Mic. 1. 8 will make thy *m*. as owls
Zech. 12. 11 In that day great *m*.
Mat. 2. 18 lam., weeping, great *m*.
2 Cor. 7. 7 when he told your *m*.
Jas. 4. 9 let laugh. be turned to *m*.
R. V. Job 3. 8 leviathan ; Isa. 51. 11
sighing ; Mic. 1. 11 wailing
Mournfully. *In sorrow.*
Mal. 3. 14 we have walked *m*. be. L..
Mouse. *Mouse.*
Lev. 11. 29 weasel, *m*., and tort.
1 Sam. 6. 4 and five golden *m*.
6. 5 your *m*. that mar land
6. 11 and the coffer with *m*. of gold
Isa. 66. 17 eating abom. and the *m*.
Mouth. *Palate.*
Job. 29. 10 tong. clear, to roof of *m*.
31. 30 Neither suffer. my *m*. to sin
34. 3 ear trieth words, *m*. tasteth
Ps. 137. 6 tongue clea. to roof of *m*.
5. 3 woman, her *m*. is smooth
8. 7 my *m*. shall speak truth
S. of S. 5. 16 His *m*. is most sweet
7. 9 thy *m*. like best wine for bel.
Lam. 4. 4 tongue cleav. to roof of *m*.
Cheek.
Ezek. 3. 26
Hos. 8. 1 Set trumpet to thy *m*.
Ps. 32. 9 *m*. must be held with bit
103. 5 sat. *m*. with good things
Throat.
Ps. 149. 6 praises of God be in *m*.
Face.
Prov. 15. 14 *m*. of fools feed. fool.
Gateway, entrance.
Dan. 3. 26 Neb. came near to *m*.
The mouth, cavity, orifice, opening.
Gen. 4. 11 opened *m*. to receive
8. 11 in her *m*. was olive leaf
29. 3 rolling stone from well's *m*.
42. 27 money it was in his sack's *m*.
Ex. 4. 11 Who made man's *m*.?
Num. 12. 8 will I speak *m*. to *m*.
22. 28 Lord opened *m*. of the ass
Deut. 11. 6 earth opened her *m*.
32. 1 and hear the words of my *m*.
Judg. 9. 38 Where is now thy *m*.
1 Sam. 1. 12 that Eli marked her *m*.
2 Sam. 22. 9 fire out of *m*. devour.
1 K. 7. 31 *m*. of it within chapter
2 K. 4. 34 put his *m*. on his *m*.
2 Chr. 18. 21 be lying spirit in *m*.
Ez. 1. 1 word of the Lord by *m*. of
Neh. 9. 20 withh. not man. from *m*.

Esth. 7. 8 and went out of king's *m.*
Job 3. 1 After this op. Job his *m.*
  15. 5 *m.* uttereth thine iniquity
Ps. 5. 19 Out of *m.* of babes and
  22. 21 Save me from lion's *m.*
Eccl. 5. 2 Be not rash with thy *m.*
S. of S. 1. 2 kiss me with k. of *m.*
Isa. 1. 20 *m.* as Lord hath spoken
Jer. 1. 9 put my words in thy *m.*
  36. 27 Baruch wrote at *m.* of Jer.
Lam. 3. 2 putteth his *m.* in dust
Ezek. 3. 3 was in my *m.* as honey
Dan. 10. 16 I op. my *m.*, and spake
Hos. 6. 5 slain by the words of *m.*
Am. 3. 12 as shep. taketh out of *m.*
Mic. 3. 5 putteth not into their *m.*
Nah. 3. 12 shall fall into the *m.* of
Zech. 9. 7 take the blood out of *m.*
Mal. 2. 6 the truth was in his *m.*
Mat. 5. 2 opened his *m.* and taught
  15. 11 Not which goeth into the *m.*
  15. 11 which cometh out of the *m.*
Luke 1. 64 *m.* was op. immediately
John 19. 29 and put it to his *m.*
Acts 1. 16 H. G., by *m.* of David
  10. 34 Peter opened his *m.*, and
Rom. 3. 14 *m.* is full of cursing and
  10. 9 confess with thy *m.* the Lord
2 Cor. 6. 11 *m.* is open unto you
Eph. 6. 19 that I may open my *m.*
Col. 3. 8 filthy com. of your *m.*
2 Thes. 2. 8 consume with sp. of *m.*
2 Tim. 4. 17 delivered out of *m.* of li.
Tit. 1. 11 *m.* must be stopped, who
Heb. 11. 33 stopped *m.* of lions
Jas. 3. 3 we put bits in horse's *m.*
1 Pet. 2. 22 nei. guile found in *m.*
Jude 16 *m.* speaketh swell. words
Rev. 1. 16 out of *m.* went sword
  13. 6 opened his *m.* in blasphemy
R. V. Job 12. 11; 34. 3 palate; Ps.
  32. 9 trappings; Isa. 19. 7 brink;
  Mat. 15. 8 ——.

Move. *Set in motion, impel, go, stir up.*
Gen. 1. 2 Spirit of G. *m.* on face of
Ex. 11. 7 not a dog *m.* his tongue
Lev. 10. 11 all that *m.* in the waters
Deut. 23. 25 shalt not *m.* sickle
Josh. 10. 21 none *m.* tongue against
  15. 18 *m.* him to ask of her father
Judg. 13. 25 Sp. of L. began to *m.*
Ruth 1. 19 city was *m.* about them
1 Sam. 1. 13 only her lips *m.*, but
2 Sam. 24. 1 *m.* David against them
2 K. 23. 18 let no man *m.* bones
1 Chr. 16. 30 that it be not *m.*
2 Chr. 18. 31 G. *m.* them to depart
Ez. 4. 15 they have *m.* sedition
Esth. 5. 9 Mordecai *m.* not for him
Job 37. 1 at this my heart is *m.*
  41. 23 thems. they cannot be *m.*
Ps. 10. 6 He ha. said, I cannot be *m.*
  46. 6 raged, kingdoms were *m.*
  112. 6 he shall not be *m.* forever
Prov. 12. 3 root of right. not be *m.*
  16. 30 *m.* his lips bringeth evil
S. of S. 5. 4 my bowels *m.* for him
Isa. 6. 4 posts of the door *m.* at the
  7. 2 heart was *m.* as trees of the
  14. 9 hell is *m.* for thee that it
  24. 19 earth is *m.* exceedingly
Jer. 4. 24 and all hills *m.* lightly
  25. 16 shall drink and be *m.* and
  49. 21 earth is *m.* at noise of their
Ezek. 47. 9 that *m.* whithersoever
Dan. 8. 7 he was *m.* with choler
Mic. 7. 17 shall *m.* out their holes
Mat. 9. 36 was *m.* with compassion
  14. 14; 18. 27; Mark 1. 41; 6. 34
Mark 15. 11 chief priests *m.* people
Acts 2. 25 that I should not be *m.*
  17. 5 but Jews *m.* with envy, took
  21. 30 city was *m.*, people ran
Col. 1. 23 be not *m.* from hope
1 Thes. 3. 3 no man be *m.* by affl.
Heb. 11. 7 *m.* with fear, prep. ark
  11. 28 kingd. which cannot be *m.*
2 Pet. 1. 21 as *m.* by Holy Ghost
Rev. 6. 14 mount. and isl. were *m.*
R. V. Gen. 9. 2 teemeth; 2 K. 21.
  8 wander; Ps. 23. 31 goeth down
  smoothly; Jer. 25. 16 reel to and
  fro; 46. 7, 8 toss themselves; 49.
  21; 50. 46 trembleth; Ezek. 47. 9
  swarmeth; Mic. 7. 17 trembling;

Mat. 14. 14; Mark 6. 34 he had
  .. on; Mat. 21. 10; Mark 15. 11
  stirred; Acts 20, 24 ——; Heb.
  12. 28 shaken
Moveable. R. V. *unstable.*
Prov. 5. 6 her ways are *m.* that
Mover. *Who moves, incites.*
Acts 24. 5 *m.* of sed. among Jews
Moving.
Gen. 1. 20 *m.* creat. that hath life
  9. 3 every *m.* thing that liveth
Job 16. 5 *m.* of thy lips assuage
John 5. 3 waiting for *m.* of waters
R. V. Job 16. 5 solace; John 5.
  3 ——
Mower. R. V. *reaper.*
Ps. 129. 7 *m.* filleth not his hand
Mowings. *Cut grass.*
Am. 7. 1 growth after king's *m.*
Mown. *Cut, reaped.*
Ps. 72. 6 like rain upon *m.* grass
Much. *In large degree.*
Gen. 30. 43 Jacob had *m.* cattle
Luke 8. 4 when *m.* peo. were gath.
  Etc., etc.
Mufflers. *Veils, wrappings.*
Isa. 3. 19 chains, bracelets, and *m.*
Mulberry trees. *Baka trees, mulberry.*
2 Sam. 5. 23 over against the *m. t.*
  5. 24. 1 Chr. 14. 14, 15
Mule. *Mule.*
Gen. 36. 24 found *m.* in wilderness
2 Sam. 13. 29 ev. man gat upon *m.*
  18. 9 Absalom rode upon *m.*
1 K. 18. 5 find grass to save *m.*
2 K. 5. 17 given two *m's* burden
Ez. 2. 66; Neh. 7. 68 *m.*, t. h. and f.
Esth. 8. 14 posts that rode on *m.*
Ps. 32. 9 Be not as horse or *m.*
Isa. 66. 20 in litters, and upon *m.*
Ezek. 27. 14 traded with horses a. *m.*
Zech. 14. 15 plague of horse, of *m.*
R. V. Gen. 36. 24 hot springs;
  Esth. 8. 14 swift steeds.
Multiplied. *Made many or great, increased.*
Ex. 11. 9 my wonders may be *m.*
Deut. 11. 21 your days may be *m.*
1 Chr. 5. 9 their cattle were *m.* in
Job 27. 14 If his children be *m.*
  35. 6 if thy transgression be *m.*
Ps. 16. 4 sorrows shall be *m.* that
  38. 19 and they that hate me are *m.*
Prov. 9. 11 thy days shall be *m.*
Isa. 59. 12 our transgressions are *m.*
Jer. 3. 16 to pass when ye be *m.* and
Ezek. 21. 15 and their ruins are *m.*
  31. 5 his boughs were *m.*, and
Dan. 4. 1 Peace be *m.* unto you
Acts 6. 1 where num. of discip. *m.*
R. V. Prov. 29. 16 increased;
  Ezek. 5. 7 are turbulent; Acts 6. 1
  multiplying.
Multiplying. *Make many or more, increase.*
Gen. 1. 22 Be fruitful, and *m.*, and
Ex. 1. 7 increased, abund., and *m.*
Lev. 26. 9 make you fruitful, and *m.*
Deut. 8. 1 that ye may live, and *m.*
Josh. 24. 3 *m.* his seed, and gave
1 Chr. 4. 27 nei. did their family *m.*
Job 9. 17 *m.* wounds without cause
  35. 16 *m.* words without knowl.
Isa. 9. 3 thou hast *m.* nation, and
Jer. 33. 22 will *m.* seed of David
Ezek. 11. 6 have *m.* your slain in
Hos. 2. 8. oil, and *m.* her silver and
  12. 10 I have *m.* visions and used
Am. 4. 4 at Gilgal *m.* transgressions
Nah. 3. 16 hast *m.* merchants above
Acts 6. 7 number of the disciples *m.*
  12. 24 word of God grew and *m.*
2 Cor. 9. 10 *m.* your seed sown and
Heb. 6. 14 multiplying I will *m.*
1 Pet. 1. 2 Grace, and peace be *m.*
Jude 2 Mercy, peace and love be *m.*
Multiplying. *Making many.*
Gen. 22. 17 in *m.* I will multiply
See also **Multiply**
Multitude. *Great number, crowd abundance.*
Gen. 16. 10 not be number for *m.*
Ex. 12. 28 mixed *m.* went up also
Lev. 25. 16 accord. to *m.* of years
Num. 11. 4 mixed *m.* was among

Deut. 1. 10 as stars of heav. for *m.*
Josh. 11. 4 as sand on shore for *m.*
1 Sam. 14. 16 and *m.* melted away
2 Sam. 6. 19 among whole *m.* of Is.
1 K. 20. 13 Hast seen this gr. *m.*?
2 K. 7. 13 they are as all the *m.*
2 Chr. 13. 8 ye be a great *m.*, and
Neh. 13. 3 separated from mixed *m.*
Esth. 5. 11 Haman told of the *m.*
Job 32. 7 *m.* of years teach wisdom
Ps. 69. 13 in *m.* of thy mercy hear
Prov. 7. 6 in *m.* of counsel. safety
Eccl. 5. 7 in *m.* of dreams vanities
Jer. 10. 13 *m.* of wat. in heavens
Ezek. 7. 14 wrath is upon all *m.*
Dan. 10. 6 voice like voice of *m.*
Hos. 10. 13 did trust in *m.* of men
Joel 3. 14 in valley of decision
Nah. 3. 3 *m.* slain, and gr. numb.
Zech. 2. 4 for *m.* of men and cattle
Mat. 4. 25 followed him great *m.*
  9. 33 *m.* marvelled, saying It was
  14. 19 commanded *m.* to sit down
  21. 8 gr. *m.* spread their garments
  23. 1 then spake Jesus to *m.*
Mark 2. 13 *m.* resorted unto him
  7. 33 he took him aside from *m.*
Luke 6. 19 *m.* sought to touch him
John 5. 13 *m.* being in that place
Acts 13. 45 when Jews saw *m.*, they
  19. 33 drew Alex. out of the *m.*
Heb. 11. 12 as stars of the sky in *m.*
Jas. 5. 20 and shall hide *m.* of sins
1 Pet. 4. 8 char. cover *m.* of sins
Rev. 7. 9 *m.* no man could number
R. V. Gen. 28. 3; 48. 4; Luke 23. 1
  company; Job. 39. 7 Jer. 3. 23;
  10. 13; 51. 16 tumult: 46. 25 Amon;
  Ps. 42. 4 throng; Prov. 20. 15
  abundance; Isa. 17. 12 ah, the up-
  roar; Jer. 12. 6 aloud; Ezek. 31.
  5; Mat. 15. many; Mark 3. 9;
  Acts 21. 34 crowd; Luke 8. 37 all
  the people; Acts 23. 7 assembly;
  Job 33. 19; Acts 21. 22 ——.
Munition. *Stronghold, bulwark.*
Isa. 29. 7 that fight against her *m.*
  33. 16 his defence sh. be *m.* of rocks
Nah. 2. 1 keep *m.*, watch the way
R. V. Is. 29. 7 strong hold
Murder (*n.*). *Murder.*
Mat. 15. 19 out of heart proc. *m.*
  19. 18 J. said, Thou shalt do no *m.*
Mark 15. 7 Barab., who had com. *m.*
Luke 23. 19 for *m.*, cast into prison
Rom. 1. 29 full of envy, *m.*, debate
Gal. 5. 21 Envyings, *m.* drunkenness
Rev. 9. 21 nei. repented they of *m.*
R. V. Mat. 19. 18 not kill; Gal. 5.
  21
Murder (*v.*). *To do murder.*
Ps. 10. 8 in secret pl. doth he *m.*
  94. 6 slay wid., *m.* fatherless
Jer. 7. 9 Will ye steal, *m.*, and com.
Hos. 6. 9 so priests *m.* in the way
Murderer. *Who murders.*
Num. 35. 26 *m.* shall be put to d.
2 K. 6. 32 this son of *m.* hath sent
  14. 6 children of *m.* he slew not
Job 24. 14 *m.* ris. with light killeth
Isa. 1. 21 lodged in it, but now *m.*
Jer. 4. 31 soul is wear. bec. of *m.*
Hos. 9. 13 bring forth children to *m.*
Mat. 22. 7 destroyed those *m.*, and
John 8. 44 was *m.* from beginning
Acts 3. 14 des. *m.* to be granted
  28. 4 No doubt this man is *m.*
1 Pet. 4. 15 let none suffer as *m.*
1 John 3. 15 no *m.* hath eternal life
Rev. 21. 8 the abominable, and *m.*
R. V. Num. 35, 16, 17, 18, 21 man-
  slayer; Hos. 9. 13 slayer; Acts
  21. 38 assassins.
Murmur. *Mutter complaint, grumble repine.*
Ex. 15. 24 people *m.* against Moses
Num. 14. 2 children of Israel *m.*
Deut. 27 ye *m.* in your tents
Josh. 9. 18 all the congregation *m.*
Ps. 106. 25 *m.* in their tents, and
Isa. 29. 24 that *m.* learn doctrine
Mat. 20. 11 *m.* against good man of
Mark 14. 5 And they *m.* against her
Luke 5. 30 scribes and Pharisees *m.*
John 6. 41 the Jews then *m.* at him
  6. 43 *m.* not among yourselves

6. 61 Jes. knew that his disciples *m*.
7. 32 Pharis. heard the people *m*.
1 Cor. 10. 10 Neither *m*., as some *m*
Murmurer. *Who murmurs.*
Jude 16 These are *m*., complainers
Murmuring. *Complaining.*
Ex. 16. 7 he heareth your *m*. ag. **L**.
Num. 14. 27 have heard *m*. of chil.
  17. 10 shalt take away their *m*.
John 7. 12 was *m*. amo. the people
Acts 6. 1 arose a *m*. of the Grecians
Phil. 2. 14 Do all things without *m*.
Murrain. *Pestilence.*
Ex. 9. 3 shall be very grievous *m*.
Muse. *Meditate, reason.*
Ps. 142. 5 I *m*. on work of thy h.
Luke 3. 15 men *m*. in hearts of John
  R. V. Luke 3. 15 reasoned
Music. *Song, praise, melody.*
1 Sam. 18. 6 with instruments of *m*.
1 Chr. 15. 16 sing. with instr. of *m*.
2-Chr. 5. 13 cymbals, and instr. of *m*.
Eccl. 12. 4 daughters of *m*. shall
Lam. 3. 63 Behold, I am their *m*.
Dan. 3. 5 *m*. fall down and worship
Am. 6. 5 invent instruments of *m*.
Luke 15. 25 drawing nigh, heard *m*.
  R. V. Lam. 3. 63 song
Musical. *Of song, melody.*
1 Chr. 16. 42 with *m*. instr's of G.
Neh. 12. 36 with *m*. instr's of David
Eccl. 2. 8 I gat *m*. instr's, all sorts
  R. V. 1 Chr. 16. 42 instr's of song
Musician. *Music leader.*
Ps. 4. title. To chief *M*.
  So Ps. 5, 6, 9, 11, 12, 13, etc.
Rev. 18. 22 voice of harpers and *m*.
  R. V. Rev. 18. 22 minstrels
Musing. *Meditating.*
Ps. 39. 3 while I was *m*. fire burned
Must. *Behoveth, necessary, requi-*
site..
Gen. 29. 26 it *m*. not be so done
Num. 23. 12 *m*. I not take heed
Deut. 4. 22 I *m*. die in this land
1 Sam. 14. 43 and lo, I *m*. die
2 Sam. 23. 3 ruling men *m*., be just
Ez. 10. 12 as should so, so *m*. we do
Mat. 16. 21 he *m*. go unto Jerusal.
Mark 8. 31 Son of man *m*. suffer
Luke 2. 49 *m*. be about my F.'s bus.
John 3. 7 Ye *m*. be born again
Acts 16. 30 what *m*. do to be saved?
Rom. 13. 5 ye *m*. needs be subject
1 Cor. 15. 52 Cor. *m*. put on incor.
2 Cor. 5. 10 *m*. appear before judg.
1 Tim. 3. 2 bishop *m*. be blameless
2 Tim. 2. 24 servant of L. *m*. strive
Tit. 1. 11 mouths *m*. be stopped
Heb. 11. 6 th. com. to G. *m*. believe
Rev. 1. 1 *m*. shortly come to pass
Mustard. *Mustard.*
Mat. 13. 31 like to grain of *m*.
  17. 20 have faith as grain of *m*. seed
Mark 4. 31; Luke 13. 19   17. 6
Muster. *Assemble, inspect.*
2 K. 25. 19 which *m*. people of land
Isa. 13. 4 Lord *m*. hosts of battle
Jer. 52. 25 who *m*. people of land
Mutter. *Murmur, Grumble.*
Isa. 8. 19 wizards that peep and *m*.
  59. 3 your tongue *m*. perverseness
Mutual. *R. V. other's.*
Rom. 1. 12 *m*. faith of you and me
Muzzle. *Stop, gag.*
Deut. 25. 4 shalt not *m*. ox when
1 Cor. 9. 9 shalt not *m*. mouth of ox
1 Tim. 5. 18 Thou shalt not *m*. ox
My. *To me, mine.*
Mat. 2. 6 rule *m*. people Israel
Mark 5. 9 *M*. name is Legion
Etc., etc.
Myrrh. *Gum, myrrh.*
Gen. 37. 25 bearing spicery and *m*.
Ex. 30. 23 of *m*. five hund. shekels
Esth. 2. 12 six mo. with oil of *m*.
Ps. 45. 8 thy garments smell of *m*.
Prov. 7. 17 perfum. my bed with *m*.
S. of S. 1. 13 bund. of *m*. is m. belov.
  5. 5 my hands dropped with *m*.
  5. 13 lips like lilies, dropping *m*.
Mat. 2. 11 presented gold and *m*.
Mark 15. 23 gave wine ming. w. *m*.
John 19. 13 br. mixt. of *m*. a. aloes
Myrtle. *Myrtle tree.*
Neh. 8. 15 go forth and fetch *m*.

Isa. 41. 19 plant in wilderness, *m*.
  55. 13 of brier shall come up *m*.
Zech. 1. 8 he stood among *m*. trees
Myself. *I, self, me.*
John, 7. 28 I am not come of *m*.
1 Cor. 4. 4 I know nothing by *m*.
Etc., etc.
Mystery. *Thing known only to*
the initiated.
Mat. 13. 11 giv. to you to know *m*.
Mark 4. 11; Luke 8. 10
Rom. 16. 25 according to rev. of *m*.
1 Cor. 2. 7 speak wis. of G. in *m*.
  13. 2 and understand all *m*. and kn.
  15. 51 Behold, I show you a *m*.
Eph. 1. 9 made known unto us *m*.
  5. 32 This is a great *m*., but
  6. 19 make known *m*. of gospel
Col. 1. 27 rich. of glo. of this *m*.
  4. 3 to speak *m*. of Christ for which
2 Thes. 2. 7 *m*. of iniq. doth alr. w'k
1 Tim. 3. 9 Holding *m*. of faith
  3. 16 great. is the *m*. of godliness.
Rev. 1. 20 *m*. of the seven stars
  17. 7 will tell thee *m*. of woman

N

Nail (*n*.).   *Claw, talon, horny sub-*
stance.
Deut. 21. 12 shave head, a. pare h. *n*.
Dan. 4. 33 his *n*. like bird's claws
  7. 19 iron, and his *n*. of brass
Pin, nail.
Judg. 4. 21 Jael took *n*. of tent, and
  4. 21 smote *n*. into his temple
  4. 22 and the *n*. was in his temples
1 Chr. 22. 3 D. prepared iron for *n*.
2 Chr. 3. 9 weight of *n*. was fif. o.
Ez. 9. 8 give *n*. in his holy place
Eccl. 12. 11 as *n*. fasten. by masters
Isa. 22. 23 I will fasten him as *n*.
  41. 7 he fasteneth it with *n*.
Jer. 10. 4 fasten it with *n*. and ham.
Zech. 10. 4 out of him came forth *n*.
John 20. 25 see in hands print of *n*.
  R. V. Judg. 4. 21, 22 tent pin
Nail. *To nail.*
Col. 2. 14 he *n*. it to his cross
Naked. *Nude, exposed, destitute.*
Gen. 2. 25 they were both *n*.
  3. 10 afraid, because I was *n*.
Ex. 32. 25 Aaron had made them *n*.
  32. 25 Moses saw people were *n*.
1 Sam. 19. 24 lay down *n*. all th. day
2 Chr. 28. 19 for he made Judah *n*.
Job 1. 21 *N*. came I out of womb
  1. 21 *n*. shall I return thither
  22. 6 stripped *n*. of their clothing
  26. 6 Hell is *n*. before him
Eccl. 5. 15 *n*. shall he return to
Isa. 20. 2 walking *n*. and barefoot
  20. 3 Isaiah walked *n*. and barefoot
  58. 7 when thou seest *n*., that
Lam. 4. 21 and shalt make thyself *n*.
Ezek. 16. 22 thou wast *n*. and bare
  18. 7 hath covered *n*. with garment
  23. 29 shall leave thee *n*. and bare
Hos. 2. 3 Lest I strip her *n*., and set
Am. 2. 16 mighty .. flee *n*. in that day
Mic. 1. 8 will go stripped and *n*.
  1. 11 Saphir, having thy shame *n*.
Hab. 3. 9 Thy bow was made *n*.
Mat. 25. 36 *N*., and ye clothed me
  25. 43 *n*., and ye clothed me not
Mark 14. 51 cloth cast about *n*. body
  14. 52 and he fled from them *n*.
John 21. 7 he was *n*. and did cast
Acts 19. 16 they fled out of house *n*.
1 Cor. 4. 11 thirst, are *n*. a. buffeted
2 Cor. 5. 3 we shall not be found *n*.
Heb. 4. 13 but all things are *n*. and
Jas. 2. 15 If brother or sister be *n*.
Rev. 3. 17 and poor, and blind, a. *n*.
  17. 16 shall make her desolate a. *n*.
  R. V. Ex. 32. 25 broken loose, let
  them loose for derision; 2 Chr.
  28. 19 dealt wantonly; Hab. 3. 9
  bare
Nakedness. *Bareness.*
Gen. 9. 22 saw the *n*. of his father
  9. 23 covered the *n*. of their father
  42. 9 spies; to see the *n*. of the land
Ex. 28. 42 breeches to cov. their *n*.
Lev. 18. 6 approach to uncover *n*.
  18. 7-19; 20. 11-21
Deut. 28. 48 and in thirst, and *n*.

1 Sam. 20. 30 confus. of mother's *n*.
Isa. 47. 3 Thy *n*. shall be uncovered
Lam. 1. 8 they have seen her *n*.
Ezek. 16. 8 thee, and covered thy *n*.
  16. 37 discov. thy *n*. unto them
  22. 10 discovered their father's *n*.
Hos. 2. 9 flax given to cover *n*.
Nah. 3. 5 will show nations thy *n*.
Hab. 2. 15 mayest look on their *n*.
Rom. 8. 35 famine, or *n*., or peril
2 Cor. 11. 27 fastings often, in *n*.
Rev. 3. 18 shame of thy *n*. appear
Name (*n*.).   *Name, appellation,*
designation, denomination.
Gen. 2. 11 *n*. of first river is Pison
  2. 20 Adam gave *n*. to all cattle
  3. 20 Adam called wife's *n*. Eve
  5. 29 And he called his *n*. Noah
  13. 4. Abram called on *n*. of Lord
  17. 15 but Sarah shall her *n*. be
  25. 26 and his *n*. was called Jacob
  30. 24 she called his *n*. Joseph
Ex. 2. 10 she called his *n*. Moses
  3. 15 Lord G., this is my *n*. for ever
  6. 3 by *n*. Jehovah was not known
  20. 7 not take *n*. of Lord in vain
  34. 14 Lord, whose *n*. is Jealous
Lev. 19. 12 shall not swear by my *n*.
Num. 1. 5 these are *n*. of men that
  1. 18 according to number of *n*.
Deut. 7. 24 shalt destr. their *n*. from
  18. 5, 7 shall minister in *n*. of Lord
  25. 10 his *n*. shall be called in Israel
Josh 19. 47 Dan, after *n*. of Dan
Judg. 13. 24 called his *n*. Samson
Ruth. 1. 2 and *n*. of his wife Naomi
1 Sam. 1. 20 she called his *n*. Samuel
  9. 2 Kish .. son, whose *n*. was Saul
  17. 23 Philis. of Gath, Goliath by *n*.
2 Sam. 7. 13 build house for my *n*.
  8. 13 David gat hima *n*. when he re.
  12. 24 he called his *n*. Solomon
1 K. 5. 5 build house unto my *n*.
2 K. 2. 24 cursed them in *n*. of Lord
1 Chr. 16. 10 Glory ye in his holy *n*.
2 Chr. 2. 1 build house for *n*. of L.
Ez. 8. 20 all were expressed by *n*.
Neh. 9. 5 blessed be thy glorious *n*.
Esth. 2. 5 whose *n*. was Mordecai
  9. 26 Purim, after the *n*. of Pur
Job 1. 1 man, whose *n*. was Job
Ps. 8. 1 how excell. thy *n*. in all earth
  54. 6 will praise thy *n*., O Lord
  68. 4 sing praises to his *n*.
  72. 17 His *n*. shall endure forever
  76. 1 his *n*. is great in Israel
  96. 2 Sing unto Lord, bless his *n*.
  105. 3 Glory ye in his holy *n*.
Prov. 18. 10 *n*. of L. is strong tower
  22. 1 good *n*. is rather to be chos.
Eccl. 7. 1 good *n*. is better than oint.
S. of S. 1. 3 thy *n*. is as ointment
Isa. 7. 14 shall call his *n*. Imman.
  9. 6 *n*. shall be called Wonderful
  25. 1 I will exalt, I will praise thy *n*.
  42. 8 I am the Lord, that is my *n*.
  54. 5 Lord of hosts is his *n*.
Jer. 16. 10 thy *n*. is great. in might
  33. 9 shall be to me *n*. of joy
Lam. 3. 55 called upon thy *n*., O L.
Ezek. 24. 2 write *n*. of the day
Dan. 1. 7 prince of eunuchs gave *n*.
Hos. 1. 4 said, called his *n*. Jezreel
Joel 2. 26 praise *n*. of L. your God,
Am. 2. 7 to profane my holy *n*.
Mic. 4. 5 will walk in *n*. of Lord
Nah. 1. 14 no more thy *n*. be sown
Zeph. 3. 20 make you a *n*. and praise
Zech. 6. 12 whose *n*. is The Branch
Mal. 1. 11 my *n*. be great among
Mat. 1. 21 shalt call his *n*. Jesus
  6. 9 Hallowed be thy *n*.
  10. 2 *n*. of the twelve apostles are
  18. 20 gather. together in my *n*.
  28. 19 baptizing in *n*. of Father
Mark 5. 9 saying, My *n*. is Legion
  13. 6 many come in my *n*., saying
Luke 1. 5 her *n*. was Elisabeth
  1. 13 And th. shalt call his *n*. John
  2. 21 his *n*. was called Jesus
John 2. 23. many believed in his *n*.
  10. 3 calleth his own sheep by *n*.
Acts 3. 6 In *n*. of Jesus Christ
  9. 15 bear my *n*. before Gentiles
Rom. 1. 5 faith among nat., for his *n*
  15. 9 confess and sing unto thy *n*.

1 Cor. 1. 13 ye baptiz. in *n.* of Paul
Eph. 1. 21 every *n.* that is named
Phil. 2. 10 at *n.* of J. ev. knee bow
Col. 3. 17 do all in *n.* of Lord J. C.
2 Thes. 1. 12 ; 3. 6
1. Tim. 6. 1 that *n.* of G. and his
2 Tim. 2. 19 that nameth *n.* of C.
Heb. 6. 12'declare *n.* unto my breth.
Jas. 2. 7 Do not blaspheme that *n.*
1 Pet. 4. 14 reproached for *n.* of C.
1 John 5. 13 believe on *n.* of Son
3 John 14 Greet the friends by *n.*
Rev. 2. 13 thou holdest fast my *n.*
19. 13 *n.* is called, Word of God
R. V. Mark 9. 41; 11. 10; 1 John
5. 13 ——; Luke 24. 18; Acts 7.
58 ; 28. 7 named

Name. (*v.*) *Say, call, designate.*
Gen. 23. 16 *n.* in audience of sons
28. 36 Is not he rightly *n.* Jacob?
48. 16 let my name be *n.* on th.
Josh. 2. 1 an harlot's house, *n.* Ra.
1 Sam. 17. 4 *n.* Goliath, of Gath
2 K. 17. 34 Jacob, whom he *n.* Israel
1 Chr. 23. 14 were *n.* of tr. of Levi
Eccl. 6. 10 hath been is *n.* already
Isa. 61. 6 be *n.* priests of the Lord
62. 2 which mouth of L. shall *n.*
Jer. 44. 26 name no more be *n.* in
Dan. 5. 12 Dan., whom k. *n.* Belt.
Am. 6. *n.* the chief of the nations
Mic. 2. 7 art *n.* The house of Jacob
Mat. 27. 57 man of Arimath., *n.* Jos.
Mark 14. 32 to place *n.* Gethsemane
Luke 1. 5 cert. priest *n.* Zacharias
1. 26 city of Galilee, *n.* Nazareth
2. 21 so *n.* of the angel before he
5. 27 Jesus saw publican, *n.* Levi
10. 38 certain woman *n.* Martha
19. 2 there was man *n.* Zaccheus
John 3. 1 man of Phar., *n.* Nicode.
Acts 5. 1 certain man *n.* Ananias
5. 34 a Pharisee, *n.* Gamaliel, a
12. 13 a damsel came, *n.* Rhoda
18. 24 a certain Jew, *n.* Apollos
Rom. 15. 20 not where C. was *n.*
1 Cor. 5. 1 forni. not *n.* among Gent.
Eph. 1. 21 far above every name *n.*
3. 15 fam. in heav. and earth *n.*
5. 3 covetousness, let it not be *n.*
2 Tim. 2. 19 that *n.* C. de. fr. iniq.
R. V. Mat. 9. 9; Mark 15. 7;
Luke 19. 2 called; John 11. 1 —
John 11. 49; Acts 24. 1 one; 1
Cor. 5. 1 even

Namely. *In this, to-wit.*
Rom. 13. 9 compre. in this say. *n.*
R. V. This word generally omitted,
where interpolated, in Italics, in
text

Napkin. *Kerchief, napkin.*
Luke 19. 20 I kept laid up in a *n.*
John 11. 44 face was bound with *n.*
20. 7 *n.*, that was about his head

Narrow. *Not broad, limited, re-
stricted, small, brief.*
Num. 22. 26 and stood in *n.* place
Josh. 17. 15 if mt. Ephr. be too *n.*
1 K. 6. 4 made window. of *n.* light
Prov. 23. 27 strange wom. is *n.* pit
Isa. 49. 19 land of destr. be too *n.*
Ezek. 40. 16 *n.* window to chamber
41. 26 *n.* wind. and palm trees
Mat. 7. 14 *n.* the way, which lead.
R. V. 1 K. 6. 4 fixed; Ezek. 40.
16; 41. 16, 26 closed; Mat. 7. 14
straitened

Narrowed. *Straitened, made
narrow.*
1 K. 6. 6 made *n.* rests round about
Isa. 28. 20 cov. *n.* than he can wrap

Narrowly. *Closely, intently.*
Job 13. 27 look. *n.* to my paths
Isa. 14. 16 shall *n.* look upon thee
R. V. Job 13. 27 markest

Nation. *People, stock, race, tribe or
tribes, organized state.*
Gen. 10. 5 after families, in their *n.*
12. 2 will make of thee a great *n.*
17. 4 shalt be father of many *n.*
25. 23 two *n.* are in thy womb, and
Ex. 34. 24 cast out *n.* before thee
Lev. 18. 28 spued out *n.* that were
Num. 23. 9 not be reck. among *n.*
Deut. 4. 7 for what *n.* is so great
11. 23 ye shall possess greater *n.*

17. 14 like all the *n.* about me
28. 50 *n.* of fierce countenance
Josh. 23. 4 divid. unto you these *n.*
Judg. 3. 1 now these are *n.* which
1 Sam. 8. 5 make us k. like all *n.*
2 Sam. 8. 11 dedicated all *n.* which
1 K. 4. 31 his fame was in all *n.*
2 K. 17. 29 every *n.* made gods of
1 Chr. 14. 17 brought fear on all *n.*
2 Chr. 15. 6 *n.* was destroyed of *n.*
Neh. 13. 26 a. many *n.* was no k.
Job 12. 23 increaseth *n.*, and des.
Ps. 22. 28 he is gov. among *n.*
113. 4 the L. is high above all *n.*
117. 1 Praise the Lord, all ye *n.*
Prov. 14. 34 Righteous. exalteth *n.*
Isa. 2. 4 he shall judge among *n.*
9. 3 Thou hast multiplied the *n.*
43. 9 Let all *n.* be gathered toget.
Jer. 1. 10 this day set thee over *n.*
Lam. 4. 17 have watched for *n.* that
Ezek. 5. 5 set it in the midst of *n.*
3. 22 thou art like young lion of *n.*
Dan. 8. 22 shall stand up out of *n.*
Hos. 9. 17 be wanderers among *n.*
Joel 3. 3 I will gather all *n.*, and will
Am. 6. 1 are named chief of *n.*
Mic. 7. 16 *n.* shall be confounded
Nah. 3. 5 will show *n.* thy naked.
Hab. 1. 6 that bitter and hasty *n.*
Zeph. 3. 6 I have cut off the *n.*
Hag. 2. 14 So is this *n.* before me
Zech. 14. 2 gath. *n.* against Jerusa.
Mal. 3. 12 all *n.* call you blessed
Mat. 24. 7 *n.* shall rise against *n.*
28. 19 teach all *n.*, baptizing them
Mark 11. 17 house be called of *n.*
Luke 7. 5 For he loveth our *n.*, and
John 11. 48 take away place and *n.*
Acts 2. 5 at Jer. men, out of every *n.*
10. 22 good report among all *n.*
Rom. 1. 5 obed. to faith among *n.*
Gal. 3. 8 In thee all *n.* be blessed
Phil. 2. 15 midst of a perverse *n.*
1 Pet. 2. 9 ye are an holy *n.*, a pecul.
Rev. 2. 26 I give power over *n.*
21. 26 bring glory and honour to *n.*
R. V, Gen. 14. 1, 9; Josh. 12 23
Goiim; Lev. 18. 26 homeborn;
Ex. 2.18; Deut. 2. 25 ; 4. 6, 19, 27 ;
14. 2 ; 28. 37 ; 30. 3 ; 1 Chr. 16.
24 ; 2 Chr. 7. 20; 13. 9 ; Neh. 1.
8 ; 19. 22 ; Ps. 96. 5 ; 106. 34;
Ezek. 38. 8 peoples; Isa. 37. 18
countries; Mark 7. 26 race; Gal.
1. 14 countrymen; Phil. 2. 15
generation

Native. *Birth.*
Jer. 22. 10 nor see his *n.* country

Nativity. *Birth, kindred.*
Gen. 11. 28 Haran died in land *n.*
Ruth. 2. 11 hast left land of thy *n.*
Jer. 46. 16 go to the land of our *n.*
Ezek. 16. 3 *n.* is land of Canaan
21. 30 created, in land of thy *n.*
23. 15 Chaldea, the l. of their *n.*
R. V. Ezek. 21 30 birth

Natural. *Produced by nature.*
Rom. 11. 21 if God spared not *n.* b.
Jas. 1. 23 behold. *n.* face in glass
Belonging to nature, native.
Deut. 34. 7 nor his *n.* fore abated
Rom. 1. 26 wom. did change *n.* use
1. 27 leaving *n.* use of women
2 Pet. 2. 12 as *n.* beasts, to be taken
Animal, sensuous.
1 Cor. 2. 14 *n.* man receiveth not
15. 44 It is sown a *n.* body, raised
15. 46 but that which is *n.*, and
R. V. 2 Pet. 2. 12 creatures with-
out reason

Naturally. *By nature.*
Phil. 2. 20 *n.* care for your state
Jude 10 but what they know *n.*
R. V. Phil. 2. 20 care truly

Nature. *Nature.*
Rom. 1. 26 change things against *n.*
2. 14 do by *n.* things contained
2. 27 uncircum. which is by *n.*
11. 24 the olive tree is wild by *n.*
11. 24 were graffed contrary to *n.*
1 Cor. 11. 14 Doth not *n.* teach
Gal. 2. 15 We who are Jews by *n.*
Eph. 2. 3 by *n.* children of wrath
Heb. 2. 16 took not *n.* of angels
Jas. 3. 6 setteth on fire course of *n.*

2 Pet. 1. 4 be partakers of div. *n.*

Naught. *Nothing, bad, worthless*
2 K. 2. 19 water is *n.*, and ground
Prov. 20. 14 it is *n.*, saith the buyer

Naughtiness. *Badness, mischief.*
1 Sam. 17. 28 the *n.* of thine heart
Prov. 11. 6 be taken in their own *n.*
Jas. 1. 21 lay apart all superfl. of *n.*
R. V. Prov. 11. 6 mischief; Jas. 1.
21 wickedness

Naughty. *Worthless, mischievous.*
Prov. 6. 12 *n.* person walketh with
17. 4 liar giveth ear to *n.* tongue
Jer. 24. 2 other basket had *n.* figs
R. V. Rom. 6. 12 worthless; 17. 4
mischievous; Jer. 24. 2 bad

Navel. *Navel, muscle.*
Job 40. 16 force is in *n.* of belly
Prov. 3. 8 shall be health to thy *n.*
S. of S. 7. 2 *n.* is like round goblet
Ezek. 16. 4 thy *n.* was not cut, nei.
R. V. Job 40. 16 muscles

Naves. R. V. *felloes.*
1 K. 7. 33 axletrees, and their *n.*

Navy. *Ships, shipping.*
1 K. 9. 26 Solomon made *n.* of ships
9. 27 Hiram sent in *n.* servants
10. 11 *n.* of Hiram that brought
10. 22 for the king had at sea a *n.*

Nay. *No, not, but, also.*
Gen. 18. 15 And he said, *N.*, but
23. 11 *N.*, my lord, hear me
Judg. 19. 22 *N.*, breth., *n.* I pray
Jer. 6. 15 *n.*, they were not ashamed
Mat. 5. 37 communica. be, Yea, *N.*
13. 29 *N.* lest, while we gather
Luke 12. 51 I tell you, *N.*, but rath.
13. 3 *N.*, but, except ye repent
16. 30 *N.*, father Abraham, but
John 7. 12 *N.*, but he deceiv. peo.
Acts 16. 37 *N.*, but let them come
Rom. 3. 27 *N.*, but by law of faith
9. 20 *N.*, O man, who art thou
1 Cor. 6. 8 *N.*, ye do wrong, and
2 Cor. 1. 17 should be yea, *n. n.*?
1. 18 our word was not yea and *n.*
Jas. 5. 12 let yea be yea, and *n. n.*
R. V. 1 K. 2. 20 deny; Judg. 19.
23 ——; John .. 12 not no ; Rom.
7. 7 howbeit

Near. *Nigh, close by.*
Gen. 19. 20 the city is *n.* to flee to
Ex. 13. 17 land of Philistines was *n.*
Lev. 21. 2 kin that is *n.* to him
Deut. 16. 21 not plant trees *n.* to a.
Josh. 15. 46 all that lay *n.* Ashdod
Judg. 20. 34 knew not evil was *n.*
2 Sam. 14. 30 Joab's field is *n.* mine
1 K. 8. 46 land of enemy, far or *n.*
2 Chr. 21. 16 Arabians, that were *n.*
Job 41. 16 One is so *n.* to another
Ps 22. 11 for trouble is *n.*, for there
119. 151 Thou art *n.*, O Lord
Prov. 10. 14 mouth of fool. is *n.* d.
Isa. 13. 22 her time is *n.* to come
51. 5 My righteousness is *n.* my
56. 1 my salvation is *n.* to come
Jer. 48. 16 calamity of Moab is *n.*
52. 25 them *n.* the king's person
Lam. 4. 18 our end is *n.*, days fulfil
Ezek. 7. 7 the day of trouble is *n.*
30. 3 is *n.*, even the day of Lord is
Dan. 9. 7 all Israel, that are *n.*
Joel 3. 14 day of L. is *n.* in valley
Obad. 15 day of Lord is *n.* upon
Zeph. 1. 14 great day of Lord is *n.*
Mat. 24. 33 know that it is *n.*, ev. at
Mark 13. 28 ye know that sum. is *n.*
John 4. 5 *n.* to parcel of ground
11. 54 unto country *n.* wilderness
Acts 10. 24 called toget. his *n.* fri.
See also **Came, Drew**, etc.
R. V. frequent changes to at, nigh
, etc.

Nearer. *Closer.*
Ruth 3. 12 is kinsman *n.* than I.
Rom. 13. 11 now is our salvation *n*

Necessary. *Needful.*
Job 23. 12 words more than *n.* for
Acts 13. 46 *n.* word of G. be spok.
15. 28 gr. burden than *n.* things
28. 10 they laded us with things *n*
1 Cor. 12. 22 members feeble are *n.*
2 Cor. 9. 5 thought it *n.* to exhort
Phil. 2. 25 supposed it *n.* to send
Tit. 3. 14 good works for *n.* uses

Heb. 9. 23 It was therefore *n.* that
R. V. 28. 10 we needed

Necessity. *Need.*
Luke 23. 17 of *n.* he must release
Acts 24. 34 have min. unto my *n.*
Rom. 12. 13 Distr. to *n.* of saints
1 Cor. 7. 37 having no *n.*, but pow.
9. 16 for *n.* is laid upon me ; yea
2 Cor. 6. 4 in afflictions, in *n.*, in
9. 7 give not grudgingly, or of *n.*
12. 10 I take pleasure in *n.* in per.
Phil. 4. 16 ye sent again unto my *n.*
Phile. 14 should not be as of *n.*
Heb. 7. 12 is made of *n.* a change
9. 16 there must of *n.* be death
R. V. Luke 23. 17 ——; Heb. 8. 3
necessary ; Phil. 4. 16 need

Neck. *Neck, throat.*
Gen. 27. 16 upon smooth of his *n.*
27. 40 sh. break yoke from off *n.*
33. 4 fell on his *n.* and kissed him
41. 42 put gold chain about his *n.*
49. 8 be in *n.* of thine enemies
Ex. 13. 13 thou shalt break his *n.*
Lev. 5. 8 wring his head from *n.*
Deut. 28. 48 put yoke upon thy *n.*
31. 27 I know thy reb. and stiff *n.*
Josh. 10. 24 put your feet upon *n.*
Judg. 8. 21 ornaments on camel's *n.*
2 Sam. 22. 41 giv. *n.* of mine enem.
2 K. 17. 14 not hear, but harden.
2 Chr. 36. 13 but he stiffened his *n.*
Neh. 9. 16 hardened their *n.*, and
Job 16. 12 he hath taken me by *n.*
39. 19 hast cloth. his *n.* wi. thun.?
41. 22 In his *n.* remain. strength
Ps. 75. 5 speak not with stiff *n.*
Prov. 29. 1 oft reprov., hardeneth *n.*
S. of S. 4. 4 *n.* is like tower of D.
7. 4 *n.* is as tower of ivory ; thine
Isa. 8. 8 he shall reach even to the *n.*
48. 4 thy *n.* is an iron sinew, and
66. 3 as if he cut off a dog's *n.*
Jer. 27. 2 yokes, put them on *n.*
30. 8 break yoke from off thy *n.*
Lam. 5. 5 Our *n.* are under persec.
Ezek. 21. 29 br. thee on *n.* of slain
Dan. 5. 7 chain of gold about *n.*
Hos. 10. 11 passed upon her fair *n.*
Mic. 2. 3 shall not remove your *n.*
Hab. 3. 13 disc. foundation to the *n.*
Mat. 18. 6 bet. mills. hang. about *n.*
Mark 9. 42 ; Luke 17. 2
Luke 15. 20 fell on *n.*, and kiss. him
Acts 15. 10 yoke on *n.* of disciples
20. 37 fell on Paul's *n.*, and kissed
Rom. 16. 4 laid down their own *n.*

Necromancer. *Magician.*
Deut. 18. 11 charmer, wizard, or *n.*

Need (*n.*). *Want, necessity.*
Deut. 15. 8 lend him suf. for his *n.*
1 Sam. 21. 15 Have I *n.* of mad men
Ez. 6. 9 that which they have *n.* of
Prov. 31. 12 sh. have no *n.* of spoil
Mat. 3. 14 I have *n.* to be baptized
Mark 11. 3 the Lord hath *n.* of him
Luke 9. 11 healed that had *n.* of h.
John 13. 29 Buy that we have *n.* of
Acts 4. 35 to ev. man as he had *n.*
1 Cor. 7. 36 if bor. require, let him
Phil. 4. 19 God shall supply your *n.*
1 Thes. 5. 1 no *n.* that I write unto
Heb. 5. 12 *n.* that one teach you
1 John 3. 17 seeth his bro. have *n.*
Rev. 21. 23 city had no *n.* of sun
1 Pet 1. 6 for a season, if *n.* be, ye

Need (*v.*). *To lack, require.*
2 Chr. 2. 16 much as thou shalt *n.*
Mat. 9. 12 whole *n.* not physician
Mark 14. 16 What *n.* we any further
Luke 15. 7 which *n.* no repentance
John 16. 30 not that any man ask
Eph. 4. 28 ha. to give to him that *n.*
1 Thes. 1. 8 *n.* not speak of any.
Rev. 22. 5 and they *n.* no candle

Needful. *Suitable, required.*
Ez. 7. 20 *n.* for the house of God
Luke 10. 42 But one thing is *n.* : and
Acts 15. 5 was *n.* to circumcise them
Phil. 1. 24 abide in flesh more *n.*
Jas. 2. 16 give not things *n.* for body
Jude 3 was *n.* for me to write unto
R. V. Jude 3 was constrained

Needle. *Needle.*
Mat. 19. 24 to go through eye of *n.*
Mark 10, 25 ; Luke 18. 25

R. V. Mat. 19. **24** ; Mark 10. **25**
needle's eye

Needlework. *Embroidery.*
Ex. 26. 36 linen, wrought with *n.w.*
Judg. 5. 30 divers colours of *n., w.*
Ps. 45. 14 brought in raiment of *n.w.*
R. V. Ex. 26. 36 ; 27. 16 ; 28. 39 ; 36.
37 ; 38. 18 ; 39. 29 work of embroid-
erer ; Judg. 5. 30 embroidery ; Ps.
45. 14 broidered work.

Needs. *Of necessity.*
Mat. 18. 7 *n.* be that offences come
Mark 13. 7 *n.*, but end shall not be
Luke 14. 18 I must *n.* go see it
John 4. 4 must *n.* go through Sam.
Acts 1. 16 script. must *n.* been fulf.
17. 3 C. must *n.* have suffered and
21. 22 mul. must *n.* come together
Rom. 13. 5 ye must *n.* be subject
2 Cor. 11. 30 If I must *n.* glory, I
R. V. Acts 17. 3 behoved ; 21.
22 ——.

Needy. *Needful, poor.*
Deut. 15. 11 open thy hand to *n.*
Job 24. 14 killeth poor and *n.*, and
Ps. 9. 18 *n.* not always be forgotten
37. 14 to cast down poor and *n.*
70. 5 But I am poor and *n.*, make
72. 13 He shall spare poor and *n.*
82. 3 do justice to afflicted and *n.*
Prov. 30. 14 to devour poor and *n.*
31. 20 she reacheth her hand to *n.*
Isa. 14. 30 the *n.* shall lie in safety
Jer. 22. 16 He judged cause of *n.*
Ezek. 16. 49 strengthen hand of *n.*
Am. 8. 4 hear, ye that swal. up *n.*
8. 6 may buy the *n.* for pair of shoes
R. V. Ps. 82. 5 destitute

Neesings. *Sneezings.*
Job 41. 18 by his *n.* light doth sh.

Neglect. *Overlook, disregard.*
Mat. 18. 17 if he shall *n.* to hear
Acts 6. 1 because widows were *n.*
Col. 2. 23 humility, and *n.* of body
1 Tim. 4. 14 *N.* not the gift in thee
Heb. 2. 3 How escape, if we *n.* sal.
R. V. Mat. 18. 17 ; refuse ; Col. 2.
23 severity of.

Negligent. *Deceived.*
2 Chr. 29. 11 My sons, be not now *n.*

Careless of.
2 Pet. 1. 12 will not be *n.* to put
R. V. 2 Pet. 1. 12 shall be ready

Neigh. *Cry aloud, bellow.*
Jer. 5. 8 *n.* after his neighbour's wife

Neighbour. *Near one, friend,*
companion.
Ex. 3. 22 ev. wom. bor. of her *n.*
20. 16 not bear false wit. against *n.*
20. 17 shalt not covet *n.'s* house
Lev. 19. 13 shalt not defraud thy *n.*
Deut. 19. 14 not remove *n.'s* land.
27. 24 cursed he that smiteth his *n.*
Josh. 20. 5 he smote *n.* unwittingly
Ruth 4. 7 plucked shoe, gave to. . *n.*
4. 17 her *n.* gave it a name .. Obed
1 Sam. 15. 28 given it to *n.* of thine
2 Sam. 12. 11 give it unto thy *n.*
1 K. 20. 35 unto *n.* in word of L.
2 K. 4. 3 bor. vessels of all thy *n.*
2 Chr. 6. 22 If man sin against *n.*
Job 12. 4 am as one mocked of *n.*
31. 9 have laid wait at *n.'s* door
Ps. 12. 2 speak van. ev. one with *n.*
79. 4 we are bec. reproach to *n.*
Prov. 3. 28 Say not unto *n.*, Go
3. 29 Devise not evil against *n.*
11. 9 hypocrite destroyeth his *n.*
14. 21 that despiseth *n.* sinneth
24. 28 Be not witness against *n.*
27. 10 bet. *n.* near, than bro. far
Eccl. 4. 4 this man is envied of *n.*
Isa. 41. 6 helped every one his *n.*
Jer. 9. 4 Take heed every one of *n.*
34. 15 proclaim. lib. ev. man to *n.*
Ezek. 23. 12 doted on Assyr. her *n.*
Hab. 2. 15 Woe to him that giv. *n.* d.
Zech. 3. 10 shall ye call ev. man *n.*
Mat. 5. 43 love thy *n.*, hate enemy
19. 19 thou shalt love *n.* as thyself
22. 39 ; Mark 12. 31 ; Luke 10. 27 ;
Rom. 13. 9 ; Gal. 5. 14 ; Jas. 2. 8
Luke 14. 12 call not thy rich *n.* lest
15. 9 she calleth her friends and *n.*
John 9. 8 *n.* . . said, Is not this he
Acts 7. 27 he that did his *n.* wrong

Rom. 13. 10 Love work. no ill to *n.*
15. 2 Let every one please his *n.*
Eph. 4. 25 speak ev. man truth wi. *n.*
Heb. 8. 11 not teach ev. man his *n.*
R. V. 1 K. 20. 35 fellow ; Ps. 15. 3 ;
Prov. 19. 4 friend ; Heb. 8. 11 fel-
low-citizen

Neighing. *Crying out.*
Jer. 8. 16 land trem. at sound of *n.*
13. 27 seen thy adulteries and *n.*

Neither. *Not either.*
Gen. 45. 6 *n.* be earing nor harvest
Mat. 7. 6 *n.* cast pearls before swine
Etc., etc.
R. V. Frequent changes to, nor

Nephew. *Son's son, grandchild,*
successor.
Judg. 12. 14 Abdon had .. thirty *n.*
Job 18. 19 neither have son nor *n.*
Isa. 14. 22 cut off from Bab. . . *n.*
1 Tim. 5. 4 if wid. have chil. or *n.*
R. V. Judg. 12. 14 ; Job 18. 19 ; Isa.
14. 22 son's sons ; 1 Tim. 5. 4
grandchildren

Nest. *Nest, bed, retreat.*
Num. 24. 21 puttest thy *n.* in rock
Deut. 32. 11 As eag. stirreth her *n.*
Job 29. 18 I shall die in my *n.*
39. 27 and make her *n.* on high?
Ps. 84. 3 the swallow *n.* for herself
104. 17 Where birds make their *n.*
Prov. 27. 8 As bird that wan. from *n.*
Isa. 10. 14 hath found *n.* in riches
16. 2 as a wan. bird cast out of *n.*
34. 15 There shall the owl make *n.*
Jer. 48. 28 like dove that maketh *n.*
Ezek. 31. 6 All fowls made their *n.*
Obad. 4 tho. set thy *n.* among stars
Hab. 2. 9 may set his *n.* on high
Mat. 8. 20 the birds of air have *n.*
Luke 9. 58

Net. *Net, woven fabric, snare.*
Ex. 27. 4 upon *n.* make bra. rings
1 K. 7. 17 made *n.* of checker work
Job 18. 8 cast into *n.* by own feet
19. 6 God compass. me with his *n.*
Ps. 9. 15 in *n.* hid is their own foot
25. 15 pluck my feet out of the *n.*
35. 8 let his *n.* hid catch himself
57. 6 prepared a *n.* for my steps
140. 5 spread *n.* by the way side
Prov. 1. 17 in vain the *n.* is spread
29. 5 flattereth, spr. *n.* for his feet
Eccl. 7. 26 wh. heart is snares and *n.*
9. 12 as fishes taken in evil *n.*
Isa. 19 8 that spr. *n.* upon waters
51. 20 streets, as wild bull in *n.*
Lam. 1. 13 hath spr. *n.* for my feet
Ezek. 12. 13 *n.* will I spr. on him
26. 14 shalt be a place to spread *n.*
32. 3 shall bring thee up in my *n.*
Hos. 5 1 and *n.* spread upon Tabor
Mic. 7. 2 they hunt . . bro. with *n.*
Hab. 1. 15 catch them in their *n.*
Mat. 4. 20 straightway left their *n.*
4. 18 Jesus saw two breth. cast. *n.*
13. 47 kingdom of heaven is like *n.*
Mark 1. 19 in ship mend. their *n.*
Luke 5. 4 let down your *n.* for dr.
5. 6 fishes, and their *n.* brake
John 21. 6 Cast *n.* on the right side
21. 11 drew *n.* full of great fishes

Nether. *Lower, under.*
Ex. 19. 17 stood at *n.* part of mt.
Deut. 24. 6 No man take *n.* mills.
Josh. 15. 19 upper springs, and *n.*
18. 13 south side of *n.* Beth.-hor.
1 K. 9. 17 built Beth.-hor. the *n.*
1 Chr. 7. 24 ; 2 Chr. 8. 5
Job 41. 24 hard as *n.* millstone
Ezek. 31. 14 to *n.* parts of earth
31. 16 be comforted in *n.* parts
32. 24 gone down into *n.* parts
R. V. Deut. 24. 6 mill

Nethermost. *Lowermost.*
1 K. 6. 6 *n.* chamber was five cubits

Nettle. *Thorn, shrub, nettle.*
Job 30. 7 under *n.* they were gath.
Prov. 24. 31 *n.* had cov. face thereof
Isa. 34. 13 *n.* in fortresses thereof
Hos. 9. 6 *n.* shall possess them
Zeph. 2. 9 breed. of *n.* and salt pits

Network. *Wreathed work, lat-*
tice.
Ex. 27. 4 shalt make grate of *n. w.*
1 K. 7. 18 rows round upon one *n. w.*

7. 41 *n. w.* to cover the two bowls
Isa. 19. 9 that weave *n.w.*, be conf.
Jer. 52. 22 with *n.w.* and pomegran.
R. V. Isa. 19. 9 white cloths

Never. *Not ever, not.*
Gen. 41. 19 such as I *n.* saw in Egy.
Judg. 2. 1 will *n.* break my covenant
Ps. 31. 1 let me *n.* be ashamed
Prov. 27. 20 Hell a. destr. are *n.* full
Isa. 13.20 It shall *n.* be inhabited
Mat. 7. 23 profess., I *n.* knew you
9. 33 It was *n.* so seen in Israel
21. 42 Did ye *n.* read in scriptures
Mark 14.21 good he h. *n.* been born
Luke 15. 29 thou *n.* gavest me kid
John 7. 46 *N.* man spake like this
11. 26 believ. in me shall *n.* die
Acts 14. 8 cripple, who *n.* walked
1 Cor. 13. 8 Charity *n.* faileth, but
Heb. 13. 5 I will *n.* leave thee, nor
2 Tim. 3. 7 Ever lear., and *n.* able
2 Pet. 1. 10 things, ye shall *n.* fail

Nevertheless. *Notwithstanding.*
Lev. 11. 4 *N.* these shall ye not eat
Mat. 29. 39 *n.* not as I will, but as
Etc., etc.
R. V. Numerous changes to, but,
howbeit, etc.

New. *Fresh, recent, new.*
Ex. 1. 8 arose a *n.* king over Egypt
Lev. 23. 16 shall offer *n.* meat off.
Num. 28. 26 bring *n.* meat offering
Deut. 22. 8 Wh. thou build *n.* house
Josh. 9. 13 these bots. of wine w. *n.*
Judg. 5. 8 They chose *n.* gods; then
1 Sam. 6. 7 therefore make *n.* cart
2 Sam. 21. 16 girded with a *n.* sword
1 K. 11. 29 clad hims. with *n.* gar.
2 K. 4. 23 nei. *n.* moon nor sabbath
1 Chr. 13. 7 carried ark in *n.* cart
2 Chr. 8. 13 on sabbaths,a. *n.* moons
Ez 3. 5 both of *n.* moons, and
Neh. 10. 39 off. of *n.* wine and oil
Job 13. 19 to burst like *n.* bottles
Ps. 33. 3 Sing unto him a *n.* song
Prov. 3. 10 presses burst w. *n.* wine
Eccl. 1. 9 is no *n.* thing under sun
S. of S. 7. 13 pleas. fruits, *n.* and old
Isa. 62. 2 shalt be called *n.* name
65. 17 I create *n.* heav., and earth
Jer. 31. 31 I will make *n.* covenant
Lam. 3. 23 They are *n.* ev. morning
Ezek. 11. 19 will put *n.* sp. in you
Hos. 2. 11 feast days, ha. *n.* moons
Joel 1. 10 wasted, *n.* wine is dried
Am. 8. 5 When will *n.* moon be gone
Hag. 1. 11 drought upon *n.* wine
Zech. 9. 17 cheerful, and *n.* wine m.
Mat. 9. 16 *n.* cloth unto old garment
Mark 1. 27 what *n.* doctrine is this?
2. 22 wine be put into *n.* bottles
Luke 22. 20 This cup is *n.* testam.
John 13. 34 A *n.* ccm. I give you
Acts 17. 19 know what th. *n.* doct.
1 Cor. 11. 25 This cup is *n.* testam.
2 Cor. 3. 6 made us min. of *n.* test.
5. 17 in Christ, he is *n.* creature
5. 17 all things are become *n.*
Gal. 6. 15 nor uncirc., but *n.* creat.
Col. 3. 10 have put on the *n.* man
Eph. 2. 15 make in himself *n.* man
Heb. 9. 15 mediator of *n.* testam.
1 Pet. 2. 2 As *n.* born babes, desire
2 Pet. 3. 13 look for *n.* heav., a. earth
1 John 2. 8 *n.* com. I write you
2 John 5 I wrote a *n.* command.
Rev. 5. 9 sung a *n.* song, saying
21. 1 I saw *n.* heaven, *n.* earth
R. V. Joel 1. 5; 3. 18 sweet; Mat.
9. 16; Mark 2. 21; Luke 5. 38
fresh; Mat. 9. 16; Mark 2. 21 undressed; Neh. 10. 39; Mat. 26. 28;
Mark 2. 22; 14. 24 ——

Newly. *Of late, freshly.*
Deut. 32. 17 gods that came *n.* up
Judg. 7. 19 had *n.* set the watch
R. V. Deut. 32. 17 up of late

Newness. *Freshness.*
Rom. 6. 4 should walk in *n.* of life
7. 6 should serve in *n.* of spirit

News. *Tidings.*
Prov. 25. 25 so is *n.* from far coun.

Next. *Nearest, immediately after.*
Gen. 17. 21 at set time in *n.* year
Ex. 12. 4 neighbour *n.* his house
Num. 11. 32 all night, and *n.* day

Deut. 21. 3 city *n.* to the slain man
1 Sam. 30. 17 unto evening of *n.* day
2 K. 6. 29 said unto her on *n.* day
1 Chr. 5. 12 Shapham *n.*, and J.
2 Chr. 28. 7 Elkanah was *n.* to king
Esth. 10. 3 Jew was *n.* to k. Ahas.
Jonah 4. 7 when morn. rose *n.* day
Mat. 27. 62 *n.* day, that followed
Mark 1. 38 Let us go into *n.* towns
Luke 9. 37 *n.* day, when they come
John 1. 29 *n.* day John seeth Jesus
Acts 7. 26 *n.* day he showed himself
R. V. Deut. 21. 3, 6 nearest; Ruth
2. 20 near; 1 Chr. 5. 12; 16. 5; 2
Chr. 31. 12; Acts 28. 13 second;
Acts 7. 26; 16. 11; 20. 15 follow-
ing, Luke 12. 12; Acts 4. 3 morrow

Nigh. *Near.*
Lev. 25. 49 any that is *n.* of kin
Num. 24. 17 behold him, but not *n.*
Deut. 4. 7 who hath God so *n.* unto
1 K. 8. 59 *n.* unto Lord our God
1 Chr. 12. 40 they that were *n.* them
Esth. 9. 20 to provinces, *n.* and far
Ps. 34. 18 Lord is *n.* unto them that
85. 9 his salvation is *n.* them that
Joel 2. 1 for the day of Lord is *n.*
Mat. 24. 32 ye know summer is *n.*
Mark 5. 21 he was *n.* unto the sea
Luke 21. 20 desolation thereof is *n.*
21. 31 kingdom of God is *n.* at hand
John 6. 4 And the passover was *n.*
11. 18 Bethany was *n.* to Jerusa.
19. 42 sepulchre was *n.* at hand
Rom. 10. 8 The word is *n.* thee
Eph. 2. 13 made *n.* by blood of C.
Phil. 2. 27 was sick *n.* unto death
Heb. 6. 8 rejected, and *n.* to cursing
R. V. Gen. 47. 29; Ex. 24. 2; Lev.
21. 3; Luke 7. 12 near; Luke 21.
20; John 6. 4; Jas. 5. 8 at hand;
Mat. 15. 8 honoureth

Night. *Night.*
Gen. 1. 5 the darkness he called *n.*
1. 16 lesser light to rule the *n.*
Ex. 12. 30 Pharaoh rose up in *n.*
Lev. 6. 9 burning upon altar all *n.*
Num. 14. 14 in pillar of fire by *n.*
Deut. 1. 33 fire by *n.* to show way
Josh. 1. 8 shall meditate day and *n.*
Judg. 6. 40 And God did so that *n.*
Ruth 3. 13 Tarry this *n.*, and it sh.
1 Sam. 15. 11 Sam. cried un. L. all *n.*
2 Sam. 17. 16 Lodge not tnis *n.* in p.
1 K. 3. 5 appear. to Sol. in dr. by *n.*
2 K. 7. 12 the king arose in the *n.*
1 Chr. 9. 33 were employed day a. *n.*
2 Chr. 7. 12 L. appear. to Sol. by *n.*
Neh. 1. 6 pray before thee day a. *n.*
Esth. 6. 1 *n.* could not king sleep
Job 3. 7 let that *n.* be solitary
20. 8 chased away as vision of *n.*
Ps. 1. 2 doth he meditate day and *n.*
19. 2 *n.* unto *n.* showeth knowled.
14. 16 the day is thine, the *n.* also
90. 4 and as a watch in the *n.*
Prov. 31. 18 cand. go. not out by *n.*
Eccl. 2. 23 heart taketh rest by *n.*
S. of S. 3. 1 By *n.* I sought him
Isa. 21. 11 Watchman, what of *n.*?
Jer. 6. 5 Arise, let us go by *n.*
36. 30 be cast out in *n.* to the frost
Lam. 2. 19 Arise, cry out in the *n.*
Dan. 5. 30 that *n.* was Belsh. king
Hos. 7. 6 their baker sleepeth all *n.*
Am. 5. 8 maketh day dark with *n.*
Obad. 5 if th. came, if robbers by *n.*
Jonah 4. 10 came up in *n.*, and per.
Zech. 1. 8 I saw by *n.*, and behold
Mat. 4. 2 fasted forty days and *n.*
28. 13 His disciples came by *n.*
Mark 5. 5 *n.* and day, he was in m.
Luke 2. 8 keep. watch ov. flock by *n.*
5. 5 Master, we have toiled all *n.*
John 3. 2 Nico. came to Jesus by *n.*
Acts 9. 25 disciples took him by *n.*
26. 7 inst. serving God day and *n.*
Rom. 13. 12 The *n.* is far spent, the
1 Cor. 11. 23 Lord Jesus, same *n.*
2 Thes. 3. 10 *N.* and day pray. ex.
5. 2 Lord so cometh thief in the *n.*
2 Thes. 3. 8 wrought wi. labour all *n.*
1 Tim. 5. 5 con. in prayers *n.* aud d.
2 Tim. 1. 3 remem. in pray. *n.* and d.
2 Pet. 3. 10 will come as thief in *n.*
Rev. 7. 15 serve him day and *n.*

21. 25 there shall be no *n.* there
R. V. Lev. 6. 20 evening; Isa.
21. 4; 59. 10 twilight; Judg. 19.
13; Mat. 27. 64; Mark 14. 27; 2
Pet. 3. 10 ——

Night-hawk. *Owl, swallow,
cuckoo.*
Lev. 11. 16 the *n. h.*, and cuckoo
Deut. 14. 15

Night season. *Night.*
Job 30. 17 pierced me in the *n. s.*
Ps. 16. 7 instruct me in the *n. s.*

Night watches. *Night.*
Ps. 63. 6 I med. on thee in *n. w.*
119. 148 prevent *n. w.* to meditate

Nine. *Nine.*
Gen. 5. 3 Adam liv. *n.* h. and th. y'rs
Ex. 38. 24 gold was tw. and *n.* tal.
Lev. 25. 8 unto thee for. and *n. y.*
Num. 34. 13 to give unto *n.* tribes
Deut. 3. 11 *n.* cubits was the length
Josh. 13. 7 inheritance un. *n.* tribes
Judg. 4. 3 had *n.* hundred chariots
2 Sam. 24. 8 came at end of *n.* mo.
2 K. 14. 2 Am. reign. tw. and *n.* y'rs
1 Chr. 3. 8 Eli. and Eliphelet, *n.*
2 Chr. 29. 1 H. reign. tw. and *n.* y.
Ez. 2. 8 children of Zattu, *n.* hun.
Neh. 11. 1 *n.* parts .. in oth. cities
Luke 17. 17 but where are the *n.*?

Nineteen. *Nine and ten.*
Gen. 11. 25 Nahor liv. h. and *n.* y'rs
Josh. 19. 38 *n.* cities with their vil.
2 Sam. 2. 30 lacked of D's ser. *n.* m.

Nineteenth. *Nine and tenth.*
2 K. 25. 8 is *n.* year of king Nebuch.
1 Chr. 24. 16 the *n.* to Pethahiah
Jer. 52. 12 was *n.* year of Nebuchad.

Ninety. *Ninety.*
Gen. 5. 9 And Enos lived *n.* years
1 Sam. 4. 15 Eli was *n.* and eight
1 Chr. 9. 6 breth., six hun. and *n.*
Ez. 2. 20 chil. of Gibhar, *n.* and f.
Neh. 7. 25 chil. of Gibeon, *n.* and f.
Jer. 52. 23 *n.* and six pomegranates
Ezek. 41. 12 length thereof *n.* cubi.
Dan. 12. 11 thou. two hun. *n.* days
Mat. 18. 12 not leave *n.* and nine
Luke 15. 7 over *n.* and nine just per.

Ninth. *Ninth.*
Lev. 25. 22 eat of fruit until *n.* y'r
Num. 7. 60 On *n.* day of Abidan
2 K. 17. 6 In *n.* year of Hoshea
1 Chr. 27. 12 *n.* captain for *n.* mo.
2 Chr. 16. 12 in thirty and *n.* year
Ez. 10. 9 It was the *n.* month, on
Jer. 39. 2 in fourth month, *n.* day
Ezek. 24. 1 Again in the *n.* year
Hag. 2. 10; Zech. 7. 1 the *n.* mo.
Mat. 2. 5 went out about *n.* hour
Mark 15. 34 at *n.* hour Jesus cried
Luke 23. 44 over earth until *n.* hour
Acts 10. 30 at *n.* hour I prayed in
Rev. 21. 20 eighth, beryl, *n.*, a topaz

Nitre. *Nitre, lye.*
Prov. 25. 20 as vinegar upon *n.*, so is
Jer. 2. 22 tho. thou wash me with *n.*
R. V. Jer. 2. 22 lye

No. *No, not any.*
Gen. 15. 3 thou hast given *n.* seed
Mat. 6. 34 Take *n.* thought for mor.
Etc., etc.

Noble. *Prince, well born, leader.*
Ex. 24. 11 *n.* of children of Israel
Num. 21. 18 *n.* of people digged it
Judg. 5. 13 have dominion over *n.*
1 K. 21. 8 *n.* that were in his city
2 Chr. 23. 20 *n.*, and gover. of peo.
Ez. 4. 10 rest whom *n.* Asnap. bro.
Neh. 5. 7 I rebuked *n.*, and rulers
Esth. 6. 9 one of king's *n.* princes
Job 29. 10 The *n.* hold their peace
Ps. 83. 11 Make their *n.* like Oreb
Prov. 8. 16 By me prin. rule, and *n.*
Eccl. 10. 17 king is the son of *n.*
Isa. 13. 2 go into the gates of the *n.*
34. 12 call *n.* thereof to kingdom
Jer. 39. 6 k. of Babylon slew all *n.*
Jonah 3. 7 by decree of k. and *n.*
Nah. 3. 18 thy *n.* shall dwell in dust
Acts 16. 11 These more n. th. those
26. 5 I am not mad, *n.* Festus
1 Cor. 1. 26 not many *n.*, are called
R. V. 43. 14 as fugitives; Jer. 30.
21 prince; Nah. 3. 18 worthless;
Acts 24. 3; 26. 25 excellent

Nobleman. *Kingly, well-born.*
Luke 19. 12 *n.* went into far country
John 4. 46 there was a certain *n.*
4. 49 the *n.* saith unto him, Sir

Noise (*n.*). *Sound, voice, din.*
Ex. 20. 18 peo. heard *n.* of trumpet
Josh. 6. 10 not shout, nor make *n.*
Judg. 5. 11 are delivered from *n.*
1 Sam. 4. 6 Philistines heard the *n.*
1 K. 1. 41 Wherefore is this *n.* of
2 K. 7. 6 *n.* of char.; *n.* of horses
1 Chr. 15. 28 making *n.* with psalte.
2 Chr. 23. 12 Ath. heard *n.* of peo.
Ez. 3. 13 the *n.* of the shout of joy
Job 36. 29 or *n.* of his tabernacle?
37. 2 Hear atten. the *n.* of his voice
Ps. 33. 3 play skilfully with loud *n.*
42. 7 Deep call. unto deep at *n.*
59. 6 they make a *n.* like a dog
66. 1 Make a joyful *n.* unto God
81. 1; 95. 1; 98. 4; 100. 1
93. 4 mightier than the *n.* of waters
Isa. 13. 4 *n.* of a multi. in mountains
Jer. 49. 21 earth is moved at the *n.*
Lam. 2. 7 made *n.* in house of Lord
Ez. 1. 24 like *n.* of great waters
Joel 2. 5 like *n.* of flame of fire
Am. 5. 23 take from me *n.* of songs
Mic. 2. 12 they shall make great *n.*
Nah. 3. 2 *n.* of whip, *n.* of wheels
Zeph. 1. 10 *n.* of cry from fish g.
Zech. 9. 15 shall drink and make *n.*
Mat. 9. 23 Je. saw people making *n.*
2 Pet 3. 10 heav. pass with great *n.*
Rev. 6. 1 heard the *n.* of thunder
R. V. Ex. 20. 18; Jer. 10. 22; Rev.
6. 1 voice; 1 Sam. 14. 19; Isa. 66.
6 tumult; Job 36. 29 thunderings;
Ps. 65. 7; Isa. 17. 12 roaring; 1
Chr. 15. 28 aloud; Ps. 55. 2 moan;
98. 4 break forth; Jer. 4. 19 dis-
quieted; Ezek. 43. 2 sound

Noise (*v.*). *Bear, spread.*
Josh. 6. 27 Joshua's fame was *n.*
Mark 2. 1 it was *n.* that he was in ho
Luke 1. 65 their sayings were *n.* ab.
Acts 2. 6 when this was *n.* abroad
R. V. Acts 2. 6 sound was heard

Noisome. *Hurtful, evil, bad.*
Ps. 91. 3 deliv. from *n.* pestilence
Ezek. 14. 15 cause *n.* beasts to pass
14. 21 send famine and *n.* beasts
Rev. 16. 2 there fell . . *n.* sore upon

None. *No one, not any.*
Gen. 23. 6 *n.* of us shall withhold
Isa. 45. 21 there is *n.* besides me
Acts 4. 12 *n.* other name under hea.
Etc., etc.

Noon. *Midday.*
Gen. 43. 16 shall dine with me at *n.*
Deut. 28. 29 grope at *n.* as the blind
2 Sam. 4. 5 Ishbosh. lay on bed at *n.*
1 K. 18. 27 at *n.*, Elijah mocked th.
2 K. 4. 20 sat on her knees till *n.*
Job 11. 17 age be clearer than *n.* d.
Ps. 55. 17 and at *n.*, will I pray and
S. of S. 1. 7 mak. flock to rest at *n.*
Isa. 16. 3 as the night in midst of *n.*
59. 10 stumble at *n.* as in the night
Jer. 6. 4 arise, and let us go up at *n.*
Am. 8. 9 cause sun to go down at *n.*
Zeph. 2. 4 drive out Ashdod at *n.*
Acts 22. 6 come nigh Damas. ab. *n.*
R. V. Job 5. 14; Ps. 55. 17 noonday

Nor. *And not, also not.*
Judg. 11. 34 had nei. son *n.* daugh.
Mat. 10. 9 Provide nei. gold *n.* silver
Heb. 13 .5 never leave thee, *n.* fors.
Etc., etc.

North. *Northward.*
Gen. 24. 18 thou shalt spread to *n.*
Ex. 26. 35 shalt put table on *n.* side
Lev. 1. 11 on the side of the altar *n.*
Num. 34. 7 this shall be *n.* border
Deut. 3. 27 lift up thine eyes *n. w.*
Josh. 8. 11 and pitched on *n.* side
Judg. 7. 11 Midianites were on *n.*
1 Sam. 14. 5 *n. w.* over against M.
1 K. 7. 25 oxen, looking towards *n.*
2 K. 16. 14 put it on *n.* side of altar
1 Chr. 9. 24 porters were toward *n.*
Job 26. 7 He stretched out the *n.*
37. 22 Fair weath. com. out of *n.*
Ps. 89. 12 *n.* and s. thou hast created
Prov. 25. 3 *n.* wind driv. away rain
Eccl. 1. 6 turneth about unto the *n.*

S. of S. 4. 16 Awake, O *n.* wind, and
Isa. 14. 31 shall come from *n.* sm.
43. 6 I will say to the *n.*, Give up
Jer. 1. 13 face thereof towards *n.*
4. 6 I will bring evil from the *n.*
Ezek. 1. 4 whirlw. came out of *n.*
Dan. 8. 4 saw the ram pushing *n. w.*
Am. 8. 12 from the *n.* even to east
Zeph. 2. 13 stretch hand against *n.*
Zech. 2. 6 flee from land of the *n.*
Luke 13. 29 they shall come from *n.*
Rev. 21. 13 on *n.*, three gates; on s

North-west.
Acts 27. 12 haven lieth toward *n. w.*

Nose. *Nose.*
Lev. 21. 18 not appr., th. hath flat *n.*
2 K. 19. 28 put my hook in thy *n.*
Job 40. 24 his *n.* pierceth through
41. 2 Canst put hook into his *n.*?
Ps. 115. 6 *n.* but they smell not
Prov. 30. 33 wring. of *n.* bring. blood
S. of S. 7. 4 *n.* is as tower of Leb.
7. 8 smell of thy *n.* like apples
Isa. 3. 21 Lord take away their *n.* j.
65. 5 These are smoke in my *n.*
Ezek. 8. 17 put branch to their *n.*
23. 25 they shall take away thy *n.*
R. V. S. of S. 7. 8 breath; Ezek.
39. 11 them that pass through

Nostril. *Nose hole.*
Gen. 2. 7 G. breathed into man's *n.*
Ex. 15. 8 with blast of *n.* wat. gath.
Num. 11. 20 eat, till come out at *n.*
2 Sam. 22. 9 went smoke out of *n.*
Job 4. 9 breath of his *n.* consumed
27. 3 the spirit of God is in my *n.*
Ps. 18. 8 went up a smoke out of *n.*
Isa. 2. 22 whose breath is in his *n.*
Lam. 4. 20 breath of *n.* was taken
Am. 4. 10 to come up unto your *n.*
R. V. Job 4. 9 anger; 39. 20 snorting

Not. *In no manner.*
Gen. 2. 5 was *n.* man to till ground
Mat. 5. 34 Swear *n.* at all; neither
Etc., etc.

Notable. *Worthy of note.*
Dan. 8. 5 and the goat had *n.* horn
Mat. 27. 16 they had a *n.* prisoner
Acts 2. 20 bef. *n.* day of L. cometh.
4. 16 *n.* miracle hath been done

Note (*n.*). *Notable.*
Rom. 16. 7 are of *n.* among apost.

Note (*v.*). *Write, mark.*
Isa. 30. 8 *n.* it in a book, that it
Dan. 10. 21 I will show which is *n.*
2 Thes. 3. 14 *n.* that man, and have
R. V. Isa. 30. 8 inscribe; Dan. 10.
21 inscribed

Nothing. *Not any thing.*
Gen. 11. 6 and *n.* will be restrained
Ex. 12. 2 seventh shall go for *n.*
Deut. 22. 26 But unto damsel do *n.*
Judg. 14. 6 he had *n.* in his hand
1 Sam. 25. 21 so that *n.* was missed
2 Sam. 24. 24 wh. doth cost me *n.*
1 K. 10. 21 it was *n.* account. of
Job 26. 7 He hangeth earth upon *n.*
Ps. 17. 3 hast tried me and find *n.*
Prov. 9. 13 foolish woman know. *n.*
Eccl. 5. 15 beggeth, and there is *n.*
Isa 34. 12 her princes shall be *n.*
Jer. 10. 24 lest thou bring me to *n.*
Lam. 1. 12 is it *n.* to you? all ye
Ezek. 13. 3 proph. th. have seen *n.*
Dan. 4. 35 inhabit. of earth as *n.*
Am. 3. 4 will lion cry, if he have *n.*
Hag. 2. 3 in comparison of it as *n.*?
Mat. 17. 20 *n.* shall be impossible
Mark 14. 61 held peace, and answ. *n.*
Luke 5. 5 toiled, and have taken *n.*
John 3. 27 man can receive *n.*, ex.
Acts 20. 20 I kept back *n.* profitab.
Rom. 14. 14 is *n.* unclean of itself
1 Cor. 4. 4 I know *n.* by myself
2 Cor. 12. 11 in *n.* am I behind the
Gal. 5. 2 Christ shall profit you *n.*
Phil. 1 20 hope, in *n.* I be ashamed
1 Tim. 6. 7 we brought *n.* into world
Tit. 1. 15 are defiled, in *n.* pure
Phil. 1. 4 without thy mind I do *n.*
Heb. 2. 8 left *n.* that is not put
Jas. 1. 4 and entire, wanting *n.*
3 John 7 taking *n.* of the Gentiles
Rev. 3. 17 sayest, I have need of *n.*

Notice. *Note, heed.*
2 Sam. 3. 36 all the people took *n.*

2 Cor. 9. 5 bounty, where. ye had *n*

Notwithstanding. *Nevertheless.*
Ex. 21. 21 *N.*, if he continue a day
Josh. 22. 19 *N.*, if land of your peo.
Judg. 4. 9 *n.* the journey that thou
2 Chr. 6. 9 *N.* thou shalt not build
Luke 10. 11 *n.*, be ye sure of this
Phil. 4. 14 *N.* ye have done well
Rev. 2. 20 *N.* I have a few things
R. V. Frequent changes to, but,
only, nevertheless, etc.

Nought. *Naught.*
Gen. 29. 15 should. th. serve for *n.*?
Deut. 28. 63 and bring you to *n.*
Neh. 4. 15 G. bro. their couns. to *n.*
Job 1. 9 Doth Job fear G. for *n.*?
Ps. 33. 10 bring. couns. of heath. to *n*
Prov. 1. 25 have set at *n.* my coun.
Isa. 41. 12 shall be as thing of *n.*
Am. 6. 13 Ye rejoice in thing of *n.*
Mal. 1. 10 do ye kindle fire for *n.*
Acts 5. 38 men, it will come to *n.*
1 Cor. 2. 6 princes, which come to *n.*
2 Thes. 3. 8 Neither eat bread for *n.*
Rev. 18. 17 in hour riches come to *n.*

Nourish. *Feed, support, cherish.*
Gen. 45. 11 there will I *n.* thee
2 Sam. 12. 3 had brought and *n.* up
Isa. 1. 2 *n.* and brought up children
44. 14 an ash, and rain doth *n.* it
Ezek. 19. 2 lioness, she *n.* her whelps
Dan. 1. 5 so *n.* them three years
Acts 7. 20 was *n.* in father's house
12. 20 their country was *n.* by the
Eph. 5. 29 *n.* and cherisheth it
1 Tim. 4. 6 *n.* in words of faith and
Jas. 5. 5 ye have *n.* your hearts as in
Rev. 12. 14 where she is *n.* for a time
R. V. Acts 12. 20 fed from

Nourisher. *Who nourishes.*
Ruth 4. 15 be *n.* of thine old age

Nourishment. R. V. *supplied*
Col. 2. 19 having *n.* ministered, knit

Novice. *Newly planted*
1 Tim. 3. 6 not *n.*, lest being lifted

Now. *At once, this moment*
Gen. 27. 37 what shall I do *n.* unto
Mat. 27. 42 let him *n.* come down

Nowadays. *These times.*
1 Sam. 25. 10 be many servts. *n. a. d.*

Number (*n.*). *Number.*
Gen. 34. 30 I being few in *n.*, they
Ex. 12. 4 according to *n.* of souls
Lev. 25. 15 According to *n.* of years
Num. 1. 18 according to *n.* of names
Deut. 4. 27 shall be left few in *n.*
Josh. 4. 5 according to *n.* of tribes
Judg. 6. 5 they . . were without *n.*
1 Sam. 6. 4 *n.* of lords of Philistines
2 Sam. 2. 15 arose and went ov. by *n.*
1 Chr. 21. 5 Joab gave sum of *n.*
2 Chr. 12. 3 people were without *n.*
Ez. 1. 9 this the *n.* of them, thirty ch.
Neh. 7. 7 *n.* of peo. of Israel was
Esth. 9. 11 the *n.* of those slain in S.
Job 38. 21 *n.* of thy days is great
Ps. 147. 4 He telleth the *n.* of stars
S. of S. 6. 8 and virgins without *n.*
Isa. 40. 26 bring. out their host by *n.*
Jer. 2. 32 forgot. me days without *n.*
Ezek. 5. 3 take thereof few in *n.*
Dan. 9. 2 Dan. understood the *n.*
Hos. 1. 10 *n.* of Israel be as sand
Joel 1. 6 nation strong, without *n.*
Mark 10. 46 disciples and *n.* of peo.
Luke 22. 3 Judas, being of the *n.*
John 6. 10 sat d., in *n.* five thousand
Acts 6. 7 *n.* of disciples multiplied
Rom. 9. 27 Though *n.* of chil. of Is.
2 Cor. 10. 12 not make ours. of *n.*
Rev. 5. 11 the *n.* was ten thousand
R. V. Mark 10. 46; Acts 1. 15 mul-
titude.

Number (*v.*). *Count, reckon.*
Gen. 16. 10 not be *n.* for multitude
Ex. 38. 25 silver of them *n.* of cong.
Lev. 25. 8 th. shalt *n.* seven sabbaths
Num. 1. 3 thou and Aaron shall *n.*
Deut. 16. 9 sev. weeks shalt thou *n.*
Josh. 8. 10 Joshua *n.* the people
Judg. 20. 15 chil. of Benj. were *n.*
1 Sam. 13. 15 Saul *n.* the people
2 Sam. 18. 1 David *n.* the people
1 K. 3. 8 that cannot be *n.*, nor coun.
2 K. 3. 6 Jehoram *n.* all Israel
1 Chr. 21. 17 command. peo. to be *n*

2 Chr. 5. 6 could not be told nor *n*.
Ez. 1. 8 *n*. them unto Sheshbazzar
Job 14. 16 now thou *n*. my steps
Ps. 90. 12 teach us to *n*. of our days
Eccl. 1. 15 is wanting cannot be *n*.
Isa. 22. 10 have *n*. house of Jerus.
Jer. 33. 22 host of heav. cannot be *n*.
Dan. 5. 26 G. hath *n*. thy kingdom
Hos. 1. 10 sand, which cannot be *n*.
Mat. 10. 30 hairs of your head are *n*.
Mark 15. 28 was *n*. with transgres.
Luke 12. 7 very hairs . . are all *n*.
Acts 1. 17 he was *n*. with us, and had
Rev. 7. 9 multitu. no man could *n*.
R. V. 2 Sam. 24. 2 sum ; Josh. 8.
10 ; 1 K. 20. 15, 26, 27 ; 2 K. 3. 6
mustered ; 1 Tim. 5. 9 enrolled.
Numbering. *Counting.*
Gen. 41. 49 corn, until he left *n*.
2 Chr. 2. 17 after *n*. wherewith Da.
Nurse (*n*.). *Nourisher.*
Gen. 24. 59 sent away Rebek. and *n*.
Ex. 2. 7 Shall I call to thee a *n*.
Ruth 4. 16 and became *n*. unto it
2 Sam. 4. 4 his *n*. took him up, fled
2 K. 11. 2 they hid him and his *n*.
2 Chr. 22 .11 put him and *n*. in bed c.
1 Thes. 2. 7 *n*. cherisheth her chil.
Nurse (*v*.). *Suckle, nourish.*
Ex. 2. 7 that she may *n*. the child
Num. 11. 12 as *n*. father beareth chi.
Isa. 60. 4 thy daughters shall be *n*.
R. V. Isa. 60. 4 carried in arms
Nurture. R. V. *chastening.*
Eph. 6. 4 br. them up in *n*. of Lord
Nut. *Nut.*
Gen. 43. 11 present, *n*. and almonds
S. of S. 6. 11 went into garden of *n*.

O.

O, Oh (*in appeal*).
Ex. 32. 31 *Oh*, this peo. have sinned
Mat. 15. 28 *O* wom. gr. is thy faith
Etc., etc.
Oak. *Oak, terebinth.*
Gen. 35. 4 Jacob hid them under *o*.
Josh. 24. 26 set it up under *o*., that
Judg. 6. 11 angel of L. sat under *o*.
2 Sam. 8. 9 head caught hold of *o*.
18. 10 saw Absalom hanged in *o*.
1 K. 13. 14 found him under an *o*.
Isa. 1. 30 ye shall be as an *o*. whose
44. 14 taketh the cypress and *o*.
Ezek. 6. 13 idols under ev. thick *o*.
Hos. 4. 13 they burn incense un. *o*.
Am. 2. 9 he was strong as the *o*.
Zech. 11. 2 howl, O ye *o*. of Bashan
Oath. *Sworn to, execration.*
Gen. 50. 25 Joseph took an *o*. of
Ex. 22. 11 *o*. of L. be between us
Lev. 5. 4 th. man pronounce wi. *o*.
Num. 5. 21 charge woman wi. an *o*.
Deut. 7. 8 because he would keep *o*.
Josh. 2. 20 will be quit of thine *o*.
Judg. 21. 5 they had made great *o*.
1 Sam. 14. 26 for peo. feared the *o*.
2 Sam. 21. 7 spared M. because of *o*.
1 K. 2. 43 Why hast not kept *o*. ?
1 Chr. 16. 16 mindful of *o*. of Israel
2 Chr. 15. 15 Judah rejoiced at *o*.
Neh. 5. 12 Neh. took *o*. of priests
Ps. 105. 9 and his *o*. unto Isaac
Eccl. 8. 2 in regard to the *o*. of God
Jer. 11. 5 That they may perf. *o*.
Ezek. 16. 59 which hast despised *o*.
Dan. 9. 11 *o*. writ. in law of Moses
Hab. 3. 9 ac. to the *o*. of the tribes
Zech. 8. 17 and love no false *o*., for
Mat. 5. 33 perform unto L. thine *o*.
26. 72 Peter, again he denied with *o*.
Mark 6. 26 sorry for his *o*'s sake
Luke 1. 73 The *o*. which he sware
Acts 2. 30 knowing G. had sworn *o*.
Heb. 6. 16 an *o*. for confirmation is
Jas. 5. 12 neither by any other *o*.
Obedience. *Hearing, submission.*
Rom. 1. 5 *o*. to faith among all
5. 19 so by *o*. of one shall many be
16. 19 your *o*. has come abroad
1 Cor. 14. 34 women to be under *o*.
2 Cor. 7. 15 he remember. *o*. of you
Phile. 21 confidence in thy *o*., I wr.
Heb. 5. 8 learned *o*. by things suf.
1 Pet. 1. 2 through sanctifi. unto *o*.
R. V. 1 Cor. 14. 34 subjection.
Obedient. *Submissive.*

Ex. 24. 7 all will we do, and be *o*.
Num. 27. 20 that congre. may be *o*.
Deut. 4. 30 if thou shalt be *o*. unto
2 Sam. 22. 45 hear, they shall be *o*.
Prov. 25. 12 w. reprover upon *o*. ear
Isa. 42. 24 nei. were they *o*. un. law
Acts 6. 7 comp. of priests were *o*.
Rom. 15. 18 wrought to make G. *o*
2 Cor. 2. 9 know whether ye be *o*.
Eph. 6. 5 Ser., be *o*. to them that
Phil. 2. 8 humb. himself, became *o*.
Tit. 2. 5 *o*. to their own husbands
1 Pet. 1. 14 As *o*. child., not fash.
R. V. Deut. 8. 20 ; Dan. 4. 30
hearken ; Num. 27. 20 ; 2 Sam. 22.
45 obey ; Tit. 2, 5, 9 subjection
Obeisance. *Bow down self.*
Gen. 37. 7 stood about, and made *o*.
37. 9 eleven stars made *o*. to
43. 28 bowed heads, and made *o*.
Ex. 18. 7 Moses went and did *o*.
2 Sam. 1. 2 fell to earth, and did *o*.
14. 4 fell on her face, and did *o*.
1 K. 1. 16 Bath. bowed, and did *o*.
2 Chr. 24. 7 came to pr., and made *o*.
Obey. *Hearken, submit.*
Gen. 22. 18 blessed, bec. thou hast *o*.
27. 8 my son, *o*. my voice according
28. 7 Jacob *o*. father and mother
Ex. 5. 2 Who is Lord, that I sh. *o*.
23. 21 Beware, and *o*. his voice
Deut. 11. 27 blessing, if ye *o*. the c.
11. 28 curse, if ye will not *o*. the c.
Josh. 5. 6 because they *o*. not voice
Judg. 2. 2 ye have not *o*. my voice
1 Sam. 8. 19 the people refused to *o*.
15. 22 to *o*. is better than sacrifice
1 K. 20. 36 because thou hast not *o*.
2 K. 18. 12 because they *o*. not voice
1 Chr. 29. 23 and all Israel *o*. him
2 Chr. 11. 4 they *o*. words of Lord
Neh. 9. 17 our fathers refused to *o*.
Job 36. 11 If they *o*. and serve him
36. 12 if th. *o*. not, they shall perish
Ps. 18. 44 they hear, they shall *o*. me
Prov. 5. 13 not *o*. voice of teachers
Isa. 11. 14 chil. of Ammon shall *o*.
Jer. 3. 25 have not *o*. voice of Lord
11. 3 Cursed be man that *o*. not
Dan. 7. 27 and all dominions shall *o*.
Zeph. 3. 2 She *o*. not the voice, she
Hag. 1. 12 Zer. *o*. voice of the Lord
Zech. 6. 15 if ye will diligently *o*.
Mat. 8. 27 even winds and sea *o*.
Mark 1. 27 spirits, and they *o*. him
Luke 17. 6 sea, and it should *o*. you
Acts 5. 29 *o*. God rather than m.
Rom. 2. 8 truth, but *o*. unrighteous.
Gal. 3. 1 that ye should not *o*. truth
Eph. 6. 1 Children, *o*. your parents
Phil. 2. 12 as ye have always *o*.
Col. 3. 22 Servants, *o*. your masters
2 Thes. 1. 8 that *o*. not the gospel
Tit. 3. 1 in mind .. to *o*. magistrates
Heb. 5. 9 salvation to all that *o*. him
Jas. 3. 3 mouths, that they may *o*.
1 Pet. 3. 1 if any *o*. not the word
3. 6 Even as Sarah *o*. Abraham
R. V. Ex. 5. 2 ; 23. 21, 22 ; Deut.
11. 27, 28 ; 28. 62 ; Josh. 24. 24 ; 1
Sam. 8. 19 ; 12. 14, 15 ; Job 36. 11,
12 ; Jer. 7. 23 ; Rom. 10. 16
hearken ; Josh. 5. 6 ; 22. 2 ; Judg.
2. 2 ; 6. 10 ; 1 Sam. 28. 21 ; Jer. 17.
23, 28 ; 2 Chr. 11. 4 hearkened ;
Jer. 11. 3 ; 12. 17 hear ; Gal.
3. 1 ——
Obeying. *Hearkening, submitting.*
Judg. 2. 17 *o*. commandments of L.
1 Sam. 15. '22 as in *o*. voice of Lord
1 Pet. 1. 22 in *o*. through the Spirit
R. V. 1 Pet. 1. 22 obedience
Object. *Speak against.*
Acts 24. 19 *o*., if th. had ought ag.
Oblation. *Offering.*
Lev. 2. 4 an *o*. of a meat offering
7. 38 to offer their *o*. to the Lord
Num. 31. 5 We have brought an *o*.
2 Chr. 31. 14 distribute of Lord
Isa. 1. 13 Bring no more vain *o*.
45. 16 peo. of land shall give *o*.
Jer. 14. 12 offer burnt off. and *o*.
Dan. 2. 46 they should offer an *o*.
Obscure. *Dark, black.*
Prov. 20. 20 lamp put in *o*. darkness
Obscurity. *Blackness, darkness.*

Isa. 29. 18 blind shall see out of *o*.
58. 10 then shall thy light rise in *o*.
59. 9 wait for light, but behold *o*.
R. V. 58. 10 ; 59. 9 darkness
Observation. *Watching.*
Luke 17. 20 king. com. not with *o*.
Observe. *Watch, heed, keep.*
Gen. 37. 11 his father *o*., saying
Ex. 12. 17 *o*. feast of unl. bread
Lev. 19. 37 shall ye *o*. my statutes
Num. 28. 2 shall ye *o*. to offer unto
Deut. 6. 3 Hear, O Israel, and *o*.
24. 8 heed, that thou *o*. dilligent.
Josh. 1. 7 that thou mayest *o*. to
Judg. 13. 14 commanded let her *o*.
2 Sam. 11. 16 when Joab *o*. the city
1 K. 20. 33 the men did diligently *o*.
2 K. 17. 37 ye shalt *o*. to do for ever
2 Chr. 7. 17 and shalt *o*. my statutes
Neh. 1. 5 mercy for them that *o*.
Ps. 107. 43 Who. is wise, and will *o*.
119. 34 yea, I shall *o*. it with my
Isa. 42. 20 Seeing, but thou *o*. not
Jer. 8. 7 the crane and swal. *o*. time
Ezek. 20. 18 nei. *o*. their judgments
Jonah 2. 8 they that *o*. lying vanities
Mat. 23. 3 whatso. they bid you *o*.
28. 20 teaching to *o*. all things
Mark 10. 20 all these have I *o*. fr.
Acts 21. 25 they *o*. no such thing
Gal. 4. 10 Ye *o*. days and months
1 Tim. 5. 21 that thou *o*. these th.
R. V. Lev. 19. 26 ; 2 K. 21. 6 ; 2
Chr. 33. 6 practise ; Deut. 16. 13 ;
2 Chr. 7. 17 ; Neh. 1. 5 ; Ps. 105.
45 keep ; Prov. 23. 26 delight in ;
Hos. 14. 8 ; John 2. 8 regard ; Gen.
37. 11 ; Mark 6. 20 kept ; Ps. 107.
43 give heed ; Hos. 13. 7 watch ;
Mat. 23. 3 ; Acts 21. 25 ——
Observer. R. V. *who practises.*
Deut. 18. 10 thou shalt not be *o*.
18. 14 these nat. hearkened to *o*.
Obstinate. *Hard, sharp.*
Deut. 2. 30 L. G. made his heart *o*.
Isa. 48. 4 I know that thou art *o*.
Obtain. *Reach, attain, acquire.*
Gen. 16. 2 I may *o*. children by her
Neh. 2. 6 I *o*. leave of the king
Esth. 2. 9 and she *o*. kind. of him
Prov. 8. 35 shall *o*. favour of Lord
12. 2 good man *o*. favour of Lord
Isa. 35. 10 they shall *o*. joy and glad.
Dan. 11. 21 he shall *o*. the kingdom
Hos. 2. 23 they had not *o*. mercy
Luke 20. 35 worthy to *o*. th. world
Acts 1. 17 had *o*. part of th. ministry
22. 28 gr. sum *o*. I this freedom
26. 22 having *o*. help of God, I
Rom. 11. 7 Israel hath not *o*. that
11. 7 the election hath *o*. it and
1 Cor. 9. 24 So run, that ye may *o*.
9. 25 do it to *o*. corruptible crown
Eph. 1. 11 we have *o*. inheritance
1 Thes. 5. 9 to *o*. salva. by our L.
1 Tim. 1. 13 but I *o*. mercy, because
2 Tim. 2. 10 that they may *o*. salva.
Heb. 1. 4 *o*. more excellent name
4. 16 grace, that we may *o*. mercy
9. 12 having *o*. eter. redemption
11. 35 might *o*. better resurrection
Jas. 4. 2 ye kill, and cannot *o*.
1 Pet. 2. 10 which had n. *o*. mercy
2 Pet. 1. 1 have *o*. precious faith
R. V. Luke 20. 35 ; 1 Cor. 9. 24 attain ; 1 Cor. 9. 25 ; Heb. 4. 16 ;
Acts 1. 17 receive ; Neh. 13. 6
asked
Obtaining. *Attaining.*
2 Thes. 2. 14 to *o*. of glory of our L.
Occasion. *Event, opportunity,
matter, cause or agency.*
Gen. 43. 18 he may seek *o*. ag. us
Deut. 22. 14 give *o*. of speech ag. h.
Judg. 9. 33 as thou shalt find *o*.
14. 4 he sought *o*. against Philis.
1 Sam. 10. 7 do as *o*. serve thee, for
2 Sam. 12. 14 given *o*. to enemies
Ez. 7. 20 shalt have *o*. to bestow
Job 33. 10 he findeth *o*. against me
Jer. 2. 24 in her *o*. who can turn
Ezek. 18. 3 not have *o*. any more
Dan. 6. 4 sought *o*. against Daniel
Rom. 7. 8 taking *o*. by command.
14. 13 put not *o*. to fall in bro's way
2 Cor. 5. 12 we give you *o*. to glo.

Gal. 5. 13 use not liberty for an o.
1 Tim. 5. 14 give none o. to adver.
1 John 2. 10 none o. of stumbling
Occasioned. *Brought about.*
1 Sam. 22. 22 o. death of all people
Occupation. *Work, trade.*
Gen. 41. 33 say, What is your o.?
Jonah 1. 8 What is thine o.? and
Acts 18. 3 hy o. were tent makers
R. V. Acts 18. 3 trade
Occupiers. *Traders, merchants.*
Ezek. 27. 27 o. of thy merchandise
Occupy. *Use, engage, fill, possess, carry on, ply.*
Ex. 38. 24 gold was o. for work
Judg. 16. 11 with new ropes never o.
Ezek. 27. 16 o. thy fairs with emer.
27. 21 they o. with thee in lambs
Luke 19. 13 said, O. till I come
1 Cor. 14. 16 o. room of unlearned
Heb. 13. 9 not prof. th. that have o.
R. V. Ex. 38. 24 used; Ezek. 27. 16, 19, 22 Luke 19. 13 trade, or traded; 1 Cor. 14. 16 filleth
Occurrent. *Falling, happening.*
1 K. 5. 4 is nei. adver. nor evil o.
Odd. *Not even.*
Num. 3. 48 o. num. to be redeemed
Odious. *Hateful.*
1 Chr. 19. 6 saw they made thems. o.
Prov. 30. 23 For o. wom wh. marr.
Odour. *Sweetness, savor.*
Lev. 26. 31 not smell sav. of sw. oil
2 Chr. 16. 14 in bed filled with o.
Esth. 2. 12 six months with sw. o.
Jer. 34. 5 shall burn o. for them
Dan. 2. 46 offer obla. and sweet o.
John 12. 3 filled with o. of ointment
Phil. 4. 18 an o. of a sweet smell
Rev. 5. 8 golden vials full of o.
18. 13 no man buyeth their o.
R. V. Jer. 34. 5 make burning; Rev. 5. 8: 18. 13 incense
Of. *Of, out of, from.*
Gen. 2. 7 God formed man o. dust
Mat. 3. 4 J. had rai. o. camel's hair
Etc., etc.
Off. *Away, not near, from.*
Gen. 24. 64 she lighted from o. cam.
Mat. 26. 58 Peter fol. him afar o.
Etc., etc.
Offence. *Sin, wrong, fault.*
Eccl. 10. 4 yielding pacifieth o.
Hos. 5. 15 till they acknowledge o.
2 Cor. 11. 7 Have I committed o.
Stumbling, stumbling block
1 Sam. 25. 31 be no o. of heart unto
Isa. 8. 14 be for rock of o. to Israel
Mat. 16. 23 thou art an o. unto me
18. 7 for it must be that o. come
Luke 17. 1 impos. but o. will come
Acts 24. 16 have consci. void of o.
Rom. 4. 25 was delivered for our o.
5. 15-20; 9. 33; 16. 17
1 Cor. 10. 32 Give none o. neither
2 Cor. 6. 3 Giving no o. in any th.
Gal. 5. 11 then is o. of cross ceased
Phil. 1. 10 be sincere and without o.
1 Pet. 2. 8 o., to th. which stumble
R. V. Mat. 16. 23; Gal. 5. 11 stumbling block; Mat. 18. 7 occasion; Rom. 4. 25; 5. 15-18 trespass; Mat. 18. 7; Luke 17. 1; Rom. 16. 17; 2 Cor. 6. 3 occasion for stumbling
Offend. *Sin, transgress, give displeasure, vex.*
Gen. 20. 9 and what have I o. thee
40. 1 had o. the king of Egypt
2 K. 18. 14 have o., return from me
2 Chr. 28. 13 we have o. against L.
Job. 34. 31 I will not o. any more
Ps. 73. 15 I should o. against genera
119. 165 which love law, nothing o.
Prov. 18. 19 A brother o. is harder
Jer. 2. 3 that devour him shall o.
Ezek. 25. 12 Edom hath greatly o.
Hos. 4. 15 har. yet, let not Judah o.
Hab. 1. 11 shall pass over and o.
Acts 25. 8 nor ag. Cæsar have I o.
Stumble, cause to stumble
Mat. 5. 29 if right eye o. pluck it
5. 30 if right hand o., cut it off
13. 57 they were o. in him. But J.
18. 6 whoso o. one of these lit. one.
Mark 6. 3 And they were o. at him

Luke 7. 23 blessed, who be not o.
John 6. 61 said, Doth this o. you?
Rom. 14. 21 whereby brother is o.
1 Cor. 8. 13 if meat make bro. to o.
2 Cor. 11. 29 is o. and I burn not?
Jas. 2. 10 keep whole law, yet o.
3. 2 For in many things we o. all
R. V. Gen. 20. 9; Jer. 37. 18; Acts 25. 8 sinned; Jer. 2. 3; Hab. 1. 11 guilty; Rom. 14. 21——. In most of the above references under the head of *Stumble*, the word stumble, stumbling or stumbleth has been introduced into R. V. text
Offender. *Sinner, erring one.*
1 K. 1. 21 I and son Sol. be count. o.
Isa. 29. 21 make man o. for word
Acts 25. 11 For if I be an o.. or
R. V. Acts 21. 11 wrong doer
Offer. *Go up toward, bring forward, present, tender, proffer.*
Gen. 8. 20 o. burnt offer. on altar
31. 54 Then Jacob o. sacrifice
Ex. 30. 9 sh. o. no strange incense
Lev. 14. 20 priest shall o. burnt off.
Num. 22. 40 Balak. o. ox. and sheep
Josh 8. 31 they o. burnt offerings
Judg. 6. 26 o burnt sac. with wood
1 Sam. 6. 14 o. kine a burnt offer.
2 Sam. 6. 17 David o. burnt offer.
1 K. 9. 25 three t. in year did Sol. o.
2 K. 3. 27 o. him a burnt offering
1 Chr. 21. 24 I will not o. burnt off.
2 Chr. 8. 12 then Sol. o. burnt off.
Ez. 3. 6 to o. burnt off. unto Lord
Job. 42. 8 o. yourself a burnt.
Ps. 66. 15 I will o. unto thee sacrifi.
Isa. 66. 3 he that o. an oblation, as
Jer. 48. 35 him that o. in high places
Ezek. 45. 1 ye shall o. oblation un. L.
Dan. 2. 46 sho. o. oblation to Daniel
Hos. 9. 4 not o. wine offer. to Lord
Am. 3. 5 Have ye o. me sacrifice
Hag. 2. 14 which they o. is unclean
Mal. 1. 7 Ye o. polluted bread upon
Mat. 5. 24 then come and o. thy gift
8. 4 o. gift Moses commanded
Mark 1. 44; Luke 5. 14
Luke 6. 29 one cheek, o. also other
Acts 7. 42 ye o. me slain beasts
8. 18. Simon o. them money
21. 16 offering be o. for every one
1 Cor. 8. 1 Now as touch. things o.
8. 4, 7, 10; 10. 19, 28
Phil. 2. 17 if I be o. upon sacrifice
2 Tim. 4. 6 now I am ready to be o.
Heb. 5. 1 that he may both o. gifts
5. 3; 8. 3; 9. 7; 10. 1; 11. 4
Jas. 2. 21 A. justified when he o.
1 Pet. 2. 5 to o. spiritual sacrifices
Rev. 8. 3 should o. with prayers
R. V. Frequent changes to, sacrifice, present, bring or brought, especially in O. T.
Offering. *Thing offered.*
Gen. 4. 3 Cain brought o. unto Lord
Ex. 24. 5 sacrificed peace o. of oxen
Lev. 1. 2 bring your o. of cattle
Num, 5. 15 he shall bring her o. for
Josh 22. 23 or if to offer peace o.
Judg. 20. 26 Israel offered b. bef. L.
1 Sam. 13. 10 had made an end of o.
2 Sam. 1. 21 nei. rain, nor fields of o.
1 K. 18. 29 proph. until time of o.
2 K. 10. 25 had made an end of o.
1 Chr. 16. 29 bring an o., and come
2 Chr. 8. 13 o. accord. to command.
Ez. 8. 25 o. of the house of our God
Neh. 10. 39 chil. of Levi bring o.
Ps. 20. 3 Lord remember all my o.
Prov. 7. 14 I have peace o. with me
Isa. 66. 20 bring o. in clean vessel
Jer. 41. 5 o. and incense in hand
Hos. 8. 13 the sacrifices of mine o.
Am. 5. 25 o. unto me sacrifices
Zeph. 3. 10 sup. shall bring mine o.
Mal. 1. 10 neither will I accept o.
Luke 21. 4 all cast in unto o. of God
Acts 21. 26 until an o. be offered
Rom. 15. 16 o. of Gent. be accept.
Eph. 5. 2 hath given himself an o.
Heb. 10. 10 through o. of body of J.
10. 18 there is no more o. for sin
R. V. Frequent changes in Lev. and Num. to oblation
Office. *Charge, oversight.*

Ex. 28. 1 minister in the priest's o.
29. 1; 30. 30; 31. 10; 39. 41; 40. 13; Lev. 7. 35; 16. 32; Num. 3. 3; Deut. 10. 6; 1 Chr. 6. 10; 2 Chr. 11. 14; Ezek. 44. 13
Gen. 41. 13 me he restored unto o.
Num. 4. 16 and to the o. of Eleazar
1 Chr. 6. 32 they waited on their o.
2 Chr. 7. 6 priests wait. on their o.
Neh. 13. 14 God, and for o. thereof
Ps. 109. 8 and let another take his o.
Luke 1. 8 he executed the priest's o
Rom. 11. 13 I magnify mine o.
12. 4 all mem. have not the same o.
1 Tim. 3. 1 desire the o. of a bishop
3. 10 let them use the o. of deacon
Heb. 7. 5 who receive o. of priest.
R. V. Neh. 13. 13 business; Rom. 11. 13 ministry; Num. 3. 10; 18. 7 priesthood; 1 Tim. 3. 10, 13 serve as deacon
Officer. *Ruler, overseer, manager, assistant.*
Gen. 41. 34 appoint o. over land
Ex. 5. 6 taskmasters and their o.
Num. 31. 14 Moses was wroth wi. o.
Deut. 16. 18 o. shalt thou make thee
Josh. 1. 10 Josh. commanded the o
1 Sam. 8. 15 give to o., and to ser.
1 K. 22. 9 king of Is. called an o.
2 K. 8. 6 king appointed certain o.
1 Chr. 28. 1 with o., and mighty men
2 Chr. 24. 11 high priest's o. came
Esth. 9. 3 o. of king helped Jews
Isa. 60. 17 will make thy o. peace
Jer. 29. 26 be o. in house of Lord
Mat. 5. 25 judge deliver thee to o.
Luke 12. 58 deliver thee to the o.
John 7. 32 priests sent o. to take him
7. 46 o. answ., Never man spake
18. 12 o. of the Jews took Jesus
Acts 5. 22 the o. found them not
5. 26 then went the captain with o.
R. V. Gen. 41. 34 overseers; 1 K. 4. 5 priest; 1 Chr. 26. 30 had oversight; Esth. 9. 3 business
Offscouring. *Scraping, refuse.*
Lam. 3. 45 hast made us as the o.
1 Cor. 4. 13 are the o. of all things
Offspring. *Issue, produce.*
Job 5. 25 thine o. as grass of earth
27. 14 his o. shall not be satisfied
31. 8 yea, let my o. be rooted out
Isa. 22. 24 shall hang upon him o.
44. 3 my blessing upon thine o.
48. 19 o. of bowels like the gravel
65. 23 the seed of blessed and o.
Acts 17. 28 for we are also his o.
Rev. 22. 16 I am the o. of David
R. V. Job 31. 8 produce
Oft. *Often.*
2 K. 4. 8 that as o. as he passed by
Mat. 9. 14 Why do Phar. fast o.?
Mark 7. 3 ex. they wash hands o.
Acts 26. 11 I punished them o. in
1 Cor. 11. 25 as o. as ye drink it
2 Cor. 11. 23 prisons, in death o.
2 Tim. 1. 16 for he o. refreshed me
Often. *Frequent.*
Prov. 29. 1 o. reprov. harden. neck
Mal. 3. 16 spake o. one to another
Mark 5. 4 he had been o. bound
Luke 5. 23 Why do disciples fast o.
2 Cor. 11. 26 o., in peril of waters
11. 27 watchings o., fastings o., in
Phil. 3. 18 of whom I have told you o
1 Tim. 5. 23 wine, for th. o. infirm.
Heb. 9. 25 he should offer hims. o.
Oftener. *More frequent.*
Acts 24. 26 he sent for him the o.
Oft, Oftentimes. *Many times.*
Job 33. 29 these th. worketh G. o. 1
Eccl. 7. 22 o. t. thine heart knoweth
Mat. 17. 15 o. t. he falleth into fire
Mark 9. 22 o. t. cast him into fire
Luke 8. 29 o. t. it had caught him
John 18. 2 Jesus o. t. resort. thithe.
Rom. 1. 13 o. t. I purposed to come
2 Cor. 8. 22 have o. t. proved dilig.
Heb. 10. 11 off. o. t. same sacrifice
Oil. *Oil, ointment.*
Gen. 28. 18 poured o. on top of it
Ex. 25. 6 spices for anointing o.
Lev. 2. 1 and shall pour o. upon it
Num 11. 8 as the taste of fresh o.
Deut. 7. 13 he will bless thine o.

1 Sam. 10. 1 Samuel took vial of o.
2 Sam. 14. 2 anoint not thys. with o.
1 K. 17. 12 I have a little o in cruse
2 K. 4. 7 sell o., and pay thy debt
1 Chr. 12. 40 brought bread and o.
2 Chr. 11. 11 store of o. and wine
Ez. 3. 7 They gave drink and o. to
Esth. 2. 12 six mo. with o. of myrrh
Job 29. 6 the rock poured me out o.
Ps. 23. 5 anointed my head with o.
  109. 18 come, like water and o.
Prov. 5. 3 mouth smoother than o.
Isa. 41. 19 plant in wildern. o. tree
Jer. 40. 10 gather ye wine and o.
Ezek. 16. 13 didst eat honey and o.
Hos. 2. 5 that give mine o. and
Joel 1. 10 up, the o. languisheth
Mic. 6. 15 not anoint the with o.
Hag. 2. 12 touch bread, wine, or o.
Mat. 25. 3 lamps, and took no o. in
  25. 4 the wise took o. in vessels
Mark 6. 13 anointed with o. many
Luke 10. 34 wounds, pouring in o.
Heb. 1. 9 anoint. th. with o. of glad.
Jas. 5. 14 anointing him with o.
Rev. 6. 6 hurt not the o. and wine

Ointment. *Oil, perfume.*
Ex. 30. 25 o. after art of apothec.
1 Chr. 9. 30 priests made o. of sp.
2 K. 20. 13 showed them precious o.
Job 41. 31 mak. sea like pot of o.
Ps. 133. 2 like prec. o. upon head
Prov. 27. 9 O. and perf. rejoi. heart
  27. 16 o. of right hand betrayeth
Eccl. 7. 1 good name is bet. than o.
  10. 1 Dead flies cause o. . st'k sav.
S. of S. 1. 3 Bec. of sav. of good o.
Isa. 1. 6 neither mollified with o.
Am. 6. 6 anoint thems. with c'f o.
Mat. 26. 7 alab. box of precious o.
Mark 14. 4 Why this waste of o.
Luke 7. 37 bro. alabast. box of o.
  23. 56 and prepared spices and o.
John 11. 2 anointed Lord with o.
  12. 3 Then took Mary pound of o.
Rev. 18. 13 no man buyeth the o.
  R. V. Ex. 30. 25 perfume ; 2 K
  20. 13 ; Ps. 123. 2 ; Isa. 1. 6 ; 39.
  2 oil

Old. *Of age, aged, ancient.*
Gen. 18. 14 Abr. and Sarah were o.
Ex. 10. 9 go with the young, and o.
Lev. 19. 32 honour face of o. man
Num. 11. 18 from tw. years o. upw.
Deut. 8. 4 Thy raiment waxed not o.
Josh. 13. 1 Josh. was o., str'k in y.
Judg. 19. 16 came o. man fr. work
1 Sam. 28. 14 An o. man cometh up
2 Sam. 5. 4 D. was thir. y'rs o. when
1 K. 12. 8 forsook couns. of o. men
2 K. 8. 17 Thir. and two y'rs o. was
1 Chr. 2. 21 mar. when threes. y'rs o.
2 Chr. 10. 6 R. took couns. with o.
Ez. 3. 8 from tw. years o. upwards
Esth. 3. 13 destr. Jews, young and o.
Job 42. 17 So Job died, being o.
Ps. 55. 19 God, he that abideth of o.
  77. 5 have considered days of o.
  143. 5 I remember the days of o.
Prov. 23. 10 Remove not o. landm.
Eccl. 4. 13 bet. wise child than o. k.
S. of S. 7. 13 pleas. fr'ts, new and o.
Isa. 61. 4 they shall build o. wastes
Jer. 6. 16 and ask for the o. paths
Lam. 5. 21 renew our days as of o.
Ezek. 23. 43 that was o. in adulter.
Mic. 5. 2 goings have been of o.
Nah. 2. 8 of o. like pool of water
Mal. 3. 4 as in the days of o., and as
Mat. 2. 16 slew chil. two years o.
  9. 16 putt. new cloth to o. garment
  9. 17 neither new wine in o. bot's
Mark 2. 21 new taketh away from o.
Luke 5. 36 new agree. not with o.
  9. 8 one of o. proph's was risen
John 3. 4 how . . be born when o. ?
Acts 21. 16 Mnason, an o. discip.
Rom. 6. 6 our o. man is crucified
1 Cor. 5. 7 Purge not o. leaven that
2 Cor. 3. 14 reading of O. Testam.
Eph. 4. 22 That ye put off o. man
Col. 3. 9 ye have put off the o. man
1 Tim. 4. 7 refuse o. wives' fables
Heb. 1. 11 they wax o. as garment
2 Pet. 1. 9 purged from his o. sins
1 John 2. 7 no new command, but o.

Jude 4 were of o. ordained to con.
Rev. 12. 9 o. serpent, called Devil
Oldness. *Antiquity.*
Rom. 7. 6 serve, not in o. of letter
Olive. *Olive, oil tree.*
Gen. 8. 11 in her mouth was o. leaf
Ex. 27. 20 bring thee pure oil o.
  Lev. 24. 2
Deut. 8. 8 a land of oil o. and hon.
Josh. 24. 13 of o. yards do ye eat
Judg. 9. 8 said to o. tree, Reign over
1 Sam. 8. 14 take v. y., and your o. y.
1 K. 6. 23 made cherubim of o. tr.
2 K. 5. 26 Is it time to rec. o. y'ds
1 Chr. 27. 28 over o. tr., and sycam.
Neh. 8. 15 Go, fetch o. branches
Job 15. 33 cast his flower as an o.
Ps. 52. 8 I am like a green o. tree
  128. 3 chil. like o. plants round
Isa. 17. 6 as the shaking of o. tree
Jer. 11. 16 thy name, A green o. tree
Hos. 14. 6 his beauty be as o. tree
Am. 4. 9 when yo. o. trees increased
Mic. 6. 15 thou shalt tread the o.
Hab. 3. 17 labour of the o. shall fail
Hag. 2. 19 o. t. hath not brought
Zech. 4. 11 what are these two o. tr.
Rom. 11. 17 being wild o. t., wert
Jas. 3. 12 Can fig t. bear o. berries ?
Rev. 11. 4 These are the two o. tr's
Olives. *Mount of*
Mat. 21. 1 come . . unto mount of O.,
  24. 3 ; 26. 30 ; Mark 11. 1 ; 14. 26 ;
Luke 19. 29 ; 22, 39 ; John 8. 1
Omega. *Last.*
Rev. 1. 8 I am Alpha, O., the begin.
R. V. Rev. 1. 11 ——— .
Omer. *Tenth of ephah.*
Ex. 16. 16 gath. an o. for every man
  16. 18, 22, 32, 33, 36
Omitted. R. V. *left undone.*
Mat. 23. 23 have o. weightier matt.
Omnipotent. R. V. *the Almighty.*
Rev. 19. 6 Lord God o. reigneth
On. *Upon, continued.*
Ex. 9. 20 o. the top of the mount
1 Sam. 19. 23 he went o. and prop.
Mat. 2. 5 setteth him o. pinnacle
Mark 4. 5 some fell o. stony ground
  Etc., etc.
Once. *One time, ever, instantly.*
Gen. 18. 32 I will speak but this o.
Ex. 30. 10 o. in y's make atonement
Lev. 16. 34 make atonem. o. a year
Deut. 7. 22 not consume them at o.
Josh. 6. 3 go round about city o.
Judg. 6. 39 I will speak but this o.
1 Sam. 26. 8 with spear to earth at o.
1 K. 10. 22 o. in three y'rs came navy
2 K. 6. 10 saved himself, not o. nor
2 Chr. 9. 21 o. came the ships or
Neh. 13. 20 lodged without Jerus. o.
Job 33. 14 G. speaketh o., yea twi.
Ps. 62. 11 God hath spoken o.
Prov. 28. 18 perv. shall fall at o.
Isa. 66. 8 shall nat. be born at o.?
Jer. 16. 21 this o. cause them to k.
Hag. 2. 6 o., it is little while, and I
Luke 23. 18 and they cried all at o.
Rom. 6. 10 he died unto sin o., but
1 Cor. 15. 6 seen of . . breth. at o.
2 Cor. 11. 25 rods, o. was I stoned
Gal. 1. 23 preach. faith o. he destr.
Eph. 5. 3 let it not be o. named
Phil. 4. 16 he sent o. and again unto
1 Thes. 2. 18 would have come o.
Heb. 7. 27 this he did o., when he
  9. 12 entered o. into holy place
  9. 28 So Christ was o. offered to
1 Pet. 3. 18 C. o. suffered for sins
Jude 3 o. delivered unto the saints
  5 though ye o. knew this, how
One. *One.*
Gen. 1. 9 be gathered unto o. place
Ex. 10. 19 remained not o. locust
Lev. 1. 26 he took o. unleav. cake
Num. 11. 19 Ye shall not eat o. day
Deut. 6. 4 Lord our God is o. Lord
Josh. 23. 10 o. man sh, chase thous.
Judg. 20. 1 was gathered as o. man
Ruth 1. 4 the name of o. was Orpah
1 Sam. 2. 34 o. day they shall die
2 Sam. 12. 1 were two men in o. city
1 K. 12. 16 now I ask o. petition
2 K. 6. 5 as o. was felling a beam
1 Chr. 1. 19 name of o. was Peleg

2 Chr. 32. 12 worship before o. altar
Ez. 10. 13 nei. is this work of o. day
Neh. 1. 2 o. of my brethren came
Esth. 8. 12 Upon o. day, in all prov.
Job 2. 10 speak. as o. of fool. wom.
  9. 3 cannot ans., o. of thousand
Ps. 14. 3 none doeth good, not o.
  27. 4 O. thing have I desired of L
Prov. 1. 14 let us have o. purse
Eccl. 4. 9 Two are better than o. because
  4. 9 Two are better than o. because
S. of S. 4. 9 with o. of thine eyes
Isa. 27. 12 shall be gathered o. by o.
Jer. 24. 2 o. basket had good figs
Ezek. 1. 15 behold o. wheel up. e.
Dan. 10, 13 Michael, o. of princes
Hos. 1. 11 appoint thems. o. head
Am. 4. 7 o. piece was rained upon
Zeph. 3. 9 serve with o. consent
Hag. 2. 1 in o. and twentieth day
Zech. 3. 9 upon o. stone be seven
Mal. 2. 10 Have we not o. father?
Mat. 6. 24 he will hate the o., and
  19. 17 none good but o., that is G.
Mark 10. 21 O. thing thou lackest
Luke 4. 40 laid his hands on ev. o.
John 10. 30 I and my Father are o.
Acts 11. 28 stood o. named Agabus
Rom. 3. 10 none righteous, no not o.
1 Cor. 8. 4 is none other God but o.
2 Cor. 11. 2 espoused you to o. hus.
Gal. 3. 28 ye are all o. in Christ
Eph. 4. 5 O. Lord, o. fa., o. baptism
Phil. 1. 27 stand fast in o. spirit
Col. 3. 15 ye are called in o. body
1 Thes. 2. 11 charged ev. o. of you
2 Thes. 1. 3 the charity of every o.
1 Tim. 2. 5 o. God, o. mediator bet.
Tit. 1. 6 the husband of o. wife
Heb. 2. 11 who are sanctif. are o.
Jas. 4. 12 There is o. lawgiver, who
2 Pet. 3. 8 thous. years as o. day
1 John 5. 8 these three agree in o.
Rev. 22. 21 every gate was o. pearl
Onion. *Onion.*
Num. 11. 5 remem. the leeks, and o.
Only. *Alone, one.*
Gen. 22. 2 Take thine o. son Isaac
Mat. 10. 42 giv. cup of cold water o
  Etc., etc.
Onward. *Forward.*
Ex. 40. 36 children of Is. went o.
Onyx. *Green beryl.*
Gen. 2. 12 there is bdellium and o.
Ex. 25. 7 O., and stones to be set
  28. 20 fourth row a beryl, and o.
1 Chr. 29. 2 ; Job 28. 16 ; Ezek
  28. 13
Open (*a.*). *Uncovered, unenclosed, unobstructed.*
Gen. 1. 20 may fly in o. firmament
Lev. 14. 7 let bird loose in o. field
Num. 19. 15 every o. vessel is un.
Josh. 8. 17 left city o. and purs. Is.
2 Sam. 11. 11 are encamp. in o. fields
1 K. 8. 29 That thine eyes may be o.
2 Chr. 7. 15 Now mine eyes shall o.
Neh. 6. 5 sent with o. let. in hand
Job 41. 14 Who can o. doors of fa.?
Ps. 5. 9 Their throat is o. sepulchre
Prov. 27. 5 o. reb. bet. than sec. l.
Isa. 28. 24 doth he o. and break c.
Jer. 5. 16 quiver is o. sepulchre
Ezek. 16. 5 wast cast out in o. field
Dan. 6. 10 windows o. in chamber
John 1. 51 ye shall see heaven o.
Acts 16. 27 keep. see. pris. doors o
2 Cor. 6. 11 our mouth is o. to you
1 Tim. 5. 24 some men's sins are o.
Heb. 6. 6 and put him to o. shame
1 Pet. 3. 12 ears are o. to prayer
Rev. 3. 8 set before thee an o. door
  10. 2 an angel had in hand book o.
R. V. Gen. 38. 14 gate of Enaim ;
  2 Cor. 3. 18 unveiled ; 1 Tim. 5.
  24 evident
Open (*v.*). *Uncover, make free, unfold, unlock.*
Gen. 8. 6 Noah o. window of the ark
  41. 56 Joseph o. all store houses
Ex. 21. 33 if man shall o. a pit
Num. 16. 30 earth o. mouth, and s.
Deut. 28. 12 L. shall o. good treas.
Josh. 10. 20 O. mouth of the cave
Judg. 4. 19 she o. bottle of milk
1 Sam. 3. 15 o. doors of house of L.

2 K. 9. 3 Then *o.* the door and flee
2 Chr. 29. 3 Hezekiah *o.* doors of
Neh. 8. 5 Ezra *o.* book in sight of
Job. 3. 1 After this *o.* Job his mouth
Ps. 39. 9 dumb, I. *o.* not my mouth
51. 15 O Lord, *o.* thou my lips
Prov. 31. 26 She *o.* mouth with wi.
S. of S. 5. 2 *O.* to me, my sister
Isa. 50. 5 L. G. hath *o.* mine ear
Jer. 50. 25 L. hath *o.* his armoury
Ezek. 37. 12 I will *o.* your graves
Dan. 10. 16 I *o.* my mouth, and sp.
Nah. 2. 6 gates of rivers shall be *o.*
Zech. 11. 1 *O.* thy doors, O Lebanon
Mal. 3. 10 if I not *o.* wind. of heav.
Mat. 3. 16 heaven were *o.* unto him
7. 7 Knock, it shall be *o.* unto you
13. 35 I will *o.* mouth in parables
Mark 7. 34 Ephphatha, that is, Be*o.*
Luke 1. 64 his mouth was *o.* immed.
John 9. 10 How were thine eyes *o.*?
10. 21 Can dev. *o.* eyes of blind?
Acts 7. 56 I see the heavens *o.*, and
1 Cor. 16. 9 gr. door and effec. is *o.*
2 Cor. 6. 11 our mouth is *o.* to you
Eph. 6. 19 that I may *o.* my mouth
Col. 4. 3 that God would *o.* us door
Heb. 4. 13 all things are *o.* to him
Rev. 3. 7 *o.*, and no man shutteth
13. 6 he *o.* mouth in blasphemy
R. V. Job 38. 17; Jer. 20. 12 revealed; Mark 1. 10 rent asunder

Opening. *To open, that is open.*
1 Chr. 9. 27 *o.* thereof every morn.
Job 12. 14 and there can be no *o.*
Prov. 1. 21 crieth, in *o.* of gates
Isa. 42. 20 *o.* ears, but heareth not
Ezek. 29. 21 will give thee *o.* of m.
R. V. Prov. 1. 21 at the entering in

Openly. *Plainly, publicly.*
Gen. 38. 21 harlot that was *o.* by
Mat. 6. 4 F... shall reward thee *o.*
Mark 7. 4 he spake that saying *o.*
John 7. 4 he seek. to be *o.* known
11. 54 Jesus walked no more *o.*
18. 20 I spake *o.* to the world
Col. 2. 15 made show of them *o.*
R. V. Gen. 38. 21 at Enaim; Mat.
6. 4, 6, 18 ——; John 7. 10; Acts
16. 37 publicly; Acts 10. 40 manifest

Operation. *Work, working.*
Ps. 28. 5 regard not *o.* of his hands
Isa. 5. 12 regard not *o.* of his hands
1 Cor. 12. 6 are diversities of *o.*
Col. 2. 12 through faith of *o.* of God
R. V. 1 Cor. 12. 6 workings; Col.
2. 12 in the, working

Opinion. *Knowledge.*
Job 32. 6 durst not show mine *o.*
32. 10 hearken; I will show mine *o.*
Judgment, conclusion.
1 K. 18. 21 halt ye between two *o*?

Opportunity. *Fit time.*
Mat. 26. 16 he sought *o.* to betray
Luke 22. 6 promised, and sought *o.*
Gal. 6. 10 as *o.*, let us do good
Phil. 4. 10 careful, but ye lack. *o.*
Heb. 11. 15 might have had *o* to

Oppose. *Place against.*
Job 30. 21 thou *o.* thyself against
Acts 18. 6 *o.* thems. and blaspheme
2. Thes. 2. 4 *o.* and exalt. himself
2 Tim. 2. 25 instruct. those that *o.*
R. V. Job 30. 21 persecutest

Opposition. *Placing against.*
1 Tim. 6. 20 avoiding *o.* of science

Oppress. *Put down, crush, burden, weigh down.*
Ex. 3. 9 the Egyptians *o.* them
23. 9 thou shalt not *o.* a stranger
Lev. 25. 14 shall not *o.* one another
Num. 10. 9 the enemy that *o.* you
Deut. 23. 16 thou shalt not *o.* serv.
Judg. 10. 8 that year they *o.* Israel
1 Sam. 12. 3 whom have I *o.*?
2 K. 13. 4 because k. of Syria *o.*
2 Chr. 16. 10 Asa *o.* some of people
Job 10. 3 is it good thou should. *o.*
Ps. 56. 1 he fighting daily *o.* me
119. 122 let not the proud *o.* me
Prov. 14. 31 that *o.* poor repr. Ma.
Isa. 53. 7 He was *o.*, and afflicted
Jer. 7. 6 If ye *o.* not stranger, the
Ezek. 22. 29 they have *o.* stranger
Hos. 12. 7 merchant, he loveth to *o.*
Am. 4. 1 kine of Bashan *o.* poor

Mic. 2. 2 so the *o.* man is in house
Zech. 7. 10 *o.* not wid., nor father.
Mal. 3. 5 wit. against those that *o.*
Acts 10. 38 healing that were *o.*
Jas. 2. 6 Do not rich men *o.* you
R. V. Lev. 25. 14, 17 wrong

Oppressed. *Burdened, wronged.*
Deut. 28. 29 thou shalt be only *o.*
Ps. 9. 9 Lord will be refuge for *o.*
103. 6 and judgment for all *o.*
Eccl. 4. 1 behold tears of the *o.*
Isa. 1. 17 relieve *o.*, judge fatherless
23. 12 O *o.* virgin, daugh. of Zion
58. 6 and to let the *o.* go free, and
Jer. 50. 33 children of Judah were *o.*
Hos. 5. 11 Ephr. is *o.* and broken
R. V. Job 35. 9 cry out; Ezek. 18.
7, 12, 16 wronged

Oppressing. *Bruising, crushing.*
Jer. 46. 16 let us go from *o.* sword
50. 16 for fear of the *o.* sword they
Zeph. 3. 1 Woe to her, the *o.* city

Oppression. *Unjust hardship, cruel imposition, tyranny.*
Ex. 3. 9 I have also seen the *o.*
Deut. 26. 7 Lord looked on our *o.*
2 K. 13. 4 he saw the *o.* of Israel
Job 36. 15 He delivered poor in *o.*
Ps. 55. 3 hear, bec. of *o.* of wicked
107. 39 are bro. low through *o.*
Eccl. 7. 7 *o.* maketh wise man mad
Isa. 5. 7 he look. for judg., beho. *o*
54. 14 thou shalt be far from *o.*
Jer. 6. 6 she is *o.* in midst of her
Ezek. 22. 29 people of land used *o.*
R. V. Ps. 12. 5 spoiling; Eccl. 7. 7
extortion; Ezek. 46. 18 ——

Oppressor. *Who oppresses.*
Job 3. 18 they hear not voice of *o.*
27. 13 this is the heritage of *o.*
Ps. 54. 3 and *o.* seek after my soul
119. 121 leave me not to mine *o.*
Prov. 3. 31 Envy thou not the *o.*
28. 16 prince, is also great *o.* but
Eccl. 4. 1 side of *o.* th. was power
Isa. 3. 12 children are their *o.*, and
9. 4 hast broken rod of his *o.* as in
14. 4 How hath the *o.* ceased! the
16. 4 *o.* are consumed out of land
Jer. 22. 3 deliver out of hand of *o.*
Zech. 9. 8 no *o.* shall pass through
R. V. Job 3. 18 taskmaster; Ps. 54.
3 violent man; Zech. 10. 4 exactor

Or. *Either, as, before.*
Gen. 31. 24 speak not good *o.* bad
Dan. 6. 24 *o.* ev. they came at but.
Rom. 12. 3 whether in body, *o.* out
Etc., etc.

Oracle. *Speaking, speaking place.*
2 Sam. 16. 23 as if man enquir. at *o.*
1 K. 6. 16 he built them for the *o.*
6. 23 within *o.* he made two cherub.
2 Chr. 3. 16 made chains, as in *o.*
Ps. 28. 2 I lift hands toward holy *o.*
Acts 7. 38 who received *o.* to give
Rom. 3. 2 to them were com. *o.* of
Heb. 5. 12 first princ. of *o.* of God
1 Pet. 4. 11 speak as the *o.* of God

Oration. *Address.*
Acts 12. 21 Herod made *o.* to them

Orator. *Speaker, charmer.*
Isa. 3. 3 L. doth tk. away eloquent *o.*
Acts 24. 1 cert. *o.* named Tertullus

Orchard. *Park, fruitful ground.*
Eccl. 2. 5 I made me gard. and *o.*
S. of S. 4. 13 plants are as *o.* of pom.
R. V. Eccl. 2. 5 parks

Ordain. *Appoint, set out, establish.*
Num. 28. 6 offering which was *o.*
1 K. 12. 32 and Jeroboam *o.* a feast
2 K. 23. 5 whom kings of Jud. had *o.*
1 Chr. 9. 2 whom Sam. the seer did *o.*
2 Chr. 11. 15 he *o.* him priest for
Esth. 9. 27 Jews *o.* feast of Purim
Ps. 8. 3 stars, which thou hast *o.*
81. 5 *o.* in Joseph for testimony
Isa. 26. 12 Lord that wilt *o.* peace
30. 33 For Tophet is *o.* of old
Jer. 1. 5 had I *o.* thee a prophet
Dan. 2. 24 king *o.* to destroy men
Hab. 1. 12 O L., thou hast *o.* them
Mark 3. 14 he *o.* twelve, that they
John 15. 16 *o.* you. that ye br. fruit
Acts 1. 22 must one be *o.* a witness
10. 42 *o.* of God to be the judge
13. 48 as were *o.* to eternal life

16. 4 decrees were *o.* of apostles
Rom. 13. 1 pow. that be are *o.* of G.
1 Cor. 2. 7 hidden wisdom God *o.*
9. 14 Even so hath the Lord *o.*
Gal. 3. 19 the law was *o.* by angels
Eph. 2. 10 which G. hath before *o.*
1 Tim. 2. 7 Wher'to I am *o.* preacher
Tit. 1. 5 sh. *o.* elders in every city
Heb. 5. 1 high priest is *o.* for men
9. 6 when these things were thus *o.*
Jude 4 of old *o.* to this condemnation
R. V. 1 Chr. 17. 9; Tit. 1. 5 appoint;
Ps. 8. 2 established; 7. 13 maketh;
Isa. 30. 33; Eph. 2. 10; Heb. 9. 6
prepared; 1 Cor. 2. 7 foreordained;
2 Chr. 11. 15; Ps. 81. 5; Jer. 1. 5;
Dan. 2. 24; Mark 3. 14; John 15.
16; Acts 14. 23; 1 Tim. 2. 7;
Heb. 5. 1; 8. 3 appointed

Order (*n.*). *Array, class, arrangement, condition.*
Gen. 22. 9 Abraham laid wood in *o.*
Ex. 40. 4 and set in *o.* the things
that are to be set
Lev. 1. 7 lay the wood in *o.* on fire
2 Sam. 17. 23 put his house in *o.*
1 K. 18. 33 Elijah put wood in *o.*
2 K. 20. 1 Set thine house in *o.* for
1 Chr. 6. 32 waited on of. ac. to *o.*
2 Chr. 8. 14 accord. to *o.* of David
Job 10. 22 land of dark. without *o.*
33. 5 set words in *o.* before me
Ps. 50 21 set them in *o.* bef... eyes
110. 4 priest after *o.* of Melchiz.
Eccl. 12. 9 the preacher set in *o.*
Isa. 44. 7 set it in *o.* for me, since I
Ezek. 41. 6 and chambers thirty in *o.*
Luke 1. 1 hand to set forth in *o.*
1. 8 exec. office in *o.* of his course
1 Cor. 14 40 Let all be done in *o.*
15. 23 every man shall rise in *o.*
Col. 2. 5 joying, and behold. your *o.*
Tit. 1. 5 I left thee to set in *o.*
Heb. 1. 6 priest, after *o.* of Melchiz.
7. 11 not be called after *o.* of A.
R. V. Ex. 40. 4; Luke 1. 1; Heb.
7. 20 ——; Ex. 26. 17 joined; 1
Chr. 15. 13; 23. 31; 2 Chr. 8. 14
ordinance

Order (*v.*). *Command.*
Ex. 27. 21 Aaron shall *o.* it from
Lev. 24. 4 He shall *o.* lamps upon
Judg. 13. 12 how shall we *o.* child. ?
2 Sam. 23. 5 cov., *o.* in all things
1 K. 20. 14 who shall *o.* the battle?
Job 13. 18 now I have *o.* my cause
37. 19 we cannot *o.* our speech
Ps. 37. 23 steps of good man are *o.*
50. 33 who *o.* conversation aright
119. 133 *o.* my steps in thy word
Isa. 9. 7 upon his kingdom to *o.* it
Jer. 46. 3 *o.* ye buckler and shield
R. V. 1 K. 20. 14 begin; Ps. 37. 23;
Isa. 9. 7 establish

Ordering. *Arrangement.*
1 Chr. 24. 19 These the *o.* of them

Ordinance. *Statute, decree.*
Ex. 12. 14 keep it a feast by *o.* forev.
15. 25 he made a statute and *o.*
Lev. 18. 3 neither walk in their *o.*
Num. 19. 2 This is the *o.* of the law
Josh. 24. 25 set them *o.* in Shech.
1 Sam. 30. 25 made it an *o.* forever
2 K. 17. 37 *o.* which he wrote for you
2 Chr. 35. 25 made them *o.* in Israel
Ez. 3. 10 after the *o.* of David, king
Neh. 10. 32 also we made *o.* for us
Job 38. 33 knowest thou *o.* of heav.
Ps. 99. 7 Kept the *o.* he gave them
119. 91 continue according to *o.*
Isa. 24. 5 the law changed the *o.*
Jer. 31. 36 if *o.* depart fr. before me
Ezek. 43. 18 these are *o.* of altar
Mal. 3. 7 are gone away from my *o.*
Luke 1. 6 walking in *o.* of the Lord
Rom. 13. 2 resist. power, resist. *o.*
1 Cor. 11. 2 Keep *o.*, as I delivered
Eph. 2. 15 command. contain. in *o.*
Col. 2. 14 Blotting out writing of *o.*
Heb. 9. 1 had *o.* of divine service
1 Pet. 2. 13 Submit to ev. *o.* of man
R. V. Lev. 18. 30; 22. 9; Mal. 3. 14
charge; Ex. 18. 20; Lev. 18. 3, 4,
30; 22. 9; Num. 9. 12, 14; 10. 8; 15.
15; 19 2; 31. 21; Ps. 99. 7 statute
or statutes; Ez. 3. 10 order; Ezek

45. 14 portion; 1 Cor. 11. 2 traditions

Ordinary. *Allowed.*
Ezek. 16. 27 dimin. thine *o.* food

Organ. R. V. *pipe.*
Gen. 4. 21 of such as handle *o.*
Job. 21. 12 rejoice at sound of the *o.*
Ps. 150. 4 praise with instr. and *o.*

Ornament. *Adornment*
Ex. 33. 4 no man put on him his *o.*
Judg. 8. 21 took *o.* on camel's neck
2 Sam. 1. 24 who put on *o.* of gold
Prov. 1. 9 *o.* of grace unto head
  4 9 give to thine head an *o.*
  25. 12 as earring of gold, and *o.*
Isa. 3. 18 will take away tinkling *o.*
  30. 22 defile *o.* of molten images
  61. 10 as bridegroom deck. with *o.*
Jer. 2. 32 Can maid forget her *o.*
Ezek. 16. 11 I decked thee with *o.*
1 Pet. 3. 4 *o.* of meek and quiet sp.
R. V. Judg. 8. 21, 26 crescents;
  Prov. 1. 9; 4. 3 chaplet; Isa. 30.
  22 plating; 61. 10 garland; 3. 20
  ankle chains; 3. 18anklets; 1 Pet.
  3. 4 apparel

Orphan. *Fatherless.*
Lam. 5. 3 We are *o.* and fatherless

Ospray. *Ospray.*
Lev. 11. 13 the ossifrage, and the *o.*
Deut. 14. 12

Ossifrage. R. V. *gier eagle.*
Lev. 11. 13 eagle, *o.,* and ospray
Deut. 14. 12

Ostrich. *Ostrich, stork.*
Job. 39. 13 or wings and feath. un. *o.*
Lam. 4. 3 cruel, like *o.* in wildern.

Other. *Another.*
Gen. 7. 10 he stayed *o.* seven days
Mat. 4. 21 he saw *o.* two brethren
  Etc., etc.

Others. *Anothers, the rest.*
Mat 5. 27 why do more than *o.?*
Mark 15. 31 mock. said, He saved *o.*
  Luke 23. 35
Phil. 2. 4 look also on things of *o.*
1 Thes. 2. 6 not yet of *o.* sought

Otherwise. *Otherway, else.*
2 Sam. 18. 13 O. I sh. have wrought
1 K. 1. 21 *O.* it sh. come to pass
2 Chr. 30. 18 yet did eat pass. *o.*
Mat. 6. 11 *o.* ye have no reward
Luke 5. 36 if *o.,* then new maketh
Rom. 11. 6 *o.* grace is no grace
Gal. 5. 10 ye will be none *o.* minded
1 Tim. 5. 25 are *o.* cannot be hid
Heb. 9. 17 *o.* it is of no strength

Ouches. *Settings.*
Ex. 28. 11 to be set in *o.* of gold.
  28. 13, 14, 25; 39. 6, 13, 16, 18

Ought (*n.*). *Aught, anything.*
Gen. 39. 6 he knew not *o.* he had
Lev. 25. 14 if ye sell *o.* to neighbour
Josh. 21 45 failed not *o.* of any th.
1 Sam. 25. 7 nei. was there *o.* miss.
2 Sam. 3. 35 if I taste bread, or *o.*
Mat. 5. 23 bro. hath *o.* against thee
Mark 11. 25 forgive, if ye have *o.*
Acts 28. 19 I had *o.* to accuse my
Phile. 18 if he oweth thee *o.,* put

Ought (*v.*). *Behooveth, owe it.*
Mat. 23 these *o.* ye have done
Mark 13. 14 stand. where it *o.* not
Luke 18. 1 men *o.* always to pray
John 4. 20 where men *o.* to worship
Acts 5. 29 We *o.* to obey God rath.
Rom. 8. 26 should pray for as we *o.*
1 Cor. 8. 2 knoweth nothing as he *o.*
2 Cor. 2. 3 of whom I *o.* to rejoice
Eph. 6. 20 speak boldly, as I *o.* to
Col. 4. 6 know how ye *o.* to answer
1 Thes. 4. 1 to walk and please G.
2 Thes. 3. 7 know how ye *o.* to fol.
1 Tim. 5. 13 sp. things they *o.* not
Tit. 1. 11 teach, things they *o.* not
Heb. 2. 1 we *o.* to give earn. heed
2 Pet. 3. 11 what .. *o.* ye to be in

Our. *Of us.*
Mat. 6. 9 *O.* F. which art in heav.
  6. 11 Give us th. day *o.* daily bread
  25. 8 for *o.* lamps are gone out
  Etc., etc.

Ourselves. *We, us.*
Num. 32. 17 we *o.* will go armed
Acts 23. 14 bound *o.* under curse
1 Cor. 11. 31 if we would judge *o.*

---

2 Cor. 1. 9 we sh. not trust in *o.*
2 Thes. 3. 9 make *o.* an ensample
Heb. 10. 25 assembling of *o.* togeth.
Rom. 15. 1 bear, not to please *o.*
1 John 1. 8 we deceive *o.,* and truth

Out. *From within.*
Gen. 24. 29. Lab. ran *o.* to the man
1 John 4. 18 perf. love cast. *o.* fear
  Etc., etc.

Outcast. *Driven out.*
Ps. 147. 2 he gathereth *o.* of Israel
Isa. 11. 12 assemble the *o.* of Israel
  16. 4 Let mine *o.* dwell with thee
Jer. 30. 17 they called thee an *o.*

Outer. *Outward, without.*
Ezek. 10. 5 heard even to *o.* court
Mat. 8. 12 cast into *o.* darkness
  22. 13; 25. 30

Outgoing. *The going out.*
Josh. 17. 9 *o.* of it were at the sea
  17. 18; 18. 19; 19. 14, 22, 29, 33
Ps. 65. 8 thou makest *o.* of morn.
R. V. In Josh., goings out

Outlandish. R. V. *strange.*
Neh. 13. 26 *o.* women caused Sol.

Outlive. *Live after.*
Judg. 2. 7 elders that *o.* Joshua

Outmost. *Outward, extreme.*
Ex. 26. 10 one curtain that is *o.*
Num. 34. 3 border be *o.* coast of

Outrageous. *Overwhelming.*
Prov. 27. 4 Wrath is cruel, anger *o.*

Outrun. *Run before.*
John 20. 4 other disc. did *o.* Peter

Outside. *Without.*
Judg . 7. 11 Gideon went to the *o*
1. K. 7. 9 *o.* toward the great court
Ezek. 40. 5 behold wall *o.* of house
Mat. 23. 25 ye make clean *o.* of cup
  23. 26; Luke 11. 39

Outstretched. *Stretched out.*
Deut. 26. 8 hand, and with *o.* arm
Jer. 21. 5 fight you with *o.* hand
  27. 5 made earth by my *o.* arm

Outward. *Without.*
Num. 35. 4 *o.* a thousand cubits
1. Sam. 16. 7 looketh on *o.* appear.
1 Chi. 26. 29 for *o.* bus. over Israel
Neh. 11. 16 Levites for *o.* business
Esth. 6. 4 Ham. come into *o.* court
Ezek. 40. 17 bro. he me into *o.* c't
Mat. 23. 27 wh. appear beautiful *o.*
2 Cor. 4. 16 tho. our *o.* man perish
Rom. 2. 18 circumcis. is *o.* in flesh
1 Pet. 3. 3 adorning not he that *o.*

Outwardly. *From without.*
Mat. 23. 58 *o.* appear righteous
Rom. 2. 28 not Jew wh. is one *o.*

Outwent. *Went before.*
Mark 6. 33 ran afoot and *o.* them

Oven. *Furnace, oven.*
Ex. 8. 3 frogs come into thine *o.*
Lev. 2. 4 bring off. baken in the *o.*
Ps. 21. 9 shall make them as fiery *o.*
Lam. 5. 10 skin was black like *o.*
Hos. 7. 4 adulterers, as *o.* heated
  7. 7 They are all hot as an *o.* and
Mal. 4. 1 that shall burn as an *o.*
Mat. 6. 30: Luke 12. 28 cast into *o.*
R. V. Ps. 21. 9; Mal. 4. 1 furnace

Over. *Above, beyond.*
Gen. 8. 1 G. made wind to pass *o.*
Num. 4. 6 shall spread *o.* it a cloth
Josh. 8. 33 *o.* against mt. Gerizim
2 Sam. 20. 21 thrown to thee *o.* wall
Eccl. 7. 16 nei. make thys. *o.* wise
S. of S. 2. 11 winter past, rain is *o.*
Mat. 2. 9 stood *o.* where child lay
Mark 15. 33 dark. *o.* whole land
Luke 2. 8 keeping watch *o.* flocks
Acts 7. 10 make him gov. *o.* Egypt
Rom. 5. 14 death reign., ev. *o.* them
Heb. 3. 6 Christ *o.* his own house
Jas. 5. 14 let them pray *o.* him
1 Pet. 3. 12 eyes of Lord are *o.* righ.
Rev. 18. 20 Rejoice *o.* her, heaven
R. V. Frequent O. T. changes to,
close by, toward, before, beside,
etc.

Over Against. *Opposite.*
Num. 8. 2 lamps *o. a.* candlestick
Deut. 32. 49 Moab, *o. a.* Jericho
1 Sam. 15. 7 Shur, is *o. a.* Egypt
Ezek. 46. 9 shall go forth *o. a.* it
Dan. 5. 5 wrote *o. a.* the candlest'k
Mat. 21. 2 Go into village *o. a.* you

Mark 12. 41 Jesus sat *o. a.* treasury
Luke 8. 26 Gadarenes, *o. a.* Galilee
Acts 20. 15 came next day *o. a.* Chios

Overcharge. *Overload.*
Luke 21. 34 lest your hearts be *o.*
2 Cor. 2, 5 that I may not *o.* you

Overcome. *Prevail, gain victory.*
Gen. 49. 19 a troop shall *o.* him
Num. 13. 13 we are well able to *o.*
2 K. 16. 5 Ahaz, but could not *o.*
S. of S. 6. 5 eyes they have *o.* me
Isa. 28. 1 valleys are *o.* with wine
Jer. 23. 9 like man whom wine *o.*
Luke 11. 22 stronger shall *o.* him
John 16. 33 I have *o.* the world
Rom. 12. 21 but *o.* evil with good
1 John 5. 5 he that *o.* the world
Rev. 12. 11 *o.* him by blood of L.
R. V. Acts 19. 16 mastered

Overdrive. *Beat, knock about.*
Gen. 33. 13 if men should *o.* them

Overflow. *Flow over.*
Deut. 11. 4 made water to *o.* them
Josh. 3. 15 for Jordan *o.* his banks
1 Chr. 12. 15 Jor., when it had *o.*
Job. 22. 16 whose foundation was *o.*
Ps. 69. 2 waters, where floods *o.* me
  69. 15 Let not the waterflood *o.* me
Isa. 8. 8 he shall *o.* and go over
  28. 17 waters *o.* the hiding places
Jer. 47. 2 waters shall *o.* the land
Dan. 11. 22 shall they be *o.* from
Joel 2. 24 fat shall *o.* with wine
R. V. Ps. 69. 15 overwhelm

Overflowed. *Flooded.*
2 Pet. 3. 6 world that was, being *o.*

Overflown. *See Overflow.*

Overflowing. *Inundation.*
Job 28. 11 He bind. floods from *o.*
  38. 25 divid. a watercourse for *o.*
Isa. 28. 2 as flood of waters *o.* shall
  30. 28 his breath, as an *o.* stream
Jer, 47. 2 north shall be *o.* flood
Ezek. 13. 11 shall be an *o.* shower
Hab. 3. 10 *o.* of water passed by
R. V. Job 28. 11 streams that
  trickle; 38. 25 waterflood; Hab.
  3. 10 tempest of water

Overlay, Overlaid. *Cover.*
Ex. 26. 32 pillors *o.* with gold
1 K. 3. 19 died, because she *o.* it
2 K. 18. 16 pil. which Hezekiah *o.*
1 Chr. 29. 4 to *o.* walls of houses
2 Chr. 3. 5 which he *o.* with gold
S. of S. 5. 14 his belly is as ivory *o.*
Heb. 9. 4 ark of the covenant *o.*

Overlaying. *Covering.*
Ex. 38. 17, 19 the *o.* of their chapt.

Overlived. *Outlived.*
Josh. 24. 31 days of eld. that *o.* J.

Over Much. *Too much.*
Eccl. 7. 16 Be not righteous *o. m*
  7. 17 Be not *o. m.* wicked
2 Cor. 2. 7 swal. up with *o. m.* sor.

Overpass. *Pass over.*
Ps. 57. 1 refuge, until calam. be *o.*
Isa. 26. 20 hide, till indigna. be *o.*
Jer. 5. 28 they *o.* deeds of wicked

Overplus. *Superfluous.*
Lev. 25. 27 restore *o.* unto the man

Overrun. *Go or pass over.*
2 Sam. 18 23 Ahimaaz *o.* Cushi
Nah. 1. 8 an *o.* flood he will make

Oversee. *Overlook.*
1 Chr. 9. 29 appointed to *o.* vessels
2 Chr. 2. 2 three th. six h. to *o.* th.

Overseer. *Overlooker.*
Gen. 39. 4 made him *o.* ov. house
2 Chr. 2. 18 *o.* to set peo. a work
Neh. 11. 9 Joel, son of Z., was t. *o.*
Prov. 6. 7 ant, having no *o.,* or
Acts 20. 28 H. G. hath made you *o.*
R. V. Acts 20. 28 bishops

Overshadow. *Overshadow.*
Mat. 17. 5 a bright cloud *o.* them
Mark 6. 7 was cloud that *o.* them
Luke 1. 35 Highest shall *o.* them
Acts 5. 15 shadow of P. *o.* them

Oversight. *Error.*
Gen. 43. 12 peradven. it was an *o.*
Charge, inspection.
Num. 3. 32 *o.* of them that keep
2 K. 12. 11 that had *o.* of the house
2 Chr. 34. 10 workmen had *o.* of
Neh. 13. 4 priest having *o.* of cham.
1 Pet. 5. 2 taking the *o.* thereof

R.[V. Num. 4. 16 charge; Neh. 13. 4 who was appointed

Overspread. *Spread over.*
Gen. 9. 19 of them was the earth o.
Dan. 9. 27 for o. of abominations
R. V. Dan. 9. 27 upon the wing

Overtake. *Reach, catch up.*
Gen. 44. 4 when thou dost o. them
Ex. 15. 9 I will pursue, I will o.
Deut. 28. 15 curses shall o. thee
Josh. 2. 5 pursue, for ye shall o.
Judg. 20. 42 but the battle o. them
1 Sam. 30. 8 thou sh. surely o. them
2 Sam. 15. 14 lest he o. us sudden.
2 K. 25. 5 Chaldeans o. Zedekiah
1 Chr. 21. 12 flee till sword o. them
Ps. 18. 37 pursued en. and o. them
Isa. 59. 9 neither doth justice o. us
Jer. 39. 5 Chaldeans o. Zedekiah
Lam. 1. 3 all her persecutors o. her
Hos. 2. 7 follow lovers, but not o. th.
Am. 9. 13 plowman shall o. reapers
Gal. 6. 1 if a man be o. in a fault
1 Thes. 5. 4 should o. you as thief

Overthrew. *See* **Overthrow.**

Overthrow (*v.*). *Throw over, overturn, break down.*
Gen. 19. 21 I will not o. this city
Ex. 14. 27 Lord o. the Egyptians
Deut. 12. 3 ye shall o. their altars
Judg. 9. 40 many were o. and wo.
2 Sam. 17. 9 some of them be o. at
1 Chr. 19. 3 for to search, and to o.
2 Chr. 14. 13 Ethiopians were o.
Job 12. 19 lead. prin. spoil., and o.
Ps. 106. 26 L. lifted his hand to o.
136. 15 o. Pharaoh and his host
141. 6 When their judges are o. **in**
Prov. 11. 11 city is o. by wicked
18. 5 not good to o. righteous in
Isa. 13. 19 as when God o. Sodom
Jer. 20. 16 as cities which Lord o.
Lam. 4. 6 was o. as in a moment
Dan. 11. 41 many countries be o.
Am. 4. 11 as G. o. Sod. and Gomor.
Jonah 3. 4 and Nineveh shall be o.
Hag. 2. 22 I will o. the chariots
Mat. 21. 12 Jesus o. tab. of mon. c.
Mark 11. 15; John 2. 15
Acts 5. 39 if of G., ye cannot o. it
1 Cor. 10. 5 were o. in wilderness
2 Tim. 2. 18 o. the faith of some
R. V. Deut. 12. 3 break down; Ps.
140. 4 thrust aside; Prov. 18. 5
turn aside; 2 Sam. 17. 9 fallen;
Job 19. 6 subverted

Overthrow (*n.*). *Thrown over.*
Gen. 19. 29 G. sent Lot out of o.
Deut. 29. 23 like o. of Sod. and Go.
Jer. 49. 18 as in the o. of Sodom
2 Pet. 2. 6 condemned th. with o.

Overtook. *See* **Overtake.**

Overturn. *Turn over or under.*
Judg. 7. 13 the tent fell and o. it
Job 9. 5 which o. them in his anger
12. 15 waters, they o. the earth
28. 9 o. mountains by the roots
34. 25 he o. them in the night, so
Ezek. 21. 27 I will o., o., o. it and

Overwhelm. *Cover over.*
Job 6. 27 ye o. the fatherless, and
Ps. 55. 5 and horror hath o. me
61. 2 thee, when my heart is o.
77. 3 I compl., and my spirit was o.
78. 53 but the sea o. their enemies
124. 4 Then waters had o. us, the
R. V. Job 6. 27 cast lots upon

Owe. *Be indebted.*
Mat. 18. 28 which o. him h. pennies
18. 28 saying, Pay me that thou o.
Luke 16. 5 How much o. th. my l.?
Rom. 13. 8 O. no man anything
Phile. 19 I do not say how thou o.

Owl. *Night-bird.*
Lev. 11. 16 o., and the night hawk
11. 17; Deut. 14. 15, 16
Job 30. 29 and a companion to o.
Ps. 102. 6 I am like o. of desert
Isa. 13. 21 and o. shall dwell there
34. 11, 13, 14, 15; 43. 20
Mic. 1. 8 make mourning as the o.
R. V. Lev. 11. 16; Deut. 14. 15;
Job 30. 29; Isa. 13. 21; 34. 13;
43. 20; Jer. 50. 39; Mic. 1. 8
ostrich. or ostriches; Isa. 34. 14

night-monster; 34. 15 arrowsnake

Own (*n.*). *To oneself.*
Lev. 14. 26 pour into his o. hand
Prov. 14. 10 heart know. his o. bit.
Dan. 11. 16 do accord. to his o. will
Luke 2. 35 pierce thro. thy o. soul
John 1. 11 his o. received him not
Acts 21. 11 bound o. hands and feet
1 Tim. 1. 2 my o. son in the faith
Tit. 1. 4 To Titus, my o. son after
R. V. In very many instances, the word is omitted.

Own (*v.*). *Possess.*
Lev. 14. 35 he that o. the house
Acts 21. 11 bind man that o. gird.

Owner. *Who owns, sir.*
Ex. 21. 28 o. of ox shall be quit
1 K. 16. 24 Shemer, o. of the hill
Job 31. 39 caused o. to lose lives
Prov. 1. 19 taketh away life of o.
Eccl. 5. 11 what good is there to o.
Isa. 1. 3 The ox knoweth his o.
Luke 19. 33 o. said, Why loose ye
Acts 27. 11 believed o. of the ship

Ox, Oxen. *Ox, bull, cow, cattle.*
Gen. 12. 16 Ab. had sheep, and o.,
Ex. 9. 3 hand of Lord is upon o.
Lev. 7. 23 shall eat no fat of o.
Num. 22. 4 as o. licketh up grass
Deut. 5. 14 not do work, nor thine o·
Josh. 6. 21 they destr. o., sheep, ass
Judg. 3. 31 slew six h. with o. goad
1 Sam. 11. 7 took o., and hewed th.
2 Sam. 6. 6 ark . . for the o. shook it
1 K. 1. 9 Adonij. slew sheep and o.
2 K. 16. 17 took sea from brasen o.
1 Chr. 12. 40 brought bread on o. and
2 Chr. 4. 3 Two rows of o. were cast
Neh. 5. 18 prep. for me daily one o.
Job 6. 5 or loweth o. over fodder?
40. 15 he eateth grass as an o.
Ps. 69. 31 shall please L. bet. than o.
Prov. 7. 22 as o. goeth to slaughter
15. 17 bet. than stalled o. and hatr.
Isa. 1. 3 o. knoweth his owner
32. 20 that send forth feet of o.
Ezek. 1. 10 four had the face of o.
Dan. 4. 33 Neb. did eat grass as o.
Am. 6. 12 will one plow with o.?
Mat. 22. 4 my o. and fat. are killed
Luke 13. 15 doth one loose o. or ass
John 5. 14 found those that sold o.
Acts 14. 13 brought o. unto gates
1 Cor. 9. 9 Doth G take care for o.?
1 Tim. 5. 18 shalt not muzzle the o.
R. V. Gen. 34. 28; Ex. 9. 3 herds;
Num 23. 1 bullocks; Deut. 14. 5
antelope; 1 Sam. 14. 14 half fur-
row's length; Jer. 11. 19 ——

P.

Pace. *Step.*
2 Sam. 6. 13 gone six p., he sacrif.

Pacified. *Quieted, appeased.*
Esth. 7. 10 Then was king's wrath p.
Ezek. 16. 63 when I am p. tow.

Pacify. *Quiet, appease.*
Prov. 16. 14 wrath, wise men will p.
21. 14 A gift in secret p. anger
Eccl. 10. 4 leave not; for yielding p.
R. V. Eccl. 10. 4 allayeth; Ezek.
16. 63 have forgiven.

Paddle. *Pin, nail.*
Deut. 23. 13 have p. on thy weapon

Paid. *Given.*
Ez. 4. 20 toll, trib., and cust. was p.

Pain (*n.*). *Pang, anguish.*
1 Sam. 4. 19 for p. came upon her
Job 14. 22 his flesh shall have p.
33. 19 He is chastened with p.
Ps. 25. 18 Look upon mine aff . . p.
48. 6 p. as a woman in travail
116. 3 p. of hell gat hold on me
Isa. 13. 8 shall be in p. as woman
21. 3 my loins are filled with p.
26. 17 wom. is in p., and cried out
Jer. 6. 24 and p. as wom. in travail
12. 13 they put themselves to p.
51. 8 Babylon, take balm for p.
Ezek. 30. 4 p. shall be in Ethiopia
30. 16 Sin shall have great p.
Mic. 4. 10 in p. and labour to bring
Nah. 2. 10 knees p. is in all loins
Acts 2. 24 hav. loosed p. of death
Rom. 8. 22 groan. and trav. in p.
Rev. 16. 10 they gnawed tongue . . p.

21. 4 neither shall be any more p̃
R. V. Nah. 2. 10 anguish; Acts 2
24 pangs

Pained. *In pain.*
Ps. 55. 4 My heart is sore p. wi. me
Isa. 23. 5 they shall be sorely p.
Jer. 4. 19 I am p. at my very heart
Joel 2. 6 people shall be much p.
Rev. 12. 2 and p. to be delivered
R. V. Joel 2. 6 anguish

Painful. *Full of pain.*
Ps. 73. 16 know it was too p. for me

Painfulness. R. V. *travail.*
2 Cor. 11. 27 In weariness and p.

Paint. *Smear, paint.*
2 K. 9. 30 she p. her face, and
Jer. 22. 14 and p. with vermilion
Ezek. 23. 40 p. thine eyes, and deck

Painting. R. V. *paint.*
Jer. 4. 30 rentest thy face with p.

Pair. *Yoke, two.*
Luke 2. 24 A p. of turtle doves, or
Rev. 6. 5 that sat had p. of balances
R. V. Rev. 6. 5 —— .

Palace. *High place.*
1 K. 16. 18 Zimri went into the p.
2 K. 15. 25 Pe. smote Pekaiah in p.
2 Chr. 36. 19 burnt all p. with fire
Ps. 48. 3 God is known in her p.
122. 7 and prosperity within thy p.
Isa. 23. 13 they raised up p. thereof
32. 14 bec. the p. shall be forsaken
34. 13 thorns shall come up in p.
Lam. 2. 5 hath swallowed all her p.
Hos. 8. 14 it shall devour the p.
Am. 1. 12 shall devour p. of Bozrah
Mic. 5. 5 when he tread in our p.

Castle, temple, palace.
1 K. 21. 1 Jezreel, hard by the p.
2 K. 20. 18 eunuch in p. of king
1 Chr. 29. 1 for p. is not for man
Ez. 4. 14 have maint. from king's p.
Neh. 1. I was in Shushan pa.
Esth. 1. 2 kingdom, in Sh. the p.
Ps. 45. 8 of myrrh, out of ivory p.
144. 12 polished, after sim. of p.
Prov. 30. 28 spider is in king's p.
S. of S. 8. 9 will build p. of silver
Isa. 13. 22 dragons in their pleas. p.
39. 7 eunuch in p. of k. of Bab.
Ezek. 25. 4 shall set th. p. in thee
Dan. 8. 2 I was at Shushan in p.
Nah. 2. 6 the p. shall be dissolved

Court, palace.
Mat. 26. 3 assembled priests to p.
26. 58 Pet. fol. J. unto high pr'ts p.
Mark 14. 66 as P. was beneath in p.
Luke 11. 21 str. man armed keep. p.
John 18. 15 went with Jesus in. p.
Phil. 1. 13 bonds manif. in all p.
R. V. 1 K. 16. 18; 2 K. 15. 25;
Neh. 2. 8; 7. 2; Hos. 8. 14 castle;
Ps. 78. 69 heights; 2 Chr. 9. 11
house; S. of S. 8. 9 turret; Am. 4.
3 Harmon; Mat. 26. 3. 29, 58;
Mark 14. 54, 66; Luke 18. 21;
John 18. 15 court; John 18. 28
judgment hall; Phil. 1. 13 præto-
rian guard; Ezek 25. 14 encamp-
ments

Pale. *Bleached, white.*
Isa. 29. 22 nei. shall face wax p.
Rev. 6. 8 looked, behold a p. horse

Paleness. *Whiteness.*
Jer. 30. 6 all faces turned into p.

Palm. *Flat, sole.*
Lev. 14. 15 pou. it into p. of hand
1 Sam. 5. 4 p. of hand were cut off
2 K. 9. 35 they found skull and p.
Isa. 49. 16 grav. thee on p. of h.
Dan. 10. 10 my knees upon p. of h.
Mat. 26. 67 smote him with p. of h.
Mark 14. 65. R. V. blows
John 18. 22 struck J. with p. of h.
R. V. John 18. 22 ——

Palm, Palm Tree.
Ex. 15. 27 Elim, where were p. t.
Lev. 23. 40 take branches of p. t.
Num. 33. 9 in Elim were p. t.
Deut. 34. 3 show him city of p. t.
Judg. 1. 16 went out of city of p. t.
4. 5 she dwelt un. p. t. of Deborah
1 K. 6. 29, 32, 35 with fig. of p. t.
7. 36; 2 Chr. 3. 5; Ezek. 40. 16
2 Chr. 3. 5 and set thereon p. t. and
28. 15 to Jericho, the city of p. t.

Neh. 8. 15 fetch ol. and *p*. branches
Ps. 92. 12 right. sh. flour. like *p. t*.
S. of S. 7. 7 thy stature is like *p. t*.
Jer. 10. 5 They are upright as *p. t*.
Ezek. 40. 22 *p. t*. were after meas.
    40. 26, 31 ; 41. 18 – 26
Joel 1. 12 *p. t*. also, and the apple
John 12. 13 Took branches of *p. t*.
Rev. 7. 9 robes, and *p*. in th. hands
Palmerworm. *Caterpillar, lo-*
    cust.
Joel 1. 4 which *p. w*. left locust eat
Am. 4. 9 the *p. w*. devoured them
Palsy. *Paralysis*.
Mat. 4. 24 that had *p*., he healed
    8. 6 my servant lieth sick of *p*.
Mark 2. 5 said to sick of *p*., Son
Luke 5. 18 behold man tak. with *p*.
Acts 8. 7 many taken with *p*., and
    R. V. Mat. 4. 24 ; Luke 5. 18, 24 ;
    Acts 8. 7 ; 9. 33 palsied
Pan. *Laver, plate, dish, pan*.
Ez. 27. 3 make *p*. to receive ashes
Lev. 2. 5 meat offering baked in *p*.
Num., 11. 8 manna, baked it in *p*.
1 Sam. 2. 14 he struck it into *p*.
2. Sam. 13. 19 she took *p*., and p.
1 Chr. 9. 31 over things made in *p*.
2 Chr. 35. 13 sod they in pots and *p*.
Ezek. 4. 3 take unto thee iron *p*.
R. V. Ex. 27. 3 ; Num. 11 8 pots
Pang. *Pain, distress, throe*.
Isa. 13. 18 *p*. sh. tak. hold of them
    26. 17 Like as wom. crieth in *p*.
Jer. 22. 23 gracious when *p*. come
    48. 41 be as heart of woman in *p*.
Mic. 4. 9 *p*. have tak. thee as wom.
Pant. *Breathe quickly, throb,*
    yearn.
Ps. 38. 10 My heart *p*., strength f.
    42. 1 *p*. after the water brooks
    119. 131 I opened my mouth, and *p*.
Isa. 21. 4 My he .rt *p*. fear affright.
Am. 2. 7 That *p*. aft. dust of earth
    R. V. Ps. 38. 10 throbbeth
Pap.   R. V. *breast*.
Ezek. 23. 21 for *p*. of thy youth
Luke 11. 27 Blessed, *p*. thou sucked
    23. 29 Bles., *p*. wh. nev. gav. suck
Rev. 1. 13 girt about *p*. with gird.
Paper. *Bushy, green*.
Isa. 19. 7 The *p*. reeds by brooks
    Paper, papyrus
2 John 12 I w'ld not write with *p*.
Parable. *Allegory, proverb*.
Num. 23. 7, 18 he took up his *p*.
Job 27. 1 Job continued his *p*. and
Ps. 49. 4 I will incline my ear to *p*.
    78. 2 I open my mouth in *p*.
Prov. 26. 7, 9 so is *p*. in m. of fools
Ezek. 17. 2 speak *p*. to house of Is.
    24. 3 utter *p*. to rebellious house
Mic. 2. 4 shall take up *p*. against
Hab. 2. 6 all these take up a *p*.
Mat. 13. 3 spake many things in *p*.
    13. 13–53 ; 15. 15 ; 21. 33 , 22. 1
    24. 32 learn a *p*. of the fig tree
Mark 3 23 he said unto them in *p*.
Luke 5. 36 he spake *p*. unto them
John 10. 6 This *p*. spake Jesus unto
Paradise. *Park, garden*.
Luke 23. 43 To-day with me in *p*.
2 Cor. 12. 4 was caught up into *p*.
Rev. 2. 7 in midst of *p*. of God
Paramour. *Unlawful husband or*
    wife.
Ezek. 23. 20 she doted upon their *p*.
Parcel. *Plot, portion, field*.
Gen. 33. 19 he bought *p*. of field
Josh. 24. 32 *p*. of gr. Jacob bought
Ruth 4. 3 Naomi selleth *p*. of land
1 Chr. 11. 13 *p*. of gr. full of barley
John 4. 5 *p*. of ground Jacob gave
    R. V. 1 Chr. 11. 13, 14 plot
Parched. *Burnt, wasted, dried*.
Lev. 23. 14 eat nei. br., nor *p*. corn
Josh. 5. 11 they did eat *p*. corn
Ruth 2. 14 he reached her *p*. corn
1 Sam. 17. 17 Take ephah of *p*. corn
2 Sam. 17. 28 Brought flour and *p. c*.
Isa. 35. 7 ground become a pool
Jer. 17. 6 *p*. places in wilderness
    R. V. Isa. 35. 7 glowing
Parchment. *Thin skin, mem-*
    brane.
2 Tim. 4. 13 bring especially the *p*.

Pardon. *Spare, forgive*.
Ex. 23. 21 not *p*. your transgressio.
    34. 9 *p*. our iniquity, and our sin
Num. 14. 19 P., I beseech thee
1 Sam. 15. 25 *p*. my sin, and turn
2 K. 5. 18 the Lord *p*. thy servant
2 Chr. 30. 18 good Lord *p*. ev. one
Neh. 9. 17 art a God ready to *p*.
Job 7. 21 why not *p*. my transgress.
Ps. 25. 11 Lord, *p*. mine iniquity
Isa. 55. 7 for he will abundantly *p*.
Jer. 5. 1 seeketh the truth, I will *p*.
    5. 7 How shall I *p*. thee for this
Lam. 3. 42 hav. tr., thou hast not *p*.
Mic. 7. 18 a God, that *p*. iniquity
Pare. *Cut, prepare*.
Deut. 21. 12 shave head, *p*. her nails
Parent. *Begetter, progenitor*.
Mat. 10. 21 children rise against *p*.
    Mark 13. 12
Luke 2. 27 *p*. brought in child Jesus
    8. 56 and her *p*. were astonished
    21. 16 shall be betrayed both by *p*.
John 9. 2 did sin, this man or his *p*.
    9. 22 These words spake his *p*.
Rom. 1. 30 evil, disobedient to *p*.
Eph. 6. 1 obey your *p*. in the Lord
Col. 3. 20 obey your *p*. in all things
1 Tim. 5. 4 require *p*., that is good
2 Tim. 3. 2 men be disobedient to *p*.
Heb. 11. 23 hid three mo. of his *p*.
Parlour. *Inner place, chamber*.
Judg. 3. 20 he was sitting in the *p*.
    3. 25 opened not the doors of *p*.
1 Sam. 9. 22 Samuel bro. th. into *p*.
1 Chr. 28. 11 gave S. pattern of *p*.
    R. V. 1 Sam. 9. 22 guest chamber ;
    1 Chr. 28. 11 chambers
Part (*n*).   *Portion, section*.
Gen. 47. 24 four *p*. be your own
Ex. 29. 26 breast shall be thy *p*.
Lev. 7. 33 right should. for his *p*.
Num. 18. 20 nei. have *p*. among th.
Deut. 10. 9 Levi hath no *p*. nor
Josh. 14. 4 gave no *p*. unto Levites
Ruth 2. 3 hap to light on *p*. of field
1 Sam. 30. 24 so shall his *p*. be
2 Sam. 20. 1 We have no *p*. in David
1 K. 16 21 Is. divided into two *p*.
2 K. 11. 7 two *p*. all that go forth
1 Chr. 12. 29 gr. *p*. had kept ward
2 Chr. 29. 16 pr. went into *p*. of h.
Neh. 3. 9 ruler of *p*. of Jerusalem
Job 26. 14 these are *p*. of his ways
    32. 17 I will answer also my *p*.
Ps. 5. 9 inward *p*. is wickedness
    51. 6 in hidden *p*. know wisdom
    118. 7 the Lord takes my *p*. with
Prov. 17. 2 shall have *p*. of inherit.
Isa. 7. 18 hiss for fly in utterm. *p*.
    44. 23 shout, ye lower *p*. of earth
Jer. 34. 18 passed between *p*. thereof
Ezek. 26. 20 in the low *p*. of earth
Dan. 2. 33 feet *p*. of iron, *p*. of cl.
Am. 7. 4 devour. deep, and eat *p*.
Mat. 2. 22 turned into *p*. of Gal.
Mark 8. 10 came into *p*. of Dalman
Luke 10. 42 Mary hath cho. good *p*.
John 13. 8 thou hast no *p*. with me
Acts 8. 21 hast neither *p*. nor let in
Rom. 11. 25 blind. in *p*. hap. to Is.
1 Cor. 13. 9 we know in *p*., and p.
2 Cor. 1. 14 acknowledged us in *p*.
Eph. 4. 9 descended into lower *p*.
Tit. 2. 8 he that is of the contrary *p*.
Heb. 2. 14 himself took *p* of same
1 Pet. 4. 14 on their *p*. he is evil
Rev. 16. 19 city divided into three *p*.
R. V. frequent changes to, por-
    tion ; and many omissions of
    word. Also many changes due
    to preceding word.
Part (*v*.).   *Divide, separate*.
Lev. 2. 6 Thou shalt *p*. it in pieces
Deut. 14. 6 every beast that *p*. hoof
Ruth 1. 17 if ought but death *p*.
2 Sam. 14. 6 was none to *p*. them
2 K. 2. 14 they *p*. hither and thith.
Job 41. 6 *p*. him among merchants ?
Ps. 22. 18 They *p*. my gar. among
Prov. 18. 18 lot *p*. between mighty
Joel 3. 2 whom they scatter and *p*.
Mat. 27. 35 crucifi., and *p*. his gar.
Mark 15. 24 ; Luke 23. 34 ; John
    19. 24
Acts 2. 45 and *p*. them to all men

Partake. *Take with, share*.
Rom. 11. 17 *p*. of root and fatness
Partaker. *Joint taker, sharer*.
Ps. 50. 18 been *p*. with adulterers
Mat. 23. 30 not been *p*. in blood
Rom. 15. 27 made *p*. of their spirit
1 Cor. 9. 10 should be *p*. of his hope
    9. 12, 13, 23 ; 10. 17, 21, 30
2 Cor. 1. 7 as ye are *p*. of suffering
Eph. 3. 6 *p*. of his promise in C.
    5. 7 Be not ye therefore *p*. with
Phil. 1. 7 ye are *p*. of my grace
Col. 1. 12 meet to be *p*. of inherit.
1 Tim. 5. 22 nei. *p*. of oth. men's sins
2 Tim. 1. 8 be thou *p*. of affliction
    2. 6 husbandman be *p*. of fruits
Heb. 2. 14 as chil. are *p*. of flesh
    3. 1 *p*. of the heavenly calling
    3. 14 we are made *p*. of Christ
    6. 4 were made *p*. of Holy Ghost
    12. 10 might be *p*. of his holiness
1 Pet. 4. 13 *p*. of Christ's suffering
    5. 1 I am also *p*. of the glory that
2 Pet. 1. 4 *p*. of the divine nature
2 John 11 that bid. God speed is *p*.
Rev. 18. 4 be not *p*. of her sins
R. V. 1 Cor. 9. 14 have their por-
    tion ; Heb 2. 14 sharers in
Parted. *Separated*.
Gen. 2. 10 river, thence it was *p*.
Job 38. 24 By what way is light *p*.
Luke 24. 51 he was *p*. from them
    See also **Part** (*v*.).
Partial.   R. V. *respect of person*.
Mal. 2. 9 have been *p*. in the law
R. V. *divided in own mind*.
Jas. 2. 4 Are ye not *p*. in yourselves
Partiality. *Divided, bearing to-*
    ward.
1 Tim. 5. 21 doing nothing by *p*.
Jas. 3. 17 without *p*., and hypocrisy
R. V. Jas. 3. 17 variance
Particular.   R. V. *severally*..
1 Cor. 12. 27 bod of C., and m. in *p*.
Eph. 5. 33 every one in *p*. love wife
Particularly. *Part by part*.
Acts 21. 19 Pet. declared *p*. things
Heb. 9. 5 we cannot now speak *p*.
R. V. Acts 21. 19 rehearsed one by
    one ; Heb. 9. 5 severally
Parties. *Persons, sides*.
Ex. 22. 9 both *p*. come bef. judges
Parting. *Mother* (idiomatic in
    A. V.).
Ezek. 21. 21 king of Bab. stood at *p*.
Partition. *Fence, division*.
1 K. 6. 21 Sol. made *p*. by chains
Eph. 2. 14 broken down wall of *p*.
R. V. 1 K. 6. 21 drew chains across
Partly. *In part*.
Dan. 2. 42 be *p*. strong, *p*. broken
1 Chr. 11. 18 divis., I *p*. believe it
Heb. 10. 33 *P*., ye were gazing stock
Partner. *In common with, sharer*.
Prov. 29. 24 *p*. with th. hat. own soul
Luke 5. 7 beckoned unto their *p*.
    5. 10 sons of Zeb., which were *p*.
2 Cor. 8. 23 Titus, he is my *p*.
Phile. 17 If thou count me a *p*.
Partridge. *Caller, partridge*.
1 Sam. 26 2) as when one hunt *p*.
Jer. 17. 11 as *p*. sitteth on eggs
Pass. *Go, occur*.
Gen. 11. 12. 6 Abram *p*. through l.
Ex. 12. 12. through land of Egypt
Lev. 18. 21 not let thy seed *p*. thro.
Num. 20. 17 Let us *p*. thro. coun.
Deut. 2. 4 Ye are to *p*. thro. coast
Josh. 3. 17 Is. *p*. ov. on dry ground
Judg. 10. 9 *p*. over Jordan to fight
1 Sam. 9. 4 Saul *p*. thro. mt. Ephr.
2 Sam. 17. 24 Absalom *p*. over Jor.
1 K. 13. 25 men *p*., and saw carcase
2 K. 4. 9 holy man of God which *p*.
1 Chr. 19. 17 David *p*. over Jordan
2 Chr. 25. 18 there *p*. by wild beast
Neh. 2. 14 no place for beast to *p*.
Job 9. 15 as brooks they *p*. away
Ps. 8. 8 *p*. through paths of the seas
    37. 36 Yet he *p*. away, and, lo, was
    144. 4 days are as shadows that *p*.
Prov. 10. 25 As whirlwind *p*. so
    22. 3 simple *p*. on, and are punish.
S. of S. 3. 4 but lit. I *p*. from them
Isa. 23. 6 *P*. ye over to Tarshish
    29. 5 as chaff that *p*. away : yea it

43. 2 When thou *p.* through waters
Jer. 5. 22 roar, yet can they not *p.*
Lam. 2. 15 All that *p.* by clap hands
Ezek. 29. 11 No foot of man shall *p.*
Dan. 11. 10 one sh. cert. *p.* through
Hos. 10. 11 I *p.* over her fair neck
Joel 3. 17 no strangers *p.* through
Am. 7. 8 I will not again *p.* by them
Jonah 2. 3 thy waves *p.* over me
Mic. 1. 11 *P.* away, inhab. of Saphir
Nah. 1. 15 wicked no m. *p.* thro. thee
Hab. 3. 10 overflow. of waters *p.* by
Zeph. 2. 15 that *p.* her shall hiss
Zech. 10. 11 *p.* thro. sea with afflic.
Mat. 5. 18 Till heaven and earth *p.*
27. 39 they that *p.* by reviled him
Mark 2. 14 as he *p.*, he saw Levi
Luke 18. 37 Jesus of Nazar. *p.* by
John 9. 1 as Jesus *p.* by, he saw man
Acts 16. 8 they *P.* Mys. came to Tr.
Rom. 5. 12 death *p.* upon all men
1 Cor. 7. 31 fashion of world *p.* away
2 Cor. 5. 17 old things are *p.* away
Eph. 3. 19 love of C., wh. *p.* knowl.
Phil. 4. 7 peace of God., *p.* underst.
Heb. 11. 29 By faith *p.* thro. R. sea
1 John 3. 14 have *p.* fr. death to life
2 Pet. 3. 10 heaven shall *p.* away
Rev. 21. 1 heaven and earth were *p.*

Passage. *Passing, ford, way.*
Num. 20. 21 Edom refused Is. *p.*
Judg. 12. 5 Gilead. took *p.* of Jordan
1 Sam. 13. 23 garrison went out to *p.*
Isa. 10. 29 They are gone over *p.*
Jer. 22. 20 lift voice, cry from the *p.*
51. 32 shew k., that *p.* are stopped
R. V. Judg. 12. 5, 6 fords : 1 Sam.
13. 23 ; 14. 4 ; Isa. 10. 29 pass or
passes ; Jer. 22. 20 Abarim

Passed. *Gone.*
Num. 33. 51 ye are *p.* over Jordan
Deut. 27. 3 when thou art *p.* over
Josh. 3. 17 when all people were *p.*
Ps. 90. 9 all our days are *p.* away
Isa. 10. 28 he is *p.* to Migron
Jer. 11. 15 holy flesh is *p.* from thee
John 5. 24 is *p.* from death unto life
Heb. 4. 14 priest, *p.* into heavens
Rev. 21. 4 for. things are *p.* away
See also **Pass.**

Passengers. R. V. *that pass through.*
Prov. 9. 15 she standeth to call *p.*
Ezek. 39. 11 give to Gog valley of *p.*

Passing. *Going.*
Judg. 19. 18 We are *p.* fr. Bethleh.
2 Sam. 15. 24 util peo. had done *p.*
2 K. 6. 26 as king of Israel was *p.*
Ps. 84. 6 *p.* through valley of Baca
Prov. 7. 8 *p.* thro. street near cor.
Isa. 31. 5 *p.* over he will preserve
Ezek. 39. 14 *p.* through land to bury
Luke 4. 30 he *p.* through midst of
Acts 5. 15 shadow of Peter *p.* by
See also **Pass.**

Passion. *Suffering.*
Acts 1. 3 show. hims. alive after *p.*
14. 15 We are men of like *p.* with
Jas. 5. 17 Elias was subj. to like *p.*

Passover. *Passing over festival.*
Ex. 12. 11 sh. eat, it is the Lord's *p.*
Lev. 23. 5 first mo. is the Lord's *p.*
Num. 9. 2 Let chil. also keep *p.*
Deut. 16. 1 Keep *p.* unto L. thy G.
Josh. 5. 11 did eat on mor. after *p.*
2 K. 23. 23 *p.* was holden in Jerus.
2 Chr. 35. 6 kill the *p.*, and sanctify
Ez. 6. 19 chil. of captiv. kept the *p.*
Ezek. 45. 21 ye shall have the *p.*
The passover institution.
Mat. 26. 2 after two days is the *p.*
Mark 14. 16 they made ready the *p.*
Luke 22. 5 have desired to eat *v.*
John 2. 13 *p.* at hand, Jesus went
18. 39 sh. release to you one at *p.*
1 Cor. 5. 7 C. our *p.* is sacrificed
Heb. 11. 28 through faith he kept *p.*

Past. *Gone by, aforetime.*
Gen. 50. 4 days of mourning were *p.*
Num. 21. 22 until we be *p.* border
Deut. 4. 32 ask now of days *p.*
1 Sam. 15. 32 Surely bit. of d. is *p.*
2 Sam. 11. 27 mourning *p.*, David
1 K. 18. 29 when midday was *p.*
Job 9. 10 doeth things *p.* find. out
17. 11 days are *p.*, purposes brok.

29. 2 Oh that I were as in mon. *p.*
Ps. 90. 4 thous y'rs. as yestr. wh. *p.*
Eccl. 3. 15 G. require. which is *p.*
S. of S. 2. 11 winter is *p.*, rain over
Jer. 8. 20 harvest is *p.*, sum. ended
Mat. 14. 15 time is now *p.*, send
Mark 16. 1 when sab. was *p.*, Mary
Luke 9. 36 voice *p.*, J. was alone
Acts 27. 9 bec. fast was already *p.*
Rom. 3. 25 for remission of sins *p.*
11. 30 ye in ti. *p.* have not believ.
11. 33 and his ways *p.* finding out
Gal. 1. 13 ye have heard in times *p.*
Eph. 2. 2 in time *p.* ye walked ac.
2 Tim. 2. 18 saying that resur. is *p.*
Phile. 11. in time *p.* unprofitable
Heb. 1. 1 spake in tim. *p.* to fathers
1 Pet. 2. 10 in time *p.* were not a p.
1 John 2. 8 bec. the darkness is *p.*
Rev. 9. 12 One woe *p.*, th. come two
R. V. Deut. 2. 10 ; Eph. 2. 2 ; Phile.
11 aforetime

Pastor. *Feeder, shepherd.*
Jer. 2. 8 *p.* transgress. against me
12. 10 *p.* have destr. my vineyard
Eph. 4. 11 gave *p.* and teachers
R. V. Jer. 2. 8 rulers ; 3. 15 ; 10. 21 ;
12. 10 ; 17. 16 ; 22. 22 ; 23. 1, 2
shepherds

Pasture. *Feeding, herbage.*
Gen. 47. 4 thy servants have no *p.*
1 K. 4. 23 twenty oxen out of *p.*
1 Chr. 4. 39 they went out to seek *p.*
Job 39. 8 range of mount. is his *p.*
Ps. 23. 2 make me to lie in green *p.*
79. 13 thy people, sheep of thy *p.*
95. 7 we are the people of his *p.*
Isa. 30. 23 cat. sh. feed in large *p.*
49. 9 their *p.* be in high places
Jer. 23. 1 scatter sheep of my *p.*
25. 36 Lord hath spoiled their *p.*
Lam. 1. 6 like harts that find no *p.*
Ezek. 34. 14 will feed th. in good *p.*
34. 31 my flock, flock of my *p.*
Hos. 13. 6 According to their *p.*, so
Joel 1. 19 devour, *p.* of wilderness
John 10. 9 in and out, and find *p.*
R. V. Isa. 49. 9 all bare heights

Pate. *Crown of head.*
Ps. 7. 16 dealing come upon own *p.*

Path. *Way, road, going.*
Gen. 49. 17 Dan be an adder in *p.*
Num. 22. 24 angel of L. stood in *p.*
Job. 19. 8 hath set dark. in my *p.*
33. 11 he marketh all my *p.*
Ps. 16. 11 shew me the *p.* of life
25. 4 O Lord, teach me thy *p.*
Prov. 3. 17 and all her *p.* are peace
4. 26 Ponder the *p.* of thy feet
Isa. 2. 3 we will walk in his path
26. 7 dost weigh the *p.* of just
Jer. 6. 16 ask for the old *p.*, where
Lam. 3. 9 he hath made my *p.* crook.
Hos. 2. 6 she shall not find her *p.*
Joel. 2. 8 sh. walk ev. one in his *p.*
Mic. 4. 2 we will walk in his *p.*
Mat. 3. 3 w. of L. make his *p.* straight
Mark 1. 3 ; Luke 3. 4
Heb. 12. 13 make strai. *p.* for feet
R. V. Num. 22. 34 hollow way ; Ps.
17. 4 ways ; Jer. 18. 15 by paths

Pathway. *Way, going.*
Prov. 12. 28 in *p.* thereof no death

Patience. *Forbearance, endurance.*
Mat. 18. 26, 29 have *p.* with me, and
Luke 8. 15 bring forth fr. with *p.*
21. 19 In *p.* possess your souls
Rom. 5. 3 tribulation worketh *p.*
5. 4 *p.* experience, experi. hope
8. 25 then do we with *p.* wait for it
2 Cor. 6. 4 ministers of God in *p.*
1 Thes. 1. 3 *p.* of hope in Lord J. C.
2 Thes. 1. 4 glory in you for your *p.*
1 Tim. 6. 11 follow after love, *p.*
2 Tim. 3. 10 thou hast known my *p.*
Tit. 2. 2 be sound in faith, in *p.*
Heb. 10. 36 For ye have need of *p.*
12. 1 let us run with *p.* the race set
Jas. 1. 3 trying of faith worketh *p.*
2 Pet. 1. 6 add to temperance *p.*, and
Rev. 1. 9 in kingdom and *p.* of J. C.

Patient. *Forbearing.*
Eccl. 7. 8 *p.* in sp. bet. than proud
Rom. 12. 12 hope, *p.* in tribulation
1 Thes. 5. 14 be *p.* toward all men

2 Thes. 3. 5 unto *p.* waiting for C.
1 Tim. 3. 3 but *p.*, not a brawler
2 Tim. 2. 24 be apt to teach, *p.*
1 Thes. 5. 14 support the weak, be *p.*
Jas. 5. 7 Be *p.*, therefore, brethren
R. V. 1 Thes. 5. 14 long suffering ;
1 Tim. 3. 3 gentle ; 2 Tim. 2. 24
forbearing.

Patiently. *Forbearingly.*
Ps. 37. 7 rest in Lord, and wait *p.*
40. 1 I waited *p.* for the Lord
Acts 26. 3 I beseech, hear me *p.*
Heb. 6. 15 after he had *p.* endured
1 Pet. 2. 2 if buffeted, take it *p.*

Patriarch. *Head of house.*
Acts 2. 29 let me freely speak of *p.*
7. 8 Jacob begat the twelve *p.*
Heb. 7. 4 *p.* Ab. ga. tenths of spoils

Patrimony. *Paternal inheritance.*
Deut. 18. 8 wh. com. of sale of *p.*

Pattern. *Shape, type, form*
Ex. 25. 9. *p.* of the tabernacle
Num. 8. 4 *p.* wh. Lord shewed M.
Josh. 22. 28 *p.* of altar of Lord
2 K. 16. 10 Ahaz sent *p.* of altar
1 Chr. 28. 11 D. gave to S. *p.* of po.
Ezek. 43. 10 let them measure *p.*
1 Tim. 1. 16 shew longsuf., for a *p.*
Tit. 2. 7 shew. thys. *p.* of good w'ks
Heb. 8. 5 accord. to *p.* shewed the
9. 23 *p.* of things in the heaven
R. V. 1 Tim. 1. 16 ; Tit. 2. 7 ensample ; Heb. 9. 23 copies

Paved. *Laid work.*
Ex. 24. 10 as it were *p.* work of st.
S. of S. 3. 10 the midst *p.* with love

Pavement. *Laid work, floor.*
2 K. 16. 17 put sea on *p.* of stone
2 Chr. 7. 3 all Is. bowed upon *p.*
Esth. 1. 6 beds were on *p.* of red
Ezek. 40. 17 *p.* made for court ar.
John 19. 13 Pil. sat in pl. called *P.*

Pavilion. *Covering, booth.*
2 Sam. 22. 12 made dark *p.* round
1 K. 20. 12 he and the kings in the *p.*
20. 16 drink. hims. drunk in *p.*
Ps. 18. 11 his *p.* round were dark
27. 5 he shall hide me in his *p.*
31. 20 keep secretly in a *p.* from
Jer. 43. 10 Nebuch. spread his *p.*

Paw (*n.*). *Palm, hand.*
Lev. 11. 27 whatev. goeth on his *p.*
1 Sam. 17. 37 del. me out *p.* of lion

Paw (*v.*). *Dig, pant.*
Job 39. 21 He *p.* in the valley, and

Pay. *Render, make complete.*
Ex. 21. 36 he shall *p.* ox for ox
Num. 20. 19 if cattle dr., I will *p.*
Deut. 23. 21 shalt not slack to *p.*
2 Sam. 15. 7 let me go *p.* my vow
1 K. 20. 39 else *p.* talent of silver
2 K. 4. 7 sell oil, *p.* thy debt and
2 Chr. 8. 8 Sol. make to *p.* tribute
Ez. 4. 13 will they not *p.* toll, tribute
Esth. 3. 9 I will *p.* ten th. tal. of sil.
Job 22. 27 thou shalt *p.* thy vows
Ps. 22. 25 I will *p.* my vows bef.
37. 21 Wicked borrow., and *p.* not
Prov. 7. 14 this day have I *p.* vows
Eccl. 5. 4 *p.* that which thou owest
Jonah 2. 9 I will pay that I vowed
Mat. 5. 26 till *p.* uttermost farthing
18. 26, 29 patience, I will *p.* thee all
23. 23 ye *p.* tithe of mint, anise, and
Luke 7. 42 they had nothing to *p.*
Rom. 13. 6 for this cause *p.* ye trib.
Heb. 7. 9 Levi *p.* tithes in Abraham
R. V. Num. 20. 19 give price ; 2
Chr. 27. 5 render

Payment. *Give back.*
Mat. 18. 25 sold all, *p.* to be made

Peace. *Quiet, ease, security.*
Gen. 15. 15 go to thy fathers in *p.*
43. 23 he said, *P.* be to you, fear not
Ex. 4. 18 Jethro said to M., Go in *p.*
Lev. 26. 6 I will give *p.* in land
Num. 25. 12 I give him cov. of *p.*
Deut. 2. 26 sent, with words of *p.*
Josh. 9. 15 Josh. made *p.* with them
Judg. 6. 23 L. said, *P.* be unto thee
1 Sam. 25. 35 Go in *p.* to th. house
2 Sam. 15. 9 king said, go in *p.*
1 K. 5. 12 was *p.* Hiram and Sol.
2 K. 18. 36 the people held their *p.*
1 Chr. 12. 18 *p.*, *p.* be unto thee
2 Chr. 34. 28 gath. to thy grave in *p.*

Ez. 9. 12 seek *p*. or wealth for ever
Neh. 5. 8 Then held they their *p*.
Esth. 9. 30 sent let. with words of *p*.
Job 5. 24 thy taberna. shall be in *p*.
13. 13 Hold your *p*., let me alone
Ps. 4. 8 lay me down in *p*., and sl.
122. 7 *p*. be within thy walls, and
Prov. 3. 7 and all her paths are *p*.
11. 12 man of underst. holdeth *p*.
Eccl. 3. 8 time of war, time of *p*.
Isa. 9. 6 Father, The Prince of *P*.
57. 21 There is no *p*., saith God
Jer. 6. 14 *P*., *P*., when there is no *p*.
23. 17 Lord said, Ye shall have *p*.
Lam. 3. 17 rem. my soul from *p*.
Ezek. 7. 25 *P*., there shall be none
Dan. 10. 19 *p*. be unto thee, be str.
Obad. 7 men at *p*. deceived thee
Mic. 3. 5 that bite with teeth, cry *p*.
Nah. 1. 15 that publisheth *p*., O J.
Hag. 2. 9 and in this place I give *p*.
Zech. 8. 19 love the truth and *p*.
Mal. 2. 6 he walked with me in *p*.
Mat. 10. 34 I came not to send *p*.
26. 63 But Jesus held his *p*.
Mark 5. 34 go in *p*., and be whole
Luke 2. 14 on e. *p*., good w. tow. m.
24. 36 and said, *P*. be unto you
John 14. 27 P. I leave with you
Acts 16. 36 now depart, go in *p*.
Rom. 1. 7 Grace to you and *p*. from
1 Cor. 7. 15 God hath call. us to *p*.
2 Cor. 1. 2 *p*. from God our Father
Gal. 6. 16 *p*. be on them, and mercy
Eph. 6. 23 *P*. be to the brethren
Phil. 4. 7 *P*., which pass. all under.
Col. 3. 15 And let *p*. of God rule
1 Thes. 5. 23 G. of *p*. sanctify you
2 Thes. 3. 16 Lord of *p*. give you *p*.
1 Tim. 1. 2 *p*., from God our Fath.
2 Tim. 2. 22 follow faith., char., *p*.
Tit. 1. 4; Phile. 3 and *p*., from God
Heb. 12. 14 Follow *p*. with all men
Jas. 2. 16 Depart in *p*., be warmed
1 Pet. 1. 2 Grace unto you, and *p*.
1 Pet. 1. 2 *p*. be multipl. unto you
2 John 3 *p*., from God the Father
Jude 2 Mercy unto you, and *p*.
Rev. 1. 4 *p*., from him which is
R. V. 1 Cor. 14. 30 silence; Rom.
10. 15

Peace offering.
Ex. 20. 24 thy *p. o*., thy sheep, oxen
Lev. 3. 1; Num. 6. 14; Deut. 27. 7;
Josh. 8. 31; Judg. 20. 26; 1 Sam.
10. 8; 2 Sam. 6. 17; 1 K. 3. 15;
2 K. 16. 13; 1 Chr. 16. 1: 2 Chr.
7. 7
Prov. 7. 14 I have *p. o*. with me
See also **Offering.**

Peaceable. *Quiet, at ease.*
Gen. 34. 21 These are *p*. with us
2 Sam. 20. 19 *p*. and faithful in Is.
1 Chr. 4. 40 land was wide and *p*.
Isa. 32. 18 peo. dwell in *p*. habita.
Jer. 25. 37 *p*. habita. are cut down
1 Tim. 2. 2 lead quiet and *p*. life
Heb. 12. 11 after it yieldeth *p*. fruit
Jas. 3. 17 wisdom is pure, then *p*.

Peaceably. *Peacefully.*
Gen. 37. 4 and could not speak *p*.
Judg. 11. 13 restore those lands *p*.
1 Sam. 16. 4 said, Comest thou *p*.?
1 K. 2. 13 Bath. said, Com. thou *p*.?
1 Chr. 12. 17 If ye be come *p*. unto
Jer. 9. 8 speaketh *p*. to neighbour
Dan. 11. 21 he shall come in *p*.
Rom. 12. 18 live *p*. with all men
R. V. Dan. 11. 21, 24 time of secur-
ity; Rom. 12. 18 at peace

Peacemaker.
Mat. 5. 9 Blessed are the *p*. for they

Peacocks. *Peacocks*
1 K. 10. 22 navy came bringing *p*.
2 Chr. 9. 21
Ostriches.
Job 39. 13 gave goodly wings to *p*.?

Pearl. *Crystal, pearl.*
Job 28. 18 no mention of cor. or *p*.
Mat. 7. 6 nei. cast *p*. before swine
13. 45. like merchant seeking *p*.
1 Tim. 2. 9 not with gold or *p*., or
Rev. 17. 4 precious stones and *p*.
R. V. Job. 28. 18 crystal

Peculiar. *Special, particular.*
Ex. 19. 5 ye shall be a *p*. treasure

Deut. 14. 2 chosen to be *p*. people
Ps. 135. 4 chosen Is. for *p*. treasure
Eccl. 2. 8 gath. *p*. treas. of kings
Tit. 2. 14 purify to hims. *p*. people
1 Pet. 2. 9 But ye are a *p*. people
R. V. Tit. 2. 14; 1 Pet. 2. 9 own
possession

Pedigree. *Birth showing.*
Num. 1. 18 declare *p*. after families

Peeled. *Pulled off, bared.*
Isa. 18. 2 to nation scattered and *p*.
Ezek. 29. 18 every shoulder was *p*.
R. V. Isa. 18. 2, 7 smooth

Peep. R. V. *chirp.*
Isa. 8. 19 wizards that *p*. and mut.
10. 14 none opened mouth or *p*.

Pelican. *Pelican.*
Lev. 11. 18; Deut. 14. 17 sw. and *p*.
Ps. 102. 6 I am like *p*. of wilderness

Pen. *Tool, reed, pen.*
Judg. 5. 14 that handle *p*. of writer
Job 19. 24 were graven with iron *p*.
Ps. 45. 1 my tongue is *p*. of writer
Isa. 8. 1 write in it with man's *p*.
Jer. 8. 8 *p*. of scribes is in vain
17. 1 written with a *p*. of iron
3 John 13 I will not with *p*. write
R. V. Judg. 5. 14 marshal's staff

Pence. *Denarii, 17 cents each.*
Mat. 18. 28 one who owed hun. *p*.
Mark 14. 5; John 12. 5 ointment
sold for more than three hun. p.
Luke 7. 41 one owed five hun. *p*.
10. 35 took out two *p*., and gave

Penny. *Denarius, 17 cents.*
Mat. 20. 2 he agreed for *p*. a day
20. 13 did not agr. with me for *p*.?
22. 19 they brought unto him a *p*.
Mark 12. 15 bring me *p*., that I may
Luke 20. 24 Show me *p*. Whose im.
Rev. 6. 6 measure of wheat for a *p*.

Pennyworth. *Penny price.*
Mark 6. 37 buy two hun. *p. w*. of br.
John 6. 7 two hun. *p. w*. of br. not s.

Pentecost. *Fiftieth day aft. Pass.*
Acts 2. 1 when day of *P*. was come
20. 16 to be at Jerusalem day of *P*.
1 Cor. 16. 8 will tarry at Eph. till *P*.

Penury. *Want, poverty.*
Prov. 14. 23 talk of lips tend. to *p*.
Luke 21. 4 she of her *p*. cast in all
R. V. Luke 21. 4 want

People. *Human beings, nation,
race, citizens, subjects.*
Gen. 11. 6 Behold the *p*. is one
47. 23 then Joseph said unto the *p*.
Ex. 1. 20 *p*. multiplied and waxed
6. 7 I will take you to me for a *p*.
Lev. 9. 22 A. lifted hand toward *p*.
26. 12 God, and ye shall be my *p*.
Num. 11. 10 Mos. heard the *p*. weep
16. 41 Ye have killed a *p*. of Lord
Deut. 4. 10 Gather me *p*. together
27. 16 all the *p*. shall say, Amen
Josh. 3. 5 Joshua said unto the *p*.
17. 17 saying, Thou art a great *p*.
Judg. 20. 31 B. went out against *p*.
Ruth 1. 16 thy *p*. shall be my *p*., and
1 Sam. 2. 24 ye make L's *p*. transg.
8. 21 Samuel heard all words of *p*.
2 Sam. 1. 4 *p*. are fled from battle
1 K. 1. 39 *p*. said, G. save king Sol.
2 K. 3. 7 my *p*. as thy *p*., my horses
1 Chr. 11. 2 shalt feed my *p*. Israel
2 Chr. 6. 3 chosen D. to be over *p*.
Ez. 2. 70 some *p*. dwelt in their cities
Neh. 1. 10 these are thy ser. and *p*.
Esth. 1. 5 king made feast unto *p*.
Job 12. 2 No doubt but ye are *p*.
Ps. 7. 8 the Lord shall judge the *p*.
28. 9 Save thy *p*., bless thine inher.
72. 4 He shall judge the poor of *p*.
Prov. 30. 25 ants are *p*. not strong
Eccl. 4. 16 is no end of all the *p*.
Isa. 3. 13 Lord standeth to judge *p*.
30. 9 that this is a rebellious *p*.
Jer. 15. 7 I will destroy my *p*. since
Lam. 1. 11 *p*. sigh, they seek bread
Ezek. 24. 18 So I spake unto the *p*.
Dan. 8. 4 shall destroy the holy *p*.
Hos. 1. 9 for ye are not my *p*. and
Joel 2. 17 Spare my *p*., O Lord
Am. 9. 10 the sinners of *p*. shall die
Obad. 13 shall not enter gate of *p*.
Jonah 1. 8 what country? of what *p*.
Mic. 1. 2 Hear, all ye *p*.; hearken

Nah. 3. 18 thy *p*. is. scat. on mount.
Hab. 2. 8 remnant of *p*. shall spoil
Zeph. 1. 11 merch. *p*. are cut down
Hag. 1. 2 *p*. say, time is not come
Zech. 13. 9 I will say, It is my *p*.
Mal. 2. 9 made you base bef. all *p*.
Mat. 1. 21 for he shall save his *p*.
4. 16 *p*. in darkness saw great light
Mark 7. 6 *p*. honoureth me with lips
Luke 2. 10 joy, which be to all *p*.
7. 16 that God hath visited his *p*.
John 11. 50 one man shall die for *p*.
Acts 3. 9 *P*. saw him praising God
28. 16 Go unto this *p*. and say
Rom. 9. 25 I will call them my *p*.
1 Cor. 10. 7 *p*. sat down to eat and
2 Cor. 6. 16 and they sh. be my *p*.
Tit. 2. 14 purify unto a peculiar *p*.
Heb. 2. 17 make reconc. for sins *p*.
2 Pet. 2. 9 ye are a peculiar *p*.
Jude 5 saved *p*. out of Egypt the
Rev. 5. 9 redeem. us out of ev. *p*.
R. V. Very frequent changes to
peoples, multitude, multitudes,
etc.,

Peradventure. *If so be, perhaps.*
Gen. 50. 15 Joseph will *p*. hate us
Ex. 32. 30 *P*. I sh. make atonem.
Josh. 9. 7 *P*. ye dwell among us
1 K. 18. 5 *p*. we may find grass
Jer. 20. 10 *p*. he will be enticed
Rom. 5. 7 *p*. for man some w'ld die
2 Tim. 2. 25 *p*. G. give th. repent.

Perceive. *See, know, understand.*
Gen. 19. 33 *p*. not when she lay do.
Deut. 29. 4 ha. not given heart to *p*.
Josh. 22. 31 *p*. Lord is among us
Judg. 6. 22 Gid. *p*. he was an angel
1 Sam. 3. 8 Eli. *p*. Lord had called
2 Sam. 12. 19 D. *p*. child was dead
1 K. 22. 33 when capt's of char. *p*.
2 K. 4. 9 I *P*. this is an holy man of
1 Chr. 14. 2 D. *P*. L. had confidence
2 Chr. 18. 32 captains of chariots *p*.
Neh. 6. 12 *P*. God had not sent him
Esth. 4. 1 Mor. *p*. all that was done
Job 9. 11 passeth, but I *p*. him not
38. 18 Hast *p*. breath of earth?
Prov. 1. 2 *p*. words of understand.
14. 7 *P*. not in him the knowledge
Eccl. 1. 17 I *P*. this is vexation
Isa. 6. 9 see ye indeed, but *p*. not
64. 4 not heard, nor *p*. by ear
Jer. 23. 18 For who hath *p*. his word
Mat. 13. 14 sh. see, and shall not *p*.
Mark 4. 12; Luke 28. 26
Mark 2. 8 Jesus *p*. in his spirit that
Luke 5. 22 when J. *p*. their thoughts
6. 41 *p*. not beam that is in own eye
John 4. 19 I *p*. thou art a prophet
Acts 10. 34 I *P*. G. is no respecter of
2 Cor. 7. 8 *p*. epist. made you sor.
Gal. 2. 9 *p*. grace given unto me
1 John 3. 16 *p*. we the love of God
R. V. Deut. 29. 4; Josh. 22. 31; 1
Sam. 3. 8; 1 John 3. 16 know;
Judg. 6. 22; 1 K. 22. 33; 2 Chr.
18. 32; Eccl. 3. 22; Luke 9. 27
saw; Neh. 6. 12; Prov. 1. 2 dis-
cern; Acts 8. 23; 14. 9; 2 Cor. 7. 8
see and seeing; Luke 6 41 con-
sidereth; Mark 12. 28 knowing;
John 12. 19 behold; Acts 23. 29
found

Perdition. *Destruction.*
John 17; 12 none lost, but son of *p*.
Phil. 1. 28 is to the token of *p*. but
2 Thes. 2. 3 revealed, the son of *p*.
1 Tim. 6. 9 wh. drown men in *p*.
Heb. 10. 39 who draw back to *p*.
2 Pet. 3. 7 and *p*. of ungodly men
Rev. 17. 8 beast shall go into *p*.
R. V. 2 Pet. 3. 7 destruction

Perfect. (v.). *Complete, finish.*
2 Chr. 8. 16 so house of G. was *p*.
Ps. 138. 8 Lord will *p*. wh. concer.
Ezek. 27. 4 build. have *p*. thy beau.
Mat. 21. 16 and thou hast *p*. praise
Luke 13. 32 third day I shall be *p*.
Heb. 10. 14 by one offer. he ha. *p*.
1 John 2. 5 in him is love of G. *p*.
4. 12 in us, and his love is *p*. in us

Perfect (a.). *Complete, finished.*
Gen. 6. 9 N. was just man and *p*.
Lev. 22. 21 be *p*. to be accepted
Deut. 18. 13 be *p*. with Lord thy G.

1 Sam. 14. 41 Saul said, Give *p*. lot
2 Sam. 22. 31 God, his way is *p*.
1 K. 8. 61 Let your heart be *p*. with
2 K. 20. 3 I walked with *p*. heart
1 Chr. 12. 38 men came with *p*. heart
2 Chr. 15. 17 the heart of Asa was *p*.
Ez. 7. 12 Artax. unto Ez., *p*. peace
Job 1. 1 that man was *p*. and upri.
8. 20 G. will not cast away *p*. man
Ps. 37. 37 *p*. man, the end is peace
139. 22 I hate them with *p*. hatred
Prov. 2. 21 the *p*. shall remain in it
4. 18 path of just shin. to *p*. day
Isa. 26. 3 keep him in *p*. peace
42. 19 who blind as he that is *p*.
Ezek. 28. 15 wast *p*. in thy ways
Mat. 5. 48 *p*., ev. as your F. is *p*.
Luke 6. 40 but every one that is *p*.
John 17. 23 that they be made *p*.
Acts 22. 3 taught accord. to *p*. man
Rom. 12. 2 good and *p*. will of G.
1 Cor. 2. 6 among th. that are *p*.
2 Cor. 12. 9 my strength is made *p*.
Gal. 3. 3 are ye made *p*. by flesh?
Eph. 4. 13 till ye come to *p*. man
Phil. 3. 12 not as tho. already *p*.
Col. 4. 12 stand *p*. in will of God
1 Thes. 3. 10 *p*. which is lacking
2 Tim. 3. 17 man of G. may be *p*.
Heb. 2. 10 capt. of sal. *p*. tho. suff.
12. 23 spirits of just men made *p*.
Jas. 1. 4 let patience have *p*. work
1 Pet. 5. 10 after suffer. made *p*.
1 John 4. 17 herein is love made *p*.
R. V. Isa. 42. 16 at peace; Acts 22.
3 strict; 24. 22 exact; Eph. 4. 13
full grown; 2 Tim. 3. 17 complete

Perfecting. *Completing.*
2 Cor. 7. 1 *p*. holi. in fear of God
Eph. 4. 12 For the *p*. of the saints

Perfection. *Completeness.*
Job 11. 7 canst find out Al. to *p*.
Ps. 50. 2 out of Zion, *p*. of beauty
119. 96 I have seen an end of *p*.
Isa. 47. 9 come upon thee in their *p*.
Luke 8. 14 and bring no fruit to *p*
2 Cor. 13. 9 we wish, even your *p*.
Heb. 6. 1 let us go on unto *p*., not
R. V. Job 28. 3 furtherest bound;
Isa. 47. 9 full measure

Perfectly. *Completely.*
Jer. 23. 20 latter days consid. it *p*.
Mat. 14. 36 touch. made *p*. whole
Acts 18. 26 expound. way of G. *p*.
1 Cor. 1. 10 be *p*. joined together
1 Thes. 5. 2 know *p*. that day of

Perfectness. *Completeness.*
Col. 3. 14 charity, is the bond of *p*.

Perform. *Do, confirm, establish..*
Gen. 26. 3 I will *p*. the oath which
Ex. 18. 18 not able to *p*. it thyself
Num. 4. 23 that enter to *p*. service
Deut. 9. 5 he may *p*. the word wh.
Ruth 3. 13 will *p*. part of kinsman
1 Sam. 3. 12 I will *p*. against Eli
2 Sam. 21. 14 keep *p*. all k. com.
1 K. 6. 12 I *p*. my word with thee
2 K. 23. 3 to *p*. words of covenant
Neh. 5. 13 that *p*. not this promise
Esth. 1. 15 she hath nót *p*. com.
Job 23. 14 he *p*. thing appointed
Ps. 21. 11 a device not able to *p*.
61. 8 that I may daily *p*. my vows
Isa. 9. 7 zeal of the L. will *p*. this
19. 21 they shall vow a vow and *p*. it
Jer. 1. 12 will hasten word to *p*.
Ezek. 37. 14 L. have spoken, and *p*.
Mic. 7. 20 wilt *p*. truth to Jacob
Nah. 1. 15 keep feasts, *p*. thy vows
Mat. 5. 33 *p*. unto Lord thine oaths
Luke 1. 20 these things shall be *p*.
2. 39 they *p*. all things according
Rom. 15. 28 when I have *p*. this, and
2 Cor. 8. 11 theref. *p*. the doing of it
Phil. 1. 6 *p*. it till day of Jesus Chr.
R. V. Gen. 26. 3; Deut. 9. 5; 1 K.
6. 12; 8. 20; 12. 15; 2 Chr. 10. 15;
Jer. 11. 5 establish, or established;
Num. 4. 23 wait upon; Deut. 23. 23;
Esth. 1. 15; Rom. 7. 18 do, or done;
2 K. 23. 3, 4; Ps. 119. 106 confirm;
Num. 15. 38; Luke 2. 39; Rom. 15.
28 accomplish; 2 Cor. 8. 11 com-
plete; Phil. 1. 6 perfect

Performance. *Completion.*
Luke 1. 45 sh. be *p*. of those things

---

2 Cor. 8. 11 *p*. out of that ye have
R. V. 2 Cor. 8. 11 completion

Perfume (*n*.). *Incense, compound.*
Ex. 30. 35 And thou shalt make it *p*.
Prov. 27. 9 Oint. and *p*. rejoic. heart
Isa. 57. 9 and didst increase thy *p*.
R. V. Ex. 30. 35, 37 incense

Perfume (*v*.). *Sprinkle scent.*
Prov. 7. 17 *p*. my bed with myrrh
S. of S. 3. 6 who is this that com. *p*.

Perhaps. *Through hap or chance.*
Acts 8. 22 *p*. thought of thy heart
2 Cor. 2. 7 lest *p*. one should swal.
Phile. 15. *p*. he departed for season
R. V. 2 Cor. 2. 7 by any means

Peril. *Danger.*
Lam. 5. 9 we gat our bread with *p*.
Rom. 8. 35 shall *p*. separate us?
2 Cor. 11. 26 *p*. of water *p*. of rob.

Perilous. R. V. *grievous.*
2 Tim. 3. 1 *p*. times shall come

Perish. *Be lost, lose away.*
Gen. 41. 36 land *p*. not thro. famine
Ex. 19. 21 and many of them *p*.
Lev. 26. 38 ye sh. *p*. among heathen
Num. 16. 33 they *p*. among congre.
Deut. 4. 26 ye shall utterly *p*. fr. off
Josh. 23. 16 ye shall *p*. quickly from
Judg. 5. 31 let all thine enemies *p*.
1 Sam. 26. 10 descend into bat., *p*.
2 Sam. 1. 27 How are weap. war *p*.
2 K. 9. 8 whole house of A. shall *p*.
Esth. 4. 16 go to king, and if I *p*., I *p*.
Job 3. 3 Let the day *p*. I was born
4. 11 the old lion *p*. for lack of prey
8. 13 the hypocrite's hope shall *p*.
Ps. 1. 6 the way of ungodly shall *p*.
102. 26 They shall *p*., thou endure
112. 10 the desire of wicked shall *p*.
Prov. 10. 28 expect. of wick. shall *p*.
19. 9 he that spreadeth lies shall *p*.
Eccl. 5. 14 riches *p*. by evil travail
Isa. 29. 14 wisdom of wise shall *p*.
Jer. 4. 9 the heart of king shall *p*.
Lam. 3. 18 my hope is *p*. from Lord
Ezek. 7. 26 law shall *p*. from priest
Dan. 2. 18 his fellows should not *p*.
Joel 1. 11 because har. of field is *p*.
Am. 3. 15 houses of ivory shall *p*.
Jonah 4. 10 came in the night and *p*.
Mic. 7. 2 good man is *p*. out of earth
Zech. 9. 5 the king shall *p*. fr. Gaza
Mat. 8. 25 saying, Lord save us, we *p*
Mark 4. 38 carest th. not that we *p*.
Luke 8. 24 Master, master, we *p*.
13. 3 except ye repent, ye shall *p*.
21. 18 not hair of your head shall *p*.
John 3. 15 who. believ. shall not *p*.
Acts 8. 20 Thy money *p*. with thee
Rom. 2. 12 sinned witho. law sh. *p*.
1 Cor. 15. 18 asleep in Christ are *p*.
2 Cor. 2. 15 savour of C. in them *p*.
Col. 2. 22 all are to *p*. with using
2 Thes. 2. 10 unrig. in them that *p*.
Heb. 1. 11 shall *p*.; thou remainest
Jas. 1. 11 and the fashion of it *p*.
1 Pet. 1. 7 more pre. than gold th. *p*.
2 Pet. 3. 6 overflowed with water, *p*.
Jude 11 *p*. in gainsaying of Core
R. V. Num. 17. 12; Jer. 48. 46 un-
done; 2 Cor. 4. 16 is decaying

Perjured. R. V. *false swearer.*
1 Tim. 1. 10 for liars, for *p*. persons

Permission. *Concession.*
1 Cor. 7. 6 but I speak this by *p*.

Permit. *Turn over on, suffer.*
Acts 26. 1 *p*. to speak for thyself
1 Cor. 13. 34 not *p*. to th. to speak
16. 7 tarry awhile, if the Lord *p*.
Heb. 6. 3 this we do, if the Lord *p*.

Pernicious. R. V. *lascivious.*
2 Pet. 2. 2 many follow their *p*. ways

Perpetual. *Continuous.*
Gen. 9. 12 covenant for *p*. genera.
Ex. 29. 9 priest's office be theirs *p*.
Lev. 3. 17 a *p*. statute for generat.
Num. 19. 21 it shall be *p*. statute
Ps. 9. 6 destruc. are come to *p*. end
Jer. 15. 18 Why is my pain *p*.
51. 39, 57 sleep *p*. sleep, not wake
Ezek. 35. 9 will make thee *p*. desol.
Hab. 3. 6 and the *p*. hills did bow
Zeph. 2. 9 Moab shall be *p*. desola.
R. V. Ps. 9. 6 forever; Jer. 50. 5;
Hab. 3. 6 everlasting [*ously*.

Perpetually. *All days, continu-*

---

1 K. 9. 3 and mine heart be there *p*.
2 Chr. 7. 16
Am. 1. 11 and his anger did tear *p*.

Perplexed. *Entangled, worried.*
Esth. 3. 15 the city Shushan was *p*.
Joel 1. 18 the herds of cattle are *p*.
Luke 9. 7 and he was *p*., because
24. 4 as they were much *p*. therea.
2 Cor. 4. 8 We were troubled and *p*.

Perplexity. *Entanglement.*
Isa. 22. 5 For it is a day of *p*. by L. G.
Mic. 7. 4 now shall be their *p*.
Luke 21. 25 distress of nat. with *p*.

Persecute. *Pursue.*
Deut. 30. 7 curses on them that *p*.
Job 19. 22 Why do ye *p*. me for G.
Ps. 7. 1 save me from them that *p*.
119. 86 they *p*. me wrongfully
Isa. 14. 6 that ruled in anger is *p*.
Jer. 29. 18 will *p*. them with sword
Lam. 3. 43 covered with anger and *p*
Mat. 5. 10 Bless. they which are *p*.
5. 44 pray for them which *p*. you
Luke 21. 12 lay hands on you, and *p*.
John 5. 16 therefore Jews *p*. Jesus
Acts 9. 4 Saul, why *p*. thou me?
22. 8 Jesus of Naz. whom thou *p*.
Rom. 12. 14 Bless th. which *p*. you
1 Cor. 4. 12 being *p*. we suffer it
2 Cor. 4. 9 *p*. but not forsaken
Gal. 1. 23 which *p*. us in times past
Phil. 3. 6 concerning zeal, *p*. church
1 Thes. 2. 15 *p*. us, and please not G.
Rev. 12. 13 dragon *p*. the woman
R. V. Ps. 7. 1, 5; 35. 3, 6; 11. 11;
83. 15; Jer. 29. 18; Lam. 3. 43, 66;
2 Cor. 4. 9 pursue, or pursued; 1
Thes. 2. 15 drave out

Persecution. *Pursuit.*
Lam. 5. 5 Our necks are under *p*.
Mat. 13. 21 when trib. and *p*. ariseth
Mark 10. 30 receive lands with *p*.
Acts 13. 50 raised *p*. against Paul
Rom. 8. 35 shall *p*. sep. us from C.?
2 Cor. 12. 10 I take pleasure in *p*.
Gal. 5. 11 why do I suffer *p*.?
2 Thes. 1. 4 and faith in all your *p*.
2 Tim. 3. 12 godly shall suffer *p*.
R. V. Acts 11. 19 tribulation

Persecutor. *Pursuer.*
Neh. 9. 11 *p*. thou threwest into de.
Ps. 7. 13 ordaineth arrows against *p*.
119. 157 Many are my *p*. and en.
142. 6 deliver me from my *p*., for
Lam. 1. 3 all her *p*. overtook her
4. 19 *p*. are swifter than eagles
1 Tim. 1. 13 Who was before a *p*.
R. V. Neh. 9. 11; Lam. 4. 19 pursuers; Ps. 7. 13 fiery shafts

Perseverance. *Endurance.*
Eph. 6. 18 with all *p*. and supplic.

Person. *Man, face, being.*
Gen. 14. 21 Give me *p*., take goods
Ex. 16. 16 according to number of *p*.
Lev. 27. 2 *p*. shall be for the Lord
Num. 31. 19 whos. hath killed any *p*.
Deut. 1. 17 not respect *p*. in judgm.
Josh. 20. 9 whosoever killeth any *p*.
Judg. 9. 4 Abimelech hired vain *p*.
1 Sam. 9. 2 not goodlier *p*. than Saul
2 Sam. 17. 11 go to battle in own *p*.
2 K. 10. 6 king's sons, being sev. *p*.
Job 13. 18 Will ye accept his *p*.?
Ps. 26. 4 I ha. not sat with vain *p*.
Prov. 28. 21 resp. of *p*. is not good
Jer. 52. 25 took seven near k's *p*.
Lam. 4. 16 resp. not *p*. of priests
Ezek. 27. 13 they traded *p*. of men
Dan. 11. 21 shall stand up vile *p*.
Jonah 4. 11 more than six sc. th. *p*.
Zeph. 3. 4 prophets are treacher. *p*.
Mal. 1. 9 will he regard your *p*.?
Mat. 22. 16 regard. not *p*. of men
Mark 12. 14
Luke 20. 21 nei. accept. *p*. of any
Acts 10. 34 G. is no respecter of *p*.
Rom. 2. 11 no resp. of *p*. with God
1 Cor. 5. 13 put away wicked *p*.
2 Cor. 2. 10 forgave I it imp. of C.
Gal. 2. 6 G. accepteth no man's *p*.
Eph. 6. 9; Col. 3. 25
Heb. 1. 3 express image of his *p*.
Jas. 2. 9 if ye have respect to *p*.
2 Pet. 2. 5 G. saved Noah, eight *p*.
Jude 16 have men's *p*. in admira.
R. V. Gen. 36. 6 Num. 5. 6 soul;

Deut. 15. 22; Ps. 49. 10 —— ;
Judg. 9. 4 fellows; Jer. 52. 25
face; Mat. 27. 24 man; Heb. 1.
3 substance

Persuade. *Move, sway, entice.*
1 K. 22. 20 Who shall *p.* Ahab
2 K. 18. 32 when he *p.* you, saying
2 Chr. 32. 15 let not Hez. *p.* you
Prov. 25. 15 long forbear. is prin. *p.*
Isa. 36. 18 lest Hezekiah *p.* you
Mat. 27. 20 priests *p.* the multitude
Luke 16. 31 nei. be *p.* though one
Acts 13. 43 who *p.* them to continue
19. 8 *p.* things concerning king
26. 28 almost thou *p.* me to be a Ch.
Rom. 8. 38 am *p.* that nei. death
15. 14 I myself also am *p.* of you
2 Cor. 5. 11 ter. of law, we *p.* men
Gal. 1. 10 do I *p.* men or God?
2 Tim. 1. 5 and I am *p.* that in thee
Heb. 6. 9 *p.* better things of you
R. V. 1 K. 22. 20 21, 22 entice; 2
Chr. 18. 2 moved; Acts 13. 43
urged; Rom. 4. 21; 14. 5 assum-
ed; Heb. 11. 13 greeted

Persuasion. *Persuasion.*
Gal. 5. 8 *p.* cometh not of him that

Pertain. *Be, belong, appertain.*
Lev. 7. 20 peace offering *p.* to Lord
Num. 31. 43 half that *p.* unto thee
Deut. 22. 5 woman not wear wh. *p.*
Judg. 6. 11 under oak that *p.* to J.
1 Sam. 27. 6 Ziklag *p.* to kings of J.
2 Sam. 9. 9 given all that *p.* to Saul
1 K. 7. 48 S, made vessels that *p.*
2 K. 24. 7 that *p.* to king of Egypt
1 Chr. 26. 32 rulers for matters *p.* G.
2 Chr. 12. 4 took cities wh. *p.* to J.
Acts 1. 3 speaking of things *p.* to
Rom. 9. 4 to whom *p.* the adoption
1 Cor. 6. 3 things that *p.* to this life
Heb. 2. 17 H. pr. in things *p.* to G.
7. 13 he *p.* to another tribe of wh.
2 Pet. 1. 3 all things that *p.* to life
R. V. Num. 4. 16 shall be; 31. 43
congregation's half; Josh. 24. 33;
1 Chr. 11. 31 of; 2 Sam. 2 15 and
for; 1 K. 7. 48 were in; Acts 1. 3
concerning; Rom. 4. 1 according;
9. 4 whose is; Heb. 7. 13 belongeth; 9. 9 touching

Perverse. *Turned over against ;
intractable, vexatious.*
Num. 22. 32 went, bec. thy way is *p.*
Deut. 32. 5 they are *p.* and crook. g.
1 Sam. 20. 30 Thou son of *p.* woman
Job 6. 30 cannot discern *p.* things?
9. 20 my mouth shall prove me *p.*
Prov. 8. 8 noth. fro. or *p.* in them
14. 2 but that is *p.* despiseth him
28. 18 but he that is *p.* shall fall
Isa. 19. 14 L. hath mingled *p.* sp.
Mat. 17. 17 O faithless and *p.* gen.
Luke 9. 41
Acts 20. 30 men arise, speak. *p.* th'gs
Phil. 2. 15 in the midst of *p.* nation
1 Tim. 6. 5 *p.* disputings of men
R. V. Job 6. 30 mischievous; Prov.
23. 33 froward; 1 Tim. 6. 5 wrang-
lings.

Perversely. *In perverse way.*
2 Sam. 19. 19 thy servant did *p.* the
1 K. 8. 47 have sinned, and done *p.*
Ps. 119. 78 they dealt *p.* with me
R. V. Ps. 119. 78 overthrown

Perverseness. *Perversity.*
Num. 23. 21 nei. hath seen *p.* in Is.
Prov. 11. 3 *p.* of transgr. shall desc.
15. 4 *p.* therein is a breach in the
Isa. 30. 12 ye trust in oppr. and *p.*
59. 3 your tongue hath muttered *p.*
Ezek. 9. 9 and the city full of *p.*
R. V. Isa. 59. 3 wickedness; Ezek.
9. 9 wresting of judgment

Pervert. *Overturn, divert, mis-
direct, mislead, corrupt.*
Ex. 23. 8 *p.* words of the righteous
Deut. 27. 14 Thou sh. not *p.* judg.
1 Sam. 8. 3 Sam's sons *p.* judgment
Job. 8. 3 Doth God *p.* judgment?
34. 12 nei. will Alm. *p.* judgment
Prov. 17. 23 tak. gift to *p.* judgm.
19. 3 foolish. of man *p.* his way
Eccl. 5. 8 if thou seest *p.* of judg.
Jer. 3. 21 they have *p.* their way
23. 36 have *p.* words of living God

Mic. 3. 9 hear this, ye that *p.* equity
Luke 23. 2 found this fel. *p.* nation
23. 14 as one that *p.* the people
Acts 13. 10 not to *p.* ways of Lord
Gal. 1. 7 some would *p.* the gospel
R. V. Deut. 24. 17; 27. 19 wrest;
Prov. 19. 3 subverteth, Eccl. 5. 8
taking away

Pestilence. *Plague, pestilence.*
Ex. 5. 3 lest ye fall on us with *p.*
Lev. 26. 25 I will send *p.* among
Num. 14. 12 will smite th. with *p.*
2 Sam. 24. 15 So L. sent *p.* upon Is.
1 K. 8. 37 if there be *p.*, blasting
1 Chr. 21. 12 Choose thee, sw. ev. *p.*
2 Chr. 7. 13 if I send *p.* among peo.
Ps. 78. 50 gave their life over to *p.*
91. 3 deliver thee from noisome *p.*
91, 6 *p.* that walketh in darkness
Jer. 21. 6 inhabitants shall die of *p.*
21. 6; 24. 10; 27. 8; 29. 17; 32. 24
Ezek. 5. 12 third part sh. die with *p.*
6. 11; 7. 15; 12. 16; 14. 19; 28.23
Am. 4. 10 I have sent you the *p.*
Hab. 3. 5 Before him went the *p.*
Mat. 24. 7 there sh. be fam. and *p.*
Luke 21. 11 earthq. sh. be, and *p.*
R. V. Mat. 24. 7 ——

Pestilent. *Plague, pernicious.*
Acts 24. 5 found this man *p.* fellow

Pestle. *Bruising tool, pestle.*
Prov. 27. 22 bray fool .. with a *p.*

Petition. *Asking, seeking, prayer.*
1 Sam. 1. 17 God grant thee thy *p.*
1 K. 2. 16 I ask one *p.* of thee
Esth. 5. 6 What is thy *p.*? it sh. be g.
7. 3 let my life be given at my *p.*
Ps. 20. 5 the Lord fulfil all thy *p.*
Dan. 6. 7 whoso. ask *p.* of any god
6. 13 maketh *p.* three times a day
1 John 5. 15 we have *p.* we desired

Pharisee. *Separate.*
Mat. 3. 7 he saw many *P.* come
See **Dictionary.**

Philosopher. *Lover of wisdom.*
Acts 17. 18 *p.* of Ep. encount. him

Philosophy. *Love of wisdom.*
Col. 2. 8 lest any spoil you th. *p.*

Phylactery. *Charm, guard.*
Mat. 23. 5 they make broad th. *p.*

Physician. *Healer, repairer.*
Gen. 50. 2 J. com. *p.* to emb. fath.
2 Chr. 16. 12 sought not L., but *p.*
Job 13. 4 ye are all *p.* of no value
Jer. 8. 22 is there no *p.* there?
Mat. 9. 12 th. be whole need not a *p.*
Mark 2. 17; 5. 31
Mark 5. 26 suff. many things of *p.*
Luke 4. 23 proverb, *P.*, heal thyself
Col. 4. 14 Luke, the beloved *P.*

Pick. *Peck.*
Prov. 30. 17 ravens shall *p.* it out

Picture. *Imagery, depicted.*
Num. 33. 52 destroy all their *p.*, and
Prov. 25. 11 like ap. of g. in *p.* of sil.
Isa. 2. 16 day of Lord be on all *p.*
R. V. Num. 33. 52 figured stones;
Isa. 2. 16 imagery

Piece. *Portion, part, fragment.*
Gen. 15. 10 laid *p.* one against an.
Ex. 29. 17 shalt cut ram in *p.*, and
Lev. 1. 6 shall flay, and cut it in *p.*
Judg. 9. 53 woman cast *p.* of millst.
1 Sam. 30. 12 they gave him *p.* of c.
2 Sam. 23. 11 *p.* of gr. full of lentiles
1 K. 11. 30 gar., Ahijah rent it in *p.*
2 K. 2. 12 Elisha rent clothes in *p.*
1 Chr. 16. 3 dealt good *p.* of flesh
2 Chr. 23. 17 peo. brake images in *p.*
Neh. 3. 20 Baruch repaired other *p.*
Job 41. 24 hard as *p.* of millstone
Ps. 58. 7 let them be as cut in *p.*
Prov. 6. 26 man is bro. to *p.* of bread
S. of S. 4. 3 temple like *p.* of pom'g.
Isa. 3. 15 beat my people to *p.*?
Jer. 37. 21 give him daily *p.* of br.
Ezek. 24. 6 bring it out *p.* by *p.*
Dan. 2. 5 ye shall be cut in *p.*, and
Hos. 3. 2 brought her fifteen *p.* of
Am. 3. 12 two legs, or *p.* of an ear
Mic. 3. 3 and chop my people in *p.*
Nah. 2. 12 lion did tear in *p.* enough
Zech. 12. 3 that burden, be cut in *p.*
Mat. 9. 16 no m. put. *p.* of new cl.
Mark 9. 21; Luke 5. 36
Acts 23. 10 lest *P.* be pulled in *p.*

See also, break, cut, dashed. etc.
R. V. Ex. 3. 7; Num. 10. 2 beaten
work; 2 Sam. 6. 19; 1 Chr. 16. 3;
Neh. 3. 11, 20 portion; 2 Sam. 23.
11; plot; 1 Sam. 2. 36 morsel; Job
40. 18 tubes; Mat. 17. 27 shekel;
Luke 14. 18 field.

Pierce. *Stab, puncture.*
Num. 24. 8 *p.* them with arrows
Judg. 5. 26 when she had *p.* and
2 K. 18. 21 go into his hand, and *p.*
Job 30. 17 My bones are *p.* in night
40. 24 his nose *p.* through snares
Ps. 22. 16 *p.* my hands and feet
Isa. 36. 6 will go into hand, and *p.*
Zech. 12. 10 look on me wh. they *p.*
Luke 2. 35 sword shall *p.* thy soul
John 19. 34 one of soldiers *p.* side
1 Tim. 6. 10 *p.* thro. with sorrows
Heb. 4. 12 word of G. quick, *p.* even
Rev. 1. 7 they also which *p.* him
R. V. Num. 24. 8 smite

Piercing. *That pierceth.*
Prov. 12. 18 speak. like *p.* of sword
Isa. 27. 1 punish lev. the *p.* serpent
R. V. Isa. 27. 1 swift

Piety. *Godliness.*
1 Tim. 5. 4 learn to show *p.* at home

Pigeon. *Dove, pigeon.*
Gen. 15. 9 Take heifer, and young *p.*
Lev. 1. 14 off. of doves, or young *p.*
Num. 6. 10 he shall bring two *p.*
Luke 2. 24 pair of doves, or two *p.*

Pile. *Heap, mass.*
Isa. 30. 33 the *p.* thereof is fire
Ezek. 24. 9 make *p.* for fire great

Pilgrimage. *Sojourning.*
Geu. 47. 9 the days of my *p.* are
Ex. 6. 4 to give them land of *p.*
Ps. 119. 54 my songs in h. of my *p.*
R. V. Ex. 6. 4 sojournings

Pilgrim. *Sojourner.*
Heb. 11. 13 they were strang. and *p.*
1 Pet. 2. 11 I beseech you as *p.*, ab.

Pill. R. V. *peel.*
Gen. 30. 37 *P.* white strakes in them
30. 38 set rods which he had *p.* be.

Pillar. *Set up, support, column.*
Gen. 19. 26 she became *p.* of salt
28. 18 and Jacob set it up for a *p.*
Ex. 13. 21 by day in *p.* of cloud
14. 19; 26. 32; 27. 10; 33. 10; 35. 11
Num. 12. 5 L. came down in *p.* of
Deut. 12. 3 overthrow altars, br. *p.*
Judg. 9. 6 by *p.* that was in Shechem
1 Sam. 2. 8 *p.* of earth are the Lord's
2 Sam. 18. 18 Ab. reared for him. *p.*
1 K. 7. 6 he made a porch of *p.*
2 K. 14. 14 the king stood by a *p.*
1 Chr. 18. 8 Sol. made *p.*, and vessels
2 Chr. 3. 17 he reared *p.* before tem.
Neh. 9. 12 led them by cloudy *p.*
Esth. 1. 6 fastened to rings and *p.*
Job 9. 6 shaketh earth and *p.* there.
26. 11 The *p.* of heaven tremble
Ps. 75. 3 I bear up the *p.* of it
99. 7 spake to them in cloudy *p.*
Prov. 9. 1 Wis. hath hewn seven *p.*
S. of S. 3. 10 He made *p.* of silver
Isa. 19. 19 at border to the Lord
Jer. 1. 18 have made thee iron *p.*
Ezek. 40. 4 there were *p.* by posts
Joel 2. 30 will show *p.* of smoke
Gal. 2. 9 C. and J., seemed to be *p.*
1 Tim. 3. 15 G., *p.* and gr. of truth
Rev. 3. 12 I make *p.* in tenp. of G.

Pillow. *Bolster, cushion.*
Gen. 28. 11 Jac. put stones for *p.*
1 Sam. 19. 13 *p.* of hair for bolster
Ezek. 13. 18 th. sew *p.* to armholes
13. 20 Behold, I am against your *p.*
Mark 4. 38 J. was asleep on a *p.*
R. V. Gen. 28. 11, 18 under his
head; Mark 4. 38 cushion

Pilot. *Guide, pilot.*
Ezek. 27. 8 wise men were thy *p.*
27. 29 all *p.* of the sea shall come

Pin. *Nail, pin, peg.*
Ex. 27. 19 make *p.* of tabernacle
Num. 3. 37 under Mer. be *p.*, cords
Judg. 16. 14 she fastened it with *p.*
Isa. 3. 22 Lord will take crisping *p.*
Ezek. 15. 3 will men take *p.* to hang
R. V. Isa. 3. 22 satchels

Pine (*v.*). *Waste away.*
Lev. 26. 31 are left shall *p.* away

Isa. 38. 12 cut me off with *p*. sick.
Lam. 4. 9 these *p*. away, stricken
Ezek. 24. 23 *p*. away for your iniq.
Mark 9. 18 gnashed teeth, *p*. away
Isa. 24. 16 my leanness; 38. 12
from the loom

Pine (*n*.).   *Pine, oil tree.*
Neh. 8. 15 fetch olive and *p*. br.
Isa. 41. 19 and *p*. and box tree
60. 13 and the *p*. tree, and box

Pinnacle.   *Little wing.*
Mat. 4. 5 ; Luke 4. 9 set. him on *p*.

Pipe (*n*.).   *Flute.*
1 Sam. 10. 5 meet prophet with *p*.
1 K. 1. 40 people piped with *p*.
Isa. 30. 29 when one goeth with *p*.
Jer. 48. 26 heart sh. sound like *p*.
Ezek. 28. 13 workmanship of thy *p*.
1 Cor. 14. 7 whether *p*. or harp
Tube, pipe.
Zech. 4. 2 sev. *p*. to seven lamps
4. 12 through the two golden *p*.
R. V. Zech. 4. 12 spouts

Pipe. (*v*.).   *Play on pipe.*
1 K. 1. 40 the people *p*. with pipes
Mat. 11. 17 We *p*., ye have not dan.
Luke 7. 32
1 Cor. 14. 7 how kno. what is *p*.?

Pipers.   R. V. *flute-players.*
Rev. 18. 22 v. of *p*. heard no more

Piss (*n*.).   R. V. *water..*
2 K. 18. 27 may drink their own *p*.
Isa. 36. 12

Piss (*v*.).   *Make water.*
1 Sam. 25. 22 any th. *p*. ag'st wall
1 K. 14. 10 cut off th. *p*. ag'st wall
16. 11 ; 21. 21 ; 2 K. 9. 8
R. V. In all above instances, man
child

Pit.   *Well, opening.*
Gen. 14. 10 and Siddim was full of *p*.
37. 20 slay him, and cast him in *p*.
Ex. 21. 33 if a man shall dig *p*.
Lev. 11. 36 a *p*. wherein is water
Num. 16. 30 go down quick into *p*.
1 Sam. 13. 6 Israelites hide in *p*.
2 Sam. 17. 9 he is hid in some *p*.
2 K. 10. 14 Jehu slew them at *p*.
1 Chr. 11. 22 Bena. slew a lion in a *p*.
Job 17. 16 They shall go down to *p*.
33. 18 He keep. back soul from *p*.
Ps. 7. 15 made *p*., and is fallen into
35. 7 they hid for me th. net in a *p*.
Prov. 23. 27 strange wom. is nar. *p*.
26. 27 Whoso. dig *p*. sh. fall there.
Eccl. 10. 8 that dig. *p*. shall fall in
Isa. 14. 15 brought to sides of *p*.
24. 17 Fear and *p*. are upon thee
Jer. 2. 6 led us through land of *p*.
48. 44 fleeth, shall fall into *p*.
Ezek. 19. 4 he was taken in their *p*.
Zeph. 2. 9 bre. of nettles, and salt *p*.
Zech. 9. 11 sent prisoners out of *p*.
Mat. 12. 11 if it fall into *p*. on sab.
Luke 14. 5 shall have ox fall into *p*.
Rev. 9. 1 was giv. key of bottoml. *p*.
R. V. Job 6. 27 make merchandise ;
17. 16 Sheol; Isa. 30. 4 abyss;
Luke 14. 5 well; Rev. 9. 1, 2, 11 ;
11. 7; 17. 8; 20. 1, 3 abyss

Pitch (*n*.).   *Pitch.*
Gen. 6. 14 pitch it within with *p*.
Ex. 2. 3 ark, she daubed it with *p*.
Isa. 34. 9 streams be turned into *p*.

Pitch (*n*.).   *Daub with pitch.*
Gen. 6. 14 thou shalt *p*. it with pitch
Settle down, encamp, fix.
Gen. 13. 12 Lot *p*. tent toward Sod.
Ex. 17. 1 Israel *p*. in Rephidim
Num. 1. 51 when the taberna. is *p*.
Deut..1. 33 search out place to *p*.
Josh. 8. 11 *p*. on north side of Ai
Judg. 6. 33 *p*. in valley·of Jezreel
1 Sam. 4. 1 Philistines *p*. in Aphek
2 Sam. 17. 26 Absalom *p*. in Gilgal
1 K. 20. 27 *p*. like two little flocks
2 K. 25. 1 Neb.·*p*. against Jerusalem
1 Chr. 15. 1 prep. place, and *p*. tent
2 Chr. 1. 4 *p*. tent for it at Jerus.
Jer. 6. 3 shepherds shall *p*. tents
Heb. 8. 2 tabernacle, which Lord *p*.
Raise or build up.
Josh. 4. 20 stones, did J. *p*. in Gil.
R. V. Gen. 13. 12 moved ; 26. 17 ;
33. 18 ; Num. 9. 17. 18 ; Judg. 18.
12 ; 2 Sam. 23. 13 ; 1 K. 20. 28, 29 ;

---

2 K. 25. 1 ; Jer. 52. 4 encamped ;
Josh. 4. 20 set up

Pitcher.   *Bottle, flagon, pitcher.*
Gen. 24. 14 Let down thy *p*., I pray
24. 15 Rebek. came out with her *p*.
Judg. 7. 16 empty *p*., lamps in *p*.
Eccl. 12. 6 or *p*. be bro. at the fount.
Lam. 4. 2 esteemed as earthen *p*.
Mark 14. 13 meet man bear. *p*. of w.
Luke 22. 10

Pitied.   *Compassioned.*
Ps. 106. 46 he made them to be *p*.

Pitiful.   *Compassionate, merc'ful.*
Lam. 4. 10 hands of *p*. women have
Jas. 5. 11 Lord is pitiful and tender
1 Pet. 3. 8 love as brethren, be *p*.
R. V. 1 Pet. 3. 8 tenderhearted

Pity (*v*.).   *Compassionate, spare.*
Deut. 13. 8 nor shall thine eye *p*.
Ps. 103. 13 as father *p*. his children
Prov. 28. 8 him that will *p*. poor
Jer. 13. 14 I will not *p*. nor spare
Lam. 2. 2 The Lord hath not *p*.
Ezek. 16. 5 none eye *p*. thee to do
Joel 2. 18 then the Lord will *p*. peo.
Zech. 11. 5 their shep's *p*. them not

Pity (*n*.).   *Compassion.*
Deut. 7. 16 th. eye shall have no *p*.
2 Sam. 12. 6 because he had no *p*.
Job 6. 14 to afflicted *p*. should be sh.
19. 21 Have *p*. upon me, have *p*.
Ps. 69. 20 look. for some to take *p*.
Prov. 19. 17 that hath *p*. on poor
Isa. 13. 18 they shall have no *p*. on
63. 9 in his *p*. he redeemed them
Jer 15. 5 who shall have *p*. on thee
Ezek. 5. 11 nei. will I have any *p*.
Am. 1. 11 Edom did cast off all *p*.
Jonah 4. 10 Thou had *p*. on gourd
Mat. 18. 33 as I had *p*. on thee
R. V. Job 6. 14 kindness ; Mat. 18. 33
mercy

Place (*v*.).   *Lay, fix, appoint.*
Ex. 18. 21 *p*. such to be rulers of
Deut. 14. 23 choose to *p*. his name
1 K. 12. 32 Jeroboam *p*. priests of
2 K. 17. 6 and *p*. them in Halah
2 Chr. 1. 14 which he *p*. in chariot
Ez. 6. 5 *p*. them in house of God
Job 20. 4 since m. was *p*. on earth
Ps. 78. 60 tent which he had *p*. am.
Isa. 5. 8 that may *p*. alone in the
Jer. 5. 22 wh. *p*. sand for the bound
Ezek. 37. 14 *p*. you in your land
Hos. 11. 11 *p*. them in their houses
Zech. 10. 6 I will bring them to *p*.

Place (*n*.).   *Site, seat, spot, situa-
tion, location.*
Gen. 1. 9 waters gather into one *p*.
Ex. 3. 5 *p*. thou standest is holy gr.
Lev. 1. 16 east part, by *p*. of ashes
Num. 9. 17 in *p*. where cloud abode
Deut. 1. 33 search *p*. to pitch tents
Josh. 5. 9 the *p*. is called Gilgal
Judg. 2. 5 they called that *p*. Boch.
Ruth. 1. 7 went forth out of the *p*.
1 Sam. 3. 2 Eli was laid in his *p*.
2 Sam. 6. 17 set it in *p*. in tabernac.
1 K. 8. 21 have set a *p*. for the ark
2 K. 6. 6. he showed him the *p*.
1 Chr. 15. 1 and prepared *p*. for ark
2 Chr. 3. 1 in *p*. D. had prepared
Ez. 1. 4 let men of his *p*. help him
Neh. 2. 14 there was no *p*. for beast
Esth. 4. 14 arise to Jews fr. anot. *p*.
Job. 7. 10 nei. sh. *p*. know him more
27. 23 shall hiss him out of his *p*.
Ps. 24. 3 shall stand in his holy *p*. ?
Prov. 15. 3 eyes of L. are on ev. *p*.
Eccl. 3. 16 I saw the *p*. of judgment
Isa. 26. 21 Lord com. out of his *p*.
Jer. 19. 3 will bring evil upon this *p*
Ezek. 3. 12 Bless. Lord from his *p*.
Dan. 2. 35 no *p*. was found for them
Hos. 5. 15 I will return to my *p*.
Joel 3. 7 *p*. whither ye sold them
Am. 4. 6 and want of bread in all *p*.
Mic. 1. 3 Lord com. out of his *p*.
Nah. 1. 8 make utter end of the *p*.
Zeph. 1. 4 I will cut Baal from his *p*.
Hag. 2. 9 in this *p*. I give peace
Zech. 14. 10 be inhabited in her *p*.
Mal. 1. 11 in ev. *p*. incense be offer.
Mat. 12. 43 he walk. through dry *p*.
27. 33 Golgotha, A *p*. of a skull
Mark 6. 32 departed into desert *p*.

Luke 4. 17 found *p*. wh. it was writ.
John 6. 10 was much grass in the *p*.
Acts 6. 14 Jesus shall destr. this *p*.
Rom. 12. 19 rather give *p*. to wrath
1 Cor. 1. 2 in every *p*. call on Jesus
2 Cor. 2. 14 knowledge in every *p*.
Eph. 4. 27 Neither give *p*. to devil
1 Thes. 1. 8 in every *p*. your faith
Heb. 12. 17 he found no *p*. of rep.
2 Pet. 1. 19 light shineth in dark *p*.
Rev. 12. 6 hath *p*. prepared of God
R. V. frequent changes, mostly
dependent on antecedent and con-
sequent words

Plague (*v*.).   *Smite, touch, plague.*
Gen. 12. 17 the Lord *p*. Pharaoh
Ex. 32. 35 the Lord *p*. the people
Josh. 24. 5 I *p*. Egypt according to
1 Chr. 21. 17 that they should be *p*.
Ps. 73. 5 neither *p*. like other men
73. 14 all day long have I been *p*.
89. 23 and I *p*. them that hate him
R. V. Ex. 32. 35 smote ; Ps. 89.
23 smite

Plague (*n*.).   *Pestilence, smiting.*
Gen. 12. 17 L. plagued Ph. with *p*.
Ex. 9. 14 I will send all my *p*. upon
Lev. 26. 21 I will bring more *p*. up.
13. 2–59 ; 14. 3–54
Num. 25. 8 *p*. was stayed from Is.
Deut. 24. 8 Take heed in *p*. of lep.
Josh. 22. 17 there was *p*. in congre.
1 Sam. 6. 4 *p*. was on you all, and
2 Sam. 24. 25 *p*. was stayed from Is.
1 K. 8. 37 whatsoever *p*. there be
1 Chr. 22. 22 may be stay. fr. peo.
2 Chr. 21 14 with *p*. will L. smite
Ps. 106. 29 *p*. brake in upon them
Jer. 19. 8 and hiss because of the *p*.
Zech. 14. 15 And so shall be the *p*.
Mark 5. 29 she was healed of the *p*.
Luke 7. 21 he cured many of their *p*.
Rev. 11. 6 to smite the earth with *p*.

Plain.   *Wilderness.*   R. V. Arabah.
Num. 22. 1 pitched in *p*. of Moab
Deut. 1. 1 *p*. over against Red Sea
Josh. 11. 2 *p*. south of Chinneroth
1 Sam. 23. 24 in *p*. south of Jesh.
2 Sam. 17. 16 Lodge not in *p*. of w.
1 K. 14. 25 from H. unto sea of *p*.
Jer. 39. 4 went out way of the *p*.
Zech. 14. 10 land sh. be turned as *p*.
Level place, valley, circuit.
Gen. 13. 10 beheld all *p*. of Jordan
Deut. 3. 10 All cities of the *p*., and
Josh. 13. 9 and all the *p*. of Medeba
Judg. 11. 33 unto *p*. of vineyards
1 Sam. 10. 3 shalt come to *p*. of Ta.
2 Sam. 18. 23 Ahi. ran by way of *p*.
1 K. 7. 46 In *p*. of Jor. did king cast
1 Chr. 27. 28 syc. t. were in low *p*.
2 Chr. 4. 17 In *p*. of Jor. king cast
Neh. 12. 28 *p*. country about Jerus.
Ps. 27. 11 and lead me in a *p*. path
Jer. 17. 26 from *p*. and fr. mount.
Am. 1. 5 cut off inhab. from *p*.
Zech. 7. 7 men inhab. south and *p*.
R. V. Gen. 12. 6 ; 13. 18 ; 14 13 ;
Judg. 4. 11 ; 9. 6 ; 1 Sam. 10. 3 oak,
or oaks ; Obad. 19 ; Zech. 7. 7 low-
land ; 2 Sam. 15. 28 fords ; Luke
6. 17 level place
Straight, clear, simple.
Gen. 25. 27 Jacob was a *p*. man
Ps. 27. 11 lead me in a *p*. path
Prov. 8. 9 *p*. to him that underst.
15. 19 way of right. be made *p*.
Isa. 28. 25 hath made *p*. the face
Jer. 48. 21 judgment come on *p*.
Hab. 2. 2 make it *p*. upon tables
Mark 7. 35 tong. loosed, he spake *p*.

Plainly.   *Clearly, distinctly.*
Ex. 21. 5 if the servant shall *p*. say
Deut. 27. 8 write words of law *p*.
1 Sam. 10. 16 told us *p*. that asses
Ez. 4. 18 letter hath been *p*. read
Isa. 32. 4 the stammerers speak *p*.
John 10. 24 if thou be C., tell us *p*.
11. 14 Jesus said unto them *p*.
16. 25 I show you *p*. of the Father
Heb. 11. 14 such things declare *p*.
R. V. 1 Sam. 2. 27 reveal ; Heb. 11.
14 make manifest

Plainness.   R. V. *boldness.*
2 Cor. 3. 12 we use gr. *p*. of speech

Plaister.   *See* **Plaster.**

Plaiting. *Platting, folding.*
1 Pet. 3. 3 let it not be *p*. of hair
Planes. *Corners, carving tools.*
Isa. 44. 13 he fitteth it with *p*., and
Planets. *Constellations.*
2 K. 23. 5 bur. incens. to S. and *p*.
Plank. *Thick board, beam.*
1 K. 6. 15 cove d the floor with *p*.
Ezek. 41. 25 were *p*. on face of por.
R. V. 1 K. 6. 15 boards; Ezek. 41.
25, 26 beams.
Plant (*n*.). *Shrub, shoot, plant.*
Gen. 2. 5 God made every *p*. of field
1 Chr. 4. 23 that dwell among *p*.
Job 14. 9 bring boughs like a *p*.
Ps. 128. 3 chil. like olive *p*. around
144. 12 sons may be as *p*. grown
S. of S. 4. 13 *p*. are orchard of pom.
Isa. 5. 7 men of J. his pleasant *p*.
17. 11 thou shalt make thy *p*. grow
Jer. 48 32 thy *p*. gone over sea
Ezek. 31. 4 riv. run. about his *p*.
34. 29 raise for th. *p*. of renown
Mat. 15. 13 *p*., my F. hath not pl.
R. V. S. of S. 4. 13 shoots; Jer. 48.
32 branches; Ezek. 31. 4; 34, 29
plantation ; 1 Chr. 4. 23 inhabi-
tants of Netaim.
Plant (*v*.). *Set in ground, sow, en-
gender, implant.*
Gen. 2. 8 God *p*. a garden eastw.
Ex. 15. 17 *p*. them in mountain of
Lev. 19. 23 *p*. all manner of trees
Num. 24. 6 trees which L. has *p*.
Deut. 28. 39 Thou shalt *p*. vineyards
2 Sam. 7. 10 peo., and will *p*. them
2 K. 19. 29 *p*. vineyards, eat fruit
1 Chr. 17. 9 *p*. them, they sh. dwell
Ps. 1. 3 like a tree *p*. by rivers of w.
94. 9 that *p*. ear, shall he not hear?
Prov. 31. 16 with fr. of hands she *p*.
Eccl. 3. 2 time to pluck wh. is *p*.
Isa. 5. 2 *p*. it with the choicest vine
40. 24 Yea, they shall not be *p*.
Jer. 2. 21 I had *p*. thee a noble vine
24. 6 I will *p*. them and not pluck
Ezek. 17. 8 It was *p*. in good soil
19. 13 she is *p*. in the wilderness
Dan. 11. 45 he shall *p*. tabernacle
Hos. 9. 13 Eph. is *p*. in a pl. place
Am. 5. 11 ye *p*. pleasant vineyards
Zeph. 1. 13 *p*. v. y., but not dr. wine
Mat. 15. 13 wh. heav. F. hath not *p*.
Mark 12. 1 certain man *p*. vineyard
Luke 13. 6 had fig t. *p*. in vineyard
Rom. 6. 5 we have been *p*. together
1 Cor. 3. 6 I have *p*., Apollos wat.
Plantation. *Planted.*
Ezek. 17. 7 water it by furrows of *p*.
Planter. *Who plants.*
Jer. 31. 5 the *p*. shall pl., and eat
Planting. *Plant, planting.*
Isa. 60. 21 people, branch of my *p*.
Mic. 1. 6 make Sam. as *p*. of vine
Plaster (*n*.). *Chalk, lime, plaster.*
Isa. 38. 21 lay it for *p*. upon the boil
Dan. 5. 5 *p*. of wall of king's palace
Plaster (*v*.). *Lime, daub, plaster.*
Lev. 14 42 ta. morter, and *p*. house
Deut. 27. 4 shalt pl. them with *p*.
Plat (*n*.). *Portion, plot.*
2 K. 9. 26 will requite thee in this *p*.
Plat (*v*.). R. V. *plaited.*
Mat. 27. 29 *p*. crown of thorns, they
Mark 15. 17; John 19. 2
Plate. *Flower, wing, plate.*
Ex. 28. 36 make *p*. of pure gold and
39. 3, 30; Lev. 8. 9; Num. 18. 36
Board, tablet.
1 K. 7. 36 on *p*. he graved cherubi.
R. V. axles
1 K. 7. 30 ev. base had *p*. of brass
Jer. 10. 9 silver spread into *p*. is
Platter. *Flat dish, board.*
Mat. 23. 25 outside of cup and *p*.
23. 26 which is within cup and *p*.
Luke 11. 39 make clean outside of *p*.
Play. *Perform, delight self, de-
ride, sport.*
Ex. 32. 6 the people rose up to *p*.
1 Sam. 18. 17 wom. ans. as they *p*.
2 Sam. 2 14 Let men arise and *p*.
2 K. 3. 15 pass, when the minstrel *p*.
1 Chr. 13. 8 David and all Israel *p*.
Job 41. 5 *p*. with him as with bird?
Ps. 33. 3 Sing song ; *p*. skilfully

---

104. 26 leviathan, thou made to *p*.
Isa. 11. 8 child shall *p*. on the hole
Ezek. 33. 32 that can *p*. on instru.
Zech. 8. 5 full of boys and girls *p*.
1 Cor. 10. 7 people rose up to *p*.
R. V. Ps. 104. 6 take pastime
Player. *Performer.*
1 Sam. 16. 16 who is a cunning *p*.
Ps. 68. 25 *p*. on instrum. followed
R. V. Ps. 68. 25 minstrel
Plea. *Cause, pleading.*
Deut. 17. 8 too hard bet. *p*. and *p*.
Plead. *Strive, urge, reason.*
Judg. 6. 31 Will ye *p*. for Baal?
1 Sam. 24. 15 The Lord *p*. my cause
Job 13. 19 Who will *p*. with me?
Ps. 35. 1 *P*. my cause, O Lord, with
119. 154 *P*. my cause, and deliver
Prov. 31. 9 *P*. cause of poor and n.
Isa. 1. 17 fatherless, *p*. for widow
51. 22 G. th. *p*. cause of his people
Jer. 2. 9 I will yet *p*. with you, sai.
Lam. 3. 58 hast *p*. cau. of my soul
Ezek. 20. 35 *P*. with you face to f.
Hos. 2. 2 *P*. with your mother, *p*.
Joel 3. 2 *P*. wi. them for my peo.
Mic. 7. 9 until he *p*. and ex. jud.
R. V. Job 16. 21 maintain right;
23. 6 contend with; Ps. 35. 1
strive ; Prov. 31 9. minister judg-
ment
Pleading. *Striving, urging.*
Job 13. 6 heark. to *p*. of my lips
Pleasant. *Desirable, grateful,
agreeable, pleasing.*
Gen. 2. 9 grow every tree that is *p*.
49. 15 he saw land that it was *p*.
2 Sam. 1. 23 Saul and Jon. were *p*.
1 K. 20. 6 whatsoever is *p*. in thine
2 K. 2 19 situation of this city is *p*.
2 Chr. 32. 27 all man. of *p*. jewels
Ps. 16. 6 lines are fall. in *p*. places
133. 1 how good and *p*. for breth.
Prov. 15. 26 words of the pure are *p*.
16. 24 *P*. words are as honeycomb
Eccl. 11. 7 *p*. for the eyes to behold
S. of S. 4. 13 an orchard wi *p*. fruits
Isa. 2. 16 ships, and *p*. pictures
17. 10 therefore plant *p*. plants
Jer. 3. 19 and give thee a *p*. land
25. 34 ye shall fall like a *p*. vessel
Lam. 1. 10 sp. hand on all *p*. things
2. 4 slew all that were *p*. to eye
Dan. 10. 3 I ate no *p*. bread neither
Hos. 9. 13 Ephraim is in a *p*. place
Joel 3. 5 have carried my *p*. things
Am. 5. 11 have plant. *p*. vineyards
Mic. 2. 9 cast out of their *p*. houses
Nah. 2. 9 glory out of *p*. furniture
Zech. 7. 14 laid the *p*. land desolate
Mal. 3. 4 Then shall offering be *p*.
R. V. Gen. 3. 6 a delight; S. of S.
4. 13; 7. 13 precious; Dan. 8. 9
glorious; Jer. 23. 10 pastures.
Pleasantness. *Delight.*
Prov. 3. 17 her ways are ways of *p*.
Please. *Delight, appear right.*
Gen. 16. 6 do unto her as it *p*. thee
Num. 24. 1 Balaam saw it *p*. Lord
Josh. 22. 33 thing *p*. chil. of Israel
Judg. 13. 23 If L. were *p*. to kill
1 Sam. 18. 26 *p*. D. to be king's son
2 Sam. 17 4 the saying *p*. Absalom
1 K. 3. 10 the speech *p*. the Lord
1 Chr. 17. 27 let it *p*. thee to bless
2 Chr. 30. 4 *p*. k. and all congrega.
Neh. 2. 6 it *p*. the king to send me
Esth. 5. 14 the thing *p*. Ham., and
Job 6. 9 even *p*. God to destroy me
Ps. 40. 13 Be *P*., O L., to deliver
115. 3 done whatsoever he hath *p*.
Prov. 16. 7 When man's ways *p*. L.
Eccl. 8. 3 he doeth whatso. *p*. him
S. of S. 2. 7 stir not up till he *p*.
Isa. 42. 21 L. is well *p*. for right.
Dan. 6. 1 *p*. Dar. to set ov. kingd.
Jonah 1. 14 hast done as it *p*. thee
Mic. 6. 7 L. be *p*. with thousands
Mal. 1. 8 will he be *p*. with thee
Mat. 3. 17 in whom I am well *p*.
Mark 1. 11; Luke 3. 22; 2 Pet. 1. 17
Acts 6. 5 saying *p*. the multitude
Rom. 8. 8 in flesh cannot *p*. God
15. 3 even Christ *p*. not himself
1 Cor. 7 32 car. how he may *p*. Lord
Gal. 1. 10 or do I seek to *p*. men?

Col. 1. 19 For it *p*. the Father that
1 Thes. 2. 4 not as *p*. men, but God
2 Tim. 3. 4 that he may *p*. him who
Tit. 2. 9 to *p*. them well in all things
Heb. 13. 16 with such sac. G. is *p*.
R. V. Gen. 16. 6 good in eyes ; 2
Chr. 3. 4 right in eyes ; Ps. 51. 19
delight in; Rom. 10. 26, 27; 1 Cor.
1. 21; Gal. 1. 15; Col. 1. 19 good
pleasure; Gal. 1. 10; Heb. 11. 5
pleasing; 1 Cor. 7. 12 content;
Acts 15. 22 seemed good; Acts
15. 34 ———
Pleasing. *Good, pleasurable.*
Esth. 8. 5 and if I be *p*. in his eyes
Hos. 9. 4 neither shall they be *p*.
Col. 1. 10 walk worthy of L. to *p*.
1 John 3. 22 do things that are *p*.
Pleasure. *Delight, good, desire.*
Gen. 18. 12 wax. old shall I have *p* ?
Deut. 23. 24 eat grapes at thine *p*.
1 Chr. 29. 17 I know thou hast *p*.
Ez. 10. 1: make confes., do his *p*.
Neh. 9. 37 have domin. at their *p*.
Esth. 1. 8 do accord. to ev. man's *p*.
Job 21. 21 what *p*. hath he in house
Ps. 5. 4 not a God that hath *p*. in w.
103. 21 bless L., ye that do his *p*.
Prov. 21. 17 that lov. *p*. shall be poor
Eccl. 5. 4 he hath no *p*. in fools
Isa. 21. 4 the night of my *p*. turned
44. 28 Cyrus shall perform my *p*.
Jer. 2. 24 ass snuffeth wind at her *p*.
Ezek. 18. 32 no *p*. in death of wick
Hos. 8. 8 Is. vessel wherein no *p*.
Hag. 1. 8 and I will take *p*. in it
Luke 8. 14 chok. with cares and *p*.
Acts 24. 27 willing to show Jews *p*.
Rom. 1. 32 have but *p*. in them that
2 Cor. 12. 10 therefore I take *p*. in
Eph. 1. 5 according to good *p*. of his
Phil. 2. 13 will and do of his good *p*.
2 Thes. 1. 11 fulfil all the ood *p*. of
1 Tim. 5. 6 that liveth in *p*. is dead
Heb. 10. 6 in sac. thou hast no *p*.
Jas. 5. 5 ye have lived in *p*. on earth
2 Pet. 2. 13 they count it *p*. to riot
Rev. 4. 11 for thy *p*. were created
R. V. Job 21. 25 good; Jer. 2. 24;
2 Thes. 1. 11 desire ; Acts 24. 27;
25. 9 gain favour; Jas. 5. 5 deli-
cately
Pledge. *Surety.*
Gen. 38. 18 What *p*., sh. I give thee?
Ex. 22. 26 take neigh. raiment to *p*.
Deut. 24. 11 shall bring out *p*. a.
1 Sam. 17. 18 breth., and take their *p*.
2 K. 18. 23 give *p*. to my l. the king
Job 24. 3 they take wid. ox for *p*.
Prov. 20. 16 take *p*. for strange wo.
Isa. 36. 8 give *p*. to my master the k.
Ezek. 18. 12 hath not restored the *p*.
Am. 2. 8 upon clothes laid to *p*.
Plenteous. *Fat, abundant.*
Gen. 41. 34 ta. fifth part in *p*. years
Deut. 28. 11 L. make th. *p*. in goods
Ps. 86. 5 L., *p*. in mercy to all them
103. 8 slow to anger, *p*. in mercy
Isa. 30. 23 and it shall be fat and *p*.
Hab. 1. 16 portion fat, their meat *p*.
Mat. 9. 37 the harvest truly is *p*.
Plenteousness. *Fulness, plenty.*
Gen. 41. 53 seven years *p*. ended
Prov. 21. 5 tho. of dill. tend to *p*.
Plentiful. *Fruitful, copious.*
Ps. 68. 9 God didst send a *p*. rain
Isa. 16. 10 joy out of the *p*. field
Jer. 2. 7 bro. you into *p*. country
48. 33 gladness is from the *p*. field
R. V. Isa. 16. 10; Jer. 48. 33 fruitful
Plentifully. *Abundantly.*
Job 26. 3 hast thou *p*. declared
Ps. 31. 23 *p*. rewardeth proud doer
Plenty. *Abundance.*
Gen. 27. 28 G. give thee *p*. of corn
Lev. 11. 36 pit, there is *p*. of water
1 K. 10. 11 great *p*. of almug trees
2 Chr. 31. 10 to eat, and have left *p*.
Job 22. 25 shalt have *p*. of silver
Prov. 3. 10 thy barns be fill. with *p*.
28. 19 that till. sh. have *p*. bread
Jer. 44. 17 then had we *p*. of victu
Joel 2. 26 eat in *p*. and be satisfied
R. V. Lev. 1. 36 gathering; Job
25 precious; 37. 23 plenteous
Plot. *Devise, design.*

Ps. 37. 12 wicked *p*. against the just

Plough (*n*.).   *Plow.*

Luke 9. 62 having put hand to *p*.

Plough, Plow.   *Break soil, till.*

Deut. 22. 10 shalt not *p*. with an ox
1 Sam. 14. 14 yoke oxen might *p*.
Judg. 14. 18 If ye had not *p*. with
Job 4. 8 that *p*. iniq., sow wicked
Ps. 129. 3 plowers *p*. on my back
Prov. 20. 4 the sluggard will not *p*.
Isa. 28. 24 Doth plowm. *p*. all day
Jer. 26. 18; Mic. 3. 12 Z. shall be *p*.
Hos. 10. 13 Ye have *p*. wickedness
Am. 6. 12 will one *p*. th. with oxen
1 Cor. 9. 10 that *p*. shall *p*. in hope

Plower.   *Who plows.*

Ps. 129. 3 *p*. made long their furrows

Plowing.   *Plowing.*

1 K. 19. 19 Elisha, who was *p*. wi.
Job 1. 14 oxen were *p*., asses feed.
Prov. 21. 4 *p*. of the wicked is sin
Luke 17. 7 having a servant *p*. or f.

Plowman.   *Plower.*

Isa. 28. 24 Doth *p*. plow all day to
Jer. 14. 4 the *p*. were ashamed
Am. 9. 13 *p*. shall overtake reaper

Ploughshare.   *Cutter, coulter.*

Isa. 2. 4; Mic. 4. 3 beat sw. into *p*.
Joel 3. 10 Beat your *p*. into swords

Pluck.   *Pull, snatch, pick.*

Gen. 8. 11 in mo. was ol. leaf *p*. off
Ex. 4. 7 and he *p*. his hand out of
Lev. 1. 16 he shall *p*. away his crop
Num. 33. 52 quite *p*. down high pl.
Deut. 23. 25 may *p*. ears with hand
Ruth 4. 7 a man *p*. off his shoe, and
2 Sam. 23. 21; 1 Chr. 11. 23 *p*. spear
  out of Egyptian's hand
2 Chr. 7. 20 I *p*. them up by roots
Ez. 9. 3 *p*. off the hair of my head
Neh. 13. 25 *p*. hair, and made swear
Job 24. 9 *p*. fatherless from breast
29. 17 *p*. the spoil out of his teeth
Ps. 52. 5 *p*. thee out of dwel. place
74. 11 thy right hand? *p*. it out of
80. 12 they which pass by do *p*. h.
Prov. 14. 1 foolish *p*. it with hand
Eccl. 3. 2 time to *p*. wh. is planted
Isa. 50. 6 them that *p*. off the hair
Jer. 12. 14 *p*. them out of their land
24. 6 will plant, and not *p*. them
Ezek. 23. 34 *p*. off thine own breasts
Dan. 7. 4 I beheld till wings we. *p*.
Am. 4. 11 as firebrand *p*. out of b.
Mic. 3. 2 who *p*. skin from them
Zech. 3. 2 is not this brand *p*. out
Mat. 5. 29; Mark 9. 47 if right eye
  offend thee, *p*. it out
Luke 6. 1 his disc. *p*. ears of corn
John 10. 28 nei. shall any *p*. them
Gal. 4. 15 have *p*. out your own eyes
Jude 12 trees, *p*. up by the roots
R. V. Ex. 4. 7 took; Lev. 1. 16
  take; Num. 33. 52 demolish;
  Ruth 4. 7 drew; Ezek. 23. 34 tear;
  Luke 17. 6 root up; Mark 5. 4
  rent; 9. 7 cast; John 10. 28, 29
  snatch

Plumb line.   *Plumbing line.*

Am. 7. 7, 8 wall made by a *p*. *l*.

Plummet.   *Stone, balance plummet.*

2 K. 21. 13 stretch over Jerusalem *p*.
Isa. 28. 17 lay righteousness to *p*.
Zech. 4. 10 shall see *p*. in hand of

Plunge.   *Dip, defile.*

Job 9. 31 sh. thou *p*. me in ditch

Poet.   *Maker, doer.*

Acts 17. 28 as cert. of your *p*. have

Point (*v*.).   R. V. *mark.*

Num. 34. 7, 8, 10 *p*. out for you m.

Point (*n*.).   *Instant, verge.*

Gen. 25. 32 I am at the *p*. to die
Mark 5. 23 daugh. lieth at *p*. of dea.
John 4. 47 he was at the *p*. of death
Sharp end.
Jer. 17. 1 written with *p*. of diam.
Ezek. 21. 15 set *p*. of sword against
Particular, detail.
Eccl. 5. 16 in all *p*. as he came, so go
Heb. 4. 15 but was in all *p*. tempted
Jas. 2. 10 offend in one *p*., is guilty

Pointed.   R. V. *threshing wain.*

Job 41. 30 he spreadeth *p*. things

Poison.   *Venom, fury.*

Deut. 32. 33 wine is *p*. of dragons

Job 6. 4 *p*. drinketh up my spirit
20. 16 He shall suck *p*. of asps
Ps. 58. 4 Their *p*. like *p*. of serpent
140. 3 adder's *p*. under their lips
Rom. 3. 13 *p*. of asps under lips
Jas. 3. 8 the tongue is evil, full of *p*.

Pole.   R. V. *standard.*

Num. 21. 8, 9 ma. serp., set it on *p*.

Policy.   *Skill, judgment.*

Dan. 8. 25 *p*. cause craft to prosp.

Polished.   *Brightened, carved.*

Ps. 144. 12 *p*. after sim. of palace
Isa. 49. 2 and made me a *p*. shaft
Dan. 10. 6 his feet like to *p*. brass
R. V. Ps. 144. 12 hewn; Dan. 10.
  6 burnished

Polishing.   *Cutting, burnishing.*

Lam. 4. 7 their *p*. was of sapphire

Poll (*n*.).   *Skull, head.*

Num. 1. 2 every male by their *p*.
1 Chr. 23. 24 as c~unted by their *p*.

Poll (*v*.).   *Cut off, shave, shear.*

2 Sam. 14. 26 when he *p*. his head
Ezek. 44. 20 they shall *p*. th. heads
Mic. 1. 16 *p*. thee for del. children

Pollute.   *Make unclean, defile.*

Ex. 20. 25 lift up tool, thou hast *p*.
Num. 18. 32 nei. *p*. the holy things
2 K. 23. 16 Josiah *p*. the altar accor.
2 Chr. 36. 14 priests *p*. house of L.
Isa. 47. 1 have *p*. mine inheritance
Jer. . 2 thou hast *p*. the land with
Lam. 2. 2 L. hath *p*. the kingdom
Ezek. 20. 31 ye *p*. yours. wi. idols
Dan. 11. 31 shall *p*. the sanctuary
Zeph. 3. 4 priests have *p*. the sanc.
Mal. 1. 7 Wherein have we *p*. thee
R. V. Jer. 7. 30 defile; Num. 18.
  23 Ezek. 7. 21, 22; 13. 19; 20.
  39; 39. 7; 44. 7; Dan. 11. 31
  profane, or profaned

Polluted.   *Defiled, made unclean.*

Ez. 2. 62 therefore were they as *p*.
Neh. 7. 64 as *p*., put fr. priesthood
Ps. 106. 38 land was *p*. with blood
Isa. 48. 11 how sh. my name be *p*.
Jer. 3. 1 shall not the land be *p*.?
Lam. 4. 14 have *p*. thems. wi. blood
Ezek. 4. 14 my soul hath not been *p*.
Hos. 6. 8 Gilead is *p*. with blood
Am. 7. 16 thou shall die in *p*. land
Mic. 2. 10 *p*., it shall destroy you
Zeph. 3. 1 Woe to her that is *p*.
Mal. 1. 7 Ye offer *p*. bread upon a.
Acts 21. 28 hath *p*. this holy place
R. V. Isa. 47. 6; 48. 11; Jer. 34.
  16; Lam. 2. 2; Ezek. 20. 9, 13, 14,
  16, 21, 22, 24 profaned; Ezek. 16
  6, 22 weltering; 2 K. 23. 16; Jer.
  2. 23; Ezek. 14. 11; 36. 18; Acts
  21. 28 defiled; Hos. 6. 8 stained,
  Am. 7. 17 unclean; Mic. 2. 10
  uncleanness

Pollution.   *Defilement.*

Ezek. 22. 10 was set apart for *p*.
Acts 15. 20 abstain from *p*. of idols
2 Pet. 2. 20 escaped the *p*. of world
R. V. 2 Pet. 2. 20 defilements

Pomegranate.   *Pomegranate.*

Ex. 28. 33 thou shall make *p*. of
Num. 13. 23 they brought of the *p*.
1 Sam. 14. 2 Saul tarried under *p*. t.
1 K. 7. 18 were upon top with *p*.
2 K. 25. 17 and *p*. upon the chapiter
2 Chr. 3. 16 S. made an hundred *p*.
S. of S. 4. 3 thy temples are like *p*.
Jer. 52. 22 *p*. were like unto these
Joel 1. 12 the *p*. trees are withered
Hag. 2. 19 *p*. hath not brought forth
R. V. 1 K. 7. 18 pillars.

Pommels.   R. V. *bowls.*

2 Chr. 4. 12 two pillars, and the *p*.

Pomp.   *Pride, show.*

Isa. 5. 14 *p*. shall descend to hell
14. 11 Thy *p*. is brought to grave
Ezek. 7. 24 will make *p*. . . to cease
30. 18; 32. 12; 33. 28
Acts 25. 23 Agrip. was come wi. *p*.
R. V. Ezek. 7. 24; 30. 18; 32. 12;
  33. 28 pride

Pond.   *Pool.*

Ex. 7. 19 stretch hand on their *p*.
Isa 19. 10 that make *p*. for fish

Ponder.   *Weigh, consider.*

Prov. 4. 26 P. path of thy feet and
5. 21 of Lord, he *p*. all his goings

---

21. 2 but the Lord *p*. the hearts
Luke 2. 19 Mary *p*. them in heart
R. V. Prov. 4. 26; 5. 6; 5. 21 level,
  and make level; 21. 2; 24. 12
  weigheth

Pool.   *Pool, pond.*

Ex. 7. 19 stretch hand on their *p*.
2 Sam. 2. 13 met by *p*. of Gibeon
1 K. 22. 38 one washed chariot in *p*.
2 K. 20. 20 he made *p*., and cond.
Neh. 2. 14 I went on to king's *p*.
Ps. 84. 6 the rain also filleth the *p*.
Eccl. 2. 6 I made me *p*. of water
S. of S. 7. 4 eyes like fish *p*. in H.
Isa. 22. 9 ye gather waters of *p*.
42. 15 and I will dry up the *p*.
Nah. 2. 8 Nineveh is of old like *p*.
John 5. 2 there is at Jerusal. a *p*.
R. V. John 5. 4; 9. 11 —

Poor.   *Needy, humble, weak, lean.*

Gen. 41. 19 kine, *p*. and ill favored
Ex. 23. 6 not wrest judgment of *p*.
Lev. 14. 21 if he be *p*. and cannot
Deut. 15. 11 For *p*. shall nev. cease
Judg. 6. 15 my fam. is *p*. in Man.
Ruth 3. 10 young men, *p*. or rich
1 Sam. 2. 8 raiseth *p*. out of dust
2 Sam. 12. 1 men. one rich, oth. *p*.
2 K. 25. 12 left *p*. to be vinedress.
Esth. 9. 22 of sending gifts to *p*.
Job 5. 16 So the poor hath hope, and
Ps. 41. 1 Bless. he that consider. *p*.
72. 13 He shall spare *p*. and needy
Prov. 10. 15 destr. of *p*. is their pov.
19. 17 th. hath pity on *p*. lend. to L.
Eccl. 4. 13 bet. *p*. ch. than fool. k.
Isa. 32. 7 devices to destroy the *p*.
Jer. 22. 16 judged cause of *p*. and
Ezek. 16. 49 strengthen hand of *p*.
Dan. 4. 27 by showing mercy to *p*.
Am. 2. 6 sold *p*. for pair of shoes
Hab. 3. 14 rejoicing to devour *p*.
Zeph. 3. 12 the *p*. shall trust in L.
Zech. 7. 10 oppress not wid. nor *p*.
Mat. 5. 3 Blessed are *p*. in spirit
26. 11 ye have *p*. always with you
Mark 12. 42 there came a *p*. widow
12. 43 *p*. wid. hath cast more in
Luke 14. 21 bring in hither the *p*.
19. 8 half my goods I give to *p*.
John 12. 6 not th. he cared for *p*.
Rom. 15. 26 contrib. for *p*. saints
2 Cor. 8. 9 he became *p*., that ye
Gal. 2. 10 that we sh. remember *p*.
Jas. 2. 2 there came in a *p*. man
2. 5 Hath not God chosen the *p*.
Rev. 3. 17 art wretched, mis.. and *p*.
13. 16 rich and *p*., and b., to rec.
R. V. In O. T., frequent changes
  to, needy

Poorer.   *Leaner, needier.*

Lev. 27. 8 If he be *p*. than they

Poorest.   *Leanest, neediest.*

2 K. 24. 14 none remained save *p*.

Poplar.   *Poplar.*

Gen. 30. 37 Jacob took rods of *p*.
Hos. 4. 13 burn incense un. *p*. and

Populous.   *Much peopled.*

Deut. 26. 5 bec. a nat. great and *p*.
Nah. 3. 8 Art thou bet. than *p*. No
R. V. Nah. 3. 8 Noamon

Porch.   *Arch, portico, vestibule,
entrance.*

Judg. 3. 23 Ehud went forth thro. *p*.
1 K. 6. 3 *p*. bef. temple of house
7. 6 he made a *p*. of pillars; the
1 Chr. 28. 11 gave Sol. pattern of *p*.
2 Chr. 29. 7 ha. shut up doors of *p*.
Ezek. 8. 16 bet. *p*. and altar were
40. 7–48; 41. 15; 44. 3; 46. 2
Mat. 26. 71 he was gone out into *p*.
Mark 14. 68 Pet. went out into *p*.
John 5. 2 is a pool having five *p*.
10. 23 Jesus walked in Sol's *p*.
Acts 3. 11 peo. ran together in *p*.
5. 12 with one accord in S's *p*.

Port.   R. V. *gate.*

Neh. 2. 13 went by night to dung *p*.

Porter.   *Gate or door keeper.*

2 Sam. 18. 26 watchman call. to *p*.
2 K. 7. 10 lepers called unto the *p*.
1 Chr. 16. 42 sons of Jed. were *p*.
2 Chr. 23. 19 he set *p*. at the gates
Ez. 7. 7 *p*. and Nethinims went up
Neh. 7. 73 the Levites and *p*. dwelt
Mark 13. 34 command. *p*. to watch

John 10. 3 To him the *p.* openeth
R. V. 1 Chr. 15. 18; 16. 38; 23. 5;
26. 1, 12, 19; 2 Chr. 8. 14 doorkeepers.

Portion. *Share, part.*
Gen. 14. 24 *p.* of men which went
Lev. 6. 17 *p.* of my offerings made
Num. 31. 36 *p.* that went out to war
Deut. 32. 9 the L.'s *p.* is his people
Josh. 17. 5 fell ten *p.* to Manasseh
1 Sam. 1. 5 unto Han. he gave a *p.*
1 K. 12. 16 wh. *p.* have we in Dav.
2 K. 9. 10 dogs eat Jezebel in *p.*
2 K. 9. 21 met him in *p.* of Naboth
2 Chr 28. 21 Ahaz took *p.* out of
Ez. 4. 16 thou shalt have no *p.* on
Neh. 2. 20 ye have no *p.*, nor right
Job 20. 29 this is *p.* of the wicked
Ps. 119. 57 Thou art my *p.*, O Lord
Prov. 31. 15 give a *p.* to maidens
Eccl. 2. 10 this was my *p.* of labour
Isa. 17. 14 This is the *p.* of them
Jer. 10. 16 The *p.* of Jacob is not
Lam. 3. 24 L. is my *p.*, saith soul
Ezek. 45. offer an holy *p.* of land
Dan. 4. 15 let his *p.* be wi. beasts
Hos. 5. 7 devour th. with their *p.*
Mic. 2. 4 changed *p.* of my people
Hab. 1. 16 by them their *p.* is fat
Zech. 2. 12 L. inherit Judah his *p.*
Mat. 24. 51 appoint him his *p.* hyp.
Luke 15. 12 give me the *p.* of goods
R. V. Josh. 17. 14; 19. 9 part; Job
26. 14 whisper Prov. 31. 15 task;
Hos. 5. 7 fields; Ezek. 45. 7; 48.
18 –

Possess. *Acquire, take possession.*
Gen. 22. 17 seed shall *p.* the gate
Lev. 20. 24 I give it you to *p.* it
Num. 13. 30 Let us go up and *p.* it
Deut. 1. 8 *p.* land which L. sware
Josh. 1. 11 L. G. giveth you to *p.* it
Judg. 11. 21 Israel *p.* all land of A.
1 K. 21. 18 whither he is gone to *p.*
2 K. 17. 24 they *p.* Samar., and dw.
1 Chr. 28. 8 that ye may *p.* land
Ez. 9. 11 land, which ye go to *p.* it
Neh. 9. 22 they *p.* land of Sihon
Job 7. 3 made to *p.* mo. of vanity
Ps. 139. 13 thou hast *p.* my reins
Prov. 8. 22 L. *p.* me in beginning
Isa. 34. 11 the bittern shall *p.* it
Jer. 32. 32 they came in and *p.* it
Ezek. 7. 24 they shall *p.* their hous.
Dan. 7. 18 *p.* the kingdom forever
Hos. 9. 6 plac., nettles shall *p.* them
Am. 2. 10 led you to *p.* land of Amo.
Obad. 17 the house of Jacob shall *p.*
Hab. 1. 6 to *p.* the dwellingplaces
Zeph. 2. 9 rem. of my people shall *p.*
Luke 18. 12 give tithes of all I *p.*
Acts 4. 32 things which he *p.* was
1 Cor. 7. 30 buy, as though they *p.*
2 Cor. 6. 10 hav. nothing, yet *p.* all
1 Thes. 4. 4 sh. know how to *p.* ves.
R. V. Job. 13. 26; Zeph. 2. 9; Zech.
8. 12 inherit

Possessed. *Having hold on.*
Josh. 13. 1 very much land to be *p.*
Jer. 32. 15 and vineyards shall be *p.*
Acts 8. 7 many that were *p.* with
16. 16 damsel *p.* wi. sp. of devina.
Demonized
Mat. 4. 24 those were *p.* with devils
8. 16, 28, 33; 9. 32; 12. 22
Mark 1. 32. 5. 15, 16; Luke 8. 36

Possession. *Holding, acquisi-
tion, occupancy.*
Gen. 23. 4 give me *p.* of burying pl.
Lev. 14. 34 Canaan, I give for *p.*
Num. 27. 4 a *p.* among the brethren
Deut. 32. 49 unto chil. of Is. for *p.*
Josh. 1. 15 return to land of your *p.*
1 Sam. 25. 2 whose *p.* were in C.
1 K. 21. 15 take *p.* of vin. of Nab.
1 Chr. 7. 28 their *p.* were Beth–el
2 Chr. 11. 14 Levites left their *p.*
Neh. 11. 3 dwelt ev. one in his *p.*
Ps. 2. 8 uttermost parts for thy *p.*
83. 12 take houses of God in *p.*
Prov. 28. 10 upright sh. have good *p.*
Eccl. 2. 7 also I had great *p.* of
Isa. 14. 23 make it *p.* for the bitter.
Ezek. 11. 15 this land given in *p.*
44. 28 shall give no *p.* in Israel
Obad. 17 Jacob shall poss. their *p.*

Mat. 19. 22; Mark 10. 22 had gr. *p.*
Acts. 2. 45 sold their *p.* and goods
Eph. 1. 14 redemp. of purchased *p.*
R. V. Num. 26. 56; Josh. 22. 7 in-
heritance.

Possessor. *Getter, owner.*
Gen. 14. 19. 22 high God, *p.* of hea.
Zech. 11. 5 Whose *p.* slay them, and
Acts 4. 34 many as were *p.* of lands

Possible. *Able, capable, may be.*
Mat. 19. 26 with G. all things are *p.*
Mark 9. 23 *p.* to him that believeth
Luke 18. 27 imp. wi. men are *p.* with
Acts 2. 24 not *p.* he shall be holden
Rom. 12. 18 If *p.*, as much as lieth
Gal. 4. 15 if *p.*, ye wo. have plucked
Heb. 10. 4 not *p.* that blood of bulls

Post. *Post, lintel.*
Ex. 12. 7 strike on the two side *p.*
Deut. 6. 9 write them on *p.* of house
Judg. 16. 3 took gate and the two *p.*
1 Sam. 1. 9 Eli sat on seat by *p.*
1 K. 6. 33 made he for the door *p.*
2 Chr. 3. 7 overlaid *p.* with gold
Prov. 8. 34 waiting at *p.* of doors
Isa. 6. 4 *p.* moved at voice of him
Ezek. 40. 9 the *p.* thereof. two cub.
40. 10–49; 41. 1, 3
Am. 9. 1 Smite, that the *p.* may sh.
Runner, carrier.
2 Chr. 30. 6 So *p.* went with letters
Esth. 3. 13 letters were sent by *p.*
8. 14 *p.* that rode upon mules and
Job 9. 25 my days are swifter than *p.*
Jer. 51. 31 One *p.* run to m. another
R. V. Ex. 12. 7 lintel; 2 Chr. 3. 7;
Ezek. 41. 21; Am. 9. 1 thresholds;
Isa. 6. 4 foundations

Posterity. *Residue.*
Gen. 45. 7 to pres. you *p.* in earth
Generation.
Num. 9. 10 If any of your *p.* shall
Descendants.
1 K. 16. 3 I will take away the *p.*
Ps. 109. 13 Let his *p.* be cut off
Dan. 11. 4 not be divided to his *p.*
Am. 4. 2 take you away, and your *p.*

Pot. *Pot, pan, cup, jar.*
Ex. 16. 3 when we sat by the flesh *p.*
Lev. 6. 28 if sodden in brazen *p.*
Judg. 6. 19 he put the broth in a *p.*
1 Sam. 2. 14 he struck it into the *p.*
1 K. 7. 45 Hiram make *p.*, and shov.
2 K. 4. 38 Set on *p.*, seethe pottage
2 Chr. 35. 13 sod they in *p.*, and cal.
Job 41. 31 mak. deep to boil like *p.*
Ps. 60. 8; 108. 9 Moab is my wash. *p.*
Prov. 17. 3 The fining *p.* is for silver
Eccl. 7. 6 as crackling under a *p.*
Jer. 1. 13 I said, I see a seething *p.*
35. 5 I set *p.* full of wine, and cups
Ezek. 24. 3 Set on *p.*, and pour wat.
Mic. 3. 3 chop in pieces, as for *p.*
Zech. 14. 20 *p.* in Lord's house like
Mark 7. 4 washing of cups, and *p.*
Heb. 9. 4 gold *p.* that had manna
R. V. Lev. 6. 28 vessel; Job 41. 31;
Mark 7. 8 —; Ps. 68. 13 sheep-
folds; 81. 6 basket; Jer. 1. 13 cal-
dron; 35. 5 bowls

Potentate. *Powerful one.*
1 Tim. 6. 15 blessed and only P.

Potsherd. *Earthenware frag-
ment.*
Job 2. 8 took *p.* to scrape himself
Ps. 22. 15 strength is dried like *p.*
Prov. 26. 23 like *p.* cov. wi. sil. dross
Isa. 45. 9. let the *p.* strive with *p.*
R. V. Prov. 26. 23 earthen vessel

Pottage. *Porridge, stew, broth.*
Gen. 25. 34 Jac. gave E. bread and *p.*
2 K. 4. 38 seethe *p.* for sons of pr.
Hag. 2. 12 if one touch bread or *p.*

Potter. *Maker, framer, potter.*
1 Chr. 4. 23 These were the *p.*, and
Ps. 2. 9 dash in pieces like *p.* ves.
Isa. 29. 16 be esteemed as *p.'s* clay
64. 8 we are the clay, thou our *p.*
Jer. 18. 4 ves. was mar. in hands of *p.*
18. 6 as clay in the *p.'s* hand, so are
Lam. 4. 2 work of hands of the *p.*
Dan. 2. 41 part of *p.'s* clay, p. of iron
Zech. 11. 13 said, Cast it unto the *p.*
Mat. 27. 7 bought wi. them *p.'s* field
Rom. 9. 21 Hath not *p.* pow. ov. cl.
Rev. 2. 27 as ves. of *p.* sh. they be

Pound. *Manah, pound.*
1 K. 10. 17 three *p.* of gold went
Ez. 2. 69 five thousand *p.* of silver
Neh. 7. 71 thous. two hun. *p.* of sil,
Mina, sum.
Luke 19. 13 deliv. ten *p.*, and said
19. 16, 18, 20, 24; 10. 25
Litra, pound.
John 12. 3 *p.* of oint. of spikenard
19. 39 aloes, about an hundred *p.*

Pour. *Make flow.*
Gen. 28. 18 *p.* oil on the top of it
Ex. 4. 9 *p.* it upon the dry land
Lev. 4. 7 *p.* blood of bullock at
Num. 5. 15 shall *p.* no oil on it
Deut. 12. 16 *p.* it on earth as water
Judg. 6. 20 angel said, *P.* out blood
1 Sam. 1. 15 *p.* out soul bef. Lord
2 Sam. 13. 9 *p.* out before him
1 K. 18. 33 *P.* it on burnt sacrifice
2 K. 3. 11 *P.* water on hands of Eli
1 Chr. 11. 18 D. would not d., but *p.*
2 Chr. 34. 21 wrath of L. is *p.* out
Job 16. 20 mine eyes *p.* out tears
Ps. 42. 4 I *p.* out my soul in me
Prov. 15. 28 mouth of w. *p.* out evil
S. of S. 1. 3 name is as oint. *p.* forth
Isa, 26. 16 *p.* prayer when chasten.
Jer. 7. 18 *p.* offer. unto other gods
Lam. 2. 4 *p.* out his fury like fire
Ezek. 7. 8 Now will I *p.* my fury
Dan. 9. 11 the curse is *p.* upon us
Hos. 5. 10 I will *p.* wrath on them
Joel 2. 28 I will *p.* out my spirit
Am. 5. 8 *p.* them out upon face of
Mic. 1. 4 as waters *p.* down a steep
Nah. 1. 6 his fury is *p.* out like fire
Zeph. 3, 8 *p.* on th. my indignation
Zech. 12. 10 will *p.* up. house of D.
Mat. 26. 7; Mark 14. 3 *p.* it on head
Luke 10. 34 *p.* in oil and wine, and
John 13. 5 he *p.* water into bason
Acts 10. 45 *p.* out gift of Holy Gh.
Rev. 16. 1 *p.* out vials of the wrath

Pourtray. *Grave.*
Ezek. 4. 1 *p.* upon it the city, ev. Jer.
8. 10; 23. 14

Poverty. *Lack, need.*
Gen. 45. 11 lest thou come to *p.*
Prov. 23. 21 glutton shall come to *p.*
30. 8 give me neither *p.* nor riches
2 Cor. 8. 2 *p.* abound. unto riches
Rev. 2. 9 I know thy works and *p.*
R. V. Prov. 11. 24; 28. 22 want

Powder. *Fine crushed, dust.*
Ex. 32. 20 Moses ground it to *p.*
Deut. 28. 24 make rain of land *p.*
2 K. 23. 6 stamped the grove to *p.*
2 Chr. 34. 7 beat. grav. images to *p.*
S. of S. 3. 6 perfum. wi. *p.* of mer.
Mat. 21. 44; Luke 20. 18 g. him to *p.*
R. V. Mat. 21. '44; Luke 20. 18
dust

Power. *Might, strength, ability,
authority.*
Gen. 21. 29 in *p.* of my hand to do
Ex– 9. 16 for to shew in thee my *p.*
Lev. 26. 19 and I will break your *p.*
Num. 14. 17 let *p.* of my l. be great
Deut. 4. 37 bro. thee out with *p.*
Josh. 8. 20 they had no *p.* to flee
1 Sam. 30. 4 wept, till had no m. *p.*
2 Sam. 22. 33 my strength and *p.*
2 K. 19. 26 inhabitan. of small *p.*
1 Chr. 29. 11 Thine, O L., is the *p.*
2 Chr. 25. 8 God hath *p.* to help
Ez. 4. 23 made them to cease by *p.*
Neh. 1. 10 hast redeem. by thy *p.*
Job 36. 22 God, he exalteth by his *p.*
Ps. 62. 11 *p.* belongeth unto God
147. 5 Great is L., and of great *p.*
Prov. 3. 27 is in *p.* of thine hand
Eccl. 4. 1 on side of oppr. was *p.*
Isa. 40. 26 for that he is strong in *p.*
Jer. 10. 12 hath made earth by his *p.*
Ezek. 30. 6 her *p.* shall come down
Dan. 8. 6 ran to him in fury of *p.*
Hos. 13. 14 will ransom thee from *p.*
Mic. 3. 8 am full of *p.* by spirit of L.
Nah. 1. 3 L. slow to ang., of great *p.*
Hab. 1. 11 imput. his *p.* to his god
Zech. 4. 6 Not by *p.*, but by my sp.
Mat. 6. 13 kingdom, and *p.*, and gl.
Mark 2. 10 Son hath *p.* to forgive
Luke 4. 6 All this *p.* will I give thee
John 1. 12 to them gave he *p.* to bec.

Acts 8. 19 Give me also this *p.*, that
Rom. 8. 38 nor *p.*, nor things pres.
1 Cor. 9. 4 Have we not *p.* to eat
2 Cor. 5. 7 excel. of *p.* may be of G.
Eph. 1. 21 far above all pr. and *p.*
Phil. 3. 10 know him, and *p.* of res.
Col. 1. 13 deliv. us fr. *p.* of darkness
1 Thes. 1. 5 in *p.*, and in Holy G.
2 Thes. 1. 11 fulfil work of fa. wi. *p.*
2 Tim. 1. 8 partakers accord. to *p.*
Tit. 3. 1 be subject to pr. and *p.*
Heb. 1. 3 uphold. all by word of *p.*
1 Pet. 1. 5 are kept by *p.* of God
2 Pet. 1. 16 *p.* and coming of L. J. C.
Jude 25 dom. and *p.*, now and for.
Rev. 4. 11 to rece. glo., hon., and *p.*
R. V. 1 Sam. 9. 1 valour; Esth. 9.
1 rule; Job 41. 12; Ps. 59. 16; Dan.
11. 6; 2 Cor. 12. 9; Eph. 6. 10
strength; Ps. 66. 7; 71. 8; 2 Thes.
1. 19 might; Hab. 2. 9 hand; Mat.
10. 1; 28. 18; Mark 3. 15; 6. 7;
Luke 4. 6, 32; 10. 19; John 17. 2;
Acts 1. 7; 1 Cor. 11. 10; 2 Cor. 13.
10; Eph. 1. 21; Rev. 2. 26; 6. 8;
8. 1; 12. 10; 13. 4, 7, 12, 15; 17. 12
authority; Luke 9. 43 majesty;
Rom. 9. 21; 1 Cor. 9. 4, 5, 6, 12; 2
Thes. 3. 9 a right; Rev. 5. 13 dominion; Mat. 6. 13; Rev. 11. 3 ——.

Powerful. *Strong, effective.*
Ps. 29. 4 the voice of the Lord is *p.*
2 Cor. 10. 10 for his letters are *p.*
Heb. 4. 12 word of G. is quick, *p.*
R. V. 2 Cor. 10. 10 strong; Heb.
4. 12 active

Practice. *Actions, habits.*
2 Pet. 2. 14 exercised with cov. *p.*

Practise. *Do habitually.*
1 Sam. 23. 9 S. secretly *d.* mischief
Ps. 141. 4 not to *p.* wicked works
Isa. 32. 6 vile per. to *p.* hypocrisy
Dan. 8. 12 and it *p.*, and prospered
Mic. 2. 1 when mor. is light they *p.*
R. V. Ps. 141. 4 occupied in; 1 Sam.
23. 9 devised; Dan. 8. 12, 24 do
pleasure.

Praise (*n.*). *P s a l m , h o m a g e ,*
thanksgiving.
Ex. 15. 11 who is like thee in *p.*
Deut. 10. 21 He is thy *p.*, thy God
Judg. 5. 3 I will sing *p.* to L. G. of
2 Sam. 22. 50 sing *p.* to thy name
1 Chr. 16. 35 may glory in thy *p.*
2 Chr. 29. 30 com. Lev. to sing *p.*
Neh. 9. 5 who is exalted above *p.*
Ps. 9. 14 I may show all thy *p.* in
27. 6 yea, I will sing *p.* unto God
47. 6; 68. 32; 75. 9; 108. 3
Prov. 27. 21 so is a man to his *p.*
Isa. 42. 8 neither my *p.* to images
Jer. 17. 14 O Lord, thou art my *p.*
Hab. 3. 3 earth was full of his *p.*
Zeph. 3. 19 get them *p.* and fame
Mat. 21. 16 thou hast perfected *p.*
Luke 18. 43 they saw it gave *p.* unto
John 9. 24 said, Give God the p.
Acts 16. 25 Paul and Silas sang *p.*
Rom. 2. 29 whose *p.* is not of men
1 Cor. 4. 5 man have *p.* of God
2 Cor. 8. 18 whose *p.* is in gospel
Eph. 1. 6 to *p.* of glory of his grace
Phil. 1. 11 unto glory and *p.* of God
1 Pet. 1. 7 found unto *p.* and honor
R. V. A few changes to, thanksgiv.

Praise (*v.*). *Extol, give thanks,*
bless, adore, glorify.
Gen. 29. 35 Now will I *p.* the Lord
Lev. 19. 24 fruit holy to *p.* Lord
Judg. 16. 24 when peo. saw, they *p.*
2 Sam. 14. 25 none to be so much *p.*
1 Chr. 16. 36 peo. said Amen, and *p.*
2 Chr. 5. 13 make one sound in *p.*
Ez. 3. 10 to *p.* Lord, after ordinance
Neh. 5. 13 to *p.* and give thanks
Ps. 22. 23 that fear the Lord, *p.* him
104. 35; 105. 45; 135. 1; 150. 1
Prov. 27. 2 let another man *p.* thee
Eccl. 4. 2 *p.* dead more th. living
S. of S. 6. 9 daught. saw and *p.* her
Isa. 62. 9 eat it, and *p.* the Lord
Jer. 20. 13 Sing unto Lord, *p.* ye L.
Dan. 4. 34 I *p.* and honoured him
Joel 2. 26 *p.* the name of the Lord
Luke 1. 64 and Zacharias *p.* God
Acts 3. 8 and leaping, and *p.* God

Rom. 15. 11 *P. L.*, all ye Gentiles
1 Cor. 11. 2 Now I *p.* you, brethren
Heb. 2. 12 in midst of ch. I sing *p.*
R. V. Many changes, especially in
Ps., to, give thanks.

Prancing. *To prance, caper.*
Judg. 5. 22 broken by means of *p.*
Nah. 3. 2 and the noise of *p.* horses

Prating. *Prattling.*
Prov. 10. 8, 10 but *p.* fool shall fall
3 John 10 *p.* ag. us wi. mal. words

Pray. *Petition, entreat, ask.*
Gen. 20. 17 Abraham *p.* unto God
Num. 11. 2 Moses *p.* unto the Lord
Deut. 9. 20 and I *p.* for Aaron also
Judg. 9. 38 Go out, I *p.*, and fight
1 Sam. 1. 12 she cont. *p.* bef. Lord
2 Sam. 7. 27 ser. found in h. to *p.*
1 K. 8. 35 they *p.* toward this place
2 K. 6. 18 Elisha *p.* unto the Lord
1 Chr. 17. 25 found in heart to *p.*
2 Chr. 7. 1 when S. made end of *p.*
Ez. 10. 1 when Ezra had *p.*, and
Neh. 1. 4 Neh. *p.* before the God
Job 42. 8 ser. Job should *p.* for you
Ps. 5. 2 God, for unto thee I *p.*
Isa. 37. 15 Hezekiah *p.* unto Lord
Jer. 7. 16 *p.* not thou for this peo.
Dan. 9. 4 *p.* unto the Lord my God
Jonah 2. 1 Jonah *p.* unto the Lord
Zech. 8. 21 go speed. to *p.* bef. Lord
Mat. 6. 6 when thou *p.*, *p.* to Fath.
Mark 14. 38 Watch ye and *p.*, lest
Luke 11. 2 when ye *p.*, say, Our Fa.
John 14. 16 I will *p.* the Father
Acts 10. 48 Th. *p.* they him to tarry
Rom. 8. 26 know not what ye *p.* for
1 Cor. 11. 4 Ev. man *p.* or prophesy.
2 Cor. 13. 7 I *p.* to G. ye do no evil
Eph. 6. 18 *P.* always with all prayer
Phil. 1. 9 I *p.*, his. love may abound
Col. 1. 9 we do not cease to *p.* for
1 Thes. 5. 17 *p.* without ceasing
2 Thes. 1. 11 we *p.* always for you
1 Tim. 2. 8 I will that men *p.* ev. w.
2 Tim. 4. 16 I *p.* God it be not laid
Heb. 13. 18 *P.* for us; for we trust
Jas. 5. 13 any afflicted? let him *p.*
1 John 5. 16 I do not say he sh. *p.*
Jude 20 building faith, *p.* Holy G.
R. V But few changes, and mostly
to, beseech, intreat.

Prayer. *A pouring out, supplica-*
tion, petition, entreating.
2 Sam. 7. 27 *p.* this prayer to thee
1 K. 8. 28 respect *p.* of thy servants
2 K. 19. 4 lift up *p.* for the remnant
2 Chr. 7. 12 said, I have heard thy *p.*
Neh. 1. 6 hear the *p.* of thy servant
Job 16. 17 also my *p.* is pure
Ps. 4. 1 G. have mercy, hear my *p.*
39. 12; 54. 2; 86. 6; 102. 1
Prov. 15. 29 he hear. *p.* of righteous
Isa. 37. 4 lift up *p.* for the remnant
Jer. 7. 16 neither lift up cry nor *p.*
Lam. 3. 8 cry, he shut. out my *p.*
Dan. 9. 17 hear *p.* of thy servant
Jonah 2. 7 my *p.* came unto thee
Hab. 3. 1 *p.* of Hab. the prophet
Mat. 21. 13 sh. be called house of *p.*
Mark 12. 40 for pre. make long *p.*
Luke 6. 12 he con. all night in *p.*
Acts 1. 14 with one accord in *p.*
Rom. 12. 12 contin. instant in *p.*
1 Cor. 7. 5 give yourselves to *p.*
2 Cor. 1. 11 helping together by *p.*
Eph. 6. 18 praying with all *p.*, and
Phil. 4. 6 and sup. with thanksgiv.
Col. 4. 2 Continue in *p.*, and watch
1 Thes. 1. 2 mention you in our *p.*
1 Tim. 5. 5 sup. and *p.* ni. and day
2 Tim. 1. 3 remem. thee in my *p.*
Phile. 22 I trust through your *p.*
Heb. 5. 7 when he had offered *p.*
Jas. 5. 16 *p.* of right. availeth much
1 Pet. 3. 12 L. ears are open unto *p.*
Rev. 5. 8 which are the *p.* of saints
R. V. Job 15. 4 devotion; Ps. 64. 1
complaint; Luke 1. 13; 2. 37; 5.
33; Rom. 10. 1; 2 Cor. 1. 11; 9.
14; Phil. 1. 4, 19; 2. Tim. 1. 3;
Jas. 5. 16; 1 Pet. 3. 12 supplication; Mat. 17. 21; 23. 14 ——

Preach. *Cry, herald, proclaim.*
Neh. 6. 7 appointed prophets to *p.*
Jonah 3. 2 *p.* the preaching I bid

Mat. 3. 1 came *p.* in the wilderness
Mark 1. 4 John did *p.* the baptism
Luke 4. 44 he *p.* in the synagogues
Acts 8. 5 Philip went down and *p.*
Rom. 10. 8 word of faith, wh. we *p*
1 Cor. 1. 23 we *p.* Christ crucified
2 Cor. 4. 5 *p.* not ourselves, but C.
Gal. 2. 2 which I *p.* among Gent.
Phil. 1. 15 Some *p.* C. ev. of envy
Col. 1. 23 was *p.* to every creature
1 Thes. 2. 9. we *p.* gospel of God
1 Tim. 3. 16 G. was *p.* unto Gentil.
2 Tim. 4. 2 *P.* the word; be inst.
1 Pet. 3. 19 he *p.* unto sp. in prison
Tell thoroughly.
Luke 9. 60 go *p.* kingdom of God
Acts 4. 2 they *p.* thro. J. the resurr.
1 Cor. 9. 14 wh. *p.* gosp. sh. live by
Phil. 1. 16 one *p.* C. of contention
Col. 1. 28 we *p.*, warning ev. man
Tell good news.
Ps. 40. 9 I have *p.* righteousness
Isa. 61. 1 to *p.* good tid. unto meek
Mat. 11. 5 poor have gospel *p.* to
Luke 4. 43 I must *p.* king. of God
Acts 5. 42 ceased not to *p.* Jesus
Rom. 1. 15 I am ready to *p.* gospel
1 Cor. 1. 17 C. sent me to *p.* gospel
2 Cor. 11. 7 *p.* to you gospel freely
Gal. 1. 9 if any man *p.* other gospel
Eph. 3. 8 I sh. *p.* among Gentiles
Heb. 4. 2 unto us was the gospel *p.*
1 Pet. 1. 12 them that have *p.* gos.
Rev. 14. 6 *p.* unto them that dwell
R. V. Ps. 40. 9; Luke 6. 90 pub-
lished; Mat. 10. 27; Luke 4. 18,
19; Acts 4. 2; 8. 5; 9. 20; 13. 5,
38; 15, 36; 17. 13; 1 Cor. 9. 14;
Phil. 1. 16, 18; Col. 1. 28 proclaim, or proclaimed; Mark 2. 2;
Acts 16. 6 speak or spake; Acts
20. 7 discoursed

Preacher. *Caller, crier, herald.*
Eccl. 1. 2 van. of van., saith the *p.*
Rom. 10. 14 how hear without *p.*?
1 Tim. 2. 7; 2 Tim. 2. 11 ord. a. *p.*
2 Pet. 2. 5 Noah, *p.* of righteous.

Preaching. *Crying, proclaiming.*
Jonah 3. 2 preach unto it the *p.*
Mat. 12. 41 they repent. at the *p.*
Luke 11. 32
Rom. 16. 25 *p.* of Jesus Christ
1 Cor. 15. 14 then is our *p.* vain, and
2 Tim. 4. 17 *p.* might be fully kn.
Tit. 1. 8 man. his word through *p.*
R. V. Acts 11. 19 speaking; 1 Cor.
1. 18 word; Tit. 1. 3; 2 Tim. 4.
17 message; 2 Cor. 10. 14 ——

Precept. *Charge, rule.*
Neh. 9. 14 commandedst them *p.*
Ps. 119. 4 commanded us to keep *p.*
119. in twenty other verses
Isa. 28. 10 *p.* upon *p.*; *p.* upon *p.*
Jer. 35. 18 ye kept all Jonadab's *p.*
Dan. 9. 5 rebelled, dep. fr. thy *p.*
Mark 10. 5 he wrote you this *p.*
Heb. 9. 19 Moses had spok. ev. *p.*
R. V. Isa. 29. 13; Neh. 9. 14;
Mark 10. 5; Heb. 9. 19 command-
ment

Precious. *Rare, costly, desirable.*
highly prized.
Gen. 24. 53 gave to moth. *p.* things
Deut. 33. 13 for *p.* things of heav.
1 Sam. 3. 1 word of the Lord was *p.*
2 Sam. 12. 30 gold with *p.* stones
1 K. 10. 10 she gave king *p.* stones
1 Chr. 20. 2 crown, *p.* stones in it
2 Chr. 3. 9 garn. house wi. *p.* stones
Ez. 1. 6 strengthened with *p.* things
Job 28. 10 eye seeth every *p.* thing
Ps. 49. 8 redemption of soul is *p.*
Prov. 3. 15 wis. is more *p.* th. rubies
Eccl. 7. 1 g. name bet. th. *p.* oint.
Isa. 13. 12 man more *p.* than gold
Jer. 20. 5 will deliv. thee *p.* things
Lam. 4. 2 The *p.* sons of Zion, com.
Ezek. 27. 20 merchant in *p.* clothes
Dan. 11. 8 carry away the *p.* vessels
1 Cor. 3. 12 gold, silver, *p.* stones
Mat. 26. 7 box of very *p.* ointment
Mark 14. 3 box of ointment, very *p.*
Jas. 5. 7 hus. waiteth for the *p.* fruit
1 Pet. 2. 7 which believe he is *p.*,
2 Pet. 1. 4 exceeding *p.* promises
Rev. 17. 4 deck. wi. gold and *p.* st.

R. V. Ps. 49. 8 ; Mark 14. 3 ; 1 Cor.
3. 12 costly ; Isa. 13. 12 rare ; Dan.
11. 8 goodly

Predestinate. R. V. *foreordain.*
Rom. 8. 29 did *p*. to be conformed
Eph. 1. 5 *p*. us unto the adoption

Pre-eminence. *Firstness, over
and above, special eminence.*
Eccl. 3. 19 man has no *p*. above
Col. 1. 18 that he might have *p*.
3 John 9 who loveth to have the *p*.

Prefer. *Give precedence.*
Esth. 2. 9 he *p*. her and her maids
Ps. 137. 6 if I *p*. not Jerus. above
Dan. 6. 3 Then was Daniel *p*. ab.
John. 1. 15 that com. after me is *p*.
Rom. 12. 10 in hon. *p*. one another
1 Tim. 5. 21 without *p*. one before
R. V. Esth. 2. 9 removed ; Dan. 6.
3 distinguished ; John 1. 15, 30
become ; 1 Tim. 5. 21 prejudice

Premeditate. *Concern.* R. V.——.
Mark 13. 11 neither do ye *p*., but

Preparation. *Making ready.*
1 Chr. 22. 5 I will now make *p*. for it
Prov. 16. 1 *p*. of the heart in man
Nah. 2. 3 flam. torches in day of *p*.
Mat. 27. 62 day that fol. day of *p*.
Mark 15. 42 because it was day of *p*.
Luke 23. 54 and that day was the *p*.
John 19. 14 it was *p*. of the passov.

Prepare. *Make ready, arrange.*
Gen. 24. 31 for I have *p*. the house
Ex. 16. 5 *p*. that which they bring
Num. 23. 4 I have *p*. seven altars
Deut. 19. 3 Thou shalt *p*. a way
Josh. 22. 26 *p*. to build us an altar
1 Sam. 7. 3 *p*. your hearts unto Lord
2 Sam. 15. 1 Absalom *p*. chariots
1 K. 5. 18 they *p*. timber and stone
1 Chr. 15. 1 D. *p*. a place for ark
2 Chr. 1. 4 place which D. had *p*.
Ez. 7. 10 for Ezra *p*. his heart
Neh. 13. 5 he had *p*. great chamber
Esth. 5. 5 unto banquet I have *p*.
Job 11. 13 *p*. thy heart toward men
Ps. 57. 6 have *p*. a net for my steps
Prov. 8. 27 when he *p*. the heavens
Isa. 14. 21 *P*. slaugh. for his childr.
Jer. 46. 14 Stand fast, and *p*. thee
Ezek. 35. 6 will *p*. thee unto blood
Dan. 2. 9 for ye have *p*. lying and c.
Hos. 2. 8 silver and gold they *p*.
Joel 3. 9 *P*. war, wake mighty men
Am. 4. 12 *p*. to meet thy God, O Is.
Jonah 1. 17 the Lord *p*. great fish
Mic. 3. 5 they *p*. war against him
Zeph. 1. 7 Lord hath *p*. a sacrifice
Mal. 3. 1 he shall *p*. way before me
Mat. 3. 3 *P*. ye the way of the Lord
Mark 14. 12 *p*. that we may eat
Luke 22. 8 Go and *p*. us the passov.
John 14. 2 I go to *p*. place for you
Rom. 9. 23 which he had afore *p*.
1 Cor. 2. 9 things which God hath *p*.
1 Tim. 2. 21 *p*. to every good work
Phile. 22 *p*. me also a lodging : for
Heb. 11. 16 he hath *p*. for them
1 Pet. 3. 20 while the ark was a *p*.
Rev. 9. 7 like horses *p*. unto battle
R. V. Many changes to, make
ready, establish, etc.

Prepared. *Made ready, established.*
Num. 21. 27 let Sihon be b'lt and *p*.
Josh. 4. 13 fort. thous. *p*. for war
2 Chr. 8. 16 all work of Sol. was *p*.
Neh. 8. 10 for whom nothing is *p*.
Prov. 21. 31 horse is *p*. ag't day of
Isa. 30. 33 for the king it is *p*. ; he
Ezek. 23. 41 bed, and table *p*. bef. it
Hos. 6. 3 his going is *p*. as morning
Nah. 2. 5 the defence shall be *p*.
Mark 14.5 up. room furnished and *p*.
See also **Prepare.**

Presbytery. *Assembled elders.*
1 Tim. 4. 14 laying on hands of *p*.

Prescribe. *Write.*
Ez. 7. 22 oil, aud salt without *p*.
Isa. 10. 1 grievousn. they have *p*.

Presence. *Face, eye, before, being,
in sight of.*
Gen. 3. 8 A. hid from *p*. of the Lord
Ex. 33. 14 My *p*. shall go with thee
Lev. 22. 3 sh. be cut off from my *p*.
Num. 20. 6 M. went fr. *p*. of assem.
Deut. 25. 9 come in *p*. of elders

Josh. 8. 32 wrote in *p*. of children
1 Sam. 18. 11 D. avoid. out of his *p*.
2 Sam. 16. 19 so will I be in thy *p*.
1 K. 12. 2 he fled from *p*. of king
2 K. 5. 27 went from his *p*. a leper
1 Chr. 16. 27 Glo. and hon. in his *p*.
2 Chr. 9. 23 kings sought *p*. of Sol.
Neh. 2. 1 not been sad in his *p*.
Esth. 1. 10 that serv. in *p*. of Ahaz.
Job 1. 12 Sat. went forth fr. *p*. of L.
Ps. 51. 11 Cast me not from thy *p*.
Prov. 17. 18 surety in *p*. of his fr.
Isa. 19. 1 idols be moved at his *p*.
Jer. 4. 26 broke down at *p*. of Lord
Ezek. 38. 20 men shake at my *p*.
Dan. 2. 27 Daniel ans. in *p*. of king
Jonah 1. 10 he fled from *p*. of Lord
Nah. 1. 5 earth is burned at his *p*.
Zeph. 1. 7 Hold peace at *p*. of Lord
Luke 15. 10 is joy in *p*. of angels
John 20. 30 did J. in *p*. of his dis.
Acts 3. 13 denied him in *p*. of Pil.
1 Cor. 1. 29 no flesh glo. in his *p*.
2 Cor. 1. 10 I Paul, in *p*. am base
Phil. 2. 12 not as in my *p*. only, but
1 Thes. 2. 17 taken for short ti. in *p*.
2 Thes. 1. 9 destr. from *p*. of Lord
Heb. 9. 24 to appear in *p*. of God
Jude 24 faultless bef. *p*. of his glory
R. V. Few changes to, before

Present (*n*). *Reward, offering.*
Gen. 32. 13 he took a *p*. for Esau
Judg. 3. 15 Is. sent a *p*. to Eglon
1 Sam. 9. 7 there is not *p*. for man
1 K. 9. 16 for a *p*. to his daughter
2 K. 8. 8 the king said, Take a *p*.
Isa. 18. 7 a *p*. brought to the Lord
Ezek. 27. 15 brought a *p*. horns of
Hos. 10. 6 for a *p*. to king Jareb

Present (*a*). *At hand, now.*
1 Sam. 13. 15 S. number. people *p*.
2 Sam. 20. 4 and be thou here *p*.
1 K. 20. 27 Israel numbered all *p*.
1 Chr. 29. 17 seen thy people *p*., to
2 Chr. 30. 21 Israel *p*. at Jerusalem
Ez. 8. 25 all Israel *p*. had offered
Esth. 5. 16 gather all the Jews *p*.
Ps. 46. 1 God is *p*. help in trouble
Luke 5. 17 power of the L. was *p*.
John 14. 25 I have spo., being *p*.
Acts 10. 33 are we all *p*. bef. God
Rom. 7. 18 to will is *p*. with me
1 Cor. 3. 22 or things *p*. or to come
2 Cor. 5. 8 willing to be *p*. with L.
Gal. 1. 4 deliver us from *p*. world
2 Tim. 4. 10 having loved *p*. world
Tit. 1. 12 live godly in the *p*. world
Heb. 9. 9 figure for the time then *p*.
2 Pet. 1. 12 established in *p*. truth

Present (*v*). *Set up, place, give.*
Gen. 46. 29 Joseph *p*. himself to fa.
Ex. 34. 2 and *p*. thyself there to me
Lev. 2. 8 when it is *p*. to the priest
Num. 3. 6 and *p*. the tribe of Levi
Deut. 31. 14 *p*. yoursel. bef. taber.
Josh. 24. 1 *p*. themselves bef. God
Judg. 6. 19 Gid. brought and *p*. it
1 Sam. 10. 19 yourselves bef. L.
Job 2. 1 Satan came to *p*. himself
Jer. 38. 26 I *p*. supplica. bef. king
Ezek. 20. 28 they *p*. provocation
Dan. 9. 18 we do not *p*. supplication
Mat. 2. 11 they *p*. unto him gifts
Luke 2. 22 bro. him to *p*. to Lord
Acts 9. 41 call. saints, *p*. her alive
Rom. 12. 1 that ye *p*. your bodies
2 Cor. 11. 2 th. I may *p*. you to C.
Eph. 5. 27 might *p*. it to himself
Col. 1. 22 *p*. you holy, unblameable
Jude 24 him that is able to *p*. you

Presently. *Now, immediately.*
1. Sam. 10. 27 not fa. to burn fat *p*.
Prov. 12. 16 fool's wrath is *p*. known
Mat. 21. 19 *p*. the fig tree withered
Phil. 2. 23 him I hope to send *p*.
R. V. Mat. 21. 19 immediately ;
26. 53 even now ; Phil. 2. 23 forth-
with.

Preserve. *Save, keep.*
Gen. 19. 32 that we may *p*. seed
Deut. 6. 24 he might *p*. us alive
Josh. 24. 17 *p*. us in all the way
1 Sam. 30. 23 Lord who hath *p*. us
2 Sam. 8. 6 L. *p*. D. whith. he went
1 Chr. 18. 6, 13
Neh. 9. 6 L. made and *p*. them all

Job 10. 12 thy visit. ha. *p*. my spirit
Ps. 31. 23 the Lord *p*. the faithful
Prov. 2. 11 discretion shall *p*. thee
Isa. 49. 6 restore the *p*. of Israel
Jer. 49. 11 I will *p*. them alive
Hos. 12. 13 by a proph. was he *p*.
Mat. 9. 17 ; Luke 5. 38 both are *p*.
Luke 17. 33 lose his life sh. *p*. it
1 Thes. 5. 23 be *p*. blameless unto
2 Tim. 4. 18 L. *p*. me unto his king.
Jude 1 sanctified, and *p*. in J. C.
R. V. 2 Sam. 8. 6, 14 ; 1 Chr. 18. 6,
13 gave victory ; Job 29. 2 ;. Prov.
2. 11 watch over ; Ps. 121. 7 keep ;
2 Tim. 4. 18 save ; Jude 1 kept ;
Luke 5. 38 ——

Preserver. R. V. *watcher.*
Job 7. 20 O thou *p*. of men ? why

Presidents. *Presidents.*
Dan. 6. 3, 4, 6, 7 over these three *p*.

Press (*n*.). *Vat.*
Prov. 3. 10 thy *p*. shall burst out
Isa. 16. 10 sh. tread no wine in *p*.
Joel 3. 13 *p*. is full, fats overflow
Hag. 2. 16 when one comes to *p*. fat
Crowd, throng.
Mark 2. 4 not come nigh for *p*., th.
Luke 8. 19
R. V. Joel 3. 13 winepress ; Mark
2. 4 ; 5. 27, 30 ; Luke 8. 19 ; 19. 3
crowd ; 8. 45 crush

Press (*v*.). *Bear down upon,
squeeze, crush, urge.*
Gen. 19. 3 he *p*. upon them greatly
Judg. 16. 16 she *p*. him with words
2 Sam. 13. 25 And he *p*. him ; how.
Esth. 8. 14 being *p*. on by the kings
Ps. 38. 2 and thy hand *p*. me sore
Ezek. 23. 3 there were th. breasts *p*.
Am. 2. 13 I am *p*. as a cart is *p*. that
Mark 3. 10 they *p*. upon him for
Luke 5. 1 *p*. upon him to hear the
Acts 18. 5 Paul was *p*. in spirit, and
2 Cor. 1. 8 we were *p*. out of meas.
Phil. 3. 14 I *p*. tow. mark for prize
R. V. Gen. 19. 3 urged ; Acts 18. 5
constrained ; 2 Cor. 1. 8 weighed
down ; Luke 16. 16 entereth vio-
lently

Presume. *Lift self, dare.*
Num. 14. 44 but they *p*. to go up
Deut. 18. 20 proph. wh. *p*. to speak
Esth. 7. 5 where is he, that durst *p*.

Presumptous. *Proud, daring.*
Ps. 19. 13 Keep thy ser. from *p*. sins
2 Pet. 2. 10 *P*. are they, selfwilled
R. V. 2 Pet. 2. 10 daring

Presumptuously. *Proudly, high-
handedly.*
Ex. 21. 14 But if a man come *p*.
Num. 15. 30 the soul that doeth *p*.
Deut. 1. 43 ye went *p*. up into hill
R. V. Num. 15. 30 with high hand

Pretence. *Pretext, show.*
Mat. 23. 14 for *p*. make long prayers
Mark 12. 40
Phil. 1. 18 whether in *p*., or truth
R. V. Mat. 23. 14 ——

Prevail. *Spread upon, gain mastery, triumph, withstand.*
Gen. 7. 18 the waters *p*., and incr.
Ex. 17. 11 M. held up hand, Is. *p*.
Num. 22. 6 peradventure I shall *p*.
Judg. 1. 35 the house of Joseph *p*.
1 Sam. 17. 50 David *p*. over Philis.
2 Sam. 24. 4 k's word *p*. ag'st Joab
1 K. 22. 22 sh. persuade him and *p*.
2 K. 25. 3 the famine *p*. in the city
1 Chr. 5. 2 Judah *p*. above brethren
2 Chr. 8. 3 and Solomon *p*. against it
Esth. 6. 13 thou sh. not *p*. ag'st him
Job 18. 9 robber sh. *p*. against him
Ps. 12. 4 with our tongue will we *p*.
Eccl. 4. 12 and if one *p*. against him
Isa. 16. 12 pray, but he shall not *p*.
Jer. 1. 19 shall not *p*. against thee
Lam. 1. 16 desol., because enemy *p*.
Dan. 11. 7 shall deal, and shall *p*.
Hos. 12. 4 had p. ov. angels and *p*.
Obad. 7 deceiv. thee, and *p*. ag'st .
Mat. 16. 18 gates of hell shall not *p*.
Luke 23. 23 voices of chief priest *p*.
John 12. 19 Perceive ye how ye *p*.
Acts 19. 20 might. grew word and *p*.
Rev. 5. 5 hath *p*. to open the book
R.V.Gen. 47. 20 ; 2 K. 25. 3 was sore

upon; Job 18.9 lay hold on; Isa.
42. 13 do mightily; Rev. 5. 5
overcome

Prevent. *Be before, stop.*
2 Sam. 22. 6 snares of death *p*. me
Job 3. 12 Why did the knees *p*. me?
Ps. 59. 10 G. of mercy shall *p*. me
Isa. 21. 14 they *p*. with their bread
Am. 9. 10 the evil shall not *p*. us
Mat. 17. 25 Jesus *p*. him, saying
1 Thes. 4. 15 Lord shall not *p*. them
R. V. Job 3. 12 receive; Ps. 88. 13
come before; 2 Sam. 22. 6, 19; Job
30. 27; Ps. 18. 5. 18 came upon;
Mat. 17. 25 spake first to

Prey. *Seized food, booty. spoil.*
Gen. 49. 9 from the *p*. my son
Num. 14. 3 our wives shall be a *p*.
Deut. 2. 35 cattle we took for a *p*.
3. 7; Josh. 8. 2; 11. 14
Judg. 5. 30 have they not divided *p*.
2 K. 21. 14 Judah shall become a *p*.
Neh. 4. 4 and give them for a *p*.
Esth. 3. 13 take the spoil for a *p*.
Job 4. 11 lion perish. for lack of *p*.
Ps. 17. 12 like as a lion greedy of *p*.
Prov. 23. 28 lieth in wait as for *p*.
Isa. 5. 29 roar and lay hold of the *p*.
Jer. 21. 9 life be unto him for a *p*.
Ezek. 7. 21 give to strang. for a *p*.
Dan. 11. 24 scatter among them *p*.
Am. 3. 4 roar, when he hath no *p*.
Nah. 2. 12 lions filled holes with *p*.
Zeph. 3. 8 until day I rise to the *p*.
R. V. Judg. 5. 30; 8. 24, 25; Esth.
9. 15, 16; Isa. 10. 2; Jer. 50. 10
spoil; Job 24. 5 meat; Prov. 23.
28 robber

Price. *Value, hire, wage.*
Lev. 25. 50 the *p*. of his sale shall be
Deut. 23. 18 not bring *p*. of a dog
2 Sam. 24. 24 will buy of thee at *p*.
1 K. 10. 28 receiv. linen yarn at *p*.
1 Chr. 21. 22 grant it me for full *p*.
2 Chr. 1. 16 mer. receiv. yarn at *p*.
Job 28. 18 *p*. of wis. is ab. rubies
Ps. 44. 12 not increase wealth by *p*.
Prov. 17. 16 *p*. in the hand of a fool
Isa. 45. 13 not for *p*., saith Lord
Jer. 15. 13 give to spoil without *p*.
Zech. 11. 12 giv. me my *p*. weighed
Mat. 13. 46 found pearl of great *p*.
Acts 4. 34 brought *p*. of the things
1 Cor. 6. 20 ye are bought with a *p*.
1 Pet. 3. 4 meek spirit of great *p*.
R. V. Deut. 23. 18 wages; Zech.
11. 12 hire

Prick. (*n.*) *Goad, prick.*
Num. 33. 55 be *p*. in your eyes and
Acts 9. 5 hard to kick against the *p*.
R. V. Acts 9. 5 ——; 26. 14 goad

Prick. (*v*) *Stick, puncture.*
Ps. 73. 21 I was *p*. in my reins
Ezek. 28. 24 *p*. brier unto h. of Is.
Acts 2. 37 they were *p*. in th. hearts

Pride. *Lifting up, conceit, exal-
tation, excellency.*
Lev. 26. 19 break *p*. of your pow.
1 Sam. 17. 28 I know thy *p*., and
2 Chr. 32. 26 Hez. humbled for *p*.
Job. 33. 17 he may hide *p*. fr. man
Ps. 10. 2 wick. in *p*. doth persec.
Prov. 16. 18 *p*. goeth bef. destruc.
Isa. 25. 11 shall br. down their *p*.
Jer. 13. 9 I will mar *p*. of Judah
Ezek. 16. 49 this was in. of Sod., *p*.
Dan. 5. 20 mind hardened in *p*.
Hos. 5. 5 the *p*. of Is. doth testify
Obad. 3 *p*. of thy heart deceived
Zeph. 2. 10 this they have for *p*.
Zech. 9. 6 will cut off *p*. of Philist.
Mark. 7. 22 out of heart proce. *p*.
1 Tim. 3. 6 being lifted up with *p*.
1 John 2. 16 *p*. of life, is not of F.
R. V. Ps. 31. 20 plottings; 1 John
2. 16 vainglory.   A few other
changes due to the context

Priest. *Prince, minister, elder,
priest.*
Gen. 14. 18 he was *p*. of high God
Ex. 3. 1 Jethro, *p*. of Midian : and
Lev. 1. 9 *p*. sh. burn all on altar
Num. 3. 3 *p*. which were anointed
Deut. 17. 9 thou shalt come unto *p*.
Josh. 3. 6 Joshua spake unto the *p*.
Judg. 17. 13 I have Lev. to my *p*.

1 Sam. 1. 19 Eli the *p*. sat on seat
2 Sam. 8. 17 Za. and Ahim. were *p*.
1 K. 1. 39 Zadok the *p*. took oil out
2 K. 12 4 Jehoash said to the *p*.
1 Chr. 15. 14 *p*. and Lev. sanctified
2 Chr. 5. 7 the *p*. brought in the ark
Ez. 2. 63 till th. stood *p*. wi. Urim
Neh. 3. 1 *p*. builded the sheep gate
Ps. 78. 64 Their *p*. fell by sword
Isa. 24. 2 with the people, so with *p*.
Jer. 4. 9 the *p*. shall be astonished
Lam. 1. 4 *p*. sigh, virgins afflicted
Ezek. 7. 26 law shall perish from *p*.
Hos. 5. 1 Hear ye this, O *p*., heark.
Joel 1. 1 Gird yours., lament, ye *p*.
Am. 7. 10 Amaz. *p*. of Beth. sent
Mic. 3. 11 *p*. thereof teach for hire
Zeph. 3. 4 *p*. have pollut. sanctuary
Hag. 2. 11 ask *p*. concerning the law
Zech. 3. 8 Hear, O Josh. the high *p*.
Mal. 2. 7 *p*. lips shall keep knowl.
Mat. 8. 4 go shew thyself to the *p*.
Mark 2. 26 is not lawful but for *p*.
Luke 3. 2 An. and Cai. were high *p*.
John 7. 32 the chief *p*. sent officers
Acts 14. 13 *p*. of Jupiter br. oxen
Heb. 5. 6 *p*. after order of Melchis.
Rev. 1. 6 hath made us *p*. unto God

Priesthood. *Priest's office.*
Ex. 40. 15 shall be an everlasting *p*.
Num. 16. 10 and seek ye the *p*.
Josh. 18. 7 *p*. of L. is their inherit.
Ez. 2. 62 as polluted, put from *p*.
Neh. 13. 29 bec. they defiled the *p*.
Heb. 7. 14 Mos. spake noth. con. *p*.
1 Pet. 2. 5 are built up an holy *p*.

Prince. *Exalted, head, leader,
captain, noble.*
Gen. 17. 20 twelve *p*. sh. he beget
Ex. 2. 14 Who made thee a *p*. and
Num. 1. 44 *p*. of Israel being twelve
Josh. 22. 14 each chief house a *p*.
Judg. 5. 3 kings; give ear, O ye *p*.
1 Sam. 2. 8 to set them among *p*.
2 Sam. 3. 38 there is a *p*. fallen in I.
1 K. 4. 2 these were the *p*. which
2 K. 24. 14 car. away Jer. and all *p*.
1 Chr. 22. 17 David command. all *p*.
2 Chr. 21. 9 Jehor. went forth wi. *p*.
Ez. 7. 28 before king's mighty *p*.
Neh. 11. 2 I broke up *p*. of Judah
Esth. 1. 3 Ahasuer. made feast to *p*.
Job 3. 15 had been at rest with *p*.
Ps. 105. 2 bind *p*. at his pleasure
Prov. 28. 2 many are the *p*. thereof.
Eccl. 10. 17 thy *p*. eat in due season
Isa. 1. 23 The *p*. are rebellious and
Jer. 26. 12 Then spake Jer. unto *p*.
Lam. 1. 6 *p*. are become like harts
Ezek. 22. 27 Her *p*. are like wolves
Hos. 7. 16 *p*. shall fall by sword
Am. 2. 3 I will slay all *p*. thereof
Zeph. 1. 8 that I will punish the *p*.
Mat. 2. 6 not least among *p*. of J.
Mark 3. 22 by *p*. of dev. cast out d.
John 14. 30 *p*. of this world cometh
Acts 5. 31 God exalted to be a *P*.
1 Cor. 2. 6 nor the wisdom of the *p*.
Eph. 2. 2 accord. to *p*. of power
Rev. 1. 5 Jesus Christ *p*. of kings
Satrap.
Dan. 3; 6. 1-7 kings sent the *p*.
R. V. Frequent changes in Kgs.
and Chrons. to, captains; In Dan.
to, satraps; In N. T. to, rulers

Princess. *Princess.*
1 K. 11. 3 S. had sev. hun. wiv., *p*.
Lam. 1. 1 *p*. among the provinces

Principal. *Chief, main part.*
Ex. 30. 23 take thou also *p*. spices
Lev. 6. 5 shall restore it in the *p*.
Num. 5. 7 recomp. tresp. with *p*.
1 K. 4. 5 son of Nathan *p*. officer
2 K. 25. 19 and the *p*. scribe of host
1 Chr. 24. 31 the *p*. fathers cast lots
Neh. 11. 17 *p*. to begin thanksgiv.
Prov. 4. 7 wisdom is the *p*. thing
Isa. 16. 8 broken down *p*. plants
Jer. 25. 35 nor *p*. of flock escape
Mic. 5. 5 raise against him *p*. men
Acts 25. 23 *p*. of the city entered
R. V. Ex. 30. 23; Neh. 11. 17 chief;
2 K. 25. 19; Jer. 52. 25 captain

Principality. *Power, rule.*
Jer. 13. 18 your *p*. shall come down
Rom 8 38 nor *p*.. nor pow. be able

Eph. 1. 12 Far above all *p*., power
Col. 2. 10 which is head of all *p*. and
Tit. 3. 1 be subject to *p*. and power
R. V. Jer. 13. 18 headtires; Eph.
1. 21 rule; Tit. 3. 1 rulers

Principle. *Element, essence.*
Heb. 5. 12 one teach you first *p*.
6. 1 *p*. of the doctrine of Christ

Print (*n.*). *Mark, impression.*
Job. 13. 27 thou set. *p*. upon heels
John 20. 25 Exc. I see *p*. of nails

Print (*v.*). *Grave, impress.*
Lev. 19. 28 sh. not *p*. any marks
Job 19. 23 O th. my words were *p*.
R. V. Job 19. 23 inscribed.

Prison. *Guarding place, place of
restraint.*
Gen. 39. 20 Potiph. put Jos. in *p*.
Judg. 16. 21 he did grind in *p*. ho.
1 K. 22. 27 Put this fellow in *p*.
2 K. 25. 29 changed his *p*. garments
2 Chr. 16. 10 Asa put H. in *p*. ho.
Neh. 12. 39 stood still in *p*. gate
Ps. 142. 7 Bring my soul out of *p*.
Isa. 42. 7 bring prisoners from *p*.
Jer. 32. 2 prophet was shut in *p*.
Mat. 4. 12 th. John was cast into *p*.
Mark 1. 14 after J. was put in *p*.
Luke 3. 20 he shut up John in *p*.
John 3. 24 John not yet cast in *p*.
Acts 5. 18 put apostles in com. *p*.
2 Cor. 11. 23 in *p*. more frequent
1 Pet. 3. 19 preach. to spirits in *p*.
Rev. 2. 10 shall cast some into *p*.
R. V. Gen. 42. 16 bound; Neh. 3.
25; Jer. 32. 2, 8, 12; 33. 1; 37. 21;
38. 6, 13, 28; 39. 14, 15 guard; Isa.
42. 7 dungeon; Acts 12. 7 cell

Prisoner. *One bound, confined,
captive.*
Gen. 39. 20 pl. where k.'s *p*. were
Num. 21. 1 took some of them *p*.
Job. 3. 18 there the *p*. rest together
Ps. 69. 33 L. despiseth not his *p*.
Isa. 10. 4 sh. bow down under *p*.
Lam. 3. 34 crush under feet all *p*.
Zech. 9. 11 I have sent for thy *p*.
Mat. 27. 16 they had notable *p*., Bar.
Mark 15. 6 released unto them *p*.
Acts 16. 25 Sang, and *p*. heard them
Rom. 16. 7 Salute And. my fellow *p*.
Col. 4. 10; Phile. 23
Eph. 3. 1 I Paul, *p*. of Jesus Christ.
2 Tim. 1. 8; Phile. 9
R. V. Num. 21. 1; Isa. 20. 4 captive;
Acts 28. 16 ——.

Private. *One's own.*
2 Pet. 1. 20 no proph. is of *p*. interp.

Privately. *Alone, by self.*
Mat. 24. 3 the disc. came to him *p*.
Mark 6. 32 they departed by ship *p*.
Luke 9. 10 he went *p*. into desert
Acts 23. 19 went wi. him aside *p*.
Gal. 2. 2 *p*. to them of reputation
R. V. Mark 6. 32 apart

Privily. *Secretly.*
Judg. 9. 31 he sent messengers *p*.
1 Sam. 24. 4 David cut S.'s robe *p*.
Ps. 10. 8 eyes *p*. set against poor
Prov. 1. 11 lurk *p*. for the innocent
Mat. 1. 19 mind. to put her away *p*.
Acts 16. 37 now do thrust us out *p*.
Gal. 2. 4 who came in *p*. to spy out
2 Pet. 2. 1 *p*. br. damnable heresies
R. V. Judg. 9. 31 craftily; Ps. 11. 2
darkness.

Privy. *Private, inner.*
Ezek. 21. 14 enter into *p*. chamber
Knowing together.
1 K. 2. 44 wickedn. th. heart is *p*. to
Acts 5. 2 his wife being *p*. to it
Pipe, penis.
Deut. 23. 1 th. hath *p*. mem. cut off
R. V. Ezek. 21. 14 ——.

Prize. *Crown, award.*
1 Cor. 9. 24 but receiveth the *p*.?
Phil. 3. 14 I press toward the *p*.

Prized. *Priced, esteemed.*
Zech. 11. 13 price that I was *p*. at

Proceed. *Go on, out or forth*
Gen. 24. 50 The thing *p*. from L.
Ex. 25. 35 br. that *p*. out of candle.
Num. 30. 2 do all that *p*. out of mo.
Deut 8. 3 *p*. out of mouth of Lord
Josh. 6. 10 word *p*. out of mouth
Judg. 11. 36 do that which *p*. out

1 Sam. 24. 13 wick. *p.* from wicked
2 Sam. 7. 12 shall *p.* out of bowels
Eccl. 10. 5 error which *p.* fr. ruler
Isa. 51. 4 for law shall *p.* from me
Jer. 9. 3 they *p.* from evil to evil
Lam. 3. 38 out of mouth *p.* not evil
Hab. 1. 4 therefore wr. judgment *p.*
Mat. 15. 19 out of heart *p.* evil tho.
    Mark 7. 21
Luke 4. 22 gracious words wh. *p.*
John 15. 26 which *p.* from Father
Acts 12. 3 he *p.* to take Peter also
Eph. 4. 29 Let no cor. communi. *p.*
2 Tim. 3. 9 they sh. *p.* no further
Jas. 3. 10 out of same mouth *p.* bles.
Rev. 11. 5 fire *p.* out of th. mouth

Process. *Cause, end, plenty.*
Gen. 4. 3 in *p.* of time C. brought
Ex. 2. 23 ca. to pass in *p.* of time
Judg. 11. 4 ; 2 Chr. 21. 19
R. V. Ex. 2. 23 course of many
    days ; Judg. 11. 4 after a while

Proclaim. *Call, herald.*
Ex. 33. 19 I will *p.* name of Lord
Lev. 25. 10 *p.* lib. throughout land
Deut. 20. 10 When thou com. *p.* p.
Judg. 7. 3 to *p.* in ears of people
1 K. 21. 9 *P.* a fast, set Naboth on
2 K. 10. 20 *p.* assembly for Baal
2 Chr. 20. 3 *p.* fast throughout Judah
Ez. 8. 21 Then I *p.* a fast there at
Esth. 6. 9 *P.*, Thus shall it be done
Prov. 12. 23 heart of fools *p.* foolish.
Isa. 61. 2 *p.* acceptable year of Lord
Jer. 3. 13 Go and *p.* these words
Joel 3. 9 *p.* this among the Gentiles
Am. 4. 5 *p.* the free offerings for
Jonah 3. 5 *p.* fast, put on sackcloth
Luke 12. 3 he *p.* upon house tops
Rev. 5. 2 saw strong angel *p.* with

Proclamation. *Voiced, cried.*
Ex. 32. 5 Aaron made *p.*, and said
1 K. 15. 22 Th. king Asa made a *p.*
2 Chr. 24. 9 J. made a *p.* through
Ez. 10. 7 made *p.* throughout Judah
Dan. 5. 29 Belshaz. made *p.* concern.
R. V. 1 K. 22. 36 cry

Procure. *Seek, do, make.*
Prov. 11. 27 that seek. good *p.* favor
Isa. 41. 21 *P.* your cause, saith Lord
Jer. 2. 17. hast thou not *p.* this
R. V. Prov. 11. 27 seeketh ; Jer.
    26. 19 commit

Profane (*a.*). *Polluted, impious.*
Lev. 21. 7 not take wife that is *p.*
Jer. 23. 11 prophet and priest are *p.*
Ezek. 21. 25 *p.* wick. prince of Is.
1 Tim. 1. 9 law is made for the *p.*
Heb. 12. 16 lest th. be any *p.* person
R. V. Ezek. 21. 25 deadly wounded ;
    22. 26 ; 44. 23 common.

Profane (*v.*). *Pollute, make common.*
Lev. 18. 21 neither *p.* name of God
Neh. 13. 17 evil do, and *p.* sabbath
Ps. 89. 39 thou hast *p.* his crown
Isa. 43. 28 I have *p.* princes of sanc.
Ezek. 36. 23 was *p.* among heathen
Am. 2. 7 maid, to *p.* my holy name
Mal. 1. 12 ye have *p.* it, in ye say
Mat. 12. 5 priests in tem. *p.* sabbath
Acts 24. 6 gone about to *p.* temple

Profaneness. *Profanity.*
Jer. 23. 15 is *p.* gone into the land

Profess. *Put before, promise, confess.*
Deut. 26. 3 I *p.* this day unto Lord
Mat. 7. 23 I *p.* I never knew you
Rom. 1. 22 *p.* themselves to be wise
2 Cor. 9. 13 glori. God for your *p.*
1 Tim. 2. 10 hast *p.* good profession
Tit. 1. 16 they *p.* they know God
R. V. 1. Tim. 6. 12 confess

Profession. *Saying same thing.*
1 Tim. 6. 12 professed a good *p.*
Heb. 3. 1 the High-Priest of our *p.*
R. V. Heb. 3. 1 ; 4. 14 ; 10. 23 confession

Profit (*u.*). *Gain, what is over*
Gen. 25. 32 what *p.* sh. birthright
Esth. 3. 8 it is not for king's *p.*
Job. 21. 15 what *p.* if we pray unto
Ps. 30. 9 what *p.* is in my blood?
Prov. 14. 23 In all lab. there is *p.*
Eccl. 1. 3 what *p.* hath man of lab.
Isa. 30. 5 nor be *p.*, but shame, and

Jer. 16. 19 things wherein is no *p.*
Mal. 3. 14 what *p.* that we kept ord.
Rom. 3. 1 what *p.* of circumcision
1 Cor. 7. 35 I speak for your own *p.*
2 Tim. 2. 14 about words to no *p.*
Heb. 12. 10 chasten., he for our *p.*

Profit (*v.*). *Make gain, profit.*
1 Sam. 12. 21 cannot *p.* nor deliver
Job 33. 27 I have sinned, it *p.* not
Prov. 11. 4 rich. *p.* not in day of wr.
Isa. 44. 9 delect. things shall not *p.*
Jer. 7. 8 lying words th. cannot *p.*
Hab. 2. 18 what *p.* graven images
Mat. 16. 26 what *p.* if he gain world
Mark 7. 11 by what, he *p.* by me
John 6. 63 quicken. flesh *p.* noth.
1 Cor. 15. 3 nor char., it *p.* nothing
Gal. 1. 14 And *p.* in Jews' religion
1 Tim. 4. 8 bodily exercise *p.* little
Heb. 4. 2 word preach. did not *p.*
Jas. 2. 14 what doth it *p.*, brethren

Profitable. *That profits, useful.*
Job 22. 2 Can ma.. be *p.* unto God
Eccl. 10. 10 wisdom is *p.* to direct
Isa. 44. 10 grav. im. is *p.* for noth.
Jer. 13. 7 girdle was *p.* for nothing
Mat. 5. 29 is *p.* for thee that one
Acts 20. 20 I kept back nothing *p.*
1 Tim. 4. 8 godliness is *p.* to all
2 Tim. 3. 16 scrip. is *p.* for doctrine
Tit. 3. 8 these things are *p.* to men
Phile. 11 but now *p.* to thee and to

Profiting. *Progress.*
1 Tim. 4. 15 that thy *p.* may appear

Profound. *Deep.*
Hos. 5. 2 are *p.* to make slander

Progenitor. *Who conceives.*
Gen. 49. 26 above bless. of my *p.*

Prognosticator. *Knower.*
Isa. 47. 13 let monthly *p.* stand up

Prolong. *Make long.*
Deut. 4. 26 shall not *p.* your days
Job 6. 11 that I should *p.* my life?
Ps. 61. 6 Thou wilt *p.* king's life
Prov. 28. 2 thy knowl. shall be *p.*
Eccl. 8. 13 nei. shall he *p.* his days
Isa. 13. 22 her days shall not be *p.*
Ezek. 12. 25 it shall be no more *p.*
Dan. 7. 12 their days were *p.* for
R. V. Job 6. 11 be patient ; Ezek.
    12. 25, 28 deferred

Promise (*n.*). *Word, assurance, hope.*
Num. 14. 34 know my breach of *p.*
1 K. 8. 56 not failed of his *p.* by the
2 Chr. 1. 9 let *p.* to D. be establish.
Neh. 5. 12 do according to this *p.*
Ps. 105. 42 remembered his holy *p.*
Luke 24. 49 I send *p.* of my Father
Acts 1. 4 but wait for *p.* of Father
Rom. 4. 13 *p.* that he should be heir
Gal. 3. 14 mi. receive *p.* of the Spirit
Eph. 1. 13 sea. with Holy Sp. of *p.*
1 Tim. 4. 8 having *p.* of the life that
2 Tim. 1. 1 according to *p.* of life
Heb. 6. 13 God made *p.* to Abrah.
2 Pet. 3. 4 wh. is *p.* of his coming
1 John 2. 25 and this the *p.* he hath

Promise. (*v.*) *Say, assure, profess.*
Ex. 12. 25 give according as he *p.*
Num. 14. 40 go unto place Lord *p.*
Deut. 1. 11 bless you, as he has *p.*
Josh. 23. 5 possess th. land as L. p.
2 Sam. 7. 28 *p.* goodness to thy ser.
1 K. 2. 24 made me an house, he *p.*
2 K. 8. 19 he *p.* him to give a light
1 Chr. 17. 26 thou hast *p.* goodness
2 Chr. 6. 10 set on throne as L. *p.*
Neh. 9. 23 concern. which thou *p.*
Esth. 4. 7 *p.* to pay to king's treas.
Jer. 32. 43 all the good I have *p.*
Mat. 14. 7 Herod *p.* with an oath
Mark 14. 11 *p.* to give him money
Luke 1. 72 mercy *p.* to our fathers
Acts 7. 5 he *p.* to give it to him for
Rom. 4. 21 what he *p.* he was able
Tit. 1. 2 *p.* before the world began
Heb. 10. 23 he is faithful that *p.*
Jas. 1. 12 Lord *p.* to them love him
1 John 2. 25 hath *p.* us eternal life
R. V. Deut. 10. 9 ; Josh. 9. 21 ; 22.
    4 ; 23. 5. 10, 15 spake unto ; Luke
    1. 72 shew mercy ; 22. 6 consented

Promote. *Make high, advance.*
Num. 22. 37 not able to *p.* thee to
Judg. 9. 9, 11 go to be *p.* over trees

Esth. 3. 1 did Ahasuerus *p.* Haman
Prov. 4. 8 exalt her. she sh. *p.* thee
Dan. 3. 30 king *p.* Shadr., Mesh.

Promotion. *Making high.*
Ps. 75. 7 *p.* cometh nei. from east
Prov. 3. 35 shame be the *p.* of fools

Pronounce. *Speak, utter.*
Lev. 5. 4 *p.* with his lips to do evil,
Judg. 12. 6 he could not *p.* it right
Neh. 6. 12. he *p.* this prophecy ag.
Jer. 11. 17 the Lord hath *p.* evil
R. V. Lev. 5. 4 utter rashly ; Jer
    18. 8 ; 34. 5 spoken

Proof. *Trial, showing.*
Acts 1. 3 showed hims. by infal. *p.*
2 Cor. 2. 9 that I might know *p.*
Phil. 2. 22 ye know the *p.* of him
2 Tim. 4. 5 make *p.* of thy ministry

Proper. R. V. *goodly.*
Heb. 11. 23 saw he was a *p.* child
Particular.
1 Chr. 29. 3 I have of own *p.* good
Own, native.
Acts 1. 19 called in the *p.* tongue
1 Cor. 7. 7 every man hath *p.* gift
R. V. 1 Cor. 7. 7 own gift from

Prophecy. *Message, prediction.*
2 Chr. 15. 8 Asa heard *p.* of Oded
Neh. 6. 12 he pronounced this *p.*
Prov. 30. 1 *P.* his mother tau. him
Dan. 9. 24 to seal vision and *p.*, and
Mat. 13. 14 in them is fulfilled the *p.*
Rom. 12. 6 whether *p.*, let us proph.
1 Cor. 13. 8 but whether there be *p.*
1 Tim. 4. 14 was given thee by *p.*
2 Pet. 1. 21 *p.* came not in old time
Rev. 19. 10 test. of J. is spirit of *p.*
R. V. Prov. 30. 1 oracle

Prophesy. *Foretell, expound.*
Num. 11. 27 Eldad and Med. do *p.*
1 Sam. 10. 11 he *p.* among prophets
1 K. 22. 12 all the prophets *p.*, so
1 Chr. 25. 1 who shall *p.* with harps
2 Chr. 18. 7 he never *p.* good to me
Ez. 6. 14 prosp. thro. *p.* of Haggai
Isa. 30. 10 *P.* not to us right things
Jer. 2. 8 the prophets *p.* by Baal
    5. 31 ; 11. 21 ; 14. 14 ; 19. 14 ; 20. 1
Ezek. 21. 9 Son of man, *p.*, and say
    25. 2 ; 28. 21, 29. 2 ; 30. 2 ; 34. 2
Joel 2. 28 sons and daugh. shall *p.*
Am. 7. 15 Lord said to me, Go, *p.*
Mic. 2. 11 I will *p.* to thee of wine
Zech. 13. 3 when any shall yet *p.*
Mat. 26. 68 *P.* unto us, thou Christ
Mark 7. 6 Well hath Es. *p.* of you
Luke 1. 67 filled with H. G., and *p.*
John 11. 51 *p.* that Jesus should die
Acts 19. 6 spake with tongues, and *p.*
1 Cor. 11. 4 every man praying or *p.*
1 Thes. 5. 20 desp. not *p.*, prove all
1 Pet. 1. 10 who *p.* of grace that
Jude 14 *P* of these, saying, Behold
Rev. 10. 11 Thou must *p.* ag. before

Prophet. *Seer, public expounder, who prophesies.*
Gen. 20. 7 restore wife, he is a *p.*
Ex. 7. 1 and Aaron shall be thy *p.*
Num. 12. 6 If th. be *p.* among you
Deut. 18. 15 G. will raise a *p.* from
Judg. 6. 8 Lord sent *d.* unto children
1 Sam. 9. 9 *p.* was bef. called seer
2 Sam. 7. 2 k. said unto Nath. the *p.*
1 K. 1. 22 Nathan the *p.* also came
2 K. 3. 11 not here a *p.* of the Lord
1 Chr. 16. 22 and do my *p.* no harm
2 Chr. 13. 22 writ. in sto. of *d.* Iddo
Ez. 9. 11 com. thy servant the *p.*
Neh. 6. 7 *p.* to preach of thee at J.
Ps. 74. 9 there is no more any *p.*
Isa. 28. 7 priest and *p.* have erred
Jer. 2. 8 the *p.* prophesied by Baal
Lam. 2. 9 *p.* find no vision from L.
Ezek. 13. 3 Woe unto the foolish *p.*
Dan. 9. 2 word came to Jer. the *p.*
Hos. 4. 5 the *p.* shall fall with thee
Am. 2. 11 raised up your sons for *p.*
Mic. 3. 5 *P.* that make my people err
Hab. 3. 1 A prayer of Hab. the *p.*
Zeph. 3. 4 Her *p.* are treacherous
Hag. 1. 1 word of L. by Hag. the *p.*
Zech. 1. 5 *p.*, do they live forever?
Mal. 4. 5 I will send Elijah the *p.*
Mat. 1. 22 fulfil. wh. was spo. by *p.*
Mark 6. 4 *p.* is not without honour
Luke 1. 70 spake by mo. of holy *p.*

John 7. 40 said, Of truth this is a *p*
Acts 3. 22 A *p*. shall the L. G. raise
Rom. 1. 2 by *p*. in holy scriptures
1 Cor. 14. 29 *p*. speak two or three
Eph. 4. 11 some *p*., some evangel.
1 Thes. 2. 15 killed L. J. and own *p*.
Tit. 1. 12 a *p*. of their own, said
Heb. 1. 1 G. spake unto fath. by *p*.
Jas. 5. 10 Take thy brethren, the *p*.
1 Pet. 1. 10 *p*. have enq. and search.
2 Pet. 2. 1 were false *p*. among peo.
1 John 4. 1 false *p*. are gone out
Rev. 20. 10 wh. is beast and false *p*.

Prophetess. *Female prophet.*
Ex. 16. 11 Miriam the *p*., sist. of A.
Judg. 4. 4 Deb. a *p*., wife of Lap.
2 K. 22. 14 went to Huldah, a *p*.
2 Chr. 34. 22 Hul. the *p*., wife of S.
Neh. 6. 14 think on *p*. Noadiah
Isa. 8. 3 I went unto the *p*., and
Luke 2. 36 Anna, a *p*., daug. of Ph.
Rev. 2. 20 Jez., wh. call. herself *p*.

Propitiation. *That appeases.*
Rom. 3. 25 God set forth to be a *p*.
1 John 2. 2 he is the *p*. for our sins

Proportion. *Space.*
1 K. 7. 36 accord. to *p*. of ev. one
Array, arrangement.
Job 41. 12 not conceal comely *p*.
Relative part.
Rom. 12. 6 accord. to *p*. of faith
R. V. 1 K. 7. 36 space

Proselyte. *Comer toward.*
Mat. 23. 15 sea and la. to ma. *p*.
Acts 2. 10 Jews and *p*. we hear

Prospect. *Face, outlook.*
Ezek. 40. 45 their *p*. was tow. south
40. 45; 42. 15; 43. 4

Prosper. *Go on, thrive, succeed.*
Gen. 24. 56 Lord hath *p*. my way
Num. 14. 41 but it shall not *p*.
Deut. 28. 29 sh. not *p*. in thy ways
Josh. 1. 7 *p*. whitherso. thou goest
Judg. 4. 24 Is. *p*., and prevailed
2 Sam. 11. 7 deman. how the war *p*.
1 K. 22. 12 Go up to Ramoth and *p*.
1 Chr. 29. 23 S. sat on throne and *p*.
2 Chr. 13. 12 fight not, ye sh. not *p*.
Ez. 5. 8 this work goeth on, and *p*.
Neh. 1. 11 *p*. thy servant this day
Job 9. 4 hardened ag. him, and *p*.
Ps. 1. 3 whatso. he doeth shall *p*.
Prov. 28. 13 that cov. sins sh. not *p*.
Eccl. 11. 6 knowest not wheth. sh. *p*.
Isa 53. 10 pleas. of L. shall *p*. in
Jer. 23. 5 a King shall reign and *p*.
Lam. 1. 5 her enemies *p*.; for Lord
Ezek. 16. 13 thou didst *p*. into king.
Dan. 6. 28 Daniel *p*. in reign of C.
1 Cor. 16. 2 lay store, as G. hath *p*.
3 John 2 *p*., even as thy soul *p*.
R. V. Ps. 73. 12 being at ease, Jer.
20. 11; 23. 5 deal wisely

Prosperity. *Good, well-being.*
Deut. 23. 6 shalt not seek their *p*.
1 K. 10. 7 *p*. exceedeth fame which
Job 15. 21 in *p*. destroyer sh. come
Ps. 122. 7 Peace within walls, and *p*.
Prov. 1. 32 *p*. of fools sh. destroy
Eccl. 7. 14 in day of *p*. be joyful
Jer. 22. 21 I spake to thee in thy *p*.
Lam. 3. 17 remov. soul; I forgat *p*.
Zech. 7. 7 when Jerusa. was in *p*.
R. V. Jer. 33. 9 peace

Prosperous. *Make to prosper.*
Gen. 24. 21 had made his journey *p*.
Josh. 1. 8 shalt make thy way *p*.
Judg. 18. 5 know wheth. way sh. *p*.
Job 8. 6 make the habitation *p*.
Isa. 48. 15 he sh. make his way *p*.
Zech. 8. 12 For the seed sh. be *p*.

Prosperously. *With prosperity.*
2 Chr. 7. 11 house, he *p*. affected
Ps. 45. 4 in thy majesty ride *p*.

Prostitute. *Pollute.*
Lev. 19. 29 Do not *p*. thy daughter

Protection. *Defence, hiding.*
Deut. 32. 38 help, and be your *p*.

Protest. *Testify.*
Gen. 43. 3 did solemnly *p*. to us
1 Sam. 8. 9 yet *p*. solemnly unto
1 K. 2. 42 king *p*. unto thee, saying
Jer. 11. 7 I earnestly *p*. unto your
Zech. 3. 6 angel of L. *p*. unto Josh.
1 Cor. 15. 31 I *p*. by your rejoicing
which

Proud. *Full of pride, haughty, vigorous, exultant.*
Job 38. 11 thy *p*. waves be stayed
Ps. 12. 3 tongue speaketh *p*. things
Prov. 15. 25 Lord will destr. h. of *p*.
Eccl. 7. 8 better than *p*. in spirit
Isa. 2. 12 day of L. on every one *p*.
Jer. 13. 15 he not *p*., L. hath spok.
Hab. 2. 5 he is *p*. man, nei. keepeth
Mal. 3. 15 now we call *p*. happy
Luke 1. 51 he hath scattered the *p*.
Rom. 1. 30 haters of G., despite., *p*.
2 Tim. 3. 2 For all men shall be *p*.
Jas. 4. 6 God resisteth the *p*. but g.
1 Pet. 5. 5
R. V. Job 26. 12 Rahab; Ps. 12. 3;
Ps. 138. 6; Prov. 6. 17; Hab 2. 5;
Rom. 1. 30; 2 Tim. 3. 2 haughty;
1 Tim. 6. 4 puffed up

Proudly. *Haughtily.*
Ex. 18. 11 *p*., he was above them
1 Sam. 2. 3 Talk no more so *p*.
Neh. 9. 10 thou knew, they dealt *p*.
Ps. 17. 10 with mouth they speak *p*.
Isa. 3. 5 chi. shall behave himself *p*.
Obad. 12 neither sh. have spoken *p*.

Prove. *Try, test.*
Gen. 42. 15 sh. be *p*. by life of Ph.
Ex. 20. 20 God is come to *p*. you
Deut. 13. 3 for Lord your God *p*.
Judg. 2. 22 thro. him I may *p*. Is.
1 Sam. 17. 39 I have not *p*. them
1 K. 10. 1 she came to *p*. him
1 Chr. 9. 1 she came to *p*. Solomon
Ps. 17. 3 Thou hast *p*. mine heart
Eccl. 2. 1 I will *p*. thee with mirth
Dan. 1. 12 *P*. thy servant, I beseech
Mal. 3. 10 *p*. me now, saith the L.
Luke 14. 19 oxen, I go to *p*. them
John 6. 6 And this he said to *p*. him
Acts 9. 22 confound. Jews, *p*. that
Rom. 12. 2 ye may *p*. which is good
2 Cor. 8. 8 to *p*. sincerity of love
Gal. 6. 4 let every man *p*. his work
Eph. 5. 10 *P*. what is accep. to L.
1 Thes. 5. 21 *P*. all things; ho. fast
1 Tim. 3. 10 these also first he *p*.
Heb. 3. 9 when your fathers *p*. me

Provender. *Fodder, food.*
Gen. 24. 25 We have *p*. enough, and
Judg. 19. 19 there is straw and *p*.
Isa. 30. 24 asses shall eat clean *p*.
R. V. Judg. 19. 21 fodder

Proverb. *Saying, similitude.*
Num. 21. 27 they that speak in . *p*
Deut. 28. 37 thou shalt become *p*.
1 Sam. 10. 12 Theref. it bec. a *p*.
1 K. 4. 32 he spake three thous. *p*.
2 Chr. 7. 20 make it to be a *p*. and
Ps. 69. 11 I became a *p*. to them
Eccl. 12. 9 preacher set in order *p*.
Jer. 24. 9 to be a *p*., and a curse
Ezek. 12. 23 sh. no more use it as *p*.
Hab. 2. 6 take up a *p*. against him
Luke 4. 23 Ye will say to me th. *p*.
John 16. 25 I sh. no more speak *p*.
2 Pet. 2. 22 happ. accord. to true *p*.
R. V. Isa 14. 4; Luke 4. 23 parable

Provide. *Look after, prepare.*
Gen. 22. 8 God will *p*. hims. lamb
Ex. 18. 21 thou shall *p*. out of all
Deut. 33. 21 *p*. first part for hims.
1 Sam. 16. 1 I have *p*. me a king
1 K. 4. 7 officers which *p*. victuals
2 Chr. 2. 7 men, whom Dav. did *p*.
Job 38. 41 Who *p*. for the raven
Ps. 78. 20 can he *p*. flesh for peo.
Prov. 6. 8 *p*. meat in summer
Mat. 10. 9 *P*. neither gold nor silv.
Luke 12. 33 *p*. yourselves bags wh.
Acts 23. 24 *p*. beasts .. set P. on
Rom. 12. 17 *P*. things hon. in sight
2 Cor. 8. 21 *P*. for honest things
1 Tim. 5. 8 if any *p*. not for own
Heb. 11. 40 having *p*. better things
R. V. Ps. 65. 9 prepared; Mat. 10. 9
get you no; Luke 12. 33 make for;
Rom. 12. 17; 2 Cor. 8. 21 take
thought for

Providence. *Forethought.*
Acts 24. 2 done to nat. by thy *P*.

Province. *Jurisdiction.*
1 K. 20. 14 men of princes of the *p*.
Ez. 2. 1 these are children of the *p*.
Neh. 11. 3 these are chief of the *p*.

Esth. 1. 1 Ahas. reigned over 127 *p*
Eccl. 2. 8 I gath. treas. of k's of *p*.
Lam. 1. 1 she was prince. among *p*.
Ezek. 19. 8 against him from the *p*.
Dan. 2. 48 made Dan. ruler over *p*.
Acts 23. 34 he asked of what *p*.

Provision. *Prepared in advance, food store, victuals, allowance.*
Gen. 42. 25 give them *p*. for way
Josh. 9. 12 bread took hot for our *p*.
1 K. 4. 22 Sol.'s *p*. for one day was
2 K. 6. 23 he prep. gr. *p*. for them
1 Chr. 29. 19 pl. for which I ma. *p*.
Ps. 132. 15 I will abund. bless her *p*.
Dan. 1. 5 king appoint. th. daily *p*.
Rom. 13. 14 make not *p*. for flesh
R. V. Dan. 1. 5 portion

Provocation. *Cause of anger, act of provoking.*
1 K. 15. 30 Jer. made Is. sin by *p*.
2 K. 23. 26 bec. of *p*. that Manass.
Neh. 9. 18 thy god wrought great *p*.
Job 17. 2 eye continue in their *p*.
Ps. 95. 8 Hard. not heart, as in *p*.
Jer. 32. 31 this city has been as *p*.
Ezek. 20. 28 pres. *p*. of their offer.
Heb. 3. 8 Hard. not hearts, as in *p*
R. V. Ps. 95. 8 at Meribah

Provoke. *Make angry or bitter.*
Ex. 23. 21 obey, and *p*. him not
Num. 14. 11 how long will peo. *p*.
Deut. 31. 20 if ye *p*. me, and break
1 Sam. 1. 6 her adversa. *p*. her sore
1 K. 14. 15 groves, *p*. Lord to anger
2 K. 23. 26 th. Manass. had *p*. him
1 Chr. 21. 1 Sat. *p*. Dav. to number
2 Chr. 28. 25 Ahaz *p*. to anger Lord
Ez. 5. 12 after fathers had *p*. God
Neh. 4. 5 for they *p*. thee to anger
Job. 12 6 that *p*. God are secure
Ps. 78. 56 they tempt. and *p*. God
Prov. 20. 2 whoso. *p*. him to anger
Isa. 1. 4 they *p*. Holy One of Israel
Jer. 7. 19 Do they *p*. me to anger?
Ezek. 8. 3 image which *p*. jealousy
Hos. 12. 14 Eph. *p*. him to anger
Luke 11. 53 to *p*. him to speak of
Rom. 10. 19 I will *p*. you to jealousy
1 Cor. 10. 22 Do we *p*. L. to jealousy
2 Cor. 9. 2 your zeal hath *p*. many
Gal. 5. 26 *p*. one another, envying
Eph. 6. 4 fathers, *p*. not children
Heb. 3. 16 some, when heard, did *p*.
R. V. Num. 14. 11, 23; 16. 30;
Deut. 31. 20; Isa. 1. 4 despise;
Deut. 32. 16; 1 Chr. 22. 1 moved,
Ps. 78. 40, 56 rebel against, Ps.
106. 7, 33, 43 were rebellious;
2 Cor. 9. 2 stirred up

Provoking. *Causing anger or sadness.*
Deut. 32. 19 bec. of *p*. of his sons
Ps. 78. 17 sinned yet more by *p*.

Prudence. *Care, wisdom.*
2 Chr. 2. 12 a son endued with *p*.
Prov. 8 12 I wisdom dwell with *p*.
Eph. 1. 8 abound. tow. us all in *p*.
R. V. 2 Chr. 2. 12 discretion; Prov.
8. 12 subtlety

Prudent. *Careful, knowing.*
1 Sam. 16. 18 D. was *p*. in matters
Prov. 12. 23 *p*. man conceal. knowl.
Isa. 5. 21 Woe to *p*. in own sight
Jer. 49. 7 is counsel per. from *p*.?
Hos. 14. 9 who is *p*., he shall know
Am. 5. 13 the *p*. shall keep silence
Mat. 11. 25 hid these things fr. *p*.
Luke 10. 21
Acts 13. 7 dep., Serg. Pau. a *p*. man
1 Cor. 1. 19 understanding of the *p*.
R. V. Isa. 3. 2 diviner; Mat. 11. 25;
Luke 10. 21; Acts 13. 7 understanding

Prudently. *R. V. wisely.*
Isa. 52. 13 my servant shall deal *p*.

Prune. *Lop off, prune.*
Lev. 25. 3 six years shalt thou *p*.
Isa. 5. 6 it shall not be *p*. nor dig.

Pruning Hooks.
Isa. 2. 4 sh. beat spears into *p*. h.
Joel 3. 10 Beat your *p*. h. into sp.
Mic. 4. 3 sh. beat spears into *p*. h.

Psalm. *Song of praise.*
1 Chr. 16. 7 David delivered this *p*.
Ps. 81. 2 Take *p*., br. hith timbrel

See Ps. in general (titles).
Luke 20. 42 David saith in bk. of *P*.
Acts 1. 20 is written in book of *P*.
1 Cor. 14. 26 ev. one of you hath *p*.
Eph. 5. 19 Speak. of yourselves in *p*.
Col. 3. 16 admon. one anoth. in *p*.
Jas. 5. 13 merry? let him sing *p*.
R. V. 1 Chr. 16. 9; Ps. 105. 2 ; Jas.
   5. 13 praises

Psalmist. *Maker of psalms,*
   singer.
2 Sam. 23. 1 David, sweet *P*. of Is.

Psaltery. *Lyre, harp.*
1 Sam. 10. 5 meet proph. with a *p*.
2 Sam. 6. 5 D. played bef. L. on *p*.
1 K. 10. 12 harps and *p*. for singers
1 Chr. 16. 5 Jeiel with *p*. and harps
2 Chr. 5. 12 Levites hav. cym. and *p*.
Neh. 12. 27 with sing., cymb., and *p*.
Ps. 33. 2. sing unto him with *p*.
Dan. 3. 5 time ye hear sound of *p*.

Publican. *Tax gatherer.*
Mat. 5. 46 do not ev. the same?
Mark 2. 15 *p*. and sinners sat tog.
Luke 3. 12 came *p*. to be baptized
R. V Mat. 5. 47 Gentiles

Publick. R. V. *public.*
Mat. 1. 19 make her a *p*. example

Publickly. R. V. *publicly.*
Acts 18. 28 conv. Jews, and that *p*.

Publish. *Say, cry out, spread*
   abroad, make to hear.
Deut. 32. 3 I will *p*. name of Lord
1 Sam. 31. 9 *p*. it in house of idols
2 Sam. 1. 20 *p*. not in st. of Askalon
Esth. 3. 14 writing was *p*. to all peo.
Ps. 26. 7 may *p*. wi. voice of thank.
Isa. 52. 7 that *p*. peace, *p*. salvation
Jer. 4. 5 Declare in Jud., *p*. in Jer.
Am. 3. 9 *P*. in palaces of Ashdod
Jonah 3. 7 *p*. thro. Nin. by decree
Nah. 1. 15 feet of him th. *p*. peace
Mark 1. 45 he began to *p*. it much
Luke 8. 39 *p*. through whole city
Acts 10. 37 was *p*. thro. all Judea
R. V. Num. 32. 3 proclaim ; 1 Sam.
   31. 9 carry tidings ; Ps. 26. 7 make
   to be heard ; Mark 13. 10 preach-
   ed ; Acts 13. 49 spread abroad

Puff. *Breathe or blow up.*
Ps. 10. 5 enemies, he *p*. at them
1 Cor. 4. 6 no one of you be *p*. up
   8. 1 knowl. *p*. up., but char. edifi.
   13. 4 char. vaunt. not, is not *p*. up
Col. 2. 18 vainly *p*. by flesh. mind

Pull. *Draw, haul, rend.*
Gen. 8. 9 Noah *p*. her unto him
1 K. 13. 4 Jerob. could not *p*. it
Ez. 6. 11 let timber be *p*. down fr.
Ps. 31. 4 *P*. me out of net laid for
Isa. 22. 19 fr. thy state *p*. th. down
Jer. 12. 3 *p*. th. like sheep for slau.
Lam. 3. 11 turned, and *p*. me to p.
Ezek. 17. 9 shall he not *p*. up roots
Am. 9. 15 sh. no more be *p*. up
Mic. 2. 8 ye *p*. off robe with garm.
Zech. 7. 11 they *p*. away shoulder
Mat. 7. 4 Let me *p*. out of the mote
Luke 6. 42 then sh. thou see to *p*.
Acts 23. 10 *P*. sh. ha. been *p*. in pi.
2 Cor. 10. 4 mighty to the *P*. down
Jude 23 And *p*. them out of the fire
R. V. Gen. 8. 9; 19. 10 brought; 1
   K. 13. 4; Luke 14. 5 draw; Ps.
   31. 4; Am. 9. 15 pluck; Jer. 1. 10;
   18. 7 break; Mic. 2. 8 strip; Mat.
   7. 4; Luke 6. 42 cast; Acts 23. 10
   torn ; 2 Cor. 10. 4 casting ; Jude
   23 snatching.

Pulpit. *High place.*
Neh, 8. 4 And Ezra stood upon a *p*.

Pulse. *Seeds, plants.*
2 Sam. 17. 28 bro. beans, parched *p*.
Dan. 1. 12, 16 let them give us *p*.

Punish. *Pain, chastise, restrain.*
Ex. 21.20 smite ser., he shall be *p*.
Lev 26. 18 I will *p*. you sev. times
Ez. 9. 13 seeing God hast *p*. us less
Prov. 21. 11 When the scorner is *p*.
   22. 3 simple pass on, and are *p*.
Isa. 10. 12 I will *p*. fr. of st. heart
Jer. 25. 12 I will *p*. k. of Babylon
Hos. 4. 9 *p*. them for their ways
Am. 3. 2 therefore I will *p*. you
Zeph. 1. 8 in day I will *p*. princes
Zech. 8. 14 As I thought to *p*. you

Acts 26. 11 I *p*. th. oft in synagogue
2 Thes. 1. 9 be *p*. with everl. destr.
2 Pet. 2. 9 reserve unjust, to be *p*.
R. V. Ex. 21. 22 fined ; Lev. 26. 18
   chastise ; 26. 24 smite ; Prov. 22.
   3 ; 27. 12 suffer for it ; Jer. 41. 44
   do judgment; Am. 3. 2 visit upon
   you ; Zech. 8. 14 do evil unto

Punishment. *Penalty.*
Gen. 4. 13 *p*. is gr. th. I can bear
Levi. 26. 41 accept *p*. of their iniq.
1 Sam. 28. 10 sh. no *p*. hap. to thee
Job. 19. 29 wrath bringeth the *p*. of
Ps. 149. 7 To ex. *p*. upon the people
Prov. 19. 19 man of wr. sh. suffer *p*.
Lam. 3, 39 man for *p*. of his sins
Ezek. 14. 10 bear *p*. of their iniq.
Zech. 14. 19 This shall be the *P*. of
Mat. 25. 46 sh. go into everlast. *P*.
2 Cor. 2. 6 Suffic. to such is this *p*.
Heb. 10. 29 of how much sorer *p*.
1 Pet. 2. 14 for the *p*. of evil doers
R. V. Prov. 19. 19 penalty; Lam.
   4. 6; Ezek. 14. 10 ——; Ezek. 14.
   10 iniquity ; Job 31. 3 disaster ; 1
   Pet, 2. 14 vengeance

Purchase (*n*.). *Acquisition.*
Gen. 49. 32 *P*. of field and of cave
Jer. 32. 11 I took evidence of the *P*.

Purchase (*v*.). *Acquire.*
Gen. 25. 10 field which Abrah. *p*.
Ex. 15. 16 over which thou hast *p*.
Lev 25. 33 if a man *p*. of Levites
Ruth. 4. 10 R. I *p*. to be my wife
Ps. 74. 2 congregation thou hast *p*.
Acts 1. 18 this man *p*. field with
1 Tim. 3. 13 *p*. to thems. good deg.
R. V. Lev. 25. 33 redeem ; Acts 1.
   18; 8. 20 obtain

Pure. *Clear, clean, refined.*
Ex. 27. 20 bring thee *p*. oil olive
Lev. 24. 7 put *p*. frankincens. upon
Deut. 32. 14 drink *p*. blood of goats
2 Sam. 22. 27 With *p*., shew thyself
1 K. 6. 20 overlaid it with *p*. gold
1 Chr. 28. 17 *p*. gold for fl. hooks
2 Chr. 9. 20 *p*. gold, none of silver
Ez. 6. 20 priests, all of them were *P*.
Job 11. 4 My doctrine is *p*., and
Ps. 24. 4 clean hands, and a *p*. heart
Prov. 15. 26 words of *p*. are pleas.
Dan. 7. 9 hair of head like *p*. wool
Mic. 6. 11 Shall I count them *p*.
Zeph. 3. 9 turn to people *p*. langu.
Mal. 1. 11 in ev. place a *p*. offering
Mat. 5. 8 Blessed are *p*. in heart
Acts 20. 26 I am *p*. from blood of
Rom. 14. 20 All things indeed are *p*.
Phil. 4. 8 whatsoever things are *p*.
1 Tim. 3. 9 Hold. faith in *p*. consc.
Tit. 1. 15 Unto *p*. all things are *p*.
Heb. 10. 22 bodies washed wi. *p*. w.
Jas. 1. 27 *P*. religion before God
1 Pet. 1. 22 love one ano. wi. *p*. heart
2 Pet. 3. 1 I stir up your *p*. minds
1 John 3. 3 purif. himself as he is *p*.
Rev. 22. 1 pure river of water of life
R. V. Ex. 30. 23 flowing; Ps. 21. 3
   fine ; Prov. 30. 5 tried ; Rom. 14.
   20 clean ; 2 Pet. 3. 1 sincere ; Rev.
   22. 1 ——

Purely. R. V. *thoroughly.*
Isa. 1. 25 I will *p*. purge away dross

Pureness. *Cleanness.*
Job 22. 30 deliver. by *p*. of hands
Prov. 22. 11 that loveth *p*. of heart
2 Cor. 6. 6 approving ourselves by *p*.

Purer. *More pure.*
Lam. 4. 7 Nazarites *p*. than snow
Hab. 1. 13 of *p*. eyes than to behold

Purge. *Cleanse, purify, pardon.*
1 Sam. 3. 14 Eli's house not be *p*.
2 Chr. 34. 3 Josiah began to *p*. Jud
Ps. 51. 7 *P*. me with hyssop and
Prov. 16. 6 By truth iniquity is *p*.
Isa. 4. 4 *p*. the blood of Jerusalem
Ezek. 20. 38 I will *p*. fr. among you
Mat. 3. 12 and he will *p*. his floor
Mark 7. 19 into the draught, *p*. all
Luke 3. 17 throughly *p*. his floor
John 15. 2 branch that bear, he *p*.
1 Cor. 5. 7 *P*. out the old leaven
2 Tim. 2. 21 If a man *p*. himself
Heb. 1. 3 when he had *p*. our sins
2 Pet. 1. 9 hath forgotten he was *p*.
R. V. Ezek. 43. 20 make atonement ;

Dan. 11. 35 purify ; Mat. 3. 12 ;
   Mark 7. 19; Luke 3. 17; John 15
   2 ; Heb. 9. 14, 22 ; 10. 2 ; 2 Pet. 1.
   9 cleanse, cleansed, clean

Purification. *Cleansing.*
Num. 19. 9 it is a *p*. for sin
2 Chr. 30 19 accord. to *p*. of sanctu.
Neh. 12. 45 porters kept ward of *p*.
Esth. 2. 12 so were days of their *p*.
Luke 2. 22 when the days of her *p*.
Acts 21. 26 accompl. of days of *p*.
R. V. Num. 19. 9, 17 sin of offering

Purified. *Cleansed.*
Num. 8. 21 Levites were *p*., and
2 Sam. 11. 4 for she was *p*. from
Ez. 6. 20 priests and Lev. were *p*.
Ps. 12. 6 as silver, *p*. seven times
Dan. 12. 10 Many shall be *p*. and

Purifier. *Cleanser.*
Mal. 3. 3 he shall sit as *p*. of silver

Purify. *Cleanse.*
Lev. 8. 15 and Moses *p*. the altar
Num. 19. 12 He shall *p*. himself
Neh. 12. 36 priests and Lev. *p*. peo.
Job 41. 25 by reas. of break. they *p*.
Isa. 66. 17 *p*. themselves in gardens
Mal. 3. 3 he sh. *p*. the sons of Levi
John 11. 55 went to Jerusalem to *p*.
Acts 21. 24 *p*. thyself with them
Tit. 2. 14 *p*. unto hims. pecu. peo.
Heb. 9. 23 patterns, should be *p*.
1 Pet. 1. 22 ye have *p*. your souls
1 John 3. 3 hath this hope *p*. hims.
R. V. Job. 41. 25 are beside ; Heb.
   9. 23 cleansed

Purifying. *Cleansing.*
Lev. 12. 4 continue in blood of *p*.
Num. 8. 7 sprinkle water of *p*. up.
1 Chr. 23. 28 in *p*. of holy things
John 2. 6 aft. manner of *p*. of Jews
Acts 15. 9 *p*. their hearts by faith
Heb. 9. 13 sanctif. to *p*. of flesh
R. V. Num. 8. 7 expiation ; Acts
   15. 9 cleansing

Purity. *Cleanliness.*
1 Tim. 4. 12 be thou an example in *p*.

Purloin. *Secrete, steal.*
Tit. 2. 10 not *p*., but shew. fidelity

Purple. *Purple.*
Ex. 25. 4 off., brass, blue, *p*., scar.
Num. 4. 13 spread *p*. cloth thereon
Judg. 8. 26 *P*. raiment that was on
2 Chr. 3. 14 made veil of *p*. and cr.
Esth. 1. 6 fastened with cords of *p*.
Prov. 31. 22 her clo. is silk and *p*.
S. of S. 7. 5 hair of thi. head like *p*.
Jer. 10. 9 blue and *p*. is their cloth.
Ezek. 27. 16 occupied in fairs wi. *p*.
Mark 15. 17 clothed him with *p*.
Luke 16. 19 rich man, clothed in *p*.
John 19. 2 put on hlm a *p*. robe
Acts 16. 14 Lydia, a seller of *p*.
Rev. 18. 16 city, that was clo. in *p*.

Purpose (*n*.). *Will, intent, desire,*
   aim.
Ruth. 2. 16 handfuls of *p*. for her
Ez. 4. 5 counsellors to frustrate *p*.
Neh. 8. 4 a pulpit made for the *p*.
Job 33. 17 withd. man from his *p*.
Prov. 20. 18 ev. *p*. is established
Eccl. 3. 1 a time to every *p*. under
Isa. 1. 11 To what *p*. is your sacrif.
Jer. 49. 30 Nebuch. conceived a *p*.
Dan. 6. 17 that *p*. be not changed
Acts 11. 23 that with *p*. of heart
Rom. 8. 28 called according to *p*.
Eph. 1. 11 according to *p*. in him
2 Tim. 1. 9 called us accord. to *p*.
1 John 3. 8 for this *p*. Son of G.
R. V. Acts 26. 18 ; 1 John 3. 8 to
   this end

Purpose (*v*.). *Will, intend, desire,*
   determine.
Gen. 27. 42 Esau *p*. to kill thee
1 K. 5. 5 I *p*. to build house of L.
2 Chr. 28. 10 *p*. to keep under J.
Ps. 17. 3 *p*. mouth sh. not transgr.
Isa. 14. 24 as I have *p*., so stand
Jer. 4. 28 I *p*. it, will not repent
Lam. 2. 8 Lord *p*. to destr. the wall
Dan. 2. 8 Daniel *p*. not to defile
Acts 19. 21 Paul *p*. to go to Jerus.
Rom. 1. 13 I *p*. to come unto you
2 Cor. 1. 17 I *p*. according to flesh
Eph. 1. 9 will which he hath *p*. in
R. V. Acts 20. 3 determined

Purse. *Bag, cup.*
Prov. 1. 14 let us all have one *p.*
Mat. 10. 9 nei. sil. nor brass in *p.*
Mark 6. 8 take no money in their *p.*
Luke 10. 4 Car. neither *p.* nor scrip
Pursue. *Follow, chase.*
Gen. 14. 14 A. armed ser. and *p.*
Ex. 14. 9 Egyptians *p.* after them
Lev. 26. 17 ye flee when none *p.*
Deut. 19. 6 Lest aveng. of blood *p.*
Josh. 2. 5 *p.* after them quickly
Judg. 4. 16 Barak *p.* after chariots
1 Sam. 23. 28 Saul returned from *p.*
2 Sam. 2. 19 Asahel *p.* after Abner
1 K. 20. 20 Syrians fled, Israel *p.*
2 K. 25. 5 Chaldees *p.* after king
2 Chr. 13. 19 Abijah *p.* after Jerobo.
Job. 13. 25 wilt thou *p.* dry stubble?
Ps. 18. 37 I have *p.* mine enemies
Prov. 28. 1 wick. flee wh. no man *p.*
Isa. 30. 16 they that *p.* you be swift
Jer. 52. 8 army of Chaldeans *p.* after
Lam. 4. 19 they *p.* us upon mount's
Ezek. 35. 6 and blood shall *p.* thee
Hos. 8. 3 Israel, the enemy shall *p.*
Am. 1. 11 Edom did *p.* his brother
Nah. 1. 8 darkness sh. *p* his enemies
R. V. Judg. 20. 45 followed; Job.
30. 15; Lam. 4. 19 chase
Pursuer. *Who pursues.*
Josh. 2. 16 mount., lest *p.* meet
Lam. 1. 6 without strength bef. *p.*
Purtenance. R. V. *inwards.*
Ex. 12. 9 roast legs wi. *p.* thereof
Push. *Shove, gore.*
Ex. 21. 32 If ox sh. *p.* manservant
Deut. 33. 17 he sh. *p.* peo. together
1 K. 22. 11 shalt thou *p.* Syrians
2 Chr. 18. 10
Job 39. 12 they *p.* away my feet
Ps. 44. 5 will *p.* down our enemies
Ezek. 34. 21 *p.* all diseased wi. horns
Dan. 8. 4 I saw the ram *p.* westward
R. V. Ex. 21. 29, 32, 36 gore; Job
30. 12 thrust aside; Dan. 11. 40
contend
Put. *Place, set.*
Gen. 2. 15 *p.* him in garden of Eden
Ex. 5. 21 *p.* sword in hand to slay
Lev. 2. 15 thou shalt *p.* oil upon it
Num. 4. 7 *p.* thereon the dishes
Deut. 28. 48 *p.* yoke on thy neck
Josh. 17. 13 they *p.* Can. to tribute
Judg. 7. 16 *p.* trump. in ev. hand
Ruth 3. 3 *p.* thy raiment upon thee
1 Sam. 17. 38 *p.* helmet on his head
2 Sam. 20. 3 *p.* them in ward, and
1 K. 2. 5 *p.* blood on his girdle that
2 K. 16. 14 *p.* it on th. n. side of altar
1 Chr. 13. 10 bec. he *p.* hand to ark
2 Chr. 9. 16 k. *p.* them in the house
Ez. 1. 7 *p.* them in house of gods
Neh. 7. 5 God *p.* into my heart to
Job. 4. 18 he *p.* no trust in his ser.
Ps. 40. 3 *p.* new song in my mouth
Prov. 23. 2 *p.* knife to thy throat
Isa. 5. 20 that *p.* darkness for light
Jer. 13. 1 *p.* it upon thy loins, and
Lam. 3. 29 *p.* his mouth in the dust
Ezek. 3. 25 shall *p.* bands on thee
Dan. 5. 19 and whom he *p.* down
Mic. 2. 12 I will *p.* them together
Zeph. 3. 19 have been *p.* to shame
Mat. 9. 17 nei. do men *p.* new wine
Mark 7. 33 *p.* finger into his ears
Luke 11. 33 hath lighted candle, *p.*
John 20. 25 *p.* finger into the print
Acts 4. 3 and *p.* the apostles in hold
Rom. 14. 13 no man *p.* stum. block
1 Cor. 15. 25 *p.* all en. under feet
2 Cor. 3. 13 which *p.* veil over face
Gal. 3. 27 baptized, have *p.* on C.
Eph. 4. 22 ye *p.* off the old man
Col. 3. 8 now ye *p.* off all these
1 Tim. 1. 12 *p.* me into ministry
2 Tim. 1. 6 I *p.* thee in remembr.
Tit. 3. 1 *p.* th. in mind to be subj.
Phile. 18 *p.* that to mine account
Heb. 8. 10 *p.* my laws into th. mind
Jas. 3. 3 *p.* bits in horses' mouths
1 Pet. 2. 15 *p.* to silence ignorance
2 Pet. 1. 14 I must *p.* off this tab.
Jude 5 will *p.* you in remembrance
Rev. 2. 24 *p.* on you none other
R. V. many changes, but chiefly
due to context

Putrefying. *Raw, open.*
Isa. 1. 6 wounds, bruises, *p.* sores
Pygarg. *Bison.*
Deut. 14. 5 the *p.*, wild ox, chamois

Q

Quails. *Quails.*
Ex. 16. 13 at even the *q.* came up
Num. 11. 31 a wind fr. L. bro. *q.*
Ps. 105. 40 peo. asked, he bro. *q.*
Quake. *Shake, tremble.*
Ex. 19. 18 whole mount *q.* greatly
1 Sam. 14. 15 spoilers trem., earth *q.*
Joel 2. 10 earth shall *q.* bef. them
Nah. 1. 5 the mountains *q.* at him
Mat. 27. 51 earth did *q.*, rocks rent
Heb. 12. 21 M. said, I fear and *q.*
Quaking. *Fearing, trembling.*
Ezek. 12. 18 eat thy bread with *q.*
Dan. 10. 7 great *q.* fell upon them
Quantity. *Content, size.*
Isa. 22. 24 hand vessels of small *q.*
R. V. every small vessel
Quarrel. *Contention, opposition.*
Lev. 26. 25 a sword sh. avenge *q.*
2 K. 5. 7 see how he seeketh *q.*
Mark 6. 19 Her. had *q.* ag'st him
Col. 3. 13 if any man have *q.* ag'st
R. V. Lev. 26. 25 execute venge-
ance; Mark 6. 19 set herself; Col.
3. 13 complain
Quarries. *Carved images.*
Judg. 3. 19, 26 E. turn. fr. *q.* by Gil.
Quarter. *Side, corner, border,
place, part.*
Gen. 19. 4 peo. from ev. *q.* to Lo.
Ex. 13. 7 no leaven seen in thy *q.*
Deut. 22. 12 make fring. on four *q.*
Josh. 15. 5 *q.* was from bay of sea
1 Chr. 9. 24 in four *q.* were porters
Isa. 47. 15 wander ev. one to his *q.*
Jer. 49. 36 winds fr. four *q.* of heav.
Ezek. 38. 6 house of Tog. of n. *q.*
Mark 1. 45 came to him from ev. *q.*
Acts 16. 3 Jews were in those *q.*
Rev. 20. 8 wh. are in four *q.* of earth
R. V. Ex. 13. 7; Deut. 22. 12 bord-
ers; 1 Chr. 9. 24 sides; Ezek. 38.
6; Acts 9. 32; 16. 3 parts; Acts
28. 7 place; Rev. 20. 8 corner
Quaternion. *File of four.*
Acts 12. 4 deliv. Peter to four *q.*
Queen. *Queen, princess, mighty
or reigning one.*
1 K. 10. 1 when *q.* of Sheb. heard
2 K. 10. 13 we salute children of *q.*
2 Chr. 9. 12 Sol. gave to *q.* of Sheba
Neh. 2. 6 king said, *q.* sitting by
Esth. 2. 4 let maid. wh. pleas. be *q.*
Ps. 45. 9 stand in gold of Ophir
S. of S. 6. 8 there are threescore *q.*
Isa. 49. 23 *q.* thy nursing mothers
Jer. 7. 18 to make cakes to *q.* of h.
Dan. 5. 10 *q.* came to banquet. h.
Mat. 12. 42 *q.* of south shall rise up
Luke 11, 31
Acts 8. 27 Candace *q.* of Ethiopia.
Rev. 18. 7 I sit a *q.*, am no widow
R. V. Jer. 13. 18: 29. 12 queen-
mother
Quench. *Extinguish, smother,
allay, quiet, subdue.*
Num. 11. 2 Mos. prayed, fire was *q.*
2 Sam. 14. 7 they shall *q.* my coal
2 K. 22. 17 wrath shall not be *q.*
2 Chr. 34. 25 my wrath sh. not be *q.*
Ps. 118. 12 are *q.* as fire of thorns
S. of S. 8. 7 waters cannot *q.* love
Isa. 43. 17 they are *q.* as tow
Jer. 4. 4 burn that none can *q.* it
Ezek. 20. 47 flame shall not be *q.*
Am. 5. 6 be none to *q.* it in Bethel
Mat. 12. 20 smo. flax sh. he not *q.*
Mark 9. 43 fire that nev. shall be *q.*
Eph. 6. 16 *q.* all the darts of wicked
1 Thes. 5. 19 *Q.* not the Spirit
Heb. 11. 34 *Q.* the violence of fire
R. V. Num. 11. 2 abated; Mark 9.
44; 45; 46
Question (*n.*). *Thing, acute say-
ing.*
1 K. 10. 1, 3 she came with hard *q.*
2 Chr. 9. 1, 2 Solom. told her all *q.*
Matter of inquiry, difference.
Mat. 22. 46 nei. durst ask more *q.*
Mark 11. 29 will ask of you one *q.*

Luke 2. 46 hearing and asking *q.*
John 3. 25 arose *q.* between some
Acts 18. 15 But if it be *q.* of words
1 Tim. 6. 4 doting about *q.* and str.
2 Tim. 2. 23 f. and unlearn. *q.* avoid
Tit. 3. 9 avoid foolish *q.*, and geneal.
R. V. 1 Tim. 1. 4; 6. 4; 2 Tim. 2.
23; Tit. 3. 9 questionings
Question (*v.*). *Seek, inquire.*
2 Chr. 31. 9 Hez. *q.* with priests
Mark 1. 27 they *q.* among thmsel.
9. 10 *q.* one with another what the
Luke 23. 9 he *q.* wi. him in words
Quick. *Alive, quickening.*
Lev. 13. 10 if there be *q.* raw flesh
Num. 16. 30 go down *q.* into the pit
Ps. 55. 15 let th. go down *q.* into hell
Acts 10. 42 orda. to be Judg. of *q.*
2 Tim. 4. 1; Heb. 4. 12; 1 Pet. 4. 5
Keen, acute, sharp.
Isa. 11. 3 make him of *q.* under.
R. V. Num. 16. 30; Ps. 55. 15;
124. 3 alive; Isa. 11. 3 his delight
shall be; Heb. 4. 12 living.
Quicken. *Preserve, keep, give.*
(said of one's life).
Ps. 71. 20 thou shalt *q.* me again
88. 18; 119. 25, 37, 40, 50; 143. 11
John 5. 21 Son *q.* whom he will
Rom. 4. 17 God, who *q.* the dead
1 Cor. 15. 45 Adam made *q.* spirit
Eph. 2. 5 *q.* us together with Christ
Col. 2. 13 hath he *q.* tog. with him
1 Tim. 6. 13 in sight of G., who *q.*
1 Pet. 3. 18 death, but *q.* by spirit
R. V. 1 Cor. 15. 45 become a life
giving.
Quickly. *With speed, in haste.*
Gen. 18. 6 make ready *q.* .. meal
Ex. 32. 8 They have turned aside *q.*
Num. 16. 46 go *q.* unto congrega.
Deut. 9. 12 get thee down *q.* from
Josh. 2. 5 pursue after them *q.*, for
Judg. 2. 17 they turn. *q.* out of way
1 Sam. 20. 19 thou shalt go down *q.*
2 Sam. 17. 16 send *q.*, and tell Dav.
2 K. 1. 11 king said, Come down *q.*
2 Chr. 18. 8 Fetch *q.* Micaiah, the
Eccl. 4. 12 cord is not *q.* broken
Mat. 5. 23 Agree with adversary *q.*
Mark 16. 8 th. went out *q.* and fled
Luke 15. 21 Go out *q.* into streets
John 13. 27 That thou doest, do *q.*
Acts 22. 18 get thee *q.* to Jerusa.
Rev. 2. 5 I will come unto thee *q.*
R. V. Mark 16. 8; Rev. 2. 5 ——
Quicksands. R. V. *Syrtis.*
Acts 27. 17 lest they fall into *q.*
Quiet (*n.*). *Rest, peace, still, calm,
silent.*
Judg. 18. 7 they dwelt *q.* and secu.
2 K. 11. 20; 2 Chr. 23. 21 city w. in *q.*
1 Chr. 4. 40 land was wide and *q.*
Job. 3. 13 should I have been *q.*
Ps. 35. 20 devise against *q.* in land
Prov. 1. 33 whoso heark., sh. be *q.*
Eccl. 9. 17 wor. of wise heard in *q.*
Isa. 7. 4 be *q.*, fear not, nei. be f't
Jer. 51. 59 Seraiah was *q.* prince
Ezek. 16. 42 fury rest, I will be *q.*
Nah. 1. 12 though *q.* be cut down
Acts 19. 36 ye ought to be *q.* and to
1 Thes. 4. 11 that ye study to be *q.*
1 Tim. 2. 2 lead *q.* and peace. life
1 Pet. 3. 4 ornament of a *q.* spirit
R. V. Nah. 1. 12 in full strength
Quietly. *Privately.*
2 Sam. 3. 27 to speak with him *q.*
Lam. 3. 26 *q.* wait for salva. of L.
Quiet (*v.*). *Set at rest.*
Job 37. 17 he *q.* the earth by wind
Ps. 131. 2 I *q.* myself as a child that
Zech. 6. 8 ha. *q.* my spirit in north
R. V. Job 37. 17 earth is still
Quietness. *Ease, rest, peace, si-
lence*
Judg. 8. 28 the country was in *q.*
1 Chr. 22. 9 I will give *q.* to Israel
Job. 20. 20 sh. not feel *q.* in belly
Prov. 17. 1 bet. dry morsel, and *q.*
Eccl. 4. 6 Better is handful with *q.*
Isa. 30. 15 in *q.* be your strength;
Acts 24. 2 by thee we enjoy gr. *q.*
2 Thes. 3. 12 wi. *q.* work, and eat
R. V. Judg. 8. 28 had rest; Acts
24. 2 much peace.

Quit (n.). *Free, innocent.*
Ex. 21. 28 owner of ox shall be *q.*
Josh. 2. 20 we will *q.* him of oath
R. V. Josh. 2. 20 guiltless
Quit (v.). *Act, be.*
1 Sam. 4. 9 *q.* yourselves like men
1 Cor. 16 13 Watch, *q.* you like men
Quite. *Wholly.*
Gen. 31. 15 *q.* devoured our money
Ex. 23. 24 *q.* break down images
Num. 17. 10 *q.* take away murmur.
2 Sam. 3. 24 Abner, he is *q.* gone
Job 6. 13 is wisdom *q.* from me?
Hab. 3. 9 thy bow made *q.* naked
R. V. Num. 17. 10 make end of;
33. 52 demolish; Ex. 23. 24 break
in pieces
Quiver (n.). *Quiver, sheath.*
Gen. 27. 3 take thy *q.* and thy bow
Job. 39. 23 *q.* rattleth against him
Ps. 127. 5 Happy man that hath *q.*
Isa. 22. 6 Elam bare *q.* wi. chariots
Jer. 5. 16 *q.* is as an open sepulchre
Lam. 3. 13 arrows of *q.* enter reins
Quiver (v.). *Shake, tremble.*
Hab. 3. 16 my lips *q.* at the voice

R.

Rabbi. *Teacher.*
Mat. 23. 8 be not ye called *R.* for
R. V. Mat. 23. 7 ——
See DICTIONARY.
Raca. *Vain.*
Mat. 5. 22 whoso. sh. say to bro., *R.*
Race. *Course, path, run.*
Ps. 19. 5 rejoi. as str. man to run *r.*
Eccl. 9. 11 the *r.* is not to the swift
1 Cor. 9. 24 they which run in a *r.*
Heb. 12. 1 let us run wi. pat. the *r.*
R. V. Ps. 19. 5 course
Rafter. *Rafter, beam.*
S. of S. 1. 17 beams cedar, *r.* of fir
Rag. *Fragment.*
Prov. 23. 21 drow. clothe man wi. *r.*
Jer. 38. 11 Ebed. took rotten *r.*
R. V. Isa. 64. 6 righteous. are as
filthy *r.*
Polluted garment.
Rage (n.). *Heat, anger, fury.*
2 K. 5. 12 Naaman turned in a *r.*
2 Chr. 16. 10 he was in *r.* with him
Job 39. 24 He swal. ground with *r.*
Ps. 7. 6 lift up thyself because of *r.*
Prov. 6. 34 jealousy is *r.* of man
Isa. 37. 28 I know thy *r.* ag'st me
Dan. 3. 13 Neb. commanded in *r.*
Hos. 7. 16 fall for *r.* of th. tongue
R. V. Job 40. 11 overflowings
Rage (v.). *Be angry, roar.*
Ps. 2. 1 Why do the heathen *r.*
Prov. 29. 9 whether he *r.* or laugh
Jer. 46. 9 Come up, *r.*, ye chariots
Nah. 2. 4 char. should *r.* in streets
R. V. Prov. 29. 9 be angry; 14. 16
beareth himself insolently
Ragged. *Jagged, broken.*
Isa. 2. 21 go into tops of *r.* rocks
Raging. *Angry, roaring.*
Ps. 89. 9 Thou rulest *r.* of the sea
Prov. 20. 1 strong drink is *r.*, and
Jonah 1. 15 sea ceased from her *r.*
Luke 8. 24 rebuked *r.* of water
Jude 13 *R.* waves of sea, foaming
R. V. Prov. 20. 1 a brawler
Rail. *Reproach, scoff.*
1 Sam. 25. 14 mess., he *r.* on them
2 Chr. 32. 17 S. wrote let. to *r.* on L.
Blaspheme, revile.
Mark 15. 29 that passed *r.* on him
Luke 23. 39 one of mal. *r.* on him
R. V. 1 Sam. 25. 14 flew upon
Railer. R. V. *reviler.*
1 Cor. 5. 11 keep not com. with *r.*
Railing. *Speaking injury.*
1 Tim. 6. 4 whereof cometh *r.*, evil
1 Pet. 3. 9 not rendering *r.* for *r.*
2 Pet. 2. 11 bring not *r.* accusation
Jude 9 not bring *r.* accusation, but
R. V. 1 Pet. 3. 9 reviling
Raiment. *Cloak, robe, garment, clothing.*
Gen. 24. 53 ser. gave *r.* to Rebek.
Ex. 21. 10 her *r.* sh. not he dimin.
Lev. 11. 32 unclean, wheth. *r.* or skin
Num. 31. 20 purify all your *r.*, and
Deut. 24. 17 nor take wid. *r.* to pl.

Josh. 22. 8 return wi. very much *r.*
Judg. 3. 16 did gird it under his *r.*
Ruth 3. 3 and put thy *r.* on thee
1 Sam. 28. 8 Saul put on other *r.*
2 K. 5. 5 Naam. took chang. of *r.*
Esth. 4. 4 she sent *r.* to clo. Mord.
Job 27. 16 Tho. he prep. *r.* as clay
Ps. 45. 14 bro. in *r.* of needlework
Isa. 14. 19 cast out as *r.* of slain
Ezek. 16. 13 thy *r.* was of fine linen
Zech. 3. 4 I will clothe thee with *r.*
Mat. 3. 4 J. had *r.* of camel's hair
Mark 9. 3 his *r.* became shining
Luke 7. 25 A man clo. in soft *r.*?
John 19. 24 they parted my *r.* . . .th.
Acts 18. 6 he shook his *r.*, and said
1 Tim. 6. 8 having food and *r.* let,
Jas. 2. 2 come a poor man in vile *r.*
Rev. 3. 5 shall be clothed in white *r.*
R. V. Ex. 22. 26, 27; Deut. 22. 3;
24. 13; Num. 31. 20; Mat. 17. 2;
27. 31; Mark 9. 3; Luke 23. 34;
John 19. 24; Acts 22. 20; Rev.
3. 5, 18; 4. 4 garment or garments;
Ps. 45. 14 broidered work; Zech.
3. 4 apparel; 1 Tim. 6. 8 covering;
Jas. 2. 2 clothing; Luke 10. 30——
Rain (n.). *Rain.*
Gen. 7. 12 *r.* was upon e. for. days
Ex. 9. 34 Phar. saw the *r.* ceased
Lev. 26. 4 will give you *r.* in seas.
1 Sam. 12. 17 call on L. to send *r.*
2 Sam. 1. 21 neither let there be *r.*
1 K. 17. 1 shall not be dew nor *r.*
2 K. 3. 17 neither shall ye see *r.*
Ez. 10. 9 trembling for the great *r.*
Job 5. 10 Who giv. *r.* upon earth
Ps. 72. 6 He sh. come down like *r.*
Prov. 25. 23 north wind driv. way *r.*
Eccl. 11. 3 if the clouds be full of *r.*
S. of S. 2. 11 the *r.* is ov. and gone
Isa. 4. 6 covert from storm and *r.*
Jer. 5. 24 fear the Lord, that giv. *r.*
Ezek. 1. 28 as bov in cloud in *r.*
Hos. 6. 3 shall come to us as the *r.*
Joel 2. 23 cause to come down *r.*
Am. 4. 7 I have withholden *r.* from
Zech. 14. 17 upon them sh. be no *r.*
Mat. 5. 45 he sendeth *r.* on just
Acts 14. 17 did good, and gave *r.*
Heb. 6. 7 earth drinketh in the *r.*
Jas. 5. 18 and the heaven gave *r.*
Rain (v.). *To rain, shower.*
Gen. 7. 4 I will cause it to *r.* on e.
Ex. 9. 23 Lord *r.* hail upon Egypt
Job 20. 23 fury, *r.* it on him eating
Ps. 11. 6 on wick. he sh. *r.* snares
Isa. 5. 6 clouds *r.* no rain upon it
Hos. 10. 12 *r.* righteousness upon
Am. 4. 7 one piece was *r.* upon
Luke 17. 29 it *r.* fire and brimstone
Jas. 5. 17 E. prayed it might not *r.*
Rev. 11. 6 *r.* not in days of proph.
Rainbow. *Rainbow.*
Rev. 4. 3; 10. 1 *r.* about the throne
Rainy. *Rainy.*
Prov. 27. 15 dropping in a *r.* day
Raise. *Lift up, cause to rise.*
Gen. 38. 8 *r.* up seed to thy broth.
Ex. 23. 1 shall not *r.* false report
Deut. 18. 15 G. will *r.* up prophet
Josh. 7. 26 *r.* ov. him heap of sto.
Judg. 2. 16 L. *r.* up judges which
Ruth 4. 5 to *r.* up the name of dead
1 Sam. 2. 8 He *r.* poor out of dust
2 Sam. 12. 11 I will *r.* evil ag'st thee
1 K. 14. 14 L. shall *r.* up a king
1 Chr. 17. 11 I will *r.* up thy seed
2 Chr. 32. 5 *r.* it up to the towers
Ez. 1. 5 all whose spirit God had *r.*
Job 19. 12 *r.* up their way against me
Ps. 41. 10 Lord be merciful, *r.* me
S. of S. 8. 5 I *r.* thee under apple tr.
Isa. 15. 5 they sh. *r.* cry of destruc.
Jer. 23. 5 will *r.* to D. a right. Br.
Ezek. 34. 29 *r.* up plant of renown
Dan. 7. 5 it *r.* up itself on one side
Hos. 6. 2 He will *r.* us up, and we
Am. 2. 11 I *r.* your sons for prophets
Mic. 5. 5 we *r.* ag'st him shepherds
Hab. 1. 6 I *r.* up the Chaldeans
Zech. 11. 16 I will *r.* up a shepherd
Mat. 3. 9 God is able of stones to *r.*
Mark 12. 19 *r.* up seed unto brother
Luke 1. 69 *r.* up horn of salvation
John 2. 19 in three days I will *r.* it

Acts 10. 40 Him G. *r.* up third day
Rom. 4. 25 was *r.* for justification
1 Cor. 6. 14 God hath *r.* up the L.
2 Cor. 1. 9 trust in G. wh. *r.* dead
Gal. 1. 1 F., who *r.* him from dead
Eph. 1. 20 he *r.* him from the dead
Col. 2. 12 G., who *r.* him from dead
1 Thes. 1. 10 he *r.* fr. dead, even J.
2 Tim. 2. 8 C., of seed of D. was *r.*
Heb. 11. 19 G. was able to *r.* him up
Jas. 5. 15 the Lord shall *r.* him up
1 Pet. 1. 21 that *r.* him from dead
R. V. Job 3. 8; 14. 12 roused; S.
of S. 8. 5 awakened; Job 50. 9;
Ez. 1. 5; Jer. 6. 22; 50. 41; 51. 11;
Joel 3. 7; Zech. 9. 13; Acts 13. 50
stir or stirred
Raiser. *Exactor.*
Dan. 11. 20 stand up a *r.* of taxes
Raising. R. V. *stir fire.*
Hos. 7. 4 bak., ceas. fr. *r.* aft. knead.
R. V. *stirring up crowd.*
Acts 24. 12 neither *r.* up the people
Raisins. *Dried fruits, clusters.*
1 Sam. 25. 18 A. took hun. clust. *r.*
2 Sam. 16. 1 asses, . . th. hun. bun. *r.*
1 Chr. 12. 40 brought bunch. of *r.*
Ram. *Male ovine animal.*
Gen. 22. 13 behold, *r.* cau. in thick.
Ex. 26. 14 for tent *r.'s* skins dyed
Lev. 8. 21 Mos. burnt *r.* on altar
Num. 7. 15 One young bul., one *r.*
Deut. 32. 14 *r.* of breed of Bashan
Josh. 6. 4 bear trump. of *r.'s* horn
1 Sam. 15. 22 heark. than fat of *r.*
2 K. 3. 4 Moab rendered hun. th. *r.*
1 Chr. 15. 26 they off. bull. and *r.*
2 Chr. 13. 9 bullock and seven *r.*
Ez. 10. 19 they off. *r.* of the flock
Job 42. 8 take you now seven *r.*
Ps. 114. 4 mountains skipped like *r.*
Isa. 1. 11 I am full of offerings of *r.*
Jer. 51. 40 will br. th. down like *r.*
Ezek. 34. 17 judge bet. *r.* and goats
Dan. 8. 4 I saw *r.* pushing westw.
Mic. 6. 7 L. be pleas. wi. thous. *r.*
R. V. Gen. 31. 10, 12 he-goats
Rampart. *Bulwark.*
Lam. 2. 8 ne made the *r.* to lament
Nah. 3. 8 whose *r.* was the sea and
Ran. *See* Run.
Rang. *See* Ring.
Range. *Row, range.*
Lev. 11. 35 wheth. oven, or *r.* for
2 K. 11. 8 he cometh within the *r.*
2 Chr. 23. 14 Have her forth of th. *r.*
Job 39. 8 *r.* of mount. is his past.
R. V. 2 K. 11. 8, 15; 2 Chr. 23. 14
ranks
Ranging. *Run to and fro.*
Pro. 28. 15 roar. lion and *r.* bear
Rank. *Vigorous.*
Gen. 41. 5, 7 seven ears, *r.* and go.
Row, order, arrangement.
Num. 2. 16 set forth in second *r.*
1 K. 7. 4, 5 light ag'st l., three *r.*
1 Chr. 12. 38 men that could keep *r.*
Mark 6. 40 sat down in *r.*, by hun.
Way, custom.
Joel 2. 7 they sh. not break their *r.*
R. V. 1 Chr. 12. 33 battle array;
Num. 2. 16, 24 ——
Ransom (n.). *Cover, price, freedom.*
Ex. 21. 30 then he sh. give for *r.*
Job 33. 24 pit, I have found a *r.*
Ps. 49. 7 None can give God a *r.*
Prov. 6. 35 He will not regard a. *r.*
Isa. 43. 3 I gave Egypt for thy *r.*
Mat. 10. 28 giv. his life *r.* for ma.
Mark. 10. 45 to give his life a *r.* for
1 Tim. 2. 6 gave himself *r.* for all
R. V. Ex. 21. 30 redemption
Ransom (v.). *Free, redeem.*
Isa. 35. 10 *r.* of the L. shall return
Jer. 31. 11 L. redeemed J., and *r.*
Hos. 13. 14 will *r.* them fr. grave
R. V. Isa. 51. 10 redeemed
Rare. *Precious.*
Dan. 2. 11 *r.* thing king requireth
Rase. *Make bare.*
Ps. 137. 7 *r.* it, even to foundations
Rash. *Hasty.*
Eccl. 5. 2 Be not *r.* with thy mouth
Isa. 32. 4 heart of *r.* shall underst.
Rashly R. V. *rash.*

Acts 19. 36 be quiet, do nothing *r*.
Rate. *Portion, measure.*
Ex. 16. 4 gath. certain *r*. every day
1 K. 16. 25 mules, *r*. year by year
2 K. 25. 30 daily *r*. for every day
2 Chr. 8. 13 after cer. *r*. every day
R. V. Ex. 16. 4 ; 2 K. 25. 30 porti.
Rather. *Better, more wisely.*
Prov. 17. 12 *r*. than fool in his folly
Mat. 10. 6 go *r*. to lost sheep of
John 3. 19 loved dark *r*. than light
Eto., etc.
R. V. Luke 11. 41 ; 12. 31 how-
beit
Rattle. *Sing, shake, rattle.*
Job 39. 32 The quiver *r*. against him
Nah. 3. 2 noise of *r*. of the wheels
Raven. *Raven, crow.*
Gen. 8. 7 Noah sent forth a *r*. wh.
Lev. 11. 15 Every *r*. after its kind
Deut. 14. 14
1 K. 17. 6 *r*. brought him bread
Job 38. 41 who provid. *r*. his food?
Ps. 147. 9 He giv. to *r*. which cry
Prov. 30. 17 *r*. of valley shall pick
S. of S. 5. 11 his locks are bla. as *r*.
Isa. 34. 11 owl and *r*. shall dwell
Luke 12. 24 Consid. *r*., th, nei. sow
Ravening. *Tearing, preying.*
Ps. 22. 13 they gasped as *r*. lion
Ezek. 22. 25 like lion *r*. the prey
Mat. 7. 15 inwa. they are *r*. wolves
Luke 11. 39 inward part full of *r*.
R. V. Luke 11. 39 extortion
Ravenous. *Snatching, tearing.*
Isa. 35. 9 nor any *r*. beast shall go
Ezek. 39. 4 give thee to *r*. birds
Ravin (*v.*). *Tear.*
Gen. 49. 27 Benj. shall *r*. as wolf
Ravin (*n.*). *Prey.*
Nah. 2. 12 lions filled dens with *r*.
Ravish. *Give heart.*
S. of S. 4. 9 Thou hast *r*. my heart
Violate, afflict.
Lam. 5. 11 They *r*. women in Zion
Isa. 13. 16 houses spoiled, wives *r*.
Zech. 14. 2 houses rifled, wives *r*.
Led astray
Prov. 5. 19, 20 be *r*. with her love
Raw. *Live, uncooked.*
Ex. 12. 9 Eat not it *r*. or sodden
Lev. 13. 10 if th. be quick *r*. flesh
1 Sam. 2. 15 not sod. flesh, but *r*.
Razor. *Knife, razor.*
Num. 6. 5 no *r*. come on his head
Judg. 16. 17 not *r*. come on mine h.
1 Sam. 1. 11. shall no *r*. come upon
Ps. 52. 2 tongue like a sharp *r*.
Isa. 7. 20 L. shave with *r*. hired
Ezek. 5. 1 take the a barber's *r*.
Reach. *Come to, stretch, extend.*
Gen. 28. 12 top of it *r*. to heaven
Ex. 26. 28 bar sh. *r*. fr. end to end
Lev. 26. 5 threshing *r*. to vintage
Num. 34 11 border shall *r*. to sea
Josh. 19 11 border *r*. to Dabbash.
Ruth 2. 14 he *r*. her parched corn
2 Chr. 28. 9 rage that *r*. to heaven
Job 20. 6 tho. head *r*. unto clouds
Prov. 31. 20 she *r*. forth her hands
Isa. 8. 8 he shall *r*. even to neck
Jer. 4. 10 sword *r*. unto the soul
Dan. 4. 11 the height *r*. to heaven
Zech. 14. 5 mountains sh. *r*. to A.
John 20. 27 *r*. hither thy finger and
2 Cor. 10. 13 meas. to *r*. unto you
Phil. 3. 13 *r*. forth unto things wh.
Rev. 18. 5 her sins have *r*. heaven
R. V. Ex. 26. 28 pass through;
Phil. 3. 13 stretching forward
Read. *Read, call.*
Ex. 24. 7 *r*. in audience of people
Deut. 17. 19 king shall *r*. therein
Josh. 8. 35 Josh. *r*. bef. congrega.
2 K. 5. 7 king of Is. *r*. the letter
2 Chr. 34. 18 Shap. *r*. it bef. king
Ez. 4. 23 letter was *r*. bef. Rehum
Neh. 8. 8 they *r*. in book of law
Esth. 6. 1 chronicles; they were *r*.
Isa. 34. 16 Seek ye the book, and *r*.
Jer. 36. 10 Then *r*. Baruch in book
Dan. 5. 7 Whoso. sh. *r*. this writing
Hab. 2. 2 that he may run that *r*. it
Mat. 21. 42 Did ye nev. *r*. in Scrip.
Mark 13. 14 let him that *r*. unders.
Luke 6. 3 Have ye not *r*. so much

John 19. 20 title *r*. many of Jews
Acts 8. 28 ennuch *r*. Es. the proph.
2 Cor. 1. 13 we write .. what ye *r*.
Eph. 3. 4 wh. ye *r*. ye may underst.
Col. 4. 16 when this epistle is *r*
1 Thes. 5. 27 epistle be *r*. unto all
Rev. 1. 3 Blessed is he that *r*. and
Reading. *Reading, calling.*
Neh. 8. 8 caused them to underst *r*.
Jer. 51. 63 when hast ma. end of *r*.
Acts 13. 15 *r*. of law and prophets
2 Cor. 3. 14 untaken away in *r*. of
1 Tim. 4. 13 give attendance to *r*.
Readiness. *Being ready.*
Acts 17. 11 received word with *r*.
2 Cor. 8. 11 there was a *r*. to will
Ready. *Prepared, apt.*
Gen. 46. 29 Jos. made *r*. his char.
Ex. 19. 11 be *r*. against third day
Nu....32. 17 we go *r*. armed before
..ut. 1. 41 ye were *r*. to go up hill
Josh. 8. 4 go not far, but be all *r*.
2 Sam. 18. 22 thou hast no tidings *r*.
2 K. 9. 21 his chariot was made *r*.
1 Chr. 28.2 made *r*. for the building
2 Chr. 35. 14 made *r*. for themselves
Ez. 7. 6 Ezra was a *r*. scribe in the
Neh. 9. 17 art a God *r*. to pardon
Esth. 3. 14 be *r*. against that day
Job 15. 24 prevail, as k. *r*. to battle
Ps. 45. 1 tongue is pen of *r*. writer
Prov. 24. 11 and those *r*. to be slain
Eccl. 5. 1 be more *r*. to hear th. give
Isa. 41. 7 it is *r*. for the soldering
Ezek. 7. 14 blown trump., to ma. *r*.
Dan. 3. 15 if ye be *r*. to worship
Hos. 7. 6 made *r*. heart like oven
Mat. 22. 4 all things are *r*., come
Mark 14. 38 The spirit truly is *r*.
Luke 12. 40 Be ye therefore *r*. also
John 7. 6 but your time is alway *r*.
Acts 21. 13 *r*. not to be bound only
Rom. 1. 15 I am *r*. to preach gospel
2. Cor. 12. 14 I am *r*. to come to you
1 Tim. 6. 18 ye be *r*. to to distribute
2 Tim. 4. 6 am now *r*. to be offered
Tit. 3. 1 Put them in mind to be *r*.
Heb. 8. 13 old is *r*. to vanish away
1 Pet. 1. 5 salva. *r*. to be revealed
Rev. 3. 2 remain, that are *r*. to die
R. V. 2 Chr. 35. 14 ; 2 Cor. 9. 2, 3
prepared ; 1 Chr. 12. 23, 24 armed
for; Mark 14. 38 willing; Acts
20. 7 intending; Heb. 8. 13 nigh;
Rev. 12. 4 about
Realm. *Kingdom.*
2 Chr. 20. 30 *r*. of Jehosh. was quiet
Ez. 7. 13 they of my *r*. who go up
Dan. 6. 1 Darius, k. ov. *r*. of Chal.
Reap. *Reap, gather.*
Lev. 19. 9 shalt not wholly *r*. cor.
Ruth 2 9. eyes be on field they *r*.
1 Sam. 8. 12 set your servants to *r*.
2 K. 19. 29 *r*., and plant vineyards
Job 4. 18 that sow wicked., *r*. same
Ps. 126. 5 that sow tears shall *r*. joy
Prov. 22. 8 that sow iniq. sh. *r*. van.
Eccl. 11. 4 regard clouds sh. not *r*.
Isa. 17. 5 *r*. ears with his arm; and
Jer. 12. 13 sown wheat, but *r*. thor.
Hos. 8. 7 reap *r*. the whirlwi.
Mic. 6. 15 sow, but thou shalt not *r*.
Mat. 6. 26 nei. do they *r*. nor gath.
Luke 12. 24 they neither sow nor *r*.
John 4. 37 One soweth, another *r*.
1 Cor. 9. 11 if we *r*. carnal things
2 Cor. 9. 6 sow. spar. sh. *r*. sparing.
Gal. 6. 7 soweth, that shall he *r*.
Jas. 5. 4 hire of labor. who *r*. fields
Rev. 14. 15 Thrust in sickle and *r*.
R. V. Lev. 23. 22 —— ; Jas. 5. 4
mowed
Reaper. *Who reaps.*
Ruth 2. 3 Ruth gleaned after the *r*.
2 K. 4. 18 child went out to the *r*.
Am. 9. 13 plowman shall overtak. *r*.
Mat. 13. 30 say to *r*., Gather tares
Reaping. *Reaping.*
1 Sam. 6. 13 *r*. harvest in the valley
Mat. 25. 24 *r*. where hast not sown
Luke 19. 22
Rear. *Set up, cause to rise*
Ex. 26. 30 thou shalt *r*. up taberna.
Lev. 26. 1 neither *r*. you up image
Num. 9. 15 day that taberna. was *r*.
2 Sam. 24. 18 Go, *r*. altar unto L.

1 K. 16. 32 he *r*. up an altar for Baal
2 K. 21. 3 Manas. *r*. altars tc Baal
2 Chr. 3. 17 Sol. *r*. pillars bef. tem.
John 2. 20 temple, wilt thou *r*. it
R. V. 2 Chr. 3. 17 set; John 2. 20
raise
Reason (*n.*). *Cause, understand-
ing.*
Gen 41. 31 plenty not know. by *r*
Ex. 3. 7 heard cry by *r*. of taskm.
Num. 9. 10 uncl. by *r*. dead body
Deut. 5. 5 afraid by *r*. of the fire
1 K. 9. 15 this is the *r*. of the levy
2 Chr. 21. 19 bow. fell by *r*. of sick.
Job 32. 11 I gave ear to your *r*.
Ps. 44. 16 For by *r*. of the enemy
Prov. 26. 16 seven men render *r*.
Eccl. 7. 25 to seek wisdom, and *r*
Isa. 49. 19 too nar. by *r*. of inhab.
Ezek. 19. 10 branches by *r*. of wat.
Dan. 8. 12 given by *r*. of transgres.
Jonah 2. 2 I cried by *r*. of affliction
John 12. 11 by *r*. many Jews went
Acts 6. 2 not *r*. we leave word of G.
Rom. 8. 20 by *r*. of him who subj.
2 Cor. 3. 10 by *r*. of glo. th. excell.
Heb. 5. 3 by *r*. hereof he ought
1 Pet. 3. 15 ask *r*. of hope in you
2 Pet. 2. 2 by *r*. of whom truth
Rev. 9. 2 darkened by *r*. of smoke
Reason (*v.*). *Reckon, discuss.*
1 Sam. 12. 7 *r*. with you before L.
Job 13. 3 I desire to *r*. with God
Isa. 1. 18 Come, let us *r*. together
Mat. 16. 7 they *r*. among themsel.
Mark 2. 8 Why *r*. ye these things
Luke 5. 21 scri. and Phr. began to *r*.
Acts 17. 2 three sabbaths Paul *r*.
Reasonable. *Rational.*
Rom. 12. 1 sacrifice, your *r*. servant
Reasoning. *Reckoning, proving*
Job. 13. 6 hear my *r*., and hearken
Mark 2. 6 scribes *r*. in th. hearts
Luke 9. 46 arose *r*. among them
Acts 28. 29 had *r*. among themselv
Rebel (*n.*). *Who rebels.*
Num. 17. 10 A.'s rod, token ag. *r*.
Ezek. 20. 38 I will purge out *r*.
Rebel (*v.*). *Turn against, resent.*
Gen. 14. 4 thirteenth year they *r*.
Num. 14. 9 *r*. not ye against Lord
Deut. 1. 26 *r*. against the command.
Josh 22. 29 G. forbid we should *r*.
1 Sam. 12. 14 if ye fear, and not *r*.
1 K. 12. 19 Is. *r*. against h. of Dav.
2 K. 1. 1 Moab *r*. against Israel
2 Chr. 13. 6 Jer. *r*. against his lord
Neh. 2. 19 will ye *r*. against king?
Job 24. 13 They are of those that *r*.
Ps. 5. 10 they have *r*. against thee
Isa. 1. 20 ye *r*., ye sh. be devoured
Jer. 52. 3 Zed. *r*. against the king
Lam. 1. 20 for I have grievously *r*.
Ezek. 2. 3 nation that hath *r*. against
Dan. 9. 5 have *r*., ev. by departing
Hos. 13. 16 she hath *r*. against God
Rebellion. *Turning against.*
Deut. 31. 27 For I know thy *r*. and
Josh. 22. 22 sh. know if it be in *r*.
1 Sam. 15. 23 *r*. is as sin of witchcr.
Ez. 4. 19 and sed. ha. been made
Neh. 9. 17 in *r*. appointed captain
Job. 34. 37 he add. *r*. unto his sin
Prov. 17. 11 evil man seeketh only *r*.
Jer. 28. 16 hast tau. *r*. against Lord
Rebellious. *Given to rebellion.*
Deut. 21. 20 son is stubborn and *r*.
1 Sam. 20. 30 son of the *r*. woman
Ez. 4. 15 this city is a *r*. city, and
Ps. 66. 7 let not *r*. exalt themselves
Isa. 30. 9 this is a *r*. people, lying
Jer. 5. 23 this people hath *r*. heart
Ezek. 2. 5 for they are a *r*. house
Rebuke (*n.*). *Reproof, chiding.*
Deut. 28. 20 Lord send on thee *r*
2 K. 19. 3 this is day of tr. and *r*.
Ps. 76. 6 At thy *r*., O G. of Jacob
Prov. 13. 11 a scorner heareth not *r*.
Eccl. 7. 5 bet. to hear *r*. of the wise
Isa. 30. 17 at *r*. of one; at *r*. of five
Jer. 15. 15 for thy sake I suffer *r*.
Ezek. 5. 15 execute judgments in *r*.
Hos. 5. 9 Eph. be des. in day of *r*.
Phil. 2. 15 without *r*., in midst of or
R. V. Phil. 2. 15 blemish ; Jer. 15
15 reproach

Rebuke (*v.*).   *Reprove, chide.*
Gen. 31. 42 hath seen and *r.* thee
Lev. 19. 17 in any wise *r.* thy neigh.
Ruth 2. 16 may glean, *r.* her not
2 Sam. 22. 16 discov. at *r.* of Lord
1 Chr. 12. 17 G. of fath. look, and *r.*
Neh. 5. 7 I *r.* nobles and rulers
Ps. 9. 5 Thou hast *r.* the heathen
Prov. 9. 8 *r.* wise man, he will love
Isa. 17. 13 God shall *r.* them, and
Am. 5. 10 hate him that *r.* in gate
Mic. 4. 3 *r.* strong nations far off
Zech. 3. 2 Lord *r.* thee, O Satan
Mal. 3. 11 I will *r.* the devourer
Mat. 8. 26 he *r.* the wind and sea
Mark 1. 25 And Jes. *r.* him, saying
Luke 4. 39 *r.* fever, and it left her
1 Tim. 5. 1 *R.* not elder, but intreat
2 Tim. 4. 2 *r.* exhort, wi. long suff.
Tit. 2. 15 exhort, *r.* with authority
Heb. 12. 5 nor faint wh. thou art *r.*
2 Pet. 2. 16 was *r.* for his iniquity
Jude 9 Mich. said, The L. *r.* thee
Rev. 3. 19 as many as I love, I *r.*
R. V. Prov. 9. 7, 8; Am. 5. 10; 1
  Tim. 5. 20; Tit. 2. 15; Rev. 3. 19
  reprove or reproveth
Rebuker.   *Who rebukes.*
Hos. 5. 2 I have been *r.* of them
Recall.   *Call back.*
Lam. 3. 21 This I *r.* to my mind
Receipt.   R. V. *place to toll.*
Mat. 9. 9 Mat. sitting at *r.* of cust.
Mark 2. 14; Luke 5. 27
Receive.   *Take, accept.*
Gen. 4. 11 *r.* bro.'s blood fr. hand
Ex. 36. 3 *r.* of Moses all offerings
Num. 23. 20 I ha. *r.* com. to bless
Deut. 9. 9 gone up into mount to *r.*
Josh. 13. 8 Gad. have *r.* their inher.
Judg. 13. 23 not have *r.* burnt off.
1 Sam. 25. 35 David *r.* of her hand
2 Sam. 18. 12 Tho. I sh. *r.* thous. sh.
1 K. 10. 28 mer. *r.* the linen yarn
2 K. 19. 14 Hez. *r.* letter of hand
1 Chr. 12. 18 Then D. *r.* them, and
2 Chr. 29. 22 priests *r.* bl., and spr.
Esth. 4. 4 raiment, but he *r.* it not
Job 2. 10 *r.* good at hand of God?
Ps. 6. 9 heard, he will *r.* my prayer
Prov. 4. 10 Hear, my son, *r.* my say.
Isa. 40. 2 she *r.* of the Lord's hand
Jer. 35. 13 Will ye not *r.* instruction
Ezek. 36. 30 ye sh. *r.* no reproach
Dan. 2. 6 ye shall *r.* of me gifts
Hos. 10. 6 Ephraim shall *r.* shame
Mic. 1. 11 he sh. *r.* of you his stan.
Zeph. 3. 7 thou wilt *r.* instruction
Mal. 2. 13 *r.* offering with good will
Mat. 10. 40 He that *r.* you, *r.* me
Mark 10. 30 he shall *r.* hund. fold
Luke 11. 10 every one that ask. *r.*
John 5. 41 I *r.* not honour fr. men
Acts 2. 38 ye sh. *r.* gift of Holy G.
Rom. 1. 5 By whom we ha. *r.* grace
1 Cor. 14. 5 that ch. may *r.* edifying
2 Cor. 6. 1 ye *r.* not grace in vain
Gal. 4. 14 *r.* me as angel of God
Eph. 6. 8 same shall he *r.* of Lord
Phil. 4. 18 having *r.* of Epaphrodi.
Col. 4. 10 Marcus, if he come *r.* h.
1 Thes. 1. 6 having *r.* word in affl.
Phile. 12 *r.* him, that is, mine own
Heb. 7. 9 who *r.* tithes, pay. tithes
Jas. 4. 3 Ye ask, and *r.* not b. ye ask
1 Pet. 4. 10 ev. man hath *r.* the gift
2 Pet. 1. 17 *r.* fr. G. hon. and glory
1 John 3. 22 wh. we ask., we *r.* of h.
2 John 4 we have *r.* a command-
  ment
Rev. 4. 11 Thou art worthy, L. to *r.*
R. V. Ex. 29. 25; 1 Sam. 12. 3; 2
  K. 12. 7, 8; John 16. 14; Heb. 7.
  6 take; Hos. 14. 2; Mark 4. 20; 1
  Thes. 2. 13 accept; Luke 9. 11;
  3 John 8 welcome; many other
  changes due to context
Receiver. R. V. *that weighs tribute.*
Isa. 33. 18 where is the *r.*?, where is
Receiving.   *Taking.*
2 K. 5. 20 in not *r.* at his hands that
Acts 17. 15 *r.* a comman. to Silas
Rom. 11. 15 wh. sh. *r.* of th. be?
Phil. 4. 15 concern. giving and *r.*
Heb. 12. 28 wheref. we *r.* a king
1 Pet. 1. 9 *r.* the end of your faith

Reckon.   *Count, calculate, con-
sider, esteem.*
Lev. 27. 18 priest sh. *r.* him money
Num. 18. 27 your off. shall be *r.*
2 Sam. 4. 2 Beeroth was *r.* to Benj.
2 K. 12. 15 they *r.* not with men
1 Chr. 5. 17 these were *r.* by gene.
2 Chr. 31. 19 were *r.* by genealogies
Ez. 8. 3 *r.* by genealogy of males
Neh. 7. 5 might be *r.* by genealog.
Ps. 4. 5 thoughts cannot be *r.* in
Isa. 38. 13 I *r.* till morning, that
Ezek. 44. 26 *r.* unto him seven days
Mat. 18. 24 wh. he had begun to *r.*
Luke 22. 37 he was *r.* am'g trans.
Rom. 4. 4 is reward not *r.* of grace
Reckoning.   *Accounting, count-
ing.*
2 K. 22. 7 there was no *r.* made
1 Chr. 23. 11 they were in one *r.*
Recommended.   *Commended.*
Acts 14. 26 whence they had been *r.*
  15. 40 being *r.* by brethren unto
R. V. Acts 14. 26 committed; 15. 40
  commended
Recompence (*n.*).   *Equal return.*
Deut. 32. 35 To me belong v. and *r.*
Job 15. 31 vanity shall be his *r.*
Hos. 9. 7 the days of *r.* are come
Joel 3. 4 will ye render me a *r.*?
Prov. 12. 14 *r.* of hand sh. be rend.
Isa. 34. 8 it is the year of *r.* for Zion
Jer. 51. 6 he will render to her *r.*
Lam. 3. 64 *r.* unto them *r.*, O Lord
Luke 14. 12 and a *r.* be made thee
Rom. 1. 27 rece. *r.* of their errors
2 Cor. 6. 13 Now for a *r.* in same
Heb. 2. 2 rece. just *r.* of reward
Recompense (*v.*).   *Give or turn
back, return, requite, repay.*
Num. 5. 7 he sh. *r.* his trespass
Ruth 2. 12 The Lord *r.* thy work
2 Sam. 19. 36 why should k. *r.* it
2 Chr. 6. 23 *r.* way upon his head
Job 34. 33 *r.* it, whe. thou refuse
Ps. 18. 24 L. *r.* me accord. to my
Prov. 20. 22 Say not, I will *r.* evil
Isa. 65. 6 I will *r.* unto th. bosom
Jer. 18. 20 sh. evil be *r.* for good?
Ezek. 7. 4 I will *r.* thy ways upon
Hos. 12. 2 accor. to doings will be *r.*
Joel 3. 4 if ye *r.* me, will I return
Luke 14. 14 they cannot *r.* thee, for
Rom. 11. 35 it sh. be *r.* unto him
2 Thes. 1. 6 to *r.* tribulat. to them
Heb. 10. 30 I will *r.* saith the Lord
R. V. Num. 5. 7, 8 restitution;
  Ezek. 7. 3, 4, 9; 11. 21; 16. 34;
  17. 19; 22. 31; 2 Chr. 6. 23; bring
  or brought; Rom. 12. 17 render
Reconcile.   *Cover, atone, reunite,
change throughout.*
Lev. 6. 30 blood is brought to *r.*
1 Sam. 29. 4 wherewi. he *r.* hims.
Ezek. 45. 20 so shall he *r.* house
Mat. 5. 24 be *r.* to thy brother, and
Rom. 5. 10 being *r.* we sh. be saved
1 Cor. 7. 11 let her be *r.* to husb.
2 Cor. 5. 20 we pray, be ye *r.* to G.
Eph. 2. 16 he might *r.* both to G.
Col. 1. 20 by him to *r.* all things
R. V. Lev. 6. 30; Ezek. 45. 20
  make atonement
Reconciliation.   *Cover, atone-
ment, propitiation.*
Lev. 8. 15 to make a *r.* upon it
2 Chr. 29. 24 made *r.* with blood
Ezek. 45. 15 to make *r.* for them
Dan. 9. 24 to make *r.* for iniquity
Heb. 2. 17 *r.* for sins of the people
R. V. Lev. 8. 15; 16. 20; Ezek. 45.
  15, 17 atonement; 2 Chr. 29. 24 sin
  offering; Heb. 2. 17 propitiation.
Record (*n.*).   *Testimony, record.*
Ez. 6. 2 therein was *r.* thus written
Esth. 6. 1 bring book of *r.* of the C.
Job 16. 19 behold, my *r.* is on high
John 1. 19 And this is the *r.* of John
2 Cor. 1. 23 I call God for a *r.* up.
Phil. 1. 8 G. is my *r.*, how I long
Gal. 4. 15 I bear you *r.* that, if pos.
1 John 5. 10 he believeth not the *r.*
3 John 12 we bear *r.*, our *r.* is true
Rev. 1. 2 who bare *r.* of word of G.
R. V. very general change to, wit-
  ness

Record (*v.*) *Testify, witness.*
Ex. 20. 24 where I *r.* my name I
Deut. 30. 19 I call heaven to *r.* this
1 Chr. 16. 4 appoint. Levites to *r.*
Neh. 12. 22 Levites were *r.* chief
Isa. 8. 2 took faithful witness. to *r.*
Acts 20. 26 I take you to *r.* th. day
R. V. Deut. 30. 19 witness; 1 Chr.
  16. 4 celebrate; Acts 20. 26 testify
Recorder.   *Who causes things
to be remembered.*
2 Sam. 8. 16 J., son of A., was *r.*
1 K. 4. 3; 2 K. 18, 18. 1 Chr. 18.
  15; 2 Chr. 34. 8; Isa. 36. 3
Recount.   R. V. *remembereth.*
Nah. 2. 5 He shall *r.* his worthies
Recover.   *Regain, repossess, re-
trieve, restore from.*
Judg. 11. 26 why did ye not *r.* them
1 Sam. 30. 18 D. *r.* all Am. took
2 Sam. 8. 3 went to *r.* his border
2 K. 8. 8 sh. I *r.* of this disease?
2 Chr. 13. 20 Nei. did Jer. *r.* str.
Ps. 39. 13 that I may *r.* strength
Isa. 11. 11 to *r.* remnant of people
Jer. 8. 22 is not health of peo. *r.*?
Hos. 2. 9 will *r.* my wool and flax
Mark 16. 18 hands on sick, they *r.*
2 Tim. 2. 26 they may *r.* themselv.
R. V. 1 Sam. 30. 19 brought back;
  Hos. 2. 9 pluck away
Red.   *Red, ruddy.*
Gen. 25. 30 Feed me with *r.* pottage
Ex. 26. 14 make cov. of sk. dyed *r.*
Num. 19. 2 bring thee a *r.* heifer
2 K. 3. 22 Moabites saw water *r.*
Esth. 1. 6 pavement of *r.*, and blue
Ps. 75. 8 wine is *r.*, full of mixture
Prov. 23. 31 Look not on w. when *r.*
Isa. 1. 18 tho. th. be *r.* like crimson
Nah. 2. 3 shield of mighty men *r.*
Zech. 1. 8 man riding on *r.* horse
Mat. 16. 2 fair weather, sky is *r.*
R. V. Ps. 75. 8 foameth
Reddish.   R. V. *reddish white.*
Lev. 13. 19 spot, white, somewh. *r.*
  13. 24, 42, 43, 49; 14. 37
Redeem.   *To free, loose.*
Gen. 48. 16 the Angel which *r.* me
Ex. 6. 6 I will *r.* you with arm. and
Lev. 25. 48 one of his breth. may *r.*
Num. 18. 15 firstborn shalt thou *r.*
Deut. 7. 8 L. hath *r.* you fr. Egyp.
Ruth 4. 6 I cannot *r.* for myself
2 Sam. 7. 23 went to *r.* for peo.
1 K. 1. 29 L. that hath *r.* my soul
1 Chr. 17. 21 whom th. *r.* out of E.
Neh. 5. 8 we have *r.* the Jews
Job 5. 20 he sh. *r.* thee from death
Ps. 103. 4 who *r.* thy life fr. destr.
Isa. 44. 23 Lord hath *r.* Jacob, and
Jer. 15. 21 and I will *r.* thee out of
Lam. 3. 58 Lord, thou hast *r.* my life
Hos. 13. 14 I will *r.* them fr. death
Mic. 4. 10 L. shall *r.* thee fr. hand
Zech. 10. 8 for I have *r.* them: and
Luke 1. 68 for he hath *r.* his people
Gal. 3. 13 C. hath *r.* us from curse
Eph. 5. 16 *R.* the time, because
Col. 4. 5 Walk in wis., *r.* the time
Tit. 2. 14 he might *r.* us from iniq.
1 Pet. 1. 18 not *r.* with corruption
Rev. 5. 9 thou hast *r.* us to God
R. V. Lev. 25. 29; 27. 27; Isa. 5.
  11; Jer. 31. 11 ransom; Lev. 25.
  29; Num. 3. 51; Ruth 4. 6 redemp-
  tion; Ps. 136. 24 delivered; Rev.
  5. 9; 14. 3, 4 purchased
Redeemer.   *Who frees.*
Job. 19. 25 I know that my *r.* liveth
Ps. 19. 14 O L., my strength and *r.*
Prov. 23. 11 for their *r.* is mighty
Isa. 41. 14 thy *r.*, mighty one of Is.
  43. 14; 44. 6; 47. 4; 48. 17; 49. 7
Jer. 50. 34 Their *r.* is strong
Redemption.   *Freeing, loosing
away.*
Lev. 25. 24 shall grant *r.* for land
Num. 3. 49 Mos. took the *r.* money
Ruth 4. 7 manner in Is. concern. *r.*
Ps. 111. 9 He sent *r.* unto his peo.
Jer. 32. 7 for the right of *r.* is thine
Luke 21. 28 your *r.* draweth nigh
Rom. 3. 24 thro. *r.* that is in Chr
1 Cor. 1. 30 C. is made unto us *r.*
Eph. 4. 30 ye are sealed unto *r.*

Col. 1. 14 In whom we have *r*. th.
Heb. 9. 12 hav. obtained eternal *r*.
Redness. *Fierceness.*
Prov. 23. 29 who hath *r*. of eyes
Redound. R. V. *abound.*
2 Cor. 4. 15 grace *r*. to glory of God
Reed. *Stalk, cane, reed.*
1 K. 14. 15 L. shall smite Is., as *r*.
2 K. 18. 21 trustest upon staff of *r*.
Job 41. 20 he lieth in covert of *r*.
Isa. 19. 6 *r*. and flags shall wither
Ezek. 42. 16 He meas. wi. measur. *r*.
Mat. 11. 7 to see? *r*. shak. by wind
Mark 15. 19 they smote him with *r*.
Luke 7. 24 A *r*. shaken by the wind
Rev. 21. 16 he meas. city with the *r*.
R. V. Isa. 19. 7 meadows
Reel. *Sway, stagger.*
Ps. 107. 27 They *r*. to and fro, stag.
Isa. 24. 20 earth shall *r*. to and fro
R. V. Isa. 24. 20 stagger
Refine. *Purify.*
1 Chr. 28. 18 for the altar *r*. gold
Isa. 25. 6 wines on the lees well *r*.
Zech. 13. 9 I will *r*. them as silver
Refiner. *Who refines.*
Mat. 3. 2 for he is like a *r*.'s fire
Reformation. *Making right.*
Heb. 9. 10 on th., until time of *r*.
Reformed. *Instructed.*
Lev. 26. 23 And if ye will not be *r*.
Refrain. *Withhold, keep back.*
Gen. 45. 1 Jos. could not *r*. himself
Esth. 5. 10 Haman *r*. himself : and
Job 7. 11 I will not *r*. my mouth
Ps. 40. 9 lo, I have not *r*. my lips, O
Prov. 10. 19 he that *r*. lips is wise
Eccl. 3. 5 time to *r*. from embracing
Isa. 42. 14 been still, *r*. myself : now
Jer. 14. 10 have not *r*. their feet
Acts 5. 38 I say, *R*. fr. these men
1 Pet. 3. 10 let him *r*. his tongue
Refresh. *Make fresh, invigorate.*
Ex. 23. 12 the stranger may be *r*.
1 Sam. 16. 23 Saul was *r*., and well
2 Sam. 16. 24 D. and peo. *r*. thems.
1 K. 13. 7 Come home, *r*. thyself
Job. 32. 20 speak, th. I may be *r*.
Prov. 25. 13 he *r*. soul of masters
Acts 27. 3 J. suffered P. to *r*. him
Rom. 15. 32 I may with you be *r*.
1 Cor. 16. 18 they have *r*. my spirits
2 Cor. 7. 13 bec. his spirit was *r*.
2 Tim. 1. 16 for he oft *r*. me, and
Phile. 7 bowels of the saints are *r*.
R. V. Rom. 15. 32 find rest
Refreshing. *Making fresh.*
Isa. 28. 12 *r*., yet they wo. not hear
Acts 3. 19 when times of *r*. come
Refuge. *Place of flight, shelter, tower, asylum.*
Num. 35. 11 appoint. you cities of *r*.
Deut. 33. 27 eternal God is thy *r*.
Josh. 20. 3 *r*. fr. avenger of blood
2 Sam. 22. 3 high tower, my *r*.
1 Chr. 6. 57 Hebron, the city of *r*.
Ps. 46. 1 G. is our *r*. and strength
Prov. 14. 26 chil. have place of *r*.
Isa. 4. 6 tabernacle for place of *r*.
Jer. 16. 19 O L., my *r*. in affliction
Heb. 6. 18 who have fled for *r*. to
R. V. Deut. 33. 27 dwelling place ;
Ps. 9. 9 high tower
Refuse (*v*.). *Decline, deny, reject, repel.*
Gen. 37. 35 but he *r*. to be comfort.
Ex. 22. 17 if her father utterly *r*.
Num. 20. 21 E. *r*. to give Is. pass.
Deut. 25. 7 bro. *r*. to raise up name
1 Sam. 8. 19 people *r*. to obey Sa.
2 Sam. 2. 23 Asa. *r*. to turn aside
1 K. 20. 35 man *r*. to smite him
2 K. 5. 16 Naaman urged, but he *r*.
Neh. 9. 17 our fathers *r*. to obey
Esth. 1. 12 queen Vashti *r*. to come
Job 34. 33 whe. thou *r*., or choose
Ps. 78. 67 he *r*. taberna. of Joseph
Prov. 1. 24 I have called, and ye *r*.
Isa. 1. 20 if ye *r*. . ye sh. be devour.
Jer. 5. 3 they have *r*. to receive cor.
Ezek. 5. 6 they ha. *r*. my judgments
Hos. 11. 5 because they *r*. to return
Zech. 7. 11 but they *r*. to hearken
Acts 7. 35 Moses whom they *r*., say.
1 Tim. 4. 7 *r*. old wives' fables
Heb. 11. 24 Mo. *r*. to be called son

R. V. 1 Sam. 16. 7 ; Ps. 118. 22 ;
Ezek. 5. 6 ; 1 Tim. 4. 4 reject or
rejected ; Prov. 10. 17 forsaketh ;
Isa. 54. 6 cast off
Refuse (*n*.). *Rejected stuff.*
1 Sam. 15. 9 every thing that was *r*.
Lam. 3. 45 Thou hast made us *r*.
Am. 8. 6 may sell the *r*. of wheat
Regard (*n*.). *Concerning.*
Eccl. 8. 2 that in *r*. to oath of God
R. V. *gave heed.*
Acts 8. 11 And to him they had *r*.
Regard (*v*.). *Attend, observe, consider, honor, keep, concern, esteem.*
Gen. 45. 20 Also *r*. not your stuff
Ex. 5. 9 let th. not *r*. vain words
Lev. 19. 31 *r*. not familiar spirits
Dent. 28. 50 not *r*. person of aged
1 Sam. 25. 25 *r*. this man of Belial
2 Sam. 13. 20 bro., *r*. not this thing
1 K. 18. 29 nei. voice, nor any th. *r*.
2 K. 3. 14 I *r*. presence of Jehosh.
1 Chr. 17. 17 *r*. me accord. to estate
Job 36. 21 Take heed, *r*. not iniq.
Ps. 28. 5 they *r*. not works of Lord
Prov. 6. 35 He will not *r*. ransom
Eccl. 5. 8 is higher than highest *r*.
Isa. 5. 12 they *r*. not work of Lord
Lam. 4. 16 Lord will no more *r*. th.
Dan. 6. 13 Daniel *r*. not thee, O k.
Am. 5. 22 nor *r*. peace offerings
Hab. 1. 5 *r*. wonder marvellously
Mal. 1. 9 will he *r*. your person ?
Mat. 22. 16 *r*. not persons of men
Mark 12. 14
Luke 18. 2 judge . . neither *r*. man
Rom. 14. 6 that *r*. day, *r*. it to Lord
Phil. 2. 30 not *r*. life, to supply lack
Heb. 8. 9 I *r*. them not, saith Lord
R. V. 2 Sam. 13. 20 take thing to
heart ; Job 39. 7 heareth ; Ps. 94. 7
consider ; Prov. 5. 2 preserve ;
Mal. 1. 9 accept ; Luke 1. 48 looked upon ; Acts 8. 11 gave heed ;
Phil. 2. 30 hazarding ; Rom. 14.6 ;
Gal. 6. 4 ——
Regeneration. *Re-creation.*
Mat. 19. 28 wh. followed me in *r*.
Tit. 3. 5 saved us by washing of *r*.
Region. *Place, section, part.*
Deut. 3. 4 *r*. of Argob, king of Og.
1 K. 4. 11 in all the *r*. of Dor
Mat. 3. 5 went to him, *r*. round J.
Mark 1. 28 fame spr. thro. all the *r*.
Luke 4. 14 ; 7. 15
Acts 8. 1 scat. through *r*. of Judea
2 Cor. 10. 16 preach in *r*. beyond
Gal. 1. 21 I came into *r*. of Syria
R. V. 1 K. 4. 11 height ; 2 Cor. 10.
16 parts
Register. *Writing, book.*
Ez. 2. 62 These sought th. *r*. am'g
Neh. 7. 5 I found *r*. of genealogy
R. V. Neh. 7. 5 the book
Rehearse. *Speak, tell back, repeat.*
Ex. 17. 14 and *r*. it in ears of Joshua
Judg. 5. 11 *r*. righ. acts of Lord
1 Sam. 17. 31 they *r*. them bef. Saul
Acts 11. 4 Peter *r*. from beginning
R. V. Acts 11. 4 began
Reign (*n*.). *Kingdom, rule.*
1 K. 6. 1 fo. year of Solomon's *r*.
2 K. 24. 12 in eighth year of his *r*.
1 Chr. 26. 31 for. year of *r*. of Dav.
2 Chr. 16. 13 ; Ez. 4. 5 ; Neh. 12.
22 ; Esth. 1. 3 ; Jer. 1. 2 ; Dan. 1. 1
Luke 3. 1 fifteenth y'r of *r*. of Tib.
Reign (*v*.). *Be king, rule.*
Gen. 37. 8 Shalt thou *r*. over us ?
Ex. 15. 18 The Lord shall *r*. for ever
Lev. 26. 17 th. hate sh. *r*. ov. you
Josh. 13. 10 k. of Amor., which *r*.
Judg. 9. 10 said, Come, *r*. over us
1 Sam. 11. 12 Who said, Sh. Saul *r*.
2 Sam. 8. 15 David *r*. ov. all Israel
1 K. 2. 11 sev. y'rs *r*. he in Hebron
2 K. 1. 17 Jehoram *r*. in his stead
1 Chr. 1. 43 these are kings that *r*.
2 Chr. 1. 13 Solomon *r*. ov. Israel
Esth. 1. 1 Ahasu. *r*. from India unto
Job 34. 30 That the hypocrite *r*. no
Ps. 47. 8 God *r*. over the heathen
Prov. 8. 15 By me kings *r*., princes
Eccl. 4. 14 out of pris. he com. to *r*.
Isa. 24. 23 when L. of hosts sh. *r*.
Jer. 23. 5 a king sh. *r*. and prosper

Mic. 4. 7 Lord shall *r*. over them
Mat. 2. 22 heard Archelaus did *r*.
Luke 1. 33 he shall *r*. over Jacob
Rom. 5. 14 death *r*. fr. Ad. to Mo.
1 Cor. 4. 8 I would to G. ye did *r*.
2 Tim. 2. 12 If we suff., we shall *r*.
Rev. 17. 18 *r*. over kings of earth
R. V. Lev. 26. 17 ; Deut. 15. 6 ;
Josh. 12. 5 ; Judg. 9. 2 ; 1 K. 4.
21 ; Rom. 15. 12 rule or ruled
Reins. *Loins, kidneys.*
Job 16. 13 he cleaveth my *r*. asund.
Ps. 26. 2 try my *r*. and my heart
Prov. 23. 16 *r*. rejoi. wh. lips speak
Jer. 11. 20 thou triest *r*. of the heart
Lam. 3. 13 caused arrow to enter *r*.
Rev. 2. 23 he which searcheth *r*.
Reject. *Despise, disapprove, throw aside, cast off.*
1 Sam. 10. 19 ye have *r*. your God
2 K. 17. 20 L. *r*. the seed of Israel
Isa. 53. 3 he is desp. and *r*. of men
Jer. 2. 37 L. ha. *r*. thy confidence
Lam. 5. 22 thou hast utterly *r*. us
Hos. 4. 6 thou hast *r*. knowledge
Mat. 21. 42 sto. which builders *r*.
Mark 12. 10 ; Luke 20. 17
Luke 7. 30 lawyers *r*. counsel of G.
Gal. 4. 14 despised not, nor *r*., but
Tit. 3. 10 after second admoni. *r*.
Heb. 6. 8 which beareth thorns is *r*.
Rejoice. *Cry or sing aloud, joy, exult, be glad.*
Ex. 18. 9 Jethro *r*. for goodness
Lev. 23. 40 ye shall *r*. before Lord
Deut. 32. 43 *R*., O ye nat. wi. peo.
Judg. 9. 19 then *r*. ye in Abimelech
1 Sam. 2. 1 bec. I *r*. in thy salvation
2 Sam. 1. 20 lest daugh. of Phil. *r*.
1 K. 5. 7 Hiram *r*. greatly, and said
2 K. 11. 20 all peo. of the land *r*.
1 Chr. 16. 32 let the fields *r*., and
2 Chr. 6. 41 let saints *r*. in goodness
Neh. 12. 43 and *r*., the wives also
Esth. 8. 15 the city of Shushan *r*.
Job 21. 12 take tim. and harp, and *r*
Ps. 97. 12 *R*. in Lord, ye righteous
Prov. 5. 18 *r*. wi. wife of thy youth
Eccl. 11. 9 *R*., young man, in youth
S. of S. 1. 4 be glad and *r*. in thee
Isa. 14. 8 Yea. th. fir. trees *r*. at these
Jer. 31. 13 sh. virgin *r*. in the dance
Ezek. 7. 12 let not buy. *r*., nor sell
Hos. 9. 1 *R*, not, O Israel, for joy
Joel 2. 21 Fear not, be glad and *r*.
Am. 6. 13 ye *r*. in thing of nought
Mic. 7. 8 *R*. not ag. me, O enemy
Hab. 1. 15 theref. th. *r*. and are glad
Zech. 2. 10 sing and *r*. O dau. of Zion
Mat. 2. 10 they *r*. wi. exceeding joy
Luke 6. 23 *R*. ye in that day, leap
John 14. 28 If ye lov. me, ye wo. *r*.
Acts 8. 39 he went on his way *r*.
Rom. 12. 15 *R*. with them that *r*.
1 Cor. 12. 26 all the mem. *r*. wi. it
2 Cor. 7. 16 I *r*. that I have confid.
Gal. 4. 27 *R*., barren that bear. not
Phil. 3. 3 we *r*. in Jesus Christ
Col. 1. 24 who *r*. in my sufferings
1 Thes. 5. 16 *r*. evermore pray
Jas. 1. 9 let bro. of low degree *r*.
1 Pet. 4. 13 *r*., as ye are partakers
2 John 4 *r*. that I found my chil.
3 John. 3 I *r*. greatly when breth.
Rev. 11. 10 that dwell on earth *r*.
R. V. 1 Sam. 2. 1 ; 1 Chr. 16. 32 ;
Ps. 9. 2 ; 60. 6 ; 68. 3, 4 ; 108. 7 ;
Isa. 13. 3 exult ; Ps. 20. 5 ; Prov.
28. 12 triumph . Ps. 96. 12 ; 98. 4.
sing for joy ; Ps. 96. 11 ; 107. 42 ;
Prov. 23. 15 ; Zech. 10. 7 ; Acts 2.
26 be glad ; Prov. 31. 25 laugheth ;
Phil. 2. 16 ; 3. 3 ; Jas. 1. 9 ; 2. 13 ;
4. 16 glory.
Rejoicing. *Joying, glorying.*
1 K. 1. 45 they are come thence *r*.
2 Chr. 23. 18 offer burnt off. with *r*.
Job 8. 21 Till he fill my lips wi. *r*.
Ps. 45. 15 with *r*. sh. they be bro.
Isa. 65. 18 I create Jerusalem a *r*.
Jer. 15. 16 joy and *r*. of mine heart
Hab. 3. 14 *r*. was as to devour poor
Zeph. 2. 15 This is the *r*. city that
Luke 15. 5 layeth it on should., *r*.
Rom. 12. 12 *r*. in hope, patient in
1 Cor. 15. 31 I protest by your *r*.

2 Cor. 1. 12 our *r*. is this, the testim.
Gal. 6. 4 then shall he have *r*. in.
Phil. 1. 26 your *r*. be more abund.
1 Thes. 2. 19 what is our crown of *r*.
Heb. 3. 6 hold fast the *r*. of hope
Jas. 4. 16 boasting all such *r*. is evi.
R. V. Job 8. 21 shouting; Ps. 107.
   22 singing; 126. 6 joy; 1 Cor. 15.
   31; 2 Cor. 1. 12, 14; Gal. 6. 4;
   Phil. 1. 26; 1 Thes. 2. 19; Heb.
   3. 6; Jas. 4. 16 glorying

Release (*n.*). *Setting free, deliverance.*
Deut. 15. 1 end of sev. y'rs make *r*.
Esth. 2. 18 he made *r*. to provinces

Release (*v.*). *Let go, free.*
Deut. 15. 2 ev. creditor shall *r*. it
Mat. 27. 15 governor was wont to *r*.
Mark 15. 16 at feast he *r*. unto them
Luke 23. 18 *r*. unto us Barabbas
John 19. 12 Pilate sought to *r*. him
R. V. Luke 23. 17 ——.

Relief. *Help, service.*
Acts 11. 29 deter. to send. *r*. to breth.

Relieve. *Make light, aid.*
Lev. 25. 35 if bro. be poor, *r*. him
Ps. 146. 9 the Lord *r*. the fatherless
Isa. 1. 17 *r*. oppr., judge fatherless
Lam. 1. 11 for meat to *r*. the soul
1 Tim. 5. 10 if she have *r*. afflicted
R. V. Lev. 25. 35; Ps. 146. 9 up-
hold; Lam. 1. 11, 16. 19 refresh

Religion. *Service, religiou.*
Acts 26. 5 aft. straitest sect of our *r*.
Jas. 1. 27 Pure *r*. undefiled bef. God

Religious. R. V. *devout.*
Acts 13. 43 many Jews and *r*. prose.
Religious, superstitious.
Jas. 1. 26 If any man seem to be *r*.

Rely. *Lean on.*
2 Chr. 13. 18 they *r*. up. the Lord G.
16. 17. Bec. thou hast *r*. on the king

Remain. *Be left, stay.*
Gen. 7. 23 Noah only *r*. alive
Ex. 8. 11 they shall *r*. in the river
Lev. 25. 52 if there *r*. but few years
Num. 11. 26 there *r*. two of the men
Deut. 3. 11 only Og k. of Bashan *r*.
Josh. 13. 2 This is the land that *r*.
Judg. 7. 3 there *r*. ten thousand
1 Sam. 11. 11 which *r*. we scattered
2 Sam. 13, 20 Tamar *r*. desolate in
1 K. 11. 16 six months did Joab *r*.
2 K. 10. 11 Jehu slew all that *r*.
1 Chr. 13. 14 ark of G. *r*. wi. family
Ez. 9. 15 for we *r*. yet escaped, as it
Job. 19. 4 my error *r*. with myself
Ps. 55. 7 would I *r*. in wilderness
Prov. 2. 21 perfect shall *r*. in land
Eccl. 2. 9 my wisdom *r*. with me
Isa. 65. 4 Which *r*. among the graves
Jer. 37. 21 Jer. *r*. in court of prison
Lam. 5. 19 Thou, O Lord, *r*. forever
Ezek. 17. 21 that *r*. shall be scatter.
Dan. 10. 8 there *r*. no streng. in me
Am. 6. 9 if there *r*. ten men in ho.
Obad 14 delivered up those that *r*.
Hag. 2. 5 my spirit *r*. among you
Zech. 5. 4 it sh. in midst of house
Mat. 14. 20 took up of frag. that *r*.
   Luke 9. 17; John 6. 12
Acts 5. 4 wh. it *r*. was it not thine
1 Cor. 7. 11 let her *r*. unmarried
2 Cor. 9. 9 his righteous. *r*. for ever
1 Thes. 4. 15 *r*. till coming of Lord
Heb. 1. 11 They sh. per. but thou *r*.
1 John 2. 24 that ye have heard *r*.
Rev. 3. 2 strengthen things which *r*.
R. V. several changes, chiefly to,
abide, or to a sense of settling,
rest

Remainder. *What is left.*
Ex. 29. 34 thou shalt burn the *r*.
Lev. 6. 16 the *r*. shall Aaron eat
2 Sam. 14. 7 nei. name nor *r*. on e.
Ps. 76. 10 *r*. of wrath sh thou restr.
R. V. Lev. 6. 16 is left; Ps. 76. 10
residue

Remaining. *Set up, stationed.*
Num. 9. 22 cloud *r*. on tabernacle
2 Sam. 21. 5 we be destroyed fr. *r*.
Left over, remnant.
Deut. 3. 3 until none was left *r*.
Josh. 11. 8 smote, till none left *r*.
2 K. 10. 11 slew, till none left *r*.
Jeb 18. 19 nei. any *r*. in dwelling

Obad. 18 there sh. not be any *r*.
John 1. 33 on which see Spirit *r*.
R. V. Num. 9. 22; John 1. 33
abiding

Remedy. *Healing.*
2 Chr. 36. 16 wrath arose, no *r*.
Prov. 29. 1 destroyed, that with. *r*.

Remember. *Print in, bear in mind, remember.*
Gen. 9. 15 I will *r*. my covenant
Ex. 20. 8 *R*. sab. day; keep it holy
Lev. 26. 42 and I will *r*. the Lord
Num. 11. 5 We *r*. the fish which
Deut. 8. 18 thou shalt *r*. L. thy G.
Josh. 1. 13 *R*. word wh. M. spake
Judg. 8. 34 Is. *r*. not L. their God
1 Sam. 1. 19 and the Lord *r*. her
2 Sam. 14. 11 let king *r*. the L. G.
2 K. 20. 3 *r*. how I have walked
1 Chr. 16. 12 *R*. his marvellous w.
2 Chr. 6. 42 *r*. the mercies of Dav.
Neh. 1. 8 word thou com. Moses
Esth. 2. 1 he *r*. Vashti, and what
Job 7. 7 O *r*. that my life is wind
Ps. 25. 7 *R*. not sins of my youth
Prov. 31. 7 drink, and *r*. his misery
Eccl. 12. 1 *r*. Creator in days of y.
S. of S. 1. 4 we will *r*. thy love m.
Isa. 63. 11 he *r*. the days of old
Jer. 14. 21 *r*., break not thy coven.
Lam. 1. 9 she *r*. not her last end
Ezek. 16. 60 I will *r*. my covenant
Hos. 2. 17 they shall no more be *r*.
Am. 1. 9 *r*. not the brotherly cov.
Jonah 2. 7 I *r*. Lord, and my pray.
Mic. 6. 5 *r*. what Balak counselled
Hab. 3. 2 O L., in wrath *r*. mercy
Zech. 10. 9 *r*. me in far countries
Mal. 4. 4 *r*. now the law of Moses
Mat. 26. 75 Peter *r*. word of Jesus
Mark 8. 18 hear not ? do ye not *r*.?
Luke 24. 8 And they *r*. his words
John 15. 20 *r*. word that I said un.
Acts 20. 31 *r*., I ceased to warn ev.
Gal. 2. 10 we should *r*. the poor
Eph. 2. 11 *r*. that ye in time past
Col. 4. 18 *R*. my bonds. Grace wi. y.
1 Thes. 2. 9 ye *r*. breth., our labour
2 Tim. 2. 8 *r*. that J. Chr. raised
Heb. 13. 3 *r*. them th. are in bonds
Jude 1. 7 *r*. words spo. of apostles
Rev. 2. 5 *r*. fr. wh. thou art fallen
R. V. Ps. 20. 7; 77. 11; S. of S. 1. 4;
Hos. 2. 17 mention

Remembrance. *Memory, recollection, memorial.*
Ex. 17. 14 put out *r*. of Amalek
Num. 5. 15 bringing iniquity to *r*.
Deut. 32. 26 I wo. make *r*. of them.
2 Sam. 18. 18 no son to keep na. in *r*.
1 K. 17. 18 come to call my sin to *r*.
Job 18. 17 His *r*. sh. per. from earth
Ps. 6. 5 in death there is no *r*.
Eccl. 1. 11 is no *r*. of former things
Isa. 43. 26 Put me in *r*.; let us plead
Lam. 3. 20 My soul hath them in *r*,
Ezek. 21. 23 call to *r*. the iniquity
Mal. 3. 16 a book of *r*. was written
Mark 11. 21 Peter calling to *r*. saith
Luke 22. 19 this do in *r*. of me
John 14. 26 br. all things to yo. *r*.
Acts 10. 31 thine alms are had in *r*.
1 Cor. 4. 17 shall bring you into *r*.
Phil. 1. 3 I thank God on every *r*.
1 Thes. 3. 6 that ye have good *r*.
1 Tim. 4. 6 if thou put breth. in *r*.
2 Tim. 1. 3 that I have *r*. of thee
Heb. 10. 3 there is a *r*. made of sins
2 Pet. 1. 12 neg. to put you in *r*.
Rev. 16. 19 Babylon came in *r*. bef.
R. V. Job 32. 12 memorable say-
ings; Isa. 57. 8 memorial; 1 Tim.
4. 6 mind.

Remission. *Sending away.*
Mat. 26. 28 blood shed for *r*. of sin
Mark 1. 4 bapt. of repent. for *r*.
Luke 1. 77 salvation by *r*. of sins
Rom. 3. 25 *r*. of sins that are past
Heb. 9. 22 without shed. blood no *r*.

Remit. *Send away.*
John 20. 23 sins ye *r*., they are *r*.

Remnant. *Left over, residue, rest, remainder.*
Lev. 2. 3 *r*. of meat off. sh. be A.'s
Deut. 3. 11 remained of *r*. of giants
Josh. 23. 12 cleave to *r*. of th. nat.

2 Sam. 21. 2 Gibeonites *r*. of Am.
1 K. 12. 23 Speak to *r*. of the people
2 K. 19. 4 lift up thy prayer for *r*.
2 Chr. 34. 9 of all the *r*. of Israel
Ez. 9. 14 sho. be no *r*. nor escaping
Neh. 1. 3 *r*. left of the captivity
Job. 22. 20 *r*. of them fire consumed
Isa. 1. 9 unless Lord left us sma. *r*.
Jer. 6. 9 they shall glean *r*. of Is.
Ezek. 5. 10 the whole *r*. will scatter
Joel 2. 32 *r*. whom Lord shall call
Am. 1. 8 *r*. of Philistines sh. perish
Mic. 2. 12 I will gath. *r*. of Israel
Hab. 2. 8 *r*. of people shall spoil
Zeph. 2. 9 *r*. of my peo. sh. possess
Hag. 1. 12 all *r*. of people obeyed
Zech. 8. 6 marvellous in eyes of *r*.
Mat. 22. 6 the *r*. took his servants
Rom. 11. 5 is *r*. accord. to election
Rev. 11. 13 the *r*. were affrighted
R. V. Lev. 2. 3 which is left; Ex.
2. 12 overhanging part; 2 K. 25. 11;
   Jer. 39. 9; Ezek. 23. 25; Mic. 5. 3
residue; Lev. 14. 18; 1 K. 12. 23;
1 Chr. 6. 70; Ez. 3. 8; Mat. 22. 6;
Rev. 11. 13: 12. 17; 19. 21 rest

Remove. *Take or move away, put off, make a change.*
Gen. 13. 18 Then Abram *r*. his tent
Ex. 8. 31 L. *r*. flies from Pharaoh
Num. 36. 9 neither sh. inherit. be *r*.
Deut. 19. 14 not *r*. neigh's landmark
Josh. 3. 1 and they *r*. from Shittim
Judg. 9. 29 then would I *r*. Abime.
1 Sam. 18. 13 Saul *r*. him from him
2 Sam. 6. 10 David would not *r*. ark
1 K. 15. 12 Asa *r*. all the idols that
2 K. 23. 27 as I have *r*. Israel and
1 Chr. 8. 6 they *r*. them to Manah.
2 Chr. 35. 12 they *r*. burnt offerings
Job. 12. 20 he *r*. speech of the trusty
Ps. 39. 10 *R*. thy stroke from me
Prov. 4. 27 *r*. thy foot from evil
Eccl. 11. 10. *r*. sorrow fr. thy heart
Isa. 13. 13 earth sh. *r*. out of place
Jer. 50. 8 *R*. out of midst of Babyl.
Lam. 1. 8 Jerusalem sinned, is *r*.
Ezek. 12. 3 *r*. thy day, thou sh. *r*.
Dan. 2. 21 he *r*. kings, set. up kings
Hos. 5. 10 like them that *r*. bound.
Joel. 2. 20. I will *r*. northern army
Am. 6. 7 banq. of them shall be *r*.
Mic. 2. 4 how hath he *r*. it from me
Zech. 3. 9 I will *r*. iniquity of land
Mat. 21. 21 say to mount. Be thou *r*.
   Mark 11. 23
Luke 22. 42 if willing, *r*. this cup
Acts 7. 4 he *r*. him into this land
1 Cor. 13. 2 that I could *r*. mount's
Gal. 1. 6 marvel ye are so soon *r*.
Rev. 2. 5 I will *r*. thy candlestick
R. V. Gen. 13. 18; Ps. 104. 5;
125. 1. Isa. 24. 20 moved; Ex.
20. 18 trembled; Num. (in all
places) journeyed; 2 Sam. 20. 12;
2 K. 17. 26; 1 Chr. 8. 6, 7; Isa.
38. 12 carried; 1 K. 15. 14; 2. K.
15. 4, 35 taken away; Job 19 10;
Isa. 33. 20 plucked up; Isa. 10. 31
fugitive; Lam. 1. 8; Ez. 7. 19
unclean; Deut. 28. 25; Jer. 15. 4;
24. 9; 29. 18; 34. 17; Ezek. 23. 46
tossed to and fro; Mat. 21. 21;
Mark 11. 23 taken up; other
changes of minor moment.

Removing. *Moving, changing.*
Gen. 30. 32 *r*. all speckled cattle
Isa. 49. 21 captive, *r*. to and fro?
Ezek. 12. 3 prepare thee stuff for *r*.
Heb. 12. 27 signifieth *r*. of things
R. V. Isa. 49. 21 wandering

Rend. *Cleave, cut, tear, split.*
Gen. 37. 29 Jacob *r*. his clothes, and
Ex. 28. 32 binding, that be not *r*.
Lev. 13. 56 he shall *r*. it out of gar.
Num. 14. 6 Josh. and Cal. *r*. cloth.
Josh. 7. 6 Joshua *r*. his clothes and
Judg. 11. 35 Jephthah *r*. his clothes
1 Sam. 15. 28 L. hath *r*. kingd. of
2 Sam. 1. 11 David took clo. and *r*.
1 K. 11. 11 I will *r*. the kingdom
2 K. 5. 7 king *r*. his clothes. and
2 Chr. 23. 13 Athaliah *r*. her clothes
Ez. 9. 3 when I heard, I *r*. gar.
Esth. 4. 1 Mordecai *r*. his clothes
Job 1. 20 Job arose and *r*. his mant

Eccl. 3. 7 time to *r*., time to sew
Isa. 64. 1 thou wouldest *r*. heavens
Jer. 4. 30 tho. thou *r*. fa. wi. paint.
Ezek. 30. 16 No shall be *r*. asunder
Hos. 13. 8 will *r*. caul of their h.
Joel 2. 13 *r*. your heart, not gar.
Mat. 7. 6 lest they turn again and *r*.
Mark 15. 38 veil of tempest was *r*.
Mat. 27. 51 ; Luke 23. 45
John 19. 24 not *r*., but cast lots for
Acts 16. 22 magistrates *r*. off clothes
R. V. Gen. 37. 33 ; Mark 9. 26 torn ;
Jer. 4. 30 enlargest

Render. *Give, return.*
Num. 18. 9 offering they *r*. to me
Deut. 32. 41 *r*. veng. to mine enem.
Judg. 9. 56 G. *r*. wickedness of A.
1 Sam. 26. 23 *r*. to ev. man his ri.
2 K. 3. 4 k. of Mid. *r*. k. of Israel
2 Chr. 32. 25 Hezekiah *r*. not again
Job 33. 26 he will *r*. his righteous.
Ps. 28. 4 *r*. to them their desert
Prov. 26. 16 men that can *r*. reason
Isa. 66. 6 voice of L. *r*. recompence
Jer. 51. 6 *r*. unto her a recompence
Lam. 3. 64 *R*. unto him a recomp
Hos. 14. 2 so we *r*. calves of lips
Joel 3. 4 will ye *r*. me recompence
Zech. 9. 12 will *r*. double to thee
Mat. 22. 21 *R*. theref. unto Cæsar
Mark 12. 17 ; Luke 20. 25
Rom. 2. 6 *r*. to ev. man according
1 Cor. 7. 3 *r*. unto wife benevolence
1 Thes. 3. 9 wh. thanks can we *r*. G.
1 Pet. 3. 9 not *r*. evil for evil
R. V. Judg. 9. 56, 57 requite ; Job.
33. 26 restoreth

Renew. *Make new, repair.*
1 Sam. 11. 14 go to Gil. *r*. kingdom
2 Chr. 15. 8 As a *r*. altar of Lord
Job 29. 20 bow was *r*. in my hand
Ps. 51. 10 *r*. right spirit within me
Isa. 41. 1 let people *r*. their strength
Lam. 5. 21 *r*. our days as of old
2 Cor. 4. 16 inward man is *r*. day by
Eph. 4. 23 be *r*. in spirit of mind
Col. 3. 10 which is *r*. in knowledge
Heb. 6. 6 If they fall away, *r*. them

Renewing. *Making new.*
Rom. 12. 2 transf. by *r*. of mind
Tit. 3. 5 regen., and *r*. of H. Ghost

Renounce. *Speak away.*
2 Cor. 4. 2 have *r*. hidden things

Renown. *Called, of name.*
Gen. 6. 4 giants of old, men of *r*.
Num. 16. 2 fa. in cong., men of *r*.
Ezek. 16. 14 *r*. went forth among
Dan. 9. 15 and hast gotten thee *r*.

Renowned. *Called, named.*
Num. 1. 16 These were *r*. of cong.
Isa. 14. 20 seed of evildoers nev. *r*.
Ezek. 23. 23 great lords and *r*.
R. V. Num. 1. 16 called ; Isa. 14,
20 named

Rent (*v*.). *See* **Rend.**
Rent (*n*.). R. V. *rope.*
Isa. 3. 24 instead of a girdle a *r*.
Torn, cut out
1 Sam. 4. 12 clothes *r*. earth on h.
2 Sam. 1. 2 ; 2 K. 18. 37 ; Isa. 36. 22 ;
Jer. 4. 15
Mat. 9. 16 ; Mark 2. 21 *r*. is worse
Luke 5. 36 the new maketh a *r*.

Repaid. *See* **Repay.**
Repair. *Renew, strengthen, build,
close.*
Judg. 21. 23 Benjamin *r*. the cities
1 K. 11. 27 Sol. *r*. breaches of city
2 K. 12. 5 let priests *r*. the breaches
1 Chr. 11. 8 and Joab *r*. rest of city
2 Chr. 33. 16 Manass. *r*. altar of L.
Ez. 9. 9 *r*. the desolation thereof
Neh. 3. 19 And next to him *r*. Ezer
Isa. 61. 4 they sh. *r*. waste cities
R. V. Judg. 21. 23 ; 2 Chr. 33. 16
built ; 2 Chr. 24. 4, 12 restore ; 32.
5 strengthened ; 33. 16 built up

Repairer, ing. *Who repairs.*
2 Chr. 24. 27 the *r*. of house of God
Isa. 58. 12 sh. be call. *r*. of breach
R. V. 2 Chr. 24. 27 rebuilding

Repay. *Pay back.*
Deut 7. 10 *r*. them to their face
Job 21. 31 wh. sh. *r*. him, wh. done ?
Jer. 21 to right. good sh. be *r*.
Isa. 59. 18 he will *r*. recompence

Luke 10. 35 when I come, I will *r*.
Rom. 12. 19 Venge. is mine, I will *r*.
Phile. 19 I will *r*. it ; I do not say
R. V. Prov. 13. 21 ; Rom. 12. 19
recompense

Repeat. R. V. *harpeth on.*
Prov. 17. 9 but he that *r*. a matter

Repent. *Have another mind.*
Mat. 3. 2 *R*., kingd. of h. at hand
Mark 1. 15 *r*., and believe gospel
Luke 11. 32 they *r*. at preach. of J.
Acts 2. 38 *R*., and be baptized
2 Cor. 12. 21 many that ha. not *r*.
Rev. 2. 5 *r*., and do the first works
To be careful with
Mat. 21. 29 but afterwards he *r*.
2 Cor. 7. 8 not *r*., though I did *r*.
Heb. 7. 21 L. sware and will not *r*.
Sigh, be sorry, rue, comfort self
Gen. 6. 6 it *r*. Lord that he made
Ex. 32. 14 L. *r*. of evil which he
Num. 23. 19 man, that he should *r*.
Deut. 32. 36 L. *r*. for his servants
Judg. 2. 18 it *r*. Lord because of
1 Sam. 15. 11 *r*. me th. I set up S.
2 Sam. 24. 16 L. *r*. him of the evil
1 K. 8. 47 *r*., and make supplica.
Job 42. 6 I abhor, and *r*. in dust
Ps. 90. 13 *r*. thee concern. thy serv.
Jer. 4. 28 I have purp., will not *r*.
Ezek. 14. 6 *R*., turn fr. your idols
Joel 2. 14 **if** he will return and *r*.
Am. 7. 3 the Lord *r*. for this ; it shall
Jonah 3. 9 God *r*. of the evil he had
Zech. 8. 14 prov. to wrath, and I *r*.
R. V. 1 K. 8. 47 turn again ; Ezek.
14. 6 ; 18. 30 return ye ; 2 Cor. 7.
8 ; regret

Repentance. *Change of mind,
concerned with, penitence.*
Hos. 13. 14 *r*. sh. be hid from eyes
Mat. 3. 8 Bring fruits meet for *r*.
Mark 2. 17 ca. to call sinners to *r*.
Luke 15. 7 ninety-nine need no *r*.
Acts 19. 4 baptized with bap. of *r*.
Rom. 2. 4 goodness of G. lead. to *r*.
2 Cor. 7. 10 godly sorrow worketh *r*.
2 Tim. 2. 25 if God will give th. *r*.
Heb. 6. 1 laying again found. of *r*.
2 Pet. 3. 9 that all should come to *r*.
R. V. Mat. 9. 13 ; Mark 2. 17 ——.

Repenting. *Being penitent.*
Jer. 15. 6 I am weary with *r*.
R. V. *compassions*
Hos. 11. 8 my *r*. are kindled together

Repetitions. *Empty speakings.*
Mat. 6. 7 when pray, use not vain *r*.

Replenish. *Fill, make full.*
Gen. 1. 28 Be fruitful, *r*. the earth
Isa. 23. 2 whom merchants have *r*.
Jer. 31. 25 ha. *r*. ev. sorrowf. soul
Ezek. 26. 2 I sh. be *r*., she laid waste
R. V. Isa. 2. 6 filled with customs

Reply. *Speak or judge back.*
Rom. 9. 20 who art thou th. *r*. ag'st

Report (*n*.). *Word, thing heard,
statement, witness.*
Gen. 37. 2 Jos. bro. father evil *r*.
Ex. 23. 1 shalt not raise false *ṗ*.
Num. 13. 32 they brought up evil *r*.
Deut. 2. 25 who sh. hear *r*. of thee
1 Sam. 2. 24 no good *r*. I hear
1 K. 10. 6 it was true *r*. I heard
2 Chr. 9. 5 true *r*. I heard in land
Neh. 6. 13 have matter for evil *r*.
Prov. 15. 30 a good *r*. maketh fat
Isa. 53. 1 Who ha. believed our *r*.
Jer. 50. 43 K. of Bab. ha. heard *r*.
John 12. 38 Who ha. believed our *r*.
Acts 6. 3 look seven men of good *r*.
Rom. 10. 16 who ha. believed our *r*.
2 Cor. 6. 8 by evil r. and good *r*.
Phil 4. 8 wh. things are of good *r*.
1 Tim. 3. 7 he must have good *r*.
Heb. 11. 2 elders obtained good *r*.
3 John 12 Demetrius hath good *r*.
R. V. Isa. 28. 19 message ; Jer. 50.
43 fame ; Prov. 15. 30 good tidings ;
1 Tim. 3. 7 testimony ; Heb. 11. 2,
39 ; 3 John 12 witness

Report (*v*.). *Say, tell, announce,
bear witness.*
Neh. 6. 19 they *r*. his good deeds
Esth. 1. 17 despise, when it be *r*.
Jer. 20. 10 R., say they, we will *r*.
Ezek. 9. 11 man with inkh. *r*. matter

Mat. 28. 15 saying is commonly *r*.
Acts 4. 23 *r*. all chief priests said
Rom. 3. 8 as we be slanderously *r*.
1 Cor. 14. 25 *r*. that God is in you
1 Tim. 5. 10 *r*. of for good works
1 Pet. 1. 12 things which are now *r*.
R. V. Neh. 6. 19 spake of ; 1 Pet. 1.
12 announced ; Mat. 28. 15 spread
abroad

Reproach (*n*.). *Blame, shame,
chiding, insult.*
Gen. 30. 23 G. hath tak. away my *r*.
Josh. 5. 9 I rolled away *r*. of Egypt
1 Sam. 11. 2 lay it for *r*. upon Is.
Neh. 2. 17 that we be no more a *r*.
Job 19. 5 plead against me my *r*.
Ps. 22. 6 a *r*. of men, and despised
Prov. 6. 33 his *r*. sh. not be wiped
Isa. 51. 7 fear not the *r*. of men
Jer. 20. 8 word of L. was made a *r*.
Lam. 5. 1 O Lord, consider our *r*.
Ezek. 5. 15 it shall be *r*. and taunt
Dan. 9. 16 thy peo. are become a *r*.
Hos. 12. 14 his *r*. sh. Lord return
Joel 2. 17 give not thy herit. to *r*.
Mic. 6. 16 ye sh. bear *r*. of people
Zeph. 2. 8 I ha. heard *r*. of Moab
Luke 1. 25 me, to take away my *r*.
Rom. 15. 3 *r*. of them that reproa.
2 Cor. 11. 21 I speak as concern. *r*.
1 Tim. 3. 7 lest he fall into *r*. and sna.
Heb. 11. 26 esteem. *r*. of C. greater
R. V. Prov. 22. 10 ignominy ; Job
20. 3 reproof ; 2 Cor. 11. 21 dis-
paragement ; 12. 10 injuries ; Isa.
43. 28 a reviling

Reproach. (*v*.) *Blame, chide, re-
vile.*
Num. 15. 30 the same *r*. the Lord
Ruth. 2. 15 Let her glean, *r*. her not
2 K. 19. 4 k. sent to *r*. living God
Neh. 6. 13 report, th. they might *r*.
Job 27. 6 my heart sh. not *r*. me
Ps. 42. 10 mine enemies *r*. me
Prov. 14. 31 that oppr. poor, *r*. M.
Isa. 37. 24 thou *r*. the Lord, and
Zeph 2. 8 they have *r*. my people
Luke 6. 22 sh. *r*. you, and cast out
Rom. 15. 3 reproa. of them th. *r*.
1 Tim. 4. 10 we lab. and suffer *r*.
1 Pet. 4. 14 if *r*. for C., hap. are ye
R. V. Num. 15. 30 blasphemeth

Reproachfully. *With reproach.*
Job 16. 10 smitten me on cheek *r*.
1 Tim. 5. 14 none occa. to spe. *r*.

Reprobate. *Rejected, condemned.*
Jer. 6. 30 *R*. sil. men sh. call th.
Rom. 1. 28 gave th. ov. to *r*. mind
2 Cor. 13. 5 C. is in you, ex. ye be *r*.
2 Tim. 3. 8 men *r*. concern. faith
Tit. 1. 16 unto every good work *r*.
R. V. Jer. 6. 30 refuse.

Reproof. *Rebuke, correction.*
Job 26. 11 are astonished at his *r*.
Ps. 38. 14 in whose mouth no *r*.
Prov. 10. 17 he th. refus. *r*. erreth
2 Tim. 3. 16 scrip. is profit. for *r*.
R. V. Job 26. 11 ; Prov. 17. 10 re-
buke

Reprove. *Reason, correct, rebuke.*
Gen. 21. 25 Ab. *r*. Abim. bec. of w.
2 K. 19. 4 *r*. words wh. L. G. heard
1 Chr. 16. 21 he *r*. k's for their sak.
Job 6. 25 but what doth arguing *r*.
Ps. 50. 8 will not *r*. thee for sacrif.
Prov. 9. 8 *R*. not scor., lest he hate
Isa. 11. 4 *r*. with equity for meek
Jer. 2. 19 thy backs l'gs. sh. *r*. thee
Hos. 4. 4 let no man *r*. another
Hab. 2. 1 what answer when *r*.
Luke 3. 19 *r*. by him for Herodias
John 3. 20 lest his deeds sho. be *r*.
Eph. 5. 11 no fellowship, rather *r*.
2 Tim. 4. 2 *r*., with long suffering
R. V. 2 K. 19. 4 ; Isa. 37. 4 ; Jer.
29. 27 rebuke ; John 16. 8 convict

Reprover. *Who reproves.*
Prov. 25. 12 so is a wise *r*. upon
Ezek. 3. 26 shall not be to them a *r*.

Reputation. *Precious, of honor.*
Eccl. 10. 1 that is in *r*. for wisdom
Acts 5. 34 Gamaliel, in *r*. am. peo.
Gal. 2. 2 but privately to them of *r*.
Phil. 2. 7 but made himself of no *r*.
R. V. Eccl. 10. 1 outweigh ; Acts 5.
34 honour of ; Gal. 2. 2 repute

Phil. 2. 7 emptied himself
Reputed. *Thought, reckoned.*
Job 18. 3 *r.* and vile in your sight?
Dan. 4. 35 inhab. of earth *r.* as noth.
R. V. Job 18. 3 become unclean
Request (*n.*). *Asking, demand.*
Judg. 8. 24 of Gid. said, I desire a *r.*
2 Sam. 14. 5 k. will perform the *r.*
Ez. 7. 6 the king granted all his *r.*
Neh. 2. 4 for wh. dost th. make *r.*
Esth. 5. 3 what is thy *r.?* it shall
Job 6. 8 Oh th. I might have my *r.*
Ps. 21. 2 hast not withh. *r.* of lips
Rom. 1. 10 *r.* for prosperous journey
Phil. 4. 6 let *r.* be ma. known to G.
R. V. Phil. 1. 4 supplication
Request (*v.*). *Seek, ask, inquire, demand, supplicate.*
Judg. 8. 26 of earrings that he *r.*
1 K. 19. 4 Elijah *r.* he might die
1 Chr. 4. 10 God granted what he *r.*
Neh. 2. 4 For wh. dost thou ma. *r.?*
Esth. 7. 7 Haman stood to make *r.*
Dan. 2. 49 Daniel *r.* of the king
Require. *Seek, inquire, demand.*
Gen. 9. 5 blood I *r.* of every beast
Ex. 12. 36 lent such things they *r.*
Deut. 10. 12 what doth L. thy G. *r.*
Josh. 22. 23 let Lord himself *r.* it
Ruth 3. 11 I will do all that thou *r.*
1 Sam. 21. 8 king's business *r.* haste
2 Sam. 3. 13 one thing I *r.* of thee
1 K. 8. 59 maintain, as mat. shall *r.*
1 Chr. 21. 3 why doth my lord *r.* this
2 Chr. 8. 14 as duty of every day *r.*
Ez. 3. 4 the custom, as every day *r.*
Neh. 5. 18 *r.* not I bread of gover.
Esth. 2. 15 she *r.* nothing but what
Ps. 40. 6 sin-offering hast th. not *r.*
Prov. 30. 7 two things have I *r.* of
Eccl. 3. 15 God *r.* th. which is past
Isa. 1. 12 who *r.* this at your hand
Ezek. 20. 40 there will I *r.* offering
Dan. 2. 11 rare thing that the king *r.*
Mic. 6. 8 what doth Lord *r.* of thee
Luke 23. 23 *r.* th. he mi. be crucif.
1 Cor. 1. 22 for the Jews *r.* a sign
R. V. Neh. 5. 18 demanded; Ex.
12. 36; Prov. 30. 7; Luke 23. 23,
25 ask; Ruth 3. 11 sayest; Eccl.
3. 15 seeketh again
Requite. *Repay.*
Gen. 50. 15 Jos. will *r.* us the evil
Deut. 32. 6 Do ye thus *r.* the Lord
Judg. 1. 7 done, so G. hath *r.* me
1 Sam. 5. 21 he ha. *r.* evil for good
2 Sam. 16. 12 Lord will *r.* me good
2 K. 9. 26 I will *r.* thee in th. plat
2 Chr. 6. 23 judge ser., by *r.* wick.
Ps. 10. 14 to *r.* it with thy hand
Jer. 51. 56 L. G. of recomp. shall *r.*
1 Tim. 5. 4 learn to *r.* their parents
R. V. 1 Sam. 25. 21 returned: Ps.
10. 14 take
Rereward. R. V. *rearward.*
Num. 10. 25 stand. of Dan was *r.*
Josh. 6. 9. *r.* aft. ark, came priests
1 Sam. 29. 2 men passed *r.* wi. Ach.
Isa. 58. 8 glo. of Lord sh. be thy *r.*
Rescue. *Take away, free.*
Deut. 28. 31 sh. ha. none to *r.* them
1 Sam. 14. 45 the people *r.* Jonathan
Ps. 35. 17 *r.* my soul fr. destruction
Dan. 6. 7 He delivereth and *r.*, and
Hos. 5. 14 I take, and none shall *r.*
Acts 23. 27 came I wi. army, and *r.*
R. V. Deut. 28. 31 save; Hos.
5. 14 deliver.
Resemblance. *Eye, appearance.*
Zech. 5. 6 their *r.* through all earth
Resemble. *Be like, liken.*
Judg. 8. 18 each *r.* children of king
Luke 13. 18 whereunto shall I *r.* it?
R. V. Luke 13. 18 liken.
Reserve. *Keep back, keep.*
Gen. 27. 36 hast thou not *r.* bless.
Num. 18. 9 the most holy things *r.*
Judg. 21. 22 we *r.* not each his wife
Ruth 2. 18 gave her that she had *r.*
2 Sam. 8. 4 *r.* of th. an hundred char.
1 Chr. 18. 4
Job. 21. 3 wick. *r.* to day of destr.
Jer. 3. 5 Will he *r.* his anger forever?
Nah. 1. 2 L. *r.* wrath for enemies
Rom. 11. 4 I have *r.* sev. thousand
Acts 25. 21 Paul appealed to be *r.*

1 Pet. 1. 4 inheritance *r.* in heaven
2 Pet. 2. 9 *r.* unjust unto judgment
Jude 6. *r.* in everlasting chains
R. V. Deut. 33. 21 seated; Judg.
21. 22 took; Ruth 2. 18; Rom.
11. 4 left; Acts 25. 21; Jude 6
kept.
Residue. *Over and above, remnant.*
Ex. 10. 5 and they shall eat the *r.*
Neh. 11. 20 *r.* of Is. were in cities
Isa. 38. 10 depriv. of *r.* of my years
Jer. 15. 9 *r.* will I deliv. to sword
Ezek. 9. 8 wilt thou destr. *r.* of Is.
Dan. 7. 7 stamped *r.* with the feet
Zeph. 2. 9 *r.* of my peo. shall spoil
Hag. 2. 2 speak to *r.* of the people
Zech. 14. 2 *r.* of peo. sh. be cut off
Mal. 2. 15 yet had he *r.* of spirit
Mark 16. 13 went and told it to *r.*
Acts 15. 17 that *r.* might seek Lord
R. V. 1 Chr. 6. 66 some; Jer. 39. 3;
Mark 16. 13 rest; Hag. 2. 2; Zech.
8. 11 remnant
Resist. *Oppose, array against.*
Zech. 3. 1 Satan at right hand to *r.*
Mat. 5. 39 That ye *r.* not evil, but
Luke 21. 15 adver., not able to *r.*
Acts 7. 51 ye do *r.* the Holy Ghost
Rom. 9. 19 who hath *r.* his will
2 Tim. 3. 8 these also *r.* the truth
Heb. 12. 4 have not *r.* unto blood
Jas. 4. 7 *R.* devil. he will flee from
1 Pet. 5. 5 G. *r.* proud, and giv. gr.
R. V. Luke 21. 15; Acts. 6. 10;
Rom. 9. 19; 13. 2; 2 Tim. 3. 8;
1 Pet. 5. 9 withstand; Zech. 3. 11
be adversary
Resolved. *Begin to know.*
Luke 16. 4 I am *r.* what to do, that
Resort. *Go, come together.*
2 Chr. 11. 13 Israel *r.* to him out of
Neh. 4. 20 *r.* ye hither unto us
Ps. 71. 3 whereunto I may con. *r.*
Mark 2. 13 multitude *r.* to him, and
John 18. 2 Jesus ofttimes *r.* thither
Acts 16. 13 spake to wom. who *r.*
R. V. Mark 10. 1; John 18. 20;
Acts 16. 13 come together
Respect (*n.*).
Gen. 4. 4 the Lord had *r.* to Abel
Ex. 2. 25 God looked and had *r.*
Lev. 29. 6 I will have *r.* unto you
1 K. 8. 28 have thou *r.* to prayer
2 K. 13. 23 the Lord had *r.* to them
2 Chr. 19. 7 nor *r.* of per. with God
Ps. 74. 20 have *r.* unto covenant
Prov. 24. 23 not good to have *r.* of p.
Isa. 17. 7 shall have *r.* to Holy One
2 Cor. 3. 10 had no glory in th. *r.*
Phil. 4. 11 I speak in *r.* of want
Col. 2. 16 let none judge in *r.* of
Heb. 11. 26 Mo. had *r.* to recomp.
Jas. 2. 1 notfaith with *r.* of persons
1 Pet. 1. 17 without *r.* of persons
R. V. Ex. 2. 25 took knowledge;
Heb. 11. 26 looked; Jas. 2. 3 regard
Respect (*v.*). *Lift up, regard.*
Lev. 19. 5 thou sh. not *r.* persons
Num. 16. 15 Moses said, *R.* not off.
Deut. 1. 17 Ye shall not *r.* persons
2 Sam. 14. 14 neither doth God *r.*
Job 37. 24 he *r.* not wise of heart
Ps. 40. 4 blessed is man that *r.* not
Isa. 17. 8 nor shall *r.* that which
Lam. 4. 16 *r.* not person of priest
R. V. Job 37. 24 regardeth
Respecter. *Acceptor.*
Acts 10. 34 God is no *r.* of persons
Respite. *Breathing spell.*
Ex. 8. 15 Pharaoh saw there was *r.*
Letting go
1 Sam. 11. 3 Give us seven days *r.*
Rest (*n.*). *Over and above, left, remainder, remnant.*
Gen. 30. 36 Jacob fed *r.* of flocks
Ex. 28. 10 names for *r.* on stone
Lev. 14. 29 *r.* of oil pur on head
Num. 31. 32 *r.* of prey wh. men had
Deut. 31. 32 *r.* of Gilead, all Bash.
Josh. 17. 2 lot for *r.* of children
Judg. 7. 6 *r.* of people bow. down
1 Sam. 13. 2 *r.* of people he sent
2 Sam. 10. 10 *r.* of peo. he delivered
1 K. 11. 41 And the *r* of the acts of

2 K. 8. 23 ; 1 Chr. 19. 11 ; 2 Chr. 13.
Neh. 2. 16 neither told it to the *r.*
Ps. 17. 14 leave *r.* of their substance
Jer. 52. 15 carried captive the *r.*
Ezek. 48. 23 *r.* of tribes from east
Dan. 2. 18 should not perish with *r.*
Mat. 27. 49 *r.* said, Let us see wheth.
Luke 12. 26 why take tho't for *r.?*
Acts 27. 44 *r.*, some on boards, and
1 Cor. 7. 12 But to the *r.* speak I
Rev. 20. 5 *r.* of dead liv. not again
Silence, quiet, ceasing, repose.
Gen. 8. 9 the dove found no *r.*
Ex. 16. 23 To morrow is *r.* of sab.
Lev. 23. 3 sev. day is sabbath of *r.*
Deut. 25. 19 God hath given thee *r.*
Josh. 1. 15 L. hath given breth. *r.*
Judg. 3. 30 land had *r.* eighty y'rs
Ruth 1. 9 L. grant you may find *r.*
2 Sam. 7. 1 Lord had given him *r.*
1 Chr. 6. 31 after that ark had *r.*
2 Chr. 15. 15 the Lord gave them *r.*
Neh. 9. 28 after they had *r.*, they
Esth. 9. 16 J. had *r.* from enemies
Job 3. 17 there the weary are at *r.*
Ps 38. 3 neither is there any *r.* in
Prov. 29. 17 and he shall give thee *r.*
Eccl. 2. 23 his heart taketh not *r.*
Isa. 14. 3 the Lord give thee *r.*
Jer. 6. 16 ye shall find *r.* for souls
Ezek. 38. 11 to them that are at *r.*
Dan. 4. 4 I Nebuchadnez. was at *r*
Mic. 2. 10 for this is not your *r.*
Zech. 9. 1 Damascus shall be the *r.*
Mat. 11. 28 Co. unto me, I give *r.*
Mark 14. 41 Sleep now, take yo. *r.*
Luke 11. 24 seeking *r.*, find. none
John 11. 13 had spoken of taking *r.*
Acts 7. 49 what is place of my *r.?*
2 Thes. 1. 7 are troub., *r.* with us
Heb. 4. 8 if J. had given them *r.*
R. V. Several changes, but none of
moment
Rest (*v.*). *Cease, be quiet, repose, put, lay or set down.*
Gen. 8. 4 ark *r.* in seventh month
Ex. 10. 14 locusts *r.* in all coasts
Lev. 25. 35 nor *r.* in sabbaths
Num. 11. 25 when sp. *r.* upon them
Deut. 5. 14 servant may *r.* as thou
Josh. 3. 13 feet shall *r.* in waters
2 Sam. 21. 10 suffer nei. birds to *r.*
1 K. 5. 4 my God hath given me *r.*
2 K. 2. 15 sp, of Elij. *r.* on Elisha
2 Chr. 14. 6 Lord had given him *r.*
Esth. 9. 22 in days wherein Jews *r.*
Job 3. 18 the prisoners *r.* together
Ps. 125. 3 rod of wicked sh. not *r.*
Prov. 14. 33 wisdom *r.* in the heart
Eccl. 7. 9 anger *r.* in bos. of fools
S. of S. 1. 7 where th. mak. flock *r.*
Isa. 57. 2 they shall *r.* in their beds
Jer. 31. 2 went to cause him to *r.*
Ezek. 5. 13 my fury to *r.* upon th.
Dan. 12. 13 thou shall *r.* and stand
Hab. 3. 16 might *r.* in day of troub.
Zeph. 3. 17 he will *r.* in. his love
Mark 6. 31 Come to desert and *r.*
Luke 10. 6 peace shall *r.* upon it
Rom. 2. 17 thou art Jew, *r.* in law
2 Cor. 12. 9 power of C. may *r.* upon
Heb. 4. 4 God did *r.* seventh day
1 Pet. 4. 14 Spirit of G. *r.* upon you
Rev. 4. 8 they *r.* not day and night
Restitution. *Exchange, restoration.*
Ex. 22. 3 he should make full *r.*
Job 20. 18 according to sub. sh. *r.* be
Acts 3. 21 until the times of *r.*
R. V. Job 20. 18 hath gotten; Acts
3. 21 restoration
Restore. *Give or turn back, make whole, place again.*
Gen. 20. 7 theref. *r.* the man his wife
Ex. 22. 1 he s. *r.* five oxen for an ox
Lev. 24. 21 that kill. beast, sh. *r.* it
Num. 35. 25 shall *r.* him to c. of ref.
Deut. 22. 2 things strayed *r.* again
Judg. 17. 4 he *r.* mon. to his moth.
1 Sam. 12. 3 ox taken, *r.* will I *r.*
2 Sam. 9. 7 will *r.* all land of Saul
1 K. 20. 34 the cities took, I will *r.*
2 K. 8. 6 saying, *R.* all that was hers
2 Chr. 8. 2 the cities Huram had *r.*
Ez. 6. 5 the vessels brought be *r.*
Neh. 5. 11 *R.*, I pray you, to them

Job 20. 10 hands shall *r*. their goods
Ps. 51. 12 *R*. me joy of thy salvation
Prov. 6. 31 he shall *r*. sevenfold
Isa. 49. 6 *r*. the preserved of Israel
Jer. 27. 22 and *r*. them to this place
Ezek. 18. 7 *r*. to debtor his pledge
Dan. 9. 25 command. to *r*. Jerus.
Joel 2. 25 I will *r*. you the years
Mat. 17. 11 Elias shall *r*. all things
Mark 3. 5 his hand was *r*. whole
Luke 19. 8 ha. ta., I *r*. him fourfold
Acts 1. 6 wilt thou *r*. the kingdom?
Gal. 6. 1 *r*. such one in meekness
Heb. 13. 19 that I may be *r*. to you
R. V. Ex. 22. 1 pay; Lev. 24. 21
make good; 25. 28 get it back; 2
Chr. 8. 2 given

Restorer. *Who restores.*
Ruth 4. 15 he shall be to thee a *r*.
Isa. 58. 12 called *r*. of paths to dw.

Restrain. *Gird in, withhold.*
Gen. 8. 2 rain from heaven was *r*.
Ex. 36. 6 So the people were *r*. from
1 Sam. 3. 13 Eli's sons vile, *r*. not
Job 15. 8 dost *r*. wisdom to thyself?
Ps. 76. 10 the wrath shalt thou *r*.
Isa. 63. 15 mercies? are they *r*.?
Ezek. 31. 15 I *r*. the floods thereof
Acts 14. 18 *r*. they the people, that
R. V. Gen. 11. 6 withholden

Restraint. *Hindrance.*
1 Sam. 14. 6 no *r*. to Lord to save

Resurrection. *Rising up.*
Mat. 22. 30 in *r*. they neither marry
Mark 12. 18 which say there is no *r*.
Luke 20. 36 being children of the *r*.
John 11. 25 Jesus said, I am the *r*.
Acts 24. 15 there shall be *r*. of dead
Rom. 6. 5 be in likeness of his *r*.
1 Cor. 15. 13 but if there be no *r*.
Phil. 3. 10 know the power of his *r*.
2 Tim. 2. 18 saying *r*. is past alr.
Heb. 11. 35 might obtain better *r*.
1 Pet. 3. 21 save us by *r*. of J. C.
Rev. 20. 5 This is the first *r*.

Retain. *Hold, restrain.*
Judg. 7. 8 *r*. those three hun. men
Job 2. 9 Dost still *r*. integrity?
Prov. 4. 4 Let th. heart *r*. my words
Eccl. 8. 8 no man th. ha. power to *r*.
Dan. 10. 8 alone, and *r*. no strength
Mic. 7. 18 God, he *r*. not his anger
John 20. 23 sins ye *r*., they are *r*.
Rom. 1. 28 did not like to *r*. God
Phile. 13 whom I would have *r*.
R. V. Job 2. 9 hold fast; Rom. 1.
28 have; Phile. 13 fain have kept.

Retire. *Turn back, withdraw.*
Judg. 20. 39 when men of Israel *r*.
2 Sam. 20. 22 from the city
Jer. 4. 6 Set up stand., *r*., stay not
R. V. Judg. 20. 39 turned; 2 Sam.
20. 22 were dispersed; Jer. 4. 6
flee for safety

Return (*n.*). *Turn back.*
Gen. 14. 17 after his *r*. fr. slaught.
1 Sam. 7. 17 his *r*. was to Ramah
1 K. 20. 22 at *r*. of y'r k. of Syria

Return (*v.*). *Turn, or come back,
give back.*
Gen. 3. 19 unto dust shalt thou *r*.
Ex. 4. 20 Moses *r*. to land of Egypt
Lev. 25. 10 *r*. ev. man to his place
Num. 16. 50 Aaron *r*. unto Moses
Deut. 1. 45 ye *r*. and wept bef. L.
Josh. 4. 18 waters of Jordan *r*. unto
Judg. 11. 39 she *r*. unto her father
Ruth 1. 8 *r*. each to mother's house
1 Sam. 17. 15 David *r*. from Saul
2 Sam. 1. 22 sword of S. *r*. not em.
1 K. 13. 13 Jer. *r*. not fr. evil ways
2 K. 20. 10 let shadow *r*. backward
1 Chr. 20. 3 people *r*. to Jerusalem
2 Chr. 31. 1 Is. *r*. to his possession
Ez. 5. 11 they *r*. us answer, saying
Neh. 4. 15 we *r*. all to the wall
Esth. 7. 8 king *r*. out of pal. gar.
Job 1. 21 Naked came, nak. sh. I *r*.
Ps. 6. 4 R., O L. deliver my soul
Prov. 26. 11 as dog *r*. to his vomit
Eccl. 12. 7 sp. sh. *r*. to G. who gave
S. of S. 6. 13 *R*., *r*., O Shul., *r*., *r*.
Isa. 10. 21 The remnant shall *r*.
Jer. 3. 22 *r*. ye backsliding childr.
Ezek. 35. 9 thy cities shall not *r*.
Dan. 11. 13 king of north shall *r*.

Hos. 2. 7 I will *r*. to first husband
Joel 2. 14 if he will *r*. and repent
Am. 4. 6 yet have ye not *r*. to me
Obad. 15 reward *r*. on own head
Mic. 5. 3 rem. of brethren shall *r*.
Zech. 1. 6 they *r*. and said, As L.
Mal. 1. 4 *r*. and build des. places
Mat. 2. 12 warned sh. not *r*. to H.
Mark 14. 40 *r*. he found th. asleep.
Luke 4. 14 And Jesus *r*. into Galilee
Acts 1. 2 Then *r*. they to Jerusalem
Gal. 1. 17 *r*. again unto Damascus
Heb. 11. 15 opportunity to have *r*.
1 Pet. 2. 25 *r*. to Shep. of souls
R. V. several unimportant changes,
chiefly to sense of, turned, came,
or bring back

Returning. *Turning back.*
Isa. 30. 15 In *r*. and rest be saved
Luke 7. 10 *r*., found servant whole
Acts 8. 28 *r*. sitting in his chariot
Heb. 7. 81 Abra. *r*. from slaughter

Reveal. *Uncover, disclose.*
Deut. 29. 29 things wh. are *r*. to us
1 Sam. 3. 21 L. *r*. himself to Sam.
2 Sam. 7. 27 hast *r*. to thy servant
Job 20. 27 heav. sh. *r*. his iniquity
Prov. 11. 13 talebearer *r*. secrets
Isa. 22. 14 *r*. in mine ears by Lord
Jer. 11. 20 unto thee I *r*. my cause
Dan. 2. 19 Then was sec. *r*. to D.
Mat. 11. 27 to whom the Son will *r*.
Luke 17. 30 day when Son is *r*.
John 12. 38 ha. arm of L. been *r*.?
Rom. 1. 18 wrath of G. is *r*. from h.
1 Cor. 3. 13 it shall be *r*. by fire
Gal. 3. 23 faith which should be *r*.
Eph. 3. 5 as now *r*. to the apostles
Phil. 3. 15 God sh. *r*. this unto you
2 Thes. 1. 7 when L. J. shall be *r*.
1 Pet. 4. 13 wh. his glory sh. be *r*.
R. V. 1 Cor. 14. 30; 2 Thes. 1. 7;
1 Pet. 4. 13 revelation

Revealer. *Unveiler.*
Dan. 2. 47 G. of gods, *r*. of secrets

Revelation. *Uncovering.*
Rom. 2. 5 *r*. of righteous judgment
1 Cor. 14. 6 I sh. speak to you by *r*.
2 Cor. 12. 7 thro. abundance of *r*.
Gal. 2. 2 I went up by *r*., and com.
Eph. 1. 17 may give you sp. of *r*.
1 Pet. 1. 13 bro. unto you, *r*. of J.
Rev. 1. 1 *r*. of J. C., which G. gave

Revellings. *Wanton festivities.*
Gal. 5. 21 works of flesh, *r*., and such
1 Pet. 4. 3 walked in *r*., banquet.

Revenge (*n.*). *Vengeance.*
Deut. 32. 42 br. beginning of *r*. on
Jer. 20. 10 we shall take *r*. on him
Ezek. 25. 15 Philistines ha. d. by *r*.
2 Chr. 7. 11 what zeal, yea what *r*.
R. V. Deut. 32. 42 leaders; 2 Cor.
7. 11 avenging

Revenge (*v.*). *Avenge.*
Jer. 15. 15 *r*. me of my persecutors
Ps. 79. 10 the *r*. of blood of serv.
Nah. 1. 2 the Lord *r*.; the Lord *r*.
2 Cor. 10. 6 readiness to *r*. all diso.
R. V. Jer. 15. 15; 2 Cor. 10. 6
avenge

Revenger. R. V. *avenger.*
Num. 35. 19-27 *r*. shall slay him
2 Sam. 14. 11 would. not suffer *r*.
Rom. 13. 4 minister of God, a *r*.

Revenue. *Income, return.*
Ez. 4. 13 thou shalt endamage *r*.
Prov. 8. 19 my *r*. better than silver
Isa. 23. 3 harvest of riv., is her *r*.
Jer. 12. 13 be ashamed of your *r*.
R. V. Jer. 12. 13 fruits

Reverence (*n.*). *Fear, bowing
down, reverence.*
2 Sam. 9. 6 Mephib. did *r*. David
1 K. 1. 31 Bathsheba did *r*. king
Esth. 3. 2 Mordecai did him not *r*.
Ps. 89. 7 to be had in *r*. of all
Heb. 12. 9 and we gave them *r*.
R. V. 2 Sam. 9. 6; 1 K. 1. 31 obeisance : Ps. 89. 7 feared above

Reverence (*v.*). *Fear, bow down,
revere.*
Lev. 19. 30 *r*. sanctuary, I am Lord
Esth. 3. 2 king's serv. *r*. Haman
Mat. 21. 37 They will *r*. my son
Mark 12. 6; Luke 20. 13
Eph. 5. 33; wife see she *r*. her husb.

R. V. Eph. 5. 33 fear
Reverend. *Feared, revered.*
Ps. 111. 9 holy and *r*. is his name
Reverse. *Make to turn back.*
Num. 23. 20 blessed; I cannot *r*. it
Esth. 8. 5 be writ. to *r*. the letters
Revile. *Rail, blaspheme.*
Ex. 22. 28 thou shalt not *r*. gods
Mat. 27. 39 that passed by *r*. him
Mark 15. 32 crucified with him *r*.
John 9. 28 they *r*. him, and said
Acts 23. 4 said, *R*. thou God's h. p.?
1 Cor. 4. 12 And being *r*., we bless
1 Pet. 2. 23 Who *r*. not again, when
R. V. Mat. 27. 39 railed on; Mark
15. 32 reproached
Reviler. *Who reviles.*
1 Cor. 6. 10 nor *r*. sh. inher. kingd.
Reviling. *Railing.*
Isa. 51. 7 nei. be afraid of their *r*.
Zeph. 2. 8 *r*. of chil. of Ammon
Revive. *Live, make to live.*
Gen. 45. 27 the spirit of Jacob *r*.
Judg. 15. 19 spirit came again, he *r*.
1 K. 17. 22 soul came again, he *r*.
2 K. 13. 21 when let down, he *r*.
Neh. 4. 2 will they *r*. the stones
Ps. 85. 6 Wilt th. not *r*. us again
Isa. 57. 15 *r*. spirit, and *r*. heart
Hos. 6. 2 Aft. two days will he *r*. us
Hab. 3. 2 O Lord, *r*. thy work in
Rom. 7. 9 command. came, sin *r*.
R. V. Ps. 85. 6 quicken; Rom. 14. 9
lived again
Reviving. *Means of life*
Ez. 9. 8, 9 give us *r*. in bondage
Revolt (*n.*). *Turn aside or against.*
Isa. 59. 13 speaking oppress. and *r*.
Revolt (*v.*). *Turn aside, rebel.*
2 K. 8. 20 In his days Edom *r*.
2 Chr. 21. 10 same time did Lib. *r*.
Jer. 5. 23 this peo. are *r*. and gone
Isa. 1. 5 ye will *r*. more and more
Revolter. *Who turns aside.*
Jer. 6. 28 They are grievous *r*.
Hos. 9. 15 all their princes are *r*.
Revolting. *Turning aside.*
Jer. 5. 23 this peo. hath *r*. heart
Reward (*n.*). *Gift, wage, recom-
pense, requital.*
Gen. 15. 1 I am thy shield, and *r*.
Num. 18. 31 it is your *r*. for serv.
Deut. 10. 17 G., who taketh not *r*.
Ruth 2. 12 full *r*. be given of Lord
2 Sam. 19. 36 why recomp. wi. su. *r*.
1 K. 13. 7 I will give thee a *r*.
Job 6. 22 Bring me? or, Give a *r*.
Ps. 58. 11 there is *r*. for righteous
Prov. 24. 20 shall be no *r*. for evil
Eccl. 4. 9 they have *r*. for labour
Isa. 45. 13 not for *r*. saith the Lord
Jer. 40. 5 captain gave Jeremiah *r*.
Ezek. 16. 34 thou giv. *r*., and no *r*.
Dan. 2 6 ye sh. receive gifts and *r*
Hos. 9. 1 *r*. upon every cornfloor
Obad. 15 thy *r*. shall return upon
Mic. 3. 11 heads there. judge for *r*.
Mat. 5. 12 great is your *r*. in heav.
Mark 9. 41 he shall not lose his *r*.
Luke 6. 35 your *r*. shall be great
Acts 1. 18 purch. field wi. *r*. of iniq.
Rom. 4. 4 to him that work. is *r*.
1 Cor. 3. 8 every man shall receive *r*.
Col. 3. 24 ye shall rec. *r*. of inherit.
1 Tim. 5. 18 labor. is worthy of *r*.
Heb. 2. 2 recei. just recomp. of *r*.
2 Pet. 2. 13 shall receive the *r*. of
2 John 8 that we receive a full *r*.
Jude 11 and ran after error for *r*.
Rev. 22. 12 my *r*. is wi. me, to give
R. V. Job 6. 22; Prov. 21. 14: Jer.
40. 5 present; Job 7. 2 wages; Ps.
40. 15; 70. 3 by reason; 94. 2
desert; Ezek. 16. 34; Hos. 2. 12;
9. 1; 1 Tim. 5. 18; 2 Pet. 2. 13;
Jude 11 hire; Obad. 15 dealing;
Col. 2. 18 prize by; 3. 24 recompense
Reward (*v.*). *Repay, recompense.*
Gen. 44. 4 have ye *r*. evil for good?
Deut. 32. 41 will *r*. them that hate
1 Sam. 24. 19 the Lord *r*. thee good
2 Sam. 22. 21 Lord *r*. me accord. to
2 Chr. 15. 7 your work shall be *r*.
Job 21. 19 he *r*. him, and he shall
Ps. 35. 12 they *r*. me evil for good

Prov. 13. 13 that feareth shall be *r*.
Isa. 3. 9 they have *r*. evil to thems.
Jer. 31. 16 for thy work shall be *r*.
Hos. 4. 9 and I will *r*. them their
Mat. 6. 4 Fath. shall *r*. thee openly
2 Tim. 4. 14 L. him accor. to work
Rev. 18. 6 *R*. her ev. as she *r*. you
R. V. 1 Sam. 24. 17; Mat. 16. 27;
2 Tim. 4. 14; Rev. 18. 6 render;
Deut. 32. 41; Mat. 6, 4, 6, 18 re-
compense; Ps. 54. 5 requite

Rewarder. *Wage giver.*
Heb. 11. 6 a *r*. of them that seek

Rib. *Rib.*
Gen. 2. 21 God took one of his *r*.
2 Sam. 2. 23 smote A. under fifth *r*.
3. 27; 4. 6; 20. 10
Dan. 7. 5 beast had *r*. in mouth
R. V. 2 Sam. 2. 23; 3. 27; 4. 6; 20.
10 in belly

Ribband. *Ribbon, thread.*
Num. 15. 38 put on the fringe a *r*.

Rich. *Wealthy, valuable.*
Gen. 13. 2 Abram was *r*. in cattle
Ex. 30. 15 *r*. shall not give more
Lev. 25. 47 if a stranger wax *r*.
Ruth 3. 10 fol. not men poor or *r*.
1 Sam. 2. 7 L. maketh poor and *r*.
2 Sam. 12. 1 two men in cit. one *r*.
Job 15. 29 he shall not be *r*., neith.
Ps. 45. 12 *r*. shall intreat thy favour
Prov. 10. 4 hand of dilig. maketh *r*.
Eccl. 5. 12 abund. of *r*. not suffer
Isa. 53. 9 he made his grave with *r*.
Jer. 9. 23 let not *r*. glory in riches
Hos. 12. 8 Ephraim said, I am *r*.
Mic. 6. 12 *r*. men thereof are full
Zech. 11. 5 blessed be L., for I am *r*.
Mat. 19. 23 *r*. man sh. hardly enter
Mark 12. 41 many *r*. cast in much
Luke 6. 24 woe unto you that are *r*.
Rom. 10. 12 same *r*.ord is *r*. to all
1 Cor. 4. 8 are f.....; now ye are *r*.
2 Cor. 6. 10 yet making many *r*.
Eph. 2. 4 God who is *r*. in mercy
1 Tim. 6. 9 *r* fall into temptation
Jas. 1. 11 so shall the *r*. man fade
Rev. 18. 3 me.·. of earth are waxed *r*.

Richer. *More opulent.*
Dan. 11. 2 the fourth shall be far *r*.

Riches. *Substance, possession, wealth, opulence.*
Gen. 31. 16 the *r*. God hath taken
Josh. 22. 8 Return with much *r*.
1 Sam. 17. 25 enrich with great *r*.
2 K. 3. 11 neither hast asked *r*.
1 Chr. 29. 12 *r*. and honour come
2 Chr. 32. 27 Hez. had exceeding *r*.
Esth. 1. 4 Ahas. showed *r*. of kingd.
Job 20. 15 he swallowed down *r*.
Ps. 37. 16 better than *r*. of wicked
Prov. 22. 1 good name rath. than *r*.
Eccl. 4. 8 nor eye satisfied with *r*.
Isa. 8. 4 *r*. of Damascus taken away
Jer. 9. 23 let not the rich glory in *r*.
Ezek. 26. 12 make a spoil of thy *r*.
Dan. 11. 2 by strength throu. his *r*.
Mat. 13. 22 decei. of *r*. choke word
Mark 4. 19; Luke 8. 14
Rom. 2. 4 or despiseth thou *r*.?
2 Cor. 8. 2 to *r*. of their liberality
Eph. 1. 7 redemption according to *r*.
Phil. 4. 19 according to *r*. in glory
Col. 1. 27 what is *r*. of the glory
1 Tim. 6. 17 nor trust in uncertain *r*.
Heb. 11. 26 reproach of C. greater *r*.
Jas. 5. 2 Your *r*. are corrupted
Rev. 5. 12 Worthy is Lamb to rec. *r*.
R. V. Gen. 36. 7; Dan. 11. 13, 24,
28 substance; Josh. 22. 8; Isa. 61.
6 wealth; Ps. 37. 16; Jer. 48. 36
abundance; Prov. 22. 16 gain

Richly. *Abundantly.*
· Col. 3. 16 let word of C. dwell *r*.
1 Tim. 6. 17 who giv. *r*. all things

Rid. *Deliver.*
Gen. 37. 22 that he might *r*. him
Ex. 6. 6 will *r*. you out of bondage
Lev. 26. 6 will *r*. beasts out of land
Ps. 82. 4 *r*. th. out hand of wicked
144. 7, 11 *r*. me, and deliver me
R. V. Gen. 37. 22 deliver; Ps. 82.
4; 144. 7, 11 rescue

Riddance. *Consuming ending.*
Lev 23. 22 th. shalt not make *r*.
Zeph 1. 18 he sh. make speedy *r*.

R. V. Lev. 23. 22 wholly reap;
Zeph. 1. 18 an end.

Ridden. *See Ride.*

Riddle. *Hidden saying.*
Judg. 14. 12 I put now *r*. unto you
Ezek. 17. 2 put forth *r*. and speak

Ride. *Ride.*
Gen. 24. 61 they *r*. upon the camels
Lev. 15. 19 what saddle he *r*. on
Num. 22. 30 ass, wh. thou hast *r*.
Deut. 32. 13 made him *r*. on hi. pl.
Judg. 5. 10 ye th. *r*. on white asses.
1 Sam. 25. 20 as she *r*. on the ass
2 Sam. 18. 9 Absalom *r*. upon mule
1 K. 18. 45 Ahab *r*. went to Jez.
2 K. 9. 16 So Jehu *r*. in chariot
Neh. 2. 12 save the beast that I *r*.
Esth. 6. 8 horse that the king *r*.
Ps. 18. 10 *r*. upon cherub, did fly
Isa. 19. 1 L. *r*. upon swift cloud
Jer. 6. 23 *r*. on horses, set in array
Hos. 14. 3 we will not *r*. on horses
Am. 2. 15 nei. sh. he th. *r*. horses
Hab. 3. 8 didst *r*. on thy horses
Hag. 2. 22 overthrow those that *r*.

Rider. *Who rides.*
Gen. 49. 17 so that *r*. shall fall
Ex. 15. 1 his *r*. hath he thrown
2 K. 18. 23 if thou be able to set *r*.
Esth. 8. 10 and he sent letters by *r*.
Job 39. 18 scorneth horse and *r*.
Isa. 36. 8 if thou be able to set *r*.
Jer. 51. 21 I break chariot and *r*.
Hag. 2. 22 hors. and *r*. sh. co. down
Zech. 10. 5 *r*. shall be confounded

Riding. *Riding.*
Num. 22. 22 he was *r*. upon ass
2 K. 4. 24 slack not thy *r*. for me
Jer. 17. 25 kings enter *r*. in char.
Ezek. 23. 6 horsemen *r*. on horses
Zech. 1. 8 man *r*. on a red horse

Ridges. *R. V. furrows.*
Ps. 65. 10 Thou waterest *r*. thereof

Rie. *R. V. spelt.*
Ex. 9. 32 wheat and *r*. not smitten
Isa. 28. 25 cast bar. and *r*. in place?

Rifled. *Spoiled, robbed.*
Zech. 14. 2 city taken, houses *r*.

Right (a.). *Not left, dexter.*
Gen. 48. 17 father laid *r*. hand on
Ex. 29. 22 take of ram *r*. should
Lev. 7. 32; Num. 18. 18
Judg. 3. 16 gird it under rai. on *r*.
1 Sam. 11. 2 thrust out your *r*. eyes
2 Sam. 20. 9 took beard wi. *r*. hand
1 K. 7. 39 five bases on *r*. side
2 K. 11. 11 from *r*. cor. of temple
2 Chr. 4. 10 he set sea on the *r*. side
Ezek. 47. 2 ran waters on *r*. side
Mat. 5. 29 if *r*. eye offend, pluck it
Luke 22. 50 and cut off his *r*. ear
John 21. 6 Cast net on *r*. side of
Acts 3. 7 he took him by *r*. hand
Rev. 1. 26 had on *r*. seven stars

Truth, upright, correct
Gen. 24. 48 which led me in *r*. way
Deut. 32. 4 G. of truth, just and *r*.
1 Sam. 12. 23 teach you the *r*. way
2 Sam. 15. 3 matter are good and *r*.
2 K. 10. 15 is thine heart *r*. as my
Ez. 8. 21 to seek of him the *r*. way
Neh. 9. 13 thou gavest *r*. judgment
Job 6. 25 how forcible are *r*. words
Ps. 19. 8 statutes of the Lord are *r*.
Prov. 4. 11 I ha. led thee in *r*. paths
Eccl. 4. 4 I consid. every *r*. work
Isa. 30. 10 proph. not to us *r*. thing
Jer. 2. 21 planted thee a *r*. seed
Hos. 14. 9 ways of the Lord are *r*.
Am. 3. 10 they know not to do *r*.
Mark 5. 15 sitting, and in *r*. mind
Luke 8. 35
Acts 4. 19 whether *r*. in si. of God

Right (n.). *Right, upright, just.*
Gen. 18. 25 shall not judge do *r*.
Deut. 21. 17 *r*. of firstborn is his
Ruth 4. 6 redeem thou my *r*. to
2 Sam. 19. 43 We have also more *r*.
1 K. 11. 33 to do that which is *r*. in
2 K. 10. 15 is thine heart *r*. as my
2 Chr. 14. 2 Asa did good and *r*.
Ps. 9. 4 hast maintained my *r*. and
Prov. 16. 13 love him that speak *r*.
Jer. 34. 15 had done *r*. in my sight
Lam. 3. 35 turn aside *r*. of man
Ezek. 21. 27 whose *r*. it is

Am. 3. 10 they know not to do *r*.
Mat. 20. 4 and what is *r*. I will give
Luke 12. 57 judge not what is *r*.
Heb. 13. 10 they have no *r*. to eat
Rev. 22. 14 have *r*. to tree of life
R. V. Many changes, chiefly due to
context.

Righteous. *Upright, just.*
Gen. 7. 1 thee have I seen *r*. before
Ex. 9. 27 L. is *r*., I and my people
Num. 23. 10 let me die death of *r*.
Deut. 25. 1 they shall justify the *r*.
1 Sam. 24. 17 thou art mo. *r*. than I
2 Sam. 4. 11 wick. ha. slain *r*. pers.
1 K. 2. 32 fell on two men more *r*.
2 K. 10. 9 Jehu said to peo. Be *r*.
Ez. 9. 15 God of Israel, thou art *r*.
Neh. 9. 8 Lord God, thou art *r*.
Job 22. 19 see it, and are glad
Ps. 5. 12 thou, Lord wilt bless *r*.
Prov. 10. 21 lips of *r*. feed many
Eccl. 3. 17 God shall judge the *r*.
Isa. 57. 1 *r*. is taken away from evil
Jer. 12. 1 *R*. art thou. O L., I plead
Lam. 1. 18 L. is *r*. I have rebelled
Ezek. 13. 22 with lies made *r*. sad
Dan. 9. 14 the Lord our God is *r*.
Am. 2. 6 they sold *r*. for silver and
Hab. 1. 4 wicked compass about *r*.
Mal. 3 18 discern bet. *r*. and wick.
Mat. 9. 13 not come to the call the *r*.
Mark 2. 17; Luke 5. 32
John 7. 24 but judge *r*. judgment
Rom. 3. 10 There is none *r*., no, not
2 Thes. 1. 6 seeing it is *r*. wi. God
1 Tim. 1. 9 law is not made for *r*.
2 Tim. 4. 8 the *r*. judge shall give
Heb. 11. 4 obt. witness he was *r*.
Jas. 5. 16 prayer of *r*. avail. much
1 Pet. 3. 12 eyes of L. are over *r*.
2 Pet. 2. 8 Lot vexed his *r*. soul
1 John 2. 1 advocate, J. C. the *r*.
Rev. 16. 5 thou art *r*., O L., which
R. V. Many changes in Job, Ps.
and Prov. to, upright

Righteously. *Rightly, justly.*
Deut. 1. 16 judge *r*. between man
Ps. 96. 10 he shall judge people *r*.
Prov. 31. 9 Open thy mouth, judge *r*.
Isa. 33. 15 He that walketh *r*., and
Jer. 11. 20 L. of h. that judgest *r*.
Tit. 2. 12 should live soberly, *r*.
1 Pet. 2. 23 to him that judgeth *r*.
R. V. Ps. 67. 4; 96. 10 with equity

Righteousness. *Rightness, justice.*
Gen. 15. 6 count. it to him for *r*.
Lev. 19. 15 in *r*. shalt thou judge
Deut. 33. 19 offer sacrifices of *r*.
1 Sam. 26. 23 L. render to ev. man *r*.
2 Sam. 22. 21 reward. me accord. *r*.
1 K. 8. 32 give according to his *r*.
2 Chr. 6. 23
Job 29. 14 I put on *r*., it clo. me
Ps. 4. 1 Hear me, God of my *r*.
Prov. 8. 8 words of mo. are in *r*.
Eccl. 7. 15 just man th. per. in *r*.
Isa. 1. 21 *r*. lodged in it, but now
Jer. 23. 6 called, The Lord our *r*.
Ezek. 14. 14 deliv. souls by their *r*.
Dan. 4. 27 break off thy sins by *r*.
Hos. 10. 12 Sow to yourselves in *r*.
Am. 5. 7 who will leave off *r*. in
Mic. 6. 5 ye may know *r*. of Lord
Zech. 8. 8 their God is truth and *r*.
Mal. 4. 2 shall Sun of *r*. arise wi.
Mat. 3. 15 becometh us to fulfil *r*.
Luke 1. 75 in *r*. bef. him all days
John 16. 8 rep. world of sin and *r*.
Acts 17. 31 will judge world in *r*.
Rom. 1. 17 therein is *r*. of God
1 Cor. 1. 1. 30 made unto us and *r*
2 Cor. 9. 9 his *r*. remain. forever
Gal. 3. 6 was account. to him for *r*.
Eph. 4. 24 aft. G. is created in *r*.
Phil. 1. 11 filled with fruits of *r*.
1 Tim. 6. 11 fol. aft *r*., godliness
2 Tim. 4. 8 laid up a crown of *r*.
Tit. 3. 5 Not by works of *r*., which
Heb. 1. 9 Thou hast loved *r*., and
Jas. 1. 20 wrath work. not *r*. of G.
1 Pet. 2. 24 dead to sins, live to *r*.
1 John 3. 7 that doeth *r*. is righte.
Rev. 19. 11 in *r*. he doth judge
R. V. Rom. 2. 26; 8. 4 ordinance;
Rom. 9. 28; 10, 3 ——

Rightly. *Rightly.*
Gen. 27. 36 Is not he *r.* named J. ?
Luke 7. 43 said, Thou hast *r.* judg.
2 Tim. 2. 15 *r.* divid. word of truth

Rigour. *Rigor, severity.*
Ex. 1. 13 chil. of Is. served with *r.*
Lev. 25. 43 thou sh. not rule wi. *r.*

Ring (*n.*). *Ring.*
Gen. 41. 42 Pharaoh took off his r.
Ex. 25. 12 th. sh. cast four *r.* of gold
26. 24; 27. 4; 28. 23; 30. 4
Num. 31. 50 bro. obla., bracelets, *r.*
Esth. 3. 10 king took *r.* from hand
S. of S. 5. 14 hands are as gold *r.*
Isa. 3. 21 shall take away the *r.*
Ezek. 1. 18 th. *r.* were full of eyes
Luke 15. 22 said, Put a *r.* on hand
Jas. 2. 2 came man with gold *r.*
R. V. Gen. 41. 42; Ex. 35. 22;
Num. 31. 50 signet ring

Ring (*v.*). *Moved, noisy.*
1 Sam. 4. 5 shout, so th. earth *r.*
1 K. 1. 45 rejoicing, so that city *r.*

Ringleader. *First leader.*
Acts 24. 5 *r.* of sect of Nazarenes

Ringstraked. *Streaked.*
Gen. 30. 35 he goats that were *r.*
30. 39, 40; 31. 8, 10, 12

Rinsed. *Submerged, rinsed*
Lev. 6. 28 be both scoured and *r.*
15. 11, 12 every vessel shall be *r.*

Riot (*n.*). *Uproar, excess.*
Tit. 1. 6 children not accused of *r.*
1 Pet. 4. 4 not to same excess of *r.*

Riot (*v.*). *Revel.*
Rom. 13. 13 walk not in *r.*, and
2 Pet. 2. 13 count it pleasure to *r.*
R. V. Rom. 13. 13 revelling; 2 Pet.
2. 13 revel.

Riotous. *Extravagant.*
Prov. 23. 20 Be not among *r.* eaters
Luke 15. 13 wasted sub. wi. *r.* living
R. V. Prov. 23. 20; 28. 7 gluttonous

Rip. *Cleave.*
2 K. 8. 12 *r.* their women wi. child
Hos. 13. 16 wo. wi. child sh. be *r.*
Am. 1. 13 they ha. *r.* wom. wi. child

Ripe. *Ripe, mature.*
Gen. 40. 10 clusters bro. *r* grapes
Ex. 22. 29 to offer thy *r.* fruits
Num. 13. 20 time of first *r.* grapes
Jer. 24. 2 like figs that are first *r.*
Joel 3. 13 sickle, for harvest is *r.*
Mic. 7. 1 my soul desired *r.* fruit
Rev. 14. 18 gather, grapes are full. *r.*

Ripening. *Ripening.*
Isa. 18. 5 and the sour grape is *r.*
Rev. 14. 15 harvest of earth is *r.*

Rise. *Arise, go up, be raised.*
Gen. 4. 8 Cain *r.* up against Abel
Ex. 24. 3 Moses *r.* up, and Joshua
Lev. 19. 32 *r.* up bef. hoary head
Num. 16. 2 they *r.* up before Moses
Deut. 2. 13 *r.* up, get over brook
Josh. 8. 7 *r.* up from the ambush
Judg. 8. 21 *R.* thou, fall upon us
Ruth. 3. 14 she *r.* bef. one co. know
1 Sam. 17. 20 D. *r.* early in morning
2 Sam. 15. 2 Absalom *r.* up early
1 K. 2. 19 king *r.* up to meet her
2 K. 3. 24 Is. *r.* and smote Moab
2 Chr. 29. 20 Hezekiah *r.* early and
Ez. 10. 6 Ez. *r.* from before house
Neh. 2. 18 Let us *r.* up and build
Job 14. 12 man lieth down, and *r.* not
Ps. 3. 1 many *r.* up against me
Prov. 28. 12 wh. wick. *r.*, man is hid.
Eccl. 12. 4 sh. *r.* at voice of bird
S. of S. 2. 10 *R.*, my love, fair one
Isa. 14. 21 they do not *r.*, nor possess
Jer. 26. 17 then *r.* up certain elders
Lam. 1. 14 I am not able to *r.* up
Dan. 8. 27 I *r.*, did k.'s business
Am. 5. 2 she shall no more *r.*, she
Obad. 1. *r.* up against her in battle
Jonah 1. 3 Jonah *r.* up to flee unto
Mic. 7. 6 daughter *r.* ag'st mother
Nah. 1. 9 affliction shall not *r.* up
Hab. 2. 7 Shall they not *r.* sudden.
Zeph. 3. 8 until day I *r.* to the prey
Mat. 20. 19 the third day he shall *r.*
Mark 3. 26 if S. sh. *r.* ag'st himself
Luke 5. 28 *r.* up, and follow. him
John 11. 23 Thy bro. shall *r.* again
Acts 10. 13 came a voice, *R.*, Peter
Rom. 14. 9 to this end C. died, and *r.*

1 Cor. 15. 13 then is Christ not *r.*
2 Cor. 5. 15 him which died, and *r.*
Col. 3. 1 if ye be *r.* from Christ
Jas. 1. 11 For sun is no sooner *r.*
R. V. Many changes to, arise; oth.
frequent but suiting context.

Rising. *Going up, rising.*
Lev. 13. 2 shall have in skin a *r.*
Num. 2. 3 east side toward *r.* sun
Deut. 4. 41 this side toward sun *r.*
Josh. 12. 1 toward *r.* of the sun
Judg. 20. 43 Gibeah, toward sun *r.*
Ps. 50. 1 fr. *r.* of sun unto going
Isa. 41, 25; Mal. 1. 11
Jer. 7. 13 *r.* up early and speaking
Lam. 3. 63 then sitting down and *r.*
Mark 9. 10 wh. *r.* fr. dead sho. mean
Luke 2. 34 *r.* of many in Israel

Rites. R. V. *statutes.*
Num. 9. 3 keep it according to *r.*

River. *That flows, stream, brook,*
flood, course, valley.
Gen. 2. 10 a *r.* went out of Eden
Ex. 2. 3 she laid it in flags by *r.*
Lev. 11. 9 whats. hath fins in *r.*
Num. 22. 5 Pathor, which is by *r.*
Deut. 1. 7 unto gr. *r.*, Euphrates
Josh. 13. 9 city that is in midst of *r.*
Judg. 5. 21 that ancient *r.*, *r.* Ki.
2 Sam. 17. 13 will draw it into *r.*
1 K. 4. 21 Solomon reigned from *r.*
2 K. 2. 12 Ab. and Ph., *r.* of Damas.
1 Chr. 1. 48 Shaul by the *r.* reigned
2 Chr. 7. 8 enter. of Hamath by *r.*
Ez. 8 21 I proclaimed fast by *r.*
Neh. 2. 9 I came to gov. beyond *r.*
Job 40. 23 he drinketh up a *r.*, and
Ps. 78. 44 turned their *r.* into blood
Prov. 5. 16 *r.* of water in streets
Eccl. 1. 7 all *r.* run into the sea
S. of S. 5. 12 as eyes of doves by *r.*
Isa. 19. 6 shall turn the *r.* far away
Jer. 2. 18 to drink waters of the *r.*?
Lam. 2. 18 let tears run like a *r.*
Ezek. 1. 1 among captives by the *r.*
Dan. 10. 4 I was by side of gr. *r.*
Joel 1. 20 *r.* of waters dried up
Am. 6. 14 unto *r.* of the wilderness
Mic. 7. 12 come from fortress to *r.*
Nah. 3. 8 was situate among the *r.*
Hab. 3. 9 didst cleave earth with *r.*
Zeph. 3. 10 beyond *r.* of Ethiopia
Zech. 10. 11 deep of *r.* shall dry
Mark 1. 5 baptized in the *r.* Jordan
John 11. 38 deep of belly sh. flow *r.*
Acts 16. 13 we went by a *r.* side
Rev. 22. 1 showed *r.* of wat. of life
R. V. Num. 34. 5; Deut. 10. 7;
Josh. 15. 4, 47; 16. 8; 17. 9;
19. 11; 1 K. 8. 65; 2 K. 24. 7;
2 Chr. 7. 8; S. of S. 5. 12; Ezek.
47. 19; Am. 6. 14; Joel 3. 18
brook or brooks; Ezek. 6. 3;
31. 12; 32. 6; 34. 13; 35. 8; 36.
4, 6; Prov. 21. 1 water courses;
Deut. 2. 24, 36; 3. 8, 12; 4. 48;
Josh. 12. 1, 2; 13. 9, 16; 2 Sam.
24. 5; 2 K. 10. 33 valley; Ex. 8. 5;
Ps. 1. 3 streams; Isa. 23. 3, 10;
Zech. 10. 11 Nile; Job 28. 10;
Ezek. 31. 4 channels

Road. R. V. *raid.*
1 Sam. 27. 10 Whith. ha. ye made *r.*

Roar. *Make noise, cry deep.*
Judg. 14. 5 lion *r.* against Samson
1 Chr. 16. 32 Let sea *r.* and fulness
Ps. 96. 11 ; 98. 7
Job 37. 4 voice *r.*, he thundereth
Ps. 104. 21 lions *r.* after their prey
Isa. 5. 29 *r.* like lions
Jer. 25. 30 L. shall *r.* from on high
Ezek. 22. 25 like *r.* lion ravening
Hos. 11. 10 *r.* like lion, wh. he *r.*
Joel 3. 16 L. shall *r.* out of Zion
Zeph. 3. 3 her princes are *r.* lions
Rev. 10. 3 angels cried, as a lion *r.*
R. V. Isa. 42. 13 shout aloud

Roaring. *Troubled, crying deep.*
Job 3. 24 my *r.* poured like water
Ps. 32. 3 bones waxed old thro. *r.*
Pr. 28. 15 as *r.* lion, so is wicked
Isa. 5. 29 shall be like a lion, th.
Ezek. 19. 7 desolate by noise of *r.*
Zech. 11. 3 voice of *r.* of lions; for
Luke 21. 25 sea and the waves *r.*
1 Pet. 5. 8 devil, as *r.* lion walk.

R. V. Isa. 31. 4 growleth
Roast. *Cook, parch.*
Ex. 12. 8 eat flesh *r.* with fire, and
Deut. 16. 7 thou shalt *r.* and eat it
1 Sam. 2. 15 Give fl. to *r.* for priest
2 Chr. 35. 13 they *r.* the passover
Prov. 12. 27 The slothful man *r.* not
Isa. 44. 16 he *r.* roast, and is satisf.
Jer. 29. 22 whom king of Babyl. *r.*

Rob. *Bereave.*
Lev. 26. 22 shall *r.* you of children
2 Sam. 17. 8 as bear *r.* of whelps
Prov. 17. 12 Let bear *r.* of whelps
Spoil, plunder, rifle.
Lev. 19. 23 shalt not *r.* neighbour
Judg. 9. 25 *r.* all that came along
1 Sam. 23. 1 Phil. *r.* thresh. floors
Ps. 119. 61 bands of wicked *r.* me
Isa. 42. 22 this is peo. *r.* and spoil.
Jer. 50. 37 sword on treas., be *r.*
Ezek. 39. 10 *r.* those that *r.* them
Mal. 3. 8 Will a man *r.* God? Yet
R. V. Ps. 119. 61 wrapped me round

Robber. *Plunderer, spoiler, taker*
of prey, burglar.
Job 12. 6 tabernacles of *r.* prosper
Isa. 42. 24 who gave Is. to the *r.*?
Jer. 7. 11 house became a den of *r.*
Ezek. 7. 22 for *r.* shall enter into it
Dan. 11. 14 *r.* of peo. exalt thems.
Hos. 6. 9 troops of *r.* wait for man
Obad. 5 If thieves came to thee, if *r.*
John 18. 40 Now Barabbas was a *r.*
2 Cor. 11. 26 perils of waters, of *r.*
R. V. Job 5. 5; 18. 9 snare; Dan.
11. 14 children of the violent

Robbery. *Snatching away, spoil-*
ing.
Ps. 62. 10 become not vain in *r.*
Prov. 21. 7 *r.* of wick. shall destroy
Isa. 61. 8 hate *r.* of burnt offering
Ezek. 22. 29 used oppr., exercised *r.*
Am. 3. 10 store up *r.* in their palaces
Nah. 3. 1 it is all full of lies and *r.*
Phil. 2. 6 thought it not *r.* to be eq.
R. V. Prov. 21. 7 violence; Nah.
3. 1 rapine

Robe. *Mantle, garment.*
Ex. 24. 8 made an ephod and *r.*
Lev. 8. 7 clothed him with the *r.*
1 Sam. 18. 4 Jon. strip. hims. of *r.*
2 Sam. 13. 18 wi. such *r.* apparelled
1 K. 22. 30 but put thou on thy *r.*
1 Chr. 15. 27 D. was clothed with *r.*
2 Chr. 18. 9 clothed in *r.*, they sat
Job 29. 14 my judgment was as *r.*
Isa. 61. 10 cov. me wi. *r.* of righte.
Ezek. 26. 16 princes lay away th. *r.*
Jonah 3. 6 king laid *r.* from him
Mic. 2. 8 ye pull off *r.* wi. garment
Mat. 27. 28 and put on him scarlet *r.*
Luke 15. 22 Bring forth the best *r.*
John 19. 2 they put on him purp. *r.*
Rev. 6. 11 *r.* were given to every one
R. V. Luke 23. 11 apparel ; John
19. 2 garment ; Rev. 22. 14 do his
commandments

Rock. *Rock.*
Ex. 17. 6 will stand bef. thee on *r.*
Num. 20. 8 speak to *r.* bef. th. eyes
Deut. 32. 31 their *r.* is not as our *R.*
Judg. 6. 21 there rose fire out of *r.*
1 Sam. 2. 2 nei. any *r.* like our God
2 Sam. 22. 3 G. of my *r.*, in him I tr.
1 K. 19. 11 L. is my *r.* and fortress
1 Chr. 11. 15 the captains went to *r.*
2 Chr. 25. 12 cast them fr. top of *r.*
Neh. 9. 15 brought water out of *r.*
Job 14. 18 *r.* is remo. out of place
Ps. 42. 9 I will say unto G. my *r.*
Prov. 30. 19 way of serpent upon *r.*
S. of S. 2. 14 my dove, in clefts of *r.*
Isa. 2. 10 enter into *r.* and hide thee
Jer. 5. 3 made faces harder than *r.*
Ezek. 24. 7 she set it on top of *r.*
Am. 6. 12 Shall horses run upon *r.*?
Obad. 3 thou that dwellest in *r.*
Nah. 1. 6 the *r.* are thrown down
Mat. 7. 25 it was founded upon *r.*
Mark 15. 46 sep. was hewn out of *r.*
Luke 8. 6 and some fell upon a *r.*
Acts 27. 29 fearing we fall upon *r.*
Rom. 9. 33 I lay a *r.* of offence
1 Cor. 10. 4 drank of that spiritual *R.*
1 Pet. 2. 8 a *r.* of offence, even to
Rev. 6. 16 said to m't's and *r.* Fall

R. V. Judg. 6. 26 stronghold ; I Sam.
14. 4 crag ; Isa. 42. 11 Sela ; Luke
6. 48 well builded ; Acts 27. 29
rocky ground

Rod. *Staff, twig, sceptre.*
Gen. 30. 37 Jacob took *r.* of poplar
Ex. 4. 20 M. took *r.* of God in hand
Lev. 27. 32 whatso. passeth under *r.*
Num. 17. 2 take of everyone a *r.*
1 Sam. 14. 27 Jona. put an end of *r.*
2 Sam. 7. 14 I will chasten with *r.*
Job 9. 34 Let him take his *r.* away
Ps. 2. 9 break them with *r.* of iron
Prov. 13. 24 that spar. *r.* hateth son
Isa. 9. 4 hast bro. *r.* of oppression
Jer. 10. 16 Is. is *r.* of his inheritance
Lam. 3. 1 seen affl. by *r.* of wrath
Ezek. 19. 12 her strong *r.* are broken
Mic. 7. 14 Feed people with thy *r.*
1 Cor. 4. 21 shall I come with a *r.*
2 Cor. 11. 25 thrice beaten with *r.*
Heb. 9. 4 Aaron's *r.* that budded
Rev. 11. 1 was given reed like a *r.*
R. V. Ps. 125. 3 sceptre ; Isa. 11. 1
shoot ; Jer. 10. 16 ; 51. 19 tribe

Rode. *See* **Ride.**

Roe. *Roe-deer, doe.*
2 Sam. 2. 18 Asa. was as a wild *r.*
1 Chr. 12. 8 swift as *r.* on mount.
Prov. 5. 19 hind, and pleasant *r.*
S. of S. 2. 7 I charge you by the *r.*
Isa. 13. 14 shall be as the chased *r.*
R. V. Prov. 5. 10 doe ; S. of S. 4. 5 ;
7. 3 fawns

Roebuck. R. V. *gazelle.*
Deut. 12. 14 may eat flesh of *r.* and
1 K. 4. 23 besides harts and *r.* and

Roll (*n.*). *Scroll, book, tablet.*
Ez. 6. 2 was found at Achmetha, a *r.*
Isa. 8. 1 take the a great *r.*, and
Jer. 36. 2 Take *r.* of book, and write
Ezek. 2. 9 *r.* of a book was therein
Zech. 5. 1 turned, behold, flying *r.*
R.V.Isa. 8.1 tablet ; Ez.6.1 archives

Roll (*v.*). *Roll, push, fold.*
Gen. 29. 3 *r.* stone from the well
Josh. 5. 9 I *r.* away repr. of Egypt
1 Sam. 14. 33 *r.* great stone unto me
Job 30. 14 in the desolation they *r.*
Isa. 34. 4 heavens sh. be *r.* together
17. 13 like *r.* thing bef. whirlwind
Jer. 51. 25 *r.* thee down from rocks
Mic. 1. 10 in house of Aph. *r.* thys.
Mat. 27. 60 he *r.* gr. stone to door
Mark 16. 4 saw stone was *r.* away
Luke 24. 2 found the stone *r.* away
Rev. 6. 14 as a scroll *r.* together
R. V. Isa. 17. 13 whirling dust

Roller. *Bandage, fold.*
Ezek. 30. 21 to put a *r.* to bind it

Roof. *Top, covering, palate.*
Gen. 19. 8 came they under my *r.*
Deut. 22. 8 make battlement for *r.*
Josh. 2. 6 brought them to the *r.*
Judg. 16. 27 on *r.* about three thou.
2 Sam. 11. 2 David walked on *r.*
Neh. 8. 16 every one upon the *r.*
Job 29. 20 tongue clea. to *r.* of m.
Ps. 137. 6 ; S. of S. 7. 9 ; Lam. 4. 4.
Ezek. 3. 26
Jer. 19. 13 upon *r.* burned incense
Mat. 8. 8 ; Luke 7. 6 not worthy th.
shouldst come under my *r.*
Mark 2. 4 they uncovered the *r.*
R. V. S. of S. 7. 9 ——.

Room. *Place, stead, place for sitting or standing.*
Gen. 24. 25 We have straw and *r.*
2 Sam. 19. 13 before me in *r.* of Joab
1 K. 2. 35 king put Ben. in J.'s room
1 Chr. 4. 41 and dwelt in their *r.*
Ps. 31. 8 hast set my feet in large *r.*
Prov. 18. 16 man's gift maketh *r.*
Mat. 23. 6 love upper. *r.* at feasts
Mark 12. 39 ; Luke 20. 46
Acts 1. 13 went into an upper *r.*
1 Cor. 14. 16 he that occupieth *r.*
R. V. 2 K. 15. 25 ; 1 Chr. 4. 41 stead ;
Ps. 31. 8 ; Luke 14. 9, 10 ; 20. 46 ;
1 Cor. 14. 16 place ; Mat. 23. 6 ;
Mark 12. 39 chief place ; Luke 14.
7. 8 chief seat ; Acts 1. 13 chamber

Root (*n.*). *Root.*
Deut. 29. 18 among you a *r.* that
Judg. 5. 14 out of Ephr. was a *r.*
2 K. 19. 30 Judah shall yet take *r.*

Job 5. 3 I have seen foolish take *r.*
Ps. 80. 9 did cause vine to take *r.*
Prov. 12. 3 *r.* of righteous shall not
Isa. 5. 24 their *r.* shall be rotten
Jer. 17. 8 spr. out her *r.* by river
Ezek. 31. 7 his *r.* was by waters
Dan. 11. 7 out of branch of her *r.*
Hos. 9. 16 Eph. smit., *r.* dried up
Am. 2. 9 yet I destroyed his *r.*
Mal. 4. 1 leave nei. *r.* nor branch
Mat. 3. 10 now axe is laid to the *r.*
Mark 4. 6 had no *r.*, it withereth
Luke 8. 13 these have no *r.*, which
Rom. 11. 16 if *r.* be holy, so branch.
1 Tim. 6. 10 love of mon. *r.* of evil
Heb. 12. 15 lest *r.* of bitter. spring
Jude 12 fruit plucked up by the *r.*
Rev. 22. 16 I am *r.* and offs. of Dav.

Root (*v.*). *To be rooted, uprooted.*
Deut. 29. 28 L. *r.* them out of land
1 K. 14. 15 he shall *r.* up Israel
Job. 31. 12 *r.* out all my increase
Ps. 52. 5 *r.* thee out of l. of living
Prov. 2. 22 transgres. sh. be *r.* out
Jer. 1. 10 to *r.* out, to pull down
Zeph. 2. 4 Ekron shall be *r.* up
Mat. 15. 13 every plant shall be *r.* up
Eph. 3. 17 *r.* and grounded in love
Col. 2. 7 *R.* and built up in him

Rope *Cord, line, rope.*
Judg. 16. 11 If they bind me wi. *r.*
2 Sam. 17. 13 then shall Is. bring *r.*
1 K. 20. 31 put *r.* upon our heads
Acts 27. 32 soldiers cut off the *r.*

Rose (*n.*). *Saffron, narcissus.*
S. of S. 2. 1 *r.* of Sharon, lily of val,
Isa. 35. 1 desert sh. blossom as *r.*

Rose (*v.*). *See* **Rise.**

Rot. *Fall away, rot.*
Num. 5. 21 L. make thy thigh to *r.*
Prov. 10. 7 name of wicked sh. *r.*
Isa. 40. 20 choos. tree th. will not *r.*
R. V. Num. 5. 21, 22, 27 fall away

Rotten. *Decayed, tattered.*
Job 13. 28 he, as *r.* thing, consum.
Jer. 38. 12 put these *r.* rags und.
Joel 1. 17 seed is *r.* under clods

Rottenness. *Putridity.*
Prov. 12. 4 th. ma. asham. is as *r.*
Isa. 5. 24 so their root sh. be as *r.*
Hos. 5. 12 be to house of Ju. as *r.*
Hab. 3. 16 *r.* ent. into my bones

Rough. *Jagged, shaggy, sharp*
Deut. 21. 4 bring heifer to *r.* val.
Isa. 27, 8 he stayeth his *r.* wind
Jer. 51. 27 come as *r.* caterpillars
Dan. 8. 21 *r.* goat is k. of Grecia
Zech. 13. 4 nei. wear a *r.* garment
Luke 3. 5 *r.* ways be ma. smooth
R. V. Zech. 13. 4 hairy

Roughly. *Sharply, fiercely.*
Gen. 42. 7 Joseph spake *r.* to him
1 Sam. 20. 10 what if fath. ans. *r.*
1 K. 12. 13 the king ans. people *r.*
2 Chr. 10. 13 king answ. them *r.*
Prov. 18. 23 the rich answereth *r.*

Round. (*adv.*). *Around, about.*
Gen. 23. 17 in borders *r.* about
Ex. 7. 24 Egyptians digged *r.* ab.
Etc., etc.

Round. (*a.*) *Circular.*
Ex. 16. 14 there lay sma. *r.* thing
1 K. 7. 35 *r.* comp. of half a cubit
2 Chr. 4. 2 molten sea, *r.* in comp.
S. of S. 7. 2 navel like *r.* goblet
Isa. 3. 18 L. take away th. *r.* tires
Luke 19. 43 enemies comp. thee *r.*
R. V. Isa. 3. 18 crescents

Rouse. *Make to rise.*
Gen. 49. 9 who shall *r.* him up ?

Rovers. *Nomads.*
1 Chr 12. 21 helped Da. ag'st *r.*

Row. (*n.*). *Row, array, course.*
Ex. 28. 17 first *r.*, a sardius, a topaz
Lev. 24. 6 sh. set them in two *r.*
1 K. 6. 36 three *r.* of hewed stone
2 Chr. 4. 3 *r.* of oxen were cast
Ez. 6. 4 three *r.* of great stones
S. of S. 1. 10 cheeks wi. *r.* of jewels
Ezek. 46. 23 boiling places und. *r.*
R. V. S. of S. 1. 10 plaits

Row (*v.*) *Row, work oar.*
Jonah 1. 13 men *r.* hard to bring
Mark 6. 48 saw them toiling in *r.*
John 6. 19 when they had *r.* about

Rower. *Who moves to and fro.*

Ezek. 27. 26 *r.* bro. thee into wa.

Royal. *Kingly, regal.*
Gen. 49. 20 he sh. yield *r.* dainties
Josh. 10. 2 Gib. was one of *r.* cit.
1 Sam. 27. 5 why dwell in *r.* city
2 Sam. 12. 26 Joab took the *r.* ci.
1 K. 10. 13 Sol. gave of *r.* bounty
2 K. 11. 1 Ath. destroyed seed *r.*
Esth. 1. 11 bring Vash. wi. crown *r.*
Isa. 62. 3 a *r.* diadem in the hand
Jer. 41. 1 Ishmael of the seed *r.*
Dan. 6. 7 to establish *r.* statute
Acts 12. 21 Herod in *r.* apparel
Jas. 2. 8 if ye fulfil the *r.* law ac
1 Pet. 2. 9 ye are a *r.* priesthood

Rub. *Break, rub.*
Luke 6. 1 *r.* them in their hands

Rubbish. *Dust, refuse.*
Neh. 4. 2 revive stones out of *r.*

Rubies. *Corals, pearls, gems.*
Job 28. 18 price of wis. is above *r.*
Prov. 3. 15 more precious than *r.*
Lam. 4. 7 more ruddy in bod. th. *r.*

Rudder. *Oar, rudder.*
Acts 27. 40 loosed the *r.* bands, and

Ruddy. *Red, ruddy.*
1 Sam. 16. 12 David, now he was *r.*
S. of S. 5. 10 belov. is white and *r.*
Lam. 4. 7 more *r.* in bod. th. rubies

Rude. *Crude.*
2 Cor. 11. 6 tho. I be *r.* in speech

Rudiment. *Element.*
Col. 2. 8 after *r.* of the world, and

Rue. *Rue.*
Luke 11. 42 ye tithe mint and *r.*

Ruin. *Fallen thing, calamity.*
2 Chr. 23. 8 they are the *r.* of him
Ps. 89. 40 brot. his str. holds to *r.*
Prov. 26. 28 flatter. mouth work *r.*
Isa. 3. 6 let *r.* be under thy hand
Ezek. 18. 30 so iniquity not be yr. *r.*
Am. 9. 11 I will raise up his *r.*, and
Luke 6. 49 *r.* of th. house was gr.
Acts 15. 16 I will build ag. the *r.*
R. V. Prov. 24. 22 destruction ;
Ezek. 21. 15 stumblings.

Ruined. *Broken down, stumbled.*
Isa. 3. 8 For Jerusalem is *r.*, and
Ezek. 36. 35 *r.* cities bec. fenced

Ruinous. *Fallen, bare, burnt.*
2 K. 19. 25 lay cities in *r.* heaps
Isa. 17. 1 Damascus sh. be *r.* heap

Rule (*n.*). *Control, measure.*
1 K. 22. 31 *r.* over Ahab's chariots
Esth. 9. 1 Jews had *r.* over them
Prov. 17. 2 wise serv. *r.* over son
Eccl. 2. 19 *r.* over all my labour
Isa. 44. 13 as carpenter stretch. *r.*
1 Cor. 15. 24 have put down all *r.*
2 Cor. 10. 13 to measure of the *r.*
Gal. 6. 16 walk according to this *r.*
Phil. 3. 16 let us walk by same *r.*
Heb. 13. 17 that have *r.* over you
R. V. K. 22. 31 command ; Prov.
25. 26 restraint ; Isa. 44. 13 line ; 2
Cor. 10. 13, 15 province

Rule (*v.*). *Have power, lead, guide, govern.*
Gen. 1. 16 greater light to *r.* day
Lev. 25. 43 shall not *r.* with rigour
Josh. 12. 2 Sihon *r.* from Aroer
Judg. 8. 22 *R.* thou over us, both
2 Sam. 23. 3 that *r.* must be just
1 K. 5. 16 officers which *r.* people
Ez. 4. 20 which *r.* over countries
Ps. 110. 2 *r.* in midst of enemies
Prov. 8. 16 princes, *r.*, and nobles
Isa. 3. 4 babes sh. *r.* over them
Lam. 5. 8 servants have *r.* over us
Ezek. 19. 14 no strong rod to *r.*
Dan. 4. 26 known that heavens *r.*
Joel 2. 17 heath. should *r.* ov. them
Zech. 6. 13 sit and *r.* on his throne
Mat. 2. 6 governor that shall *r.* over
Mark 10. 42 are accounted to *r.* ov.
Col. 3. 15 peace of G. *r.* in hearts
1 Tim. 3. 5 know not how to *r.* ho.
Rev. 2. 27 he *r.* with a rod of iron
R. V. Ezek. 22. 33 be king ; Mat.
2. 6 be shepherd ; Ruth 1. 1 judged

Ruler. *Leader, head, prince, prefect, magistrate.*
Gen. 41. 43 Phar. made Joseph *r.*
Ex. 22. 28 thou shalt not curse *r.*
Num. 13. 2 ev. one *r.* among them
Deut. 1. 13 I will make them *r.* ov

1 Sam. 25. 30 ha. appointed thee *r*.
2 Sam. 7. 8 I took thee to be *r*. ov.
1 K. 1. 35 I appointed Solomon *r*.
2 K. 11. 4 Jehoiada fetched *r*. over
1 Chr. 27. 31 these were *r*. of subj.
2 Chr. 35. 8 *r*. of the house of God
Ez. 10. 14 let *r*. of congregation
Neh. 7. 2 gave Hanani. *r*. of palace
Esth. 3. 12 to *r*. of every people
Ps. 2. 2 *r*. take counsel together
Prov. 23. 1 so is wick. *r*. over poor
Eccl. 10. 4 if spirit of the *r*. rise up
Isa. 1. 10 hear word of L. *r*. of S.
Jer. 51. 46 vio. of land, *r*. ag'st *r*.
Ezek. 23. 23 capts. and *r*., gr. lords
Dan. 2. 10 no *r*. ask. such things
Hos. 4. 18 *r*. with shame do love
Mic. 5. 2 out of thee shall come *r*.
Mat. 9. 18 there came a certain *r*.
Mark 5. 22 one of *r*.'s of synagogue
Luke 23. 35 *r*. also derided him
John 7. 26 do the *r*. know Christ?
Acts. 3. 17 ye did it, as also did *r*.
Rom. 13. 3 *r*., not a terror to good
Eph. 6. 12 against *r*. of darkness
1 Tim. 3. 4 one that *r*. his own house
R. V. Gen. 43. 16 steward; Num.
  13. 2; 1 Sam. 25. 30; 2 Sam. 6.
  21; 7. 8; 1 K. 1. 35; 1 Chr. 2. 12;
  5. 2; 11. 2; 17. 7; 28. 4; 2 Chr.
  6. 5; 11. 22; 29. 20; Ez. 10. 14;
  Neh. 11. 1; Esth. 3. 12; 8. 9; 9.
  3 prince or princes; 1 K. 11. 28;
  Neh. 7. 2 charge; 2 K. 25. 22;
  Mark 13. 9; Luke 21. 12 governor;
  2 Chr. 26. 11 officer; 2 Sam. 8. 18;
  20. 26 priest; Gen. 41. 43; Mat.
  24. 45, 47; 25. 21, 23 set; Deut.
  1. 13; Isa. 29. 10 heads; 1 Chr.
  26. 32 overseers; Jer. 51. 23, 28,
  57 deputies.

Ruling. *To rule.*
2 Sam. 23. 3 just, *r*. in fear of God
Jer. 22. 30 *r*. any more in Judah
1 Tim. 3. 12 *r*. their children and

Rumbling. *Noise.*
Jer. 47. 3 at the *r*. of his wheels

Rumour. *What is heard.*
2 K. 19. 7 he shall hear a *r*., and
Isa. 37. 7 he shall hear a *r*., and
Jer. 49. 14 I have heard *r*. from L.
Ezek. 7. 26 and *r*. shall be upon *r*.
Obad. 1 we heard *r*. from the Lord
Mat. 24. 6 sh. hear of wars and *r*.
Mark 13. 7 of wars and *r*. of wars
Luke 7. 17 And *r*. of him went forth
R. V. Jer. 49. 14 tidings

Rump. R. V. *fat tail.*
Ex. 29. 22 shalt take of the ram *r*.
Lev. 3. 9 *r*., it shall he take off hard

Run. *Go in or on, flow, move
  swiftly, rush.*
Gen. 18. 2 he *r*. to meet them from
Ex. 9. 23 fire *r*. along the ground
Lev. 15. 25 if it *r*. beyond the time
Num. 11. 27 there *r*. a young man
Josh. 7. 2 Josh. sent mes., they *r*.
Judg. 7. 21 host *r*., cried, and fled
1 Sam. 4. 12 there *r*. man to Benj.
2 Sam. 18. 23 he said unto him, *R*.
1 K. 19. 20 left oxen, *r*. after Elij.
2 K. 4. 26 *R*. now, to meet her
2 Chr. 16. 9 eyes of L. *r*. to and fro
Job 16. 14 he *r*. on me like giant
Ps. 119. 32 I *r*. way of commandm.
Prov. 1. 16 For their feet *r*. to evil
Eccl. 1. 7 all rivers *r*. into the sea
S. of S. 1 4 we will *r*. after thee
Isa. 40. 31 sh. *r*., and not be weary
Jer. 12. 5 if thou ha. *r*. wi. footmen
Ezek. 31. 4 wi. her riv. *r*. around
Dan. 8. 6 and *r*. into him in the fury
Joel 2. 7 they *r*. like mighty men
Am. 6. 12 Shall horses *r*. upon rock?
Hab. 2. 2 he may *r*. that readeth
Hag. 1. 9 *r*. every man to his house
Nah. 2. 4 they *r*. like lightnings
Zech. 2. 4 *R*., speak to this man
Mat. 8. 32 swine *r*. violently down
Mark 10. 17 there came one *r*., and
Luke 15. 20 *r*., and fell on his neck
Acts 3. 11 all the people *r*. together
Rom. 9. 16 nor of him that *r*., but G.
1 Cor. 9. 24 *r*. that ye may obtain
Gal. 5. 7 Ye *r*. well; who did hinder

Phil. 2. 16 I have not *r*. in vain
Heb. 12. 1 *r*. wi. patience the race
1 Pet. 4. 4 strange ye *r*. not with
Jude 11 *r*. after the error of Balaam
Rev. 9. 9 of many horses *r*. to battle
R. V. Judg. 18. 25 fall; 1 Sam. 17.
  17 carry quickly; Am. 5. 24 roll;
  Joel 2. 9 leap upon; Mat. 9. 17 is
  spilled

Running. *Flowing.*
Lev. 15. 2 when man hath *r*. issue
Prov. 5. 15 *r*. water out of own well
R. V. Lev. 15. 2; 22. 4 issue

Rush (*n*.). *Reed.*
Job 8. 11 Can *r*. gr. without mire?
Isa. 9. 14 L. will cut off br. and *r*.

Rush (*v*.). *Push, run violently.*
Judg. 9. 44 Abimelech *r*. forward
Isa. 17. 13 nations sh. *r*. like waters
Jer. 8. 6 as the horse *r*. into battle
Acts 19. 29 they *r*. with one accord

Rushing *Shaking, wasting, rush-
  ing.*
Isa. 17. 12 woe to multitude and *r*.
Jer. 47. 3 at the *r*. of his chariots
Ezek. 3. 12 I heard voice of gr. *r*.
Acts 2. 2 sound from h. as of *r*. wind

Rust. *Eating, rust.*
Mat. 6. 19 wh. *r*. doth not corrupt
Jas. 5. 3 *r*. of them shall be witness

Rye. *See Rie.*

S

Sabachthani. *Hast thou forsaken
  me?*
Mat. 27. 46 s.? that is to say, My G.
Mark 15. 34.

Sabbath. *Cessation, sabbath.*
Ex. 16. 23 To mor. is rest of holy *s*.
  20. 8 Rem. *s*. day to keep it holy
Lev. 16. 31 It sh. be *s*. of rest unto
Num. 28. 10 burnt offering of ev. *s*.
Deut. 5. 4 seventh day is *s*. of Lord
2 K. 4. 23 is nei. new moon nor *s*.
1 Chr. 9. 32 bread, prepare it ev. *s*.
2 Chr. 36. 21 the land had enjoyed *s*.
Neh. 10. 31 wo. not buy on the *s*.
Ps. 92 (tit.) A Song for the *s*. day
Isa. 1. 13 new moons and *s*. l cann.
Lam. 1. 7 adversaries did mock at *s*.
Ezek. 10. 12 I gave *s*. to be sign
Hos. 2. 11 make to cease her *s*. and
Am. 8. 5 when will the *s*. be gone?
Mat. 12. 1 Jesus went on the *s*. day
Mark 3. 4 lawful to do good on *s*.
Luke 4. 31 taught th. on the *s*. days
Acts 13. 14 went into synag. on *s*.
John 7. 23 If man on the *s*. receive
Acts 1. 12 fr. Jerus. *s*. day's journey
R. V. Lev. 23. 24, 39 solemn rest;
  Lam. 1. 7 desolations

Sack. *Vessel, bag sack.*
Gen. 42. 25 res. ev. man's mon. to *s*.
Lev. 11. 32 unclean, whet. skin or *s*.
Josh. 9 4 and took old *s*. upon asses
R. V. Gen. 42. 25 vessels

Sackcloth. *Dress of sackcloth.*
Gen. 37. 34 Jacob put *s*. upon loins
2 Sam. 3. 31 gird you with *s*., and
1 K. 20. 32 they girded *s*. upon loins
2 K. 19. 2 he sent Eli. covered wi *s*.
1 Chr. 21. 6 elders of Is. clothed in *s*.
Neh. 9. 1 Is. assembled with *s*. on
Esth. 4. 1 Mord. put on *s*. wi. ashes
Job. 16. 15 I sewed *s*. on my skin
Ps. 69. 11 I made *s*. my garment
Isa. 3 24 stomacher, a girding of *s*.
Jer. 4. 8 gird you with *s*. and howl
Lam. 2. 10 they girded thems. wi. *s*.
Ezek. 7. 18 also gird thems. with *s*.
Dan. 9. 3 seek L. with *s*. and ashes
Joel 1. 8 like virgin girded with *s*.
Am. 8. 10 I will bring *s*. upon loins
Jonah 3. 5 peo. of Nineveh put on *s*.
Mat. 11. 21; Luke 10. 13 repent. in *s*.
Rev. 6. 12 sun became black as *s*.

Sacrifice (*n*.). *Slaughtered, offer-
  ing.*
Gen. 31. 54 Jac. offered *s*. on mount
Ex. 12. 27 it is *s*. of Lord's passover
Lev. 3. 3 he shall offer *s*. of peace
Num. 6. 17 he shall offer ram for *s*.
Deut. 32. 38 which did eat fat of *s*.
Josh. 22. 26 not for offerings nor *s*.
Judg. 6. 26 offer *s*. with the wood of
1 Sam. 1. 21 offer unto L. yearly *s*.

---

2 Sam. 15. 12 sent, while he offer. *s*
1 K. 8. 63 Sol. offered *s*. of peace
2 K. 5. 17 offer neither offer. nor *s*
1 Chr. 29. 21 they sac. *s*. unto Lord
2 Chr. 7. 1 peo. offered *s*. before L.
Ez. 9. 4 I sat until the evening *s*.
Neh. 12. 43 they off. *s*., and rejoiced
Ps. 4. 5 Offer the *s*. of righteousness
Prov. 15. 8 *s*. of wicked is abomina.
Eccl. 5. 1 than to give *s*. of fools
Isa. 34. 6 the Lord hath *s*. in Bozrah
Jer. 7. 21 Put your offerings unto *s*.
Ezek. 20. 28 they off. there their *s*.
Dan. 9. 27 he sh. cause *s*. and obla.
Hos. 6. 6 I desired mercy, not *s*.
Am. 4. 4 bring yo. *s*. every morning
Jonah 1. 16 men offered *s*. unto L.
Zeph. 1. 7 the L. hath prepared *s*.
Mal. 1. 8 And if ye offer blind for *s*.
Mat. 9. 13 I will have mercy, not *s*.
Mark 9. 49 every *s*. shall be salted
Luke 2. 24 offer a *s*. accor. to law
Acts 7. 41 they offered *s*. to idols
Rom. 12. 1 present your bodies *s*.
1 Cor. 8. 4 offered in *s*. unto idols
Eph. 5. 2 offering and *s*. to God
Phil. 2. 17 if I be offer. upon the *s*.
Heb. 5. 1 offer both gifts and *s*.
1 Pet. 2. 5 to offer up spiritual *s*.
R. V. In O. T. frequent changes to,
  offering, oblation

Sacrifice (*v*.). *To slaughter, offer-*
Ex. 3. 18 that we may *s*. to Lord
Lev. 9. 4 peace off. to *s*. before L.
Deut 16. 2 thou sh. *s*. the passover
Josh. 8. 31 they *s*. peace offering
Judg. 2. 5 they *s*. there unto Lord
1 Sam. 16. 5 I am come to *s*. to L.
2 Sam. 6. 13 David *s*. oxen and fatl.
1 K. 3. 2 the people *s*. in high places
2 K. 12. 3 peo. *s*. and burnt incense
1 Chr 21. 28 when David saw, he *s*.
2 Chr. 28. 23 he *s*. to g. of Damascus
Ez. 4. 2 we do *s*. unto him since
Neh. 4. 2 San. spake; will they *s*.?
Ps. 54. 6 I will freely *s*. unto thee
Eccl. 9. 2 things come to him th. *s*.
Isa. 65. 3 people that *s*. in gardens
Ezek. 16. 20 thou *s*. to be devoured
Hos. 8. 13 They *s*. flesh for sacrifice
Jonah 2. 9 I will *s*. unto thee with
Zech. 14. 21 all that *s*. shall come
Mal. 1. 14 *s*. unto L. corrupt thing
1 Cor. 5. 7 C. our passover is *s*. for
Rev. 2. 14 eat things *s*. unto idols

Sacrilege. R. V. *rob temples.*
Rom. 2. 22 dost thou commit *s*.?

Sad. *Rueful, morose, grieved.*
Gen. 40. 6 J. looked, they were *s*.
1 Sam. 1. 18 counten. no more *s*.
1 K. 21. 5 Why is thy spirit so *s*.
Neh. 2. 2 why is thy countenance *s*.
Ezek. 13. 22 whom I ha. not made *s*.
Mat. 6. 16 be not of *s*. countenance
Mark 10. 22 he was *s*. at the saying
Luke 24. 17 as ye walk, and are *s*.
R. V. Ezek. 13. 22 grieved; Mark
  10. 22 countenance fell

Saddle (*n*.). *Riding seat.*
Lev. 15. 9 wh. saddle he rideth upon

Saddle (*v*.). *Bind up, girth.*
Gen. 22. 3 Abrah. rose and *s*. ass
Num. 22. 21 And Balaam *s*. his ass
Judg. 19. 10 with him two asses *s*.
2 Sam. 19. 26 I will *s*. me an ass
1 K. 2. 40 Shimei *s*. his ass, and
2 K. 4. 24 she *s*. an ass, and said

Sadly. *Morosely.*
Gen. 40. 7 Wherefore look ye so *s*.

Sadness. *Gloom, grief.*
Eccl. 7. 3 for by *s*. of countenance

Safe. *Secure, in safety.*
1 Sam. 12. 11 and ye dwelled *s*.
2 Sam. 18. 29 Is the young man *s*.?
Job 21. 9 their houses *s*. from fear
Ps. 119. 117 hold me up, I sh. be *s*.
Prov. 18. 10 righteous run., and is *s*.
Isa. 5. 29 carry the prey away *s*.
Ezek. 34 27 shall be *s*. in the land
Luke 15. 27 he had received him *s*.
Acts 23. 24 they bring him *s*. to F.
Phil. 3. 1 to write, for you it is *s*.
R. V. Ezek. 34. 27 secure; 2 Sam.
  18. 29, 32 well with

Safeguard. *Ward, guard.*
1 Sam. 22. 23 with me thou be in *s*.

Safely. *Securely.*
Ps. 78. 53 And he led them on *s.*
Prov. 1. 33 who heark. sh. dwell *s.*
Isa. 41. 3 pursued, and passed *s.*
Hos. 2. 18 I will make them lie *s.*
Zech. 14. 11 Jerusalem shall be *s.*
Acts 16. 23 jailor to keep them *s.*
R. V. Prov. 1. 33 ; 3. 23 ; Ezek.
28. 26 ; 34. 25, 28 ; 38. 8, 11, 14 ;
39. 26 securely

Safety. *Security.*
Lev. 25. 18 ye shall dwell in *s.*
Deut. 33. 28 Israel shall dwell in *s.*
Job 11. 18 shall take thy rest in *s.*
Ps. 12. 5 I will set him in *s.* from
Prov. 11. 14 in mul. of counsel. is *s.*
Isa. 14. 30 needy sh. lie down in *s.*
Acts 5. 23 prison shut with all *s.*
1 Thes. 5. 3 shall say, Peace and *s.*
R. V. Job 3. 26 ease ; 24. 23 security ;
Prov. 21. 31 victory

Saffron. *Saffron, crocus.*
S. of S. 4. 14 spikenard and *s.*, cala.

Said. *See* **Say.**

Sail (*n.*). *Sail, sign, gear.*
Isa. 33. 23 they could not spread *s.*
Ezek. 27. 7 spreadest to be thy *s.*
Acts 27. 17 strak. *s.*, so were driven
R. V. Acts 27. 17 gear

Sail (*v.*). *Sail.*
Luke 8. 23 as they *s.*, he fell asleep
Acts 20. 3 as he was about to *s.*

Sailing. *Navigating.*
Acts 27. 9 *s.* was now dangerous
R.V. Acts 27.9 voyage ; 21. 2 crossing

Sailors. R. V. *mariners.*
Rev. 18. 17 and *s.* stood afar off

Saint. *Set apart, pious, holy.*
Deut. 33. 3 his *s.* are in thy hand
1 Sam. 2. 9 He will keep feet of *s.*
2 Chr. 6. 41 and let thy *s.* rejoice
Job 5. 1 to which of *s.* wilt turn?
Ps. 30. 4 Sing unto Lord, O ye *s.*
Prov. 2. 8 preserveth way of his *s.*
Dan. 7. 22 judgment was given to *s.*
Hos. 11. 12 Judah is faithful with *s.*
Zech. 14. 5 God sh. come, and all *s.*
Mat. 27. 52 man. *s.* which slept arose
Acts 9. 32 he came down to the *s.*
Rom. 1. 7 in Rome, called to be *s.*
1 Cor. 1. 2 sanctified, called to be *s.*
2 Cor. 1. 1 *s.* which are in Achaia
Eph. 1. 1 *s.* which are at Ephesus
Phil. 4. 21 Sal. every *s.* in C. Jesus
Col. 1. 26 is made manifest to *s.*
1 Thes. 3. 13 coming of L. with *s.*
2 Thes. 1. 10 be glorified in his *s.*
1 Tim. 5. 10 have washed the *s.* feet
Phile. 7 bowels of *s.* are refreshed
Heb. 6. 10 ye have ministered to *s.*
Jude 3. faith once delivered to *s.*
Rev. 8. 3 offer it with prayers of *s.*
R. V. Deut. 33. 2 ; 1 Sam. 2. 9 ; Job
5. 11 ; 15. 15 ; Ps. 89. 5, 7 ; Dan.
8. 13 ; Hos. 11. 12 ; Zech. 14. 5 ;
Jude 14 holy one, or ones ; Rev.
15. 3 ages

Saith. *See* **Say.**

Sake. *Purpose, regard, because of.*
Gen. 8. 21 nor curse gr. for man's *s.*
Ex. 18. 8 to Egypt for Israel's *s.*
Num. 25. 11 was zealous for my *s.*
1 Sam. 23. 10 destr. city for my *s.*
2 Sam. 5. 12 exalt kingd. for Is. *s.*
1 K. 8. 41 cometh for thy name's *s.*
Neh. 9. 31 for thy great mercies' *s.*
Job 19. 17 intreat. for children's *s.*
Ps. 23. 3 leadeth me for name's *s.*
Isa. 37. 35 for own *s.* and David's
Jer. 14. 7 do thou it for name's *s.*
Ezek. 20. 9 wrought for my nam. *s.*
Dan. 9. 17 shine on, for Lord's *s.*
Mat. 5. 11 evil ag. you for my *s.*
Mark 4. 17 persecution for word's *s.*
Luke 6. 22 for the Son of man's *s.*
John 12. 9 came not for Jesus' *s.*
Acts 9. 16 suffer for my name's *s.*
Rom. 4. 23 written for his *s.* alone
1 Cor. 4. 10 we are fools for C.'s *s.*
2 Cor. 4. 5 your serv. for Jesus' *s.*
Eph. 4. 32 G. for C's. *s.* hath forg.
Phil. 1. 29 also to suffer for his *s.*
1 Thes. 1. 5 for love's *s.*, 1 beseech
1 Pet. 2. 13 ; 1 John 2. 12 ; 2 John
2 ; 3 John 7 ; Rev. 2. 3

Sale. *A selling.*
Lev. 25. 27 count the years of *s.*
Deut. 18. 8 that which cometh of *s.*

Salt (*n. a.*). *Salt.*
Gen. 19. 26 she became pillar of *s.*
Lev. 2. 13 shalt thou season with *s.*
Num. 18. 19 it is a covenant of *s.*
Josh. 3. 16 the sea, even the *s.* sea
Judg. 9. 45 and sowed it with *s.*
2 Sam. 8. 13 smi. Syr. in val. of *s.*
2 K. 2. 20 cruse, and put *s.* therein
1 Chr. 18. 12 slew Ed. in val. of *s.*
2 Chr. 25. 11 Amaz. went to v. of *s.*
Ez. 6. 9 they have need of *s.*, wine
Job 6. 6 unsav. eaten without *s.*
Jer. 17. 6 in a *s.* land not inhabited
Ezek. 43. 24 priests cast *s.* on them
Zeph. 2. 9 Moab shall be as *s.* pits
Mat. 5. 13 Ye are *s.* of the earth
Mark 9. 5 Have *s.* in yourselves
Luke 14. 34 S. is good, but if the *s.*
Col. 4. 6 speech be season. with *s.*
Jas. 3. 12 yield *s.* water and fresh

Salt (*v.*). *To salt.*
Ezek. 16. 4 thou wast not *s.* at all
Mat. 5. 19 wherewith shall it be *s.*
Mark 9. 49 ev. one sh. be *s.* wi. fire
R. V. Mark 9. 49 ——.

Saltness. *Saltiness.*
Mark 9. 50 if salt. have lost his *s.*

Salutation. *Greeting, embrace.*
Mark 12. 38 scribes who love *s.*
Luke 1. 41 when Eliz. heard the *s.*
1 Cor. 16. 21 greet you, the *s.* of
Col. 4. 18 The *s.* by hand of me Paul
2 Thes. 3. 17 *s.* of P. wi. own hand

Salute. *Greet, embrace.*
Judg. 18. 15 Danites came and *s.*
1 Sam. 25. 14 D. sent messeng. to *s.*
2 Sam. 8. 10 sent his son to *s.* D.
2 K. 10. 13 we go to *s.* the children
Mat. 5. 47 if ye *s.* brethren only
Mark 15. 18 and began to *s.* him
Luke 10. 4 *s.* no man by the way
Acts 18. 22 when he *s.* the church
Rom. 16. 9 S. Urb. our helper in C.
1 Cor. 16. 19 Aquila and Priscil. *s.*
2 Cor. 13. 13 All the saints *s.* you
Phil. 4. 21 S. every saint in C. J.
Col. 4. 10 A. my fel. prisoner *s.* you
2 Tim. 4. 19 S. Prisca and Aquila
Tit. 3. 15 All with me *s.* thee
Phile. 23 There *s.* thee Epaphras
Heb. 13. 24 They of Italy *s.* you
1 Pet. 5. 13 church at Babylon *s.* you
3 John 14 Our friends *s.* thee
R. V. Judg. 18. 15 ask. of his welfare

Salvation. *Safety, ease.*
Gen. 49. 18 I have waited for thy *s.*
Ex. 14. 13 see the *s.* of the Lord
Deut. 32. 15 light. est. Rock of *s.*
1 Sam. 2. 1 because I rejoice in thy *s.*
2 Sam. 22. 51 He is the tower of S.
1 Chr. 16. 35 Save us, G. of our *s.*
2 Chr. 20. 17 see *s.* of Lord with you
Job 13. 16 He also shall be my *s.*
Ps. 3. 8 *s.* belongeth unto the Lord
Isa. 12. 2 Lord Jehovah is my *s.*
Jer. 3. 23 in the Lord is *s.* of Israel
Lam. 3. 16 and quietly wait for *s.*
Jonah 2. 9 S. is of the Lord
Mic. 7. 7 I will wait for God of *s.*
Hab. 3. 18 I joy in God of my *s.*
Zech. 9. 9 he is just and having *s.*
Luke 2. 30 eyes have seen thy *s.*
John 4. 22 worship, *s.* is of Jews
Acts 13. 26 to you is this *s.* sent
Rom. 1. 16 it is power of G. unto *s.*
2 Cor. 1. 6 your consolation and *s.*
Eph. 1. 13 heard gospel of your *s.*
Phil. 1. 19 this shall turn to my *s.*
1 Thes. 5. 8 helmet the hope of *s.*
2 Thes. 2. 13 chosen to *s.* thro. sanct.
Heb. 1. 14 who shall be heirs of *s.*
1 Pet. 1. 5 kept thro. faith unto *s.*
2 Pet. 3. 15 long suffer. of L. is *s.*
Jude 3 to write to you of com. *s.*
Rev. 19. 1 S., glory, honour, power
R. V. 1 Sam. 11. 13 ; 2 Sam. 22. 51 ;
Ps. 68. 20 deliverance ; 1 Sam. 19. 5
victory ; Jer. 3. 23 help ; 2 Cor.
1. 6 ——

Same. *Even he, it, they, etc.*
Gen. 19. 37 *s.* is father of Moabites
Lev. 23. 20 *s.* soul will I destroy
2 K. 8. 22 Lib. revolt. at *s.* time

Ez. 5. 16 then came *s.* Sheshbaz.
Ps. 75. 8 he poureth out of the *s.*
Ezek. 10. 16 *s.* wheels also turned
Dan. 7. 21 *s.* horn made war with
Mat. 13. 1 *s.* day went Jesus out
Mark 3. 35 *s.* is my bro. and sister
Luke 9. 48 least, *s.* sh. be greatest
John 1. 2 *s.* was in beg. with God
Acts 1. 11 *s.* Jesus, which is taken
Rom. 9. 17 *s.* purp. have I raised
1 Cor. 1. 10 be joined in *s.* mind
2 Cor. 2. 3 I wrote *s.* unto you, wh.
Eph. 6. 8 *s.* sh. he receive of Lord
Phil. 4. 2 that they be of *s.* mind
Jas. 3. 2 the *s.* is a perfect man and
1 Pet. 2. 7 *s.* is ma. head of corner
Rev. 3. 5 *s.* shall be clo. in white

Sanctification. *Setting apart, separation, devoted to.*
1 Cor. 1. 30 of G. is made to us *s.*
1 Thes. 4. 3 will of G., even yo. *s.*
2 Thes. 2. 13 chos. to salva. thro. *s.*
1 Pet. 1. 2 elect, thro. *s.* of the spirit

Sanctify. *To set apart, separate.*
Gen. 2. 3 G. blessed sev. day, and *s.*
Ex. 13. 2 S. unto me all firstborn
Lev. 20. 8 I am the Lord which *s.*
Num. 7. 1 *s.* tabernacle instrum.
Deut. 15. 19 thou sh. *s.* unto Lord
Josh. 7. 13 *s.* the people, and say
1 Sam. 7. 1 and *s.* Eleazar his son
1 Chr. 23. 13 sho *s.* most hol. things
2 Chr. 29. 5 *s.* house of Lord God
Neh. 3. 1 they *s.* it, and set up the
Job 1. 5 Job sent and *s.* them, and
Isa. 8. 13 *s.* Lord of hosts himself
Jer. 1. 5 before thou camest, I *s.*
Ezek. 36. 23 I shall be *s.* in you
Joel 2. 16 Gather peo... *s.* congrega.
Mat. 23. 17 or temple that *s.* gold
John 17. 17 *s.* them thro. thy truth
Acts 20. 32 inherit. among them *s.*
Rom. 15. 16 being *s.* by H. Ghost
1 Cor. 1. 2 to them *s.* in Christ J.
Eph. 5. 26 might *s.* and cleanse it
1 Thes. 5. 23 God of peace *s.* you
1 Tim. 4. 5 it is *s.* of G. and prayer
2 Tim. 2. 21 be vessel unto hon., *s.*
Heb. 2. 11 who are *s.* are all one
1 Pet. 3. 15 *s.* L. G. in your hearts
Jude 1 to them th. are *s.* by God
R. V. Gen. 2. 3 ; 2 Chr. 7. 16, 20
hallowed ; Deut. 5. 12 keep it
holy ; 1 Sam. 21. 5 be holy ; Isa
13. 3 consecrated ; Joel 1 beloved.

Sanctuary. *Place set apart.*
Ex. 25. 8 let them make me a *s.*
Lev. 12. 4 nor come into the *s.* un.
Num. 3. 28 keeping charge of the *s.*
Josh. 24. 26 oak that was by the *s.*
1 Chr. 22. 19 build ye *s.* of L. God
2 Chr. 26. 18 go out of the *s.* for
Neh. 10. 39 where are vessels of *s.*
Ps. 63. 2 as I have seen thee in the *s.*
Isa. 8. 14 and he shall be for a *s.*
Jer. 17. 12 throne is place of our *s.*
Lam. 4. 1 stones of *s.* are poured
Ezek. 11. 16 I be unto them as *s.*
Dan. 8. 11 place of *s.* was cast down
Am. 7. 9 *s.* of Is. shall be laid waste
Heb. 8. 2 minister of *s.*, and of tab.
R. V. Ezek. 45. 2 ; Heb. 9. 2 ; 13.
11 holy place

Sand. *Sand.*
Gen. 41. 49 Joseph gath. corn as *s.*
Ex. 2. 12 Egyptian, hid him in *s.*
Deut. 33. 19 suck treasures hid in *s.*
Josh. 11. 4 people, as *s.* on seashore
Judg. 7. 12 their camels were as *s.*
1 Sam. 13. 5 peo. as *s.* on seashore
2 Sam. 17. 11 all Israel be gath. as *s.*
1 K. 4. 20 as *s.* by sea for nultitude
Job 6. 3 it would be heavier than *s.*
Ps. 78. 27 fowls like as *s.* of the sea
Prov. 27. 3 stone is heavy, *s.* weighty
Isa. 10. 22 tho. thy people be as *s.*
Jer. 5. 22 placed *s.* for bound of sea
Hos. 1. 10 Israel shall be as the *s.*
Hab. 1. 9 shall gather captivity as *s.*
Mat. 7. 26 man built house on *s.*
Rom. 9. 27 chil. of Is. be as the *s.*
Heb. 11. 12 as *s.* which is by shore
Rev. 13. 1 I stood on *s.* of the sea

Sandal. *Sandal.*
Mark 6. 9 but be shod with *s.*, and
Acts 12. 8 gird thyself, gird thy *s.*

Sang. *See Sing.*
Sank. *See Sink.*
Sap. *Fat, life.*
Ps. 104. 16 trees of Lord full of *s.*
Sapphire. *Sapphire.*
Ex. 24. 10 paved work of *s.* stone
Job 28. 6 stones are the place of *s.*
S. of S. 5. 14 ivory overlaid with *s.*
Isa. 54. 11 lay foundations with *s.*
Lam. 4. 7 their polishing was of *s.*
Ezek. 10. 1 over them .. a *s.* stone
Rev. 21. 19 foundation of wall was *s.*
Sardine. R. V. *sardius.*
Rev. 4. 3 to look upon like a *s.* stone
Sardius. *Ruby, sardine.*
Ex. 28. 17 first row shall be a *s.*
Ezek. 28. 13 prec. sto. thy cover., *s.*
Rev. 21. 20 sixth, *s.* ; seventh, chrys.
Sardonyx. *Sardonyx.*
Rev. 21. 20 fifth, *s.* ; sixth, sardius
Sat. *See Sit.*
Satan. *Adversary.*
Job 1. 6 and *s.* came also among
See DICTIONARY.
Satiate. *Fill, satisfy.*
Jer. 31. 14 I will *s.* soul of priests
31. 25 I have *s.* my weary soul
46. 10 sh. be *s.* and made drunk
Satisfaction. R. V. *ransom.*
Num. 35. 31 sh. take no *s.* for life
Satisfy. *Fill, supply fully.*
Ex. 15. 9 lust be *s.* upon them
Lev. 26. 26 shall eat, and not be *s.*
Deut. 14. 29 and shall eat and be *s.*
Ps. 22. 26 meek shall eat and be *s.*
Prov. 12. 11 tilleth land shall be *s.*
Eccl. 1. 8 eye is not *s.* with seeing
Isa. 58. 11 *s.* thy soul is drought
Jer. 50. 10 that spoil her shall be *s.*
Lam. 5. 6 have given hand to be *s.*
Ezek. 7. 19 they shall not *s.* souls
Joel 2. 19 send corn, ye shall be *s.*
Am. 4. 8 drink, but they were not *s.*
Mic. 6. 14 shall eat, but not be *s.*
Hab. 2. 5 as death, cannot be *s.* but
Mark 8. 4 whence can man *s.* these
R. V. Prov. 12. 11 have plenty;
18. 20 filled
Satisfying. *Filling.*
Prov. 13. 25 righteous eateth to *s.*
Col. 2. 23 not in honour to the *s.*
R. V. Col. 2. 23 indulgence
Satyr. *Hairy thing, goat.*
Isa. 13. 21 owls shall dwell there, *s.*
34. 14 the *s.* shall cry to his fellow
Save (*prep. and conj.*). *Unless, except.*
Josh. 11. 13 burned none, *s.* Hazor
Mat. 11. 27 nei. know. the F. *s.* Son
Luke 18. 19 none good, *s.* one, God
John 6. 46 *s.* he which is of God he
Etc. etc.
Save (*v.*). *Keep alive, give safety.*
Gen. 12. 12 but they will *s.* thee al.
Ex. 14. 30 Lord *s.* Israel that day
Num. 31. 15 have ye *s.* all women
Deut. 20. 16 shalt *s.* alive nothing
Josh. 10. 6 come quickly, and *s.* us
Judg. 21. 14 gave wives they had *s.*
1 Sam. 27. 11 D. *s.* nei. man nor wo.
2 Sam. 3. 18 I will *s.* my people
1 K. 1. 12 thou mayest *s.* own life
2 K. 14. 27 he *s.* them from Jerobo.
1 Chr. 16. 35 *S.* us G. of our salva.
2 Chr. 32. 22 the Lord *s.* Hezekiah
Neh. 6. 11 go into the temple to *s.*
Job 5. 15 he *s.* the poor from sword
Ps. 6. 4 oh *s.* me for thy mercies'
Prov. 20. 22 wait on Lord, he sh. *s.*
Isa. 33. 22 Lord is King, he will *s.*
Jer. 15. 20 I am with thee to *s.* thee
Lam. 4. 17 nation that could not *s.*
Ezek. 13. 18 will ye *s.* souls alive
Hos. 1. 7 will *s.* them by Lord G.
Hab. 1. 2 even cry, thou wilt not *s.*
Zeph. 3. 19 will *s.* her that halteth
Zech. 10. 6 I will *s.* house of Jos.
Mat. 1. 21 he shall *s.* his people
Mark 8. 35 who. will *s.* life. sh. los.
Luke 7. 50 Thy faith has *s.* thee
John 12. 27 F., *s.* me fr. this hour
Acts 16. 30 what must I do to be *s.*
Rom. 5. 9 we shall be *s.* fr. wrath
1 Cor. 3. 15 he himself shall be *s.*
2 Cor. 2. 15 sweet savor in them *s.*
Eph. 2. 8 by grace are ye *s.* through

1 Thes. 2. 16 Gent., that they be *s.*
2 Thes. 2. 10 truth, they mi. be *s.*
1 Tim. 1. 15 J. ca. into world to *s.*
2 Tim. 1. 9 hath *s.*, and called us
Tit. 3. 5 *s.*, by wash of regeneration
Heb. 7. 25 he is able also to *s.* them
Jas. 4. 12 one lawgiver, able to *s.*
1 Pet. 3. 21 ev. baptism doth also *s.*
Jude 5 have *s.* people out of land
2 Pet. 2. 5 *s.* Noah, the eighth person
Rev. 21. 24 nations *s.*, walk in light
Saving. *Giving safety.*
Ps. 20. 6 with *s.* strength of hand
Heb. 11. 7 prepared ark to *s.* of
Rev. 2. 17 *s.* he that receiveth it
R. V. Ps. 28. 8 stronghold
Saviour. *Who saves, preserver,*
2 Sam. 22. 3 and my refuge, my *s.*
2 K. 13. 5 the Lord gave Israel a *s.*
Neh. 9. 27 thou gavest them *s.*, who
Ps. 106. 21 They forgat God their *s.*
Isa. 43. 3 G., Holy One of Is., thy *s.*
Jer. 14. 8 the hope of Israel, the *s.*
Hos. 13. 4 there is no *s.* beside me
Obad. 21 *s.* shall come up on Zion
Luke 1. 47 sp. rejoi. in God my *S.*
John 4. 42 this is the Christ, the *S.*
Acts 13. 23 God raised unto Is. a *S.*
Eph. 5. 23 Christ, he is *S.* of body
Phil. 3. 20 whence we look for a *S.*
1 Tim. 4. 10 who is *S.* of all men
2 Tim. 1. 10 man. by appear. of *S.*
Tit. 1. 4 and L. Jesus Christ our *S.*
2 Pet. 1. 11 kingd. of our L. and *S.*
1 John 4. 14 Fath. sent Son to be *S.*
Jude 25 the only wise God our *S.*
Savour. *Smell, odor, flavor.*
Gen. 8. 21 Lord smelled a sweet *s.*
Ex. 5. 21 ye have made *s.* abhorred
Jer. 17. 6 burn the fat for sweet *s.*
Num. 15. 3 make sweet *s.* unto L.
Ez. 6. 10 offer sacrifices of sweet *s.*
S. of S. 1. 3 *s.* of thy good ointment
Ezek. 20. 41 I accept you wi. sw. *s.*
Joel 2. 20 his ill *s.* shall come up
Mat. 5. 13 ; Luke 14. 34 if salt lost *s.*
2 Cor. 2. 15 we are sweet *s.* of Chr.
Eph. 5. 2 sacrifice to G. for sweet *s.*
Savourest. R. V. *mindest.*
Mat. 16. 23 ; Mark 8. 33 *s.* not th.
Savoury. *Tasteful.*
Gen. 27. 4 make me *s.* meat such as
27. 31 he had also made *s.* meat
Saw (*v.*). *See See.*
Saw (*n.*). *Saw.*
2 Sam. 12. 31 put them under *s.*, and
1 K. 7. 9 stones, sawed with *s.*
1 Chr. 20. 3 cut themselves with *s.*
Isa. 10. 15 shall *s.* magnify itself
Saw (*v.*). *To saw.*
1 K. 7. 9 costly stones *s.* with saw
Heb. 11. 37 they were *s.* asunder
Say. *Lift voice, speak.*
Gen. 1. 3 God *s.*, Let there be light
Ex. 32. 7 Lord *s.* unto Moses, go
Lev. 10. 19 A. *s.* unto M., Behold
Num. 14. 35 Lord *s.*, I will do it
Deut. 11. 21 as Lord of thy fathers *s.*
Josh. 5. 14 What *s.* my lord to serv.
Judg. 6. 27 did as the Lord had *s.*
1 Sam. 4. 20 women that stood by *s.*
2 Sam. 7. 20 what can Dav. *s.* more
1 K. 13. 7 king *s.* unto man of God
2 K. 1. 3 angel of Lord *s.* to Elijah
1 Chr 22. 11 build house, as he ha. *s.*
2 Chr. 18. 15 *s.* noth. but the truth
Ez. 8. 17 I told them what should *s.*
Esth. 6. 10 take apparel, as thou *s.*
Job 1. 5 Job *s.*, may be sons ha. si.
Ps. 2. 7 the Lord hath *s.* unto me
Eccl. 2. 15 I *s.* in my heart, that
Isa. 58. 9 and he sh. *s.*, Here I am
Jer. 23. 17 L. *s.* Ye sh. have peace
Ezek. 2. 8 son of man hear wh. I *s.*
Dan. 6. 21 Then *s.* Dan. unto king
Mat. 7. 4 how wilt thou *s.* to bro.
Mark 9. 6 he wist not what to *s.*
Luke 12. 19 I will *s.* to my soul
John 8. 26 I ha. man. things to *s.*
Acts 3. 22 ye hear what he shall *s.*
Rom. 7. 7 what *s.*? Is the law sin *?*
1 Cor. 14. 16 how shall be *s.* Amen
2 Cor. 12. 6 For I will *s.* the truth
Heb. 5. 11 have many things to *s.*
Jas. 4. 15 for that ye ought to *s.* If
the Lord will

R. V. Frequent changes to, speak, tell, etc.
Saying. *Word, speaking*
Gen. 37. 11 his fath. observed the *s*
Num. 14. 39 Moses told these *s.*
Deut. 1. 23 the *s.* pleased me well
1 Sam. 18. 8 the *s.* displeased Saul
2 Sam. 17. 4 *s.* pleased Absalom
1 K. 2. 38 Shimei said, *s.* is good
2 K. 5. 14 according to *s.* of man
1 Chr. 21. 19 D. went at *s.* of Gad
2 Chr. 13. 22 his *s.* are writ. in story
Esth. 1. 21 the *s.* pleased the king
Ps. 49. 4 open my dark *s.* on harp
Prov. 1. 6 underst. dark *s.* of wi.
Jonah 4. 2 was not this my *s.* when
Mat. 7. 24 whoso. heareth these *s.*
Mark 8. 32 he spake that *s.* openly
Luke 1. 29 she was troubled at *s.*
John 4. 37 herein is that *s.* true
Acts 6. 5 *s.* pleased whole multit.
Rom. 13. 9 comprehend. in this *s.*
1 Cor. 15. 54 be brought to pass *s.*
1 Tim. 1. 15 This is a faithful *s.*
2 Tim. 2. 11 It is a faithful *s.* : For
Tit. 3. 8 faithful *s.*, and th. things
Rev. 22. 6 *s.* faithful and true : and
R. V. Many changes, chiefly to, word, or words.
Scab. *Scab, scurvy.*
Lev. 13. 2 have in skin of flesh a *s.*
Deut. 28. 27 L. smite thee with *s.*
Isa. 3. 17 the L. will smite with a *s*
R. V. Deut. 28. 27 scurvy.
Scabbard. *Sheath.*
Jer. 47. 6 Put up thyself into thy *s.*
Scaffold. *Pulpit.*
2 Chr. 6. 13 S. had made braz. *s.*
Scale. (*v.*) *Climb up over.*
Prov. 21. 22 wise man *s.* city of mi
Scales. *Armor, scales.*
Lev. 11. 9 whatso. hath fins and *s.*
Deut. 14. 9 th. have *s.* sh. ye eat
Job 41. 15 His *s.* are his pride
Ezek. 29. 4 cause fish to stick to *s.*
Acts 9. 18 fell from his eyes as *s.*
Balances.
Isa. 40. 12 weighed mountains in *s.*
Scall. *Scall, scab.*
Lev. 13. 30 it is dry *s.*, ev. leprous
13. 31–37; 14. 54
Scalp. *Pate, top of head.*
Ps. 68. 21 G. shall wound hairy *s.*
Scant. *Lean, scanty.*
Mic. 6. 10 *s.* measure is abominable
Scapegoat. R. V. *for Azazel.*
Lev. 16. 8 other lot for the *s. g.*
16. 10, 26
Scarce. *Hardly.*
Gen. 27. 30 Jacob was yet *s.* gone
Acts 14. 18 these sayings *s.* restrain
R. V. Acts 27. 7 with difficulty
Scarcely. *Hardly.*
Rom. 5. 7 *s.* for righteous one die
1 Pet. 4. 18 if righteous *s.* be saved
Scarceness. *Scarcity.*
Deut. 8. 9 shall eat bread without *s.*
Scare. *Frighten.*
Job 7. 14 thou *s.* me with dreams
Scarlet. *Crimson, purple.*
Gen. 38. 28 and bound a *s.* thread
Ex. 25. 4 blue and purple, and *s.*
Lev. 14. 4 and cedar wood, and *s.*
Num. 4. 8 shall spread cloth of *s.*
Josh. 2. 18 bind line of *s.* thread
2 Sam. 1. 24 S. who cloth. you in *s.*
Prov. 31. 21 household clo. with *s*
S. of S. 4. 3 Thy lips like thread of *s*
Isa. 1. 18 though your sins be as *s.*
Lam. 4. 5 brought up in *s.* embrace
Dan. 5. 7 be clothed with *s.*, and
Nah. 2. 3 the valiant men are in *s.*
Mat. 27. 28 and put on him *s.* robe
Heb. 9. 19 took water, and *s.* wool
Rev. 17. 4 arrayed in purple and *s.*
R. V. Dan. 5. 7, 16, 29 purple
Scatter. *Spread, disperse.*
Gen. 11. 8 Lord *s.* them abroad from
Ex. 5. 12 the people were *s.* abroad
Lev. 26. 33 I will *s.* you am. heath.
Num. 16. 37 sh. thou the fire yonder
Deut. 4. 27 L. sh. *s.* you am. nations
1 Sam. 13. 11 I saw people were *s.*
2 Sam. 18. 8 the battle was *s.* over
1 K. 22. 17 said, I saw all Israel *s.*
2 K. 25. 5 and all his army were *s*

2 Chr. 18. 16 did see all Israel s.
Neh. 1. 8 I will s. you abroad, am.
Esth. 3. 8 There is certain people s.
Job 37. 11 he s. his bright cloud
Ps. 18. 14 he sent out arrows and s.
Prov. 11. 24 that s., yet increaseth
Isa. 41. 16 whirlwind shall s. them
Jer. 10. 21 their flocks shall be s.
Ezek. 5. 10 remnant of thee I s.
Dan. 4. 14 hew down tree, s. fruit
Joel 3. 2 whom they have s among
Nah. 3. 18 people is s. on mountain
Hab. 3. 14 came as whirlwind to s.
Zech. 1. 19 horns which s. Judah
Mat. 12.30 th. gath. not with me s.
Luke 1. 51 he hath s. the proud
John 10. 12 wolf catcheth, and s.
Acts 8. 1 they were all s. abroad
Jas. 1. 1 twelve tribes which are s.
1 Pet. 1. 1 strangers s. thro. Pont.
R. V. 2 Sam. 18. 8; Job 37. 1
spread; Ps. 60. 1 broken down;
Prov. 20. 26 winnoweth; Isa. 18. 2
tall; 30. 30 a blast; Dan. 12. 2
breaking in pieces; Ezek. 12. 15;
Acts. 5. 36 disperse; Jas. 1. 1; 1
Pet. 1. 1 the Dispersion

Scent. *Smell, memory.*
Job 14. 9 through s. of water bad
Jer. 48. 11 his s. is not changed
Hos. 14. 7 s. shall be as the wine

Sceptre. *Reed, rod, staff, insignia of power.*
Gen. 49. 10 s. sh. not depart fr. Jud.
Num. 24. 17 s. shall rise out of Isra.
Esth. 5. 2 king held out to Esther s.
Ps. 45. 6 s. of thy kingdom is right.
Isa. 14. 5 Lord hath broken the s.
Ezek. 19. 11 she had rods for the s.
Am. 1. 5 cut off him that holdeth s.
Zech. 10. 11 s. of Egypt shall depart
Heb. 1. 8 s. of righteousness is the s.

Schism. *Rent, division.*
1 Cor. 12. 25 there should be no s.

Scholar. *One taught.*
1 Chr. 25. 8 as well teacher as s.
Mal. 2. 12 Lord will cut off the s.
R. V. Mal. 2. 12 that answereth

School. *School.*
Acts 19. 9 disputing daily in the s.

Schoolmaster. R. V. *tutor.*
Gal. 3. 24, 25 the law was our s.

Science. *Knowledge.*
Dan. 1. 4 in wisd., understanding s.
1 Tim. 6. 20 avoid. oppositions of s.
R. V. 1 Tim. 6. 20 knowledge

Scoff. *Deride.*
Hab. 1. 10 they shall s. at the kings

Scoffer. R. V. *mocker.*
2 Pet. 3. 3 shall come in last days s.

Scorch. *Wither, parch.*
Mat. 13. 6; Mark 4. 6 they were s.
Heb. 16. 8 power given to s. men

Scorn (n.). *Contempt, disdain.*
2 K. 19. 21 and laughed thee to s.
Esth. 3. 6 s. to lay hands on Mord.
Job 22. 19 innocent laugh. th. to s.
Ps. 22. 7; Isa. 37. 22; Ezek. 23. 32
Hab. 1. 10 the princes shall be a s.
R. V. Job 12. 4 laughing stock;
Hab. 1. 10 derision

Scorn (v.). *Deride.*
Job 39. 7 He s. multitude of the city
Prov. 3. 24 he s., but giveth grace
Ezek. 16. 31 harlot, in that thou s.
R. V. Prov. 19. 28 mocketh at

Scorner. *Who scorns or scoffs.*
Prov. 1. 22 s. delight in scorning
Isa. 29. 20 and the s. is consumed
Hos. 7. 5 he stretched hand with s.

Scornful. *Scoffing, derisive.*
Ps. 1. 1 nor sitteth in the seat of s.
Prov. 29. 8 s. bring. city into snare
Isa. 28. 14 hear word of Lord, ye s.

Scorning. *Scoffing.*
Job 34. 7 Job, who drink. s. like wa.
Ps. 123. 4 filled with s. of those at
Prov. 1. 22 s. delight in their scorn.

Scorpion. *Scorpion.*
Deut. 8. 15 through wilder. where s.
1 K. 12. 11 I will chastise you with s.
2 Chr. 10. 11 will chas. you with s.
Ezek. 2. 6 thou dost dwell among s.
Luke 11. 12 will he offer him s.?
Rev. 9. 3 as s. of earth have power

Scoured. *Cleaned.*

Lev. 6. 28 it shall be s. and rinsed

Scourge (n.). *Scourge, whip.*
Josh. 23. 13 s. in sides, and thorns
Job 5. 21 thou sh. be hid from s.
Isa. 10. 26 Lord shall stir up a s.
John 2. 15 made s. of small cords

Scourge (v.). *To whip, flog.*
Lev. 19. 20 maid, she shall be s.
Mat. 10. 17 will s. you in synagog.
Mark 10. 34 shall mock him, and s.
Luke 18. 33 s., and put him to d.
John 19. 1 Pil. took J., and s. him
Acts 22. 24 shall be examined by s.
Heb. 11. 36 others had trial of s.
R. V. Lev. 19. 20 punished

Scrabble. *Scribble.*
1 Sam. 21. 13 s. on doors of gate

Scrape. *Scrape.*
Lev. 14. 41 cause house to be s.
Job 2. 8 Job took him potsherd to s.
Ezek. 26. 4 I will also s. her dust

Screech Owl. R. V. *night monster.*
Isa. 34. 14 s. o. also shall rest there

Scribe. *Writer, numberer, clerk.*
2 Sam. 8. 17 Seraiah was the s.
1 K. 4. 3 Elihoreph and Ahiah s.
2 K. 12. 10 k.'s s. and priest came
1 Chr. 2. 55 the families of the s.
2 Chr. 34. 13 of Lev. there were s.
Ez. 7. 6 Ezra, he was a ready s.
Neh. 8. 1 they spake to Ez. the s.
Esth. 3. 12 then were k.'s s. called
Isa. 33. 18 where is the s.? where
Jer. 36. 32 gave it to Baruch the s.
Mat. 15. 1 Then came to Jesus s.
Mark 1. 22 he taught them not as s.
Luke 5. 21 s. and Pharisees began
John 8. 3 s. and Pharisees brought
Acts 4. 5 s. gath. against apostles
1 Cor. 1. 20 where is the s.? where
R. V. Isa. 33. 18 that counted;
Mat. 23. 14; 26. 3; Luke 11. 44

Scrip. *Bag, purse, wallet.*
1 Sam. 17. 40 D. put stones in s.
Mat. 10. 10 nor s. for your journey
Mark 6. 8; Luke 9. 3; 10. 4
Luke 22. 25 I sent you without s.
R. V. Mat. 10. 10; Mark 6. 8;
Luke 9. 3; 10. 4; 22. 35, 36 wallet

Scripture. *Writing, thing written.*
Dan. 10. 21 which is noted in the s.
Mat. 21. 42 Did ye never read s.
Mark 12. 24 ye know not the s., nei.
Luke 4. 21 This day is s. fulfilled
John 5. 39 Search the s.; for in th.
Acts 1. 16 this s. must needs have
Rom. 4. 3 For what saith the s.?
1 Cor. 15. 3 C died according to s.
Gal. 3. 8 s., foreseeing that God
1 Tim. 5. 18 s. saith, Th. sh. not m.
2 Tim. 3. 16 s. is given by inspira.
Jas. 2. 8 royal law according to s.
1 Pet. 2. 6 it is contained in the s.
2 Pet. 1. 20 no s. is of priv. interp.
R. V. Dan. 10. 21 writing; 2 Tim.
3. 15 holy writing; Mark 15. 28 —

Scroll. *Roll, book.*
Isa. 34. 4 heav. sh. be rolled as s.
Rev. 6. 14 heaven departed as a s.

Scull. *See* **Skull.**

Scum. R. V. *rust.*
Ezek. 24. 6 woe to pot whose s. is
24. 12 s. went not forth out of her

Scurvy. *Scurvy.*
Lev. 21. 20 not appr. man th. be s.

Sea. *Sea.*
Gen. 1. 10 the waters called he S.
Ex. 10. 19 cast them into the Red s.
Lev. 11. 9 whatsoever hath fins in s.
Num. 34. 6 shall have s. for border
Deut. 3. 17 fr. Chin. to s. of plain
Josh. 15. 5 east border was salt s.
Judg. 7. 12 as sand of s. for multi.
1 Sam. 13. 5 peo. as sand on the s.
2 Sam. 22. 16 channels of s. appear
1 K. 5. 9 convey them by s. in floats
2 K. 14. 25 he restored coast to s.
1 Chr. 18. 8 Sol. made the brazen s.
2 Chr. 4. 6 the s. was for the priests
Ez. 3. 7 bring cedar trees to the s.
Neh. 9. 11 went through midst of s.
Esth. 10. 1 and upon isles of the s.
Job 7. 12 Am I a s., or a whale, that

Ps. 24. 2 he ha. founded it upon s.
Prov. 8. 29 he gave to s. his decree
Eccl. 1. 7 the rivers run into the s.
Isa. 5. 30 roar, like roaring of s.
Jer. 51. 42 s. is come upon Babylon
Lam. 2. 13 for thy breach is like s.
Ezek. 26. 3 s. cause waves to come
Dan. 7. 3 beasts came up from s.
Hos. 4. 3 fishes of s. be taken away
Joel 2. 20 with face toward east s.
Am. 5. 8 calleth for waters of the s.
Jonah 1. 4 Lord sent wind into s.
Mic. 7. 12 shall come from s. to s.
Nah. 1. 4 He rebuketh the s., and
Hab. 3. 15 Thou didst walk thro. s.
Zeph. 1. 3 I will consum. fish. of s.
Hag. 2. 6 will shake heaven and s.
Zech. 9. 10 dominion from s. to s.
Mat. 8. 26 he arose and rebuked s.
Mark 1. 16 as he walked by the s.
Luke 17. 6 be thou planted in the s.
John 6. 1 Jesus went over s. of Gal.
Acts 27. 38 cast wheat into the s.
Rom. 9. 27 number be as sand of s.
1 Cor. 10. 1 fathers passed through s.
2 Cor. 11. 26 in perils in the s. in
Heb. 11. 29 by faith pass. thro. R. s.
Jas. 1. 6 like waves of the s. driven
Jude 13 waves of the s., foaming
Rev. 4. 6 before the throne was a s.

Seafaring. *Sea going.*
Ezek. 26. 17 inhabited of s. men

Sea Monsters. R. V. *jackals.*
Lam. 4. 3 s. m. drawn out the breath

Seal (n.). *Signet, impression.*
1 K. 21. 8 sealed them with his s.
Job. 38. 14 turned as clay to the s.
1 Cor. 9. 2 s. of mine apostleship
2 Tim. 2. 19 having s., Lord know.
Rev. 6. 1 Lamb opened one of s.

Seal (v.). *Close up, impress.*
Deut. 32. 34 Is not this s. among
1 K. 21. 8 she wrote letters, and s.
Neh. 10. 1 those that s. were Neh.
Esth. 8. 8 s. it with the king's ring
Job 14. 17 My transgr. is s. in bag
S. of S. 4. 12 spring shut, fountain s.
Isa. 8. 16 bind testimony, s. law
Jer. 32. 10 subsc. evid., and s. it
Ezek. 28. 12 thou s. sum of wisd.
Dan. 12. 9 words are closed and s.
Mat. 27.66 ma. sepulc. sure, s. stone
John 6. 27 him hath God the F. s.
2 Cor. 1. 22 hath s. us, and given
Eph. 1. 13 ye were s. with Hol. Sp.
Rev. 22. 10 S. not sayings of proph.
R. V. Rev. 7. 5–8 —

Seam. *Seam.*
John 19. 23 the coat was without s.

Search (n.). *Seeking, inquiry.*
Deut. 13. 14 make s., and ask diligently
Ez. 6. 1 s. was made in h. of the rolls
Job 8. 8 prepare thyself to the s.
Ps. 64. 6 accomplish a diligent s.
Jer. 2. 34 not found it by secret s.
R. V. Job 38, 16 recesses

Search (v.). *Seek, inquire.*
Gen. 31. 34 Laban s. all the tent
Lev. 27. 33 not s. whe. it be good
Num. 10. 33 to s. out resting place
Deut. 1. 22 they sh. s. out the land
Josh. 2. 2 came men to s. country
Judg. 18. 2 they said, Go, s. land
1 Sam. 23. 23 that I will s. him out
2 Sam. 10. 3 city, and spy it out
1 K. 20. 6 they sh. s. thine house
2 K. 10. 23 S., look there be here
1 Chr. 19. 3 his servants came to s.
Job 39. 8 he s. after green thing
Ps. 64. 6 They s. out iniquities
Prov. 2. 4 s. for her as for treasures
Eccl. 7. 25 to s. and seek wisdom
Jer. 17. 10 I the Lord, s. the heart
Lam. 3. 40 let us s. and try our ways
Ezek. 34. 11 I will both s. my sheep
Am. 9. 3 will s. and take them out
Obad. 6 how things of Es. s. out
Zeph. 1. 12 s. Jerus. with candles
Mat. 2. 8 s. dil. for young child
John 5. 39 S. the scriptures, for in th.
Acts 17. 11 Bereans s. the scriptures
Rom. 8. 27 that s. hearts knoweth
1 Cor. 2. 10 the spirit s. all things
1 Pet. 1. 10 the prophets have s. dil.
Rev. 2. 23 I am he which s. reins
R. V. Gen. 31. 34, 37 felt about;

Num. 10. 33; Deut. 1. 33 seek;
Num. 13. 2, 21, 32; 14. 6, 7, 34, 36,
38; Deut. 1. 24 spy or spied out;
Acts 17. 11 examining
Searching. *Spying, seeking.*
Num. 13. 25 return. from *s.* of land
Judg. 5. 16 divisions of Reuben *s.*
Job 11. 7 canst thou by *s.* find G. ?
Prov. 20. 27 *s.* inw. parts of belly
Isa. 40. 28 no *s.* of his understand.
1 Pet. 1. 11 *s.* wh. time Sp. of C.
R. V. Num. 13. 25 spying out
Seared. R. V. *branded in.*
1 Tim. 42 consc. *s.* with hot iron
Season (*n.*). *Time, appointed or
set period, division of year*
Gen. 1. 14 let them be signs, for *s.*
Ex. 18. 26 judged people at all *s.*
Lev. 26. 4 I will give you rain in *s.*
Num. 9. 2 keep passov. at appoi. *s.*
Deut. 16. 6 at *s.* thou came. forth
Josh. 24. 7 ye dw. in wild. long *s.*
2 K. 4. 16 this *s.*, embrace a son
1 Chr. 21. 29 altar, at that *s.* at Gib.
2 Chr. 15. 3 for long *s.* Israel hath
Job 5. 26 as corn cometh in his *s.*
Ps. 1. 3 that bringeth fruit in his *s.*
Prov. 15 23 word spo. in *s.*, good
Eccl. 10. 17 princes eat in due *s.*
Ezek. 34. 26 cau. showers to co. in *s.*
Dan. 2. 21 he chang. times and *s.*
Hos. 2. 9 and wine in *s.* thereof
Mat. 21. 41 sh. render fruits in *s.*
Mark 12. 2 at *s.* he sent to husb.
Luke 4. 13 devil departed for a *s.*
John 5. 4 angel went at certain *s.*
Acts 24. 25 when I ha. conveni. *s.*
2 Cor. 7. 8 sorry, though but for a *s.*
Gal. 6. 9 for in due *s.* we shall reap
1 Thes. 5. 1 of *s.*, ye ha. no need
2 Tim. 4. 2 be instant in *s.*, out of
Phile. 15 he departed for a *s.*, that
Heb. 11. 25 pleas. of sin for a *s.*
1 Pet. 1. 6 rejoice, though for a *s.*
Rev. 6. 11 should rest yet a little *s.*
R. V. Josh. 24. 7 days; 1 Chr. 21,
29; Luke 23. 8; Acts 20. 18; Rev.
6. 11; 20. 3 time; Acts 19. 22; 1
Pet. 1. 6 while; John 5. 4 ——
Season (*v.*). *Salt, prepare.*
Lev. 2. 13 shalt thou *s.* with salt
Mark 9. 50 wherewith will ye *s.* **it**
Luke 14. 34 wherew. sh. it be *s.* ?
Col. 4. 6 speech be with grace, *s.*
Seat (*n.*). *Sitting place, throne.*
Judg. 3. 20 Eg. rose out of his *s.*
1 Sam. 1. 9 Eli sat upon a *s.* by a post
2 Sam. 23. 8 Tachmonite sat in *s.*
1 K. 2. 19 a *s.* set for king's mother
Esth. 3. 1 set his *s.* ab. all princes
Job 29. 7 prepared my *s.* in street
Ps. 1. 1 nor sitteth in *s.* of scornful
Prov. 9. 14 she sit. at door on a *s.*
Ezek. 28. 2 I sit in the *s.* of God
Am. 6. 3 and cau. *s.* of viol. to come
Mat. 23. 2 Phar. sit in Moses' *s.*
Mark 11. 15 Jesus overthrew the *s.*
Luke 11. 43 ye love uppermost *s.*
Rev. 2. 13 dwell., where Satan's *s.*
R. V. K. 2. 19; Luke 1. 52; Rev.
2. 13; 4. 4; 11. 16; 13. 2; 16. 10
throne or thrones
Seated (*v.*). R. V. *reserved.*
Deut. 33. 21 lawgiver, was he *s.*, and
Second. *Next after first.*
Gen. 1. 8 ev. and mor. were *s.* day
Ex. 2. 13 and when he went out *s.* d.
Lev. 5. 10 offer *s.* for burnt offer.
Num. 10. 6 wh. ye blow alarm *s.* t.
Josh. 6. 14 *s.* day compassed city
Judg. 20. 25 Benj. went forth *s.* day
1 Sam. 20. 34 eat no meat *s.* of mo.
2 Sam. 14. 29 Absa., he se a *s.* time
1 K. 6. 1 month of Zif is *s.* month
2 K. 9. 19 he went *s.* on horseback
1 Chr. 15. 18 brethren of *s.* d gr e
2 Chr. 30. 2 keep passover *s.* month
Ez. 3. 8 *s.* mo. began Zerubbabel
Neh. 8. 13 on *s.* day were gathered
Esth. 2. 14 she returned to *s.* house
Job 42. 14 the name of *s.*, Kezia
Eccl. 4. 8 alone and there is not a *s.*
Isa. 11. 11 L. sh. set his hand *s.* ti.
Jer. 1. 13 word of L. came a time
Ezek. 10. 14 *s.* face was f. of man
Dan. 7. 5 a *s.*, like to a bear, and it

Jonah 3. 1 word cam. to J. *s.* time
Hag. 1. 15 In *s.* year of Darius the
Zeph. 1. 10 an howling from the *s.*
Zech. 6. 2 in *s.* char. black horses
Mat. 22. 39 and the *s.* is like unto it
Mark 14. 72 *s.* time the cock crew
Luke 20. 30 *s.* took her to wife, and
John 4. 54 This is *s.* miracle that
Acts 10. 15 voice spake a *s.* time
1 Cor. 15. 47 the *s.* man is the Lord
2 Cor. 1. 15 might have a *s.* benefit
Tit. 3. 10 first and *s.* admonition
Heb. 9. 28 ap. *s.* time without sin
2 Pet. 3. 1 *s.* epistle, I now write
Rev. 2. 11 not be hurt of *s.* death
Secondarily. *Second.*
1 Cor. 12. 28 God hath *s.* prophets
Secret. *Hidden, thing hidden.*
Gen. 49. 6 come not into their *s.*
Deut. 29. 29 *s.* things belong to L.
Judg. 3. 19 I have a *s.* errand unto
1 Sam. 19. 2 abide in a *s.* place, and
Job. 15. 8 Hast heard the *s.* of God ?
Ps. 18. 11 made dark. his *s.* place
Prov. 9. 17 bread eat. in *s.* is pleas.
Eccl. 12. 14 judgment, wi. ev. *s.* th.
S. of S. 2. 14. in *s.* places of stairs
Isa. 45. 19 I have not spoken in *s.*
Jer. 13. 17 soul should weep in *s.* p.
Lam. 3. 10 and as a lion in *s.* places
Ezek. 7. 22 sh. pollute my *s.* place
Dan. 2. 9 *s.* was revealed to Daniel
Am. 3. 7 revealeth *s.* to servants
Mat. 6. 4 That alms may be in *s.*
Mark 4. 22 neither anything kept *s.*
Luke 8. 17 noth. is *s.* that sh. not
John 7. 10 he went, as it were in *s.*
Rom. 216 G. sh. judges *s.* of men
1 Cor. 14. 25 thus are *s.* of heart ma.
Eph. 5. 12 thi. done of them in *s.*
R. V. Gen. 49. 6 council; Judg.
13. 18 wonderful; Job 40. 13; Ps.
19. 12; Prov. 27. 5; Eccl. 12. 14;
Mat. 13. 35 hidden; Ps. 10. 8; 27.
5; 31. 20; S. of S. 2. 14 covert;
Ps. 18. 11 hiding; Job 20. 26
treasures; Mat. 24. 26 inner;
Luke 11. 33 cellar.
Secretly. *Hiddenly, covertly.*
Gen. 31. 27 wheref. did. th. flee *s.*
Deut. 27. 24 he that smi. neigh. *s.*
Josh. 2. 1 Josh. sent men to spy *s.*
1 Sam. 18. 22 Commune with D. *s.*
2 Sam. 12. 12 For thou didst it *s.*
2 K. 17. 9 did *s.* things not right
Job. 31. 27 heart ha. been *s.* enticed
Ps. 10. 6 He lieth in wait *s.* as a lion
Jer. 38. 16 Zed. the king sware *s.*
Hab. 3. 14 to devour the poor *s.*
John 11. 28 called M. her sister *s.*
R. V. 1 Sam. 23. 9—— ; Ps. 10. 9
the covert
Sect *Choice, party.*
Acts 5. 17 which is *s.* of Sadducees
15. 5; 24. 5; 26. 5; 28. 22
Secure (*a.*). *Safe, confident.*
Judg. 8. 11 smote, the host was *s.*
Job 11. 18 thou shalt be *s.*, bec.
Secure (*v.*). R. V. *rid you of care.*
Mat. 28. 14 will persua., and *s.* you
Securely. *Safely, confidently.*
Prov. 3. 29 seeing he dwelleth *s.*
Mic. 2. 8 pass by *s.* as men averse
Security. *Enough.*
Acts 17. 9 when they had taken *s.*
Sedition. *Rising up.*
Ez. 4. 15 they ha. moved *s.* in city
Luke 23. 19 for *s.* made in the city
Acts 24. 5 mover of *s.* among Jews
Gal. 5. 20 works of the flesh are, *s.*
R. V. Luke 23. 19; Acts 24. 5 in-
surrection; Gal. 5. 20 divisions
Seduce. *Make to err, lead astray*
2 K. 21. 9 Manasseh *s.* them to do
Prov. 12. 26 way of the wicked *s.*
Isa. 19. 13 they have also *s.* Egypt
Ezek. 13. 10 they have *s.* my people
Mark 13. 22 false proph's rise to *s.*
1 Tim. 4. 1 giving heed to *s.* spir.
1 John 2. 26 concer. them that *s.*
Rev. 2. 20 Jezebel to *s.* my serv.
R. V. Isa. 19. 13; Mark 13. 22; 1
John 2. 26 go or lead astray
Seducers. R. V. *impostors.*
2 Tim. 3. 13 and *s.* shall wax worse
and worse

See. *See, behold, look, consider,
perceive, discern, know.*
Gen. 1. 4 God *s.* the light, was good
Ex. 24. 11 *s.* God, and did eat and dr.
Lev. 9. 24 when peo. *s.*, they shout.
Num. 13. 18 *s.* the land, what it is
Deut. 1. 28 we have *s.* Anakims
Josh. 3. 3 when ye *s.* ark of coven.
Judg. 1. 24 spies *s.* man co. forth
Ruth 2. 18 *s.* wh. she had gleaned
1 Sam. 3. 2 eyes dim. he co. not *s.*
2 Sam. 6. 16 *s.* king David leaping
1 K. 22. 17 I *s.* Israel scattered upon
2 K. 2. 12 And he *s.* him no more
1 Chr. 19. 10 Joab *s.* battle was set
2 Chr. 9. 3 Sheba had *s.* the wisdom
Ez. 3. 12 that had *s.* the first house
Neh. 4. 11 shall not know, nei. *s.*
Esth. 3. 5 H. *s.* Mord. bowed not
Job 5. 3 ha. *s.* foolish taking root
Ps. 34. 8 *s.* that the Lord is good
Prov. 26. 12 *S.* thou a man wise in
Eccl. 1. 8 eye is not satisfied with *s.*
S. of S. 7. 12 *s.* if the vine flourish
Isa. 6. 1 *s.* also L. siiting on throne
Jer. 2. 31 *s.* ye word of the Lord
Lam. 1. 11 *s.*, O L., and consider
Ezek. 1. 27 I *s.* as colour of amber
Dan. 8. 15 I Dan., had *s.* the vision
Hos. 5. 13 When Eph. *s.* his sickness
Joel 2. 28 your young men shall *s.*
Am. 6. 2 Pass ye to Calneh and *s.*
Jonah 3. 10 G. *s.* their works, that
Mic. 6. 9 the man of wisdom shall *s.*
Hab. 3. 10 the mountains *s.* thee
Zeph. 3. 15 thou sh. not *s.* evil more
Hag. 2. 3 and how do ye *s.* it now ?
Zech. 1. 8 I *s.*, behold man riding
Mal. 1. 5 your eyes shall *s.*, and
Mat. 2. 2 have *s.* his star in the east
Mark 1. 10 he *s.* heavens opened
Luke 2. 30 eyes ha. *s.* thy salvation
John 1. 33 *s.* the spirit descending
Acts 2. 31 nei. flesh did *s.* corruption
Rom. 1. 11 I long to *s.* you, that
1 Cor. 2. 9 eye hath not *s.*, nor ear
Gal. 1. 19 other apostles *s.* I none
Phil. 2. 28 when ye *s.* him again, ye
Col. 2. 1 have not *s.* my face in flesh
1 Thes. 2. 17 endeav. the more to *s.*
1 Tim. 6. 16 whom no man hath *s.*
2 Tim. 1. 4 Gr. desiring to *s.* thee
Heb. 11. 23 *s.* he was a proper child
Jas. 5. 11 have *s.* end of the Lord
1 Pet. 1. 8 having not *s.*, ye love
1 John 4. 12 No man hath *s.* God
3 John 14 trust I shall short. *s.* thee
Rev. 1. 7 every eye shall *s.* him
Seed. *Seed, progeny.*
Gen. 1. 11 whose *s.* is upon earth
Ex. 16. 31 it was like coriander *s.*
Lev. 11. 38 if water be put upon *s.*
Num. 24. 7 shall be in many waters
Deut. 10. 15 chose th. *s.* after them
Josh. 24. 3 multiplied *s.*, ga. Isaac
Ruth 4. 12 of L. Lord shall give
1 Sam. 8. 15 he will take tenth of *s.*
2 Sam. 7. 12 I will set up thy *s.*
1 K. 11. 14 he was of the king's *s.*
2 K. 7. 20 L rejected *s.* of Israel
1 Chr. 6. 13 O ye *s.* of Israel
2 Chr. 22. 10 she destroyed *s.* royal
Ez. 2. 59 they co. not show their *s.*
Neh. 9. 2 *s.* of Israel separated
Esth. 6. 13 If Mor. be of *s.* of Jews
Job 21. 8 their *s.* is established in
Ps. 18. 50 to D., and his *s.* forever.
Prov. 11. 21 *s.* of right. sh. be deliv.
Eccl. 11. 6 In morning sow thy *s.*
Isa. 6. 13 holy *s.* shall be substance
Jer. 2. 21 I planted thee a right *s.*
Ezek. 17. 5 he took of *s.* of land
Dan. 2. 43 they ming. thems. with *s.*
Am 9. 13 sh. overtake that soweth *s.*
Joel 1. 17 *s.* is rotten under clods
Hag. 2. 19 Is the *s.* yet in the barn ?
Zech. 8. 12 the *s.* sh be prosperous
Mal. 2. 3 I will corrupt your *s.*, and
Mat. 13. 2 th. sow. good *s.* is Son
Mark 4. 31 like grain of mustard *s.*
Luke 1. 55 to A., to his *s.* forever
John 7. 42 Chr. com. of *s.* of David
Acts 13. 23 of this man's *s.* ha. God
Rom. 9. 7 In Israel thy *s.* be called
1 Cor. 15. 38 to ev. *s.* his own body
2 Cor. 11. 22 are they *s.* of Abrah.

Gal. 3. 17 to A. and *s.* were promis.
2 Tim. 2. 8 Remem. L.at J. C. of *s.*
Heb. 11. 18 in Is. thy *s.* be called
1 Pet. 1.23 born, not of corruptible *s.*
1 John 3. 9 his *s.* remaineth in him
Rev. 12. 17 ma. war wi. remnant of *s.*

Seeing. *After that, since, see.*
Ex. 23. 9 *s.* ye w　strangers in la.
Judg. 19. 23 *s.* this man is come
1 K. 1. 48 mine eyes even *s.* it
Job 14. 5 *s.* his days are determined
Prov. 20. 12 the hearing ear, *s.* eye
Isa. 33. 15 shutteth eyes from *s.* evil
Ezek. 21. 4 *s.* I will cut from thee
Dan. 2. 47 *s.* thou couldest reveal
Luke 1. 34 *s.* I know not a man
Acts 2. 15 *s.* it is but third hour
Rom. 3. 30 *s.* it is one God which
1 Cor. 14. 16 *s.* he understands not
2 Cor. 11. 18 *S.* man. glo. aft. flesh
2 Thes. 1. 6 *S.* it is righteous thing
Heb. 5. 11 *s.* ye are dull of hearing

Seek. *Search, inquire.*
Gen. 37. 16 said, I *s.* my brethren
Ex. 4. 24 met and Lord *s.* to kill him
Lev. 19. 31 neither *s.* after wizards
Num. 15. 39 *s.* not after own heart
Deut. 4. 29 thou shalt *s.* the Lord
Josh. 2. 22 pursuers *s.* them through.
Judg. 14. 4 *s.* occasion against Phil.
Ruth 3. 1 shall I not *s.* rest for thee
1 Sam. 9. 3 Kish said, Go *s.* asses
2 Sam. 21. 2 Saul *s.* to slay them
1 K. 1. 3 they *s.* for a fair damsel
2 K. 6. 19 I will bring man ye *s.*
1 Chr. 14. 8 Phil. went to *s.* David
2 Chr. 11. 16 set hearts to *s.* Lord
Ez. 2. 62 these *s.* their register amo.
Neh. 2. 10 come man to *s.* welfare
Esth. 3. 6 Haman *s.* to destr. Jews
Ps. 27. 8 thy face, Lord, will I *s.*
Prov. 14. 6 A scorner *s.* wisdom
Eccl. 7. 29 they have *s.* inventions
S. of S. 3. 1 I *s.* him whom soul lov.
Isa. 40. 20 he *s.* cunning workman
Jer. 2. 24 that *s.* her will not weary
Lam. 1. 11 people sigh, they *s.* bread
Ezek. 7. 25 they shall *s.* peace, and
Dan. 9. 3 *s.* by prayer and supplica.
Hos. 10. 12 it is time to *s.* Lord
Am. 8. 12 run to and fro to *s.* word
Nah. 3. 7 whence sh. I *s.* comforters
Zeph. 2. 3 *S.* ye Lord, all ye meek
Zech. 8. 22 nat. sh. come to *s.* Lord
Mal. 2. 7 they should *s.* the law at
Mat. 6. 33 *s.* first kingdom of God
Mark 8. 11 *s.* a sign from heaven
Luke 2. 49 How is it ye *s.* me?
John 5. 18 Jews *s.* more to kill him
Acts 10. 21 I am he whom ye *s.*
Rom. 2. 7 *s.* for glory and honour
1 Cor. 10. 24 Let no man *s.* his own
2 Cor. 12. 14 I *s.* not yours, but you
Gal. 1. 10 do I *s.* to please men?
Phil. 2. 21 For all *s.* their own, not
Col. 3. 10 *s.* things which are above
1 Thes. 2. 6 Nor of men *s.* we glory
2 Tim. 1. 17 he *s.* me very diligently
Heb. 11. 6 rewarder of th. that *s.*
1 Pet. 5. 8 *s.* whom he may devour
Rev. 9. 6 in tho. days men *s.* death

Seem. *Appear, think.*
Gen. 19. 14 *s.* as one that mocked
Lev. 14. 35 It *s.* as it were plague
Josh. 9. 25. as it *s.* good and right
Judg. 19. 24 do what *s.* good unto
1 Sam. 18. 23 *S.* it to you light thing
2 Sam. 3. 19 that *s.* good to Israel
1 K. 21. 2 or, if it *s.* good to thee
Esth. 3. 11 also to do as it *s.* good
Jer. 18. 4 as *s.* good to the potter
Mat. 11. 26 even so, it *s.* good in thy
Luke 1. 3 It *s.* good to me also
Acts 15. 28 it *s.* good to Holy Ghost
1 Cor. 3. 18 if any man *s.* to be wise
2 Cor. 10. 9 not *s.* as if I wo. terrify
Gal. 2. 9 James and John who *s.*
Heb. 4. 1 if any *s.* to come short
Jas. 1. 26 if any man *s.* religious

Seemly. *Comely.*
Prov. 19. 10 Delight is not *s.* for foo!
26. 1 honour is not *s.* for a fool

Seen. *See* See

Seer. *Beholder, scer.*
1 Sam. 9. 9 Come, let us go to the *s.*
2 Sam. 24. 11 came to prophet, D's *s.*

2 K. 17. 13 by all prophets, and *s.*
1 Chr. 21. 9 L. spake to Gad, D's *s.*
2 Chr. 29. 30 words of Asaph the *s.*
Isa. 30. 10 say to the *s.,* See not
Am. 7. 12 said, O thou *s.,* flee thee
Mic. 3. 7 then shall *s.* be ashamed

Seethe. *Boil, cook.*
Ex. 16. 23 and *s.* that ye will *s.*
Deut. 14. 21 not *s.* kid in mo.'s milk
1 Sam. 2. 13 ca., while flesh was *s.*
2 K. 4. 38 *s.* pottage for the sons of
Job 41. 20 smoke as out of a *s.* pot
Jer. 1. 13 what seest? I see *s.* pot
Ezek. 24. 5 let them *s.* the bones
Zech. 14. 21 pot, take, and *s.* therein

Seize. *Take hold, grip.*
Josh. 8. 7 rise from ambush, *s.* city
Job 3. 6 let darkness *s.* úpon it, let
Ps. 55. 15 Let death *s.* upon them
Jer. 49. 24 and fear hath *s.* on her
Mat. 21. 38 let us *s.* his inheritance
R. V. Josh. 8. 7; Mat. 21. 38 take

Selah. *Musical note or pause.*
Ps. 3. 2 no help for him in God. *S.*
So in Ps. 3. 4, 8; 4. 2; 7. 5, etc.

Self. *Very, selfish.*
Gen. 7. 13 *s.* same day entered Noah
Ex. 12. 51 *s.* sa. day it came to pass
Deut. 32. 48 L. sp. unto M. *s.* sa. day
Josh. 5. 11 did eat corn *s.* same day
Mat. 8. 13 was healed *s.* same hour
2 Cor. 5. 5 wrought for *s.* sa. thing
Tit. 1. 7 bishop must not be *s.* w.
2 Pet. 2. 10 Presumptuous, *s.* w.
See also, self *with her, him, it, mine,*
my, them, thy, your, our, etc.

Sell. *Sell, dispose of.*
Gen. 25. 31 *s.* me thy birthright
Ex. 21. 7 if a man *s.* his daughter
Lev. 25. 14 if thou *s.* to neighbour
Deut. 2. 28 sh. *s.* meat for money
Judg. 2. 14 *s.* th. into ha. of enem.
Ruth 4. 3 *s.* a parcel of land which
1 Sam. 12. 9 *s.* them unto Sisera
1 K. 1. 20 *s.* thyself to work evil
2 K. 17. 17 *s.* themselves to do evil
Neh. 5. 8 will ye ever *s.* brethren?
Ps. 44. 12 *s.* thy people for nought
Prov. 23. 23 Buy truth, and *s.* it not
Isa. 50. 1 to whom I have *s.* you?
Ezek. 48. 14 they shall not *s.* of it
Joel 3. 8 I will *s.* your sons and dau.
Am. 2. 6 *s.* the righteous for silver
Nah. 2. 4 *s.* nat. thro. whoredoms
Zech. 11. 5 they *s.* them say, Bless.
Mat. 19. 21 go *s.* that thou hast, and
Mark 11. 15 J. cast out them that *s.*
Luke 22. 36 let him *s.* his garment
John 2. 14 found th. that *s.* doves
Acts 5. 1 Ananias *s.* a possession
Heb. 12. 16 for morsel *s.* birthright
Rev. 13. 17 th. no man mi. buy or *s.*
R. V. Jas. 4. 13 trade

Seller. *Who sells.*
Neh. 13. 20 *s.* lodged without Jerus.
Isa. 24. 2 as wi. buyer, so with *s.*
Ezek. 7. 12 let not the *s.* mourn
Acts 16. 14 Lydia, a *s.* of purple

Selvedge. *Edge, end.*
Ex. 26. 4 from *s.* in the coupling
36. 11 edge of one curtain from *s.*

Selves. *One another.*
Mark 8. 16 they reasoned among *t. s.*
Luke 4. 36 spake among *t. s.,* saying
John 6. 43 Murmur not among *y. s.*
Acts 20. 30 of *o. s.* shall men rise
2 Cor. 8. 5 gave their *o. s.* to Lord
2 Tim. 3. 2 be lovers of their *o. s.*
1 Thes. 5. 11 comfort *y. s.* together
Jas. 1. 22 only deceiving your *o. s.*

Senate. *Assembly of elders.*
Acts 5. 21 called *s.* of Is. together

Senator. *Elder, senior.*
Ps. 105. 22 and teach his *s.* wisdom

Send. *Make to go, give.*
Gen. 24. 7 *s.* his angel before thee
Ex. 3. 10 I will *s.* thee to Pharaoh
Lev. 26. 36 I will *s.* a faintness into
Num. 13. 17 Moses *s.* them to spy
Deut. 9. 23 Lord *s.* you fr. Kadesh
Josh. 7. 2 Josh. *s.* men from Jericho
Judg. 4. 6 she *s.* and called Barak
1 Sam. 4. 4 the people *s.* to Shiloh
2 Sam. 3. 12 Abner *s.* mes. to Dav.
1 K. 5. 2 Sol. *s.* to Hiram, saying
2 K. 1. 9 king *s.* him captain of fif.

1 Chr. 13. 2 let us *s.* unto brethren
2 Chr. 2. 13 I have *s.* cunning man
Ez. 8. 16 Then *s.* I for Eliezer
Neh. 2. 6 it pleased king to *s.* me
Esth. 4. 4 she *s.* raiment to Mord.
Job 1. 5 Job *s.* and sanctified them
Ps. 43. 3 *s.* out thy light and truth
Prov. 9. 3 hath *s.* forth her maidens
Isa. 9. 8 Lord *s.* a word into Jacob
Jer. 7. 25 I *s.* you all my servants
Lam. 1. 13 he *s.* fire into my bones
Ezek. 2. 3 I *s.* thee to children of Is.
Dan. 6. 22 God hath *s.* his angel
Hos. 8. 14 I *s.* fire upon the cities
Joel 2. 19 I will *s.* you corn, wine
Am. 7. 10 *s.* to Jerobo. k. of Israel
Mic. 6. 4 *s.* before Mos. and Aaron
Hag. 1. 22 as Lord God had *s.* him
Zech. 2. 9 Lord of hosts hath *s.* me
Mal. 4. 5 I will *s.* you Elijah the
Mat. 2. 16 Herod *s.* forth, and slew
10. 16 I *s.* you forth as sheep in
Mark 1. 2 I *s.* my messeng. before
14. 13 he *s.* forth two disciples
Luke 7. 20 John Baptist ha. *s.* us
22. 35 I send you without purse
John 1. 6 was a man *s.* from God
6. 57 living Father hath *s.* me, and
Acts 3. 20 he shall *s.* Jesus Christ
Rom. 10. 15 how preach, except *s.*
1 Cor. 1. 17 C. *s.* me not to baptize
2 Cor. 9. 3 Yet have I *s.* brethren
Eph. 6. 22 I ha. *s.* you for the same
Phil. 2. 19 I trust in Lord J. to *s.*
Col. 4. 8 whom I have *s.* for same
1 Thes. 3. 5 I *s.* to know your faith
2 Thes. 2. 11 G. sh. *s.* them delus.
2 Tim. 4. 12 Tychicus have I *s.* to E.
Tit. 3. 12 I shall *s.* Artemas to thee
1 Pet. 1. 12 wi. H. G. *s.* from heav.
1 John 4. 9 G. *s.* his only beg. Son
Rev. 1. 11 *s.* it to seven churches
R. V. Gen. 12. 20 brought; Judg.
5. 15 rushed forth; other changes
of slight moment, and chiefly dependent on antecedent or consequent word

Sending. *Making to go.*
2 Sam. 13. 16 evil in *s.* me away is
Esth. 9. 19 *s.* portions one to anoth.
Ps. 78. 49 cast on th. trouble by *s.*
Isa. 7. 25 be forth *s.* of oxen
R. V. 2 Sam. 13. 16 putting me
forth; Ps. 78. 49 band of evil

Sense. *Meaning.*
Neh. 8. 8 they read b'k, and gave *s.*
Mental power.
Heb. 5. 14 have their *s.* exercised

Sensual. *Animal, sensuous.*
Jas. 3. 15 This wisdom is earthly, *s.*
Jude 19 *s.,* having not the Spirit

Sent. *See* Send.

Sentence. *Saying, words, judg-*
ment, word of the law.
Deut. 17. 10 do according to the *s.*
Ps. 17. 2 let my *s.* come forth from
Prov. 16. 10 *s.* is in lips of the king
Eccl. 8. 11 bec. *s.* is not executed
Jer. 4. 12 now I give *s.* against th.
Dan. 5. 12 showing of hard *s.,* and
Luke 23. 24 And Pilate gave *s.* that
Acts 15. 19 my *s.* is, we trouble not
2 Cor. 1. 9 had *s.* of dea. in oursel.
R. V. Jer. 4. 12; Acts 15. 19 judg-
ment

Separate (*a.*). *Apart, cut off.*
Gen. 49. 26 *s.* from his brethren
Josh. 16. 9 *s.* cit. for chil. of Eph.
Ezek. 41. 12 build. before *s.* place
2 Cor. 6. 17 be ye *s.,* saith the Lord
Heb. 7. 26 undefiled, *s.* fr. sinners

Separate (*v.*). *Part, set apart.*
Gen. 13. 9 *s.* thyself from me; if
Ex. 33. 16 so shall we be *s.,* I and
Lev. 15. 31 ye *s.* children of Israel
Num. 8. 14 thus ye *s.* the Levites
Deut. 8. 10 L. *s.* the tribe of Levi
1 K. 8. 53 *s.* th. to be inheritance
1 Chr. 25. 1 David *s.* to the service
2 Chr. 25. 10 Amaz. *s.* them, to put
Ez. 8. 24 I *s.* twelve chief priests
Neh. 13. 3 *s.* fr. Is. the mixed
Prov. 19. 4 poor is *s.* fr. neighbour
Isa. 56. 3 Lord hath utterly *s.* me
Jer. 37. 12 Jer. went to *s.* himself
Ezek. 14. 7 strang. wh. *s.* himself

Hos. 9. 10 went and *s.* themselves
Zech. 7. 3 in fifth month, *s.* myself
Mat. 25. 32 *s.* them as a shepherd
Luke 6. 22 blessed when men *s.*
Acts 13. 2 *S.* me Barn. and Saul
19. 9 Paul *s.* the disciples, dis. daily
Rom. 1. 1 apostle, *s.* unto gospel
8. 35 who sh. *s.* us fr. love of C.
Gal. 1. 15 *s.* me fr. moth's womb
Jude 19 they who *s.* themselves
R. V. Num. 6. 2 make special ; Jer.
37. 12 receive his portion ; Hos. 4.
14 go apart ; 9. 10 consecrated

Separation. *Put apart, impurity.*
Lev. 12. 2 according to days of *s.*
Num. 6. 4 days of *s.* eat nothing
19. 13 wat. of *s.* was not sprinkled
Ezek. 42. 20 make *s.* between sanct.
R. V. Lev. 12. 2 impurity

Sepulchre. *Burying place.*
Mat. 23. 27 for ye are like whited *s.*
Rom. 3. 13 Th. throat is an open *s.*
Tomb, monument.
Mat. 23. 29 garnish *s.* of righteous
Mark 15. 46 and laid him in a *s.*
Luke 11. 47 ye build *s.* of prophets
John 19. 42 the *s.* was nigh at hand
Acts 2. 29 and his *s.* is with us
Grave.
Gen. 23. 6 in the choice of our *s.*
Deut. 34, 6 no man knoweth of his *s.*
Judg. 8. 32 Gid. was buried in the *s.*
1 Sam. 10. 2 two men by Rachel's *s.*
2 Sam. 2. 32 bur. him in *s.* of fath.
1 K. 13. 22 carcase sh. not co. to *s.*
2 K. 13. 21 they cast the man into *s.*
2 Chr. 16. 14 buried him in own *s.*
Neh. 2. 3 place of my father's *s.*
Ps. 5. 9 their throat is open *s.*, they
Isa. 22. 16 thou hast hewed out *s.*
Jer. 5. 16 Their quiver is as open *s.*
R. V. Mat. 23. 29 ; 27. 60 ; 28. 8 ;
Mark 15. 46 ; 16. 2, 3, 5, 8 ; Luke
11. 47 ; 23. 53, 55 ; 24. 1, 2, 9, 12,
22, 24 ; John 19. 41,42 ; 20. 1–11 ;
Acts 2. 29 ; 7. 16 ; 13. 29 tomb or
tombs.

Seraphim. *Burning things.*
Isa. 6. 2 throne, above it stood the *s.*
6. 6 Then flew one of the *s.* un. me

Sergeant. *Rod holder.*
Acts 16. 35, 38 magistrates sent *s.*

Serpent. *Serpent, creeping thing, dragon, reptile.*
Gen. 3. 1 the *s.* was more subtil than
Ex. 4. 3 rod became *s.* ; Mos. fled
Num. 21. 6 Lord sent *s.* among peo.
Deut. 8. 15 wherein were fiery *s.*
2 K. 18. 4 break in pieces brazen *s.*
Job 26. 13 hand formed crooked *s.*
Ps. 58. 4 poison is like poison of *s.*
Prov. 23. 32 at last it bit. like a *s.*
Eccl. 10. 8 break. hedge, *s.* sh. bite
Isa. 14. 29 his fruit sh. be fiery *s.*
Jer. 8. 17 will send *s.*, cockatrices
Am. 5. 19 the wall and a *s.* bit him
Mic. 7. 17 shall lick dust like a *s.*
Mat. 8. 10 will ye give him a *s.*
Mark 16. 18 They shall take up *s.*
Luke 10. 19 power to tread on *s.*
John 3. 14 M. lifted *s.* in wilder.
1 Cor. 10. 9 and were destroyed of *s.*
2 Cor. 11. 3 as the *s.* beguiled Eve
Jas. 3. 7 every kind of *s.* is tamed
Rev. 12. 9 that old *s.*, called Devil
R. V. Deut. 32. 24 crawling things ;
Jas. 3. 7 creeping things

Servant. *Server, bondman, slave, minister, hired one, attendant.*
Gen. 9. 25 *s.* of *s.* shall he be unto
26. 19 Isaac's *s.* digged in valley
Ex. 14. 31 believed L. and his *s.*
21. 20 And if a man smite his *s.*
Lev. 25. 6 for thee and for thy *s.*
Num. 12. 7 My *s.* Moses is not so
Deut. 15. 17 he sh. be thy *s.* for ev.
Josh. 1. 2 Moses my *s.* is dead ; now
Judg. 6. 27 Gid. took ten of his *s.*
1 Sam. 16. 17 Saul said unto his *s.*
2 Sam. 2. 31 *s.* of D. had smit. Ben.
1 K. 1. 19 Sol. thy *s.* ha. he not ca.
2 K. 4. 1 thy *s.* my husband is dead
1 Chr. 2. 34 Shesh. had *s.*, an Egy.
2 Chr. 24. 9 *s.* of G. laid upon Is.
Ez. 2. 55 children of Solomon's *s.*
Neh. 1. 10 these are thy *s.* and peo.

Esth. 1. 3 Ahazu. made feast unto *s*
Job 1. 8 Hast considered my *s.* Job
Ps. 31. 16 ma. face to shine upon *s.*
Prov. 11. 29 fool sh. be *s.* to wise
Eccl. 10. 7 I ha. seen *s.* upon horses
Isa. 24. 2 as wi. *s.*, so with master
Jer. 2. 14 Is Israel a *s.*? home born
Lam. 5. 8 *S.* have ruled over us
Ezek. 37. 24 David my *s.* sh. be k.
Dan. 1. 13 as th. seest, deal with *s.*
Joel 2. 29 on *s.* will I pour spirit
Am. 3. 7 he revealed secrets to *s.*
Mic. 6. 4 redeem. out of house of *s.*
Hag. 2. 23 I take thee, Zerub., my *s.*
Zech. 3. 8 I will bring forth my *s.*
Mal. 1. 6 son hon. father, *s.* master
Mat. 10. 25 and *s.* be as his lord
25. 23 Well done, good and faith. *s*
Mark 14. 47 smote *s.* of hi. priest
Luke 2. 29 now let thy *s.* depart
John 13. 16 *s.* is not gr. than lord
Acts 16. 17 *s.* of the most hi. God
Rom. 1. 1 Paul a *s.* of Jesus Christ
1 Cor. 7. 22 called, being free, is *s.*
2 Cor. 4. 5 your *s.* for Jesus' sake
Gal. 4. 7 thou art no more a *s.* but
Eph. 6. 5 *S.*, be obedient to them
Phil. 2. 7 took on him form of *s.*
Col. 4. 12 Epaphras is *s.* of Christ
1 Tim. 6. 1 Let *s.* count own mast.
2 Tim. 2. 24 *s.* of L. must not strive
Tit. 2. 9 exhort *s.* to be obedient
Phile. 16. not as *s.*, but above a *s.*
Heb. 3. 5 Mos. was faithful as a *s.*
Jas. 1. 1 James, a *s.* of God and
1 Pet. 2. 16 us'g liberty as *s.* of God
2 Pet. 2. 19 they are the *s.* of corr.
Jude 1 Jude, the *s.* of Jesus Christ
Rev. 19. 5 Praise God, all ye his *s.*
R. V. Gen. 26. 14 household ; 44.
10, 16, 17 bondmen ; Gen. 14. 14 ;
1 Sam. 24. 7 men ; 1 Sam. 16. 18 ;
25. 19 ; 2 Sam. 21. 2 young men ;
Ex. 33. 11 ; Num. 11. 28 ; Mark
9. 35 minister ; Deut. 15. 18 hireling ; 2 K. 10. 19 worshippers ; Ez.
2. 65 ; Eccl. 2. 7 menservants ; Mat.
26. 58 ; Mark 14. 54 officers ; John
8. 34, 35 ; 1 Cor. 7. 21, 22, 23 ; Gal.
4. 1. 7 ; 1 Pet. 2. 16 ; 2 Pet. 2. 19
bondservant

Serve. *Give service, minister.*
Gen. 29. 20 Jac. *s.* sev. y's for Rach.
Ex. 3. 12 *s.* G. upon this mountain
Lev. 25. 40 *s.* thee to year of jubilee
Num. 4. 24 families of Gersh. to *s.*
Deut. 6. 13 fear L. thy God, and *s.*
Josh. 22. 5 *s.* him with all humility
Judg. 2. 11 children of Is. *s.* Baal
1 Sam. 7. 3 *s.* him, he will deliver
2 Sam. 10. 19 ma. peace wi. Is., and *s.*
1 K. 4. 21 *s.* Solomon all the days
2 K. 17. 41 *s.* their graven images
1 Chr. 28. 9 *s.* him with per. heart
2 Chr. 7. 19 go and *s.* other gods
Neh. 9. 35 they have not *s.* thee
Esth. 1. 10 chamberlain that *s.*
Job 21. 15 Almighty, that we sho. *s.*
Ps. 2. 11 *S.* the Lord with fear, and
Isa. 19. 23 Egyp. sh. *s.* with Assyr.
Jer. 5. 19 so shall ye *s.* strangers
Ezek. 20. 39 *s.* ye ev. one his idols
Dan. 3. 12 they *s.* not thy gods, nor
Hos. 12. 12 Israel *s.* for a wife, and
Zeph. 3. 9 call upon the Lord, to *s.*
Mal. 3. 14 said, It is vain to *s.* God
Mat. 6. 24 Ye cannot *s.* G. and mam.
Luke 16. 13 No ser. can *s.* two mast.
John 12. 2 ma. him sup., Martha *s.*
Acts 20. 19 *S.* G. with all humility
Rom. 1. 25 *s.* creature mo. th. Crea.
Gal. 5. 13 by love *s.* one another
Phil. 2. 22 he ha. *s.* wi. me in gospel
Col. 3. 24 for ye *s.* the Lord Christ
1 Thes. 1. 9 *s.* living and true God
2 Tim. 1. 3 thank God, whom I *s.*
Tit. 3. 3 *s.* divers lusts and pleasures
Rev. 7. 15 *s.* him day and night
R. V. Gen. 39. 4 ; 40. 4 ; 2 Chr. 29.
11 ; Esth. 1. 10 ; Ps. 101. 6 ; Isa.
56. 6 minister ; 19. 23 worship ;
Jer. 40. 10 ; 52. 12 stand before ;
Ezek. 48. 18, 19 labour in

Service. *Serving, ministration.*
Gen. 29. 27 we give thee this for *s.*
Ex. 11. 25 Wh. mean ye by this *s.*

Num. 3. 7 to do *s.* of tabernacle
Josh. 22. 27 do the *s.* of the Lord
1 K. 12, 4 make grievous *s.* lighter
1 Chr. 9. 19 Korahites were over *s.*
2 Chr. 31. 2 every man accord. to *s.*
Ez. 8. 20 princes appointed for *s.*
Neh. 10. 32 for *s.* of house of God
Ps. 104. 14 grow, and herbs for *s.*
Jer. 22. 13 useth his neighbour's *s.*
Ezek. 29. 18 army to serve gr. *s.*
John 16. 2 think he doeth God *s.*
Rom. 12. 1 sacrifice, your reason. *s.*
2 Cor. 9. 12 administra. of this *s.*
Gal. 4. 8 we did *s.* unto th. which
Eph. 6. 7 wi. good will doing *s.* as
Phil. 2. 17 off. on sacrifice and *s.*
1 Tim. 6. 2 do *s.* because beloved
Heb. 9. 1 ordinances of divine *s.*
Rev. 2. 19 I know thy works and *s.*
R. V. Ex. 35. 19 ; 39. 1, 41 ; 1 Chr.
9. 28 ministering ; Num. 4. 47 ; 8.
24 work ; Rom. 15. 31 ministra-
tion ; Gal. 4. 8 bondage ; Rev. 2. 19
ministry ; 2 Cor. 11.8 minister unto

Servitor. R. V. *servant.*
2 K. 4. 43 his *s.* said, What, sho. I

Servitude. *Service.*
2 Chr. 10. 4 griev. *s* of thy father
Lam. 1. 3 Judah gone because of *s.*
R. V. 2 Chr. 10. 4 service

Set. *Place, fix.*
Gen. 1. 17 G. *s.* them in firmament
Ex. 25. 30 *s.* on table shewbread
Lev. 26. 11 *s.* tabernac. among you
Num. 8. 13 *s.* Levites before Aaron
Deut. 1. 8 I ha. *s.* land before you
Josh. 8. 12 *s.* th. to lie in ambush
Judg 20. 29 Israel *s.* liers in wait
1. Sam. 12. 13 L. ha. *s.* k. over you
2 Sam. 12. 20 they *s.* bread bef. him
1 K. 2. 15 Is. *s.* their faces on me
2 K. 4. 10 let us *s.* him there a bed
1 Chr. 11. 25 D. *s.* him ov. his guard
2 Chr. 4. 10 he *s.* sea on right side
Ez. 4. 10 *s.* in cities of Samaria
Neh. 4. 9 *s.* a watch against them
Esth. 2. 17 *s.* crown on her head
Job 28. 3 He *s.* an end to darkness
Ps. 19. 4 In them he *s.* tabernacle
Prov. 1. 25 *s.* at nought my counsels
Eccl. 3. 11 ha. *s.* would in th. heart
S. of S. 8. 6 *S.* me as seal on heart
Isa. 21. 6 *s.* watch., let him declare
Jer. 32. 20 ha. *s.* signs and wonders
Lam, 3. 6 ha. *s.* me in dark places
Ezek. 4. 2 *s.* the camp against it
Dan. 9. 3 I *s.* my face unto L. God
Hos. 11. 8 sh. I set thee as Zeboim ?
Am. 7. 8 I will *s.* a plumb line in
Obad. 4. *s.* thy nest among the stars
Nah. 3. 6 *s.* thee as gazing stock
Hab. 2. 9 may *s.* his nest on high
Zech. 3. 5 *s.* fair mitre on his head
Mat. 25. 33 *s.* sheep on right hand
Mark 9. 36 child, *s.* him in midst
Luke 4. 9 *s.* him on pinnacle of tem.
John 2. 10 doth *s.* forth good wine
Acts 13. 9 Paul *s.* his eyes on him
Rom. 14. 10 *s.* at nought brother
1 Cor. 4. 9 God *s.* forth apostles
Eph. 1. 20 *s.* him at right hand
Heb. 2. 7 *s.* over work of hands
Rev. 3. 8 *s.* bef. thee an open door
R. V. Frequent changes, chiefly
due to antecedent and consequent
words.

Setter. *Teller forth.*
Acts 17. 18 *s.* forth of strange gods

Setting. *Filling, placing.*
Ex. 28. 17 set in it *s.* of stones
Ezek. 43. 8 in their *s.* of threshold
Mat. 27. 66 sealing sto., *s* watch
Luke 4. 40 when sun was *s.*, they
R. V. Mat. 27. 66 the guard being
with them.

Settle. *Sink down, fix.*
1 K. 8. 13 built a *s.* place for thee
2 K. 8. 11 he *s.* his countenance
1 Chr. 17. 14 will *s.* him in house
Ps. 65. 10 thou *s.* furrows thereof
Prov. 8. 25 before mounts. were *s.*
Jer. 48. 11 he hath *s.* on his lees
Ezek. 36. 11 *s.* you aft. old estates
Zeph. 1. 12 punish men *s.* on lees
Luke 21. 14 *S.* it in your hearts
Col. 1. 23 faith, grounded and *s.*

1 Pet. 5. 10 God of all grace *s.* you
A border
Ezek. 43. 17 *s.* fourteen cubits long
R. V. Ezek. 36. 11 cause to be in-
  habited; 1 Pet. 5. 10 ——.
Seven. *Seven.*
Gen. 29. 20 J. serv. *s.* y's for Rachel
Ex. 12. 15 *s.* days eat unl. bread
Lev. 4. 6 sprinkle blood *s.* times
Num. 8. 2 *s.* lamps shall give light
Deut. 16. 15 *S.* days keep sol. feast
Josh. 6. 4 compass the city *s.* times
Judg. 12. 9 Ib. judged Is. *s.* years
Ruth 4. 15 bet. to thee th. *s.* sons
1 Sam. 2. 5 the barren hath born *s.*
2 Sam. 5. 5 D. reigned ov. J. *s.* y's
1 K. 6. 38 was *s.* years in building
2 K. 5. 10 wash in Jordan *s.* times
1 Chr. 19. 18 Dav. slew *s.* thousand
2 Chr. 7. 8 Sol. kept feast *s.* days
Ez. 2. 5 chil. of Arah, *s.* hundred
Neh. 7. 68 horses, *s.* hun. and thirty
Esth. 1. 5 king made feast *s.* days
Job 1. 2 born unto him *s.* sons and
Ps. 119. 164 *s.* times a day I praise
Prov. 9. 1 she ha. hewn *s.* pillars
Eccl. 11. 2 Give a portion to *s.* and
Isa. 4. 1 *s.* wom. ta. hold one man
Jer. 15. 9 that ha. born *s.* languish.
Ezek. 3. 15 sat astonished *s.* days
Dan. 9. 25 unto Mess. sh. be *s.* w'ks
Mic. 5. 5 raise ag'st him *s.* sheph.
Zech. 3. 9 on stone sh. be *s.* eyes
Mat. 15. 36 he took the *s.* loaves
Mark 12. 20 there were *s.* brethren
Luke 20. 31 in like manner the *s.*
Acts 6. 3 look ye out *s.* men of
Rom. 11. 14 I ha. reserved *s.* thous.
Rev. 1. 4 John to the *s.* churches
2. 1 ; 3. 1 ; 4. 5 ; 5. 1 ; 8. 2 ; 10. 3.
Sevens. *Seven.*
Gen. 7. 2 clean beasts take by *s.*
Seventeen. *Ten and seven.*
Gen. 37. 2 Jos. being *s.* years old
Jer. 32. 9 Jer. weighed *s.* shekels
Seventeenth. *Tenth and seventh.*
Gen. 7. 11 on *s.* day the fountains
8. 4 ark rested on *s.* day of mo.
Seventh. *Seventh.*
Gen. 2. 2 on *s.* day God ended work
Ex. 20. 10 *s.* day is sabbath of Lord
Lev. 23. 3 *s.* day is sabbath of rest
Num. 6. 9 the *s.* day he shall shave it
Deut. 15. 12 on *s.* day let him go
Josh. 6. 4 *s.* day ye shall compass
Judg. 14. 15 came to pass on *s.* day
1 K. 8. 2 Ethanim is the *s.* month
2 K. 11. 4 *s.* year Jehoiada sent and
1 Chr. 2. 15 Oz. the sixth, David *s.*
2 Chr. 5. 3 feast was in *s.* month
Ez. 3. 1 when *s.* month was come
Neh. 8. 2 on first day of *s.* month
Esth. 1. 10 *s.* day, heart of k. was
Jer. 28. 17 Hanan. died in *s.* month
Ezek. 45. 25 in *s.* mo. do the like
Hag. 2. 1 in *s.* month came Lord
Zech. 7. 5 mourned fifth and *s.* mo.
Seventy. *Seven tens.*
Gen. 4. 24 truly Lamech *s.* and sev.
Ex. 1. 5 souls that came were *s.*
Num. 11. 25 gave it to *s.* elders
Judg. 9. 56 slaying his *s.* brethren
2 Sam. 24. 15 there died of peo. *s.*
2 K. 10. 1 Ahab had *s.* sons in Sam.
1 Chr. 21. 14 there fell of Is. *s.* th.
Ez. 2. 5 childr. of Arah, sev. hun. *s.*
Neh. 7. 39 priests, nine hundred *s.*
Esth. 9. 16 slew of foes *s.* five th.
Isa. 23. 15 Tyre sh. be forgot. *s.* yr.
Jer. 25. 11 nations sh. serve *s.* years
Ezek. 41. 22 porah wall. was *s.* cub. br'd
Zech. 7. 5 when ye fasted *s.* years
Mat. 18. 22 times; but, Until *s.* ti.
Luke 10. 1 Lord appointed other *s.*
Sever. *Part, separate.*
Ex. 8. 22 And I will *s.* in that day
Lev. 20. 26 I *s.* you from other peo.
Deut. 4. 41 Moses *s.* three cities
Judg. 4. 11 Heber *s.* from Kenites
Ezek. 39. 14 *s.* out men of employ
Mat. 13. 49 *s.* wicked from the just
R. V. Lev. 20. 26; Deut. 4. 41 sep-
  arated
Several. *Separate.*
Num. 28. 13 *s.* tenth deal of flour
2 K. 15. 15 Az. dwelt in *s.* house

2 Chr. 26. 21 *s.* house, being a leper
Mat. 25. 15 according to *s.* ability
Rev. 21. 21 ev. *s.* ga. was of pearl
Severally. *Separately.*
1 Cor. 12. 11 divi. to every man *s.*
Severity. *Cutting off.*
Rom. 11. 22 on them which fell, *s.*
Sew. *Sew, fasten.*
Gen. 3. 7 they *s.* fig leaves together
Job 14. 17 thou *s.* up mine iniquity
Eccl. 3. 7 time to rend, time to *s.*
Ezek. 13 18 woe to wom. th. *s.* pil.
Mark 2. 21 no man *s.* new cloth on
R. V. Job 14. 17 fasteneth
Shade. *Shadow, defence.*
Ps. 121. 5 Lord is thy *s.* upon right
Shadow. *Shadow, defence.*
Gen. 19. 8 came under *s.* of my roof
Judg. 9. 15 put your trust in my *s.*
2 K. 20. 9 shall the *s.* go forward ?
1 Chr. 29. 15 our days are as a *s.*
Job 14. 2 he fleeth also as a *s.*, and
Ps. 17. 8 hide me under *s.* of wings
102. 11 my days are like a *s.*
Eccl. 6. 12 life he spendeth as a *s.*
S. of S. 2. 3 I sat under *s.* wi. deli.
Isa. 4. 6 shall be tabernacle for *s.*
Jer. 48. 45 under the *s.* of Heshbon
Lam. 4. 20 Under his *s.* we sh. live
Ezek. 31. 6 und. his *s.* dwelt nations
Dan. 4. 12 beasts of field had *s.* und.
Hos. 4. 13 bec. *s.* thereof is good
Jonah 4. 5 Jon. sat under it in the *s.*
Mark 4. 32 fowls lodge under *s.* of it
Acts 5. 15 *s.* of Peter mi. overshad.
Col. 2. 17 are *s.* of things to come
Heb. 8. 5 serve unto *s.* of heaven
Jas. 1. 17 wi. whom no *s.* of turn.
Great shade or shadow.
Job 3. 5 darkness and *s.* of death
Ps. 23. 4 thro. valley of *s.* of death
Isa. 9. 2 dwell in land of *s.* of death
Am. 5. 8 turn. *s.* of d. into morning
Mat. 4. 16 sat in the reg. and *s.* of d.
Luke 1. 79 in darkness and in *s.* of d.
Shadowing. *Overshadowing.*
Isa. 18. 1 Woe to land *s.* wi. wings
Ezek. 31. 3 a cedar with *s.* shroud
Heb. 9. 5 over it the cherubim *s.*
R. V. Isa. 18. 1 rustling; Heb. 9.
  5 overshadowing.
Shady. R. V. *lotus.*
Job 40. 21, 22 lieth under *s.* trees
Shaft. *Arrow, haft.*
Isa. 49. 2 he made me a polished *s.*
R. V. *base, pedestal.*
Ex. 25 31 his *s.*, and branches
Num. 8. 4 beaten gold, unto the *s.*
Shake. *Move, wave, tremble, dash,*
  drive or force off.
Lev. 26. 36 sound of *s.* leaf shall
Judg. 16. 20 I will go and *s.* myself
2 Sam. 6. 6 hold, for oxen *s.* ark
22. 8 the earth *s.* and trembled
1 K. 14. 15 smite Is., as a reed *s.*
2 K. 19. 21 daug. of Jer. ha. *s.* head
Neh. 5. 13 even thus be he *s.* out
Job 4. 14 fear made my bones to *s.*
Ps. 18. 7 founda. of hills were *s.*
46. 3 mountains *s.* wi. the swelling
68. 8 earth *s.*, heavens also dropp.
Isa. 13. 13 I will *s.* the heavens
Jer. 23. 9 broken, all my bones *s.*
Ezek. 26. 10 walls shall *s.* at noise
38. 20 men shall *s.* at my presence
Dan. 4. 14 *s.* off leaves, scat. fruit
Joel 3. 16 heaven and earth shall *s.*
Am. 9. 1 door, that the posts may *s.*
Hag. 2. 7 I will *s.* all nations, and
Zech. 2. 9 I will *s.* hand on them
Mat. 10. 14 *s.* off dust of your feet
Mark 6. 11 ; Luke 9. 5
Mat. 11. 7 see ? reed *s.* with wind
Mark 13. 25 pow. in heav. sh. be *s.*
Luke 6. 38 good meas. pressed, *s.*
Acts 28. 5 he *s.* off the beast into fire
2 Thes. 2. 2 be not soon *s.* in mind
Heb. 12. 26 I *s.* not the earth only
Rev. 6. 13 fig tree, when *s.* of wind
R. V. Lev. 26. 36 driven; Job 16. 12
  dashed; Isa. 13. 13 ; Heb. 12. 26
  make tremble; Mat. 28. 4 quake.
Shaking. *Moving, shaking.*
Job 41. 29 he laugh. at *s.* of spear
Ps. 44. 14 *s.* of head among people
Isa. 17. 6 as the *s.* of an ollve tree

19. 16 because of *s.* of the hand
30. 32 battles of *s.* will he fight
Ezek. 37. 7 noise, and behold a *s.*
38. 19 there shall be a great *s.* in
R. V. Job 41. 29 rushing; Ezek.
  37. 7 an earthquake
Shall. *Am to, is to, are to.*
2 Chr. 15. 7 your work *s.* be reward.
Mat. 16. 27 Son of man *s.* come in
Etc., etc.
Shambles. *Market place.*
1 Cor. 10. 25 whatsoever is sold in *s.*
Shame (*n.*). *Reproach, confusion,*
  dishonor.
Ex. 32. 25 made naked to their *s.*
Judg. 18. 7 none mi. put them to *s.*
1 Sam. 20. 34 fath. had done him *s.*
2 Sam. 13. 13 sh. I cause *s.* to go ?
2 Chr. 32. 21 retur. wi. *s.* of father
Job 8. 22 hate, sh. be clothed with *s.*
Ps. 4. 2 how long turn glory to *s.* ?
40. 14 let them be put to *s.* that
119. 31 O Lord put me not to *s.*
Prov. 10. 5 th. sleep in har. caus *s.*
13. 5 wicked man cometh to *s.*
Isa. 20. 4 uncovered to *s.* of Egypt
Jer. 3. 24 *s.* devoured labour of fath.
Ezek. 7. 18 *s.* shall be on all faces
Dan. 12. 2 Awake, some to *s.* and
Hos. 4. 7 change their glory to *s.*
Obad. 10 for viol., *s.* shall cov. thee
Mic. 1. 11 pass away, hav. *s.* naked
Nah. 3. 5 I will show kingds. thy *s.*
Hab. 2. 10 thou hast consulted *s.*
Zeph. 3. 5 unjust knoweth no *s.*
Luke 14. 9 begin with *s.* to take the
Acts 5. 41 counted wor. to suffer *s.*
1 Cor. 6. 5 I speak to your *s.*, Is it so,
11. 14 long hair, it is a *s.* unto him
Eph. 5. 12 *s.* even to speak of thing
Phil. 3. 19 whose glory is their *s.*
Heb. 6. 6 and put him to an open *s.*
12. 2 endured cross, despising *s.*
Jude 13 foaming out their own *s.*
Rev. 3. 18 th. *s.* of thy nakedness
R. V. Ex. 32. 25 derision ; Jer. 2 ;
  35. 4 ; 40. 14 ; 44. 9 ; 109. 29 ; Acts
  5. 41 ; 1 Cor. 11. 14 dishonour ;
  Ps. 83. 16 confusion ; 83. 17 con-
  founded ; Prov. 25. 10 revile ; Jer.
  3. 24 ; Hos. 9. 10 ; 1 Cor. 14. 35
  shameful ; Mic. 2. 6 reproaches.
Shame (*v.*). *To shame.*
Gen. 38. 23 take it . . lest we be *s.*
2 Sam. 19. 5 thou hast *s.* the faces
Ps. 14. 6 have *s.* counsel of the pool
1 Cor. 4. 14 I write these to *s.* you
Shamefacedness. R. V. *shame-*
  fastness, (i. e. modesty).
1 Tim. 2. women adorn with *s.*
Shameful. *Make ashamed.*
Jer. 11. 13 set up altars to *s.* things
Hab. 2. 16 *s.* spewing on thy glory
Shamefully. *Disgracefully.*
Hos. 2. 5 conceived them, done *s.*
Mark 12. 4 sent him away *s.* hand.
Luke 20. 11 entreated him *s.*, sent
1 Thes. 2. 2 and were *s.* entreated
Shamelessly. *Publicly.*
2 Sam. 6. 20 fellows *s.* uncovered
Shape (*n.*). *Form, likeness.*
Luke 3. 22 H. G. descend. in bod. *s.*
John 5. 37 voice, nor seen his *s.*
Rev. 9. 7 *s.* of locusts like horses
R. V. Luke 3. 22; John 5. 37 form
Shape (*v.*). *Form.*
Ps. 51. 5 I was *s.* in iniquity ; and
Share. *Cutter, mattock.*
1 Sam. 13. 20 to sharp. ev. m. his *s.*
Sharp. *Pointed, keen.*
Ex. 4. 25 Zipporah took a *s.* stone
Josh. 5. 2 Make thee *s.* knives, and
1 Sam. 14. 4 *s.* rocks on one side
Job 41. 30 *S.* stones are under him
Ps. 45. 5 Thine arrows are *s.* in heart
57. 4 and their tongue a *s.* sword
Prov. 5. 4 her end is *s.* as sword
Isa. 41. 15 ma. thee *s.* thresh. instr.
Ezek. 5. 1 take thee a *s.* knife, take
Acts 15. 39 the contention was so *s.*
Rev. 1. 16 out of mo. went *s.* sword
2. 12 ; 14. 14 ; 19. 15
R. V. Josh. 5. 2, 3 flint ; 1 Sam.
  14. 4 rocky ; Job 41. 30 threshing
  wain ; Ex. 4. 25 ——
Sharpen. *Make sharp.*

1 Sam. 13. 20 s. ev. man his share
Job 16. 9 mine enemy s. his eyes
Ps. 140. 3 they s. their tongues like
Prov. 27. 17 Iron s. iron; so man
Ezek. 21. 9 sword is s., and furb.
R. V. 1 Sam. 13. 21 set

Sharper. *Keener, worse.*
Mic. 7. 4 most upright s. than thorn
Heb. 4. 12 word of God s. than sw.
R. V. Mic. 7. 4 worse

Sharply. *Strongly, severely.*
Judg. 8. 1 Eph. did chide wi. Gid. s.
Tit. 1. 13 rebuke them s. that they

Sharpness. R. V. *deal sharply,*
2 Cor. 13. 10 being present, I use s.

Shave. *Cut off, shear, shave.*
Gen. 41. 14 Jos. s., changed raiment
Lev. 13. 33 but scall shall he not s.
14. 8, 9; 21. 5
Num. 6. 9 then he shall s. his head
6. 18 Naz. shall s. head of separ.
Deut. 21. 12 s. her head, pare nails
Judg. 16. 19 cau. him to s. locks
2 Sam. 10. 4 s. half of their beards
1 Chr. 19. 4 s., and cut off garments
Job 1. 20 Job rent mantle, s. head
Isa. 7. 20 Lord s. with a razor that
Ezek. 44. 20 Nei. shall they s. head
Acts 21. 24 that they may s. heads
R. V. Num. 8. 7 cause razor to
pass over

Shaven. *Shaved.*
Lev. 13. 33 He shall be s., but scall
Num. 6. 19 after hair of sep. is s.
Judg. 16. 17 if I be s., str. will go
Jer. 41. 5 fourscore men, beards s.
1 Cor. 11. 5 even as if she were s.
11. 6 shame for woman to be s.

She. *This or that (woman).*
Gen. 2. 12 s. gave me of the tree
Mat. 26. 12 s. poured this ointment
Luke 2. 3 6 Anna, s. was of great
Etc., etc.
Female
Gen. 12. 16 Phar. had oxen, s. asses
Job 1. 3 substance was oxen, s. asses

Sheaf. *Thing bound, sheaf.*
Gen. 37. 7 and, lo, my s. arose and
Lev. 23. 11 wave s. bef. the Lord
Deut. 24. 19 hast forgot s. in field
Ruth 2. 7 gath. aft. reap. among s.
Neh. 13. 15 on sab. bringing in s.
Job 24. 10 take away s. fr. hungry
Ps. 126. 6 rejoicing, bring. his s.
Am. 2. 13 as a cart that is full of s.
Mic. 4. 12 L. sh. gather them as s.
Zech. 12. 6 govern. like torch in s.

Shear. *Cut off, shear.*
Gen. 31. 19 Laban went to s. sheep.
Deut. 15. 19 nor s. firstl. of sheep
1 Sam. 25. 2 Nabal was s. sheep

Shearer. *Who shears.*
Gen. 38. 12 Ju. went to sheep s.
1 Sam. 25, 7 I heard thou hast s.
Isa. 53. 7 as sheep bef. s. is dumb
Acts 8. 32 like lamb dumb bef. s.

Shearing House
2 K. 10. 12, 14 Jehu was at the s. h.

Sheath. *Scabbard, sheath.*
1 Sam. 17. 51 D. dr. sword out of s.
2 Sam. 20. 8 sword fastened in s.
1 Chr. 21. 27 angel put sword in s.
Ezek. 21. 3 draw sw. out of his s.
John 18. 11 Put up thy sw. into s.

Shed. *Pour out.*
Gen. 9. 7 Whoso s. man's blood, by
Lev. 17. 4 he hath s. blood, and
Num. 35. 33 by blood of him th. s.
Deut. 21. 17 hands ha. not s. blood
1 Sam. 25. 31 thou hast s. blood
2 Sam. 20. 10 s. bowels to ground
1 K. 2. 31 innocent blood, Joab s.
2 K. 21. 16 Manass. s. innoc. blood
2 Chr. 28. 3 man of war. s. blood
Ps. 79. 3 blood they s. like water
Prov. 1. 16 ma. haste to s. blood
Isa. 59. 7 haste to s. innoc. blood
Jer. 7. 6 and s. not innocent blood
Lam. 4. 13 have s. blood of the just
Isa. 33. 25 lift up eyes, s. blood
Joel 3. 19 Lec. they s. innoc. blood
Mat. 26. 28 my bl. is s. for many
Mark 14. 24 bl. of new test., is s.
Luke 22. 20 bl., wh. is s. for you
Acts 22. 20 bl. of Stephen was s.
Rom. 3. 15 feet swift to s. blood

Tit. 3. 6 H. G., s. on us abundant.
Heb. 9. 22 without s. of bl. no re.
Rev. 16. 6 ha. s. blood of saints
R. V. Ex. 22. 2, 3; 1 Sam. 25. 26,
33 bloodguiltiness; Ezek. 35. 5
given over to; Ezek. 36. 18;
Luke 22. 20; Acts 2. 33; Tit. 3.
6; Rev. 16. 6 poured out

Shedder. *Who pours out.*
Ezek. 18. 10 beget son, s. of blood

Sheep. *Sheep.*
Gen. 4. 2 Abel was a keeper of s.
Ex. 9. 3 hand of Lord is upon thy s.
Lev. 1. 10 if his offering be of s.
Num. 22. 40 Balak offer. ox and s.
Deut. 14. 4 ye shall eat ox, the s.
Josh. 7. 24 Josh. took Achan, his s.
Judg. 6. 4 Midianites left neither s.
1 Sam. 8. 17 will take tenth of the s.
2 Sam. 7. 8 I took thee from fol. s.
1 K. 1. 9 Adonij. slew s. and oxen
2 K. 5. 26 Is it a time to receive s.
1 Chr. 12. 40 bro. ox. and s. abund.
2 Chr. 14. 15 Asa carried fr. E. s.
Neh. 3. 1 they builded the s. gate
Job 1. 16 fire fallen, burned up s.
Ps. 79. 13 peo., and s. of thy pasture
S. of S. 6. 6 thy teeth as flock of s.
Isa. 53. 6 like s. have gone astray
Jer. 50. 6 people hath been lost s.
Ezek. 34. 11 I will both search my s.
Hos. 12. 12 for a wife he kept s.
Joel 1. 18 flocks of s. made desol.
Mic. 5. 8 as a young lion among s.
Zech. 13. 7 the s. shall be scattered
Mat. 7. 15 which come in s.'s cloth.
10. 6 go rather to lost s. of h. of Is.
Mark 14. 27 smite shep., s. sh. scat.
Luke 15. 6 I have found my s. lost
John 10. 2 he is shep. of the s.
10. 15 I lay down my life for the s.
21. 16 Jesus saith, Feed my s.
Acts 8. 32 led as s. to the slaughter
Rom. 8. 36 we are accounted as s.
Heb. 13. 20 Jesus, gr. shepherd of s.
1 Pet. 2. 25 ye were as s. going astr.
Rev. 18. 13 none buyeth s., horses
R. V. Gen. 34. 28; Ex. 9. 3; Lev.
22. 21; Num. 31. 28; Deut. 7. 13;
15. 19; 28. 4, 18, 51; 1 Sam. 8, 17;
Ps. 49. 17 flock or flocks; S. of S.
4. 2; 6. 6 ewes; John 10. 4 his
own; 10. 14 mine own

Sheep Cote. *Sheep cote.*
1 Sam. 24. 3 Saul ca. to s. c. by t. way
2 Sam. 7. 8 I took thee from s. c.
1 Chr. 17. 7 I took thee from s. c.

Sheep Fold. *Sheep court, cote*
Num. 32. 16 we will build s. f. here
Judg. 5. 16 Why abodest am. s. f.?
Ps. 78. 70 D. took him from s. f.
John 10. 1 ent. not by door into s. f.

Sheep Market.
John 5. 2 at Jerusalem by s. m.

Sheep Master. *Herdsman.*
2 K. 3. 4 king of Moab was a s. m.

Sheepskin.
Heb. 11. 37 they wandered in s. sk.

Sheet. *Linen piece.*
Judg. 14. 12 I give you thirty s.
Acts 10. 11 great s. knit at corners
R. V. Judg. 14. 12 linen garments

Shekel. *Shekel, piece.*
Gen. 23. 15 land worth four hun. s.
Ex. 21. 32 give their master thirty s.
Lev. 5. 15 after s. of the sanctuary
Num. 3. 47 even take five s. apiece
Deut. 22. 29 damsel's fath. fifty s.
Josh. 7. 21 spoils, two hun. s. silv.
Judg. 8. 26 rings, sev. teen hund. s.
1 Sam. 17. 7 coat, five thousand s.
2 Sam. 24. 4 threshing floor, fift. s.
2 K. 7. 1 meas. of flour sold for s.
1 Chr. 21. 25 D.ga. Or. six hund. s.
2 Chr. 3. 9 wei. of nails was fif. s.
Neh. 5. 15 gov. had taken forty s.
Jer. 32. 9 bou. field for sev. teen s.
Ezek. 4. 10 by weight, twenty s.
Am. 8. 5 ephah small, the s. great
R. V. Ex. 30. 23, 24——; Judg. 17.
2, 3, 4, 10; 2 Sam. 18. 11, 12 pieces.

Shelter. *Safety.*
Job 24. 8 emb. rock for want of s.
Ps. 61. 3 thou hast been s. for me
R. V. Ps. 61. 3 refuge

Shepherd. *Sheep feeder, herder.*

Gen. 49. 24 then. the s., stone of Is.
Ex. 2. 17 s. came, drove them away
Num. 27. 17 be not as sheep. no s.
1 Sam. 17. 40 five stones in s.'s bag
2 Chr. 18. 16 scat. as sheep, no s.
Ps. 23. 1 L. is my s., I sh. not w't
Eccl. 12. 11 assem., giv. fr. one s.
S. of S. 1. 8 feed kids bes. s.'s tents
Isa. 44. 28 He is my s., sh. perform
Jer. 6. 3 s. with flocks shall come
Ezek. 34. 2 sho. not s. feed flocks
Am. 1. 2. habita. of s. shall mourn
Mic. 5. 5 raise ag'st him seven s.
Nah. 3. 18 Thy s. slumber, O king
Zeph. 2. 6 coasts be cottages for s.
Zech. 10. 3 anger kindled ag'st s
Mat. 25. 32 as s. divid. his sheep
Mark 6. 34 as sheep not having s.
Luke 2. 20 s. returned, glorifying
John 10. 2 that entereth in .. is the s.
10. 14 I am the good s., and kn.
Heb. 11. 20 our L. J., that great s.
1 Pet. 2. 25 now returned unto s.

Sherd. *Potsherd.*
Isa. 30. 14 shall not be found a s.
Ezek. 23. 34 thou sh. break the s.

Sheriffs. *Prefects.*
Dan. 3. 2, 3 Neb. sent to gather s.

Shew (*v.*). *See* **Show.**

Shew (*n.*). *Show.*
Ps. 39. 6 ev. man walk. in vain s.
Gal. 6. 12 as desire to make fair s.
Col. 2. 15 made s. of them openly

Shew Bread. *Show bread, bread
of arrangement or faces.*
Ex. 25. 30 set upon the tables s.
Num. 4. 7 on tab. of s. b. they sh.
1 Sam. 21. 6 was no bread but s. b.
1 K. 7. 48 tab. of gold, whereon s. b.
1 Chr. 28. 16 ga. gold for tab. of s. b.
2 Chr. 2. 4 for the continual s. b.
Neh. 10. 33 for the service of s. b.
Mat. 12. 4 David did eat the s. b.
Mark 2. 26; Luke 6. 4
Heb. 9. 2 tabern. wherein was s. b.

Shewing. *Showing.*
Ps. 78. 4 s. to generation to come
S. of S. 2. 9 s. himself thro. lattice
Dan. 5. 12 and s. of hard sentences
Luke 1. 80 in desert till day of s.
R. V. Ps. 78. 4 telling; S. of S.
2. 9 sheweth; Luke 1. 80 bringing

Shield. R. V. *javelin.*
1 Sam. 17. 45 Thou comest with s
Job 39, 23 glittering spear and s.
Shield, buckler, armor.
Gen. 15. 1 Fear not, I am thy s.
Deut. 33. 29 Lord, the s. ot help
Judg. 5. 8 was there s. seen among
1 Sam. 17. 7 one bear. s. went bef.
2 Sam. 8. 7 David took s. of gold
1 K. 14. 27 Rehobo. made brazen s.
2 K. 11. 10 priests gave David s.
1 Chr. 12. 24 chil. of Jud. th. bare s.
2 Chr. 11. 12 in every city he put s.
Neh. 4. 16 half held spears and s.
Ps. 3. 3 But thou, O Lord, art a s.
28. 7 Lord is my strength and s.
Prov. 30. 5 s. to them that trust
Isa. 21. 5 arise, princes, anoint s.
Jer. 46. 3 order ye buckler and s.
51. 11 make bri. arrows, gath. s.
Ezek. 23. 24 set against thee s. and
Nah. 2. 3 s. of mighty made red
Eph. 6. 16 above all, tak. s. of faith

Shine. *Make light, shine.*
Ex. 34. 30 skin of his face s. and
Num. 6. 25 Lord made his face to s.
Deut. 33. 2 Lord s. forth fr. mt. P.
2 K. 3. 22 sun s. upon the water
Job 25. 5 even the moon, it s. not
37. 15 causeth light of cloud to s.
Ps. 50. 2 perfec. of beauty, God s.
80. 1 O shepherd of Israel, s. forth
Prov. 4. 18 s. more .. unto per. day
Eccl. 8. 1 man's wis. mak. face s.
Isa. 9. 2 upon them hath light s.
60. 1 Arise, s., thy light has come
Jer. 5. 28 are waxen fat, they s.
Ezek. 43. 2 earth s. with his glory
Dan. 12 3 they that be wise shall s.
Mat. 5. 16 Let your light so s bef.
Luke 17. 24 as the lightning s. unto
John 1. 5 light s. in darkness; and
5. 35 He was burning and s. light
Acts 9. 3 suddenly th. s, round ab't

22. 6 there *s.* gr. light round ab't
2 Co. 4. 4 lest light of C. should *s.*
Phil. 2. 15 among whom ye *s.* as
2 Pet. 1. 19 as light th. *s.* in darkness
1 John 2. 8 the true light now *s.*
Rev. 18. 23 candle shall *s.* no more
R. V. Mat. 24. 27 is seen ; Job 25.
   25 no brightness

Shining. *Brightness, glistening.*
2 Sam. 23. 4 grass springing by *s.*
Prov. 4. 18 path of just is as *s.* light
Isa. 4. 5 the *s.* of a fire by night
Joel 2. 10 stars shall withdraw *s.*
Hab. 3. 11 at *s.* of thy glittering
Mark 9. 3 his raiment became *s.*
Luke 11. 36 *s.* of a candle giveth
Acts 26. 13 above bright. of sun *s.*
R. V. Mark 9. 3 glistering ; Luke
   24. 4 dazzling

Ship. *Ship, vessel, boat.*
Gen. 49. 13 Zebul. a haven for *s.*
Num. 24. 24 *s.* shall come from Ch.
Deut. 28. 68 L. shall bring th. wi. *s.*
Judg. 5. 17 did Dan remain in *s.?*
1 K. 9. 26 Sol. made a navy of *s.*
2 Chr. 8. 18 Hur. sent by servants *s.*
Job 9. 26 they pass. as the swift *s.*
Ps. 48. 7 breakest *s.* of Tarshish
Prov. 30. 19 the way of *s.* in the sea
Isa. 2. 16 day of L. on *s.* of Tarshish
   33. 21 no gallant *s.* shall pass by
Ezek. 27. 9 all *s.* of sea with mar.
   30. 9 shall messengers go forth in *s.*
Dan. 11. 30 *s.* of Chittim shall come
   11. 40 king shall co. with many *s.*
Jonah 1. 3 Jonah found a *s.* going
Mat. 4. 21 in a *s.* with Zebedee
8. 24 *s.* was covered with waves
Mark 1. 19 in the *s.* mending nets
   4. 38 in the hinder part of *s.* asleep
Luke 5. 7 filled, *s.* began to sink
Acts 20. 38 accompanied him to *s.*
   21. 2 *s.* sailing over into Phenicia
Jas. 3. 4 *s.* though they be great
Rev. 8. 9 third part of *s.* destroyed
18. 17 company in *s.* stood afar off
R. V. Ezek. 27. 5 ; Mark 4. 38 ——;
   Mat. 4. 21, 22 ; 8. 23, 24 ; 9. 1 ; 13.
   2 ; 14. 13, 29, 32, 33 ; 15. 39 ; Mark
   1. 19, 20 ; 3. 9 ; 4. 1, 36, 37 ; 5. 2,
   18. 21 ; 6. 32, 45, 47, 51, 54 ; 8. 10
   13, 14 ; Luke 5. 2, 3, 7, 11 ; 8. 22,
   37 ; John 6. 17, 19, 21, 24 ; 21. 3, 6,
   8 boat or boats ; Acts 27. 41 vessel ;
   Acts 27. 18 throw overboard freight

Ship Boards. *Ship planks.*
Ezek. 27. 5 made thy *s. b.* of fir tree
Ship Master. *Pilot, owner.*
Jonah 1. 6 *s. m.* came to him, said
Acts 27. 11 centurion believ. *m.* of *s.*
Rev. 18. 17 *s. m.* and sailors cried
Ship Men. *Sailors.*
1 K. 9. 27 Hiram sent *s. m.* that had
Acts 27. 27, 30 *s. m.* were ab. to flee
R. V. Acts 27. 27 sailors
Shipping. R. V. *boats.*
John 6. 24 they also took *s.,* and
Shipwreck. *Shipwreck.*
2 Cor. 11. 25 thrice I suffered *s.*
1 Tim. 1. 19 concer. faith made *s.*
Shittah Tree. R. V. *acacia.*
Isa. 41. 19 I will plant the *s. t.*
Shittim. R. V. *acacia.*
Ex. 25. 10 make an ark of *s.* wood
   38. 1 he made the altar of *s.* wood
Deut. 10. 3 I made ark of *s.* wood
Shivers. *Fragments.*
Rev. 2. 27 ves. of potter bro. to *s.*
Shock. *Bunch, stack, shock.*
Judg. 15. 5 Samson burnt up the *s.*
Job 5. 26 like as *s.* of corn cometh
Shod. *Furnished with shoes.*
2 Chr. 28. 15 took captives, *s.* them
Ezek. 16. 10 I *s.* thee with badg. sk.
Mark 6. 9 be *s.* with sandals, put
Eph. 6. 15 *s.* with prepar. of gospel
Shoe. *Shoe.*
Ex. 3. 5 put *s.* from off thy feet
Deut. 25. 9 loose his *s.* from feet
Josh. 9. 5 old *s.* clouted on thy feet
Ruth 4. 7 a man plucked off his *s.*
1 K. 2. 5 put blood in *s.* on his feet
Ps. 60. 8 over Edom will I cast *s.*
S. of S. 7. 1 How beau. thy feet wi. *s.*
Isa. 5. 27 nor latchet of *s.* be broken
Ezek. 24. 23 your *s.* upon your feet

Am. 2. 6 sold poor for a pair of *s.*
Mat. 3. 11 *s.* am not worthy to bear
Mark 1. 7 latchet of whose *s.* I am
Luke 3. 16 ; John 1. 37 ∙ Acts 13. 25
Luke 10. 4 Car. neither scrip nor *s.*
Acts 7. 33 Put off *s.* from thy feet
R. V. Deut. 33. 25, bars ; S. of S.
   7. 1 sandals.
Shoe Latchet.
Gen. 14. 23 not take ev. to a *s. l.*
Isa. 5. 27 nor *l.* of their *s.* be broken
John 1. 27 *s. l.* not worthy to loos.
Shone. *See* **Shine.**
Shook. *See* **Shake.**
Shoot. *Cast, throw, send forth.*
Gen. 49. 23 the archers *s.*
Ex. 36. 33 made middle bar to *s.*
Num. 21. 30 we have *s.* at them
1 Sam. 20. 36 as lad ran, he *s.* arrow
2 Sam. 11. 20 Knew ye not th. wo. *s.*
2 K. 13. 17 Elisha said *S.,* and he *s.*
1 Chr. 5. 18 able to *s.* with bow
2 Chr. 35. 23 archers *s.* at Josiah
Job 8. 16 branch *s* forth in garden
Ps. 11. 2 may privily *s.* at upright
   64. 7 G. sh. *s.* at them with arrows
Isa. 27. 8 measur. when it *s.* forth
Jer. 9. 8 tongue is an arrow *s.* out
Ezek. 31. 14 nei. *s.* top am. boughs
Am. 7. 1 in beginning of the *s.* up
Mark 4. 32 must. seed *s.* branches
Luke 21. 30 When they now *s.* forth
R. V. Ex. 36. 33 pass through ; Ps.
   58. 7 aimeth ; Isa. 27. 8 sendest
   away : Ezek. 31. 14 set ; Mark
   4. 32 set
Shooter. *Who shoots.*
2 Sam. 11. 24 *s.* shot from off wall
Shore. *Lip, edge, beach.*
Gen. 22. 17 as sand upon the sea *s.*
Ex. 14. 30 saw Egyptian dead on *s.*
Josh. 15. 2 bord. from *s.* of salt sea
Judg. 5. 17 Asher continu. on sea *s.*
1 Sam. 13. 5 people as sand on *s. s.*
1 K. 9. 26 Eloth on *s.* of Red sea
Jer. 47. 7 against Ashkelon and *s. s.*
Mat. 13. 2 multitude stood on the *s.*
Mark 6. 53 came to land, drew to *s.*
John 21. 4 Jesus stood on the *s.*; but
Acts 21. 5 we kneeled down on *s.*
Heb. 11. 12 as sand wh. is by sea *s.*
R. V. Josh. 15. 2 uttermost part ;
   Judg. 5. 17 haven ; Mat. 13. 2, 48 ;
   John 21. 4 ; Acts 21. 5 ; 27. 39, 40
   beach
Shorn. *Sheared.*
S. of S. 4. 2 like sheep th. are ev. *s.*
Acts 18. 18 hav. *s.* head in Cenchrea
1 Cor. 11. 6 not cov., let her be *s.*
Short. *Little, brief.*
Num. 11. 23 Is L's hand waxen *s. ?*
Job 17. 12 light *s.* bec. of darkness
   20. 5 triumphing of wicked is *s.*
Ps. 89. 47 Remem how *s.* my time
Rom. 9. 28 will cut it *s.* in righteous.
1 Cor. 7. 29 breth., the time is *s.*
1 Thes. 2. 17 taken from you *s.* time
Rev. 12. 12 know. he hath *s.* time
Shortened. *Cut off, made short.*
Ps. 89. 45 days of youth thou *s.*
Prov. 10. 27 years of wick. sh. be *s.*
Isa. 50. 2 Is my hand *s.* at all
   59. 1 the Lord's hand is not *s.*
Mat. 24. 22 except those days be *s.*
Mark 13. 20 except that Lord had *s.*
Shorter. *Shorter.*
Isa. 28. 20 the bed is *s.* than man
Shortly. *Soon, quickly.*
Gen. 41. 32 G. will *s.* br. it to pass
Jer. 27. 16 vessels sh. *s.* be brought
Ezek. 7. 8 I *s.* pour out my fury
Acts 25. 4 that he would depart *s.*
Rom. 16. 20 G. sh. bruise Satan *s.*
1 Cor. 4. 19 I will come to you *s.*
Phil. 2. 19 I trust to send Timo. *s.*
1 Tim. 3. 14 hope. to co. to thee *s.*
2 Tim. 4. 9 Do dilig. to come *s.*
Heb. 13. 23 if he come, I see
2 Pet. 1. 14 *s.* I must put off this
3 John 14 trust I sh. *s.* see thee
Rev. 1. 1 things wh. must *s.* come
R. V. 2 Pet. 1. 14 swiftly
Shot. *See* **Shoot.**
Should. *Be about.*
Mat. 26. 35 Tho. I *s.* die with thee
Mark 10. 32 tell th. what *s.* happen

Luke 9. 31 *s.* accomplish at Jerus.
John 6. 71 he that *s.* betray him
   Etc., etc.
R. V. Frequent changes to, would,
   may, might, etc.
Shoulder. *Shoulder, arm, thigh.*
Gen. 9. 23 laid garments upon *s.*
Ex. 12. 34 bound in clothes upon *s.*
Lev. 7. 32 right *s.* give to priest
Num. 7. 9 sons of Ko. bear on *s.*
Deut. 33. 12 he sh. dwell between *s.*
Josh. 4. 5 take every man sto. on *s.*
Sudg. 9. 48 Abi. laid bow on his *s.*
1 Sam. 17. 6 target of brass bet. *s.*
1 Chr. 15. 15 Levites bare ark on *s.*
2 Chr. 35. 3 not a burden upon *s.*
Neh. 9. 29 withd. *s.,* harden. neck
Job 31. 36 I wo. take it on my *s.*
Ps. 81. 6 I removed sh. from burden
Isa. 9. 4 hast broken staff of his *s.*
   11. 14 shall fly on *s.* of Philistines
Ezek. 12. 7 I bare it upon my *s.*
   29. 18 head bald, every *s.* peeled
Zech. 7. 11 pulled away *s.,* stopped
Mat. 23. 4 burdens, lay them on *s.*
Luke 15. 5 lay. it on *s.,* rejoicing
R. V. Ex. 29. 22, 27 ; Lev. 7. 32, 33,
   34 ; 8. 25, 26 ; 9. 21 ; 10. 14, 15 ;
   Num. 6. 20 ; 18. 18 ; 1 Sam. 9. 24
   thigh ; Ex. 28. 12 ; 39. 7 shoulder
   pieces
Shout (*n.*). *Loud outcry.*
Num. 23. 21 *s.* of k. is among them
Josh. 6. 5 people *s.* with a great *s.*
1 Sam. 4. 5 Israel *s.* with great *s.*
2 Chr. 13. 15 men of Ju. gave a *s.*
Ez. 3. 11 peo. shouted with great *s.*
Ps. 47. 5 God is gone up with a *s.*
Jer. 25. 30 Lord shall give a *s.* as
Acts 12. 22 peo. gave a *s.,* saying
1 Thes. 4. 16 L. sh. descend wi. a *s.*
Shout. (*v.*). *Cry out, shout.*
Ex. 32. 18 not voice of them th. *s.*
Lev. 9. 24 when all peo. saw, th. *s.*
Josh. 6. 10 not *s.,* nor make noise
Judg. 15. 14 Philist. *s.* against him
1 Sam. 4. 5 when ark came, Is. *s.*
2 Chr. 13. 15 as the men of Judah *s.*
Ez. 3. 11 all people *s.* wi. gr. shout
Job 38. 7 sons of God *s.* for joy
Ps. 47. 1 *s.* to God with triumph
Isa. 44. 23 *s.,* ye low. parts of earth
Jer. 31. 7 *s.* among chief of nations
Lam. 3. 8 I *s.,* he shutteth prayer
Zeph. 3. 14 *s.,* O. Is., be glad and
Zech. 9. 9 *s.,* O daugh. of Jerusal.
R. V. Lam. 3. 8 call for help
Shouting. *Shouting.*
2 Sam. 6. 15 brought up ark wi. *s.*
2 Chr. 15. 14 sware to Lord with *s.*
Job 39. 25 smelleth battle, and *s.*
Prov. 11. 10 wicked per., there is *s.*
Isa. 16. 10 no singing, neither be *s.*
Jer. 20. 16 hear th. *s.* at noontide
Ezek. 21. 22 lift up the voice wi. *s.*
Am. 2. 2 M. sh. die in tum. and *s.*
Zech. 4. 7 br. forth headsto. with *s.*
R. V. Isa. 16. 10 joyful noise
Shovel. *Shovel.*
Ex. 27. 3 shall make pans and *s.*
Num. 4. 14 altar, put on it the *s.*
1 K. 7. 40 Hir. made lavers and *s.*
2 K. 25. 14 *s.* he took, the snuffers
2 Chr. 4. 11 Huram made pots and *s.*
Isa. 30. 24 been winnowed with *s.*
Jer. 52. 18 Chal. carried to Bab. *s.*
Show (*n.*). *see* **Show.** (*n.*).
Show (*v.*). *Tell, declare, reveal,
explain, present to view.*
Gen. 12. 1 land that I will *s.* thee
Ex. 33. 19 I *s.* mercy on whom I
Lev. 24. 12 mind of L. might be *s.*
Num. 13. 26 *s.* them fruit of land
Deut. 5. 5 *s.* you the word of Lord
Josh. 2. 12 I ha. *s.* you kindness
Judg. 6. 17 *s.* me sign thou talkest
1 Sam. 15. 6 ye *s.* kindness to chil.
2 Sam. 2. 6 L. *s.* kindness and truth
1 K. 3. 6 *s.* unto thy serv. David
2 K. 22. 10 the scribe *s.* the king
1 Chr. 19. 2 I *s.* kindness to Hanum
2 Chr. 16. 9 to *s.* himself strong in
Ez. 2. 59 could not *s.* father's house
Esth. 2. 10 Esth. had not *s.* people
Job 11. 6 he would *s.* thee secrets
Ps. 19. *y* firma. *s.* his handywork

85. 7 s. us thy mercy, O Lord, and
Prov. 28. 24 must s. himself friend.
Isa. 30. 30 s. the lighting down of
Jer. 32. 18 Thou s. lovingkindness
Ezek. 43. 10 s. the house to Israel
Dan. 2. 2 call magicians to s. king
Am. 7. 1 Thus hath the Lord God s.
Mic. 7. 15 I s. marvellous things
Nah. 3. 5 s. nations thy nakedness
Hab. 1. 3 Why dost s. me iniquity
Zech. 1. 20 Lord s. me carpenters
Mat. 4. 8 s. him kingdoms of world
Mark 14. 15 he will s. you up. room
Luke 20. 24 S. penny. Whose im.
John 2. 18 What signs s. thou us
Acts 7. 3 come into land I s. thee
Rom. 2. 15 s. work of law written
1 Cor. 11. 26 ye do s. Lord's death
2 Cor. 8. 24 s. proof of your love
Eph. 2. 17 s. exceeding riches of
1 Thes. 1. 9 for they themselves s.
1 Tim. 6. 15 in his times he shall s.
2 Tim. 2. 15 s. thyself appr. of God
Tit. 3. 2 but gentle, s. all meekness
Heb. 6. 11 every one s. diligence
Jas. 2. 18 s. faith without thy works
2 Pet. 1. 14 as our L. J. C. hath s.
1 John 1. 2 s. to your eternal life
Rev. 4. 1 I will s. thee things wh.
R. V. frequent changes, chiefly to,
tell, declare, manifest, etc

Shower. *Rain.*
Deut. 32. 2 my speech distil as s.
Job 24. 8 the poor are wet with s.
Ps. 65. 10 thou make it soft with s.
Jer. 3. 3 s. have been withholden
Ezek. 13. 11 shall be overflowing s.
34. 26 there shall be s. of blessing
Mic. 5. 7 Jac. sh. be as s. on grass
Zech. 10. 1 Lord shall give them s
Luke 12. 54 say, There cometh s.

Shrank. R. V. *hip.*
Gen. 32. 32 eat not sinew which s.

Shred. *Split.*
2 K. 4. 39 gourds s. them into pot

Shrines. *Inner places.*
Acts 19. 24 silversmith, wh. ma. s.

Shroud. *Bough.*
Ezek. 31. 3 cedar, wi. shadowing s.

Shrubs. *Shrub, bush.*
Gen. 21. 15 Ha. cast child under s.

Shun. ◻*Decline, avoid.*
Acts 20. 27 not s. to declare to you
2 Tim. 2. 16 s. profane babblings
R. V. Acts 20. 27 shrank

Shut. *Close, shut.*
Gen. 19. 6 Lot s. door after him
Ex. 14. 3 wilderness hath s. them
Lev. 13. 4 priest shall s. up him
Num. 12. 15 Miriam was s. fr. camp
Deut. 15. 7 s. hand fr. poor bro.
Josh. 6. 1 Jericho was s. up because
Judg. 3. 23 Ehud. s. doors of parlour
1 Sam. 1. 5 L. had s. up her womb
2 Sam. 20. 3 were s. up unto day of
1 K. 4. 5 s. door on her and sons
2 K. 17. 4 king of Assyr. s. him up
2 Chr. 7. 13 If I s. heav. be no rain
Neh. 6. 10 let us s. doors of temple
Job 3. 10 it hath s. up sea ?
Ps. 69. 15 let not pit s. her mouth
Prov. 17. 28 that s. lips is a man
Eccl. 12. 4 doors sh. be s. in streets
S. of S. 4. 12 sister, a spring s. up
Isa. 6. 10 s. th. eyes; lest they see
Jer. 32. 2 the proph. was s. in court
Lam. 3. 8 when I cry he s. out pray.
Ezek. 44. 1 gate of sanctua. was s.
Dan. 12. 4 s. up words, seal book
Mat. 6. 6 s. thy door, pray in secr.
Luke 4. 25 heav. was s. three years
John 20. 26 came J., came being s.
Acts 5. 23 prison truly found we s.
Gal. 3. 23 s. up unto faith which
1 John 3. 17 s. his bowels of compas.
Rev. 3. 8 open door, no man can s.
R. V. Deut. 32. 30 delivered

Shutting *Closing.*
Josh. 2. 5 about time of s. of gate

Shuttle. *Weaving part.*
Job 7. 6 swifter than a weaver's s.

Sick. *Sick, diseased.*
Gen. 48. 1 Behold, thy father is s.
Lev. 15. 33 that is s. of her flowers
1 Sam. 19. 14 she said, He is s.
2 Sam. 12. 15 L. struck ch., was s.

1 K. 14. 1 son of Jeroboam fell s.
2 K. 1. 2 Ahaz fell down, was s.
2 Chr. 32. 4 Hez. was s. unto death
Neh. 2. 2 why sad, thou art not s.
Ps. 35. 13 s., my cloth. was sackclo.
Prov. 13. 12 Hope def. mak. heart s.
S. of S. 2. 5 comfort, I am s. of love
Isa. 1. 5 whole head is s., heart faint
Jer. 14. 18 that are s. with famine
Ezek. 34. 4 nei. healed wh. was s.
Dan. 8. 27 Daniel fainted, and was s.
Hos. 7. 5 princes have made him s.
Mic. 6. 13 I made thee s. in smiting
Mal. 1. 8 offer s., is it not evil ?
Mat. 4. 24 they brought unto him s.
Mark 6. 5 that he laid hands on s.
Luke 7. 2 centurion's serv. was s.
John 11. 1 cert. man s., named Laz.
Acts 5. 15 brought s into the streets
Phil. 2. 26 had heard he had been s.
2 Tim. 4. 20 Tro. I left at Mil. s.
Jas. 5. 14 s. ? let him call elders
R. V. Prov 23. 35 hurt; Mic. 6. 13
wound ; Luke 7. 10 ——; 5. 24;
Acts 9. 33 palsied

Sickle. *Reapinghook.*
Deut. 16. 9 begin. to put the s. to
Jer. 15. 16 cut off him th. hand. s.
Joel 3. 13 Put in s., harvest is ripe
Mark 4. 29 immedi. he put. in s.
Rev. 14. 14 and in hand a sharp s.
14. 18 Thrust in sharp s., gather

Sickly. *Not strong.*
1 Cor. 11. 30 many are weak and s.

Sickness. *Disease, infirmity.*
Ex. 23. 25 I will take s. away from
Lev. 20. 18 if lie wi. wom. having s.
Deut. 7. 15 Lord will take away s.
1 K. 17. 17 his s. was so sore, that
2 K. 13. 14 Now Elisha was fallen s.
2 Chr. 21. 15 thou sh. have great s.
Ps. 41. 3 wilt make all his bed in s.
Eccl. 5. 17 sor. and wrath with s.
Isa. 38. 9 Hez. recovered of his s.
Hos. 5. 13 When Eph. saw his s.
Mat. 4. 23 Jesus went healing all s.
John 11. 4 this s. is not unto death

Sicknesses. *Diseases.*
Deut. 28. 59 sore s. of long contin.
Mat. 8. 17 took infirm., bare our s.
Mark 3. 15 have power to heal s.
R. V. Mat. 8. 17 diseases ; Mark 3.
15 ——;

Side. *Round about.*
Num. 16. 27 from taberna. on every s
Judg. 7. 18 blow trumpet on ev. s.
1 Sam. 12. 11 hand of enemies ev. s.
1 K. 5. 4 God ha. given rest on ev. s.
1 Chr. 22. 18 ; 2 Chr. 14. 7
Job 19. 10 destroyed me on every s.
Ps. 12. 8 wicked walk on every s.
Jer. 6. 25 sword of en. on every s.
Ezek. 16. 33 come to thee on ev. s.
Edge, margin, side.
Gen. 6. 16 the door of ark set in s.
Ex. 2. 5 maidens walked by river's s.
Lev. 5. 9 shall sprinkle s. of altar
Num. 21. 13 pitched on s. of Arnon
Deut. 1. 5 on this s. Jordan, Moab
Josh. 23. 13 scourges in s., thorns
Judg. 2. 3 be as thorns in your s.
1 Sam. 14. 4 sharp rock on one s.
2 Sam. 2. 16 thrust sword in fel. s.
1 K. 4. 24 he had peace on all s.
2 K. 9. 23 come up to s. of Lebanon
1 Chr. 6. 78 on other s. of Jordan
2 Chr. 4. 10 Set the sea on right s.
Ez. 8. 36 to the governors on this s.
Job 18. 12 destructio. ready at his s.
Ps. 91. 7 thousand shall fall at s.
Isa. 37. 24 I come up to s. of Leb.
Jer. 6. 22 nat. raised from s. of earth
Ezek. 4. 8 sh. not turn from one s.
Dan 7. 5 raised up itself on one s.
Mat. 13. 14 seeds fell by the way s.
Mark 2. 13 he went forth by sea s.
Luke 8. 22 go over unto the other s.
John 20. 25 thrust hand into my s.
Acts 16. 13 on sab. went by riv. s.
2 Cor. 4. 8 are troubled on every s.
R. V. Many changes frequent, due mostly
to context ; as, other side, beyond,
etc.

Siege. *Besiege, fortress.*
Deut. 20. 19 to employ them in s.
1 K. 15. 27 Nadab laid s. to Gibbe.

2 Chr. 32. 10 abide in s. of Jerusalem
Isa. 29. 3 I will lay s. aguinst thee
Jer. 19. 9 eat flesh of friend in s.
Ezek. 4. 2 lay s., build fort against
Mic. 5. 1 he hath laid s. against us
Nah. 3. 14 Draw the water for the s.
Zech. 12. 2 when they shall be in s.

Sieve. *Sifter.*
Isa. 30. 28 sift nations with the s.
Am. 9. 9 as the corn is sifted in s.

Sift. *Shake, sift.*
Isa. 30. 28 to sift nations with sieve
Am. 9. 9 like as corn is s. in sieve
Luke 22. 31 Sat. desired he may s.

Sigh (n.). *Sigh.*
Lam. 1. 22 for my s. are many

Sigh (v.). *Sigh, groan.*
Ex. 2. 23 Is. s. by reason of bond.
Job 3. 24 s. cometh before I eat
Ps. 31. 10 spent my years with s.
Isa. 21. 2 the s. I have made cease
24. 7 all the merry hearted do s.
Jer. 45. 3 I fainted in my s. and I
Lam. 1. 11 peo. s., they seek bread
Ezek. 21. 7 say, Wheref. s. thou ?
Mark 8. 12 s. deeply in his spirit
R. V. Jer. 45. 3 groaning

Sight. *Vision, appearance, eye,
spectacle.*
Gen. 2. 9 every tree pleasant to s.
Ex. 24. 17 s. of glory of Lord was
Lev. 13. 4 in s. not deep. th. skin
Num. 13. 13 in own s. as grasshop.
Deut. 12. 25 do right in s. of Lord
Josh. 4. 14 L. magnified Josh. in s.
Judg. 6. 1 Is. did evil in s. of L.
Ruth 2. 13 Let me find fa. in thy s.
1 Sam. 29. 9 thou art good in my s.
2 Sam. 2. 9 cut enemies out of s.
1 K. 11. 6 Sol did evil in s. of Lord
2 K. 17. 23 L. remov. Is. out of s.
1 Chr. 22. 8 ha. shed blood in my s.
2 Chr. 24. 2 Joash did right in s. of
Neh. 8. 5 Ez. op. book in s. of all
Esth. 2. 15 Esther obt. favour in s.
Job 25. 5 stars not pure in his s.
Ps. 5. 5 foolish not stand in thy s.
Prov. 1. 17 in vain net spread in s.
Eccl. 6. 9 Bet. s. of eyes than wand.
Isa. 26. 17 so ha. we been in thy s.
Jer. 4. 1 put abom. out of my s.
Ezek. 10. 2 went in my s. to fill
Dan. 4. 20 s. thereof to all the earth
Hos. 6. 2 we shall live in his s.
Am. 9. 3 tho. they be hid from s.
Jonah 2. 4 I am cast out of thy s.
Mal. 2. 17 that doeth ev. is good s.
Mat. 11. 5 The blind receive th. s.
Mark 10. 52 received s., followed J.
Luke 18. 41 that I may receive s.
John 9. 11 washed, and received s.
Acts 9. 9 was three days without s.
Rom. 12. 17 Prov. things hon. in s.
2 Cor. 5. 7 we walk by faith, not s.
Gal. 3. 11 no man just. in s. of G.
Col. 1. 22 unreprovable in his s.
1 Thes. 1. 3 in s. of God our Fath.
Heb. 13. 21 wellpleasing in his s.
Jas. 4. 10 hum. yours. in s. of God
1 John 3. 22 things pleas. in his s.
Rev. 13. 13 mak. fire to come in s.
R. V. Many changes to, eyes, pres-
ence, appearance, etc.

Sign (n.). *Sign, signal, token.*
Gen. 1. 14 let th. be for s. and sea.
Ex. 4. 9 if they will not believe s.
Num. 16. 38 they sh. be a s. to Is.
Deut. 6. 22 L. shewed s. and won.
Josh. 4. 6 this be a s. among you
Judg. 6. 17 shew me s. thou talkest
1 Sam. 2. 34 this shall be s. to you
1 K. 13. 3 he gave s. the same day
2 K. 19. 29 this shull be s. to thee
2 Chr. 32. 24 and he gave him a s.
Neh. 9. 10 sh. s. and wond. on Phar.
Ps. 74. 4 they set up ensigns for s.
Isa. 7. 4 Lord shall give you a s.
Jer. 10. 2 and not be dismayed at s.
Ezek. 14. 8 ma. him s. and proverb
Dan. 6. 27 he work. s. and wonders
Mat. 12. 38 Master, we wo. see s.
Mark 8. 12 There sh. no s. be given
Luke 2. 12 this shall be s. to you
John 2. 18 Wh. s. showest thou us
Acts 28. 11 ship, whose s. was Castor
Rom. 4. 11 he rec. s. of circumcis.

1 Cor. 1. 22 the Jews require a *s.*
2 Cor. 12. 12 *s.* of apost. w. wrought
2 Thes. 2. 9 working of Sat. with *s.*
Heb. 2. 4 God bearing wit. with *s.*
Rev. 15. 1 I saw another *s.* in heaven
Sign (*v.*).   *Write, note.*
Dan. 6. 9 Darius *s.* the writing
6. 10 Dan. knew the writing was *s.*
Signet.   *Seal, signet.*
Gen. 38. 25 whose are these, the *s.*
Ex. 28. 11 like engraving of a *s.*
Jer. 22. 24 though Coniah were *s.*
Dan. 6. 17 the king sealed it with *s.*
Hag. 2. 24 I will ma. thee as a *s.*
Signification.   *Sense, meaning.*
1 Cor. 14. 10 and none is without *s.*
Signify.   *Declare, manifest.*
John 12. 33 *s.* by what death he
Acts 21. 26 to *s.* accomplishment of
Heb. 9. 8 Hly. Gh. *s.* that the way
1 Pet. 1. 11 the spirit in them did *s.*
Rev. 1. 1 *s.* it by angel to servant
R. V. Acts 21. 26 declaring ; 1 Pet.
1. 11 point out
Silence.   *Stillness, quietness.*
Judg. 3. 19 O k. ; who said, Keep *s.*
Job 4. 16 there was *s.*, I heard voice
Ps. 31. 18 lying lips be put to *s.*
39. 2 I was dumb with *s.*, I held
94. 17 my soul had alm. dwelt in *s.*
Eccl. 3. 7 time to keep *s.* ti. to speak
Isa. 41. 1 keep *s.* bef. me, O islands
Jer. 8. 14 Lord God hath put us to *s.*
Lam. 3. 28 sitteth alone, keeping *s.*
Am. 5. 13 the prudent shall keep *s.*
Hab. 2. 20 let earth keep *s.* bef. you
Mat. 22. 34 he put Sadduc. to *s.*
Acts 15. 12 all the multitude kept *s.*
1 Cor. 14. 28 keep *s.* in the church
14. 34 Let wom. keep *s.* in church
1 Tim. 2. 11 let woman learn in *s.*
1 Pet. 2. 15 may put to *s.* ignorance
Rev. 8. 1 there was *s.* in heaven
R. V. Ps. 31. 18 dumb ; Isa. 15. 1
nought ; 62. 6 take no rest ; Acts
22. 2 quiet ; 1 Tim. 2. 11, 12 quietness
Silent.   *Still, without voice.*
1 Sam. 2. 9 wick. sh. be *s.* in darkn.
Ps. 22. 2 I cry in night, am not *s.*
39. 2 w. dumb wi. *s.* held my peace
Isa. 47. 5 sit thou *s.*, and get thee
Jer. 8. 14 let us be *s.* there, for Lord
Zech. 2. 13 Be *s.*, O all flesh, bef. L.
R. V. Ps. 28. 1 deaf unto.
Silk.   *Silk.*
Prov. 31. 22 tap., her clothing is *s.*
Ezek. 16. 10 I covered thee with *s.*
Rev. 18. 12 no man buyeth her *s.*
R. V. Prov. 31. 22 fine linen
Silly.   *Simple, foolish.*
Job 5. 2 envy slayeth the *s.* one
Hos. 7. 11 Ephr. is like a *s.* dove
2 Tim. 3. 6 lead captive *s.* women
Silver.   *Silver, silverling.*
Gen. 13. 2 Abram was rich in *s.*
Ex. 20. 23 shall not ma. gods of *s.*
Lev. 5. 15 estima. by shekels. of *s.*
Num. 7. 13 his off. was *s.* charger
Deut. 7. 25 thou sh. not desire *s.*
Josh. 7. 21 they are hid, *s.* under
Judg. 17. 2 behold, *s.* is with me
1 Sam. 2. 36 crouch for *s.* and bre.
2 Sam. 8. 10 Joram bro. vessels of *s.*
1 K. 10. 21 none of *s.*, it was noth.
2 K. 16. 8 Ahaz took *s.* and gold
1 Chr. 18. 10 Tou sent vessels of *s.*
2 Chr. 1. 15 king made *s.* at Jerusal.
Ez. 1. 4 let men help him wi. *s.*
Neh. 5. 15 gov. had for. shek. of *s.*
Job 3. 15 princes fill. houses with. *s.*
22. 25 thou sh. have plenty of *s.*
Ps. 12. 6 as *s.* tried in a furnace
66. 10 hast tried us, as *s.* is tried
115. 4 their idols are *s.* and gold
Prov. 3. 14 wisd. is better than *s.*
10. 20 tongue of just is choice *s.*
25. 11 like ap. of go. in pict. of *s.*
Eccl. 2. 8 I gathered me also *s.*
12. 6 or ever the *s.* cord be loosed
S. of S. 8. 9 will build a palace of *s.*
Isa. 1. 22 Thy *s* is become dross
48. 10 refined thee, but not with *s.*
Jer. 10. 4 deck it with *s.* and gold
Ezek. 7. 19 sh. cast *s.* into streets
Dan. 2. 32 his breast and arms of *s.*

Hos. 2. 8 I multiplied her *s.* and g.
Joel 3. 5 ye have taken my *s.* and go
Am. 2. 6 they sold righteous for *s.*
Nah. 2. 9 Take ye the spoil of *s.*
Hab. 2. 19 it is laid over with *s.*
Zeph. 1. 11 that bear *s.* are cut off
Hag. 2. 8 *s.* is mine, gold is mine
Zech. 6. 11 take *s.* and make crowns
Mal. 3. 3 purge them as gold and *s.*
Mat. 10. 9 Provide nei. gold nor *s.*
26. 15 cov. for thirty pieces of *s.*
Acts 3. 6 *s.* and gold have I none
19. 24 Demetrius made *s.* shrines
1 Cor. 3. 12 build on this found., *s.*
2 Tim. 2. 20 are ves. of *s.* and gold
Jas. 5. 3 your go. and *s.* is cankered
1 Pet. 1. 18 not redeemed as with *s.*
Rev. 9. 20 not wor. idols of g. and *s.*
R. V. Josh. 24. 32 ; 2 K. 22. 4
money ; 1 Chr. 28. 17 bowl
Silverlings.   *Coin, shekel.*
Isa. 7. 23 vines at a thousand *s.*
Silversmith.   *Worker in silver.*
Acts 19. 24 Demetrius a *s.* made
Similitude.   *Likeness, form.*
Num. 12. 8 *s.* of L. sh. he behold
Deut. 4. 12 heard voi., but saw no *s.*
2 Chr. 4. 3 under it was *s.* of oxen
Ps. 106. 20 changed glory into *s.*
Dan. 10. 16 one like *s.* sons of men
Rom. 5. 14 after *s.* of A.'s trangres.
Heb. 7. 15 after *s.* of Melchisedec
Jas. 3. 9 men made after *s.* of God
Comparisons.
Hos. 12. 10 I ha. spoken and used *s.*
R. V. Num. 12. 8 ; Deut. 4. 12, 12,
16 form ; Ps. 144. 12 fashion ; 106.
20 ; Rom. 5. 14 ; Jas. 3. 9 likeness ; Heb. 7. 15 if .. likewise
Simple.   *Plain, artless, innocent, foolish.*
Ps. 19. 7 Lord maketh wise the *s.*
Prov. 1. 4 to give subtilty to the *s.*
8. 5 O ye, *s.*, understand wisdom
27. 12 but *s.* pass on, and are pun.
Ezek. 45. 20 do for him that is *s.*
Rom. 16. 18 fair speeches deceive *s.*
R. V. Rom. 16. 18 innocent
Simplicity.   *Plainness, innocence.*
2 Sam. 15. 11 they went in their *s.*
Prov. 1. 22 How lo. will yove *s.* ? *s.*
Rom. 12. 8 that giveth, do it with
2 Cor. 1. 12 in *s.* had conversatione
11. 3 corrupted from *s.* that is in C.
R. V. Rom. 2. 8 liberality ; 2 Cor.
1. 12 holiness
Sin (*n.*).   *Sin, error, offence, guilt, trespass, transgression.*
Gen. 4. 7 not well, *s.* lieth at door
Ex. 10. 17 forgive my *s.* this once
Lev. 4. 3 if priest *s.* according to *s.*
Num. 16. 26 lest ye be consum. in *s.*
Deut. 15. 9 cry to Lord, if it be *s.*
Josh. 24. 19 G. will not forg. your *s.*
1 Sam. 2. 17 *s.* of young men was gr.
2 Sam. 12. 13 L. ha. put away thy *s.*
1 K. 8. 34 L., forg. *s.* of thy people
2 K. 3. 3 Jeh. cleaved to *s.* of Jer.
2 Chr. 28. 13 ye add more to our *s.*
Neh. 1. 6 confess *s.* of child. of Israel
Job 20. 11 his bones are full of *s.*
Ps. 25. 7 Remem. not *s.* of my youth
51. 2 Wash, and cleanse me from *s.*
Prov. 10. 16 life, fruit of wick. to *s.*
14. 34 *s.* is reproach to any people
21. 4 plowing of the wicked is *s.*
Isa. 3. 9 they declare their *s.* as Sod.
Jer. 17. 1 *s.* of Jud. is writ. wi. pen
Lam. 4. 22 dau., he will disc. thy *s.*
Ezek. 3. 20 he shall die in his *s.*
Dan. 4. 27 break off *s.* by righteous.
Hos. 4. 8 They eat up *s.* of my peo.
Am. 5. 12 I know your mighty *s.*
Mic 1. 13 she is the beginning of *s.*
Zech. 13. 1 fount. open. to Jerus. f. *s.*
Mat. 1. 21 he sh. save peo. from *s.*
9. 5 say, Thy *s.* be forgiven thee
Mark 2. 5 Son, thy *s.* be forg. the.
Luke 5. 21 Who can forg. *s.* but God
John 1. 29 wh. tak. away *s.* of world
Acts 7. 60 lay not *s.* to their charge
Rom. 3. 20 by law is knowl. of *s.*
5. 12 *s.* ent. wor. and death by *s.*
14. 23 whatsoever is not faith is *s.*
1 Cor. 15. 3 Christ died for our *s.*
2 Cor. 5. 21 made him be *s.* for us

Gal. 1. 4 Who gave hims. for our *s.*
Eph. 2. 1 quick. who were dead in *s.*
Col. 1. 14 even the forgiveness of *s.*
1 Thes. 2. 16 to fill up the *s.* alway
2 Thes. 2. 3 man of *s.* be revealed
1 Tim. 3. 22 nei. parta. of o. men's *s.*
2 Tim. 3. 6 lead women laden wi. *s.*
Heb. 3. 13 be hardened through *s.*
Jas. 1. 15 it bring. forth *s.*, and *s.*
1 Pet. 2. 22 did no sin, nei. guile
2 Pet. 1. 9 he was purged fr. old *s.*
1 John 1. 7 blood of J. cleans. fr. *s.*
Rev. 18. 5 her *s.* ha. reach. to heaven
R. V. Prov. 10. 12, 19 ; 28. 13 transgression ; 14. 9 Jer. 51. 5 guilt ; 2
Chr. 28. 10 ; Eph. 1. 7 ; 2. 5 ; Col.
2. 13 trespasses ; Col. 2. 11 ; 1 John
2. 2 ——.
Sin.   *Err, go astray.*
Gen. 20. 6 I withheld thee from *s.*
Ex. 10. 16 I ha. *s* against Lord G.
Lev. 4. 2 if soul *s.* thro. ignorance
Num. 22. 34 Balaam said, I have *s.*
Josh. 7. 20 I have *s.* against Lord
1 Sam. 19. 4 Let not k. *s.* ag. serv.
2 Sam. 12. 13 D. sa. to Nath., I ha. *s.*
1 K. 8. 50 forgive peo. that have *s.*
2 K. 17. 7 children of Israel had *s.*
1 Chr. 21. 8 I have *s.* greatly, bec.
2 Chr. 6. 22 If man *s.* ag. neighbour
Neh. 1. 6 I and fath's house have *s.*
Job 1. 22 Job *s.* not. nor charged G.
Ps. 41. 4 heal my soul, for I have *s.*
Prov. 14. 21 that despiseth neigh. *s.*
Eccl. 7. 20 not a just man that *s.* not
Isa. 43. 27 fath. hath *s.* and thy teac.
Jer. 3. 25 we have *s.* against Lord
Lam. 1. 8 Jerus. hath grievously *s.*
Ezek. 18. 4, 20 soul that *s.*, it sh. die
Dan. 9. 5 *s.*, and committed iniquity
Hos. 4. 7 as th. increased, so they *s.*
Mic. 7. 9 I bear indig. of L. bec. I *s.*
Hab. 2. 20 consult. shame and ha. *s*
Zeph. 1. 17 they ha. *s.* against the L.
Mat. 27. 4 I *s.* in that I betrayed
Luke 15, 18, 21 I ha. *s.* ag. Heaven
John 5. 14 *s.* no more, lest worse co.
Rom. 6. 15 *s.* bec. not under law ?
1 Cor. 6. 18 that commit. fornica. *s.*
2 Cor. 12. 21 I bewail which have *s.*
Eph. 4. 26 Be ye angry, and *s.* not
1 Tim. 5. 20 them that *s.* rebuke
Tit. 3. 11 *s.*, being condemned of self
Heb. 10. 26 if we *s.* wilfully after
2 Pet. 2. 4 G. spared not angels th. *s.*
1 John 2. 1 these write I th. ye *s.* not
R. V. Lev. 4. 13 err
Sin offering.
Ex. 29. 36 every day bullock for *s. o.*
Lev. 6. 25 This the law of the *s. o.*
2 Chr. 29. 21 ; Ez. 6. 17 ; Neh. 10.
33 ; Ps. 40. 6 ; Ezek. 40. 39
Since.   *From, seeing that.*
Gen. 46. 30 *s.* I have seen thy face
Josh. 2. 12 *s.* I ha. shewed kindness
Mat. 24. 21 *s.* begin. of the world
Etc., etc.
Sincere.   *Pure, true, genuine.*
Phil. 1. 10 be *s.* and without offence
1 Pet. 2. 2 as babes desire *s.* milk
R. V. 1 Pet. 2. 2 spiritual
Sincerely.   *Plainly, truly.*
Judg. 9. 16 if ye ha. done tru. and *s.*
Phil. 1. 16 one preach Christ not *s.*
R. V. Judg. 9. 16 uprightly ; Phil. 1.
16 —— but transferred to vs. 17
Sincerity.   *Plainness, truth, genuineness.*
Josh. 24. 14 serve him in *s.* and tr.
1 Cor. 5. 8 with unleav. bread of *s.*
2 Cor. 1. 12 in godly *s.* we have had
Eph. 6. 24 that love Lord J. C. in *s.*
Tit. 2. 7 showing uncov., gravity, *s.*
R. V. Eph. 6. 24 uncorruptness ;
Tit. 2. 7 ——
Sinew.   *Nerve, sinew.*
Gen. 32. 32 chil. of Is. eat not of *s.*
Job 10. 11 fenced me wi. bo. and *s.*
30. 17 bones are pierced, *s.* take no
Isa. 48. 4 thy neck is an iron *s.*
Ezek. 37. 6 I will lay *s.* upon you
R. V. Job 30. 17 gnaw
Sinful.   *Erring, in sin.*
Num. 32. 14 an increase of *s.* men
Isa. 1. 4 *s.* nation, a people laden
Am. 9. 8 eyes of L. on *s.* kingdom

Mark 8. 38 ashamed in *s.* generat.
Luke 5. 8 for I am a *s.* man, O L.
Rom. 7. 13 sin might bec. exceed. *s.*

Sing. *Sing, praise.*
Ex. 15. 1 *s.*, Mos. and child. of Is.
Num. 21. 17 Is. *s.* song, Spr. up, O.
Judg. 5. 1 Then *s.* Deb. and Barak
1 Chr. 16. 23 *S.* unto L., all the earth
Job 29. 13 caus. widow's heart to *s.*
38. 7 morning stars *s.* together, and
Ps. 13. 6 I will *s.* unto the Lord
21. 13; 27. 6; 33. 3; 59. 16
98. 1 *s.* unto the Lord a new song
Prov. 29. 6 righteous *s.* and rejoice
Isa. 24. 14 *s.* for majesty of Lord
49. 13 *S.*, O heav. ; be joyful earth
Jer. 20. 13 *S.* unto L., praise ye L.
Ezek. 27. 25 ships of Tarsh. did *s.*
Hos. 2. 15 sh. *s.* as in days of youth
Zeph. 3. 14 *S.*, O daughter of Zion
Zech. 2. 10 *S.*, and rejoice, O daugh.
Mat. 26. 30 when they had *s.* hymn
Mark 14. 26 And when they had *s.*
Acts 16. 25 Silas prayed and *s.* prais.
Rom. 15. 9 I will confess and *s.*
1 Cor. 14. 15 I will *s.* with the spirit
Eph. 5. 19 *s.* and making melody
Col. 3. 16 *s.* with grace in heart to
Heb. 2. 12 in midst of church I *s.*
Jas. 5. 13 Is any merry ? let him *s.*
Rev. 5. 9 And they *s.* a new song
15. 3 they *s.* the song of Moses the
R. V. Ps. 30. 4 ; 33. 2 ; 57. 9 ; 71. 22,
23 ; 98. 5 ; 101. 1 sing praises ;
Isa. 24. 14 shout ; Hos. 2. 15 make
answer

Singed. *Scorched.*
Dan. 3. 27 nor was hair of head *s.*

Singer. *Who sings.*
1 K. 10. 12 made psalteries for *s.*
1 Chr. 6. 33 Heman a *s.* son of Joel
2 Chr. 5. 1 Levites which were *s.*
Ez. 2. 41 The *s.*, children of Asaph
Neh. 7. 1 *s.* and Levites were ap.
Ps. 68. 25 *s.* went bef., the players
Eccl. 2. 8 I gat me men *s.*, and wo.
Ezek. 40. 44 chamb. of *s.* in court
Hab. 3. 19 *s.* on my stringed instr.
R. V. Hab. 3. 19 musician

Singing. *Singing.*
1 Sam. 18. 6 wom. came *s.* and dan.
2 Sam. 19. 35 the voice of *s.* men
1 Chr. 6. 32 they ministered with *s.*
2 Chr. 23. 18 offer burnt off. with *s.*
Ez. 2. 65 am. them two hun. *s.* men
Neh. 12. 27 kept dedication wi. *s.*
Ps. 100. 2 come bef. his presence *s.*
S. of S. 2. 12 time of *s.* birds is come
Isa. 14. 7 they break forth in *s.*
16. 10 in vineyards shall be no *s.*
Zeph. 3. 17 joy over thee with *s.*
Eph. 5. 19 *s.* and making melody
Col. 3. 16 *s.* with grace in heart
R. V. 1 Chr. 6. 32 ; 13. 8 songs

Single. *Unspotted.*
Mat. 6. 22 if therefore eye be *s.*
Luke 11. 34 eye *s.*, bod. full of light

Singleness. *Not duplicate.*
Acts 2. 46 wi. gladness and *s.* of h.
Eph. 6. 5 with. fear, in *s.* of heart
Col. 3. 22 in *s.* of heart, fearing God

Singular. R. V. *accomplish.*
Lev. 27. 2 man shall make *s.* vow

Sink. *Go down.*
Ex. 15. 10 sea covered them, they *s.*
1 Sam. 17. 49 stone *s.* into his fore.
2 K. 9. 24 smote Jehor., he *s.* down
Ps. 69. 2 I *s.* in deep mire, where
69. 14 Deliver me, let me nct *s.*
Jer. 51. 64 Thus shall Babylon *s.*
Mat. 14. 30 begin. to *s.*, he cried
Luke 5. 7 so that they began to *s.*
9. 44 Let these sayings *s.* down
Acts 20. 9 he *s.* wi. sleep, and fell

Sinned. *See* Sin (*v.*),

Sinner. *Who sins.*
Gen. 13. 13 men of Sodom were *s.*
1 Sam. 15. 18 utterly des. *s.* of Am.
Ps. 1. 1 nor standeth in way of *s.*
Prov. 1. 10 if *s.* ent. consent not
Eccl. 2. 26 he giveth travail
Isa. 1. 28 destr. of *s.* be together
33. 14 The *s.* in Zion are afraid
Am. 9. 10 *s.* shall die by the sword
Mat. 9. 10 many *s.* sat do. wi. him
Mark 2. 17 to call *s.* to repentance

Luke 6. 32 *s.* love those love them
John 6. 16 can *s.* do miracles?
Rom. 5. 8 wh. we were *s.*, C. died
Gal. 2. 15 Jews, not *s.* of Gentiles
1 Tim. 1. 9 the law is made for *s.*
Jas. 4. 8 cleanse your hands, ye *s.*
Jude 15 speeches wh. *s.* have spok.
R. V. Luke 13. 4 offenders

Sir. *Lord, master, man.*
Gen. 43. 20 *S.*, we ca. to buy food
Mat. 13. 27 *S.*, didst not thou sow
John 4. 15 *S.*, give me this water
Acts 16. 30 *S.*, wh. do to be saved
Rev. 7. 14 said to him, *S.*, thou kn.
R. V. Gen. 43. 20 ; Rev. 7. 14 my
lord

Sister. *Sister.*
Gen. 30. 1 Rachel envied her *s.*, and
Ex. 15. 20 Miriam, *s.* of Aaron
Lev. 18. 18 nei. take wife to her *s.*
Num. 26. 59 A., M., Miriam their *s.*
Deut. 27. 22 Cursed, that lieth wi. *s.*
Josh. 2. 13 save alive my bro. and *s.*
Judg. 15. 2 is not her younger *s.* fa.
2 Sam. 13. 1 son of D. had fairer *s.*
1 K. 11. 19 *s.* of Taph. the queen
2 K. 11. 2 *s.* of Ahaziah took Joash
1 Chr. 1. 39 Timna was Lotan's *s.*
2 Chr. 22. 11 she was *s.* of Ahaziah
Job 17. 14 Thou art my mother and *s.*
Prov. 7. 4 wisdom, Thou art my *s.*
S. of S. 4. 12 garden inclosed is my *s.*
Jer. 3. 7 treacher. *s.*, Judah saw it
Ezek. 16. 45 thou art the *s.* of my *s.*
Hos. 2. 1 Say unto your *s.*, Ruham.
Mat. 12. 50 same is my bro. and *s.*
Mark 6. 3 are not his *s.* with us?
Luke 10. 39 she had *s.* called Mary
John 11. 5 J. loved Mar., and her *s.*
Acts 23. 16 Paul's *s.'s* son heard of
Rom. 16. 1 I com. to you P. our *s.*
1 Cor. 7. 15 a *s.* is not und. bondage
Col. 4. 10 Marcus, *s.'s* son to Barn.
1 Tim. 5. 2 entreat the younger *s.*
Jas. 2. 15 If brother or *s.* be naked
2 John 13 chil. of thy elect *s.* greet
R. V. 1 Chr. 7. 15 ; 1 Cor. 9. 15
wife ; Col. 4. 10 cousin

Sister-in-Law. *Brother's wife.*
Ruth 1. 15 thy *s. i. l.* is gone back

Sit. *Brood, hatch.*
Jer. 17. 11 As partridge *s.* on eggs
Sit, seat, set, rest.
Gen. 19. 1 Lot *s.* in gate of Sodom
Ex. 2. 15 Moses *s.* down by well
Lev. 15. 4 ev. thing whereon he *s.*
Num. 32. 6 breth. go to war, ye *s.*
Deut. 17. 18 when he *s.* on throne
Judg. 3. 20 Eg. was *s.* in sum. parl.
Ruth 2. 14 she *s.* beside the reapers
1 Sam. 4. 13 Eli *s.* upon a seat
2 Sam. 18. 24 David *s.* bet. two gates
1 K. 1. 46 Sol. *s.* on throne of kingd.
2 K. 1. 9 he *s.* on the top of an hill
1 Chr. 17. 16 king came and *s.* bef. L.
2 Chr. 18. 18 I saw L. *s.* on throne
Ez. 9. 4 I *s.* astonied till the evening
Neh. 1. 4 that I *s.* down and wept
Esth. 1. 2 Ahazuerus *s.* on throne
Job 2. 8 took potsherd, and *s.* down
Ps. 1. 1 nor *s.* in seat of scornful
110. 1 *S.* thou at my right hand
Prov. 9. 14 she *s.* in door of house
Eccl. 10. 6 the rich *s.* in low places
S. of S. 2. 3 I *s.* under his shadow
Isa. 14. 13 I *s.* on mt. of congrega.
52. 2 *s.* down, O Jerus., loose thys.
Jer. 15. 17 I *s.* not in assem. of m.
Lam. 1. 1 How doth city *s.* solitary
Ezek. 28. 2 I *s.* in the seat of God
Dan. 7. 9 Ancient of days did *s.*
Joel 3. 12 there will I *s.* to judge
Jonah 3. 6 k. of Nineveh *s.* in ashes
Mic. 4. 4 *s.* every man und. his vine
Zech. 1. 11 and all the earth *s.* still
Mal. 3. 3 he shall *s.* as a refiner
Mat. 4. 16 peo. wh. *s.* in dark. saw
26. 69 Peter *s.* without in palace
Mark 12. 36 *S.* thou on my ri. hand
Luke 14. 31 what k. *s.* not down first
John 9. 8 he that *s.* and begged?
Acts 2. 3 like as of fire, it *s.* on each
1 Cor. 10. 7 people *s.* down to eat
Col. 3. 1 Christ *s.* on right **hand**
Eph. 2. 6 *s.* together in heav. places
2 Thes. 2. 4 he as God *s.* in temple

Heb. 1. 3 *s.* on ri. hand of Majesty
Jas. 2. 3 *s.* here in a good place
Rev. 20. 4 thrones, they *s.* on them

Sith. *If.*
Ezek. 35. 6 *s.* thou ha. not hated bl.

Sitting. *Seated.*
1 K. 10. 5 and *s.* of his servants
2 K. 4. 38 sons of prophets were *s.*
2 Chr. 18. 18 I saw L. *s.* on throne
Neh. 2. 6 the queen also *s.* by him
Esth. 5. 13 Mord. *s.* at king's gate
Ps. 139. 2 knowest my down *s.* and
Jer. 38. 7 king *s.* in gate of Benjamin
Lam. 3. 63 behold their *s.* down
Mat. 20. 30 blind men *s.* by way
Mark 16. 5 they saw young man *s.*
Luke 2. 46 *s.* in midst of doctors
John 2. 14 changers of money *s.*
Acts 2. 2 house where they were *s.*
Rev. 4. 4 I saw tw. four elders *s.*
R. V. Mat. 21. 5 riding

Sitting Place.
2 Chr. 9. 18 stays each side *s. p.*

Situate. *Placed, fixed.*
1 Sam. 14. 5 front was *s.* northward
Ezek. 27. 3 art *s.* at entry of sea
Nah. 3. 8 No, *s.* among the rivers
R. V. 1 Sam. 14. 5 rose up ; Ezek.
27. 3 dwellest

Situation. *Seat, elevation.*
2 K. 2. 19 *s.* of this city is pleasant
Ps. 48. 2 beautiful for *s.*, joy of earth
R. V. Ps. 48. 2 elevation

Six. *Six.*
Gen. 7. 6 Noah was *s.* hun. y'rs old
Ex. 20. 9 *S.* days shalt thou labor
Lev. 25. 3 *S.* years shalt sow fields
Job 5. 19 sh. deliv. thee in *s.* troub.
Prov. 6. 16 *s.* things doth Lord hate
Mat. 17. 1 after *s.* days Jesus ta. P.
Luke 13. 14 *s.* da. men o't to work
Jchn 2. 6 waterpots of stone, after
Acts 11. 12 *s.* breth. accompanied
Jas. 5. 17 by space of *s.* years and
Rev. 4. 8 beasts had each *s.* wings

Sixth. *Sixth.*
Gen. 1. 31 ev. and mor. were *s.* day
Josh. 19. 32 *s.* lot ca. to chil. of N.
Mat. 20. 5 he went out ab. *s.* hour
Mark 15. 33 *s.* hour, there was dark.
Luke 1. 26 *s.* month Gab. was sent
John 4. 6 it was about the *s.* hour
Acts 10. 9 P. went to pray ab. *s.* ho.
Rev. 6. 12 when he had op. *s.* seal

Sixteen. *Ten and six.*
Gen. 46. 18 she bare Jacob *s.* souls
Ex. 26. 25 their sockets of silver, *s.*
Num. 31. 46 *s.* thousand persons
Josh. 19. 22 *s.* cities with villages
1 Chr. 4. 27 Shimei had *s.* sons and
2 Chr. 26. 3 *S.* years old was Uzziah
Acts 27. 37 two hun. threesc. *s.* souls

Sixty. *Six tens.*
Gen. 5. 15 Mah. lived *s.* five years
Lev. 27. 3 twenty years old to *s.*
Num. 7. 88 rams for sac. were *s.*
Mat. 13. 8 ; Mark 4. 8 s.me *s.* fold

Size. *Measure, form.*
Ex. 36. 9 curtains were of one *s.*
1 K. 6. 25 cherubim were of one *s.*
1 Chr. 23. 29 for all measure and *s.*
R. V. Ex. 36. 9, 15 measure ; 1 K.
6. 25 ; 7. 37 form

Skilful. *Having skill.*
1 Chr. 5. 18 sons of Re. *s.* in war
2 Chr. 2. 14 man *s.* to work in gold
Ezek. 21. 31 gi. you into ha. of *s.*
Dan. 1. 4 children *s.* in all wisdom,
Am. 5. 16 as are *s.* of lamentation

Skilfully. *With skill.*
Ps. 33. 3 Sing a new song ; play *s.*

Skilfulness. *Skill.*
Ps. 78. 72 guided th. by *s.* of hand

Skill (*n.*). *Knowledge, dexterity.*
Eccl. 9. 11 nor favour to men of *s.*
Dan. 1. 17 G. gave them *s.* in learn.

Skill (*v.*). *To know how.*
1 K. 5. 6 not any can *s.* to hew
2 Chr. 2. 7 send man can *s.* to grave

Skin. *Skin.*
Gen. 3. 21 L. G. make coats of *s.*
Ex. 22. 27 cov. is his raiment for *s.*
Lev. 7. 8 priest shall have the *s.*
Num. 4. 6 put on cov. of badgers' *s.*
Job 2. 4 *S.* for *s.*, all man hath
30. 30 My *s.* is black upon me

Ps. 102. 5 my bones cleave to my *s.*
Jer. 13. 23 Can Ethiop. chan. his *s.*
Lam. 3. 4 my *s.* ha. made me old
Ezek. 37. 6 I will cover you with *s.*
Mic. 3. 2 who pluck of their *s.* fr.
Mark 1. 6 John, with girdle of *s.*
Heb. 11. 37 wandered ab. in goat *s.*
R. V. Ex. 16. 10; 36. 19; Num. 4.
  6, 8, 10, 11, 12, 14, 25; Ezek. 16.
  10 sealskin; Job 18. 13 body;
  Ps. 102. 5 flesh; Mark 1. 6 leath-
  ern girdle

Skip. *Spring, leap, dance.*
Ps. 29. 6 He ma. th. to *s.* like calf
  114. 4 mountains *s.* like rams
S. of S. 2. 8 cometh *s.* upon hills
Jer. 48. 27 spakest, thou *s.* for joy
R. V. Jer. 48. 27 waggest the head

Skirt. *Wing, hem, skirt.*
Deut. 22. 30 not discov. father's *s.*
Ruth 3. 9 spread *s.* over handmaid
1 Sam. 15. 27 he laid hold upon *s.*
Ps. 133. 2 down to *s.* of garments
Jer. 2. 34 in *s.* is found blood of
Lam. 1. 9 Her filthiness is in her *s.*
Ezek. 16. 8 I spread my *s.* ov. thee
Nah. 3. 5 I will discover thy *s.*
Hag. 2. 12 with his *s.* touch bread
Zech. 8. 23 men sh. ta. hold of *s.*

Skull. *Skull, poll.*
Judg. 9. 53 mill sto, to break his *s.*
2 K. 9. 35 no more of her than *s.*
Mat. 27. 33 that is, place-of a *s.*
Mark 15. 22 Golgotha, place of a *s.*
John 19. 17 he went to pl. called *s.*

Sky. *Cloud, heaven.*
Deut. 33. 26 rideth in excell. on *s.*
2 Sam. 22. 12 waters, and clouds of *s.*
Job 37. 18 Hast thou spread out *s.*
Ps. 77. 17 the *s.* sent out a sound
Isa. 45. 8 let *s.* pour righteousness
Jer. 51. 9 judgment is lifted to *s.*
Mat. 16. 2 fair weather, *s.* is red
Luke 12. 56 ye discern face of *s.*
Heb. 11. 12 as stars of *s.* in multi.
R. V. Mat. 16. 2, 3; Luke 12. 56;
  Heb. 11. 12 heaven

Slack (*adj.*). *Loose, slow, remiss.*
Deut. 7. 10 he will not be *s.* to him
Josh. 18. 3 How long *s.* to possess
Prov. 10. 4 poor th. deal wi. *s.* hand
Zeph. 3. 16 Let not thine hand be *s.*
2 Pet. 3. 9 L. not *s.* conc. promise

Slack (*v.*). *Delay, loosen, slow.*
Deut. 23. 21 shalt not *s.* to pay it
Josh. 10. 6 *S.* not hand fr. servants
2 K. 4. 24 *s.* not thy riding for me
Hab. 1. 4 law is *s.,* and judgment

Slackness. *Slowness.*
2 Pet. **3.** 9 as some men count *s.*

Slain. *Put to death, pierced, slaughtered.*
Gen. 34. 27 sons of Jac. ca. upon *s.*
Lev. 26. 17 ye sh. be *s.* bef. enemies
Num. 19. 16 whoso. turneth one *s.*
Deut. 21. 1 If one be found *s.* in
Josh. 11. 6 deliv. them *s.* before Is.
Judg. 20. 4 husband of woman *s.*
1 Sam. 4. 11 two sons of Eli were *s.*
2 Sam. 1. 19 beauty of Israel is *s.*
1 K. 11. 15 Joab gone up to bury *s.*
2 K. 3. 23 the kings are surely *s.*
1 Chr. 5. 22 there fell down many *s.*
2 Chr. 13. 17 fell *s.* of Is. five hund.
Esth. 7. 4 for we are sold to be *s.*
Ps. 89. 10 broken Rahab, as one *s.*
Prov. 24. 11 those ready to be *s.*
Isa. 22. 2 thy *s.* not *s.* with sword
Jer. 9. 1 weep day and night for *s.*
Lam. 2. 20 shall the prophets be *s.*
Ezek. 6. 7 *s.* fall in midst of you
Dan. 11. 26 many shall fall down *s.*
Nah. 3. 3 there is multitude of *s.*
Zeph. 2. 12 Ethiopians, ye sh. be *s.*
Acts 7. 42 ye offer. to me *s.* beasts
Heb. 11. 37 were *s.* with the sword
R. V. Lev. 26. 17; Deut. 1. 1
  smitten

Slain (*v.*). *See* **Slay.**

Slander (*n.*). *Evil report.*
Num. 14. 36 by bring. a *s.* on land
Ps. 31. 13 I have heard *s.* of many
Prov. 10. 18 that utter. *s.* is a fool
Jer. 6. 28 revolters, walking with *s.*
R. V. Num. 14. 36 evil report;
  Ps. 31. 13 defaming

Slander (*n.*). *Defame.*
2 Sam. 19. 27 he hath *s.* thy servant
Ps. 50. 20 thou *s.* thine own mother
101. 5 *s.* neighbour, cut him off

Slanderer. *Accuser, devil.*
1 Tim. 3. 11 wives, be grave, not *s.*

Slang. *See* **Sling** (*v.*).

Slaughter. *Slaying, killing.*
Gen. 14. 17 return from *s.* of Chedor.
Josh. 10. 10 L. slew them with gr. *s*
Judg. 11. 33 Jeph. smote A. with *s.*
1 Sam. 4. 10 there was very great *s.*
2 Sam. 1. 1 David was ret. from *s.*
1 K. 20. 21 Slew Syrians with gr. *s.*
2 Chr. 13. 17 his people slew wi. *s.*
Esth. 9. 5 wi. stroke of sword and *s.*
Ps. 44. 22 counted as sheep for *s.*
Prov. 7. 22 as an ox goeth to the *s.*
Isa. 27. 7 is he slain according to *s.*
Jer. 7. 32 nor Hinnom, but val. of *s.*
Ezek. 21. 15 it is wrapped up for *s.*
Hos. 5. 2 revolters profound for *s.*
Obad. 9 mount E. be cut off by *s.*
Zech. 11. 7 I will feed flock of *s.*
Acts 8. 32 He was led as sheep to *s.*
Rom. 8. 36 accounted sheep for *s.*
Heb. 7. 1 Abr. returning from *s.*
Jas. 5. 5 hearts, as in days of *s.*

Slave. *Body, slave.*
Jer. 2. 14 a serv.? a homeborn *s.*?
Rev. 18. 13 buy horses, chariots, *s.*

Slay. *Smite, put to death.*
Gen. 4. 8 Cain rose ag. A. and *s.* h.
Ex. 13. 15 Lord *s.* all the firstborn
Lev. 20 15 if man lie with beast *s.*
Num. 14. 16 he hath *s.* th. in wild.
Deut. 9. 28 he bro. th. out to *s.* them
Josh. 8. 24 Is. made an end of *s.*
Judg. 7. 25 they *s.* Oreb on rock
1 Sam. 22. 21 Saul had *s.* L's priests
2 Sam. 3.30 Joab and Abish. *s.* Abner
1 K. 16. 11 he *s.* house of Baasha
2 K. 10. 11 Jehu *s.* house of Ahab
1 Chr. 10. 2 Philist. *s.* Jonathan
2 Chr. 26. 8 Pekah *s.* son of Rem.
Neh. 4. 11 *s.,* cause work to cease
Esth. 9. 10 sons of Haman *s.* they
Job 20. 16 viper's tongue sh. *s.* th.
Ps. 37. 32 wicked seeketh to *s.* him
  59. 11 *S.* not, lest my people forget
Prov. 1. 32 turn. of simple sh. *s.*
Isa. 11. 4 with breath of lips he *s.*
Jer. 15. 3 sword to *s.,* dogs to tear
Lam. 3. 43 thou hast *s.* not pitied
Ezek. 9. 6 *S.* utter. old and young
Dan. 3. 22 flame of the fire *s.* men
Hos. 6. 5 *s.* th. by words of mouth
Am. 4. 10 young men have I *s.* wi.
Zech. 11. 5 Whose possessor *s.* them
Mat. 2. 16 Herod *s.* all children
Luke 9. 22 *s.,* be raised third day
John 5. 16 Jews sought to *s.* him
Acts 2. 23 by wicked hands ha. *s.*
Rom. 7. 11 sin deceived, by it *s.*
Eph. 2. 16 having *s.* the enmity th.
1 John 3. 12 And wheref. *s.* he him?
Rev. 2. 13 faithful martyr, who *s.*
  5. 12 Worthy is the Lamb that *s.*
R. V. Many changes to, kill, smote,
  put to death, etc.

Slayer. *Who slays.*
Num. 35. 11 that *s.* may flee thither
Deut. 19. 6 lest avenger pursue *s.*
Josh. 20. 5 shall not deliver up *s.*
Ezek. 21. 11 sword, to give it to *s.*
R. V. In. Num. Deut. and Josh.
  manslayer

Sleep (*n.*). *Sleep.*
Gen. 28. 16 Jac. awak. out of his *s.*
Judg. 16. 14 S. wak. out of his *s.*
1 Sam. 26. 12 a deep *s.* from God
Job 14. 12 nor be raised out of *s.*
Ps. 13. 3 lest I sleep the *s.* of death
Prov. 3. 24 thy *s.* shall be sweet
  6. 10 a little *s.,* a little slumber
Eccl. 5. 12 *s.* of lab. man is sweet
Isa. 29. 10 L. pour. on you deep *s.*
Jer. 31. 26 my *s.* was sweet to me
Dan. 2. 1 his *s.* brake from him
Zech. 4. 1 man wakened out of *s.*
Mat. 1. 24 J. being raised from *s.*
Luke 9. 32 they were heavy with *s.*
John 11. 11 awake him out of *s.*
Acts 16. 27 keeper awak. out of *s.*
Rom. 13. 11 ti. to awake out of *s.*

Sleep (*v.*). *Sleep, slumber.*

Gen. 28. 11 Jacob lay down to *s.*
Ex. 22. 27 wherein shall he *s.*?
Deut. 24. 12 not *s.* with his pledge
Judg. 16. 19 ma. him *s.* on her kn.
1 Sam. 26. 7 S. lay *s.* within trench
2 Sam. 11. 9 Uriah *s.* at door of hou.
1 K. 2. 10 David *s.* with his fathers
2 K. 8. 24 Joram *s.* with his fathers
2 Chr. 9. 31 Sol. *s.* with his fathers
Esth. 6. 1 night could not king *s.*
Job. 7. 21 now shall I *s.* in dust
Ps. 4. 8 I will lay me down in *s.*
Prov. 4. 16 For they *s.* not, except
  6. 9 How long wilt *s.* O sluggard
Eccl. 5. 12 abun. of rich not suf. to *s.*
Isa. 5. 27 non shall slumber nor *s.*
Jer. 51. 57 they sh. *s.* perpet. sleep
Ezek. 34. 25 they dwell safely and *s.*
Dan. 12. 2 many that *s.* in the dust
Hos. 7. 6 their baker *s.* all night
Mat. 9. 24 maid is not dead but, *s.*
Mark 14. 41 *S.* now, take your rest
Luke 22. 46 Why *s.*? rise and pray
John 11. 11 our friend Lazarus *s.*
Acts 12. 6 Pet. was *s.* bet. two sold.
1 Cor. 11. 30 many weak, and may *s.*
Eph. 5. 14 Awake, thou that *s.*
1 Thes. 5. 6 let us not *s.,* as others
R. V. Isa. 56. 10 dreaming

Sleight. *Artifice.*
Eph. 4. 14 and carried by *s.* of men

Slept. *See* **Sleep**

Slew. *See* **Slay**

Slide. *Slip, fail.*
Deut. 32 35 foot sh. *s.* in due time
Ps. 26. 1 trusted in L., sh. not *s.*
  37. 31 none of his steps shall *s.*
Jer. 8. 5 is peo. of Jerus. *s.* back
Hos. 4. 16 Is. *s.* back as a heifer
R. V. Ps. 26. 1 without wavering;
  Hos. 4. 16 behaved stubbornly.

Slightly. *Lightly.*
Jer. 6. 14 healed hurt of my peo. *s.*

Slime (*v.*). *Bitumen.*
Gen. 11. 3 *s.* had they for morter
  14. 10 vale of Sid. full of *s.* pits
Ex. 2. 3 she daubed the ark with *s.*

Sling (*n.*). *Sling.*
1 Sam. 17. 40 *s.* was in his hand
  17. 50 David prevailed with a. *s.*
2 Chr. 26. 14 Uzziah prepared *s.*
Prov. 26. 8 that bind. stone in *s.*

Sling (*v.*). *Sling out.*
Judg. 20. 16 ev. one th. co. *s.* stones
1 Sam. 17. 49 D. *s.,* and smo. Philist.
  22. 29 then shall he *s.* as out of
Jer. 10. 18 I will *s.* out inhabitants

Slinger. *Who slings.*
2 K. 3. 25 howbeit, *s.* went about

Slingstones. *Stones for slingers.*
Job 41. 28 *s.* s. turned into stubble
Zech. 9. 15 they sh. subdue with. *s.s*

Slip (*n.*). *Branch, cutting.*
Isa. 17. 10 sh. set it with strange *s.*

Slip (*v.*), *Slide, slip.*
Deut. 19. 5 head *s.* from the helve
1 Sam. 19. 10 D. *s.* out of S.'s pres.
2 Sam. 22. 37 my feet did not *s.*
Job 12. 5 he that is ready to *s.*
Ps. 17. 5 th. my footsteps *s.* not
  73. 2 my steps had well nigh *s.*
Heb. 2. 1 lest we sho. let them *s.*
R. V. H b. 2. 1 drift away

Slippery. *Smooth.*
Ps. 35. 6 let way be dark and *s.*
  73. 18 didst set them in *s.* places
Jer. 23. 12 th way sh. be as *s.* ways

Slothful. *Sluggish, idle.*
Judg. 18. 9 be not *s.* to poss. land
Prov. 12. 24 *s.* sh. be under tribute
  15. 19 way of *s.* is as a hedge
  18. 9 *s.* is brother to great waster
  26. 15 *s.* man hid. hand in bosom
Mat. 25. 26 wicked and *s.* servant
Rom. 12. 11 Not *s.* in bus., fervent
Heb. 6. 12 ye be not *s.,* but follow.
R. V. Prov. 15. 19; 19. 24; 22. 13;
  26. 13, 14, 15 sluggard; 18. 9 slack;
  Heb. 6. 12 sluggish.

Slothfulness. *Sloth.*
Prov. 19. 15 *S.* casteth into sleep
Eccl. 10. 18 by *s.* building decayeth

Slow. *Sluggish, idle.*
Ex. 4. 10 but I am *s.* of speech
Neh. 9. 17 thou art G., *s.* to anger
Ps. 103. 8 L. is grac., *s.* to anger

Prov. 14. 29 *s.* to wrath, of great
  15. 18 *s.* to anger appeaseth strife
Joel 2. 13 *s.*; Jonah 4. 2; Nah.1. 3
Luke 24. 25 *s.* of heart to believe
Tit. 1. 12 Cretians are *s.* bellies
Jas. 1. 19 be *s.* to hear, *s.* to speak
R. V. Tit. 1. 12 idle

Slowly. *Slowly.*
Acts 27. 7 had sailed *s.* many days

Sluggard. *Sloth ful.*
Prov. 6. 6 Go to the ant, thou *s.*
  6. 9 How long wilt sleep, O *s.*?
  13. 4 The soul of the *s.* desireth
  20. 4 *s.* will not plow by reason
  26. 16 *s.* is wiser in own conceit.

Sluice. *Hire, wage.*
Isa. 19. 10 all that make *s.* for fish
R. V. That work for hire be grieved
  in soul.

Slumber (*n.*). *Sleep, rest.*
Ps. 132. 4 not give *s.* to eyelids
Prov. 6. 4 Gi. sleep to eyes, nor *s.*
  6. 10 little *s.*, folding of hands
Rom. 11. 8 G. ha. given spirit of *s.*
R. V. Rom. 11. 8 stupor

Slumber (*v.*). *Sleep, nod.*
Ps. 121. 3 th. keep. thee will not *s.*
Isa. 5. 27 none shall *s.* nor sleep
Nah. 3. 18 Thy shepherds *s.*, O k.
Mat. 25. 5 bridegr. tarried they *s.*
2 Pet. 2. 3 their damnation *s.* not

Slumbering. *Sleeping.*
Job 33. 15 when sleep falleth in *s.*

Small. *Little, few, fine.*
Gen. 19. 11 smote men, *s.* and great
Ex. 18. 22 ev. *s.* matter shall judge
Lev. 16. 12 sweet incense beaten *s.*
Num. 32. 41 Jair took the *s.* towns
Deut. 1. 17 hear *s.* as well as great
1 Sam. 30. 2 they slew not, gr. or *s.*
2 Sam. 7. 19 *s.* thing in thy sight, O.
1 K. 2. 20 I desire *s.* petition of thee
2 K. 23. 2 all people, *s.* and great
1 Chr. 26. 13 cast lots, *s.* and great
2 Chr. 18. 30 Fight not wi. *s.* or gr.
Esth. 1. 20 husban. hon. to gr. and *s.*
Job. 15. 11 Are consolations of G. *s.*
Ps. 115. 13 He will bless *s.* and gr.
  119. 141 I am *s.* and despised
Prov. 24. 10 faint, thy strength is *s.*
Isa. 1. 9 had left to us *s.* remnant
Jer. 49. 15 ma. thee *s.* am. heathen
Ezek. 16. 20 Is whoredoms *s.* matter
Dan. 11.23 become strong wi. *s.* peo.
Am. 8. 5 making eph. *s.*, shek. gr.
Obad. 2 made thee *s.* among heath.
Zech. 4. 10 despis. day of *s.* things
Acts 12. 18 no *s.* stir. am. soldiers
1 Cor. 4. 3 with me it is a *s.* thing
Jas. 3. 4 they turned with *s.* helm
Rev. 20. 12 saw dead, *s.* and gr , st.
R. V. Deut. 9. 21 fine; Job. 36. 27
  draweth up; 37. 6 shower of ; Jer.
  44. 28 few ; Mark 3. 9; Acts 19. 24
  little; Num. 32. 41; John 2. 15;
  6. 9———.

Smallest. *Least.*
1 Sam. 9. 21 Benj. of *s.* of tribes

Smart. *Suffer.*
Prov. 11. 15 surety for str. sh. *s.*

Smell (*n.*). *Savor, odor.*
Gen. 27. 27 Is. smelled *s.* of raim.
S, of S. 2. 13 tender grape give *s.*
Isa. 3. 24 instead of sweet *s.* stink
Dan. 3. 27 nor *s.* of fire passed on
Hos. 14. 6 and his *s.* as Lebanon
Phil. 4. 18 scent and od. of sweet *s.*
R. V. Isa. 3.24 spices; S. of S. 1.
  12; 2. 13; 7. 13 fragrance

Smell (*v.*). *Scent, smell.*
Gen. 8. 21 Lord *s.* a sweet savour
Ex. 30. 38 make like to that to *s.*
Lev. 26. 31 will not *s.* your odours
Job 39. 25 he *s.* the battle afar off
Ps. 45. 8 thy garments *s.* of myrrh
  115. 6 noses have they, they *s.* not
S. of S. 5. 5 fingers wi. sw. *s.* myrrh
Am. 5. 21 not *s.* in your assemblies
1 Cor. 12. 17 hear., where were *s.*?
Eph. 5. 2 sacrif. for sw. *s.* savour
R. V. Am. 5. 21 take no delight; S.
  of S. 5. 5, 13 liquid.

Smite. *Strike, plague, kill.*
Gen. 8. 21 nei. will I *s.* any more
Ex. 2. 13 Wherefore *s.* thou thy fel.
  12. 29 Lord *s.* all the firstborn in

Num. 14. 12 I will *s.* with pestilence
Deut. 2. 33 we *s.* him and his sons
Josh. 7. 5 the men of Ai *s.* of them
Judg. 1. 8 Jud. had *s.* it wi. sword
1 Sam. 4. 8 these Gods *s.* Egyptians
2 Sam. 2. 31 serv. of D. had *s.* Benj.
1 K. 14. 15 the Lord shall *s.* Israel
2 K. 2. 8 And Elijah *s.* the waters
1 Chr. 18. 1 David *s.* the Philistines
2 Chr. 14. 14 they *s.* all the cities
Neh. 13. 25 I *s.* certain of them
Esth. 9. 5 Jews *s.* all their enemies
Job 2. 7 Satan *s.* Job with boils
Ps. 3. 7 thou hast *s.* all enemies
  105. 33 He *s.* their vines and fig tr.
  121.6 the sun sh. not *s.* thee by day
Prov. 19. 25 *S.* scorner, simple be.
S. of S. 5.7 they *s.* me, they wound.
Isa. 10. 24 he sh. *s.* thee with rod
Jer. 2. 20 In vain ha. I *s.* children
Lam. 3. 30 giv. cheek to him th. *s.*
Ezek. 5. 2 *s.* about it with knife
Dan. 8. 7 *s.* ram, and brake horns
Hos. 6. 1 he hath *s.*, he will bind
Am. 4. 9 I ha. *s.* you wi. blasting
Jonah 4. 7. *s.* gourd th. it withered
Mic. 5. 1 they *s.* judge of Israel
Hag. 2. 17 I *s.* you with mildew
Zech. 9. 4 *s.* her power in the sea
Mal. 4. 6 lest I *s.* earth wi. curse
Mat. 26. 31 I will *s.* the shepherd
Mark 14. 47 *s.* servant of high pr.
Luke 22. 64 who is it that *s.* thee?
John 18. 23 J. ans., Why *s.* th. me?
Acts 12. 7 angel *s.* Pet. on the side
2 Cor. 11. 20 if man *s.* you on face
Rev. 11. 6 power to *s.* the earth
R. V. 1 Sam. 23. 5 slew ; 2 Sam. 10.
  15, 19 put to the worse ; 2 Chr. 22.
  5 wounded ; Mat. 24. 49; Luke
  12. 63 beat; Mat. 26. 51; Luke
  22. 64; John 18. 10; 19. 3 struck

Smiter. *Who smites.*
Isa. 50. 6 I gave my back to the *s.*

Smith. *Carver, artificer.*
1 Sam. 13. 19 there was no *s.* found
Isa. 54. 16 I have created the *s.*
Worker in iron.
Isa. 44. 12 *s.* with tongs worketh
Smith, metal worker
2 K. 24. 14 Neb. carried away all *s.*
Jer. 29. 2 *s.* were departed fr. Jer.

Smitten. *See* Smite.
Smoke (*n.*). *Smoke, vapor.*
Gen. 19. 28 *s.* of country went up
Ex. 19. 18 *s.* thereof ascended as
Josh. 8. 20 *s.* of Ai ascended up
Judg. 20. 38 make great flame wi. *s.*
2 Sam. 22. 9 went *s.* out of nostrils
Job 41. 20 out of nostril goeth *s.*
Ps. 37. 20 wicked consumed into *s.*
  102. 3 my days are consum. like *s.*
  119. 83 I am like a bottle in the *s.*
Prov. 10. 26 as *s.* to eyes, so slug.
S. of S. 3. 6 Who com. like pil. of *s.*
Isa. 4. 5 a cloud and *s.* by day, and
Hos. 13. 3 and as *s.* out of chimney
Joel 2. 30 and fire, and pillars of *s.*
Nah. 2. 13 I burn her chariots in *s.*
Acts 2. 19 and fire, and vapour of *s.*
Rev. 8. 4. *s.* of the incense ascended
  15. 18 temple was filled with *s.*
  19. 3 her *s.* rose for ever and ever

Smoke. (*v.*). *To smoke.*
Deut. 29. 20 anger of Lord shall *s.*
Ps. 74. 1 why doth thine anger *s.*
  104. 32 he toucheth hills, they *s.*

Smoking. *Smoking.*
Gen. 15. 17 behold a *s.* furnace and
Ex. 20. 18 people saw mountain *s.*
Isa. 7. 4 tails of *s.* firebrands, for
Mat. 12. 20 *s.* flax not be quenched

Smooth. (*adj.*). *Not rough, plain.*
Gen. 27. 11 Esau is hairy, I am *s.*
1 Sam. 17. 40 D. chose five *s.* stones
Isa. 30. 10 speak unto us *s.* things
  57. 6. among *s.* stones of stream
Luke 3. 5 rough ways be made *s.*

Smooth. (*v.*). *Make smooth.*
Isa. 41. 7 he that *s.* with hammer

Smoother. *More smooth.*
Ps. 55. 11 words were *s.* th. butter
Prov. 5. 3 her mouth is *s.* than oil

Smote. *See* Smite.
Snail. *Snail, lizard.*
Lev. 11. 30 the lizard, the *s.*, mole

Ps. 58. 8 As *s.*, let every one pass
R. V. Lev. 11. 30 sand-lizard

Snare. (*n.*) *Cord, gin, net, pit,*
  toil, device.
Ex. 10. 7 How long sh. th. man be *s*
  23. 33 it will surely be a *s.* unto
Deut. 7. 16 that will be *s.* to thee
Josh. 23. 13 they sh. be *s.* and traps
Judg. 2. 3 their gods sh. be a *s.*
1 Sam. 18. 21 she may be *s.* to him
2 Sam. 22. 6 *s.* of death prevented
Job 22. 10 *s.* are round about thee
Job 40. 24 Behemoth's nose pier. *s.*
Ps. 11. 6 on wicked he sh. rain *s.*
  38. 12 seeking life, lay *s.* for me
  64. 5 commune to lay *s.* privily
Prov. 13. 14 to depart for *s.* of death
  18. 7 fool's lips are *s.* of his soul
  29. 25 The fear of man bringeth *s.*
Eccl. 9. 12 as birds are caught in *s.*
Isa. 8. 14 *s.* to inhab. of Jerusalem
  24. 17 pit, the *s.* are upon thee
Jer. 18. 12 digged pit, and hid *s.*
Lam. 3. 47 a *s.* is come upon us
Ezek. 12. 13 he sh. be tak. in my *s.*
Hos. 5. 1 ye have been *s.* on Miz.
Am. 3. 5 Can bird fall in a *s.* upon
Luke 21. 35 as a *s.* shall it come
Rom. 11. 9 Let their table be ma. *s.*
1 Cor. 7. 35 may cast *s.* upon you
1 Tim. 3. 7 lest he fall into *s.* of d.
  6. 9 rich, fall into a *s.* and lusts
2 Tim. 2. 26 may recover out of *s.*
R. V. Job 18. 8 toils ; 18. 10 noose;
  Prov. 29. 8 flame; Lam. 3. 47 pit.
Jer. 5. 26 lie in wait

Snare (*v.*). *Catch in snare.*
Deut. 7. 25 lest thou be *s.* therein
Ps. 9. 16 wicked is *s.* in work of
Prov. 6. 2 *s.* wi. words of thy mouth
  12. 13 wicked is *s.* by transgression
Eccl. 9. 12 so men *s.* in an evil time
Isa. 8. 15 many shall fall and be *s.*
  42. 22 they are all *s.* in holes

Snatch. *Pluck, cut off.*
Isa. 9. 20 he shall *s.* on right hand

Sneeze. *Sneeze.*
2 K. 4. 35 the child *s.* seven times

Snorting. *Snorting.*
Jer. 8. 16 *s.* of horses was heard

Snout. *Nose.*
Prov. 11. 22 as jewel in swine's *s.*

Snow. *Snow.*
Ex. 4. 6 his hand was leprous as *s.*
Num. 12. 10 Miriam became as *s.*
2 Sam. 23.20 in pit in time of *s.*
2 K. 5. 27 Gehazi went white as *s.*
Job 6. 16 and wherein the *s.* is hid
  9. 30 If I wash with *s.* water
  24. 19 Drought and heat cons. *s.*
  37. 6 he saith to *s.* Be on earth
Ps. 51. 7 I shall be whiter than *s.*
  147. 16 He giveth *s.* like wool
Prov. 25. 13 As cold of *s.* in harvest
  26. 1 as *s.* in summer, so honour
  31. 21 She is not afraid of the *s.*
Isa. 1. 18 sins scarlet, white as *s.*
Jer. 18. 14 Will man leave *s.* of Leb
Lam. 4. 7 Naz. were purer than *s.*
Dan. 7. 9 garment was white as *s.*
Mat. 28. 3. his raiment white as *s.*
Mark 9. 3 rai. exceeding white as *s*
Rev. 1. 14 his hairs white as *s.*

Snowy R. V. *time of snow.*
1 Chr. 11. 22 slew a lion on *s.* day

Snuff. *Inhale, snuff.*
Jer. 2. 24 a wild ass *s.* up wind
  14. 6 they *s.* wind like dragons
Mal. 1. 14 ye have *s.* at it, saith L.
R. V. Jer. 14. 6 pant for air

Snuff Dish. *Dish for snuff.*
Ex. 25. 38 *s. d.* shall be of gold
Num. 4. 9 cover his tongs, and *s. d.*

Snuffers. *Tongs, forceps.*
Ex. 37. 23 he made *s.* of pure gold
  1 K. 7. 50; 2 Chr. 4. 22
2 K. 12. 13 not made *s.* of the money
Jer. 52. 18 Chaldeans took away *s.*

So. *Thus,* etc.
Gen. 1. 5 he said, O. sh. thy seed
Mat. 5. 16 Let your light *s.* shine
  Etc., etc.
R. V. Many changes, chiefly to,
  and, thus, etc. Many omissions of
  the word.

Soaked. R.V. *Drunken.*

Isa. 34. 7 land sh. be *s*. wi. blood
Soap. *See* **Sope.**
Sober. *Temperate, sedate, prudent, sound-minded.*
2 Cor. 5. 13 whether we be *s*., it is
1 Thes. 5. 6 let us watch and be *s*.
1 Tim. 3. 2 be *s*., of good behaviour
Tit. 1. 8 lover of good men, *s*., just
1 Pet. 1. 13 be *s*., hope to the end
R. V. 2 Cor. 5. 13 ; 2 Tim. 3. 2 ;
 Tit. 1. 8 soberminded ; 1 Tim. 3.
 11 ; Tit. 2. 2 temperate ; 1 Pet. 4.
 7 of sound mind ; Tit. 2. 4 ——.
Soberly. *Temperately, soundly.*
Rom. 12. 3 think *s*., accord. as God
Tit. 2. 12 we should live *s*., right.
Sober Minded. *Sound-minded.*
Tit. 2. 6 Young men, ex. to be *s. m.*
Soberness. *Sobriety.*
Acts 26. 25 speak forth words of *s*.
Sobriety. *Soundness of mind.*
1 Tim. 2. 9 adorn themselves with *s*.
2. 15 continue in holiness with *s*.
Socket. *Hollow, socket.*
Ex. 26. 19 make forty *s* of silver
27. 10 ; 35. 11 ; 36. 24 ; 38. 10
Num. 3. 36 *s*. thereof, and all vessels
S. of S. 5. 15 as pillars on *s*. of gold
Sod. *Boil, cook.*
Gen. 25. 29 Jacob *s*. pottage ; Esau
Ex. 12. 9 Eat not of it raw, nor *s*.
Lev. 6. 28 ves. wherein is *s*. be brok.
Num. 6. 19 priest sh. ta. *s*. shoulder
1 Sam. 2. 15 he will not ha. *s*. flesh
2 Chr. 35. 13 offer. *s*. they in pots
Lam. 4. 10 women have *s*. children
Sodering. *Joining.*
Isa. 41. 7 It is ready for the *s*.
Sodomite. *Devotee, unclean.*
Deut. 23. 17 no *s*. of sons of Israel
1 K. 14. 24 there were *s*. in land
2 K. 23. 7 he brake the house of *s*.
Soever. *If.*
Mark 6. 10 in what pl. *s*. ye enter
Soft. *Melted, tender.*
Job 23. 16 God maketh my heart *s*.
Ps. 65. 10 makest it *s*. with showers
Prov. 15. 1 *s*. ans. tur. away wrath
25. 15 *s*. tongue breaketh the bone
Mat. 11. 8 ; Luke 7. 25 in *s*. raiment
R. V. Job 23. 16 faint
Softer. *Tenderer.*
Ps. 55. 21 words were *s*. than oi¹
Softly. *Gently, quietly.*
Gen. 33. 14 I will lead on *s*., as cat.
Judg. 4. 21 Joel went *s*. unto him
Ruth 3. 7 she came *s*., and uncovered
1 K. 21. 27 Ahab heard and went *s*.
Isa. 8. 6 waters of Shiloah go *s*.
38. 15 I shall go *s*. all my years
Acts 27. 13 the south wind blew *s*.
Soil. *Land, ground.*
Ezek. 17. 8 was planted in good *s*.
Sojourn. *Dwell, abide.*
Gen. 12. 10 Ab. went to Egypt to *s*.
Ex. 12. 48 when stranger shall *s*.
Lev. 17. 12 nei. any stranger that *s*.
Num. 9. 14 if a stranger shall *s*.
Deut. 26. 5 he went to Egy. and *s*.
Josh 20. 9 cities for strangers that *s*.
Judg. 17. 7 Levite, he is *s*. in Bethle.
Ruth 1. 1 El. went to *s*. in Moab
1 K. 17. 20 widow with whom I *s*.
2 K. 8. 1 *s*. wheresoever thou canst
Ez. 1. 4 who. remaineth where he *s*.
Ps. 105. 23 Jac. *s*. in land of Ham
Isa. 23. 7 her feet s.i. car. her to *s*.
Jer. 43. 2 Go not to Egypt to *s*.
Lam. 4. 15 they shall no more *s*. th.
Ezek. 47. 23 in what tribe strange. *s*.
Acts 7. 6 seed should *s*. in strange
Heb. 11. 9 by faith he *s*. in land
Sojourner. *Settler, dweller.*
Gen. 23 4 I am a *s*. with you
Lev. 22. 10 *s*. of priest sh. not eat
Num. 35. 15 six cities a ref. for *s*.
2 Sam. 4. 3 *s*. there till this day
1 Chr. 29. 15 we are strangers and *s*.
Sojourning. *Abiding.*
Ex. 12. 40 the *s*. of Israel was four
Judg. 19. 1 Levite *s*. on mt. Ephr.
1 Pet. 1. 17 pass time of *s*. in fear
Solace. *Rejoice.*
Prov. 7. 18 Come, let us *s*. ourselves
Sold. *Made sale of.*
Ex. 22. 3 then he shall be *s*, for theft

Lev. 25. 23 land sh. not be *s*. for ev.
Deut. 15. 12 or Heb. woman be *s*.
Neh. 5. 8 Jews, *s*. unto heathen
Esth. 7. 4 we are *s*., I and my people
Ps. 105. 17 Joseph, *s*. for a servant
Jer. 34. 14 Heb., which ha. been *s*.
Mat. 18. 25 lord com. him to be *s*.
Mark 14. 5 it might have been *s*.
Luke 12. 6 spar. *s*. for two farthings
John 12. 5 Why not oint. *s*. for
Acts 4. 37 Joses, having land, *s*. it
Rom. 7. 14 am carnal, *s*. und. sin
See also **Sell.**
Soldier. *Man of war.*
1 Chr. 7. 4 *s*., six and thirty thous.
2 Chr. 25. 13 *s*. fell upon the cities
Ez. 8. 22 I am ashamed to requ. *s*.
Isa. 15. 4 the *s*. of Moab shall cry
Mat. 27, 27 *s*. of gov. took Jesus
Mark 15. 16 *s*. led him away into
Luke 23. 36 the *s*. also mocked him
John 19. 2 *s*. platted crown of thorns
Acts 12. 6 P. was sleeping bet. *s*.
2 Tim. 2. 4 chosen him to be a *s*.
Phil. 2. 25 Epaphrod. my fellow *s*.
Phile. 2 Ap. and Ar. our fellow *s*.
R. V. Chr. 7. 4 host ; 2 Chr. 25. 13 ;
 Isa. 15. 4 men ; 1 Chr. 7. 11 ; Mat.
 27. 27 ——.
Sole. *Palm, sole.*
Gen. 8. 9 dove found no rest for *s*.
Deut. 28. 35 *s*. of foot to top of h.
Josh. 4. 18 *s*. of priest's feet lifted
2 Sam. 14. 25 fr. *s*. of foot to crown
1 K. 5. 3 until L. put th. under *s*.
2 K. 19. 24 wi. *s*. of feet I dried
Job 2. 7 smote Job from *s*. of feet
Isa. 60. 14 bow thems. down at *s*.
Ezek. 1. 7 *s*. of feet was like *s*. of a
Mal. 4. 3 sh. be ashes under your *s*.
Solemn. *Set, appointed.*
Lev. 23. 36 it is a *s*. assembly
Num. 10. 10 in your *s*. days, and
Deut. 16. 8 sev. day be *s*. assembly
2 K. 10. 20 Proclaim a *s*. assembly
2 Chr. 2. 4 on *s*. feasts of the Lord
Neh. 8. 18 eighth day a *s*. assembly
Ps. 81. 3 appoint., on our *s*. feasts
Isa. 1. 13 iniquity, ev. *s*. meeting
Lam. 1. 4 none come to *s*. feasts
Ezek. 36. 38 as flock in *s*. feasts
Hos. 9. 5 What wi. ye do in the *s*. day
Joel 1. 14 calls *s*. assem., gath. elders
Am. 5. 21 not smell in *s*. assemblies
Nah. 1. 15 keep thy *s*. feasts, per.
Zeph. 3. 18 gath. them for *s*. assem.
Mal. 2. 3 ev. dung of your *s*. feasts
R. V. Num. 10. 10 ; 15. 3 ; 2 Chr. 2.
 4 ; 8. 13 set ; Ezek. 36. 38 ; 46. 9 ap-
 pointed ; Deut. 16. 5 ; Nah. 1.15—
Solemnity. *Appointed.*
Deut. 31. 10 *s*. of the year of release
Isa. 30. 29 the night, when a holy *s*.
33. 20 upon Zion, the city of our *s*.
Ezek. 45. 17 in sabbaths, in all *s*.
R. V. Deut. 31. 10 set time ; Isa. 30.
 29 feast ; Ezek. 45. 17 appointed
 feasts
Solemnly. *With testimony.*
Gen. 43. 3 The man did *s*. protest
1 Sam. 8. 9 protest *s*. unto them
Solitary. *Separate, lonely.*
Ps. 68. 6 God setteth *s*. in families
Lam. 1. 1 How doth the city sit *s*.
Silent.
Job 3. 7 let that night be *s*., let no
30. 3 For w. and famine they were *s*
Dry, desolate, desert.
Ps. 107. 4 they wandered in *s*. way
Isa. 35. 1 the *s*. place shall be glad
Mark 1. 35 departed into *s*. place
R. V. Job 3. 7 barren ; 30. 3 gaunt ;
 Ps. 107. 4 ; Mark 1. 35 desert
Solitarily. *Alone.*
Mic. 7. 14 which dwell in woods
Some. *One, about, thing or number indefinite.*
Gen. 37. 20 and cast him into *s*. pit
Mat. 13. 5 *S*. fell on stony places
Mark 7. 2 they saw *s*. disciples eat
Etc., etc.
R. V. many omissions of word
Somebody. *Someone.*
Luke 8. 46 *S*. hath touched me
Acts 5. 36 Theudas boasting to be *s*.
Something. *Certain thing.*

Mark 5. 43 that *s*. should be given
Luke 11. 54 and seeking to catch *s*.
John 13. 29 he shall give *s*. to poor
Acts 3. 5 expecting to receive *s*.
Gal. 6. 3 man think himself to be *s*.
Sometime, es. *Aforetime, once.*
Eph. 2. 13 ye who were *s*. afar off
Col. 3. 7 in the which ye walked *s*.
Tit. 3. 3 we also were *s*. foolish
1 Pet. 3. 20 Which *s*. were disobed.
R. V. Eph. 2. 13 ; 5.8 once ; Tit. 3.
 3 ; 1 Pet. 3. 20 aforetime
Somewhat. *More or less.*
Lev. 4. 22 when a ruler hath done *s*.
1 K. 2. 14 he said, I have *s*. to say
2 K. 5. 20 I will run and take *s*.
Luke 7. 40 I have *s*. to say to them
Acts 23. 20 inquire *s*. more perfectly
Rom. 15. 24 if first I be *s*. filled
2 Cor. 5. 12 may have *s*. to answer
Gal. 2. 6 these who seemed to be *s*.
Heb. 8. 3 this man have *s*. to offer
Rev. 2. 4 I have *s*. against thee bec.
R. V. Lev. 13. 6, 21, 26, 28, 56 ; 2
 Chr. 10. 10 ——
Son. *Son, boy child, offspring, descendant.*
Gen. 6. 10 Noah begat three *s*.
17. 19 Sarah shall bare thee a *s*.
27. 24 Art thou my very *s*. Esau?
35. 22 the *s*. of Jacob were twelve
Ex. 4. 20 Mos. took his wife and *s*.
30. 30 anoint Aaron and his *s*., and
Lev. 8. 6 M brought A. and his *s*.
Num. 3. 10 appoint A. and his *s*.
Deut. 1. 28 ha. seen *s*. of Anakims
Josh. 1. 1 Lord spake to J. *s*. of N.
24. 33 Eleazar *s*. of Aaron died
Judg. 6. 11 his *s*. G. threshed wheat
Ruth 4. 17 there is *s*. born to Naomi
1 Sam. 1. 8 am I not bet. th. ten *s*.
10. 21 Saul *s*. of Kish was taken
17. 17 Jesse said to David his *s*.
2 Sam. 1. 13 I am *s*. of a stranger
8. 18 David's *s*. were chief rulers
19. 4 my *s*. Absalom, O A., my *s*.
1 K. 2. 1 he charged Solomon his *s*.
11. 43 Rehoboam his *s*. reigned
2 K. 1. 17 Je. reigned, he had no *s*.
10. 1 Ahab had seventy *s*. in Sam.
1 Chr. 23. 1 he made S. his *s*. king
2 Chr. 27. 9 Ahaz his *s*. reigned
Ez. 3. 9 Then stood Jeshua with *s*.
Neh. 1. 9 I words of N. *s*. of Hach.
Esth. 9. 14 they hanged Ham. ten *s*.
Job 38. 7 *s*. of God shouted for joy
Ps. 2. 7 my *s*. ; this day ha. I begot.
72. 20 prayers of David *s*. of Jesse
Prov. 1. 8 *s*., hear instruc. of father
5. 1 *s*., attend unto thy wisdom
10. 1 wise *s*. maketh glad father
13. 24 that spareth rod hateth *s*.
Eccl. 1. 1 words of Preach., *s*. of D.
S. of S. 2. 3 so is my belov. among *s*.
Isa. 1. 1 vision of Isaiah *s*. of Amoz
14. 12 O Lucifer, *s*. of morning
Jer. 1. 1 words of Jer. *s*. of Hilkiah
36. 14 Baruch *s*. of Ner. took roll
Lam. 4. 2 The precious *s*. of Zion
Ezek. 1. 3 Ezekiel the *s*. of Buzi
Dan. 10. 10 his *s*. shall be stirred
Hos. 13. 13 he is an unwise *s*. ; for
Joel 3. 8 I will sell your *s*. and your
Am. 2. 11 I raised your *s*. for proph.
Jonah 1. 1 came to J. *s*. of Amittai
Mic. 7. 6 the *s*. dishonoureth father
Zeph. 1. 1 Zeph. the *s*. of Cushi
Hag. 2. 4 be strong, *s*. of Josedech
Zech. 1. 1 Zecha. *s*. of Barachiah
Mal. 1. 6 A *s*. honoureth his father
Mat. 1. 1 Jesus C., the *s*. of David
3. 17 This is my beloveth *S*., in
26. 2 the *S*. of man is betrayed
Mark 1. 1 gospel of J. C., *s*. of G.
3. 17 Boanerges, *s*. of thunder
Luke 1. 13 Elizabeth shall bear *s*.
4. 41 thou art Christ, *s*. of God
15. 11 A certain man had two *s*.
John 1. 45 Jesus of Naz., *s*. of God
19. 26 saith to moth., behold thy *s*.
Acts 8. 37 I believe J. C. is *s*. of G.
Rom. 1. 3 his *s*. Jesus C. our Lord
1 Cor. 15. 28 then sh. *S*. be subject
2 Cor. 6. 18 ye sh. be my *s*. and dau.
Gal. 2. 20 I live by faith of the *S*.
Eph. 3. 5 made known to *s*. of men

Phil. 2. 22 as *s.* wi. fath., he served
Col. 1. 13 translated to kingd. of *s.*
1 Thes. 1. 10 to wait for *S.* fr. heav.
2 Thes. 2. 3 man of sin, *s.* of perdi.
1 Tim. 1. 2 Unto Tim., my *s.* in faith
2 Tim. 2. 1 my *s.*, be strong in grace
Titus 1. 4 To Titus, mine own *s.*
Phile. 10 beseeeh thee for *s.* Onesi.
Heb. 1. 5 he shall be to me a *S.*
12. 5 *s.*, despise not chastening
Jas. 2. 21 offered Isaac his *s.* upon
1 Pet. 5. 13 salut., so doth M. my *s.*
2 Pet. 1. 17 This is my beloved *S.*
1 John 3. 2 now we are *s.* of God
2 John 9 he hath both Father and *S.*
Rev. 1. 13 one like unto *S.* of man
R. V. Gen. 23. 3, 16, 20 ; 25. 10 ; 32.
22 ; Num. 21. 8, 18, 22 ; Deut. 4.
1 ; 2 Chr. 21. 7 ; Mark 13. 12 ;
John 1. 12 ; 1 Cor. 4. 14, 17 ; Col.
3. 6 ; Phil. 2. 15, 22 ; 1 Tim. 1. 18 ;
2 Tim. 1. 2 ; 2. 1 ; Tit. 1. 4 ; Phile.
10 ; 1 John 3. 1, 2 child or children :
Num. 1. 20 ; 26. 5 firstborn ; 2
Sam. 23. 6 ungodly ; Acts 3. 13, 26
Servant ; Col. 4. 10 cousin ; Gen.
36. 15 ; Isa. 56. 3, 6 ; Mat. 18. 11 ;
24. 36 ; 25. 13 ; Luke 9. 56 ; John
12. 4 ; Acts 8. 37 ; 1 John 5. 13 ——
Song. *Singing, praising, ode.*
Gen. 31. 27 sent thee away with *s.*
Ex. 15. 1 then sang Moses this *s.*
15. 2 Lord is my strength and *s.*
Num. 21. 17 Is. sang this *s.*, Spring
Deut. 31. 22 Moses wrote this *s*
Judg. 5. 12 utter *s.* ; arise, Barak
2 Sam. 22. 1 D. spake words of th. *s.*
1 K. 4. 32 his *s.* were thousand and fi.
1 Chr. 6. 31 D. set ov. service of *s.*
2 Chr. 29. 27 *s.* of L. began with the.
Neh. 12. 46 in days of D. were *s*
Job 30. 9 now am I their *s.* ; yea
35. 10 G., who giveth *s.* in night
Ps. 33. 3 Sing unto him a new *s.*
69. 12 I was the *s.* of drunkards
See titles to 30 ; 48 ; 65 ; 66 etc.
Prov. 25. 20 sing *s.* to heav. heart
Eccl. 7. 5 man to hear *s.* of fools
S. of S. 1. 1 *S.* of *s.*, which is Solo.
Isa. 5. 1 *s.* of my beloved touching
24. 9 shall not drink wine with a *s.*
38. 20 sing *s.* to string. instrument
Lam. 3. 14 I was their *s.* all day
Ezek. 26. 13 I cause thy *s.* to cease
Am. 8. 3 of temple sh. be howlings
Eph. 5. 19 in psalms, spiritual *s.*
Col. 3. 16 hymns and spiritual *s.*
Rev. 5. 9 And they sung a new *s.*
14. 3 no man could learn that *s.*
R. V. 1 Chr. 25. 7 ; Isa. 35. 10
singing
Soon. *When, quickly.*
Ex. 2. 18 ye are come so *s.* to day
Deut. 4. 26 ye sh *s.* utterly perish
Job. 32. 22 my Maker would *s.* take
Ps. 37. 2 they shall *s.* be cut down
90. 10 *s.* cut off, and we flee away
106. 13 They *s.* forgot his works
Prov. 14. 17 *s.* angry deal. foolishly
Ezek. 23. 16 as *s.* as she saw them
Mat. 21. 20 How *s.* is fig t. withered
Acts 12. 18 Now as *s.* as it was day
Gal. 1. 6 so *s.* removed from him
2 Thes. 2. 2 be not *s.* sha. in mind
Tit. 1. 7 not self-wil., not *s.* angry
R. V. Ps. 68. 31 haste to ; Mat. 21.
20 immediately ; Gal. 1. 6 ; 2 Thes.
2. 2 quickly ; Josh. 3. 13 ; 2 Sam.
6. 18 ; Mark 14. 45 ; Luke 1. 44 ;
15. 30 ; 23. 7 ; John 16. 21 ; Acts
10. 29 ; Rev. 10. 10 ; 12. 4 when
Sooner. *More swiftly.*
Heb. 13. 19 restored to you the *s.*
Jas. 1. 11 the sun is no *s.* risen
R. V. Jas. 1. 11 ——.
Soothsayer. *Diviner.*
Josh. 13. 22 Baalam son of Beor, *s.*
Isa. 2. 6 they are *s.* like Philistines
Dan. 5. 7 the king cried to bring *s.*
Mic. 5. 12 shalt have no more *s.*
Soothsaying. *Divining.*
Acts 16. 16 bro. masters' gain by *s.*
Sop. *Morsel.*
John 13. 26 He it is to wh. I give *s.*
13. 27 after *s.* Satan entered him
Sope. *Soap.*

Jer. 2. 22 wash, and take much *s.*
Mal. 3. 2 for he is like fuller's *s.*
Sorcerer. *Magician, wizard, enchanter.*
Ex. 7. 11 Pha. called wise men and *s.*
Isa. 57. 3 draw hither, sons of *s.*
Jer. 27. 9 hearken not to your *s.*
Dan. 2. 2 Neb. command. to call *s.*
Mal. 3. 5 be swift witness against *s.*
Acts 13. 6 they found a certain *s.*
13. 8 Elymas the *s.* so his name
Rev. 21. 8 *s.* sh. have part in lake
22. 15 For without are dogs and *s.*
Sorcery. *Magic.*
Acts 8. 9 who beforetime used *s.*
Sorceries. *Enchantments.*
Isa. 47. 9 come on thee for thy *s.*
Acts 8. 11 he bewitched them wi. *s.*
Rev. 9. 21 nei. repented of their *s.*
Sore (*n.*). *Plague, ulcer, pain.*
Gen. 34. 25 third day, when were *s.*
Lev. 13. 42 if a white reddish *s.*
2 Chr. 6. 29 ev. one know his own *s.*
Job. 5. 18 he maketh *s.* and bindeth
Ps. 38. 11 friends stand aloof fr. *s.*
77. 2 my *s.* ran in the night
Isa. 1. 6 bruises and putrefying *s.*
Luke 16. 20 Laz. at gate, full of *s.*
Rev. 16. 2 there fell a grievous *s.*
R. V. Lev. 13. 42, 43 ; 2 Chr. 6. 28,
29 ; Ps. 38. 11 plague
Sore (*adj.*). *Evil, much, heavy, very, grievous.*
Gen. 20. 8 the men were *s.* afraid
Ex. 14. 10 chil. of Is. were *s.* afraid
Num. 22. 3 Moab was *s.* af. of peo.
Deut. 6. 22 showed signs gr. and *s.*
Josh. 9. 24 we were *s.* afr. of lives
Judg. 10. 9 Israel was *s.* distressed
1 Sam. 17. 24 men of Is. were *s.* afr.
2 Sam. 2. 17 was *s.* battle that day
1 K. 17. 17 his sickness was so *s.*
2 K. 3. 26 saw the battle was *s.*
1 Chr. 10. 4 *s.* afr. So Saul took sw.
2 Chr. 35. 23 aw. ; for I am *s.* wonnd.
Job 2. 7 Sat. smote Job with *s.* boils
Ps. 6. 3 My soul is also *s.* vexed
38. 8 I am feeble and *s.* broken
Eccl. 5. 13 *s.* evil which I have seen
Isa. 64. 9 Be not wroth very *s.*, O L.
Jer. 52. 6 famine was *s.* in the city
Ezek. 21. 10 sharp. to ma. *s.* slaugh.
Mic. 2. 10 destroy wi. *s.* destruction
Mat. 17. 6 fell on their face, *s.* afraid
Sore (*adv.*). *Hardly, grievously, greatly, weighty.*
Gen. 19. 9 pressed *s.* upon the man
2 Sam. 13. 36 king also wept very *s.*
2 K. 20. 3 And Hezekiah wept *s.*
2 Chr. 28. 19 transgr. *s.* against Lord
Ez. 10. 1 for the people wept very *s.*
Dan. 6. 14 king was *s.* displeased
Zech. 1. 2 L. ha. been *s.* displeased
Mat. 17. 15 he is a lunatic, *s.* vexed
Mark 6. 51 and they were *s.* amazed
Acts 20. 37 And they all wept *s.*, and
Sorely. *Greatly.*
Isa. 23. 5 *s.* pained at report of T.
Sorer. *Worse.*
Heb. 10. 29 how much *s.* punishment
Sorrow (*n.*). *Pain, grief, affliction, mourning.*
Gen. 42. 38 hairs with *s.* to grave
Ex. 15. 14 *s.* take hold of inhabitants.
Lev. 26. 16 terror cause *s.* of heart
Deut. 28. 65 L. shall give *s.* of mind
2 Sam. 22. 6 *s.* of hell compas. me
1 Chr. 4. 9 bec. I bare him with *s.*
Neh. 2. 2 nothing else but *s.* of hea.
Esth. 9. 22 was turned from *s.* to joy
Job 3. 10 hid not *s.* from mine eyes
Ps. 13. 2 having *s.* in my heart daily
32. 10 many *s.* shall be to wicked
Prov. 10. 10 that winketh caus. *s.*
10. 22 L. maketh rich, addeth no *s.*
23. 29 Who hath woe ? who ha. *s.*?
Eccl. 1. 18 incr. knowl. increas. *s.*
Isa. 53. 3 man of *s.*, acquainted with
Jer. 30. 15 thy *s.* is incurable for
Lam. 1. 18 hear, and behold my *s.*
Ezek. 23. 33 filled wi. drunk. and *s.*
Dan. 10. 16 by vision *s.* are turned
Hos. 13. 13 *s.* of travail. wom. shall
Mat. 24. 8 these are beginning of *s.*
Mark 13. 8 these are beginning of *s.*
Luke 22. 45 found them sleep. for *s.*

John 16. 20 *s.* shall be turned to joy
Rom. 9. 2 I have *s.* in my heart
2 Cor. 7. 10 godly *s.* work. repent.
Phil. 2. 27 lest I have *s.* upon *s.*
1 Tim. 6. 10 pierced thems. with *s.*
Rev. 18. 17 no widow, sh. see no *s.*
R. V. Gen. 3. 17 ; Ps. 127. 2 toil ;
Ex. 15. 14 pangs ; Deut. 28. 65
pining ; Job 3. 10 trouble ; 41. 22
terror ; Job 6. 10 ; Jer. 30. 15 ; 45. 3 ;
51. 29 ; Rom. 9. 2 pain ; 2 Sam.
22. 6 ; Ps. 18. 4, 5 ; 116. 3 cords ;
Ps. 55. 10 mischief ; Isa. 5. 30
distress ; Isa. 29. 2 lamentation ;
Mat. 24. 8 ; Mark 13. 8 travail ;
Rev. 18. 7 ; 21. 4 mourning
Sorrow (*v.*). *Grieve, make sad.*
1 Sam. 10. 2 thy father *s.* for you
Jer. 31. 12 th. shall not *s.* any more
Hos. 8. 10 sh. *s.* for the burden of k.
2 Cor. 7. 9 that ye *s.* to repentance
1 Thes. 4. 13 that ye *s.* not as others
Sorrowful. *Grieved, sad, pained.*
1 Sam. 1. 15 woman of a *s.* spirit
Job 6. 7 things refus. are as *s.* meat
Ps. 69. 29 But I am poor and *s.*
Prov. 14. 13 in laughter heart is *s.*
Jer. 31. 25 replenish. every *s.* soul
Zeph. 3. 18 gather them that are *s.*
Zech. 9. 5 Gaza shall be very *s.*
Mat. 26. 22 they were exceeding *s.*
Mark 14. 34 My soul is exceeding *s.*
Luke 18. 24 wh. Jesus saw he was *s.*
John 16. 20 and ye shall be *s.*, but
2 Cor. 6. 10 *s.*, yet alway rejoicing
Phil. 2. 28 that I may be less *s.*
Sorrowing. *Pained.*
Luke 2. 48 I have sought thee *s.*
Acts 20. 38 *S.* for the words which
Sorry. *Grieved, sad.*
1 Sam. 22. 8 none of you that is *s.*
Neh. 8. 10 nei. be *s.*, for joy of L.
Ps. 38. 18 I will be *s.* for my sin
Isa. 51. 19 who shall be *s.* for thee?
Mat. 17. 23 they were exceeding *s.*
Mark 6. 26 the king was exceeding *s.*
2 Cor. 2. 2 For if I make you *s.*
R. V. Neh. 8. 10 ; Mat. 14. 9 grieved ; Isa. 51. 19 bemoaned
Sort. *Kind, class, in part, species, manner.*
Gen. 6. 19 two of every *s.* in ark
Deut. 22. 11 garment of divers *s.*
1 Chr. 24. 5 divid. one *s.* with anoth.
Ez. 4. 8 wrote to Ar. after this *s.*
Neh. 5. 18 store of all *s.* of wine
Ps. 78. 45 He sent divers *s.* of flies
Eccl. 2. 8 instruments, that of all *s.*
Ezek. 27. 24 thy merchants in all *s.*
39. 4 unto rav. birds of every *s.*
Acts 17. 5 lewd fellows of baser *s.*
Rom. 15. 15 wri. boldly in some *s.*
1 Cor. 3. 13 try work of wh. *s.* it is
2 Cor. 7. 11 sorrow. after godly *s.*
2 Tim. 3. 6 this *s.* creep into houses
3 John 6 journey after a godly *s.*
R. V. Deut. 22. 11 mingled stuff ;
Ps. 78. 45 ; 105. 31 swarms ; Dan.
1. 10 own age ; Acts 17. 5 rabble ;
Rom. 15. 15 measure
Sottish. *Thick headed.*
Jer. 4. 22 they are *s.* children, and
Sought. *See* Seek.
Soul. *Soul, breath, life.*
Gen. 2. 7 and man became a living *s.*
12. 13 *s.* sh. live because of thee
Ex. 12. 15 that *s.* shall be cut off
Lev. 4. 2 If *s.* sin through ignorance
17. 12 No *s.* of you shall eat blood
26. 43 their *s.* abhorred my statutes
Num. 11. 6 now our *s.* is dried away
Deut. 4. 9 keep thy *s.* diligently lest
6. 5 love Lord with all thy *s.*, and
Josh. 11. 11 they smote all the *s.*
Judg. 5. 21 O my *s.*, thou ha. trod.
1 Sam. 1. 10 she was in bitter. of *s.*
18. 3 he loved him as his own *s.*
2 Sam. 5. 8 are hated of David's *s.*
1 K. 1. 29 that hath redeem. my *s.*
2 K. 4. 27 her *s.* is vexed within her
1 Chr. 22. 10 set your *s.* to seek L
2 Chr. 6. 38 if they return with *s.*
Job 10. 1 my *s.* is weary of my life
19. 2 How long vex my *s.*, and
Ps. 6. 3 My *s.* also is sore vexed
11. 1 how say ye to my *s.*. Flee

22. 20 Deliver my s. from sword
26. 9 gather not my s. wi. sinners
57. 1 my s. trusteth in thee : yea,
86. 4 unto thee do I lift up my s.
104. 1 Bless the Lord, O my s. O
Prov. 11. 30 he that win. s. is wise
13. 4 s. of diligent sh. be made fat
18. 7 fool's lips are snare of his s.
27. 7 full s. loatheth honeycomb
Eccl. 2. 3 his s. be not fill. wi. good
S. of S. 3. 6 s. failed when he spake
Isa. 1. 14 your feasts my s. hateth
58. 11 satisfy my s. in drought and
Jer. 5. 9 shall my s. be avenged and
51. 45 deliver ye every man his s.
Lam. 3. 4 L. is my portion, saith s.
Ezek. 3. 19 thou hast deliver. my s.
18. 4 the s. that sinneth it shall die
Hos. 9. 4 bread of s. sh. not come
Jonah 2. 7 my s. fainted within me
Mic. 7. 1 my s. desired ripe fruit
Hab. 2. 10 hast sinned against thy s.
Zech. 11. 8 my s. lothed them, and
Mat. 10. 28 but not able to kill the s
11. 29 ye shall find rest for your s.
26. 38 My s. is exceed. sorrowful
Mark 8. 36 gain world, lose own s.
8. 37 what shall a man give for s.
12. 30 love the Lord with all thy s.
Luke 1. 46 my s. doth magnify L.
12. 19 I will say to my s., Soul,
12. 20 this night thy s. be required
John. 12. 27 Now is my s. troubled
Acts 2. 27 not leave my s. in hell
Rom. 13. 1 Let every s. be subject
1 Cor. 15. 45 Adam was made liv. s.
2 Cor. 1. 23 call for record on my s.
1 Thes. 2. 8 imparted on s. to you
Heb. 6. 19 we have as anchor of s.
Jas. 1. 21 word, able to save your s.
1 Pet. 1. 22 ye ha. purified your s.
2 Pet. 2. 8 vexed his s. day to day
3 John 2 even as thy s. prospereth
Rev. 16. 3 every s. died in the sea
R. V. Lev. 17. 11; Num. 16. 38;
Sam. 26. 21; Job. 31. 30; Prov.
22. 23; Mat. 16. 26; Mark 8. 36,
37 life or lives; Lev. 4. 2; 5. 1, 2,
4, 15, 17; 6. 2; 7. 21 any one;
Num. 15. 27 one person; Job 30.
15 honour; Prov. 19. 18 heart;
Hos. 9. 4 appetite; Ps. 16. 2; Jer.
5. 41; Mark 12. 23 ——
Sound (n.). *Voice, sound.*
Ex. 28. 35 and his s. shall be heard
Lev. 26. 36 s. of leaf shall chase
Josh. 6. 5 when ye hear s. of trump.
2 Sam. 5. 24 wh. ye hear s. of going
1 K. 1. 40 earth rent with the s.
2 K. 6. 32 is not s. of master's feet
1 Chr. 15. 28 with s. of the cornet
2 Chr. 5. 13 one s. heard in praising
Neh. 4. 20 in what place ye hear s.
Job 15. 21 dreadful s. in his ears
21. 12 rejoice at the s. of the organ
Ps. 47. 5 gone up wi. s. of trumpet
77. 17 water, skies sent out a s.
92. 3 sing upon harp with sol. s.
Eccl. 12. 4 s. of grinding is low, and
Jer. 4. 21 see standard, hear the s.
50. 22 s. of battle is in the land
Ezek. 10. 5 s. of cherubim's wings
26. 13 s. of harp shall be no more
Dan. 3. 5 at what time ye hear s.
Am. 2. 2 Moab shall die with s.
Mat. 24. 31 his angels with great s.
John 3. 8 hearest s., canst not tell
Acts 2. 2 there came s. from heaven
Rom. 10. 18 s. went into all earth
1 Cor. 14. 7 thi. without life giv. s.
Heb. 12. 19 not come to s. of trum.
Rev. 1. 15 as the s. of many waters
R. V. Job. 39. 24; John 3. 8; 1
Cor. 14. 7, 8; Rev. 1. 15; 18. 22
voice
Sound (adj.). *Healthy, perfect.*
Ps. 119. 80 Let my heart be s. in
Prov. 2. 7 He layeth up s. wisdom
3. 21 Keep s. wisdom and discre.
14. 30 s. heart is life of flesh : but
Luke 15. 27 received him safe and s.
1 Cor. 14. 7 give a distinction in s.
1 Tim. 1. 10 contra. to s. doctrine
2 Tim. 1. 7 G. has giv. us s. minds
1. 13 Hold fast form of s. words
Tit. 1. 9 may be able by s. doctrine

2. 2 that aged men be s. in faith
R. V. Ps 119. 80 perfect ; 2 Tim.
1. 7 discipline
Sound (v.). *Blow, make noise.*
Ex. 19. 19 the trumpet s. long, and
Lev. 25. 9 sh. ye make trump. to s.
Num. 10. 7 ye shall not s. an alarm
1 Chr. 15. 19 were appointed to s.
2 Chr. 13. 14 priests s. wi. trumpets
Neh. 4. 18 he that s. the trumpet
Isa. 16. 11 my bowels s. like harp
Jer. 48. 36 heart shall s. for Moab
Joel 2. 1 s. alarm on holy mount.
Mat. 6. 2 do not s. trumpet before
Luke 1. 44 voice of salutation s.
1 Cor. 15. 52 the trumpet shall s.
1 Thes. 1. 8 from you s. word of L.
Rev. 8. 7 first angel s., there fol.
Search, take soundings.
1 Sam. 20. 12 when I ha. s. my fath.
Acts 27. 28 s., found it tw. fathoms
Sounding. *Make noise.*
2 Chr. 5. 12 hun. and tw. priests s.
Isa. 63. 15 where is s. of thy bowels
Ezek. 7. 7 not the s. of mountains
1 Cor. 13. 1 not charity, as s. brass
R. V. Isa. 63. 15 yearning ; Ezek.
7. 7 joyful shouting
Soundness. *Wholeness.*
Ps. 38. 3 no s. in my flesh because
Isa. 1. 6 even unto the head is no s.
Acts 3. 16 giv. him this perfect s.
Sour. *Acid, turned.*
Isa. 18. 5 the s. grape is ripening
Jer. 31. 29 fathers ha. eat. s. grape
Ezek. 18. 2 fath. have eat. s. grapes
Hos. 4. 18 Their drink is s., they
R. V. Isa. 18. 5 ——
South. *South, right hand.*
Gen. 13. 1 Abram went into the s.
Ex. 26. 18 make boards on s. side
Num. 13. 22 they ascend. by the s.
Deut. 1. 7 take your journey in s.
Josh. 10. 40 Josh. smote count. of s.
Judg. 1. 15 thou hast giv. me s. land
1 Sam. 27. 10 D. said, Ag. s. of Jud.
2 Sam. 24. 7 they went to s. of Jud.
1 K. 7. 25 three looking toward s.
1 Chr. 9. 24 toward e. w. n. and s.
2 Chr. 4. 10 he set sea over ag. s.
Job 9. 9 Pleiades, and chamb. of s.
Ps. 78. 26 he brought in s. wind
S. of S. 4. 16 Awake, O n. wind ; s.
Isa. 21. 1 As whirlwinds in the s.
Jer. 13. 19 cities of s. sh. be shut
Ezek. 20. 47 say to forest of the s.
Dan. 11. 9 king of the s. shall come
Obad. 19 they of S. sh. poss. mount
Zech. 14. 10 fr. G. to R. s. of Jeru.
Mat. 12. 42 queen of s. shall rise
Luke 12. 55 when ye see s. wi. blow
Acts 27. 12 lying toward s. west
Rev. 21. 13 on the s. three gates
Southward. *Southerly.*
Gen. 13. 14 L said to A. Look s.
Num. 13. 17 get ye up this way s.
Josh. 15. 1 the wilderness of Zin s
1 Sam. 14. 5 s. over against Gibeah
1 Chr. 26. 17 north. four a day, s.
Ezek. 47. 19 this is the south side s.
Dan. 8. 4 I saw the ram pushing s.
R. V. Num. 13. 17 by the South ;
Josh. 15. 21 in the South ; I Sam.
14. 5 on the south
Sow (n.). *Sow, swine.*
2 Pet. 2. 22 s. washed to her wallow.
Sow (v.). *Sow, send, scatter.*
Gen. 26. 12 Is. s. in land same year
Ex. 23. 10 six years thou sh. s. land
Lev. 19. 19 not s. wi. mingled seed
Deut. 11. 10 wh. thou s. thy seed
21. 4 valley neither eared nor s.
Judg. 6. 3 so it was, wh. Is. had s.
2 K. 19. 29 and in third year, s. ye
Job 4. 8 plow iniquity, s. wicked.
Ps. 97. 11 Light is s. for righteous
126. 5 s. in tears, shall reap in joy
Prov. 22. 8 s. iniq. sh. reap vanity
16. 28 A froward man s. strife
Eccl. 11. 6 In morning s. thy seed
Isa. 28. 24 Doth plowman plow to s.
Jer. 4. 3 Break fallow ground and s.
31. 27 I will s. the house of Israel
Ezek. 36. 9 ye shall be tilled and s.
Hos. 8. 7 they have the s. wind, and
Am. 9. 13 plow. overtake him that s.

Mic. 6. 15 shalt s. but sh. not reap
Nah. 1. 14 no more of thy name be s.
Hag. 1. 6 s. much, bring in little
Zech. 10. 9 I will s. th. am'g people
Mat. 6. 26 they s. not, neither reap
13. 37 that s. good seed is the Son
Mark 4. 14 The sower s. the word
Luke 8. 5 A sower went out to s.
John 4. 36 he that s. and reapeth
1 Cor. 15. 42 It is s. in corruption
15. 43 It is s. in dishonour, rai. in gl.
15. 44 It is s. in the natural body
2 Cor. 9. 6 He which s. sparingly
Gal. 6. 7 whatsoev. man s., that sh.
Jas. 3. 18 righteous. is s. in peace
R. V. Prov. 16. 28 scattereth
Sower. *Who sows.*
Isa. 55. 10 it may give seed to s.
Jer. 50. 16 cut off s. from Babylon
Mat. 13. 18 hear ye the parable of s.
Mark 4. 14 The s. soweth the word
2 Cor. 9. 10 ministereth seed to s.
Sowing. *Sown, seed.*
Lev. 11. 37 if carcase fall on any s.
26. 5 the vintage shall reach to s. t.
Space. *Period, distance.*
Gen. 29. 14 abode with him s. of mo
32. 16 and put a s. betwixt drove
Lev. 25. 8 s. of the seven sabbaths
Deut. 2. 14 s. in which we came
Josh. 3. 4 shall be s. bet. you and it
Ez. 9. 8 now for little s. grace hath
Ezek. 40. 12 s. bet. little chambers
Luke 22. 59 about s. of one hour
Acts 5. 7 the s. of three hours after
5. 34 put the apostles forth little s.
Rev. 2. 21 I gave her s. to repent
R. V. Lev. 25. 8; Deut. 2. 14 days ;
Ez. 9. 8 moment ; Jer. 28. 11 —— ;
Ezek. 40. 12 border ; Acts 5. 34;
Rev. 17. 10 while ; Acts 15. 33;
Rev. 2. 21 time ; Jas. 5. 17 for ;
Rev. 14. 20 as far as
Spake. *See Speak.*
Span (n.). *Span, stretched hand.*
Ex. 28. 16 s. shall be length thereof
1 Sam. 17. 4 height six cubits and s.
Isa. 40. 12 meted out heaven with s.
Lam. 2. 20 women eat chil. s. long
Ezek. 43. 13 the edge shall be a s.
R. V. Lam. 2. 20 dandled
Span (v.). *R. V. spread out.*
Isa. 48. 13 my hand hath s. heavens
Spare. *Shelter, pity, withhold, forbear.*
Gen. 18. 24 wilt thou destroy not s.
Deut. 13. 8 neither shall thou s.
1 Sam. 15. 3 s. them not, but slay
2 Sam. 21. 7 king s. Mephibosheth
2 K. 5. 20 master hath s. Naaman
Neh. 13. 22 S. me accor. to mercy
Job 6. 10 let him not s., I have not
30. 10 and s. not to spit in my face
Ps. 72. 13 shall s. the poor and needy
78. 50 he s. not soul from death
Prov. 13. 24 that s. rod hateth son
Isa. 9. 19 no man shall s. brother
Jer. 13. 14 I will not pity, nor s.
Ezek. 5. 11 neither shall mine eye s.
Joel 2. 17 S. thy people, O Lord
Jonah 4. 11 should I not s. Ninev.
Hab. 1. 17 not s. to slay nations
Mal. 3. 17 s. th., as man s. his own
Acts 20. 29 enter, not s. the flock
Rom. 8. 32 that s. not his own Son
1 Cor. 7. 28 have trouble, I s. you
2 Cor. 1. 23 to s. you I came not
2 Pet. 2. 4 if God s. not the angels
R. V. Ps. 72. 13; Jonah 4. 11 have
pity on ; Prov. 21. 26 withholdeth
Sparingly. *Scantily.*
2 Cor 9. 6 who sow. s. sh. reap s
Spark. *Brand, fiery point.*
Job 5. 7 trouble, as s. fly upward
Isa. 1. 31 tow, maker of it as a s.
R. V. Isa. 50. 11 firebrands
Sparkle. *Flash, be brilliant.*
Ezek. 1. 7 s. like burnished brass
Sparrow. *Bird, sparrow.*
Ps. 84. 3 s. hath found an house
102. 7 as a s. alone upon house top
Mat. 10. 29 more val. than many s.
Luke 12. 6 five s. sold for two farth.
Spat. *See Spit.*
Speak. *Say, lift voice.*
Gen. 9. 8 God s. unto Noah, saying

Ex. 7. 8 the Lord *s.* unto Moses
Lev. 21. 1 *S.* unto the sons of Aaron
Num. 17. 12 chil. of Is. *s.* unto Mo.
Deut. 1. 9 I *s.* to you at that time
Josh. 1. 1 the Lord *s.* unto Joshua
Judg. 8. 9 he *s.* to men of Penuel
1 Sam. 7. 3 Sam. *s.* to house of Is.
2 Sam. 24. 17 David *s.* unto the L.
1 K. 1. 11 Nathan *s.* to Bath-sheba
2 K. 19. 10 Thus sh. ye *s.* to Hezek.
1 Chr. 15. 16 D. *s.* to chief of Levi.
2 Chr. 1. 2 Solom. *s.* unto all Israel
Ez. 8. 22 we had *s.* unto the king
Neh. 8. 1 *s.* to Ezra to bring the law
Esth. 4. 10 Esth. *s.* to Hatach, and
Job 3. 2 And Job *s.* and said, Let
Ps. 29. 9 in his temple every one *s.*
Prov. 6. 13 he *s.* with his feet, he
Eccl. 3. 7 silence, and a time to *s.*
S. of S. 2. 10 My beloved *s.*, and said
Isa. 24. 3 for Lord hath *s.* this word
Jer. 28. 2 Thus *s.* the Lord of hosts
Ezek. 31. 2 *s.* unto Phar. k. of Egy.
Dan. 1. 3 king *s.* unto Ashpenaz
Hos. 2. 14 I will *s.* comfort. to her
Joel 3. 8 for the Lord hath *s.* it
Am. 3. 1 Hear word the L. hath *s.*
Obad. 18 for the Lord hath *s.* it
Jonah 2. 10 Lord *s.* unto the fish
Mic. 4. 4 mouth of Lord hath *s.* it
Zeph. 3. 13 rem. of Is. sh. not *s.* lies
Hag. 1. 13 *s.* Hag. the L's. messen.
Zech. 2. 4 *s.* to this young man, say.
Mat. 13. 34 without par. *s.* he not
Mark 1. 34 suffered not devils to *s.*
Luke 14. 3 Jesus *s.* unto the lawyers
John 7. 39 this *s.* he of the spirit
Acts 2. 29 let me freely *s.* to you
Acts 2. 4 began to *s.* wi. oth. tongues
Rom. 6. 19 I *s.* after manner of men
1 Cor. 2. 7 we *s.* the wisdom of God
2 Cor. 4. 13 we believe, therefore *s.*
Gal. 3. 15 I *s.* after manner of men
Eph. 5. 32 I *s.* concerning Christ
Phil. 4. 11 Not *s.* in respect of want
Col. 4. 4 manifest, as I ought to *s.*
1 Thes. 2. 2 we are bold in G. to *s.*
1 Tim. 2. 7 I *s.* the truth in Christ
Tit. 2. 15 These things *s.*, and exhort
Heb. 11. 4 by it he, being dead, yet *s.*
Jas. 1. 19 be swift to hear, slow to *s.*
1 Pet. 2. 12 they *s.* ag'st you as evil
2 Pet. 1. 21 men of G. *s.* as moved
1 John 4. 5 therefore *s.* they of world
2 John 12 I trust to come to you *s.*
3 John 14 see thee, and we shall *s.*
Jude 16 mouth *s.* swelling words
Rev. 1. 12 turned to see voice th. *s.*
R. V. Many changes, chiefly to, say, said, answered, spoken, utter

Speaker. *Who speaks.*
Ps. 140. 11 let not evil *s.* be estab.
Acts 14. 12 because he was chief *s.*

Speaking. *Saying.*
Gen. 24. 15 before he had done *s.*
Deut. 11. 19 *s.* of them when thou
Esth. 10. 3 and *s.* peace to his seed
Job 4. 2 who can withhold self fr. *s.*
Isa. 58. 13 nor *s.* thine own words
Dan. 7. 8 and mouth *s.* great things
Mat. 6. 7 shall be heard for much *s.*
Acts 14. 3 they abode, *s.* boldly in
2 Cor. 13. 3 proof of Chr. *s.* in me
Eph. 4. 31 let evil *s.* be put away
1 Tim. 4. 2 *S.* lies in hypocrisy
1 Pet. 2. 1 laying aside all evil *s.*

Spear. *Javelin, lance, spear.*
Josh. 8. 18 Josh. stretched out the *s.*
Judg. 5. 8 was there *s.* seen among
1 Sam. 26. 12 D. took *s.* and cruse
2 Sam. 1. 6 Saul leaned upon his *s.*
2 K. 11. 10 did priest give David's *s.*
1 Chr. 11. 11 lifted *s.* aga. three hun.
2 Chr. 23. 9 priest deliv. *s.* and buck.
Neh. 4. 13 set peo. wi. *s.* and bows
Job 39. 23 rattleth against him, the *s.*
  41. 29 Leviathan laugheth at the *s.*
Ps. 35. 3 Draw out also the *s.*, and
  46. 9 he cutteth the *s.* in sunder
Isa. 2. 4 beat *s.* into pruninghooks
Jer. 46. 4 furbish *s.*, put on the brig.
Ezek. 39. 9 shall burn *s.* with fire
Joel 3. 10 Beat pruninghooks into *s.*
Mic. 4. 3 sh. beat *s.* into pru. hooks
Nah. 3. 3 lift sword and glitter. *s.*
Hab. 3. 11 at shining of glittering *s.*

John 19. 34 sol. wi. *s.* pier. his side
R. V. Josh. 8. 18, 26 ; Job 41. 29 javelin ; 2 Sam. 23. 8 ———

Spearmen. *Reeds, spearmen.*
Ps. 68. 30 Rebuke the company of *s.*
Acts 23. 23 ma. ready two hun. *s.*
R. V. Ps. 68. 30 the reeds

Special. *Peculiar, chiefly.*
Deut. 7. 6 L. chosen thee a *s.* peo.
Acts 19. 11 God wrought *s.*mir. by

Specially. *Most of all.*
Acts 25. 26 I bro. him *s.* before thee
1 Tim. 4. 10 Sav., *s.* of tho. th. bel.
Tit. 1. 10 *s.* they of circumcision
Phile. 16. brother beloved, *s.* to me

Speckled. *Speckled, spotted, sorrel.*
Gen. 30. 32 removing the *s.* cattle
Jer. 12. 9 heritage is to me as *s.* bird
Zech. 1. 8 red horses, *s.* and white
R. V. Ps. Zech. 1. 8 sorrel

Spectacle. *Show, theatre.*
1 Cor. 4. 9 we are made *s.* to world

Sped. *See Speed.*

Speech. *Saying, word, talk.*
Gen. 11. 1 who. earth was of one *s.*
Ex. 4. 10 M. said, I am slow of *s.*
Num. 12. 8 speak not in dark *s.*
Deut. 32. 2 my *s.* shall distil as dew
2 Sam. 19. 11 *s.* of Is. is come to k.
1 K. 3. 10 Sol's *s.* pleased the Lord
Job 13. 17 Hear diligently my *s.* and
Ps. 19. 2 day unto day uttereth *s.*
Prov. 17. 7 Excel. *s.* becom. not fool
S. of S. 4. 3 thy *s.* is comely ; thy t.
Isa. 28. 23 hearken, and hear my *s.*
Jer. 31. 23 shall use this *s.* in Jud.
Ezek. 1. 24 the *s.* as noise of an host
Hab. 3. 2 O L., I have heard thy *s.*
Mat. 26. 73 thy *s.* bewrayeth thee
Mark 14. 70 thy *s.* agreeth thereto
John 8. 43 Why not unders. my *s.*?
Acts. 14. 11 saying in *s.* of Lycao.
Rom. 16. 18 by fair *s.* deceive hearts
1 Cor. 2. 1 ca. not with excel. of *s.*
2 Cor. 11. 6 rude in *s.* not in knowl.
Col. 4. 6 Let your *s.* be with grace
Tit. 2. 8 sound *s.* cannot be cond.
Jude 15. convince them of hard *s.*
R. V. 2 Sam. 14. 20 matter ; 2 Chr. 32. 18 language ; S. of S. 4. 3 mouth ; Ezek. 1. 24 tumult ; Hab. 3. 2 report ; 1 Cor. 4. 19 word ; Jude 15 things

Speechless. *Without breath, dumb.*
Mat. 22. 12 how camest? he was *s.*
Luke 1. 22 Zacharias remained *s.*
Acts 9. 7 the men with him stood *s.*
R. V. Luke 1. 22 dumb

Speed (*n.*). *Haste, progress.*
Gen. 24. 12 O L., send me good *s.*
1 Sam. 20. 38 Jon.cried, Make *s.* h.
2 Sam. 15. 14 *s.* lest he overtake us
1 K. 12. 18 Reho. made *s.* to get up
Ez. 6. 12 let it be done with *s.*
Isa. 5. 26 they come with *s.* swiftly
Acts 17. 15 come to him with all *s.*
2 John 10 receiv. not, nei. bid God *s.*
R. V. Ez. 6. 12 all diligence ; 2 John 10, 11 greeting.

Speed (*v.*). *Find.*
Judg. 5 30 Have they not sped?

Speedy. *Hasty.*
Zeph. 1. 18 he shall make *s.* riddance
R. V. *end, yea, terrible end.*

Speedily. *In haste.*
2 Sam. 17. 16 *s.* pass over ; lest king
Ez. 6. 13 king sent, so they did *s.*
Ps. 69. 17 I am in trouble, hear *s.*
Eccl. 8. 11 sent. is not executed *s.*
Isa. 58. 8 health sh. spring forth *s.*
Zech. 8. 21 let us go *s.* and pray bef.
R. V. Gen. 44. 11 hasted ; 2 Sam.17. 16 in any wise ; 2 Chr. 35. 13 quickly ; Ez. 6. 13 ; 7. 17, 21, 26 with diligence ; Ps. 143 7 make haste.

Spend. *Pay out, pass, exhaust.*
Gen. 21. 15 water w. *s.* in the bottle
Lev. 26. 20 strength be *s.* in vain
Deut. 32. 23 I will *s.* mine arrows
Judg. 19. 11 the day was far *s.* ; and
1 Sam. 9. 7 bread is *s.* in our vessels
Job 21. 13 they days in wealth
Ps. 31. 10 my life is *s.* with grief
  90. 9 we *s.* years as tale that is told
Prov. 29. 3 keep. co. with harlots *s.*

Eccl. 6. 12 life he *s.* as a shadow?
Isa. 49. 4 *s.* my strength for nought
Jer. 37. 2 all bread in cit. were *s.*
Mark 5. 26 had *s.* all that she had
Luke 15. 14 And when he had *s.* a.
Acts 18. 23 aft. he had *s.* some time
Rom. 13. 12 night far *s.*, day at hand
2 Cor. 12. 15 I will gladly *s.* for you
R. V. Ps. 90. 9 bring to an end ;
Prov. 21. 20 swalloweth ; 29. 3 wasteth

Spent. *see* **Spend.**
Spew. *see* **Spue.**

Spice (*n.*). *Spice, spicery.*
Gen. 43. 11 carry man a present, *s.*
Ex. 30. 24 Take unto thee sweet *s.*
1 K. 10. 2 wi. camels that bare *s.*
2 K. 20 13 Hez. showed them the *s.*
1 Chr. 9. 29 appoint. to oversee *s.*
2 Chr. 9. 9 queen of Sh. gave S. *s.*
S. of S. 4. 14 aloes, with all chief *s.*
Ezek. 27. 22 occupied thy fairs w. *s.*
Mark 16. 1 had bought sweet *s.*
Luke 23. 56 returned, and prepar. *s.*
John 19. 40 wound it in. lin. wi. *s.*
R. V. Gen. 43. 11 spicery ; 1 K. 10. 15

Spice (*v.*). *To spice.*
S. of S. cause thee to drink *s.* wine
Ezek. 24. 10 flesh, and *s.* it well
R. V. Ezek. 24. 10 make thick the broth

Spicery. *Spices.*
Gen 37. 25 with camels bearing *s.*

Spider. *Spider.*
Job 8. 14 trust shall be a *s.* web
Isa. 29. 5 eggs, and weave *s.* web
R. V. *lizard*
Prov. 30. 28 *s.* tak. hold wi. hands

Spied. *see* **Spy**

Spies. *Walkers, searchers.*
Gen. 42. 9 Joseph said. Ye are *s.*
Josh. 6. 23 men that were *s.* went
1 Sam. 26. 4 David sent out *s.* and
2 Sam. 15. 10 Absalom sent *s.* thro.
R. V. *Atharim*
Num. 21. 1 Is. came by way of *s.*
Who spy
Luke 20. 20 sent forth *s.*, which
Heb. 11. 31 when she had receiv. *s.*
R. V. Judg. 1. 24 watchers

Spikenard. *Nard.*
S. of S. 1. 12. my *s.* send. forth *s.*
Mark 14. 3 box of ointment of *s.*
John 12. 3 pound of ointment of *s.*

Spill. *Pour out.*
Gen. 38. 9 Onan *s.* seed on ground
2 Sam. 14. 14 as water *s.* on ground
Mark 2. 22 wine is *s.*, and bottles
Luke 5. 37 burst bottles, and be *s.*
R. V. Mark 2. 22 perisheth

Spilt. *See* **Spill.**

Spin. *Spin.*
Ex. 35. 25 woman wise hear. did *s.*
Mat. 6. 28 ; Luke 12. 27 nei. do th. *s.*

Spindle. R. V. *distaff.*
Prov. 31. 19 She lay. hands to the *s.*

Spirit. *Breath, wind, spirit.*
Gen. 1. 2 *S.* of God moved on water
Ex. 31. 3 filled him with *s.* of God
Num. 5. 14 if *s.* of jealousy come
Deut. 34. 9 Joshua was full of *s.*
Josh. 5. 1 nei. was there *s.* in them
Judg. 6. 34 *s.* of L. came up. Gideon
1 Sam. 1. 15 I am woman of sor. *s.*
2 Sam. 23. 2 *s.* of Lord spake by me
1 K. 10. 5 was no more *s.* in her
2 K. 2. 15 *s.* of Elij. did rest on Eli.
1 Chr. 5. 26 G. stirred up *s.* of Pul
2 Chr. 15. 1 *s.* of G. came on Azar.
Ez. 1. 1 Lord stirred up *s.* of Cyrus
Neh. 9. 20 gavest thy *s.* to instruct
Job 27. 3 *s.* of G. is in my nostrils
Ps. 51. 10 renew a ri. *s.* within me
Prov. 16. 18 haughty *s.* before a fall
Eccl. 1. 14 all is van. and vex. of *s.*
Isa. 19. 3 the *s.* of Egypt shall fail
Jer. 51. 11 L. raised *s.* of the king
Ezek. 3. 12 *s.* took me up, I heard
Dan. 2. 1 Nebu. *s.* was troubled
Hos. 5. 4 *s.* of whoredom in midst
Joel 2. 28 pour *s.* on all flesh ; and
Mic. 2. 7 is *s.* of Lord straitened?
Hag. 1. 14 L. stirred *s.* of Zerubba.
Zech. 4. 6 Not by mi., but by my *s.*
Mal. 2. 15 take heed to your *s.*, and

Mat. 3. 16 saw *S.* of G. descending
Mark 3. 30 He hath an unclean *s.*
Luke 2. 27 he ca. by *S.* into temple
John 3. 5 Except man be born of *S.*
Acts 7. 59 Lord Jesus, receive my *s.*
Rom. 8. 2 law of *S.* of life in Christ
1 Cor. 2. 10 *S.* searcheth all things
2 Cor. 2. 13 I had no rest in my *s.*
Gal. 4. 6 God hath sent *S.* of Son
Eph. 1. 13 ye are sealed wi. Holy *S.*
Phil. 1. 27 that ye stand in one *s.*
Col. 2. 5 yet am I with you in *s.*
1 Thes. 5. 19 Quench not the *S.*
2 Thes. 2. 2 nei. by *s.*, nor by word
1 Tim. 4. 1 th. *S.* speaketh expressly
2 Tim. 4. 22 L. J. C. be with thy *s.*
Phile. 25 grace be with your *s.*
Heb. 1. 7 Who maketh his angels *s.*
Jas. 2. 26 body without *s.* is dead
1 Pet 4. 6 live accord. to God in *s.*
1 John 4. 1 believe not every *s.*, but
Jude 19 sensual, having not the *s.*
Rev. 1. 10 I was in *s.* on Lord's day
R. V. Ps. 104. 4; Eccl. 1. 14, 17; 2.
11, 17, 26; 4. 4, 6, 16: 6. 9; 11. 5;
Zech. 6. 5; Heb. 1. 7 wind or
winds; Isa. 40. 7; 59. 19; 2 Thes.
2. 8; Rev. 11. 1 breath; Mat.
14. 26; Mark 6. 49 apparition;
Acts 18. 5 by word; Eph. 5. 9
light; Luke 2. 40; 9. 55; Rom.
8. 1; 1 Cor. 6. 20; 1 Tim. 4. 12;
1 Pet. 1. 22

Spiritual.   *Of the spirit.*
Hos. 9. 7 the *s.* man is mad, for
Rom. 7. 14 we know the law is *s.*
1 Cor. 9. 11 sown unto you *s.* things
Gal. 6. 1 ye which are *s.* restore
Eph. 1. 3 blessed us with *s.* bless.
Col. 1. 9 filled with *s.* understand.
1 Pet. 2. 5 are built up a *s.* house

Spiritually.   *Minding of spirit.*
Rom. 8. 6 to be *s.* minded is life
1 Cor. 2. 14 they are *s.* discerned
Rev. 11. 8 which *s.* is called Sod.

Spit.   *Spit.*
Lev. 15. 8 hath issue *s.* upon him
Num. 12. 14 if fath. had *s.* in face
Deut. 25. 9 she shall *s.* in his face
Job 30. 10 spare not to *s.* in face
Isa. 50. 6 I hid not my face from *s.*
Mat. 26. 67 Then they *s.* in his face
Luke 18. 32 spite. entr., *s.* on him
John 9. 6 spoken, he *s.* on ground

Spite.   *Anger, grudge.*
Ps. 10. 14 beholdest mischief and *s.*

Spitefully.   R. V. *shamefully.*
Mat. 22. 6 they entreated them *s.*
Luke 18. 32 shall be *s.* entreated

Spittle.   *Spit.*
1 Sam. 21. 13 let his *s.* fall down
Job 7. 19, alone, till I swallow .
John 9. 6 he made clay of *s.* and

Spoil (*n.*).   *Prey, booty, plunder,*
thing captured.
Gen. 49. 27 at night sh. divide *s.*
Ex. 15. 19 en. said, I will divide *s.*
Num. 31. 11 they took all the *s.*
Deut. 3. 7 *s.* of cities, we took for
Josh. 7. 21 saw among *s.* a garment
Judg. 5. 30 necks of th. that take *s.*
1 Sam. 14. 32 people flew up. the *s.*
2 Sam. 3. 22 Joab bro. in great *s.*
1 K. 3. 23 therefore, Moab, to the *s.*
1 Chr. 20. 2 fr. Rab. he brought *s.*
2 Chr. 14. 13 carried away much *s.*
Ez. 9. 7 kings ha. been deli. to *s.*
Esth. 9. 10 on *s.* laid not th. hand
Job 29. 17 I plucked *s.* out of teeth
Ps. 68. 12 th. tarried at ho. divid. *s.*
Prov. 1. 13 *s.* we fill houses with *s.*
Isa. 8. 4 *s.* of Samaria sh. be taken
Jer. 50. 10 Chaldea shall be a *s.*
Ezek. 38. 13 Art thou co. to take *s.?*
Dan. 11. 24 scatter among them *s.*
Nah. 2. 9 *s.* of silver, *s.* of gold
Hab. 2. 17 cover, and *s.* of beasts
Zech. 2. 9 shall be a *s.* to servants
Luke 11. 22 tak. and divid. his *s.*
Heb. 7. 4 Abrah. gave tenth of *s.*
R. V. Num. 31. 53; 2 Chr. 14. 13
booty ; Job 29. 17 prey; Prov. 31.
11 gain; Isa. 25. 11 craft ; Hab.
2. 17 destruction.

Spoil (*v.*).   *Snatch, seize, capture,*
destroy, plunder.

Gen. 34. 27 sons of Jacob *s.* city
Ex. 3. 22 ye shall *s.* the Egyptians
Deut. 28. 29 sh. be oppressed and *s.*
Judg. 2. 14 hand of spoilers that *s.*
1 Sam. 14. 36 *s.* them until morning
2 Sam. 23. 10 people returned to *s*
2 K. 7. 16 people *s.* the tents of Syr.
2 Chr. 14. 14 they *s.* all the cities
Job 12. 19 leadeth princes away *s.*
Ps. 44. 10 they which hate us *s.*
Prov. 22. 23 L. will *s.* soul of those
S. of S. 2. 15 lit. foxes that *s.* vines
Isa. 11. 14 sh. *s.* them of the east
Jer. 4. 13 Woe unto us ! we are *s.*
Ezek. 23. 46 I give them to be *s*
Hos. 10. 2 break altars, *s.* images
Am. 3. 11 thy palaces shall be *s.*
Mic. 2. 4 and say, We be utterly *s.*
Hab. 2. 8 thou hast *s.* many nations
Nah. 2. 9 Take ye the *s.* of silver
Zeph. 2. 9 my people shall *s.* them
Zech. 2. 8 sent to nations which *s.*
Mat. 12. 29 then he will *s.* his house
Mark 3. 27 enter house and *s.* goods
Col. 2. 8 *s.* you through philosophy

Spoiling.   *Destroying.*
Ps. 35. 12 good to the *s.* of my soul
Isa. 22. 4 *s.* of daughter of my peo.
Jer. 48. 3 voice from Horonaim *s.*
Hab. 1. 3 *s.* and violence before me
Heb. 10. 34 joyful *s.* of your goods
R. V. Ps. 35. 12 bereaving

Spoken.   *Said, told, uttered.*
1 K. 18. 24 peo. said, It is well *s.*
Job 32. 4 E. waited till Job had *s.*
Ps. 87. 3 Glo. things are *s.* of thee
S. of S. 8. 8 when she sh. be *s.* for
Obad. 12 neither sho. thou have *s.*
Mat. 1. 22 which was *s.* of the Lord
Mark 5. 36 J. heard word th. was *s.*
Luke 18. 34 nei. knew the things *s.*
Acts 13. 45 things wh. were *s.* by P.
Rom. 1. 8 your faith is *s.* of thro.
Heb. 12. 19 ent. th. word not be *s.*
R. V. Some changes, chiefly to,
said, spake, etc.

Spokes.   *Spokes.*
1 K. 7. 33 felloes, their *s.*, all molten

Spokesman.   *Mouthman.*
Ex. 4. 16 he sh. be thy *s.* to people

Sponge.   *Sponge.*
Mat. 27. 48 one ran and took a *s.*
Mark 15. 36 one ran and filled a *s.*
John 19. 29 filled *s.* with vinegar

Spoon.   *Hollow thing, pan.*
Ex. 25. 29 shalt make dishes and *s.*
Num. 4. 7 put there. dishes and *s.*
1 K. 7. 50 Sol. made *s.* of pu. gold
2 K. 25. 14 Chaldees took away *s.*
2 Chr. 4. 22 *s.*, and censers, of gold
Jer. 52. 18 bowls, and the *s.* took th.

Sport (*n.*).   *Play, derision.*
Judg. 16. 25 that he may make us *s.*
Prov. 10. 23 *s.* to fool to do mischief

Sport (*v.*).   *Play, mock.*
Gen. 26. 8 Isaac was *s.* wi. Rebek.
Isa. 57. 4 against whom do ye *s.*
1 Pet. 2. 13 *s.* with own deceivings
R. V. 2 Pet. 2. 13 revelling

Spot.   *Stain, blot, blemish.*
Lev. 13. 4 If bright *s.* be white
Num. 19. 2 bring heifer without *s.*
Deut. 32. 5 *s.* is not *s.* of his chil.
Job 11. 15 lift thy face without *s.*
S. of S. 4. 7 there is no *s.* in thee
Job 13. 23 can leopard change *s.?*
Eph. 5. 27 glori. church, not hav. *s.*
1 Tim. 6. 14 Keep com. without *s.*
Heb. 9. 14 offer. himself without *s.*
1 Pet. 1. 19 lamb without blem. or *s.*
2 Pet. 2. 13 *S.* they are and blem.
Jude 12 *s.* in your feasts of charity
R. V. Num. 28. 3, 9, 11 ; 29. 17, 26;
Deut. 32. 5 ; Heb. 9. 14 blemish;
Lev. 13. 39 tetter; Jude 12 hidden
rocks

Spotted.   *Spotted, stained.*
Gen. 30. 32 removing all *s.* cattle
Jude 29 hating garment *s.* by flesh

Spouse.   R. V. *bride.*
S. of S. 4. 8 Come from Leb. my *s.*
Hos. 4. 13 *s.* shall commit adultery

Sprang.   *See Spring.*

Spread.   *Stretch or go out, forth,*
abroad or over, scatter.
Gen. 33. 19 where he had *s.* his tent

Ex. 9. 29 I will *s.* hands to Lord
Lev. 13. 7 if scab *s.* much in the skin
Num. 4. 6 shall *s.* over it a cloth
Deut. 32. 11 as eagle *s.* her wings
Judg. 15. 9 Philist *s.* thems. into L
Ruth 3. 9 *s.* skirt over handmaid
1 Sam. 30. 16 th. were *s.* upon earth
2 Sam. 17. 19 *s.* ground corn there.
1 K. 8. 7 cherubim *s.* their wings
2 K. 19. 14 Hez. *s.* it before Lord
1 Chr. 14. *s* Philistines *s.* themsel.
2 Chr. 26. 8 Uzziah's name *s.* abroad
Ex. 9. 5 *s.* out my hands unto Lord
Job 36. 30 he *s.* his light upon it
Ps. 37. 35 *s.* himself like bay tree
105. 39 He *s.* clouds for covering
140. 5 have *s.* net by the way side
Prov. 1. 17 in vain the net is *s.* in
39. 5 flattering neighbour *s.* a net
Isa. 14. 11 worm is *s.* under thee
25. 7 veil that is *s.* over all nations
Jer. 8. 2 shall *s.* them before the sun
Lam. 1. 10 adversary *s.* out his hand
Ezek. 16. 8 I *s.* my skirt over thee
Hos. 7. 12 I *s.* my net upon them
Joel 2. 2 as morn. *s.* upon mount's
Heb. 1. 8 horsemen sh. *s.* themsel.
Zech. 1. 17 cities shall be *s.* abroad
Mal. 2. 3 will *s.* dung on yo. feasts
Mat. 21. 8 multit. *s.* their garments
Mark 1. 28 his fame *s.* thro. Galilee
Luke 19. 36 *s.* their clothes in way
Acts 4. 17 but that it *s.* no further
R. V. 2 Sam. 17. 19 strewed ; 1 Chr.
14. 9 made raid; Job 9. 8 stretcheth;
Mark 1. 28 went out; 6. 14 become
known ; 1 Thes. 1. 8 gone forth

Spreading.   *Spreading.*
Job 36. 29 understand *s.* of clouds?
Ps. 37. 35 I have seen wicked *s.*
Ezek. 17. 6 and became a *s.* vine

Sprig.   *Shoot, twig, branch.*
Isa. 18. 5 he shall both cut off the *s.*
Ezek. 17. 6 a vine, and shot forth *s.*

Spring (*n.*).   *Going up.*
1 Sam. 9. 26 about *s.* of day Sam.
Shoot, plant.
Ezek. 17. 9 wither in leaves of her *s.*
Fountain, source, slope.
Deut. 4. 49 plain under *s.* of Pisgah
Josh. 10. 40 smote all country of *s.*
Judg. 1. 15 Gi. me blessing, also *s.*
2 K. 2. 21 he went forth to the *s.*
Job 38. 16 Hast thou entered into *s.*
Ps. 104. 10 He send *s.* into valleys
Prov. 25. 26 troub. fount., corrupt *s.*
S. of S. 4. 12 spouse, is *s.* shut up
Isa. 41. 18 will ma. dry land *s.* of w.
Jer. 51. 36 I will make her *s.* dry
Hos. 13. 15 his *s.* shall become dry
R. V. Deut. 4. 49; Josh. 10. 40;
12. 8 slopes; Ps. 87. 7; Jer. 51.
36 fountains

Spring (*v.*).   *Go, break or shoot*
forth, sprout, leap.
Gen. 41. 6 seven thin ears *s.* up
Lev. 13. 42 it is leprosy *s.* up in his
Num. 21. 17 Is. sang, *S.* up, O well
Judg. 19. 25 when day began to *s.*
1 K. 4. 33 hyssop *s.* out of the wall
2 K. 19. 29 shall eat that which *s.* of
Job 5. 6 neither doth trouble *s.* out
Ps. 85. 11 Truth sh. *s.* out of earth
92. 7 the wicked *s.* as the grass
Isa. 45. 8 let righteousness *s.* up
Hos. 10. 4 judg. *s.* up as hemlock
Joel 2. 22 pastures of wilder. do *s.*
Mat. 13. 7 thorns *s.* up and choked
Mark 4. 5 and immediately it *s.* up
Luke 8. 6 as soon as it was *s.* up
Acts 16. 29 called for light, *s.* in
Heb. 7. 14 our Lord *s.* out of Juda
R. V. Lev. 13. 42 breaking out;
Mat. 13. 7 ; Luke 8. 6, 7, 8 grew ;
Mark 4. 8 growing

Springing.   *Living, growing,*
leaping, sprouting.
Gen. 26. 19 found well of *s.* water
2 Sam. 23. 4 as tender grass *s.* out
Ps. 65. 10 thou blessest *s.* thereof
John 4. 14 a well of water *s.* up
Heb. 12. 15 lest root of bitterness *s.*

Sprinkle.   *Sprinkle.*
Ex. 9. 8 let M. *s.* it toward heaven
Lev. 1. 5 *s.* blood round about upon
Num. 19. 21 he that *s.* wat. of sepa.

2 K. 9. 33 her blood was s. on wall
2 Chr. 29. 22 priests s. it on altar
Job 2. 12 s. dust on their heads
Isa. 63. 3 their blood shall be s. up.
Ezek. 36. 25 I s. cl. water upon you
Heb. 11. 28 he kept passover, and s.
1 Pet. 1. 2 unto obedience and s.

Sprout. *Change, spring.*
Job 14. 7 tree, that it will s. again
Sprung. *See* **Spring** (*v.*).
Spue. *Vomit, eject.*
Lev. 18. 28 as it s. out the nations
Jer 25. 27 Drink, be drunken and s.
Hab. 2. 16 s. shall be on thy glory
Rev. 3. 16 s. thee out of my mouth
R. V. Lev. 18. 28; 20. 22 vomit
Spun. *Spinned.*
Ex. 35. 35 bro. which they had s.
Spy. *See, search, traverse.*
Ex. 2. 11 he s. Egyptian smiting
Num. 21. 32 Moses sent to s. out J.
Josh. 2. 1 sent men to s. secretly
Judg. 18. 2 Dan sent men to s. land
2 Sam. 10. 3 to search city, and s.
2 K. 9. 17 he s. company of Jehu
1 Chr. 19. 3 overthrow, and s. land
Gal. 2. 4 who came privily to s.
Square (*n.*). *Side, square.*
1 K. 7. 5 doors and posts were s.
Ezek. 45. 2 in breadth, s. round ab.
R. V. Ezek. 14. 16, 17 sides
Square (*v.*). *Make square.*
Ezek. 41. 21 posts of temple were s.
Stability. *Stability.*
Isa. 33. 6 knowledge s. of thy times
Stable. *Fold, standing.*
Ezek. 25. 5 make Rab. s. for camels
Established, firm
2 Chr. 16. 30 the world shall be s.
Stablish. *Make firm, establish.*
2 Sam. 7. 13 I will s. the throne of
1 Chr. 18. 3 went to s. his dominion
2 Chr. 17. 5 Lord s. his kingdom
Esth. 9. 21 To s. this among them
Ps. 119. 38 S. thy word unto serv.
Hab. 2. 12 Woe to him that s. city
Rom. 16. 25 that is of pow. to s. you
2 Cor. 1. 21 us with you in Chr.
Col. 2. 7 built, and s. in the faith
1 Thes. 3. 13 s. your hearts unblame.
2 Thes. 2. 17 s. you in ev. good work
Jas. 5. 8 be patient, s. your hearts
1 Pet. 5. 10 make you per., s., stren.
R. V. 2 Sam. 7. 13; 1 Chr. 17. 12; 2
Chr. 7. 18; establish; Esth. 9. 21
enjoin; Ps. 119. 33 confirm
Stacks. R. V. *shocks.*
Ex. 22. 6 s. of corn be consumed
Staff. *Bar, rod, handle, stay, stave,*
sceptre.
Gen. 32. 10 wi. my s. I passed Jor.
Ex. 12. 11 with yo. s. in your hand
Num. 13. 23 between two on a s.
Judg. 6. 21 put forth the end of s.
1 Sam. 17. 7 s. of spear like beam
2 Sam. 3. 29 that leaneth on a s.
2 K. 4. 29 Gird loins, take my s.
Ps. 23. 4 thy rod and s. comf. me
Isa. 3. 1 L. will take from Ju. s.
Jer. 48. 17 how is strong s. broken
Ezek. 29. 6 have been a s to Israel
Hos. 4. 12 their s. declar. to them
Zech. 8. 4 every man with his s.
Mark 6. 8 take nothing, save a s.
Heb. 11. 21 lean. on top of his s.
Stagger. *Reel, waver.*
Job 12. 25 s. like a drunken man
Ps. 107. 20 reel to and fro, and s.
Isa. 19. 14 as a drunken man s.
Rom. 4. 20 s. not at promise of God
Stain. *Pollute, stain.*
Job 3. 5 and shadow of death s. it
Isa. 23. 9 the pride of all glory
R. V. Job. 3. 5 claim it
Stairs. *Ascent, steps.*
1 K. 6. 8 went up with winding s.
2 K. 9. 13 under him on top of s.
Neh. 9. 4 then stood on s. Jeshua
S. S. 2. 14 in secret places of the s.
Ezek. 43. 17 s. sh. look toward east
Acts 21. 40 Paul stood on the s.
R. V. Ezek. 40. 6; 43. 17 steps; S.
of S. 2. 14 steep place
Stake. *Pin, nail, stake.*
Isa. 33. 20 not one of s. removed
Stalk. *Stem, cane, reed.*

Gen. 41. 5 seven ears on one s.
Josh. 2. 6 hid them with s. of flax
Hos. 8. 7 no s., bud yield no meal
R. V. Hos. 8. 7 standing corn
Stall. *Feeding place, manger,*
crib.
1 K. 4. 26 Sol. had for. thousand s.
2 Chr. 32. 28 s. for beasts, and cotes
Am. 6. 4 and calves out of the s.
Hab. 3. 17 shall be no herd in s.
Mal. 4. 2 sh. grow as calves of s.
Luke 13. 15 loose his ox from the s.
Stalled. *Fattened.*
Prov. 15. 17 than s. ox and hatred
Stammerer. *Who stammers.*
Isa. 32. 4 tongue of s. read. to spe.
Stammering. R. V. *strange.*
Isa. 28. 11 s. lips and another tong.
Stamp. *Tread down, trample.*
Deut. 9. 21 burnt it, s. it, ground it
2 Sam. 22. 43 did s. them as mire
2 K. 23. 6 and s. it small to powder
2 Chr. 15. 16 Asa cut down idol, s.
Jer. 47. 3 the s. of hoofs of horses
Ezek. 25. 6 thou hast s. with feet
Dan. 7. 7 it break in pieces, and s.
R. V. 2 Chr. 15. 16 made dust of;
Dan. 8. 7, 10 trample
Stanch. *Set, check.*
Luke 8. 44 her issue of blood s.
Stand. *Cessation.*
Ezek. 39. 7 their loins to be at a s.
Stand. *To set, place, stand.*
Gen. 18. 2 lo, three men s. by him
Ex. 2. 17 Moses s. up and helped
Lev. 9. 5 congreg. drew near and s.
Num. 9. 8 S. still, and I will hear
Deut. 5. 5 I s. bet. Lord and you
Josh. 3. 13 they sh. s. upon heap
Judg. 6. 31 Joash said to all that s.
1 Sam. 6. 20 Who is able to s. bef.
2 Sam. 1. 10 I s. upon him, and slew
1 K. 1. 2 let her s. before the king
2 K. 2. 7 they two s. by Jordan
1 Chr. 21. 1 Satan s. up against Is.
2 Chr. 4. 4 It s. on twelve oxen
Ez. 3. 9 Then s. Jeshua with sons
Neh. 8. 4 scribe s. upon a pulpit
Esth. 6. 5 Haman s. in the court
Job. 29. 8 the aged arose, and s. up
Ps. 26. 12 foot s. in an even place
Prov. 12. 7 house of right. shall s.
Eccl. 8. 3 s. not in an evil thing
S. of S. 2. 9 he s. behind our wall
Isa. 3. 13 Lord s. to judge people
Jer. 18. 20 I s. before thee to speak
Ezek. 3. 23 glory of the L. s. there
Dan. 2. 2 came and s. before king
Hos. 10. 9 Is. sinned; there they s.
Am. 2. 15 nei. s. that handleth bow
Obad. 11 In day thou s. on oth. side
Mic. 5. 4 s. and feed in strength of
Nah. 1. 6 Who s. bef. his indigna.
Hab. 3. 6 He s., and measured ear.
Zech. 1. 8 he s. among myrtle trees
Mal. 3. 2 who s. wh. he appeareth?
Mat. 6. 5 they love to pray s. in syn.
Mark 3. 2 kingd. divided cannot s.
Luke 18. 11 Phar. s. and prayed
John 1. 26 there s. one among you
Acts 1. 11 men of Gal., why s. ye
Rom. 9. 11 that purp. of G. mi. s.
1 Cor. 16. 13 s. fast in the faith
2 Cor. 1. 24 for by faith ye s.
Eph. 6. 14 S., hav. your loins girt
Phil. 1. 27 ye s. fast in one spirit
Col. 4. 12 that ye may s. perfect
1 Thes. 3. 8 if ye s. fast in the Lord
2 Thes. 2. 15 s. fast, ho. to traditions
2 Tim. 2. 19 founda. of G. s. sure
Heb. 10. 11 priest s. daily minister.
Jas. 5. 9 Judge s. before the door
1 Pet. 5. 12 grace of G. where. ye s.
Rev. 3. 20 I s. at door and knock
R. V. Several changes, but chiefly
due to words before and after.
Standard. *Banner, ensign, sail.*
Num. 1. 52 every man by his own s.
Isa. 59. 19 Sp. of L. shall lift up s.
Jer. 4. 6 Set up the s. toward Zion
Standing. *Setting, not lying.*
Ex. 22. 6 so s. corn be consumed
Lev. 26. 1 neither rear up s. image
Num. 22. 23 angel of the Lord s.
Judg. 15. 5 let them go into s. corn
1 Sam. 22. 6 his serv. were s. about

Ps. 69. 2 deep mire, where is no s.
Am. 9. 1 I saw L. s. upon the altar
Mic. 1. 11 sh. receive of you his s.
Zech. 6. 5 go forth s. before Lord
Heb. 9. 8 first tabernacle was yet s.
Stank. *See* **Stink.**
Star. *Star.*
Gen. 1. 16 God made lights, s. also
Ex. 32. 13 will mult. your seed as s.
Num. 24. 17 sh. co s. out of Jacob
Deut. 1. 10 ye are as s. of heaven
Judg. 5. 20 s. fought against Sisera
1 Chr. 27. 23 wo. increase Is. like s.
Neh. 4. 21 ris. of morn. till s. appear
Job. 38. 7 morning s. sang together
Ps. 136. 9 moon and s. to rule night
Eccl. 12. 2 while sun or s. be not
Isa. 14. 13 exalt throne above s.
Jer. 31. 35 the ordinances of the s.
Ezek. 32. 7 cover heav., ma. s. dark
Dan. 8. 10 cast down s. to ground
Joel 2. 10 s. shall withdraw shining
Am. 5. 8 Seek him that ma. seven s.
Obad. 4 tho. thou set nest among s.
Nah. 3. 16 mul. merchants above s.
Mat. 2. 2 we ha. seen s. in the east
Mark 13. 25 s. of heaven shall fall
Luke 21. 25 shall be signs in the s.
Acts 27. 20 neither sun nor s appear.
1 Cor. 15. 41 another glory of the s.
Heb. 11. 12 as s. of sky in multitude
2 Pet. 1. 19 day dawn, and day s. ar.
R. V. Am. 5. 8 Pleiades
Star Gazer. *Star viewer.*
Isa. 47. 13 let the s. g. stand up
Stare. *See, fix gaze.*
Ps. 22. 17 bones, they look and s. up
State. *Station, condition.*
2 Chr. 24. 13 set house of God in s.
Esth. 1. 7 wine, according to the s.
Ps. 39. 5 man at best s. is vanity
Prov. 27. 23 Be dil. to kn. s. of flocks
Isa. 22. 19 from thy s. he pull thee
Mat. 12. 45 last s. worse than first
Luke 11. 26 s. of that man is worse
Phil. 2. 19 comfort, I know your s.
Col. 4. 7 my s. shall Tych. declare
R. V. Esth. 1. 7; 2. 18 bounty; Ps.
39. 5 estate; Isa. 22. 19 station;
Col. 4. 7 affairs
Stately. *Noble, grand.*
Ezek. 23. 41 satest upon a s. bed
Station. R. V. *office.*
Isa. 22. 19 I will drive thee from s.
Stature. *Measure, length, height.*
Num. 13. 32 we saw men of great s.
1 Sam. 16. 7 Look not on hei. of s.
2 Sam. 21. 20 was a man of great s.
1 Chr. 11. 23 slew Egyptian of gr. s.
S. of S. 7. 7 thy s. is like palm tree
Isa. 10. 33 high of s. shall be hewn
Ezek. 19. 11 her s. was exalted am.
Mat. 6. 27 Wh. can add cubit to s.?
Luke 2. 52 J. incr. in wisd. and s.
Eph. 4. 13 measure of s. of fulness
Statute. *Decree, statute.*
Gen. 26. 5 Abraham kept my s.
Ex. 27. 21 It shall be s. for ever
Lev. 18. 5 Ye shall keep my s., and
Num. 19. 21 it sh. be perpetual s.
Deut. 4. 1 hearken, O Is., unto s.
Josh. 24. 25 set them a s. in Shech.
1 Sam. 30. 25 he made s. and ord.
2 Sam. 22. 23 as for s., I did not d.
1 K. 2. 3 to keep s. and command.
2 K. 17. 8 Is. walked in s. of heath.
1 Chr. 22. 13 takest heed to fulfil s.
2 Chr. 7. 19 if ye forsake my s. and
Ez. 7. 10 to teach in Israel s. and ju.
Neh. 1. 7 they have not kept the s.
Ps. 119. 48 I will meditate in thy s.
Jer. 44. 10 neither walked in my s.
Ezek. 20. 25 I gave them also s.
Dan. 6. 15 no decree or s. be chang'd
Zech. 1. 6 s., which I commanded
Mic. 6. 16 the s. of Omri are kept
Mal. 4. 4 Remember the law with s.
Staves. *Bars, rods, staffs.*
Ex. 25. 13 make s. of shittim wood
Num. 4. 6 and shall put in the s.
1 Sam. 17. 43 comest to me with s.
1 Chr. 15. 15 L. carried ark with s.
Hab. 3. 14 didst strike with his s.
Zech. 11. 7 I took unto me two s.
Mat. 10. 10 provide nei. shoes nor s.
Mark 14. 43 com. multitude with s.

Luke 9. 3 Take neither scrip nor *s.*
R. V. Mat. 10. 10; Luke 9. 3 staff
Stay (*n.*). *Support, stand.*
Lev. 13. 5 if the plague be at a *s.*
2. Sam. 22. 19 the Lord was my *s.*
1 K. 10. 19 were *s.* on either side
2 Chr. 9. 18 two lions standing by *s*
Ps. 18. 18 but the Lord was my *s.*
Isa. 3. 1 Lord doth take away the *s.*
Stay (*v.*). *Stand, wait, uphold, support, cease, delay.*
Gen. 8. 10 he *s.* other seven days
Ex. 9. 28 ye shall *s.* me no longer
Lev. 13. 23 if spot *s.* in his place
Num. 16. 50 and the plague was *s.*
Josh. 10. 19 *s.* ye not but pursue
1 Sam. 15. 16 *S.*, I will tell thee wh.
2 Sam. 17. 17 Jonath. *s.* by En-rogel
Ruth 1. 13 would ye *s.* for them
1 K. 22. 35 k. was *s.* in his chariot
2 K. 4. 6 not vessel. And the oil *s.*
1 Chr. 21. 22 plague be *s.* fr. people
Job 38. 11 here shall thy waves be *s.*
38. 37 who *s.* bottles of heaven
Ps. 106. 30 and so the plague was *s.*
Prov. 28. 17 sh. flee ; let no man *s.*
S. of S. 2. 5 *S.* me wi. flagons, com.
Isa. 10. 20 shall no more again *s.*
Lam. 4. 6 and no hands *s.* on her
Ezek. 31. 15 the great waters were *s.*
Dan. 4. 35 none can *s.* his hand, nor
Hos. 13. 13 sho. not *s.* long in place
Hag. 1. 10 heaven is *s.* from dew
Luke 4. 42 people came and *s.* him
Acts 19. 22 he himself *s.* in Asia
R. V. 1 Sam. 24. 7 checked ; Job
38. 37 pour out
Stead. *In place of.*
Gen. 22. 13 off. in the *s.* of his son
2 Cor. 5. 20 pray you in Christ's *s.*
Phile. 13 in thy *s.* he ministered
R. V. Phile. 13 behalf
Steady. *Stable.*
Ex. 17. 12 his hands were *s.* until
Steal. *Steal, go furtively.*
Gen. 31. 19 Rachel had *s.* images
Ex. 20. 15 Thou shalt not *s.*
Lev. 19. 11 not *s.*, nei. deal falsely
Deut. 24. 7 If a man be found *s.*
Josh. 7. 11 have *s.*, and dissembled
2 Sam. 15. 6 Ab. *s.* hearts of men
2 K. 11. 2 Jeh. *s.* him fr. k's sons
Job. 27. 20 a tempest *s.* him away
Prov. 9. 17 *S.* waters are sweet, and
Jer. 7. 9 Will ye *s.*, commit adulter.
Hos. 4. 2 By *s.*, they break out, and
Obad. 5 would they had not *s.* till
Zech. 5. 3 that *s.* shall be cut off
Mat. 6. 19 thieves break thro. and *s.*
Mark 10. 19 Do not *s.*, Do not bear
Luke 18. 20 not *s.*, not bear fal. wit.
John 10. 10 thief co. not, but to *s.*
Rom. 2. 21 sho. not *s.*, dost thou *s.* ?
Eph. 4. 28 Let him th. *s. s.* no more
Stealth. *Furtively.*
2 Sam. 19. 3 people gat them by *s.*
Stedfast. *Firm, steady.*
Job 11. 15 yea, thou shalt be *s.* and
Ps. 78. 8 spirit was not *s.* with God
Dan. 6. 26 living God, *s.* for ever
1 Cor. 7. 37 th. stand. *s.* in his heart
2 Cor. 1. 7 And our hope of you is *s.*
Heb. 6. 10 anchor, both sure and *s.*
1 Pet. 5. 9 Whom resist *s.* in faith
R. V. Ps. 78. 37 faithful ; Heb. 3.
14 firm
Stedfastly. *Firmly, steadily.*
Ruth 1. 18 saw she was *s.* minded
2 K. 8. 11 settled his countenance *s.*
Luke 9. 51 *s.* set to go to Jerusalem
Acts 1. 10 looked *s.* toward heaven
2 Cor. 3. 7 chil. of Is. could not *s.*
R. V. Acts 6. 15 ; 14. 9 fastening his
eyes upon
Stedfastness. *Stability.*
Col. 2. 5 *s.* of your faith in Christ
2 Pet. 3. 17 lest ye fall from your *s.*
Steel. R. V. *brass.*
2 Sam. 22. 35 a bow of *s.* is broken
Job 20. 24 bow of *s.* sh. strike him
Ps. 18. 34 bow of *s.* is brok. by arm
Jer. 15. 12 shall iron break the *s.* ?
Steep. *Steep, descent.*
Ezek. 38. 20 *s.* places shall fall
Mic. 1. 4 waters pour. down *s.* place
Mat. 8. 32 swine ran down *s.* place

Mark 5. 13 ; Luke 8. 33
Stem. R. V. *stock.*
Isa. 11. 1 a rod out of *s.* of Jesse
Step (*n.*). *Going, tread, footstep, ascent, stair.*
Ex. 20. 26 nei. sh. thou go up by *s.*
1 Sam. 20. 3 but *s.* bet. me and death
2 Sam. 22. 37 Thou ha. enlarg. my *s.*
1 K. 10. 19 The throne had six *s.*
2 Chr. 9. 18 were six *s.* to the throne
Job 23. 11 My foot hath held his *s.*
Ps. 37. 31 none of his *s.* shall slide
Prov. 5. 5 her *s.* ta. hold on hell
Isa. 26. 6 *s.* of needy shall tread
Jer. 10. 23 not in man to direct *s.*
Lam. 4. 18 They hunt our *s.*, that
Ezek. 40. 22 went unto it by sev. *s.*
Dan. 11. 43 Ethiop. sh. beat his *s.*
Rom. 4. 12 walk in *s.* of that faith
1 Cor. 12. 18 walked we not in *s.* ?
1 Pet. 2. 21 ye shall follow his *s.*
R. V. Ps. 27. 23 goings ; 85. 13
footsteps
Step (*v.*). *Go.*
John 5. 4 who. *s.* in was ma. whole
5. 7 another *s.* down before me
Stern. *Hinder part.*
Acts 27. 29 cast anchors out of *s.*
Steward. *Over house, head, chief.*
Gen. 15. 2 *s.* of my house is Eliez.
1 K. 16. 9 drunk in house of his *s.*
1 Chr. 28. 1 David assembled his *s.*
Mat. 20. 8 l. of viney. sa. to his *s.*
Luke 16. 1 cert. rich man had a *s.*
1 Cor. 4. 1 *s.* of mysteries of God
Tit. 1. 7 bishop be blameless, as *s.*
1 Pet. 4. 10 good *s.* of grace of God
R. V. 1 Chr. 28. 1 rulers
Stewardship. *House rule.*
Luke 16. 2 give account of thy *s.*
Stick (*n.*). *Stick, fagot.*
Num. 15. 32 found man th. gath. *s.*
1 K. 17. 10 wom. was gathering *s.*
2 K. 6. 6 cut down *s.* and cast it
Lam. 4. 8 it is become like a *s.*
Ezek. 37. 13 take *s.*, write upon it
Acts 28. 3 Paul gath. bundle of *s.*
Stick (*v.*). *Cleave, fasten, protrude.*
1 Sam. 26. 7 his spear *s.* in ground
Job 33. 21 bones not seen to *s.* out
Ps. 38. 2 thine arrows *s.* fast in me
119. 31 I ha. *s.* to thy testimonies
Prov. 18. 24 friend th. *s.* clo. th. bro.
Ezek. 29. 4 cau. fish to *s.* to scales
Acts 27. 41 the forepart *s.* fast
R. V. Ps. 119. 31 cleave ; Acts
27. 41 struck
Stiff. *Hard, stiff.*
Jer. 17. 23 but made their neck *s.*
Stiff-hearted. *Hard of heart.*
Ezek. 2. 4 impud. children and *s. h.*
Stiff-necked. *Hardened, stubborn.*
Ex. 32. 9 this peo. is a *s. n.* people
Deut. 10. 16 and be no more *s. n.*
2 Chr. 30. 8 not *s. n.*, as your faith.
Ps. 75. 5 speak not with a *s. n.*
Jer. 17. 23 but made their neck *s.*
Acts 7. 51 Ye *s. n.* and uncircum.
Stiffened. *Make hard.*
2 Chr. 36. 13 he *s.* neck, and hard.
Still (*adj., adv.*). *Yet, quiet.*
Gen. 12. 9 A. journey., going on *s.*
Ex. 15. 16 they sh. be *s.* as a stone
Lev. 13. 57 if it appear *s.* in gar.
Num. 14. 38 Josh. and C. lived *s.*
Judg. 18. 9 land good, are ye *s.* ?
2 Sam. 14. 32 to have been there *s.*
1 K. 19. 12 after fire *s.* small voice
Ps. 23. 2 lead. me beside *s.* waters
46. 10 Be *s.*, know that I am God
Isa. 42. 14 I have been *s.*, and refain.
Jer. 8. 14 why do we sit *s.* ? assem-
Mark 4. 39 said to sea, Peace, be *s.*
Rev. 22. 11 unj., let him be unjust *s.*
Still (*v.*). *Calm, quiet.*
Num. 13. 30 Cal. *s.* people bef. Mos.
Neh. 8. 11 Levites *s.* all the people
Ps. 65. 7 which *s.* noise of the seas
89. 9 the waves arise, thou *s.* them
Sting (*n.*). *Goad, spur, sting.*
1 Cor. 15. 55 O death, wh. is thy *s.* ?
Rev. 9. 10 th. were *s.* in their tails
Sting (*v.*). *Cut, sting.*
Prov. 23. 32 serp., and *s.* like adder

Stink (*n.*). *Smell, rottenness.*
Isa. 3. 24 instead smell, shall be *s.*
Joel 2. 20 his *s.* shall come up and
Am. 4. 10 made *s.* of your camps
R. V. Isa. 3 24 rottenness
Stink (*v.*). *Stink, abhorred.*
Gen. 34. 30 troub. me, to make me *s.*
Ex. 7. 18 fish die, the river shall *s.*
2 Sam. 10. 6 Ammon saw they me *s.*
Ps. 38. 5 My wounds *s.*, are corrupt
Eccl. 10. 1 Dead flies can. *s.* savour
Isa. 50. 2 fish *s.*, there is no water
John 11. 39 L. by this time he *s.*
Stir (*n.*). *Cry, tumult.*
Isa. 22. 2 full of *s.* a tumultuous city
Acts 12. 18 *s.* among soldiers
19. 23 arose no small *s.* about that
R. V. Isa. 22. 2 shoutings
Stir (*v.*). *Awake, move, rouse.*
Ex. 35. 21 Every one whose heart *s.*
Num. 24. 9 lion, who sh. *s.* him up
Deut. 32. 11 As an eagle *s.* up nest
1 Sam. 26. 19 If Lord ha. *s.* thee up
1 K. 11. 14 L. *s.* up advers. to Sol.
1 Chr. 5. 26 G. *s.* up spirit of Pul
2 Chr. 36. 22 L. *s.* up sp. of Cyrus
Job 41. 10 None th. dare *s.* him up
Ps. 35. 23 *S.* up thyself, and awake
Prov. 15. 18 wrathful man *s.* strife
S. of S. 2. 7 *s.* not, nor awak. my love
Isa. 10. 26 L. shall *s.* up a scourge
Dan. 11. 25 *s.* his power and courage
Hag. 1. 14 L. *s.* spirit of Zerubbabel
Luke 23. 5 He *s.* up the people
Acts 17. 16 his sp. was *s.* with. him
2 Tim. 1. 6 thou *s.* up gift of God
2 Pet. 3. 1 I *s.* up your pure minds
R. V. Num. 24. 9 rouse ; 1 K.
11. 14, 23 raised ; Dan. 11. 10 war ;
Acts 13. 50 urged on ; 17. 16 provoked.
Stock. *Root, race, stem.*
Lev. 25. 47 *s.* of the stranger's family
Job 14. 8 *s.* thereof die in ground
Isa. 44. 19 fall down to *s.* of tree ?
Jer. 2. 27 to *s.*, Thou art my father
Hos. 4. 12 peo. ask coun. at their *s.*
Acts 13. 26 children of *s.* of Abraham
Phil. 3. 5 of *s.* of Is., tribe of Benj.
Wood, fetter.
Job 13. 27 puttest my feet in the *s.*
Jer. 20. 3 bro. Jeremi. out of the *s.*
Prov. 7. 22 as fool to correct. of *s.*
Acts 16. 24 made th. feet fast in *s.*
R. V. Jer. 29. 26 shackles
Stole, Stolen. See Steal.
Stomach. *Stomach.*
1 Tim. 5. 23 use lit. wine for *s.* sake
Stomacher. *Festive garment.*
Isa. 3. 24 instead of a *s.*, sackcloth
Stone (*n.*). *Stone.*
Gen. 11. 3 brick for *s.*, slime for mor.
Ex. 15. 5 sank into bottom as a *s.*
Lev. 14. 42 And they sh. take other *s.*
Num. 14. 10 bade stone them with *s.*
Deut. 4. 13 wrote th. on tables of *s.*
Josh. 4. 5 take up every man a *s.*
Judg. 20. 16 ev. one could sling *s.*
1 Sam. 7. 12 Sam. took a *s.* and set
2 Sam. 16. 6 And he cast *s.* at David
1 K. 5. 18 they prep. timber and *s.*
2 K. 3. 19 mar good land with *s.*
1 Chr. 20. 2 were precious *s.* in it
2 Chr. 1. 15 made go. precious as *s.*
Ez. 5. 8 is builded with great *s.* and
Neh. 4. 2 will they revive the *s.* out
Job 14. 19 The waters wear the *s.*
Ps. 91. 12 lest dash thy foot ag. *s.*
118. 22 *S.* refus. bec. head of cor
Prov. 17. 8 A gift is as precious *s.*
Eccl. 10. 9 Who. removeth *s.* sh. be
Isa. 8. 14 for a *s.* of stumbling, and
27. 9 *s.* of the altar as chalk *s.* that
Jer. 43. 9 Take gr. *s.* in thine hand
Lam. 3. 58 they cast a *s.* upon me
Ezek. 16. 40 sh. stone thee with *s.*
Dan. 2. 34 sawest till *s.* was cut
Mic. 1. 6 will pour down *s.* thereof
Hab. 2. 11 s sh. cry out of the wall
Hag. 2. 15 *s.* upon *s.* in the temple
Zech. 3. 9 For behold *s.* I have laid
Mat. 3. 9 God is able of these *s.* to
7. 9 bread, will he give him a *s.*
Mark 12. 10 *s.* wh. build. reject. is
Luke 24. 2 found the *s.* rolled away
John 8. 7 without sin, cast *s.* at her

11. 41 Then they took away *s.* from
Acts 4. 11 *s.* wh. was set at nought
1 Cor. 3. 12 if any man build pr. *s.*
2 Cor. 3. 7 writ. and engraved in *s.*
1 Pet. 2. 6 lay in Sion ch. corner *s.*
Rev. 4. 3 was to look on sardine *s.*
R. V. Ex. 4. 25 flint; Job 40. 17
  thighs; Ps. 137. 9 rock; Isa. 34.
  11 plummet; Mark 12. 4 ——;
  John 1. 42 Peter

Stone (*v.*).   *To stone.*
Ex. 8. 26 will they not *s.* us?
Lev. 20. 2 people of land sh. *s.* him
Deut. 13. 10 sh. *s.* him that he die
Josh. 7. 25 after they had *s.* them
1 Sam. 30. 6 people spake of *s.* him
1 K. 21. 10 carry him out, and *s.*
2 Chr. 10. 18 chil. of Israel *s.* him
Ezek. 16. 40 they shall *s.* thee, and
Mat. 21. 35 husbandmen *s.* another
Mark 12. 4 and at him they cast *s.*
Luke 13. 34 kill. prophets, *s.* them
John 11. 8 Jews sought to *s.* thee
Acts 7. 59 *s.* Stephen, calling on G.
2 Cor. 11. 25 once *s.*, thrice shipw.
Heb. 11. 37 *s.*, were sawn asunder

Stone Squarers.   R. V. *Gebalites.*
1 K. 5. 18 builders did hew, and *s. s.*

Stony.   *Rugged.*
Ps. 141. 6 overthrown in *s.* places
Ezek. 11. 19 I will take *s.* heart out
Mat. 13. 5 some fell on *s.* places
Mat. 13. 20; Mark 4. 5, 16
R. V. Mat. 13. 5, 20; Mark 4. 5, 16
  rocky

Stood.   *See* **Stand.**

Stool.   R. V. *birthstool.*
Ex. 1. 16 When ye see them on *s.*

Chair.
2 K. 4. 10 set for him bed, and *s.*

Stoop.   *Bend, bow.*
Gen. 49. 9 he *s.*, couched like lion
1 Sam. 24. 8 D. *s.* wi. face to earth
2 Chr. 36. 17 no compass on him *s.*
Job 9. 13 helpers do *s.* under him
Prov. 12. 25 Heav. in heart ma. it *s.*
Isa. 46. 1 Bel boweth down, Nebo *s.*
Mark 1. 7 I am not worthy to *s.*
Luke 24. 12 *s.*, he beheld linen cloth
John 8. 8 he *s.* down, and wrote
R. V. 1 Sam. 24. 8; 28. 14 bowed

Stop.   *Shut, restrain, stop.*
Gen. 8. 2 windows of heaven were *s.*
Lev. 15. 3 or flesh be *s.* from issue
1 K. 18. 44 that the rain *s.* thee not
2 K. 3. 19 and *s.* all wells of water
2 Chr. 32. 30 Hez. *s.* the upper water
Neh. 4. 7 breaches began to be *s.*
Job 5. 16 the poor hope, iniquity *s.*
Ps. 58. 4 like the deaf adder that *s.*
Prov. 21. 13 Whoso *s.* ears at the cry
Isa. 33. 15 that *s.* his ears f. hearing
Jer. 51. 32 the passages are *s.*, and
Zech. 7. 11 refused, *s.* their ears
Rom. 3. 19 that every mouth be *s.*
Acts 7. 57 cried out loud, and *s.*
2 Cor. 11. 10 no man *s.* me of boast
Tit. 1. 11 whose mouths must be *s.*
Heb. 11. 33 *s.* the mouths of lions
R. V. Jer. 51. 32 surprised

Store (*n.*).   *Deposit, reserve.*
Gen. 41. 36 food shall be for *s.* to
Lev. 26. 10 and ye shall eat old *s.*
Deut. 28. 5 Blessed basket and *s.*
1 K. 10. 10 of spices very great *s.*
1 Chr. 27. 25 over *s.* houses in field
2 Chr. 8. 6 s. cities that Solomon had
Neh. 5. 18 *s.* of all sorts of wine
Ps. 33. 7 layeth depth in *s.* houses
Jer. 50. 26 open her *s.* houses; cast
Nah. 2. 9 for there is none end of *s.*
Mal. 3. 10 Bring tithes into *s.* houses
Luke 12. 24 nei. *s.* house nor barn
1 Cor. 16. 2 let every one lay in *s.*
R. V. Deut. 28. 5, 17 kneading-
  trough

Store (*v.*).   *Treasure up.*
Am. 3. 10 who *s.* vio. and robbery

Stories.   *Going up.*
Gen. 6. 16 with second and third *s.*
Ezek. 41. 16 galleries three *s.* over
Am. 9. 6 buildeth his *s.* in heaven
R. V. Am. 9. 6 chambers

Stork.   *Kite, heron, stork.*
Lev. 11. 19 sh. not eat *s.*, the heron
Deut. 14. 18 the *s.* after her kind

Ps. 104. 17 *s.*, fir trees her home
Jer. 8. 7 the *s.* knoweth her times
Zech. 5. 9 they had wings like th. *s.*

Storm.   *Tempest, whirlwind.*
Job 21. 18 as chaff that *s.* carrieth
Ps. 85. 15 make them afraid with *s.*
Isa. 4. 6 as covert from *s.* and rain
Ezek. 38. 9 Thou shalt come like *s.*
Nah. 1. 3 Lord hath his way in *s.*
Mark 4. 37 there arose a great *s.*
Luke 8. 23 there came *s.* of wind
R. V. Isa. 29. 6 whirlwind

Stormy.   *Whirlwindy.*
Ps. 107. 25 He raiseth the *s.* wind
Ezek. 13. 13 will rend it wi. *s.* wind

Story.   R. V. *commentary.*
2 Chr. 13. 22 writ. in *s.* of prophets
  24. 27 in *s.* of book of the kings

Stout.   *Great, strong.*
Job 4. 11 *s.* lion's whelps are scat.
Isa. 9. 9 that say in the *s.* of heart
Dan. 7. 20 look more *s.* th. fellows
Mal. 3. 13 words ha. been *s.* ag. me

Stout-hearted.   *Great of heart.*
Ps. 76. 5 *s. h.* are spoiled, they ha.
Isa. 46. 12 Hearken to me, ye *s. h.*

Stoutness.   *Greatness.*
Isa. 9. 9 they say in the *s.* of heart

Straight.   *Direct, plain.*
Josh. 6. 5 ascend *s.* up before him
1 Sam. 6. 12 kine took the *s.* way
2 Chr. 3. 20 bro. it *s.* to west. side
Ps. 5. 8 mak. way *s.* bef. my face
Prov. 4. 25 let eyelids look *s.* bef.
Eccl. 1. 15 crooked cannot be m. *s.*
Isa. 42. 16 I make crook. things *s.*
Jer. 31. 9 walk by the waters in *s.*
Ezek. 1. 7 their feet were *s.* feet
Mat. 3. 3 Prep., make his paths *s.*
Mark 1. 3; Luke 3. 4; John 1. 23
Luke 13. 13 she was made *s.* and
Acts 9. 11 go into street called S.
Heb. 12. 13 make *s.* paths for feet
R. V. Isa. 45. 2 plain

Straightway.   *Immediately.*
1 Sam. 9. 13 ye shall *s.* find him
Prov. 7. 22 He goeth after her *s.*
Dan. 10. 17 *s.* remained no strength
Mat. 4. 20 And they *s.* left their nets
Mark 5. 42 *s.* the damsel arose and
Luke 14. 5 will *s.* pull him out
John 13. 32 God shall *s.* glorify him
Acts 5. 10 then fell she down *s.* at
Jas. 1. 24 *s.* forget. what manner
R. V. Luke 8. 55; Acts 5. 10; 16.
  33 immediately; Mark 2.2; 7.35;
  Luke 5. 39 ——

Strain.   *Filter.*
Mat. 23. 24 guides, wh. *s.* at gnat

Strait.   *Distress.*
1 Sam. 13. 6 saw they were in a *s.*
2 Sam. 24. 14 I am in a great *s.* let
1 Chr. 21. 13 gr. *s.*, let me fall now
Job 36. 16 remove thee out of *s.*
Lam. 1. 3 overtook her between *s.*
Phil. 1. 23 I am in *s.* betwixt two

Narrow, contracted.
2 K. 6. 1 place we dwell in is too *s.*
Isa. 49. 20 place is too *s.* for me
Mat. 7. 13 Enter ye in at *s.* gate
Luke 13. 14 Strive to enter *s.* gate
R. V. Isa. 49. 20 distress; Mat. 7. 13,
  14; Luke 13. 24 narrow

Straighten.   *Distress, constrain.*
Job 37. 10 breadth of waters is *s.*
Prov. 4. 12 thy steps shall not be *s.*
Ezek. 42. 6 building was *s.* more
Jer. 19. 9 seek lives shall *s.* them
Mic. 2. 7 is spirit of the Lord *s.*?
Luke 12. 50 how am I *s.* till it be
2 Cor. 6. 12 not *s.* in us, *s.* in your

Straightest.   *Strictest.*
Acts 26. 5 aft *s.* sect of our religion

Straitly.   *Strictly.*
Gen. 43. 7 man asked us *s.* our state
Josh. 6. 1 Jericho was *s.* shut up
Mark 1. 43 he *s.* charged him and
Acts 4. 17 let us *s.* threaten them
R. V. Mat. 9. 30; Mark 1. 43
  strictly; Mark 3. 12; 5. 43 much;
  Luke 9. 21 but; Acts 4. 17 ——

Straitness.   *Distress.*
Deut. 28. 53 eat flesh of sons in *s.*
Job 36. 16 place wh. there is no *s.*
Jer. 19. 9 eat flesh of friend in *s.*

Straitest.   *Most strict.*

Acts 26. 5 after *s.* sect of religion
Strake.   *Struck, lowered.*
Acts 27. 17 they fearing, *s.* sail, and
Strakes.   *Streaks.*
Gen. 30. 37 pilled white *s.* in them
Lev. 14. 37 if plague be with hol. *s.*
Strange.   *Not own, foreign, un-*
  known, unfamiliar, new.
Gen. 42. 7 Joseph made himself *s.*
Ex. 2. 22 been stranger in a *s.* land
Lev. 10. 1 N. and A. offered *s.* fire
Judg. 11. 2 thou art son of *s.* woman
1 K. 11. 1 k. loved many *s.* women
2 K. 19. 24 I have drunk *s.* waters
Ez. 10. 2 tresp., taken *s.* wives
Neh. 13. 27 transg., marry. *s.* wives
Ps. 114. 1 went from peo. of *s.* lang.
Prov. 21. 8 the way of man is *s.*
Isa. 17. 10 and shalt set with *s.* lips
Jer. 2. 21 how turned into *s.* vine
Ezek. 3. 5 sent to peo. of *s.* speech
Hos. 8. 12 were counted a *s.* thing
Zeph. 1. 8 clothed with *s.* apparel
Luke 5. 26 We have seen *s.* things
Acts 7. 6 sojourn in a *s.* land; and
Heb. 11. 9 sojourn as in *s.* country
1 Pet. 4. 4 they think it *s.* ye run
Jude 7 as Sodom going after *s.* flesh
R. V. Job 31. 3 disaster; 19. 13
  hardly with; Prov. 21. 8 crooked;
  Judg. 11. 2 another; Zeph. 1. 8;
  Acts 26. 11 foreign; Heb. 11. 9
  not his own

Strangely.   *Not knowingly.*
Deut. 32. 27 adversaries behaved *s.*

Stranger.   *Foreigner, sojourner,*
  alien, one unknown.
Gen. 15. 13 seed shall be *s.* in land
Ex. 12. 43 no *s.* shall eat thereof
Lev. 19. 33 if *s.* sojourn in land
Num. 16. 40 that no *s.* off. incense
Deut. 10. 19 Love *s.*, for we are *s.*
Josh. 8. 33 as well *s.*, as he born
Judg. 19. 12 not turn to city of *s.*
Ruth 2. 10 of me, seeing I am a *s.*
2 Sam. 1. 13 I am the son of a *s.*
1 K. 3. 18 there was no *s.* with us
1 Chr. 22. 2 *s.* were in land of Is.
2 Chr. 2. 17 Solomon numbered *s.*
Neh. 13. 30 cleansed I them of *s.*
Job 31. 32 *s.* did not lodge in street
Ps. 94. 6 They slay widow and *s.*
Prov. 5. 10 Lest *s.* be fill. wi. wealth
Eccl. 6. 2 not power to eat, a *s.* eat.
Isa. 56. 3 nei. let son of *s.* speak
Jer. 14. 8 why be as a *s.* in land
Lam. 5. 2 inher. is turn. *s.* houses
Ezek. 7. 21 I give it in. hand of *s.*
Hos. 7. 9 *s.* devoured his strength
Joel 3. 17 shall no *s.* pass through
Obad. 11 in the day that *s.* carried
Mal. 3. 5 that turn aside *s.* from
Mat. 17. 25 tribute? of chil. or *s.*
Luke 24. 18 Art thou *s.* in Jerusalem
John 10. 5 *s.* will they not follow
Acts 2. 10 *s.* of Rome, Jews and pr.
Eph. 2. 12 *s.* from cov. of promise
1 Tim. 5 10 if she have lodged *s.*
Heb. 11. 13 confessed they were *s.*
1 Pet. 1. 1 to *s.* scat. thro. Pontus
3 John 5 whatso. thou doest to *s.*
R. V. Gen. 17. 8; 28. 4; 36. 7; 37.
  1 sojournings; Ex. 12. 43; Prov.
  5. 10; Ezek. 44. 7, 9 alien; Ex. 2.
  22; 12, 19; Lev. 25. 47; 1 Chr.
  16. 19; Ps. 105. 12; 119. 19; Jer.
  14. 8; Acts 2. 10; 7. 29; 1 Pet. 2.
  11 sojourner; Deut. 17. 15; 23.
  20; 29. 22 foreigner; Isa. 5. 17
  wanderers; 29. 5 foes; Obad. 12
  of his disaster.

Strangle.   *Choke, suffocate.*
Job 7. 15 my soul chooseth *s.* and
Nah. 2. 12 the lion did tear and *s.*
Acts 15. 20 abstain from things *s.*

Straw.   *Straw.*
Gen. 24. 25 have *s.* and provender
Ex. 5. 7 no more give the people *s.*
Judg. 19. 19 th. is *s.* and provender
1 K. 4. 28 Barley and *s.* for horses
Job 41. 27 He esteemeth *s.* as iron
Isa. 11. 7 lion shall eat *s.* like ox

Straw (*v.*).   *See* **Strew.**

Stream.   *Flowing, brook, river,*
  channel, valley.
Ex. 8. 5 Stretch thy rod over the *s.*

Num. 21. 15 *s.* of brooks that goeth
Job 6. 15 as *s.* of brooks they pass
Ps. 78. 16 He brot. *s.* out of rock
S. of S. 4. 15 liv. waters *s.* fr. Leb.
Isa. 11. 15 smite it in the seven *s.*
Dan. 7. 10 fiery *s.* issued forth fr.
Am. 5. 24 righteous. as mighty *s.*
Luke 6. 48 *s.* beat vehemently on
R. V. Ex. 7. 19; 8. 5 rivers; Num.
21. 15 slope; Job 6. 15 channel;
Isa. 27. 12 brook; 57. 6. valley

Street. *Walking place, broad place.*
Gen. 19. 2 will abide in *s.* all night
Deut. 13. 16 in midst of *s.* thereof
Josh. 2. 19 whoso. sh. go out in. *s.*
Judg. 19. 15 he sat him down in *s.*
2 Sam. 1. 20 pub. it not in *s.* of A.
1 K. 20. 34 sh. make *s.* in Damasc.
2 Chr. 29. 4 gath. them unto east *s.*
Ez. 10. 9 people sat in *s.* of house
Neh. 8. 1 into *s.* before the gate
Esth. 4. 6 went to Mord. unto *s.* of
Job 29. 7 I prep. my seat in the *s.*
Ps. 18. 42 cast them out as dirt in *s.*
Prov. 1. 20 she utter. her voice in *s.*
Eccl. 12. 4 doors shall be shut in *s.*
S. of S. 3. 2 go about the city in *s.*
Isa. 5. 25 carcases were torn in *s.*
59. 14 truth is fallen in the *s.*
Jer. 9. 21 cut off young men fr. *s.*
Lam. 2. 11 sucklings swoon in the *s.*
Ezek. 7. 19 sh. cast their silver in *s.*
Dan. 9. 25 the *s.* sh. be built again
Am. 5. 16 Wailing sh. be in all *s.*
Mic. 7. 10 trodden down as mi. of *s.*
Zeph. 3. 6 I made their *s.* waste
Zech. 9. 3 and gold as mire of the *s*
Mat. 6. 5 pray stand. in cor. of *s.*
Mark 6. 56 they laid the sick in *s.*
Luke 10. 10 go your ways into *s.*
Acts 9. 11 go into *s.* called Straight
Rev. 11. 8 dead bodies sh. lie in *s.*
21. 21 *s.* of city was pure gold
R. V. 2 Chr. 29. 4; 32. 6; Ez.
10. 9; Neh. 8. 1, 3, 16; Esth.
4. 6; Prov. 1. 20; 7. 12; Isa.
15. 3; Am. 5. 16 broad place or
way; Ps. 144. 13 fields; Mark 6.
56 market place

Strength. *Might, power, force.*
Gen. 4. 12 ground sh. not yield *s.*
Ex. 15. 2 the L. is my *s.* and song
Lev. 26. 20 your *s.* be spent in vain
Num. 23. 22 he ha. *s.* of an unicorn
Deut. 21. 17 he is beginning of his *s.*
Josh. 11. 13 cities th. stood in th. *s.*
Judg. 16. 5 see wh. his gr. *s.* lieth
1 Sam. 2. 9 by *s.* sh. no man prevail
2 Sam. 22. 40 hast girded me wi. *s.*
1 K. 19. 8 went in the *s.* of meat
2 K. 18. 20 I have *s.* for the war
1 Chr. 16. 11 Seek the L. and his *s.*
2 Chr. 13. 20 Nei. did J. recover *s.*
Neh. 4. 10 *s.* of bearer of burdens is
Job 12. 13 With him is wis. and *s.*
Ps. 71. 16 I will go in *s.* of L. God
Prov. 20. 29 glo. of young men is *s.*
Eccl. 9. 16 wisdom is better than *s.*
Isa. 49. 5 and my G. shall be my *s.*
Jer. 16. 19 my *s.*, and my fortress
Lam. 1. 14 hath made my *s.* to fall
Ezek. 30. 18 pomp of her *s.* sh. c.
Dan. 2. 37 a kingdom, power, and *s.*
Hos. 7. 9 Strang. ha. devour. his *s.*
Joel 3. 16 *s.* of children of Israel
Am. 6. 13 not take horns by our *s.*
Mic. 5. 4 sh. stand and feed in *s.*
Nah. 3. 9 E. and Eg. were her *s.*
Hag. 2. 22 will destr. *s.* of kingdom
Zech. 12. 5 inhab. of Jer. be my *s.*
Mark 12. 30 love L. with all thy *s.*
Luke 1. 51 he shewed *s.* with arm
Acts 3. 7 feet and bones received *s.*
Rom. 5. 6 wh. we were yet witho. *s.*
1 Cor. 15. 56 the *s.* of sin is the law
2 Cor. 12. 9 my *s.* is made perfect
Heb. 11. 11 Sarah herself receiv. *s.*
Rev. 12. 10 Now is come salv. and *s.*
R. V. Job 12. 13; 39. 19; Ps. 80. 2;
Prov. 8. 14; 24. 5; Rev. 5. 12
might; Ps. 18. 2; 144. 1; Isa. 26. 4
rock; Ps. 60. 7; 108. 8 defence;
Ps. 31. 4; 37. 39; Prov. 10. 29;
Isa. 23. 4, 14; 25. 4; Ezek. 30. 15;
Nah. 3. 11 strong hold; Ps. 33. 17;

Ezek. 24. 21; 30. 18; 33. 28; 1 Cor.
15. 56; 2 Cor. 12. 9; Heb. 11. 11;
Rev. 3. 8; 12. 10 power

Strengthen. *Make strong.*
Gen. 48. 2 Israel *s.* himself, and sat
Deut. 3. 28 charge Joshua, *s.* him
Judg. 3. 12 Lord *s.* Eglon, the king
1 Sam. 23. 16 Jona. *s.* hand in God
2 Sam. 2. 7 let your hands be *s.* and
1 K. 20. 22 Go, *s.* thyself, and mark
1 Chr. 11. 10 who *s.* themselves wi.
2 Chr. 1. 1 Sol. son of David was *s.*
Ez. 1. 6 all that were about th. *s.*
Neh. 6. 9 Now, O God, *s.* my hands
Job 4. 3 and thou hast *s.* the weak
Ps. 41. 3 Lord will *s.* him upon bed
Prov. 8. 28 he *s.* fount. of the deep
Eccl. 7. 19 Wisdom *s.* wise mo. than
Isa. 22. 21 clo. him wi. robe, and *s.*
Jer. 23. 14 they *s.* hands of ev. doers
Ezek. 30. 24 I will *s.* arms of kings
Dan. 10. 19 I was *s.*, and said, Let
Hos 7. 15 I have *s.* their arms, yet
Am. 5. 9 That *s.* the spoiled against
Zech. 10. 6 I will *s.* house of Judah
Luke 22. 43 there appear. an angel *s.*
Acts 9. 19 received meat, he was *s.*
Eph. 3. 16 *s.* with might by Spirit
Col. 1. 11 *S.* with all might, accord.
Phil. 4. 13 thro. Christ which *s.* me
2 Tim. 4. 17 L. stood with me. and *s.*
1 Pet. 5. 10 make you per., stab., *s.*
Rev. 3. 2 Be watchful, *s.* the things
R. V. Ps. 41. 3 support; Ezek. 30. 25
hold up; Luke 22. 32; Acts 18. 23;
Rev. 3. 2 stablish

Stretch. *Spread out, extend.*
Gen. 22. 10 Abr. *s.* forth his hand
Ex. 7. 5 I *s.* mine hand upon Egypt
Deut. 4. 34 mighty hand, *s.* out arm
Josh. 8. 18 *S.* out spear in thy hand
1 Sam. 26. 11 L. forbid I shou. *s.* forth
2 Sam. 24. 16 angel *s.* out his hand
1 K. 8. 42 and of thy *s.* out arm
2 K. 21. 13 *S.* ov. Jer. line of Sama.
1 Chr. 21. 16 angel with a sword *s.*
2 Chr. 6. 32 hand, and thy *s.* out arm
Job. 15. 25 he *s.* out hand ag. God
Ps. 104. 2 who *s.* heav. like a curtain
Prov. 31. 20 she *s.* hand to the poor
Isa. 8. 8 *s.* out of his wings shall fill
Jer. 10. 20 none to *s.* my tent more
Lam. 2. 8 he hath *s.* out a line, he
Ezek. 25. 13 *s.* mine hand upon Ed.
Dan. 11. 42 sh. *s.* hand on countries
Hos. 7. 5 he *s.* hand with scorners
Am. 6. 4 *s.* thems. on their couches
Zech. 1. 16 line sh. be *s.* on Jerus.
Mat. 12. 49 he *s.* hand tow. disci.
Mark 3. 5 *S.* hand. And he *s.* it.
Luke 22. 53 ye *s.* no hands against
John 21. 18 thou sh. *s.* forth hands
Acts 4. 30 By *s.* forth hands to heal
Rom. 10. 21 All day I *s.* my hands
2 Cor. 10. 14 we *s.* not ourselv's be
R. V. Ex. 3. 20; 9. 15; 1 Sam. 24.
6; 26. 9, 11, 23; 2 Sam. 1. 14;
Job 30. 24; Acts 12. 1 put; Ex.
25. 20; Ps. 44. 20; 88. 9; 136. 6;
143. 6; Prov. 31. 20; Isa. 10. 8;
Rom. 10. 21 spread, or spread
forth.

Strew. *Scatter, sprinkle.*
Ex. 32. 20 ground calf, *s.* it on wat.
2 Chr. 34. 4 he *s.* it upon the graves
Mat. 21. 8 cut branches and *s.* them
Mark 11. 8 branches of trees, and *s.*

Stricken. *Smitten, going on in.*
Gen. 24. 1 Ab. was old. and well *s.*
Josh. 13. 1 Josh. was old and *s* in
1 K. 1. 1 David was old *s.* in years
Isa. 1. 5 Why sho. we be *s.* more
Lam. 4. 9 *s.* for want of the fruits
Luke 1. 7 and both well *s.* in years

Strife. *Contention.*
Gen. 13. 7 was *s.* between herdmen
Num. 27. 14 *s.* of the congregation
Deut. 1. 12 How can I bear your *s.*
Judg. 12. 2 I and my peo. were at *s.*
2 Sam. 19. 9 all people were at *s.*
Ps. 80. 6 ma. *s.* unto our neighbour
Prov. 15. 18 wrathful man stir. up *s.*
Isa. 58. 4 ye fast for *s.* and debate
Jer 15. 10 ha. borne me a man of *s.*
Ezek. 47. 19 fr. Tamar to wat. of *s.*
Hab. 1. 3 there are that raise up *s.*

Luke 22. 24 there was *s.* among th.
Rom. 13. 13 walk honestly, not in *s.*
1 Cor. 3. 3 there is among you *s.*
2 Cor. 12. 20 envyings, wraths, *s.*
Gal. 5. 20 wrath, *s.*, seditions, her.
Phil. 2. 3 Let noth. be done thro. *s.*
1 Tim. 6. 4 doting ab. quest. and *s.*
2 Tim. 2. 23 avoid, know. they ge. *s.*
Heb. 6. 16 oath for con. is end of *s.*
Jas. 3. 16 where envying and *s.* is
R. V. Ps. 106. 32 Meribah; Prov.
15. 18; 26. 20; Luke 22. 24 contention; 2 Cor. 12. 20; Gal. 5. 20;
Phil. 2. 3; Jas. 3. 14, 16 faction;
1 Tim. 6. 4 disputes

Strike. *Smite, strike.*
Ex. 12. 7 *s.* it on two side posts and
Judg. 5. 26 when she had *s.* through
1 Sam. 2. 14 *s.* it into pan, or kettle
2 Sam. 12. 15 L. *s.* chi. th. U's wife
2 K. 5. 11 *s.* his hand over the place
2 Chr. 13. 20 Jeroboam, Lord *s.* him
Job 20. 24 bow of steel shall *s.* him
Ps. 110. 5 Lord shall *s.* through k.
Prov. 17. 26 nor to *s.* princes for e.
Jer. 5. 3 L. thou hast *s.* them, but
Hab. 3. 14 didst *s.* thro. wi. staves
Mat. 26. 51 one *s.* serv. of high pr.
Mark 14. 65 ser. did *s.* him wi. han.
Luke 22. 64 they *s.* him on the face
John 18. 22 *s.* Jesus wi. palm of h.
To loose, let go.
Acts 27. 17 *s.* sail, and were driven
Rev. 9. 5 Scorp., when he *s.* a man
R. V. Ex. 12. 7 put; Deut. 21. 4
break; 2 K. 5. 11 wave; Hab. 3.
14 pierce; Mark 14. 65 received
blows; 2 Chr. 13. 20; Mat. 26. 51
smote; Luke 22. 64 ——

Striker. *Reviler, striker.*
1 Tim. 3. 3 Not given to wine, no *s.*
Tit. 1. 7 no *s.*, not given to fil. lucre

String. *Cord, bond.*
Ps. 11. 2 make ready arrow on *s.*
33. 2 psaltery and instr. of ten *s.*
Mark 7. 35 *s.* of his tongue was loos.
R. V. Ps. 21. 12 bowstrings; Mark
7. 35 bond

Stringed. *With strings.*
Ps. 150. 4 praise him with *s.* instru.
Isa. 38. 20 sing songs to *s.* instrument
Hab. 3. 19 singer on *s.* instrument

Strip. *Take or put off.*
Gen. 37. 23 they *s.* Jos. out of coat
Ex. 33. 6 *s.* thems. of their ornam.
Num. 20. 28 M. *s.* A. of his garments
1 Sam. 18. 4 Jon *s.* himself of robe
: Chr. 10. 8 Phil. ca. to *s.* the slain
2 Chr. 20. 25 jewels wh. they *s.* off
Job 19. 9 He ha. *s.* me of my glory
Isa. 32. 11 *s.* you, and make you bare
Ezek. 16. 39 they sh. *s.* thee of clo.
Hos. 2. 3 Lest I *s.* her naked, and
Mat. 27. 28 they *s.* Jesus, put on
Luke 10. 30 which *s.* him of raiment

Stripe. *Stroke, beating, blow.*
Ex. 21. 25 wound for wound, *s.* for *s.*
Deut. 25. 3 Forty *s.* he may gi. him
2 Sam. 7. 14 with. of chi. of men *s.*
Ps. 89. 32 will visit iniquity with *s.*
Prov. 17. 10 hundred *s.* into a fool
19. 29 *s.* are prepared for fools
Isa. 53. 5 with his *s.* we are healed
Luke 12. 48 commit things wor. of *s.*
Acts 16. 33 washed *s.*; was baptized
2 Cor. 6. 5 In *s.*, in imprisonments
1 Pet. 2. 24 by whose *s.* ye were h.
R. V. Prov. 20. 30 strokes

Stripling. *A youth.*
1 Sam. 17. 56 Enq. whose son *s.* is

Stripped. *Spoiled, robbed.*
Mic. 1. 8 I will go *s.* and naked
See also **Strip.**

Strive. *Contend, endeavor.*
Gen. 26. 20 herdmen of Ger. did *s.*
Ex. 21. 22 two men of Heb. *s.* togeth.
Lev. 24. 10 son and man of Is. *s.* t.
Num. 20. 13 bec. chil. of Is. *s.* tog.
Deut. 25. 11 When men *s.* together
Judg. 11. 25 did he ev. *s.* ag. Israel
2 Sam. 14. 6 two *s.* together in field
Job 33. 13 Why dost thou *s.* ag. him?
Ps. 35. 1 Plead, L., wi. them th. *s.*
Prov. 3. 30 *s.* not without cause
Isa. 41. 11 th. *s.* wi. thee sh. perish
Jer. 50. 24 thou ha. *s.* against Lord

Dan. 7. 2 winds of heaven *s.* upon
Hos. 4. 4 let no man *s.* nor reprove
Mat. 12. 19 He shall not *s.*, nor cry
Luke 13. 24 *S.* to enter strait gate
John 6. 32 Jews *s.* among themsel.
Acts 7. 26 M. shew. hims. as th *s.*
Rom. 15. 20 I *s.* to preach gospel
1 Cor. 9. 25 ev. man th. *s.* for mast.
Phil. 1. 27 with one mind *s.* togeth.
Col. 1. 29 *s.* accord. to his working
2 Tim. 2. 24 serv. of L. must not *s.*
Heb. 12. 4 not resisted unto blood, *s.*
R. V. Ex. 21. 18; 2 Tim. 2. 5 con-
tend; Rom. 15. 20 making it my
aim.

Strivings. *Contentions.*
2 Sam. 22. 44 hast del. me from *s.* of
Ps. 18. 43 hast delivered me from *s.*
Tit. 3. 9 avoid *s.* about the law; for
R. V. Tit. 3. 9 fightings

Stroke. *Blow, smiting, plague.*
Deut. 17. 8 hard between *s.* and *s.*
Esth. 9. 5 smote all enemies with *s.*
Job 23. 2 *s.* is heavier th. groaning
Ps. 39. 10 Remove thy *s.* from me
Prov. 18. 6 his mouth calleth for *s.*
Isa. 30. 26 healeth *s.* of their wound
Ezek. 24. 16 desire of eyes with a *s.*
R. V. Prov. 18. 6 stripes

Strong. *Mighty, hard, robust,
having strength.*
Gen. 49. 14 Issachar is a *s.* ass cou.
Ex. 6. 1 with a *s.* hand shall he let
Num. 20. 20 Ed. came with a *s.* hand
Deut. 2. 36 not one city too *s.* for
Josh. 14. 11 I am as *s.* this day as
Judg. 14. 14 out of *s.* came sweet.
1 Sam. 14. 52 when S. saw *s.* man
2 Sam. 3. 6 Abner made himself *s.*
1 K. 8. 42 shall hear of thy *s.* hand
2 Chr. 11. 12 he made the cities *s.*
Neh. 9. 25 And they took *s.* cities
Job 8. 2 words be like a *s.* wind
Ps. 19. 5 rejoiceth as *s.* man to run
Prov. 7. 26 *s.* men been slain by her
Eccl. 9. 11 battle is not to the *s.*
S. of S. 8. 6 for love is *s.* as death
Isa. 8. 7 L. bringeth waters, *s.* and
Jer. 21. 5 will fight with a *s.* arm
Ezek. 3. 14 hand of the Lord was *s.*
Dan. 4. 11 tree grew and was *s.*
Joel. 3. 10 let the weak say, I am *s.*
Am. 2. 14 *s.* sh. not streng. his force
Mic. 4. 3 shall rebuke *s.* nations
Nah. 2. 1 watch, make thy loins *s.*
Hag. 2. 4 be *s.* O Zer., be *s.* O Josh.
Mat. 12. 29 how enter *s.* man's ho.
Mark 3. 27 except he bind *s.* man
Luke 1. 80 child grew, and waxed *s.*
Acts 3. 16 thro. faith made man *s.*
Rom. 4. 20 *s.* in faith, giving glory
1 Cor. 16. 13 quit you like men, be *s.*
2 Cor. 12. 10 wh. weak, th. am I *s.*
Eph. 6. 10 brethr., be *s.* in the Lord
2 Tim. 2. 1 my son, be *s.* in grace
Heb. 6. 18 we mi. ha. *s.* consolation
1 John 2. 14 writ. you, bec. ye are *s.*
Rev. 5. 2 I saw *s.* angel proclaim.
R. V. Few changes to mighty, val-
iant, etc.

Stronger. *More strong.*
Gen. 25. 23 one people shall be *s.*
Num. 13. 31 not able, they are *s.*
Judg. 14. 18 what is *s.* th. a lion?
2 Sam. 3. 1 David waxed *s.* and *s.*
1 K. 20. 23 we shall be *s.* than they
Job 17. 9 cl. hands sh. be *s.* and *s.*
Ps. 105. 24 he made them *s.* than
Jer. 20. 7 thou art *s.* than I, and
Luke 11. 22 wh. a *s.* th. he come
1 Cor. 11. 25 weak. of G. is *s.* than

Strongest. *Strongest.*
Prov. 30. 30 wh. is *s.* am. beasts

Strong Hold. *Fenced place for-
tress.*
Num. 13. 19 whe. in tents or *s. h.*
Judg. 6. 2 Is. ma. caves and *s. h.*
1 Sam. 23. 14 David abode in *s. h.*
2 K. 8. 12 their *s. h.* set on fire, and
2 Chr. 11. 11 Rehob. fortified *s. h.*
Ps. 89. 40 brought his *s. h.* to ruin
Isa. 23. 11 to destroy *s. h.* thereof
Jer. 48. 18 spoiler sh. destroy *s. h.*
Lam. 2. 5 Lord destroyed his *s. h.*
Dan. 11. 24 his devices against *s. h.*
Mic. 4. 8 *s. h.* of daughter of Zion

Nah. 1. 7 L. a *s. h.* in day of troub.
Hab. 1. 10 shall deride every *s. h.*
Zech. 9. 3 Tyrus did build a *s. h.*
2 Cor. 10. 4 mi. to pulling downs. *h.*

Strongly. *With strength.*
Ez. 6. 3 let foundations be *s.* laid

Strove. *See Strive.*
Struck. *See Strike.*
Struggle. *Contend, make effort.*
Gen. 25. 22 children *s.* togeth. with.

Stubble. *Straw, stubble.*
Ex. 5. 12 gather *s.* instead of straw
Job 13. 25 wilt th. pursue dry *s.*?
Ps. 83. 13 make them as *s.* before
Isa. 5. 24 as fire devoureth the *s.*
Jer. 13. 24 I will scatter them as *s.*
Joel 2. 5 fire that devoureth the *s.*
Obad. 18 house of Esau for *s.* and
Nah. 1. 10 they shall be devour. as *s.*
Mal. 4. 1 that do wick., shall be *s.*
1 Cor. 3. 12 on the found., hay, *s.*

Stubborn. *Refractory, wilful.*
Deut. 21. 18 if a man have a *s.* son
Judg. 2. 19 ceased not from *s.* ways
Ps. 78. 8 not as fath., a *s.* generation
Prov. 7. 11 She is loud and *s.*; her
R. V. Prov. 7. 11 wilful

Stubbornness. *Hardness, stiffness.*
Deut. 9. 27 look not to *s.* of people
1 Sam. 15. 23 *s.* is as iniquity and

Stuck. *See Stick.*
Studs. *Knobs.*
S. of S. 1. 11 borders of gold, with *s.*

Study. *Apply mind.*
Prov. 15. 28 heart of righteous *s.*
Eccl. 12. 12 much *s.* is a weariness
1 Thes. 4. 11 that ye *s.* to be quiet
2 Tim. 2. 15 *S.* to show thys. appr.
R. V. 2 Tim. 2. 15 give diligence

Stuff. *Goods, baggage.*
Gen. 31. 37 thou searched all my *s.*
Ex. 22. 7 if man deliv. *s.* to keep
Josh. 7. 11 put it am. their own *s.*
1 Sam. 10. 22 hid himself am. the *s.*
Neh. 13. 8 cast forth *s.* of Tobiah
Ezek. 12. 3 prep. *s.* for removing
Luke 17. 31 house top, *s.* in house
R. V. Luke 17. 31 goods

Stumble. *Trip, strike, against.*
1 Sam. 2. 4 that *s.* girded wi. strength
1 Chr. 13. 9 hold ark; for the oxen *s.*
Ps. 27. 2 to eat my flesh, they *s.*
Prov. 4. 12 runneth, thou sh. not *s.*
Isa. 5. 27 None sh. be weary nor *s.*
Jer. 50. 32 proud shall *s.* and fall
Dan. 11. 19 he shall *s.* and fall, and
Nah. 3. 3 they *s.* upon their corpses
Mal. 2. 8 they sh. *s.* in their walk
John 11. 10 man walk in night, he *s.*
Rom. 9. 32 they *s.* at that *s.* stone
1 Pet. 2. 8 to them wh. *s.* at word
R. V. Prov. 24. 17 is overthrown

Stumbling. *Striking against.*
Lev. 19. 14 sh. not put *s.* bl. before
Isa. 8. 14 be for stone of *s.* to Israel
Jer. 6. 21 lay *s.* bl. bef. this people
Zeph. 1. 3 I will consume the *s.* bl.
Rom. 9. 32 they st. at that *s.* stone
1 Cor. 1. 23 unto the Jews a *s.* block
1 Pet. 2. 8 stone of *s.*, rock of offence
1 John 2. 10 is no. occas. of *s.* in him

Stump. *Rooty part.*
1 Sam. 5. 4 only *s.* of D. was left
Dan. 4. 15 leave *s.* of roots in earth
4. 26 command. to leave *s.* of tree

Subdue. *Put down, humble, con-
quer.*
Gen. 1. 28 replen. the earth, and *s.* it
Num. 32. 22 land be *s.* bef. the Lord
Deut. 20. 20 bulwarks, until be *s.*
Josh. 18. 1 land was *s.* before them
Judg. 3. 30 Moab was *s.* that day
1 Sam. 7. 13 the Philistines were *s.*
2 Sam. 8. 11 gold of nations he *s.*
1 Chr. 22. 18 land is *s.* before Lord
Neh. 9. 24 *s.* bef. them the inhabit.
Ps. 18. 47 God avengeth me, and *s.*
Isa. 45. 1 to *s.* nations before him
Dan. 7. 24 he shall *s.* three kings
Mic. 7. 19 he will *s.* our iniquities
Zech. 9. 15 devour, *s.* wi. sling stones
1 Cor. 15. 28 all sh. be *s.* unto him
Phil. 3. 21 he is able to *s.* all things
Heb. 11. 33 Who thro. faith *s.* kingd.
R. V. Deut. 20. 20 fall; Dan. 7. 24

put down; Mic. 7. 19 tread under
foot; Zech. 9. 15 tread down; r
Cor. 15. 28; Phil. 3. 21 subject

Subject. *Subdued, placed under.*
Luke 2. 51 Jesus was *s.* unto them
Rom. 8. 7 it is not *s.* to law of God
1 Cor. 14. 32 spirit of proph. are *s.*
Eph. 5. 24 as church is *s.* unto C.
Tit. 3. 1 Put th. in mind to be *s.* to
Heb. 2. 15 all lifetime *s.* to bondage
1 Pet. 2. 18 Ser., be *s.* to yo. masters
R. V. Rom. 13. 5; Tit. 3. 1; 1 Pet.
2. 18 in subjection

Subjected. *Placed under.*
Rom. 8. 20 who. ha. *s.* same in hope

Subjection. *Holding under, bondage.*
Ps. 106. 42 they were brou. into *s.*
Jer. 34. 11 and brou. them into *s.*
1 Cor. 9. 27 bring it into *s.*; lest
2 Cor. 9. 13 glorify God for your *s.*
Gal. 2. 5 we gave place by *s.*, not
1 Tim. 2. 11 wom. learn with all *s.*
Heb. 2. 5 put in *s.* world to come
1 Pet. 3. 1 wives, be in *s.* to husb.
R. V. 1 Cor. 9. 27 bondage; 2 Cor.
9. 13 obedience

Submit. *Put or set under, yield.*
Gen. 16. 9 Return to mistr., and *s.*
2 Sam. 22. 45 Strang. sh. *s.* thems.
1 Chr. 29. 24 sons of Da. *s.* to Sol.
Ps. 66. 3 enemies shall *s.* to thee
Rom. 10. 3 not *s.* to righteousness
1 Cor. 16. 16 ye *s.* yours. unto such
Eph. 5. 21 *S.* yours. one to another
Col. 3. 18 Wives, *s.* to yo. husbands
Heb. 13. 17 Obey them, and *s.* yo.
Jas. 4. 7 *S.* yours. theref. to God
1 Pet. 2. 13 *S.* yours. to ev. ordin.
R. V. Rom. 10. 3; Eph. 5. 21, 22;
1 Cor. 16. 16; Col. 3. 18; Jas.
4. 7; 1 Pet. 2. 13; 5. 5 be subject
or subjection

Suborn. *Bring under, induce.*
Acts 6. 11 they *s.* men, which said

Subscribe. *Write.*
Isa. 44. 5 anoth. shall *s.* with hand
Jer. 32. 10 I *s.* the evi. and sealed it
32. 12 witnesses that *s.* the book

Substance. *Strength, thing,
goods, possession, life quality.*
Gen. 7. 4 I will destroy every liv. *s.*
13. 6 their *s.* was great, so they
Deut. 11. 6 swal. them and all *s.*
Josh. 14. 4 gave Lev. cities for *s.*
1 Chr. 27. 31 these were rulers of *s.*
2 Chr. 21. 17 carried away all the *s.*
Ez. 10. 8 all his *s.* sho. be forfeited
Job 1. 3 Job's *s.* was sev. th. sheep
20. 18 accor. to *s.* the restitution
Ps. 17. 14 leave their *s.* to babes
Prov. 12. 27 *s.* of dil. man is prec.
S. of S. 8. 7 if a man gi. *s.* for love
Isa. 6. 13 as oak, wh. *s.* is in them
Jer. 15. 13 Thy *s.* will I go to spoil
Hos. 12. 8 I have found me out *s.*
Obad. 13 nor laid hands on their *s.*
Mic. 4. 13 consecrate their *s.* to L.
Luke 8. 3 min. to him of their *s.*
Heb. 11. 1 fai. is *s.* of things hoped
R. V. Gen. 7. 4, thing; Deut. 11. 6
living thing; Gen. 36. 6; Heb.
10. 34 possession; Ps. 139. 15
frame; Prov. 10. 3 desire; Isa.
6. 13 stock; Hos. 12. 8 wealth;
Heb. 11. 1 assurance

Subtil. *Wise, crafty, wily.*
Gen. 3. 1 serpent more *s.* than any
2 Sam. 13. 3 Jonadab was a *s.* man
Prov. 7. 10 harlot, and *s.* of heart
R. V. Prov. 7. 10 wily

Subtilly. *Craftily.*
1 Sam. 23. 22 told me he deal. *s*
Ps. 105. 25 to deal *s.* with servant
Acts 7. 19 dealt *s.* with our kindred

Subtilty. *Deceit, guile, craft.*
Gen. 27. 35 thy bro. came with *s.*
2 K. 10. 19 Jehu did it in *s.*, to the
Prov. 1. 4 to give *s.* to the simple
Mat. 26. 4 might take Jesus by *s.*
Acts 13. 10 O full of *s.* and mischief
2 Cor. 11. 3 ser. beguil. E. thro. *s.*
R. V. Gen. 27. 35; Acts 13. 10
guile; 2 Cor. 11. 3 craftiness

Suburb. *Surrounding, place about
a city.*

Lev. 25. 34 field of *s.* not be sold
Num. 35. 2 to Levites *s.* for cities
Josh. 14. 4 with *s.* for their cattle
2 K. 23. 11 by the chamber in the *s.*
1 Chr. 5. 16 dwelt in *s.* of Sharon
2 Chr. 11. 14 the Lev. left their *s.*
Ezek. 27. 28 *s.* shall shake at sound
R. V. 2 K. 23. 11 precincts

Subvert. *Overturn, pervert.*
Lam. 3. 36 To *s.* a man in his cause
Acts 15. 24 *s.* souls, saying, Ye must
2 Tim. 2. 14 but to *s.* of hearers
Tit. 1. 11 who *s.* houses, teaching
R. V. Tit. 1. 11 overthrow : 3. 11 perverted

Succeed. *Possess, take place of.*
Deut. 2. 12 chil. of Esau *s.* them
25. 6 first born sh. *s.* his bro. dead
R. V. Deut. 12. 29 possessest

Success. *Prosperous result.*
Josh. 1. 7 thou shalt have good *s.*

Succour. *Gird about, help.*
2 Sam. 8. 5 Syrians came to *s.* Had.
2 Cor. 6. 2 in day of salva. have I *s.*
Heb. 2. 18 able to *s.* them tempted

Succourer. *Helper, protector.*
Rom. 16. 2 she ha. been *s.* of many

Such. *As he, she, it, this, etc.*
Gen. 41. 19 *s.* as I nev. saw in Egy.
Mat. 19. 14 of *s.* is kingd. of heaven
Etc., etc.

Suck (*n.*). *To suckle.*
Gen. 21. 7 Sarah given children *s.*
1 Sam. 1. 23 Han. gave her son *s.*
1 K. 3. 21 I rose to give child *s.*
Lam. 4. 3 sea monsters give *s.* to
Mat. 24. 19 woe to th. that give *s.*
Mark 13. 17 Luke 21. 23
Luke 23. 29 paps that nev. gave *s.*

Suck (*v.*). *Drain, suck.*
Deut. 33. 19 they sh. *s.* of abunda.
Job 3. 12 why breasts I should *s.?*
20. 16 shall *s.* the poison of asps
39. 30 her young ones *s.* up blood
S. of S. 8. 1 *s.* breasts of my mother
Isa. 60. 16 sh. suck milk of Gentiles
Ezek. 23. 34 sh. drink it and *s.* it out
Joel 2. 16 gath. those that *s.* breasts
Luke 11. 27 blessed are paps th. *s.*
R. V. Ezek. 23. 34 drain

Sucking. *That sucks.*
Num. 11. 12 as fa. beareth *s.* child
1 Sam. 7. 9 Samuel took a *s.* lamb
Isa. 11. 8 *s.* ch. play on hole of asp
Lam. 4. 4 tongue of *s.* child cleav.

Suckling. *That sucks.*
Deut. 32. 25 *s.* with man of gray
1 Sam. 15. 3 stay infant and *s.*, ox
Ps. 8. 2 out of mo. of babes and *s.*
Jer. 44. 7 to cut off child and *s.*
Lam. 2. 11 *s.* swoon in the streets
Mat. 21. 16 out of mo. of bab. and *s.*

Sudden. *Quick, in instant.*
Job 22. 10 *s.* fear troubleth thee
Prov. 3. 25 Be not afraid of *s.* fear
1 Thes. 5. 3 then *s.* destr. cometh

Suddenly. *Quickly, instantly.*
Num. 6. 9 if any man die very *s.*
Josh. 10. 9 Josh. came unto them *s.*
2 Sam. 15. 14 lest he overtake us *s.*
2 Chr. 29. 36 the thing was done *s.*
Job 5. 3 *s.* I cursed his habitation
Ps. 6. 10 let them be ashamed *s.*
Prov. 6. 15 he shall be broken *s.*
Eccl. 9. 12 it falleth *s.* upon them
Isa. 29. 5 it shall be at an inst. *s.*
Jer. 4. 20 *s.* are my tents spoiled
Hab. 2. 7 shall they not rise up *s.*
Mal. 3. 1 the Lord shall *s.* come
Mark 13. 36 Lest, com. *s.* he find
Luke 9. 39 and he *s.* crieth out, and
Acts 9. 3 *s.* there shined about him
1 Tim. 5. 22 Lay hands *s.* on no man
R. V. Deut. 7. 4 ; 2 Sam. 15. 14
quickly ; 1 Tim. 5. 22 hastily

Sue. R. V. *Go to law.*
Mat. 5. 40 if any man *s.* thee at law

Suffer. *Permit, endure, bear with.*
Gen. 20. 6 therefore *s.* I thee not
Ex. 22. 18 sh. not *s.* witch to live
Lev. 19. 17 and not *s.* sin upon him
Num. 21. 23 Sih. would not *s.* Is.
Deut. 8. 3 and he *s.* thee to hunger
Josh. 10. 19 *s.* them not to enter c.
Judg. 16. 26 *S.* that I feel pillars
1 Sam. 24. 7 *s.* them not to rise ag.

2 Sam. 21. 10 *s.* nei. birds to rest
1 K. 15. 17 not *s.* any to go out or
1 Chr. 16. 21 *s.* no man to do wr.
Esth. 3. 8 not for k's profit to *s.*
Job 9. 18 not *s.* me to take breath
Ps. 9. 13 consider trouble I *s.* of
Prov. 19. 15 idle soul sh. *s.* hunger
Eccl. 5. 6 *s.* not thy mouth to cause
Jer. 15. 15 for thy sake I *s.* rebuke
Ezek. 44. 20 nor *s.* locks to grow
Mat. 19. 14 J. said, *S.* little chil.
Mark 1. 34 *s.* not devils to speak
Luke 9. 5 *s.* me first to bury my
Acts 17. 3 Chr. must needs have *s.*
Rom. 8. 17 if so be we *s.* with him
1 Cor. 4. 12 being persecuted, we *s.*
2 Cor. 1. 6 sufferings which we *s.*
Gal. 3. 4 ye *s.* things in vain ?
Phil. 1. 29 given to believe and *s.*
1 Thes. 3. 4 told you, we should *s.*
2 Thes. 1. 5 kingdom, for wh. ye *s.*
1 Tim. 4. 10 we both labour and *s.*
2 Tim. 2. 12 If we *s.*, we sh. reign
Heb. 13. 12 J. *s.* without the gate
1 Pet. 2. 21 Christ also *s.* for us
Jas. 5. 10 an exam. of *s.* affliction
Jude 7 example, *s.* vengeance of
Rev. 2. 20 bec. thou *s.* that woman
R. V. Lev. 22. 16 cause ; Lev. 19.
17 ; Prov. 19. 19 ; Mat. 17. 17 ;
Mark 9. 19 ; Luke 9. 41 ; 1 Cor. 9.
12 ; 2 Cor. 11. 19, 20 ; Heb. 13.
22 bear, or bear with ; Luke 8. 32
give leave ; 12. 39 left ; 1 Cor. 4.
12 ; 2 Tim. 2. 12 endure ; 1 Tim.
2. 12 permit ; 4. 10 strive.

Suffering. *Affliction.*
Rom. 8. 18 I reckon that the *s.* of
2 Cor. 1. 5 as *s.* of Christ abound in
Phil. 3. 10 fellowship of his *s.* being
Col. 1. 24 rejoice in my *s.* for you
Heb. 2. 9 *s.* of death, crown. wi. glo.
1 Pet. 4. 13 are partakers of C's. *s.*

Suffice. *Be enough.*
Num. 11. 22 sh. herds be sl. to *s.*
Deut. 3. 26 Let it *s.* ; speak no more
Judg. 21. 14 wives, they *s.* th. not
Ruth 2. 14 she did eat, and was *s.*
1 K. 20. 10 dust of Samaria shall *s.*
John 14. 8 Lord, show us F., it *s.* us
1 Pet. 4. 3 For the time past may *s.*

Sufficiency. *Enough, adequacy.*
Job 20. 22 In the fulness of his *s.*
2 Cor. 3. 5 but our *s.* is of God

Sufficient. *Enough, adequate.*
Ex. 36. 7 the stuff they had was *s.*
Deut. 15. 8 thou shalt lend him *s.*
Prov. 25. 16 eat so much as is *s.* for
Isa. 40. 16 Leban. is not *s.* to burn
Mat. 6. 34 *S.* unto day is evil there.
Luke 14. 28 whether he have *s.* to
John 6. 7 bread is not *s.* for them
2 Cor. 12. 9 My grace is *s.* for thee

Sufficiently. *Enough.*
Isa. 23. 18 to eat *s.* and for clothing

Suit. *Plea.*
2 Sam. 15. 4 ev. man which hath *s.*
Job. 11. 19 many make *s.* unto thee
Outfit, clothing.
Judg. 17. 10 give thee *s.* of apparel
Isa. 3. 22 changeable *s.* of apparel
R. V. Isa. 3. 22 festival robes

Sum (*n.*). *Amount, number.*
Ex. 30. 12 take *s.* of the children
Num. 1. 2 Ta. ye *s.* of congregation
2 Sam. 24. 9 Joab gave *s.* of number
Esth. 4. 7 *s.* of mon. Ham. promised
Ps. 139. 17 O G ! how great is the *s.*
Ezek. 28. 12 Thou sealest up the *s.*
Dan. 7. 1 Daniel told *s.* of dream
Acts 22. 28 Wi. great *s.* obtained I
Heb. 8. 1 *s.* : We have such an high
R. V. Ex. 21. 30 ransom ; Acts 7. 16
price ; Heb. 8. 1 chief point

Sum (*v.*). *Count up.*
2 K. 22. 4 that he may *s.* the silver

Summer. *Summer.*
Gen. 8. 22 *s.* and winter, day and
Judg. 3. 20 Eg. was sit. in *s.* parl.
2 Sam. 16. 1 hundred of *s.* fruits
Ps. 32. 4 turned into drought of *s.*
Prov. 10. 5 th. gath. in *s.* is a wise s.
Isa. 28. 4 as hasty fruits before *s.*
Jer. 8. 20 harvest is past, *s.* is end.
Dan. 2. 35 li. chaff of *s.* threshing
Am. 8. 2 said, A basket of *s.* fruit

Mic. 7. 1 when they gather. *s.* fruit
Zech. 14. 8 in *s.* and w. shall it be
Mat. 24. 32 ye know that *s.* is nigh
Mark 13. 28 ; Luke 21. 30

Sumptuously. *Brilliantly.*
Luke 16. 19 rich man which fared *s.*

Sun. *Sun.*
Gen. 15. 12 when *s.* was going down
Ex. 16. 21 when the *s.* waxed hot, it
Lev. 22. 7. *s.* down, he shall be clean
Num. 2. 3 hang them again. the *s.*
Deut. 4. 19 lest when thou seest *s.*
Josh. 10. 12 *S.*, stand still on Gib.
Judg. 5. 31 that love be as the *s.*
1 Sam. 11. 9 *s.* be hot, ye have help
2 Sam. 2. 24 pursued, *s.* went down
1 K. 22. 36 about going down of *s.*
2 K. 3. 22 *s.* shone upon the water
2 Chr. 18. 34 *s.* going down he died
Neh. 7. 3 not ga. be op. till *s.* hot
Job 8. 16 He is green before the *s.*
Ps. 84. 11 L. G. is a *s.* and shield
Eccl. 1. 9 no new thing under the *s.*
S. of S. 6. 10 fair as moon, clear as *s.*
Isa. 24. 23 then *s.* sh. be ashamed
Jer. 8. 2 spread them before the *s.*
Ezek. 32. 7 I will cov. *s.* wi. cloud
Joel 2. 10 *s.* and moon sh. be dark
Dan. 6. 14 lab. till going down of *s.*
Am. 8. 9 cau. *s.* to go do. at noon
Jonah 4. 8 *s.* did arise. *s.* beat upon
Hab. 3. 11 *s.* and moon stood still
Mic. 3. 6 *s.* go down ov. prophets
Nah. 3. 17 *s.* ariseth they flee away
Mal. 1. 11 fr. rising of *s.*, to going
Mat. 5. 45 he maketh his *s.* to rise
Mark 4. 6 *s.* up, it was scorched
Luke 21. 25 sh. be signs in the *s.*
Acts 2. 20 *s.* sh. be turn. to dark.
1 Cor. 15. 41 th. is one glory of *s.*
Eph. 4. 26 let not *s.* go down on
Jas. 1. 11 the *s.* is no sooner risen
Rev. 6. 12 *s.* became as sackcloth
21. 23 the city had no need of *s.*

Sunrising. *Rising of sun.*
Num. 21. 11 wilderness, toward *s.*
Deut. 4. 41 ; Josh. 1. 15 ; Judg.
20. 43

Sunder. *Apart, in two.*
Ps. 46. 9 cutteth the spear in *s.*
Isa. 27. 9 chalk stones beaten in *s.*
Nah. 1. 13 I will burst bonds in *s.*
Luke 12. 46 and wi' cut him in *s.*
R. V. Luke 12. 46 asunder

Sundered. *Parted.*
Job. 41. 17 stick, they cannot be *s.*

Sundry. R. V. *divers portion.*
Heb. 1. 1 God who at *s.* times and

Sung. *see* **Sing.**

Sup. *Sip up, take supper..*
Hab. 1. 9 their faces shall *s.* up as
Luke 17. 8 ma. ready . . I may *s.*
1 Cor. 11. 25 took cup, when he *s.*
Rev. 3. 20 I will *s.* with him, he
R. V. Hab. 1. 9 set eagerly

Superfluity. R. V. *overflowing.*
Jas. 1. 21 lay apart filthi. and *s.*

Superfluous. *Overmuch.*
Lev. 21. 18 flat nose, anything *s.*
2 Cor. 9. 1 is *s.* for me to wri. you

Superscription. *Written on or over.*
Mat. 22. 20 Whose is image and *s.*
Mark 15. 26 *s.* of his accu. was wr.
Luke 23. 38 *s.* also was written over

Superstition. R. V. *religion.*
Acts 25. 19 questions ag. him of *s.*

Superstitious. *Over reverent.*
Acts 17. 22 in all thi. ye are too *s.*

Supper. *Evening meal.*
Mark 6. 21 Herod made *s.* to lords
Luke 22. 20 also the cup aft. *s.*, say.
John 12. 2 made him *s.* ; and Mar.
1 Cor. 11. 20 not to eat Lord's *s.*
Rev. 19. 9 that are called to the *s.*

Supplant. *Trip, displace.*
Gen. 27. 36 hath *s.* me twice times
Jer. 9. 4 every bro. will utterly *s.*

Supple. R. V. *cleanse.*
Ezek. 16. 4 nei. washed to *s.* thee

Suppliant. *Worshipper.*
Zeph. 3. 10 my *s.* shall bring off.

Supplication. *Entreaty, prayer.*
1 Sam. 13. 12 I have not made *s.*
1 K. 8. 28 have thou respect to his *s.*
2 Chr. 6. 21 hearken to *s.* of serv.

Bsth. 4. 8 make *s.* for her people
Job 8. 5 make thy *s.* to Almighty
Ps. 6. 9 The Lord hath heard my *s.*
Isa. 45. 14 they shall make *s.* to thee
Jer. 3. 21 weeping and *s.* of Israel
Dan. 9. 3 10 seek by prayer and *s.*
Hos. 12. 4 and made *s.* unto him
Zech. 12. 10 spirt of grace and of *s.*
Acts 1. 14 accord in prayer and *s.*
Eph. 6. 18 with all prayer and *s.*
Phil. 4. 6 but in every thing by *s.*
1 Tim. 2. 1 *s.* be made for all men
Heb. 5. 7 he offered prayer and *s.*
Supplied. *See* **Supply.**
Supply (*v.*). *Add to, make full.*
1 Cor. 16. 17 what lacking they *s.*
2 Cor. 9. 12 *s.* want of the saints
Phil. 2. 30 *s.* your lack of service
Eph. 4. 16 that wh. every joint *s.*
R. V. 2 Cor. 9. 12 filleth measure
Supply (*n.*). *Store, supply.*
2 Cor. 8. 14 be a *s.* for their want
Phil. 1. 19 *s.* of spirit of Jesus C.
Support. *Hold up, help.*
Acts 20. 35 ye ought to *s.* the weak
1 Thes. 5. 14 *s.* the weak, be patient
R. V. Acts 20. 35 help
Suppose. *Think, reckon.*
2 Sam. 13. 32 Let not my lord *s.* th.
Mat. 20. 10 they *s.* they should have
Mark 6. 49 *s.* it had been a spirit
Luke 3. 23 as was *s.* son of Joseph
John 20. 15 *s.* him to be gardener
Acts 7. 25 *s.* his breth. would have
1 Cor. 7. 26 I *s.* that this is good
2 Cor. 11. 5 I *s.* I was not behind
Phil. 2. 25 *s.* it necessary to send
1 Tim. 6. 5 *s.* that gain is godliness
1 Pet. 5. 12 a faithful brother as I
R. V. Luke 12. 51 ; 13. 2 ; 1 Cor.
7. 26 ; Heb. 10. 29 think ; 2 Cor.
11. 5 reckon ; 1 Pet. 5. 12 account
him.
Supreme. *Over, above.*
1 Pet. 2. 13 whether to th. king, as *s.*
Sure. *Firm, secure, certain.*
Gen. 23. 17 the borders were made *s.*
Ex. 3. 19 I am *s.* k. will not let you
Num. 32. 23 be *s.* yo. sin will find
1 Sam. 2. 35 will build him *s.* house
2 Sam. 1. 10 was *s.* he could not live
1 K. 11. 38 and build thee a *s.* house
Neh. 9. 38 we make a *s.* covenant
Ps. 19. 7 testimony of the Lord is *s.*
Prov. 6. 3 and make *s.* thy friend
Isa. 33. 16 his waters shall be *s.*
Dan. 4. 26 thy kingdom shall be *s.*
Mat. 27. 64 sepulchre be made *s.*
Luke 10. 11 be ye *s.* of this, that
John 6. 69 we believe and are *s.*
Acts 13. 34 I give *s.* mercies of D.
Rom. 15. 29 I am *s.* when I come
2 Tim. 2. 19 found. of G. stand *s.*
Heb. 6. 19 both *s.* and stedfast, and
2 Pet. 1. 10 ma. call. and election *s.*
R. V. Prov. 6. 3 importune ; Ex. 3.
19 ; 1 Sam. 20. 7 ; Luke 10. 11 ;
John 6. 69 ; 16. 30 ; Rom. 2. 2 ; 15
29 know ; 2 Tim. 2. 19 firm
Surely. *Truly, for, of a certain.*
Gen. 28. 16 *S.* the L. is in this place
Ex. 2. 14 *S.* this thing is known
Num. 14. 35 I will *s.* do it unto all
1 Sam. 15. 32 *S.* bit. of death past
2 Sam. 12. 5 done this shall *s.* die
1 K. 11. 2 *s.* they turn away heart
Job 34. 12 *s.* G. will not do wickedly
Prov. 10. 9 walk. upright. walk. *s.*
Isa. 49. 4 *s.* my judg. is with the L.
Jer. 4. 10 *s.* thou hast deceived this
Mat. 26. 73 *S.* thou art one of them
Mark 14. 70 ; Luke 4. 23 ; John 17.
8 ; Acts 12. 11 ; Heb. 6. 14 ; Rev.
22. 20
R. V. Many changes to, for, of a
truth, etc.
Surety. *Certainty.*
Gen. 15. 13 know of a *s.* thy seed
Acts 12. 11 of a *s.* Lord sent angels
Security, pledge, bail.
Gen. 43. 9 I will be *s.* for him
Job 17. 3 put me in a *s.* with thee
Ps. 119. 122 Be *s.* for thy servant for
Prov. 6. 1 if thou be *s.* for thy friend
Heb. 7. 22 so was Jesus made *s.* of
R. V. Acts 12. 11 truth

Suretyship. *Security, pledge.*
Prov. 11. 15 that hateth *s.* is sure
Surfeiting. *Debauch, headache.*
Luke 21. 34 hearts be everch. wi. *s.*
Surmisings. *Suspicions.*
1 Tim. 6. 4 whereof cometh evil *s.*
Surname (*n.*). *Added name.*
Mat. 10. 3 Leb. whose *s.* was Thad.
Acts 10. 5 Sim whose *s.* is Peter
R. V. Mat. 10. 3 —— ; Acts 15. 37
who was called
Surname (*v.*). *Add name.*
Isa. 44. 5 *s.* himself by name of Is.
Mark 3. 16 And Si on he *s.* Peter
Luke 22. 3 udas *s.* Iscariot, being
Acts 1. 23 Barabbas, wh. was *s.* Jus.
R. V. Luke 22. 3 ; Acts 15. 22 called
Surprise. *Catch hold suddenly.*
Isa. 33. 14 fearfuln. *s.* hypocrites
J r. 48. 41 the strong h lds are *s.*
51. 41 how is the praise of earth *s.*?
Sustain. *Support, uphold.*
Gen. 27. 37 with corn have I *s.* him
1 K. 17. 9 commanded a widow to *s.*
Neh. 9. 1 forty years didst *s.* them
Ps. 3. 5 I awaked, the Lord *s.* me
Prov. 18. 14 spirit of man will *s.*
Isa. 59. 16 righteousness, it *s.* him
R. V. Isa. 59. 16 upheld
Sustenance. *Food. that sustains.*
Judg. 6. 4 Midian. left no *s.* for Is'
2 Sam. 19. 32 Barzillai provided *s.*
Acts 7. 11 our fathers found no *s.*
Swaddle. *Swathe, dandle.*
Lam. 2. 22 those I ha. *s.* and brou.
Ezek. 16. 4 not salted at all, nor *s.*
R. V. Lam. 2. 22 dandled
Swaddling. *Wrapped, swathed.*
Job 38. 9 I ma. darkness a *s.* band
Luke 2. 7 wrapped him in *s.* clothes
Swallow (*v.*). *Take down throat,*
make disappear, devour.
Ex. 7. 12 Aaron's rod *s.* their rod
Num. 16. 30 earth op. mouth and *s.*
Deut. 11. 6 how earth *s.* them up
2 Sam. 17. 16 lest king be *s.* up
Job 5. 5 robber *s.* their substance
Ps. 21. 9 L. sh. *s.* them in his wrath
Prov. 1. 12 *s.* them alive as grave
Eccl. 10. 12 lips of fool *s.* himself
Isa. 25. 8 *s.* up death in victory
Jer. 51. 34 he *s.* me up like dragon
Lam. 2. 2 L. ha. *s.* all habitations
Ezek. 36. 3 they have *s.* you up
Hos. 8. 8 Israel is *s.* up, now shall
Am. 8. 8 how that *s.* up needy
Obad. 16 and they shall *s.* down
Jonah 1. 17 L. prepar. fish to *s.* Jo.
Mat. 23. 24 stra. at gnat, *s.* camel
1 Cor. 15. 54 Death is *s.* up in vic.
2 Cor. 2. 7 such one should be *s.* up
Rev. 12. 16 earth *s.* up the flood
R. V. Job 5. 5 gapeth for ; Hab.
1. 13 devoureth
Swallow (*n.*). *Swallow, pigeon,*
crane.
Ps. 84. 3 the *s.* hath found a nest
Prov. 26. 2 as *s.* by flying, so curse
Isa. 38. 14 Like *s.*, so did I chatter
Jer. 8. 7 crane and *s.* observe times
Swan. R. V. *horned owl.*
Lev. 11. 18 not eaten, *s.* peli., eagle
Deut. 14. 16 not eat, owl. gr. owl, *s.*
Sware. *See* **Swear.**
Swarm. *Company, collection.*
Ex. 8. 21 I will send *s.* of flies on
Judg. 14. 8 a *s.* of bees and honey
Swear. *Make oath, take oath.*
Gen. 21. 24 Abraham said, I will *s.*
Ex. 13. 5 land L. *s.* to thy fathers
Lev. 19. 12 not *s.* by my na. falsely
Num. 30. 2 if man *s.* to bind soul
Deut. 1. 8 possess land wh. L. *s.*
Josh. 6. 22 bring out wom., as ye *s.*
Judg. 15. 12 *S.*, ye will not fall on
1 Sam. 19. 6 Saul *s.*, As L. liveth
2 Sam. 3. 35 Dav. *s.*, So do G. to me
1 K. 1. 30 I *s.* unto thee by L. God
2 K. 25. 24 Geda. *s.* to them, and
2 Chr. 15. 14 they *s.* unto the Lord
Ez. 10. 5 Ezra made all Israel to *s.*
Neh. 13. 25 I made them *s.* by God
Ps. 89. 3 I ha. *s.* unto D. my serv.
Eccl. 9. 2 he that *s.*, as he that fear.
Isa. 3. 7 In that day shall he *s.*
Jer. 38. 16 Zed. *s.* secretly to Jer.

Hos. 4. 15 nei. go up to Beth., nor *s*
Am. 8. 14 *s.* by the sin of Samaria
Mic. 7. 20 perform truth thou ha. *s.*
Zeph. 1. 5 that *s.* by L., *s.* by Mal.
Mat. 5. 34 I say, *S.* not at all, nei.
Mark 14. 71 he began to curse and *s.*
Luke 1. 73 oath he *s.* to our father
Acts 2. 30 knowing that God had *s.*
Heb. 3. 11 So I *s.* in my wrath, if
Jas. 5. 12 *s.* not, neither by heav., nei.
Rev. 10. 6 *s.* by him that liv. for ever
R. V. Ex. 6. 8 lifted up my hand
Swearing. *Adjuration, swearing.*
Lev. 5. 1 soul sin, hear voice of *s.*
Jer. 23. 10 bec. of *s.*, land mourn.
Hos. 4. 2 by *s.*, lying, and stealing
R. V. Lev. 5. 1 adjuration
Swearer. *Who swears.*
Mal. 3. 5 witness against false *s.*
Sweat. *Sweat.*
Gen. 3. 19 in *s.* of face eat bread
Ezek. 44. 18 anything th. causeth *s.*
Luke 22. 44 *s.* as drops of blood
Sweep. *Sweep.*
Judg. 5. 21 riv. Kish. *s.* them away
Prov. 28. 3 *s.* rain leaveth no food
Isa. 14. 23 *s.* it wi. besom of destr.
Jer. 46. 15 Why val. men *s.* away?
Mat 12. 44 he findeth it *s.* and gar.
Luke 15. 8 doth not *s.* the house
Sweet. *Sweet, spiced, pleasing.*
Gen. 8. 21 Lord smelled a *s.* savour
Ex. 30. 7 A. shall burn *s.* incense
Lev. 6. 15 burn on altar for *s.* sav.
Num. 4. 16 to office of El. *s.* incense
2 Sam. 23. 1 D., *s.* psalmist of Isr.
2 Chr. 2. 4 burn bef. him *s.* incense
Neh. 8. 10 eat the fat, drink the *s.*
Esth. 2. 12 six months wi. *s.* odonrs
Job 21. 33 clods of valley sh. be *s.*
Ps. 55. 14 took *s.* counsel together
Prov. 9. 17 stolen waters are *s.*, and
Eccl. 5. 12 sleep of lab. man is *s.*
S. of S. 2. 14 *s.* thy voice, thy count.
Isa. 5. 20 put bitter for *s.*, *s.* for bit.
Jer. 6. 20 *s* cane from far country
Mic. 6. 15 *s.* wine, but not dr. wine
Mark 16. 1 brought *s.* spices, that
2 Cor. 2. 15 are unto G. a *s.* savour
Eph. 5. 2 sacri. to G. for *s.* savour
Phil. 4. 18 an odour of a *s.* smell
Jac. 3. 11 pl., *s.* waters and bitter?
Rev. 10. 9 in thy mouth *s.* as honey.
R. V. Jer. 6. 20 pleasing ; Mark
16. 1
Sweeter. *More sweet.*
Judg. 14. 18 what is *s.* than honey?
Ps. 19. 12 thy word *s.* than honey
Sweetly. *Agreeably.*
Job 24. 20 worms sh. feed *s.* on him
S. of S. 7. 9 wine, tha. goeth down *s*
R. V. S. of S. 7. 9 smoothly
Sweetness. *Sweetness.*
Judg. 14. 14 out of strong came *s*
Prov. 16. 21 *s.* of lips incr. learning
Ezek. 3. 3 in mouth as honey for *s.*
Swell. *Make to rise, dilate.*
Num. 5. 21 thigh rot. and belly to *s.*
Deut. 8. 4 neither did thy foot *s.*
Neh. 9. 41 forty years feet *s.* not
Swelling. *Rising, puffing up.*
Ps. 46. 3 mount. shake wi. the *s.*
Isa. 30. 13 as a breach, *s.* in a wall
Jer 12. 5 how do in *s.* of Jordan?
2 Cor. 12. 20 lest there be *s.*, tumul.
2 Pet. 2. 18 they speak gr. *s.* words
Jude 16 mouth speaketh *s.* words
R. V. Jer. 12. 5 ; 49. 19 ; 50. 44
pride
Swept. *See* **Sweep.**
Swerve. *Turn from course.*
1 Tim. 1. 6 having *s.* turned aside
Swift. *Speedy, rapid, quick.*
Deut. 28. 49 nation, *s.* as eag. flieth
1 Chr. 12. 8 *s.* as roes on mountains
Job 9. 26 passed away as *s.* ships
Prov. 6. 18 feet *s.* run. to mischief
Eccl 9. 11 race is not to *s.*, nor bat.
Isa. 18. 2 Go, .. messeng., to nations
Jer. 2. 23 *s.* dromedary traversing
Am. 2. 14 flight *s.* perish from *s.*
Mic. 1. 13 bind chariot to *s.* beast
Mal. 3. 5 witness ag. sorcerers
Rom. 3. 15 feet *s.* to shed blood
Jas. 1. 19 every man be *s* to hear
2 Pet. 2. 1 sh. bring *s.* destruction

Swim. *Make to float, swim.*
2 K. 6. 6 thither, and the iron did *s*.
Ps. 6. 6 night ma. I my bed to *s*.
Isa. 25. 11 as he that *s*. spreadeth
Ezek. 47. 5 waters to *s*. in a river
Acts 27. 42 lest any should *s*. out
Swine. *Hog, hogs.*
Lev. 11. 7 *s*. though he divide hoof
Deut. 14. 8 *s*. bec. he divide. hoof
Prov. 11. 22 As jewel in a *s*. snout
Isa. 65. 4 eat *s*. flesh, and broth of
Mat. 7. 6 nei. cast pearls before *s*.
Mark 5. 11 was a herd of *s*. feeding
Luke 8. 33 devils entered into *s*.
R. V. Mat. 8. 32 ——; Mark 5. 14
  them
Swollen. *Swelled.*
Acts 28. 6 looked wh. he sh. ha. *s*.
Swoon. *Enfeeble, faint.*
Lam. 2. 11 children *s*. in the street
2. 12 they *s*. as the wounded in str.
Sword. *Sword, weapon.*
Gen. 24. 70 by thy *s*. sh. thou live
Ex. 5. 21 put a *s*. in their hand
Lev. 26. 25 I will bring *s*. on you
Num. 22. 29 were *s*. in mine hand
Deut. 32. 25 *s*. without, terror with.
Josh. 5. 13 stood with his *s*. drawn
Judg. 7. 18 *s*. of the L. and Gideon
1 Sam. 13. 22 neither *s*. nor spear
2 Sam. 1. 22 *s*. of S. returned not
1 K. 3. 24 bring *s*., they brought *s*.
2 K. 11. 20 they slew Ath. with *s*.
1 Chr. 10. 4 S. took *s*., fell upon it
2 Chr. 20. 9 ev. com. on us, as th. *s*.
Ez. 9. 7 kings are delivered to *s*.
Neh. 4. 18 ev. one had his *s*. gird.
Esth 9. 5 Jews smote ene. with *s*.
Job 5. 15 he sav. the poor from *s*.
Ps. 22. 20 Deliv. my soul fr. the *s*.
Prov. 5. 4 end, sharp as two edg. *s*.
S. of S. 3. 8., hold *s*., expert in war
Isa. 1. 20 ye sh. be devour. with *s*.
Jer. 2. 30 yo'1 *s*. devoured prophets
Lam. 5. 9 bec. of *s*. of wilderness
Ezek. 5. 17 I will bring *s*. upon thee
Dan. 11. 33 they shall fall by the *s*.
Hos. 2. 18 I will break bow and *s*.
Joel 3. 10 Beat ploughshares into *s*.
Am. 7. 11 Jerobo. sh. die by the *s*.
Mic. 4. 3 sh. beat *s*. into ploughsh.
Nah. 2. 13 *s*. sh. devour young lions
Zeph. 2. 12 Ethio. be slain by my *s*.
Hag. 2. 22 ev. one by *s*. of his bro.
Zech. 13. 7 Awake, *s*.. ag. my shep.
Mat. 10. 34. not send peace, but a *s*.
Mark 14. 47 one of them drew a *s*.
Lnke 21. 24 shall fall by edge of *s*.
John 18. 10 Pet. having a *s*. drew it
Acts 16. 27 he drew his *s*. and wo.
Rom. 13. 4 he beareth not *s*. in vain
Eph. 6. 17 *s*. of spirit, is the word
Heb. 2. 12 sharper than two edg. *s*.
Rev. 6. 4 was giv. to him a great *s*.
R. V. Job 2. 25 point; Joel 2. 8
  weapons
Sworn. *See* **Swear.**
Sycamine. *Mulberry or fig.*
Luke 17. 6 say to *s*., Be plucked
Sycamore. *Mulberry or fig.*
2 K. 10. 27 cedars ma. he to be as *s*.
1 Chr. 27. 28 over *s*. tr. was Baal-h.
2 Chr. 1. 15 cedar tr. made he as *s*.
Ps. 78. 47 He destroyed their *s*. tr.
Isa. 9. 10 the *s*. are cut down, but
Am. 7. 14 and a gatherer of *s*. fruit
Luke 19. 4 Zaccheus climbed *s*. t.
Synagogue. *Meeting place.*
Ps. 74. 8 they ha. burned all *s*. of G.
Mat. 4. 23 Jes. went teaching in *s*.
Mark 1. 21 he entered *s*. and taught
Luke 4. 16 he went into *s*. on sab.
John 18. 20 I ever taught in the *s*.
Acts 6. 9 there arose cert. of the *s*.
Rev. 2. 9 but are the *s*. of Satan
R. V. Acts 13. 42 ——

T

Taber. *Beat daintily.*
Nah. 2. 7 doves, *t*. on their breasts
Tabernacle. *Tent, covering, dwelling place,*
Ex. 27. 21 the *t*. of the congregation
Lev. 1. 1 L. spake out of *t*. of cong.
Num. 9. 17 cloud was ta. up fr. *t*.
Deut. 16. 13 observe the feast of *t*.

Josh. 22. 19 wherein L.'s *t*. dwell
2 Sam. 7. 6 waiked in tent and *t*.
1 K. 2. 28 Joab fled to *t*. of Lord
1 Chr. 6. 48 Levites for serv. of *t*.
2 Chr. 1. 5 put brazen altar before *t*.
Ez. 3. 4 They kept the feast of *t*.
Job 18. 6 light shall be dark in his *t*.
Ps. 61. 4 I'will abide in thy *t*. for ev.
Prov. 14. 11 *t*. of upright sh. flourish
Isa. 4. 6 shall be *t*. for a shadow
Jer. 10. 20 My *t*. is spoiled, all my
Lam. 2. 4 in *t*. of daughter of Zion
Ezek. 37. 27 my *t*. sh. be with them
Dan. 11. 45 he sh. plant *t*. of palace
Hos. 9. 6 thorns sh. be in their *t*.
Am. 9. 11 will raise up *t*. of David
Mal. 2. 12 L. cut off man out of *t*.
Mat. 17. 4 let us ma. here three *t*.
Mark 9. 5; Luke 9. 33
John 7. 2 feast of *t*. was at hand
Acts 7. 43 ye took up *t*. of Moloch
2 Cor. 5. 1 if house of *t*. be dissolved
Heb. 8. 2 true *t*., wh. Lord pitched
2 Pet. 1. 14 I must put off my *t*.
Rev. 21. 3 *t*. of God is with men
R. V. In O. T. nearly always, tent
  or tents; Luke 16. 9; Acts 7. 46
  habitation
Table. *Tablet, board, table.*
Ex. 24. 12 I give thee *t*. of stone
Lev. 24. 6 six in a row, upon pure *t*.
Num. 3. 31 their charge sh. be the *t*.
Deut. 4. 13 he wrote th. on two *t*.
Judg. 1. 7 k. gath. meat under my *t*.
1 Sam. 20. 34 J. arose fr. *t*. in anger
2 Sam. 9. 7 sh. eat bread at my *t*.
1 K. 4. 27 all that came to Sol's *t*.
2 K. 4. 10 set for him bed and *t*.
1 Chr. 28. 16 likewise sil. for the *t*.
2 Chr. 4. 8 He made also ten *t*., and
Neh. 5. 17 at my *t*. hun a. fifty Jews
Job. 36. 16 wh. should be set on *t*.
Ps. 78. 19 can G. furn. *t*. in wildern.
Prov. 9. 2 she hath furnished her *t*.
S. of S. 1. 12 While k. sit. at his *t*.
Isa. 21. 5 Prep. *t*., watch in watch
Jer. 17. 1 grav. on *t*. of their heart
Ezek. 39. 20 shall be filled at my *t*.
Dan. 11. 27 sh. speak lies at one *t*.
Hab. 2. 2 make it plain on *t*. that he
Mal. 1. 12 *t*. of the L. is polluted
Mat. 21. 12 overthrew *t*. of mon. ch.
Mark 7. 28 dogs under *t*. eat of
Luke 22. 21 betrayeth me is on *t*.
John 13. 28 no man at the *t*. knew
Acts 6. 2 leave word of G. a. serv. *t*.
Rom. 11. 9 Let their *t*. be ma. snare
1 Cor. 10. 21 cannot be par. of L.'s *t*.
2 Cor. 3. 3 not in *t*. of sto., but fl.
Heb. 9. 2 wherein was *t*. of covenant
R. V. Isa. 30. 8; Luke 1. 63 tablet;
  Mark 7. 4 ——; John 12. 2 meat
Tablet. *Bracelet, buckle.*
Ex. 35. 22 men and wom. brought *t*.
Num. 31. 50 oblation of rings and *t*.
Scent box
Isa. 3. 20 I will take away the *t*.
Writing tablet.
Luke 1. 63 he asked for a writing *t*.
R. V. Ex. 35. 22; Num. 31. 50 arm-
  lets; Isa. 3. 20 perfume boxes
Tabret. *Timbrel.*
Gen. 31. 27 have sent thee with *t*.
1 Sam. 10. 5 from high place with *t*.
Job 17. 6 aforetime I was as a *t*.
Isa. 24. 8 The mirth of *t*. ceaseth
Jer. 31. 4 again be adorned with *t*.
Ezek. 28. 13 workmanship of thy *t*.
R. V. 1 Sam. 10. 5; 18. 6 timbrel
Taches. R. V. *clasps.*
Ex. 26. 6 make fifty *t*. of gold and
  26. 11, 33; 35. 11; 36. 13; 39. 33
Tackling. *Ship gear.*
Isa. 33. 23 Thy *t*. are loosed, could
Acts 27. 19 the third day cast out *t*.
Tail. *Rear, caudal part.*
Ex. 4. 4 put out hand, take it by *t*.
Deut. 28. 13 L. sh. ma. thee h., not *t*.
Judg. 15 4. foxes, turned *t*. to *t*.
Job 40. 17 He moveth his *t*. like a
Isa. 9. 14 cut off tr. Is. head and *t*.
Rev. 9. 10 had *t*. like unto scorpions
Take. *Take, receive, capture.*
Gen. 2. 15 L. G. *t*. the man, and put
Ex. 6. 7 I will *t*. you for a people
Lev. 8. 10 M. *t*. the anointing oil

Num. 32. 42 Nobah went and *t*. K.
Deut. 1. 23 I *t*. twelve men of you
Josh. 10. 28 Josh. *t*. Mak., and sm.
Judg. 1. 18 Judah *t*. Gaza wi. coast
Ruth 4. 13 Boaz *t*. Ruth, she was w.
1 Sam. 14. 47 Saul *t*. kingd. over Is.
2 Sam. 5. 7 D. *t*. stronghold of Zion
1 K. 9. 16 Phar. had go. and *t*. Gezer
2 K. 2. 8 Elijah *t*. his mantle, and
1 Chr. 10. 4 Saul *t*. sword, fell on it
2 Chr. 16. 6 Asa the k. *t*. all Judah
Ez. 10. 44 these had *t*. strange wives
Neh. 5. 2 we *t*. up corn for th., that
Esth. 6. 10 Make haste, *t*. the ap.
Job 1. 21 Lord gave, the Lord ha. *t*.
Ps. 81. 2 *T*. psalm, bring hith. tim.
Prov. 1. 19 which *t*. away *l*ife of own
  16. 32 better than he that *t*. city
Eccl. 5. 15 shall *t*. noth. of his labour
S. of S. 5. 7 Keepers *t*. away my v.
Isa. 8. 4 spoil of Samaria shall be *t*.
Jer. 3. 14 I will *t*. you one of a city
Lam. 5. 13 They *t*. yo. men to grind
Ezek. 3. 12 the spirit *t*. me up, and
Dan. 11. 31 *t*. away daily sacrifice
Hos. 2. 17 *t*. away names of Baalim
Joel 3. 5 ye have *t*. my sil. and go.
Am. 5. 11 *t*. fr. him burd. of wheat
Jonah 1. 15 *t*. Jonah, cast him forth
Mic. 2. 9 children have ye *t*. away
Hab. 2. 6 *t*. up a parable against
Zeph. 3. 15 L. hath *t*. away judgm.
Zech. 6. 11 *t*. sil. and go., make cro.
Mal. 2. 3 one sh. *t*. you away wi. it
Mat. 5. 40 *t*. coat, let him ha. cloak
Mark 2. 9 *t*. up thy bed, go thy way
Luke 9. 3 *T*. noth. for your journey
John 1. 29 Lamb of G., wh. *t*. away
Acts 1. 20 His bishopric let ano. *t*.
Rom. 7. 8 *t*. occas. by the comman.
1 Cor. 6. 15 sh. I *t*. members of C.
2 Cor. 11. 8 I robbed ch., *t*. wages
Gal. 5. 15 *t*. heed ye be not consum.
Phil. 2. 7 *t*. on him form of servant
1 Thes. 2. 17 *t*. fr. you for short time.
2 Thes. 2. 7 till he be *t*. out of way
1 Tim. 3. 5 how *t*. care of church
2 Tim. 2. 26 who are *t*. captive by
Heb. 9. 9 he *t*. blood of calves and
2 Pet. 1. 19 do well that ye *t*. heed
1 John 3. 5 manif. to *t*. away sins
Rev. 5. 7 he came and *t*. the book
R. V. The frequent changes are
  mostly due to context; as, Mat.
  6. 25 take no thought, becomes,
  be not anxious, etc.
Taking. *Taking.*
2 Chr. 19. 7 respect. nor *t*. of gifts
Jer. 50. 46 noise of *t*. of Babylon
Hos. 11. 3 go, *t*. them by their arms
Tale. *Narrative, story, talk.*
Ps. 90. 9 spend years as a *t*. told
Ezek. 22. 9 carry *t*. to shed blood
Luke 24. 11 th. words seemed as *t*.
Number, count.
1 Sam. 18. 27 foreski. in *t*. to king
1 Chr. 9. 28 bring vessels in by *t*.
Quantity. measure.
Ex. 5. 8 And the *t*. of brick which
R. V. Luke 24. 11 talk
Tale-bearer. *Slanderer, whisperer.*
Lev. 19. 16 not go up and do. as *t*. b.
Prov. 11. 13 A *t*. b. reveal. secrets
  18. 8 words of *t*. b. are as wounds
R. V. Prov. 18. 8; 26. 20, 22
  whisperer
Talent. *Weight, cake, balance.*
Ex. 25. 39 Of *t*. of gold sh. make it
2 Sam. 12. 30 crown, wei. thereof *t*
1 K. 9. 14 Hir. sent to k. six sc. *t*.
2 K. 15. 19 Men. ga. Pul thous. *t*.
1 Chr. 19. 6 Ammon sent thous. *t*.
2 Chr. 25. 9 what do for hundr. *t*.
Ez. 8. 26 I weighed .. *t*. of silver
Esth. 3. 9 I will pay ten thous. *t*.
Zech. 5. 7 there was lifted up a *t*.
Mat. 18. 24 one owed ten thous. *t*.
  25. 15, 16, 20, 22, 24, 25, 28
Rev. 16. 21 ev. stone weight of a *t*.
Talitha. *Maiden, damsel.*
Mark 5. 41 he said unto her, *T*. cu.
Talk (*n*.). *Speech, mouth, lip.*
Job 11. 2 man full of *t*. be justified?
Prov. 14. 23 *t*. tendeth to penury
Eccl. 10. 13 end of *t*. is mischievo.

Mat. 22. 15 mi. entangle him in *t.*

Talk (*v.*).   *Speak, meditate.*
Gen. 4. 8 C. *t.* with A. his brother
Ex. 33. 9 the Lord *t.* with Moses
Num. 11. 17 I will come do. and *t.*
Deut. 5. 4 L. *t.* wi. you face to face
Judg. 6. 17 show me a sign thou *t.*
1 San. 2. 3 *T.* no more so proudly
1 K. 1. 14 while thou *t.* with king
2 K. 2. 11 as they went on, and *t.*
1 Chr. 16. 9 *t.* ye of all his works
2 Chr. 25. 16 it came to pass as he *t.*
Esth. 6. 14 while they were *t.* with
Job 13. 7 will ye *t.* deceitfully?
Ps. 69. 26 and they *t.* to the grief of
Prov. 24. 2 their lips *t.* of mischief
Jer. 12. 1 let me *t.* of thy judgments
Ezek. 33. 30 chil. of thy peo. are *t.*
Dan. 9. 22 informed me, *t.* with me
Zech. 1. 9 angel that *t.* wi. me said
Mat. 17. 3 appeared M. and E. *t.*
Mark 6. 50 he *t.* with them, and sai.
Luke 24. 14 they *t.* of these things
John 4. 2 marv. he *t.* with woman
Acts 20. 11 *t.*, even till break of day
Rev. 4. 1 as a trumpet *t.* with me
R. V. Several changes and nearly
  all to, speak or spake
Talker.   *Who talks.*
Ezek. 36. 3 taken up in the lips of *t.*
Tit. 1. 10 For there are many vain *t.*
Talking.   *Talking, musing.*
1 K. 18. 27 either is *t.*, or pursuing
Job 29. 9 princes refrained from *t.*
Eph. 5. 4 filthiness, nor foolish *t.*
R. V. 1 K. 18. 27 musing
Tall.   *High.*
Deut. 2. 10 peo. great, many, and *t.*
2 K. 19. 23 ; Isa. 37. 24 cut down *t.*
  cedars
Taller.   *Higher.*
Deut. 1. 28 peo. greater and *t.* than
Tame.   *Subdue, tame.*
Mark 5. 4 neither could man *t.* him
Jas. 3. 8 the tongue can no man *t.*
Tanner.   *Who tans hides.*
Acts 9. 43 Pe. tarried with Si. a *t.*
  10. 6 He lodgeth with Simon a *t.*
Tapestry.   *Covering.*
Prov. 7. 16 decked bed wi. cov. of *t.*
  31. 22 She maketh coverings of *t.*
Tare (*v.*).   See **Tear.**
Tares.   *Darnel, weed.*
Mat. 13. 25 his enemy sowed *t.* am'g
  13. 26, 27, 29, 30, 36, 38, 40
Target.   *Javelin, buckler.*
1 Sam. 17. 6 of brass bet. should.
1 K. 10. 16 Sol. made two hundr. *t.*
2 Chr. 14. 8 army that bare *t.* and
R. V. 1 Sam. 17. 6 javelin ; 2 Chr.
  14. 8 bucklers
Tarry.   *Stay, delay, abide.*
Gen. 19. 2 *t.* all night, wash feet
Ex. 24. 14 *T.* for us, until we come
Lev. 14. 8 *t.* out of tent seven days
Num. 22. 19 *t.* ye here this night
Judg. 5. 28 why *t.* wheels of chariot?
Ruth 3. 13 *T.* this night, and in m.
1 Sam. 10. 8 he *t.* sev. days accord.
2 Sam. 18. 14 said Joab, I may not *t.*
1 K. 9. 3 open the door, flee, *t.* not
1 Chr. 19. 5 *T.* in Jer. till beards gr.
Ps. 40. 17 art my help, make no *t.*
Prov. 23. 30 that *t.* long at the wine
Isa. 46. 13 m salvation shall not *t.*
Jer. 14. 8 turyth to *t.* fosr a night
Mic. 5. 7 as the showers that *t.* not
Hab. 2. 3 vision come, it will not *t*
Mat. 25. 5 While the bridegroom *t.*
Mark 14. 34 *t.* here, watch with me
Luke 2. 43 Jesus *t.* in Jerusalem
John 3. 22 he *t.* wi. th. and baptiz.
Acts 9. 43 P. *t.* many days in Joppa
1 Cor. 16. 8 I will *t.* at Ephesus till
1 Tim. 3. 15 if I *t.* long thou may.
Heb. 10. 37 will come, and not *t.*
R. V. Lev. 14. 8 dwell ; 1 Sam. 14. 2 ;
  2 Sam. 15. 29 ; 2 K. 14. 10 ; Mat.
  26. 38 ; Mark 14. 34 ; Luke 24. 29 ;
  John 4. 40 ; Acts 9. 43 ; 18. 20
  abide or abode ; Ps. 101. 7 be estab-
  lished ; Hab. 2. 3 delay ; Acts 20.
  5 ; 27. 33 ; 1 Cor. 11. 38 wait or
  wating ; Acts 15. 33 spent time ;
  Acts 20. 15 ——.
Task.   *Matter, part.*

Ex. 5. 13 Fulfil works, your daily *t.*
  5. 14 Wherefore not fulfil your *t.*
Task=master.   *Overseer.*
Ex. 1. 11 they did set ov. them *t. m.*
  3. 7 heard cry by reason of th. *t. m.*
Taste (*n.*).   *Taste, palate.*
Ex. 16. 31 manna, *t.* of it like wafers
Num. 11. 8 *t.* was as *t.* of fresh oil
Job 6. 6 any *t.* in while of an egg?
Ps. 119. 103 sweet thy word to *t.*
Prov. 24. 13 honey co., sweet to *t.*
S. of S. 2. 3 fruit was sweet to *t.*
Jer. 48. 11 his *t.* remained in him
Taste (*v.*).   *Taste, experience.*
1 Sam. 14. 24 none of peo. *t.* any fo.
2 Sam. 19. 35 can ser. *t.* wh. I eat
Job 12. 11 doth not mouth *t* meat
Ps. 34. 8 O *t.* and see Lord is good
Dan. 5. 2 Belshaz. whiles he *t.* wi.
Jonah 3. 7 nor flock *t.* any thing
Mat. 27. 34 wh. he had *t.* thereof
Mark 9. 1 some sh. not *t.* of death
Luke 14. 24 none bidden *t.* of sup.
John 2. 9 ruler *t.* wat. made wine
Col. 2. 21 touch not, *t.* not, han. not
Heb. 2. 9 sho. *t.* death for ev. man
  6. 4 have *t.* of the heavenly gift
1 Pet. 2. 3 If so be ye have *t.* that
Tattler.   *Idle talker.*
1 Tim. 5. 13 not only idle, but *t.*
Taught.   See **Teach.**
Taunt.   *Reproach, byword.*
Jer. 24. 9 I deliver them to be a *t.*
Ezek. 5. 15 so it be repro. and *t.*
Taunting.   *Reproving.*
Hab. 2. 6 take up *t.* proverb against
Tax (*v.*).   *Register, value, levy.*
2 K. 23. 35 Jehoiakin *t.* the land
Luke 2. 1 decree that world be *t.*
  2. 3 all went to be *t.*, ev. one into
R. V. Luke 2. 1, 3, 5 enrol
Tax (*n.*).   *Exaction.*
Dan. 11. 20 stand up a raiser of *t.*
Taxation.   *Registry, valuation.*
2 K. 23. 35 exacted accor. to his *t.*
Taxing.   R. V. *enrolment.*
Luke 2. 2 *t.* first made when Cy.
Acts 5. 37 rose up J. in days of *t.*
Teach.   *Make to know, teach.*
Ex. 4. 15 I they what ye shall do
Lev. 10. 11 that ye *t.* chil. of Israel
Deut. 33. 10 *t.* Jac. thy judgments
Judg. 13. 8 *t.* us what we shall do
1 Sam. 12. 23 I will *t.* good and ri.
2 Sam. 1. 18 bade *t.* chil. of Judah
1 K. 8. 36 *t.* them the good way
2 K. 17. 28 *t.* they sh. fear the L.
2 Chr. 6. 27 *t.* them the good way
Ez. 7. 10 to *t.* in Israel statutes
Neh. 8. 9 Levites that *t.* the people
Job 6. 24 *T.*, I will hold tongue
Ps. 27. 11 *T.* me thy way, O Lord
Prov. 4. 11 I ha. *t.* thee in wisdom
Eccl. 12. 9 preacher was wise, he *t.*
Isa. 2. 3 he will *t.* us of his ways
Jer. 9. 5 they *t.* tongue to speak
Ezek. 44. 23 *t.* my people the differ.
Dan. 1. 4 whom they mi. *t.* learning
Hos. 10. 11 Eph. is heifer that is *t.*
Mic. 3. 11 priests thereof *t.* for hire
Hab. 2. 19 dumb st., Arise, it sh. *t.*
Mat. 4. 23 *t.* in synag. and praying
  5. 2 opened his mouth, and *t.* them
Mark 1. 21 he entered synag. and *t.*
  9. 31 he *t.* disciples, and said unto
Luke 4. 31 he *t.* them on sab. days
  12. 12 Holy Ghost shall *t.* you
John 7. 14 J. went into tem. and *t.*
  8. 28 as my Father hath *t.* me, I
Acts 1. 1 Jesus began to do and *t.*
Rom. 2. 21 another, *t.* not self?
1 Cor. 11. 14 Doth not nature *t.* you
Gal. 1. 12 nei. *t.*, but by revelation
Eph. 4. 21 heard, and have been *t.*
Col. 1. 28 warning every man, and *t.*
2 Thes. 2. 15 tradi. ye have been *t.*
1 Tim. 2. 12 I suffer not wom. to *t.*
2 Tim. 2. 2 who shall be able to *t.*
Tit. 1. 11 *t.* things, they ought not
Heb. 5. 12 he ha. need th. one *t.* you
1 John 2. 27 ye need not man *t.* you
Rev. 2. 14 *t.* Balac to cast st. before
R. V. 1 Sam. 12. 23 ; Ps. 25. 8, 12 ;
  Acts 22. 3 ; 1 Cor. 14. 19 instruct ;
  Jer. 28. 16 ; 29. 32 spoken ; Mat.
  28. 19 make disciples ; Acts 16. 21

---

set forth ; Tit. 2. 4 train
Teacher.   *Who teaches.*
1 Chr. 25. 8 small as great, *t.* as the
Ps. 119. 99 more underst. than *t.*
Prov. 5. 13 not obeyed voice of *t.*
Isa. 30. 20 thine eyes shall be thy *t*
Hab. 2. 18 molten image, *t.* of lies
John 3. 2 we know thou art a *t.*
Acts 13. 1 were certain proph. and *t.*
Rom. 2. 20 confident thou art a *t.*
1 Cor. 12. 29 all prophets? are all *t*
Eph. 4. 11 and some, pastors and *t.*
1 Tim. 2. 7 *t.* of Gentiles in faith
2 Tim. 1. 11 and *t.* of the Gentiles
Tit. 2. 3 not giv. to wine, *t.* of good
Heb. 5. 12 forti. ye ought to be *t.*
2 Pet. 2. 1 be false *t.* among you
R. V. Isa. 43. 27 interpreters
Teaching.   *Instructing.*
2 Chr. 15. 3 Is. without *t.* priests
Jer. 32. 33 rising early and *t.* them
Mat. 4. 23 Jesus went about Gal. *t*
Mark 7. 7 *t.* commandment of men
Luke 23. 5 *t.* throughout all Jewry
Acts 5. 25 the apostles *t.* the peo.
Rom. 12. 7 he that teacheth on *t.*
Col. 1. 28 warning and *t.* ev. man
Tit. 1. 11 *t.* things they ought not
Tear.   *Cleave, rend, pull violently,*
  lacerate.
Gen. 44. 28 Surely he is *t.* in pieces
Ex. 22. 13 If it be *t.* in pieces, let
Deut. 33. 20 *t.* arm with crown of
Judg. 8. 7 I will *t.* yo. fl. wi. thor.
2 Sam. 13. 31 K. arose, *t.* his gar.
1 K 13. 28 not eat. car., nor *t.* ass
2 K. 2. 24 *t.* forty two children of
Job 16. 9 He *t.* me in his wrath
Ps. 7. 2 Lest he *t.* soul like lion
Isa. 5. 25 carcases were *t.* in streets
Jer. 15. 3 sw. to slay, dogs to *t.*
Ezek. 13. 21 yo. kerchiefs will I *t.*
Hos. 5. 14 I will tear and go away
Am. 1. 11 his anger did *t.* perpetu.
Mic. 5. 8 young lion *t.* in pieces
Nah. 2. 12 lion did *t.* enough for
Zech. 11. 16 shepherd sh. *t.* claws
Mal. 1. 13 bro. that which was *t.*
Mark 1. 26 when uncl. sp. had *t. h.*
Luke 9. 39 *t.* him that he foameth
  9. 42 devil threw him, and *t.* him
R. V. 2 Sam. 13. 31 rent ; Jer. 16.
  17 break bread ; Mark 9. 18 dash-
  eth down ; Isa. 5. 25 refuse ; Mal.
  1. 13 taken by violence
Tears.   *Tears.*
2 K. 20. 5 heard prayer, seen thy *t.*
Esth. 8. 3 Esther besought him w. *t.*
Job 16. 20 mine eye pour. out *t.*
Ps. 6. 6 I water my couch with *t.*
  42. 3 My *t.* have been my meat
  126. 5 th. sow in *t.* sh. reap in joy
Eccl. 4. 1 behold the *t.* of such as
Isa. 16. 9 I will water thee with *t.*
  25. 8 Lord G. will wipe away *t.*
Jer. 9. 1 mine eyes a fountain of *t.*
  13. 17 weep, and run down wi. *t.*
Lam. 1. 2 her *t.* are on her cheeks
  2. 18 let *t.* run down like a river
Ezek. 24. 16 nei. sh. thy *t.* run down
Mal. 2. 13 cover. altar of L. with *t.*
Mark 9. 24 father cried, said wi. *t.*
Luke 7. 38 to wash his feet with *t.*
  7. 44 she washed my feet with *t.*
Acts 20. 19 Serving the L. with *t.*
2 Cor. 2. 4 I wrote you wi. many *t*
2 Tim. 1. 4 being mindful of thy *t*
Heb. 5. 7 offered supplica. with *t.*
Rev. 7. 17 G. sh. wipe away all *t.*
R. V. Mark 9. 24 ——
Teat.   *Breast, teat.*
Isa. 32. 12 they shall lament for *t.*
Ezek. 23. 3 bruised *t.* of th. virgins
  23. 21 bruising thy *t.* by Egyptia.
Tedious.   *Cutting in, tiresome.*
Acts 24. 4 that I be not *t.* to thee
Teeth.   See **Tooth.**
Teil Tree.   R. V. *terebinth.*
Isa. 6. 13 as a *t. t.*, and as an oak
Tekel.   *Weighed.*
Dan. 5. 27 *T.* ; art weig in balances
Tell.   *Lift voice, say, speak, talk*
  out, declare.
Gen. 3. 11 Who *t.* th. thou wa. nak.
Ex. 4. 28 M. *t.* A. all words of L.
Lev. 14. 35 that owneth house sh. *t.*

Num. 11. 27 ran young man and *t.*
Deut. 32. 7 elders, th. will *t.* thee
Josh. 7. 19 *t.* me wh. th. hast done
Judg. 9. 7 when th. *t.* it to Jotham
Ruth 3. 4 he will *t.* thee what to do
1 Sam. 3 . 18 Sam. *t.* him ev. whit
2 Sam. 1. 20 *T.* it not in Gath, pub.
1 K. 10. 3 Sol. *t.* her all questions
2 K. 4. 2 What do for thee? *t.* me
1 Chr. 17. 10 I *t.* thee L. will build
2 Chr. 34. 18 scribe *t.* king, saying
Ez. 8. 17 *t.* them what should say
Neh. 2. 12 nei. *t.* I any man what
Esth. 4. 12 *t.* to Mor. Esth's words
Job 1. 15 I only am escaped to *t.*
Ps. 50. 12 If hungry, I would not *t.*
Prov. 30. 4 na., if thou canst *t.* ?
Eccl. 6. 12 who can *t.* what sh. 'be
S. of S. 1. 7 *T.* me, wh. soul loveth
Isa. 19. 12 let th. *t.* me now, and let
Jer. 48. 20 t. Ar., th. M. is spoiled
Ezek. 24. 19 not *t.* us what things
Dan. 2. 4 *t,* thy servant the dream
Joel 1. 3 *T.* ye your children of it
Jonah 1. 8 *T.*, pray, for wh. cause
Mat. 8. 4 See th. *t.* no man, but go
Mark 5. 19 *t.* them how gr. things
Luke 22. 6, 7 Art thou the C.? *t.* us
John 10. 25 *t.* you, ye believe not
Acts 12. 14 *t.* how P. stood bef. gate
2 Cor. 12. 2 whe. in body, cannot *t.*
Gal. 4. 21 *t.* me, ye that desire to
Phil. 3. 18 *t.* you oft., and now *t.* you
1 Thes. 3. 4 *t.* you bef. we sh. suffer
2 Thes. 2. 5 when with you, I *t.* you
Heb. 11. 32 time would fail to *t.*
Jude 18 *t.* you there sho. be mock.
R. V. Frequent changes to, speak,
   say, shew, etc.

Telling.   *Numbering, narrating.*
Judg. 7. 15 Gid. heard *t.* of dream
2 Sam. 11. 19 made an end of *t.* mat.
2 K 8. 5 as he was *t.* the king how.

Temper.   *Moisten, mingle.*
Ex. 29. 2 unleavened *t.* with oil
Ezek. 46. 14 oil, to *t.* wi. fine flour
1 Cor. 12. 24 G. ha. *t.* body togeth.
R. V. Ex. 29. 2 mingled ; 32. 35
   seasoned ; Ezek. 46. 14 moisten

Temperance.   *Self-restraint.*
Acts 24. 25 And as he reasoned of *t.*
Gal. 5. 23 *t.* ; ag. such is no law
2 Pet. 1. 6 add to know. *t.*, and to *t.*

Temperate.   *Continent, prudent.*
1 Cor. 9. 25 striv. for mastery is *t.*
Tit. 1. 8 bishop be sober, holy, *t.*

Tempest.   *Storm, whirlwind.*
Job 9. 17 he breaketh me with a *t.*
27. 20 *t.* steal. him away in night
Ps. 11. 6 on wicked sh. he rain *t.*
55. 8 I hasten from storm and *t.*
Isa. 28. 2 which is a *t.* of hail
54. 11 O afflicted, tossed with *t.*
Am. 1. 14 *t.* in day of whirlwind
Jonah 1. 4 was a mighty *t.* in sea
Mat. 8. 24 there arose a *t.* in sea
Acts 27. 18 exceed. tossed with *t.*
Heb. 12. 18 nor unto darkness and *t.*
2 Pet. 2. 17 clouds carried with a *t.*
R. V. Ps. 11. 6 burning wind ; Acts
27. 18 ; 2 Pet. 2. 17 storm

Tempestuous.   *Stormy.*
Ps. 50. 30 shall be *t.* round about
Jonah 1. 11, 13, sea wrought, and *t.*
Acts 27. 14 arose against *t.* wind

Temple.   *House, palace, sanctuary,*
   dwelling, place.
1 Sam. 3. 3 lamp of G. went out in *t.*
2 Sam. 22 7 hear my voice out of *t.*
1 K. 6. 3 porch bef. of the house
2 K. 18. 16 cut gold from doors of *t.*
1 Chr. 6. 10 priest's office in the *t.*
2 Chr. 36. 7 put vessels in *t.* at B.
Ez. 4. 1 they builded *t.* unto Lord
Neh. 6. 10 let us shut doors of *t.*
Ps. 11. 4 The Lord is in his holy *t.*
Isa. 6. 1 and his train filled the *t.*
Jer. 7. 4 lying, saying, The *t.* of L.
Ezek. 41. 1 he bro. me to the *t.*, and
Dan. 5. 2 Nebuch. had ta. out of *t.*
Hos. 8. 14 forgot. Maker, build. *t.*
Joel 3. 5 into *t.* my goodly things
Am. 8. 3 songs of *t.* sh. be howlings
Jonah 2. 4 look toward thy holy *t.*
Mic. 1. 2 be witness fr. his holy *t.*
Hab. 2. 20 The Lord is in his holy *t.*

Hag. 2. 15 laid upon sto. in the *t.*
Zech. 6. 12 he sh. build *t.* of Lord
Mal. 3. 1 sh. sudden. come to his *t.*
Mat. 4. 5 set. him on pinnacle of *t.*
21. 12 Jesus went into *t.* of God
Mark 11. 11 entered Jer. and into *t.*
Luke 2. 27 he ca. by spirit into *t.*
19. 47 he taught daily in the *t.*
John 2. 14 found in *t.* th. sold oxen.
7. 28 Then cried Jesus in the *t.*
Acts 3. 10 at Beautiful gate of *t.*
26. 21 Jews caught me in the *t.*
1 Cor. 3. 16 know ye are the *t.* of G.
3. 17 for the *t.* of God is holy
2 Cor. 6. 16 ye are *t.* of living God
Eph. 2. 21 grow. into *t.* in the Lord
2 Thes. 2. 4 he as God sitteth in th. *t.*
Rev. 3. 12 I make pillar in *t.* of
21. 22 God Al. and Lamb are the *t.*
Upper cheeks, temples
Judg. 4. 21 smote nail into his *t.*
S. of S. 4. 3 thy *t.* are like pomegran.
R. V. 1 K. 11. 10, 11, 13 ; 1 Chr. 6.
10 ; 10. 10 ; 2 Chr. 23. 10 ; Acts 7.
48 house or houses ; Hos. 8. 14
palaces ; Mat. 23. 35 ; 27. 5 ; Luke
11. 51 sanctuary

Temporal.   *For a time.*
2 Cor. 4. 18 for things seen are *t.*

Tempt.   *Try, test, prove.*
Gen. 22. 1 God did *t.* Abraham
Ex. 17. 2 wherefore do ye *t.* Lord?
Num. 14. 22 have *t.* me ten times
Deut. 6. 16 ye shall not *t.* the Lord
Ps. 78. 18 they *t.* God in th. heart
Isa. 7. 12 neither will I *t.* the Lord
Mal. 3. 15 that *t.* G. are delivered
Mat. 4. 1 then was J. led to be *t.*
19. 3 Pharisees came unto him, *t.*
Mark 1. 13 was for. days *t.* of Satan
Luke 10. 25 lawyer stood up and *t.*
John 8. 6 This they said, *t.* him
Acts 15. 10 why *t.* ye God, to put
1 Cor. 7. 5 that Satan *t.* ye not for
Gal. 6. 1 consider., lest thou be *t.*
1 Thes. 3. 5 lest tempter ha. *t.* you
Heb. 2. 18 he ha. suffer., being *t.*
11. 37 were sawn asunder, were *t.*
Jas. 1. 13 no man say wh. *t.*, I am *t.*
R. V. Luke 20. 23 ——

Temptation.   *Trial, proof.*
Deut. 4. 34 take nation by *t.*, signs
Ps. 95. 8 in day of *t.* in wilderness
Mat. 6. 13 and lead us not into *t.*
26. 41 pray, that ye enter not into *t.*
Mark 14. 38 ; Luke 22. 40, 46
Luke 4. 13 when devil ended all *t.*
Acts 20. 19 serv. God with many *t.*
1 Cor. 10. 13 hath no *t.* taken you
Gal. 4. 14 *t.* in my fl. ye desp. not
1 Tim. 6. 9 that be rich fall into *t.*
Heb. 3. 8 in day of *t.* in wilderness
Jas. 1. 2 joy when ye fall into *t.*
1 Pet. 1. 6 are in heaviness thro. *t.*
2 Pet. 2. 9 how deliv. godly out of *t.*
Rev. 3. 10 keep thee fr. hour of *t.*
R. V. Ps 95. 8 Massah ; Acts 20.
19 ; Rev. 3. 10 trial

Tempter.   *Prover.*
Mat. 4. 3 And when *t.* came to him
1 Thes. 3. 5 by means *t.* tempted

Ten.   *Ten.*
Gen. 16. 3 Ab. dwelt *t.* years in C.
Ex. 26. 1 ma. tab. wi. *t.* curtains
Lev. 26. 26 *t.* wom. sh. bake bread
Num. 7. 14 spoon of *t.* sh. of gold
Deut. 10. 4 first writing, the *t.* com.
Josh. 17. 5 fell *t.* por. to Manasseh
Judg. 6. 27 Gid. took *t.* of his serv.
Ruth 1. 4 dwelt there ab. *t.* years
1 Sam. 1. 8 am not I bet th. *t.* sons
2 Sam. 18. 3 art wor. *t.* thous. of us
1 K. 7. 38 made he *t.* lav. of brass
2 K. 20. 11 bro. shad. *t.* deg. back
1 Chr. 29. 7 of sil. *t.* thous. talents
2 Chr. 4. 8 He made also *t.* tables
Ez. 1. 10 basons, fo. hundred and *t.*
Neh. 4. 12 they said unto us *t.* times
Esth. 9. 13 let Ham's *t.* sons be ha.
Job 19. 3 *t.* ti. ha. ye reproach. me
Ps. 3. 6 not be afraid of *t.* thousand
92. 3 Upon instrum. of *t.* strings
Eccl. 7. 19 more th. *t.* mighty men
Isa. 5. 10 *t.* a. of viney. sh. yield
Jer. 41. 1 Ishmael, *t.* men with him
Ezek. 41. 1 breadth of door *t.* cub.

Dan. 1. 12 Prove thy serv. *t.* days
Am. 6. 9 remain *t.* in one house
Hag. 2. 16 measures, th. were but *t*
Zech. 8. 23 *t.* men sh. take hold out
Mat. 25. 1 *t.* virgins, took lamps
Mark 10. 41 when *t.* heard it, they
Luke 15. 8 wh. wom., hav. *t.* pieces
19. 16 thy pound gained *t.* pounds
Acts 25. 6 when he had tar. *t.* days
1 Cor. 4. 15 tho. ye ha. *t.* thou. ins.
Jude 14 L. cometh with *t.* thousand
Rev. 17. 12 the *t.* horns, are *t.* kings

Tend.   *Aim, conduce.*
Prov. 10. 16 labour of righteous *t.*
21. 5 diligent *t.* to plenteousness

Tender.   *Soft, pitiful, merciful.*
Gen. 18. 7 Abraham fetched a calf *t.*
29. 17 Leah was *t.* eyed, but Rach.
Deut. 28. 54 man that is *t.* among
2 Sam. 23. 4 as *t.* grass springing
2 K. 22. 19 Bec. thine heart was *t.*
1 Chr. 22. 5 my son is young and *t.*
2 Chr. 13. 7 Rehobo. was *t.* hearted
Job 14. 7 *t.* branch will not cease
Prov. 4. 3 I was my father's son, *t.*
S. of S. 2 13 the vines wi. *t.* grape
Isa. 47. 1 no more be called *t.* and
Ezek. 17. 22 I will crop off a *t.* one
Dan. 1. 9 G. bro. Dan. into *t.* love
Mat. 24. 32 Wh. his branch is yet *t.*
Mark 13. 28 Wh. her branch is yet *t.*
Luke 1. 78 Thro. *t.* mercy of our G.
Eph. 4. 32 be kind to one ano., *t.* h.
Jas. 5. 11 L. is pitiful, of *t.* mercy
R. V. S. of S. 2. 13, 15 ; 7. 12 in
blossom ; Dan. 1. 9 compassion ;
Jas. 5. 11 merciful

Tenderness.   *Softness.*
Deut. 28. 26 set foot on gro. for *t.*

Tenons.   *Hands, projections.*
Ex. 26. 17 Two *t.* be in one board
26. 19 ; 36. 22. 24

Tenor.   *Mouth, drift.*
Gen. 43. 7 according to *t.* of words
Ex. 34. 27 after *t.* of these words

Tent.   *Tent, booth, tabernacle.*
Gen. 4. 20 fa. of such as dwell in *t.*
9. 21 Noah was uncovered in *t.*
13. 12 Lot pitched his *t.* toward S.
26. 17 Isaac pitched his *t.* in val.
Ex. 18. 7 M. and Jeth. came to *t.*
33. 8 stood every man at *t.* door
40. 19 he spread *t.* over tabernacle
Lev. 14. 8 tarry out of *t.* sev. days
Num. 9. 15 cloud cov, *t.* of testim.
Deut. 1. 27 ye murmur. in your *t.*
Josh. 3. 14 people removed from *t.*
Judg 4. 17 Sisera fled to *t.* of Jael
1 Sam. 4. 10 fled every man to his *t.*
2 Sam. 16. 22 they spread Absal. a *t.*
1 K. 12. 16 to your *t.*, O Israel ; now
2 K. 7. 8 lepers went into one *t.*
1 Chr. 15. 1 Da. pitched a *t.* for ark
2 Chr. 1. 4 he pitched *t.* for it at J.
Ez. 8. 15 we abode in *t.* three days
Ps. 69. 25 let none dwell in their *t.*
84. 10 th. dwell in *t.* of wickedness
S. of S. 1. 5 comely as *t.* of Kedar
Isa. 38. 12 age remo. as shepherd's *t.*
Jer. 10. 20 none to stretch forth *t.*
Hab. 3. 7 I saw the *t.* of Cushan
Zech. 12. 7 L. sh. save *t.* of Judah
R. V. Gen. 26. 17 ; 33. 18 ; Num.
9. 17, 18, 20 ; Ez. 8. 15 encamped ;
Num. 25. 8 pavilion ; Num. 13.
19 ; 1 Sam. 17. 53 ; 2 K. 7. 16 ; 2
Chr. 31. 2 camp or camps ; 2 Sam.
11. 11 booths

Tenth.   *One of ten, tithe, tenth.*
Gen. 28. 22 surely give *t.* to thee
Ex. 16. 36 omer is *t.* part of eph.
Lev. 27. 32 *t.* shall be holy to L.
Num. 18. 21 given childr. of L. *t.*
Deut. 23. 2 to *t.* genera. not enter
Josh. 4. 19 ca. out of Jor. on *t.* day
1 Sam. 8. 15 king take *t.* of seed
2 K. 25. 1 it came to pass in *t.* day
1 Chr. 12. 13 Jer. the *t.*, Mach. el.
Ez. 10. 16 sat first day of *t.* month
Esth. 2. 16 *t.* month, month of *T.*
Isa. 6. 13 yet in it shall be a *t.* and
Jer. 32. 1 in *t.* year of Zedekiah
Ezek. 45. 14 offer *t.* part of a bath
Zech. 8. 19 the fast of *t.*, shall be to
John 1. 39 it was about the *t.* hour
Heb. 7. 2 To whom Ab. gave *t.* p.

Rev. 11. 13 t. part of the city fell
Tent-maker.
Acts 18. 3 by occupa. were t. m.
Teraphim. *Home gods, nourishers*
Judg. 17. 5 Micah made ephod a t.
18. 14 there is in these houses t.
Hos. 3. 4 Is. shall abide without t.
Termed. *Said, called.*
Isa. 62. 4 no more be t. Forsaken
Terrace. *Raised place.*
2 Chr. 9. 11 ma. of algum trees t.
Terrestrial. *Earthly.*
1 Cor. 15. 40 bodies t., glory of t.
Terrible. *Fearful, dreadful.*
Ex. 34. 10 t. thing I will do with
Deut. 7. 21 G., a mighty God and t.
Judg. 13. 6 count. of angel, very t.
2 Sam. 7. 23 do for you gr. things, t.
Neh. 1. 5 the t. God, that keepeth
Job. 37. 22 with God is t. majesty
Ps. 47. 2 the Lord most high is t.
66. 3 t. art thou in thy works
S. of S. 6. 4 t. as army wi. banners
Isa. 13. 11 lay low haughtin. of t.
29. 20 t. one is brought to nought
Jer. 20. 11 L. is wi. me mighty t.
Lam. 5. 10 because of t. famine
Ezek. 1. 22 as colour of t. crystal
Dan. 2. 31 form of image was t.
Joel 2. 11 Lord is great and very t.
Hab. 1. 7 Chaldeans are t. and
Zeph. 2. 11 L. will be t. unto them
Heb. 12. 21 so t. was sight that
R. V. Lam. 5. 10 burning; Dan. 7.
7 powerful; Heb. 12. 21 fearful
Terribleness. *Fear inspiring.*
Deut. 26. 8 L. brought us with t.
1 Chr. 17. 21 make thee a name of t.
Jer. 49. 16 Thy t. ha. deceived thee
Terribly. R. V. *mightily.*
Isa. 2. 19 aris° to shake t. earth
Nah. 2. 3 fir trees sh. be t. shaken
Terrify. *Frighten, make afraid.*
Deut. 20. 3 not tremble, nei. be t.
Job 3. 5 let blackness of day t. it
7. 14 thou. t. me through visions
Luke 21. 9 hear of wars, be not t.
24. 37 they were t. and affrighted
2 Cor. 10. 9 not seem as if I wo. t.
Phil. 1. 28 in noth. t. by adversity
R. V. Job 9. 34 make afraid
Terror. *Fear, dread, terror.*
Gen. 35. 5 t. of G. was upon cities
Lev. 26. 16 I will app. over you t.
Deut. 32. 25 sword without, t. with.
Josh. 2. 9 your t. if fallen upon us
Job 6. 4 t. of God set themselves
18. 11 t. shall make him afraid
24. 17 they are in the t. of death
Ps. 55. 4 t. of death are fallen on
73. 19 are utterly consumed with t.
Isa. 10. 33 L. will lop bough wi. t.
19. 17 Judah shall be a t. to Egypt
Jer. 20. 4 ma. thee a t. to thyself
Lam. 2. 22 hast called in day my t.
Ezek. 26. 21 I will make thee a t.
Rom. 13. 3 rulers not t. to good
2 Cor. 5. 11 knowing the t. of Lord
1 Pet. 3. 14 be not afraid of th. t.
R. V. 2 Cor. 5. 11; 1 Pet. 3. 14
fear
Testament. R. V. *covenant.*
Mat. 26. 28 this is my blood of the
new t., which; Mark 14. 24
Luke 22. 20 This cup is the new t.
in my blood, which; 1 Cor. 11. 25
1 Cor. 3. 6 made minis. of new t.
Heb. 7. 22 ma. surety of a better t.
9. 15 he is mediator of new t. for
9. 20 This is the blood of new t.
Rev. 11. 19 in temple ark of his t.
Testator. R. V. *he that made it.*
Heb. 9. 16 of neces. be death of t.
9. 17 no strength while t. liveth
Testify. *Bear witness.*
Ex. 21. 29 it hath been t. to owner
Num. 35. 30 one witness sh. not t.
Deut. 8. 19 I t. that ye shall perish
Ruth 1. 21 Lord hath t. against me
2 Sam. 1. 16 mouth ha. t. ag. thee
2 K. 17. 13 yet L. t. against Israel
2 Chr. 24. 19 prophets t. ag. them
Neh. 9. 26 slew prophets which t.
Job 15. 6 own lips t. against thee
Ps. 50. 7 t. against thee; I am God
Isa. 59. 12 our sins t. against us

Jer. 14. 7 our iniquities t. against us
Hos. 5. 5 the pride of Israel doth t.
Am. 3. 13 t. in the house of Jacob
Mic. 6. 3 I wearied thee? t. ag. me
Luke 16. 28 send Laza. that he t.
John 3. 11 We t. that we ha. seen
4. 44 Jesus t. that prophet hath no
Acts 2. 40 with oth. words did he t.
20. 21 T. to Jews and to Greeks
1 Cor. 15. 15 we have t. of G. that
Gal. 5. 3 I t. to every man circum.
Eph. 4. 17 this I say, and t. in Lord
1 Thes. 4. 6 we forewarned, you t.
1 Tim. 2. 6 who gave himself to be t.
Heb. 2. 6 one in a certain place t.
1 Pet. 1. 11 it t. the sufferings of
1 John 4. 14 we ha. seen and do t.
3 John 3 brethren came and t. of
Rev. 22. 16 I Jesus sent angel to t.
R. V. John 2. 25; 3. 11, 32; 5. 39;
15. 26; 21. 24; Heb. 11. 14; 1 John
4 bear witness; 1 Cor. 15. 15;
Heb. 7. 17 witnessed
Testimony. *Witness, evidence.*
Ex. 16. 34 Aaron laid it before the t.
25. 16; 26. 33; 27. 21; 30. 6; 31. 7
Lev. 16. 13 mercy seat is upon the t.
Num. 1. 50 Levites over taber. of t.
Deut. 4. 45 These are the t. and stat.
Josh. 4. 16 priests bear the ark of t.
Ruth 4. 7 gave neighbour, this was t.
1 K. 2. 3 to keep his t., as written
2 K. 17. 15 his t. which he testified
1 Chr. 29. 19 to keep thy com., thy t.
2 Chr. 23. 11 crown, and gave him t.
Neh. 9. 34 nor kings hearken to t.
Ps. 19. 7 the t. of the Lord is sure
78. 5 he established a t. in Jacob
119. 167 my soul hath kept thy t.
Isa. 8. 16 Bind up t., seal the law
Jer. 44. 23 nor in his statutes, nor t,
Mat. 8. 4 and offer the gift for a t.
Mark 6. 11 shake off dust for a t.
Luke 5. 14 as M. comman., for a t.
John 3. 32 no man receiveth his t.
Acts 14. 3 which ga. t. unto the word
1 Cor. 1. 6 as t. of C. was confirmed
2 Cor. 1. 12 the t. of our conscience
2 Thes. 1. 10 bec. our t. was believ.
2 Tim. 1. 8 Be not ashamed of t. of L
Heb. 3. 5 for a t. of those things which
Rev. 1. 2 bare record of t. of J. C.
R. V. Ruth 4. 7 attestation; John
3. 32, 33; 8. 17; 21. 24 witness;
Acts 13. 22; 14. 3; Heb. 11. 5 bear
witness; 1 Cor. 2. 1 mystery
Tetrarch. *Ruler of a fourth.*
Mat. 14. 1 Herod the t. heard of Je.
Luke 3. 19 H. the t., being reproved
Acts 13. 1 bro. up wi. Herod the t.
Than. *Or that, but.*
Mat. 11. 22 more tol. for Tyre, t. you
Luke 3. 13 exact no more t. appoi.
Etc., etc..
Thank (n.). *Gratitude, blessing.*
2 Sam. 22. 50 I give t. to thee, O L.
1 Chr. 16. 41 to give t. to L., bec.
2 Chr. 31. 2 to minister, and give t.
Ez. 3. 11 in praising and giving t.
Neh. 12. 31 companies wh. gave t.
Ps. 6. 5 in grave who shall give t.
92. 1 good thing to give t. unto
Dan. 6. 10 he prayed, and gave t.
Mat. 26. 27 Je. took cup and gave t.
Mark 8. 6 seven loaves and gave t.
Luke 2. 38 Anna gave t. to the Lord
John 6. 11 when he had given t.
Acts 27. 35 bread, and gave t. to G.
Rom. 14. 6 for he giveth God t.
1 Cor. 11. 24 had given t., he brake
2 Cor. 1. 11 it may be giv. by many
Eph. 1. 16 Cease not to give t. for
Col. 1. 3 give t. to God and Father
1 Thes. 1. 2 give t. to God always
2 Thes. 2. 13 bound to give t. alway
Heb. 13. 15 offer praise, giving t.
Rev. 4. 9 give t. to him on throne
R. V. Heb. 13. 15 confession
Thank (v.). *Express gratitude, bless.*
2 Sam. 14. 22 and Joab t. the king
1 Chr. 16. 4 to t. and praise L. God
Dan. 2. 23 I t. thee, and praise
Mat. 11. 25 J. said, I t. thee, O F.
Luke 18. 11 t., I am not as oth. men
John 11. 41 Father, I t. thee thou

Acts 28. 15 when P. saw, he t. God
Rom. 1. 8 t. God through J. C. for
1 Cor. 1. 4 I t. God on your behalf
Phil. 1. 3 I t. God on remem. of you
1 Thes. 2. 13 For this cause t. we G.
2 Thes. 1. 3 bound to t. G. always
1 Tim. 1. 12 I t. C. J. our L., who
2 Tim. 1. 3 I t. G., whom I serve fr
Phile. 4 I t. G., making mention of
Thankful. *Give thanks.*
Ps. 100. 4 be t. to him, and bless
Rom. 1. 21 glorifi. not, nei. were t.
Col. 3. 15 let peace rule, be ye t.
R. V. Ps. 100. 4; Rom. 1. 21 give
thanks
Thankfulness. *Gratitude.*
Acts 24. 3 We accept with all t.
Thankworthy. R. V. *acceptable.*
1 Pet. 2. 19 t. if man endure grief
Thanksgiving. *Giving thanks.*
Lev. 7. 12 If he offer it for a t. then
Neh. 11. 17 to begin t. in prayer
Ps. 26. 7 publish with voice of t.
100. 4 enter into his gates with t.
Isa. 51. 3 t. and melo. found there
Jer. 30. 19 out of them proceed t.
Am. 4. 5 offer a sacrifice of t. with
Jonah 2. 9 sacrifice wi. voice of t.
2 Cor. 4. 15 thro. t. grace redound
Phil. 4. 6 let your requests
Col. 2. 7 abounding therein with t.
1 Tim. 4. 3 God to be recei. with t.
Rev 7. 12 t. and hon. be to our G.
Thank-offering. *See Offering.*
That. *Which, so that.*
Gen. 1. 31 God saw t. he had made
Mat. 1 22 t. it might be fulfilled
8. 8 Lord, I am not worthy t. thou
Etc., etc.
The. *These, this, etc.*
Luke 24. 21 to day is t. third day
Gal. 2. 18 if I build again t. things
Etc., etc.
Theatre. *Show, spectacle.*
Acts 19. 29 they rushed into the t.
19. 31 wo. not adventure into the t.
Thee. *Thou.*
Gen. 16. 6 do to her as it please. t.
Mat. 5. 29 if eye offend t., pluck
Etc., etc.
Theft. *Stealing.*
Ex. 22. 3 he shall be sold for his t.
Mat. 15. 19 out of the heart proceed evil thoughts, t.; Mark 7. 22
Rev. 9. 21 nei. repented they of t.
Their. *Theirs, of him, it, them, etc.*
Lev. 18. 10 t. is thine own naked.
Mat. 5. 3 t. is kingdom of heaven
Etc., etc.
Them. *They (objective).*
Mark 9. 16 What question ye wi. t.?
John 19. 24 parted raim. among t.
Etc., etc.
Themselves. *Selves.*
Ezek. 43. 26 they sh. consecrate t.
Mat. 9. 3 the scribes said within t.
Etc., etc.
Then. *That time, in truth.*
Ez. 4. 9 T. wrote Rehum the chan.
Mat. 12. 28 t. the king. of G. is co.
Rom. 10. 17 So t. faith co. by hear.
Etc. etc.
Thence. *From there.*
Gen. 11. 8 scattered them from t.
Mat. 11. 1 he departed t. to teach
John 4. 43 he departed t., and went
Etc. etc.
Thenceforth. *From this time.*
Lev. 22. 27 from eighth day and t.
Mat. 5. 13 it is t. good for nothing
There. *That place, here.*
Gen. 2. 8 t. he put the man who.
Mat. 2. 13 be t. till I bring word
John 12. 26 where I am, t. sh. my
Etc. etc.
Thereat. *At that.*
Ex. 30. 19 wash hands and feet t.
Mat. 7. 13 many th. be wh. go in t.
Thereby. *Through it, therein.*
Gen. 24. 14 t. shall I know thou ha.
Job 22. 21 where I am, t. ye may be
Jer. 51. 43 nei. doth man pass t.
John 12. 4 Son mi. be glorified t.
Eph. 2. 16 having slain enmity t.
Heb. 12. 15and t. many be defiled

1 Pet. 2. 2 word, th. ye may grow *t.*
Thereabout. *Concerning.*
Luke 24. 4 were much perplexed *t.*
Therefore. *Also, for this, but.*
1 Sam. 12. 16 *t.* see this gr. thing
Ez. 4. 14 *t.* have we certified the
Acts 10. 20 Arise *t.*, get thee down,
Rom. 8. 12 *T.*, breth., we are debt.
2 Cor. 4. 13 believed, *t.* ha. spoken
Therein. *In there or it.*
Ex. 40. 3 put *t.* ark of testimony
Lev. 10. 1 put fire *t.*, incense there.
Luke 10. 9 heal the sick that are *t.*
Acts 17. 24 made world and all *t.*
Eph. 6. 20 th. *t.* I may speak bold.
2 Pet. 3. 10 works *t.* sh. be burned
Rev. 21. 22 I saw not temple *t.*, for
Thereof. *Concerning, of it.*
1 K. 17. 13 make me *t.* little cake
Mat. 12. 36 they sh. give account *t.*
Luke 22. 1 I will not more eat *t.*
Thereon. *On it.*
Ez. 6. 11 set up, let him be hang. *t.*
Mat. 21. 19 ca. to it, found noth. *t.*
Mark 11. 13 might find any thing *t.*
John 12. 14 found young ass, sat *t.*
Rev. 6. 4 power to him that sat *t.*
Thereout. *Out from.*
Lev. 2. 2 shall. take *t.* his handful of
Thereto. *To it.*
Ps. 119. 9 his way? by tak. heed *t.*
Thereunto. *With this view.*
Eph. 6. 18 watching *t.* wi. persever.
1 Thes. 3. 3 th. we are appointed *t.*
1 Pet. 3. 9 knowing ye are *t.* called
Therewith. *In it, with it.*
1 Tim. 6. 8 having food let us *t.* be
Jas. 3. 9 *T.* bless we G., and *t.* curse
3 John 10 not content *t.*, nei. doth
These. *This (pl.).*
Gen. 2. 4 *T.* are gen. of the heavens
Mat. 13. 53 wh. J. fin. *t.* parables
Etc., etc.
They. *All these or those.*
Gen. 3. 7 knew that *t.* were naked
Mat. 5. 4 mourn, *t.* sh. be comforted
John 5. 39 Search the scriptures, *t.*
Etc., etc.
Thick. *Dense, not thin.*
Ex. 10. 22 was *t.* darkness in land
Lev. 23. 40 the boughs of *t.* trees
Deut. 32. 15 fat, thou art grown *t.*
2 Sam. 18. 9 mule went under *t.* bo.
1 K. 7. 26 it was hand breadth *t.*
Neh. 8. 15 fetch branches of *t.* trees
Job 15. 26 runneth upon *t.* bosses
Ps. 74. 5 had lifted axes on *t.* trees
Ezek. 6. 13 slain under every *t.* oak
Hab. 2. 6 lad. himself with *t.* clay
Luke 11. 29 people gather *t.* togeth.
Thicker. *More thick.*
1 K. 12. 10 My little f. sh. be *t.* **than**
2 Chr. 10. 10
Thicket. *Thick growth, jungle.*
Gen. 22. 13 a ram caught in a *t.*
1 Sam. 13. 6 Israel did hide in *t.*
Isa. 9. 18 sh. kindle in the *t.* of for.
Jer. 4. 7 lion is come up from his *t.*
Thickness. *Distance through.*
2 Chr. 4. 5 *t.* of it was handbreadth
Jer.. 52. 21 *t.* thereof four fingers
Ezek. 4. 19 *t.* of wall five cubits
Thief. *Who steals, robber.*
Ex. 22. 2 If *t.* be found breaking
Deut. 24. 7 that *t.* shall die; and
Job 24. 14 the murderer is as a *t.*
Ps. 50. 18 when thou sawest a *t.*
Prov. 6. 30 not desp. *t.* if he steal
29. 24 partner with *t.* hateth soul
Isa. 1. 23 princes are compan. of *t.*
Jer. 2. 26 as a *t.* is ashamed when
49. 9 *t.* by night, they will destroy
Hos. 7. 1 *t.* com. in. troop of robbers
Joel 2. 9 enter at windows like *t.*
Obad. 5 If *t.* came, if robbers by
Zech. 5. 4 sh. enter into house of *t.*
Mat. 6. 19 where *t.* break through
Mark 11. 17 My house, ye have
    made it a den of *t.* ; Luke 19. 46
Luke 12. 33 where no *t.* approacheth
John 10. 1 same is a *t.* and robber
1 Cor. 6. 10 *t.* shall not inherit king.
1 Thes. 5. 2 day of L. cometh as a *t.*
1 Pet. 4. 15 let none suffer as a *t.*
2 Pet. 3. 10 day of L. cometh as a *t*
Rev. 3. 3 I will co. on thee as a *t.*

R. V. Mat. 21. 13 ; 26. 55 ; 27. 38,
    44 ; Mark 11. 17 ; 14. 48 ; 15. 27 ;
    Luke 10. 30, 36 ; 19. 46 ; 22. 52
    robber, or robbers
Thigh. *Thigh, leg.*
Gen. 24. 2 Put thy hand under my *t.*
Ex. 28. 42 from loins even unto *t.*
Num. 5. 21 Lord make thy *t.* to rot
Judg. 15. 8 he smote them hip and *t.*
Ps. 45. 3 Gird sword upon thy *t.*
S. of S. 7. 1 they *t.* are like jewels
Isa. 47. 2 make bare leg, uncover *t.*
Jer. 31. 19 I smote upon my *t.* ; I
Ezek. 21. 12 howl, smite upon thy *t.*
Dan. 2. 32 his belly and *t.* of brass
Rev. 19. 16 hath on his *t.* a name
R V. Isa. 47. 2 leg
Thin. *Lean, small, not thick.*
Gen. 41. 6 sev. *t.* ears and blasted
    41. 27 seven *t.* and ill favoured kine
Ex. 30. 3 they beat gold into *t.* plates
Lev. 13. 30 if there be yellow *t.* hair
1 K. 7. 29 additions made of *t.* work
Isa. 17. 4 glory of Jacob be made *t.*
R. V. Gen. 41. 27 lean ; 1 K. 7. 29
    hanging
Thine. *Thy.*
Gen. 14. 23 take any thing that is *t.*
Lev. 10. 15 it shall be *t.*, thy sons
1 K. 3. 26 let neither be mine nor *t.*
1 Chr. 12. 18 *t.* are we, David and
Ps. 119. 94 I am *t.*, save me, for I
Mat. 7. 4 and beam is in *t.* own eye
Mark. 2. 11 go thy way into *t.* house
Luke 22. 42 not thy will, but *t.*, be d.
John 17. 10 mine are *t.*, *t.* are mine
Acts 5. 4 sold, was it not *t.* own
Rom. 10. 6 Say not in *t.* heart, Who
1 Tim. 5.23 wine, for *t.* oft. infirmi.
Phile. 19 owest to me *t.* own self
Heb. 1. 10 heav. are works of *t.* h.
Rev. 3. 18 anoint *t.* eyes with salve
R. V. Many changes to, thy
Thing. *Word, matter, object.*
Gen. 14. 23 I will not take any *t.*
Ex. 20. 17 nor *t.* that is thy neigh's
Lev. 8. 5 *t.* which Lord commanded
Num. 16. 30 if Lord made a new *t.*
Deut. 11. 14 *t.* thou ha. spo. is good
Josh. 21. 45 failed not of *t.* spoken
Judg. 6. 29 Who hath done this *t.*
Ruth 3. 18 till he have finished *t.*
1 Sam. 2. 23 Why do ye such *t.* ? for
2 Sam. 11. 25 Let not this *t.* displease
1 K. 20. 9 but this *t.* I may not do
2 K. 8. 13 he should do this great *t.*
1 Chr. 4. 22 And these are ancient *t.*
2 Chr. 12. 12 in Judah *t.* went well
Ez. 9. 3 heard *t.*, I rent my garment
Neh. 6. 8 no such *t.* as thou sayest
Esth. 2. 4 the *t.* pleased the king
Job 15. 11 is th. secret *t.* wi. thee ?
Ps. 2. 1 why do peo. imagine a vain *t.*
    101. 3 I set no wicked *t.* bef. eyes
Prov. 22. 18 For it is a pleasant *t.*
Eccl. 1. 8 all *t.* are full of labour
Isa. 38. 7 L. will do this *t.* that he sp
Jer. 7. 23 this *t.* commanded I them
Lam. 2. 13 what *t.* take to witness
Ezek. 11. 25 spake all .. that Lord
Dan. 10. 1 *t.* was reveal. to Daniel
Hos. 6. 10 I have seen a horrible *t.*
Joel 3. 5 into temp. my goodly *t.*
Am. 6. 13 rejoice in a *t.* of nought
Obad. 6. how are *t.* of E. searched
Mic. 7. 15 show to him marvel. *t.*
Zech. 4. 10 despise day of small *t.*
Mat. 4. 9 All these *t.* I give thee
    13. 34 these *t.* spake J. unto multi.
Mark 2. 8 Why reason ye these *t.*
    13. 4 when shall these *t.* be ? and
Luke 5. 27 after these *t.* he went fo.
    12. 31 all *t.* sh. be added unto you
John 1. 28 These *t.* were do. in B.
    50. 20 Father sheweth Son all *t.*
Acts 12. 17 shew these *t.* unto Jam.
1 Cor. 1. 10 I beseech, sp. some *t.*
2 Cor. 5. 5 wro. us for self same *t.*
Eph. 5. 6 of these *t.* cometh wrath
Phil. 4. 8 praise, think on these *t.*
2 Thes. 2. 5 wi. you, I told you *t.* ?
1 Tim. 4. 11 These *t.* com. and teach
2 Tim. 1. 12 cause, I suffer these *t.*
Tit. 2. 15 These *t.* speak and exhort
Heb. 7. 13 he of who. *t.* are spoken
Jas. 3. 10 these *t.* ought not so be

2 Pet. 1. 9 that lack. these *t.* is blind
1 John 1. 4 these *t.* write we to you
Rev. 22. 8 I John saw these *t.*, and
See also creeping, holy, base, great,
    hoped for, those, weak, etc.
R. V. The changes are chiefly due
    to antecedent and consequent
    words. There are many omis-
    sions of the word.
Think. *Consider, reckon, conceive,*
    review, remember, believe.
Gen. 48. 11 had not *t.* to see thy fa.
Ex. 34. 2 L. repented of evil he *t.*
Num. 24. 11 I *t.* to promote thee to
Deut. 19. 19 as he *t.* to have done
Judg. 15. 2 *t.* thou hadst hated her
Ruth 4. 4 And I *t.* to advertise thee
1 Sam. 18. 25 S. *t.* to make Dav. fall
2 Sam. 5. 6 *D.* cannot come hither
2 K. 5. 11 *t.*, He will surely come
1 Chr. 19. 3 *T.* thou David doth h.
2 Chr. 13. 18 ye *t.* to withstand k.
Neh. 6. 2 they *t.* to do me mischief
Esth. 6. 6 Haman *t.* in his heart, to
Job 31. 1 why sho. I *t.* upon a maid ?
Ps. 40. 17 yet the Lord *t.* upon me
    48. 9 We ha. *t.* of thy lov. kindness
Prov. 23. 7 as he *t.* in heart, so is
Eccl. 8. 17 a wise man *t.* to kn. it
Isa. 14. 24 as I *t.*, so come to pass
Jer. 29. 11 I know thoughts I *t.*
Ezek. 38. 10 shall *t.* an evil thought
Dan. 7. 25 *t.* to change ti. and laws
Jonah 1. 6 if so be that God will *t.*
Zech. 1. 6 Like as Lord of hosts *t.*
Mal. 3. 16 that feared the L., an *t.*
Mat. 3. 9 not to say within yours.
    22. 42 Saying, What *t.* ye of Chr. ?
Mark 14. 64 heard blasph.; wh. *t.*
Luke 13. 4 *t.* ye they were sinners
John 5. 39 *t.* ye have eternal life
Acts 10. 9 but *t.* he saw a vision
Rom. 12. 3 highly than he oug. to *t.*
1 Cor. 13. 11 I *t.* as a child ; but
2 Cor. 10. 2 *t.* to be bold ag. some
Gal. 6. 3 if man *t.* hims. something
Eph. 3. 20 above all we ask or *t.*
Phil. 1. 7 it is meet for thee to *t.*
1 Thes. 3. 1 *t.* it good to be left at
Jas. 4. 5 Do ye *t.* that script. saith
1 Pet. 4. 4 wherein they *t.* strange
2 Pet. 1. 13 I *t.* it meet as long as
R. V. Gen. 50. 10 meant ; Ex. 32.
    14 ; Esth. 6. 6 said ; 2 Sam. 14. 13 ;
    Ezek. 38. 10 devise ; 2 Chr. 11. 32
    was minded ; Neh. 5. 19 remem-
    ber ; Job 31. 1 look ; 42. 2 pur-
    pose ; Ezek. 38. 10 device ; Luke
    9. 47 ; 12. 17 reasoned ; Luke
    19. 11 ; Acts 13. 25 suppose ; Acts
    26. 8 ; Heb. 10. 29 judged ; Rom.
    2. 3 reckon ; 2 Cor. 3. 5 ; 12. 16
    account ; 10. 7 consider ; 10. 11
    reckon
Third. *Third.*
Gen. 1. 13 eve. and morn. we. *t.* day
Ex. 19. 1 In the *t.* month, when
Lev. 19. 6 oug. to remain till *t.* day
Num. 2. 24 go forward in *t.* rank
Deut. 23. 8 in their *t.* generation
Josh. 19. 10 *t.* lot came for Zebulon
Judg. 20. 30 Is. went up on *t.* day
1 Sam. 3. 8 Lord call. Sam. *t.* time
2 Sam. 3. 3 *t.* Absalom, son of M.
1 K. 6. 6 *t.* was seven cubits broad
2 K. 11. 6 And a *t.* part at the gate
1 Chr. 27. 5 *t.* captain of the host
2 Chr. 23. 4 *t.* part ent. on sabbath
Neh. 10. 32 *t.* part of sh. for service
Esth. 5. 1 came to pass on *t.* day
Job 42. 14 name of *t.*, Keren-hap.
Isa. 37. 30 *t.* year sow ye, and reap
Jer. 38. 14 in *t.* entry in the house
Ezek. 10. 14 and *t.* the face of a lion
Dan. 2. 39 *t.* kingdom of brass, wh.
Hos. 6. 2 day he will raise us up
Zech. 6. 3 in *t.* char. white horses
Mat. 16. 21 be raised again the *t.* day
Mark 15. 25 it was the *t.* hour, and
Luke 18. 33 *t.* day he sh. rise again
John 2. 1 *t.* day th. was a marriage
Acts 10. 40 Him G. raised up *t.* day
1 Cor. 15. 4 he rose again the *t.* day
Rev. 4. 7 *t.* beast had face like man
Thirst (*n.*). *Thirst.*
Ex. 17. 3 kill us and chil. with *t.*

Deut. 28. 48 serve enemies in *t.*
Judg. 15. 18 now I shall die for *t.*
2 Chr. 32. 11 persuade to die by *t.*
Neh. 9. 15 broug. water for their *t.*
Job 24. 11 tread wi. press., suffer *t.*
Ps. 69. 21 in my *t.* gave me vinegar
Isa. 5. 13 multi. dried up with *t.*
Jer. 2. 25 withh. thy throat from *t.*
Lam. 4. 4 cleaveth to mouth for *t.*
Hos. 2. 3 naked, slay her with *t.*
Am. 8. 11 not fam., nor *t.* for water
2 Cor. 11. 27 in hunger and *t.,* in

Thirst (*v.*). *Be thirsty.*
Ex. 17. 3 people *t.* there for water
Ps. 42. 2 my soul *t.* for God, for
Isa. 49. 10 shall not hunger nor *t.*
Mat. 5. 6 hunger and *t.* after right.
John 4. 13 drink. of this water *t.*
4. 14 who. drinketh shall never *t.*
19. 28 after this, Jesus saith, I *t.*
1 Cor. 4. 11 to this present hour we *t.*
Rev. 7. 16 th. shall not *t.* any more

Thirsty. *Athirst.*
Judg. 4. 19 give me water, I am *t.*
2 Sam. 17. 29 people is *t.* in wilder.
Ps. 63. 1 longeth for thee in *t.* land
Prov. 25. 21 if he be *t.,* gi. him dr.
25. 25 as water to *t.* soul, So is
Isa. 65. 13 drink, but ye shall be *t.*
Ezek. 19. 13 she is planted in *t.* gr.
Mat. 25. 35 I was *t.,* ye gave drink
R. V. Ps. 63. 1 ; 143. 6 weary ; Mat.
25. 37 athirst

Thirteen. *Three and ten.*
Gen. 17. 25 Ishmael was *t.* years old
Num. 29. 13 shall offer *t.* bullocks
Josh. 19. 6 *t.* cities and their villages
1 K. 7. 1 building house *t.* years
1 Chr. 6. 60 cities through families *t.*
Ezek. 40. 11 length of gate *t.* cubits

Thirteenth. *Three and tenth.*
Gen. 14. 4 in *t.* year they rebelled
1 Chr. 24. 13 The *t.* to Huppah, the
Esth. 3. 12 on *t.* day of first month
Jer. 25. 3 From the *t.* year of Josiah

Thirtieth. *Thirty.*
2 K. 15. 13 reign in nine and *t.* year
2 Chr. 15. 19 five and *t.* years of A.
Neh. 5. 14 two and *t.* year of Arta.

Thirty. *Thirty.*
Gen. 6. 15. height of ark *t.* cubits
Num. 4. 3 from *t.* years old and up
Judg. 14. 12 will give you *t.* sheets
1 Sam. 9. 22 Saul sat among *t.* per.
2 Sam. 5. 4 David was *t.* years old
1 K. 4. 22 provision was *t.* measures
Jer. 38. 10 Take hence *t.* men from
Ezek. 41. 6 side chambers were *t.*
Zech. 11. 12 weigh. for my price *t.*
Mat. 13. 8 brought forth some *t.*
27. 3 Judas brought ag. *t.* pieces
Mark 4. 8 some *t.,* some sixty, some
Luke 3. 23 began to be *t.* years
John 6. 19 rowed tw. or *t.* furlongs

Thirty one.
Josh. 12. 24 kings of J. subdued *t. o.*
1 K. 16. 23 in the *t. o.* year of Asa

Thirty Two.
Num. 31. 40 L.'s tribu. *t. t.* persons

Thirty Three.
Gen. 46. 15 sons and daughters *t. t.*
Lev. 12. 4 bl. of purifying *t. t.* days

Thirty Four.
Gen. 11. 16 Eber lived *t. f.* years

Thirty Five.
2 Chr. 3. 15 pillars of *t. f.* cubits

Thirty Six.
Josh. 7. 5 men of Ai sm. *t. s.* of Is

Thirty Seven.
2 Sam. 23. 39 Uriah, *t. s.* in all

Thirty Eight.
Deut. 2. 14 over Zered *t. e.* years
John 5. 5 had infirmity *t. e.* years

Thirty Ninth.
2 Chr. 16. 12 Asa in *t. n.* year dis.

This. *That is here.*
Gen. 2. 23 *T.* is bone of my bones
Mat. 1. 22 Now all *t.* was done, th.
Etc., etc.

Thistle. *Thorn, bramble, thicket.*
Gen. 3. 18 *t.* shall it bring forth to
2 K. 14. 9 *t.* was in Lebanon wild
2 Chr. 25. 18 passed and trode do. *t.*
Job 31. 40 let *t.* grow inst. of wheat
Hos. 10. 8 *t.* come up on th. altars
Mat. 7. 16 do men gath. figs of *t.?*

Thither. *Hither, this way.*
1 Sam. 10. 22 if any man sh. come *t.*
Jer. 50. 5 with their faces *t.* ward
That way, hence
Deut. 1. 37 Thou shalt not go in *t.*
Mat 2. 22 Herod was afraid to go *t.*
Mark 6. 33 and ran afoot *t.* out of
Luke 17. 37 *t.* will eag. be gathered
John 18. 2 J. ofttimes resorted *t.*
Acts 17. 13 came *t.,* and stirred up
Rom. 15. 14 to be bro. on my way *t.*

Thongs. *Straps.*
Acts 22. 45 th. bound him with *t.*

Thorn. *Brier, bramble, thorn.*
Gen. 3. 18 *T.* shall it bring forth
Ex. 22. 6 If fire catch in *t.,* so that
Num. 33. 55 pricks, and *t.* in y. sides
Josh. 23. 13 sh. be *t.* in your eyes
Judg. 8. 7 will tear your flesh wi. *t.*
2 Sam. 23. 6 all as *t.* thrust away
2 Chr. 33. 11 took Manass. am. th. *t.*
Job 41. 2 or bore his jaw with *t.?*
Ps. 58. 9 Bef. your pots can feel *t.*
Prov. 15. 19 slothful as hedge of *t.*
Eccl. 7. 6 as crack. of *t.* under pot
S. of S. 2. 2 As lily among *t.,* so is
Isa. 7. 19 they shall rest upon *t.*
34. 13 *t.* shall come up in palaces
Jer. 12. 13 sown wheat, sh. reap *t.*
Ezek. 2. 6 tho. briers a. *t.* be wi. thee
Hos. 2. 6 will hedge thy way wi. *t.*
Mic. 7. 4 upright sharper than *t.* h.
Nah. 1. 10 be folden together as *t.*
Mat. 7. 16 Do men gath. grapes of *t.*
Mark 4. 7 some fell among *t.,* and
Luke 6. 44 of *t.* men not gather figs
John 9. 2 soldiers plat. crown of *t.*
2 Cor. 12. 7 was giv. me *t.* in flesh
Heb. 6. 8 wh. beareth *t.* and briers
R. V. 2 Chr. 33. 11 in chains ; Job
41. 2 hook

Thoroughly. *Entirely.*
Ex. 21. 19 cause him to be *t.* healed
2 K. 11. 18 his images break they *t.*

Those. *That* (*pl.*).
Gen. 6. 4 giants in earth in *t.* days
Mat. 3. 1 In *t.* days came John Bap.
Etc., etc.

Thou. *Thyself.*
Gen. 3. 14 *t.* art cursed ab. all cattle
Mat. 2. 6 *t.* Beth., in land of Juda
Etc., etc.

Though. *If, as if, even if.*
Job 13. 15 *T.* he slay me, yet I trust
Mat. 26. 35 *T.* I sho. die, yet will I

Thought (*v.*). *See* Think.

Thought (*n.*). *A thinking, judg-
ment, design, purpose.*
Gen. 6. 5 imagina. of *t.* of his heart
Deut. 15. 9 not a *t.* in thy wick. heart
Judg. 5. 15 for Reub. were great *t.*
1 Sam. 9. 5 lest my father take *t.*
Chr. 28. 9 Lo, understandeth all *t.*
Job 4. 13 in *t.* from visions of night
20. 2 my *t.* cause me to answer
Ps. 10. 4 after God is not in all his *t.*
94. 11 L. knoweth the *t.* of man
139. 17 How precious thy *t.* unto
Prov. 24. 9 *t.* of foolishness is sin
Eccl. 10. 20 Curse not k., no not *t.*
Isa. 55. 8 for my *t.* are not your *t.*
Jer. 4. 14 how long sh. vain *t.* lodge
Ezek. 38. 10 thou sh. think evil *t.*
Dan. 5. 10. let not thy *t.* trouble thee
Am. 4. 15 declareth to man his *t.*
Mic. 4. 12 they know not *t.* of L.
Mat. 15. 19 out of h. proc. evil *t.*
Mark 13. 11 take no *t.* beforehand
Luke 5. 22 Jesus perceived their *t.*
Acts 8. 22 if *t.* of thy heart may be
Rom. 2. 15 *t.* meanwhile accusing
1 Cor. 3. 20 L. knoweth the *t.* of
2 Cor. 10. 5 bri. into captiv. ev. *t.*
Heb. 4. 12 God is a discerner of *t.*
Jas. 2. 4 become judges of evil *t.*
R. V. Judg. 5. 15 resolves ; Prov.
15. 26 devices ; Jer. 23. 20 intents ;
Luke 5. 22 ; 24. 38 ; 1 Cor. 3. 20
reasonings. The phrases, take
thought, or, take no thought, be-
come, be anxious, or, be not anxious

Thousand. *Thousand.*
Gen. 24. 60 be thou mother of *t.*
Ex. 34. 7 keeping mercy for *t.,* for.
Num. 1. 16 tribes of f., heads of *t.*

Deut. 5. 10 showing mercy unto *t.*
Josh. 4. 13 forty *t.* prepared for w.
Judg. 1. 4 slew in Bezek ten *t.* men
1 Sam. 13. 2 Saul chose three *t.* men
2 Sam. 10. 18 D. slew for. *t.* horse.
1 K. 4. 32 he spake three *t.* prov.
2 K. 14. 7 He slew of Edom ten *t.*
1 Chr. 7. 1 ch. fathers and cap. of *t.*
2 Chr. 1. 2 captains of *t.* and hun.
Ez. 2. 37 children Immer, a *t.* fifty
Neh. 3. 13 *t.* cubits on the wall un.
Esth. 3. 9 I will pay ten *t.* talents
Job 9. 3 not answer him one of a *t.*
Ps. 50. 10 cattle npon a *t.* hills
90. 4 *t.* years in thy sight are but
Eccl. 6. 6 though he live a *t.* years
S. of S. 4. whereon hang *t.* bucklers
Isa. 30. 17 *t.* sh. flee at the rebuke
60. 2 A little shall become a *t.*
Jer. 32. 18 show. lov. kind. unto *t.*
Ezek. 45. 1 length of five and tw. *t.*
Dan. 5. 1 made a feast to *t.* lords
Am. 5. 3 The city went out by a *t*
Mic. 6. 7 Will the L. be pleas. wi. *t.*
Mat. 14. 21 had eaten were five *t.*
Mark 8. 9 ; Luke 9. 14 ; John 6. 10
Acts 19. 19 found it fifty *t.* pieces
1 Cor. 10. 8 fell three and twent. *t.*
2 Pet. 3. 8 and *t.* years as one day
Jude 14 Lord cometh with ten *t.* of
Rev. 20. 2 Sat., bound him a *t.* ye.

Thread. *String, thread.*
Gen. 14. 23 not take fr. *t.* to latch.
Josh. 2. 18 bind scar. *t.* in window
Judg. 16. 12 br. ropes fr. arms as *t.*
S. of S, 4. 3 Thy lips like *t.* of scarlet
R. V. Judg. 16. 9 string

Threaten. *Menace, threaten.*
Acts 4. 17 let us straitly *t.* them
9. 1 Saul, yet breathing out *t.*
Eph. 6. 9 do same th., for bearing *t.*
1 Pet. 2. 23 wh. he suff., he *t.* not

Three. *Three.*
Gen. 6. 10 Noah begat *t.* sons, Shem
Ex. 2. 2 child, she hid him *t.* mo.
Lev. 25. 21 bring forth fruit *t.* years
Num. 12. 4 Come ye *t.* unto tabern.
Deut. 19. 2 separate *t.* cit. for thee
Josh. 1. 11 within *t.* days ye pass
Judg. 1. 20 expelled *t.* sons of Anak
1 Sam. 11. 11 S. peo. in *t.* compan.
2 Sam. 18. 14 he took *t.* darts in h.
1 K. 4. 32 he spake *t.* thou. proverbs
2 K. 2. 17 they sought *t.* days, but
1 Chr. 10. 6 Saul died, and his *t.* sons
2 Chr. 13. 2 Abijah reigned *t.* years
Ez. 8. 15 abode we in tents *t.* days
Neh. 2. 11 I ca. to Jer., th. *t.* days
Esth. 4. 16 nei. eat not dr. *t.* days
Job 2. 11 wh. Job's *t.* friends heard
Prov. 30. 15 *t.* things are nev. satis.
30. 29 be *t.* things which go well
Isa. 17. 6 or *t.* berries in the top of
Jer. 36. 23 when Jeh. read *t.* leaves
Ezek. 40. 10 *t.* on this side, *t.* on th.
Dan. 10. 2 D. was mourn. *t.* weeks
Am. 4. 4 bring tithes after. *t.* years
Jonah 1. 17 in belly of fish *t.* days
Zech. 11. 8 *T.* shepherds I cut off
Mat. 12. 40 so Son be *t.* da. in earth
18. 20 where two or *t.* are gathered
Mark 8. 31 after *t.* days rise again
Luke 4. 25 heav. was shut *t.* years
13. 21 hid in *t.* measures of meal
John 2. 19 in *t.* days I will raise it
Acts 9. 9 was *t.* da. without sight
1 Cor. 13. 13 faith, ho., char., th. *t.*
2 Cor. 13. 1 in mo. of *t.* witnesses
Gal. 1. 18 aft. *t.* y's I went to Jeru.
1 Tim. 5. 19 but bef. two or *t.* wit.
Heb. 11. 23 M. was hid *t.* months
Jas. 5. 17 by the space of *t.* years
1 John 5. 8 *t.,* and these *t.* are one
Rev. 6. 6 *t.* mea. of barley for penny

Threefold. *Threefold.*
Eccl. 4. 12 *t.* cord not quic. brok.

Threescore. *Sixty.*
Gen. 25. 26 Isaac was *t.* years old
Ex. 15. 27 wells, *t.* and ten palm *t.*
Lev. 12. 5 continue *t.* and six days
Num. 31 39 the L.'s tribute was *t.*
Deut. 3. 4 *t.* cities. all the region
Josh. 13. 30 are in Bashan, *t.* cities
Judg. 8. 30 G. had *t.* and ten sons
1 Sam. 6. 19 fif. thous. *t.* ten men
2 Sam. 2. 31 three hun. *t.* men died

1 K. 4. 13 *t.* gr. cities with walls
2 K. 25. 19 took *t.* men of the people
1 Chr. 2. 21 married wh. he was *t.*
2 Chr. 11. 21 Reho. took *t.* concub.
Ez. 2. 9 Zac., seven hund. and *t.*
Neh. 7. 72 *t.* and sev. priests garm
Ps. 90. 10 days of our years *t.* ten
S. of S. 6. 8 There are *t.* queens, and
Isa. 7. 8 within *t.* five years sh. Ep.
Jer. 52. 25 took *t.* men of the people
Ezek. 40. 14 made posts of *t.* cubits
Dan. 9. 26 after *t.* and two weeks
Luke 24. 13 was fr. Jer. *t.* furlongs
Acts 7. 14 kindred, *t.* and fifteen
1 Tim. 5. 9 not widow be ta. und. *t.*
Rev. 13. 18 his num. is six h. and *t.*

Thresh. *Tread down, beat off.*
Judg. 6. 11 G. *t.* wheat by wi. press
2 K. 13. 7 made them like dust by *t.*
1 Chr. 21. 20 Now Ornan was *t.* w.
Isa. 41. 15 thou sh. *t.* the mountains
Jer. 51. 33 floor, it is time to *t.* her
Am. 1. 3 bec. they have *t.* Gilead
Mic. 4. 13 Arise and *t.*, O dau. of Z.
Hab. 3. 12 didst *t.* heath. in anger
1 Cor. 9. 10 *t.* in hope, be partaker
R. V. Judg. 6. 11 beating out ; Jer.
   51. 33 trodden

Threshing. *Treading, beating.*
Gen. 50. 10 came to *t.* floor of Atad
Lev. 26. 5 *t.* shall reach to vintage
Num. 18. 27 tho. it were corn of *t.* fl.
Ruth 3. 2 he win. barley in *t.* floor
2 Sam. 23. 1 fight, and rob *t.* floors
2 Sam. 24. 22 behold, *t.* instr. and
1 Chr. 21. 23 the *t.* instr. for wood
2 Chr. 3. 1 prep. in *t.* floor of Ornan
Isa. 28. 27 not threshed wi. *t.* instr.
Jer. 51. 33 daug. of Bab. like *t.* fl.
Am. 1. 3 thresh. Gil. with *t.* instr.
Dan. 2. 35 like chaff of summer *t.*

Threshold. *Sill, entrance.*
Judg. 19. 27 her hands were on *t.*
1 Sam. 5. 4 hands cut off on the *t.*
1 K. 14. 17 came to *t.*, child died
Neh. 12. 25 keeping ward at the *t.*
Ezek. 9. 3 glory of G. gone up to *t.*
Zeph. 2. 14 desolation shall be in *t.*
R. V. Neh. 12. 25 storehouses

Threw. *See* **Throw.**

Thrice. *Three times.*
Ex. 34. 23 *T.* in y'r sh. men ch. ap.
2 K. 13. 18 Smite on gr. ; he smote *t.*
Mat. 26. 34 thou shalt deny me *t.*
   Mark 14. 30 ; Luke 22. 61
Luke 22. 34 sh. *t.* deny thou knewest
John 13. 38 till th. ha. denied me *t.*
Acts 10. 16 was done *t.*, and vessel
2 Cor. 11. 25 *t.* beat., suf. shipwreck

Throat. *Throat, gullet*
Ps. 5. 9 their *t.* is open sepulchre
Prov. 23. 2 put a knife to thy *t.*, if
Jer. 2. 25 withh. thy *t.* from thirst
Mat. 18. 28 servant took him by *t.*
Rom. 3. 13 Their *t.* is open sepulchre

Throne. *Seat for king, judge,*
priest.
Gen. 41. 40 in *t.* will I be greater
Ex. 11. 5 first born, that sit. on his *t.*
Deut. 17. 18 when he sitteth on *t.*
1 Sam. 2. 8 make them inherit *t.*
2 Sam. 3. 10 to set *t.* of D. ov. Israel
1 K. 1. 13 S. shall sit upon my *t.*
   2. 12 Then sat Sol. on *t.* of David
2 K. 13. 13 Jerobo. sat upon his *t.*
1 Chr. 17. 12 will stablish his *t.* forev.
2 Chr. 6. 10 I am set on *t.* of Israel
Neh. 3. 7 unto *t.* of the governor
Esth. 1. 2 Ahaz. sat on *t.* of his king.
Job 26. 9 hold. back face of his *t.*
Ps. 11. 4 the Lord's *t.* is in heaven
   45. 6 Thy *t.*, O G., is for ev. and ev.
Prov. 16. 12 *t.* is estab. by righteous.
Isa. 6. 1 saw Lord sitting upon a *t.*
   66. 1 heav. is my *t.*, earth my foot.
Jer. 3. 17 sh. call Jerus. *t.* of Lord
Lam. 5. 19 thy *t.* fr. genera. to gen.
Ezek. 1. 26 likeness of *t.*, as appear.
Dan. 7. 9 *t.* was like fiery flame and
Jonah 3. 6 K. of Nin. rose fr. his *t.*
Hag. 2. 22 I will overth. *t.* of king.
Zech. 6. 13 sh. be a priest on his *t.*
Mat. 5. 34 nei. by heav., it is G.'s *t.*
Luke 1. 32 L. sh. gi. him *t.* of fath.
Acts 2. 30 raise C. to sit on his *t.*
Col. 1. 16 whether they be *t.*, or

Heb. 4. 16 come boldly to *t.* of grace
Rev. 1. 4 sev. spirits are bef. his *t.*
   20. 11 saw a great white *t.*, and

Throng. *Press, squeeze.*
Mark 5. 31 seest multitude *t.* thee
Luke 8. 42 as he went the people *t.*
R. V. Luke 8. 45 press

Through. *Into and out.*
Ex. 36. 33 he made bar to shoot *t.*
Mat. 19. 24 easier for cam. to go *t.*
By reason of.
Luke 1. 78 *T.* tender mercy of God
John 15. 3 are clean *t.* the word

Throughly. *Thoroughly.*
Gen. 11. 3 make brick, burn them *t.*
Job 6. 2 my grief were *t.* weighed
Ps. 51. 2 wash me *t.* from iniquity
Jer. 7. 5 if ye *t.* amend your ways
Ezek. 16. 9 I *t.* washed away blood
Mat. 3. 12 will *t.* purge his floor
Luke 3. 17 *t.* purge his floor, and
R. V. 2 Cor. 11. 6 —— ; 2 Tim. 3. 17
   completely

Throw. *Fling, hurl, cast, impel,*
make to tumble.
Ex. 15. 21 horse and rider ha. he *t.*
Judg. 2. 2 shall *t.* down their altars
2 Sam. 16. 13 Shi. *t.* stones at David
1 K. 19. 10 Is ha. *t.* do. th. altars
2 K. 9. 33 So they *t.* Jezebel down
2 Chr. 31. 1 *t.* down high places
Neh. 9. 11 persecutors *t.* into deep
Jer. 1. 10 over nat., to *t.* down, to b.
Lam. 2. 2 ha. *t.* down in his wrath
Ezek. 38. 20 mounts. shall *t.* down
Mic. 5. 11 will *t.* down thy strongh.
Nah. 1. 6 rocks are *t.* down by him
Mal. 1. 4 they build, I shall *t.* down
Mat. 24. 2 one sto. sh. not be *t.* down
   Mark 13. 2 ; Luke 21. 6
Mark 12. 42 and she *t.* in two mites
Luke 9. 42 the devil *t.* him down
Acts 22. 23 cried, *t.* dust into the air
Rev. 18. 21 gr. cit. Baby. be *t.* down
R. V. Judg. 2. 2 ; 6. 32 ; Jer. 33. 4 ;
   Nah. 1. 6 ; break or broken ; Jer.
   1. 10 ; 31. 28 overthrow ; Rev.
   18. 21 cast

Throwing. R. V. *Stone in hand.*
Num. 35. 17 if he smite with *t.* stone

Thrown. *See* **Throw.**

Thrust. *Drive, cast, pierce, push.*
Ex. 11. 1 he sh. surely *t.* you out
Num. 25. 8 Phin. *t.* them through
Deut. 33. 27 he sh. *t.* out enemy
Judg. 9. 41 Zeb. *t.* out Gaal and bre.
1 Sam. 31. 4 Draw sw., *t.* me thro.
2 Sam. 18. 14 *t.* them through Absal.
1 K. 2. 27 Sol. *t.* out Abiathar from
2 K. 4. 27 Gehazi came to *t.* her
1 Chr. 10. 4 Draw sword, *t.* me thro.
2 Chr. 26. 20 Uzziah, they *t.* out thro.
Job 32. 13 say, God *t.* him down
Ps. 118. 13 th. hast *t.* sore at me
Isa. 13. 15 every one sh. be *t.* thro.
Jer. 51. 4 they that are *t.* through
Ezek. 16. 40 *t.* thee thro. wi. swords
Joel 2. 8 neither sh. one *t.* another
Zech. 13. 3 sh. *t.* him thro. when he
Luke 4. 29 *t.* him out of the city
John 20. 25 *t.* my hand into his side
Acts 7. 27 th. did wrong *t.* him away
Heb. 12. 20 stoned or *t.* through
Rev. 14. 15 *T.* in sickle, and reap
R. V. Deut. 13. 5, 10 draw ; Judg.
   6. 38 pressed ; 9. 41 ; 11. 2 drave ;
   Job 32. 13 vanquished ; 1 Sam. 11.
   2 ; Luke 5. 3 ; John 20. 25, 27 put ;
   Luke 4. 29 ; Acts 16. 24, 37 ; Rev.
   14. 19 cast ; Luke 10. 15 brought ;
   Acts 27. 39 drive ; Heb. 12. 20 —— ;
   Rev. 14. 15, 18 send forth

Thumb. *Thumb.*
Ex. 29. 20 put it on *t.* of right hand
Lev. 8. 23, 24 ; 14. 14, 17, 25, 28
Judg. 1. 6 cau. him and cut off *t.*

Thunder (n). *Thunder, voice.*
Ex. 9. 23 the Lord sent *t.* and hail
1 Sam. 7. 10 Lord thundered with *t.*
Job. 26. 14 *t.* of his pow. who unders.
   39. 25 smelleth. *t.* of captains afar
Ps. 77. 18 voice of thy *t.* in heaven
   81. 7 answ. in secret pl. of the *t.*
Isa. 29. 6 sh. be visited of L. wi. *t.*
Mark 3. 17 Boanerges, is sons of *t.*
Rev. 4. 5 out of throne proceed. *t.*

   19. 6 as voice of mighty *t.*, saying
R. V. 39. 19 quivering mane

Thunder (v.). *To thunder.*
1 Sam. 2. 10 out of heav. sh. he *t.*
2 Sam. 22. 14 The L. *t.* from heaven
Job 37. 4 he *t.* with voice of excell.
Ps. 18. 3 L. also *t.* in the heavens
John 12. 29 people heard it, said it *t.*

Thunderbolt. *Heated thing.*
Ps. 78. 48 gave their flocks to *t.*

Thus. *So, this manner.*
Gen. 24. 30 *T.* spake the man to me
Mat. 2. 5 *t.* it is written by prophet
Luke 18. 11 Phar. stood and pray. *t.*
Rom. 9. 20 Why ha. thou ma. me *t.*?
Rev. 9. 17 *t.* I saw horses in vision
R. V. many changes to, so, and, etc.

Thy. *Of thee.*
Mat. 1. 20 fear not to take *t.* wife
Mark 5. 9 asked, What is *t.* name ?
Etc., etc.

Thyine. *Thya tree.*
Rev. 18. 22 merchandise of *t.* wood

Thyself. *Thee, own self.*
Gen. 13. 9 separate *t.* I pray thee
Mat. 4. 6 If S. of G., cast *t.* down
Mark 1. 44 shew *t.* to priest, and
Luke 4. 23 prov., Physician, heal *t.*
John 1. 22 what sayest thou of *t.*?
Acts 16. 28 P. cried, Do *t.* no harm
Rom. 13. 9 love thy neighbour as *t.*
Gal. 6. 1 consid. *t.*, lest be tempted
1 Tim. 4. 7 exercise *t.* unto godliness
2 Tim. 2. 15 Stu. ly to shew *t.* approv.
Tit. 2. 7 shew. *t.* pattern of works
Jas. 2. 8 shalt love neighbour as *t.*

Tide. *Time.*
Josh 8. 29 hanged on tree till ev. *t.*
2 Sam. 11. 2 ca. to pass in ev. *t.*, th.
Isa. 17. 14 behold at ev. *t.* trouble
Jer. 20. 16 hear shout. at noon *t.*

Tidings. *News, report, word.*
Gen. 29. 13 Laban heard *t.* of Jacob
Ex. 33. 4 when people heard evil *t.*
1 Sam. 4. 19 Phine. wife heard *t.*
2 Sam. 4. 4 when *t.* came of Saul
1 K. 2. 28 Then *t.* came to Joab
1 Chr. 10. 9 to carry *t.* unto idols
Ps. 142. 7 not be afraid of evil *t.*
Jer. 20. 15 cursed that brought *t.*
Ezek. 21. 7 answer, For the *t.*, bec.
Dan. 11. 44 *t.* out of east, trouble
Luke 1. 19 Gab., shew thee glad *t.*
Acts 11. 22 *t.* of these things came
Rom. 10. 15 bring glad *t.* of good
R. V. 1 Sam. 11. 4, 5, 6 word ; Acts
   11. 22 report

Tie. *Fasten, bind.*
Ex. 39. 31 *t.* unto it lace of blue
1 Sam. 6. 7 *t.* kine to the cart, and
2 K. 7. 10 horses *t.*, and asses *t.*
Prov. 6. 21 and *t.* about thy neck
Mat. 21. 2 and ye shall find an ass *t.*
   Mark 11. 2, 4 ; Luke 19. 30

Tile. *Brick.*
Ezek. 4. 1 son of man, take thee a *t.*

Tiling. R. V. *tiles.*
Luke 5. 19 let him down through *t.*

Till. *Up to, until.*
Gen. 3. 19 eat bread, *t.* thou return
Dan. 2. 34 sawest *t.* stone be cut
John 21. 22 that he tarry *t.* I come

Till (v.) *Work, cultivate.*
Gen. 2. 5 not a man to *t.* the ground
2 Sam. 9. 10 servants shall *t.* land
Prov. 12. 11 th. *t.* land sh. be satisf.
Jer. 27. 11 *t.* it, and dwell therein
Ezek. 36. 34 desolate land sh. be *t.*

Tillage. *Working, cultivation.*
1 Chr. 27. 26 did work of field for *t.*
Neh. 10. 37 Lev. have tithes for *t.*
Prov. 13. 23 food is in *t.* of the poor

Tiller. *Worker.*
Gen. 4. 2 Cain was *t.* of the ground

Timber. *Wood, beam, tree.*
Ex. 31. 5 cunning, in carving of *t.*
Lev. 14. 45 shall break down the *t.*
1 K. 5. 18 so they prepared *t.* and st
   1 Chr. 22. 14 ; 2 Chr. 2. 9
Ez. 5. 8 *t.* is laid in the walls, and
Neh. 2. 8 give me *t.* to ma. beams
Ezek. 26. 12 sh. lay thy stones and *t.*
Hab. 2. 11 beam out of *t.* answer
Zech. 5. 4 consume it wi. *t.* thereof
R. V. Ex. 31. 5 wood ; 1 Chr 14. 1
   cedar trees ; Ez. 6. 11 beam

Timbrel. *Tabret, timbrel.*
Ex. 15. 20 Miriam took *t.* in hand
Judg. 11. 34 daughter came with *t.*
2 Sam. 6. 5 Is. played bef. L. wi. *t.*
Job 21. 12 They take *t.* and harp
Ps. 68. 25 damsels playing with *t.*

Time. *Duration, period, season, in number.*
Gen. 4. 3 in *t.* it came to pass, th.
Ex. 21. 19 shall pay for loss of *t.*
Lev. 16. 2 come not at all *t.* into
Num. 20. 15 dwelt in Egypt long *t.*
Deut. 3. 23 I besought L. at that *t.*
Josh. 11. 18 Josh. made war long *t.*
Judg. 14. 8 after a *t.* he returned
Ruth. 2. 14 meal *t.* come thou hither
1 Sam. 14. 18 ark th. *t.* was with Is.
2 Sam. 7. 11 since *t.* I commanded
1 K. 8. 65 that *t.* Sol. held feast
2 K. 5. 26 is it a *t.* to receive money
1 Chr. 9. 25 to come from *t.* to *t.*
2 Chr. 7. 8 same *t.* Sol. kept feast
Ez. 10. 13 it is a *t.* of much rain
Neh. 4. 22 same *t.* I said to people
Esth. 1. 13 wise men, wh. knew th. *t.*
Job. 19. 3 ten *t.* ye reproached me
Ps. 34. 1 bless the Lord at all *t.*
Prov. 17. 17 A friend lov. at all *t.*
Eccl. 3. 2 a *t.* to be born, a *t.* to die
S. of S. 2. 12 *t* of sing. birds is come
Isa. 13. 22 her *t.* is near to come
Jer. 8. 7. crane observe *t.* of coming
Ezek. 4. 11 *t.* of *t.* sh. thou drink
Dan. 2. 8 I know ye would gain *t.*
Hos. 10. 12 it is *t.* to seek the Lord
Joel 3. 11 in that *t.*, I sh. bring ag.
Am. 5. 13 silence in that *t.*, every *t.*
Mic. 3. 4 hide his face at that *t.*
Hag. 1. 2 *t.* has not come, *t.* that
Zech. 10. 1 Ask of Lord rain in *t.*
Mat. 8. 29 co. to torment us bef. *t.*
Mark 1. 15 The *t.* is fulfilled, and
Luke 21. 8 the *t.* draweth near, go
John 7. 6 My *t.* is not yet come
Acts 3. 19 *t.* of refresh. shall come
Rom. 9. 9 At this *t.* will I come
1 Cor. 4. 5 judge nothing bef. the *t.*
2 Cor. 6. 2 now is the accepted *t.*
Gal. 4. 10 Ye observe da., mo., and *t.*
Eph. 1. 10 dispen. of fulness of *t.*
Col. 4. 5 Walk in wisd., redeem. *t.*
1 Thes. 2. 17 ta. fr. you for short *t.*
2 Thes. 2. 6 mi. be reveal. in his *t.*
1 Tim. 2. 6 to be testified in due *t.*
2 Tim. 4. 6 *t.* of my depart. at hand
Tit. 1. 3 in *t.* manifested his word
Heb. 4. 16 gra. to help in *t.* of need
Jas. 4. 14 that appeareth a little *t.*
1 Pet. 1. 11 what manner of *t.* Sp.
Rev. 12. 14 for a *t.*, and *t.* a. half a *t.*
R. V. many changes to, day, season, hour. So, many to suit context, as
Mat. 4. 6 at any time, to, haply

Tin. *Tin.*
Num. 31. 22 *t.* that may abide fire
Isa. 1. 25 will take away all thy *t.*
Ezek. 12. 18 they are brass and *t.*

Tingle. *Sting, quiver, ring.*
1 Sam. 3. 11 ears of every one sh. *t.*
2 K. 21. 12; Jer. 19. 3

Tinkle. *Sound, clang.*
Isa. 3. 16 making *t.* with their feet
1 Cor. 13. 1 I am bec. as *t.* cymbal
R. V. 1 Cor. 13. 1 clanging

Tip. *Point, tip.*
Ex. 29. 20 blood, put on *t.* of ri. ear
Lev. 8. 23, 24; 14. 14, 17, 25, 28
Luke 16. 24 dip *t.* of finger in water

Tire (*n.*). *Ornament, headdress.*
Isa. 3. 18 L. will take away their *t.*
Ezek. 24. 17 bind *t.* of thine head

Tire (*v.*). *Attire, dress.*
2 K. 9. 30 Jezebel *t.* her head and

Tithe (*n*). *Tenth.*
Gen. 14. 20 Abr. gave Melchiz. *t.*
Lev. 27. 30 the *t.* of land is Lord's
Num. 18. 24 *t.* I have given to Lord
Deut. 12. 17 not eat *t.* of thy corn
2 Chr. 31. 5 *t.* of all brought they
Neh. 10. 37 *t.* of ground to Levites
Am. 4. 4 bring yo. sacrifices and *t.*
Mal. 3. 10 Bring *t.* into storehouses
Mat. 23. 23 pay *t.* of mint, anise
Luke 18. 12 I give *t.* of all I poss.
Heb. 7. 5 ha. command. to take *t.*
Tithe (*v.*). *Give tenth.*

Deut. 14. 22 thou shalt *t.* increase
Luke 11. 42 ye *t.* mint and rue

Title. *Inscription, monument.*
2 K. 23. 17 what *t.* is that I see?
Job 32. 22 nor give flat. *t.* to man
John 19. 19 P. wrote a *t.* and put
R. V. 2 K. 23. 17 monument.

Tittle. *Little mark or dot.*
Mat. 5. 18 one *t.* shall in no wise
Luke 16. 17 one *t.* of law to fail

Toe. *Foot thumb, toe.*
Ex. 29. 20 upon gr. *t.* of right foot
Lev. 8. 24 on great *t.* of right feet
Judg. 1. 6 cut off thumbs and gr. *t.*
2 Sam. 21. 20 and on every foot six *t.*
1 Chr. 20. 6 fingers and *t.* were tw.
Dan. 2. 42 *t.* of feet were part iron

Together. *As one, with each other.*
Gen. 26. 6 went both of them *t.*
Ex. 19. 8 all the people answered *t.*
Deut. 22. 10 not plow ox and ass *t.*
Josh. 9. 2 gathered themselves *t.*
Judg. 19. 6 they did eat and drink *t.*
1 Sam. 17. 10 that we may fight *t.*
2 Sam. 2. 13 met *t.* by pool of Gib.
1 K. 3. 18 were *t.*; th. was no stranger
1 Chr. 10. 6 Saul died, household *t.*
Ez. 4. 3 we *t.* will build unto Lord
Neh. 6. 2 come, let us meet *t.* in v.
Job 17. 16 our rest *t.* is in the dust
Ps. 55. 14 We took sweet couns. *t.*
Isa. 1. 31 they shall both burn *t.*
Jer. 41. 1 did eat bread *t.* in Miz.
Lam. 2. 8 ram. and wall; th. lang. *t.*
Hos. 1. 11 chil. of Is. be gather. *t.*
Mic. 2. 12 put them *t.* as sheep of B.
Zech. 10. 4 came every oppressor *t.*
Mat. 22. 34 Phar. were gathered *t.*
Luke 17. 35 Two women grinding *t.*
John 21. 2 were *t.* Simon and Peter
Acts 14. 1 went *t.* into synagogue
Rom. 3. 12 are *t.* bec. unprofitable
1 Cor. 7. 5 come *t.*, that Sat. tempt
1 Thes. 4. 17 be caught up *t.* with

Toil (*n.*). *Labor, trial.*
Gen. 5. 29 conc. our work and *t.*

Toil (*v.*). *Try, labor.*
Mat. 6. 28 lilies, they *t.* not, neither do they spin; Luke 12. 27
Mark 6. 48 saw then *t.* in rowing
Luke 5. 5 we have *t.* all the night
R. V. Mark 6. 48 distressed

Token. *Sign, signal.*
Gen. 9. 12 This is *t.* of the covenant
Ex. 12. 13 blood sh. be to you for a *t.*
Num. 17. 10 kept for *t.* ag. rebels
Josh. 2. 12 and give me a true *t.*
Job 21. 29 do ye not know their *t.*
Ps. 65. 8 They are afraid at thy *t.*
Isa. 44. 25 frustrateth *t.* of the liars
Mark 14. 44 Ju. had given th. a *t.*
Phil. 1. 28 evident *t.* of perdition
2 Thes. 1. 5 *t.* of righteous judgment
R. V. Ex. 13. 16; Ps. 135. 9 sign

Told. *See* **Tell.**

Tolerable. *Sufferable.*
Mat. 10. 15 mo. *t.* for land of Sodom
Mark 6. 11; Luke 10. 12
Mat. 11. 22; Luke 10. 14 *t.* for Tyre
R. V. Mark 6. 11 —

Toll. R. V. *tribute.*
Ez. 4. 13 will they not pay *t.*, tribute

Tomb. *Heap, monument, burying place, sepulchre.*
Job. 21. 33 shall remain in the *t.*
Mat. 8. 28 with devils com. out of *t.*
Mark 5. 2, 3, 5; Luke 8. 27
Mat. 27. 60 Jos. laid body in own *t.*
Mark 6. 29 corpse, laid it in a *t.*
R. V. Mat. 23. 29 sepulchres

Tongs. *Tongs, snuffers.*
Ex. 25. 38 ma. *t.* thereof of gold
Num. 4. 9 cov. *t.* with cloth of blue
1 K. 7. 49 lamps, and *t.* of gold
2 Chr. 4. 21 the *t.*, made he of gold
Isa. 6. 6 coal he had taken with *t.*

Tongue. *Tongue, language.*
Gen. 10. 5 ev. one after his own *t.*
Ex. 4. 10 I am slow of speech and *t.*
Deut. 28. 49 whose *t.* not unders.
Josh. 10. 21 none moved his *t.* agai.
Judg. 7. 5 lappeth of water with *t.*
2 Sam. 23. 2 his word was in my *t.*
Esth. 7. 4 if sold, I had held my *t.*
Job 5. 21 be hid from scourge of *t.*
Ps. 5. 9 they flatter with their *t.*

Prov. 10. 20 *t.* of the just is as silver
S. of S. 4. 11 milk are under thy *t.*
Isa. 3. 8 bec. their *t.* is against Lord
Jer. 9. 3 they bend their *t* like bow
Lam. 4. 4 *t.* of suck. child cleaveth
Ezek. 3. 26 I will ma. thy *t.* cleave
Dan. 1. 4 learning and *t.* of Chald.
Hos. 7. 16 princes fall for rage of *t.*
Am. 6. 10 Hold thy *t.*; for we may
Mic. 6. 12 their *t.* is deceitful in
Hab. 1. 13 holdest *t.* when wicked
Zeph. 3. 13 nei. deceit. *t.* be found
Zech. 14. 12 th. *t.* consume in mouth
Mark 7. 33 spit, and touched his *t.*
Luke 1. 64 his *t.* loosed, he spake
John 5. 2 called in Heb. *t.*, Bethes.
Acts 2. 4 began to sp. wi. other *t.*
Rom. 14. 11 ev. *t.* sh. confess God
1 Cor. 12. 10 to ans. divers kinds of *t.*
Phil. 2. 11 ev. *t.* sh. confess that J.
Jas. 3. 5 the *t.* is a little member
1 Pet. 3. 10 let him refr. *t.* from evil
1 John 3. 8 not love in word, nei. *t.*
Rev. 5. 9 redeemed out of every *t.*
R. V. Ez. 4. 17; Esth. 7. 4; Job 6. 24; 13. 19; Am. 6. 10 peace; Acts 2. 8; 21. 40; 22. 2; 26. 14 language; Rev. 9. 11; 16. 16 ——.

Took; *See* **Take.**

Tool. *Weapon.*
Ex. 20. 25 if thou lift up thy *t.* upon it
Vessel, thing.
1 K. 6. 7 nor any *t.* of iron heard

Tooth. *Tooth.*
Gen. 49. 12 eyes red, and *t.* white
Ex. 21. 24 Eye for eye, *t.* for *t.*, hand
Lev. 24. 20 *t.* for *t.*; as he ha. cause
1 Sam. 2. 13 hook of three *t.* in ha.
Job 4. 10 *t.* of young lion are broken
19. 20 escaped with skin of my *t.*
Ps. 3. 7 hast brok. *t.* of the ungodly
Prov. 10. 26 As vinegar to the *t.*, and
S. of S. 6. 6 *t.* are as flock of sheep
Jer. 31. 29 chil's. *t.* are set on edge
Lam. 3. 16 ha. brok. my *t.* wi. gravel
Dan. 7. 7 beast had great iron *t.*
Joel 1. 6 whose *t.* are *t.* of a lion
Mic. 3. 5 bite wi. *t.*, and cry, Peace
Zech. 9. 7 abomination from bet. *t.*
Mat. 8. 12 shall be gnashing of *t.*
13. 42; 22. 13; 24. 51; Luke 13. 28
Mark 9. 18 gnash. wi. *t.*, pineth away
Acts 7. 54 gnashed on him with th. *t.*
Rev. 9. 8 *t.* were as the *t.* of lions

Top. *Roof, crown, highest part.*
Gen. 8. 5 *t.* of mount's were seen
Ex. 19. 20 L. came on *t.* of Sinai
Num. 14. 40 got into *t.* of mountain
Deut. 3. 27 Get thee into *t.* of Pis.
Josh. 15. 8 border went to *t.* of mo.
Judg. 6. 26 build altar on *t.* of rock
1 Sam. 26. 13 D. stood on *t.* of hill
2 Sam. 16. 22 spr. tent on *t.* of house
1 K. 7. 16 set on *t.* of the pillars
2 K. 1. 9 Elijah sat on *t.* of an hill
1 Chr. 14. 15 in *t.* of mulberry trees
2 Chr. 3. 15 chapiter on *t.* of each of
Esth. 5. 2 Esth. touch. *t.* of sceptre
Job. 24. 24 cut off as the *t.* of ears
Ps. 72. 16 corn on *t.* of mountains
Prov. 8. 2 she stand. in *t.* of high
S. of S. 4. 8 look from *t.* of Amana
Isa. 30. 17 as beacon on *t.* of mount.
Lam. 2. 19 faint for hunger in *t.* of
Ezek. 17. 4 cropp. *t.* of young twigs
Hos. 4. 13 sacrif. on *t.* of mountains
Joel 2. 5 noise of chariots on *t.* of m.
Am. 1. 2 *t.* of Carmel shall wither
Nah. 3. 10 dashed at *t.* of streets
Zeph. 1. 16 worship host on house *t.*
Zech. 4. 2 with bowl upon *t.* of it
Mat. 27. 51 rent from *t.* to bottom
Mark 13. 15 on house *t.* not go down
Luke 12. 3 proclaimed on house *t.*
John 19. 23 woven from *t.* through.
Heb. 11. 21 worsh., le. on *t.* of staff
R. V. Ex. 28. 32 head; Deut. 28. 35; 33. 16 crown; Judg. 15. 8, 11 cleft; Judg. 9. 51; 1 K. 23. 12 roof; Ezek. 24. 7, 8; 26. 4, 14 bare

Topaz. *Topaz, emerald.*
Ex. 28. 17 shall be *t.*, and a carbuncle
Job. 28. 19 *t.* of Ethi. not equal it
Ezek. 28. 13 *t.* was thy covering
Rev. 21. 20 beryl; the ninth, a *t*

Torch. *Light, torch, lamp.*

Nah. 2. 3 chariots sh. be with *t.*
Zech. 12. 6 make govern. like a *t.*
John 18. 3 Judas cometh with *t.* and
R. V. Nah. 2. 3 flash with steel
Torment (*n.*). *Anguish, torture.*
Mat. 4. 24 tak. with disease and *t.*
Luke 16. 23 lifted eyes, being in *t.*
1 John 4. 18 because fear hath *t.*
Rev. 9. 5 th. *t.* was as *t.* of scorpions
R. V. 1 John 4. 18 punishment
Torment (*v.*). *Try, make to suffer.*
Mat 8. 6 servant lieth grievously *t.*
Mark 5. 7 I adjure thee *t.* me not
Luke 8. 28 I beseech thee, *t.* not
Heb. 11. 37 destitute, afflicted, *t.*
Rev. 9. 5 should be *t.* five months
R. V. Luke 16. 24, 25 in anguish ;
Heb. 11. 37 evil entreated
Tormentors. *Who torment.*
Mat. 18. 34 lord deliver. him to *t.*
Torn. *See* **Tear.**
Tortoise. R. V. *great lizard.*
Lev. 11. 29 the *t.* shall be unclean
Tortured. *Beaten.*
Heb. 11. 35 oth. were *t.*, not accept.
Toss. *Shake, drive, agitate.*
Ps. 109. 23 I am *t.* up and down as
Prov. 21. 6 a vanity *t.* to and fro
Isa. 22. 18 He will . . and *t.* thee like
Jer. 5. 22 though waves *t.* themsel.
Mat. 14. 24 ship was *t.* with winds
Acts 27. 18 exceed. *t.* with tempest
Eph. 4. 14 children, *t.* to and fro
Jas. r. 6 that wavereth, is li. wave *t.*
R. V. Prov. 21. 6 driven ; Mat.
14. 24 distressed ; Acts 27. 18
laboured
Tossings. *Movings, tossings.*
Job 7. 4 I am full of *t.*, to and fro
Totter. *Waver, be unsteady.*
Ps. 62. 3 ye shall be as a *t.*, fence
Touch. *Be or come in contact,*
touch, made to feel with.
Gen. 3. 3 neither *t.* it, lest ye die
Ex. 19. 13 sh. not an hand *t.*, it, but
Lev. 5. 2 if soul *t.* any unclean thing
Num. 5. 14 sh. not *t.* any holy thing
Deut. 14. 8 not eat flesh, nor *t.* dead
Josh. 9. 19 therefore we may not *t.*
Judg. 6. 21 angel of L. *t.* the flesh
Ruth 2. 9 that they shall not *t.* thee
1 Sam. 10. 26 whose hearts G. had *t.*
2 Sam. 14. 10 he shall not *t.* thee
1 K. 6. 27 wing of one *t.* one wall
2 K. 13. 21 *t.* the bones of Elisha
1 Chr. 16. 22 *T.* not mine anointed
Esth. 5. 2 Esther *t.* top of sceptre
Job 2. 5 *t.* his bone and flesh, he
Ps. 104. 32 he *t.* hills, they smoke
Prov. 6. 29 who *t.* her, not innocent
Isa. 6. 7 lo, this hath *t.* thy lips and
Jer. 1. 9 Then the Lord *t.* my mouth
Lam. 4. 15 unclean ; depart, *t.* not
Ezek. 7. 10 wither when east wind *t.*
Dan. 8. 5 he goat *t.* not the ground
Hos. 4. 2 break, and blood *t.* blood
Am. 9. 5 Lord of hosts that *t.* land
Hag. 2. 12 if one with skirt *t.* bread
Zech. 2. 8 th. *t.* you *t.* apple of eye
Mat. 8. 3 J. put forth hand and *t.*
Mark 5. 28 If I may *t.* his clothes
Luke 8. 45 Jesus said, Who *t.* me ?
John 20. 17 *T.* me not ; I am not yet
Acts 27. 3 next day we *t.* at Sidon
1 Cor. 7. 1 good not to *t.* a woman
2 Cor. 6. 17 *t.* not the unclean thing
Col. 2. 21 *T.* not, taste not, hand. not
Heb. 4. 15 priest wh. cannot be *t.*
1 John 5. 18 wicked one *t.* him not
Touching. *Concerning.*
Jer. 22. 11 thus saith L. *t.* Shallum
Mat. 18. 19 *t.* anything they sho. ask
Acts 24. 21 *T.* the resurrection of
Rom. 11. 28 but as *t.* the election
1 Cor. 8. 1 as *t.* things offer. idols
Phil. 3. 5 as *t.* the law, a Pharisee
Col. 4. 10 *t.* whom ye received com.
2 Thes. 3. 4 confidence in the L. *t.*
R. V. 1 Cor. 8. 1 ; 1 Thes. 4. 9 con-
cerning
Tow. *Flax refuse.*
Judg. 16. 9 as thread of *t.* is broken
Isa. 1. 31 the strong shall be as *t.*
R. V. Isa. 43. 17 flax
Toward. *In direction of, unto.*
Gen. 18. 16 men rose, looked *t.* Sod.

Ex. 28. 27 *t.* the forepart thereof
Num. 21. 20 Pisgah, look. *t.* Jeshi.
1 Sam. 20. 41 David arose out *t.* the
2 Sam. 15. 23 *t.* way of the wildern.
1 K. 8. 44 pray to Lord *t.* the city
2 K. 25. 4 k. went way *t.* the plain
2 Chr. 6. 34 pray to thee *t.* the city
Ezek. 20. 46 set thy face *t.* the south
Dan. 6. 10 windows open *t.* Jerusa.
Mat. 28. 1 began to dawn *t.* first day
Mark 6. 34 moved wi. compassion *t.*
Luke 2. 14 peace, good will *t.* men
John 6. 17 went over sea *t.* Caper.
Acts 1. 10 looked stedf. *t.* heaven
Rom. 12. 16 same mind one *t* ano.
1 Cor. 7. 36 behav. uncom. *t.* virgin
2 Cor. 1. 18 word *t.* you was not yea
Gal. 2. 8 mighty in me *t.* Gentiles
Eph. 2. 7 kindness *t.* us thro. Chr.
Phil. 2. 30 sup. lack of ser. *t.* me
Col. 4. 5 Walk in wisdom *t.* them
1 Thes. 5. 14 weak, be patient *t.* all
2 Thes. 1. 3 charity of all *t.* each
Phile. 5 faith, thou hast *t.* L. God
Heb. 6. 10 love, wh. ye ha. show. *t.*
1 Pet. 3. 21 answ. of good consc. *t.*
1 John 3. 21 have we confid. *t.* God
R. V. many changes to, unto, **to,**
in, and similar prepositions
Towel. *Cloth, linen.*
John 13. 4 he riseth, and took a *t.*
Tower. *High structure, secure*
place, bulwark, citadel.
Gen. 11. 4 let us build a city, and *t.*
Judg. 8. 17 he beat do. *t.* of Penuel
2 Sam. 22. 51 he is *t.* of salvation
2 K. 9. 17 stood a watchman on *t.*
2 Chr. 26. 9 Uzziah built *t.* in Jeru.
Neh. 3. 1 to *t.* of Meah th. sancti.
Ps. 61. 3 a strong *t.* from enemy
Prov. 18. 10 the Lord is a strong *t.*
S. of S. 4. 4 Thy neck is li. *t.* of D.
Isa. 32. 14 forts and *t.* sh. be dens
Jer. 31. 38 fr. *t.* of Han. unto gate
Ezek. 30. 6. fr. *t.* of Syene sh. fall
Mic. 4. 8 thou, O *t.* of the flock,
Zech. 14. 10 *t.* of Han. to k's wine
Hab. 2. 1 I will set me up on the *t.*
Zeph. 3. 6 ha. cut off nations ; th. *t.*
Mat. 21. 23 digged wineps. bu. a *t.*
Mark 12. 1 built *t.*, let it to husb.
Luke 13. 4 eighteen, on wh. *t.* fell
R. V. 2 K. 5. 24 hill ; Zeph. 1. 16 ;
3. 6. battlements
Town. *City, town, village.*
Gen. 25. 16 sons of Ish., by their *t.*
Num. 32. 41 Jair took small *t.*
Deut. 3. 5 unwalled *t.* a gr. many
Josh. 13. 30 coast, all the *t.* of Jair
Judg. 11. 26 Is. dwelt in Hesh. *t.*
1 Sam. 16. 4 elders of the *t.* tremb.
1 K. 4. 13 to him pertained *t.* of Jair
1 Chr. 2. 23 he took Aram, wi. *t.* of
Esth. 9. 19 Jews dwelt in unwall. *t.*
Jer. 19. 15 bring on her *t.* the evil
Hab. 2. 12 Woe to him th. build. *t.*
Zech. 2. 4 sh. be as *t.* without walls
Mat. 10. 11 whatsoever *t.* ye enter
Mark 8. 27 J. went into *t.* of Cesar.
Luke 9. 6 went thro. *t.* preaching
John 11. 1 Bethany, *t.* of Mary and
R. V. Gen. 25. 16 ; 1 Chr. 2. 23 ;
Zech. 2. 4 ; Mark 8. 23, 26, 27 ;
Luke 5. 17 ; 9. 6, 12 ; John 11. 1,
30 ; 7. 42 village or villages ; 1
Sam. 27. 5 cities
Town Clerk. *Scribe, writer.*
Acts 19. 35 when *t. c.* appeas. peo.
Trade (*n.*). *Occupation.*
Gen. 46. 32 their *t.* been to feed c.
Trade (*v.*). *Go about, traffic.*
Gen. 34. 10 dwell and *t.* ye therein
Ezek. 27. 12 Tarsh. *t.* in thy fairs
Mat. 25. 16 five talents, went and *t.*
Luke 19. 15 every man gained by *t.*
Rev. 18. 17 as *t.* by sea, stood afar
Tradition. *Handing down.*
Mat. 15. 2 why do dis. transgr. *t.*
Mark 7. 3 holding to *t.* of elders
Gal. 1. 14 Zealous of *t.* of my fath.
2 Thes. 2. 15 hold *t.* ye been tau.
1 Pet. 1. 18 received by *t.* fr. father
R. V. 1 Pet. 1. 18 handed down
Traffic (*n.*). *Trade.*
1 K. 10. 15 had of *t.* of merchants
Ezek. 17. 4 car. it into land of *t.*

Traffic (*v.*). *To trade.*
Gen. 42. 34 ye shall *t.* in the land
Traffickers. *Traders, pedlers.*
Isa. 23 8 *t.* are the honourable of
Train (*n.*). *Force, company.*
1 K. 10. 2 to Jerus. with great *t.*
Skirt extension
Isa. 6 1 L., his *t.* filled the temple
Train (*v.*). *Rear, instruct.*
Gen. 14. 14 Abram armed *t.* serv.
Prov. 22. 6 *T.* chi. in way he sh. go
Traitor. *A giver over, betrayer.*
Luke 6. 16 Jud. Iscar. which was *t.*
2 Tim. 3. 4 in last days men be *t.*
Trample. *Tread upon.*
Ps. 91. 13 the dragon *t.* under feet
Isa. 63. 3 I will *t.* them in my fury
Mat. 7. 6 lest th. *t.* th. under feet
Trance. *Ecstasy.*
Num. 24. 4 *t.*, but hav. eyes open
Acts 10. 10 ready, he fell into a *t.*
R. V. Num. 24. 4, 16 down
Tranquillity. *Serenity, ease.*
Dan. 4. 27 be a length. of thy *t.*
Transfer. *Carry over.*
1 Cor. 4. 6 I ha. in fig. *t.* to myself
Transfigured. *Transformed.*
Mat. 17. 2 ; Mark 9. 2 was *t.* bef. t.
Transform. *Give different form.*
Rom. 12. 2 be ye *t.* by renewing
2 Cor. 11. 13 *t.* thems. into apostles
R. V. 2 Cor. 11. 13, 14, 15 fashion
Transgress. *Step over, rebel, de-*
ceive, trespass.
Num. 14. 41 Wherefore *t.* comman.
Deut. 26. 13 I have not *t.* comman.
Josh. 7. 11 they have *t.* my coven.
Judg. 2. 20 this peo. hath *t.* my cov.
1 Sam. 2. 24 make L.'s people to *t.*
1 K. 8. 50 wherein they have *t.* ag.
2 K. 18. 12 but *t.* his covenant, and
1 Chr. 5. 25 they *t.* against the God
2 Chr. 26. 16 he *t.* ag. the L. his G.
Ez. 10. 10 Ye have *t.* and taken st.
Neh. 1. 8 If ye *t.*, I will scatter
Esth. 3. 3 Why *t.* the king's comm.
Ps. 17. 3 purpose. mouth sh. not *t.*
Prov. 28. 21 for bread that man *t.*
Isa. 43. 27 thy teachers have *t.* ag.
Jer. 2. 8 the pastors *t.* against me
Lam. 3. 42 We have *t.* and rebelled
Ezek. 2. 3 they and their fa. have *t.*
Dan. 9. 11 all Is. have *t.* thy law
Hos. 7. 13 because they have *t.*
Am. 4. 4 Come to Bethel, and *t.* ; at
Hab. 2. 5 he *t.* by wine, is proud
Zeph. 3. 11 wherein thou hast *t.* ag.
Mat. 15. 2 Why do thy disciples *t.*
Luke 15. 29 neither *t.* I at any time
1 John 3. 4 committeth sin *t.* law
2 John 9. nor *t.* thy commandments
R. V. 1 Chr. 2. 7 ; 5. 25 ; 2 Chr. 12.
2 ; 26. 16 ; 28. 19 ; 36. 14 ; Ez. 10
10 ; Neh. 1. 8 ; 13. 27 ; Hos. 7. 13
trespass ; 1 Sam. 14. 33 ; Ps. 25. 3 .
Hab. 2. 5 dealt treacherously ; Jer.
2. 20 serve ; 1 John 3. 4 doeth
lawlessness ; 2 John 9 goeth on-
ward.
Transgressing. *Stepping over.*
Deut. 17. 2 wickedn., in *t.* coven.
Isa. 59. 13 in *t.* and lying ag. Lord
Transgression. *Overstepping,*
trespass, deceit, rebellion
Ex. 23. 21 will not pardon your *t.*
Lev. 16. 16 atonement because of *t.*
Josh. 24. 19 will not forgive your *t.*
1 Sam. 24. 11 is nei. *t.* in my hand
1 K. 8. 50 forgive people their *t.*
1 Chr. 9. 1 carried to Babyl. for *t.*
2 Chr. 29. 19 Ahaz cast away in *t.*
Ez. 10. 6 mourned bec. of their *t.*
Job 13. 23 ma. me to know my *t.*
Ps. 32. 1 blessed wh. *t.* is forgiven
Prov. 12. 13 wicked is snared by *t.*
Isa. 50. 1 your *t.* is your mother
Jer. 5. 6 because their *t.* are many
Lam. 1. 5 multitude of her *t.* gone
Ezek. 33. 12 deliver in day his *t.*
Dan. 12 ag. sacri. by reason of *t.*
Am. 1. 3 For three *t.* of Damascus
Mic. 1. 5 For *t.* of Jacob is all this
Acts 1. 25 fr. which Jud. by *t.* fell
Rom. 4. 15 wh. no law is, is no *t.*
Gal. 3. 19 It was added because of *t.*
1 Tim. 2. 14 woman dece. was in *t.*

Heb. 2. 2 every *t.* receiv. recomp.
1 John 3. 4 for sin is *t.* of the law
R. V. Josh. 22. 22; 1 Chr. 10. 13;
Ez. 9. 4; 10. 6; 2 Chr. 29. 19 tres-
pass; 1 John 3. 4 lawlessness
Transgressor. *Stepper over, de-*
ceiver, treacherous one, trespasser
Ps. 37. 38 *t.* sh. be destroyed toget.
Prov. 2. 22 *t.* shall be rooted out
Isa. 1. 28 destruction of *t.* together
Dan. 8. 23 *t.* are come to the full
Hos. 14. 9 but *t.* shall fall therein
Mark 15. 28 he was num. with *t.*
Luke 22. 37 he was reckoned am. *t.*
Gal. 2. 18 build, I ma. myself a *t.*
Jas. 2. 9 are convin. of law as *t.*
R. V. Prov. 2. 22; 11. 3, 6; 13. 2,
15; 21. 18; 22. 12; 23. 28 treacher-
ous; 26. 10 that pass by.
Translate. *Bear up over.*
2 Sam. 3. 10 *t.* kingdom from Saul
Col. 1. 13 *t.* us into kingd. of Son.
Heb. 11. 5 Enoch was *t.*, that he
Translation. *Putting up over.*
Heb. 11. 5 bef. *t.* he had this testim.
Transparent. *Appearing through.*
Rev. 21. 21 pure gold, as it were *t.*
Trap. *Snare, trap.*
Josh. 23. 13 shall be snares and *t.*
Job 18. 10 snare is laid for h., and *t.*
Ps. 69. 22 welfare, let become a *t.*
Jer. 5. 26 wicked, they set a *t.*, th.
Rom. 11. 9 let their table be ma. *t.*
Travail (*n.*). *Bringing forth, pain,*
toil, weariness, distress.
Gen. 38. 27 pass, in time of her *t.*
Ex. 18. 8 told Jethro all *t.* by way
Num. 20. 14 know. all the *t.* th. ha.
Ps. 48. 6 and pain, as of woman in *t.*
Eccl. 1. 13 sore *t.* G. given to men
Isa. 53. 1 sh. see of *t.* of his soul
Jer. 4. 31 voice as of a woman in *t.*
Lam. 3. 5 compas. with gall and *t.*
Mic. 4. 9 pangs as a woman in *t.*
John 16. 21 woman *t.* hath sorrow
1 Thes. 2. 9 for ye rememb. our *t.*
2 Thes. 3. 8 wro. wi. *t.* night and day
R. V. Eccl. 4. 4 labour; 5. 14 ad-
venture
Travail (*v.*). *Bring forth, be*
pained.
Gen. 35. 16 Rachel *t.*, she had hard
1 Sam. 4. 19 she bowed her. and *t.*
Job 15. 20 wick. man *t.* with pain
Ps. 7. 14 behold, he *t.* with iniq.
Isa. 23. 4 I *t.*, nor bring children
Jer. 31. 8 her that *t.* with child
Hos. 13. 13 sor. of *t.* wom. sh. co.
Mic. 5. 3 break forth and cry, th. *t.*
Rom. 8. 22 and *t.* in pain together
Gal. 4. 27 break forth thou that *t.*
Rev. 12. 2 *t.* in birth, and pained
Travel (*n.*). *Journeying.*
Acts 19. 29 Paul's companion in *t.*
Travel (*v.*). *To go, walk, journey.*
Prov. 6. 11 poverty co. as one th. *t.*
Isa. 21. 13 O ye *t.* comp. of Dedan.
Mat. 25. 14 heaven is as a man *t.*
Acts 11. 19 Ste. *t.* as far as Phenice
2 Cor. 8. 19 cho. of churches to *t.*
R. V. Prov. 6. 11; 24. 34 a robber;
Isa. 63. 1 marching; Mat. 25. 14
going
Traveller. *Who goes, wayfarer.*
Judg. 5. 6 *t.* walked thro. by ways
2 Sam. 12. 4 came *t.* to rich man
Job 31. 32 I open. my doors to *t.*
Traversing. *Passing over.*
Jer. 2. 23 a dromedary *t.* her ways
Treacherous. *Deceitful.*
Isa. 21. 2 *t.* dealeth treacherously
Jer. 3. 8 her *t.* sister Judah feared
Zeph. 3. 4 proph. are light and *t.*
Treacherously. *Deceitfully.*
Judg. 9. 23 men of Shechem. de. *t.*
Isa. 33. 1 deal. *t.* they dealt not *t.*
Jer. 3. 20 as a wife *t.* departeth fr.
Lam. 1. 2 her friends have dealt *t.*
Hos. 5. 7 they dealt *t.* against Lord
Hab. 1. 13 look. on them th. deal *t.*
Mal. 2. 11 Judah hath dealt *t.*, and
Treachery. *Deceit.*
2 K. 9. 23 there is *t.*, O Ahaziah
Tread. *Trample, tread.*
Deut. 1. 36 give land he ha. *t.* on
Josh. 1. 3 ev. place your foot sh. *t.*

49

Judg. 5. 21 thou hast *t.* do. strength
1 Sam. 5. 5 *t.* on thresh. of Dagon
2 K. 7. 17 peo. *t.* upon him in gate
2 Chr. 25. 18 beast *t.* down thistle
Job 9. 8 *t.* on the waves of the sea
Ps. 7. 5 let him *t.* down my life
Isa. 10. 6 *t.* th. down like the mire
Jer. 48. 33 none sh. *t.* with shouting
Lam. 1. 15 *t.* virgin, daughter of Ju.
Ezek. 34. 18 ye must *t.* wi. your feet
Dan, 7. 23 sh. *t.* it down, and br. it
Hos. 10. 11 Eph. loveth to *t.* corn
Am. 5. 11 your *t.* is upon the poor
Mic. 1. 3 L. will *t.* on high places
Nah. 3. 14 *t.* morter, make brick.
Zech. 10. 5 which *t.* their enemies
Mal. 4. 3 ye shall *t.* down wicked
Mat. 5. 13 cast out, be *t.* under foot
Luke 10. 19 power to *t.* on serpents
1 Cor. 9. 9 not muzzle the ox that *t.*
Heb. 10. 29 *t.* under foot Son of G.
Rev. 11. 2 cit. sh. they *t.* und. foot
R. V. Isa. 1. 12; Am. 5. 11 trample
Treader. *Who treads.*
Isa. 16. 10 *t.* shall tread out no wine
Am. 9. 13 the *t.* of grapes him that
Treason. *Conspiracy, betrayal.*
1 K. 16. 20 acts of Zim., and his *t.*
2 Chr. 23. 13 rent her clo., said. *T.*, *t.*
Treasure (*n.*). *Thing laid up,*
valued, set store by.
Gen. 43. 23 God hath given you *t.*
Ex. 1. 11 built Pharaoh *t.* cities
Deut. 28. 12 L. shall open good *t.*
1 K. 7. 15 put am. *t.* of the house
2 K. 12. 18 took gold was found in *t.*
1 Chr. 26. 20 Ahi. was over the *t.* of
2 Chr. 12. 9 took away *t.* of house
Ez. 7. 20 bestow it on k's *t.* house
Neh. 7. 70 Tirs. gave to *t.* thousand
Job 38. 22 hast seen *t.* of the hail
Ps. 17. 14 belly thou fillest with *t.*
Prov. 15. 6 in house of right. is *t.*
Isa. 33. 6 fear of the Lord is his *t.*
Jer. 15. 13 thy *t.* will I give to spoil
Ezek. 28. 4 gotten gold into thy *t.*
Dan. 1. 2 bro. ves. into the *t.* house
Hos. 13. 15 he shall spoil *t.* of all
Mic. 6. 10 Are yet *t.* of wickedness
Mat. 6. 19 Lay not up *t.* on earth
Mark 10. 21 thou sh. ha. *t.* in heav.
Luke 12. 34 where *t.* is, there heart
Acts 8. 27 eunuch had charge of *t.*
2 Cor. 4. 17 *t.* in earthen vessels
Col. 2. 3 in whom are hid *t.* of wis.
Heb. 11. 26 gr. rich. th. *t.* of Egypt
Jas. 5. 3 have heaped *t.* for last day
R. V. 1 Chr. 26. 20, 22, 24, 26; 27. 25;
Job 38. 22; Prov.8. 21; Jer. 10. 3;
51. 16 treasuries; Jer. 41. 8 stores
hidden
Treasure (*v.*). *Store up.*
Isa. 23. 18 it shall not be *t.* up nor
Rom. 2. 5 *t.* up wrath against day of
Treasurer. *Treasure keeper.*
Ez. 1. 8 by the hand of Mith. the *t.*
Neh. 13. 13 I made *t.* ov. the treas.
Isa. 22. 15 Go. get thee unto this *t.*
Dan. 3. 2 Nebuch. gathered the *t.*
Treasury. *Treasure place.*
Josh. 6. 19 sil. sh. co. into *t.* of Lord
1 Chr. 9. 26 Levites were over the *t.*
2 Chr. 32. 27 Hez. made *t.* for silver
Neh. 13, 12 brought tithe unto the *t.*
Esth. 3. 9 silver, bring it into k's *t.*
Ps. 135. 7 bringeth wind out of *t.*
Jer. 38. 11 went into hou. under *t.*
Mat. 27. 6 is not lawful to put in *t.*
Mark 12, 41 J. sat over against *t.*
Luke 21. 1 saw rich cast. gifts in *t.*
John 8. 20 words spake Jesus in *t.*
Treatise. *Word, discourse.*
Acts 1.1 former *t.* I ma., O Theoph.
Tree. *Tree, wood, timber.*
Gen. 1. 29 I have given you every *t.*
Ex. 9. 25 the hail brake every *t.*
Lev. 19. 23 planted all manner of *t.*
Num. 24. 6 as *t.* of lign aloes wh.
Deut. 16. 21 not plant grove of *t.*
Josh. 8. 29 k. of Ai he hanged on *t.*
Judg. 9. 10 *t.* said to fig *t.*, Come
1 Sam. 22. 6 Saul abode under *t.*
2 Sam. 5. 11 H. sent to D. cedar *t.*
1 K. 4 33 he spake of *t.* from cedar
2 K. 3. 25 they felled the good *t.*
1 Chr. 16. 33 Th. sh. *t.* of wood sing

769

2 Chr. 2. 8 Send cedar *t.* out of Leb.
Ez. 3. 7 bring cedar *t.* fr. Lebanon
Neh. 10. 35 bring first fr. of fruit *t.*
Esth. 2. 23 were both hanged on a *t.*
Job 14. 7 hope of a *t.*, if cut down
Ps. 1. 3 be like a *t.* planted by river
Prov. 11. 30 fruit of righteous is a *t.*
Eccl. 2. 5 I planted *t.* of all kinds
S. of S. 2. 3 As apple am. *t.* of woods
Isa. 7. 2 as *t.* of the wood are moved
Jer. 2. 20 und. green *t.* th. wanderest
Ezek. 15. 2 W. vine *t.* mo. th. any *t.*
Dan. 4. 14 Hew *t.*, cut off branches
Joel 1. 12 *t.* of field are withered
Mat. 3. 10 every *t.* that bringeth not
forth good fruit, 7. 19; Luke 3. 9
Mat. 2. 18 others cut down bran. of
t. and strewed; Mark 11. 8
Mark 8. 24 I see men as *t.* walk
Luke 21. 29 behold fig *t.* and all *t.*
Acts 5. 30 whom ye hanged on a *t.*
Gal. 3. 13 Cur. ev. one th. hang. on *t.*
1 Pet. 2. 24 Who bare our sins on *t.*
Jude 12 *t.* whose fruit withereth
Rev. 2. 7 give to eat of the *t.* of life
Num. 6. 4 grapevine; Num. 24. 6;
1. K. 4. 33; Isa. 66. 17; Rom. 11.
17——; 1 K. 6. 23, 31–34 wood;
1 K. 5. 10; 2 K. 19. 23; 2 Chr. 1.
15; 9. 27 cedars; Isa. 6. 13 tere-
binth; Ezek. 31. 14 mighty ones
Tremble. *Shake, quiver.*
Gen. 27. 33 Isaac *t.* very exceeding,
Ex. 19. 16 people in the camp *t.*
Deut. 2. 25 nations sh. *t.* because
Judg. 5. 4 earth *t.*, heavens dropped
1 Sam. 4. 13 Eli's heart *t.* for ark
2 Sam. 22. 8 the earth shook and *t.*
Ez. 10. 3 that *t.* at commandment
Job 26. 11 pillars of heaven *t.* and
Ps. 60. 2 hast made the earth to *t.*
Eccl. 12. 3 keepers of house sh. *t.*
Isa. 32. 11 *T.*, women th. are at ease
Jer. 4. 24 *t.*, and all the hills moved
Ezek. 26. 18 sh. isles *t.* in the day
Dan. 5. 19 peo. *t.* and feared before
Hos. 11. 11 *t.* as bird out of Egypt
Joel 2. 1 let all inhabit. of land *t.*
Am. 8. 8. Sh. not land *t.* for this
Hab. 3. 10 mount's saw thee, they *t.*
Mark 16. 8 they fled; for they *t.* and
Acts 24. 25 as he reasoned, Felix *t.*
Jas. 2. 19 the devils believe and *t.*
R. V. Hab. 3. 10 were afraid; Acts
24. 25 was terrified.
Trembling. *Fearing, quaking.*
Ex. 15. 15 men, *t.* sh. take hold upon
Deut. 28. 65 sh. give thee a *t.* heart
1 Sam. 14. 15 was *t.*, a very great *t.*
Job 4. 14 Fear came upon me and *t.*
Ps. 2. 11 Serve L., and rejoice wi. *t.*
Isa. 51. 17 hast drunk. of cup of *t.*
Jer. 30. 5 We ha. heard a voice of *t.*
Ezek. 12. 18 dr. thy water wi. *t.* and
Hos. 13. 1 when Ephraim sp. *t.*, her
Zech. 12. 2 I will ma. Jer. a cup of *t.*
Mark 5. 33 the woman fearing and *t.*
Luke 8. 47 came *t.*, and falling down
Acts 9. 6 he *t.* and astonished said
1 Cor. 2. 3 was wi. you in fear and *t.*
2 Cor. 7. 15 wi. fear and *t.* ye receiv.
Eph. 6. 5 be obedi., wi. fear and *t.*
Phil. 2. 12 work out salva. with *t.*
R. V. Job 21. 6 horror; Isa. 51. 17,
22 staggering . Zech. 12. 2 reeling
Trench. *Rampart, bulwark.*
1 Sam. 26. 5 Saul lay in the *t.*, and
2 Sam. 20. 15 bank, it stood in the *t.*
Luke 19. 43 enemies sh. cast *t.* about
Ditch, conduit
1 K. 18. 32 he made a *t.* about altar
R. V. 1 Sam. 17. 20; 26. 5, 7 place
of wagons; 2 Sam. 20. 15 rampart;
Luke 19. 43 bank
Trespass (*n.*). *Falling aside, tran-*
gression, guilt.
Gen. 31. 36 Wh. my *t.* ? wh. my sin
Ex. 22. 9 For all manner of *t.*, whe.
Lev. 5. 15 If a soul commit *t.*, and
Num. 5. 7 he shall recomp. his *t.*
1 Sam. 25. 28 forgive *t.* of ha. maid
2 K. 12. 16 *t.* mon. was not brought
1 Chr. 21. 3 why cause *t.* to Israel?
2 Chr. 24. 18 wrath ca. for their *t.*
Ez. 9. 6 our *t.* is grown to heaven
Ps. 68. 21 such as goeth on in *t.*

Ezek. 17. 20 I will plead for his *t.*
Dan. 9. 7 bec. of *t.* they trespassed
Mat. 6. 14 if ye forgive men their *t.*
Mark 11. 25 yo. F. may forgi. yo. *t.*
2 Cor. 5. 19 not imput. their *t.* unto
Eph. 2. 1 you who were dead in *t.*
Col. 2. 13 quickened, forgiven all *t.*
R. V. Gen. 50. 17 transgression;
Num. 5. 7, 8; Lev. 6. 5; 22. 16;
1 Chr. 21. 3; 2 Chr. 19. 10; Ez. 9.
7, 13; 10. 10, 19 guilt or guilty; 2
Chr. 24. 18; Ez. 6. 15; 9. 6, 15;
Ps. 68. 21 guiltiness; Mat. 8. 35;
Mark 11. 26——.
Trespass (*v.*). *Trangress, err, sin, become guilty.*
Lev. 5. 19 he ha. cert. *t.* ag. Lord
Num. 5. 7 recomp. ag. whom he *t.*
Deut. 32. 51 Bec. ye *t.* against me
1 K. 8. 31 If man *t.* ag. his neighbour
2 Chr. 19. 10 this do, ye sh. not *t.*
Ez. 10. 2 We have *t.* ag. our God
Ezek. 14. 13 land sin. ag. me by *t.*
Dan. 9. 7 bec. they have *t.* against
Hos. 8. 1 they *t.* against my law
Mat. 18. 15 if bro. *t.*, tell him fault
Luke 17. 3 if brother *t.*, rebuke him
R. V. 2 Chr. 19. 10 be guilty; 1 K.
8. 31; Mat. 18. 5; Luke 17. 3, 4
sin
Trial. *Proof, test.*
Job 9. 23 laugh at *t.* of innocent
Ezek. 21. 13 *t.*, and what if the sw.
2 Cor. 8. 2 How in *t.* of affliction
Heb. 11. 36 others had *t.* of mock.
1 Pet. 1. 7 *t.* of your faith might
R. V. 2 Cor. 8. 2 ; 1 Pet. 1. 7 proof
Tribe. *Tribe, rod, staff.*
Gen. 49. 28 these are twelve *t.* of Is.
Ex. 39. 14 name accord. to tw. *t.*
Lev. 24. 11 daugh. of Dib., *t.* of D.
Num. 1. 4 shall be man of every *t.*
Deut. 1. 15 I took chief of your *t.*
Josh. 13. 2 Mos. ga. inherit. to *t.*
Judg. 21. 6 is one *t.* cut off fr. Is.
1 Sam. 9. 21 Benj., smallest of *t.*
2 Sam. 5. 1 Then ca. *t.* of Is. to D.
1 K. 11. 31 I will gi. ten *t.* to thee
2 K. 17. 18 none left but *t.* of Jud.
1 Chr. 27. 22 These were prin. of *t.*
2 Chr. 6. 5 I chose no city am. *t.*
Ez. 6. 17 accord. to num. of the *t.*
Ps. 78. 55 made *t.* of Is. to dwell
Isa. 19. 13 they that are stay of *t.*
Ezek. 37. 19 take *t.* of Is. his fel.
Hos. 5. 9 am. *t.* of Is. ha. I made
Hab. 3. 9 to oaths of *t.* ev. thy wo.
Zech. 9. 1 eyes of man, as *t.* of Israel
Mat. 24. 30 then sh. *t.* of e. mourn
Luke 22. 30 judging tw. *t.* of Israel
Acts 13. 21 Saul, of *t.* of Benjamin
Rom. 11. 1 I am Is. of *t.* of Benjam.
Phil. 3. 5 stock of Is., *t.* of Benjam.
Heb. 7. 14 of which *t.* M. sp. noth.
Jas. 1. 1 to tw. *t.* wh. are scattered
Rev. 5. 5 lion of *t.* of Jud., root of
Tribulation. *Distress, affliction.*
Deut. 4. 30 wh. in *t.*, if thou turn
Judg. 10. 14 deliver you in ti. of *t.*
1 Sam. 10. 19 saved you out of *t.*
Mat. 24. 21 For then shall be gr. *t.*
Mark 13. 24 in those days, after *t.*
John 16. 33 In world ye shall ha. *t.*
Acts 14. 22 must though *t.* enter
Rom. 5. 3 we glory in *t.* also, kn.
2 Cor. 1. 14 Who comf. us in our *t.*
Eph. 3. 13 des. ye faint not at my *t.*
2 Thes. 1. 6 recomp. *t.* to th. suffer
Rev. 1. 9 John, your compan. in *t.*
R. V. Judg. 10. 14; 1 Sam. 10. 19 distress; 2 Cor. 1. 4; 7. 4; 1 Thes. 1. 4; 3. 4; 2 Thes. 1. 6 affliction
Tributary. *Under tribute.*
Deut. 20. 11 the people shall be *t.*
Judg. 1. 30 the Canaanites became *t.*
Lam. 1. 1 and how is she become *t.*
Tribute. *Burden, levy, tax.*
Gen. 49. 15 Issa. bec. servant to *t.*
Num. 31. 28 levy *t.* to Lord for men
Deut. 16. 10 wi. *t.* of free will offer.
Josh. 17. 13 put the Canaanit. to *t.*
2 Sam. 20. 24 Adoram was ov. the *t.*
1 K. 4. 6 on those did Sol. levy *t.*
2 K. 23. 33 Pharaoh put land to *t.*
2 Chr. 8. 8 them did S. ma. to pay *t.*
Ez. 4. 13 will they not pay toll, *t.*,

Neh. 5, 4 borrow. money for k.'s *t.*
Esth. 10. 1 Ahazuerus laid *t.* upon
Prov. 12. 24 slothful sh. be under *t.*
Mat. 17. 24 Doth not yo. m. pay *t.*?
22. 17 Is it lawful to give *t.* unto
Cæsar; Mark 12. 14; Luke 20. 22
Rom. 13. 6 for this cause pay ye *t.*
R. V. Gen. 49. 15; Josh. 16. 10;
17. 13; Judg. 1. 28; Prov. 12. 24
task work; 1 K. 4. 6; 9. 21; 12.
18; 2 Chr. 10. 18 levy; 2 Chr. 8.
8 bond servants; Mat. 17. 24 half shekel
Trickle. R. V. *poureth..*
Lam. 3. 49 Mine eye *t.* down, and
Tried. *see* **Try.**
Trim. *Make go well.*
Jer. 2. 33 Why *t.* way to seek love?
Clip, put in order.
2 Sam. 19. 24 M. had not *t.* beard
Mat. 25. 7 virgins *t.* their lamps
Triumph. *Overcome, glory, shout.*
Ex. 15. 1 for he hath *t.* gloriously
2 Sam. 1. 20 lest uncircumcised *t.*
Job 20. 5 That *t.* of wicked is short
Ps 47. 1 shout unto God with *t.*
2 Cor. 2. 14 causeth us to *t.* in C.
Col. 2. 15 made show of *t.* over
R. V. Ps. 60. 8; 108. 9 shout
Trode. Trodden. *See* **Tread.**
Troop. *Force, band, company.*
Gen. 30. 11 Leah said, A *t.* com., and
1 Sam. 30. 8 Shall I pursue this *t.*?
2 Sam. 3. 22 Joab ca. fr. pursuing *t.*
Job 19. 12 His *t.* came togeth., and
Ps. 18. 29 by thee I ha. run thro. *t.*
Isa. 65. 11 prepare tab. for that *t.*
Jer. 18. 22 sh. bring a *t.* suddenly
Hos. 6. 9 as *t.* of robbers wait f. men
Am. 9. 6 ha. founded his *t.* in earth
Mic. 5. 1 O daughter of *t.*, he hath
R. V. Gen. 30. 11 fortunate; 2 Sam.
2. 25 band; Job 6. 19 caravans;
Isa. 65. 11 Fortune; Am. 9. 6 vault upon
Trouble (*n.*). *Distress, sorrow, calamity, straitness.*
Deut. 31. 17 *t.* shall befall them
2 K. 19. 3 This day is a day of *t.*
1 Chr. 22. 14 in my *t.* I prepared
2 Chr. 15. 4 they in *t.* did turn to L.
Neh. 9. 32 let not all *t.* seem little
Job. 5. 7 man born to *t.*, as sparks fly
Ps. 9. 9 Lord a refuge in times of *t.*
Prov. 11. 8 right. is deliv. out of *t.*
Isa. 1. 14 they are *t.* unto me, I am
Jer. 2. 27 in *t.* will say, Save us
Lam. 1. 21 enemies heard of my *t.*
Ezek. 7. 7 the day of *t.* is near, and
Dan. 12. 1 there shall be time of *t.*
Nah. 1. 7 strong hold in day of *t.*
Hab. 3. 16 mi. rest in the day of *t.*
Zeph. 1. 15 a day of *t.* and distress
Mark 13. 8 shall be famines and *t.*
1 Cor. 7. 28 shall have *t.* in flesh
2 Cor. 1. 4 to comfort wh. are in *t.*
2 Tim. 2. 9 I suffer *t.* as evil doer
R. V. 1 Chr. 22. 14; Ps. 9. 13; 31. 7,
9; 2 Cor. 1. 4, 8 affliction; 2 Chr.
15. 4; Job 15. 24; Ps. 59. 16; 66.
14, 17; 102. 2; Isa. 8. 22 distress;
2 Chr. 29. 8 tossed to and fro; Neh.
9. 32 travail; Job 34. 29 condemn;
Ps. 41. 1 evil; Ps. 78. 33; Isa. 17.
14 terror; Ps. 3. 1; 13. 4; 60. 11
adversaries; Isa. 22. 5 discomfiture; 65. 23 calamity; Jer. 8.
15; 14. 19 dismay; Ezek. 7. 7
tumult; Acts 20. 10 make no ado;
1 Cor. 7. 28 tribulation; 2 Tim. 2.
9 hardship; Mark 13. 8 -——.
Trouble (*v.*). *Vex, disturb, trouble.*
Gen. 34. 30 *t.* me to make me stink
Ex. 14. 24 L. *t* host of Egyptians
Josh. 6. 18 lest ye *t.* camp of Israel
Judg. 11. 35 one of th. that *t.* me
1 Sam. 28. 11 saw th. he was sore *t.*
2 Sam. 4. 1 all Israelites were *t.*
1 K. 18. 17 Art th. he th. *t.* Israel?
2 K. 6. 11 the king of Syria was *t.*
2 Chr. 32. 18 they cried to *t.* them
Ez. 4. 4 people *t.* them in building
Job 4. 5 toucheth thee, thou art *t.*
Ps. 38. 6 I am *t.*, I am bowed down
Prov. 11. 17 th. is cruel *t.* own flesh
Isa. 57. 20 wick. are like the *t.* sea

Jer. 31. 20 my bowels are *t.* for him
Lam. 1. 20 bowels *t.*, heart is turned
Ezek. 28. 16 isles in sea shall be *t.*
Dan. 5. 9 Th. was Belshaz. greatly *t.*
Zech. 10. 2 *t.* because no shepherd
Mat. 2. 3 Herod was *t.* at Jerus.
Mark 14. 6 Let her alone; why *t.* h.?
Luke 11. 7 *T.* me not, door is shut
John 14. 1 Let not your heart be *t.*
Acts 15. 19 *t.* people and rulers
2 Cor. 7. 5 we are *t.* on every side
Gal. 6. 17 hencef. let no man *t.* me
2 Thes. 1. 7 to you that are *t.*, rest
Heb. 12. 15 lest bitterness *t.* you
1 Pet. 3. 14 not af. of terror, nor *t.*
R. V. Ex. 14. 24 discomfited; Job
34. 20 shaken; Ps. 38. 5 pained;
77. 3 disquieted; 77. 16 trembled;
48. 5; 83. 17; Ezek. 26. 18 dismay-
ed; Zech. 10. 2; 2 Thes. 1. 7 af-
flicted.
Troubler. *Who troubles.*
1 Chr. 2. 7 Achar, the *t.* of Israel
Troubling. *Trembling, agitating.*
Job 3. 17 There wicked cease fr. *t.*
John 5. 4 step. in after *t.* of water
R. V. John 5. 4 ——
Troublous. *Distressful.*
Dan. 9. 25 sh. be built in *t.* times
Trough. *Gutter, trough.*
Gen. 24. 20 emptied pitcher into *t.*
Ex. 2. 16 they filled the *t.* to water
Trow. *Think.*
Luke 17. 9 thank serv.? I *t.* not
Truce Breakers. R. V. *implac-
able.*
2 Tim. 3. 3 last days shall be *t. b.*
True. *Of a truth, real, sincere.*
Gen. 42. 11 we are *t.* men, thy serv.
Deut. 17. 4 it be *t.*, and thing cert.
Josh. 2. 12 and give me a *t.* token
2 Sam. 7. 28 God, thy words be *t.*
1 K. 22. 16 tell noth. but which is *t.*
2 Chr. 15. 3 Is. ha. been wi. *t.* God
Neh. 9. 13 and gavest them *t.* laws
Ps. 19. 9 judgments of Lord are *t.*
Jer. 42. 5 the Lord be a *t.* witness
Dan. 3. 14 is it *t.* O Shadrach, do
Zech. 7. 9 execute *t.* judgment, and
Mat. 22. 16 we know th. thou art *t.*
Luke 16. 11 com. to trust *t.* riches
John 3. 33 set to his seal th. G. is *t.*
Acts 12. 9 and wist not th. it was *t.*
Rom. 3. 4 let G. be *t.*, ev. man liar
2 Cor. 1. 18 as God is *t.*, our word
Phil. 4. 8 whatsoever things are *t.*
1 Thes. 1. 9 turn fr. idols to *t.* God
1 Tim. 3. 1 This is a *t.* saying, If
Tit. 1. 13 This witness is *t.* where f.
Heb. 8. 2 *t.* tabernacle which Lord
1 Pet. 5. 12 this is *t.* grace of God
2 Pet. 2. 22 according to *t.* proverb
1 John 5. 20 this is the *t.* God
3 John 12. we know our rec. is *t.*
Rev. 3. 7 saith holy, he that is *t.*
R. V. 2 Cor. 1. 18; 1 Tim. 3. 1
faithful
Truly. *Surely, truly.*
Num. 14. 21 *t.* as I live, saith Lord
Ps. 116. 16 *t.*, I am thy servant
Prov. 12. 22 deal *t.* are his delight
Mat. 27. 54 *t.* this was Son of God
Luke 20. 21 teachest way of God *t.*
John 4. 18 no husb. saidst thou *t.*
R. V. changes are mostly to, surely indeed, etc.
Trump. *Trumpet.*
1 Cor. 15. 52 at last *t.* dead shall
1 Thes. 4. 16 L. sh. descend with *t*
Trumpet. *Trumpet.*
Ex. 19. 16 voice of *t.* exceed. loud
Lev. 25. 9 make *t.* sound through.
Num. 10. 2 Make two *t.* of silver
Josh. 6. 4 priests sh. blow with *t.*
Judg. 7. 16 he put *t.* in ev. man's ha.
1 Sam. 13. 3 blew *t.* througho. land
2 Sam. 2. 28 Joab blew *t.*, all people
1 K. 1. 34 blow ye with the *t.*, and
2 K. 9. 13 blew *t.*, say., Joab is king
1 Chr. 15. 24 did blow wi. *t.* bef. ark
2 Chr. 5. 13 they lift voice with *t.*
Ez. 3. 10 priest in apparel with *t.*
Neh. 4. 18 th. sounded *t.* was by m
Job 39. 25 He saith am. *t.*, Ha, ha!
Ps. 81. 3 Blow up *t.* in new moon, in
Isa. 18. 3 when he bloweth *t.*, hear

Jer. 6. 1 blow the *t.* in Tekoa, and
Ezek. 33. 3 blow *t.*, warn the people
Hos. 8. 1 Set the *t.* to thy mouth, He
Joel 2. 1 Blow ye the *t.* in Zion, and
Am. 2. 2 sh. die wi. sound of the *t.*
Zeph. 1. 16 day of *t.* and alarm. ag.
Zech. 9. 14 God sh. blow *t.*, and shall
Mat. 24. 31 angels wi. gr. sound of *t.*
1 Cor. 14. 8 if *t.* gi. uncertain sound
Heb. 12. 19 sound of *t.*, and th. voice
Rev. 1. 20 heard great voice, as of *t.*

Trumpeters. *Who trumpet.*

2 K. 11. 14 and *t.* stood by the king
2 Chr. 5. 13 *t.* and singers were as
Rev. 18. 22 voice of *t.* heard no mo.

Trust (*n.*). *Confidence, hope.*

Job 8. 14 whose *t.* sh. be a spider's
Ps. 71. 5 O L. G., my *t.* fr. my youth
Prov. 22. 19 thy *t.* may be in Lord
Isa. 30. 3 *t.* in Egypt your confusion
Luke 16. 11 who co. to yo. *t.* riches?
2 Cor. 3. 4 such *t.* have we thro. C.
1 Tim. 1. 11 gospel, com. to my *t.*

Trust (*v.*). *Lean on, believe, be confident, take refuge, hope.*

Deut. 28. 52 walls down, where. th. *t.*
Judg. 11. 20 Sih. *t.* not Is. to pass
Ruth 2. 12 under whose wings to *t.*
2 Sam. 22. 3 G. my rock, in him I *t.*
Judg. 20. 36 *t.* unto liers in wait wh.
1 K. 18. 20 on whom dost thou *t.*?
2 K. 18 5 He *t.* in L. G. of Israel
1 Chr. 5. 20 bec. they put *t.* in him
2 Chr. 32. 10 Whereon do ye *t.*, that
Job 40. 23 *t.* he can draw up Jordan
Ps. 4. 5 and put your *t.* in the Lord
Prov. 28. 26 th. *t.* in own heart is fool
Isa. 12. 2 I will *t.*, and not be afraid
Jer. 7. 4 *T.* ye not in lying words
Ezek. 16. 15 didst *t.* in th. own beau.
Dan. 3. 28 deliv. serv. th. *t.* in him
Hos. 10. 13 bec. thou did. *t.* in way
Am. 6. 1 that *t.* in mountain of Sa.
Mic. 7. 5 *t.* ye not in a friend, put
Nah. 1. 7 Lord knoweth them th. *t.*
Hab. 2. 18 the maker of his work *t.*
Zeph. 3. 12 shall *t.* in name of Lord
Mat. 12. 21 in his na. sh. Gentiles *t.*
Mark 10. 24 them that *t.* in riches
Luke 11. 22 armour wherein he *t.*
John 5. 45 Moses, in whom ye *t.*
1 Cor. 16. 7 but I *t.* to tarry a while
2 Cor. 1. 9 sho. not *t.* in ourselves
Phil. 2. 19 I *t.* in L. J. to send Tim.
Eph 1. 12 who first *t.* in Christ
1 Thes. 2. 4 to be put in *t.* wi. gospel
1 Tim. 4. 10 we *t.* in the living God
Phile. 22 I *t.* that thro. yo. prayers
Heb. 13. 18 *t.* we have good consci.
1 Pet. 3. 5 holy wom., who *t.* in G.
2 John 12 I *t.* to come unto you
3 John 14 *t.* I shall shortly see thee
R. V. Ruth 2. 12 ; Ps. 36. 7 ; 37. 40 ;
61. 4 ; 91. 4 ; Isa. 14. 32 take refuge ; Mat. 12. 21 ; Luke 24. 21 ;
Rom. 15. 12, 24 ; 1 Cor. 16. 7 ;
2 Cor. 1. 10, 13 ; 5. 11 ; 13. 6 ; Eph.
1. 12 ; Phil. 2. 19 ; 1 Tim. 4. 10 ;
6. 17 ; Phile. 22 ; 2 John 12 ; 3 John
14, hope or hoped ; 2 Cor. 3. 4 ;
Phil. 3. 4 confidence ; Heb. 13. 18
persuaded

Trusty. *Steady.*

Job 12. 20 removeth speech of *t.*

Truth. *Truth, stability, reality.*

Gen. 24. 27 not left dest. mas. of *t.*
Ex. 18. 21 men of *t.*, hating covet.
Deut. 13. 14 if it be *t.*, and thing c.
Josh. 24. 14 serve him in sinc. and *t.*
Judg. 9. 15 If in *t.* ye anoint. me k.
1 Sam. 12. 24 serve him in *t.* wi. all
2 Sam. 2. 6 L. shewed kindness in *t.*
1 K. 2. 4 to walk before me in *t.*
2 K. 20. 3 I walked bef. thee in *t.*
2 Chr. 18. 15 say noth. but *t.* to me
Esth. 9. 30 wi. words of peace and *t.*
Ps. 26. 3 and I have walked in thy *t.*
Prov. 12. 19 lip of *t.* sh. be establi.
23. 23 Buy the *t.*, and sell it not
Eccl. 12. 10 written, was words of *t.*
Isa. 59. 14 *t.* is fallen in the street
Jer. 4. 2 L. liveth, in *t.*, in judgment
Dan. 8. 12 it cast down *t.* to ground
Hos. 4. 1 is no *t.*, nor mercy, nor k.
Mic. 7. 20 shall perform *t.* to Jacob
Zech. 8. 3 Jerus. be call. city of *t.*

Mal. 2. 6 law of *t.* was in his mouth
Mat. 15. 27 *T.*, L., yet dogs eat of the
Mark 5. 33 and told him all the *t.*
Luke 4. 25 of a *t.*, many widows were
John 1. 17 grace and *t.* ca. by J. C.
Acts 26. 25 speak words of *t.* and s.
Rom. 9. 1 I say *t.* in Christ, I lie not
1 Cor. 5. 8. unleavened bread of *t.*
2 Cor. 11. 10 As the *t.* of C. is in me
Gal. 2. 5 th. *t.* of gospel mi. continue
Eph. 4. 25 speak ev. man *t.* wi. nei.
Phil. 1. 18 whether in pretence, or *t.*
Col. 1. 5 ye heard bef. in word of *t.*
2 Thes. 2. 10 received not love of *t.*
1 Tim. 2. 4 come to knowl. of *t.*
2 Tim. 2. 15 right. divid. word of *t.*
Tit. 1. 1 to acknowledging of the *t.*
Heb. 10. 26 ha. receiv. knowl. of *t.*
Jas. 1. 18 begat he us wi. word of *t.*
1 Pet. 1. 22 purified in obeying *t.*
2 Pet. 2. 2 way of *t.* evil spok. of
1 John 1. 8 dec. ours., *t.* not in us
2 John 3 Grace be with you, in *t.*
2 John 1. Gaius, wh. I love in *t.*
R. V. Deut. 32. 4 ; Ps. 33. 4 ; 89.
49 ; 98. 3 ; 119. 30 faithfulness

Try. *Prove, test.*

Deut. 21. 5 shall every stroke be *t.*
Judg. 7. 4 I will *t.* them for thee
2 Sam. 22. 31 word of the L. is *t.*
1 Chr. 29. 17 I know, my G., thou *t.*
2 Chr. 32. 31 G. left him, to *t.* him
Job 12. 11 Doth not ear *t.* words?
Ps. 26. 2 *t.* my reins and my heart
Isa. 28. 16 I lay in Zion a *t.* stone
Jer. 12. 3 thou hast *t.* my heart tow.
Lam. 3. 40 search and *t.* our ways
Dan. 11. 35 to *t.* them, to purge, a.
Zech. 13. 9 will *t.* them as gold is *t.*
1 Cor. 3. 13 fire *t.* ev. man's work
1 Thes. 2. 4 pleasing G. wh. *t.* hea.
Heb. 11. 17 Abra., when he was *t.*
Jas. 1. 12 when *t.*, he shall receive
1 Pet. 1. 7 though it be *t.* with fire
1 John 4. 1 *t.* spirits whether of G.
Rev. 2. 2 hast *t.* them which say
R. V. Dan. 11. 35 refine ; 1 Cor. 3.
13 ; 1 Pet. 4. 12 ; 1 John 4. 1
prove

Trying. *Proving, testing.*

Jas. 1. 3 *t.* of faith work. patience

Tumble. *Turn over.*

Judg. 7. 13 a cake *t.* into the host

Tumult. *Noise, uproar.*

1 Sam. 4. 14 wh. noise of this *t.*?
2 Sam. 18. 29 I saw *t.*, but knew
2 K. 19. 28 *t.* come unto mine ears
Ps. 83. 2 thine enemies make a *t.*
Isa. 33. 3 at noise of *t.* people fled
Jer. 11. 16 with noise of a great *t.*
Hos. 10. 14 *t.* rise among people
Am. 2. 2 Moab shall die with *t.*
Zech. 14. 13 *t.* fr. Lord amo. them
Mat. 27. 24 rather a *t.* was made
Mark 5. 38 he seeth *t.*, and them
Acts 21. 34 not kn. certainly for *t.*
2 Cor. 6. 5 in imprisonments, in *t.*
R. V. 2 K. 19. 28 ; Isa. 37. 29 ar-
rogancy ; Acts 21. 34 uproar

Tumultuous. *Noisy, turbulent.*

Isa. 13. 4 a *t.* noise of kingdoms
Jer. 48. 45 devour head of *t.* ones

Turn (*n.*). *Time, row.*

Esth. 2. 12 ev. maid's *t.* was come

Turn (*v.*). *Turn, alter, direct.*

Gen. 24. 49 that I may *t.* to right
Ex. 7. 23 Phar. *t.*, went into house
Lev. 19. 4 *T.* ye not unto idols, nor
Num. 14. 25 *t.*, get you into wilder.
Deut. 1. 7 *T.* you, take your journ.
Josh. 7. 26 Lord *t.* from his anger
Judg. 18. 21 So they *t.* and departed
Ruth. 1. 11 *T.*, my daughters, why
1 Sam. 15. 31 Sam. *t.* ag. after Saul
2 Sam. 2. 19 Asahel *t.* not fr. fol.
1 K. 17. 3 Get thee hence, *t.* eastw.
2 K. 5. 12 Naaman *t.* went away
1 Chr. 10. 14 *t.* kingdom unto Dav.
2 Chr. 12. 12 wrath of L. *t.* fr. him
Ez. 6. 22 *t.* heart of k. of Assyria
Neh. 9. 35 nei. *t.* fr. wicked works
Esth. 9. 1 tho. it was *t.* to contrary
Job 5. 1 to wh. of saints wilt th. *t.*?
Ps. 9. 17 wicked sh. be *t.* into hell
Prov. 15. 1 soft ans. *t.* away wrath
Eccl. 3. 20 and all *t.* to dust again

S. of S. 6. 5 turn thine eyes fr. me
Isa. 1. 25 I will *t.* my hand on thee
Jer. 2. 27 they *t.* their back to me
Lam. 1. 20 my heart is *t.* within me
Ezek. 4. 8 not *t.* from one side to
Dan. 9. 16 let thine anger be *t.* aw.
Hos. 7. 8 Ephraim is a cake not *t.*
Joel 2. 31 sun sh. be *t.* into darkness
Am. 6. 12 ye have *t.* judgment into
Jonah 3. 9 repent, *t.* fr. fierce anger
Mic. 7. 19 He will *t.* ag., ha. comp.
Nah. 2. 2 L. ha. *t.* away excellency
Hab. 2. 16 cup shall be *t.* unto thee
Zeph. 3. 20 I *t.* back your captivity
Zech. 10. 9 live with chil., *t.* again
Mal. 2. 6 did *t.* many from iniquity
Mat. 5. 39 cheek, *t.* to him other
Mark 5. 30 Jesus *t.* about in press
Luke 1, 17 to *t.* hearts of fathers
John 16. 20 sorrow shall *t.* into joy
Acts 9, 25 th. dwelt in Lyd. *t.* to L.
Rom. 11. 26 *t.* away ungodlin. of J.
2 Cor. 3. 16 when it sh. *t.* to the L.
Gal. 4. 9 how *t.* ye ag. to the weak
Phil. 1. 19 this sh. *t.* to my salva.
1 Thes. 1. 9 how he *t.* to G. fr. idols
1 Tim. 5. 15 some already *t.* aside
2 Tim. 1. 14 were in Asia to be *t.*
Tit. 1. 14 men, th. *t.* fr. the truth
Heb. 12. 25 if we *t.* aw. fr. him th.
Jas. 4. 9 let laughter be *t.* to sor.
2 Pet. 2. 21 *t.* fr. the holy command.
Jude 4 *t.* grace of G. into lascivious.
Rev. 11. 6 to *t.* waters into blood
R. V. changes are chiefly to, return,
change, and other words depend-
on context.

Turning. *Turning.*

2 K. 21. 13 wipe Jer. as a dish, *t.*
2 Chr. 36. 13 hardened heart fr. *t.*
Prov. 1. 32 the *t.* away of simple
Isa. 29. 16 your *t.* of things upside
Mic. 2. 4 *t.* away he hath divided
Acts 3. 26 to bless you in *t.* you
Jas. 1. 17 with wh. is no sha. of *t.*

Turtle. *Turtle-dove.*

Gen. 15. 9 take me a *t.* dove, and
Lev. 1. 14 sh. bring off. of *t.* dove
12. 6 a young pigeon, or a *t.* dove
Num. 6. 10 he shall bring two *t.*
Ps. 74. 19 deliv. not soul of *t.* dove
S. of S. 2. 12 voice of *t.* is heard in l.
Jer. 8. 7 *t.* and crane observe time
Luke 2. 24 sacri. pair of *t.* doves

Tutors. R. V. *guardians.*

Gal. 4. 12 a child is under *t.* and

Twain. *Two.*

1 Sam. 18. 21 be my son in law *t.*
2 K. 4. 33 shut door upon them *t.*
Isa. 6. 2 with *t.* he covered his face
Jer. 34. 18 they cut the calf in *t.*, and
Ezek. 21. 19 both *t.* sh. come forth
Mat. 5. 41, a mile, go with him *t.*
Mark 10. 8 they are no more *t.*, but
Eph. 2. 15 make in himself of *t.*

Twelfth. *Two and tenth.*

1 K. 19. 19, oxen, he with the *t.*
Rev. 21. 20 *t.* founda. was amethyst

Twelve. *Two and ten.*

Gen. 14. 4 *t.* years they served C.
Ex. 15. 27 Elim, where were *t.* well;
Lev. 24. 15 thou sh. bake *t.* cakes
Deut. 1. 23 I took *t.* men of you
Josh. 4. 3 Take out of Jor. *t.* stone;
2 Sam. 2. 15 arose *t.* of Benjamin
1 K. 7. 25 the sea stood on *t.* oxen
Neh. 5. 14 *t.* years not eaten bread
Mat. 9. 20 wom. was disea. *t.* year;
Mark 3. 14 And he ordained *t.* that
5. 42 she was of the age of *t.* year;
Luke 2. 42 when Jesus was *t.* year;
John 6. 70 Have I not cho. you *t.*
1 Cor. 15. 5 And was seen of the *t.*
Rev. 12. 1 on head cro. of *t.* stars

Twenty. *Twice ten.*

Gen. 18. 31 shall be found *t.* there, I
Ex. 30. 14 fr. *t.* years old, and above
2 K. 4. 42 brought man *t.* loaves
Ez. 8. 27 weighed *t.* basons of gold
Zech. 5. 2 length of roll *t.* cubits

Twice. *Two times.*

Gen. 41. 32 dream was doubled *t.*
Ex. 16. 5 and it shall be *t.* as much
1 K. 11. 9 had appeared to him *t.*
2 K. 6 10 and saved not once nor *t.*
Neh. 13. 20 with. Jeru. once or *t.*

Job 33. 14 God speak. once, yea *t*.
Ps. 62. 11 *t*. have I heard this that
Mark 14. 30 before the cock crow *:*.
Luke 18. 12 I fast *t*. in the week
Jude 12 trees *t*. dead, plucked up

Twig. *Shoot, suckling.*
Ezek. 17. 4 H cropped top of his *t*.

Twilight. *Dim light.*
1 Sam. 30. 17 D. smote them from *t*.
2 K. 7. 5 lepers rose up in the *t*. to
Job 3. 9 Let stars of the *t*. be dark
Prov. 7. 9 went to her house in *t*.
Ezek. 12. 6 carry it forth in the *t*.
R. V. Ezek. 12. 6, 7, 12 dark

Twined. *Twisted.*
Ex. 26. 1 ten curtains of *t*. linen

Twinkling. *Gleaming.*
1 Cor. 15. 52 changed, in *t*. of eye

Twins. *Double, twofold.*
Gen. 25. 24 days fulfilled, behold *t*.
S. of S. 4. 5 are like roes that are *t*.

Two. *Two, pair.*
Gen. 1. 16 God made *t*. great lights
Mat. 6. 24 No man can ser. *t*. mast.
Etc., etc.

Twofold. *Doubly.*
Mat. 23. 15 *t*. more the child of hell

U.

Unaccustomed. *Untaught.*
Jer. 31. 18 as bullock *u*. to yoke

Unadvisedly. *Babblingly.*
Ps. 106. 33 spake *u*. with his lips

Unawares. *Not knowing, unexpected.*
Gen. 31. 20 Jacob stole *u*. to Laban
Num. 34. 11 killeth any person *u*.
Deut. 4. 42 sho. kill neighbour *u*.
Josh. 20. 3 the slayer that killeth *u*.
Ps. 35. 8 destruc. come on him *u*.
Luke 21. 34 day come on you *u*.
Gal. 2. 4 false breth. *u*. brought
Heb. 13. 2 some enterta. angels *u*.
Jude 4 For certain men crept in *u*.
R. V. Num. 35. 11, 15; Josh. 20. 3,
9; unwittingly, Luke 21. 34 suddenly; Gal. 2. 4; Jude 4 privily.

Unbelief. *Distrust, disobedience.*
Mat. 13. 58 works, because of *u*.
Mark 9. 24 I bel., help thou mine *u*.
Rom. 3. 3 sh. *u*. make faith with.
1 Tim. 1. 13 did it ignorantly in *u*.
Heb. 4. 6 ent. not in because of *u*.
R. V. Mat. 17. 20 little faith; Rom.
11. 30, 32; Heb. 4. 6, 11 disobedience; Rom. 3. 3 want of faith.

Unbeliever. *Disbeliever.*
Luke 12. 46 his portion with the *u*.
1 Cor. 6. 6 goeth to law before *u*.
2 Cor. 6. 14 unequally yoked wi. *u*.
R. V. Luke 12. 46 unfaithful

Unbelieving. *Not believing.*
Acts 14. 2 *u*. Jews stirred Gentiles
1 Cor. 7 14 *u*. husband is sanctified
Tit. 1. 15 unto *u*. is nothing pure
Rev. 21. 8 *u*. ha. their part in lake
R. V. Acts 14. 2 disobedient

Unblameable, y. *Blameless.*
Col. 1. 22 to present you ho. and *u*.
1 Thes. 2. 10 how *u*. we behaved
R. V. Col. 1. 22 without blemish

Uncertain, ly. *Not certain.*
1 Cor. 9. 26 run, not as *u*., so fight
1 Tim. 6. 17 nor trust in *u*. riches

Unchangeable. *Without change.*
Heb. 7. 24 hath an *u*. priesthood

Uncircumcised. *Not circumcised.*
Gen. 17. 14 *u*. chi. sh. be cut off
Ex. 6. 12 hear, who am of *u*. lips?
Lev. 19. 23 three years sh. be as *u*.
Josh. 5. 7 they were *u*., because th.
Judg. 14. 3 goest to ta. wife of *u*.
1 Sam. 17. 26 who is this *u*. Philist.
2 Sam. 1. 20 lest daugh. *u*. triumph,
1 Chr. 10. 4 lest *u*. come and abuse
Isa. 52. 1 no more come to the *u*.
Jer. 6. 10 their ear is *u*., th. cannot
Ezek. 28. 10 shalt die deaths of *u*.
Acts 7. 51 stiff necked *u*. in hearts
Rom. 4. 11 faith he had being *u*.
1 Cor. 7. 18 let him not become *u*.

Uncircumcision. *Uncircumcision.*
Rom. 2. 25 circumcis. is made *u*.
1 Cor. 7. 18 Is any called in *u*.? let
Gal. 2. 7 gospel of *u*. committed
Eph. 2. 11 who are called *u*. by

Col. 2. 13 being dead in sins and *u*.

Uncle. *Uncle. relation.*
Lev. 10. 4 Uzziel, the *u*. of Aaron
1 Sam. 10. 14 Saul's *u*. said to him
1 Chr. 27. 32 D.'s *u*. was counsellor
Jer. 32. 9 bought field of H., my *u*.
Am. 6. 10 man's *u*. take him up

Unclean. *Defiled, offensive.*
Lev. 5. 2 if soul touch any *u*. thing
Num. 6. 7 He sh. not make hims. *u*.
Deut. 12. 15 *u*. and clean may eat
Josh. 22. 19 if yo. possession be *u*.
Judg. 13. 4 eat not any *u*. thing
Ez. 9. 11 land ye go to pos. is *u*.
Job 36. 14 hypocrites is among *u*.
Eccl. 9. 2 one event to clean and *u*.
Isa. 6. 5 I am a man of *u*. lips
Lam. 4. 15 Depart ye; it is *u*., de.
Ezek. 22. 26 between clean and *u*.
Hos. 9. 3 they shall eat *u*. things
Hag. 2. 13 If *u*. by dead body, touch
Mat. 10. 1 power against *u* spirits
Mark 1. 26 when *u*. sp. had torn him
Luke 9. 42 Jesus rebuked the *u*. sp.
Acts 10. 28 I sh. not call any man *u*.
Rom. 14. 14 nothing is *u*. of itself
1 Cor. 7. 14 else were your chil. *u*.
2 Cor. 6. 17 touch not the *u*. thing
Eph. 5. 5. no *u*. person hath inheri.
Heb. 9. 13 of heifer sprinkling *u*.
Rev. 16. 13 I saw *u*. sp. like frogs

Uncleanness. *Defilement.*
Lev. 5. 3 if he touch *u*. of man
Num. 5. 19 not gone aside to *u*.
Deut. 23. 10 by reason of *u*, that
2 Sam. 11. 4 purified from her *u*.
2 Chr. 29. 16 priests brought out *u*.
Ez. 9. 11 filled the land with their *u*.
Ezek. 36. 29 I will save you fr. *u*.
Zech. 13. 1 fountain opened for *u*.
Mat. 23. 27 full of bones and *u*.
Rom. 1. 24 G. also gave th. to *u*.
2 Cor. 12. 21 and not repented of *u*.
Gal. 5. 19 works of the flesh are *u*.
Col. 3. 5 mortify fornication, *u*.
1 Thes. 2. 3 exhortation not of *u*.
2 Pet. 2. 10 that walk in lust of *u*.
R. V. 2 Pet. 2. 10 defilement

Unclothed. *Not clothed.*
2 Cor. 5. 4 not that we would be *u*.

Uncomely. R. V. *unseemly.*
1 Cor. 12. 23 *u*. parts ha. comeliness

Uncondemned. *Not judged.*
Acts 16. 37 ha. beaten us openly *u*.

Uncorruptible. *Incorruptible.*
Rom. 1. 23 changed th. glory of th. *u*.

Uncorruptness. *Incorruption.*
Tit. 2. 7 in doctrine, shewing *u*.

Uncover. *Reveal, make bare.*
Gen. 9. 21 Noah was *u*. in his tent
Lev. 10. 6 *U*. not your heads, nei.
Num. 5. 18 priest sh. *u*. wom.'s head
Deut. 27. 20 bec. he *u*. fath. skirt
Ruth 3. 7 came softly and *u*. feet
2 Sam. 6. 20 *u*. himself as vain fel.
Isa. 47. 2 *u*. thy locks, *u*. the thigh
Jer. 49. 10 I ha. *u*. his secret place
Ezek. 4. 7 there arm shall be *u*.
Hab. 2. 16 let thy foreskin be *u*.
Zeph. 2. 14 he sh. *u*. the cedar work
Mark 2. 4 they *u*. roof wh. he was
1 Cor. 11. 5 prophesi. with head *u*.
R. V. Lev. 21. 6, 10; Num. 5. 18
let hair go loose; Isa. 47. 2 remove;
Hab. 2. 16 circumcised; Zeph. 2.
14 laid bare; 1 Cor. 11. 5, 13 unveiled

Unction. R. V. *anointing.*
1 John 2. 20 ye ha. an *u*. fr. Hol. O.

Undefiled. *Pure, perfect.*
Ps. 119. 1 Blessed are *u*. in the way
S. of S. 5. 2 love, my dove, my *u*.
Heb. 13. 4 marriage is honora., b. *u*.
Jas. 1. 27 pure religion and *u*. befo.
1 Pet. 1. 4 inher. incorruptible, *u*.
R. V. Ps. 119. 1 perfect

Under. *Beneath.*
Gen. 1. 7 *u*. firmam. from waters
Mat. 5. 15 Nei. put it *u*. a bushel
Etc., etc.

Undergirding. *Support.*
Acts 27. 17 used helps, *u*. the ship

Undersetter. *Shoulder, corner.*
1 K. 7. 30 the four corners had *u*.

Understand. *Know fully, discern.*
Gen. 11. 7 may not *u*. one another

Num. 16. 30 *u*. these provoked L.
Deut. 28. 49 tong. thou sh. not *u*.
2 K. 18. 26 Speak in Syrian, we *u*.
1 Chr. 28. 19 the Lord made me to *u*.
Job 28. 23 God *u*. the way thereof
Ps. 19. 12 Who can *u*. his errors?
Prov. 28. 5 Evil men *u*. not judg.
Isa. 6. 9 Hear ye indeed, but *u*. not
Jer. 9. 12 Who is wise, that may *u*.?
Ezek. 3. 6 words thou canst not *u*.
Dan. 8. 16 make this man to *u*. vis.
Hos. 14. 9 Who is wise he shall *u*.
Mic. 4. 12 nei. *u*. counsel of Lord
Mat. 26. 10 When J. *u*. it, he said
Mark 8. 21 How is it ye do not *u*.?
Luke 2. 50 they *u*. not the saying
John 12. 16 These things *u*. not dis.
Acts 8. 26 sh. hear, and sh. not *u*.
Rom. 3. 11 There is none that *u*.,
1 Cor. 13. 11 wh. child, I *u*. as a ch.
Eph. 5. 17 *u*. what the will of Lord
Phil. 1. 12 I wo. ye sh. *u*., brethren
1 Tim. 1. 7 *u*. nei. what they say, n.
Heb. 11. 3 Thro. faith we *u*. that t.
2 Pet. 2. 12 evil of thi. they *u*. not
R. V. Gen. 41. 15 hearest; Deut.
9. 3, 6 know; Neh. 8. 13 give attention; Ps. 19. 12; Dan. 9. 25
discern; 11. 33 be wise; Ps. 73
17; 94. 8; 107. 43; Isa. 44. 18 consider; Ps. 81. 5; 1 Cor. 13. 2;
Phil. 1. 12 know or knew; Mat.
15. 17; 26. 10; John 8. 27; 12.
40; Rom. 1. 20; Eph. 3. 14 perceive; Acts 23. 27 learned; 1 Cor.
13. 11 felt

Understanding *Intelligence, knowledge, wisdom.*
Ex. 31. 3 Bez., I ha. filled him w. *u*.
Deut. 4. 6 this is your wis. and *u*.
1 K. 3. 11 hast asked for thyself *u*.
1 Chr. 22. 12 L. gi. thee wis. and *u*.
2 Chr. 2. 12 wise son endued wi. *u*.
Ez. 8. 18 they brought man of *u*.
Job 28. 12 where is the place of *u*.?
Ps. 47. 7 sing ye praises with *u*.
Prov. 4. 5 get *u*.! forget it not; n.
16. 22 *U*. is a wellspring of life
Eccl. 9. 11 nor *u*. to men of *u*.
Isa. 11. 2 sp. of *u*. shall rest upon
Jer. 51. 15 stretch. out heaven by *u*
Ezek. 28. 4 wi. thy *u*. thou hast
Dan. 1. 17 Dan. had *u*. in visions
Hos. 13. 2 made idols ac. to th. *u*.
Obad. 7 there is no *u*. in him
Mat. 15. 16 Are ye yet without *u*.
Mark 12. 23 to love him with *u*.
Luke 2. 47 were astonished at his *u*.
Rom. 1. 31 without *u*, cov. breakers
1 Cor. 1. 19 bring to nothing the *u*.
Eph. 1. 18 eyes of *u*. being enlight.
Phil. 4. 7 peace, wh. passeth all *u*.
Col. 1. 9 be filled with spiritual *u*.
2 Tim. 2. 7 the Lord give thee *u*.
1 John 5. 20 Son ha. giv. us an *u*.
Rev. 13. 18 Let him th. ha. *u*. count
R. V. Ez. 8. 16 teachers; 8. 18 discretion; Prov. 17. 28 prudent; 10.
13 discernment; Dan. 11. 35 wise;
Luke 1. 3 accurately; 24. 45; 1
Cor. 14. 20 mind; Eph. 1. 18
heart

Understood. See **Understand.**

Undertake. *Take in hand.*
Esth. 9. 23 Jews *u*. to do as they
Isa. 38. 14 I am oppress., *u*. for me
R. V. Isa. 38. 14 be surety

Undo. *Loose, bring to grief.*
Num. 21. 29 art *u*., O peo. of Chem.
Josh. 11. 15 Joshua left nothing *u*.
Isa. 6. 5 Woe is me! for I am *u*.
Zeph. 3. 19 I will *u*. all that afflict
R. V. Zeph. 3. 19 deal with

Undone. See **Undo.**

Undressed. *Untrimmed.*
Lev. 25. 5 nei. gath. gra. of vine *u*.

Unequal, ly. *Not equal.*
Ezek. 18. 25 Is., are not yo. ways *u*.?
2 Cor. 6. 14 be not yoked *u*. with

Unfaithful, ly. *Deceitful.*
Ps. 78. 57 turned back, and dealt *u*
Prov. 25. 19 confid. in an *u*. man
R. V. Ps. 78. 57 treacherously

Unfeigned. *Real.*
2 Cor. 6. 6 by H. Ghost, by love *u*.
1 Tim. 1. 5 pure heart, of faith *u*.

2 Tim. 1. 5 I call to remembr. *u.*
1 Pet. 1. 22 *u.* love of the brethren
Unfruitful. *Not fruitful.*
Mat. 13. 22 choke word, he beco. *u.*
Mark 4. 19 choke word, it beco. *u.*
1 Cor. 14. 14 my understanding is *u.*
Eph. 5. 11 ha. no fellowsh. with *u.*
Tit. 3. 14 works, that th. be not *u.*
2 Pet. 1. 8 nei. be barren nor *u.*
Ungird. *Loosen.*
Gen. 24. 32 he *u.* his camels, and
Ungodliness. *Irreverence.*
Rom. 1. 18 a. all *u.* and unrighteous.
2 Tim. 2. 16 will increase unto *u.*
Tit. 2. 12 denying *u.* and worldly
Ungodly. *Impious, wicked.*
2 Sam. 22. 5 *u.* men ma. me afraid
2 Chr. 19. 2 Shouldest thou help *u.*
Job 16. 11 G. ha. deliv. me to the *u.*
Ps. 1. 6 way of the *u.* shall perish
Prov. 16. 27 *u.* man diggeth up evil
19. 28 *u.* witness scorneth judgment
Rom. 5. 6 in due time C. died for *u.*
1 Tim. 1. 9 the law is for the *u.*
1 Pet. 4. 18 where shall *u.* appear.
2 Pet. 2. 5 bringing the flood on *u.*
Jude 4 *u.* men, turn. grace of God
R. V. Prov. 16. 27; 19. 28 worthless;
2 Chr. 19. 2; Job 34. 18; Ps. 1. 1, 4,
5, 6; 3. 7; 78. 12 wicked
Unholy. *Not holy, common.*
Lev. 10. 10 differ. bet. holy and *u.*
1 Tim. 1. 9 law was made for *u.*
2 Tim. 3. 2 men be unthankful *u.*
Heb. 10. 29 counted blood cov. *u.*
R. V. Lev. 10. 10 the common
Unicorn. R. V. *wild ox.*
Num. 23. 22 he hath strength of *u.*
Deut. 33. 17 horns like horns of *u.*
Job 39. 10 canst bind *u.* in furrow?
Ps. 29. 6 Lebanon and Sirion like *u.*
Isa. 34. 7 the *u.* shall come down
Unite. *Join.*
Gen. 49. 6 honour, be not thou *u.*
Ps. 86. 11 *u.* my heart to fear thy
Unity. *Oneness.*
Ps. 133. 1 for brethren to dwell in *u.*
Eph. 4. 3 Endeavouring to keep *u.*
Unjust. *Unrighteous.*
Ps. 43. 1 O deliver me from *u.* man
Prov. 11. 7 hope of *u.* man perish.
Zeph. 3. 5 *u.* knoweth no shame
Mat. 5. 45 send. rain on just and *u.*
Luke 16. 8 L. com. the *u.* steward
Acts 24. 15 resurrec. of just and *u.*
1 Cor. 6. 1 go to law before *u.*, and
1 Pet. 3. 18 suffered, the just for *u.*
2 Pet. 2. 9 res. *u.* to day of judgment
Rev. 22. 11 th. is *u.*, let him be *u.* s.
R. V. Prov. 28. 8 — ; 11. 7 iniquity; Luke 16. 8, 10; 18. 6; 1 Cor.
6. 1; 1 Pet. 3. 18; 2 Pet. 2. 9;
Rev. 22. 11 unrighteous.
Unjustly. *Wrongfully.*
Ps. 82. 2 How long will ye judge *u.*
Isa. 26. 10 in land of upri. deal *u.*
R. V. Isa. 26. 10 wrongfully
Unknown. *Not known.*
Acts 17. 23 inscript., To the *u.* God
1 Cor. 14. 14 if I pray in *u.* tongue
2 Cor. 6. 9 As *u.*, yet well known
Gal. 1. 22 *u.* by face unto churches
Unlade. *Unload.*
Acts 21. 3 ship was to *u.* burden
Unlawful. *Not lawful.*
Acts 10. 28 it is an *u.* thing for man
2 Pet. 2. 8 vexed soul with *u.* deeds
R. V. 2 Pet. 2. 8 lawless.
Unlearned. *Ignorant.*
Acts 4. 13 perceived they were *u.*
1 Cor. 14. 16 occupieth room of *u.*
2 Tim. 2. 23 avoid *u.* questions avoid
2 Pet. 3. 16 they that are *u.* wrest
R. V. 2 Tim. 2. 23; 2 Pet. 3. 16 ignorant
Unleavened. *Without leaven.*
Gen. 19. 3 did bake *u.* bread, and
Ex. 12. 8 roast wi. fire and *u.* bread
Lev. 2. 5 shall be of fine flour *u.*
Num. 6. 19 priest take one *u.* cake
Deut. 16. 3 seven days eat *u.* bread
Josh. 5. 11 eat old corn of land *u.*
Judg. 6. 19 Gid. made ready *u.* cak.
1 Sam. 28. 24 and did bake *u.* bread
1 K. 23. 9 they did eat *u.* bread
1 Chr. 23. 29 for the *u.* cakes, and

2 Chr. 8. 13 in feast of *u.* bread
Ez. 6. 22 kept feast of *u.* bread
Ezek. 45. 21 sov. days; *u.* br. shall
Mat. 26. 17 day of fea. of *u.* bread
Mark 14. 1 feast of pass and *u.* br.
Luke 22. 1 f. of *u.* br. drew nigh
Acts 12. 3 were days of *u.* bread
1 Cor. 5. 7 new lump, as ye are *u.*
Unless. *Except.*
Lev. 22. 6 not eat, *u.* he wash flesh
Num. 22. 33 *u.* she turned from thee
1 Cor. 15. 2 *u.* ye ha. believ. in vain
Unloose. *Loose.*
Mark 1. 7 shoes I am not worthy
to *u.* ; Luke 3. 16; John 1. 27
Unmarried. *Not wedded.*
1 Cor. 7. 8 I say to *u.*, abide ev. as I
Unmerciful. *Without mercy.*
Rom. 1. 31 without affection, *u.*
Unmindful. *Forgetful.*
Deut. 32. 18 Rock th. begat th. *u.*
Unmoveable. *Immovable.*
Acts 27. 41 forepart remained *u.*
1 Cor. 15. 58 breth., be stedfast, *u.*
Unoccupied. *Unused.*
Judg. 5. 6 the highways were *u.*
Unperfect. *Imperfect.*
Ps. 139. 16 eyes did see, yet being *u.*
Unprepared. *Not prepared.*
2 Cor. 9. 4 *u.*, we sho. be ashamed
Unprofitable. *Useless, hurtful.*
Job. 15. 3 Sho. reason wi. *u.* talk?
Mat. 25. 30 cast *u.* ser. into dark.
Luke 17. 10 We are *u.* ser., we ha.
Rom. 3. 12 they are tog. become *u.*
Tit. 3. 9 strivings, for they are *u.*
Phile. 11 wh. in time past was *u.*
Heb. 13. 17 not wi. grief. th. is *u.*
Unprofitableness. *Useless.*
Heb. 7. 8 the weakness and *u.* th.
Unpunished. *Free, innocent.*
Prov. 11. 21 wicked sh. not be *u.*
19. 5 false witness sh. not be *u.*
Jer. 49. 12 go *u.*? thon sh. not go *u.*
Unquenchable. *Not quenchable.*
Mat. 3. 12 not burn the chaff with
u. fire, Luke 3. 17
Unreasonable. *Irrational.*
Acts 25. 27 it seemeth *u.* to send
2 Thes. 3. 2 delivered from *u.* men
Unrebukeable. R. V. *without
reproach.*
1 Tim. 6. 14 keep this command. *u.*
Unreproveable. *Blameless.*
Col. 1. 22 to present you holy, *u.*
Unrighteous. *Perverse, unjust.*
Ex. 23. 1 put not hand to be an *u.*
Job 27. 7 riseth against me be as *u.*
Ps. 71. 4 deliv. out of hand of *u.*
Isa. 10. 1 woe to th. that decree *u.*
Luke 16. 11 not faithful in *u.* mat.
Rom. 3. 5 is G. *u.*, who tak. ven.?
1 Cor. 6. 9 *u.* shall not inherit the
Heb. 6. 10 God is not *u.* to forget
Unrighteously. *Perversely.*
Deut. 25. 16 all that do *u.* are ab.
Unrighteousness. *Iniquity.*
Lev. 19. 15 no *u.* in judgment
Ps. 92. 15 there is no *u.* in him
Jer. 22. 13 that build. house by *u.*
Luke 16. 19 friends of mam. of *u.*
John 7. 18 is true, no *u.* in him
Rom. 1. 29 Being filled with all *u.*
1 Cor. 6. 9 know ye that *u.* shall
2 Cor. 6. 14 righteousness with *u.*
2 Thes. 2. 10 wi. deceivable. of *u.*
Heb. 8. 12 be merciful to their *u.*
2 Pet. 2. 13 sh. receive reward of *u.*
1 John 1. 9 cleanse us from all *u.*
R. V. 2 Cor. 6. 14; Heb. 8. 12 iniquity; 2 Pet. 2. 13, 15 wrong
doing
Unripe. *Not ripe.*
Job 15. 33 shall shake off *u.* grape
Unruly. *Lawless.*
1 Thes. 5. 14 warn th. that are *u.*
Tit. 1. 10 many *u.* and vain talkers
Jas. 3. 8 the tongue is an *u.* evil
R. V. 1 Thes. 5. 14 disorderly ; Jas.
3. 8 restless
Unsatiable. *Without satiety.*
Ezek. 16. 28 because thou wast *u.*
Unsavory. R. V. *no savour.*
Job 6. 6 be eat. without salt?
Unsearchable. *Not searchable.*
Job 5. 9 G. doeth great th. and *u.*

Ps. 145. 3 Lord his greatness is *u.*
Prov. 25. 3 the heart of kings is *u.*
Rom. 11. 33 how *u.* are his judgm.
Eph. 3. 8 preach *u.* riches of Ch.
Unseemly. *Not meet.*
Rom. 1. 27 work. that which is *u.*
1 Cor. 13. 5 doth not behave its. *u.*
Unshod. *Barefoot.*
Jer. 2. 25 withh. foot fr. being *u.*
Unskilful. R. V. *without experience.*
Heb. 5. 13 ev. one th. use. mi. is *u.*
Unspeakable. *Untold.*
2 Cor. 9. 15 thanks to G. for his *u.*
1 Pet. 1. 8 ye rejoice with joy *u.*
Unspotted. *Clean.*
Jas. 1. 27 to keep himself *u.* from
Unstable. *Not stedfast.*
Gen. 49. 4 *u.* as water, not excel
Jas. 1. 8 double minded man is *u.*
2 Pet. 3. 16 are unlearned and *u.*
R. V. 2 Pet. 2. 14; 3. 16 unstedfast
Unstopped. *Opened.*
Isa. 35. 5 ears of deaf shall be *u.*
Untaken. *Not taken.*
2 Cor. 3. 14 remain. veil *u.* away
Untempered. *Not tempered.*
Ezek. 13. 10 daubed wi. *u.* morter
Unthankful. *Ungrateful.*
Luke 6. 35 he is kind unto the *u.*
2 Tim. 3. 2 disobedi. to parents, *u.*
Until. *See* Till.
Untimely. *Out of time.*
Job 3. 16 or as a hidden *u.* birth
Ps. 58. 8 iike *u.* birth of a woman
Eccl. 6. 3 an *u.* birth is better than
Rev. 6. 13 as fig tree casteth *u.* figs
R. V. Rev. 6. 13 unripe
Unto. *See* To.
Untoward. R. V. *crooked*
Acts 2. 40 Save fr. this *u.* genera.
Unwalled. *Open.*
Deut. 3. 5 *u.* towns a great many
Esth. 9. 19 Jews dw. in *u.* towns
Ezek. 38. 11 go to land of *u.* villages
Unwashen. *Unwashed.*
Mat. 15. 20 to eat with *u.* hands
Mark 7. 2 defiled, that is *u.*, hands
R. V. Mark 7. 5 defiled
Unwise. *Not wise.*
Deut. 32. 6 O foolish people and *u.*?
Hos. 13. 13 he is an *u.* son, for he
Rom. 1. 14 debtor to wise and *u.*
Eph. 5. 17 be not *u.*, but underst.
R. V. Rom. 1. 14 ; Eph. 5. 17 foolish
Unwittingly. *Not knowing.*
Lev. 14. 4 if eat of holy things *u.*
Josh. 20. 3 that killeth a person *u.*
R. V. Josh. 20. 3, 5 unawares
Unworthy. *Not worthy.*
Acts 13. 46 judge yourselves *u.* of
1 Cor. 6. 2 *u.* to judge small mat.?
Unworthily. *Not worthy.*
1 Cor. 11. 27 drink cup of the L. *u.*
Upbraid. *Reproach.*
Judg. 8. 15 wi. whom he did *u.* me
Mat. 11. 20 Then began he to *u.*
Mark 16. 14 he *u.* th. with unbel.
Jas. 1. 5 giveth liberally, and not
Uphold. *Support, maintain.*
Job 4. 4 Thy words have *u.* him
Ps. 37. 17 the Lord *u.* the righteous
Prov. 29. 23 honour sh. *u.* the humb.
Isa. 41. 10 I will *u.* thee wi. ri. hand
Ezek. 30. 6 that *u.* Egypt sh. fall
Heb. 1. 3 *u.* all things by word of
Upon. *On, unto, to.*
Gen. 22. 12 Lay not hand *u.* the lad
Mat. 3. 16 like dove, and lighting *u.*
Etc., etc.
Upper. *Above.*
2 K. 18. 17 by conduit of the *u.* pool
Ezek. 42. 5 *u.* chamb. were shorter
Mark 14. 15 show you large *u.* room
Acts 1. 13 went into an *u.* room
Uppermost. *Highest.*
Gen. 40. 17 in *u.* basket there was
Isa. 17. 6 in top of the *u.* bough
Mat. 23. 6 they love the *u.* rooms at
feasts, Mark 12. 39 ; Luke 11. 43
R. V. Mat. 23. 6; Mark 12. 39;
Luke 11. 43 chief
Upright. *Upright, perfect.*
Gen. 37. 7 my sheaf arose, stood *u.*
Lev. 26. 13 and made you go *u.*
1 Sam. 29. 6 thou hast been *u.* with

2 Sam. 22. 24 I was *u.* before him
2 Chr. 29. 34 Levites were more *u.*
Job 1. 1 that man was perfect and *u.*
Ps. 25. 8 Good and *u.* is the Lord
Prov. 2. 21 *u.* sh. dwell in the land
Eccl. 7. 29 G. ha. made man *u.*, but
Isa. 26. 7 thou, most *u.*, dost weigh
Dan. 8. 18 touched, and set me *u.*
Mic. 7. 4 *u.* is sharper than thorn
R. V. 2 Sam. 22. 24, 26; Job 12. 4;
    Ps. 18. 23, 25; 19. 13; 37. 18;
    Prov. 11. 20; 28. 10; 29. 10 perfect

Uprightly. *Upright.*
Ps. 15. 2 th. walketh *u.* shall abide
Prov. 2. 7 buckler to th. walk *u.*
Isa. 33. 15 speak. *u.* sh. dwell high
Am. 5. 10 abhor him that speak. *u.*
Mic. 2. 7 to him that walketh *u.*
Gal. 2. 14 that they walked not *u.*
R. V. Prov. 2. 7 integrity

Uprightness. *Rightness.*
1 K. 3. 6 walked before thee in *u.*
1 Chr. 29. 17 and hast pleasure in *u.*
Job 4. 6 and the *u.* of thy ways?
Ps. 9. 8 judgment to people in *u.*
Prov. 2. 13 Who leave paths of *u.*
Isa. 26. 7 The way of the just is *u.*
R. V. Job 4. 6; Prov. 28. 6 integrity

Uprising. *Rising up.*
Ps. 139. 2 my downsitting and *u.*

Uproar. *Tumult, riot.*
1 K. 1. 41 noise of city in an *u.*
Mat. 26. 5 lest there be an *u.* am.
Mark 14. 2 lest th. be *u.* of people
Acts 17. 5 set all the city in an *u.*
R. V. Mat. 26. 5; Mark 14. 2 tu-
    mult; Acts 19. 40 riot; 21. 31 con-
    fusion; 21. 38 sedition.

Upside Down. *Face upward.*
2 K. 21. 13 dish, and turning it *u. d.*
Ps. 146. 9 wicked he turneth *u. d.*
Isa. 24. 1 Lord turneth earth *u. d.*
Acts 17. 6 have turned world *u. d.*

Upward. *Upward, high, on high.*
Gen. 7. 20 *u.* did waters prevail
Ex. 38. 26 twenty years old and *u.*
Judg. 1. 36; 1 Chr. 23. 3; 2 Chr.
    31. 16; Ez. 3. 8;
Eccl. 3. 21 sp. of man that goeth *u.*
Isa. 37. 31 root downward, fruit *u.*
Ezek. 1. 11 wings were stretched *u.*
Hag. 2. 15 consider from this day *u.*

Urge. *Press.*
Gen. 33. 11 Jacob *u.* Esau, and he
Judg. 16. 16 *u.* th. his soul was vex.
2 K. 2 17 they *u.* him till ashamed
Luke 11. 53 Pharis. began to *u.* him
R. V. Luke 11. 53 press

Urgent. *Pressing.*
Ex. 12. 33 Egyptians were *u.* on
Dan. 3. 22 king's command. was *u.*

Us (*n.*). *We* (*objective*).
Ex. 10. 25 must give *u.* sacrifices
Mat. 1. 23 interpr. is, G. is with *u.*
Etc., etc.

Use (*n.*). *Service.*
Lev. 7. 24 be used in any other *u.*
Deut. 26. 14 aught for unclean *u.*
2 Sam. 1. 18 teach Judah *u.* of bow
1 Chr. 28. 15 to *u.* of candlestick
Rom. 1. 26 did change natural *u.*
Eph. 4. 29 good to *u.* of edifying
2 Tim. 2. 21 meet for master's *u.*
Tit. 3. 14 works for necessary *u.*
Heb. 5. 14 by *u.* ha. senses exerci.
R. V. 2 Sam. 1. 18 song

Use (*v.*). *Employ, turn to account,
treat, to be wont.*
Lev. 19. 26 neither *u.* enchantments
Num. 10. 2 *u.* trumpets for calling
1 Chr. 12. 2 could *u.* right hand
Jer. 23. 31 *u.* th. tongues and say
Ezek. 12. 23 no mo. *u.* it as proverb
Mat. 6. 7 *u.* not vain repetitions
Acts 14. 5 to *u.* apostles despitefully
Rom. 3. 13 with tongues *u.* deceit
1 Cor. 9. 12 have not *u.* this power
2 Cor. 1. 17 did I *u.* lightness? or
Gal. 5. 13 *u.* not liberty for occasion
1 Thes. 2. 5 *u.* we flattering wor.
1 Tim. 3. 13 ha *u.* office of deacon
Heb. 10. 33 companions were so *u.*
1 Pet. 4. 9 *u.* hospitality one to an.

Using. *Use.*
Col. 2. 22 wh. are to perish with *u.*
1 Pet. 2. 16 no° *u.* liber. for cloke

Usurp. *Take self power.*
1 Tit. 2. 12 not to *u.* auth. ov. man

Usurer. *Who exacts.*
Ex. 22. 25 not to be to him as an *u.*

Usury. *Exaction, interest.*
Ex. 22. 25 nei. sh. lay upon him *u.*
Lev. 25. 36 Take thou no *u.* of him
Deut. 23. 19 shall not lend upon *u.*
Neh. 5. 10 let us leave off this *u.*
Ps. 15. 5 putteth not his money to *u.*
Prov. 28. 8 He that by *u.* increaseth
Isa. 24. 2 as with taker of *u.*, so with
Jer. 15. 10 neither lent on *u.*, nor
Ezek. 18. 13 Hath giv. forth up. *u.*
Mat. 25. 27 ha. received own wi. *u.*
Luke 19. 23 requi. mine own wi. *u.*
R. V. Mat. 25. 27; Luke 19. 23 in-
    terest.

Utmost. *Ena, furthest.*
Gen. 49. 26 *u.* bound of the hills
Num. 22. 41 mi. see *u.* of the peo.
Deut. 30. 4 driven out to *u.* parts
Jer. 9. 26 in *u.* corners, that dwell
Luke 11. 31 she came fr. *u.* parts
R. V. Deut. 34. 2 hinder; Joel 2. 20
    western; Luke 11. 31 ends

Utter (*adj.*). *Total, last degree.*
1 K. 20. 42 I appointed to *u.* destr.
Nah. 1. 8 make *u.* end of the place
Zech. 14. 11 no more *u.* destruction
R. V. *outer.*
Ezek. 40. 31 arches were tow. *u.* co.
    41. 1; 43. 19; 46. 20. 47. 2

Utter (*v.*). *Speak.*
Lev. 5. 1 if he do not *u.* it, then he
Num. 30. 6 or *u.* ought of her lips
Josh. 2. 20 if thou *u.* our business
Judg. 5. 12 Awake, Deb., *u.* a song
2 Sam. 22. 14 L., m. H. *u.* his voice
Job 8. 10 Sh. not they *u.* words out
Ps. 19. 2 Day unto day *u.* speech
Prov. 10. 18 that *u.* sland. is a fool
Eccl. 5. 2 not heart be hasty to *u.*
Isa. 32. 6 to *u.* error against the Lord
Jer. 1. 16 I will *u.* my judgments
Ezek. 24. 3 *u.* a parab. unto rebel.
Joel 2. 11 Lord shall *u.* his voice
Am. 1. 2 L. will *u.* voice from Jerus.
Mic. 7. 3 he *u.* mischievous desire
Hab. 3. 10 the deep *u.* his voice, and
Mat. 13. 25 I will *u.* things kept
Rom. 8. 26 groan. wh. cannot be *u.*
1 Cor. 14. 9 exc. ye *u.* by the tongue
2 Cor. 12. 4 not lawf. for man to *u.*
Heb. 5. 11 many th. hard to be *u.*
Rev. 10. 3 seven thunders *u.* voices

Utterly. *Entirely, surely.*
Ex. 17. 14 *u.* put out remembrance
Judg. 15. 2 thought th. *u.* hated her
1 Sam. 15. 3 smite Am., *u.* destroy
Ps. 73. 19 *u.* consumed with terrors
Isa. 2. 18 idols he shall *u.* abolish
Hos. 1. 6 I will *u.* take them away

Uttermost. *End, extremity.*
Ex. 26. 4 make in the *u.* edge of
Num. 11. 1 consumed in *u.* parts
Josh. 15. 1 Zin was the *u.* part of
1 Sam. 14. 2 S. tarried in *u.* part of
2 K. 7. 5 to the *u.* camp of Syria
Neh. 1. 9 cast out into *u.* part of
Ps. 2. 8 give *u.* parts for possession
Isa. 7. 18 hiss for fly in *u.* part of
Mat. 5. 26 till hast paid *u.* farthing
Mark 13. 27 gath. elect from *u.* part
Acts 24. 22 I will know *u.* of your
1 Thes. 2. 16 wrath is come to *u.*
Heb. 7. 25 able to save to the *u.*
R. V. Ex. 26. 4; 36. 11, 17; 2 K. 7.
    5, 8 outmost; Deut. 11. 24 hinder;
    Josh. 15. 5 end; Mat. 5. 26 last.

V.

Vagabond. *Wanderer.*
Gen. 4. 12 Cain, a *v.* sh. thou be in
Ps. 109. 10 Let his children be *v.*
Acts 19. 13 certain of the *v.* Jews
R. V. Gen. 4. 12 wanderer; Acts
    19. 13 strolling

Vail. *See* **Veil.**

Vain. *Empty, profitless, proud,
showy, false.*
Ex. 20. 7 not take name of L. in *v.*
Lev. 26. 16 ye shall sow seed in *v.*
Deut. 32. 47 For it is not a *v.* thing
Judg. 9. 4 Abim. hired *v.* persons
1 Sam. 25. 21 in *v.* have I kept all

---

2 Sam. 6. 20 one of the *v.* fellows
2 K. 17. 5 became *v.* and went up
2 Chr. 13. 7 gath. unto him *v.* men
Job 9. 29 If wicked, labour I in *v.*
Ps. 39. 6 they are disquieted in *v.*
Prov. 31. 30 Fav. deceitf., beauty *v.*
Eccl. 6. 12 all days of his *v.* life wh
Isa. 1. 13 Bring no more *v.* oblations
Jer. 6. 29 the founder melteth in *v.*
Lam. 2. 14 proph. ha. seen *v.* things
Ezek. 6. 10 I have not said in *v.* th.
Zech. 10. 2 they comfort in *v.*, theref.
Mal. 3. 14 It is *v.* to serve God
Mat. 6. 7 use not *v.* repetitions
Acts 4. 25 people imagine *v.* things
Rom. 1. 21 bec. *v.* in imagination
1 Cor. 3. 20 thoughts of wise are *v.*
2 Cor. 6. 1 not grace of God in *v.*
Gal. 2. 2 lest I should run in *v.*
Eph. 5. 6 no man dec. wi. *v.* words
Phil. 2. 16 run not in *v.*, nei. labour
Col. 2. 8 spoil you through *v.* deceit.
1 Thes. 3. 5 and our labour be in *v.*
1 Tim. 6. 20 avoiding *v.* babblings
2 Tim. 2. 16 shun *v.* babblings, for
Tit. 3. 9 strivings are unprof. and *v.*
Jas. 1. 26 this man's religion is *v.*
1 Pet. 1. 18 redeemed fr. *v.* conversa.
R. V. Ex. 5. 9 lying; Job 35. 16;
    Ps. 89. 47; Isa. 49. 4; Jer. 10. 3;
    23. 15; 51. 58; Lam. 2. 14; Isa.
    49. 4 vanity; Jer. 4. 14 evil; Isa.
    45. 18 waste; Eph. 5. 6 empty;
    Gal. 2. 21 nought; 1 Tim. 6. 20;
    2 Tim. 2. 16——

Vain Glory. *Pride.*
Gal. 5. 26 not be desirous of *v. g.*
Phil. 2. 3 nothing done thro. *v. g.*

Vainly. *Ix varity.*
Col. 2. 18 *v.* puffed up by fleshly

Vale. *Lowland.*
Gen. 14. 3 kings in the *v.* of Siddom
Deut. 1. 7 in the hills and in the *v.*
1 K. 10. 27 cedars as sycamore in *v.*
Jer. 33. 13 in cities of *v.* shall flocks
R. V. Deut. 1. 7; Josh. 10. 40; 1 K.
    10. 27; 2 Chr. 1. 15; Jer. 33. 13
    lowland

Valiant. *Mighty, worthy.*
1 Sam. 18. 17 be thou *v.* for me, and
2 Sam. 17. 10 and he also that is *v.*
1 K. 1. 42 thou art *v.* man, and
1 Chr. 7. 2 sons of T. were *v.* men
S. of S. 3. 7 threescore *v.* men of
Isa. 33. 7 their *v.* ones shall cry
Jer. 46. 15 Why are thy *v.* swp. aw.
Nah. 2. 3 *v.* men are in scarlet
Heb. 11. 34 through faith waxed *v.*
R. V. 1 K. 1. 42; 1 Chr. 7. 2, 5;
    11. 26; 28. 1; L. of S. 3. 7; Heb.
    11. 34 mighty; Jer. 46. 15 strong.

Valiantest. *Mightiest.*
Judg. 21. 10 tw. thou. men of th. *v.*

Valiantly. *Strongly, bravely.*
Num. 24. 18 and Israel shall do *v.*
1 Chr. 19. 13 and let us behave *v.*
Ps. 60. 12 Thro. G. we shall do *v.*

Valley. *Cleft place, gorge, plain,
slope, lowland.*
Gen. 14. 17 *v.* of Sha., king's dale
Num. 32. 9 they went into the *v.* E.
Deut. 34. 3 plain in *v.* of Jericho
Josh. 8. 11 *v.* between th. and Ai
1 Sam. 17. 2 men pitch. by *v.* of E.
2 Sam. 23. 13 Phil. pitch. in *v.* of R.
2 K. 14. 7 slew Ed. in *v.* of salt
1 Chr. 4. 39 went unto e. side of *v.*
2 Chr. 20. 26 was call., The *v.* of B.
Neh. 2. 13 I went by gate of the *v.*
Job 21. 33 clods of *v.* sh. be sweet
Ps. 23. 4 I wa. thro. *v.* of sh. of de.
Prov. 30. 17 ravens of *v.* pick out
S. of S. 6. 11 went to see fr. of *v.*
Isa. 17. 5 that gath. ears in *v.* of R.
Jer. 2. 23 See thy way in the *v.*
Ezek. 37. 1 in the *v.* full of bones
Hos. 1. 5 bow of Is. in *v.* of Jezr.
Joel 3. 2 bring them into *v.* of Jeh.
Zech. 12. 11 Is. chased them unto *v.*
Luke 3. 5 Every *v.* shall be filled
R. V. Josh. 9. 1; 11. 2, 16; 12. 8;
    15. 33; Judg. 1. 9; Jer. 32. 44
    lowland.

Valour. *Might, valiant.*
Josh. 10. 7 all mighty men of *v.*
Judg. 3. 29 ten thousand men of *v.*

1 K. 11. 28 Jeroboam, a man of *v.*
2 K. 5. 1 Naaman was mighty in *v.*
1 Chr. 12. 28 Zadok, man mi. of *v.*
2 Chr. 17. 17 Eliada a man of *v.*
Neh. 11. 14 breth., mighty men of *v.*

Value (*n.*).   *Weight, price.*
Job 13. 4 all physicians of no *v.*
Mat. 10. 31 ye are of more value
  than many sparrows ; Luke 12. 7

Value (*v.*).   *Weight, price.*
Lev. 27. 8 the priest shall *v.* him
Job 28. 16 cannot be *v.* with gold
Mat. 27. 9 pri. of him that was *v.*

Vanish.   *Disappear.*
Job 7. 9 cloud is consum., and *v.*
Isa. 51. 6 heav. sh. *v.* like smoke
Jer. 49. 7 is their wisdom *v.*?
Luke 24. 31 he *v.* out of their sight
1 Cor. 13. 8 knowledge, it shall *v.*
Heb. 8. 13 waxeth old, ready to *v.*
Jas. 4. 14 life is a vapour that *v.*

Vanity.   *Emptiness, pride, folly, iniquity.*
Deut. 32. 21 prov. me to ang. wi. *v.*
1 K. 16. 13 provok. L. wi. their *v.*
2 K. 17. 15 they followed *v.*, and
Job 7. 16 alone, for my days are *v.*
Ps. 10. 7 under tong. misch. and *v.*
Prov. 22. 8 sow. iniq. shall reap *v.*
Eccl. 1. 2 *V.* of *v.*, saith P., *v.* of *v.*
  2. 11 all is *v.* and vexation of spirit
  7. 6 laughter of fool. This is *v.*
Isa. 5. 18 draw iniq. wi. cords of *v.*
Jer. 2. 5 have walked after *v.*, and
Ezek. 13. 6 have seen *v.* and lying
Hos. 12. 11 *v.*, they sacri. bullocks
Jonah 2. 8 that observe *v.* forsake
Hab. 2. 13 weary themsel. for *v.*
Zech 10. 2 the idols have spoken *v.*
Acts 14. 15 ye should turn from *v.*
Rom. 8. 20 creature ma. subject to *v.*
Eph. 4. 17 walk not as Gent, in *v.*
2 Pet. 2. 18 speak gr. words of *v.*
R. V. Job 15. 35; Ps. 10. 7 ini-
  quity ; Prov. 21. 6 vapour; 22. 8
  calamity : Isa. 57. 13 breath; 58.
  9 wickedly ; Jer. 10. 8 idols ; Acts
  14. 15 vain things

Vapour.   *Thing lifted up, breath, cloud, smoke.*
Job 36. 27 pour rain accord. to *v*
Ps. 135. 7 He cau. the *v.* to ascend
Acts 2. 19 signs, blood, fire, and *v.*
Jas. 4. 14 what is your life? **a *v.***

Variableness.   *Change.*
Jas. 1. 17 no *v.*, nei. sh. of turning

Variance.   *At two, strife.*
Mat. 10. 35 am co. to set man at *v.*
Gal. 5. 20 works of the flesh, are, *v.*
R. V. Gal. 5. 20 strife

Vaunt.   *Boast, brag self.*
Judg. 7. 2 last Is. *v.* themselves
1 Cor. 13. 4 charity *v.* not itself

Vehement.   R. V. *sultry.*
Jonah 4. 8 G. prep. *v.* east wind

Great, strong.
S. of S. 8. 6 which ha. most *v.* fla.
2 Cor. 7. 11 what *v.* desire, wh. zeal
R. V. 2 Cor. 7. 11 ——

Vehemently.   *Strongly, loudly.*
Mark 14. 31 he spake the more *v.*
Luke 6. 48 stream beat *v.* on house
  23. 10 stood and *v.* accused him
R V. Luke 6. 48, 49 brake

Veil.   *Covering, curtain.*
Gen. 24. 65 she took a *v.*, and cov.
Ex. 26. 31 make *v.* of blue and pur.
Lev. 21. 23 he sh. no go in unto *v.*
Num. 4. 5 take down the cover. *v.*
Ruth 3. 15 Bring *v.* thou hast on
2 Chr. 3. 14 he made the *v.* of blue
S. of S. 5. 7 keep. took away my *v.*
Isa. 3. 23 L. will take away the *v.*
Mat. 27. 51 *v.* of the temple was
  rent in twain, Mark 15. 38; Luke
  23. 45
2 Cor. 3. 13 not as M., wh. put a *v.*
Heb. 6. 19 wh. entereth within *v.*

Vein.   R. V. *mine.*
Job 28. 1 there is a *v.* for silver

Vengeance.   *Retribution.*
Gen. 4. 15 *v.* shall be ta. sev. fold
Deut. 32. 35 To me belongeth *v.*
Judg. 11. 36 the L. hath taken *v.*
Ps. 94. 1 G.. to whom *v.* belongeth
Prov. 6. 34 not spare in day of *v.*

Isa. 34. 8 it is the day of Lord's *v.*
Jer. 11. 20 let me see thy *v.* on them
Lam. 3. 60 hast seen all their *v.*
Ezek. 25. 14 I will lay *v.* on Edom
Mic. 5. 15 I will exec. *v.* in anger
Nah. 1. 2 L. will ta. *v.* on adversar.
Luke 21. 22 these be the days of *v.*
Acts 28. 4 *v.* suffereth not to live
Rom. 12. 19 *V.* is mine, I will repay
2 Thes. 1. 8 In fire taking *v.* on th.
Heb. 10. 30 *v.* belongeth unto me
Jude 7. suffering *d.* of eternal fire
R. V. Acts 28. 4 justice; Jude 7
  punishment

Venison.   *Hunted meat.*
Gen. 27. 5 Esau went to hunt *v.*

Venom.   *Poison.*
Deut. 32. 33 Th. wine is *v.* of asps

Venomous.   *Poisonous.*
Acts 28. 4 barbarians saw *v.* beast

Vent.   *Opening.*
Job 32. 19 as wine wh. hath no *v.*

Venture.   *Simply, chance.*
1 K. 22. 34 a certain man drew a
  bow at a *v.*; 2 Chr. 18. 33.

Verified.   *Made true.*
Gen. 42. 20 so sh. your words be *v.*
1 K. 8. 26 and let thy word be *v.*
2 Chr. 6. 17 let thy word be *v.*, wh.

Verily.   *Truly.*
Gen. 42. 21 We are *v.* guilty conc.
Mat. 5. 18 *v.* I say unto you, Till
Acts 19. 4 John *v.* baptized with
Heb. 3. 5 Moses *r.* was faithful
  Etc., etc.

Verity.   *Truth.*
Ps. 111. 7 wor. of his hands are *v.*
1 Tim. 2. 7 teacher in faith and *v.*

Vermilion.   *Red, ochre.*
Jer. 22. 14 cieled, painted with *v.*
Ezek. 23. 14 images portr. with *v.*

Very.   *Really, selfsame, exceeding.*
Gen. 1. 31 behold, it was *v.* good
Mat. 18. 31 they were *v.* sorry, and
1 Thes. 5. 23 *v.* G. of peace sanc. you
  Ete., etc.

Vessel.   *Utensil, vessel.*
Gen. 43. 11 take fruits in your *v.*
Ex. 27. 3 all *v.* thou shalt make
Lev. 8. 11 anointed altar and all *v.*
Num. 18. 3 sh. not come nigh the *v.*
Deut. 23. 24 not put any in thy *v.*
Josh. 6. 19 all *v.* are consecrated
Ruth 2. 9 athirst, go unto the *v.*
1 Sam. 9. 7 bread is spent in our *v.*
2 Sam. 8. 10 Joram bro. *v.* of gold
1 K. 7. 45 these *v.*, wh. Hir. made
2 K. 4. 3 borrow thee *v.*, empty *v.*
1 Chr. 9. 28 had charge of minist. *v.*
2 Chr. 4. 18 Sol. made all these *v.*
Ez. 1. 7 the king brought forth *v.*
Neh. 10. 39 where are *v.* of sanctu.
Esth. 1. 7 gave drink in *v.* of gold
Ps. 31. 12 I am like a broken *v.*
Prov. 25. 4 come forth *v.* for finer
Isa. 66. 20 bring offering in clean *v.*
Jer. 14. 3 returned with *v.* empty
Ezek. 4. 9 put them in one *v.* and
Dan. 1. 2 bro. *v.* into the treasury
Hos. 8. 8 *v.* wherein is no pleasure
Hag. 2. 16 draw *v.* out of the press
Mat. 13. 48 gathered good into *v.*
Mark 11. 16 th. any man sho. car. *v.*
Luke 8. 16 cov. it wi. *v.*, or putteth
John 19. 29 was set *v.* full of vineg.
Acts 9. 15 he is a chosen *v.* unto me
Rom. 9. 21 ma. one *v.* to hon., anot.
2 Cor. 4. 7 treasure in earthen *v.*
1 Thes. 4. 4 poss. his *v.* in santific.
2 Tim. 2. 21 shall be *v.* into honour
Heb. 9. 21 taber. and all the *v.* of
1 Pet. 3. 7 to wife as to weaker *v.*
Rev. 2. 27 as *v.* of potter be broken
R. V. Ex 27. 19; 39. 40; Num. 3. 36
  instruments; Ex. 40. 9; Num. 1. 50;
  4. 15, 16; 1 Chr. 9. 29 furniture

Vestment.   *Dress, attire.*
2 K. 10. 22 Bring *v.* for worshippers

Vestry.   *Wardrobe.*
2 K. 10. 22 said unto him over the *v.*

Vesture.   *Clothing, raiment, attire, wrap.*
Gen. 41. 42 arrayed him in *v.* of lin.
Deut. 22. 12 make fringes on thy *v.*
Ps. 22. 18 and cast lots upon my *v.*

Mat. 27. 35 on my *v.* they cast lots
John 19. 24 for my *v.* th. cast lots
Heb. 1. 12 as a *v.* sh. fold them up
Rev. 19. 13 clo. with *v.* dipped in
R. V. Mat. 27. 35 —— ; Heb. 1. 12
  mantle; Rev. 19. 16 garment.

Vex.   *Trouble, cross, distress, oppress, crush, destroy.*
Ex. 22. 21 shalt not *v* a stranger
Lev. 19. 23 if stranger shalt not *v.*
Num. 25. 17 *V.* Midian., smite them
Judg. 10. 8 they *v.* and oppr. childr.
1 Sam. 14. 47 Saul *v.* his enemies
2 Sam. 12. 18 how will he *v.* himse.
2 K. 4. 27 for her soul is *v.* within
2 Chr. 15. 6 G. did *v.* th. wi. adver.
Neh. 9. 27 into hands of en., who *v.*
Job 19. 2 How long will ye *v.* soul
Ps. 6. 20 L., heal, my bones are *v.*
Isa. 7. 6 go up ag. Judah, and *v.* it
Ezek. 32. 9 I will *v.* hearts of peo.
Hab. 2. 7 not awake that *v.* thee
Mat. 15. 22 daugh. is *v.* with devil
Luke 6. 18 were *v.* wi uncl. spirits
Acts 12. 1 k. stretched hands to *v.*
2 Pet. 2. 7 del. Lot, *v.* with filthy
R. V. Neh. 9. 27; 2 Pet. 2. 7 dis-
  tressed ; Isa. 63. 10 grieved; Ezek.
  22. 7 wronged ; Luke 6. 18 troubled

Vexation.   *Trouble, striving.*
Deut. 28. 20 L. sh. send on thee *v.*
2 Chr. 15. 5 *v.* were on inhabitants
Eccl. 1. 14 all is van. and *v.* of spirit
Isa. 65. 14 shall howl for *v.* of spirit
R. V. Deut. 28. 20 discomfiture ;
  Isa. 28. 19 nought, throughout
  Eccl. striving

Vial.   *Vial, flask, bowl, bason.*
1 Sam. 10. 1 Sam. took a *v.* of oil,
Rev. 5. 8 golden *v.* full of odours
  15. 7; 16. 1-17; 17. 1* 21. 9
R. V. In Rev. bowl or bowls

Victory.   *Ease, triumph.*
2 Sam. 19. 2 *v.* was turn. into mourn.
1 Chr. 29. 11 th., O L., is *v.*, and m.
Ps. 98. 1 holy arm hath got. him *v.*
Isa. 25. 8 He swal. up death in *v.*
Mat. 12. 20 send judgment unto *v.*
1 Cor. 15. 54 Death is swal. up in *v.*
  15. 55 O grave, where is thy *v.*
1 John 5. 4 this is *v.* that overcom.
Rev. 15. 2 had gotten *v.* over beast

Victuals.   *Food, provisions.*
Gen. 14. 11 took *v.*, went their way
Ex. 12. 39 nei. had they prepared *v.*
Lev. 25. 37 not lend him thy *v.* for
Deut. 23. 19 usury of *v.* usury of
Josh. 1. 11 Prep., *v.*, within three d.
Judg. 7. 8 So peo. took *v.* in hand
1 Sam. 22. 10 gave *v.* and sword
1 K. 4. 7 provided *v.* for the king
Neh. 10. 31 bring *v.* on the sabbath
Jer. 40. 5 capt. of guard ga. him *v.*
Mat. 14. 15 go into villag., buy *v.*
Luke 9. 12 go into towns, get *v.*
R. V. Josh. 9 14 provision; Mat.
  14. 15 food

View.   *Look upon, consider.*
Josh. 2. 1 Go, *v.* land, even Jerich.
2 K. 2. 7 and stood to *v.* afar off
Ex. 8. 15 I *v.* people and priests
Neh. 2. 13 I *v.* the walls of Jerus.
R. V. Josh. 7. 2 spy out

Vigilant.   *Watchful.*
1 Tim. 3. 2 a bishop then must be *v.*
1 Pet. 5. 8 Be sober, be *v.*, because
R. V. 1 Tim 3. 2 temperate ; 1 Pet.
  5. 8 watchful

Vile.   *Low, wicked, unclean.*
Deut. 25. 3 lest thy brother seem *v.*
Judg. 19. 24 do not so *v.* a thing
1 Sam. 15. 9 *v.* and refuse, they des.
2 Sam. 6. 22 I will yet be more *v.*
Job 18. 3 why are we reputed *v.*?
Ps. 15. 4 *v.* person is contemned
Isa. 32. 5 *v.* per. shall be no more
Jer. 15. 19 take prec. from the *v.*
Lam. 1. 11 consid., for I am bec. *v.*
Dan. 11. 21 shall stand a *v.* person
Nah. 1. 14 make grave, thou art *v.*
Rom. 1. 26 God gave them up to *v.*
Phil. 3. 21 Who shall change our *v.*
Jas. 2. 2 a poor man in *v.* raiment
R. V. Judg. 19. 24 folly; Job 18. 3
  unclean ; 40. 4 small account; Ps.
  15. 4 reprobate; Dan. 11. 21 con-

Vilely. *With loathing.*
2 Sam. 1. 21 shield is v. cast away
Viler. R. V. *scourged out.*
Job 30. 8 they were v. than earth
Vilest. *Most vile.*
Ps. 12. 8 when v. men are exalted
Village. *Court, hamlet, town.*
Ex. 8. 13 frogs died out of the v.
Lev. 25. 31 houses of v. counted
Num. 21. 32 they took the v. there.
Josh. 13. 23 inher., the cities and v.
Judg. 5. 7 v., they ceased in Israel
1 Sam. 6. 18 fenced cities, and v.
1 Chr. 4. 32 their v. were, Etam
Neh. 6. 2 meet in one of the v.
Esth. 9. 19 Jews of v., that dwelt
Ps. 10. 8 sit. in lurking pl. of the v.
S. of S. 7. 11 let us lodge in the v.
Isa. 42. 11 the v., Kedar doth inhab.
Ezek. 38. 11 to land of unwall. v.
Hab. 3. 14 did. strike head of his v.
Mat. 9. 35 Jesus went about all v.
Mark 6. 6 went about v., teaching
Luke 8. 1 he went through every v.
R. V Ex. 8. 13 courts; Num.
21. 25, 32; 2 Chr. 28. 18; Neh. 11. 31
towns; Judg. 5. 11 rule.
Villany. *Folly, vileness.*
Isa. 32. 6 vile person will speak v.
Jer. 29. 23 Because th. ha. com. v.
R. V. Jer. 29. 23 folly
Vine. *Vine, branch.*
Gen. 40. 9 behold, a v. before me
Lev. 25. 5 nei. gath. grapes of thy v.
Num. 20. 5 no place of figs or v.
Deut. 8. 8 land of wheat, bar., v.
Judg. 9. 12 trees said to v., Reign
1 K. 4. 25 every man under his v.
2 K. 18. 31 eat ev. man of own v.
Job 15. 33 shake off gr. as the v.
Ps. 78. 47. destr. their v. with hail
S. of S. 2. 13 v. give a good smell
Isa. 5. 2 planted it with choicest v.
Jer. 2. 21 I plant. thee a noble v.
Ezek. 15. 6 As v. among trees of the
Hos. 10. 1 Israel is an empty v.
Joel 1. 7 he hath laid my v. waste
Mic. 4. 4 sit every man under his v.
Hab. 3. 17 neither fruit be in the v.
Hag. 2. 19 v. hath not bro. forth
Zech. 8. 12 the v. sh. give her fruit
Mal. 3. 11 nei. sh. v. cast her fruit
Mat. 26. 29 I will not drink of fruit
of v.; Mark 14. 25; Luke 22. 18
John 15. 1 I am the true v., and
Jas. 3. 12 berries? either a v., figs?
Rev. 14. 18 gath. clusters of the v.
R. V. Rev. 14. 19 vintage
Vine Dressers
2 K. 25. 12 left poor of l. to be v. *d.*
2 Chr. 26. 10 had v. d. in the mounts.
Isa. 61. 5 sons of aliens your v. d.
Joel 1. 11 be ashamed, O ye v. d.
Vinegar. *Sour wine.*
Num. 6. 3. Naz. shall drink no v.
Ruth. 2. 14 dip thy morsel in the v.
Ps. 69. 21 th. gave me v. to drink
Prov. 10. 26 as v. to teeth, and as
Mat. 27. 48 sponge, filled it with v.
Mark 15. 36; Luke 23. 36; John
19. 29
R. V. Mat. 27. 34 wine
Vineyard. *Vineyard.*
Gen. 9. 20 Noah, he planted a v.
Ex. 22. 5 if cause v. to be eaten
Lev. 19. 10 shall not glean thy v.
Num. 16. 14 not giv. inher. of v.
Deut. 6. 11 he swore to give thee v.
Josh. 24. 13 of v. ye plant. not ye eat
Judg. 9. 27 gath. their v., and trode
1 Sam. 8. 14 will ta. yo. fields, and v.
1 K. 21. 2 Give me your v., that
2 K. 18. 32 a land of bread and v.
1 Chr. 27. 27 over v. was Shimei
Neh. 5. 3 have mortgaged our v.
Job 24. 18 behold. not way of v.
Ps. 80. 15 v. thy ri. hand ha. plant.
Prov. 24. 30 I went by v. of man
Eccl. 2. 4 houses, I planted me v.
S. of S. 1. 6 own v. have I not kept
Isa. 1. 8 Z. is left as cottage in v.
Jer. 12. 10 pastors destroyed my v.
Ezek. 28. 26 build houses, and pl. v.
Hos. 2. 15 I will give her her v.
Am. 5. 11 ye ha. planted pleas. v.

Mic. 1. 6 make Sa. as planti. of v.
Zeph. 1. 13 sh. plant v. but not dr.
Mat. 20. 1 hire labor. into his v.
Luke 20 15 they cast him out of v.
1 Cor. 9. 7 who pl. v., and eateth
Vintage. *Harvest, product.*
Lev. 26. 5 shall reach unto the v.
Judg. 8. 2 better than v. of Abiez.
Job 24. 6 they gath. v. of wicked
Isa. 32. 10 the v. shall fail, the ga.
Jer. 48. 32 spoiler is fall. upon v.
Mic. 7. 1 I am as gleanings of v.
Zech. 11. 2 forest of the v. is come
Viol. *Lyre, lute.*
Isa. 5. 12 harp, v. tabret, and pipe
Am. 5. 23 I will not hear mel. of v.
R. V. Isa. 5. 12 lute
Violate. R. V. *done violence.*
Ezek. 22. 26 Her priests v. my law
Violence. *Snatching, force, fury.*
Gen. 6. 11 earth was filled with v.
Lev. 6. 2 or thing tak. away by v.
2 Sam. 22. 3 thou savest me from v.
Ps. 11. 5 th. lov. v. his soul hateth
Prov. 4. 17 they drink the wine of v.
Isa. 60. 18 V. sh. no more be heard
Jer. 6. 7 v. and spoil is heard in
Ezek. 7. 11 V. is risen up into a rod
Joel 3. 19 for v. ag. the childr. of
Am. 3. 10 who store up v. and rob.
Obad. 10 For v. against thy broth.
Jonah. 3. 8 turn ev. one from the v.
Mic. 6. 12 rich men are full of v.
Hab. 1. 2 cry out unto thee of v.
Zeph. 1. 9 fill mast. houses with v.
Mal. 2. 16 cov. v. with his garment
Mat. 11. 12 kingd. of heav. suff. v.
Luke 3. 14 Do v. to no man, neith.
Acts 5. 26 brought them without v.
Heb. 11. 34 Quenched the v. of fire
Rev. 18. 21 wi. v. sh. that gr. city
R. V. Lev. 6. 2 robbery; Mic. 2. 2
seize; Acts 24. 7 ——; Heb. 11.
34 power; Rev. 18. 21 mighty fall
Violent. *Snatching, furious.*
2 Sam. 22. 49 hast del. me fr. v. m.
Ps. 7. 16 v. dealing sh. come down
Prov. 16. 29 v. man entice. neigh.
Eccl. 5. 8 if thou seest v. pervert
Mat. 11. 12 the v. take it by force
Violently. *Forcefully.*
Gen. 21. 25 A.'s servants had v. ta.
Lev. 6. 4 sh. restore wh. he took v.
Deut. 28. 31 ass shall be v. taken
Job 20. 19 hath v. taken a house
Lam. 2. 6 ha. v. tak. away his tab.
Mat. 8. 32 ran v. down steep place
Mark 5. 13; Luke 8. 33
R. V. Lev. 6. 4 by robbery; Mat.
8. 32; Mark 5. 13; Luke 8. 33
rushed
Viper. *Viper.*
Job 20. 16 v. tongue sh. slay him
Isa. 30. 6 whence co. v and serpts.
Mat. 3. 7 O generation of v.
Luke 3. 7 gen. of v., who ha. warn.
Acts 28. 3 ca. a. v. out of the heat
Virgin. *Unmarried female.*
Gen. 24. 43 then when v. com. forth
Ex. 22. 17 pay accord. to dow. of v.
Lev. 21. 14 ta. v. of his own people
Deut. 22. 19 bro. evil name upon v
Judg. 21. 12 th. found four hund. v.
2 Sam. 13. 2. Tamar; she was a v.
1 K. 1. 2 sought for the king a v.
2 K. 19. 21 v., the daugh. of Zion
Esth. 2. 2 Let there be v. sought
Ps. 45. 14 v. her companions that
S. of. S. 1. 3 therefore do the v. love
Isa. 7. 14 v. sh. conceive, bare son
Jer. 31. 21 O v. of Is., turn again to
Lam. 1. 4 priests sigh, v. are afflict.
Joel 1. 8 Lament like v. girded wi.
Am. 5. 2 The v. of Israel is fallen
Mat. 1. 23 a v. shall be with child
Luke 1. 27 the v.'s name was Mary
Acts 21. 9 man had four daugh., v.
1 Cor. 7. 28 if v. marry, not sinned
2 Co. 11. 2 I may present you as v.
Rev. 14. 4 not defiled, they are v.
Virginity. *Maidenhood.*
Lev. 21. 13 take a wife in her v.
Deut. 22. 15 br. tok. of damsel's v.
Judg. 11. 37 bewail my v., I and
Ezek. 23. 3 bruised teats of their v.
Luke 2. 36 lived sev. y'rs fr. her v.

Virtue. *Strength, power.*
Mark 5. 30 knowing th. v. had gone
Luke 6. 19 th. went v. out of him
Phil. 4. 8 if there be any v., and
2 Pet. 1. 5 add to your faith v.; and
R. V. Mark 5. 30; Luke 6. 19; 8.
46 power.
Virtuous. *Strong, worthy.*
Ruth 3. 11 thou art a v. woman
Prov. 12. 4 A v. woman is a crown
31. 10 Who can find a v. woman?
Virtuously. *Worthily.*
Prov. 31. 29 Many daugh. ha. do. v.
Visage. *Face, appearance.*
Isa. 52. 14 his v. was marred more
Lam. 4. 8 v. is blacker than a coal
Dan. 3. 19 form of his v. was chan.
Visible. *That may be seen.*
Col. 1. 16 all things v. and invisib.
Vision. *Sight, thing seen.*
Gen. 15. 1 L. came to Ab. in a v.
Num. 12. 6 make myself kn. in v.
1 Sam. 3. 15 S. feared to show E. v.
2 Sam. 7. 17 accor. to v., so did Na.
1 Chr. 17. 15 accor. to v. so did Na.
2 Chr. 32. 33 are writ. in v. of Isa.
Job 20. 8 be chased as v. of night
Ps. 89. 19 sp. in v. to thy Ho. One
Prov. 29. 18 wh. no v. peo. perish
Isa. 1. 1 v. of Isaiah son of Amoz
Jer. 14. 14 they proph. a false v.
Lam. 2. 9 her prophets find no v.
Ezek. 7. 26 sh. seek v. of prophets
Dan. 1. 17 D. had understand. of v.
Hos. 12. 10 I have multiplied v. and
Obad. 1 The v. of Obadiah. Thus
Mic. 3. 6 ye shall not have a v.
Nah. 1. 1 book of v. of Nahum the
Hab. 2. 2 Write v., make it plain
Mat. 17. 9 Tell the v. to no man
Luke 1. 22 perch. he had seen a v.
Acts 2. 17 young men shall see v.
2 Cor. 12. 1 I come to v. and revela.
Rev. 9. 17 I saw horses in the v.
R. V. Ezek. 8. 4 appearance; Acts
9. 12
Visit. *Look in on, inspect.*
Gen. 21. 1 L. v. Sarah as he said
Ex. 3. 16 I have surely v. you, and
Lev. 18. 25 I v. the iniquity thereof
Num. 14. 18 v. iniq. of fath. upon
Deut. 5. 9 v. iniq. of fathers upon
Judg. 15. 1 Sam v. wife with a kid
Ruth 1. 6 L. had v. his peo. in giv.
1 Sam. 2. 22 L. v. Han., so she could
Job 5. 24 shalt v. thy habitation
Ps. 17. 3 thou hast v. me in night
Prov. 19. 23 sh. not be v. with evil
Isa. 23. 17 L. will v. Tyre, and she
Jer. 3. 16 nei. sh. they v. it, neither
Lam. 4. 22 he will v. thine iniquity
Ezek. 38. 8 after many days be v.
Hos. 2. 13 v. on her days of Baalim
Am. 3. 14 I will v. altars of Bethel
Zeph. 2. 7 L. their G. shall v. them
Zech. 11. 16 not v. those cut off
Mat. 25. 36 was sick, and ye v. me
Luke 7. 16 God hath v. his people
Acts 15. 14 God did v. the Gentiles
Heb. 2. 6 or son of man, that th. v.
Jas. 1. 27 To v. the fatherless and
Vocation. R. V. *calling.*
Eph. 4. 1 walk worthy of the v.
Voice. *Voice, sound.*
Gen. 3. 8 heard v. of the Lord God
Ex. 3. 18 shall hearken to thy v.
Lev. 5. 1 if soul hear v. of swear.
Num. 14. 1 congrega. lifted their v.
Deut. 1x. Heard v. of yo. words
Josh. 5. 6 th. obey. not v. of Lord
Judg. 2. 2 ye ha. not obey. my v.
Ruth 1. 9 lifted up v., and wept
1 Sam. 1. 13 her v. was not heard
2 Sam. 3. 32 king lifted up his v.
1 K. 17. 22 Lord heard v. of Elijah
2 K. 7. 10 neither v. of man, but
1 Chr. 15. 16 by lift. up v. with joy
2 Chr. 20. 19 praise L. with loud v.
Ez. 3. 12 many wept with a loud v
Neh. 9. 4 cried with v. unto the L.
Job 4. 16 and I heard a v., saying
Ps. 18. 6 heard my v. out of temple
Prov. 1. 20 Wisdom uttereth her v.
Eccl. 5. 3 fool's v. is kn. by multit.
S. of S. 2. 12 v. of turtle is heard in
Isa. 6. 4 posts of door moved at v.

Jer. 3. 13 ye ha. not obeyed my *v.*
Lam. 3. 56 heard my *v.*, hide not
Ezek. 1. 24 as *v.* of the Almighty
Dan. 8. 16 heard *v.* bet. the banks
Joel 2. 11 Lord shall utter his *v.*
Am. 1. 2 L. will utter *v.* from Jeru.
Jonah 2. 2 cried, thou heard my *v.*
Mic. 6. 1 let the hills hear thy *v.*
Nah. 2. 7 lead as with *v.* of doves
Hab. 3. 16 my lips quivered at the *v.*
Zeph. 2. 14 *v.* sh. sing in windows
Hag. 1. 12 obeyed *v.* of Lord God
Zech. 11. 3 *v.* of the roaring of lions
Mat. 3. 3 *v.* of one cry. in wilder.
Mark 1. 11 came *v.* fr. hea., saying
Luke 1. 42 she spake with loud *v.*
John 1. 23 I am *v.* of one crying
Acts 7. 3 *v.* of L. came upon him
1 Cor. 14. 10 are many kinds of *v.*
Gal. 4. 20 I des. to change my *v.*
1 Thes. 4. 16 with *v.* of archangel
Heb. 12. 26 whose *v.* shook earth
2 Pet. 1. 17 came such a *v.* to him
Rev. 1. 12 I turned to see the *v.*

Void. *Vacant, empty.*
Gen. 1. 2 e. was with. form, and *v.*
Num. 30. 12 if husb. made them *v.*
Deut. 32. 28 a nat. *v.* of counsel
1 K. 22. 10 *v.* place in ent. of gate
2 Chr. 18. 9 in a *v.* pl. at entering
Ps. 89. 39 hast made *v.* the cove.
Prov. 11. 12 *v.* of wisd. despiseth
Isa. 55. 11 not return unto me *v.*
Jer. 19. 7 will ma. *v.* counsel of Jud.
Nah. 2. 10 She is empty, and *v.*, and
Rom. 3. 31 Do we make *v.* the law
1 Cor. 9. 15 make my glorying *v.*

Volume. *Roll, scroll.*
Ps. 40. 7 in *v.* of book it is written
Heb. 10. 7 in *v.* of book it is writ.

Voluntary. *Willing.*
Lev. 1. 3 shall offer it of *v.* will
Ezek. 46. 12 prepare a *v.* burnt off.

Voluntarily. *Willingly.*
Ezek. 46. 12 prepare offerings *v.*

Vomit (*n.*). *Ejected matter.*
Prov. 26. 11 dog return. to his *v.*
Isa. 19. 14 man stagger. in his *v.*
Jer. 48. 26 Moab sh. wallow in *v.*

Vomit (*v.*). *To eject.*
Lev. 18. 25 land *v.* out her inhabi.
Job 20. 15 shall *v.* them up again
Prov. 23. 18 morsel eat. sh. thou *v.*
Jonah 2. 10 it *v.* Jonah on dry land

Vow (*n.*). *Vow.*
Gen. 28. 20 *v.*, saying, If G. will be
Lev. 7. 16 if sacrifice of offer. be a *v.*
Num. 6. 2 *v.* of a Nazarite, to separ.
Deut. 23. 18 br. price of dog for *v.*
Judg. 11. 30 Jephthah vowed a *v.*
1 Sam. 1. 11 Hannah vowed a *v.*
2 Sam. 15. 7 let go and pay my *v.*
Job 22. 27 thou shalt pay the *v.*
Ps. 22. 25 I will pay my *v.* before
Prov. 7. 14 this day I paid my *v.*
Eccl. 5. 4 when thou vowest a *v.*
Isa. 19. 21 they sh. vow a *v.* to L.
Jer. 44. 25 will surely perf. our *v.*
Jonah 1. 16 men fear. L. made *v.*
Nah. 1. 15 keep feasts, perform *v.*
Acts 18. 18 head, for he had a *v.*

Vow (*v.*). *Vow.*
Gen. 28. 20 Jacob *v.* a vow, saying
Lev. 27. 8 accord. to ability that *v.*
Num. 6. 21 law of N. who hath *v.*
Deut. 23. 22 if forbear to *v.*, no sin
Judg. 11. 30 Jephthah *v.* a vow
Ps. 132. 2 He *v.* to the mighty God
Eccl. 5. 4 pay which thou hast *v.*
Jonah 2. 9 I will pay that I have *v.*
Mal. 1. 14 cursed be deceiver th. *v.*

Voyage. *A sailing, course.*
Acts 27. 10 this *v.* will be with hurt

Vulture. *Kite, vulture.*
Lev. 11. 14 the *v.*, after his kind
Deut. 14. 13 the glede, kite, the *v.*
Job 28. 7 path *v.* eye hath not seen
Isa. 34. 15 there sh. *v.* be gathered
R. V. Lev. 11. 14; Deut. 14. 13;
Isa. 34. 15 kite ; Job 28. 7 falcon's

W.

Wafer. *Thin cake.*
Ex. 16. 31 taste of it was like *w.*
Lev. 2. 4 or *w.* anointed with oil
Num. 6. 19 priest shall take one *w.*

Wag. *Move, shake.*
Jer. 18. 16 ev. one sh. *w.* his head
Lam. 2. 15 *w.* heads at dau. of J.
Mat. 27. 39 they reviled on him *w.*
  their heads ; Mark 15. 29.
R. V. Jer. 18. 16 shake

Wages. *Hire, reward.*
Gen. 29. 15 tell me, wh. sh. *w.* be?
Ex. 2. 9 nurse it, I will gi. thee *w.*
Lev. 19. 13 *w.* of hired not abide
Jer. 22. 13 useth service without *w.*
Ezek. 29. 18 had no *w.*, nor his army
Luke 3. 14 be content with your *w.*
John 4. 36 that reapeth receiv. *w.*
Rom. 6. 23 the *w.* of sin is death
2 Cor. 11. 8 I robbed ch., taking *w.*
2 Pet. 2. 15 who lov. *w.* of unright.
R. V. 2 Pet. 2. 15 hire

Wagon. *Cart, chariot.*
Gen. 45. 19 take you *w.* out of Egy.
Num. 7. 6 Moses took *w.* and oxen

Wail. *Smite breast,cry out,lament.*
Jer. 9. 19 *w.* is heard out of Zion
Ezek. 7. 11 nei. sh. be *w.* for them
Mat. 13. 42 be *w.* and gnash. of teeth
Mark 5. 38 he seeth them th. *w.* gr.
Rev. 1. 7 all kind. of earth shall *w.*
R. V. Mat. 13. 42, 50 weeping
  Rev. 1. 7 mourn

Wait (*v.*). *Stand still, await, expect, attend on.*
Gen. 49. 18 I have *w.* for thy salva.
Num. 3. 10 Aa. and sons shall *w.*
1 K. 20. 38 prophets depart., and *w.*
2 K. 6. 33 what sho. I *w.* for Lord
1 Chr. 6. 32 they *w.* on their office
2 Chr. 7. 6 priests *w.* on their offices
Job 29. 23 *w.* for me as for the rain
Ps. 25. 5 on thee do I *w.* all the day
Prov. 20. 22 *w.* on L., he sh. save t.
Isa. 8. 17 I will *w.* upon the Lord
Jer. 14. 22 we will *w.* upon thee; for
Lam. 3. 25 L. is good to th. that *w.*
Ezek. 19. 5 saw that she had *w.*
Dan. 12. 12 blessed is he that *w.*
Hos. 6. 9 as troop of robbers *w.*
Mic. 5. 7 as showers that *w.* not
Mark 3. 9 ship should *w.* on him
Luke 2. 25 *w.* for consola. of Israel
John 5. 3 *w.* for moving of waters
Acts 17. 16 P. *w.* for them at Athens
Rom. 8. 19 *w.* for manifes. of sons
1 Cor. 1. 7 *w.* for coming of Lord J.
Gal. 5. 5 we through the Spirit *w.*
1 Thes. 1. 10 *w.* for his Son fr. hea.
1 Pet. 3. 20 long suffer. of God *w.*
R. V. Job 17. 13; Isa. 59. 9; Ps.
  128. 2 ; Luke 12. 36 look

Wait. (*n.*). *Watch, ambush.*
Num. 35. 20 if hurl by lay. of *w.*
Job 38. 40 abide in cov. to lie in *w.*?
Ps. 71. 10 th. lie in *w.* for my soul
Jer. 9. 8 in heart he layeth his *w.*
R. V. Ps. 71. 10; Jer. 5. 26 watch;
  Judg. 9. 35 ambush

Wake. *Stir, rouse, rise, awake.*
Ps. 77. 4 th. holdest mine eyes *w.*
S. of S. 5. 2 I sleep but my hea. *w.*
Isa. 50. 4 he *w.* mine ear to hear
Jer. 51. 39 sleep perpe. sleep. not *w.*
1 Thes. 5. 10 wheth. we *w.* or sleep
R. V. Ps. 77. 4 watching ; Joel 3.
  9. 12 stir, or bestir

Walk. (*n.*). *Going, way.*
Ezek. 42. 4 bef. chambers was a *w.*
Nah. 2. 5 shall stumble in their *w.*

Walk. (*v.*) *Go on, tread.*
Gen. 5. 22 Enoch *w.* with G. after
Ex. 2. 5 maidens *w.* along riv. side
Lev. 26. 12 I will *w.* am. you, and
Josh. 5. 6 chil. of Is. *w.* forty y'rs
Judg. 5. 6 travellers *w.* thro. byways
1 Sam. 2. 35 *w.* bef. mine anoi. for
2 Sam. 7. 6 *w.* in tent and tabernac.
1 K. 3. 14 as thy father D. did *w.*
2 K. 10. 31 Jehu took no heed to *w.*
1 Chr. 17. 6 I have *w.* wi. all Israel
2 Chr. 6. 16 ta. heed, to *w.* in my l.
Job 22. 14 he *w.* in circuit of heaven
Ps. 12. 8 The wicked *w.* on ev. side
Prov. 13 20 th. *w.* wi. wise men sh.
Eccl. 2. 14 the fool *w.* in darkness
Isa. 3. 16 *w.* and minc. as they go
Jer. 3. 17 nor *w.* after imagination
Lam. 5. 18 Z., the foxes *w.* upon it.
Ezek. 5. 7 ha. not *w.* in my statutes

Hos. 5. 11 he *w.* after the command.
Joel 2. 8 they shall *w.* in his path
Am. 3. 3 Can two *w.* togeth., except
Mat. 4. 18 J., *w.* on sea of Gal., saw
Mark 2. 9 Arise, take up bed, and *w.*
Luke 11. 44 the men that *w.* over
John 10. 23 Jesus *w.* in the temple,
Acts 3. 9 all the people saw him *w.*
Rom. 6. 4 sho. *w.* in newness of life
1 Cor. 7. 17 as L. call., so let him *w.*
2 Cor. 5. 7 we *w.* by faith, not sight
Gal. 5. 16 *W.* in the Spirit, and ye s.
Eph. 5. 2 *w.* in love, as Christ loved
Phil. 3. 18 many *w.*, of wh. I ha. b
Col. 1. 10 might *w.* worthy of the **L**
1 Thes. 4. 12 That ye may *w.* hon.
2 Thes. 3. 11 some wh. *w.* disorderly
1 Pet. 5. 8 devil, *w.* about seeking
1 John 1. 6 and *w.* in dark., we lie
2 John 6 *w.* after his commandment
3 John 3 *even* as thou *w.* in truth
Jude 16 *w.* after their own lusts
Rev. 3. 4 they shall *w.* with me in

Wall. *Wall, fence, inclosure.*
Ex. 14. 22 waters were a *w.* unto
Num. 13. 28 cities are *w.*, very great
Deut. 1. 28 cit. are *w.* up to heaven
Josh. 2. 15 and she dwelt upon *w.*
1 Sam. 25. 16 They were a *w.* unto
2 Sam. 11. 21 why went ye nigh *w.*?
1 K. 4. 33 hyssop th. springs of *w.*
2 Chr. 25. 23 brake down *w.* of Jer.
Ps. 62. 3 a bowing *w.* shall ye be
Prov. 18. 11 as high *w.* in conceit
S. of S. 8. 9 If she be a *w.*, we will
Isa. 60. 18 sh. call thy *w.* Salvation
Jer. 1. 18 brazen *w.* ag. whole land
Lam. 2. 18 O *w.* of Zion, let tears
Ezek. 8. 8 Son of man, dig in the *w.*
Dan. 9. 25 street sh. be built, and *w.*
Am. 1. 7 will send a fire on the *w.*
Hab. 2. 11 stone sh. cry out of the *w.*
Acts 9. 25 let him down by the *w.*
Heb. 11. 30 By faith *w.* of Jeric. fell
Rev. 21. 14 *w.* had twelve founda.
R. V. Gen. 49. 6 ox ; Num. 13. 28;
  22. 24 ; Deut. 1. 28 : Isa. 5. 5 ; Hos.
  2. 6 fence or fenced ; 1 K. 21 23
  rampart

Wallow. *Roll, reel.*
2 Sam. 21. 12 Amasa *w.* in blood in
Jer. 6. 26 gird with sackcloth, *w.*
Ezek. 27. 30 they shall *w.* in ashes
Mark 9. 20 fell on the ground, and *w.*
2 Pet. 2. 22 and sow washed to her *w.*

Wander. *Go on, move about, go astray, err.*
Gen. 20. 13 G. caused me to *w.* from
Num. 14. 33 chil. sh. *w.* in wildern.
Deut. 27. 18 maketh the blind to *w.*
Job. 15. 23 he *w.* abroad for bread
Ps. 59. 15 *w.* up and down for meat
Prov. 27. 8 as bird *w.* from her nest
Isa. 16. 3 bewray not him that *w.*
Jer. 2. 20 under green tree thou *w.*
Ezek. 34. 6 My sheep *w.* thro. mo.
1 Tim. 5. 13 *w.* from house to house
Heb. 11. 37 *w.* about in sheepskins
Jude 13 *w.* stars to wh. is reserved

Wanderer. *Who wanders.*
Jer. 48. 12 I will send to him *w.*
Hos. 9. 17 sh. be *w.* among nations

Want (*n.*). *Need, lack.*
Deut. 28. 57 she shall eat th. for *w.*
Judg. 19. 20 all thy *w.* lie on me
Job 24. 8 they embrace rock for *w.*
Ps. 34. 9 no *w.* to them that fear
Prov. 10. 21 fools die for *w.* of wis.
Mark 12. 44 of her *w.* cast in all
Luke 15. 14 he began to be in *w.*
2 Cor. 8. 14 abundance for their *w.*
R. V. Prov. 10. 21 lack ; Phil. 2. 25
  need

Want (*v.*). *To need, lack.*
Deut. 15. 8 lend him which he *w.*
2 K. 10. 19 prophets, let none be *w.*
Ps. 23. 1 shepherd, I shall not *w.*
Prov. 13. 25 belly of wicked sh. *w.*
S. of S. 7. 2 like goblet that *w.* not
Isa. 34. 16 none shall *w.* her mate
Jer. 33. 17 D. sh. nev. *w.* man to sit
Ezek. 4. 17 may *w.* bread and water
John 2. 3 *w.* wine, mother of Jesus
2 Cor. 11. 9 wh. I *w.*, I was charged

Tit. 1 5 set in order the things *w*.
R. V. Prov. 28. 16; Eccl. 6. 2; Jas.
1. 4 lack or lacking

Wanton. *Loose, lewd.*
Isa. 3. 16 daugh., walk with *w*. eyes
1 Tim. 5. 11 to wax *w*. against Chr.
Jas. 5. 5 have lived and been *w*.
R. V. Jas. 5. 5 take pleasure

Wantonness. *Lewdness.*
Rom. 13. 13 not in chamber. and *w*.
2 Pet. 2. 18 allure through much *w*.
R. V. 2 Pet. 2. 18 lasciviousness

War (*n.*). *Battle, fight, war.*
Gen. 14. 2 these made *w*. with Bera.
Ex. 15. 3 The Lord is a man of *w*.
Josh. 11. 18 Josh. made *w*. long ti.
Judg. 11. 4 Ammon made *w*. ag. Is.
2 Sam. 1. 27 How are weap. of *w*.
1 K. 2. 5 and shed the blood of *w*.
1 Chr. 5. 10 in days of S. made *w*.
Job 10. 17 changes and *w*. are ag.
Ps. 49. 6 He ma. *w*. to cease unto
Prov. 24. 6 by wise coun. ma. thy *w*.
Eccl. 3. 8 time of *w*., time of peace
S. of S. 3. 8 hold swords, being .. *w*.
Isa. 2. 4 nei. sh. learn *w*. any more
Jer. 4. 19 hast heard alarm of *w*.
Ezek. 17. 17 nor Phar. make in *w*.
Joel. 3. 9 let all the men of *w*. draw
Mat. 24. 6 shall hear of *w*. and rum.
of *w*., Mark 13. 7; Luke 21. 9
Luke 23. 11 Her. wi. men of *w* set
Jas. 4. 1 whence *w*. and fight. am.
Rev. 11. 7 beast sh. make *w*. again.
R. V. Deut. 21. 10; Judg. 21. 22;
2 Chr. 6. 34; Jer. 6. 23 battle.

War (*v.*). *To fight, wage war.*
Josh. 24. 9 Balak *w*. against Israel
2 Sam. 22. 35 He teach. my h. to *w*.
2 K. 19. 8 k. of Assyr. *w*. ag. Lib.
2 Chr. 26. 6 Uzziah *w*. ag. Philist.
Isa. 41. 12 *w*. ag. thee be as nothing
Rom. 7. 23 a law in my memb., *w*.
2 Cor. 10. 3 do not *w*. after flesh
1 Tim. 1. 18 mi. *w*. a good warfare
Jas. 4. 1 lusts th. *w*. in members
1 Pet. 2. 11 lusts, wh. *w*. ag. soul

Ward. *Guard, keep.*
Gen. 40. 3 he put them in *w*. in ho.
Lev. 24. 12 they put him in *w*., that
2 Sam. 20. 3 put them in *w*., fed th.
1 Chr. 12. 29 had kept *w*. of Saul
Isa. 21. 8 I am set in my *w*. whole
Jer. 37. 13 capt. of the *w*. was th.
Ezek. 19. 9 put him in *w*. in chains
Acts 12. 10 past first and second *w*.
R. V. 1 Chr. 25. 8; 26. 12 charge;
Ezek. 19. 9 cage.

Wardrobe. *Clothes keep.*
2 K. 22. 14 Shallum, the keeper of
the . , 2 Chr. 34. 22

Ware (*v.*). *Aware.*
Acts 14. 6 were *w*. of it, and fled to
2 Tim. 4. 15 of coppersmith be *w*.

Ware. *See Wear.*

Ware (*n.*). *Thing for sale, article.*
Jer. 10. 17 gath. up *w*. out of land
Ezek. 27. 16 by reas. of multi. of *w*.

Warfare. *War waging, strife.*
Isa. 40. 2 her *w*. is accomplished
1 Cor. 9. 7 Who goeth *w*. any time
2 Cor. 10. 4 weap. of *w*. not carnal
1 Tim. 1. 18 might. war a good *w*.

Warm (*adj.*). *Not cold.*
2 K. 3. 34 flesh of child waxed *w*.
Job 6. 17 they *w*. warm, th. vanish
Isa. 44. 15 ta. thereof, and *w*. him.

Warm (*v.*). *To warm.*
Job 31. 20 were not *w*. wi. fleece
Isa. 44. 16 saith, Aha, I am *w*., I
Mark 14. 67 she saw Pet. *w*. hims.
Jas. 2. 16 be ye *w*. and filled, not.

Warn. *Notify, admonish.*
2 K. 6. 10 the man of God *w*. him
2 Chr. 19. 10 sh. *w*. they tresp. not
Ps. 19. 11 by them is servant *w*.
Mat. 2. 12 Joseph being *w*. of God
Luke 3. 7 O gen. of vip., who ha. *w*.
Acts 20. 31 I ceased not to *w*. ev.
1 Cor. 4. 14 beloved sons, I. *w*. you
1 Thes. 5. 14 th. that are unruly
R. V. Acts 20. 31; 1 Cor. 4. 14; 1
Thes. 5. 14 admonish

Warning. *Admonition.*
Jer. 6. 10 to whom sh. I give *w*.?
Col. 1. 28 *w*. ev. man, and teaching

Warp. *Long threads.*
Lev 13. 48 wheth. in the *w*. or woof

Warrior. *Who battles.*
1 K. 12. 21 chosen men, wh. were *w*.
Isa. 9. 5 battle of *w*. is with noise

Was. *See Am.*

Wash. *Cleanse, bathe.*
Gen. 18. 4 *w*. feet, and rest yourselv.
Ex. 2. 5 daugh. of Ph. come do. to *w*.
Num. 19. 7 priest sh. *w*. his clothes
Ruth 3. 3 *w*. thyself and anoint thee
2 Sam. 12. 20 David arose and *w*. and
1 K. 22. 38 one *w*. chariot in pool
2 K. 5. 10 *w*. in Jordan sev. times
Job 9. 30 if I *w*. myself with water
Ps. 51. 2 *w*. me from mine iniquity
Prov. 30. 12 not *w*. from filthiness
S. of S. 5. 12 eyes are *w*. with milk
Isa. 1. 16 *W*., you, make you cl., put
Jer. 2. 22 tho. thou *w*. with nitre
Mat. 27. 24 P. *w*. hands bef. multitu.
Mark 7. 3 except they *w*., eat not
Luke 7. 44 but she hath *w*. my feet
John 13. 10 is *w*. need. not save to
Acts 16. 33 took them, *w*. stripes
1 Cor. 6. 11 ye are *w*., ye are sanctif.
1 Tim. 5. 10 if she *w*. saint's feet
Rev. 1. 5 that *w*. us from our sins
R. V. Ex. 2. 5 ; Lev. 14. 8, 9 ; 15. 16 ;
16. 4, 24; 22. 6; Deut. 23. 11 ; 2
Sam. 11. 2; John 13. 10 bathe;
Luke 7. 38, 44 wet ; Rev. 1. 5 loosed

Washing. *Cleansing.*
S. of S. 4. 2 sheep wh. go up fr. *w*.
Mark 7. 4 *w*. of cups and tables
Eph. 5, 26 cleanse with *w*. of water
Tit. 3. 5 saved us by *w*. of regenera.

Washpot. *Pot for washing.*
Ps. 60. 8; 108. 9 Moab is my *w. p.*

Wast. *See Am.*

Waste (*n.*). *Wilderness, desert.*
Jer. 49. 13 Bozrah shall bec. a *w*.
Mic. 2. 8 pass as men averse to *w*.
Loss, destruction
Mat. 26. 8 what purpose is this *w*.
Mark 14. 4 Why this *w*. of ointment

Waste (*adj.*). *Dry, desolate.*
Deut. 32. 10 found him in *w*. wild.
Job 30. 3 fleeing into the *w*. wild.
Isa. 24. 1 Lord maketh the earth *w*.
Jer. 2. 15 lions made his land *w*.
Ezek. 5. 14 I will make Jerusal. *w*.

Waste (*v.*). *Destroy, consume.*
Num. 14. 33 till your carcas. be *w*.
Deut. 2. 14 the men of war were *w*.
1 K. 17. 14 barrel of meal not *w*.
Job 14. 10 man dieth, and *w*. away
Ps. 80. 13 boar of wood doth *w*.
Prov. 19. 26 he that *w*. his father
Isa. 6. 11 till cities be *w*. without
Jer. 44. 6 are *w*. and desolate as
Joel 1. 10 the field is *w*., corn is *w*.
Luke 15. 13 *w*. subst. wi. riot. liv.

Wasteness. *Desolation.*
Zeph. 1. 15 a day of *w*. and desola.

Waster. *Destroyer.*
Prov. 18. 9 brother to a great *w*.
Isa. 54. 16 I created *w*. to destroy
R. V. Prov. 18. 9 destroyer

Watch (*n.*). *Watch, guard.*
Ex. 14. 24 in morn. *w*. L. looked
Judg. 7. 19 middle *w*. had set *w*.
2 K. 11. 6 so shall ye keep the *w*.
Job 7. 12 am I a sea, that set *w*.?
Ps. 63. 6 when I meditate in *w*.
Jer. 51. 12 ma. the *w*. strong, set
Lam. 2. 19 in beginning of the *w*.
Mat. 24. 43 wh. *w*. thief wo. come
Mark 6. 48 about fourth *w*. of ni.
Luke 2. 8 shepherds keeping *w*. ov.

Watch (*v.*). *Look out, guard.*
1 Sam. 19. 11 Saul sent to *w*. Dav.
Ez. 8. 29 w. ye, keep vessels till
Job 14. 16 dust not *w*. ov. my sin?
Ps. 102. 7 I *w*., I am as a sparrow
Isa. 21. 5 *w*. in the watchtower, eat
Jer. 5. 6 a leop. sh. *w*. over cities
Lam. 4. 17 we have *w*. for a nation
Mat. 24. 42 *W*. for ye kn. not what
Mark 13. 35; Luke 21. 36; Acts
20. 31
1 Cor. 16. 13 *W*., stand fast in faith
1 Thes. 5. 6 not sleep, let us *w*. and
2 Tim. 4. 5 *w*. thou in all things
Heb. 13. 17 they *w*. for your souls
Rev. 16. 15 blessed is he that *w*.

Watcher. *Who watches.*
Jer. 4. 16 published that *w*. come
Dan. 4. 13 *w*. and holy one came

Watchful. *Wakeful.*
Rev. 3. 2 be *w*., strengthen things

Watching. *Guarding, looking out*
1 Sam. 4. 13 E. sat by way side in
Prov. 8. 34 heareth me, *w*. daily at
Mat. 27. 54 were with him *w*. Jesus
2 Cor. 6. 5 in labours, in *w*., in fast.

Watchman. *Watcher.*
2 Sam. 18. 25 *w*. cried, told king
2 K. 9. 17 stood *w*. on the tower
Ps. 127. 1 *w*. waketh but in vain
S. cf S. 3. 3 *w*. that go about the c.
Isa. 21. 11 *W*., wh. of the night? *W*.
Jer. 6. 17 set *w*. over you, saying
Ezek. 3. 17 made thee *w*. unto the h.
Hos. 9. 8 *w*. of Ephr. was with God

Watch Tower.
2 Chr. 20. 24 Judah came tow. *w. t.*
Isa. 21. 5 watch in *w. t.* eat, drink

Water (*n.*). *Water.*
Gen. 1. 2 sp. of G. mo. on face *w*.
Ex. 2. 10 Bec. I drew him out of *w*.
Num. 5. 17 take holy *w*., put into *w*.
Josh. 3. 13 rest in the *w*. of Jordan
Judg. 1. 15 gi. me also springs of *w*.
1 Sam. 7. 6 gathered and drew *w*.
1 K. 13. 19 did eat bread drank *w*.
2 Chr. 18. 26 feed him wi. *w*. of af.
Ez. 10. 6 eat no bread, nor drink *w*.
Job. 8. 11 can flag gr. without *w*.?
Ps. 23. 2 leadeth me beside still *w*.
Prov. 5. 15 drink *w*. of out of cistern
Eccl. 11. 1 cast thy br. upon the *w*.
S. of S. 4. 15 as well of *w*. streams
Isa. 1. 22 thy wine mixed with *w*.
Jer. 2. 13 forsa. fount. of living *w*.
Lam. 2. 19 pour out heart like *w*.
Ezek. 4. 17 may want bread and *w*.
Hos. 2. 5 lov. that gave me my *w*.
Am. 8. 11 not fam. nor thirst of *w*.
Jonah 2. 5 *w*. compassed me about
Zech. 14. 8 liv. *w*. sh. go. fr. Jerus.
Mat. 3. 11 I baptize you with *w*.
Mark 14. 13 bearing a pitcher of *w*.
Luke 8. 23 ship was filled with *w*.
John 2. 11 fill water pots with *w*.
Acts 1. 5 John baptized with *w*.
Eph. 5. 26 cleanse wi. wash. of *w*.
1 Tim. 5. 23 Drink no longer *w*., but
Heb. 9. 19 took *w*. and scarlet wool
Jas. 3. 12 yield salt *w*. and fresh
1 Pet. 3. 20 few souls saved by *w*.
1 John 5. 6 is he that came by *w*.

Water (*v.*). *To water.*
Gen. 2. 10 out of Eden to *w*. garden
Deut. 11. 10 *w*. it with thy foot, as
Ps. 6. 6 I *w*. couch with my tears
Prov. 11. 25 liberal soul sh. be *w*.
Eccl. 2. 6 to *w*. wood that bringeth
Isa. 58. 11 sh. be like a *w*. garden
Jer. 31. 12 soul sh. be a *w*. garden
Ezek. 32. 6 will *w*. it wi. my blood
1 Cor. 3. 6 I planted, Apollos *w*.

Watering. *For water.*
Gen. 30. 38 set rods in *w*. troughs
Job 37. 11 by *w*. he wearieth clouds
Luke 13. 15 and lead him aw. to *w*.

Water Pot. *Water vessel.*
John 2. 6 set there six *w. p.* of sto.

Wave (*n.*). *Rolling thing, billow.*
Job 38. 11 sh. thy proud be. be stay.
Ps. 42. 7 *w*. are gone over me
Isa. 48. 18 righteous. as *w* of sea
Jer. 5. 22 tho. *w*. tossed, not prevail
Ezek. 26. 3 as sea causeth his *w*.
Jonah 2. 3 thy *w*. passed over me
Mat. 8. 24 ship was cover. with *w*.
Luke 21. 25 the sea and *w*. roaring
Acts 27. 41 part was brok. with *w*.
Jas. 1. 6 wavering is like *w*. of sea
Jude 13 raging *w*. of sea, foaming

Wave (*v.*). *Shake, wave.*
Ex. 29. 24 shalt *w*. them for offer.
Lev. 8. 29; Num. 5. 25; 6. 20

Wave (*adj.*). *Waved.*
Ex. 29. 24 for *w*. off. before Lord
Lev. 7. 30; Num. 6. 20; 18. 11, 18

Waver. *Incline, hesitate.*
Heb. 10. 23 hold faith without *w*.
Jas. 1. 6 ask in faith, nothing *w*.
R. V. Jas. 1. 6 doubteth

Wax (*n.*). *Wax.*
Ps. 22. 14 my heart is like *w*., it is

Mic. 1. 4 be cleft as *w.* before fire
Wax (*v.*). *Become, grow.*
Gen. 26. 13 Isaac *w.* great, and went
Ex. 1. 7 chil. of Israel *w.* exceeding
Num. 11. 23 Is L.'s hand *w.* short?
Deut. 8. 4 their raiment *w.* not old
Josh. 23. 1 Joshua *w.* old, stricken
1 Sam. 3. 2 eyes began to *w.* dim
2 K. 4. 34 flesh of child *w.* warm
Esth. 9. 4 Mord. *w.* greater and gr.
Job 6. 17 they *w.* warm, they van.
Ps. 32. 3 bones *w.* old thro. roaring
Isa. 17. 4 fatness of flesh *w.* lean
Jer. 6. 24 our hands *w.* feeble; ang.
Ezek. 16. 7 increased and *w.* great
Mat. 13. 15 people's heart *w.* gross
Luke 1. 80 child *w.* strong in spirit
Acts 13. 46 Paul and Bar. *w.* bold
Heb. 11. 34 who *w.* valiant in fight
Rev. 18. 3 merchants *w.* rich thro.
R. V. Gen. 41. 56; Josh. 23. 1
was; Acts 13. 46 spake out
Way. *Going, path, road, passage, journey, distance, direction*
Gen. 3. 24 flaming sword to keep *w.*
Josh. 1. 8 sh. make my *w.* prosper.
Judg. 2. 17 they turned out of *w.*
Ruth 1. 7 went on the *w.* to return
2 Sam. 2. 24 by *w.* of wild. of Gib.
1 K. 2. 2 I go the *w.* of all earth
2 Chr. 6. 16 chil. ta. heed to th. way
Ez. 8. 21 to seek a right *w.* for us
Neh. 9. 12 to give th. light in the *w.*
Job 3. 23 Why light to man who. *w.*
Ps. 18. 21 I have kept *w.* of the L.
Prov. 3. 17 Her *w.* are *w.* of pleas.
Eccl. 11. 9 walk in *w.* of thine heart
Isa. 2. 3 he will teach us his *w.*
Lam. 2. 4 The *w* of Zion do mourn
Ezek. 3. 18 to warn wick. fr. his *w.*
Jonah 3. 8 let th. turn from evil *w.*
Hag 1. 5 saith L., Consider yo. *w.*
Zech. 1. 2 Turn ye now fr. evil *w.*
Mat. 3. 3 Prepare ye *w.* of the L.
Mark 1. 2 which sh. prep. *w.* befo.
Luke 1. 79 to guide feet in *w.* of p.
John 1. 23 Make straight *w.* of L.
Rom. 11. 33 his *w.* past finding out
1 Cor. 12. 31 show I more excell. *w.*
1 Thes. 3. 11 J. C., direct our *w.*
Heb. 10. 20 By new and living *w.*,
Rev. 15. 3 just and true are thy *w.*
Wayfaring. *Journeying.*
Isa. 35. 8 *w.* man, tho. fool, sh. not
Jer. 9. 2 a lodging place of *w.* men
Waymark. *Sign.*
Jer. 31. 21 set thee up *w. m.*, make
Way Side. *By the way.*
1 Sam. 4. 13 Eli. sat by *w. s.* watch.
Ps. 140. 5 ha. spread net by the *w. s.*
We. *Ourselves, us.*
Gen. 19. 13 we will destr. this place
Mat. 6. 12 debts, as *w.* forg. debtors
Etc., etc.
Weak. *Feeble, poor.*
Judg. 6. 15 then shall I be *w.*, and
2 Sam. 3. 39 I am *w.* though anoint.
Job 4. 3 hast strengthened *w.* hands
Ps. 6. 2 have mercy, O L. I am *w.*
Is. 14. 10 art thou become *w.* as we?
Ezek. 7. 17 knees sh. be *w.* as water
Mat. 26. 41 sp. will., but flesh is *w.*
Acts 20. 35 ye ought to support *w.*
Rom. 4. 19 being not *w.* in faith
1 Cor. 1. 27 *w.* things to confound
Gal. 4. 9 turn ye to *w.* elements?
1 Thes. 5. 14 support *w.*, be patient
Weaken. *To make weak.*
Ez. 4. 4 people of land *w.* Judah
Job 12. 21 he *w.* strength of mighty
Ps. 102. 23 *w.* my strength in way
Isa. 14. 12 which didst *w.* the nati.
R. V. Job 12. 21 looseth; Isa. 14.
12 lay low.
Weaker. *More weak.*
2 Sam. 3. 1 Saul's house *w.* and *w.*
1 Pet. 3. 7 honour wife as *w.* vessel
Weakness. *Lacking strength.*
1 Cor. 1. 25 *w.* of G. is strong. than
2 Cor. 12. 9 strength is perf. in *w.*
Wealth. *Substance, riches, prosperity, might.*
Gen. 34. 29 sons of Ja. took th. *w.*
Ruth 2. 1 a kinsman, man of *w.*
1 Sam. 2. 32 see enemy in all *w.*
2 K. 15. 20 exacted of men of *w.*

2 Chr. 1. 11 thou hast not asked *w.*
Job 21. 13 spend their days in *w.*
Ps. 19. 4 *W.* maketh many friends
Prov. 10. 15 a man's *w.* is his city
Eccl. 5. 19 to whom G. hath giv. *w.*
1 Cor. 10. 24 seek ev. man anoth. *w.*
R. V. Ez. 9. 12; Job 21. 13 prosperity; Esth. 10. 3; 1 Cor. 10. 24
good; Prov. 5. 10 strength.
Wealthy. *Full, rich, at ease.*
Ps. 66. 12 brought us into a *w.* place
Jer. 49. 31 get up into *w.* nations
R. V. Jer. 49. 31 at ease.
Wean. *Win off, alienate.*
Gen. 21. 8 Isaac grew and was *w.*
1 K. 11. 20 whom T. *w.* in Ph.'s ho.
Ps. 131. 2 my soul is as a *w.* child
Isa. 11. 8 *w.* child shall put hand on
Weapon. *Arm, instrument.*
Gen. 27. 3 take thy *w.*, thy quiver
Deut. 1. 41 gird. on ev. man his *w.*
Judg. 18. 11 men appointed with *w.*
2 Sam. 1. 27 How are *w.* of war per.
2 K. 11. 8 ev. man with *w.* in hand
Job 20. 24 shall flee from iron *w.*
Eccl. 9. 18 Wisdom is better than *w.*
Isa. 13. 5 and *w.* of his indignation
Jer. 21. 4 I will turn back th. *w.* of
Ezek. 39. 10 sh. burn *w.* with fire
2 Cor. 10. 4 *w.* of warf. not carnal
Wear. *Waste away, decline.*
Job 14. 19 The waters *w.* the stones
Luke 9. 12 day began to *w.* away
Bear clothing.
Deut. 22. 11 not *w.* gar. of div. color
1 Sam. 2. 28 to *w.* an ephod before
Isa 4. 1 Eat our bread, *w.* apparel
Zech. 13. 4 nei. *w.* a rough garment
Mat. 11. 8 that *w.* soft clothing are
Luke 8. 27 had dev., *w.* no clothing
John 19. 6 Then ca. Jesus, *w.* crown
1 Pet. 3. 3 let it not be *w.* of gold
Jas. 2. 3 him that *w.* gay clothing
Weary (*adj.*). *Faint, vexed, heavily pressed, despondent.*
Gen. 27. 46 Rebek. said, I am *w.*
Job 3. 17 wicked cease, *w.* be at rest
Ps. 6. 6 I am weary with groaning
Prov. 3. 11 be not *w.* of L.'s correc.
Jer. 2. 24 th. seek her will not *w.*
Gal. 6. 9 not be *w.* in well doing
Weary (*v.*). *Tire, make faint.*
Gen. 19. 11 *w.* thems. to find door
Job 37. 11 he *w.* the thick cloud
Eccl. 10. 15 foolish *w.* every one of
Isa. 43. 23 not *w.* thee with incense
Jer. 4. 31 soul is *w.* bec. of murder.
Ezek. 24. 12 she *w.* herself with lies
Mal. 2. 17 wherein have we *w.* him
John 4. 6 J. being *w.* sat on well
Heb. 12. 3 lest ye be *w.* and faint
R. V. Job 37. 11 ladeth
Weariness. *Labor, fatigue.*
Eccl. 12. 12 study is *w.* of the flesh
Mal. 1. 3 said, What a *w.* is it!
Wearisome. *Miserable.*
Job. 7. 3 *w.* nights are appointed
Weasel. *Weasel, mole.*
Lev. 11. 29 *w.*, and mouse, uncl.
Weather. *Sky condition.*
Job. 37. 22 Fair *w.* co. out of north
Prov. 25. 20 take. gar. in cold *w.*
Mat. 16. 2 fair *w.*, for sky is red
R. V. Job 37. 22 splendour
Weave. *Weave, plait.*
Ex. 28. 32 have binding of *w.* work
Judg. 16. 13 If thou *w.* seven locks
2 K. 23. 7 *w.* hangings for grove
Isa. 19. 9 th. *w.* nets sh. be confound.
Weaver. *Who weaves.*
Ex. 35. 35 all man. of work of the *w.*
1 Sam. 17. 7 spear like a *w.* beam
Job 7. 6 days swifter th. *w.* shuttle
Isa. 38. 12 cut off like *w.* my life
Web. *Woven thing.*
Job 8. 14 trust shall be a spider's *w.*
Isa. 59. 6 *w.* sh. not bec. garments
Wedding. R. V. *marriage feast.*
Mat. 22. 3 were bidden to the *w.*
Luke 12. 36 will return from the *w.*
Wedge. *Tongue.*
Josh. 7. 21 Achan saw a *w.* of gold
Isa. 13. 12 than golden *w.* of Ophir
Wedlock. *Wedded estate.*
Ezek. 16. 38 as women that br. *w.*
Weeds. *Weeds.*

Jonah 2. 5 *w.* were about my head
Week. *Seven, sabbath to sabbath.*
Gen. 29. 27 fulfil her. *w.*, we will
Deut. 16. 9 Sev. *w.* sh. thou numb.
Jer. 5. 24 he reserve. appointed *w.*
Dan. 10. 2 D. was mourn. three *w.*
Mat. 28. 1 tow. first day of the *w.*
Mark 16. 2; Luke 24. 1; John 20. 1
1 Cor. 16. 2 on first day of *w.*, let
Weep. *Weep, shed tears, wail.*
Gen. 29. 11 Jacob lifted voi. and *w.*
Ex. 2. 6 and, behold, the babe *w.*
Num. 11. 4 children of Is. *w.* again
Ruth 1. 9 she kissed them, and *w.*
1 Sam. 1. 8 why *w.* thou? why eat.
2 Sam. 1. 24 daugh. of Is., *w.* ov. S.
Neh. 1. 4 I sat down and *w.*, and
Esth. 4. 3 great mourning and *w.*
Job 27. 15 his widows shall not *w.*
Ps. 30. 5 *w.* may endure for a night
Eccl. 3. 4 time to *w.*, time to laugh
Isa. 30. 19 thou shalt *w.* no more, he
Jer. 13. 17 my soul sh. *w.* in secret
Lam. 1. 2 She *w.* sore in the night
Ezek. 24. 23 ye sh. not mourn nor *w.*
Mat. 2. 18 Rachel *w.* for her child.
Mark 5. 39 why make ado and *w.*
Luke 13. 28 sh. be *w.* and gnashing
John 11. 31 She goeth to grave to *w.*
Acts 9. 39 widows stood by him *w.*
Rom. 12. 15 and *w.* wi. them that *w*
Phil. 3. 18 told you often, now *w.*
Jas. 5. 1 *w.* for your miseries that
Weigh. *Strike balance, ponder.*
Gen. 23. 16 Abr. *w.* to Eph. silver
1 Sam. 2. 3 by him actions are *w.*
Job 6. 2 Oh that my grief were *w.*
Ps. 58. 2 ye *w.* violence of hands
Prov. 16. 2 the Lord *w.* the spirits
Isa. 26. 7 thou dost *w.* path of just
Dan. 5. 37 thou art *w.* in balance
Weight. *Weight.*
Gen. 43. 21 money in sack full *w.*
Lev. 19. 35 do no unrighteous. in *w.*
Deut. 25. 13 sh. not have divers *w.*
Judg. 8. 26 *w.* of golden earrings
1 Sam. 17. 5 *w.* of coat was five thou.
2 K. 25. 16 the brass was without *w.*
1 Chr. 28. 14 he gave gold by *w.*
Job 28. 25 make *w.* for the winds
Prov. 11. 1 a just *w.* is his delight
Ezek. 4. 10 thy meat sh. be by *w.*
2 Cor. 4. 17 a more exceeding *w.* of
Heb. 12. 1 let us lay aside every *w.*
Weighty. *Of weight.*
Prov. 27. 3 stone is heavy, sand *w.*
2 Cor. 10. 10 letters say they, are *w.*
Weightier. *Heavier.*
Mat. 23. 23 ha. omitted *w.* matters
Welfare. *Good, peace.*
Gen. 43. 27 asked them of their *w.*
Neh. 2. 10 man to seek *w.* of Israel
Job 30. 15 and my *w.* passeth away
Ps. 69. 22 should have been for *w.*
R. V. 1 Chr. 18. 10 salute; Ps. 69. 22
peace
Well (*n.*). *Cistern, pit, well, spring, fountain.*
Gen. 21. 9. she saw a *w.* of water
Ex. 2. 5 Moses sat down by a *w.* of
Josh. 18. 15 went to *w.* of Nephtoah
1 Sam. 19. 22 came to gr. *w.* in Sec.
2 K. 3. 19 ye shall stop *w.* of water
Neh. 9. 25 took *w.* digged, vineyards
Ps. 84. 6 passing Baca, make it a *w.*
S. of S. 4. 15 a *w.* of waters fr. L.
Isa. 12. 3 draw out of *w.* of salva.
John 4. 6 Now Jacob's *w.* was th.
2 Pet. 2. 17 These are *w.* without
R. V. Gen. 24. 13, 16, 29, 30, 42,
43; 49. 22; Josh. 18. 15; 2 K. 3.
19, 25; Prov. 10. 11 fountain or
fountains; Ex. 15. 27; Judg. 7.
1; Ps. 84. 6; 2 Pet. 2. 17 spring
or springs; Deut. 6. 11; 2 K. 26.
10; Neh. 9. 25 cisterns
Well. (*adv.*). *Good, rightly, much, sincerely.*
Gen. 4. 7 if thou dost not *w.*, sin
Ex. 4. 14 I know he can speak *w.*
Judg. 14. 3 for she pleaseth me *w.*
Ruth 3. 1 that it maybe *w.* wi. thee
2 Sam. 18. 28 and said, All is *w.*
Ps. 49. 18 thou doest *w.* to thyself
Eccl. 8. 12 *w.* with them fear God
Isa. 3. 10 it shall be *w.* with him

Jer. 40. 4 I will look *w*. to thee
Mat. 25. 21 *w*. done, good and faith.
Mark 12. 6 sent his *w*. beloved son
Luke 20. 39 Mas., thou hast *w*. said
1 Tim. 5. 17 elders that rule *w*. be
Wen. *Running sore.*
Lev. 22. 22 having a *w*. or scurvy
Wench. *Maid servant.*
2 Sam. 17. 17 *w*. went and told th.
Went. *See* **Go.**
Wept. *See* **Weep.**
Were. *If was.*
Num. 22. 29 would *w*. sw. in hand
Ps. 14. 2 if *w*. any th. did understand
Etc., etc.
West. *Setting of sun.*
Gen. 28. 14 shall spread abroad to *w*.
Deut. 33. 23 possess the *w*. and sou.
Josh. 15. 12 *w*. bor. was to gr. sea
Ps. 103. 12 as far as east is from *w*.
Isa. 11. 14 fly on Philist. tow. *w*.
Ezek. 48. 1 his sides east and *w*.
Dan. 8. 5 a he goat came from *w*.
Mat. 8. 11 many sh. come from *w*.
Luke 12. 54 cloud sh. rise out of *w*.
Westward. *Sunsetward.*
Gen. 13. 14 A. looked east. and *w*.
Deut. 3. 27 lift up thine eyes *w*.
Dan. 8. 4 I saw a ram pushing *w*.
Wet. *Wet, moist.*
Job 24. 8 th. are *w*. with showers
Dan. 4. 15 let it be *w*. with dew
Whale. *Sea monster, dragon.*
Gen. 1. 21 God created great *w*., and
Job 7. 12 am I a sea, or a *w*., that
Ezek. 3. 2 th. art as *w*. in the seas
Mat. 12. 40 Jon. was th. days in *w*.
R. V. Gen. 1. 21 ; Job 7. 12 sea
monster, or s. Ezek. 3. 2 dragons
What. *That which, say.*
Gen. 4. 10 *W*. hast thou done? vo.
Mat. 7. 9 *w*. man is there of you
Etc., etc.
Whatsoever. *What ever, all.*
Gen. 8. 19 *w*. creep. upon the earth
Mark 6. 22 Ask of me *w*. thou wilt
Etc., etc.
Wheat. *Corn, grain, wheat.*
Gen. 30. 14 R. went in days of *w*.
Ex. 9. 32 *w*. and rie not smitten
Deut. 8. 8 land of *w*. and barley
1 Sam. 12. 17 is it not *w*. har. to day?
1 Chr. 21. 10 Ornan was thresh. *w*.
Job 31. 40 thist. grow instead of *w*.
Ps. 81. 16 fed them wi. finest of *w*.
Prov. 27 22 bray a fool among *w*.
Isa. 28. 25 cast in the principal *w*.
Jer. 12. 13 sown *w*. but shall reap
Ezek. 4. 9 Take unto thee *w*., and
Mat. 3. 12 gath. his *w*. into garner
Luke 22. 31 th. he may sift you *w*.
John 12. 24 Ex. a corn of *w*. fall
1 Cor. 15. 37 may ch. of *w*. or of so.
R. V. Num. 18. 12 corn; Prov. 27.
22 bruised corn.
Wheaten. *Of wheat.*
Ex. 29. 2 ta, wafers made of *w*. fl.
Wheel. *Rolling thing, wheel.*
Ex. 14. 25 took off th. chariot *w*.
Judg. 5. 28 why tarry *w*. of chariots
Ps. 83. 13 make them like a *w*., as
Eccl. 12. 6 *w*. brok. at the cistern
Isa. 5. 28 their *w*. like a whirlwind
Ezek. 1. 15 one *w*. upon the earth
Dan. 7. 9 and his *w*. as burning fire
R. V. Ps. 83. 13 whirling dust;
Ezek. 23, 24 ; 26. 10 wagons
Whelp. *Son, young of.*
Gen. 49. 9 Judah is a lion's *w*. ; fr.
2 Sam. 17. 8 as a bear robbed of *w*.
Job 4. 11 lion's *w*. are scattered ab.
Jer. 28. 8 *w*. have not trodden it
Nah. 2. 12 lion did tear for his *w*.
R. V. Job 28. 8 proud beasts
When. *That time, what time.*
Ps. 94. 8 fools, *w*. will ye be wise?
Eccl. 8. 7 who can tell *w*. it will be?
Whence. *From where.*
Gen. 16. 8 *w*. camest thou? whither
John 7. 28 and ye know *w*. I am
Whensoever. *When.*
Mark 14. 7 *w*. ye will ye may do th.
Rom 15. 24 *W*. I take my journ. in.
Where. *What place.*
Gen. 3. 9 God said to Adam, *W*.
art thou

Mat. 6. 20 *w*. thieves do not break
Etc., etc.
Whereabout. *About where.*
1 Sam. 21. 2 let no man know *w*. I
Whereas. *Since, in view.*
Gen. 31. 37 *W*. thou hast searched
1 Pet. 2. 12 *w*. they speak ag. you
Whereby. *By this or what.*
Gen. 15. 8 *w*. shall I know that
Luke 1. 78 *w*. the day spring from
Wherefore. *For what, therefore.*
Gen. 10. 9 *W*. it is said, Even as Ni.
Mat. 7. 20 *W*. by their fruits ye sh.
Etc., etc.
Wherein. *In that.*
Gen. 7. 15 *w*. is the breath of life
1 Pet. 3. 20 *w*. few souls were saved
Whereof. *Of which.*
Num. 5. 3 camps in the midst *w*.
1 Cor. 7. 1 concerning things *w*. ye
Whereon. *On which.*
Ex. 3. 5 place *w*. thou standest is
Whereto. *Whither.*
Isa. 55. 11 sh. prosper *w*. I sent it
Whereupon. *On which.*
Acts 24. 18 *W*. cer. Jews from Asia
Wheresoever. *In what place.*
Luke 17. 37 *W*. the body is, thither
Whereto. *To what end.*
Col. 1. 29 *W*. I also labour, striving
Wherewith. *With which.*
Gen. 24. 41 the blessing *w*. his fath.
Heb. 10. 29 *w*. he was sanctified
Wherewithal. *With which.*
Mat. 6. 31 *W*. shall we be clothed
Whet. *Sharpen, roll.*
Ps. 64. 3 *w*. their tongues like sword
Eccl. 10. 10 and he do not *w*. the
Whether. *Or, in case.*
Ex. 21. 31 *W*. he have gored a son
Mat. 26. 63 tell *w*. thou be Christ
Which. *That.*
Gen. 1. 7 waters *w*. were above the f.
John 21. 25 other things *w*. Jesus
While. *What time, time.*
Gen. 29. 9 *w*. he yet spake wi. them
Mat. 13. 21 not root, dureth for a *w*.
Whip. *Rod, scourge, whip.*
1 K. 12. 11 fa. chast. you with *w*.
Prov. 26. 3 *w*. for horse, bri. for ass
Whirl. *Go round, twist.*
Eccl. 1. 6 wind *w*. about continually
Whirlwind. *Whirlwind.*
2 K. 2. 1 ta. Elijah to heaven by *w*,
Job 37. 9 out of south cometh *w*.
Ps. 58. 9 take th. away as in a *w*.
Prov. 1. 27 destruction com. as a *w*.
Jer. 23. 19 a *w*. of L. is gone forth
Dan. 11. 40 come aga. him like *w*.
Hos. 8. 7 sown wind, shall reap *w*.
R. V. Job 37. 9; Isa. 17. 13 ; 29. 6
storm ; Jer. 23. 19; 25. 32 ; 30. 23
tempest
Whisper. *Speak low.*
Ps. 41. 7 All that hate me *w*. toget.
Isa. 29. 4 speech sh. *w*. out of dust
Whisperer. *Talebearer, detractor.*
Prov. 16. 28 a *w*. separateth friends
Rom. 1. 29 full of deceit malig., *w*.
Whisperings. *Mutterings.*
2 Cor. 12. 20 lest there be deb., *w*.
Whit. *Bit.*
Deut. 13. 16 burn spoil thereof ev. *w*.
2 Cor. 11. 5 I was not a *w*. behind
White (*n. adj.*). *White, fine, clear.*
Gen. 49. 12 his teeth be *w*. as milk
Ex. 16. 31 like as coriander seed, *w*.
Num. 12. 10 Mir. leprous, *w*. as sn.
Judg. 5. 19 ye th. ride on *w*. asses
Esth. 8. 15 Mord. went out in *w*.
Job 6. 6 any taste in *w*. of egg?
Ps. 68. 14 it was *w*. as snow in Sal.
Eccl. 9. 8 let thy garments be *w*.
Isa. 1. 18 sins shall be *w*. as snow
Ezek. 27. 18 D. traded in *w*. wool
Dan. 7. 9 garment was *w*. as snow
Mat. 5. 36 make hair *w*. or black
Mark 16. 5 saw a man clothed in *w*.
Luke 9. 29 and his raiment was *w*.
John 4. 35 fields are *w*. to harvest
Rev. 7. 14 made *w*. in blood of Lamb
White (*v*.). *Make white.*
Mat. 23. 27 scribes like *w*. sepulc.
Mark 9. 3 no fuller can *w*. them
Whiter. *More white.*

Ps. 51. 7 I shall be *w*. than snow
Lam. 4. 7 Nazarites *w*. than milk
Whither. *To which.*
1 Sam. 10. 14 Saul said, *W*. went ye
Heb. 11. 8 he went not knowing *w*.
See **Go, goest,** *etc.*
Whithersoever. *Wherever.*
Prov. 17. 8 *w*. it turneth it prosper.
Mat. 8. 19 ; Luke 9. 57 follow *w*. go.
Rev. 14. 4 follow Lord *w*. he goest
Who. *Which one.*
Gen. 36. 1 gen. of Esau, *w*. is Edom
Mat. 3. 7 *w*. ha. warned you to flee
Etc., etc.
Whole. *Entire, sound.*
Ex. 12. 6 *w*. assembly of congrega.
Deut. 27. 6 build altar of *w*. stone
Josh. 10. 13 not to go down a *w*. day
Job 5. 18 and his hands made *w*.
Mat. 9. 12 th. that be *w*., need not a
physician ; Mark 2. 17; Luke 5. 31
Mark 8. 36 if he gain the *w*. world
Acts 19. 29 *w*. city filled wi. confus.
1 Cor. 5. 6 lit. leaven leav. *w*. lump
Wholesome. *Healing, healthy.*
Prov. 15. 4 *w*. tongue is tree of life
1 Tim. 6. 3 consent not to *w*. words
R. V. 1 Tim. 6. 3 sound
Wholly. *Entirely.*
Deut. 1. 36 Caleb *w*. follow. the L.
1 Thes. 5, 23 God sanctify you *w*.
1 Tim. 4. 15 gi. thyself *w*. to them
Whom. *Which, who.*
Gen. 2. 8 put man *w*. he had formed
Mat. 16. 13 *W*. do men say th. I am
Whomsoever. *Whoso.*
Mat. 11. 27 *w*. the Son will reveal
Luke 4. 6 and to *w*. I will I give it
Whore. *Fornicator, harlot.*
Lev. 21. 7 not take wife that is *w*.
Prov. 23. 27 a *w*. is a deep ditch
Isa. 57. 3 seed of adulterer and *w*.
Jer. 3. 3 thou hast a *w*. forehead
Ezek. 16. 33 they give gifts to *w*.
Rev. 17. 1 judgment of the great *w*.
R. V. Lev. 19. 29; 21. 7, 9; Deut.
22. 21 ; 23. 17; Judg. 19.2 ; Ezek.
16. 28, 33 ; Rev. 17. 1, 15, 16; 19. 2
harlot
Whoredom. *Fornication.*
Gen. 38. 24 she is with child by *w*.
Num. 25. 1 peo. began to commit *w*.
2 K. 9. 22 *w*. of thy mother Jezeb.
Jer. 3. 2 polluted land with thy *w*.
Ezek. 16. 20 Is thy *w*. small matter
Whoremonger. *Fornicator.*
Eph. 5. 5 no *w*. hath any inherit.
1 Tim. 1. 10 law made for *w*., liars
Heb. 13. 4 *w*. and adulterers God
Rev. 21. 8 *w*. have their part in lake
Whoring. *Fornicating.*
Ex. 34. 15 go a *w*. after their gods
Num. 15. 39 eyes, ye use to go a *w*.
Judg. 8. 27 Is. went thither a *w*. aft.
1 Chr. 5. 35 *w*. after gods of people
Ps. 73. 27 destroy all that go a *w*.
Ezek. 23. 30 bec. th. hast gone a *w*.
Whorish. *Lewd.*
Prov. 6. 26 by means of *w*. women
Ezek. 6. 9 brok. with her *w*. heart
Whose. *Of whom.*
Gen. 1. 11 *w*. seed is upon the earth
Mat. 22. 20 *W*. is this image and sup.
Whosoever. *Whoever.*
Mat. 11. 12 *w*. hath., to him be giv.
Rev. 22. 27 *w*. will, let him take
Why. *Wherefore, for what.*
Jer. 25. 13 turn, *w*. will ye die?
Acts 14. 15 *w*. do ye these things?
Wicked. *Evil, bad, perverse.*
Gen. 13. 13 men of Sod. were *w*. and
Ex. 23. 7 I will not justify the *w*.
Deut. 23. 9 keep thee fr. ev. *w*. thing
1 Sam. 2. 9 *w*. be silent in darkness
2 Sam. 4. 11 *w*. ha. slain righteous
Neh. 9. 35 nei. turned they from *w*.
Job 3. 17 There *w*. cease fr. troubl.
Ps. 9. 17. *w*. sh. be turned into hell
Prov. 4. 19 *w*. of *w*. is as darkness
Eccl. 8. 13 it sh. not be well w. the *w*.
Isa. 3. 11 Woe to *w*. ! it sh. be ill w.
Jer. 5. 26 am. my peo. are found *w*.
Ezek. 8. 9 beho. the *w*. abominations
Mal. 4. 3 ye shall tread down the *w*.
Mat. 13. 38 tares are children of *w*.
Luke 19. 22 judge thee, thou *w*. s.

Acts 2. 23 by *w.* hands ha. crucified
1 Cor. 5. 13 put away that *w.* person
Eph. 6. 16 to quench darts of the *w.*
Col. 1. 21 and enemies by *w.* works
2 Thes. 3. 2 delivered from *w.* men
2 Pet. 3. 17 led away wi. error of *w.*
1 John 2. 13 ye have overco. *w.* one
R. V. Frequent changes to, evil, unrighteous, etc.

Wickedly. *Evilly, wrongly.*
Gen. 19. 7 I pray you, do not so *w.*
1 Sam. 12. 25 if ye shall still do *w.*
2 Sam. 22. 22 I ha. not *w.* departed
2 Chr. 6. 37 done amiss, and dealt *w.*
Job 13. 7 Will ye speak *w.* of God?
Ps. 74. 3 the enemy hath done *w.*
Mal. 4. 1 that do *w.* be as stubble

Wickedness. *Evil, iniquity.*
Gen. 6. 5 God saw *w.* was great in
Lev. 19. 29 land become full of *w.*
2 Sam. 3. 39 reward acc. to his *w.*
1 K. 1. 52 if *w.* be found in him
Job. 4. 8 that sow *w.* reap same
Ps. 5. 4 that hath pleasure in *w.*
Prov. 4. 17 they eat the bread of *w.*
Eccl. 7. 15 prolong. life in his *w.*
Isa. 47. 10 hast trusted in thy *w.*
Jer. 4. 14 wash thine heart from *w.*
Lam. 1. 22 let *w.* come befo. thee
Ezek. 16. 57 Bef. thy *w.* was discov.
Hos. 10. 13 plough *w.,* reaped ini.
Mat. 22. 18 Jesus perceived their *w.*
Mark 7. 22 out of heart proceed *w.*
Luke 11. 39 inw. part is full of *w.*
Acts 25. 5 man, if any *w.* in him.
Rom. 1. 29 being filled wi. all *w.*
1 Cor. 5. 8 leaven of malice and *w.*
Eph. 6. 12 ag. *w.* in high places
R. V. The changes are chiefly to,
evil, unrighteousness, etc.

Wide. *Broad, ample.*
Deut. 15. 8 sh. open hand *w.* unto
1 Chr. 4. 40 land was *w.,* and quiet
Ps. 104. 25 this great and *w* sea
Prov. 13. 3 th. ope. *w.* his lips shall
Jer. 22. 14 will build me a *w.* house
Mat. 7. 13 *w.* is gate to destruction

Wideness. R. V. *breadth.*
Ezek. 41. 10 the *w.* of twenty cubits

Widow. *Bereft of husband.*
Ex. 22. 22 shalt not afflict any *w.*
Num 30. 9 vow of *w* stand against
Deut. 10. 18 ex. judgment of the *w.*
2 Sam. 14. 5 I am a *w.* woman, and
Job 22. 9 hast sent *w.* away empty
Ps. 94. 6 th. slay *w.* and stranger
Isa. 1. 17 fatherless, plead for the *w.*
Jer. 7. 6 if ye oppress not the *w.*
Lam. 1. 1 how is she bec. as a *w.*
Zech. 7. 10 oppress not the *w.,* nor
Mat. 23. 14 for ye devour *w.* houses
    Mark 12. 40 ; Luke 20. 47
Acts 6. 1 because *w.* were neglected
1 Cor. 7. 8 I said to *w.,* It is good
1 Tim. 5. 3 honour *w.* that are *w.*
Jas. 1. 27 religion is to visit *w.*

Widowhood. *State of widow.*
Gen. 38. 19 put on garments of *w.*
Isa. 47. 9 shall come in one day *w.*

Wife. *Wedded woman, spouse, con-
sort.*
Gen. 2. 24 sh. a man cleave to his *w.*
Ex. 20. 17 not covet neighbour's *w.*
Deut. 22. 30 sh. not ta. father's *w.*
Judg. 4. 4 *w.* of Lap. judged Isra.
Ruth 1. 2 name of his *w.* was Nao.
1 Sam. 2. 20 Eli bless. Elk. and *w.*
2 K. 5. 2 she waited on Naam.'s *w.*
2 Chr. 8. 11 *w.* sh. not dw. in house
Esth. 5. 10 Haman called for his *w.*
Job 19. 17 breath is stra. to my *w.*
Ps. 128. 3 *w.* shall be a fruitful vine
Prov. 5. 18 rejoi. wi. *w.* of thy youth
Eccl. 9. 9 Live joyfully wi. *w.* whom
Jer. 3. 1 If a man put away his *w.*
Ezek. 16. 32 as *w.* th. com. adultery
Mat. 1. 6 that had been *w.* of Urias
Mark 1, 30 S.'s *w.'s* moth. lay sick
Luke 1. 13 *w.* Elis. sh. bear a son
1 Cor. 7. 2 let ev. man have own *w.*
Eph. 5. 22 *W.,* submit unto husba.
Col. 3. 19 Husbands, love your *w.*
1 Tim. 3. 2 bishop be hus. of one *w.*
1 Pet. 3. 1 won by conversat. of *w.*
Rev. 21. 9 sh. the bride, Lamb's *w.*
R. V. Ex. 19. 15 ; Lev. 21. 7 ; Judg.

21. 14 ; Ez. 10. 2, 10, 11, 14, 17, 18 ;
Neh. 12. 43 ; 13. 23, 27 ; 1 Tim. 3.
11 ; 1 Pet. 3. 7 woman or women ;
Mat. 19. 29 ; 22. 25 ; Mark 10. 29 ;
Luke 17. 27 ; 20. 30 ——

Wild. *Untamed, uncultivated.*
Gen. 16. 12 Ish. will be a *w.* man
Lev. 26. 22 will send *w.* beasts am.
2 Sam 2. 18 light of foot as *w.* roe
2 K. 4. 39 foun:l *w.* vine, and gath.
Job 39. 15 the *w.* beast may break
Ps. 80. 13 *w.* beasts doth devour it
Isa. 13. 22 *w.* beast of isl. sh. cry
Jer. 50. 39 *w.* beasts of desert dwell
Mat. 3. 4 ; Mark 1. 6 his meat,, *w.*

Wilderness. *Desert, desolate
place, plain.*
Gen. 16. 7 found her by fount. in *w.*
Lev. 16. 22 let go the goat in the *w.*
Num. 1. 1 L. spake to M. in *w.* of S.
Deut. 8. 16 fed thee in *w.* wi. manna
Josh. 5. 6 walked forty years in *w.*
Judg. 8. 7 tear fl. wi. thorns of *w.*
1 K. 2. 34 Joab was buried in the *w.*
2 Chr. 8. 4 Sol. built Tadmor in *w.*
Job 1. 19 came gr. wind fr. the *w.*
Ps. 78. 19 Can G. furn. table in *w.?*
Prov. 21. 19 bet. to dwell in *w.* th.
S. of S. 3. 6 Who that com. out *w.*
Isa. 14. 17 made the world as a *w.*
Jer. 2. 24 wild ass used to the *w.*
Lam. 4. 3 cruel, like ostriches of *w.*
Ezek. 6. 14 more desol. than *w.* to.
Hos. 9. 10 found Is. like grapes *w.*
Joel 1. 19 ha. devour. pastures of *w.*
Am. 2. 10 led you for. y'rs thro. *w.*
Mat. 3. 1 John, preaching in the *w.*
Mark 1. 3 voi. of one cry. in the *w.*
Luke 7. 24 Wh. went into *w.* to see
John 3. 14 M. lift. up serp. in *w.*
Acts 7. 30 appear. to him in the *w.*
2 Cor. 11. 26 oft. in perils in the *w.*
Heb. 3. 17 whose carcases fell in *w.*
R. V. Job 30. 3 dry ground ; Ps.
107. 40 waste ; Am. 6. 14 Arabah ;
Ps. 78. 17 ; Prov. 21. 19 ; Isa. 33.
9 ; Jer. 51. 43 ; Mat. 15. 43 ; Mark
8. 14 ; Luke 5. 16 ; 8. 29 desert, or
desert place

Wiles. *Deceits, artifices.*
Num. 25. 18 they vex you with *w.*
Eph. 6. 11 able to stand ag. the *w.*

Willily. *Craftily.*
Josh. 9. 4 Gibeonites did work *w.*

Wilfully. *Willingly.*
Heb. 10. 26 if we sin *w.* after we

Will. (*n.*) *Wish, desire.*
Gen. 49. 6 in self *w.* they digged do.
Ez. 7. 18 to do after *w.* of yo. God
Ps. 40. 8 I delight to do thy *w.,* O G.
Mat. 6. 10 Thy *w.* be done in earth
Mark 3. 35 Who. sh. do the *w.* of G.
Luke 11. 2 Thy *w.* be do., as in hea.
John 6. 39 this the Father's *w.* wh.
Acts 21. 14 The *w.* of the L. be done
Rom. 12. 2 accept. and per. *w.* of G.
2 Cor. 8. 5 unto us by the *w.* of God
Eph. 1. 9 made kn. myst. of his *w.*
Col. 1. 9 filled wi. knowl. of his *w.*
1 Thes. 4. 3 For this is the *w.* of G.
Heb. 10. 7 Lo, I come to do thy *w.*
1 Pet. 2. 15 For so is the *w.* of God
1 John 2. 17 th. do. *w.* of G. abid.

Will (*v.*). *Be willing, about to be.*
Ruth 3. 13 if he *w.* do part of kins.
Job 13. 3 let come on me what *w.*
Prov. 21. 1 turn. it whither he *w.*
Am. 7. 8 I *w.* not again pass by th.
Mat. 8. 3 said, I *w.,* be thou clean
    Mark 1. 41 ; Luke 5. 13
Acts 9. 6 wh. *w.* th. have me to do?
Rom. 7. 18 to *w.* is present with me
1 Cor. 4. 19 I come to you, if L. *w.*
Phil. 2. 13 G. work. bo. to *w.* and do.
2 Tim. 3. 12 all that *w.* live godly
Jas. 2. 20 *w.* thou know, O vain *w.*
3 John 13 I *w.* not with ink and pen
R. V. Changes of the pure auxiliary
are to, would, should, shall, etc.

Willing. *Wishing, meaning to.*
Ex. 3. 5 whosoever is of a *w.* heart
1 Chr. 28. 9 serve G. with *w.* mind
Ps. 110. 3 thy people shall be *w.*
Mat. 26. 41 spirit is *w.,* fl. is weak
John 5. 35 ye were *w.* to rejoice in
Rom. 9. 22 if G. *w.* to show wrath

2 Cor. 5. 8 *w.* rather to be absent
Heb. 6. 17 *w.* to show heirs of prom.
2 Pet. 3. 9 not *w.* any should perish
R. V. Ex. 35. 29 free will ; Job 39.
9 content ; Mark 15. 15 ; 2 Pet.
3. 9 wishing ; Luke 10. 29 ; 23. 20 ;
Acts 24. 27 ; 25. 9 ; 27. 43 : Heb.
13. 18 desiring ; 1 Thes. 2. 8 well
pleased ; Heb. 6. 17 being minded.

Willingly. *Freely, so minded.*
Ex. 25. 2 every man that gives *w.*
Judg. 5. 2 peo. *w.* offer. themselves
Neh. 11. 2 that *w.* offered themsel.
Prov. 31. 13 she work. *w.* wi. hands
Lam. 3. 33 he doth not afflict *w.*
Rom. 8. 20 subj. to vanity not *w.*
2 Cor. 9. 17 if I do this *w.,* a rewar.
Phile. 14 not as of necess., but *w.*

Willow. *Willow, salix, ozier.*
Job 40. 22 *w.* of brook comp. him
Ps. 137. 2 hanged our harps on *w.*
Ezek. 17. 5 has set it as a *w.* tree

Wilt. *See* Will (*v.*).

Wimples. R. V. *shawls.*
Isa. 3. 22 take aw. mantles and *w.*

Win. *Gain, take.*
2 Chr. 32. 1 he thought to *w.* them
Phil. 3. 8 that I may *w.* Christ
1 Pet. 3. 1 may without word be *w.*
R. V. Phil. 3. 8 gain

Wind (*n.*). *Wind.*
Ex. 10. 13 the east *w.* brought locusts
2 Sam. 22. 11 seen on wings of the *w.*
Job 1. 19 came *w.* fr. the wilderness
Ps. 1. 4 like chaff wh. *w.* driveth
Prov. 25. 14 Who. boast. is like *w.*
Eccl. 11. 4 th. obser. *w.* sh. not sow
Ezek. 5. 2 third part sh. scat. in *w.*
Dan. 7. 2 four *w.* of heaven strove
Jonah 1. 4 L. sent *w.* into the sea
Mat. 7. 25 *w.* blew, beat on house
Mark 4. 41 even the *w.* obey him ?
Luke 7. 24 A reed shaken wi. th. *w.*
John 3. 8 *w.* bloweth where it list.
Eph. 4. 14 car. ab. wi. ev. *w.* of doc.
R. V. Isa. 27. 8 blast ; Jer. 14. 6
air ; Hos. 13. 15 breath.

Wind (*v.*). *Go round, twist, tie.*
John 19. 40 *w.* it in linen clothes
Acts 5. 6 *w.* him up, and carried h.
R. V. Ezek. 41. 7 encompass

Window. *Open place, outlook.*
Gen. 7. 11 *w.* of heav. were opened
Josh. 2. 15 let down by cord thr. *w.*
Judg. 5. 28 moth. looked out thr. *w.*
1 Sam. 19. 12 Mic. let Dav. thro. *w.*
Prov. 7. 6 at *w.* of my ho. I looked
Isa. 24. 18 *w.* fr. on high are opened
Acts 20. 9 sat in *w.* a young man
R. V. Gen. 6. 16 light ; 1 K. 7. 4,
5 prospects ; Isa. 54. 12 pinnacles.

Windy. *With wind.*
Ps. 55. 8 hasten from the *w.* storm

Wine. *Grape-juice, syrup.*
Gen. 9. 24 Noah awoke fr. his *w.,*
Lev. 10. 9 do not drink *w.* nor stro.
Deut. 32. 33 *w.* is poison of dragons
1 Sam. 1. 14 put away *w.* from thee
2 K. 18. 32 a land of corn and *w.*
2 Chr. 11. 11 put store of oil and *w.*
Neh. 2. 1 *w.,* and I took up the *w.*
Job. 32. 19 my belly is as *w.* which
Ps. 60. 3 to dr. *w.* of astonishment
Prov. 21. 1 *W.* is mocker, str. dr.
23. 31 Look not on *w.* wh. it is red
Mat. 9. 17 Nei. put new *w.* in o. bot.
Mark 15. 23 ga. *w.* ming. wi. myrrh
Luke 1. 15 dr. nei. *w.* nor str. drink
John 2. 3 wanted *w.* ; have no *w.*
Rom. 14. 21 nei. eat fl., nor dr. *w.*
1 Tim. 5. 23 use lit. *w.* for stomach's
Tit. 2. 3 not given to *w.* teachers
Rev. 6. 6 see th. hurt not oil and *w.*
R. V. Num. 18. 12 ; Mic. 6. 15 vin-
tage ; Num. 28. 7 drink ; Sam. 6
19 ; 1 Chr. 16. 3 ; Hos. 3. 1 raisins.

Wine-bibber. *Wine sucker.*
Mat. 11. 19 Behold a man gluttonous and *w. b.* ; Luke 7. 34.

Wine Fat. *Wine vat, or press.*
Isa. 63. 2 like him treadeth *w. f.*
Mark 12. 1 digged a place for *w. f.*

Wine-press. *Wine-press or
trough.*
Num. 18. 27 thro. fulness of *w. p.*
Judg. 6. 11 thresh. wheat by *w. p.*

Isa. 63. 3 I have trod. *w. b.* alone
Lam. 1. 15 trodden Jud. as in *w. p*
Mat. 21. 33 and digged *w. p.* in it
Rev. 14. 19 cast it into *v. p.* of wrath
Wing. *Wing, pinion.*
Ex. 19. 4 I bare you on eagles' *w.*
Ruth 2. 12 under whose *w.* thou art
2 Sam. 22. 11 seen on *w.* of the wind
Job 39. 13 gavest *w.* to the peacock?
Ps. 17. 8 hide me un. sh. of thy *w.*
Prov. 23. 5 riches make thems. *w.*
Mat. 23. 37 as hen gathereth her
  chickens under her *w.*; Luke 13. 34
R. V. Deut. 32. 11 pinions
Winged. *With wings.*
Gen. 1. 21 G. created every *w.* fowl
Wink. *Move eyelid.*
Job 15. 12 wh. do thy eyes *w.* at?
Ps. 35. 19 *w.* with eye th. hate me
Prov. 6. 13 wicked man *w.* wi. eye
R. V. *overlook*
Acts 17. 30 ignorance God *w.* at
Winnow. *Scatter, spread.*
Ruth 3. 2 Boaz *w.* barley to night
Isa. 30. 24 ha. been *w.* with shovel
Winter (*n.*). *Winter.*
Gen. 8. 22 and *w.* shall not cease
Ps. 74. 17 ha. made summer and *w.*
S. of S. 2. 11 *w.* is past, rain is over
Mat. 24. 20 pray that your flight be
  not in *w.*; Mark 13. 18
2 Tim. 4. 21 do dilig. to. co. bef. *w.*
Winter (*v.*).
Isa. 18. 6 beasts shall *w.* on them
1 Cor. 16. 6 *w.* with you, that ye may
Tit. 3. 12 I determined there to *w.*
Winter House.
Jer. 36. 22 the king sat in the *w. h.*
Wipe. *Rub, cleanse, blot out.*
2 K. 21. 13 *w.* Jerusalem as a dish
Luke 7. 38 woman did *w.* them with
  hairs of head ; John 11. 2
Rev. 7. 17 G. sh. w. away all tears
Wire. *Wire, thread.*
Ex. 39. 3 gold plates, cut into *w.*
Wisdom. *Understanding, knowledge, skill, prudence.*
Deut. 34. 9 Joshua was full of *w.*
1 K. 4. 29 God gave Solomon *w.*
1 Chr. 22. 12 the Lord give thee *w.*
2 Chr. 9. 23 ail so. Sol. to hear *w.*
Job 28. 28 fear of the L., that is *w.*
Ps. 37. 30 mo. of right. speaketh *w.*
Prov. 1. 7 fools despise *w.* and ins.
Isa. 29. 14 *w.* of wise shall perish
Jer. 9. 23 let not wise glory in *w.*
Mic. 6. 9 the man of *w.* shall see
Mat. 13. 54 Whence ha. this man *w.*
Mark 6. 2 what *w.* is this which is
Luke 2. 52 Jesus increased in *w.*
Acts 7. 22 Moses was learned in *w.*
1 Cor. 3. 19 *w.* of world is foolishness
Col. 1. 28 teach every man in all *w.*
R. V. 1 Chr. 22. 12 discretion ; Job
  36. 5 ; Ps. 136. 5 ; Prov. 10. 21 ;
  Eccl. 10. 3 understanding ; Prov.
  1. 3 wise dealing ; 8. 5 subtilty ; 8.
  14 knowledge ; Dan. 2. 14 prudence
Wise. *Knowing, prudent.*
Gen. 3. 6 a tree to make one *w.*
Ex. 7. 11 Phar. called the *w.* men
1 K. 2. 9 thou art *w.* man, and kn.
2 Chr. 2. 12 given to David a *w.* son
Job 5. 13 He ta. *w.* in own craftin.
Ps. 2. 10 be *w.* now, O ye kings
Prov. 3. 7 be not *w.* in own eyes
Eccl. 2. 14 *w.* man's eyes are in head
Isa. 5. 21 woe to them that are *w.*
Dan. 2. 21 God giv. wisdom to *w.*
Mat. 2. 1 ca. *w.* men from the east
Luke 12. 42 Who is that *w.* steward
Rom. 1. 14 I am debtor to the *w.*
Eph. 5. 15 walk not as fools, but *w.*
1 Tim. 1. 17 king eternal, only *w.* G.
Jude 25 To only *w.* G. our Saviour
Thus, way, surely.
Mat. 1. 18 birth of *C.* was this *w.*
Luke 18. 17 he shall in no *w.* enter
John 6. 37 will in no *w.* cast out
R. V. 1 Chr. 26. 14 discreet ; Prov.
  1. 5 sound ; 1 Tim. 1. 17 ; Jude
  25 —— ; Lev. 19. 17 ; Deut. 21. 23
  surely ; Rom. 10. 6 thus
Wisely. *With wisdom.*
Ex. 1. 10 let us deal *w.* with them
1 Sam. 18. 5. D. behaved himself *w.*

Ps. 58. 5 voice charming never so *w.*
Prov. 16. 20 handleth a matter *w.*
Luke 16. 8 becau. he had done *w.*
Wiser. *More wise.*
1 K. 4. 31 S. was *w.* than all men
Job 35. 11 mak. us *w.* than fowls
Ps 119. 98 made me *w.* th. enemies
Luke 16. 8 in their generation *w.*
1 Cor. 1. 25 fool. of G. *w.* than men
Wish (*n.*). *Desire.*
Job 33. 6 I am according to thy *w.*
Wish (*v.*). *Desire, pray for.*
Job 31. 30 *w.* a curse to his soul
Ps. 40. 14 put to shame that *w.* evil
Acts 27. 29 cast anchors, *w.* for day
Rom. 9. 3 co. *w.* myself accursed
3 John 2. 1 *w.* thou mayest prosper
Ps. 40. 14 delight ; Jonah 4. 8 re-
  quested ; 2 Cor. 13. 9 ; 3 John 2
  pray
Wist. *Know.*
Ex. 16. 15 they *w.* not what it was
Mark 9. 6 he *w.* not what to say
Luke 2. 49 *w.* ye not that I must be
Wit. *That is, namely.*
Gen. 24. 21 to *w.*, whether L. made
2 Cor. 5. 19 To *w.*, G. was in C., rec.
Witch. R. V. *sorcerer.*
Ex. 22. 18 not suffer a *w.* to live
Deut. 18. 10 not be among you a *w.*
Witchcraft. R. V. *sorcery.*
1 Sam. 15. 23 rebelli. is as sin of *w.*
Mic. 5. 12 cut off *w.* out of land
Gal. 5. 20 works of the flesh are *w.*
With. *With.*
Gen. 4. 8 And Cain talked *w.* Abel
Mark 12. 30 *w.* all my heart, and *w.*
Etc., etc.
Withal. *With, together.*
1 K. 19. 1 *w.* Elijah slain prophets
Acts 25. 27 not *w.* to signi. crimes
Withdraw. *Draw away.*
1 Sam. 14. 19 S. said to priests, *W.*
Job. 9. 13 if God will not *w.* anger
Ps. 74. 11 why *w.*, thy right hand?
Prov. 25. 17 *w.* from neighb. s house
Ezek. 20. 22 I *w.* mi. hand, and wro.
Mat. 12. 15 J. knew, he *w.* himself
Mark 3. 7 J. *w.* with his disciples
Luke 22. 41 *w.* about a stone's cast
Gal. 2. 12 when they come, he *w.*
Wither. *Dry up, fade away.*
Gen. 41. 23 And, behold, sev. ears *w.*
Job. 8. 12 flag *w.* before any herb
Ps. 1. 3 his leaf also shall not *w.*
Isa. 15. 6 the hay is *w.*, the grass
Jonah 4. 7 smote gourd that it *w.*
Mat. 12. 10 man wh. had hand *w.*
Mark 4. 6 bec. it had no root, it *w.*
Luke 8. 6 soon as sprung up, it *w.*
John 15. 6 cast forth as branch, *w.*
1 Pet. 1. 24 grass *w.*, and the flower
Withhold. *Keep back, restrain.*
Gen. 20. 6 I *w.* thee fr. sinning ag.
1 Sam. 25. 26 the Lord hath *w.* thee
Job 4. 2 who can *w.* from speaking
Ps. 21. 2 not *w.* request of his lips
Prov. 23. 13 *W.* not correc. fr. child
Jer. 3. 3 the showers have been *w.*
2 Thes. 2. 6 now ye know what *w.*
R. V. Job 42. 2 ; 2 Thes. 2. 6 restrain
Within. *Inside, among.*
Gen. 60. 14 pitch it *w.* and without
Mat. 3. 9 think not to say *w.* yours
Without. *Outside, apart from.*
Ezek. 2. 10 was writ. within and *w.*
Mat. 13. 34 *w.* parab. spake he not
Withs. *Cords, strings.*
Judg. 16. 7 if they bind me with *w.*
Withstand. *Stand against.*
Num. 22. 32 angel went to *w.* Ba.
Esth. 9. 2 no man could *w.* them
Eccl. 4. 12 if one prevail, two sh. *w.*
Acts 11. 17 what I, th. I cou. *w.* God
Gal. 2. 11 I *w.* him to the face, bec.
2 Tim. 3. 8 Jan. and Jam. *w.* Moses
Witness (*n.*). *Who testifies, proof.*
Gen. 31. 44 for *w.* bet. me and thee
Deut. 5. 20 Nei. bear false *w.* against
Josh. 22. 27 be *w.* bet. us and you
Ruth 4. 11 the elders said, We are *w.*
1 Sam. 12. 5 they answered, He is *w.*
Job 16. 8 wrinkles, a *w.* against me
Ps. 27. 12 false *w.* are risen ag. me
Prov. 24. 28 Be not *w.* ag. neighbor
Jer. 29. 23 I am a *w.*, saith the Lord

Mat. 26. 65 wh. need have we of *w.*?
Mark 14. 59 nei. did their *w.* agree
Luke 24. 48 ye are *w.* of these things
John 1. 7 came to bear *w.* of Light
Acts 1. 8 be *w.* unto me in Jerusal.
Rom. 1. 9 G. my *w.*, whom I serve
1 Thes. 2. 10 Ye are *w.*, and G. also
2 Tim. 2. 2 ha. heard of me am. *w.*
Tit. 1. 13 This *w.* is true. Wheref.
Heb. 10. 15 H. G. also is a *w.* to us
1 Pet. 5. 1 *w.* of the suffering of C.
1 John 5. 6 the spirit th. beareth *w.*
Rev. 1. 5 J. C., who is faithful *w.*
Witness (*v.*). *Testify, show, prove.*
1 Sam. 12. 3 here I am, *w.* aga. me
Isa. 3. 9 countenance *w.* agai. them
Lam. 2. 13 what shall I take to *w.*?
Mat. 26. 62 what is it wh. these *w.*
  against thee ; Mark 14. 60
Rom. 3. 21 being *w.* by law and pro.
Heb. 7. 8 of whom it is *w.* he liveth
Witty. *Knowing.*
Prov. 8. 12 I find out *w.* inventions
Wittingly. *Intelligently.*
Gen. 48. 14 Is. guid. his hand *w.*
Wives. *See* **Wife.**
Wizard. *Knowing one, conjurer.*
Deut. 18. 11 sh. not be am. you *w.*
1 Sam. 28. 3 Saul put away the *w.*
Isa. 8. 19 *w.* that peep and mutter
Woe. *Sorrow, misery, grief.*
Num. 21. 29 *W.* un. thee, Moab! th.
Mat. 11. 21 *W.* un. thee, Chora. *w.*
Etc., etc.
Wolf. *Jackal, wolf.*
Gen. 49. 27 Ben. shall ravin as a *w.*
Isa. 11. 6 *w.* shall dwell with lamb
Jer. 5. 6 *w.* of evening spoil them
Ezek. 22. 27 her princ. are like *w.*
Mat. 7. 15 but inwardly they are *w.*
Luke 10. 3 send you forth amo. *w.*
John 10. 12 hirel. seeth *w.* coming
Acts 20. 29 *w.* sh. ent. among you
Woman. *Woman, female.*
Gen. 2. 23 she shall be called *W.*
Lev. 12. 2 If *w.* ha. conceived seed
Num. 5. 22 the *w.* shall say, Amen
Josh. 2. 4 *w.* took men, hid them
Ruth 1. 5 *w.* was left of her sons
1 Sam. 1. 15 am *w.* of sorrowf. spir.
1 K. 3. 17 I and this *w.* dwell in
2 Chr. 24. 7 Athal., that wicked *w.*
Neh. 13. 26 outland. *w.* cause sin
Job 14. 1 M born of *w.* . few days
Ps. 48. 6 pain as of a *w.* in travail
Prov. 9. 13 A foolish *w.* is clamor.
Isa. 4. 1 sev. *w.* ta. hold of one man
Jer. 7. 18 *w.* knead dough, to make
Mat. 5. 28 whoso looketh on a *w.*
Mark 10. 12 if *w.* put away husb.
Luke 7. 39 what man. of *w.* is this?
John 2. 4 *W.*, wh. ha. I to do wi. th.?
Acts 16. 14 a cert. *w.* named Lydia
Rom. 1. 26 *w.* did change nat. use
1 Cor. 14. 34 let *w.* keep silence
Gal. 4. 4 sent his S., made of a *w.*
1 Thes. 5. 3 com. as travail on *w.*
1 Tim. 2. 12 I suff. not *w.* to teach
Heb. 11. 35 *w.* receiv. dead raised
1 Pet. 3. 5 manner holy *w.* adorn.
Womb. *Hollow place, matrix, belly, body.*
Gen. 25. 23 Two nat. are in thy *w.*
Deut. 7. 13 will bless fr. of thy *w.*
Ruth 1. 11 and more sons in *w.*?
1 Sam. 1. 5 L. had shut up her *w.*
Job 1. 21 Nak. ca. I out of mo. *w.*
Ps. 22. 9 who took me out of *w.*
Prov. 31. 2 and what, the son of *w.*?
Isa. 49. 1 L. ha. called me fr. th. *w.*
Hos. 12. 3 took bro. by heel in *w.*
Mat. 19. 12 so born from moth. *w.*
Luke 1. 31 sh. conceive in thy *w.*
John 3. 4 can he enter mother's *w.*
Acts 3. 2 man, lame fr. mother's *w*
Rom. 4. 19 nei. deadn. of Sara's *w*
Gal. 1. 15 who separ. me fr. mo. *w.*
R. V. Deut. 7. 13 body
Won. *See* **Win.**
Wonder (*n.*). *Sign, miracle, prodigy, amazement.*
Ex. 3. 20 smite Egypt with my *w.*
Josh. 3. 5 Lord will do *w.* among
1 Chr. 16. 12 Remember his *w.*, and
Job 9. 10 G. do *w.* without number
Ps. 71. 7 I am as a *w.* unto many

Isa. 8. 16 children are for *w.* in Is.
Jer. 32. 20 set signs and *w.* in Eg.
Mat. 24. 24 For false Christs shall show signs and *w.*, Mark. 13. 22
John 4. 48 Except ye see signs, *w.*
Acts 2. 22 approved of God by *w.*
2 Cor. 12. 12 in signs, and *w.* and
2 Thes. 2. 9 coming in signs and *w.*
Heb. 2. 4 God bear. witness with *w.*
R. V. Rev. 12. 1, 3 sign

Wonder. (*v.*) *Be amazed, aston-ished.*
Gen. 24. 21 *w.* at her, held peace
Jer. 4. 9 and the prophets shall *w.*
Mat 15. 31 multitude *w.* when they
Mark 6. 51 they were am. and *w.*
Luke 11. 14 dumb spake, and p. *w*,
Acts 7. 31 When Moses saw, he *w.*
Rev. 13. 3 and all the world *w.* after
R. V. Gen. 24. 21 looked stedfastly;
Mark 6. 51 ——; Luke 8. 25 ; 11.
14 marvelled ; Acts 8. 13 amazed

Wonderful. *Wondrous, mighty.*
Deut. 28. 59 will make plagues *w.*
2 Sam. 1. 26 thy love to me was *w.*
Job 42. 3 uttered things too *w.* for
Ps. 139. 6 knowl. is too *w.* for me
Prov. 30. 18 three thi. are too *w.*
Isa. 9. 6 his name sh. be called *w.*
Mat. 21. 15 saw the *w.* things he did
Acts 2. 11 speak the *w.* works of G.
R. V. Ps. 78. 4 wondrous ; Mat. 7. 22 Acts 2. 21 mighty.

Wonderfully. *In wondrous man-ner.*
Ps. 139 14 am fearfully and *w.* made
Dan. 8. 24 he shall destroy *w.*, and

Wondrous. *Marvellous.*
Job 37. 14 Consid. *w.* works of G.
Ps. 71. 17 I declared thy *w.* works
Jer. 21. 2 accord. to his *w.* works
R. V. 1 Chr. 16. 9 ; Ps. 105. 2 mar-vellous

Wondrously. *Marvellously.*
Judg. 13. 19 and the angel did *w.*,
Joel 2. 26 Lord dealt *w.* with you

Wont. *Accustomed.*
Num. 22. 30 was I ev. *w.* to do so
2 Sam. 20. 18 *w.* to speak in old ti.
Dan. 3. 19 sev. times more th. w *w.*
Mat. 27. 15 gov. was *w.* to release
Mark 10. 1 as he was *w.*, he taught
Luke 22. 39 went, as he was *w.* to

Wood. *Wood, tree, forest.*
Gen. 6. 14 Make ark of gopher *w.*
Ex. 38. 1 he ma. altar of shittim *w.*
Josh. 9. 21 be hewers of *w.* and draw.
1 Sam. 6. 14 they clave *w.* of cart
2 K. 2. 24 two she bears out of *w.*
1 Chr. 22. 4 Tyre bro. much cedar *w.*
Neh. 8. 4 Ez. stood on pulpit of *w.*
Job 41. 27 esteem. brass as rotten *w.*
Ps. 80. 13 boar of the *w.* doth waste
Prov. 26. 20 no *w.*, the fire goeth out
S. of S. 2. 3 apple *t.* am. trees of *w.*
Isa. 7. 2 as trees of *w.* are moved
Jer. 5. 14 I will make this people *w.*
1 Cor. 3. 12 this foundation, *w.*, hay
Rev. 9. 20 not worship idols of *w.*
R. V. Deut. 19. 5 ; Josh. 17. 18 ; 1 Sam. 14. 25, 26 ; Ps. 83. 14 ; Eccl. 2. 6 ; Isa. 7. 2 ; Mic. 7. 14 forest ; 1 Chr. 22. 4 trees ; Ex. 26. 32, 37 ; 36. 36 ; Ps. 141. 7 —— .

Woof. *Cross thread, filling.*
Lev. 13. 48 wheth. plague be in *w.*

Wool. *Wool.*
Judg. 6. 37 put fleece of *w.* in floor
Ps. 147 16 Lord giveth snow like *w.*
Prov. 31. 13 She seeketh *w.* and flax
Isa. 1. 18 sins like crim., be as *w.*
Dan. 7. 9 hair of head like pure *w.*
Heb. 9. 19 he took the blood and *w.*
Rev. 1. 14 hairs were white like *w.*

Woollen. *Of wool.*
Lev. 13. 48 in warp or woof of *w.*
Deut. 22. 11 not wear a garm. of *w.*

Word. *Saying, speech, matter.*
Gen. 15. 14 *w.* of Lord ca. upon him
Ex. 4. 28 M. told A. *w.* of the Lord
Lev. 10. 7 did accord. to. *w.* of Mos.
Num. 11. 24 M. told peo. *w.* of Lord
Deut. 1. 1 these be the *w.* wh. M. spake
Josh. 3. 9 hear *w.* of Lord your God
Judg. 2 4 angel of L. spa. these *w.*
1 Sam. 4. 1 *w.* of Sam. came to Is.

2 Sam. 7. 4 *w.* of L. came to Nath.
2 K. 3. 12 *w.* of the L. is with him
20. 19 Good is *w.* of the L. which
1 Chr. 16. 15 be ye mindful of *w.*
Ez. 1. 1 *w.* of L. by mou'h of Jer.
Neh. 1. 1 *w.* of Neh. son of Hach.
Job 2. 13 sat, and none spake a *w.*
Ps. 19. 14 let *w.* of my mouth be
Prov. 1. 6 understand *w.* of the wise
Isa. 1. 10 Hear *w.* of L., ye rul. of
Jer. 1. 1 *w.* of Jer. son of Hilkiah
Ezek. 12. 25 *w.* shall come to pass
Hos. 6. 5 slain th. by *w.* of mouth
Jonah 3. 6 *w.* came to k. of Nineveh
Zeph. 2. 5 *w.* of Lord is against you
Mal. 2. 17 wearied L. with your *w.*
Mat. 4. 4 not live by bread, but *w.*
Mark 4. 14 sower soweth the *w.*
Luke 3. 4 as written in book of *w.*
John 1 1 In beginning was the *W.*
Acts 2. 22 men of Is. hear these *w.*
Rom. 9. 9 this is the *w.* of promise
1 Cor. 1. 17 not with wisdom of *w.*
Gal. 5. 14 all law is fulf. in one *w.*
Eph. 5. 26 cleanse *w.* vain *w.*
Phil. 2. 16 holding forth *w.* of life
Col. 3. 16 let *w.* of C. dwell in you
1 Thes. 2. 5 nei. used we flatter. *w.*
1 Tim. 4. 5 is sanctified by *w.* of G.
2 Tim. 4. 2 Preach *w.*, be instant in
Tit. 2. 5 that *w.* of G. be not blasph.
Heb. 4. 12 *w.* of G. is quick, and po.
Jas. 1. 22 But be ye doers of the *w.*
1 Pet. 1. 23 born again by *w.* of God
2 Pet. 1. 19 We ha. sure *w.* of proph.
Jude 17 remem. ye the *w.* spoken
Rev. 1. 2 Who bare record of the *w.*
R. V. Num. 4. 45 ; Josh. 19. 50 ; 22. 9 commandment ; Deut. 8. 3 ; 2 K. 23. 16 ; John 7. 9 ; 8. 30 ; 9. 22, 40 ; 17. 1 thing ; 2 Sam. 19. 14 1 K. 2. 42 ; Luke 20. 26 ; John 12. 47, 48 saying ; 1 K. 13. 26 mouth ; 1 Chr. 21. 12 answer ; Jonah 3. 6 tidings ; Mat. 2. 13 tell ; Luke 4. 4 ; Acts 28. 29 ; 1 John 5. 7 —— .

Work (*n.*). *Work, act, deed, doing, business.*
Gen. 2. 2 sev. day G. ended his *w.*
Ex. 20. 9 six days sh. thou do *w.*
Num. 4. 3 to do *w.* in the tabernac.
Josh. 24. 31 had known *w.* of the L.
Judg. 2. 7 had seen gr. *w.* of Lord
1 Sam. 8. 8 Accord. to all *w.* which
2 K. 19. 18 the *w.* of men's hands
1 Chr. 4. 23 dwelt wi. k. for his *w.*
2 Chr. 4. 11 Huram finished the *w.*
Neh. 4. 19 The *w.* is gr. and large
Job. 1. 10 ha. blessed *w.* of his hands
Ps. 19. 1 firm. show. thy handy *w.*
Prov. 16. 3 Commit thy *w.* unto L.
Eccl. 1. 14 I have seen all the *w.*
Isa. 2. 8 worsh. *w.* of own hands
Jer. 10. 15 are vanity, *w.* of errors
Lam. 3. 64 Render accor. to *w.* of
Dan. 9. 14 righteous in all his *w.*
Jonah 3. 10 God saw their *w.*, that
Mat. 5. 16 th. may see your good *w.*
Mark 13. 34 to every man his *w.*, and
John 6. 29 This is the *w.* of God
Acts 9. 36 wom. was full of good *w*
Rom. 2. 4 if A. were justified by *w*
1 Cor. 9. 1 are not ye my *w.* in Lord
Gal. 2. 16 man is not justifi. by *w.*
Eph. 2. 9 not of *w.*, lest man boast
Phil. 2. 30 Bec. for the *w.* of Christ
Col. 1. 10 being fruitful in good *w.*
2 Thes. 2. 17 stab. you in ev. good *w.*
2 Tim. 1. 9 not accord. to *w.*, but
Tit. 2. 7 show. thys. pat. of good *w.*
Heb. 1. 10 heav. are *w.* of thy hands
Jas. 1. 4 let pati. have perfect *w.*
1 Pet. 1. 7 judgeth accor. to man's *w.*
Rev. 2. 9 know thy *w.*, and tribula.
R. V. Ex. 35. 33, 35 workmanship ; Prov. 11. 18 wages ; Isa. 40. 10 ; 49. 4 ; 61. 8 ; 62. 11 recompense ; Ps. 77. 11 ; 141. 4 ; Mat. 16. 27 deeds ; Rom. 11. 6 grace ; Heb. 13. 21 thing.

Work (*v.*). *Do, toil, labor.*
Ex. 34. 21 six days thou shalt *w.*,
1 K. 21. 20 sold thyself to *w.* evil
Job 23. 9 on left hand wh. he *w.*
Ps. 15. 2 *w.* righteousness, dwell
Prov. 11. 18 wicked *w.* deceit. *w.*

Isa. 19. 9 they that *w.* in fine flax
Ezek. 33. 26 ye *w.* abomination
Dan. 6. 27 *w.* signs and wonders
Hos. 6. 8 city of them th. *w.* iniquity
Mic. 2. 1 devise iniquity, and *w.* evil
Hab. 1. 5 *w.* a work in your days
Mat. 7. 23 depart, ye th. *w.* iniquity
Luke 13. 14 six days men o't to *w.*
John 5. 17 My Father *w.* hitherto
Acts 10. 35 he that *w.* righteousness
Rom. 2. 10 to ev. man that *w.* good
1 Cor. 16. 10 he *w.* work of the Lord
Eph. 2. 2 spirit that *w.* in children
Phil. 2. 13 it is God wh. *w.* in you
Col. 1. 29 which *w.* in me mightily
1 Thes. 2. 13 effectually *w.* in you
Jas. 1. 3 trying of faith *w.* patience

Worker. *Who works.*
1 K. 7. 14 father was a *w.* in brass
2 Cor. 6. 1 as *w.* together with him
Phil. 3. 2 dogs, beware of evil *w.*

Work-fellow. *Fellow-worker.*
Rom. 16. 21 my *w. f.* salute you

Working. *Doing, laboring.*
Ps. 52. 3 like a razor *w.* deceitful.
Isa. 28. 29 the Lord excellent in *w*
Mark 16. 20 the Lord *w.* with them
1 Cor. 4. 12 *w.* with our own hands
Eph. 1. 19 according to *w.* of power
Col. 1. 29 his *w.* wh. worketh in me
Heb. 13. 21 *w.* that wh. is pleasing
Rev. 16. 14 spir. of devils *w.* mirac.

Workman. *Worker.*
Ex. 35. 35 work work of cunning *w.*
2 Chr. 24. 13 so the *w.* wrought
S. of S. 7. 1 work of a cunning *w.*
Isa. 40. 19 *w.* melteth an image
Jer. 10. 3 work of *w.* with the ax
Hos. 8. 6 made it, not of God
Mat. 10. 10 *w.* is worthy of meat
Acts 19. 25 with *w.* of like occupa.
2 Tim. 2. 15 a *w.* not to be ashamed

Workmanship. *Work, workers art.*
Ex. 31. 3 and in all manner of *w.*
2 K. 16. 10 according to *w.* thereof
Ezek. 28. 13 *w.* of tabrets prepared
Eph. 2. 10 we are his *w.* in C. Je.

World. *Age, time, dispensation.*
Mat. 12. 32 neither in this *w.*, neith.
13. 39 harvest is end of the *w.*, and
13. 40 so sh. it be in end of this *w.*
28. 20 wi. you alway unto end *w.*
Mark 4. 19 cares of this *w.*, and de.
10. 30 in *w.* to come eternal life
Luke 18. 30 in *w.* to co. everl. life
20. 34 children of this *w.* marry, and
Rom. 12. 2 be not conformed to *w*
1 Cor. 1. 20 where is disputer of *w.* ?
2 Cor. 4. 4 god of this *w.* h. blinded
Gal. 1. 4 deliver us fr. this evil *w.*
Eph. 1. 21 not only in this *w.*, but
1 Tim. 6. 17 Charge rich in this *w.*
2 Tim. 4. 10 having loved pres. *w.*
Tit. 2. 12 live soberly in this *w.*
Heb. 1. 2 by whom he made the *w.*
11. 3 Through faith we underst. *w.*

Duration, indefinite time.
Ps. 73. 12 ungodly, who prosper in *w.*
Eccl. 3. 11 ha. set *w.* in their hearts
Isa. 45. 17 not asham., *w.* without
64. 4 for since beginning of *w.*
Luke 1. 70 prophets, since *w.* began
John 9. 32 Since *w.* began was not
Rom. 16. 25 secret since the *w.* be.
1 Cor. 8. 13 eat no flesh whi. *w.* st.
Eph. 3. 21 all ages, *w.* without end
2 Tim. 1. 9 giv. in C. J. since *w.*
Tit. 1. 2 promised before the *w.* be.

Land, earth, world.
1 Sam. 2. 8 Lord hath set the *w.* up
2 Sam. 22. 16 founda. of *w.* appear.
1 Chr. 16. 30 *w.* also. sh. be stable
Job 18. 18 sh. be chased out of *w.*
34. 13 who hath disposed the *w.*
37. 12 may do on the face of *w.*
Ps. 9. 8 he shall judge the *w.* in
17. 14 deliver from men of the *w.*
22. 27 ends of *w.* shall remember
24. 1 and the *w.* is the Lord's
33. 8 inhabit. of *w.* stand in awe
89. 11 founded *w.* and its fulness
Prov. 8. 26 nor made dust of the *w.*
Isa. 13. 11 I will punish *w.* for evil
14. 17 made the *w.* as a wildern.
14·21 nor fill the *w.* with cities

24. 4 *w.* languisheth and fadeth
Jer. 10. 12 he ha. established the *w.*
Lam. 4. 12 *w.* would not ha. belie.
Nah. 1. 5 *w.*, and all that dw. ther.
Mat. 4. 8 show. him king'd's of *w.*
5. 14 Ye are the light of the *w.*
13. 38 The field is the *w.* ; the s.
16. 26 if shall gain the whole *w.*
18. 7 Woe unto *w.* bec. of offences
Mark 16. 15 Go to all *w.* and preach
Luke 11. 50 shed fr. foundation of *w.*
John 1. 10 He was in *w. w.*knew not
1. 29 wh. taketh away sin of the *w.*
3. 16 For God so loved the *w.*, that
3. 19 light is come into the *w.*, and
4. 42 indeed Chr., Saviour of the *w.*
8. 12 I am the light of the *w.*
8. 23 ye are of this *w.*, I am not
12. 47 not to judge *w.*, but save *w.*
16. 33 In *w.* ye have tribulation
18. 36 My kingdom is not of this *w.*
Acts 17. 6 have turned the *w.* upside
17. 31 in which he will judge *w.*
19. 27 Asia and *w.* worshippeth
24. 5 among Jews throughout *w.*
Rom. 3. 6 how sh. G. judge the *w.*
3. 19 all the *w.* may become guilty
5. 12 as by one man sin entered *w.*
1 Cor. 1. 20 G. ma. foolish wis. of *w.*
1. 21 *w.* by wisdom knew not God
1. 19 wisdom of *w.* is foolishness
4. 13 are made as filth of the *w.*
7. 31 fashion of *w.* passeth away.
2 Cor. 7. 10 sorrow of *w.* work. death
Gal. 4. 3 in bond under elem. of *w.*
6. 14 *w.* is crucified unto me
Eph. 1. 4 before the foundation of *w.*
2. 12 no hope without God in *w.*
Phil. 2. 15 shine as lights in the *w.*
Col. 1. 6 as it is in all the *w.*
2. 8 after rudiments of the *w.*
1 Tim. 1. 15 C. ca. into *w.* to save
6. 7 we bro. nothing into this *w.*
Heb. 2. 5 ha. put in subjec. the *w.*
11. 38 of whom *w.* was not worthy
Jas. 1. 27 keep unspotted fr. the *w.*
3. 6 tongue is a *w.* of iniquity
1 Pet. 1. 20 before foundation of *w.*
2 Pet. 2. 5 spared not the old *w.*, but
1 John 2. 16 all in the *w.* is of the *w.*
4. 17 as he is, so are we in *w.*
2 John 7 deceivers are ent. in *w.*
Rev. 12. 9 Satan deceiveth whole *w.*
13. 3 *w.* wondered after the beast
R. V. Ps. 22. 27 ; Isa. 62. 11 ; Rev.
13. 13 earth] ; 1 Cor. 10. 11 ; Eph.
3. 9 ; Heb. 6. 5 ; 9. 26 age or ages;
Isa. 60. 4 of old ; Mat. 12. 32 that
which is ; Rom. 16. 25 ; 2 Tim.
1. 9 ; Tit. 1. 2 time eternal ; John
17. 12 —— .

Worldly. *Of the world.*
Tit. 2. 12 ungodliness and *w.* lusts
Heb. 9. 1 first cov. had *w.* sanct.

Worm. *Creeping thing, worm.*
Ex. 16. 24 neither any *w.* therein
Deut. 28. 39 the *w.* shall eat them
Job 7. 5 clothed with *w.* and dust
19. 26 though *w.* destroy his body
21. 26 and *w.* shall cover them
24. 20 *w.* feed sweetly on him
25. 6 man is a *w.*, son of man *w.*
Ps. 22. 6 I am a *w.*, and no man
Isa. 14. 11 *w.* is spread under thee
41. 14 Fear not, thou *w.* Jacob
51. 8 *w.* sh. eat them like wool
66. 24 their *w.* shall not die
Jonah 4. 7 a *w.* smote the gourd
Mark 9. 44 Where their *w.* dieth not
Acts 12. 23 Herod was eaten of *w.*
R. V. Mic. 7. 17 crawling thing ;
Job 19. 26 ; Mark 9. 44, 46 —— .

Wormwood. *Hemlock, wormwood.*
Deut. 29. 18 a root that beareth *w.*
Prov. 5. 4 her end is bitter as *w.*
Lam. 3. 15 ha. ma. me drunk. wi *w.*
Am. 5. 7 who turn judgment to *w.*
Rev. 8. 11 name of star called *w.*

Worse. *More ill or evil.*
Gen. 19. 9 deal *w.* with thee than
2 Sam. 19. 7 *w.* th. all that befel
2 K. 14. 12 Jud. was put to the *w.*
Jer. 7. 26 did *w.* th. their fathers
Mat. 12. 45 last state of that man
is *w.* than first ; Luke 11. 26

Mark 2. 21 and the rent is ma. *w.*
1 Cor. 8. 8 if we eat not, are we *w.*
2 Tim. 3. 13 seducers shall wax *w.*
Worship. *Bow, esteem, glory.*
Gen. 22. 5 I and the lad will go *w.*
24. 26 Abr. bowed down and *w.* L.
24. 52 Abr's servant *w.* the Lord
Ex. 4. 31 they bowed heads and *w.*
33. 10 all the peo. rose up and *w.*
34. 14 thou sh. *w.* no other god
Deut. 4. 19 lest th. be driven to *w.*
8. 19 if thou *w.* other gods, 11. 16
26. 10 and *w.* before Lord thy G.
Josh. 5. 14 did *w.*, and said to him
Judg. 7. 15 *w.* and ret. into the host
1 Sam. 1. 3 to *w.* and sac. unto L.
1. 28 and he *w.* the Lord there
15. 31 turn. aft. Saul ; and Saul *w.*
2 Sam. 12. 20 ca. into ho. of L. *w.*
15. 32 D. co. to mount., wh. he *w.*
1 K. 5. 6 serve other gods and *w.*
11. 33 *w.* Ashtoreth the goddess
22. 53 he served Baal, and *w.* him
2 K. 17. 16 *w.* all host of heaven
17. 36 L. ye fear, him shall ye *w.*
18. 22 sh. *w.* bef. altar in Jerusal.
1 Chr. 16 29 *w.* L. in beauty of ho.
29. 20 bow. do. their heads and *w.*
2 Chr. 7. 3 *w.* and praised the L.
29. 28 all the congregation *w.*
32. 12 Ye shall *w.* bef. one altar
Neh. 8. 6 *w.* L. with their faces
9. 6 the host of heaven *w.* thee
Job 1. 20 fell upon ground and *w.*
Ps. 5. 7 will *w.* toward thy temple
45. 11 he is thy L., *w.* thou him
81. 9 neither *w.* any strange god
95. 6 let us *w.* and bow down
97. 7 boast of idols, *w.* him all ye
99. 5 exalt the Lord our G., and *w.*
106. 19 Made a calf in Hor., and *w.*
138. 2 will *w.* toward his ho. temp
Isa. 2. 8 *w.* work of th. own hands
27. 13 *w.* Lord in the holy mount
44. 15 yea, he mak. a god, and *w.*
49. 7 princes also shall *w.*, because
Jer. 7. 2 enter these gates to *w.* L.
13. 20 *w.* oth. gods, be as a girdle
25. 6 go not after other gods to *w.*
44. 19 did we *w.* her without men ?
Ezek. 8. 16 thy *w.* the sun toward
46. 2 he shall *w.* at the threshold
46. 9 that ent. to *w.* by north gate
Dan. 3. 6 fall down and *w.* the golden image
3. 6, 7, 10, 11, 12, 14, 15, 28
Mic. 5. 13 thou shalt no more *w.*
Zeph. 1. 5 that *w.* host of heaven
2. 11 men shall *w.* him, every one
Zech. 14. 16 go fr. y'r to y'r to *w.*
Mat. 2. 2 star, and are come to *w.*
2. 8 that I may come *w.* him also
4. 9 if thou wilt fall down and *w.*
4. 10 Thou shalt *w.* the L. thy G.
8. 2 there came a leper and *w.*
9. 18 came a certain ruler and *w.*
15. 25 Then came she and *w.*, say.
28. 17 when they saw him, they *w.*
Mark 7. 7 in vain do they *w.* me
15. 19 bowing their knees, *w.* him
Luke 4. 7 If thou wilt *w.* in this mount
24. 52 *w.* him, and ret. to Jerusa.
John 4. 20 fath.'s *w.* in this mount.
4. 23 shall *w.* the Father in spirit
4. 24 that *w.* him must *w.* him in
9. 38 said, L., I believe, and he *w.*
Acts 7. 43 figures wh. ye ma. to *w.*
8. 27 had come to Jerusalem to *w.*
10. 25 fell do. at his feet and *w.* him
24. 14 se *w.* I God of my fathers
Rom. 1. 25 *w.* creature more than
1 Cor. 14. 25 fal. down he will *w.* G.
Phil. 3. 3 which *w.* G. in the spirit
2 Thes. 2. 4 called G., or that is *w.*
Heb. 1. 6 let angels of God *w.* him
11. 21 Jacob *w.* leaning on staff
Rev. 3. 9 will make them come *w.*
4. 10 *w.* him that liveth for ever
9. 20 they should not *w.* devils
11. 1 and them that *w.* therein
13. 8 all that dwell on earth sh. *w.*
14. 7 *w.* him that made heaven
19. 10 I fell at his feet to *w.* him
20. 4 souls that had not *w.* beast
R. V. 2 K. 17. 36 bow ; Luke 14.
10 glory ; Acts 7. 42 ; 17. 25 ; 24.
14 serve

Worshipper. *Who worships.*
2 K. 10. 19 destroy the *w.* of Baal
10. 21 all *w.* of Baal came, so that
10. 23 wi. you none but *w.* of Baal
John 4. 23 *w.* sh. worship in spirit
9. 31 if any man be a *w.* of God
Acts 19. 35 Ephesus is a *w.* of D.
Heb. 10. 2 because *w.* once purged
R. V. Acts 19. 35 temple keeper
Worshipping. *To worship.*
2 K. 19. 37 was *w.* in ho. of Nisroch
2 Chr. 20. 18 Ju. fell down *w.* Lord
Isa. 37. 38 as he was *w.* in house of
Mat. 20. 20 Zeb's chil. ca. *w.* him
Col. 2. 18 beguile you in *w.* of ang
Worst. *Most evil.*
Ex. 7. 24 bring *w.* of the heathen
Worth. *Value, price.*
Gen. 23. 9 much money as it is *w.*
Lev. 27. 23 priest sh. reckon to h. *w.*
Deut. 15. 18 he hath been *w.* double
2 Sam. 18. 3 thou art *w.* ten thousand
1 K. 21. 2 gi. thee *w.* of it in money
Job. 24. 25 make speech nothing *w.*
Prov. 10. 20 heart of wicked lit. *w.*
Ezek. 30. 2 Howl, ye, Woe *w.*day. ?
Worthies. *Honorable.*
Nah. 2. 5 He shall recount his *w.*
Worthily. *Deservingly.*
Ruth 4. 11 do thou *w.* in Ephratah
Worthy. *Deserving, of worth.*
Gen. 32. 10 I am not *w.* of mercies
Deut. 19. 6 he was not *w.* of death
25. 2 if wick., man be *w.* to be beat.
1 Sam. 1. 5 he gave a *w.* portion
26. 16 ye are *w.* to die, because ye
1 K. 1. 52 If he will show hims. *w.*
2. 26 for thou art *w.* of death, but
Jer. 26. 11 This man is *w.* to die, for
26. 16 This man is *w.* to die for
Mat. 3. 11 shoes I am not *w.* to bear
10. 10 workman is *w.* of his meat
22. 8 which were bidden not *w.*
Mark 1. 7 shoes not *w.* to unloose
Luke 3. 16 ; John 1. 27 ; Acts 13. 25
Luke 3. 8 fruits *w.* of repentance
7. 4 That he was *w.* for whom he
10. 7 labourer is *w.* of his hire
15. 19 no mo. *w.* to be call. thy son
21. 36 that ye may be accounted *w.*
Acts 23. 29 but nothing *w.* of death
24. 2 we. deeds are done to nation
Rom. 1. 32 wh. com. things *w.* of d.
8. 18 suff. not *w.* to be compared
Eph. 4. 1 th. ye walk *w.* of voca*t*ion
Col. 1. 10 ye might walk *w.* of Lord
1 Thes. 2. 12 would walk *w.* of God
2 Thes. 1. 5 be counted *w.* of king.
1 Tim. 5. 17 Let elders be counted *w.*
5. 18 labourer is *w.* of his reward
Heb. 3. 3 this man was counted *w.*
10. 29 shall he be thought *w.*, who
Jas. 2. 7 blaspheme that *w.* name
Rev. 3. 4 in white, for they are *w.*
4. 11 art *w.* O L., to receive glory
5. 2 Who is *w.* to open the book
5. 12 *W.* is Lamb that was slain
R. V. 1 Sam. 1. 5 double ; Luke
21. 36 prevail ; Jas. 2. 7 honourable
Wot. *Know, perceive*
Gen. 21. 26 I *w.* not who ha. done
44. 15 *w.* ye not th. I can divine ?
Ex. 32. 1 we *w.* not wh. is become
Num. 22. 6 *w.* he wh. thou blessed
Josh. 2. 5 whith. men went I *w.* not
Acts 3. 17 I *w.* thro. ignorance ye did
Rom. 11. 2 *W.* ye not what script.
Phil. 1. 22 what choose I *w.* not
R. V. Gen. 21. 26 ; 44. 15 ; Ex. 32
1, 23 ; Num. 22. 6 know.
Would. *Will, wish.*
Gen. 30. 34 *w.* it mi. be according to
Ex. 16. 3 *W.* to God we had died
Num. 11. 29 *W.* G. all the L.'s peo.
Deut. 28. 67 *W.* G. it were even, and
Josh. 7. 7 *w.* G. we had been con.
Judg. 9. 29 *w.* G. this peo. were un.
1 Sam. 2. 25 bec. Lord *w.* slay them
2 Sam, 18. 33 *w.* I had died for thee
2 K. 4. 13 *w.* thou be spok. for to k.
Ps. 35. 25 Ah ! so *w.* we ha. it ; yet
Dan. 5. 19 king, whom he *w.* he slew
Mat. 2. 18 Rach. *w.* not be comfort.
5. 42 him that *w.* borrow of thee
Mark 3. 13 call. to him who. he *w.*
John 1. 43 Jesus *w.* go into Galilee

Rom. 1. 13 I *w.* not have you ignor.
7. 15 for what I *w.*, that do I not
1 Cor. 7. 7 *w.* all men were as I
2 Cor. 1. 8 we *w.* not ha. you ignor.
Gal. 3. 2 This *w.* I learn of you
Col. 1. 27 To whom G. *w.* ma. kno.
1 Thes. 2. 18 we *w.* ha. come to you
2 Thes. 3. 10 if any *w.* not work,
Phile. 14 without mind *w.* I do no.
Heb. 10. 5 Sac. and off. thou *w.* not
Rev. 3. 15 I *w.* thou wert co. or hot
18. 8 words of talebearer are as *w.*
23. 29 hath *w.* without cause?
R. V. Many changes to, did, could,
  may, should, was about. etc.

Wound (*n.*). *Hurt, injury, cut*
Ex. 21. 25 *w.* for *w.*, stripe for stri.
1 K. 22. 35 blood ran out of *w.*
2 K. 8. 29 J. went to be heal. of *w.*
2 Chr. 22. 6 because of the *w.* given
Job 9. 17 and multiplied my *w.*
  34. 6 my *w.* is incurable without
Ps. 38. 5 My *w.* stink, are corrupt
  147. 3 and bindeth up their *w.*
Prov. 6. 33 *w.* and dishon. sh. he get
  27. 6 Faithful are *w.* of a friend
Isa. 1. 6 no soundness in it, but *w.*
  30. 26 healeth the stroke of th. *w.*
Jer. 6. 7 before me is grief and *w.*
Hos. 5. 13 Jud. saw his *w.* could
Obad. 7 have laid a *w* under thee
Mic. 1. 9 for her *w.* is incurable
Zech. 13. 6 Wh. th. *w.* in thy hands?
Luke 10. 34 bound *w.*, pouring oil
Rev. 13. 3 his deadly *w.* was healed
  R. V. Prov. 18. 8; 26. 22 dainty
  morsels; Obad. 7 snare; Rev. 13.
  3, 12 death stroke

Wound (*v.*). *Smite, cut, pierce, bruise.*
Judg. 9. 40 many were over... and *w.*
1 Sam. 17. 52 *w.* of Philist. fell do.
1 K. 20. 37 in smiting he *w.* him
1 Chr. 10. 3 Saul was *w.* of archers
2 Chr. 35. 23 Have away; for I .. *w.*
  13. 14 which had the *w.* by a sword
Job 5. 18 *w.*, and hands ma. whole
Ps. 18. 38 I have *w.* them, that they
Prov. 7. 26 she ha. cast do. many *w.*
Isa. 51. 9 art not it that *w.* dragon?
Jer. 30. 14 I *w.* thee with wound of
Lam. 2. 12 swooned as *w.* in streets
Zech. 13. 6 *w.* in house of my friend
Mark 12. 4 and *w.* him in the head
Luke 10. 30 *w.* him, departed, leav.
Acts 19. 16 they fled, naked and *w.*
1 Cor. 8. 12 *w.* their weak consci.
Rev. 13. 3 saw heads as it were *w.*
  R. V. 2 Sam. 22. 39; Ps. 18. 38; 32.
  39; 110. 6; Rev. 13. 13 smite or
  smitten through; 1 Sam. 31. 3; 1
  Chr. 10. 3 distressed; Isa. 51. 9
  pierced; Luke 10. 30 beat.
Wound (*v.*). *Bind, tie. See* **Wind.**
Wounding. *Hurt.*
Gen. 4. 23 slain a man to my *w.*
Woven. *Weaved.*
John 19. 23 coat was with. seam, *w.*
Wrap. *Roll, fold, draw around.*
Gen. 38. 14 Tamar *w.* herself, and sat
1 K. 19. 13 E. *w.* his face in mantle
Job 8. 17 roots are *w.* about heap
Ezek. 21. 15 swo. is *w.* for slaugh.
Jonah 2. 5 weeds *w.* about my head
Mat. 27. 59 Jos. *w.* body in linen
  Mark 15. 46· Luke 23. 53
John 20. 7 napkin *w.* together in
  R. V. Ezek. 21. 15 pointed; Mark
  15. 46 wound; John 20. 7 rolled up
Wrath. *Anger, heat, fury.*
Gen. 39. 19 that his *w.* was kindled
Num. 1. 53 no *w.* upon the congrega.
Deut. 29. 23 overthrew in ang. a. *w.*
Josh. 9. 20 lest *w.* be upon us, bec.
2 Sam. 11. 20 if the king's *w.* arise
2 K. 22. 13 great is *w.* of the Lord
2 Chr. 12. 7 my*w.* sh. not be poured
Neh. 13. 18 ye bring mo. *w.* upon Is.
Job 5. 2 for *w.* killeth foolish man
Ps. 2. 5 sh. speak to them in his *w.*
Prov. 11. 4 Rich. pr. not in day of *w.*
Eccl. 5. 17 sor. and *w.* wi. sickness
Isa. 9. 19 Thro. *w.* of Lord of hosts
Jer. 7. 29 forsak. genera. of his *w.*
Lam. 2. 2 ha. thrown down in his *w.*
Ezek. 7. 12 *w.* is upon all multitude

Hos. 5. 10 I will pour out my *w.* **up.**
Am. 1. 11 he kept his *w.* forever
Hab. 3. 2 O L., in *w.* remem. mercy
Zeph. 1. 15 That day is a day of *w.*
Mat. 3. 7 warn. you to flee from *w.*
Luke 4. 28 heard, were filled with *w.*
John 3. 36 *w.* of G. abideth on him
Acts 19. 28 they were full of *w.*, and
Rom. 1. 18 *w.* of G. is revealed fr.
2 Cor. 12. 20 lest there be debates, *w.*
Gal. 5. 20 works of flesh, *w.*, strife
Eph. 2. 3 by nature childr. of *w.*
Col. 3. 6 *w.* of G. com. on children
1 Thes. 1. 10 del us fr. *w.* to come
1 Tim. 2. 8 lift. hands without *w.*
Heb. 3. 11 I sware in my *w.*, They
Jas. 1. 19 slow to sp., slow to *w.*
Rev. 6. 16 hide us fr. *w.* of Lamb
  R. V. Num. 11. 33; Deut. 11. 17; 2
  Chr. 29. 10; 30. 8; Job 36. 13; 40.
  11; Ps. 55. 3; 78. 31; Prov. 14. 29;
  Jer. 44. 8 anger; Deut. 32. 27
  provocation; Job. 5. 2; Prov. 12.
  16; 27. 3 vexation; Ps. 58. 9 burning
Wrathful. *Angry, fierce.*
Ps. 69. 24 let *w.* anger take hold
Prov. 15. 18 a *w.* man stir. strife
  R. V. Ps. 69. 24 fierceness
Wreath (*n.*). *Band, wreath.*
1 K. 7. 17 *w.* of work, for chapiters
2 Chr. 4. 12 *w.* to cov. the pommels
  R. V. 2 Chr. 4. 12, 13 network
Wreath (*v.*). *Knit together, wrap.*
Ex. 28. 14 chains, of *w.* work ma. th.
2 K. 25. 17 pillar of *w.* work he
  R. V. 2 K. 25. 17 network; Lam. 1.
  14 knit together
Wrest. *Turn aside, twist, distort.*
Ex. 23. 2 after many to *w.* judgment
Ps. 56. 5 Ev. day th. *w.* my words
2 Pet 3. 16 th. that are unstable *w.*
Wrestle. *Grapple, contend.*
Gen. 30. 8 Rach. said, Wi. *w.* ha. I *w.*
Eph. 6. 12 we *w.* not against flesh
Wretched *Miserable.*
Rom. 7. 24 O *w.* man that I am
Rev. 3. 17 know. not thou art *w.*
Wretchedness. *Badness.*
Num. 11. 15 let me not see my *w.*
Wring. *Twist, turn, strain.*
Lev. 1. 15 *w.* off his head, burn it
Judg. 6. 38 *w.* the dew out of fleece
Ps. 73. 10 waters of cup are *w.* out
Prov. 30. 33 *w.* of nose bri. blood
Isa. 51. 17 ha. *w.* out dregs of cup
Wrinkle. *Crease, wrinkle.*
Job 16. 8 th. hast filled me with *w.*
Eph. 5. 27 not having spot or *w.*
Write. *Inscribe, write.*
Ex. 17. 14 *W.* this for mem. in book
Num. 5. 23 priest sh. *w.* these curses
Deut. 4. 13 *w.* them on tab. of sto.
Josh. 8. 32 Josh. *w.* copy of the law
1 Sam. 10. 25 Sam. *w.* it in a book
2 Sam. 11. 14 *W.* a letter to Joab
1 K. 21. 8 she *w.* let. in A.'s name
2 K. 10. 1 Jehu *w.* letters, and sent
2 Chr. 26. 22 Isaiah the prophet *w.*
Neh. 9. 38 make covenant, and *w.* it
Esth. 8. 5 *w.* to destroy the Jews
Job 13. 26 *w.* bitter things agai. me
Ps. 87. 6 L. sh. count, when he *w.*
Prov. 3. 3 *w.* them on tab. of heart
Isa. 8. 1 *w.* in it with man's pen
Jer. 22. 30 *W.* ye this man childless
Ezek. 24. 2 *W.* thee name of the day
Hos. 8. 12 ha. *w.* the great things of
Hab. 2. 2 *W.* vision, made it plain
Mark 14. 4 suff. to *w.* bill of divorce.
Luke 1. 3 seemed good to me to *w.*
John 1. 45 found him, of wh. M. *w.*
Acts 15. 23 *w.* letters aft. this man.
Rom. 15. 15 I have *w.* the mo. bold.
1 Cor. 4. 14 I *w.* not to shame you
2 Cor. 1. 13 we *w.* none oth. things
Gal. 6. 11 how large let. I have *w.*
Phil. 3. 1 To *w.* same things to you
1 Thes. 4. 9 need not that I *w.* you
1 Tim. 3. 14 I *w.* unto thee, hoping
Phile. 19 *w.* it. wi. mine own hand
Heb. 8. 10 *w.* them in their hearts
1 John 1. 4 these things *w.* we that
2 John 12 Hav. many thi. to *w.* you
3 John 9 I *w.* unto the church
Jude 3 I gave diligence to *w.* you
Rev. 1. 11 Wh. thou seest, *w.* in b.

Writer. *Scribe, who writes.*
Judg. 5. 14 that handle pen of *w.*
Ps. 45. 1 tongue is pen of ready *w.*
Ezek. 9. 2 *w.* inkhorn by his side
  R. V. Judg. 5. 14 marshal's staff
Writing. *To write, written.*
Ex. 32. 16 the *w.* was the *w.* of God
Deut. 10. 4 wrote accor. to first *w.*
1 Chr. 28. 19 ma. me underst. in *w.*
Ez. 1. 1 Cyrus ma. proclama. in *w.*
Esth. 1. 22 sent. let. according to *w.*
Isa. 38. 9 *w.* of Hez. king of Judah
Ezek. 13. 9 not in *w.* of ho. of Israel
Mat. 5. 31 give her a *w.* of divor.
John 5. 47 if ye believe not his *w.*
  R. V. Mat. 19. 7 bill
Writing Table. *Tablet.*
Luke 1. 63 Zach. asked for a *w. t.*
Written. *Inscribed, wrote.*
Ex. 31. 18 *w.* with the finger of G.
Deut. 9. 10 *w.* wi. the finger of God
Josh. 1. 8 do all that is *w.* therein
2 Sam. 1. 18 it is *w.* in book of Ja.
1 K. 2. 3 as is *w.* in law of Moses
2 K. 1. 18; 1 Chr. 9. 1; 2 Chr. 9.
  29; Esth. 10. 2
1 Chr. 4. 41 these *w.* by name came
2 Chr. 13. 22 *w.* in the story of Id.
Ez. 3. 2 as *w.* in the law of Moses
Neh. 6. 6 *w.*, It is reported among
Esth. 1. 19 *w.* am. laws of Persians
Job 19. 23 Oh th. my *w.* were *w.*
Ps. 40. 7 in vol. of book it is *w.*
Prov. 22. 20 have not I *w.* to thee
Eccl. 12. 20 wh. was *w.* was upright
Isa. 4. 3 that is *w.* among the living
Jer. 17. 1 sin of Jud. *w.* with pen
Ezek. 2. 10 *w.* within and without
Dan. 5. 24 and this writing was *w.*
Mal. 3. 16 book of remem. was *w.*
Mat. 2. 5 thus it is *w.* by prophet
Mark 1. 2 *w.*, I send messenger be.
Luke 2. 33 As *w.* in law of the L.
John 2. 17 disc. remem. it was *w.*
Acts 1. 20 is *w.* in book of Psalms
Rom. 1. 17 *w.*, The just sh. li. by fa.
1 Cor. 1. 19 *w.*, I will destroy wis. of
2 Cor. 3. 2 Ye are our epistle *w.*
Gal. 3. 10 *w.*, Cursed is ev. one that
Heb. 10. 7 in vol. of the book is *w.*
1 Pet. 1. 16 *w.*, Be ye holy, I am H.
Rev. 1. 3 keep things which are *w.*
R, V. Few changes, and chiefly to,
  wrote
Wrong (*n., adj.*). *Evil, injury, not right.*
Gen. 16. 5 my *w.* be upon thee
Judg. 11. 27 *w.* to war against me
1 Chr. 12. 17 no *w.* in my hands
Job 19. 7 cry out of *w.*, not heard
Ps. 105. 14 suf. no man to do th. *w.*
Jer. 22. 3 do no *w.*, no violence
Lam. 3. 59 thou hast seen my *w.*
Mat. 20. 13 Friend, I do thee no *w.*
Acts 7. 24 see. one of th. suffer *w.*
1 Cor. 6. 7 why not rather take *w.*?
2 Cor. 7. 12 cause th. had done *w.*
Col. 3. 25 doeth *w.*, receive for *w.*
  R. V. Jer. 22. 13 injustice; Hab. 1. 4
  perverted
Wrong (*v.*). *To wrong, work injury.*
Prov. 8. 36 th. sinneth *w.* own soul
2 Cor. 7. 2 we have *w.* no man
Wrongfully. *Unjustly, not rightly.*
Job 21. 27 devices ye *w.* imagine
Ps. 35. 19 let not enemi. *w.* rejoice
1 Pet. 2. 19 endure grief, suffer *w.*
Wrote. *See* **Write.**
Wroth. *Heated, wrathy, angry.*
Gen. 4. 5 and Cain was very *w.*
Deut. 3. 26 L. was *w.* with me for
Josh. 22. 18 wi. whole congrega.
1 Sam. 18. 8 Saul was very *w.*, and
2 Sam. 3. 8 then Ab. was very *w.*
2 K. 5. 11 Naaman was *w.*, and
2 Chr. 16. 10 Asa was *w.* with seer
Ps. 18. 70 shaken, bec. he was *w.*
Isa. 28. 21 *w.*, as in val. of Gibeon
Jer. 37. 15 princes were *w.* wi. Jer.
Mat. 2. 16 Herod was exceeding *w.*
Rev. 12. 17 dragon was *w.* wi. wom.
Wrought. *Do, work.*
Gen. 34. 7 Shechem *w.* folly in **Is.**
Deut. 13. 14 such abomination is *w.*

Josh. 7. 15 she ha. *w.* folly in Israel
1 Sam. 11. 13 to day L. *w.* salvation
2 Sam. 18. 13 I sho. ha. *w.* falsehood
1 K. 5. 16 ruled over peo. that *w.*
2 K. 3. 2 Jehor. *w.* ev. in si. of Lord
1 Chr. 22. 2 masons to hew *w.* stones
2 Chr. 21. 6 Jehoram *w.* evil in si.
Job 12. 9 hand of L. hath *w.* this
Ps. 31. 19 hast *w.* for them that
Eccl. 2. 11 works my hands had *w.*
Isa. 26. 12 th. hast *w.* works in us
Jer. 11. 15 she *w.* le " dness wi. many
Ezek. 20. 9 I *w.* for my na.'s sake
Dan. 4. 2 wond. that God hath *w.*
Mat. 20. 12 have *w.* but one hour
Mark 14. 6 *w.* a good work on me
John 3. 21 mani. th. are *w.* in God
Acts 5. 12 were signs *w.* am. people
Rom. 15. 18 Ch. ha. not *w.* by me
2 Cor. 5. 5. *w.* us for same thi. God
Gal. 2. 8 th. *w.* effectually in Peter
Eph. 1. 20 which he *w.* in Christ
Pet. 4. 3 to have *w.* will of Gentiles
R. V. Ex. 26. 36; 27. 16; 36. 1 work;
Deut. 17 2 doeth; 1 K. 16. 25; 2
K. 3. 2; 2 Chr. 21. 6; 34. 13 did;
2 Sam. 18. 13 dealt; Jonah. 1. 11
grow; Ps. 78. 43 set; Mat. 20. 12
spent; 2 Thes. 3. 8 working.
Wrung. *See* **Wring.**

Y.

Yarn. R. V. *droves.*
1 K. 10. 28 S. bro. out of E. linen *y.*
2 Chr. 1. 16 merchants rec. linen *y.*
Ye. *You, yourselves.*
Gen. 40. 7 Wheref. look *y.* so sadly
Mat. 5. 13 *Y.* are the salt of earth
Etc., etc.
Yea. *Verily, indeed, truly.*
Gen. 20. 6 *Y.* I know th. thou didst
Mat. 5. 37 let your com. be *Y., y.*
Etc., etc.
Year. *Year.*
Gen. 1. 14 be for seasons, days, *y.*
Ex. 7. 7 Mos. was fourscore *y.* old
Lev. 12. 6 sh. bring lamb of first *y.*
Num. 1. 3 Fr. twenty *y.* old upwar.
Deut. 8. 2 G. led thee for *y.* in wild.
Josh. 5. 6 chil. of Is. walk. forty *y.*
Judg. 3. 11 land had rest forty *y.*
Ruth 1. 1 dwelt there about ten *y.*
1 Sam. 1. 7 he did so *y.* by *y.*, when
2 Sam. 14. 28 A. dw. two *y.* in Jer.
1 K. 5. 11 Sol. gave to Hir. *y.* by *y.*
2 K. 1. 17 in second *y.* of Jehoram
1 Chr. 21. 12 Either th. *y.* famine, or
2 Chr. 8. 13 three times in *y.*; or
Ez. 1. 1 in first *y.* of Cyrus of Per.
Neh. 1. 1 twent. *y.*, I was in Shus.
Esth. 1. 3 third *y.* he ma. a decree
Job 10. 5 are thy *y.* as man's days
Ps. 90. 4 thous. *y.* in thy si. are but
90. 10 our *y.* are threesc. *y.* and ten
Prov. 10. 27 *y.* of wick. sh. be short
Eccl. 6. 3 so that his *y.* be many
Isa. 6. 1 In *y.* Uz. died I saw Lord
Jer. 17. 8 not care. in *y.* of drought
Ezek. 1. 2 fifth *y.* of king Jehoiac.
Dan. 1. 5 so nourish. them three *y.*
Joel 2. 2 ev. to *y.* of many generati.
Am. 1. 1 two *y.* bef. the earthquake
Mic. 6. 6 come wi. calves of a *y.* old?
Hab. 3. 2 thy work in midst of *y.*
Hag. 1. 1 in second *y.* of Da., came
Zech. 14. 16 go up *y.* to *y.* to worsh.
Mal. 3. 4 offerings, as in former *y.*
Mat. 9. 20 an issue of bl. twenty *y.*
Mark 5. 42 she was age of twelve *y.*
Luke 4. 19 To preach accep. *y.* of L.
John 2. 20 For six *y.* was th. tem. in
Acts 4. 22. the man was ab. fort. *y.*
Rom. 15. 23 hav. gr. desire many *y.*
2 Cor. 8. 10 but to be forward a *y.*
Gal. 1. 18 aft. three *y.* went to Jer.
1 Tim. 5. 9 to num. und. threesc. *y.*
Heb. 1. 12 and thy *y.* shall not fail
2 Pet. 3. 8 and thous. *y.* as one day
Rev. 20. 2 Sa., bound him thous. *y.*
Yearn. *Burn, desire.*
Gen. 43. 30 his bowels did *y.* on bro.
1 K. 3. 26 her bowels *y.* upon son
Yell. *Make noise, growl.*
Jer. 2. 15 lions roar. on him, and *y.*
51. 38 roar like lions; th. shall *y.*
R. V. Jer. 51. 38 growl

Yellow. *Yellow, green, light.*
Lev. 13. 36 priest not seek for *y.* hair
Ps. 68. 13 dove covered with *y.* gold
Yes. *Truly, verily.*
Mat. 17. 25 He saith, *Y.*. And when
Mark 7. 28 *Y.*, L.; yet the dogs un.
Rom. 3. 29 of Gentiles? *Y.*, of Gent.
Yesterday. *Day before, former time.*
Ex. 5. 14 why not fufilled task *y.*
1 Sam. 20. 27 co. nei. *y.* nor to day
2 Sam. 15. 20 Whereas thou ca. b. *y.*
2 K. 9. 26 seen *y.* blood of Naboth
Job 8. 9 are of *y.* and know nothing
Ps. 90. 4 a thousand years, but as *y.*
John 4. 52 *Y.*, the fever left him
Heb. 13. 8 same *y.*, to day, for ever
Yesternight. *Night before.*
Gen. 19. 34 I lay *y.* with my father
31. 29 G. of your fathers spake *y.*
Yet. *Still.*
Mat. 17. 5 While he *y.* spake, beho.
John 7. 33 *Y.* a little while I am
Gal. 2. 20 *y.* not I, but C. speaketh
Etc., etc.
Yield. *Give, bring forth.*
Gen. 1. 11 tree *y.* fr. after its kind
Lev. 25. 19 land shall *y.* her fruit
Num. 17. 8 rod of Aa. *y.* almonds
Deut. 11. 17 land *y.* not her fruit
2 Chr. 30. 8 *y.* yourselves unto Lord
Neh. 9. 37 it *y.* increase to kings
Ps. 67. 6 shall earth *y.* her increase
Prov. 12. 12 root of right. *y.* fruit
Eccl. 10. 4 *y.* pacifi. great offences
Isa. 5. 10 ten acres sh. *y.* one bath
Jer. 17. 8 nei. shall cease fr. *y.* fruit
Ezek. 34. 27 earth sh. *y.* her increas
Hos. 8. 7 the bud shall *y.* no meal
Joel 2. 22 fig tree and vi. *y.* strength
Hab. 3. 17 altho. fields *y.* no meat
Mat. 27. 50 Jesus *y.* up the ghost
Mark 4. 7 choked it, it *y.* no frnit
Acts 23. 21 do not thou *y.* to them
Rom. 6. 13 but *y.* yourselv. unto G.
Heb. 12. 11 it *y.* peaceable fruit
Jas. 3. 12 no fount. *y.* bo. salt wat.
Rev. 22. 2 tree of life *y.* her fruit
R. V. Num. 17. 8 bare; Acts 5. 10 gave; Rom. 16. 19 presented
Yoke (n.). *Bar, pair.*
Gen. 27. 40 break *y.* from his neck
Lev. 26. 13 brok. bands of your *y.*
Num. 19. 2 on which nev. came *y.*
Deut. 28. 48 put *y.* of iron on thy n.
1 Sam. 11. 7 they took a *y.* of oxen
1 K. 12. 4 Thy fa. ma. our *y.* griev.
2 Chr. 10. 11 I will put mo. to yo. *y.*
Job 1. 3 J. had fiv. hun. *y.* of oxen
Isa. 9. 4 hast brok. *y.* of his burden
Jer. 2. 20 of old I ha. broken thy *y.*
Lam. 1. 14 *y.* of my transg. is bound
Ezek. 30. 18 break there *y.* of Egypt
Hos. 11. 4 as they had taken off *y.*
Nah. 1. 13 now will I break his *y.*
Mat. 11. 30 For my *y.* is easy, and
Luke 14. 19 I boug. fiv. *y.* of oxen
Acts 15. 10 put *y.* on disciples' neck
Gal. 5. 1 be not entangled with *y.*
1 Tim. 6. 1 as many as under *y.*
R. V. 27. 2; 28. 10, 12. 13 bar or bars; 1 Sam. 14. 14 ——— .
Yoke. (*v.*) *Couple.*
2 Cor. 6. 14 Be not unequally *y.*
Yoke Fellow. *Companion.*
Phil. 4. 3 I entreat thee, true *y.*
Yonder. *There, that place.*
Gen. 22. 5 I and the lad will go *y.*
Num. 16. 37 scat. thou the fire *y.*
Mat. 17. 20 Remove hence to *y.* p.
You. *You.*
Mat. 26. 11 ha. poor always wi. *y.*
Mark 14. 7; John 13. 8; etc., etc.
Young. *Lately born, not old.*
Gen. 15. 9 Take me dove and *y.* pi.
Ex. 10. 9 go with our *y.* and with
Lev. 9. 2 *y.* calf for a sin offering
Num. 6. 10 shall bring two *y.* pige.
Deut. 22. 6 not take dam wi. the *y.*
Josh. 6. 21 destr. all in cit. *y.* and
Judg. 9. 54 *y.* man thrust him thro.
Ruth 2. 15 Boaz comman. his *y.* m.
1 Sam. 1. 24 Shiloh; the child w. *y.*
2 Sam. 1. 5 D. said unto the *y.* man
1 K. 11. 28 S. seeing *y.* man that he
2 K. 4. 22 Send one of the *y.* men
1 Chr. 22. 5 Sol. is *y.* and tender

2 Chr. 13. 7 Reho. was *y.* and ten.
Ez. 6. 9 *y.* bullocks for burnt off.
Esth. 13 to kill all Jews, *y.* and old
Job 29. 8 *y.* men saw me, and hid
Ps. 37. 25 I ha. been *y.*, now am o.
Prov. 1. 4 to *y.* man knowl. and d.
S. of S. 2. 9 beloved is like a *y.* ha.
Isa. 13. 18 bows sh. dash *y.* to piec.
Jer. 51. 22 break in piec. old and *y.*
Lam. 2. 21 *y.* and old lie on ground
Ezek. 9. 6 Slay utterly old and *y.*
Joel 2. 28 your *y.* men sh. see visi.
Zech. 9. 27 Corn sh. ma. *y.* men ch.
Mat. 19. 20 *y.* man saith unto him
Mark 14. 51 followed him a *y.* man
Luke 7. 14 *Y.* man, I say unto thee
John 21. 18 When *y.*, thou gird. th.
Acts 5. 10 *Y.* men found her dead
Tit. 2. 4 may teach the *y.* women to
1 John 2. 13 I write you, *y.* men,
R. V. 1 Sam. 20. 22 boy; Mark 7. 25; 10. 13 little; Acts 20. 12 lad
Younger. *Less old.*
Gen. 9. 24 know what *y.* son done
Judg. 1. 13 the *y.* brother took it
1 Sam. 14. 49 Saul's *y.* daughter
1 Chr. 24. 31 against *y.* brethren
Job 30. 1 that are *y.* than I, have
Ezek. 16. 46 thy *y.* sister is Sodom
Luke 15. 12 *y.* said, Gi. me portion
1 Tim. 5. 1 entreat *y.* as brethren
1 Pet. 5. 5 *y.* submit to the elder
Youngest. *Least old.*
Gen. 42. 13 *y.* is with our father
Josh. 6. 26 in *y.* son sh. set up gates
Judg. 9. 5 Jotham, *y.* son. was left
1 Sam 16. 11 there remains yet *y.*
2 Chr. 21. 17 none left save the *y.*
Your, Yours. *Of you.*
Mat. 5. 12 for great is *y.* reward
Luke 6. 20 *y.* is the kingdom of G.
Etc., etc.
Yourselves. *Your (intensive).*
Gen. 45. 5 be not angry with *y.*
Mat. 6. 19 Lay not for *y.* treasures
Etc., etc.
Youth. *Young years.*
Gen. 8. 21 man's heart is evil fr. *y.*
Lev. 22. 13 in fa.'s house as in *y.*
Num. 30. 16 in *y.* in her fa.'s house
1 Sam. 17. 33 a man of war fr. *y.*
2 Sam. 19. 7 evil befel thee from *y.*
1 K. 18. 12 I fear the L. from my *y.*
Job 13. 26 possess iniqu. of my *y.*
Ps. 25. 7 remember not sins of *y.*
Prov. 5. 18 rejoi. wi. wife of thy *y.*
Isa. 40. 30 even the *y.* shall faint
Jer. 3. 4 thou art guide of my *y.*
Lam. 3. 27 he bear yoke in his *y.*
Ezek. 4. 14 not polluted fr. my *y.*
Hos. 2. 15 sing, as in days of her *y.*
Joel 1. 8 as virgin for husband of *y.*
Zech. 13. 5 taught to keep cat. fr. *y.*
Mal. 2. 14 bet. thee and wife of *y.*
Mat. 19. 20 these things have I kept from *y.*; Mark 10. 20; Luke 18. 21
Acts 26. 4 manner of life fr. my *y.*
1 Tim. 4. 12 no man despi. thy *y.*
R. V. Job 29. 4 ripeness; 30. 12 rabble.
Youthful. *Young.*
2 Tim. 2. 22 Flee also *y.* lusts; but

Z

Zeal. *Ardor, fervor.*
2 Sam. 21. 2 to slay them in his *z.*
2 K. 10. 16 see my *z.* for the Lord
Ps. 69. 9 *z.* of thy ho. eaten me up
Isa. 9. 7 *z.* of L. will perform this
Ezek. 5. 13 I have spoken it in *z.*
John 2. 17 *z.* of ho. eaten me up
Rom. 10. 2 they have a *z.* of God
2 Cor. 7. 11 yea, what *z.*, what rev.
Phil. 3. 6 Concerning *z.*, persecut.
Col. 4. 13 hath a great *z.* for you
Zealous. *Ardent, fervent.*
Num. 25. 11 he was *z.* for my sake
Acts 21. 20 they are all *z.* of law
1 Cor. 14. 12 *z.* of spiritual gifts
Gal. 1. 14 exceed. *z.* of the traditions
Rev. 3. 19 be *z.* theref. and repent
R. V. Num. 25. 11, 13 jealous
Zealously. *Ardently.*
Gal. 4. 17 *z.* affect you, but not well
Zion. *Fortress.*
2 Sam. 5. 7 D. took strongh. of *Z.*
See DICTIONARY.